CASS & BIRNBAUM'S GUIDE TO AMERICAN COLLEGES

CASS & BIRNBAUM'S GUIDE TO AMERICAN COLLEGES

16TH EDITION

MELISSA CASS AND JULIA CASS-LIEPMANN

Editors

HarperPerennial
A Division of HarperCollins*Publishers*

Earlier editions of this work were published under the title *Comparative Guide to American Colleges.*

Cass & Birnbaum's Guide to American Colleges. 16th Edition. Copyright © 1994 by Melissa K. Cass and Julia Cass-Liepmann. All rights reserved. Printed in the United States of America. No part of this book may be used or reproduced in any manner whatsoever without written permission except in the case of brief quotations embodied in critical articles and reviews. For information address HarperCollins*Publishers*, Inc., 10 East 53rd Street, New York, New York 10022.

HarperCollins books may be purchased for educational, business, or sales promotional use. For information, please write to: Special Markets Department, HarperCollins Publishers, Inc., 10 East 53rd Street, New York, New York 10022.

FIRST EDITION

Designed by Alma Hochhauser Orenstein

ISSN 1075-3443
ISBN 0-06-273295-1

94 95 96 ❖/CW 10 9 8 7 6 5 4 3 2 1

For Ryan, Barbara, Megan, David, Alexander, and Peggy

Contents

A Note of Appreciation

The authors are grateful to the many critics who have offered wide-ranging suggestions for the improvement of the *Guide.* Some of the new kinds of information provided in recent editions reflect these suggestions. Many opportunities for offering more useful information to the college-bound students remain, however, and additional suggestions will be most welcome from readers of *Cass and Birnbaum's.*

We wish to express our special thanks to the thousands of college administrators and students who provided information for this volume. Although information on which the *Guide* is based is drawn from many sources, the data received directly from the institutions themselves are most helpful in preparing complete and accurate descriptions. Aware as we are of the many demands on the time of college administrators, we are especially appreciative of their cooperation in making the *Guide* as useful a tool as possible for students, counselors, and parents. Although we must be held solely accountable for all errors—either of omission or of commission—this work would not have been possible without the aid and counsel of a large number of individuals in higher education and in the nation's secondary schools.

The authors are also indebted to a great many people for assistance in preparation of this volume. Special thanks must go to Lou Aubain, Linda Fichera, Kathy Fowler, Alex Rodriguez, Wilfredo Ramirez, and Christina Tartaglia for their invaluable assistance in the production of the book.

Introduction

The purpose of this volume is to help high school juniors and seniors choose a college. It was conceived nearly 30 years ago as a consumer's guide to the approximately 1,500 four-year, regionally accredited colleges in the nation. It contains many kinds of information, some published *only* in this guide.

A consumer's guide must do two things that set it apart from others. First, it must change as students change, adding new information to meet the interests and expectations of each new generation of students, for each has somewhat different needs.

Second, a consumer's guide must provide comparative data that will allow the "customers", whether students or parents, to make informed choices among colleges. These data are given in an effort to indicate the essential nature of the college. No attempt is made to reach a judgment on whether a school is "good" or "bad," for such a judgment is virtually meaningless except in relation to a particular student and his or her special needs.

It is important that students take the time to identify their own individual needs before and during the college choice process. With the help of their parents and guidance counselors, students should make a dispassionate appraisal of themselves, their abilities and their aspirations, their strengths and their weaknesses. Then they can identify on a realistic basis those colleges that are appropriate to their own tastes and talents.

Using This Guide

The following pages describe and explain the information provided in the descriptions of colleges. The data presented have been selected to illuminate specific characteristics of individual institutions. Some were selected because they provide factual information about the nature and personality of an institution. Others offer a more specifically comparative or analytical approach to a college; still others bear directly on questions of special interest to students.

The descriptions of individual colleges vary in length, depth of characterization, and the amount of analytical data provided. Among the determining factors are:

The reluctance of a college to reveal comparative and analytical information about itself. Many institutions are eager to make known all kinds of information about themselves. A few are less willing to make public even basic data. Without full information, it is impossible to analyze a school and provide a complete comparative description.

Some institutions are not susceptible to analytical treatment. The comparative approach to colleges is not appropriate for specialized institutions of higher learning such as seminaries, and music and art institutions. In such cases, only a short description is given.

Note: This book is not a measure of the overall quality of colleges, which are institutions far too complex to be ranked by simple statistical data.

The nation's colleges are vital, growing, ever-changing institutions. Any statistics that attempt to encompass them are like snapshots of an object in motion. By the time the camera shutter has clicked, the picture has changed. But institutions do not change their essential natures with such speed, and this volume is able to characterize the colleges it describes so that students and their parents can determine those of special interest. However, the catalogs of individual institutions should always be consulted to obtain additional factual information and the most recent statistics.

Brief Description and Capsule

A brief description of each college is followed by a capsule of information that includes founding date, enrollment, relative cost, application deadline, and other data. (For universities with significant graduate and professional school enrollment, total undergraduate and graduate enrollment is given.) No accrediting information is given, since all colleges in this volume are accredited by the appropriate regional accrediting association.

Admission

The first question prospective applicants are likely to ask about a college in which they are interested is, "Can I get in?" Even for highly qualified individuals the answer may vary. Either because the institution in question has received far more qualified applications than they have slots available or because the admissions office considers criteria other than the solely academic in the admissions process.

However, by carefully considering the admissions data, prospective students can determine whether their academic credentials entitle them to consideration by a given college, whatever the selectivity. And for less selective institutions they can judge, in a rough way at least, what the odds for acceptance are.

Cass and Birnbaum's Selectivity Index. The first yardstick of its kind to measure the quality of a college's student body, the Selectivity Index was introduced in the *Comparative Guide's* first edition in 1964, and has been widely imitated in various forms. It categorizes colleges according to the academic potential of their students and suggests the difficulty a student may have in being accepted by a particular college and, once accepted, the academic competition he or she will meet.

The selectivity index categorizes the several hundred colleges for which objective data are available as "selective," "selective (+)," "very selective," "very (+) selective," "highly selective," "highly (+) selective," and "among the most selective in the country." These categories are general, but they are based on statistical and other factual information: the percentage of applicants accepted by the college, the average test scores of recent freshman classes, the ranking of recent freshmen in their high school classes, and other related data that measure the scholastic potential of the student body. *This index is a crucial measure of the academic quality of a college because, as research on higher education indicates, an institution of higher learning can never be much better than its student body—and is not likely to be much worse.* (When a college does not have this kind of information about itself, or declines to make the information public, no judgment is made. This fact explains why a few institutions of substantial quality are not given a selectivity ranking.)

SAT/ACT scores are just one factor considered by most colleges in admissions. While useful, they are sometimes misinterpreted. For this reason, the College Entrance Examination Board, the publisher of the SATs and The American Council on Education have asked colleges to stop publishing average test scores and instead publish only ranges of scores. In most cases this is given as the "middle fifty percent range" of test scores, i.e., 25% of the entering freshmen scored below this range, 25% scored above this range.

Some schools have complied with the request of the Board and Council and others have not. Therefore reports on test scores in this edition of the *Guide* vary somewhat from school to school.

The Scholastic Aptitude Test (SAT) of the College Entrance Examination Board is scored on a scale of 200 to 800, while the American College Test (ACT) of the American College Testing Program is on a scale of 1 to 36. Not all colleges require entering students to take one of these tests, and even those that do require one or the other are relying far less on the results than in the past.

In many cases, additional information about SAT scores is also given. The percentage of students scoring above 500, above 600, and above 700—on both verbal and mathematical—gives the reader a clear view of the distribution of scores of the freshman class.

For the colleges that have compiled test scores or ranges for their freshman classes and are willing to publish them, data on the 1993–94 freshman class are given. Prospective applicants can check their own test scores against the average scores or range in any institution that interests them—keeping in mind that this is an *average of the scores of the entire freshman class, not a cut-off point.* They should then read carefully the other admissions information on the college to determine what other factors are likely to be important—either positively or negatively—in consideration of their application.

Capable students with special talents and qualities of intellect and spirit should not allow themselves to be turned away from consideration of the more selective schools by the high average test scores reported. Most of the leading institutions in the nation are not playing the "numbers game," but are seeking a varied student body that reflects nonintellective qualities as well as academic excellence.

Some large universities admit students separately to the undergraduate professional schools and colleges within the institution. In these cases, admissions data are given for the individual schools and colleges. Students sometimes take advantage of the varied selectivity of these schools and colleges to improve their academic record and to transfer to a more competitive division after a year or two at the university.

Specific admission requirements are given only briefly in most cases for several reasons. First, such requirements are similar for most colleges. They include a standard pattern of college-preparatory subjects: English, social studies, science, mathematics, and foreign language. Second, the exact combination of high school courses is far less important to most colleges than a strong scholastic record that clearly demonstrates the student's capacity for college-level work. Few colleges will not make exceptions to their specific requirements for clearly capable applicants whom they find attractive. Third, some professional and specialized institutions have special requirements. In these cases, the general nature of the requirements is noted and the reader is referred to the institution's catalog. Where no admissions data are given, the reader may assume that high school graduation with an average record is all that is specifically required.

Required is a section which lists the admissions tests and other procedures demanded by individual colleges. They may include standardized test scores (SAT or ACT), ACH or SAT II (achievement tests in individual subject areas administered by the College Entrance Examination Board—sometimes the required subject fields are specified by the college, sometimes they are left to the applicant), interviews (some institutions require an interview with applicants on campus or with a representative of the college), essays, and occasionally, special requirements such as religious affiliation.

New to this edition is *Criteria considered in admissions.* The criteria are ranked in order of importance and include high school academic record, standardized test scores, recommendations, extracurricular activities, etc. This provides the student with an overview of the relative importance given different data and other information by an individual institution.

Included with the academic admissions criteria are the nonacademic factors which may play a role in the admissions process. Colleges place varying degrees of emphasis on special talents, alumni children, diverse student body, religious affiliation and other factors. While no one factor can transform a weak applicant into a strong one, a competent student who fulfills a college's desire for geographic diversity or who possesses a desired special talent may have the edge over another equally qualified applicant.

Entrance programs is a section which lists a number of special programs and opportunities available to entering students. They include: advanced placement (many colleges allow degree credit or advanced course placement to students who have completed college-level studies in high school), early admission (some colleges admit exceptionally able students before graduation from high school), early decision (some colleges will take action on the applications of well-qualified students who apply early in the fall or winter of the student's senior year), midyear admission (many colleges admit freshmen at the beginning of each semester, quarter, or trimester; others admit them only at the beginning of the fall term), deferred admission (after acceptance, the college allows students to defer actual enrollment for one or more terms).

Apply gives the date by which institutions expect to receive applications if they are to be considered for entrance the following fall. Each college sets its own date and, as admissions pressures decline, the final date on which institutions will accept applications tends to be more flexible. Students applying for early admission or early decision should consult the catalog of the institution for the final date by which they must apply. *Rolling admissions* describes a policy under which applications are evaluated as soon as they are received and acceptances sent to successful candidates on a continuing basis until all freshman places are filled. In all cases, an early application is far more likely to receive thoughtful attention than a late one.

Transfers. A large number of students each year search for a college other than the one they are attending, a college that will better meet their maturing needs. The information given in this section is designed to help students who have already completed one or more years of undergraduate work to select the "second school of their choice."

Students should remember that they will change during their college years. The desire to move to another college may indicate a poor initial choice of college, increasing maturity that requires greater challenge for the individual, or newly developed career goals that can be better served by another institution.

Academic Environment

Once prospective applicants have determined their chance of admission to a particular institution, they will want to know more about the educational milieu that awaits them there—the range of academic opportunity, the intensity of the pressures they will encounter, and some measure of their chance for scholastic success. Part of the answer to these questions is provided by the data on the academic quality of the student body (see above). This is a measure of the academic competition a student will meet. It needs to be supplemented, however, by a wide range of other information given in this section. Some of this is simple, self-explanatory, factual information about the college; some of it is more complicated analytical data which need to be explained in some detail:

Degrees offered shows the range of study available at the institution: associate degrees (usually 2-year programs), bachelors-the traditional 4-year degree, masters and doctoral degrees.

Average undergraduate class size is given as a percent of classes within certain size ranges. In some cases an overall average is given as well as, or instead of, a range. In general, introductory level classes are likely to be larger while upper division classes will have fewer students. Some schools pride themselves on small classes throughout the four years.

The percent of entering freshmen who graduate in 4 or 5 years has become increasingly important as budget cuts at many institutions reduce the frequency with which required courses are offered. Many students have told us that it has become difficult to fulfill graduation requirements within four years. It should also be remembered that a significant number of students take a year or two off in the course of their academic career to work, travel, or pursue other interests. Therefore, the prospective student would do well to inquire carefully of the colleges on their short list about the ease with which a student can graduate within a given length of time.

The percent who return for their sophomore year provides some insight into the nature of the student body and the academic environment. A high dropout rate may indicate rigorous academic standards, low entrance requirements, or some other special factor. At many state colleges, entrance is guaranteed by law to all high school graduates within the state, however, some colleges with an open admissions policy maintain scholastic standards by dropping substantial numbers of students during their freshman and sophomore years.

Special programs lists opportunities offered students either outside the college or within it. Several such programs need explanation. Many colleges offer special programs which combine undergraduate and professional studies. Thus, "3–2 engineering" means that after 3 years of successful undergraduate study a student may transfer to an engineering school and complete work for his professional degree in 2 additional years. The undergraduate institution confers the student's undergraduate degree (usually a BA or BS) either at the end of the first year of successful professional study or upon completion of his studies when the professional degree is conferred. In recent years, a number of variations on the 3–2 program concept have appeared involving BA/BS undergraduate degrees, undergraduate/graduate and undergraduate/professional programs. A variety of accelerated programs are included which allow capable students to combine the senior year of high school with the freshman year of college. "Washington Semester," which is sponsored by American University in Washington, D.C., offers students on other campuses an opportunity to spend a semester in the nation's capital studying and observing government in action. "United Nations Semester" is a similar program, sponsored by Drew University. Junior-year or study-abroad programs are noted but usually not described in detail. These programs vary widely from one college to another and should be checked carefully in each college catalog. Cooperative work/study programs in which practical job experience in industry, business, or government is integrated with the student's classroom work are available at many colleges and universities. Further information about such programs can be obtained from the National Commission for Cooperative Education, Northeastern University, Boston, Massachusetts 02115. Also included with this section are brief descriptions of the programs especially geared to the adult student (over 21 years of age).

Calendar. Many colleges have experimented with new ways to organize the academic year in place of the traditional semester or quarter systems. Some have also switched back to the traditional semester system. Of the many variations, two are especially popular: the 3–3 calendar divides the academic year into three terms with three subjects studied each term; the 4–1–4 calendar allows for two terms of four months each, divided by a one-month interterm that is often used for experimental projects. In other cases, the length of terms is stated in weeks rather than months—a few colleges have opted for 7-week terms, for instance.

Undergrate Degrees Conferred

Undergraduate degrees conferred gives the percentage of graduates during the academic year 1991–92 (the most recent year for which data are available) who majored in different broad fields of study (social science, engineering, humanities, etc.) at each college. In an effort to provide consistency and avoid ambiguity, this information is given as compiled by the United States Department of Education. These data provide insight into the focus of student interests and a view of where the college allocates its resources. At a college where a very high percentage of students major in liberal studies, the campus culture and ambiance of campus life are likely to be somewhat different than one where a large majority of students major in vocational/professional areas. Even though both colleges may claim to be liberal arts colleges, they are actually very different—in their allocation of personnel and resources, in the educational function they perform, in the nature of the student body, and in the temper of the student culture. Each performs a valuable, but different, educational function, and serves best rather different kinds of students. However, the strongly motivated, self-directed student will find opportunities for obtaining the kind of education he wants at either institution.

Comparative Listing of Majors Index supplements Undergraduate Degrees Conferred data by listing every college (in alphabetical order) that actually conferred degrees in specific major fields. Among the physical sciences, for instance, a prospective student can see what colleges conferred degrees in Astronomy,

Molecular Physics, Oceanography, etc. (each subject listed separately). The index also gives the number of degrees in each subject actually conferred by each college in a recent year. This comparative data, which indicates the size of departments, also suggests, though it does not document, departmental strength. It also avoids listing "paper majors," in which a college rarely confers a degree and for which it has limited or no regular faculty.

Doctoral degrees conferred suggest the range and scope of graduate and professional study that takes place on campus. The presence of a strong graduate department in a university is often reflected in the department of the undergraduate college. It is also true, in some cases, that graduate departments that are devoted primarily to research and to developing professionals at the doctoral level largely ignore the undergraduate department.

Graduates Career Data

Just as the Selectivity Index and SAT/ACT scores measure the "in put" of a college, Graduates Career Data is a measure of the "out put." Perhaps the ultimate measure of a college is the success of its graduates. This section gives the percent of graduates going on to graduate school and to medical, law, dental, and business schools, as well as the specific professional schools that enroll them most frequently. It also gives the percent of 1992–93 graduates who are employed and the fields or corporations where the largest numbers of graduates found employment.

A description of *Career Development Services* offered by the institution details services offered to students to aid them in choosing and pursuing a career. These services vary considerably from institution to institution, but in many cases the services go far beyond senior year job placement and students would be well advised to seek out the office in their freshman year. At their best, a college's career planning office will help a student explore his or her various study and career options and will help the student find opportunities to "try out" a given career.

Faculty

The faculty is the second most important factor—after the student body—in determining the nature and quality of a college, yet it is one of the most difficult of all aspects of an institution to assess.

The percentage of faculty holding the doctorate is generally accepted in higher education as an important factor. Doctoral degrees earned at the nation's major graduate institutions usually confer greater status on their holders than comparable degrees earned at lesser institutions. There is little objective evidence to prove that a degree earned at one institution guarantees greater competence than a similar degree earned at another, but the fact that certain institutions enjoy greater professional status implies that the most competent students—and future professors—will be attracted to them.

The percent of undergraduate classes taught by tenured faculty indicates the use or absence of teaching assistants. A dazzling constellation of senior faculty are of little benefit to the lowly undergraduate if he or she is taught only by teaching assistants.

In response to requests by students we have added the percent of teaching faculty who are female and minority.

Student Body

Information on the geographical, racial, and religious composition of the student body suggests the diversity of the student body and the variety of life-styles available. Many colleges place substantial emphasis on attracting a diverse student body, since learning takes place just as surely—and just as importantly—outside the classroom as inside it. These institutions believe that a heterogeneous student body in which different racial, religious, economic groups and varied geographical areas are represented offers the best training ground for life in our pluralist society, in which vastly different cultures meet, live and work together. On the other hand, a substantial number of fine colleges, notably those with close religious affiliation or control, prefer a more homogeneous campus climate.

The *average age of undergraduate students* is given here when it differs from the traditional 18–22 age range.

Religious Orientation

A great number of the nation's colleges were founded by religious denominations and a significant proportion of them still maintain affiliation with some church group, even when they are no longer controlled by the church. But the closeness of denomination ties—and their influence on campus life and culture—varies from one school to another. In many cases, church affiliation is largely formal and traditional and has little impact on day-to-day college life. In others there is a deep and strong religious commitment which is reflected in virtually every aspect of college life.

In this section, the religious studies and the religious observances required of students are included, as well as the percent of students affiliated with the specific church. (*See* pages xxxiii–xxxvi for listing of colleges by religious affiliation.)

Campus Life

Greatly expanded in response to many requests from students and parents, this section offers subjective information (as well as objective data) about the "atmosphere" on campus.

Every student lives two lives at college—an academic life and a social life (which includes both the informal, peer-group learning that is an extension of the classroom, and social/recreational activities)—and it is sometimes a question as to which is the more "educational." But both the academic and the social milieu in which a student lives are important to his or her development. The college provides, or fails to provide, a rich environment for stimulating the development of young scholars—and young human beings.

Since the nation's colleges are located in every conceivable kind and size of community, students who are considering going to another, unfamiliar part of the country for college should be careful to look before they leap. The shock of going from an urban to a rural setting (or vice versa) or from one climate extreme to another can adversely affect a student's experience. Student's should consider what they like and don't like about where they are before narrowing down their choices of college.

If they come from an urban area where museums, the theater, and the concert hall have become regular adjuncts to their daily lives, a small town many miles from a metropolitan center may appear to them to be a cultural desert. Even if the college makes a relatively successful effort to compensate for its cultural isolation, some urban-bred students may remain dissatisfied. Others may find the relative quiet to be an advantage. Students from small towns and small high schools should also consider the potential culture shock they could encounter in an urban environment or a large and possibly bureaucratic institution.

The percentage of students living on campus is likely to be most important in urban and suburban institutions where a high proportion of students commute. Student life on campus is bound to be profoundly affected by large numbers of students who attend classes during the day and then leave for home. On the other hand, if the college is a very large one, a substantial number of students may live on campus and, even though they might represent a minority of the student body, the institution may offer an active, satisfactory campus environment.

The percentage of students leaving the campus on weekends is important for the students from another part of the country, since some colleges draw most of their students from a relatively limited area. Although a high percentage of the students live on campus, many of them regularly go home on weekends. Students from several hundred miles away, unless they have friends who take them home with them, may find themselves on a relatively deserted campus once Friday afternoon classes are over.

Annual Costs

Annual costs givcs information on tuition and fees and room and board for the year 1993–94, the percentage of students receiving financial aid, the average amount of assistance, and any special programs a college may have to help parents to pay college costs. We have added the number of scholarships awarded, by the institution, for academic merit, special talents, and need.

The rapid rise in the cost of higher education in recent decades has made four years of college a major investment for most American families. Costs have become a significant factor in college choice.

Many students and parents assume that the high tuition costs in higher education today preclude attendance at most private schools. This is not necessarily so, many high-quality colleges are prepared to meet the actual financial needs of students they want to enroll. Students and parents should study carefully the data given on the percent of students receiving financial aid and the average amount of assistance they receive. They should also contact the financial aid officer, as early as possible, for more detailed information and advice.

A substantial number of colleges have devised ingenious programs of prepayment, deferred payment and loans that can be especially helpful to middle-class families. These are listed briefly under the rubric *Meeting Costs* in the Annual Costs section of college descriptions.

Degrees Granted

The abbreviations for degrees granted by individual institutions are listed as a reference and explained below.

AA	Associate of Arts
AB, BA	Bachelor of Arts
ABT	Bachelor of Arts in Teaching
BA, AB	Bachelor of Arts
BAcc	Bachelor of Accounting
BArch	Bachelor of Architecture
BApA	Bachelor of Applied Art
BApAS	Bachelor of Applied Arts and Sciences
BAEd	Bachelor of Arts in Education
BAE1Ed	Bachelor of Arts in Elementary Education
BAGEd	Bachelor of Arts in General Education
BAGS	Bachelor of Arts in General Studies
BAM	Bachelor of Arts in Music
BAR	Bachelor of Arts in Religion
BApS	Bachelor of Applied Science
BASecEd	Bachelor of Arts in Secondary Education
BATh	Bachelor of Arts in Theology
BBA	Bachelor of Business Administration
BBEd	Bachelor of Business Education
BCom	Bachelor of Commerce
BCA	Bachelor of Creative Arts
BCE	Bachelor of Civil Engineering
BChE	Bachelor of Chemical Engineering
BCM	Bachelor of Church Music
BCS	Bachelor of College Studies
BE	Bachelor of Engineering
BEd	Bachelor of Education
BEE	Bachelor of Electrical Engineering
BES	Bachelor of Engineering Science
BET	Bachelor of Engineering Technology
BFA	Bachelor of Fine Arts
BFAEd	Bachelor of Fine Arts Education
BGS	Bachelor of General Studies
BHum	Bachelor of Humanities
BIA	Bachelor of Industrial Administration
BID	Bachelor of Industrial Design
BIE	Bachelor of Industrial Engineering
BIM	Bachelor of Industrial Management
BIS	Bachelor of Individual Studies
BLA	Bachelor of Liberal Arts
BLArch	Bachelor of Landscape Architecture
BLS	Bachelor of Liberal Studies
BM	Bachelor of Music
BME	Bachelor of Mechanical Engineering
BMEd	Bachelor of Music Education
BMTh	Bachelor of Musical Therapy
BPh	Bachelor of Philosophy
BPHEd	Bachelor of Physical Education
BPS	Bachelor of Professional Studies
BREd	Bachelor of Religious Education
BS	Bachelor of Science
BSA	Bachelor of Science in Administration
BSAcc	Bachelor of Science in Accounting
BSAg	Bachelor of Science in Agriculture
BSAv	Bachelor of Science in Aviation
BSAEd	Bachelor of Science in Art Education
BSAJ	Bachelor of Science in Administration of Justice
BSB	Bachelor of Science in Business
BSBA	Bachelor of Science in Business Administration
BSBEd	Bachelor of Science in Business Education
BSBehavSci	Bachelor of Science in Behavioral Science
BSChem	Bachelor of Science in Chemistry
BSCom	Bachelor of Science in Commerce
BSCor	Bachelor of Science in Corrections
BSCrim	Bachelor of Science in Criminology
BSChE	Bachelor of Science in Chemical Engineering
BSCE	Bachelor of Science in Civil Engineering
BSCrimJ	Bachelor of Science in Criminal Justice

BSE Bachelor of Science in Engineering
BSEd Bachelor of Science in Education
BSEcBA Bachelor of Science in Economics and Business Administration
BSEE Bachelor of Science in Electrical Engineering
BSE1Ed Bachelor of Science in Elementary Education
BSEnvH Bachelor of Science in Environmental Health
BSES Bachelor of Science in Engineering Science
BSEnvStud Bachelor of Science in Environmental Studies
BSF Bachelor of Science in Forestry
BSFS Bachelor of Science in Foreign Service
BSGA Bachelor of Science in Governmental Administration
BSGS Bachelor of Science in General Studies
BSHEc Bachelor of Science in Home Economics
BSHEd Bachelor of Science in Health Education
BSHPhEd Bachelor of Science in Health and Physical Education
BSHS Bachelor of Science in Health Science/Studies
BSIE Bachelor of Science in Industrial Engineering
BSIEd Bachelor of Science in Industrial Education
BSIT Bachelor of Science in Industrial Technology
BSL Bachelor of Science in Languages, Bachelor of Science in Linguistics
BSLE Bachelor of Science in Law Enforcement
BSLPS Bachelor of Science in Liberal Professional Studies
BSM Bachelor of Science in Music
BSME Bachelor of Science in Mechanical Engineering
BSMEd Bachelor of Science in Music Education
BSMIS Bachelor of Science in Management Information Science
BSMT Bachelor of Science in Medical Technology
BSN Bachelor of Science in Nursing
BSOA Bachelor of Science in Office Administration
BSOE Bachelor of Science in Occupational Education
BSPharm Bachelor of Science in Pharmacy
BSPA Bachelor of Science in Professional Arts
BSPhEd Bachelor of Science in Physical Education
BSPhT Bachelor of Science in Physical Therapy
BSR Bachelor of Science in Recreation
BSRT Bachelor of Science in Radiologic Technology
BSS Bachelor of Special Studies
BSSecEd Bachelor of Science in Secondary Education
BSecS Bachelor of Secretarial Science
BST Bachelor of Science in Technology
BSTE Bachelor of Science in Textile Engineering
BSTIEd Bachelor of Science in Trade and Industrial Education
BSTM Bachelor of Science in Technology of Management
BSVHEc Bachelor of Science in Vocational Home Economics
BSVTEd Bachelor of Science in Vocational–Technical Education
BSocW Bachelor of Social Welfare/Work
BT Bachelor of Technology
BTE Bachelor of Technology Engineering
BTh Bachelor of Theology
BUS Bachelor of University Studies
BVA Bachelor of Visual Arts
BVEd Bachelor of Vocational Education
MA Master of Arts
MAEd Master of Arts in Education
MAT Master of Arts in Teaching
MBS Master of Business Administration
ME Master of Engineering
MFA Master of Fine Arts
MM Master of Music
MMEd Master of Music Education
MS Master of Science
PhD Doctor of Philosophy

Abbreviations

ACCK	Associated Colleges of Central Kansas
ACH	Achievement Tests of College Entrance Examination Board
ACM	Associated Colleges of Midwest
ACT	American College Testing Program
CCFL	College Center of the Finger Lakes
CLEP	College Level Examination Program
COSIP	College Science Improvement Program of National Science Foundation
CSC	California State College
CSCA	Central States College Association
CSU	California State University
CUNY	City University of New York
GED	General Education Development Tests
GLCA	Great Lakes Colleges Association
IUPUI	Indiana University–Purdue University at Indianapolis
LSACU	Lake Superior Association of Colleges and Universities
MIT	Massachusetts Institute of Technology
NHCUC	New Hampshire College and University Council
NHEC	Nassau Higher Education Consortium
NYU	New York University
ROTC	Reserve Officer Training Corps A—Army; AF—Air Force; N—Navy and Marine
RPI	Rensselaer Polytechnic Institute
SAM	Single Application Method
SAT	Scholastic Aptitude Test of the College Entrance Examination Board
SCAT	School and College Ability Test
SUNY	State University of New York
UC	University of California
USC	University of Southern California

Religious Index

African Methodist Episcopal

Edward Waters College
Livingstone College (African M.E. Zion)
Morris Brown College
Paul Quinn College
Wilberforce University

American Baptist

Alderson-Broaddus College
Benedict College (Indep.)
Eastern College
Florida Memorial College
Franklin College of Indiana (Indep.)
Grand Rapids Baptist College
Judson College (Ill.)
Kalamazoo College (Indep.)
Linfield College (Indep.)
Ottawa University
Shaw University
Sioux Falls College
Virginia Union University
William Jewell College

Assemblies of God

Bethany College
Evangel College
Northwest College
Southern California College
Southeastern College of the Assemblies of God
Southwestern Assemblies of God College

Christian Methodist Episcopal

Lane College
Miles College
Texas College

Christian and Missionary Alliance

Nyack College
Simpson College (Ca.)

Christian Reform

Calvin College
Dordt College

Church of the Brethren

Ashland College
Bridgewater College (Va.) (Indep.)
Elizabethtown College
Juniata College (Indep.)
La Verne University of (Indep.)
Manchester College
McPherson College

Church of Christ

Abilene Christian College
David Lipscomb College
Freed-Hardman College
Harding College
Lubbock Christian College
Michigan Christian College
Oklahoma Christian U. (Indep.)
Pepperdine University (Indep.)

Church of God

Anderson College
Findlay College
Lee College
Mid-America Bible College
Warner Pacific College
Warner Southern College

Church of the Nazarene

Eastern Nazarene College
Mid-America Nazarene College
Mount Vernon Nazarene College
Northwest Nazarene College
Olivet Nazarene College
Point Loma College
Southern Nazarene University
Trevecca Nazarene College

Disciples of Christ

Barton College
Bethany College (W.V.)(Indep.)
Butler University (Indep.)
Chapman University
Culver-Stockton College
Eureka College
Hiram College (Indep.)
Jarvis Christian College
Lynchburg College (Indep.)
Northwest Christian College
Phillips University
Texas Christian University (Indep.)
Transylvania University (Indep.)

Episcopal

Kenyon College
Saint Augustine's College
Saint Paul's College
South, University of the Voorhees College

Free Methodist

Greenville College (Indep.)
Roberts Wesleyan College
Seattle Pacific University
Spring Arbor College

Jewish

Baltimore Hebrew College (Indep.)
Gratz College (Indep.)
Jewish Theological Seminary of America (Conservative)
Judaism, University of (Conservative)
Spertus College of Judaica (Indep.)
Yeshiva University (Indep.)

Latter-day Saints

Brigham Young University
Brigham Young University-Hawaii Campus
Graceland College (Reorganized Latter-day Saints)
Park College (Reorganized Latter-day Saints)

Evangelical Lutheran Church in America

Augsburg College
Augustana College (Ill.)
Augustana College (S.D.)
Bethany College (Ks.)
Capital University
Carthage College
Concordia College (Moorhead, Mn.)
Dana College
Gettysburg College (Indep.)
Grand View College
Gustavus Adolphus College
Lenoir Rhyne College
Luther College
Midland Lutheran College
Muhlenberg College
Newberry College
Pacific Lutheran University (Indep.)
St. Olaf College
Susquehanna University
Texas Lutheran College
Thiel College
Upsala College
Wagner College (Indep.)
Wartburg College
Wittenberg University

Lutheran-Missouri Synod

Concordia University (Ca.)
Concordia College (Il.)
Concordia College (Mi.)
Concordia College (N.Y.)
Concordia College, St. Paul (Mn.)
Concordia College (Or.)
Concordia University (Wi.)
Concordia College (Nb.)
St. John's College (Ks.)
Valparaiso University

Mennonite

Bethel College (Ks.)
Bluffton College
Eastern Mennonite College
Goshen College

Mennonite Brethren

Fresno Pacific College
Tabor College

Moravian

Moravian College
Salem College

Nondenominational Protestant-Independent

Asbury College
Azusa Pacific University
Berry College (Ga.)
Biola College
Gordon College
John Brown University
King's College (N.Y.)
Lancaster Bible College
LeTourneau College
Milligan College
Northwestern College (Mn.)
Oral Roberts University
Patten College
Philadelphia College of Bible
Rio Grande College
Taylor University
Westmont College
Wheaton College (Ill.)
William Jennings Bryan College)

Presbyterian Church, U.S.A.

Agnes Scott College (Indep.)
Alma College
Arkansas College
Austin College
Barber-Scotia College
Beaver College (Indep.)
Belhaven College
Blackburn College
Bloomfield College
Buena College
Carroll College (Wi.)
Coe College (Indep.)
Davidson College
Davis and Elkins College
Dubuque, University of (Indep.)
Grove City College
Hampden-Sydney College
Hanover College (Indep.)
Hastings College
Huron College
Idaho, College of
Inter American University of Puerto Rico (Indep.)
Jamestown College
Johnson C.Smith University (Indep.)
King College
Knoxville College
Lafayette College
Lake Forest College (Indep.)
Lewis and Clark College (Indep.)
Lindenwood (Indep.)
Malcalester College
Mary Baldwin College
Maryville College (Tn.)(Indep.)
Millikin University
Missouri Valley College
Monmouth College (ill.)
Muskingum College (Indep.)
Occidental College of the
Pikeville College
Presbyterian College
Queens College (N.C.)
Rhodes College

St. Andrews Presbyterian College
Schreiner College
Sheldon Jackson College
Sterling College
Stillman College
Trinity University (Tx.)(Indep.)
Tusculum College
Warren Wilson College (Indep.)
Waynesburg College
Westminster College (Mo.)(Indep.)
Westminster College (Pa.)
Whitworth College
Wilson College
Wooster, College of (Indep.)

Reformed Church in America

Central University of Iowa
Hope College (Indep.)
Northwestern College (Ia.)

Reformed Presbyterian

Covenant College
Geneva College

Roman Catholic

Albertus Magnus College
Allentown College of St. Francis de Sales (Indep.)
Anna Maria College
Aquinas College
Assumption College
Avila College
Barat College (Indep.)
Barry College (Fl.)
Bayamon Central University
Bellarmine College
Belmont Abbey College
Benedictine College
Boston College
Brescia College
Briar Cliff College (Ia.)
Cabrini College
Caldwell College
Calumet College
Canisius College (Indep.)
Cardinal College (Mt.)(Indep.)
Catholic University of America (Indep.)
Catholic University of Puerto Rico
Chaminade College of Honolulu
Chestnut Hill College (Indep.)
Christian Brothers College (Indep.)
Clarke College (Ia.)
Conception Seminary College
Creighton University (Indep.)
Dallas, University of
Dayton, University of (Indep.)
De Paul University
Detroit Mercy University of (Indep.)
Divine Word College
Dominican College of San Rafael (Indep.)
Duquesne University
Edgewood College (Indep.)
Emmanuel College (Indep.)
Fairfield University
Felician College
Fontbonne College (Indep.)
Fordham University (Indep.)
Gannon College
Georgetown University
Georgian Court College
Gonzaga University
Great Falls, College of
Gwynedd-Mercy College (Indep.)
Holy Apostles College
Holy Cross, College of the
Holy Family College (Pa.)
Holy Names College (Indep.)
Holy Redeemer College
Illinois Benedictine College
Immaculata College (Indep.)
Incarnate Word College
Iona College (Indep.)
John Carroll University
Kansas Newman College
King's College (Pa.)
La Roche College
La Salle College (Indep.)
Le Moyne College
Lewis University
Loras College
Loretto Heights College (Indep.)
Lourdes College
Loyola Marymount University (Indep.)
Loyola University, New Orleans

St. Norbert College (Indep.)
Saint Peter's College
Saint Rose, College of (Indep.)
St. Scholastica, College of
St. Thomas University of (Mn.)
St. Thomas, University of (Tx.)
Saint Vincent College
Saint Xavier College
Salve Regina University
San Diego, University of (Indep.)
San Francisco, University of
Santa Clara University (Indep.)
Santa Fe, College of
Scranton, University of
Seattle University
Seton Hall University
Seton Hall College (Indep.)
Siena Heights College
Silver Lake College
Spalding College (Indep.)
Spring Hill College
Steubenville, College of
Stonehill College (Indep.)
Thomas Aquinas College
Thomas More College
Trinity College (D.C.)
Trinity College (V.T.)
Ursuline College (Indep.)
Villanova University
Viterbo University (Indep.)
Wadhams Hall
Walsh University
Wheeling College
Xavier University (Oh.)(Indep.)
Xavier University of Louisiana

Seventh-Day Adventist

Andrews University
Atlantic Union College
Columbia Union College
Loma Linda University
Oakwood College
Pacific Union College
Southern College of Seventh Day Adventists
Southwestern Adventist College
Union College (Nb.)
Walla Walla College

Society of Friends

Earlham College
Friends University
George Fox College
Guilford College
Haverford College (Indep.)
Malone College
William Penn College
Wilmington College

Southern Baptist

Averett College
Baylor University
Belmont College
Blue Mountain College
Bluefield College
California Baptist College
Campbell University
Campbellsville College
Carson-Newman College
Cumberland College
Dallas Baptist College
East Texas Baptist College
Furman University
Gardner-Webb College
Georgetown College (Ky.)
Grand Canyon College
Hannibal-LaGrange College
Hardin-Simmons University
Houston Baptist University
Howard Payne University
Judson College (Al.)
Louisiana College
Mars Hill College
Mary Hardin-Baylor, University of
Mercer University
Mercer University in Atlanta
Meredith College
Missouri Baptist College
Mobile College
Oklahoma Baptist University
Ouachita Baptist University
Palm Beach Atlantic College
Richmond, University of
Samford University
Shorter College
Southwest Baptist College
Stetson University (Indep.)

Tift College
Union University (Tn.)
Wake Forest University
Wayland Baptist University
William Carey College
Wingate College

United Church of Christ

Catawba College
Cedar Crest College
Defiance College
Doane College (Indep.)
Drury College (Indep.)
Elmhurst College
Elon College
Franklin and Marshall College (Indep.)
Heidelberg College
Hood College (Indep.)
Lakeland College
Northland College (Indep.)
Pacific University (Indep.)
Talladega College
Ursinus College (Indep.)
Yankton College

United Church of Christ, United Methodist

Dillard University (Indep.)
Huston-Tillotson College

United Methodist

Adrian College
Alaska Pacific College
Albion College
Albright College
Allegheny College (Indep.)
American University (Indep.)
Baker University
Baldwin-Wallace College
Bennett College
Bethune-Cookman College
Birmingham-Southern College
Centenary College of Louisiana
Central Methodist College
Claflin College
Clark College (Ga.)
Columbia College (S.C.)
Cornell College (Ia.)(Indep.)
Dakota Wesleyan University
Denver, University of (Indep.)
DePauw University (Indep.)
Dickinson College (Pa.)(Indep.)
Drew University (Indep.)
Duke University (Indep.)
Emory and Henry College
Emory College
Evansville, University of
Ferrum College
Florida Southern College
Greensboro College
Hamline University
Hendrix College
High Point College
Huntington College (Al.)(Indep.)
Illinois Wesleyan University (Indep.)
Indiana Wesleyan University
Indianapolis, University of
Iowa Wesleyan College
Kansas Wesleyan
Kendall College
Kentucky Wesleyan College
LaGrange College
Lambuth College
Lebanon Valley College
Lycoming College
MacMurray College (Indep.)
McKendree College
McMurry College
Methodist College
Millsaps College
Morningside College
Mount Union College
Nebraska Wesleyan University (Indep.)
North Carolina Wesleyan College
North Central College
Ohio Northern University
Ohio Wesleyan University (Indep.)
Oklahoma City University
Otterbein City University
Pfeiffer College
Philander Smith College
Puget Sound, University of (Indep.)
Randolph-Macon College (Indep.)
Randolph-Macon Women's College (Indep.)

Rust College
Shenandoah College and Conservatory of Music
Simpson College (Ia.)(Indep.)
Southern Methodist University
Southwestern Christian College
Southwestern College (Ks.)
Southwestern University (Tx.)
Tennessee Wesleyan College
Texas Wesleyan College
Union College (Ky.)
Virginia Wesleyan College
Wesley College
Wesleyan College (Ga.)(Indep.)
West Virginia Wesleyan College
Wiley College
Willamette University
Wofford College

Wesleyan Church of America

Bartlesville Wesleyan College
Central Weselayn College
Houghton College
Marion College

Other

Academy of the New Church (Church of New Jerusalem)
Aurora College (Advent Christian/Indep.)
Baptist Bible College of Pennsylvania (Baptist)
Bethel College (In.)(Missionary)
Bethel College (Mn.)(Baptist General Conference)
Bethel College (Tn.)(Cumberland Presbyterian)
California Lutheran College (American Lutheran, Lutheran Church of America)
Cedarville College (Oh.)(Baptist)
Columbia Bible College and Seminary
Dr. Martin Luther College (Evangelical Luthern Synod)
Erksine College (Associate Reformed Presbyterian/Indep.)
Grace College (Fellowship of Grace Brethren)
Hellenic College (Greek Orthodox)
Huntington College (In.)(United Brethren in Christ)
Illinois College (United Church of Christ, United Presbyterian/Indep.)
Johnson Bible College (Christian Church)
LeMoyne-Owen College (Tn.) (Baptist, United Church of Christ)
Liberty University (Baptist)
Messiah College (Brethren in Christ)
Morris College (Baptist)
Mount Olive College (Original Free Will Baptist)
North Park College (Evangelical Covenant)
Oakland City College (Baptist)
Olivet College (United Church of Christ, Congregational Church/Indep.)
Pacific Christian College (Christian Churches, Churches of Christ)
Paine College (Christian Methodist Episcopal, United Methodist)
Piedmont College (Congregational Christian Churches)
Principia College (Christian Science/Indep.)
Rocky Mountain College (United Church of Christ, United Methodist, United Presbyterian)
Southwestern College of Christian Ministries (Pentacostal Holiness)
Tougaloo College (Disciples of Christ, United Church of Christ)
Trinity College (Ill.) (Evangelical Free Church)
Urbana College (Swedenborgian)
(Virginia Intermont College (General Baptist Association)
Western Baptist College (Regular Baptist)

The College Selection Index

The College Selection Index is a grid designed to answer four basic questions in the college selection process:

- What kind of education will I receive?
- Can I get in?
- Can I afford it?
- What will it be like when I get there?

The goal of the Index is to enable you to quickly find those schools that meet your individual needs—academically, financially and socially.

Whether you are seeking a small, moderately-priced liberal arts school in rural Pennsylvania or an engineering/technical school located in a major metropolitan area in California, you can begin your search with the College Selection Index. By consulting those variables in the Index that are most critical to you, you will be able to compile a list of schools that meet your personal needs and requirements. Once you have compiled your list, you are ready to consult the text of this book—the college descriptions—to make comparative, in-depth evaluations of the schools you have chosen.

The Index is comprised of more than 40 variables—from location, institutional control and campus setting to type of curriculum, entrance difficulty, average annual cost, size of the undergraduate student body and the characteristics of the students that comprise it.

Since arrangement of the colleges in the Index is alphabetical by state, then by college name within the state, the College Selection Index doubles as a geographical index. The institutional control follows the name of each college.

What Kind of Education Will I Receive?

In this category, colleges are classified by the general type of curriculum they offer. Here, you will be able to locate the business schools, engineering schools, schools of fine arts, liberal arts schools and schools that prepare students for a profession in religion. Multipurpose, multidimensional schools—the major universities—are grouped in the "comprehensive" category. The criteria used to identify the "type of school" is largely based on the types of degrees generally conferred by the colleges.

Can I Get In?

These entrance difficulty levels are drawn from the original Cass & Birnbaum selectivity index. Introduced 30 years ago, the Cass & Birnbaum selectivity index was the first yardstick of its kind to measure the quality of a college's student body. It categorizes colleges according to the academic potential of its students and suggests the difficulty a student may have in being accepted. For more information about the Cass & Birnbaum selectivity index, see the Introduction.

Can I Afford It?

The three fiscal categories (less than $10,000; $10,000 to $20,000; greater than $20,000) reflect the annual tuition and fees only. Figures for room and board are included in the individual college descriptions. Figures are given for in-state tuition and fees. Tuition and fees at public institutions are typically higher for out-of-state students. Consult the individual college descriptions for this information.

The category "> 50% of students receive financial aid" is a barometer of the availability of financial aid. The average amount of financial assistance can be found in the individual college descriptions.

What Will It Be Like When I Get There?

Perhaps no factor is more important to prospective college students than campus environment. Is it a commuter school or do most students live in campus dorms? Are most of the students from in-state or is the student body demographically diverse? Are undergrads mostly male, mostly female or is it a coed school? What is the academic climate like? Is it a Greek school?

The function of this category is to give you insight into each school's community, campus and academic environments.

Campus setting describes the size of community in which the college is located. In most cases, the schools have supplied this information to the editors.

Four ranges are used to gauge the size of the undergraduate enrollment—based on the total number of students enrolled in degree programs in Fall 1993. Included is a "very small" category (under 1,000 students) for students seeking a more personalized campus experience.

Under "campus life," you will be able to identify the parochial schools (where more than 75% of the students are from in-state), the dorm schools (where more than 50% of the students live in college-related housing), the academically serious schools (where more than 20% of the graduates pursue postgraduate work) and the Greek schools (where more than a quarter of the students belong to fraternities or sororities).

Because our objective in presenting the College Selection Index is to simplify the sometimes complicated process of choosing a college, we have made every effort to keep the Index as simple as possible. As such, it should only be used as a starting point for students and their parents in their search for the "right" school.

COLLEGE SELECTION INDEX

	What Kind of Education Will I Receive?						Can I Get In?					Can I Afford It?				What Will It Be Like When I Get There?													
	Type of School						Entrance Difficulty					Average Annual Cost				Campus Setting			Undergrad Enrollment				Student Body			Campus Life			
	Liberal Arts	Business	Engineering/Technical	Fine Arts	Seminary/Bible/Rabbinical/Talmudic	Comprehensive	Most Selective	Highly Selective	Very Selective	Selective	Non-selective	> $20,000	$10,000 to $20,000	< $10,000	> 50% of students receive aid	Urban	Suburban	Rural	Large (< 20,000 students)	Medium (10,000 to 20,000 students)	Small (1,000 to 10,000 students)	Very Small (< 1,000 students)	Coed	Male/Mostly Male (80% or more)	Female/Mostly Female (80% or more)	> 75% of undergrads from in-state	> 50% live in college-related housing	> 20% of grads pursue postgrad work	> 25% belong to fraternity/sorority
Alabama																													
Alabama Agricultural and Mechanical Univ *State*						●					●			●	●		●				●		●						
Alabama State Univ *State*						●					●			●	●		●			●			●				●		
Auburn Univ at Montgomery *State*						●					●			●	●		●				●		●						
Auburn Univ *State*						●			●					●		●				●			●					●	●
Birmingham-Southern Coll *Methodist*	●									●			●		●		●				●		●				●	●	●
Huntingdon Coll *Independent*	●										●			●	●		●					●	●			●	●	●	●
Jacksonville State Univ *State*	●										●			●				●			●		●			●		●	
Judson Coll *Southern Baptist*	●										●			●	●			●				●			●	●	●	●	
Livingston Univ *State*						●					●			●	●			●			●		●						
Miles Coll *Christian Methodist Episcopal*	●										●			●	●		●					●	●						
Oakwood Coll *Seventh-day Adventist*	●										●			●	●		●				●		●				●		
Samford Univ *Southern Baptist*						●					●			●	●		●				●		●				●	●	●
Southeastern Bible Coll *Independent*					●									●	●		●					●	●			●			
Spring Hill Coll *Roman Catholic*	●									●			●		●	●					●		●				●	●	●
Talladega Coll *United Church of Christ*	●										●			●	●			●				●	●				●	●	●
Troy State Univ *State*	●										●			●	●		●				●		●			●			●
Tuskegee Univ *Independent*						●					●			●				●			●		●				●		
Univ of Alabama *State*						●					●			●		●				●			●			●		●	
Univ of Alabama at Birmingham *State*						●					●			●		●				●			●			●		●	
Univ of Alabama in Huntsville *State*						●					●			●		●					●		●			●			
Univ of Mobile *Southern Baptist*	●										●			●	●		●				●		●			●		●	
Univ of Montevallo *State*	●										●			●	●	●					●		●			●		●	●
Univ of North Alabama *State*						●					●			●	●	●					●		●			●			
Univ of South Alabama *State*						●					●			●	●	●				●			●			●			●
Alaska																													
Alaska Pacific Univ *United Methodist*	●										●			●		●					●		●			●	●		

COLLEGE SELECTION INDEX

	What Kind of Education Will I Receive? Type of School						Can I Get In? Entrance Difficulty					Can I Afford It? Average Annual Cost				What Will It Be Like When I Get There? Campus Setting			Undergrad Enrollment				Student Body			Campus Life			
	Liberal Arts	Business	Engineering/Technical	Fine Arts	Seminary/Bible/Rabbinical/Talmudic	Comprehensive	Most Selective	Highly Selective	Very Selective	Selective	Non-selective	> $20,000	$10,000 to $20,000	< $10,000	> 50% of students receive aid	Urban	Suburban	Rural	Large (> 20,000 students)	Medium (10,000 to 20,000 students)	Small (1,000 to 10,000 students)	Very Small (< 1,000 students)	Coed	Male/Mostly Male (80% or more)	Female/Mostly Female (80% or more)	> 75% of undergrads from in-state	> 50% live in college-related housing	> 20% of grads pursue postgrad work	> 25% belong to fraternity/sorority
Alaska (cont.)																													
Sheldon Jackson Coll *Presbyterian*	●										●			●	●			●				●	●				●		
Univ of Alaska, Anchorage *State*						●					●			●		●				●			●			●			
Univ of Alaska, Fairbanks *State*	●										●			●	●	●					●		●			●			
Univ of Alaska, Southeast *State*	●													●			●				●		●			●			
Arizona																													
Arizona State Univ Main Campus *State*						●					●			●			●		●				●						
Grand Canyon Univ *Southern Baptist*	●										●			●	●	●					●		●			●			
Northern Arizona Univ *State*						●					●			●	●			●		●			●			●	●		
Prescott Coll *Independent*	●										●			●	●		●					●	●						
Southwestern Conservative Baptist Bible Coll *Conservative Baptist*					●						●			●	●	●						●	●				●		
Univ of Arizona *State*						●			●					●	●	●				●			●						
Arkansas																													
Arkansas Coll *Presbyterian*	●								●				●		●			●				●	●			●			●
Arkansas State Univ *State*						●					●			●	●	●					●		●			●			
Arkansas Tech Univ *State*	●										●			●	●		●				●		●			●			●
Harding Univ *Church of Christ*	●									●				●	●			●			●		●				●	●	
Henderson State Univ *State*	●										●			●	●			●			●		●			●			
Hendrix Coll *United Methodist*	●								●					●	●		●					●	●			●	●	●	
John Brown Univ *Independent*	●										●			●	●			●				●	●				●		
Ouachita Baptist Univ *Southern Baptist*	●										●			●	●		●				●		●			●	●	●	
Philander Smith Coll *United Methodist*	●										●			●	●	●						●	●			●		●	
Southern Arkansas Univ *State*						●					●			●				●			●		●			●			
Univ of Arkansas, Pine Bluff *State*						●					●			●		●					●		●			●			
Univ of Arkansas at Little Rock *State*						●					●			●	●	●				●			●			●			
Univ of Arkansas at Monticello *State*						●					●			●	●		●				●		●			●	●		
Univ of Arkansas *State*						●					●			●	●	●				●			●			●			●

COLLEGE SELECTION INDEX

	What Kind of Education Will I Receive?						Can I Get In?					Can I Afford It?				What Will It Be Like When I Get There?													
	Type of School: Liberal Arts	Business	Engineering/Technical	Fine Arts	Seminary/Bible/Rabbinical/Talmudic	Comprehensive	Entrance Difficulty: Most Selective	Highly Selective	Very Selective	Selective	Non-selective	Average Annual Cost: > $20,000	$10,000 to $20,000	< $10,000	> 50% of students receive aid	Campus Setting: Urban	Suburban	Rural	Undergrad Enrollment: Large (> 20,000 students)	Medium (10,000 to 20,000 students)	Small (1,000 to 10,000 students)	Very Small (< 1,000 students)	Student Body: Coed	Male/Mostly Male (80% or more)	Female/Mostly Female (80% or more)	Campus Life: > 75% of undergrads from in-state	> 50% live in college-related housing	> 20% of grads pursue postgrad work	> 25% belong to fraternity/sorority
Arkansas (cont.)																													
Univ of Central Arkansas *State*	●										●			●		●		●				●		●			●		
Univ of the Ozarks *Presbyterian Church*	●										●			●	●			●				●	●					●	
Williams Baptist Coll *Southern Baptist*	●										●			●	●			●				●	●			●	●		
California																													
Academy of Art Coll *Independent*				●									●		●	●					●		●				●		
Armstrong Univ *Independent*		●									●		●			●						●	●						
Art Center Coll of Design *Independent*				●									●				●				●		●						
Azusa Pacific Univ *Independent*	●										●		●		●		●				●		●			●			
Bethany Bible Coll *Assemblies of God*					●												●												
Biola Univ *Independent*	●										●		●		●		●				●		●						
California Baptist Coll *Southern Baptist*					●						●		●				●					●	●				●		
California Coll of Arts and Crafts *Independent*				●									●			●					●		●						
California Institute of Technology *Independent*			●				●					●			●		●				●		●				●	●	
California Institute of the Arts *Independent*				●																									
California Lutheran Coll *Lutheran*	●										●		●		●		●				●		●			●	●	●	
California Lutheran Univ *Lutheran*	●										●									●			●			●	●	●	
California Maritime Academy *State*			●								●			●	●		●					●		●		●	●		
California Polytechnic State Univ/San Luis Obispo *State*						●				●				●			●			●			●			●			
California State Polytechnic Univ/Pomona *State*			●							●				●			●			●			●			●		●	
Chapman Univ *Disciples of Christ*	●										●	●			●		●				●		●						●
Christian Heritage Coll *Baptist*	●												●		●		●					●	●				●		
Claremont McKenna Coll *Independent*	●							●				●			●		●					●	●				●	●	
Cogswell Polytechnical Coll *Independent*			●								●			●			●					●		●		●			
Coll of Notre Dame *Independent*	●										●		●		●		●					●	●			●		●	
Concordia Univ, California *Independent (Lutheran-Missouri Synod)*	●										●		●		●		●					●	●			●	●		
CSC/Bakersfield *State*	●	●								●				●		●					●		●			●			

COLLEGE SELECTION INDEX

	What Kind of Education Will I Receive?						Can I Get In?					Can I Afford It?				What Will It Be Like When I Get There?													
	Type of School						Entrance Difficulty					Average Annual Cost				Campus Setting			Undergrad Enrollment				Student Body			Campus Life			
	Liberal Arts	Business	Engineering/Technical	Fine Arts	Seminary/Bible/Rabbinical/Talmudic	Comprehensive	Most Selective	Highly Selective	Very Selective	Selective	Non-selective	> $20,000	$10,000 to $20,000	< $10,000	> 50% of students receive aid	Urban	Suburban	Rural	Large (> 20,000 students)	Medium (10,000 to 20,000 students)	Small (1,000 to 10,000 students)	Very Small (< 1,000 students)	Coed	Male/Mostly Male (80% or more)	Female/Mostly Female (80% or more)	> 75% of undergrads from in-state	> 50% live in college-related housing	> 20% of grads pursue postgrad work	> 25% belong to fraternity/sorority
California (cont.)																													
CSC/San Bernardino *State*						●				●				●			●				●		●			●			
CSC/Stanislaus *State*						●				●				●				●			●		●			●		●	
CSU/Chico *State*						●				●				●	●		●			●			●			●			
CSU/Dominguez Hills *State*						●				●				●		●					●		●						
CSU/Fresno *State*	●									●				●			●			●			●			●			
CSU/Fullerton *State*						●				●			●			●					●		●			●			
CSU/Hayward *State*						●				●				●			●			●			●			●			
CSU/Long Beach *State*						●				●				●			●		●				●						
CSU/Los Angeles *State*						●				●				●		●				●			●			●			
CSU/Northridge *State*						●				●				●			●		●				●			●			
CSU/Sacramento *State*						●				●				●		●				●			●			●			
CSU/San Bernardino *State*	●									●				●			●			●			●						
CSU/San Diego State Univ *State*						●				●				●			●		●				●			●			
CSU/San Francisco State Univ *State*						●				●				●		●				●			●			●			
CSU/San Jose State Univ *State*	●									●				●		●				●			●			●			
CSU/Sonoma State Univ *State*	●									●				●			●				●		●			●			
CSU/Stanislaus *State*	●	●				●				●				●				●			●		●			●		●	
Dominican Coll of San Rafael *Independent*	●	●									●		●		●		●					●	●			●			
Fresno Pacific Coll *Mennonite Brethren*	●										●			●	●	●						●	●			●	●		
Fresno State Coll *State*																													
Golden Gate Univ *Independent*		●									●			●		●						●	●			●			
Harvey Mudd Coll *Independent*			●				●						●		●		●					●	●				●	●	
Holy Names Coll *Independent*	●										●		●		●		●					●	●					●	
Humboldt State Univ *State*	●									●				●			●				●		●			●			
Humphreys Coll *Independent*		●												●	●		●					●			●				
John F. Kennedy Univ *Independent*	●	●												●			●					●	●						

COLLEGE SELECTION INDEX

California (cont.)

College	What Kind of Education Will I Receive?						Can I Get In?					Can I Afford It?				What Will It Be Like When I Get There?													
	Type of School						Entrance Difficulty					Average Annual Cost				Campus Setting			Undergrad Enrollment				Student Body			Campus Life			
	Liberal Arts	Business	Engineering/Technical	Fine Arts	Seminary/Bible/Rabbinical/Talmudic	Comprehensive	Most Selective	Highly Selective	Very Selective	Selective	Non-selective	> $20,000	$10,000 to $20,000	< $10,000	> 50% of students receive aid	Urban	Suburban	Rural	Large (> 20,000 students)	Medium (10,000 to 20,000 students)	Small (1,000 to 10,000 students)	Very Small (< 1,000 students)	Coed	Male/Mostly Male (80% or more)	Female/Mostly Female (80% or more)	> 50% live in college-related housing	> 75% of undergrads from in-state	> 20% of grads pursue postgrad work	> 25% belong to fraternity/sorority
Loma Linda Univ *Seventh-day Adventist*	●					●					●			●	●	●						●	●						
Louise Salinger Academy of Fashion *Independent*													●			●						●	●						
Loyola Marymount Univ *Independent*						●				●			●		●		●				●		●			●			
Menlo Coll *Independent*	●										●		●				●					●	●				●		
Mills Coll *Independent*	●								●				●		●	●						●			●		●		
Mount St. Mary's Coll *Independent*	●										●		●		●	●						●			●	●	●		
National Univ *Independent*	●										●			●		●					●		●						
New Coll of California *Independent*	●										●			●	●	●					●		●			●			
Occidental Coll *Independent*	●							●					●		●	●					●		●				●	●	
Pacific Christian Coll *Christian Churches, Churches of Christ*	●										●			●	●	●						●	●				●	●	
Pacific Union Coll *Seventh-day Adventist*						●					●		●		●			●				●	●			●	●		
Patten College *Independent*	●													●	●	●						●	●			●		●	
Pepperdine Univ *Independent*	●								●				●		●		●				●		●				●	●	●
Pitzer Coll *Independent*	●							●					●		●		●					●	●				●	●	
Point Loma Nazarene Coll *Nazarene*	●										●			●	●	●					●		●			●	●		
Pomona Coll *Independent*	●						●						●		●		●				●		●				●	●	
Sacramento State Coll *State*																													
Saint John's Coll *Roman Catholic*					●									●	●		●					●		●		●	●	●	
Saint Joseph's Coll Seminary *Roman Catholic*	●																							●					
Saint Mary's Coll of California *Roman Catholic*	●									●			●		●		●				●		●			●	●	●	
San Diego State Univ *State*																													
San Francisco Art Institute *Independent*				●																									
San Francisco Conservatory of Music *Independent*				●																									
Santa Clara Univ *Independent*						●			●				●		●		●				●		●				●	●	●
Scripps Coll *Independent*						●				●			●				●					●			●		●	●	
Simpson Coll *Christian and Missionary Alliance*	●																												

COLLEGE SELECTION INDEX

	What Kind of Education Will I Receive?						Can I Get In?					Can I Afford It?				What Will It Be Like When I Get There?													
	Type of School						Entrance Difficulty					Average Annual Cost				Campus Setting			Undergrad Enrollment				Student Body			Campus Life			
	Liberal Arts	Business	Engineering/Technical	Fine Arts	Seminary/Bible/Rabbinical/Talmudic	Comprehensive	Most Selective	Highly Selective	Very Selective	Selective	Non-selective	> $20,000	$10,000 to $20,000	< $10,000	> 50% of students receive aid	Urban	Suburban	Rural	Large (> 20,000 students)	Medium (10,000 to 20,000 students)	Small (1,000 to 10,000 students)	Very Small (< 1,000 students)	Coed	Male/Mostly Male (80% or more)	Female/Mostly Female (80% or more)	> 75% of undergrads from in-state	> 50% live in college-related housing	> 20% of grads pursue postgrad work	> 25% belong to fraternity/sorority
California (cont.)																													
Southern California Coll *Assemblies of God*	•										•			•	•	•						•	•			•	•		
Stanford Univ *Independent*						•	•						•		•		•				•		•				•	•	•
Thomas Aquinas Coll *Roman Catholic*	•										•		•		•			•				•	•				•	•	
UC/Berkeley *State*									•					•	•	•			•				•			•		•	
UC/Davis *State*						•			•					•	•		•			•			•			•		•	
UC/Irvine *State*	•								•					•		•				•			•			•		•	
UC/Los Angeles *State*						•			•					•		•			•				•			•		•	
UC/Riverside *State*	•					•			•					•			•				•		•			•		•	
UC/San Diego *State*	•								•					•			•			•			•			•		•	
UC/Santa Barbara *State*	•								•					•			•			•			•			•	•	•	•
UC/Santa Cruz *State*	•								•					•	•		•			•		•			•		•		
United States International Univ *Independent*	•								•		•		•		•		•				•		•			•	•		
Univ of Judaism *Conservative Jewish*	•													•	•		•					•	•				•	•	
Univ of La Verne *Independent*	•	•									•		•		•		•				•		•			•			
Univ of Redlands *Independent*						•			•				•		•		•				•		•				•		
University of San Diego *Independent*						•				•			•		•	•					•		•					•	•
Univ of San Francisco *Roman Catholic*	•										•		•		•	•					•		•				•	•	
Univ of Southern California *Independent*						•				•			•		•	•				•			•				•		•
Univ of the Pacific *Independent*						•				•			•		•		•				•		•			•	•	•	•
West Coast Univ *Independent*		•									•			•		•					•		•			•			
Westmont Coll *Independent*	•									•			•		•		•				•		•			•	•	•	
Whittier Coll *Independent*	•									•			•		•		•				•		•				•	•	•
Woodbury Univ *Independent*		•										•		•		•	•						•	•			•		
Colorado																													
Adams State Coll *State*	•									•				•	•		•				•		•			•			
Beth-El Coll of Nursing *Independent*														•	•	•						•			•	•			

COLLEGE SELECTION INDEX

	What Kind of Education Will I Receive? — Type of School						Can I Get In? — Entrance Difficulty					Can I Afford It? — Average Annual Cost				What Will It Be Like When I Get There? — Campus Setting			Undergrad Enrollment				Student Body			Campus Life			
	Liberal Arts	Business	Engineering/Technical	Fine Arts	Seminary/Bible/Rabbinical/Talmudic	Comprehensive	Most Selective	Highly Selective	Very Selective	Selective	Non-selective	> $20,000	$10,000 to $20,000	< $10,000	> 50% of students receive aid	Urban	Suburban	Rural	Large (< 20,000 students)	Medium (10,000 to 20,000 students)	Small (1,000 to 10,000 students)	Very Small (< 1,000 students)	Coed	Male/Mostly Male (80% or more)	Female/Mostly Female (80% or more)	> 75% of undergrads from in-state	> 50% live in college-related housing	> 20% of grads pursue postgrad work	> 25% belong to fraternity/sorority
Colorado (cont.)																													
Colorado Coll *Independent*	●											●			●	●					●		●				●	●	●
Colorado School of Mines *State*			●					●						●	●		●				●		●					●	●
Colorado State Univ *State*						●				●				●			●			●			●			●			
Colorado Technical Coll *Independent*			●								●			●			●				●			●		●			
Fort Lewis Coll *State*	●										●			●	●			●			●		●					●	
Mesa State Coll *State*	●										●			●	●	●					●		●			●			
Metropolitan State Coll *State*						●					●			●	●	●					●		●			●			
Regis Univ *Roman Catholic*	●										●		●		●		●				●	●	●				●		
United States Air Force Academy *Federal*			●						●						●		●				●		●				●		
Univ of Colorado, Colorado Springs *State*						●				●				●		●					●		●			●			
Univ of Colorado, Denver *State*	●	●	●	●		●				●				●		●					●		●			●		●	
Univ of Colorado at Boulder *State*						●			●					●	●		●			●			●					●	●
Univ of Denver *Independent*						●				●			●		●	●					●		●				●	●	●
Univ of Northern Colorado *State*						●					●			●	●		●				●		●			●			
Univ of Southern Colorado *State*	●		●								●			●	●		●				●		●			●			
Western State Coll of Colorado *State*	●										●			●	●			●			●		●						
Connecticut																													
Albertus Magnus Coll *Roman Catholic*	●										●		●		●		●					●	●				●	●	
Bridgeport Engineering Institute *Independent*			●								●			●		●						●	●						
Central Connecticut State Univ *State*						●					●			●			●			●			●			●			
Charter Oak State Coll *State*	●																●				●		●			●			
Connecticut Coll *Independent*	●							●					●		●		●				●		●				●	●	
Eastern Connecticut State Univ *State*						●					●			●	●		●				●		●			●	●	●	
Fairfield Univ *Independent*						●			●				●		●		●				●		●				●		
Holy Apostles Coll *Roman Catholic*	●										●			●			●					●		●					
Quinnipiac Coll *Independent*	●	●								●			●		●		●				●		●				●	●	

COLLEGE SELECTION INDEX

	What Kind of Education Will I Receive?						Can I Get In?					Can I Afford It?				What Will It Be Like When I Get There?													
	Type of School						Entrance Difficulty					Average Annual Cost				Campus Setting			Undergrad Enrollment				Student Body			Campus Life			
	Liberal Arts	Business	Engineering/Technical	Fine Arts	Seminary/Bible/Rabbinical/Talmudic	Comprehensive	Most Selective	Highly Selective	Very Selective	Selective	Non-selective	> $20,000	$10,000 to $20,000	< $10,000	> 50% of students receive aid	Urban	Suburban	Rural	Large (> 20,000 students)	Medium (10,000 to 20,000 students)	Small (1,000 to 10,000 students)	Very Small (< 1,000 students)	Coed	Male/Mostly Male (80% or more)	Female/Mostly Female (80% or more)	> 75% of undergrads from in-state	> 50% live in college-related housing	> 20% of grads pursue postgrad work	> 25% belong to fraternity/sorority
Connecticut (cont.)																													
Sacred Heart Univ *Roman Catholic*						●					●		●		●		●				●		●				●	●	
Saint Joseph Coll *Independent*	●									●			●		●		●					●			●		●		
Southern Connecticut State Univ *State*	●										●			●		●					●		●			●			
Teikyo Post Coll *Independent*	●										●		●		●		●					●	●						
Trinity Coll *Independent*	●							●					●		●	●					●		●				●		●
United States Coast Guard Academy *Federal*			●						●						●		●					●	●				●		
Univ of Bridgeport *Independent*						●					●		●		●	●						●	●				●	●	
Univ of Connecticut *State*						●				●				●				●		●			●			●	●		
Univ of Hartford *Independent*						●					●		●		●		●				●		●						
Univ of New Haven *Independent*	●		●								●		●		●		●				●		●						
Wesleyan Univ *Independent*	●						●						●		●			●			●		●				●		
Western Connecticut State Univ *State*	●										●			●	●		●				●		●			●	●	●	
Yale Univ *Independent*	●						●							●	●	●					●		●				●	●	
Delaware																													
Delaware State Univ *State*						●					●			●		●					●		●				●		●
Goldey Beacom Coll *Independent*		●									●			●		●					●		●						
Univ of Delaware *State*						●			●					●	●		●			●			●						
Wesley Coll *United Methodist*		●									●			●	●	●						●	●				●		
Wilmington Coll *Independent*						●					●			●		●						●	●			●		●	
District of Columbia																													
American Univ *Independent*	●							●				●			●		●				●		●				●	●	●
Catholic Univ of America *Independent*	●								●				●		●	●					●		●				●	●	
Corcoran School of Art *Independent*				●												●													
Gallaudet Coll *Independent*	●										●			●		●					●		●				●	●	●
George Washington Univ *Independent*						●		●					●		●	●					●		●				●	●	●
Georgetown Univ *Roman Catholic*	●						●						●		●	●					●		●				●	●	

COLLEGE SELECTION INDEX

	What Kind of Education Will I Receive?						Can I Get In?					Can I Afford It?				What Will It Be Like When I Get There?													
	Type of School						Entrance Difficulty					Average Annual Cost				Campus Setting			Undergrad Enrollment				Student Body			Campus Life			
	Liberal Arts	Business	Engineering/Technical	Fine Arts	Seminary/Bible/Rabbinical/Talmudic	Comprehensive	Most Selective	Highly Selective	Very Selective	Selective	Non-selective	> $20,000	$10,000 to $20,000	< $10,000	> 50% of students receive aid	Urban	Suburban	Rural	Large (> 20,000 students)	Medium (10,000 to 20,000 students)	Small (1,000 to 10,000 students)	Very Small (< 1,000 students)	Coed	Male/Mostly Male (80% or more)	Female/Mostly Female (80% or more)	> 75% of undergrads from in-state	> 50% live in college-related housing	> 20% of grads pursue postgrad work	> 25% belong to fraternity/sorority
District of Columbia (cont.)																													
Howard Univ *National and Independent*	●										●			●	●	●					●		●					●	
Mount Vernon Coll *Independent*	●										●		●			●						●			●		●		
Southeastern Univ *Independent*	●										●			●		●						●	●						
Trinity Coll *Roman Catholic*	●									●			●				●					●			●		●		
Univ of the District of Columbia *Municipal*	●					●					●			●		●					●		●			●			
Florida																													
Barry Univ *Roman Catholic*	●										●		●		●		●				●		●						
Bethune-Cookman Coll *United Methodist*	●										●			●	●	●					●		●			●	●	●	
Eckerd Coll *Independent*	●								●				●		●		●				●		●				●	●	
Edward Waters Coll *African Methodist Episcopal*	●	●				●					●			●		●						●	●			●			
Flagler Coll *Independent*	●										●			●	●		●				●		●				●		
Florida Agricultural and Mechanical Univ *State*			●								●			●	●		●				●		●						
Florida Baptist Theological Coll *Southern Baptist*					●									●	●			●				●		●				●	
Florida Bible Coll *Independent*					●									●				●				●	●			●			
Florida Christian Coll *Churches of Christ*					●									●			●					●	●			●			
Florida Institute of Technology *Independent*			●			●			●				●		●		●				●		●				●		
Florida Memorial Coll *American Baptist*	●										●			●		●					●		●						
Florida Southern Coll *United Methodist*	●										●			●			●				●		●			●	●	●	●
Florida State Univ *State*						●			●					●		●				●			●			●		●	●
Hobe Sound Bible Coll *Independent*					●									●	●		●					●	●				●		
Jacksonville Univ *Independent*						●					●		●		●		●				●		●						●
New Coll of the Univ of South Florida *Independent/State*	●							●						●	●	●						●	●				●	●	
Nova Univ *Independent*						●					●			●	●		●				●		●					●	
Palm Beach Atlantic Coll *Southern Baptist*	●										●			●	●	●					●		●					●	
Ringling School of Art *Independent*				●																									
Rollins Coll *Independent*	●								●				●		●		●				●		●					●	●

COLLEGE SELECTION INDEX

	What Kind of Education Will I Receive?						Can I Get In?					Can I Afford It?				What Will It Be Like When I Get There?													
	Type of School						Entrance Difficulty					Average Annual Cost				Campus Setting			Undergrad Enrollment				Student Body			Campus Life			
	Liberal Arts	Business	Engineering/Technical	Fine Arts	Seminary/Bible/Rabbinical/Talmudic	Comprehensive	Most Selective	Highly Selective	Very Selective	Selective	Non-selective	> $20,000	$10,000 to $20,000	< $10,000	> 50% of students receive aid	Urban	Suburban	Rural	Large (> 20,000 students)	Medium (10,000 to 20,000 students)	Small (1,000 to 10,000 students)	Very Small (< 1,000 students)	Coed	Male/Mostly Male (80% or more)	Female/Mostly Female (80% or more)	> 75% of undergrads from in-state	> 50% live in college-related housing	> 20% of grads pursue postgrad work	> 25% belong to fraternity/sorority
Florida (cont.)																													
Rollins Coll *Independent*	•								•				•		•		•				•		•					•	•
Saint Leo Coll *Independent*	•										•			•	•			•			•		•				•		•
Southeastern Coll of the Assemblies of God *Assemblies of God*					•						•			•	•		•				•		•				•	•	
Stetson Univ *Southern Baptist*	•			•					•				•		•		•				•		•			•	•	•	•
Univ of Central Florida *State*						•				•				•			•			•			•			•			
Univ of Florida *State*						•			•					•	•		•		•				•			•			•
Univ of Miami *Independent*						•			•				•		•		•				•		•					•	•
Univ of South Florida *State*						•					•			•		•				•			•			•			
Univ of Tampa *Independent*	•										•		•			•					•		•				•		•
Warner Southern Coll *Church of God*	•										•			•	•			•				•	•			•		•	
Webber Coll *Independent*		•									•			•	•														
Georgia																													
Agnes Scott Coll *Independent*	•								•				•		•	•						•			•		•	•	
Albany State Coll *State*	•										•			•	•	•					•		•			•			•
Armstrong State Coll *State*	•										•			•		•					•		•			•			
Atlanta Coll of Art *Independent*				•						•			•			•						•	•						
Atlanta Univ Center *State*						•																							
Augusta Coll *State*	•										•			•		•					•		•						
Berry Coll *Independent*	•									•			•		•			•			•		•			•	•	•	
Brenau Univ *Independent*						•					•		•		•		•				•				•	•	•	•	•
Clark Atlanta Univ *United Methodist*	•										•			•		•					•		•				•		•
Clayton State Coll *State*	•													•			•				•		•			•			
Columbus Coll *State*	•										•			•		•					•		•			•			
Covenant Coll *Reformed Presbyterian*	•									•				•	•			•				•	•				•		
Emory Univ *United Methodist*	•	•							•				•		•		•				•		•				•	•	•
Fort Valley State Coll *State*						•					•			•	•			•			•		•			•	•		

COLLEGE SELECTION INDEX

	What Kind of Education Will I Receive?						Can I Get In?					Can I Afford It?				What Will It Be Like When I Get There?													
	Type of School						Entrance Difficulty					Average Annual Cost				Campus Setting			Undergrad Enrollment				Student Body			Campus Life			
Georgia (cont.)	Liberal Arts	Business	Engineering/Technical	Fine Arts	Seminary/Bible/Rabbinical/Talmudic	Comprehensive	Most Selective	Highly Selective	Very Selective	Selective	Non-selective	> $20,000	$10,000 to $20,000	< $10,000	> 50% of students receive aid	Urban	Suburban	Rural	Large (> 20,000 students)	Medium (10,000 to 20,000 students)	Small (1,000 to 10,000 students)	Very Small (< 1,000 students)	Coed	Male/Mostly Male (80% or more)	Female/Mostly Female (80% or more)	> 75% of undergrads from in-state	> 50% live in college-related housing	> 20% of grads pursue postgrad work	> 25% belong to fraternity/sorority
Georgia Coll *State*	●	●				●					●			●		●					●		●			●			●
Georgia Institute of Technology *State*			●						●					●	●	●					●		●						●
Georgia Southern Coll *State*	●										●			●	●		●				●		●			●	●		
Georgia Southwestern Coll *State*						●					●			●		●				●			●			●		●	●
Georgia State Univ *State*						●				●				●		●				●			●			●		●	●
Kennesaw State Coll *State*	●	●									●			●			●				●		●			●			
Lagrange Coll *United Methodist*	●										●			●	●		●					●	●			●		●	●
Life Coll *Independent*	●													●			●				●		●						
Medical Coll of Georgia *State*														●	●	●						●			●				
Mercer Univ Atlanta *Southern Baptist*	●										●			●		●						●	●						
Mercer Univ *Southern Baptist*						●					●		●		●	●					●		●				●		●
Morehouse Coll *Independent*	●										●			●	●	●					●			●			●		
Morris Brown Coll *African Methodist Episcopal*	●										●			●	●	●					●		●				●		
North Georgia Coll *State*	●										●			●	●			●			●		●			●		●	●
Oglethorpe Univ *Independent*	●								●				●		●		●					●	●				●	●	●
Paine Coll *United Methodist, Christian Methodist Episcopal*	●										●			●	●	●						●	●			●	●	●	
Piedmont Coll *Congregational Christian Churches*	●										●			●	●			●				●	●			●			
Savannah State Coll *State*						●					●			●	●	●					●		●			●			
Shorter Coll *Southern Baptist*	●										●			●	●		●				●		●			●	●	●	●
Southern Coll of Technology *State*			●								●			●			●				●		●			●			
Spelman Coll *Independent*	●										●			●	●	●					●		●			●	●		
Thomas Coll *Independent*	●										●			●			●					●	●			●			
Toccoa Falls Coll *Independent*					●						●			●	●			●				●	●				●	●	
Univ of Georgia *State*						●			●					●	●	●				●			●			●			●
Valdosta State Coll *State*	●										●			●	●	●					●		●			●			
Wesleyan Coll *Independent*	●										●		●		●		●					●			●		●	●	

COLLEGE SELECTION INDEX

	What Kind of Education Will I Receive? Type of School						Can I Get In? Entrance Difficulty					Can I Afford It? Average Annual Cost				What Will It Be Like When I Get There? Campus Setting			Undergrad Enrollment				Student Body			Campus Life			
	Liberal Arts	Business	Engineering/Technical	Fine Arts	Seminary/Bible/Rabbinical/Talmudic	Comprehensive	Most Selective	Highly Selective	Very Selective	Selective	Non-selective	> $20,000	$10,000 to $20,000	< $10,000	> 50% of students receive aid	Urban	Suburban	Rural	Large (< 20,000 students)	Medium (10,000 to 20,000 students)	Small (1,000 to 10,000 students)	Very Small (< 1,000 students)	Coed	Male/Mostly Male (80% or more)	Female/Mostly Female (80% or more)	> 75% of undergrads from in-state	> 50% live in college-related housing	> 20% of grads pursue postgrad work	> 25% belong to fraternity/sorority
Georgia (cont.)																													
West Georgia Coll *State*	●										●			●				●			●		●			●			●
Hawaii																													
Brigham Young Univ—Hawaii Campus *Latter-Day Saints*	●										●			●	●			●			●		●				●		
Chaminade Univ of Honolulu *Roman Catholic*						●					●		●		●		●				●		●						
Hawaii Pacific Univ *Independent*						●					●			●		●	●				●		●					●	
Univ of Hawaii at Hilo *State*						●					●			●			●				●		●			●			
Univ of Hawaii at Manoa *State*						●					●			●		●				●			●			●			
Idaho																													
Albertson Coll *Independent*	●												●		●		●					●	●			●	●	●	●
Boise State Univ *State*	●										●			●		●				●			●			●			
Idaho State Univ *State*						●					●			●	●			●			●		●			●			
Lewis-Clark State Coll *State*	●										●			●	●		●				●		●						
Northwest Nazarene Coll *Nazarene*	●	●		●	●	●					●			●	●	●					●		●				●		
Univ of Idaho *State*						●				●				●	●			●			●		●					●	●
Illinois																													
American Conservatory of Music *Independent*				●												●						●	●						
Augustana Coll *Lutheran*	●								●				●		●	●					●		●			●	●	●	●
Aurora Univ *Independent*	●										●		●		●		●				●		●			●			
Barat Coll *Independent*						●					●		●		●	●		●					●	●			●	●	●
Blackburn Coll *Presbyterian*	●										●			●	●		●					●	●						
Bradley Univ *Independent*						●				●			●		●	●					●		●			●			●
Chicago State Univ *State*	●					●					●			●		●					●		●						
Coll of St. Francis *Roman Catholic*						●					●			●	●		●					●	●			●	●		
Columbia Coll *Independent*						●					●		●		●	●	●				●		●		●	●			
Concordia Univ, Illinois *Lutheran-Missouri Synod*	●										●			●			●				●		●				●	●	
DePaul Univ *Roman Catholic*						●				●			●			●					●		●			●	●		

COLLEGE SELECTION INDEX

	What Kind of Education Will I Receive? Type of School						Can I Get In? Entrance Difficulty					Can I Afford It? Average Annual Cost				What Will It Be Like When I Get There? Campus Setting			Undergrad Enrollment				Student Body			Campus Life			
	Liberal Arts	Business	Engineering/Technical	Fine Arts	Seminary/Bible/Rabbinical/Talmudic	Comprehensive	Most Selective	Highly Selective	Very Selective	Selective	Non-selective	> $20,000	$10,000 to $20,000	< $10,000	> 50% of students receive aid	Urban	Suburban	Rural	Large (> 20,000 students)	Medium (10,000 to 20,000 students)	Small (1,000 to 10,000 students)	Very Small (< 1,000 students)	Coed	Male/Mostly Male (80% or more)	Female/Mostly Female (80% or more)	> 75% of undergrads from in-state	> 50% live in college-related housing	> 20% of grads pursue postgrad work	> 25% belong to fraternity/sorority
Illinois (cont.)																													
Eastern Illinois Univ *State*						●					●			●	●			●			●		●			●	●		●
Elmhurst Coll *United Church of Christ, 1871*						●					●			●	●		●				●		●			●			●
Eureka Coll *Disciples of Christ*	●										●		●		●			●				●	●			●	●		●
Greenville Coll *Independent*	●										●			●	●			●				●	●						
Illinois Benedictine Coll *Roman Catholic*	●									●			●		●		●				●		●			●			
Illinois Coll *Independent*	●									●				●	●	●						●	●			●	●		
Illinois Institute of Technology *Independent*			●						●				●		●	●					●		●			●	●	●	●
Illinois State Univ *State*						●					●			●				●		●			●			●	●		
Illinois Wesleyan Univ *Independent*	●			●					●				●		●	●					●		●			●	●	●	●
Intl. Academy of Merchandising and Design *Independent*														●		●						●			●	●			
Judson Coll *American Baptist*	●										●			●	●		●					●	●				●	●	
Kendall Coll *Methodist*	●	●									●			●	●		●					●	●			●			
Knox Coll *Independent*	●								●				●		●			●			●		●				●	●	●
Lake Forest Coll *Independent*	●								●				●		●		●					●	●				●	●	●
Lewis Univ *Roman Catholic*						●					●		●		●		●				●		●			●		●	●
Loyola Univ of Chicago *Roman Catholic*						●			●				●		●	●					●		●			●			
MacMurray Coll *Independent*	●										●			●	●		●					●	●			●	●		
McKendree Coll *United Methodist*	●										●			●	●			●				●	●			●			●
Millikin Univ *Presbyterian Church*	●	●		●					●				●		●	●					●		●			●	●	●	●
Monmouth Coll *Presbyterian Church*	●									●			●		●			●				●	●			●	●	●	●
Moody Bible Institute *Independent*					●									●		●					●		●			●			
National Louis Univ *Indpendent*						●					●			●	●		●				●		●			●		●	
North Central Coll *United Methodist*						●			●				●		●		●				●		●			●	●	●	
North Park Coll *Evangelical Covenant*	●									●			●		●	●						●	●				●	●	
Northeastern Illinois Univ *State*						●					●			●	●	●					●		●			●			
Northern Illinois Univ *State*	●		●	●		●					●			●	●			●		●			●			●	●		●

COLLEGE SELECTION INDEX

	What Kind of Education Will I Receive?						Can I Get In?					Can I Afford It?				What Will It Be Like When I Get There?													
	Type of School						Entrance Difficulty					Average Annual Cost				Campus Setting			Undergrad Enrollment				Student Body			Campus Life			
	Liberal Arts	Business	Engineering/Technical	Fine Arts	Seminary/Bible/Rabbinical/Talmudic	Comprehensive	Most Selective	Highly Selective	Very Selective	Selective	Non-selective	> $20,000	$10,000 to $20,000	< $10,000	> 50% of students receive aid	Urban	Suburban	Rural	Large (> 20,000 students)	Medium (10,000 to 20,000 students)	Small (1,000 to 10,000 students)	Very Small (< 1,000 students)	Coed	Male/Mostly Male (80% or more)	Female/Mostly Female (80% or more)	> 75% of undergrads from in-state	> 50% live in college-related housing	> 20% of grads pursue postgrad work	> 25% belong to fraternity/sorority
Illinois (cont.)																													
Northwestern Univ *Independent*						●		●					●		●	●	●			●			●				●	●	●
Olivet Nazarene Coll *Church of the Nazarene*	●										●			●	●	●					●		●				●	●	
Parks Coll of St. Louis Univ *Roman Catholic*			●								●			●	●		●				●			●			●	●	●
Principia Coll *Independent*	●								●				●		●			●				●	●				●		
Quincy Univ *Independent*	●								●					●	●	●					●		●				●	●	
Rockford Coll *Independent*	●										●		●		●	●						●	●			●	●		
Rockford Coll *Independent*	●										●		●		●	●						●	●			●	●		
Roosevelt Univ *Independent*	●										●			●	●	●					●		●			●			
Roosevelt Univ *Independent*	●										●			●	●	●					●		●			●			
Rosary Coll *Roman Catholic*	●									●			●		●		●					●	●			●			
Saint Xavier Univ *Roman Catholic*	●										●		●		●	●					●		●						
School of the Art Institute of Chicago *Independent*				●									●		●	●					●		●						
Shimer Coll *Independent*	●										●		●		●		●					●	●						
Southern Illinois Univ at Carbondale *State*						●					●			●	●			●		●			●			●	●	●	
Southern Illinois Univ/Edwardsville *State*						●					●			●	●		●				●		●			●			
Spertus Coll of Judaica *Independent*					●																								
Trinity Christian Coll *Christian, Reformed*	●										●			●			●					●	●				●		
Trinity Coll *Independent*	●										●			●	●		●					●	●				●		
Univ of Chicago *Independent*						●	●					●			●	●					●		●				●	●	
Univ of Illinois at Chicago *State*						●					●			●	●	●				●			●			●		●	
Univ of Illinois at Urbana-Champaign *State*						●	●							●	●		●		●				●			●		●	●
Vandercook Coll of Music *Independent*					●										●		●						●	●					
Western Illinois Univ *State*							●					●			●	●			●			●		●			●	●	●
Wheaton Coll *Independent*		●								●				●		●		●				●		●				●	●
Indiana																													
Anderson Univ *Church of God*						●					●		●		●	●					●		●				●	●	

COLLEGE SELECTION INDEX

Indiana (cont.)

College	Liberal Arts	Business	Engineering/Technical	Fine Arts	Seminary/Bible/Rabbinical/Talmudic	Comprehensive	Most Selective	Highly Selective	Very Selective	Selective	Non-selective	> $20,000	$10,000 to $20,000	< $10,000	> 50% of students receive aid	Urban	Suburban	Rural	Large (> 20,000 students)	Medium (10,000 to 20,000 students)	Small (1,000 to 10,000 students)	Very Small (< 1,000 students)	Coed	Male/Mostly Male (80% or more)	Female/Mostly Female (80% or more)	> 75% of undergrads from in-state	> 50% live in college-related housing	> 20% of grads pursue postgrad work	> 25% belong to fraternity/sorority
	What Kind of Education Will I Receive? Type of School						**Can I Get In?** Entrance Difficulty					**Can I Afford It?** Average Annual Cost				**What Will It Be Like When I Get There?** Campus Setting			Undergrad Enrollment				Student Body			Campus Life			
Ball State Univ *State*						●					●			●	●		●			●			●			●			●
Bethel Coll *Missionary*	●										●		●		●		●				●		●			●			
Butler Univ *Independent*	●								●				●		●		●				●		●			●	●		●
Calumet Coll of Saint Joseph *Roman Catholic*	●										●			●	●	●						●	●						
DePauw Univ *Independent*	●								●				●		●			●			●		●				●	●	●
Earlham Coll *Society of Friends*	●								●				●		●		●				●		●				●		
Franklin Coll of Indiana *Independent*	●										●		●		●		●					●	●			●	●		●
Goshen Coll *Mennonite*	●									●				●	●			●				●	●				●	●	
Grace Coll *Grace Brethen*	●										●			●	●			●				●	●				●		
Hanover Coll *Independent*	●								●					●	●			●			●		●				●	●	●
Huntington Coll *United Brethen*	●				●						●			●	●			●				●	●				●	●	
Indiana Institute of Technology *Independent*		●	●								●			●		●						●	●				●	●	
Indiana State Univ *State*						●					●			●	●	●					●		●			●		●	●
Indiana Univ at Kokomo *State*	●										●			●		●					●		●			●			
Indiana Univ at South Bend *State*	●										●			●		●					●		●			●			
Indiana Univ Bloomington *State*	●									●				●	●		●		●				●				●		
Indiana Univ East *State*	●										●			●	●	●					●		●			●			
Indiana Univ Northwest *State*	●										●			●		●					●		●			●			
Indiana Univ Southeast *State*	●										●			●			●				●		●			●			
Indiana Univ—Purdue Univ at Fort Wayne *State*						●					●			●	●		●				●		●			●			
Indiana Univ—Purdue Univ at Indianapolis *State*						●					●			●		●					●		●			●			
Indiana Wesleyan Univ *Wesleyan*	●										●			●	●		●					●	●			●			
Manchester Coll *Church of the Brethen*	●										●			●	●			●			●		●			●	●		
Marian Coll *Roman Catholic*	●										●			●	●	●						●	●			●			
Martin Univ *Independent*	●										●			●	●	●						●	●			●		●	
Oakland City Coll *Baptist*	●										●			●	●			●				●	●			●	●		

COLLEGE SELECTION INDEX

What Kind of Education Will I Receive? · Can I Get In? · Can I Afford It? · What Will It Be Like When I Get There?

	Type of School						Entrance Difficulty					Average Annual Cost				Campus Setting			Undergrad Enrollment				Student Body			Campus Life			
	Liberal Arts	Business	Engineering/Technical	Fine Arts	Seminary/Bible/Rabbinical/Talmudic	Comprehensive	Most Selective	Highly Selective	Very Selective	Selective	Non-selective	> $20,000	$10,000 to $20,000	< $10,000	> 50% of students receive aid	Urban	Suburban	Rural	Large (> 20,000 students)	Medium (10,000 to 20,000 students)	Small (1,000 to 10,000 students)	Very Small (< 1,000 students)	Coed	Male/Mostly Male (80% or more)	Female/Mostly Female (80% or more)	> 75% of undergrads from In-state	> 50% live in college-related housing	> 20% of grads pursue postgrad work	> 25% belong to fraternity/sorority
Indiana (cont.)																													
Purdue Univ/Calumet Campus *State*	●		●								●			●		●					●		●			●			
Purdue Univ *State*						●			●					●		●			●				●					●	
Rose-Hulman Institute of Technology *Independent*			●					●					●		●		●				●			●			●		●
Saint Francis Coll *Roman Catholic*	●										●			●	●	●						●	●			●	●		
Saint Joseph's Coll *Roman Catholic*	●										●		●		●			●				●	●				●		
Saint Mary's Coll *Roman Catholic*	●									●			●		●		●				●				●		●	●	
Saint Mary-of-the-Woods Coll *Roman Catholic*	●										●		●		●		●					●			●		●		
Saint Meinrad Coll *Roman Catholic*					●									●	●			●				●		●			●	●	
Taylor Univ *Independent*	●										●		●		●			●			●		●				●		
Tri-State Univ *Independent*			●								●			●				●				●	●				●	●	●
Univ of Evansville *United Methodist*	●									●			●		●		●				●		●				●	●	●
Univ of Indianapolis *State*						●					●		●		●		●				●		●			●			
Univ of Notre Dame *Independent*						●		●					●		●		●				●		●				●	●	
Univ of Southern Indiana *State*	●	●	●								●			●	●		●				●		●			●			●
Valparaiso Univ *Lutheran-Missouri Synod*						●			●				●		●			●			●		●				●	●	●
Wabash Coll *Independent*	●									●			●				●				●		●		●	●	●	●	
Iowa																													
Briar Cliff Coll *Roman Catholic*	●										●		●		●		●				●		●				●		
Buena Vista Coll *Presbyterian*						●					●		●		●			●			●		●			●	●		
Central Coll *Reformed Church*	●			●									●				●				●		●						
Clarke Coll *Roman Catholic*	●										●		●		●	●						●	●				●		
Coe Coll *Independent*	●								●				●		●	●					●		●				●	●	●
Cornell Coll *Independent*	●								●				●		●			●			●		●				●	●	●
Divine Word Coll *Roman Catholic*	●				●																								
Dordt Coll *Christian Reformed*	●										●			●	●			●			●		●				●		
Drake Univ *Independent*						●			●				●		●		●				●		●				●		●

COLLEGE SELECTION INDEX

	What Kind of Education Will I Receive?						Can I Get In?					Can I Afford It?				What Will It Be Like When I Get There?													
	Type of School						Entrance Difficulty					Average Annual Cost				Campus Setting			Undergrad Enrollment				Student Body			Campus Life			
	Liberal Arts	Business	Engineering/Technical	Fine Arts	Seminary/Bible/Rabbinical/Talmudic	Comprehensive	Most Selective	Highly Selective	Very Selective	Selective	Non-selective	> $20,000	$10,000 to $20,000	< $10,000	> 50% of students receive aid	Urban	Suburban	Rural	Large (> 20,000 students)	Medium (10,000 to 20,000 students)	Small (1,000 to 10,000 students)	Very Small (< 1,000 students)	Coed	Male/Mostly Male (80% or more)	Female/Mostly Female (80% or more)	> 75% of undergrads from in-state	> 50% live in college-related housing	> 20% of grads pursue postgrad work	> 25% belong to fraternity/sorority
Iowa (cont.)																													
Graceland Coll *RLDS Church*	●				●									●	●			●				●	●				●		
Grand View Coll *State*	●										●			●		●					●		●						
Grinnell Coll *Independent*	●							●					●		●		●				●		●				●		
Iowa State Univ *State*						●			●					●	●		●			●			●			●			●
Iowa Wesleyan Coll *United Methodist*	●										●			●	●			●				●	●				●		
Loras Coll *Roman Catholic*	●									●			●		●	●					●		●				●		
Luther Coll *Evangelical Lutheran Church in America*	●								●				●		●			●			●		●				●	●	
Maharishi International Univ *Independent*											●		●		●			●				●	●					●	
Morningside Coll *United Methodist*	●									●			●		●		●					●	●			●			
Mount Mercy Coll *Roman Catholic*	●										●			●	●		●					●	●			●			
Mount Saint Clare Coll *Roman Catholic*	●										●			●	●			●				●	●						
Northwestern Coll of Iowa *Reformed Church*	●										●			●	●			●			●		●				●		
Simpson Coll *Independent*	●										●		●		●		●				●		●			●	●		●
St. Ambrose Coll *Roman Catholic*	●										●			●	●	●					●		●						
Teikyo Marycrest Univ *Roman Catholic*	●										●		●		●			●				●	●				●		
Teikyo Westmar Univ *United Methodist*	●										●		●		●			●				●	●				●		
Univ of Dubuque *Independent*	●										●		●		●		●				●		●				●		
Univ of Iowa *State*						●			●					●	●		●			●			●						●
Univ of Northern Iowa *Iowa*	●									●				●	●		●			●			●			●			
Upper Iowa Univ *Independent*		●									●			●				●			●		●				●		
Vennard Coll *Interdenominational*					●									●				●				●	●				●		
Wartburg Coll *Evangelical Lutheran in America*	●									●			●		●			●			●		●				●		
William Penn Coll *Friends*	●										●		●		●			●				●	●			●	●		
Kansas																													
Bethany Coll *Lutheran*	●										●		●		●			●				●	●				●		
Baker Univ *United Methodist*	●										●		●		●		●					●	●				●	●	●

COLLEGE SELECTION INDEX

	What Kind of Education Will I Receive?						Can I Get In?					Can I Afford It?				What Will It Be Like When I Get There?													
	Type of School						Entrance Difficulty					Average Annual Cost				Campus Setting			Undergrad Enrollment				Student Body			Campus Life			
	Liberal Arts	Business	Engineering/Technical	Fine Arts	Seminary/Bible/Rabbinical/Talmudic	Comprehensive	Most Selective	Highly Selective	Very Selective	Selective	Non-selective	> $20,000	$10,000 to $20,000	< $10,000	> 50% of students receive aid	Urban	Suburban	Rural	Large (> 20,000 students)	Medium (10,000 to 20,000 students)	Small (1,000 to 10,000 students)	Very Small (< 1,000 students)	Coed	Male/Mostly Male (80% or more)	Female/Mostly Female (80% or more)	> 75% of undergrads from in-state	> 50% live in college-related housing	> 20% of grads pursue postgrad work	> 25% belong to fraternity/sorority
Kansas (cont.)																													
Barclay Coll *Friends Church*					•									•	•			•				•	•				•		
Benedictine Coll *Independent*	•									•			•		•			•				•	•				•		
Bethel Coll *Mennonite*	•										•		•		•		•					•	•						
Emporia State Univ *State*						•					•			•	•	•					•		•			•			•
Fort Hays State Univ *State*						•					•			•	•		•				•		•			•			
Franklin Univ *Independent*	•	•	•			•					•			•		•					•		•			•			
Friends Univ *Friends*	•										•			•	•	•					•		•			•			
Kansas Newman Coll *Roman Catholic*	•										•			•	•	•						•	•			•			
Kansas State Univ *State*						•					•			•	•		•			•			•			•			•
Kansas Wesleyan Univ *United Methodist*	•										•			•	•		•					•	•			•			
Manhattan Christian Coll *Independent Christian Church*					•									•	•		•					•	•						
McPherson Coll *Brethen*	•										•			•	•			•				•	•				•		
Mid-America Nazarene Coll *Nazarene*	•										•			•			•				•		•						
Ottawa Univ *American Baptist*	•										•			•	•		•					•	•					•	
Pittsburg State Univ *State*						•					•			•	•			•			•		•			•			
Saint Mary Coll *Roman Catholic*	•										•			•	•		•					•	•						
Southwestern Coll *United Methodists*	•										•			•	•			•				•	•			•	•		
Sterling Coll *Presbyterian*	•			•							•			•	•			•				•	•				•		
Tabor Coll *Mennonite Brethen*	•										•			•	•			•				•	•				•		
Univ of Kansas-Lawrence *State*						•				•				•			•			•			•						•
Washburn Univ of Topeka *City*						•					•			•		•					•		•			•			
Wichita State Univ *State*						•					•			•		•					•		•			•		•	
Kentucky																													
Alice Lloyd Coll *Independent*	•										•			•	•			•				•	•			•	•		
Asbury Coll *Independent*	•										•			•	•		•					•	•				•		
Bellarmine Coll *Roman Catholic*						•			•				•		•		•				•		•			•		•	

COLLEGE SELECTION INDEX

	What Kind of Education Will I Receive?						Can I Get In?					Can I Afford It?				What Will It Be Like When I Get There?													
	Type of School						Entrance Difficulty					Average Annual Cost				Campus Setting			Undergrad Enrollment				Student Body			Campus Life			
	Liberal Arts	Business	Engineering/Technical	Fine Arts	Seminary/Bible/Rabbinical/Talmudic	Comprehensive	Most Selective	Highly Selective	Very Selective	Selective	Non-selective	> $20,000	$10,000 to $20,000	< $10,000	> 50% of students receive aid	Urban	Suburban	Rural	Large (> 20,000 students)	Medium (10,000 to 20,000 students)	Small (1,000 to 10,000 students)	Very Small (< 1,000 students)	Coed	Male/Mostly Male (80% or more)	Female/Mostly Female (80% or more)	> 75% of undergrads from in-state	> 50% live in college-related housing	> 20% of grads pursue postgrad work	> 25% belong to fraternity/sorority
Kentucky (cont.)																													
Berea Coll *Independent*	●									●				●	●			●			●		●				●	●	
Brescia Coll *Roman Catholic*	●										●			●	●		●					●	●			●		●	
Campbellsville Coll *Southern Baptist*	●										●			●				●				●	●						
Centre Coll *Independent*	●							●					●		●		●					●	●				●	●	●
Cumberland Coll *Baptist*	●										●			●	●			●			●		●				●	●	
Eastern Kentucky Univ *State*						●					●			●	●	●				●			●			●	●		●
Georgetown Coll *Southern Baptist*	●										●			●	●		●				●		●			●	●		●
Kentucky State Univ *State*	●										●			●	●		●				●		●			●			
Kentucky Wesleyan Coll *United Methodist*	●										●			●	●		●					●	●			●		●	●
Morehead State Univ *State*						●					●			●	●			●			●		●			●			●
Murray State Univ *State*						●					●			●	●			●			●		●			●	●	●	●
Northern Kentucky Univ *State*						●					●			●		●					●		●			●			
Pikeville Coll *Presbyterian Church*	●										●			●	●			●				●	●			●	●	●	
Spalding Univ *Independent*	●										●			●	●	●						●	●			●			
Thomas More Coll *Roman Catholic*	●										●			●			●					●	●				●	●	
Transylvania Univ *Independent*	●								●				●		●	●						●	●			●	●	●	●
Union Coll *United Methodist*	●										●			●	●			●				●	●					●	
Univ of Kentucky *State*						●					●			●	●		●			●			●			●			●
Univ of Louisville *State*						●					●			●	●	●					●		●			●			
Western Kentucky Univ *State*						●					●			●	●	●				●			●			●		●	
Louisiana																													
Centenary Coll of Louisiana *United Methodist*	●								●				●		●		●					●	●				●	●	●
Dillard Univ *Independent*	●										●			●	●	●					●		●				●	●	●
Grambling State Univ *State*						●					●			●	●			●			●		●				●	●	
Grantham Coll of Engineering *Independent*			●											●			●					●		●				●	
Louisiana Coll *Southern Baptist*	●					●					●			●	●	●		●		●		●	●			●	●		●

COLLEGE SELECTION INDEX

	What Kind of Education Will I Receive?						Can I Get In?					Can I Afford It?				What Will It Be Like When I Get There?													
	Type of School						Entrance Difficulty					Average Annual Cost				Campus Setting			Undergrad Enrollment				Student Body			Campus Life			
	Liberal Arts	Business	Engineering/Technical	Fine Arts	Seminary/Bible/Rabbinical/Talmudic	Comprehensive	Most Selective	Highly Selective	Very Selective	Selective	Non-selective	> $20,000	$10,000 to $20,000	< $10,000	> 50% of students receive aid	Urban	Suburban	Rural	Large (> 20,000 students)	Medium (10,000 to 20,000 students)	Small (1,000 to 10,000 students)	Very Small (< 1,000 students)	Coed	Male/Mostly Male (80% or more)	Female/Mostly Female (80% or more)	> 75% of undergrads from in-state	> 50% live in college-related housing	> 20% of grads pursue postgrad work	> 25% belong to fraternity/sorority
Louisiana (cont.)																													
Louisiana State Univ in Shreveport *State*						●					●			●			●				●		●			●			
Louisiana Tech Univ *State*			●								●			●	●		●				●		●			●			
Loyola Univ, New Orleans *Roman Catholic*	●									●			●		●	●					●		●					●	●
McNeese State Univ *State*						●					●			●	●		●				●		●			●	●		
Nicholls State Univ *State*	●										●			●	●	●					●		●			●			
Northeast Louisiana Univ *State*						●					●			●	●	●					●		●			●			
Northwestern State Univ of Louisiana *State*						●					●			●	●			●			●		●			●			●
Our Lady of Holy Cross Coll *Roman Catholic*	●										●			●	●	●						●	●			●			
Saint Joseph Seminary Coll *Roman Catholic*	●																												
Southeastern Louisiana Univ *State*	●										●			●				●			●		●			●			
Southern Univ in New Orleans *State*	●										●			●	●	●					●		●						
Southern Univ *State*						●					●			●	●	●					●		●			●		●	
Tulane Univ *Independent*						●		●					●		●	●					●		●				●	●	●
Univ of New Orleans *State*						●					●			●		●					●		●			●			
Univ of Southwestern Louisiana *State*						●					●			●	●	●				●			●			●			
Xavier Univ of Louisiana *Roman Catholic*	●										●		●					●	●										
Maine																													
Bates Coll *Independent*	●							●				●					●				●		●				●		
Bowdoin Coll *Independent*	●							●				●					●				●		●				●	●	●
Colby Coll *Independent*	●							●				●						●			●		●				●		
Coll of the Atlantic *Independent*										●			●		●		●					●	●					●	
Husson Coll *Independent*		●												●	●	●						●	●			●	●		●
Maine Coll of Art *Independent*				●									●		●	●						●	●						
Maine Maritime Academy *State*			●								●			●	●			●				●		●			●		
Saint Joseph's Coll *Roman Catholic*	●										●			●	●			●				●	●				●	●	
Thomas Coll *Independent*		●									●			●		●						●	●				●		

COLLEGE SELECTION INDEX

	What Kind of Education Will I Receive?						Can I Get In?					Can I Afford It?				What Will It Be Like When I Get There?													
	Type of School						Entrance Difficulty					Average Annual Cost				Campus Setting			Undergrad Enrollment				Student Body			Campus Life			
	Liberal Arts	Business	Engineering/Technical	Fine Arts	Seminary/Bible/Rabbinical/Talmudic	Comprehensive	Most Selective	Highly Selective	Very Selective	Selective	Non-selective	> $20,000	$10,000 to $20,000	< $10,000	> 50% of students receive aid	Urban	Suburban	Rural	Large (> 20,000 students)	Medium (10,000 to 20,000 students)	Small (1,000 to 10,000 students)	Very Small (< 1,000 students)	Coed	Male/Mostly Male (80% or more)	Female/Mostly Female (80% or more)	> 75% of undergrads from in-state	> 50% live in college-related housing	> 20% of grads pursue postgrad work	> 25% belong to fraternity/sorority
Maine (cont.)																													
Unity Coll *Independent*		●										●			●				●				●	●					●
Univ of Maine at Farmington *State*						●					●			●	●			●			●		●			●			
Univ of Maine at Fort Kent *State*	●										●			●	●			●				●	●			●		●	
Univ of Maine at Machias *State*	●					●					●			●	●			●				●	●			●	●		●
Univ of Maine at Orono *State*	●									●				●	●			●			●		●			●			
Univ of Maine at Presque Isle *State*	●										●			●	●			●				●	●			●			
Univ of New England *Independent*						●					●		●		●			●				●	●						
Univ of Southern Maine *State*	●									●				●	●	●	●				●		●			●			
Westbrook Coll *Independent*		●									●		●		●	●						●	●				●		
Maryland																													
Baltimore Hebrew Coll *Independent*					●									●	●	●													
Bowie State Univ *State*	●										●			●	●		●				●		●			●			
Capitol Coll *Independent*			●								●		●		●		●					●		●		●		●	
Coll of Notre Dame of Maryland *Roman Catholic*	●										●		●		●		●				●				●		●		
Columbia Union Coll *Seventh-day Adventist*	●										●			●	●		●				●		●						
Coppin State Coll *State*	●										●			●		●					●		●			●		●	
Frostburg State Coll *State*	●										●			●	●			●			●		●			●			●
Goucher Coll *Independent*	●								●				●		●		●					●			●		●	●	
Hood Coll *Independent*						●				●			●		●	●						●			●		●	●	
Loyola Coll *Roman Catholic*	●								●				●		●		●				●		●						
Maryland Institute, Coll of Art *Independent*				●									●		●	●						●	●						
Morgan State Univ *State*	●					●					●			●	●	●					●		●						
Mount Saint Mary's Coll *Independent*						●				●			●		●			●			●		●				●	●	
Salisbury State Univ *State*	●										●			●	●	●					●		●			●			
Sojourner–Douglas Coll *Independent*	●										●			●		●						●	●			●			
Southwest Baptist Coll *Southern Baptist*						●					●			●				●			●		●				●		

COLLEGE SELECTION INDEX

	What Kind of Education Will I Receive?						Can I Get In?					Can I Afford It?				What Will It Be Like When I Get There?												
	Type of School						Entrance Difficulty					Average Annual Cost				Campus Setting			Undergrad Enrollment				Student Body			Campus Life			
	Liberal Arts	Business	Engineering/Technical	Fine Arts	Seminary/Bible/Rabbinical/Talmudic	Comprehensive	Most Selective	Highly Selective	Very Selective	Selective	Non-selective	> $20,000	$10,000 to $20,000	< $10,000	> 50% of students receive aid	Urban	Suburban	Rural	Large (> 20,000 students)	Medium (10,000 to 20,000 students)	Small (1,000 to 10,000 students)	Very Small (< 1,000 students)	Coed	Male/Mostly Male (80% or more)	Female/Mostly Female (80% or more)	> 75% of undergrads from in-state	> 50% live in college-related housing	> 20% of grads pursue postgrad work	> 25% belong to fraternity/sorority
Maryland (cont.)																													
St. John's Coll *Independent*	●						●						●		●	●						●	●				●	●	
St. Mary's Coll of Maryland *State*	●								●					●	●			●			●		●			●	●	●	
St. Mary's Seminary and Univ *Roman Catholic*					●						●			●	●	●						●		●					
The Johns Hopkins Univ *Independent*	●						●						●		●	●					●		●				●	●	●
Towson State Univ *State*						●					●			●			●				●		●			●		●	
United States Naval Academy *Federal*			●						●						●		●				●			●			●		
Univ of Maryland, Eastern Shore *State*	●										●			●	●			●			●		●				●	●	
Univ of Maryland Baltimore County *State*						●					●			●			●				●		●			●		●	
Univ of Maryland *State*						●				●				●	●		●		●				●				●	●	●
Washington Bible Coll *Non-denominational*					●									●			●					●	●						
Washington Coll *Independent*	●									●			●		●			●				●	●				●	●	●
Western Maryland Coll *Independent*	●									●			●		●			●			●		●				●	●	●
Massachusetts																													
American International Coll *Independent*	●										●		●		●	●					●		●				●	●	●
Amherst Coll *Independent*	●						●					●					●				●		●				●	●	
Anna Maria Coll *Roman Catholic*	●										●		●		●		●				●		●			●	●	●	
Assumption Coll *Roman Catholic*	●									●			●		●	●					●		●				●	●	
Atlantic Union Coll *Seventh-day Adventist*					●						●		●		●		●					●	●				●		
Babson Coll *Independent*		●								●		●					●				●		●				●		
Bentley Coll *Independent*						●				●			●		●		●				●		●				●	●	●
Berklee Coll of Music *Independent*													●			●					●			●					
Boston Coll *Roman Catholic*						●			●			●			●		●				●		●				●	●	
Boston Conservatory of Music *Independent*													●			●						●	●						
Boston Univ *Independent*						●			●			●			●	●				●			●				●	●	
Bradford Coll *Independent*	●										●		●		●	●						●	●				●	●	
Brandeis Univ *Independent*	●							●				●			●		●				●		●				●	●	

COLLEGE SELECTION INDEX

What Kind of Education Will I Receive? — Type of School | Can I Get In? — Entrance Difficulty | Can I Afford It? — Average Annual Cost | What Will It Be Like When I Get There? — Campus Setting, Undergrad Enrollment, Student Body, Campus Life

College	Liberal Arts	Business	Engineering/Technical	Fine Arts	Seminary/Bible/Rabbinical/Talmudic	Comprehensive	Most Selective	Highly Selective	Very Selective	Selective	Non-selective	> $20,000	$10,000 to $20,000	< $10,000	> 50% of students receive aid	Urban	Suburban	Rural	Large (> 20,000 students)	Medium (10,000 to 20,000 students)	Small (1,000 to 10,000 students)	Very Small (< 1,000 students)	Coed	Male/Mostly Male (80% or more)	Female/Mostly Female (80% or more)	> 75% of undergrads from in-state	> 50% live in college-related housing	> 20% of grads pursue postgrad work	> 25% belong to fraternity/sorority
Massachusetts (cont.)																													
Bridgewater State Coll *State*						●					●			●			●				●		●			●			
Clark Univ *Independent*	●								●			●			●	●					●		●				●	●	
Coll of Our Lady of the Elms *Roman Catholic*	●										●			●	●	●						●			●		●		
Coll of the Holy Cross *Roman Catholic/Jesuit*	●							●					●		●		●				●		●				●	●	
Curry Coll *Independent*	●										●		●		●		●					●	●				●		
Eastern Nazarene Coll *Nazarene*	●										●			●	●		●					●	●				●		
Emerson Coll *Independent*	●										●		●		●	●					●		●						
Emmanuel Coll *Independent*	●										●		●		●	●						●			●		●		
Fitchburg State Coll *State*	●										●			●	●		●				●		●			●	●		
Framingham State Coll *State*	●										●			●	●		●				●		●			●	●		
Gordon Coll *Independent*	●									●			●		●		●				●		●				●		
Hampshire Coll *Independent*	●								●			●			●			●			●		●					●	
Harvard Coll *Independent*	●						●						●		●	●					●			●			●	●	
Hebrew Coll *Independent*														●			●					●	●			●			
Hellenic Coll *Greek Orthodox*	●										●			●	●	●						●	●				●		
Lesley Coll *Independent*						●					●		●		●	●						●			●				
Massachusetts Coll of Art *State*				●										●	●	●					●		●			●			
Massachusetts Institute of Technology *Independent*			●				●						●		●	●					●		●				●	●	●
Massachusetts Maritime Academy *State*			●								●			●	●		●					●		●		●	●		
Merrimack Coll *Roman Catholic*	●										●		●		●		●				●		●				●	●	
Mount Holyoke Coll *Independent*	●							●					●		●		●				●				●		●	●	
New England Conservatory of Music *Independent*				●																									
Nichols Coll *Independent*	●	●									●			●	●			●				●	●			●	●		
North Adams State Coll *State*	●										●			●	●			●			●		●			●	●		
Northeastern Univ *Independent*						●				●			●		●	●				●			●						
Pine Manor Coll *Independent*	●										●		●				●					●			●		●		

COLLEGE SELECTION INDEX

	What Kind of Education Will I Receive?						Can I Get In?					Can I Afford It?				What Will It Be Like When I Get There?													
	Type of School						Entrance Difficulty					Average Annual Cost				Campus Setting			Undergrad Enrollment				Student Body			Campus Life			
	Liberal Arts	Business	Engineering/Technical	Fine Arts	Seminary/Bible/Rabbinical/Talmudic	Comprehensive	Most Selective	Highly Selective	Very Selective	Selective	Non-selective	> $20,000	$10,000 to $20,000	< $10,000	> 50% of students receive aid	Urban	Suburban	Rural	Large (> 20,000 students)	Medium (10,000 to 20,000 students)	Small (1,000 to 10,000 students)	Very Small (< 1,000 students)	Coed	Male/Mostly Male (80% or more)	Female/Mostly Female (80% or more)	> 75% of undergrads from In-state	> 50% live in college-related housing	> 20% of grads pursue postgrad work	> 25% belong to fraternity/sorority
Massachusetts (cont.)																													
Plymouth State Coll *State*	●										●			●	●			●			●		●				●		
Radcliffe Coll *Independent*	●						●						●		●	●					●				●		●	●	
Regis Coll *Independent*	●										●		●		●		●					●			●	●	●		
Saint John's Seminary *Roman Catholic*	●																												
Salem State Coll *State*						●					●			●	●		●				●		●			●			
Simmons Coll *Independent*						●				●			●		●	●					●				●		●	●	
Simon's Rock of Bard Coll *Independent*	●								●				●		●			●				●	●				●		
Smith Coll *Independent*	●							●					●				●				●				●		●	●	
Springfield Coll *Independent*	●										●		●		●	●					●		●						
St. Hyacinth Coll-Seminary *Roman Catholic*	●													●				●				●		●		●			
Tufts Univ *Independent*	●							●					●		●		●				●		●				●	●	
Univ of Massachusetts—Boston *State*						●					●			●	●	●					●		●			●		●	
Univ of Massachusetts—Dartmouth *State*						●					●			●	●		●				●		●			●			
Univ of Massachusetts—Lowell *State*						●					●			●	●	●					●		●			●			
Univ of Massachusetts/Amherst *State*						●				●				●	●			●		●			●			●	●	●	
Wellesley Coll *Independent*	●						●						●		●		●				●				●		●	●	
Wentworth Institute of Technology *Independent*			●											●	●	●					●			●					
Western New England Coll *Independent*	●										●			●	●	●					●		●				●		
Westfield State Coll *State*	●										●			●	●		●				●		●			●	●		
Wheaton Coll *Independent*	●									●			●		●			●			●		●				●	●	
Wheelock Coll *Independent*	●										●		●		●	●						●			●		●		
Williams Coll *Independent*	●						●						●		●			●			●		●				●	●	
Worcester Polytechnic Institute *Independent*			●					●					●		●		●				●		●				●	●	●
Worcester State Coll *State*	●										●			●	●		●				●		●			●			
Michigan																													
Adrian Coll *Methodist*	●								●				●		●		●				●		●			●	●	●	●

COLLEGE SELECTION INDEX

	What Kind of Education Will I Receive? (Type of School)						Can I Get In? (Entrance Difficulty)					Can I Afford It? (Average Annual Cost)				What Will It Be Like When I Get There? (Campus Setting)			(Undergrad Enrollment)				(Student Body)			(Campus Life)			
	Liberal Arts	Business	Engineering/Technical	Fine Arts	Seminary/Bible/Rabbinical/Talmudic	Comprehensive	Most Selective	Highly Selective	Very Selective	Selective	Non-selective	> $20,000	$10,000 to $20,000	< $10,000	> 50% of students receive aid	Urban	Suburban	Rural	Large (> 20,000 students)	Medium (10,000 to 20,000 students)	Small (1,000 to 10,000 students)	Very Small (< 1,000 students)	Coed	Male/Mostly Male (80% or more)	Female/Mostly Female (80% or more)	> 75% of undergrads from in-state	> 50% live in college-related housing	> 20% of grads pursue postgrad work	> 25% belong to fraternity/sorority
Michigan (cont.)																													
Albion Coll *United Methodist*	●								●				●		●		●				●		●			●		●	●
Alma Coll *Presbyterian*	●									●			●		●		●				●		●			●	●	●	●
Andrews Univ *Seventh-day Adventist*					●						●		●					●			●		●				●	●	
Aquinas Coll *Roman Catholic*	●										●		●		●	●					●		●			●	●		
Baker Coll of Flint *Independent*		●	●											●		●					●		●			●			
Calvin Coll *Christian Reformed*	●					●				●			●		●		●				●		●				●	●	
Center for Creative Studies *Independent*													●		●	●						●					●		
Central Michigan Univ *State*	●										●			●	●			●		●			●			●			
Concordia Coll, Ann Arbor *Lutheran-Missouri Synod*	●												●		●		●					●	●			●	●		
Eastern Michigan Univ *State*						●					●			●	●		●			●			●			●		●	
Ferris State Coll *State*						●					●			●	●			●			●		●			●			
GMI Engineering and Management Institute *Independent*			●						●				●		●	●					●		●				●	●	●
Grace Bible Coll *Grace Gospel Fellowship*					●									●	●		●					●	●				●		
Grand Rapids Baptist Coll *Baptist*	●										●			●			●					●	●			●	●		
Grand Valley State Univ *State*	●										●			●	●		●				●		●			●			
Great Lakes Christian Coll *Church of Christ*	●													●	●		●					●	●			●	●		
Hillsdale Coll *Independent*	●								●				●		●			●			●		●				●	●	●
Hope Coll *Independent*	●									●			●		●		●				●		●			●			
Kalamazoo Coll *American Baptist*	●								●				●		●		●				●		●				●	●	
Kendall Coll of Art and Design *Independent*				●										●	●	●						●	●			●			
Lake Superior State Univ *State*	●										●			●	●	●					●		●						
Lawrence Technological Univ *Independent*		●	●								●			●	●		●				●		●						
Madonna Univ *Roman Catholic*	●										●			●			●				●		●			●			
Marygrove Coll *Independent*	●										●			●	●	●						●			●				
Michigan Christian Coll *Church of Christ*	●										●			●			●					●	●				●		
Michigan State Univ *State*						●				●				●			●		●				●			●		●	

COLLEGE SELECTION INDEX

	What Kind of Education Will I Receive?						Can I Get In?					Can I Afford It?				What Will It Be Like When I Get There?													
	Type of School						Entrance Difficulty					Average Annual Cost				Campus Setting			Undergrad Enrollment				Student Body			Campus Life			
	Liberal Arts	Business	Engineering/Technical	Fine Arts	Seminary/Bible/Rabbinical/Talmudic	Comprehensive	Most Selective	Highly Selective	Very Selective	Selective	Non-selective	> $20,000	$10,000 to $20,000	< $10,000	> 50% of students receive aid	Urban	Suburban	Rural	Large (> 20,000 students)	Medium (10,000 to 20,000 students)	Small (1,000 to 10,000 students)	Very Small (< 1,000 students)	Coed	Male/Mostly Male (80% or more)	Female/Mostly Female (80% or more)	> 75% of undergrads from in-state	> 50% live in college-related housing	> 20% of grads pursue postgrad work	> 25% belong to fraternity/sorority
Michigan (cont.)																													
Michigan Technological Univ *State*			●						●					●	●			●			●		●			●	●		●
Northern Michigan Univ *State*						●					●			●	●			●			●		●			●			
Northwood Institute—Midland Campus *Independent*		●									●			●	●	●					●		●				●		●
Oakland Univ *State*						●					●			●			●				●		●			●			
Olivet Coll *Independent*	●			●	●						●		●		●			●				●	●				●		
Sacred Heart Seminary *Roman Catholic*					●																								
Saginaw Valley State Univ *State*	●										●			●	●	●					●		●			●			
Siena Heights Coll *Roman Catholic*	●										●			●	●		●					●	●			●			
Spring Arbor Coll *Free Methodist*	●										●			●	●			●				●	●			●			
St. Mary's Coll *Independent*	●										●			●	●		●					●	●			●		●	●
Univ of Detroit Mercy *Independent*						●				●				●	●	●					●		●			●		●	●
Univ of Michigan—Dearborn *State*						●				●				●			●				●		●			●			
Univ of Michigan—Flint *State*	●										●			●		●					●		●			●			
Univ of Michigan *State*						●		●						●		●			●				●				●		●
Wayne State Univ *State*						●					●			●	●	●				●			●			●			
Minnesota																													
Western Michigan Univ *State*						●					●			●	●	●				●			●			●			
Augsburg Coll *Lutheran*	●										●		●		●	●					●		●			●	●		
Bethel Coll *Baptist*	●										●		●	●			●				●		●				●		
Cardinal Stritch Coll *Roman Catholic*	●										●		●				●					●	●			●			
Carleton Coll *Independent*	●							●				●			●			●			●		●				●	●	
Coll of Associated Arts *Independent*				●										●	●	●						●	●			●			
Coll of Saint Benedict *Indpendent*	●									●			●		●			●			●				●	●	●	●	
Coll of St. Catherine *Roman Catholic*	●									●			●		●		●				●				●	●		●	
Coll of St. Scholastica *Roman Catholic*	●										●		●		●		●				●		●					●	
Concordia Coll, St. Paul *Lutheran-Missouri Synod*	●										●		●		●	●					●		●			●			

COLLEGE SELECTION INDEX

	What Kind of Education Will I Receive?						Can I Get In?					Can I Afford It?				What Will It Be Like When I Get There?													
	Type of School						Entrance Difficulty					Average Annual Cost				Campus Setting			Undergrad Enrollment				Student Body			Campus Life			
	Liberal Arts	Business	Engineering/Technical	Fine Arts	Seminary/Bible/Rabbinical/Talmudic	Comprehensive	Most Selective	Highly Selective	Very Selective	Selective	Non-selective	> $20,000	$10,000 to $20,000	< $10,000	> 50% of students receive aid	Urban	Suburban	Rural	Large (> 20,000 students)	Medium (10,000 to 20,000 students)	Small (1,000 to 10,000 students)	Very Small (< 1,000 students)	Coed	Male/Mostly Male (80% or more)	Female/Mostly Female (80% or more)	> 75% of undergrads from in-state	> 50% live in college-related housing	> 20% of grads pursue postgrad work	> 25% belong to fraternity/sorority
Minnesota (cont.)																													
Concordia Coll at Moorhead *Evangelical Lutheran Church*	•								•				•		•		•				•		•				•	•	
Crown Coll *Christian Missionary Alliance*					•									•	•		•					•	•						
Dr. Martin Luther Coll *Wisconsin Evangelical Lutheran Synod*														•	•			•				•	•				•		
Gustavus Adolphus Coll *Evangelical Lutheran Church in America*	•								•				•		•		•				•		•				•	•	•
Hamline Univ *United Methodist*	•								•				•		•	•					•		•						
Macalester Coll *Presbyterian Church*	•								•				•		•	•					•		•					•	
Mankato State Univ *State*						•					•			•	•			•			•		•			•			
Minneapolis Coll of Art and Design *Independent*				•									•		•	•						•	•						
Minnesota Bible Coll *Christian Churches/Churches of Christ*					•									•	•		•					•	•				•	•	
Moorhead State Univ *State*						•				•				•	•	•					•		•						
North Central Bible Coll *Assemblies of God*	•													•	•	•						•	•				•		
Northwestern Coll *Independent*	•										•		•		•		•				•		•				•		
Saint John's Univ *Independent*	•									•			•		•			•			•			•		•	•	•	
Saint Mary's Coll *Roman Catholic*	•										•		•		•			•			•		•				•		
Southwest State Univ *State*	•		•								•			•	•			•			•		•				•		
St. Cloud State Univ *State*						•					•			•	•	•				•			•			•			
St. Olaf Coll *Evangelical Lutheran Church in America*	•								•				•		•			•			•		•				•	•	
Univ of Minnesota—Duluth *State*		•										•			•	•			•			•		•			•	•	•
Univ of Minnesota—Morris *State*		•								•					•	•			•			•		•			•	•	•
Univ of Minnesota *State*							•			•					•	•	•			•				•					
Univ of St. Thomas *Roman Catholic*		•				•					•			•		•	•					•		•			•		
Winona State Univ *State*							•					•			•	•			•			•		•				•	•
Mississippi																													
Alcorn State Univ *State*	•										•			•	•		•				•		•			•	•		
Belhaven Coll *Presbyterian*	•										•			•	•	•					•		•			•			
Blue Mountain Coll *Southern Baptist*	•										•			•				•				•			•	•			

COLLEGE SELECTION INDEX

	What Kind of Education Will I Receive?						Can I Get In?					Can I Afford It?				What Will It Be Like When I Get There?													
	Type of School						Entrance Difficulty					Average Annual Cost				Campus Setting			Undergrad Enrollment				Student Body			Campus Life			
	Liberal Arts	Business	Engineering/Technical	Fine Arts	Seminary/Bible/Rabbinical/Talmudic	Comprehensive	Most Selective	Highly Selective	Very Selective	Selective	Non-selective	> $20,000	$10,000 to $20,000	< $10,000	> 50% of students receive aid	Urban	Suburban	Rural	Large (> 20,000 students)	Medium (10,000 to 20,000 students)	Small (1,000 to 10,000 students)	Very Small (< 1,000 students)	Coed	Male/Mostly Male (80% or more)	Female/Mostly Female (80% or more)	> 75% of undergrads from in-state	> 50% live in college-related housing	> 20% of grads pursue postgrad work	> 25% belong to fraternity/sorority
Mississippi (cont.)																													
Delta State Univ *State*						●					●			●				●			●		●			●		●	●
Jackson State Univ *State*						●					●			●	●	●					●		●			●	●		
Millsaps Coll *United Methodist*	●								●				●		●	●					●		●				●	●	●
Mississippi Coll *Southern Baptist*	●										●			●	●		●				●		●			●	●		
Mississippi State Univ *State*						●					●			●	●			●			●		●			●	●		●
Mississippi Univ for Women *State*	●										●			●	●		●				●		●			●			●
Mississippi Valley State Univ *State*	●										●			●	●			●			●		●			●	●		
Rust Coll *United Methodist*	●										●			●	●			●			●		●				●		
Tougaloo Coll *United Church of Christ, Disciples of Christ*	●										●			●			●				●		●			●	●	●	
Univ of Mississippi *State*						●					●			●	●			●			●		●				●		●
Univ of Southern Mississippi *State*						●					●			●	●		●				●		●			●	●		
Wesley Coll *Congregational Methodist Church*					●				●					●	●			●				●	●				●		
William Carey Coll *Southern Baptist*		●									●			●	●	●					●		●			●	●		
Missouri																													
Avila Coll *Catholic*						●					●		●		●		●				●		●						
Central Methodist Coll *United Methodist*	●										●		●		●			●				●	●			●			●
Central Missouri State Univ *State*						●					●			●	●			●		●			●			●			
Coll of the Ozarks *Independent*	●										●			●	●			●			●		●				●		
Columbia Coll *Disciples of Christ*	●										●		●		●	●						●	●			●		●	
Conception Seminary Coll *Roman Catholic*					●																								
Culver-Stockton Coll *Disciples of Christ*	●										●			●	●			●				●	●						●
Deaconess Coll of Nursing *Independent*														●	●	●						●			●				
Drury Coll *Independent*	●									●				●	●	●					●		●			●		●	●
Evangel Coll *Assemblies of God*	●										●			●		●					●		●						
Fontbonne Coll *Independent*	●										●			●	●		●				●		●			●			
Hannibal-Lagrange Coll *Southern Baptist*	●										●			●				●				●	●			●			

COLLEGE SELECTION INDEX

	What Kind of Education Will I Receive?						Can I Get In?					Can I Afford It?				What Will It Be Like When I Get There?													
	Type of School						Entrance Difficulty					Average Annual Cost				Campus Setting			Undergrad Enrollment				Student Body			Campus Life			
	Liberal Arts	Business	Engineering/Technical	Fine Arts	Seminary/Bible/Rabbinical/Talmudic	Comprehensive	Most Selective	Highly Selective	Very Selective	Selective	Non-selective	> $20,000	$10,000 to $20,000	< $10,000	> 50% of students receive aid	Urban	Suburban	Rural	Large (> 20,000 students)	Medium (10,000 to 20,000 students)	Small (1,000 to 10,000 students)	Very Small (< 1,000 students)	Coed	Male/Mostly Male (80% or more)	Female/Mostly Female (80% or more)	> 75% of undergrads from in-state	> 50% live in college-related housing	> 20% of grads pursue postgrad work	> 25% belong to fraternity/sorority
Missouri (cont.)																													
Harris-Stowe State Coll *City*											•			•	•	•						•	•			•			
Kansas City Art Institute *Independent*				•																									
Lincoln Univ *State*						•					•			•	•			•			•		•			•			
Lindenwood Coll *Independent*	•										•			•	•		•				•		•			•			•
Maryville Univ-St. Louis *Independent*	•	•		•		•					•			•			•				•		•			•			
Missouri Baptist Coll *Southern Baptist*	•										•			•	•		•				•		•			•			
Missouri Southern State Coll *State*	•										•			•	•		•				•		•			•			
Missouri Valley Coll *Presbyterian Church*	•										•			•	•			•			•		•				•		•
Missouri Western State Coll *State/District*	•	•		•		•					•			•	•		•				•		•			•		•	
Northeast Missouri State Univ *State*	•									•				•	•			•			•		•					•	•
Northwest Missouri State Univ *State*						•					•			•	•			•			•		•					•	•
Park Coll *Reorganized Latter Day Saints*	•										•			•	•		•					•	•					•	
Research Coll of Nursing *Roman Catholic*											•			•	•	•						•			•	•	•		
Rockhurst Coll *Independent*						•			•					•	•	•					•		•				•		•
Rockhurst Coll *Independent*						•			•					•	•	•					•		•				•		•
Saint Louis Univ *Independent*	•					•				•			•		•	•					•		•				•	•	•
Southeast Missouri State Univ *State*						•					•			•	•			•			•		•			•	•		
Southwest Missouri State Univ *State*						•					•			•			•			•			•			•			
St. Louis Coll of Pharmacy *Independent*									•					•	•	•						•	•						
Stephens Coll *Independent*	•										•		•		•	•					•				•		•	•	
Univ of Missouri—Columbia *State*						•			•					•	•	•				•			•			•			•
Univ of Missouri—Kansas City *State*						•			•					•	•	•					•		•			•			
Univ of Missouri—Rolla *State*			•						•					•	•			•			•		•			•			•
Univ of Missouri—St. Louis *State*						•					•			•	•		•				•		•				•		
Washington Univ *Independent*						•		•					•				•				•		•				•	•	
Webster Univ *Independent*	•										•			•	•		•				•		•			•			

COLLEGE SELECTION INDEX

	What Kind of Education Will I Receive? Type of School						Can I Get In? Entrance Difficulty					Can I Afford It? Average Annual Cost				What Will It Be Like When I Get There? Campus Setting			Undergrad Enrollment				Student Body			Campus Life			
	Liberal Arts	Business	Engineering/Technical	Fine Arts	Seminary/Bible/Rabbinical/Talmudic	Comprehensive	Most Selective	Highly Selective	Very Selective	Selective	Non-selective	> $20,000	$10,000 to $20,000	< $10,000	> 50% of students receive aid	Urban	Suburban	Rural	Large (> 20,000 students)	Medium (10,000 to 20,000 students)	Small (1,000 to 10,000 students)	Very Small (< 1,000 students)	Coed	Male/Mostly Male (80% or more)	Female/Mostly Female (80% or more)	> 75% of undergrads from in-state	> 50% live in college-related housing	> 20% of grads pursue postgrad work	> 25% belong to fraternity/sorority
Missouri (cont.)																													
Westminster Coll *Independent*	●									●				●	●			●				●	●				●		●
William Jewell Coll *Baptist*	●									●				●	●		●				●		●			●	●	●	●
William Woods Univ *Independent*	●										●			●	●			●				●			●			●	●
Montana																													
Carroll Coll *Independent*	●										●		●		●			●			●		●				●	●	
Coll of Great Falls *Roman Catholic*	●										●			●	●	●						●	●			●			
Eastern Montana Coll *State*						●					●			●	●	●					●		●			●			
Montana Coll of Mineral Science and Technology *State*		●	●								●			●	●		●				●		●			●	●		
Montana State Univ *State*						●					●			●	●			●			●		●						
Northern Montana Coll *State*	●										●			●	●			●			●		●			●			
Pembroke State Univ *State*	●										●			●				●			●		●			●			
Rocky Mountain Coll *Presbyterian, Methodist, United Church of Christ*	●										●			●	●		●					●	●						
Rocky Mountain Coll *Presbyterian, Methodist, United Church of Christ*	●										●			●	●		●					●	●						
Univ of Montana *State*	●			●		●					●			●	●	●					●		●			●			
Western Montana Coll of the Univ of Montana *State*	●										●			●	●			●			●		●			●			
Nebraska																													
Bellevue Coll *Independent*	●	●									●			●			●					●	●			●			
Bemidji State Univ *State*	●										●			●	●			●			●		●			●			
Chadron State Coll *State*	●										●			●	●			●			●		●						
Clarkson Coll *Episcopalian*	●													●			●					●	●			●			
Coll of Saint Mary *Independent*	●										●			●	●	●						●	●			●			
Concordia Coll, Seward *Lutheran-Missouri Synod*	●													●	●			●				●	●						
Creighton Univ *Independent*						●			●				●		●	●					●		●					●	●
Dana Coll *Evangelical Lutheran Church*	●										●			●	●			●				●	●				●	●	
Doane Coll *Independent*	●										●			●	●			●				●	●			●	●	●	●
Hastings Coll *Presbyterian Church*	●										●			●	●			●				●	●			●	●	●	●

COLLEGE SELECTION INDEX

	What Kind of Education Will I Receive?						Can I Get In?					Can I Afford It?				What Will It Be Like When I Get There?													
	Type of School						Entrance Difficulty					Average Annual Cost				Campus Setting			Undergrad Enrollment				Student Body			Campus Life			
	Liberal Arts	Business	Engineering/Technical	Fine Arts	Seminary/Bible/Rabbinical/Talmudic	Comprehensive	Most Selective	Highly Selective	Very Selective	Selective	Non-selective	> $20,000	$10,000 to $20,000	< $10,000	> 50% of students receive aid	Urban	Suburban	Rural	Large (> 20,000 students)	Medium (10,000 to 20,000 students)	Small (1,000 to 10,000 students)	Very Small (< 1,000 students)	Coed	Male/Mostly Male (80% or more)	Female/Mostly Female (80% or more)	> 75% of undergrads from in-state	> 50% live in college-related housing	> 20% of grads pursue postgrad work	> 25% belong to fraternity/sorority
Nebraska (cont.)																													
Midland Lutheran Coll *Evangelical Lutheran Church in America*	●										●			●	●		●					●	●			●	●		●
Nebraska Wesleyan Univ *Independent*	●								●					●	●	●					●		●			●	●		●
Peru State Coll *State*	●										●			●	●			●			●		●			●			
Union Coll *Seventh-day Adventist*	●										●			●		●						●	●				●		
Univ of Nebraska at Omaha *State*						●					●			●	●	●					●		●			●			
Univ of Nebraska—Kearney *State*											●			●	●			●			●		●			●			
Univ of Nebraska—Lincoln *State*						●				●				●	●	●				●			●			●			●
Wayne State Coll *State*	●										●			●	●			●			●		●			●	●		
York Coll *Church of Christ*	●										●			●	●			●				●	●				●		
Nevada																													
Morrison Coll *Independent*		●												●	●	●						●	●			●			
Sierra Nevada Coll *Independent*	●										●			●				●			●		●						
Univ of Nevada—Las Vegas *State*	●										●			●	●	●					●		●			●			
Univ of Nevada—Reno *State*	●		●								●			●	●	●					●		●			●			
New Hampshire																													
Colby-Sawyer Coll *Independent*						●					●		●		●			●				●	●				●	●	
Coll for Lifelong Learning *State*	●										●			●				●				●	●			●	●	●	●
Daniel Webster Coll *Independent*	●										●		●		●	●						●	●				●		
Dartmouth Coll *Independent*	●						●						●					●			●		●				●	●	●
Franklin Pierce Coll *Independent*	●										●		●					●			●		●				●		
Keene State Coll *State*	●										●			●	●		●				●		●				●	●	●
New England Coll *Independent*	●										●		●					●				●	●				●		●
New Hampshire Coll *Independent*	●	●									●		●		●		●					●	●				●		
Notre Dame Coll *Independent*	●										●			●	●		●					●	●					●	
Rivier Coll *Independent*	●										●			●			●					●			●	●		●	
Saint Anselm Coll *Roman Catholic*	●									●			●		●		●				●		●				●	●	

COLLEGE SELECTION INDEX

	What Kind of Education Will I Receive? — Type of School						Can I Get In? — Entrance Difficulty					Can I Afford It? — Average Annual Cost				What Will It Be Like When I Get There? — Campus Setting			Undergrad Enrollment				Student Body			Campus Life			
	Liberal Arts	Business	Engineering/Technical	Fine Arts	Seminary/Bible/Rabbinical/Talmudic	Comprehensive	Most Selective	Highly Selective	Very Selective	Selective	Non-selective	> $20,000	$10,000 to $20,000	< $10,000	> 50% of students receive aid	Urban	Suburban	Rural	Large (> 20,000 students)	Medium (10,000 to 20,000 students)	Small (1,000 to 10,000 students)	Very Small (< 1,000 students)	Coed	Male/Mostly Male (80% or more)	Female/Mostly Female (80% or more)	> 75% of undergrads from In-state	> 50% live in college-related housing	> 20% of grads pursue postgrad work	> 25% belong to fraternity/sorority
New Hampshire (cont.)																													
Univ of New Hampshire *Independent*						•			•					•	•			•		•			•				•		
New Jersey																													
Bloomfield Coll *Presbyterian*	•										•		•				•				•		•						
Caldwell Coll *Roman Catholic*	•										•		•		•	•					•		•			•			
Camden Coll of Arts and Sciences *State*	•										•			•	•	•					•		•			•		•	
Centenary Coll *Independent*						•					•		•		•			•				•			•	•	•		•
Coll of Engineering *State*			•						•					•	•		•				•		•			•	•	•	
Coll of Nursing *State*										•				•	•	•						•			•	•		•	
Coll of Pharmacy *State*									•					•	•		•					•	•			•	•	•	
Coll of Saint Elizabeth *Roman Catholic*	•										•		•		•		•					•			•	•	•		
Cook Coll *State*									•					•	•		•				•		•			•	•	•	
Douglass Coll *State*	•									•				•	•		•				•				•	•	•	•	
Drew Univ *Independent*	•								•				•		•		•				•		•				•	•	
Fairleigh Dickinson Univ *Independent*						•					•		•		•		•			•			•			•	•		
Felician Coll *Roman Catholic*	•										•			•			•					•			•	•			•
Georgian Court Coll *Roman Catholic*	•										•			•			•					•			•	•		•	
Jersey City State Coll *State*						•					•			•	•	•					•		•			•		•	
Kean Coll of New Jersey *State*	•										•			•			•		•			•							
Livingston Coll *State*	•										•			•	•		•				•		•			•		•	
Mason Gross School of the Arts *State*				•							•			•	•		•					•	•			•	•	•	
Monmouth Coll *Independent*	•										•		•		•		•				•		•			•	•		•
Montclair State Coll *State*						•				•				•	•		•				•		•			•			
New Jersey Institute of Technology *State/City*			•			•			•					•	•	•					•			•		•			•
Newark Coll of Arts and Sciences *State*	•									•				•	•	•					•		•			•		•	
Princeton Univ *Independent*						•	•						•				•				•		•				•	•	
Ramapo Coll of New Jersey *State*	•										•			•			•				•		•			•			

COLLEGE SELECTION INDEX

	What Kind of Education Will I Receive? — Type of School						Can I Get In? — Entrance Difficulty					Can I Afford It? — Average Annual Cost				What Will It Be Like When I Get There? — Campus Setting			Undergrad Enrollment				Student Body			Campus Life			
	Liberal Arts	Business	Engineering/Technical	Fine Arts	Seminary/Bible/Rabbinical/Talmudic	Comprehensive	Most Selective	Highly Selective	Very Selective	Selective	Non-selective	> $20,000	$10,000 to $20,000	< $10,000	> 50% of students receive aid	Urban	Suburban	Rural	Large (> 20,000 students)	Medium (10,000 to 20,000 students)	Small (1,000 to 10,000 students)	Very Small (< 1,000 students)	Coed	Male/Mostly Male (80% or more)	Female/Mostly Female (80% or more)	> 75% of undergrads from in-state	> 50% live in college-related housing	> 20% of grads pursue postgrad work	> 25% belong to fraternity/sorority
New Jersey (cont.)																													
Rider Coll *Independent*	●	●									●		●		●		●				●		●			●	●		
Rowan Coll of New Jersey *State*	●										●			●	●		●				●		●						
Rutgers Coll *State*	●								●					●	●		●				●		●			●	●	●	
Rutgers—The State Univ of New Jersey *State*						●								●	●	●			●				●						
Saint Peter's Coll *Roman Catholic*	●										●			●	●	●					●		●			●		●	
Seton Hall Univ *Roman Catholic*						●					●		●		●		●				●		●			●	●	●	●
Thomas A. Edison State Coll *State*							●					●			●	●	●					●		●					●
Trenton State Coll *State*						●				●				●	●		●				●		●			●	●	●	
Univ Coll *State*	●										●			●	●	●						●	●			●			
Upsala Coll *Lutheran*	●										●		●			●					●		●			●	●		●
William Paterson Coll *State*	●										●			●			●				●		●			●			
New Mexico																													
Coll of Santa Fe *Roman Catholic*	●										●			●	●		●					●	●					●	
Coll of the Southwest *Independent*	●										●			●	●			●				●	●			●		●	
Eastern New Mexico Univ *State*						●					●			●	●			●			●		●				●		
New Mexico Highlands Univ *State*	●										●			●	●			●			●		●			●			
New Mexico Institute of Mining and Technology *State*			●						●					●	●			●				●	●			●		●	
New Mexico State Univ *State*											●			●	●	●					●		●						
St. John's Coll *Independent*	●						●						●		●		●					●					●	●	
Univ of New Mexico *State*						●					●			●	●	●				●			●			●			
Western New Mexico Univ *State*	●										●			●	●			●			●		●			●	●		
New York																													
Adelphi Univ *Independent*	●										●		●				●				●		●			●		●	
Albany Coll of Pharmacy *Independent*											●		●		●	●						●	●			●			●
Alfred Univ *Independent*						●		●				●			●			●			●		●				●	●	●
Audrey Cohen Coll *Independent*	●	●												●	●	●						●	●			●		●	

COLLEGE SELECTION INDEX

	What Kind of Education Will I Receive? — Type of School						Can I Get In? — Entrance Difficulty					Can I Afford It? — Average Annual Cost				What Will It Be Like When I Get There? — Campus Setting			Undergrad Enrollment				Student Body			Campus Life			
	Liberal Arts	Business	Engineering/Technical	Fine Arts	Seminary/Bible/Rabbinical/Talmudic	Comprehensive	Most Selective	Highly Selective	Very Selective	Selective	Non-selective	> $20,000	$10,000 to $20,000	< $10,000	> 50% of students receive aid	Urban	Suburban	Rural	Large (> 20,000 students)	Medium (10,000 to 20,000 students)	Small (1,000 to 10,000 students)	Very Small (< 1,000 students)	Coed	Male/Mostly Male (80% or more)	Female/Mostly Female (80% or more)	> 75% of undergrads from in-state	> 50% live in college-related housing	> 20% of grads pursue postgrad work	> 25% belong to fraternity/sorority
New York (cont.)																													
Bard Coll *Independent*	●								●				●		●			●			●		●				●	●	
Barnard Coll *Independent*	●							●				●			●	●					●				●		●	●	
Bernard M. Baruch Coll *City*	●	●									●			●		●				●			●			●			
Brooklyn Coll *City*	●					●					●			●		●					●		●			●		●	
Canisius Coll *Independent*	●									●			●			●					●		●			●		●	
City Coll *City*						●					●			●		●					●		●			●		●	
City Coll *State*						●								●		●				●			●			●			
City Univ of New York *State*						●								●		●				●			●			●			
Clarkson Univ *Independent*		●						●				●			●			●			●		●				●		●
Colgate Univ *Independent*	●							●				●			●			●			●		●				●	●	●
Coll of Insurance *Independent*		●									●		●			●						●	●				●		
Coll of Mount Saint Vincent *Independent*	●										●		●		●	●						●	●			●	●		
Coll of New Rochelle *Independent*						●					●		●		●		●					●			●	●	●	●	
Coll of Saint Rose *Independent*	●									●				●		●					●		●			●	●		
Coll of Staten Island *City*						●					●			●		●				●			●			●			
Columbia Coll *Independent*	●						●					●				●					●		●				●	●	
Columbia—Sch Engineering & Applied Sci *Independent*			●					●				●				●					●		●				●	●	
Columbia—School of General Studies *Independent*	●												●			●					●		●					●	
Concordia Coll, Bronxville *Lutheran-Missouri Synod*	●										●			●	●		●					●	●				●		
Cornell Univ *Independent*						●	●						●		●			●		●			●				●	●	●
D'Youville Coll *Independent*	●										●			●	●	●					●		●			●	●		
Daemen Coll *Independent*	●										●			●	●		●				●		●			●			●
Dominican Coll of Blauvelt *Roman Catholic*						●					●			●	●		●					●	●					●	
Dowling Coll *Independent*						●					●			●	●		●				●		●			●		●	
Elmira Coll *Independent*	●										●		●		●		●				●		●				●	●	
Eugene Lang Coll of the New School for Social Research *Independent*	●			●					●				●		●	●						●	●						

COLLEGE SELECTION INDEX

	What Kind of Education Will I Receive? Type of School						Can I Get In? Entrance Difficulty					Can I Afford It? Average Annual Cost				What Will It Be Like When I Get There? Campus Setting			Undergrad Enrollment				Student Body			Campus Life			
	Liberal Arts	Business	Engineering/Technical	Fine Arts	Seminary/Bible/Rabbinical/Talmudic	Comprehensive	Most Selective	Highly Selective	Very Selective	Selective	Non-selective	> $20,000	$10,000 to $20,000	< $10,000	> 50% of students receive aid	Urban	Suburban	Rural	Large (> 20,000 students)	Medium (10,000 to 20,000 students)	Small (1,000 to 10,000 students)	Very Small (< 1,000 students)	Coed	Male/Mostly Male (80% or more)	Female/Mostly Female (80% or more)	> 75% of undergrads from in-state	> 50% live in college-related housing	> 20% of grads pursue postgrad work	> 25% belong to fraternity/sorority
New York (cont.)																													
Five Towns Coll *Independent*						•								•	•		•					•	•			•		•	
Fordham Univ *Independent*	•	•							•				•		•	•					•		•				•	•	
Hamilton Coll *Independent*	•							•					•		•			•			•		•				•	•	•
Hartwick Coll *Independent*	•									•			•		•			•			•		•					•	•
Herbert H. Lehman Coll *City*						•					•			•		•					•		•			•			
Hobart and William Smith Colls *Independent*	•								•				•		•			•			•		•				•	•	•
Hofstra Univ *Independent*	•								•				•		•		•				•		•				•	•	•
Houghton Coll *Wesleyan*	•								•					•	•			•			•		•				•	•	
Hunter Coll *City*	•			•							•			•	•	•				•			•			•			
Iona Coll *Independent*	•										•			•	•		•				•		•			•			
Ithaca Coll *Independent*	•									•			•		•			•			•		•				•		
Jewish Theological Seminary of America *Conservative Jewish*					•									•		•													
John Jay Coll of Criminal Justice *City*											•			•		•					•		•			•			
Juilliard School *Independent*				•																									
Keuka Coll *Independent*	•										•			•	•			•				•	•			•	•		
King's Coll *Independent*	•										•			•	•		•					•	•				•		
Laboratory Institute of Merchandising *Independent*											•			•	•	•						•			•				
Le Moyne Coll *Roman Catholic*	•								•				•		•		•				•		•			•	•	•	
LIU–Brooklyn Campus *Independent*						•					•		•		•	•					•		•			•		•	
LIU–C. W. Post Coll *Independent*						•					•		•		•		•				•		•				•	•	
LIU–Southampton Coll *Independent*	•										•		•		•			•			•		•				•	•	
Manhattan Coll *Independent*						•				•			•		•		•				•		•			•		•	
Manhattan School of Music *Independent*				•									•		•	•						•	•					•	
Manhattanville Coll *Independent*	•					•			•				•		•		•				•		•				•	•	
Marist Coll *Independent*	•										•		•		•		•				•		•				•		
Marymount Coll *Independent*	•										•		•		•		•					•			•		•	•	

COLLEGE SELECTION INDEX

	What Kind of Education Will I Receive? Type of School						Can I Get In? Entrance Difficulty					Can I Afford It? Average Annual Cost				What Will It Be Like When I Get There? Campus Setting			Undergrad Enrollment				Student Body			Campus Life			
	Liberal Arts	Business	Engineering/Technical	Fine Arts	Seminary/Bible/Rabbinical/Talmudic	Comprehensive	Most Selective	Highly Selective	Very Selective	Selective	Non-selective	> $20,000	$10,000 to $20,000	< $10,000	> 50% of students receive aid	Urban	Suburban	Rural	Large (> 20,000 students)	Medium (10,000 to 20,000 students)	Small (1,000 to 10,000 students)	Very Small (< 1,000 students)	Coed	Male/Mostly Male (80% or more)	Female/Mostly Female (80% or more)	> 75% of undergrads from in-state	> 50% live in college-related housing	> 20% of grads pursue postgrad work	> 25% belong to fraternity/sorority
New York (cont.)																													
Marymount Manhattan Coll *Independent*	•										•			•	•	•						•			•	•			
Medaille Coll *Independent*	•										•			•	•	•						•	•			•			
Medgar Evers Coll *City*	•										•			•		•					•	•	•						
Mercy Coll *Independent*	•										•			•	•		•				•		•			•			
Molloy Coll *Roman Catholic*						•					•			•	•		•				•		•			•		•	
Mount Saint Mary Coll *Independent*	•										•			•	•		•				•		•				•	•	
Nazareth Coll of Rochester *Independent*	•										•		•		•		•				•		•			•	•	•	
New School for Soc. Res./Parsons School of Des. *Independent*				•					•				•		•	•					•		•						
New York City Technical Coll *City*			•											•	•	•					•		•			•			
New York Institute of Technology *Independent*	•		•	•		•					•			•	•	•	•				•		•			•			
New York Univ *Independent*						•			•				•		•	•				•			•				•	•	
Niagara Univ *Independent*	•					•					•		•		•		•				•		•			•			
Nyack Coll *Christian and Missionary Alliance*	•	•			•						•			•	•		•					•	•						
Pace Univ Westchester *Independent*	•										•		•		•		•				•		•				•		
Pace Univ *Independent*						•					•		•		•	•					•		•			•			
Polytechnic Univ *Independent*			•						•				•		•	•	•				•			•		•			•
Pratt Institute *Independent*				•						•			•		•	•					•		•				•		
Queens Coll *City*	•										•			•		•				•			•			•			
Rensselaer Polytechnic Institute *Independent*			•			•		•					•		•	•					•		•				•		•
Roberts Wesleyan Coll *Free Methodist*	•										•			•	•		•					•	•			•	•		
Rochester Institute of Technology *Independent*						•				•			•		•		•				•		•				•		
Russell Sage Coll *Independent*						•				•			•		•	•					•				•	•	•		
Sarah Lawrence Coll *Independent*	•								•				•		•		•					•	•				•		
School of Visual Arts *Independent*				•																									
Siena Coll *Independent*	•									•			•		•		•				•		•			•	•	•	
Skidmore Coll *Independent*	•								•				•		•			•			•		•				•	•	

COLLEGE SELECTION INDEX

	What Kind of Education Will I Receive?						Can I Get In?					Can I Afford It?				What Will It Be Like When I Get There?													
	Type of School						Entrance Difficulty					Average Annual Cost				Campus Setting			Undergrad Enrollment				Student Body			Campus Life			
	Liberal Arts	Business	Engineering/Technical	Fine Arts	Seminary/Bible/Rabbinical/Talmudic	Comprehensive	Most Selective	Highly Selective	Very Selective	Selective	Non-selective	> $20,000	$10,000 to $20,000	< $10,000	> 50% of students receive aid	Urban	Suburban	Rural	Large (> 20,000 students)	Medium (10,000 to 20,000 students)	Small (1,000 to 10,000 students)	Very Small (< 1,000 students)	Coed	Male/Mostly Male (80% or more)	Female/Mostly Female (80% or more)	> 75% of undergrads from in-state	> 50% live in college-related housing	> 20% of grads pursue postgrad work	> 25% belong to fraternity/sorority
New York (cont.)																													
St. Bonaventure Univ *Independent*						●				●				●	●			●			●		●			●	●	●	
St. Francis Coll *Independent*	●										●			●	●	●					●		●			●		●	
St. John Fisher Coll *Independent*	●									●				●	●		●				●		●			●	●		
St. John's Univ *Independent*						●					●			●	●	●			●				●			●			
St. Joseph's Coll *Independent*	●										●			●	●	●						●	●			●		●	●
St. Lawrence Univ *Independent*	●								●				●		●			●			●		●				●	●	●
St. Thomas Aquinas Coll *Independent*	●										●			●	●		●				●		●					●	
State Univ Coll at Brockport *State*						●					●			●	●		●				●		●			●	●	●	
State Univ Coll at Buffalo *State*						●					●			●	●	●					●		●			●			
State Univ Coll at Cortland *State*	●										●			●	●			●			●		●			●	●		
State Univ Coll at Fredonia *State*	●									●				●	●			●			●		●			●	●	●	
State Univ Coll at Geneseo *State*	●								●					●	●			●			●		●			●	●	●	
State Univ Coll at New Paltz *State*						●				●				●	●						●		●			●			
State Univ Coll at Old Westbury *State*	●										●			●			●				●		●			●	●	●	
State Univ Coll at Oneonta *State*	●									●				●	●			●			●		●			●	●		
State Univ Coll at Oswego *State*	●	●								●				●	●	●					●		●			●	●	●	
State Univ Coll at Plattsburgh *State*	●									●				●	●		●				●		●			●	●	●	
State Univ Coll at Potsdam *State*	●								●					●	●			●			●		●			●		●	●
State Univ of New York at Albany *State*	●								●					●	●	●				●			●			●	●	●	●
State Univ of New York at Albany *State*						●			●					●	●	●				●			●			●	●	●	●
State Univ of New York at Binghamton *State*						●			●					●	●		●				●		●			●			●
State Univ of New York at Buffalo *State*						●			●					●	●		●			●			●			●	●	●	●
State Univ of New York at Stony Brook *State*						●			●					●	●		●				●		●			●		●	
State Univ of New York Maritime Coll *State*										●				●	●	●						●		●			●		
SUNY Coll at Purchase *State*	●					●			●					●	●		●				●		●			●	●	●	●
SUNY-Empire State Coll *State*	●										●			●							●		●			●			

COLLEGE SELECTION INDEX

	What Kind of Education Will I Receive?						Can I Get In?					Can I Afford It?				What Will It Be Like When I Get There?													
	Type of School						Entrance Difficulty					Average Annual Cost				Campus Setting			Undergrad Enrollment				Student Body			Campus Life			
	Liberal Arts	Business	Engineering/Technical	Fine Arts	Seminary/Bible/Rabbinical/Talmudic	Comprehensive	Most Selective	Highly Selective	Very Selective	Selective	Non-selective	> $20,000	$10,000 to $20,000	< $10,000	> 50% of students receive aid	Urban	Suburban	Rural	Large (> 20,000 students)	Medium (10,000 to 20,000 students)	Small (1,000 to 10,000 students)	Very Small (< 1,000 students)	Coed	Male/Mostly Male (80% or more)	Female/Mostly Female (80% or more)	> 75% of undergrads from in-state	> 50% live in college-related housing	> 20% of grads pursue postgrad work	> 25% belong to fraternity/sorority
New York (cont.)																													
SUNY-Fashion Institute of Technology *State*				●							●			●		●					●				●	●		●	
Syracuse Univ *Independent*						●			●				●		●	●				●			●				●	●	●
The Coll of White Plains of Pace Univ *Indpendent*	●										●		●		●		●					●	●						
The Cooper Union for the Advancement of Science and Art *Independent*						●	●							●	●	●						●	●					●	
Touro Coll *Independent*	●									●				●		●					●		●			●	●	●	
Union Coll *Independent*	●							●					●		●		●				●		●				●	●	●
United States Merchant Marine Academy *Federal*									●													●							
United States Military Academy *Federal*			●						●						●		●				●			●			●		
Univ of Rochester *Indpendent*						●		●					●		●		●				●		●				●	●	●
Utica Coll of Syracuse Univ *Independent*	●									●			●		●	●					●		●				●		
Vassar Coll *Independent*	●							●					●		●		●				●		●				●	●	
Wadhams Hall Seminary-Coll *Roman Catholic*					●									●				●				●		●			●		
Wagner Coll *Independent*						●					●		●		●		●				●		●				●	●	●
Webb Institute of Naval Architecture *Independent*			●								●			●	●		●					●	●						
Wells Coll *Independent*	●								●				●		●			●				●			●		●	●	
Yeshiva Univ *Independent*						●			●				●		●	●					●		●				●	●	
York Coll *City*	●										●			●	●	●					●		●			●			
North Carolina																													
Appalachian State Univ *State*					●					●			●			●			●			●			●		●		
Atlantic Christian Coll *Independent*	●													●			●				●		●						
Barber-Scotia Coll *Presbyterian*	●										●			●	●			●				●	●			●	●		●
Barton Coll *Disciples of Christ*	●												●		●		●				●		●			●			
Belmont Abbey Coll *Roman Catholic*	●										●		●		●		●					●	●						●
Bennett Coll *United Methodist*	●										●			●	●	●						●			●				
Campbell Univ *Southern Baptist*	●										●		●		●			●			●		●						
Catawba Coll *United Church of Christ*	●										●		●		●		●					●	●						

COLLEGE SELECTION INDEX

North Carolina (cont.)

	What Kind of Education Will I Receive?						Can I Get In?					Can I Afford It?				What Will It Be Like When I Get There?													
	Type of School						Entrance Difficulty					Average Annual Cost				Campus Setting			Undergrad Enrollment				Student Body			Campus Life			
	Liberal Arts	Business	Engineering/Technical	Fine Arts	Seminary/Bible/Rabbinical/Talmudic	Comprehensive	Most Selective	Highly Selective	Very Selective	Selective	Non-selective	> $20,000	$10,000 to $20,000	< $10,000	> 50% of students receive aid	Urban	Suburban	Rural	Large (> 20,000 students)	Medium (10,000 to 20,000 students)	Small (1,000 to 10,000 students)	Very Small (< 1,000 students)	Coed	Male/Mostly Male (80% or more)	Female/Mostly Female (80% or more)	> 75% of undergrads from in-state	> 50% live in college-related housing	> 20% of grads pursue postgrad work	> 25% belong to fraternity/sorority
Davidson Coll *Presbyterian*	●							●					●		●		●				●		●				●	●	●
Duke Univ *Independent*			●		●		●						●			●				●			●				●	●	●
East Carolina Univ *State*						●					●			●		●				●			●			●			●
East Coast Bible Coll *Church of God*					●									●			●					●	●						
Elon Coll *United Church of Christ*	●										●			●	●		●				●		●					●	●
Fayetteville State Univ *State*						●					●			●	●	●					●		●			●	●		
Gardner-Webb Univ *Southern Baptist*	●										●			●	●		●				●		●			●	●		
Greensboro Coll *United Methodist*	●										●			●			●					●	●				●		
Guilford Coll *Friends*	●								●				●				●				●		●				●		
High Point Coll *United Methodist*	●										●			●	●		●				●		●				●		●
John Wesley Coll *Independent*					●									●	●	●						●	●			●			
Johnson C. Smith Univ *Independent*	●										●			●	●	●					●		●				●	●	●
Lenoir Rhyne Coll *Evangelical Lutheran Church in America*	●					●					●		●		●	●					●		●				●	●	●
Livingstone Coll *African Methodist Episcopal Zion*	●										●			●	●		●					●	●				●		
Mars Hill Coll *Southern Baptist*	●										●			●	●			●			●		●				●	●	●
Meredith Coll *Southern Baptist*	●										●			●			●				●				●	●	●		
Methodist Coll *United Methodist*	●										●			●	●		●				●		●						
Mount Olive Coll *Original Free Will Baptist*	●										●			●	●			●				●	●			●			
North Carolina Agricultural and Tech. State Univ *State*			●			●					●			●	●	●					●		●						
North Carolina Central Univ *State*	●										●			●	●	●					●		●			●	●	●	
North Carolina School of the Arts *State*				●																									
North Carolina State Univ *State*	●	●	●						●					●			●			●			●			●		●	●
North Carolina Wesleyan Coll *United Methodist*	●										●			●	●		●					●	●					●	
Pfeiffer Coll *United Methodist*	●										●			●	●			●				●	●				●		
Queens Coll *Presbyterian*	●										●		●		●	●						●	●				●	●	●
Saint Augustine's Coll *Episcopal*	●										●			●	●	●					●		●				●	●	

COLLEGE SELECTION INDEX

	What Kind of Education Will I Receive? Type of School						Can I Get In? Entrance Difficulty					Can I Afford It? Average Annual Cost				What Will It Be Like When I Get There? Campus Setting			Undergrad Enrollment				Student Body			Campus Life			
	Liberal Arts	Business	Engineering/Technical	Fine Arts	Seminary/Bible/Rabbinical/Talmudic	Comprehensive	Most Selective	Highly Selective	Very Selective	Selective	Non-selective	> $20,000	$10,000 to $20,000	< $10,000	> 50% of students receive aid	Urban	Suburban	Rural	Large (> 20,000 students)	Medium (10,000 to 20,000 students)	Small (1,000 to 10,000 students)	Very Small (< 1,000 students)	Coed	Male/Mostly Male (80% or more)	Female/Mostly Female (80% or more)	> 75% of undergrads from in-state	> 50% live in college-related housing	> 20% of grads pursue postgrad work	> 25% belong to fraternity/sorority
North Carolina (cont.)																													
Salem Coll *Moravian*	●									●				●	●	●						●			●		●		
Shaw Univ *American Baptist*	●										●			●	●	●					●		●				●		
St. Andrews Presbyterian Coll *Presbyterian*	●										●			●	●			●				●	●				●		
Univ of North Carolina at Asheville *State*	●									●				●		●					●		●			●			
Univ of North Carolina at Chapel Hill *State*	●							●						●		●				●			●			●	●		
Univ of North Carolina at Charlotte *State*						●					●			●		●				●			●			●			
Univ of North Carolina at Greensboro *State*						●				●				●		●					●		●			●			
Univ of North Carolina at Wilmington *State*	●										●			●		●					●		●			●			
Wake Forest Univ *Southern Baptist*	●								●				●			●					●		●				●	●	
Warren Wilson Coll *Presbyterian*	●										●			●				●				●	●				●		
Western Carolina Univ *State*						●					●			●				●			●		●			●	●		●
Wingate Coll *Southern Baptist*		●									●			●	●			●			●		●				●		
Winston-Salem State Univ *State*						●					●			●	●		●				●		●			●	●		
North Dakota																													
Dickinson State Coll *State*	●	●		●		●					●			●	●			●			●		●			●			
Jamestown Coll *Presbyterian Church*	●										●			●	●			●				●	●				●		
Mayville State Univ *State*	●	●									●			●	●			●				●	●				●		
Minot State Univ *State*	●	●		●							●			●	●			●			●		●			●			
North Dakota State Univ *State*						●					●			●	●	●					●		●						●
Trinity Bible Coll *Assembly of God*					●						●			●				●				●	●						
Univ of Mary *Roman Catholic*	●										●			●	●		●				●		●			●	●		
Univ of North Dakota *State*	●										●			●	●	●					●		●						
Valley City State Coll *State*	●										●			●	●			●				●	●			●			
Ohio																													
Antioch Coll *Independent*	●									●			●		●		●					●	●				●		
Ashland Coll *Brethen*	●										●		●		●		●				●		●			●	●		●

COLLEGE SELECTION INDEX

Ohio (cont.)

	What Kind of Education Will I Receive?						Can I Get In?					Can I Afford It?				What Will It Be Like When I Get There?												
	Type of School						Entrance Difficulty					Average Annual Cost				Campus Setting			Undergrad Enrollment				Student Body			Campus Life			
	Liberal Arts	Business	Engineering/Technical	Fine Arts	Seminary/Bible/Rabbinical/Talmudic	Comprehensive	Most Selective	Highly Selective	Very Selective	Selective	Non-selective	> $20,000	$10,000 to $20,000	< $10,000	> 50% of students receive aid	Urban	Suburban	Rural	Large (> 20,000 students)	Medium (10,000 to 20,000 students)	Small (1,000 to 10,000 students)	Very Small (< 1,000 students)	Coed	Male/Mostly Male (80% or more)	Female/Mostly Female (80% or more)	> 75% of undergrads from in-state	> 50% live in college-related housing	> 20% of grads pursue postgrad work	> 25% belong to fraternity/sorority
Baldwin-Wallace Coll *United Methodist*	●										●		●		●		●				●		●			●	●	●	●
Bluffton Coll *Mennonite*	●										●		●				●					●	●			●	●		
Bowling Green State Univ *State*	●										●			●			●			●			●			●	●		
Capital Univ *Lutheran*						●				●			●		●		●				●		●			●			
Case Western Reserve Univ *Independent*						●		●					●		●	●					●		●					●	●
Cedarville Coll *Baptist*	●										●		●		●			●			●		●				●		
Central State Univ *State*	●										●			●				●			●		●			●	●		
Cleveland Institute of Art *Independent*				●									●		●	●						●	●						
Cleveland Institute of Music *Independent*				●									●		●	●						●	●					●	
Cleveland State Univ *State*						●					●			●	●	●				●			●			●			
Coll of Mount St. Joseph *Independent*	●										●			●	●		●				●		●			●			
Coll of Wooster *Independent*	●								●				●		●			●			●		●				●	●	●
Columbus Coll of Art and Design *Independent*													●		●	●					●		●						
Defiance Coll *United Church of Christ*	●										●			●	●		●					●	●			●	●		
Denison Univ *Independent*	●									●			●		●			●			●		●				●		●
Dyke Coll *Independent*		●												●	●	●						●	●			●			
Franciscan Univ of Steubenville *Roman Catholic*	●									●				●	●		●				●		●				●		
Heidelberg Coll *United Church of Christ*	●									●			●		●		●					●	●			●	●	●	●
Hiram Coll *Independent*	●								●				●		●			●				●	●			●	●	●	
John Carroll Univ *Roman Catholic*						●					●		●		●		●				●		●				●	●	●
Kent State Univ *State*						●					●			●	●			●	●				●			●			
Kenyon Coll *Episcopal*	●							●					●		●			●			●		●				●	●	●
Lake Erie Coll *Independent*	●										●			●	●		●					●	●			●			
Lourdes Coll *Roman Catholic*	●										●			●			●					●			●	●			
Malone Coll *Evangelical Friends Church*	●										●			●	●		●				●		●			●			
Marietta Coll *Independent*	●									●			●		●		●				●		●				●		

COLLEGE SELECTION INDEX

	What Kind of Education Will I Receive? Type of School						Can I Get In? Entrance Difficulty					Can I Afford It? Average Annual Cost				What Will It Be Like When I Get There? Campus Setting			Undergrad Enrollment				Student Body			Campus Life			
	Liberal Arts	Business	Engineering/Technical	Fine Arts	Seminary/Bible/Rabbinical/Talmudic	Comprehensive	Most Selective	Highly Selective	Very Selective	Selective	Non-selective	> $20,000	$10,000 to $20,000	< $10,000	> 50% of students receive aid	Urban	Suburban	Rural	Large (> 20,000 students)	Medium (10,000 to 20,000 students)	Small (1,000 to 10,000 students)	Very Small (< 1,000 students)	Coed	Male/Mostly Male (80% or more)	Female/Mostly Female (80% or more)	> 75% of undergrads from in-state	> 50% live in college-related housing	> 20% of grads pursue postgrad work	> 25% belong to fraternity/sorority
Ohio (cont.)																													
Miami Univ *State*	●									●				●				●		●			●				●	●	●
Mount Union Coll *United Methodist*	●										●		●		●		●				●		●			●	●	●	●
Mount Vernon Nazarene Coll *Church of the Nazarene*	●										●			●	●		●				●		●			●	●	●	
Muskingum Coll *Presbyterian Church USA*	●										●		●		●			●			●		●			●	●		●
Notre Dame Coll of Ohio *Roman Catholic*	●										●			●	●	●						●			●	●	●		
Wilmington Coll *Friends*	●										●			●	●			●			●		●			●		●	●
Wright State Univ *State*						●					●			●			●				●		●			●			
Xavier Univ *Independent*	●									●			●		●		●				●		●				●	●	
Youngstown State Univ *State*						●					●			●	●	●					●		●			●			
Oklahoma																													
Bartlesville Wesleyan Coll *Wesleyan Church*	●										●			●	●		●					●	●						
Cameron Univ *State*						●					●			●		●					●		●			●			
East Central Univ *State*						●					●			●	●			●			●		●			●	●		
Langston Univ *State*	●		●								●			●				●			●		●			●	●		
Mid-America Bible Coll *Independent*					●									●	●	●						●	●				●		
Northeastern State Univ *State*						●					●			●	●			●			●		●			●			
Northwestern Oklahoma State Univ *State*	●										●			●	●			●			●		●			●			
Oklahoma Baptist Univ *Southern Baptist*	●										●			●	●		●				●		●				●	●	
Oklahoma Christian Univ of Science and Arts *Independent*	●										●			●	●	●					●		●				●		
Oklahoma City Univ *United Methodist*	●										●			●	●	●					●		●					●	
Oklahoma Panhandle State Univ *State*	●										●			●				●			●		●			●			
Oklahoma State Univ *State*						●					●			●	●			●		●			●			●			●
Oral Roberts Univ *Independent*	●										●			●	●		●				●		●				●	●	
Phillips Univ *Disciples of Christ*	●										●			●	●	●						●	●				●		
Southeastern Oklahoma State Univ *State*	●										●			●	●			●			●		●			●			
Southern Nazarene Univ *Nazarene*	●										●			●	●	●						●	●					●	

COLLEGE SELECTION INDEX

	What Kind of Education Will I Receive?						Can I Get In?					Can I Afford It?				What Will It Be Like When I Get There?													
	Type of School						Entrance Difficulty					Average Annual Cost				Campus Setting			Undergrad Enrollment				Student Body			Campus Life			
	Liberal Arts	Business	Engineering/Technical	Fine Arts	Seminary/Bible/Rabbinical/Talmudic	Comprehensive	Most Selective	Highly Selective	Very Selective	Selective	Non-selective	> $20,000	$10,000 to $20,000	< $10,000	> 50% of students receive aid	Urban	Suburban	Rural	Large (> 20,000 students)	Medium (10,000 to 20,000 students)	Small (1,000 to 10,000 students)	Very Small (< 1,000 students)	Coed	Male/Mostly Male (80% or more)	Female/Mostly Female (80% or more)	> 75% of undergrads from in-state	> 50% live in college-related housing	> 20% of grads pursue postgrad work	> 25% belong to fraternity/sorority
Oklahoma (cont.)																													
Southwestern Coll of Christian Ministries *Pentecostal Holiness*					●						●			●	●	●						●	●					●	
Southwestern Oklahoma State Univ *State*	●										●			●	●			●			●		●			●	●		
Univ of Central Oklahoma *State*						●					●			●			●			●			●			●			
Univ of Oklahoma *State*						●					●			●	●		●			●			●			●			●
Univ of Science and Arts of Oklahoma *State*	●										●			●	●			●			●		●			●			
Univ of Tulsa *Independent*						●			●					●	●	●					●		●					●	●
Oregon																													
Concordia Coll, Portland *Lutheran-Missouri Synod*	●												●				●					●	●						
Eastern Oregon State Coll *State*	●										●			●	●			●			●		●						
Eugene Bible Coll *Open Bible Churches*					●									●	●		●					●	●					●	
George Fox Coll *Quaker*	●										●		●		●		●				●		●				●	●	
Lewis and Clark Coll *Independent*	●								●				●		●		●				●		●					●	
Linfield Coll *American Baptist*	●					●					●		●		●			●			●		●					●	●
Marylhurst Coll for Lifelong Learning *Roman Catholic*	●										●			●	●		●					●	●			●			
Mount Angel Seminary *Roman Catholic*	●																					●							
Northwest Christian Coll *Churches of Christ/Disciples of Christ*	●													●	●		●					●	●					●	
Oregon Health Sciences Univ *State*											●					●													
Oregon Institute of Technology *State*			●								●			●	●			●			●		●						
Oregon State Univ *State*	●		●								●			●	●			●		●			●			●		●	●
Pacific Northwest Coll of Art *Independent*				●										●	●	●						●	●						
Pacific Univ *Independent*	●										●		●		●		●					●	●				●		●
Portland State Univ *State*						●					●			●	●	●					●		●			●			
Reed Coll *Independent*	●						●						●				●				●		●				●	●	
Southern Oregon State Coll *State*	●	●		●		●					●			●	●		●	●			●		●						
Univ of Oregon *State*						●				●				●	●	●				●			●						
Univ of Portland *Independent*						●					●		●		●		●				●		●						

COLLEGE SELECTION INDEX

	What Kind of Education Will I Receive?						Can I Get In?					Can I Afford It?				What Will It Be Like When I Get There?													
	Type of School						Entrance Difficulty					Average Annual Cost				Campus Setting			Undergrad Enrollment				Student Body			Campus Life			
	Liberal Arts	Business	Engineering/Technical	Fine Arts	Seminary/Bible/Rabbinical/Talmudic	Comprehensive	Most Selective	Highly Selective	Very Selective	Selective	Non-selective	> $20,000	$10,000 to $20,000	< $10,000	> 50% of students receive aid	Urban	Suburban	Rural	Large (> 20,000 students)	Medium (10,000 to 20,000 students)	Small (1,000 to 10,000 students)	Very Small (< 1,000 students)	Coed	Male/Mostly Male (80% or more)	Female/Mostly Female (80% or more)	> 75% of undergrads from in-state	> 50% live in college-related housing	> 20% of grads pursue postgrad work	> 25% belong to fraternity/sorority
Oregon (cont.)																													
Warner Pacific Coll *Church of God*	●										●			●		●						●	●						
Western Baptist Coll *Independent*	●				●						●			●	●		●					●	●				●		
Western Oregon State Coll *State*	●					●					●			●	●			●			●		●			●	●		
Willamette Univ *United Methodist*	●								●						●	●					●		●				●	●	●
Pennsylvania																													
Academy of the New Church *Church of New Jerusalem*					●					●				●			●					●	●						
Albright Coll *United Methodist*	●								●				●		●		●					●	●				●	●	●
Allegheny Coll *United Methodist*	●								●			●			●		●				●		●				●	●	●
Allentown Coll of St. Francis De Sales *Roman Catholic*	●										●		●		●			●			●		●				●		
Alvernia Coll *Roman Catholic*	●										●			●	●	●					●		●			●	●		
Baptist Bible Coll and Seminary of Pennsylvania *Baptist*					●									●	●	●						●	●				●		
Beaver Coll *Independent*	●										●		●		●		●				●		●			●			
Bloomsburg Univ of Pennsylvania *State*	●										●			●	●			●			●		●			●			
Bryn Mawr Coll *Independent*	●						●					●					●				●				●		●	●	
Bucknell Univ *Independent*	●							●				●			●			●			●		●				●	●	●
Cabrini Coll *Roman Catholic*	●										●		●		●		●				●		●				●		
California Univ of Pennsylvania *State*						●					●			●			●				●		●			●			
Carlow Coll *Roman Catholic*	●										●		●		●	●						●			●	●			
Carnegie Mellon Univ *Independent*						●			●			●			●						●		●				●	●	●
Cedar Crest Coll *United Church of Christ*	●									●			●		●		●				●				●	●	●	●	
Chatham Coll *Independent*	●									●			●		●	●						●			●	●	●	●	
Chestnut Hill Coll *Independent*	●									●			●		●		●					●			●	●	●		
Cheyney Univ of Pennsylvania *State*	●										●			●	●		●				●		●			●	●		
Clarion Univ of Pennsylvania *State*	●										●			●	●			●			●		●			●			
Coll Misericordia *Roman Catholic*	●										●		●		●		●					●	●				●		
Delaware Valley Coll of Science and Agriculture *Independent/State*											●		●		●		●				●		●				●		

COLLEGE SELECTION INDEX

Pennsylvania (cont.)

	What Kind of Education Will I Receive?						Can I Get In?					Can I Afford It?				What Will It Be Like When I Get There?													
	Type of School						Entrance Difficulty					Average Annual Cost				Campus Setting			Undergrad Enrollment				Student Body			Campus Life			
	Liberal Arts	Business	Engineering/Technical	Fine Arts	Seminary/Bible/Rabbinical/Talmudic	Comprehensive	Most Selective	Highly Selective	Very Selective	Selective	Non-selective	> $20,000	$10,000 to $20,000	< $10,000	> 50% of students receive aid	Urban	Suburban	Rural	Large (> 20,000 students)	Medium (10,000 to 20,000 students)	Small (1,000 to 10,000 students)	Very Small (< 1,000 students)	Coed	Male/Mostly Male (80% or more)	Female/Mostly Female (80% or more)	> 75% of undergrads from in-state	> 50% live in college-related housing	> 20% of grads pursue postgrad work	> 25% belong to fraternity/sorority
Dickinson Coll *Independent*	●								●				●		●		●				●		●				●	●	●
Drexel Univ *Independent/State*						●			●				●		●	●					●		●				●		●
Duquesne Univ *Roman Catholic*						●				●			●		●	●					●		●			●	●	●	●
East Stroudsburg Univ of Pennsylvania *State*						●					●			●	●			●			●		●			●			
Eastern Coll *American Baptist*	●										●		●		●		●				●		●					●	
Edinboro Univ of Pennsylvania *State*						●					●			●	●			●			●		●			●			●
Elizabethtown Coll *Church of the Brethen*	●								●				●		●		●				●		●				●		
Franklin and Marshall Coll *Independent*	●							●				●			●		●				●		●				●	●	●
Gannon Univ *Roman Catholic*	●										●		●		●	●					●		●			●	●	●	
Geneva Coll *Reformed Presbyterian*	●										●			●	●		●				●		●			●	●	●	
Gettysburg Coll *Independent*	●								●				●					●			●		●				●	●	●
Gratz Coll *Jewish*																													
Grove City Coll *United Presbyterian*	●								●					●	●			●			●		●				●		●
Gwynedd-Mercy Coll *Independent*						●					●		●		●		●					●	●			●			
School of Sciences and Human Resources *Independent*														●	●	●						●	●			●			
Haverford Coll *Independent*	●						●						●				●				●		●				●	●	
Holy Family Coll *Roman Catholic*	●										●			●	●	●					●		●			●			
Immaculata Coll *Roman Catholic*	●										●			●			●					●			●	●			
Indiana Univ of Pennsylvania *State*						●				●				●	●			●		●			●			●			●
Juniata Coll *Independent*	●								●				●		●			●			●		●			●	●	●	
King's Coll *Roman Catholic*	●										●		●		●	●					●		●						
Kutztown Univ *State*						●					●			●	●			●			●		●			●	●		
La Roche Coll *Roman Catholic*						●					●			●	●		●					●	●			●		●	
La Salle Univ *Independent*	●	●							●				●		●	●					●		●				●		●
Lafayette Coll *Presbyterian Church*	●							●					●				●				●		●				●	●	●
Lancaster Bible Coll *Independent*					●									●	●		●					●	●						

COLLEGE SELECTION INDEX

	What Kind of Education Will I Receive? Type of School						Can I Get In? Entrance Difficulty					Can I Afford It? Average Annual Cost				What Will It Be Like When I Get There? Campus Setting			Undergrad Enrollment				Student Body			Campus Life			
	Liberal Arts	Business	Engineering/Technical	Fine Arts	Seminary/Bible/Rabbinical/Talmudic	Comprehensive	Most Selective	Highly Selective	Very Selective	Selective	Non-selective	> $20,000	$10,000 to $20,000	< $10,000	> 50% of students receive aid	Urban	Suburban	Rural	Large (> 20,000 students)	Medium (10,000 to 20,000 students)	Small (1,000 to 10,000 students)	Very Small (< 1,000 students)	Coed	Male/Mostly Male (80% or more)	Female/Mostly Female (80% or more)	> 75% of undergrads from in-state	> 50% live in college-related housing	> 20% of grads pursue postgrad work	> 25% belong to fraternity/sorority
Pennsylvania (cont.)																													
Lebanon Valley Coll *United Methodist*	●									●			●		●			●				●	●			●	●		●
Lehigh Univ *Independent*						●		●					●		●		●				●		●				●		●
Lincoln Univ of Pennsylvania *Independent/State*	●										●			●	●			●			●		●				●		
Lock Haven Univ of Pennsylvania *State*	●										●			●	●		●				●		●			●			
Lycoming Coll *United Methodist*	●										●		●		●		●				●		●			●	●		●
Mansfield Univ of Pennsylvania *State*						●					●			●	●			●			●		●			●	●		
Marywood Coll *Independent*	●										●		●		●		●				●		●			●			
Mercyhurst Coll *Independent*	●										●			●	●		●				●		●				●		
Messiah Coll *Brethen in Christ*	●								●					●	●		●				●		●				●	●	
Millersville Univ of Pennsylvania *State*	●									●				●	●		●				●		●			●	●		
Moore Coll of Art *Independent*				●									●		●	●						●			●		●		
Moravian Coll *Moravian*	●									●			●		●	●					●		●				●		●
Muhlenberg Coll *Evangelical Lutheran Church in America*	●								●				●		●		●				●		●				●	●	●
Neumann Coll *Roman Catholic*	●										●			●	●		●					●	●			●			
Pennsylvania State Univ *State*						●		●						●	●		●		●				●			●			●
Philadelphia Coll of Art *Independent*				●																									
Philadelphia Coll of Bible *Independent*					●						●			●	●		●					●	●						
Philadelphia Coll of Pharmacy and Science *Independent*									●				●		●	●					●		●				●	●	
Philadelphia Coll of Textiles and Science *Independent*						●					●		●		●		●				●		●						
Point Park Coll *Independent*	●										●			●	●	●					●		●			●			
Robert Morris Coll *Independent*		●									●			●	●		●				●		●			●			
Rosemont Coll *Roman Catholic*	●							●					●		●		●					●			●		●	●	
Saint Charles Borromeo Seminary *Roman Catholic*					●																			●					
Saint Francis Coll *Roman Catholic*	●										●		●		●			●			●		●				●		●
Saint Joseph's Univ *Roman Catholic*						●				●			●		●	●					●		●				●	●	●
Saint Vincent Coll *Roman Catholic*	●										●		●		●			●			●		●			●	●	●	

COLLEGE SELECTION INDEX

	What Kind of Education Will I Receive? — Type of School						Can I Get In? — Entrance Difficulty					Can I Afford It? — Average Annual Cost				What Will It Be Like When I Get There? — Campus Setting			Undergrad Enrollment				Student Body			Campus Life			
	Liberal Arts	Business	Engineering/Technical	Fine Arts	Seminary/Bible/Rabbinical/Talmudic	Comprehensive	Most Selective	Highly Selective	Very Selective	Selective	Non-selective	> $20,000	$10,000 to $20,000	< $10,000	> 50% of students receive aid	Urban	Suburban	Rural	Large (> 20,000 students)	Medium (10,000 to 20,000 students)	Small (1,000 to 10,000 students)	Very Small (< 1,000 students)	Coed	Male/Mostly Male (80% or more)	Female/Mostly Female (80% or more)	> 75% of undergrads from in-state	> 50% live in college-related housing	> 20% of grads pursue postgrad work	> 25% belong to fraternity/sorority
Pennsylvania (cont.)																													
Seton Hill Coll *Independent*	●										●		●		●		●					●			●	●	●	●	
Shippensburg Univ *State*	●									●				●	●			●			●		●			●	●		●
Slippery Rock Univ *State*	●										●			●	●			●			●		●			●			
Swarthmore Coll *Independent*	●		●				●						●		●		●				●		●				●	●	
Temple Univ *Indpendent/State*						●				●				●	●	●				●			●						
Thiel Coll *Lutheran*	●										●		●		●			●				●	●			●	●		●
Univ of Pennsylvania *Independent/State*						●	●						●			●					●		●				●		●
Univ of Pittsburgh, Bradford Campus *State-related*	●										●			●	●			●				●	●			●	●		
Univ of Pittsburgh *State-related*						●			●					●	●	●				●			●			●		●	
Univ of Scranton *Roman Catholic*	●					●				●			●		●	●					●		●				●	●	
Univ of the Arts *Independent*				●							●		●		●	●					●		●						
Ursinus Coll *Independent*	●								●				●		●		●				●		●				●	●	●
Villanova Univ *Roman Catholic*						●			●				●		●		●				●		●				●	●	●
Washington and Jefferson Coll *Independent*	●									●			●		●		●				●		●				●	●	●
Waynesburg Coll *Presbyterian*	●										●			●	●			●			●		●			●			
West Chester Univ of Pennsylvania *State*						●					●			●	●		●				●		●			●	●		
Westminster Coll *Presbyterian*	●									●			●		●			●			●		●			●	●		●
Widener Univ *Independent*						●				●			●		●		●				●		●				●		●
Wilkes Univ *Independent*	●										●		●		●	●					●		●			●	●	●	
Wilson Coll *Independent*	●										●		●		●		●					●			●		●	●	
York Coll of Pennsylvania *Independent*						●					●			●	●		●				●		●				●	●	●
Puerto Rico																													
Bayamon Central Univ *Roman Catholic*	●										●			●							●		●			●			
Conservatorio de Musica de Puerto Rico *State*				●																									
Inter American Univ of Puerto Rico *Independent*	●					●					●			●	●	●			●				●			●			
Pontifical Catholic Univ of Puerto Rico *Roman Catholic*	●										●			●	●	●					●		●			●	●		

COLLEGE SELECTION INDEX

	What Kind of Education Will I Receive? Type of School						Can I Get In? Entrance Difficulty					Can I Afford It? Average Annual Cost				What Will It Be Like When I Get There? Campus Setting			Undergrad Enrollment				Student Body			Campus Life			
	Liberal Arts	Business	Engineering/Technical	Fine Arts	Seminary/Bible/Rabbinical/Talmudic	Comprehensive	Most Selective	Highly Selective	Very Selective	Selective	Non-selective	> $20,000	$10,000 to $20,000	< $10,000	> 50% of students receive aid	Urban	Suburban	Rural	Large (> 20,000 students)	Medium (10,000 to 20,000 students)	Small (1,000 to 10,000 students)	Very Small (< 1,000 students)	Coed	Male/Mostly Male (80% or more)	Female/Mostly Female (80% or more)	> 75% of undergrads from in-state	> 50% live in college-related housing	> 20% of grads pursue postgrad work	> 25% belong to fraternity/sorority
Puerto Rico (cont.)																													
Univ of Puerto Rico *Commonwealth*						•					•			•		•			•				•			•			
Univ of Sacred Heart *Independent*	•										•			•		•					•		•			•	•		
Rhode Island																													
Brown Univ *Independent*	•						•					•				•					•		•				•	•	
Bryant Coll *Independent*		•								•			•		•		•				•		•				•	•	•
Providence Coll *Roman Catholic*	•								•				•		•	•					•		•				•	•	
Rhode Island Coll *State*	•										•			•		•					•		•			•			
Rhode Island School of Design *Independent*				•					•				•		•	•					•		•				•		
Roger Williams Coll *Independent*	•										•		•		•		•				•		•				•	•	•
Salve Regina Univ *Roman Catholic*						•					•		•		•		•				•		•				•	•	
Univ of Rhode Island *State*						•				•				•	•			•			•		•				•		•
South Carolina																													
Benedict Coll *American Baptist*	•										•			•		•					•		•			•	•		
Central Wesleyan Coll *Wesleyan*	•										•		•			•			•				•	•				•	•
Claflin Coll *United Methodist*	•										•			•			•					•	•						
Clemson Univ *State*						•			•					•	•			•		•			•				•		•
Coastal Carolina Univ *State*						•					•			•	•		•				•		•						
Coker Coll *Independent*	•										•		•		•			•				•	•			•		•	
Coll of Charleston *State*	•										•			•	•	•					•		•			•		•	•
Columbia Bible Coll and Seminary *Independent*					•									•	•		•					•	•				•		
Columbia Coll *United Methodist*	•										•		•		•		•				•				•	•	•		
Converse Coll *Independent*	•									•			•		•	•						•			•		•	•	
Erskine Coll *Presbyterian*	•										•		•		•			•				•	•			•	•	•	•
Francis Marion Coll *State*	•										•			•	•			•			•		•			•			
Furman Univ *Independent*	•								•				•		•		•				•		•				•	•	•
Lander Univ *State*	•										•			•				•			•		•			•			

COLLEGE SELECTION INDEX

	What Kind of Education Will I Receive?						Can I Get In?					Can I Afford It?				What Will It Be Like When I Get There?													
	Type of School						Entrance Difficulty					Average Annual Cost				Campus Setting			Undergrad Enrollment				Student Body			Campus Life			
	Liberal Arts	Business	Engineering/Technical	Fine Arts	Seminary/Bible/Rabbinical/Talmudic	Comprehensive	Most Selective	Highly Selective	Very Selective	Selective	Non-selective	> $20,000	$10,000 to $20,000	< $10,000	> 50% of students receive aid	Urban	Suburban	Rural	Large (> 20,000 students)	Medium (10,000 to 20,000 students)	Small (1,000 to 10,000 students)	Very Small (< 1,000 students)	Coed	Male/Mostly Male (80% or more)	Female/Mostly Female (80% or more)	> 75% of undergrads from in-state	> 50% live in college-related housing	> 20% of grads pursue postgrad work	> 25% belong to fraternity/sorority
South Carolina (cont.)																													
Limestone Coll *Independent*	●										●			●	●		●					●	●			●			
Morris Coll *Baptist*	●										●			●	●		●					●	●			●	●		
Newberry Coll *Lutheran*	●										●			●	●		●					●	●			●	●		●
Presbyterian Coll *Presbyterian*	●								●				●		●			●			●		●				●	●	●
South Carolina State Coll *State*	●										●			●				●			●		●			●	●		
The Citadel *State*						●				●				●	●		●				●			●			●	●	
Univ of South Carolina at Aiken *State*	●										●			●			●				●		●			●			
Univ of South Carolina at Spartanburg *State*						●					●			●			●				●		●			●			
Univ of South Carolina *State*						●					●			●	●	●				●			●			●	●		●
Voorhees Coll *Episcopal*	●										●			●	●			●				●	●			●	●	●	●
Winthrop Univ *State*						●					●			●		●					●		●			●			●
Wofford Coll *United Methodist*	●									●			●		●	●					●		●				●	●	●
South Dakota																													
Augustana Coll *Lutheran*	●								●				●		●	●						●	●				●	●	●
Black Hills State Univ *State*	●										●			●	●			●			●		●			●			
Dakota State Coll *State*	●										●		●		●		●				●		●				●	●	
Dakota Wesleyan Univ *State*	●										●			●	●			●				●	●			●	●		
Huron Univ *Independent*	●										●			●	●			●				●	●						
Mount Marty Coll *Roman Catholic*	●										●			●	●			●				●			●		●		
Northern State Coll *State*	●										●			●	●	●					●		●			●			
Sinte Glesko Univ *Independent*	●										●			●	●			●				●	●			●			
Sioux Falls Coll *American Baptist*	●										●			●	●	●						●	●						
South Dakota School of Mines and Technology *State*			●							●				●	●		●				●		●				●	●	
South Dakota State Univ *State*	●					●					●			●	●			●			●		●			●	●		
Univ of South Dakota *State*						●					●			●	●			●			●		●				●		●

COLLEGE SELECTION INDEX

	What Kind of Education Will I Receive?						Can I Get In?					Can I Afford It?				What Will It Be Like When I Get There?													
	Type of School						Entrance Difficulty					Average Annual Cost				Campus Setting			Undergrad Enrollment				Student Body			Campus Life			
	Liberal Arts	Business	Engineering/Technical	Fine Arts	Seminary/Bible/Rabbinical/Talmudic	Comprehensive	Most Selective	Highly Selective	Very Selective	Selective	Non-selective	> $20,000	$10,000 to $20,000	< $10,000	> 50% of students receive aid	Urban	Suburban	Rural	Large (> 20,000 students)	Medium (10,000 to 20,000 students)	Small (1,000 to 10,000 students)	Very Small (< 1,000 students)	Coed	Male/Mostly Male (80% or more)	Female/Mostly Female (80% or more)	> 75% of undergrads from in-state	> 50% live in college-related housing	> 20% of grads pursue postgrad work	> 25% belong to fraternity/sorority
Tennessee																													
Austin Peay State Univ *State*						●					●			●	●	●					●		●			●			
Belmont Univ *Southern Baptist*	●										●			●	●	●					●		●						
Bethel Coll *Presbyterian*	●										●			●	●			●				●	●					●	
Carson-Newman Coll *Southern Baptist*	●										●			●	●			●			●		●				●	●	
Christian Brothers Coll *Independent*	●								●				●		●	●					●		●			●	●		●
Crichton Coll *Independent*	●	●				●					●			●	●		●					●	●						
David Lipscomb Univ *Church of Christ*	●										●			●	●	●					●		●				●		●
East Tennessee State Univ *State*						●					●			●		●					●		●			●			
Fisk Univ *Independent*	●										●			●	●	●						●	●				●		
Freed-Hardeman Coll *Independent*	●										●			●	●			●			●		●						●
Johnson Bible Coll *Christian Church*					●									●	●			●				●	●				●		
King Coll *Presbyterian Church*	●									●				●	●		●					●	●						
Knoxville Coll *Presbyterian Church*	●										●			●	●	●					●		●				●		
Lambuth Coll *United Methodist*	●										●			●	●	●						●	●			●			●
Lane Coll *Christian Methodist Episcopal*	●										●			●	●	●						●	●				●		●
Lee Coll *Church of God*	●										●			●	●		●				●		●				●		
Lemoyne-Owen Coll *United Church of Christ, Baptist*	●										●			●	●	●					●		●			●			
Lincoln Memorial Univ *Independent*						●					●			●	●			●				●	●					●	
Maryville Coll *Independent*	●										●		●		●		●					●	●				●	●	
Memphis Coll of Art *Independent*				●										●	●	●						●	●						
Memphis State Univ *State*						●					●			●	●	●				●			●			●			
Middle Tennessee State Univ *State*						●					●			●	●		●			●			●			●			
Milligan Coll *Church of Christ*	●										●			●	●		●					●	●				●		
Rhodes Coll *Presbyterian*	●								●				●		●		●				●		●				●	●	●
Southern Coll of Seventh-Day Adventists *Seventh-day Adventist*	●										●			●	●			●			●		●				●	●	
Tennessee State Univ *State*						●					●			●	●	●					●		●			●			

COLLEGE SELECTION INDEX

	What Kind of Education Will I Receive?						Can I Get In?					Can I Afford It?				What Will It Be Like When I Get There?													
	Type of School						Entrance Difficulty					Average Annual Cost				Campus Setting			Undergrad Enrollment				Student Body			Campus Life			
	Liberal Arts	Business	Engineering/Technical	Fine Arts	Seminary/Bible/Rabbinical/Talmudic	Comprehensive	Most Selective	Highly Selective	Very Selective	Selective	Non-selective	> $20,000	$10,000 to $20,000	< $10,000	> 50% of students receive aid	Urban	Suburban	Rural	Large (< 20,000 students)	Medium (10,000 to 20,000 students)	Small (1,000 to 10,000 students)	Very Small (< 1,000 students)	Coed	Male/Mostly Male (80% or more)	Female/Mostly Female (80% or more)	> 75% of undergrads from in-state	> 50% live in college-related housing	> 20% of grads pursue postgrad work	> 25% belong to fraternity/sorority
Tennessee (cont.)																													
Tennessee Technological Univ *State*			●								●			●	●			●			●		●			●			●
Tennessee Wesleyan Coll *United Methodist*	●										●			●	●			●				●	●						
Trevecca Nazarene Coll *Nazarene*	●										●			●		●					●		●				●		
Tusculum Coll *Presbyterian*	●										●			●	●		●					●	●			●	●		
Union Univ *Southern Baptist*	●										●			●			●				●		●			●	●	●	●
Univ of Tennessee at Chattanooga *State*						●					●			●	●	●					●		●			●			
Univ of Tennessee at Martin *State*	●										●			●	●			●			●		●			●	●	●	●
Univ of Tennessee *State*						●				●				●	●	●				●			●			●	●		●
Univ of the South *Episcopal*	●							●					●					●			●		●				●	●	●
Vanderbilt Univ *Independent*						●		●					●		●	●					●		●				●	●	●
William Jennings Bryan Coll *Independent*	●										●			●	●			●				●	●				●		
Texas																													
Abilene Christian Univ *Church of Christ*						●					●		●		●	●					●		●					●	
Angelo State Univ *State*	●										●			●		●					●		●			●			
Austin Coll *Presbyterian*	●								●				●		●		●				●		●			●	●	●	●
Baylor Univ *Baptist*						●				●				●	●	●					●		●			●			●
Concordia Lutheran Coll *Lutheran-Missouri Synod*	●										●			●	●	●						●	●			●			
Dallas Baptist Univ *Southern Baptist*	●										●			●	●	●						●	●			●			
East Texas Baptist Univ *Southern Baptist*	●										●			●				●				●	●			●	●		
East Texas State Univ *State*						●					●			●				●			●		●			●			
Hardin-Simmons Univ *Southern Baptist*	●										●			●	●	●					●		●			●			
Houston Baptist Univ *Southern Baptist*	●										●			●	●		●				●		●			●			
Howard Payne Univ *Southern Baptist*	●										●			●	●		●				●		●					●	●
Huston-Tillotson Coll *United Methodist, United Church of Christ*	●										●			●	●	●						●	●			●			●
Incarnate Word Coll *Roman Catholic*	●										●			●	●	●					●		●			●			
Jarvis Christian Coll *Disciples of Christ*	●										●			●	●			●				●	●						

COLLEGE SELECTION INDEX

	What Kind of Education Will I Receive?						Can I Get In?					Can I Afford It?				What Will It Be Like When I Get There?												
	Type of School						Entrance Difficulty					Average Annual Cost				Campus Setting			Undergrad Enrollment				Student Body			Campus Life			
	Liberal Arts	Business	Engineering/Technical	Fine Arts	Seminary/Bible/Rabbinical/Talmudic	Comprehensive	Most Selective	Highly Selective	Very Selective	Selective	Non-selective	> $20,000	$10,000 to $20,000	< $10,000	> 50% of students receive aid	Urban	Suburban	Rural	Large (> 20,000 students)	Medium (10,000 to 20,000 students)	Small (1,000 to 10,000 students)	Very Small (< 1,000 students)	Coed	Male/Mostly Male (80% or more)	Female/Mostly Female (80% or more)	> 75% of undergrads from in-state	> 50% live in college-related housing	> 20% of grads pursue postgrad work	> 25% belong to fraternity/sorority
Texas (cont.)																													
Lamar Univ *State*	•		•								•			•	•		•				•		•			•			
Letourneau Univ *Independent*						•					•			•	•	•						•	•				•		
Lubbock Christian Univ *Church of Christ*	•										•			•	•		•					•	•						•
McMurry Coll *United Methodist*	•										•			•	•	•					•		•			•			•
Midwestern State Univ *State*	•										•			•		•					•		•			•			
Our Lady of the Lake Univ of San Antonio *Roman Catholic*	•										•			•	•	•					•				•				
Paul Quinn Coll *African Methodist Episcopal*	•										•			•	•	•					•		•			•	•		
Prairie View Agricultural and Mechanical Univ *State*						•					•			•	•			•			•		•			•	•	•	•
Rice Univ *Independent*						•	•							•	•	•					•		•				•	•	
Sam Houston State Univ *State*						•					•			•			•				•		•			•	•		
Schreiner Coll *Presbyterian*	•										•			•	•			•				•	•			•	•	•	
Southern Methodist Univ *Independent*	•								•				•		•		•				•		•				•	•	•
Southwest Texas State Univ *State*	•										•			•			•			•			•			•			
Southwestern Adventist Coll *Seventh-day Adventist*	•										•			•	•		•					•	•						
Southwestern Assemblies of God Coll *Assemblies of God*					•						•			•	•		•					•	•						
Southwestern Christian Coll *Independent*					•																								
Southwestern Univ *United Methodist*	•								•				•		•		•				•		•			•	•	•	•
St. Edward's Univ *Independent*	•										•			•	•	•					•		•			•	•		
St. Mary's Univ of San Antonio *Roman Catholic*	•		•								•			•	•		•				•		•			•	•		•
Stephen F. Austin State Univ *State*	•										•			•	•			•		•			•			•	•		•
Tarleton State Univ *State*	•										•			•	•			•			•		•			•			
Texas A & M at Galveston *State*										•				•			•				•		•				•		
Texas A & M Univ–Kingsville *State*	•										•			•	•		•				•		•			•			
Texas A & M Univ *State*						•				•				•	•	•			•				•			•	•		
Texas Christian Univ *Independent*						•				•				•	•	•					•		•					•	•
Texas Coll *Christian Methodist Episcopal*	•										•			•	•	•						•	•				•		

COLLEGE SELECTION INDEX

	What Kind of Education Will I Receive?						Can I Get In?					Can I Afford It?				What Will It Be Like When I Get There?													
	Type of School						Entrance Difficulty					Average Annual Cost				Campus Setting			Undergrad Enrollment				Student Body			Campus Life			
	Liberal Arts	Business	Engineering/Technical	Fine Arts	Seminary/Bible/Rabbinical/Talmudic	Comprehensive	Most Selective	Highly Selective	Very Selective	Selective	Non-selective	> $20,000	$10,000 to $20,000	< $10,000	> 50% of students receive aid	Urban	Suburban	Rural	Large (> 20,000 students)	Medium (10,000 to 20,000 students)	Small (1,000 to 10,000 students)	Very Small (< 1,000 students)	Coed	Male/Mostly Male (80% or more)	Female/Mostly Female (80% or more)	> 75% of undergrads from in-state	> 50% live in college-related housing	> 20% of grads pursue postgrad work	> 25% belong to fraternity/sorority
Texas (cont.)																													
Texas Lutheran Coll *Evangelical Lutheran Church in America*	●										●			●	●			●				●	●			●	●	●	●
Texas Southern Univ *State*						●					●			●	●	●					●		●			●		●	●
Texas Tech Univ *State*											●			●		●				●			●			●		●	
Texas Wesleyan Univ *United Methodist*						●					●			●		●					●		●						
Texas Woman's Univ *State*						●					●			●	●	●					●				●	●			
Trinity Univ *Independent*	●							●					●		●	●					●		●				●	●	●
Univ of Dallas *Roman Catholic*	●								●				●		●		●				●		●				●	●	
Univ of Houston *State*						●					●			●		●				●			●			●			
Univ of Mary Hardin-Baylor *Southern Baptist*	●	●		●							●			●	●			●			●		●			●	●	●	
Univ of North Texas *State*	●					●					●			●		●				●			●			●			
Univ of St. Thomas *Roman Catholic*	●									●				●	●	●						●	●			●			
Univ of Texas at Arlington *State*						●					●			●	●		●			●			●			●			
Univ of Texas at Austin *State*						●		●						●	●	●			●				●			●			●
Univ of Texas at El Paso *State*	●			●							●			●	●	●				●			●			●			
Univ of Texas at San Antonio *State*						●					●			●	●		●				●		●			●			
Univ of Texas—Pan American *State*						●					●			●	●		●				●		●			●			
Wayland Baptist Univ *Southern Baptist*	●										●			●	●			●			●		●			●	●	●	
West Texas State Univ *State*						●					●			●	●			●			●		●						
Wiley Coll *United Methodist*		●									●			●	●			●				●	●				●		●
Utah																													
Brigham Young Univ *Latter-Day Saints*						●			●					●	●		●		●				●				●	●	
Southern Utah Univ *State*	●										●			●	●			●			●		●			●			
Univ of Utah *State*						●					●			●	●	●				●			●			●		●	
Utah State Univ *State*	●										●			●	●	●				●			●			●			
Weber State Coll *State*	●										●			●		●					●		●			●			
Westminster Coll of Salt Lake City *Independent*	●										●			●	●		●				●		●			●		●	

COLLEGE SELECTION INDEX

	What Kind of Education Will I Receive?						Can I Get In?					Can I Afford It?				What Will It Be Like When I Get There?													
	Type of School						Entrance Difficulty					Average Annual Cost				Campus Setting			Undergrad Enrollment				Student Body			Campus Life			
	Liberal Arts	Business	Engineering/Technical	Fine Arts	Seminary/Bible/Rabbinical/Talmudic	Comprehensive	Most Selective	Highly Selective	Very Selective	Selective	Non-selective	> $20,000	$10,000 to $20,000	< $10,000	> 50% of students receive aid	Urban	Suburban	Rural	Large (> 20,000 students)	Medium (10,000 to 20,000 students)	Small (1,000 to 10,000 students)	Very Small (< 1,000 students)	Coed	Male/Mostly Male (80% or more)	Female/Mostly Female (80% or more)	> 75% of undergrads from in-state	> 50% live in college-related housing	> 20% of grads pursue postgrad work	> 25% belong to fraternity/sorority
Vermont																													
Bennington Coll *Independent*	●								●			●			●			●				●	●				●		
Burlington Coll *Independent*	●													●	●	●						●	●			●		●	
Castleton State Coll *State*	●										●			●	●			●			●		●				●		
Champlain Coll *Independent*		●											●			●					●		●			●			
Coll of St. Joseph *Independent*	●										●			●	●			●				●	●				●		
Goddard Coll *Independent*	●										●		●		●			●				●	●				●	●	
Green Mountain Coll *Independent*	●										●		●		●			●					●				●	●	
Johnson State Coll *State*	●										●			●	●			●			●		●				●		
Lyndon State Coll *State*	●										●			●	●			●			●		●				●		
Marlboro Coll *Independent*	●								●				●		●		●					●	●				●	●	
Middlebury Coll *Independent*	●							●				●						●			●		●				●		
Norwich Univ *Independent*						●					●		●		●			●			●		●				●		
Saint Michael's Coll *Roman Catholic*	●					●				●			●		●		●				●		●				●		
Southern Vermont Coll *Independent*	●										●			●	●		●					●	●				●		
Trinity Coll of Vermont *Roman Catholic*	●										●		●		●		●					●			●	●	●		
Univ of Vermont *State*						●				●				●	●	●					●		●				●		
Virginia																													
Averett Coll *Southern Baptist*	●										●		●		●	●					●		●			●			●
Bluefield Coll *Southern Baptist*	●										●		●		●		●					●	●			●			
Bridgewater Coll *Independent*	●										●			●			●				●		●			●	●		
Christendom Coll *Roman Catholic*	●												●					●				●	●				●		
Christopher Newport Coll *State*						●					●			●			●				●		●			●			
Christopher Newport Univ *State*						●					●			●			●				●		●			●			
Clinch Valley Coll of the Univ of Virginia *State*	●										●			●				●			●		●			●	●		
Coll of William and Mary *State*						●		●						●				●			●		●				●		●
Eastern Mennonite Coll and Seminary *Mennonite*	●										●			●	●			●				●	●				●		

COLLEGE SELECTION INDEX

Virginia (cont.)

	What Kind of Education Will I Receive?						Can I Get In?					Can I Afford It?				What Will It Be Like When I Get There?													
	Type of School						Entrance Difficulty					Average Annual Cost				Campus Setting			Undergrad Enrollment				Student Body			Campus Life			
	Liberal Arts	Business	Engineering/Technical	Fine Arts	Seminary/Bible/Rabbinical/Talmudic	Comprehensive	Most Selective	Highly Selective	Very Selective	Selective	Non-selective	> $20,000	$10,000 to $20,000	< $10,000	> 50% of students receive aid	Urban	Suburban	Rural	Large (> 20,000 students)	Medium (10,000 to 20,000 students)	Small (1,000 to 10,000 students)	Very Small (< 1,000 students)	Coed	Male/Mostly Male (80% or more)	Female/Mostly Female (80% or more)	> 75% of undergrads from in-state	> 50% live in college-related housing	> 20% of grads pursue postgrad work	> 25% belong to fraternity/sorority
Emory and Henry Coll *United Methodist*	•								•					•				•				•	•						
Ferrum Coll *United Methodist*						•					•			•	•			•			•		•			•	•		
George Mason Univ *State*						•			•					•			•				•		•			•			
Hampden-Sydney Coll *Presbyterian Church*	•								•				•		•			•				•		•			•		•
Hampton Univ *Independent*	•										•			•				•			•		•				•		
Hollins Coll *Independent*	•								•				•		•		•					•			•		•	•	
James Madison Univ *State*						•			•					•				•			•		•						•
Liberty Univ *Baptist*	•										•			•	•	•				•			•				•		
Longwood Coll *State*	•	•									•			•	•			•			•		•			•	•		•
Lynchburg Coll *Independent*	•					•					•		•		•		•				•		•				•	•	•
Mary Baldwin Coll *Presbyterian Church*	•										•		•		•		•					•			•		•	•	
Mary Washington Coll *State*						•			•					•	•		•				•		•			•	•	•	
Marymount Univ *Roman Catholic*						•					•		•		•		•				•		•				•		
Norfolk State Univ *State*	•										•			•	•	•					•		•						
Old Dominion Univ *State*						•					•			•	•		•				•		•			•			
Radford Coll *State*						•					•			•			•				•		•			•		•	•
Randolph-Macon Coll *Independent*	•								•				•				•				•		•				•	•	•
Randolph-Macon Woman's Coll *Independent*	•								•				•		•		•					•			•		•	•	
Roanoke Coll *Independent*	•									•			•		•		•				•						•	•	•
Saint Paul's Coll *Episcopal*	•										•			•	•			•				•	•				•		
Shenandoah Coll and Conservatory of Music *United Methodist*	•	•		•		•					•			•	•			•				•	•				•		•
Sweet Briar Coll *Independent*	•									•			•		•			•				•			•		•	•	
Univ of Richmond *Baptist*						•			•				•		•		•				•		•				•	•	•
Univ of Virginia *State*	•							•						•	•		•			•			•				•	•	•
Virginia Commonwealth Univ *State*						•				•				•		•				•			•			•			
Virginia Intermont Coll *Baptist*	•										•			•		•						•	•				•		

COLLEGE SELECTION INDEX

	What Kind of Education Will I Receive? — Type of School						Can I Get In? — Entrance Difficulty					Can I Afford It? — Average Annual Cost				What Will It Be Like When I Get There? — Campus Setting			Undergrad Enrollment				Student Body			Campus Life			
	Liberal Arts	Business	Engineering/Technical	Fine Arts	Seminary/Bible/Rabbinical/Talmudic	Comprehensive	Most Selective	Highly Selective	Very Selective	Selective	Non-selective	> $20,000	$10,000 to $20,000	< $10,000	> 50% of students receive aid	Urban	Suburban	Rural	Large (> 20,000 students)	Medium (10,000 to 20,000 students)	Small (1,000 to 10,000 students)	Very Small (< 1,000 students)	Coed	Male/Mostly Male (80% or more)	Female/Mostly Female (80% or more)	> 75% of undergrads from In-state	> 50% live in college-related housing	> 20% of grads pursue postgrad work	> 25% belong to fraternity/sorority
Virginia (cont.)																													
Virginia Military Institute *State*			●								●			●	●			●			●			●			●		
Virginia Polytechnic and State Univ *State*						●		●						●	●			●		●			●			●	●		●
Virginia State Univ *State*						●					●			●				●			●		●				●	●	
Virginia Union Univ *American Baptist*	●										●			●		●					●		●				●	●	
Virginia Wesleyan Coll *United Methodist*	●										●		●		●	●					●		●				●	●	●
Washington and Lee Univ *Independent*	●							●					●					●			●		●				●	●	●
Virgin Islands																													
Univ of the Virgin Islands *Public*	●										●			●	●		●				●		●			●	●	●	
Washington																													
Central Washington Univ *State*	●										●			●				●		●			●			●			
City Univ *Independent*	●	●									●			●		●					●		●						
Cornish Coll of the Arts *Independent*				●																									
Eastern Washington Univ *State*						●					●			●			●				●		●			●			
Evergreen State Coll *State*						●				●				●			●				●		●			●			
Gonzaga Univ *Roman Catholic*						●				●			●		●	●					●		●					●	
Heritage Coll *Independent*	●										●			●	●			●				●	●			●			
Northwest Coll *Assemblies of God*	●	●			●									●	●		●					●	●				●		
Pacific Lutheran Univ *Independent*	●			●					●				●		●		●				●		●				●		
Puget Sound Christian Coll *Independent Christian Church/Churches of Christ*					●						●			●	●		●					●	●					●	
Saint Martin's Coll *Roman Catholic*	●					●					●		●		●		●					●	●			●			
Seattle Pacific Univ *Free Methodist*	●									●			●		●	●					●		●						
Seattle Univ *Roman Catholic*						●				●			●		●	●					●		●			●			
Univ of Puget Sound *Independent*	●								●				●		●		●				●		●				●	●	●
Univ of Washington *State*						●				●				●		●			●				●			●		●	●
Walla Walla Coll *Seventh-day Adventist*	●		●								●			●	●			●			●		●				●		
Washington State Univ *State*						●					●			●				●		●			●			●			

COLLEGE SELECTION INDEX

	What Kind of Education Will I Receive? Type of School						Can I Get In? Entrance Difficulty					Can I Afford It? Average Annual Cost				What Will It Be Like When I Get There? Campus Setting			Undergrad Enrollment				Student Body			Campus Life			
	Liberal Arts	Business	Engineering/Technical	Fine Arts	Seminary/Bible/Rabbinical/Talmudic	Comprehensive	Most Selective	Highly Selective	Very Selective	Selective	Non-selective	> $20,000	$10,000 to $20,000	< $10,000	> 50% of students receive aid	Urban	Suburban	Rural	Large (> 20,000 students)	Medium (10,000 to 20,000 students)	Small (1,000 to 10,000 students)	Very Small (< 1,000 students)	Coed	Male/Mostly Male (80% or more)	Female/Mostly Female (80% or more)	> 75% of undergrads from in-state	> 50% live in college-related housing	> 20% of grads pursue postgrad work	> 25% belong to fraternity/sorority
Washington (cont.)																													
Western Washington Univ *State*						●				●				●	●		●				●		●			●	●		
Whitman Coll *Independent*	●								●				●		●			●			●		●				●	●	●
Whitworth Coll *Presbyterian*						●				●			●		●		●				●		●				●		
West Virginia																													
Alderson-Broaddus Coll *American Baptist*	●										●		●		●			●				●	●				●		
Bethany Coll *Independent*	●									●			●		●			●				●	●				●	●	●
Bluefield State Coll *State*						●					●			●				●			●		●			●			
Concord Coll *State*	●													●	●			●			●		●			●			●
Davis and Elkins Coll *Presbyterian*	●										●			●	●			●				●	●				●		●
Fairmont State Coll *State*	●	●	●	●							●			●	●		●				●		●			●			●
Glenville State Coll *State*	●										●			●	●			●			●		●			●			
Marshall Univ *State*						●					●			●	●	●					●		●			●			
Salem Teikyo Univ *Independent*	●										●			●				●				●	●				●		●
Shepherd Coll *State*	●								●					●			●				●		●				●	●	●
Univ of Charleston *Independent*	●										●		●		●		●				●		●			●		●	●
West Liberty State Coll *State*	●										●			●	●			●			●		●				●		●
West Virginia Institute of Technology *State*			●								●			●				●			●		●			●			
West Virginia State Coll *State*	●										●			●	●		●				●		●			●			
West Virginia Univ *State*						●			●					●	●	●				●			●					●	●
West Virginia Wesleyan Coll *United Methodist*	●										●		●		●			●			●		●				●	●	●
Wheeling Jesuit Coll *Roman Catholic*						●					●		●		●		●					●	●				●	●	
Wisconsin																													
Alverno Coll *Roman Catholic*	●										●		●		●		●				●				●	●			
Bellin Coll of Nursing *Independent*														●		●						●			●	●			
Beloit Coll *Independent*	●								●				●		●		●				●		●				●	●	
Carroll Coll *Presbyterian*	●									●			●		●		●				●		●			●	●		●

COLLEGE SELECTION INDEX

	What Kind of Education Will I Receive?						Can I Get In?					Can I Afford It?				What Will It Be Like When I Get There?													
	Type of School						Entrance Difficulty					Average Annual Cost				Campus Setting			Undergrad Enrollment				Student Body			Campus Life			
	Liberal Arts	Business	Engineering/Technical	Fine Arts	Seminary/Bible/Rabbinical/Talmudic	Comprehensive	Most Selective	Highly Selective	Very Selective	Selective	Non-selective	> $20,000	$10,000 to $20,000	< $10,000	> 50% of students receive aid	Urban	Suburban	Rural	Large (> 20,000 students)	Medium (10,000 to 20,000 students)	Small (1,000 to 10,000 students)	Very Small (< 1,000 students)	Coed	Male/Mostly Male (80% or more)	Female/Mostly Female (80% or more)	> 75% of undergrads from in-state	> 50% live in college-related housing	> 20% of grads pursue postgrad work	> 25% belong to fraternity/sorority
Wisconsin (cont.)																													
Carthage Coll *Lutheran*	●										●		●		●	●					●		●				●		●
Concordia Univ Wisconsin *Lutheran-Missouri Synod*	●										●			●	●		●					●	●						
Edgewood Coll *Independent*	●										●			●	●	●						●	●			●			
Lakeland Coll *United Church of Christ*	●										●			●	●			●			●		●			●	●		
Lawrence Univ *Independent*	●								●				●		●	●					●		●				●	●	●
Marian Coll of Fond Du Lac *Roman Catholic*	●										●			●	●		●				●		●			●	●		
Marquette Univ *Roman Catholic*	●								●				●		●	●					●		●					●	
Milwaukee School of Engineering *Independent*			●								●		●		●	●					●			●			●	●	●
Mount Mary Coll *Independent*	●										●			●	●	●						●			●	●			
Mount Senario Coll *Independent*	●										●			●	●			●				●	●			●			
Northland Coll *Independent*	●										●			●	●			●				●	●						
Ripon Coll *Independent*	●								●				●		●			●				●	●				●	●	●
Saint Francis Seminary, School of Pastoral Mininstry *Roman Catholic*																													
Silver Lake Coll of the Holy Family *Roman Catholic*	●										●			●	●			●				●	●			●		●	
St. Norbert Coll *Roman Catholic*	●					●				●			●		●		●				●		●				●		
Univ of Wisconsin—Eau Claire *State*	●	●									●			●	●			●			●		●			●			
Univ of Wisconsin—Green Bay *State*	●										●			●	●	●					●		●			●			
Univ of Wisconsin—La Crosse *State*	●										●			●		●					●		●			●			
Univ of Wisconsin—Madison *State*						●			●					●	●	●			●				●				●	●	
Univ of Wisconsin—Milwaukee *State*	●	●	●	●							●			●		●				●			●			●			
Univ of Wisconsin—Oshkosh *State*	●	●									●			●				●			●		●			●	●		
Univ of Wisconsin—Parkside *State*		●	●								●			●		●					●		●			●			
Univ of Wisconsin—Platteville *State*	●		●								●			●	●			●			●		●			●	●		
Univ of Wisconsin—River Falls *State*						●					●			●	●		●				●		●				●		
Univ of Wisconsin—Stevens Point *State*						●					●			●	●			●			●		●			●			
Univ of Wisconsin—Stout *State*																													

COLLEGE SELECTION INDEX

	What Kind of Education Will I Receive? Type of School						Can I Get In? Entrance Difficulty					Can I Afford It? Average Annual Cost				What Will It Be Like When I Get There? Campus Setting			Undergrad Enrollment				Student Body			Campus Life			
	Liberal Arts	Business	Engineering/Technical	Fine Arts	Seminary/Bible/Rabbinical/Talmudic	Comprehensive	Most Selective	Highly Selective	Very Selective	Selective	Non-selective	> $20,000	$10,000 to $20,000	< $10,000	> 50% of students receive aid	Urban	Suburban	Rural	Large (> 20,000 students)	Medium (10,000 to 20,000 students)	Small (1,000 to 10,000 students)	Very Small (< 1,000 students)	Coed	Male/Mostly Male (80% or more)	Female/Mostly Female (80% or more)	> 75% of undergrads from in-state	> 50% live in college-related housing	> 20% of grads pursue postgrad work	> 25% belong to fraternity/sorority
Wisconsin (cont.)																													
Univ of Wisconsin—Superior *State*	●										●			●	●	●					●		●						
Univ of Wisconsin—Whitewater *State*		●				●					●			●	●		●				●		●			●	●	●	
Viterbo Coll *Independent*	●										●			●	●	●					●		●				●		
Wisconsin Lutheran Coll *Wisconsin Evangelical Lutheran Synod*	●										●			●	●		●					●	●			●	●		
Wittenberg Univ *Lutheran*	●								●				●		●		●				●		●				●	●	●
Wyoming																													
Univ of Wyoming *State*						●					●			●	●			●			●		●						

CASS & BIRNBAUM'S GUIDE TO AMERICAN COLLEGES

Description of Colleges

Abilene Christian University

Abilene, Texas 79699 (915) 674-2653

A church-related university, located in a metropolitan area of 112,000, 150 miles west of the Dallas-Fort Worth metroplex. Emphasis on the Bible and "teachings of Christ as they apply to the problems of the 20th century." Most convenient major airport: Abilene Municipal.

Founded: 1906	**Total Enrollment:** 4,069
Affiliation: Church of Christ	**Cost:** < $10K
UG Enrollment: 1,439 M, 1,450 W (full-time); 242 M, 254 W (part-time)	**% Receiving Financial Aid:** 70%
	Admission: Non-selective
	Application Deadline: July 1

Admission. Graduates of accredited high schools with 2.0 minimum GPA eligible; 95% of applicants accepted, 64% of these actually enroll; 39% of freshmen graduate in top fifth of high school class, 59% in top two-fifths. Average freshman scores: SAT, 430 verbal, 490 mathematical; ACT, 21 composite. *Required:* SAT or ACT. Criteria considered in admissions, in order of importance: high school academic record, standardized test scores, recommendations. *Entrance programs:* early decision, early admission, advanced placement. *Apply* by July 1. *Transfers* welcome; 200 enrolled 1993–94.

Academic Environment. Degrees offered: associates, bachelors, masters, doctoral. Graduation requirements include 12 semester hours of English, 9 of humanities, 3 of math, 3 of fine arts, 15 of Bible. *Majors offered:* international studies available in many departments. Current honors student finds her classes "wonderful, exciting," but notes that "not all departments are equally funded." Average undergraduate class size: 15% under 20, 80% 20–40, 5% over 40. About 46% of students entering as freshmen graduate eventually; 70% of freshmen return for sophomore year. Current students agree that computer facilities are ample, even during finals. *Special programs:* 3–2 engineering, cross registration with Hardin-Simmons and McMurry. Adult programs include Bachelor of Applied Studies for students over 25. *Calendar:* semester, summer school.

Undergraduate degrees conferred (610). 21% were in Business and Management, 18% were in Education, 11% were in Communications, 6% were in Theology, 5% were in Life Sciences, 5% were in Psychology, 4% were in Social Sciences, 4% were in Health Sciences, 3% were in Public Affairs, 3% were in Visual and Performing Arts, 3% were in Multi/Interdisciplinary Studies, 3% were in Computer and Engineering Related Technology, remainder in 17 other fields.

Graduates Career Data. Advanced studies pursued by 35% of students; 16% enter graduate school; 4% enter medical school; 1% enter dental school; 3% enter law school; 11% enter business school. Medical schools typically enrolling largest number of graduates include Southwestern, Baylor, U. of Texas-Galveston; dental schools include Baylor, U. of Texas-San Antonio; law schools include Baylor, U. of Texas, Pepperdine; business schools include U. of Texas, Texas A&M. University reports all 1992–1993 graduates seeking employment are employed. Fields typically hiring largest numbers of graduates include education, accounting and social work. Career Development Services: "There are counseling and career development services from the freshman year through placement after graduation."

Faculty. About 76% of faculty hold PhD or equivalent. About 63% of undergraduate classes taught by tenured faculty. About 22% of teaching faculty are female; 3% minority.

Student Body. About 65% of students from in state; 77% West, 8% South, 4% Midwest, 3% Middle Atlantic, 2% Northwest, 2% New England, 4% Foreign. An estimated 80% of students reported as Protestant, 10% Catholic; 4% Afro-American, 4% Hispanic, 9% other minority. Average age of undergraduate student: 23.

Religious Orientation. University is a church-related institution, "but not church-governed"; 5 courses in religion required of all students; 75% of students affiliated with the Church of Christ. "A sincere effort is made to weave Christianity into every facet of college life."

Varsity Sports. Men (Div.II): Baseball, Basketball, Cross Country, Football, Golf, Soccer, Tennis, Track. Women (Div.II): Basketball, Cross Country, Tennis, Track, Volleyball.

Campus Life. Current students report social life centers around on-campus activities: gym, library, campus center, movies (on- and off-campus). They also appreciate the "positive Christian atmosphere" and the "fellowship, love and support" found on campus.

About 38% of men, 44% of women live in traditional dormitories; no coed dormitories; rest live in off-campus housing or commute. Freshmen given preference in college housing if all students cannot be accommodated. No intervisitation in men's and women's dormitory rooms. There are no fraternities or sororities. About 50% of resident students leave campus on weekends.

Annual Costs. Tuition and fees, $7,170; room and board, $3,090; estimated $500 other, exclusive of travel. About 70% of students receive financial aid; average amount of assistance, $7,278. Assistance is typically divided 40% scholarship/grant, 40% loan, 20% work. University reports 510 scholarships awarded on basis of academic merit alone, 315 for special talents alone, 500 for need alone. Meeting costs: university offers prepayment of tuition, savings account, and investment account.

Academy of Art College

San Francisco, California 94105

An independent college of art affiliated with the University of San Francisco and offering bachelors and masters degree programs. College has "state-of-the-art" computing, photography, and motion picture facilities. Half the undergraduate student body is minority; a third is of foreign origin. Graduates typically find work in advertising, publishing, graphic design, and photography.

Founded: 1929	**Affiliation:** Independent

Academy of the New Church

Bryn Athyn, Pennsylvania 19009

A church-related institution, the college is devoted to teaching its students in the light of Swedenborgian New Church beliefs, and to preparing ministers and teachers for the church.

Founded: 1876
Affiliation: Church of New Jerusalem

Adams State College

Alamosa, Colorado 81102 **(800) 824-6494 or (719) 589-7712**

A state-supported college, located in a city of 8,500, 230 miles southwest of Denver. Most convenient major airport: Alamosa Regional.

Founded: 1921
Affiliation: State
UG Enrollment: 874 M, 941 W (full-time); 53 M, 149 W (part-time)
Total Enrollment: 2,353
Cost: < $10K
% Receiving Financial Aid: 82%
Admission: Selective
Application Deadline: Aug. 1

Admission is selective. Graduates of state-accredited high schools with minimum 2.0 GPA in 15 college preparatory units who rank in top two-thirds of class eligible; others given individual consideration; 90% of applicants accepted, 41% of these actually enroll; 33% of freshmen graduate in top fifth of high school class, 67% in top two-fifths. Average freshman ACT scores: 21.2 composite. *Required:* ACT or SAT. Criteria considered in admissions, in order of importance: high school academic record, standardized test scores, writing sample, recommendations, extracurricular activities. *Out-of-state* freshman applicants: college welcomes students from out of state. State limits out-of-state enrollment. No special requirements for out-of-state applicants. About 98% of out-of-state applicants accepted, 41% of these actually enroll. *Apply* by August 1; rolling admissions. *Transfers* welcome; 129 enrolled 1993–94.
Academic Environment. Degrees offered: associates, bachelors, masters. About 39% of requirements for graduation are elective; 40% of courses must be upper division. About 40% of students entering as freshmen graduate within four years. Average undergraduate class size: 75% between 20–40, 25% over 40. *Special programs:* CLEP, independent study, honors, undergraduate research, 3-year degree, individualized majors. *Calendar:* semester, summer school.
Undergraduate degrees conferred (252). 34% were in Business and Management, 23% were in Multi/Interdisciplinary Studies, 10% were in Social Sciences, 10% were in Psychology, 5% were in Education, 4% were in Mathematics, 4% were in Life Sciences, 4% were in Letters, 3% were in Physical Sciences, remainder in 2 other fields.
Graduates Career Data. According to most recent data available, full-time graduate or professional study pursued by 12% of students immediately after graduation. Professional schools typically enrolling largest numbers of graduates include Adams State C., U. of Colorado, Colorado State U. *Careers in business and industry* pursued by 40% of graduates.
Faculty. About 67% of faculty hold PhD or equivalent terminal degree. About 80% of undergraduate classes taught by tenured faculty.
Varsity Sports. Men (NCAA, Div.II): Basketball, Cross Country, Football, Golf, Track, Wrestling. Women (NCAA, Div.II): Basketball, Cross Country, Softball, Track, Volleyball.
Campus Life. College seeks a national student body; 80% of students from in state; almost all from North Central states. An estimated 24% of students reported as Hispanic, 2% as Black, 3% other minority, according to most recent data available.

About 30% of men, 24% of women live in traditional dormitories; 4% of men, 3% of women in coed dormitories, 9% of men, 11% of women live in college apartments; rest commute. There are no fraternities or sororities on campus. About 25% of resident students leave campus on weekends.
Annual Costs. Tuition and fees, $1,650 (out-of-state, $4,848); room and board, $3,450; estimated $2,000 other, exclusive of travel. About 82% of students receive financial aid; average amount of assistance, $4,138. Assistance is typically divided 47% scholarship/grant, 40% loan, 13% work. College reports 820 scholarships awarded for academic merit alone, 280 for special talents, 105 for need. *Meeting Costs:* college offers deferred payment plan.

Adelphi University

Garden City, New York 11530 **(516) 663-1100**

The oldest liberal arts college on Long Island, like many liberal arts institutions Adelphi supplements its traditional concern for the arts and sciences with professional/vocational studies. It also offers strong programs in the performing arts. The 75-acre campus is located in a community of 25,400, 25 miles east of New York City in suburban Nassau County, within walking distance of the Long Island Rail Road. Most convenient major airports: La Guardia/Kennedy.

Founded: 1896
Affiliation: Independent
UG Enrollment: 1,171 M, 2,070 W (full-time); 482 M, 1,143 W (part-time)
Total Enrollment: 8,535
Cost: $10K–$20K
% Receiving Financial Aid: 66%
Admission: Selective
Application Deadline: March 1

Admission is selective. About 66% of applicants accepted, 42% of these actually enroll; 44% of freshmen graduate in top fifth of high school class, 70% in top two-fifths. *Required:* SAT or ACT; recommendations, interview recommended. *Non-academic factors* considered in admissions: special talents, alumni children, diverse student body, extracurricular activities. *Entrance programs:* early decision, early admission, midyear admission, deferred admission, advanced placement. About 9% of entering students from private schools, 14% from parochial schools. *Apply* by March 1. *Transfers* welcome.
Academic Environment. Students "have an equal say" on University Council which advises on matters related to student and academic life. Core curriculum exposes students to issues of modern civilization (4 courses), and to issues pertaining to nature society and culture, art and expression (7 courses). Senior seminar and a writing course are also required. *Undergraduate studies* offered by College of Arts and Sciences, schools of Banking and Money Management, Business Administration, Education, Nursing, Social Work, University College. *Majors offered* in Arts and Sciences in addition to usual studies include anthropology, art, art education, communications, dance, fine arts, interdisciplinary studies, Latin American studies, medical technology, music, recreation and human performance science, theater arts, social welfare, speech arts, ABLE degree program for adults.

About 68% of students entering as freshmen graduate within 5 years; 12% of freshmen do not return for sophomore year. *Special programs:* honors, CLEP, independent study, study abroad, undergraduate research, joint degree programs in dentistry and optometry, 3–2 engineering, Hy Weinberg Center for Speech and Communication Disorders. *Calendar:* semester, summer school.
Undergraduate degrees conferred (1,086). 38% were in Business and Management, 12% were in Social Sciences, 8% were in Health Sciences, 8% were in Education, 6% were in Life Sciences, 6% were in Public Affairs, 5% were in Communications, 5% were in Psychology, 4% were in Visual and Performing Arts, 3% were in Letters, remainder in 6 other fields.
Graduates Career Data. *Full-time graduate or professional study* pursued immediately after graduation by 64% of students. *Careers in business and industry* pursued by 85–90% of business graduates. Corporations typically hiring largest numbers of graduates include Big 8 accounting firms and large banks.
Faculty. About 85% of faculty hold PhD or equivalent.
Student Body. According to most recent data available, 93% of students from New York; 97% Middle Atlantic. An estimated 54% of students reported as Catholic, 17% Jewish, 16% Protestant, 13% other; 10% Black, 5% Hispanic, 3% Asian, 4% other minority.
Varsity Sports. Men (Div.II): Baseball, Basketball, Lacrosse (I), Soccer (I). Women (Div.II): Basketball, Soccer, Softball (I), Tennis.
Campus Life. System of dormitory self-governance permits student "participation" in developing regulations governing student social life. With the exception of one residence hall all dormitories are coed by room, floor or wing, with 24-hour intervisitation policy.

About 6% of women live in traditional dormitories; 31% of men, 22% of women in coed dormitories; 8% of men, 6% of women in off-campus housing; 61% of men, 66% of women commute. Freshmen given preference in college housing if all students cannot be accommodated. There are 7 fraternities, 5 sororities on campus which about 10% of men, 10% of women join; they provide no residence facilities. About 60% of students leave campus on weekends.

Annual Costs. Tuition and fees, $12,300; room and board, $6,000. According to most recent data available, about 66% of students receive financial aid; assistance is typically divided 53% scholarship, 28% loan, 19% work. University reports some scholarships awarded on the basis of academic merit alone. *Meeting Costs:* university offers a deferred payment plan.

Adrian College

Adrian, Michigan 49221 (517) 265-5161

A church-related college located in a town of 20,400 in southeastern Michigan, 75 miles southwest of Detroit. Most convenient major airport: Toledo, Ohio.

Founded: 1859
Affiliation: United Methodist
UG Enrollment: 509 M, 527 W (full-time); 35 M, 64 W (part-time)
Cost: $10K–$20K
% Receiving Financial Aid: 90%
Admission: Selective (+)
Application Deadline: Rolling

Admission is selective (+). About 77% of applicants accepted, 31% of these actually enroll; 35% of freshmen graduate in top fifth of high school class, 66% in top two-fifths. Average freshman ACT scores: 22.7, 23.4 W composite. *Required:* SAT or ACT. Criteria considered in admissions, in order of importance: high school academic record, standardized test scores, recommendations, extracurricular activities, writing sample; other factors considered: diverse student body, religious affiliation and/or commitment, special talents, alumni children. Entrance program: midyear admission. About 10% of entering students from private schools, 30% from parochial schools. *Apply:* rolling admissions. *Transfers* welcome; 35 enrolled 1993–94.

Academic Environment. *Degrees:* associates, bachelors. About 91% of general education requirements for graduation are elective; distribution requirements numerous. *Majors offered* include environmental science, management information systems. Current and recent students appreciate the "real world" experience of their professors, as well as their helpfulness and accessibility. Students are less happy with limited choice of majors. About 47% of students entering as freshmen graduate within four years, 58% eventually; 79% of freshmen return for sophomore year. Average class size: 95% under 20, 4% 20–40. *Special programs:* individually designed majors, study abroad, internships, May Term (4 week interdisciplinary course), fashion design with FIT and American College in London, 3–2 engineering. *Calendar:* semester, May Term, summer school.

Undergraduate degrees conferred (197). 25% were in Business and Management, 16% were in Social Sciences, 14% were in Education, 10% were in Letters, 7% were in Mathematics, 6% were in Life Sciences, 4% were in Foreign Languages, 4% were in Visual and Performing Arts, 4% were in Psychology, 4% were in Home Economics, 3% were in Computer and Engineering Related Technology, 3% were in Philosophy and Religion, remainder in Physical Sciences.

Graduates Career Data. Advanced studies pursued by 24% of graduates; 22% enter graduate school. About 66% of 1992–93 graduates employed. Fields typically hiring largest numbers of graduates include business, education, biology. Career Development Services: interview preparation, on-campus recruitment, alumni assistance in career search.

Faculty. About 75% of faculty hold PhD or equivalent. About 70% of undergraduate classes taught by tenured faculty. About 36% of teaching faculty are female; less than 2% minority.

Student Body. About 79% of students from in state; 95% Midwest, 2% foreign. An estimated 69% of students reported as Protestant, 27% Catholic, rest unaffiliated or other; 6% Black, 5% other minority.

Religious Orientation. Adrian is a church-related institution; 15% of students reported affiliated with Methodist Church. No religious study required of students.

Varsity Sports. Men (Div.III): Baseball, Basketball, Cross Country, Football, Golf, Soccer, Swimming, Tennis, Track. Women (Div. III): Basketball, Cross Country, Golf, Soccer, Softball, Swimming, Tennis, Track, Volleyball.

Campus Life. Recent student reports 65% of students participate in varsity sports, 90% play intramurals. Other students report active interest in campus organizations and activities; one notes that small size of campus allows students to have leadership positions they might not have at a larger school.

About 11% of men, 26% of women live in traditional dormitories; 47% of men, 35% of women in coed dormitories; 9% of men, 6% of women live in off-campus college-related housing; 19% of men, 19% of women commute. There are 5 fraternities, 3 sororities on campus which about 30% of men, 30% of women join; 14% of men, 14% of women live in fraternities and sororities. About 50% of students leave campus on weekends.

Annual Costs. Tuition and fees, $10,800; room and board, $3,540; estimated $1,000 other, exclusive of travel. About 90% of students receive financial aid; average amount of assistance, $9,548. Assistance is typically divided 10% scholarship, 41% grant, 47% loan, 2% work. College reports 124 scholarships awarded on the basis of academic merit alone, 32 for special talents. *Meeting Costs:* Michigan Loan Program; college expresses a "commitment to meet the financial need for students who wish to attend."

Agnes Scott College

Decatur, Georgia 30030 (404) 371-6000

A small, liberal arts college for women, Agnes Scott attracts an above-average student body, and is increasingly seeking a national representation, although its students are still principally from the South. Founded by Presbyterians, it has always been independent of religious control, while maintaining close ties with the church. Located in a community of 18,000, within metropolitan Atlanta, the 100-acre campus is easily accessible by all transportation. Most convenient major airport: Hartsfield (Atlanta).

Founded: 1889
Affiliation: Independent (Presbyterian)
UG Enrollment: 510 W (full-time); 1 M, 62 W (part-time)
Total Enrollment: 600
Cost: $10K–$20K
% Receiving Financial Aid: 96%
Admission: Very (+) Selective
Application Deadline: March 1

Admission is very (+) selective. About 84% of applicants accepted, 39% of these actually enroll; 81% of freshmen graduate in top fifth of high school class, 96% in top two-fifths. Average freshman SAT scores: range of middle 50%: 470–600 verbal; 490–610 mathematical. *Required:* SAT or ACT, essay. Criteria considered in admissions, in order of importance: high school academic record, standardized test scores, recommendations, writing sample, extracurricular activities. *Entrance programs:* early decision, early admission, mid-year admission, deferred admission, advanced placement. *Apply* by March 1. *Transfers* welcome; 13 enrolled for 1993–94.

Academic Environment. Degrees offered: bachelors, masters. Program of liberal arts studies designed for serious, academically inclined student. Low student-faculty ratio fosters extensive contact with professors. Graduation requirements include 2 semesters English composition, 1 semester each math, natural science, social science, fine arts, literature, history or classical civilization, religious or philosophical thought; foreign language to intermediate level; 4 semesters physical education. Maximum of 8 semester hours may be elected on a Pass/Fail basis by juniors and seniors. Strong honor system allows exams to be self-scheduled and unproctored. *Majors offered* include art/psychology, economics and business, Art History-Bible and Religion, creative writing, classical languages and literature, studio art, student-designed majors, interdisciplinary majors in international relations and Latin American studies. Average undergraduate class size: 84% under 20, 16% 20–40. Computer facilities reported as "outstanding"; one port per student in residence halls.

About 60% of students entering as freshmen graduate eventually; 80% of freshmen return for sophomore year. *Special programs:* independent study, honors, study abroad, preparatory program for business, Washington Semester, Georgia Legislative internship, Exchange Programs with Mills College and Sharp women science research associates, PLEN, over 300 internships available, cross registration with 17 other institutions in the University Center in Georgia, 3–2 programs in engineering, information and computer science, indus-

trial management, management science, biotechnology, and architecture. Adult programs: Return to College Program for students over 21; they attend regular classes. *Library:* "one of 5 largest Robert Frost collections in U.S." Calendar: semester.
Undergraduate degrees conferred (105). 32% were in Social Sciences, 17% were in Psychology, 16% were in Letters, 10% were in Visual and Performing Arts, 7% were in Foreign Languages, 5% were in Multi/Interdisciplinary Studies, 5% were in Life Sciences, 3% were in Physical Sciences, remainder in 4 other fields.
Graduates Career Data. Advanced studies pursued by 46% of graduates; 33% enter graduate school; 7% enter law school; 2% dental school. Law schools typically enrolling largest numbers of graduates include Emory, U. of Georgia, Georgia State; dental schools include U. of North Carolina. About 67% of 1992–1993 graduates employed. Fields typically hiring largest numbers of graduates include education, non-profit organizations.
Faculty. About 97% of faculty hold PhD or equivalent. About 64% of classes taught by tenured faculty. About 59% of teaching faculty are female; 6% Black, 6% other minority.
Student Body. About 51% of students from in state; 90% South, 4% foreign. An estimated 46% of students reported as Protestant, 10% Catholic, 15% other or unaffiliated. An estimated 12% of students are Black, 3% Hispanic, 6% other, 3% international.
Religious Orientation. Agnes Scott "has always maintained a close relationship to the Presbyterian Church, but is not controlled or supported by it." A one semester course in religious or philosophical thought required for BA.
Varsity Sports. Women (DIV III) Basketball, Cross Country, Soccer, Tennis, Volleyball.
Campus Life. First seven weeks freshmen have 12 PM curfew Monday through Thursday. All students have own dorm entry key. Intervisitation limited. Students socialize with Georgia Tech and Emory men; some student desire reported for "more casual opportunities to meet men."

About 88% of women live in dormitories; rest commute. There are no sororities on campus. About 25% of resident students leave campus on weekends.
Annual Costs. Tuition and fees, $12,135; room and board, $5,000; estimated $950 other, exclusive of travel. About 96% of first-year students receive financial aid; average amount of assistance, $10,973. Assistance is typically divided 64% scholarship/grant, 24% loan, 12% work. College reports 246 scholarships awarded on the basis of academic merit alone, 3 for special talents, 269 for need.

University of Akron

Akron, Ohio 44325 **(216) 972-7100**

A state-supported university, located in a city of 265,000, 35 miles south of Cleveland, Akron has long had an international reputation for its departments of chemistry and polymer science and for special work carried on in the Institute of Polymer Science. Most convenient major airport: Hopkins International (Cleveland).

Founded: 1870
Affiliation: State
UG Enrollment: 7,500 M, 7,500 W (full-time); 4,100 M, 4,600 W (part-time)
Total Enrollment: 27,671
Cost: < $10K
% Receiving Financial Aid: 50%
Admission: Non-selective
Application Deadline: March 1

Admission. Graduates of accredited high schools with minimum 2.5 GPA eligible; others admitted on basis of high school record and ACT or SAT scores. About 77% of applicants accepted, 67% of these actually enroll; 32% of freshmen graduate in top quarter of high school class, 62% in top half, according to most recent data available. Average freshman scores: SAT, 412 M, 394 W verbal, 479 M, 422 W mathematical; ACT, 19 M, 18 W composite, 19 M, 17 W mathematical, according to most recent data available. *Required:* interview for 6-year BS/MD program. *Out-of-state* freshman applicants: state does not limit out-of-state enrollment. Requirements for out-of-state applicants: 3.0 GPA, 20 ACT composite score, 1000 combined SAT score. *Entrance programs:* mid-year and summer admission, rolling admission, advanced placement. About 9% of entering students from private or parochial schools. *Apply:* March 1 recommended for students requesting campus housing. *Transfers* welcome; 958 accepted 1992–1993.

Academic Environment. Degrees offered: associates, bachelors, masters, doctoral. Students are members of University Council and student observers are present at meetings of trustees. Administration reports 34% of courses required for graduation are elective. *Undergraduate studies* offered by Buchtel College of Arts and Sciences, colleges of Business Administration, Education, Engineering, Fine and Applied Arts, Nursing; most students enroll in General College for first 2 years and complete program of general studies. Average class size: 90% between 20–40.

About 50% of students entering as freshmen graduate eventually; 70% of freshmen return for sophomore year, according to most recent data available. *Special programs:* CLEP, independent study, undergraduate research, study abroad, honors, co-op/internships in most majors, 5-year optional cooperative work/study program in engineering, credit by examination. *Calendar:* semester, summer school.
Undergraduate degrees conferred (2,712). 27% were in Business and Management, 15% were in Education, 8% were in Health Sciences, 7% were in Social Sciences, 7% were in Engineering, 4% were in Visual and Performing Arts, 4% were in Communications, 4% were in Home Economics, 3% were in Engineering and Engineering Related Technology, 3% were in Life Sciences, 3% were in Psychology, remainder in 9 other fields.
Graduates Career Data. Full-time advanced studies pursued immediately after graduation by 15% of students, according to most recent data available. *Careers in business and industry* pursued by 55% of graduates, according to most recent data available
Faculty. About 52% of faculty hold PhD or equivalent.
Student Body. About 85% of students from Ohio. An estimated 9% of students reported are Black, 5% other minority, according to most recent data available[+*+] aided through Developmental Services program providing tutoring, remedial courses, etc.; Afro-American studies program and Black Cultural Center.
Varsity Sports. Men (Div.I): Baseball, Basketball, Cross Country, Golf, Football, Riflery, Soccer, Softball, Tennis, Track. Women (Div.I): Basketball, Cross Country, Riflery, Softball, Tennis, Track, Volleyball.
Campus Life. Campus primarily for commuters. Students allowed cars on campus; state laws regarding drinking enforced. About 4% of men, 5% of women live in traditional dormitories; 1% of each live in coed dormitories; 16% of men, 13% of women live in off-campus housing; 78% of men, 79% of women commute. Freshmen given preference in college housing if all students cannot be accommodated. There are 16 fraternities, 10 sororities on campus which about 9% of men, 6% of women join; 2% of men, 1% of women live in fraternities and sororities. About 40% of resident students leave campus on weekends.
Annual Costs. Tuition and fees, $3,039 (out-of-state, $7,575); room and board, $3,660; estimated $1,410 other, exclusive of travel. About 50% of students receive financial aid; average amount of assistance, $3,670. Assistance is typically divided 9% scholarship, 30% loan, 27% work.

Alabama Agricultural and Mechanical University

Normal, Alabama 35762 **(205) 851-5000**

A state-supported, land-grant institution, located in a small community near Huntsville (pop. 137,800); founded as a college for Negroes and still serving a predominantly black student body.

Founded: 1875
Affiliation: State
UG Enrollment: 1,899 M, 2,074 W (full-time); 128 M, 162 W (part-time)
Total Enrollment: 5,593
Cost: < $10K
% Receiving Financial Aid: 74%
Admission: Non-selective

Admission. Graduates of accredited high schools eligible; 68% of applicants accepted, 51% of these actually enroll. Average freshman ACT scores: 16.5 M, 16.7 W. Required: SAT or ACT. Entrance programs: early admission, mid-year admission, deferred admission. Criteria considered in admissions, in order of importance: high school academic record, standardized test scores, recommendations, writing sample, extracurricular activities. Out-of-state freshman applicants: university seeks students from out-of-state. State does not limit out-of-state enrollment. Transfers welcome; 189 first time transfers enrolled 1993–94.

Academic Environment. Degrees offered: associates, bachelors, masters, doctoral. About 42–45 credit hours in general education are required for graduation. Average undergraduate class size: 38% under 20, 60% 20–40. About 21% of students entering as freshmen graduate within 5 years. Special programs: CLEP, independent study, undergraduate research, engineering, pre-veterinary medicine, pre-nursing, cross registration with U. of Alabama Huntsville, Oakwood College, Calhoun Community College. Adult program: Bachelor of Technical Studies allows for practical and work experiences. *Calendar:* semester, summer school.

Undergraduate degrees conferred (344). 27% were in Business and Management, 16% were in Education, 7% were in Computer and Engineering Related Technology, 7% were in Engineering and Engineering Related Technology, 6% were in Communications Technologies, 5% were in Marketing and Distribution, 4% were in Agricultural Sciences, 4% were in Life Sciences, 3% were in Physical Sciences, 3% were in Home Economics, 3% were in Mathematics, remainder in 11 other fields.

Graduates Career Data. *Careers in business and industry* pursued by 57% of graduates, according to most recent data available. Career Development Services offer placement, internships, work-study, co-op, mock interviews, on-campus recruitment and career development.

Faculty. About 59% of faculty hold PhD or equivalent. About 35% of teaching faculty are female; 57% Black, 2% Hispanic, 18% other minority.

Student Body. About 71% of students from Alabama; 75% from South, 15% from Midwest, 3% West, 5% foreign.

Varsity Sports. Men (Div.II): Baseball, Basketball, Cross Country, Football, Soccer (I), Tennis, Track. Women (Div.II): Basketball, Cross Country, Track, Volleyball.

Campus Life. About 36% of men, 40% women live in traditional dormitories; no coed dormitories; rest commute. There are 4 fraternities, 3 sororities on campus; they provide no residential facilities.

Annual Costs. Tuition and fees, $1,650 (out-of-state $3,200); room and board, $2,550; estimated $500 other, exclusive of travel. About 74% of students receive financial aid; average amount of assistance, $3,704. Assistance typically divided 4% scholarship, 48% grant, 35% loan, 4% loan, 8% assistantship, 1% other. University reports 331 scholarships awarded on the basis of academic merit alone, 225 for special talents, 465 for need alone.

Alabama State University

Montgomery, Alabama 36195 (205) 293-4290

A state-supported institution, located in a city of 133,400; founded as a college for Negroes and still serving a predominantly black student body. Most convenient major airport: Dannelly Field.

Founded: 1874
Affiliation: State
Total Enrollment: 4,478 M, W (full-time)
Cost: < $10K
Admission: Non-selective
Application Deadline: June 15

Admission. Graduates of accredited high schools with 16 units (11 in academic subjects) and C average eligible; graduates of non accredited schools and GED graduates admitted conditionally. About 98% of applicants accepted, 41% of these actually enroll. *Required:* ACT or SAT. *Out-of-state* students welcome. *Apply* by June 15. *Transfers* welcome.

Academic Environment. *Degrees:* AB, BFA, BS, BM. About 40–50% of general education credits for graduation are required; distribution requirements fairly numerous. About 20–25% of students entering as freshmen graduate eventually; 55% of freshmen do not return for sophomore year. *Special programs:* CLEP. *Calendar:* quarter, summer school.

Undergraduate degrees conferred (252). 16% were in Education, 15% were in Business and Management, 12% were in Protective Services, 11% were in Computer and Engineering Related Technology, 10% were in Business (Administrative Support), 8% were in Life Sciences, 8% were in Communications, 4% were in Public Affairs, 4% were in Psychology, 4% were in Mathematics, 3% were in Social Sciences, 3% were in Parks and Recreation, remainder in 4 other fields.

Varsity Sports. Men (Div.IAA): Baseball, Basketball, Cross Country, Football, Golf, Javelin, Tennis, Track. Women (Div.IAA): Basketball, Tennis, Track, Volleyball.

Student Body. According to most recent data available, 65% of students from in state; 75% South, 15% Middle Atlantic. An estimated 97% of students reported as Black.

Campus Life. About 29% of men, 43% of women live in traditional dormitories; rest live in off-campus housing or commute. No intervisitation in men's and women's dormitory rooms.

Annual Costs. Tuition and fees, $1,608 (out-of-state, $3,108); room and board, $2,110. About 80% of students receive financial aid; assistance is typically divided 15% scholarship, 30% loan, 55% work.

The University of Alabama

Tuscaloosa, Alabama 35487 (205) 348-5666

A state-supported university, located in Tuscaloosa, a city of 72,800, 50 miles southwest of Birmingham, the University of Alabama comprises 9 undergraduate colleges and schools and a number of graduate and professional divisions. Most convenient major airport: Birmingham Municipal.

Founded: 1831
Affiliation: State
UG Enrollment: 6,928 M, 6,821 W (full-time); 731 M, 863 W (part-time)
Total Enrollment: 19,494
Cost: < $10K
% Receiving Financial Aid: 34%
Admission: Non-selective
Application Deadline: April 15

Admission. High school graduates with 2.0 GPA in 16 units and minimum SAT/ACT scores of 950/21 eligible; 78% of applicants accepted, 46% of these actually enroll. Average freshman ACT scores: 23.2 composite. *Required:* ACT or SAT. *Out-of-state* freshman applicants: university seeks students from out of state. State does not limit out-of-state enrollment. No special requirements for out-of-state applicants; 79% of applicants accepted, 54% of these enrolled. *Entrance programs:* mid-year admission, advanced placement. *Apply* by April 15 for priority; rolling admissions. *Transfers* welcome.

Academic Environment. Degrees offered: bachelors, masters, doctoral. Recent student cites "top quality professors, honors programs, mentor programs" as academic strengths. Requirements for graduation include 2 units each English composition, math, natural science, social studies, and foreign language or computer science, 4 units humanities. *Majors offered* in addition to usual arts and sciences include health care management, international business concentration, public archaeology, sports training, student-designed interdisciplinary majors. Average undergraduate class size: 45% under 20, 41% 20–40, 14% over 40. Current student feels some classes are "fairly large," but a recent student notes that many large lecture classes also have labs and discussion groups.

About 51% of students entering as freshmen graduate eventually; 81% of freshmen return for sophomore year. *Special programs:* CLEP, independent study, study abroad, honors, Marine Science Institute, combined programs with arts and sciences (in occupational therapy, physical therapy or radiology), cooperative work/study program, undergraduate research, 3-year degree, individualized majors, 3–2 pharmacy, Interim Term offers primarily creative and experimental courses, National Student Exchange, cross registration. Adult program: external degree. *Calendar:* semester, interim term, summer school.

Undergraduate degrees conferred (2,650). 27% were in Business and Management, 13% were in Communications, 12% were in Education, 8% were in Engineering, 7% were in Social Sciences, 5% were in Health Sciences, 4% were in Home Economics, 4% were in Multi/Interdisciplinary Studies, 4% were in Psychology, 4% were in Letters, 3% were in Life Sciences, remainder in 16 other fields.

Graduates Career Data. Graduate schools typically enrolling largest numbers of graduates include U. of Alabama according to most recent data available. Corporations typically hiring largest numbers of graduates include Arthur Andersen, AmSouth, Ernst & Young, Parisians, according to most recent data available. Career development services include interest and aptitude exploration surveys, resume development, internships, on-campus interviewing, resume referral for students and alumni.

Faculty. About 86% of faculty hold PhD or equivalent. About 39% of undergraduate classes taught by tenured faculty. About 31% of teaching faculty are female; 7% minority.
Student Body. About 68% of students from in state; 91% South, 3% Midwest, 2% New England, 3% foreign. An estimated 12% of students reported as Black, 5% other minority. Average age of undergraduate student: 22.
Varsity Sports. Men (Div.I): Baseball, Basketball, Cross Country, Football, Golf, Swimming & Diving, Tennis, Track. Women (Div.I): Basketball, Cross Country, Golf, Gymnastics, Swimming & Diving, Tennis, Track, Volleyball. Student interest fairly strong in intercollegiate athletics.
Campus Life. Students report shopping, restaurants and entertainment all available within walking distance. Cars allowed but parking is a problem. On-campus activities, including intramural sports, recreation center, and cultural events, reported adequate "to occupy the student's every minute."

About 37% of undergraduates live in traditional dormitories or on-campus apartments; no coed dormitories; rest live in off-campus housing or commute. Intervisitation in men's and women's dormitory rooms limited. There are 27 fraternities, 19 sororities on campus which about 14% of men, 26% of women join; 5% of men, 9% of women live in fraternities and sororities.
Annual Costs. Tuition and fees, $2,172 (out-of-state, $5,424); room and board, $3,530; estimated $2,000 other ("depends on student"), exclusive of travel. About 34% of students receive financial aid (75% of financial aid applicants); average amount of assistance, $4,161. Assistance is typically divided 13% scholarship, 12% grant, 73% loan, 3% work. University reports some scholarships awarded on the basis of academic merit alone. *Meeting Costs:* university offers PLUS, non-subsidized loans, various state programs.

The University of Alabama at Birmingham

Birmingham, Alabama 35294 **(205) 934-8221**

The University of Alabama at Birmingham includes Academic Affairs as well as an Academic Health Center with a variety of schools in medicine, dentistry, optometry, nursing, health related professions and public health; and the UAB Graduate School. Most convenient major airport: Birmingham Municipal.

Founded: 1969
Affiliation: State
UG Enrollment: 3,144 M, 3,816 W (full-time); 2,235 M, 2,463 W (part-time)
Total Enrollment: 15,913
Cost: < $10K
% Receiving Financial Aid: 35%
Admission: Non-selective

Admission. High school graduates with 16 units (12 in academic subjects) and 2.0 GPA eligible; 71% of applicants accepted, 75% of these actually enroll. Average freshman ACT scores: 22 M, 21 W composite. *Out-of-state* freshman applicants: State does not limit out-of-state enrollment; no special requirements for out-of-state applicants; 359 out-of-state undergraduate students enrolled. States from which most out-of-state students are drawn: Georgia, Florida, Mississippi, Tennessee. Criteria considered in admissions: standardized tests, high school academic record. *Entrance programs:* early admission, mid-year admission, deferred admission, advanced placement. *Apply* by no specific deadline. *Transfers* welcome; 1,313 enrolled 1993–94.
Academic Environment. Degrees offered: bachelors, masters, doctoral. Academic Affairs (formerly University College) has schools of Business, Education, Engineering, Arts and Humanities, Natural Sciences and Mathematics, Social and Behavioral Sciences. Each school offers undergraduate and graduate programs. Core curriculum required for graduation includes courses in math, English, computers, history, science, political science, foreign culture, and ethical reasoning. About 15% of entering freshmen graduate within four years, 40% eventually; 67% of freshmen return for sophomore year. *Special programs:* CLEP, honors, cross registration, individualized majors, cooperative education, study abroad, special services program, "mini-terms" are available in September and December. *Calendar:* quarter, summer school.
Undergraduate degrees conferred (1,324). 24% were in Business and Management, 17% were in Education, 13% were in Health Sciences, 6% were in Engineering, 6% were in Allied Health, 5% were in Social Sciences, 5% were in Life Sciences, 4% were in Psychology, 4% were in Protective Services, 3% were in Computer and Engineering Related Technology, 3% were in Communications, 3% were in Public Affairs, remainder in 7 other fields.
Graduates Career Data. Advanced studies pursued by 15–20% of students. Corporations typically hiring largest numbers of graduates include area hospitals, Alabama Power, Central Bank, Bell South. Career Center services include aptitude testing, resume/interview workshops, on-campus recruiting, career resource area.
Faculty. About 86% of faculty hold PhD or equivalent. About 29% of teaching faculty are female; 13% minority.
Varsity Sports. Men (Div.I): Baseball, Basketball, Cross Country, Football, Golf, Soccer, Tennis, Track. Women (Div.I): Basketball, Cross Country, Golf, Tennis, Track, Volleyball.
Student Body. About 95% of students from Alabama; 97% from South; 2% foreign. An estimated 21% of students reported as Black, 6% Asian, 4% other minority. Average age of undergraduate student is 25.
Campus Life. Campus is designed for commuting students, although some dormitory space available for single students in high-rise buildings on campus. About 8% of men, 8% of women live on campus; rest commute. There are 11 fraternities, 7 sororities on campus which about 6% of men, 5% of women join; fraternities and sororities provide no residence facilities.
Annual Costs. Tuition and fees, $2,358 (out-of-state, $4,458), room and board, $5,175; estimated $1,920 other, exclusive of travel. About 35% of students receive financial aid; average amount of assistance, $4,900. Assistance is typically divided 9% scholarship, 21% grant, 64% loan, 6% work. University reports 824 scholarships awarded on the basis of academic merit alone, 200 for special talents, 35 for need.

University of Alabama in Huntsville

Huntsville, Alabama 35899 **(800) 824-2255**

A state-supported institution, the Huntsville campus is part of the University of Alabama system; located in a city of 137,800.

Founded: 1950
Affiliation: State
UG Enrollment: 1,449 M, 1,278 W (full-time); 1,694 M, 1,700 W (part-time)
Total Enrollment: 8,271
Cost: < $10K
% Receiving Financial Aid: 33%
Admission: Non-selective
Application Deadline: Aug. 15

Admission. High school graduates with 16 units (12 in academic subjects) and acceptable high school average eligible; 70% of applicants accepted, 50% of these actually enroll. *Required:* SAT or ACT. Average freshman scores: SAT, 474 M, 426 W verbal, 566 M, 490 W mathematical; ACT 24.1 M, 22 W composite. *Out-of-state* freshman applicants: university seeks students from out of state. State does not limit out-of-state enrollment. No special requirements for out-of-state applicants. States from which most out-of-state students are drawn: Tennessee, Georgia, Florida, Mississippi. Criteria considered in admissions: standardized tests, high school academic record. *Entrance programs:* early admission, mid-year admission, deferred admission, advanced placement. *Apply* by August 15. *Transfers* welcome; 403 enrolled 1993–94.
Academic Environment. Degrees offered: bachelors, masters, doctoral. Graduation requirements include courses in science, social science, English Composition, Survey of Literature, Origins and Development of the Contemporary World, foreign language, fine arts, humanities; one course in mathematics, statistics, computer science, or philosophy also required. *Majors offered* include: optical science, electrical engineering, computer engineering, civil and environmental engineering. About 65% of freshman return for sophomore year. Average undergraduate class size: 55% under 20, 35% 20–40, 10% over 40. *Special programs:* cross-registration, internship/cooperative programs. *Calendar:* quarter, summer school.
Undergraduate degrees conferred (674). 35% were in Engineering, 28% were in Business and Management, 11% were in Health Sciences, 4% were in Letters, 4% were in Physical Sciences, 4% were in Computer and Engineering Related Technology, 3% were in Education, 3% were in Visual and Performing Arts, remainder in 5 other fields.

Faculty. About 89% of faculty hold PhD or equivalent. About 40% of undergraduate classes taught by tenured faculty. About 29% of teaching faculty are female; 1% Black, 1% Hispanic, 9% other minority.
Student Body. About 90% of students from in state; 2% Midwest, 2% Middle Atlantic, 1% West, 5% Foreign. About 78% are Protestant, 10% Catholic, 1% Jewish, 6% unaffiliated, 5% other. An estimated 8% are Black, 4% Asian, 2% Hispanic, 3% other minority. Average age of undergraduate student: 26.
Varsity Sports. Men (Div.II): Basketball, Crew, Cross Country, Ice Hockey, Soccer, Tennis. Women (Div.II): Basketball, Crew, Cross Country, Tennis, Volleyball.
Campus Life. Campus is designed for commuting students. About 6% of men, 7% of women live in coed dormitories; 3% each in off-campus housing; rest commute. There are 5 fraternities, 5 sororities on campus with 11% of men, 7% of women join; fraternities and sororities provide no residence facilities. About 25% of resident students leave campus on weekends.
Annual Costs. Tuition and fees, $2,418 (out-of-state, $4,836); room and board, $3,390; estimated $1,800 other, exclusive of travel. About 33% of students receive financial aid; average amount of assistance, $2,100. Assistance is typically divided 20% scholarship, 30% grant, 20% loan, 30% work. University reports 550 scholarships awarded on the basis of academic merit alone, 120 for special talents.

Alaska Pacific University

Anchorage, Alaska 99508 (907) 564-8248

A small, liberal arts institution, Alaska Pacific is proud of being the only private university in the state. Most convenient major airport: Anchorage.

Founded: 1959
Affiliation: United Methodist
Total Enrollment: 1,751 M, W, (full-time)
Cost: < $10K
% Receiving Financial Aid: 41%
Admission: Non-selective
Application Deadline: Aug. 15

Admission. High school graduates with minimum 2.5 GPA or equivalent, and minimum combined score of 800 SAT or 17 ACT composite eligible; 55% of applicants accepted, 44% of these actually enroll. *Required:* SAT or ACT. *Apply* by August 15. *Transfers* welcome.
Academic Environment. *Degrees:* AB. *Majors offered* include hospitality management, Pacific Rim studies, see also undergraduate degrees conferred (below). About 40% of students entering as freshmen do not return for sophomore year. *Special programs:* study abroad, independent study, internship, pre-engineering program. Adult programs: BA in Organizational Administration with minimum 16 month, 39 semester hour required residency.
Undergraduate degrees conferred (139). 72% were in Business and Management, 12% were in Education, 8% were in Psychology, 4% were in Liberal/General Studies, remainder in 4 other fields.
Student Body. According to most recent data available, 95% of students from Alaska. An estimated 52% of students reported as Protestant, 16% Catholic, 29% unaffiliated, 2% other; 5% Black, 3% Hispanic, 3% Asian, 8% Native American, 5% other minority.
Campus Life. About 47% of men, 53% of women live in coed dormitories; rest live in off-campus housing or commute. Freshman are given preference in college housing if all students cannot be accommodated. There are no fraternities or sororities on campus.
Annual Costs. Tuition and fees, $6,930; room and board, $4,050. About 41% of students receive financial aid. University reports some scholarships awarded on the basis of academic merit alone.

University of Alaska, Anchorage

Anchorage, Alaska 99508 (907) 786-1525

The Anchorage campus of the University of Alaska, composed of the Anchorage Community College and Anchorage Senior College, is located in the state's largest city, population 49,216. Most convenient major airport: Anchorage International.

Founded: 1954
Affiliation: State
UG Enrollment: 2,100 M, 2,500 W (full-time); 3,398 M, 4,953 W (part-time)
Total Enrollment: 20,183
Cost: < $10K
Admission: Non-selective
Application Deadline: April 1

Admission. Graduates of accredited high schools with GPA of 2.5 or higher eligible. *Required:* SAT or ACT. No restrictions on out-of-state applicants. *Apply* through late registration; April 1 preferred. *Transfers* welcome.
Academic Environment. *Degrees:* AB, BBA, BEd, BM, BS, BT. *Library:* 358,000 volumes; other materials include Alaskana Collection. Calendar: semester, summer school.
Undergraduate degrees conferred (434). 25% were in Business and Management, 19% were in Education, 12% were in Health Sciences, 9% were in Social Sciences, 6% were in Psychology, 5% were in Communications, 4% were in Letters, 4% were in Public Affairs, 3% were in Visual and Performing Arts, 3% were in Multi/Interdisciplinary Studies, remainder in 6 other fields.
Varsity Sports. Men (Div.II): Basketball, Cross Country, Hockey (I), Swimming, Alpine Skiing, Nordic Skiing. Women (Div.II): Basketball, Alpine Skiing, Gymnastics, Nordic Skiing, Volleyball.
Student Body. About 75% of students from Alaska. An estimated 3% of students reported as Black, 2% Hispanic, 3% Asian, 5% Native American, according to most recent data available.
Campus Life. About 1% of men, 1% of women live in apartment-style dormitories; rest commute.
Annual Costs. Tuition and fees, $1,788 (out-of-state, $5,116). University reports some scholarships awarded on the basis of academic merit alone.

University of Alaska, Fairbanks

Fairbanks, Alaska 99775 (907) 474-7821

Established as an agricultural college and school of mines, the University of Alaska has become a multi-campus land- and sea-grant institution. The 2,250-acre main campus is located 4 miles northwest of Fairbanks (pop. 28,000), second largest city in the state. Campuses are also located in Bethel, Nome, and Kotzebue. Most convenient major airport: Fairbanks International.

Founded: 1917
Affiliation: State
UG Enrollment: 1,622 M, 1,637 W (full-time); 1,363 M, 2,367 W (part-time)
Total Enrollment: 7,676
Cost: < $10K
% Receiving Financial Aid: 62%
Admission: Non-selective
Application Deadline: Aug. 1

Admission. High school graduates with minimum 2.0 GPA eligible; others admitted on basis of ACT; 86% of applicants accepted, 65% of those actually enroll. Average freshman scores, according to most recent data available: SAT, 460 M, 446 W verbal, 499 M, 455 W mathematical; ACT (enhanced), 21 M, 20 W composite, 20 M, 18 W mathematical. *Required:* ACT. *Out-of-state* freshman applicants: university welcomes out-of-state students. About 69% of applicants accepted, 55% enroll. *Entrance programs:* midyear admission, advanced placement. *Apply* by August 1. *Transfers* welcome.
Academic Environment. Fairbanks offers a broad range of undergraduate studies in the arts, sciences and professions. Education and business management are popular majors. In addition, as the major research center for Alaska, the university offers unusual opportunities for studies relating to the northern environment, including engineering, fisheries science, geological engineering, natural resources management, physical sciences, petroleum engineering, rural development, Russian studies, and wildlife management. It is also the state's center for study in Alaskan native cultures and languages. *Undergraduate studies* offered by colleges of Liberal Arts, Natural Sciences, Rural Alaska; and the following professional schools, Agriculture and Land Resource Management, Career and Continuing Education, Engineering, Management, Mineral Engineering. About 54% of general education requirements for graduation are elective; distribution requirements fairly numerous. *Special programs:* CLEP, honors, undergraduate research, study

abroad, independent study, individualized majors. *Calendar:* semester, summer school.

Undergraduate degrees conferred (488). 16% were in Education, 15% were in Business and Management, 11% were in Social Sciences, 10% were in Engineering, 6% were in Public Affairs, 6% were in Letters, 5% were in Psychology, 5% were in Renewable Natural Resources, 4% were in Life Sciences, 4% were in Protective Services, 4% were in Communications, 3% were in Visual and Performing Arts, 3% were in Physical Sciences, remainder in 6 other fields.

Graduates Career Data. *Full-time graduate or professional study* pursued immediately after graduation by 20% of students. *Careers in business and industry* pursued by 66% of graduates. Corporations typically hiring largest numbers of graduates include ARCO, Standard Oil, Boeing.

Faculty. About 62% of faculty hold PhD or equivalent.

Student Body. According to most recent data available, 91% of students from in state, 94% West/Northwest, 2% North Central, 1% each Middle Atlantic, New England, South. An estimated 2% of students reported as Black, 1% Hispanic, 3% Asian, 14% Native American, 11% other minority.

Varsity Sports. Men (Div. II): Basketball, Cross Country (running), Cross Country (skiing), Hockey (I), Riflery. Women (Div. II): Basketball, Cross Country (running), Cross Country (skiing), Riflery, Volleyball.

Campus Life. About 3% of men, 3% of women live in traditional dormitories; 20% of men, 15% of women in coed dormitories; rest live in off-campus housing or commute. Intervisitation in men's and women's dormitory rooms limited. Sexes segregated in coed dormitories by floor. There are no fraternities or sororities. About 60% of resident students leave campus on weekends. Cars permitted, but university warns students of limited number of headbolt heater outlets on campus.

Annual Costs. Tuition and fees, $2,214 (out-of-state, $5,542); room and board, $3,220. About 62% of students receive financial aid. Assistance is typically divided 30% scholarship, 70% loan. University reports some scholarships awarded on the basis of academic merit alone. *Meeting Costs:* university offers Permanent Fund Dividend Savings Plan.

University of Alaska, Southeast

Juneau, Alaska 99801 **(907) 789-4457**

A small, public institution serving a primarily part-time, commuter student body, offering degrees in Business and Management, Education, Renewable Natural Resources, Liberal/General Studies, and Life Sciences. University of Alaska Southeast is located in the state capital. Formerly known as University of Alaska, Juneau.

Founded: 1972
Affiliation: State
Total Enrollment: 4,420 M, W, (full- and part-time)
Cost: < $10K

Albany College of Pharmacy

Albany, New York 12208 **(518) 445-7221**

An independent institution located in the state capital, Albany College of Pharmacy offers a specialized curriculum. Most convenient major airport: Albany County.

Founded: 1881
Affiliation: Independent
Total Enrollment: 244 M, 396 W (full-time)
Cost: < $10K
% Receiving Financial Aid: 85%
Admission: Non-selective
Application Deadline: Rolling

Admission. High school graduates with 16 credits eligible; 73% of applicants accepted, 53% of these actually enroll; 70% of freshmen graduate in top quarter of high school. Average freshman SAT scores: 460 M, 550 W. *Required:* SAT or ACT. Criteria considered in admissions, in order of importance: high school academic record, standardized test scores, recommendations, extracurricular activities. *Entrance programs:* early decision, advanced placement, rolling admission. *Apply:* rolling admissions. Transfers welcome; 43 enrolled 1993–94.

Academic Environment. Degrees offered: bachelors. *Majors offered* include: five-year programs professionally accredited in pharmacy. Approximately 92% of students entering as freshmen graduate within five years; 85–90% return for sophomore year. *Special programs:* cross registration with 15 local colleges.

Undergraduate degrees conferred (139). 100% were in Health Sciences.

Graduates Career Data. Advanced studies pursued by 12% of graduates.

Faculty. About 90% of faculty hold PhD or equivalent. About 95% of undergraduate classes taught by tenured faculty. About 5% of teaching faculty are female; 2% minority.

Student Body. About 90% of students from in state; 94% Middle Atlantic, 3% New England, 1% South, 2% Foreign.

Varsity Sports. Men (NAC): Basketball, Golf, Skiing, Soccer. Women (NAC): Basketball, Golf, Skiing, Soccer.

Campus Life. About 10% of students live in coed dormitories; 30% in off-campus college housing; 60% commute. There are 3 fraternities, 1 sorority on campus which about 65% of men, 65% of women join.

Annual Costs. Tuition and fees, $8,700; room and board, $4,500; estimated $700 other, exclusive of travel. About 85% of students receive financial aid; average amount of assistance, $1,200..

Albany State College

Albany, Georgia 31705 **(912) 439-4650**

A state-supported college, located in a city of 72,600, 175 miles south of Atlanta; founded as a college for Negroes, Albany State serves primarily the people of its own community and Southwest Georgia.

Founded: 1903
Affiliation: State
Total Enrollment: 2,459 M, W (full-time)
Cost: < $10K
% Receiving Financial Aid: 78%
Admission: Non-selective
Application Deadline: May 15

Admission. Graduates of approved high schools with 16 units (9 in academic subjects) eligible; 56% of applicants accepted, 56% of these actually enroll. *Required:* SAT or ACT, interview in some cases. *Out-of-state* freshman applicants: college seeks students from out of state. State does not limit out-of-state enrollment. No special requirements for out-of-state applicants. *Apply* by May 15. *Transfers* welcome.

Academic Environment. *Degrees:* AB, BS, BBA. No general education requirements for graduation are elective; distribution requirements fairly numerous. About 75% of students entering as freshmen graduate eventually; 2% of freshmen do not return for sophomore year. *Special programs:* CLEP, independent study, study abroad, honors, cooperative education program. *Calendar:* quarter, summer school.

Undergraduate degrees conferred (204). 25% were in Business and Management, 14% were in Protective Services, 13% were in Education, 11% were in Health Sciences, 10% were in Allied Health, 5% were in Psychology, 3% were in Social Sciences, 3% were in Public Affairs, 3% were in Letters, 3% were in Business (Administrative Support), 3% were in Mathematics, remainder in 4 other fields.

Varsity Sports. Men (Div.II): Baseball, Basketball, Cross Country, Football, Track. Women (Div.II): Basketball, Cross Country, Tennis, Track, Volleyball.

Campus Life. According to most recent data available; 98% of students from South, 2% Northwest. An estimated 81% of students reported to be Black, 1% other minority. About 10% of men, 23% of women live in traditional dormitories; no coed dormitories; rest commute. Intervisitation in men's dormitory rooms limited; no intervisitation in women's dormitory rooms. There are 4 fraternities, 4 sororities on campus which about 10% of men, 12% of women join; they provide no residence facilities.

Annual Costs. Tuition and fees, $1,773 (out-of-state, $3,153); room and board, $2,475. College reports some scholarships awarded on the basis of academic merit alone.

State University of New York at Albany

(See State University of New York)

Albertson College

Caldwell, Idaho 83605 **(208) 459-5500**

A small, church-related, liberal arts college, located in a town of 16,000, 25 miles west of Boise. Formerly known as College of Idaho. Most convenient major airport: Boise Municipal.

Founded: 1891
Affiliation: Independent (Presbyterian Church (USA))
Total Enrollment: 330 M, 348 W (full-time); 21 M, 20 W (part-time)
Cost: $10K–$20K
% Receiving Financial Aid: 89%
Admission: Non-selective
Application Deadline: February 15

Admission. Graduates of accredited high schools eligible; 82% of applicants accepted, 33% of these actually enroll. Average freshman scores: SAT, 487 verbal, 524 mathematical; ACT, 24 composite. *Required:* SAT or ACT, essay. Criteria considered in admissions, in order of importance: high school academic record, standardized test scores, recommendations, extracurricular activities, writing sample; other factors considered: alumni children, diverse student body, special talents. *Apply:* rolling admissions; February 15 preferred. *Transfers* welcome; 53 enrolled 1993–94.

Academic Environment. Degrees offered: bachelors, (masters programs being phased out) . Core requirements include English, Western civilization, fine and performing arts, literature, natural sciences, mathematics, philosophy, religion, social sciences, and physical education. About 50% of freshmen graduate within four years, 55% eventually; 15% of freshmen do not return for sophomore year. *Special programs:* study abroad, 3–2 programs in engineering, cross registration with Northwest Nazarene. *Calendar:* semester, 6-week winter session, summer school.

Undergraduate degrees conferred (104). 20% were in Business and Management, 18% were in Life Sciences, 15% were in Social Sciences, 13% were in Psychology, 11% were in Education, 7% were in Multi/Interdisciplinary Studies, 5% were in Visual and Performing Arts, 3% were in Physical Sciences, 3% were in Mathematics, 3% were in Letters, remainder in Philosophy and Religion.

Graduates Career Data. Advanced studies pursued by 50% of students.

Faculty. About 71% of faculty hold PhD or equivalent. About 75% of undergraduate classes taught by tenured faculty. About 36% of teaching are female; 1% ethnic minority.

Varsity Sports. Men (NAIA): Baseball, Basketball, Skiing (NCSA-NW) , Soccer. Women (NAIA): Skiing (NCSA-NW) , Soccer, Tennis, Volleyball.

Campus Life. About 78% of students from in state; 88% Northwest, 6% West; 5% foreign. Albertson is a church-related institution; 3 units of religion required of all students; attendance at chapel services voluntary. College notes that its church relationship is cherished and maintained, although the college is nonsectarian in spirit and in instruction.

About 11% of women live in traditional dormitories; 46% of men, 35% of women live in coed dormitories; rest commute. There are 3 fraternities, 3 sororities on campus which about 20% of men, 20% of women join; 1% of men live in fraternities.

Annual Costs. Tuition and fees, $13,000; room and board, $3,000. About 89% of students receive financial aid; average amount of assistance, $8,510. Assistance is typically divided 45% scholarship/grant, 40% loan, 15% work.

Albertus Magnus College

New Haven, Connecticut 06511 **(800) 578-9160**

A Catholic, liberal arts college, Albertus Magnus is located on a 50-acre campus in a wooded area on the outskirts of New Haven (pop. 126,100) .

Founded: 1925
Affiliation: Roman Catholic
Total Enrollment: 150 M, 300 W (full-time); 50 M, 176 W (part-time)
Cost: $10K–$20K
% Receiving Financial Aid: 74%
Admission: Non-selective
Application Deadline: Rolling

Admission. High school graduates with minimum 2.5 GPA in 16 academic units eligible; 90% of applicants accepted, 60% of these actually enroll; 20% of freshmen graduate in top fifth of high school class, 50% in top two-fifths. Average freshmen SAT scores: 410 verbal, 460 mathematical. *Required:* SAT or ACT; interview recommended. Criteria considered in admissions, in order of importance: high school academic record, standardized test scores, recommendations, extracurricular activities. *Entrance programs:* early admission, mid-year admission, deferred admission. *Apply:* rolling admissions. *Transfers* welcome.

Academic Environment. Degrees offered: associates, bachelors, masters. Tri-session calendar recently introduced. Graduation requirements include 2 sessions English, 1 each math, science, fine arts, foreign language, and religion, choice of 4 out of 5 social and behavioral sciences. *Majors offered* include art therapy, international business, teacher preparation, social gerontology, communications, health care management, human services, criminal justice. Average undergraduate class size: 90% under 20, 10% 20–40.

About 70% of students entering as freshmen graduate eventually; 80% of freshmen return for sophomore year. *Special programs:* CLEP, career internships, January term, independent study, junior year abroad, undergraduate research; cross registration with Quinnipiac, Palear School of Art, numerous interdepartmental majors. *Calendar:* tri-session.

Undergraduate degrees conferred (127). 34% were in Business and Management, 17% were in Letters, 17% were in Communications, 10% were in Social Sciences, 8% were in Psychology, 5% were in Visual and Performing Arts, 3% were in Multi/Interdisciplinary Studies, 3% were in Liberal/General Studies, remainder in 3 other fields.

Graduates Career Data. Advanced studies pursued by 40% of students; 8% attend law school; 10% attend business school; 2% attend medical school. About 50% of 1992–93 graduates employed.

Faculty. About 95% of faculty hold PhD or equivalent. About 70% of undergraduate classes taught by tenured faculty.

Student Body. About 70% of students from in state; 90% New England, 3% Middle Atlantic, 1% Midwest, 1% South, 5% foreign. An estimated 75% of students Catholic, 25% other.

Religious Orientation. Albertus Magnus is a church-related institution; six hours of religious studies required of all students.

Varsity Sports. Men (Div.III): Baseball, Basketball, Cross Country, Diving, Soccer, Swimming, Tennis, Track. Women (Div.III): Basketball, Cross Country, Softball, Swimming, Tennis, Volleyball.

Campus Life. Cars permitted for all. Use of alcoholic beverages on campus governed by state law. Cultural and intellectual opportunities offered by the community supplemented by campus activities.

About 60% of students live in dormitories; rest commute. About 40% of resident students leave campus on weekends. There are no fraternities or sororities on campus.

Annual Costs. Tuition and fees, $11,560 (for 2 15-credit sessions; $13,920 for 3 sessions); room and board, $4,720; estimated $750 other, exclusive of travel. About 74% of students receive financial aid; average amount of assistance, $6,000. Assistance is typically divided 40% scholarship/grant, 40% loan, 20% work. College reports 25 scholarships awarded on basis of academic merit alone.

Albion College

Albion, Michigan 49224 **(800) 858-6770**

A church-related, liberal arts college, highly regarded in the Middle West, located in a community of 11,000, 90 miles west of Detroit and 175 miles east of Chicago. Most convenient major airport: Detroit Metropolitan.

Founded: 1835
Affiliation: United Methodist
Total Enrollment: 832 M, 822 W (full-time)
Cost: $10K–$20K
% Receiving Financial Aid: 81%
Admission: Very (+) Selective
Application Deadline: April 1

Admission is very (+) selective. About 90% of applicants accepted, 29% of these actually enroll; 58% of freshmen graduate in top fifth of high school class, 83% in top two-fifths. Average freshman scores: SAT, 536 M, 530 W verbal, 605 M, 559 W mathematical; 70% of freshman score above 500 on verbal, 29% above 600, 2% above 700; 81% score above 500 on mathematical, 32% above 600, 15% above 700; ACT, 25 composite. *Required:* SAT or ACT, essay. Criteria considered in admissions, in order of importance: high school academic record, standardized test scores, recommendations, extracurricular activities, writing sample; other factors considered: special talents, alumni children, diverse student body, religious affiliation and/or commitment. *Entrance programs:* mid-year admission, rolling admission. *Apply* by April 1. *Transfers* welcome; 33 enrolled 1993–94.

Academic Environment. Degrees offered: associates, bachelors. Administration source reports "a great deal of student involvement in curricular planning." Student body characterized as strongly concerned with both scholarly/intellectual interests and occupational/professional goals. College places emphasis on the importance of liberal arts in the context of pre-professional education. Relations with professors in and out of class reported by student leader to be "excellent, close." Graduation requirements include 13 course core and category requirements, writing competency exam. *Majors offered* in addition to usual arts and sciences include mathematics/economics, international studies, interdepartmental and student-designed majors. Average undergraduate class size: 51% under 20, 41% 20–40, 8% over 40.

About 70% of entering freshmen graduate eventually; 84% of freshmen return for sophomore year. *Special programs:* CLEP, honors, undergraduate research, study abroad, independent study, Gerald R. Ford Institute for Public Service, professional management and human services programs, GLCA, 3–2 engineering, education and nursing, Basic Ideas program for freshmen, intensive humanities program, upperclass course in community relations. *Calendar:* semester.

Undergraduate degrees conferred (401). 45% were in Social Sciences, 19% were in Letters, 10% were in Life Sciences, 6% were in Psychology, 5% were in Physical Sciences, 4% were in Mathematics, 3% were in Visual and Performing Arts, remainder in 5 other fields.

Graduates Career Data. Advanced studies pursued by 35% of students; 17% enter graduate school; 4% enter medical school; 9% enter law school; 2% enter business school. Medical schools typically enrolling largest numbers of graduates include Wayne State, Michigan State; law schools include Detroit College of Law, Wayne State, U. of Detroit. Fields typically hiring largest numbers of graduates include accounting, banking, sales/marketing; corporations include Arthur Andersen, Coopers & Lybrand, National Bank of Detroit, Comerica. Comprehensive career services include career guidance, SIGI-Plus, career testing, job search assistance, on-campus interviews.

Faculty. About 96% of faculty hold PhD or equivalent. About 74% of undergraduate classes taught by tenured or tenure track faculty. About 25% of teaching faculty are female; 8% minority.

Student Body. About 85% of students from within state; 95% from Midwest, less than 2% foreign. An estimated 41% of students reported as Protestant, 27% Catholic, 19% unaffiliated, 13% other; 4% Black, 6% other minority.

Religious Orientation. Albion College is a church-related institution, makes no religious demands on students; 14% of students reported affiliated with the United Methodist Church.

Varsity Sports. Men (Div.III): Baseball, Basketball, Cross Country, Diving, Football, Golf, Soccer, Swimming, Tennis, Track. Women (Div. III): Basketball, Cross Country, Diving, Golf, Soccer, Softball, Swimming, Tennis, Track, Volleyball.

Campus Life. Cars allowed for upperclassmen; student leader reports parking inadequate for residential students. No public possession or consumption of alcohol. Albion has a strong fraternity/sorority system, but relations with independents are said to be good. College has a Union Board which sponsors "many dances, concerts, coffee houses, etc." Students reported to be very interested in intramurals (most popular: football) .

About 57% of men, 84% of women live in coed dormitories; 5% of men, 13% of women live in off-campus college-related housing; rest commute. Sexes segregated in coed dormitories by wing, floor or suite. There are 6 fraternities, 6 sororities on campus which about 52% of men, 48% of women join; 35% of men live in fraternities; sororities provide no residence facilities. About 30% of resident students leave campus on weekends.

Annual Costs. Tuition and fees, $13,676; room and board, $4,588; estimated $1,300 other, exclusive of travel. About 81% of students receive financial aid; average amount of assistance, $11,944. Assistance is typically divided 71% scholarship/grant, 22% loan, 7% work. College reports 778 scholarships awarded on the basis of academic merit alone, 119 for special talents alone. *Meeting Costs:* college offers monthly payment plan, deferred payment plan, alternative loan payments.

Albright College

Reading, Pennsylvania 19612-5234 (215) 921-7512

Albright is a small denominational liberal arts college, with a strong pre-professional emphasis. It is located on an 110-acre campus in a city of 87,600, about 55 miles northwest of Philadelphia. Most convenient major airport: Philadelphia International.

Founded: 1856
Affiliation: United Methodist
Total Enrollment: 435 M, 450 W (full time)
Cost: $10K–$20K
% Receiving Financial Aid: 90%
Admission: Very Selective
Application Deadline: Feb. 15

Admission is very selective. About 75% of applicants accepted, 30% of these actually enroll; 51% of freshmen graduate in top fifth of high school class, 85% in top two-fifths. Average freshman SAT scores: 523 M, 525 W verbal, 581 M, 571 W mathematical (1991–92) . *Required:* SAT, essay; recommendation and interview strongly recommended. Criteria considered in admissions, in order of importance: high school academic record, extracurricular activities, recommendations, writing sample, standardized test scores; other factors considered: diverse student body, special talents. *Entrance programs:* early admission, mid-year admission, advanced placement, deferred admission. About 14% of entering students from private schools, 15% parochial schools. *Apply* by February 15. *Transfers* welcome. 25 enrolled for 1993–94.

Academic Environment. Degrees offered: bachelors. Temple U. maintains graduate extension center on campus, offering advanced courses in education, psychology, and MSW program; St. Joseph's U. offers MBA and Hospital Administration programs on campus. One student feels "the academic program has a lot of things to pick from." Another student reports that professors teach only three classes "which gives them more time to give students outside help and to make the classes more comprehensive." Administration reports 20% of courses required for graduation; distribution requirements fairly numerous: 2 courses philosophy or religion, 2 courses each English, social sciences, 1 course each arts, history, 2 semesters science, additional course in humanities, foreign language proficiency. Average undergraduate class size: 90% under 20; 10% 20–40. Current student notes "it is a small campus and the teachers are always around."

About 72% of students entering as freshmen graduate within four years; 92% of freshmen return for sophomore year. *Special programs:* CLEP, January term, independent study, study abroad, undergraduate research, Washington Semester, 3–2 programs in forestry and environmental management, natural resources. *Calendar:* 4–1–4, summer school.

Undergraduate degrees conferred (307). 33% were in Business and Management, 13% were in Life Sciences, 11% were in Psychology, 10% were in Letters, 9% were in Social Sciences, 5% were in Computer and Engineering Related Technology, 4% were in Health Sciences, 3% were in Mathematics, 3% were in Home Economics, remainder in 6 other fields.

Graduates Career Data. Advanced studies pursued by 50% of graduates. Medical schools typically enrolling largest numbers of graduates include Temple, Jefferson; dental schools include Temple; law schools include Dickinson, Temple; business schools include Wharton, Purdue, Northeastern. Employers typically hiring largest numbers of graduates include AT&T, IBM, U.S. Government. Career development services include career and alumni workshops, referral services, resume book, on-campus recruitment.

Faculty. About 80% of faculty hold PhD or equivalent.

Student Body. About 45% of students from in state; 84% from Middle Atlantic, 10% New England, 3% foreign. An estimated 22% of students reported as Protestant, 51% Catholic, 6% Jewish, 18% unaffiliated, 3% other; 4% as Black, 2% Asian, 2% Hispanic, 2% other minority.

Religious Orientation. Albright is a church-related institution; 1 course in philosophy or religion required of all students. Chaplain, Sunday worship services available to students. College "seeks to make possible intellectual development in an atmosphere of Christian ideals."
Varsity Sports. Men (Div.III): Baseball, Basketball, Cross Country, Football, Golf, Soccer, Swimming, Tennis, Track, Wrestling. Women (Div.III): Basketball, Cross Country, Golf, Field Hockey, Softball, Swimming, Tennis, Track, Volleyball.
Campus Life. One student reports "We are in a city, so I think students tend to keep activities on campus more." Another student, from NY, considers location to be more of a small town. Time spent outside of classes reported, by one student, as "extracurricular activities, work, work, work, and partying." Another student generally concurs, but adds sports, shopping, skiing, and movies to the list.

About 85% of students live on campus; 3% live in off-campus housing; 12% commute. There are 5 fraternities, 4 sororities on campus which about 25% of men, 25% of women join. About 5% of resident students leave campus on weekends.
Annual Costs. Tuition and fees, $15,010; room and board, $4,250; estimated $1,000 other, exclusive of travel. About 90% of students receive financial aid; average amount of assistance, $4,600. Assistance is typically 50% scholarship. College reports some scholarships awarded on the basis of academic merit alone.

Alcorn State University

Lorman, Mississippi 39096 (601) 877-6147

The oldest land-grant college founded for Negroes in the U.S., Alcorn State still serves a predominantly black student body. Campus is located 17 miles southwest of Port Gibson (pop. 2,600) and 45 miles south of Vicksburg. Most convenient major airport: Jackson Municipal Airport.

Founded: 1871
Affiliation: State
UG Enrollment:
Total Enrollment: 3,244 M, W (full-time)
Cost: < $10K
% Receiving Financial Aid: 85%
Admission: Non-selective
Application Deadline: June 30

Admission. Graduates of accredited high schools with 15 acceptable units eligible; 58% of applicants accepted, 73% of these actually enroll; 20% of freshmen graduate in top fifth of their high school class, 45% in top two-fifths. *Required:* SAT or ACT. *Out-of-state* freshman applicants: university welcomes students from out of state. State does not limit out-of-state enrollment. Special requirements for out-of-state applicants; ACT score of 15 or above, combined SAT of 720 or above. About 47% of out-of-state applicants accepted, 51% of these actually enroll. *Apply* by June 30. *Transfers* welcome.
Academic Environment. *Degrees:* AB, BS. *Special programs:* honors, cooperative education, developmental education, Eight College Consortium. About 42% of entering freshmen graduate eventually; 32% of freshmen do not return for sophomore year. *Calendar:* semester, summer school. *Miscellaneous:* A ROTC.
Undergraduate degrees conferred (269). 22% were in Business and Management, 19% were in Education, 9% were in Life Sciences, 7% were in Health Sciences, 7% were in Social Sciences, 6% were in Engineering and Engineering Related Technology, 5% were in Communications, 4% were in Physical Sciences, 4% were in Business (Administrative Support), 3% were in Home Economics, 3% were in Agricultural Sciences, 3% were in Agribusiness and Agricultural Production, remainder in 4 other fields.
Graduates Career Data. *Full-time graduate or professional study* pursued by 16% of students immediately after graduation; 3% each enter dental, law and business schools. *Careers in business and industry* pursued by 62% of graduates.
Varsity Sports. Men (Div. 1): Baseball, Basketball, Cross Country, Football, Golf, Tennis, Track. Women (Div. 1): Basketball, Cross Country, Tennis, Track, Volleyball.
Campus Life. According to most recent data available; 83% of students from in state; 93% from South. An estimated 92% of students reported as Black, 1% other minority.

About 90% of men, 74% of women live in traditional dormitories; no coed dormitories; rest commute. There are 4 fraternities, 4 sororities on campus which about 5% of men, 6% of women join; they provide no residence facilities.

Annual Costs. Tuition and fees, $2,376 (out-of-state, $4,336); room and board, $2,098. About 85% of students receive financial aid. University reports some scholarships awarded on the basis of academic merit alone. *Meeting Costs:* university offers Parent PLUS Loan.

Alderson-Broaddus College

Philippi, West Virginia 26416 (304) 457-1700

A church-related college, located in a community of 3,000, 110 miles south of Pittsburgh, Alderson-Broaddus asserts that it "takes its church-relatedness seriously, but not from a narrow sectarian point of view."

Founded: 1871
Affiliation: American Baptist
Total Enrollment: 712 M, W (full-time)
Cost: < $10K
% Receiving Financial Aid: 87%
Admission: Non-selective
Application Deadline: Rolling

Admission. High school graduates with 15 units, 2.0 GPA in college preparatory subjects and minimum of 18 ACT or 800 SAT eligible; 75% of applicants accepted, 40% of these actually enroll; 90% of freshmen graduate in top half of high school class. *Required:* ACT or SAT (ACT preferred); interview "preferred", required for physician's assistant program. *Apply:* rolling admission. *Transfers* welcome.
Academic Environment. On-campus hospital available for 4-year paramedical programs. *Degrees:* AB, BS. Requirements for graduation include a Liberal Arts CORE, a Liberal Arts minor, and additional directed electives. About 59% of students entering as freshmen graduate eventually; 31% of freshmen do not return for sophomore year. *Special programs:* CLEP, independent study, study abroad. *Calendar:* semester, summer session.
Undergraduate degrees conferred (115). 31% were in Allied Health, 18% were in Health Sciences, 16% were in Education, 6% were in Business and Management, 5% were in Public Affairs, 4% were in Life Sciences, 3% were in Social Sciences, 3% were in Psychology, 3% were in Theology, 3% were in Computer and Engineering Related Technology, 3% were in Communications, remainder in 3 other fields.
Varsity Sports. Men (NAIA): Baseball, Basketball, Soccer, Tennis. Women (NAIA): Basketball, Tennis, Volleyball.
Student Body. According to most recent data available, 59% of students from in state; 65% North Central, 24% Middle Atlantic. An estimated 58% of students reported as Protestant, 14% Catholic, 14% unaffiliated, 15% other; 3% Black, 1% Hispanic, 1% Asian, 2% other minority.
Religious Orientation. Alderson-Broaddus is a church-related institution; 1 course in religion required of all students; attendance at regular chapel services recommended.
Campus Life. Cars permitted except for freshmen. Use or possession of alcoholic beverages by a student is a violation of college policy.

About 70% of men, 60% of women live in traditional dormitories; no coed dormitories; rest commute. Freshmen are given preference in college housing if all students cannot be accommodated. Intervisitation in men's and women's dormitory rooms limited. There are 4 fraternities, 3 sororities on campus which about 13% of men, 6% of women join; they provide no residence facilities. About 60% of resident students leave campus on weekends.
Annual Costs. Tuition and fees, $9,838; room and board, $3,180. About 87% of students receive financial aid. College reports some scholarships awarded on the basis of academic merit alone. *Meeting Costs:* college offers Academic Management Services.

Alfred University

Alfred, New York 14802 (607) 871-2115

A private institution, Alfred includes the Liberal Arts College, Colleges of Business Administration, Professional Studies, Division of Electrical, Industrial and Mechanical Engineering, and Graduate School, as well as the state-supported College of Ceramics, which includes a Division of Ceramic Engineering and Science, and a School of Art and Design. The College of Ceramics, a unit of the State University of New York, offers the largest ceramic engineering program in the world. Although primarily a liberal arts institution, the professional influence on campus is substantial. Taking advantage of the rural setting, the university offers an environmental studies major which provides an interdepartmental approach to "the application of basic knowledge to problems of man and his environment." Located in a community of 2,500, Alfred's 232-acre main campus is about 70 miles south of Rochester, in the foothills of the Allegheny Mountains. Most convenient major airport: Rochester.

Founded: 1836	**Total Enrollment:** 2,326
Affiliation: Independent	**Cost:** $10K–$20K
UG Enrollment: 1,029 M, 801 W (full-time); 55 M, 55 W (part-time)	**% Receiving Financial Aid:** 65%
	Admission: Highly Selective
	Application Deadline: Feb. 15

Admission is highly selective for Engineering and Science (Ceramics); very selective for Engineering and Science (Industrial, Mechanical, Electrical) , Professional Studies; selective (+) for Liberal Arts; selective for Art and Design (Ceramics) , Business Administration. For all schools, 66% of applicants accepted, 27% of these actually enroll; 61% of freshmen graduate in top fifth of high school class, 89% in top two-fifths. Average freshman scores: SAT, 530 M, 537 W verbal, 601 M, 574 W mathematical; ACT, 26 M, 26 W composite.

For Liberal Arts (348 M, 354 W, f-t; 17 M, 67 W, p-t) , 70% of applicants accepted, 21% of these actually enroll; 60% of freshmen graduate in top fifth of high school class, 92% in top two-fifths. Average freshman SAT scores: 536 M, 553 W verbal, 570 M, 574 W mathematical; ACT, 26 M, 26 W composite, 26 M, 26 W mathematical (according to most recent data available) .

For Art and Design (Ceramics) , (144 M, 231 W, f-t, 4 M, 3 W, p-t) , 50% of applicants accepted, 49% of these actually enroll; 48% of freshmen graduate in top fifth of high school class, 87% in top two-fifths. Average freshman SAT scores: 499 M, 519 W verbal, 544 M, 548 W mathematical; ACT, 23 M, 24 W composite, 25 M, 25 W mathematical (according to most recent data available) .

For Business Administration (162 M, 110 W, f-t, 5 M, 12 W, p-t) , 67% of applicants accepted, 20% of these actually enroll; 80% of freshmen graduate in top fifth of high school class, 97% in top two-fifths. Average freshman SAT scores: 544 M, 492 W verbal, 597 M, 558 W mathematical; ACT, 25 M, 24 W composite, 26 M, 25 W mathematical (according to most recent data available) .

For Engineering and Science (Ceramics) , (285 M, 74 W, f-t, 13 M, 1 W, p-t) , 74% of applicants accepted, 55% of these actually enroll; 83% of freshmen graduate in top fifth of high school class, 97% in top two-fifths. Average freshman SAT scores: 522 M, 501 W verbal, 648 M, 605 W mathematical; ACT, 27 M, 25 W composite, 27 M, 27 W mathematical (according to most recent data available) .

For Engineering and Science (Industrial, Mechanical, Electrical) , (83 M, 16 W, f-t, 7 M, 1 W, p-t) , 65% of applicants accepted, 18% of these actually enroll; 53% of freshmen graduate in top fifth of high school class, 90% in top two-fifths. Average freshman SAT scores: 536 M, 655 W verbal, 615 M, 615 W mathematical; ACT, 26 M, 26 W composite, 27 M, 26 W mathematical (according to most recent data available) .

For College of Professional Studies (Education) (6 M, 32 W, f-t; 7 M, 101 W, p-t) , 50% of applicants accepted, 13% of these actually enroll; all of freshmen graduate in top fifth of high school class. Average freshman SAT scores: 460 M, 550 W verbal, 550 M, 580 W mathematical (according to most recent data available) .

Required: SAT, essay, transcripts, recommendations, portfolio for art students. Criteria considered in admissions, in order of importance: high school academic record, recommendations, extracurricular activities, writing sample, standardized test scores; other factors considered: special talents, alumni children, diverse student body. *Entrance programs:* early decision, early admission, mid-year admission, deferred admission. About 17% of entering students from private schools. *Apply* by February 15. *Transfers* welcome; 150 enrolled 1993–94.

Academic Environment. Degrees offered: bachelors, masters, doctoral. Current student cites small classes, accessible faculty, and friendly people as strengths of the school. He also finds the business program rigorous and relevant. Administration reports requirements for graduation vary by curriculum; general education requirements for Liberal Arts in Basic Competencies and Areas of Knowledge. *Majors offered* include ceramic engineering, ceramic science, glass science engineering, health care planning and management, industrial engineering, interdepartmental programs in environmental studies, international studies. Average undergraduate class size: 18.

About 72% of students entering as freshmen graduate eventually; 92% of freshmen return for sophomore year. Student reports "Alfred spends more per student than most large universities on library resources. Computers are easy to find and always available." Special programs: CLEP, independent study, study abroad, international baccalaureate, 3–2 forestry, 3–2 engineering, accelerated programs, double majors, student designed majors, cross registration with SUNY College of Technology. *Calendar:* early semester, summer school.

Undergraduate degrees conferred (324). 22% were in Business and Management, 20% were in Health Sciences, 9% were in Social Sciences, 8% were in Education, 6% were in Psychology, 5% were in Engineering, 5% were in Life Sciences, 4% were in Communications, 3% were in Protective Services, 3% were in Visual and Performing Arts, 3% were in Liberal/General Studies, 3% were in Mathematics, remainder in 7 other fields.

Graduates Career Data. Advanced studies pursued by 30% graduates; 3% enter medical school; 1% enter dental school; 5% enter law school; 11% enter business school. Medical schools typically enrolling largest numbers of graduates include Rochester, Tufts; dental schools include Tufts; law schools include Cornell, Hofstra, SUNY; business schools include NYU, Rochester, Clarkson. About 51% of 1992–93 graduates employed. Employers typically hiring largest numbers of graduates include Corning Glass Works, Eastman Kodak, IBM, Arthur Andersen. *Career Counseling Program* offers career guidance and job placement services.

Faculty. About 87% of faculty hold PhD or equivalent. About 80% of undergraduate classes taught by tenured faculty. About 24% of teaching faculty are female.

Student Body. About 70% of students from in state; foreign students from 31 different countries. An estimated 26% of students reported as Protestant, 48% Catholic, 7% Jewish, 19% unaffiliated; 78% as Black, 2% Hispanic, 2% Asian, 6% other minority.

Religious Orientation. Alfred is an independent institution, makes no religious demands on students. Local clergy representing an interdenominational Protestant church, Roman Catholic church, Quakers, Jews, and Seventh Day Baptists "share in an ecumenical ministry to students."

Varsity Sports. Men (Div.III): Basketball, Cross Country, Diving, Equestrian, Football, Golf, Lacrosse, Skiing, Soccer, Swimming, Tennis, Track. Women (Div.III): Basketball, Cross Country, Diving, Equestrian, Golf, Lacrosse, Skiing, Soccer, Swimming, Tennis, Track, Volleyball.

Campus Life. One student reports that the university brings many activities to campus. "there is also a wide range of clubs and organizations to get involved in. With only 2,000 undergraduate students, it is easy to get involved and become a leader. Sometimes I find myself too busy." Same student enjoys a "pick-up game of basketball with friends and professors and writing for the campus newspaper." He also notes that "when students are not participating in extracurricular activities, they STUDY." Off-campus activities reported to include dinner at a professor's house and trips to Buffalo or Rochester for musicals and sporting events.

About 75% of men, 75% of women live in coed dormitories; 5% of men, 3% of women live in off-campus housing; 3% of men, 5% of women commute. Sexes segregated in coed dormitories by floor or room. There are 7 fraternities, 4 sororities on campus which about 20% of men, 17% of women join; 17% of men, 14% of women live in fraternities and sororities. About 10% of resident students leave campus on weekends.

Annual Costs. Tuition and fees, $16,048; room and board, $5,006; estimated $400 other, exclusive of travel. About 65% of students receive financial aid; average amount of assistance, $9,200. Assistance is typically divided 75% scholarship, 15% loan, 10% work. University reports "several" scholarships awarded on the basis of academic merit alone. *Meeting Costs:* university offers budget plan, 0% institutional loan program, prepayment options.

Alice Lloyd College

Pippa Passes, Kentucky 41844 **(606) 368-2101**

Founded in 1913 as a primary school, Alice Lloyd became a college in 1923 designed to serve students in the surrounding area. Its stated goal is to prepare students to return to their home area and serve there as community leaders. Students are drawn primarily from 67 counties in 4 adjacent states. Most convenient major airport: Lexington, Kentucky

Founded: 1923
Affiliation: Independent
Total Enrollment: 529 M, W (full-time)
Cost: < $10K
% Receiving Financial Aid: 100%
Admission: Non-selective
Application Deadline: Aug. 1

Admission. High school graduates or the equivalent eligible. Preference given to students who are perceived to be potential leaders. About 40% of applicants accepted, 38% of these actually enroll. Average freshmen ACT scores, according to most recent data available: 20 M, 19.8 W composite. *Apply* by August 1; rolling admissions. *Transfers* welcome.
Academic Environment. College confers both associate and baccalaureate degrees.
Undergraduate degrees conferred (75). 75% were in Education, 12% were in Business and Management, 9% were in Life Sciences, 4% were in Social Sciences.
Campus Life. College does not actively recruit outside of its target area, although it does welcome a limited number of others to provide some diversity. College is not denominational, but "makes some religious and patriotic as well as strong work ethic demands on students." Alice Lloyd is "in a very rural area". About 80% of the men, 80% of the women live in traditional dormitories. All students, teachers and staff eat in one common dining hall, one of the traditions of the school.
Annual Costs. All students are expected to work for the college a minimum of 10 hours a week. In return for the work the college assumes all of the tuition costs of approximately $7,500 and most students will be expected to contribute $2,480 to cover the cost of room and board, although the latter can be met by the college if needed.

Allegheny College

Meadville, Pennsylvania 16335 **(814) 332-4351 or (800) 521-5293**

Allegheny has for years been a high quality, traditional, liberal arts college, with a strong reputation for pre-professional preparation. College attracts a diverse student body. Allegheny is non-sectarian in its religious philosophy but has had an historic association with the United Methodist Church. It is located in a town of 14,000, 90 miles north of Pittsburgh and 90 miles east of Cleveland. Most convenient major airport: Pittsburgh or Erie.

Founded: 1815
Affiliation: Independent (United Methodist)
Total Enrollment: 848 M, 898 W (full-time)
Cost: $10K–$20K
% Receiving Financial Aid: 74%
Admission: Very (+) Selective
Application Deadline: Feb. 15

Admission is very (+) selective. About 71% of applicants accepted, 26% of these actually enroll; 70% of freshmen graduate in top fifth of high school class, 91% in top two-fifths. Average freshmen scores: SAT, middle 50% of class score 450–560 verbal, 520–630 mathematical; 57% of freshmen score above 500 on verbal, 14% above 600, 1% above 700; 86% score above 500 on mathematical, 38% above 600, 6% above 700; ACT: 22–27 composite. *Required:* SAT or ACT, essay, 2 recommendations. Criteria considered in admissions, in order of importance: high school academic record; standardized test scores; recommendations, extracurricular activities, and "personal qualities/character" considered of equal importance; writing sample. Other factors considered include alumni children, diverse student body, special talents. *Entrance programs:* early decision, early admission, mid-year admission, advanced placement, deferred entrance. About 20% of entering students from private and parochial schools. *Apply* by February 15. *Transfers* welcome; 15 enrolled 1993–94.
Academic Environment. Degrees offered: bachelors. Graduation requirements include a 1-semester freshman seminar; 3-course clusters in arts/humanities, natural sciences, and social sciences; sophomore writing course; and special concentration or minor outside the division of the major. Several student reports indicate students are encouraged to "think about areas that aren't in our majors." "There is a lot of latitude to explore multidisciplinary interests (e.g., chemistry major with theatre minor and psychology concentration) ." There is "a lot of interaction between the professor and students," "a lot of active learning," and "a lot more personal attention" [than at larger institutions]. Writing is stressed at all levels, culminating in a senior thesis or project, which "prepares students for masters-level research." Average undergraduate class size: 74% under 20, 23% 20–40, 3% over 40.

About 74% of students entering as freshmen graduate eventually; 88% of freshmen return for sophomore year. *Special programs:* CLEP, independent study, study abroad, undergraduate research, GLCA, 3-year degree, individualized majors, internships, joint and double majors, Washington Semester, 3–2 programs in engineering, environmental management, forestry, nursing, 2–2, 3–2, and 3–1 programs in 5 allied health fields, 3–3 physical therapy, 3–4 doctoral program in nursing. *Library:* special collections include extensive Lincoln materials. *Calendar:* "early" semester (break at Christmas) , summer school.
Undergraduate degrees conferred (452). 36% were in Social Sciences, 14% were in Psychology, 12% were in Letters, 9% were in Life Sciences, 6% were in Communications, 6% were in Multi/Interdisciplinary Studies, 4% were in Visual and Performing Arts, 4% were in Physical Sciences, 4% were in Mathematics, 3% were in Foreign Languages, remainder in 2 other fields.
Graduates Career Data. Advanced studies pursued by 29% of graduates; 5% enter medical school; 1% enter dental school; 2% enter law school; 2% enter business school. Medical schools typically enrolling largest numbers of graduates include Temple, Penn State, Hahnemann, U. of Pittsburgh; dental schools include U. of Pittsburgh; law schools include Dickinson, Cornell; business schools include U. of Pittsburgh, Case Western. About 67% of 1992–93 graduates employed. Fields typically hiring largest numbers of graduates include insurance, banking, and manufacturing. Career development services include group and individual counseling, internships and externships (observation) , resume/interview workshops, library resources, alumni/parent network, planning newsletters and workshops.
Faculty. About 91% of faculty hold doctorate or appropriate terminal degree; substantial number earned at leading institutions. About 47% of classes taught by tenured faculty. About 32% of teaching faculty are female; 8% minority.
Student Body. About 53% of students from in-state; 72% Middle States, 14% Midwest, 7% New England, 2% South, 2% West, 3% foreign. An estimated 35% of students reported as Protestant, 41% Catholic, 2% Jewish, 13% unaffiliated, 8% other; 3% as Black, 1% Hispanic, 2% Asian.
Religious Orientation. Allegheny has a traditional association with the United Methodist Church, but is non-sectarian and makes no religious demands on students. Places of worship available on campus and in immediate community for major faiths.
Varsity Sports. Men (Div.III): Baseball, Basketball, Cycling Club, Cross Country, Diving, Fencing Club, Football, Golf, Ice Hockey Club, Soccer, Swimming, Tennis, Track (indoor/outdoor) . Women (Div.III): Basketball, Cross Country, Diving, Soccer, Softball, Swimming, Tennis, Track (indoor/outdoor) , Volleyball. About half of the 20 teams nationally rank in Div. III every year.
Campus Life. One recent student comments that Allegheny students "study hard and play hard." Another feels "the campus is practically self-contained. [with] a lot of activities—social, cultural, etc." There is some feeling that the local town is small, but Erie, about 35 minutes away, "makes up for it." Another recent student notes "A very nice college community atmosphere is maintained." Cars discouraged, but permitted for all except freshmen (may keep but not operate) and financial aid recipients (must have special permission) . Alcoholic beverages "strictly" prohibited under age 21, or by anyone in public areas; "dry rush." Intervisitation governed by the living units themselves.

About 9% of men, 41% of women live in traditional dormitories; 48% of men, 30% of women in coed dormitories; 26% of men, 29% of women live in off-campus housing; less than 1% commute from home. Housing guaranteed all 4 years to anyone participating in "room draw." Sexes segregated in coed dormitories by wing or floor. There are 5 fraternities, 5 sororities on campus which about 25% of men, 30% of women join; 17% of men live in fraternities; sororities provide no residence facilities. About 10% of resident students leave campus on weekends.
Annual Costs. Tuition and fees, $16,700; room and board, $4,320; estimated $800 other, exclusive of travel. About 74% of students receive need-based financial aid; average amount of need-based

assistance, $16,700. Assistance is typically divided 71% scholarship/grant, 21% loan, 9% work. College reports up to 100 institutional scholarships awarded on the basis of academic merit and special talents alone, about 1,200 for need. Meeting Costs: college offers guaranteed tuition plan for prepayment.

Allentown College of St. Francis De Sales

Center Valley, Pennsylvania 18034 **(215) 282-4443**

A church-related, co-educational, liberal arts college, conducted by the Oblate Fathers of St. Francis de Sales, located in a rural community 7 miles from both Allentown and Bethlehem. Most convenient major airports: Allentown-Bethlehem-Easton.

Founded: 1964
Affiliation: Independent (Roman Catholic)
UG Enrollment: 436 M, 503 W (full-time, day program); 107 M, W (part-time)
Total Enrollment: 2,167
Cost: < $10K
% Receiving Financial Aid: 90%
Admission: Non-selective
Application Deadline: Aug. 1

Admission. High school graduates with 16 units in academic subjects eligible; 65% of applicants accepted, 37% of these actually enroll; 38% of freshmen graduate in top fifth of high school class, 66% in top two-fifths. Average freshman SAT scores: 470 verbal, 515 mathematical; 34% of freshmen score above 500 on verbal, 8% above 600; 56% score above 500 on mathematical, 19% above 600, 1% above 700. *Required:* SAT; on-campus interview strongly encouraged. Criteria considered in admissions, in order of importance: high school academic record, standardized test scores, recommendations, extracurricular activities; other factors considered: special talents. About 6% of entering students from private schools, 53% from parochial schools. *Apply* by August 1: rolling admissions. *Transfers* welcome; 47 enrolled 1993–94.
Academic Environment. Degrees offered:bachelors, masters. Core requirements include a course called Communication and Thought, as well as 2 semesters of theology, foreign language or foreign cultures, 3 semesters of physical education, 4 in humanities, 4 in Modes of Thinking, and 1 semester Values Seminar. Unusual majors offered include business communications, dance, medical technology, theater, sports administration. Average undergraduate class size: 18; 60% of classes under 20, 35% between 20–40, 5% over 40. Students report that the professors and administrators are readily available to assist students with any problems they encounter. About 60% of students entering as freshmen graduate within four years, 62% eventually; 15% of freshmen do not return for sophomore year. *Special programs:* CLEP, independent study, study abroad, honors program, undergraduate research, January term, cooperative programs including cross-registration through 6 members of Lehigh Valley Association, internships available in all majors. Adult programs: accelerated degree program. *Calendar:* semester.
Undergraduate degrees conferred (312). 32% were in Business and Management, 13% were in Marketing and Distribution, 8% were in Computer and Engineering Related Technology, 7% were in Visual and Performing Arts, 7% were in Health Sciences, 6% were in Protective Services, 5% were in Psychology, 5% were in Social Sciences, 4% were in Home Economics, 3% were in Life Sciences, 3% were in Liberal/General Studies, 3% were in Letters, remainder in 5 other fields.
Graduates Career Data. Advanced studies pursued by 10% of graduates according to a study of 1991–92 graduates; 6% enter business school. About 86% of 1991–92 graduates employed. Career Development Services include counseling, internships, career preparation and resume seminars, on-campus recruitment.
Faculty. About 72% of faculty hold PhD or equivalent. About 27% of undergraduate classes taught by tenured faculty. About 40% of teaching faculty are female.
Varsity Sports. Men (Div.III): Baseball, Basketball, Cross Country, Golf, Soccer, Tennis, Track. Women (Div.III): Basketball, Cross Country, Softball, Tennis, Track, Volleyball.
Student Body. College does not seek a national student body; 65% of students from in state; 96% from Middle Atlantic, 2% South, 1% Foreign. An estimated 85% of students reported as Catholic, 14% Protestant; 1% Black, 2% Hispanic, 1% Asian.
Religious Orientation. College is a church-related institution; 2 courses each in theology, philosophy required of all students.
Campus Life. About 80% of students live in traditional dormitories; rest live in off-campus housing or commute. Intervisitation in men's and women's dormitory rooms limited. There is 1 sorority on campus which about 20% of women join. About 35% of resident students leave campus on weekends.
Annual Costs. Tuition and fees, $9,270; room and board, $4,620; estimated $500 other, exclusive of travel. About 90% of students receive financial aid; average amount of assistance, $8,000. Assistance is typically divided 50% scholarship/grant, 40% loan, 10% work. *Meeting Costs:* college offers loan programs.

Alma College

Alma, Michigan 48801 **(517) 463-7139 or (800) 321-ALMA**

A small, liberal arts college, founded by the Presbyterian Synod of Michigan, Alma is the only Presbyterian college in Michigan. It is, however, now controlled by a self-perpetuating Board of Trustees. "An active concern for the moral, spiritual and ethical aspects of life is, "nevertheless, still "encouraged." The campus is located in a town of 9,800, 45 miles north of Lansing. Most convenient major airports: Capital City (Lansing) or Tri-City (Saginaw).

Founded: 1886
Affiliation: Presbyterian Church (USA)
Total Enrollment: 564 M, 742 W (full-time)
Cost: $10K–$20K
% Receiving Financial Aid: 95%
Admission: Selective
Application Deadline: March 1

Admission is selective. About 85% of applicants accepted, 36% of these actually enroll; 66% of freshmen graduate in top fifth of high school class, 91% in top two-fifths. Average freshman ACT scores: 26 composite. *Required:* ACT or SAT. Criteria considered in admissions, in order of importance: standardized test scores, high school academic record, recommendations, writing sample, extracurricular activities; other factors considered: special talents, diverse student body. *Entrance programs:* early decision, mid-year admission, deferred admission, advanced placement. *Apply* by March 1. *Transfers* welcome; 27 enrolled 1993–94.
Academic Environment. Degrees offered: bachelors. As a part of the liberal arts curriculum, students must show proficiency in writing and mathematical skills and are required to complete course work in the humanities, natural sciences and social sciences. *Majors offered* in addition to usual arts and sciences include art and design, biochemistry, international business, communications, exercise and health science, pre-engineering, and religious studies. Student reports call professors "very energetic and very personable." They also report that students are "friendly" and "helpful", even academically. Average undergraduate class size: 50% under 20; 40% 20–40, 10% over 40; student:faculty ratio 15:1.

About 57% of students entering as freshmen graduate within four years, 70% eventually; 88% of freshmen return for sophomore year. *Special programs:* CLEP, independent study, study abroad, honors, undergraduate research, 3-year degree, individualized majors, public affairs and public policy programs, pre-engineering, African Studies Program, internships, Spring Term in May features intensive study and travel, cross-registration with Stillman.
Undergraduate degrees conferred (261). 23% were in Business and Management, 18% were in Social Sciences, 10% were in Life Sciences, 9% were in Health Sciences, 7% were in Education, 6% were in Visual and Performing Arts, 6% were in Physical Sciences, 5% were in Psychology, 5% were in Letters, 5% were in Foreign Languages, 3% were in Philosophy and Religion, 3% were in Mathematics, remainder in Computer and Engineering Related Technology.
Graduates Career Data. Advanced studies pursued by 27% of 1990–91 graduates; 4% enter medical school; 1% enter dental school; 12% enter law school; 6% enter business school. Medical schools typically enrolling largest numbers of graduates include Michigan State, U. of Michigan; law schools include Cornell, Duke, Harvard; business schools include Northwestern, U. of Chicago, U. of Indiana. College reports over 95% of those who apply are accepted for medical and law school placement. About 65% of 1990–91 graduates

employed. Corporations typically hiring largest numbers of graduates include Andersen Consulting, National Bank of Detroit, Ernst & Young, K-Mart Corporation. Career development services include career counseling, placement assistance, resume writing assistance, on-campus interviewing, interview techniques.

Faculty. About 84% of faculty hold PhD or equivalent. About 60–65% of undergraduate classes taught by tenured faculty. About 32% of teaching faculty are female; 3% ethnic minority.

Student Body. About 94% of students from in state; 97% Midwest, 1% foreign. An estimated 39% of students reported as Protestant, 25% Catholic, 1% Jewish, 31% unaffiliated, 4% other; 2% Black, 1% Hispanic, 3% other minority.

Religious Orientation. Alma is a church-related institution, affiliated with the Presbyterian Church, U.S.A. Interdenominational chapel service and Roman Catholic mass available on campus, Jewish services 18 miles away. About 18% students are Presbyterian. No religious course study required.

Varsity Sports. Men (Div.III): Baseball, Basketball, Cross Country, Diving, Football, Golf, Soccer, Swimming, Tennis, Track. Women (Div. III): Basketball, Cross Country, Diving, Golf, Soccer, Softball, Swimming, Tennis, Track, Volleyball.

Campus Life. Student leader notes that this "is a very small campus, allowing lots of campus involvement and providing many student leadership opportunities." Administration source reports "most students find Alma's campus safe and secure." College hosts the Highland Festival each spring, "one of the largest Scottish gatherings in North America." Interest in fraternities/sororities and athletics remains strong. About 40% of students participate in varsity sports, 25% in performing arts. Cars allowed. College seeks to provide "a smoke-free environment." Students required to live in college residences. No dorm hours, residence halls are locked at midnight, students have keys. Intervisitation hours: 9 am to 1 am weekdays, 2:30 am Friday, Saturday.

About 32% of men, 26% of women live in traditional dormitories; 42% of men, 51% of women in coed dormitories; 2% of men, 6% of women live in off-campus housing; 14% of men, 12% of women commute. Freshmen given preference in college housing if all students cannot be accommodated. Sexes segregated in coed dormitories by wing or floor. There are 5 fraternities, 4 sororities on campus which about 40% of men, 4% of women join; 10% of men, 5% of women live in fraternities and sororities. About 40% of resident students leave campus on weekends.

Annual Costs. Tuition and fees, $12,041; room and board, $4,334; estimated $1,425 other, exclusive of travel. About 95% of students receive financial aid; average amount of assistance, $8,500. Assistance is typically divided 70% scholarship, 24% loan, 6% work. College reports "unlimited" scholarships awarded on the basis of academic merit, special talents, and need. *Meeting Costs:* college offers variety of payment plans and loans.

Alvernia College

Reading, Pennsylvania 19607 **(215) 777-0525**

A church-related, liberal arts college conducted by the Bernardine Sisters, located near a city of 87,600, 56 miles northwest of Philadelphia. Most convenient major airport: Philadelphia.

Founded: 1958
Affiliation: Roman Catholic
Total Enrollment: 1,243 M, W (full-time); 147 M, 330 W (part-time)
Cost: < $10K
% Receiving Financial Aid: 85%
Admission: Non-selective
Application Deadline: Rolling

Admission. Graduates of accredited high schools with 16 units, GPA of 2.0 (2.5 for some programs) or higher and minimum combined SAT score of 800 or ACT of 17, eligible; 82% of applicants accepted, 58% of these actually enroll; 10% of freshmen graduate in top fifth of high school class, 40% in top two-fifths. *Required:* SAT or ACT. About 56% of entering students from private schools, 15% from parochial schools. *Apply:* rolling admissions. *Transfers* welcome.

Academic Environment. *Degrees:* AB, BS. Unusual majors offered include addiction studies, criminal justice, physical therapy assistant. About 25% of students entering as freshmen do not return for sophomore year. *Calendar:* semester, summer school.

Undergraduate degrees conferred (139). 40% were in Business and Management, 14% were in Education, 6% were in Social Sciences, 6% were in Allied Health, 6% were in Communications, 5% were in Protective Services, 5% were in Computer and Engineering Related Technology, 4% were in Letters, 4% were in Psychology, 3% were in Life Sciences, remainder in 6 other fields.

Varsity Sports. Men (Div.III): Baseball, Basketball, Cross Country, Golf, Tennis. Women (Div.III): Basketball, Cross Country, Field Hockey, Golf, Softball, Tennis, Volleyball.

Campus Life. According to most recent data available, 85% of students from in state; 95% Middle Atlantic. Alvernia is a church-related institution; daily Mass offered. About 8% of men, 11% of women live in coed dormitories (segregated by wing); rest live in off-campus housing or commute. No intervisitation in men's or women's dormitory rooms. There are no fraternities or sororities. About 30% of students leave campus on weekends.

Annual Costs. Tuition and fees, $8,474; room and board, $4,000. About 85% of students receive financial aid; assistance is typically divided 20% scholarship, 60% loan, 20% work. College reports some scholarships awarded on the basis of academic merit alone. *Meeting Costs:* college offers a payment plan.

Alverno College

Milwaukee, Wisconsin 53234 **(414) 382-6100**

A liberal arts college for women, conducted by the Sisters of St. Francis, located on a 50-acre campus, 10 miles from downtown Milwaukee. Alverno also runs a large Weekend College offering full- and part-time programs for adult learners. Most convenient major airport: General Mitchell International (Milwaukee).

Founded: 1887
Affiliation: Independent (Roman Catholic)
UG Enrollment: 1,317 W (full-time); 1,235 W (part-time)
Total Enrollment: 2,552
Cost: < $10K
% Receiving Financial Aid: 85%
Admission: Non-selective
Application Deadline: Aug. 1

Admission. Graduates of accredited high schools with minimum 2.0 GPA in 12 units (10 in academic subjects) eligible; 63% of applicants accepted, 32% of these actually enroll. Average freshman ACT scores: 20. *Required:* ACT, high school records, college's own entrance assessment. *Entrance programs:* mid-year admission, advanced placement, rolling admission. *Apply* by August 1. *Transfers* welcome, 112 enrolled 1993–94.

Academic Environment. *Degrees:* bachelors. Graduation requirements include competency levels in each of 8 "abilities": communication, problem solving, analysis, valuing, social interaction, global perspectives, effective citizenship, and aesthetic responsiveness. *Majors offered* include music therapy, art therapy, dance and movement studies, nuclear medicine technology. Average undergraduate class size: 25% under 20, 55% between 20–40, 20% over 40. About 52% of students entering as freshmen graduate within four years; 90% of freshmen return for sophomore year. *Special programs:* CLEP, study abroad, art students may take courses at Milwaukee Institute of Art and Design, 3–2 programs in engineering, off-campus experiential learning internships. Adult programs: Weekend College offered in Business, Professional Communication and BSN completion. *Calendar:* semester, summer school.

Undergraduate degrees conferred (293). 42% were in Business and Management, 20% were in Communications, 17% were in Health Sciences, 12% were in Education, 3% were in Psychology, remainder in 8 other fields.

Graduates Career Data. Full-time advanced studies pursued immediately after graduation by 7% of students, 30% eventually. About 90% of 1992–93 graduates employed. Employers typically hiring largest numbers of graduates include Arthur Anderson, Miller Brewing, Milwaukee Public Schools, St. Lukes Hospital. Career Development Services include comprehensive resource center, career counselors, computer search programs.

Faculty. About 81% of faculty hold PhD or equivalent. About 48% of undergraduate classes taught by tenured faculty. About 71% of teaching faculty are female; 6% black, 3% other.

Student Body. About 96% of students from in state; 98% Midwest; 1% Foreign. An estimated 46% of students reported as 25% Catholic,

24% Protestant, 30% other; 15% Black, 5% Hispanic, 5% other minority. Average age of undergraduate student: 24.
Religious Orientation. Alverno is a church-related institution; religious study required. Places of worship available on campus for Catholics, in immediate community for Protestants.
Campus Life. With downtown Milwaukee 12 miles from campus and 5 colleges nearby, students have available wide range of cultural activities to supplement those on campus. Cars allowed. About 11% of women live in traditional dormitories; rest commute. There are no sororities on campus. About 75% of resident students leave campus on weekends.
Annual Costs. Tuition and fees, $7,884; room and board, $3,460; estimated $550 other, exclusive of travel. About 85% of students receive financial aid; average amount of assistance, $3,500–4,000. College reports scholarships available for academic merit, special talents, and need.

American Conservatory of Music

Chicago, Illinois 60602

An independent school of music, offering bachelors, masters, and doctoral degree programs.

Founded: 1886 — **Affiliation:** Independent

American International College

Springfield, Massachusetts 01109 — **(413) 737-7000**

An independent college, located in a city of 160,000, 90 miles west of Boston. Most convenient major airport: Bradley International.

Founded: 1885
Affiliation: Independent
UG Enrollment: 658 M, 523 W (full-time); 141 M, 110 W (part-time)
Total Enrollment: 1,543
Cost: < $10K
% Receiving Financial Aid: 66%
Admission: Non-selective
Application Deadline: Rolling

Admission. Graduates of approved high schools with 16 units (12 in academic subjects) eligible; 77% of applicants accepted, 21% of these actually enroll; 27% of freshmen graduate in top fifth of high school class, 67% in top two-fifths. *Required:* SAT or ACT. *Entrance programs:* early admission, midyear admission, deferred admission, advanced placement. About 15% of entering students from private schools, 15% from parochial schools. *Apply:* rolling admissions. *Transfers* welcome.
Academic Environment. *Degrees:* BA, BSBA, BSEd, BSN. About 21% of general education requirements for graduation are elective; distribution requirements fairly numerous. Unusual majors offered include international business, computer information systems. About 68% of students entering as freshmen graduate eventually; 19% of freshmen do not return for sophomore year. *Special programs:* CLEP, independent study, study abroad, honors, undergraduate research, 3-year degree. *Calendar:* semester, 5-week intersession, summer school.
Undergraduate degrees conferred (287). 44% were in Business and Management, 15% were in Education, 9% were in Protective Services, 8% were in Social Sciences, 7% were in Psychology, 6% were in Health Sciences, 3% were in Liberal/General Studies, remainder in 8 other fields.
Graduates Career Data. *Full-time graduate or professional study* pursued by 27% of students immediately after graduation; 15% enter business school, according to most recent data available.
Varsity Sports. Men (Div.II): Baseball, Basketball, Cross Country, Football, Golf, Hockey, Soccer, Tennis. Women (Div.II): Basketball, Cross Country, Soccer, Softball, Tennis, Volleyball.
Campus Life. According to most recent data available, 70% of students from New England, 20% Middle Atlantic.

About 37% of men, 40% of women live in traditional dormitories; 33% of men, 25% of women in coed dormitories; 30% of men, 35% of women commute. Sexes segregated in coed dormitories by floor. Freshmen are given preference in college housing if all students can not be accommodated. There are 4 fraternities, 3 sororities on campus, which about 15% each men, women join, they provide no residence facilities. About 35% of students leave campus on weekends.
Annual Costs. Tuition and fees, $9,414; room and board, $4,553. About 66% of students receive financial aid; assistance is typically divided 55% grant, 30% loan, 15% work. College reports some scholarships awarded on the basis of academic merit alone.

American University

Washington, D.C. 20016 — **(202) 885-6000**

American University, which serves as headquarters for the "Washington Semester," is a cosmopolitan institution, attracting an unusually diverse student body from all 50 states and more than 130 foreign countries. University includes: College of Arts and Sciences (which comprises more than twenty teaching units includes School of Communication, School of Education, Kogod College of Business Administration, School of Public Affairs, School of International Service, and Washington College of Law. The 78-acre campus is located in a residential section of northwest Washington. Most convenient major airport: Washington National.

Founded: 1893
Affiliation: Independent
UG Enrollment: 2,016 M, 3,024 W (full-time); 209 M, 313 W (part-time)
Total Enrollment: 11,692
Cost: $10K–$20K
% Receiving Financial Aid: 60%
Admission: Highly Selective
Application Deadline: Feb. 1

Admission is highly selective. For all schools, 70% of applicants accepted, 33% of these actually enroll; 60% of freshmen graduate in top fifth of high school class, 85% in top two-fifths. Average freshman SAT scores: 550 M, 570 W verbal; 580 M, 560 W mathematical; ACT, 27 M, 26 W composite. *Required:* SAT or ACT, essay; ACHs in English, mathematics and foreign languages recommended for placement. University offers a comprehensive support program for a limited number of learning disabled students. Applicants are evaluated according to their individual backgrounds and needs. Criteria considered in admissions, in order of importance: high school academic record, standardized test scores, writing sample, extracurricular activities, recommendations; other factors considered: special talents, alumni children. *Entrance programs:* early decision, early admission, advanced placement. About 45% of entering students from private and parochial schools. *Apply* by February 1. *Transfers* welcome, 450 enrolled 1993–94.
Academic Environment. *Degrees:* bachelors, masters, doctoral. The distinguished faculty includes experts and scholars of national and international reputation. University makes use of personnel resources of Washington for all its programs. The international student population reinforces university's emphasis on international aspects of all its programs. Students must complete rigorous distribution requirements which include 6 semester hours in each of 5 areas: creative arts, Traditions That Shape the Western World, International and Intercultural Experience, Social Institutions and Behavior, natural sciences; also required are a 2-course sequence in English. Courses outside major may be taken Pass/Fail. Average undergraduate class size: 24.

About 67% of students entering as freshmen graduate within four years, 70% eventually; 89% of freshmen return for sophomore year. *Special programs:* CLEP, cooperative education, independent study, study abroad, honors, undergraduate research, "Selected Topics" courses, cross-registration with Washington consortium universities, a variety of summer workshops abroad, world capitals program in Copenhagen, Brussels, Rome, Vienna, London, Paris, Beijing, Buenos Aires, Poland, Budapest, Santiago, Chile, Prague, numerous off-campus internships in Washington area, interdisciplinary majors. Adult programs: APEL Program enables adults to earn undergraduate academic credit for life experience through work, military, community service, etc. *Calendar:* semester, summer school.
Undergraduate degrees conferred (1,349). 39% were in Social Sciences, 19% were in Business and Management, 12% were in Communications, 8% were in Protective Services, 5% were in Psychology, 4% were in Visual and Performing Arts, 3% were in Letters, 3% were in Area and Ethnic Studies, remainder in 8 other fields.
Graduate Career Data. Advanced studies pursued by 60% of students. Career Center offers career counseling, placement, coop education, career fairs, alumni network.

Faculty. About 90% of faculty hold PhD or equivalent. About 98% of undergraduate classes taught by tenured faculty.
Student Body. About 5% of students from Washington D.C.; 32% Middle Atlantic, 15% New England, 8% Midwest, 7% South, 7% West, 4% Northwest, 12% Foreign. About 30% of students reported as Protestant, 30% Catholic, 20% Jewish, 5% Muslim, 15% other; 8% as Black, 5% Hispanic, 4% Asian, 2% other minority.
Religious Orientation. American is loosely affiliated with the United Methodist Church; makes no religious demands on students. Places of worship available on campus for all major faiths.
Varsity Sports. Men (Div.I): Basketball, Cross Country, Golf, Soccer, Swimming, Tennis, Wrestling. Women (Div.I): Basketball, Cross Country, Field Hockey, Lacrosse, Soccer, Swimming, Tennis, Volleyball.
Campus Life. Student body strongly oriented to both scholarly/intellectual interest and occupational/professional goals. Campus culture is varied and many-faceted, supplements the multiple cultural and intellectual facilities of metropolitan Washington. Student leader reports a very healthy student government which provides services for extra-curricular activities. Administration source reports emphasis on needs of commuters and international students. Administration suggests that some students may be uncomfortable in the very heterogeneous environment provided by the university, but that students, typically, "form their own small friendship or interest groups." Parking at a premium on campus; cars permitted for all except freshman and sophomore residents. Some smoking restrictions. Alcohol not permitted in residence halls. Dormitories are all coed, with sexes segregated either by floor or room.

About 65% of men, 65% of women live in coed dormitories; 30% of men and 30% of women live in off-campus college-related housing; rest commute. Freshmen guaranteed college housing, normally, all students who want campus housing can be accommodated. There are 7 fraternities, 7 sororities on campus which about 20% of men, 15% of women join. Fraternities and sororities provide no residence facilities. About 10% of resident students leave campus on weekends.
Annual Costs. Tuition and fees, $15,326; room and board, $6,022; estimated $2,500 other, exclusive of travel. About 70% of students receive financial aid; average amount of assistance, $9,300. University provides financial aid and extensive honor scholarship program. Assistance is typically divided 53% scholarship, 30% loan, 17% work according to most recent data available. University reports 200+ scholarships awarded on the basis of academic merit alone. *Meeting Costs:* university offers Family Finance Center, installment payment plans.

Amherst College

Amherst, Massachusetts 01002 (413) 542-2328

One of the most highly esteemed liberal arts colleges in the country, Amherst prides itself on its devotion to undergraduate instruction with faculty emphasis on teaching as well as research. Coeducational since 1975–76, the 100-acre main campus is located in the small (pop. 20,300) New England town of the same name. Hampshire College and the University of Massachusetts are also located there. Nearby Smith and Mt. Holyoke complete the 5-college consortium of which Amherst is a member. Most convenient major airport: Bradley International.

Founded: 1821
Affiliation: Independent
Total Enrollment: 888 M, 697 W (full-time)
Cost: $10K–$20K
% Receiving Financial Aid: 45%
Admission: Most Selective
Application Deadline: Dec. 31

Admission is among the most selective in the country. About 23% of applicants accepted, 43% of these actually enroll; 90% of freshmen graduate in top tenth of high school class. Average freshman SAT scores: 633 M, 645 W verbal, 697 M, 669 W mathematical; 95% of freshmen score above 500 on verbal, 75% above 600, 24% above 700; 99% score above 500 on mathematical, 86% above 600, 52% above 700. *Required:* any 3 ACH, 2 essays. Criteria considered in admissions, in order of importance: high school academic record, recommendations, and writing sample considered of equal importance; test scores and extracurricular activities considered equally; other factors considered: special talents, diverse student body, alumni children. *Entrance programs:* early decision. About 37% of entering students from private schools, 5% from parochial. *Apply* by December 31. *Transfers* welcome, 13 enrolled 1993–94.
Academic Environment. Degrees offered: bachelors. All entering freshmen are required to take 2 courses, one each semester, in a program called Introduction to Liberal Studies (ILS). The ILS courses, each taught by 3 to 5 faculty, are designed to expose freshmen "to the wide range of learning that takes place at the college." Each student also has a faculty adviser during the first 2 years and a major department adviser during the last 2. Number of students preparing for traditional careers of Amherst graduates—business, medicine, law—affects academic climate. Five College Cooperative Program (with Hampshire, U. of Massachusetts, Mt. Holyoke, and Smith) expands academic resources and opportunities. Fewer graduates now go directly to graduate and professional schools than in the past. Reasons include need to earn and save to pay for graduate study and the preference of graduate business schools for applicants with two to three years of work experience. Highly motivated students with clearly defined professional objectives likely to be most successful. *Majors offered* in addition to usual studies include: law, jurisprudence & social thought. Average undergraduate class size: 22–25 students.

About 97% of students entering as freshmen graduate within five years; 98% of freshmen return for sophomore year. *Special programs:* independent study, study abroad, honors, undergraduate research, Twelve College Exchange, field study, January term, cross registration with Smith, Mt. Holyoke, Hampshire College and U. Mass. *Calendar:* semester, open January term (no-credit).
Undergraduate degrees conferred (447). 30% were in Social Sciences, 19% were in Letters, 11% were in Area and Ethnic Studies, 8% were in Foreign Languages, 7% were in Visual and Performing Arts, 6% were in Psychology, 6% were in Physical Sciences, 6% were in Life Sciences, 3% were in Philosophy and Religion, 3% were in Multi/Interdisciplinary Studies, remainder in 2 other fields.
Graduates Career Data. Advanced studies pursued within 5 years after graduation by 85% of students; 29% enter graduate school, 7% enter medical school, 6% enter law school. Medical schools typically enrolling largest numbers of graduates include Johns Hopkins, Harvard, Cornell; law schools include Harvard, Yale, Columbia; business schools include Harvard, Stanford, Wharton. About 63% of 1992–93 graduates employed. Fields typically hiring largest numbers of graduates include business, education, science/health, and government/law. Career development services include career counseling, on-campus recruitment, resume/interview workshops, minority mentoring program, internships, law, medical, and graduate school advising.
Faculty. More than 77% of faculty hold PhD or equivalent. About 29% of teaching faculty are female; 5% are Black, 2% Hispanic, 4% other minority.
Student Body. About 11% of students from in state; 19% New England, 34% Middle Atlantic, 13% Midwest, 19% Northwest, 12% South, 5% Foreign. An estimated 7% of students reported are Black, 8% Hispanic, 11% Asian. *Minority group students:* Amherst has for many years welcomed students from minority groups who are capable of handling college's rigorous academic program; no special academic provisions; Black Cultural Center organized by Afro-American Society.
Varsity Sports. Men (Div.III): Baseball, Basketball, Cross Country, Diving, Football, Golf, Ice Hockey, Lacrosse, Soccer, Swimming, Tennis, Track. Women (Div.III): Basketball, Cross Country, Diving, Field Hockey, Golf, Lacrosse, Soccer, Swimming, Tennis, Track, Volleyball.
Campus Life. Amherst is now fully co-educational, although men still outnumber women. Students at Amherst have responded to current campus concerns, but this is not an activist campus. College is 90 miles from Boston and a substantial distance from other cultural centers. This factor probably offset by beauty of college's rural setting which so many contemporary students find attractive. Cultural and intellectual resources of the area increased by fact that the sister institutions of the Five College group are all located within a radius of 7 miles. High interest reported in both cultural and athletic activities—80% of students are said to participate in intramural and varsity sports. Only specific rules governing student conduct are concerned with academic responsibilities. Recently small number of juniors and seniors permitted to live off campus. Visitation procedures estab-

lished by each residential unit. Cars allowed for all except scholarship students.

About 98% of students live in coed dormitories; 2% commute. There are no fraternities or sororities on campus. About 5% of resident students leave campus on weekends.

Annual Costs. Tuition and fees, $19,152; room and board, $5,000; estimated $1,958 other, exclusive of travel. About 45% of students receive financial aid; average amount of assistance, $18,259. Assistance is typically divided 76% grant, 16% loan, 8% work. College reports scholarships awarded only on the basis of need. *Meeting Costs:* college offers various payment plans, parent loan programs.

Anderson University

Anderson, Indiana 46011 (317) 641-4082

A church-related university, located in a city of 70,800, 40 miles northeast of Indianapolis. While the university welcomes all eligible students, "it is expected that each student will conduct himself as a Christian citizen." Formerly known as Anderson College. Most convenient major airport: Indianapolis.

Founded: 1917
Affiliation: Church of God
UG Enrollment: 713 M, 1,014 (full-time); 83 M, 218 W (part-time)
Total Enrollment: 1,889
Cost: < $10K
% Receiving Financial Aid: 90%
Admission: Non-selective
Application Deadline: Rolling

Admission. Graduates of accredited high schools who rank in top three-quarters of class (preferably top half) eligible; 79% of applicants accepted, 83% of these actually enroll; 50% of freshmen graduate in top fifth of high school class, 76% in top two-fifths. Average freshman scores, according to most recent data available: SAT, 420 verbal, 470 mathematical; ACT, 21 composite, 20 mathematical. *Required:* SAT or ACT, interview, 2 personal references. *Apply:* rolling admissions. *Transfers* welcome.

Academic Environment. *Degree:* AB, BSN. Unusual majors offered include athletic training, family science, graphic design, medical technology, nursing, Christian ministries, glass program (Art). About 65% of students entering as freshmen graduate within four years; 25% of freshmen do not return for sophomore year. *Special programs:* CLEP, independent study, study abroad (85% of students participate) , honors, undergraduate research, individualized majors, 2–3 engineering, Center for Public Service. *Calendar:* semester, January term, summer school.

Undergraduate degrees conferred (272). 22% were in Education, 20% were in Business and Management, 8% were in Marketing and Distribution, 6% were in Public Affairs, 6% were in Visual and Performing Arts, 5% were in Psychology, 4% were in Communications, 3% were in Social Sciences, 3% were in Life Sciences, 3% were in Letters, 3% were in Theology, remainder in 10 other fields.

Graduates Career Data. *Full-time graduate or professional study* pursued by 20% of students immediately after graduation; 5% enter seminary. *Careers in business and industry* pursued by 20% of graduates.

Faculty. About 60% of faculty hold PhD or equivalent.

Varsity Sports. Men (NAIA) , Baseball, Basketball, Cross Country, Football, Golf, Soccer, Tennis, Track. Women (NAIA) , Basketball, Cross Country, Softball, Tennis, Track, Volleyball.

Campus Life. According to most recent data available, 59% of students from Indiana; 90% of students from North Central. Anderson is a church-related institution; 6 semester hours of Bible, 3 hours each of religion, philosophy, attendance at twice weekly chapel services required of all students.

About 40% of men, 60% of women live in traditional dormitories; 2% each live in off-campus housing; rest commute. Intervisitation in men's and women's dormitory rooms limited to scheduled open houses. There are no fraternities or sororities. About 40% of resident students leave campus on weekends.

Annual Costs. Tuition and fees, $9,520; room and board, $3,400. About 90% of students receive financial aid; assistance is typically divided 53% scholarship, 38% loan, 9% work. University reports some scholarships awarded on the basis of academic merit alone. *Meeting Costs:* university offers 10-month budget plan, no finance charge.

Andrews University

Berrien Springs, Michigan 49104 (616) 471-3303

A small church-related university, located in a village of 2,000, 20 miles north of South Bend, Indiana, Andrews conducts several manufacturing and other enterprises in which many students work part-time. Although not mandatory that students be members of the Seventh-day Adventist Church, they must be comfortable within university's "religious, social, and cultural atmosphere."

Founded: 1874
Affiliation: Seventh-day Adventist
UG Enrollment: 767 M, 856 W (full-time); 119 M, 153 W (part-time)
Total Enrollment: 2,510
Cost: $10K–$20K
% Receiving Financial Aid:
Admission: Non-selective
Application Deadline: Rolling

Admission. Graduates of approved high schools with 10 units in academic subjects and C average eligible; 58% of applicants accepted, 67% of these actually enroll; 29% of freshmen graduate in top fifth of high school class, 56% in top two-fifths. *Required:* ACT. About 66% of entering students from private schools. *Apply:* rolling admissions. *Transfers* welcome.

Academic Environment. *Degrees:* BA, BS, BATh, BBA, BET, BFA, BSAEd, BSIT, BSMT, BM. About 35% of general education requirements for graduation are elective; distribution requirements fairly numerous. About 52% of entering students graduate eventually. *Special programs:* CLEP, independent study, study abroad, honors, undergraduate research, individualized majors. *Calendar:* quarter, summer school.

Undergraduate degrees conferred (352). 16% were in Health Sciences, 14% were in Life Sciences, 13% were in Business and Management, 7% were in Education, 6% were in Psychology, 5% were in Letters, 5% were in Architecture and Environmental Design, 5% were in Multi/Interdisciplinary Studies, 4% were in Philosophy and Religion, 3% were in Communications, remainder in 15 other fields. *Doctoral degrees:* Education 10, Theology 10, Psychology 2, Philosophy and Religion 1.

Graduates Career Data. *Full-time graduate or professional study* pursued immediately after graduation by 23% of students. *Careers in business and industry* pursued by 66% of graduates.

Student Body. According to most recent data available, 54% of students from North Central, 16% Middle Atlantic. An estimated 90% of students reported as Protestant; 14% Black, 6% Hispanic, 5% Asian, 18% other minority.

Campus Life. Andrews is a church-related institution; 18 credits of religion, attendance at chapel and worship services required of all students. About 55% of men, 56% of women live in traditional dormitories; no coed dormitories; rest live in off-campus housing or commute. No intervisitation in men's or women's dormitory rooms. There are no fraternities or sororities.

Annual Costs. Tuition and fees, $11,250; room and board, $3,990. University reports some scholarships awarded on the basis of academic merit alone.

Angelo State University

San Angelo, Texas 76909 (915) 942-2042

A state-supported university, located in a city of 80,000 in West Texas. Most convenient major airport: Mathis Field (San Angelo).

Founded: 1928
Affiliation: State
UG Enrollment: 2,055 M, 2,376 W (full-time); 612 M, 853 W (part-time)
Total Enrollment: 5,383
Cost: < $10K
% Receiving Financial Aid: 43%
Admission: Non-selective
Application Deadline: Aug. 16

Admission. Graduates of accredited high schools who rank in top quarter of class or meet minimum combined class rank and ACT/SAT score requirements eligible, others considered for provisional admission; 56% of applicants accepted, 60% of these actually enroll; 58% of freshmen graduate in top quarter of high school class, 90% in top half. Average freshman scores, according to most recent data available: SAT, 436 M, 437 W verbal, 512 M, 473 W mathematical; ACT, 22.8 M, 23.6 W composite. *Required:* ACT or SAT. *Out-of-state* freshman applicants: university welcomes students from out of state. State does not limit out-of-state enrollment. No special requirements for out-of-state applicants. *Apply* by August 16. *Transfers* welcome.

Academic Environment. *Degrees:* AB, BS, BBA, BMEd, BSN. About 50% of general education requirements for graduation are elective; distribution requirements fairly numerous. *Special programs:* CLEP, International Studies Program (summers) , 3–2 physics-electrical engineering with U. of Texas at El Paso. About 44% of freshmen do not return for sophomore year. *Calendar:* semester, summer school.

Undergraduate degrees conferred (703). 31% were in Business and Management, 29% were in Education, 6% were in Social Sciences, 6% were in Psychology, 5% were in Computer and Engineering Related Technology, 4% were in Letters, 3% were in Visual and Performing Arts, 3% were in Agricultural Sciences, remainder in 7 other fields.

Faculty. About 69% of faculty hold PhD or equivalent.

Varsity Sports. Men (Div.II): Basketball, Cross Country, Football, Track. Women (Div.II): Basketball, Cross Country, Track, Volleyball.

Campus Life. According to most recent data available, 95% of students from Texas. An estimated 12% of students reported as Hispanic, 5% Black, 3% other minority. Angelo State makes no religious demands on students. About 25% of men, 24% of women live in traditional dormitories; rest commute. Intervisitation in men's and women's dormitory rooms limited. Freshmen given preference in college housing if all students cannot be accommodated. There are 4 fraternities, 2 sororities on campus which 4% of men, 2% of women join; they provide no residence facilities. About 33% of resident students leave campus on weekends.

Annual Costs. Tuition and fees, $1,489 (out-of-state, $5,569); room and board, $3,592. About 43% of students receive financial aid, assistance is typically divided 30% scholarship, 27% grants, 37% loan, 6% work. University reports some scholarships awarded on the basis of academic merit alone.

Anna Maria College

Paxton, Massachusetts 01612 **(508) 849-3300 or (800) 344-1154**

A small, church-related, liberal arts college, Anna Maria is administered by the Sisters of Saint Anne and is located in a town of 3,800, 8 miles west of Worcester, Massachusetts, the second largest city in New England. Most convenient major airport: Worcester.

Founded: 1946
Affiliation: Roman Catholic
UG Enrollment: 175 M, 219 W (full-time); 104 M, 195 W (part-time)
Total Enrollment: 1,850
Cost: $10K–$20K
% Receiving Financial Aid: 80%
Admission: Non-selective
Application Deadline: Sept. 1

Admission. High school graduates with 16 units eligible; 80% of applicants accepted without condition, 35% of these actually enroll; 11% of freshmen graduate in top fifth of high school class, 47% in top three-fifths. Average freshman SAT scores: 408 verbal, 417 mathematical. *Required:* SAT or ACT, essay, portfolio for art, audition for music. *Non-academic factors* considered in admissions: special talents, alumni children, diverse student body. About 30% of entering students from parochial schools. *Apply* by September 1. *Transfers* welcome, 20 M, 36 W accepted 1993–94.

Academic Environment. *Degrees:* bachelors. Programs offered: marketing, studio art, criminal justice, music performance, Spanish, pre-med, pre-dentistry, finance, history, art therapy, music education, music therapy, medical technology, paralegal studies, psychology, social work. *Special programs:* CLEP, independent study, study abroad, 3-year degree, individualized majors, cooperative programs through Worcester Consortium. *Calendar:* semester.

Undergraduate degrees conferred (97). 32% were in Business and Management, 18% were in Education, 13% were in Protective Services, 7% were in Public Affairs, 5% were in Visual and Performing Arts, 5% were in Liberal/General Studies, 4% were in Allied Health, 3% were in Psychology, 3% were in Health Sciences, 3% were in Computer and Engineering Related Technology, remainder in 4 other fields.

Graduates Career Data. *Careers in business and industry* pursued by 57% of graduates.

Faculty. About 33% of faculty hold PhD.

Religious Orientation. Anna Maria is a church-related institution; 4 courses in religious studies, ethics, or philosophy required of all students.

Student Body. About 75% of students from Massachusetts; 6% Foreign.

Varsity Sports. Men (Div.III): Baseball, Basketball, Golf, Soccer, Tennis. Women (Div.III): Basketball, Cross Country, Field Hockey, Golf, Soccer, Tennis.

Campus Life. About 25% of men, 50% of women live in traditional dormitories; rest commute. Freshmen given preference in college housing if all students cannot be accommodated. There are no fraternities or sororities on campus. About 50% of resident students leave campus on weekends.

Annual Costs. Tuition and fees, $10,600; room and board, $5,200. About 80% of students receive financial aid; average amount of assistance, $9,700. Assistance is typically divided 59% scholarship/grant, 36% loan, 5% work. College reports some scholarships awarded on the basis of academic merit alone. *Meeting Costs:* college offers Academic Management Tuition Plan, Tuition Management Services, budget payment plans, loans to parents, credit card payment plan.

Antioch College

Yellow Springs, Ohio 45387 **(513) 767-6400**

One of the oldest experimental and innovative liberal arts colleges in the country, Antioch has established a national network of centers and programs throughout the country and abroad. Located in a village of 4,600, the 100-acre main campus adjoining a 1,000-acre nature preserve is 19 miles east of Dayton.

Founded: 1852
Affiliation: Independent
Total Enrollment: 2,782 M, W
Cost: $10K–$20K
% Receiving Financial Aid: 74%
Admission: Selective (+)
Application Deadline: March 1

Admission is selective (+). About 82% of applicants accepted, 34% of these actually enroll. Average freshman SAT scores, according to most recent data available: 556 M, 505 W verbal, 535 M, 501 W mathematical. *Required:* essay, recommendations; SAT, ACT, interview recommended. *Non-academic factors* considered in admissions: diverse student body, involvement, independence, self-direction. *Entrance programs:* early decision, early admission, midyear admission, deferred admission, rolling admissions. *Apply* by March 1, recommended. *Transfers* welcome.

Academic Environment. Antioch's work/study program sets it apart from most other colleges; 3 12-week quarters; one-third of the student body is on co-op while the remaining students study on campus. Similar experience possible during an optional year of study and work abroad. General education program "emphasizes mastery of knowledge and skill areas." The bachelor's degree may be earned in either 4 or 5 years. Academic program consists of 3 principal features, each considered essential: (1) academic studies, (2) work or other educational experience, (3) student involvement in college's "democratic government." Students who appear most successful at Antioch are those who are self-directed, self-motivated, and emotionally self-sufficient, with ability to tolerate frequent changes of environment. *Degrees:* AB, BS. *Majors offered* within six academic institutes: Arts, Humanities, Communications and Media Arts, Human Development, Social and Management Studies, and Science and Technology. Concentrations in both disciplinary and interdisciplinary programs are available in the Institutes.

About 53% of students entering as freshmen graduate eventually; 15% of freshmen do not return for sophomore year. *Special programs:* CLEP, independent study (possible also during off-campus job period) , study abroad, undergraduate research, individualized majors, programs of GLCA, environmental field programs, cross-registration through Southwestern Ohio Council for Higher Education, member of NHCUC, 3–2 program in engineering with Washington U.. Adult programs: Antioch offers programs designed specifically for adult learners at campuses in Yellow Springs, Ohio, Los Angeles and Santa Barbara, California, and in Seattle, Washington. *Calendar:* 4- or 5-year, 4-quarter.

Undergraduate degrees conferred (81). 21% were in Visual and Performing Arts, 11% were in Liberal/General Studies, 10% were in Social Sciences, 6% were in Psychology, 6% were in Physical Sciences, 6% were in Letters, 6% were in Education, 5% were in Public Affairs, 5% were in Life Sciences, 5% were in Foreign Languages, 5% were in Communications, 5% were in Business and Management, remainder in 5 other fields.

Faculty. About 67% of teaching faculty hold doctorate.

Student Body. According to most recent data available, 22% of students from in state; 41% North Central, 25% Middle Atlantic, 12% New England, 12% South, 7% West/Northwest. An estimated 8% of students reported as Black, 2% Hispanic, 4% other minority.

Religious Orientation. Antioch is an independent, nonsectarian college. Religious activities arranged by interested students and faculty members. Rockford Chapel (built in the form of Friends meeting house) available "for contemplation, worship, small meetings, and weddings." Places of worship available in immediate community for Catholics and Protestants; synagogues located in nearby Springfield, Dayton.

Campus Life. Antioch students have long had a significant voice in policy decisions of every kind—and have enjoyed a large degree of personal freedom, limited by few specific regulations. Conscious effort to balance the demands of community with those of individuality. For instance, catalog states that "Antiochians are expected to think about the consequences of their actions for themselves, others, and the College. Anything that hinders or exploits other people or the College or that offends good taste is undesirable [ELLIPSE] the College has the right at any time to exercise its powers of summary dismissal." Antioch's plentiful student activities appear to be diverse. Nearest major cultural centers are Dayton (19 miles away) , and Columbus and Cincinnati, each 60 miles from campus. No formal intercollegiate sports; when student interest develops, a sports club is formed to participate informally with nearby colleges. Unmarried students expected to live in dormitories their first two years. Cars permitted for all.

About 93% of students live in coed dormitories; rest in off-campus housing. Sexes segregated in dormitories by floor or room. There are no fraternities or sororities.

Annual Costs. Tuition and fees, $16,356; room and board, $3,176. About 74% of students receive financial aid; assistance is typically divided 59% scholarship, 24% loan, 17% work. College reports some scholarships awarded on the basis of academic merit alone. *Meeting Costs:* college offers monthly payment plans.

Appalachian State University

Boone, North Carolina 28608 **(704) 262-2000**

A state-supported institution, located in the Blue Ridge Mountains, in a town of 8,800, 100 miles northwest of Charlotte. Most convenient major airport: Greensboro (2 hours).

Founded: 1899
Affiliation: State
UG Enrollment: 4,841 M, 5,073 W (full-time); 365 M, 414 W (part-time)
Total Enrollment: 11,641
Cost: < $10K
% Receiving Financial Aid: 42%
Admission: Non-selective
Application Deadline: Mar. 31

Admission. Graduates of accredited high schools eligible; 64% of applicants accepted, 26% of these actually enroll; 50% of freshmen graduate in top fifth of high school class, 87% in top two-fifths. Average freshman scores: SAT, 466 M, 475 W verbal, 535 M, 507 W mathematical. *Required:* SAT or ACT. Criteria considered in admissions, in order of importance: high school academic record, standardized test scores, writing sample, extra curricular activities, recommendations; other factors considered: special talents, diverse student body. *Out-of-state* freshman applicants: university seeks students from out of state. State limits out-of-state enrollment to 18% of entering class. No special requirements for out-of-state applicants. About 52% of out-of-state students accepted, 26% enroll. *Apply* by March 31. *Transfers* welcome; 835 enrolled 1993–94.

Academic Environment. *Degrees:* bachelors, masters, doctoral. Core requirements include courses in English, humanities, social sciences, natural sciences, mathematics, physical education. Average undergraduate class size: 46% under 20, 45% between 20–40, 10% over 40. About 31% of students entering as freshmen graduate within four years, 56% eventually; 86% of freshmen return for sophomore year. *Special programs:* CLEP, independent study, study abroad, honors, undergraduate research, 3-year degree, individualized majors, 3–2 engineering, medical technology program. Adult programs: special Adult Academic Advisor. *Calendar:* semester, summer school.

Undergraduate degrees conferred (2,100). 25% were in Business and Management, 21% were in Education, 11% were in Communications, 8% were in Social Sciences, 5% were in Protective Services, 5% were in Psychology, 3% were in Home Economics, 3% were in Computer and Engineering Related Technology, 3% were in Letters, 3% were in Visual and Performing Arts, 3% were in Parks and Recreation, remainder in 10 other fields.

Graduates Career Data. Advanced studies pursued by 20% of graduates. About 75% of 1992–93 graduates employed. Fields typically hiring largest numbers of graduates include consumer sales, banking, accounting, computer information systems. Career Development Center provides career information, assistance with resume writing, interviewing skills and job search techniques, on-campus recruitment, employer information, credentials service, and career counseling.

Faculty. About 95% of faculty hold PhD or equivalent. About 29% of teaching faculty are female; less than 3% ethnic minority.

Student Body. About 89% of students from North Carolina; 98% South, less than 1% foreign. An estimated 71% of students reported as Protestant, 9% Catholic, 18% unaffiliated, 1% other; 4% Black, 2% other minority. Average age of undergraduate student: 22.

Varsity Sports. Men (Div.IAA,SC): Baseball, Basketball, Cross Country, Football, Golf, Soccer, Tennis, Track, Wrestling. Women (Div.I,SC): Basketball, Cross Country, Football, Field Hockey, Golf, Soccer, Tennis, Track.

Campus Life. About 4% of men, 15% of women live in traditional dormitories; 28% of men, 25% of women in coed dormitories; rest commute. Intervisitation in men's and women's dormitory rooms varies according to housing option chosen. There are 11 fraternities, 7 sororities on campus, 5% men join, 2% women join. Freshmen given preference in college housing if all students can not be accommodated. About 20% of resident students leave campus on weekends.

Annual Costs. Tuition and fees, $1,458 (out-of-state, $7,524); room and board, $2,540; estimated $1,000 other, exclusive of travel. About 42% of students receive financial aid; average amount of assistance, $2,600. Assistance is typically divided 39% scholarship, 48% grant, 46% loan, 6% work. *Meeting Costs:* university offers PLUS Loans, accepts credit cards.

Aquinas College

Grand Rapids, Michigan 49506 **(616) 459-8281**

A Catholic college, founded by the Dominican Sisters of Grand Rapids, located in a residential section of a city of 450,000. Most convenient major airport: Kent County International.

Founded: 1922
Affiliation: Roman Catholic
UG Enrollment: 478 M, 813 W (full-time); 306 M, 621 W (part-time)
Total Enrollment: 1,784
Cost: $10K–$20K
% Receiving Financial Aid: 90%
Admission: Non-selective
Application Deadline: Aug. 1

Admission. Graduates of accredited high schools with 15 units, 2.5 average, and minimum ACT score of 18 eligible; 97% of applicants accepted, 41% of these actually enroll; 32% of freshmen graduate in top fifth of high school class, 72% in top two-fifths. Average freshman ACT scores, according to most recent data available: 21 M, 19 W composite, 20 M, 18 W mathematical. *Required:* ACT or SAT. *Non-academic factors* considered in admissions: leadership, extracurricular activities. *Entrance programs:* midyear admissions, deferred admission, advanced placement, rolling admissions. About 28% of entering students from parochial schools. *Apply* by August 1. *Transfers* welcome.

Academic Environment. Aquinas offers alternative plans for meeting liberal education requirements for degree: the Distribution Plan in which there are fairly numerous distribution guidelines for selecting the required 48 semester hours of liberal education and the Contractual Plan under which a student may pursue personal educational objectives through developing (and getting approved) a course of study. *Degrees:* AB, BS, BFA, BAGEd, BSBA, BM, BMEd. Unusual majors offered include gerontology cognate. About 50% of students entering as freshmen graduate eventually; 73% of freshmen return for sophomore year. *Special programs:* CLEP, independent study, study abroad, undergraduate research, individualized majors, career development programming, co-op program, field experience semester. *Calendar:* semester, minisession, summer school.

Undergraduate degrees conferred (385). 39% were in Business and Management, 10% were in Communications, 9% were in Social Sciences, 7% were in Liberal/General Studies, 5% were in Letters, 5% were in Education, 4% were in Psychology, 4% were in Life Sciences, 3% were in Philosophy and Religion, 3% were in Mathematics, 3% were in Computer and Engineering Related Technology, 3% were in Visual and Performing Arts, remainder in 4 other fields.

Faculty. About 48% of faculty hold PhD or equivalent.

Varsity Sports. Men (NAIA, I): Baseball, Basketball, Cross Country, Golf, Soccer, Tennis, Track (Indoor/Outdoor). Women (NAIA, I): Basketball, Cross Country, Softball, Tennis, Track (Indoor/Outdoor) , Volleyball.

Campus Life. According to most recent data available, 97% of students from in state, almost all from North Central. An estimated 17% of students reported as Protestant, 47% Catholic, 2% unaffiliated, 34% other; 5% Black, 2% Hispanic, 10% other minority. About 44% of men, 53% of women live in coed dormitories; rest live in off-campus housing or commute. There are no fraternities or sororities. About 30% of students leave campus on weekends.

Annual Costs. Tuition and fees, $10,402; room and board, $4,124. About 90% of students receive financial aid; assistance is typically divided 60% scholarship, 30% loan, 10% work. College reports some scholarships awarded on the basis of academic merit alone. *Meeting Costs:* college offers monthly payment plan.

Arizona State University Main Campus

Tempe, Arizona 85287-0112 (800) 252-ASU1

Arizona State today includes 11 undergraduate and graduate colleges and professional divisions. The main campus is located in a city of 140,000, in the metropolitan Phoenix area, and enjoys official status as an arboretum with more than 115 species of trees suited to the arid Arizona climate. Arizona State University West Campus is now a separately accredited institution. Most convenient major airport: Phoenix Sky Harbor International.

Founded: 1885
Affiliation: State
UG Enrollment: 11,664 M, 10,929 W (full-time); 3,876 M, 3,709 W (part-time)
Total Enrollment: 41,250
Cost: < $10K
% Receiving Financial Aid: 65%
Admission: Selective
Application Deadline: April 15

Admission is selective. Arizona graduates of accredited high schools who rank in top half of class or with a minimum ACT composite score of 21 or SAT of 430 verbal, 450 mathematical or high school GPA of 2.5 eligible (higher class rank and test scores required for Engineering and Computer Science applicants; class rank in top 5%, ACT of 29 or SAT of 1,250 required for Honors College); 81% of applicants accepted, 36% of these actually enroll; 41% of freshmen graduate in top fifth of high school class, 70% in top two-fifths. Average freshman scores: SAT, 453 verbal, 521 mathematical; ACT 23 composite. *Required:* SAT or ACT. *Out-of-state* freshman applicants: university seeks students from out of state. *Out-of-state* enrollment not limited. Requirement for out-of-state applicants: rank in top quarter of class or a minimum ACT composite score of 23 or SAT of 1,010 or high school GPA of 3.0; 3,316 out-of-state students enrolled 1993–94. States from which most out-of-state students are drawn: California, Illinois, New York, New Jersey. Criteria considered in admissions, in order of importance: standardized test scores and high school record, recommendations, extracurricular activities. *Entrance programs:* midyear admission, advanced placement, rolling admissions. *Apply* by April 15 for priority; earlier if hoping for on-campus housing. *Transfers* welcome; 4,428 enrolled 1993–94.

Academic Environment. Degrees offered: bachelors, masters, doctoral. Minimum of 35 hours of approved general studies courses required of all students. *Undergraduate studies* offered by colleges of Architecture and Environmental Design, Business, Education, Engineering and Applied Sciences, Fine Arts, Liberal Arts and Sciences, Nursing, Public Programs, Social Work. Honors College offers challenging living/learning environment for 1,000 students; advanced students take graduate courses for honors credit. Unusual majors offered include purchasing/materials management, energy systems engineering, interdisciplinary studies, bioengineering. New emphasis in theatre including acting, design directing, history/theory and criticism, theatre for youth, and theatre management. Strongest programs reported to be business, engineering, education, and fine arts. Recent student reports that though 100 level courses tend to be large, 200 level courses were "no larger than 30 students."

About 15% of students entering as freshmen graduate within four years, 50% eventually; 70% of freshmen return for sophomore year. *Special programs:* 3–2 engineering, CLEP, independent study, honors, study abroad, undergraduate research, 3-year degree, January term, graduate courses for undergraduate credit, interdisciplinary studies, centers for American Studies, Asian Studies, Family Life, Indian Education, Latin American studies, cooperative programs with American Graduate School of International Management. *Calendar:* semester, January term, summer school.

Undergraduate degrees conferred (5,912). 28% were in Business and Management, 12% were in Social Sciences, 9% were in Education, 8% were in Communications, 6% were in Engineering, 5% were in Psychology, 5% were in Visual and Performing Arts, 4% were in Protective Services, 4% were in Engineering and Engineering Related Technology, 3% were in Letters, 3% were in Health Sciences, remainder in 14 other fields.

Graduates Career Data. *Careers in business and industry* pursued by 60% of graduates (1990–91). Career development services include co-op education, internships, career classes, interest inventory, on-campus interviews, resume assistance, alumni services, career fairs and workshops, job hotline, resume referrals.

Faculty. About 93% of faculty hold PhD or equivalent. About 41% of undergraduate class taught by tenured faculty. About 28% of teaching faculty are female; 2% Black, 5% Hispanic, 7% other minority.

Student Body. University seeks a national/international student body; 69% of students from in state; 79% West, 6% Midwest, 4% New England, 3% foreign. An estimated 9% of students reported as Hispanic, 3% African-American, 4% Asian, 6% other minority. Average age of undergraduate student: 23.

Varsity Sports. Men (Div.1): Baseball, Basketball, Cross Country, Diving, Football, Golf, Swimming, Tennis, Track, Volleyball, Wrestling. Women (Div.1): Basketball, Cross Country, Diving, Golf, Gymnastics, Softball, Swimming, Tennis, Track, Volleyball.

Campus Life. Recent and current students agree that "everything a student may need is within walking distance [of the campus]." Both also regard the climate and the community as pluses. Though only a small percentage of students actually live on campus, the number (3,000) is significant.

Less than 2% of students live in traditional or coed dormitories; rest live in off-campus housing or commute. About 8% of men, 5% of women join fraternities and sororities; 800 students live in fraternities and sororities.

Annual Costs. Tuition and fees, $1,844; (out-of-state, $7,350); room and board, $4,600; estimated $700 other, exclusive of travel. ASU is committed to meeting the demonstrated financial need of accepted students. Scholarships available based on academic merit and athletics, as well as need. *Meeting Costs:* university offers parent loan program.

University of Arizona

Tucson, Arizona 85721 (602) 621-3237

A land-grant institution, the University of Arizona, possibly because of tradition, location, and climate, has a far more cosmopolitan student body than most state universities. It is located on a 304-acre campus in a residential area of Tucson (pop. 500,000) , which has attracted a substantial number of talented people in the arts on whom the university can and does draw. Most convenient major airport: Tucson International.

Founded: 1885
Affiliation: State
UG Enrollment: 11,005 M, 10,659 W (full-time); 2,486 M, 2,408 W (part-time)
Total Enrollment: 35,279
Cost: < $10K
% Receiving Financial Aid: 60%
Admission: Selective (+)
Application Deadline: April 1

Admission is selective (+) , varies somewhat among various colleges. For all schools, Arizona graduates who rank in top quarter of class, with minimum 3.0 HS GPA, ACT composite score of 25 or combined SAT of 1010 are eligible; 80% of applicants accepted, 40% of these actually enroll; 20% of freshmen graduate in top fifth of high school class, 33% in top two-fifths. Average freshman scores: SAT (combined) , 990; ACT, 23.

Required: ACT or SAT. Criteria considered in admissions, in order of importance: high school academic record, standardized test scores, writing sample, recommendations, extracurricular activities; other factors considered: special talents, diverse student body. *Out-of-state* freshman applicants: university welcomes students from out of state. Requirements for admissions more selective for out-of-state applicants. States from which most out-of-state students are drawn: California, Illinois, Texas. *Entrance programs:* early admission, midyear admission, deferred admission. *Apply* by April 1 (final deadline, preference given to early applications); rolling admissions. *Transfers* welcome; 2,491 enrolled in 1993–94.

Academic Environment. Degrees offered: bachelors, masters, doctoral. *Undergraduate studies* offered to freshmen in Agriculture, Architecture, Arts and Sciences, Business and Public Administration, Engineering and Mines; juniors may be admitted to programs in Education, Health Related Professions, Pharmacy, and Nursing. Arizona is a large research university and offers a wide variety of programs and majors; unusual majors offered include the nationally recognized program in arid land studies as well as astronomy, fishery biology, Latin American studies, Mexican American studies, microbiology, optical sciences, Oriental studies, Portuguese, race track management, wildlife biology. The strongest programs are reported to be in the sciences and engineering.

About 42% of students entering as freshmen graduate within five years, 55% eventually; 75% of freshmen return for sophomore year. *Special programs:* CLEP, independent study, study abroad, honors, undergraduate research, graduate courses open to some students, 3–2 MBA, internships/cooperative work study available in "many departments". *Calendar:* semester, summer school.

Undergraduate degrees conferred (4,226). 21% were in Business and Management, 13% were in Social Sciences, 10% were in Engineering, 7% were in Letters, 6% were in Education, 5% were in Multi/Interdisciplinary Studies, 5% were in Psychology, 5% were in Communications, 5% were in Life Sciences, 4% were in Visual and Performing Arts, 3% were in Architecture and Environmental Design, 3% were in Home Economics, 3% were in Health Sciences, remainder in 13 other fields. *Doctoral degrees:* Physical Sciences 55, Education 45, Biological Sciences 32, Social Sciences 12, Engineering 23, Agriculture and Natural Resources 22, Foreign Languages 6, Letters 9, Psychology 12, Fine and Applied Arts 8, Mathematics 2, Business and Management 9, Health Sciences 11, Allied Health 7, Area and Ethnic Studies 2, Philosophy and Religion 3, Renewable Natural Resources 2, Parks and Recreation 1.

Graduates Career Data. *Full-time graduate or professional study* pursued immediately after graduation by 35% of students. *Careers in business and industry* pursued by 70% of graduates. Corporations typically hiring largest numbers of graduates include IBM, Arthur Anderson, Rockwell International. *Career Counseling Program:* Liberal arts majors urged to seek interviews with business/industry representatives who visit campus. Help provided in preparing for interviews.

Faculty. About 95% of faculty hold PhD or equivalent. About 25% teaching faculty are female; 12% ethnic minority.

Student Body. About 70% of students from in state. Average age of undergraduate student: 22.

Varsity Sports. Men (Div.I): Baseball, Basketball, Cross Country, Football, Golf, Swimming/Diving, Tennis, Track. Women (Div.I): Basketball, Cross Country, Golf, Gymnastics, Softball, Swimming/Diving, Tennis, Track, Volleyball.

Campus Life. High student interest reported in varsity sports (most popular: football, basketball, baseball) and intramurals (most popular: flag football, softball, tennis).

Large majority of students live off-campus or commute. About 18% of students live in traditional dormitories; 6% in coed dormitories; 44% live in off-campus housing; 25% commute. Intervisitation in men's and women's dormitory rooms limited. There are 27 fraternities, 19 sororities on campus which about 12% of men, 12% of women join; 7% of students live in fraternities and sororities. About 35% of resident students leave campus on weekends.

Annual Costs. Tuition and fees, $1,840 (out-of-state, $7,346); room and board, $3,968; estimated $625 other, exclusive of travel. About 60% of students receive financial aid; average amount of assistance, $1,800. Assistance is typically divided 23% scholarship, 11% grant, 33% loan, 32% work. University reports scholarships awarded on the basis of academic merit and/or financial need.

Arkansas College

Batesville, Arkansas 72503 **(501) 793-9813 or (800) 423-2542 (out-of-state)**

A small, church-related, liberal arts college, located on a 136-acre campus in a city of about 10,000 in the foothills of the Ozarks, 90 miles northeast of Little Rock. Most convenient major airport: Little Rock.

Founded: 1872
Affiliation: Presbyterian
Total Enrollment: 233 M, 297 W (full-time); 72 M, 116 W (part-time)
Cost: < $10K
% Receiving Financial Aid: 93%
Admission: Selective (+)
Application Deadline: Mar. 1

Admission is selective (+). About 47% of applicants accepted, 50% of these actually enroll; 67% of freshmen graduate in top fifth of high school class, 93% in top two-fifths. Average freshman ACT scores: 24.2 men, 24.9 women composite. *Required:* ACT or SAT, essay; interview recommended. Criteria considered in admissions, in order of importance: high school academic record, standardized test scores, extracurricular activities, recommendations, writing sample; other factors considered: special talents, alumni children, diverse student body, religious affiliation and/or commitment. *Entrance programs:* early admission, midyear admission, advanced placement. *Apply* by March 1; rolling admissions. *Transfers* welcome; 29 enrolled 1993–94.

Academic Environment. Degrees offered: bachelors. Requirements for graduation include 8 credits in math and science, 6 each in English, history, and world literature, 3 each in college algebra, social science, fine arts, and religion and philosophy, 2 semesters physical education. New program in politics recently added. Unusual majors include hospital administration. Current students enthuse about benefits of small classes, close relations with faculty and opportunities for student research; limited number of majors seen as a weakness, but not serious.

About 35% of students entering as freshmen graduate within four years, 37% eventually; 75% of freshmen return for sophomore year. *Special programs:* January Term, study abroad (some financial aid available) , 3–2 and 2–2 engineering, cooperative education. Average undergraduate class size: 69% of classes under 20; 28% between 20–40; student-faculty ratio of 11:1. *Calendar:* 4–1–4, summer school.

Undergraduate degrees conferred (88). 27% were in Business and Management, 26% were in Education, 11% were in Life Sciences, 7% were in Psychology, 6% were in Letters, 6% were in Marketing and Distribution, 3% were in Public Affairs, 3% were in Physical Sciences, 3% were in Communications, remainder in 5 other fields.

Graduates Career Data. Advanced studies pursued by 13% of students immediately after graduation. About 35% of 1992–93 graduates employed. Career Development Office instructs students in interview skills; also offered: co-op education, internship opportunities, interest inventories, on-campus interviews, and personal career counseling.

Faculty. About 79% of faculty hold PhD or equivalent. About 19% of undergraduate classes taught by tenured faculty. About 26% of teaching faculty are female; 4% ethnic minority.

Student Body. About 80% of students from in state; 87% South. An estimated 79% of students reported as Protestant, 6% Catholic, 16% unaffiliated; 4% Black, 2% other minority.

Religious Orientation. College is a church-related institution. About 7% of students reported affiliated with Presbyterian Church; 1 course in religion required of students.

Varsity Sports. Men (NAIA II): Baseball, Basketball, Cross Country, Golf, Tennis, Track. Women (NAIA II): Basketball, Cross Country, Tennis, Track, Volleyball.
Campus Life. Small-town setting focuses student life on campus activities. Current students report many social and entertainment events offered on-campus. Greek life reported as active, but open to all students.

About 77% men, 68% women live in traditional dormitories; no coed dormitories; rest commute. Intervisitation in men's and women's dormitory rooms limited. There are 4 fraternities, 3 sororities on campus which 25% of men, 21% of women join; they provide no residence facilities. About 20% of resident students leave campus on weekends.
Annual Costs. Tuition and fees, $8,060; room and board, $3,536; estimated $1,030 other, exclusive of travel. About 93% of students receive financial aid; average amount of assistance, $8,737. Assistance is typically divided 35% scholarship, 34% grant, 23% loan, 8% work. College reports 282 scholarships awarded on the basis of academic merit alone, 35 for special talents. *Meeting Costs:* college offers early payment plan. College reports that the decision to admit a student is made without regard to financial aid needs.

Arkansas State University

State University, Arkansas 72467 — (800) 643-0080, (800) 382-3030 (out-of-state)

A state-supported university located in Jonesboro, a city of just under 50,000, near Ozark recreational areas and Memphis, Tennessee. Most convenient major airport: Memphis, Tennessee..

Founded: 1909
Affiliation: State
UG Enrollment: 3,266 M, 3,946 W (full-time); 682 M, 1,025 W (part-time)
Total Enrollment: 9,888
Cost: < $10K
% Receiving Financial Aid: 65%
Admission: Non-selective
Application Deadline: 30 days before registration

Admission. High school graduates (or GED) with high school GPA of 2.0 and ACT score of 19 eligible; students with ACT of 24, or GPA of 2.25 for 8 semesters (2.6 for 7 semesters) admitted unconditionally; those with lower GPA and test scores may be admitted with restricted registration (contact Admissions Office for details); 97% of applicants accepted, 60% of these actually enroll. Average freshman ACT scores: 20.95 M, 21.09 W composite. *Required:* ACT. Criteria considered in admissions, in order of importance: standardized test scores, high school academic record. *Out-of-state* freshman applicants: university seeks students from out of state. State does not limit out-of-state enrollment. No special requirements for out-of-state applicants; 97% of out-of-state applicants accepted, 47% of these actually enroll. States from which most of out-of-state students are drawn: Missouri, Tennessee, Texas. Entrance programs: early decision, early admission, deferred admission, advanced placement. *Apply* by 30 days prior to registration. *Transfers* welcome; 739 enrolled 1993–94.
Academic Environment. Degrees offered: associates, bachelors, masters, doctoral. *Undergraduate studies* offered by colleges of Agriculture, Arts and Sciences, Business, Communications, Education, Fine Arts, Nursing & Health Professions, University College, and departments of Engineering, and Military Science. Graduation requirements include 6 hours of English, 11 hours of natural science and mathematics, 15 hours of social sciences, 10 hours of arts and humanities, 2 hours of physical education. About 16% of students entering as freshmen graduate within four years, 30% eventually; 63% of freshmen return for sophomore year. Average undergraduate class size: 46% under 20, 39% between 20–40, 15% over 40. *Special programs:* CLEP, study abroad, honors. *Calendar:* semester, summer school.
Undergraduate degrees conferred (1,070). 31% were in Education, 25% were in Business and Management, 8% were in Communications, 6% were in Health Sciences, 5% were in Computer and Engineering Related Technology, 4% were in Social Sciences, 3% were in Psychology, remainder in 15 other fields.
Graduates Career Data. Office of Career Planning and Placement Services assists students and alumni in career choices and job searches. Services include on-campus interviews, credential service, job listings, counseling, outreach programs (resume writing, interviewing skills, business etiquette), job fairs, computerized matching and information center.
Faculty. About 73% of faculty hold PhD or equivalent. About 55% of undergraduate classes taught by tenured faculty. About 37% of teaching faculty are female; 4% Black, 4% other minority.
Student Body. About 84% of students from Arkansas; 93% from Midwest, 3% foreign. An estimated 11% of students reported as Black, 3% Asian, 2% other minority. Average age of undergraduate students: 23.
Varsity Sports. Men (Div.IA): Baseball, Basketball, Football, Golf, Track. Women (Div.IA): Basketball, Tennis, Track, Volleyball.
Campus Life. About 14% of men, 15% of women live in traditional dormitories; no coed dormitories; rest live in off-campus housing or commute. There are 12 fraternities, 8 sororities on campus. About 80% of resident students leave campus on weekends.
Annual Costs. Tuition and fees (based on 12 semester hours), $1,632 (out-of-state, $3,096); room and board, $2,330; estimated $500–750 other, exclusive of travel. About 65% of students receive financial aid. Assistance is typically divided 14% scholarship, 44% grant, 28% loan, 13% work.

Arkansas Tech University

Russellville, Arkansas 72801 — (501) 968-0343

A state-supported university, located in a community of 14,000, 75 miles northwest of Little Rock and 85 miles east of Fort Smith.

Founded: 1909
Affiliation: State
Total Enrollment: 1,596 M, 1,814 W (full-time)
Cost: < $10K
% Receiving Financial Aid: 60%
Admission: Non-selective

Admission. High school graduates eligible; 15 units with recommendation of principal may be substituted for high school graduation; almost all applicants accepted, 56% actually enroll; 56% of entering freshmen graduate in top quarter of high school class, 81% in top half. Average freshman ACT scores: 19.8 M, 20.0 W composite. *Required:* ACT, minimum HS GPA. Criteria considered in admissions, in order of importance: high school academic record, standardized test scores, recommendations. *Out-of-state* freshman applicants: university seeks students from out of state. State does not limit out-of-state enrollment. No special requirements for out-of-state applicants. *Apply* through registration period. *Transfers* welcome.
Academic Environment. Degrees offered: associates, bachelors, masters. Core requirements include 6 hours English/communications, 3 hours mathematics, 8–12 hours sciences, 6 hours fine arts/humanities, 6 hours social sciences, and 2 hours physical education or military service. Arkansas Tech offers unique programs in Fisheries and Wildlife, General Engineering, Recreation and Park Administration, and Hospitality Management. The Arkansas Mining and Minerals Institute is also located on the campus. About 23% of students entering as freshmen graduate within four years; 65% of freshmen return for sophomore year. *Special programs:* CLEP, independent study, honors, internships, undergraduate research, individualized majors. *Calendar:* semester, summer school.
Undergraduate degrees conferred (485). 28% were in Education, 21% were in Business and Management, 10% were in Social Sciences, 6% were in Physical Sciences, 5% were in Health Sciences, 5% were in Renewable Natural Resources, 4% were in Letters, 4% were in Agribusiness and Agricultural Production, 3% were in Psychology, remainder in 10 other fields.
Graduates Career Data. Fields typically employing largest numbers of graduates include business, marketing, computer systems. Career Development Services include resume writing, videos for interview preparation, graduate school information, Career Fair, out-of-state and in-state job listings.
Faculty. About 59% of faculty hold PhD or equivalent. About 63% of undergraduate classes taught by tenured faculty. About 32% of teaching faculty are female; 4% ethnic minority.
Student Body. About 98% of students from Arkansas. An estimated 60% of students reported as Protestant, 5% Catholic, 4% other, 30% unaffiliated or not reported; 3% Black, 2% other minority. Average age of undergraduate students: 25.

Varsity Sports. Men (Div.IA): Baseball, Basketball, Football, Golf. Women (Div.IA): Basketball, Volleyball.
Campus Life. About 28% of men, 19% of women live in traditional dormitories; rest live in off-campus housing or commute. There are 6 fraternities and 4 sororities on campus, which about 18% of men, 14% of women join. About 80% of resident students leave campus on weekends.
Annual Costs. Tuition and fees, $1,710 (out-of-state, $3,360); room and board, $2,490; estimated $1,450 other, exclusive of travel. About 60% of students receive financial aid, average amount of assistance, 2,490. Assistance is typically divided: 22% scholarship, 33% grant, 36% loan, 5% work. University reports 400 scholarships awarded on the basis of academic merit alone, 300 for special talents.

University of Arkansas

Fayetteville, Arkansas 72701 (501) 575-5346

The state's major university, located in a city of 35,000, in northwest Arkansas, the University of Arkansas offers undergraduate, graduate, and professional degrees in a wide variety of fields. Most convenient major airport: Fayetteville Municipal/Tulsa (OK) International.

Founded: 1971
Affiliation: State
UG Enrollment: 5,708 M, 4,708 W (full-time); 766 M, 983 W (part-time)
Total Enrollment: 12,329
Cost: < $10K
% Receiving Financial Aid: 57%
Admission: Non-selective
Application Deadline: Aug. 15

Admission. High school graduates with minimum GPA of 2.5, 13 units in college preparatory courses, or ACT of 18 (or combined SAT of 770) eligible; 98% of applicants accepted. Average freshman ACT scores, according to most recent data available: 23 M, 22 W composite, 22 M, 21 W mathematical. *Required:* ACT or SAT. *Out-of-state* freshman applicants: university seeks students from out of state. State does not limit out-of-state enrollment. No special requirements for out-of-state applicants. About 98% of applicants accepted, 36% of these enroll. *Apply* by August 15 (April 1 for financial assistance); rolling admissions. *Transfers* welcome.
Academic Environment. Administration reports 30% of courses required for graduation are elective; distribution requirements fairly numerous. *Undergraduate studies* offered by colleges of Arts and Sciences, Agriculture and Home Economics, Business Administration, Education, Engineering, schools of Nursing, Pharmacy. *Majors offered* in Arts and Sciences in addition to usual studies include anthropology, architecture, bacteriology, geography, journalism, social welfare, BA in Computer Science (more general applications in the liberal arts than the BS).

About 36% of students entering as freshmen graduate within six years; 33% of freshmen do not return for sophomore year. *Special programs:* CLEP, independent study, study abroad, honors, undergraduate research, individualized majors, senior thesis option, Fulbright College Scholars Program—a 4-year interdisciplinary honors program, 3–3 law program with UA School of Law, students may substitute first year of medical or dental work for last year of bachelor degree. *Calendar:* semester, summer school.
Undergraduate degrees conferred (1,710). 28% were in Business and Management, 15% were in Engineering, 13% were in Education, 8% were in Communications, 5% were in Social Sciences, 3% were in Psychology, 3% were in Life Sciences, 3% were in Architecture and Environmental Design, 3% were in Agricultural Sciences, remainder in 16 other fields. *Doctoral degrees:* Education 41, Business and Management 20, Psychology 10, Physical Sciences 9, Agriculture and Natural Resources 25, Social Sciences 1, Letters 6, Engineering 7, Biological Sciences 4, Mathematics 1.
Faculty. About 79% of faculty hold PhD or equivalent.
Student Body. According to most recent data available, 82% of students from in state; 89% North Central; 2.3% foreign students 1990–91. An estimated 5% of students reported as Black, 7% other minority.
Varsity Sports. Men (Div.IA): Baseball, Basketball, Cross Country, Football, Golf, Swimming & Diving, Tennis, Track. Women (Div.IA): Basketball, Soccer, Swimming & Diving, Tennis, Track.
Campus Life. Cars allowed for all. Possession and use of alcohol not permitted on campus, in any university-related housing, or at official functions.

About 13% of men, 12% of women live in traditional dormitories; 5% of men, 7% of women in coed dormitories; 73% of men, 72% of women live in off-campus housing or commute. Freshmen given preference in college housing if all students cannot be accommodated. Intervisitation in men's and women's dormitory rooms limited. Sexes segregated in coed dormitories by floor. There are 21 fraternities, 12 sororities on campus which about 20% of men, 21% of women join; 9% of men, 10% of women live in fraternities and sororities.
Annual Costs. Tuition and fees, $1,838 (out-of-state, $4,862); room and board, $3,300. About 57% of students receive financial aid; assistance is typically divided 24% scholarship, 43% loan, 9% work. University reports some scholarships awarded on the basis of academic merit alone.

University of Arkansas at Little Rock

Little Rock, Arkansas 72204 (501) 569-3000

A state-supported institution primarily concerned with serving the educational needs of the state. Most convenient major airport: Little Rock.

Founded: 1927
Affiliation: State
UG Enrollment: 2,660 M, 3,219 W (full-time); 1,686 M, 2,426 W (part-time)
Total Enrollment: 12,070
Cost: < $10K
% Receiving Financial Aid: 77%
Admission: Non-selective
Application Deadline: Aug. 1

Admission. Graduates of approved high schools with C average or minimum ACT/SAT of 19/750 eligible; others admitted by examination; 75% applicants accepted, 68% of these actually enroll. Average freshman ACT scores: 19 composite. *Required:* SAT, ACT or SCAT. Criteria considered in admissions: high school academic record, standardized test scores. *Out-of-state* freshman applicants: university seeks students from out of state. State does not limit out-of-state enrollment. No special requirements for out-of-state applicants; 63% of applicants accepted, 81% enroll. States from which most out-of-state students are drawn: Texas, Oklahoma, Louisiana. *Entrance programs:* early decision, early admission, deferred admission. *Apply* by August 1. *Transfers* welcome; 1,047 enrolled 1993–94.
Academic Environment. Degrees offered: associates, bachelors, masters, doctoral. Graduation requirements include 9 hours written and oral literacy, 3 hours math and statistics, 8 hours lab science, 6 hours arts, 3 hours world humanities, 6 hours world history, 3 hours U.S. traditions, 6 hours individual cultures and societies. *Special programs:* CLEP, honors, independent study, study abroad, individualized majors, January term, cross registration with U. of Arkansas Medical School, internship/cooperative work-study programs available. *Calendar:* semester, summer school.
Undergraduate degrees conferred (751). 26% were in Business and Management, 10% were in Communications, 8% were in Social Sciences, 8% were in Psychology, 7% were in Protective Services, 6% were in Liberal/General Studies, 6% were in Education, 5% were in Letters, 4% were in Engineering and Engineering Related Technology, 4% were in Life Sciences, 4% were in Computer and Engineering Related Technology, 3% were in Business (Administrative Support), 3% were in Visual and Performing Arts, remainder in 5 other fields.
Graduates Career Data. Graduate study pursued by 24% of students (1990–91). About 93% of graduates employed. Career Development Services include aptitude testing, group and individual counseling, placement services, resume and interview workshops, on-campus recruitment, and library resources.
Faculty. About 47% of faculty hold PhD or equivalent. About 43% of teaching faculty are female; 5% are Black, 4% other minority.
Varsity Sports. Men (NCAA Div.I): Baseball, Basketball, Cross Country, Golf, Soccer, Swimming/Diving, Tennis, Track, Volleyball, Water Polo. Women (NCAA Div.I): Cross Country, Golf, Soccer, Swimming/Diving, Tennis, Track.
Student Body. About 95% of students from Arkansas. An estimated 15% of students reported as Black, 6% other minority. Average age of undergraduate student: 26.
Campus Life. About 4% of students live in coed dormitories; 97% commute. There are 6 fraternities, 5 sororities on campus which about 5% of men, 3% of women join; they provide no residence facilities.

Annual Costs. Tuition and fees, $2,246 (out-of-state, $5,222); room and board, $2,390. About 77% of students receive financial aid. University reports 77% of scholarships awarded on the basis of need alone. *Meeting Costs:* University offers Tuition Deferment Plan.

University of Arkansas at Monticello

Monticello, Arkansas 71655 **(501) 460-1026**

A state-supported institution, located near a community of 9,000, 100 miles southeast of Little Rock. Most convenient major airport: Little Rock.

Founded: 1909
Affiliation: State
Total Enrollment: 2,111 M, W (full-time)
Cost: < $10K
% Receiving Financial Aid: 70%
Admission: Non-selective
Application Deadline: Aug. 18

Admission. Graduates of accredited high schools with 15 units eligible; 77% of applicants accepted, 84% of these actually enroll. *Required:* ACT. *Out-of-state* freshmen applicants: state does not limit out-of-state enrollment. No special requirements for out-of-state applicants. *Apply* by August 18. *Transfers* welcome.
Academic Environment. *Degrees:* AB, BS. About 50–90% of general education requirements for graduation are elective; distribution requirements fairly numerous. Unusual majors offered include forestry, agriculture. About 35% of students entering as freshmen graduate eventually; 48% of freshmen do not return for sophomore year. *Special programs:* 3–2 programs in agricultural education, allied health. *Calendar:* semester, summer school.
Undergraduate degrees conferred (213). 28% were in Business and Management, 28% were in Education, 9% were in Letters, 9% were in Agricultural Sciences, 8% were in Renewable Natural Resources, 4% were in Social Sciences, 3% were in Business (Administrative Support), remainder in 7 other fields.
Faculty. About 57% of faculty hold PhD or equivalent.
Varsity Sports. Men (NAIA): Baseball, Basketball, Cross Country, Football, Track. Women (NAIA): Basketball, Track, Cross Country.
Campus Life. According to most recent data available, 91% of students from in state; 94% North Central, 6% South. An estimated 17% of students reported as Black, 2% other minority.

About 38% of men, 18% of women live in traditional dormitories; no coed dormitories; rest live in off-campus housing or commute. Limited visitation in men's or women's dormitory rooms. Freshmen given preference in college housing if all students cannot be accommodated. There are 8 fraternities, 4 sororities on campus which about 13% of men, 7% of women join; they provide no residence facilities. About 79% of resident students leave campus on weekends.
Annual Costs. Tuition and fees, $1,464 (out-of-state, $3,384); room and board, $2,200. About 70% of students receive financial aid; assistance is typically divided 15% scholarship, 45% grant, 25% loan, 15% work. University reports some scholarships awarded on the basis of academic merit alone. *Meeting Costs:* university offers installment plan for all room and board costs; out-of-state fees may be waived for students from contiguous states of Mississippi, Louisiana, and Texas.

University of Arkansas, Pine Bluff

Pine Bluff, Arkansas 71601 **(501) 541-6558**

A state-supported, land-grant college, located in a city of 65,115, 42 miles southeast of Little Rock; founded as a college for Negroes and still serving a multi-ethnic student body.

Founded: 1873
Affiliation: State
Total Enrollment: 3,003 M, W (full-time)
Cost: < $10K
Admission: Non-selective
Application Deadline: Aug. 15

Admission. Graduates of accredited high schools with 15 units (8 in academic subjects) eligible; others admitted by examination. *Required:* SAT or ACT. *Out-of-state* freshman applicants: university seeks students from out of state. State does not limit out-of-state enrollment. No special requirements for out-of-state applicants. *Apply* by August 15. *Transfers* welcome.
Academic Environment. *Degrees:* BA, BS. About 45% of students entering as freshmen graduate eventually. *Calendar:* semester, summer school.
Undergraduate degrees conferred (312). 25% were in Business and Management, 21% were in Education, 10% were in Protective Services, 5% were in Health Sciences, 4% were in Public Affairs, 4% were in Letters, 4% were in Home Economics, 4% were in Social Sciences, 4% were in Engineering and Engineering Related Technology, 4% were in Life Sciences, 4% were in Computer and Engineering Related Technology, 3% were in Agribusiness and Agricultural Production, 3% were in Psychology, remainder in 5 other fields.
Varsity Sports. Men (NAIA I/NCAA II): Basketball, Cross Country, Football, Golf, Tennis, Track. Women (NAIA I): Basketball, Cross Country, Track, Volleyball.
Student Body. About 83% of students from in state, 93% North Central, 4% South. An estimated 80% of students are Black, 2% other minority, according to most recent data available.
Campus Life. About 12% of men, 13% of women live in traditional dormitories; no coed dormitories; rest live in off-campus housing or commute. No intervisitation in men's or women's dormitory rooms. There are 7 fraternities, 7 sororities on campus which about 4% of men, 4% of women join; they provide no residence facilities.
Annual Costs. Tuition and fees, $1,464 (out-of-state, $3,384); room and board, $2,194.

Armstrong University

Berkeley, California 94704 **(510) 848-2500**

A small, private university offering business-oriented degree programs. Student body is predominantly international, from more than 25 countries.

Founded: 1918
Affiliation: Independent
UG Enrollment: 25 M, 18 W (full-time)
Total Enrollment: 115
Cost: < $10K
Admission: Non-selective
Application Deadline: Rolling

Admissions. About 96% of applicants accepted, 20% actually enroll. Criteria considered in admissions, in order of importance: high school academic record, recommendations, writing sample. *Entrance programs:* early decision, early admission, mid-year admission, deferred admission, advanced placement. *Apply:* rolling admission.
Academic Environment. Degrees offered: associates, bachelors, masters. Degree programs offered in business administration, certificate programs in computer technology, English as a Second Language. Programs are supported by a "state-of-the-art" computer learning center. Average undergraduate class size: 96% under 20, 4 20–40. *Special programs:* January Term, English as a Second Language (ESL).
Faculty. About 50% of faculty hold PhD or equivalent. About 36% of teaching faculty are female; 9% Black, 14% Hispanic, 18% other minority.
Student Body. About 6% of students from in state, 94% foreign. An estimated 2% of student reported as Black, 3% Hispanic, 82% Asian. Average age of undergraduate student: 25.
Campus Life. Campus is located in downtown Berkeley, close to public transportation and UC Berkeley, and 15 miles from San Francisco. About 10% of men live in off-campus, college-related housing; rest of men, all women commute.
Annual Costs. Tuition and fees, $5,985; room and board, $5,550; estimated $1,950 other, exclusive of travel.

Armstrong State College

Savannah, Georgia 31419 **(912) 927-5320**

A state-supported, commuter college, offering 4- and 2-year degree programs; located in a city of 200,000. Most convenient major airport: Savannah.

Founded: 1935
Affiliation: State
Total Enrollment: 3,780 M, W (full-time)
Cost: < $10K
% Receiving Financial Aid: 27%
Admission: Non-selective
Application Deadline: 5 days before quarter

Admission. Graduates of accredited high schools or equivalent eligible; 96% of applicants accepted, 93% of these actually enroll. Required: SAT or ACT. *Out-of-state* freshman applicants: college welcomes students from out of state. State does not limit out-of-state enrollment. No special requirements for out-of-state applicants. All out-of-state applicants accepted, 68% enroll. *Entrance programs:* early admission, midyear admission, deferred admission. *Apply* by 5 days prior to quarter. *Transfers* welcome.
Academic Environment. *Degrees:* AB, BS, BSElEd, BSMT, BSEd, BMEd. About 60% of general education requirements for graduation are elective; no distribution requirements. About 45% of students entering as freshmen graduate eventually; 35% of freshmen do not return for sophomore year. *Calendar:* quarter, summer school.
Undergraduate degrees conferred (311). 28% were in Education, 17% were in Health Sciences, 15% were in Liberal/General Studies, 8% were in Social Sciences, 8% were in Protective Services, 6% were in Letters, 5% were in Psychology, 3% were in Life Sciences, 3% were in Physical Sciences, 3% were in Visual and Performing Arts, 3% were in Computer and Engineering Related Technology, remainder in 2 other fields.
Varsity Sports. Men (Div.II): Baseball, Basketball, Cross Country, Tennis. Women (Div.II): Basketball, Swimming, Tennis, Volleyball.
Student Body. College does not seek a national student body; 95% of students from Georgia; 99% South. An estimated 16% of students reported as Black, 2% other minority, according to most recent data available.
Campus Life. About 5% each of men, women live in coed dormitories, rest live in off-campus housing or commute. There are no fraternities, 2 sororities on campus which about 5% of women join; they provide no residence facilities.
Annual Costs. Tuition and fees, $1,569 (out-of-state, $2,949); room and board, $3,306. About 27% of students receive financial aid; assistance is typically divided 54% scholarship, 38% loan, 8% work. College reports some scholarships awarded on the basis of academic merit alone.

Arnold and Marie Schwartz College of Pharmacy and Health Sciences

(See Long Island University, Brooklyn Center)

Art Center College of Design

Pasadena, California 91103

An independent, professional college of art and design, offering studies in communications design, industrial design, illustration, advertising design, photography, TV-film and fine arts. Degrees granted are BFA, BS, MFA, MS.

Founded: 1930
Affiliation: Independent

School of the Art Institute of Chicago

Chicago, Illinois 60603

An independent, professional institution, the Art Institute offers BFA and MFA degree programs of study in fine arts, design, crafts and teacher education.

Founded: 1866
Affiliation: Independent

University of the Arts

Philadelphia, Pennsylvania 19102 (215) 875-4808

The first and only university dedicated solely to professional training in the visual and performing arts, the University of the Arts is the product of the merger of the Philadelphia College of Art and the Philadelphia College of the Performing Arts, and includes the Shubert Theatre. Most convenient major airport: Philadelphia..

Founded: 1987
Affiliation: Independent
Total Enrollment: 1,359 M, W (full-time); 34 M, 73 W (part-time)
Cost: $10K–$20K
% Receiving Financial Aid: 83%
Admission: Non-selective
Application Deadline: April 1

Admission. Graduates of accredited high schools or equivalent eligible; 63% of applicants accepted, 51% of these actually enroll. *Required:* SAT or ACT, interview, portfolio review or audition. *Non-academic factors* considered in admissions: special talents, alumni children, diverse student body. *Apply* by April 1. *Transfers* welcome.
Academic Environment. *Degrees:* BFA, BM, BS. The university is located in the heart of the city's artistic community. Academic studies required for graduation vary by program from 18–45 credits in humanities, language and literature, art history, social studies, philosophy and science, and related arts. *Special programs:* exchange programs with other art schools.
Campus Life. About 47% of students from in state; 82% Middle Atlantic, 7% New England. An estimated 8% of students reported as Black, 3% Hispanic, 5% Asian, according to most recent data available.

About 22% of men, 23% of women live in coed dormitories; rest commute. Freshmen given preference in college housing if all students cannot be accommodated. There are no fraternities or sororities. About 30% of resident students leave campus on weekends.
Annual Costs. Tuition and fees, $12,170. About 83% of students receive financial aid; assistance is typically divided 50% scholarship, 25% loan, 25% work. College reports some scholarships awarded on the basis of academic merit alone. *Meeting Costs:* college offers monthly payment plans.

Asbury College

Wilmore, Kentucky 40390 (800) 888-1818

An interdenominational, co-educational college, "open to those who desire training in a Christian atmosphere"; located in a village of 3,500, 15 miles south of Lexington. Most convenient major airport: Lexington—Bluegrass..

Founded: 1890
Affiliation: Independent
Total Enrollment: 1,048 M, W (full-time)
Cost: < $10K
% Receiving Financial Aid: 88%
Admission: Non-selective
Application Deadline: Aug. 15

Admission. Graduates of accredited high schools with C average, minimum SAT scores of 380 verbal, 360 math or ACT composite of 18 eligible; others given individual consideration; 81% of applicants accepted, 68% of these actually enroll; 48% of freshmen graduate in top fifth of high school class, 68% in top two-fifths. *Required:* ACT or SAT, minister's recommendation, personal reference. Non-academic factor considered in admissions: religious affiliation and/or commitment. *Entrance programs:* early decision, early admission, midyear admission, deferred admission, advanced placement. *Apply* by August 15 (preferred). About 21% of entering students from private schools. *Transfers* welcome.
Academic Environment. *Degrees:* BA, BS. About 47% of general education requirements for graduation are elective; no distribution requirements. Programs recently added include: intercultural studies, journalism. About 67% of students entering as freshmen graduate eventually; 12% of freshmen do not return for sophomore year. *Special programs:* CLEP, honors, independent study, study abroad, Christian College Coalition, Wesleyan Urban Coalition, 3–3 nursing, 3–1 programs in medical technology with three different institutions. *Calendar:* quarter, summer school, December term.

Undergraduate degrees conferred (201). 19% were in Education, 14% were in Theology, 10% were in Business and Management, 10% were in Social Sciences, 8% were in Psychology, 7% were in Public Affairs, 6% were in Letters, 5% were in Visual and Performing Arts, 5% were in Life Sciences, 4% were in Communications Technologies, remainder in 6 other fields.
Faculty. About 60% of faculty hold PhD or equivalent.
Varsity Sports. Men (NAIA): Soccer, Baseball, Tennis; (NAIA/NCCAA) Cross Country; (NCAA III) Swimming. Women (Div.III): Volleyball, Swimming, Tennis; (NCAA/NCCAA): Cross Country.
Student Body. About 47% of students from South, 35% North Central, 12% Middle Atlantic. An estimated 87% of students reported as Protestant; 4% as minority according to most recent data available.
Religious Orientation. Asbury is an independent institution; follows Methodist doctrine, but not supported by the church; 8 quarter hours of Bible required of all students; "religious life of vital nature" on campus.
Campus Life. About 82% of men, 83% of women live in traditional dormitories; no coed dormitories; rest live in off-campus housing or commute. Freshmen given preference in college housing if all students cannot be accommodated. No intervisitation in men's or women's dormitory rooms. There are no fraternities or sororities. About 10% of students leave campus on weekends.
Annual Costs. Tuition and fees, $8,445; room and board, $2,660. About 88% of students receive financial aid; assistance is typically divided 52% scholarship, 38% loan, 10% work. College reports some scholarships awarded on the basis of academic merit alone. *Meeting Costs:* college offers budget and deferred payment plans.

Ashland College

Ashland, Ohio 44805 **(419) 289-5052**

A private college that concentrates on the education of the "whole individual" within the context of a Judeo-Christian-oriented college environment. Ashland is located in a community of 20,000, 60 miles southwest of Cleveland. Most convenient major airport: Cleveland.

Founded: 1878
Affiliation: Brethren
UG Enrollment: 744 M, 907 W (full-time); 162 M, 349 W (part-time)
Total Enrollment: 3,863
Cost: $10K–$20K
% Receiving Financial Aid: 95%
Admission: Non-selective
Application Deadline: Aug. 21

Admission. High school graduates with 16 units (13 in academic subjects) eligible; selects applicants on basis of individual potential irrespective of race or religion; 86% of applicants accepted, 35% of these actually enroll. *Required:* SAT or ACT; interview strongly recommended. *Non-academic factors* considered in admissions: special talents, alumni children. *Entrance programs:* early admission, midyear admission, deferred admission, advanced placement. *Apply* by August 21; rolling admissions. *Transfers* welcome.
Academic Environment. *Degrees:* AB, BS, BSEd, BSBA, BM, BFA. About 33% of general education credits for graduation are required; distribution requirements fairly numerous. Unusual majors offered include toxicology, broadcast sales and station management. About 50% of students entering as freshmen graduate within 4 years; 30% of freshmen do not return for sophomore year. *Special programs:* CLEP, independent study, study abroad, honors, undergraduate research, 3–2 programs in engineering, art, home economics/human development, intersession and mini-mester tours. *Calendar:* 4–1–4, summer school.
Undergraduate degrees conferred (434). 31% were in Education, 27% were in Business and Management, 9% were in Protective Services, 8% were in Marketing and Distribution, 4% were in Communications, 3% were in Visual and Performing Arts, 3% were in Psychology, remainder in 13 other fields.
Faculty. About 44% of faculty hold PhD or equivalent.
Student Body. About 86% of students from in state, 89% North Central, 7% Middle Atlantic. An estimated 56% of students reported as Protestant, 27% as Catholic, 1% as Jewish, 16% unaffiliated, other; 6% as Black, 1% Hispanic, according to most recent data available.
Varsity Sports. Men (Div.II): Baseball, Basketball, Cross Country, Football, Golf, Soccer, Swimming, Tennis, Track, Wrestling. Women (Div.II): Basketball, Cross Country, Softball, Swimming, Tennis, Track, Volleyball.
Religious Orientation. Ashland is a church-related institution; 3–4 hours of Bible history required of all students. Religious clubs on campus include Coalition for Christian Outreach, Newman Club.
Campus Life. Cars permitted. About 49% of men, 62% of women live in traditional dormitories; 18% of men, 15% of women live in coed dormitories; 18% of men, 22% of women live in off-campus housing or commute. Freshmen given preference in college housing if all students cannot be accommodated. Intervisitation in men's and women's dormitory rooms limited. There are 5 fraternities, 4 sororities on campus which about 30% of men, 35% of women join; 15% of men live in fraternities; sororities provide no residence facilities. About 50% of students leave campus on weekends.
Annual Costs. Tuition and fees, $10,933; room and board, $4,520. About 95% of students receive financial aid; assistance typically divided 65% scholarship, 32% loan, 3% work. College reports some scholarships awarded on the basis of academic merit alone. *Meeting Costs:* college offers participation in private budget plans, family discount.

College of Associated Arts

St. Paul, Minnesota 55102

An independent college offering bachelors programs in fine and applied arts; located in an historic neighborhood and housed in an old mansion.

Founded: 1924 **Affiliation:** Independent

Assumption College

Worcester, Massachusetts 01615-0005 **(508) 752-5615**

Long a Catholic college for men, and the only American college founded by the Augustinians of the Assumption, Assumption is now fully co-educational, with women sharing all academic and student extracurricular activities on the 140-acre campus located in a residential section of Worcester (pop. 180,000), midway between Boston and Springfield. Most convenient major airports: Worcester Municipal, Logan (Boston).

Founded: 1917
Affiliation: Roman Catholic
UG Enrollment: 727 M, 1,044 W (full-time)
Total Enrollment: 2,197
Cost: $10K–$20K
% Receiving Financial Aid: 64%
Admission: Selective
Application Deadline: March 1

Admission is selective. About 69% of applicants accepted, 27% of these actually enroll; 25% of freshmen graduate in top fifth of high school class, 59% in top two-fifths. Average freshman SAT scores, according to most recent data available: 450 M, 440 W verbal, 500 M, 470 W mathematical; 24% of freshman score above 500 on verbal, 2% above 600; 47% score above 500 on mathematical, 1% above 600. *Required:* SAT. *Non-academic factors* considered in admissions: alumni children, special talents. *Entrance programs:* early decision, early admission, midyear admission, advanced placement, deferred admission. About 5% of entering students from private schools, 35% from parochial schools. *Apply* by March 1. *Transfers* welcome.
Academic Environment. Administration reports 70% of courses required for graduation are elective; distribution requirements, however, fairly numerous: 2 courses each in 7 of 8 academic areas. *Degree:* AB. *Majors offered* in 21 fields including usual arts and sciences, foreign affairs, social and rehabilitation services. College reports its French Institute is "one of the largest academic resource centers on French tradition located in English-speaking North America."

About 75% of students entering as freshmen graduate eventually; 10% of freshmen do not return for sophomore year. *Special programs:* CLEP, study abroad, optional January interterm, 3-year degree, "limited" individualized majors, cooperative programs through Worcester Consortium, 3–2 in engineering with Worcester Polytechnic, study at Merrill-Palmer Institute. Adult programs: Center for Continuing and Professional Education. *Calendar:* semester, summer school.

Undergraduate degrees conferred (526). 30% were in Business and Management, 15% were in Social Sciences, 13% were in Letters, 11% were in Psychology, 10% were in Allied Health, 8% were in Health Sciences, 4% were in Liberal/General Studies, remainder in 7 other fields.
Graduates Career Data. *Full-time graduate or professional study* pursued immediately after graduation by 44% of students; 2% enter medical school; 5% enter dental school; 5% enter law school; 7% enter business school, according to most recent data available. Medical schools typically enrolling largest numbers of graduates include U. of Massachusetts; dental schools include Tufts; law schools include Suffolk, Boston College; business schools include Assumption, Babson. *Careers in business and industry* pursued by 17% of graduates. Corporations typically hiring largest numbers of graduates include big six accounting firms, Digital, State Mutual Insurance Co.. *Career Counseling Program* designed specifically for liberal arts students. Liberal arts majors urged to seek interviews with business/industry representatives who visit campus. Help provided in preparing for interviews. Alumni reported as helpful in both career guidance and job placement.
Faculty. About 86% of faculty hold PhD or equivalent.
Student Body. About 60% of students from Massachusetts; 92% New England. *Minority group students:* financial aid available.
Religious Orientation. Assumption is a church-related institution; 2 courses in both religion and philosophy required of all students as part of general studies program. College chaplain, daily Mass available. Non-Catholic students "encouraged to join in the life of the church or temple of their choice in Worcester." No religious clubs on campus. Places of worship available on campus for Catholics, in immediate community for all major faiths.
Varsity Sports. Men (Div.II): Baseball, Basketball, Crew, Cross Country, Football(III), Hockey, LaCrosse, Soccer, Tennis, Track, Volleyball. Women (Div.II): Basketball, Cross Country, Field Hockey, Softball, Tennis, Track, Volleyball.
Campus Life. Interest reported high in both varsity athletics (most popular: basketball, football, hockey, baseball, softball, field hockey) and in intramurals (most popular: basketball, volleyball, softball). Cars allowed for all students; parking permits required; parking reported as adequate for both commuting and resident students. Alcohol allowed in residence halls for those of legal age. Some restrictions on intervisitation.

About 22% of men, 14% of women live in traditional dormitories; 60% of men, 68% of women live in coed dormitories; rest live in off-campus housing or commute. There are no fraternities or sororities. About 25% of resident students leave campus on weekends.
Annual Costs. Tuition and fees, $11,595; room and board, $5,670. About 64% of students receive financial aid; assistance is typically divided 60% scholarship, 30% loan, 10% work. College reports scholarships awarded only on the basis need. Meeting Costs. College offers monthly payment plans.

Atlanta College of Art
Atlanta, Georgia 30309

An independent, professional college of visual arts, the college offers the BFA in communication design (including advertising design, graphic design, and illustration), drawing, electronic arts (including computer art, computer graphics, and video), interior design, painting, printmaking, and sculpture.

Founded: 1928 **Affiliation:** Independent

Atlanta University Center
Atlanta, Georgia 30314

The Atlanta University Center consists of 6 institutions on adjoining campuses which maintain their individual independence, but cooperate closely in the exchange of students and faculty and the common use of certain facilities. All are institutions that were founded to provide higher education for Negroes. The 6 institutions are: Atlanta University, a graduate and professional school; Morehouse College, an undergraduate institution for men; Spelman College, an undergraduate school for women; Clark College and Morris Brown College, both co-educational, church-affiliated institutions; and the Interdenominational Theological Center, a professional school for training religious leaders. (See separate alphabetical listings for the undergraduate colleges.)

Atlantic Christian College
(see Barton College)

College of the Atlantic
Bar Harbor, Maine 04609 (207) 288-5015

An unusual small college with a curriculum focused almost exclusively on the study of ecology, located in a famous village on the Maine shore. Most convenient major airport: Bangor International.

Founded: 1969
Affiliation: Independent
UG Enrollment: 92 M, 121 W (full-time); 12 M, 10 W (part-time)
Total Enrollment: 225
Cost: $10K–$20K
% Receiving Financial Aid: 60%
Admission: Selective
Application Deadline: March 1

Admission is selective. About 70% of applicants accepted, 44% of these actually enroll; 50% of freshmen graduate in top fifth of high school class, 90% in top two-fifths. Average freshman scores: SAT, 563 M, 563 W verbal; 580 M, 544 W mathematical; 91% score above 500 on verbal, 22% above 600, 5% above 700; 74% score above 500 on mathematical, 22% above 600, 5% above 700; ACT, 28 composite. *Required:* essay; interview recommended. Criteria considered in admissions, in order of importance: high school academic record, writing sample, "passion for a College of the Atlantic-type of education"; other factors considered: special talents, diverse student body, extracurricular activities, alumni children. About 14% of entering students from private schools, 9% from parochial schools. *Entrance programs:* early decision, advanced placement. *Apply* by March 1; rolling admissions. *Transfers* welcome; 70 enrolled 1993–94.
Academic Environment. Degrees offered: bachelors, masters. College offers unusual program geared to the study of different aspects of human ecology. Recent student stresses that program is "self-directed, self-motivated" and that because of this it "is not for everyone." She also notes the "wide variety of courses are offered." All programs are interdisciplinary; fields include public policy, marine biology, environmental design and education, ecology, oceanography, elementary and secondary science education, as well as more traditional academic disciplines related to the central theme of human ecology. Graduation requirements include 2 courses each from 3 resource areas: environmental science, human studies, arts and design; 1 human ecology core course, 1 Western Civilization course, required 10-week internship, final project, human ecology essay. Average undergraduate class size: 90% under 20, 9% between 20–40, 1% over 40. *Special programs:* study abroad, cross registration with U. of Maine. About 45% of entering students graduate within four years, 63% eventually; 90% of freshmen return for sophomore year. *Library:* recent student notes that though library is small it offers "good supplementary programs (inter-library loan)." Calendar: 3 ten-week terms, summer school.
Undergraduate degrees conferred (45). 100% were in Multi/Interdisciplinary Studies.
Graduates Career Data. Advanced study pursued by 45% of graduates; of those 70% enter graduate school, 10% enter law school, 5% enter business school, 3% enter medical school, 12% to other programs. Law schools typically enrolling largest numbers of graduates include: Vermont Law School. About 90% of 1992–93 graduates employed. Career development services provided.
Faculty. About 85% of faculty hold PhD or equivalent. All undergraduate classes taught by tenured faculty. About 30% of teaching faculty are female.
Student Body. About 20% of students are from Maine; 35% New England, 35% Middle Atlantic, 12% West/Northwest, 4% each Midwest, South, 8% foreign. An estimated 2% of students reported as minority, according to most recent data available.

Campus Life. Bar Harbor is isolated, especially in the winter, but the college offers weekly movies, speakers, dances, etc. to offset this. Acadia National Park is COA's "backyard", most students take advantage of this for canoeing, kayaking, mountain biking and cross-country skiing. In addition the college Outing Club organizes many trips throughout the year. About 10% of men, 10% of women live in coed dormitories; 5% live in off-campus college-related housing; rest commute. Freshmen given preference in college housing if all students cannot be accommodated. There are no fraternities or sororities. About 5% of resident students leave campus on weekends.
Annual Costs. Tuition and fees, $13,287; room and board $3,860; $870 other, exclusive of travel. About 60% of students receive financial aid; average amount of assistance, $12,880. Assistance is typically divided 60% grant, 33% loan, 7% work. College reports all scholarships awarded on the basis of need alone. *Meeting Costs:* college offers installment billing, college short-term loans.

Atlantic Union College

South Lancaster, Massachusetts 01561 (508) 368-2235

A church-related college, located in a village of 2,700, 40 miles west of Boston. Most convenient major airport: Logan (Boston).

Founded: 1882
Affiliation: Seventh-day Adventist
Total Enrollment: 970 M, W (full-time); 39 M, 159 W (part-time)
Cost: $10K–$20K
% Receiving Financial Aid: 80%
Admission: Non-selective
Application Deadline: August 1

Admission. Graduates of accredited high schools with C average in college preparatory program eligible; others given individual consideration. About 69% of freshmen applicants accepted, 82% of these actually enroll. *Required:* SAT or ACT, recommendations. About 52% of entering students from parochial schools, 6% from private schools. *Apply* by August 1; rolling admissions. *Transfers* welcome.
Academic Environment. *Degrees:* BA, BS. Unusual majors offered include sacred music, majors recently added include life science and natural science. *Special programs:* January Term, study abroad, English Language Institute. Adult programs: Continuing Education Program and Adult Degree Program. *Calendar:* semester, intercession, summer school.
Undergraduate degrees conferred (103). 14% were in Education, 13% were in Business and Management, 9% were in Psychology, 9% were in Theology, 9% were in Philosophy and Religion, 8% were in Health Sciences, 7% were in Visual and Performing Arts, 7% were in Life Sciences, 6% were in Public Affairs, 5% were in Letters, 5% were in Computer and Engineering Related Technology, 4% were in Business (Administrative Support), 3% were in Mathematics, remainder in 3 other fields.
Student Body. College does not seek a national student body; 51% from in state. An estimated 78% of students reported as Seventh Day Adventist, 18% unaffiliated, 4% other; 23% Black, 14% Hispanic, 3% Asian, 13% other minority, according to most recent data available.
Religious Orientation. Atlantic Union is a church-related institution; 12 hours of religion, attendance at chapel required of all students.
Campus Life. About 19% of men, 32% of women live in traditional dormitories; no coed dormitories; rest live in off-campus housing or commute. Freshmen given preference in college housing if all students cannot be accommodated. No intervisitation in men's or women's dormitory rooms.
Annual Costs. Tuition and fees, $10,700; room and board, $3,550. About 80% of students receive financial aid; assistance is typically divided 35% scholarship, 40% loan, 25% work. College reports some scholarships awarded on the basis of academic merit alone.

Auburn University

Auburn University, Alabama 36849 (205) 844-4080

A state-supported university, located on a 1,871-acre main campus in a community of 28,000, 60 miles east of Montgomery. Most convenient major airports: Atlanta (GA), Montgomery (AL), Columbus (GA).

Founded: 1856
Affiliation: State
UG Enrollment: 9,464 M, 7,810 W (full-time); 1,106 M, 613 W (part-time)
Total Enrollment: 19,979
Cost: < $10K
% Receiving Financial Aid: 45%
Admission: Very Selective
Application Deadline: Sept. 1

Admission is very selective. About 79% of applicants accepted, 73% of these actually enroll; 49% of freshmen graduate in top fifth of high school class, 76% in top two-fifths. Average freshman scores, according to most recent data available: SAT, 510 M, 507 W verbal, 592 M, 561 W mathematical; 54% of freshmen score above 500 on verbal, 14% above 600, 1% above 700; 85% score above 500 on mathematical, 46% above 600, 8% above 700; ACT, 24.6 M, 23.9 W composite, 24.3 M, 22.7 W mathematical. *Required:* ACT or SAT, minimum GPA of 2.0. *Out-of-state* freshman applicants: University welcomes students from out-of-state. State limits out-of-state enrollment based on availability of facilities and faculty. Higher admissions requirements for out-of-state applicants. About 70% of out-of-state applicants accepted, 44% enroll. *Non-academic factors* considered in admissions: alumni children, diverse student body, preference given to in-state students. *Entrance programs:* midyear admission, advanced placement, deferred admission. About 10% of entering students from private schools, 7% from parochial. *Apply* by September 1; rolling admissions but early application is strongly encouraged. *Transfers* welcome.
Academic Environment. Pressures for academic achievement appear moderate. Administration reports percentage of electives required for graduation varies with curriculum. *Undergraduate studies* offered by colleges of Liberal Arts, Agriculture, Business, Education, Engineering, Sciences and Mathematics, schools of Architecture, Forestry, Human Sciences, Nursing; upper class students admitted to school of Pharmacy, college of Veterinary Medicine. *Majors offered* in addition to usual arts and sciences include foreign language, international trade, communication disorders, geological engineering and molecular biology; unusual majors in aviation management, foreign language/international trade, building science, fashion merchandising. Computer science and computer engineering majors offered.

About 65% of students entering as freshmen graduate eventually; 85% of freshmen return for sophomore year. *Special programs:* CLEP, independent study, study abroad, honors, 3-year degree, freshman tutorial program, study partners, cooperative work/study program (in most curricula), 3–2 engineering, 5-year education program allows a student to complete a degree in a non-education field then enter a 1-year program leading to M.Ed. and teacher certification. Adult programs: OTA (Over Traditional Age) support group. *Library:* includes U.S. Map Repository. *Calendar:* quarter, summer school.
Undergraduate degrees conferred (3,879). 30% were in Business and Management, 18% were in Engineering, 10% were in Education, 5% were in Social Sciences, 5% were in Health Sciences, 4% were in Communications, 3% were in Psychology, 3% were in Life Sciences, 3% were in Letters, 3% were in Visual and Performing Arts, remainder in 16 other fields. *Doctoral degrees:* Education 38, Psychology 18, Agriculture and Natural Resources 13, Biological Sciences 9, Engineering 6, Letters 5, Physical Sciences 3, Mathematics 2.
Graduates Career Data. According to most recent data available, full-time graduate or professional study pursued immediately after graduation by 40% of students; 1% enter medical school; less than 1% enter dental school; 4% enter law school; 9% enter business school. Medical and dental schools typically enrolling largest numbers of graduates include U. of Alabama; law schools include U. of Alabama, Cumberland, Georgia, Yale. *Careers in business and industry* pursued by 60% of graduates. Corporations typically hiring largest numbers of graduates include Intergraph, Pratt & Whitney, Alabama Power, Big Eight Accounting Firms.
Faculty. About 80% of faculty hold PhD or equivalent.
Student Body. University welcomes a national student body; 60% of students from Alabama; 94% South, 2% each North Central, Middle Atlantic. An estimated 81% of students reported as Protestant, 13% Catholic, 3% unaffiliated, 3% other; 4% Black, 2% other minority, according to most recent data available.
Varsity Sports. Men (Div.I-A): Baseball, Basketball, Football, Golf, Swimming, Tennis, Track. Women (Div.I-A): Basketball, Golf, Gymnastics, Swimming, Tennis, Track, Volleyball.

Campus Life. Most men and three-quarters of women live off-campus—a factor that obviously influences lifestyles of those living on campus. "Numerous" all-college activities are reportedly "heavily participated in by all students." High interest reported in fraternities/sororities, intramural sports (most popular: football, basketball, softball, volleyball) and varsity sports (most popular: football, basketball-men's and women's). Dorm visitation hours and curfew regulations determined by residents of each dorm. Cars permitted; parking reported as adequate for both commuting and resident students. Possession or use of alcohol on campus prohibited.

About 8% of men, 25% of women live in traditional dormitories; no coed dormitories; 85% of men, 75% of women live in off-campus housing or commute. There are 31 fraternities, 18 sororities on campus which about 20% of men, 32% of women join; 7% of men live in fraternities; sororities use designated dormitory facilities. About 15% of resident students leave campus on weekends.

Annual Costs. Tuition and fees, $1,950 (out-of-state, $5,850); room and board, $3,873. About 45% of students receive financial aid; assistance is typically divided 30% scholarship, 53% loan, 17% work. University reports some scholarships awarded on the basis of academic merit alone.

Auburn University at Montgomery

Montgomery, Alabama 36117-3596 (205) 244-3000

A campus of Auburn University, AUM is a commuter institution designed to serve students from the immediate area. Most convenient major airport: Montgomery.

Founded: 1967
Affiliation: State
UG Enrollment: 1,405 M, 2,070 W (full-time); 807 M, 1,134 W (part-time)
Total Enrollment: 6,407
Cost: < $10K
% Receiving Financial Aid: 62%
Admission: Non-selective
Application Deadline: Sept. 1

Admission. High school graduates with 16 units and C average eligible; others admitted by examination. About 88% of freshmen applicants accepted, 65% of these actually enroll. Average freshman ACT scores: 21.2 M, 20.2 W composite. *Required:* SAT or ACT, minimum HS GPA 2.0. *Out-of-state* students: state does not limit out-of-state enrollment. States from which most out-of-state students are drawn: Georgia, Florida. *Entrance programs:* early decision, early admission, mid-year admission, deferred admission, advanced placement, rolling admission. *Apply* by September 1. *Transfers* welcome.

Academic Environment. *Degrees:* bachelors, masters, doctoral (joint with Auburn U.). Graduation requirements include 10 hours each English, science, and world history, and 5 hours math. *Special programs:* CLEP, individualized majors, study abroad, cross registration with Huntingdon College and Faulkner U., internships and cooperative education programs available. Average undergraduate class size: 41% under 20; 53% between 20–40, 6% over 40. *Library:* includes more than 1,000,000 government documents. *Calendar:* quarter, summer school.

Undergraduate degrees conferred (691). 35% were in Business and Management, 20% were in Education, 6% were in Liberal/General Studies, 6% were in Health Sciences, 5% were in Communications, 5% were in Protective Services, 4% were in Social Sciences, 4% were in Psychology, 3% were in Computer and Engineering Related Technology, remainder in 6 other fields.

Graduates Career Data. Career Development Center offers resource library, counseling, assessment and testing, seminars to assist with resume preparation, interviewing skills, and job search, on-campus recruitment,

Faculty. About 74% of faculty hold PhD or equivalent. About 36% of teaching faculty are female; 4% Black, 5% other minority.

Student Body. Almost all students from South. An estimated 20% of students reported as Black, 3% other minority. Average age of undergraduate students: 24.

Varsity Sports. Men (NAIA): Baseball, Basketball, Soccer, Tennis. Women (NAIA): Basketball, Tennis.

Campus Life. About 9% of men, 8% of women live in coed dormitories; rest live in off-campus housing or commute. There are 5 fraternities and 6 sororities on campus; 3% of men join, 4% of women join.

Annual Costs. Tuition and fees, $1,800 (out-of-state, $5,400); room only, $1,590; estimated $1,960 other, exclusive of travel. About 62% of students receive financial aid. College reports 177 scholarships awarded on the basis of academic merit alone, 47 for special talents, 4 for need alone.

Audrey Cohen College

New York, New York 10014

A small, highly innovative institution that offers full-time baccalaureate and master degree programs designed to train professionals in business management and human services while they are working full-time. The college attracts an adult minority student body. The school integrates classwork with fieldwork, and learning can be applied, tested, documented, and assessed in the field. Because three full semesters are offered annually, students can complete their bachelors in two years and eight months, the masters degree in one year. Formerly known as College for Human Services.

Augsburg College

Minneapolis, Minnesota 55454 (612) 330-1001

A church-related, liberal arts college, located in a residential area of downtown Minneapolis, near the HHH Metrodome and the University of Minnesota. Most convenient major airport: Minneapolis-St. Paul International.

Founded: 1869
Affiliation: Evangelical Lutheran Church in America
UG Enrollment: 681 M, 781 W (full-time); 72 M, 114 W (part-time)
Total Enrollment: 3,000
Cost: $10K–$20K
% Receiving Financial Aid: 82%
Admission: Non-selective
Application Deadline: Aug. 1

Admission. High school graduates with 2.5 GPA who rank in top half of high school class eligible; 77% of applicants accepted, 39% of these actually enroll; 32% graduate in top fifth of high school class, 54% in top two-fifths. Average freshman scores: SAT, 460 verbal, 580 mathematical; ACT, 21.6 composite. *Required:* SAT or ACT, essay. Criteria considered in admissions, in order of importance: high school academic record, standardized test scores, recommendations, writing sample, extracurricular activities; other factors considered: special talents, diverse student body, religious affiliation and/or commitment, alumni children. *Entrance programs:* midyear admission, deferred admission. *Apply* by August 1; rolling admissions. *Transfers* welcome; 157 enrolled 1993–94.

Academic Environment. *Degrees:* bachelors, masters. Graduation requirements include 21–24 courses in 8 "perspectives" (liberal arts) as well as 9–12 courses in major. Current and recent students cite "helpful faculty" and small class size as strengths. About 33% of entering freshman graduate within four years; 78% of freshmen return for sophomore year. *Special programs:* CLEP, independent study, study abroad, honors, undergraduate research, individualized majors, January Interim, "metro-urban" studies program, coop education, dual-degree program in occupational therapy, 3–2 engineering, cross registration with 5 ACTC schools. Adult programs: Weekend College with every-other-weekend format enrolls more than 1,200 adult learners. Average undergraduate class size: 17; 77% of classes under 20, 23% between 20–40. *Calendar:* 4–1–4, summer school, weekend college.

Undergraduate degrees conferred (414). 30% were in Business and Management, 17% were in Education, 12% were in Communications, 7% were in Social Sciences, 6% were in Health Sciences, 5% were in Letters, 5% were in Psychology, 4% were in Physical Sciences, 3% were in Public Affairs, 3% were in Computer and Engineering Related Technology, remainder in 7 other fields.

Graduates Career Data. Advanced studies pursued by 11% of graduates. About 78% of 1991–92 graduates are employed. Fields typically hiring largest numbers of graduates include business, social work, education; specific employers include 3M, Norwest Banks, West Publishing. College reports that "We provide a full range of career development assessments and employment assistance services to students and all programs of the college."

Faculty. About 68% of faculty hold PhD or equivalent. About 47% of teaching faculty are women; 3% Black, 3% American Indian, 3% Asian, 2% Hispanic.

Student Body. About 77% of students from Minnesota; 81% Midwest, foreign 7%. An estimated 61% of students reported as Protestant, 19% Catholic, 19% other; 12% Asian, 5% Black, 2% Native American, 1% Hispanic, 1% other minority. Average age of undergraduate student: 22.
Religious Orientation. Augsburg is a church-related institution; 3 courses in religion required of all students; attendance at chapel services voluntary. About 43% students affiliated with the Lutheran church. Places of worship available on campus and within walking distance for 3 major faiths.
Varsity Sports. Men (Div.III): Baseball, Basketball, Cross Country, Football, Golf, Hockey, Soccer, Tennis, Track, Wrestling. Women (Div.III): Basketball, Cross Country, Soccer, Softball, Tennis, Track, Volleyball.
Campus Life. Recent and current students agree that the urban location of the campus provides easy access for off-campus recreation. Studying and partying also reported to be frequent activities, outside of class time.

About 60% each of men, women live in coed dormitories; 35% each in annex housing; rest commute. Sexes segregated by floor in freshman dormitory; by apartment in others. Freshmen are given preference in college housing if all students cannot be accommodated. There are no fraternities or sororities. About 30% of resident students leave campus on weekends.
Annual Costs. Tuition and fees, $11,404; room and board, $4,204; estimated $1,450 other, exclusive of travel. About 82% of students receive financial aid; average amount of assistance, $11,700. Assistance is typically divided 55% scholarship and grant, 40% loan, 5% work. College reports 4 scholarships awarded on the basis of academic merit alone, 2 for special talents (for new students); several academic ability scholarships for returning students.

Augusta College

Augusta, Georgia 30910 (404) 737-1405

A state-supported, liberal arts, commuter college, located in a city of 59,900. Most convenient major airport: Atlanta Hartsville.

Founded: 1925
Affiliation: State
UG Enrollment: 1,025 M, 1,605 W (full-time); 552 M, 1,138 W (part-time)
Total Enrollment: 4,652
Cost: < $10K
% Receiving Financial Aid: 32%
Admission: Non-selective
Application Deadline: Aug. 15

Admission. High school graduates with 14 units in college preparatory courses eligible; 78% of applicants accepted. Average freshman SAT scores, according to most recent data available: 410 M, 390 W verbal, 450 M, 415 W mathematical. *Required:* SAT or ACT. *Out-of-state* freshman applicants: college welcomes students from out of state. State does not limit out-of-state enrollment. No special requirements for out-of-state applicants. About 74% of applicants accepted, 61% enroll. *Apply* by August 15. *Transfers* welcome.
Academic Environment. *Degrees:* AB, BS, BBA, BM, BSEd. About 15% of general education requirements for graduation are elective; distribution requirements fairly numerous. About 10% of students entering as freshmen graduate eventually; 69% of freshmen return for sophomore year. *Special programs:* CLEP, independent study, study abroad, undergraduate research. *Calendar:* quarter, summer school.
Undergraduate degrees conferred (351). 32% were in Business and Management, 16% were in Social Sciences, 15% were in Education, 9% were in Communications, 8% were in Psychology, 6% were in Life Sciences, 4% were in Computer and Engineering Related Technology, 4% were in Letters, remainder in 4 other fields.
Graduates Career Data. *Careers in business and industry* pursued by 55–60% of graduates according to most recent data available. Corporations typically hiring largest numbers of graduates include Cameron & Barkly, C & S Bank, Georgia Power.
Faculty. About 61% of faculty hold PhD or equivalent.
Student Body. About 75% of students from Georgia; 97% South; 39 foreign students 1990–91. An estimated 15% of students reported as Black, 3% Asian, 2% other minority, according to most recent data available.
Varsity Sports. Men (Div.I): Baseball, Basketball, Cross Country, Golf, Soccer, Tennis. Women (Div. I): Basketball, Cross Country, Softball, Tennis, Swimming, Volleyball.
Campus Life. About 2% of men 4% of women live in off-campus college-related housing, rest commute. There are 2 fraternities, 3 sororities on campus which about 1% of men, less than 1% of women join; they provide no residence facilities.
Annual Costs. Tuition and fees, $1,593 (out-of-state, $2,973). About 32% of students receive financial aid. College reports some scholarships awarded on the basis of academic merit alone.

Augustana College

Rock Island, Illinois 61201-2296 (309) 794-7000

A church-related liberal arts institution, Augustana is the first of the colleges founded by Scandinavian Lutherans in America. Today the college attracts an able student body of diverse religious, ethnic, social and economic backgrounds, mainly from the Upper Midwest. The wooded 115-acre campus is in the "Quad Cities", an urban area of 380,000 on the Mississippi River, 160 miles west of Chicago. Most convenient major airport: Quad City Airport.

Founded: 1860
Affiliation: Evangelical Lutheran Church of America
Total Enrollment: 857 M, 1,131 W (full-time)
Cost: < $10K
% Receiving Financial Aid: 91%
Admission: Very Selective
Application Deadline: May 1

Admission is very selective. About 88% of applicants accepted, 30% of these actually enroll; 62% of freshmen graduate in top fifth of high school class, 87% in top two-fifths. Average freshman ACT scores: 25 M, 25 W composite; middle fifty percent of students scored between 23–28. *Required:* SAT or ACT; interview recommended for all, required for some. Criteria considered in admissions, in order of importance: high school academic record, standardized test scores, extracurricular activities, recommendations, writing sample, interview; other factors considered: diverse student body, special talents, alumni children. *Entrance programs:* early decision, early admission, deferred admission, midyear admission, advanced placement. *Apply* by May 1; rolling admissions. *Transfers* welcome; 91 enrolled 1993–94.
Academic Environment. Degree offered: bachelors. Pre-professional preparation reported to be "outstanding." For example, "premeds have a 90–94% acceptance rate; virtually 100% of pre-law and business applicants accepted by graduate schools." Students have representation on Board of Trustees and on committees which carry on academic and administrative work of the college. Students reported to be about equally concerned with occupational/professional goals and scholarly/intellectual interests. Student leader comments that college's academic strength lies in its "traditional liberal arts concentrations." Administration reports graduation requirements in addition to completion of major include 5 specific courses (English, foreign language, religion, cross-cultural perspectives, and physical education) and 40% of credits from 5 distribution categories: fine arts, literature and language, humanities, natural sciences, social sciences. *Majors offered* include usual arts and sciences, accounting, business administration, computer science, geography, medical technology, Scandinavian, speech therapy; interdisciplinary studies (Asian, environmental, area studies, urban). New programs include African-American Studies, ethics, Latin American Studies, women's studies. New Augustana Library and extensive computer services are given high marks by students. Average undergraduate class size (not including independent study): 66% of classes under 20, 30% between 20–40, 4% above 40.

About 63% of students entering as freshmen graduate within four years, 68% eventually; 86% of freshmen return for sophomore year. *Special programs:* independent and directed studies, full-quarter and micro (half-term) internships, study abroad (including fall terms, summer programs, exchange programs with foreign universities, and international internship placements), honors, undergraduate research, 3-year degree "possible," some individualized majors, credit by examination, "Foundations" is an interdisciplinary, team-taught program offered to honors students; 3–2 programs in engineering, forestry, landscape architecture, occupational therapy, and environmental management, medical technology and cyto-technology with structured program of clinical experience. *Calendar:* quarter, summer school.
Undergraduate degrees conferred (519). 24% were in Business and Management, 15% were in Life Sciences, 13% were in

Letters, 13% were in Social Sciences, 11% were in Education, 8% were in Psychology, 4% were in Visual and Performing Arts, 3% were in Physical Sciences, 3% were in Foreign Languages, remainder in 5 other fields.

Graduates Career Data. Advanced study pursued by 35% of students; 4% enter medical school; less than 1% enter dental school; 4% enter law school; 2% enter business school. Medical schools typically enrolling largest numbers of graduates include U. of Iowa, Chicago College of Osteopathic Medicine; law schools include Valparaiso, U. of Iowa, DePaul; business schools include Northern Illinois U., Loyola. About 58% of 1992–93 graduates employed. Fields typically employing largest numbers of graduates include accounting, education, retail management, marketing/sales. Career Development Services include extensive personalized internship program; seminars in job search skills, resume writing, networking, and graduate school application process; Career Fairs; computerized job-line; Alumni Mentor Program; testing and assessment; information center. Alumni reported as helpful in both career guidance and job placement.

Faculty. About 83% of the faculty hold doctorate or equivalent. About 65% of undergraduate classes taught by tenured faculty. About 38% of teaching faculty are female; 8% ethnic minorities.

Student Body. About 80% of students from in state; 92% North Central; 3% foreign students. An estimated 60% of students reported as Protestant, 26% Catholic, 12% unaffiliated; 3% as Black, 2% Hispanic, 2% Asian. *Minority group students:* special scholarships and grants, tutoring aid available. Human Relations Committee exerts leadership in dealing with racial issues on campus.

Religious Orientation. Augustana is a church-related institution; 1 course in religion required of all students; attendance at chapel services voluntary. The Campus Ministry staff includes a Lutheran pastor and a Catholic priest, both full-time. Protestant and Catholic services are held weekly.

Varsity Sports. Men (NCAA Div.III): Baseball, Basketball, Cross Country, Football, Golf, Soccer, Swimming, Tennis, Track, Wrestling. Women (NCAA Div.III): Basketball, Cross Country, Soccer, Softball, Swimming, Tennis, Track, Volleyball.

Campus Life. Student Bill of Rights and Student Judiciary assure student input in decisions regarding campus community. High interest reported in both intramural and varsity sports; 80% of freshmen "lettered' in high school. Cars allowed; possession or use of alcoholic beverages on campus forbidden; "it is expected" that there will be no drinking "at Augustana parties where minors are present." Intervisitation hours determined by each residence group within limits of campus schedule; rules governing intervisitation enforced "judiciously." Student leader comments that "We like it here. This is a church-related college which holds strong ties to the members and philosophy of Swedish-American Lutheranism." However, a majority of students come from other faiths or are unaffiliated with any church.

About 20% of men, 22% of women live in traditional dormitories; 43% of men, 44% of women live in coed dormitories; 3% of men, 3% of women live in off-campus college-related housing; rest live in other off-campus housing or commute. Freshmen are given preference in college housing if all students cannot be accommodated. There are 7 fraternities, 7 sororities on campus which about 35% of men, 35% of women join; they provide no residence facilities. About 20% of resident students leave campus on weekends.

Annual Costs. Tuition and fees, $8,808; room and board, $2,994; estimated $1,200 other, exclusive of travel. About 91% of students receive financial aid; average amount of assistance, $9,695. Assistance is typically divided 51% scholarship/grant, 38% loan, 11% work. College reports 730 scholarships awarded on the basis of academic merit alone, 220 for special talents, 959 for need. *Meeting Costs:* college offers prepayment plan, PLUS Loans, monthly payment plans.

Augustana College

Sioux Falls, South Dakota 57197 (605) 336-5516

A church-related, liberal arts, and pre-professional college, located on a 100-acre campus in a city of 100,000. Most convenient major airport: Joe Foss Field (Sioux Falls).

Founded: 1860
Affiliation: Evangelical Lutheran Church of America
Total Enrollment: 485 M, 855 W (full-time); 133 M, 219 W (part-time)
Cost: $10K–$20K
% Receiving Financial Aid: 93%
Admission: Selective (+)
Application Deadline: May 1

Admission is selective (+). About 95% of applicants accepted, 41% of these actually enroll; 46% of freshmen graduate in top fifth of high school class, 74% in top two-fifths. Average freshman ACT scores: 23 M, 22 W composite. *Required:* SAT or ACT. Criteria considered in admissions, in order of importance: high school academic record, standardized test scores, writing sample, recommendations, extracurricular activities. *Entrance programs:* deferred admission, advanced placement. *Apply* by May 1; rolling admissions. *Transfers* welcome; 114 enrolled 1993–94.

Academic Environment. Degrees offered: associates, bachelors, masters. Unusual majors offered include aviation administration, education of the hearing impaired. Average undergraduate class size: 20% under 20, 60% between 20–40, 20% over 40. Administration reports many opportunities for internships and employment in Sioux Falls. Current and recent students cite accessible faculty and challenging academic program as strengths.

About 53% of students entering as freshmen graduate within four years; 75% of freshmen return for sophomore year. *Special programs:* CLEP, independent study, study abroad, honors, undergraduate research, 3-year degree, individualized majors, 4–2 and 3–2 programs in engineering, 3–2 programs in physical therapy and occupational therapy. Adult programs: "selection" of evening courses available to accommodate adult learners. *Calendar:* 4–1–4, summer school.

Undergraduate degrees conferred (361). 22% were in Business and Management, 19% were in Education, 11% were in Social Sciences, 9% were in Health Sciences, 7% were in Letters, 6% were in Communications, 6% were in Life Sciences, 4% were in Psychology, 3% were in Visual and Performing Arts, 3% were in Computer and Engineering Related Technology, 3% were in Physical Sciences, remainder in 6 other fields.

Graduates Career Data. Advanced studies pursued by 20% of graduates; 3% enter medical school; 3% enter law school; 1% each enter business and dental schools. Medical schools typically enrolling largest numbers of graduates include USD, U. of Minnesota; law schools include USD, U. of Nebraska. About 90% of 1992–93 graduates employed. Fields typically hiring largest numbers of graduates include school systems, private business. Career and Placement Office offers workshops and seminars for career planning and interview skills.

Faculty. About 51% of faculty hold PhD or equivalent. About 75% of undergraduate classes taught by tenured faculty. About 31% of teaching faculty are female; 2% ethnic minority.

Student Body. About 72% of students from in state; 91% Midwest, 3% West. An estimated 77% of students reported as Protestant, 17% Catholic, 2% unaffiliated; 1% Black, 2% other minority.

Religious Orientation. Augustana is a church-related institution; 2 courses in religion required of all students. About 76% of students reported affiliated with Evangelical Lutheran Church.

Varsity Sports. Men (Div.II): Baseball, Basketball, Cross Country, Football, Track, Wrestling. Women (Div.II): Basketball, Cross Country, Softball, Track, Volleyball.

Campus Life. Students report that campus is in "a nice neighborhood" and is "close to shopping, the arts, parks, etc." College sponsors "comedians, movies, dances every weekend." Sports are also reported to be popular.

About 59% of men, 41% of women live in coed dormitories; rest live in off-campus housing or commute. Intervisitation in men's and women's dormitory rooms limited. Sexes segregated in coed dormitories by wing or floor. There are local societies on campus; they provide no residence facilities. About 25% of resident students leave campus on weekends.

Annual Costs. Tuition and fees, $10,300; room and board, $3,120; estimated $1,000 other, exclusive of travel. About 93% of students receive financial aid; average amount of assistance, $9,000. Assistance is typically divided 25% scholarship, 20–25% grant, 30% loan, 15% work. College reports some scholarships awarded on the basis of academic merit or special talents alone.

Aurora College

See Aurora University

Aurora University

Aurora, Illinois 60506 (708) 896-1975

Founded by the Advent Christian Church, Aurora is now independent and non-denominational. The 26-acre campus is located in a residential section of a city of 80,000, part of a high-tech corridor, 40 miles southwest of Chicago. Formerly known as Aurora College. Most convenient major airport: Chicago.

Founded: 1893
Affiliation: Independent
UG Enrollment: 404 M, 591 W (full-time); 405 M, 532 W (part-time)
Total Enrollment: 1,932
Cost: < $10K
% Receiving Financial Aid: 90%
Admission: Non-selective
Application Deadline: Rolling

Admission. Graduates of accredited high schools with a minimum 2.0 GPA in 15 units of college preparatory curriculum and minimum combined SAT score of 840 or ACT composite of 20 eligible; 56% of applicants accepted, 41% of these actually enroll; 29% of freshmen graduate in top fifth of high school class, 51% in top two-fifths. Average freshman scores: ACT, 21 M, 21 W composite. *Required:* SAT or ACT, essay. Criteria considered in admissions, in order of importance: standardized test scores, high school academic record, recommendations, extracurricular activities, writing sample. *Apply:* rolling admissions. *Transfers* welcome; 150 enrolled 1993–94.

Academic Environment. Degrees offered: bachelors, masters. Current student enjoys university's 30–1 student-teacher ratio, lecture/discussion format of classes, and trimester system. Graduation requirements include: 4 courses each in humanities, natural science/math, social/behavioral sciences, and 3 courses in communications. *Special programs:* study abroad, fall semester in the American West, extensive internship program, cross registration with Illinois Benedictine, North Central, 3–2 program in engineering. Adult programs: Life Experience/Education Assessment Program. *Calendar:* 3 11-week terms, summer school.

Undergraduate degrees conferred (315). 23% were in Business and Management, 19% were in Health Sciences, 10% were in Education, 8% were in Psychology, 7% were in Public Affairs, 7% were in Computer and Engineering Related Technology, 6% were in Communications, 5% were in Social Sciences, 4% were in Protective Services, 3% were in Business (Administrative Support), remainder in 6 other fields.

Graduates Career Data. *Full-time graduate or professional study* pursued by 11% of students immediately after graduation. *Careers in business and industry* pursued by 85% of graduates.

Faculty. About 56% of faculty hold PhD or equivalent.

Student Body. About 96% of students from Illinois. An estimated 70% of students reported as Protestant, 23% Catholic, 4% unaffiliated, 3% other; 14% Black, 6% Hispanic, 4% Asian.

Religious Orientation. Although Aurora is now non-denominational, "The Christian faith is the foundation on which Aurora College has been built." No specific religious demands made on students, however.

Varsity Sports. Men (Div.III): Baseball, Basketball, Football, Golf, Soccer, Tennis. Women (Div.III): Basketball, Softball, Tennis, Volleyball.

Campus Life. Sporting events and student functions reported as popular; studying and working also important. Current student characterizes campus as "very conservative."

About 13% of men, 11% of women live in traditional dormitories; rest live in off-campus college-related housing or commute. Freshmen given preference in college housing if all students cannot be accommodated. Intervisitation in men's and women's dormitory rooms limited. There are 4 fraternities, 6 sororities on campus which about 20% of men, 20% of women join; they provide no residence facilities. About 40% of resident students leave campus on weekends.

Annual Costs. Tuition and fees, $9,700; room and board, $3,681; estimated $500 other, exclusive of travel. About 90% of students receive financial aid; average amount of assistance, $7,165. Assistance is typically divided 59% scholarship/grant, 37% loan, 4% work. College reports 37 scholarships awarded on the basis of academic merit alone. *Meeting Costs:* college offers monthly payment plan, installment payment plan, term payment plan.

Austin College

Sherman, Texas 75090 (903) 813-2387 or (800) 442-5363

A small, church-related, liberal arts college, located in a community of 30,000, Austin has developed an innovative education program that allows students the option of a fairly structured course of study or greater flexibility in selecting the courses to be pursued. The 65-acre main campus is located 60 miles north of Dallas. Most convenient major airport: Dallas-Fort Worth.

Founded: 1849
Affiliation: Presbyterian
UG Enrollment: 542 M, 576 W (full-time)
Total Enrollment: 1,171
Cost: $10K–$20K
% Receiving Financial Aid: 86%
Admission: Selective (+)
Application Deadline: Rolling

Admission is selective (+). About 84% of applicants accepted, 36% of these actually enroll; 62% of freshmen graduate in top fifth of high school class, 89% in top two-fifths. Average freshman scores: SAT, 495 M, 501 W verbal, 567 M, 545 W mathematical; 50% of freshmen score above 500 on verbal, 15% above 600, 2% above 700; 70% score above 500 on mathematical, 31% above 600, 8% above 700; ACT, 23 M, 26 W composite. *Required:* SAT or ACT, essay; interview strongly recommended. Criteria considered in admissions, in order of importance: high school academic record, standardized test scores, interview; other factors considered: recommendations, extracurricular activities, writing sample, special talents, diverse student body. *Entrance programs:* early admission, midyear admission, deferred admission, advanced placement. About 10% of entering students from private schools. *Apply* by December 1, February 1, or March 15 for decision within 2 weeks. *Transfers* welcome; 59 enrolled 1993–94.

Academic Environment. Degrees offered: bachelors, masters. Educational program emphasizes individualization through a mentor/student relationship. Students encouraged to take major responsibility in working out their education. Two degree options offered: Basic and Special. A student choosing the Basic program must take four foundation courses and complete one course in each of eight designated sets that comprise the exploration dimension. Students must also take 7–11 courses in a major. Under the Special option emphasis is on flexibility and there are no required courses. Four major core courses taken by most students: (a) Communication/Inquiry, a freshman seminar in which students explore a contemporary topic, and (b) a 3-course interdisciplinary Heritage of Western Culture sequence. Communication/Inquiry includes a 4-day orientation program for freshmen before the start of classes, monitors entering students' skills needed for academic success, and provides a faculty mentor for each student. Average undergraduate class size: 58% under 20, 37% between 20–40, 5% over 40. Recent student says "The primary focus of the faculty here is teaching. [they] are very high caliber, yet very accessible and approachable."

About 70% of students entering as freshmen graduate eventually; 81% of freshmen return for sophomore year. *Special programs:* CLEP, independent study, study abroad, honors, undergraduate research, 3-year degree, January Term includes courses on- and off-campus emphasizing experiential learning, Washington Semester, 5-year BA/MA teacher education program, 3–2 engineering. *Calendar:* 4–1–4, summer school.

Undergraduate degrees conferred (312). 24% were in Social Sciences, 16% were in Psychology, 14% were in Business and Management, 10% were in Life Sciences, 8% were in Letters, 7% were in Communications, 4% were in Foreign Languages, 4% were in Visual and Performing Arts, 4% were in Philosophy and Religion, 3% were in Physical Sciences, 3% were in Education, remainder in 2 other fields.

Graduates Career Data. Advanced studies pursued by 42% of graduates; 8% enter teachers program; 6% enter medical school; 3% enter business school; 2% enter law school. Graduate programs typically enrolling largest numbers of graduates include Austin College Teachers Program; medical schools include U. of Texas at San Antonio, Austin, Galveston. About 42% of 1992–93 graduates employed. Employers typically hiring largest numbers of graduates include Electronic Data Systems, Texas Instruments, Farmers Insurance. Career Development Program provides career testing, computerized career information, individual counseling, and various workshops. College actively solicits alumni help in both career guidance and job placement; alumni network also provides internships, summer jobs.

Faculty. About 98% of faculty hold PhD or equivalent. About 61% of undergraduate classes taught by tenured faculty. About 19% of teaching faculty are female; 5% minority.

Student Body. About 91% of students from Texas; 97% from South, 1% foreign. An estimated 57% of students reported as Protestant, 15% Catholic, 19% unaffiliated, 8% other; 5% as Black, 9% Hispanic, 5% Asian, 3% other minority. *Minority group students:* peer counseling provided.

Religious Orientation. Austin is a church-related institution with a nonsectarian curriculum; several voluntary worship services on campus each week; students are encouraged "to explore their religious values and participate in religious activities on and off campus." About 10% of students reported affiliated with Presbyterian Church.

Varsity Sports. Men (TIAA, Div.II): Baseball, Basketball, Football, Golf, Soccer, Swimming (AEW), Tennis, Track. Women (TIAA Div. II): Basketball, Swimming (AEW), Tennis, Track, Volleyball.

Campus Life. Recent student found college to be "a very close-knit environment. Great people, great education, great fun." He also cited the "incredible variety and diversity of extracurricular activities; from community service to sports to arts." Through membership on joint student/faculty committees students have voice in determining campus social regulations. Intervisitation determined by each residence hall within college parameters (10 am to midnight, Sunday-Thursday; to 2 am, Friday, Saturday). Dallas, 60 miles away, offers attractions of a major metropolitan center. Lake Campus, 20 miles north on Lake Texoma, provides recreational facilities. Motor vehicles permitted. Drinking permitted only in dormitory rooms or College "PUB" by those of legal age. Gambling forbidden. College expects students to avoid "the use of obscenity, indecent exposure, and similar behavior."

About 43% of men, 41% of women live in traditional dormitories; 22% of men, 26% of women in coed dormitories; rest live in off-campus housing or commute. Freshmen given preference in college housing if all students cannot be accommodated. There are 9 fraternities, 6 sororities on campus which about 19% of men, 21% of women join; they provide no residence facilities. About 30% of resident students leave campus on weekends.

Annual Costs. Tuition and fees, $10,865; room and board, $4,134; estimated $1,800 other, exclusive of travel. About 86% of students receive financial aid; average amount of assistance, $8,874. Assistance is typically divided 56% scholarship/grant, 37% loan, 7% work. College reports 430 scholarships awarded on the basis of academic merit alone. *Meeting Costs:* college offers family contribution loans plus college endowment.

Austin Peay State University

Clarksville, Tennessee 37043 (615) 648-7661

A state-supported institution, located in a city of 50,000, 47 miles northwest of Nashville. Most convenient major airport: Nashville International.

Founded: 1927
Affiliation: State
UG Enrollment: 1,573 M, 2,164 W (full-time); 838 M, 605 W (part-time)
Total Enrollment: 6,942
Cost: < $10K
% Receiving Financial Aid: 59%
Admission: Non-selective
Application Deadline: April 18

Admission. High school graduates with a GPA of 2.75 or ACT composite of 16 eligible, others admitted under "controlled admission policy"; 87% of applicants accepted, 75% of these actually enroll. *Required:* ACT. *Out-of-state* freshman applicants: university welcomes students from out of state; no special requirements for out-of-state applicants. *Apply* by April 18. *Transfers* welcome.

Academic Environment. *Degrees:* AB, BS, BFA, BSEd. About 30–50% of general education requirements for graduation are elective; distribution requirements fairly numerous. Programs recently added include engineering technology major; industrial technology major recently dropped. About 32% of students entering as freshmen graduate eventually; 50% of freshmen return for sophomore year. *Calendar:* quarter, summer school.

Undergraduate degrees conferred (568). 25% were in Education, 21% were in Business and Management, 10% were in Health Sciences, 7% were in Visual and Performing Arts, 6% were in Social Sciences, 6% were in Psychology, 5% were in Architecture and Environmental Design, 4% were in Letters, remainder in 10 other fields.

Varsity Sports. Men (Div.IA): Baseball, Basketball, Cross Country, Football (IAA), Golf, Tennis. Women (Div.IA): Basketball, Cross Country, Golf, Softball, Tennis, Volleyball.

Student Body. University does not seek a national student body; 89% of students from Texas. An estimated 84% of students reported as Protestant, 9% Catholic, 2% Jewish, 5% other; 15% Black, 3% Hispanic, 2% other minority, according to most recent data available.

Campus Life. About 11% of men, 11% of women live in traditional dormitories; 10% men, 11% women in coed dormitories; rest commute. Intervisitation in dormitory rooms limited. There are 10 fraternities, 7 sororities on campus which about 10% of men, 6% of women join.

Annual Costs. Tuition and fees, $1,800 (out-of-state, $5,582); room and board, $2,860. About 59% of students receive financial aid; assistance is typically divided 49% scholarship, 39% loan, 12% work. University reports some scholarships awarded on the basis of academic merit alone. *Meeting Costs:* university offers PLUS.

Averett College

Danville, Virginia 24541 (804) 791-5600 or (800) AVE-RETT

A church-related college, Averett is located in the residential area of a community of 60,000. Most convenient major airports: Danville; Greensboro (NC).

Founded: 1854
Affiliation: Southern Baptist
UG Enrollment: 334 M, 443 W (full-time); 294 M, 294 W (part-time)
Total Enrollment: 2,024
Cost: < $10K
% Receiving Financial Aid: 87%
Admission: Non-selective
Application Deadline: Aug. 1

Admission. High school graduates with 2.0 GPA, and rank in 60th percentile of class eligible; 88% of applicants accepted, 40% of these actually enroll; 11% of freshmen graduate in top fifth of high school class, 45% in top two-fifths. Average freshman SAT scores: 419 M, 427 W verbal, 493 M, 452 W mathematical. *Required:* SAT. Criteria considered in admissions, in order of importance: high school academic record, standardized test scores, extracurricular activities, leadership record, special talents, personal qualities, recommendations. *Entrance programs:* early admission, midyear admission, deferred admission, advanced placement. *Apply* by August 1. *Transfers* welcome; 115 enrolled 1993–94.

Academic Environment. Degrees offered: associates, bachelors, masters. College operates on an early semester with May term calendar which allows students attending all 3 terms to graduate in 3 years. Requirements for graduation include 9 hours English, 6 hours fine arts, 15 hours history and social science, 6 hours religion and philosophy, and 3 hours IDS. Unusual majors include equestrian studies, aviation studies. About 33% of entering students graduate within four years; 75% of freshmen return for sophomore year. Average undergraduate class size: 98% under 20. *Special programs:* study abroad, internships and cooperative work/study programs. Adult programs: AACE, Accelerated degree completion programs offered in business; IDEAL, individualized learning contracts. *Calendar:* 4–4–1, summer school.

Undergraduate degrees conferred (255). 47% were in Business and Management, 15% were in Education, 5% were in Social Sciences, 4% were in Psychology, 4% were in Life Sciences, 3% were in Communications, 3% were in Mathematics, remainder in 13 other fields.

Graduates Career Data. Full-time advanced studies pursued by 11% of students immediately after graduation. *Careers in business and industry* pursued by 85% of graduates, according to most recent data available. Career Development Services include aptitude testing,

on-campus recruitment, counseling, placement service, resume/interview workshops, and library resources.
Faculty. About 77% of faculty hold PhD or equivalent. About 32% of teaching faculty are female; 4% ethnic minority.
Student Body. About 76% of students from in state; 82% South, 11% Middle Atlantic, 2% New England, 3% foreign. An estimated 58% of students reported as Protestant, 13% Catholic, 29% other; 12% as Black, 4% Asian, 4% other minority.
Religious Orientation. Averett is a church-related institution; 6 hours of religion or philosophy required of all students. About 38% of students reported affiliated with the Baptist Church.
Varsity Sports. Men (Div.III): Basketball, Cross Country, Golf, Horsemanship (IHSA), Soccer, Tennis. Women (Div.III): Basketball, Cross Country, Horsemanship (IHSA), Soccer, Softball, Tennis, Volleyball.
Campus Life. About 44% of students live in coed dormitories; rest commute. Freshmen given preference in college housing if all students cannot be accommodated. Intervisitation in men's and women's dormitory rooms limited. There are 2 fraternities, 1 sorority, which about 15% men, 12% women join; they provide no residence facilities. About 50% of resident students leave campus on weekends.
Annual Costs. Tuition and fees, $9,710; room and board, $3,900. About 87% of students receive financial aid; average amount of assistance, $8,000. Assistance is typically divided 68% scholarship/grant, 30% loan, 13% work. College reports scholarships awarded on the basis of academic merit alone, as well as need. *Meeting Costs:* college offers non-need based loans, 10-month payment plan.

Avila College

Kansas City, Missouri 64145-1698 (816) 942-8400

A church-related college, conducted by the Sisters of St. Joseph of Carondelet, located in a city of 507,100. Most convenient major airport: Kansas City International.

Founded: 1916
Affiliation: Roman Catholic
UG Enrollment: 179 M, 472 W (full-time); 123 M, 367 W (part-time)
Total Enrollment: 1,389
Cost: < $10K
% Receiving Financial Aid: 85%
Admission: Non-selective
Application Deadline: Rolling

Admission. Graduates of accredited high schools with 16 units (12 in academic subjects) who rank in top half of class eligible; 78% of applicants accepted, 28% of these actually enroll; 34% of freshmen graduate in top fifth of high school class, 74% in top two-fifths. Average freshman scores: SAT, 412 M, 472 W verbal, 471 M, 482 W mathematical; ACT, 21 composite. *Required:* ACT. Criteria considered in admissions, in order of importance: high school academic record, standardized test scores, writing sample, recommendations, extracurricular activities. About 15% of entering students from parochial schools. *Apply:* rolling admissions. *Transfers* welcome; 140 enrolled 1993–94.
Academic Environment. Degrees offered: bachelors, masters. Graduation requirements include 3 hours each in writing, communication, mathematics, literature, Western Civilization, and art, theatre, or music, 9 hours/2 areas in Philosophy and Theology, 6 hours in foreign language, 7 hours/2 areas in natural science, including lab, 9 hours/3 areas in economics, political science, psychology, and sociology. Unusual majors include graphic design, radiology technology, social work. About 34% of students entering as freshmen graduate within four years, 49% eventually; 62% of freshmen return for sophomore year. Average undergraduate class size: 82% under 20, 18% 20–40. *Special programs:* CLEP, study abroad, Weekend College, Elder Hostel, internship /cooperative work-study, student exchange, Washington Center, enrichment programs. Adult programs: evening and Saturday classes. *Calendar:* semester, summer school.
Undergraduate degrees conferred (186). 27% were in Business and Management, 9% were in Visual and Performing Arts, 9% were in Psychology, 8% were in Health Sciences, 8% were in Education, 7% were in Marketing and Distribution, 6% were in Social Sciences, 5% were in Letters, 5% were in Public Affairs, 4% were in Communications, 3% were in Liberal/General Studies, 3% were in Allied Health, 3% were in Business (Administrative Support), remainder in 5 other fields.
Graduates Career Data. Advanced studies pursued by 18% of graduates. About 90% of 1992–93 graduates employed by July of 1993. Fields typically hiring largest numbers of graduates include: data processing/information systems, sales/accounting, nursing, education. Career Development Services include job postings and search strategies, interview skills, computerized resume writing, graduate school searches and GRE/GMAT preparation.
Faculty. About 69% of faculty hold PhD or equivalent. About 68% of undergraduate classes taught by continuous appointment faculty. About 63% of teaching faculty are female; 5% ethnic minority.
Student Body. About 68% of students come from within the state; 95% Midwest, 4% foreign. An estimated 37% of students reported as Catholic, 63% as other; 9% as Black, 2% Hispanic, 5% other minority. Average age of undergraduate student: 24.
Religious Orientation. Avila is a church-related institution; no courses in religion required of students. About 37% of students reported affiliated with Catholic Church.
Varsity Sports. Men (NAIA): Baseball, Basketball, Soccer. Women (NAIA): Basketball, Soccer, Softball, Volleyball.
Campus Life. Current student finds her fellow students to be non-traditional and diverse. She notes that the small size of the school allows her to be involved "in many activities at the same time."

About 8% of men, 14% of women live in coed dormitories; rest commute. Freshmen given preference in college housing if all students cannot be accommodated. Intervisitation in men's and women's dormitory rooms limited. There are no fraternities or sororities. About 33% of resident students leave campus on weekends.
Annual Costs. Tuition and fees, $8,530; room and board, $3,600; estimated $1,600 other, exclusive of travel. About 85% of students receive financial aid; average amount of assistance, $7,540. Assistance is typically divided 25% scholarship, 25% grant, 40% loan, 10% work. College reports 125 scholarships awarded on the basis of academic merit alone, 212 for special talents, 350 for need. *Meeting Costs:* college offers Guaranteed Tuition Plan (freezes tuition at first year rate).

Azusa Pacific University

Azusa, California 91702 (818) 812-3016

A private, interdenominational liberal arts college, located in the San Gabriel Valley communities of Azusa and Glendora, 30 miles east of Los Angeles. Most convenient major airport: Ontario International.

Founded: 1899
Affiliation: Independent
UG Enrollment: 639 M, 805 W (full-time)
Total Enrollment: 3,869
Cost: $10K–$20K
% Receiving Financial Aid: 80%
Admission: Non-selective
Application Deadline: Rolling

Admission. High school graduates eligible; 88% of applicants accepted, 51% of these actually enroll. *Required:* SAT, minimum HS GPA, essay, 1 personal and 1 academic reference. Criteria considered in admissions, in order of importance: writing sample, high school academic record, recommendations, standardized test scores, extracurricular activities. *Apply:* rolling admissions. *Transfers* welcome.
Academic Environment. Degrees offered: associates, bachelors, masters. Graduation requirements include 3 units community ministry, 15 Bible, 2 health, 9 communication, 3 fine arts, 4 physical education, 24 religion and philosophy, 9–10 social science, 11–13 science/math. One recent student praises "small Christian environment" and small class size (18:1 faculty-student ratio). About 38% of students entering as freshmen graduate within four years; 73% of freshmen return for sophomore year. *Special programs:* May Term, study abroad, 2–2 and 3–2 engineering. Adult programs: degree completion program for business and management. *Calendar:* 4–4–1, summer school.
Undergraduate degrees conferred (304). 18% were in Business and Management, 10% were in Psychology, 9% were in Visual and Performing Arts, 9% were in Social Sciences, 9% were in Liberal/General Studies, 9% were in Communications, 8% were in Health Sciences, 6% were in Public Affairs, 5% were in Philosophy

and Religion, 4% were in Education, 4% were in Letters, remainder in 7 other fields.

Graduates Career Data. University Career Center offers individual and group seminars on resume writing, interviewing, job search, and sponsors Career Days.

Faculty. About 48% of faculty hold PhD or equivalent. About 39% of teaching faculty are female.

Student Body. About 79% of students from in state; almost all West/Northwest. An estimated 63% of students reported as Protestant, 6% Catholic, 22% unaffiliated, 9% other; 3% as Black, 5% Hispanic, 16% Asian, 1% Native American, according to most recent data available. Average age of undergraduate student: 22.

Religious Orientation. University is an independent institution seeking "to train its students for Christian life and service"; 24 units of religion and philosophy, 3 units of community ministry required of all students.

Varsity Sports. Men (NAIA): Baseball, Basketball, Cross Country, Football, Soccer, Tennis, Track. Women (NAIA): Basketball, Cross Country, Soccer, Softball, Tennis, Track, Volleyball.

Campus Life. Recent students cite sports(varsity and intramural), as well as "hanging out" and "random fun things" as favorite campus activities. Parking is mentioned as a problem.

About 62% of students live in traditional dormitories; rest live in off-campus housing or commute. Intervisitation in dormitory rooms during limited, posted hours (at the residential director's discretion). There are no fraternities or sororities on campus. About 50% of resident students leave campus on weekends.

Annual Costs. Tuition and fees, $11,084; room and board, $3,950. About 80% of students receive financial aid; average amount of assistance: $7,000. Assistance is typically divided 25% scholarship, 50% loan, 25% work. University reports some scholarships awarded on the basis of academic merit alone. *Meeting Costs:* university offers PLUS Loans.

Babson College

Wellesley, Massachusetts 02157 **(617) 239-5522 or (800) 488-3696**

An independent, highly respected business college, with a strong MBA program, located in Wellesley, a Boston suburb of 29,000. Most convenient major airport: Logan (Boston).

Founded: 1919
Affiliation: Independent
UG Enrollment: 1,065 M, 615 W (full-time)
Total Enrollment: 3,235
Cost: $10K–$20K
% Receiving Financial Aid: 49%
Admission: Selective (+)
Application Deadline: February 1

Admission is selective (+). About 57% of applicants accepted, 36% of these actually enroll; 58% of freshmen graduate in top fifth of high school class, 84% in top two-fifths. Range of freshman SAT scores: middle 50% score between 430–530 on verbal, 520–630 on mathematical. *Required:* SAT or ACT, 2 ACH (for course placement only), 2 essays; interview recommended. Criteria considered in admissions, in order of importance: high school academic record, standardized test scores, extracurricular activities, writing sample, recommendations; other factors considered: special talents, alumni children, diverse student body. *Entrance programs:* early decision, early admission, advanced placement. About 36% of entering students from private schools, 11% from parochial schools. *Apply* by February 1. *Transfers* welcome; 65 enrolled 1993–94.

Academic Environment. Degrees offered: bachelors, masters. Although business and management-related course work is central to Babson's undergraduate experience, there is a commitment to a strong liberal arts foundation as evidenced by the graduation requirements which include a management core of 13 business-related courses, a liberal arts core of 13 courses and concentrations, and 6 electives in either management or liberal arts. The Cluster Program, required of all first-year students, encourages interdisciplinary study. A new pilot program allows first-year students working in teams to actually launch and manage a small business and use the profits to support a community service project. Average undergraduate class size: 29; 32% of classes under 20, 47% between 20–40, 21% over 40 (maximum class size: 42). About 84% of entering students graduate within four years, 85% eventually; 94% of freshmen return for sophomore year. *Special programs:* January term, Management Consulting Field Experience internships (Career Services office lists over 700 internship opportunities), study abroad, cross-registration with Brandeis, Regis, Pine Manor, Wellesley. *Calendar:* semester, optional January term, summer term.

Undergraduate degrees conferred (515). 85% were in Business and Management, 14% were in Communications, remainder in Area and Ethnic Studies.

Graduates Career Data. Advanced studies pursued by 4% graduates. Fields typically hiring largest numbers of graduates include public accounting firms, retail, commercial banking, investment banking. Career Development Services include career/interest assessment, workshops/seminars, counseling, career resource library, on-campus recruitment, corporate database, internships, alumni directories.

Faculty. About 93% of faculty hold PhD or equivalent. About 41% of undergraduate classes taught by tenured faculty. About 25% of teaching faculty are female; 2% Black, 3% Hispanic, 4% other (international, etc.).

Student Body. About 41% of students from within state; 55% New England, 21% international. An estimated 2% of students reported as Black, 3% Hispanic, 6% Asian, 28% other minority (including non-resident alien and international students).

Varsity Sports. Men (Div.III): Baseball, Basketball, Cross Country, Diving, Golf, Hockey, Lacrosse, Skiing, Soccer, Swimming, Tennis. Women (Div.III): Basketball, Cross Country, Diving, Field Hockey, Lacrosse, Skiing, Soccer, Softball, Swimming, Tennis, Volleyball.

Campus Life. Current student observes that student time outside of class is spent "studying during the week, partying on the weekend." He also laments the need for a car to go shopping. About 8% of men live in traditional residence halls; 72% of men, all women live in coed residence halls. There are 4 fraternities, 2 sororities, which about 10% of men, 8% of women join; they provide no residence facilities. About 25% of resident students leave campus on weekends.

Annual Costs. Tuition and fees, $16,445; room and board, $6,715; estimated $1,450 other, exclusive of travel. About 49% of students receive financial aid; average amount of assistance, $14,427. Assistance is typically divided 2% scholarship, 60% grant, 28% loan, 10% work. College reports 20 scholarships awarded on the basis of academic merit alone. *Meeting Costs:* college offers payment plans, parent loan programs.

Baker University

Baldwin City, Kansas 66006 **(800) 873-4282**

A small, church-related institution located in a community of 3,000, 45 miles southwest of Kansas City. Most convenient major airport: Kansas City International.

Founded: 1858
Affiliation: United Methodist
Total Enrollment: 1,558 M, W (full-time)
Cost: < $10K
% Receiving Financial Aid: 91%
Admission: Non-selective
Application Deadline: Rolling

Admission. Graduates of accredited high schools with C average and rank in top half of high school class eligible; 77% of applicants accepted, 54% of these actually enroll; 41% of freshmen graduate in top quarter of high school class, 71% in top half. *Required:* SAT or ACT; interview suggested. *Apply:* rolling admissions. *Transfers* welcome.

Academic Environment. *Degrees:* AB, BS, BMEd, BBA. Interdisciplinary core curriculum (4 courses) thematically organized, centered on six important contexts. About 50% of general education requirements for graduation are elective; distribution requirements fairly numerous. Unusual majors offered include international business. About 65% of entering students graduate eventually; 24% of freshmen do not return for sophomore year. *Special programs:* CLEP, independent study, study abroad, honors, undergraduate research, individualized majors, 3–2 engineering programs. *Calendar:* 4–1–4, summer school.

Undergraduate degrees conferred (208). 46% were in Business and Management, 15% were in Education, 8% were in Psychology, 8% were in Social Sciences, 7% were in Communications, 5% were in Life Sciences, 3% were in Letters, remainder in 7 other fields.

Graduates Career Data. According to most recent data available, full-time graduate or professional study pursued by 20% of students immediately after graduation. *Careers in business and industry* pursued by 69% of graduates.
Varsity Sports. Men (NAIA, Div. II): Baseball, Basketball, Cross Country, Football, Golf, Soccer, Tennis, Track. Women (NAIA, Div.II): Basketball, Cross Country, Softball, Tennis, Track, Volleyball.
Student Body. About 66% of students from in state. An estimated 57% of students reported as Protestant, 22% as Catholic, 19% unaffiliated, 10% other; 10% as minorities, according to most recent data available.
Religious Orientation. Baker is a church-related institution; however, no courses in religion required.
Campus Life. About 41% of men, 46% of women live in traditional dormitories and upper classmen coed dormitories; 18% of men, 15% of women live in off-campus housing or commute. Freshmen are given preference in college housing if all students cannot be accommodated. Intervisitation in men's and women's dormitory rooms limited. There are 4 fraternities, 4 sororities on campus which about 57% of men, 56% of women join; 31% of men, 39% of women live in fraternities and sororities.
Annual Costs. Tuition and fees, $8,234; room and board, $4,050. About 91% of students receive financial aid. University reports some scholarships awarded on the basis of academic merit alone. *Meeting Costs:* 10 Month Tuition Plan.

Baker College of Flint

Flint, Michigan 48507

An independent college enrolling over 10,000 students on seven campuses across the state: Flint, Muskegon, Owosso, Port Huron, Cadillac, Mount Clemens, and Auburn Hills. While not all programs are offered at each campus, the college as a whole offers more than sixty programs from diplomas and certificates to associates and bachelor degrees in career- and employment-oriented programs. Bachelor level programs available on Flint campus include business administration, aviation management, graphic communication, health information management, interior design, industrial management, occupational therapy.

Founded: 1911 **Affiliation:** Independent

Baldwin-Wallace College

Berea, Ohio 44017 (216) 826-2222

A church-related, liberal arts college, located on a 52-acre campus in a suburban community of 22,400, 14 miles southwest of Cleveland. Most convenient major airport: Cleveland Hopkins.

Founded: 1845
Affiliation: United Methodist
UG Enrollment: 1,042 M, 1,541 W (full-time); 530 M, 1,025 W (part-time)
Total Enrollment: 3,637
Cost: $10K–$20K
% Receiving Financial Aid: 98%
Admission: Non-selective
Application Deadline: July 1

Admission. High school graduates with GPA of 3.0, SAT of 950, or ACT of 21 composite eligible. About 75% of applicants accepted, 47% of these actually enroll; 46% of freshmen graduate in top fifth of high school class, 78% in top two-fifths. Freshman scores, according to most recent data available: SAT, middle 50% range 390–490 M, 400–520 W verbal, 440–570 M, 430–560 W mathematical; ACT, middle 50% range 18–24 M, 19–25 W composite. *Required:* SAT or ACT; interview recommended. *Non-academic factors* considered in admissions: special talents, diverse student body, teacher recommendations, student activities. *Entrance programs:* advanced placement. About 2% of entering students from private schools, 13% from parochial schools. *Apply:* rolling admissions; recommended by July 1. *Transfers* welcome.
Academic Environment. Core curriculum stipulates that 68 credit hours (of the 186 required for graduation) must be distributed among humanities, social sciences, math/statistics/computers, physical education, and international studies. Seniors take comprehensive exams or equivalent. *Degrees:* AB, BS, BSEd, BM, BMEd. Unusual, new, or notable majors include: music therapy, criminal justice, international studies. About 70% of entering freshmen graduate eventually, 205% of freshmen do not return for sophomore year. *Special programs:* CLEP, humanities year, independent study, study abroad, honors, individualized majors, 3–2 engineering, master degree program in biology with Case Western Reserve, combined program with Duke School of Forestry, United Nations Semester, Washington Semester. Adult programs: Baldwin-Wallace enrolls approximately 1,500 undergraduate adult students in evening, weekend and certificate programs. *Calendar:* quarter, summer school.
Undergraduate degrees conferred (927). 49% were in Business and Management, 13% were in Education, 6% were in Social Sciences, 6% were in Communications, 6% were in Psychology, 4% were in Visual and Performing Arts, 4% were in Letters, remainder in 11 other fields.
Faculty. About 75% of faculty hold PhD or equivalent.
Graduates Career Data. According to most recent data available, full-time graduate or professional study pursued immediately after graduation by 30% of students; 1% enter medical school; 1% enter law school; 3% enter business school. Medical and dental schools typically enrolling largest numbers of graduates include Case Western Reserve, Ohio State, Ohio U.; law schools include Cleveland Marshall, Ohio State; business schools include Baldwin-Wallace, Cleveland State, Case Western Reserve. *Careers in business and industry* pursued by 63% of graduates. Corporations typically employing largest numbers of graduates include Ernst & Young, Price Waterhouse, Ameritrust, National City Bank. *Career Counseling Program* includes interview and resume workshops, career day, placement orientation; award winning career appraisal center, on-campus interviewing. Alumni participate actively in both career guidance and job placement.
Faculty. About 75% of faculty hold PhD or equivalent.
Student Body. College seeks a national student body; 85% of students from in state; 12% Middle Atlantic, 1% each New England, South, West. An estimated 30% of students reported as Protestant, 47% Catholic, 23% other or unaffiliated; 5% as Black, 1% other minority, according to most recent data available. *Minority group students:* Cleveland Scholarship Program; Experimental Learning Center; Black Culture adjacent to campus.
Religious Orientation. Baldwin-Wallace is a church-related institution, but makes no religious demands on students. Places of worship available on campus for Protestants, in immediate community for 3 major faiths.
Varsity Sports. Men (Div.III): Baseball, Basketball, Cross Country, Football, Golf, Soccer, Swimming, Tennis, Track, Wrestling. Women (Div. III): Basketball, Cross Country, Soccer, Softball, Swimming, Tennis, Track, Volleyball.
Campus Life. Administration source describes campus as "an informal, friendly place." She adds that B-W is a "sleepy liberal arts college by day, bustling part-time undergraduate and graduate program by night—one that provides diverse opportunities to a diverse student body." Regulations governing campus life relatively free; all students have keys to their residence halls; intervisitation noon to midnight Sunday-Thursday, noon to 2 am Friday and Saturday.

About 9% of women live in traditional dormitories, 15% of men, 15% of women live in coed dormitories, 13% of men, 22% of women commute. There are 6 fraternities, 8 sororities on campus; 28% of men, 21% of women join; 14% of men, 12% of women live in fraternities and sororities. About 30% of students leave campus on weekends.
Annual Costs. Tuition and fees, $10,980; room and board, $4,230. About 98% of students receive financial aid; assistance is typically divided 61% grant/scholarship, 32% loan, 7% work. College reports some scholarships awarded on the basis of academic merit alone.

Ball State University

Muncie, Indiana 47306 (317) 285-8300 (out-of-state) 1-800-482-4BSU (in state)

A state-supported university, located in a city of 78,000, 56 miles northeast of Indianapolis. Campus facilities include a planetarium and an art museum. Most convenient major airport: Indianapolis.

Founded: 1918
Affiliation: State
UG Enrollment: 7,496 M, 8,652 W (full-time); 924 M, 1,283 W (part-time)
Total Enrollment: 20,717
Cost: < $10K
% Receiving Financial Aid: 70%
Admission: Non-selective
Application Deadline: March 1

Admission. Graduates of accredited high schools who rank in top half of class, with minimum combined SAT of 800 or 19 ACT composite eligible; 81% of applicants accepted, 41% of these actually enroll; 46% of freshmen graduate in top fifth of high school class, 60% in top two-fifths. Average freshman scores: SAT, 422 M, 419 W verbal; 494 M, 454 W mathematical; ACT, 20.8 M, 21.1 W composite. Criteria considered in admissions, in order of importance: high school academic record, strength of high school curriculum, standardized test scores, recommendations. *Required:* SAT or ACT. *Out-of-state* freshman applicants: university actively seeks out-of-state students. State does not limit out-of-state enrollment. No special requirements for out-of-state students. *Entrance programs:* deferred admission. *Apply* by March 1; rolling admissions. *Transfers* welcome; 779 enrolled in 1993–94.

Academic Environment. *Degrees:* associates, bachelors, masters, doctoral. Core requirements include five core courses and an additional 26 hours of distribution requirements from different areas. Special Programs: study abroad, BS-MBA program, 3–2 program in engineering, internship/cooperative work-study programs. About 50% of students entering as freshmen graduate within six years; 77% of freshmen return for sophomore year. Average undergraduate class size: 31. *Calendar:* semester, summer school.

Undergraduate degrees conferred (2,848). 21% were in Business and Management, 17% were in Education, 10% were in Communications, 8% were in Social Sciences, 6% were in Health Sciences, 6% were in Architecture and Environmental Design, 4% were in Visual and Performing Arts, 4% were in Protective Services, 3% were in Letters, 3% were in Psychology, 3% were in Home Economics, remainder in 14 other fields. *Doctoral degrees:* Education 64, Letters 6, Fine and Applied Arts 8, Social Sciences 6, Biological Sciences 2.

Graduates Career Data. Advanced studies pursued by 13% of graduates. About 69% of 1991–92 graduates employed. Fields typically hiring largest number of graduates include education, wholesale/retail trade, finance, insurance, real estate, health care. Career Development Service coordinates all campus employment opportunities, provides assistance with job search including resume preparation.

Faculty. About 66% of faculty hold PhD or equivalent. About 98% of undergraduate classes taught by tenured faculty. About 38% of teaching faculty are female.

Student Body. University seeks a national student body; about 89% of students from in state; 397 foreign students 1993–94. An estimated 5% of students reported as Black, 6% other minority.

Varsity Sports. Men (Div.IA): Baseball, Basketball, Cross Country, Diving, Football, Golf, Swimming, Tennis, Track, Volleyball. Women (Div.IA): Basketball, Cross Country, Diving, Field Hockey, Gymnastics, Softball, Swimming.

Campus Life. Ball State offers Wellness Residence Halls giving students the opportunity to live in a healthy environment conducive to making positive life-style choices. These halls feature a tobacco-free environment, fitness center, wellness and nutrition programming and education. About 23% of men, 30% of women live in traditional dormitories, 9% of men, 7% of women in coed dormitories; 65% of men, 63% of women live in off-campus housing; rest commute. Freshmen given preference in college housing if all students cannot be accommodated. Intervisitation in men's and women's dormitory rooms limited. Sexes segregated in coed dormitories by floor. There are 20 fraternities, 18 sororities on campus; which about 13% of men, 13% of women join; 13% of men live in fraternities; sororities provide no residential facilities.

Annual Costs. Tuition and fees, $2,656 (out-of-state, $6,584); room and board, $3,376; estimated $1,000 other, exclusive of travel. About 70% of students receive financial aid; average amount of assistance, $3,500. Assistance is typically divided 50% scholarship, 25% loan, 25% work, according to most recent data available. University reports scholarships available for academic merit alone, athletics, and several departmental scholarships.

Baltimore Hebrew College

Baltimore, Maryland 21215

A private institution offering graduate and undergraduate programs in Judaica and Hebraica with concentrations in Hebrew literature, Bible, Rabbinic literature, Jewish history, philosophy, and political science. Specializing in Jewish Studies; nontheological.

Founded: 1919
Affiliation: Independent

Baptist Bible Institute

Graceville, Florida 32440

A small theological college founded by the Florida Baptist Convention, the Institute offers programs in theology, religious education and religious music.

Founded: 1943
Affiliation: Florida Baptist Convention

Baptist Bible College and Seminary of Pennsylvania

Clarks Summit, Pennsylvania 18411

A small religious institution devoted to preparing students for careers in churches, Christian schools, and agencies.

Affiliation: Baptist

Barat College

Lake Forest, Illinois 60045 **(312) 234-3000**

Founded as a liberal arts college for women, affiliated with the Religious of the Sacred Heart, Barat is now governed by a lay board of trustees and recently began admitting male students. The 30-acre campus is located in a community of 15,600, 28 miles north of Chicago. Most convenient major airport: Chicago O'Hare.

Founded: 1858
Affiliation: Independent
Total Enrollment: 90 M, 305 W (full-time); 46 M, 264 W (part-time)
Cost: < $10K
% Receiving Financial Aid: 70%
Admission: Non-selective
Application Deadline: Rolling

Admission. High school graduates eligible; 70% of applicants accepted, 68% of these actually enroll; 21% of freshmen graduate in top fifth of high school class, 40% in top two-fifths. *Required:* SAT or ACT; interview recommended. Non-academic factor considered in admissions: special talents. *Entrance programs:* midyear admission, deferred admission, advanced placement. About 8% of entering students from private schools, 14% from parochial schools. *Apply:* rolling admissions. *Transfers* welcome.

Academic Environment. College offers individually planned programs, interdisciplinary studies. Students encouraged to design individualized majors. Some distribution requirements. *Degrees:* AB, BFA, BS. *Majors offered* include usual arts and sciences, art therapy, dance therapy, humanities, international studies, theatre/dance, management/business, psychology/education (elementary, secondary, early childhood special education), BSN completion for RNs. About 70–80% of students entering as freshmen graduate eventually; 20% of freshmen do not return for sophomore year. *Special programs:* CLEP, independent study, study abroad, undergraduate research, individualized majors, cross-registration with Lake Forest College, internships, January Term (graphic design), LD program for students with learning disabilities. *Calendar:* semester, summer school.

Undergraduate degrees conferred (82). 34% were in Business and Management, 20% were in Education, 10% were in Multi/Interdisciplinary Studies, 7% were in Visual and Performing Arts, 7% were in Letters, 7% were in Communications, 6% were in Social Sciences, 4% were in Psychology, remainder in 3 other fields.
Graduates Career Data. According to most recent data available, full-time graduate or professional study pursued immediately after graduation by 35% of students; 5% enter law school; 5% enter business school. *Careers in business and industry* pursued by 60% of graduates. Corporations typically hiring largest numbers of graduates include Abbott Laboratories, Baxter Travenol, Marriott hotels.
Faculty. About 60% of faculty hold PhD or equivalent.
Student Body. College seeks a national student body; 85% of students from in state; 90% North Central. An estimated 60% of students reported as Catholic, 30% Protestant, 5% Jewish, 5% unaffiliated; 14% as Black, 9% Hispanic, 5% Asian, according to most recent data available. *Minority group students:* Black Student Union and International Club "for social activities."
Religious Orientation. For many years a Roman Catholic institution, Barat is now under secular control and open to all faiths "in the ecumenical spirit of Vatican II." No religious activities required of students "but opportunities are provided for developing relevant liturgies and participating in the search for religious awareness." Places of worship available on campus for Catholics, in immediate community for all faiths.
Varsity Sports. Men (NAIA): Basketball. Women (NAIA): Volleyball.
Campus Life. Administration reports "fewer regulations in favor of encouraging students to take responsibility for their own decisions and choices"; rules concerning women's dorm hours, visitation, and so on in place. Visitors must leave dorms by 1 am week nights, 3 am weekends. Cars permitted for all. About 59% of men, 46% of women live in traditional dormitories; rest commute. There are no fraternities or sororities. About 20% of resident students leave campus on weekends.
Annual Costs. Tuition and fees, $9,830; room and board, $4,300. About 70% of students receive financial aid; assistance is typically divided 40% scholarship, 30% loan, 30% work. College reports some scholarships awarded on the basis of academic merit alone.

Barber-Scotia College

Concord, North Carolina 28025 (704) 786-5171

A church-related college, located in a community of 18,500, 22 miles north of Charlotte; founded as a college for Negroes and still serving a predominantly Black student body.

Founded: 1867
Affiliation: Presbyterian Church (USA)
Total Enrollment: 354 M, 356 W (full-time)
Cost: < $10K
% Receiving Financial Aid: 80%
Admission: Non-selective

Admission. Graduates of accredited high schools with 16 units (10 in academic subjects) eligible; graduates of non-accredited schools admitted by examination; 95% of applicants accepted, 60% of these actually enroll; 20% of freshmen graduate in top fifth of their high school class, 50% in top two-fifths. *Required:* SAT or ACT, minimum high school GPA of 2.0, interview. Criteria considered in admissions, in order of importance: high school academic record, recommendations, extracurricular activities, standardized test scores, writing sample; other factors considered: special talents, alumni children, diverse student body, religious affiliation and/or commitment. *Apply:* no specific deadline. *Transfers* welcome; 68 enrolled 1993–94.
Academic Environment. Degrees offered: associates, bachelors. All students required to take General Studies curriculum. Average undergraduate class size: about 30% of classes under 20, 65% 20–40. About 56% of students entering as freshmen graduate within four years; 25% of freshmen do not return for sophomore year. *Special programs:* January Term, study abroad, internships and cooperative work/study programs available. *Calendar:* semester.
Undergraduate degrees conferred (40). 68% were in Business and Management, 28% were in Social Sciences, 3% were in Parks and Recreation, 3% were in Multi/Interdisciplinary Studies.
Faculty. About 80% of faculty hold PhD or equivalent. About 90% of classes taught by tenured faculty. About 44% of teaching faculty are female; 70% Black, 12% other ethnic minority.
Varsity Sports. Men (NAIA): Basketball, Gymnastics, Tennis, Track, Volleyball. Women (NAIA): Basketball, Gymnastics, Tennis, Track, Volleyball.
Student Body. College seeks a national student body; 75% of students from in state; 90% South, 2% foreign.
Religious Orientation. Barber-Scotia is a church-related institution; 3 hours of religion required of all students; attendance urged at chapel and vesper services.
Campus Life. About 40% each of men, women live in traditional dormitories; no coed dormitories; 40% of men, 50% of women live in off-campus college related housing, rest commute. No intervisitation in men's or women's dormitory rooms. There are 6 fraternities, 4 sororities, which about 45% of men, 70% of women join.
Annual Costs. Tuition and fees, $4,200; room and board, $2,612; estimated $1,600 other, exclusive of travel. About 80% of students receive financial aid. Assistance typically includes scholarship and work/study program. College reports 10 scholarships awarded on the basis of academic merit alone, 20 for special talents alone.

Barclay College

Haviland, Kansas 67059

A small college of the Friends Church, Barclay offers specialized programs in the Bible and ministries. The college is located in a rural community of 800.

Founded: 1917
Affiliation: Friends

Bard College

Annandale-on-Hudson, New York 12504 (914) 758-7472

Bard is a small, well-known liberal arts college located about 150 miles north of New York City. Once an Episcopalian institution, it is now independent but still retains essentially historic ties with the church as a member of the Association of Episcopal Colleges. Bard administers Simon's Rock Early College, an institution that accepts students after their sophomore year in high school. Simon's Rock retains its separate identity (see separate listing). Bard is located north of New York City, in a village of about 1,450 overlooking the Hudson River. The 600-acre campus lies on the eastern side of the river adjacent to a 400-acre wildlife preserve. Most convenient major airports: Albany, New York City area.

Founded: 1860
Affiliation: Independent
UG Enrollment: 1,023 M, W (full-time)
Total Enrollment: 1,173
Cost: $10K–$20K
% Receiving Financial Aid: 66%
Admission: Very (+) Selective
Application Deadline: February 15

Admission is very (+) selective. About 53% of applicants accepted, 39% of these actually enroll; 60% of freshmen graduate in top fifth of high school class, 90% in top two-fifths. Average freshman SAT scores (not required): approximately 1200 combined verbal, mathematical. *Required:* for Immediate Decision Plan: seminar and interview; for traditional application: essays, recommendations; SAT or ACT optional, interview strongly recommended. *Non-academic factors* considered of major importance in admissions: special talents, extracurricular involvement, volunteer/employment activities, diverse student body. *Entrance programs:* early admission, midyear admission, special one-day admission program (Immediate Decision Plan), deferred admission. About 30% of entering students from private schools, 10% parochial. *Apply* by February 15 for traditional application. *Transfers* welcome.
Academic Environment. Bard has a national student body, drawing students from every part of the country. Pressures for acad-

emic achievement do not appear intense. Tutorials are a strong tradition at Bard and, although not required, represent half of the courses taught each year. Some distribution requirements: 2 semester courses in each of 4 divisions by graduation. All incoming freshmen must attend 3-week pre-semester "Workshop in Language and Thinking" in August, emphasis is on writing, and 2 freshmen seminars: fall concentrates on ancient Greece (Homer, Herodotus, Plato), spring deals with the origins of modern politics and society in Europe and America in the 18th and 19th centuries. Other requirements: Moderation (process through which a major is selected), Junior Conference, Senior Project. *Degree:* BA. *Majors offered* include arts and sciences, anthropology, drama and dance, creative writing, film, independent major, Russian studies. Classes are small and students report that it is easy to get to know the faculty. The strongest programs are reported to be in language and literature, and fine and performing arts.

About 70% of students entering as freshmen graduate within 5 years; 18% of freshmen do not return for sophomore year. *Special programs:* independent study, study abroad, undergraduate research, 3-year degree, credit for off-campus work "if judged of intellectual or artistic value," intensive German language immersion, 3–2 engineering with Columbia, 3–2 MBA with Rochester, 3–2 MS in forestry and environmental studies with Duke, 3–2 MPA with Syracuse, 3–2 MSW with Hunter, Pennsylvania, 3–2 public health with Yale, 3–2 city and regional planning and 2–3 architecture with Pratt, accelerated law program with Benjamin Cardoza. *Calendar:* semester, winter field period.

Undergraduate degrees conferred (211). 38% were in Visual and Performing Arts, 34% were in Social Sciences, 18% were in Letters, 6% were in Multi/Interdisciplinary Studies, 3% were in Liberal/General Studies.

Graduates Career Data. According to most recent data available, full-time graduate or professional study pursued immediately after graduation by 50% of students. Medical schools typically enrolling largest numbers of graduates include Einstein; law and business schools include NYU, Hunter, Columbia. *Careers in business and industry* pursued by 45% of graduates. *Career Counseling Program:* students urged to seek interviews with business/industry representatives who visit campus. Help provided in preparing for interviews. Alumni reported as helpful in both career guidance and job placement.

Faculty. About 90% of faculty hold doctorate or equivalent.

Student Body. College seeks a national student body; 30% of students from in state; 50% Middle Atlantic, 21% New England, 8% West. An estimated 10% of students reported as Protestant, 10% Catholic, 25% Jewish, 50% unaffiliated, 5% other; 9–10% as minority, according to most recent data available.

Religious Orientation. College originally chartered as an institution of the Episcopal Church "today is independent and enrolls students of all races and faiths." Regular Sunday chapel services. Major Jewish holidays recognized. Chapel committee, Jewish Services Committee, and chaplain responsible for religious activities on campus. Places of worship available in immediate community for major faiths.

Varsity Sports. Men (NAIA): Basketball, Cross Country, Soccer, Tennis, Volleyball. Women (NAIA): Basketball, Cross Country, Soccer, Softball, Tennis, Volleyball.

Campus Life. Bard is small, somewhat isolated, and self-sufficient. Community life on campus is considered "too close" by some students. On the other hand, Bard students are virtually free of all specific social restrictions; subject to discipline or dismissal, however, if they interfere with functioning of college or disrupt community living on the campus. Cars permitted; parking reported as adequate. New York City, 2 hours away by car or train, offers students an infinite variety of cultural and recreational opportunities. Unlike many schools, security is not a major concern at Bard.

About 85% of students live on-campus (90% in coed housing); rest live in off-campus housing or commute. Sexes segregated in coed dormitories by room. Freshmen given preference in college housing if all students cannot be accommodated. There are no fraternities or sororities. About 20% of students leave campus on weekends.

Annual Costs. Tuition and fees, $15,710; room and board, $5,160; estimated $800 other, exclusive of travel. About 55% of students receive financial aid. Assistance is typically divided 70% scholarship, 20% loan, 10% work. College reports some scholarships awarded on the basis of academic merit alone.

Barnard College

(See Columbia University)

Barrington College

(See Gordon College)

Barry University

Miami Shores, Florida 33161 **(305) 899-3100**

A church-related, liberal arts university, conducted by the Dominican Sisters of Adrian, Michigan, Barry is located on 85 acres in suburban Miami Shores. Most convenient major airport: Miami.

Founded: 1940
Affiliation: Roman Catholic
UG Enrollment: 600 M, 900 W (full-time); 1,120 M, 1,600 W (part-time)
Total Enrollment: 6,850
Cost: $10K–$20K
% Receiving Financial Aid: 65%
Admission: Non-selective
Application Deadline: Rolling

Admission. High school graduates with minimum of 16 academic units and C+ average in academic subjects eligible. About 73% of students applying for admission are accepted; 50% of freshman graduate in the top fifth of their high school class. Average freshman scores: SAT, 424 M, 427 W verbal; 478 M, 454 W mathematical; ACT, 19 M, 20 W composite. Criteria considered in admissions, in order of importance: standardized test scores, high school academic record, recommendations, extra curricular activities, writing sample; other factors considered: special talents, alumni children. *Required:* SAT or ACT; essay. *Entrance programs:* early decision. *Apply:* rolling admissions. About 50% of entering students are from private/parochial schools. *Transfers* welcome.

Academic Environment. Degrees offered: bachelors, masters, doctoral. Adult Programs: Continuing Education programs offered. *Special programs:* study abroad, 3–2 program in engineering, Washington Internship. According to most recent data about 55% of students entering as freshmen graduate eventually; 20% of freshmen do not return for sophomore year. *Calendar:* semester, summer school.

Undergraduate degrees conferred (911). 56% were in Liberal/General Studies, 12% were in Business and Management, 11% were in Health Sciences, 4% were in Social Sciences, 3% were in Education, 3% were in Life Sciences, remainder in 15 other fields.

Faculty. About 75% of faculty hold PhD or equivalent.

Student Body. According to most recent data available, 70% of students from Florida, 15% Middle Atlantic. An estimated 18% of students reported as Black, 25% Hispanic, 2% Asian.

Religious Orientation. Barry is a church-related institution; 9 hours of philosophy or religious studies required of all students. Religious Affairs Committee coordinates religious activities on campus.

Sports Varsity. Men (Div.II): Baseball, Basketball, Crew, Cross Country, Golf, Soccer, Tennis. Women (Div.II): Basketball, Crew, Cross Country, Soccer, Softball, Tennis, Volleyball.

Campus Life. Rules governing student conduct are moderate; curfew for all resident students midnight Sunday through Thursday; self-regulated hours on Friday and Saturday. There is one male dormitory, three female dormitories, three coed dormitories; 14% of men, 26% of women live in dormitories. No intervisitation in women's dormitory rooms. There is 1 fraternity and 3 sororities on campus.

Annual Costs. Tuition and fees, $12,000; room and board, $6,000. About 65% of students receive financial aid. Assistance is typically divided 33% scholarship, 33% loan, 33% work. University reports some scholarships awarded on the basis of academic merit alone.

Bartlesville Wesleyan College

Bartlesville, Oklahoma 74006 **(918) 335-6151**

A private, Christian, liberal arts college, sponsored to provide education "within a Christian environment." The 36-acre campus is located in a community of 40,000, 50 miles north of Tulsa. Most convenient major airport: Tulsa.

Founded: 1905
Affiliation: Wesleyan Church (Western Zone)
Total Enrollment: 205 M, 303 W (full-time)
Cost: < $10K
% Receiving Financial Aid: 95%
Admission: Non-selective
Application Deadline: Rolling

Admission. High school graduates with minimum combined SAT score of 700 or ACT composite score of 15, GPA of 2.0 eligible. About 53% of applicants accepted; 33% of freshmen graduate in top fifth of their high school class, 92% in top two-fifths. Average freshman ACT scores: 21 M, 22 W composite, 20 M, 20 W mathematical. *Required:* SAT or ACT. Criteria considered in admissions, in order of importance: high school academic record, standardized test scores; other factors considered: extra curricular activities, alumni children, religious affiliation and/or commitment. About 95% of freshman come from public schools. *Apply:* rolling admissions. *Transfers* welcome; 36 enrolled 1993–94.
Academic Environment. Degrees offered: associates, bachelors. Average undergraduate class size: 90% under 20, 10% 20–40. Adult programs: Management of Human Resources for those 25 years and older who have completed 70 hours of undergraduate work. *Special programs:* study abroad; internship/cooperative work-study. According to most recent data available an estimated 50% of students entering as freshmen graduate eventually; 76% return for sophomore year.
Undergraduate degrees conferred (76). 39% were in Business and Management, 24% were in Education, 7% were in Social Sciences, 7% were in Psychology, 7% were in Philosophy and Religion, 5% were in Computer and Engineering Related Technology, 4% were in Theology, 4% were in Life Sciences, 4% were in Letters.
Graduates Career Data. Fields typically employing largest numbers of graduates are education and business. Career Development Services: Learning Resource Center offers personal inventory testing, job placement services available for some fields.
Faculty. About 40% of faculty hold PhD or equivalent. About 30% of teaching faculty are female.
Student Body. An estimated 43% of students from in state; 88% from the Midwest, 5% foreign students 1993–94. Average age of undergraduate student: 27. An estimated 87% of students reported as Protestant, 4% Catholic, 9% unaffiliated; 4% Black, 10% other minority.
Religious Orientation. Bartlesville is a church-related institution; about 37% of students affiliated with the Wesleyan church; 3 courses in religion are required.
Varsity Sports. Men (NAIA/NCCAA): Basketball, Soccer. Women (NAIA/NCCAA): Basketball, Soccer, Volleyball.
Campus Life. About 48% of men, 52% of women live in traditional dormitories; rest commute.
Annual Costs. Tuition and fees, $6,350; room and board, $3,050; estimated $1,000 other. About 95% of students receive financial aid. According to most recent data available assistance is typically divided 30% scholarship, 30% loan, 30% work. College reports some scholarships awarded on the basis of academic merit alone.

Barton College

Wilson, North Carolina 27893 **(919) 399-6300 or (800) 345-4973**

A church-related, liberal arts college, with professional programs in teacher education, business, education of the hearing impaired, and nursing. Affiliated with the Christian Church (Disciples of Christ), Barton is located in a city of 35,000, 45 miles east of Raleigh. Formerly known as Atlantic Christian College. Most convenient major airport: Raleigh-Durham International.

Founded: 1902
Affiliation: Disciples of Christ
Total Enrollment: 376 M, 733 W (full-time); 154 M, 351 W (part-time)
Cost: < $10K
% Receiving Financial Aid: 80%
Admission: Non-selective
Application Deadline: July 31

Admission. Graduates of accredited high schools with 12 in academic subjects eligible; 83% of applicants accepted, 31% of these actually enroll; 20% of freshmen graduate in top fifth of high school class, 44% in top two-fifths. Average freshman SAT scores: 396 verbal, 444 mathematical. *Required:* SAT. Criteria considered in admissions, in order of importance: high school academic record, standardized test scores, recommendations, writing sample, extracurricular activities; other factors considered: special talents. *Apply* by July 31; rolling admissions. *Transfers* welcome; 224 enrolled 1993–94.
Academic Environment. Degrees offered: bachelors. Core requirements include 15 hours in humanities and fine arts, 6 in social sciences, 11 in natural sciences and mathematics, 6–9 in writing proficiency, 3–4 in computational proficiency, 6–9 in global and cross cultural perspective, 2 in sports science, and 2 from Barton College Seminar. Unusual, new or notable majors include education of the deaf and hard of hearing, international studies, nursing, communications, social work, music recording technology, environmental science. About 70% of students entering as freshmen graduate within four years; 7% of freshmen do not return for sophomore year. Average undergraduate class size: 40% under 20, 59% 20–40, 1% over 40. *Special programs:* CLEP, January Term, study abroad, 3–2 program in medical technology, internships. Adult programs: Weekend College. *Calendar:* semester, summer school.
Undergraduate degrees conferred (300). 36% were in Business and Management, 20% were in Health Sciences, 17% were in Education, 6% were in Public Affairs, 5% were in Social Sciences, 3% were in Psychology, 3% were in Mathematics, 3% were in Communications, remainder in 7 other fields.
Graduates Career Data. Fields typically employing largest numbers of graduates include corporate areas, education systems, medical facilities. Career Development Services include interest inventories, resume writing workshops, interview technique seminars, group and individual counseling, on-campus recruitment, placement services, internship programs, library resources, job-fairs.
Faculty. About 61% of faculty hold PhD or equivalent. About 48% of undergraduate classes taught by tenured faculty. About 48% of teaching faculty are female; 7% ethnic minorities.
Student Body. About 83% of students from in state, 85% South, 13% Middle Atlantic; 1% foreign. An estimated 73% of students reported as Protestant, 7% Catholic, 17% unaffiliated; 11% Black, 1% Hispanic, 1% Asian, 3% other minority.
Religious Orientation. Barton is a church-related institution; 1 course in religion required of all students.
Varsity Sports. Men (NAIA 26): Baseball, Basketball, Golf, Soccer, Tennis. Women (NAIA 26): Basketball, Soccer, Softball, Tennis, Volleyball.
Campus Life. Students report that they are kept busy studying, but the small town of Wilson "offers a warm atmosphere and there are several other colleges nearby" to complement the college sponsored activities and clubs. About 23% of men, 24% of women live in traditional dormitories; 12% of men, 10% of women live in coed dormitories; 57% of men, 66% of women commute. There are 4 fraternities, 3 sororities on campus which about 6% of men, 6% of women join; 8% of men live in fraternities; sororities provide no residence facilities.
Annual Costs. Tuition and fees, $7,363; room and board, $3,326; estimated $1,933 other, exclusive of travel. About 80% of students receive financial aid; average amount of assistance, $6,475. Assistance is typically divided 24% scholarship, 30% grant, 39% loan, 7% work. College reports 324 scholarships awarded on the basis of academic merit alone, 140 for special talents alone, 182 for need alone. *Meeting Costs:* college offers Parent PLUS Loans, CONCERN Loans.

Bates College

Lewiston, Maine 04240 **(207) 786-6000**

Long a small, high-quality liberal arts college serving a regional clientele, Bates has broadened its appeal and now attracts students from other regions of the country as well as abroad.

Although still drawing substantial numbers from the Northeast its student body has become a heterogeneous one. Located in a city of 41,800, the 100-acre campus is 35 miles north of Portland and 135 miles northeast of Boston. Most convenient major airport: Portland.

Founded: 1855
Affiliation: Independent
Total Enrollment: 1,515 M, W (full-time)
Cost: > $20K
% Receiving Financial Aid: 50%
Admission: Highly Selective
Application Deadline: Feb. 1

Admission is highly selective. About 42% of applicants accepted, 33% of these actually enroll; 80% of freshmen graduate in top fifth of high school class, 96% in top two-fifths. Average freshman SAT scores, middle fifty percent range: 560–630 verbal, 590–670 mathematical; 93% of freshmen score above 500 on verbal, 46% above 600, 5% above 700; 97% score above 500 on mathematical, 72% above 600, 17% above 700. *Required:* SAT or ACT, 3 ACH including English, essay; interview strongly recommended. *Non-academic factors* considered in admissions: special talents, diverse student body, geographical diversity, alumni children. *Entrance programs:* early decision, early admission, midyear admission, advanced placement, deferred admission. About 30% of entering students from private schools, 5% from parochial schools. *Apply* by February 1. *Transfers* welcome.

Academic Environment. Pressures for academic achievement appear fairly intense. Students may complete degree requirements in 3 years by taking 5 courses each semester and 3 "short term" units of concentrated study during 5-week term in May and early June. No extra charge for acceleration so student may save nearly quarter of cost for degree by taking 3-year option. Students have some influence on curriculum decisions through Faculty-Student Committees. Administration reports general education requirements include 3 semesters each science and social science, 5 semesters humanities, 1 semester quantitative techniques. All freshmen take 2 semesters physical education. *Degrees:* AB, BS. *Majors offered* include usual arts and sciences, anthropology, geology, rhetoric, theater, women's studies. Strongest programs reported to be in the sciences, art, religion, psychology, English and political science.

About 86% of students entering as freshmen graduate within four years, 90% eventually; 2% of freshmen do not return for sophomore year. *Special programs:* independent study, study abroad, honors, undergraduate research, 3-year degree, individualized majors, off-campus projects, 3–2 engineering with Columbia, RPI, Case Western, Washington U.. *Calendar:* 4–4–1 (semester, 5-week short term).

Undergraduate degrees conferred (402). 35% were in Social Sciences, 13% were in Psychology, 12% were in Letters, 8% were in Visual and Performing Arts, 6% were in Multi/Interdisciplinary Studies, 6% were in Life Sciences, 5% were in Foreign Languages, 5% were in Physical Sciences, 4% were in Philosophy and Religion, 3% were in Communications, remainder in 2 other fields.

Graduates Career Data. According to most recent data available, full-time graduate or professional study pursued immediately after graduation by 20% of students; 2% enter medical school; 3% enter law school; 2% enter business school. Medical schools typically enrolling largest numbers of graduates include Georgetown, Tufts, Johns Hopkins; dental schools include Tufts; law schools include U. of Maine, Boston U., U. of Pennsylvania; business schools include U. of Chicago, Yale, Tuck. Career Counseling Program: Student assessment of program reported as "excellent!" for both career guidance and job placement by recent student leader. Alumni reported as "very!" helpful in both career guidance and job placement.

Faculty. About 95% of faculty hold doctorate or appropriate terminal degree; most earned at nation's top graduate institutions.

Student Body. College seeks a national student body; 13% of students from in state; 55% New England, 23% Middle Atlantic, 6% North Central, 5% West/Northwest. An estimated 30% of students reported as Protestant, 34% Catholic, 6% Jewish, 20% unaffiliated, 10% other; 3% as Black, 1% Hispanic, 4% Asian, 3% other minority, according to most recent data available.

Religious Orientation. Founded by the Freewill Baptist Church, Bates has long been nondenominational, makes no religious demands on students. Religious clubs on campus include Newman, Intervarsity, Christian Science, Hillel, Canter bury. Places of worship available on campus for 3 major faiths.

Varsity Sports. Men (Div.III): Baseball, Basketball, Cross Country, Diving, Football, Lacrosse, Skiing (I), Soccer, Squash, Swimming, Tennis, Track. Women (Div.III): Basketball, Cross Country, Diving, Field Hockey, Golf, Lacrosse, Skiing (I), Soccer, Softball, Squash, Swimming, Tennis, Track, Volleyball.

Campus Life. Students have a strong voice in determining policy. Several living styles available, ranging from no visitation, no visitation during the weekday, and limited visitation. Regulations concerning alcohol and drugs conform to civil law. Cars permitted on campus. Campus may be considered far from urban centers by some students. Lewiston, however, provides opportunities for career internships in hospitals, law firms, schools, and the like. Bates is described by an administration source as a "friendly place with strong, albeit informal, academic focus."

About 21% of students live in traditional dormitories; 79% live in coed dormitories. Sexes segregated in coed dormitories by wing, floor, or room. There are no fraternities or sororities. About 25% of students leave campus on weekends.

Annual Costs. Comprehensive fee, $23,990. About 50% of first-year students receive financial aid. College reports scholarships awarded only on the basis of need. *Meeting Costs:* College offers 10-month payment option, Supplemental Loan Program of Maine Educational Loan Authority.

Bayamáon Central University

Bayamáon, Puerto Rico 00621 (809) 786-3030

A church-related institution, Bayamáon Central is primarily a commuter college. Spanish is language of instruction, though all students are expected to have a knowledge of English since they may be required to use English texts and reference materials. Most convenient major airport: International Luis Munoz (San Juan).

Founded: 1961
Affiliation: Roman Catholic
Total Enrollment: 909 M, 1,423 W (full-time); 125 M, 167 W (part-time)
Cost: < $10K
% Receiving Financial Aid: 10%
Admission: Non-selective
Application Deadline: April 15

Admission. High school graduates eligible. About 76% of applicants accepted, 79% of these actually enroll. *Required:* SAT, interview. *Apply* by April 15. *Transfers* welcome.

Academic Environment. *Degrees:* AB, BS, BBA. About 25% of general education requirements for graduation are elective; distribution requirements fairly numerous. New programs in elementary education and communications recently added. *Calendar:* semester, summer school.

Undergraduate degrees conferred (238). 27% were in Education, 23% were in Health Sciences, 19% were in Business and Management, 5% were in Philosophy and Religion, 5% were in Computer and Engineering Related Technology, 5% were in Life Sciences, 4% were in Business (Administrative Support), 4% were in Psychology, 3% were in Public Affairs, 3% were in Physical Sciences, remainder in Multi/Interdisciplinary Studies.

Varsity Sports. Men (LAICRE): Basketball, Chess, Cross Country, Decathlon, Table Tennis, Track, Volleyball. Women (LAICRE): Basketball, Chess, Cross Country, Table Tennis, Track, Volleyball.

Campus Life. University seeks a national student body; almost all students from Puerto Rico. Bayamáon Central is a church-related institution. There are no dormitories; 30% of men, 20% of women live in off-campus housing; rest commute. There are no fraternities or sororities.

Annual Costs. Tuition and fees, $2,350; estimated $1,200 other, exclusive of travel. About 10% of students receive financial aid; assistance is typically divided 85% scholarship, 11% loan, 4% work. College reports all scholarships awarded on the basis of need.

Baylor University

Waco, Texas 76798 (817) 755-1811

Although Baylor attracts students from all parts of the country, more than three-quarters of them come from the Southwest, giving the institution a distinctly regional flavor. The campus is located in a city of 110,000 on the banks of the Brazos River in central Texas. About 381 students enrolled in Baylor schools of Dentistry and Nursing in Dallas, and the Academy of Health Sciences in San Antonio. Most convenient major airport: Waco Regional.

Founded: 1845
Affiliation: Baptist
UG Enrollment: 4,446 M, 5,473 W (full-time)
Total Enrollment: 12,194
Cost: < $10K
% Receiving Financial Aid: 66%
Admission: Selective
Application Deadline: Rolling

Admission is selective. According to most recent data available about 70% of freshmen graduate in top quarter of high school class. Freshman scores: SAT, Interquartile Range, 940–1140; 45% score above 500 on verbal, 12% above 600, 1% above 700; 80% score above 500 on mathematical, 35% above 600, 9% above 700; ACT, Interquartile Range, 21–25 composite. Criteria considered in admissions, in order of importance: high school class rank, standardized test scores, academic record, recommendations, extracurricular activities, writing sample; other factors considered: special talents, alumni children, diverse student body, religious affiliation and/or commitment. *Required:* ACT or SAT, essay. *Entrance programs:* early admission, midyear admission, advanced placement. *Apply:* rolling admissions. *Transfers* welcome; 471 enrolled Fall, 1993.

Academic Environment. Several students recently queried consider the student-faculty ratio, the small class size, the attendence policy, and the accessibility of faculty to be strengths of the academic program. Degrees offered: bachelors, masters, doctoral. Core requirements include 12 semester hours of English, 3 of math, 6–9 fine arts, 3–16 foreign language, 12 science, 18 social science, 4 physical education, and 2 semester courses of Chapel-Forum(lecture series). *Undergraduate studies* offered by the College of Arts and Sciences, schools of Business, Education, Music, Nursing. *Majors offered* in addition to usual arts and sciences include anthropology, environmental studies, foreign service, home economics, journalism, communications, clinical gerontology, neuroscience, taxation, health education, biblical and related languages, museum studies. Undergraduate programs recently added: health/fitness studies, health science studies.

About 72% of students entering as freshmen graduate eventually; 85% of freshmen return for sophomore year. Adult programs: cooperative program with MCC and the Baylor Hankamer School of Business leading to the BBA degree. Designed as a night program for those already in the work force. *Special programs:* January term, study abroad, 3–2 programs in BA/JD, BBA/JD, forestry, law, optometry, architecture, dentistry, medical technology, medicine. *Calendar:* semester, summer school.

Undergraduate degrees conferred (2,253). 26% were in Business and Management, 19% were in Education, 7% were in Marketing and Distribution, 7% were in Social Sciences, 7% were in Communications, 6% were in Life Sciences, 5% were in Psychology, 5% were in Letters, 4% were in Health Sciences, remainder in 18 other fields. *Doctoral degrees:* Psychology 15, Education 9, Physical Sciences 7, Letters 3.

Graduates Career Data. Career Development Services include workshops, seminars, independent research, group and individual career counseling, internships, development of letter-writing, resume and interviewing skills, assessment, on-campus interviewing, referral program, career resources library, and job listings.

Faculty. About 33% of the teaching faculty are female.

Student Body. About 78% of students from in state; 1% foreign. An estimated 75% of students reported as Protestant, 12% Catholic, 5% other, 9% non specified; 4% as Black, 6% Hispanic, 6% Asian.

Religious Orientation. Baylor is a church-related institution; 2 courses in religion required of all students.

Varsity Sports. Men (Div.I): Baseball, Basketball, Cross Country, Football(IA), Golf, Tennis, Track. Women (Div.I): Basketball, Cross Country, Golf, Tennis, Track, Volleyball.

Campus Life. Intervisitation limited to specific times. Alcohol prohibited on campus or at any university function. Cars allowed for all. Several recent students describe the students, faculty and administration as very conservative. Nearest major cultural center, Dallas, is 100 miles from campus, students agree that this creates an atmosphere conducive to study during the week, but allows for weekend trips to Dallas, Austin and Houston.

According to most recent data available about 32% of students live in traditional dormitories; no coed dormitories; rest commute. There are 17 fraternities, 13 sororities which about 20% of men, 25% of women join; they provide no residence facilities.

Annual Costs. Tuition and fees, $7,070; room and board, $3,920; estimated $1,946 other, exclusive of travel. About 66% of students receive financial aid. University reports some scholarships awarded on the basis of academic merit alone.

Beaver College

Glenside, Pennsylvania 19038 **(215) 572-2900 or (800) 776-BEAVER**

Founded as a liberal arts college for women, Beaver has been coeducational for many years. Although historically related to the Presbyterian Church, it is nonsectarian "in spirit and in practice." In addition to liberal arts and science studies, the college offers majors in many career-oriented programs. Beaver is located in one of Philadelphia's northern suburbs (pop. 17,400). Most convenient major airport: Philadelphia International.

Founded: 1853
Affiliation: Independent (Presbyterian)
UG Enrollment: 222 M, 650 W (full-time); 161 M, 365 W (part-time)
Total Enrollment: 2,387
Cost: $10K–$20K
% Receiving Financial Aid: 73% freshman, 64% else
Admission: Non-selective
Application Deadline: Rolling

Admission. About 85% of applicants accepted, 30% of these actually enroll; 43% of freshmen graduate in top fifth of high school class. Average freshman SAT scores: 30% score above 500 on verbal, 3% above 600, 1% above 700; 58% score above 500 on mathematical, 16% above 600, 3% above 700. Criteria considered in admissions, in order of importance: high school academic record, recommendations, standardized test scores, extra curricular activities, writing sample; other factors considered: special talents, alumni children. *Required:* SAT, essay; interview recommended. *Entrance programs:* early decision, early admission, midyear admission, deferred admission, advanced placement. About 14% of entering students from private schools, 16% from parochial schools. *Apply:* rolling admissions. *Transfers* welcome; 123 enrolled 1993–94.

Academic Environment. Curriculum built on premise that liberal and career education are intertwined. Opportunities in all majors for internships, apprenticeships, cooperative education placements, independent study, and in some fields, cooperative student-faculty research. Geographic location permits use of New York City, Washington D.C. as well as Philadelphia as part of the learning laboratory. Administration reports 25% of courses devoted to distribution requirements which include 2 courses in English (unless exempted), 2 semesters of the same laboratory science, 2 semesters foreign language. Degrees offered: associates, bachelors, masters. Unusual majors offered include science illustration, art therapy, interior design, actuarial studies, international studies, London Preview. Average undewrgraduate class size: 17. About 71% of entering freshmen graduate within four years; 85% of freshmen return for sophomore year. Adult programs: special orientation programs, "Bridge" course which focuses on adjustment issues for the non-traditional learner. *Special programs:* study abroad; 3–2 in engineering; Washington Internship; Appalachian semesters; 3–4 in optometry; 4+2 program in physical therapy. *Calendar:* 4–1–4.

Undergraduate degrees conferred (217). 18% were in Psychology, 15% were in Business and Management, 12% were in Education, 12% were in Life Sciences, 11% were in Computer and Engineering Related Technology, 9% were in Visual and Performing Arts, 8% were in Social Sciences, 5% were in Communications, 3% were in Letters, remainder in 5 other fields.

Graduates Career Data. Advanced studies pursued by 17% of students; 7% enter graduate school in the arts and sciences; 3% enter medical, law or business schools; many enter Beaver's M.S. program in physical therapy. About 90% of 1992–93 graduates employed. Large numbers of graduates typically enter health related professions. Career Development Services include aptitude testing, placement service, resume and interview workshops, on-campus recruitment, individual counseling, internships, coop education, library resources, SIGI computer system, alumni career contact service.

Faculty. About 85% of faculty hold PhD or equivalent. About 54% of undergraduate classes taught by tenured faculty. About 49% of teaching faculty are female.

Student Body. College seeks a regional student body; 78% of students from in state; 97% Middle Atlantic, 2% New England, 1% South; 27 foreign students 1993–94. An estimated 29% of students reported as Protestant, 35% Catholic, 6% Jewish; 9% Black, 2% Hispanic, 2% Asian, 1% other minority. Average age of undergraduate student: 23.
Religious Orientation. Beaver is historically church-related, but nonsectarian in spirit and practice.
Varsity Sports. Men (NCAA Div.III) Baseball, Basketball, Cross Country, Equestrian (IHSA), Ski Club, Soccer, Tennis, Volleyball. Women (NCAA Div.III): Basketball, Cross Country, Equestrian (IHSA), Field Hockey, Lacrosse, Soccer, Softball, Tennis, Volleyball.
Campus Life. Located in the northern suburbs of Philadelphia, the college offers easy access to the social and cultural facilities of the city; within 100 miles of both New York and Washington. College makes effort to draw on resources of all 3 areas for regular curricular, as well as extracurricular, activities.

About 24% of women live in traditional dormitories; 76% of students live in coed dormitories; rest commute. Sexes segregated in coed dormitories by wing or floor. There are no fraternities or sororities. About 25% of resident students leave campus on weekends.
Annual Costs. Tuition and fees, $12,250; room and board, $5,150; estimated $900 other, exclusive of travel. About 73% of freshman, 64% of continuing students, receive financial aid; average amount of assistance, $11,042. Assistance is typically divided 60% scholarship, 30% loan, 10% work. College awards some scholarships for distinguished scholars and academic achievement, and 69% for need alone.

Belhaven College

Jackson, Mississippi 39202 (601) 968-5940

A church-related college, Belhaven is located in a residential area of the state capital (pop. 300,000). As part of the school's Christian environment, faculty are all members of some evangelical church. Most convenient major airport: Hawkins Field.

Founded: 1883
Affiliation: Presbyterian Church (USA)
UG Enrollment: 313 M, 423 W (full-time); 135 M, 212 W (part-time)
Total Enrollment: 1,083
Cost: < $10K
% Receiving Financial Aid: 92%
Admission: Non-selective
Application Deadline: Rolling

Admission. Graduates of accredited high schools with GPA of 2.5, minimum SAT/ACT of 830/19 eligible, others admitted by committee decision; 79% of applicants accepted, 61% of these actually enroll; 51% of entering freshman graduate in the top fifth of high school class; 74% in top two-fifths. Average freshman scores: SAT, 467 verbal, 455 mathematical; ACT, 23 composite. Criteria considered in admissions, in order of importance: high school academic record, standardized test scores, recommendations, extra curricular activities, writing sample; other factors considered: special talents. *Required:* ACT or SAT. *Entrance programs:* early admission, advanced placement. *Apply:* rolling admissions. *Transfers* welcome; 180 enrolled 1993–94.
Academic Environment. Degrees offered: bachelors. Core requirements include 6 hours of English composition, 3 hours speech, 8 hours religion, 6 hours literature, 3 hours mathematics, 7 hours science, 9 hours history. Adult programs: EDGE program offers credit for experience in work and military. *Special programs:* January term, 3–2 in engineering, internship/work study. *Calendar:* semester, summer school.
Undergraduate degrees conferred (143). 38% were in Business and Management, 17% were in Education, 13% were in Psychology, 8% were in Letters, 8% were in Life Sciences, 4% were in Visual and Performing Arts, 3% were in Theology, 3% were in Social Sciences, 3% were in Computer and Engineering Related Technology, remainder in 2 other fields.
Graduates Career Data. About 72% of 1992–93 graduates employed. Employers typically hiring the largest number of graduates include Skytel, Sanderson Farms, A. G. Edwards. Career Development Services include mentoring program, internships, full and part-time employment, interest inventory testing, resume and interviewing workshops.
Faculty. About 80% of faculty hold PhD or equivalent. All undergraduate classes taught by tenured faculty.
Student Body. College does not seek a national student body; 88% of students from Mississippi.
Religious Orientation. Belhaven is a church-related institution; three religious courses are required of all students.
Varsity Sports. Men (NAIA): Baseball, Basketball, Cross Country, Golf, Soccer, Tennis. Women (NAIA): Basketball, Cross Country, Softball Club, Tennis.
Campus Life. About 30% of students live in traditional dormitories; rest commute. Freshmen given preference in college housing if all students cannot be accommodated. No intervisitation in men's or women's dormitory rooms. There are no fraternities or sororities on campus. About 33% of resident students leave campus on weekends.
Annual Costs. Tuition and fees, $6,980; room and board, $2,580; estimated $600 for books. About 92% of students receive financial aid; average amount of assistance $3,000. College reports some scholarships awarded on the basis of academic merit alone.

Bellarmine College

Louisville, Kentucky 40205-0671 (800) 535-1133

A church-related, liberal arts college where more than two-thirds of students major in business and management, accounting, and nursing. Bellarmine is located in a city of 900,000. Most convenient major airport: Standiford Field (Louisville).

Founded: 1950
Affiliation: Roman Catholic
UG Enrollment: 489 M, 709 W (full-time); 178 M, 427 W (part-time)
Total Enrollment: 2,338
Cost: < $10K
% Receiving Financial Aid: 79%
Admission: Selective (+)
Application Deadline: Aug. 1

Admission is selective (+). About 88% of applicants accepted, 44% of these actually enroll; 39% of freshmen graduate in top tenth of high school class, 63% in top fourth. Average freshman scores: 480 M, 462 W verbal, 540 M, 500 W mathematical; 42% score above 500 on verbal, 12% above 600; 63% score above 500 on mathematical, 21% above 600, 3% above 700; ACT, 23 M, 23.6 composite. *Required:* ACT or SAT, essay, college preparatory curriculum. Criteria considered in admissions, in order of importance: high school academic record, standardized test scores, extra curricular activities, recommendations, writing sample; other factors considered: special talents. *Entrance programs:* mid-year admission, deferred admission. According to most recent data available about 2% of entering students from private schools, 35% from parochial schools. *Apply* by August 1; rolling admissions. *Transfers* welcome.
Academic Environment. Degrees offered: bachelors, masters. Core requirements include 2 courses in each of English composition, world literature, social sciences, western civilization, natural sciences; 3 courses each in philosophy and theology; 1 course in each of mathematics, art history, music literature, and senior seminar. Average undergraduate class size: 38% under 20, 60% between 20–40, 2% over 40. Adult programs: B.S. in Commerce with either a Business Administration or Accounting emphasis - evening classes. Special Programs: study abroad, cross registration, internships. About 60% of students entering as freshmen graduate within 4 years, 65% eventually; 75% of freshmen return for sophomore year. Library materials include: Thomas Merton Collection. *Calendar:* semester, summer school.
Undergraduate degrees conferred (307). 38% were in Business and Management, 16% were in Health Sciences, 9% were in Communications, 7% were in Social Sciences, 7% were in Psychology, 5% were in Life Sciences, 5% were in Education, 4% were in Liberal/General Studies, 3% were in Visual and Performing Arts, remainder in 7 other fields.
Graduates Career Data. Advanced studies pursued by 30% of students; of these, 30% enter graduate school, 10% enter medical school, 10% enter dental school, 10% enter law school, 40% enter business school. Medical, dental and law schools typically enrolling largest numbers of graduates include U. of Louisville, U. of Kentucky; business schools include Bellarmine, U. of Kentucky. About 89% of 1992–93 graduates employed. Fields typically hiring largest number of graduates include accounting, retail management, nursing, and sales. Career Development Services include career planning and testing, internships, workshops, on-campus recruiting.

Faculty. About 82% of faculty hold PhD or equivalent. About 65% of undergraduate classes taught by tenured faculty. About 41% of teaching faculty are female; 5% minority.
Student Body. College seeks a national student body; about 80% of students from in state; 7% South, 8% Midwest, 1% New England, 1% West, 1% foreign students. An estimated 30% of students reported as Protestant, 65% Catholic, 5 other or unaffiliated; 2% Black, 1% Hispanic, 1% Asian, 1% other minority.
Religious Orientation. Bellarmine is a church-related institution; 9 hours of theology required of all students. Campus chapel provides a regular schedule of masses and other religious services.
Varsity Sports. Men (Div.II): Baseball, Basketball, Cross Country, Golf, Soccer, Tennis, Track. Women (Div.II): Basketball, Cross Country, Field Hockey, Soccer, Softball, Tennis, Track, Volleyball.
Campus Life. About 30% of students live in traditional or coed dormitories; rest live in off-campus housing or commute. There is one fraternity, which provides no residential facilities; no sororities. About 50% of residential students leave campus on weekends.
Annual Costs. Tuition and fees, $8,272; room and board, $2,655; estimated $750 other, exclusive of travel. About 79% of students receive financial aid; average amount of assistance, $6,565. Assistance is typically divided 32% scholarship, 24% grant, 38% loan, 6% work. College reports 396 scholarships awarded on the basis of academic merit alone and 300 for special talents.

Bellevue College

Bellevue, Nebraska 68005 **(402) 291-8100**

A coeducational, business administration and liberal arts college, Bellevue is located in the Omaha metropolitan area.

Affiliation: Independent
Total Enrollment: 238 M, 271 W (full-time)
Cost: < $10K
Admission: Non-selective

Admission. Graduates of high school or equivalent who ranked in the top two-thirds of their graduating class eligible; others considered on an individual basis; all applicants accepted, all enrolled. *Required:* interview.
Academic Environment. *Degrees:* BA, BFA. All students must complete core curriculum consisting of required courses in the humanities, social sciences, behavioral sciences, modern languages, natural sciences and mathematics.
Undergraduate degrees conferred (413). 86% were in Business and Management, 3% were in Social Sciences, 3% were in Psychology, 3% were in Marketing and Distribution, remainder in 6 other fields.
Varsity Sports. Men (NAIA): Baseball, Basketball. Women (NAIA): Golf, Volleyball.
Campus Life. About 95% of students from Nebraska. College has no residence facilities.
Annual Costs. Tuition and fees, $3,100.

Bellin College of Nursing

Green Bay, Wisconsin 54305-3400

An independent college of nursing, Bellin offers a bachelors program. Students admitted as freshmen take two years of general education courses at University of Wisconsin-Green Bay; 50% of new students are transfers.

Founded: 1909
Affiliation: Independent

Belmont Abbey College

Belmont, North Carolina 28012 **(800) 523-2355**

A coeducational college operated by the Benedictine community of Belmont Abbey, the school is located in a community of 5,000, 10 miles west of Charlotte. Belmont Abbey cooperates closely with nearby Sacred Heart College. Most convenient major airport: Charlotte-Douglas International.

Founded: 1876
Affiliation: Roman Catholic
UG Enrollment: 334 M, 375 W (full-time)
Total Enrollment: 867
Cost: < $10K
% Receiving Financial Aid: 78%
Admission: Non-selective
Application Deadline: August 15

Admission. Graduates of approved high schools graduating in top half of class with GPA of 2.0 and SAT of 800 eligible; others admitted by examination; 78% of applicants accepted, 23% of these actually enroll; 35% of freshmen graduate in top fifth of high school class, 44% in top two-fifths. Average freshman scores: SAT, 420 M, 420 W verbal, 463 M, 463 W mathematical; 37% of freshmen score above 500 on verbal, 1% above 600; 49% score above 500 on mathematical, 4% above 600; ACT, 21 M; 21 W composite. Criteria considered in admissions, in order of importance: high school academic record, standardized test scores, writing sample, recommendations. *Required:* SAT or ACT; interview recommended. *Entrance programs:* early decision, early admission, mid-year admission, advanced placement. According to most recent data available about 25% of entering students from private schools, 40% from parochial schools. *Apply* by: August 15; rolling admissions. *Transfers* welcome.
Academic Environment. Degrees offered: bachelors, masters. Several students recently polled find the academic program to be challenging and rewarding, they list the small class sizes and the accessibility of faculty as the greatest strengths. Core requirements include 3 courses in English, 2 in mathematics, 3 in philosophy, 2 in religion, 2 in foreign language, 2 in history, 2 in social sciences, 2 in lab sciences, and Great Books Seminar. Average undergraduate class size: 75% under 20, 25% between 20–40. Adult programs: evening school offers 5 majors. *Special programs:* study abroad, 3–2 in engineering. About 36% of students entering as freshmen graduate within 4 years; 71% of freshman return for sophomore year. *Calendar:* semester.
Undergraduate degrees conferred (172). 52% were in Business and Management, 15% were in Education, 12% were in Social Sciences, 5% were in Computer and Engineering Related Technology, 4% were in Parks and Recreation, 3% were in Letters, remainder in 6 other fields.
Faculty. About 85% of faculty hold PhD or equivalent. About 52% of undergraduate classes taught by tenured faculty.
Student Body. About 63% of students from North Carolina; 79% South, 13% Middle Atlantic, 1% New England, 1% Midwest, 1% West, 4% Foreign. An estimated 40% of students reported as Catholic, 50% as Protestant, 7% unaffiliated, 3% Muslim; 6% Black, 1% Hispanic, 1% Asian, 5% other minority. Average age of undergraduate student: 23.
Religious Orientation. Belmont Abbey has a strong Catholic heritage; 2 courses in theology required of all students.
Varsity Sports. Men (NAIA II): Baseball, Basketball, Cross Country, Golf, Soccer, Tennis. Women (NAIA II): Basketball, Cross Country, Soccer, Softball, Tennis, Volleyball.
Campus Life. About 44% of men, 44% of women live in co-ed dormitories; rest commute. There are 5 fraternities, 3 sororities on campus which about 40% of men, 40% of women join. About 15% of resident students leave campus on weekends.
Annual Costs. Tuition and fees, $7,134 ($8,284 for out-of-state students); room and board, $4,506; estimated $1,520 other, exclusive of travel. About 78% of students receive financial aid. College reports 40 scholarships awarded on the basis of academic merit alone and 25 for special talents.

Belmont University

Nashville, Tennessee 37212 **(615) 385-6785**

A church-related, liberal arts college, located on a 30-acre campus in the capital of Tennessee. Most convenient major airport: Nashville International.

Founded: 1951
Affiliation: Southern Baptist
Total Enrollment: 851 M, 1,113 W (full-time)
Cost: < $10K
% Receiving Financial Aid: 75%
Admission: Non-selective
Application Deadline: July 30

Admission. Graduates of accredited high schools with C average in 10 academic units and rank in top half of class eligible; 78% of applicants accepted, 45% of these actually enroll. Average freshman scores: SAT, 501 M, 476 W verbal, 525 M, 492 W mathematical; ACT, 24 M, 23 W composite. *Required:* SAT or ACT; interview only if requested by college. *Apply* by July 30. *Transfers* welcome; 379 enrolled 1993–94.

Academic Environment. Degrees offered: bachelors, masters. About 21% of general education requirements for graduation are elective; distribution requirements fairly numerous. Average undergraduate class size: 67% under 20, 31% 20–40, 2% over 40. About 53% of students entering as freshmen graduate within four years; 34% of freshmen do return for sophomore year. *Special programs:* CLEP, study abroad, 3–2 engineering. *Calendar:* semester, summer school.

Undergraduate degrees conferred (379). 28% were in Business and Management, 10% were in Education, 9% were in Health Sciences, 9% were in Marketing and Distribution, 8% were in Psychology, 7% were in Visual and Performing Arts, 5% were in Social Sciences, 5% were in Philosophy and Religion, 4% were in Letters, 4% were in Communications, remainder in 8 other fields.

Student Body. College seeks a national student body; 72% of students from in state; 5% foreign. An estimated 77% of students reported as Protestant, 9% as Catholic, 12% as unaffiliated; 2% as Black, 8% other ethnic minorities.

Religious Orientation. Belmont is a church-related institution; 6 semester hours of Bible, 10 convocational and cultural life credits required of all students.

Varsity Sports. Men (NAIA): Baseball, Basketball, Cross Country, Golf, Soccer, Tennis. Women (NAIA): Basketball, Cross Country, Golf, Softball, Tennis, Volleyball.

Campus Life. There are 3 male and 2 female traditional dormitories. Townhouses for men and women to be completed by Fall 1994. About 30% of men, 25% of women live in dormitories; rest commute. Freshmen are given preference in college housing if all students cannot be accommodated. There are two fraternities and two sororities.

Annual Costs. Tuition and fees, $7,100; room and board, $3,610; estimated $1,480 other, exclusive of travel. About 75% of students receive financial aid; average amount of assistance, $6,368. College reports some scholarships awarded on the basis of academic merit alone.

Beloit College

Beloit, Wisconsin 53511 **(608) 363-2500 (out-of-state) (800) 356-075**

Ostensibly a small, traditional midwestern liberal arts college, Beloit has twice in the past twenty-five years introduced imaginative changes in its calendar and curriculum to meet emerging changes in higher education. The major programs of the experimental years have been retained as the college returned to a more traditional pattern. However, in many ways Beloit remains a less conventional school than other top midwestern colleges primarily because of the great diversity of its student body and the variety of off-campus work and educational experiences it makes available to its students. Although college is historically related to the United Church of Christ, it has always been nonsectarian and welcomes students of all races and creeds. Located in a community of 36,000, the 65-acre campus is about 70 miles southwest of Milwaukee. Most convenient major airports: Chicago, Milwaukee, Madison.

Founded: 1846
Affiliation: Independent
UG Enrollment: 485 M, 638 W (full-time)
Total Enrollment: 1,211
Cost: $10K–$20K
% Receiving Financial Aid: 83%
Admission: Very Selective
Application Deadline: March 15

Admission is very selective. About 77% of applicants accepted, 30% of these actually enroll; 43% of freshmen graduate in top fifth of high school class, 75% in top two-fifths. Average freshman scores: SAT, 549 verbal, 575 mathematical; 73% freshmen score above 500 on verbal, 31% above 600, 2% above 700; 83% score above 500 on mathematical, 40% over 600, 11% above 700; ACT, 26 M, 26 W composite. Criteria considered in admissions, in order of importance: high school academic record, writing sample, extra-curricular activities, recommendations, standardized test scores; other factors considered: special talents, diverse student body. *Required:* SAT or ACT, essay. *Entrance programs:* early decision, early admission, midyear admission, deferred admission, advanced placement. About 20% of freshmen from private schools, 80% public schools. *Apply* preferably by March 15; rolling admissions. *Transfers* welcome; 40 enrolled 1993–94.

Academic Environment. Degrees offered: bachelors, masters. Pressures for academic achievement appear moderately intense; however, administration source claims "the emphasis is on learning, not grades." Majority of students reported as academically, intellectually inclined and majors selected clearly indicate a liberal arts centered student body with few degrees conferred in professional/vocational areas. Faculty adviser system for freshmen aims to develop "a deep and genuine intellectual relationship." Curriculum is organized into 3 divisions: social sciences, natural sciences and mathematics, arts and humanities. Students expected to take courses in each area as well as meet proficiency requirements in English composition (a "writing intensive" course) and participate in the First Year Initiative (FYI) Program of freshmen seminars in addition to courses in their major/interdisciplinary minor or double major program. Continued emphasis on experiential learning offers a wide range of field terms, internships, summer jobs, study in various programs on- and off-campus, which help to broaden students' personal and vocational experience and interests. Students may select among 46 fields of concentration or set up their own programs of study. Students participate as members of faculty Academic Senate and sit on major senate committees. Average undergraduate class size: 80% under 20, 18% between 20–40, 2% over 40. *Special programs:* study abroad; 3–2 programs in engineering, nursing, social services, forestry, enviromental management, medical technology, MBA.

About 68% of students entering as freshmen graduate eventually; 97% of freshmen return for sophomore year. *Special programs:* honors, independent study, study abroad (choice of seminars of 20 students under Beloit professor, cooperative programs conducted in English, or individual study), undergraduate research, ACM sponsored programs, Porter Scholars, credit by examination, archaeological and geological field schools, astronomy, Washington Semester, dual-degree and combined-degree programs in nursing, medical technology, business, engineering, forest and environmental management, social work, teaching, conditional early acceptance to Medical College of Wisconsin. *Calendar:* semester.

Undergraduate degrees conferred (243). 42% were in Social Sciences, 16% were in Letters, 9% were in Psychology, 8% were in Visual and Performing Arts, 8% were in Life Sciences, 4% were in Physical Sciences, 4% were in Foreign Languages, 3% were in Mathematics, remainder in 4 other fields.

Graduates Career Data. Advanced studies pursued by 31% of students; 2% enter medical or dental school; 3% enter law school; 2% enter business school. Medical schools typically enrolling largest numbers of graduates include U. of Wisconsin, Medical College of Wisconsin, Washington U.; law schools include U. of Wisconsin, U. of Chicago; business schools include Chicago, Northwestern, Washington U. *Careers in business and industry* pursued by 40% of graduates. Corporations typically hiring largest numbers of graduates include Peace Corps, Arthur Andersen, American National Bank, McCann Erickson. Career Development Services include placement service, alumni job network, SIGI, internships, field terms, experiential learning.

Faculty. About 94% of faculty hold PhD or equivalent. About 52% of undergraduate classes taught by tenured faculty. About 30% of teaching faculty are female; 6% minorities.

Student Body. College seeks a national student body; about 22% of students from in state; 66% Midwest, 10% international. An estimated 60% of students reported as Protestant, 25% Catholic, 10% Jewish; 3% as Black, 3% Asian, 2% Hispanic, 10% other minority. *Minority group students:* special counseling, tutoring, activity programs through Educational Development Program and Skills Center, and precollegiate programs starting in elementary school; "need-blind" admissions.

Religious Orientation. Founded by members of the Congregational and Presbyterian churches, Beloit has always been nonsectarian by charter and makes no religious demands on students.

Varsity Sports. Men (Div.III): Baseball, Basketball, Cross Country, Diving, Football, Golf, Soccer, Swimming, Tennis, Track. Women

(Div.III): Basketball, Cross Country, Diving, Soccer, Softball, Swimming, Tennis, Track, Volleyball.
Campus Life. Students have significant role in determining policy and planning programs. Students expected to live in residence halls for six terms (3 years). Housing includes traditional and coed dormitories (with sexes segregated by wing, floor, or room), plus fraternity and special interest group houses. Despite distance from major cultural center, only 4% of students reported to leave campus on weekends, apparently because of the wide variety of events college provides; campus is 50 miles from Madison, 90 miles from Chicago.

About 23% men, 36% women live in traditional dormitories (including single-sex floors of coed dorms); 46% of men, 48% of women live in coed dormitories; 5% of men, 6% of women live in off-campus housing; 8% of each commute. There are 4 fraternities, 2 sororities which about 10% of men, 5% of women join; 18% of students live in fraternities and 2% in sororities. About 4% of students leave campus on weekends.
Annual Costs. Tuition and fees, $15,430; room and board, $3,520; estimated $1,050 other, exclusive of travel. About 83% of students receive financial aid; average amount of assistance, $11,783. Assistance is typically divided 49% scholarship, 21% grant, 20% loan, 10% work. College reports 76 scholarships for academic merit alone, 832 for need alone. College offers broad program of grants, loans, and work opportunities, including "moral obligation" scholarships involving a moral but not a legal obligation to repay in future years.

Bemidji State University

Bemidji, Minnesota 56601 (218)755-2040

A state-supported university, located in a city of 11,500, 150 miles west of Duluth. Most convenient major airport: Minneapolis/St. Paul.

Founded: 1913
Affiliation: State
UG Enrollment: 1,683 M, 1,762 W (full-time); 353 M, 660 W (part-time)
Total Enrollment: 5,017
Cost: < $10K
% Receiving Financial Aid: 95%
Admission: Non-selective
Application Deadline: Aug. 15

Admission. Minnesota graduates of high school who rank in top half of class or score 21.0 or score minimum of 21 on ACT eligible; others given individual consideration; 73% of applicants accepted, 64% of these actually enroll; 28% of freshmen graduate in top fifth of high school class, 58% in top two-fifths. Average freshman ACT scores: 21.1 M, 21.0 W composite. *Required:* ACT. Criteria considered in admissions, in order of importance: high school academic record, standardized test scores, recommendations, extracurricular activities, writing sample. *Out-of-state* freshman applicants: university seeks students from out of state. State does not limit out-of-state enrollment, no special requirements. *Apply* by August 15; rolling admissions. *Transfers* welcome, 526 enrolled 1993–94.
Academic Environment. Degrees offered: associates, bachelors, masters. Core requirements include courses in freshman English, humanities, social sciences, physical sciences, liberal education activities, and physical education. Computer literacy required of all students. *Majors offered* in addition to usual studies include accounting, aquatic biology, criminal justice, technical illustration commercial design, model building, nursing, engineering, physics. About 31% of students entering as freshmen do not return for sophomore year. *Special programs:* study abroad, internships, 3–1 program in medical technology, cross registration through state system. *Calendar:* quarter, summer school.
Undergraduate degrees conferred (665). 35% were in Education, 15% were in Business and Management, 6% were in Protective Services, 6% were in Visual and Performing Arts, 6% were in Social Sciences, 5% were in Engineering and Engineering Related Technology, 4% were in Psychology, 4% were in Life Sciences, 4% were in Public Affairs, 3% were in Communications, remainder in 13 other fields.
Faculty. About 70% of faculty hold PhD or equivalent. About 26% of teaching faculty are female; 4% ethnic minorities.
Student Body. University seeks a national student body; about 89% of students from in state; 93% Midwest, 6% foreign. Average age of undergraduate student: 25.
Varsity Sports. Men (NAIA-NCAA Div. II): Basketball, Baseball, Football, Golf, Hockey, Track. Women (NAIA-NCAA Div. II): Basketball, Softball, Tennis, Track, Volleyball.
Campus Life. About 30% of students live in coed dormitories; rest commute. Freshmen given preference in college housing if all students cannot be accommodated. Sexes segregated in dormitories by floor; intervisitation unlimited. There are 4 fraternities on campus which about 1% of men, 1% of women join; they provide no residence facilities. About 50% of resident students leave campus on weekends.
Annual Costs. Tuition and fees, $2,516 (out-of-state, $4,808); room and board, $2,672; estimated $2,500 other, exclusive of travel. About 95% of students receive financial aid. University reports some scholarships awarded on the basis of academic merit alone. *Meeting Costs:* university offers PLUS Loans.

Benedict College

Columbia, South Carolina 29204 (803)253-5143

An independent college with a long association with the Baptist church, Benedict retains "a Christian orientation," but is "increasingly nonsectarian." The college is located in a city of 101,229, was founded as a college for Negroes and still serves a predominantly Black student body. Most convenient major airport: Columbia Metropolitan.

Founded: 1870
Affiliation: American Baptist
Total Enrollment: 503 M, 1012 W (full-time)
Cost: < $10K
Admission: Non-selective
Application Deadline: Rolling

Admission. Graduates of approved high schools with 19 units (preferably 16 in academic subjects) eligible; others admitted by examination; open admissions; 69% of applicants accepted, 52% of these actually enroll. Non-academic factor considered in admissions: special talents. *Apply:* rolling admissions. *Transfers* welcome.
Academic Environment. *Degrees:* BA, BS. About 43% of general education requirements for graduation are elective; no distribution requirements. About 76% of students entering as freshmen graduate eventually; 39% of freshmen do not return for sophomore year. *Special programs:* 3–2 programs available with Clemson, Georgia Tech., Southern Technical Institute. *Calendar:* semester, summer school.
Undergraduate degrees conferred (152). 30% were in Business and Management, 13% were in Protective Services, 11% were in Education, 9% were in Public Affairs, 7% were in Physical Sciences, 7% were in Computer and Engineering Related Technology, 6% were in Social Sciences, 5% were in Communications, 5% were in Life Sciences, 3% were in Marketing and Distribution, remainder in 3 other fields.
Graduates Career Data. According to most recent data available, full-time graduate or professional study pursued immediately after graduation by 19% of students; 5% enter business school.
Varsity Sports. Men (NAIA): Baseball, Basketball, Cross Country, Tennis, Track. Women (NAIA): Basketball, Cross Country, Softball, Volleyball.
Campus Life. College seeks a national student body; 85% of students from in state. An estimated 72% of students reported as Protestant, 2% Catholic, 27% unaffiliated or other; 99% Black. Benedict is a church-related institution; campus religious programs and services directed by the College Minister.

About 78% of students live in traditional dormitories; no coed dormitories; rest live in off-campus housing or commute. No intervisitation in men's or women's dormitory rooms. Freshmen given preference in college housing if all students cannot be accommodated. There are 4 fraternities, 4 sororities on campus which about 6% of men, 10% of women join; they provide no residence facilities.
Annual Costs. Tuition and fees, $5,534; room and board, $2,892. About 85% of students receive financial aid. College reports some scholarships awarded on the basis of academic merit alone.

Benedictine College

Atchison, Kansas 66002-1499 (913) 367-5340

A Benedictine, Roman Catholic, residential and liberal arts college located in a town of 13,000, 50 miles northwest of Kansas City.

Founded: 1971
Affiliation: Roman Catholic
UG Enrollment: 421 M, 292 W (full-time)
Total Enrollment: 780
Cost: < $10K
% Receiving Financial Aid: 98%
Admission: Non-selective
Application Deadline: Aug. 1

Admission. About 98% of applicants accepted, 38% of these actually enroll; 34% of freshmen graduate in top fourth of high school class, 61% in top half. Average freshman ACT scores: 22.3 composite. Criteria considered in admissions, in order of importance: high school academic record, standardized test scores, class rank, recommendations, extra curricular activities; other factors considered: diverse student body. *Required:* ACT minimum of 18 (or SAT 700 combined); minimum HS GPA of 2.0, and rank in top half of high school class. *Entrance programs:* midyear admission. About 68% of freshman are from private or parochial schools. *Apply* by: August 1, rolling admissions. *Transfers* welcome; 45 enrolled 1993–94.
Academic Environment. Degrees offered: bachelors. Core requirements include 3 courses in religion, philosophy, foreign language, 2 in world civilization, social sciences, and 1 each in English composition, literature, mathematics, natural sciences, fine arts, and physical education. Unusual majors offered include astronomy, sports management, athletic training. Average undergraduate class size: 20% under 20, 60% between 20–40, 20% over 40. Adult programs: Institute for Religious Studies provides theological education for ministers, Catholic school teachers, religious educators, and other interested adults. *Special programs:* study abroad; 3–2 programs in engineering, medical technology, physical therapy, occupational therapy, individualized majors. About 43% of students entering as freshmen graduate eventually; 60% of freshmen return for sophomore year. *Calendar:* semester.
Undergraduate degrees conferred (129). 25% were in Business and Management, 21% were in Social Sciences, 17% were in Education, 9% were in Life Sciences, 9% were in Letters, 5% were in Communications, 4% were in Mathematics, remainder in 7 other fields.
Graduates Career Data. Advanced studies pursued by 17% of students; 2% medical school; 2% law school. About 83% of 1992–93 graduates employed. Fields typically hiring largest numbers of graduates include business, accounting, education, social services, technical. Career Development Services include assessment, counseling, emplpoyment fairs, career days, interviewing days, printed resources, Job Guarantee Program, alumni network, job listings.
Faculty. About 86% of faculty hold PhD or equivalent. About 39% of teaching faculty are female; 6% Hispanic, 1% other minority.
Student Body. About 62% of students from in state, 91% Midwest, 2% South, 2% West, 1% Northwest, 3% foreign; 13% Protestant, 65% Catholic, 16% unaffiliated, 6% other; 3% Black, 5% Hispanic, 2% other minority.
Religious Orientation. Benedictine College is a church-related institution; 3 courses in religion are required of all students.
Varsity Sports. Men (NAIA II): Baseball, Basketball, Football, Golf, Soccer, Tennis. Women (NAIA): Basketball, Soccer, Softball, Tennis, Track, Volleyball.
Campus Life. About 90% of men, 90% of women live in traditional dormitories; no coed dormitories; rest live in off-campus housing or commute. Intervisitation in men's and women's dormitory rooms limited. There are no fraternities or sororities. About 25% of residential students leave campus on weekends.
Annual Costs. Tuition and fees, $9,080; room and board, $3,750. About 98% of students receive financial aid; average amount of assistance, $6,500. Assistance is typically divided 20% schoalrship, 10% grant, 65% loan, 5% work. College reports 20 scholarships awarded for academic merit alone, 18 for special talents, 2 for need.

Bennett College

Greensboro, North Carolina 27401 **(919) 370-8624**

A church-related college for women, located in a city of 150,000. Most convenient major airport: Piedmont International

Founded: 1873
Affiliation: United Methodist
Total Enrollment: 569 W (full-time)
Cost: < $10K
% Receiving Financial Aid: 78%
Admission: Non-selective
Application Deadline: Aug. 1

Admission. High school graduates with 16 units (12 in academic subjects) eligible. About 72% of applicants accepted, 59% of these actually enroll. Average freshman ACT scores, according to most recent data available: 12 composite, 12 mathematical. *Required:* SAT or ACT, essay. *Apply* by August 1; rolling admissions. *Transfers* welcome.
Academic Environment. *Degrees:* BA, BS, BFA. *Special programs:* CLEP, independent study, Greensboro Regional Consortium for High Education, dual degree program in engineering with NC A & T. *Calendar:* semester.
Undergraduate degrees conferred (65). 32% were in Business and Management, 17% were in Life Sciences, 14% were in Multi/Interdisciplinary Studies, 12% were in Education, 6% were in Mathematics, 5% were in Psychology, 3% were in Public Affairs, 3% were in Letters, 3% were in Computer and Engineering Related Technology, remainder in 3 other fields.
Graduates Career Data. According to most recent data available, full-time graduate or professional study pursued by 20% of students immediately after graduation. *Careers in business and industry* pursued by 20% of graduates.
Faculty. About 52% of faculty hold PhD or equivalent.
Campus Life. College seeks a national student body; 41% of students from South, 41% Middle Atlantic. About 85% of women live in traditional dormitories; rest commute.
Annual Costs. Tuition and fees, $6,011; room and board, $2,250. About 78% of students receive financial aid; average amount of assistance, 60% of tuition and fees. Assistance is typically divided 20% scholarship, 65% loan, 39% work. College reports some scholarships awarded on the basis of academic merit alone.

Bennington College

Bennington, Vermont 05201 **(802) 442-6349**

Bennington was founded as an experimental college on the premise that "learning should be acquired actively and personally; and that an undergraduate education should be not merely a preparation for graduate school or a career, but an experience valuable in itself and the model for a lifelong vocation of learning." The college has always included the visual and performing arts as an integral part of the academic program. The 550-acre campus is located at the foot of the Green Mountains, 4 miles from a town of 18,000 in southwest Vermont, about 40 miles northeast of Albany, New York. Most convenient major airport: Albany, New York.

Founded: 1932
Affiliation: Independent
Total Enrollment: 186 M, 279 W (full-time)
Cost: > $20K
% Receiving Financial Aid: 80%
Admission: Very Selective
Application Deadline: Jan. 1

Admission is very selective. About 62% of applicants accepted, 38% of these actually enroll; 47% of freshmen graduate in top fifth of high school class, 85% in top two-fifths. Average freshman SAT scores; 565 verbal, 551 mathematical, middle fifty percent range: SAT, 520–620 verbal, 500–600 mathematical; ACT, 25 composite. Criteria considered in admissions, in order of importance: writing sample, interview, high school academic record, recommendations, extra curricular activities, standardized test scores; other factors considered: special talents, alumni children. *Required:* SAT or ACT, essay, interview. *Entrance programs:* early decision, early admission, midyear admission, deferred admission. *Apply* by January 1 (regular decision); November 15 (early decision). *Transfers* welcome; 63 enrolled 1993–94.
Academic Environment. With faculty members serving as advisors Bennington students are expected "to construct both the overall shape of their academic program and their individual majors." Bennington's 7:1 student/faculty ratio doubtless contributes to the interaction and individualized attention students consider the greatest academic strength of the college. College calls attention to small classes, access to the seminar and tutorial format in the junior and senior year, and to the off-campus 8-week cooperative work program, in which all students participate each year. Standard course patterns, examinations, and other hallmarks of traditional college conspicuously absent at Bennington. Outstanding characteristic is heavy concentration on the arts in the curriculum, however, natural sciences and social sciences are reported to be very strong and gain-

ing popularity as majors. Students are evaluated with written comments by the faculty. Grades are not given. Although there are no specific required courses, there is "a required balance": each student must include work from 4 different divisions in first 2 years and complete by graduation 1 year beyond introductory level in each of 3 disciplines, as well as a senior project or thesis.

Degree offered: bachelors. Average undergraduate class size: 95% under 20. *Special programs:* independent study, study abroad, individualized majors, group and individual tutorials. About 62% of students entering as freshmen graduate eventually; 85% of freshmen return for sophomore year. *Calendar:* semester, 8-week nonresident winter term.

Undergraduate degrees conferred (157). 50% were in Visual and Performing Arts, 30% were in Letters, 15% were in Social Sciences, 6% were in Multi/Interdisciplinary Studies.

Graduates Career Data. According to most recent data available, full-time graduate or professional study pursued by 30% of students immediately after graduation. *Careers in business and industry* pursued by 13% of graduates. Career Development Services include assistance with resume and cover letter production, job placement and graduate school application.

Faculty. About 40% of faculty hold PHD or equivalent.

Student Body. About 6% of students from in state; 24% Middle Atlantic, 30% New England, 12% West, 7% Northwest, 7% South, 8% Midwest, 12% foreign students. An estimated 7% of students reported as Black, 2% Hispanic, 9% Asian American. *Minority group students:* financial aid available through Educational Opportunity Grants Program and College Work-Study Program.

Religious Orientation. Bennington is an independent institution, makes no religious demands on students; little evidence that religion is a major concern on campus.

Campus Life. Students have almost total control over campus social life. College conceives of itself as a "small but open community" in which everyone is expected to participate in decision making. A student judicial council handles most cases governing student conduct. Bennington is significantly influenced by its isolation, the nearest major cultural centers, Boston and New York, are 200 miles away, but students report that there are always many cultural and academic activities on campus. Coed intramural and informal intercollegiate sports: soccer, tennis, volleyball. Cars permitted. Limited number of upper-class students may choose to live off campus.

About 98% each of men, women live in coed dormitories; rest live in off-campus college-related housing. Freshmen given preference in college housing if all students cannot be accommodated. Intervisitation in men's and women's dormitory rooms unlimited; sexes segregated by room. There are no fraternities or sororities. An estimated 5% of students leave campus on weekends.

Annual Costs. Comprehensive fee, $24,850, estimated $1,000 other, exclusive of travel. About 80% of students receive financial aid; average amount of assistance, $14,000. Assistance is typically divided 74% scholarship, 18% loan, 8% work. College reports scholarships awarded only on the basis of need.

Bentley College

Waltham, Massachusetts 02254 (617) 891-2244

An independent, professional institution, offering programs in accounting, business, and the liberal arts, located on a 110-acre campus in a suburb of 61,600, 9 miles from Boston. Most convenient major airport: Logan (Boston).

Founded: 1917
Affiliation: Independent
UG Enrollment: 2,087 M, 1,773 W (full-time); 645 M, 897 W (part-time)
Total Enrollment: 7,150
Cost: $10K–$20K
% Receiving Financial Aid: 53%
Admission: Selective
Application Deadline: Mar. 10

Admission is selective. About 63% of applicants accepted, 39% of these actually enroll; 47% of freshmen graduate in top fifth of high school class, 87% in top two-fifths. *Non-academic factors* considered in admissions: special talents, diverse student body, alumni children. About 8% of entering students from private schools, 14% from parochial schools. *Required:* SAT or ACT; interview recom mended. *Apply* by March 10. *Transfers* welcome.

Academic Environment. *Degrees:* BA, BS, BA/MBA. About 47% of general education requirements for graduation are elective; distribution requirements fairly numerous. Bentley is committed to the integration of computers into the curriculum; computer literacy required of all students. All entering freshmen required to lease microcomputer. College facilitates student ownership. Facilities reported as adequate to meet student demand. About 75% of entering students graduate eventually; 10% of freshmen do not return for sophomore year. *Special programs:* study abroad, directed study of specialized topic, internships, departmental honors. *Calendar:* semester.

Undergraduate degrees conferred (997). 89% were in Business and Management, 4% were in Computer and Engineering Related Technology, 3% were in Communications, 3% were in Liberal/General Studies, remainder in 2 other fields.

Graduates Career Data. *Careers in business and industry* pursued by 95% of graduates. Corporations typically hiring largest numbers of graduates include Digital Equipment Corp., Raytheon, Peat Marwick.

Varsity Sports. Men (Div.II): Baseball, Basketball, Cross Country, Football (III), Golf, Hockey, Soccer, Tennis, Track, Swimming. Women (Div. II): Basketball, Cross Country, Field Hockey, Softball, Tennis, Volleyball, Track.

Campus Life. About 57% of students from in state; 84% New England. An estimated 65% of students reported as Catholic, 20% Protestant, 5% Jewish, 7% unaffiliated, 3% other; 2% Black, 4% Hispanic, 2% Asian, according to most recent data available.

About 69% of men, 73% of women live in coed dormitories or apartments; rest live in off-campus housing or commute. Freshmen given preference in college housing if all students cannot be accommodated. There are 6 fraternities and 4 sororities, which 15% of men, 10% of women join; they provide no residence facilities.

Annual Costs. Tuition and fees, $12,880; room and board, $5,200. About 53% of students receive financial aid; assistance is typically divided 59% scholarship, 33% loan, 8% work. College reports some scholarships awarded on the basis of academic merit alone. *Meeting Costs:* college offers tuition prepayment plan, installment payment plan.

Berea College

Berea, Kentucky 40404 (606) 986-9341

Primarily for residents of the Southern Appalachian region, the college is located in a town of 9,000 in the Cumberland Mountains. Berea operates a varied labor program in which all students participate to meet a substantial portion of college expenses. Most convenient major airport: Bluegrass Field (Lexington).

Founded: 1855
Affiliation: Independent
Total Enrollment: 690 M, 850 W (full-time)
Cost: < $10K
% Receiving Financial Aid: 100%
Admission: Selective
Application Deadline: Rolling

Admission is selective. College gives preference to qualified applicants from families of modest income who live in 338 mountain counties in 9 Southern Appalachian states. About 33% of applicants accepted, 76% of these actually enroll; 53% of freshmen graduate in top fifth of high school class, 79% in top two-fifths. Average freshman scores: SAT, 453 M, 476 W verbal, 532 M, 496 W mathematical; 37% score above 500 on verbal, 8% above 600; 57% score above 500 on mathematical; 23% above 600, 2% above 700; ACT, 21.8 M, 22.7 W composite. Criteria considered in admissions, in order of importance: high school class rank and academic record, standardized test scores, writing sample, recommendations, extra curricular activities. *Required:* SAT or ACT, parents' financial statement, essay. *Entrance programs:* mid-year admission. About 7% of freshman are from private or parochial schools. *Apply:* rolling admissions. *Transfers* welcome; 53 enrolled 1993–94.

Academic Environment. Degrees offered: bachelors. College places emphasis on cross-disciplinary learning; core requirements include course work in quantitative reasoning, religion, natural science, physical science, cultural areas, fine arts, and wellness. About 54% of students entering as freshmen graduate eventually; 73% of freshmen return for sophomore year. *Special programs:* January term, independent study, study abroad, individualized majors, 3–2 engineering. *Calendar:* 4–1–4, summer school.

Undergraduate degrees conferred (281). 16% were in Business and Management, 13% were in Social Sciences, 10% were in Education, 9% were in Letters, 6% were in Agricultural Sciences, 5% were in Psychology, 5% were in Physical Sciences, 5% were in Visual and Performing Arts, 5% were in Engineering and Engineering Related Technology, 5% were in Life Sciences, 5% were in Vocational Home Economics, 5% were in Foreign Languages, 3% were in Home Economics, 3% were in Health Sciences, remainder in 4 other fields.

Graduates Career Data. According to most recent data available, full-time graduate or professional study pursued by 20% of students immediately after graduation. Career Development Services include counseling, resume and interviewing workshops, student employment opportunities, career fairs, summer job opportunities.

Faculty. About 81% of faculty hold PhD or equivalent. About 71% of full-time faculty are tenured. About 38% of teaching faculty are female; 11% minority.

Student Body. About 48% of students from in-state, 80% of students from Southern Appalachian mountain area. College tries to use 20% out-of-territory quota to secure students from other areas; 6% foreign students 1993–94. An estimated 9% of students reported as Black, 8% other minority.

Religious Orientation. Berea is a nondenominational, independent institution, makes some religious demands on students; one course in religion is required, and attendance at 10 convocation events each semester required of all students.

Varsity Sports. Men (NAIA): Baseball, Basketball, Cross Country (coed), Golf(coed), Soccer(coed), Swimming (coed), Tennis, Track. Women (NCAA Div.III): Cross Country (coed), Field Hockey, Golf (coed), Slow Pitch Softball, Swimming (coed), Tennis, Volleyball.

Campus Life. About 86% of men, 83% of women live in traditional dormitories; no coed dormitories; 2% of men, 3% of women live in off-campus housing; rest commute. There are no fraternities or sororities.

Annual Costs. No tuition; fees, $183; room and board, $2,700; estimated $1,187 other, exclusive of travel. All students work a minimum of 10 hours a week at labor assignments in lieu of tuition and earn at least one-third of expenses.

Berklee College of Music

Boston, Massachusetts 02215

A private, professional school of contemporary music offering programs leading to a BM degree or professional diploma in composition, arranging, music education, film scoring, or music business/management. Specialized programs include: commercial arranging, music production and engineering, music synthesis, film scoring. Its primary purpose is to prepare students for careers in music.

Founded: 1945 **Affiliation:** Independent

Bernard M. Baruch College

(See City University of New York)

Berry College

Rome, Georgia 30149 **(404) 236-2215**

An independent, nonsectarian, Christian institution located in the suburbs of Rome (pop. 79,800), 65 miles northwest of Atlanta. Most convenient major airport: Atlanta.

Founded: 1902
Affiliation: Independent
Total Enrollment: 1,657 M, W (full-time)
Cost: < $10K
% Receiving Financial Aid: 92%
Admission: Selective
Application Deadline: 30 days before term

Admission is selective. About 55% of applicants accepted, 42% of these actually enroll; 46% of freshmen graduate in top fifth of high school class, 88% in top two-fifths. *Required:* SAT or ACT; interview recommended. *Entrance programs:* early decision, early admission, midyear admission, deferred admission, advanced placement. *Apply* by 30 days prior to beginning of term. *Transfers* welcome.

Academic Environment. *Degrees:* AB, BS, BM. About 46% of general education requirements for graduation are elective; distribution requirements fairly numerous. *Majors offered* include communications, fashion merchandising. About 50% of entering students graduate eventually; 28% of freshmen do not return for sophomore year. *Library:* select depository for government documents. *Calendar:* quarter, summer school.

Undergraduate degrees conferred (248). 92% were in Visual and Performing Arts, 8% were in Education.

Graduates Career Data. *Full-time graduate or professional study* pursued immediately after graduation by 26% of students, according to most recent data available. Medical and dental schools typically enrolling largest numbers of graduates include Medical College of Georgia; law schools include U. of Georgia, Emory; business schools include Georgia State, U. of Georgia, Berry. *Careers in business and industry* pursued by 48% of graduates. Corporations typically hiring largest numbers of graduates include Trust Company Bank, First Wachovia Corp., State Farm Insurance. *Career Counseling Program* includes course entitled Career Development, computer assisted career guidance counseling, Career Day, job shadowing program. Alumni reported to be active in career guidance and job placement.

Faculty. About 81% of faculty hold PhD or equivalent.

Student Body. College seeks a national student body; 79% of students from in state; 94% South. An estimated 72% of students reported as Protestant, 9% Catholic, 3% other; 2% Black, 2% other minority,according to most recent data available.

Religious Orientation. Berry is a nonsectarian institution with a Christian environment; 1 course in either religion or philosophy required of all students; Sunday service available.

Varsity Sports. Men (NAIA): Baseball, Basketball, Cross Country, Soccer, Tennis. Women (NAIA): Basketball, Cross Country, Soccer, Tennis.

Campus Life. About 80% of men, 78% of women live in traditional dormitories; no coed dormitories; rest live in off-campus housing or commute. Freshmen given preference in college housing if all students cannot be accommodated. Intervisitation in men's and women's dormitory rooms limited. There are no fraternities or sororities. About 20–40% of students leave campus on weekends.

Annual Costs. Tuition and fees, $6,450; room and board, $3,116; estimated $1,460 other, exclusive of travel. About 92% of students receive financial aid; assistance is typically divided 35% scholarship, 30% loan, 35% work. College reports some scholarships awarded on the basis of academic merit alone. *Meeting Costs:* all students are assured work opportunities.

Bethany Bible College

Santa Cruz, California 95066

A church-related institution, the college is devoted to preparing students for various church ministries as well as public and private elementary education.

Founded: 1919 **Affiliation:** Assemblies of God

Bethany College

Lindsborg, Kansas 67456 **(913) 227-3311**

A church-related, liberal arts college, located in a community of 3,500 in the Smoky Valley region of central Kansas, 75 miles north of Wichita. Most convenient major airport: Wichita Mid-Continent.

Founded: 1881
Affiliation: Evangelical Lutheran Church in America
Total Enrollment: 381 M, 325 W (full-time)
Cost: < $10K
% Receiving Financial Aid: 97%
Admission: Non-selective
Application Deadline: Rolling

Admission. High school graduates with 16 units eligible; 93% of applicants accepted, 24% of these actually enroll. Average freshman ACT scores: 22.9 composite. Criteria considered in admissions, in order of importance: high school academic record, standardized test scores, writing sample, recommendations. *Required:* minimum ACT composite score of 19 and H.S. GPA of 2.5. *Entrance programs:* midyear admission. About 18% of freshman come from private schools. *Apply:* rolling admissions. *Transfers* welcome; 71 enrolled 1993–94.

Academic Environment. Degrees offered: bachelors. Average undergraduate class size: 80% under 20, 15% between 20–40; 5% over 40. *Special programs:* January term; 3–2 programs in aerospace, electrical, mechanical & industrial engineering, experience-based education. About 32% of students entering as freshmen graduate in 4 years; 76% of freshmen return for sophomore year. *Calendar:* 4–1–4.

Undergraduate degrees conferred (147). 35% were in Education, 22% were in Business and Management, 7% were in Social Sciences, 6% were in Psychology, 6% were in Parks and Recreation, 5% were in Life Sciences, 4% were in Visual and Performing Arts, 4% were in Public Affairs, 3% were in Computer and Engineering Related Technology, remainder in 5 other fields.

Graduates Career Data. Advanced studies pursued by 19% of students; 12% enter graduate school, 1% law school, 2% medical school, 2% business school, 2% other. About 94% of 1992–93 graduates employed. Employers typically hiring largest number of graduates include schools, businesses, and social service agencies. Career Development Services include career library, assistance with resume preparation and interviewing skills, computerized self-assessment programs, alumni network for job placement.

Faculty. About 64% of faculty hold PhD or equivalent. All undergraduate classes taught by tenured faculty. About 28% of teaching faculty are female; 2% minority.

Student Body. College seeks a national student body; about 67% of students from Kansas; 86% from Midwest, 5% South, 4% West, 2% Northwest, 3% foreign. An estimated 59% of students reported as Protestant, 23% as Catholic, 17% as unaffiliated or other; 4% as Black, 3% Hispanic, 2% Asian, 4% other minority.

Religious Orientation. Bethany is a church-related institution; 2 courses in religion required of all students; chapel services voluntary.

Varsity Sports. Men (NAIA, Div.II): Baseball, Basketball, Cross Country, Football, Golf, Soccer, Tennis, Track. Women (NAIA, Div.II): Basketball, Cross Country, Golf, Soccer, Softball, Tennis, Track, Volleyball.

Campus Life. About 43% of students live in traditional dormitories; 42% in coed dormitories; 15% commute. There are 3 fraternities, 3 sororities on campus which about 10% of men, 10% of women join; they provide no residence facilities. About 15% of resident students leave campus on weekends.

Annual Costs. Tuition and fees, $8,000; room and board, $3,265. About 97% of students receive financial aid; average amount of assistance, $7,600. Assistance is typically divided 52% scholarship, 38% loan, 10% work, according to most recent data available. College reports some scholarships awarded on the basis of academic merit alone.

Bethany College

Bethany, West Virginia 26032 (304) 829-7600

A small, liberal arts college, with an "historical affiliation" with the Christian Church (Disciples of Christ), located in a village of 800, 40 miles southwest of Pittsburgh. Most convenient major airport: Pittsburgh (PA).

Founded: 1840
Affiliation: Independent (Disciples of Christ)
Total Enrollment: 364 M, 380 W (full-time)
Cost: $10K–$20K
% Receiving Financial Aid: 78%
Admission: Selective
Application Deadline: Rolling

Admission is selective. About 82% of applicants accepted, 39% of these actually enroll; 33% of freshmen graduate in top fifth of high school class, 63% in top two-fifths. Average freshman scores, according to most recent data available: SAT middle fifty percent range, 420–500 verbal, 450–540 mathematical; 38% of freshman score above 500 on verbal, 11% above 600, 1% above 700; 46% score above 500 on mathematical, 16% above 600, 2% above 700; ACT, 21.2 composite. *Required:* SAT or ACT, essay, minimum high school GPA; interview recommended. Criteria considered in admissions, in order of importance: high school academic record, recommendations, standardized test scores, extracurricular activities, writing sample, interview. *Entrance programs:* early decision, early admission, midyear admission, deferred admission, advanced placement. About 8% of entering students from private schools, 28% from parochial schools. *Apply:* rolling admissions. *Transfers* welcome.

Academic Environment. Degrees offered: bachelors. Core requirements include 4 practicum assignments, and 32 credits from 8 general studies areas, senior year project and comprehensive examination (both written and oral). *Majors offered* include usual arts and sciences, applied mathematics, communications, education, fine arts, theater, environmental science, international studies. Average undergraduate class size: 15.

About 85% of students entering as freshmen graduate eventually; 11% of freshmen do not return for sophomore year. *Special programs:* CLEP, honors, independent study, study abroad, undergraduate research, "completely voluntary" January interterm, individualized majors, Washington Semester, United Nations Semester, 3–2 programs in engineering. *Calendar:* 4–1–4.

Undergraduate degrees conferred (171). 22% were in Communications, 16% were in Social Sciences, 16% were in Psychology, 9% were in Business and Management, 7% were in Letters, 6% were in Education, 4% were in Physical Sciences, 4% were in Philosophy and Religion, 4% were in Liberal/General Studies, 3% were in Public Affairs, remainder in 6 other fields.

Graduates Career Data. Advanced studies pursued by 32% of graduates; 4% enter medical school; 8% enter law school; 5% enter business school. Medical schools typically enrolling largest numbers of graduates include Ohio State; law schools include West Virginia U.; business schools include U. of Pittsburgh. About 99% of 1992–93 graduates employed. Fields typically hiring largest numbers of graduates include radio/TV, advertising/PR, education, sales. Career Development Services include resume and interview preparation, employer visits, alumni network, transportation to career fairs.

Faculty. About 75% of faculty hold PhD or equivalent. About 98% of undergraduate classes taught by tenured faculty.

Student Body. College seeks a national student body; 20% of students from in state; 48% Middle Atlantic, 15% New England, 15% Midwest, 8% South, 6% West, 5% foreign. An estimated 65% of students reported as Protestant, 30% Catholic, 3% Jewish, 1% unaffiliated, 1% other; 8% as Black, 2% Asian, 3% Hispanic, 2% other minorities.

Religious Orientation. Although an independent college, "with complete freedom from sectarian control," Bethany has a continuing relationship with the Disciples of Christ; makes no religious demands on students. Both rabbi and Catholic priest teach in religion department. Religious clubs on campus include Newman, Jewish Fellowship, Canterbury; Encounter coordinates religiously oriented service activities on campus. Places of worship available on campus and in immediate community for major faiths.

Varsity Sports. Men (Div.III): Baseball, Basketball, Cross Country, Football, Golf, Soccer, Swimming/Diving, Tennis, Track. Women (Div.III): Basketball, Cross Country, Golf, Soccer, Softball, Swimming/Diving, Tennis, Track, Volleyball.

Campus Life. Students enjoy considerable freedom in their personal and social activities within the fairly broad regulations of the college. After freshman year students live in small residence units; each of the 19 units determines house rules (including intervisitation hours), sponsors social or educational programs. Cars allowed for students in good standing. Pittsburgh is an hour away, Wheeling, W.Va. a half hour; most social life takes place on campus.

About 62% of men, 77% of women live in traditional dormitories; 2% men, 2% women live in coed dormitories; 1% of men, 1% of women commute. Freshmen given preference in college housing if all students cannot be accommodated. There are 6 fraternities, 4 sororities on campus which about 50% of men, 50% of women join; 35% men, 20% of women live in fraternities and sororities. About 20% of resident students leave campus on weekends.

Annual Costs. Tuition and fees, $14,000; room and board, $4,500. About 78% of students receive financial aid, average amount of assistance, $9,850. Assistance is typically divided 20–50% scholarship, 60–65% grant, 15–20% loan, 10–15% work. College reports 35% of scholarships awarded on the basis of academic merit alone, 20% for special talents, 48% for need. *Meeting Costs:* college offers monthly payment plan.

Beth-El College of Nursing

Colorado Springs, Colorado 80917-5338

A specialized college, offering associates, bachelors, and masters degrees in nursing. Students take a year of general education classes at other local colleges.

Founded: 1904 **Affiliation:** Independent

Bethel College

Mishawaka, Indiana 46545 (219) 257-3339

A small, church-related, liberal arts college, located on a 62-acre suburban campus in the twin city (pop. 45,000) of South Bend. Most convenient major airport: Michiana Regional.

Founded: 1947
Affiliation: Missionary
UG Enrollment: 312 M, 421 W (full-time); 133 M, 269 W (part-time)
Total Enrollment: 1,158
Cost: < $10K
% Receiving Financial Aid: 85%
Admission: Non-selective
Application Deadline: Rolling

Admission. Graduates of accredited or commissioned high schools, preferably with 12 units in college preparatory subjects, who rank in top half of class eligible; others admitted on probation. About 84% of applicants accepted, 64% of these actually enroll. About 30% of freshmen graduate in top fifth of high school class, 55% in top two-fifths. Average freshman scores: SAT, 28% of freshmen score above 500 on verbal, 3% above 600; 43% score above 500 on mathematical, 19% above 600, 3% above 700. Criteria considered in admissions, in order of importance: high school academic record, standardized test scores, recommendations, extra curricular activities, writing sample; other factors considered: "Christian commitment." *Required:* SAT or ACT. *Apply:* rolling admissions. *Transfers* welcome; 67 enrolled 1993–94.
Academic Environment. Degrees offered: associates, bachelors, masters. Several students recently polled list small class sizes and "solid Christian perspective" as strengths of the college. About 75% of students entering as freshmen graduate within four years; 70% of freshmen return for sophomore year. Adult programs: Organizational Management for students 25 years or older, accepts previous college work and work experience for credit allowing completion of bachelor's degree in one year; special tuition breaks and evening/weekend classes. *Special programs:* study abroad, internships, 3–2 in engineering. *Calendar:* trimester.
Undergraduate degrees conferred (122). 66% were in Business and Management, 15% were in Education, 5% were in Psychology, 5% were in Health Sciences, remainder in 7 other fields.
Faculty. About 48% of faculty hold PhD or equivalent. About 45% of teaching faculty are female; 4% minority.
Student Body. About 82% of students from Indiana; 93% Midwest, 1% foreign students. An estimated 82% of students reported as Protestant, 11% Catholic, 7% unaffiliated; 13% Black, 1% Asian American. Average age of undergraduate student: 28.
Religious Orientation. Bethel is a church-related institution; 3 courses in religion, attendance at 3 weekly chapel services required of all students.
Varsity Sports. Men (NCCAA/NAIA): Baseball, Basketball, Cross Country, Golf, Soccer, Tennis. Women (NCCAA): Basketball, Cross Country, Softball, Tennis, Volleyball.
Campus Life. About 35% of men, 28% of women live in traditional dormitories; no coed dormitories; rest commute. There are no fraternities or sororities. About 35% of resident students leave the campus on weekends.
Annual Costs. Tuition and fees, $8,700; room and board, $2,900. About 85% of students receive financial aid; average amount of assistance, $6,704. Assistance is typically divided 28% scholarship/grant, 55% loan, 17% work. College reports 179 scholarships awarded on the basis of academic merit alone and 61 for special talents.

Bethel College

North Newton, Kansas 67117 (800) 522-1887 or (316) 283-2500

A church-related, liberal arts college, located on the northern edge of Newton (pop. 15,000), 35 miles north of Wichita. Most convenient major airport: Mid-Continent (Wichita).

Founded: 1887
Affiliation: Mennonite
Total Enrollment: 234 M, 303 W (full-time); 44 M, 57 W (part-time)
Cost: < $10K
% Receiving Financial Aid: 97%
Admission: Non-selective
Application Deadline: Rolling

Admission. Graduates of accredited high schools who rank in top half of class accepted; others admitted if score in top two-thirds on standardized tests; some given individual consideration; 67% of applicants accepted; 55% of these actually enroll. About 19% of entering students graduate in top tenth of high school class, 35% in top fourth, 64% in top half. Average freshman ACT scores: 22.5 composite. Criteria considered in admissions, in order of importance: standardized test scores, high school academic record, recommendations, writing sample, extra curricular activities; other factors considered: special talents, alumni children, religious affiliation and/or commitment. *Required:* ACT (SAT acceptable); interview recommended. *Entrance programs:* early decision, early admission, midyear admission. *Apply:* rolling admissions. *Transfers* welcome; 71 enrolled 1993–94.
Academic Environment. Degrees offered: bachelors. Core requirements include 40–58 credit hours in communications, natural sciences, humanities, social sciences, global awareness, health management, religious studies. Average undergraduate class size: 79% under 20, 18% between 20–40, 3% over 40. Adult programs: RN Outreach - degree completion program for RN's to obtain BSN primarily through off-campus video lectures. *Special programs:* study abroad, January term, cross registration, 3–2 program in engineering, Mexico Internship Program. About 35% of students entering as freshmen graduate within 4 years; 85% of freshmen return for sophomore year. *Calendar:* 4–1–4, summer school.
Undergraduate degrees conferred (125). 17% were in Business and Management, 12% were in Health Sciences, 11% were in Public Affairs, 10% were in Visual and Performing Arts, 10% were in Education, 8% were in Social Sciences, 6% were in Multi/Interdisciplinary Studies, 5% were in Philosophy and Religion, 5% were in Letters, 4% were in Life Sciences, 3% were in Physical Sciences, 3% were in Mathematics, remainder in 4 other fields.
Graduate Career Data. Advanced studies pursued by 8% of students. About 52% of 1992–93 graduates employed. Fields typically hiring largest number of graduates include nursing, education.
Faculty. About 80% of faculty hold PhD or equivalent. About 90% of undergraduate classes taught by tenured faculty. About 41% of teaching faculty are female; 1% minority. Career Development Services include one full-time staff member, SIGI computerized career planning system.
Student Body. About 60% of students from Kansas; 85% Midwest, 1% New England, 4% South, 4% West, 1% Northwest, 5% foreign. An estimated 81% of students reported as Protestant, 9% as Catholic, 5% unaffiliated, 4% other. Average age of undergraduate student: 24.
Religious Orientation. Bethel is a church-related institution, affiliated with the General Conference Mennonite Church; 2 religious courses are required, attendance at biweekly convocations required of all students; chapel service voluntary.
Varsity Sports. Men (NAIA Div.II): Basketball, Football, Soccer, Tennis, Track. Women(NAIA Div.II): Basketball, Tennis, Track, Volleyball.
Campus Life. About 35% of students live in traditional dormitories; 24% in coed dormitories; 5% live in off-campus housing; 36% commute. There are no fraternities or sororities. About 25% of resident students leave campus on weekends.
Annual Costs. Tuition and fees, $8,000; room and board, $3,350; estimated $1,000 other, exclusive of travel. About 97% of students receive financial aid; average amount of assistance, $5,400. Assistance is typically divided 40% scholarship/grant, 53% loan, 17% work. College reports 160 freshman scholarships based on academic merit, 140 based on need.

Bethel College

St. Paul, Minnesota 55112 (612) 638-6242, Aid 638-6241

A church-related, liberal arts college, Bethel gives preference to applicants from Conference Baptist churches. The campus is located in a residential area midway between St. Paul and Minneapolis. Most convenient major airport: Minneapolis/St. Paul.

Founded: 1871
Affiliation: Baptist
Total Enrollment: 1,939 M, W (full-time); 40 M, 77 W (part-time)
Cost: < $10K
Admission: Non-selective
Application Deadline: Rolling

Admission. Graduates of accredited high schools who rank in top half of class eligible; 88% of applicants accepted, 65% of these actually enroll; 49% of freshmen graduate in top fifth of high school class, 78% in top two-fifths. Required: SAT, PSAT or ACT; "reputation as a person with evangelical Christian standards of faith and practice similar to those of Bethel College," pastor's reference. College notes that "students who will insist upon the use of tobacco or alcoholic beverages or participation in activities inconsistent with a Christian commitment are advised not to apply for admission." *Apply:* rolling admissions. *Transfers* welcome.
Academic Environment. *Degree:* AB. About 96% of general education requirements for graduation are elective; distribution requirements limited. *Computer Science* courses offered; none required; major offered. Facilities reported as adequate to meet student demand. About 79% of students entering as freshmen graduate eventually; 8% of freshmen do not return for sophomore year. *Special programs:* January Term, study abroad, adult degree program, 3–2 engineering, American Studies (Washington, DC), urban studies (San Francisco). *Library:* 140,000 volumes and microforms, 640 periodicals, member of CLIC; hours until 10:15 PM (5 PM on weekends). *Calendar:* 4–1–4.
Undergraduate degrees conferred (390). 24% were in Education, 23% were in Business and Management, 11% were in Health Sciences, 8% were in Psychology, 7% were in Social Sciences, 5% were in Communications, 4% were in Life Sciences, 4% were in Public Affairs, 4% were in Theology, 3% were in Physical Sciences, 3% were in Visual and Performing Arts, 3% were in Letters, remainder in 4 other fields.
Varsity Sports. Men (Div.III): Baseball, Basketball, Cross Country, Football, Golf, Hockey, Soccer, Tennis, Track. Women (Div.III): Basketball, Cross Country, Tennis, Track, Volleyball.
Student Body. According to most recent data available, 64% of students from in state; 91% North Central, 4% South. An estimated 98% of students reported as Protestant, 2% Catholic; 2% minority.
Religious Orientation. Bethel is owned and operated by the Baptist General Conference of America; 12 credits in Christianity and philosophy required of all students; daily chapel services available. Participation in Christian service encouraged. Places of worship available on campus for Protestants, in immediate community for 3 major faiths.
Campus Life. About 53% of men, 56% of women live in traditional dormitories; rest live in off-campus housing or commute. Freshmen given preference in college housing if all students cannot be accommodated. Intervisitation in men's and women's dormitory rooms limited. There are no fraternities or sororities. About 60% of students leave campus on weekends.
Annual Costs. Tuition and fees, $9,250; room and board, $3,380; estimated $1,370 other, exclusive of travel. About 89% of students receive financial aid; assistance is typically divided 59% scholarship, 32% loan, 9% work. College reports some scholarships awarded on the basis of academic merit alone. *Meeting Costs:* college offers monthly payment plan.

Bethel College

McKenzie, Tennessee 38201 (901) 352-5321

A church-related college, owned and operated by the Cumberland Presbyterian Church, located in a community of 5,048, 120 miles northeast of Memphis.

Founded: 1842
Affiliation: Presbyterian Church (USA)
Total Enrollment: 675 M, W (full-time)
Cost: < $10K
Admission: Non-selective
Application Deadline: September 20

Admission. Graduates of approved high schools with 11 academic units or rank in top two-thirds of class eligible; others admitted by examination. *Required:* ACT. *Apply* by September 20. *Transfers* welcome.
Academic Environment. *Degrees:* AB, BS. Personal and Cultural Enrichment (PACE) program requires 52 quarter hours credit in Liberal studies. About 60% of students entering as freshmen graduate eventually; 30% of freshmen do not return for sophomore year. *Special programs:* CLEP, 3-year degree, independent study, honors, interdisciplinary majors. *Calendar:* quarter, summer school.
Undergraduate degrees conferred (50). 30% were in Business and Management, 18% were in Social Sciences, 12% were in Education, 10% were in Letters, 6% were in Psychology, 6% were in Philosophy and Religion, 4% were in Physical Sciences, 4% were in Mathematics, 4% were in Life Sciences, remainder in 3 other fields.
Varsity Sports. Men (NAIA III): Baseball, Basketball, Golf. Women (NAIA III): Basketball, Tennis, Volleyball.
Student Body. College seeks a national student body; 87% of students from South.
Religious Orientation. Bethel is a church-related institution; 6 quarter hours of Bible required of all students; attendance at weekly chapel services and daily vespers voluntary. Religious clubs on campus include Newman, Koinonia, Vesper Group.
Campus Life. About 54% of men, 56% of women live in traditional dormitories; no coed dormitories; rest live in off-campus housing or commute. There are 4 fraternities, 5 sororities on campus; they provide no residence facilities. About 70% ("peak") of students leave campus on weekends.
Annual Costs. Tuition and fees, $5,250; room and board, $2,650.

Bethune-Cookman College

Daytona Beach, Florida 32114 (904) 255-1401

A church-related college, located in a city of 100,000, 90 miles south of Jacksonville; founded as a college for Negroes and still serving a predominantly black student body. Most convenient major airport: Daytona Beach.

Founded: 1904
Affiliation: United Methodist
Total Enrollment: 868 M, 1,260 W (full-time); 31 M, 51 W (part-time)
Cost: < $10K
% Receiving Financial Aid: 92%
Admission: Non-selective
Application Deadline: July 30

Admission. Graduates of accredited high schools with 15 units (9 in academic subjects) eligible; 70% of applicants accepted, 51% of these actually enroll; 20% of freshmen graduate in top fifth of high school class, 45% in top two-fifths. Average freshman ACT scores: 16 composite. *Required:* minimum HS GPA, essay, recommendations. Criteria considered in admissions, in order of importance: high school academic record, recommendations, writing sample, standardized test scores, extracurricular activities; other factors considered: special talents. *Entrance programs:* early decision, early admission, midyear admission, deferred admission, advanced placement. *Apply* by July 30; rolling admissions. *Transfers* welcome; 32 enrolled 1993–94.
Academic Environment. Degrees offered: bachelors. General education requirements include 54 credit hours with courses in psychology, English, mathematics, humanities, religion, speech, biological sciences, physical sciences, African American history, and physical education. Computer literacy required of all students. *Majors offered* in addition to usual studies include hospitality management. Average class size: 40% under 20, 50% 20–40, 10% over 40. About 20% of students entering as freshmen graduate within four years, 42% eventually; 67% of freshmen return for sophomore year. *Special programs:* January Term, study abroad, honors, Talent Search, Student Support Services Program, 3–2 engineering, internships and cooperative work/study programs. *Calendar:* semester, summer school.

Undergraduate degrees conferred (326). 46% were in Business and Management, 13% were in Education, 10% were in Protective Services, 8% were in Communications, 6% were in Psychology, 6% were in Social Sciences, 4% were in Health Sciences, remainder in 8 other fields.
Graduates Career Data. Advanced studies pursued by 23% of graduates; 2% enter law school, 9% enter business school. Graduate and professional schools typically enrolling largest numbers of graduates include U. of Florida, Howard U., Nova U., Stetson. About 70% of 1992–93 graduates employed. Employers typically hiring largest numbers of graduates include IBM, Southern Bell, local school districts, retailers. Career Development Services include counseling, career library, on-campus recruitment, SIGI computerized career guidance system, graduate school advisement, career related work experience and summer employment programs, career fairs, Teacher Recruitment Fair, credential file service.
Faculty. About 94% of faculty hold PhD or equivalent. About 25% of undergraduate classes taught by tenured faculty. About 41% of teaching faculty are female; 56% Black, 12% other ethnic minorities.
Student Body. About 83% of students from in state; 87% South, 5% Middle Atlantic, 3% foreign. An estimated 70% of students reported as Protestant, 5% Catholic, 25% other; 96% as Black, 3% other ethnic minority.
Religious Orientation. Bethune-Cookman is a church-related institution; 6 hours of religion and philosophy required of all students. Freshmen must attend religious activities on campus; optional for upperclassmen.
Varsity Sports. Men (Div.I): Baseball, Basketball, Cross Country, Football (IAA), Golf, Tennis, Track. Women (Div.I): Basketball, Cross Country, Softball, Tennis, Track, Volleyball.
Campus Life. About 56% of men, 57% of women live in traditional dormitories; no coed dormitories; rest commute. Freshmen given preference in college housing if all students cannot be accommodated. Intervisitation in men's and women's dormitory rooms limited. There are 4 fraternities, 4 sororities which 2% of men, 5% of women join. About 40% of resident students leave campus on weekends.
Annual Costs. Tuition and fees, $5,165; room and board, $3,210; estimated $2,500 other, exclusive of travel. About 92% of students receive financial aid; average amount of assistance, $6,700. Assistance is typically divided 12% scholarship, 42% grant, 40% loan, 6% work. College reports 40 scholarships awarded on the basis of academic merit alone, 310 for special talents, 35 for need alone. *Meeting Costs:* college offers PLUS loans, deferred payment plan.

Biola University

La Mirada, California 90639 (213) 903-4752

An independent institution, strongly committed to the evangelical Christian viewpoint, located in a community of 40,000, 22 miles southeast of Los Angeles. Most convenient major airport: Los Angeles International.

Founded: 1908
Affiliation: Independent
Total Enrollment: 2,419 M, W (full-time); 52 M, 53 W (part-time)
Cost: $10K–$20K
% Receiving Financial Aid: 70%
Admission: Non-selective
Application Deadline: June 1

Admission. About 75% of applicants accepted, 57% of these actually enroll. Average freshman scores, according to most recent data available: SAT, 460 M, 459 W verbal, 531 M, 496 W mathematical; ACT, 23 M, 23 W composite, 22 M, 24 W mathematical. *Required:* SAT or ACT; interview on or off-campus, pastor's reference. Non-academic factor considered in admission: Christian commitment. *Apply* by June 1; rolling admissions. *Transfers* welcome.
Academic Environment. *Degrees:* AB, BS, BM. About 20% of general education requirements for graduation are elective; distribution requirements fairly numerous. About 77% of students entering as freshmen graduate eventually; 17% of freshmen do not return for sophomore year. *Special programs:* CLEP, independent study, study abroad, dual degree in engineering with USC. *Calendar:* 4–1–4, summer school.
Undergraduate degrees conferred (329). 15% were in Social Sciences, 14% were in Business and Management, 12% were in Education, 12% were in Communications, 11% were in Theology, 10% were in Psychology, 8% were in Visual and Performing Arts, 4% were in Letters, 4% were in Health Sciences, 4% were in Life Sciences, 4% were in Computer and Engineering Related Technology, remainder in 3 other fields.
Graduates Career Data. *Full-time graduate or professional study* pursued immediately after graduation by 35% of students according to most recent data available.
Faculty. About 60% of faculty hold PhD or equivalent.
Student Body. According to most recent data available, university seeks a national student body; 70% of students from in state, 93% from West/Northwest. Almost all students reported as Protestant; 3% Black, 4% Hispanic, 13% Asian, 1% other minority.
Religious Orientation. Biola is an interdenominational, independent institution, theologically conservative; 30 units of Bible and doctrine, attendance at weekly chapel services required of all students. Students expected to devote 3 hours weekly to Christian service with area churches.
Varsity Sports. Men (NAIA): Baseball, Basketball, Cross Country, Soccer, Track. Women (NAIA): Basketball, Cross Country, Tennis, Track, Volleyball.
Campus Life. About 50% of students live in traditional dormitories; no coed dormitories; rest live in off-campus housing or commute. Freshmen given preference in college housing if all students cannot be accommodated. No intervisitation in men's or women's dormitory rooms. There are no fraternities or sororities.
Annual Costs. Tuition and fees, $11,388; room and board, $4,736. About 70% of students receive financial aid; assistance is typically divided 60% scholarship, 25% loan, 15% work. University reports some scholarships awarded on the basis of academic merit alone. *Meeting Costs:* university offers student need grants.

Birmingham-Southern College

Birmingham, Alabama 35254 (800) 523-5793

Birmingham-Southern characterizes itself as a liberal arts college of Christian heritage and outlook. It does not, however, impose any denominational, racial, or ethnic restrictions on faculty, staff, or student body. The college is located on a 200-acre campus, 3 miles from the center of the Birmingham metropolitan area of 900,000. Most convenient major airport: Birmingham Municipal.

Founded: 1856
Affiliation: United Methodist
UG Enrollment: 627 M, 749 W (full-time); 65 M, 141 W (part-time)
Total Enrollment: 1,673
Cost: $10K–$20K
% Receiving Financial Aid: 84%
Admission: Selective (+)
Application Deadline: March 1

Admission is selective (+). About 73% of applicants accepted, 48% of these actually enroll; 61% of freshmen graduate in top fifth of high school class, 85% in top two-fifths. Average freshman scores: SAT, 515 verbal, 535 mathematical; ACT, 26 composite. *Required:* SAT or ACT, essay. Criteria considered in admissions, in order of importance: high school academic record, standardized test scores, special talents, extracurricular activities, recommendations, writing sample. *Entrance programs:* early decision, midyear admission, deferred admission. About 75% of entering students from private schools, 5% from parochial schools. *Apply* by March 1. *Transfers* welcome; 66 enrolled 1993–94.
Academic Environment. Pressures for academic achievement moderately strong. Administration source characterizes student body as strongly concerned with occupational/professional goals, a judgment documented by the most popular majors: business, accounting, and allied health professions. College "expects its graduates to have attained certain fundamental skills: the ability to read critically, to write articulately" and to master mathematical and scientific concepts. To this end a variety of studies are required. Computer literacy required of all students. Virtually every division of the college uses the computer "with academic program." Degrees offered: bachelors, masters. *Majors offered* include usual arts and sciences, international business management, human resources development, visual and performing arts. Center for Leadership Studies was begun in 1991 to increase the understanding of leadership within the liberal arts context. Center stresses the importance of service work and provides opportunities in and out of the classroom for students to analyze leadership theories, reflect on leadership experience, and meet with community leaders. Average undergraduate class size: 65% under 20, 32% 20–40, 3% over 40.

About 69% of students entering as freshmen graduate within four

years; 8% of freshmen do not return for sophomore year. *Special programs:* CLEP, January Term, independent study, study abroad, honors, undergraduate research, individualized majors, Washington Semester, 3–2 programs in engineering, nursing. Adult programs: Evening adult studies program. *Calendar:* 4–1–4, summer school.
Undergraduate degrees conferred (332). 43% were in Business and Management, 10% were in Social Sciences, 8% were in Psychology, 7% were in Visual and Performing Arts, 6% were in Letters, 6% were in Life Sciences, 5% were in Multi/Interdisciplinary Studies, 5% were in Education, 4% were in Mathematics, 3% were in Computer and Engineering Related Technology, remainder in 3 other fields.
Graduates Career Data. Advanced studies pursued immediately after graduation by 31% of students; 8% enter medical school; 4% enter law school. Graduate and professional schools typically enrolling largest numbers of graduates include U. of Alabama. About 53% of 1993 graduates are employed full-time, 9% part-time, 1% entered military. Employers typically hiring largest numbers of graduates include banks, accounting firms, school districts, churches. Career Development Services include counseling for 3 phases of career development: identifying and evaluating, gathering information, reflecting and deciding.
Faculty. About 81% of faculty hold PhD or equivalent. About 40% of undergraduate classes taught by tenured faculty. About 39% of teaching faculty are female; 4% ethnic minorities.
Student Body. College seeks a national student body; 71% of students from in state; 91% South, 2% foreign. An estimated 80% of students reported as Protestant, 8% Catholic; 12% as Black, 2% Asian, 2% other ethnic minorities.
Religious Orientation. Birmingham-Southern is a church-related institution, makes no religious demands on students. Places of worship available in immediate community for 3 major faiths. Services held in college chapel each Monday at 6:00 PM.
Varsity Sports. Men (NAIA): Baseball, Basketball, Soccer, Tennis. Women (NAIA): Tennis, (Soccer as of Fall, 1995).
Campus Life. Dormitories may have limited or unlimited intervisitation hours depending on the option chosen by students and parents. All students under 21 who do not live within commuting distance of the college must live in the dormitories.

About 60% of men, 75% of women live in traditional dormitories; 9% of men, 5% of women live in coed dormitories; 16% of men, 12% of women live in off-campus college related housing. There are 6 fraternities, 7 sororities on campus which about 62% of men, 70% of women join; 15% of men live in fraternities; 8% of women live in sororities. About 20% of resident students leave campus on weekends.
Annual Costs. Tuition and fees, $11,019; room and board, $3,670; estimated $1,000 other, exclusive of travel. About 84% of students receive financial aid; average amount of assistance, $7,200. Assistance is typically divided 35% scholarship, 30% grant, 20% loan, 15% work. College reports 300 scholarships awarded on the basis of academic merit alone, (including the McWane Honors Scholarship which offers full tuition and an $8,000 per year stipend); 42 awarded on the basis of special talents alone. *Meeting Costs:* college offers monthly payment plan.

Biscayne College

(See St. Thomas University)

Bishop Clarkson College

(See Clarkson College)

Black Hills State University

Spearfish, South Dakota 57799-9501 **(605) 642-6343 or (800) 255-2478**

A state-supported college, located in a community of 11,000, in a mountain valley at the mouth of Spearfish Canyon in the Northern Black Hills. Most convenient major airport: Rapid City Regional.

Founded: 1883
Affiliation: State
Total Enrollment: 1,161 M, 1,614 W (full-time)
Cost: < $10K
% Receiving Financial Aid: 75%
Admission: Non-selective
Application Deadline: Rolling

Admission. South Dakota graduates of approved high schools who rank in top two-thirds of class or score 20 on ACT composite eligible; others admitted by examination; 100% of applicants accepted, 60% of these actually enroll; 17% of freshmen graduate in top fifth of high school class, 40% in top two-fifths. Average freshman scores: ACT, 19 M, 19 W composite. *Required:* ACT, minimum HS GPA, class rank. *Out-of-state* freshman applicants: university welcomes out-of-state students. Requirement for out-of-state applicants: rank in top half of class or score of 20 on ACT composite. State does not limit out-of-state enrollment. *Entrance programs:* early admission, advanced placement. *Apply* by: registration day, rolling admissions. *Transfers* welcome; 419 enrolled 1993–94.
Academic Environment. Degrees offered: associates, bachelors, masters. About 48% of general education requirements for graduation are elective; core requirements include courses in English, speech, psychology, mathematics, science, health, social sciences, arts & letters, humanities. Unusual majors offered include physical wellness management, tourism, library media. Average undergraduate class size: 30% under 20, 50% between 20–40, 20% over 40. *Special programs:* CLEP, independent study, study abroad, honors, individualized majors, some 3–2 programs. About 70% of students entering as freshmen graduate eventually; 50% of freshmen return for sophomore year. *Calendar:* semester, summer school.
Undergraduate degrees conferred (339). 42% were in Education, 26% were in Business and Management, 11% were in Social Sciences, 5% were in Psychology, 3% were in Life Sciences, remainder in 9 other fields.
Graduates Career Data. Largest numbers of graduates employed by school districts, accounting firms, businesses. Career Development Services include resume writing, interviewing techniques, on-campus recruitment, Career Fair.
Faculty. About 63% of faculty hold PhD or equivalent. About 25% of teaching faculty are female; 1% minority.
Student Body. About 85% of students from in state; 8 foreign students 1993–94. Average age of undergraduate student: 28.
Varsity Sports. Men (NAIA II): Basketball, Cross Country, Football, Track, Rodeo(NIRA). Women (NAIA II): Basketball, Cross Country, Track, Volleyball, Rodeo(NIRA).
Campus Life. About 10% of men, 10% of women live in traditional dormitories; 30% of men, 30% of women in coed dormitories; rest live in off-campus housing or commute. Freshmen given preference in college housing if all students cannot be accommodated. Intervisitation in men's and women's dormitory rooms limited. Sexes segregated in coed dormitories by wing or floor. There is 1 fraternity, 1 sorority on campus,which about 2% men, 2% women join; they provide no residence facilities. About 50% of resident students leave campus on weekends.
Annual Costs. Tuition and fees, $2,220 (out-of-state, $3,892); room and board, $2,397; estimated $600 other, exclusive of travel. About 75% of students receive financial aid. Assistance is typically divided 50% grant/scholarship, 46% loan, 5% work. College reports some scholarships awarded on the basis of academic merit alone.

Blackburn College

Carlinville, Illinois 62626 **(217) 854-3231**

A small, liberal arts college, Blackburn is unusual for its student-operated Work Study Program instituted in 1913. Every student devotes 15 hours weekly to maintaining college buildings, cooking and serving meals, aiding staff, even constructing new facilities. Program helps keep costs down for both college and students. The 80-acre campus is located in a town of 5,700, 40 miles south of Springfield and 60 miles northeast of St. Louis, Missouri. Most convenient major airport: St. Louis.

Founded: 1837
Affiliation: Presbyterian Church (USA)
Total Enrollment: 465 M, W (full-time); 5 M, 10 W (part-time)
Cost: < $10K
% Receiving Financial Aid: 88%
Admission: Non-selective
Application Deadline: August

Admission. About 64% of applicants accepted, 40% of these actually enroll. Average freshman scores, according to most recent data available: SAT, 444 verbal, 486 mathematical; ACT: 19.5 composite. *Required:* SAT or ACT; "each student must be willing to take part in life and work of the college." Entrance programs: early admission, deferred admission. *Apply* by August; rolling admissions. *Transfers* welcome.
Academic Environment. Students have a role in college governance (including representation on faculty committees). Administration reports 40% of courses required for graduation are elective; distribution requirements include 8 semester hours in natural sciences, 9 semester hours each in social sciences and humanities, one course each in philosophy and religion. *Degree:* AB. *Majors offered* in 27 fields of arts and sciences including elementary education, special education, medical technology, public administration, computer science, Japanese studies.

About 47% of students entering as freshmen graduate eventually; about 35% of freshmen do not return for sophomore year. *Special programs:* CLEP, honors, undergraduate research, study abroad, independent study, individualized majors, credit by examination, Washington Semester, Mexico Semester, foreign culture option (as substitute for proficiency in foreign language), 3–2 program in engineering with Washington U.. Adult programs: Graduate Teacher Education program. *Calendar:* semester.
Undergraduate degrees conferred (95). 28% were in Business and Management, 17% were in Education, 15% were in Social Sciences, 11% were in Psychology, 7% were in Life Sciences, 5% were in Computer and Engineering Related Technology, 3% were in Visual and Performing Arts, 3% were in Public Affairs, 3% were in Letters, remainder in 4 other fields.
Graduates Career Data. According to most recent data available, full-time graduate or professional study pursued immediately after graduation by 13% of students. *Careers in business and industry* pursued by 62% of graduates. Corporations typically hiring largest numbers of graduates include McDonnell Douglas, EDS, State Farm.
Faculty. About 79% of faculty hold PhD or equivalent.
Student Body. According to most recent data available, 75% of students from in state; 90% North Central, 5% from South. An estimated 45% of students reported as Protestant, 30% Catholic, 1% Jewish, 20% unaffiliated, 4% other; 18% as Black, 1% Hispanic, 4% Asian.
Religious Orientation. Blackburn is a church-related institution; 6 hours of philosophy and religion required of all students; attendance at Sunday chapel services voluntary. Interdenominational Protestant services on campus each week.
Varsity Sports. Men (Div.III): Baseball, Basketball, Cross Country, Football, Golf, Soccer, Swimming, Tennis, Track, Wrestling. Women (Div. III): Basketball, Cross Country, Soccer, Softball, Swimming, Tennis, Track, Volleyball.
Campus Life. Intervisitation regulations set by each dormitory without restriction. Motor vehicles allowed for all students. College allows possession or use of alcohol by those of legal age (21) in student rooms only. Those living in residence hall are required to participate in Work Program.

About 20% of men, 47% of women live in traditional dormitories, 66% of men, 27% of women live in coed dormitories; rest commute. There are no fraternities or sororities. About 5% of students leave campus on weekends.
Annual Costs. Tuition and fees, $8,120; room and board, $1,000. About 88% of students receive financial aid; assistance is typically divided 70% scholarship, 25% loan, 5% work. College reports all scholarships awarded on the basis of need. *Meeting Costs:* all resident students required to work 15 hours on-campus in student-managed work program for which they receive $2,000 work grant.

Bloomfield College

Bloomfield, New Jersey 07003 **(201) 748-9000**

A church-related, liberal arts college, located in a community of 55,000, 15 miles from New York City. Most convenient major airport: Newark International.

Founded: 1868
Affiliation: Presbyterian Church (USA)
Total Enrollment: 1,858 M, W (full-time)
Cost: < $10K
Admission: Non-selective
Application Deadline: Rolling

Admission. High school graduates with 16 units, GPA of 2.0 and minimum combined SAT of 750 (850 for Nursing) eligible; 69% of applicants accepted, 39% of these actually enroll; 12% of freshmen graduate in top fifth of high school class, 42% in top two-fifths. *Required:* SAT or ACT; interview strongly recommended. *Apply:* rolling admissions. *Transfers* welcome.
Academic Environment. *Degree:* BA. About 33% of general education requirements for graduation are elective; distribution requirements limited. *Majors offered* in addition to usual studies include pre-chiropractic. About 40% of students entering as freshmen graduate eventually; 35% of freshmen do not return for sophomore year. *Special programs:* CLEP, independent study, honors, undergraduate research, study abroad, individualized majors, 3–2 programs in cytotechnology, medical technology, toxicology. *Calendar:* 4–1–4, summer school.
Undergraduate degrees conferred (153). 41% were in Business and Management, 20% were in Social Sciences, 13% were in Health Sciences, 8% were in Computer and Engineering Related Technology, 7% were in Life Sciences, 4% were in Psychology, 3% were in Letters, 3% were in Multi/Interdisciplinary Studies, remainder in 3 other fields.
Varsity Sports. Men (NAIA): Baseball, Basketball, Soccer. Women (NAIA): Basketball, Softball, Volleyball.
Student Body. According to most recent data available, 95% of students from New Jersey. An estimated 50% of students reported as Black, 7% Hispanic, 2% Asian.
Religious Orientation. Bloomfield is a church-related institution; makes no religious demands on students.
Campus Life. About 21% of men, 18% of women live in traditional dormitories; 70% of men, 70% of women commute. Freshmen given preference in college housing if all students cannot be accommodated. Intervisitation in men's and women's dormitory rooms unlimited; sexes segregated by floor. There are 4 fraternities, 4 sororities on campus, which about 14% of men, 17% of women join; 9% of men, 12% of women live in fraternities, sororities. About 50% of resident students leave campus on weekends.
Annual Costs. Tuition and fees, $8,050; room and board, $4,100. About 71% of students receive financial aid; assistance is typically divided 47% scholarship, 40% loan, 13% work. College reports some scholarships awarded on the basis of academic merit alone. *Meeting Costs:* college offers "lenient" deferment arrangements.

Bloomsburg University of Pennsylvania

Bloomsburg, Pennsylvania 17815 **(717) 389-4000**

A state-supported university, located in a town of 11,500, 80 miles north of Harrisburg, near Pocono resorts. Most convenient major airport: Wilkes Barre/Scranton International.

Founded: 1839
Affiliation: State
UG Enrollment: 2,249 M, 3,599 W (full-time); 347 M, 598 W (part-time)
Total Enrollment: 7,375
Cost: < $10K
% Receiving Financial Aid: 66%
Admission: Non-selective

Admission. Graduates of accredited high schools with 16 units in academic subjects eligible; 45% of applicants accepted, 34% of these actually enroll; 40% of freshmen graduate in top fifth of high school class, 85% in top two-fifths. Average freshman scores: SAT, 461 M, 467 W verbal, 542 M, 515 W mathematical; 31% of freshman score above 500 on verbal, 3% above 600; 66% score above 500 on mathematical, 15% above 600, 1% above 700. Criteria considered in admissions, in order of importance: standardized tests, high school academic record, personal characteristics. *Required:* SAT. *Out-of-state* freshman applicants: state limits out-of-state enrollment to 10–12% of entering class. *Entrance programs:* early admission, advanced placement, University Scholars Program. *Apply:* no specific date. *Transfers* welcome; 313 enrolled 1993–94.
Academic Environment. Degrees offered: associates, bachelors, masters. Core requirements include 12 semester hours each of humanities, social sciences, natural sciences and mathematics; 9 semester hours in communication; 3 semester hours each in quantitative-analytical reasoning, values, ethics and responsible decision

making, and fitness and recreation skills. *Special programs:* CLEP, independent study, study abroad, undergraduate research, work-study internships for credit, Cooperative Studies Program, 3–2 programs in engineering. About 43% of students entering as freshmen graduate in 4 years; 86% of freshmen return for sophomore year. *Calendar:* semester, summer school.

Undergraduate degrees conferred (1,240). 27% were in Education, 27% were in Business and Management, 9% were in Social Sciences, 6% were in Letters, 4% were in Psychology, 4% were in Health Sciences, 3% were in Life Sciences, 3% were in Computer and Engineering Related Technology, 3% were in Business (Administrative Support), 3% were in Allied Health, 3% were in Mathematics, remainder in 7 other fields.

Graduate Career Data. Advanced studies pursued by 15% of students. About 73% of 1991–92 graduates employed. Fields typically hiring largest numbers of graduates include: accounting, elementary education, business administration, nursing. Career Development Services include career counseling and planning assistance to students and alumni, career library, job search workshops, seminars & job fair programs, credential files, on-campus interviewing, SIGI-PLUS.

Faculty. About 61% of faculty hold PhD or equivalent. About 35% of teaching faculty are female; 5% Black, 1% Hispanic, 5% other minority.

Student Body. University welcomes a national student body; about 90% of students from in state, 99% Middle Atlantic; 53 foreign students 1993–94. An estimated 3% of students reported as Black, 1% Hispanic, 1% Asian, 1% other minority. Average age of undergraduate: 22.

Varsity Sports. Men (Div.II): Baseball, Basketball, Cross Country, Football, Soccer, Swimming, Tennis, Track, Wrestling (Div.I). Women (Div.II): Basketball, Cross Country, Field Hockey, Lacrosse, Soccer, Softball, Swimming, Tennis, Track.

Campus Life. About 10% of men, 17% of women live in traditional dormitories; 2% of men, 2% of women in coed dormitories; rest commute. Intervisitation in men's and women's dormitory rooms limited. There are 10 fraternities, 10 sororities which about 12% of men, 15% of women join.

Annual Costs. Tuition and fees, $3,458 (out-of-state, $7,856); room and board, $2,854. About 66% of students receive financial aid; average amount of assistance, $3,800. Assistance is typically divided 6% scholarship, 31% grant, 52% loan, 11% work.

Blue Mountain College

Blue Mountain, Mississippi 38610 **(601) 685-4161**

A church-related college for women, located in a village of under 1,000, 70 miles southeast of Memphis. Men in church-related vocations admitted as commuters.

Founded: 1873	**Cost:** < $10K
Affiliation: Southern Baptist	**Admission:** Non-selective
Total Enrollment: 317 M, W (full- and part-time)	**Application Deadline:** July 31

Admission. Graduates of accredited high schools eligible; 80% of applicants accepted, 64% of these actually enroll. *Required:* ACT or SAT recommended. *Apply* by July 31. *Transfers* welcome.

Academic Environment. *Degrees:* AB, BS, BM, BSEd. About 26% of general education requirements for graduation are elective; distribution requirements fairly numerous. About 43% of students entering as freshmen graduate eventually; 40% of freshmen do not return for sophomore year. *Special programs:* CLEP, independent study, honors. *Calendar:* semester, summer school.

Undergraduate degrees conferred (87). 61% were in Education, 10% were in Social Sciences, 7% were in Theology, 5% were in Psychology, 5% were in Life Sciences, 3% were in Letters, 3% were in Business (Administrative Support), remainder in 3 other fields.

Graduates Career Data. *Full-time graduate or professional study* pursued immediately after graduation by 13% of students according to most recent data available.

Varsity Sports. Women (NAIA): Basketball, Tennis.

Student Body. College does not seek a national student body; 89% of students from in state, 98% South. An estimated 99% of students reported as Protestant; 3% Black, 1% Asian according to most recent data available.

Religious Orientation. Blue Mountain is owned and controlled by the Mississippi Baptist Convention; 6 semester hours of Bible required of all students.

Campus Life. About 48% of women live in dormitories; no coed dormitories; rest of women, all men live in off-campus housing or commute. No intervisitation in women's dormitory rooms. There are no fraternities or sororities. About 67% of students leave campus on weekends.

Annual Costs. Tuition and fees, $3,248; room and board, $2,030. *Meeting Costs:* college offers deferred payment plan, sibling tuition discounts.

Bluefield College

Bluefield, Virginia 24605 **(703) 326-3682**

For many years a co-educational junior college which sent nearly all its graduates on to senior colleges, Bluefield is now accredited as a 4-year institution offering both associate and baccalaureate degrees. Most convenient major airport: Roanoke.

Founded: 1922	**Cost:** < $10K
Affiliation: Southern Baptist	**% Receiving Financial Aid:** 90%
Total Enrollment: 341 M, 424 W (full-and part-time)	**Admission:** Non-selective
	Application Deadline: Rolling

Admission. Graduates of accredited high schools with minimum GPA of 2.0 eligible; 94% of applicants accepted, 50% of these actually enroll; 44% of freshmen graduate in top fourth of their high school class, 74% in top half. Criteria considered in admissions, in order of importance: high school academic record, recommendations, extra curricular activities; other factors considered: special talents, alumni children. *Required:* interview. *Apply:* rolling admissions until August 15. *Transfers* welcome; 59 enrolled 1993–94.

Academic Environment. Degrees offered: associates, bachelors. Core requirements include 51–53 credit hours. Unusual majors offered include equestrian studies, business administration with emphasis in computer information systems. Average undergraduate class size: 18. About 64% of freshmen return for sophomore year. *Special programs:* study abroad, internships/cooperative work study programs. Adult programs: credit for experience, Management of Human Resources degree program geared to adult students.

Undergraduate degrees conferred (55). 42% were in Business and Management, 18% were in Education, 9% were in Social Sciences, 5% were in Protective Services, 5% were in Psychology, 5% were in Philosophy and Religion, 5% were in Life Sciences, 5% were in Liberal/General Studies, 4% were in Mathematics.

Graduates Career Data. *Full-time graduate or professional study* pursued by 10% of students immediately after graduation, 5% attend theological seminaries, according to most recent data available. Career Development Services: full-time Director of Career Development.

Faculty. About 65% of faculty hold PhD or equivalent. No tenured faculty; about 21% of teaching faculty are female.

Varsity Sports. Men (NAIA): Baseball, Basketball, Golf, Soccer, Tennis. Women (NAIA): Basketball, Softball, Tennis, Volleyball.

Campus Life. About 80% of students from in state; 95% from South; 10 foreign students 1993–94. An estimated 94% of students reported as Protestant, 6% Catholic; 3% of students reported as Black, 2% other minority.

About 40% each of men, women live in traditional dormitories, rest commute. There are 3 fraternities which about 20% of men join; no sororities, according to most recent data available.

Annual Costs. Tuition and fees, $6,500; room and board, $4,100. About 90% of students receive financial aid, average amount of assistance, $2,738. College reports some scholarships awarded on the basis of academic merit alone.

Bluefield State College

Bluefield, West Virginia 24701 **(304) 327-4000**

A state-supported college, located in a community of 22,000, 120 miles southeast of Charleston. Most convenient major airport: Mercer County (Bluefield).

Founded: 1895
Affiliation: State
Total Enrollment: 622 M, 841 W (full-time); 484 M, 654 W (part-time)
Cost: < $10K
% Receiving Financial Aid: 44%
Admission: Non-selective
Application Deadline: Rolling

Admission. Graduates of accredited high schools eligible, open admissions; 80% of applicants accepted, 62% of these actually enroll; 10% of freshmen graduate in top fifth of high school class, 35% in top two-fifths. Average freshman ACT scores: 17.5 M, 18.1 W composite. *Required:* ACT. Criteria considered in admissions: high school academic record, standardized test scores. *Out-of-state* freshman applicants: college actively seeks out-of-state students. State does not limit out-of-state enrollment. About 94% of out-of-state applicants accepted, 34% of these actually enroll. *Entrance programs:* early decision, early admission, midyear admission, deferred admission, advanced placement. *Apply:* rolling admissions until June 1. *Transfers* welcome; 304 enrolled 1993–94.
Academic Environment. Degrees offered: associates, bachelors. Core requirements include 40 hours of general studies. Average undergraduate class size: 40% under 20, 50% 20–40, 10% over 40. About 39% of entering students graduate eventually; 58% of freshmen return for sophomore year. Adult programs: Regents Bachelor of Arts - Life Experience Program. Special program: CLEP. *Calendar:* semester, summer school.
Undergraduate degrees conferred (237). 24% were in Business and Management, 23% were in Education, 17% were in Multi/Interdisciplinary Studies, 14% were in Engineering and Engineering Related Technology, 10% were in Protective Services, 4% were in Social Sciences, 4% were in Computer and Engineering Related Technology, 3% were in Health Sciences, remainder in Letters.
Graduates Career Data. Advanced studies pursued by 10% of students. About 85% of 1992–93 graduates employed. Fields typically hiring largest numbers of graduates include health related, computer science, engineering/technology, business.
Varsity Sports. Men (NAIA): Baseball, Basketball, Cross Country, Golf, Tennis. Women (NAIA): Basketball, Cross Country, Softball, Tennis.
Student Body. College does not seek a national student body; 92% of students from West Virginia, all from Middle Atlantic.
Campus Life. College primarily for commuters; no residence facilities. There are 4 fraternities, 2 sororities on campus which about 2% of men, 1% of women join.
Annual Costs. Tuition and fees, $1,836 (out-of-state, $4,202); estimated $800 other, exclusive of travel. About 44% of students receive financial aid; average amount of assistance, $2,000. Assistance is typically divided 10% scholarship, 40% grant, 40% loan, 10% work. College reports 50 scholarships awarded on the basis of academic merit alone, 40 for special talents, 10 based on need.

Bluffton College

Bluffton, Ohio 45817 (419) 358-3000

A church-related college, supported by the General Conference Mennonite Church, located in a town of 3,600, 60 miles south of Toledo. Most convenient major airports: Dayton, Toledo.

Founded: 1899
Affiliation: Mennonite
Total Enrollment: 665 M, W (full-time); 68 M, 42 W (part-time)
Cost: < $10K
% Receiving Financial Aid: 92%
Admission: Non-selective
Application Deadline: Aug. 1

Admission. Graduates of accredited high schools with 16 units eligible; preference given those in top half of class; applicants not usually considered if in lower third of class; 73% of applicants accepted, 34% of these actually enroll; 50% of freshmen graduate in top fifth of high school class, 86% in top two-fifths. Average freshman scores, according to most recent data available: SAT, 453 M, 443 W verbal, 511 M, 519 W mathematical; ACT, 22 M, 23 W composite. *Required:* SAT or ACT, recommendations; interview recommended. *Apply* by August 1; rolling admissions. *Transfers* welcome.
Academic Environment. *Degrees:* AB, BSN, BSMT. About 60–65% of general education requirements for graduation are elective; distribution requirements limited. Unusual majors offered include peace and conflict studies. About 65% of students entering as freshmen graduate within four years; 30% of freshmen do not return for sophomore year. *Special programs:* CLEP, independent study, study abroad, honors, undergraduate research, 3-year degree, individualized majors. Adult programs: Bluffton in Industry program. *Calendar:* quarter, summer school.
Undergraduate degrees conferred (144). 31% were in Business and Management, 22% were in Education, 9% were in Parks and Recreation, 8% were in Social Sciences, 5% were in Health Sciences, 4% were in Home Economics, 3% were in Visual and Performing Arts, 3% were in Psychology, 3% were in Mathematics, 3% were in Communications, remainder in 6 other fields.
Faculty. About 59% of faculty hold PhD or equivalent.
Varsity Sports. Men (NCAA III): Baseball, Basketball, Cross Country, Football, Golf, Soccer, Tennis, Track. Women (NCAA III): Basketball, Cross Country, Soccer, Softball, Tennis, Track, Volleyball.
Student Body. College seeks a national student body; 89% of students from in state. An estimated 67% of students reported as Protestant, 19% Catholic, 14% unaffiliated; 2% Black, according to most recent data available.
Religious Orientation. Bluffton is a church-related institution, makes no religious demands on students.
Campus Life. About 93% each of students live in traditional dormitories; no coed dormitories; rest commute. Freshmen given preference in college housing if all students cannot be accommodated. Intervisitation in men's and women's dormitory rooms limited. There are no fraternities or sororities. About 50% of students leave campus on weekends.
Annual Costs. Tuition and fees, $9,226; room and board, $3,726. About 92% of students receive financial aid; assistance is typically divided 50% scholarship/grant, 36% loan, 14% work. College reports some scholarships awarded on the basis of academic merit alone. *Meeting Costs:* college offers Tuition Equalization Program (guarantees tuition to be equal to average state school).

Boise State University

Boise, Idaho 83725 (208) 385-1156

A state-supported, liberal arts college offering 2- and 4-year programs; located in state capital (pop. 99,100). Most convenient major airport: Boise.

Founded: 1932
Affiliation: State
UG Enrollment: 3,207 M, 3,658 W (full-time); 2,030 M, 2,704 W (part-time)
Total Enrollment: 14,194
Cost: < $10K
Admission: Non-selective
Application Deadline: July 31

Admission. Graduates of accredited high schools with 15 units eligible; 89% of applicants accepted, 68% of these actually enroll. Average freshman scores, according to most recent data available: ACT, 19.3 M, 18.3 W composite, 17.2 M, 15.1 W mathematical. *Required:* ACT or SAT. *Out-of-state* freshman applicants: university welcomes out-of-state students. *Apply* by July 31. *Transfers* welcome.
Academic Environment. *Degrees:* AB, BS, BBA, BFA, BM, BSN. About 14% of general education credits for graduation are required; distribution requirements fairly numerous. *Special programs:* CLEP, independent study, study abroad, honors. *Calendar:* semester, summer school.
Undergraduate degrees conferred (918). 29% were in Business and Management, 18% were in Education, 12% were in Social Sciences, 7% were in Communications, 6% were in Health Sciences, 5% were in Visual and Performing Arts, 4% were in Multi/Interdisciplinary Studies, 3% were in Protective Services, 3% were in Psychology, remainder in 11 other fields.
Graduates Career Data. *Careers in business and industry* pursued by 85% of graduates, according to most recent data available.
Faculty. About 60% of faculty hold PhD or equivalent.
Varsity Sports. Men (Div.I): Basketball, Cross Country, Football (AA), Golf, Tennis, Track, Wrestling. Women (Div.I): Basketball, Cross Country, Gymnastics, Tennis (II), Track and Field, Volleyball.
Student Body. College does not seek a national student body; 91% of students from in state, 95% West.

Campus Life. Boise State makes no religious demands on students. About 8% of men, 8% of women live in coed dormitories; 92% of men, 92% of women live in off-campus housing or commute. Intervisitation in men's and women's dormitory rooms limited. There are 2 fraternities, 4 sororities on campus; less than 1% of men live in fraternities.
Annual Costs. Tuition and fees, $1,480 (out-of-state, $4,530); room and board, $3,240. About 50% of students receive financial aid; assistance is typically divided 46% scholarship/grant, 48% loan, 6% work. College reports some scholarships awarded on the basis of academic merit alone. *Meeting Costs:* college offers deferred payment plans.

Boston College

Chestnut Hill, Massachusetts 02167 (617) 552-3100

Founded as a college by the Jesuits, Boston College is now a major, co-educational university, listed among the most prestigious Catholic institutions, offering a full complement of nationally-ranked academic programs. The college is located in the residential suburb of Chestnut Hill, 6 miles from the heart of Boston and has easy access to the city by public transportation. Most convenient major airport: Logan Airport (Boston).

Founded: 1863
Affiliation: Roman Catholic
UG Enrollment: 4,182 M, 4,625 W (full-time)
Total Enrollment: 14,440
Cost: $10K–$20K
% Receiving Financial Aid: 61%
Admission: Very (+) Selective
Application Deadline: January 10

Admission is very (+) selective. For all schools, 47% of applicants accepted, 35% of these actually enroll. Average freshman SAT scores: middle fifty percent range, 520–610 verbal, 600–690 mathematical; 83% of freshman score above 500 on verbal, 34% above 600, 2% above 700; 98% score above 500 on mathematical, 75% above 600, 21% above 700.

Required: SAT or ACT, 3 ACH including English and mathematics I or II, personal essays; interview recommended. Criteria considered in admissions, in order of importance: high school academic record, standardized test scores, extra curricular activities, writing sample, recommendations; other factors considered: diverse student body, special talents, alumni children. *Entrance programs:* early action, early admission, midyear admission, advanced placement, deferred admission, honors program. About 13% of entering students from private schools; 29% from parochial schools. *Apply* by: January 10 for preliminary application, January 25 secondary application. *Transfers* welcome; 271 enrolled 1993–94.
Academic Environment. Degrees offered: bachelors, masters, doctoral. High student interest reported in both scholarly/intellectual and occupational/professional concerns. College has a tradition of preparing substantial numbers of students for professional training in medicine, law, and teaching. College also includes a strong nursing program and a variety of scholarship and special interest programs. Students have influence on curriculum decisions and also sit on long-range academic and fiscal planning committees. Core requirements include two courses in each of history, philosophy, natural sciences, social sciences, theology; one course in each of fine arts, literature, writing, mathematics, cultural diversity; other requirements vary with department. *Majors offered* in addition to usual arts and sciences include: accounting, computer science, fine arts, international studies, linguistics, management, nursing, education, special education, studio art, theater for teaching, nursing BS to MS program, minors in German Studies, and Faith, Peace and Justice. Average undergraduate class size: 38% under 20, 44% 20–40, 18% over 40. Extensive modern computer facilities on campus.

About 84% of students entering as freshmen graduate within four years, 88% within six years; 7% of freshmen do not return for sophomore year. *Special programs:* honors, CLEP, independent study, study abroad including Irish Studies Program, and Abbey Theatre Program, undergraduate research, 3-year degree, individualized majors, Black and Third World studies, French and Spanish Immersion program, Presidential Scholars Program, Scholars of the College, PULSE Program, Russian and East European Center, cross-registration with Boston-area institutions, combined BA/MSW, 3-2 program in engineering, internships in communications and political science. *Calendar:* semester, summer school.

Undergraduate degrees conferred (2,362). 28% were in Business and Management, 24% were in Social Sciences, 12% were in Letters, 7% were in Communications, 7% were in Psychology, 6% were in Education, 4% were in Health Sciences, 3% were in Life Sciences, remainder in 9 other fields. *Doctoral degrees:* Education 28, Social Sciences 11, Psychology 16, Letters 2, Physical Sciences 6, Biological Sciences 4, Foreign Languages 2, Theology 1, Philosophy and Religion 4.
Graduates Career Data. Advanced studies pursued by 29% of students; 4% enter medical or dental school, 8% enter law school, 4% enter business school. Medical or dental schools typically enrolling largest numbers of graduates include Tufts, Georgetown, U. of Massachusetts, U. of Connecticut, Dartmouth; law schools include Boston College, Suffolk, New England School of Law, Georgetown. About 62% of 1992–93 graduates employed. Career Development Services include assistance in all facets of career decision-making and job-hunting through individual counseling and workshops; computerized career guidance system, alumni career service and network, a credential service, video-taped practice interviews, resume and cover letter critiques, career fairs, graduate school advising, job search workshops and career panels. Assessment of program reported as "very strong" for both career guidance and job placement. Alumni reported as helpful in both career guidance and job placement; recent student leader reports "great network of BC alumni in Boston."
Faculty. About 95% of faculty hold PhD or equivalent. About 60% of undergraduate classes are taught by tenured faculty. About 31% of teaching faculty are female.
Student Body. College seeks a national student body; 31% of students from in state; 47% New England, 30% Middle Atlantic, 6% North Central, 4% foreign. An estimated 77% of students reported as Catholic, 9% Protestant, 9% unaffiliated, 3% other; 3% as Black, 5% Hispanic, 7% Asian, 3% other minority or unknown. *Minority group students:* Black Forum, Organization for Latin American Affairs, Asian Students Intercultural Club.
Religious Orientation. Boston College is a Jesuit institution; 2 courses in theology (chosen from a wide variety of Christian and other world religions) required of all students.
Varsity Sports. Men (Div.I): Baseball, Basketball, Cross Country, Diving, Fencing, Football, Golf, Hockey, Lacrosse, Sailing, Skiing, Soccer, Swimming, Tennis, Indoor and Outdoor Track, Waterpolo, Wrestling. Women (Div.I): Basketball, Cross Country, Diving, Field Hockey, Fencing, Golf, Lacrosse, Sailing, Skiing, Soccer, Softball, Swimming, Tennis, Track, Volleyball.
Campus Life. Boston College supplements its rigorous academic program with intense competition in Division I sports, one of only three universities with Division I football, basketball and hockey. Students report they have significant role in determining regulations governing student conduct—they have substantial representation on the university-wide governance committees. Almost three quarters of students now reside on campus. Rich cultural resources of Boston easily available; Theater Arts Center on campus. Cars permitted for juniors and seniors only; college considers "unacceptable" the unauthorized use of alcoholic beverages in campus facilities; 24-hour parietals, cohabitation "strictly prohibited."

About 1% of women live in traditional dormitories; 73% of all undergraduates live in coed dormitories; rest live in off-campus housing or commute. Freshmen given preference in college housing if all students cannot be accommodated. There are no fraternities or sororities.
Annual Costs. Tuition and fees, $16,006; room and board, $6,700; estimated $1,300 other, exclusive of travel. About 61% of students receive financial aid; average amount of assistance, $15,095. Assistance is typically divided 62% scholarship/grant, 28% loan, 10% work. College reports about 10 scholarships per class awarded on the basis of academic merit alone, about 100 for special talents, about 800 based on need.

Boston Conservatory of Music

Boston, Massachusetts 02215

An independent college of performing arts, offering music, dance, musical theater, opera, and voice therapy. The BFA, BM, MFA, and MM degrees and 4-year diploma conferred. Thirty-hour core in liberal arts required for graduation.

Founded: 1867
Affiliation: Independent

Boston State College

(See University of Massachusetts, Boston)

Boston University

Boston, Massachusetts 02215 (617) 353-2300

Boston University is located in the Back Bay area of Boston on the Charles River, an urban location which provides access to the city's extensive cultural resources. The university is increasing the number of students from outside the Northeast and is attracting an increasingly international student body. A wide variety of undergraduate and graduate degree programs are offered by the university's numerous schools and colleges. Most convenient major airport: Logan

Founded: 1839
Affiliation: Independent
UG Enrollment: 6,392 M, 7,537 W (full-time); 291 M, 275 W (part-time)
Total Enrollment: 28,594
Cost: $10K–$20K
% Receiving Financial Aid: 67%
Admission: Very (+) Selective
Application Deadline: Jan. 15

Admission is among the most selective in the country for the limited 6-year LA/Medical Education and 7-year LA/Dental programs; very (+) selective for Liberal Arts, Communication, Engineering; very selective for Education, Management, Allied Health Professions, Arts; selective for Metropolitan College School of Hospitality. For all schools, 64% of applicants accepted, 29% of these actually enroll; 70% of freshmen graduate in top fifth of high school class, 94% in top two-fifths. Average freshman SAT scores: 551 M, 546 W verbal, 624 M, 583 W mathematical; 74% score above 500 on verbal, 28% above 600, 3% above 700; 90% score above 500 on mathematical, 53% above 600, 13% above 700.

For Liberal Arts (2,458 M, 3,407 W f-t), 67% of applicants accepted, 21% of these actually enroll; 70% of freshmen graduate in top fifth of high school class, 94% in top two-fifths. Average freshmen SAT scores: 551 M, 546 W verbal, 624 M, 583 W mathematical; 70% score above 500 on verbal, 20% above 600, 2% above 700; 88% score above 500 on mathematical, 47% above 600, 11% above 700.

For Allied Health Professions (1,519 M, 607 W f-t), 45% of applicants accepted, 57% of these actually enroll; 79% of freshmen graduate in top fifth of high school class, 98% in top two-fifths. Average freshman SAT scores: 513 M, 540 W verbal, 623 M, 597 W mathematical; 63% score above 500 on verbal, 14% above 600; 79% score above 500 on mathematical, 36% above 600, 4% above 700.

For the Arts (231 M, 382 W f-t), 46% of applicants accepted, 27% of these actually enroll; 44% of freshmen graduate in top fifth of high school class, 71% in top two-fifths. Average freshmen SAT scores: 532 M, 520 W verbal, 585 M, 517 W mathematical; 60% score above 500 on verbal, 15% above 600; 62% score above 500 on mathematical, 26% above 600, 7% above 700.

For General Studies (608 M, 667 W, f-t), 60% of applicants accepted, 34% of these actually enroll; 15% of freshmen graduate in top fifth of high school class, 37% in top two-fifths. Average freshman SAT scores: 461 M, 440 W verbal, 521 M, 468 W mathematical; 19% score above 500 on verbal, 2% above 600; 42% score above 500 on mathematical, 10% above 600.

For Communication (504 M, 966 W f-t), 65% of applicants accepted, 29% of these actually enroll; 62% of freshmen graduate in top fifth of high school class, 91% in top two-fifths. Average freshman SAT scores: 550 M, 556 W verbal, 604 M, 566 W mathematical; 77% score above 500 on verbal, 21% above 600, 1% above 700; 84% score above 500 on mathematical, 37% above 600, 5% above 70.

For Education (66 M, 377 W f-t), 69% of applicants accepted, 34% of these actually enroll; 76% of freshmen graduate in top fifth of high school class, 92% in top two-fifths. Average freshman SAT scores: 500 M, 535 W verbal, 552 M, 582 W mathematical; 63% score above 500 on verbal, 19% above 600; 79% score 500 on mathematical, 36% above 600, 4% above 700.

For Engineering (1,141 M, 294 W f-t), 78% of applicants accepted, 23% of these actually enroll; 79% of freshmen graduate in top fifth of high school class, 96% in top two-fifths. Average freshman SAT scores: 543 M, 543 W verbal, 655 M, 630 W mathematical; 67% score above 500 on verbal, 23% above 600, 3% above 700; 97% score above 500 on mathematical, 72% above 600, 25% above 700.

For Management (999 M, 631 W f-t), 57% of applicants accepted, 27% of these actually enroll; 65% of freshmen graduate in top fifth of high school class, 87% in top two-fifths. Average freshman SAT scores: 507 M, 510 W verbal, 602 M, 601 W mathematical; 54% score above 500 on verbal, 9% above 600; 92% score above 500 on mathematical, 49% above 600, 7% above 700.

For Metropolitan College School of Hospitality Administration (76 M, 135 W f-t), 66% of applicants accepted, 37% of these actually enroll; 50% of freshmen graduate in top fifth of high school class, 86% in top two-fifths. Average freshman SAT scores: 475 M, 511 W verbal, 578 M, 557 W mathematical; 39% score above 500 on verbal, 4% above 600, 4% above 700; 73% score above 500 on mathematical, 38% above 600, 3% above 700.

For 6-year Liberal Arts/Medical Education (83 M, 48 W, f-t), 11% of applicants accepted, 48% of these actually enroll; all freshmen graduate in top fifth of high school class. Average freshman SAT scores: 655 M, 674 W verbal, 741 M, 730 W mathematical; all score above 500 on verbal, 91% above 600, 17% above 700; all score above 600 on mathematical, 86% above 700.

Required: SAT or ACT; some programs require SAT II subject tests, some require interview. Criteria considered in admissions, in order of importance: high school academic record, standardized test scores, recommendations, writing sample, extra curricular activities; other factors considered: portfolio/audition (for School of the Arts only). *Entrance programs:* early decision, early admission, midyear admission, deferred admission, advanced placement. About 19% of entering students from private schools, 13% from parochial schools. *Apply* by January 15, November 15 for early decision. *Transfers* welcome; 591 enrolled 1993–94.

Academic Environment. Pressures for academic achievement vary among the different schools and colleges from mild to relatively rigorous. Student attitudes also vary widely from strenuously intellectual and scholarly to the more socially oriented. Students, like those on many other campuses, are increasingly concerned with whether the high cost of a college education "will guarantee job success after graduation." Administration reports 30–40% of courses required for graduation are elective; distribution requirements fairly numerous: in Liberal Arts, for example, requirements include foreign language proficiency, English composition (unless exempted), mathematics, divisional studies or an integrated eight course Core Curriculum in addition to the field of concentration. Degrees offered: bachelors, masters, doctoral. *Undergraduate studies* offered by colleges of Liberal Arts, Engineering, Allied Health Professions, General Studies, schools of Communication, the Arts (Theatre Arts, Visual Arts, Music), Education, Management, Metropolitan College, 6-year Liberal Arts/Medical Education Program and a 7-year Liberal Arts/Dental Program. *Majors offered* in Liberal Arts cover a wide range of studies including international relations, mathematical astronomy, Soviet and East European Studies. New programs include College of Liberal Arts Honors Program, environmental studies, East Asian studies, Latin American studies, biotechnology, biochemistry and molecular biology, 5-year BS/MSPT (physical therapy). Average undergraduate class size is 28; 45% under 20, 41% 20–40, 14% over 40; of the classes held in the freshmen and sophomore years, 65% have fewer than 30 students.

About 71% of students entering as freshmen graduate eventually; 15% of freshmen do not return for sophomore year. *Special programs:* January term, study abroad, honors, undergraduate research, accelerated degree programs, combined Bachelors/Masters degree programs, collaborative dual-degree programs, cooperative education programs, cross-registration with Boston College, Tufts, Hebrew College, and Brandeis, 3–2 engineering programs with 18 schools, 2–2 engineering programs with 15 schools, internships available in most professions in the Boston area and throughout the world, international student exchange program, Washington semester. Adult programs: Metropolitan College offers full and part time degree and non-degree programs in the evenings. *Calendar:* semester, summer school.

Undergraduate degrees conferred (3,667). 19% were in Business and Management, 18% were in Social Sciences, 17% were in Communications, 9% were in Engineering, 8% were in Psychology, 5% were in Visual and Performing Arts, 5% were in Letters, 4% were in Life Sciences, 3% were in Education, 3% were in

Allied Health, remainder in 9 other fields. *Doctoral degrees*: Education 64, Social Sciences 29, Psychology 44, Letters 5, Life Sciences 32, Physical Sciences 15, Health Professions 10, Theology 10, Mathematics 3, Visual and Performing Arts 5, Interdisciplinary Studies 39, Area Studies 5, Foreign Languages 2, Philosophy and Religion 9, Business and Management 4.

Faculty. About 82% of faculty hold PhD or equivalent. About 30% of undergraduate classes taught by tenured faculty. About 27% of teaching faculty are female.

Student Body. University seeks a national student body; 23% from in state; 34% New England, 26% Middle Atlantic, 7% Midwest, 9% West, 9% South, 15% foreign students. An estimated 39% of students reported as Catholic, 20% Protestant, 15% Jewish, 11% other; 4% as African-American, 5% Hispanic, 13% Asian-American.

Religious Orientation. Founded as a school of theology under Methodist auspices, BU is now an independent institution and welcomes all races and religions; no compulsory religious studies or observances.

Varsity Sports. Men (Div.I): Baseball, Basketball, Crew, Cross Country, Football (IAA), Golf, Ice Hockey, Soccer, Swimming and Diving, Tennis, Indoor and Outdoor Track, Wrestling. Women (Div.I): Basketball, Crew, Cross Country, Field Hockey, Swimming and Diving, Tennis, Indoor and Outdoor Track.

Campus Life. There is no "typical" BU student. Students represent all 50 states and more than 120 different countries, reflecting many lifestyles, ranging from the very traditional–conservative to the very liberal. Individual residential units tend to attract students of similar lifestyles, making for relatively homogeneous groupings and providing a pluralist solution to what might otherwise become a source of conflict. Parking remains a serious problem; resident students are not allowed to bring cars on campus. BU is an urban university, with the advantages and disadvantages of a city. The wealth of cultural activities available to students in the Boston-Cambridge area rivals that of any location in the country. Recent student reports that "...Boston encourages academic growth. Going to school in the academic capital of America has obvious advantages. I gave up the rolling greens and got a better all around education." Campus life is so diverse that there is little agreement even among student leaders concerning the issues of particular concern and activities of special interest. It is clear, however, that student involvement in decision making is largely limited to regulations governing student conduct. Unlimited intervisitation; "self-imposed curfews" for all students. Unmarried freshmen under 21 must live in residence halls.

Less than 1% of men, 4% of women live in traditional dormitories; 58% of men, 58% of women in coed dormitories; 3% of men, 3% of women commute; rest live in off-campus housing. There are 7 national fraternities, 9 national sororities on campus, which about 5% of men, 8% of women join.

Annual Costs. Tuition and fees, $17,650; room and board, $6,480; estimated $465 for books and supplies, $1,200 other, exclusive of travel. About 67% of undergraduate students receive financial aid; average freshman award, $16,626. Assistance is typically divided 68% gift, 22% loan, 11% work. University reports 1,549 scholarships awarded on the basis of academic merit alone, 182 athletic scholarships per year, 135 fine arts scholarships, 6,582 need-based scholarships.

Bowdoin College

Brunswick, Maine 04011 **(207) 725-3000**

Bowdoin, Maine's oldest institution of higher learning, was for many years one of the nation's top-flight liberal arts colleges for men; it became co-educational in the fall of 1970. Located in a town of 20,000, the 110-acre campus is 25 miles northeast of Portland. Most convenient major airport: Portland International Jetport.

Founded: 1794
Affiliation: Independent
Total Enrollment: 749 M, 741 W (full-time)
Cost: $10K–$20K
% Receiving Financial Aid: 36%
Admission: Highly (+) Selective
Application Deadline: January 15

Admission is highly (+) selective. About 30% of applicants accepted, 41% of these actually enroll; 93% of freshmen graduate in top fifth of high school class, 99% in top two-fifths(of those reporting). Average freshman SAT scores: 570 M, 580 W verbal, 660 M, 620 W mathematical; 86% score above 500 on verbal, 39% above 600, 3% above 700; 95% score above 500 on mathematical, 68% above 600, 24% above 700 (test scores are optional; approximately 77% of entering students submit them). Criteria considered in admissions, in order of importance: high school academic record, recommendations, writing sample, extra curricular activities, standardized test scores; other factors considered: diverse student body, geographical distribution, alumni children, special talents. *Required:* high school record, essay, English teacher recommendation, references "important"; test scores optional; interview recommended. *Entrance programs:* early decision, deferred admission, sophomore and junior transfers. About 46% of entering students from private or parochial schools. *Apply* by January 15. *Transfers* welcome; 6 enrolled 1993–94.

Academic Environment. Core distribution requirements include 2 courses in each of: natural sciences and mathematics, social and behavioral sciences, humanities and fine arts, non-Eurocentric studies. Pressures for academic achievement appear moderately intense. Substantial numbers of students prepare for traditional professions: medicine, law, and, business. Strong departments reported to be biology, chemistry, economics, English, art history, languages, and the bio/chem program. Degree offered: bachelors. *Majors offered* include usual arts and sciences, Afro-American studies, Arctic studies, Asian studies, chemical physics, environmental studies, Theatre Arts (dance and performance), self-designed majors, interdisciplinary majors. Programs in women's studies and Africana studies recently added. Average undergraduate class size: 64% under 20, 25% 20–40, 11% over 40.

About 90% of students entering as freshmen graduate within eventually; 4% of freshmen do not return for sophomore year. *Special programs:* independent study, study abroad (including Consortium for East-West Cultural and Academic Exchange), honors, undergraduate research fellowships, freshman writing/literature seminars, senior seminars, various specialized centers (such as Bowdoin Scientific Station), Twelve College Exchange, 3–2 programs in law and engineering. *Calendar:* semester.

Undergraduate degrees conferred (376). 40% were in Social Sciences, 13% were in Life Sciences, 10% were in Letters, 9% were in Foreign Languages, 8% were in Visual and Performing Arts, 5% were in Physical Sciences, 4% were in Psychology, 4% were in Philosophy and Religion, 3% were in Mathematics, 3% were in Area and Ethnic Studies, remainder in Multi/Interdisciplinary Studies.

Graduates Career Data. Advanced studies pursued by 32% of students; 15% enter law school, 3% enter medical or dental schools. About 33% of 1993 graduates employed. Career Development Services include assessment, internships, summer jobs, job shadowing program, career workshops. Student assessment of program reported as good for both career guidance and job placement. Bowdoin Advisory Service, a national network of alumni, parents, and friends of the college reported as helpful in both career guidance and job placement.

Faculty. About 95% of faculty hold PhD or equivalent. About 55% of undergraduate classes taught by tenured faculty. About 35% of teaching faculty are female; 3% African American, 4% Asian American.

Student Body. About 15% of students from in state; 52% New England, 21% Middle Atlantic, 9% Midwest, 8% West, 5% South, 3% foreign. An estimated 3% of students reported as African American, 3% Hispanic American, 7% Asian American, 3% other minority.

Religious Orientation. Bowdoin for a half century had close ties with the Congregational Church, has been independent since 1908, makes no religious demands on students.

Varsity Sports. Men (Div.III): Baseball, Basketball, Cross Country, Football, Hockey (ECAG East), Lacrosse, Skiing, Soccer, Swimming, Tennis, Track. Women (Div.III): Basketball, Cross Country, Field Hockey, Ice Hockey, Lacrosse, Skiing, Soccer, Softball, Squash, Swimming, Tennis, Track, Volleyball. Coed: Golf.

Campus Life. Student leader reports that "because of its smallness students, faculty and staff are close, and because of its remote location members of the college community seek most of their intellectual and social needs on campus, making the campus very active." Interest in varsity and intramural athletics and in fraternities remains high at Bowdoin. Student body functions under an honor system and a social code, with a minimum of specific regulations. One administration source asserts that "there is a student Social Code which is designed to protect students' behavior from infringing on the rights of other students." Enforcement of regulations concerning drinking and use of cars reported as "judicious" by administration.

About 70% of men, 80% of women live in coed dormitories or college apartments; 15% of men, 12% of women commute. There are 8 coed fraternities on campus which 37% of students join; 15% of men, 8% of women live in fraternities.

Annual Costs. Tuition and fees, $18,300; room and board, $5,855; estimated $1,150 other, exclusive of travel. About 36% of students receive financial aid; average amount of assistance, $16,450. Assistance is typically divided 4% scholarship, 73% grant, 16% loan, 5% work. College reports scholarships awarded only on the basis of need.

Bowie State University

Bowie, Maryland 20715 (301) 464-6570

A state-supported college, located on a 237-acre campus in a town of 33,695, 18 miles northwest of Washington, D.C.; founded as a college for Blacks, but now fully integrated. Most convenient major airport: Baltimore/Washington International.

Founded: 1865
Affiliation: State
UG Enrollment: 799 M, 1,161 W (full-time); 317 M, 602 W (part-time)
Total Enrollment: 3,672
Cost: < $10K
% Receiving Financial Aid: 53%
Admission: Non-selective
Application Deadline: April 1

Admission. High school graduates or GED holders eligible; 59% of applicants accepted, 53% of these actually enroll; 8% graduate in top fifth of high school class, 43% in top two-fifths. Average freshman SAT scores, according to most recent data available: 347 M, 349 W verbal, 395 M, 372 W mathematical. *Required:* SAT, minimum 2.0 GPA. *Out-of-state* freshman applicants: university seeks students from out of state. State limits out-of-state enrollment to 10% of entering class; 48% of out-of-state applicants accepted, 45% actually enrolled. No special requirements for out-of-state applicants. *Apply* by April 1. *Transfers* welcome.

Academic Environment. *Degrees:* BA, BS. About 60% of general education requirements for graduation are elective; distribution requirements fairly numerous. About 26% of freshmen do not return for sophomore year. *Special programs:* CLEP, cooperative education, honors, independent study, undergraduate research, individualized majors, handicapped student services, academic support programs, 2+2 in technology, 3–2 engineering with George Washington U., U. of Maryland, Howard, dual degree in dentistry with U. of Maryland. *Calendar:* semester, summer school.

Undergraduate degrees conferred (266). 37% were in Business and Management, 14% were in Education, 11% were in Social Sciences, 6% were in Public Affairs, 6% were in Health Sciences, 6% were in Communications Technologies, 5% were in Psychology, 5% were in Computer and Engineering Related Technology, 3% were in Communications, 3% were in Mathematics, remainder in 4 other fields.

Graduates Career Data. *Full-time graduate or professional study* pursued by 15% of students immediately after graduation; 8% attend business school, according to most recent data available.

Varsity Sports. Men (Div.II): Baseball, Basketball, Football, Tennis, Track. Women (Div.II): Basketball, Softball, Tennis, Track, Volleyball.

Student Body. University does not seek a national student body; 84% of students from in state; 92% Middle Atlantic. An estimated 65% of students reported as Black, 1% Hispanic, 3% Asian, 4% other minority, according to most recent data available.

Campus Life. About 18% of men, 20% of women live in traditional dormitories; rest commute. Freshmen given preference in college housing if all students cannot be accommodated. Intervisitation in men's and women's dormitory rooms limited. Sexes segregated in coed dormitories by floor. There are 5 fraternities, 4 sororities on campus; they provide no residence facilities. About 30% of resident students leave campus on weekends.

Annual Costs. Tuition and fees, $2,736 (out-of-state, $5,128); room and board, $3,799. About 53% of students receive financial aid; assistance is typically divided 57% scholarship, 27% loan, 16% work. College reports some scholarships awarded on the basis of academic merit alone. *Meeting Costs:* college offers Academic Management Service.

Bowling Green State University

Bowling Green, Ohio 43403 (419) 372-2086

A state-supported institution, located in a town of 21,800, 23 miles south of Toledo. University maintains the Firelands Campus at Huron. Most convenient major airport: Toledo.

Founded: 1910
Affiliation: State
Total Enrollment: 16,248 M, W (full-time)
Cost: < $10K
Admission: Non-selective
Application Deadline: February 1

Admission. High school graduates with 17 units (13 in academic subjects) eligible; 68% of applicants accepted, 46% of these actually enroll; 40% of freshmen graduate in top fifth of high school class, 79% in top two-fifths. *Required:* ACT or SAT. *Out-of-state* freshman applicants: university welcomes students from out of state. State does not limit out-of-state enrollment. About 70% of out-of-state applicants accepted, 34% actually enroll. *Non-academic factors* considered in admissions: special talents, diverse student body. *Entrance programs:* early decision, midyear admission, advanced placement. *Apply* by February 1; December 15 for Business Administration. *Transfers* welcome.

Academic Environment. *Undergraduate studies* offered by colleges of Arts and Sciences (including Schools of Art and Speech Communication), Business Administration (including School of Journalism), Education (including School of Technology), Health and Community Services (including School of Nursing), College of Musical Arts. *Majors offered* in addition to usual studies include popular culture. About 15–30% of general education requirements for graduation are elective; distribution requirements fairly numerous. About 60% of entering students graduate eventually; 19% of freshmen do not return for sophomore year. *Special programs:* CLEP, independent study, study abroad, honors, 3-year degree, individualized majors. *Calendar:* semester, summer school.

Undergraduate degrees conferred (2,902). 24% were in Business and Management, 22% were in Education, 8% were in Communications, 7% were in Health Sciences, 5% were in Social Sciences, 3% were in Visual and Performing Arts, 3% were in Life Sciences, 3% were in Psychology, remainder in 21 other fields. *Doctoral degrees:* Letters 6, Psychology 18, Education 14, Biological Sciences 3, Communications 4, Fine and Applied Arts 4, Social Sciences 3, Area and Ethnic Studies 5, Mathematics 1.

Faculty. About 77% of faculty hold PhD or equivalent.

Student Body. College does not seek a national student body; 92% of students from in state.

Varsity Sports. Men (Div. I): Baseball, Basketball, Cross Country, Football, Golf, Gymnastics, Soccer, Swimming/Diving, Tennis, Track. Women (Div. I): Basketball, Cross Country, Golf, Gymnastics, Softball, Swimming/Diving, Tennis, Track, Volleyball.

Campus Life. About 10% of men, 30% of women live in traditional dormitories; 32% men, 21% women in coed dormitories; 52% of men, 45% of women live in off-campus housing or commute. Freshmen given preference in college housing if all students cannot be accommodated. Intervisitation in men's and women's dormitory rooms limited. Sexes segregated in coed dormitories by floor or wing. There are 23 fraternities, 18 sororities on campus which about 22% of men, 16% of women join; 7% of men, 4% of women live in fraternities and sororities. About 25% of resident students leave campus on weekends.

Annual Costs. Tuition and fees, $3,334 (out-of-state, $7,308); room and board, $3,478. About 55% of students receive financial aid. University reports some scholarships awarded on the basis of academic merit alone. *Meeting Costs:* university offers installment payment plan.

Bradford College

Bradford, Massachusetts 01835 (508) 372-7161

A small, co-educational, liberal arts college. The 70-acre campus is located in a community that is now part of the city of Haverhill in northeastern Massachusetts. Most convenient major airport: Logan (Boston).

Founded: 1803
Affiliation: Independent
Total Enrollment: 214 M, 305 W (full-time)
Cost: $10K–$20K
% Receiving Financial Aid: 71%
Admission: Non-selective
Application Deadline: Rolling

Admission. High school graduates eligible; 75% of applicants accepted, 28% of these actually enroll; 22% of freshmen graduate in top fifth of high school class, 56% in top two-fifths. *Required:* essay, guidance counselor recommendation; interview recommended. *Non-academic factors* considered in admissions: special talents, diverse student body, alumni children. About 15% of entering students from private schools. *Apply* by no specific deadline, rolling admissions. *Transfers* welcome; 87 accepted 1993–94.

Academic Environment. Degrees offered: bachelors. The Bradford Plan mandates studies in communication skills (7 credits), general education (26 credits), and a comprehensive major including a senior project; in addition students are strongly urged to complete a practical minor and an off-campus internship. Several recent students list small class sizes and accessibility of faculty as strengths of the Bradford program. Average undergraduate class size: about 70% under 20, 30% 20–40. *Special programs:* CLEP, independent study, honors, undergraduate research, study abroad, individualized majors, one-to-one tutorial freshman program, credit internships, English Language Institute, College Learning Program. *Calendar:* semester.

Undergraduate degrees conferred (68). 100% were in Multi/Interdisciplinary Studies.

Graduates Career Data. *Full-time graduate or professional study* pursued by 20% of students immediately after graduation. *Careers in business and industry* pursued by 80% of graduates.

Student Body. College seeks a national student body; 40% of students from in state; 75 foreign students 1993–94.

Varsity Sports. Men: Basketball, Lacrosse, Soccer, Volleyball. Women: Basketball, Softball, Volleyball.

Campus Life. About 80% of students live in single sex or coed dormitories; rest commute. Freshmen guaranteed space in college housing. There are no fraternities or sororities.

Annual Costs. Tuition and fees, $13,220; room and board, $6,120; estimated $1,300 other, exclusive of travel. About 70% of students receive financial aid; average amount of assistance, $14,000. Assistance is typically divided 71% scholarship, 26% loan, 3% work. College reports 40 scholarships awarded on the basis of academic merit alone.

Bradley University

Peoria, Illinois 61625 (309) 676-7611

An independent university, located in a residential area of a city of 180,000, midway between Chicago and St. Louis. Most convenient major airport: Greater Peoria Airport.

Founded: 1897
Affiliation: Independent
UG Enrollment: 2,285 M, 2,246 W (full-time); 279 M, 364 W (part-time)
Total Enrollment: 6,024
Cost: $10K–$20K
% Receiving Financial Aid: 82%
Admission: Selective (+)
Application Deadline: Aug. 1

Admission is selective (+). About 91% of applicants accepted, 31% of these actually enroll; 50% of freshmen graduate in top fifth of high school class, 74% in top two-fifths. Average freshman scores: SAT, 530 verbal, 590 mathematical; 64% of freshman score above 500 on verbal, 26% above 600, 4% above 700; 87% score above 500 on mathematical, 49% above 600, 15% above 700; ACT, 25 composite. *Required:* SAT or ACT. Criteria considered in admissions, in order of importance: high school academic record, standardized test scores, recommendations, extracurricular activities, writing sample; other factors considered: Special talents, alumni children, diverse student body. *Entrance programs:* early decision, advanced placement. *Apply* by August 1; rolling admissions. *Transfers* welcome; 513 enrolled 1993–94.

Academic Environment. Degrees offered: bachelors, masters. *Undergraduate studies* offered by colleges of Liberal Arts and Sciences, Business Administration, Communications and Fine Arts, Engineering and Technology, Education and Health Sciences, Institute of International Studies. *Majors offered* in addition to usual studies include international business, international studies, computer engineering, elementary education-liberal arts double major. About 35% of general education requirements for graduation are elective; general education requirements for all students. Several recent students report that the classes are small, the faculty is accessible, and library and computer facilities are excellent. Average undergraduate class size: 47% of classes under 16, 44% 16–35, 9% over 35. About 38% of students entering as freshmen graduate within four years, 64% eventually; 20% of freshmen do not return for sophomore year. *Special programs:* CLEP, cooperative education, independent study, study abroad, honors, undergraduate research, individualized majors, Scholar's Program. *Calendar:* semester, summer school.

Undergraduate degrees conferred (1,050). 25% were in Business and Management, 14% were in Engineering, 13% were in Communications, 10% were in Education, 8% were in Engineering and Engineering Related Technology, 7% were in Social Sciences, 5% were in Psychology, 3% were in Health Sciences, 3% were in Visual and Performing Arts, remainder in 10 other fields.

Graduates Career Data. Advanced studies pursued by 16% of students. About 89% of 1992–93 graduates employed. Corporations typically hiring largest numbers of graduates include Caterpillar, Inc., Arthur Andersen, Motorola, State Farm Insurance. Career Development Services include assistance with resume writing, interviewing techniques, Career Fairs, networking. Alumni reported as active in both career guidance and job placement.

Faculty. About 81% of faculty hold PhD or equivalent. About 30% of teaching faculty are female; 2% Black, 1% Hispanic, 6% other ethnic minorities.

Student Body. University seeks a national student body; 75% of students from in state; 1% foreign.

Varsity Sports. Men (Div.I): Baseball, Basketball, Cross Country, Golf, Soccer, Swimming, Tennis. Women (Div.I): Basketball, Cross Country, Golf, Softball, Tennis, Volleyball.

Campus Life. Cars permitted, except for freshmen. All full-time, non-veteran freshmen and sophomores under 21 must live in dormitories. About 1% of men live in traditional dormitories; 17% of men, 22% of women live in coed dormitories. Freshmen given preference in college housing if all students cannot be accommodated. Intervisitation in men's and women's dormitory rooms unlimited. Sexes segregated in coed dormitories by floor. There are 18 fraternities, 11 sororities on campus which about 40% of men, 30% of women join; 8% of men, 4% of women live in fraternities and sororities.

Annual Costs. Tuition and fees, $10,360; room and board, $4,200; estimated $2,000 other, exclusive of travel. About 82% of students receive financial aid; average amount of assistance, $7,196. Assistance is typically divided 25% scholarship, 35% grant, 34% loan, 6% work. University reports 955 scholarships awarded on the basis of academic merit alone, 377 for special talents alone, 2,400 for need alone. *Meeting Costs:* university offers deferred payments, monthly payment plan.

General Institutional Data. College newspaper: The Bradley Scout. Percent of annual budget derived from tuition: 79%. Total unrestricted endowment: $6,000,000.

Brandeis University

Waltham, Massachusetts 02254-9110 (617) 736-3500

The only nonsectarian institution of higher learning in the U.S. founded by the American Jewish community, Brandeis is a small research university with an integrated graduate and undergraduate faculty affording undergraduate opportunities for contact with scholars "working at the frontier of their fields." Located nine miles west of Boston in a suburban community of 58,000, the 235-acre campus contains numerous buildings of modern design, created by leading contemporary architects. Most convenient major airport: Logan Airport (Boston).

Founded: 1948
Affiliation: Independent
UG Enrollment: 1,312 M, 1,507 W (full-time)
Total Enrollment: 3,938
Cost: $10K–$20K
% Receiving Financial Aid: 60%
Admission: Highly (+) Selective
Application Deadline: January 1

Admission is highly (+) selective. About 65% of applicants accepted, 30% of these actually enroll; 71% of freshmen graduate in top fifth of high school class, 95% in top two-fifths. Average freshman SAT scores: middle fifty percent range, 530–640 verbal, 580–690 mathematical. According to most recent data available 93% of freshmen score above 500 on verbal, 56% above 600, 5% above 700; 97% score above 500 on mathematical, 70% above 600, 16% above 700. *Required:* SAT and 3 ACH (including English) or ACT, essay; interview recommended. Criteria considered in admissions, in order of importance: high school academic record, recommendations, extra curricular activities, writing sample, standardized test scores; other factors considered: diverse student body, alumni children, special talents. *Entrance programs:* early decision, midyear admission, deferred admission, Adult Scholar Program. About 28% of entering students from private schools. *Apply* by: Part I by January 1, Part II by February 1. *Transfers* welcome; 83 enrolled 1993–94.

Academic Environment. Brandeis is in many ways a rigorously traditional liberal arts college. This dimension is in sharp contrast to other aspects of student life on campus which tend to be more relaxed. Student influence is felt through joint faculty/student committees and student membership on the board of trustees. In recent years at Brandeis, as at many other schools, undergraduates have become more career oriented. Although emphasis on scholarly and intellectual pursuits remains strong, vocational and professional interests are rising. Numerous studies in Judaism available; focus cultural rather than religious. The core curriculum requires successful completion of 3 semester courses from a single cluster to be selected from at least 2 different schools of the University, seminar in Humanistic Inquiries with writing lab, 1 course designated as writing intensive, 1 course designated quantitative reasoning, up to 3 courses in a foreign language, 1 course from each of creative arts, humanities, science, and social sciences, and up to 2 non-credit physical education courses and a swim test. Degrees offered: bachelors, masters, doctoral. *Majors offered* include usual arts and sciences, African and Afro-American studies, anthropology, fine arts, Latin American studies, linguistics and cognitive science, Near Eastern and Judaic studies, theater arts, double majors and independent concentrations available; new department of Neuroscience recently added. Average undergraduate class size: median class size of 16, 75% of classes under 27.

About 78% of students entering as freshmen graduate within 4 years, 82% eventually; approximately 10% do not return for sophomore year. *Special programs:* independent study, study abroad, honors, undergraduate research, individualized majors, internships, premed, pre-law, various specialized centers (such as Feldberg Computer Center), 4-year BA/MA combined programs in biochemistry, chemistry, mathematics, physics, history, biology, 5-year program in international economics and finance, Near Eastern and Judaic studies, theatre arts, cross-registration agreements with Tufts, Wellesley, Boston U., Boston College, Babson, Bentley. Adult programs: Brandeis Adult Scholars Option (over 25); usually part-time, special support services offered. *Calendar:* semester.

Undergraduate degrees conferred (752). 41% were in Social Sciences, 14% were in Psychology, 13% were in Letters, 11% were in Area and Ethnic Studies, 9% were in Life Sciences, 3% were in Philosophy and Religion, 3% were in Visual and Performing Arts, remainder in 5 other fields. *Doctoral degrees:* Social Sciences 13, Public Affairs and Services 31, Biological Sciences 12, Physical Sciences 11, Letters 6, Mathematics 9, Area Studies 2, Psychology 2, Fine and Applied Arts 2.

Graduates Career Data. Full-time advanced studies pursued immediately after graduation by 36% of students; 8% enter medical or dental school; 15% enter law school; 3% enter business school. Medical schools typically enrolling largest numbers of graduates include NYU, Albert Einstein, Mt. Sinai; dental schools include Boston U., Tufts; law schools include Harvard, U. of Penn., Columbia, NYU; business schools include Harvard, Stanford, Chicago, Wharton, Columbia. About 50% of 1993 graduates employed. Fields typically hiring largest numbers of graduates include banking, consulting, human services, and public policy and government. Career Development Services include "guidance and support in career preparation"; job banks, on-campus interviewing, resume preparation and referral, careers library, career panels, internships, community professional and business sponsors with students on campus. Student assessment of program reported as good for both career guidance and job placement. Alumni reported as helpful in both career guidance and job placement; student leader reports "there are a significant number of networks with alumni."

Faculty. About 93% of faculty hold doctorate. About 32% of teaching faculty are female.

Student Body. About 26% of students from in state; 36% Middle Atlantic, 36% New England, 8% West/Northwest, 7% Midwest, 5% South, 5% foreign. An estimated 4% of students reported as Black, 3% Hispanic, 9% Asian. Educationally disadvantaged students: both academic and financial aid; transitional year prepares potential students, provides private tutors, assistance in academic life adjustment.

Religious Orientation. University is a Jewish-sponsored nonsectarian institution; makes no religious demands on students. Student religious organizations associated with the 3 chapels, 1 for each major faith, symbolically located in a triangle on campus. Each chapel has an appointed chaplain who works with one of the student religious groups.

Varsity Sports. Men (Div.III): Baseball, Basketball, Cross Country, Fencing, Golf, Swimming & Diving, Tennis, Track. Women (Div. III): Basketball, Cross Country, Fencing, Softball, Swimming & Diving, Tennis, Track, Volleyball.

Campus Life. Control over student personal and social life on campus largely in student hands, with some "staff support and guidance" from the office of the Dean of Student Affairs; Brandeis is notably free of in loco parentis regulations. Kosher food service available for those wishing it. University enforces state regulations on the consumption of alcohol. Student life at Brandeis is influenced by the wealth of intellectual and cultural offerings and facilities available on campus and in the Boston–Cambridge area. Easy access to Boston and to transportation facilities to NYC and elsewhere offers additional attraction. Outstanding facilities on campus include Slosberg Music Center, Spingold Theater Arts Center, and Feldberg Computer Center, National Center for Complex Systems, Gosman Sports and Convocation Center. Greatest student interest reported in intramural sports, cultural activities, social and campus activism, and community service.

About 91% of students live in coed dormitories; rest live in off-campus housing or commute. Freshmen and sophomores are guaranteed college housing. Intervisitation in men's and women's dormitory rooms unlimited; sexes segregated by wing, floor or room. There are no fraternities or sororities. About 10% of students leave campus on weekends.

Annual Costs. Tuition and fees, $18,955; room and board, $6,630; estimated $1,410 other, exclusive of travel. About 60% of students receive financial aid; average amount of assistance, $18,300. Assistance is typically divided 74% scholarship, 19% loan, 7% work. University reports about 50 scholarships per year awarded on the basis of academic merit alone, 1,300 based on need.

Brenau University

Gainesville, Georgia 30501 (404) 534-6100

Brenau started as a small, liberal arts college for women, but has expanded to include coeducational day programs in fine arts and nursing, and a variety of evening and weekend programs specifically catering to the non-traditional adult student population. Brenau still maintains the Women's College as a separate division. Brenau is located in a community of 43,000, 50 miles northeast of Atlanta. Most convenient major airport: Atlanta-Hartsfield International.

Founded: 1878
Affiliation: Independent
UG Enrollment: 111 M, 806 W (full-time); 162 M, 317 W (part-time)
Total Enrollment: 1,800
Cost: < $10K
% Receiving Financial Aid: 81%
Admission: Non-selective
Application Deadline: Rolling

Admission. For Women's College, graduates of accredited high schools with 16 units eligible; 75% of applicants accepted, 55% of these actually enroll; 19% of freshman graduate in top fifth of high school class, 40% in top two-fifths. Average freshman SAT scores: 445 verbal; 472 mathematical. *Required:* SAT or ACT; interview recommended. Criteria considered in admissions, in order of importance: high school academic record, standardized test scores, recommendations, extra curricular activities; other factors considered: special talents. About 19% of entering students from private schools, 1% from parochial schools. *Entrance programs:* early decision, early admission, mid-year admission, deferred admission, advanced placement. *Apply*: rolling admissions. *Transfers* welcome; 320 enrolled 1993–94.

Academic Environment. *Degrees:* Bachelors, Masters. The Women's College offers usual arts and sciences as well as programs in education, business administration, public administration, music, art (including interior design), dance, theatre, applied mathematics, communication, and several pre-professional programs. Core requirement of 65 quarter hours includes courses in English, behavioral sciences, mathematics, humanities, fine arts, lab science, social sciences. Adult programs: university offers programs designed for non-traditional students in education, business administration and public administration. Internships required for most majors. Average undergraduate class size: 89% under 20, 10% 20–40. About 52% of students entering as freshmen graduate eventually; 40% of freshmen do not return for sophomore year. *Calendar:* quarter, summer school.

Undergraduate degrees conferred (341). 36% were in Business and Management, 24% were in Education, 10% were in Health Sciences, 7% were in Protective Services, 5% were in Public Affairs, 5% were in Communications, 4% were in Visual and Performing Arts, 3% were in Architecture and Environmental Design, remainder in 7 other fields.

Graduates Career Data. Advanced studies pursued by about 50% of graduates. Career Development Services include resume preparation, courses, Career Day.

Faculty. About 80% of faculty hold PhD or equivalent; no tenure system. About 51% of teaching faculty are female; 3% African American.

Student Body. About 90% of students from South, 3% Midwest, 5% foreign students 1993–94. An estimated 9% of students reported African American, 4% other minority, according to most recent data available.

Varsity Sports. Women (NAIA): Tennis.

Campus Life. About 50% of students in Women's College live in dormitories; all other programs are non-residential. There are 8 sororities on campus which about 60% of women join; 20% live in sororities.

Annual Costs. Tuition and fees, $8,840; room and board, $5,894. About 81% of students receive financial aid; average amount of assistance, $6,131. College reports 5 scholarships awarded on the basis of academic merit alone, 40 for special talents, 120 for need.

Brescia College

Owensboro, Kentucky 42301 **(502) 686-4241 or (800) 264-1234**

A church-related, liberal arts college, founded by the Ursuline Sisters, located in a city of 55,000, 110 miles southwest of Louisville, and 50 miles southeast of Evansville, Indiana. Most convenient major airport: Dress Regional Airport (Evansville, Il).

Founded: 1925
Affiliation: Roman Catholic
Total Enrollment: 168 M, 284 W (full-time); 82 M, 167 W (part-time)
Cost: < $10K
% Receiving Financial Aid: 95%
Admission: Non-selective
Application Deadline: Rolling

Admission. High school graduates with GPA of 2.0 eligible; about 85% of applicants accepted, 38% of these actually enroll; 32% of entering freshmen graduated in top fifth of high school class, 61% in top two-fifths. Average freshman ACT score: 22 composite. *Required:* SAT or ACT; interview recommended. Criteria considered in admissions, in order of importance: high school academic record, standardized test scores, recommendations, extracurricular activities. *Apply*: rolling admissions. *Transfers* welcome; 65 enrolled 1993–94.

Academic Environment. Degrees offered: associates, bachelors, masters. About 50% of general education requirements for graduation are elective; distribution requirements fairly numerous. *Majors offered* in addition to usual studies include communication sciences and disorders, special education, graphic design, ministry formation, business emphasis in marketing, human resource management, social work. About 33% of entering students graduate within four years, 60% eventually; 33% of freshmen do not return for sophomore year. *Special programs:* cross registration with Kentucky Wesleyan, 3–3 program in Doctor of Nursing with Case Western Reserve. Adult programs: weekend college modules. Average undergraduate class size: 79% under 20, 21% 20–40. *Calendar:* semester, summer school.

Undergraduate degrees conferred (94). 26% were in Education, 21% were in Business and Management, 11% were in Social Sciences, 10% were in Life Sciences, 9% were in Visual and Performing Arts, 5% were in Letters, 4% were in Psychology, 3% were in Multi/Interdisciplinary Studies, 3% were in Liberal/General Studies, 3% were in Computer and Engineering Related Technology, remainder in 3 other fields.

Graduates Career Data. Advanced studies pursued by 25% of graduates. Professional schools typically enrolling largest numbers of graduates include U. of Kentucky, U. of Louisville, Western Kentucky U.

Faculty. About 34% of faculty hold PhD or equivalent. About 49% of teaching faculty are female.

Student Body. College seeks a national student body; 86% of students from in state; 1% foreign. An estimated 2% of students reported as Black, 1% Hispanic, 1% Asian, 1% Native American.

Religious Orientation. Brescia is a church-related institution; about 60% of students reported to be affiliated with Roman Catholic Church; 6 hours of religious studies required of all students.

Varsity Sports. Men (NAIA): Basketball, Golf, Soccer, Tennis. Women (NAIA): Basketball, Softball, Volleyball.

Campus Life. About 20% of students live in traditional dormitories; rest live in off-campus housing or commute. There are no fraternities or sororities.

Annual Costs. Tuition and fees, $6,700; room and board, $3,100; estimated $1,000 other, exclusive of travel. About 95% of students receive financial aid; assistance is typically divided 6% scholarship, 36% grant, 55% loan, 3% work. College reports some scholarships are available on the basis of academic merit alone. *Meeting Costs:* college offers payment plan.

Briar Cliff College

Sioux City, Iowa 51104 **(712) 279-5200**

A church-related, liberal arts college, founded by the Sisters of St. Francis of the Holy Family, located in a city of 86,000. Most convenient major airport: Sioux Gateway.

Founded: 1930
Affiliation: Roman Catholic
Total Enrollment: 258 M, 480 W (full-time); 108 M, 322 W (part-time)
Cost: < $10K
% Receiving Financial Aid: 97%
Admission: Non-selective
Application Deadline: Rolling

Admission. Graduates of accredited high schools with 16 units eligible; 98% of applicants accepted, 45% of these actually enroll; 36% of freshmen graduate in top fifth of high school class, 67% in top two-fifths. Average freshman SAT scores: 440 M, 330 W verbal, 440 M, 380 W mathematical; ACT, 21.3 M, 22.7 W composite. *Required:* SAT or ACT. Criteria considered in admissions, in order of importance: high school academic record, standardized test scores, recommendations. About 31% of entering students from parochial schools, according to most recent data available. *Apply*: rolling admissions. *Transfers* welcome; 137 enrolled 1993–94.

Academic Environment. Degrees offered: associates, bachelors. In addition to usual arts and sciences, Briar Cliff offers programs in nursing, human resource management, and writing. All general education requirements for graduation are elective; distribution requirements fairly numerous. About 47% of students entering as freshmen graduate eventually; 29% of freshmen do not return for sophomore year. *Special programs:* CLEP, independent study, study abroad, individualized majors, "extensive" internship programs, 3–2 engineering with Iowa State. Adult programs: Weekend College and evening classes. Calendar. 3–3.

Undergraduate degrees conferred (236). 25% were in Business and Management, 23% were in Health Sciences, 10% were in Public Affairs, 7% were in Psychology, 5% were in Letters, 5% were in Communications, 4% were in Multi/Interdisciplinary Studies, 4% were in Education, 3% were in Theology, 3% were in Life Sciences, 3% were in Visual and Performing Arts, 3% were in Social Sciences, remainder in 5 other fields.

Graduates Career Data. Advanced studies pursued immediately after graduation by 9% of students. About 82% of 1992 graduates

employed. Career Development Services include aptitude testing, on-campus recruitment, placement services, resume and interview workshops, internships and cooperative education programs, Career Expo, graduate school information and exam preparation.
Faculty. About 65% of faculty hold PhD or equivalent. About 44% of teaching faculty are female.
Student Body. About 71% of students from Iowa; 90% from NorthCentral. An estimated 46% of students reported as Catholic, 15% Protestant, 39% unreported; 2% Black, 2% Hispanic, 5% other minority. Average age of undergraduate students: 26.
Religious Orientation. Briar Cliff is a church-related institution but makes no religious demands on students; daily Mass offered.
Varsity Sports. Men (NAIA): Baseball, Basketball, Golf, Soccer. Women (NAIA): Basketball, Golf, Soccer, Softball, Volleyball.
Campus Life. The 70-acre campus rests on a hill that enables Briar Cliff to function as its own community.

About 28% of full-time students live in traditional dormitories; 36% live in coed dormitories (sexes segregated by floor); rest commute. There are no fraternities or sororities.
Annual Costs. Tuition and fees, $9,930; room and board, $3,445. About 97% of current freshmen receive financial aid; average amount of assistance, $8,400. Assistance is typically divided 36% scholarship/grant, 42% loan, 18% work. College reports some scholarships awarded on the basis of academic merit alone.

Bridgeport Engineering Institute

Fairfield, Connecticut 06430 (203) 259-5717

A private independent, engineering institution which offers programs in electrical, mechanical, and manufacturing engineering.

Founded: 1924
Affiliation: Independent
Total Enrollment: 276 M, W (full- and part-time)
Cost: < $10K
Admission: Non-selective
Application Deadline: August 31

Admission. About 73% of applicants accepted, all of these actually enroll; 7% of freshmen graduate in the top fifth of their high school class, 42% in top two-fifths. *Required:* on-campus interview. *Apply* by August 31. *Transfers* welcome.
Academic Environment. *Degrees:* BS. Almost all graduates are employed by business and industry. Corporations typically hiring largest numbers of graduates include United Technologies, Perkin Elmer, Pitney Bowes.
Undergraduate degrees conferred (64). 100% were in Engineering.
Campus Life. About 95% of students are from Connecticut. An estimated 30% of students reported as Protestant, 35% Catholic, 15% Jewish, 20% unaffiliated; 5% Black, 4% Hispanic according to most recent data available. Institute offers no residential facilities.
Annual Costs. Tuition and Fees, $5,780. About 10% of students receive financial aid. Assistance is typically 100% scholarship. College reports some scholarships awarded on the basis of academic merit alone.

University of Bridgeport

Bridgeport, Connecticut 06601 (203) 576-4000

An independent university, located on an 86-acre campus in a city of 156,500, 60 miles northeast of New York City; also includes Junior College of Connecticut.

Founded: 1927
Affiliation: Independent
Total Enrollment: 258 M 269 W (full-time); 126 M, 186 W (part-time)
Cost: $10K–$20K
% Receiving Financial Aid: 69%
Admission: Non-selective
Application Deadline: August 1

Admission. For all schools graduates of accredited high schools with 16 units eligible; 74% of applicants accepted, 35% of these actually enroll. Average freshman SAT scores: 423 M, 421 W verbal, 510 M, 472 W mathematical. *Required:* SAT, ACH in English (also language for Arts and Sciences if continuing study; mathematics I for majors in health professions, sciences, mathematics); audition or portfolio for Fine Arts; interview for some programs. Criteria considered in admissions, in order of importance: high school academic record, standardized test scores, recommendations, writing sample, extracurricular activities; other factors considered: diverse student body, special talents, alumni children. *Entrance programs:* early decision, early admission, midyear admission, advanced placement, deferred admission. *Apply* by August 1; rolling admissions. *Transfers* welcome; 113 enrolled 1993–94.
Academic Environment. Degrees offered: associates, bachelors, masters, doctoral. *Undergraduate studies* offered by colleges of Science and Engineering, Health Sciences, Arts and Humanities, and Business and Public Management. *Majors offered* in addition to usual studies include dental hygiene, graphic design, journalism, medical technology, oceanography-mathematics, oceanography-physics, respiratory technology, theater arts. Core requirements include 6 credits in English Composition, 3 in oral communication, 3 in mathematics, 3 in fine arts, 6 in humanities, 6 in natural sciences, 6 in social sciences, and 3 credit Capstone Seminar. Average undergraduate class size: 85% of classes under 20, 13% between 20–40, 2% over 40. About 50% of entering students graduate eventually; 70% of freshmen return for sophomore year. *Special programs:* CLEP, independent study, honors, study abroad, undergraduate research, internships, cross registration with Sacred Heart U. and Fairfield. Adult programs: IDEAL, a degree completion program for the adult learner with 39 prior college credits. *Calendar:* semester, spring mini-mester, summer school.
Undergraduate degrees conferred (357). 24% were in Business and Management, 20% were in Multi/Interdisciplinary Studies, 16% were in Engineering, 8% were in Visual and Performing Arts, 7% were in Marketing and Distribution, 4% were in Allied Health, 3% were in Computer and Engineering Related Technology, 3% were in Communications, 3% were in Psychology, remainder in 8 other fields.
Graduates Career Data. Advanced studies pursued by 33% of graduates; 2% enter medical school; 5% enter chiropractic school; 5% enter law school; 10% enter business school. *Career Counseling Program* offers help with resumes, preparation for interviews, career guidance and career placement services, on-campus interviewing. Student assessment of program reported as good for career guidance and fair for job placement. Alumni reported, by recent student leader, as not helpful in either career guidance or job placement. Co-operative education program (work/study) considered one of university's "strongest assets."
Faculty. About 82% of faculty hold PhD or equivalent. About 59% of undergraduate classes taught by tenured faculty. About 16% of teaching faculty are female; 2% Black, 1% Hispanic, 13% Asian.
Student Body. About 58% of students from in state, 60% New England, 11% Middle Atlantic, 27% foreign. An estimated 17% of students reported as Black, 4% Asian, 9% Hispanic.
Varsity Sports. Men (Div.II): Baseball, Basketball, Cross Country, Soccer, Volleyball. Women (Div.II): Basketball, Cross Country, Gymnastics, Soccer, Softball.
Campus Life. Both men and women have 24-hour open houses ("provided majority of floor and residence halls want it"). University includes group ombudsman committee on which faculty, administration, and student body are equally represented.

About 65% of men, 58% of women live in coed dormitories; rest live in off-campus housing or commute. Freshmen given preference in college housing if all students cannot be accommodated. There are 3 fraternities, 3 sororities on campus which about 5% of men, 5% of women join. About 25% of resident students leave campus on weekends.
Annual Costs. Tuition and fees, $12,445; room and board, $6,540. About 69% of students receive financial aid; average amount of assistance, $15,542. Assistance is typically divided 65% scholarship, 17% grant, 14% loan, 4% work. University reports 206 scholarships awarded on the basis of academic merit alone, 79 for special talents, 381 for need. *Meeting Costs:* university offers deferred payment plans.

Bridgewater College

Bridgewater, Virginia 22812 (703) 828-2501

Historically associated with the Church of the Brethren, Bridgewater is an independent, liberal arts college, located in a town of 3,500, 130 miles southwest of Washington, D.C.

Founded: 1880
Affiliation: Independent (Brethren)
Total Enrollment: 927 M, W (full-time)
Cost: $10K–$20K
Admission: Non-selective
Application Deadline: June 1

Admission. Graduates of accredited high schools with college preparatory courses eligible; 81% of applicants accepted, 45% of these actually enroll; 36% of freshmen graduate in top fifth of high school class, 62% in top two-fifths. *Required:* SAT. *Apply* by June 1. *Transfers* welcome.
Academic Environment. *Degrees:* AB, BS. About 95% of general education requirements for graduation are elective; distribution requirements fairly numerous. About 60% of students entering as freshmen graduate eventually; 25% of freshmen do not return for sophomore year. *Special programs:* independent study, study abroad, honors, undergraduate research, optional 3-week interterm, 3-year degree. *Calendar:* 3–3–1–3, summer session.
Undergraduate degrees conferred (196). 29% were in Business and Management, 18% were in Education, 15% were in Social Sciences, 10% were in Life Sciences, 6% were in Home Economics, 5% were in Psychology, 5% were in Letters, 4% were in Physical Sciences, 3% were in Visual and Performing Arts, remainder in 6 other fields.
Graduates Career Data. *Full-time graduate or professional study* pursued immediately after graduation by 15% of students, according to most recent data available.
Varsity Sports. Men (Div.III): Baseball, Basketball, Cross Country, Football, Golf, Tennis, Track. Women (Div.III): Basketball, Field Hockey, Lacrosse, Softball, Tennis, Volleyball.
Student Body. College does not actively seek a national student body; 81% of students from Virginia, 83% South, 14% Middle Atlantic.
Religious Orientation. Bridgewater is an independent institution; two courses in biblical studies required, attendance at 7 convocations per term required of all students. Religious clubs on campus include Baptist, Brethren Student Fellowship, Lutheran, Wesley, Westminster.
Campus Life. About 79% of men, 82% of women live in traditional dormitories; no coed dormitories; rest commute. Freshmen given preference in college housing if all students cannot be accommodated. Intervisitation in men's and women's dormitory rooms limited. There are no fraternities or sororities. About 40% of students leave campus on weekends.
Annual Costs. Tuition and fees, $10,770; room and board, $4,530. College reports some scholarships awarded on the basis of academic merit alone.

Bridgewater State College

Bridgewater, Massachusetts 02324 (617) 697-8321

A state-supported, liberal arts and teachers college, located in a community of 11,800, 30 miles south of Boston.

Founded: 1840
Affiliation: State
Total Enrollment: 6,203 M, W (full-time)
Cost: < $10K
Admission: Non-selective
Application Deadline: March 1

Admission. Graduates of accredited high schools with 16 credits and at least average record eligible. *Required:* SAT. *Apply* by March 1. *Transfers* welcome.
Academic Environment. *Degrees:* AB, BSEd. *Special programs:* study abroad, honors, undergraduate research. *Library:* 89,000 volumes, open-stack privileges. *Calendar:* semester.
Undergraduate degrees conferred (1,184). 37% were in Education, 21% were in Business and Management, 9% were in Social Sciences, 7% were in Psychology, 6% were in Letters, 4% were in Visual and Performing Arts, 4% were in Transportation and Material Moving, 3% were in Public Affairs, 3% were in Communications, remainder in 7 other fields.
Student Body. About 99% of students from New England. *Minority group students:* special financial and academic provisions.
Campus Life. About 10% of men, 19% of women live in traditional dormitories; rest live in off-campus housing or commute. Intervisitation hours established by residents of each dormitory and "approved by the president of the college." About 40% of resident students leave campus on weekends.
Annual Costs. Tuition and fees, $3,000 (out-of-state, $6,864); room and board $3,590.

Brigham Young University

Provo, Utah 84602 (801) 378-5000

A large university, dedicated primarily to serving the young people of the Mormon Church, located in a city of 79,000, 45 miles south of Salt Lake City. The university also has a branch campus on Hawaii. Most convenient major airport: Salt Lake International.

Founded: 1875
Affiliation: Latter-Day Saints
UG Enrollment: 13,062 M, 13,316 W (full-time); 616 M, 637 W (part-time)
Total Enrollment: 30,547
Cost: < $10K
% Receiving Financial Aid: 60%
Admission: Selective (+)
Application Deadline: Feb. 15

Admission is selective (+). About 73% of applicants accepted, 80% of these actually enroll; 81% of freshmen graduate in top fifth of their high school class, 97% in top two-fifths. Average freshman ACT scores: 27.4 M, 26.2 W composite. *Required:* ACT, "student commitment and confidential report", interview. Criteria considered in admissions, in order of importance: high school academic record, standardized test scores, interview, recommendations, extra curricular activities, writing sample; other factors considered: special talents, religious affiliation and/or commitment, exceptional creativity, or "other unusual preparation for university study." Entrance programs: early admission, advanced placement. *Apply* by February 15; rolling admissions. *Transfers* welcome; 1,196 enrolled 1993–94.
Academic Environment. Degrees offered: bachelors, masters, doctoral. Pressures for academic achievement appear moderate; atmosphere, however, is oriented toward scholarly pursuits as well as toward development of immediately marketable skills. *Undergraduate studies* offered by colleges of Biological and Agricultural Sciences, Education, Engineering Sciences and Technology, Family, Home, and Social Sciences, Fine Arts and Communications, Humanities, Nursing, Physical and Mathematical Sciences, Physical Education, School of Management. *Majors offered* include usual arts and sciences, in wide range of fields; 102 degree programs available; unusual majors include construction management, physical plant administration. Administration reports very strong programs in accounting and languages. Core requirements include courses in intensive writing, mathematics or foreign language, history of civilization, American history, biological science, physical science, physical education, health and religion. Average undergraduate class size: 38; 33% of classes under 20, 41% 20–40, 26% over 40.

About 65% of men, 48% of women entering as freshmen graduate eventually; about 80% of entering students return for sophomore year. More than 75% of men, 11% of women serve a 2-year mission for the LDS Church and this requires 7 years from point of entry as freshmen to graduation. *Special programs:* study abroad, Washington Seminar, international internships, cooperative education internships. *Calendar:* 4–4–2–2 (3 16-week semesters, with 3rd semester divided in half).
Undergraduate degrees conferred (4,962). 16% were in Education, 15% were in Business and Management, 11% were in Social Sciences, 6% were in Foreign Languages, 6% were in Engineering, 5% were in Communications, 5% were in Letters, 5% were in Psychology, 5% were in Vocational Home Economics, 5% were in Visual and Performing Arts, 4% were in Area and Ethnic Studies, 3% were in Life Sciences, remainder in 13 other fields. *Doctoral degrees:* Education 49, Psychology 9, Home Economics 10, Engineering 11, Physical Sciences 10, Biological Sciences 1, Social Sciences 4, Agriculture and Natural Resources 1, Fine and Applied Arts 3, Letters 1, Interdisciplinary Studies 1, Law 144, Physical Education 10.
Graduates Career Data. Advanced studies pursued immediately after graduation by 25% of students. About one-third of graduates employed at time of graduation. Fields typically hiring largest numbers of graduates include accounting, computer science, and education. Career Development Services include counseling, job listings,

on-campus recruitment and interviewing, vocational interest testing and advisement.
Faculty. About 78% of faculty hold PhD or equivalent. About 17% of teaching faculty are female; 3% minority.
Student Body. About 32% of students from Utah; 49% of students from Mountain states, 25% Pacific, 6% foreign students 1993–94. An estimated 99% of students reported as Latter Day Saints; 3% Asian, 2% Hispanic, less than 1% Black, 7% other minority.
Religious Orientation. Brigham Young is a church-related institution; 14 courses in religion required for graduation.
Varsity Sports. Men (Div.IA): Baseball, Basketball, Cross Country, Football, Golf, Gymnastics, Skiing, Swimming/Diving, Tennis, Track, Volleyball, Wrestling. Women (Div.I): Basketball, Cross Country, Golf, Gymnastics, Skiing, Swimming/Diving, Tennis, Track, Volleyball.
Campus Life. Code of Student Conduct, applying to non-Mormons as well, "extends to a student's life both on and off campus"; prohibitions include use of tea, coffee, alcoholic beverages, tobacco. University regulations concerning women's dorm hours and public behavior between the sexes enforced "rigorously." Administration and students report that the campus is great for those who love outdoor activities; close to skiing, hiking, fishing, hunting, water sports, biking.

About 13% of men, 17% of women live in traditional dormitories; no coed dormitories; the rest live in off-campus housing or commute. Intervisitation in men's and women's dormitory rooms limited. There are no fraternities or sororities.
Annual Costs. Tuition and fees, $2,200 (non-members of the church, $3,300); room and board, $3,450. About 60% of students receive financial aid; average amount of assistance, $3,550. Assistance is typically divided 39% scholarship, 46% Pell grant, 14% loan. University reports 1,725 scholarships awarded on the basis of academic merit alone, 635 for special talents, 1,965 other.

Brigham Young University—Hawaii Campus

Laie, Hawaii 96762 (808) 293-3738

Brigham Young University-Hawaii Campus is located in a town of 3,000, 28 miles north of Honolulu on Oahu. Most convenient major airport: Honolulu International.

Founded: 1955
Affiliation: Latter-Day Saints
Total Enrollment: 772 M, 1,038 W (full-time); 92 M, 126 W (part-time)
Cost: < $10K
Admission: Non-selective
Application Deadline: March 31

Admission. Graduates of approved high schools with 12 units in academic subjects eligible; 70% of applicants accepted, 84% of these actually enroll. Average freshman ACT scores: 21 M, 21 W composite. *Required:* ACT, minimum high school GPA of 2.5, essay, interview (off-campus interviews arranged); adherence to code of behavior: students will be "honest, courteous, chaste, and modest, and must abstain from use of alcohol, tobacco, and drugs." Criteria considered in admissions, in order of importance: high school academic record, standardized test scores, recommendations, writing sample, extra curricular activities; other factors considered: special talents, religious affiliation and/or commitment. *Apply* by March 31. *Transfers* welcome; 565 enrolled 1993–94.
Academic Environment. Degrees offered: associates, bachelors. About 53% of general education requirements for graduation are elective; distribution requirements fairly numerous. About 20% of entering students graduate eventually; 46% of freshmen do not return for sophomore year. Average undergraduate class size: 100% of classes 20–40. *Special programs:* Teacher Professional Diploma Program. *Calendar:* 4–4–2, summer school.
Undergraduate degrees conferred (189). 39% were in Business and Management, 18% were in Education, 9% were in Marketing and Distribution, 6% were in Social Sciences, 6% were in Computer and Engineering Related Technology, 5% were in Business (Administrative Support), 4% were in Public Affairs, 3% were in Visual and Performing Arts, 3% were in Life Sciences, 3% were in Home Economics, remainder in 3 other fields.
Faculty. About 60% of faculty hold PhD or equivalent. About 95% of classes taught by tenured faculty. About 31% of teaching faculty are female.
Student Body. About 28% of students from Hawaii, 20% "other island nations of the South Pacific," 26% mainland U.S., 20% Orient. An estimated 95% of students reported as Latter-day Saints; 1% Black, 2% Hispanic, 33% Asian, 32% other minority.
Religious Orientation. College is a church-related institution; 1 course in religion required each term.
Varsity Sports. Men (NAIA): Basketball, Cross Country, Golf, Swimming, Tennis, Track. Women (NAIA): Cross Country, Softball, Tennis, Track, Volleyball.
Campus Life. About 48% of men, 63% of women live in traditional dormitories, 23% of men, 4% of women live in off-campus college-related housing, rest commute. About 5% of resident students leave campus on weekends.
Annual Costs. Tuition and fees, $2,375; room and board, $4,375; estimated $2,000 other, exclusive of travel. About 70% of students receive financial aid; average amount of assistance, $1,000.

State University College at Brockport

(See State University of New York)

Brooklyn College

(See City University of New York)

Brooklyn College of Pharmacy

(See Long Island University—Brooklyn Center)

Brown University

Providence, Rhode Island 02912 (401) 863-2378

Brown, the seventh oldest institution of higher learning in the country, is a fully integrated co-educational university. Although an eminent graduate institution, Brown considers itself a university college with major emphasis on undergraduate instruction. The 40-acre main campus is located in a residential area of Providence.

Founded: 1764
Affiliation: Independent
UG Enrollment: 7,291 M, W (undergraduate)
Cost: $10K–$20K
% Receiving Financial Aid:
Admission: Most Selective
Application Deadline: Jan. 1

Admission is among the most selective in the country. About 21% of applicants accepted, 52% of these actually enroll; 90% of freshmen graduate in top fifth of high school class, 98% in top two-fifths according to most recent data available (University declines to provide current admissions data). *Required:* SAT or ACT, any 3 ACH. *Non-academic factors* considered in admissions: diverse student body, special talents; geographical distribution, alumni children, athletic ability considered. *Entrance programs:* early action, midyear admission (transfers only), advanced placement, deferred admission. *Apply* by January 1. *Transfers* welcome.
Academic Environment. Brown has no distribution requirements permitting cross-disciplinary concentrations and "satisfactory" or "no credit" grades for all courses. The almost complete freedom offered by the innovative curriculum has been maintained despite the pressures attendant on admission to graduate school—a factor which caused a return to letter grades. Most students take advantage of 1 or more of the options open to them during their undergraduate years and the program appears to have substantial support from cur-

rent students as well as graduates. Single faculty teaches both graduates and undergraduates. Very able students may select program that permits completion of AB and MA degrees in 4 years. Special 7-year medical program leads to MD degree. Program in Liberal Medical Education combines the current 4-year MD program and the special 7-year program into a single 8-year continuum which incorporates the undergraduate years. Administration source reports strong academic programs include premed, computer science, art, history, engineering, mathematics and classics. *Degrees:* AB, BS. *Majors offered* include usual arts and sciences, applied mathematics, Asian studies, chemistry, engineering, international relations, linguistics; many interdepartmental and special concentrations. Most students cite the academic freedom as the greatest strength of the Brown program, but one recent student adds "the wit and enthusiasm of faculty" as well as the diversity of course offerings. One student warns that "...if you are not self-motivated this curriculum is not for you."

About 92% of students entering as freshmen graduate eventually; 4–5% of freshmen do not return for sophomore year. *Special programs:* independent study, study abroad, honors, individualized majors, 5-year AB/BS, seminar-type "modes of thought" courses for freshmen, interdisciplinary studies, cooperative arrangement with Rhode Island School of Design. *Library:* 1,966,160 volumes, 15,200 periodicals, 250 special collections. *Calendar:* semester.

Undergraduate degrees conferred (1,520). 29% were in Social Sciences, 10% were in Letters, 9% were in Life Sciences, 7% were in Multi/Interdisciplinary Studies, 6% were in Area and Ethnic Studies, 6% were in Engineering, 6% were in Visual and Performing Arts, 5% were in Psychology, 5% were in Business and Management, 3% were in Philosophy and Religion, 3% were in Mathematics, 3% were in Computer and Engineering Related Technology, 3% were in Foreign Languages, remainder in 5 other fields. *Doctoral degrees:* Physical Sciences 30, Social Sciences 17, Letters 20, Mathematics 18, Foreign Languages 4, Engineering 13, Area Studies 6, Biological Sciences 11, Psychology 4, Computer and Information Sciences 2, Fine and Applied Arts 3, Philosophy and Religion 8.

Graduates Career Data. Full-time graduate study pursued immediately after graduation by 25% of students according to most recent data available; 34% enter medical school; 17% enter law school; 3% enter business school. Medical schools typically enrolling largest numbers of graduates include NYU, Albert Einstein, Mt. Sinai; law schools include NYU, Columbia, Boston U.; business schools include Harvard, U. of Chicago. *Careers in business and industry* pursued by 65% of graduates. Corporations hiring largest numbers of graduates include AT&T, IBM, Goldman Sachs, General Electric. *Career Counseling Program:* Alumni reported as helpful in both career guidance and job placement.

Faculty. Nearly all faculty hold doctorate; very high percentage earned at nation's top graduate schools.

Student Body. According to most recent data available, 5% of students from in state, 20% New England, 35% Middle Atlantic, 12% North Central, 6% West, 8% South, 2% Northwest. An estimated 22% of students reported as Protestant, 22% Catholic, 22% Jewish, 30% unaffiliated, 5% other; 7% Black, 6% Hispanic, 12% Asian, less than 1% Native American. *Minority group students:* academic support services, counseling, and financial aid available to all students. Third World Center and other clubs and groups attract interest of minority students.

Religious Orientation. Founded by Baptists, Brown is now independent and is proud of long tradition of religious freedom; makes no religious demands on students. Religious clubs on campus include University Christian Movement, Hillel, Christian Science. Facilities for worship available on campus for 3 major faiths.

Varsity Sports. Men (Div.I): Baseball, Basketball, Crew, Cross Country, Football (IAA), Ice Hockey, Lacrosse, Soccer, Swimming/Diving, Tennis, Track, Water Polo, Wrestling. Women (Div.I): Basketball, Crew, Cross Country, Field Hockey, Ice Hockey, Lacrosse, Soccer, Softball, Squash, Swimming/Diving, Tennis, Track, Volleyball.

Campus Life. Students most likely to feel at home on campus reported to be "socially conscious, intellectually and academically adventurous, community-minded." Least at home students who are "passive; rigid academically and intellectually." Students are encouraged to develop their own codes of conduct, subject to a few overriding university restrictions, such as observance of state laws governing firearms, alcohol, and drugs. Administration reports that "Brown is the most liberal of the Ivies....Key to Brown is diversity and freedom across the board." Recent student reports that the largest organization on campus is the Brown Community Outreach program, she adds, "most Brown students participate in some form of community service in the Providence area." Social and cultural life enriched by facilities available in Providence and the more extensive, as well as more distant opportunities offered in Boston. Most students appear, however, to stay on campus or in Providence. Permission to use cars granted to resident students in order of class (seniors first).

About 3% each of men and women live in traditional dormitories; 70% of men, 75% of women in coed dormitories; 19% each of men and women in off-campus housing or commute. Freshmen given preference in college housing if all students cannot be accommodated. Intervisitation in men's and women's dormitory rooms unlimited. Sexes segregated in coed dormitories either by wing, room or floor. There are 10 fraternities, 2 sororities on campus which about 8% of men, 3% of women join; 8% of men, 3% of women live in fraternities and sororities. About 5% of students leave campus on weekends.

Annual Costs. Tuition and fees, $19,006; room and board, $5,612. About 40% of students receive financial aid. Assistance is typically divided 65% scholarship, 23% loan, 12% work. University reports scholarships awarded only on the basis of need. *Meeting Costs:* university offers parent loan plans, SHARE.

Bryan College

(See William Jennings Bryan College)

Bryant College

Smithfield, Rhode Island 02917 (401) 232-6000

An independent, professional college of business administration and business education; located on a 387-acre campus in a town of 20,000, 12 miles from Providence. Most convenient major airport: T.F. Green (Warwick, RI).

Founded: 1863	**Total Enrollment:** 4,154
Affiliation: Independent	**Cost:** $10K–$20K
UG Enrollment: 1,472 M, 1,084 W (full-time); 378 M, 623 W (part-time)	**% Receiving Financial Aid:** 58%
	Admission: Selective
	Application Deadline: Rolling

Admission is selective. About 80% of applicants accepted, 36% of these actually enroll; 32% of freshman graduate in top fifth of high school class, 71% in top two-fifths. Average freshman SAT scores: 463 M, 461 W verbal, 594 M, 552 W mathematical; 21% of freshmen score above 500 on verbal; 65% score above 500 on mathematical, 20% above 600, 2% above 700. *Required:* SAT or ACT; interview recommended. Criteria considered in admissions, in order of importance: high school academic record, standardized test scores, recommendations, extra curricular activities; other factors considered: diverse student body, special talents, alumni children. About 19% of entering students from parochial schools. *Entrance programs:* early decision, early admission, midyear admission, deferred admission, advanced placement. *Apply:* rolling admissions; prior to Christmas recommended. *Transfers* welcome; 156 enrolled 1993–94.

Academic Environment. Degrees offered: associates, bachelors, masters. *Majors offered* in addition to usual studies include actuarial mathematics, business communications. Core requirements include computer information systems, economics, mathematics, statistics, business, accounting, college writing, humanities, and electives in liberal arts and science. About 76% of entering students graduate eventually; 14% of freshmen do not return for sophomore year. Average undergraduate class size: about 23% under 20, 70% 20–40, 7% above 40. Adult programs: variety of graduate degree programs. *Special programs:* January term, study abroad, internships, 5-year BS/MBA. *Calendar:* semester, winter and summer intersessions, summer school.

Undergraduate degrees conferred (833). 91% were in Business and Management, 6% were in Computer and Engineering Related Technology, remainder in 3 other fields.

Graduates Career Data. Advanced studies pursued by about 5% of students immediately after graduation, 30% eventually. *Careers in* *business and industry* pursued by about 95% of graduates. Employers typically hiring largest numbers of graduates include accounting firms, computer firms. Career Development Services include non-credit career development course, developmental programming, on-campus recruitment.

Faculty. About 84% of faculty hold PhD or equivalent. About 48% of undergraduate classes taught by tenured faculty. About 22% of teaching faculty are female; 2% Black, less than 2% Hispanic, 5% other minority.

Student Body. About 16% of students from in state; 82% New England, 13% Middle Atlantic, 4% foreign. An estimated 60% of students reported as Catholic, 18% Protestant, 5% Jewish, 12% unaffiliated, 3% other; 2% Black, 2% Hispanic, 2% Asian, 2% other minority.

Varsity Sports. Men (NCAA Div.II): Baseball, Basketball, Cross Country, Golf, Soccer, Tennis, Track. Women (NCAA Div.II): Basketball, Cross Country, Soccer, Softball, Tennis, Track, Volleyball.

Campus Life. About 5% of women live in traditional dormitories; 79% of men, 82% of women in coed dormitories; 12% of men, 8% of women live in off-campus housing or commute. There are 8 fraternities, 5 sororities on campus, which about 15% of men, 12% of women join; 10% of men, 5% of women live in fraternities and sororities. About 20% of resident students leave campus on weekends.

Annual Costs. Tuition and fees, $12,120; room and board, $6,216; estimated $1,200 other, exclusive of travel. About 58% of students receive financial aid; average amount of assistance, $10,647. Assistance is typically divided 54% grant, 34% loan, 12% work. College reports 100 scholarships awarded on the basis of academic merit alone, 22 for special talents, 1,473 based on need.

Bryn Mawr College

Bryn Mawr, Pennsylvania 19010 (215) 526-5150

Bryn Mawr, one of the most eminent colleges for women in the country, is actually a quasi-university with 2 co-educational graduate schools offering masters and doctoral degrees in 17 departments and programs and a Graduate School of Social Work and Social Research. It is linked closely in the undergraduate college in both course offerings and social life with nearby Haverford, second of the three Quaker-founded colleges in the area. Ties with the other member of the trio, Swarthmore, are not so uniformly close. The college's 136-acre campus is located in a suburban community of 5,700, 11 miles west of Philadelphia. Most convenient major airport: Philadelphia International.

Founded: 1885
Affiliation: Independent
UG Enrollment: 1,182 W (full-time)
Total Enrollment: 1,881
Cost: $10K–$20K
% Receiving Financial Aid: 43%
Admission: Most Selective
Application Deadline: January 15

Admission is among the most selective in the country. About 53% of applicants accepted, 41% of these actually enroll; 83% of freshmen graduate in top fifth of high school class; 96% in top two-fifths. Freshman SAT scores, according to most recent data available: 90% of freshmen score above 500 on the verbal, 64% above 600, 16% above 700; 94% score above 500 on mathematical, 66% above 600, 14% above 700. *Required:* SAT, 3 ACH including English composition, interview (on- or off-campus). *Non-academic factors* considered in admissions: special talents, diverse student body, "evidence of intellectual curiosity." *Entrance programs:* early decision, early admission, advanced placement, deferred admission. *Apply* by January 15. *Transfers* welcome.

Academic Environment. Close cooperation with Haverford is an important feature of life at Bryn Mawr. Each semester 50% of students take advantage of cross-registration between the two colleges. Some departments are federated; most departments plan curriculum jointly to expand opportunities and avoid duplication. Cooperative programs with Swarthmore and the U. of Pennsylvania and exchange programs with other colleges also expand opportunities. Elected student representatives on the Board of Trustees and students serve on faculty committees including the Committee of Admissions. Despite extremely capable student body, demands of college are so rigorous that few can coast during freshman year. Influence of the small but highly regarded graduate programs may account for the relatively large number of female scholars the college has produced. Administration reports 70% of courses required for graduation are elective; distribution requirements, however, fairly numerous: 2 semesters work in each of 4 broad fields, English composition, proficiency in foreign language and mathematics. *Degree:* AB. *Majors offered* include usual arts and sciences, anthropology, classical and Near Eastern archaeology; number of interdepartmental major areas. New programs include: East Asian studies, comparative literature; new minors include feminist and gender studies, neuro and behavioral sciences.

About 83% of students entering as freshmen graduate eventually; 4% of freshmen do not return for sophomore year. *Special programs:* independent study, study abroad, honors, undergraduate research, interdepartmental courses, summer institutes at Avignon, Madrid, Florence, Pushkin Institute in Moscow, Center for Classical Studies in Rome, guest senior year, cooperative programs with Haverford, Swarthmore, U. of Penn., 3–2 engineering with CalTech, U. of Penn., BA/MCP in city and regional planning with U. of Penn.. Adult programs: continuing education programs, post-baccalaureate programs. *Library:* 866,213 titles, 1,960 periodicals, rare book collection, archaeological library, on-line computer library center. *Calendar:* semester.

Undergraduate degrees conferred (295). 31% were in Social Sciences, 15% were in Foreign Languages, 15% were in Letters, 7% were in Life Sciences, 7% were in Physical Sciences, 6% were in Psychology, 5% were in Mathematics, 4% were in Philosophy and Religion, 4% were in Visual and Performing Arts, 3% were in Multi/Interdisciplinary Studies, remainder in 2 other fields. *Doctoral degrees:* Public Affairs and Services 4, Social Sciences 6, Education 5, Biological Sciences 3, Fine and Applied Arts 4, Foreign Languages 2, Letters 2, Psychology 1, Physical Sciences 1, Philosophy and Religion 2.

Graduates Career Data. According to most recent data available, full-time graduate study pursued immediately after graduation by 38% of students; 5% enter medical school; 6% enter law school; 4% enter business school. Medical schools enrolling largest numbers of graduates include U. of Pennsylvania, Medical College of Pennsylvania, Case Western, Mt. Sinai; law schools include Harvard, Temple, George Washington, Boston U.; business schools include Wharton, Harvard, NYU. *Careers in business and industry* pursued by 24% of graduates. Corporations typically hiring largest numbers of graduates include Anderson Consulting, Chase Manhattan, Metropolitan Life, Prudential.

Faculty. About 98% of faculty hold doctorate; majority earned at nation's leading graduate schools.

Student Body. College seeks a national student body; 15% of students from in state; 37% Middle Atlantic, 17% South, 15% West/Northwest, 10% North Central, 12% New England; 9% foreign. An estimated 4% Black, 14% Asian, 3% Hispanic, according to most recent data available. Disadvantaged students: "strong financial aid program" and supportive programs such as writing clinic, tutoring available to all students.

Religious Orientation. Founded by members of Society of Friends, Bryn Mawr is now nonsectarian and independent; no compulsory religious studies or observances. Places of worship available in immediate community for major faiths.

Varsity Sports. Women (Div.III): Basketball, Cross Country, Field Hockey, Lacrosse, Soccer, Swimming & Diving, Tennis, Volleyball.

Campus Life. Most social and extracurricular activities shared with Haverford students (campus 1 mile away). Unlimited meal exchange and regular intercampus bus service make commuting between the colleges convenient. Numerous residences on both campuses are coed and students at Bryn Mawr and Haverford "are very free to determine their own lifestyles." Formal regulations minimal. Cars permitted on campus to all but freshmen. Smoking prohibited in designated areas; student drinking policy enforced through honor system. Dorm hours and intervisitation regulated by students. Public transportation to center of Philadelphia takes 20 minutes; service every half hour.

About 77% of women live in traditional dormitories; 11% in coed dormitories; rest live in off-campus housing or commute. Intervisitation in men's and women's dormitory rooms unlimited. Sexes segregated in coed dormitories by room. There are no sororities.

Annual Costs. Tuition and fees, $17,660; room and board, $6,450. About 43% of students receive financial aid; assistance is typically divided 71% grant/scholarship, 19% loan, 9% work. College reports scholarships awarded only on the basis of need. *Meeting Costs:* college offers tuition loan programs, and prepaid tuition plans.

Bucknell University

Lewisburg, Pennsylvania 17837 (717) 523-1271

A private, co-educational university, founded by Baptists, Bucknell has long been popular with students from the Mid-Atlantic states. The university offers concentrations in the arts and sciences, education, management, and continues its well-known engineering program. Located in a community of 18,000, the 300-acre campus is 60 miles north of Harrisburg. Most convenient major airports: Harrisburg, Williamsport.

Founded: 1846
Affiliation: Independent
UG Enrollment: 1,730 M, 1,596 W (full-time)
Total Enrollment: 3,600
Cost: $10K–$20K
% Receiving Financial Aid: 59%
Admission: Highly Selective
Application Deadline: January 1

Admission is highly selective. About 58% of applicants accepted, 23% of these actually enroll; 79% of freshmen graduate in top fifth of high school class, 97% in top two-fifths. Average freshman SAT scores: middle fifty percent range, 510–590 verbal, 590–670 mathematical; 74% of freshmen score above 500 on verbal, 22% above 600, 1% above 700; 96% score above 500 on mathematical, 65% above 600, 18% above 700. *Required:* SAT or ACT, audition for music applicants. Criteria considered in admissions, in order of importance: high school academic record, recommendations, standardized test scores, extra curricular activities, writing sample; other factors considered: alumni children, diverse student body, special talents. *Entrance programs:* early decision, early admission, advanced placement, deferred admission. About 32% of entering students from private or parochial schools. *Apply* by January 1. *Transfers* welcome "insofar as space permits"; 48 enrolled 1993–94.

Academic Environment. Degrees offered: bachelors, masters. The university has traditional strength in the engineering sciences, but administration source reports strong programs also in the sciences, social sciences and humanities, all of which emphasize undergraduate cooperative research with faculty, and English which features a national poetry center. Bucknell offers five first-year residential colleges: the arts college, the international college, the humanities college, the environmental college and the college of social justice. Core requirements include First Year Foundation Seminar, 4 courses in humanities, 2 courses in social sciences, 2 courses in natural sciences and mathematics, 1 course in Natural & Fabricated Worlds, 1 course in Human Diversity, and a Capstone (senior year) course or experience. Administration reports additional requirements differ substantially for various degree programs. Majors offered include usual arts and sciences, accounting, animal behavior, cell biology, international relations, management, education (elementary, early childhood, secondary, research), engineering, environmental studies, Latin American studies, geography, geology, Japanese studies, theater and drama. Relations between students and faculty said to be excellent, "neither too distant nor too close." Average undergraduate class size: 56% of classes under 20, 30% 20–40, 14% over 40.

About 88% of students entering as freshmen graduate within four years, 90% eventually; 4% of freshmen do not return for sophomore year. *Special programs:* study abroad (including summer, semester, and junior year programs), BS/MS programs in sciences, BA/BS in engineering. *Calendar:* semester, summer school.

Undergraduate degrees conferred (844). 31% were in Social Sciences, 13% were in Engineering, 12% were in Business and Management, 9% were in Life Sciences, 8% were in Letters, 5% were in Psychology, 4% were in Education, 4% were in Physical Sciences, 4% were in Visual and Performing Arts, 3% were in Mathematics, remainder in 5 other fields.

Graduates Career Data. Advanced studies pursued immediately after graduation by 28% of students; 4% enter medical school; 5% enter law school; 3% enter business school. Medical schools typically enrolling largest numbers of graduates include Penn, Penn State, Jefferson; dental schools include Pittsburgh, Temple; law schools include Georgetown, Virginia, Cornell, Dickinson; business schools include Tuck, Wharton, NYU. About 67% of 1992–93 graduates employed. Corporations typically hiring largest numbers of graduates include American Express, Anderson Consulting, Cooper & Lybrand, The MPY Company. Career Development Services include computer linked career search, on-campus recruitment.

Faculty. About 96% of faculty hold PhD or equivalent. About 69% of undergraduate classes taught by tenured faculty. About 28% of teaching faculty are female; 5% minority.

Student Body. University seeks a national student body; 33% of students from in state; 72% Middle Atlantic, 16% New England, 5% Midwest, 2% foreign. An estimated 38% of students reported as Protestant, 34% Catholic, 4% Jewish, 20% unaffiliated, 4% other; 3% as Black, 2% Hispanic, 3% Asian, 3% other minority.

Varsity Sports. Men (Div.I): Baseball, Basketball, Crew, Cross Country, Diving, Football (AA), Golf, Lacrosse, Soccer, Swimming, Tennis, Track, Wrestling. Women (Div.I): Basketball, Crew, Cross Country, Diving, Field Hockey, Lacrosse, Soccer, Softball, Swimming, Tennis, Track, Volleyball.

Campus Life. Campus life reflects the varied tastes and interests of a heterogeneous student body that includes traditional fraternity types and sports enthusiasts, as well as those interested in poetry readings, foreign films, cultural events, intellectual and social issues. However, administration and recent students agree that Bucknell students are very much a "middle of the road" group politically and socially. Only freshmen must live in residence halls. Cars allowed for upperclass students. Use of alcoholic beverages limited to students over 21 in fraternity houses and dormitory rooms. Fraternities have recently adopted an invitation-only, "closed party" system to help prevent underage drinking.

About 5% of men, 10% of women live in traditional dormitories; 72% of men, 88% of women in coed dormitories; 2% of men, 2% of women live in off-campus housing or commute. Freshmen given preference in college housing if all students cannot be accommodated. Intervisitation in men's and women's dormitory rooms determined by each hall. Sexes segregated in coed dormitories by wing, floor or room. There are 12 fraternities, 8 sororities on campus which about 52% of men, 58% of women join; 21% of men live in fraternities. About 5% of resident students leave campus on weekends.

Annual Costs. Tuition and fees, $17,730; room and board, $4,590; estimated $1,500 other, exclusive of travel. About 59% of students receive financial aid; average amount of assistance, $12,000. Assistance is typically divided 55% grant, 33% loan, 12% work. University reports scholarships awarded only on the basis of need.

Buena Vista College

Storm Lake, Iowa 50588 (800) 383-9600 or (712) 749-2235

A church-related, liberal arts college, located near the shores of 3,200-acre Storm Lake, in a "progressive college town" of 9,000, 75 miles east of Sioux City. Most convenient major airport: Sioux City, Iowa.

Founded: 1891
Affiliation: Presbyterian Church (USA)
Total Enrollment: 475 M, 493 W (full-time); 22 M, 33 W (part-time)
Cost: $10K–$20K
% Receiving Financial Aid: 93%
Admission: Selective (+)
Application Deadline: May 1

Admission is selective (+). About 80% of applicants accepted, 41% of these actually enroll; 43% of freshmen graduate in top fifth of high school class, 74% in top two-fifths. Average freshman SAT scores: 493 M, 513 W verbal, 523 M, 501 W mathematical. *Required:* SAT or ACT; interview recommended. Criteria considered in admissions, in order of importance: high school academic record, standardized test scores, recommendations, extracurricular activities, writing sample; other factors considered: special talents, alumni children. About 4% of entering students from private or parochial schools. *Entrance programs:* early decision, early admission, midyear admission. *Apply* by May 1; February 1 for priority; rolling admissions. *Transfers* welcome; 63 enrolled 1993–94.

Academic Environment. Degrees offered: bachelors. General education requirements include 36 hours in humanities, sciences, arts and English. Computer literacy required of all students. Academic and Cultural Events Series allows students to earn credit for attending lectures and classical performances. *Majors offered* in addition to usual arts and sciences include teacher education, international business, management/entrepreneurship, corporate communication, pre-medicine, pre-law, accounting; new program in arts management recently added. Average undergraduate class size: 68% of classes under 20, 27% between 20–40, 5% over 40; student/faculty ratio of 14:1. About 54% of students entering as freshmen graduate within four years, 62% eventually; 26% of freshmen do not return for sophomore year. *Special programs:* CLEP, January term, independent study, study abroad, individualized majors, internships and work-study programs, 3–2 engineering, dental school early admit program with U. of Iowa. *Calendar:* 4–1–4, summer school.

Undergraduate degrees conferred (722). 43% were in Business and Management, 26% were in Education, 10% were in Multi/Interdisciplinary Studies, 6% were in Communications, 5% were in Psychology, 3% were in Social Sciences, remainder in 9 other fields.

Graduates Career Data. Advanced studies pursued by 16% of graduates. Graduate and professional schools typically enrolling largest numbers of graduates include U. of Iowa, Drake. About 95% of 1992–93 graduates employed. Fields typically hiring largest numbers of graduates include education, accounting, finance/banking, marketing. Career Development Services include interest surveys, resume and interviewing workshops, career days, on-campus recruitment, internships, computer networks for sharing resumes with employers.

Faculty. About 65% of faculty hold PhD or equivalent. About 70% of classes are taught by tenured faculty. About 44% of teaching faculty are female; 9% ethnic minorities.

Student Body. College seeks a national student body; 76% of students from Iowa, 94% from Midwest; 5% foreign. An estimated 65% of students reported as Protestant, 26% Catholic, 5% unaffiliated; 7% ethnic minorities.

Varsity Sports. Men (Div.III): Baseball, Basketball, Cross Country, Diving, Football, Golf, Swimming, Tennis, Track, Wrestling. Women (Div.III): Basketball, Cross Country, Diving, Golf, Softball, Swimming, Tennis, Track, Volleyball.

Religious Orientation. Buena Vista is a church-related institution; makes no religious demands on students; attendance at convocation optional.

Campus Life. About 70% of students live in traditional dormitories; 10% of students in coed dormitories; 5% live in off-campus college related housing; rest commute. Freshmen given preference in college housing if all students cannot be accommodated. Intervisitation in men's and women's dormitory rooms limited. There are no fraternities or sororities. About 50% of resident students leave campus on weekends.

Annual Costs. Tuition and fees, $12,565; room and board, $3,585; estimated $450 other, exclusive of travel. About 93% of students receive financial aid; average amount of assistance, $12,258. Assistance is typically divided 64% scholarship/grant, 30% loan, 6% work. College reports some scholarships awarded for academic merit alone, special talents alone, and for need alone.

State University College at Buffalo

(See State University of New York)

State University of New York at Buffalo

(See State University of New York)

Burlington College

Burlington, Vermont 05401 (802) 862-9616

A small, liberal arts institution, Burlington serves primarily underprivileged adults in Chittenden County. Most convenient major airport: Burlington International.

Founded: 1972
Affiliation: Independent
Total Enrollment: 28 M, 43 W (full-time); 35 M, 55 W (part-time)
Cost: < $10K
% Receiving Financial Aid: 80%
Admission: Non-selective
Application Deadline: 2 weeks before classes

Admission. Open admissions policy; almost all applicants accepted, 89% of these actually enroll. Criteria considered in admissions, in order of importance: interview, recommendations, writing sample; other factors considered: "readiness for success in non-traditional structure/program", first generation [LBRK]to attend[RBRK] college. *Required:* interview. *Apply* by 2 weeks prior to start of classes. *Transfers* welcome; 21 enrolled 1993–94.

Academic Environment. Degrees offered: associates, bachelors. *Majors offered* include transpersonal psychology, feminist studies, human services, individualized majors, contract-based learning. All programs are designed for adult learners, Independent Degree Program designed for continuing students with 60 credits of previous college work. *Special programs:* 8-week summer term, internships, independent study, cross registration programs.

Undergraduate degrees conferred (32). 38% were in Psychology, 19% were in Multi/Interdisciplinary Studies, 16% were in Visual and Performing Arts, 16% were in Education, 6% were in Business and Management, 3% were in Social Sciences, 3% were in Communications.

Graduates Career Data. Advanced studies pursued by 51% of graduates. Career Development Services provided.

Faculty. About 8% of faculty hold PhD or equivalent (varies).

Campus Life. University does not actively seek a national student body; 90% of students from Vermont. An estimated 5% of students reported as Black, 2% other minorities. College provides no housing.

Annual Costs. Tuition and fees, $7,500. About 80% of students receive financial aid; average amount of assistance, $6,214. Assistance is typically divided 36% grant, 48% loan, 16% work.

Butler University

Indianapolis, Indiana 46208 (317) 283-9255

An independent, liberal arts institution, Butler offers students a wide variety of majors including numerous pre-professional programs. Butler's 290-acre campus includes twenty-one buildings, playing fields, Holcomb Observatory and Planetarium, a formal botanical garden and a nature preserve, all just 7 miles from the center of Indianapolis (pop. 769,400).

Founded: 1855
Affiliation: Independent
UG Enrollment: 1,071 M, 1,547 W (full-time)
Total Enrollment: 3,733
Cost: $10K–$20K
% Receiving Financial Aid: 82%
Admission: Selective (+)
Application Deadline: Rolling

Admission is selective (+). About 86% of applicants accepted, 34% of these actually enroll; 61% of freshmen graduate in top fifth of high school class, 84% in top two-fifths. Average freshman scores: SAT, 480 M, 492 W verbal, 525 M, 550 W mathematical; about 46% of freshmen score above 500 on verbal, 11% above 600, 2% above 700; 70% score above 500 on mathematical, 30% above 600, 4% above 700; ACT, 24 M, 26 W composite. *Required:* SAT or ACT, essay; interview suggested; audition required in music, dance, and radio-TV. Criteria considered in admissions, in order of importance: high school academic record, standardized test scores, writing sample, recommendations, extra curricular activities; other factors considered: special talents (for fine arts), diverse student body, alumni children, leadership skills, motivation, career potential. *Entrance programs:* early decision, early admission, midyear admission, advanced placement. About 10% of entering students from private schools, 10% from parochial schools. *Apply:* rolling admissions. *Transfers* welcome; 124 enrolled 1993–94.

Academic Environment. Degrees offered: bachelors, masters. Butler offers students majors in 54 academic fields through the colleges of Liberal Arts and Sciences, Education, Business Administration, Pharmacy, and Jordan College of Fine Arts. Core requirements include courses in oral and written communication and comprehension, computer literacy, physical education and interdisciplinary studies, as well as distribution requirements in humanities, fine arts, social sciences, natural sciences and quantitative reasoning. Majors offered in addition to usual arts and sciences include actuarial science, American studies, computer science, international management, journalism, arts administration, piano pedagogy, radio and television, theater, and voice. In addition, Butler offers pre-professional programs in dentistry, engineering, forestry, law, medicine, optometry, veterinary medicine. Butler's Irwin Library houses basic research tools, the rare books collection, archives, and the National Track and Field Hall of Fame Library. In 1992 Butler began operation of a non-commercial, educational television station.

About 60% of entering students graduate within four years, 65% eventually; 19% of freshmen do not return for sophomore year. Average undergraduate class size: 54% of classes under 20, 39% 20–40, 7% over 40. *Special programs:* CLEP, independent study, many study abroad options, honors, internships and cooperative work/study programs in College of Business Administration, undergraduate research, 3-year degree, individualized majors. *Calendar:* semester, summer session and post-summer session.

Undergraduate degrees conferred (481). 20% were in Business and Management, 16% were in Education, 16% were in Health Sciences, 16% were in Communications, 7% were in Visual and Performing Arts, 6% were in Social Sciences, 4% were in Letters, 3% were in Home Economics, 3% were in Physical Sciences, remainder in 7 other fields.

Graduates Career Data. Advanced studies pursued by 15% of students immediately after graduation. University reports that Butler graduates who apply to medical and dental schools across the nation average a 90% acceptance rate. About 70% of 1992–93 graduates employed. Fields typically hiring largest numbers of graduates include accounting, pharmacy, education. Career Development Services include aptitude testing, placement services, resume/interviewing workshops, on-campus recruitment, individual counseling, internships and cooperative education programs, library resources.

Faculty. About 80% of faculty hold PhD or equivalent. About 75% of undergraduate classes are taught by tenured faculty, there are no teaching assistants. About 27% of teaching faculty are female; 7% minorities.

Student Body. University seeks a national student body; 75% of students from Indiana, 92% Midwest, 3% Middle Atlantic, 2% New England. An estimated 54% of students reported as Protestant, 28% Catholic, 1% Jewish, 10% unaffiliated; 5% Black, 2% other minority.

Religious Orientation. Butler is an independent institution with historic ties to the Christian Church (Disciples of Christ), makes no religious demands on students.

Varsity Sports. Men (Div.I): Baseball, Basketball, Cross Country, Football (II), Golf, Lacrosse, Soccer, Swimming, Tennis, Track, Volleyball. Women (Div.I): Basketball, Cross Country, Soccer, Softball, Swimming, Tennis, Track.

Campus Life. Students and administration describe the student body, faculty and administration as conservative. The Student Government Association acts as liaison between students and faculty and administration. Butler students can take advantage of more than 100 different activities on campus, including, but not limited to, social groups, religious organizations, service clubs, honorary societies, performance groups, fraternities and sororities, intramural and varsity athletics. In addition, the city of Indianapolis offers students a wide range of cultural and recreational activities.

About 45% of men, 50% of women live in coed dormitories; 17% of men, 13% of women live in off-campus housing or commute. Coed dormitories segregated by wing. There are 8 fraternities, 9 sororities on campus which about 26% of men, 22% of women join; 38% of men, 37% of women live in fraternities and sororities. About 50% of resident students leave campus on weekends.

Annual Costs. Tuition and fees, $12,280; room and board, $4,140; estimated $1,200 other, exclusive of travel. About 82% of students receive financial aid; average amount of assistance, $10,000. Assistance is typically divided 55% scholarship, 35% loan, 10% work. University reports 558 scholarships awarded on the basis of academic merit alone, 448 awarded for special talents, 1,271 based on need.

Cabrini College

Radnor, Pennsylvania 19087-3699 (215) 971-8552

A church-related college, conducted by the Missionary Sisters of the Sacred Heart, located in a Main Line suburb of Philadelphia.

Founded: 1957
Affiliation: Roman Catholic
UG Enrollment: 245 M, 581 W (full-time); 90 M, 350 W (part-time)
Total Enrollment: 1,557
Cost: $10K–$20K
% Receiving Financial Aid: 88%
Admission: Non-selective
Application Deadline: Rolling

Admission. Graduates of accredited high schools with 17–21 units in academic subjects and 80% grade average who rank in top half of class eligible; others admitted on evidence of ability; 70% of applicants accepted, 26% of these actually enroll; 19% of freshmen graduate in top fifth of high school class, 46% in top two-fifths. Average freshman SAT scores, according to most recent data available: 453 M, 452 W verbal, 488 M, 466 W mathematical. *Required:* SAT or ACT, recommendation; interview highly recommended. *Apply:* rolling admissions. *Transfers* welcome.

Academic Environment. *Degrees:* AB, BS, BSEd. About 50% of general education requirements for graduation are elective; some distribution requirements. About 55% of students entering as freshmen graduate within five years; 20% of freshmen do not return for sophomore year. *Special programs:* CLEP, independent study, study abroad, individualized majors. Adult programs: assessment of prior learning program, credit for life experience, CLEP, DANTES exams. *Calendar:* semester, summer school.

Undergraduate degrees conferred (184). 32% were in Business and Management, 29% were in Education, 13% were in Communications, 6% were in Social Sciences, 3% were in Psychology, 3% were in Life Sciences, 3% were in Liberal/General Studies, remainder in 9 other fields.

Graduates Career Data. According to most recent data available, full-time graduate or professional study pursued immediately after graduation by 9% of students; 5% enter law school, 3% enter business school.

Varsity Sports. Men (NCAA Div. III): Basketball, Cross Country, Soccer, Tennis. Women (Div. III): Cross Country, Field Hockey, Softball, Tennis, Volleyball.

Student Body. College does not seek a national student body; 98% of students from Middle Atlantic. An estimated 80% of students reported as Catholic, 9% as Protestant, 1% as Jewish; 2% as Black, 1% Hispanic, 2% as other minorities, according to most recent data available.

Religious Orientation. Cabrini is a church-related institution; 6 credits in religion required of all Catholic students.

Campus Life. About 64% of students live in traditional dormitories; rest commute. Intervisitation in women's dormitory rooms limited. There is one service "sorority" on campus, which about 9% of men and women join.

Annual Costs. Tuition and fees, $10,200; room and board, $5,790. About 88% of students receive financial aid; assistance is typically divided 35% scholarship, 60% loan, 5% work. College reports some scholarships awarded on the basis of academic merit alone. *Meeting Costs:* college offers installment payment plan, various loan programs.

Caldwell College

Caldwell, New Jersey 07006 (201) 228-4424

A church-related, liberal arts college, previously for women only, became co-educational in 1986, conducted by the Sisters of St. Dominic, located in a town of 8,700, 20 miles west of New York City. Most convenient major airport: Newark.

Founded: 1939
Affiliation: Roman Catholic
Total Enrollment: 240 M, 453 W (full-time); 185 M, 683 W (part-time)
Cost: < $10K
% Receiving Financial Aid: 67%
Admission: Non-selective
Application Deadline: Rolling

Admission. High school graduates with 16 units in college preparatory subjects, minimum high school GPA of 2.0, and rank in top half of high school class eligible; 60% of applicants accepted, 35% of these actually enroll; 24% of freshmen graduate in top fifth of high school class, 47% in top two-fifths. Average freshman SAT scores: 440 verbal, 470 mathematical. *Required:* SAT or ACT, interview. Criteria considered in admissions, in order of importance: standard-

ized test scores, high school academic record, recommendations, extra curricular activities; other factors considered: special talents. About 30% of entering students from private or parochial schools. *Entrance programs:* midyear admission. *Apply:* rolling admissions. *Transfers* welcome; 211 enrolled 1993–94.
Academic Environment. Degrees offered: bachelors, masters. Strongest programs reported to be business and education. Core requirements include 15 credits in religion, 6 credits each in English, history, foreign language, social sciences, mathematics, 3 credits in science, 4 credits in fine arts, 2 credits in communications, 1 credit in physical education. About 50% of students entering as freshmen graduate eventually; 20% of freshmen do not return for sophomore year. Average undergraduate class size: 59% of classes under 20, 40% 20–40, 1% over 40. *Special programs:* CLEP, independent study, study abroad, honors, undergraduate research, optional January interterm, internships/cooperative work-study programs, 3-year degree. Adult programs: continuing education for matriculating and non-matriculating students, External Degree program including study by mail, phone, interview with mentor; orientation each semester. *Calendar:* semester, summer school.
Undergraduate degrees conferred (133). 51% were in Business and Management, 13% were in Education, 12% were in Psychology, 8% were in Social Sciences, 7% were in Letters, 4% were in Life Sciences, remainder in 5 other fields.
Graduates Career Data. Advanced studies pursued by 11% of graduates. About 79% of 1992–93 graduates employed. Career Development Services include career education and counseling, vocational testing, on-campus Career Information Day.
Faculty. About 36% of faculty hold PhD or equivalent. About 54% of teaching faculty are female; 9% minorities.
Student Body. About 79% of students from in state; 81% Middle Atlantic, 17% foreign. An estimated 66% of students reported as Catholic, 20% Protestant, 9% unaffiliated, 2% other; 10% as Black, 6% Hispanic, 2% Asian, 17% other minority.
Varsity Sports. Men: Basketball, Golf, Soccer, Tennis. Women (Div.III): Basketball, Softball, Tennis.
Religious Orientation. Caldwell is a church-related institution; 5 courses in religious studies and philosophy required of all students.
Campus Life. About 39% of men, 32% of women live in coed dormitories; rest commute. No intervisitation in women's dormitory rooms. There are no fraternities or sororities on campus. About 70% of resident students leave campus on weekends.
Annual Costs. Tuition and fees, $8,460; room and board, $4,400; estimated $1,325 other, exclusive of travel. About 67% of students receive financial aid; average amount of assistance, $8,089. Assistance is typically divided 66% scholarship/grant, 25% loan, 9% work. College reports 94 scholarships awarded on the basis of academic merit alone, 31 for special talents, 207 based on need.
General Institutional Data. College newspaper: The Kettle. Total unrestricted endowment: $43,000.

California Baptist College

Riverside, California 92504 **(714) 689-5771**

A church-related college, located in a city of 140,100, 50 miles east of Los Angeles.

Founded: 1950
Affiliation: Southern Baptist
Total Enrollment: 693 M, W (full-time)
Cost: < $10K
% Receiving Financial Aid:
Admission: Non-selective
Application Deadline: Rolling

Admission. Graduates of accredited high schools with 800 SAT or 16 ACT composite, or 2.0 GPA eligible; others admitted by examination or on basis of potential for college work; 75% of applicants accepted, 45% of these actually enroll; 28% of freshmen graduate in top fifth of high school class, 55% in top two-fifths. *Required:* SAT or ACT, "satisfactory evidence of good moral character." *Apply:* rolling admissions. *Transfers* welcome.
Academic Environment. *Degrees:* AB, BS. About 46% of general education requirements for graduation are elective; distribution requirements fairly numerous. About 68% of students entering as freshmen graduate eventually; 30% of freshmen do not return for sophomore year. *Special programs:* CLEP, honors, 3-year degree. *Calendar:* semester, summer school.
Undergraduate degrees conferred (87). 32% were in Business and Management, 17% were in Education, 14% were in Social Sciences, 11% were in Philosophy and Religion, 10% were in Psychology, 7% were in Visual and Performing Arts, 5% were in Communications, 3% were in Letters.
Graduates Career Data. *Careers in business and industry* pursued by 50% of graduates, according to most recent data available.
Varsity Sports. Men (NAIA): Baseball, Basketball, Soccer. Women (NAIA): Basketball, Volleyball.
Campus Life. College seeks a national student body; 72% of students from California. An estimated 83% of students reported as Protestant, 5% Catholic, 3% unaffiliated, 9% other; 8% Black, 6% Hispanic, 4% Asian, 9% other minority, according to most recent data available.
Religious Orientation. California Baptist is a church-related institution; 9 hours of religion or philosophy required of all students; attendance at chapel is required.
Campus Life. About 42% of men, 57% of women live in traditional dormitories; 15% of men, 9% of women live in married student housing, rest commute. No intervisitation in men's or women's dormitory rooms. There are no fraternities or sororities. About 50% of resident students leave campus on weekends.
Annual Costs. Tuition and fees, $7,848; room and board, $5,352. About 87% of students receive financial aid; assistance is typically divided 32% scholarship, 63% loan, 5% work. College reports some scholarships awarded on the basis of academic merit alone.

California College of Arts and Crafts

Oakland, California 94618

An independent, professional visual arts institution, the college specializes in the education and training of artists, designers, and architects, and offers the BFA, BArch. and MFA degrees.

Founded: 1907
Affiliation: Independent

California Institute of Technology

Pasadena, California 91125 **(818) 356-6341**

Caltech is the most prestigious scientific–technological institution in the U.S.—and it was also the first scientific institution to insist that undergraduates devote at least 20% of their course time to humanistic and cultural studies. Caltech has been co-educational since 1970. The 124-acre campus is located in a residential area 1 mile from downtown Pasadena (pop. 119,000), 12 miles from Los Angeles. Most convenient major airport: Los Angeles International.

Founded: 1891
Affiliation: Independent
UG Enrollment: 662 M, 238 W (full-time)
Total Enrollment: 1,977
Cost: $10K–$20K
% Receiving Financial Aid: 75%
Admission: Most Selective
Application Deadline: January 1

Admission is among the most selective in the country. About 24% of applicants accepted, 45% of these actually enroll; all freshmen graduate in top fifth of high school class. Average freshman SAT scores: 660 verbal, 750 mathematical; all freshmen score above 500 on verbal, 84% above 600, 21% above 700; all score above 600 on mathematical, 93% above 700. *Required:* SAT, 3 ACH (mathematics II, English Composition and choice of biology, chemistry, or physics), 3 recommendations, essay. Criteria considered in admissions, in order of importance: high school academic record, standardized test scores, recommendations, extra curricular activities, writing sample; other factors considered: commitment to science. About 20% of entering students from private schools. *Entrance programs:* early action, early admission, deferred admission. *Apply* by January 1. *Transfers* welcome; 12 enrolled 1993–94.
Academic Environment. Degrees offered: bachelors, masters, doctoral. Caltech has equally strong commitments to the sciences, pure and applied mathematics, and to engineering. It provides opportunities for independent study with no set requirements and for individual student to devise his or her own curriculum in confer-

ence with faculty committee. Exchange programs with nearby liberal arts colleges also open doors to students. One student leader calls attention to the "rapid pace" of academic life. The student body is among the 2 or 3 most able in the U.S. With an extraordinarily rigorous scientific–technical curriculum and a student body proficient in verbal as well as mathematical skills, competition is intense. Core requirements include 2 years mathematics, 2 years physics, 1 year chemistry, 1 year chemistry lab, 1 year additional lab class, humanities electives. Student interests in scholarly/intellectual pursuits rivaled by career-oriented concerns. Students who leave Caltech reported to be "those who have lost interest in sciences." About half of students on campus enrolled in graduate studies. Classes usually small, 90% of classes have enrollment under 20, many of them seminars. Majors offered include applied physics, astronomy, biology, chemical engineering, chemistry, economics, engineering and applied science, English, geological sciences, history, mathematics, physics, and social sciences, independent studies. *Computer Science:* computer literacy not required (nearly all students are, however, computer literate); major offered. Students not required to own microcomputer. University facilitates student ownership. Facilities reported as adequate to meet student demand; all student rooms can accommodate terminals linked to mainframe; "several" terminals in each dorm, "many" in library and labs.

About 75% of students entering as freshmen graduate within four years, 80% within five years; 5% of freshmen do not return for sophomore year. *Special programs:* independent study, undergraduate research, individualized majors, 3–2 engineering, numerous internship/cooperative work-study programs, exchange programs with Occidental, Scripps, Art Center College of Design. *Library:* 440,000 volumes, 6,300 periodicals, extensive collections of microforms, government documents, archives, maps; open-stack privileges; hours until 1 am. *Calendar:* quarter.

Undergraduate degrees conferred (165). 86% were in Visual and Performing Arts, 14% were in Architecture and Environmental Design. *Doctoral degrees:* Physical Sciences 53, Engineering 60, Biological Sciences 9, Mathematics 9, Social Sciences 3, Computer and Information Sciences 5.

Graduates Career Data. Advanced studies pursued immediately after graduation by 61% of students. About 16% of 1992–93 graduates employed. Industries typically hiring largest numbers of graduates include Aerospace, Computers, Electronics, Instruments. Career Development Services include counseling, mock interviews, job fairs, placement services. Alumni reported as helpful in both career guidance and job placement.

Faculty. All faculty hold PhD or equivalent; overwhelming proportion from leading graduate institutions. All undergraduate classes taught by tenured faculty. About 10% of faculty are female.

Student Body. Institute does not seek a national student body; 30% of students from California; 47% West/Northwest, 19% South, 14% Midwest, 20% Middle Atlantic/New England, according to most recent data available. An estimated 27% of students reported as Asian, 5% Hispanic, less than 2% other minority. *Minority group students:* active recruitment, as well as academic and financial "encouragement given to promising minority students."

Varsity Sports. Men (Div. III): Baseball, Basketball, Crew, Fencing, Golf, Soccer, Swimming, Tennis, Track, Water Polo. Women (Div. III): Cross Country, Fencing, Tennis, Track, Volleyball.

Campus Life. Students enjoy considerable latitude in determining policies governing campus life. An honor system, monitored by a Student Board of Control, governs both academic and Non-academic affairs affecting students. Students are said to "desire more time to plan and participate in social activities with other colleges." Student social life influenced by 3:1 ratio of men to women. Many cultural and intellectual opportunities available both on campus and in surrounding Pasadena and Los Angeles areas. Intramural sports reported to be very popular. Residence facilities arranged in 7 undergraduate and 4 graduate houses, each administered autonomously by its own elective Excom (legislative body that makes decisions on conduct of house members, social events, etc.) and an upperclass committee appointed by the Excom.

About 80% of students live in coed dormitories; 20% live in off-campus housing or commute. All-female campus housing available. Housing is guaranteed all four years; freshmen required to live on-campus. Intervisitation in men's and women's dormitory rooms unlimited. There are no fraternities or sororities. "Very few" resident students leave campus on weekends.

Annual Costs. Tuition and fees, $16,110; room and board, $6,135; estimated $1,350 other, exclusive of travel. About 75% of students receive financial aid; average amount of assistance, $15,082. Assistance is typically divided 78% grant, 17% loan, 5% work. Institute reports all scholarships awarded on the basis of need.

California Institute of the Arts

Valencia, California 91355

An independent institution consisting of 5 schools (Art/Design, Dance, Music, Theater, Film/Video) for professional training in all the performing and visual arts, and offering the BFA and MFA degrees.

Founded: 1961 **Affiliation:** Independent

California Lutheran College

(See California Lutheran University)

California Lutheran University

Thousand Oaks, California 91360 (805) 492-2411

A church-related, liberal arts university with a "Christian atmosphere," located in a community of 100,000, 50 miles northwest of Los Angeles. Formerly known as California Lutheran College. Most convenient major airport: Los Angeles International.

Founded: 1959
Affiliation: Lutheran
UG Enrollment: 645 M, 778 W (full-time); 201 M, 231 W (part-time)
Total Enrollment: 2,963
Cost: $10K–$20K
% Receiving Financial Aid: 85%
Admission: Non-selective
Application Deadline: June 1

Admission. Graduates of approved and accredited high schools with 12 academic units eligible; others given individual consideration; 76% of applicants accepted, 48% of these actually enroll; 22% of freshmen graduate in top fifth of high school class, 38% in top two-fifths. Average freshman SAT scores: 440 M, 433 W verbal, 514 M, 483 W mathematical; 23% of freshmen score above 500 on verbal, 53% score above 500 mathematical. *Required:* SAT or ACT, essay, academic recommendation. Criteria considered in admissions, in order of importance: high school academic record, writing sample, standardized test scores, recommendations, extra curricular activities; other factors considered: special talents, alumni children, diverse student body, religious affiliation and/or commitment. Entrance programs available: mid-year admission, deferred admission, advanced placement. *Apply* by June 1; rolling admissions. *Transfers* welcome; 215 enrolled 1993–94.

Academic Environment. Degrees offered: bachelors, masters. Core curriculum is a writing intensive, integrated liberal arts program including courses in general studies, gender and ethnic studies, and computer technology. About 55% of entering students graduate within four years, 60% eventually; 21% of freshmen do not return for sophomore year. Adult programs: accelerated evening programs with degrees offered in business administration, accounting, and computer science. *Special programs:* CLEP, honors, undergraduate research, independent study, study abroad, 3–2 engineering. Calendar: 4–1–4, summer school.

Undergraduate degrees conferred (369). 34% were in Business and Management, 12% were in Education, 9% were in Psychology, 8% were in Social Sciences, 8% were in Communications, 6% were in Marketing and Distribution, 5% were in Letters, 5% were in Life Sciences, 4% were in Visual and Performing Arts, 3% were in Protective Services, 3% were in Computer and Engineering Related Technology, remainder in 5 other fields.

Graduates Career Data. Advanced studies pursued by 35% of students; 15% enter graduate school, 4% enter medical school, 1%

enter dental school, 4% enter law school, 10% enter business school. Medical schools typically enrolling largest numbers of graduates include: U of Utah, Ohio State U., Loma Linda U., UC San Diego; law schools include: UC Davis, Pepperdine, U. of Denver; business schools include: CLU. Employers typically hiring largest numbers of graduates include Ernst and Young, Deluxe Check Printers, and Prudential-Rache. Career Development Services include counseling, interest inventory, resume and interviewing techniques, on-campus recruitment.

Faculty. About 72% of faculty hold PhD or equivalent. About 34% of teaching faculty are female; 2% Black, 6% Hispanic, 2% other minority.

Student Body. About 82% of students from California; 84% West, 3% Northwest, 1% Middle Atlantic, 1% Midwest, 1% South, 10% foreign. An estimated 48% of students reported as Protestant, 21% as Catholic, 1% as Jewish, 1% as Muslim, 27% unaffiliated; 3% as Black, 11% Hispanic, 4% Asian, 1% other minority.

Varsity Sports. Men (NCAA Div.III): Baseball, Basketball, Cross Country, Football, Golf, Soccer, Tennis, Track. Women (NAIA Div.III): Basketball, Cross Country, Soccer, Softball, Tennis, Track, Volleyball.

Religious Orientation. California Lutheran is a church-related institution, owned by the Evangelical Lutheran Church in America; 2 courses in religion required of all students; attendance at chapel services voluntary.

Campus Life. About 55% of students live in coed dormitories; rest live in off-campus housing or commute. There are no fraternities or sororities. About 25% of resident students leave campus on weekends.

Annual Costs. Tuition and fees, $12,040; room and board, $5,200; estimated $2,500 other, exclusive of travel. About 85% of students receive financial aid; average amount of assistance, $9,772. Assistance is typically divided 30% scholarship, 30% grant, 30% loan, 10% work. University reports 350 scholarships awarded on the basis of academic merit alone, 100 for special talents, 600 based on need.

California Maritime Academy

Vallejo, California 94590 **(707) 648-4200**

A state-supported professional academy established to train officers for the Merchant Marine. The campus is located in a community of 110,000, north of San Francisco. Most convenient major airports: Oakland or San Francisco.

Founded: 1929
Affiliation: State
Total Enrollment: 430 M, 57 W (full-time)
Cost: < $10K
% Receiving Financial Aid: 55%
Admission: Non-selective
Application Deadline: Mar. 15

Admission. About 65% of applicants accepted, 34% of these actually enroll. Freshman SAT scores: 34% of entering freshmen score above 500 on verbal, 10% above 600, 1% above 700; 57% score above 500 on mathematical, 15% above 600, 1% above 700. Criteria considered in admissions, in order of importance: high school academic record, standardized test scores, recommendations, writing sample, extra curricular activities; other factors considered: diverse student body. *Required:* SAT or ACT. *Out-of-state* freshman applicants: academy welcomes out-of-state students. State does not limit out-of-state enrollment. About 17% of entering students from private schools. *Apply* by March 15; rolling admissions. *Transfers* welcome; 30 enrolled 1993–94.

Academic Environment. Degree offered: bachelors. Unusual majors offered include marine transportation, marine engineering technology; business administration recently added. Current student notes that required Fire School and annual 2-month Sea Training provide valuable training and experience. About 71% of entering students graduate eventually; 15% of freshmen do not return for sophomore year. Average undergraduate class size: 38% under 20, 47% 20–40, 15% over 40.

Undergraduate degrees conferred (86). 42% were in Military Sciences, 40% were in Engineering, 19% were in Business and Management.

Graduates Career Data. *Careers in business and industry* pursued by 94% of graduates. About 70% of 1992–93 graduates employed. Corporations typically hiring largest numbers include Chevron Shipping, Military Sealift, Arco Marine.

Faculty. About 40% of faculty hold PhD or equivalent. About 85% of classes taught by tenured faculty. About 12% of teaching faculty are female; 5% minority.

Student Body. About 88% of students from California; 96% West; 6 foreign students 1993–94.

Campus Life. About 80% of men, 95% of women live on campus in coed dormitories (segregated by wing), rest commute. Approximately 45% of resident students leave campus on weekends.

Annual Costs. Tuition and fees, $2,548 (out-of-state, $8,138); room and board, $4,770; estimated $500 other, exclusive of travel. About 55% of students receive financial aid; average amount of assistance, $4,600. Assistance is typically divided 40% grant, 50% loan, 10% work. Academy reports 15 scholarships awarded on the basis of academic merit alone.

California University of Pennsylvania

California, Pennsylvania 15419 **(412) 938-4404**

A state-supported university, serving western Pennsylvania, located in a town of 6,600, 35 miles south of Pittsburgh. Most convenient major airport: Greater Pittsburgh International.

Founded: 1852
Affiliation: State
Total Enrollment: 6,711 M, W (full-time)
Cost: < $10K
Admission: Non-selective
Application Deadline: August 1

Admission. Graduates of accredited high schools eligible; 72% of applicants accepted, 52% of these actually enroll; 18% of freshmen graduate in top fifth of high school class, 44% in top two-fifths. *Required:* SAT; interview recommended. *Out-of-state* freshman applicants: university welcomes students from out of state. State does not limit out-of-state enrollment. No special requirements for out-of-state applicants. About 84% of applicants accepted, 50% enroll. *Non-academic factors* considered in admissions: special talents. *Apply* by August 1. *Transfers* welcome.

Academic Environment. *Degrees:* BA, BS, BSEd. *Majors offered* in liberal arts, science and technology programs, education, health related fields, management technology, athletic training. About 30% of general education requirements for graduation are elective; distribution requirements fairly numerous. About 50% of students entering as freshmen graduate eventually; 22% of freshmen do not return for sophomore year. *Special programs:* CLEP, study abroad, individualized majors, 3–2 engineering. *Calendar:* semester, summer school.

Undergraduate degrees conferred (928). 35% were in Education, 17% were in Business and Management, 8% were in Social Sciences, 7% were in Letters, 6% were in Engineering and Engineering Related Technology, 4% were in Psychology, 4% were in Public Affairs, 3% were in Life Sciences, 3% were in Health Sciences, remainder in 14 other fields.

Graduates Career Data. *Careers in business and industry* pursued by 70% of graduates, according to most recent data available. Corporations typically hiring largest numbers of graduates include Westinghouse, JC Penney, International Telemarketing Service.

Faculty. About 57% of faculty hold PhD or equivalent.

Student Body. University seeks a national student body; 90% of students from in state; 98% from Middle Atlantic. An estimated 44% of students reported as Protestant, 50% as Catholic, 3% as Jewish, 3% unaffiliated or other; 7% as Black, 1% as Hispanic, 1% other minority, according to most recent data available.

Varsity Sports. Men (Div.II): Baseball, Basketball, Cross Country, Football, Rugby, Soccer, Track, Wrestling. Women (Div.II): Basketball, Cross Country, Rugby, Softball, Tennis, Track, Volleyball.

Campus Life. About 26% of students live in traditional dormitories; no coed dormitories; 69% live in off-campus housing or commute. Freshmen given preference in college housing if all students cannot be accommodated. Intervisitation in men's and women's dormitory rooms limited. There are 12 fraternities, 9 sororities on campus which about 10% of men, 8% of women join; 5% of students live in fraternities and sororities. About 80% of resident students leave campus on weekends.

Annual Costs. Tuition and fees, $3,384 (out-of-state, $6,778); room and board, $3,460. About 65% of students receive financial aid; assistance is typically divided 42% scholarship, 49% loan, 9% work. University reports some scholarships awarded on the basis of academic merit alone.

The California State University System

Most convenient major airport: San Francisco and/or Los Angeles.

California has the most completely developed state system of higher education in the nation. It consists of an extensive network of 2-year colleges, which any high school graduate in the state may enter; the State University system of 19 campuses, which accepts students who graduate in the top third of their high school class; and the University of California, which, at the undergraduate level, accepts high school graduates with B average and combined score of 2,500 on SAT and 3 ACH. The state universities vary rather widely in the programs they offer, the nature of campus life, and the number of out-of-state students they enroll. All, however, accept out-of-state students, and some actively seek such students in an effort to provide a more cosmopolitan environment for learning. These universities offer extensive liberal arts programs in which a progressively larger number of students enroll, but business administration and teacher education are also popular programs. Many campuses offer experimental programs such as off-campus degrees, weekend colleges, and "self-paced learning programs."

Descriptions of the 19 campuses that make up the California State University system follow in alphabetical order.

Admission. Although some differences in the nature of student body are discernible among the universities, admission to all of them is selective. Policy governing admission is common to all. *Required:* SAT or ACT; all will accept either test for determination of admission eligibility. Some may require admitted students to take a test other than that originally submitted before enrollment. Eligibility determined by weighted combination of grade point average and test scores; California residents must have eligibility index placing them in top third of state's high school graduates. *Out-of-state* freshman enrollment not limited to a certain percentage by state; however, out-of-state enrollment in some programs maybe restricted or priority given to residents. Requirements for out-of-state applicants: grade point average and test score equivalent to top sixth of California high school graduates. *Apply:* very early for some programs; rolling admissions until quotas filled; where quotas filled for entering freshmen and transfer students, applications redirected to campuses with enrollment still open. *Transfers* welcome; graduates of California community colleges and veterans given priority.

Religious Orientation. The California State University system makes no religious demands on students. Religious clubs for students and other facilities available on or near all campuses.

California Polytechnic State University/San Luis Obispo

San Luis Obispo, California 93407 (805) 756-1111

Cal Poly/San Luis Obispo is located on a 5,000-acre campus in a coastal city of 43,000, midway between Los Angeles and San Francisco.

Founded: 1901
Affiliation: State
Total Enrollment: 7,971 M, 5,593 W (full-time)
Cost: < $10K
% Receiving Financial Aid: 43%
Admission: Selective
Application Deadline: Nov. 30

Admission is selective. (See also California State University and Colleges System.) About 35% of applicants accepted; 81% of these actually enroll. Average freshman SAT scores: 451 verbal; 553 mathematical. Criteria considered in admissions, in order of importance: high school academic record, standardized test scores. *Apply* by November 30. *Transfers:* 1,131 enrolled 1992–93.

Academic Environment. Degrees offered: bachelors, masters. Emphasis on "occupational-centered curricula." Work in major field started in freshman year and pursued concurrently with a program of required general education courses. Students are represented on "every policy making council or committee in the university." Core requirements include 14 quarter units in communication in the English language, 18 in the physical universe, 18 in arts and humanities, 18 in social, political, and economic systems, and 6 in technology. Undergraduate studies offered by schools of Agriculture, Architecture and Environmental Design, Business, Liberal Arts, Engineering and Technology, Professional Studies and Education, Science and Mathematics. *Majors offered* in 49 BS programs, 6 BA fields, and architecture. Average undergraduate class size: 21.

About 59% of entering students graduate eventually; 17% of freshmen do not return for sophomore year. *Special programs:* study abroad, internship/cooperative education programs. *Calendar:* quarter, summer school.

Undergraduate degrees conferred (2,700). 20% were in Engineering, 13% were in Business and Management, 8% were in Social Sciences, 7% were in Agribusiness and Agricultural Production, 7% were in Architecture and Environmental Design, 6% were in Engineering and Engineering Related Technology, 5% were in Home Economics, 5% were in Letters, 4% were in Life Sciences, 4% were in Agricultural Sciences, 4% were in Liberal/General Studies, 3% were in Psychology, remainder in 9 other fields.

Graduates Career Data. Advanced studies pursued by 16% of students. Careers in engineering, agriculture, business and liberal arts pursued by 77% of graduates. Career Development Services include counseling, testing, assistance with interviewing skills and resume preparation, on-campus recruitment.

Faculty. About 63% of faculty hold PhD or equivalent. About 88% of classes taught by tenured faculty. About 22% of teaching faculty are female; 14% minority.

Student Body. About 91% of students are from California. Average age of undergraduate student: 23.3.

Varsity Sports. Men (Div.II): Baseball, Basketball, Crew, Cross Country, Football, Gymnastics, Rodeo, Skiing, Soccer, Swimming, Tennis, Track, Volleyball, Wrestling. Women (Div.II): Basketball, Cross Country, Gymnastics, Rodeo, Skiing, Soccer, Softball, Swimming, Tennis, Track, Volleyball, Rodeo.

Campus Life. Recent student comments, "The ocean is five minutes away; the mountains are five minutes away; what else can you ask for? The town is small, no building is taller than five stories, and Farmer's Market is every Thursday night. It's the best small town anywhere!"

About 8% of men, 7% of women live in traditional or co-ed dormitories; 84% men, 88% women in college-related off-campus housing. There are 27 fraternities, 8 sororities on campus, which about 8% men, 5% women join; 8% of men, 5% of women live in fraternities and sororities.

Annual Costs. Tuition and fees, $2,217 (out-of-state, $9,597); room and board, $4,763; estimated $1,962 other, exclusive of travel. About 43% of students receive financial aid. Assistance is typically divided 30% scholarship, 47% grant, 20% loan, 3% work. University reports 3 scholarships awarded on special talents alone.

CSC/Bakersfield

Bakersfield, California 93311-1099 (805) 664-3036

The newest campus in the system, Bakersfield enrolled its first classes in 1970. The 375-acre campus is located in a city of 150,000, north of Los Angeles and east of San Luis Obispo. Most convenient major airport: Meadows Field.

Founded: 1965
Affiliation: State
UG Enrollment: 1,166 M, 1,772 W (full-time); 412 M, 631 W (part-time)
Total Enrollment: 4,192
Cost: < $10K
Admission: Selective
Application Deadline: Rolling

Admission. (See also California State University System.) About 56% of applicants accepted, 60% of these actually enroll. Average freshman scores: SAT, 420 M, 389 W verbal, 435 M, 431 W mathematical; ACT, 21 composite. *Required:* SAT or ACT, minimum HS GPA of 2.0, college preparatory course pattern. *Entrance programs:* early decision, early admission, midyear admission, advanced placement. *Out-of-state* freshman applicants: university welcomes out-of-state students; no limit; somewhat more selective admission requirements. *Apply:* rolling admissions. *Transfers* welcome; 617 enrolled 1993–94.

Academic Environment. University's academic villages integrate classrooms, lounge, study areas, and dormitory rooms which are grouped in a single part of the campus. Administration reports one-third each of courses required for graduation are general education, major/minor, elective. Degrees offered: bachelors, masters. *Majors offered* in 30 fields including anthropology, business administration, criminal justice, fine arts, health sciences, nursing, physical education, religious studies, petroleum land studies. Average undergraduate class size: 100% of classes between 20–40. About 28% of students entering as freshmen graduate within five years. *Special programs:* January Term, CLEP, independent study, study abroad, honors, individualized majors, credit by examination, experimental learning credit, modularized courses, ethnic and area studies (Black, Chicano, Asian, Latin-American), internships, cross registration within CSU system. *Calendar:* 3–3, summer school.

Undergraduate degrees conferred (701). 24% were in Business and Management, 22% were in Liberal/General Studies, 11% were in Social Sciences, 6% were in Education, 6% were in Psychology, 5% were in Letters, 5% were in Health Sciences, 4% were in Communications, 3% were in Public Affairs, remainder in 9 other fields.

Graduates Career Data. Career Development Services include centralized placement office which offers counseling, works in cooperation with academic departments, maintains active program of relations with business, industry, government, and education.

Faculty. About 80% of faculty hold PhD or equivalent. About 38% of teaching faculty are female; 3% Black, 12% Hispanic, 7% other ethnic minorities.

Varsity Sports. Men (Div.II): Basketball, Soccer, Swimming/Diving, Track, Wrestling(Div. I). Women (Div.II): Softball, Swimming/Diving, Tennis, Track, Volleyball.

Student Body. University seeks a national student body; 97% of students from California; 1% out-of-state, 2% foreign. Average age of undergraduate student: 26.

Campus Life. Very small percentage of students live on campus; residence facilities still limited.

About 1% of men, 2% of women in coed dormitories; rest live in off-campus housing or commute. Freshmen given preference in college housing if all students cannot be accommodated. Intervisitation in men's and women's dormitory rooms limited. Sexes segregated in coed dormitories by floor. There are 3 fraternities and 4 sororities, which about 1% each of men, women join; they provide no residence facilities.

Annual Costs. Tuition and fees, $1,692 (out-of-state, $9,072); room and board, $3,710. About 40% of students receive financial aid; average amount of assistance, $3,500. Assistance is typically divided 5% scholarship, 45% grant, 45% loan, 5% work. University reports 130 scholarships awarded on the basis of academic merit alone, 170 for special talents.

CSC/San Bernardino

(See CSU/San Bernardino)

CSC/Stanislaus

(See CSU/Stanislaus)

California State Polytechnic University/Pomona

Pomona, California 91768-4019 (714) 869-2000

A former ranch, the large 1,400-acre campus of Cal Poly/Pomona is located in a city of 104,000, 40 minutes east of downtown Los Angeles. Most convenient major airport: Ontario (CA).

Founded: 1938
Affiliation: State
Total Enrollment: 14,758 M, W (full-time)
Cost: < $10K
Admission: Selective
Application Deadline: Rolling

Admission. (See also California State University and Colleges System.) About 63% of applicants accepted, 63% of these actually enroll. *Out-of-state* freshman applicants: university welcomes out-of-state students. About 47% of out-of-state applicants accepted. *Entrance programs:* early decision, early admission, midyear admission, advanced placement. *Apply:* rolling admissions. *Transfers* welcome.

Academic Environment. *Degrees:* AB, BS. Students begin work in major field as first-quarter freshmen. *Majors offered* in limited arts and sciences, broad range of sciences and professional/vocational fields including electrical and computer engineering, hotel and restaurant management, international agriculture, landscape architecture, urban planning.

About 31% of students entering as freshmen graduate eventually; 27% of freshmen do not return for sophomore year. *Special programs:* CLEP, independent study, study abroad, honors, undergraduate research, credit by examination. *Calendar:* quarter, summer quarter.

Undergraduate degrees conferred (2,861). 38% were in Business and Management, 18% were in Engineering, 6% were in Liberal/General Studies, 6% were in Architecture and Environmental Design, 4% were in Engineering and Engineering Related Technology, 4% were in Social Sciences, 4% were in Psychology, 3% were in Computer and Engineering Related Technology, 3% were in Life Sciences, remainder in 13 other fields.

Graduates Career Data. According to most recent data available, full-time graduate or professional study pursued immediately after graduation by 22% of students; 19% enter business school. *Careers in business and industry* pursued by 69% of graduates. Corporations typically hiring largest numbers of graduates include Rockwell International, General Dynamics, Hughes Aircraft.

Varsity Sports. Men (Div.II): Baseball, Basketball, Cross Country, Soccer, Tennis, Track. Women (Div.II): Basketball, Cross Country, Soccer, Softball (I), Tennis, Track, Volleyball.

Student Body. University does not seek a national student body; 97% of students from California. An estimated 4% of students reported as Black, 14% Hispanic, 21% Asian. *Minority group students:* special grants, tutoring programs, residence hall programs.

Campus Life. About 4% of men, no women live in traditional dormitories; 4% of men, 6% of women in coed dormitories; rest live in off-campus housing or commute. Freshmen given preference in college housing if all students can not be accommodated. Intervisitation in men's and women's dormitory rooms unlimited. Sexes segregated in coed dormitories by wing. There are 13 fraternities, 7 sororities, 2 coed fraternities. About 30% of resident students leave campus on weekends.

Annual Costs. Tuition and fees, $1,523 (out-of-state, $8,903); room and board, $5,526. About 25% of students receive financial aid; assistance typically divided 60% scholarship, 36% loan, 4% work. University reports some scholarships awarded on the basis of academic merit alone.

CSU/Chico

Chico, California 95929-0850 (916) 898-6321

Second oldest in the system, the greater Chico area is a community of 76,500, 100 miles north of Sacramento. Most convenient major airport: Chico Municipal, Sacramento.

Founded: 1889
Affiliation: State
UG Enrollment: 5,910 M, 5,915 W (full-time); 686 M, 665 W (part-time)
Total Enrollment: 14,707
Cost: < $10K
% Receiving Financial Aid: 63%
Admission: Selective
Application Deadline: Nov. 30

Admission is selective. (See also California State University System.) About 81% of applicants accepted, 33% of these actually enroll. Average freshman scores (1992): SAT, 420 M, 421 W verbal, 501 M, 462 W mathematical; ACT, 20 M, 21 W composite. Criteria considered in admissions, in order of importance: high school academic record, standardized test scores. Required: SAT or ACT. *Entrance programs:* early decision, early admission. *Out-of-state* freshman applicants: university welcomes out-of-state students; 65% accepted, 77% of these actually enroll. *Apply* by November 30 for priority; rolling admission. *Transfers:* 1,901 enrolled 1993–94.

Academic Environment. Degrees offered: bachelors, masters. *Undergraduate studies* offered by colleges of Agriculture, Behavioral and Social Sciences, Business, Communications and Education, Engineering, Humanities and Fine Arts, Natural Sciences, Professional Studies; also Area and Interdisciplinary Program. *Majors offered* include usual arts and sciences, anthropology, construction management, geography, international relations, microbiology, communications, nursing, social welfare, computer engineering, industrial technology. Adult Programs: 60+ (if over 60 years of age can enroll for a small fee if working towards a degree); Encore Re-entry program. Average undergraduate class size: 42% under 20, 48% 20–40, 10% over 40.

About 54% of entering students graduate eventually; 19% of freshmen do not return for sophomore year. *Special programs:* January term, independent study, study abroad, honors in English, external degree programs (Shasta, Yuba, Lassen Colleges), exchange with U. of New Hampshire, individualized majors, Planned Educational Leave, credit by examination, cooperative education program. *Calendar:* semester, summer school.

Undergraduate degrees conferred (2,880). 20% were in Business and Management, 14% were in Social Sciences, 11% were in Communications, 11% were in Liberal/General Studies, 7% were in Engineering, 6% were in Psychology, 6% were in Education, 4% were in Health Sciences, 3% were in Parks and Recreation, 3% were in Home Economics, remainder in 14 other fields.

Graduates Career Data. Corporations typically hiring largest numbers of graduates include Hewlett Packard, Macy's, Tandem. Career Development Services: on-campus recruiting, seminars, job notification, placement file service, reference materials, placement for teachers, employment counseling, career planning and Career Exploration Center.

Faculty. About 66% of faculty hold PhD or equivalent. All undergraduate classes taught by tenured faculty. About 34% of teaching faculty are female; 10% minority.

.Student Body. University seeks a national student body; about 95% of students from California, 5% foreign. An estimated 3% of undergraduate students reported as Black, 8% Hispanic, 5% Asian, 9% other minority. *Minority group students:* Educational Opportunity Program, Ethnic and Women's Studies program, Mexican American Studies program. Average age of undergraduate student: 23.

Varsity Sports. Men (Div.II): Baseball, Basketball, Cross Country, Football, Soccer, Track & Field. Women (Div.II): Basketball, Cross Country, Soccer, Softball, Track & Field, Volleyball.

Campus Life. Recent student comments, "...Chico is still small enough to make you feel at home. The people are friendly, the air is clean, the crime rate is low and the professors are accessible. Chico provides an ideal atmosphere for learning because the college is the most influential factor in the town." About 4% of men, 6% of women live in coed dormitories; rest commute. Most students live near campus and commute, but Chico is considered a residential campus. Sexes segregated in coed dormitories by floor. There are 18 fraternities, 12 sororities on campus; about 12% each men and women join.

Annual Costs. Tuition and fees, $1,782 (out-of-state, $9,162); room and board, $4,364; estimated $1,926 other, exclusive of travel. About 63% of students receive financial aid; average amount of assistance, $1,638.

CSU/Dominguez Hills

Carson, California 90747 **(213) 516-3600**

One of the California State University campuses, Dominguez Hills is located on the historic Rancho San Pedro in the southwest portion of the Los Angeles metropolitan area. University is primarily for commuters.

Founded: 1960
Affiliation: State
Total Enrollment: 1,467 M, 2,083 W (full-time)
Cost: < $10K
Admission: Selective
Application Deadline: Rolling

Admission. (See also California State University System.) About 76% of applicants accepted, 47% of these actually enroll. All students graduate in top third of their high school class. *Entrance programs:* early decision, early admission, midyear admission. *Out-of-state* freshman applicants: university welcomes out-of-state students. *Apply:* rolling admissions. *Transfers* welcome.

Academic Environment. Administration reports 20% of courses required for graduation are elective. *Undergraduate studies* offered by schools of Education, Humanities and Fine Arts, Science, Mathematics and Technology, Social and Behavioral Sciences, Management. *Degrees:* BA, BS. *Majors offered* include usual arts and sciences, analytic chemistry, anthropology, management, earth and marine sciences, geography, linguistics, medical technology, organic biochemistry, physical chemistry, physical education, speech, theater arts, 20th century thought and expression, urban and environmental management.

About 50% of students entering as freshmen graduate eventually; 15% of freshmen do not return for sophomore year. *Special programs:* CLEP, honors, independent study, study abroad, undergraduate research, credit by examination. Calendar: 3 terms, summer school.

Undergraduate degrees conferred (906). 34% were in Business and Management, 10% were in Social Sciences, 9% were in Multi/Interdisciplinary Studies, 8% were in Public Affairs, 7% were in Psychology, 6% were in Liberal/General Studies, 5% were in Computer and Engineering Related Technology, 4% were in Health Sciences, 4% were in Visual and Performing Arts, 3% were in Communications, 3% were in Letters, remainder in 8 other fields.

Faculty. About 90% of faculty hold PhD or equivalent.

Varsity Sports. Men (Div.II): Baseball, Basketball, Golf, Soccer. Women (Div.II): Basketball, Soccer, Softball, Volleyball.

Campus Life. University seeks a national student body; almost all students from West/Northwest. An estimated 35% of students reported as Black, 11% Hispanic, 13% Asian, 2% other minority, according to most recent data available. *Minority group students:* Mexican American, Afro-American programs. About 3% of students live in university-owned apartments; rest commute.

Annual Costs. Tuition and fees, $1,959 (out-of-state, $9,339); room and board $4,287. University reports some scholarships awarded on the basis of merit.

CSU/Fresno

Fresno, California 93740-0047 **(209) 278-2287**

Fresno is located on a 220-acre main campus in a city of 510,500 in the heart of the San Joaquin Valley. An additional 1,190 acres contains "one of the best-equipped agricultural plants in the West." Most convenient major airport: Fresno Air Terminal.

Founded: 1911
Affiliation: State
UG Enrollment: 6,474 M, 7,020 W (full-time)
Total Enrollment: 18,017
Cost: < $10K
% Receiving Financial Aid: 39%
Admission: Non-selective
Application Deadline: September 9

Admission. (See also California State University and Colleges System.) About 79% of applicants accepted, 31% of these actually enroll. Average freshman SAT scores: 393 verbal, 458 mathematical, according to most recent data available. Criteria considered in admissions, in order of importance: high school academic record, standardized test scores. *Entrance programs:* early decision, early admission, midyear admission, advanced placement, 60+ program, reentry, high school early admission for minority students. *Out-of-state* freshman applicants: university welcomes out-of-state students. *Out-of-state* enrollment for Nursing and Physical Therapy programs limited. *Apply* by September 9. *Transfers:* 2,001 enrolled 1993.

Academic Environment. Degrees offered: bachelors, masters, doctoral. *Undergraduate studies* offered by schools of Agricultural Sciences and Technology, Business and Administrative Sciences, Education and Human Development, Engineering, Health and Social Work, Arts and Humanities, Natural Sciences, Social Sciences. *Majors offered* include usual arts and sciences, various agricultural fields, anthropology, business, communicative disorders, computer science, criminology, engineering, geography, health science, home economics, industrial arts, industrial technology, journalism, liberal studies, linguistics, microbiology, nursing, physical education, physical therapy, telecommunications, recreation administration, Russian, social welfare, surveying engineering, theatre arts. Administration reports 40% of courses required for graduation are elective.

About 56% of entering students graduate within 6 years; 20% of freshmen do not return for sophomore year. *Special programs:* CLEP, independent study, study abroad, honors, individualized majors,

credit by examination, weekend university, Asian studies program, Armenian studies courses, Moss Landing marine laboratories. Adult programs: Reentry Program, Weekend University. *Calendar:* semester, summer school.
Undergraduate degrees conferred (2,976). 23% were in Business and Management, 20% were in Liberal/General Studies, 7% were in Social Sciences, 6% were in Engineering, 5% were in Health Sciences, 5% were in Education, 5% were in Letters, 4% were in Psychology, 4% were in Agricultural Sciences, 3% were in Communications, 3% were in Engineering and Engineering Related Technology, remainder in 14 other fields.
Faculty. About 88% of faculty hold PhD or equivalent.
Student Body. About 95% of students from California. An estimated 19% of students reported as Hispanic, 4% Black, 8% Asian, 2% Native American, according to most recent data available. *Minority group students:* Educational Opportunity Program, ethnic studies; financial, academic, social aid available, retention programs in some departments. Average age of undergraduate student: 21.5.
Varsity Sports. Men (Big West): Baseball, Basketball, Football, Golf, Swimming, Tennis, Track, Wrestling (PAC 10). Women (Big West): Basketball, Softball, Volleyball.
Campus Life. College provides some residential facilities; large majority of students live off campus. About 2% of women live in traditional dormitories; 5% of men, 3% of women live in coed dormitories; 93% of men, 94% of women commute. There are 13 fraternities, 8 sororities on campus; about 2% of men, 1% of women live in fraternities and sororities.
Annual Costs. State fees, $1,648 (out-of-state tuition and fees, $7,552); room and board, $4,302; estimated $500 books. About 39% of students receive financial aid. Assistance is typically divided 67% scholarship/grant, 30% loans, 3% work. University reports some scholarships awarded on the basis of academic merit.

CSU/Fullerton

Fullerton, California 92634 (714) 773-2370

Located on a 225-acre campus in a city of 100,395, 30 miles southeast of Los Angeles, traditionally a university for commuters, Fullerton now reports more than half of its students living in off-campus housing rather than at home.

Founded: 1957	**Cost:** < $10K
Affiliation: State	**Admission:** Selective
Total Enrollment: 5,332 M, 6,815 W (full-time)	**Application Deadline:** Rolling

Admission. (See also California State University and Colleges System.) About 76% of applicants accepted, 38% of these actually enroll. Average freshman scores: SAT, 407 M, 387 W verbal, 503 M, 455 W mathematical; ACT, 22 M, 20 W composite. Criteria considered in admissions, in order of importance: high school academic record, standardized test scores, recommendations. *Entrance programs:* early decision, early admission, midyear admission, advanced placement. *Out-of-state* freshman applicants: university welcomes out-of-state students; about 50% of out-of-state applicants accepted, 50% of these enroll. *Transfers* welcome; 2,322 enrolled 1993–94.
Academic Environment. Administration reports 30% of courses required for graduation are elective. Degrees offered: bachelors, masters. *Majors offered* include usual arts and sciences, anthropology, business administration, child development, communications, computer science, criminal justice, earth science, engineering, ethnic studies, geography, human services, liberal studies, linguistics, nursing, physical education, religious studies, Russian area studies, speech communication and pathology, theater arts.

About 19% of students entering as freshmen graduate within four years, 61% eventually; 27% of freshmen do not return for sophomore year. *Special programs:* CLEP, independent study, study abroad, honors, credit by examination, individualized majors, cross registration with other CSU campuses. *Calendar:* semester, summer school. *Miscellaneous:* A ROTC (on campus), AF ROTC (with UCLA).
Undergraduate degrees conferred (3,990). 32% were in Business and Management, 12% were in Communications, 9% were in Social Sciences, 8% were in Education, 6% were in Psychology, 5% were in Visual and Performing Arts, 4% were in Engineering, 4% were in Letters, 4% were in Liberal/General Studies, 3% were in Computer and Engineering Related Technology, 3% were in Protective Services, remainder in 9 other fields.
Graduates Career Data. Career Development Services include career and personal counseling; seminars and workshops covering resume writing, job search techniques, interview skills; on-campus recruitment.
Faculty. About 88% of faculty hold PhD or equivalent. About 28% of teaching faculty are female; 3% Black, 4% Hispanic, 12% other ethnic minority.
Student Body. University does not seek a national student body; 98% of students from California. *Minority group students:* special financial, academic, social provisions; Afro-American, Chicano Studies programs.
Varsity Sports. Men (NCAA): Baseball, Basketball, Cross Country, Fencing, Football, Golf, Gymnastics, Soccer, Tennis, Wrestling. Women (WCAA): Basketball, Cross Country, Fencing, Golf, Gymnastics, Softball, Tennis, Volleyball.
Campus Life. Fullerton is largely a commuter school; 85% of students travel 5 miles or more to campus. About 1% of students live in on-campus apartments, rest live in off-campus apartments or commute. Student government is "very service oriented." There are 13 fraternities, 7 sororities on campus, which about 8% of men, 4% of women join. Almost all students leave campus on weekends.
Annual Costs. Tuition and fees, $1,622 (out-of-state, $9,002). University reports scholarships awarded on the basis of need alone.

CSU/Hayward

Hayward, California 94542 (415) 881-3811

Primarily a commuter college, Hayward is located on a 354-acre campus in the foothills overlooking San Francisco Bay.

Founded: 1957	**Cost:** < $10K
Affiliation: State	**Admission:** Selective
Total Enrollment: 10,281 M, W (full-time)	**Application Deadline:** Rolling

Admission. (See also California State University and Colleges System.) About 59% of applicants accepted, 66% of these actually enroll; 46% of freshmen graduate in top fifth of high school class, 100% in top two-fifths. Entrance program: advanced placement. *Out-of-state* freshman applicants: university welcomes out-of-state students. *Transfers* welcome.
Academic Environment. Administration reports 20% of courses required for graduation are elective. *Degrees:* BA, BS. *Majors offered* include usual arts and sciences, anthropology, ethnic studies, business administration, computer science, geography, human development, Latin American studies, liberal studies, statistics; special major also possible.

Special programs: independent study, study abroad, credit by examination. Calendar: quarter, summer quarter and session.
Undergraduate degrees conferred (2,025). 38% were in Business and Management, 11% were in Liberal/General Studies, 9% were in Psychology, 8% were in Social Sciences, 5% were in Computer and Engineering Related Technology, 5% were in Health Sciences, 4% were in Letters, 3% were in Life Sciences, 3% were in Visual and Performing Arts, 3% were in Education, 3% were in Protective Services, 3% were in Communications, remainder in 7 other fields.
Faculty. About 80% of faculty hold PhD or equivalent.
Varsity Sports. Men (NCAC, Div. II): Baseball, Basketball, Cross Country, Football, Soccer, Swimming, Tennis, Track, Volleyball; (CCIJA): Judo. Women (NCAC): Basketball, Cross Country, Soccer, Softball, Swimming, Tennis, Track, Volleyball; (CCIJA): Judo.
Student Body. University does not seek a national student body; 90% of students from California. An estimated 10% of students reported as Black, 18% Asian, 6% Hispanic, 4% Native American or other minority, according to most recent data available. *Minority group students:* Educational Opportunity Program, Ethnic Studies department and major.
Campus Life. Most students commute; "fewer than 200 walk to campus." About 3% of students live in off-campus, coed dormitory; rest commute. There are 3 fraternities and 2 sororities, which about 1% of men, 1% of women join.
Annual Costs. Tuition and fees, $1,423 (out-of-state, $8,803). University reports scholarships awarded only on the basis of need.

CSU/Humboldt State University

Arcata, California 95521 (707) 826-4402

Located 290 miles north of San Francisco on Arcata Bay, "heart of the Redwood Empire," Humboldt has School of Natural Resources, offering interrelated programs of study in fisheries, oceanography, forestry, wildlife management, watershed management, and natural resources. Most convenient major airport: Arcata/Eureka.

Founded: 1913
Affiliation: State
Total Enrollment: 7,166 M, W (full-time)
Cost: < $10K
Admission: Selective
Application Deadline: Rolling

Admission. (See also California State University System.) About 46% of applicants accepted, 75% of these actually enroll; all freshmen graduate in top third of high school class. *Out-of-state* freshman applicants: university welcomes out-of-state students. About 72% of applicants accepted, 52% enroll. *Apply*: rolling admissions. *Transfers* welcome.
Academic Environment. *Degrees:* AB, BS. *Majors offered* include usual arts and sciences, geography, home economics, industrial arts, journalism, religious studies, speech pathology/audiology, theater arts, zoology, professional and occupational curricula including business, environmental resources engineering, environmental ethics, nursing, oceanography, social work, speech-communication, national resources fields.

About 41% of entering students graduate eventually; 26% of students entering as freshmen do not return for sophomore year. *Special programs:* CLEP, study abroad, individualized majors. *Calendar:* semester, summer extension.
Undergraduate degrees conferred (961). 14% were in Social Sciences, 11% were in Liberal/General Studies, 10% were in Renewable Natural Resources, 9% were in Life Sciences, 8% were in Visual and Performing Arts, 8% were in Business and Management, 7% were in Psychology, 6% were in Letters, 4% were in Education, 4% were in Health Sciences, 3% were in Physical Sciences, 3% were in Communications, 3% were in Multi/Interdisciplinary Studies, 3% were in Foreign Languages, remainder in 7 other fields.
Graduates Career Data. *Careers in business and industry* pursued by 66% of students. *Career Counseling Program:* workshops, job listings, outreach, classes, video tapes, internships, some co-op positions, on-campus interviews. Alumni reported as not helpful in career guidance or job placement.
Faculty. About 71% of faculty hold PhD or equivalent.
Varsity Sports. Men (Div.II): Basketball, Cross Country, Football, Soccer, Track, Wrestling. Women (Div.II): Basketball, Cross Country, Swimming, Softball, Track, Volleyball.
Student Body. University does not seek a national student body; 97% of students from California. An estimated 2% of students reported as Black, 2% Hispanic, 2% Asian, 3% Native American, 3% other minority, according to most recent data available.
Campus Life. Student population largely from out of area—perhaps attracted by combination of relatively stable campus life and specialized curricula in natural resources fields. Another factor maybe identified by a student leader who asserts that "the environment is similar to that of the Garden of Eden in places." Rules governing student life include provision for up to 24-hour intervisitation (with policies established by each residence unit). About 21% of men, 16% of women live in coed dormitories; 78% of men, 84% of women live in off-campus housing. There are 2 fraternities, 3 sororities, which about 2% men, 2% women join. Less than 1% of resident students leave campus on weekends.
Annual Costs. Tuition and fees, $1,468 (out-of-state, $8,848). About 45% of students receive financial aid; assistance is typically divided 43% scholarship/grant, 50% loan, 6% work. University reports some scholarships awarded on the basis of academic merit alone.

CSU/Long Beach

Long Beach, California 90840 (213) 498-4141

One of the largest of the system, Long Beach is located on a 322-acre campus on the outskirts of a city of 381,209, 25 miles southwest of Los Angeles.

Founded: 1949
Affiliation: State
Total Enrollment: 22,611 M, W (full-time)
Cost: < $10K
Admission: Selective
Application Deadline: Rolling

Admission. (See also California State University and Colleges System.) About 53% of applicants accepted, 58% of these actually enroll; 98% of freshmen graduate in top third of high school class. *Out-of-state* freshman applicants: university welcomes out-of-state students. About 42% of applicants accepted, 37% enroll. *Non-academic factors* considered in admissions: special talents, diverse student body. *Entrance programs:* early admission, midyear admission, advanced placement. *Transfers* welcome.
Academic Environment. Experimental courses, suggested by students or faculty, are designed "to encourage educational innovation." Administration reports 33% of courses required for graduation are elective. *Undergraduate studies* offered by schools of Applied Arts and Sciences, Business Administration, Education, Engineering, Fine Arts, Humanities, Social and Behavioral Sciences. *Majors offered* in addition to usual studies include administration of travel and tourism, anthropology, entomology, food service system administration, geography, journalism, marine biology, microbiology, radio–TV, social welfare, theater arts.

About 33% of students entering as freshmen graduate eventually; 30% of freshmen do not return for sophomore year. *Special programs:* CLEP, study abroad, honors, undergraduate research, independent study, credit by examination, acceleration, Asian studies, Center for Latin American Studies, Ocean Studies Consortium. *Calendar:* early semester, winter and summer sessions.
Undergraduate degrees conferred (4,273). 21% were in Business and Management, 10% were in Liberal/General Studies, 9% were in Engineering, 8% were in Letters, 8% were in Social Sciences, 7% were in Visual and Performing Arts, 7% were in Psychology, 5% were in Communications, 4% were in Protective Services, 4% were in Health Sciences, 3% were in Home Economics, 3% were in Education, 3% were in Engineering and Engineering Related Technology, remainder in 11 other fields.
Graduates Career Data. According to most recent data available, full-time graduate or professional study pursued immediately after graduation by 10% of students. Corporations typically hiring largest numbers of graduates include Rockwell, Hughes, Northrop, McDonnell Douglas, TRW.
Faculty. About 81% of faculty hold PhD or equivalent.
Varsity Sports. Men (Div.I): Baseball, Basketball, Cross Country, Fencing, Football(IA), Golf, Swimming, Tennis, Track, Volleyball, Water Polo. Women (Div.I): Basketball, Cross Country, Fencing, Golf, Gymnastics, Softball, Soccer, Swimming, Tennis, Track, Volleyball.
Student Body. University is largely nonresidential in character; 96% of students from California. An estimated 25% of students reported as Protestant, 25% Catholic, 3% Jewish, 40% unaffiliated; 5% Black, 9% Hispanic, 15% Asian, 9% other minority, according to most recent data available.
Campus Life. About 1% each men, women live in traditional dormitories, 3% of men, 4% of women live in coed dormitories; 95% of men, 94% of women commute. There are 15 fraternities, 11 sororities on campus which about 7% of men, 4% of women join; 1% each live in fraternities and sororities. About 60% of resident students leave campus on weekends.
Annual Costs. Tuition and fees, $1,423 (out-of-state, $8,803); room and board, $4,800. University reports some scholarships awarded on the basis of academic merit alone.

CSU/Los Angeles

Los Angeles, California 90032 (213) 343-3901

Primarily a commuter institution, CSU/Los Angeles' urban campus is located just a few miles from the center of Los Angeles. Most convenient major airport: Los Angeles International.

Founded: 1947
Affiliation: State
Total Enrollment: 13,793 M, W (full-time)
Cost: < $10K
Admission: Selective
Application Deadline: August 7

Admission. (See also California State University System.) About 58% of applicants accepted, 100% of freshmen graduate in top third of high school class. *Out-of-state* freshman applicants: university welcomes out-of-state students. *Entrance programs:* early admission, midyear admission, advanced placement, early entrance. *Apply* by August 7. *Transfers* welcome.

Academic Environment. Administration reports 20% of courses required for graduation are elective. *Undergraduate studies* offered by schools of Natural and Social Sciences, Business and Economics, Education, Engineering and Technology, Arts and Letters. *Majors offered* in Natural and Social Sciences in addition to usual range of studies include Afro-American Studies, anthropology, biochemistry, biophysics, Chicano Studies, geography, Latin American studies, microbiology, health and human services, computer information systems, business administration option in production and operations management.

Special programs: independent study, study abroad, honors, 3-year degree, individualized majors, cooperative education program, internship in public service, Center for Asian and African Studies, credit by examination. *Calendar:* quarter, summer quarter.

Undergraduate degrees conferred (1,670). 32% were in Business and Management, 10% were in Education, 8% were in Engineering, 6% were in Health Sciences, 6% were in Social Sciences, 5% were in Computer and Engineering Related Technology, 5% were in Protective Services, 4% were in Psychology, 4% were in Visual and Performing Arts, 3% were in Letters, 3% were in Communications, 3% were in Engineering and Engineering Related Technology, remainder in 12 other fields.

Faculty. About 90% of faculty hold PhD or equivalent.

Varsity Sports. Men (Div.II): Baseball, Basketball, Cross Country, Swimming & Diving, Soccer, Tennis, Track, Water Polo. Women (Div. II): Basketball, Cross Country, Swimming & Diving, Tennis, Track, Volleyball.

Student Body. University does not seek a national student body; 94% of students from California. An estimated 11% of students reported as Black, 28% Hispanic, 29% Asian, 1% Native American, according to most recent data available.

Campus Life. Almost completely a commuter institution, student life centers around fraternity houses and other campus organizations; interest in intercollegiate athletics growing and intramurals remain popular. The university population averages over 26 years of age; 75% of students work at least part-time. About 3% of men, 3% of women live in coed dormitories; rest live off-campus and commute. Freshmen given preference in college housing if all students cannot be accommodated. There are 5 fraternities, 5 sororities on campus which about 2% each of men, women join.

Annual Costs. Tuition and fees, $1,428 (out-of-state, $7,332). University reports some scholarships awarded on the basis of academic merit alone.

CSU/Northridge

Northridge, California 91330 (818) 885-3700

Northridge is located on a 350-acre campus in the northwestern part of the San Fernando Valley in suburban Los Angeles. Most convenient major airport: Los Angeles International.

Founded: 1956
Affiliation: State
Total Enrollment: 21,460 total graduate and undergraduate
Cost: < $10K
% Receiving Financial Aid: 21%
Admission: Selective
Application Deadline: November 30

Admission. (See also California State University System.) About 84% of applicants accepted; all freshmen graduate in the top third of their high school class. Average freshman SAT scores, according to most recent data available: 400 verbal, 465 mathematical. *Entrance programs:* early admission, midyear admission, advanced placement. *Out-of-state* freshman applicants: university welcomes out-of-state students. *Out-of-state* enrollment limited to 3%; certain majors closed to out-of-state students. *Apply* by November 30; rolling admissions. *Transfers* welcome.

Academic Environment. *Degrees:* AB, BM, BS. *Majors offered* include usual arts and sciences, Afro-American studies, Asian-American Studies, anthropology, business administration, computer science, theatre, engineering, biochemistry, environmental chemistry, geography, health sciences, home economics, journalism, Mexican American studies, radio–TV–film, recreation administration.

About 36% of students entering as freshmen graduate eventually; 27% of freshmen do not return for sophomore year. *Special programs:* January Interim Term, CLEP, study abroad, honors, undergraduate research, individualized majors, accelerated residence credit program. Adult programs: Adult Reentry program, counseling services. *Calendar:* early semester, summer school.

Undergraduate degrees conferred (4,024). 22% were in Business and Management, 12% were in Social Sciences, 9% were in Liberal/General Studies, 9% were in Letters, 7% were in Psychology, 7% were in Communications, 6% were in Visual and Performing Arts, 6% were in Engineering, 5% were in Education, 5% were in Health Sciences, 3% were in Life Sciences, remainder in 10 other fields.

Graduates Career Data. According to most recent data available, full-time graduate or professional study pursued immediately after graduation by 17% of students. *Careers in business and industry* pursued by 72% of graduates.

Faculty. About 83% of faculty hold PhD or equivalent.

Varsity Sports. Men (Div.II): Baseball, Basketball, Cross Country, Football, Golf, Soccer, Swimming/Diving, Track, Volleyball. Women (Div.II): Basketball, Cross Country, Softball, Swimming/Diving, Tennis, Track, Volleyball.

Student Body. University does not seek a national student body; 97% of students from California. An estimated 13% of students reported as Hispanic, 13% Asian, 6% Black, 9% other minority, according to most recent data available. *Minority group students:* 2 campus houses (for Chicano and Black students); Educational Opportunity Program; academic departments.

Campus Life. Campus is primarily commuter oriented. About 5% of men, 6% of women live in coed dormitories; 94% of men, 93% of women live in off-campus housing or commute. Freshmen given preference in college housing if all students cannot be accommodated. There are 19 fraternities, 11 sororities on campus; less than 1% each live in fraternities and sororities.

Annual Costs. Tuition and fees, $2,002 (out-of-state, $9,382); room and board, $5,340. About 21% of students receive financial aid. University reports some scholarships awarded on the basis of academic merit alone.

CSU/Sacramento

Sacramento, California 95819 (916) 454-6111

Located in the state capital, Sacramento's 288-acre campus borders the American River in the eastern section of the city (pop. 254,400).

Founded: 1947
Affiliation: State
Total Enrollment: 19,450 M, W (full-time)
Cost: < $10K
Admission: Selective
Application Deadline: Rolling

Admission. (See also California State University and Colleges System.) About 61% of applicants accepted, 67% of these actually enroll; 75% of freshmen graduate in top fifth of high school class, 98% in top two-fifths. *Transfers* welcome.

Academic Environment. Administration reports 34% of courses required for graduation are elective. Student leader asserts government majors benefit from location in state capital, praises quality of program in criminal justice. *Undergraduate studies* offered by schools of Arts and Sciences, Business and Public Administration, Education, Engineering, Social Work. *Majors offered* include usual arts and sciences, anthropology, corrections, drama, ethnic studies, geography, journalism, home economics, police science and administration, social welfare, environmental resources, nursing.

About 40% of students entering as freshmen graduate eventually; 15% of freshmen do not return for sophomore year. *Special programs:* CLEP, independent study, study abroad, honors, undergraduate research, credit by examination. *Calendar:* early semester, summer school.

Undergraduate degrees conferred (3,691). 28% were in Business and Management, 9% were in Social Sciences, 9% were in Liberal/General Studies, 9% were in Communications, 8% were in Engineering, 6% were in Protective Services, 5% were in Psychology, 5% were in Education, 3% were in Health Sciences, 3% were in Letters, remainder in 14 other fields.

Varsity Sports. Men (Div.II): Baseball, Basketball, Cross Country, Football, Golf, Soccer, Swimming, Tennis, Track. Women (Div. II): Basketball, Cross Country, Golf, Gymnastics, Softball, Swimming, Tennis, Track.
Student Body. University does not seek a national student body; 94% of students from California.
Campus Life. Campus life influenced by high percentage of commuters; about a third of students are married. Students enjoy location of campus which is "within driving distance of the beach, Lake Tahoe, Reno, etc." About 5% of men, 5% of women live in coed dormitories; rest live in off-campus housing or commute. Intervisitation in men's and women's dormitory rooms unlimited. Sexes segregated in coed dormitories by wing or floor. About 50% of students leave campus on weekends.
Annual Costs. Tuition and fees, $1,420 (out-of-state, $8,800); room and board, $4,618. University reports some scholarships awarded on the basis of academic merit alone.

CSU/San Bernardino

San Bernardino, California 92407-2397 (909) 880-5000

A commuter campus, San Bernardino is located on 430 acres in a city of 104,300, 70 miles east of Los Angeles. Most convenient major airport: Ontario International.

Founded: 1960
Affiliation: State
UG Enrollment: 2,932 M, 4,214 W (full-time)
Total Enrollment: 12,121
Cost: < $10K
Admission: Selective
Application Deadline: May 1

Admission. (See also California State University System.) Criteria considered in admissions: high school academic record, standardized test scores. *Entrance programs:* early admission, midyear admission.. *Out-of-state* freshman applicants: university welcomes out-of-state students. *Apply* by May 1 for first priority. *Transfers* welcome; 87 enrolled 1993–94.
Academic Environment. Administration reports 30% of courses required for graduation are elective. Student leader reports: "Small classes provide excellent and informal academic atmosphere." Degrees offered: bachelors, masters. *Majors offered* include usual arts and sciences, anthropology, drama, geography, paralegal studies, biochemistry, health science options in community health education, school health, environmental health and safety, health administration, food and nutrition, industrial technology, commercial music.

About 33% of students entering as freshmen graduate eventually; 10% of freshmen do not return for sophomore year. *Special programs:* CLEP, honors, independent study, study abroad, undergraduate research, individualized majors, credit by examination. *Calendar:* 3–3, summer school.
Undergraduate degrees conferred (1,354). 32% were in Business and Management, 27% were in Liberal/General Studies, 10% were in Social Sciences, 9% were in Psychology, 3% were in Letters, 3% were in Life Sciences, 3% were in Computer and Engineering Related Technology, 3% were in Visual and Performing Arts, 3% were in Communications, remainder in 11 other fields.
Graduates Career Data. According to most recent data available, full-time graduate or professional study pursued immediately after graduation by 16% of students. *Careers in business and industry* pursued by 58% of graduates. Career Development Services include workshops on resume writing, interviewing skills, job search strategies. Conducts Career Fair and Careers in Education Job Fair, administers student part-time employment program.
Faculty. About 98% of faculty hold PhD or equivalent.
Student Body. University does not seek a national student body; 86% students from California. An estimated 8% of students reported as Black, 19% Hispanic, 9% Asian, 6% other ethnic minorities. *Minority group students:* Educational Opportunity Program.
Varsity Sports. Men (Div.II): Baseball, Basketball, Golf, Soccer, Swimming. Women (Div.II): Basketball, Soccer, Softball, Swimming, Volleyball.
Campus Life. University provides limited residential facilities. About 3% of students live in dormitories; rest commute. Freshmen given preference in college housing if all students cannot be accommodated. Intervisitation in men's and women's dormitory rooms unlimited. Sexes segregated in coed dormitories by wing or floor. There are 4 fraternities, 4 sororities, which about 3% of men, 2% of women join; they provide no residence facilities. About 50% of resident students leave campus on weekends.
Annual Costs. Tuition and fees, $1,598 (out-of-state, $7,502); room and board, $4,457; estimated $2,500 other, exclusive of travel. University reports all scholarships awarded on the basis of need.

CSU/San Diego State University

San Diego, California 92182 (619) 594-5200

Third oldest campus in the system, San Diego is the most southern. The 300-acre campus is located in a city of 770,000, 10 miles inland from the Pacific Ocean and a short distance from mountainous desert country. Most convenient major airport: San Diego.

Founded: 1897
Affiliation: State
UG Enrollment: 10,568 M, 11,299 W (full and part-time)
Total Enrollment: 27,573
Cost: < $10K
Admission: Selective
Application Deadline: Rolling

Admission. (See also California State University System.) About 70% of applicants accepted, 53% of these actually enroll. Average freshman scores: SAT, 408 verbal, 474 mathematical; ACT, 21 composite. Criteria considered in admissions, in order of importance: high school academic record, standardized test scores. *Required:* SAT or ACT, minimum high school GPA 2.0. *Out-of-state* freshman applicants: university welcomes out-of-state students, admission requirements somewhat higher. *Entrance programs:* midyear admission, advanced placement. *Apply:* rolling admissions. *Transfers* welcome.
Academic Environment. Administration reports 70% of courses needed for graduation are required. Degrees offered: bachelors, masters, doctoral. *Majors offered* include usual arts and sciences, Afro-American studies, anthropology, Asian studies, astronomy, geography, journalism, Latin American studies, Mexican American studies, microbiology, Russian studies, social welfare; degree programs in applied arts and sciences, business administration, education, engineering, nursing, social work. Average undergraduate class size: 35.

About 47% of entering students graduate eventually. *Special programs:* study abroad, January term. *Calendar:* semester, summer school.
Undergraduate degrees conferred (5,642). 23% were in Business and Management, 13% were in Liberal/General Studies, 10% were in Social Sciences, 7% were in Psychology, 7% were in Letters, 6% were in Engineering, 5% were in Public Affairs, 5% were in Education, 4% were in Communications, 4% were in Visual and Performing Arts, 3% were in Health Sciences, 3% were in Protective Services, remainder in 11 other fields. *Doctoral degrees:* Life Sciences 2, Education 2, Physical Sciences 1. Average undergraduate class size: 35% under 20.
Faculty. About 88% of faculty hold PhD or equivalent.
Student Body. About 90% of students from California. An estimated 5% of students reported as Black, 13% Hispanic, 7% Asian, 19% other minority. Average age of undergraduate student: 24.
Varsity Sports. Men (Div.I): Baseball, Basketball, Football(IA), Soccer, Tennis, Volleyball. Women (Div.I): Basketball, Cross Country, Soccer, Softball, Tennis, Track, Volleyball.
Campus Life. About 12% of students live in coed residence halls; 30% live in off-campus housing; 50% commute. There are 17 fraternities, 12 sororities on campus; 8% of students live in fraternities and sororities.
Annual Costs. Tuition and fees, $1,742 (out-of-state, $7,892); room and board, $4,000–7,000; estimated $3,000 other, exclusive of travel. About 40% of students receive financial aid. Scholarships awarded on basis of academic merit and special talents.

CSU/San Francisco State University

San Francisco, California 94132 (415) 338-2017

San Francisco was established as a teacher training institution, but is now a major collegiate institution offering a wide range of baccalaureate and masters degree programs. The university is located on a 100-acre campus in the southwestern section of San Francisco. Most convenient major airport: San Francisco International.

Founded: 1899
Affiliation: State
Total Enrollment: 19,755 (full-time)
Cost: < $10K
% Receiving Financial Aid: 25%
Admission: Selective
Application Deadline: Nov. 1

Admission. (See also California State University System.) About 60% of applicants accepted, 48% of these actually enroll. Average freshman scores, according to most recent data available: SAT, 416 M, 409 W verbal, 500 M, 459 W mathematical; ACT, 22 M, 21 W composite, 21 M, 21 W mathematical. *Required:* SAT or ACT. *Entrance programs:* midyear admission, deferred admission, advanced placement. *Out-of-state* freshman applicants: university welcomes out-of-state students. Requirements for out-of-state students slightly higher than for residents; 51% of applicants accepted, 54% of these enroll. *Apply* by November 1; rolling admissions. *Transfers* welcome.

Academic Environment. Administration reports 35% of courses required for graduation are elective. *Undergraduate studies* offered by schools of Humanities, Behavioral and Social Sciences, Business, Creative Arts, Education, Ethnic Studies, Sciences and Health, Physical Education, Recreation and Leisure Studies. *Majors offered* include broad range of arts and sciences and vocational and professional fields, anthropology, black studies, LaRaza studies, geography, international relations, social welfare, urban studies, nursing, film, radio–TV, hospitality management, industrial technology.

Special programs: study abroad, credit by examination for Experiential Learning. *Calendar:* semester, summer school.

Undergraduate degrees conferred (3,871). 29% were in Business and Management, 11% were in Social Sciences, 8% were in Psychology, 7% were in Letters, 7% were in Communications, 6% were in Visual and Performing Arts, 6% were in Liberal/General Studies, 4% were in Health Sciences, 4% were in Education, 3% were in Life Sciences, 3% were in Home Economics, 3% were in Engineering, remainder in 10 other fields. *Doctoral Degrees:* Education 3.

Varsity Sports. Men (NCAA, Div.II): Baseball, Basketball, Cross Country, Football, Soccer, Swimming, Track, Wrestling. Women (NCAA, Div.II): Basketball, Cross Country, Soccer, Softball, Swimming, Track, Volleyball.

Student Body. University does not seek a national student body; majority of students from San Francisco area, 94% from California. An estimated 7% of students reported as Black, 8% Hispanic, 29% Asian, 3% other minority, according to most recent data available.

Campus Life. San Francisco State is primarily a commuter institution. However, residence facilities for more than 1,000 students are provided on campus. Students have major influence in determining campus regulations. There are 10 fraternities, 10 sororities on campus.

Annual Costs. Tuition and fees, $1,424 (out-of-state, $8,804); room and board, $4,474. About 25% of students receive financial aid; assistance is typically divided 47% scholarship/grant, 46% loan, 7% work. University reports some scholarships awarded on the basis of academic merit alone.

CSU/San Jose State University

San Jose, California 95192 (408) 924-1000

Oldest of the system, San Jose State is located on a 64-acre campus in the heart of "Silicon Valley," in a city of more than 500,000, 51 miles south of San Francisco and 30 miles from the Pacific Ocean.

Founded: 1857
Affiliation: State
UG Enrollment: 7,199 M, 7,193 W (full-time); 3,678 M, 3,585 W (part-time)
Total Enrollment: 27,057
Cost: < $10K
Admission: Selective
Application Deadline: Rolling

Admission. (See also California State University and Colleges System.) About 79% of applicants accepted, 17% of these actually enroll. Average freshman scores: SAT, 379 M, 362 W verbal, 490 M, 440 W mathematical; ACT, 20 M, 18 W composite. Criteria considered in admissions, in order of importance: high school academic record, standardized test scores; other factors considered: special talents. *Out-of-state* freshman applicants: university welcomes out-of-state students. About 48% of out-of-state applicants accepted, 39% enroll. *Entrance programs:* early admission, midyear admission. *Transfers* welcome; 3,760 enrolled 1993–94.

Academic Environment. Degrees offered: bachelors, masters. *Undergraduate studies* offered by schools of Humanities and the Arts, Applied Arts and Sciences, Business, Education, Engineering, Science, Social Science, and New College. *Majors offered* include broad range of arts and sciences and professional/vocational fields, including advertising, Afro-American studies, Chinese, computer engineering, computer science/math, conservation, law enforcement, nursing, penology, photography, public relations, radio–TV broadcasting, speech pathology and audiology, weather communications; special majors also available. Average undergraduate class size: lower division, 30% under 20, 52% 20–39, 18% 40 or more; upper division, 39% under 20, 47% 20–39, 14% 40 or more. About 4% of students entering as freshmen graduate within four years, 42% eventually; about 21% do not return for sophomore year.

Special programs: CLEP, January Term, study abroad, independent study. Calendar: semester, summer school.

Undergraduate degrees conferred (3,677). 23% were in Business and Management, 9% were in Social Sciences, 8% were in Communications, 8% were in Engineering, 6% were in Visual and Performing Arts, 5% were in Engineering and Engineering Related Technology, 5% were in Psychology, 5% were in Health Sciences, 4% were in Liberal/General Studies, 4% were in Letters, 3% were in Education, 3% were in Computer and Engineering Related Technology, 3% were in Life Sciences, 3% were in Protective Services, remainder in 11 other fields.

Graduates Career Data. About 79% of 1992–93 graduates employed. Career Development Services include career counseling, information, help with job search strategies, job line and placement services. Alumni reported as helpful in both career guidance and job placement.

Faculty. About 78% of faculty hold PhD or equivalent. About 32% of tenured full-time faculty are female; 3% Black, 6% Hispanic, 11% other ethnic minorities.

Varsity Sports. Men (Div.I): Baseball, Basketball, Football(I-A), Golf, Gymnastics, Soccer, Tennis, Wrestling. Women (Div.I): Basketball, Golf, Gymnastics, Softball, Swimming/Diving, Tennis, Volleyball.

Student Body. About 97% of students from California; 2% foreign. An estimated 5% of students reported as Black, 13% Hispanic, 26% Asian, 15% other minorities.

Campus Life. Although a small percentage of the student body lives on campus (about 1,500 students), San Jose is not truly a commuter school since the overwhelming majority live off-campus, but not at home. Thus campus life is relatively active, though not within the framework of dormitory living. Recently completed Recreation and Events Center gets "high usage."

There are 14 fraternities, 7 sororities on campus which about 9% of men, 4% of women join; 2% of men, 1% of women live in fraternities and sororities.

Annual Costs. Tuition and fees, $1,724 (out-of-state, $7,628); room and board, $4,956; estimated $3,024 other, exclusive of travel. About 35% of students receive financial aid; average amount of assistance, $3,783. Assistance is typically divided 6% scholarship, 16% grant, 48% loan, 30% work. University reports some scholarships awarded on the basis of special talents alone.

CSU/Sonoma State University

Rohnert Park, California 94928 (707) 664-2778

Located in a semi-rural area, Sonoma is within an hour's drive of San Francisco. University has adopted cluster school system "in an attempt to combat swelling numbers"; university includes Sonoma School of Arts and Sciences, Hutchins School of Liberal Studies, schools of Environmental Studies, Expressive Arts. Most convenient major airport: San Francisco.

Founded: 1960
Affiliation: State
UG Enrollment: 1,676 M, 2,563 W (full-time); 501 M, 758 W (part-time)
Total Enrollment: 7,405
Cost: < $10K
% Receiving Financial Aid: 60%
Admission: Selective
Application Deadline: Nov. 30

Admission is selective. (See also California State University System.) About 36% of applicants accepted, 22% of these actually enroll. Average freshman scores: SAT, 486 verbal, 482 mathematical; ACT, 22 composite. *Required:* SAT is required if GPA is less than 3.0. *Out-of-state* freshman applicants: university welcomes out-of-state students; requirements for admission slightly higher than for residents. *Apply* by November 30. *Transfers* welcome; 1,117 enrolled 1993–94.

Academic Environment. Administration reports 35% of courses required for graduation are elective. Degrees offered: bachelors, masters. *Majors offered* include usual arts and sciences, Afro-American studies, anthropology, geography, environmental studies, liberal studies-expressive arts, management, Mexican American studies, nursing, physical education, theater arts, urban studies, India studies. Average undergraduate class size: 20.

About 27% of students entering as freshmen graduate within four years; 21% of freshmen return for sophomore year. *Special programs:* CLEP, January Term, independent study, study abroad, individualized majors, credit by examination, internships and field-based programs, double majors, dual enrollment, BS/MBA, BS/MPA, teacher prep program, variety of certificate programs available. *Calendar:* 4–1–4, summer school.

Undergraduate degrees conferred (1,113). 23% were in Business and Management, 15% were in Psychology, 12% were in Social Sciences, 11% were in Liberal/General Studies, 6% were in Visual and Performing Arts, 6% were in Multi/Interdisciplinary Studies, 5% were in Letters, 4% were in Life Sciences, 3% were in Communications, 3% were in Health Sciences, 3% were in Physical Sciences, 3% were in Computer and Engineering Related Technology, remainder in 6 other fields.

Graduates Career Data. Advanced studies pursued by 15% of graduates. Graduate and professional schools typically enrolling largest numbers of graduates include U. of California and California State U. Employers typically hiring largest numbers of graduates include Bank of America, Deloitte & Touche, Hewlett Packard, Kaiser, Sonoma County. Career Development Services include field experience, community involvement program, internships, employment services. Student assessment of program reported as good for both career guidance and job placement.

Faculty. About 76% of faculty hold PhD or equivalent. About 37% of teaching faculty are female.

Student Body. University does not seek a national student body; 94% of students from California; 5% foreign. An estimated 4% of students reported as Black, 3% Asian, 8% Hispanic, 15% other minority. *Minority group students:* EOP, tutoring available. Average age of undergraduate student: 23.

Varsity Sports. Men (Div.II): Baseball, Basketball, Football, Soccer. Women (Div.II): Basketball, Softball, Soccer, Volleyball.

Campus Life. The average student characterized by student leader as "independent, self-motivated." About 6% of men, 6% of women live in coed dormitories; 24% of men, 54% of women live in off-campus, college related housing; rest live in other off-campus housing or commute. Freshmen given preference in college housing if all students cannot be accommodated. There are 6 fraternities and 9 sororities on campus, which about 3% of men, 4% of women join. About 25% of resident students leave campus on weekends.

Annual Costs. Tuition and fees, $1,746 (out-of-state, $9,126); room and board, $5,250. About 60% of students receive financial aid. University reports a limited number of scholarships awarded on the basis of academic merit alone. *Meeting Costs:* university offers PLUS Loans.

CSU/Stanislaus

Turlock, California 95382 (209) 667-3256

Stanislaus is located on a 230-acre campus in a community of 24,000 in the northern San Joaquin Valley, midway between San Francisco and Yosemite National Park. Most convenient major airport: Modesto.

Founded: 1957
Affiliation: State
UG Enrollment: 1,433 M, 1,960 W (full-time); 416 M, 765 W (part-time)
Total Enrollment: 5,857
Cost: < $10K
% Receiving Financial Aid: 35%
Admission: Selective
Application Deadline: Aug. 1

Admission. (See also California State University and Colleges System.) About 70% of applicants accepted, 60% of these actually enroll; 50% of freshman graduate in top fifth of their high school class, 85% in top two-fifths. Criteria considered in admissions, in order of importance: high school academic record, standardized test scores, recommendations, extra curricular activities; other factors considered: special talents, diverse student body. *Required:* SAT or ACT; eligibility index combines test scores and GPA. *Out-of-state* freshman applicants: university welcomes out-of-state students; state does not limit out-of-state enrollment; admission requirements somewhat more selective. *Entrance programs:* early decision, early admission, midyear admission, deferred admission, advanced placement. *Apply* by August 1; rolling admission. *Transfers* welcome; 2,700 enrolled 1993–94.

Academic Environment. Degrees offered: bachelors, masters. *Majors offered* include usual arts and sciences, anthropology, applied studies, business administration, cognitive studies, drama, fine arts, geology. Core requirements for undergraduate liberal arts: 48 units general education/breadth requirement. Administration reports 40% of courses required for graduation are elective. Adult programs: Re-entry Services Program. Average undergraduate class size: 30% under 20, 50% 20–40, 20% over 40.

About 65% of students entering as freshmen graduate eventually; 20% of freshmen do not return for sophomore year. *Special programs:* CLEP, independent study, study abroad, individualized majors, credit by examination, ethnic studies, Winter Term (single course immersion), Stockton Center, cooperative education, television course delivery system. *Calendar:* 4–1–4, summer school.

Undergraduate degrees conferred (815). 28% were in Liberal/General Studies, 20% were in Business and Management, 13% were in Social Sciences, 6% were in Psychology, 5% were in Health Sciences, 5% were in Letters, 5% were in Education, 3% were in Life Sciences, 3% were in Computer and Engineering Related Technology, 3% were in Visual and Performing Arts, remainder in 7 other fields.

Graduates Career Data. Advanced studies pursued by 60% of students.

Faculty. About 87% of faculty hold PhD or equivalent. About 60% of undergraduate classes taught by tenured faculty. About 34% of teaching faculty are female; 5% Black, 6% Hispanic, 7% other minority.

Student Body. About 90% of students from California; 95% West, 5% foreign. Average age of undergraduate student: 25.

Varsity Sports. Men (Div.III): Baseball, Basketball, Cross Country, Golf, Soccer, Track. Women (Div.III): Basketball, Cross Country, Softball, Track, Volleyball.

Campus Life. About 65% of students live in coed dormitories, 35% live in off-campus college-related housing. There are 3 fraternities, 2 sororities. About 50% of resident students leave campus on weekends.

Annual Costs. Tuition and fees, $1,636 (out-of-state, $2,460); room and board, $4,810; estimated $1,879 other, exclusive of travel. About 35% of students receive financial aid; assistance is typically divided 2% scholarship, 28% grant, 70% loan, 5% work. University reports 205 scholarships awarded on the basis of academic merit alone, 11 based on need.

University of California

Berkeley, California 94720

The University of California, an enormous institution with 9 campuses offering undergraduate, graduate, and professional studies, forms the apex of the nation's largest and most elaborate higher education structure. Complementing the university is the 19-campus State University and Colleges System and an extensive network of 2-year colleges. Much of the luster of the university comes from the eminence of the faculty at the oldest campus at Berkeley and the next oldest campus at Los Angeles. However, each of the other campuses, at Davis, Irvine, Riverside, San Diego, Santa Barbara, and Santa Cruz, in its own fashion, is a unique institution. An additional campus at San Francisco is devoted exclusively to the health sciences.

Admission to the university's undergraduate campuses is very selective and uniform throughout system. California residents who complete specified high school subjects with an over-all average of 3.30 are eligible. (If average is below 3.29 but above 2.77, student must also earn progressively higher scores on the required SAT or ACT the lower his grade point average.) Other California residents may be admitted if combined SAT score is 1,100 (or ACT score is 26) and total score on ACH is 1,650 (with minimum of 500 on each ACH). *Required:* SAT or ACT, 3 ACH including English Composition, mathematics, and choice of social studies, foreign language, science, or English Literature. *Out-of-state* freshman enrollment not specifically limited by state. Requirements for out-of-state applicants: average of 3.4 or higher in required subjects; admission by examination possible for those scoring 1,730 on 3 ACH instead of 1,650 required for residents. *Out-of-state* transfer applicants must offer average of 2.8 or higher. *Apply* from November 1 to 30. Students may apply to as many as 8 campuses of the University using one application form. Meeting admissions requirements does not guarantee admission to the campus or program of choice as many attract more qualified applicants than can be accommodated. When quotas are filled applications are redirected to campuses with enrollments still open.

Faculty. On most campuses, majority of faculty hold doctorate or equivalent training.

Religious Orientation. The university, as a state institution, is prohibited from making any religious demands on students; religious clubs for students and other facilities available on or near all campuses.

UC/Berkeley

Berkeley, California 94720 **(510) 642-6000**

Berkeley is the largest and most prestigious of the 8 undergraduate campuses of the university. The national and international stature of its graduate and professional schools adds further to its reputation. Out-of-state applicants are welcomed, but "may be given low priority if applying in highly competitive area." Nevertheless, many continue to apply; New York, Massachusetts, and Illinois are heavily represented among out-of-state students. The campus is located in a city of 114,000, across the bay from San Francisco. Most convenient major airport: Oakland/San Francisco.

Founded: 1855
Affiliation: State
UG Enrollment: 11,512 M, 10,201 W (full-time)
Total Enrollment: 21,713
Cost: < $10K
% Receiving Financial Aid: 51%
Admission: Very (+) Selective
Application Deadline: Novmeber 30

Admission is very (+) selective. (See also University of California.) About 42% of applicants accepted, 39% of these actually enroll; 75% of freshmen graduate with high school GPA of 3.5 or above, 41% 4.0; 95% graduate in top fifth of their high school class. Average freshman SAT scores: 564 verbal, 654 mathematical. *Required:* SAT or ACT, essay. Criteria considered in admissions, in order of importance: high school academic record and standardized test scores, writing sample and extracurricular activities; other factors considered: special talents, diverse student body, non-standard grading system, reentry, residency. *Entrance programs:* midyear admission (junior transfers only), advanced placement. About 13% of entering students from private schools, 73% from California public schools, 14% other. *Apply* by November 30. *Transfers* welcome; 1,474 enrolled 1993–94.

Academic Environment. Virtually every conceivable college offering is available. Pressures for academic achievement are as great or greater than on the other campuses of the university. Current students are somewhat younger and more pragmatically inclined than classes in the recent past. Characterized as "competent, competitive, and practiced at handling stress." Size of university creates gulf between students, faculty, and administration; some efforts now to remedy this. Students who are self-directed and highly motivated have best chance of surviving until graduation. Administration reports 25–44% of courses required for graduation are elective; some distribution requirements in Letters and Science, however; 8 courses in fields outside general area of major (provision for exemption from some course work through advanced placement tests), course sequence in reading and composition (unless exempt). *Undergraduate studies* offered by colleges of Letters and Science, Chemistry, Engineering, Environmental Design, Natural Resources; schools of Business Administration, Journalism, Optometry all require junior standing for admission. *Majors offered* include studies in 121 academic departments and special programs; 4 types of majors programs available in Letters and Science: departmental, group, field, individual.

About 36% of students entering as freshmen graduate within four years, 78% within six years; 9% of freshmen do not return for sophomore year. *Special programs:* CLEP, independent study, study abroad, honors, undergraduate research, individualized majors, experimental collegiate program, ethnic studies, combined programs with professional schools at Berkeley and San Francisco as well as other UC campuses, interdisciplinary studies. Adult programs: Reentry Program. *Calendar:* semester, summer school.

Undergraduate degrees conferred (5,681). 29% were in Social Sciences, 11% were in Engineering, 10% were in Letters, 9% were in Multi/Interdisciplinary Studies, 9% were in Life Sciences, 5% were in Psychology, 4% were in Business and Management, 4% were in Architecture and Environmental Design, 3% were in Physical Sciences, remainder in 14 other fields. *Doctoral degrees:* Engineering 128, Social Sciences 99, Biological Sciences 86, Physical Sciences 121, Education 37, Mathematics 45, Letters 27, Psychology 18, Agriculture and Natural Resources 16, Architecture and Environmental Design 10, Interdisciplinary Studies 24, Foreign Languages 18, Health Professions 18, Fine and Applied Arts 9, Business and Management 5, Public Affairs and Services 4, Computer and Information Sciences 14, Area Studies 4, Library Science 4, Law 1, Liberal/General Studies 1.

Graduates Career Data. According to most recent data available, full-time graduate or professional study pursued immediately after graduation by 26% of students; 93% intend to pursue advanced studies; 75% of UC-Berkeley graduates who apply to medical school are accepted. *Careers in business and industry* pursued by 59% of graduates.

Faculty. About 95% of faculty hold PhD or equivalent. About 19% of faculty are female; 12% ethnic minorities.

Student Body. University welcomes out-of-state students; 90% of students from California; 4% undergraduate foreign students. An estimated 36% of undergraduate students reported as Asian, 6% Black, 14% Hispanic, 9% other minority.

Varsity Sports. Men (Div.I): Baseball, Basketball, Crew, Cross Country, Diving, Football, Golf, Gymnastics, Rugby, Soccer, Swimming, Tennis, Track, Water Polo. Women (Div.I): Basketball, Crew, Cross Country, Field Hockey, Gymnastics, Soccer, Softball, Swimming, Tennis, Track, Volleyball.

Campus Life. Berkeley, as one student leader reports, "is not a 'Rah! Rah!' school." It is a serious place where political activities are very important, though coed intramural sports and varsity athletics are increasingly popular. There is very little contact between faculty and students other than in the classroom. Nevertheless, Berkeley remains an intellectually stimulating and culturally rich campus, with activities available for every interest and taste.

About 25% of undergraduate students live in campus housing; rest live in off-campus housing or commute. Freshmen are given preference in college housing if all students cannot be accommodated. Intervisitation in men's and women's dormitory rooms unlimited. There are 41 fraternities, 15 sororities on campus.

Annual Costs. Tuition and fees, $3,970 (out-of-state, $11,688); room and board, $6,025. About 51% of students receive financial aid; average amount of assistance, $5,400. University reports "very few" scholarships awarded on the basis of academic merit alone. *Meeting Costs:* University offers various loan programs.

UC/Davis

Davis, California 95616 **(916) 752-2971**

Founded as an agricultural experiment farm and farm school, Davis is the only campus of the university that confers more than a token number of degrees in agricultural subjects. Largest division is College of Letters and Science, and university includes rapidly growing College of Engineering. UC/Davis also includes a graduate division and highly acclaimed professional schools of Management, Law, Medicine and Veterinary Medicine. The campus is located in a community of 44,000, 15 miles west of Sacramento, 72 miles northeast of San Francisco. Most convenient major airport: Sacramento Metropolitan.

Founded: 1906
Affiliation: State
UG Enrollment: 8,169 M, 8,559 W (full-time); 250 M, 228 W (part-time)
Total Enrollment: 22,486
Cost: < $10K
% Receiving Financial Aid: 57%
Admission: Very Selective
Application Deadline: Nov. 30

Admission is very selective. (See also University of California.) About 70% of applicants accepted, 27% of these actually enroll. Average freshman SAT scores: 491 M, 481 W verbal, 615 M, 559 W mathematical; 49% of freshmen score above 500 on verbal, 13% above 600, 1% above 700; 84% score above 500 on mathematical, 50% above 600, 13% above 700. *Required:* SAT or ACT, 3 ACH including English Composition and Mathematics 1,2, or 2C. Criteria considered in admissions, in order of importance: high school academic record, standardized test scores, writing sample, extracurricular activities; other factors considered: special talents, diverse student body, "personal experiences that have affected applicants educational achievements." Entrance programs: early admission, deferred admission, advanced placement. *Out-of-state* freshman applicants: university welcomes out-of-state students. *Apply* by November 30. *Transfers* welcome; 1,448 new transfers enrolled fall 1993.

Academic Environment. Pressures for academic achievement are fairly intense. Land-grant/agricultural college image gradually fading as overwhelming proportion of undergraduate students enroll in College of Letters and Science which enrolls 7,809 undergraduates; College of Agriculture and Environmental Sciences enrolls 3,823, the Division of Biological Sciences, enrolls 3,276, College of Engineering enrolls 2,298. General education requirements are designed to expose students to a variety of disciplines and methods, and to encourage development of analytical reasoning and clear communication skills; they include three courses from each of three areas: civilization and culture, contemporary societies, and nature and environment. UC/Davis offers nearly 100 undergraduate majors, including anthropology, bacteriology, biochemistry, dramatic art, geography, genetics, Oriental languages, physiology; interdepartmental majors in Afro-American studies, international relations, linguistics, classical civilization, women's studies, Chicano studies. Unusual, new or notable majors include fiber and polymer science, population biology, biological systems engineering, fermentation science. Programs with the strongest reputations are in the sciences, including animal science, agricultural economics, biology, engineering, botany, food science, pre-vet and pre-med, although the studio art program is also nationally recognized.

About 29% of students entering as freshmen graduate within four years, 75% eventually; 9% of freshmen do not return for sophomore year. *Special programs:* independent study, study abroad, honors, undergraduate research, 3-year degree, individualized majors, internships and cooperative work/study programs, summer sessions international and UC/Davis Washington Center. *Calendar:* quarter, summer school.

Undergraduate degrees conferred (3,122). 18% were in Social Sciences, 16% were in Life Sciences, 11% were in Engineering, 8% were in Psychology, 8% were in Letters, 7% were in Agribusiness and Agricultural Production, 7% were in Multi/Interdisciplinary Studies, 4% were in Home Economics, 4% were in Visual and Performing Arts, 3% were in Agricultural Sciences, remainder in 12 other fields.

Doctoral degrees: Biological Sciences 107, Physical Sciences 36, Engineering 23, Agriculture and Natural Resources 22, Social Sciences 11, Foreign Languages 3, Letters 6, Mathematics 3, Psychology 8, Multi/Interdisciplinary Studies 2, Health Sciences 1, Philosophy and Religion 2.

Graduates Career Data. Advanced studies pursued by 43% of students; 5% enter medical school; 4% enter law school; 3% enter business school. Graduate and professional schools typically enrolling largest numbers of graduates include other UC campuses. *Careers in business and industry* pursued by 55% of graduates. Typical fields of employment include sales/marketing, finance/accounting/banking, engineering, biological/health sciences. Career Development Services include workshops and seminars on career trends, career search techniques, identification of skills and interests, individual and group advising, career related field experiences. Alumni reported as helpful in career guidance and job placement.

Faculty. About 98% of faculty hold PhD or equivalent. About 23% of teaching faculty are female; 2% Black, 3% Hispanic, 9% other ethnic minorities.

Student Body. About 96% of students from California; 1% foreign students. An estimated 19% of students reported as Asian American, 4% African American, 10% Hispanic American, 6% other minority.

Varsity Sports. Men (Div. II): Baseball, Basketball, Cross Country, Football, Golf, Soccer, Swimming, Tennis, Track, Wrestling. Women (Div. II): Basketball, Cross Country, Gymnastics, Soccer, Softball, Swimming, Tennis, Track, Volleyball.

Campus Life. Located in a now "relatively urban" area, Davis is characterized by one student leader as a "safe" UC campus where most students are "primarily academically involved." Regulations governing campus social life quite free, and another student notes that "faculty and administration are always ready to negotiate changes." Cars permitted, parking by permit only (and, reportedly, inadequate for commuters); campus core closed to vehicular traffic at all times. Administration source suggests "bring your bike to Davis [ELLIPSE] the city of Davis claims more than 40,000 bicycles—more bikes per capita than any other city in the U.S." Public transportation in city of Davis; regular bus service provided by student government, Greyhound Bus, and Amtrak. Drinking allowed for students over 21 in residence halls.

According to most recent data available, about 2% of men, 2% of women live in traditional dormitories; 25% of men, 30% of women live in coed dormitories; 45% of men, 42% of women live in off-campus housing; 13% of men, 13% of women commute. The university guarantees residence hall housing for all entering undergraduate students and not less than 25% of all students. There are 31 fraternities, 20 sororities, which about 12% of men, 9% of women join.

Annual Costs. Tuition and fees, $3,712 (out-of-state, $11,411); room and board, $5,822; estimated $2,334 other, exclusive of travel. About 57% of students receive financial aid; average amount of assistance, $1,681 (undergraduate). Assistance is typically divided 9% scholarship, 44% grant, 44% loan, 3% work-study. University reports 1,334 scholarships awarded on the basis of academic merit alone.

UC/Irvine

Irvine, California 92717 **(714) 856-6703**

Irvine is one of the smaller, but fastest growing, campuses of the University of California system. Undergraduate arts and sciences are organized into 6 basic schools: Biological Sciences, Engineering, Fine Arts, Humanities, Physical Sciences, and Social Sciences. The campus also includes a Graduate School of Management and the UCI/California College of Medicine. Campus spreads over 1,510 acres in the city of Irvine (pop. 60,000), some 5 miles from the Pacific Ocean beaches. Most convenient major airport: John Wayne Orange County.

Founded: 1960
Affiliation: State
UG Enrollment: 6,501 M, 7,181 W (full-time)
Total Enrollment: 15,337
Cost: < $10K
% Receiving Financial Aid: 40%
Admission: Very Selective
Application Deadline: Rolling

Admission is very selective. (See also University of California.) About 21% of applicants accepted, 94% of these actually enroll; all freshmen graduate in top fifth of high school class. Average freshman SAT scores, according to most recent data available: 466 verbal, 568 mathematical. Non-academic factor considered in admissions: diverse student body. *Entrance programs:* midyear admission, deferred admission, advanced placement. About 11% of entering students from private schools. *Out-of-state* freshman applicants: university welcomes out-of-state students; 5% of applicants accepted, 5% enroll. *Transfers* welcome.

Academic Environment. Student academic interests are reported to be almost equally divided between scholarly/intellectual pursuits and the desire to prepare for an occupation or career. Interdisciplinary work stressed by the schools of arts and sciences. Students have some influence on academic affairs, according to student leader. Administration reports they are "encouraged to participate with faculty on Academic Senate and administrative committees." All students must take 3 4-unit courses each in writing, natural science, social and behavioral science, and Humanistic Inquiry; and 3 4-unit courses in foreign language, linguistics, logic, mathematics, or computer science. *Majors offered* include usual arts and sciences, dance, drama, engineering, fine arts, linguistics, inter-school majors in comparative culture (African, American, Asian, Black, Chicano, Latin American), information and computer science, social ecology.

About 57% of students entering as freshmen graduate eventually; 9% of freshmen do not return for sophomore year. *Special programs:* study abroad, honors, undergraduate research, 3–2 BA/MBA. *Calendar:* quarter, summer school.

Undergraduate degrees conferred (2,762). 23% were in Social Sciences, 19% were in Life Sciences, 14% were in Multi/Interdisciplinary Studies, 12% were in Psychology, 7% were in Engineering, 6% were in Computer and Engineering Related Technology, 6% were in Letters, 5% were in Visual and Performing Arts, 3% were in Physical Sciences, remainder in 3 other fields. *Doctoral degrees:* Physical Sciences 21, Biological Sciences 18, Social Sciences 8, Psychology 3, Computer and Information Sciences 6, Health Sciences 1, Interdisciplinary Studies 5, Engineering 7, Letters 7, Mathematics 1, Foreign Languages 2, Philosophy and Religion 1, Business and Management 1, Area and Ethnic Studies 2.

Graduates Career Data. According to most recent data available, full-time graduate or professional study pursued by 36% of students immediately after graduation; 6% enter medical school; 5% enter other health profession; 11% enter law school. Corporations typically hiring largest numbers of graduates include: Andersen Consulting, Baxter Health Care, Hewitt & Assoc., Hughes, McDonnell Douglas, Rockwell. Career Development Services include separate counselor for liberal arts students. Alumni reported as helpful in both career guidance and job placement.

Faculty. About 95% of faculty hold PhD or equivalent.

Student Body. Most students from within state, but university welcomes out-of-state and foreign students; 97% of students from California. An estimated 34% of students reported as Asian, 3% as Black, 9% as Hispanic, 9% other minority, according to most recent data available.

Varsity Sports. Men (Div.IA): Baseball, Basketball, Crew, Cross Country, Golf, Sailing, Soccer, Swimming, Tennis, Track, Volleyball, Water Polo. Women (Div.IA): Basketball, Cross Country, Soccer, Swimming, Tennis, Track, Volleyball.

Campus Life. University is essentially a commuter school; 70% of students commute. Regulations governing student social life very free; 24-hour intervisitation, drinking subject only to state law. Circular plan of campus building facilitates close-in parking. Student leader reports the need for a program which would "integrate commuters with on-campus students."

Less than 1% of women live in traditional dormitories; 6% of men, 6% of women in coed dormitories; rest live in off-campus housing or commute. There are 16 fraternities, 12 sororities on campus which about 13% of men and 13% of women join; they provide no residence facilities.

Annual Costs. Tuition and fees, $3,074 (out-of-state, $10,773); room and board, $5,383. About 40% of students receive financial aid—average amount, $3,455. University reports some scholarships awarded on the basis of academic merit alone.

UC/Los Angeles

Los Angeles, California 90024 (213) 825-3101

The largest campus of the University of California, UCLA ranks as one of the major graduate and undergraduate institutions in the U.S. It is located in Westwood, a suburb of Los Angeles, 5 miles from the Pacific Ocean. Most convenient major airport: Los Angeles International.

Founded: 1881
Affiliation: State
UG Enrollment: 11,852 M, 12,255 W (full-time)
Total Enrollment: 32,399

Cost: < $10K
% Receiving Financial Aid: 48%
Admission: Very Selective
Application Deadline: Rolling

Admission is very selective. (See also University of California.) About 43% of applicants accepted, 37% of these actually enroll. Average freshman SAT scores, according to most recent data available: 518 M, 509 W verbal, 636 M, 589 W mathematical; 59% of freshman score above 500 on verbal, 22% above 600, 2% above 700; 82% score above 500 on mathematical, 60% above 600, 20% above 700. *Required:* SAT or ACT. *Entrance programs:* early admission, deferred admission, advanced placement. About 21% of entering students from private schools. *Out-of-state* freshman applicants: university welcomes out-of-state students; admissions requirements GPA 3.4 or above, SAT combined score of 1100 or above; 29% of applicants accepted, 24% of these enroll. *Transfers* welcome.

Academic Environment. Students have "advisory role" only in academic decision making. Pressures for academic achievement intense, but do not equal those at Berkeley. UCLA has 69 departments, 13 schools and colleges and is well-known for its vast network of organized research units, which include various institutes, centers for area programs, comparative programs, laboratories, museums. As in other top ranking graduate institutions, junior faculty, who often have the closest contact with undergraduates especially in their first two years, are recruited from among the most talented graduates of the first-rate graduate departments. University life influenced by large number of commuting students. *Undergraduate studies* offered by colleges of Letters and Science, Fine Arts, schools of Engineering and Applied Science, Nursing. *Majors offered* in Letters and Science, in addition to wide range of usual studies, include ancient Near Eastern civilization, anthropology, Arabic, astronomy, bacteriology, Chinese, geography, Hebrew, Indo-European studies, Japanese, linguistics and East Asian languages, meteorology, motion picture/TV, Portuguese, Scandinavian languages, theater, world arts and cultures; interdepartmental majors in earth physics and exploration geophysics, Latin American studies, premedical studies, public service. New programs include: applied linguistics, BS in computer science, TESL; programs recently dropped include nonrenewable natural resources, Russian linguistics.

About 64% of entering students graduate within 5 years; 6% of freshmen do not return for sophomore year. *Special programs:* independent study, internships, study abroad, honors, undergraduate research, individualized majors. *Library:* 6,156,761 titles, 96,676 periodicals, 6,769,895 other materials; open-stack collection for undergraduates in College Library; there are 19 different libraries on campus. *Calendar:* quarter, summer school.

Undergraduate degrees conferred (5,105). 41% were in Social Sciences, 13% were in Psychology, 10% were in Letters, 7% were in Life Sciences, 7% were in Visual and Performing Arts, 6% were in Engineering, 4% were in Mathematics, 3% were in Multi/Interdisciplinary Studies, remainder in 7 other fields. *Doctoral Degrees:* Social Sciences 69, Psychology 28, Life Sciences 47, Letters 40, Visual and Performing Arts 18, Mathematics 17, Engineering 44, Multi/Interdisciplinary Studies 10, Physical Sciences 57, Foreign Languages 14, Health Sciences 21, Philosophy and Religion 2, Area and Ethnic Studies 2, Business and Management 13, Education 51, Computer and Information Sciences 8, Library and Archival Sciences 1, Architectural and Environmental Design 4, Public Affairs 3.

Graduates Career Data. According to most recent data available, full-time graduate or professional study pursued immediately after graduation by 59% of students; 9% enter medical school; 2% enter dental school; 18% enter law school; 7% enter business school. *Careers in business and industry* pursued by 63% of graduates.

Faculty. All of "ladder faculty" hold PhD or equivalent.

Student Body. University does not actively seek a national student body; 93% of students from California. An estimated 7% of students reported as Black, 13% Hispanic, 18% Asian, 1% Native American, 3% Filipino, 1% other minority, according to most recent data available.

Varsity Sports. Men (NCAA): Baseball, Basketball, Crew, Cross Country, Football, Golf, Gymnastics, Soccer, Swimming, Tennis, Track, Volleyball, Water Polo. Women (NCAA): Basketball, Crew, Cross Country, Golf, Gymnastics, Softball, Swimming, Tennis, Track, Volleyball.

Campus Life. Regulations governing student social life relatively free; high proportion of students live off campus. Rich cultural and social resources of Los Angeles easily available as well as a very wide range of activities on campus. Student interest in varsity and intramural athletics, as well as fraternities and sororities reported to be high. Cars allowed but campus parking severely limited; university encourages use of bicycles, motor scooters, motorcycles (no registration required).

About 17% of students live in coed dormitories; 64% live in off-campus housing or commute. Freshmen given preference in college housing if all students cannot be accommodated. Sexes segregated in dormitories by room. There are 31 fraternities, 18 sororities on campus which about 16% of men, 17% of women join; 19% of students live in fraternities and sororities.

Annual Costs. Tuition and fees, $3,899 (out-of-state, $11,598); room and board, $5,410. About 48% of students receive financial aid; assistance is typically divided 30% scholarship/grant, 50% loan, 20% work. University reports some scholarships awarded on the basis of academic merit alone.

UC/Riverside

Riverside, California 92521 **(909) 787-3411**

The Riverside campus, originally founded as a citrus experiment station, was converted in 1954 to a college of letters and science to provide a small, high-quality, liberal arts college for the University of California System. Studies offered by College of Natural and Agricultural Sciences and College of Humanities and Social Sciences. A new College of Engineering recently added. Campus is located in a city of 170,100, 50 miles east of Los Angeles. Most convenient major airport: Ontario.

Founded: 1954
Affiliation: State
UG Enrollment: 3,293 M, 3,629 W (full-time)
Total Enrollment: 8,677
Cost: < $10K
% Receiving Financial Aid: 47%
Admission: Very Selective
Application Deadline: November 30

Admission is very selective. (See also University of California.) About 77% of applicants accepted, 19% of these actually enroll; 90% of freshmen graduate in top fifth of their high school class, 95% in top two-fifths. Average freshman SAT scores: 453 M, 431 W verbal, 579 M, 513 W mathematical; 31% of freshmen score above 500 on verbal, 8% above 600, 1% above 700; 67% score above 500 on mathematical, 31% above 600, 9% above 700. Criteria considered in admissions, in order of importance: high school academic record, standardized test scores, extra curricular activities, writing sample, recommendations; other factors considered: special talents, diverse student body. *Required:* SAT or ACT, 3 ACH, minimum GPA (depending on test score), essay. *Entrance programs:* early admission, advanced placement, high school/university program. About 12% of entering students from private schools. *Out-of-state* freshman applicants: university welcomes out-of-state students, 3.4 GPA required. *Apply* by November 30; rolling admissions. *Transfers* welcome; 614 enrolled 1993–94.

Academic Environment. Degrees offered: Bachelors, Masters, Doctoral. *Majors offered* include usual arts and sciences, administrative studies, anthropology, biochemistry, business administration, ethnic studies, classical studies, computer science, entomology, geography, geophysics, Latin American studies, liberal studies, linguistics, environmental science, plant science, soil science, statistics, theater. The Biomedical Sciences Program (a joint program with UCLA) leads to medical degree in 7 years. New majors include women's studies, Asian studies, creative writing.

Pressures for academic achievement can be quite intense. Approximately 17% of students on campus are graduate students. Largest academic programs are bio-med (premed) and the other "hard sciences." Administrative studies and political science also reported as strong. Administration reports about 88% of courses required for graduation are elective; distribution requirements fairly numerous and vary with each college.

About 70% of students entering as freshmen graduate eventually; 11% of freshmen do not return for sophomore year. *Special programs:* January Term at College of William and Mary, independent study, study abroad programs in 29 countries, honors, undergraduate research, individualized majors, 7-year BS/MD program with UCLA School of Medicine. Adult programs: University Extension Program, counseling, Reentry Coordinator. Average undergraduate class size: 22. *Calendar:* quarter, summer school.

Undergraduate degrees conferred (1,035). 22% were in Business and Management, 17% were in Life Sciences, 16% were in Social Sciences, 8% were in Multi/Interdisciplinary Studies, 7% were in Psychology, 7% were in Liberal/General Studies, 6% were in Letters, 3% were in Visual and Performing Arts, 3% were in Computer and Engineering Related Technology, 3% were in Physical Sciences, 3% were in Health Sciences, remainder in 5 other fields. *Doctoral degrees:* Biological Sciences 48, Social Sciences 21, Mathematics 3, Education 11, Physical Sciences 18, Agriculture and Natural Resources 8, Foreign Languages 1, Letters 4, Psychology 8.

Graduates Career Data. Advanced studies pursued immediately after graduation by 47% of students (up to 70% within five years); 15% enter medical school; 3% enter dental school; 4% enter law school; 5% enter business school. Medical schools typically enrolling largest numbers of graduates include UCLA, UCSF, UCI; dental schools include Loma Linda, UCLA, Northwestern; law schools include UC Davis, UCLA, Hastings; business schools include UC Riverside, UCLA, Claremont. About 50% of 1993 graduates employed. Corporations typically hiring largest numbers of graduates include Hughes, Aerojet Electro Systems, General Dynamics. Career Development Services include separate counselors for different fields, vocational testing, career seminars and workshops, internships/coop education placements, graduate and professional school application, on-campus interviews, interview and resume preparation, career information library, individual and group counseling. Alumni reported as helpful in both career guidance and job placement.

Faculty. About 98% of faculty hold PhD or equivalent.

Student Body. University does not actively seek a national student body; 97% of students from California. An estimated 4% of students reported as Black, 14% Hispanic, 37% Asian, 1% other minority. *Minority group students:* Black Studies and Chicano Studies programs, financial, academic, social programs, variety of agencies provide aid and support for minority students. Average age of undergraduate student: 21.

Varsity Sports. Men (Div.II): Baseball, Basketball, Cross Country, Karate, Tennis, Water Polo. Women (Div.II): Basketball, Cross Country, Karate, Softball, Tennis, Volleyball.

Campus Life. Wide range of cultural and social activities on campus. Los Angeles, 50 miles away, is available for those who seek the resources of a large city. Campus ombudsman available to students whose problems are "not receiving adequate consideration." Intervisitation in men's and women's dormitory rooms unlimited, "but hours of visitation are voted on by each floor"; sexes segregated by room.

About 30% of students live in either coed dormitories or fraternities and sororities; 70% off-campus housing or commute. Housing guaranteed for new students for three years. There are 14 fraternities, 12 sororities on campus, which 10% of men, 14% of women join.

Annual Costs. Tuition and fees, $3,748 (out-of-state, $11,447; room and board, $5,430; estimated $738 books. About 47% of students receive financial aid. University reports some scholarships awarded on the basis of academic merit alone.

UC/San Diego

La Jolla, California 92093 **(619) 534-3160**

The University of California, San Diego (UCSD) is one of nine campuses of the University of California system. The campus rests on the bluffs of La Jolla (pop. 28,800), overlooking the Pacific Ocean. Opened as a marine station in 1912, the campus became home to the world-famous Scripps Institution of Oceanography. UCSD enrolled its first undergraduate students in 1964. The university's undergraduate program is administered through a five-college system modeled after the Cambridge and Oxford systems. Each college—Revelle, Muir, Third, Warren, and Fifth—has its own set of general education requirements, and its own faculty and administrative and advising staff. Students, however, may pursue any UCSD major through any of the five colleges. Most convenient major airport: San Diego International.

Founded: 1964
Affiliation: State
UG Enrollment: 7,596 M, 6,728 W (full-time)
Total Enrollment: 16,780
Cost: < $10K
% Receiving Financial Aid: 33%
Admission: Very Selective
Application Deadline: Rolling

Admission is very selective. (See also University of California.) About 56% of applicants accepted, 28% of these actually enroll; 90% of freshmen graduate in top tenth of high school class; all in top fifth. Average freshman SAT scores, according to most recent data available: 540 M, 540 W verbal, 620 M, 620 W mathematical; 64% of freshman score above 500 on verbal, 22% above 600, 2% above 700; 86% score above 500 on mathematical, 58% above 600, 16% above

700. *Entrance programs:* early decision, early admission, deferred admission. *Non-academic factors* considered in admissions: special talents, diverse student body. About 10% of entering students from private schools, 5% from parochial schools. *Out-of-state* freshman applicants: university welcomes out-of-state students. *Out-of-state* enrollment limited to 10% of student body; 50% of applicants accepted, 25% enroll. *Transfers* welcome.

Academic Environment. The 5 colleges that make up UC/ San Diego differ substantially in philosophy and requirements for graduation. Revelle's program is designed to give student exposure to all branches of learning; breadth requirements "extensive and explicit." Muir's program is designed for student "who desires considerable freedom of choice among their courses and who will accept the responsibility for helping to plan their own curriculum." Third College's academic focus is on understanding the factors which determine societal change and development and the alleviation of contemporary social problems. Earl Warren College is more career oriented with emphasis on professional and pre-professional training. Fifth College provides an emphasis on international studies and foreign languages; students are encouraged to study abroad. *Degrees:* AB, BS. *Majors offered* include usual arts and sciences, acoustic information processing, anthropology, applied mathematics, applied physics, bioengineering, cognitive science, electromechanics, individualized majors, information and computer science, Judaic studies, linguistics, microbiology, optical information processing, Russian literature, visual arts.

About 60% of entering students graduate eventually; 14% of freshmen do not return for sophomore year. *Special programs:* independent study, internships, study abroad, freshman/faculty discussion groups. *Calendar:* quarter, summer school.

Undergraduate degrees conferred (2,677). 25% were in Social Sciences, 16% were in Life Sciences, 13% were in Engineering, 9% were in Psychology, 7% were in Communications, 5% were in Visual and Performing Arts, 5% were in Business and Management, 4% were in Letters, 4% were in Multi/Interdisciplinary Studies, 4% were in Mathematics, 4% were in Physical Sciences, remainder in 4 other fields. *Doctoral degrees:* Physical Sciences 42, Biological Sciences 31, Psychology 6, Engineering 17, Foreign Languages 5, Mathematics 5, Fine and Applied Arts 3, Letters 12, Social Sciences 24, Computer and Information Science 1, Philosophy and Religion 5.

Graduates Career Data. According to most recent data available, full-time graduate study pursued immediately after graduation by 30% of students of which 17% enter medical school; 9% enter dental school; 14% enter law school; 3% enter business school; 9% enter engineering school. Professional schools typically enrolling largest numbers of graduates include University of California, University of San Diego. *Careers in business and industry* pursued by 70% of graduates. Corporations typically hiring largest numbers of graduates include Hewlett Packard, Arthur Andersen, Hybritech, McDonnell-Douglas. *Career Counseling Program* offers services to all students. Alumni reported as helpful in both career guidance and job placement.

Faculty. About 90% of faculty hold PhD or equivalent.

Student Body. University seeks a national student body; 92% of students from California; 98% West/Northwest. An estimated 3% of students reported as Black, 8% Hispanic, 14% Asian, 11% other minority, according to most recent data available.

Varsity Sports. Men (Div.III): Baseball, Basketball, Crew, Cross Country, Fencing, Coed Golf, Soccer, Swimming, Tennis, Track, Volleyball, Water Polo. Women (Div.III): Basketball, Crew, Cross Country, Fencing, Coed Golf, Soccer, Softball, Swimming, Tennis, Track, Volleyball, Water Polo.

Campus Life. Extensive recreational and cultural opportunities of San Diego easily accessible to students. Laguna Mountains to the east provide year-round camping and hiking; Mexico is within an hour's drive of the campus. Modest student interest in varsity athletics, but more than 60% of students participate in intramural sports. Students have significant role in determining campus social regulations.

About 31% of men, 32% of women live in coed residence facilities; 60% of men, 59% of women live in off-campus housing or commute. Freshmen given preference in college housing if all students cannot be accommodated. Intervisitation in men's and women's dormitory rooms unlimited. There are 12 fraternities, 6 sororities; which 9% each men, women join; 9% each men and women live in fraternities or sororities.

Annual Costs. Tuition and fees, $4,008 (out-of-state, $11,707); room and board, $6,562. About 33% of students receive financial aid; assistance typically divided 5% scholarship, 41% loan, 4% work. University reports some scholarships awarded on the basis of academic merit alone. *Meeting Costs:* PLUS loans available.

UC/Santa Barbara

Santa Barbara, California 93106 (805) 893-2881

Santa Barbara is the fourth largest of the university's campuses. The university attracts students from all parts of the U.S. and many foreign countries. Location of the campus on the Pacific Ocean is a prime asset. Components consist of colleges of Letters and Science, Creative Studies, Engineering, Graduate School of Education, and Graduate Division. Located on an 815-acre promontory, the campus is 2 miles from the town of Goleta and 10 miles from city of Santa Barbara (pop. 74,000). Most convenient major airport: Santa Barbara.

Founded: 1891
Affiliation: State
UG Enrollment: 7,942 M, 8,033 W (full-time)
Total Enrollment: 18,519
Cost: < $10K
% Receiving Financial Aid: 21%
Admission: Very Selective
Application Deadline: Rolling

Admission is very selective. (See also University of California.) About 59% of applicants accepted, 25% of these actually enroll; 90% of freshmen graduate in top fifth of high school class, 95% in top two-fifths. Average freshman SAT scores, according to most recent data available: 502 M, 490 W verbal, 607 M, 554 W mathematical; 50% of freshman score above 500 on verbal, 12% above 600, 1% above 700; 82% score above 500 on mathematical, 46% above 600, 8% above 700. *Non-academic factors* considered in admissions: special talents. Entrance program: midyear admission. About 17% of entering students from private schools. *Out-of-state* freshman applicants: university welcomes out-of-state students. *Transfers* welcome.

Academic Environment. Burgeoning graduate departments on campus are stimulating higher standards for undergraduate divisions. College of Creative Studies is a small, separate academic unit with a special curriculum and specially selected students who give evidence "of a capacity for independent, concentrated, and sustained work in one or more fields of study. [ELLIPSE]" Santa Barbara is a coastal campus with a major interest in the marine sciences. The student body's academic bent is described as primarily scholarly and intellectual. Campus is home to the Institute for Theoretical Physics, National Center for Geographic Information and Analysis, Interdisciplinary Humanities Center, Center for Robotic Systems, Ocean Engineering Lab, Center for Risk Studies and Safety, Compound Semiconductor Research Center. Administration reports percent of courses required for graduation varies by program; distribution requirements fairly numerous for AB (but some may be taken passed/not passed): 8 units English reading and composition, 12 units science, mathematics and technology, 12 units social sciences, 12 units civilization and thought, 16 units arts and literature, proficiency in foreign language. *Degrees:* AB, BS, BM, BSE. *Majors offered* in Letters and Science in addition to usual studies include anthropology, aquatic biology, Asian studies, biochemistry/molecular biology, black studies, dance, dramatic art, ecology and evolution, environmental studies, film studies, geography, history of public policy, Latin American and Iberian Studies, linguistics, and women's studies.

About 62% of students entering as freshmen graduate eventually; 14% of freshmen do not return for sophomore year. *Special programs:* independent study, study abroad, individualized majors, credit by examination. *Library:* 1,900,000 titles; other materials include government documents, technical reports, satellite imagery collections, map collection, and other special collections; open-stack privileges. *Calendar:* quarter, summer school.

Undergraduate degrees conferred (3,853). 25% were in Social Sciences, 12% were in Business and Management, 11% were in Multi/Interdisciplinary Studies, 8% were in Psychology, 8% were in Letters, 6% were in Communications, 6% were in Engineering, 5% were in Life Sciences, 5% were in Visual and Performing Arts, 3% were in Law, remainder in 9 other fields. *Doctoral degrees:* Social Sciences 30, Education 23, Physical Sciences 32, Biological Sciences 18, Engineering 13, Fine and Applied Arts 9, Mathematics 6, Foreign

Languages 1, Psychology 6, Letters 5, Interdisciplinary Studies 2, Health Professions 3, Philosophy and Religion 5.

Graduates Career Data. According to most recent data available, full-time graduate or professional study pursued immediately after graduation by 31% of students; 2% enter medical school or dental school; 4% enter law school; 2% enter business school. Medical and dental schools typically enrolling largest numbers of graduates include UC campuses; law schools include Hastings, Santa Clara, McGeorge. *Careers in business and industry* pursued by 42% of graduates.

Faculty. All permanent faculty hold PhD or equivalent.

Student Body. University does not seek a national student body; 94% of students from California. An estimated 3% of students reported as Black, 11% Asian, 10% Hispanic, 3% other minority, according to most recent data available.

Varsity Sports. Men (Div.I): Baseball, Basketball, Cross Country, Football(III), Golf, Gymnastics, Soccer, Swimming, Tennis, Track, Volleyball, Water Polo. Women (Div.I): Basketball, Cross Country, Gymnastics, Soccer, Softball, Swimming, Tennis, Track, Volleyball.

Campus Life. Very high proportion of students live in the Isla Vista community, bordering the campus, which offers opportunities to develop a wide range of lifestyles. Extensive variety of cultural and social activities on campus supplemented by resources of the city of Santa Barbara, 10 miles from campus. Frequent municipal buses serve campus. Motor vehicles permitted; freshmen, sophomores, and juniors living off campus within 1 mile of campus boundary (including Isla Vista) not allowed to buy season campus parking permits for cars or motorcycles; limited parking allowed on a daily basis.

About 59% of students live in on-campus housing including coed residence halls and family student housing; 41% of students live in off-campus housing or commute. Freshmen given preference in college housing if all students cannot be accommodated. There are 12 fraternities, 12 sororities on campus which about 17% of men, 17% of women join; 6% of students live in fraternities and sororities.

Annual Costs. Tuition and fees, $2,953 (out-of-state, $10,652); room and board, $5,780. About 21% of students receive financial aid. University reports some scholarships awarded on the basis of academic merit alone.

UC/Santa Cruz

Santa Cruz, California 95064 **(408) 429-4008**

Santa Cruz was established to provide an opportunity for innovation and experimentation within the huge University of California system. Students affiliate with one of the 8 small residential colleges of liberal arts and sciences but take courses campus-wide. The 2,000-acre campus overlooks Santa Cruz (pop. 44,000) and Monterey Bay, 75 miles south of San Francisco.

Founded: 1965
Affiliation: State
UG Enrollment: 3,996 M, 4,887 W (full-time); 251 M, 302 W (part-time)
Total Enrollment: 9,860
Cost: < $10K
% Receiving Financial Aid: 59%
Admission: Very Selective
Application Deadline: Rolling

Admission is very selective. (See also University of California.) About 35% of applicants accepted, 51% of these actually enroll; all freshmen graduate in top third of high school class. *Entrance programs:* midyear admission, advanced placement. *Out-of-state* freshman applicants: university welcomes out-of-state students. *Out-of-state* enrollment not limited but priority given to residents. *Transfers* welcome.

Academic Environment. Santa Cruz was designed to offer quality undergraduate instruction with close student/ faculty communication and an innovative attitude toward higher education. All grading is pass/no record in conjunction with written evaluation. (Letter grades are available as an option, in addition to evaluations, in certain cases.) Administration reports 50% of courses required for graduation are elective; nature of courses required vary from college to college; required courses, however, are designed to meet university distribution requirements. Many students take advantage of the options of joint, double, or individualized majors; field studies, independent studies, and apprentice teaching are also important curriculum components. Life sciences and social sciences reported to be among the strongest academic offerings. A small graduate program offers both MA and PhD degrees. *Degree:* BA. *Majors offered* include usual arts and sciences, American studies, community studies, East Asian studies, environmental studies, information and computer sciences, Latin American studies, modern society and social thought, psychobiology, women's studies.

About 38% of students entering as freshmen graduate within five years; 20% of freshmen do not return for sophomore year. *Special programs:* academic reentry, CLEP, honors, independent study, study abroad, undergraduate research, credit by petition, field study, student-taught courses. Organized research units: Center for South Pacific studies, Center for Coastal Marine studies, Lick Observatory. *Calendar:* quarter, summer school (including intensive language study).

Undergraduate degrees conferred (1,915). 24% were in Social Sciences, 17% were in Multi/Interdisciplinary Studies, 13% were in Psychology, 12% were in Life Sciences, 9% were in Letters, 9% were in Visual and Performing Arts, 3% were in Physical Sciences, 3% were in Area and Ethnic Studies, 3% were in Engineering, remainder in 5 other fields. *Doctoral degrees:* Physical Sciences 13, Biological Sciences 14, Letters 5, Psychology 7, Interdisciplinary Studies 6, Computer and Information Sciences 1, Mathematics 1, Social Sciences 3.

Graduates Career Data. According to most recent data available, full-time graduate or professional study pursued immediately after graduation by 35% of students. *Careers in business and industry* pursued by 60% of graduates. *Career Counseling Program:* student assessment of program reported as good for both career guidance and job placement.

Faculty. About 95% of faculty hold PhD or equivalent.

Student Body. University welcomes a national student body; 89% of students from California. An estimated 16% of students reported as Asian, 2% Black, 6% Hispanic, 1% Native American, according to most recent data available.

Varsity Sports. Men: Baseball, Basketball, Cross Country, Fencing, Football, Martial Arts, Racquetball, Rugby, Sailing, Tennis. Women: Baseball, Basketball, Cross Country, Fencing, Football, Martial Arts, Racquetball, Rugby, Sailing, Tennis.

Campus Life. Student leader reports that "outdoor, environmentally concerned, politically active individuals" are likely to feel most at home on campus. Another student leader remarks that students typically transfer out "because of the liberal politics or slow-lane lifestyle here." Student social and dormitory life reported—by both students and administration—as subject only to student regulation. Cars are discouraged and parking facilities kept to minimum. Students walk or bike to and from classes; minibuses connect colleges and core facilities; frequent city bus service runs through campus. Students pay quarterly fee and "may ride anywhere in the transit district at no additional charge." Campus is located in one of the most attractive areas of the California coast.

About 15% of students live in traditional or coed dormitories; 9% in college apartments; 1% in RV park; rest live in off-campus housing or commute. Freshmen given preference in college housing if all students cannot be accommodated. There are no fraternities or sororities. About 25% of students leave campus on weekends.

Annual Costs. Tuition and fees, $3,023 (out-of-state, $10,722); room and board, $5,805. About 59% of students receive financial aid; assistance is typically divided 51% scholarship, 30% loan, 19% work. University reports some scholarships awarded on the basis of academic merit alone.

Calumet College of Saint Joseph

Whiting, Indiana 46394 **(219) 473-4215**

A church-related institution, conducted by the Society of the Precious Blood, Calumet is a commuter college, located in a city of 105,000, 10 miles from Chicago. Most convenient major airport: Midway/O'Hare.

Founded: 1951
Affiliation: Roman Catholic
Total Enrollment: 794 M, W (full-time)
Cost: < $10K
% Receiving Financial Aid: 52%
Admission: Non-selective
Application Deadline: Rolling

Admission. Graduates of approved high schools with 15 units (10 in college preparatory subjects) and two of the following eligible: rank in top half of class, C average, IQ of 110; 86% of applicants accepted, 79% of these actually enroll; 12% of freshmen graduate in top fifth of high school class, 29% in top two-fifths. Average freshman scores, according to most recent data available: SAT, 346 M, 344 W verbal, 352 M, 330 W mathematical; ACT, 17 M, 16 W composite. *Required:* SAT or ACT. *Apply:* rolling admissions. *Transfers* welcome.

Academic Environment. *Degrees:* AB, BS. About 60 hours of general education requirements for graduation; distribution requirements fairly numerous. *Special programs:* CLEP, independent study, study abroad, honors, individualized majors, accelerated summer programs, alternate scheduling (intensive study). Adult programs: Degree Completion Program (complete BA in one year for students with 60+ credits), credit for life experience, evening and weekend degree programs, off-campus sites, accelerated summer programs. *Calendar:* semester, summer school.

Undergraduate degrees conferred (161). 76% were in Business and Management, 4% were in Education, 4% were in Computer and Engineering Related Technology, 4% were in Public Affairs, 4% were in Communications, remainder in 6 other fields.

Faculty. About 45% of faculty hold PhD or equivalent.

Student Body. About 66% of students from in-state; almost all from North Central. An estimated 60% of students reported as Protestant, 35% Catholic, 5% other; 22% Black, 13% Hispanic, according to most recent data available.

Religious Orientation. College is a church-related institution; 9 hours of theology required of all students, daily Mass offered.

Campus Life. No dormitories on campus. There are no fraternities or sororities on campus.

Annual Costs. Tuition and fees, $4,250. About 52% of students receive financial aid. College reports some scholarships awarded on the basis of academic merit alone. *Meeting Costs:* college offers institutional grants and scholarships.

Calvin College

Grand Rapids, Michigan 49546 **(800) 748-0122 or (616) 957-6106**

A church-related, liberal arts college, Calvin admits students affiliated with its sponsoring church as well as other Christian traditions; located in a city of 500,000. Most convenient major airport: Kent County International.

Founded: 1876
Affiliation: Christian Reformed
Total Enrollment: 1,539 M, 1,862 W (full-time)
Cost: < $10K
% Receiving Financial Aid: 63%
Admission: Selective
Application Deadline: Rolling

Admission is selective. About 85% of applicants accepted, 60% of these actually enroll; 49% of freshmen graduate in top fifth of high school class, 76% in top two-fifths. Average freshman scores: SAT, 505 verbal, 567 mathematical; 55% of freshmen score above 500 on verbal, 19% above 600, 3% above 700; 73% score above 500 on mathematical, 42% above 600, 15% above 700; ACT, 25.1 M, 24.2 W composite. Criteria considered in admissions, in order of importance: high school academic record, standardized test scores, recommendations, extra curricular activities, writing sample. *Required:* ACT (SAT accepted), essay. About 62% of entering students from private schools. *Entrance programs:* midyear admission. *Apply:* rolling admissions. *Transfers* welcome; 132 enrolled 1993–94.

Academic Environment. Degrees offered: bachelors, masters. *Majors offered* in addition to usual arts and sciences include geology, telecommunications, occupational therapy; new programs include film studies, minor in third world studies. Core requirements include courses in history, philosophy, math, economics or political science, psychology or social science, science, literature or fine arts, religion, and competency in written and spoken rhetoric, physical education, and at least 1 foreign language. Several students agree that the strengths of Calvin include the variety of majors and educational opportunities, the accessibility of the faculty, the advising system, the small class size, interactive education, and the "integration of faith and learning".

About 65% of students entering as freshmen graduate within five years; 17% of freshmen do not return for sophomore year. Average undergraduate class size: 48% under 20, 47% 20–40, 5% over 40. Adult programs: degree completion program for students over 25 years old with 2 years of college already completed. *Special programs:* study abroad, January interim term, credit by examination, business department cooperative programs. *Calendar:* 4–1–4, summer school.

Undergraduate degrees conferred (869). 16% were in Business and Management, 16% were in Education, 11% were in Social Sciences, 10% were in Letters, 7% were in Psychology, 5% were in Visual and Performing Arts, 5% were in Health Sciences, 5% were in Engineering, 5% were in Communications, 4% were in Life Sciences, 3% were in Foreign Languages, 3% were in Public Affairs, remainder in 8 other fields.

Graduates Career Data. Advanced studies pursued by 22% of students; 2% enter medical school, 3% enter business school. Professional schools typically enrolling largest numbers of graduates include Wayne State U., U. of Michigan, Michigan State U. About 75% of 1993 graduates employed. Fields typically employing largest numbers of graduates include education, business, engineering. Career Development Services include exploration of resources and talents of students, computerized career informational system, placement services.

Faculty. About 83% of faculty hold PhD or equivalent. About 65% of classes taught by tenured faculty. About 17% of teaching faculty are female; 4% minorities.

Student Body. College seeks a national student body; 53% of students from in state; 74% Midwest, 3% Middle Atlantic, 3% New England; 7% West, 1% South, 1% Northwest, 11% foreign students. An estimated 97% of students reported as Protestant, 1% Catholic, 1% unaffiliated, 2% other; 1% Black, 3% Asian, 2% other minority.

Religious Orientation. Calvin is the college of the Christian Reformed Church; 63% of students are affiliated with this church; 6 courses in religion required of all students; attendance at chapel services is voluntary. Religious organizations on campus include Bible study groups, Inter Varsity group.

Varsity Sports. Men (NCAA Div.III): Baseball, Basketball, Cross Country, Diving, Golf, Soccer, Swimming, Tennis, Track. Women (NCAA Div. III): Basketball, Cross Country, Diving, Golf, Soccer, Softball, Swimming, Tennis, Track, Volleyball.

Campus Life. Cars allowed; parking described by administration source as adequate, though recent student leader disagrees. Alcohol not permitted on campus or at college-related activities. Freshmen and sophomores expected to live in college housing if they do not live at home.

About 53% of men, 60% of women live in traditional dormitories or campus apartments (available for upperclassmen); about 40% of men, 33% of women live in off-campus college-related housing, 7% each men and women commute. Intervisitation in men's and women's dormitory rooms limited. There are no fraternities or sororities. About 20% of resident students leave campus on weekends.

Annual Costs. Tuition and fees, $9,450; room and board, $3,570; estimated $1,050 other, exclusive of travel. About 63% of students receive financial aid; average amount of assistance, $7,500. Assistance is typically divided 27% scholarship, 33% grant, 32% loan, 8% work. College reports 1,200 scholarships awarded on the basis of academic merit alone, 850 awarded on the basis of need, 26 awarded for special talents, 200 awarded based on a combination of academic merit and need.

Camden College of Arts and Sciences

(See Rutgers—The State University of New Jersey)

Cameron University

Lawton, Oklahoma 73505 **(405) 581-2230**

A state-supported university, located in a city of 85,000, 100 miles southwest of Oklahoma City. Most convenient major airport: Lawton Municipal.

Founded: 1908
Affiliation: State
UG Enrollment: 1,496 M, 1,940 W (full-time); 1,029 M, 1,149 W (part-time)
Total Enrollment: 5,969
Cost: < $10K
% Receiving Financial Aid: 48%
Admission: Non-selective
Application Deadline: First week of classes

Admission. Oklahoma graduates of accredited high schools with C average or who rank in top three-quarters of class, or comparable rank on composite ACT score eligible; others admitted "on probation'; 96% of applicants accepted, 73% of these actually enroll. Average freshman ACT scores: 20 M, 22 W composite. Criteria considered in admissions, in order of importance: standardized test scores, high school academic record; other factors considered: special talents. *Required:* ACT. *Out-of-state* freshman applicants: university does not seek students from out of state. State does not limit out-of-state enrollment. Requirement for out-of-state applicants: rank in top half of class or comparable rank on composite ACT score; 97% of out-of-state applicants accepted. *Apply* by first week of classes, rolling admission. *Transfers* welcome; 179 enrolled 1993–94.
Academic Environment. Degrees offered: associates, bachelors, masters. About 8% of general education requirements for graduation are elective; distribution requirements fairly numerous. About 72% of students entering as freshmen graduate eventually; 6% of freshmen do not return for sophomore year. Average undergraduate class size: 3% 20–40, 97% over 40. *Calendar:* semester, summer school.
Undergraduate degrees conferred (451). 24% were in Education, 23% were in Business and Management, 12% were in Social Sciences, 10% were in Visual and Performing Arts, 4% were in Psychology, 4% were in Engineering and Engineering Related Technology, 4% were in Agricultural Sciences, 4% were in Letters, 3% were in Life Sciences, 3% were in Home Economics, remainder in 5 other fields.
Faculty. About 57% of faculty hold PhD or equivalent. About 97% of classes taught by tenured faculty. About 32% of teaching faculty are female.
Student Body. University does not seek a national student body; 88% of students are from Oklahoma. An estimated 15% of students reported as Black, 5% Hispanic, 2% Asian, 6% Native American. Average age of undergraduate students: 27.
Varsity Sports. Men (NAIA-Div.II): Baseball, Basketball, Golf, Tennis. Women (NAIA-Div.II): Basketball, Softball, Tennis, Volleyball.
Campus Life. About 4% of men, 6% of women live in traditional dormitories; rest live in off-campus housing or commute. Limited intervisitation in men's or women's dormitory rooms. Sexes segregated in coed dormitory by floor. There are 2 fraternities, 3 sororities on campus which 4% of men and 6% of women join; they provide no residence facilities. About 6% of resident students leave campus on weekends.
Annual Costs. Tuition and fees, $1,700 (out-of-state, $3,000); room and board, $2,200; estimated $1,500 other, exclusive of travel. About 48% of students receive financial aid, average amount of assistance $5,250. Assistance is typically divided 9% scholarship, 71% grant, 14% loan, 6% work. University reports 178 scholarships awarded on the basis of academic merit, 56 awarded for special talents.

Campbell University

Buies Creek, North Carolina 27506 (910) 893-1320

A church-related college, located in a village of 3,100, 30 miles southeast of Raleigh, the state capital, and Fayetteville.

Founded: 1887
Affiliation: Southern Baptist
Total Enrollment: 905 M, 1,139 W (full-time)—main campus
Cost: < $10K
% Receiving Financial Aid: 88%
Admission: Non-selective
Application Deadline: August 1

Admission. Graduates of approved high schools with 12 units in academic subjects eligible; 64% of applicants accepted, 46% of these actually enroll; 19% of freshmen graduate in top fifth of high school class, 47% in top two-fifths. Freshman SAT scores: 25% above 500 verbal, 5% about 600; 41% above 500 mathematical, 12% above 600. Criteria considered in admissions, in order of importance: high school academic record, standardized test scores, extra curricular activities, recommendations. *Required:* 800 or above on SAT (or comparable ACT), C+ average. *Apply* by August 1, rolling admission. *Transfers* welcome; 247 enrolled 1993–94.
Academic Environment. Degrees offered: associates, bachelors, masters, doctoral. Distribution requirements fairly numerous. About 62% of students entering as freshmen graduate eventually; 22% of freshmen do not return for sophomore year. *Special programs:* CLEP, independent study, 3–2 Business, 3–3 Law, internship required for some majors. *Calendar:* semester, summer school.
Undergraduate degrees conferred (428). 32% were in Business and Management, 18% were in Social Sciences, 14% were in Education, 7% were in Communications, 4% were in Business (Administrative Support), 4% were in Home Economics, 3% were in Psychology, 3% were in Philosophy and Religion, 3% were in Protective Services, 3% were in Life Sciences, remainder in 7 other fields.
Faculty. About 77% of faculty hold PhD or equivalent. About 33% of teaching faculty are female.
Student Body. About 62% of students are from North Carolina; 50 states and 36 foreign countries represented. About 28% of students are Protestant, 12% are Catholic, 58% other; 8% Black, 3% Hispanic, 1% Asian, 2% other minority.
Religious Orientation. Campbell is a church-related institution; course in religion, attendance at twice-weekly "cultural enrichment program" required of all students; attendance at church services encouraged.
Varsity Sports. Men (NCAA Div.I): Baseball, Basketball, Cross Country, Golf, Soccer, Tennis, Track, Wrestling. Women (NCAA Div.I): Basketball, Cross Country, Golf, Soccer, Softball, Tennis, Track, Volleyball.
Campus Life. About 77% of men, 73% of women live in traditional dormitories; no coed dormitories; rest live in off-campus housing or commute. No intervisitation in men's or women's dormitory rooms. There are no fraternities, or sororities. Over 40 clubs and organizations on campus.
Annual Costs. Tuition and fees, $8,024; room and board, $2,850; estimated $900 other, exclusive of travel. About 88% of students receive financial aid; average amount of assistance, $6,800.

Campbellsville College

Campbellsville, Kentucky 42718 (502) 465-8158

A church-related college, located in a community of 10,000, 80 miles south of Louisville.

Founded: 1906
Affiliation: Southern Baptist
Total Enrollment: 900 M, W (full-time)
Cost: < $10K
Admission: Non-selective
Application Deadline: September 5

Admission. Graduates of accredited high schools with C average or ACT composite score of 16 or minimum combined SAT score of 700 eligible. *Required:* ACT (SAT acceptable). *Apply* by September 5. *Transfers* welcome.
Academic Environment. *Degrees:* AB, BS, BM. About 75% of general education requirements for graduation are elective; distribution requirements fairly numerous. About 54% of students entering as freshmen graduate eventually; 28% of freshmen do not return for sophomore year. *Special programs:* CLEP, independent study, study abroad, honors. *Calendar:* semester, summer school.
Undergraduate degrees conferred (86). 37% were in Education, 27% were in Business and Management, 15% were in Social Sciences, 5% were in Psychology, 5% were in Theology, 3% were in Mathematics, 3% were in Life Sciences, remainder in 3 other fields.
Student Body. College seeks a national student body; 81% of students from South, 17% North Central, 3% Middle Atlantic.
Religious Orientation. Campbellsville is a church-related institution; 6 hours of Bible or philosophy required of all students; attendance at weekly chapel services voluntary; regular church attendance urged for all students and faculty.
Campus Life. About 51% of men, 60% of women live in traditional dormitories; no coed dormitories; rest commute. No intervisitation in men's or women's dormitory rooms. There are no fraternities or sororities.
Annual Costs. Tuition and fees, $5,720; room and board, $3,000.

Canisius College

Buffalo, New York 14208 **(716) 888-2200**

A liberal arts college founded by the Jesuits, Canisius is now governed by an independent board of trustees. The campus is located about 3 miles from the downtown district of the city (pop. over 300,000). Most convenient major airport: Buffalo International.

Founded: 1870
Affiliation: Independent (Roman Catholic)
UG Enrollment: 1,636 M, 1,339 W (full-time); 287 M, 263 W (part-time)
Total Enrollment: 4,920
Cost: $10K–$20K
% Receiving Financial Aid: 80%
Admission: Selective
Application Deadline: Rolling

Admission is selective. About 80% of applicants accepted, 30% of these actually enroll; 34% of freshmen graduate in top fifth of high school class, 59% in top two-fifths. Average freshman scores: SAT, 448 verbal, 510 mathematical; 26% of freshman score above 500 on verbal, 5% above 600; 54% score above 500 on mathematical, 19% above 600, 3% above 700; ACT, 23 composite. *Required:* SAT or ACT. Criteria considered in admissions, in order of importance: high school academic record, standardized test scores, recommendations, writing sample, extracurricular activities; other factors considered: special talents, alumni children. *Entrance programs:* early admission, midyear admission, deferred admission, advanced placement. About 30% of entering students from private or parochial schools. *Apply:* rolling admissions. *Transfers* welcome; 222 enrolled 1993–94.

Academic Environment. Students reported to have some voice in curriculum decision making through joint student/faculty committees; do not have role in selection and promotion of faculty. Core requirements include general studies in literature, religion and philosophy, as well as area studies in natural sciences, social sciences, art and literature, history, philosophy, religious studies, mathematics, and languages. Degrees offered: associates, bachelors, masters. *Majors offered* include usual arts and sciences, accounting, biochemistry, education, management. New programs include: Spanish, elementary/early secondary education, athletic training major, computer information systems concentration. Average undergraduate class size: 22% under 20, 77% between 20–40, 1% over 40.

About 41% of entering students graduate within four years, 53% eventually; 7% of freshmen do not return for sophomore year. *Special programs:* honors, undergraduate research, independent study, study abroad, individualized majors, 2–3 programs in engineering, 2–2 in environmental science and forestry with SUNY Syracuse, "early assurance" with SUNY Buffalo Medical and Dental, 7-year BA/BS-DDS with SUNY Buffalo Dental, 4-1 BA/MBA, other joint degree programs with SUNYAB Dental School, Ohio College of Podiatric Medicine, and SUNY College of Optometry. Adult programs: new Center for Adult Admission and Academic Services offers programs for adult learners designed to assist adults as they enter or return to higher education; Center for Professional Development offers NYS approved programs in real estate and insurance; Center for Entrepreneurship. *Library:* on-line and CD-ROM database searching; allied operations include TV Studio, A-V Services and Archives. *Calendar:* semester, summer school.

Undergraduate degrees conferred (616). 38% were in Business and Management, 25% were in Social Sciences, 9% were in Letters, 8% were in Psychology, 5% were in Life Sciences, 4% were in Education, 4% were in Computer and Engineering Related Technology, remainder in 8 other fields.

Graduates Career Data. Advanced studies pursued by 22% of graduates; 3% enter medical school; 3% enter law school; 2% enter business school. Medical and dental school typically enrolling largest numbers of graduates include SUNY Buffalo; law schools include SUNY Buffalo, Albany, Akron, Thomas Cooley; business schools include SUNY Buffalo, Canisius. About 67% of 1992 graduates employed. Fields typically employing largest numbers of graduates include accounting, education, financial services, sales/marketing. Career Development Services include interest testing of all freshmen, professional career counseling on individual basis, SIGIPLUS computerized system, on-campus recruitment, interview preparation. Alumni reported as helpful in career guidance.

Faculty. About 93% of faculty hold PhD or equivalent. About 74% of undergraduate classes taught by tenured faculty. About 20% of teaching faculty are female; 5% ethnic minority.

Student Body. About 92% of students from New York; 94% Middle Atlantic, 2% New England, 3% foreign. An estimated 59% of students reported as Catholic, 7% Protestant, 33% not reporting; 5% as Black, 2% other minority.

Religious Orientation. Canisius was founded as a Jesuit institution, now governed by independent board of trustees; 3 courses in religion required of all students; attendance at religious services voluntary. Places of worship available on campus for both Catholics and other religious denominations.

Varsity Sports. Men (Div.I): Baseball, Basketball, Crew, Cross Country, Football (IAA), Golf, Hockey(NCAA/ECAC), Lacrosse, Soccer, Swimming, Tennis, Track. Women (Div. I): Basketball, Crew, Cross Country, Soccer, Softball, Swimming, Tennis, Track, Volleyball. Coed: Cheerleading, Rifle. A variety of club sports are also popular on campus including Rugby, Lacrosse.

Campus Life. Students from more than 20 states and 30 foreign countries contribute to campus life, although Canisius still serves primarily a regional, commuting student body.

About 27% of students live on campus; 73% commute. On-campus housing is guaranteed for all four years. There are 2 fraternities, 2 sororities, 8 honor societies, and 2 business fraternities on campus. About 33% of resident students leave campus on weekends.

Parking regulations constitute sole restriction on use of cars. Consumption of alcoholic beverages limited to approved campus functions and designated areas in residence halls. Intervisitation permitted.

Annual Costs. Tuition and fees, $10,270; room and board, $5,240; estimated $1,600 other, exclusive of travel. About 80% of students receive financial aid; average amount of assistance, $9,678. Assistance is typically divided 62% scholarship/grant, 31% loan, 7% work. College reports 10–15 scholarships awarded on the basis of academic merit alone, full and partial grants for special talents. *Meeting Costs:* College offers Tuition Plan.

Capital University

Columbus, Ohio 43209 **(800) 289-6289**

A Lutheran-related university, located in the suburban community of Bexley (pop. 14,000), 3 miles from the capital city of 665,000. The institution includes the Conservatory of Music, School of Nursing, Law School, College of Arts and Sciences, Adult Degree Program and the Graduate School of Administration. Most convenient major airport: Port Columbus.

Founded: 1830
Affiliation: Lutheran
UG Enrollment: 585 M, 960 W (full-time)
Total Enrollment: 3,824
Cost: $10K–$20K
% Receiving Financial Aid: 97%
Admission: Selective
Application Deadline: August 1

Admission is selective. About 79% of applicants accepted, 32% of these actually enroll; 58% of freshmen graduate in top fifth of high school class, 86% in top two-fifths. Average freshman scores: SAT, 465 verbal, 510 mathematical; ACT, 23 composite. *Required:* SAT or ACT, audition for Conservatory; interview recommended. Criteria considered in admission, in order of importance: high school academic record, standardized test scores, recommendations, extracurricular activities; other factors considered: special talents, diverse student body. *Apply* by August 1; rolling admissions. *Transfers* welcome; 128 enrolled 1993–94.

Academic Environment. Graduation requirements include 36-hour common core curriculum. Students seem very happy with quality of teaching, personal attention from faculty and field experiences; not as happy with tuition increases. Degrees offered: bachelors, masters. Unusual, new, or notable majors include: music industry, organizational communications, philosophy, sports medicine, athletic training.

About 65% of students entering as freshmen graduate within four years; 82% of freshmen return for sophomore year. *Special programs:* independent study, study abroad, honors, undergraduate research, credit by examination, 3–2 programs in engineering and in occupational therapy, cross registration with Ohio State,

Columbus State, Otterbein. Adult programs: evening degree programs offered in Columbus, Cleveland, and Dayton. *Calendar:* early semester.

Undergraduate degrees conferred (467). 16% were in Business and Management, 15% were in Education, 14% were in Multi/Interdisciplinary Studies, 13% were in Health Sciences, 5% were in Public Affairs, 5% were in Communications, 4% were in Social Sciences, 4% were in Liberal/General Studies, 3% were in Visual and Performing Arts, 3% were in Letters, 3% were in Psychology, 3% were in Computer and Engineering Related Technology, remainder in 7 other fields.

Graduates Career Data. Advanced studies pursued by 17% of graduates; 2% enter medical or dental school; 4% enter law school; 3% enter business school, 20% attend seminary. About 71% of graduates employed. Career Development Services offer career counseling, resume writing and interviewing workshops.

Faculty. About 78% of faculty hold PhD or equivalent. About 3% of teaching faculty are Black, 1% other minority.

Student Body. About 90% of students from in state; 93% from Midwest; 2% Middle Atlantic, 1% South, 1% New England, 3% foreign. An estimated 65% of students reported as Protestant, 20% Catholic, 1% Jewish, 9% unaffiliated, 5% other; 6% as Black, 2% Asian, 3% other minority.

Religious Orientation. Capital is Lutheran-related; 2 courses in religion required; 22% of students affiliated with this church. Students and staff "urged to participate" in chapel services, but not required.

Varsity Sports. Men (Div.III): Baseball, Basketball, Football, Golf, Soccer, Tennis, Wrestling. Women (Div.III): Basketball, Soccer, Softball, Tennis, Volleyball.

Campus Life. Students report social life is divided between on-campus activities, work or work/study, and visits to nearby Ohio State University. Regulations governing campus life fairly liberal; intervisitation restricted. Cars permitted; on-campus parking permit required.

About 70% of men, 70% of women live in traditional dormitories; rest commute. All upper class dormitories are coed. Freshmen given preference in college housing if all students cannot be accommodated. There are 6 fraternities, 6 sororities on campus which about 30% of men, 30% of women join; they provide no residence facilities. About 25% of resident students leave campus on weekends.

Annual Costs. Tuition and fees, $12,500; room and board, $3,910; estimated $1,500 other, exclusive of travel. About 97% of students receive financial aid; average amount of assistance, $7,500. Assistance is typically divided 35% scholarship, 34% grant, 20% loan, 10% work. University reports number of scholarships awarded for each: academic merit, special talents, and need, "varies."

Capitol College

Laurel, Maryland 20708 (301) 953-3200

An engineering college located in a small suburban community about 10 miles from Washington, D.C.

Affiliation: Independent
Total Enrollment: 768 M, W (full-time); 433 M, 49 W (part-time)
Cost: < $10K
% Receiving Financial Aid: 56%
Admission: Non-selective
Application Deadline: Rolling

Admission. High school graduates eligible; admissions based on SAT, high school transcript, and GPA. *Required:* interview recommended. *Apply:* rolling admissions. *Transfers* welcome.

Academic Environment. *Degree:* BS. College offers 4-year programs in electronic engineering technology, computer engineering technology, telecommunications technology, technical communications, management of telecommunications systems. About 29% of entering students graduate eventually. *Calendar:* semester, summer school.

Undergraduate degrees conferred (106). 91% were in Engineering and Engineering Related Technology, 8% were in Engineering, remainder in Business and Management.

Graduates Career Data. Advanced studies pursued by 22% of graduates. *Careers in business and industry* pursued by all graduates. Corporations typically hiring largest numbers of graduates include Singer Link Co., E-Systems Melpar, Litton-Amecom.

Campus Life. On-campus apartment-style housing available.

Annual Costs. Tuition and fees, $8,013. About 56% of students receive financial aid. College reports some scholarships awarded on the basis of academic merit alone. *Meeting Costs:* college offers Maryland Supplemental Loan Program.

Cardinal Stritch College

Milwaukee, Wisconsin 53217 (414) 352-5400

A church-related college, owned by the Sisters of St. Francis of Assisi, located near Lake Michigan in the Fox Point-Glendale suburb of Milwaukee (pop. 750,000). Most convenient major airport: General Mitchell International.

Founded: 1937
Affiliation: Roman Catholic
UG Enrollment: 223 M, 569 W (full-time); 313 M, 225 W (part-time)
Total Enrollment: 1,105
Cost: < $10K
% Receiving Financial Aid: 79%
Admission: Non-selective
Application Deadline: Aug. 1

Admission. High school graduates with 15 units who rank in top half of class, with ACT/SAT of 18/800 and GPA of 2.0 eligible; 79% of applicants accepted, 61% of these actually enroll; 27% of freshmen graduate in top fifth of high school class, 54% in top two-fifths. Average freshman scores: ACT, 21.8 M, 22.7 W composite. *Required:* SAT or ACT. Criteria considered in admissions, in order of importance: high school academic record, standardized test scores, writing sample, recommendations, extracurricular activities. About 17% of entering students from parochial schools. *Apply* by August 1; rolling admissions. *Transfers* welcome; 159 enrolled 1993–94.

Academic Environment. Degrees offered: associates, bachelors, masters. Graduation requirements include 15 credits in philosophy/religious studies/history, 6 credits in social sciences, 7–8 credits in math/natural science, 14–15 credits in literature/fine arts, 9–15 credits in communication. Average undergraduate class size: 90% under 20.

About 57% of entering freshmen graduate within four years; 78% of freshmen return for sophomore year. *Special programs:* CLEP, independent study, study abroad, undergraduate research. Adult programs: Evening accelerated undergraduate and graduate programs offered in business and management, PMA Program, Returning Student Seminar. *Calendar:* semester, summer school.

Undergraduate degrees conferred (479). 72% were in Business and Management, 10% were in Education, 4% were in Health Sciences, 3% were in Philosophy and Religion, 3% were in Visual and Performing Arts, 3% were in Communications, 3% were in Social Sciences, remainder in 6 other fields.

Graduates Career Data. Advanced studies pursued by 12% of graduates. Career Development Services incude career counseling, career resource library, job search assistance, job campaign, and resume and interviewing assistance.

Faculty. About 35% of faculty hold PhD or equivalent. About 75% of teaching faculty are female.

Student Body. About 93% of students from Wisconsin; 98% Midwest. An estimated 54% of students reported as Catholic, 22% Protestant, 2% Jewish, 22% other; 8% of students are Black, 3% Hispanic, 2% Asian, 5% other.

Religious Orientation. Cardinal Stritch is a church-related institution; 2 courses in religious study required of all students.

Varsity Sports. Men (NAIA): Baseball, Basketball, Soccer. Women (NAIA): Basketball, Cross Country, Soccer, Softball, Volleyball.

Campus Life. About 26% of men and 18% of women live in traditional dormitories; rest live in off-campus housing or commute. Freshmen given preference in college housing if all students cannot be accommodated. Intervisitation in dormitory rooms limited. There are no fraternities or sororities on campus. About 20% of resident students leave campus on weekends.

Annual Costs. Tuition and fees, $7,680; room and board, $3,480; estimated $1,700 other, exclusive of travel. About 79% of students receive financial aid; average amount of assistance, $8,000, according to most recent data available. Assistance is typically divided 47% scholarship, 33% loan, 20% work.

Carleton College

Northfield, Minnesota 55057 **(800) 995-2275**

Carleton is one of the nation's most widely known and respected liberal arts colleges, outstanding for the number of scientists, university teachers, and members of the professions it has produced. The college historically has attracted a national student body of high quality and a distinguished faculty. Today, its semirural, small-town location and its easy access to Minneapolis/St. Paul, 40 miles away, offer the best of both worlds. Most convenient major airport: Minneapolis-St. Paul.

Founded: 1866
Affiliation: Independent
UG Enrollment: 833 M, 845 W (full-time)
Total Enrollment: 1,678
Cost: $10K–$20K
% Receiving Financial Aid: 65%
Admission: Highly (+) Selective
Application Deadline: February 1

Admission is highly (+) selective. About 58% of applicants accepted, 31% of these actually enroll; 90% of freshmen graduate in top fifth of high school class, 98% in top two-fifths. Average freshman scores: SAT, 83% of freshmen score above 500 on verbal, 56% above 600, 12% above 700; 86% score above 500 on mathematical, 71% above 600, 30% above 700; ACT, 29 composite. *Required:* SAT or ACT; 3 ACH including English recommended, essay, interview recommended. Criteria considered in admissions, in order of importance: high school academic record, recommendations, writing sample, extracurricular activities, standardized test scores; other factors considered: special talents, alumni children, diverse student body. *Entrance programs:* early decision, early admission, advanced placement, deferred admission. About 16% of entering students from private schools, 3% parochial schools. *Apply* by February 1. *Transfers* welcome; 31 enrolled 1993–94.

Academic Environment. Administration and student sources agree that at least 80% of the student body is primarily oriented toward scholarly and intellectual interests. Those who feel most at home at Carleton reported to be those who have diverse interests, are intellectually curious and are content with athletics and social activities as supplements to academics. Students who are not "well prepared academically," prefer "an urban environment, or a primarily social environment" are most likely to leave before graduation, though few do so. Student leader reports that those who need help have free tutoring and other academic support systems available. The academic pace is described as "intense" with three ten-week terms, but students are also described (by a student) as "supportive" of each other. Student contact with professors is said to be frequent and informal in faculty homes as well as offices. Graduation requirements include 3 courses in math/science, 3 in social sciences, 2 in humanities, 2 in arts, foreign language competency, writing requirement, and one course in non-Western civilization. Extensive study abroad program; 60% of students participate. Degrees offered: bachelors. Unusual, new, or notable majors include: international relations, technology and public policy studies, Chinese language and literature, Medieval studies, cognitive studies, computer science major, several interdisciplinary programs. Average undergraduate class size: 73% under 20, 23% between 20–40, 4% over 40.

About 84% of students entering as freshmen graduate within four years, 89% eventually; 95% of freshmen return for sophomore year. *Special programs:* honors, independent study, study abroad, undergraduate research, individualized majors, numerous opportunities for off-campus domestic and overseas study, off-campus programs in Australia and Nepal, programs of ACM, urban teaching, freshman seminars, credit by examination, senior colloquia, cross-registration with St. Olaf, Washington Semester, Princeton Critical Languages program, area studies (Asian, Latin American), 3–2 engineering, 3–3 law, 3–2 nursing. *Calendar:* 3–3.

Undergraduate degrees conferred (457). 33% were in Social Sciences, 14% were in Physical Sciences, 14% were in Letters, 8% were in Visual and Performing Arts, 6% were in Life Sciences, 6% were in Psychology, 5% were in Philosophy and Religion, 5% were in Area and Ethnic Studies, 4% were in Foreign Languages, remainder in 3 other fields.

Graduates Career Data. Advanced studies pursued by 25% of students immediately after graduation, 75% within five years; 16% enter graduate school; 3% enter medical school; 3% enter law school; 2% enter business school; 1% enter dental school. About 64% of 1992–93 graduates employed. Fields typically hiring largest numbers of graduates include education, science research, social services. Career Development Services include a full range of counseling, assessment inventories, alumni shadowing, job fairs and job search preparation, assistance with internships and access to Alumni Career Network.

Faculty. About 96% of faculty hold PhD or equivalent. About 32% of teaching faculty are female; 4% Black, 2% Hispanic, 4% Asian.

Student Body. About 23% of students from in state; 52% Midwest, 19% New England/Middle Atlantic, 18% West/Northwest, 9% South, 2% foreign. An estimated 3% of students reported as Black, 9% Asian, 3% Hispanic, 1% other minority. "Carleton is committed to diversity—geographical, socio-economic, racial and religious." Minority group students: special advisers for minority students, black studies program (including a major), SOUL lounge in Student Union, scholarships, grants-in-aid, student work, loans; establishment of black dance troupe, singing, literary, dramatic groups.

Religious Orientation. Founded by the Congregational Church, Carleton is now independent and nonsectarian; makes no religious demands on students.

Varsity Sports. Men (Div.III): Baseball, Basketball, Cross Country, Diving, Football, Golf, Skiing, Soccer, Swimming, Tennis, Track, Wrestling. Women (Div.III): Basketball, Cross Country, Diving, Golf, Skiing, Soccer, Softball, Swimming, Tennis, Track, Volleyball.

Campus Life. Few students leave campus on weekends despite small town environment and the availability of frequent bus service to Minneapolis/St. Paul. Student cooperative sponsors a full calendar of social and cultural events on campus. Students reported to be concerned about "the number... and mix of different social events, i.e., rock dances and square dances," and that a wide range is provided. All dormitories coed, with some single sex floors available. Dorms open 24 hours a day, there does not appear to be a security problem. Few cars permitted (essentially no student-owned cars); restrictions on cars brings mixed response from students—some feel it contributes to "provincialism" of campus, others strongly support them because they reinforce "the residential aspect of Carleton." Carleton has a very diverse student body in a cohesive community with students playing an important role in administrative and academic decisions, including faculty selection. According to a student source, "Carleton students take... studies seriously, enjoy Carleton, and do have social lives."

About 78% of men, 74% of women live in coed dormitories; 14% of men, 17% of women live in off-campus college-related housing; 8% of men, 9% of women live in other off-campus housing. Freshmen given preference in college housing if all students cannot be accommodated. Sexes segregated in coed dormitories by floor or room. There are no fraternities or sororities on campus. About 5% of resident students leave campus on weekends.

Annual Costs. Tuition and fees, $18,405; room and board, $3,750; estimated $1,000 other, exclusive of travel. About 65% of students receive financial aid; average amount of need-based assistance, $14,500. Assistance is typically divided 65% scholarship/grant, 22% loan, 13% work. College reports 70–80 scholarships awarded on the basis of academic merit alone, 250 on need alone. *Meeting Costs:* college offers prepayment plan, monthly payment plans.

Carlow College

Pittsburgh, Pennsylvania 15213 **(800) 333-CARLOW or (412) 578-6059**

A church-related, liberal arts college, founded by the Sisters of Mercy. Primarily for women, college accepts men as matriculating students. The 13-acre campus is located in the Oakland section of Pittsburgh (pop. 400,000), 10 minutes from the downtown area. Most convenient major airport: Greater Pittsburgh International.

Founded: 1929
Affiliation: Roman Catholic
UG Enrollment: 74 M, 733 W (full-time); 75 M, 938 W (part-time)
Total Enrollment: 1,863
Cost: < $10K
% Receiving Financial Aid: 89%
Admission: Non-selective
Application Deadline: Rolling

Admission. High school graduates with 18 units (14 in academic subjects) and B average eligible; 81% of applicants accepted, 53% of these actually enroll. College emphasizes that admission is based on careful review of all applicant's credentials. *Required:* SAT or ACT; interview recommended. Criteria considered in admissions, in order of importance: high school academic record, "personality," recommendations, extracurricular activities, standardized test scores, writing sample; other factors considered: special talents, alumni children. *Entrance programs:* early admission, advanced placement. *Apply:* rolling admissions. *Transfers* welcome; 100 enrolled 1993–94.

Academic Environment. Degrees offered: bachelors, masters. Unusual, new, or notable majors include: early childhood/elementary education, special education, medical marketing, theology, individually designed independent majors.

About 56% of students entering as freshmen graduate eventually; 70% of freshmen return for sophomore year. *Special programs:* independent study, internships, CLEP, credit for life experience, field placement, study abroad, honors, undergraduate research, credit by examination, cross-registration with 9 other Pittsburgh colleges and universities; nursing program "uses a wide variety of acute and long-term care facilities for clinical experience"; Montessori, kindergarten and non-graded elementary school run by college on campus. Adult programs: Weekend College, Carlow Accelerated Program (evening classes), Carlow Hill College. *Library:* special collections include Black Studies Collection, Peace Studies Collection, Career Resources Center. *Calendar:* semester, summer school.

Undergraduate degrees conferred (168). 35% were in Health Sciences, 20% were in Business and Management, 15% were in Communications, 8% were in Education, 5% were in Liberal/General Studies, 4% were in Life Sciences, 4% were in Psychology, 4% were in Multi/Interdisciplinary Studies, remainder in 4 other fields.

Faculty. About 38% of faculty hold PhD or equivalent.

Student Body. About 97% of students from in state; less than 1% foreign. An estimated 24% of students reported as Catholic, 10% Protestant, 61% unknown, 6% other; 10% Black, less than 1% each Hispanic, Asian, American Indian. *Minority group students:* special adviser and counselor to Black students; United Black Students Association; Advisor to International Students. Average age of undergraduate student: 31.

Religious Orientation. Carlow is a church-related institution; 1 course in theology required of all students; attendance at religious services voluntary.

Varsity Sports. Women (NAIA): Basketball, Crew, Volleyball.

Campus Life. Location in Oakland area enhances campus life. Many cultural and educational opportunities within walking distance of college. Cars usually not permitted for resident students because of severe shortage of parking space on campus. Alcohol prohibited in residence halls; limited visitation.

About 60% of female day students live in dormitories; rest commute. Freshmen given preference in college housing if all students cannot be accommodated. There are no fraternities or sororities on campus. About 50% of resident students leave campus on weekends.

Annual Costs. Tuition and fees, $9,650; room and board, $4,264; estimated $1,000 other, exclusive of travel. About 89% of students receive financial aid; average amount of assistance, $8,100. Assistance typically divided 20% scholarship, 40% grant, 30% loan, 10% work. College reports 127 scholarships awarded on the basis of academic merit alone, 130 on special talents alone, 369 on need alone. *Meeting Costs:* college offers tuition payment plans, parent loans.

Carnegie Mellon University

Pittsburgh, Pennsylvania 15213 (412) 268-2082

Carnegie Mellon University is the result of the merger of the Carnegie Institute of Technology and the Mellon Institute (a prestigious research institution). The university consists of a college of engineering (Carnegie Institute of Technology), a College of Humanities and Social Sciences, a college of science (Mellon College of Science), a College of Fine Arts, and a number of graduate and research units. The university is located 5 miles from the heart of Pittsburgh on a 103-acre main campus. Most convenient major airport: Pittsburgh.

Founded: 1900
Affiliation: Independent
UG Enrollment: 2,640 M, 1,760 W (full-time)
Total Enrollment: 7,000
Cost: $10K–$20K
% Receiving Financial Aid: 63%
Admission: Very (+) Selective
Application Deadline: February 1

Admission is very (+) selective. For all schools, 60% of applicants accepted, 24% of these actually enroll; 80% of freshmen graduate in top fifth of high school class, 91% in top two-fifths. Average freshman scores: SAT, 77% of freshmen score above 500 on verbal, 32% above 600, 3% above 700; 92% score above 500 on mathematical, 73% above 600, 32% above 700; ACT, 85% score above 25 on composite, 15% score between 19–24.

For Carnegie Institute, 64% of applicants accepted, 22% of these actually enroll; 88% of freshmen graduate in top fifth of high school class, 97% in top two-fifths. Average freshmen SAT scores: 79% of freshmen score above 500 on verbal, 31% above 600, 3% above 700; 99% score above 500 on mathematical, 92% above 600, 49% above 700, according to most recent data available.

For Mellon College of Science, 62% of applicants accepted, 22% of these actually enroll; 78% of freshmen graduate in top fifth of high school class, 95% in top two-fifths. Average freshmen SAT scores: 80% of freshmen score above 500 on verbal, 32% above 600, 6% above 700; all score above 500 on mathematical, 88% above 600, 42% above 700, according to most recent data available.

For Humanities and Social Sciences, 74% of applicants accepted, 22% of these actually enroll; 62% of freshmen graduate in top fifth of high school class, 87% in top two-fifths. Average freshman SAT scores: 69% of freshmen score above 500 on verbal, 28% above 600, 3% above 700; 88% score above 500 on mathematical, 53% above 600, 11% above 700, according to most recent data available.

For Fine Arts, 38% of applicants accepted, 38% of these actually enroll; 55% graduate in top fifth of high school class, 84% in top two-fifths. Average freshmen SAT scores: 63% of freshmen score above 500 on verbal, 24% above 600, 1% above 700; 74% score above 500 on mathematical, 45% above 600, 9% above 700, according to most recent data available.

For Industrial Management, 57% of applicants accepted, 26% of these actually enroll; 82% of freshmen graduate in top fifth of high school class, 96% in top two-fifths. Average freshmen SAT scores: 85% of freshmen score above 500 on verbal, 63% above 600, 12% above 700; 98% score above 500 on mathematical, 75% above 600, 25% above 700, according to most recent data available.

Required: SAT I and SAT II, English and math, or ACT; portfolio (for art), portfolio or project (for design), audition (for drama, music); interview (on or off-campus) strongly recommended. *Entrance programs:* early decision, early admission. *Apply* by February 1. *Transfers* welcome; 111 enrolled 1993–94.

Academic Environment. Pressures for academic achievement appear fairly rigorous for Carnegie Institute of Technology and Mellon College of Science. Common freshman year for engineering and science students. All candidates for BS degree at CIT and MCS must complete a core curriculum of at least 8 courses offered by the College of Humanities and Social Sciences. A somewhat more extensive general education distribution curriculum is required of students in the College of Humanities and Social Sciences. College of Fine Arts has few distribution requirements. Degrees offered: bachelors, masters, doctoral. Unusual, new, or notable majors include: double majors in physics or mathematics with English, history, or languages. Computer literacy required of all except Fine Arts students. Average undergraduate class size: 33% under 20, 30% between 20–40, 33% over 40.

About 93% of freshmen return for sophomore year. *Special programs:* study abroad, individualized majors, Washington Semester, cross-registration with PGH Council on Higher Education. *Calendar:* semester, summer school.

Undergraduate degrees conferred (875). 27% were in Engineering, 16% were in Visual and Performing Arts, 10% were in Business and Management, 10% were in Social Sciences, 8% were in Mathematics, 8% were in Letters, 4% were in Computer and Engineering Related Technology, 4% were in Architecture and Environmental Design, 4% were in Physical Sciences, 3% were in Life Sciences, 3% were in Psychology, remainder in 3 other fields.

Graduates Career Data. Advanced studies pursued by 30% of graduates; 17% enter graduate school; 3% enter medical school; 3% enter law school; 7% enter business school. About 90% of 1992–93 graduates using Career Center employed. Career Center offers counseling services, summer job search workshops, job location and development assistance, resume referrals, and coordinate senior job placement.

Faculty. About 89% of faculty hold PhD or equivalent; more than one-third earned at nation's top graduate schools. About 98% of undergraduate classes taught by tenured faculty.

Student Body. About 27% of students from in state; 40% Middle Atlantic, 20% New England, 10% South, 10% West, 5% Northwest; 10% foreign. An estimated 7% of students reported as Black, 8% Hispanic, 15% Asian, 20% other minority.
Religious Orientation. Carnegie Mellon is an independent institution, makes no religious demands on students. Committee on Religious Affairs (including chaplains and advisers to university-recognized religious groups) advises university on religious life and activities.
Varsity Sports. Men (Div.III): Basketball, Crew, Cross Country, Football, Golf, Soccer, Swimming, Tennis, Track. Women (Div.III): Basketball, Crew, Cross Country, Soccer, Swimming, Tennis, Track, Volleyball.
Campus Life. Student reports indicate "There is plenty to do around here." Recreational sports are "a favorite pastime"; and "the College of Fine Arts is always putting something on, and these productions are very popular with the students." Pittsburgh is also easily accessible. Attitude toward drugs "corrective rather than punitive." Use of alcohol subject to state law, but alcoholic beverages may be served at "a closed house party" with guests by invitation only. Administration reports "campus regulations are based on the adult responsibility and attitudes of its student population." Campus security is reported to be "not an issue."

About 10% of men live in traditional dormitories; 50% of men, 60% of women in coed dormitories; 17% each live in off-campus housing; 3% each commute. Freshmen required to live in university housing. Sexes segregated in coed dormitories by wing, floor or room. There are 14 fraternities, 5 sororities on campus which about 31% each men, women join. About 1% of resident students leave campus on weekends.
Annual Costs. Tuition and fees, $17,125; room and board, $5,515; estimated $1,550 other, exclusive of travel. About 63% of students receive financial aid; average amount of assistance, $14,000. Assistance is typically divided 60% scholarship, 25% loans, 15% work.

Carroll College

Helena, Montana 59625 **(406) 447-4300**

A church-related college, conducted by the diocese, located in the state capital (pop. 30,000). Most convenient major airport: Helena.

Founded: 1909
Affiliation: Independent (Roman Catholic)
Total Enrollment: 426 M, 667 W (full-time); 91 M, 231 W (part-time)
Cost: < $10K
% Receiving Financial Aid: 80%
Admission: Non-selective
Application Deadline: July 1

Admission. Graduates of accredited high schools with 15 units (10 in academic subjects) eligible; 93% of applicants accepted, 53% of these actually enroll; 51% of freshmen graduate in top fifth of high school class, 73% in top two-fifths. Average freshman ACT scores: 23 composite. *Required:* SAT or ACT; essay. Criteria considered in admissions, in order of importance: high school academic record, standardized test scores, recommendations, writing sample, extracurricular activities; other factors considered: special talents, alumni children, diverse student body, religious affiliation and/or commitment. About 10% of entering students from parochial schools, 25% private schools. *Entrance programs:* advanced placement. *Apply* by July 1; rolling admission. *Transfers* welcome, 29 enrolled 1993–94.
Academic Environment. Graduation requirements include 6 credits in theology, 6 in philosophy, 10 in communication, 3 each in literature, fine arts, mathematics, natural science, and history, and 9 in social sciences. Degrees offered: associates, bachelors. Unusual, new, or notable majors include: TESOL (Teaching English to Speakers of Other Languages), computer science-software engineering. Average undergraduate class size: 54% under 20, 36% between 20–40, 10% over 40.

About 50% of students entering as freshmen graduate within four years, 70% eventually; 74% of freshmen return for sophomore year. *Special programs:* study abroad, cooperative education, 3–2 engineering, computer science, and occupational therapy. *Calendar:* semester, summer term.

Undergraduate degrees conferred (183). 20% were in Business and Management, 13% were in Education, 10% were in Psychology, 10% were in Health Sciences, 10% were in Public Affairs, 8% were in Social Sciences, 8% were in Life Sciences, 5% were in Communications, 4% were in Letters, 4% were in Mathematics, remainder in 6 other fields.
Graduates Career Data. Advanced studies pursued by 36% of graduates; 6% enter medical school; 1% enter dental school; 5% enter law school; 3% enter business school. Medical schools typically enrolling the largest numbers of graduates include U.of Washington; dental schools include U. of Minnesota; law schools include: U. of Montana; business schools include U. of Montana. About 45% of 1992–93 graduates employed. Fields typically employing largest numbers of graduates include: business, education, nursing.
Faculty. About 50% of faculty hold PhD or equivalent. About 63% of undergraduate classes taught by tenured faculty. About 33% of the teaching faculty are female; 3% minority.
Student Body. About 70% of students from Montana; 94% West/Northwest, 6% foreign. An estimated 60% of students reported as Catholic; 1% Black, 1% Hispanic, 1% Asian, 5% other minority.
Religious Orientation. Carroll is a church-related institution; 2 religious courses required of all students.
Varsity Sports. Men (NAIA,Div.I): Basketball, Football. Women (NAIA,Div.I): Basketball, Volleyball.
Campus Life. About 10% of men, 33% of women live in traditional dormitories; 39% men, 5% women live in coed dormitories; rest commute. Freshmen given preference in college housing if all students cannot be accommodated. Intervisitation in men's and women's dormitory rooms limited. There are no fraternities or sororities on campus. About 30% of students leave campus on weekends.
Annual Costs. Tuition and fees, $7,760; room and board, $3,650; estimated $1,000 other, exclusive of travel. About 80% of students receive financial aid; average amount of assistance, $7,190. Assistance is typically divided 28% scholarship, 17% grant, 73% loan, 18% work. College reports 317 scholarships awarded on the basis of academic merit alone, 124 on special talents alone, 513 on need alone. *Meeting Costs:* college offers deferred payment plan.

Carroll College

Waukesha, Wisconsin 53186 **(414) 524-7220**

A small, liberal arts college, Carroll is affiliated with the United Presbyterian Church, but is not sectarian in outlook or enrollment. The 36-acre campus is located in a residential community of 47,000, 18 miles west of Milwaukee. Most convenient major airport: Mitchell Field (Milwaukee).

Founded: 1846
Affiliation: United Presbyterian
Total Enrollment: 576 M, 919 W (full-time)
Cost: $10K–$20K
% Receiving Financial Aid: 90%
Admission: Selective
Application Deadline: March 15

Admission is selective. About 90% of applicants accepted, 44% of these actually enroll. Average freshman scores, according to most recent data available: ACT, 22.8 M, 22.3 W composite. *Required:* SAT or ACT. *Non-academic factors* considered in admissions: special talents, alumni children, diverse student body, extracurricular participation. *Entrance programs:* early admission, midyear admission, deferred admission, advanced placement. *Apply* by March 15; rolling admissions. *Transfers* welcome.
Academic Environment. Students have a major voice in curriculum decision making through joint student/faculty committees. Administration reports considerable flexibility in requirements for graduation (Experimental Program for selected students eliminates all but one basic religion course and one language course requirement, individually designed major an option for all students); distribution requirements remain for most. *Degrees:* AB, BS, BSMT. *Majors offered* include usual arts and sciences, accounting, business administration, international relations, medical technology, social welfare, artificial intelligence, fitness management.

About 65% of students entering as freshmen graduate within four years; 20% of freshmen do not return for sophomore year. *Special programs:* CLEP, independent study, study abroad, credit by examination, Washington Semester, United Nations Semester, programs of CSCA, 3–2 engineering, 3-year degree, individualized majors, new cultural experience. *Calendar:* 4–1–4, summer school.

Undergraduate degrees conferred (350). 20% were in Health Sciences, 19% were in Business and Management, 9% were in Social Sciences, 9% were in Communications, 8% were in Psychology, 8% were in Education, 7% were in Visual and Performing Arts, 5% were in Letters, 5% were in Computer and Engineering Related Technology, 3% were in Life Sciences, 3% were in Public Affairs, remainder in 6 other fields.

Graduates Career Data. According to most recent data available, advanced studies pursued by 12% of graduates; 2% enter medical school; 1% enter law school. Graduate and professional schools enrolling largest numbers of graduates include UW, Marquette, Medical College of Wisconsin. *Careers in business and industry* pursued by 40% of graduates. Corporations typically hiring largest numbers of graduates include Northwestern Mutual, Marshall & Ilsley, General Electric Medical Systems.

Faculty. About 71% of faculty hold doctorate.

Student Body. About 88% of students from in state; 15% foreign. An estimated 49% of students reported as Protestant, 37% Catholic; 3% Black, 27% Hispanic, 2% other minority, according to most recent data available.

Religious Orientation. Carroll is a church-related institution; completion of 1 course in religion and attendance at 3 "confrontations" and 3 assemblies yearly required of all students. Religious clubs on campus include Committee on Religious Life, Intervarsity, denominational clubs. Places of worship available on campus for all major faiths.

Varsity Sports. Men (Div.III): Baseball, Basketball, Cross Country, Football, Golf, Swimming & Diving, Tennis, Track, Wrestling. Women (Div.III): Basketball, Cross Country, Golf, Softball, Swimming & Diving, Tennis, Track, Volleyball.

Campus Life. Students allowed considerable freedom and self-governance, including alternate-floor coed dorm option. All non-commuters required to live in residence halls except seniors. Rules for women the same as for men; open intervisitation (visitors must be escorted). Alcohol permitted in rooms for those of legal age (21). Student interest in fraternities/sororities strong, but declining; student interest in intercollegiate athletics strong and on rise for women's athletics. Waukesha growing as cultural center; Milwaukee about 18 miles from campus.

About 16% of women live in traditional dormitories; 55% of men, 55% of women live in coed dormitories; 34% of men, 29% of women live in off-campus housing or commute. Freshmen given preference in college housing if all students cannot be accommodated. There are 5 fraternities, 4 sororities on campus which about 24% of men, 18% of women join; 11% of men live in fraternities; sororities provide no residence facilities.

Annual Costs. Tuition and fees, $11,790; room and board, $3,740. About 90% of students receive financial aid; assistance is typically divided 67% scholarship, 25% loan, 8% work. College reports some scholarships awarded on the basis of academic merit alone. *Meeting Costs:* college offers flexible payment plans.

Carson-Newman College

Jefferson City, Tennessee 37760 (615) 471-3223

A church-related college, located in a town of 6,000, 30 miles east of Knoxville. Most convenient major airport: McGhee-Tyson (Knoxville).

Founded: 1851
Affiliation: Southern Baptist
Total Enrollment: 1,945 M, W (full-time)
Cost: < $10K
% Receiving Financial Aid: 88%
Admission: Non-selective
Application Deadline: May 1

Admission. High school graduates with 16 units with a GPA of 2.0, rank in top half of class, and ACT of 17.0 eligible; 82% of applicants accepted, 50% of these actually enroll; 50% of freshmen graduate in top fifth of high school class. Average freshman ACT scores, according to most recent data available: 21.8 composite. *Required:* ACT, pastor's recommendation. *Non-academic factors* considered in admissions: special talents, alumni children, religious affiliation and/or commitment. *Apply* by May 1. *Transfers* welcome.

Academic Environment. *Degrees:* AB, BM, BS, BSN. About 50% of general education requirements for graduation are elective. About 44% of students entering as freshmen graduate eventually; 69% of freshmen return for sophomore year. *Special programs:* CLEP, independent study, study abroad, London Semester, honors, undergraduate research, optional May miniterm, Center for Baptist Studies, Center for Educational Service to Appalachia, Wellness Center, Church Music Center. *Calendar:* early semester, summer school.

Undergraduate degrees conferred (376). 23% were in Business and Management, 16% were in Education, 13% were in Social Sciences, 8% were in Psychology, 7% were in Life Sciences, 7% were in Communications, 5% were in Visual and Performing Arts, 4% were in Home Economics, 3% were in Letters, remainder in 9 other fields.

Graduates Career Data. Advanced studies pursued by 25% of graduates; 5% enter medical school; 5% enter seminary. *Careers in business and industry* pursued by 25% of graduates.

Faculty. About 63% of faculty hold PhD or equivalent.

Student Body. About 67% of students from Tennessee; 92% from South. An estimated 91% of students reported as Protestant, 2% Catholic, 7% unaffiliated; 3% Black, 1% other minority, according to most recent data available.

Religious Orientation. Carson-Newman is a church-related institution; strong Baptist religious emphasis on campus; 6 semester hours of religion, attendance at weekly chapel services required of all students. Student religious groups on campus all Baptist.

Varsity Sports. Men (NAIA): Baseball, Basketball, Cross Country, Football, Golf, Tennis, Track, Wrestling. Women (NAIA): Basketball, Cross Country, Softball, Tennis, Track, Volleyball.

Campus Life. About 58% of students live in traditional dormitories; no coed dormitories; rest live in off-campus housing or commute. Intervisitation in men's and women's dormitory rooms limited to special occasions only. There are no fraternities or sororities. About 65% of students leave campus on weekends.

Annual Costs. Tuition and fees, $7,850; room and board, $3,000; estimated $2,200 other, exclusive of travel. About 88% of students receive financial aid. Assistance is typically divided 25% grants, 25% scholarship, 40% loan, 10% work. College reports some scholarships awarded on the basis of academic merit alone. *Meeting Costs:* college offers AMS payment plan, Sibling Discount.

Carthage College

Kenosha, Wisconsin 53140 (414) 551-6000

A church-related, liberal arts college, located in a city of 78,000, midway between Chicago and Milwaukee. The 75-acre campus is on the shore of Lake Michigan. Most convenient major airports: Milwaukee, O'Hare (Chicago).

Founded: 1847
Affiliation: Lutheran
Total Enrollment: 642 M, 762 W (full-time); 179 M, 391 W (part-time)
Cost: $10K–$20K
% Receiving Financial Aid: 92%
Admission: Non-selective
Application Deadline: May 1

Admission. High school graduates with 14 academic units who rank in top half of class eligible; 85% of applicants accepted, 31% of these actually enroll; 36% of freshmen graduate in top fifth of high school class, 63% in top two-fifths. Average freshman scores: SAT, 460 M, 460 W verbal, 514 M, 490 W mathematical; 34% of freshman score above 500 on verbal, 9% above 600; 46% freshman score above 500 on mathematical, 30% above 600, 5% above 700; ACT, 22 M, 23 W composite. *Required:* SAT or ACT; interview suggested. Criteria considered in admissions, in order of importance: high school academic record, standardized test scores, extracurricular activities, recommendations; other factors considered: special talents, alumni children, diverse student body, religious affiliation and/or commitment. *Entrance programs:* early decision, early admission, midyear admission, deferred admission, advanced placement. About 20% of freshmen from private schools. *Apply* by May 1; rolling admissions. *Transfers* welcome; 94 enrolled 1993–94.

Academic Environment. Degrees offered: bachelors, masters. Graduation requirements include 4 semesters of heritage studies, 1 of history or philosophy, 1 of literature, 1 of fine arts, 2 of sciences, 1 of mathematics, 2 of social sciences, 2 of religious studies, and 2 7-week courses in physical education. Unusual majors offered: exercise and sports science. Average undergraduate class size: 20.

About 50% of students entering as freshmen graduate within four years, 60% eventually; 72% of freshmen return for sophomore year. *Special programs:* 3–2 engineering, 3–2 occupational therapy, independent study, study abroad, honors. Adult programs: evening/weekend program, advising, 4 undergraduate majors can be fully completed evenings/weekends. *Calendar:* 4–1–4, summer school.

Undergraduate degrees conferred (234). 41% were in Business and Management, 17% were in Education, 9% were in Social Sciences, 6% were in Protective Services, 4% were in Visual and Performing Arts, 3% were in Psychology, 3% were in Philosophy and Religion, 3% were in Public Affairs, 3% were in Physical Sciences, 3% were in Parks and Recreation, remainder in 5 other fields.

Graduates Career Data. Advanced studies pursued by 17% of graduates; 11% enter graduate school. About 95% of 1992–93 graduates employed. Fields typically employing largest numbers of graduates include accounting, business administration, elementary education, marketing. Career Development Services offers resume writing workshops, on-campus recruitment and interviewing, information on graduate schools, career fairs and career counseling.

Faculty. About 89% of faculty hold PhD or equivalent. About 51% of undergraduate classes taught by tenured faculty. About 29% of the teaching faculty are female.

Student Body. About 64% of students from Wisconsin; 98% Midwest. An estimated 58% of students reported as Protestant, 27% Catholic, 1% Jewish; 6% as Black, 2% Hispanic, 1% Asian.

Religious Orientation. Carthage is a church-related institution; 21% of students affiliated with this church; 2 courses in religion required of all students; attendance at weekly chapel services required unless there is a religious conflict.

Varsity Sports. Men (Div.III): Baseball, Basketball, Cross Country, Football, Golf, Swimming, Tennis, Track, Wrestling. Women (Div.III): Basketball, Cross Country, Golf, Softball, Swimming, Tennis, Track, Volleyball.

Campus Life. About 26% of women live in traditional dormitories; 90% men, 64% of women live in coed dormitories; 10% of men, 10% of women commute. Freshmen given preference in college housing if all students cannot be accommodated. Intervisitation in men's and women's dormitory rooms limited. There are 8 fraternities, 4 sororities on campus which about 18% of men, 25% of women join; fraternities and sororities are located in wings of residence halls. About 25% of resident students leave campus on weekends.

Annual Costs. Tuition and fees, $12,400; room and board, $3,595; estimated $1,500 other, exclusive of travel. About 92% of students receive financial aid; average amount of assistance, $10,100. Assistance is typically divided 32% scholarship, 22% grant, 41% loan, 5% work. College reports 115 scholarships awarded on the basis of academic merit alone, 54 on special talents alone, 14 on need alone. *Meeting Costs:* college offers Budget Payment Plan, and various other methods of financing.

Case Western Reserve University

Cleveland, Ohio 44106 (216) 368-4450

Case Western Reserve was created through the federation of Case Institute of Technology, a school of engineering and science with a national reputation, and Western Reserve University, a liberal arts and professional institution of high regional repute. Today Case Western Reserve is an independent research university comprised of a college of arts and sciences, a graduate school, and professional schools of dentistry, engineering, law, management, medicine, nursing, and social work. Undergraduates are admitted to the university, not to the separate colleges, and may pursue interests in arts and sciences, management, and engineering. The 128-acre main campus is located in Cleveland's University Circle, home of many of the city's major cultural institutions, including a nationally known symphony orchestra and art museum. Most convenient major airport: Cleveland Hopkins International.

Founded: 1826
Affiliation: Independent
UG Enrollment: 1,823 M, 1,228 W (full-time); 220 M, 293 W (part-time)
Total Enrollment: 9,276
Cost: $10K–$20K
% Receiving Financial Aid: 83%
Admission: Highly Selective
Application Deadline: Feb. 15

Admission is highly selective. About 81% of applicants accepted, 23% of these actually enroll; 89% of freshmen graduate in top fifth of high school class, 99% in top two-fifths. Average freshman scores: SAT, middle 50% range, 510–640 verbal, 610–730 mathematical; 79% of freshmen score above 500 on verbal, 43% above 600, 9% above 700; 97% score above 500 on mathematical, 80% above 600, 44% above 700; ACT, middle 50% range, 26–31 composite. *Required:* SAT or ACT; writing sample. Criteria considered in admissions, in order of importance: high school academic record/standardized test scores given equal rank, recommendations/extracurricular activities/writing sample given equal rank; special talents, skills and abilities, and diverse student body, also considered. *Entrance programs:* early decision, early admission, midyear admission, deferred admission, advanced placement. About 30% of entering students from private and parochial schools. *Apply* by February 15. *Transfers* welcome; 132 enrolled 1993–94.

Academic Environment. Undergraduate students pursue degrees through 1 of 3 core programs. The Case Core emphasizes the sciences, mathematics, and computer sciences with elective courses in the liberal arts and leads to a BS in engineering, mathematics, the sciences, or management science. The Western Reserve Core leads to a BA in the humanities, arts, social sciences, or natural sciences, as well as a BS in accountancy, management, nutrition, art and music education, or medical technology. The Lambda (liberal arts/mathematics-based alternative) Core curriculum combines mathematics, computing technology, and liberal arts for students looking toward careers that demand quantitative skills as well as the broad perspective gained through liberal arts courses. Degrees offered: bachelors, masters, doctoral. Unusual, new, or notable majors include: anthropology, astronomy, biotechnology, dramatic arts, medical technology, nursing, nutrition, polymer science, statistics. Joint programs in music and art with Cleveland Institute of Music, and Cleveland Institute of Art.

About 72% of students entering as freshmen graduate eventually; 91% of freshmen return for sophomore year. Average undergraduate class size: 53% 20 or under, 29% 21–40, 18% over 40. *Special programs:* independent study, undergraduate research, individualized majors, study abroad, Washington Semester, integrated graduate and professional studies at CWR (law, management, nursing, social work, dentistry), "senior year in absentia" for students admitted to other medical or dental schools, 6-year dental program, co-op education (in engineering, science, management, accountancy), Minority Engineers Industrial Opportunity Program, professional practicum (in liberal arts, management, accountancy), 3–2 programs (engineering, astronomy, biochemistry), cross registration with schools in Cleveland area. *Calendar:* early semester (2 4-month semesters, fall semester begins in late August), summer school.

Undergraduate degrees conferred (619). 39% were in Engineering, 11% were in Social Sciences, 11% were in Business and Management, 9% were in Psychology, 8% were in Physical Sciences, 7% were in Life Sciences, 5% were in Letters, 3% were in Visual and Performing Arts, remainder in 10 other fields.

Graduates Career Data. Advanced studies pursued by 39% of 1991–92 graduates; 8% of students enter medical school; 1% enter dental school; 5% enter law school; 4% enter business school. Medical schools typically enrolling largest numbers of graduates include CWRU, Ohio State, Johns Hopkins; dental schools include CWRU, Ohio State; law schools include CWRU, Ohio State; business schools include CWRU, Cleveland State. About 53% of 1991–92 graduates employed. Employers typically hiring largest numbers of graduates include Andersen Consulting, Ernst & Young, Lincoln Electric. Office of Career Planning and Placement offers resume and interview workshops, career counseling, aptitude testing, internships and cooperative education, on-campus interviewing, and a library of occupational and employer information.

Faculty. About 97% of faculty hold PhD or equivalent. About 53% of undergraduate classes taught by tenured faculty. About 27% of teaching faculty are female.

Student Body. About 62% of students from in state; 69% Midwest, 14% Middle Atlantic, 2% New England, 4% South; 8% foreign. An estimated 7% of students reported as Black, 2% Hispanic, 10% Asian, 5% other minority. Disadvantaged students: university offers "academic support services and intense counseling."

Varsity Sports. Men (Div.III): Baseball, Basketball, Cross Country, Diving, Fencing, Football, Golf, Soccer, Swimming, Tennis, Track, Wrestling. Women (Div.III): Basketball, Cross Country, Diving, Fencing, Soccer, Swimming, Tennis, Track, Volleyball.

Campus Life. A single Office of Student Affairs oversees housing and extracurricular activities for students. Students appear to have substantial control over most aspects of campus social life; participate directly in representative assemblies. Cars allowed; rules for alcoholic beverages conform to state laws. Off-campus housing possible for students over 21.

About 3% of students live in traditional dormitories; 52% of students live in coed dormitories; 16% live in off-campus housing; 15% commute. All students are guaranteed college housing. Intervisitation in men's and women's dormitory rooms unlimited. There are 18 fraternities, 5 sororities on campus which about 40% of men, 20% of women join; 30% of students live in fraternities and sororities. About 15% of resident students leave campus on weekends.

Annual Costs. Tuition and fees, $15,320; room and board, $4,590; estimated $1,650 other, exclusive of travel. About 83% of students receive financial aid (including outside scholarships); average amount of assistance, $14,280. Assistance is typically divided 60% scholarship, 26% loan, 14% work. University reports 275 scholarships awarded to Fall 1993 freshmen on the basis of academic merit alone, 3 on special talents alone. *Meeting Costs:* university offers Tuition Stabilization Program, tuition stays at current rate when 4 years of tuition is prepaid, also offers a loan feature for all or portion of funds to be borrowed to participate in Tuition Stabilization Program.

Castleton State College

Castleton, Vermont 05735 **(802) 468-5611**

A state-supported college, located in the center of the Green Mountains, in a village of 2,800, 12 miles west of Rutland. Most convenient major airport: Rutland County.

Founded: 1787
Affiliation: State
UG Enrollment: 758 M, 808 W (full-time); 101 M, 202 W (part-time)
Total Enrollment: 2,089
Cost: < $10K
% Receiving Financial Aid: 75%
Admission: Non-selective
Application Deadline: Rolling

Admission. Graduates of accredited high schools with 16 units (12 in academic subjects) eligible; 75% of applicants accepted, 40% of these actually enroll; 18% of freshmen graduate in top fifth of their high school class, 41% in top two-fifths. Average freshman scores: SAT, 423 verbal, 473 mathematical; ACT 21 composite. *Required:* SAT or ACT; essay. Criteria considered in admissions, in order of importance: high school academic record, standardized test scores, writing sample, recommendations, extracurricular activities; other factors considered: special talents, diverse student body. *Out-of-state* freshman applicants: college actively seeks students from out-of-state; 69% accepted, 38% enrolled. *Out-of-state* enrollment limited to 50% of entering class. States from which most out-of-state students are drawn from New York, Massachusetts, Connecticut, New Jersey. About 15% of freshman come from private or parochial schools. *Apply:* rolling admissions. *Transfers* welcome; 178 enrolled 1993–94.

Academic Environment. Graduation requirements include 2 courses each: communication, math, science, 3 courses in literature and the arts, choice of 1 course in computers, foreign cultures, history, philosophy/psychological analysis, or social analysis, 2 courses in "Soundings" (cultural exposure to noted speakers, plays, and concerts). Degrees offered: associates, bachelors, masters. Small class size and faculty who are "willing to help" and "very down to earth" cited as particular strengths by students. Unusual, new, or notable majors include: athletic training, exercise technology, geology, criminal justice, corporate communications. About 71% of freshmen return for sophomore year. Average undergraduate class size: 15% under 20. *Special programs:* CLEP, independent study, study abroad, 3–2 engineering, work-study programs. *Calendar:* semester, summer school.

Undergraduate degrees conferred (223). 23% were in Business and Management, 22% were in Education, 11% were in Communications, 7% were in Visual and Performing Arts, 6% were in Protective Services, 5% were in Social Sciences, 4% were in Letters, 4% were in Multi/Interdisciplinary Studies, 3% were in Psychology, 3% were in Allied Health, remainder in 7 other fields.

Graduates Career Data. Advanced studies pursued by 22% of graduates; 10% enter business school. About 93% of 1991–92 graduates employed.

Faculty. About 84% of faculty hold PhD or equivalent. About 58% of undergraduate classes taught by tenured faculty. About 35% of the teaching faculty are female; 2% Black, 2% Hispanic, 4% other minority.

Student Body. About 60% of students from in state; 85% New England, 13% Middle Atlantic. An estimated 2% of students reported as minority.

Varsity Sports. Men (Div.III): Baseball, Basketball, Cross Country, Lacrosse, Soccer, Tennis. Women (Div.III): Basketball, Cross Country, Lacrosse, Soccer, Softball, Tennis.

Campus Life. College is located in the Green Mountains. "An ideal location for those who love the outdoors and like all four seasons", according to administration source. Students agree that hiking, biking, rollerblading, skiing are popular.

About 49% of men, 51% of women live in coed dormitories; 38% of men, 34% of women live in off-campus housing; rest commute. Freshmen given preference in college housing if all students can not be accommodated. Intervisitation in freshmen women's dormitory rooms limited. There are no fraternities or sororities on campus. About 10–12% of resident students leave campus on weekends.

Annual Costs. Tuition and fees, $4,208 (out-of-state, $8,360); room and board, $4,640; estimated $1,000 other, exclusive of travel. About 75% of students receive financial aid; average amount of assistance, $5,117. Assistance is typically divided 37% scholarship, 53% loan, 10% work. College reports 20–30 scholarships awarded on the basis of academic merit and special talents alone. *Meeting Costs:* college offers AMS.

Catawba College

Salisbury, North Carolina 28144 **(704) 637-4402**

A church-related college, located in a town of 28,000, 40 miles northeast of Charlotte. Most convenient major airport: Charlotte, NC.

Founded: 1851
Affiliation: United Church of Christ
Total Enrollment: 482 M, 433 W (full-time)
Cost: < $10K
% Receiving Financial Aid: 85%
Admission: Non-selective
Application Deadline: Rolling

Admission. Graduates of accredited high schools with 16 units (12 in academic subjects) with GPA of 2.00 and SAT combined score of 700 eligible; 81% of applicants accepted, 33% of these actually enroll; 16% of freshmen graduate in top fifth of high school class, 43% in top two-fifths. Average freshman SAT scores: 22% of freshmen scored above 500 on verbal, 2% above 600; 43% of freshmen scored above 500 on mathematical, 11% above 600. *Required:* SAT, essay. Criteria considered in admissions, in order of importance: high school academic record, standardized test scores, writing sample, extracurricular activities, recommendations; other factors considered: alumni children, diverse student body, religious affiliation and/or commitment. *Entrance programs:* early admission, midyear admission, deferred admission, advanced placement. *Apply:* rolling admissions. *Transfers* welcome; 54 enrolled 1993–94.

Academic Environment. Graduation requirements include courses in math, science, humanities, foreign language, fine arts, and physical fitness. Degrees offered: bachelors. Unusual, new, or notable majors include: sports medicine, environmental science, international relations. About 32% of entering students graduate within four years, 45% eventually; 70% of freshmen return for sophomore year. Average undergraduate class size: 50% under 20, 45% 20–40, 5% over 40. *Special programs:* CLEP, study abroad, independent study, 3-year degree, individualized majors, 3–2 programs in medical technology, forestry and environmental studies. *Calendar:* early semester, summer school.

Undergraduate degrees conferred (194). 30% were in Business and Management, 19% were in Education, 10% were in Communications, 8% were in Visual and Performing Arts, 7% were in Social Sciences, 6% were in Letters, 6% were in Psychology, 4% were in Parks and Recreation, 3% were in Life Sciences, 3% were in Law, remainder in 6 other fields.

Graduates Career Data. Advanced studies pursued by 10% of graduates. About 70% of 1992–93 graduates employed. Career Development Services include aptitude testing, counseling, resume and interview workshops, and internships.

Faculty. About 85% of faculty hold PhD or equivalent. About 35% of teaching faculty are female.
Student Body. About 51% of students from in state; an estimated 7% reported as Black, 2% Hispanic, 1% Asian, 1% other minority.
Religious Orientation. Catawba is a church-related institution; attendance at 2 convocations and a number of other college-sponsored events required of all students each year.
Varsity Sports. Men (NCAA Div. II): Baseball, Basketball, Cross Country, Football, Golf, Lacrosse, Soccer, Tennis. Women (NCAA Div.II): Basketball, Cross Country, Diving, Field Hockey, Soccer, Softball, Swimming, Tennis, Volleyball.
Campus Life. About 68% of men, 57% of women live in traditional dormitories; rest live in off-campus housing or commute. Freshmen given preference in college housing if all students cannot be accommodated. Intervisitation in men's and women's dormitory rooms limited. There are no fraternities or sororities on campus. About 30% of resident students leave campus on weekends.
Annual Costs. Tuition and fees, $9,000; room and board, $3,950; estimated $1,000 other, exclusive of travel. About 85% of students receive financial aid; average amount of assistance, $6,082. Assistance typically divided 30% scholarship, 16% grant, 38% loan, 15% work. *Meeting Costs:* college offers payment plan.

Catholic University of America

Washington, D.C. 20064 (202) 319-5305

Founded as a national university by the Roman Catholic Bishops of the U.S., all curricula, with the exception of philosophy and religion, are now under lay rather than religious control. The student body remains predominantly Catholic, however. The university was founded as a graduate institute, but the undergraduate student body now makes up more than a third of the total enrollment. The 190-acre campus is located in the northeastern section of the nation's capital, 3 miles from downtown Washington. Most convenient major airport: Washington National.

Founded: 1887
Affiliation: Independent (Roman Catholic)
UG Enrollment: 979 M, 1,180 W (full-time); 82 M, 129 W (part-time)
Total Enrollment: 6,147
Cost: $10K–$20K
% Receiving Financial Aid: 40%
Admission: Very Selective
Application Deadline: February 15

Admission is very selective. For all schools, 85% of applicants accepted, 34% of these actually enroll; 36% of freshmen graduate in top fifth of high school class, 66% in top two-fifths. Average freshman SAT scores: 55% of freshmen score above 500 on verbal, 17% above 600, 2% above 700; 75% score above 500 on mathematical, 31% above 600, 6% above 700.

Required: SAT or ACT, essay, ACH (for Arts and Sciences: English, mathematics, choice of science, language; for Engineering and Architecture: English, mathematics II, science—preferably physics; for Nursing: English, mathematics, science; for Music: English), audition for Music; interview strongly recommended. Criteria considered in admissions, in order of importance: high school academic record, standardized test scores, recommendations; writing sample and extracurricular activities considered of equal importance; other factors considered: diverse student body, special talents, alumni children. *Entrance programs:* early admission, advanced placement, deferred admission. *Apply* by February 15. *Transfers* welcome; 161 enrolled 1993–94.
Academic Environment. Degrees offered: bachelors, masters, doctoral. Although traditional ecclesiastical control of the university has been weakened, changes in the academic environment have been less dramatic than on some similar campuses. There are indications, however, that students have some voice in curriculum and related matters. Student-organized course evaluations also influence faculty. Student body characterized as somewhat concerned with scholarly/intellectual pursuits, but very strongly oriented toward career goals. Desire of students for a School of Business to replace the business department in Arts and Sciences reported. General education requirements include 4 courses in religion and religious education, 4 in philosophy, 1 or 2 English composition, 3 in humanities, 4 in languages and literature, 4 in mathematics and natural sciences, and 4 in social and behavioral sciences. *Majors offered* include usual arts and sciences, accounting, anthropology, architecture, area studies, chemical physics, computer science, drama, elementary education, engineering, construction engineering, medical technology, nursing, social work, interdisciplinary major in medieval and Byzantine studies. New program in Communication Studies recently added. University Honors Program for selected students offers seminar style classes. Average undergraduate class size: 45% of classes under 20, 33% between 20–40, 2% over 40.

About 59% of students entering as freshmen graduate within four years, 74% eventually; 15% do not return for sophomore year. *Special programs:* CLEP, study abroad, honors, undergraduate research, 3-year degree, individualized majors, junior and senior seminars (required in Arts and Sciences), cross-registration through Washington Consortium, 3–2 programs in civil engineering and architecture. *Calendar:* semester, summer school.
Undergraduate degrees conferred (745). 28% were in Social Sciences, 13% were in Architecture and Environmental Design, 11% were in Business and Management, 9% were in Health Sciences, 7% were in Engineering, 7% were in Letters, 6% were in Visual and Performing Arts, 5% were in Psychology, 4% were in Philosophy and Religion, 3% were in Education, remainder in 7 other fields.
Graduates Career Data. Advanced studies pursued by 45% of graduates; 10% enter law school, 2% enter medical school. *Careers in business and industry:* Corporations typically hiring largest numbers of graduates include Ernst & Young, Continental Corp. *Career Counseling Program* reported to be good. Student leader enthuses "we have a great career guidance program with programs, workshops and available jobs at all times." Alumni said to be active in both career guidance and job placement, offering "lectures, interviews and one on one guidance."
Faculty. About 95% of faculty hold PhD or equivalent. About 33% of undergraduate classes are taught by tenured faculty. About 30% of teaching faculty are female; 11% ethnic minorities.
Student Body. About 41% of students from Middle Atlantic, 12% New England, 31% South, 4% Midwest, 2% West; 10% foreign. An estimated 90% of students reported as Catholic, 5% Protestant, 2% other, 3% unaffiliated; 7% Black, 5% Asian, 3% Hispanic.
Religious Orientation. Strong Catholic atmosphere on campus but students of all races and creeds welcome. All undergraduate students in Arts and Sciences take 4 courses each in religion, philosophy; non-Catholics take separate courses in religion and are excused from religious observances. Places of worship available on campus for Catholics, in immediate community for all faiths.
Varsity Sports. Men (Div.III): Baseball, Basketball, Cross Country, Football, Soccer, Swimming, Tennis, Track. Women (Div. III): Basketball, Cross Country, Field Hockey, Soccer, Softball, Swimming, Tennis, Track, Volleyball.
Campus Life. Student leader characterizes typical C.U. student as "friendly, energetic, responsible, and also very Catholic," but adds "my friends that aren't Catholic don't feel misplaced." Cars allowed, campus registration required; drinking permitted in residence halls and campus pub in compliance with D.C. laws. Strong interest expressed in "all intramural sports," most popular: football, softball, basketball.

About 11% of men, 19% of women live in traditional dormitories; 38% of men, 34% of women live in coed dormitories; rest commute. There is 1 fraternity, 1 sorority on campus.
Annual Costs. Tuition and fees, $13,614; room and board, $6,220; estimated $1,580 other, exclusive of travel. About 40% of students receive financial aid; average amount of assistance, $12,178. Assistance is typically divided 56% scholarship/grant, 40% loan, 4% work. University reports 323 scholarships awarded on the basis of academic merit alone, 80 for special talents, 877 for need. *Meeting Costs:* university offers Concern loan program, 12-month payment plan.

Catholic University of Puerto Rico

(see Pontifical Catholic University of Puerto Rico)

Cedar Crest College

Allentown, Pennsylvania 18104 (215) 437-4471

An independent college affiliated with the United Church of Christ, Cedar Crest offers a combination of pre-professional career preparation and liberal arts. Cooperative activities with five other neighboring private colleges expand opportunities. The 84-acre campus is a national arboretum, located in a residential section of a city of 109,500, 55 miles north of Philadelphia and 90 miles west of New York City. Most convenient major airport: Allentown-Bethlehem-Easton.

Founded: 1867	**Cost:** $10K–$20K
Affiliation: United Church of Christ	**% Receiving Financial Aid:** 90%
Total Enrollment: 18 M, 773 W (full-time); 74 M, 680 W (part-time)	**Admission:** Selective
	Application Deadline: August 1

Admission is selective. About 80% of applicants accepted, 31% of these actually enroll; 39% of freshmen graduate in top fifth of high school class, 68% in top two-fifths. Average freshman scores: SAT, 469 verbal, 489 mathematical; 33% of freshmen score above 500 on verbal, 7% above 600, 1% above 700; 42% of freshmen score above 500 on mathematical, 7% above 600, 2% above 700; ACT, 24 composite. *Required:* SAT or ACT, essay. Criteria considered in admissions, in order of importance: high school academic record, standardized test scores, recommendations, writing sample, extracurricular activities; other factors considered: special talents, alumni children, diverse student body. *Entrance programs:* early admission, midyear admission, deferred admission, advanced placement. *Apply* by August 1; rolling admissions. *Transfers* welcome; 100 enrolled 1993–94.

Academic Environment. Students are voting members on a majority of faculty committees and on the Board of Trustees. Graduation requirements include 3 credit writing course, 6 credits international language, Junior Seminar, 9 credits each in humanities, Historical Societal, arts, and 8 credit lab science. Students reports academic strengths are: "approachable, reasonable professors and administrators" and the real life experience of their professors. Degrees offered: bachelors. Unusual, new, or notable majors include: genetic engineering, nursing, nuclear medicine, medical technology, paralegal studies. Average undergraduate class size: 78% under 20; 20% 20–40, 2% over 40.

About 59% of students entering as freshmen graduate within four years, 63% eventually; 83% of freshmen return for sophomore year. *Special programs:* CLEP, honors, undergraduate research, independent study, study abroad, interdisciplinary majors, self-designed majors, cooperative programs including cross-registration through members of Lehigh Valley Association, internships, acceleration, Washington Semester, India Semester, Harrisburg Urban Semester, teacher certification program, 3–2 programs (engineering, industrial management, computer and information science, and health systems management), English as Second Language. Adult programs: numerous degree and certification evening programs available. *Calendar:* semester.

Undergraduate degrees conferred (179). 24% were in Health Sciences, 14% were in Business and Management, 12% were in Education, 11% were in Psychology, 7% were in Social Sciences, 6% were in Communications, 4% were in Visual and Performing Arts, 4% were in Letters, 3% were in Life Sciences, remainder in 9 other fields.

Graduates Career Data. Advanced studies pursued by 26% of graduates; 4% enter business school; 2% enter law school; 2% enter medical school. Medical schools typically enrolling largest numbers of graduates include Hahneman U.; law schools include U. of Pennsylvania; business schools include Villanova, U. of Pennsylvania. About 90% of 1992–93 graduates employed. Employers typically hiring largest numbers of graduates include Air Products, hospitals, KPMG Peat Marwick. Career Development Services include career counseling, career courses and workshops, resume bank and critique service, resume production service, job listings, career resource library, on-campus recruiting, and SIGI-Plus computerized career guidance system.

Faculty. About 78% of faculty hold PhD or equivalent. About 61% of teaching faculty are female.

Student Body. About 83% of students from in state; 94% Middle Atlantic, 2% New England, 3% foreign. An estimated 50% of students reported as Protestant, 40% Catholic, 1% Jewish, 1% Muslim, 6% unaffiliated, 2% other; 2% Black, 2% Hispanic, 2% Asian, 1% other minority. *Minority group students:* financial aid and tutoring as needed.

Religious Orientation. Cedar Crest is a church-related institution, but makes no religious demands on students; 10% of students affiliated with the church.

Varsity Sports Women (NCAA Div.III): Basketball, Cross Country, Field Hockey, Lacrosse, Tennis, Track, Volleyball.

Campus Life. Proximity to other colleges enhances student life, while allowing students the advantages of a small, women's college, especially access to leadership positions, and community spirit. Cars allowed for all students; students over 21 permitted to drink at parties and in dormitory rooms. Three intervisitation options open to students ranging from limited hours to complete freedom.

About 85% of women live in dormitories; rest commute. There are no sororities on campus. About 30% of students leave campus on weekends.

Annual Costs. Tuition and fees, $13,720; room and board, $5,210; estimated $1,500 other, exclusive of travel. About 90% of students receive financial aid; average amount of assistance, $12,000. Assistance is typically divided 7% scholarship, 60% grant, 28% loan, 5% work. College reports 126 scholarships awarded on the basis of academic merit alone, 4 for special talents alone, 512 for need alone. *Meeting Costs:* college offers parent loan program, monthly payment plan, sibling grants (to families with students enrolled), special loans with "forgiveness" for education and nursing majors.

Cedarville College

Cedarville, Ohio 45314 **(513) 766-2211**

Cedarville is a Baptist college which offers a "liberal arts curriculum (LBRK)which(RBRK) is coupled with an evangelical, conservative theological position in regard to doctrine and patterns of conduct." Most convenient major airport: Dayton.

Founded: 1887	**Cost:** < $10K
Affiliation: Baptist	**% Receiving Financial Aid:** 75%
Total Enrollment: 950 M, 1,246 W (full-time)	**Admission:** Non-selective
	Application Deadline: Rolling

Admission. Admissions committee "bases its choice" on (1) the applicant's "evidence of personal faith in Jesus Christ" and having lived a Christian life; (2) his academic ability and rank in class; (3) his scholastic ability as shown by the ACT or SAT. About 83% of applicants accepted, 57% of these actually enroll; about 45% of freshmen graduate in top fifth of high school class; 73% in top two fifths. Average freshman scores: SAT, 491 M, 481 W verbal, 544 M, 507 W mathematical; ACT, 24 M, 23 W composite. About 43% of freshman from parochial schools. *Apply:* rolling admissions. *Transfers* welcome; 102 enrolled in 1993–94.

Academic Environment. Graduation requirements include 80–90 quarter hours of writing, humanities, science, and social science. Degrees offered: associates, bachelors. *Special programs:* honors, study abroad. About 49% of entering students graduate within four years, 55% eventually; 80% of freshmen return for sophomore year. *Calendar:* quarter, summer school.

Undergraduate degrees conferred (289). 25% were in Business and Management, 19% were in Education, 11% were in Health Sciences, 9% were in Communications, 8% were in Theology, 8% were in Psychology, 4% were in Mathematics, 4% were in Social Sciences, 3% were in Letters, remainder in 5 other fields.

Graduates Career Data. Advanced studies pursued by 18% of 1991–92 graduates. About 80% of 1991–92 graduates employed. Career Development Services include interest testing, workshops and library of resources.

Faculty. About 52% of faculty hold PhD or equivalent. About 51% of undergraduate classes taught by tenured faculty. About 28% of teaching faculty are female; 2% Black, 1% Hispanic, 2% other minority.

Student Body. About 35% of students from in state; 63% Midwest, 21% Middle Atlantic, 6% New England, 5% South, 2% West, 1% foreign. All students reported as Protestant; 1% Black, 3% other minority.

Religious Orientation. College is a church-related institution; 63% of students affiliated with this church; 12 courses in Biblical education required of all students.

Varsity Sports. Men (NAIA Div.I): Baseball, Basketball, Cross Country, Golf, Soccer, Tennis, Track. Women (NAIA Div.I): Basketball, Cross Country, Softball, Tennis, Track, Volleyball.

Campus Life. Students under 25 expected to live in campus residence halls unless they are living at home. About 79% of men, 87% of women live in traditional dormitories; rest live in off-campus housing or commute. Freshmen given preference in college housing if all students cannot be accommodated. There are no fraternities or sororities on campus.

Annual Costs. Tuition and fees, $6,959; room and board, $3,756; estimated $1,570 other, exclusive of travel. About 75% of students receive financial aid; average amount of assistance, $7,725. College reports 400 scholarships awarded on the basis of academic merit alone, 30 on special talents alone.

Centenary College

Hackettstown, New Jersey 07840 (201) 852-1400

Long a prestigious 2-year college for women, with a strong liberal arts transfer program, Centenary now also offers 4-year specialized baccalaureate degree programs. The college went coed in April of 1988; residence halls and a sports program for men have been in place since 1989. The campus is located in a town of 16,000, 52 miles west of New York City. Most convenient major airports: Newark, New York City area.

Founded: 1867
Affiliation: Independent
Total Enrollment: 899 M, W (full-time); 99 M, 356 W (part-time)
Cost: < $10K
% Receiving Financial Aid: 75%
Admission: Non-selective
Application Deadline: Rolling

Admission. Graduates of accredited high schools with GPA of 2.5 eligible. About 92% of applicants accepted; 15% of freshmen graduate in top fifth of high school class, 42% in top two-fifths. Average freshman SAT scores, according to most recent data available: 350 M, 380 W verbal, 360 M, 400 W mathematical. *Required:* SAT or ACT; interview strongly recommended. *Non-academic factors* considered in admissions: special talents. *Apply:* rolling admissions. *Transfers* welcome.

Academic Environment. *Degrees:* BA, BS, BFA. Degree programs offered in art and graphic design, communications, computer science, education, equine studies, fashion design, fashion merchandising/retailing, liberal arts, business administration/management, psychology, computer technology. About 50% of entering students graduate within four years; 25% of freshmen do not return for sophomore year. *Calendar:* semester.

Undergraduate degrees conferred (123). 32% were in Business and Management, 17% were in Liberal/General Studies, 15% were in Psychology, 11% were in Letters, 7% were in Agribusiness and Agricultural Production, 6% were in Architecture and Environmental Design, 5% were in Computer and Engineering Related Technology, 5% were in Marketing and Distribution, remainder in Communications.

Graduates Career Data. *Careers in business and industry* pursued by 54% of graduates.

Faculty. About 80% of faculty hold PhD or equivalent terminal degree.

Student Body. About 75% of students from New Jersey. An estimated 12% of students reported as Black, 3% Hispanic, according to most recent data available.

Varsity Sports. Men: Basketball, Soccer. Women: Basketball, Cross Country, Equine Riding Team, Softball, Swimming, Tennis, Volleyball.

Campus Life. About 44% of men, 53% of women live in traditional dormitories; 16% of men, 6% of women live in coed dormitories; rest commute. Housing is guaranteed for four years. There are 3 sororities, 1 fraternity, which about 21% of women, 18% of men join. About 57% of students leave campus on weekends.

Annual Costs. Tuition and fees, $11,500; room and board, $5,400. About 75% of students receive financial aid; average amount of assistance, 60–70% of need. Assistance is typically divided 50% scholarship, 40% loan, 10% work. College reports some scholarships awarded on the basis of academic merit alone. *Meeting Costs:* college offers tuition funding agencies, PLUS Loans.

Centenary College of Louisiana

Shreveport, Louisiana 71104 (318) 869-5131

A Methodist college, located in a metropolitan area of 300,000. Most convenient major airport: Shreveport Regional.

Founded: 1825
Affiliation: United Methodist
UG Enrollment: 345 M, 430 W (full-time)
Total Enrollment: 1,026
Cost: < $10K
% Receiving Financial Aid: 82%
Admission: Selective (+)
Application Deadline: May 1

Admission is selective (+). About 87% of applicants accepted, 40% of these actually enroll; 50% of freshmen graduate in top fifth of high school class, 72% in top two-fifths. Average freshman scores: SAT, 500 verbal, 550 mathematical; 53% of freshmen score above 500 on verbal, 16% above 600, 2% above 700; 67% score above 500 on mathematical, 32% above 600, 2% above 700; ACT, 24.5 composite. *Required:* SAT or ACT, minimum HS GPA 2.5, essay, recommendations, interview. Criteria considered in admissions, in order of importance: high school academic record, standardized test scores, writing sample, recommendations, interview, extracurricular activities; other factors considered: special talents, alumni children. *Entrance programs:* early admission, midyear admission, deferred admission, advanced placement. About 35% of entering students from private schools, 15% parochial. *Apply* by May 1; rolling admissions. *Transfers* welcome, 49 enrolled 1993–94.

Academic Environment. Graduation requirements include 2 courses in English, 2 in General Education, 1 in exercise science, 2 in lab sciences, 1–2 in mathematics, 3 in art, music, theater, speech or foreign language, 4 in religion, history and philosophy, 3 in economics, political science, psychology, or sociology; students must also have a service learning experience, experience in another culture, and career exploration. Supportive faculty and diverse student body considered strengths by student source; administration source adds high medical/law school acceptance rate. Degrees offered: bachelors, masters. Unusual, new, or notable majors include: biophysics, geology, biochemistry.

About 40% of students entering as freshmen graduate within four years, 53% within five years; 73% of freshmen return for sophomore year. *Special programs:* CLEP, independent study, study abroad, honors, undergraduate research, individualized majors, 3–2 programs in engineering, forestry, speech and language pathology. *Calendar:* semester, May module, summer school.

Undergraduate degrees conferred (170). 19% were in Social Sciences, 15% were in Education, 15% were in Business and Management, 9% were in Life Sciences, 9% were in Physical Sciences, 8% were in Psychology, 6% were in Letters, 5% were in Visual and Performing Arts, 5% were in Multi/Interdisciplinary Studies, 4% were in Theology, 4% were in Foreign Languages, remainder in 2 other fields.

Graduates Career Data. Advanced studies pursued by 31% of graduates; 12% enter medical school; 4% enter law school; 2% enter business school; 1% enter dental school. About 50% of 1992–93 graduates employed. Career Development Center starts working with students in the freshman year and offers seminars in interviewing techniques, resume workshops, and career and major exploration.

Faculty. About 92% of faculty hold PhD or equivalent. About 22% of teaching faculty are female; 3% Hispanic.

Student Body. About 60% of students from in state; an estimated 66% of students reported as Protestant, 17% Catholic, 1% Jewish, 13% unaffiliated, 3% other; 6% Black, 2% Hispanic, 2% Asian, 5% other minority.

Religious Orientation. Centenary is a church-related institution. Students are required to take 1 religious course.

Varsity Sports. Men (Div.I): Baseball, Basketball, Cross Country, Golf, Soccer, Tennis, Track. Women (Div.I): Cross Country, Gymnastics, Soccer, Softball, Tennis, Track, Volleyball.

Campus Life. Shreveport offers city ballet company, and symphony, while college theatre department has productions throughout the year. Greek influence reported "small, but positive" and "Greeks here don't party all the time—they take academics seriously."

About 56% of men, 67% of women live in traditional dormitories; no coed dormitories; rest live in off-campus housing or commute. Intervisitation in men's and women's dormitory rooms limited. There are 4 fraternities, 2 sororities on campus which about 24% of men, 24% of women join. About 10% of resident students leave campus on weekends.

Annual Costs. Tuition and fees, $8,446; room and board, $3,200; estimated $1,200 other, exclusive of travel. About 82% of students receive financial aid; average amount of assistance, $7,300.

College reports 112 scholarships awarded on the basis of academic merit alone, 71 for special talents alone, 109 for need alone. *Meeting Costs:* college offers guaranteed tuition plan.

Center for Creative Studies

Detroit, Michigan 48202

A private, professional college of art and design, the Center for Creative Studies is located in the heart of Detroit's University Cultural Center. Degree programs offered include: Graphic Communication, Industrial Design, Photography, Fine Arts, and Transportation Design. Graduates typically employed by arts companies, advertising agencies, photography studios, and the auto industry.

Founded: 1906 **Affiliation:** Independent

Central College

Pella, Iowa 50219 **(800) 458-5503**

A church-related, liberal arts university located in a community of 9,000, 45 minutes southeast of Des Moines. Most convenient major airport: Des Moines International.

Founded: 1853
Affiliation: Reformed Church
Total Enrollment: 643 M, 855 W (full-time)
Cost: $10K–$20K
% Receiving Financial Aid: 97%
Admission: Selective (+)
Application Deadline: Aug. 1

Admission is selective (+). About 87% of applicants accepted, 36% of these actually enroll; 53% of freshmen graduate in top fifth of high school class, 69% in top two-fifths. Average freshman ACT scores: 23 composite. *Required:* SAT or ACT; interview recommended. Criteria considered in admission, in order of importance: high school academic record, standardized test scores, recommendations, writing samples, extracurricular activities; other factors considered: special talents, alumni children, diverse student body, religious affiliation and/or commitment. *Entrance programs:* mid-year admission, deferred admission, advanced placement. *Apply* by August 1; rolling admissions. *Transfers* welcome; 49 enrolled 1993–94.

Academic Environment. Student observes that the trimester system "enables us to study 3 topics intensely for 10 weeks, and then move on to a completely new schedule." However, she also notes that "the study is intense and much work is expected to be done outside the classroom." Administration reports 17% of courses required for graduation are elective. All departments have English proficiency standards, verbal and written, that must be met by majors before graduation. Degrees offered: bachelors. Unusual, new, or notable majors include: interdisciplinary concentrations in pre-medical science, linguistics, recreation, international management, urban studies, international studies.

About 63% of students entering as freshmen graduate within four years, 72% eventually; 82% of freshmen return for sophomore year. Average undergraduate class size: 15% of classes under 20; 80% 20–40, 5% over 40. *Special programs:* honors, independent study, study abroad (50% of students study abroad at some point), undergraduate research, individualized majors, credit by examination, Urban Term, "numerous" internship programs, cooperative urban teacher education program, 3–2 engineering, 3–2 occupational therapy, 3–4 architecture. *Calendar:* 3 by 3, summer school.

Undergraduate degrees conferred (389). 26% were in Business and Management, 15% were in Education, 12% were in Social Sciences, 8% were in Communications, 8% were in Psychology, 7% were in Liberal/General Studies, 5% were in Life Sciences, 4% were in Foreign Languages, 4% were in Mathematics, 3% were in Letters, 3% were in Physical Sciences, 3% were in Computer and Engineering Related Technology, remainder in 5 other fields.

Graduates Career Data. Advanced studies pursued by 16% of graduates; 3% enter medical school; 2% enter law school; 1% enter business school. Medical and dental schools typically enrolling largest numbers of graduates include U. of Iowa; law schools include U. of Iowa, Drake; business schools include U. of Iowa, Thunderbird, Drake U. About 99% of 1992–93 graduates employed. Employers typically hiring largest numbers of graduates include Principal Financial Group, Pella Corp., Ernst and Young, Allied Insurance. Career Development Services include lifetime credential assistance, mock interviews, career library, early assistance with career planning through testing and courses.

Faculty. About 86% of faculty hold PhD or equivalent. About 44% of undergraduate classes taught by tenured faculty. About 42% of teaching faculty are female; 2% Black, 2% Hispanic, 6% other minority.

Student Body. About 76% of students from in state; 89% Midwest, 4% West, 1% each New England, Middle Atlantic, South, Northwest, 3% foreign. An estimated 74% of students reported as Protestant, 18% Catholic, 1% Jewish, 5% unaffiliated, 2% other; 1% as Black, 2% Hispanic, 2% Asian, 1% other minority. *Minority group students:* greater leniency in dealing with those with academic problems; Coalition for a Multicultural Campus has a special social and cultural budgets.

Religious Orientation. Central is a church-related institution; 8% of students affiliated with this church; 1 course in religion required of all students; attendance at nondenominational chapel services voluntary.

Varsity Sports. Men (Div.III): Baseball, Basketball, Cross Country, Football, Golf, Soccer, Tennis, Track, Wrestling. Women (Div.III): Basketball, Cross Country, Golf, Softball, Tennis, Track, Volleyball.

Campus Life. Both student leader and administration source agree that social life is not active; sponsored social activities attract some students, but this is not a "party" school. Athletic program, both varsity and intramural attract the most student interest. Intervisitation hours "limited" and student leader reports they are sometimes seen as too stringent. Alcohol forbidden on campus or at college functions; cars allowed for all.

About 76% of men, 54% of women live in traditional dormitories; 9% of men, 38% of women live in coed dormitories; 2% each of men, women live in off-campus housing or commute. Freshmen given preference in college housing if all students cannot be accommodated. Sexes segregated in coed dormitories by floor. There are 4 fraternities, 2 sororities on campus which about 12% of men, 5% of women join; 12% of men, 5% of women live in fraternities and sororities. About 15% of students leave campus on weekends.

Annual Costs. Tuition and fees, $10,365; room and board, $3,660; estimated $700 other, exclusive of travel. About 97% of students receive financial aid. Average amount of assistance $9,333. Assistance is typically divided 69% scholarship and grant, 23% loan, 8% work. University reports unlimited scholarships awarded on the basis of academic merit alone, talents alone and need alone. *Meeting Costs:* university offers a monthly payment plan.

University of Central Arkansas

Conway, Arkansas 72035 **(501) 450-5000**

A state-supported university, located in a town of 15,500, 30 miles northwest of Little Rock.

Founded: 1908
Affiliation: State
UG Enrollment: 2,968 M, 4,434 W (full-time); 454 M, 665 W (part-time)
Total Enrollment: 8,521
Cost: < $10K
% Receiving Financial Aid: 60%
Admission: Non-selective
Application Deadline: Aug. 15

Admission. Graduates of accredited high schools with 15 units (11 in academic subjects) eligible. About 83% of applicants accepted, 64% of these actually enroll. Average freshman ACT scores: 21.7 composite. *Required:* ACT. Criteria considered in admissions, in order of importance: standardized test scores, high school academic record. *Out-of-state* freshman applicants: State does not limit out-of-state enrollment, no special requirements. *Apply* by August 15. *Transfers* welcome; 400 enrolled 1993–94.

Academic Environment. Degrees offered: associates, bachelors, masters. About 80% of general education credits for graduation are required; distribution requirements fairly numerous. About 25% of entering students graduate within four years, 30% eventually; 63% of entering freshmen return for sophomore year. *Calendar:* semester, summer school.

Undergraduate degrees conferred (812). 31% were in Education, 25% were in Business and Management, 10% were in Allied Health, 7% were in Social Sciences, 5% were in Letters, 4% were in Business (Administrative Support), 4% were in Psychology, 3% were in Life Sciences, 3% were in Health Sciences, remainder in 11 other fields.
Graduates Career Data. Advanced studies pursued by 15% of graduates; 5% enter business school. *Careers in business and industry* pursued by 50% of graduates.
Student Body. About 96% of students from Arkansas; 97% from South, 3% foreign. An estimated 85% of students reported as Protestant, 10% Catholic, 5% unaffiliated; 12% Black, 1% Hispanic, 1% Asian, 1% Native American, according to most recent data available.
Varsity Sports. Men (NAIA): Basketball, Football. Women (NAIA): Basketball, Volleyball.
Campus Life. About 22% of men, 24% of women live in traditional dormitories; no coed dormitories; rest live in off-campus housing or commute. Parking reported to be a significant problem. Freshmen given preference in college housing if all students cannot be accommodated. There are 9 fraternities, 8 sororities on campus which about 18% of men, 20% of women join. About 70% of resident students leave campus on weekends.
Annual Costs. Tuition and fees, $1,700 (out-of-state, $3,274); room and board, $1,450. About 60% of students receive financial aid; average amount of assistance, $3,400. Assistance is typically divided 19% scholarship, 36% grant, 37% loan, 9% work. University reports 14 scholarships awarded on the basis of academic merit alone, 4 for special talents.

Central Connecticut State University

New Britain, Connecticut 06050 (203) 827-7543

A state-supported university including separate schools of Arts and Sciences, Business, Education and Professional Studies, and Technology. Located in a city of 74,240, 9 miles southwest of Hartford. Most convenient major airport: Bradley International.

Founded: 1849
Affiliation: State
UG Enrollment: 3,079 M, 3,315 W (full-time); 1,870 M, 2,011 W (part-time)
Total Enrollment: 12,665
Cost: < $10K
% Receiving Financial Aid: 20%
Admission: Non-selective
Application Deadline: May 1

Admission. Graduates of accredited high schools with 16 units, 12 in academic subjects, eligible; about 60% of applicants accepted, 36% of these actually enroll; 18% of freshmen graduate in top fifth of high school class, 48% in top two-fifths. Average freshman SAT scores: 419 verbal, 462 mathematical. *Required:* SAT; interview optional. Criteria considered in admissions, in order of importance: high school academic record, class rank, standardized test scores, recommendations, writing sample, extracurricular activities. *Out-of-state* freshman applicants: university welcomes out-of-state students. State does not limit out-of-state enrollment. No special requirements for out-of-state students. *Apply* by May 1; rolling admissions. *Transfers* welcome; 689 enrolled 1993–94.
Academic Environment. Degrees offered: bachelors, masters. *Majors offered* include usual arts and sciences, anthropology, business studies, computer science, East Asian studies, education, geography, international studies, engineering technology, management information systems, medical technology, nursing education, office administration, public administration. General education requirements include 62 of 122 required credits for graduation. Average undergraduate class size: 55% of classes under 20, 41% between 20–40, 3% over 40.

About 40% of students entering as freshmen graduate within four years, 45% eventually; 27% of freshmen do not return for sophomore year. *Special programs:* January term, study abroad, independent study, undergraduate research, individualized majors, Cooperative Education Program, honors, cross registration with other Connecticut State University system schools, special student services for learning disabled students. *Calendar:* semester, summer school.
Undergraduate degrees conferred (1,404). 41% were in Business and Management, 13% were in Education, 9% were in Engineering and Engineering Related Technology, 7% were in Communications, 7% were in Social Sciences, 5% were in Psychology, 3% were in Health Sciences, remainder in 12 other fields.
Graduates Career Data. Advanced studies pursued by 19% of graduates; 5% enter business schools. Graduate and professional schools typically enrolling largest numbers of graduates include U. of Connecticut, Central Connecticut State, Hartford Graduate Center, U. of Hartford. About 80% of students responding to survey of 1992–93 graduates employed. Employers typically hiring largest numbers of graduates include United Technologies, Aetna Insurance, Travelers Insurance, ITT Hartford, State of Connecticut. Career Development Services include workshops on resume writing, interviewing techniques, job search strategies, and employment information; coop education and intern programs also available.
Faculty. About 73% of faculty hold PhD or equivalent. About 5% of teaching faculty are Black, 4% Hispanic, 6% other minority.
Student Body. About 94% of students from in state; 97% New England, 1% Middle Atlantic; 2% foreign. An estimated 43% of students reported as Catholic, 10% Protestant, 2% Jewish, 41% unaffiliated; 7% as Black, 4% Hispanic, 2% Asian, 3% other minority. *Minority group students:* financial provisions through variety of governmental programs; college–community liaison for minority groups; admissions officers with "special interest" in encouraging applications from qualified black and Spanish-speaking students; student social groups including organization of Afro and Black students.
Varsity Sports. Men (Div.I): Baseball, Basketball, Cross Country, Football, Golf, Gymnastics, Soccer, Swimming, Tennis, Track, Wrestling. Women (Div.I): Basketball, Cross Country, Golf, Softball, Swimming, Tennis, Track, Volleyball.
Campus Life. Campus still attracts large number of commuters. Rules governing student life have not changed substantially in recent years. Intervisitation possible within scheduled hours. Cars permitted.

About 25% of students live in dormitories; rest live in off-campus housing or commute. Intervisitation in men's and women's dormitory rooms limited. Sexes segregated in coed dormitories by wing, floor or room. There are no fraternities or sororities on campus. About 75% of resident students leave campus on weekends.
Annual Costs. Tuition and fees, $1,754 (out-of-state, $5,678); room and board, $1,770–$1,990; estimated $1,023 other, exclusive of travel. About 28% of students receive financial aid; average amount of assistance, $4,700. Assistance is typically divided 14% scholarship, 31% grant, 52% loan, 3% work. University reports 453 scholarships awarded on the basis of academic merit alone, 131 for special talents alone, 2,570 for need alone. *Meeting Costs:* university offers Academic Management Services.

University of Central Florida

Orlando, Florida 32816 (407) 823-2000

A state-supported institution, located in east-central Florida; the region has a population of approximately 2,000,000. Most convenient major airport: Orlando International.

Founded: 1963
Affiliation: State
UG Enrollment: 5,807 M, 6,375 W (full-time); 3,167 M, 3,181 W (part-time)
Total Enrollment: 23,333
Cost: < $10K
% Receiving Financial Aid: 56%
Admission: Selective
Application Deadline: Mar. 15

Admission is selective. About 42% of applicants accepted, 64% of these actually enroll. Average freshman scores: SAT, 437 M, 425 W verbal, 553 M, 495 W mathematical; 33% of freshmen score above 500 on verbal, 6% above 600, 4% above 700; 64% of freshmen score above 500 on mathematical, 17% above 600, 4% above 700; ACT, 23 M, 24 W composite. *Required:* SAT or ACT, 2.6 minimum GPA. Criteria considered in admissions, in order of importance: high school academic record, standardized test scores, extracurricular activities, recommendations. *Out-of-state* freshman applicants: state does not limit out-of-state enrollment. States from which most out of state students are drawn: New Jersey, New York, Massachusetts. *Entrance programs:* early admission, rolling admission. *Apply* by March 15. *Transfers* welcome; 3,206 enrolled 1993–94.
Academic Environment. *Undergraduate studies* offered by colleges of Business Administration, Education, Engineering, Liberal

Studies, Health Related Professions, Arts and Sciences. Degrees offered: associates, bachelors, masters, doctoral. About 10% of general education requirements for graduation are elective; distribution requirements fairly numerous. New majors include: motion picture technology.

About 24% of entering students graduate within four years, 47% within six years; 70% of freshmen return for sophomore year. Average undergraduate class size: lower lecture: 44, upper lecture: 35. *Special programs:* CLEP, honors, independent study, study abroad, internship, credit by examination, reduced credit-hour degree. *Calendar:* semester, summer school.

Undergraduate degrees conferred (3,611). 26% were in Business and Management, 17% were in Education, 10% were in Liberal/General Studies, 9% were in Engineering, 8% were in Communications, 5% were in Psychology, 4% were in Social Sciences, 3% were in Engineering and Engineering Related Technology, 3% were in Health Sciences, remainder in 13 other fields.

Graduates Career Data. Advanced studies pursued by 9% of graduates. Career Development Services include individualized counseling about current and projected trends in the job market, resume advice and critiquing, computerized career guidance, career planning mini-classes, resume referrals at employers' request, on-campus interviews, list of job opportunities, interviewing tips, and help in organizing job search.

Faculty. About 80% of faculty hold PhD or equivalent. About 58% of undergraduate classes taught by tenured faculty. About 25% of teaching faculty are female; 3% Black, 3% Hispanic, 8% other minority.

Student Body. About 93% of students from in state, 3% foreign. An estimated 5% of students reported as Black, 8% Hispanic, 4% Asian. Average age of undergraduate student: 24.

Varsity Sports. Men (Div.I): Baseball, Basketball, Cross Country, Football, Golf, Soccer, Tennis, Track. Women (Div.I): Basketball, Cross Country, Golf, Soccer, Tennis, Track, Volleyball.

Campus Life. About 8% of each live in traditional or coed dormitories; rest commute. Freshmen given preference in college housing if all students cannot be accommodated. Intervisitation in men's and women's dormitory rooms limited. There are 13 fraternities, 14 sororities on campus which about 9% of men, 6% of women join.

Annual Costs. Tuition and fees, $1,756, (out-of-state, $6,659); room and board, $4,305; estimated $2,670 other, exclusive of travel. About 56% of students receive financial aid; assistance typically divided 12% scholarship, 24% grant, 55% loan, 9% work. *Meeting Costs:* PLUS loan for parents, supplemental loans, prepaid tuition plan.

Central Methodist College

Fayette, Missouri 65248 (816) 248-3391

A church-related college, including the Swinney Conservatory of Music, located in a town of 3,500, 50 miles northwest of Jefferson City. Most convenient major airport: Columbia Regional.

Founded: 1854
Affiliation: United Methodist
Total Enrollment: 440 M, 480 W (full-time)
Cost: < $10K
% Receiving Financial Aid: 89%
Admission: Non-selective
Application Deadline: Aug. 1

Admission. High school graduates with 15 units in academic subjects and GPA of 2.0 eligible; nongraduates with GED considered; 81% of applicants accepted, 44% of these actually enroll; 27% of freshmen graduate in top fifth of high school class, 55% in top two-fifths. Average freshman ACT scores: 19 M, 21 W composite. *Required:* ACT. Criteria considered in admission, in order of importance: high school academic record, standardized test scores. *Entrance programs:* early decision, early admission, midyear admission, rolling admission. *Apply* by August 1. *Transfers* welcome; 41 enrolled 1993–94.

Academic Environment. Degrees offered: associates, bachelors. Graduation requirements include 4 units of English, 3 of math, 2 units each of science, foreign language, social science, and humanities. About 30% of students entering as freshmen graduate within four years, 50% eventually; 67% of freshman return for sophomore year. *Special programs:* CLEP, independent study, study abroad, honors, undergraduate research, optional January interim, BSN completion program, cross-registration with Mid-Missouri Associated Colleges, 3–3 law, 3–2 and 2–2 engineering, 3–2 physical therapy, 3–1 medical technology. *Calendar:* 4–1–4, summer school.

Undergraduate degrees conferred (99). 25% were in Education, 25% were in Business and Management, 9% were in Multi/Interdisciplinary Studies, 6% were in Life Sciences, 5% were in Communications, 4% were in Visual and Performing Arts, 4% were in Social Sciences, 4% were in Psychology, 4% were in Mathematics, 4% were in Health Sciences, 4% were in Computer and Engineering Related Technology, 3% were in Philosophy and Religion, remainder in Letters.

Graduates Career Data. Advanced studies pursued by 19% of graduates. About 30% of 1992–93 graduates employed. Fields typically employing largest numbers of graduates include nursing, education, business, accounting. Career Development Services include job hunting assistance, job fairs, resume preparation and job listings.

Faculty. About 50% of faculty hold PhD or equivalent.

Student Body. About 89% of students from in state; 91% Midwest, 5% Middle Atlantic, 2% New England, 2% Northwest, less than 1% foreign. An estimated 76% of students reported as Protestant, 18% Catholic; 7% Black, 1% Hispanic, 1% Asian, 1% other minority.

Religious Orientation. Central Methodist is a church-related institution; no religious studies required of students.

Varsity Sports. Men: Baseball, Basketball, Football, Golf, Skiing, Soccer, Swimming, Tennis, Track, Volleyball. Women: Basketball, Cross Country, Golf, Soccer, Softball, Swimming, Tennis, Track, Volleyball.

Campus Life. About 80% of students live in traditional dormitories; no coed dormitories; rest commute. Freshmen given preference in college housing if all students cannot be accommodated. Intervisitation in men's and women's dormitory rooms limited. There are 5 fraternities, 5 sororities on campus which about 50% of men, 60% of women join; they provide no residence facilities. About 50% of resident students leave campus on weekends.

Annual Costs. Tuition and fees, $8,050; room and board, $3,370; estimated $3,000 other, exclusive of travel. About 89% of students receive financial aid; average amount of assistance, $6,800. Assistance typically divided: 30% scholarship, 20% grant, 40% loan, 10% work. College reports 437 scholarships awarded on the basis of academic merit, 392 for special talents, 311 for need. *Meeting Costs:* college offers Loan Grant Program.

Central Michigan University

Mount Pleasant, Michigan 48859 (517) 774-3076

A state-supported university, located in a town of 24,000, 70 miles north of Lansing. Most convenient major airport: Midland, Bay City, Saginaw.

Founded: 1892
Affiliation: State
UG Enrollment: 5,777 M, 7,259 W (full-time); 565 M, 829 W (part-time)
Total Enrollment: 16,252
Cost: < $10K
% Receiving Financial Aid: 65%
Admission: Non-selective
Application Deadline: Mar. 1

Admission. High school graduates with acceptable records or satisfactory ACT scores eligible; 86% of applicants accepted, 41% of these actually enroll. Average freshman ACT scores: 21 composite. *Required:* ACT (SAT acceptable). Criteria considered in admission, in order of importance: high school academic record, standardized test scores, recommendations. *Out-of-state* freshman applicants: university seeks students from out-of-state. State does not limit out-of-state enrollment. No special requirements for out-of-state applicants. *Apply* by March 1. *Transfers* welcome; 1,174 enrolled 1993–94.

Academic Environment. University includes a residential honors college. Degrees offered: bachelors, masters, doctoral. Specific course and distribution requirements vary with major. About 17% of students entering as freshmen graduate within four years, 56% eventually; 74% of freshmen return for sophomore year. *Special programs:* CLEP, independent study, study abroad, honors, undergraduate research, joint program in engineering with Michigan Technological U.. Adult programs: Continuing Certification for Elementary and Secondary Teachers, Extended Degree Program. *Calendar:* semester, summer school.

Undergraduate degrees conferred (3,140). 26% were in Business and Management, 11% were in Education, 9% were in Letters, 7% were in Social Sciences, 5% were in Psychology, 5% were in Communications, 4% were in Parks and Recreation, 4% were in Vocational Home Economics, 4% were in Mathematics, 3% were in Life Sciences, 3% were in Allied Health, 3% were in Visual and Performing Arts, remainder in 13 other fields.
Graduate Career Data. Career Development Services include on-campus interviews, mock interviews, career information library and resume tips.
Faculty. About 73% of faculty hold PhD or equivalent. About 65% of undergraduate classes taught by tenured faculty. About 35% of teaching faculty are female; 4% Black, 7% other minority.
Student Body. About 98% of students from in state; 99% Midwest; less than 1% foreign. An estimated 3% of students reported as Black, 5% other minority.
Varsity Sports. Men (NCAA): Baseball, Basketball, Cross Country, Football, Wrestling. Women (NCAA): Basketball, Cross Country, Gymnastics, Softball, Volleyball.
Campus Life. About 37% of men, 35% of women live in traditional and coed dormitories; 38% of men, 46% of women live in off-campus college related housing; 12% of men, 9% of women commute. Freshmen given preference in college housing if all students cannot be accommodated. Intervisitation in men's and women's dormitory rooms limited, unlimited depending on student choice of dormitory. There are 17 fraternities, 13 sororities on campus which about 12% of men, 10% of women join.
Annual Costs. Tuition and fees, $2,901 (out-of-state, $7,132); room and board, $3,836; estimated $1,600 other, exclusive of travel. About 65% of students receive financial aid.

Central Missouri State University

Warrensburg, Missouri 64093 **(816) 543-4290**

A state-supported university, located in a town of 15,000, 50 miles southeast of Kansas City. Most convenient major airport: Kansas City.

Founded: 1871
Affiliation: State
UG Enrollment: 3,925 M, 4,169 W (full-time); 758 M, 838 W (part-time)
Total Enrollment: 11,282
Cost: < $10K
% Receiving Financial Aid: 67%
Admission: Non-selective
Application Deadline: Rolling

Admission. High school graduates eligible; lower portion of the class may be admitted on probation; 88% of applicants accepted, 34% these actually enroll; 25% of freshmen graduate in top fifth of high school class, 53% in top two-fifths. Average freshmen ACT scores: 20.5 composite. *Required:* ACT or SAT, minimum high school rank in upper two thirds of class. Criteria used in admissions, in order of importance: high school rank, standardized test scores, high school academic record. *Out-of-state* freshman applicants: university seeks students from out-of-state. Requirement for out-of-state applicants: rank in upper two-thirds of class, and ACT scores in upper two-thirds percentile. About 33% of out-of-state applicants enrolled. States from which most out-of-state students are drawn: Illinois, Kansas, Iowa, Nebraska. *Entrance programs:* early decision, early admission, midyear admission, deferred admission, advanced placement. *Apply:* rolling admissions. *Transfers* welcome; 987 enrolled Fall, 1993.
Academic Environment. Graduation requirements include 6 semester hours of English/grammar, 3 of oral communication, 3–5 of mathematics, 3–5 of lab science, 6 of humanities, 9 of history/government/social science, 3 of multicultural studies, 2–3 of technology, 4–6 of individual development. Degrees offered: associates, bachelors, masters. Unusual, new, or notable majors include: aviation, criminal justice, graphics, safety science and technology, social gerontology, speech pathology and audiology. About 38% of entering students graduate eventually; 60% of freshmen return for sophomore year. Average undergraduate class size: 35. *Special programs:* CLEP, independent study, study abroad, honors, 3-year degree, individualized majors, 3–2 engineering. *Calendar:* semester, summer school.
Undergraduate degrees conferred (1,406). 24% were in Business and Management, 19% were in Education, 13% were in Engineering and Engineering Related Technology, 9% were in Protective Services, 6% were in Communications, 5% were in Precision Production, 3% were in Social Sciences, 3% were in Psychology, 3% were in Health Sciences, remainder in 15 other fields.
Graduates Career Data. About 84% of 1991–92 graduates employed. Fields typically employing largest numbers of graduates include industrial safety, computer science, management/marketing, and graphics. Career Planning and Placement Office provides information and assistance to students for research and selection of individual career paths; assists students and alumni in preparation for entering work force.
Faculty. About 70% of faculty hold PhD or equivalent. About 32% of teaching faculty are female; 1% Black, 1% Hispanic, 5% other minority.
Student Body. About 93% of students from in state; 96% Midwest; 2% foreign. An estimated 7% of students reported as Black, 5% other minority. Average age of undergraduate: 22.7.
Varsity Sports. Men: Baseball, Basketball, Cross Country, Football, Golf, Track, Wrestling. Women: Basketball, Cross Country, Softball, Track, Volleyball.
Campus Life. About 26% of men, 21% of women live in traditional and coed dormitories; about 70% of men, 76% of women commute. Sexes segregated in coed dormitories by wing or floor. There are 14 fraternities, 12 sororities on campus which about 12% of men, 11% of women join; 4% of men, 3 of women live in fraternities and sororities.
Annual Costs. Tuition and fees, $2,160 (out-of-state, $4,320); room and board, $2,978; estimated $2,550 other, inclusive of travel. About 67.5% of students receive financial aid; average amount of assistance, $3,405. Assistance is typically divided 12% scholarship; 31% grant; 54% loan; 2% work. University reports 1,442 scholarships awarded on the basis of academic merit alone, 1,250 for special talents alone. *Meeting Costs:* university offers budget payment plan, fee reductions for alumni children, use of credit cards.

University of Central Oklahoma

Edmond, Oklahoma 73034 **(405) 341-2980**

A state-supported university, located in a city of 51,000, 12 miles north of Oklahoma City. Most convenient major airport: Will Rogers World (Oklahoma City).

Founded: 1890
Affiliation: State
UG Enrollment: 3,463 M, 4,293 W (full-time); 1,812 M, 2,624 W (part-time)
Total Enrollment: 15,901
Cost: < $10K
% Receiving Financial Aid: 31%
Admission: Non-selective
Application Deadline: Aug. 1

Admission. Oklahoma graduates of accredited high schools with 11 units in academic subjects and GPA of 2.7, rank in upper two-thirds of class, or score 15 on ACT composite (or 710 on SAT combined) eligible; 97% of applicants accepted, 41% of these actually enroll; 6% of freshmen graduate in top fifth of high school class, 36% in top two-fifths. Average freshmen ACT scores: 21.3 M, 20.6 W composite. *Required:* ACT or SAT, minimum HS GPA. Criteria considered in admissions, in order of importance: standardized test scores, high school academic record, extracurricular activities, recommendations; other factors considered include special talents. *Out-of-state* freshman applicants: university seeks students from out-of-state. States from which most out-of-state students drawn: Texas, Kansas. *Entrance programs:* early decision, early admission, midyear admission. *Apply* by August 1; rolling admission. *Transfers* welcome; 1,732 enrolled in 1993–94.
Academic Environment. Graduation requirements include 6 hours of English, 6 of social studies, 6–8 of science, 5 of humanities, 4 of health/physical education, 3 of math. Degrees offered: bachelors, masters. About 13% of students entering as freshmen graduate within four years, 23% eventually; 47% of freshman return for sophomore year. Unusual, new, or notable majors include: funeral science, actuarial science. *Special programs:* CLEP, independent study. *Calendar:* semester, summer school.
Undergraduate degrees conferred (1,785). 32% were in Education, 23% were in Business and Management, 6% were in Computer and Engineering Related Technology, 5% were in Social

Sciences, 5% were in Letters, 4% were in Marketing and Distribution, 4% were in Health Sciences, 4% were in Communications, 3% were in Protective Services, 3% were in Home Economics, 3% were in Psychology, remainder in 10 other fields.
Graduate Career Data. Career Development Services offer resume writing and interviewing workshops, and on-campus interviews.
Faculty. About 66% of faculty hold PhD or equivalent. About 37% of teaching faculty are female; 5% Black, 1% Hispanic, 7% other minorities.
Student Body. About 90% of students from in state; 7% foreign. An estimated 7% of students reported as Black, 1% Hispanic, 2% Asian, 10% other minority. Average age of undergraduate student: 26.
Varsity Sports. Men (Div.II): Baseball, Basketball, Cross Country, Football, Golf, Tennis, Track, Wrestling. Women (Div.II): Basketball, Cross Country, Softball, Tennis, Track, Volleyball.
Campus Life. About 8% of men, 8% of women live in traditional dormitories; no coed dormitories; 90% of men, 90% of women live in commute. There are 7 fraternities, 5 sororities on campus which 2% of men, 2% of women join; 2% each live in fraternities and sororities.
Annual Costs. Tuition and fees, $1,497 (out-of-state, $3,559); room and board, $2,150. About 31% of students receive financial aid, average amount of assistance, $2,503. Assistance typically divided: 5% scholarship; 45% grant; 40% loan; 10% work.

Central State University

Wilberforce, Ohio 45384 **(513) 376-1351**

A state-supported university, located in a small village 4 miles northeast of Xenia (pop. 25,400) and 18 miles east of Dayton; founded as a college for Negroes but now aims to serve "all people in our society regardless of race."

Founded: 1887
Affiliation: State
Total Enrollment: 3,623 M, W (full-time)
Cost: < $10K
Admission: Non-selective
Application Deadline: April 1

Admission. All Ohio graduates of accredited high schools accepted; nonresidents limited to those "who have demonstrated high academic promise." Required: ACT. *Apply* by April 1. *Transfers* welcome.
Academic Environment. *Degrees:* AB, BS, BSEd. *Special programs:* honors, cross-registration through Dayton-Miami Valley Consortium. *Calendar:* quarter, summer school.
Undergraduate degrees conferred (254). 28% were in Business and Management, 11% were in Education, 9% were in Marketing and Distribution, 9% were in Communications, 8% were in Social Sciences, 7% were in Computer and Engineering Related Technology, 6% were in Psychology, 5% were in Mathematics, 3% were in Engineering, 3% were in Engineering and Engineering Related Technology, remainder in 8 other fields.
Student Body. About 80% of students from Ohio.
Campus Life. About 56% of men, 48% of women live in dormitories; rest commute. Intervisitation in men's and women's dormitory rooms limited. There are 4 fraternities, 3 sororities on campus.
Annual Costs. Tuition and fees, $3,588 (out-of-state, $7,176); room and board, $3,753. About 70% of students receive financial aid.

Central State University

(See University of Central Oklahoma)

Central Washington University

Ellensburg, Washington 98926 **(509) 963-1211**

A state-supported university, located in a semi-urban town of 14,000, 100 miles east of Seattle. Most convenient major airport: Yakima

Founded: 1891
Affiliation: State
UG Enrollment: 2,902 M, 3,048 W (full-time); 438 M, 587 W (part-time)
Total Enrollment: 7,660
Cost: < $10K
% Receiving Financial Aid: 60%
Admission: Non-selective
Application Deadline: Feb. 1

Admission. Graduates of accredited Washington high schools with 14.5 units in academic subjects and a 2.5 average eligible; those with 2.0 average considered if space permits; 68% of applicants accepted, 54% of these actually enroll. About 33% of entering freshmen graduate in top fifth of their high school class, 66% in top two-fifths. Average freshman SAT scores, according to most recent data available: 429 M, 413 W verbal, 488 M, 441 W mathematical. *Required:* Washington Pre-College Test, SAT, or ACT. *Out-of-state* freshman applicants: university seeks students from out of state. State limits out-of-state enrollment to 15% of total new students. Requirement for out-of-state applicants: 2.5 average. *Apply* by February 1. *Transfers* welcome.
Academic Environment. *Degrees:* BA, BS, BM, BAEd. Foreign language requirement, also demonstration of minimum competency levels in basic academic skills required. About 45% of students entering as freshmen graduate eventually; 25% of freshmen do not return for sophomore year. *Special programs:* honors, individualized majors, study abroad. *Calendar:* quarter, summer school.
Undergraduate degrees conferred (1,759). 32% were in Business and Management, 22% were in Education, 9% were in Social Sciences, 5% were in Protective Services, 4% were in Psychology, 3% were in Communications, 3% were in Visual and Performing Arts, 3% were in Engineering and Engineering Related Technology, remainder in 16 other fields.
Faculty. About 75% of faculty hold PhD or equivalent.
Student Body. About 97% of students from Washington. An estimated 1% of students reported as Black, 3% Hispanic, 2% Asian, 2% Native American, 1% other minority, according to most recent data available. Central Washington U. makes no religious demands on students.
Varsity Sports. Men (NAIA Div.I): Baseball, Basketball, Cross Country, Football, Golf, Swimming, Tennis, Track, Wrestling. Women (NAIA Div.I): Basketball, Cross Country, Swimming, Tennis, Track, Volleyball.
Campus Life. About 2% of students live in traditional dormitories; 38% of students in coed dormitories; 9% live in on-campus apartments; 51% live in off-campus housing or commute. Sexes segregated in coed dormitories by wing, floor or room. There are no fraternities or sororities.
Annual Costs. Tuition and fees, $1,971 (out-of-state, $6,948); room and board, $3,673. About 60% of students receive financial aid. Assistance is typically divided 25% scholarship, 25% loan, 50% work. University reports some scholarships awarded on the basis of academic merit alone.

Central Wesleyan College

Central, South Carolina 29630 **(803) 639-4099**

A small, church-related college located in a community midway between Charlotte and Atlanta. Most convenient major airport: Greenville-Spartanburg Jetport.

Founded: 1906
Affiliation: Wesleyan
Total Enrollment: 1,067 M, W (full-time)
Cost: < $10K
% Receiving Financial Aid: 93%
Admission: Non-selective
Application Deadline: Aug. 1

Admission. High school graduates with 16 units and C average eligible; 85% of applicants accepted, 73% of these actually enroll; 20% of freshmen graduate in top fifth of high school class, 40% in top two-fifths. Average freshmen SAT scores, according to most recent data available: 390 M, 390 W verbal, 430 M, 380 W mathematical. *Required:* SAT or ACT; interview required "in rare situations." Non-academic factors considered in admissions: "willingness to live in harmony with college rules.." *Apply* by August 1; rolling admissions. *Transfers* welcome.
Academic Environment. *Degrees:* AB, BS. About 30% of general education requirements for graduation are elective; distribution

requirements fairly numerous. *Majors offered* in addition to usual studies include youth ministries/music, management of human resources. About 40% of students entering as freshmen graduate eventually; 35% of freshmen do not return for sophomore year. *Special programs:* CLEP, independent study, Leadership Education for Adult Professionals (LEAP), study abroad, cooperative programs at Clemson U. including nursing. *Calendar:* semester, summer school.

Undergraduate degrees conferred (215). 67% were in Business and Management, 13% were in Philosophy and Religion, 7% were in Education, 5% were in Letters, 3% were in Psychology, remainder in 5 other fields.

Graduates Career Data. According to most recent data available, advanced studies pursued by 45% of graduates; 10% enter business school, 15% enter seminary. *Careers in business and industry* pursued by 50% of graduates.

Faculty. About 60% of faculty hold PhD or equivalent.

Student Body. About 70% of students from in state; 95% from South. An estimated 98% of students reported as Protestant, 1% Catholic; 10% reported as Black, 2% Asian, according to most recent data available.

Religious Orientation. Central Wesleyan is a church-related institution; 9 hours of Bible, 3 hours in philosophy required of all students; attendance at church services is "encouraged."

Varsity Sports. Men (NAIA, Div. I, & NCCAA): Baseball, Basketball, Golf, Soccer. Women (NAIA, Div. I, & NCCAA): Basketball, Softball, Volleyball.

Campus Life. About 40% of men, 50% of women live in traditional dormitories; no coed dormitories; rest commute. Freshmen given preference in college housing if all students cannot be accommodated. No intervisitation in men's or women's dormitory rooms. There are no fraternities or sororities. About 40% of resident students leave campus on weekends.

Annual Costs. Tuition and fees, $8,100; room and board, $3,080. About 93% of students receive financial aid; assistance is typically divided 34% scholarship, 44% loan, 8% work. *Meeting Costs:* college offers prepaid tuition plan.

Centre College

Danville, Kentucky 40422 **(606) 238-5350**

One of the nation's older colleges, Centre has an illustrious past and eminent alumni and has long been one of the South's leading colleges. College leads the nation in percentage of alumni providing financial support (70% in recent years). Founded under Presbyterian auspices, Centre is now governed by an independent board of trustees. Located in a town of 13,000, the 75-acre campus is 85 miles southeast of Louisville and 35 miles from Lexington. Most convenient major airport: Lexington, KY.

Founded: 1819
Affiliation: Independent
Total Enrollment: 493 M, 459 W (full-time)
Cost: $10K–$20K
% Receiving Financial Aid: 65%
Admission: Highly Selective
Application Deadline: March 1

Admission is highly selective. About 87% of applicants accepted, 33% of these actually enroll; 60% of freshmen graduate in top fifth of high school class, 95% in top two-fifths. Average freshman scores, middle 50% range: SAT, 480–590 verbal, 500–650 mathematical; ACT, 25–29 composite. *Required:* SAT or ACT; interview encouraged (required for scholarship applicants). Criteria considered in admissions, in order of importance: high school academic record, standardized test scores, recommendations, extracurricular activities, writing sample; other factors considered: special talents, diverse student body. *Entrance programs:* early decision, early admission, mid-year admission, advanced placement, deferred admission. About 15% of entering students from private schools, 10% parochial. *Apply* by March 1. *Transfers* welcome; 20 enrolled 1993–94.

Academic Environment. Students report great satisfaction with academic program. Specific strengths reported to be "challenging" classes, "wonderful" "caring" faculty, and a "broad-based program that prepares students for the 'real world'". "The thing I like best about Centre is the openness to individuality. We are allowed mental freedom and this helps us prepare for the future [while] enriching our knowledge of culture, arts, and society." General education requirements for graduation are intended to equip students "with skills needed to pursue a lifetime of learning." All students take courses (some specified) chosen from 6 broad "contexts": The Aesthetic Context (3 courses), The Scientific Context (3 courses), The Social Context (3 courses), The Cross-Cultural Context (1 course), The Context of Fundamental Questions (2 courses), and The Integrative Context (1 course). In addition, the College's Basic Skills requirements mandate competency in mathematics, expository writing, and a foreign language; these skills may be shown by proficiency or courses. Degrees offered: bachelors. Unusual, new, or notable majors include: biochemistry and molecular biology, chemical physics, dramatic art, psychobiology, anthropology, international relations.

About 72% of students entering as freshmen graduate within four years, 79% eventually; 90% of freshmen return for sophomore year. Average undergraduate class size: 18–21. *Special programs:* CLEP, independent study, study abroad, undergraduate research, individualized majors, January/February interterm (used primarily for special seminars, independent research, intensive language study, off-campus programs), 3–2 engineering. *Calendar:* 4–2–4, summer school.

Undergraduate degrees conferred (209). 31% were in Social Sciences, 19% were in Life Sciences, 15% were in Letters, 7% were in Physical Sciences, 6% were in Foreign Languages, 6% were in Psychology, 6% were in Mathematics, 5% were in Visual and Performing Arts, 3% were in Philosophy and Religion, remainder in 2 other fields.

Graduates Career Data. Advanced studies pursued by 50% of graduates within 2 years; 8% enter law school; 5% enter medical school; 3% enter business school. About 45% of 1992–93 graduates employed.

Faculty. About 95% of faculty hold PhD or equivalent. About 60% of undergraduate classes taught by tenured faculty.

Student Body. About 65% of students from in state; 92% South, 6% North Central; 4% foreign. An estimated 3% of students reported as Black, 1% Hispanic, 2% Asian. *Minority group students:* limited funds available for special aid; Black Student Union.

Religious Orientation. Centre is "no longer officially related to the Presbyterian churches."

Varsity Sports. Men (Div. III): Baseball, Basketball, Cross Country, Diving, Football, Golf, Soccer, Swimming, Tennis, Track. Women (Div.III): Basketball, Cross Country, Diving, Field Hockey, Golf, Soccer, Softball, Swimming, Tennis, Track, Volleyball.

Campus Life. Students enjoy considerable freedom in their personal and social activities within the fairly broad regulations of the college. Students at Centre characterized by college as "highly motivated and very able academically; active in athletics [LBRK]50% on a varsity team by graduation, 90% in intramurals[RBRK], student government, Greek organizations, arts, etc." Student elected social board sponsors and organizes campus-wide activities; Norton Center for the Arts includes glass-blowing and print-making capabilities. Cars allowed. Regulations concerning drinking conform to state law; prohibited on campus for those under 21. Intervisitation not allowed for first term freshmen; some limitations for others.

About 20% of men, 54% of women live in traditional residence halls; 42% of men, 36% of women in coed residence halls; 7% of men, 10% of women live in off-campus housing or commute. Freshmen are required to live in college housing. Sexes segregated in coed dormitories by floor. There are 6 fraternities, 3 sororities on campus which about 60% of men, 50% of women join; 55% of men live in fraternities; sororities provide no residence facilities. About 10% of resident students leave campus on weekends.

Annual Costs. Tuition and fees, $11,600; room and board, $4,250; estimated $900 other, exclusive of travel. About 65% of students receive financial aid. Assistance is typically divided 65% scholarship; 35% grant, work and loan. *Meeting Costs:* college offers payment plans with no interest charge.

Chadron State College

Chadron, Nebraska 69337 **(308) 432-6000**

A state-supported college, located in a town of 6,000, in the Pine Ridge country of northwest Nebraska and 60 minutes south of the Black Hills. Most convenient major airport: Rapid City, SD.

Founded: 1910
Affiliation: State
UG Enrollment: 877 M, 1,045 W (full-time); 191 M, 382 W (part-time)
Total Enrollment: 3,439
Cost: < $10K
% Receiving Financial Aid: 90%
Admission: Non-selective
Application Deadline: Rolling

Admission. Graduates of approved and accredited high schools admitted; 100% of applicants accepted, 60% of these actually enroll. About 28% of freshmen graduate in top fifth of high school class, 54% in top two-fifths. Average freshman ACT score: 20.7 composite. *Required:* ACT. Criteria considered in admissions, in order of importance: high school academic record, standardized test scores. *Out-of-state* freshman applicants: college seeks students from out of state. State does not limit out-of-state enrollment. Requirement for applicants from noncontiguous states: rank in top half of class. About 99% of out-of-state applicants accepted. *Apply:* rolling admissions. *Transfers* welcome; 203 enrolled 1993–94.
Academic Environment. Degrees offered: associates, bachelors, masters. Core requirements include 6 hours each of composition, science, history; 3 hours each of communications, mathematics, humanities, arts, government, health/wellness, social cultural studies, global studies, ethics; 2 hours of physical activities. About 69% of students entering as freshmen graduate eventually; 20% of freshmen do not return for sophomore year. Average undergraduate class size: 75% of classes under 20, 15% between 20–40, 10% over 40. *Special programs:* CLEP, independent study, internship programs. Adult programs: "Serious Adult Students" Orientation, counseling, lounge, peer support. *Calendar:* semester, summer school.
Undergraduate degrees conferred (263). 27% were in Business and Management, 27% were in Education, 6% were in Protective Services, 5% were in Social Sciences, 5% were in Life Sciences, 4% were in Mathematics, 4% were in Home Economics, 3% were in Physical Sciences, 3% were in Letters, 3% were in Visual and Performing Arts, 3% were in Psychology, remainder in 6 other fields.
Graduates Career Data. Advanced studies pursued by 8% of graduates. About 90% of 1992–93 graduates employed. Fields typically employing largest numbers of graduates include business and education.
Faculty. About 82% of faculty hold PhD or equivalent. About 33% of teaching faculty are female; 3% minorities.
Student Body. About 72% of students from Nebraska; 94% of students from Midwest; 1% foreign. An estimated 1% of students reported as Black, 3% Hispanic, 1% Asian, 4% other minorities. Average age of undergraduate student: 25.
Varsity Sports. Men (NAIA Div.II): Basketball, Football, Track, Wrestling. Women (NAIA, Div.II): Basketball, Golf, Track, Volleyball.
Campus Life. About 16% of men, 15% of women live in traditional dormitories; no coed dormitories; rest commute. Freshmen given preference in college housing if all students cannot be accommodated. Intervisitation in men's and women's dormitory rooms limited. There are no sororities or fraternities. About 35% of resident students leave campus on weekends.
Annual Costs. Tuition and fees, $1,575 (out-of-state, $2,670); room and board, $2,516. About 90% of students receive financial aid; average amount of assistance, $2,045. Assistance is typically divided 13% scholarship, 34% grant, 43% loan, 10% work. College reports 608 scholarships awarded on the basis of academic merit alone, 61 awarded for need alone. *Meeting Costs:* College offers installment plan for room and board.

Chaminade University of Honolulu

Honolulu, Hawaii 96816 **(808) 735-4735**

A church-related college, operated by the Society of Mary (Marianists), located in a city of 1,000,000.

Founded: 1955
Affiliation: Roman Catholic
UG Enrollment: 766 (full-time); 1,154 (part-time)
Total Enrollment: 2,452
Cost: < $10K
% Receiving Financial Aid: 60%
Admission: Non-selective
Application Deadline: Rolling

Admission. High school graduates with 15 units in academic subjects eligible with 2.0 GPA minimum; 88% of applicants accepted, 38% of these actually enroll. Average freshmen scores: SAT, 440 verbal, 480 math; ACT, 19 composite. *Required:* SAT or ACT; essay required. Criteria considered in admissions, in order of importance: high school academic record, standardized test scores, writing sample, recommendations, extracurricular activities. *Apply:* rolling admissions. *Transfers* welcome; 168 students enrolled 1993–94.
Academic Environment. Graduation requirements include 61–62 credits including 9 upper division credits outside the major. Degrees offered: associates, bachelors, masters. *Majors offered* include: interior design, criminal justice, early childhood education with a Montessori emphasis. Average undergraduate class size: 75% under 20, 25% 20–40. *Special programs:* internships, individualized majors, learning center with tutorials, study abroad, 3–2 engineering, cross registration with other Hawaii schools. About 70% of freshman return for sophomore year. *Calendar:* traditional/accelerated semester, summer school.
Undergraduate degrees conferred (222). 35% were in Business and Management, 12% were in Social Sciences, 11% were in Protective Services, 10% were in Multi/Interdisciplinary Studies, 7% were in Education, 7% were in Architecture and Environmental Design, 5% were in Computer and Engineering Related Technology, 5% were in Communications, 4% were in Psychology, remainder in 4 other fields.
Graduate Career Data. Career Development Services offer resume and interview workshops, interest inventory tests, internships, job fairs on campus, and job referrals.
Student Body. About 45% of students from in state, 35% from mainland, 20% foreign and Trust Territory. An estimated 42% of students reported as Catholic; 44% as Asian, 35% White, 4% Black, 1% Hispanic, 15% other minority.
Religious Orientation. Chaminade is a church-related institution; 6 hours of religion/theology required of all students.
Varsity Sports. Men (NCAA II): Basketball, Cross Country, Tennis, Water polo (NCAA I). Women (NAIA): Cross Country, Softball, Tennis, Volleyball.
Campus Life. About 35% of students live in traditional and coed dormitories; rest live in off-campus housing or commute. Intervisitation in men's and women's dormitory rooms limited. Sexes segregated in coed dormitories by apartment. About 10% of resident students leave campus on weekends. There are no fraternities or sororities on campus. About 10% of resident students leave campus on weekends.7
Annual Costs. Tuition and fees, $9,900; room and board, $4,300; estimated $1,000 other, exclusive of travel. About 60% of students receive financial aid; average amount of assistance, $7,000. Assistance is typically divided 10% scholarship, 20% grant, 50% loan, 20% work. University reports 10 scholarships awarded on basis of academic merit alone, 10 for special talents alone, 39 for merit/need. *Meeting Costs:* University offers CUH Study Grant.

Champlain College

Burlington, Vermont 05402

Primarily a two-year business college, Champlain offers bachelors degrees in business and accounting; college is developing four-year programs in professional studies.

Founded: 1878
Affiliation: Independent

Chapman University

Orange, California 92666 **(714) 997-6711**

A private, liberal arts college, located in a city of 90,000, 32 miles southeast of Los Angeles, Chapman administers Semester at Sea, a shipboard program of travel/study. Most convenient major airports: Los Angeles International, John Wayne.

Founded: 1861
Affiliation: Disciples of Christ
UG Enrollment: 720 M, 942 W (full-time)
Total Enrollment: 2,930
Cost: $10K–$20K
% Receiving Financial Aid: 67%
Admission: Non-selective
Application Deadline: March 1

Admission. High school graduates with academic average of 2.5 and minimum combined SAT score of 760 eligible; 81% of applicants accepted, 48% of these actually enroll; 39% of freshmen graduate in top fifth of high school class, 66% in top two-fifths. Average freshman scores: SAT, 443 M, 454 W verbal, 503 M, 492 W mathematical; ACT, 22 M, 23 W composite. *Required:* SAT or ACT, essay, HS GPA of 2.5, recommendation; interview recommended. Criteria considered in admissions, in order of importance: high school academic record, standardized test scores, writing sample, extracurricular activities, recommendations. About 24% of entering students from private schools. *Apply* by March 1, rolling admissions. *Transfers* welcome, 346 enrolled 1993–94.

Academic Environment. Degrees offered: bachelors, masters. *Majors offered* include usual arts and sciences, communications, computer science, peace studies, environmental studies, food science and nutrition, film and TV production, business, music, education, English/writing, religion. Basic core requirements include 6 credits writing, 3 in oral communication, Algebra II, 4 in physical education and 4 credit Freshman Seminar; general education requirements include 9 credits in humanities, 10 in natural sciences, 9 in social sciences, 6 in foreign language, 3 in Cultural Heritage and 3 in Diversity, in addition all juniors take writing proficiency exam. Students find small classes and personal attention to be strengths of the academic program. Average undergraduate class size: 56% of classes under 20, 40% between 20–40, 4% over 40.

About 41% of students entering as freshmen graduate eventually; 29% of freshmen do not return for sophomore year. *Special programs:* CLEP, independent study, study abroad, honors, undergraduate research, optional January interterm, individualized majors, extensive internship programs. *Calendar:* 4–1–4, summer school.

Undergraduate degrees conferred (330). 43% were in Business and Management, 16% were in Communications, 12% were in Liberal/General Studies, 7% were in Letters, 6% were in Psychology, 5% were in Social Sciences, 4% were in Visual and Performing Arts, remainder in 9 other fields.

Faculty. About 81% of faculty hold PhD or equivalent. About 49% of undergraduate classes taught by tenured faculty. About 34% of teaching faculty are female; 2% Black, 3% Hispanic, 4% other ethnic minorities.

Student Body. University seeks a national student body; according to most recent data available; 65% of students from California; 85% West. An estimated 16% of students reported as Protestant, 20% Catholic, 2% Jewish, 62% unaffiliated; 5% as Black, 9% Asian, 10% Hispanic, 5% other minority.

Religious Orientation. Chapman is a church-related institution, affiliated with the Christian Church (Disciples of Christ); attendance at chapel services voluntary.

Varsity Sports. Men (Div.III): Baseball, Basketball, Cross Country, Football, Golf, Lacrosse, Soccer, Tennis, Track. Women (Div.III): Basketball, Cross Country, Diving, Soccer, Softball, Swimming, Tennis, Track, Volleyball.

Campus Life. The suburban south coast area location offers students ocean sports/activities 15 minutes from campus, and mountain sports/activities only 1 hour from campus. College characterized by student leaders as "toward the conservative end of the spectrum." All undergraduates under 21 required to live in college-approved housing unless living at home. About 32% of students live in coed dormitories; 9% live in off-campus college-related housing; rest commute. Intervisitation in coed dormitories unlimited; sexes segregated by room. There are 5 fraternities and 4 sororities, which about 21% men, 16% women join. About 60% of resident students leave campus on weekends.

Annual Costs. Tuition and fees, $16,328; room and board, $5,780; estimated $1,700 other, exclusive of travel. About 67% of students receive financial aid; average amount of assistance, $16,500. Assistance is typically divided 15% scholarship, 43% grant, 38% loan, 4% work. College reports 376 scholarships awarded on the basis of academic merit alone, 124 for special talents, 864 for need alone.

College of Charleston

Charleston, South Carolina 29412 (803) 792-5670

Long one of the oldest independent, liberal arts institutions in the U.S., the College of Charleston became state-supported in 1970. The campus lies in the heart of Charleston (pop. 75,000), one of the South's most historic cities. Most convenient major airport: Charleston Metropolitan.

Founded: 1770
Affiliation: State
UG Enrollment: 2,585 M, 4,266 W (full-time); 537 M, 663 W (part-time)
Total Enrollment: 10,566
Cost: < $10K
% Receiving Financial Aid: 56%
Admission: Non-selective
Application Deadline: June 1

Admission. About 66% of applicants accepted, 40% of these actually enroll; 44% of freshmen graduate in top fifth of high school class, 79% in top two-fifths. Average freshman scores: SAT, 491 M, 488 W verbal, 557 M, 516 W mathematical; 42% score above 500 on verbal, 9% above 600, 1% above 700; 68% score above 500 on mathematical, 15% above 600, 3% above 700; ACT, 21 M, 20 W composite. *Required:* SAT or ACT. Criteria considered in admissions, in order of importance: high school academic record, standardized test scores, recommendation, extracurricular activities, writing sample; other factors considered: special talents, diverse student body. *Out-of-state* freshman applicants: college actively seeks students from out-of-state. State does not limit out-of-state enrollment. Special requirements for out-of-state applicants for international students only. About 54% out-of-state freshman students accepted, 57% of these actually enrolled. States from which most out-of-state students are drawn: Georgia, North Carolina, Virginia. *Entrance programs:* early decision, early admission, mid-year admission, deferred admission, advanced placement. About 28% of students are from private schools. *Apply* by June 1. *Transfers* welcome; 800 students enrolled 1993–94.

Academic Environment. Graduation requirements include 6 hours of English, 6 of history, 8 of natural science, 6 of mathematics, 0–12 of foreign language, 6 of social science, 12 of humanities. Degrees offered: bachelors, masters. Marine biology reported to be very strong program; other natural sciences also take advantage of the environmental resources of the area.

About 37% of entering freshmen graduate within four years, 48% eventually; 82% of freshmen return for sophomore year. *Special programs:* CLEP, internships, study abroad, 3-year degree, Maymester term, 3–2 engineering, cross registration with Citadel, Medical U. of South Carolina, early admission to medical or dental school (3+1), Trident Technical, Charleston Southern U. Adult programs: welcome and orientation sessions every two months; incentive grants and learning strategies course. Average undergraduate class size: 26. *Calendar:* semester, summer school.

Undergraduate degrees conferred (906). 24% were in Business and Management, 20% were in Social Sciences, 14% were in Education, 10% were in Life Sciences, 9% were in Letters, 8% were in Psychology, 6% were in Visual and Performing Arts, 3% were in Physical Sciences, 3% were in Mathematics, remainder in 3 other fields.

Graduate Career Data. Advanced studies pursued by 33% of graduates; 21% enter graduate school; 3% enter medical school; 3% enter law school; 1% enter dental school. Graduate and professional schools typically enrolling largest numbers of graduates include Medical U. of South Carolina. About 90% of 1992–93 graduates employed. Fields typically hiring largest numbers of graduates include business/industry, education, government/military. Career Development Services offer interest and skill inventories, career planning sessions, resource library including computer databases.

Faculty. About 86% of faculty hold PhD or equivalent. About 40% of undergraduate classes taught by tenured faculty. About 35% of teaching faculty are female; 7% minority.

Student Body. About 77% of students from in state; 2% foreign. An estimated 8% of students reported as Black, 4% other minority. Average age of undergraduate student: 22.5.

Varsity Sports. Men: Baseball, Basketball, Cross Country, Equestrian, Golf, Soccer, Swimming, Tennis. Women: Basketball, Cross Country, Equestrian, Golf, Soccer, Softball, Swimming, Tennis, Volleyball.

Campus Life. Nature of campus life affected by large percentage of commuters. Location in the city, yet only 20 minutes from the beach, reported by students to provide "a lot for students to do." Visitation in the dormitories limited; cars allowed, but "not needed" according to student source.

About 10% of men, 22% of women live in traditional dormitories; 4% men, 2% women in coed dormitories; 4% men, 5% women live in college-owned historic houses; 81% men, 70% women live in commute. Freshmen given preference in college housing if all students cannot be accommodated. There are 11 fraternities, 9 sororities on campus which about 18% of men, 18% of women join; 1% of each live in fraternities and sororities. About 45% of resident students leave campus on weekends.

Annual Costs. Tuition and fees, $2,950 (out-of-state, $5,900); room and board, $3,300; estimated $2,255 other, exclusive of travel. About 56% of students receive financial aid; average amount of assistance, $4,711. Assistance is typically divided 7% scholarship, 27% grant, 47% loan, 19% work. College reports 125 scholarships awarded on the basis of academic merit alone, 60 scholarships for special talents alone. *Meeting Costs:* college offers tuition plan, academic management services, prepayment plans.

University of Charleston

Charleston, West Virginia 25304 **(304) 357-4750** **(800) 995-4682**

An independent university, located in the capital city (pop. 80,000). Most convenient major airport: Yeager (Charleston).

Founded: 1888
Affiliation: Independent
UG Enrollment: 246 M, 525 W (full-time); 179 M, 432 W (part-time)
Total Enrollment: 1,434
Cost: < $10K
% Receiving Financial Aid: 75%
Admission: Non-selective
Application Deadline: Rolling

Admission. Graduates of approved high schools with 16 academic units and C average who rank in top half of class eligible. About 77% of applicants accepted, 35% of these actually enroll; 48% of freshmen graduate in top fifth of high school class, 74% in top two-fifths. Average freshman scores: SAT, 445 M, 441 W verbal, 520 M, 489 W mathematical; 44% score above 500 on verbal, 9% above 600, 48% above 500 on mathematical, 18% above 600, 9% above 700; ACT, 21 composite. *Required:* SAT or ACT. Criteria considered in admissions, in order of importance: high school academic record and standardized test scores rank equally as most important, recommendation and extracurricular activities rank equally, and as do writing sample and interview. *Entrance programs:* early decision, mid-year admission, advanced placement. *Apply:* rolling admissions; Health Sciences: Dec. 31. *Transfers* welcome; 196 students enrolled 1993–94.

Academic Environment. Graduation requirements include courses in arts and humanities, social sciences, natural sciences, and human services. Degrees offered: associates, bachelors, masters. *Majors offered* include: sports medicine, interior design, political science, environmental science, education, respiratory care, nursing, radiology. Average undergraduate class size: 67% under 20, 27% 20–40, 6% over 40. About 52% of entering freshman graduate within four years, 54% eventually; 74% of freshman return for sophomore year. *Special programs:* CLEP, independent study, honors, study abroad, internships. *Calendar:* semester, 3-week spring intersession, summer school.

Undergraduate degrees conferred (137). 26% were in Business and Management, 20% were in Health Sciences, 10% were in Military Sciences, 6% were in Social Sciences, 6% were in Psychology, 6% were in Life Sciences, 6% were in Architecture and Environmental Design, 5% were in Education, 4% were in Liberal/General Studies, 4% were in Communications, remainder in 5 other fields.

Graduates Career Data. Advanced studies pursued by 33% of graduates. About 62% of 1992–93 graduates employed. Fields typically hiring largest numbers of graduates include nursing, business, radiology. Career Development Services offer Myers-Briggs analysis, SIGI Plus, in-class presentations on career development, and individual counseling.

Faculty. About 60% of faculty hold PhD or equivalent. About 60% of teaching faculty are female; 2% Hispanic.

Student Life. About 87% of students from in state; 90% Middle Atlantic, 3% New England, 2% Midwest, 1% each South, West, Northwest, 2% foreign. An estimated 32% of students are Protestant, 8% Catholic, 1% Jewish, 1% Muslim, 1% other, 57% "not given"; 3% Black, 1% Hispanic, 2% Asian, 3% "not given." Average age of undergraduate student: 27.

Varsity Sports. Men(Div.II): Baseball, Basketball, Crew, Golf, Soccer, Tennis. Women(Div.II): Basketball, Crew, Golf, Soccer, Softball, Tennis, Volleyball.

Campus Life. Campus is located in the state capitol; in the words of one student: "we are just minutes from anything." About 27% of men, 14% of women live in coed dormitories; rest commute. Freshmen given preference in college housing if all students cannot be accommodated. Intervisitation in men's and women's dormitory rooms limited. There are 3 fraternities, 2 sororities on campus which about 31% of men, 17% of women join; they provide no residence facilities. About 40% of resident students leave campus on weekends.

Annual Costs. Tuition and fees, $9,250; room and board, $3,480; estimated $900 other, exclusive of travel. About 75% of students receive financial aid; average amount of assistance, $8,250. Assistance is typically divided 40% grant, 55% loan, 5% work. College reports 175 scholarships awarded on the basis of academic merit alone, 200 for special talents alone, 300 for need alone. *Meeting Costs:* college offers payment plans, privately financed loans.

Charter Oak State College

Farmington, Connecticut 06032-1934

Charter Oak State College was established by the State of Connecticut to provide a way for adults to complete an associates or bachelors degree outside the classroom. There is no campus, however, there is a main office in Farmington and four regional offices in the state. Applicants must have 9 credits off college-level work; credit may be earned by testing, correspondence courses, and other non-traditional methods, as well as through transfer from another college.

Founded: 1973
Affiliation: State

Chatham College

Pittsburgh, Pennsylvania 15232 **(412) 365-1290** **(800) 837-1290**

Like a number of other women's colleges, Chatham is combining liberal arts studies with pre-professional programs. Its neighboring institutions, Carnegie-Mellon, Pittsburgh, and Duquesne play a significant role in the social life of Chatham students. The college's 55-acre campus is located in a residential area, some 20 minutes by bus or car from downtown Pittsburgh. Most convenient major airport: Pittsburgh International..

Founded: 1869
Affiliation: Independent
UG Enrollment: 469 W (full-time); 132 W (part-time)
Total Enrollment: 621
Cost: $10K–$20K
% Receiving Financial Aid: 85%
Admission: Selective
Application Deadline: Rolling

Admission is selective. About 93% of applicants accepted, 46% of these actually enroll; 55% of freshmen graduate in top fifth of high school class, 80% in top two-fifths. Average freshmen scores: SAT, 491 verbal, 481 mathematical; 44% score above 500 on verbal, 16% above 600, 44% score above 500 on mathematical, 10% above 600; ACT, 22 composite. *Required:* SAT or ACT, essay; interview highly recommended. Criteria considered in admissions, in order of importance: high school academic record, writing sample, recommendation, standardized test scores, extracurricular activities; other factors considered: special talents, diverse student body. *Entrance programs:* early admission, mid-year admission, deferred admission. *Apply:* rolling admission. *Transfers* welcome; 55 enrolled 1993–94.

Academic Environment. Student reports small classes a plus: they can't "hide in a sea of faces. That keeps a student on her toes." But same student laments the "un-academic" student body and would like more academic challenges. Another student is more content with the relaxed atmosphere. January interim program for experimentation, travel, and for internships in numerous agencies, laboratories, corporations and organizations in and around Pittsburgh; the entire junior class will travel abroad and study in groups of 20 with 2 faculty instructors (cost included in regular tuition). Graduation requirements include 7 core courses, with some selection: 2 writing courses, 1st year interim, 2 courses on Western and non-Western society, 1 lab science, 1 course in human values, proficiencies in reading, mathematics, and computer literacy. Degrees offered: bachelors, masters. *Majors offered* include art history, media arts, accounting, administration of justice, communications, arts management, education, engineering, environmental studies, European studies, global policy, pre-law, pre-med, pre-dentistry, occupational therapy, physical therapy, veterinary science. Average undergraduate class size: 86% under 20, 12% 20–40, 2% over 40.

About 50% of students entering as freshmen graduate eventually, 77% of freshmen return for sophomore year. *Special programs:* January term, study abroad, cross registration with 9 Pittsburgh colleges and universities, 3–2 engineering, early admission to medical school (3+1). Adult programs: Gateway Program for women 7 or more years out of high school. *Calendar:* 4–1–4.

Undergraduate degrees conferred (84). 19% were in Communications, 18% were in Business and Management, 17% were in Social Sciences, 12% were in Psychology, 7% were in Visual and Performing Arts, 7% were in Letters, 5% were in Public Affairs, 5% were in Mathematics, 4% were in Philosophy and Religion, 4% were in Life Sciences, remainder in 2 other fields.

Graduates Career Data. Advanced studies pursued by 28% of graduates; 8% enter graduate school, 7% enter law school, 7% enter business school, 5% enter medical school, 1% enter seminary. Medical schools typically enrolling largest numbers of graduates include U. of Pittsburgh; laws schools include U. of Pittsburgh, Duquesne U., Dickinson; business schools include Carnegie Mellon, U. of Pittsburgh. About 50% of 1992–93 graduates employed. Fields and employers typically hiring largest numbers of graduates include television/cable, U. of Pittsburgh, human service agencies. Career Development Services offer testing, personality/interest, internships, resume assistance, mock interviews, alumnae networking, mentor program, graduate school admissions test simulations, and on-campus recruitment.

Faculty. About 93% of faculty hold PhD or equivalent. About 70% of undergraduate classes taught by tenured faculty. About 60% of teaching faculty are female; 2% Black.

Student Body. About 80% of students from in state; 86% Middle Atlantic, 5% South, 1% each New England, South, 1% West/Northwest, 6% foreign.

Varsity Sports. Women: Basketball, Soccer, Softball, Volleyball.

Campus Life. Security factors rather than in loco parentis tradition main consideration in administration's regulations. Students enjoy "the safety and security of a beautiful, rural-type setting" and add that it is "very quiet" on campus. Pittsburgh has a student population of 60,000; students can augment their social life at other nearby campuses. Seniors and 2nd term juniors may have cars; others require special permission. Intervisitation not limited.

About 78% of women live in traditional dormitories; rest commute. There are no sororities on campus. About 30% of resident students leave campus on weekends.

Annual Costs. Tuition and fees, $12,780; room and board, $5,230; estimated $1,250 other, exclusive of travel. About 85% of students receive financial aid; average amount of assistance, $12,237. Assistance is typically divided 18% scholarship, 44% grant, 26% loan, 12% work. College reports 99 scholarships awarded on the basis of academic merit alone, 22 for special talents alone, 164 for need alone. *Minority group students:* financial aid according to need.

Chestnut Hill College

Philadelphia, Pennsylvania 19118-2695 (215) 248-7001

A church-related, liberal arts college, conducted by the Sisters of St. Joseph, Chestnut Hill is located on a 45-acre campus in a suburban residential area of metropolitan Philadelphia. Most convenient major airport: Philadelphia International.

Founded: 1924
Affiliation: Independent (Roman Catholic)
UG Enrollment: 518 W (full-time); 44 M, 253 W (part-time)
Total Enrollment: 1,213
Cost: < $10K
% Receiving Financial Aid: 70%
Admission: Selective
Application Deadline: March 15

Admission is selective. About 74% of applicants accepted, 50% of these actually enroll; 51% of freshmen graduate in top fifth of high school class, 79% in top two-fifths. Average freshman SAT scores: 495 verbal, 483 mathematical; 54% of freshmen score above 500 on verbal, 10% above 600; 55% score above 500 on mathematical, 13% above 600. *Required:* SAT or ACT, essay. Criteria considered in admissions, in order of importance: high school academic record, recommendations, standardized test scores, writing sample, extracurricular and/or community activities; other factors considered: "demonstration of short term goals." Entrance programs: early admission, deferred admission, advanced placement. About 59% of entering students from private schools or parochial schools. *Apply* by March 15 for priority on financial aid; rolling admissions. *Transfers* welcome; 12 enrolled fall, 1993.

Academic Environment. Students influence academic decision making through inclusion on College Council and other faculty and administrative committees. Distribution requirements include 11 hours in natural sciences (8 in lab science), 9 hours in social sciences, 21 hours in humanities, 6 hours in religious studies, 6 hours beyond elementary level foreign language, 1 hour in Freshman Seminar, 3 hours in 2 writing courses, 2 hours in physical education and swimming test. Degrees offered: associates, bachelors, masters. *Majors offered* include usual arts and sciences, elementary education, Montessori Teacher Training, fine arts and technology, communications and technology, molecular biology, biochemistry, pre-medical, pre-dental, pre-law, pre-veterinary. New Technology Center opened in 1991 offering 125 IBM, Apple Macintosh stations, CD-ROM, on-line databases. Average undergraduate class size: 15, (upper level classes 8–12).

About 89% of students entering as freshmen graduate eventually; 15% of freshmen do not return for sophomore year. *Special programs:* CLEP, independent study, honors, 4 study abroad options, 3-year degree, individualized majors, Exchange program with 10 other members of the Sisters of St. Joseph College Consortium, cross-registration with nearby LaSalle College, dual-degree programs with Thomas Jefferson U., Pennsylvania College of Podiatric Medicine. Adult programs: Re-Entry At Chestnut Hill Program for adult students. *Library:* special collections include Irish Collection, Morton collection of first editions. *Calendar:* semester.

Undergraduate degrees conferred (104). 29% were in Education, 20% were in Social Sciences, 15% were in Business and Management, 11% were in Psychology, 7% were in Letters, 6% were in Life Sciences, 6% were in Foreign Languages, 3% were in Visual and Performing Arts, 3% were in Mathematics, remainder in Physical Sciences.

Graduates Career Data. Advanced studies pursued by 13% of graduates. Medical schools typically enrolling largest numbers of graduates include Medical College of Pennsylvania, U. of Pennsylvania School of Veterinary Medicine; dental schools include Temple; law schools include Dickinson, Temple, Villanova. Fields typically employing largest numbers of graduates include chemical processing, pharmaceuticals, education, insurance and financial services. *Career Counseling Program* provides guidance and information on careers, professions and employment opportunities; offers workshops, on-campus recruitment, credentials service, SIGI computerized guidance system; coordinates coop program and internships. Student assessment of program reported as good for career guidance and good to fair for job placement. Alumni reported as "sometimes" helpful in career guidance and job placement.

Faculty. About 71% of faculty hold PhD or equivalent. About 77% of full-time undergraduate teaching faculty are female; 3% ethnic minorities.

Student Body. College seeks a national student body; 76% of students from Pennsylvania; 90% Middle Atlantic, 4% South, 3% foreign. About 59% of students reported as Catholic, 11% Protestant, 26% undeclared; 10% Black, 7% Hispanic, 3% Asian.

Religious Orientation. Chestnut Hill has a strong Catholic tradition; 6 semester hours of religious studies required of all students. Religious clubs on campus include Liturgy Club, Charismatic Prayer Group. Places of worship available on campus for Catholics, in immediate community for all faiths.

Varsity Sports. Women (NCAA Div.III): Basketball, Field Hockey, Lacrosse, Softball, Tennis, Volleyball.

Campus Life. Recent student leader reports "there is more freedom given to students...we receive the support of the faculty and administration in our endeavors—which makes this a very warm and friendly environment." Male visitors are welcome in various lounges and in dormitory rooms during set hours. Cars or motorbikes permitted for all.

About 67% of women live in dormitories; rest live in off-campus housing or commute. Freshmen given preference in college housing

if all students cannot be accommodated. There are no sororities. About 40% of resident students leave campus on weekends.
Annual Costs. Tuition and fees, $9,750; room and board, $4,775; estimated $675 other, exclusive of travel. About 70% of students receive need-based financial aid, 20% receive academic merit and other non-need-based aid; average amount of assistance, $6,000. College reports that 12% of first year students receive full-tuition scholarships awarded on the basis of academic merit alone, 20% of first year students receive partial scholarships based on academic merit.

Cheyney University of Pennsylvania

Cheyney, Pennsylvania 19319 (215) 399-2275

A state-supported university, located in a village of 750, 24 miles from Philadelphia; founded as a college for Negroes and still serving a predominantly black student body.

Founded: 1837
Affiliation: State
Total Enrollment: 689 M, 830 W (full-time)
Cost: < $10K
% Receiving Financial Aid: 83%
Admission: Non-selective
Application Deadline: June 30

Admission. Graduates of approved high schools with satisfactory SAT or ACT scores eligible; others admitted by examination; 69% of applicants accepted, 26% of these actually enroll. *Required:* SAT. Criteria considered in admissions, in order of importance: high school academic record, standardized test scores, writing sample, recommendation, extracurricular activities; other factors considered: special talents, alumni children, diverse student body. *Out-of-state* freshman applicants: college welcomes students from out-of-state. State does not limit out-of-state enrollment. No special requirements for out-of-state applicants; 71% accepted, 21% actually enrolled. States from which most of out-of-state students are drawn: New York, New Jersey. *Entrance programs:* early admission, mid-year admission. *Apply* by June 30. *Transfers* welcome; 58 students enrolled 1993–94.
Academic Environment. Degrees offered: bachelors, masters. Graduation requirements include 6 credits in communication, humanities, science, and social science, 4 credits in health and physical education, and 3 credits in mathematics. About 25% of students entering as freshmen graduate eventually. *Special programs:* January term, study abroad, cross registration with West Chester, internships. *Calendar:* semester, summer school.
Undergraduate degrees conferred (133). 32% were in Business and Management, 17% were in Social Sciences, 10% were in Education, 10% were in Communications, 5% were in Psychology, 5% were in Parks and Recreation, 5% were in Engineering and Engineering Related Technology, 4% were in Life Sciences, 4% were in Home Economics, 3% were in Computer and Engineering Related Technology, remainder in 4 other fields.
Graduate Career Data. Advanced studies pursued by 9% of graduates. About 84% of 1992–93 graduates are employed. Career Development Services make available employment and educational opportunities to students.
Faculty. About 52% of faculty hold PhD or equivalent. About 77% of undergraduate classes taught by tenured faculty. About 40% of teaching faculty are female; 58% Black, 1% Hispanic, 13% other minority.
Student Body. About 80% of students from in state; 96% Middle Atlantic. An estimated 97% of students reported are Black, 1% Hispanic, 1% other minority.
Varsity Sports. Men: Basketball, Cross Country, Football, Soccer, Tennis, Track, Wrestling. Women: Basketball, Cross Country, Tennis, Track, Volleyball.
Campus Life. About 65% of men, 64% of women live in traditional dormitories; rest commute. Freshmen given preference in college housing if all students cannot be accommodated. Intervisitation in men's and women's dormitory rooms limited. There are 4 fraternities, 4 sororities on campus which about 6% of men, 6% of women join; they provide no residence facilities.
Annual Costs. Tuition and fees, $2,954 (out-of-state, $7,352); room and board, $3,686; estimated $500 other, exclusive of travel. About 83% of students receive financial aid; average amount of assistance, $2,542. Assistance is typically divided 53% scholarship, 34% loan, 13% work. Meeting Costs: university offers installment plans, accepts credit cards.

Chicago State University

Chicago, Illinois 60628 (312) 995-2513

A state-supported, commuter university, located in Chicago. Most convenient major airport: Midway.

Founded: 1867
Affiliation: State
UG Enrollment: 837 M, 1,702 W (full-time)
Total Enrollment: 5,128
Cost: < $10K
% Receiving Financial Aid: 80%
Admission: Non-selective
Application Deadline: Rolling

Admission. High school graduates eligible; 64% of applicants accepted, 45% of these actually enroll; 28% of freshmen graduate in top fifth of high school class, 47% in top two-fifths. *Required:* ACT, class rank. *Out-of-state* freshman applicants: university welcomes out-of-state students. State does not limit out-of-state enrollment; 41% of applicants accepted, 25% enroll. *Apply:* rolling admissions. *Transfers* welcome.
Academic Environment. *Degrees:* AB, BS, BSEd. About 35% of general education requirements for graduation are elective; distribution requirements fairly numerous. *Special programs:* CLEP, independent study, honors, study abroad, University Without Walls, Chicago Consortium of Colleges and Universities, individualized curriculum program, Board of Governors Program for Adults. *Calendar:* year-round trimester.
Undergraduate degrees conferred (503). 26% were in Multi/Interdisciplinary Studies, 19% were in Business and Management, 13% were in Education, 7% were in Social Sciences, 5% were in Health Sciences, 5% were in Allied Health, 5% were in Protective Services, 4% were in Psychology, 3% were in Computer and Engineering Related Technology, remainder in 9 other fields.
Varsity Sports. Men (NCAA, Div.I): Baseball, Basketball, Cross Country, Soccer, Tennis, Track, Wrestling. Women (NCAA, Div.I): Basketball, Cross Country, Tennis, Track, Volleyball.
Student Body. University does not seek a national student body; 98% of students from Illinois. An estimated 81% of students reported as Black, 3% Hispanic, 1% Asian, 2% other minority, according to most recent data available.
Annual Costs. Tuition and fees, $2,198 (out-of-state, $5,894). About 80% of students receive financial aid; assistance is typically divided 50% scholarship, 25% loan, 25% work. University reports some scholarships awarded on the basis of academic merit alone. *Meeting Costs:* university offers deferred payment plan.

University of Chicago

Chicago, Illinois 60637 (312) 702-8650

Chicago has long been among the most highly esteemed institutions of higher learning in the country. In addition to a strong undergraduate arts and sciences program, Chicago has 10 graduate and professional schools of high repute. Far from being ignored, as at many large universities where the emphasis is placed on prestigious graduate schools, Chicago's undergraduates benefit substantially from the many opportunities for their own research and for participating in faculty research projects and in the wealth of 3–2 programs within the university as well as at other top institutions. Students can arrange joint BA/MA programs in most fields. The 175-acre campus is located in a residential neighborhood on Chicago's South Side. Most convenient major airports: Midway, O'Hare.

Founded: 1891
Affiliation: Independent
UG Enrollment: 1,924 M, 1,442 W (full-time)
Total Enrollment: 10,867
Cost: $10K–$20K
% Receiving Financial Aid: 66%
Admission: Most Selective
Application Deadline: January 15

Admission is among the most selective in the country. About 47% of applicants accepted, 31% of these actually enroll; 89% of freshmen graduate in top fifth of high school class. Average freshman scores, middle 50% range: SAT, 570–680 verbal, 630–672 mathematical; ACT, 27–31 composite. *Required:* SAT or ACT, essay. Criteria considered in admission, in order of importance: high school academic record, class rank, writing sample, recommendations and extracurricular activities rank equally, standardized test scores; other factors considered: special talents. *Entrance programs:* early decision. About 23% of entering students from private schools, 8% parochial. *Apply* by January 15. *Transfers* welcome; 67 students enrolled 1993–94.

Academic Environment. The university college offers a highly competitive academic culture. Students are expected to be proficient in both verbal and mathematical skills. They are also expected to come prepared to act as adults and to assume primary responsibility for their own academic careers. Those who are so prepared have available as fine an academic experience as they will find at any university college in the country. Those who require a more protected and supportive environment are likely to experience difficulties. Aware of this problem, the college has instituted "a strong advisory program [LBRK]in which[RBRK] 17 full-time advisers are on staff to help students plan their academic programs." Student body is characterized by both administration and student source as primarily scholarly and intellectual. Students looking for a "party" school and the "pre-professional" student are reported to be least at home on campus. Faculty are reported to be responsive to students who ask questions, initiate discussions, and visit during office hours. Some student concern regarding increased use of teaching assistants. University considers the undergraduate Core Curriculum a significant strength; student source concurs, he found the two year sequence "immensely helpful in selecting a major, and acclimating oneself to the rigorous academic program here." Students in all collegiate divisions required to achieve competence in 4 areas (humanities, and the biological, physical, and social sciences), usually by taking year-long courses in each division as well as year-long courses in a civilization (Western or non-Western), mathematics beyond pre-calculus, a foreign language, and a one quarter course in art or music. Credit for these Common Core courses may be given through Advanced Placement credit or the College's own placement exams. Degrees offered: bachelors, masters, doctoral. *Majors offered* include anthropology, environmental studies, Indian civilization, East Asian or Near Eastern languages and civilizations, linguistics, public policy, Russian civilization, South Asian studies, "many" interdisciplinary opportunities; "Law, Letters and Society" recently introduced. Average undergraduate class size: 69% under 20, 24% 20–40, 7% over 40.

About 75% of students entering as freshmen graduate within four years, 88% within five years; 91–95% of freshmen return for sophomore year. *Special programs:* study abroad, joint BA/MA or BS/MS in biology/biochemistry, chemistry/biochemistry, economics, geography, linguistics, math, Romance languages and literatures, social sciences, 3–2 in business, law, public policy and social work, early medical school admission program available. *Library:* special undergraduate reading rooms; "extensive use" by undergraduates of graduate library facilities. *Calendar:* 4 quarters including optional summer session.

Undergraduate degrees conferred (857). 34% were in Social Sciences, 11% were in Letters, 11% were in Life Sciences, 8% were in Psychology, 7% were in Physical Sciences, 6% were in Mathematics, 5% were in Public Affairs, 4% were in Philosophy and Religion, 4% were in Area and Ethnic Studies, 4% were in Multi/Interdisciplinary Studies, remainder in 4 other fields. *Doctoral degrees:* Social Sciences 90, Physical Sciences 36, Life Sciences 26, Letters 17, Philosophy and Religion 36, Theology 1, Visual and Performing Arts 10, Psychology 9, Education 21, Health Sciences 6, Foreign Languages 6, Area and Ethnic Studies 6, Multi/interdisciplinary Studies 1, Business 6, Public Affairs and Services 11, Library Science 3, Mathematics 6.

Graduates Career Data. Advanced studies pursued by 33% of graduates immediately, 95% within five years; immediately: 17% enter graduate school; 7% enter medical school; 6% enter law school; 1% enter business school. Professional school enrolling largest number of graduates include several major national and international institutions. About 61% of 1992–93 graduates employed. Fields typically hiring largest numbers of graduates include business and industry, academic/research, finance, teaching. Career Development Services offers assistance to students on career planning, job search strategies, employment opportunities, graduate degree programs, extensive career library, individual counseling, employer recruiting program, resume writing and interviewing workshops, and alumni contact files for major national cities available to all students.

Faculty. All faculty hold PhD or equivalent. About 47% of undergraduate classes taught by tenured faculty.

Student Body. About 26% of students from in state; 46% Midwest, 21% Middle Atlantic, 17% West, 6% South, 6% New England, 4% foreign. An estimated 5% of undergraduate students reported as Black, 4% Hispanic, 26% Asian, 1% other minority.

Varsity Sports. Men (Div.III): Baseball, Basketball, Cross Country, Fencing, Football, Soccer, Swimming, Tennis, Track, Wrestling. Women (Div.III): Basketball, Cross Country, Soccer, Softball, Swimming, Tennis, Track, Volleyball.

Campus Life. The dormitories have progressively taken on more of the quality of a supportive house system. Students have virtually complete freedom in determining their own social life, both on and off campus. Freshmen required to live in College Houses unless commuting from home or excused for specific reasons. Senior faculty and their families live in the principal college residence halls. All College Houses are coed, however, single-sex floors are available; 24-hour intervisitation policy. Although the university is located in Chicago's South Side, 10 minutes from the Loop, its large campus offers more of a traditional collegiate setting than do many urban institutions. Facilities of many kinds are available on campus for cultural and recreational as well as academic activity. A varied calendar of cultural and intellectual activities on campus is supplemented by facilities of metropolitan Chicago. Students' problem is not that of finding desirable activities, but of making a choice among many alternatives: one student laments, "The lack of free time to just do nothing." Students who, because of taste or experience, do not wish a highly cosmopolitan environment, may find life at Chicago overwhelming.

About 66% of students live in coed dormitories; 31% live in off-campus college-related housing; 3% each commute. Housing guaranteed for all four years for all students. Sexes segregated in coed College Houses either by wing, floor or room. There are 9 fraternities, 2 sororities which about 10% of men, 3% of women join; they provide no residence facilities. About 3% of resident students leave campus on weekends.

Annual Costs. Tuition and fees, $17,910; room and board, $6,130; estimated $1,208 other, exclusive of travel. About 66% of students receive financial aid; average amount of assistance, $12,931. *Meeting Costs:* university offers monthly payment plan, prepaid tuition plan. *Minority group students:* financial and academic help available.

Chico State College

(See California State University/Chico)

Christ College, Irvine

(See Concordia University, Irvine, California)

Christendom College

Front Royal, Virginia 22630 **(703) 636-2900**

A small, liberal arts college, offering a "rigorous program of studies in an authentically Catholic atmosphere." Campus is located on the Shenandoah River, 1 hour from Washington, DC, and near the Blue Ridge Mountains.

Founded: 1979
Affiliation: Roman Catholic
Total Enrollment: 60 M, 83 W (full-time)
Cost: < $10K
Admission: Non-selective
Application Deadline: April 1

Admission. High school graduates "of good moral character", who show ability to do "serious intellectual work at the college level" eligible. *Required:* SAT or ACT, 3 essays, 2 recommendations; interview recommended. *Non-academic factors* considered in admissions: religious affiliation and/or commitment, special talents, extracurricular activities. *Entrance programs:* early decision, midyear admission, rolling admission. *Apply* by April 1. *Transfers* welcome; 8 enrolled 1993–94.

Academic Environment. Degrees offered: associates, bachelors. Graduation requirements include 6 semesters of philosophy, 5 of English, 6 of theology, 2 of political science, 3 of history, 1 of mathematics, 4 of a foreign language. *Majors offered* include theology, philosophy, history, political science and economics, English language and literature, French. Average undergraduate class size: 85% under 20, 15% 20–40. About 88% of freshmen return for sophomore

year. *Special programs:* Institute in Rome, Summer Institute, Christendom in Dublin, internships.
Faculty. About 90% of faculty hold PhD or equivalent.
Student Body. All students reported as Catholic; 1% as Black, 3% Hispanic.
Religious Orientation. College is a church-related institution; 6 courses in religious studies required of all students. Attendance at religious activities not required, however, College "encourages a generous participation in its spiritual life."
Campus Life. About 93% of men, 97% of women live in traditional dormitories; rest commute. About 4% of resident students leave campus on weekends.
Annual Costs. Tuition and fees, $8,200; room and board, $3,400; estimated $450 other, exclusive of travel.

Christian Brothers College

Memphis, Tennessee 38104 (901) 722-0205

A church-related college, but now independently controlled, conducted by the Christian Brothers, located in a city of 874,000. Most convenient major airport: Memphis International.

Founded: 1871
Affiliation: Independent (Roman Catholic)
Total Enrollment: 1,652 M, W (full-time); 145 M, 184 W (part-time)
Cost: < $10K
% Receiving Financial Aid: 72%
Admission: Selective (+)
Application Deadline: August 1

Admission is selective (+). About 92% of applicants accepted, 41% of these actually enroll. About 43% of freshmen graduate in top fifth of high school class, 69% in top two-fifths. Average freshman scores, according to most recent data available: SAT, 500 M, 462 W verbal, 563 M, 496 W mathematical; 79% of freshman score above 500 on verbal, 8% above 600, 1% above 700; 59% score above 500 on mathematical, 30% above 600, 4% above 700; ACT, 24.2 M, 22.6 W composite, 23.5 M, 21.3 W mathematical. *Required:* SAT or ACT. *Entrance programs:* early admission, midyear admission, advanced placement. About 8% of entering students from private schools, 30% from parochial schools. *Apply* by August 1; rolling admissions. *Transfers* welcome.
Academic Environment. *Degrees:* BS. About 27% of general education requirements for graduation are required but specific requirements vary widely with major. About 45% of students entering as freshmen graduate eventually; 27% of freshmen do not return for sophomore year. *Majors offered* in addition to usual studies include computer science, telecommunications/information systems management, English for corporate communications and management. *Special programs:* CLEP, independent study, study abroad, honors, under graduate research, 3-year degree, individualized majors, 3–1 medical technology program, Greater Memphis Consortium. *Calendar:* semester, summer school.
Undergraduate degrees conferred (275). 46% were in Business and Management, 23% were in Engineering, 7% were in Psychology, 6% were in Physical Sciences, 4% were in Communications, 3% were in Life Sciences, 3% were in Computer and Engineering Related Technology, 3% were in Social Sciences, remainder in 5 other fields.
Faculty. About 72% of faculty hold PhD or equivalent.
Graduates Career Data. According to most recent data available, full-time graduate or professional study pursued immediately after graduation by 24% of students; 2% enter medical school, 2% enter law school, 19% enter business school. Professional schools typically enrolling largest numbers of graduates include U. of Tennessee Memphis, Memphis State U.. *Careers in business and industry* pursued by 93% of graduates. Corporations typically hiring largest numbers of graduates include Anderson Consulting, Shell Oil, Procter & Gamble.
Varsity Sports. Men (NAIA): Baseball, Basketball, Soccer, Tennis. Women (NAIA): Basketball, Tennis, Volleyball.
Student Body. College does not actively seek a national student body; 76% of students from in state; 85% South, 9% North Central. An estimated 55% of students reported as Protestant, 28% Catholic, 15% unaffiliated, 2% other; 20% Black, 5% other minority, according to most recent data available.
Religious Orientation. Christian Brothers is a church-related institution that reflects the fundamental principals of the Catholic Church, but makes no religious demands on students.
Campus Life. About 16% of men; 13% of women live in traditional dormitories; no coed dormitories; rest live in off-campus housing or commute. Intervisitation in men's and women's dormitory rooms limited. There are 5 fraternities, 3 sororities, 1 coed fraternity on campus which about 20% of men, 10% of women join; they provide no residence facilities.
Annual Costs. Tuition and fees, $8,090; room and board, $3,080. About 72% of students receive financial aid; assistance is typically divided 45% scholarship, 35% loan, 20% work. College reports some scholarships awarded on the basis of academic merit alone. *Meeting Costs:* College offers campus grants and loans.

Christian Heritage College

El Cajun, California 92019 (619) 440-3041

A church-related liberal arts college founded by the Scott Memorial Baptist Church, Christian Heritage draws the great majority of its students from the West Coast.

Founded: 1970
Affiliation: Scott Memorial Baptist Church
Total Enrollment: 290 M, W (full-time)
Cost: < $10K
Admission: Non-selective
Application Deadline: June 1

Admission. About 96% of applicants accepted, 51% of these actually enroll; 22% of freshmen graduate in top fifth of high school class, 45% in top two-fifths. *Required:* SAT or ACT, interview (off-campus arrangements can be made). Non-academic factor considered in admissions: religious affiliation and/or commitment. About 60% of entering students from private schools or parochial schools. *Apply* by June 1. *Transfers* welcome.
Academic Environment. *Degrees:* BA, BS. Nearly half of students major in Bible Studies or counseling psychology. Requirements for graduation include 10 credits in Apologetics and 12 credits in Bible Studies. About 27% of students entering as freshmen graduate eventually; 40% of freshmen do not return for sophomore year.
Undergraduate degrees conferred (64). 30% were in Education, 23% were in Psychology, 17% were in Theology, 11% were in Business and Management, 8% were in Social Sciences, 8% were in Home Economics, remainder in 2 other fields.
Student Body. About 60% of students from in state; 90% from West, 5% Northwest. All students reported as Protestant; 2% Black, 3% Hispanic, 2% Asian.
Campus Life. About 40% of men, 50% of women live in traditional dormitories; rest commute.
Annual Costs. Tuition and fees, $7,900; room and board, $3,900. About 65% of students receive financial aid; assistance is typically divided 50% grant, 25% scholarship, 15% loan, 10% work. College reports some scholarships awarded on the basis of academic merit alone.

Christopher Newport College

(See Christopher Newport University)

Christopher Newport University

Newport News, Virginia 23606 (804) 594-7015 or (800) 333-4CNU

Founded as a state-supported, commuter institution, Christopher Newport is now a comprehensive university and seeks a national student body. Formerly known as Christopher Newport College. Most convenient major airport: Newport News—Williamsburg.

Founded: 1960
Affiliation: State
UG Enrollment: 1,135 M, 1,775 W (full-time); 759 M, 990 W (part-time)
Total Enrollment: 4,756
Cost: < $10K
% Receiving Financial Aid: 45%
Admission: Non-selective
Application Deadline: Aug. 1

Admission. Graduates of accredited high schools with 16 units and C average eligible; 87% of applicants accepted, 60% of these actually enroll; 37% of freshmen graduate in top quarter of high school class, 80% in top half. Average freshman SAT scores: 430 M, 410 W verbal, 481 M, 437 W mathematical. *Required:* SAT, essay; interview recommended. *Out-of-state* freshman applicants: college seeks students from out-of-state. No special requirements for out-of-state applicants. About 90% of out-of-state applicants accepted, 50% enroll. States from which most out-of-state students are drawn: North Carolina, New Jersey, Texas. *Entrance programs:* early decision, early admission, mid-year admission, advanced placement. *Apply* by August 1. *Transfers* welcome; 1,133 enrolled 1993–94.

Academic Environment. Graduation requirements: area requirements include English, math, foreign language, humanities, natural science, social science, and physical education/health. Degrees offered: bachelors, masters. *Majors offered* include applied physics, Japanese studies, international business, music/theater. Average undergraduate class size: 34% under 20, 52% 20–40, 14% over 40. About 11% of entering freshmen graduate within four years, 46% eventually; 73% of freshman return for sophomore year. *Special programs:* CLEP, study abroad, 3–2 in forestry and environmental studies with Duke, cross registration with Tidewater area colleges, internships with NASA, Fort Eustis, Fort Monroe, CEBAF, Rauch, Witt & Company. *Calendar:* semester, summer school.

Undergraduate degrees conferred (640). 43% were in Business and Management, 17% were in Education, 7% were in Social Sciences, 7% were in Public Affairs, 6% were in Computer and Engineering Related Technology, 5% were in Psychology, 4% were in Letters, 3% were in Life Sciences, remainder in 7 other fields.

Graduate Career Data. Advanced studies pursued by 15% of graduates. About 96% of 1991–92 graduates employed. Fields typically hiring largest numbers of graduates include Newport News public schools, Hampton schools, NASA. Career Development Services offer career counseling, career resource center, employment support services, corporate recruitment program, student employment program, job listings, computer software for career planning, career information days.

Faculty. About 84% of faculty hold PhD or equivalent. About 30% of undergraduate classes taught by tenured faculty. About 33% of teaching faculty are female; 6% Black, 1% Hispanic, 7% other minority.

Student Body. About 94% of students from in state; 95% South, 2% New England, 2% Middle Atlantic, 1% foreign. An estimated 13% of students reported as Black, 2% Hispanic, 3% Asian, 1% other minority. Average age of undergraduate student: 26.5.

Varsity Sports. Men (Div.III): Baseball, Basketball, Cross Country, Golf, Sailing, Soccer, Tennis, Track. Women (Div.III): Basketball, Cross Country, Sailing, Softball, Tennis, Track, Volleyball.

Campus Life. One coed dormitory will open Fall, 1994 for 440 students. There are 5 fraternities, 4 sororities on campus which 12% men join, 9% women join.

Annual Costs. Tuition and fees, $3,196 (out-of-state, $7,860); room and board $4650; an estimated $1,750 other, excluding travel. About 45% of students receive financial aid; average amount of assistance, $3,690. Assistance is typically divided 36% scholarship, 56% loan, 8% work. University reports 11 scholarships awarded on the basis of academic merit alone, 1 for special talents, 23 for need/academic merit. *Meeting Costs:* university offers various loan programs and AMS payment plan.

Church College of Hawaii

(See Brigham Young University—Hawaii Campus)

University of Cincinnati

Cincinnati, Ohio 45221 (513) 556-1100

A state-supported institution, the University of Cincinnati offers instruction in 7 undergraduate colleges, law, medicine, and graduate studies. The university also offers 2-year programs at Clermont General and Technical College, Raymond Walters General and Technical College, College of Pharmacy, Ohio College of Applied Science (which also offers 4-year technology programs), and University College. Most convenient major airport: Greater Cincinnati International.

Founded: 1819
Affiliation: State
UG Enrollment: 5,672 M, 5,364 W (full-time); 1,090 M, 941 W (part-time)
Total Enrollment: 18,676
Cost: < $10K
Admission: Selective
Application Deadline: Rolling

Admission is selective for McMicken College of Arts and Sciences, colleges of Design, Architecture, and Art, Engineering, Nursing and Health, Business Administration, College–Conservatory of Music. For all schools, 81% of applicants accepted, 35% of these actually enroll. Average freshman scores: SAT, 471 M, 456 W verbal, 563 M, 497 W mathematical; 35% of freshman score above 500 on verbal, 7% above 600; 66% score above 500 on mathematical, 30% above 600, 6% above 700; ACT, 24 M, 23 W composite.

For Arts and Sciences (2,100 M, 2,382 W, full-time), 70% of applicants accepted, 39% of these actually enroll; 36% of freshmen graduate in top fifth of high school class, 68% in top two-fifths. Average freshman scores: SAT, 446 M, 435 W verbal, 512 M, 471 W mathematical; ACT, 22.1 M, 21.5 W composite, 21.8 M, 20.5 W mathematical, according to most recent data available.

For Design, Architecture, Art, and Planning (560 M, 637 W, full-time), 42% of applicants accepted, 51% of these actually enroll; 55% of freshmen graduate in top fifth of high school class, 82% in top two-fifths. Average freshman scores: SAT, 514 M, 512 W verbal, 599 M, 543 W mathematical; ACT, 25.3 M, 24.4 W composite, 25.9 M, 23.2 W mathematical, according to most recent data available.

For Engineering (1,418 M, 260 W, full-time), 75% of applicants accepted, 44% of these actually enroll; 74% of freshmen graduate in top fifth of high school class, 94% in top two-fifths. Average freshman scores: SAT, 518 M, 504 W verbal, 627 M, 580 W mathematical; ACT, 26.5 M, 26.2 W composite, 27.3 M, 26.8 W mathematical, according to most recent data available.

For Nursing and Health, (37 M, 418 W, full-time), 94% of applicants accepted, 47% of these actually enroll; 60% of freshmen graduate in top fifth of high school class, 93% in top two-fifths. Average freshman scores: SAT, 511 M, 466 W verbal, 551 M, 524 W mathematical; ACT, 24.7 M, 21.9 W composite, 22.9 M, 20.8 W mathematical, according to most recent data available.

For Music (269 M, 318 W, full-time), 46% of applicants accepted, 56% of these actually enroll; 35% of freshmen graduate in top fifth of high school class, 62% in top two-fifths. Average freshman scores: SAT, 489 M, 491 W verbal, 529 M, 523 W mathematical; ACT, 22.9 M, 21.8 W composite, 21.1 M, 19.9 W mathematical, according to most recent data available.

For Business Administration (1,232 M, 804 W, full-time), 87% of applicants accepted, 38% of these actually enroll; 56% of freshmen graduate in top fifth of high school class, 87% in top two-fifths. Average freshman scores: SAT, 471 M, 449 W verbal, 567 M, 519 W mathematical; ACT, 24.0 M, 22.7 W composite, 567 M, 519 W mathematical, according to most recent data available.

For Education (326 M, 860 W, full-time), 84% of applicants accepted, 41% of these actually enroll; 30% of freshmen graduate in top fifth of high school class, 63% in top two-fifths. Average freshman scores: SAT, 415 M, 422 W verbal, 466 M, 447 W mathematical; ACT, 19.8 M, 19.8 W composite, 18.5 M, 18.7 W mathematical, according to most recent data available.

For Applied Science (461 M, 64 W full-time), 87% of applicants accepted, 63% of these actually enroll; 29% of freshmen graduate in top fifth of high school class, 52% in top two-fifths. Average freshman scores: SAT, 420 M, 392 W verbal, 524 M, 481 W mathematical; ACT, 21.0 M, 20.0 W composite, 21.6 M, 20.2 W mathematical, according to most recent data available.

Required: SAT or ACT, audition for music or dance, Dental Hygiene Aptitude Test for dental hygiene students. *Non-academic factors* considered in admissions: special talents (for music and art). *Out-of-state* freshman applicants: university welcomes out-of-state students. State does not limit out-of-state enrollment. No special requirements for out-of-state applicants. *Apply:* rolling admissions; December 1 for assured consideration. *Transfers* welcome; 1,030 enrolled 1993–94.

Academic Environment. Degrees offered: associates, bachelors, masters, doctoral. Pressures for academic achievement vary widely among the different colleges and courses of study. University is well known for its cooperative education program. Administration reports for Arts and Sciences 50% of courses required for graduation are elective; distribution requirements fairly numerous. *Undergraduate studies* offered to freshmen in 8 colleges listed above. *Majors offered* in Arts and Sciences in addition to usual studies include anthropology, computer science, foreign affairs, geography, medical technology, speech pathology and audiology, theater arts. Administration reports all undergraduate classes have less than 20 students.

About 40% of students entering as freshmen graduate within four years; 30% of freshmen do not return for sophomore year. *Special programs:* study abroad (including spring quarter in Salamanca, Spain, and German work/study program), honors, undergraduate research, independent study, Washington Semester, Afro-American studies, cooperative work/study program (in Engineering, Business Administration, Design, Architecture, and Art), combined degree programs (arts/medicine or education), 3-year MA program for selected juniors interested in college teaching; affiliation with Art Academy of Cincinnati, Cincinnati Speech and Hearing Center, Hebrew Union College. *Calendar:* quarter, summer school.

Undergraduate degrees conferred (3,022). 24% were in Business and Management, 13% were in Engineering, 8% were in Social Sciences, 8% were in Education, 8% were in Health Sciences, 6% were in Visual and Performing Arts, 5% were in Communications, 4% were in Engineering and Engineering Related Technology, 4% were in Architecture and Environmental Design, 3% were in Life Sciences, 3% were in Psychology, 3% were in Home Economics, remainder in 12 other fields.

Graduates Career Data. Career Development Services include interview preparation, resume assistance, on-campus interviewing.

Faculty. About 78% of faculty hold PhD or equivalent.

Student Body. About 93% of students from Ohio. An estimated 7% of students reported as Black, 3% Asian, 1% Hispanic, 1% other minority.

Varsity Sports. Men (Div.I): Baseball, Basketball, Cross Country, Football(IA), Golf, Soccer, Softball, Swimming, Tennis, Track. Women (Div.I): Basketball, Cross Country, Soccer, Swimming, Tennis, Track, Volleyball.

Campus Life. Interest in fraternities/sororities and varsity athletics increasing. Regulations governing student life relaxed somewhat in recent years. Alcohol policies conform to state law; cars allowed.

About 4% of men, 4% of women live in traditional dormitories; 3% of men, 4% of women live in coed dormitories; rest live in off-campus housing or commute, according to most recent data available. Freshmen outside commuting distance given preference in college housing if all students cannot be accommodated. Sexes segregated in coed dormitories by floor. There are 24 fraternities, 11 sororities on campus.

Annual Costs. Tuition and fees, $3,558 (out-of-state, $8,712); room and board, $4,431; estimated $1,100 other, exclusive of travel. Financial aid ranges from $300 to full tuition. College reports some scholarships awarded on the basis of academic merit alone.

The Citadel

Charleston, South Carolina 29409 (800) 868-1842

A unique institution, The Citadel is a state-supported college providing a liberal arts education "reinforced by the best features of a military environment." The 100-acre campus is located 3 miles from historic, downtown Charleston in a metropolitan area of 250,000. Most convenient major airport: Charleston International.

Founded: 1842
Affiliation: State
Total Enrollment: 2,000 M (full-time)
Cost: < $10K
% Receiving Financial Aid: 50%
Admission: Selective
Application Deadline: June 1

Admission is selective. Graduates of accredited high schools who "conform to the ethical standards and discipline of cadet life" eligible; 83% of applicants accepted, 49% of these actually enroll; 29% of freshmen graduate in top fifth of high school class, 61% in top two-fifths. Average freshman scores: SAT, 460 verbal, 520 mathematical; ACT, 22 composite. *Required:* combined SAT minimum of 800 or ACT of 20, ACH in mathematics, HS GPA of 2.0; on-campus interview recommended. Criteria considered in admissions, in order of importance: high school academic record, standardized test scores, extracurricular activities, recommendations. *Out-of-state* freshman applicants: college seeks students from out of state. State does not limit out-of-state enrollment; no special requirements. *Apply* by June 1; rolling admissions. *Transfers* welcome; 15% of student body are transfers.

Academic Environment. Degrees offered: bachelors (AB, BS, BSBA, BSCE, BSEE). *Majors offered* include usual arts and sciences, business administration, computer science, education, engineering (civil and electrical). Core requirements include 2 years foreign language, 2 years lab science, 1 year Western civilization, 4 years English, 1 year mathematics, 2 years physical science; computer literacy required of all students; other requirements vary with program. Average undergraduate class size: 65% of classes under 20, 35% between 20–40.

About 65% of students entering as freshmen graduate within four years, 70% eventually; 18% of freshmen do not return for sophomore year. *Special programs:* CLEP, honors, study abroad, independent study. *Calendar:* semester, summer school.

Undergraduate degrees conferred (485). 34% were in Business and Management, 29% were in Social Sciences, 8% were in Engineering, 7% were in Life Sciences, 6% were in Education, 5% were in Psychology, 4% were in Letters, remainder in 4 other fields.

Graduates Career Data. Advanced studies pursued by 40% of graduates. About 70% of 1992–93 graduates employed. Fields typically hiring largest numbers of graduates include U.S. Armed Forces, banking, engineering, sales.

Faculty. About 90% of faculty hold PhD or equivalent. About 90% of undergraduate classes taught by tenured faculty. About 20% of teaching faculty are female.

Student Body. About 50% of students from South Carolina; 78% from South, 8% Midwest, 4% Middle Atlantic, 2% foreign. An estimated 78% of students reported as Protestant, 21% Catholic; 7% as Black, 1% Asian, 1% Hispanic, 2% other minority.

Religious Orientation. The Citadel is a state institution, offering a nonsectarian program "founded on a solid religious life." Places of worship available on campus for major faiths.

Varsity Sports. Men (Div.IA): Baseball, Basketball, Cross Country, Football (IAA), Golf, Soccer, Tennis, Track, Wrestling.

Campus Life. College operates within "framework of a military program." Leave is limited. All cadets housed in barracks; veterans may live in off-campus housing. There are no fraternities. About 30% of resident students leave campus on weekends.

Annual Costs. Tuition and fees, $2,697, (out-of-state, $6,432); room and board, $3,859; estimated $3,260 other, exclusive of travel (for freshmen, $700 for uniforms). About 50% of students receive financial aid; average amount of assistance, $5,000–6,000. Assistance is typically divided 20% scholarship, 20% grant, 60% loan, 10% work. College reports 115 scholarships awarded on the basis of academic merit alone, 25 full four-year academic scholarships awarded to each freshman class. *Meeting Costs:* college offers ten month payment plan.

City College

(See City University of New York)

City University

Bellevue, Washington 98008 (206) 643-2000

A small university designed primarily for working adults, City University enrolls about one-third of its students in full-time undergraduate programs.

Affiliation: Independent
UG Enrollment: 98 M, 117 W (full-time); 723 M, 1,011 W (part-time)
Total Enrollment: 4,566
Cost: < $10K
Admission: Non-selective
Application Deadline: Rolling

Admissions. Open enrollment; all high school diploma holders (or equivalent) admitted. *Entrance programs:* advanced placement. *Apply:* rolling admissions. Most students transfer some credit from previous college experience.

Academic Environment. Degrees offered: associates, bachelors, masters. Primary emphasis of school is business, with a liberal arts core. Graduation requirements include minimum of 55 credits distributed as follows: 15 credits in humanities, 15 in social sciences, 15 in natural sciences, 5 in mathematics, 5 in college writing. Strong use of adjunct professional faculty. Average undergraduate class size: 87% of classes under 20, 13% between 20–40.
Undergraduate degrees conferred (241). 91% were in Business and Management, 4% were in Computer and Information Sciences, 4% were in Law, remainder in 1 other field.
Campus Life. A commuter institution, City University provides no residential facilities. About 90% of graduates find employment in business and industry.
Annual Costs. Tuition and fees, $6,575.

City University of New York

New York, New York 10021

The City University of New York (CUNY), the largest municipal university system in the United States, includes 4 well-known liberal arts colleges that offer baccalaureate degrees—Brooklyn, City, Hunter and Queens colleges—and 5 other fully accredited 4-year institutions, each of which has its own special focus and character—Baruch, John Jay, Lehman, Staten Island and York. The university also includes 7 community colleges, (one of which, Medgar Evers, is also accredited to offer some 4-year programs), a technical college and a graduate school as well as schools of law and medicine. Each of the 4-year institutions operates its undergraduate program with a large degree of autonomy. See separate alphabetical listings below.

Admission Requirements vary somewhat among the 4-year colleges. There is full articulation between the 2-year colleges (where an open admissions policy is followed) and the 4-year colleges. Anyone with an associate degree is guaranteed transfer to one of CUNY's 4-year institutions.

Minority group students: CUNY operates "the largest university-sponsored program in the nation to aid disadvantaged high school youth" to enter and stay in college through the College Discovery Program and Operation SEEK (Search for Education, Evaluation, and Knowledge).

Bernard M. Baruch College

New York, New York 10010 **(212) 725-3158**

Baruch College, a separate institution in the CUNY system, includes schools of Liberal Arts and Sciences, and Education, but its School of Business remains the largest component, providing professional training in business and public administration. The commuter college is located in mid-Manhattan. Most convenient major airport: La Guardia.

Founded: 1919	**Cost:** < $10K
Affiliation: City	**Admission:** Non-selective
Total Enrollment: 15,351 M, W (full-time)	**Application Deadline:** June 15

Admission. (See also City University of New York.) 82% applicants accepted, 51% of these actually enroll. *Out-of-state* freshman applicants: university welcomes out-of-state students. State does not limit out-of-state enrollment; 83% of applicants accepted, 50% actually enroll. *Required:* SAT or ACT optional. *Apply* by June 15. *Transfers* welcome.
Academic Environment. *Degrees:* BA, BBA, BSEd. About 32% of general education requirements for graduation are elective; distribution requirements fairly numerous. *Special programs:* 4[1/2] year BBA/MBA program in accounting, 4-year BBA/MBA program in statistics, premed program, program in actuarial sciences, bi-cultural/bilingual (Hispanic) program in International Business, programs in arts management and musical enterprise management, CLEP, honors, study abroad, independent study, individualized majors. Calendar: semester, summer school.
Undergraduate degrees conferred (1,720). 79% were in Business and Management, 6% were in Computer and Engineering Related Technology, 3% were in Psychology, 3% were in Social Sciences, remainder in 10 other fields.
Faculty. About 80% of faculty hold PhD or equivalent.
Varsity Sports. Men: Archery, Baseball, Basketball, Bowling, Fencing, Soccer, Swimming, Tennis, Volleyball. Women: Archery, Basketball, Bowling, Fencing, Swimming, Tennis, Volleyball.
Campus Life. Student body drawn primarily from New York City; 95% of students from New York State. An estimated 16% of students reported as Protestant, 47% Catholic, 5% Jewish, 23% unaffiliated, 9% other; 24% Black, 23% Hispanic, 18% Asian, 21% Native American, 3% other minority. College provides no residence facilities.
Annual Costs. Tuition and fees, $2,552, (out-of-state, $5,152. About 70% of students receive financial aid; assistance is typically divided 40% scholarship, 40% loan, 20% work. College reports some scholarships awarded on the basis of academic merit alone.

Brooklyn College

Brooklyn, New York 11210 **(718) 780-5051**

Brooklyn College is a large, municipal institution, serving primarily the Greater New York area. Its 26-acre campus is located in the borough after which it is named. Most convenient major airport: John F. Kennedy International.

Founded: 1930	**Cost:** < $10K
Affiliation: City	**Admission:** Non-selective
Total Enrollment: 15,629 M, W (full-time)	**Application Deadline:** Rolling

Admission. (See also City University of New York.) High school graduates with an 80 academic average, 900 combined SAT score, or rank in top third of high school class eligible; about 60% of applicants accepted, 64% of these actually enroll. *Out-of-state* freshman applicants: university welcomes out-of-state students. State does not limit out-of-state enrollment; about 58% of accepted applicants enroll. *Apply:* rolling admissions; January 15 recommended. *Transfers* welcome.
Academic Environment. Pressures for academic achievement appear moderately strong. Undergraduate degree programs offered by Schools of Education, Humanities, Performing Arts, Science, Social Science, Liberal Arts, Continuing Higher Education. *Degrees:* BA, BS. About 70% of requirements for graduation are prescribed; distribution requirements vary with school. *Special programs:* independent study, study abroad, honors, undergraduate research, 3-year degree, individualized majors, 3–2 engineering with City College, combined programs with Center for Health Sciences at Brooklyn (including BA/MD, BS in nursing, and 5 other health related fields), 4-year combined BA/MA program in biology, chemistry, psychology, and physics, credit by examination, Scholar's Program. *Calendar:* semester.
Undergraduate degrees conferred (1,096). 24% were in Business and Management, 20% were in Education, 14% were in Social Sciences, 10% were in Psychology, 6% were in Letters, 6% were in Computer and Engineering Related Technology, 5% were in Communications, 3% were in Visual and Performing Arts, remainder in 9 other fields.
Graduates Career Data. According to most recent data available, full-time graduate or professional study pursued immediately after graduation by 39% of students. *Careers in business and industry* pursued by 79% of graduates. Corporations typically hiring largest numbers of graduates include Goldman Sacks, Laventhal, Arthur Young, Price Waterhouse.
Faculty. About 79% of faculty hold PhD or equivalent.
Student Body. College does not seek a national student body; 97% of students from New York. An estimated 21% of students reported as Black, 9% Hispanic, 7% Asian, 1% other minority, according to most recent data available.
Varsity Sports. Men (Div.I): Baseball, Basketball, Cross Country, Football (III), Soccer, Swimming, Tennis, Track, Wrestling. Women (Div.I): Basketball, Cross Country, Fencing, Softball, Swimming, Tennis, Track, Volleyball.
Campus Life. Brooklyn and the Greater New York area combine to offer full range of cultural opportunities. A commuter college, Brooklyn provides no residence facilities. There are 9 fraternities, 3 sororities on campus which about 4% of men, 2% of women join.
Annual Costs. Tuition and fees, $2,605, (out-of-state, $5,205). About 65% of students receive financial aid. College reports some scholarships awarded on the basis of academic merit alone.

City College

New York, New York 10031 **(212) 650-6977**

A well-known municipal institution serving the Greater New York area, City College has 9 divisions. The campus houses the College of Liberal Arts and Sciences, schools of Engineering, Architecture and Environmental Studies, Education, Nursing, and Bio-Medical Education, and the centers for Legal Education, Performing Arts, Worker Education, and Vocational Teacher Education. Most convenient major airport: LaGuardia.

Founded: 1847
Affiliation: City
UG Enrollment: 4,682 M, 3,799 W (full-time); 1,345 M, 1,377 W (part-time)
Total Enrollment: 14,832
Cost: < $10K
% Receiving Financial Aid: Varies
Admission: Non-selective
Application Deadline: January 15

Admission. (See also City University of New York.) High school graduates with academic average of 80, rank in top half of high school class, or have combined SAT of 900 eligible. About 73% of applicants accepted, 46% of these actually enrolled; 8% of freshmen graduate in top tenth of high school class, 50% in top half. *Out-of-state* applicants: University welcomes out-of-state students. State does not limit out-of-state enrollment. Most out-of-state students are international students. Criteria considered in admission, in order of importance: high school academic record, class rank, standardized test scores. *Entrance programs:* early admission, mid-year admission, advanced placement. *Apply* by January 15 for freshmen, March 15 for transfer students. *Transfers* welcome, 990 enrolled 1993–94.

Academic Environment. Administration reports, for Liberal Arts and Sciences, 54% of courses required for graduation are elective; distribution requirements fairly numerous. Degrees offered: bachelors, masters. *Majors offered* include: geophysics, theatre and dance, urban and ethnic studies, secondary science, math education, early childhood education, physician assistant program, accelerated 7 year BS/MD, 6 year BA/JD. About 80% of freshman return for sophomore year. *Special programs:* independent study, study abroad, honors, credit by examination, cross registration with sister CUNY colleges, internships. Calendar: semester, summer school.

Undergraduate degrees conferred (1,227). 19% were in Engineering, 10% were in Social Sciences, 10% were in Architecture and Environmental Design, 10% were in Education, 8% were in Liberal/General Studies, 7% were in Life Sciences, 6% were in Computer and Engineering Related Technology, 6% were in Psychology, 6% were in Visual and Performing Arts, 5% were in Health Sciences, 3% were in Letters, remainder in 9 other fields.

Graduates Career Data. Advanced studies pursued by 40% of graduates; 10% enter graduate school; 15% enter medical school; 10% enter engineering programs, 3% enter law school; 2% enter business school.

Faculty. About 80% of faculty hold PhD or equivalent. About 29% of teaching faculty are female; 14% Black, 4% Hispanic, 5% other minority.

Student Body. About 85% of students from in state. Average age of undergraduate student: 26.

Varsity Sports. Men (Div.III): Baseball, Basketball, Cross Country, Diving, Fencing, Gymnastics, Lacrosse, Soccer, Swimming, Track, Wrestling. Women (Div.III): Cross Country, Diving, Fencing, Softball, Swimming, Tennis, Track, Volleyball.

Campus Life. Metropolitan New York offers widest possible range of cultural events in addition to campus activities. No dormitory facilities available; City College is a commuter institution.

Annual Costs. Tuition and fees, $2,543 (out-of-state, $5,143); estimated $3,275 other expenses. College reports 25 scholarships awarded on the basis of academic merit alone.

Herbert H. Lehman College

Bronx, New York 10468 **(718) 960-8131**

Formerly the Bronx campus of Hunter College, Lehman has been a separate CUNY unit since 1968. Most convenient major airport: LaGuardia.

Founded: 1931
Affiliation: City
UG Enrollment: 1,276 M, 2,724 W (full-time)
Total Enrollment: 9,955
Cost: < $10K
Admission: Non-selective
Application Deadline: Rolling

Admission. (See also City University of New York.) High school graduates with academic average of 80, rank in top third of high school class, or have combined SAT of 900 eligible; about 67% of applicants accepted, 56% of these actually enroll. About 30% of freshmen graduate in top fifth of high school class, all in top two-fifths. *Out-of-state* freshman applicants: college welcomes out-of-state students. State does not limit out-of-state enrollment. All applicants accepted, 51% enroll. *Entrance programs:* early admission, midyear admission, deferred admission, advanced placement. About 3% of entering students from private schools, 23% from parochial schools. *Apply:* rolling admissions. *Transfers* welcome.

Academic Environment. *Degrees:* AB, BS, BFA. About 48% of general education requirements for graduation are elective; new core curriculum, distribution requirements fairly numerous. Unusual programs include: corporate training, program for deaf and hearing impaired. *Special programs:* CLEP, independent study, study abroad, honors, undergraduate research, 3-year degree, individualized majors, combined 4-year baccalaureate/master's program. *Calendar:* semester, summer school. *Miscellaneous:* Phi Beta Kappa, Golden Key.

Undergraduate degrees conferred (853). 22% were in Social Sciences, 15% were in Health Sciences, 14% were in Psychology, 11% were in Business and Management, 7% were in Computer and Engineering Related Technology, 6% were in Public Affairs, 5% were in Letters, 5% were in Education, 4% were in Liberal/General Studies, remainder in 8 other fields.

Graduates Career Data. According to most recent data available, full-time graduate or professional study pursued immediately after graduation by 29% of students. *Careers in business and industry* pursued by 40% of graduates. Corporations typically hiring largest numbers of graduates include New York City government, Montefiore Hospital, IBM, Citibank.

Faculty. About 86% of faculty hold PhD or equivalent.

Varsity Sports. Men (Div.III): Baseball, Basketball, Cross Country, Judo, Soccer, Softball, Swimming, Track, Volleyball. Women (Div.III): Cross Country, Track, Volleyball.

Campus Life. College does not seek a national student body; 98% of students from New York. An estimated 48% of students reported as Catholic, 33% Protestant, 3% Jewish, 11% unaffiliated, 5% other; 33% Black, 34% Hispanic, 2% Asian, 1% other minority, according to most recent data available. No dormitory facilities available; Lehman is a commuter institution. There are no fraternities, 1 sorority.

Annual Costs. Tuition and fees, $2,560 (out-of-state, $5,160). About 85% of students receive financial aid. College reports some scholarships awarded on the basis of academic merit alone. Meeting costs: college offers PLUS Loans.

Hunter College

New York, New York 10021 **(212) 772-4490**

Founded as a teacher training college for women, Hunter gradually expanded its offerings to include full range of liberal arts and became co-educational in 1950. The Park Avenue campus offers both graduate and undergraduate studies. Schools of Nursing, Health Sciences and Social Work at other locations in the city. Most convenient major airport: Kennedy or LaGuardia.

Founded: 1870
Affiliation: City
UG Enrollment: 2,112 M, 5,584 W (full-time); 1,823 M, 4,447 W (part-time)
Cost: < $10K
% Receiving Financial Aid: 75%
Admission: Non-selective
Application Deadline: Rolling

Admission. (See also City University of New York.) High school graduates with academic average of 80, rank in top third of high school class, or have minimum of 900 combined SAT score eligible. *Entrance programs:* mid-year admission, deferred admission, advanced placement. *Transfers* welcome.

Academic Environment. Pressures for academic achievement appear moderate. Graduation requirements include 10–12 credits in

lab science and math, 9 credits in literature, 12 credits in foreign language, 9 credits in humanities and arts, 12 credits in social sciences, 1 credit in gymnastics. Degrees offered: bachelors, masters. About 52% of students entering as freshmen graduate within four years, 75% of freshmen return for sophomore year. *Special programs:* accelerated BA/MA programs in anthropology, economics, history, music, physics, English, biopharmacology, and mathematics. BA/MS in sociology and social research. CLEP, independent study, study abroad, honors, undergraduate research, individualized majors, 3–2 engineering with City College. *Calendar:* semester, summer school.
Undergraduate degrees conferred (1,587). 22% were in Social Sciences, 15% were in Psychology, 9% were in Letters, 9% were in Health Sciences, 8% were in Communications, 7% were in Visual and Performing Arts, 6% were in Business and Management, 4% were in Liberal/General Studies, 3% were in Foreign Languages, 3% were in Computer and Engineering Related Technology, 3% were in Allied Health, remainder in 7 other fields.
Graduate Career Data. Career Development Services offer on campus recruitment, internships, career counseling, resume assistance, and job referrals.
Faculty. About 85% of faculty hold PhD or equivalent.
Student Body. About 94% of students from in state, 3% from out-of-state, 3% foreign. An estimated 24% of students reported as Black, 24% Hispanic, 14% Asian. Average age of undergraduate students: 28.
Varsity Sports. Men (Div.III): Basketball, Fencing, Swimming, Tennis, Wrestling. Women (Div.III): Basketball, Fencing, Swimming, Track, Volleyball.
Campus Life. Less than 2% of students live on-campus; rest commute.
Annual Costs. Tuition and fees, $2,450 (out-of-state, $5,050), room only, $3,200. About 75% of students receive financial aid.

John Jay College of Criminal Justice

New York, New York 10019 **(212) 489-5080**

A specialized, commuter institution, located in mid-Manhattan, offering degree programs for criminal justice agency personnel, civilian students interested in public service careers, and liberal arts major. College accepts out-of-state students on a space-available basis.

Founded: 1964
Affiliation: City
Total Enrollment: 8,522 M, W (full-time)
Cost: < $10K
Admission: Non-selective
Application Deadline: Rolling

Admission. (See also City University of New York.) About 59% of applicants accepted actually enroll. *Apply:* rolling admissions. *Transfers* welcome.
Academic Environment. *Degrees:* AB, BS. New programs include: legal studies, security management. *Calendar:* semester, summer school.
Undergraduate degrees conferred (479). 57% were in Protective Services, 20% were in Social Sciences, 11% were in Psychology, 9% were in Public Affairs, remainder in 2 other fields.
Faculty. About 80% of faculty hold PhD or equivalent.
Varsity Sports. Men (Div.III): Baseball, Basketball, Tennis. Women (Div.III): Basketball, Softball, Tennis.
Campus Life. About 98% of students from New York City area. An estimated 36% of students reported as Black, 27% Hispanic, 3% Asian, 1% Native American, according to most recent data available. No dormitories on campus.
Annual Costs. Tuition and fees, $2,554 (out-of-state, $5,154). About 80% of students receive financial aid; assistance is typically divided 60% scholarship, 20% loan, 20% work. College reports some scholarships awarded on the basis of academic merit alone.

Medgar Evers College

Brooklyn, New York 11225 **(718) 735-1946**

Named after the widely respected civil rights leader who was killed in 1963, Medgar Evers offers both 2 and 4-year programs. It is located in central Brooklyn, a predominantly black community, and is designed primarily to serve the higher education needs of the surrounding area.

Founded: 1969
Affiliation: City
Total Enrollment: 3,924 M, W (full-time)
Cost: < $10K
Admission: Non-selective
Application Deadline: Rolling

Admission. (See also City University of New York.) About 97% of applicants accepted, 63% of these actually enroll. *Apply:* rolling admissions. *Transfers* welcome.
Academic Environment. *Degrees:* BA, BS. About 80% of general education requirements for graduation are elective; distribution requirements fairly numerous. *Special programs:* SEEK/College Discovery, adult and continuing education, work-study, computer-assisted instruction, internships, independent study, undergraduate research. *Calendar:* semester, summer school.
Undergraduate degrees conferred (146). 33% were in Business and Management, 26% were in Health Sciences, 22% were in Education, 9% were in Public Affairs, 7% were in Psychology, 3% were in Life Sciences.
Varsity Sports. Men (Div.III): Basketball, Cross Country, Soccer, Track. Women (Div.III): Track, Volleyball.
Campus Life. College does not seek a national student body; 96% of students from New York. An estimated 85% of students reported as Protestant, 7% Catholic, 2% unaffiliated, 6% other; 88% Black, 2% Oriental, 8% other minority, according to most recent data available. No dormitories on campus. There are no fraternities or sororities.
Annual Costs. Tuition and fees, $2,150 (out-of-state, $2,726). About 85% of students receive financial aid. *Meeting Costs:* college is participant in New York State Parental Loan Program and Federal Guaranteed Student Loans.

New York City Technical College

Brooklyn, New York 11201 **(718) 643-8595**

A recently accredited technical college of the City University of New York, New York Technical is a commuter institution located in Brooklyn. Most convenient major airport: JFK International.

Founded: 1946
Affiliation: City
Total Enrollment: 10,309 M, W (full-time)
Cost: < $10K
% Receiving Financial Aid: 85%
Admission: Non-selective
Application Deadline: Jan. 15

Admissions. Graduates of accredited high schools or the equivalent eligible; 54% of accepted applicants actually enroll. *Out-of-state* freshman applicants: university welcomes out-of-state students. State does not limit out-of-state enrollment; 43% of accepted out-of-state applicants enroll. *Apply* by January 15. *Transfers* welcome.
Academic Environment. *Degree:* BT. *Special programs:* study abroad. About 11% of students entering as freshmen graduate eventually from four year programs, other leave after receiving associate degrees.
Undergraduate degrees conferred (27). 100% were in Business and Management.
Campus Life. About 97% of students from New York. An estimated 55% of students reported as Black, 21% Hispanic, 8% Asian, 1% Native American, according to most recent data available. All students commute.
Annual Costs. Tuition and fees, $2,499 (out-of-state, $5,099). About 85% of students receive financial aid. College reports all scholarships awarded on the basis of need. *Meeting Costs:* college offers Parent PLUS Loans.

Queens College

Flushing, New York 11367 **(718) 997-5600**

A large, municipal, commuter college, located in the borough of Queens. Most convenient major airport: Kennedy or LaGuardia.

Founded: 1937
Affiliation: City
UG Enrollment: 3,780 M, 5,048 W (full-time); 2,044 M, 3,638 W (part-time)
Total Enrollment: 16,268
Cost: < $10K
% Receiving Financial Aid: 41%
Admission: Non-selective
Application Deadline: Aug. 1

Admission. (See also City University of New York.) About 65% of applicants accepted, 50% of these actually enroll; about 38% of freshmen graduate in top fifth of their high school class, 68% in top two-fifths. *Apply* by August 1; rolling admissions. *Transfers* welcome.
Academic Environment. *Degrees:* AB, BM. *Majors offered* include usual arts and sciences, anthropology, communication arts and sciences, computer science, drama and theater, Hebrew, home economics, Latin American studies, linguistics, Portuguese. About 40% of students entering as freshmen graduate eventually; 30% of freshmen do not return for sophomore year. *Special programs:* CLEP, independent study, honors, undergraduate research, individualized majors, credit by examination, 4-year AB/MA in anthropology, philosophy, physics, political science, music (4[1/2] years), 3–2 and 2–2 engineering with City College, Columbia, New York Polytechnic, Pratt Institute. Adult programs: Adult Collegiate Education Program for highly motivated over 25 years old. *Calendar:* semester, summer school.
Undergraduate degrees conferred (1,738). 22% were in Social Sciences, 18% were in Business and Management, 12% were in Education, 10% were in Letters, 10% were in Communications, 7% were in Psychology, 6% were in Computer and Engineering Related Technology, 4% were in Visual and Performing Arts, 4% were in Home Economics, remainder in 7 other fields.
Faculty. About 87% of faculty hold PhD or equivalent.
Campus Life. College does not seek a national student body; about 93% of students from New York. College serves a commuter population.
Annual Costs. Tuition and fees, $2,631 (out-of-state, $5,231. About 41% of students receive financial aid; assistance is typically divided 86% scholarship, 12% loan, 2% work. College reports some scholarships awarded on the basis of academic merit alone. *Meeting Costs:* college offers various state, federal and college programs.

College of Staten Island

Staten Island, New York 10301 (718) 982-2000

The College of Staten Island was formed in 1976 through the merger of Richmond College, an upper-division institution offering the last two years of a baccalaureate program, and the two-year Staten Island Community College. In the academic year 1993–94 CSI moved to a new 204-acre campus which includes five new buildings featuring state-of-the-art facilities and equipment. Most convenient major airport: Newark, JFK, LaGuardia.

Founded:
Affiliation: City, 1955
UG Enrollment: 2,683 M, 3,266 W (full-time); 1,816 M, 3,071 W (part-time)
Total Enrollment: 12,050
Cost: < $10K
% Receiving Financial Aid: 40%
Admission: Non-selective
Application Deadline: July 1

Admission. (See also City University of New York.) High school graduates with academic average of 80 or rank in top two-thirds of high school class eligible for 4-year program; others admitted to 2-year program; all eligible applicants accepted. *Out-of-state* freshman applicants: college welcomes out-of-state students. State does not limit out-of-state enrollment. *Apply* by July 1; rolling admissions. *Transfers* welcome; 548 enrolled fall, 1993.
Academic Environment. Degrees offered: associates, bachelors, masters, doctoral (through CUNY Graduate School). College offers wide range of liberal arts majors as well as professional/vocational programs in computer science, engineering science, business, and nursing. Core curriculum includes English and physical education and courses from each of three general areas: science/technology/mathematics, social sciences/history/philosophy, and humanities. About 13% of entering students graduate within four years, 25% eventually; 30% of freshmen do not return for sophomore year. *Special programs:* study abroad, 3–2 in business and social work. *Calendar:* semester, summer school.
Undergraduate degrees conferred (805). 30% were in Business and Management, 18% were in Psychology, 13% were in Social Sciences, 9% were in Health Sciences, 7% were in Liberal/General Studies, 6% were in Letters, 4% were in Computer and Engineering Related Technology, 4% were in Engineering, 3% were in Visual and Performing Arts, remainder in 6 other fields.
Graduates Career Data. Career Development Services include career counseling, placement service, resume/interview workshops, on-campus recruitment, paid internships, library resources.
Faculty. About 78% of faculty hold PhD or equivalent. About 33% of teaching faculty are female; 4% Black, 2% Hispanic, 4% other minorities.
Varsity Sports. Men (Div.III): Baseball, Basketball, Soccer, Tennis. Women (Div.III): Basketball, Softball, Tennis, Volleyball.
Campus Life. About 95% of students from New York. An estimated 11% of students reported as Black, 7% Hispanic, 8% Asian, 2% other minority. Average age of undergraduate student: 27. No dormitories on campus.
Annual Costs. Tuition and fees, $2,559 ($5,159 out-of-state). About 40% of students receive financial aid, average amount of assistance, $1,600. All resident senior or community college first-time freshmen who enroll in any CUNY undergraduate degree program on or after June 1, 1992 will be entitled to a waiver of 100% of all resident tuition charges for the final semester of study culminating in a baccalaureate degree, one time only.

York College

Jamaica, New York 11451 (718) 262-2165

One of the senior colleges of CUNY, York is a small liberal arts, commuter college located in the borough of Queens. Most convenient major airport: JFK or LaGuardia Airport.

Founded: 1966
Affiliation: City
Total Enrollment: 5,505 M, W (full-time); 880 M, 2,085 W (part-time)
Cost: < $10K
% Receiving Financial Aid: 56%
Admission: Non-selective
Application Deadline: Rolling

Admission. (See also City University of New York.) About 60% of those accepted actually enroll. *Apply:* rolling admissions. *Transfers* welcome.
Academic Environment. *Degrees:* AB, BS, BSN. About 40% of general education requirements for graduation are elective; distribution requirements fairly numerous. *Special programs:* CLEP, independent study, study abroad, honors, undergraduate research, individualized majors, interdisciplinary majors. *Calendar:* semester, summer school.
Undergraduate degrees conferred (494). 43% were in Business and Management, 16% were in Education, 10% were in Public Affairs, 8% were in Social Sciences, 7% were in Psychology, 4% were in Health Sciences, 3% were in Allied Health, remainder in 8 other fields.
Faculty. About 75% of faculty hold PhD or equivalent.
Varsity Sports. Men (Div.III): Basketball, Soccer, Tennis, Track, Volleyball. Women (Div.III): Basketball, Cheerleading, Track, Volleyball.
Campus Life. College seeks a national student body; 90% of student body from New York State. An estimated 66% of students reported as Black, 15% Hispanic, 11% Asian, according to most recent data available. No dormitories on campus.
Annual Costs. Tuition and fees, $2,534 (out-of-state, $5,134). About 56% of students receive financial aid, assistance is typically divided 70% scholarship, 13% loan, 17% work. College reports some scholarships awarded on the basis of academic merit alone.

Claflin College

Orangeburg, South Carolina 29115 (803) 534-2710

A church-related college, located in a town of 15,000; founded as a college for Negroes and still serving a predominantly black student body.

Founded: 1869
Affiliation: United Methodist
Total Enrollment: 347 M, 604 W (full-time)
Cost: < $10K
Admission: Non-selective
Application Deadline: June 1

Admission. Graduates of accredited high schools or equivalent with 16 units eligible; 58% of freshman applicants accepted, 41% of these actually enroll. *Required:* SAT or ACT. *Apply* by June 1. *Transfers* welcome; 32 enrolled 1993–94.

Academic Environment. Degrees offered: bachelors. About 82% of general education credits for graduation are required; distribution requirements fairly numerous. *Calendar:* semester.

Undergraduate degrees conferred (80). 26% were in Business and Management, 25% were in Social Sciences, 21% were in Education, 6% were in Mathematics, 6% were in Life Sciences, 5% were in Visual and Performing Arts, 5% were in Philosophy and Religion, 3% were in Physical Sciences, 3% were in Letters.

Student Body. About 83% of students from South, 9% Middle Atlantic, 3% New England, 2% foreign; an estimated 96% of students reported as Black, 3% other ethnic minority.

Religious Orientation. Claflin is a church-related institution; 2 courses in religion required of all students.

Varsity Sports. Men: Basketball, Tennis, Track. Women: Basketball, Softball, Tennis, Track, Volleyball.

Campus Life. About 75% of men, 75% of women live in traditional dormitories; no coed dormitories; rest live in off-campus housing or commute. There are 4 fraternities, 4 sororities on campus.

Annual Costs. Tuition and fees, $4,412; room and board, $2,400.

The Claremont Colleges

Claremont, California 91711

A cluster of institutions with limited enrollment and varied curricula, The Claremont Colleges share many central services, permit students to take courses at any member college, and combine to provide a variety of cultural and extracurricular programs. Together, Claremont McKenna (formerly Claremont Men's College), Harvey Mudd, Pitzer, Pomona, Scripps, and The Claremont Graduate School seek to offer the facilities of a large university while maintaining the environment of small, residential colleges. Each of the 6 schools is separate, with its own faculty, administration, curriculum, and student body. The 6 schools, in order of founding are:

Pomona, with about 1,500 students, is the largest of the undergraduate colleges. Founded in 1887, it is co-educational and offers all majors in the liberal arts and sciences (see separate alphabetical listing).

Scripps, founded in 1926, enrolls about 650 women and offers special opportunities in humanities and the fine arts (see separate alphabetical listing).

Claremont McKenna, founded as Claremont Men's College in 1946, enrolls almost 900 students in public affairs programs, nearly half in economics and political science (see separate alphabetical listing).

Harvey Mudd, founded in 1955, is co-educational, enrolls about 600 students, and specializes in science and engineering (see separate alphabetical listing).

Pitzer, founded in 1963 and newest of the Claremont group, is a co-educational liberal arts college for about 800 students. It places special emphasis on the social and behavioral sciences (see separate alphabetical listing).

The Claremont Graduate School, founded in 1925, offers advanced work to selected undergraduates at the other 5 colleges as well as to its own 1,700 students. It grants master's degrees in 18 fields and the doctorate in 14.

Claremont University Center is the coordinating body for the group, responsible for intercollegiate organization and planning.

Central Programs and Services include a 1,750,000-volume library system, 2,600-seat auditorium, bookstore, computer facility, minority studies centers, and health and counseling services as well as a variety of concert and theater events.

Affiliated Institutions. Five other institutions share library facilities and, in some cases, faculty: the School of Theology at Claremont, Rancho Santa Ana Botanic Garden, Francis Bacon Foundation Library, the Center for California Public Affairs, and the Robert J. Bernard Biological Field Station.

Religious Orientation. All of the Claremont Colleges are independent and nonsectarian, making no religious demands on students; religious activities on campus are voluntary and coordinated by 3 college-appointed chaplains: a minister, a rabbi, and a priest. Places of worship are available for all major faiths in nearby communities.

The 6 campuses are contiguous, and are located in a small college town of 35,000, 35 miles east of Los Angeles.

Claremont McKenna College

Claremont, California 91711
(See also The Claremont Colleges) (909) 621-8088

Third of the Claremont Colleges to be founded, Claremont McKenna College is a liberal arts institution where more than half of the students major in economics or government. There are 16 other arts and science majors offered, but college considers itself especially suitable for students pointing toward careers in law, government, politics, foreign service, business, finance or management. Most convenient major airport: Ontario.

Founded: 1946
Affiliation: Independent
Total Enrollment: 522 M, 365 W (full-time)
Cost: $10K–$20K
% Receiving Financial Aid: 72%
Admission: Highly (+) Selective
Application Deadline: Feb. 1

Admission is highly (+) selective. About 41% of applicants accepted, 30% of these actually enroll; 89% of freshmen graduate in top fifth of high school class, 98% in top two-fifths. Average freshman scores: SAT, 600 verbal, 670 mathematical; 94% of freshmen score above 500 on verbal, 56% above 600, 4% above 700; 99% score above 500 on mathematical, 82% above 600, 37% above 700; ACT, 28 composite. *Required:* SAT or ACT; two essays, transcripts, recommendations. Criteria considered in admissions, in order of importance: high school academic record, standardized test scores, extracurricular activities, recommendation, writing sample; other factors considered: special talents, alumni children, diverse student body. *Entrance programs:* early decision, early admission, mid-year admission, deferred admission. About 30% of entering students from private or parochial schools. *Apply* by February 1. *Transfers* welcome; 44 enrolled 1993–94.

Academic Environment. Students are reported to be somewhat more concerned with career goals than those at Pomona and less interested in pure science than those at Harvey Mudd; rather, they are concerned "with the economic and political forces and problems of the world." Students frequently enter graduate schools of business as well as law and medical schools. The professional schools they attend are, typically, among the most prestigious in the country. Main curriculum emphasis on government and economics. Course distribution patterns relatively defined: 2 courses from humanities areas, 2 from sciences, 3 from economics, political science, history, and psychology, 1 course in mathematics including instruction in computer use, 1 course in English composition, 4 semesters physical education. *Degree:* BA. *Majors offered* include usual arts and sciences, Asian studies, international management, Latin American studies, management engineering (5-year program with Stanford and Harvey Mudd, one of the Claremont Colleges), PPE (politics, philosophy and economics), psychobiology, philosophy and public affairs, science and management. Degrees offered: bachelors. *Majors offered* include: environmental, economics and politics (EEP), management/engineering, politics, philosophy and economics (PPE). Average undergraduate class size: 66% under 20, 33% 20–40, 1% over 40.

About 81% of students entering freshmen graduate within four years, 84% eventually; 92% of freshmen return for sophomore year. *Special programs:* study abroad, independent study, honors, undergraduate research, individualized majors, internships, 3–2 management-engineering, cross registration with other Claremont colleges. *Calendar:* semester.

Undergraduate degrees conferred (235). 63% were in Social Sciences, 9% were in Psychology, 7% were in Letters, 5% were in Multi/Interdisciplinary Studies, 5% were in Mathematics, 3% were in Life Sciences, 3% were in Philosophy and Religion, 3% were in Engineering, remainder in 3 other fields.

Graduates Career Data. Advanced studies pursued by 75–80% of graduates; an estimated 20% enter graduate school; 25% enter law school; 25% enter business school; 5% enter medical school; 1% enter dental school. Fields typically hiring largest numbers of graduates include consulting, accounting, finance, government. Career Development Services offer interviewing, internships, research opportunities, and "many" other services.

Faculty. All of faculty hold PhD or equivalent. About 23% of teaching faculty are female.

Student Body. About 63% of students from in state; 73% West, 11% Northwest, 4% Midwest; 3% South, 3% Middle Atlantic, 2% New England, 4% foreign. An estimated 6% of students reported as Black, 12% Hispanic, 19% Asian.
Varsity Sports. Men (NCAA Div.III): Baseball, Basketball, Cross Country, Diving, Football, Golf, Lacrosse, Soccer, Swimming, Tennis, Track, Volleyball, Water Polo. Women (NCAA Div.III): Basketball, Cross Country, Diving, Golf, Lacrosse, Soccer, Softball, Swimming, Tennis, Track, Volleyball, Water Polo.
Campus Life. Campus life at Claremont McKenna enriched by facilities and activities of other colleges of the Claremont group, which are supplemented by opportunities in Los Angeles, 32 miles away. Student leader characterizes student body as primarily concerned with marketable skills, but also with a healthy interest in social activities. Strong interest reported in both intramural and varsity sports. Most popular intramurals: inner tube water polo, basketball; varsity sports: soccer, water polo, football, basketball. Student-run campus escort service available.

About 96% of students live in coed dormitories; rest live in off-campus housing or commute. All students are guaranteed housing. Residence halls house 60–75 students each. Intervisitation in dormitory rooms unlimited. There are no fraternities or sororities on campus. About 5% of resident students leave campus on weekends.
Annual Costs. Tuition and fees, $16,400; room and board, $5,750; estimated $1,350 other, exclusive of travel. About 72% of students receive financial aid; "all need is met," average amount of assistance, $15,509. College reports 30 prizes awarded per entering class based on academic merit alone.

Clarion University of Pennsylvania

Clarion, Pennsylvania 16214 (814) 226-2000

A state-supported university, Clarion is located in a town of 6,100, 90 miles north of Pittsburgh.

Founded: 1866
Affiliation: State
UG Enrollment: 1,969 M, 2,859 W (full-time); 186 M, 419 W (part-time)
Total Enrollment: 5,881
Cost: < $10K
% Receiving Financial Aid: 74%
Admission: Non-selective
Application Deadline: Rolling

Admission. High school graduates with GPA of 2.0 eligible; about 91% of applicants accepted, 48% of these actually enroll; 17% of freshmen graduate in top fifth of high school class, 43% in top two-fifths. Average freshman SAT scores: 412 verbal, 448 mathematical. *Required:* SAT or ACT, essay; interview recommended; auditions for some majors. Criteria considered in admissions, in order of importance: high school academic record, standardized test scores, extracurricular activities, recommendations, writing sample; other factors considered: special talents. *Out-of-state* freshman applicants are welcome. State limits out-of-state enrollment. *Apply:* rolling admissions. *Transfers* welcome; 350 enrolled 1993–94.
Academic Environment. Degrees offered: associates, bachelors, masters. Administration reports 30–60% of courses needed for graduation are required; numerous distribution requirements for teacher education curriculum. *Majors offered* include usual arts and sciences, business fields, 7 specialized teacher education curricula including environmental education, computer science, library science, music education, special education, mental retardation, nursing, speech pathology and audiology. About 57% of students entering as freshmen graduate eventually; 21% of freshmen do not return for sophomore year. *Special programs:* CLEP, January Term, independent study, study abroad, honors, undergraduate research, 3-year degree, acceleration, credit by examination. *Calendar:* semester, summer school.
Undergraduate degrees conferred (952). 31% were in Business and Management, 24% were in Education, 10% were in Communications, 7% were in Health Sciences, 5% were in Psychology, 3% were in Letters, 3% were in Social Sciences, 3% were in Mathematics, 3% were in Life Sciences, remainder in 8 other fields.
Graduates Career Data. Advanced studies pursued by 11% of students. About 63% of 1992–93 graduates employed. Career Development Services include helping students to make informed career and educational decisions, preparing them for the job search, helping students with the transition from college to career.
Faculty. About 57% of faculty hold PhD or equivalent. About 39% of teaching faculty are female; 8% ethnic minorities.
Student Body. University does not seek a national student body; 94% of students from Pennsylvania. *Minority group students:* precollege experience program; attempt made to meet financial needs; academic year guidance and tutorial services.
Varsity Sports. Men (Div.II): Baseball, Basketball, Cross Country, Football, Golf, Swimming, Track, Wrestling (Div. I). Women (Div.II): Basketball, Cross Country, Softball, Swimming, Tennis, Track, Volleyball.
Campus Life. About 2% of men, 7% of women live in traditional dormitories; 13% of men, 13% of women in coed dormitories; rest live in off-campus housing or commute. Sexes segregated in coed dormitories by floor. There are 11 fraternities, 9 sororities on campus which about 13% of men, 9% of women join.
Annual Costs. Tuition and fees, $3,710 (out-of-state, $8,108); room and board, $3,200.About 74% receive financial aid, average amount of assistance, $4,061. Assistance is typically divided 6% scholarship, 33% grant, 55% loan, 6% work. University reports some scholarships awarded on the basis of academic merit alone. *Meeting Costs:* Academic Management Service.

Clark College

(See Clark Atlanta University)

Clark Atlanta University

Atlanta, Georgia 30314 (404) 681-3080

A church-related college, located in a city of 1,700,000; part of the Atlanta University Center. Founded as a college predominantly for Negroes, Clark is now operated for the benefit of all qualified students.

Founded: 1869
Affiliation: United Methodist
Total Enrollment: 3,723 M, W (full-time)
Cost: < $10K
Admission: Non-selective
Application Deadline: Rolling

Admission. High school graduates with 16 acceptable units eligible; others considered individually; 75% of applicants accepted. About 10% of freshmen graduate in top fifth of high school class, 32% in top two-fifths. *Required:* SAT or ACT. *Apply:* rolling admissions. *Transfers* welcome.
Academic Environment. *Degrees:* AB, BS, BSHEc, BSMT. About 40% of general education requirements for graduation are elective; distribution requirements fairly numerous. About 29% of students entering as freshmen graduate within four years. *Special programs:* independent study, study abroad, honors, undergraduate research, individualized majors. *Calendar:* semester, May interim, summer school.
Undergraduate degrees conferred (595). 45% were in Social Sciences, 17% were in Psychology, 7% were in Business and Management, 7% were in Letters, 6% were in Visual and Performing Arts, 4% were in Life Sciences, 3% were in Foreign Languages, remainder in 8 other fields.
Varsity Sports. Men (NCAA Div.II): Basketball, Cross Country, Football, Tennis, Track. Women (NCAA Div.II): Basketball, Cross Country, Tennis, Track.
Student Body. College seeks a national student body; 73% of students from South, 9% North Central, 8% Middle Atlantic. An estimated 96% of student body is reported as Black, according to most recent data available.
Religious Orientation. Clark is a church-related institution; one course in religion and philosophy required of all students; attendance at weekly chapel services not required. Religious clubs on campus include Philoi, YM-YWCA, Christian Fellowship of Faith and Action.

Campus Life. About 24% of men, 31% of women live in traditional dormitories; 18% of men, 23% of women live in coed dormitories; rest live in off-campus housing or commute. Intervisitation in men's and women's dormitory rooms limited. There are 4 fraternities, 4 sororities on campus which about 18% of men, 14% of women join; they provide no residence facilities.
Annual Costs. Tuition and fees, $7,460; room and board, $4,200.

Clark University

Worcester, Massachusetts 01610 **(508) 793-7431**

Founded as a graduate school, Clark now regards itself as a research university with a liberal arts college. The undergraduate college, established in 1902, participates in and benefits from the research orientation; sixty percent of graduates go on to earn advanced degrees. The 52-acre campus is located in the heart of a city of 176,000, about 40 miles west of Boston, and in a neighborhood of Victorian mansions that the university has renovated for its building needs, rather than building new. Most convenient major airport: Worcester or Boston.

Founded: 1887
Affiliation: Independent
UG Enrollment: 809 M, 1,090 W (full-time)
Total Enrollment: 2,617
Cost: $10K–$20K
% Receiving Financial Aid: 60%
Admission: Very (+) Selective
Application Deadline: February 15

Admission is very (+) selective. About 71% of applicants accepted, 22% of these actually enroll; 56% of freshmen graduate in top fifth of high school class. Average freshman SAT scores: middle 50% range: 470–570 verbal, 510–620 mathematical. *Required:* SAT or ACT, minimum 3.0 GPA; essay. Criteria considered in admissions, in order of importance: high school academic record, standardized test scores, recommendation, extracurricular activities, writing sample; other factors considered: special talents, alumni children, diverse student body. *Entrance programs:* early decision, early admission, midyear admission, advanced placement, deferred admission. About 33% of entering students from private or parochial schools. *Apply* by February 15. *Transfers* welcome; 104 enrolled 1993–94.
Academic Environment. Students have membership on virtually all university committees including Admission, Financial Aid, and Academic Board. Representatives of administration and student body agree that stress at Clark is placed on creating "an intellectually serious environment with strong emphasis on scholarly effort and achievements." Academic life characterized as "somewhat traditional." Student body characterized as primarily scholarly/intellectual with a modest minority primarily concerned with occupational/professional goals. Opportunities to take courses at graduate level are available as well as opportunity for undergraduate independent study and research. Graduation requirements include Program of Liberal Studies: 2 critical thinking courses in 2 categories—verbal expression and formal analysis—and six perspectives courses "designed to broaden students' awareness of a variety of issues and points of view within the liberal arts." First year students are not required to take any particular courses, however, they are strongly encouraged to take the critical thinking courses. There is a first year seminar series, whose faculty member serves as the students' academic advisor through their sophomore year. Degrees offered: bachelors, masters, doctoral. Clark offers 28 undergraduate majors (including a self-designed major), and students can augment their programs with interdisciplinary concentrations or department-based minors. Unusual majors offered include: environmental studies, race and ethnic relations, Jewish studies and cultural identities and global processes; personalized study program. Average undergraduate class size: 67% under 20, 24% 20–40, 8% over 40; faculty to student ratio of 1 to 11.

About 68% of students entering as freshmen graduate within four years, 77% eventually; 85% of freshmen return for sophomore year. *Special programs:* internships in environmental studies in Israel, study abroad, honors, undergraduate research, self-designed and interdisciplinary majors, cooperative programs through Worcester Consortium, pass/no record option for 1 course each of 4 semesters, 5-year BA/MBA, BA/MA in biology, environmental affairs, international development, 3–2 in engineering with Columbia U., cross registration with Worcester Consortium for Higher Education. Adult programs: College of Professional and Continuing Education. *Calendar:* semester system, plus one 4 week module at the end of the spring semester at the Clark University Center in Europe (optional), summer school.
Undergraduate degrees conferred (609). 31% were in Social Sciences, 17% were in Psychology, 14% were in Business and Management, 10% were in Life Sciences, 5% were in Visual and Performing Arts, 4% were in Liberal/General Studies, 4% were in Multi/Interdisciplinary Studies, 4% were in Letters, 3% were in Mathematics, 3% were in Computer and Information Sciences, 3% were in Philosophy and Religion, remainder in 3 other fields. *Doctoral degrees:* Social Sciences 7, Education 5, Psychology 6, Biological Sciences 3, Physical Sciences 3.
Graduates Career Data. Advanced studies pursued by 32% of graduates immediately after graduation, 60% eventually; 6% enter business school; 4% enter law school; 3% enter medical or dental schools. Clark ranks in the top 10% of colleges and universities whose graduates earned PhDs in the sciences or engineering. Medical schools typically enrolling largest numbers of graduates include Tufts; dental schools include Harvard; law schools include U. of Chicago, Northeastern; business schools include Pace, U. of Buffalo, U. of Hartford. Fields typically hiring largest numbers of graduates include insurance/banking, communication/journalism, environmental affairs. Career Development Services offer on campus recruitment, counseling, career fair, mock interviews, university network, and resume workshops, employment reference library, advising committees to assist with graduate and professional school application process.
Faculty. About 99% of faculty hold PhD or equivalent. About 44% of undergraduate classes taught by tenured faculty. About 31% of teaching faculty are female; 1% Black, 1% Hispanic, 7% other minority.
Student Body. About 34% of students from in state; 54% New England, 20% Middle Atlantic, 4% West, 3% South, 15% foreign. An estimated 17% of students reported as Protestant, 25% Catholic, 22% Jewish; 2% Black, 2% Hispanic, 4% Asian, 12% other.
Varsity Sports. Men (Div.III): Baseball, Basketball, Crew, Cross Country, Diving, Lacrosse, Soccer, Swimming, Tennis. Women (Div.III): Basketball, Crew, Cross Country, Diving, Field Hockey, Soccer, Softball, Swimming, Tennis, Volleyball.
Campus Life. Clark enjoys both the advantages and the contemporary disadvantages of an urban institution. Regulations governing student life are minimal, largely influenced by student desires; for instance, parietal rules are determined by vote of residents of each dormitory, and after freshman year students allowed to live off campus if they wish. Students most likely to feel at home on campus are those who are "academically motivated, liberal minded." Heavy partiers and the very conservative are less likely to feel comfortable. Despite urban location, the state's best ski runs are nearby and Cape Ann and Cape Cod are within weekend driving distance. Cars are permitted on campus after freshman year. Student Activities Center includes a pool and field house, as well as a Craft Center.

About 54% of students live in traditional dormitories; 6% live in coed dormitories; 7% live in off-campus housing; 33% commute. Freshmen are required to live in college housing. Sexes segregated in coed dormitories by wing or floor. There are no fraternities or sororities on campus.
Annual Costs. Tuition and fees, $17,000; room and board, $4,400; estimated $1,200 other, exclusive of travel. About 60% of students receive financial aid; average amount of assistance, $14,992. Assistance is typically divided 56% scholarship, 8% grant, 29% loan, 7% work. University reports 100 scholarships awarded only on the basis of academic merit alone, 996 for need alone. *Meeting Costs:* university offers monthly payment plan, institutionally subsidized parental loans.

Clarke College

Dubuque, Iowa 52001 **(800) 255-2255 or (319) 588-6316**

Clarke is a church-related, liberal arts college, founded by the Sisters of Charity of the Blessed Virgin Mary. Formerly a college for women, Clarke is now co-educational. The college is located on a 60-acre campus in a city of 63,000, 185 miles west of Chicago. Most convenient major airport: O'Hare International (Chicago).

Founded: 1843
Affiliation: Roman Catholic
UG Enrollment: 192 M, 412 W (full-time); 97 M, 253 W (part-time)
Total Enrollment: 980
Cost: $10K–$20K
% Receiving Financial Aid: 93%
Admission: Non-selective
Application Deadline: Rolling

Admission. Graduates of accredited high schools with minimum 2.0 GPA eligible; 74% of applicants accepted, 61% of these actually enroll; 37% of freshmen graduate in top fifth of high school class, 66% in top two-fifths. Average freshman ACT score median range: 21–26 composite. *Required:* SAT or ACT, essay; recommendation from high school counselor or teacher. Criteria considered in admissions, in order of importance: high school academic record, writing sample, recommendation, standardized test scores.

Entrance programs: early admission, mid-year admission, deferred admission, advanced placement. About 25% of entering students from private, 23% parochial schools. *Apply:* rolling admissions. *Transfers* welcome; 77 enrolled 1993–94.

Academic Environment. Single-discipline, multidiscipline, or contract majors available in 36 areas. Requirements for graduation include 3 hours in English composition, 6 in skills, 3 in computer literacy, 6 in religious studies, 6 in philosophy, 9 in humanities/arts, 9 in social science, 6 in foreign language or multicultural studies. Degrees offered: associates, bachelors, masters. Average undergraduate class size: 18; lab size, 16; lecture, 25.

About 44% of students entering as freshmen graduate within four years, 54% eventually; 75% of freshmen return for sophomore year. *Special programs:* CLEP, independent study, study abroad, undergraduate research, cooperative education, internships, 3–2 in engineering, cross registration with Loras College, U. of Dubuque. Adult programs: Accelerated degree programs in business management, marketing, CIS, BSN completion, communications. *Calendar:* semester, summer school (3 sessions).

Undergraduate degrees conferred (124). 25% were in Business and Management, 15% were in Visual and Performing Arts, 11% were in Computer and Engineering Related Technology, 10% were in Education, 9% were in Health Sciences, 6% were in Public Affairs, 6% were in Communications, 3% were in Social Sciences, 3% were in Psychology, 3% were in Physical Sciences, 3% were in Letters, remainder in 4 other fields.

Graduates Career Data. Advanced studies pursued by 14% of graduates; 12% enter graduate school; 2% enter law school. Graduate or professional schools typically enrolling largest numbers of graduates include U. of Illinois. About 81% of 1992–93 graduates employed. Fields typically hiring largest numbers of graduates include public relations, management, computer programming, education. Career Development Services offer career planning, employment opportunities, job search workshops, on campus recruitment, cooperative education program, teacher placement, and career fairs.

Faculty. About 63% of faculty hold PhD or equivalent. About 43% of undergraduate classes taught by tenured faculty. About 62% of teaching faculty are female; 2% Black, 2% other minority.

Student Body. About 60% of students from in state; 95% Midwest, 1% each New England, Middle Atlantic, South, West, foreign. An estimated 64% of students reported as Catholic, 30% Protestant, 6% unaffiliated; 6% as Black, 3% Hispanic, 2% other minority. Average age of undergraduate student: 24.

Religious Orientation. Clarke is a Catholic institution; 64% of students affiliated with the church; campus ministry coordinates religious activities. Daily mass is available but not required; six hours in religious studies required of all students.

Varsity Sports. Men (NAIA): Baseball, Basketball, Cross Country, Golf, Skiing, Soccer, Tennis, Volleyball. Women (NAIA): Basketball, Cross Country, Golf, Skiing, Soccer, Tennis, Volleyball.

Campus Life. About 63% of women live in traditional dormitories; 75% of men, and 12% of women live in coed dormitories; rest commute. Intervisitation in women's dormitory rooms limited. There are no fraternities or sororities on campus. About 20% of students leave campus on weekends.

Annual Costs. Tuition and fees, $10,455; room and board, $3,500; estimated $1,200 other, exclusive of travel. About 93% of students receive financial aid; average amount of assistance, $9,285. Assistance is typically divided 34% scholarship, 24% grant, 27% loan, 15% work. College reports all scholarships awarded on the basis of academic merit alone. *Meeting Costs:* college offers McElroy Loan Program.

Clarkson College

Omaha, Nebraska 68131

An independent, professional college of nursing, conferring a bachelor of science in nursing, and several programs for re-entering professionals to upgrade nursing degrees. Clarkson now also offers programs for physical therapy assistant and occupational therapy assistant. Virtually all students are drawn from within Nebraska or nearby states. Formerly known as Bishop Clarkson College.

Founded: 1888
Affiliation: Episcopalian

Clarkson University

Potsdam, New York 13699-5615 (315) 268-6479

Clarkson is an engineering and technical school which also offers programs in the sciences and management. Clarkson enrolls large number of transfers from two-year colleges with which it has "articulation agreements." The campus is located in a town of 10,000, 135 miles north of Syracuse. Most convenient major airports: Syracuse, NY or Montreal, Canada.

Founded: 1896
Affiliation: Independent
UG Enrollment: 1,812 M, 520 W (full-time); 34 M, 19 W (part-time)
Total Enrollment: 2,772
Cost: $10K–$20K
% Receiving Financial Aid: 90%
Admission: Very (+) Selective
Application Deadline: Feb. 15

Admission is very (+) selective. About 90% of applicants accepted, 29% of these actually enroll; 61% of freshmen graduate in top fifth of high school class, 87% in top two-fifths. Average freshman scores: SAT, 509 M, 540 W verbal, 613 M, 597 W mathematical; 56% of freshmen score above 500 on verbal, 52% above 600, 4% above 700; 94% score above 500 on mathematical, 83% above 600, 11% above 700. *Required:* SAT or ACT; ACH, interview, essay recommended. Criteria considered in admissions, in order of importance: high school academic record, extracurricular activities, recommendation, standardized test scores, writing sample; other factors considered: special talents, alumni children, diverse student body. *Entrance programs:* early decision, early admission, mid-year admission, deferred admission, advanced placement. *Apply* by February 15; rolling admission. *Transfers* welcome; 154 enrolled 1993–94.

Academic Environment. Pressures for academic achievement are moderate to intense; greater in engineering than in management and industrial distribution. Despite efforts to increase offerings in the humanities, students major in the technical areas. All students required to take at least 1 course in each of 3 schools: Arts and Sciences, Engineering, and Management; 2 courses in Science, 1 in computer programming, and 6 in liberal studies including humanities and social sciences. Degrees offered: bachelors, masters, doctoral. Average undergraduate class size: 26% under 20; 35% 20–40, 39% over 40.

About 64% of students entering as freshmen graduate within four years, 74% eventually; 85% of freshmen return for sophomore year. *Special programs:* CLEP, study abroad, individualized majors, cross-registration with St. Lawrence U., 4–1 MBA, 3–2 engineering. *Calendar:* semester, summer school.

Undergraduate degrees conferred (778). 56% were in Engineering, 17% were in Business and Management, 16% were in Multi/Interdisciplinary Studies, 3% were in Computer and Engineering Related Technology, remainder in 8 other fields.

Graduates Career Data. Advanced studies pursued by 18% of graduates; 8% enter business school; 1% each enter medical or law school; 8% other. About 67% of 1992–93 graduates employed. Employers typically hiring largest numbers of graduates include IBM, General Electric, Procter & Gamble, Texas Instrument. Career Development Services offer career counseling, career development workshops, job search workshops, career and graduate planning library, student credential files and scheduling of employment interviews.

Faculty. About 90% of faculty hold PhD or equivalent. About 40% of undergraduate classes taught by tenured faculty. About 12% of teaching faculty are female; 21% minority.

Student Body. About 74% of students from in state; 16% New England, 1% each Middle Atlantic, Midwest, South, West, Northwest, 4% foreign. An estimated 20% of students reported as Protestant, 40% Catholic, 1% Jewish, 32 unaffiliated; 2% Black, 2% Asian, 5% other minority.

Varsity Sports. Men (Div.III): Baseball, Basketball, Cross Country, Diving, Golf, Ice Hockey (I), Lacrosse, Skiing, Soccer, Swimming, Tennis. Women (Div.III): Basketball, Cross Country, Diving, Lacrosse, Skiing, Soccer, Swimming, Tennis, Volleyball.

Campus Life. In the words of one student leader: "If a student is interested in engineering or science and would like a nice quiet campus, then this has got to be the place." Strong interest in hockey and intramural sports, as well as hiking, skiing, skating, and mountain biking. Cultural and recreational opportunities supplemented by those at nearby SUNY College at Potsdam and, to lesser extent, St. Lawrence U. and 2-year SUNY campus at Canton. Motor vehicles allowed for all except freshmen. Students, other than fraternity members and commuters, expected to live in residence halls; exemptions granted on basis of seniority.

About 22% of men, 17% women live in traditional dormitories; 27% of men, 29% of women live in coed dormitories; 22% of men, 17% of women live in on-campus apartments; 22% of men, 30% of women commute. Freshmen given preference in college housing if all students cannot be accommodated. Sexes segregated in coed dormitories by floor or room. Unlimited intervisitation. There are 14 fraternities, 3 sororities on campus which about 23% of men, 28% of women join; 12% of men, 4% of women live in fraternities and sororities.

Annual Costs. Tuition and fees, $15,383; room and board, $5,322; estimated $500 other, exclusive of travel. About 90% of students receive financial aid; average amount of scholarship, $12,380. Assistance is typically divided 5% scholarship, 54% grant, 38% loan, 3% work. University reports 140 scholarships awarded on the basis of special talents alone, 1,700 for need alone. *Meeting Costs:* university offers loan option.

Clayton State College

Morrow, Georgia 30260

A state supported commuter college offering associates and bachelor's degree programs in career-oriented areas. College is located 10 miles south of Atlanta.

Founded: 1969 **Affiliation:** State

Clemson University

Clemson, South Carolina 29634 (803) 656-2287

A state-supported, land-grant institution, located in a town of 9,000, 30 miles southwest of Greenville. Most convenient major airport: Greenville-Spartanburg.

Founded: 1889
Affiliation: State
UG Enrollment: 6,599 M, 5,156 W (full-time); 476 M, 294 W (part-time)
Total Enrollment: 16,614
Cost: < $10K
% Receiving Financial Aid: 55–60%
Admission: Selective (+)
Application Deadline: June 1

Admission is selective (+). About 65% of applicants accepted, 44% of these actually enroll; 64% of freshmen graduate in top fifth of high school class, 90% in top two-fifths. Average freshman scores: SAT, 490 M, 483 W verbal, 585 M, 541 W mathematical. *Required:* SAT or ACT. *Out-of-state* freshman applicants: university seeks students from out-of-state. State limits out-of-state enrollment. Requirements for out-of-state applicants vary by major; 60% applicants accepted, 20% enroll. Criteria considered in admissions, in order of importance: high school academic record, standardized test scores, major, state residency. About 20% of freshman from private or parochial schools. *Entrance programs:* mid-year admission, advanced placement. *Apply* by June 1 for freshmen; rolling admission. *Transfers* welcome; 646 enrolled 1993–94.

Academic Environment. Graduation requirements include 9 hours in composition and speaking skills, 6 in mathematics, 11 in science and technology, 6 in humanities, 6 in social sciences. Administration source characterizes student body as primarily concerned with professional/occupational interests, and degrees conferred suggest concern for marketable skills and career goals. *Undergraduate studies* offered by colleges of Liberal Arts, Agricultural Sciences, Architecture, Education, Engineering, Forest and Recreation Resources, Commerce and Industry, Nursing, and Sciences. Degrees offered: bachelors, masters, doctoral. *Majors offered* in over 65 curricula in arts and sciences, professional and vocational fields. Average undergraduate class size: 57% under 20,, 37% 20–40, 6% over 40.

About 71% of students entering as freshmen graduate eventually, 87% of freshmen return for sophomore year. *Special programs:* honors, cooperative education, study abroad. *Calendar:* semester, summer school.

Undergraduate degrees conferred (2,330). 23% were in Business and Management, 20% were in Engineering, 11% were in Education, 7% were in Marketing and Distribution, 7% were in Social Sciences, 5% were in Architecture and Environmental Design, 4% were in Life Sciences, 3% were in Parks and Recreation, 3% were in Psychology, 3% were in Letters, remainder in 9 other fields.

Graduates Career Data. About 34% of 1992–93 graduates employed. Fields typically hiring largest numbers of graduates include engineering, business and finance, education, nursing. Career Development Services offer counseling, employer recruitment, job fairs, career library and resume preparation.

Faculty. About 82% of faculty hold PhD or equivalent. About 60–65% of undergraduate classes taught by tenured faculty. About 28% of teaching faculty are female.

Student Body. About 73%% of students from in state. An estimated 9% of students reported as Black, 1% Asian, 9% other minority. *Minority group students:* special academic and social provisions.

Varsity Sports. Men (Div.I): Baseball, Basketball, Cross Country, Diving, Football, Golf, Soccer, Swimming, Tennis, Track, Wrestling. Women (Div.I): Basketball, Cross Country, Diving, Soccer, Swimming, Tennis, Track, Volleyball.

Campus Life. Strong interest reported in varsity sports (most popular: football, basketball, soccer), intramural sports (most popular: flag football, softball), sponsored social activities, general student organizations such as honorary and professional clubs. Students most likely to feel at home on campus: academically-talented, socially-interested, traditional-aged student; least likely to feel at home: non-traditional (older) student. Cars allowed, but administration source notes students feel parking is inadequate.

About 32% of men, 43% of women live in traditional dormitories; 17% live in apartments; 51% of men, 40% of women commute. Intervisitation in men's and women's dormitory rooms limited. There are 20 fraternities, 14 sororities on campus which about 15% of men, 25% of women join.

Annual Costs. Tuition and fees, $2,954 (out-of-state, $7,896); room and board, $3,610; estimated $3,325 other, exclusive of travel. About 55–56% of students receive financial aid; average amount of assistance, $3,300. Assistance is typically divided 19% scholarship, 32% loan, 14% work. University reports 2,300 scholarships awarded on the basis of academic merit alone. *Meeting Costs:* university offers payment plan.

Cleveland Institute of Art

Cleveland, Ohio 44106

An independent, professional college of art, located in Cleveland's University Circle, the Institute offers a 5-year program leading to the BFA in 14 majors fields as well as a 4-year program in art education in cooperation with Case Western Reserve.

Founded: 1882 **Affiliation:** Independent

Undergraduate degrees conferred (72). 90% were in Visual and Performing Arts, 6% were in Allied Health, 4% were in Architecture and Environmental Design.

Cleveland Institute of Music

Cleveland, Ohio 44106

An independent, professional conservatory of music offering bachelor and master of music degrees as well as the Doctor of Musical Arts degree. Institute offers joint program with adjacent Case Western Reserve University.

Founded: 1920 **Affiliation:** Independent

Undergraduate degrees conferred (43). 100% were in Visual and Performing Arts.

Cleveland State University

Cleveland, Ohio 44115 (216) 687-3755

Largely an institution for commuters, Cleveland State is located in the heart of Cleveland. Cooperative work/study programs optional in all fields. Most convenient major airport: Cleveland Hopkins (also Cleveland Amtrak).

Founded: 1964
Affiliation: State
UG Enrollment: 3,887 M, 4,051 W (full-time); 2,028 M, 2,000 W (part-time)
Total Enrollment: 17,137
Cost: < $10K
% Receiving Financial Aid: 51%
Admission: Non-selective
Application Deadline: 2 weeks before term

Admission. High school graduates who graduate in top three–fifths of class with acceptable SAT or ACT score eligible; Ohio residents with lower qualifications admitted to Student Development Program. Almost all applicants accepted, 52% of these actually enroll. Average freshman scores: SAT, 412 M, 404 W verbal, 465 M, 415 W mathematical; ACT, 20.3 M, 19.0 W composite. *Required:* SAT or ACT. Criteria considered in admissions, in order of importance: Ohio residence, standardized test scores, high school academic record. *Out-of-state* freshman applicants: state does not limit out-of-state enrollment. Special requirements for out-of-state applicants: rank in top half of high school class, ACT above 18 composite. *Apply* by 2 weeks prior to beginning of term; rolling admissions. *Transfers* welcome; 1,068 enrolled 1993–94.

Academic Environment. Degrees offered: bachelors, masters, doctoral. *Undergraduate studies* offered by colleges of Arts and Sciences, Business Administration, Education, Urban Affairs, Fenn College of Engineering. General education requirements include 24 credits in language and intellectual skills, 20 credits in humanities, 8 credits in fine arts, 12 credits in natural sciences, 20 credits in social and behavioral sciences.

About 26% of students entering as freshmen graduate within four years, 38% within six years; 47% of freshmen do not return for sophomore year. *Special programs:* CLEP, independent study, study abroad, internships and cooperative work-study programs, cross registration with 14 local colleges and universities. *Calendar:* quarter, summer school.

Undergraduate degrees conferred (1,639). 30% were in Business and Management, 10% were in Communications, 9% were in Engineering, 9% were in Social Sciences, 7% were in Education, 6% were in Psychology, 5% were in Public Affairs, 4% were in Allied Health, 4% were in Engineering and Engineering Related Technology, 3% were in Letters, remainder in 10 other fields.

Faculty. About 98% of faculty hold PhD or equivalent. About 25% of teaching faculty are female; 7% Black, 2% Hispanic, 11% other ethnic minorities.

Varsity Sports. Men (Div.I): Baseball, Basketball, Cross Country, Diving, Golf, Soccer, Swimming, Tennis, Track. Women (Div.I): Basketball, Cross Country, Diving, Soccer, Softball, Swimming, Tennis, Track, Volleyball.

Student Body. University seeks a national student body; 98% of students from within state. Average age of undergraduate student: 25.7.

Campus Life. Coed housing available for limited number of students; 98% of students commute. Intervisitation in men's and women's coed residence hall rooms unlimited; sexes segregated by room. There are 8 fraternities, 8 sororities on campus which about 1% of men, 1% of women join.

Annual Costs. Tuition and fees, $3,126 (out-of-state, $6,252); room and board, $4,161. About 51% of students receive financial aid; average amount of assistance, $3,374. Assistance is typically divided 3% scholarship, 70% grant, 18% loan, 9% work.

Clinch Valley College

(See University of Virginia)

Coastal Carolina College

(See University of South Carolina at Coastal Carolina)

Coe College

Cedar Rapids, Iowa 52402 (319) 399-8500 (800) 332-8404

A small, independent, liberal arts college, located in a residential section of a city of 150,000, 225 miles west of Chicago, Coe has continued to improve curriculum offerings in an effort to attract a national student body. Most convenient major airport: Cedar Rapids Municipal.

Founded: 1851
Affiliation: Independent (Presbyterian Church (USA))
Total Enrollment: 513 M, 614 W (full-time); 90 M, 115 W (part-time)
Cost: $10K–$20K
% Receiving Financial Aid: 90%
Admission: Selective (+)
Application Deadline: Rolling

Admission is selective (+). About 74% of applicants accepted, 37% of these actually enroll; 50% of freshmen graduate in top fifth of high school class, 85% in top two-fifths. Average freshman scores: SAT, 490 M, 510 W verbal, 600 M, 530 W mathematical; 52% of freshmen score above 500 on verbal, 14% above 600; 71% score above 500 on mathematical, 35% above 600, 11% above 700; ACT, 25 composite. *Required:* SAT or ACT; essay. Criteria considered in admissions, in order of importance: high school academic record, standardized test scores, recommendation, writing sample, extracurricular activities; other factors considered: alumni children, diverse student body. *Entrance programs:* early decision, mid-year admission, deferred admission. About 15% of entering students from private schools. *Apply:* rolling admission. *Transfers* welcome; 79 enrolled 1993–94.

Academic Environment. Graduation requirements include first year seminar in one of 20 subject areas, distribution courses in fine arts, natural sciences, humanities, and Western and foreign culture course work; students have a variety of courses to chose from for core requirements. Student leader and administration source agree student body is primarily concerned with scholarly/intellectual interests. Pressures for academic achievement appear moderate. Degrees offered: bachelors, masters. Average class size: 68% under 20, 31% 20–40, 1% over 40.

About 68% of students entering as freshmen graduate within four years, 73% eventually; 82% of freshmen return for sophomore year. *Special programs:* CLEP, independent study, study abroad, honors, undergraduate research, 3-year degree, individualized majors, January interterm, 3–2 engineering, 3–2 MSW with U. of Chicago, 3–4 architecture with Washington U., cross registration with Mt. Mercy College and U. of Iowa. Adult programs: Evening degree program, second baccalaureate degree students over 25 are eligible for reduced tuition. *Calendar:* 4–1–4, summer school.

Undergraduate degrees conferred (248). 34% were in Business and Management, 11% were in Social Sciences, 9% were in Visual and Performing Arts, 9% were in Health Sciences, 8% were in Psychology, 7% were in Education, 6% were in Computer and Engineering Related Technology, 5% were in Letters, 4% were in Life Sciences, 3% were in Physical Sciences, 3% were in Mathematics, remainder in 3 other fields.

Graduates Career Data. Advanced studies pursued by 26% of graduates; 12% enter graduate school; 6% enter business school; 5% enter law school; 2% enter medical school; 1% enter dental school. Medical schools typically enrolling largest numbers of graduates include U. of Iowa; law schools include U. of Iowa, Creighton, Washington U.; business schools include U. of Iowa, Ohio State, Washington U. About 92% of 1992–93 graduates employed. Fields typically hiring largest numbers of graduates include business/finance, sales/marketing, research, education, communications. Career Development Services offer resume/interview workshops, library resources internships, on campus recruitment, and individual career counseling.
Faculty. About 85% of faculty hold PhD or equivalent. About 70% of undergraduate classes taught by tenured faculty. About 29% of teaching faculty are female; 2% Black, 1% Hispanic, 1% other minority.
Student Body. About 58% of students from in state; 85% Midwest, 3% South, 3% West, 2% Middle Atlantic, 1% New England, 5% foreign.

Minority group students: Educational Development Counseling Program.
Varsity Sports. Men (Div.III): Baseball, Basketball, Cross Country, Diving, Football, Golf, Soccer, Softball, Swimming, Tennis, Track, Wrestling. Women (Div.III): Basketball, Cross Country, Diving, Soccer, Softball, Swimming, Tennis, Track, Volleyball.
Campus Life. Students report "many" extracurricular activities to chose from, both on-campus and off. Student Activities Committee offers variety of concerts, comedians, other groups also sponsor activities, "so there's almost always something going on." Freshmen required to live on campus. Upperclassmen may select "varied living accommodations on and off campus." Cars allowed. Alcohol permitted only in student rooms.

About 37% of men, 44% of women live in traditional dormitories; 27% of men, 30% of women in coed dormitories; 13% of men, 5% of women live in college-related housing; 22% of men, 21% of women commute. Sexes segregated in coed dormitories by floor. There are 4 fraternities, 3 sororities on campus which about 30% of men, 30% of women join, less than 1% of men live in fraternities, sororities provide no residential facilities. About 25% of resident students leave campus on weekends.
Annual Costs. Tuition and fees, $12,805; room and board, $4,280; estimated $500–800 other, exclusive of travel. About 90% of students receive financial aid; average amount of assistance, $11,989. Assistance is typically divided 66% scholarship/grant, 25% loan, 9% work. College reports unlimited scholarships awarded on the basis of merit, unlimited for special talents alone. Meeting costs: college offers tuition discount plan, biannual plan, 10-month payment plan.

Cogswell Polytechnical College

Cupertino, California 95014 **(408) 252-5550**

A small school of technology, Cogswell offers programs to prepare students for careers in business and industry. Most convenient major airport: San Jose International.

Founded: 1887
Affiliation: Independent
Total Enrollment: 146 M, 19 W (full-time); 180 M, 23 W (part-time)
Cost: < $10K
Admission: Non-selective
Application Deadline: August 1

Admission. Graduates of accredited high schools with 2.3 average eligible. College recommends "strong math and science course work." About 80% of applicants accepted, 78% of these actually enroll. Criteria considered in admissions, in order of importance: high school academic record, recommendations, standardized test scores. *Entrance programs:* early admission, midyear admission, deferred admission, advanced placement. *Apply* by August 1; rolling admissions. *Transfers* welcome; 40 accepted 1993–94.
Academic Environment. Degrees offered: associates, bachelors. Programs offered in civil/structural, electronic, mechanical, and safety/fire protection engineering technology; music engineering technology, computer and video imaging. About 60% of students entering as freshmen graduate within four years; 15% of freshmen do not return for sophomore year. Average undergraduate class size: all classes have less than 20 students.
Undergraduate degrees conferred (26). 69% were in Engineering and Engineering Related Technology, 27% were in Protective Services, 4% were in Engineering.
Graduates Career Data. About 97% of 1992–93 graduates employed, most by engineering firms. Corporations typically hiring largest numbers of graduates include Lockheed, Hewlett Packard, Ford Aerospace, Varian Corp..
Faculty. About 48% of faculty hold PhD or equivalent. All undergraduate classes taught by tenured faculty. About 20% of teaching faculty are female.
Annual Costs. Tuition and fees, $6,600; estimated $1,000 other costs, exclusive of travel. Financial aid: average amount of assistance, $5,000. Assistance is typically divided 10% scholarship, 10% grant, 80% loan. College reports 15 scholarships awarded on the basis of academic merit alone.

Coker College

Hartsville, South Carolina 29550 **(803) 383-8050**

A small, independent, liberal arts college, located in a town of 8,000, 70 miles northeast of Columbia. Most convenient major airport: Columbia Metropolitan.

Founded: 1908
Affiliation: Independent
Total Enrollment: 284 M, 406 W (full-time); 116 M, 106 W (part-time)
Cost: < $10K
% Receiving Financial Aid: 90%
Admission: Non-selective
Application Deadline: August 1

Admission. High school graduates with 18 units (12 in academic subjects) who rank in top half of class, with GPA of 2.0, and score above 850 on combined SAT or 20 on ACT eligible; 74% of applicants accepted, 62% of these actually enroll. About 31% of the freshman graduate in the top fifth of their high school class, 66% in the top two-fifths. Average freshman scores: SAT, 427 M, 463 W verbal, 473 M, 463 W mathematical; 21% score above 500 on verbal, 8% above 600; 38% score above 500 on mathematical, 5% above 600. *Required:* SAT or ACT, interview, essay. Criteria considered in admissions, in order of importance: high school academic record, standardized test scores, interview, recommendations, writing sample, extra curricular activities; other factors considered: diverse student body. *Entrance programs:* midyear admission, advanced placement. About 15% of entering students are from private schools. *Apply* by: August 1; rolling admissions. *Transfers* welcome; 126 enrolled 1993–94.
Academic Environment. *Degrees:* bachelors. Core requirements for liberal arts program of 46 semester hours including foreign language, history, literature, creative and performing arts, mathematics, science, social science, fine arts. Average undergraduate class size: 99% under 20. Several recent students list small classes and faculty accessibility as strengths of the academic program. About 46% of students entering as freshmen graduate within four years, 57% eventually; 81% of freshmen return for sophomore year. *Special programs:* study abroad, numerous internship and cooperative work-study programs, cross-registration with Central College. Adult programs: Evening College, military program. *Calendar:* quarter, summer school.
Undergraduate degrees conferred (132). 23% were in Education, 23% were in Business and Management, 22% were in Social Sciences, 11% were in Marketing and Distribution, 7% were in Visual and Performing Arts, 7% were in Psychology, remainder in 4 other fields.
Graduates Career Data. About 97% of the 1992–93 graduates are employed. Career Development Services include testing, individualized programs, job fairs, career days.
Faculty. About 76% of faculty hold PhD or equivalent. About 42% of classes taught by tenured faculty. About 28% of teaching faculty are female; 6% Black, 2% Hispanic.
Student Body. About 86% of students from in state; 94% from South, 2% foreign. An estimated 31% Black, 1% Hispanic, 2% other minority. Average age of undergraduate student: 27.
Religious Orientation. Coker is a nonsectarian, independent institution "dedicated to the ideals of Christian education"; attendance at chapel services not required.

Varsity Sports. Men (NAIA Div.II): Baseball, Basketball, Golf, Soccer, Tennis. Women (NAIA Div.II): Basketball, Soccer, Softball, Tennis, Volleyball.
Campus Life. About 32% of men, 34% of women live in coed dormitories; rest commute. There are no fraternities or sororities. About 36% of students leave campus on weekends.
Annual Costs. Tuition and fees, $9,510; room and board, $4,280; estimated $1,000 other, exclusive of travel. About 90% of students receive financial aid, average amount of assistance: $7,494. Assistance is typically divided 26% scholarship, 31% grant, 41% loan, 2% work. College reports 80 scholarships awarded on the basis of academic merit alone, 130 on special talents alone, 80 on need alone.

Colby College

Waterville, Maine 04901-4799 (207) 872-3000

Colby is one of a small number of New England colleges whose solid reputation as liberal arts institutions have made them attractive to students. Colby has, for a number of years, sought students from other parts of the country, though not at the expense of alumni children who make up 5% of the student body. The 714-acre campus includes a nature preserve, miles of cross-country trails, and a pond that is cleared of snow in the winter for ice skating. It is located on the outskirts of a community of 18,200. Most convenient major airport: Portland, Maine.

Founded: 1813
Affiliation: Independent
Total Enrollment: 810 M, 910 W (full-time)
Cost: $10K–$20K
% Receiving Financial Aid: 47%
Admission: Highly Selective
Application Deadline: Jan. 15

Admission is highly selective. About 46% of applicants accepted, 37% of these actually enroll; 76% of freshmen graduate in top fifth of high school class, 96% in top two-fifths. Average freshman SAT scores: 570 M, 530 W verbal, 650 M, 620 W mathematical; 90% of freshmen score above 500 on verbal, 40% above 600, 3% above 700; 91% score above 500 on mathematical, 65% above 600, 10% above 700; ACT, 27 composite. *Required:* SAT or ACT, 3 ACH including EN or ES, essay; interview and campus visit recommended. Criteria considered in admissions, in order of importance: high school academic record, extra curricular activities, recommendations, standardized test scores; other factors considered: special talents, diverse student body, alumni children. Entrance programs: early decision, early admission, midyear admission(for transfers only), advanced placement, deferred admission. About 29% of entering students from private schools, 8% from parochial schools. *Apply* by: January 15; November 1 and January 1 for early decision. *Transfers* welcome; 26 enrolled 1993–94.
Academic Environment. Degrees offered: bachelors. Pressures for academic achievement appear strong, but not overwhelming. Core requirements include 2 semester courses in each of 3 divisions: humanities, social sciences, natural sciences; foreign language proficiency, English composition, and 1 full year physical education. A student may earn up to 15 credits on a pass/fail basis; another 15 credits may be earned in independent field experience programs. All students must enroll in 3 on- or off-campus January programs during 4 years at Colby. Many January programs offered for regular academic credit. *Majors offered* include usual arts and sciences, administrative science, performing arts, science technology studies, and a variety of interdisciplinary majors including African American studies, legal studies, women's studies, international studies, environmental studies, and regional studies. Strongest majors reported to be government, English, economics, biology, and American studies; programs in creative writing, foreign studies and foreign languages also have excellent reputations.

About 86% of students entering as freshmen graduate within four years, 92% eventually; 96% of freshmen return for sophomore year. Average undergraduate class size: 60% under 20, 34% 20–40, 6% over 40. *Special programs:* January Program of Independent Study, study abroad, honors, undergraduate research, Senior Scholars, 3–2 program in engineering with Dartmouth, credit by examination, Washington Semester, field experience, student-designed majors. Adult programs: Non-traditional degree program. *Library:* selected depository for federal documents; special collections in literature; open-stack privileges; separate science and art libraries. *Calendar:* 4–1–4.

Undergraduate degrees conferred (462). 39% were in Social Sciences, 12% were in Letters, 10% were in Life Sciences, 9% were in Area and Ethnic Studies, 7% were in Psychology, 5% were in Business and Management, 5% were in Visual and Performing Arts, 5% were in Foreign Languages, 3% were in Physical Sciences, 3% were in Philosophy and Religion, remainder in 2 other fields.
Graduates Career Data. Advanced studies pursued immediately after graduation by 14% of students; 1% enter medical school, 4% enter law school. Medical schools typically enrolling largest numbers of graduates include U. Vermont, Columbia; law schools include Boston College, Boston U., Suffolk. George Washington U.. About 52% of 1992–93 graduates employed. Fields typically hiring largest numbers of graduates include economics, consulting, business, environmental science. Career Development Services tailored to the liberal arts graduate which include recruiting, interviewing, consortia in five locations, counseling, resource library and SIGI computer system. Student assessment of program reported as good for both career guidance and job placement. Alumni reported as active in both career guidance and job placement.
Faculty. About 98% of faculty hold PhD or equivalent. About 40% of teaching faculty are female; 7% minority.
Student Body. About 12% of students from in state; 60% New England, 18% Middle Atlantic, 7% Midwest, 9% West/Northwest, 4% South, 3% foreign. An estimated 2% of students reported as Black, 2% Hispanic, 3% Asian, 2% other minority. *Minority group students:* "extensive assistance—in most cases covering full need"—available to those requiring financial help.
Religious Orientation. Founded by Baptists and "proud of its heritage," Colby has long been an independent institution and makes no religious demands on students. Administration reports "considerable" student participation in on-campus religious life. Ecumenical team ministry (rabbi, Catholic priest, Protestant minister) is active. Chapel activities coordinated by the chaplain. Places of worship available on campus and in immediate community for major faiths.
Varsity Sports. Men (Div.III): Baseball, Basketball, Crew, Cross Country, Football, Golf, Ice Hockey, Lacrosse, Skiing (downhill & cross country, Div.I), Soccer, Squash, Swimming, Tennis, Track. Women (Div.III): Basketball, Crew, Cross Country, Field Hockey, Golf, Ice Hockey, Lacrosse, Skiing (downhill & cross country, Div.I), Soccer, Softball, Squash, Swimming, Tennis, Track, Volleyball.
Campus Life. Colby is an ideal school for those with a love of the outdoors—one-third of the students belong to the Outing Club. Student leader notes that "College's location in rural Maine allows us to enjoy the changing seasons yet not be so isolated that we can't spend weekends in Portland (1 1/2 hours away) or Boston (3 1/4 hours). But she also adds that "people who aren't flexible to dramatic weather changes may find it difficult." A quarter of the students are active in the performing arts where they may direct and produce their own plays, act, and manage technical aspects of production. The Colby Art Museum maintains a permanent collection and prominent traveling exhibits. For several years students have had considerable autonomy in determining regulations governing dormitories. Possession of alcoholic beverages prohibited for those under 21 (in accordance with state law). College "encourages temperance" and where "drinking leads to disruptive behavior, a student faces sanctions." Cars permitted for all students, including freshmen.

About 91% of men, 94% of women live in coed dormitories; rest commute. There are no fraternities or sororities on campus. About 16% of resident students leave campus on weekends.
Annual Costs. Tuition and fees, $18,690; room and board, $5,540; estimated $1,300 other, exclusive of travel. About 47% of students receive financial aid; average amount of assistance, $14,400. Assistance is typically divided 81% grant, 12% loan, 7% work. College reports scholarships awarded only on the basis of need.

Colby-Sawyer College

New London, New Hampshire 03257 (603) 526-3700 or (800) CSC-1015

A small, independent, coed institution, the college offers 4-year programs in several fields including liberal arts, business, health professions. The 80-acre campus is located in a rural village of 2,400, 35 miles northeast of Concord. Most convenient major airport: Logan (Boston).

Founded: 1837
Affiliation: Independent
Total Enrollment: 229 M, 425 W (full-time)
Cost: $10K–$20K
% Receiving Financial Aid: 55%
Admission: Non-selective
Application Deadline: Rolling

Admission. Graduates of accredited high schools with college preparatory program eligible; 85% of applicants accepted, 35% of these actually enroll. Average freshman SAT scores: 850 combined verbal, mathematical. *Required:* SAT or ACT, essay, 2 recommendations; interview strongly recommended. Criteria considered in admissions, in order of importance: high school academic record, writing sample, interview, standardized test scores, recommendations, extra curricular activities; other factors considered: diverse student body, special talents, alumni children. *Entrance programs:* mid-year admission, deferred admission, advanced placement. About 12% of entering students from private school, 12% parochial schools. *Apply:* rolling admissions; February 15 for financial aid. *Transfers* welcome: 15–20 enrolled 1993–94.

Academic Environment. Degrees offered: associates, bachelors. *Majors offered* in addition to usual studies include graphic design, communications, sports science. Internships and cooperative work-study programs required for most majors, strongly recommended for all. Facilities include new state-of-the-art IBM and Macintosh computer laboratories. Students and administration report that the size of the school allows for very small classes and promotes faculty-student interaction. Average undergraduate class size: under 20. About 65% of entering freshmen return for sophomore year. *Special programs:* CLEP, independent study, study abroad, individualized majors, cooperative programs through NHCUC. Adult programs: continuing education for older students. *Calendar:* 4–1–4.

Undergraduate degrees conferred (67). 33% were in Business and Management, 16% were in Health Sciences, 16% were in Education, 10% were in Visual and Performing Arts, 9% were in Psychology, 7% were in Area and Ethnic Studies, 6% were in Allied Health, remainder in Life Sciences.

Graduates Career Data. Advanced studies pursued by about 35% of graduates. About 65% of 1992–93 graduates employed. Career Development Services are available all four years.

Faculty. About 85% of faculty hold PhD or equivalent. About 50% of teaching faculty are female.

Student Body. About 25% of students from in state; 75% of students from New England, 1% Foreign.

Varsity Sports. Men (Div.III): Basketball, Equestrian, Lacrosse, Skiing(Alpine), Soccer, Tennis, Volleyball. Women (Div.III): Basketball, Equestrian, Lacrosse, Soccer, Skiing(Alpine), Tennis, Volleyball.

Campus Life. About 25% of women live in traditional dormitories; 75% each men and women live in coed dormitories, rest live in off-campus housing or commute. Freshmen given preference in college housing if all students cannot be accommodated. Cars are not permitted for freshmen. There are no fraternities or sororities.

Annual Costs. Comprehensive fee (tuition and room and board), $18,500; estimated $500 other, exclusive of travel. About 55% of students receive financial aid. Assistance is typically divided 33% grant, 33% loan, 33% work. College reports about 5% of aid awarded on the basis of academic merit alone, about 95% on the basis of need alone.

Colgate University

Hamilton, New York 13346 **(315) 824-7401**

Colgate is one of a small number of venerable liberal arts institutions that have, for more than 100 years, prepared Americans for business, the professions, and teaching. Its alumni are strong supporters of the school, both financially and otherwise. College continues to enjoy a strong tradition of good teaching. The 1,400-acre campus is located in a scenic, rural setting on a hillside in Central New York State's Chenango Valley. Hamilton, a town of 2,500, is 30 miles southwest of Utica and 38 miles southeast of Syracuse. Most convenient major airport: Syracuse (46 miles away).

Founded: 1819
Affiliation: Independent
Total Enrollment: 1,299 M, 1,353 W (full-time)
Cost: $10K–$20K
% Receiving Financial Aid: 63%
Admission: Highly (+) Selective
Application Deadline: Jan. 15

Admission is highly (+) selective. About 52% of applicants accepted, 29% of these actually enroll; 82% of freshmen graduate in top fifth of high school class. Median SAT scores for middle 50% of accepted students: 546–638 verbal, 603–700 mathematical; 83% of freshmen score above 500 on verbal, 37% above 600, 3% above 700; 94% score above 500 on mathematical, 67% above 600, 18% above 700; ACT: 25.4–29.3 composite. *Required:* can choose from 3 options: SAT and 3 ACH, ACT, or 5 ACH; essay. Criteria considered in admissions, in order of importance: high school academic record, standardized test scores, recommendations, writing sample, extra curricular activities; other factors considered: diverse student body, special talents, alumni children. *Entrance programs:* early decision, midyear admission, deferred admission. About 31% of entering students from private schools. About 31% of entering freshmen come from private schools. *Apply* by January 15. *Transfers* welcome: 17 enrolled Fall, 1993; 5 expected Spring, 1994.

Academic Environment. A very able student body, equipped to deal with increasing competition, reinforce institutional efforts to maintain academic standards. Competition is intense enough to stimulate those who are looking forward to seeking admission to the more prestigious graduate and professional schools. Student leader reports that "Academics are the main concern at Colgate, often to the exclusion of other activities." Core requirements include a six course distribution requirement, 4 general education courses, foreign language proficiency, first-year seminar. Degrees offered: bachelors, masters. *Majors offered* include usual arts and sciences, astrogeophysics, Native American studies, international relations, peace and world order studies, neuroscience, marine science, Asian studies, biochemistry.

About 87% of students entering as freshmen graduate within four years, 90% eventually; 95% of freshmen return for sophomore year. *Special programs:* CLEP, independent study, 3-year degree, 4-year BA/MA, honors, undergraduate research, individualized majors, 2 Washington study groups, semester exchange programs, 4-year AB/MA, 3–2 programs in engineering, 3–4 program in architecture, study groups abroad (London for economics, history, English; France, Spain, India, Japan, Israel, Soviet Union, Yugoslavia). Average undergraduate class size: 48% under 20, 47% 20–40, 5% over 40. *Library:* special collections; archives; open-stack privileges. *Calendar:* semester.

Undergraduate degrees conferred (686). 40% were in Social Sciences, 14% were in Letters, 11% were in Philosophy and Religion, 7% were in Life Sciences, 5% were in Physical Sciences, 5% were in Area and Ethnic Studies, 5% were in Psychology, 4% were in Foreign Languages, 4% were in Visual and Performing Arts, remainder in 5 other fields.

Graduates Career Data. Full-time advanced studies pursued immediately after graduation by 26% of students, 50% within one year, 80% within five years; 3% enter medical school; 9% enter law school; 2% enter business school. Medical schools typically enrolling largest numbers of graduates include U. of Rochester, SUNY, U. of Virginia; law schools include Boston U., Georgetown, Harvard, Albany Law; dental schools include SUNY, Tufts; other schools include Veterinary Medical Cornell. About 53% of 1992–93 graduates are employed. Corporations typically hiring largest numbers of graduates include Arthur Andersen, Chase Manhattan, Chem Bank, Merrill Lynch. Career Development Services include complete range of planning and placement services. Student assessment of program reported as good for both career guidance and job placement. Alumni reported as active in both career guidance and job placement.

Faculty. About 98% of faculty hold doctorate or appropriate terminal degree. About 38% of teaching faculty are female; 4% Black, 2% Hispanic, 9% other minority.

Student Body. About 34% of students from in state; 55% Middle Atlantic, 22% New England, 7% Midwest, 4% South, 8% West/Northwest, 3% foreign. An estimated 5% of students reported as Black, 3% Hispanic, 5% Asian, 3% other minority. *Minority group students:* special scholarship funds; tutoring; cultural center for third-world students (including library).

Religious Orientation. Baptist in origin, Colgate is now an independent institution and nonsectarian. Chapel House for personal meditation open to all faiths. All groups represented in Colgate Religious Association, which sponsors lectures, service programs, various religious projects.

Varsity Sports. Men (Div.I): Basketball, Cross Country, Football (IAA), Golf, Hockey, Lacrosse, Soccer, Swimming & Diving, Tennis, Track. Women (Div.I): Basketball, Cross Country, Field Hockey, Lacrosse, Soccer, Softball, Swimming & Diving, Tennis, Track, Volleyball. It is unusual for a quality liberal arts institution to field both men's and women's teams in Division I varsity competition.

Campus Life. About 42% of men, 40% of women live in coed dormitories; 18% of men, 27% of women in off-campus college-related housing; 16% of men, 23% of women live in private apartments; less than 1% commute. There are 9 fraternities, 4 sororities, which about 45% of men, 35% of women join; 23% of men, 9% of women live in fraternities and sororities. Less than 5% of students leave campus on weekends.

Annual Costs. Tuition and fees, $18,620; room and board, $5,400; estimated $1,330 other, exclusive of travel. About 63% of students receive financial aid; average amount of assistance, $15,600. Assistance is typically divided 82% grant, 12% loan, 6% work. University reports scholarships awarded only on the basis of need. *Meeting Costs:* university offers tuition prepayment options, in addition to parent loan programs and deferred payments plans.

Colorado College

Colorado Springs, Colorado 80903 **(719) 389-6344 or (800) 542-7214**

Colorado College is a private liberal arts institution located in a region of the Rocky Mountains that has become increasingly attractive to students from all sections of the country. Established two years before Colorado became a state to bring classical New England scholarship to the western wilderness, the college is proud of its origins. The 90-acre campus is located in the residential section of a city of 200,000 in a metropolitan area of 320,000, 70 miles south of Denver. Most convenient major airport: Colorado Springs Municipal.

Founded: 1874
Affiliation: Independent
Total Enrollment: 922 M, 965 W (full-time)
Cost: $10K–$20K
% Receiving Financial Aid: 55%
Admission: Very (+) Selective
Application Deadline: Jan. 15

Admission is very (+) selective. About 49% of applicants accepted, 31% of these actually enroll; 78% of freshmen graduate in top fifth of high school class, 97% in top two-fifths. Average freshman SAT scores, middle fifty percent range: 1090–1270 combined verbal, mathematical; 81% of freshmen score above 500 on verbal, 35% above 600, 4% above 700; 92% score above 500 on mathematical, 59% above 600, 14% above 700. *Required:* SAT or ACT; essay. Criteria considered in admissions, in order of importance: high school academic record, standardized test scores, writing sample, extra curricular activities, recommendations; other factors considered: diverse student body, special talents, alumni children, "commitment, quality of activities." Entrance programs: deferred admission, advanced placement, early admission, Common Application Form, summer matriculation (about 10–15% of freshman class "starts in summer, leaves in fall, returns again in January"); midyear admission for transfers only. About 25% of entering students from private schools, 3% from parochial schools. *Apply* by January 15. *Transfers* welcome: 68 enrolled 1993–94.

Academic Environment. College has the unique Colorado College Plan, a schedule under which students take only one course at a time in a seminar setting, and professors teach only one. Each block lasts for 3 1/2 weeks, then there is a 4 1/2 day break, then students return to begin a new block. There are 8 blocks in an academic year and an optional 1/2 block. Students and faculty report that the plan intensifies and enhances classroom discussion and student participation, opportunities for field studies and on-site learning, as well as independent study. Students appear to be involved in determining curriculum policy in many departments through student/faculty committees. Students also sit on Board of Trustees committees for educational policy and development. Grading system offers option of letter grade, no credit, or pass/no credit. Administration reports all courses required for graduation are elective; students must, however, fulfill departmental requirements for a major; general education requirements: at least 3 courses in each of the 3 major divisions: humanities, social sciences and natural sciences; and 2 "alternative perspectives" courses. Students also have the option of completing a thematic minor. Degrees offered: bachelors, masters. *Majors offered* include usual arts and sciences, anthropology, comparative literature, economics with optional business concentration, fine arts with drama concentration, geology, medical technology, all-college major in liberal arts and sciences, various interdisciplinary majors including Southwest studies, environmental studies; new programs in biochemistry and environmental geology recently added.

About 71% of students entering as freshmen graduate within four years, 80% eventually; 92% of freshmen return for sophomore year. Average undergraduate class size: 79% under 20, 22% 20–40. Student/faculty ratio is 13:1. *Special programs:* independent study, study abroad, honors, undergraduate research, individualized majors, programs of ACM, summer introductory geology in Rocky Mountains, study at universities in Japan, Manchester or Germany, Freshman Seminar Program, Southwestern Studies Program, off-campus studies, 3–2 programs in engineering, Teacher Certification Program, urban semester in Chicago, consortial semester in Russia. *Calendar:* 8 3½-week "blocks" (semester change after 4th block).

Undergraduate degrees conferred (478). 39% were in Social Sciences, 17% were in Letters, 10% were in Life Sciences, 9% were in Multi/Interdisciplinary Studies, 8% were in Visual and Performing Arts, 5% were in Physical Sciences, 4% were in Liberal/General Studies, 3% were in Philosophy and Religion, 3% were in Foreign Languages, remainder in 2 other fields.

Graduates Career Data. Full-time advanced studies pursued immediately after graduation by about 30% of students, within 3 years an additional 25% enter graduate programs; 5% enter law school, 5% enter medical school, 3% enter business school. Medical schools typically enrolling large number of graduates include U. of Colorado, Dartmouth, Mayo, Vanderbilt; law schools include Denver U., U. of Colorado, Columbia U., Georgetown; other schools include U. of Chicago, Duke, U. of California schools. Career Development Services include resume writing, interviewing skills, job search, on-campus recruitment, career fairs, graduate school information. Alumni reported to be helpful in both career counseling and job placement.

Faculty. About 96% of faculty PhD or equivalent. About 70% of undergraduate classes taught by tenured faculty. About 33% of teaching faculty are female.

Student Body. About 30% of students from in state; 48% Midwest, 14% West, 12% New England, 7% Northwest, 10% South, 6% Middle Atlantic, 3% Foreign. An estimated 2% of students reported as Black, 5% Hispanic, 3% Asian, 5% other minority, 10% unreported.

Varsity Sports. Men (Div.III): Baseball, Basketball, Cross Country, Football, Golf, Ice Hockey (I), Lacrosse, Soccer, Swimming, Tennis, Track. Women (Div.III): Basketball, Cross Country, Soccer (I), Swimming, Tennis, Track, Volleyball.

Campus Life. Administration source characterizes student body as primarily oriented to occupational/professional interests, with fairly strong interest in scholarly/intellectual goals as well as the arts. Option of single-sex dorm versus coed dorm available to all students. Visitation policy (up to 24 hours) determined by majority vote in each dorm area, except for those areas designated for non visitation. Cars permitted for all; seniors may live off campus. Cultural and social campus programs developed jointly by students and faculty. Colorado Springs is a cultural oasis, part of a metropolitan area of 300,000. Wide range of intercollegiate and intramural sports for men and women, including ice hockey (most popular campus sport) for both men and women students.

About 11% of men, 16% of women live in traditional dormitories; 58% of men, 68% of women live in coed dormitories; 16% of each men, women live in off-campus housing or commute. Freshmen given preference in college housing if all students cannot be accommodated. Sexes segregated in coed dormitories by wing, floor or room. There are 4 fraternities, 4 sororities on campus which about 20% of men, 20% of women join; 15% of men live in fraternities; sororities provide no residence facilities.

Annual Costs. Tuition and fees, $15,942; room and board, $4,096; estimated $450 books. About 55% of students receive financial aid; average amount of assistance, $12,600. Assistance is typically divided 62% scholarship/grant, 28% loan, 10% work. College reports 76 scholarships awarded on the basis of academic merit alone, 30 for special talents alone, and 923 for need alone.

Colorado School of Mines

Golden, Colorado
80401-1873

(800) 245-1060 (in state)
(800) 446-9488 (out-of-state)

Enjoying an international reputation for the education of engineers in fields related to mineral resources, Colorado School of Mines is characterized by some as the foremost school of mineral engineering. The 207-acre campus is located in a town of 9,000 in the heart of a Rocky Mountain mineral-producing area, 13 miles west of Denver. Most convenient major airport: Denver International Airport.

Founded: 1874
Affiliation: State
UG Enrollment: 1,585 M, 483 W (full-time)
Total Enrollment: 3,093
Cost: < $10K
% Receiving Financial Aid: 85%
Admission: Highly Selective
Application Deadline: May 1

Admission is highly selective. About 79% of applicants accepted, 41% of these actually enroll; 88% of freshmen graduate in top fifth of high school class, all in top two-fifths. Average freshman scores: SAT, 550 verbal, 650 mathematical; 77% of freshmen score above 500 on verbal, 12% above 600, 1% above 700; all score above 500 on mathematical, 80% above 600, 10% above 700; ACT, 28 composite. *Required:* SAT or ACT, rank upper 1/3 of high school class. Criteria considered in admissions, in order of importance: high school academic record, standardized test scores, recommendations, extra curricular activities; other factors considered: special talents, diverse student body. *Out-of-state* freshman applicants: school actively seeks students from out of state. State does not limit out-of-state enrollment. No special requirements for out-of-state applicants; about 80% of applicants accepted. *Entrance programs:* midyear admission, deferred admission, advanced placement. *Apply* by May 1; financial aid deadline, March 1; rolling admissions. *Transfers* welcome: 108 enrolled 1993–94.

Academic Environment. Student body is well prepared, curriculum is demanding, as one student puts it, "If you are not willing to give up a lot of your social life and work extremely hard on a continual basis, you don't belong at Mines." The teaching plant and library are well equipped, but students recommend having your own personal computer since the network is crowded. Objectives of the school are strictly professional, there is very little interest in anything other than engineering. Students are motivated by the knowledge that Mines has an excellent reputation and graduates are eagerly recruited by industry. There is some concern about the narrowness of the curriculum. Common freshman year for all curricula. Administration reports 6% of courses required for graduation are elective; distribution requirements include year freshman English, minimum of 2 semesters humanities or social sciences, 4 semesters physical education. Degrees offered: bachelors, masters, doctoral. Majors include engineering aspects of chemistry, geology, geophysics, mathematics, metallurgy, mining, physics. Average undergraduate class size: 20% under 20, 60% 20–40, 20% over 40.

About 35% of students entering as freshmen graduate within four years, 65% eventually; 85% of freshmen return for sophomore year. *Special programs:* CLEP, honors, graduate courses open to qualified seniors, study abroad. *Library:* 395,000 volumes, 2,500 periodicals, other materials include special collections and government documents. *Calendar:* semester, 6-week summer field trip, summer school.

Undergraduate degrees conferred (276). 90% were in Engineering, 7% were in Mathematics, 4% were in Physical Sciences.

Graduates Career Data. Advanced studies pursued by 20% of students (1992–93). About 80% of 1992–93 graduates employed. Fields typically employing largest numbers of graduates include petroleum, energy, construction, environmental, chemical processing, foods, pharmaceuticals; specific employers include Exxon, Dow Chemical, Fluor Daniel, US West, Environmental Scientists & Engineers, Inc.. Career development services offered: workshop provides job counseling, scheduling interviews with industry and government representatives.

Faculty. More than 90% of faculty hold PhD or equivalent. All classes taught by tenure track faculty. About 10% of teaching faculty are female; 3% minority.

Student Body. About 69% of students from in state; 76% West/Northwest, 1% New England, 1% Middle Atlantic, 5% South, 3% Midwest, 14% foreign. An estimated 52% of students are Protestant, 21% Catholic, 5% Jewish, 2% Muslim, 15% unaffiliated, 5% other. An estimated 2% of students reported as Black, 4% Hispanic, 3% Asian, 1% Native American. *Minority group students:* special scholarships and financial aid grants available. Special summer programs are run for Chicano students.

Varsity Sports. Men (NCAA Div.II): Baseball, Basketball, Cross Country, Football, Golf, Lacrosse, Soccer, Swimming, Tennis, Track, Wrestling. Women (NCAA Div.II): Basketball, Cross Country, Softball, Swimming, Track, Volleyball.

Campus Life. Both students and administration describe the political philosophy that characterizes student body, faculty, and administration as conservative. Appointment of a Director of Student Activities reportedly helped stimulate more active social life. However, student source reports that there is not enough social life "at school or nearby." Interest in fraternities and intercollegiate and intramural sports reported as high. Denver offers wide range of social and cultural opportunities. Cars permitted for all; intervisitation during specified hours.

About 10% of men live in dormitories; 14% of men, 24% of women live in coed dormitories; 5% of men, 5% of women live in off-campus college-related housing; 56% of men, 56% of women live in other off-campus housing or commute. There are 7 fraternities, 2 sororities on campus which about 19% of men, 20% of women join; 15% of men, 15% of women live in fraternities and sororities.

Annual Costs. Tuition and fees, $4,366 (out-of-state, $11,962); room and board, $4,050; estimated $1,900 other, exclusive of travel. About 85% of students receive financial aid; average amount of assistance $6,000. Assistance is typically divided 10% scholarship, 37% grant, 45% loan, 8% work. School reports 300 scholarships awarded on the basis of academic merit alone, 350 awarded on special talents alone, 1,200 awarded on need alone.

Colorado State University

Fort Collins, Colorado 80526 (303) 491-6909

A land-grant college and state university, with 3 campuses located in or near Fort Collins (pop. 78,000), 65 miles north of Denver, Colorado State offers programs with strong emphasis on the biological sciences, as well as liberal arts studies.

Founded: 1870
Affiliation: State
Total Enrollment: 20,795 M, W (full-time)
Cost: < $10K
Admission: Selective
Application Deadline: Rolling

Admission is selective for colleges of Engineering, Forestry and Natural Resources, Natural Science, Veterinary Medicine and Biomedical Sciences, Agricultural Science, Arts, Humanities and Social Sciences.

For Engineering (920 M, 190 W, full-time): according to most recent data available, 80% of applicants accepted, 40% of these actually enroll; 62% of freshmen graduate in top fifth of high school class, 92% in top two-fifths. Average freshman scores: SAT, 485 M, 473 W verbal, 607 M, 579 W mathematical; 37% of freshmen score above 500 on verbal, 6% above 600; 91% score above 500 on mathematical, 48% above 600, 7% above 700; ACT, 26.4 M, 26.3 W composite, 27.2 M, 26.7 W mathematical.

For Forestry and Natural Resources (646 M, 294 W, full-time): according to most recent data available, 59% of applicants accepted, 56% of these actually enroll; 45% of freshmen graduate in top fifth of high school class, 80% in top two-fifths. Average freshman scores: SAT, 499 M, 517 W verbal, 550 M, 546 W mathematical; 52% of freshmen score above 500 on verbal, 20% above 600; 70% score above 500 on mathematical, 28% above 600, 6% above 700; ACT, 23.8 M, 23.3 W composite, 23.3 M, 22.1 W mathematical.

For Natural Sciences (1,035 M, 975 W, full-time): according to most recent data available, 64% of applicants accepted, 48% of these actually enroll; 48% of freshmen score in top fifth of high school class, 91% in top two-fifths. Average freshman scores: SAT, 473 M, 469 W verbal, 562 M, 513 W mathematical; 32% of freshmen score above 500 on verbal, 7% above 600; 62% score above 500 on mathematical, 21% above 600, 3% above 700; ACT, 24.8 M, 24.1 W composite, 24.8 M, 23.1 W mathematical.

For Veterinary Medicine and Biomedical Sciences (207 M, 344 W, full-time): according to most recent data available, 72% of applicants accepted, 52% of these actually enroll; 51% of freshmen graduate in top fifth of high school class, 82% in top two-fifths. Average freshman scores: SAT, 478 M, 487 W verbal, 547 M, 502 W mathematical; 41% of freshmen score above 500 on verbal, 5% above 600; 55% score above 500 on mathematical, 18% above 600; ACT, 24.4 M, 24.2 W composite, 24.2 M, 22.6 W mathematical.

For College of Agricultural Sciences (306 M, 384 W, full-time): according to most recent data available, 69% of applicants accepted, 54% of these actually enroll; 49% of freshmen graduate in top fifth of high school class, 85% in top two-fifths. Average freshman scores: SAT, 477 M, 485 W verbal, 528 M, 519 W mathematical; 34% score above 500 on verbal, 3% above 600; 62% score above 500 on mathematical, 9% above 600; ACT, 24.0 M, 24.9 W composite, 24.2 M, 23.0 W mathematical.

For College of Business (627 M, 490 W, full-time): according to most recent data available, 50% of applicants accepted, 51% of these actually enroll; 41% of freshmen graduate in top fifth of high school class, 89% in top two-fifths. Average freshman scores: SAT, 436 M, 432 W verbal, 528 M, 504 W mathematical; 16% of freshmen score above 500 on verbal, 1% above 600; 58% score above 500 on mathematical, 15% above 600; ACT, 23.4 M, 22.8 W composite, 23.1 M, 22.4 W mathematical.

For College of Applied Human Sciences (890 M, 1,977 W, full-time): according to most recent data available, 48% of applicants accepted, 58% of these actually enroll; 47% of freshmen graduate in top fifth of high school class, 85% in top two-fifths. Average freshman scores: SAT, 458 M, 444 W verbal, 542 M, 489 W mathematical; 26% of freshmen score above 500 on verbal, 1% above 600; 46% score above 500 on mathematical, 7% above 600; ACT, 23.1 M, 22.9 W composite, 22.2 M, 22.1 W mathematical.

For College of Arts, Humanities and Social Sciences (1,460 M, 1,586 W, full-time): according to most recent data available, 49% of applicants accepted, 45% of these actually enroll; 37% of freshmen graduate in top fifth of high school class, 43% in top two-fifths. Average freshman scores: SAT, 478 M, 491 W verbal, 523 M, 508 W mathematical; 40% of freshmen score above 500 on verbal, 10% above 600; 54% score above 500 on mathematical, 19% above 600; ACT, 24.1 M, 23.8 W composite, 22.6 M, 21.8 W mathematical.

Required: SAT or ACT. *Out-of-state* freshman applicants: university welcomes students from out of state. No special requirements for out-of-state applicants. About 73% of applicants accepted, 24% enroll. *Entrance programs:* early decision, midyear admission, advanced placement. *Apply:* rolling admissions. *Transfers* welcome.

Academic Environment. Administration reports percentage of elective courses varies considerably by major. *Undergraduate studies* offered in 9 colleges listed above. *Majors offered* include usual arts and sciences, professional and vocational fields, atmospheric sciences, biomedical sciences, communication disorders, environmental health, industrial construction management, microbiology, technical journalism.

Special programs: independent study, study abroad (cooperative programs), honors, optional January interterm, cooperative education. *Calendar:* early semester, summer term.

Undergraduate degrees conferred (2,935). 17% were in Business and Management, 12% were in Social Sciences, 10% were in Home Economics, 6% were in Engineering, 6% were in Life Sciences, 5% were in Psychology, 5% were in Engineering and Engineering Related Technology, 4% were in Agricultural Sciences, 4% were in Letters, 3% were in Education, 3% were in Visual and Performing Arts, 3% were in Renewable Natural Resources, 3% were in Communications, 3% were in Computer and Engineering Related Technology, remainder in 11 other fields.

Student Body. University seeks a national student body; 81% of students from Colorado, 83% North Central, 7% West/ Northwest.

Varsity Sports. Men (Div.I): Baseball, Basketball, Cross Country, Football, Golf, Tennis, Track, Wrestling. Women (Div.I): Basketball, Cross Country, Golf, Softball, Swimming, Tennis, Track, Volleyball.

Campus Life. Students reported to be most at home on campus: academically motivated, enjoy a variety of social and outdoor recreational activities. Least at home: socially motivated one who seeks an urban pace. Alcohol permitted in accordance with state laws. Cars allowed for all. All freshmen under 21 required to live in residence halls or with approved housing groups. Administration source characterizes students as "generally responsible, conservative, and participative in matters surrounding university policy making."

About 30% of men, 33% of women live in coed dormitories; 70% of men, 67% of women live in off-campus housing or commute. Intervisitation in men's and women's dormitory rooms unlimited; sexes segregated by floor or suite. There are 12 fraternities, 9 sororities on campus which about 10% each of men, women join; 4% of men, 5% of women live in fraternities and sororities.

Annual Costs. Tuition and fees, $2,510 (out-of-state, $7,676); room and board, $4,140. About 45% of students receive financial aid. University reports some scholarships awarded on the basis of academic merit alone. *Meeting Costs:* university offers deferred payment plan which permits payment of tuition in two equal installments.

Colorado Technical College

Colorado Springs, Colorado 80907 (719) 598-0200

A technical institution, Colorado Tech offers programs in engineering, computer science and management leading to associate, baccalaureate, and masters degrees. All programs are designed for working adults, most students are pursuing their educational goals on a part-time basis. Most convenient major airport: Colorado Springs.

Founded: 1965
Affiliation: Independent
UG Enrollment: 398 M, 76 W (full-time); 572 M, 138 W (part-time)
Total Enrollment: 1,487
Cost: < $10K
Admission: Non-selective
Application Deadline: 2 weeks before quarter

Admission. High school graduates or equivalent eligible; 86% of applicants accepted, 77% of these actually enroll. *Required:* SAT or ACT, 4 ACH. *Entrance programs:* midyear admission, advanced placement, rolling admission. *Apply* by 2 weeks prior to quarter. *Transfers* welcome: 159 enrolled 1993–94.

Academic Environment. Degrees offered: associates, bachelors, masters. *Majors offered* include engineering, computer science, logistics systems, management. Average undergraduate class size: 68% under 20, 32% 20–40.

Undergraduate degrees conferred (138). 42% were in Engineering and Engineering Related Technology, 20% were in Computer and Engineering Related Technology, 20% were in Business and Management, 18% were in Engineering.

Graduates Career Data. Advanced studies pursued by 8% of students. About 95% of 1992–93 graduates employed. Graduates are typically employed by engineering, computer science, systems management firms including Digital Corp., IBM, Ford Aerospace, Honeywell, Computer Science Corp., Martin Marietta. Career Development Services include career fairs, resume service, career library, professional development course.

Faculty. About 38% of faculty hold PhD or equivalent; no tenure system. About 17% of teaching faculty are female; 4% minority.

Student Body. About 95% of students from in state. An estimated 6% of students reported as Black, 5% Hispanic, 3% Asian, 11% other minority. Average age of undergraduate students: 26; almost all students are part-time, working adults.

Campus Life. Colorado Tech is a commuter institution, provides no residence facilities.

Annual Costs. Tuition and fees, $7,740 for 12 months, $5,805 for 9 months; estimated annual costs for books and fees, $1,040 for 12 months, $780 for 9 months. College reports some scholarships awarded on the basis of academic merit alone.

University of Colorado at Boulder

Boulder, Colorado 80309 (303) 492-6301

The University of Colorado is as often considered a national institution as it is a state university; a substantial percentage of its students comes from other states and foreign countries. Its location, climate, cosmopolitan student body, and faculty make it attractive to students from all over the country. The 600-acre campus is located in a city of 90,000, 25 miles northwest of Denver. Other Colorado University campuses are located in Denver (10,677 enrollment), Colorado Springs (5,724 enrollment), and the Health Sciences Center in Denver (2,305). Most convenient major airport: Denver.

Founded: 1876
Affiliation: State
UG Enrollment: 12,399 M, 10,388 W (full-time); 1,177 M, 1,049 W (part-time)
Total Enrollment: 25,013
Cost: < $10K
% Receiving Financial Aid: 69%
Admission: Very Selective
Application Deadline: Feb. 15

Admission is very selective. About 66% of applicants accepted, 37% of these actually enroll; 54% of freshmen graduate in top fifth of high school class, 87% in top two-fifths. Average freshman scores middle fifty percent range: SAT, 440–540 verbal, 500–630 mathematical; ACT, 22–28 enhanced composite. *Required:* SAT or ACT. Criteria considered in admissions, in order of importance: high school academic record, standardized test scores, personal essay, recommendations, extracurricular activities; other factors considered: special talents, alumni children, diverse student body. *Out-of-state* freshman applicants: university welcomes students from out of state. State limits out-of-state enrollment, 45% of freshmen class from out-of-state. Special requirements for out-of-state applicants: more competitive. *Entrance programs:* midyear admission, deferred admission, advanced placement. *Apply* by February 15; rolling admissions. *Transfers* welcome; 2,334 enrolled fall, 1993.

Academic Environment. Degrees offered: bachelors, masters, doctoral. Pressures for academic achievement vary widely within the university; in general, appear moderate. Student leader and administration source agree that students are primarily concerned about preparation for careers. Colorado, however, is a state university where academic accomplishment is quite respectable and opportunity even greater. Talented students may participate in honors program, undergraduate research opportunities and several residential academic programs. *Undergraduate studies* offered by colleges of Architecture and Planning, Arts and Sciences, Business and Administration, Music, Engineering and Applied Science, Environmental Design, schools of Education, Journalism, Nursing, (freshmen admitted only to 5 colleges listed). Academic programs having strong national reputations include psychology, biology, chemistry and biochemistry, physics, engineering, music, astrophysical and space sciences. *Majors offered* in over 150 areas including aerospace engineering sciences, area studies (African and Middle Eastern, Asian, Central and East European, East Asian, Latin American), anthropology, Chinese, communication and theater, entrepreneurship/small business, environmental conservation, environmental design, dance, fine arts, kinesiology, linguistics, international affairs, Japanese, Russian, tourism and recreation, communication disorders and speech science, women's studies. Administration reports no specific courses required for graduation. The College of Arts and Sciences includes two sets of general education requirements: skills acquisition and content area of study. These include foreign language; quantitative reasoning and mathematics; written communication; critical thinking, historical context; literature and the Arts; natural science; contemporary societies; ideas and values. *Computer Science:* computer literacy not required of all students, although virtually all students become computer literate. Facilities reported as adequate to meet student demand; more than 1,200 terminals/PCs available in 36 sites; all dorm rooms and offices able to connect to VAX network on ISN. Ratio of undergraduate teaching faculty to students is 1 to 22; 33% of introductory level classes have 20–40 students.

About 35% of students entering as freshmen graduate within four years, 64% within six years; 20% of freshmen do not return for sophomore year. *Special programs:* 3 academic residential programs, Academic Access Institute for educationally disadvantaged students, CLEP, support for learning disabled Arts and Sciences freshmen, independent study, study abroad, honors, undergraduate research, individualized majors, combined 2-degree programs (business with engineering, foreign languages). *Calendar:* semester, summer school.

Undergraduate degrees conferred (4,110). 21% were in Social Sciences, 17% were in Business and Management, 10% were in Communications, 9% were in Engineering, 8% were in Psychology, 6% were in Letters, 5% were in Life Sciences, 4% were in Visual and Performing Arts, remainder in 11 other fields. *Doctoral degrees:* Education 30, Social Sciences 25, Physical Sciences 46, Psychology 15, Engineering 19, Biological Sciences 16, Business and Management 7, Letters 10, Communications 10, Fine and Applied Arts 10, Foreign Languages 3, Health Professions 2, Mathematics 1, Computer and Information Sciences 1, Philosophy and Religion 3.

Graduates Career Data. Advanced studies pursued by 30% of students. About 60% of 1992–93 graduates "expect to be employed." Fields typically hiring the largest number of graduates include marketing/sales, communications, electrical engineering, computer/information science. Career Development Services include job bank, job fairs, on-campus interviewing, career library, resume application, cooperative education, research referral to employers.

Faculty. About 99% of faculty have doctorate or equivalent. About 26% of teaching faculty are female.

Student Body. University seeks a national student body; 67% of students from Colorado; 71% West, 9% North Central, 7% South, 6% Middle Atlantic, 5% New England; 1,054 foreign students 1993–94. An estimated 2% of students reported as Black, 6% Hispanic, 6% Asian, 7% other minority. *Minority group students:* special aid and tutorial programs for Black, Mexican American, Migrant, Asian, and American Indian students.

Varsity Sports. Men (Div. IA, Big Eight): Basketball, Cross Country, Football, Golf, Skiing, Tennis, Track. Women (Div. IA, Big Eight): Basketball, Cross Country, Skiing, Tennis, Track, Volleyball.

Campus Life. Because of its size and its fairly cosmopolitan faculty and student body, the university provides an unusual array of social and cultural activities; Boulder, too, is reported to be "fairly comprehensive culturally"; for those students who desire more big city opportunities, Denver is just 25 miles from campus. Cars permitted for all students. Freshmen are required to live in residence halls for 2 semesters. Dorm doors locked at midnight. Administration source reports regulations concerning alcohol and drugs comply with state law; smoking permitted only in designated areas.

About 28% of men and women live in coed dormitories; 63% of men, 63% of women live in off-campus housing or commute. Freshmen given preference in college housing if all students can not be accommodated. Intervisitation in men's and women's dormitory rooms unlimited. Sexes segregated in coed dormitories by floor or wing. There are 26 fraternities, 14 sororities on campus which about 15% of men, 16% of women join; 10% of men, 10% of women live in fraternities and sororities.

Annual Costs. Tuition and fees, $2,580 (out-of-state, $12,086); room and board, $3,830; estimated $1,910 other, exclusive of travel. About 69% of students receive financial aid; average amount of assistance., $6,000; 50% hold part-time jobs. University reports 1,800 scholarships awarded on the basis of academic merit alone, 195 athletic scholarships.

University of Colorado, Colorado Springs

Colorado Springs, Colorado 80933 (719) 593-3000

A comprehensive institution for commuters. Most convenient major airport: Colorado Springs.

Founded: 1965
Affiliation: State
UG Enrollment: 1,112 M, 1,458 W (full-time); 631 M, 938 W (part-time)
Total Enrollment: 5,724
Cost: < $10K
% Receiving Financial Aid: 21%
Admission: Selective
Application Deadline: July 1

Admission is selective. About 75% of applicants accepted, 60% of these actually enroll; 31% of freshmen graduate in top fifth of high school class, 74% in top two-fifths. Average freshman scores, middle fifty percent range: SAT, 850–1040 combined verbal, mathematical; ACT, 20–25.5 composite, 19.5–25.5 mathematical. *Required:* SAT or ACT. Criteria considered in admissions, in order of importance: high school academic record, class rank, standardized test scores, recommendations. *Out-of-state* freshman applicants: university actively seeks students from out-of-state. State does not limit out-of-state enrollment. *Apply* by July 1 (Fall), December 1 (Spring); rolling admissions. *Transfers* welcome; 448 enrolled 1993–94.

Academic Environment. Degrees offered: bachelors, masters, doctoral. Core requirements include English and computer literacy, other requirements vary with program.

Undergraduate degrees conferred (526). 32% were in Business and Management, 16% were in Social Sciences, 11% were in Psychology, 10% were in Communications, 9% were in Engineering, 5% were in Computer and Engineering Related Technology, 4% were in Letters, 3% were in Multi/Interdisciplinary Studies, 3% were in Life Sciences, remainder in 5 other fields.

Faculty. About 90% of faculty hold PhD or equivalent. About 25% of teaching faculty are female.

Student Body. About 85% of students from in state; 45 foreign students 1992–93. An estimated 2% of students reported as Black, 5%

Hispanic, 3% Asian, 3% other minority. Average age of undergraduate students: 27.
Varsity Sports. Men (NCAA Div.II): Basketball, Golf, Soccer, Tennis. Women (NCAA Div.II): Basketball, Softball, Tennis, Volleyball.
Campus Life. Colorado is a commuter institution, provides no residence facilities.
Annual Costs. Tuition and fees, $2,269 (out-of-state, $7,369). About 21% of students receive financial aid. Assistance is typically divided 11% scholarship, 52% loan, 38% work. University reports some scholarships awarded on the basis of academic merit alone.

University of Colorado, Denver

Denver, Colorado 80217-3364 (303) 556-2398

One of four institutions in the University of Colorado system, CU-Denver is a non-residential, urban campus located in downtown Denver.

Founded: 1912
Affiliation: State
UG Enrollment: 1,746 M, 1,955 W (full-time); 1,153 M, 1,200 W (part-time)
Total Enrollment: 10,677
Cost: < $10K
% Receiving Financial Aid: 29%
Admission: Non-selective
Application Deadline: Rolling

Admission. About 47% of applicants accepted, 46% of these actually enroll; 47% of freshmen graduate in top fifth of high school class, 81% in top two-fifths. Average SAT scores: 41% score above 500 on verbal, 15% above 600, 3% above 700; 50% score above 500 on mathematical, 15% above 600, 3% above 700. *Required:* SAT or ACT, minimum GPA. Criteria considered in admissions, in order of importance: high school academic record, standardized test scores, and class rank considered of equal importance; recommendations also considered. *Entrance programs:* midyear admission. *Apply:* rolling admissions. *Transfers* welcome; 1,110 enrolled 1993–94.
Academic Environment. Degrees offered: bachelors, masters, doctoral. Programs offered in Liberal Arts, Architecture and Planning, Business, Education, Engineering, Fine Arts, and the Graduate School of Public Affairs. Graduation requirements include 9 credit hours in writing/speech, 3 in mathematics, 9 in behavioral sciences, 9 in social sciences, 6 in humanities, 3 in arts, and 3 in multicultural diversity. *Special programs:* January Term, study abroad, cross-registration, internship/work-study.
Graduates Career Data. Advanced studies pursued by 37% of graduates. About 88% of 1992–93 graduates employed. Career Development Services include resume services, job fairs, mock interviews, job bank services, job library.
Faculty. About 96% of faculty hold PhD or equivalent. About 30% of teaching faculty are female; 5% Hispanic, 9% other minority.
Student Body. About 96% of students from in state, 2% foreign. An estimated 3% of students reported as Black, 7% Hispanic, 6% Asian, 10% other minority. Average age of undergraduate student: 26.
Campus Life. Campus is located in downtown Denver; all students commute.
Annual Costs. Tuition and fees, $1,955 (out-of-state, $8,916); estimated $510 other, exclusive of travel. About 29% of students receive financial aid; average amount of assistance, $5,034. Assistance is typically divided 4% scholarship, 7% grant, 69% loan, 10% work. University reports 359 scholarships awarded on the basis of academic merit alone.

Columbia Bible College and Seminary

Columbia, South Carolina 29230 (803) 754-4100

A Bible college with an emphasis on "biblical inerrancy, world missions, victorious Christian living, academic excellence, and total life training." Most convenient major airport: Columbia Metropolitan.

Founded: 1923
Affiliation: Independent
Total Enrollment: 208 M, 168 W (full-time); 32 M, 29 W (part-time)
Cost: < $10K
% Receiving Financial Aid: 59%
Admission: Non-selective
Application Deadline: Rolling

Admission. High school graduates with minimum GPA of 2.0 eligible; 83% of applicants accepted, 47% of these actually enroll; 27% of freshmen graduate in top fifth of high school class, 53% in top two fifths. *Required:* SAT or ACT. Criteria considered in admissions, in order of importance: high school academic record, standardized test scores, recommendations, writing sample, extra curricular activities. Entrance program: midyear admission. *Apply:* rolling admissions. *Transfers* welcome; 63 enrolled Fall 1993.
Academic Environment. Degrees offered: associates, bachelors, masters. Programs in psychology and biblical languages recently added. About 60% of students entering as freshmen graduate eventually; 65% return for sophomore year. *Special programs:* January term, study abroad, Midlands Technical school (1 & 2 year programs).
Undergraduate degrees conferred (112). 100% were in Theology.
Faculty. About 56% of faculty hold PhD or equivalent; no tenure system. About 28% of teaching faculty are female; 4% minority.
Religious Orientation. Columbia is a multi-denominational bible college. Thirteen courses in religion required of all students.
Student Body. About 36% of students from in state; 69% from South, 9% Middle Atlantic, 6% Midwest, 7% West/Northwest, 6% foreign. All students reported as Protestant; 6% Black, 1% Hispanic, 1% Asian, 6% other minority. Average age of undergraduate students: 24.
Campus Life. About 49% of men, 68% of women live in traditional dormitories; rest live in off-campus housing or commute.
Annual Costs. Tuition and fees, $6,150; room and board, $3,262, estimated $2,458 other, exclusive of travel. About 59% of students receive financial aid, average amount of assistance $4,924. Assistance is typically divided 2% scholarship, 39% grant, 54% loan, 5% work. College reports 20 scholarships awarded for merit alone, 15 for special talents alone, 47 for need alone.

Columbia College

Chicago, Illinois 60605 (312) 663-1600

An independent, nonresidential institution, located in downtown Chicago, providing "unique opportunities for its role in educating students in the creative and public arts." Most convenient major airport: O'Hare.

Founded: 1890
Affiliation: Independent
Total Enrollment: 5,505 M, W (full-time); 945 M, 1,050 W (part-time)
Cost: < $10K
Admission: Non-selective
Application Deadline: Rolling

Admission. High school graduates eligible; 90% of applicants accepted, 44% of these actually enroll. *Required:* SAT or ACT (optional). *Apply:* rolling admissions. *Transfers* welcome.
Academic Environment. *Degree:* AB. *Special programs:* CLEP, independent study, 3-year degree. About 35% of students entering as freshmen graduate eventually; 35% of freshmen do not return for sophomore year. *Calendar:* semester, intensive midterm, summer school.
Undergraduate degrees conferred (665). 100% were in Liberal/General Studies.
Campus Life. College seeks a national student body; 98% of students from in state. An estimated 24% of students reported as Black, 8% Hispanic, 4% Asian, 1% Native American, according to most recent data available. No dormitories on campus. There are no fraternities or sororities.
Annual Costs. Tuition and fees, $6,654.

Columbia College

Columbia, Missouri 65216 (314) 875-7352

An independent, co-educational liberal arts/career college, located in a city of 70,000, midway between Kansas City and St. Louis. Most convenient major airport: Lambert Field (St. Louis).

Founded: 1851
Affiliation: Independent
UG Enrollment: 288 M, 402 W (full-time); 64 M, 82 W (part-time)
Total Enrollment: 836
Cost: < $10K
% Receiving Financial Aid: 60%
Admission: Non-selective
Application Deadline: Aug. 20

Admission. High school graduates with 15 units eligible; 99% of applicants accepted, 47% of these actually enroll. About 13% of freshmen graduate in top fifth of high school class, 26% in top two-fifths. Average freshman ACT scores: 20.7 M, 20.0 W composite. *Required:* ACT or SAT; interview required if GPA below 2.0. *Apply* by August 20; rolling admissions. *Transfers* welcome; 109 enrolled 1993–94.

Academic Environment. Degrees offered: associates, bachelors, masters. General education requirements include 9 hours of basic skills, 18 hours of humanities (3 disciplines), 8 hours mathematics/science, 9 hours social perspectives (3 disciplines). Unusual, new or notable programs include commercial investment real estate, travel administration, fashion merchandising and design, meeting and convention planning, social work. *Special programs:* CLEP, independent study, study abroad, honors, extended studies program, American Experience (2–8 week programs for international students), cross registration. Average undergraduate class size: 50% of classes under 20, 50% between 20–40. *Calendar:* semester, summer school; 8-week evening sessions.

Undergraduate degrees conferred (553). 68% were in Business and Management, 8% were in Psychology, 8% were in Liberal/General Studies, 5% were in Protective Services, 5% were in Social Sciences, remainder in 4 other fields.

Graduates Career Data. Advanced studies pursued by 25% of students. Fields typically employing the largest numbers of graduates include business, education, criminal justice. Career Development Services include career counseling, placement service, resume/interview workshops, salary negotiation, library resources, graduate school information.

Faculty. About 73% of faculty hold PhD or equivalent. About 50% of undergraduate classes taught by tenured faculty, 90% by full-time faculty. About 31% of teaching faculty are female; 11% minorities.

Varsity Sports. Men (NAIA): Basketball, Golf, Soccer. Women (NAIA): Golf, Softball, Volleyball.

Student Body. College seeks a national student body; 76% of students from Missouri; 82% from Midwest, 14% foreign. An estimated 21% of students reported as Protestant, 7% Catholic, 2% Jewish; 9% Black, 22% other minority.

Campus Life. About 18% of women (full-time day students) live in traditional dormitories; 14% men, 5% women live in coed dormitories; rest live in off-campus housing or commute. Full-time freshmen and sophomores required to live on campus. Intervisitation in men's and women's dormitory rooms limited. There are 5 honorary and 1 service fraternities for men and women, 1 social fraternity for men, 1 sorority. About 50% of resident students leave campus on weekends.

Annual Costs. Tuition and fees, $7,900; room and board, $3,524; estimated $1700 other, exclusive of travel. About 60% of students receive financial aid; average amount of assistance, $8,700. Assistance is typically divided 25% scholarship, 12% grant, 58% loan, 5% work. College reports some scholarships awarded on the basis of academic merit alone, some for special talents, some for need.

Columbia College

Columbia, South Carolina 29203 (803) 786-3012

A church-related four-year college for women located in a city of 350,000. Most convenient major airport: Columbia.

Founded: 1854
Affiliation: United Methodist
UG Enrollment: 968 W (full-time); 241 W (part-time)
Total Enrollment: 1,238
Cost: < $10K
% Receiving Financial Aid: 86%
Admission: Non-selective
Application Deadline: May 1

Admission. Graduates of accredited high schools with 18 units (16 in academic subjects) and C average or better eligible; 84% of applicants accepted, 39% of these actually enroll; 40% of freshman graduate in top fifth of class, 67% top two-fifths. Average freshman SAT scores: 413 verbal, 438 mathematical. *Required:* SAT or ACT; interview optional. Criteria considered in admissions, in order of importance: high school academic record, standardized test scores, recommendations; other factors considered: special talents. Entrance program: early admission. *Apply* preferably by May 1; rolling admissions. *Transfers* welcome; 91 enrolled 1993–94.

Academic Environment. Degrees offered: bachelors, masters. General education requirements vary with program: 62 hours for AB, 41 for Music, 31 for Nursing. Average undergraduate class size: 20. Students list small class sizes, one-on-one interaction with faculty, and free tutoring as strengths of the academic program. *Special programs:* honors, independent study, study abroad, contractual studies, interdisciplinary majors, practicum, optional May session, internships. About 52% of students entering as freshmen graduate within four years. Adult programs: Women's Evening College, programs in business administration, public affairs, second degree and health services degrees. *Calendar:* early semester, summer school.

Undergraduate degrees conferred (200). 33% were in Education, 20% were in Business and Management, 11% were in Public Affairs, 9% were in Multi/Interdisciplinary Studies, 8% were in Visual and Performing Arts, 4% were in Life Sciences, 4% were in Psychology, 3% were in Mathematics, 3% were in Social Sciences, 3% were in Letters, remainder in 6 other fields.

Faculty. About 62% of faculty hold PhD or equivalent. About 70% of classes taught by tenured faculty. About 55% of teaching faculty are female.

Student Body. About 90% of students from in state; 93% from South, 3% Middle Atlantic, 1% each New England, Midwest, Northwest, foreign. An estimated 81% of students reported as Protestant, 7% Catholic, 4% other, 8% unaffiliated.

Religious Orientation. Columbia is a church-related institution; 2 religious courses required. About 22% of students are affiliated with United Methodist church.

Varsity Sports. Women (NAIA): Tennis, Volleyball.

Campus Life. About 62% of women live in traditional dormitories; rest commute. Freshmen given preference in college housing if all students can not be accommodated. There are no sororities. About 50% of resident students leave campus on weekends.

Annual Costs. Tuition and fees, $9,750; room and board, $3,770. About 86% of students receive financial aid; average amount of assistance, $8,807. Assistance is typically divided 15% scholarship, 38% grant, 42% loan, 5% work. College reports 306 scholarships awarded on the basis of academic merit alone, 185 for special talents, 410 for need alone.

Columbia Union College

Takoma Park, Maryland 20912 (301) 891-4234

Columbia is one of the "charter members" of the Ivy League, but unlike its companion schools, it left behind its earlier aristocratic pretensions and associations, for the most part, as it became one of the nation's most productive university establishments. Columbia College, a leading undergraduate (now) coed college, and the School of Engineering and Applied Science are the two principal undergraduate divisions of Columbia University. A different and wholly separate undergraduate division of the University is the School of General Studies, which exists to serve part-time and non-traditional students. Barnard College, one of the nation's top women's liberal arts colleges, is an autonomous affiliate of the University. Columbia University also maintains fourteen first-rate graduate and professional schools. The influence of these schools on undergraduate life and study cannot be ignored, for the percentage of Columbia College graduates going on to graduate and professional study is one of the highest in the country.

Columbia is an urban university, located on the upper west side of Manhattan in an area that has undergone significant population changes in recent years, but which also includes a cluster of major cultural, religious, and educational institutions. Venturesome students can learn not only from their collegiate studies but also from the proximity of the university to the very heart of Manhattan's ethnic diversity. Most convenient major airports: Newark, LaGuardia, Kennedy.

A church-related college, located in a suburban community of 18,500, adjacent to Washington, D.C. College reports it views community around the campus "as its special mission field"; most academic programs "geared to meeting this goal." Most convenient major airport: Washington National.

Founded: 1904
Affiliation: Seventh-day Adventist
Total Enrollment: 1,211 M, W (full-time); 259 M, 473 W (part-time)
Cost: < $10K
% Receiving Financial Aid: 71%
Admission: Non-selective
Application Deadline: Rolling

Admission. Graduates of accredited high schools with 18 units and C average may be admitted by certificate; 71% of applicants accepted, 45% of these actually enroll. Average freshman scores, according to most recent data available: SAT, 436 M, 432 W verbal, 472 M, 419 W mathematical; ACT, 19 M, 20 W composite. *Required:* SAT or ACT, interview. *Non-academic factors* considered in admissions: religious affiliation and/or commitment. *Apply:* rolling admissions. *Transfers* welcome.

Academic Environment. *Degrees:* AB, BS. Programs offered include: business, allied health, communications, journalism, engineering, nursing. About 45% of freshmen do not return for sophomore year. *Special programs:* CLEP, independent study, study abroad, undergraduate research, 3–2 program in engineering with U. of Maryland. Adult programs: Evening program for those already having 60+ credits, also External Correspondence Program. *Calendar:* semester, summer school.

Undergraduate degrees conferred (238). 57% were in Business and Management, 18% were in Psychology, 8% were in Health Sciences, 3% were in Theology, 3% were in Mathematics, 3% were in Education, remainder in 9 other fields.

Faculty. About 45% of faculty hold PhD or equivalent.

Varsity Sports. Men (Div.III): Basketball, Cross Country, Soccer. Women (Div.III): Basketball, Tennis, Track, Volleyball.

Student Body. College does not seek a national student body; 44% of students from Maryland, almost all from Middle Atlantic. An estimated 36% of students reported as Black, 4% Hispanic, 8% Asian, 4% other minority, according to most recent data available.

Religious Orientation. Columbia Union is a church-related institution; 12 hours of religion, attendance at 75% of chapel services each semester required of all students.

Campus Life. About 22% of men, 24% of women live in traditional dormitories; no coed dormitories; rest live in off-campus housing or commute. No intervisitation in men's or women's dormitory rooms. There are no fraternities or sororities. About 25% of students leave campus on weekends.

Annual Costs. Tuition and fees, $9,760; room and board, $3,450. About 71% of students receive financial aid; assistance is typically divided 30% scholarship, 40% loan, 30% work. College reports some scholarships awarded on the basis of academic merit alone. *Meeting Costs:* college offers payment plan.

Columbia University

New York, New York 10027

Columbia has a central body, the University Senate, which brings students, faculty, administration, staff, and alumni together to develop policy on important campus issues.

Total Enrollment: 19,000 (excluding Barnard College)

Undergraduate degrees conferred (1,377). 35% were in Social Sciences, 17% were in Engineering, 15% were in Letters, 5% were in Philosophy and Religion, 4% were in Life Sciences, 3% were in Foreign Languages, 3% were in Visual and Performing Arts, 3% were in Health Sciences, 3% were in Psychology, 3% were in Area and Ethnic Studies, remainder in 6 other fields. *Doctoral degrees:* Social Sciences 79, Engineering 48, Humanities 73, Natural Sciences 93, Education 45, Health Professions 20, Architecture and Environmental Design 2, Law 2, Social Work 18, Library Science 8.

Columbia College

(See Columbia Univeristy) (212) 854-2521

Columbia College, long an eminent private nonsectarian institution for men, first admitted women in the Fall of 1983. It is the only Ivy League school located in New York City; Barnard, its sister institution, will remain a school for women only. Students from all 50 states and many foreign countries are attracted to its campus in Manhattan by the easy access it offers to the largest aggregate of theaters, museums and libraries in the country.

Founded: 1754
Affiliation: Independent
Total Enrollment: 1,783 M, 1,664 W (full-time)
Cost: $10K–$20K
% Receiving Financial Aid: 53%
Admission: Most Selective
Application Deadline: January 1

Admission is among the most selective in the country. About 30% of applicants accepted, 42% of these actually enroll; about 77% of freshmen graduate in top tenth of high school class, 92% in top fifth. Freshman scores, middle fifty percent range: SAT, 600–700 verbal, 650–750 mathematical. *Required:* SAT or ACT, 3 ACH including English Composition, essay; interview strongly recommended (off-campus interviews with alumni arranged all over the U.S. and in many foreign countries). Columbia reports that the single most important factor considered in the admissions process is the high school academic record (rigor of program taken and grades received), other factors considered include standardized test scores, teacher's and counselor's recommendations, essay and personal history, extracurricular distinction, and personal interview. *Entrance programs:* early decision, deferred admission, advanced placement. According to most recent data available, about 33% of entering students from private schools; 11% from parochial schools. *Apply* by January 1; November 1 for early decision. *Transfers* accepted in fall and spring; 72 enrolled fall, 1993.

Academic Environment. Pressures for academic achievement are intense. Columbia College, smallest of the Ivy League colleges, has the advantages of being one part of a large university. The many attractions of New York City, while offering unrivaled educational opportunities, may prove overwhelming for some who would feel more at home in a small-town, small-college environment. Student leader reports that "Relations with professors in core courses and advanced courses are very good," but there is little contact in some introductory level courses. Campus orientation tends to be both scholarly and intellectual. The Columbia Core Curriculum includes 6 semester long courses where "students examine the seminal works of Western civilization - works of moral and religious philosophy, social science, literature, music, art, sculpture and architecture - and in small, seminar-style classes discuss these works with each other and their instructor." Requirements also include two additional courses in non-Western cultures or contemporary issues, a writing course called Logic and Rhetoric, foreign language proficiency, three semesters of science, and two semesters of physical education. Degrees offered: bachelors. Majors and concentrations offered in more than 50 areas including many joint degree programs with other schools within the University and numerous interdepartmental majors including ancient studies, biochemistry, biology-psychology, biophysics, urban studies, women's studies, African-American studies. Columbia College departments registering the largest numbers of majors are English, history, political science, economics and psychology.

About 80% of students entering as freshmen graduate within four years, 90% within six years; 96% of freshmen return for sophomore year. *Special programs:* independent study, study abroad in France, Japan, and UK, undergraduate research, individualized majors, graduate courses (some for graduate credit), special achievement tests, combined programs with School of Engineering and Applied Science, 5 year AB/MIA with School of International Affairs; AB/MFA with School of the Arts in film, writing, and theatre, joint BA/MMusic with Juilliard. *Calendar:* semester, summer school.

Graduates Career Data. More than 90% of Columbia College graduates will eventually pursue advanced studies. Approximately 25% of a typical graduating class will attend law school, about 15% medical school; more than 90% of Columbia College graduates who apply to medical, law and business schools are accepted. Graduate and professional schools typically enrolling largest numbers of graduates include Columbia, Harvard, Yale, Stanford. *Career Counseling Program* designed specifically for liberal arts students. Liberal arts majors urged to seek interviews with business/industry representatives who visit campus. Help provided in preparing for interviews. Alumni reported as active in both career guidance and job placement.

Faculty. All of faculty hold doctorate. The student to faculty ratio is 7:1. About 29% of full-time faculty are female; 19% minority.

Student Body. College seeks a national student body; about 20% of students from New York; 45% Middle Atlantic, 13% New England, 14% West, 10% Midwest, 12% South, 5% foreign. About 8% of students reported as African American, 19% Asian, 9% Latino/Latina.
Varsity Sports. Men (Div.I): Baseball, Basketball, HW/LW Crew, Cross Country, Fencing, Football (IIA), Golf, Soccer, Swimming and Diving, Tennis, Track (Indoor & Outdoor), Wrestling. Women (Div.I): Archery, Basketball, Crew, Cross Country, Fencing, Soccer, Swimming and Diving, Tennis, Track (Indoor & Outdoor), Volleyball.
Campus Life. With the wide diversity of the student body, Columbia College offers a full range of cultural activities. College largely serves as its own cultural center, although rich resources of New York City are easily accessible to those who desire them. Regulations governing student conduct very relaxed; coed dormitories with Barnard; 24-hour intervisitation in effect. Cars permitted, but parking is a serious problem at Columbia. Freshmen not required to live on campus, but may do so if they desire (90% do).

More than 88% of students live in residence halls, most of the rest live in nearby alternatives such as fraternity houses or religious residences. All Columbia buildings are coeducational, although single-sex accommodations for women are available. All students are guaranteed housing for 4 years. Freshmen are required to live on campus unless commuting from home. Sexes segregated in coed dormitories by floor or room. There are 12 men's fraternities, 5 coed fraternities, and 7 sororities on campus which about 18% of men, 8% of women join.
Annual Costs. Tuition and fees, $17,500; room and board, $6,610; estimated $1,500 other, exclusive of travel. About 53% of students receive financial aid; average grant is $10,000, average aid package, $16,000; every package includes loan and a job ("self-help"). College reports admissions are need-blind and scholarships awarded only on the basis of need.

Columbia—School of Engineering and Applied Science (undergraduate division)

(See Columbia Univeristy) (212) 954-2521

A small engineering school within a large university, the school requires all students to receive 2 years of strong liberal arts study before beginning their specialized studies.

Founded: 1864
Affiliation: Independent
Total Enrollment: 806 M, 202 W (full-time)
Cost: $10K–$20K
% Receiving Financial Aid: 60%
Admission: Highly (+) Selective
Application Deadline: January 1

Admission is highly (+) selective. About 51% of applicants accepted, 39% of these actually enroll; 79% of freshmen graduate in top tenth of high school class, 94% in top fifth. Average freshman SAT scores: middle fifty percent range 550–700 on verbal; 73% score above 700 on mathematical. *Required:* SAT or ACT, 3 ACH (English, mathematics, choice of chemistry or physics); interview strongly recommended (off-campus interviews with alumni arranged all over the U.S. and in many foreign countries). Columbia reports that the single most important factor considered in the admissions process is the high school academic record (rigor of program taken and grades received), other factors considered include standardized test scores, teacher's and counselor's recommendations, essay and personal history, extracurricular distinction, and personal interview. *Entrance programs:* early decision, deferred admission, advanced placement. According to most recent data available, about 33% of entering students from private schools; 11% from parochial schools. *Apply* by January 1; November 1 for early decision. *Transfers* accepted in fall only; 14 enrolled 1993.
Academic Environment. SEAS students take a selection of the Core Curriculum courses described under Columbia College, and the writing course, Logic and Rhetoric; in addition, one course each in economics and computer science, a 1 point course meant to familiarize them with specific engineering disciplines and departments, and 2 semesters of physical education. In total, a minimum of 28 points out of 124 required for graduation will be liberal arts credits. Degree offered: bachelors. *Majors offered* include wide range of technical and professional programs.

About 84% of students entering as freshmen graduate within four years; 89% of freshmen return for sophomore year. *Special programs:* honors, undergraduate research, 3-year degree, individualized majors, qualified undergraduates may take graduate courses, 3–2 engineering with 84 liberal arts colleges, variety of joint programs with other schools within the university. *Calendar:* semester.
Graduates Career Data. Full-time graduate study pursued by 30% of students immediately after graduation according to most recent data available. *Careers in business and industry* pursued by 70% of graduates. Alumni reported as active in both career guidance and job placement, though students don't always take advantage of alumni assistance according to recent student leader.
Student Body. School seeks a national student body; 40 states, the District of Columbia, Puerto Rico and 48 foreign countries are represented in the current student body. Of the students reporting ethnic origin: 48% Asian American, 4% African American, 5% Latino/Latina.
Varsity Sports. Men (Div.I): Baseball, Basketball, Crew, Cross Country, Fencing, Football, Golf, Soccer, Swimming, Tennis, Track, Wrestling. Women (Div.I): Archery, Basketball, Crew, Cross Country, Fencing, Soccer, Swimming, Tennis, Track, Volleyball.
Campus Life. More than 88% of students live in residence halls, most of the rest live in nearby alternatives such as fraternity houses or religious residences. All Columbia buildings are coeducational, although single-sex accommodations for women are available. All students are guaranteed housing for 4 years. Freshmen are required to live on campus unless commuting from home. Sexes segregated in coed dormitories by floor or room. There are 12 men's fraternities, 5 coed fraternities, and 7 sororities on campus which about 18% of men, 8% of women join.
Annual Costs. Tuition and fees, $17,500; room and board, $6,610; estimated $1,500 other, exclusive of travel. About 65% of students receive financial aid; average grant is $12,000; average aid package, $18,000; every package includes loan and a job ("self-help"). College reports admissions are need-blind and scholarships awarded only on the basis of need. (No financial aid is available for students who are not U.S. citizens or permanent residents.)

Barnard College

(See Columbia Univeristy) (212) 854-2014

Barnard is a small women's college within Columbia University. It provides the intimacy of a small liberal arts college with the vast resources of a large prestigious university. Barnard and Columbia students may share classes, libraries, space in dormitories and extracurricular activities. The college occupies 4 acres in the heart of upper Manhattan. The small, well-defined autonomous campus is located on Broadway, directly across from the Columbia University campus.

Founded: 1889
Affiliation: Independent
Total Enrollment: 2,121 W (full-time)
Cost: $10K–$20K
% Receiving Financial Aid:
Admission: Highly (+) Selective
Application Deadline: Jan. 15

Admission is highly (+) selective. About 48% of applicants accepted, 44% of these actually enroll; 83% of freshmen graduate in top fifth of high school class, all in top two-fifths. Average freshman SAT scores: 600 verbal, 620 mathematical; 94% of freshmen score above 500 on verbal, 50% above 600, 6% above 700; 98% score above 500 on mathematical, 66% above 600, 13% above 700. *Required:* SAT and 3 ACH (including English composition or literature) or ACT; essay; interview "strongly recommended." Criteria considered in admissions, in order of importance: high school academic record, recommendations, standardized test scores, writing sample, extra curricular activities; other factors considered: special talents, alumnae children, diverse student body. *Entrance programs:* early decision, midyear admission. About 43% of entering students from private or parochial schools. *Apply* by January 15. *Transfers* welcome; 91 enrolled 1993–94.
Academic Environment. Pressures for academic achievement are intense and standards are high. Student body almost equally concerned with scholarly/intellectual interests and preparation for careers. Impact of intellectual and cultural resources of New York

City on college environment very strong. Cross-registration with Columbia gives Barnard students access to a tremendous variety of courses. Course of study quite varied, flexible and academically traditional. Administration reports distribution requirements include 2 semesters laboratory science; 4 semesters of foreign language (unless exemption granted); 1 semester first-year seminar; 1 semester first-year English; 4 semester courses in humanities or social sciences outside the major; 1 semester quantitative reasoning; 4 semester courses dealing with geographic and cultural diversity are required but may include courses taken to satisfy other requirements; 2 semesters physical education also required. Degree offered: bachelors. *Majors offered* in addition to usual arts and sciences include anthropology, architecture, linguistics, Oriental studies, statistics, area studies (Asia, Latin America, Russia, Western Europe); interdepartmental majors include American studies, ancient studies, environmental studies, program in the arts, medieval and renaissance studies, urban studies, women's studies. Strongest programs reported to be English, creative writing, political science, economics, art history, premed, foreign languages, religion, psychology and women's studies. Average undergraduate class size: 78% under 20, 15% 20–40, 7% over 40.

About 81% of students entering as freshmen graduate within four years, 87% eventually; 95% of freshmen return for sophomore year. *Special programs:* honors, independent study, study abroad, undergraduate research, 3-year degree (by petition only in individual cases), individualized majors, interdepartmental majors, satisfaction of requirements by examination, Senior Scholar Program, graduate courses (some for graduate credit), many combined programs with Columbia professional schools, double degree program in Judaic studies with Jewish Theological Seminary. *Calendar:* semester.

Undergraduate degrees conferred (528). 36% were in Social Sciences, 16% were in Letters, 10% were in Psychology, 8% were in Visual and Performing Arts, 8% were in Area and Ethnic Studies, 5% were in Life Sciences, 5% were in Philosophy and Religion, 5% were in Liberal/General Studies, remainder in 6 other fields.

Graduates Career Data. Advanced studies pursued by 36% of students; 6% enter medical school; 1% enter dental school; 7% enter law school; 1% enter business school. Medical schools typically enrolling largest numbers of graduates include Columbia, NYU, Albert Einstein, Mt. Sinai School of Medicine, Cornell, Harvard; dental schools include Columbia, U. of Pennsylvania, Boston U., NYU; law schools include NYU, Columbia, Fordham, Yale, Cardozo, U. Chicago, Harvard; business schools include Columbia, Harvard, Wharton. About 65% of 1992–93 graduates employed. Fields typically hiring largest numbers of graduates include banking-finance, education, publishing/journalism, broadcasting. Career Development Services include thousands of paid and unpaid internship listings, career classes, on-campus interviewing, career fairs, resume assistance, career panels weekly, alumnae shadowing program. Student assessment of program reported as good for both career guidance and job placement. Alumnae reported as active in both career guidance and job placement.

Faculty. About 98% of faculty hold PhD or equivalent. About 65% undergraduate classes taught by tenure-track faculty. About 61% of teaching faculty are female.

Student Body. About 42% of students from in state; 64% Middle Atlantic, 12% New England, 6% Midwest, 9% West, 5% South, 4% foreign. About 4% of students are Black, 6% Hispanic, 25% Asian, 5% other. *Minority group students:* The Higher Education Opportunity Program provides counseling, tutoring, and financial assistance to economically and financially disadvantaged N.Y. State women. Minority ethnic groups have numerous organizations.

Varsity Sports. Women (NCAA Div.I): Basketball, Crew, Cross Country, Fencing, Hockey (ice and field), Lacrosse, Soccer, Softball, Swimming and Diving, Tennis, Track, Volleyball.

Campus Life. College imposes few restrictions on social life of students. Regulation of housing and political activity achieved through joint student/faculty/administration discussions. Barnard benefits from all the rich resources of New York City so easily available to students, as well as from its proximity and affiliation with Columbia University.

About 45% of women live in traditional dormitories, 45% in coed dormitories; 10% commute. There are no sororities.

Annual Costs. Tuition and fees, $17,756; room and board, $7,736; estimated $1,400 other, exclusive of travel. About 60% of students receive financial aid; average amount of assistance, $18,700. Assistance is typically divided 74% grant, 17% loan, 9% work. College reports scholarships awarded only on the basis of need.

Columbia—School of General Studies

(See Columbia University) (212) 280-2752

The School of General Studies is the liberal arts division of the university for adult men and women, as well as for younger students who work full-time. It shares all facilities with the other undergraduate colleges of Columbia.

Founded:
Affiliation: Independent
Total Enrollment: 323 M, 246 W (full-time) 745 M, 960 W (part-time)
Cost: $14,972
Application Deadline: Rolling

Admission. About 51% of applicants accepted, 81% of these actually enroll. *Required:* high school or college transcript, autobiographical statement, General Studies aptitude exam, interview. *Non-academic factors* considered in admissions: special talents. *Entrance programs:* midyear admission, deferred admission. *Apply:* rolling admissions. *Transfers* welcome.

Academic Environment. Some 1,300 day and evening courses are offered throughout the academic year; 500 during the summer session. Faculty are shared with Columbia College, the Graduate School of Arts and Sciences, and the School of International and Public Affairs. *Degrees:* AB, BS.

Special programs: study abroad, independent study, qualified students may take graduate courses. *Calendar:* semester.

Graduates Career Data. Full-time graduate study pursued by 80% of students immediately after graduation.

Varsity Sports. Available at Columbia College and Barnard.

Campus Life. General Studies students come from all walks of life, some to begin or continue their education, others to prepare for switching careers. This is a commuter institution, most students commute; some off-campus housing available through the university.

Annual Costs. Tuition and fees, $14,972; estimated $900 for books and supplies. University reports all scholarships awarded on the basis of need. *Meeting Costs:* school offers PLUS program.

Columbus College

Columbus, Georgia 31907-5645 (706) 568-2035

A state-supported, commuter institution, located in a city of 191,000. Most convenient major airport: Atlanta, Georgia.

Founded: 1958
Affiliation: State
UG Enrollment: 1,134 M 1,739 W (full-time); 609 M, 1,127 W (part-time)
Total Enrollment: 5,241
Cost: < $10K
% Receiving Financial Aid: 40%
Admission: Non-selective
Application Deadline: Sept. 2

Admission. Graduates of accredited high schools with minimum GPA of 1.8 eligible; 75% of applicants accepted, 85% of these actually enroll. Average freshman SAT scores: 418 verbal, 464 mathematical. *Required:* SAT (minimum 350 verbal, 350 mathematical), or ACT. Criteria considered in admissions, in order of importance: standardized test scores, high school academic record. *Out-of-state* freshman applicants: does not seek students from out-of-state. State does not limit out-of-state enrollment. *Entrance programs:* early admission, midyear admission, deferred admission. *Apply* by September 2; rolling admissions. *Transfers* welcome; 322 enrolled 1993–94.

Academic Environment. Degrees offered: associates, bachelors, masters, Specialist in Education. Core requirements include 2 semesters of English, 3 hours in speech/communications, 3 hours of physical education, and pass the Georgia Regents Exam. Average undergraduate class size: 40% under 20, 60% 20–40. *Special programs:* CLEP, honors, undergraduate research, independent study, study abroad, joint enrollment, internships, Regents Engineering Transfer Program with Georgia Tech. Adult programs: re-entry program, study skills, adult/student support team. *Calendar:* quarter, summer school.

Undergraduate degrees conferred (388). 22% were in Business and Management, 19% were in Education, 12% were in Health Sciences, 10% were in Liberal/General Studies, 8% were in Protective Services, 6% were in Social Sciences, 5% were in Letters, 4% were in Psychology, 4% were in Mathematics, 3% were in Visual and Performing Arts, 3% were in Computer and Engineering Related Technology, remainder in 4 other fields.
Graduates Career Data. Fields typically employing largest numbers of graduates include education, banking and finance, local and federal government, local industries. Career Development Services include workshops on resume and interviewing skills, career planning and placement, assistance in finding full and part-time jobs for students and alumni.
Faculty. About 64% of faculty hold PhD or equivalent. About 99% of undergraduate classes taught by tenured faculty. About 34% of teaching faculty are female.
Student Body. College does not seek a national student body; 80% of students from in state; 95% from South. Average age of undergraduate students: 26.
Varsity Sports. Men (Div.II): Baseball, Basketball, Cross Country, Golf, Tennis. Women (Div.II): Basketball, Cross Country, Softball, Tennis, Volleyball.
Campus Life. Columbus is primarily a commuter institution; there are on-campus apartments which can house 232 people, filled on a first come first served basis. There are 4 fraternities, 4 sororities, which about 4% men, 3% women join. About 25% of resident students leave campus on weekends.
Annual Costs. Tuition and fees, $1,601 (out-of-state, $4,364); $3,291 room and board; estimated $700 other, exclusive of travel. About 40% of students receive financial aid. College reports some scholarships awarded on the basis of academic merit alone.

Columbus College of Art and Design

Columbus, Ohio 43215

A specialized college of visual arts, offering bachelor degree programs. CCAD is one of the oldest and largest continuously-run art colleges in the country.

Founded: 1879 **Affiliation:** Independent

Conception Seminary College

Conception, Missouri 64433

A church-related college of liberal arts, Conception Seminary is devoted to preparing men who are investigating a possible call to ministry or for the Roman Catholic priesthood to the level of the AB degree.

Founded: 1873 **Affiliation:** Roman Catholic

Undergraduate degrees conferred (13). 69% were in Philosophy and Religion, 23% were in Psychology, 8% were in Social Sciences.

Concord College

Athens, West Virginia 24712 **(304) 384-5248**

A state-supported college, located in a village of 1,300, 90 miles southwest of Charleston. Most convenient major airport: Yeager (Charleston, WV).

Founded: 1872
Affiliation: State
Total Enrollment: 890 M, 1,236 W (full-time); 283 M, 551 W (part-time)
Cost: < $10K
% Receiving Financial Aid: 64%
Admission: Non-selective
Application Deadline: Rolling

Admission. Graduates of approved high schools with 17 units, college preparatory program, and a "C" average or better; 96% of applicants accepted, 60% of these actually enroll. Average freshman ACT scores: 19.9 M, 20.2 W composite. *Required:* SAT or ACT. Criteria considered in admissions, in order of importance: high school academic record, standardized test scores, recommendations, writing sample, extra curricular activities. *Out-of-state* freshman applicants: college actively seeks students from out-of-state. State does not limit out-of-state enrollment. Entrance program: early admission, midyear admission, advanced placement. *Apply:* rolling admissions. *Transfers* welcome; 216 enrolled 1993–94.
Academic Environment. Degrees offered: associates, bachelors. Core requirements include 6 hours English, 6 hours literature, 12 hours social sciences, 6 hours fine arts, 14–15 hours mathematics and natural sciences. *Majors offered* in addition to usual studies include travel industry management, social work. *Special programs:* January term, cross registration with Bluefield State, internships in commercial art, travel industry management and social work. Average undergraduate class size: 5% under 20, 90% 20–40, 5% over 40. About 28% of students entering as freshmen graduate within four years, 41% eventually; 55% of freshmen return for sophomore year. *Calendar:* semester, summer school.
Undergraduate degrees conferred (359). 34% were in Education, 19% were in Business and Management, 9% were in Marketing and Distribution, 7% were in Public Affairs, 6% were in Multi/Interdisciplinary Studies, 4% were in Psychology, 4% were in Visual and Performing Arts, 4% were in Social Sciences, remainder in 8 other fields.
Graduates Career Data. Advanced studies pursued by 23% of students; 2% enter law school; 5% enter business school; 2% enter medical school; 2% enter dental school. Business schools typically enrolling largest numbers of graduates include WVU, VPI, WV College of Graduate Studies. Fields typically employing largest numbers of graduates include business, education, travel, communications.
Faculty. About 52% of faculty hold PhD or equivalent. About 70% of undergraduate classes taught by tenured faculty. About 3% of teaching faculty are ethnic minorities.
Student Body. College seeks a national student body; 91% of students from in state; 94% Middle Atlantic; 1% New England; 1% Midwest; 2% South; 1% West; 1% foreign students. An estimated 40% of student body reported as Protestant, 15% Catholic, 40% unaffiliated, 5% other; 4% Black, 1% Hispanic, 1% other minority. Average age of undergraduate students: 26.
Varsity Sports. Men (NCAA Div.II): Baseball, Basketball, Cross Country, Football, Golf, Tennis. Women (NCAA Div.II): Basketball, Cross Country, Golf, Softball, Tennis, Volleyball.
Campus Life. About 45% of men, 40% of women live in traditional dormitories; rest commute. Intervisitation in men's and women's dormitory rooms limited. There are 5 fraternities, 4 sororities on campus which about 15% of men, 15% of women join. About 60% of resident students leave campus on weekends.
Annual Costs. Tuition and fees, $1,936 (out-of-state, $4,106); room and board, $3,168; estimated $1,000 other, exclusive of travel. About 64% of students receive financial aid; average amount of assistance, $3,700. Assistance is typically divided 30% scholarship, 35% grant, 29% loan, 6% work. College reports 300 scholarships awarded on the basis of academic merit alone, 50 for special talents, 32 for need.

Concordia College, Ann Arbor

Ann Arbor, Michigan 48105 **(313) 995-7322**

A church-related, liberal arts college, Concordia also offers teacher education. Most convenient major airport: Detroit Metropolitan.

Founded: 1963
Affiliation: Lutheran-Missouri Synod
Total Enrollment: 218 M, 344 W (full-time)
Cost: < $10K
% Receiving Financial Aid: 89%
Admission: Non-selective
Application Deadline: September 1

Admission. High school graduates with minimum GPA of 2.25, combined SAT of 700, or ACT composite of 18 eligible; 88% of applicants accepted, 50% of these actually enroll; 38% of freshman graduate in top fifth of high school class; 58% in top two-fifths.

Average freshman scores: SAT, 460 M, 500 W verbal, 530 M, 470 W mathematical; 44% of freshman score above 500 on verbal, 3% above 600; 57% score above 500 on mathematical, 32% above 600; ACT, 20 composite. *Required:* SAT or ACT. Criteria considered in admissions, in order of importance: high school academic record, standardized test scores, recommendations, extra curricular activities; other factors considered: diverse student body, special talents, religious affiliation and/or commitment. *Entrance programs:* midyear admission, advanced placement. About 6% of entering students come from private schools, 13% parochial schools. *Apply* by September 1; rolling admissions. *Transfers* welcome; 39 enrolled 1993–94.

Academic Environment. Degrees offered: associates, bachelors. Average undergraduate class size: 80% under 20, 19% 20–40, 1% over 40. *Special programs:* study abroad in England, Austria. Adult programs: Human Resources Administration and Health Care Administration are offered as accelerated degree completion programs.

Undergraduate degrees conferred (152). 54% were in Business and Management, 20% were in Education, 9% were in Theology, 5% were in Letters, 4% were in Visual and Performing Arts, 3% were in Life Sciences, remainder in 4 other fields.

Faculty. About 55% of faculty hold PhD or equivalent. About 71% of undergraduate classes taught by tenured faculty. About 33% of teaching faculty are female; 1% ethnic minority.

Student Body. College seeks a national student body; 77% of students from in state; 92% Midwest; 4% New England, 1% each Middle Atlantic, South, West, Foreign. An estimated 85% of students reported as Protestant, 3% Catholic, 12% unaffiliated or not reported; 9% Black, 1% Asian.

Religious Orientation. Concordia is a church-related institution; 50% of students are affiliated with the church; 3 religious courses are required of all students.

Varsity Sports. Men (NAIA Div.III): Baseball, Soccer, Basketball (Div.II). Women (NAIA Div.III): Basketball, Baseball, Volleyball.

Campus Life. About 69% of men, 69% of women live in traditional dormitories; rest commute. Freshmen given preference in college housing if all students cannot be accommodated. There are no fraternities or sororities. About 15% of resident students leave campus on weekends.

Annual Costs. Tuition and fees, $9,480; room and board, $4,180; estimated $1,000 other, exclusive of travel. About 89% of students receive financial aid; average amount of assistance, $5,160. Assistance is typically divided 25% scholarship, 42% grant, 29% loan, 4% work. College reports there are some scholarships awarded on the basis of academic merit alone, some for special talents.

Concordia College, Bronxville

Bronxville, New York 10708 (800) 937-2655

A church-related college "offering a holistic approach to liberal arts education necessary for careers and vocations, marked by self-fulfillment and service to church and society." Most convenient major airport: LaGuardia, JFK.

Founded: 1881
Affiliation: Lutheran-Missouri Synod
Total Enrollment: 491 M, W (full-time); 33 M, 136 W (part-time)
Cost: < $10K
% Receiving Financial Aid: 71%
Admission: Non-selective
Application Deadline: Rolling

Admission. High school graduates who give satisfactory evidence of ability to pursue college level work eligible; 59% of applicants accepted, 56% of these actually enroll. About 13% of freshmen graduate in top fifth of high school class, 47% in top two-fifths. Average freshmen SAT scores, according to most recent data available: 410 verbal, 447 mathematical. *Required:* SAT or ACT, interview (on or off campus), audition for music majors. *Non-academic factors* considered in admissions: special talents, diverse student body, religious affiliation and/or commitment, co-curricular activities. About 8% of entering students from private schools, 35% from parochial schools. *Apply:* rolling admissions. *Transfers* welcome.

Academic Environment. AB, BS. About 43% of students entering as freshmen graduate eventually; 20–35% of freshmen do not return for sophomore year. *Special programs:* study abroad, exchange program with Rocky Mountain College (Billings, MT), consortium majors with other Westchester colleges. *Calendar:* 4–1–4.

Undergraduate degrees conferred (74). 22% were in Business and Management, 20% were in Education, 16% were in Social Sciences, 11% were in Public Affairs, 9% were in Mathematics, 5% were in Liberal/General Studies, 5% were in Letters, 4% were in Philosophy and Religion, 3% were in Life Sciences, remainder in 3 other fields.

Faculty. About 45% of faculty hold PhD or equivalent.

Varsity Sports. Men (NCAA, Div. II): Baseball, Basketball, Soccer, Tennis, Volleyball. Women (NCAA, Div. II): Basketball, Softball, Tennis, Volleyball.

Student Body. About 66% of students from in state; 74% Middle Atlantic, 4% from New England. An estimated 38% of students reported as Protestant, 37% Catholic, 17% unaffiliated, 8% other; 12% Black, 5% Hispanic, 9% Asian, according to most recent data available.

Religious Orientation. Concordia is a church-related institution; "classes in theology form an integral part of each student's academic program."

Campus Life. About 67% of men, 70% of women live in traditional dormitories; remainder commute. "All students whose legal residence is not within a reasonable commuting distance, live in college residences." There are no fraternities or sororities. About 25% of resident students leave campus on weekends.

Annual Costs. Tuition and fees, $9,370; room and board, $4,330. About 71% of students receive financial aid, assistance is typically divided 75% scholarship, 23% loan, 2% work. College reports some scholarships awarded on the basis of academic merit alone. *Meeting Costs:* college offers AMS and Tuition Plan.

Concordia College at Moorhead

Moorhead, Minnesota 56562 (218) 299-3004

A church-related, liberal arts college, located in a community of 32,220, directly across the Red River from Fargo, North Dakota (pop. 65,000). Concordia has joined with neighboring Moorhead State and North Dakota State in a program of cross-registration and shared facilities. Most convenient major airport: Fargo, ND.

Founded: 1891
Affiliation: Evangelical Lutheran Church
Total Enrollment: 1,167 M, 1,790 W (full-time)
Cost: < $10K
% Receiving Financial Aid: 83%
Admission: Selective (+)
Application Deadline: Rolling

Admission is selective (+). About 90% of applicants accepted, 47% of these actually enroll; 48% of freshmen graduate in top fifth of high school class, 77% in top two-fifths. Average freshman scores: SAT, middle fifty percent range, 420–560 M, 440–570 W verbal, 470–630 M, 460–590 W mathematical; 47% of freshman score above 500 on verbal, 13% above 600, 3% above 700; 63% score above 500 on mathematical, 30% above 600, 7% above 700; ACT, middle fifty percent range, 20–27 M, 21–27 W composite. *Required:* SAT or ACT, two recommendations. Criteria considered in admissions, in order of importance: high school academic record, standardized test scores, recommendations, extra curricular activities, writing sample; other factors considered: diverse student body, special talents, alumni children, religious affiliation and/or commitment. *Entrance programs:* early admission, deferred admission, advanced placement. *Apply:* rolling admissions. *Transfers* welcome; 104 enrolled 1993–94.

Academic Environment. Pressures for academic achievement appear moderate. Core requirements include 1 year English, 1 semester liberal arts course, 2 semesters religion, distribution requirements of 7 courses out of five areas, two half semester courses in physical education, and "integration course". Administration source characterizes student body as strongly oriented toward vocational/professional goals; student source sees student body as equally concerned with career goals and scholarly/intellectual pursuits. Degrees offered: bachelors. *Majors offered* in 34 areas including German Institute, immersion language program. Average undergraduate class size: 46% under 20, 47% 20–40, 7% over 40.

About 62% of students entering as freshmen graduate within four years, 70% eventually; 84% of freshmen return for sophomore year.

Special programs: CLEP, independent study, study abroad programs through language departments and archaeological expedition, honors, undergraduate research, individualized majors, optional May seminars in Europe, urban studies (Chicago), internships and cooperative work/study programs, Washington Semester, acceleration, exchange with Fort Lewis College, Tri-College (Concordia, NDSU, Moorhead State), 3–2 programs in engineering and architecture, Institute of German Studies (1 year total immersion program). Adult programs: ACCORD (Adults Continuing Education at Concordia). *Calendar:* semester, summer school.

Undergraduate degrees conferred (639). 17% were in Business and Management, 16% were in Education, 10% were in Social Sciences, 8% were in Life Sciences, 7% were in Communications, 7% were in Psychology, 6% were in Health Sciences, 6% were in Foreign Languages, 6% were in Letters, 5% were in Visual and Performing Arts, 3% were in Public Affairs, 3% were in Mathematics, remainder in 5 other fields.

Graduates Career Data. Advanced studies pursued by 40% of students; 5% enter medical school; 4% enter law school; 3% enter business school; 1% enter dental school. Graduate and professional schools typically enrolling largest numbers of graduates include U. of Minnesota, U. of North Dakota. About 75% of 1992–93 graduates employed. Fields typically hiring largest numbers of graduates include teaching, management, health care, finance, accounting, banking. Career Development Services provided through the Center for Educational Counseling and Growth, through academic department sponsored seminars and workshops, and through the Placement Office which assists students in evaluating career objectives and contacting prospective employers, services includes computer assisted guidance system, cooperative education, Volunteers in Placement, job fairs, seminars. Alumni reported as helpful in both career guidance and job placement.

Faculty. About 73% of faculty hold PhD or equivalent. About 36% of teaching faculty are female; 5% ethnic minority.

Student Body. College seeks a national student body; 62% of students from in state; 85% Midwest, 9% West; 4% foreign students. An estimated 79% of students reported as Protestant, 13% Catholic, 6% unaffiliated, 2% other; 2% Asian, 2% other ethnic minority.

Religious Orientation. Concordia is a church-related institution; about 55% of students are affiliated with the Evangelical Lutheran Church in America; 2 courses in religion required of all students; attendance at daily chapel services expected. Places of worship available on campus for 3 major faiths.

Varsity Sports. Men (NCAA Div.III): Baseball, Basketball, Cross Country, Football, Golf, Hockey, Soccer, Tennis, Track, Wrestling. Women (NCAA Div. III): Basketball, Cross Country, Golf, Soccer, Softball, Tennis, Track, Volleyball.

Campus Life. Strong interest among substantial majority of students reported in religious activities and in the arts. Regulations governing campus life reported by student leader as "moderately strict." Alcohol and drugs prohibited on campus; alcoholic products not advertised on campus. Most of campus is smoke-free; tobacco products not sold or advertised on campus. Cars permitted; parking reported as adequate.

About 37% men, 44% women live in traditional dormitories; 17% men, 18% women live in coed dormitories; rest live in off-campus housing. Freshmen given preference in college housing if all students cannot be accommodated. There are no fraternities or sororities on campus. There are 3 brother–sister societies on campus; they provide no residence facilities. About 15% of resident students leave campus on weekends.

Annual Costs. Tuition and fees, $9,700; room and board, $3,050; estimated $1,050 other, exclusive of travel. About 83% of students receive financial aid; average amount of assistance, $7,928. Assistance is typically divided 63% scholarship/grant, 30% loan, 7% work. College reports 45 scholarships awarded on the basis of academic merit alone, 34 for special talents, 2,009 for need alone.

Concordia College, Portland

Portland, Oregon 97211 **(503) 280-8501 or (800) 321-9371**

Concordia is a church-related institution located in northeast Portland, a city of 400,000. Most convenient major airport: Portland.

Founded: 1905
Affiliation: Lutheran-Missouri Synod
Total Enrollment: 369 M, 442 W (full-time); 66 M, 140 W (part-time)
Cost: < $10K
Admission: Non-selective
Application Deadline: Rolling

Admission. High school graduates with cumulative high school average of 2.25 in college prep program, minimum verbal SAT of 400, or ACT composite of 18 eligible; 69% of applicants accepted, 39% of these actually enroll; 35% of freshman graduate in top fifth of high school class, 56% in top two-fifths. Average freshman scores: SAT, 434 verbal, 466 mathematical; ACT, 19 composite. Entrance program: early admission, mid-year admission, advanced placement. *Apply:* rolling admissions. *Transfers* welcome; 196 enrolled 1993–94.

Academic Environment. Degrees offered: associates, bachelors. Core requirements include 12 quarter hours of communication, 15 humanities, 15 religion, 8 natural sciences, 6 fine arts, 6 social sciences, 4 mathematics, 4 physical education. *Majors offered* in addition to usual arts and sciences include business, international business, health care/social work, education, theological studies. About 55% of entering freshmen return for sophomore year. Average undergraduate class size: 65% under 20, 31% 20–40, 4% over 40. Adult programs: accelerated degree programs designed for business executives, health care providers.

Undergraduate degrees conferred (149). 50% were in Business and Management, 31% were in Education, 11% were in Health Sciences, 5% were in Liberal/General Studies, 3% were in Public Affairs, remainder in Philosophy and Religion.

Faculty. About 52% of faculty hold PhD or equivalent. About 23% of teaching faculty are female.

Student Body. About 67% of students from in state; 87% from Northwest, 3% West, 9% foreign. About 45% of students reported as Protestant, 4% Catholic, 51% not reporting; 2% Black, 1% Hispanic, 2% Asian, 9% international, 18% other minority. Average age of undergraduate student: 27; 48% of student body over 25 years of age.

Religious Orientation. Concordia is a church-related college, "worship is placed at the center of life and activities at Concordia; 4 religious course are required of all students.

Varsity Sports. Men (NAIA): Baseball, Basketball, Soccer. Women (NAIA): Basketball, Softball, Volleyball.

Campus Life. About 20% of men and women live in traditional dormitories; 20% of men and women live in off-campus housing; rest commute. There are no fraternities or sororities on campus. About 10% of resident students leave campus on weekends.

Annual Costs. Tuition and fees, $9,300; room and board, $3,000; estimated $500 other, exclusive of travel. College reports scholarships awarded only on the basis of need.

Concordia College, St. Paul

St. Paul, Minnesota 55104 **(612) 641-8233**

A four-year liberal arts college, owned and operated by the Lutheran Church-Missouri Synod, which offers programs in pre-seminary studies, and preparation for directors of Christian education and teachers in both parochial and public schools, as well as two- and four-year liberal arts programs in a variety of pre-professional areas. Concordia also offers a degree completion program for adult learners.

Founded: 1893
Affiliation: Lutheran-Missouri Synod
Total Enrollment: 476 M, 573 W (full-time); 65 M, 116 W (part-time)
Cost: < $10K
% Receiving Financial Aid: 75%
Admission: Non-selective
Application Deadline: August 15

Admissions. High school graduates with minimum GPA of 2.0 eligible; 70% of applicants accepted, 52% of these actually enroll; 24% of freshman graduate in top fifth of high school class, 49% in top two-fifths. Freshman ACT composite scores: 18–23. *Required:* ACT. Criteria considered in admissions, in order of importance: high school academic record, standardized test scores, writing sample, recommendations, extra curricular activities. *Entrance pro-*

grams: midyear admission, advanced placement. About 12% of entering students from private schools, 7% parochial schools. *Apply* by August 15; rolling admissions. *Transfers* welcome; 243 enrolled 1993–94.

Academic Environment. Degrees offered: associates, bachelors, masters. Average undergraduate class size: 40% under 20, 48% 20–40, 2% over 40. About 24% of entering students graduate within four years, 38% eventually; 63% of freshman return for sophomore year. *Special programs:* study abroad, cross registration with neighboring colleges, many degree programs offer internship/cooperative work-study programs. Adult programs: degree completion programs offered in Organizational Management and Marketing.

Faculty. About 75% of faculty hold PhD or equivalent. About 75% of undergraduate classes taught by tenured faculty. About 22% of teaching faculty are female; 4% Black, 2% other ethnic minority.

Student Body. About 85% of students from in state. An estimated 74% of students reported as Protestant, 17% Catholic, 3% unaffiliated, 6% other; 6% Black, 7% Asian, 1% Hispanic. Average age of undergraduate student: 23.

Religious Orientation. Concordia is a church-related institution; 46% of students are affiliated with Lutheran church; 3 courses in religion required of all students.

Varsity Sports. Men: Baseball, Basketball, Cross Country, Football, Soccer, Track. Women: Basketball, Cross Country, Softball, Track, Volleyball.

Campus Life. About 46% men, 44% women live in traditional dormitories; 5% men, 4% women live in off-campus college related housing; rest commute. About 65% of resident students leave campus on weekends.

Annual Costs. Tuition and fees, $9,720; room and board, $3,480; estimated $1,500 other, exclusive of travel. About 75% of students receive financial aid; average amount of assistance, $10,523. Assistance is typically divided 60% scholarship/grant, 27% loan, 13% work. College reports 60 awarded for academic merit alone, 1 for music, rest awarded on basis of need.

Undergraduate degrees conferred (323). 56% were in Business and Management, 22% were in Education, 5% were in Psychology, 4% were in Theology, 4% were in Multi/Interdisciplinary Studies, 3% were in Social Sciences, remainder in 6 other fields.

Concordia College, Seward

Seward, Nebraska 68434 **(402) 643-7233**

A church-related college, conducted by the Lutheran Church—Missouri Synod primarily for the preparation and training of students for professional work in the Lutheran Church, but also offering programs in teacher education, the liberal arts, and pre-professional training.

Founded: 1894
Affiliation: Lutheran-Missouri Synod
Total Enrollment: 358 M, 459 W (full-time)
Cost: < $10K
% Receiving Financial Aid: 93%
Admission: Non-selective
Application Deadline: August 1

Admission. High school graduates eligible; 88% of applicants accepted, 47% of these actually enroll. Average freshman ACT scores: 22.5 composite. *Required:* ACT or SAT. Criteria considered in admissions: high school academic record, standardized test scores. *Apply* by August 1; rolling admissions. *Transfers* welcome; 40 enrolled 1993–94.

Academic Environment. Degrees offered: bachelors, masters. About 60% of students are studying for church-related professions such as Lutheran teachers, pre ministerial and directors of Christian education programs. About 66% of entering students graduate within five years. *Special programs:* study abroad, cross registration with University of Nebraska-Lincoln, internships and cooperative work/study programs in teacher education, business and director of Christian education programs.

Student Body. About 37% of students from in state; 80% Midwest, 8% West/Northwest, 6% South, 2% New England, 2% Middle Atlantic, 1% foreign. An estimated 87% of students reported as affiliated with Lutheran Church. About 4% of students reported as ethnic minorities.

Annual Costs. Tuition and fees, $8,506; room and board, $3,270; estimated $1,650 other, exclusive of travel. About 93% of students receive financial aid; average amount of assistance, $4,491. Assistance is typically divided 17% scholarship, 18% grant, 63% loan, 2% work. College reports some scholarships awarded on the basis of academic merit alone.

Undergraduate degrees conferred (135). 65% were in Education, 6% were in Psychology, 6% were in Business and Management, 4% were in Social Sciences, 3% were in Precision Production, 3% were in Theology, 3% were in Communications, remainder in 6 other fields.

Concordia Lutheran College

Austin, Texas **(512) 452-7661**

A small liberal arts college located in the state capital, Concordia Lutheran also offers professional/occupational programs.

Founded: 1926
Affiliation: Lutheran-Missouri Synod
Total Enrollment: 200 M, 300 W (full-time)
Cost: < $10K
% Receiving Financial Aid: 70%
Admission: Non-selective
Application Deadline: August 15

Admission. High school graduates with minimum 750 combined SAT or 17 composite ACT and 2.5 GPA eligible; 69% of applicants accepted, 57% of these actually enroll; 34% of freshmen graduate in top fifth of high school class, 67% in top two-fifths. *Required:* ACT or SAT. *Apply* by August 15. *Transfers* welcome.

Academic Environment. Degree offered: bachelors. Concordia Lutheran offers majors in general studies, Mexican-American studies, behavioral sciences, business, church music, communications, environmental science, teacher education, pre-seminary studies. About 55% of entering freshmen do not return for sophomore year.

Student Body. About 91% of students from Texas; 95% North Central. An estimated 76% of students reported as Protestant, 14% Catholic, 5% unaffiliated, 5% other; 5% Black, 8% Hispanic, 1% other minority.

Campus Life. About 21% of men, 23% of women live in traditional dormitories; 14% of men, 9% of women in coed dormitories; rest commute.

Annual Costs. Tuition and fees, $6,400; room and board, $3,500; estimated $1,450 other, exclusive of travel. About 70% of students receive financial aid; average amount of assistance, $4,580. College reports some scholarships awarded on the basis of academic merit alone.

Undergraduate degrees conferred (76). 28% were in Business and Management, 26% were in Education, 25% were in Communications, 12% were in Liberal/General Studies, 7% were in Social Sciences, 3% were in Physical Sciences.

Concordia Teachers College

(See Concordia University, Illinois)

Concordia University, California

Irvine, California 92715 **(714) 854-8002**

A small, church-related liberal arts college, part of the ten campus Concordia University system, located in a community of 50,000 about 50 miles south of Los Angeles. Formerly known as Christ College, Irvine. Most convenient major airports: John Wayne (Santa Ana), Los Angeles.

Founded: 1972
Affiliation: Independent (Lutheran-Missouri Synod)
Total Enrollment: 252 M, 389 W (full-time); 26 M, 72 W (part-time)
Cost: $10K–$20K
% Receiving Financial Aid: 75%
Admission: Non-selective
Application Deadline: June 30

Admission. High school graduates with 2.8 GPA eligible; about 72% of applicants accepted, 29% of these actually enroll. Average freshman scores: SAT, 420 verbal, 485 mathematical; ACT, 22 composite. *Required:* SAT or ACT. Criteria considered in admissions, in order of importance: high school academic record, standardized test scores, recommendations, extracurricular activities; other factors considered: diverse student body, religious affiliation and/or commitment, special talents. *Apply* by June 30. *Transfers* welcome; 103 enrolled 1993–94.

Academic Environment. Degrees offered: bachelors, masters. About 45% of entering students graduate within four years; 19% of freshmen do not return for sophomore year. Library materials include children's collection, curriculum lab. *Special programs:* study abroad, cross registration, Teacher Credential Program.

Undergraduate degrees conferred (103). 100% were in Unknown.

Graduates Career Data. According to most recent data available, full-time graduate or professional study pursued immediately after graduation by 34% of students. *Careers in business and industry* pursued by 36% of graduates. Career Development Services include assessment, assistance with resume and interviewing skills, job search.

Varsity Sports. Men (NAIA, Div. I): Baseball, Basketball, Cross Country, Soccer. Women (NAIA, Div. I): Basketball, Cross Country, Softball, Volleyball.

Student Body. About 80% of students from in state; 10% foreign. An estimated 3% of students reported as Black, 7% Hispanic, 12% Asian, 2% other minorities.

Religious Orientation. Concordia is a church-related institution; 3 courses in religion required of all students.

Campus Life. About 69% of students live in campus apartments; rest commute. Freshmen given preference in college housing if all students cannot be accommodated. There are no fraternities or sororities.

Annual Costs. Tuition and fees, $10,440; room and board, $4,230; estimated $1,455 other, exclusive of travel. About 75% of students receive financial aid; average amount of assistance, $8,000. Assistance is typically divided 20% scholarship, 30% grant, 40% loan, 10% work. College reports some scholarships awarded on the basis of academic merit alone. *Meeting Costs:* college offers two monthly payment plans and loans.

Concordia University, Illinois

River Forest, Illinois 60305 **(800) 735-2668 or (708) 209-3100**

A church-related, liberal arts institution, Concordia offers 4-year programs as well as graduate programs in education, counseling, human services, and church music. Formerly known as Concordia Teachers College. Most convenient major airport: O'Hare International (Chicago).

Founded: 1864
Affiliation: Lutheran-Missouri Synod
UG Enrollment: 387 M, 781 W (full-time); 31 M, 114 W (part-time)
Total Enrollment: 2,497
Cost: < $10K
Admission: Non-selective
Application Deadline: Rolling

Admission. High school graduates with minimum ACT score 20 or rank in upper half of graduating class eligible; 76% of applicants accepted, 46% of these actually enroll; 47% of freshmen graduate in top fifth of high school class. Average freshman ACT scores: 23 M, 23 W composite. Criteria considered in admissions, in order of importance: high school academic record, extra curricular activities, standardized test scores, recommendations; other factors considered: special talents, alumni children, diverse student body, religious affiliation and/or commitment. About 33% of students entering from private schools. *Apply* by 1 week prior to term, rolling admissions. *Transfers* welcome; 151 enrolled 1993–94.

Academic Environment. Degrees offered: bachelors, masters. Unusual majors offered include advertising design. Average undergraduate class size: 20. About 80% of students entering as freshmen graduate within four years; 83% of freshmen return for sophomore year. Adult programs: Concordia Organizational Management Program, degree completion program for adults over 25.

Undergraduate degrees conferred (205). 49% were in Education, 11% were in Psychology, 10% were in Business and Management, 8% were in Health Sciences, 4% were in Social Sciences, 3% were in Public Affairs, 3% were in Allied Health, 3% were in Theology, 3% were in Communications, remainder in 4 other fields.

Graduates Career Data. Advanced studies pursued by 25% of students; 8% enter seminary. Career Development Services offered through the Office of Career Counseling and Placement.

Faculty. About 61% of faculty hold PhD or equivalent. About 58% of undergraduate classes taught by tenured faculty.

Student Body. College seeks a national student body; 67% of students from in state; 11% foreign students. An estimated 74% of students reported as Protestant, 20% Catholic, 16% Black, 2% Hispanic, 3% Asian.

Religious Orientation. Concordia is a church-related institution; about 51% of students are affiliated with the church; 3 religious courses are required of all students.

Varsity Sports. Men (NCAA III): Baseball, Basketball, Cross Country, Football, Tennis, Track, Wrestling. Women (NCAA III): Basketball, Cross Country, Softball, Tennis, Track.

Campus Life. About 35% of women live in traditional dormitories; 100% of men, 65% of women live in coed dormitories. There are no fraternities or sororities. About 40% of resident students leave campus on weekends.

Annual Costs. Tuition and fees, $8,576; room and board, $4,035; estimated $1,400 other, exclusive of travel. College reports some scholarships awarded on the basis of academic merit alone.

Concordia University Wisconsin

Mequon, Wisconsin 53097 **(414) 243-4300**

Long a church-related 2-year college, Concordia now also offers baccalaureate and masters degree programs. The campus is located 15 minutes north of downtown Milwaukee, on Lake Michigan.

Founded: 1881
Affiliation: Lutheran-Missouri Synod
Total Enrollment: 394 M, 294 W (full-time); 36 M, 41 W (part-time)
Cost: < $10K
% Receiving Financial Aid: 85%
Admission: Non-selective
Application Deadline: August 15

Admission. High school graduates with 16 credits (11 in basic liberal arts) and C average eligible; others may be admitted provisionally. About 81% of applicants accepted, 45% of these actually enroll; 26% of freshman graduate in top fifth of high school class, 51% in top two-fifths. Average freshman ACT scores: 21 composite. *Required:* ACT. Criteria considered in admissions, in order of importance: high school academic record, standardized test scores, recommendations, extra curricular activities, writing sample. *Apply* by August 15; rolling admissions. *Transfers* welcome; 94 enrolled 1993–94.

Academic Environment. Degrees offered: associates, bachelors, masters. Concordia offers programs for "students who are preparing for vocations in the several ministries of the church and for various professional and business careers in the community." New programs include occupational therapy, justice and public policy. Core requirements include 50.5 credits including courses in theology, humanities, cross culture, social science, sciences, communication, mathematics, physical education. Average undergraduate class size: 71% under 20, 24% 20–40, 5% over 40. About 61% of entering freshmen graduate eventually; 75% of freshman return for sophomore year. *Special programs:* required January term, study abroad, 3–2 engineering. Adult programs: Degree completion programs in BSN, Liberal Arts, Health Care Administration. *Calendar:* 4–1–4.

Undergraduate degrees conferred (175). 41% were in Business and Management, 20% were in Education, 18% were in Health Sciences, 7% were in Theology, 3% were in Public Affairs, remainder in 7 other fields.

Faculty. About 65% of faculty hold PhD or equivalent. About 25% of teaching faculty are female; 10% Black.

Student Body. About 60% of students from in state; 86% from Midwest, 2% each South, West, Northwest, 8% foreign students. An

estimated 60% of students reported as Protestant, 20% Catholic, 10% other; 6% Black, 8% Asian, 2% Hispanic.
Religious Orientation. Concordia is a church-related institution; 60% of students are affiliated with Lutheran Church; 3 religious courses required of all students.
Varsity Sports. Men (NAIA): Baseball, Basketball, Cross Country, Football, Golf, Soccer, Tennis, Track, Wrestling. Women (NAIA): Basketball, Cross Country, Softball, Tennis, Track, Volleyball.
Campus Life. About 63% of men, 51% of women live in traditional dormitories, remainder live in off-campus housing or commute, according to most recent data available. There are no fraternities or sororities on campus. Campus is alcohol-free. Students and administration characterize the student body, faculty and administration as conservative. About 50% of resident students leave campus on weekends.
Annual Costs. Tuition and fees, $9,300; room and board, $3,400; estimated $2,000 other, exclusive of travel. About 85% of students receive financial aid; average amount of assistance, $6,500. Assistance is typically divided 10% scholarship, 35% grant, 50% loan, 5% work. College reports 2 scholarships awarded on the basis of academic merit alone, various grants based on need.

Connecticut College

New London, Connecticut 06320-4195 (203) 439-2200

Connecticut College, a high-quality liberal arts institution, was originally a prestigious women's college but has been co-educational since 1969. The 702-acre campus, which includes a 450-acre arboretum, overlooks the Long Island Sound and is located 2 miles from the center of New London (pop. 32,000), 125 miles from New York City, and 100 miles from Boston. Most convenient major airport: Hartford, CT, Providence, RI or Groton, CT.

Founded: 1911
Affiliation: Independent
Total Enrollment: 699 M, 931 W (full-time); 91 M, 141 W (part-time)
Cost: $10K–$20K
% Receiving Financial Aid: 54%
Admission: Highly Selective
Application Deadline: January 15

Admission is highly selective. About 51% of applicants accepted, 28% of these actually enroll; 77% of students graduate in top fifth of high school class, 99% in top two-fifths. Average SAT scores: 90% of students score above 500 on verbal, 50% above 600, 5% above 700; 96% score above 500 on mathematical, 68% above 600, 15% above 700. *Required:* SAT or ACT, 3 ACH including English Composition, essay; interview strongly recommended. Criteria considered in admissions, in order of importance: high school academic record, standardized test scores, writing sample, recommendations, extra curricular activities; other factors considered: diverse student body, alumni children, special talents, character. *Entrance programs:* early decision, advanced placement, deferred admission. About 40% of entering students from private schools, 6% from parochial schools. *Apply* by January 15; early decision by November 15. *Transfers* welcome; 36 enrolled 1993–94.
Academic Environment. Students appear to favor majors in the social and behavioral sciences rather than the natural sciences and mathematics that have become so popular on many campuses. Majors with the greatest enrollment include government, history, English, and psychology. Other highly rated programs include art, dance, theater, the Center for International Studies and the Liberal Arts, and the Center for Conservation Biology and Environmental Studies. Interdisciplinary programs are offered in American studies, Asian studies, classical civilization, Italian studies, medieval studies, modern European studies, Russian and East European studies, urban affairs. The theater department makes use of the college's association with National Theatre Institute of O'Neill Foundation in Waterford, Connecticut. Students may design, with committee approval, their own interdisciplinary major programs. Administration reports no specific courses required for graduation; but a distribution of courses is required among eight broad disciplinary areas, including demonstration of proficiency in a foreign language. Freshmen may take the Freshman Focus, a writing-intensive program designed to promote critical thinking. Under Connecticut College's honor code, students can take self-scheduled, unproctored exams any time during a 10-day exam period.

Degrees offered: bachelors, masters. Computer facilities include Fairlight music system, foreign language computer lab, VAX. Average undergraduate class size: 17; 66% of classes under 20, 29% 20–40, 5% over 40. About 84% of students entering as freshmen graduate within four years, 92% eventually; 92% of freshmen return for sophomore year. *Special programs:* independent study, study abroad, honors, undergraduate research, individualized majors, Twelve College Exchange, single-course exchange with U.S. Coast Guard Academy, Trinity, Wesleyan and National Theatre Institute, summer programs in marine biology, and the arts, Williams College-Mystic Seaport program in American marine studies, member Institute of European Studies, 3–2 program in engineering. Adult programs: Return to College program. *Calendar:* early semester.
Undergraduate degrees conferred (495). 42% were in Social Sciences, 9% were in Visual and Performing Arts, 8% were in Letters, 8% were in Psychology, 6% were in Life Sciences, 6% were in Foreign Languages, 6% were in Area and Ethnic Studies, 4% were in Philosophy and Religion, 4% were in Home Economics, 4% were in Multi/Interdisciplinary Studies, remainder in 2 other fields.
Graduates Career Data. Advanced studies pursued by 22% of students; 3% enter medical school; 2% enter law school; 2% enter business school. Medical schools typically enrolling largest numbers of graduates include U. of Connecticut, Yale, Tufts; law schools include George Washington, NYU, Boston U.. About 74% of 1992–93 graduates employed. Career Development Services include testing and vocational appraisal, counseling, assistance with resume and interview preparation, visits from prospective employers.
Faculty. About 94% of faculty hold PhD or equivalent. About 42% of teaching faculty are female; 7% ethnic minorities.
Student Body. College seeks a national student body; 29% of students from in state; 49% New England, 24% Middle Atlantic, 9% South, 7% West/Northwest, 6% Midwest, 5% foreign. An estimated 30% of students reported as Protestant, 26% Catholic, 10% Jewish, 4% other; 4% Black, 2% Hispanic, 2% Asian, 11% other minority. *Minority group students:* Minority Cultural Center.
Varsity Sports. Men (Div.III): Basketball, Crew, Cross Country, Diving, Ice Hockey, Lacrosse, Sailing, Soccer, Squash, Swimming, Tennis, Track. Women (Div.III): Basketball, Crew, Cross Country, Diving, Field Hockey, Lacrosse, Sailing, Soccer, Squash, Swimming, Tennis, Track, Volleyball.
Campus Life. Each dormitory sends a representative to the Student Government Association which regulates dorm life, most student activities, and includes a judiciary board which deals with the honor code. All dorms have a mix of students from the 4 classes. All students are guaranteed a single room after the first year. Drinking regulations conform to state law. Parking privileges on campus for all. Students, with parental consent, may petition to live off campus. Students report that most of the social life is centered on campus, New London is not a college town, but many students take advantage of the easy access to Connecticut beaches, Boston and New York City.

About 98% each of men, women live in coed dormitories; 1% each live in off-campus college related housing; 1% each commute. Sexes segregated in coed dormitories either by floor or room. There are no fraternities or sororities.
Annual Costs. Tuition and fees, $18,130; room and board, $6,030; estimated $100 other, exclusive of travel. About 54% of students receive financial aid; average amount of assistance, $12,953. Assistance is typically divided 79% grant, 18% loan, 3% work. College reports all scholarships awarded only on the basis of need.

University of Connecticut

Storrs, Connecticut 06268 (203) 486-2000

The only land-grant institution in Connecticut, the university has experienced a spectacular increase in students, quality of faculty, and general reputation. It now comprises 16 schools and colleges (12 of which are located at Storrs, the remainder at Hartford and Farmington) and 4 2-year regional campuses. At the graduate and professional level university includes schools of Law, Social Work, Medicine, Dentistry, and Center for Insurance, Education and Research. Significant numbers of applications are now being received from out-of-state students. The main campus of 2,000 acres is located in a rural community of 10,700, 8 miles from Willimantic. Most convenient major airport: Bradley International

Founded: 1881
Affiliation: State
UG Enrollment: 5,310 M, 5,453 W (full-time); 370 M, 349 W (part-time)
Total Enrollment: 16,457
Cost: < $10K
Admission: Selective (+)
Application Deadline: April 1

Admission is selective (+). About 67% of applicants accepted, 33% of these actually enroll; 48% of freshmen graduate in top fifth of high school class, 86% in top two-fifths. Average freshman SAT scores: 480 verbal, 500 mathematical; 42% of freshmen score above 500 on verbal, 8% above 600; 74% score above 500 on mathematical, 32% above 600, 7% above 700. *Required:* SAT. Criteria considered in admissions, in order of importance: high school academic record, standardized test scores, extracurricular activities, writing sample, recommendations; other factors considered: special talents. *Out-of-state* freshman applicants: state does not limit out-of-state enrollment. No special requirements for out-of-state applicants; 64% applicants accepted, 22% enroll. *Entrance programs:* deferred admission, midyear admission. *Apply* by April 1. *Transfers* welcome; 600 enrolled 1993–94.

Academic Environment. There is some effort to involve students in curriculum decision making—students represented on "most university committees." Center for Educational Innovation offers individualized majors. Students allowed, after counseling, as much as 3 semesters' leave without readmission problems. Pressures for academic achievement vary considerably among the various schools and colleges, as well as among departments. *Undergraduate studies* offered by colleges of Liberal Arts and Sciences, Agriculture and Natural Resources, schools of Allied Health Professions, Engineering, Fine Arts, Home Economics, Nursing, Pharmacy (5-year program); 2 years of college work required for schools of Education and Business Administration. Core requirements for College of Liberal Arts and Sciences include specific studies in foreign language, expository writing, mathematics, literature and the arts, culture and modern society, philosophical analysis, science, and technology. *Majors offered* in Liberal Arts and Sciences, in addition to wide range of studies include anthropology, Latin American studies, statistics, Women's studies. Average undergraduate class size: 30.

About 69% of students entering as freshmen graduate eventually; 13% of freshmen do not return for sophomore year. *Special programs:* CLEP, independent study, study abroad, honors, undergraduate research, 3-year degree, individualized majors, urban semester, cooperative education, student services for learning disabled. Adult programs: Separate dormitory floor available for older students. Calendar: semester, summer school.

Undergraduate degrees conferred (3,470). 19% were in Social Sciences, 14% were in Business and Management, 13% were in Letters, 8% were in Engineering, 6% were in Psychology, 6% were in Home Economics, 5% were in Liberal/General Studies, 5% were in Health Sciences, 4% were in Life Sciences, 4% were in Visual and Performing Arts, 4% were in Education, remainder in 13 other fields.

Graduates Career Data. Advanced studies pursued by 15% of students. Career Development Services include counseling, on-campus interviews.

Faculty. About 90% of faculty hold PhD or equivalent. About 24% of teaching faculty are female.

Student Body. University welcomes out-of-state students. About 85% of students from Connecticut, almost all from New England and Middle Atlantic. An estimated 3% of students reported as Black, 3% Hispanic, 4% Asian, 5% other minority.

Varsity Sports. Men (Div.I): Baseball, Basketball, Cross Country, Football (IAA), Golf, Hockey (II), Soccer, Swimming, Tennis, Track. Women (Div. I): Basketball, Cross Country, Soccer, Softball, Swimming, Tennis, Track, Volleyball.

Campus Life. Student life at Storrs characterized by campus representatives as reasonably free. Procedures outlining student rights and responsibilities reflect decreasing role of university in loco parentis. Intervisitation hours in all dormitory residences set in September by vote of residents without prior limitation. Enforcement up to individual dormitory. Wide range of intellectual and cultural activities available on campus, supplemented by resources of Hartford, just 25 miles away. Freshmen and sophomores under age of 21 not allowed motor vehicles on campus; parking space for others assigned by seniority of student. University proscribes "intoxicating liquor in any of the dormitories, educational facilities, and public premises when they are in use by minors." Juniors, seniors, and those over 21 may live off campus.

About 65% of students live in traditional or coed dormitories; 35% of students live in off-campus housing or commute. Freshmen given preference in college housing if all students cannot be accommodated. Sexes segregated in coed dormitories by floor. There are 16 fraternities, 9 sororities which about 10% of students join. About 30% of resident students leave campus on weekends.

Annual Costs. Tuition and fees, $4,290 (out-of-state, $11,410); room and board, $4,878; estimated $700 other, exclusive of travel. About 50% of students receive financial aid; average amount of assistance, $2,375. University reports some scholarships awarded on the basis of academic merit alone. *Meeting Costs:* University offers Knight Tuition Plan, Connecticut College Savings Bond Plan.

Conservatorio de Musica de Puerto Rico

Hato Rey, Puerto Rico 00918

The Conservatorio offers degree programs in music education as well as in music as a performing art.

Founded: 1959
Affiliation: State

Undergraduate degrees conferred (26). 65% were in Visual and Performing Arts, 35% were in Education.

Converse College

Spartanburg, South Carolina 29302 **(803) 596-9040**

An independent, liberal arts college for women, Converse also includes a well-known School of Music which accepts a limited number of men, only as graduate students. The 70-acre campus is located in a city of 47,000, 70 miles southwest of Charlotte, North Carolina. Most convenient major airport: Greenville/Spartanburg.

Founded: 1889
Affiliation: Independent
UG Enrollment: 660 W (full-time); 80 W (part-time)
Total Enrollment: 1,106
Cost: $10K–$20K
% Receiving Financial Aid: 80%
Admission: Selective (+)
Application Deadline: April 1

Admission is selective (+). About 92% of applicants accepted, 37% of these actually enroll; 80% of freshmen graduate in top fifth of high school class. Average freshman SAT scores: 517 verbal, 505 mathematical, according to most recent data available. *Required:* SAT. Criteria considered in admissions, in order of importance: high school academic record, standardized test scores, recommendations, extra curricular activities; other factors considered: special talents. *Entrance programs:* advanced placement. About 30% of entering students from private or parochial schools. *Apply* by April 1. *Transfers* welcome; 17 enrolled 1993–94.

Academic Environment. Pressures for academic achievement appear moderate. Calendar offers option of independent study or practical experience either on or off campus. Core requirements include one course in each of English composition, literature, mathematics, Western culture, two courses in each of science, social science, humanities, physical education, and four in foreign language. Degrees offered: bachelors, masters. Average undergraduate class size: 80% under 20, 20% 20–40.

About 61% of students entering as freshmen graduate eventually; 76% of freshmen return for sophomore year. *Special programs:* CLEP, credit by examination, honors, study abroad, independent study, 3-year degree, internships and cooperative work/study programs available in most disciplines, 5-year 2-degree medical program, education for the deaf (in cooperation with South Carolina School for the Deaf and Blind), cross-registration with neighboring Wofford. Adult programs: Converse II, program has special entrance requirements and fee payment, students are mixed in classes with traditional students, evening programs available in business. *Calendar:* 4–2–4, summer school.

Undergraduate degrees conferred (165). 21% were in Business and Management, 18% were in Visual and Performing Arts, 18% were in Education, 12% were in Social Sciences, 7% were in Letters, 7% were in Architecture and Environmental Design, 6% were in Psychology, 3% were in Life Sciences, 3% were in Foreign Languages, remainder in 4 other fields.
Graduates Career Data. Advanced studies pursued by 20% of students; 5% enter medical school, 5% enter law school, 5% enter business school. About 70% of 1992–93 graduates employed. Career Development Services include counseling, resume and interview preparation workshops, internship programs, placement services. Alumnae reported as active in both career guidance and job placement.
Faculty. About 85% of faculty hold PhD or equivalent. About 70% of undergraduate class taught by tenured faculty. About 27% of teaching faculty are female; 5% Hispanic.
Student Body. College seeks a national student body; 45% of students from in state; 75% South. An estimated 95% of students reported as Protestant, 4% Catholic, 1% Jewish; 6% as Black, 3% Hispanic, 1% Asian, according to most recent data available.
Varsity Sports. Women (NAIA): Basketball, Cross Country, Tennis, Volleyball.
Campus Life. Office of Career Services offers career/life counseling to students and alumnae. Visitation recently liberalized. Beer and wine sold in Rathskeller; alcohol prohibited elsewhere on campus. Cars permitted. About 80% of women live in dormitories; rest commute. There are no sororities.
Annual Costs. Tuition and fees, $12,050 room and board, $3,700. About 80% of students receive financial aid. College reports 15 scholarships awarded on the basis of academic merit alone, 8 for special talents.

Cook College

(See Rutgers—The State University of New Jersey)

The Cooper Union for the Advancement of Science and Art

New York, New York 10003 (212) 353-4120

Founded more than 100 years ago by Peter Cooper as a tuition-free institution for U.S. residents irrespective of race, color, or creed, Cooper Union is able to attract a small, highly capable student body for training in architecture, engineering, and fine arts. The co-educational college is located in the heart of Manhattan on the Lower East Side. Most convenient major airports: LaGuardia, Kennedy, Newark.

Founded: 1859
Affiliation: Independent
UG Enrollment: 634 M, 326 W (full-time); 10 M, 16 W (part-time)
Total Enrollment: 1,075
Cost: Fees, $300
% Receiving Financial Aid: 100%
Admission: Most Selective
Application Deadline: Jan. 1

Admission is among the most selective in the country.

For Engineering (400 M, 88 W), 13% of applicants accepted, 67% of these actually enroll. Average freshman SAT scores: 600 verbal, 740 mathematical; 72% of freshmen score above 500 on verbal, 35% above 600, 7% above 700; all score above 600 on mathematical, 63% above 700.

For Architecture (127 M, 67 W), 8% of applicants accepted, 86% of these actually enroll. Average freshman SAT scores: 520 verbal, 540 mathematical; 54% of freshmen score above 500 on verbal, 9% above 600; 75% freshmen score above 500 on mathematical, 20% above 600, 5% above 700.

For Art (129 M, 139 W), 9% of applicants accepted, 96% of these actually enroll. Average freshman SAT scores: 540 verbal, 460 mathematical; 59% of freshmen score above 500 on verbal, 23% above 600, 2% above 700; 57% score above 500 on mathematical, 19% above 600, 6% above 700.

Engineering students carefully selected on basis of academic performance and standardized test scores; selection of art and architecture students based on "perceived artistic talent."

Required for Engineering applicants: SAT or ACT, ACH in physics or chemistry, mathematics (level I or II), essay. Required for Art and Architecture applicants: SAT or ACT, essay, portfolio, Cooper Union's own entrance tests. *Entrance programs:* early decision, early admission, deferred admission, advanced placement. *Apply* by January 1 for Architecture, by January 10 for Art, February 1 for Engineering. *Transfers* welcome; 39 enrolled 1993–94.
Academic Environment. Pressures for academic achievement intense. Cooper Union's graduates rank high in accomplishment. Students represented on all curriculum committees, but do not have role in selection and promotion of faculty. Core requirements include a sequence in humanities and social sciences; 6 credits in Studies in Literature, 6 credits in the Making of the Modern World. Degrees offered: bachelors, masters. *Majors offered* include 4 engineering fields, interdisciplinary engineering, fine arts, architecture.

About 77% of students entering as freshmen graduate eventually; 13% of freshmen do not return for sophomore year. *Special programs:* CLEP, undergraduate research, study abroad including art school exchange programs, cross registration with NYU and New School, individualized majors, internships and cooperative work/study programs. *Calendar:* semester.
Undergraduate degrees conferred (176). 52% were in Engineering, 36% were in Visual and Performing Arts, 13% were in Architecture and Environmental Design.
Graduates Career Data. Advanced studies pursued by 55% of graduates; 3% enter medical school; 3% enter law school; 1% enter business school. About 35% of 1992–93 graduates are employed. Fields typically hiring largest numbers of graduate include engineering, computer science, architecture, design. Career Development Services include counseling, internship programs, on-campus engineering recruitment, resume and interviewing workshops.
Faculty. About 80% of faculty hold PhD or equivalent.
Student Body. About 60% of students from New York; 80% Middle Atlantic, 4% New England, 4% West/Northwest, 3% Midwest, 3% South, 7% Foreign. An estimated 8% of students reported as Black, 9% Hispanic, 27% Asian, 6% other ethnic minority.
Campus Life. Few regulations governing student conduct. Location of campus in the Greenwich Village area between the East and West villages presents extraordinary opportunities for urban experience—both positive and negative. Recently Cooper Union built its first dormitory, and the changeover from commuter school to partly-residential school is changing the campus environment. The location of the school and the extremely intense work load tend to limit campus-based social life, but there are many school-sponsored parties, intramural sports, and student organized activities and trips.

About 17% of men, 18% of women live in the new coed dormitory, the rest live in off-campus housing or commute. There are 3 fraternities; 2 sororities; which about 6% of men, 5% of women join.
Annual Costs. Fees, $300; room and board, $8,700; estimated $2,982 other, exclusive of travel. All students receive full tuition scholarships; 43% receive further aid. Cooper Union reports all scholarships awarded on the basis of academic merit alone.

Coppin State College

Baltimore, Maryland 21216-3698 (410) 333-5990

A state-supported institution, located in metropolitan Baltimore; founded as a college for training African American teachers, and its present focus is on the needs of the minority and economically disadvantaged students from Baltimore City. Most convenient major airport: Baltimore/Washington.

Founded: 1900
Affiliation: State
UG Enrollment: 869 M, 1,293 W (full-time); 203 M, 551 W (part-time)
Total Enrollment: 3,267
Cost: < $10K
% Receiving Financial Aid: 88%
Admission: Non-selective
Application Deadline: July 15

Admission. High school graduates eligible; college prep curriculum not required; non graduates admitted by examination. About 52% of freshmen applicants accepted; 54% of these actually enroll. Average freshman SAT scores: 376 verbal, 406 mathematical. *Required:* SAT, minimum HS GPA. Criteria considered in admissions, in order of importance: high school academic record, standardized test scores, recommendations, extracurricular activities, writing sample; other factors considered: special talents, alumni children. *Out-of-state* freshman applicants: college seeks students from out of state. State does not limit out-of-state enrollment. No special requirements for out-of-state applicants. About 58% applicants accepted, 41% enroll. *Apply* by July 15; rolling admissions. *Transfers* welcome; 276 enrolled fall, 1993.

Academic Environment. Degrees offered: bachelors, masters. Coppin offers 15 majors and an honors program; programs include management, media arts, nursing, education, as well as several pre-professional and dual degree programs. Core requirements include courses in English; mathematics, logic or philosophy; history; social sciences; physical education and health. About 73% of students entering as freshmen return for sophomore year. Coppin's students are a mix of recent high school graduates; employed persons pursuing higher education part-time by day, evening, or weekend; and professionals seeking to improve skills or to change careers. *Special programs:* CLEP, honors, January Term, study abroad, independent study, dual degree programs in engineering, dentistry, pharmacy; internships. Average undergraduate class size: 24. *Calendar:* semester, summer school.

Undergraduate degrees conferred (208). 22% were in Business and Management, 18% were in Health Sciences, 11% were in Protective Services, 11% were in Psychology, 10% were in Education, 7% were in Social Sciences, 5% were in Letters, 4% were in Public Affairs, 3% were in Mathematics, 3% were in Physical Sciences, 3% were in Computer and Engineering Related Technology, remainder in 2 other fields.

Graduates Career Data. Advanced studies pursued by 34% of recent graduates. Employers typically hiring largest numbers of graduates include public school systems, health care facilities, correctional institutions and services, business. Career Development Services include information services for awareness and planning, employer contacts, placement services, opportunities for experiential learning.

Faculty. About 64% of full-time faculty hold PhD or equivalent. About 45% of full-time teaching faculty are female; 64% Black, 1% Hispanic, 8% other ethnic minorities.

Student Body. About 82% of students from Maryland; most from Middle Atlantic states, 2% foreign. An estimated 91% of students reported as Black, 2% other ethnic minority. Average age of undergraduate student: 25.

Varsity Sports. Men (Div.II): Baseball, Basketball, Cross Country, Swimming, Tennis, Track, Wrestling. Women: Basketball, Cross Country, Softball, Swimming, Tennis, Track, Volleyball.

Campus Life. Coppin opened its coed dormitory in 1993 and now about 8% of men, 7% of women live on campus; rest commute. There are 3 fraternities, 5 sororities on campus.

Annual Costs. Tuition and fees, $2,605 (out-of-state, $4,677); room and board, $4,540. About 88% of students receive financial aid; average amount of assistance, $3,256. Assistance is typically divided 20% scholarship, 45% grant, 25% loan, 10% work. College reports 85 honors scholarships awarded, 10 for achievement, 6 for opportunity, and 17 for "options".

Corcoran School of Art

Washington, D.C. 20006

A college of art and design, Corcoran is located in the nation's capital. Degrees are conferred in graphic design, photography, and other fine arts.

Undergraduate degrees conferred (62). 100% were in Visual and Performing Arts.

Cornell College

Mount Vernon, Iowa 52314 (800) 747-1112

One of a number of small, Midwestern, liberal arts colleges that welcome students from all parts of the country, Cornell maintains ties to the Methodist Church, but makes no specific religious demands on its students. The campus of over 100 acres is located in a community of 3,500, 15 miles east of Cedar Rapids. Most convenient major airport: 15 miles east of Cedar Rapids.

Founded: 1853
Affiliation: Independent (United Methodist)
Total Enrollment: 478 M, 662 W (full-time)
Cost: $10K–$20K
% Receiving Financial Aid: 80%
Admission: Very Selective
Application Deadline: March 1

Admission is very selective. About 85% of applicants accepted, 30% of these actually enroll; 57% of freshmen graduate in top fifth of high school class, 27% in top two-fifths. Average freshman scores: SAT, 520 verbal, 560 mathematical; 58% of freshmen score above 500 on verbal, 24% above 600, 4% above 700; 80% above 500 on mathematical, 30% above 600, 8% above 700; ACT, 25 composite. *Required:* ACT or SAT, essay, recommendation. Criteria considered in admissions, in order of importance: high school academic record, recommendations, writing sample, extracurricular activities, standardized test scores; other factors considered: special talents, alumni children. *Entrance programs:* early decision, mid-year admission, deferred admission, advanced placement. *Apply* by March 1. *Transfers* welcome; 21 enrolled 1993–94.

Academic Environment. Under the Block Plan the academic year is divided into nine terms, each 3[1/2] weeks long. Students enroll in one course each term, and must complete eight terms per year. The ninth term may be taken at no additional cost, and may be used for the enrichment of the student's educational experience, to gain practical experience through internships, or to meet the requirements for graduation more quickly. Students consider the one-course-at-a-time program a real strength of the academic program: "it allows for a lot of individual attention", but it also "really makes you prioritize your time and stop procrastinating." Four degree programs offer student option of traditionally structured course of study or a nontraditional combination of regular courses, independent study, work-service, and travel. Student works out course of study with advisor to achieve individualized goals. Distribution requirements for BA fairly numerous: 1 course in English, 2 in social sciences, 3 in humanities, 1 in fine arts, 1–4 in foreign language, 1 in mathematics, 2 in science, 1 in physical education. Degrees offered: bachelors. *Majors offered* include: English, economics and business, psychology, biology, education, politics, international business. Average undergraduate class size: 65% under 20, 35% 20–40.

About 65% of students entering as freshmen graduate eventually, 75% of freshmen return for sophomore year. *Special programs:* CLEP, independent study, study abroad, undergraduate science research, individualized majors, Washington Semester, programs of ACM, East Asian studies in Tokyo, semester exchange with Fisk U., Rust, or U. of Puerto Rico, cooperative degree program in nursing and medical technology with Rush U. (Chicago), 3–2 engineering, environmental management, natural resource management, occupational therapy. *Calendar:* nine 3[1/2] week terms.

Undergraduate degrees conferred (246). 37% were in Social Sciences, 9% were in Visual and Performing Arts, 9% were in Life Sciences, 8% were in Philosophy and Religion, 8% were in Letters, 8% were in Education, 7% were in Foreign Languages, 6% were in Psychology, 3% were in Physical Sciences, 3% were in Computer and Engineering Related Technology, remainder in Mathematics.

Graduates Career Data. Advanced studies pursued by 35% of graduates; 65% within 5 years. Professional schools typically enrolling largest numbers of graduates include U. of Iowa. About 60% of 1992–93 graduates employed. Fields typically hiring largest numbers of graduates include education, economics and business, psychology, international business/relations. Career Development Services offer individual counseling, resume writing, and work with Iowa Private Placement Consortium.

Faculty. About 76% of faculty hold PhD or equivalent. About 85–90% of undergraduate classes taught by faculty. About 22% of teaching faculty are female.

Student Body. About 27% of students from in state; 74% Midwest, 16% Northwest, 4% Northwest, 2% Middle Atlantic, 1% New England, 1% South, 3% foreign. An estimated 25% of students reported as Protestant, 20% Catholic, 1% Jewish, 44% unaffiliated, 10% other, according to most recent data available; 3% Black, 2% Hispanic, 2% Asian, 2% other minority.

Varsity Sports. Men (NCAA Div.III): Baseball, Basketball, Cross Country, Football, Golf, Soccer, Swimming, Tennis, Track, Wrestling. Women (NCAA Div.III): Basketball, Cross Country, Soccer, Softball, Swimming, Tennis, Track, Volleyball.

Campus Life. Interest in intramural sports reported as very strong, most popular intramural sports are basketball and volleyball; varsity sports: football (men) and volleyball (women). Cedar Rapids and Iowa City, 15 and 20 miles away, are nearest metropolitan centers. Cars permitted but "not considered a necessity." Possession and use of alcoholic beverages now allowed in residence halls for those of legal age. Intervisitation permitted within designated hours. Key permits available to students for use after residence halls are locked. Students expected to live in college housing.

About 33% of men, 22% of women live in traditional dormitories; 10% of men, 20% of women live in coed dormitories; rest live in off-campus college-related housing or commute. About 35% men join fraternities, 35% women join sororities. Freshmen given preference in college housing if all students cannot be accommodated. About 10–15% of resident students leave campus on weekends.

Annual Costs. Tuition and fees, $14,228; room and board, $4,197; estimated $1,500 other, exclusive of travel. About 80% of students receive financial aid; average amount of assistance, $13,000. Assistance is typically divided 69% gift aid, 24% loan, 7% work. *Minority group students:* "special attention given to financial needs of all low income students." College reports 500+ scholarships awarded on the basis of academic merit alone. *Meeting Costs:* college offers extended payment plan, prepayment plan to lock in tuition.

Cornell University

Ithaca, New York 14853 **(607) 255-5241**

Cornell University is both New York State's land-grant university and an eminent private institutional member of the Ivy League. The university includes four privately supported colleges: Architecture, Art and Planning, Arts and Sciences, Engineering, and the School of Hotel Administration, as well as the state-supported schools: Agriculture and Life Sciences, Human Ecology, and Labor Relations. The 740-acre campus is located in a small city of 40,000 in central New York. Most convenient major airport: Syracuse.

Founded: 1865
Affiliation: Independent
UG Enrollment: 6,878 M, 5,935 W (full-time)
Total Enrollment: 18,449
Cost: $10K–$20K
% Receiving Financial Aid: 70%
Admission: Most Selective
Application Deadline: January 1

Admission is among the most selective in the country for College of Arts and Sciences; highly (+) selective for New York State College of Agriculture and Life Sciences, College of Engineering, New York State School of Industrial and Labor Relations; highly selective for colleges of Architecture, Art, and Planning, School of Hotel Administration; very (+) selective for New York State College of Human Ecology. For all schools, 27% of applicants accepted, 50% of these actually enroll; 81% of freshmen reporting class rank graduate in top fifth of high school class, 95% in top two-fifths. Average freshman scores: SAT, 88% of freshman score above 500 on verbal, 50% above 600; 98% score above 500 on mathematical, 87% above 600, 47% above 700.

For Arts and Sciences (2,184 M, 1,808 W), 34% of applicants accepted, 35% of these actually enroll; 86% of freshmen graduate in top tenth of high school class, 95% in top fifth. Average freshman SAT scores: 92% of freshmen score above 500 on verbal, 65% above 600, 13% above 700; 99% score above 500 on mathematical, 91% above 600, 49% above 700.

For Agriculture and Life Sciences (1,582 M, 1,507 W), 32% of applicants accepted, 62% of these actually enroll; 87% of freshmen graduate in top tenth of high school class, 98% in top fifth. Average freshman SAT scores: 86% of freshmen score above 500 on SAT verbal, 42% above 600, 4% above 700; 98% score above 500 on mathematical, 79% above 600, 33% above 700.

For Architecture, Art and Planning (255 M, 223 W), 26% of applicants accepted, 60% of these actually enroll; 82% of freshmen graduate in top fifth of high school class, 97% in top two-fifths. Average freshman SAT scores: 79% of freshmen score above 500 on verbal, 30% above 600, 1% above 700; 94% score above 500 on mathematical, 76% above 600, 27% above 700. Large majority of students enrolled in 5-year program, limited number in 4-year.

For Engineering (1,904 M, 513 W), 53% of applicants accepted, 41% of these actually enroll; 81% of freshmen graduate in top tenth of high school class, 97% in top fifth. Average freshman SAT scores: 87% of freshmen score above 500 on verbal, 46% above 600, 6% above 700; 100% score above 550 on mathematical, 99% above 600, 72% above 700.

For Human Ecology (363 M, 886 W), 32% of applicants accepted, 63% of these actually enroll; 85% of freshmen graduate in top tenth of high school class, 98% in top fifth. Average freshman SAT scores: 90% of freshmen score above 500 on verbal, 48% above 600, 5% above 700; 98% score above 500 on mathematical, 79% above 600, 36% above 700.

For Industrial and Labor Relations (348 M, 282 W), 47% of applicants accepted, 76% of these actually enroll; 93% of freshmen graduate in top fifth of high school class, 99% in top two-fifths. Average freshman SAT scores: 92% of freshmen score above 500 on verbal, 51% above 600, 4% above 700; 99% score above 500 on mathematical, 71% above 600, 24% above 700.

For Hotel Administration (370 M, 313 W), 35% of applicants accepted, 81% of these actually enroll; 80% of freshmen graduate in top fifth of high school class, 99% in top two-fifths. Average freshman SAT scores: 70% of freshmen score above 500 on verbal, 26% above 600, 1% above 700; 96% score above 500 on mathematical, 63% above 600, 18% above 700.

Required: SAT or ACT, 3 ACH in different subjects, including English (with or without composition), for Arts and Sciences, English, mathematics, chemistry or physics or biology for Engineering, English and mathematics for Industrial and Labor Relations, and Human Ecology; interview for Architecture, Fine Arts, and Planning, Hotel Administration, Industrial and Labor Relations. Criteria considered in admissions, in order of importance: high school academic record (first), then standardized test scores, recommendations, extracurricular activities, and writing sample all receive equal ranking; other factors considered: special talents, alumni children. *Entrance programs:* early decision (except Hotel Administration, Industrial and Labor Relations), early admission, mid-year admission, deferred admission, advanced placement, rolling admission (notification for several units). *Apply* by January 1; by November 10 for early decision. *Transfers* welcome; 454 enrolled 1993–94.

Academic Environment. Undergraduate study at college of Architecture, Art, and Planning leads to professional degree after 5 years. (BArch). Students in Engineering may apply to continue for a fifth year for a professional degree of Master of Engineering. Graduation requirements in Arts and Sciences include 2 semesters freshman writing seminars, 2 courses each from biological/physical sciences, social sciences/history, humanities/expressive arts, mathematics/computer science; foreign language proficiency; 2 semesters physical education. All colleges require at least one semester of a first year writing seminar. Degrees offered: bachelors, masters, doctoral.

About 88% of students entering as freshmen graduate eventually; 97% of freshmen return for sophomore year. *Special programs:* independent study, study abroad, honors, undergraduate research, individualized majors, College Scholar Program, Greek civilization program for selected freshmen and sophomores, college program in Engineering (permitting individualized majors), management internship in Hotel Administration, acceleration, combined programs among various Cornell colleges. *Calendar:* semester, January Term, summer school.

Undergraduate degrees conferred (1,992). 27% were in Engineering, 23% were in Social Sciences, 10% were in Business and Management, 7% were in Life Sciences, 7% were in Letters, 4% were in Architecture and Environmental Design, 4% were in Psychology, 4% were in Physical Sciences, 3% were in Computer and Engineering Related Technology, 3% were in Visual and Performing Arts, 3% were in Area and Ethnic Studies, remainder in 4 other fields. *Doctoral degrees:* Physical Sciences 47, Social Sciences 24, Engineering 77, Letters 19, Architecture and Environmental Design 3, Business and Management 4, Psychology 8, Mathematics 7, Fine and Applied Arts 5, Biological Sciences 13, Foreign Languages 16, Computer and Information Sciences 9, Philosophy and Religion 2, Law 1.

Graduates Career Data. Advanced studies pursued by 32% of students immediately following graduation; 11% enter graduate school, 7% enter medical school; 6% enter law school; 1% enter business school. Medical schools typically enrolling largest numbers of graduates include Cornell, U. of Pennsylvania; law schools include NYU. Corporations typically hiring largest numbers of graduates include Andersen Consulting, Proctor & Gamble, Chase Manhattan, AT&T. Career Development offers a full range of services including counseling, placement, recruiting and diagnostic testing.

Faculty. About 96% of faculty hold PhD or equivalent. About 99% of undergraduate classes taught by faculty, tenured and non-tenured. About 18% of teaching faculty are female.

Student Body. About 48% of students from in state.

An estimated 5% of students reported as Black, 5% Hispanic, 13% Asian, 5% other minority, according to most recent data available. *Minority group students:* Office of Minority Educational Affairs coordinates support services, including tutoring and social facilities, for minorities and others in need of assistance; minority student clubs reported to be among the most active student organizations on campus.

Varsity Sports. Men (Div.I): Baseball, Basketball, Crew, Cross Country, Diving, Equestrian, Football, Golf, Ice Hockey, Lacrosse, Soccer, Swimming, Tennis, Track, Wrestling. Women (Div.I): Basketball, Crew, Cross Country, Diving, Equestrian, Ice Hockey, Field Hockey, Lacrosse, Soccer, Softball, Swimming, Tennis, Track, Volleyball.

Campus Life. Student social life at Cornell is quite free and includes a wide variety of lifestyles. The Office of Ombudsman is designed to help resolve complaints against the university. A wide variety of cultural and recreational activities are available on campus. Student leader reports, "This university has so many different things happening it is impossible to be bored." The university provides a major share of the community's intellectual and cultural activities; Cornell Daily Sun is Ithaca's only morning newspaper and provides coverage of national and international events. In addition to varsity sports, Cornell has an extensive intramural program including cross-country skiing, sailing, broomstick polo, etc. Visitation policies set by the individual housing units, but university warns that "visitation does not mean continued residence." Drinking permitted, subject to state law.

About 76% of students live in school housing. Freshmen given preference in college housing if all students can not be accommodated. There are 47 fraternities, 18 sororities on campus which about 32% of men, 28% of women join. About 10% of resident students leave campus on weekends.

Annual Costs. Tuition for endowed units, $18,226; for statutory units, $7,426, (out-of-state, $14,106); room and board, $5,963. About 70% of students receive financial aid; average amount of need-based Cornell grant for first year students, $11,750. Cornell "has a need-blind admissions policy and is committed to meeting 100% of a students demonstrated need." Meeting Costs: university offers Cornell Installment Plan, Multiple Year Tuition Payment.

Cornish College of the Arts

Seattle, Washington 98102

A 4-year college of the visual and performing arts, offering a very focused environment for students who wish to pursue careers as artists.

Undergraduate degrees conferred (81). 100% were in Visual and Performing Arts.

State University College at Cortland

(See State University of New York)

Covenant College

Lookout Mountain, Georgia 30750 (800) 637-2687 or (706) 820-1560

Covenant College is a "Christian liberal arts institution" whose stated purpose is: "That in all things Christ might have preeminence." Campus is located on Lookout Mountain in the northwest corner of Georgia, overlooking Chattanooga, Tennessee. Most convenient major airport: Chattanooga, Tennessee.

Founded: 1955
Affiliation: Reformed Presbyterian
Total Enrollment: 273 M, 332 W (full-time)
Cost: < $10K
% Receiving Financial Aid: 93%
Admission: Selective (+)
Application Deadline: May 1

Admission is selective (+). About 78% of applicants accepted, 42% of these actually enroll; 38% of entering freshmen graduate in top fifth of their high school class, 71% in top two-fifths. Average freshman scores: SAT, 52% of freshman score above 500 on verbal, 24% above 600, 3% above 700; 72% score above 500 on mathematical, 31% above 600, 8% above 700; ACT, 25 composite. *Required:* SAT or ACT, interview, essay. Criteria considered in admissions, in order of importance: standardized test scores and "profession of Christian faith by student or parent" rank equally as most important, high school academic record and recommendations rank equally. *Apply* by May 1 for priority; rolling admissions. *Transfers* welcome; 46 enrolled 1993–94.

Academic Environment. Degrees offered: associates, bachelors, masters. Graduation requirements include 12 hours Bible, English composition, 2 hours microcomputer applications, 4 hours mathematics, 3 hours each physical education, speech, foreign language (or demonstrate proficiency), 4 hours lab science, 22 hours cultural courses, 3 hours art, literature, philosophy, or music. Average undergraduate class size: 37% under 20; 44% 20–40, 19% over 40. About 40% of students entering as freshmen graduate eventually, 74% of freshmen return for sophomore year. *Special programs:* undergraduate research, study abroad, independent study, Au Sable Trails Institute in Michigan, American Studies Program in Washington, D.C., 3–2 engineering with Georgia Institute of Technology, May Term. Adult programs: Quest Program - Adult Completion, minimum of 60 college credits, 5 years work experience; program completion in 13 months. *Calendar:* early semester, summer school.

Undergraduate degrees conferred (101). 26% were in Education, 14% were in Social Sciences, 10% were in Theology, 9% were in Letters, 8% were in Multi/Interdisciplinary Studies, 7% were in Business and Management, 6% were in Psychology, 4% were in Computer and Information Sciences, 4% were in Life Sciences, 4% were in Physical Sciences, 3% were in Visual and Performing Arts, 3% were in Parks and Recreation, 2% were in Philosophy and Religion.

Graduates Career Data. Office of Career Planning and Placement offers career guidance through individual counseling testing, SIGI Plus workshops, career/life planning course. Placement services available to assist graduating seniors in locating employment, writing resumes, and pursuing graduate study programs.

Faculty. About 73% of faculty hold PhD or equivalent. About 23% undergraduate classes taught by tenured faculty. About 3% of teaching faculty are female; 3% Black.

Student Body. About 19% of students from in state; 59% South, 12% West, 11% New England, 7% Plains, 6% Great Lakes, 4% foreign. About 98% of students reported as Protestant; 3% Black.

Religious Orientation. Covenant is a church-related institution; 64% of students affiliated with this church; 3 courses in religious studies required of all students; attendance at daily chapel services expected.

Varsity Sports. Men (NCCAA): Basketball (Div.II), Cross Country, Soccer (NAIA). Women (NCCAA): Basketball, Cross Country, Volleyball.

Campus Life. About 83% of men, 81% women live in traditional dormitories; rest commute. No intervisitation in men's or women's dormitory rooms. About 2% of resident students leave campus on weekends. There are no fraternities or sororities on campus.

Annual Costs. Tuition and fees, $9,310; room and board, $3,744, estimated $500 other, exclusive of travel. About 93% of students receive financial aid, average amount of assistance, $5,401. Assistance is typically divided 61% scholarship/grant, 26% loans and 13% work. College reports 224 scholarships awarded on the basis of academic merit alone; 182 special talents alone; 273 for need alone.

Creighton University

Omaha, Nebraska 68178 (402) 280-2703

A relatively small university conducted by Jesuits, Creighton is now under predominantly lay control. School is noted for its strong preprofessional training and for the number of students who continue professional training within the university. The campus is located in a metropolitan area of 614,300. Most convenient major airport: Eppley Airfield (Omaha).

Founded: 1878
Affiliation: Independent (Roman Catholic)
UG Enrollment: 1,577 M, 1,999 W (full-time); 224 M, 393 W (part-time)
Total Enrollment: 5,434
Cost: $10K–$20K
% Receiving Financial Aid: 75%
Admission: Very Selective
Application Deadline: August 1

Admission is very selective for colleges of Arts and Sciences, Business Administration. For all schools, 90% of applicants are accepted, 38% of these actually enroll; 47% of freshmen graduate in top fifth of high school class, 76% in top two-fifths. Average freshman ACT scores, according to most recent data available: 23 composite.

Required: ACT or SAT. *Entrance programs:* midyear admission. About 40% of entering students from private schools; 1% from parochial schools. *Apply* by August 1; rolling admissions. *Transfers* welcome.

Academic Environment. Pressures for academic achievement appear moderate. Administration reports 40–50% of courses are elective. *Undergraduate studies* offered by colleges of Arts and Sciences, Business Administration, and Nursing; professional schools of Dentistry, Law, Medicine, Pharmacy require previous college work for entrance. *Majors offered* in addition to usual arts and sciences include classical civilization, creative writing, business communications, dance, education, journalism, medical technology, radiologic technology, exercise science, management information systems, ministry, occupational therapy, organizational communication, statistics, theater, exercise science, ministry.

About 65% of students entering as freshmen graduate eventually; 18% of freshmen do not return for sophomore year. *Special programs:* CLEP, independent study, study abroad, 2–3 engineering with Detroit, 3–3 in business administration and law. Adult programs: University offers credit and non-credit programs for non-traditional students. *Calendar:* early semester (first semester starts third week in August), summer school.

Undergraduate degrees conferred (783). 21% were in Business and Management, 18% were in Health Sciences, 10% were in Social Sciences, 9% were in Psychology, 9% were in Life Sciences, 6% were in Allied Health, 5% were in Communications, 4% were in Physical Sciences, 3% were in Letters, 3% were in Mathematics, remainder in 9 other fields.

Graduates Career Data. According to most recent data available, full-time graduate or professional study pursued immediately after graduation by 40% of students; 11% enter medical school; 4% enter dental school; 9% enter law school; 1% enter business school. Medical, dental, law, and business schools typically enrolling largest numbers of graduates include Creighton. *Careers in business and industry* pursued by 23% of graduates. Corporations typically hiring largest numbers of graduates include Applied Communications, Price Waterhouse, Union Pacific Railroad, Arthur Andersen. *Career Counseling Program:* serves all students; ongoing effort to attract employers for liberal arts students reported. Student assessment of program reported as good for career guidance but only fair for job placement. Alumni reported to provide some help in both career guidance and job placement.

Faculty. About 81% of faculty hold PhD or equivalent.

Student Body. University seeks a national student body; 39% of students from Nebraska; 80% from North Central, 9% West, 5% Northwest. An estimated 64% of students reported as Catholic, 22% Protestant, 12% unaffiliated, 2% other; 3% as Black, 3% Hispanic, 4% Asian, 4% other minority, according to most recent data available.

Religious Orientation. Creighton is an independent institution with a "Roman Catholic orientation"; 6 hours of theology required; attendance at religious services voluntary. Protestant chaplain available on campus. Places of worship available on campus for Catholics, in immediate community for all major faiths.

Varsity Sports. Men (Div.IA): Baseball, Basketball, Cross Country, Golf, Soccer, Tennis. Women (Div.IA): Basketball, Cross Country, Golf, Soccer, Softball, Tennis.

Campus Life. Recent student leader and administration source agree students are primarily concerned with occupational goals. Cars allowed on campus. Intervisitation during specified hours (1 am weekdays, 2 am weekends); smoking limited to designated areas and private living quarters. Alcohol permitted only for those of legal age (21); no controlled substances allowed—subject to disciplinary review. Seniors from outside the city may choose to live in campus residence halls or off campus.

About 4% of women live in traditional dormitories; 32% of men, 31% of women in coed dormitories; 67% of men, 65% of women live in off-campus housing or commute. Freshmen given preference in college housing if all students cannot be accommodated. Sexes segregated in coed dormitories by wing. There are 7 fraternities, 4 sororities on campus which about 22% of men, 20% of women join; 1% of men live in fraternities; sororities provide no residence facilities. About 25% of resident students leave campus on weekends.

Annual Costs. Tuition and fees, $10,252; room and board, $4,178. About 75% of students receive financial aid. University reports some scholarships awarded on the basis of academic merit alone. *Meeting Costs:* university offers 10-month payment plan.

Crichton College

Memphis, Tennessee 38112-4319 (901) 458-7526

An independent Bible/Christian liberal arts institution, Crichton is located in Memphis, a city of 700,000. Most convenient major airport: Memphis.

Affiliation: Independent
Total Enrollment: 114 M, 100 W (full-time)
Cost: < $10K
% Receiving Financial Aid: 85%
Admission: Non-selective
Application Deadline: 2 weeks before registration

Admission. Christian graduates of accredited high schools eligible; 91% of applicants accepted, 79% of these actually enroll. Average freshman ACT scores, according to most recent data available: ACT, 14.9 M, 15.4 W composite, 15.4 M, 12.6 W mathematical. *Required:* ACT, students must be Christians. *Apply* by two weeks prior to registration. *Transfers* welcome.

Academic Environment. *Degrees:* AB, BS, BME. Each degree program is composed of 3 curriculum areas: Bible-theology core (30 hours), general education core (46 hours), and a departmental major. About 20% of students entering as freshmen graduate eventually. *Calendar:* semester, January Term.

Student Body. About 69% of students from in state; 85% South, 12% North Central. An estimated 99% of students reported as Protestant, 1% Catholic; 36% Black, 1% other minority, according to most recent data available.

Religious Orientation. Chrichton is a church-related institution; 30 hours in Bible-theology required of all students.

Undergraduate degrees conferred (28). 39% were in Education, 29% were in Theology, 21% were in Psychology, 11% were in Business and Management.

Campus Life. About 4% men, 4% women live in traditional dormitories; rest commute. About 7% of students leave campus on weekends.

Annual Costs. Tuition and fees, $4,750. About 85% of students receive financial aid. College reports some scholarships awarded on the basis of academic merit alone. *Meeting Costs:* college offers PLUS loans.

Crown College

St. Bonifacius, Minnesota 55375

A small Christian college, founded by the Christian and Missionary Alliance. Crown College offers associate and baccalaureate degree programs.

Founded: 1916
Affiliation: The Christian Missionary Alliance

Culver-Stockton College

Canton, Missouri 63435 (314) 288-5221

A church-related, liberal arts college, affiliated with the Christian Church (Disciples of Christ), located in a town of 2,500, 20 miles north of Quincy, Illinois. Most convenient major airport: Quincy, Illinois.

Founded: 1853
Affiliation: Disciples of Christ
Total Enrollment: 360 M, 632 W (full-time)
Cost: < $10K
% Receiving Financial Aid: 94%
Admission: Non-selective
Application Deadline: May 1

Admission. Graduates of accredited high schools with C average or rank in top half of class accepted; those with less than C average may be admitted conditionally; 70% of applicants accepted, 25% of these actually enroll. About 46% of freshmen graduate in top fifth of high school class, 78% in top two-fifths. *Required:* SAT or ACT, rank in top half of HS class, minimum HS GPA of 2.0; for nursing GPA of 3.0, ACT of 20. Criteria considered in admissions, in order of importance: high school academic record, standardized test scores, recommendations, extracurricular activities, writing sample; other factors considered: religious affiliation and/or commitment. *Entrance programs:* deferred admission, advanced placement. *Apply* by May 1; rolling admissions. *Transfers* welcome; 68 enrolled 1993–94.

Academic Environment. Degrees offered: bachelors. Distribution requirements include courses in humanities, fine arts, natural sciences, social sciences, mathematics and language; specific core requirements include English composition, speech, personal computer, Christian Heritage. About 38% of students entering as freshmen graduate within four years, 46% eventually; 66% of freshman return for sophomore year. Average undergraduate class size: 63% of classes under 20, 29% between 20–40, 8% over 40. *Special programs:* CLEP, independent study, honors, study abroad, undergraduate research, 3–2 programs in pre-engineering, occupational therapy, MBA, internships available in most fields. Adult programs: evening and weekend programs offered. *Calendar:* semester, 3-week May interim, summer school.

Undergraduate degrees conferred (168). 30% were in Business and Management, 26% were in Education, 11% were in Health Sciences, 7% were in Psychology, 4% were in Visual and Performing Arts, 4% were in Social Sciences, 4% were in Protective Services, 4% were in Parks and Recreation, 4% were in Communications, 3% were in Letters, remainder in 4 other fields.

Graduates Career Data. Advanced studies pursued by 9% of students; 2% enter law school. Graduate and professional schools typically enrolling largest numbers of graduates include U. of Missouri, Western Illinois U., Sangamon State U. About 94% of 1992–93 graduates employed. Fields typically hiring the largest number of graduates include small entrepreneur businesses, education, nursing. Career Development Services include individual and group counseling, on-campus recruitment, credential files, job placement.

Faculty. About 62% of faculty hold PhD or equivalent. About 38% of undergraduate classes taught by tenured faculty. About 17% of teaching faculty are female; 7% Black, 2% Hispanic, 2% other minorities.

Student Body. College seeks a national student body; about 53% of students from in state; 94% Midwest, 1% foreign. An estimated 49% of students reported as Protestant, 23% Catholic, 30% unaffiliated; 4% as Black, 1% other minority.

Religious Orientation. Culver-Stockton is a church-related institution; 3 hours in religion required of all students.

Varsity Sports. Men (NAIA): Baseball, Basketball, Football, Golf, Soccer, Tennis. Women (NAIA): Basketball, Softball, Tennis, Volleyball.

Campus Life. About 41% men, 40% women live in traditional dormitories; no coed dormitories. There are 5 fraternities, 3 sororities on campus which about 48% of men, 27% of women join; 8% of men live in fraternities and 8% of women live in sororities.

Annual Costs. Tuition and fees, $7,650; room and board, $3,500; estimated $800 other, exclusive of travel. About 94% of students receive financial aid; average amount of assistance, $7,250. Assistance is typically divided 50% scholarship, 20% grant, 25% loan, 5% work. College reports 665 scholarships awarded on the basis of academic merit alone, 422 for special talents. *Meeting Costs:* college offers Academic Management Service.

Cumberland College

Williamsburg, Kentucky 40769 **(606) 549-2200 or (800) 343-1609**

A church-related college, located in a community of 3,700, 101 miles south of Lexington. Most convenient major airport: Knoxville, TN; Lexington, KY.

Founded: 1889
Affiliation: Southern Baptist
UG Enrollment: 601 M, 705 W (full-time); 33 M, 89 W (part-time)
Total Enrollment: 1,518
Cost: < $10K
% Receiving Financial Aid: 90%
Admission: Non-selective
Application Deadline: Rolling

Admission. Graduates of accredited high schools eligible; others admitted by examination. About 79% of applicants accepted, 40% of these actually enrolled; 33% of freshmen graduated in top fifth of high school class, 89% in top two fifths. Average freshman scores: SAT, 420 verbal, 470 mathematical; ACT, 21 composite. *Required:* SAT or ACT, essay. Criteria considered in admissions, in order of importance: high school academic record, standardized test scores, writing samples, recommendations, extracurricular activities; other factors considered: special talents. *Apply:* rolling admissions. *Transfers* welcome; 79 students enrolled 1993–94.

Academic Environment. Graduation requirements includc 7 courses in personal development, 4 in symbolics/communications, 6 in natural and social sciences. Degrees offered: bachelors, masters. Average undergraduate class size: 48% under 20, 50% 20–40, 2% over 40. *Special programs:* study abroad. About 60% of students entering as freshmen graduate eventually; 65% of freshmen return for sophomore year. *Calendar:* semester, summer school.

Undergraduate degrees conferred (230). 25% were in Education, 20% were in Business and Management, 11% were in Computer and Engineering Related Technology, 10% were in Social Sciences, 6% were in Mathematics, 5% were in Letters, 5% were in Psychology, 5% were in Life Sciences, 4% were in Allied Health, remainder in 6 other fields.

Graduate Career Data. Advanced studies pursued by 55% of graduates. About 90% of 1992–93 graduates employed. Fields typically hiring largest numbers of graduates include education, business, computer information systems. Career Development Services include on-campus recruitment with over 125 companies in 1992–93.

Faculty. About 42% of faculty hold PhD or equivalent. About 39% of undergraduate classes taught by tenured faculty. About 36% of teaching faculty are female; 4% minority.

Student Body. About 52% of students from in state; 80% South, 20% Midwest. An estimated 90% of students reported Protestant, 5% Catholic; 6% as Black, 1% Hispanic, 2% other minority.

Religious Orientation. Cumberland is a church-related institution; 6 hours of religion, attendance at weekly chapel/convocation required of all students.

Varsity Sports. Men (Div.I): Baseball, Basketball, Cross Country, Football (Div.II), Golf, Soccer, Swimming, Tennis, Track. Women (Div.I): Basketball, Cross Country, Golf, Soccer, Softball, Swimming, Tennis, Track, Volleyball.

Campus Life. Students agree that the small town and rural campus atmosphere enhance their study habits. Popular extracurricular activities include intramurals, campus clubs, and community service.

About 55% of men, 63% of women live in traditional dormitories; rest live in off-campus housing or commute. About 40% of resident students leave campus on weekends.

Annual Costs. Tuition and fees, $6,230; room and board, $3,526, estimated $1,000 other, exclusive of travel. About 90% of students receive financial aid; average amount of assistance, $6,000. Assistance is typically divided 36% grant, 39% loan, 25% work. College reports 633 scholarships awarded on the basis of academic merit alone, 135 for special talents alone, 43 for need alone. *Meeting Costs:* college offers monthly payment plan.

Curry College

Milton, Massachusetts 02186 **(617) 333-0500 or (800) 669-0686**

A small, independent, liberal arts college, located in a Boston suburb of 24,000. Most convenient major airport: Logan (Boston).

Founded: 1879
Affiliation: Independent
Total Enrollment: 424 M, 456 W (full-time)
Cost: $10K–$20K
% Receiving Financial Aid: 50%
Admission: Non-selective
Application Deadline: April 1

Admission. Graduates of approved high schools with 16 units eligible; 76% of applicants accepted, 30% of these actually enroll. Average freshman scores: SAT, 380 verbal, 420 mathematical. *Required:* SAT or ACT, essay, recommendation. Criteria considered in admissions, in order of importance: high school academic record, recommendations, writing sample, extracurricular activities, standardized test scores; other factors considered: special talents, alumni children, diverse student body. About 30% of entering students from private schools. *Entrance programs:* early decision, early admission, midyear admission, deferred admission, advanced placement. *Apply* by April 1; rolling admission. *Transfers* welcome; 102 enrolled 1993–94.
Academic Environment. Degrees offered: bachelors, masters. Graduation requirements include courses in writing, literature, fine arts, psychology, sociology, politics and history, philosophy, science, and communication. Unusual majors offered include: justice studies. Average undergraduate class size: 21. About 70% of freshmen return for sophomore year. *Special programs:* CLEP, independent study, study abroad, individually initiated major, cross registration with Stonehill. Adult Programs: continuing education department. *Calendar:* semester, summer school.
Undergraduate degrees conferred (210). 27% were in Communications, 26% were in Business and Management, 10% were in Health Sciences, 10% were in Education, 10% were in Social Sciences, 9% were in Psychology, 3% were in Letters, remainder in 4 other fields.
Graduate Career Data. Career Development Services offer assistance with resume writing, job listings, job options, and an annual career fair.
Student Body. About 59% of students from in state; 74% New England, 4% foreign. An estimated 3% of students reported as Black, 2% Hispanic, 1% Asian, 19% other minority.
Faculty. About 67% of faculty hold PhD or equivalent. About 56% of teaching faculty are female.
Varsity Sports. Men (Div.III): Baseball, Basketball, Football, Ice Hockey, Lacrosse, Soccer, Tennis. Women (Div.III): Basketball, Soccer, Softball, Tennis.
Campus Life. About 65% of students live in coed dormitories; rest commute. Intervisitation in men's and women's dormitory rooms unlimited. Sexes segregated in coed dormitories by floor. There are no fraternities or sororities on campus. About 30% of resident students leave campus on weekends.
Annual Costs. Tuition and fees, $13,100; room and board, $5,000; estimated $1,200 other, exclusive of travel. About 50% of students receive financial aid; average amount of assistance, $8,000.

C. W. Post Center

(See Long Island University)

Daemen College

Amherst, New York 14226 **(800) 462-7652 (in-state)**
(716) 839-8225 (out-of-state)

Daemen is a private, coeducational, career-oriented liberal arts college. The 37-acre campus is located in a suburban area of Buffalo (pop. 462,800). Most convenient major airport: Buffalo International.

Founded: 1947
Affiliation: Independent
UG Enrollment: 433 M, 824 W (full-time); 116 M, 417 W (part-time)
Total Enrollment: 1,802
Cost: < $10K
% Receiving Financial Aid: 92%
Admission: Non-selective
Application Deadline: Rolling

Admission. High school graduates eligible. *Required:* SAT or ACT; on-campus interview recommended. Criteria considered in admissions, in order of importance: high school academic record, standardized test scores, recommendations, extracurricular activities. *Entrance programs:* early decision, early admission, deferred admission. *Apply:* rolling admission. *Transfers* welcome; 258 enrolled 1993–94.
Academic Environment. Graduation requirements: all students complete a core requirement of 45 hours, with courses in arts, composition, economics/sociology, government/history, literature, math, philosophy/religious studies, psychology. Degrees offered: bachelors, masters. Average undergraduate class size: 18 24 students. *Special programs:* CLEP, independent study, study abroad, co-op education. *Calendar:* semester.
Undergraduate degrees conferred (215). 52% were in Allied Health, 10% were in Health Sciences, 8% were in Education, 7% were in Business and Management, 6% were in Marketing and Distribution, 3% were in Multi/Interdisciplinary Studies, 3% were in Social Sciences, 3% were in Public Affairs, 3% were in Letters, remainder in 4 other fields.
Graduates Career Data. Advanced studies pursued by 10% of graduates. About 80% of 1992–93 graduates employed. Fields typically hiring largest numbers of graduates include physical therapy, business, education, nursing. Career Development Services provides assistance through workshops, career counseling and assessment, field experiences, job listings, and extensive career library.
Faculty. About 78% of faculty hold PhD or equivalent. About 27% of undergraduate classes taught by tenured faculty. About 46% of teaching faculty are female.
Student Body. About 88% of students from in state, 3% foreign.
Varsity Sports. Men (NAIA): Basketball. Women (NAIA): Basketball.
Campus Life. Student life influenced by large percentage of commuters on campus. Provision for limited visitation hours. Alcohol permitted in accordance with state law (must be 21). About 28% of students live in traditional dormitories; 12% of men, 14% of women live in fraternities or sororities; rest commute. There are 2 fraternities, 4 sororities on campus.
Annual Costs. Tuition and fees, $8,650; room and board, $4,350; estimated $600 other, exclusive of travel. About 92% of students receive financial aid; average amount of assistance, $6,000. *Meeting Costs:* college offers Daemen Parent Loan Program.

Dakota State College

Madison, South Dakota 57042 **(605) 256-5139**

A state-supported college, located in a community of 6,300, affiliated administratively with the University of South Dakota. Most convenient major airport: Joe Foss Field (Sioux Falls).

Founded: 1881
Affiliation: State
Total Enrollment: 959 M, W (full-time); 124 M, 379 W (part-time)
Cost: < $10K
% Receiving Financial Aid: 58%
Admission: Non-selective
Application Deadline: Rolling

Admission. South Dakota graduates of accredited high schools who rank in top two-thirds of class eligible; others admitted by examination; 93% of applicants accepted, 67% of these actually enroll; 15% of freshmen graduate in top fifth of high school class, 32% in top two-fifths. Average freshman ACT scores, according to most recent data available: 19 M, 19 W composite, 19 M, 18 W mathematical. *Required:* ACT. *Out-of-state* freshman applicants: college does not seek students from out of state. State does not limit out-of-state enrollment. About 59% of applicants accepted, 75% of these enroll. Requirement for out-of-state applicants: rank in top half of class or score in top half on ACT composite. *Apply:* rolling admissions. *Transfers* welcome.
Academic Environment. *Degrees:* BS, BSEd. About 43% of general education requirements for graduation are elective; distribution requirements fairly numerous. *Majors offered* in addition to usual studies include fine arts management, physical health management, technology management. *Special programs:* CLEP, study abroad, independent study, credit by examination. *Calendar:* semester, summer school.
Undergraduate degrees conferred (127). 45% were in Business and Management, 27% were in Education, 20% were in Computer and Engineering Related Technology, 6% were in Health Sciences, remainder in 3 other fields.
Graduates Career Data. According to most recent data available, full-time graduate or professional study pursued by 3% of students immediately after graduation. *Careers in business and industry* pursued by 84% of graduates.

Faculty. About 21% of faculty hold PhD or equivalent.
Varsity Sports. Men (Div.III): Basketball, Cross Country, Football, Track. Women (Div.III): Basketball, Cross Country, Track, Volleyball.
Student Body. College does not seek a national student body; 93% of students from South Dakota. Less than 3% of students reported as minorities according to most recent data available.
Campus Life. About 11% of men, 9% of women live in traditional dormitories; 4% of men, 8% of women in coed dormitories; rest live in off-campus housing or commute. Intervisitation in men's and women's dormitory rooms limited. Sexes segregated in coed dormitories by floor. There are no fraternities or sororities. About 30% of students leave campus on weekends.
Annual Costs. Tuition and fees, $2,139 (out-of-state, $2,863); room and board, $2,480. About 58% of students receive financial aid; assistance is typically divided 50% scholarship/grant, 38% loan, 12% work. College reports some scholarships awarded on the basis of academic merit alone.

Dakota Wesleyan University

Mitchell, South Dakota 57301-4398 **(605) 995-2650**

A small, church-related, liberal arts institution, located in a town of 15,000, 70 miles west of Sioux Falls. Most convenient major airport: Sioux Falls, SD.

Founded: 1885
Affiliation: United Methodist
Total Enrollment: 618 M, W (full-time); 27 M, 119 W (part-time)
Cost: < $10K
% Receiving Financial Aid: 87%
Admission: Non-selective
Application Deadline: Rolling

Admission. Graduates of accredited high schools with rank in top half of class "who give evidence of good moral character and future promise are immediately eligible"; others given individual consideration; 84% of applicants accepted, 64% of these actually enroll. About 17% of freshmen graduate in top fifth of their high school class, 36% in top two-fifths. Average freshman ACT scores, according to most recent data available: 19.0 M, 19.5 W composite, 17.7 M, 17.0 W mathematical. *Required:* SAT or ACT. *Apply* by first day of classes; rolling admissions. *Transfers* welcome.
Academic Environment. *Degrees:* AB, BMEd. About 65% of students entering as freshmen graduate within four years; 30% of freshmen do not return for sophomore year. *Special programs:* 3–2 in engineering with South Dakota State. *Calendar:* 4–1–4, summer school.
Undergraduate degrees conferred (95). 25% were in Business and Management, 20% were in Education, 12% were in Social Sciences, 12% were in Psychology, 11% were in Public Affairs, 9% were in Life Sciences, 5% were in Mathematics, 4% were in Letters, remainder in Communications.
Graduates Career Data. According to most recent data available, full-time graduate or professional study pursued by 17% of students immediately after graduation. *Careers in business and industry* pursued by 25% of graduates.
Faculty. About 41% of faculty hold PhD or equivalent.
Varsity Sports. Men (NAIA Div.II): Baseball, Basketball, Cross Country, Football, Golf, Tennis, Track. Women (NAIA Div.II): Basketball, Cross Country, Tennis, Track, Volleyball.
Student Body. College seeks a national student body; 85% of students from South Dakota; 97% North Central. An estimated 50% of students reported as Protestant, 46% Catholic, 10% other; 1% Black, 1% Asian, 10% Native American, according to most recent data available.
Religious Orientation. Dakota Wesleyan is a church-related institution, makes no religious demands on students.
Campus Life. About 47% of men live in traditional dormitories; 10% of men, 27% of women live in coed dormitories; rest commute. Freshmen given preference in college housing if all students cannot be accommodated. Intervisitation in men's and women's dormitory rooms limited. There are no fraternities or sororities. About 75% of resident students leave campus on weekends.
Annual Costs. Tuition and fees, $7,110; room and board, $2,600. About 87% of students receive financial aid; assistance is typically divided 46% scholarship/grant, 46% loan, 8% work. University reports some scholarships awarded on the basis of academic merit alone. *Meeting Costs:* university offers various payment plans, loan programs, and scholarships.

Dallas Baptist University

Dallas, Texas 75211-9800 **(214) 333-5360**

A church-related, liberal arts college, located on a 200-acre campus in southwest Dallas. Formerly known as Dallas Baptist College. Most convenient major airport: Dallas-Fort Worth.

Founded: 1898
Affiliation: Southern Baptist
UG Enrollment: 393 M, 363 W (full-time)
Total Enrollment: 1,626
Cost: < $10K
% Receiving Financial Aid: 83%
Admission: Non-selective
Application Deadline: Rolling

Admission. Acceptance based on combination of test scores, class rank and high school grades; 98% of applicants accepted, 36% of these actually enroll; 46% graduate in top quarter of high school class, 72% in top half. *Required:* SAT or ACT. *Apply:* rolling admissions. *Transfers* welcome.
Academic Environment. *Degrees:* BA, BS, BBA, BCA, BM. About 40% of general education requirements for graduation are elective; distribution requirements fairly numerous. *Special programs:* Bachelor of Career Arts based on life and work experience, study abroad. *Calendar:* 4–1–4, plus long and short winter terms, summer school.
Undergraduate degrees conferred (388). 45% were in Business and Management, 10% were in Education, 8% were in Protective Services, 7% were in Liberal/General Studies, 6% were in Philosophy and Religion, 5% were in Computer and Engineering Related Technology, 5% were in Health Sciences, 3% were in Transportation and Material Moving, remainder in 9 other fields.
Varsity Sports. Men (NAIA): Baseball, Basketball. Women (NAIA): Volleyball.
Student Body. University seeks a national student body; about 85% of students from in Texas. An estimated 60% of students reported as Protestant, 8% Catholic, 33% other; 22% Black, 4% Hispanic, 3% Asian, 1% Native American, according to most recent data available.
Religious Orientation. Dallas Baptist is a church-related institution; 33 hours of religion over 4 years, certain semesters of attendance at weekly chapel services required of all students.
Campus Life. About 9% of men, 8% of women live in traditional dormitories; no coed dormitories; 3% live in off-campus university related housing; rest commute. No intervisitation in men's or women's dormitory rooms. About 60% of resident students leave campus on weekends.
Annual Costs. Tuition and fees, $6,000; room and board, $3,130. About 83% of students receive financial aid; assistance is typically divided 49% scholarship, 34% loan, 17% work. College reports some scholarships awarded on the basis of academic merit alone. *Meeting Costs:* college offers Parent PLUS Loans.

University of Dallas

Irving, Texas 75062 **(214) 721-5000**

A small, church-related institution, the University of Dallas is located on a 750-acre campus in a city of 150,000, on the northwest boundary of Dallas. Most convenient major airport: Dallas-Fort Worth.

Founded: 1955
Affiliation: Roman Catholic
UG Enrollment: 494 M, 564 W (full-time); 28 M, 45 W (part-time)
Total Enrollment: 2,901
Cost: $10K–$20K
% Receiving Financial Aid: 86%
Admission: Very (+) Selective
Application Deadline: Feb. 1

Admission is very (+) selective. About 86% of freshmen applicants accepted, 42% of these actually enroll; 65% of freshmen graduate in top fifth of high school class, 88% in top two-fifths. Average freshman scores: SAT, 544 M, 542 W verbal, 603 M, 572 W mathematical; 74% of freshman score above 500 on verbal, 25% above 600, 3% above 700; 84% score above 500 on mathematical, 43% above 600, 7% above 700; ACT, 27 M, 26 W composite. *Required:* SAT or ACT, essay, recommendation; interview recommended. Criteria considered in admissions, in order of importance: high school academic record, standardized test scores, writing sample, extracurricular activities, recommendations, personality and "intangible qualities"; other factors considered: special talents, alumni children, diverse student body. *Entrance programs:* early action, early admission, midyear admission, deferred admission, advanced placement. *Apply* by February 1. *Transfers* welcome; 85 enrolled 1993–94.

Academic Environment. Administration source characterizes student body as overwhelmingly scholarly/intellectual in their interests. Graduation requirements include 12 credits each in philosophy, English, 9 credits in math or fine arts, 6–8 credits in science, 3–14 credits in foreign language, 6 credits each in Western civilization, American civilization, and theology, 3 credits each in politics, and economics. Degrees offered: bachelors, masters, doctoral. *Majors offered* include: English, chemistry, physics, politics, business leaders of tomorrow, pre-med. Average undergraduate class size: 65% under 20, 31% 20–40, 4% over 40.

About 53% of entering freshmen graduate within four years, 62% eventually; 84% of freshmen return for sophomore year. *Special programs:* study abroad (all sophomores may spend semester at U. of Dallas Rome campus, 85% of students participate), undergraduate research, optional interterm, cross registration with U. of Texas-Arlington, -Dallas, Washington U., 5-year MBA program. *Calendar:* semester, summer school.

Undergraduate degrees conferred (197). 28% were in Social Sciences, 18% were in Life Sciences, 18% were in Letters, 10% were in Philosophy and Religion, 8% were in Visual and Performing Arts, 7% were in Psychology, 4% were in Education, 3% were in Physical Sciences, 3% were in Foreign Languages, remainder in 2 other fields.

Graduates Career Data. Advanced studies pursued by 49% of graduates; 2% enter medical school; 3% enter law school; 2% enter business school. Career Development Services offers career library, job listings and internship opportunities, career counseling, resume/cover letter preparation, development of interviewing skills and job search techniques, and a career development course.

Faculty. About 95% of faculty hold PhD or equivalent. About 17% of teaching faculty are female; 2% Black, 3% other minority.

Student Body. About 64% of students from in state; 16% Midwest, 9% West, 8% South; 5% New England, 4% foreign. An estimated 68% of students reported as Catholic, 13% Protestant, 1% Jewish, 1% Muslim, 15% unaffiliated, 1% other; 1% Black, 13% Hispanic, 10% Asian, 5% other minority.

Religious Orientation. Dallas is a church-related institution; 68% of students affiliated with this church; 2 courses in theology required.

Varsity Sports. Men: Basketball, Golf, Tennis. Women: Basketball, Tennis, Volleyball.

Campus Life. Students disagree about most popular on-campus activities: the freshman with an "un-declared" major says students "sit and talk, watch movies, go to parties, campus dances, dinners with religious groups, etc." The sophomore pre-med student says students spend their leisure time "studying", although she does concede that off-campus "movies, concerts, and dances" are available. Downtown Dallas, 12 miles from campus, offers numerous social and cultural opportunities to supplement campus activities. All freshmen expected to live in residence halls. Intervisitation "rigidly restricted (weekends 6 PM-1 am)." Cars permitted.

About 29% of men, 37% of women live in traditional dormitories; 25% of men, 20% of women live in coed dormitories; 13% of men, 8% of women in college-related off-campus housing; rest commute. About 30% of resident students leave campus on weekends. There are no fraternities or sororities on campus.

Annual Costs. Tuition and fees, $10,200; room and board, $4,783; estimated $1,200 other, exclusive of travel. About 86% of students receive financial aid; average amount of assistance, $11,438. Assistance is typically divided 54% scholarship/grant, 30% loan, 16% work. College reports 356 scholarships awarded on the basis of academic merit alone, 271 for special talent alone. *Meeting Costs:* college offers payment plans.

Dana College

Blair, Nebraska 68008 **(402) 426-7222 or (800) 444-3262**

A church-related, liberal arts college, located in a town of 7,000, 18 miles north of Omaha. Dana is the only 4-year college in U.S. founded by Danish immigrants; "Dana" is the poetic word for Denmark.

Founded: 1884
Affiliation: Evangelical Lutheran Church
Total Enrollment: 252 M, 298 W (full-time)
Cost: < $10K
% Receiving Financial Aid: 97%
Admission: Non-selective
Application Deadline: Rolling

Admission. High school graduates with minimum 2.0 GPA and ACT of 19 or SAT of 790, who rank in top half of class accepted; others considered individually; 84% of applicants accepted, 39% of these actually enroll; 25% of freshmen graduate in top fifth of high school class, 55% in top two-fifths. Average freshman scores: ACT, 21.5 composite. *Required:* ACT or SAT. Criteria considered in admissions, in order of importance: high school academic record, standardized test scores, writing sample, recommendation, extracurricular activities. About 25% of freshman from parochial schools. *Entrance programs:* early admission. *Apply:* rolling admissions. *Transfers* welcome; 44 enrolled 1993–94.

Academic Environment. Degrees offered: bachelors. Graduation requirements include up to 17 hours of baseline competencies called "Skills for Living in a Global and Technological Community"; 15 liberal arts core hours called "The Shared Experience" which includes the start of each students' portfolio, which they will add to throughout their college experience; and 18 hours of distribution courses. *Majors offered* include: social work and teacher education, Danish language studies, biology, business communications, art. Average class size: 82% under 20, 17% 20–40, 1% over 40. About 32% of students entering as freshmen graduate within four years, 45% eventually; 64% of freshmen return for sophomore year. *Special programs:* CLEP, independent study, study abroad, honors, undergraduate research, 3-year degree, individualized majors. Adult program: Weekend College. *Calendar:* semester, January interim, summer school.

Undergraduate degrees conferred (92). 27% were in Business and Management, 24% were in Education, 10% were in Social Sciences, 10% were in Communications Technologies, 7% were in Public Affairs, 5% were in Life Sciences, 3% were in Visual and Performing Arts, 3% were in Physical Sciences, 3% were in Foreign Languages, remainder in 4 other fields.

Graduate Career Data. Advanced studies pursued by 21% of graduates; 8% enter graduate school; 4% enter medical school; 1% enter dental school; 1% enter law school; 4% enter business school. Medical schools typically enrolling largest numbers of graduates include: U. of Nebraska; dental schools include Creighton; law schools include U. of Nebraska, Lincoln; business schools include U. of Nebraska, U. of Iowa. About 98% of 1992–93 graduates employed. Fields typically hiring largest numbers of graduates include education, social work, business, communications. Career Development Services offer alumni career panels, mock interviews, career fairs, on campus interviews, resume writing assistance, internship assistance, graduate career tracking.

Faculty. About 45% of faculty hold PhD or equivalent. About 78% of undergraduate classes taught by tenured faculty. About 27% of teaching faculty are female; 1% Black, 1% other minority.

Student Body. About 52% of students from in state; 83% Midwest, 6% West, 4% South, 2% Middle Atlantic, 5% foreign. An estimated 68% are reported as Protestant, 24% Catholic, 3% unaffiliated, 4% other; 8% Black, 1% Hispanic, 2% Asian, 4% other minority.

Religious Orientation. Dana is a church-related institution; 40% of students affiliated with this church; 1 course in religious studies required of students.

Varsity Sports. Men (NAIA Div.II): Baseball, Basketball, Cross country, Football, Golf, Soccer, Tennis, Track, Wrestling. Women (NAIA Div.II): Basketball, Cross country, Golf, Soccer, Softball, Tennis, Track, Volleyball.

Campus Life. Intramurals, campus activates, and organizations occupy students outside of classes, however, students agree that on weekends "everyone goes home." About 14% of women live in traditional dormitories; 85% of men, 76% of women live in coed dormitories; rest commute. There are no fraternities or sororities on campus.

Annual Costs. Tuition and fees, $8,780; room and board, $3,130; estimated $1,600 other, exclusive of travel. About 97% of students receive financial aid; average amount of assistance, $8,500. College reports over 300 scholarships awarded on the basis of academic merit alone, over 150 for special talents alone, 78% for need alone.

Daniel Webster College

Nashua, New Hampshire 03063 **(603) 883-3556**

Founded as the New England Aeronautical Institute, offering 2-year programs in aeronautics and aerospace, the college has now been accredited as a 4-year institution and has adopted the name of its former liberal arts division. Most convenient major airport: Manchester, NH.

Founded: 1965	**Cost:** $10K–$20K
Affiliation: Independent	**% Receiving Financial Aid:** 62%
Total Enrollment: 742 M, W (full-time)	**Admission:** Non-selective
	Application Deadline: April 1

Admission. Graduates of accredited high school with 16 credits eligible; 81% of applicants accepted, 35% of these actually enroll; 16% of freshmen graduate in top fifth of high school class, 47% in top two-fifths. *Required:* SAT, school recommendations; interview strongly recommended. *Non-academic factors* considered in admissions: diverse student body, alumni children. *Apply* by April 1. *Transfers* welcome.

Academic Environment. College primarily oriented toward programs in aviation (including air traffic control, flight training), business and management and computer science. About 65% of entering freshmen graduate eventually; 10% of freshmen do not return for sophomore year.

Undergraduate degrees conferred (106). 60% were in Transportation and Material Moving, 28% were in Business and Management, 11% were in Computer and Engineering Related Technology.

Graduates Career Data. *Careers in business and industry* pursued by 100% of graduates. Corporations typically hiring largest numbers of graduates include Digital, Sanders Associates, many airlines.

Varsity Sports. Men (college has applied for NCAA Div.III): Baseball, Basketball, Cross Country, Soccer. Women (college has applied for NCAA Div.III): Basketball, Softball, Volleyball.

Student Body. About 20% of students from in state; 80% New England, 15% Middle Atlantic. An estimated 5% of students reported as Black, 3% Hispanic, 1% Asian, according to most recent data available.

Campus Life. College is located in a city of 60,000, 35 miles northwest of Boston. About 70% of men, 75% of women live in traditional dormitories; rest commute. Freshmen given preference in college housing if all students cannot be accommodated. Percent of students leaving campus on weekends "varies by season of year."

Annual Costs. Tuition and fees, $11,852 (flight training fees are extra); room and board, $4,656. About 62% of students receive financial aid, assistance is typically divided 25–50% scholarship, 33% loan, 25% work. College reports all scholarships awarded on the basis of need. *Meeting Costs:* college offers Academic Management Service.

Dartmouth College

Hanover, New Hampshire 03755 **(603) 646-2875**

Dartmouth is primarily an undergraduate college, but also encompasses a number of graduate programs and several professional schools, including a 3-year medical program. Like its fellow all-male Ivy League schools, Dartmouth is now solidly coeducational. The college maintains a year-round program which enables it to accommodate a larger number of students. The campus is located in a small rural New England town, 135 miles northwest of Boston. Most convenient major airport: Logan (Boston, 2 hours away).

Founded: 1769	**Cost:** $10K–$20K
Affiliation: Independent	**% Receiving Financial Aid:** 44%
UG Enrollment: 2,162 M, 1,626 W (full-time)	**Admission:** Most Selective
Total Enrollment: 4,939	**Application Deadline:** January 1

Admission is among the most selective in the country. About 26% of applicants accepted, 52% of these actually enroll; 90% of freshmen graduate in top fifth of high school class. Average freshman SAT scores: 640 verbal, 710 mathematical; all freshman score above 500 on verbal, 54% above 600, 16% above 700; 98% above 500 on mathematical, 89% above 600, 56% above 700. *Required:* SAT or ACT, any 3 ACH, essay, counselor recommendation. Criteria considered in admissions, in order of importance: high school academic record, recommendation, standardized test scores, extracurricular activities, writing sample; other factors considered: special talents, alumni children. About 32% of entering students from private schools, 5% parochial. *Entrance programs:* early decision. *Apply* by January 1; November 10 early decision. *Transfers* not accepted.

Academic Environment. Students have a multiplicity of interests, but are reported to be primarily concerned with academic achievement and career goals—an orientation that is supplemented by substantial interest in sports, social activities and the arts. College prides itself on the fact that all senior faculty members teach introductory courses as well as more specialized offerings. Student leader reports that "professors, for the most part, are firmly committed to teaching, not research," but also complains that they are "too isolated-not accessible on an informal basis." With year-round calendar consisting of 4 co-equal terms, bachelor's degree requires completion of 11 terms (3 courses each term), including participation in at least 1 summer term. Students may combine on-campus terms and vacation periods for wide variety of attendance options. Some difficulty has been encountered, however, in reconciling needs of students during a full-year calendar and summer vacation plans of faculty. Graduation requirements include 12 distributives across 10 academic fields. Degrees offered: bachelors, masters, doctoral.

About 96% of students entering as freshmen graduate within four years; 97% of freshmen return for sophomore year. *Special programs:* CLEP, independent study, study abroad, honors, undergraduate research, 3-year degree, individualized majors, Twelve College Exchange, freshman seminars, inter-divisional college courses, cooperative program in urban studies with MIT, Native American studies, Senior fellows program, combined programs with Dartmouth professional schools, interdisciplinary programs. *Calendar:* 4 terms.

Undergraduate degrees conferred (1,019). 41% were in Social Sciences, 15% were in Letters, 8% were in Engineering, 7% were in Psychology, 5% were in Visual and Performing Arts, 5% were in Philosophy and Religion, 5% were in Life Sciences, 5% were in Foreign Languages, 4% were in Physical Sciences, remainder in 4 other fields.

Graduates Career Data. Advanced studies pursued by 21% of graduates; 6% enter medical school; 5% enter law school; less than 1% enter business school. Career Development Services include on-campus interviews, interview preparation.

Faculty. About 94% of faculty hold PhD or equivalent; all undergraduate classes taught by tenured faculty.

Student Body. About 4% of students from in state; 29% New England, 29% Middle Atlantic, 17% West, 10% Midwest, 10% South, 5% foreign. An estimated 7% of students reported as Black, 4% Hispanic, 9% Asian, 2% Native American. *Minority group students:* Black and Native American residential and social centers; "various scholarship opportunities. College makes a special effort to balance what would otherwise be injustices in admissions and financial aid policies."

Varsity Sports. Men (Div.I): Baseball, Basketball, Crew, Cross Country, Diving, Equestrian, Football(IAA), Golf, Ice Hockey, Lacrosse, Skiing, Soccer, Swimming, Tennis, Track, Volleyball. Women (Div.I): Basketball, Crew, Cross Country, Diving, Equestrian, Field Hockey, Golf, Ice Hockey, Lacrosse, Skiing, Soccer, Swimming, Tennis, Track, Volleyball.

Campus Life. Students have primary responsibility for governing campus social life. College is distant from the cultural and intellectual facilities of any major metropolitan center; largely dependent on campus activities such as athletics, Greek system, clubs and organizations. Student reports campus location promotes interest in swimming, biking, hiking, backpacking and skiing. The college's Hopkins Center adds to the scope and variety of performing arts available to the entire region. College also furnishes the local community with a daily newspaper and radio station. Dartmouth "requires students to observe the recognized standards of morality, good order, and gentlemanly behavior in their rooms and elsewhere." Dormitory life, in other respects, wholly self-governed. Most unmarried undergraduates live in residence; those living off campus must register with Student Housing Office. Cars permitted for all except freshmen. Public drinking not allowed.

About 76% of students live in coed dormitories; 2% in off-campus college-related housing; 8% in other off-campus housing. Freshmen

given preference in college housing if all students cannot be accommodated. Sexes segregated in coed dormitories either by floor or suite. There are 17 fraternities, 9 sororities, and 5 coed fraternities; 60% of students join fraternities and sororities; 14% of students live in fraternities and sororities.
Annual Costs. Tuition and fees, $18,375; room and board, $5,979; estimated $1,590 other, exclusive of travel. About 44% of students receive financial aid. College reports scholarships awarded only on the basis of need. *Meeting Costs:* college offers Dartmouth Education Loan Corporation loans, Dartmouth Education Association loans, need blind admissions.

David Lipscomb University

Nashville, Tennessee 37204-3951 (615) 269-1776

A church-related university, "dedicated to the building of Christian character," located on a 65-acre campus in a residential section of Nashville. Formerly known as David Lipscomb College. Most convenient major airport: Nashville International.

Founded: 1891
Affiliation: Church of Christ
Total Enrollment: 2,109 M, W (full-time); 168 M, 203 W (part-time)
Cost: < $10K
% Receiving Financial Aid: 71%
Admission: Non-selective
Application Deadline: May 15

Admission. Graduates of approved high schools with 15 units (9 in academic subjects) eligible; 89% of applicants accepted; 72% of these actually enroll. About 42% of freshmen graduate in top fifth of high school class, 92% in top two-fifths. *Required:* SAT or ACT. *Apply* by May 15 for priority; rolling admissions. *Transfers* welcome.
Academic Environment. *Degrees:* BA, BS. About 35% of general education requirements for graduation are elective; distribution requirements fairly numerous. About 50% of students entering as freshmen graduate within four years; 25% of freshmen do not return for sophomore year. *Special programs:* CLEP, independent study, study abroad, 3–2 programs in engineering, nursing, and medical technology. Adult programs: Courses leading to business/accounting degree offered at non-traditional times. *Calendar:* semester, summer school.
Undergraduate degrees conferred (431). 24% were in Business and Management, 16% were in Education, 9% were in Marketing and Distribution, 8% were in Letters, 8% were in Life Sciences, 6% were in Social Sciences, 5% were in Psychology, 3% were in Physical Sciences, 3% were in Home Economics, 3% were in Visual and Performing Arts, 3% were in Theology, remainder in 10 other fields.
Graduates Career Data. According to most recent data available, full-time graduate or professional study pursued immediately after graduation: 3% enter medical school; 3% enter law school; 3% enter business school. *Careers in business and industry* pursued by 75% of graduates.
Faculty. About 71% of faculty hold PhD or equivalent.
Varsity Sports. Men (NAIA): Baseball, Basketball, Cross Country, Golf, Tennis, Track. Women (NAIA): Basketball, Tennis.
Student Body. University seeks a national student body; 65% of students from Tennessee; 87% South, 10% North Central, 1% Middle Atlantic; 17 foreign students 1990–91. An estimated 99% of students reported as Protestant; 3% Black, less than 1% other minority, according to most recent data available.
Religious Orientation. David Lipscomb is a church-related institution; strong religious emphasis on campus. Each student has a class in the Bible every day; attendance at daily chapel services required of all students.
Campus Life. About 48% of men, 54% of women live in traditional dormitories; no coed dormitories; rest commute. Freshmen given preference in college housing if all students can not be accommodated. No intervisitation in men's or women's dormitory rooms. There are 7 fraternities, 8 sororities; which about 21% of men, 18% of women join. About 60% of students leave campus on weekends.
Annual Costs. Tuition and fees, $6,285; room and board, $3,190. About 71% of students receive financial aid; assistance is typically divided 37% grant/scholarship, 48% loan, 15% work. College reports some scholarships awarded on the basis of academic merit alone. *Meeting Costs:* university offers payment plan.

Davidson College

Davidson, North Carolina 28036 (704) 892-2000

Largely traditional in its approach to education, Davidson boasts that more of its students have achieved doctorates and gone on to become college teachers than any other institution in the region. The 450-acre campus is located in a village of 3,000, 20 miles north of Charlotte. An additional 106-acre lake campus is just 3 miles north of the main campus. Most convenient major airport: Charlotte, NC (24 miles).

Founded: 1837
Affiliation: Presbyterian
Total Enrollment: 865 M, 736 W (full-time)
Cost: $10K–$20K
% Receiving Financial Aid: 60%
Admission: Highly (+) Selective
Application Deadline: Jan. 15

Admission is highly (+) selective. About 40% of applicants accepted, 47% of these actually enroll; 91% of freshmen graduate in top fifth of high school class, all in top two-fifths. Average freshman scores: SAT, middle 50% range 530–630 verbal, 600–700 mathematical; 86% of freshmen score above 500 on verbal, 46% above 600, 6% above 700, 95% score above 500 on mathematical, 76% above 600, 25% above 700; ACT middle 50% range 27–31 composite. *Required:* SAT or ACT, essay; ACH and interview "strongly recommended." Criteria considered in admissions: high school academic record considered of most importance; other factors considered: standardized test scores, recommendations, writing sample, extracurricular activities, alumni children, diverse student body, special talents. *Entrance programs:* early decision, deferred admission. About 40% of entering students from private schools. *Apply* by January 15. *Transfers* welcome; 8 enrolled 1993–94.
Academic Environment. Davidson has the distinction of having produced the third largest number of Rhodes Scholars among liberal arts colleges, exceeded only by Swarthmore and Williams. As in many other top flight academic institutions currently, students have become more concerned with professional/occupational goals in addition to scholarly/intellectual interests. Most popular major: economics, followed by English and premed studies. Administration reports that students who feel most at home on campus are "goal oriented, highly ambitious, bright...with some social skills." Center for Special Studies, comprising 2% of student body, offers individualized academic planning and study, freeing participants from traditional requirements. Students have some influence on curriculum decision making, none on faculty hiring and promotion. Pressures for academic achievement appear intense. High percentage of graduates go on to medicine and law. Core requirements include courses in literature, fine arts, history, religion and philosophy, natural sciences and mathematics, social sciences, cultural diversity, and physical education. Students may participate in an "extended studies" program (individually designed courses). Degree offered: bachelors. *Majors offered* include usual arts and sciences. Average undergraduate class size: 20.

About 89% of students entering as freshmen graduate within four years, 91% eventually; 3–4% of freshmen do not return for sophomore year. *Special programs:* independent study, study abroad, honors, undergraduate research, individualized majors, Washington Semester, South Asia studies program, Career/Service Program of Non-academic off-campus experience for 1 or more terms, spring term in classics abroad, field work in psychology, 3–2 engineering. *Calendar:* semester.
Undergraduate degrees conferred (343). 39% were in Social Sciences, 14% were in Letters, 11% were in Life Sciences, 7% were in Psychology, 7% were in Foreign Languages, 6% were in Philosophy and Religion, 5% were in Visual and Performing Arts, 4% were in Physical Sciences, 4% were in Mathematics, remainder in 2 other fields.
Graduates Career Data. About 88% of 1993 graduates intend to pursue advanced studies; 14% entered medical school; 15% entered law school; 10% entered business school. Medical schools typically enrolling largest numbers of graduates include UNC-Chapel Hill, Bowman Gray, Duke; dental schools include U. of North Carolina; law schools include UNC-Chapel Hill, Duke, Wake Forest, U. of Virginia; business schools include UNC-Chapel Hill, U. of Virginia, Wharton, Harvard. About 40% of 1993 graduates are employed. Fields typically employing largest numbers of graduates include business, health, law, education. Career Development Services

include career counseling, resume/interview workshops, on-campus recruitment, information meetings, job fairs.

Faculty. About 97% of faculty hold PhD or equivalent. About 63% of undergraduate classes taught by tenured faculty. About 25% of teaching faculty are female; 3% Black, 4% Hispanic, 2% other ethnic minorities.

Student Body. College seeks a national student body; 25% of students from in state; 55% South, 12% Middle Atlantic, 5% New England. An estimated 70% of students reported as Protestant, 12% Catholic, 11% unaffiliated; 4% as Black, 2% Hispanic, 4% Asian.

Religious Orientation. Davidson is a church-related institution. College has "regarded the Christian faith as central to its life since it was established." One semester of religion required of all students. Religious clubs on campus include Y Service Corp., Davidson Christian Fellowship, Fellowship of Catholic Students. Places of worship available on campus and in immediate community for Protestants and Catholics, 20 miles away for Jews.

Varsity Sports. Men (Div.IAA): Baseball, Basketball, Cross Country, Football, Golf, Soccer, Swimming, Tennis, Track, Wrestling. Women (Div.IAA): Basketball, Cross Country, Field Hockey, Lacrosse, Soccer, Swimming, Tennis, Track, Volleyball.

Campus Life. Students are primarily responsible for decisions concerning social life. Strong interest in fraternities and eating clubs still reported. Students now select their eating club or fraternity rather than the reverse. Women have eating houses in lieu of sororities. Relations between Greeks and independents said to be good; most parties open to all students. Some administration concern reported with "the amount of social life." No student discontent reported with social facilities; some concern with residential facilities which are said to be "Spartan and old." Graduation requirements include "proficiency in one team, one water-related, and two lifetime sports." All students may use motor vehicles. Most popular intramural sports: flicker ball(a form of touch football) and basketball. Most popular varsity sports: basketball, soccer, tennis, volleyball. Alcoholic beverages allowed for those over 21; drug users face mandatory counseling; prosecution for dealers. Special permission needed to live off campus.

About 50% of men, 40% of women live in traditional dormitories; 35% of men, 52% of women in coed dormitories; 14% of men, 9% of women live in off-campus housing or commute. Freshmen given preference in college housing if all students cannot be accommodated. Sexes segregated in coed dormitories by floor. There are 6 (nonselective) fraternities, 2 women only eating clubs, 2 coed eating clubs on campus, about 65% of men join fraternities, 1% of men live in fraternities, 24% of women join eating clubs, 23% of students join coed eating clubs.

Annual Costs. Tuition and fees, $16,263; room and board, $4,774. About 60% of students receive financial aid; average amount of assistance, $12,400. Assistance is typically divided 15% scholarship, 57% grant, 18% loan, 10% work. College reports 210 scholarships awarded on the basis of academic merit alone, 50 for special talents, 425 for need. *Meeting Costs:* college offers referral to outside agencies for payment plans.

Davis and Elkins College

Elkins, West Virginia 26241 (304) 636-5850

A church-related, liberal arts college, located in a town of 10,000 in the foothills of the Allegheny Mountains, 135 miles south of Pittsburgh. Most convenient major airports: Dulles (Washington, DC), Pittsburgh.

Founded: 1904
Affiliation: Presbyterian
Total Enrollment: 311 M, 443 W (full-time)
Cost: < $10K
% Receiving Financial Aid: 65%
Admission: Non-selective
Application Deadline: Rolling

Admission. Graduates of recognized high schools, preferably with 12 academic units in college preparatory courses, eligible; 86% of applicants accepted, 37% of these actually enroll; 22% of freshmen graduate in top fifth of high school class, 48% in top two-fifths. Average freshman scores: SAT, 399 verbal; 437 mathematical; ACT 19 composite. *Required:* SAT or ACT. Criteria considered in admissions, in order of importance: high school academic record, standardized test scores, recommendation. *Entrance programs:* early admission, midyear admission, deferred admission, advanced placement, rolling admission. *Apply:* rolling admissions. *Transfers* welcome; 75 enrolled 1993–94.

Academic Environment. Degrees offered: associates, bachelors. Graduation requirements include 6 hours English composition, 2 hours physical education, 5 hours fine arts, 3 hours literature, 3 hours math, 12 hours historical studies, 7 hours natural sciences, 6 hours social sciences. *Majors offered* include: fashion merchandising, recreation management and tourism. Average undergraduate class size: 35% under 20, 60% 20–40, 5% over 40. About 65% of freshmen return for sophomore year. *Special programs:* CLEP, independent study, contract degree programs, study abroad, undergraduate research, 3-year degree, 3–2 in forestry, engineering, occupational therapy; "heavy stress on off-campus learning experiences." Adult program: Mentor Assisted Adult Program (MAP). *Calendar:* 4–1–4, summer school.

Undergraduate degrees conferred (112). 24% were in Business and Management, 18% were in Education, 9% were in Marketing and Distribution, 7% were in Health Sciences, 6% were in Life Sciences, 6% were in Communications, 4% were in Social Sciences, 4% were in Psychology, 4% were in Letters, 4% were in Visual and Performing Arts, 3% were in Physical Sciences, 3% were in Allied Health, remainder in 5 other fields.

Faculty. About 62% of faculty hold PhD or equivalent. About 45% of undergraduate classes taught by tenured faculty. About 43% of teaching faculty are female, 1% Black, 3% other minority.

Student Body. About 60% of students from in state; 93% from Middle Atlantic, 3% New England, 3% South, 1% Midwest, 2% foreign. An estimated 65% of students reported as Protestant, 20% Catholic, 1% Jewish, 5% unaffiliated, 9% other; 4% Black, 1% Hispanic, 2% Asian, 3% other minority. Average age of undergraduate student: 22.

Religious Orientation. Davis and Elkins is a church-related institution, jointly supported by the United Presbyterian Church and the Presbyterian Church in the U.S.; 1 course in religious studies required.

Varsity Sports. Men (Div.II): Baseball, Basketball, Cross Country, Golf, Soccer, Tennis. Women: (NCAA Div.I), Field Hockey, (Div.II), Basketball, Cross Country, Softball, Tennis.

Campus Life. Distance from major metropolitan areas focuses student social life on campus activities and clubs; students also spend time skiing, camping, hiking, fishing.

About 60% of students live in traditional dormitories; rest commute. Freshmen given preference in college housing if all students cannot be accommodated. Intervisitation in men's and women's dormitory rooms limited for new students. There are 3 fraternities, 2 sororities on campus which about 20% each of men, women join. About 25% of students leave campus on weekends.

Annual Costs. Tuition and fees, 8,980; room and board, $4,250; estimated $1,000 other, exclusive of travel. About 65% of students receive financial aid; average amount of assistance, $6,500. Assistance is typically divided 45% scholarship/grant, 40% loan, 15% work. *Meeting Costs:* college offers parent loans and AMS.

University of Dayton

Dayton, Ohio 45469 (800) 837-7433

A church-related university, founded by the Society of Mary, Dayton is now under the control of a predominantly lay board of trustees. The university is on a 110-acre main campus in a metropolitan area of 942,000. Most convenient major airport: Dayton International.

Founded: 1850
Affiliation: Independent (Roman Catholic)
UG Enrollment: 3,085 M, 2,804 W (full-time); 391 M, 282 W (part-time)
Total Enrollment: 10,660
Cost: $10K–$20K
% Receiving Financial Aid: 93%
Admission: Selective
Application Deadline: Rolling

Admission is selective. About 85% of applicants accepted, 30% actually enroll. About 43% of freshmen graduate in top fifth of high school class, 71% in top two-fifths. Average freshman scores: SAT, 504 verbal, 578 mathematical; ACT, 25 composite. *Required:* SAT or ACT; interview encouraged. Criteria considered in admissions, in order of importance: high school academic record (including courses taken, GPA, and class rank), standardized test scores, recommendation, extracurricular activities, writing sample. About 46% of entering students from private and parochial schools. *Entrance programs:* early decision, midyear admission, deferred admission, advanced placement, summer trial admission. *Apply:* rolling admissions. *Transfers* welcome.

Academic Environment. *Undergraduate studies* offered by College of Arts and Sciences, schools of Business Administration, Education, Engineering. Degrees offered: bachelors, masters, doctoral. *Majors offered* include: environmental geology, education, visual communication design, exercise science and fitness management, various engineering and technology fields, performing and visual arts. Graduation requirements include courses in history, philosophy, religious studies, English. Accessible faculty, challenging curriculum, and study abroad program reported as strengths. Average undergraduate class size: 27; 35% under 20, 31% 20–40, 6% over 40.

About 67% of students entering as freshmen graduate within five years; 85% of freshmen return for sophomore year. *Special programs:* CLEP, independent study, study abroad, honors and scholars programs, Third World Immersion, undergraduate research, 3-year degree, dual degree programs with Wilberforce U. and Thomas More College, cooperative education, individualized majors, cross registration through Dayton-Miami Valley Consortium. *Calendar:* early semester, split third term, (including spring–summer term of 2 6-week units).

Undergraduate degrees conferred (1,548). 23% were in Business and Management, 14% were in Engineering, 12% were in Communications, 10% were in Education, 8% were in Engineering and Engineering Related Technology, 6% were in Psychology, 6% were in Social Sciences, 3% were in Protective Services, 3% were in Visual and Performing Arts, 3% were in Computer and Engineering Related Technology, 3% were in Letters, remainder in 13 other fields.

Graduates Career Data. Career Placement Center offers interviewing techniques, resume writing, job search, internships, cooperative education, on-campus recruitment and career counseling to all students and alumni.

Faculty. About 85% of faculty hold PhD or equivalent. About 98% of undergraduate classes taught by tenured faculty. About 21% of teaching faculty are female.

Student Body. About 55% of students from in state; majority from Midwest, 1% foreign. An estimated 71% of students reported as Catholic, 14% Protestant, 7% unaffiliated, 9% other; 4% Black, 2% Hispanic, 1% Asian, 1% other minority.

Religious Orientation. University is an independent institution, with a strong Catholic heritage; 71% of students affiliated with the church; 4 courses in religion or philosophy required; attendance at religious services optional.

Varsity Sports. Men (Div.I): Baseball, Basketball, Crew, Cross Country, Football (Div.IAA), Golf, Soccer, Tennis, Wrestling. Women (Div.I): Golf, Soccer, Softball, Tennis, Volleyball.

Campus Life. Campus is "secluded enough and pretty", but also "centrally located, with easy access to downtown and various malls, restaurants, bars and movie theaters," as well as state parks and camp grounds. Varsity and intramural sports, concerts, dances and other campus activities reported popular. Residential students not permitted cars without special permission; others, including faculty and staff, must purchase permit; parking is "often a major problem," according to student report. Alcohol allowed for students over 21; use of drugs not allowed, disciplinary action will be taken. Each residence unit decides intervisitation policies within limits established by university guidelines.

Almost half of the student body lives in traditional dormitories or suite type residence halls; upper class students live in university-owned houses, suites, and apartments; rest commute. All students guaranteed housing all four years. There are 14 fraternities, 10 sororities on campus which about 17% of men, 20% of women join; 1% of students live in fraternities and sororities. About 10% of resident students leave campus on weekends.

Annual Costs. Tuition and fees, $11,090; room and board, $4,030; estimated $1,000 other, exclusive of travel. About 93% of students receive financial aid; average amount of assistance, $4,030. Assistance is typically divided 28% scholarship/grant, 22% loan, 14% work. University reports 1,800 scholarships awarded on the basis of academic merit alone. *Meeting Costs:* university offers low interest monthly payment plan.

Deaconess College of Nursing

St. Louis, Missouri 63139 (314) 768-3044

A small professional college of nursing, Deaconess is controlled by an independent board, although it is affiliated with the United Church of Christ. The campus is located in a metropolitan area of 2.5 million. Most convenient major airport: St. Louis.

Founded: 1889
Affiliation: Independent
UG Enrollment: 24 M, 255 W (full-time); 8 M, 104 W (part-time)
Total Enrollment: 391
Cost: < $10K
% Receiving Financial Aid: 90%
Admission: Non-selective
Application Deadline: Rolling

Admission. High school graduates who rank in top third of high school class eligible; 60% of applicants accepted, 50% of these actually enroll; 26% of freshmen graduate in top fifth of high school class, 58% in top two-fifths. Average freshman scores: ACT, 22.1 composite. *Required:* SAT or ACT, essay. Criteria considered in admissions, in order of importance: high school academic record, standardized test scores, recommendation, writing sample, extracurricular activities; other factors considered: special talents. About 22% of entering students from private schools. *Apply:* rolling admissions. *Transfers* welcome; 83 enrolled 1993–94.

Academic Environment. Degrees offered: associates, bachelors. College also offers an RN-BSN completion program. *Majors offered* include: LPN to RN Bridge Program. Average undergraduate class size: 8% under 20, 80% 20–40, 12% over 40. About 65% of students entering as freshmen graduate within four years, 70% eventually; 87% of freshmen return for sophomore year. *Special programs:* cross registration with Fontbonne.

Graduate Career Data. Advanced studies pursued by 9% of graduates; 6% enter graduate school; 3% enter business school. All 1992–93 graduates employed. Fields typically hiring largest numbers of graduates include hospitals, health care agencies. Career Development Services offer on-campus recruitment, counseling, internships, library resources, resume/interview workshops.

Faculty. About 11% of faculty hold PhD or equivalent. About 96% of teaching faculty are female; 4% Afro-American.

Student Body. About 72% of students from in state; 98% Midwest, less than 1% foreign. An estimated 38% of students reported as Protestant, 47% Catholic, 15% unaffiliated; 8% Black, 2% Asian. Average age of undergraduate student: 23.

Campus Life. About 25% of women live in traditional dormitories; 19% of men live in off-campus college-related housing; rest commute. There are no fraternities or sororities.

Annual Costs. Tuition and fees, $6,160; room and board, $3,200; estimated $1,000 other, exclusive of travel. About 90% of students receive financial aid; average amount of assistance, $4,500. Assistance is typically divided 40% scholarship, 35% grants, 80% loan, 5% work. College reports 100 scholarships awarded on the basis of academic merit alone, 48 for need alone. *Meeting Costs:* college offers institutional loans, working scholarships, tuition reimbursement.

Defiance College

Defiance, Ohio 43512 (419) 783-2330

A small, church-related, liberal arts college, located in a town of 17,000, 50 miles southwest of Toledo. Most convenient major airport: Toledo Express.

Founded: 1850
Affiliation: United Church of Christ
UG Enrollment: 339 M, 306 W (full-time); 110 M, 179 W (part-time)
Total Enrollment: 934
Cost: < $10K
% Receiving Financial Aid: 85%
Admission: Non-selective
Application Deadline: Rolling

Admission. High school graduates with minimum 2.0 GPA in 14 academic units eligible; others given individual consideration; 79% of applicants accepted, 43% of these actually enroll; 21% of freshmen graduate in top fifth of high school class, 44% in top two-fifths.

Average freshman scores: SAT, 381 verbal, 438 mathematical; ACT, 18.8 composite. *Required:* SAT or ACT; interview recommended. Criteria considered in admissions, in order of importance: high school academic record, standardized test scores, class rank, writing sample, recommendation, extracurricular activities; other factors considered: special talents, alumni children, diverse student body, religious affiliation and/or commitment. *Apply:* rolling admissions. *Transfers* welcome; 57 enrolled 1993–94.

Academic Environment. Degrees offered: associates, bachelors, masters. About 80% of general education requirements for graduation are elective; distribution requirements fairly numerous. *Majors offered* include: environmental science, restoration ecology. Average undergraduate class size: 20% under 20, 69% 20–40, 3% over 40. About 29% of students entering as freshmen graduate within four years, 50% eventually; 62% of freshmen return for sophomore year. *Special programs:* cooperative education, internships, independent study, self-designed majors, study abroad, field experiences, 3–2 engineering. Adult programs: weekend degree completion program. *Library:* Indian Wars Collection, President Eisenhower collection room. *Calendar:* 4–1–4, summer school.

Undergraduate degrees conferred (155). 33% were in Business and Management, 28% were in Education, 8% were in Public Affairs, 8% were in Health Sciences, 5% were in Psychology, 4% were in Protective Services, 4% were in Mathematics, 4% were in Communications, remainder in 6 other fields.

Graduates Career Data. Advanced studies pursued by 8% of graduates; 4% enter graduate schools; 4% enter business schools. Corporations typically hiring largest numbers of graduates include Ernst & Young, K-Mart, Cooper Tire. Career Development Services include programs on resume writing and interview skills, counseling, and career guidance computer system.

Faculty. About 56% of faculty hold PhD or equivalent. About 80% of undergraduate classes taught by tenured faculty. About 49% of teaching faculty are female.

Student Body. About 91% of students from in state, 96% Midwest, 2% South, 1% New England, 1% foreign. An estimated 29% of students reported as Protestant, 21% Catholic, 20% unaffiliated, 5% United Church of Christ; 10% Black, 2% Hispanic. Average age of undergraduate student: 22.

Religious Orientation. Defiance is a church-related institution; 5% of students affiliated with the church.

Varsity Sports. Men (NCAA): Baseball, Basketball, Cross Country, Football, Golf, Soccer, Tennis, Track. Women (NCAA): Basketball, Cross Country, Soccer, Tennis, Track, Volleyball.

Campus Life. About 42% of men, 23% of women students live in traditional dormitories; no coed dormitories; rest commute. Intervisitation in men's and women's dormitory rooms limited. There are 3 fraternities, 3 sororities on campus which about 6% of men, 8% of women join; 1% of each men and women students live in fraternities or sororities.

Annual Costs. Tuition and fees, $9,950; room and board, $3,530; estimated $1,000 other, exclusive of travel. About 85% of students receive financial aid. Assistance is typically divided 30% scholarship, 23% grant, 40% loan, 7% work. College reports "unlimited" scholarships awarded on the basis of academic merit alone and need alone, 4 for special talents alone. *Meeting Costs:* college offers monthly payment plan, guaranteed tuition plan.

Delaware State University

Dover, Delaware 19901 **(302) 736-4917**

A state-supported, land-grant university, located in the state capital (pop.25,000); founded as a college for Negroes, but now fully integrated. Most convenient major airport: Philadelphia.

Founded: 1891	**Cost:** < $10K
Affiliation: State	**% Receiving Financial Aid:** 48%
Total Enrollment: 2,882 M, W (full-time); 170 M, 263 W (part-time)	**Admission:** Non-selective
	Application Deadline: June 1

Admission. Graduates of approved high schools with 15 units (10 in academic subjects) and C average eligible; others admitted by examination; 62% of applicants accepted, 52% of these actually enroll. *Out-of-state* freshman applicants: state limits out-of-state enrollment to 30% of entering class. No special requirements for out-of-state applicants. About 58% of out-of-state applicants accepted, 44% of these actually enroll. *Apply* by June 1. *Transfers* welcome.

Academic Environment. *Degrees:* AB, BS. About 20% of general education requirements for graduation are elective; distribution requirements fairly numerous. About 25% of students entering as freshmen graduate eventually; 45% of freshmen do not return for sophomore year. *Majors offered* in addition to usual studies include aircraft systems management, airway science management, computer science, hotel restaurant management, dietetics. *Special programs:* honors, undergraduate research, study abroad, 3–2 engineering. *Calendar:* semester, summer school.

Undergraduate degrees conferred (229). 45% were in Business and Management, 22% were in Education, 6% were in Social Sciences, 4% were in Physical Sciences, 4% were in Health Sciences, 3% were in Psychology, 3% were in Life Sciences, 3% were in Renewable Natural Resources, remainder in 8 other fields.

Faculty. About 57% of full-time faculty hold PhD or equivalent.

Varsity Sports. Men (Div.I): Baseball, Basketball, Cross Country, Football(IAA), Tennis, Track, Wrestling. Women (Div.I): Basketball, Cross Country, Tennis, Track, Volleyball.

Student Body. University seeks a national student body; 63% of students from in state; 96% Middle Atlantic. An estimated 85% of students reported as Protestant, 10% Catholic; 60% Black, 4% other minority, according to most recent data available.

Campus Life. About 36% of men, 39% of women live in traditional dormitories; no coed dormitories; rest commute. Intervisitation in men's and women's dormitory rooms limited. There are 3 fraternities, 3 sororities on campus which about 40% of men, 21% of women join. Fraternities and sororities provide no residence facilities.

Annual Costs. Tuition and fees, $1,788 (out-of-state, $2,668); room and board, $3,454. About 48% of students receive financial aid; assistance is typically divided 63% scholarship, 17% loan, 10% work. College reports some scholarships awarded on the basis of academic merit alone. *Meeting Costs:* University offers deferred payment plan.

University of Delaware

Newark, Delaware 19716 **(302) 831-8123**

A privately controlled, state-assisted, land, sea, and space-grant university, located on a 1,000-acre main campus in a town of 25,600, 14 miles southwest of Wilmington and 40 miles south of Philadelphia. Most convenient major airport: Philadelphia.

Founded: 1743	**Total Enrollment:** 18,015
Affiliation: State	**Cost:** < $10K
UG Enrollment: 5,824 M, 7,663 W (full-time); 633 M, 812 W (part-time)	**% Receiving Financial Aid:** 50%
	Admission: Selective (+)
	Application Deadline: Mar. 1

Admission is selective (+). About 31% of applicants accepted actually enroll; 47% of freshmen graduate in top fifth of high school class, 83% in top two-fifths. Average freshman SAT scores: middle 50% range, 990–1150 combined. *Required:* SAT or ACT; essay for honors consideration. Criteria considered in admissions, in order of importance: high school academic record, standardized test scores, writing sample for honors consideration; recommendation, extracurricular activities, other factors considered: alumni children, diverse student body. *Out-of-state* freshman applicants: university welcomes students from out-of-state. Requirements for out-of-state applicants include higher SAT scores and high school percentile rank than for Delaware residents. States from which most out-of-state students are drawn: New Jersey, Pennsylvania, New York, Maryland, Connecticut, Virginia. About 23% of entering students from parochial or independent schools. *Entrance programs:* early decision, early admission, deferred admission, midyear admission, advanced placement. *Apply* by March 1; rolling admission. *Transfers* welcome.

Academic Environment. Administration reports percentage of electives required for graduation varies from college to college;

graduation requirements for liberal arts program include freshman English, a course in multicultural or gender related topic, math and foreign language courses, 12–13 credits in each discipline: creative arts and humanities, study of culture and institutions over time, empirically-based study of human beings and their environment, and natural phenomena. Student leader comments that since classes are very large, students must take the initiative in order to have contact with faculty. Administration source reports that "almost all of approximately 1,000 faculty teach undergraduate courses and more than half offer research opportunities to undergraduates." Undergraduate studies offered in 103 fields by colleges of Arts and Sciences, Agricultural Sciences, Business and Economics, Education, Engineering, Human Resources, Nursing; Physical Education, Athletics, and Recreation. Degrees offered: bachelors, masters, doctoral. *Majors offered* include: art conservation, women's studies, athletic training. Average undergraduate class size: 48% under 20, 39% 20–40, 13% over 40, 3% over 100.

About 50% of students entering as freshmen graduate within four years, 70% eventually; 86% of freshmen return for sophomore year. *Special programs:* independent study, undergraduate research, study abroad, honors, winter session, individualized majors, double majors, National Student Exchange, 5½-year BS engineering/MBA, 4-year BA/MA in engineering, credit by examination. *Calendar:* semester, 5-week winter session, summer school.

Undergraduate degrees conferred (3,150). 22% were in Social Sciences, 15% were in Business and Management, 11% were in Education, 7% were in Psychology, 7% were in Letters, 7% were in Engineering, 6% were in Home Economics, 6% were in Life Sciences, 4% were in Communications, 3% were in Visual and Performing Arts, remainder in 15 other fields.

Graduates Career Data. Advanced studies pursued by 18% of students within one year of graduation; 4% enter law school, 3% enter business school, 1% enter medical. Medical schools typically enrolling largest numbers of graduates include Jefferson Medical, U. of Maryland, U. of Pennsylvania; dental schools include Temple U., U. of Maryland, U. of Pennsylvania; law schools include Widener, Villanova, Seton Hall. Corporations typically hiring largest numbers of graduates include DuPont, AT&T, Chase Manhattan, "Big 6" accounting firms. Career Development Services offer job placement, assistance with resume writing and interview skills, and career library.

Faculty. About 83% of faculty hold PhD or equivalent. About 31% of teaching faculty are female; 3% Black, 12% other minority.

Student Body. About 42% of students from in state; 90% Middle Atlantic, 5% New England, 1% Midwest, 1% South, 1% West, 1% Northwest, 1% foreign. An estimated 42% of students reported as Catholic, 30% Protestant, 11% Jewish, 14% unaffiliated, 3% other; 5% Black, 2% Asian, 1% other minority. *Minority group students:* special financial and academic programs including Upward Bound and Academic Advancement Office programs; Black Student's Union, Minority Student Programming Advisory Board, Center for Black Culture for social and academic programs.

Varsity Sports. Men (Div.I): Baseball, Basketball, Cross Country, Diving, Football, Golf, Lacrosse, Soccer, Swimming, Tennis, Track. Women (Div.I): Basketball, Cross Country, Diving, Field Hockey, Lacrosse, Soccer, Softball, Swimming, Tennis, Track, Volleyball.

Campus Life. There is provision on campus for several lifestyles, including unlimited intervisitation. Cars on campus not generally permitted; alcohol permitted in student rooms and at approved functions for students over 21. Single freshmen required to live in university residence halls. Most popular intramural sports reported as basketball, football, softball and volleyball.

About 53% of students live on campus in traditional dormitories, coed dormitories and fraternities and sororities; 40% live in off-campus college-related housing; rest commute. Sexes segregated in coed dormitories either by floor or suite. There are 24 fraternities, 14 sororities on campus, which about 10% men, 14% women join. About 25% of resident students leave campus on weekends.

Annual Costs. Tuition and fees, $3,550 (out-of-state, $9,650); room and board, $4,030; estimated $1,800 other, exclusive of travel. About 50% of students receive financial aid; average amount of assistance for freshmen, $3,200. University reports 550 scholarships awarded on the basis of academic merit alone for freshman only, 174 for special talents alone.

Delaware Valley College of Science and Agriculture

Doylestown, Pennsylvania 18901 (215) 345-1500

An independent, state-aided, professional school, located in a community of 8,300, 30 miles north of Philadelphia. College operates its own farms. Most convenient major airport: Philadelphia.

Founded: 1896
Affiliation: Independent/State
Total Enrollment: 1,808 M, W (full-time)
Cost: $10K–$20K
% Receiving Financial Aid: 78%
Admission: Non-selective
Application Deadline: Rolling

Admission. Graduates of approved high schools with 15 units, preferably in academic subjects, eligible; 81% of applicants accepted, 37% of these actually enroll. About 17% of freshmen graduate in top fifth of high school class, 38% in top two-fifths. Average freshman SAT scores, according to most recent data available: 375 M, 419 W verbal, 424 M, 450 W mathematical. *Required:* minimum combined SAT of 900; interview. *Non-academic factors* considered in admissions: special talents, alumni children. *Apply:* rolling admissions. *Transfers* welcome.

Academic Environment. *Degree:* BS. About 10% of general education requirements for graduation are elective; distribution requirements fairly numerous. All students required to obtain 24 weeks of occupational experience related to major. About 50% of students entering as freshmen graduate eventually; 25% of freshmen do not return for sophomore year. Adult programs: continuing education programs offered. *Calendar:* semester, summer school.

Undergraduate degrees conferred (223). 33% were in Business and Management, 27% were in Agricultural Sciences, 23% were in Agribusiness and Agricultural Production, 12% were in Life Sciences, 3% were in Computer and Engineering Related Technology, remainder in Physical Sciences.

Graduates Career Data. Careers in business and industry pursued by 90% of students immediately after graduation, according to most recent data available.

Varsity Sports. Men (Div.III): Baseball, Basketball, Cross Country, Equitation, Football, Golf, Lacrosse, Soccer, Track, Wrestling. Women (Div.III): Basketball, Cross Country, Equitation, Field Hockey, Golf, Softball, Track, Volleyball.

Student Body. About 72% of students from in state; 96% Middle Atlantic. An estimated 5% of students reported as Black, 1% Asian, according to most recent data available.

Campus Life. About 60% of men, 62% of women live in traditional dormitories; 10% men, 13% of women live in coed dormitories; rest commute. Intervisitation in men's and women's dormitory rooms limited. There are 2 fraternities on campus. About 75% of resident students leave campus on weekends.

Annual Costs. Tuition and fees, $11,645; room and board, $4,785. About 78% of students receive financial aid; assistance is typically divided 52% scholarship, 38% loan, 10% work. College reports some scholarships awarded on the basis of academic merit alone.

Delta State University

Cleveland, Mississippi 38733 (601) 846-3000

A state-supported college, located in a community of 13,300, 110 miles south of Memphis. Most convenient major airport: Greenville, MS.

Founded: 1925
Affiliation: State
Total Enrollment: 1,216 M, 1,612 W (full-time); 169 M, 335 W (part-time)
Cost: < $10K
Admission: Non-selective
Application Deadline: Rolling

Admission. Mississippi graduates of accredited high schools with 15 units and score of 15 on ACT composite eligible; others admitted by examination; 97% of freshmen applicants accepted, 88% of these actually enroll. Average freshman scores: ACT, 19.7 composite.

Required: ACT. Criteria considered in admissions, in order of importance: standardized test scores, high school academic record, recommendations, extracurricular activities. *Out-of-state* freshman applicants. No special requirements for out-of-state applicants; 93% of applicants accepted, 87% enroll. *Apply*: rolling admissions. *Transfers* welcome; 552 enrolled 1993–94.

Academic Environment. Degrees offered: bachelors, masters, doctoral. About 40% of general education requirements for graduation are elective; distribution requirements fairly numerous. *Majors offered* in addition to usual studies include commercial aviation, computer science, audiology/speech pathology. About 28% of students entering as freshmen graduate within four years; 24% of entering freshmen do not return for sophomore year. Special programs: CLEP, honors, study abroad, independent study, cross registration with Westfield State College in Massachusetts. *Calendar:* semester, summer school.

Undergraduate degrees conferred (582). 42% were in Business and Management, 20% were in Education, 5% were in Health Sciences, 5% were in Social Sciences, 4% were in Protective Services, 4% were in Transportation and Material Moving, 4% were in Life Sciences, remainder in 12 other fields.

Graduates Career Data. Advanced studies pursued by 24% of graduates; 4% enter medical school, 3% enter dental school, 10% enter business school. Graduate and professional schools enrolling largest numbers of graduates include U. of Mississippi. About 60% of 1992–93 graduates employed. Fields employing largest numbers of graduates include education, business, nursing. Career Planning and Placement Office offers assistance to students and alumni.

Faculty. About 56% of faculty hold PhD or equivalent. About 38% of teaching faculty are female; 7% Black, 1% other ethnic minorities.

Varsity Sports. Men (Div.II): Baseball, Basketball, Football, Golf, Rifle, Swimming. Women (Div.II): Basketball, Rifle, Swimming, Tennis.

Student Body. University does not seek a national student body; 94% of students from Mississippi; 98% South. An estimated 23% of students reported as Black, 1% other minority.

Campus Life. About 41% of men, 37% of women live in traditional dormitories; no coed dormitories; rest commute. No intervisitation in men's or women's dormitory rooms. There are 8 fraternities, 6 sororities on campus which about 24% of men, 25% of women join and live in designated sections of the dormitories. About 80% of resident students leave campus on weekends.

Annual Costs. Tuition and fees, $2,194 (out-of-state, $4,428); room and board, $1,880; estimated $300 other, exclusive of travel. Financial aid: average amount of assistance, $3,500. Assistance is typically divided 45% scholarship/grant, 45% loan, 10% work. University reports some scholarships awarded on the basis of academic merit alone.

Denison University

Granville, Ohio 43023 **(800) 336-4766 or (614) 587-0810**

Despite its designation as a university, Denison is primarily a high-quality, liberal arts college with a national student body. The 250-acre campus is located in a small town (pop. 4,000) 27 miles east of Columbus, the state capital. Most convenient major airport: Columbus.

Founded: 1831
Affiliation: Independent
Total Enrollment: 862 M, 973 W (full-time)
Cost: $10K–$20K
% Receiving Financial Aid: 62%
Admission: Selective (+)
Application Deadline: Feb. 1

Admission is selective (+). About 82% of applicants accepted, 23% of these actually enroll; 48% of freshmen graduate in top fifth of high school class, 72% in top two-fifths. Average freshman scores: SAT, 460–570 verbal; 520–630 mathematical; 56% of freshman score above 500 on verbal, 14% above 600, 2% above 700; 94% score above 500 on mathematical, 39% above 600, 7% above 700; ACT, middle 50% range, 25–29 composite. *Required:* SAT or ACT. Criteria considered in admissions, in order of importance: high school academic record, standardized test scores, writing sample, extracurricular activities, recommendation; other factors considered: special talents, alumni children, diverse student body. *Entrance programs:* early decision, early admission, midyear admission, advanced placement, deferred admission. About 20% of entering students from private schools, 12% from parochial schools. *Apply* by February 1. *Transfers* welcome; 19 enrolled 1993–94.

Academic Environment. Student representatives are voting members on most faculty committees (faculty salary, promotion, and tenure are exceptions). Graduation requirements include 2 writing courses, women/minority studies, 3 semesters in science, 2 in fine arts, foreign language proficiency, oral proficiency, and several fields of inquiry. One student applauded the general education requirements for the exposure to a range of subjects, while another, a transfer student, felt they were too rigid and restrictive. All students responding were extremely lavish in their overall praise of the academic program at Denison. Degrees offered: bachelors. *Majors offered* in addition to usual studies include biochemistry, PPE (Philosophy, Politics, and Economics), black studies, computer science, environmental studies, dance, sociology/anthropology, theater and cinema, area studies (Latin America, France, Germany, East Asian). Academic programs receiving national recognition include math and computer science, economics, psychology, sciences, philosophy, writing. Average undergraduate class size: 67% under 20, 32% 20–40, 1% over 40.

About 75% of students entering as freshmen graduate within four years, 78% eventually, 85% of freshmen return for sophomore year. *Special programs:* CLEP, May Term, independent study, study abroad, honors, undergraduate research, individualized majors, programs of GLCA, directed study, junior and senior fellows, Washington Semester, study at Merrill–Palmer Institute, exchange with Howard, Fisk, or Morehouse, combined programs (with U. of Chicago leading to master's, with Duke School of Forestry, 3–2 engineering, environmental management and forestry, natural resources, medical technology, occupational therapy; 4–3 dentistry with Case Western Reserve, with Duke and U. of North Carolina in physical therapy, with Washington U. in occupational therapy); May term internships. *Calendar:* 4–4–1.

Undergraduate degrees conferred (528). 38% were in Social Sciences, 13% were in Letters, 9% were in Life Sciences, 8% were in Psychology, 8% were in Foreign Languages, 6% were in Visual and Performing Arts, 5% were in Communications, 5% were in Philosophy and Religion, remainder in 5 other fields.

Graduates Career Data. Advanced studies pursued by 15% of students immediately after graduation; 10% enter graduate school; 1% enter medical school; less than 1% enter dental school; 3% enter law school; 1% enter business school. Medical schools typically enrolling largest numbers of graduates include Ohio State, Western Reserve, U. of Cincinnati; law schools include National, Ohio State. Corporations typically hiring largest numbers of graduates include Leo Burnett Advertising, Chubb Group Of Insurance Co., Bank One, Andersen Consulting. Career Development Services offer career advising, workshops, assessment, on campus recruitment, professional school advising, career fairs, alumni network, library resources.

Faculty. About 97% of faculty hold PhD or equivalent. About 50% of undergraduate classes taught by tenured faculty. About 34% of teaching faculty are female; 3% Black, 1% Hispanic, 2% other minority.

Student Body. About 38% of students from in state; 54% Midwest, 22% Middle Atlantic, 7% New England, 11% South, 2% West, 1% Northwest, 3% foreign. An estimated 48% of students reported as Protestant, 26% Catholic, 2% Jewish, 13% unaffiliated, 11% other; 5% Black, 3% Asian, 2% Hispanic. *Minority group students:* generous scholarship funds designated for minority students; black admissions counselor; foreign students adviser; a number of courses in minority group studies offered; special library funds for speakers, programs, films, etc., on Black America; provisions for social activities available through Black Student Union.

Religious Orientation. Denison is an independent institution founded by American Baptists.

Varsity Sports. Men (Div.III): Baseball, Basketball, Cross Country, Diving, Football, Golf, Lacrosse, Soccer, Swimming, Tennis, Track. Women (Div.III): Basketball, Cross Country, Diving, Field Hockey, Lacrosse, Soccer, Swimming, Tennis, Track, Volleyball.

Campus Life. Recent student leader asserts "Students are given much power on campus, which enhances the development of leadership skills." Students agree that on-campus social life is active, with sports, campus organizations, and Greek activities all vying for students' attention. Intervisitation permitted in all areas of residence under student-determined rules. Cars allowed for all but freshmen.

Drinking age is 21; social events are monitored. Smoking guidelines recently added; drugs not allowed. On campus residency required for most students; lottery for a limited number to live off-campus. Most popular intramural sports: football, soccer, speedball; varsity sports: football, lacrosse (both men's and women's).

About 10% of men, 30% of women live in traditional dormitories; 55% of men, 66% of women live in coed dormitories; 2% of men, 2% of women live in off-campus housing; rest commute. Housing guaranteed for all students. Sexes segregated in coed dormitories by floor or room. There are 11 fraternities, 8 sororities on campus which about 56% of men, 58% of women join; 31% of men live in fraternities. About 10% of resident students leave campus on weekends.

Annual Costs. Tuition and fees, $16,730; room and board, $4,420; estimated $1,100 other, exclusive of travel. About 62% of students receive financial aid; average amount of assistance, $13,600. Assistance is typically divided 20% scholarship, 48% grant, 20% loan, 12% work. University reports 353 scholarships awarded on the basis of academic merit alone, 37 for special talents alone. *Meeting Costs:* university offers variety of payment plans.

University of Denver

Denver, Colorado 80208 **(303) 871-2036**

An independent university maintaining "an official connection" with its founding church, Denver has always welcomed students of all races and faiths. D.U. is the only private university in the state and includes the Colleges of Arts and Sciences and Business Administration. Attracting a broadly representative student body, the university is located 6 miles from the heart of Denver. Most convenient major airport: Stapleton International.

Founded: 1864
Affiliation: Independent (United Methodist)
Total Enrollment: 6,681 M, W (full-time)
Cost: $10K–$20K
% Receiving Financial Aid: 60%
Admission: Selective
Application Deadline: August 1

Admission is selective. For all schools, 70% of applicants accepted, 34% of these actually enroll; 44% of freshmen graduate in top fifth of high school class, 70% in top two-fifths. *Required:* recommended SAT or ACT, two recommendations, interview. *Non-academic factors* considered in admission: special talents. *Entrance programs:* early admission, midyear admission, advanced placement, deferred admission. *Apply* by August 1. *Transfers* welcome.

Academic Environment. Administration reports one-third of courses required for graduation are elective; distribution requirements for AB fairly numerous. *Undergraduate studies* offered by Colleges of Arts and Sciences and Business Administration. *Degrees:* AB, BS, BFA, BM, BMEd, BSChem, BSBA. *Majors offered* in addition to usual studies include anthropology, computer science, education, environmental science, geography, Latin American studies, mass communications, speech pathology and audiology, theater. Students report that small classes and accessible faculty help to create an atmosphere conducive to learning.

About 65% of entering freshman graduate within four years; 13% of freshmen do not return for sophomore year. *Special programs:* CLEP, independent study, study abroad, honors, undergraduate research, December interterm, credit by examination, student foreign work-exchange program in business, 5-year 2-degree programs in arts or business, 3–2 BA/MBA, 3–2 Engineering/MBA. Calendar: quarter, 3-week interterm, summer school.

Undergraduate degrees conferred (654). 45% were in Business and Management, 15% were in Social Sciences, 7% were in Psychology, 7% were in Communications, 6% were in Visual and Performing Arts, 5% were in Life Sciences, 4% were in Letters, remainder in 11 other fields.

Graduates Career Data. *Full-time graduate or professional study* pursued by 50% of students immediately after graduation, according to most recent data available. Although 65% of students are reported as professionally/vocationally oriented in their studies and majors, the counseling program is designed for liberal arts students as well; offering career exploration seminars, active placement service and cooperative education program. Alumni reported as helpful in both career guidance and job placement.

Faculty. About 88% of full-time faculty hold PhD or equivalent.

Student Body. University seeks a national student body; 30% of students from in state; 50% North Central, 10% New England, 10% Middle Atlantic. An estimated 35% of students reported as Protestant, 25% Catholic, 20% Jewish, 20% unaffiliated or other; 4% as Black, 2% Asian, 6% Hispanic, according to most recent data available.

Religious Orientation. Denver is an independent institution with ties to the United Methodist Church, makes no religious demands on students. Religious clubs on campus include Hillel, Episcopal, Christian Science, Deseret, Gamma Delta, Pioneer Christian Fellowship, Methodist, Newman. Places of worship available in immediate community for all faiths.

Varsity Sports. Men (NAIA, Div. I): Ice Hockey, Lacrosse, (Div.II): Baseball, Basketball, Soccer, Swimming, Tennis. Women (Div.II): Basketball, Gymnastics(Div. I), Swimming, Soccer, Tennis, Volleyball.

Campus Life. Student body is cosmopolitan. Unlike many institutions with a substantial out-of-state enrollment, Denver does not require students to live in university residences. Use of alcohol on campus limited; use off campus regulated by local and state laws. Cars allowed for all.

About 45% of students live in coed dormitories; 15% of students live in off-campus housing; 10% commute. Freshmen given preference in college housing if all students cannot be accommodated. Intervisitation in men's and women's dormitory rooms unlimited; sexes segregated by wing. There are 9 fraternities, 5 sororities on campus which about 30% of men, 27% of women join; 30% of men and women live in fraternities and sororities. About 10% of students leave campus on weekends. Freshmen are given preference in college housing if all students cannot be accommodated.

Annual Costs. Tuition and fees, $13,572; room and board, $4,302. About 60% of students receive financial aid. University reports some scholarships awarded on the basis of academic merit alone. *Meeting Costs:* university offers installment plan.

DePaul University

Chicago, Illinois 60604 **(312) 362-8000**

A church-related, urban university, founded by the Vincentian Fathers, DePaul offers undergraduate programs at its Lincoln Park Campus in a residential area in Chicago's North Side and at the downtown Lewis Center in the Loop. Most convenient major airport: O'Hare (Chicago).

Founded: 1898
Affiliation: Roman Catholic
UG Enrollment: 2,669 M, 3,400 W (full-time); 1,364 M, 2,355 W (part-time)
Total Enrollment: 16,479
Cost: $10K–$20K
Admission: Selective
Application Deadline: August 1

Admission is selective. About 73% of applicants accepted, 35% of these actually enroll; 27% of freshmen graduate in top fifth of high school class, 57% in top two-fifths. Average freshman scores: combined SAT, 1065; ACT, 24.5 composite. *Required:* SAT or ACT; auditions in music and theatre; interview recommended. Criteria considered in admissions, in order of importance: high school academic record, standardized test scores, writing sample, extracurricular activities, recommendations; other factors considered: diverse student body, special talents. *Entrance programs:* early admission, midyear admission, deferred admission. About 27% of entering freshman from private and parochial schools. *Apply* by August 1; rolling admissions. *Transfers* welcome; 1,103 enrolled 1993–94.

Academic Environment. Degrees offered: bachelors, masters, doctoral. About 50% of general education credits are required for graduation; distribution requirements fairly numerous. Freshmen admitted directly to College of Commerce, School of Music, The Theatre School, and the College of Liberal Arts and Sciences; students enroll as juniors in the School of Education. *Majors offered* in Liberal Arts and Sciences in addition to usual studies include Afro-American studies, computer science, environmental sciences, geography, Latin-American studies, Jewish studies, nursing, theatre arts, travel and tourism, recording and sound technology, international studies, health law administration. New program in software engineering recently added.

About 60% of students entering as freshmen graduate within five years, according to most recent data available. *Special programs:* CLEP, independent study, study abroad, honors, undergraduate research, 3-year degree, pre-law programs, 3–2 engineering with Detroit, Illinois, Southern California, Chicago Consortium of Colleges and Universities. Adult programs: Non-traditional adult degree programs available through School for New Learning which allows students to set their own educational goals and design their own curriculum. *Calendar:* quarter, summer school.

Undergraduate degrees conferred (1,586). 49% were in Business and Management, 11% were in Multi/Interdisciplinary Studies, 9% were in Social Sciences, 6% were in Communications, 5% were in Visual and Performing Arts, 5% were in Computer and Engineering Related Technology, 4% were in Psychology, 3% were in Education, remainder in 8 other fields.

Graduates Career Data. Professional programs enrolling largest numbers of graduates are business and law. Career Development Services include on-campus interviewing, career planning services, and placement services.

Faculty. About 77% of faculty hold PhD or equivalent.

Student Body. University seeks a national student body; 84% of students from in state. An estimated 12% of students reported as Black, 10% Hispanic, 6% Asian, 3% other minority.

Religious Orientation. DePaul is a church-related institution; two non-denominational courses required. Places of worship available on campus for Catholics, in immediate community for all major faiths.

Varsity Sports. Men (Div.I): Baseball, Basketball, Cross Country, Golf, Soccer, Swimming, Tennis, Track. Women (Div.I): Basketball, Cross Country, Soccer, Softball, Swimming, Tennis, Track, Volleyball.

Campus Life. University is primarily a commuter institution; majority of evening students are older and nontraditional. Cars allowed, parking permits required. Some areas marked as non-smoking; drugs not allowed, except with doctor's prescription. Administration source describes students as having "strong pragmatic interest in their particular major."

About 8% of men, 10% of women live in coed dormitories; rest commute. Freshmen given preference in college housing if all students cannot be accommodated. There are 5 fraternities, 5 sororities on campus; they provide no residence facilities.

Annual Costs. Tuition and fees, $10,590; room and board, $5,030. *Meeting Costs:* university offers budget programs.

DePauw University

Greencastle, Indiana 46135 **(317) 658-4000**

Although a university in name, DePauw has for generations remained a quality liberal arts college that also includes a small school of music. Nearly half the student body studies off campus for a semester, mostly in foreign programs. The 175-acre campus is located in a town of 8,900, 40 miles west of Indianapolis. Most convenient major airport: Indianapolis International.

Founded: 1837
Affiliation: Independent (United Methodist)
Total Enrollment: 897 M, 1,086 W (full-time)
Cost: $10K–$20K
% Receiving Financial Aid: 64%
Admission: Very Selective
Application Deadline: February 15

Admission is very selective. About 83% of applicants accepted, 31% of these actually enroll; 69% of freshmen graduate in top fifth of high school class, 92% in top two-fifths. Average freshman scores: SAT, middle 50% range, 460–580 verbal, 510–650 mathematical; 60% above 500 on verbal, 21% above 600, 1% above 700; 82% above 500 on mathematical, 46% above 600, 10% above 700; ACT, 24–28 composite. *Required:* SAT or ACT; interview strongly recommended; audition for School of Music. Criteria considered in admissions, in order of importance: high school academic record, standardized test scores, recommendation, writing sample, extracurricular activities; other factors considered: special talents, alumni children, diverse student body. *Entrance programs:* early notification. About 7% of entering students from private schools, 10% parochial. *Apply* by February 15. *Transfers* welcome; 15 enrolled 1993–94.

Academic Environment. Graduation requirements include competency in oral communication, quantitative reasoning and writing, and distribution requirements in six areas. Majority of students reported concerned with occupational/professional goals. *Undergraduate studies* offered by College of Liberal Arts, schools of Music, Nursing. Degrees offered: bachelors. *Majors offered* include: women's studies, black studies, Asian studies; student may design interdisciplinary major combining a number of disciplines. "Fifth Year Program" allows outstanding graduates to take a fifth year of classes as long as the subjects are outside the undergraduate major. Students cite flexibility (of the academic program), concerned faculty and study abroad opportunities as strengths. Average undergraduate class size: 71% under 20, 27% 20–40, 2% over 40.

About 79% of students entering as freshmen graduate eventually, 90% of freshmen return for sophomore year. *Special programs:* independent study, study abroad, honors, undergraduate research, Winter Term, area minor in business and public service (including internships), Washington Semester, United Nations Semester, New York Semester in the arts, Science Research Fellows Program, 3–2 engineering, nursing, medicine, medical technology. *Calendar:* 4–1–4.

Undergraduate degrees conferred (574). 31% were in Social Sciences, 16% were in Letters, 13% were in Communications, 7% were in Psychology, 7% were in Visual and Performing Arts, 5% were in Education, 5% were in Life Sciences, 3% were in Foreign Languages, 3% were in Health Sciences, 3% were in Physical Sciences, 3% were in Mathematics, remainder in 4 other fields.

Graduates Career Data. Advanced studies pursued by 30% of graduates; 15% enter graduate school; 4% enter medical school; 1% enter dental school; 6% enter law school. About 60% of 1992–93 graduates are employed. Corporations typically hiring largest numbers of graduates include Arthur Andersen, Eli Lilly, Arvin Industries, The Northern Trust. Career Development Services offer aptitude testing, counseling groups, placement services, resume/interview workshops, on-campus recruitment, internships and cooperative education, and library resources.

Faculty. About 82% of faculty hold PhD or equivalent. About 28% of teaching faculty are female; 1% Black, 1% Hispanic, 3% other minority.

Student Body. About 40% of students from in state; 70% Midwest, 12% West, 8% South, 3% Northwest, 2% each Middle Atlantic, New England, 3% foreign. An estimated 60% of students reported as Protestant, 21% as Catholic, 1% Jewish, 8% unaffiliated, 11% other; 7% Black, 3% Hispanic, 2% Asian, 2% international students.

Religious Orientation. DePauw is a church-related institution, but independently controlled; 17% of students affiliated with the church; attendance voluntary at chapels and convocations.

Varsity Sports. Men (Div.III): Baseball, Basketball, Cross Country, Football, Golf, Soccer, Swimming, Tennis, Track, Wrestling. Women (Div.III): Basketball, Cross Country, Field Hockey, Golf, Soccer, Swimming, Tennis, Track, Volleyball.

Campus Life. DePauw remains a fraternity/sorority school with very high proportion of students living in Greek-letter society houses. Inevitably campus social life is dominated by these institutions, though alternatives for independents are reported to "flourish" in co-educational residence halls. High interest in intramural sports reported; most popular: football (men's and women's), basketball, volleyball. Somewhat less interest in varsity sports; most popular, football and basketball. Administration reports more than half the student body volunteers for community service each year. Cars permitted for all students. No smoking allowed in classrooms; alcohol limited to student rooms; drugs considered illegal and prohibited.

About 41% of students live in coed dormitories; 2% of men, 7% of women live in off-campus housing; 6% men, 8% women commute. Freshmen given preference in college housing if all students cannot be accommodated. There are 13 fraternities, 10 sororities on campus which about 82% of men, 78% of women join; 51% of men and 44% of women live in fraternities and sororities.

Annual Costs. Tuition and fees, $13,700; room and board, $4,830; estimated $1,300 other, exclusive of travel. About 64% of students receive financial aid; average amount assistance $10,731. Assistance is typically divided 32% scholarship, 45% grant, 18% loan, 5% work. University reports 549 scholarships awarded on the basis of academic merit alone, 254 for special talents alone, 814 for need alone.

University of Detroit Mercy

Detroit, Michigan 48221 **(313) 927-1245**

An urban university, founded by Jesuits, Detroit is now governed by a board of trustees with lay representation. The University of Detroit and Mercy College of Detroit have consolidated into one institu-

tion. All current programs, policies, and procedures are being reexamined and are subject to change. The 70-acre main campus is located in the northwest section of Detroit. Most convenient major airport: Detroit City Airport or Detroit Metropolitan Airport.

Founded: 1877
Affiliation: Independent (Roman Catholic)
UG Enrollment: 1,198 M, 1,340 W (full-time); 543 M, 1,807 W (part-time)
Total Enrollment: 5,426
Cost: < $10K
% Receiving Financial Aid: 60%
Admission: Selective (+)
Application Deadline: August 1

Admission is selective (+). About 79% of applicants accepted, 45% of these actually enroll; 39% of freshmen graduate in top fifth of high school class, 65% in top two-fifths. Average freshman scores, according to most recent data available: SAT, 491 verbal, 531 W mathematical; ACT, 22.5 composite.

Required: ACT (preferred) or SAT; interview recommended. *Non-academic factors* considered in admissions: geographical distribution; special talents, alumni children, diverse student body. *Entrance programs:* early decision, early admission, midyear admission, advanced placement. About 40% of entering freshman from private or parochial schools. *Apply* by August 1; rolling admissions. *Transfers* welcome.

Academic Environment. Liberal Arts curriculum eliminates predetermined course requirements and permits student with faculty guidance to select an individualized program; core curriculum required for development of values and competence in basic skills. Administration reports 25% of courses needed for graduation in Liberal Arts are required (other colleges range 25–75%). Required two semester co-op program said to aid students in finding jobs during school and after graduation; "hands-on experience to go along with the diploma." Both administration and student leader characterize student body overwhelmingly oriented toward vocational/professional goals. Strongest academic programs reported to be engineering, architecture, and business administration. *Undergraduate studies* offered to freshmen by 5 colleges and schools listed above. *Majors offered* in Liberal Arts in addition to usual studies include computer science, dental hygiene, journalism, medical technology, performing arts, radio–TV; interdepartmental and intercollegiate majors such as urban studies also available.

About 60% of students entering as freshmen graduate eventually; about 18% of entering freshmen do not return for sophomore year. *Special programs:* CLEP, independent study, honors (Liberal Arts), study abroad, individualized majors, cross-registration with Marygrove, Madonna, 1–1 College Accelerated Program, combined BA/JD, and BS/DDS with U. of Detroit Mercy Dental and Law Schools. Adult programs: The Outer Drive Campus is devoted to the needs of the non-traditional, mid-career/adult student. *Calendar:* trimester, summer school.

Undergraduate degrees conferred (792). 22% were in Health Sciences, 20% were in Business and Management, 10% were in Engineering, 9% were in Social Sciences, 7% were in Allied Health, 5% were in Communications, 3% were in Protective Services, 3% were in Letters, 3% were in Architecture and Environmental Design, 3% were in Psychology, 3% were in Life Sciences, remainder in 12 other fields.

Graduates Career Data. According to most recent data available, full-time graduate or professional study pursued immediately after graduation by about 20% of students. Graduate and professional schools typically enrolling largest numbers of graduates include U. of Detroit Mercy, Wayne State, U. of Michigan. *Careers in business and industry* pursued by 90% of graduates. Corporations typically hiring largest numbers of graduates include Ford, General Motors, Chrysler Corp. Career Development Services: Student assessment of career counseling program reported as good for both career guidance and job placement. Alumni reported as helpful in both career guidance and job placements.

Faculty. About 92% of faculty hold PhD or equivalent terminal degree in their field.

Student Body. University seeks a national student body; 85% of students from in state, 90% North Central, 7% New England. An estimated 60% of students reported as Catholic, 25% Protestant, 3% Jewish, 2% unaffiliated, 10% other; 26% as Black, 2% Asian, 1% each Hispanic, Native American, 8% other minority, according to most recent data available.

Religious Orientation. Detroit is Catholic in heritage; most curricula require 6–9 credits in philosophy or theology. No required religious observances. Religious clubs on campus include Knights of Columbus, Campus Ministries. Places of worship available on campus for all major faiths.

Varsity Sports. Men (Div.I): Baseball, Basketball, Cross Country, Fencing, Golf, Riflery, Soccer, Tennis, Track. Women (Div.I): Basketball, Cross Country, Fencing, Track, Softball.

Campus Life. There are no curfews and 24-hour intervisitation option possible subject to vote of resident unit. Regulations on cars, alcohol, smoking, and drugs conform to state law. High percentage of commuters has strong influence on campus life; students who live on-campus said to be "close-knit."

About 20% of students live in coed dormitories; 79% of students commute. Sexes segregated in coed dormitories by floor or room. There are 14 fraternities, 3 sororities on campus which about 20% of men, 11% of women join; 1% of students live in fraternities or sororities. About 20% of students leave campus on weekends.

Annual Costs. Tuition and fees, $8,550; room and board, $3,192. About 60% of students receive financial aid. University reports some scholarships awarded on the basis of academic merit alone.

DeVry Institutes

Oakbrook Terrace, Illinois 60181-4624

DeVry Institutes is composed of 11 DeVry Institute of Technology campuses in the United States and Canada. They offer applications-oriented programs, including electronic technology, computer information systems, business operations, telecommunications management, and accounting. Degrees offered: certificate, diploma, associates, bachelors, masters. Classes offered day, evening, and Saturday; not all programs offered at all campuses. Campuses in Addison (Illinois), Atlanta (Georgia), Chicago (Illinois), Columbus (Ohio), Dallas (Texas), Kansas City (Missouri), Los Angeles (California), Phoenix (Arizona), Woodbridge, (New Jersey); Calgary, Toronto (Canada).

Dickinson College

Carlisle, Pennsylvania 17013-2896 (717) 245-1231

A small, liberal arts, co-educational college, Dickinson was founded before the Revolution. College is strongly committed to injecting an international dimension into the entire curriculum, emphasizing both foreign languages and cultures. The 87-acre main campus (a 19-acre recreation area is nearby) is located in a town of 20,000, on the western edge of greater Harrisburg. Most convenient major airport: Harrisburg International.

Founded: 1773
Affiliation: Independent
Total Enrollment: 805 M, 1,084 W (full-time)
Cost: $10K–$20K
% Receiving Financial Aid: 59%
Admission: Very (+) Selective
Application Deadline: Feb. 20

Admission is very (+) selective. About 84% of applicants accepted, 19% of these actually enroll; 58% of freshmen graduate in top fifth of high school class, 91% in top two-fifths. Average freshman SAT scores: 59% of freshmen score above 500 on verbal, 15% above 600, 1% above 700; 77% score above 500 on mathematical, 31% above 600, 2% above 700; middle fifty percent range for accepted applicants: 480–590 verbal, 530–640 mathematical. *Required:* SAT or ACT, essay, recommendations; interview highly recommended. Criteria considered in admissions, in order of importance: high school academic record, personality and intangible qualities, recommendations, extra curricular activities, writing sample, standardized test scores; other factors considered: special talents, alumni children, diverse student body, geographic distribution. *Entrance programs:* early decision, early admission, midyear admission, advanced placement, deferred admission. About 25% of entering freshmen from private schools, 7% from parochial schools. *Apply* by: February 20, early decision plan I, December 15, early decision plan II, February 1. *Transfers* welcome; 65 enrolled 1993–94.

Academic Environment. College's commitment to an international focus is reflected in the fact that Dickinson graduates more language majors than any other small private college in the entire nation, more than 25% of students study abroad, and satellite "dishes" on campus receive foreign language and cultural programs from overseas. Foreign language and multicultural houses on campus with resident assistants from countries hosting college's student abroad programs add strength to the international focus. Dickinson has also been distinguished by its well-known pre-law program as well as its success in preparing students for medical school, dental school and graduate business programs. Degree offered: bachelors. *Majors offered* in addition to usual arts and sciences include environmental studies, American studies, East Asian Studies, international studies, interdepartmental concentrations, Judaic studies, Latin American studies, policy studies, Russian and Soviet area studies, 11 foreign languages: Chinese, French, Greek, German, Hebrew, Italian, Japanese, Latin, Portuguese, Russian, Spanish. Core requirements include 3 courses in each of 3 divisions plus freshman seminar and 1 course in comparative civilizations, foreign language proficiency, 3 semesters physical education. Introductory chemistry and mathematics courses are now patterned after the nationally-acclaimed introductory Workshop Physics course developed by Dickinson Professor Priscilla Laws.

Average undergraduate class size: 61% under 20, 37% between 20–40, 2% over 40. About 86% of students entering as freshmen graduate eventually; 87% of freshmen return for sophomore year. *Special programs:* independent study, internships, study abroad, honors, undergraduate research, 3-year degree, individualized majors, marine studies, Washington Semester, Appalachian Semester, South Asian Studies program, cross-registration programs with Franklin & Marshall and Gettysburg College, 3–2 Binary Engineering, and recently established linkage programs with Monterey Institute of International Studies, American Graduate School of International Management, and Rutgers Graduate School of Management, guaranteeing admission to students whose performance at Dickinson meets specified requirements. *Calendar:* semester, summer school.

Undergraduate degrees conferred (523). 35% were in Social Sciences, 18% were in Foreign Languages, 12% were in Letters, 7% were in Psychology, 6% were in Visual and Performing Arts, 6% were in Public Affairs, 6% were in Area and Ethnic Studies, 5% were in Life Sciences, 3% were in Physical Sciences, remainder in 4 other fields.

Graduates Career Data. Advanced studies pursued by 58% of students; 5% enter medical school or dental school; 13% enter law school; 10% enter business school. Medical schools typically enrolling largest numbers of graduates include Pennsylvania State U., Temple, U. of Pennsylvania; dental schools include Temple, Tufts; law schools include U. of Pittsburgh, William and Mary, Columbia; business schools include U. of Pennsylvania, Duke, Rutgers. About 95% of those seeking employment had it within six months of graduating. Employers typically hiring largest numbers of graduates include Merck, Arthur Anderson, J.P. Morgan, Sharp & Dohme, First Boston Book, IBM, U.S. Department of Energy, Procter & Gamble, Chubb Insurance, Bell Atlantic, Hershey Corp. Graduates reported to have very high acceptance rate at medical and law schools. Career Development Services include assessment and counseling workshops & programs, placement services, career fairs consortium with other liberal arts schools, and peer career consultants who assist students with job search process; seniors may participate in the recruiting program which includes over 300 organizations and corporations. Alumni reported as helpful in both career guidance and job placement.

Faculty. About 99% of faculty hold PhD or equivalent. About 50% of undergraduate classes taught by tenured faculty. About 38% of teaching faculty are female; about 8% minority.

Student Body. About 38% of students from in state; 67% Middle Atlantic, 19% New England, 7% South, 2% Midwest, 1% West, 1% Northwest, 3% foreign. An estimated 38% of students reported as Protestant, 28% Catholic, 12% Jewish, 18% unaffiliated, 4% other; 2% Black, 3% Asian, 2% Hispanic. *Minority group students:* social and academic counseling; cultural house.

Religious Orientation. Now independent of religious affiliation, Dickinson was founded by Presbyterians and for many years related to the Methodist Church.

Varsity Sports. Men (MAC Div.III): Baseball, Basketball, Cross Country, Diving, Football(Centennial Conf.III), Golf, Indoor Track, Lacrosse, Soccer, Swimming, Tennis, Track. Women (MAC Div. III): Basketball, Cross Country, Diving, Field Hockey, Indoor Track, Lacrosse, Soccer, Softball, Swimming, Tennis, Track, Volleyball.

Campus Life. All freshmen (except for the very small number of commuters) and "most" upperclassmen "expected" to live in dormitories. Each residence hall formulates its own rules "in consultation with the Office of Educational Services." Cars permitted for all students. Alcohol limited to those over 21. Smoking restricted to out-of-doors; permitted in individual offices and dorm rooms by consent of roommates. Drugs prohibited. Student body almost evenly divided between independents and members of fraternities/sororities. Some tensions reported, but relations "mostly good." Relatively isolated from a major cultural center, college provides on campus substantial range of cultural and extracurricular activity. In Harrisburg, Baltimore, Washington, and Philadelphia (18, 90, 100, 120 miles, respectively, from campus) popular cultural offerings available to students, through frequent college-sponsored trips. Most popular intramural sports: rugby, ice hockey, volleyball, softball: varsity sports for men and women: soccer, basketball, swimming, for men: football, for women: field hockey.

About 4% of men, 18% of women live in traditional dormitories; 47% of men, 55% of women in coed dormitories; 21% of men, 18% of women in college related off-campus housing; rest commute. Freshmen given preference in college housing if all students cannot be accommodated. Sexes segregated in coed dormitories either by wing or floor. There are 9 fraternities, 5 sororities on campus which about 30% of men, 40% of women join; 27% of men live in fraternities, 8% of women live in sororities. Very small percentage of students leave campus on weekends.

Annual Costs. Tuition and fees, $17,775; room and board, $4,930; estimated $900 other, exclusive of travel. About 59% of students receive financial aid; average amount of assistance, $15,882. Assistance is typically divided 4% scholarship, 54% grant, 36% loan, 7% work. College reports 30 scholarships awarded to upperclassmen in recognition of academic merit and campus community service; all other financial aid is awarded on basis of need.

Dickinson State College

Dickinson, North Dakota 58601 (701) 227-2175

A state-supported college, located in a town of 20,000, 100 miles west of Bismarck. Most convenient major airport: Bismarck.

Founded: 1918
Affiliation: State
Total Enrollment: 589 M, 789 W (full-time); 60 M, 175 W (part-time)
Cost: < $10K
% Receiving Financial Aid: 80%
Admission: Non-selective
Application Deadline: Rolling

Admission. North Dakota graduates of accredited or approved high schools with 17 units and GPA minimum of 2.0 eligible; 95% of applicants accepted; about 15% of entering freshmen graduate in top fifth of their high school class, 35% in top two-fifths. Average freshmen ACT scores: 21.1 M, 20.8 W composite. *Required:* interview for nursing, ACT (preferred) or SAT. Criteria considered in admissions, in order of importance: high school academic record, standardized test scores, class rank, recommendations; other factors considered: diverse student body, extra-curricular activities, special talents. *Out-of-state* freshman applicants: college actively seeks out-of-state students. State does not limit out-of-state enrollment. Requirement for out-of-state applicants: GPA of 2.0 and minimum ACT composite score of 15. About 95% of applicants accepted. *Apply:* by registration; rolling admissions. *Transfers* welcome; 174 enrolled 1993–94.

Academic Environment. Degrees offered: associates, bachelors. Dickinson State offers programs in liberal arts, business, fine arts, agriculture, and nursing. About 15% of general education requirements for graduation are elective; distribution requirements fairly numerous. About 75% of freshmen return for sophomore year. Average undergraduate class size: 30% under 20, 60% 20–40, 10% over 40; faculty-student ration of 1:18. *Special programs:* study abroad, internships in business and agriculture. *Calendar:* quarter, summer school.

Undergraduate degrees conferred (187). 50% were in Education, 33% were in Business and Management, 5% were in Life Sciences, 4% were in Liberal/General Studies, 4% were in Health Sciences, remainder in 4 other fields.

Graduates Career Data. Advanced studies pursued by 7% of students. About 94% of 1992–93 graduates employed. Career Development Services provided by Learning Resource Center.

Faculty. About 45% of faculty hold PhD or equivalent. About 26% of classes taught by tenured faculty. About 40% of teaching faculty are female; 3% minority.

Varsity Sports. Men (NAIA, Div. II): Baseball, Basketball, Cross Country, Football, Golf, Tennis, Track, Wrestling. Women (NAIA): Basketball, Cross Country, Golf, Tennis, Track, Volleyball.
Student Body. College seeks a national student body; 79% of students from North Dakota; 95% Western region, 2% foreign. An estimated 50% of students reported as Protestant, 35% Catholic, 1% Jewish, 13% unaffiliated, 1% other; 3% minority, according to most recent data available.
Campus Life. About 12% of students live in traditional dormitories; 10% live in coed dormitories; rest live in off-campus housing or commute. About 60% of resident students leave campus on weekends.
Annual Costs. Tuition and fees, $1,782 (out-of-state, $4,462); room and board, $2,010; estimated $600 other, exclusive of travel. About 80% of students receive financial aid; average amount of assistance, $2,879. Assistance is typically divided 5% scholarship, 38% grant, 54% loan, 6% work. College reports 440 scholarships awarded on the basis of academic merit alone, 139 for special talents, 3 based on need alone.
General Institutional Data. College newspaper: Western Concept. Percent of annual budget derived from tuition: 30%.

Dillard University

New Orleans, Louisiana 70122 **(504) 283-8822**

A church-related institution, located in a city of 593,500; founded as a college for Negroes and still serving a predominantly black student body.

Founded: 1869
Affiliation: Independent
Total Enrollment: 1,662 M, W (full-time)
Cost: < $10K
% Receiving Financial Aid: 85%
Admission: Non-selective
Application Deadline: July 1

Admission. Graduates of recognized high schools with 15 acceptable units eligible; 68% of applicants accepted, 62% of these actually enroll; 16% of freshmen graduate in top fifth of high school class, 44% in top two-fifths. *Required:* SAT or ACT. *Apply* by July 1. *Transfers* welcome.
Academic Environment. About 55% of entering students graduate eventually; 45% within four years. *Degrees:* AB, BSN. About 52% of general education requirements for graduation are elective; distribution requirements fairly numerous. *Special programs:* CLEP, study abroad, honors, undergraduate research, 3-year degree. *Calendar:* semester, summer school.
Undergraduate degrees conferred (227). 25% were in Business and Management, 15% were in Health Sciences, 10% were in Education, 7% were in Protective Services, 7% were in Allied Health, 6% were in Social Sciences, 5% were in Life Sciences, 4% were in Psychology, 4% were in Letters, 4% were in Computer and Engineering Related Technology, 4% were in Communications, 4% were in Physical Sciences, 3% were in Mathematics, 3% were in Public Affairs, remainder in Visual and Performing Arts.
Graduates Career Data. According to most recent data available, full-time graduate or professional study pursued by 25% of students immediately after graduation. *Careers in business and industry* pursued by 42% of graduates.
Faculty. About 46% of full-time faculty hold PhD or equivalent.
Varsity Sports. Men (NAIA): Basketball; Women (NAIA): Basketball.
Student Body. University seeks a national student body; 77% of students from South, 8% North Central. An estimated 80% of student reported as Protestant, 19% as Catholic, 1% other; 100% as Black, according to most recent data available.
Religious Orientation. Dillard maintains ties with the United Church of Christ and United Methodist Church; makes no religious demands on students. Religious clubs on campus include Baptist, Methodist, Newman.
Campus Life. About 45% of men, 51% of women live in traditional dormitories; no coed dormitories; rest commute. No intervisitation in men's or women's dormitory rooms. There are 4 fraternities, 4 sororities on campus which about 20% of men, 9% of women join; they provide no residence facilities. About 5% of students leave campus on weekends.
Annual Costs. Tuition and fees, $6,400; room and board, $3,750. About 85% of students receive financial aid. Assistance is typically divided 38% scholarship, 45% loan, 17% work. University reports some scholarships awarded on the basis of academic merit alone.

University of the District of Columbia

Washington, D.C. 20008 **(202) 274-5000**

The university was formed in the fall of 1976 through the merger of Washington's three public colleges: The Federal City College, District of Columbia Teachers College, both four-year institutions, and the two-year Washington Technical Institute. The university is a co-educational, land-grant institution with satellite campuses at various sites in the Metropolitan Area.

Founded: 1976
Affiliation: Municipal
Total Enrollment: 1,664 M, 1,994 W (full-time); 2,641 M, 3,686 W (part-time)
Cost: < $10K
% Receiving Financial Aid: 20%
Admission: Non-selective
Application Deadline: June 14

Admission. High school graduates (or GED) eligible; open admissions policy; 99% of applicants accepted, 44% of these actually enroll. Out-of-city freshman applicants: university welcomes out-of-city students. City does not limit out-of-city enrollment. About 90% of freshmen come from public schools, 5% private schools, 5% parochial schools. *Apply* by June 14; rolling admissions. *Transfers* welcome.
Academic Environment. Degrees offered: associates, bachelors, masters. About 64% of general education requirements for graduation are elective; distribution requirements fairly numerous. About 28% of the students entering as freshmen graduate eventually; 30% of freshmen return for sophomore year. Adult programs: Adult and Continuing Education and Cooperative Extension. *Calendar:* quarter, summer school.
Undergraduate degrees conferred (564). 26% were in Business and Management, 11% were in Computer and Engineering Related Technology, 10% were in Social Sciences, 8% were in Education, 6% were in Visual and Performing Arts, 6% were in Engineering, 4% were in Health Sciences, 4% were in Architecture and Environmental Design, 3% were in Protective Services, 3% were in Psychology, 3% were in Life Sciences, 3% were in Construction Trades, remainder in 13 other fields.
Graduate Career Data. Advanced studies pursued by 6% of students. Fields typically hiring largest number of graduates include business & management, education, engineering. Career Development Services include assisting students and alumni in planning for entry into meaningful careers based upon their interests, aptitudes, and skills.
Faculty. About 52% of faculty hold PhD or equivalent. About 34% of teaching faculty are female; 49% Black, 2% Hispanic, and 23% other minority.
Student Body. About 87% of students from D.C.; 91% Middle Atlantic, 2% South, 1% West, 1% Northwest; 4% Foreign. According to most recent data available an estimated 80% of students reported as Black, 12% other minority. Average age of undergraduate students: 29.
Varsity Sports. Men (NCAA Div.II): Baseball, Basketball, Racquetball, Soccer, Swimming, Tennis, Track, Volleyball. Women (NCAA Div.II): Basketball, Racquetball, Swimming, Tennis, Track, Volleyball.
Campus Life. There are no dormitories on campus. There are 2 fraternities, 2 sororities, which about 3% of men, 3% of women join.
Annual Costs. Tuition and fees, $974 (out-of-district, $3,566); estimated $1,550 other, exclusive of travel. About 20% of students receive financial aid; average amount of assistance, $1,262. Assistance is typically divided 10% scholarship, 55% grant, 30% loan, 5% work. University reports 60 scholarships awarded for academic merit alone, 100 for special talents, 341 for need.

Divine Word College

Epworth, Iowa 52045

A church-related, liberal arts college and seminary, owned by the Divine Word Missionaries, which prepares young men to be priests or brothers.

Founded: 1912
Affiliation: Roman Catholic

Doane College

Crete, Nebraska 68333 (402) 826-8222

An independent, liberal arts college, maintaining "a viable association" with the United Church of Christ, Doane maintains a traditional campus in Crete, a town of 5,000, 25 miles southwest of Lincoln, as well as a campus in Lincoln primarily for non-traditional (adult) students. Most convenient major airport: Lincoln, Nebraska.

Founded: 1872
Affiliation: Independent (United Church of Christ)
UG Enrollment: 388 M, 444 W (full-time Crete campus)
Total Enrollment: 1,576
Cost: < $10K
% Receiving Financial Aid: 93%
Admission: Non-selective
Application Deadline: June 1

Admission. Graduates of recognized high schools (or GED) eligible; 89% of applicants accepted, 34% of these actually enroll. About 39% of freshmen graduate in top fifth of high school class, 75% in top two- fifths. Average freshman scores: ACT, 23.5 M, 22.7 W composite, 23.0 M, 21.5 W mathematical. *Required:* ACT, interview, art students must submit a portfolio, music and drama students must audition. Criteria considered in admissions, in order of importance: high school academic record, standardized test scores, recommendations, extra curricular activities; other factors considered: special talents, alumni children. *Entrance programs:* early decision, early admission, midyear admission, deferred admission, advanced placement. About 20% of freshman come from private or parochial schools. *Apply* by June 1; rolling admissions. *Transfers* welcome; 24 enrolled 1993–94.

Academic Environment. Degrees offered: bachelors masters. The Doane Plan requires courses in 8 categories: Heritage studies, contemporary issues, international/multicultural, natural sciences, quantitative reasoning, communication, health and well being. *Majors offered* include English as a Second Language. Adult programs: Intensive 8-week sessions are held usually at night or Saturday mornings on the Lincoln campus. *Special programs:* January term, independent study, honors, study abroad, student-designed majors, accelerated programs, double majors, 3–2 program in engineering. About 50% of students entering as freshmen graduate eventually; 74% of freshmen return for sophomore year. Average undergraduate class size: 58% under 20, 38% between 20–40, 4% over 40. *Calendar:* 4–1–4, limited summer school.

Undergraduate degrees conferred (5). 40% were in Social Sciences, 40% were in Multi/Interdisciplinary Studies, 20% were in Philosophy and Religion.

Graduates Career Data. Advanced studies pursued by 34% of students; 1% enter dental school, 3% enter law school. Career Development Services include career counseling, printed resources, internships, placement services.

Faculty. About 70% of full-time faculty hold PhD or equivalent. About 43% of undergraduate classes taught by tenured faculty. About 34% of teaching faculty are female; 2% minority.

Student Body. About 81% of students from in state; 94% Midwest, 1% Middle Atlantic, 1% West, 1% Northwest, 3% Foreign. An estimated 63% of students reported as Protestant, 25% Catholic, 3% unaffiliated, 12% not reporting; 1% Black, 1% Hispanic, 1% Asian.

Varsity Sports. Men (NAIA Div.II): Baseball, Basketball, Cross Country, Football, Golf, Tennis, Track. Women (NAIA Div.II): Basketball, Cross Country, Golf, Softball, Tennis, Track, Volleyball.

Campus Life. All unmarried students under the age of 22 expected to live on campus if not living at home with parents. About 36% of students live in traditional dormitories; 52% of students live in coed dormitories; rest commute. Intervisitation in men's and women's dormitory rooms limited. Sexes segregated in coed dormitories by wing. There are 5 local fraternities, 4 local sororities which about 30% of men, 36% of women join; they provide no residence facilities.

Annual Costs. Tuition and fees, $9,390; room and board, $2,830; estimated $1,350 other, exclusive of travel. About 93% of students receive financial aid; average amount of assistance, $7,900. Assistance is typically divided 36% scholarship, 19% grant, 41% loan, 4% work. College reports 991 scholarships awarded on the basis of academic merit alone, 613 for special talents, 491 for need.

Dominican College of Blauvelt

Orangeburg, New York 10962 (914) 359-7800

A small, independent, co-educational college, located in a suburban community, 17 miles from New York City. Most convenient major airports: Stewart (Newburgh, NY), Newark, NJ.

Founded: 1952
Affiliation: Roman Catholic
Total Enrollment: 243 M, 530 W (full-time); 203 M, 660 W (part-time)
Cost: < $10K
% Receiving Financial Aid: 65%
Admission: Non-selective
Application Deadline: August 15

Admission. Graduates of accredited high schools with 16 units in academic subjects eligible; 91% of applicants accepted, 33% of these actually enroll. About 5% of freshmen graduate in top fifth of high school class, 13% in top two-fifths. *Required:* SAT, interview. *Entrance programs:* early decision, advanced placement. *Apply* by August 15; rolling admissions. About 36% of freshmen come from parochial schools, 4% private schools. *Transfers* welcome; 147 enrolled in 1993–94.

Academic Environment. Degrees offered: associates, bachelors. Core requirements include 36–39 credits in General Education Curriculum. Average undergraduate class size: 80% under 20, 20% between 20–40. About 50% of students entering as freshmen graduate eventually; 70% of freshmen return for sophomore year. *Special programs:* January term, independent study, honors, credit by examination, 3–2 in engineering. Adult programs: evening ACCEL and Weekend College. *Calendar:* semester, summer school, Weekend College.

Undergraduate degrees conferred (262). 38% were in Business and Management, 16% were in Health Sciences, 12% were in Allied Health, 10% were in Psychology, 6% were in Social Sciences, 6% were in Public Affairs, 3% were in Letters, 3% were in Education, 3% were in Computer and Engineering Related Technology, remainder in 2 other fields.

Graduate Career Data. Advanced studies pursued by 40% of students(1991). About 89% of 1992–93 graduates employed. Fields typically hiring the largest number of graduates include health-care, business, education.

Faculty. About 43% of faculty hold PhD or equivalent. About 60% of undergraduate classes taught by tenured faculty. About 62% of teaching faculty are female; 10% minority.

Student Body. About 70% of students from New York; 98% from Middle Atlantic; 2% New England. An estimated 9% of students reported as Black, 7% Hispanic, 3% Asian. Average age of undergraduate student: 30.

Varsity Sports. Men (NAIA/ECAC): Baseball, Basketball, Golf, Soccer. Women (NAIA/ECAC): Basketball, Soccer, Softball, Volleyball.

Religious Orientation. Dominican College is a church- related institution, but makes no religious demands on students.

Campus Life. About 5% of men and 5% of women live in coed dormitories; 2% live in off-campus college related housing; rest commute. There are no fraternities or sororities.

Annual Costs. Tuition and fees, $8,060; room and board, $5,400; estimated $2,400 other, exclusive of travel. About 65% of students receive financial aid; average amount of assistance, $2,400. Assistance is typically divided 34% scholarship/grant, 64% loan, 2% work. College reports 62 scholarships awarded on the basis of academic merit alone, 52 for special talents, 61 for need.

Dominican College of San Rafael

San Rafael, California 94901-8008 (415) 457-4440

An independent and Catholic co-educational liberal arts college, Dominican of San Rafael receives "no direct support from Church or State." Today the college environment is ecumenical, yet "its history and distinctive character are rooted in the traditions of the Dominican Order." The wooded campus is located in a town of 46,800, 20 miles north of San Francisco. Most convenient major airport: San Francisco International.

Founded: 1890
Affiliation: Independent (Roman Catholic)
UG Enrollment: 150 M, 498 W (full-time); 20 M, 130 W (part-time)
Total Enrollment: 1,098
Cost: $10K–$20K
% Receiving Financial Aid: 76%
Admission: Non-selective
Application Deadline: August 15

Admission. Graduates of accredited high schools with 15 units eligible; 81% of applicants accepted, 43% of these actually enroll. Average freshman SAT scores: 432 verbal, 452 mathematical. *Required:* SAT, essay. Criteria considered in admissions, in order of importance: high school academic record, standardized test scores, recommendations, extra curricular activities, writing sample; other factors considered: special talents; college prefers minimum 2.5 average in academic subjects and combined SAT score of 800 (ACT composite 19) but considers each applicant individually on basis of present motivation and potential. *Required:* SAT, essay. Entrance programs: early admission, midyear admission, deferred admission, advanced placement. About 6% of entering students from private schools, 12% from parochial schools. *Apply* by August 15; rolling admissions. *Transfers* welcome; 130 enrolled 1993–94.

Academic Environment. Degrees offered: bachelors, masters. Most highly enrolled majors include nursing, psychology, business, biology, liberal studies (for prospective elementary education teachers), international studies. Dominican also offers graduate programs in counseling psychology, education, and Pacific Basin Studies. Core requirements include 6 units in religious heritage, 3 units in each of human nature, verbal expression, natural world, quantitative reasoning, cultural perspectives, human relationships, creativity in the arts, and a 12 unit colloquium experience in cultural heritage. About 41% of students entering as freshmen graduate eventually. Average undergraduate class size: 67% under 20, 29% between 20–40, 4% over 40. Adult programs: Pathways program for working adults, must be 23 or over. *Special programs:* CLEP, independent study, study abroad, undergraduate research, individualized majors, internship program, interim courses. *Calendar:* semester, summer school.

Undergraduate degrees conferred (79). 19% were in Social Sciences, 14% were in Psychology, 14% were in Health Sciences, 13% were in Business and Management, 11% were in Letters, 10% were in Multi/Interdisciplinary Studies, 6% were in Visual and Performing Arts, 4% were in Mathematics, 4% were in Life Sciences, 3% were in Philosophy and Religion, 3% were in Education.

Graduates Career Data. Advanced studies pursued by 18% of students; 6% enter teaching credential programs. About 71% of 1992–93 graduates employed. Fields typically hiring the largest number of graduates include business, health. Career Development Services include interest testing, career counseling, resume-writing and interviewing workshops, job fairs.

Faculty. About 58% of undergraduate full-time faculty hold PhD or equivalent. About 50% of undergraduate classes taught by full-time faculty (no tenure system). About 61% of teaching faculty are female; 10% minority.

Student Body. About 94% of students from California; 96% West/Northwest, 3% Foreign. An estimated 10% of students reported as Protestant, 34% Catholic, 3% other, 53% unaffiliated; 6% Black, 10% Hispanic, 10% Asian, 1% Native American. Average age of undergraduate student: about 40% of undergraduates are 18–24 years old, large evening/weekend program for working adults.

Religious Orientation. College is a church-related institution; 6 units of religious studies required of all students; religious exercises optional.

Varsity Sports. Men (NAIA): Basketball, Cross Country, Tennis, Volleyball. Women (NAIA): Basketball, Cross Country, Tennis, Volleyball.

Campus Life. About 25% of students live in coed dormitories; rest commute. There are no fraternities or sororities. About 50% of resident students leave campus on weekends.

Annual Costs. Tuition and fees, $12,180; room and board, $5,680; estimated $1,962 other, exclusive of travel. About 76% of students receive financial aid. Assistance is typically divided 53% scholarship or grant, 31% loan, 16% work. College reports financial aid is awarded on the basis of need and merit.

Dordt College

Sioux Center, Iowa 51250 (712) 722-6081

A church-related, liberal arts college, located in a community of 5,500, 45 miles northeast of Sioux City. Students expected "to express the Christian faith positively in their general conduct and life style." Most convenient major airport: Sioux City or Sioux Falls.

Founded: 1957
Affiliation: Christian Reformed
Total Enrollment: 511 M, 537 W (full-time)
Cost: < $10K
% Receiving Financial Aid: 98%
Admission: Non-selective
Application Deadline: August 25

Admission. Graduates of approved high schools with 15 units (minimum of 8 in academic subjects) eligible; 93% of applicants accepted, 54% of these actually enroll. About 41% of freshmen graduate in top fifth of high school class, 73% in top two-fifths. Average freshmen ACT scores: 23 M, 23 W composite. *Required:* ACT, minimum H.S. GPA of 2.0. Criteria considered in admissions, in order of importance: high school academic record, standardized test scores, recommendations, extra curricular activities; other factors considered: religious affiliation and/or commitment. About 58% of freshmen students come from private school, 2% parochial schools. *Apply* by August 25; rolling admissions. *Transfers* welcome; 50 enrolled 1993–94.

Academic Environment. Degrees offered: associates, bachelors. Core requirements include 14 out of 40 courses, taken from three academic divisions: social sciences, natural sciences, and the arts; computer literacy also required. Students and administration describe the political philosophy of the student body, faculty and administration as conservative. About 58% of students entering as freshmen graduate within four years; 85% of freshmen return for sophomore year. Average undergraduate class size: 65% under 20, 30% between 20–40, 5% over 40. *Special programs:* CLEP, independent study, individualized majors, study abroad, national business internship, Chicago Metropolitan Program, American Studies in Washington, D.C., Latin American Studies Program, AuSable Institute of Environmental Studies, Los Angeles Film Studies, Russian Studies, Netherland Studies. *Calendar:* semester.

Undergraduate degrees conferred (179). 21% were in Education, 20% were in Business and Management, 10% were in Public Affairs, 8% were in Letters, 6% were in Communications, 5% were in Visual and Performing Arts, 5% were in Psychology, 4% were in Social Sciences, 4% were in Engineering, 4% were in Agricultural Sciences, 3% were in Life Sciences, 3% were in Computer and Engineering Related Technology, remainder in 7 other fields.

Graduates Career Data. Advanced studies pursued by 18% of students; 2% enter medical school; 2% enter law school; 4% enter business school. About 96% of 1992–93 graduates employed. Fields typically hiring largest number of graduates include education, business, engineering, agriculture. Career Development Services include career counseling, career workshops, resume writing, job seeking skills, on-campus interviewing, interest testing, job information.

Faculty. About 65% of faculty hold PhD or equivalent. All of undergraduate classes taught by tenured faculty. About 18% of teaching faculty are female.

Student Body. College seeks a national student body; 38% of students from within the state; 62% Midwest, 10% West, 8% Northwest, 2% New England, 2% South, 1% Middle Atlantic, 15% Foreign. Almost all students reported as Protestant; 1% Black, 2% Asian, 1% Hispanic. Average age of undergraduate students: 22.

Religious Orientation. Dordt is a church-related institution; 1 course in theology is required in core curriculum, 1 course in philosophy required, also 1 senior level course in "discipleship." Twice-weekly chapel services are not mandatory.

Varsity Sports. Men (NAIA): Baseball, Basketball, Cross Country, Golf, Hockey, Soccer, Tennis, Track. Women (NAIA): Basketball, Cross Country, Softball, Tennis, Track, Volleyball.

Campus Life. Dordt is in the process of adding dormitory and recreational facilities. Several students comment on the friendly atmosphere both on-campus and in the town. About 38% each of men, women live in traditional dormitories; 15% each of men, women live in coed dormitories; 32% men, 37% women live in off-campus housing; rest commute. There are no fraternities or sororities. About 30% of resident students leave campus on weekends.

Annual Costs. Tuition and fees, $9,250; room and board, $2,440; estimated $400 other, exclusive of travel. About 98% of students receive financial aid; average amount of assistance, $7,800. Assistance is typically divided 20% scholarship, 20% grant, 20% loan, 8% work. College reports 210 scholarships awarded on the basis of academic merit alone for freshmen and transfers, 51 for special talents. All scholarships are renewable.

Douglass College

(See Rutgers—The State University of New Jersey)

Dowling College

Oakdale, New York 11769 (516) 244-3030

An independent, liberal arts college, located on a former Vanderbilt waterfront estate in a Long Island village of 7,300, 50 miles east of New York City.

Founded: 1959
Affiliation: Independent
Total Enrollment: 4,695 M, W (full-time)
Cost: < $10K
% Receiving Financial Aid: 78%
Admission: Non-selective
Application Deadline: Rolling

Admission. High school graduates with 16 units (all in academic subjects) eligible; 80% of applicants accepted, 51% of these actually enroll; 26% of freshmen graduate in top fifth of high school class, 56% in top two-fifths. *Required:* SAT or ACT; interview recommended. *Apply:* rolling admissions. *Transfers* welcome.
Academic Environment. Bachelor's program in aeronautics uses facilities of MacArthur Airport at Islip. Business internship available in cooperative BBA program. *Degrees:* BA, BS, BBA, BSLPS. About 5% of general education requirements for graduation are elective; no distribution requirements. About 55% of students entering as freshmen graduate eventually; 28% of freshmen do not return for sophomore year. *Special programs:* CLEP, independent study, study abroad. *Calendar:* semester, January special studies period, summer school.
Undergraduate degrees conferred (792). 42% were in Business and Management, 15% were in Education, 13% were in Liberal/General Studies, 9% were in Social Sciences, 5% were in Psychology, 4% were in Computer and Engineering Related Technology, 3% were in Visual and Performing Arts, 3% were in Letters, 3% were in Engineering, remainder in 4 other fields.
Faculty. About 68% of full-time faculty hold PhD or equivalent.
Varsity Sports. Men (Div.II): Baseball, Basketball, Golf, Lacrosse, Soccer, Tennis. Women (Div.II): Basketball, Softball, Tennis, Volleyball.
Student Body. College seeks a national student body; 99% of students from New York, according to most recent data available.
Campus Life. About 10% of men, 10% of women live in coed dormitories; rest commute. There are no fraternities or sororities.
Annual Costs. Tuition and fees, $8,690. About 78% of students receive financial aid. Assistance is typically divided 30% scholarship, 40% loan, 30% work. College reports some scholarships awarded on the basis of academic merit alone. *Meeting Costs:* college offers SHELF loans, parent loans, various payment plans.

Dr. Martin Luther College

New Ulm, Minnesota 56073-3300

An institution sponsored by the Wisconsin Evangelical Lutheran Synod, Dr. Martin Luther College is devoted solely to a curriculum of elementary and secondary teacher education that prepares students for careers in the teaching ministry of the church's school system.

Affiliation: Wisconsin Evangelical Lutheran Synod

Undergraduate degrees conferred (83). 100% were in Education.

Drake University

Des Moines, Iowa 50311 (515) 271-3181

Drake University is a relatively small, independent university which includes a number of undergraduate and professional schools. The campus is located in a residential setting just ten minutes from downtown Des Moines. Most convenient major airport: Des Moines.

Founded: 1881
Affiliation: Independent
UG Enrollment: 1,486 M, 1,983 W (full-time); 248 M, 543 W (part-time)
Total Enrollment: 6,333
Cost: $10K–$20K
% Receiving Financial Aid: 80%
Admission: Selective (+)
Application Deadline: March 1

Admission is selective (+). For all schools, 92% of applicants accepted, 33% of these actually enroll; 62% of freshmen graduate in top fifth of high school class, 84% in top two-fifths. Average freshman scores: SAT, 488 M, 503 W verbal, 562 M, 539 W mathematical; 65% above 500 verbal, 26% above 600, 8% above 700; 44% above 500 mathematical, 11% above 600, 1% above 700; ACT, 25 M, 25 W composite. *Required:* SAT or ACT, essay, counselor recommendation; interview recommended. Criteria considered in admissions, in order of importance: high school academic record, standardized test scores, recommendations, writing sample, extra curricular activities. *Entrance programs:* early admission, midyear admission, advanced placement, deferred admission. About 5% of entering students from private schools, 14% from parochial schools. *Apply* by: March 1; rolling admissions. *Transfers* welcome; 339 enrolled 1993–94.
Academic Environment. Drake prides itself on "blending liberal arts and professional education." Core requirements include courses in composition, language and communication skills, humanities, natural sciences and social sciences. *Undergraduate studies* offered to freshmen by colleges of Arts and Sciences, Business and Public Administration, Education, schools of Journalism and Mass Communication, Fine Arts, and Pharmacy and Health Sciences. Degrees offered: bachelors, masters, doctorate. *Majors offered* in addition to usual liberal arts include actuarial science, astronomy, computer science, geography, graphic design/commercial art, international relations, magazine journalism, medical technology, music business, musical theatre, nursing completion program, pharmacy, public administration. Average undergraduate class size: 22% under 20, 64% between 20–40, 14% over 40. Students list small class size, faculty accessibility, many opportunities for internships, and Drake's "Mac-in-the-room" program (MacIntosh computer in every room on campus, guaranteeing every student easy access) as strengths of the university. Drake is a member of nationwide consortium that shares in the development and exchange of instructional software. The library is currently under renovation, with plans for expansion.

About 62% of students entering as freshmen graduate within four years, 67% eventually; 80% of freshmen return for sophomore year. *Special programs:* CLEP, independent study, study abroad, 3-year degree, individualized majors, credit by examination, Intensive English as a Second Language Program, Washington Semester, United Nations Semester, 3–2 engineering, Honors program, cross registration programs. Adult programs: accelerated studies for adult students offers junior and senior level courses in accounting, management, and general business for degree completion. *Calendar:* early semester, summer school.
Undergraduate degrees conferred (768). 22% were in Business and Management, 16% were in Communications, 14% were in Health Sciences, 11% were in Social Sciences, 6% were in Education, 6% were in Letters, 5% were in Visual and Performing Arts, 5% were in Psychology, 4% were in Life Sciences, 3% were in Liberal/General Studies, remainder in 9 other fields.
Graduates Career Data. Advanced studies pursued by 18% of students; 2% enter medical school; 1% enter dental school; 6% enter law school; 5% enter business school. Medical schools typically enrolling largest numbers of graduates include U. of Iowa, Washington, Northwestern; law schools include U. of Iowa, Drake, U. of Illinois; business schools include U. of Iowa, U. of Illinois, Drake. About 98% of 1992–93 graduates employed. Corporations typically hiring largest numbers of graduates include Principal Financial Group, Peat Marwick, Arthur Andersen, various school districts.

Faculty. About 93% of faculty hold PhD or equivalent. About 64% of undergraduate classes taught by tenured faculty. About 28% of teaching faculty are female; 7% minority.

Student Body. University seeks a national student body; 33% of students from in state; 82% Midwest, 1% New England, 3% Middle Atlantic, 2% South, 6% West, 1% Northwest, 5% Foreign. An estimated 36% of students reported as Protestant, 22% Catholic, 5% Jewish; 5% Black, 3% Asian, 7% other minority. *Minority group students:* Drake Black Afro-American Society, Black Cultural Center; Minority Student Adviser, Los Estudiantes.

Varsity Sports. Men (Div.I): Basketball, Cross Country, Football (IAA), Golf, Soccer, Tennis, Track. Women (Div.I): Basketball, Cross Country, Softball, Tennis, Track, Volleyball.

Campus Life. Cars allowed for all. Smoking restricted to designated areas, 2 buildings are smoke-free. Alcohol may be served at recognized functions; legal age, 21; drugs prohibited. Residence in university-approved houses required for all students for the first two years following high school graduation.

About 39% of men, 47% of women live in coed dormitories; 27% of men, 23% of women live in off-campus college-related housing; 18% of men, 18% of women commute. There are 11 fraternities, 10 sororities on campus which 35% of men, 28% of women join; 16% of men, 12% of women live in fraternities and sororities. About 8% of resident students leave campus on weekends.

Annual Costs. Tuition and fees, $12,780; room and board, $4,520 ($275 reduction for students who bring their own Apple Macintosh, IBM or IBM compatible PC); estimated $2,050 other, exclusive of travel. About 80% of students receive financial aid; average amount of assistance, $13,900. Assistance is typically divided 55% scholarship/grant, 35% loan, 10% work. University reports 1,372 scholarships awarded on the basis of academic merit alone, 360 for special talents, 1,391 for need.

Drew University

Madison, New Jersey 07940 **(201) 408-DREW**

One of a small number of liberal arts institutions located in and around New York City, Drew combines proximity to the nation's major cultural center with the quiet of a semirural campus. The university includes, besides the College of Liberal Arts, a well-known Methodist theological seminary and a graduate school. College sponsors United Nations Semester open to students from all parts of the country. The 150-acre campus is located in a town of 18,000, about 27 miles west of New York. Most convenient major airport: Newark.

Founded: 1866
Affiliation: Independent (United Methodist)
UG Enrollment: 599 M, 801 W (full-time); 24 M, 66 W (part-time)
Total Enrollment: 2,068
Cost: $10K–$20K
% Receiving Financial Aid: 75%
Admission: Very (+) Selective
Application Deadline: February 15

Admission is very (+) selective. About 76% of applicants accepted, 23% of these actually enroll; 65% of freshmen graduate in top fifth of high school class, 88% in top two-fifths. Average freshman SAT scores, according to most recent data available: 557 M, 559 W verbal, 610 M, 584 W mathematical; 75% of freshmen score above 500 on verbal, 39% above 600, 6% above 700; 85% score above 500 on mathematical, 47% above 600, 15% above 700. *Required:* SAT or ACT; interview recommended. *Non-academic factors* considered in admissions: diverse student body, special talents, alumni children, minorities. *Entrance programs:* early decision, early admission, midyear admission, advanced placement, deferred admission. About 34% of entering students from private or parochial schools. *Apply* by February 15. *Transfers* welcome.

Academic Environment. Pressures for academic achievement appear moderately intense. Majority of students reported to be primarily oriented toward scholarly/intellectual interest with a substantial minority primarily concerned with occupational/professional goals. General education requirements mandate demonstrated ability to write clearly, computer literacy, completion of one year of a foreign language, a freshman seminar and, in addition to fulfilling requirements for a major, completion of basic courses in the liberal arts. Grading policy eliminates all grades below C, the level that must be achieved to receive credit for courses; former pass/fail option now pass/no credit. *Degree:* AB. *Majors offered* include usual arts and sciencces, anthropology, behavioral science, botany, psychology, Russian area studies, theater arts, zoology. *Computer Science* courses offered; none required (but computer literacy required through non-credit series of workshops); major offered, designed for science and engineering. Every student receives a microcomputer, printer, and software. A software library with over 500 programs and CD/ROM with 1,484 shareware programs is maintained with a full-time software librarian, as well as an aid station to offer assistance and answer questions. Facilities reported as adequate to meet student demand.

About 79% of students entering as freshmen graduate eventually; 8% of freshmen do not return for sophomore year. *Special programs:* CLEP, independent study, study abroad, honors, optional January interterm, field work programs, undergraduate research, individualized majors, semesters in London or Washington (for political science), Brussels (for international organization and trade), New York City (for art), Oxford (for religion), 5 year BA/MA with Duke School of Forestry, 3–2 engineering with Georgia Tech, Stevens, and Washington U., business internship, semester in marine biology at U. of Miami, business administration and state teacher certification program with College of St. Elizabeth. Adult programs: Continuing University Education program for students who previously interrupted their studies. *Calendar:* semester, optional January interterm, summer session.

Undergraduate degrees conferred (355). 42% were in Social Sciences, 16% were in Letters, 11% were in Psychology, 9% were in Life Sciences, 6% were in Visual and Performing Arts, 4% were in Multi/Interdisciplinary Studies, 3% were in Foreign Languages, 3% were in Physical Sciences, 3% were in Computer and Engineering Related Technology, remainder in 4 other fields.

Graduates Career Data. Aaccording to most recent data available, full-time graduate or professional study pursued immediately after graduation by 28% of students; 4% enter medical school; 1% enter dental school; 7% enter law school; 1% enter business school. Medical and dental schools typically enrolling largest numbers of graduates include U. MDNJ, Robert Wood Johnson; law schools include Rutgers, NYU, Seton Hall, Temple, U. of Connecticut; business schools include Rutgers, NYU. *Careers in business and industry* pursued by 65% of graduates. Corporations typically hiring largest numbers of graduates include Prudential Insurance, Chubb Insurance, National Westminster Bank. Career Development Services: Student assessment of program reported as good for career guidance and fair for job placement. Alumni reported as active in career guidance and job placement according to administration.

Faculty. About 90% of faculty hold doctorate or equivalent terminal degree.

Student Body. University seeks a national student body; 54% of students from in state; 75% Middle Atlantic, 16% New England. An estimated 5% of students reported as Black, 3% Hispanic, 3% Asian, less than 1% other minority, according to most recent data available.

Religious Orientation. Drew is an independent institution, but retains "an historic and continuing association" with the United Methodist Church. Attendance at biweekly chapel services voluntary. Religious clubs on campus include Interfaith Council, Hillel, Newman, Alpha and Omega Christian Fellowship, Canterbury. Places of worship available on campus and in immediate community for Catholics and Protestants.

Varsity Sports. Men (Div.III): Baseball, Basketball, Cross Country, Equestrian, Fencing, Lacrosse, Soccer, Tennis. Women (Div.III): Basketball, Cross Country, Equestrian, Fencing, Field Hockey, Lacrosse, Soccer, Softball.

Campus Life. Drinking on campus permitted in accordance with state laws; each dormitory determines its own intervisitation policy. No fraternities or sororities; high interest reported in varsity athletics and intramural sports. Most popular varsity sport for men: soccer, lacrosse, basketball; for women: field hockey, lacrosse, basketball. Most popular intramurals: play football, softball, volleyball. All students live on campus except commuters. Cars permitted only for seniors in good standing and not receiving financial aid. Proximity to New York City offers many opportunities for college to import talent to perform on campus, as well as for students to avail themselves of the city's rich offerings.

About 18% of men, 23% of women live in traditional dormitories; 75% of men, 70% of women live in coed dormitories; rest live in off-campus housing or commute. Freshmen given preference in college housing if all students cannot be accommodated. Sexes segregated in coed dormitories by wing, floor or room. There are no fraternities or sororities. About 30% of students leave campus on weekends.

Annual Costs. Tuition and fees, $18,058; room and board, $5,348. About 75% of students receive financial aid. University reports some scholarships awarded on the basis of academic merit alone.

Drexel University

Philadelphia, Pennsylvania 19104 (215) 895-6727

Drexel is a privately supported, co-educational institution located in the University City section of West Philadelphia. The University includes the Colleges of Business Administration, Engineering, Arts and Sciences, the Nesbitt College of Design Arts, the College of Information Studies, and the Evening College. Still substantially a commuter institution, the number of residential students is rising. Most convenient major airport: Philadelphia International.

Founded: 1891
Affiliation: Independent/State
UG Enrollment: 4,359 M, 2,188 W (full-time); 1,634 M, 629 W (part-time)
Total Enrollment: 11,594
Cost: $10K–$20K
% Receiving Financial Aid: 70%
Admission: Very Selective
Application Deadline: May 1

Admission is very selective for colleges of Engineering, selective for College of Business and Administration, Nesbitt College of Design Arts, College of Arts and Sciences.

For all schools, 91% of applicants accepted, 37% of these actually enroll; 42% of freshmen graduate in top fifth of high school class, 71% in top two-fifths. Average freshmen SAT scores, according to most recent data available: middle fifty percent range, 410–520 verbal, 500–620 mathematical.

For Engineering (2,138 M, 368 W (full-time)), 91% of applicants accepted, 39% of these actually enroll; 58% of freshmen graduate in top fifth of high school class, 82% in top two-fifths. Average freshman SAT scores: 477 M, 470 W verbal, 601 M, 585 W mathematical; 34% of freshman score above 500 on verbal, 6% above 600; 85% score above 500 on mathematical, 45% above 600, 10% above 700, according to most recent data available.

For Business and Administration, (1,447 M, 836 W (full-time)), 91% of applicants accepted, 37% of these actually enroll; 32% of freshmen graduate in top fifth of high school class, 59% in top two-fifths. Average freshman SAT scores: 450 M, 435 W verbal, 542 M, 491 W mathematical; 20% of freshman score above 500 on verbal, 3% above 600; 55% score above 500 on mathematical, 19% above 600, 3% above 700, according to most recent data available.

For Nesbitt College of Design Arts, (135 M, 538 W (full-time)), 91% of applicants accepted, 39% of these actually enroll; 24% of freshmen graduate in top fifth of high school class, 57% in top two-fifths. Average freshman SAT scores: 449 M, 451 W verbal, 506 M, 496 W mathematical; 22% of freshman score above 500 on verbal, 3% above 600; 47% score above 500 on mathematical, 11% above 600, according to most recent data available.

For Arts and Sciences, (508 M, 402 W (full-time)), 92% of applicants accepted, 29% of these actually enroll; 32% of freshmen graduate in top fifth of high school class, 63% in top two- fifths. Average freshman SAT scores: 484 M, 456 W verbal, 564 M, 504 W mathematical; 32% of freshman score above 500 on verbal, 7% above 600; 58% score above 500 on mathematical, 22% above 600, 5% above 700, according to most recent data available.

For Information Sciences, (130 M, 44 W (full-time)), 95% of applicants accepted, 66% of these actually enroll; 50% of freshmen graduate in top fifth of high school class, 79% in top two-fifths. Average freshman SAT scores: 513 M, 386 W verbal, 576 M, 532 W mathematical; 48% of freshman score above 500 on verbal, 9% above 600, 4% above 700; 74% score above 500 on mathematical, 26% above 600, according to most recent data available.

Required: SAT or ACT, 3 ACH for Engineering (English, mathematics I or II, science), interview desired. *Non-academic factors* considered in admissions: alumni children, diverse student body, special talents, extra-curricular activities, work experience. *Entrance programs:* early decision, early admission, deferred admission, advanced placement, midyear admission. *Apply* by May 1; rolling admissions. *Transfers* welcome.

Academic Environment. Some increase in student influence in curriculum decision making through student/faculty committees. Pattern remains quite traditional in some of the colleges—especially Engineering. The Humanities and Technology Program offers flexibility to student whose interests change in the course of his undergraduate studies. Pressures for academic achievement appear to vary from moderate to moderately strong—greatest in colleges of Science and Engineering. Curricula in these colleges offered only in 5-year cooperative work/study program, alternating 6-month periods of study on campus and employment in industry—available after freshman year; cooperative plan optional in other colleges. *Degrees:* BS, BSBA. *Majors offered* include 5 fields of engineering, biological sciences, chemistry, computer science, environmental science, mathematics, physics, business administration, commerce and engineering, nutrition and food, human behavior and development, design, photography, humanities, social sciences and information studies.

About 60% of students entering as freshmen graduate eventually; 25% of freshmen do not return for sophomore year. *Special programs:* CLEP, honors, undergraduate research, individualized majors, 5-year BS/MS cooperative education programs, 3–3 engineering with Lincoln U. *Calendar:* 4 quarters.

Undergraduate degrees conferred (1,407). 45% were in Business and Management, 34% were in Engineering, 6% were in Computer and Engineering Related Technology, 4% were in Architecture and Environmental Design, 3% were in Marketing and Distribution, remainder in 15 other fields.

Graduates Career Data. *Careers in business and industry:* Corporations typically hiring largest numbers of graduates include General Electric, IBM, DuPont.

Faculty. About 93% of faculty hold PhD or equivalent.

Student Body. University seeks "regional" student body; 66% of students from Pennsylvania; 97% from Middle Atlantic. An estimated 6% of students reported as Black, 12% Asian, 2% Hispanic, according to most recent data available.

Varsity Sports. Men (Div.I): Baseball, Basketball, Crew, Cross Country, Golf, Lacrosse, Soccer, Swimming, Tennis, Track, Wrestling. Women (Div.I): Badminton, Basketball, Field Hockey, Lacrosse, Softball, Swimming, Tennis, Volleyball.

Campus Life. Although number of residential students is rising, student life at Drexel still largely typical of many urban community institutions. Location of campus makes for easy access to Philadelphia's many cultural attractions. Cars discouraged for freshmen; parking scarce.

About 63% of men, 37% of women live in coed dormitories; 20% of men, 51% of women in off-campus housing or commute. Freshmen given preference in college housing if all students cannot be accommodated. Intervisitation in men's and women's dormitory rooms unlimited; sexes segregated by floor. There are 14 fraternities, 5 sororities on campus which about 17% of men, 12% of women join, about 17% of men, 12% of women live in fraternities and sororities. About 60% of residential students leave campus on weekends.

Annual Costs. Tuition and fees, $12,326; room and board, $6,500. About 70% of students receive financial aid. University reports some scholarships awarded on the basis of academic merit alone.

Drury College

Springfield, Missouri 65802 (417) 873-7879

A small, liberal arts college, founded by Congregationalists, Drury is located on a 40-acre campus in the heart of the Ozarks, in a residential area of a city of 125,000. Most convenient major airports: Springfield, St. Louis, Kansas City.

Founded: 1873
Affiliation: Independent (United Church of Christ)
UG Enrollment: 490 M, 575 W (full-time)
Total Enrollment: 1,453
Cost: < $10K
% Receiving Financial Aid: 85%
Admission: Selective
Application Deadline: Aug. 1

Admission is selective. About 97% of applicants accepted, 45% of these actually enroll; 55% of freshmen graduate in top fifth of high school class, 78% in top two-fifths. Average freshman scores: SAT, 511 M, 365 W verbal; 550 M, 542 W mathematical; ACT, 24.2 M, 24.9 W composite. *Required:* SAT or ACT, essay, interview, reference from high school guidance counselor. Criteria considered in admissions, in order of importance: high school academic record, standardized test scores, recommendations, writing sample, class rank. *Entrance programs:* early admission, midyear admission, advanced placement. About 14% of entering students from private or parochial schools. *Apply* by: August 1; rolling admissions. *Transfers* welcome; 90 enrolled 1993–94.

Academic Environment. Drury offers 28 programs of study with students having opportunities to conduct research in the science departments; internships are encouraged in most areas. Drury prides itself on successful placements in the job market as well as graduate and professional programs. All students (except BMEd) must complete 51 hours of liberal arts foundation courses. Degrees offered: bachelors, masters. *Majors offered* include usual arts and sciences, architecture (5-year), business administration, education, law enforcement, medical technology, nursing, international studies.

About 52% of students entering as freshmen graduate eventually; 19% of freshmen do not return for sophomore year. Average undergraduate class size: 44% of classes under 20, 56% 20–40. *Special programs:* CLEP, honors, independent study, study abroad, undergraduate research, January winter term (3 required for graduation), May Term, Washington Semester, exchange with Grambling, cooperative urban teacher education program, credit by examination, internships, theater artist program, international business administration program, pre-engineering and pre-occupational therapy with Washington U., pre-medical scholars with St. Louis U. (early acceptance). *Calendar:* 4–1–4, summer school.

Undergraduate degrees conferred (297). 25% were in Business and Management, 13% were in Education, 11% were in Communications, 10% were in Social Sciences, 9% were in Psychology, 7% were in Life Sciences, 6% were in Health Sciences, 5% were in Visual and Performing Arts, 5% were in Letters, 4% were in Architecture and Environmental Design, remainder in 5 other fields.

Graduates Career Data. Advanced studies pursued by 29% of students; 6% enter medical school; 2% enter dental school; 3% enter law school; 3% enter business school. Medical schools typically enrolling largest numbers of graduates include St. Louis U., U. of Missouri-Columbia; law schools include U. of Missouri, Washburn; business schools include Drury College, Southwest Missouri State, U. of Illinois. About 65% of 1992–93 graduates employed. Career Development Services include aptitude testing, counseling, workshops, placement service, on-campus recruitment, internships and cooperative work-study, graduate and professional school information. Alumni reported as helpful in both career guidance and job placement.

Faculty. About 93% of faculty hold PhD or equivalent. About 80% of undergraduate classes taught by tenured faculty. About 24% of teaching faculty are female.

Student Body. College seeks a national student body; 84% of students from Missouri; 92% North Central, 4% foreign. An estimated 62% of students reported as Protestant, 10% Catholic, 3% Jewish, 35% unaffiliated; 1% as Black, 5% other minority.

Religious Orientation. Drury is an independent institution with traditional affiliation with the United Church of Christ, one course in religion required of all students.

Varsity Sports. Men (NCAA Div. I, NAIA Div. II): Basketball, Golf, Soccer, Swimming, Tennis. Women (NAIA): Soccer, Swimming, Tennis, Volleyball.

Campus Life. Administration reports "shared governance at all levels of policy making." Key privileges for women except freshmen who have midnight curfew (1 am on weekends). Alcohol not allowed on campus.

About 25% of men, 25% of women live in traditional dormitories; no coed dormitories; rest commute. There are 4 fraternities, 4 sororities on campus which about 39% of men, 42% of women join; 10% of men live in fraternities; sororities provide no residence facilities. About 40% of resident students leave campus on weekends.

Annual Costs. Tuition and fees, $8,760; room and board, $3,380; estimated $1,000 other, exclusive of travel. About 85% of students receive financial aid; average amount of assistance, $4,600. Aid is typically broken down, $3,000 scholarship, $600 loan, $1,000 work. College reports 700 scholarships awarded on the basis of academic merit alone, 225 for special talents, 550 for need.

University of Dubuque

Dubuque, Iowa 52001 **(319) 589-3200**

An independent institution, with historic ties to the Presbyterian Church (USA), located in a city of 66,000, 180 miles west of Chicago. Most convenient major airport: O'Hare (Chicago), or Dubuque Regional.

Founded: 1852
Affiliation: Independent (Presbyterian Church (USA))
Total Enrollment: 1,016 M, W (full-time); 63 M, 149 W (part-time)
Cost: $10K–$20K
% Receiving Financial Aid: 82%
Admission: Non-selective
Application Deadline: June 1

Admission. High school graduates with 15 units (10 in academic subjects) who rank in top 60% of class and score 15 on ACT composite eligible; 94% of applicants accepted, 27% of these actually enroll. About 32% of freshmen graduate in top fifth of high school class, 72% in top two-fifths. Average freshmen ACT scores, according to most recent data available: 21.9 composite. *Required:* SAT or ACT. *Apply* by June 1; rolling admissions. *Transfers* welcome.

Academic Environment. *Degrees:* AB, BS, BM, BSBA. About 67% of general education requirements for graduation are elective; distribution requirements fairly numerous. About 32% of freshmen do not return for sophomore year. *Special programs:* CLEP, independent study, study abroad, undergraduate research, individualized majors, cross-registration with nearby Clarke and Loras colleges, 3–3 college seminary plan. Adult programs: Tri-College Degree, weekend accelerated classes. *Calendar:* semester, summer school.

Undergraduate degrees conferred (134). 30% were in Business and Management, 14% were in Health Sciences, 13% were in Education, 10% were in Transportation and Material Moving, 10% were in Psychology, 8% were in Social Sciences, 4% were in Life Sciences, 4% were in Letters, 3% were in Multi/Interdisciplinary Studies, remainder in 4 other fields.

Faculty. About 68% of faculty hold PhD or equivalent.

Varsity Sports. Men (Div.III): Baseball, Basketball, Cross Country, Football, Golf, Tennis, Track, Wrestling. Women (Div.III): Basketball, Golf, Softball, Tennis, Track, Volleyball.

Student Body. University seeks a national student body; 59% of students from in state; 87% North Central. An estimated 27% of students reported as Protestant, 50% Catholic, 13% unaffiliated; 9% Black, 15% Asian, 2% Hispanic, 1% Native American, according to most recent data available.

Religious Orientation. University is a private institution, with ties to Presbyterian Church; makes no religious demands on students; "allows complete freedom of religious choice." Courses in religion optional in general education program; attendance at chapel services not required.

Campus Life. About 60% of students live in traditional dormitories; 40% live in off-campus housing or commute. Intervisitation in men's and women's dormitory rooms limited; women must be escorted. There are 7 fraternities, 3 sororities on campus which about 10% of men, 5% of women join; they provide no residence facilities. About 70% of students leave campus on weekends.

Annual Costs. Tuition and fees, $10,530; room and board, $3,620. About 82% of students receive financial aid. University reports some scholarships awarded on the basis of academic merit alone.

Duke University

Durham, North Carolina 27706 **(919) 684-3214**

Duke has become a truly national institution with half again as many students drawn from the Middle Atlantic states as from its own home region, the South, and substantial numbers from every area of the country. Its once strong religious affiliation is now characterized as "United Methodist affinity without control by the church." The traditional separation of the East Campus (Woman's College) and the main West Campus changed with merger of Trinity and Woman's College; men and women housed on both. Duke is located at the southwest edge of Durham, a city of 100,000, about 250 miles southwest of Washington, D.C.

Founded: 1838
Affiliation: Independent (United Methodist)
Total Enrollment: 10,579 M, W (full-time)
Cost: $10K–$20K
% Receiving Financial Aid: 37%
Admission: Most Selective
Application Deadline: January 15

Admission is among the most selective in the country for Trinity College, School of Engineering. For all schools, 26% of applicants accepted, 47% of these actually enroll; 71% of freshmen graduate in top fifth of high school class; 67% of entering freshmen from public schools, 33% from private and parochial schools.

For Trinity (2,691 M, 2,386 W), 21% of applicants accepted, 45% of these actually enroll; 95% graduate in top fifth of high school class, all in top two-fifths. Average freshman scores: SAT, 626 M, 621 W verbal, 691 M, 652 W mathematical; 95% of freshmen score above 500 on verbal, 70% above 600, 14% above 700; 99% score above 500 on mathematical, 87% above 600, 42% above 700, according to most recent data available.

For Engineering (650 M, 205 W), 33% of applicants accepted, 40% of these actually enroll; 98% graduate in top fifth of high school class, all in top two-fifths. Average freshman scores: SAT, 620 M, 615 W verbal, 730 M, 701 W mathematical; 97% of freshmen score above 500 on verbal, 66% above 600, 12% above 700; all score above 500 on mathematical, 99% above 600, 77% above 700, according to most recent data available.

Required: SAT, 3 ACH including English composition (mathematics for engineers). *Non-academic factors* considered in admissions: diverse student body, special talents, alumni children, athletics. *Entrance programs:* early decision, midyear admission, deferred admission, advanced placement. *Apply* by January 15. *Transfers* welcome.

Academic Environment. Student body is primarily oriented toward occupational/professional goals. Strongest academic programs reported to be in the natural sciences. University has, for many years, been actively recruiting students of high ability. High percentage of graduates go on to medical and law schools. Pressures for academic achievement are intense. Curriculum allows students to complete degree requirements in 3 years by attending an early summer session for 2 years; also includes alternative Program II for highly qualified students who design individualized plans of study. For Program I students, 4 semester courses (at least 2 at advanced level) are required in a division outside the major field, 2 courses in the third division, participation in several types of "small group learning experiences." Distribution requirements include science, history, literature courses, and foreign language requirement. *Degrees:* AB, BS, BSE. *Majors offered* include usual arts and sciences, engineering (civil, electrical, mechanical, biomedical), film and video, human development, neurosciences, primatology.

About 90% of students entering as freshmen graduate eventually; 3% of freshmen do not return for sophomore year. *Special programs:* independent study, study abroad, honors, undergraduate research, 3-year degree, individualized majors, double majors, interdisciplinary majors, reading-out of introductory courses, distinguished professors seminars, semester at Classical Center in Rome, student-organized house courses, living/learning corridors, combined programs with Duke schools of Forestry, Law, and Business, reciprocal arrangements with neighboring state universities. *Calendar:* semester, summer school.

Undergraduate degrees conferred (1,566). 36% were in Social Sciences, 11% were in Engineering, 11% were in Psychology, 8% were in Letters, 8% were in Life Sciences, 6% were in Public Affairs, 5% were in Multi/Interdisciplinary Studies, 3% were in Physical Sciences, 3% were in Visual and Performing Arts, remainder in 5 other fields.

Graduates Career Data. According to most recent data available, full-time graduate study pursued immediately after graduation by 45% of students; 9% enter medical school; 1% enter dental school; 16% enter law school; 2% enter business school. Medical schools typically enrolling largest numbers of graduates include Duke, Baylor, Emory; dental schools include U. of North Carolina; law schools include Harvard, Duke, Washington U.; business schools include Duke, Chicago, Columbia. Career Development Services: Student assessment of program reported as fair for career guidance and good for job placement. Alumni reported as actively helpful in both career guidance and job placement.

Faculty. Overwhelming proportion of faculty hold doctorate; large majority earned at nation's leading graduate institutions.

Student Body. University seeks a national student body; 12% of students from in state; 33% South, 39% Middle Atlantic, 8% New England, 10% North Central, 9% West/Northwest. An estimated 28% of students reported as Protestant, 12% Catholic, 6% Jewish, 54% unaffiliated; 5% as Black, 2% Hispanic, 4% Asian, according to most recent data available.

Religious Orientation. Duke maintains some of its traditional ties with the United Methodist Church, but is now essentially an independent institution, makes no religious demands on students. Denominations with chaplains assigned to Duke include Baptist, Catholic, Episcopal, Jewish, Lutheran, Methodist, Presbyterian, United Campus Christian Fellowship. Places of worship available on campus for major faiths.

Varsity Sports. Men (Div.I): Baseball, Basketball, Cross Country, Fencing, Football, Golf, Lacrosse, Soccer, Swimming, Tennis, Track, Wrestling. Women (Div.I): Basketball, Cross Country, Fencing, Field Hockey, Golf, Swimming, Tennis, Track, Volleyball.

Campus Life. Student social life and regulations are under virtually complete student control with a few limitations. Smoking is restricted in some areas, including Medical Center. Alcohol limited to those over 21; public occasions must be registered and alternative beverages provided. Illegal drugs are "strictly prohibited." Students allowed to live off campus after freshman year; but on-campus housing available all four years. Although Greeks dominate campus social life and there is little interaction with independents, the latter are numerous enough to make up a separate world. Wide range of intellectual, cultural, and recreational activities offered on campus. Cultural facilities of U. of North Carolina at Chapel Hill, North Carolina State U., and North Carolina Central University at Durham, all within 25 miles. Student leader reports that "the strong extracurricular environment enables students to learn as much outside as in the classroom." Intervisitation allowed with consent of roommate; quiet hours apply except weekend evenings.

About 16% of men, 41% of women live in traditional dormitories; 32% of men, 36% of women in coed dormitories; 27% of men, 23% of women live in university-owned apartments, off-campus housing or commute. All undergraduate students are guaranteed housing. Sexes segregated in coed dormitories by wing or floor. There are 21 fraternities, 13 sororities on campus which about 40% of men, 40% of women join. About 25% of men live in fraternities, sororities provide no residential facilities. Less than 1% of resident students leave campus on weekends.

Annual Costs. Tuition and fees, $17,160; room and board, $5,550. University reports some scholarships awarded on the basis of academic merit alone. *Meeting Costs:* university offers deferred tuition payments, guaranteed tuition plan (four years at freshman rate), SHARE, work-study.

Duquesne University

Pittsburgh, Pennsylvania 15282 **(412) 434-6220**

A church-related, urban university, conducted by the Congregation of the Holy Ghost, Duquesne is located on a 40-acre campus in a city of 520,100. Most convenient major airport: Greater Pittsburgh International.

Founded: 1878
Affiliation: Roman Catholic
UG Enrollment: 1,754 M, 2,254 W (full-time); 299 M, 322 W (part-time)
Total Enrollment: 8,015
Cost: $10K–$20K
% Receiving Financial Aid: 78%
Admission: Selective
Application Deadline: July 1

Admission is selective for College of Liberal Arts and Sciences, schools of Business Administration, Music. For all schools, 89% of applicants accepted, 43% of these actually enroll; 51% of freshmen graduate in top fifth of high school class, 74% in top two-fifths. Average freshman scores, according to most recent data available: SAT, 400–520 verbal, 440–590 mathematical; 34% of freshmen score above 500 on verbal, 5% above 600; 56% score above 500 on mathematical, 23% above 600; ACT, 20–25 composite, 18–26 mathematical.

Required: SAT (preferred), or ACT, audition theory test for music; interview welcomed. *Non-academic factors* considered in admissions: special talents (for music school), leadership qualities. *Entrance programs:* early decision, early admission, advanced placement. About 45% of entering students from private schools. *Apply* by July 1; rolling admissions. *Transfers* welcome.

Academic Environment. Pressures for academic achievement appear moderate. Student body characterized by administration as equally concerned with professional/occupational goals and scholarly/intellectual interests. Curriculum in Liberal Arts and Sciences substitutes required area of study for specified courses; numerous distribution requirements. *Undergraduate studies* offered in 6 schools listed above. *Majors offered* in Liberal Arts and Sciences in addition to usual studies include computer science, journalism, music therapy.

About 53% of students entering as freshmen graduate within four years, 71% eventually; 11% of freshmen do not return for sophomore year. *Special programs:* CLEP, independent study, study abroad, honors, 3-year degree, individualized majors, credit by examination, cross-registration with 8 other Pittsburgh colleges and universities, 3–2 engineering. *Calendar:* semester, summer school.

Undergraduate degrees conferred (915). 26% were in Business and Management, 20% were in Health Sciences, 18% were in Education, 10% were in Communications, 6% were in Social Sciences, 4% were in Psychology, 3% were in Letters, 3% were in Protective Services, remainder in 8 other fields.

Graduates Career Data. According to most recent data available, full-time graduate or professional study pursued by 44% of students immediately after graduation; 2% enter medical school; 8% enter law school; 12% enter business school. Law schools typically enrolling largest numbers of graduates include Duquesne, Dickinson, U. of Pittsburgh; business schools include Duquesne. *Careers in business and industry* pursued by 54% of graduates. Corporations typically hiring largest numbers of graduates include Westinghouse, Pittsburgh National, Mellon Bank, USX.

Faculty. About 78% of faculty hold PhD or equivalent.

Student Body. University seeks a national student body; 83% of students from in state; 90% Middle Atlantic; 138 foreign students 1990–91. An estimated 12% of students reported as Protestant, 75% Catholic, 2% Jewish; 2% Black, 1% Hispanic, 1% Asian, according to most recent data available.

Religious Orientation. Duquesne is a church-related institution; 9 credits total required in theology and philosophy. No courses or religious services compulsory for students of other faiths. Protestant and Jewish clergymen available through chaplain's office. Religious clubs on campus include Hillel, Association of Eastern Christian Students, St. Paul's Seminary Guild. Places of worship available on campus for Catholics, in immediate community for all faiths.

Varsity Sports. Men (Div.I): Baseball, Basketball, Cross Country, Football (III), Golf, Rifle, Swimming & Diving, Tennis. Women (Div.I): Basketball, Cross Country, Golf, Rifle, Swimming & Diving, Tennis, Track, Volleyball.

Campus Life. Both student and administration representatives report active role of undergraduates as voting members of "virtually every university committee." Limited intervisitation only in freshmen women's dorms. Alcohol (beer) limited to those over 21. No smoking in public areas. Use of drugs results in disciplinary and/or criminal action.

About 41% of men, 41% of women live in traditional dormitories; 49% each of men, women commute. Freshmen given preference in college housing if all students cannot be accommodated. There are 8 fraternities, 8 sororities on campus which about 13% of men, 14% of women join; 10% each men, women live in fraternities and sororities.

Annual Costs. Tuition and fees, $11,320; room and board, $5,114. About 78% of students receive financial aid; assistance is typically divided 35% scholarship, 55% loan, 10% work. University reports some scholarships awarded on the basis of academic merit alone. *Meeting Costs:* University offers deferred payment plan, Knight Plan, PLUS Loans.

Dyke College

Cleveland, Ohio 44115

A private, independent four-year college specializing in business-related programs. Dyke offers diploma, certificate, associates and baccalaureate degree programs with various study options ranging from full day classes to evening/weekend programs, accelerated management degree, external degree, and cooperative education programs.

Founded: 1848 **Affiliation:** Independent

D'Youville College

Buffalo, New York 14201 **(716) 881-7600**

Founded as liberal arts college for women by the Grey Nuns, D'Youville is now an independent, co-educational institution under predominantly lay control, located in a city of 462,800. Most convenient major airport: Buffalo.

Founded: 1908
Affiliation: Independent
UG Enrollment: 290 M, 784 W (full-time); 66 M, 270 W (part-time)
Total Enrollment: 1,796
Cost: < $10K
% Receiving Financial Aid: 92%
Admission: Non-selective
Application Deadline: Aug. 1

Admission. Graduates of approved high schools with 16 units in college preparatory subjects and GPA of 2.0 or better, and combined SAT of 800 or better eligible; requirements for physical therapy, occupational therapy, dietetics, and nursing slightly higher; 60% of applicants accepted, 24% of these actually enroll; 18% graduate in top fifth of high school class, 47% in top second fifth. Average freshman scores: SAT, 435 verbal, 497 mathematical; 20% above 500 verbal, 1% above 600; 55% above 500 mathematical, 10% above 600; ACT, 22 composite. *Required:* SAT or ACT; interview recommended. Criteria considered in admissions, in order of importance: high school academic record, standardized test scores, recommendations, extra curricular activities; other factors considered: special talents. About 15% of freshmen from parochial schools, 5% private schools. *Apply* by: August 1 for Fall, rolling admissions. *Transfers* welcome; 243 enrolled 1993–94.

Academic Environment. Degrees offered: bachelors, masters. *Majors offered* include physician assistant, dual degree programs. Core requirements include 5 courses in humanities, 2 each in English and natural sciences, 1 each in philosophy or religion, history, sociology, psychology, economics or political science, math or computer science. Average undergraduate class size: 30. About 19% of students entering as freshmen graduate within four years, 38% eventually; 77% of freshmen return for sophomore year. *Special programs:* CLEP, independent study, study abroad, individualized majors, 5-year BS/MS programs in dietetics, physical therapy, and occupational therapy. *Calendar:* semester, summer school.

Undergraduate degrees conferred (169). 31% were in Health Sciences, 24% were in Allied Health, 17% were in Education, 16% were in Business and Management, 4% were in Public Affairs, remainder in 5 other fields.

Graduates Career Data. Advanced studies pursued by 12% of students; majority of students pursue careers in education and health related fields. About 93% of 1992–93 graduates employed. Fields typically hiring the largest number of graduates include physical therapy, occupational therapy.

Faculty. About 59% of faculty hold PhD or equivalent. About 57% of teaching faculty are female; 5% minority.

Student Body. College does not seek a national student body; 76% of students from New York; 79% Middle Atlantic, 3% New England, 18% Foreign. Average age of undergraduate student: 24.

Religious Orientation. D'Youville is a college with a Catholic heritage. Places of worship available on campus for Catholics, in immediate community for 3 major faiths.

Varsity Sports. Men (Div.III): Basketball. Women (Div.III): Basketball, Volleyball.

Campus Life. Campus has history of involvement in city projects and affairs. About 75% of women, 25% of men live in coed dormitories; rest live in off-campus housing or commute. Freshmen given preference in college housing if all students cannot be accommodated. Intervisitation in men's and women's dormitory rooms limited. There are no fraternities or sororities.

Annual Costs. Tuition and fees, $8,720; room and board, $4,130; estimated $1,330 other, exclusive of travel. About 92% of students receive financial aid; average amount of assistance, $5,500. Assistance is typically divided 73% scholarship, 10% loan, 17% work, according to most recent data available. College reports 76 scholarships awarded for academic merit alone, 21 for special talents, 330 for need.

Earlham College

Richmond, Indiana 47374 **(317) 983-1600**
toll-free, (800) EARLHAM

Earlham is a small, midwestern Quaker college that has attracted a national student body with its traditional "Living Fellowship," which emphasizes teaching and individual self-development. The 800-acre campus is located on the outskirts of a community of 40,000, 40 miles west of Dayton and 70 miles east of Indianapolis. Most convenient major airport: Dayton, Ohio.

Founded: 1847
Affiliation: Society of Friends
Total Enrollment: 1,144 M, W (full-time)
Cost: $10K–$20K
% Receiving Financial Aid: 72%
Admission: Very (+) Selective
Application Deadline: Feb. 15

Admission is very (+) selective. About 74% of applicants accepted, 36% of these actually enroll; 54% of freshmen graduate in top fifth of high school class, 83% in top two-fifths. Average freshman scores, according to most recent data available: SAT, middle fifty percent range, 500–620 verbal, 490–620 mathematical; ACT 26 composite. *Required:* SAT or ACT. *Non-academic factors* considered in admissions: special talents. *Entrance programs:* early decision, early admission, deferred admission. About 28% of entering freshmen from private or parochial schools. *Apply* by February 15. *Transfers* welcome.

Academic Environment. Campus climate is characterized as "intellectual" rather than merely "academic." Students participate in decisions concerning curriculum as well as faculty hiring and promotion. Student leader notes that "students carry a great deal of responsibility, and usually exercise it rationally." Academic program is rigorous, but is tempered by college's commitment to cooperative learning. Varied opportunities for group tutorials, independent study, study abroad (60% study in 20 countries). Off-campus internships related to academic interests for upperclassmen. Administration reports 50% of courses required for graduation are elective; distribution requirements, however, fairly numerous: of 36 term courses needed for graduation, 4 in humanities core program, 2 in social sciences, 1 in fine arts, 4 in natural sciences; competency in physical education, 3 terms or proficiency in a foreign language. *Degree:* AB. *Majors offered* include usual arts and sciences, African-American studies, computer science, Japanese studies, professional option, fine arts, human development and social relations, International studies, management, peace and global studies, museum studies, women's studies.

About 75–80% of students entering as freshmen graduate eventually; 9% of freshmen do not return for sophomore year. *Special programs:* CLEP, independent study, study abroad, undergraduate research, individualized majors, programs of GLCA, freshman seminars, tutorials, study at Merrill–Palmer Institute, winter term programs (in Washington and New York), off-campus marine biology studies (U. of South Florida) and tropical ecology (Caribbean), Center for East Asian Language and Area Studies, Wilderness pre-terms, academic pre-terms, intensive French, German, Japanese and Spanish programs, Southwest Field Studies winter term off-campus, 3–2 programs in engineering, forestry, architecture, business, nursing. *Calendar:* 3–3. *Miscellaneous:* Phi Beta Kappa.

Undergraduate degrees conferred (244). 22% were in Social Sciences, 14% were in Letters, 13% were in Life Sciences, 9% were in Foreign Languages, 8% were in Physical Sciences, 7% were in Multi/Interdisciplinary Studies, 6% were in Area and Ethnic Studies, 5% were in Visual and Performing Arts, 5% were in Psychology, 5% were in Business and Management, 3% were in Philosophy and Religion, remainder in 3 other fields.

Graduates Career Data. According to most recent data available, full-time graduate study pursued immediately after graduation by 28% of students (50% within five years of graduation); 4% enter law school. Law schools typically enrolling largest numbers of graduates include Ohio State, U. of Michigan. *Careers in business and industry* pursued by 17% of graduates. Career Counseling Center is described by administration source as "active." Alumni reported as helpful in both career guidance and job placement.

Faculty. About 88% of teaching faculty hold doctorate or equivalent.

Student Body. College seeks a national student body; 17% from in state; 25% from North Central, 33% from Middle Atlantic, 12% from South, 15% from New England. An estimated 40% of students reported as Protestant, 10% Catholic, 4% Jewish, 44% unaffiliated; 4% as Black, 2% Hispanic, 2% Asian, 16% other minority, according to most recent data available.

Religious Orientation. Earlham is a church-related institution, affiliated with the Society of Friends but nonsectarian in policy and practice; "no discrimination in admission on the basis of religion." Two courses in philosophy and/or religion required of all students; voluntary attendance at convocations which sometimes deal with religious themes. Religious clubs on campus include Young Friends, Jewish Students Collective, Christian Fellowship, Deputations, Bahai Club, Meetinghouse Cabinet. Places of worship available in immediate community for 3 major faiths.

Varsity Sports. Men (NCAC, Div.III): Baseball, Basketball, Cross Country, Football, Golf, Soccer, Tennis, Track. Women (NCAC): Basketball, Cross Country, Field Hockey, Lacrosse, Soccer, Softball, Tennis, Track, Volleyball.

Campus Life. Campus operates by consensus with a strong Quaker foundation. There is considerable student/faculty/administration interaction. Administration source refers to the "openness, friendliness, and informality" that characterize campus life. Residence in dormitories expected of freshmen; most sophomores, many juniors and seniors also living in dormitories. Smoking discouraged on-campus; alcohol and drugs not permitted on-campus. Located an hour away from any major cultural center, college seeks to overcome isolation with moderately active calendar of cultural and intellectual events.

About 63% of students live in coed dormitories; 20% live in college-related off-campus housing, 17% live in other off-campus housing. Freshmen given preference in college housing if all students cannot be accommodated. Sexes segregated in coed dormitories either by wing, floor or room. There are no fraternities or sororities. A "very small" number of students leave campus on weekends.

Annual Costs. Tuition and fees, $15,326; room and board, $4,056. About 72% of students receive financial aid. Assistance is typically divided 84% scholarship, 12% loan, 5% work. College reports some scholarships awarded on the basis of academic merit alone.

East Carolina University

Greenville, North Carolina 27858-4353 **(919) 757-6640**

A state-supported institution, located in a city of 50,000, 86 miles east of Raleigh. Most convenient major airport: Pitt-Greenville, or Raleigh-Durham.

Founded: 1907
Affiliation: State
UG Enrollment: 5,875 M, 7,293 W (full-time); 709 M, 893 W (part-time)
Total Enrollment: 17,729
Cost: < $10K
Admission: Non-selective
Application Deadline: March 15

Admission. Graduates of accredited high schools with 20 units eligible; 69% of applicants accepted, 38% of these actually enroll. About 35% of freshmen graduate in top fifth of high school class, 74% in top two-fifths. Average freshman SAT scores: 435 M, 434 W verbal, 503 M, 473 W mathematical; 17% above 500 verbal, 2% above 600; 44% above 500 mathematical, 8% above 600. *Required:* SAT or ACT; minimum H.S. GPA. Criteria considered in admissions, in order of importance: high school academic record, standardized test scores; other factors considered: special talents, diverse student body. *Out-of-state* freshman applicants: university welcomes students from out of state. State limits out-of-state enrollment to 18% of entering class. Requirements for out-of-state applicants; slightly higher SAT scores and predicted grade average. About 56% of applicants accepted, 30% enroll. States from which most out-of-state students are drawn include Virginia, Maryland, New Jersey. Entrance programs: advanced placement. *Apply* by: March 15; rolling admissions. Transfers welcome; 1,355 enrolled 1993–94.

Academic Environment. Degrees offered: bachelors, masters, doctoral. Core requirements include 43 semester hours including English, library science, sciences, social sciences, mathematics, humanities, fine arts, health and physical education. Average undergraduate class size: 44% under 20, 40% between 20–40, 16% over 40. About 16% of students entering as freshmen graduate within four years, 50% eventually; 78% of freshmen return for sophomore year.

Special programs: independent study, study abroad, internships, honors. *Calendar:* semester, summer school.
Undergraduate degrees conferred (2,207). 22% were in Education, 18% were in Business and Management, 8% were in Social Sciences, 6% were in Health Sciences, 6% were in Visual and Performing Arts, 6% were in Home Economics, 5% were in Psychology, 5% were in Communications, 4% were in Letters, 3% were in Parks and Recreation, 3% were in Life Sciences, remainder in 10 other fields.
Faculty. About 80% of faculty hold PhD or equivalent. About 33% of teaching faculty are female; 8% minority.
Student Body. University seeks a national student body; 85% of students from in state; 93% South, 5% Middle Atlantic,less than 1% Foreign. An estimated 72% of students reported as Protestant, 13% Catholic, 10% unaffiliated, 6% other; 9% Black, 3% other minority. Average age of undergraduate student: 22.
Varsity Sports. Men (Div.IA): Baseball, Basketball, Cross Country, Diving, Football, Golf, Soccer, Swimming, Tennis, Track. Women (Div.IA): Basketball, Cross Country, Diving, Fastpitch Softball, Soccer, Swimming, Tennis, Track, Volleyball.
Campus Life. About 16% of men, 18% of women live in traditional dormitories; 9% of men, 10% of women live in coed dormitories; 73% of men, 70% of women commute. There are 22 fraternities, 12 sororities on campus which about 15% of men, 15% women join; 2% of men, 2% of women live in fraternities and sororities.
Annual Costs. Tuition and fees, $1,366 (out-of-state, $7,432); room and board, $3,150. Average financial aid package, $5,586. Assistance is typically divided 28% scholarship, 17% grant, 54% loan, 1% work. University reports 90 scholarships awarded for academic merit alone, 459 for special talents; none based on need alone.

East Central University

Ada, Oklahoma 74820 (405) 332-8000

A state-supported institution, located in a community of 20,000, 85 miles southeast of Oklahoma City. Most convenient major airport: Will Rogers International (Oklahoma City).

Founded: 1909
Affiliation: State
UG Enrollment: 1,376 M, 1,909 W (full-time); 217 M, 339 W (part-time)
Total Enrollment: 4,257
Cost: < $10K
% Receiving Financial Aid: 75%
Admission: Non-selective

Admission. Oklahoma graduates of accredited high schools with 2.7 average, rank in top two-thirds of class, or score of 16 on ACT eligible. About 29% of freshmen graduate in top quarter of high school class; 36% in top half. Average freshman ACT scores 19.97 composite. *Required:* SAT or ACT. *Out-of-state* freshman applicants: university welcomes students from out of state. State does not limit out-of-state enrollment. Requirement for out-of-state applicants: 2.0 GPA from last school attended. About 90% of applicants accepted, 84% enroll. *Entrance programs:* early admission. *Apply* before enrollment. *Transfers* welcome.
Academic Environment. Degrees offered: bachelors, masters. About 14% of general education requirements for graduation are elective; distribution requirements fairly numerous. About 53% of students entering as freshmen graduate eventually; 41% of freshmen do not return for sophomore year, according to most recent data available. *Majors offered* in addition to usual studies include business administration, accounting, elementary education, nursing, engineering technology. *Special programs:* CLEP, independent study, Ardmore Higher Education Center, Westfield Exchange Programs. *Calendar:* semester, summer school.
Undergraduate degrees conferred (591). 26% were in Education, 21% were in Business and Management, 8% were in Health Sciences, 6% were in Engineering, 5% were in Social Sciences, 5% were in Protective Services, 5% were in Life Sciences, 3% were in Computer and Engineering Related Technology, 3% were in Letters, 3% were in Public Affairs, 3% were in Mathematics, remainder in 8 other fields.
Graduates Career Data. According to most recent data available, full-time graduate or professional study pursued by 12% of students immediately after graduation. *Careers in business and industry* pursued by 60% of graduates.
Faculty. About 64% of faculty hold PhD or equivalent. About 60% of undergraduate classes taught by tenured faculty. About 28% of teaching faculty are female.
Varsity Sports. Men (NAIA, Div. I): Baseball, Basketball, Football, Golf, Tennis, Track. Women (NAIA, Div. I): Basketball, Tennis.
Student Body. University seeks a national student body; 98% of students from Oklahoma. An estimated 2% of students reported as Black, 3% Native American, 2% other minority, according to most recent data available. Average age of undergraduate student: 25.
Campus Life. About 60% men, 40% women live in coed dormitories; rest live in off-campus housing or commute. There are 4 fraternities, 3 sororities on campus which about 8% of men, 8% of women join. About 80% of resident students leave campus on weekends.
Annual Costs. Tuition and fees, $1,490 (out-of-state, $3,553); room and board, $2,068; estimated $150–250 other, exclusive of travel. About 75% of students receive financial aid; average amount of assistance, $2,000. University reports some scholarships awarded on the basis of academic merit alone.

East Coast Bible College

Charlotte, North Carolina 28214

A small church-related college, offering associate and baccalaureate degree programs. Campus is located 7 miles west of Charlotte.

Founded: 1976
Affiliation: Church of God

East Stroudsburg University of Pennsylvania

East Stroudsburg, Pennsylvania 18301 (717) 424-3211

A state-supported institution located in a town of 7,900, 80 miles west of New York City. Most convenient major airport: Allentown-Bethlehem-Easton.

Founded: 1893
Affiliation: State
UG Enrollment: 1,731 M, 2,216 W (full-time); 283 M, 328 W (part-time)
Total Enrollment: 5,403
Cost: < $10K
% Receiving Financial Aid: 75%
Admission: Non-selective
Application Deadline: March 1

Admission. Graduates of approved high schools eligible; 58% of applicants accepted, 37% of these actually enroll. About 18% of freshmen graduate in top fifth of high school class, 57% in top two-fifths. Average freshman SAT scores: middle 50% range, 380–460 verbal, 420–520 mathematical. *Required:* SAT or ACT. Criteria considered in admissions, in order of importance: high school academic record, standardized test scores, recommendations, extracurricular activities; other factors considered: special talents, alumni children, diverse student body. *Out-of-state* freshman applicants: university welcomes students from out of state. State limits out-of-state enrollment. No special requirements for out-of-state applicants. About 47% of applicants accepted, 28% enroll. *Apply* by March 1. *Transfers* welcome; 439 enrolled 1993–94.
Academic Environment. Degrees offered: associates, bachelors, masters. *Majors offered* include usual arts and sciences, hospitality management, geography, speech pathology (and audiology), programs in both elementary and secondary education, physical education, and health sciences, environmental studies, hotel, restaurant and tourism management. Core requirements include English composition, physical education, 15 credits in each of Arts and Sciences, Social Sciences, 9 credits electives. Average undergraduate class size: 41% of classes under 20, 47% between 20–40, 12% over 40.

About 25% of students entering as freshmen graduate within four years, 50% eventually; 34% of freshmen do not return for sophomore year. *Special programs:* CLEP, independent study, honors, National Student Exchange, 3–2 programs in engineering, pharmacy, internships available in most fields. Calendar: semester, summer school.

Undergraduate degrees conferred (807). 34% were in Education, 14% were in Business and Management, 12% were in Social Sciences, 6% were in Life Sciences, 6% were in Letters, 5% were in Psychology, 4% were in Communications Technologies, 3% were in Health Sciences, 3% were in Computer and Engineering Related Technology, 3% were in Parks and Recreation, remainder in 7 other fields.
Graduates Career Data. According to most recent data available, full-time graduate or professional study pursued by 9% of students immediately after graduation. *Careers in business and industry* pursued by 56% of graduates. Career Development Services include career counseling, resume/interview workshops, on-campus interviewing, job listings, library resources.
Faculty. About 65% of faculty hold PhD or equivalent. About 65% of undergraduate classes taught by tenured faculty. About 37% of teaching faculty are female; 6% Black, 2% Hispanic, 3% other ethnic minorities.
Student Body. College welcomes a national student body; 78% of students from in state; 98% Middle Atlantic, 1% foreign. *Minority group students:* special recruitment, financial aid package; reduced academic load and some tutoring; "particular attention to satisfactory adjustment."
Varsity Sports. Men (Div.II): Baseball, Basketball, Cross Country, Football, Soccer, Tennis, Track, Volleyball, Wrestling(Div. I). Women (Div.II): Basketball, Cross Country, Field Hockey, Lacrosse, Soccer, Softball, Tennis, Track, Volleyball.
Campus Life. About 45% of men, 47% of women live in traditional or coed dormitories; rest live in off-campus housing or commute. Freshmen given preference in college housing if all students cannot be accommodated. Intervisitation in men's and women's dormitory rooms limited. There are 9 fraternities, 8 sororities, which less than 10% of students join; less than 1% of men live in fraternities, sororities provide no housing facilities. About 50% of students leave campus on weekends. .
Annual Costs. Tuition and fees, $3,664 (out-of-state, $8,062); room and board, $3,222. About 75% of students receive financial aid; average amount of assistance, $4,000. Assistance is typically divided 3% scholarship, 33% grant, 56% loan, 8% work. College reports some scholarships awarded on the basis of academic merit alone. *Meeting Costs:* university offers Academic Management Services.

East Tennessee State University

Johnson City, Tennessee 37614 **(615) 929-4112**

A state-supported university, located in the foothills of the southern Appalachian mountains, in a city of 40,000, 100 miles northeast of Knoxville. Most convenient major airport: Tri Cities Regional.

Founded: 1909
Affiliation: State
UG Enrollment: 2,931 M, 3,775 W (full-time); 951 M, 1,689 W (part-time)
Total Enrollment: 11,272
Cost: < $10K
% Receiving Financial Aid: 47%
Admission: Non-selective
Application Deadline: Aug. 1

Admission. Graduates of accredited high schools with 14 required high school units and GPA of 2.3 or better or minimum ACT score of 19, or age 21 or older eligible; 82% of applicants accepted, 48% of these actually enroll. About 29% of freshman graduate in top fifth of high school class, 59% in top two-fifths. Average freshman scores: SAT, 400 verbal, 450 mathematical. *Required:* SAT or ACT, 14 required high school units. *Out-of-state* freshman applicants: university welcomes out-of-state students. State does not limit out-of-state enrollment. Requirements for out-of-state applicants: no probationary admission, satisfactory ACT or SAT scores. States from which most out of state students are drawn include Virginia, North Carolina, South Carolina. *Entrance programs:* early admission. *Apply* by: August 1; rolling admissions. *Transfers* welcome; 592 enrolled 1993–94.
Academic Environment. Degrees offered: associates, bachelors, masters, doctoral. General education requirements for graduation vary with program; distribution requirements fairly numerous. Average undergraduate class size: 40% under 20, 43% between 20–40, 17% over 40. About 20% of entering students graduate within four years, 40% eventually; 75% of freshmen return for sophomore year. *Special programs:* study abroad, cross registration with Milligan College, cooperative work-study. Adult programs: Bachelor of General Studies - no specific major. *Calendar:* semester, summer school.
Undergraduate degrees conferred (1204). 27% were in Business and Management, 17% were in Education, 8% were in Health Sciences, 7% were in Social Sciences, 7% were in Engineering and Engineering Related Technology, 5% were in Psychology, 4% were in Protective Services, 4% were in Communications, 4% were in Letters, 3% were in Public Affairs, 3% were in Life Sciences, 3% were in Home Economics, remainder in 10 other fields.
Graduates Career Data. Advanced studies pursued by 12% of students; 4% enter business school, 4% enter medical or dental school, 2% enter law school. About 92% of 1992–93 graduates employed. Fields typically hiring largest numbers of graduates include nursing, education, business, technical, allied health, liberal arts. Career Development Services include computer job matching, job data base access, resume design, cooperative education, job search seminars, job fairs, alumni job network.
Faculty. About 82% of faculty hold PhD or equivalent. About 60% of undergraduate classes taught by tenured faculty. About 35% of teaching faculty are female, 7% minority.
Student Body. About 86% of students from in state; 97% South; 1% Foreign. An estimated 4% of students reported as Black, 6% other minority; 75% Protestant, 10% Catholic, 1% Jewish, 1% Muslim, 10% unaffiliated, 3% other. Average age of undergraduate student: 25.
Varsity Sports. Men (Div.I): Baseball, Basketball, Cross Country, Football (IAA), Golf, Tennis, Track. Women (Div.I): Basketball, Cross Country, Golf, Tennis, Track, Volleyball.
Campus Life. East Tennessee State is primarily a commuter school. About 18% of men, 16% of women live in traditional dormitories; no coed dormitories; rest commute. There are 8 fraternities, 4 sororities on campus which about 5% of men, 6% of women join; 2% of men live in fraternities; sororities provide no residence facilities. About 60% of resident students leave campus on weekends.
Annual Costs. Tuition and fees, $1,680 (out-of-state, $5,480); room and board, $3,120; estimated $2,400 other, exclusive of travel. About 47% of students receive financial aid, average amount of assistance, $3,167. Assistance is typically divided 7% scholarship, 43% grant, 43% loan, 7% work. University reports 347 scholarships awarded for academic merit alone, 457 for special talents, 158 athletic scholarships awarded.

East Texas Baptist University

Marshall, Texas 75670 **(214) 935-7963**

A church-related college, located in a community of 25,000, 35 miles west of Shreveport, Louisiana. Most convenient major airports: Shreveport (LA), Dallas (TX).

Founded: 1912
Affiliation: Southern Baptist
Total Enrollment: 957 M, W (full-time)
Cost: < $10K
Admission: Non-selective
Application Deadline: Rolling

Admission. Graduates of accredited high schools with 16 units (10 in academic subjects) who rank in top half of class or score 15 on ACT composite admitted; others with lower ACT scores are usually given conditional admission. *Required:* SAT or ACT. *Apply:* rolling admissions. *Transfers* welcome.
Academic Environment. *Degrees:* AB, BAS, BS, BM. About 10% of general education requirements for graduation are elective; distribution requirements fairly numerous. About 30% of students entering as freshmen graduate eventually; 45% of freshmen do not return for sophomore year. *Special programs:* CLEP, independent study, honors, study skills. *Calendar:* 4–1–4, May term, summer school.
Undergraduate degrees conferred (150). 25% were in Education, 24% were in Business and Management, 20% were in Philosophy and Religion, 11% were in Social Sciences, 8% were in Letters, 4% were in Life Sciences, remainder in 6 other fields.
Varsity Sports. Men (NAIA): Baseball, Basketball, Golf, Tennis. Women (NAIA): Basketball.

Student Body. College does not seek a national student body; 87% of students from in state; 95% South.
Religious Orientation. East Texas Baptist is a church-related institution; 9 hours of religion, attendance at biweekly chapel services required of freshmen, sophomore, and transfer students.
Campus Life. About 52% of men, 61% of women live in traditional dormitories; no coed dormitories; rest live in off-campus housing or commute. No intervisitation in men's or women's dormitory rooms. There are no fraternities or sororities. About 40% of students leave campus on weekends.
Annual Costs. Tuition and fees, $5,100; room and board, $2,780. *Meeting Costs:* college offers Deferred Payment Plan without interest.

East Texas State University

Commerce, Texas 75428 (214) 886-5081

A state-supported university, located in a rural town of 10,000, 65 miles northeast of Dallas. East Texas also operates the Metroplex Center in Dallas which offers graduate programs in education and business. Most convenient major airport: Dallas-Fort Worth.

Founded: 1889
Affiliation: State
UG Enrollment: 1,744 M, 2,271 W (full-time); 1,350 M, W (part-time)
Total Enrollment: 8,038
Cost: < $10K
Admission: Non-selective
Application Deadline: 2 weeks before term

Admission. Graduates of accredited high schools admitted on basis of high school grades and ACT composite score of 18 or combined SAT score of 800; 65% of applicants accepted, 50% of these actually enroll. About 25% of freshmen graduate in top fifth of high school class, 51% in top two-fifths. Average freshman scores: SAT, 415 M, 408 W verbal, 493 M, 442 W mathematical; ACT, 21.5 M, 20.8 W composite. *Required:* SAT or ACT. Criteria considered in admissions, in order of importance: high school academic record, standardized test scores. *Out-of-state* freshman applicants: university welcomes out-of-state students. State does not limit out-of-state enrollment. *Entrance programs:* early decision, early admission, midyear admission. *Apply* by 2 weeks prior to term. *Transfers* welcome; 1,073 enrolled 1992.
Academic Environment. Degrees offered: bachelors, masters, doctoral. Core requirements include 6 semester hours each of English Composition, history, physical science, Capstones; 3 each of mathematics, speech; 8 of sciences, and 4 of physical education. Unusual, new or notable majors include BS in printing. About 17% of students entering as freshmen graduate within four years, 35% eventually. *Special programs:* CLEP, independent study, honors, study abroad, undergraduate research, individualized majors, field-based study, cross registration with U. of North Texas, ETSU, and Texarkana. *Calendar:* semester, summer school.
Undergraduate degrees conferred (1010). 44% were in Education, 18% were in Business and Management, 6% were in Social Sciences, 5% were in Psychology, 5% were in Visual and Performing Arts, 3% were in Letters, 3% were in Computer and Engineering Related Technology, remainder in 15 other fields.
Faculty. About 83% of full-time faculty hold PhD or equivalent. About 28% of teaching faculty are female; 4% Black, 2% Hispanic, 3% other ethnic minorities.
Varsity Sports. Men (NCAA/Div.II): Basketball, Cross Country, Football, Golf, Track. Women (NCAA/Div.II): Basketball, Cross Country, Golf, Track, Volleyball.
Student Body. University seeks a national student body; 96% of students from in state; 2% foreign. An estimated 12% of students reported as Black, 3% Hispanic, 2% other minority.
Campus Life. About 10% each of men, women live in traditional dormitories; 4% of men, 3% of women live in coed dormitories; rest live in off-campus housing or commute, according to most recent data available. Intervisitation in men's and women's dormitory rooms limited. There are 9 fraternities, 8 sororities on campus. Freshmen given preference in college housing if all students cannot be accommodated. About 70% of resident students leave campus on weekends.
Annual Costs. Tuition and fees, $1,596 (out-of-state, $5,676); room and board, $3,500. University reports some scholarships awarded on the basis of academic merit alone.

Eastern College

St. Davids, Pennsylvania 19087-3696 (215) 341-5810

A small, church-related, liberal arts college, Eastern College is located on a 100-acre campus on Philadelphia's Main Line, 12 miles northwest of the city. Most convenient major airport: Philadelphia International.

Founded: 1932
Affiliation: American Baptist
UG Enrollment: 423 M, 634 W (full-time); 93 M, 262 W (part-time)
Total Enrollment: 1,842
Cost: $10K–$20K
% Receiving Financial Aid: 85%
Admission: Non-selective

Admission. High school graduates who rank in top half of class, eligible; 77% of applicants accepted, 47% of these actually enroll; 33% of freshmen graduate in top fifth of high school class, 62% in top two-fifths. Average freshman SAT scores: 452 verbal, 479 mathematical; 33% above 500 verbal, 6% above 600, 1% above 700; 44% above 500 mathematical, 14% above 600, 1% above 700; ACT, 23 composite. *Required:* SAT or ACT, essay. Criteria considered in admissions, in order of importance: high school academic record, class rank, standardized test scores, writing sample, extra curricular activities, recommendations; other factors considered: special talents, alumni children, religious affiliation and/or commitment. *Entrance programs:* deferred admission, early admission, midyear admission. *Apply* by: no specific deadline. *Transfers* welcome; 82 enrolled 1993–94.
Academic Environment. Degrees offered: associates, bachelors, masters. *Majors offered* in addition to usual arts and sciences include BSN for RN's only, organizational management, school health services. Core requirements include Biblical foundations, theological/philosophical foundations, mathematics, English writing, health and wellness, symbolic language, literature and the arts, cross-cultural learning, our heritage, government and economics, the individual and social systems, natural sciences, and a capstone. Students list faculty accessibility, small classes, and Christian environment as strengths of the college. Average undergraduate class size: 30.

About 43% of students entering as freshmen graduate within four years, 50% eventually; 73% of freshmen return for sophomore year. *Special programs:* CLEP, independent study, study abroad, honors, undergraduate research, optional winter term, individualized majors, cross registration with Cabrini and Rosemont, internships, Degree Completion Program. Adult programs: organizational management for students at least 25 years of age with demonstrable work experience and a minimum of 60 transferable semester hours. *Calendar:* semester, summer school.
Undergraduate degrees conferred (189). 40% were in Business and Management, 19% were in Education, 10% were in Psychology, 8% were in Social Sciences, 6% were in Health Sciences, 5% were in Letters, 4% were in Public Affairs, 3% were in Theology, remainder in 5 other fields.
Graduates Career Data. Advanced studies pursued by 25% of students; 10% of those enter law school; 90% other. About 93% of 1992–93 graduates employed. Career Development Services include group and individual counseling, careers library, on-campus recruitment, resume workshops, resume preparation. Alumni reported as active in career guidance.
Faculty. About 38% of faculty hold PhD or equivalent. About 46% of teaching faculty are female; 8% Black, 3% Hispanic, 2% other minority.
Student Body. College seeks a national student body; 69% of students from in state; 89% Middle Atlantic, 4% New England, 3% Foreign. An estimated 34% of students reported as Protestant, 17% Catholic, 25% unaffiliated, 23% other; 11% as Black, 2% Asian, 2% Hispanic, 2% other minority. Average age of undergraduate student: 26 (including non-traditional undergraduate students).
Religious Orientation. Eastern College is a church-related institution; 9 hours of religion required. Attendance at Sunday services urged.
Varsity Sports. Men (NCCAA/PAC): Baseball, Basketball, Cross Country, Soccer, Tennis, Volleyball. Women (NCCAA/PAC): Basketball, Cross Country, Field Hockey, Lacrosse, Soccer, Softball, Tennis, Volleyball.

Campus Life. Moderately strict rules governing student life include prohibition of alcohol for students on campus; smoke-free campus. Dancing at college functions permitted with prior approval. Cars must be registered. Intervisitation in dormitory rooms limited to up to twelve hours per week. Rules concerning student conduct enforced "judiciously."

About 39% of students live in coed dormitories; rest commute. Dormitories segregated by floor. There are no fraternities or sororities on campus. About 65% of resident students leave campus on weekends.

Annual Costs. Tuition and fees, $11,120; room and board, $4,757; estimated $236 other, exclusive of travel. About 85% of students receive financial aid. College reports some scholarships awarded on the basis of academic merit alone.

Eastern Connecticut State University

Willimantic, Connecticut 06226 (203) 456-5286

A state-supported university, located in a city of 22,000, 28 miles from both Hartford and New London. Most convenient major airport: Bradley, Windsor Locks.

Founded: 1889
Affiliation: State
Total Enrollment: 1,269 M, 1,497 W (full-time); 1,001 M, 1,519 W (part-time)
Cost: < $10K
% Receiving Financial Aid: 60%
Admission: Non-selective
Application Deadline: May 1

Admission. Graduates of approved high schools with 16 units (12 in college preparatory subjects) and GPA of 2.5 eligible; 73% of applicants accepted, 44% of these actually enroll; 20% of entering freshmen graduate in top fifth of high school class, 70% in top two-fifths. Average freshman SAT scores: 430 M, 440 W verbal, 470 M, 450 W mathematical. *Required:* SAT. Criteria considered in admissions, in order of importance: high school academic record, standardized test scores, recommendations, extra curricular activities. *Out-of-state* freshman applicants: college welcomes out-of-state students. State does not limit out-of-state enrollment. No special requirements for out-of-state applicants. About 70% of applicants accepted, 31% enroll. Most out-of-state students are drawn from New England and Middle Atlantic states. *Entrance programs:* early admission, midyear admission, deferred admission, advanced placement. About 11% of freshmen come from parochial schools. *Apply* by: May 1; rolling admissions. *Transfers* welcome; 334 enrolled 1993–94.

Academic Environment. Degrees offered: associates, bachelors, masters. Majors in addition to usual arts and sciences include accounting, early childhood education. Core requirements include courses in Western and non-Western traditions, humanities, literature, sciences, mathematics, social sciences, writing, computer science, and physical education. Average undergraduate class size: 25% under 20, 65% between 20–40, 10% over 40. About 40% of entering freshmen graduate within four years, 50% eventually; 78% return for sophomore year. *Special programs:* CLEP, independent study, study abroad, honors, 3-week winter intersession, cross registration with U. of Connecticut, cooperative work/study programs. Adult programs: Bachelor of General Studies, a self-designed academic program. *Calendar:* semester, summer school.

Undergraduate degrees conferred (673). 32% were in Business and Management, 16% were in Education, 13% were in Social Sciences, 9% were in Psychology, 7% were in Communications, 6% were in Liberal/General Studies, 5% were in Letters, 3% were in Life Sciences, 3% were in Computer and Engineering Related Technology, remainder in 5 other fields.

Graduates Career Data. Advanced studies pursued by 32% of students. About 82% of 1992–93 graduates employed. Career Development Services include a full range of career planning and job placement services for students and alumni.

Faculty. About 78% of faculty hold PhD or equivalent.

Student Body. College does not seek a national student body; 89% from the state, 92% from New England; 4% Foreign.

Varsity Sports. Men (NCAA Div.III): Baseball, Basketball, Cross Country, Soccer, Track. Women (NCAA/Div.III): Basketball, Cross Country, Soccer, Track, Volleyball.

Campus Life. About 60% of men, 60% of women live in coed dormitories or on campus apartments; 20% live in off-campus college-related housing; rest commute. Intervisitation in men's and women's dormitory rooms limited. Sexes segregated in coed dormitories by floor. There are no fraternities or sororities.

Annual Costs. Tuition and fees, $2,946 (out-of-state, $7,658); room and board, $4,020; estimated $500 other, exclusive of travel. About 60% of students receive financial aid; average amount of assistance, $5,700. Assistance is typically divided 60% grant/scholarship, 20% loan, 20% work. University reports 11 scholarships awarded for academic merit alone, 150 for need.

Eastern Illinois University

Charleston, Illinois 61920-3099 (217) 581-2223

A state-supported institution, located in a community of 20,000, 180 miles south of Chicago. Most convenient major airport: Indianapolis (IN).

Founded: 1895
Affiliation: State
UG Enrollment: 4,187 M, 4,974 W (full-time); 305 M, 540 W (part-time)
Total Enrollment: 11,395
Cost: < $10K
% Receiving Financial Aid: 65%
Admission: Non-selective
Application Deadline: Rolling

Admission. High school graduates with 12 units in college preparatory subjects and rank in top half of class with ACT composite score of 18, or rank in top 75% of class with ACT of 22 eligible; 76% of applicants accepted, 37% of these actually enroll; 25% of freshmen graduate in top fifth of high school class, 64% in top two-fifths. Average freshman ACT scores: 22 composite. *Required:* ACT (SAT accepted). Criteria considered in admissions, in order of importance: standardized test scores, high school academic records; other factors considered: diverse student body. *Out-of-state* freshman applicants: university does not actively seek students from out-of-state. State does not limit out-of-state enrollment. No special requirements for out-of-state applicants. Most out-of state students come from the Midwest. *Entrance programs:* early admission, midyear admission, advanced placement. *Apply* by 10 days before registration; rolling admissions. *Transfers* welcome; 1,155 enrolled 1993–94.

Academic Environment. Degrees offered: bachelors, masters. *Majors offered* in addition to usual arts and sciences include athletic training, industrial technology, business education, accounting, computer management, finance, marketing, management, home economics, industrial technology, communication disorders and sciences, music, theater arts. Core requirements include 40–46 hours of courses in language; quantitative reasoning and problem solving; scientific awareness; foreign languages; cultural experience; foundations of civilizations; human behavior, social interaction, and well-being; U.S. Constitution; and a senior seminar. About 53% of students entering as freshmen graduate eventually. *Special programs:* CLAP, study abroad, honors, 3–2 in engineering. Adult programs: Board of Governors, BA. *Calendar:* semester, summer school.

Undergraduate degrees conferred (2116). 22% were in Education, 14% were in Business and Management, 14% were in Social Sciences, 11% were in Letters, 8% were in Psychology, 7% were in Home Economics, 5% were in Life Sciences, 4% were in Multi/Interdisciplinary Studies, 3% were in Visual and Performing Arts, remainder in 11 other fields.

Faculty. About 73% of faculty hold PhD or equivalent. About 75% of undergraduate classes taught by tenured faculty. About 33% of teaching faculty are female; 8% minority.

Student Body. University does not seek a national student body; 98% of students from Illinois; 108 foreign students 1993–94. An estimated 5% of students reported as Black, 2% Hispanic, 2% other minority.

Varsity Sports. Men (Div.I): Baseball, Basketball, Cross Country, Football(IAA), Golf, Soccer, Swimming, Tennis, Track, Wrestling. Women (Div.I): Basketball, Cross Country, Softball, Swimming, Tennis, Track, Volleyball.

Campus Life. About 19% of students live in traditional dormitories; 22% in coed dormitories; 11% of students live in other on-campus housing; 48% commute. Intervisitation in men's and women's dormitory rooms limited. Sexes segregated in coed dormitories by wing. There are 16 fraternities, 12 sororities, which about 18% of men, 16% of women join. About 25% of resident students leave campus on weekends.

Annual Costs. Tuition and fees, $2,600 (out-of-state, $6,296); room and board, $2,948; estimated $1,420 other, exclusive of travel. About

65% of students receive financial aid (1992–93); average amount of assistance, $3,194. Assistance is typically divided 49% scholarship/grant, 34% loan, 17% work. University reports some scholarships awarded on the basis of academic merit alone.

Eastern Kentucky University

Richmond, Kentucky 40475 **(606) 622-2106**

A state-supported university, located in a town of 17,000, 26 miles southeast of Lexington. Most convenient major airport: Bluegrass (Lexington).

Founded: 1906
Affiliation: State
Total Enrollment: 15,003 M, W (full-time); 831 M, 1,288 W (part-time)
Cost: < $10K
% Receiving Financial Aid: 71%
Admission: Non-selective

Admission. Kentucky graduates of accredited high schools eligible; all applicants accepted, 50% actually enroll. About 26% graduate in top fifth of high school class, 53% in top two-fifths. *Required:* ACT. *Out-of-state* freshman applicants: university seeks students from out of state. State limits out-of-state enrollment to 15–20% of entering class. Requirements for out-of-state applicants: rank in top half of class, 19 on ACT, 840 combined SAT. *Apply:* no specific deadline. *Transfers* welcome.
Academic Environment. *Undergraduate studies* offered by colleges of Arts and Sciences, Business, Education, Applied Arts and Technology. About 10–15% of general education requirements for graduation are elective; distribution requirements fairly numerous. *Majors offered* in addition to usual studies include fire and safety engineering technology, police administration, special education with emphasis in interpreting for deaf. About 35% of students entering as freshmen graduate eventually; 35% of freshmen do not return for sophomore year. *Special programs:* CLEP, independent study, study abroad, honors, undergraduate research, individualized majors, 3–2 engineering, 3–4 pre-veterinary. *Calendar:* semester, summer school.
Undergraduate degrees conferred (1576). 22% were in Education, 15% were in Business and Management, 13% were in Protective Services, 6% were in Communications, 6% were in Social Sciences, 5% were in Health Sciences, 4% were in Allied Health, 4% were in Psychology, 4% were in Engineering and Engineering Related Technology, 3% were in Computer and Engineering Related Technology, remainder in 15 other fields.
Varsity Sports. Men (Div.IA): Baseball, Basketball, Cross Country, Football(IAA), Golf, Tennis, Track. Women (Div.IA): Basketball, Cross Country, Field Hockey, Tennis, Track, Volleyball.
Student Body. University seeks a national student body. About 85% of students from in state. An estimated 6% of students reported as Black, 2% other minority, according to most recent data available.
Campus Life. About 33% of men, 61% of women live in traditional dormitories; 3% each men, women live in coed dormitories; rest commute. Freshmen given preference in college housing if all students cannot be accommodated. Intervisitation in men's and women's dormitory rooms limited to open houses. There are 15 fraternities, 12 sororities on campus which about 11% of men, 12% of women join; they provide no residence facilities. About 60% of resident students leave campus on weekends.
Annual Costs. Tuition and fees, $1,460 (out-of-state, $4,140); room and board, $3,046. About 71% of students receive financial aid. College reports some scholarships awarded on the basis of academic merit alone.

Eastern Mennonite College and Seminary

Harrisonburg, Virginia 22801 **(703) 433-8771**

A Christian college affiliated with the Mennonite Church, located in a town of 30,000 in the Shenandoah Valley, 120 miles southwest of Washington D.C. Most convenient major airport: Dulles International (Washington D.C.).

Founded: 1917
Affiliation: Mennonite
Total Enrollment: 375 M, 528 W (full-time)
Cost: < $10K
% Receiving Financial Aid: 98%
Admission: Non-selective
Application Deadline: Aug. 1

Admission. Graduates of accredited high schools who rank in top half of class and have minimum combined SAT of 750 or ACT composite score of 17 are eligible; 91% of applicants accepted, 52% of these actually enroll. About 40% of freshmen graduate in top two-fifths of high school class. Average freshman scores: SAT, 500 M, 469 W verbal, 548 M, 486 W mathematical; ACT, 23 M, 22 W composite. *Required:* SAT or ACT, acceptance of college's "standards of personal lifestyle consistent with New Testament teaching"; interview recommended. *Apply* by August 1; rolling admissions. *Transfers* welcome; 72 enrolled 1993–94.
Academic Environment. Degrees offered: associates, bachelors, masters. General education requirements for graduation include 12 semester hours in humanities, 10 in Bible studies, 5 in communications, 6 in mathematics/sciences, 9 in cross cultural studies, 1 in physical education. *Majors offered* in addition to usual studies include food service administration, camping, recreation, & youth ministries, community nutrition, international agriculture; new programs recently added in international business, biochemistry. About 21% of students entering as freshmen do not return for sophomore year. Average undergraduate class size: 47% of classes under 20, 43% between 20–40, 10% over 40. *Special programs:* independent study, study abroad in Europe, Latin America, Middle East, honors (sociology), summer seminars in other countries, study-service in Washington D.C., 3–2 program in engineering. Calendar: 3 11-week terms, summer school.
Undergraduate degrees conferred (211). 18% were in Education, 15% were in Business and Management, 10% were in Liberal/General Studies, 9% were in Public Affairs, 9% were in Life Sciences, 8% were in Health Sciences, 7% were in Letters, 6% were in Psychology, 4% were in Social Sciences, 4% were in Theology, 3% were in Agribusiness and Agricultural Production, 3% were in Computer and Engineering Related Technology, remainder in 5 other fields.
Graduates Career Data. Advanced studies pursued by 5% of graduates. Career Development Services include resources for career exploration, job listings, on-campus interviews, credential file service, training in job search techniques, newsletter.
Varsity Sports. Men (NCAA/Div.III): Baseball, Basketball, Cross Country, Soccer, Tennis, Track, Volleyball. Women (NCAA/Div.III): Basketball, Cross Country, Field Hockey, Fastpitch Softball, Track, Volleyball.
Student Body. College seeks a national student body; 34% of students from in state. An estimated 98% of students reported as Protestant, 1% Catholic, 1% unaffiliated; 3% Black, 2% Hispanic, 2% Asian.
Religious Orientation. Eastern Mennonite is a church-related institution; strong Christian emphasis on campus. Courses in faith development, attendance at chapel services required of all students. Prohibited: smoking, drinking, dancing, gambling, and abusive language.
Campus Life. About 53% of men, 59% of women live in traditional dormitories; no coed dormitories; rest live in off-campus housing or commute. No intervisitation in men's or women's dormitory rooms. There are no fraternities or sororities. About 25% of resident students leave campus on weekends.
Annual Costs. Tuition and fees, $9,100; room and board, $3,600; estimated $1,200 other, exclusive of travel. About 98% of students receive financial aid; average amount of assistance, $8,000. Assistance is typically divided 25% grant, 10% scholarship, 50% loan, 15% work. College reports 400 scholarships awarded on the basis of academic merit alone, 250 for need alone.

Eastern Michigan University

Ypsilanti, Michigan 48197 **(313) 487-3060**

A state-supported university, located in a community of 80,000, 30 miles west of Detroit. Most convenient major airport: Detroit Metropolitan.

Founded: 1849
Affiliation: State
UG Enrollment: 5,524 M, 7,445 W (full-time); 2,509 M, 3,476 W (part-time)
Total Enrollment: 25,000
Cost: < $10K
% Receiving Financial Aid: 75%
Admission: Non-selective
Application Deadline: July 1

Admission. Graduates of accredited high schools with acceptable academic records eligible; others admitted on basis of standardized test scores; 81% of applicants accepted; 35% of these actually enroll. Average freshman scores: SAT, 465 verbal, 480 mathematical; ACT, 21 composite. *Required:* SAT or ACT, art students must submit a portfolio, music students must audition. Criteria considered in admissions, in order of importance: high school academic record, standardized test scores, recommendations, extra curricular activities, writing sample. *Out-of-state* freshman applicants: university welcomes students from out of state. State does not limit out-of-state enrollment. No special requirements for out-of-state applicants. States from which most out-of-state students are drawn include Ohio. *Entrance programs:* advanced placement. About 10% of students come from private or parochial schools. *Apply* by July 1; rolling admissions. *Transfers* welcome; 1,957 enrolled 1993–94.
Academic Environment. Degrees offered: bachelors, masters, doctoral. *Undergraduate studies* offered by colleges of Arts and Sciences, Business, Education. *Majors offered* include: facility management, Japanese language and culture, hospitality management, language and world business, African-American studies, accounting information systems, polymers and coatings. Core requirements include 65 credits selected from 5 core areas: symbolics and communication, science/technology, social sciences, arts, and humanities. About 68% of students entering as freshmen return for sophomore year. *Special programs:* CLEP, January term, independent study, study abroad, honors, individualized majors, 3–2 in forestry, Weekend University, continuing education, corporate contract learning, regional learning centers, cross registration programs, internships and cooperative work-study programs. *Calendar:* semester, summer school.
Undergraduate degrees conferred (2939). 21% were in Education, 16% were in Business and Management, 9% were in Social Sciences, 6% were in Letters, 4% were in Health Sciences, 4% were in Visual and Performing Arts, 4% were in Computer and Engineering Related Technology, 4% were in Psychology, 4% were in Public Affairs, 4% were in Engineering and Engineering Related Technology, 4% were in Allied Health, 3% were in Life Sciences, 3% were in Marketing and Distribution, remainder in 16 other fields.
Graduates Career Data. Advanced studies pursued by 30% of students. About 80% of 1992–93 graduates employed. Fields typically hiring largest number of graduates include public teaching, business, psychology. Career Development Services include resume writing, interview skills, career placement, search, on campus job fairs, industry affiliation, co-ops, internships, screening, aptitude testing.
Faculty. About 78% of faculty hold PhD or equivalent. About 79% of undergraduate classes taught by tenured faculty.
Student Body. University does not seek a national student body; 90% of students from Michigan, 98% from Midwest. An estimated 7% of students reported as Black, 1% Hispanic, 1% Asian, 4% other minority, according to most recent data available. Average age of undergraduate student: 24.
Varsity Sports. Men (Div.I): Baseball, Basketball, Cross Country, Diving, Football, Golf, Soccer, Swimming, Tennis, Track, Wrestling. Women (Div.I): Basketball, Cross Country, Diving, Gymnastics, Softball, Swimming, Tennis, Track, Volleyball.
Campus Life. About 12% of women live in traditional dormitories; 16% of men and women in coed dormitories; 20% live in off-campus housing; 47% commute. Intervisitation in men's and women's dormitory rooms limited. There are 18 fraternities, 9 sororities on campus, which about 6% of men, 4% of women join; 5% of men and women live in fraternities and sororities.
Annual Costs. Tuition and fees, $2,700 (out-of-state, $6,600 - Ohio residents pay in-state tuition); room and board, $4,031; estimated $2,000–2,500 other, exclusive of travel. About 75% of students receive financial aid; average amount of assistance, $3,000. Assistance is typically divided 27% scholarship/grant, 44% loan, 29% work. College reports some scholarships awarded on the basis of academic merit alone.

Eastern Montana College

Billings, Montana 59101 **(406) 657-2158**

A state-supported college, located in a city of 95,000. Most convenient major airport: Billings Logan Field..

Founded: 1925
Affiliation: State
UG Enrollment: 902 M, 1,578 W (full-time); 304 M, 563 W (part-time)
Total Enrollment: 3,732
Cost: < $10K
Admission: Non-selective
Application Deadline: August 25

Admission. Graduates of accredited Montana high schools with GPA of 2.0 admitted; 98% of applicants accepted, 65% of these actually enroll. Average freshman scores: SAT, 421 verbal, 464 mathematical; ACT, 20.1 M, 19.9 W composite. *Required:* ACT recommended (for placement only). *Out-of-state* freshman applicants: college welcomes students from out of state. State does not limit out-of-state enrollment. Requirements for out-of-state applicants: GPA of 2.0. *Apply* by August 25. *Transfers* welcome; 400 enrolled 1993–94.
Academic Environment. Degrees offered: associates, bachelors, masters. General education requirements include 44–54 credits. About 6% of students entering as freshmen graduate within four years, 26% eventually, about 53% of freshmen do not return for sophomore year. *Special programs:* CLEP, independent study, undergraduate research, 3-year degree. *Calendar:* quarter, summer school.
Undergraduate degrees conferred (510). 37% were in Business and Management, 36% were in Education, 8% were in Allied Health, 5% were in Psychology, 4% were in Communications, 4% were in Social Sciences, remainder in 6 other fields.
Graduates Career Data. Advanced studies pursued by 7% of students. About 76% of 1992–93 graduates employed.
Faculty. About 84% of faculty hold PhD or equivalent. About 33% of teaching faculty are female.
Varsity Sports. Men (NCAA/Div.II): Basketball, Cross Country, Golf, Tennis. Women (NCAA/Div.II): Basketball, Cross Country, Tennis, Volleyball.
Student Body. College seeks a national student body; 92% of students from in state.
Campus Life. About 12% of students live in dormitories; rest commute. Freshmen required to live on campus first year. Intervisitation in men's and women's dormitory rooms limited. Sexes segregated in coed dormitories by floor. There is 1 fraternity, 1 sorority on campus.
Annual Costs. Tuition and fees, $1,916 (out-of-state, $5,556); room and board, $3,260; estimated $1,025 other, exclusive of travel.

Eastern Nazarene College

Quincy, Massachusetts 02170 **(617) 773-2373**

A church-related college, offering "a liberal arts program with Christian perspectives," located in a suburban city of 83,000, 7 miles south of Boston.

Founded: 1900
Affiliation: Nazarene
Total Enrollment: 244 M, 367 W (full-time)
Cost: < $10K
% Receiving Financial Aid: 78%
Admission: Non-selective
Application Deadline: Aug. 1

Admission. High school graduates with recommendations of high school and pastor eligible; 79% of applicants accepted; 49% of these actually enroll. About 27% of freshmen graduate in top fifth of high school class, 47% in top two-fifths. Average freshmen SAT scores: 33% score above 500 on verbal, 11% above 600; 57% score above 500 on mathematical, 23% above 600, 6% above 700. *Required:* SAT or ACT, acceptance of college code (each student "voluntarily agrees to abstain from the use of alcoholic beverages and tobacco and attendance at dances and theater"). Criteria considered in admissions, in order of importance: high school academic record, standardized test scores, recommendations, extra curricular activities, writing sample. *Entrance programs:* early admission, midyear admission, advanced placement. *Apply* by: August 1; rolling admission. *Transfers* welcome; 32 enrolled 1993–94.
Academic Environment. Degrees offered: associates, bachelors, masters. Core requirements include 16 courses. Unusual majors include sports therapy. About 41% of students entering as freshmen graduate within four years, 55% eventually; 69% of freshmen return for sophomore year. Adult programs: LEAD, a degree completion 22-month evening course for business administration (605 students currently enrolled). *Special programs:* CLEP, independent study,

study abroad, undergraduate research, January term, 3–2 programs in engineering, pharmacy. *Calendar:* 4–1–4, summer school.

Undergraduate degrees conferred (124). 19% were in Education, 16% were in Business and Management, 9% were in Psychology, 8% were in Philosophy and Religion, 7% were in Public Affairs, 7% were in Communications, 6% were in Social Sciences, 6% were in Physical Sciences, 6% were in Life Sciences, 5% were in Letters, remainder in 6 other fields.

Faculty. About 62% of faculty hold PhD or equivalent. About 25% of teaching faculty are female; 2% black, 4% Hispanic, 6% other minority.

Student Body. College does not seek a national student body; 42% from Massachusetts, 60% of students from New England, 29% Middle Atlantic, 1% Midwest, 4% South, 2% West, 4% Foreign. An estimated 87% of students reported as Protestant, 6% Catholic, 6% unreported, 1% other; 5% Black, 4% Asian, 1% Hispanic, 3% other minority.

Religious Affiliation. Eastern Nazarene is a church-related institution; strong religious emphasis on campus; required 4-year core curriculum includes 3 courses in religion. Attendance required at 3 chapel services weekly; regular church attendance expected.

Varsity Sports. Men (NAIA & NCCAA/Div.III): Baseball, Basketball, Cross Country, Soccer, Tennis. Women (NAIA & NCCAA/Div.III): Basketball, Cross Country, Softball, Tennis, Volleyball.

Campus Life. About 75% of men, 75% of women live in traditional dormitories; no coed dormitories; rest commute. No intervisitation in men's or women's dormitory rooms. There are no fraternities or sororities. About 30% of resident students leave campus on weekends.

Annual Costs. Tuition and fees, $8,270; room and board, $3,400; estimated $1,000 other, exclusive of travel. About 78% of students receive financial aid; average amount of assistance for freshmen in 1993, $6,237. College reports some scholarships awarded on the basis of academic merit alone.

Eastern New Mexico University

Portales, New Mexico 88130 — (505) 562-2178 or (800) 367-3668

A state-supported university, located in a rural town of 10,564, 120 miles southwest of Amarillo, Texas. Most convenient major airports: Lubbock or Amarillo (TX).

Founded: 1928
Affiliation: State
UG Enrollment: 1,444 M, 1,927 W (full-time)
Total Enrollment: 3,939
Cost: < $10K
% Receiving Financial Aid: 87%
Admission: Non-selective
Application Deadline: August 1

Admission. Graduates of accredited high schools with 15 units and either 2.5 GPA or satisfactory score on standardized test eligible; 95% of applicants accepted; 67% of these actually enroll. Average freshman scores: ACT, 20.3 M, 20.4 W composite. *Required:* SAT or ACT. Criteria considered in admissions, in order of importance: high school academic record, standardized test scores, recommendations, writing sample, extra curricular activities. *Out-of-state* freshman applicants: university seeks students from out of state. State does not limit out-of-state enrollment. No special requirements for out-of-state applicants. About 98% of out-of-state students accepted, 85% of these actually enroll. States from which most out-of-state students are drawn include Texas, California, Colorado. *Entrance programs:* early admission, midyear admission, deferred admission, advanced placement. *Apply* by: August 1; rolling admission. *Transfers* welcome; 376 enrolled 1993–94.

Academic Environment. Degrees offered: associates, bachelors, masters. *Undergraduate studies* offered by colleges of Liberal Arts and Sciences, Business, Education, Technology and Fine Arts. Core requirements include courses in communications, sciences, mathematics, human social behavior, humanities, fine arts, physical well-being. Unusual majors include public relations. About 30% of students entering as freshmen graduate within four years, 50% eventually; 67% of freshmen return for sophomore year. Average undergraduate class size: 68% under 20, 30% between 20–40, 2% over 40. *Special programs:* CLEP, study abroad, honors, internships/cooperative education programs, undergraduate research. Adult programs: Bachelor of University Studies adult re-entry program. *Calendar:* semester, May interterm, summer school.

Undergraduate degrees conferred (473). 33% were in Education, 16% were in Business and Management, 10% were in Social Sciences, 5% were in Communications, 5% were in Visual and Performing Arts, 5% were in Liberal/General Studies, 5% were in Computer and Engineering Related Technology, 4% were in Mathematics, 3% were in Psychology, remainder in 11 other fields.

Faculty. About 87% of faculty hold PhD or equivalent. About 83% of undergraduate classes taught by tenured faculty. About 36% of teaching faculty are female; 1% Black, 5% Hispanic, 5% other minority.

Student Body. University seeks a national student body; 70% of students from in state; 79% West, 5% South, 10% Midwest, 2% Mid Atlantic, 1% New England, 1% Northwest 2% Foreign students. An estimated 25% of students reported as Protestant, 67% Catholic, 1% Jewish, 7% unaffiliated; 5% Black, 20% Hispanic, 1% Asian, 2% other minority. Average age of undergraduate student: 26.

Varsity Sports. Men (NCAA,Div.II): Baseball, Basketball, Football, Rodeo. Women (NCAA,Div.II): Basketball, Rodeo, Tennis, Volleyball.

Campus Life. About 42% of men, and 28% women live in traditional dormitories; 39% of men, 44% of women in coed dormitory; 6% of men, 8% of women live in off-campus housing; 12% of men, 18% of women commute. There are 5 fraternities, 3 sororities on campus which about 10% of men, 8% of women join; 1% of men live in fraternities, 2% of women live in sororities. About 35% of resident students leave campus on weekends.

Annual Costs. Tuition and fees, $1,443 (out-of-state, $5,283); room and board, $2,713. About 87% of students receive financial aid; average amount of assistance, $1,312. Assistance is typically divided 4% scholarship, 75% grant, 20% loan, 1% work. University reports 135 scholarships awarded for academic merit alone, 42 for special talents.

Eastern Oregon State College

LaGrande, Oregon 97850 — (503) 962-3496

A state-supported college, located in a town of 10,000, 260 miles east of Portland. Most convenient major airport: Pendleton.

Founded: 1929
Affiliation: State
Total Enrollment: 876 M, 1,004 W (full-time); 80 M, 136 W (part-time)
Cost: < $10K
% Receiving Financial Aid: 80%
Admission: Non-selective
Application Deadline: August 1

Admission. Graduates of high schools with 14 units of college preparatory courses and 2.0 average for all course work or combined SAT scores of 890 (ACT composite score of 20) eligible; non-graduates admitted if meeting other requirements; 47% of applicants accepted, 65% of these actually enroll. *Required:* SAT or ACT. Criteria considered in admissions, in order of importance: high school academic record, extra curricular activities, recommendations; other factors considered: special talents. *Out-of-state* freshman applicants: college welcomes students from out of state. State limits out-of-state enrollment to 25% of entering class. *Entrance programs:* early decision. *Apply* by: August 1; rolling admission. *Transfers* welcome; 255 enrolled 1993–94.

Academic Environment. Degrees offered: associates, bachelors, masters. Core requirements include 15 credits in each of humanities; social sciences; natural sciences; art, language, and logic. About 60% of students entering as freshmen graduate eventually; 60% of freshmen for sophomore year. *Special programs:* study abroad, bilingual education, external degree, National Student Exchange, 3–2 engineering. *Calendar:* quarter, summer school.

Undergraduate degrees conferred (294). 26% were in Liberal/General Studies, 25% were in Multi/Interdisciplinary Studies, 19% were in Business and Management, 6% were in Social Sciences, 6% were in Education, 4% were in Psychology, 3% were in Public Affairs, remainder in 6 other fields.

Faculty. About 54% of faculty hold PhD or equivalent.

Student Body. College seeks a national student body; 70% of students from Oregon; 2% Foreign. An estimated 1% of students reported as Black, 3% Hispanic, 3% Asian, 6% other minority. Average age of undergraduate student: 22.

Varsity Sports. Men (NAIA,Div.II): Baseball, Basketball, Cross Country, Football, Rodeo (NCRA), Skiing (NCSA), Track. Women

(NAIA): Basketball, Cross Country, Rodeo(NCRA), Skiing (NCSA), Track, Volleyball.

Campus Life. About 13% of students live in traditional dormitories; 6% in coed dormitories; rest live in off-campus housing or commute, according to most recent data available. About 30% of resident students leave campus on weekends.

Annual Costs. Tuition and fees, $2,595; room and board, $3,495; estimated $1,650 other, exclusive of travel. About 80% of students receive financial aid. College reports 2 scholarships awarded for academic merit alone, 1 for special talents.

Eastern Washington University

Cheney, Washington 99004 (509) 359-2397

A state-supported university, located in a community of 7,000, 16 miles southwest of Spokane. Most convenient major airport: Spokane International.

Founded: 1890
Affiliation: State
UG Enrollment: 2,895 M, 3,666 W (full-time); 250 M, 309 W (part-time)
Total Enrollment: 8,431
Cost: < $10K
Admission: Non-selective
Application Deadline: July 1

Admission. Graduates of accredited high schools with 2.5 average or rank in top half of class after 6 semesters eligible; others given individual consideration; 85% of applicants accepted, 41% of these actually enroll. Average freshman scores: SAT, middle 50% range, 350–470 verbal, 400–520 mathematical; ACT, 18–23 composite. Entrance program: midyear admission, advanced placement. *Out-of-state* students: no special requirements, no limits. *Apply* by July 1; February 15 for priority. *Transfers* welcome; 1,638 enrolled 1993–94.

Academic Environment. Degrees offered: bachelors, masters. About 33% of general education requirements for graduation are elective; distribution requirements fairly numerous. About 76% of entering freshmen return for sophomore year. *Special programs:* honors, individualized majors, study abroad, internships, credit by examination, Indian Education Program. *Calendar:* quarter, summer school.

Undergraduate degrees conferred (1547). 24% were in Education, 19% were in Business and Management, 10% were in Liberal/General Studies, 6% were in Psychology, 6% were in Social Sciences, 5% were in Health Sciences, 4% were in Communications, 4% were in Allied Health, 4% were in Parks and Recreation, 3% were in Life Sciences, 3% were in Letters, remainder in 12 other fields.

Graduates Career Data. Advanced studies pursued by 14% of graduates. About 67% of 1992–93 graduates employed. Career Planning and Placement Office offers credentials file maintenance, on-campus interviews, on-line interest assessment, counseling.

Varsity Sports. Men (NCAA I): Basketball, Cross Country, Football (IAA), Golf, Tennis, Track. Women (NCAA Div.I): Basketball, Cross Country, Golf, Tennis, Track, Volleyball.

Student Body. University seeks a national student body; 90% of students from in state; 5% foreign.

Campus Life. About 16% each of men, women live in coed dormitories; 84% each live in off-campus housing or commute. Freshmen given preference in college housing if all students cannot be accommodated. Intervisitation in men's and women's dormitory rooms unlimited. There are 6 fraternities, 7 sororities on campus which about 4% of men, 5% of women join.

Annual Costs. Tuition and fees, $2,256 (out-of-state, $7,974); room and board, $3,799. About 45% of students receive financial aid; assistance is typically divided 36% scholarship, 57% loan, 7% work. College reports some scholarships awarded on the basis of academic merit alone.

Eckerd College

St. Petersburg, Florida 33711 (813) 864-1166

An independent liberal arts college, founded by the Presbyterian Church, Eckerd has a national student body. The 281-acre, waterfront campus is located in a city of 300,000 in the Tampa Bay area. Most convenient major airport: Tampa International.

Founded: 1958
Affiliation: Independent
Total Enrollment: 677 M, 715 W (full-time)
Cost: $10K–$20K
% Receiving Financial Aid: 82%
Admission: Very Selective
Application Deadline: April 15

Admission is very selective. About 77% of applicants accepted, 33% of these actually enroll; 58% of freshmen graduate in top fifth of high school class, 82% in top two-fifths. Average freshman scores: SAT, 517 verbal, 559 mathematical; 58% of freshmen score above 500 on verbal, 17% above 600, 1% above 700; 78% score above 500 on mathematical, 31% above 600, 5% above 700; ACT, 25.1 composite. *Required:* SAT or ACT, essay, recommendation. Criteria considered in admissions, in order of importance: high school academic record, standardized test scores, extracurricular activities, recommendations, writing sample; other factors considered: special talents, demonstrated leadership/service. *Entrance programs:* early admission, midyear admission, advanced placement, deferred admission. About 20% of entering students from private, 5% from parochial schools. *Apply* by April 15; rolling admissions. *Transfers* welcome; 76 enrolled 1993–94.

Academic Environment. Key features of educational program: (1) a "mentorship" program which supplants faculty advisorship, aimed at intimate knowledge, understanding, and support of students; (2) an Autumn Term, a three week program of orientation, socialization, and planning for incoming freshmen; (3) a values-oriented program of general education: Western Civilization program in freshman year, interdisciplinary seminars during sophomore and junior years, senior seminars exploring major value issues confronting individuals, professions, and societies in the future; (4) Academy of Senior Professionals—an adjacent residential campus for retired professionals whose members provide teaching, career and personal counseling opportunities for undergraduates. Degree requirements include demonstrated competency in writing, one year of foreign language, and one course in mathematics or computer science. Degrees offered: bachelors. *Majors offered* include marine science, environmental studies, comparative education studies, diplomacy and international relations, and women's and gender studies. Average undergraduate class size: 20; 60% under 20, 35% 20–40, 5% over 40.

About 60% of students entering as freshmen graduate within four years, 67% eventually; 85% of freshmen return for sophomore year. *Special programs:* CLEP, independent study, study abroad, undergraduate research, individualized majors, January Term (an independent project on- or off-campus, internship or study abroad), 3–2 engineering, internships in management, human development, international business. Adult programs: Program for Experienced Learners includes degree completion program for students over 25 with weekend and evening offerings, independent study and credit for experiential learning. *Calendar:* 4–1–4, summer school.

Undergraduate degrees conferred (462). 41% were in Business and Management, 18% were in Psychology, 11% were in Social Sciences, 6% were in Life Sciences, 5% were in Letters, 3% were in Area and Ethnic Studies, 3% were in Visual and Performing Arts, remainder in 10 other fields.

Graduates Career Data. Advanced studies pursued by 45% of graduates; 17% enter graduate school; 13% enter business school; 8% enter law school; 5% enter medical school; 1% enter dental school. Medical schools typically enrolling largest numbers of graduates include U. of Florida, Penn State, Vanderbilt; dental schools include U. of Florida; law schools include U. of Florida, Columbia, American U.; business schools include U. of Florida, Emory, American Graduate School of International Management. About 55% of 1992–93 graduates employed. Fields typically hiring largest numbers of graduates include business, public service/government, marine/environmental agencies. Career Development Services include interest testing, resume writing, alumni networks, Academy of Senior Professionals career counseling and networking, on-campus interviewing.

Faculty. About 95% of faculty hold PhD or equivalent. About 65% of undergraduate classes taught by tenured faculty. About 31% of teaching faculty are female; 4% Black, 6% Hispanic, 3% other minority.

Student Body. About 30% of students from in state; 20% Middle Atlantic, 17% New England, 10% Midwest, 7% South, 5% West, 1% Northwest, 10% Foreign. An estimated 45% of students reported as Protestant, 30% Catholic, 2% Jewish, 15% unaffiliated, 1% Muslim,

7% other; 3% Black, 3% Hispanic, 2% Asian, 1% other minority. *Minority group students:* Black Society.

Religious Orientation. Eckerd is an independent institution, founded by 2 Presbyterian synods and covenanted to the Presbyterian Synod of the South. Eckerd considers itself "a Christian community" open to students of all faiths; 20% of students affiliated with the church.

Varsity Sports. Men (Div.II): Baseball, Basketball, Cross Country, Golf, Soccer, Tennis. Women (Div.II): Basketball, Cross Country, Softball, Tennis, Volleyball.

Campus Life. Students report campus is slightly isolated from St. Petersburg (one student notes an advantage: "we can generally be loud without bothering our neighbors"), so social life is focused primarily on campus activities. Another student observes, "The weather is always nice, the beach is 5 minutes away, and the waterfront is right in our backyard." Alcohol allowed in selected areas for those over 21, no "kegs" permitted on campus; drugs "not permitted"; smoking permitted in dormitories only. Cars permitted for all. Pets allowed. High interest reported in intramural sports (most popular: flag football, basketball, volleyball); milder interest in varsity sports (most popular: men's basketball, baseball, women's volleyball).

About 38% of men, 39% of women live in traditional dormitories; 37% of men, 38% of women in coed dormitories; 25% of men, 23% of women commute. Freshmen given preference in college housing if all students cannot be accommodated. Intervisitation in men's and women's dormitory rooms unlimited. Sexes segregated in coed dormitories by floor. There are no fraternities or sororities on campus. About 5% of resident students leave campus on weekends.

Annual Costs. Tuition and fees, $14,930; room and board, $3,925; estimated $1,200 other, exclusive of travel. About 82% of students receive financial aid; average amount of assistance, $12,800. Assistance is typically divided 35% scholarship, 35% grant, 23% loan, 7% work. College reports 200 scholarships awarded on the basis of academic merit alone; 50 for special talents alone; 850 for need alone. *Meeting Costs:* college offers payment plan through private agency, PLUS Loans, TERI Loans.

Edgecliff College

(See Xavier University (Ohio))

Edgewood College

Madison, Wisconsin 53711 (608) 257-4861

Edgewood College, founded by the Dominican Sisters, is located in a city of 173,300. Most convenient major airport: Madison.

Founded: 1927
Affiliation: Independent (Roman Catholic)
UG Enrollment: 225 M, 601 W (full-time); 159 M, 415 W (part-time)
Total Enrollment: 1,787
Cost: < $10K
% Receiving Financial Aid: 87%
Admission: Non-selective
Application Deadline: August 1

Admission. High school graduates with 16 units (12 in academic subjects) eligible; 83% of applicants accepted, 56% of these actually enroll. Average freshmen ACT scores: 21.2 composite. *Required:* SAT or ACT. Criteria considered in admissions, in order of importance: high school academic record, standardized test scores, recommendations, writing sample, extracurricular activities; other factors considered: special talents. About 25% of entering students from private schools. *Entrance programs:* rolling admissions. *Apply* by August 1. *Transfers* welcome; 190 enrolled 1993–94.

Academic Environment. Degrees offered: associates, bachelors, masters. Graduation requirements include 2 semesters college-level composition; math, logic, speech, foreign language. *Majors offered* include art therapy, music. Average undergraduate class: 65% under 20, 31% 20–40. About 40% of students graduate within 4 years; 80% of freshman return for sophomore year. *Special programs:* CLEP, independent study, credit for prior learning, study abroad, honors, optional January winterim, internships, individualized majors, cross registration with U. Wisconsin at Madison, 3–2 pre-engineering. Adult programs: Weekend Degree Program, meets 2 weekends per month. *Calendar:* 4–1–4, summer school.

Undergraduate degrees conferred (94). 46% were in Business and Management, 17% were in Education, 9% were in Social Sciences, 7% were in Health Sciences, 4% were in Protective Services, 3% were in Philosophy and Religion, 3% were in Letters, 3% were in Computer and Engineering Related Technology, remainder in 5 other fields.

Graduate Career Data. Advanced studies pursued immediately after graduation by 50% of students; 34% enter graduate schools; 16% enter business schools. Business schools typically enrolling the largest numbers of graduates include Edgewood, U. of Wisconsin-Madison. Employers typically hiring largest numbers of graduates include CUNA Service Group, hospitals and clinics, State of Wisconsin, St. Mary's Hospitals. Career Development Services include resume writing, interview skills, developmental materials, SIGI plus, computerized job matching system.

Faculty. About 68% of faculty hold PhD or equivalent. About 28% of undergraduate classes taught by tenured faculty. About 48% of teaching faculty are female; 2% Black, 5% other minority.

Student Body. About 85% of students from in state; 95% Midwest, 5% foreign. An estimated 15% of students reported as Protestant, 42% Catholic, 56% unknown or other; 2% Black, 1% Hispanic, 4% Asian, 24% other or unknown.

Religious Orientation. Edgewood is an independent institution with a strong Catholic heritage. Attendance at Mass not required; no religious course study required.

Varsity Sports. Men: Baseball, Basketball, Golf, Soccer, Tennis. Women: Basketball, Golf, Soccer, Softball, Tennis, Volleyball.

Campus Life. Students report proximity to Madison (city and university) provides extensive recreational activities, however they also note that campus is "not too close" [to the city] and is "very safe and beautiful."

About 13% of men, 16% of women live in traditional dormitories; 4% of men, 3% of women live in co-ed dormitories; 2% of men, 7% of women live in off-campus college-related housing; rest commute. Freshmen given preference in college housing if all students cannot be accommodated. Intervisitation in men's and women's dormitory rooms limited. Sexes segregated in coed dormitories by wing or suite. There are no fraternities or sororities on campus. About 50% of resident students leave campus on weekends.

Annual Costs. Tuition and fees, $8,000; room and board, $3,700; estimated $1,800 other, exclusive of travel. About 87% of students receive financial aid; average amount of assistance, $8,000. Assistance is typically divided 30% scholarship, 30% grant, 30% loan, 10% work. College reports 125 scholarships awarded on the basis of academic merit alone; 125 for special talents alone; 250 for need alone. *Meeting Costs:* college offers installment payment plan.

Edinboro University of Pennsylvania

Edinboro, Pennsylvania 16444 (814) 732-2761

A state-supported university located in a community of 6,000, 18 miles south of Erie. Most convenient major airport: Erie International.

Founded: 1857
Affiliation: State
Total Enrollment: 2,751 M, 3,567 W (full-time); 290 M, 527 W (part-time)
Cost: < $10K
% Receiving Financial Aid: 82%
Admission: Non-selective
Application Deadline: Rolling

Admission. Graduates of approved high schools eligible; 70% of applicants accepted, 44% of these actually enroll. *Required:* SAT or ACT; audition for prospective music majors. Criteria considered in admissions, in order of importance: high school academic record, standardized test scores, extracurricular activities, recommendations; other factors considered: special talents, diverse student body, alumni children. *Out-of-state* freshman applicants: university seeks students from out-of-state. State limits out-of-state enrollment to 10% of entering class. No special requirements for out-of-state applicants; about 69% of applicants accepted, 24% enroll. *Entrance programs:* midyear admission, deferred admission, advanced placement, rolling admission. *Apply:* rolling admissions. *Transfers* welcome; 659 enrolled 1993–94.

Academic Environment. Degrees offered: associates, bachelors, masters. About 50% of general education requirements for graduation are elective; distribution requirements fairly numerous. About 49% of students entering as freshmen graduate eventually; 72% of freshmen return for sophomore year. *Special programs:* CLEP, independent study, honors, disabled students program, study abroad, program in nutrition with Mercyhurst, 3–2 engineering. Adult programs: Opportunity College provides special scheduling and advisement services for adult students. *Calendar:* semester, summer school.

Undergraduate degrees conferred (969). 26% were in Education, 15% were in Business and Management, 9% were in Communications, 8% were in Visual and Performing Arts, 7% were in Psychology, 6% were in Protective Services, 4% were in Health Sciences, 4% were in Social Sciences, 4% were in Public Affairs, 3% were in Physical Sciences, 3% were in Computer and Engineering Related Technology, remainder in 9 other fields.

Faculty. About 56% of faculty hold PhD or equivalent. About 34% of teaching faculty are female; 3% are Black, 1% Hispanic, 6% other minority.

Student Body. About 87% of students from in state, 2% Foreign. An estimated 4% of students reported as Black, 1% Hispanic, 1% Asian, 2% other minority. Average age of undergraduate student: 23.

Varsity Sports. Men (Div.II): Baseball, Basketball, Cross Country, Football, Golf, Swimming, Tennis, Track, (Div.I) Wrestling. Women (Div.II): Basketball, Cross Country, Softball, Swimming, Tennis, Track, Volleyball.

Campus Life. About 31% of men, 30% of women live in coed dormitories; 28% men, 25% women live in off-campus college-related housing; rest commute. Freshmen given preference in college housing if all students cannot be accommodated. Intervisitation in men's and women's dormitory rooms limited. There are 7 fraternities, 5 sororities on campus, which about 10% of men, 15% of women join.

Annual Costs. Tuition and fees, $3,531; (out-of-state, $7,929); room and board, $3,650; estimated $1,230 other, exclusive of travel. About 82% of students receive financial aid, average amount of assistance, $4,140. Assistance is typically divided 1% scholarship, 33% grant, 60% loan, 6% work.

Edward Waters College

Jacksonville, Florida 32209

An accredited 4-year college, founded as an institution for the education of Black youth, Edward Waters has programs in the liberal arts, teacher education, and business.

Founded: 1866
Affiliation: African Methodist Episcopal

Undergraduate degrees conferred (79). 100% were in Unknown.

Elizabeth City State University

Elizabeth City, North Carolina 27909 **(919) 335-3305**

A state-supported institution, located in a town of 14,800, 45 miles south of Norfolk; founded as a college for Negroes and still serving a predominantly Black student body. Most convenient major airport: Norfolk (VA) (45 miles away).

Founded: 1891
Affiliation: State
Total Enrollment: 1,702 M, W (full-time)
Cost: < $10K
% Receiving Financial Aid: 90%
Admission: Non-selective
Application Deadline: Aug. 1

Admission. Graduates of accredited high schools with 20 units (15 in academic subjects) with GPA of 2.0 eligible; others given consideration; 59% of applicants accepted, 58% of these actually enroll. About 11% of freshmen graduate in top fifth of high school class, 26% in top two-fifths. *Required:* SAT. *Out-of-state* freshman applicants: university welcomes students from out of state. State limits out-of-state enrollment to 18% of entering class. About 43% out-of-state applicants accepted, 45% of these enroll. *Non-academic factors* considered in admissions: special talents, alumni children. *Apply* by August 1. *Transfers* welcome.

Academic Environment. *Degrees:* BA, BS, BSEd. About 37% of general education requirements for graduation are elective; distribution requirements fairly numerous. About 45% of students entering as freshmen graduate eventually; 30% of freshmen do not return for sophomore year. *Majors offered* in addition to usual studies include computer science, music industry studies, studio art; minor in airway science. *Special programs:* CLEP, honors, cooperative education, extended day/weekend program, BEEP & special services. *Calendar:* semester, summer school.

Undergraduate degrees conferred (221). 33% were in Business, 25% were in Education, 10% were in Social Sciences, 8% were in Protective Services, 6% were in Computer and Information Sciences, 5% were in Letters, 4% were in Life Sciences, 4% were in Physical Sciences, 3% were in Mathematics, reminder in 2 other fields.

Varsity Sports. Men (Div. II): Baseball, Basketball, Football, Tennis, Track, Wrestling. Women (Div. II): Basketball, Cheerleading, Softball, Tennis, Track, Volleyball.

Student Body. According to most recent data available, 82% of students from North Carolina. An estimated 98% of students reported as Protestant; 76% Black.

Campus Life. According to most recent data available, about 40% of men, 60% of women live in traditional dormitories; no coed dormitories; rest live in off-campus housing or commute. Freshmen given preference in college housing if all students cannot be accommodated. Intervisitation in men's and women's dormitory rooms limited. There are 5 fraternities, 4 sororities on campus which about 3% of men, 4% of women join; they provide no residence facilities. About 50% of resident students leave campus on weekends.

Annual Costs. Tuition and fees, $1,184 (out-of-state, $6,202); room and board, $2,648. About 90% of students receive financial aid, according to most recent data available. University reports some scholarships awarded on the basis of academic merit alone. *Meeting Costs:* university offers Incentive Scholars for residents in 16 county region of northeastern North Carolina, and time payment plans.

Elizabethtown College

Elizabethtown, Pennsylvania 17022 **(717) 367-1000**

A church-related, liberal arts college, Elizabethtown is located on a 180-acre campus in a community of 10,000, 20 miles from Harrisburg and Lancaster, 100 miles from Philadelphia and Baltimore. Most convenient major airport: Harrisburg International.

Founded: 1899
Affiliation: Church of the Brethren
UG Enrollment: 504 M, 981 W (full-time); 126 M, 177 W (part-time)
Total Enrollment: 1,788
Cost: $10K–$20K
% Receiving Financial Aid: 82%
Admission: Selective (+)
Application Deadline: Rolling

Admission is selective (+). About 75% of applicants accepted, 23% of these actually enroll; 61% of freshmen graduate in top fifth of high school class, 85% in top two-fifths. Average freshman scores: SAT, 492 verbal, 546 mathematical; 46% of freshmen score above 500 on verbal, 8% above 600; 73% score above 500 on mathematical, 27% above 600, 5% above 700. *Required:* SAT or ACT, essay, recommendations; interview required for occupational therapy, recommended for others; audition required for music. Criteria considered in admissions, in order of importance: high school academic record, standardized test scores, recommendations, extracurricular activities, writing sample; other factors considered: diverse student body, alumni children, special talents, religious affiliation. *Entrance programs:* early admission, midyear admission, deferred admission, advanced placement. *Apply:* rolling admissions; December 15 for Occupation Therapy. *Transfers* welcome; 34 enrolled 1993–94.

Academic Environment. Graduation requirements include a freshman seminar, a junior/senior colloquium, 3 credit hours of the Power of Language, 3–4 of math, 3 of Creative Expression, 6 of Cultural Heritage, 3–4 of Foreign Cultures, 3 of the Natural World, 6 of the Social World, 3 of Values and Choice, 3 of Physical Well Being. Degrees offered: bachelors. New or notable majors offered include: occupational therapy, music therapy, international business.

About 65% of students entering as freshmen graduate eventually; 80% of freshmen return for sophomore year. Special programs:

CLEP, honors, independent study, internship, study abroad, undergraduate research, 3-year degree, 3–2 engineering with Penn State, 3–2 environmental management and forestry with Duke, 2–2 allied health with Thomas Jefferson, study at Merrill–Palmer Institute. Adult programs: Welcome Back Program for adults with previous college experience. *Calendar:* semester, summer school.

Undergraduate degrees conferred (362). 29% were in Business and Management, 16% were in Education, 13% were in Communications, 10% were in Allied Health, 6% were in Psychology, 5% were in Health Sciences, 5% were in Social Sciences, 4% were in Public Affairs, 4% were in Letters, remainder in 7 other fields.

Graduates Career Data. Full-time advanced studies pursued within 8 months of graduation by 16% of students; 3% enter medical school; 3% enter law school, 2% enter business school; less than 1% enter dental school. About 70% of 1992–93 graduates employed. Employers typically hiring largest numbers of graduates include AMP, Coopers & Lybrand, Ernst & Young, HERCO, EDS. Career Development Services include resume development, interviewing skills, job search, major/career exploration, externships, job fair and on-campus interviewing.

Faculty. About 70% of faculty hold PhD or equivalent. About 66% of undergraduate classes taught by tenured faculty. About 25% of teaching faculty are female.

Student Body. About 62% of students from in state, 92% Middle Atlantic; 4% New England, 1% South, 2% Foreign. An estimated 49% of students reported as Protestant, 34% Catholic, 1% Jewish, 8% unaffiliated; 2% as Black, 1% Hispanic, 2% Asian. Social organizations for Black and international students.

Religious Orientation. Elizabethtown is a church-related institution; 3% of students affiliated with the church; no religious demands on students.

Varsity Sports. Men (Div.III): Baseball, Basketball, Cross Country, Golf, Soccer, Swimming, Tennis, Wrestling. Women (Div.III): Basketball, Cross Country, Field Hockey, Golf, Soccer, Softball, Swimming, Tennis, Volleyball.

Campus Life. Relative distance from urban attractions (10–20 minutes from Hershey, Harrisburg and Lancaster) focuses student attention on college programing. Students agree college does a "good job" of bringing in entertainment. More than 50 clubs, movies, nightclub, dances, and "some form of special event every weekend" on campus. Athletics and day trips to ski areas, the Poconos, and the beach also popular. Alcohol prohibited to students under 21; not permitted in public areas; all students may have cars.

About 40% of men, 35% of women live in traditional dormitories; 40% of men, 50% of women live in coed dormitories, 5% of each live in off-campus college-related housing; rest live in off-campus housing or commute. Freshmen given preference in college housing if all students cannot be accommodated. There are no fraternities or sororities on campus. About 20% of resident students leave campus on weekends.

Annual Costs. Tuition and fees, $13,600; room and board, $4,250; estimated $1,250 other, exclusive of travel. About 82% of students receive financial aid; average amount of assistance, $11,092. Assistance is typically divided 65% scholarship/grant, 25% loan, 10% work. College reports 464 scholarships awarded on the basis of academic merit alone; 759 for need alone. *Minority group students:* special provisions for financial aid. *Meeting Costs:* college offers 10-month payment plan.

Elm College

(See College of Our Lady of the Elms)

Elmhurst College

Elmhurst, Illinois 60126 (708) 617-3400

A church-related, liberal arts college, "open to students of all faiths," located in a suburban community of 45,000, 17 miles west of downtown Chicago. Most convenient major airport: O'Hare International (Chicago).

Founded: 1871
Affiliation: United Church of Christ
UG Enrollment: 575 M, 1,030 W (full-time); 427 M, 655 W (part-time)
Total Enrollment: 2,687
Cost: < $10K
% Receiving Financial Aid: 55%
Admission: Non-selective
Application Deadline: August 15

Admission. Graduates of accredited high schools with 16 units and rank in top half of class; ACT test scores above 20 or GPA of "C" or better eligible; 70% of applicants accepted, 40% of these actually enroll; 35% of freshman graduate in top fifth of high school class, 68% in top two fifths. Average freshman scores: ACT, 20.8 composite. *Required:* SAT or ACT; interview recommended. Criteria considered in admissions, in order of importance: high school academic record, standardized test scores, recommendations, extracurricular activities, writing sample; other factors considered: special talents, alumni children, diverse student body. About 19% of entering students from parochial schools. *Entrance programs:* midyear admission, rolling admission. *Apply* by August 15. *Transfers* welcome; 369 enrolled 1993–94.

Academic Environment. Degrees offered: bachelors. Graduation requirements include 10–12 courses divided between 6 categories. *Majors offered* include athletic training, urban studies, arts management, music business, church music, environmental management. Average undergraduate class size: 70% under 20, 30% 20–40.

About 44% of students entering as freshmen graduate within four years, 65–70% eventually; 73% of freshmen return for sophomore year. *Special programs:* CLEP, independent study, study abroad, honors, individualized majors, 3–2 engineering, Washington semester. Adult programs: Elmhurst Management Program for working adults, weekend option. *Calendar:* 4–1–4, summer school.

Undergraduate degrees conferred (745). 52% were in Business and Management, 12% were in Education, 10% were in Health Sciences, 5% were in Social Sciences, 4% were in Psychology, 4% were in Letters, 4% were in Liberal/General Studies, remainder in 9 other fields.

Graduates Career Data. Advanced studies pursued by 6% of graduates immediately, 13% within one year; 8% enter business school. Employers typically hiring largest numbers of graduates include Allstate Insurance, AT&T, Motorola, Walgreen Drugs, UPS, Performance Analytics, Chicago area hospitals.

Faculty. About 80% of faculty hold PhD or equivalent. About 10% of teaching faculty are female; 1% Black, 1% Hispanic, 1% other minority.

Student Body. About 98% of students from in state. An estimated 18% of students reported as Protestant, 38% Catholic, 35% unaffiliated, 9% other; 5% Black, 3% Hispanic, 4% Asian.

Religious Orientation. Elmhurst is a church-related institution; 3% of students affiliated with the church; course in religion required of all students as a liberal arts as well as a religious requirement; attendance at weekly ecumenical Sunday services voluntary.

Varsity Sports. Men (Div.III): Baseball, Basketball, Cross Country, Football, Golf, Tennis, Track, Wrestling. Women (Div.III): Cross Country, Golf, Softball, Tennis, Track, Volleyball.

Campus Life. About 14% of men, 16% of women live in traditional dormitories or in coed dormitories; rest live in off-campus housing or commute. Freshmen given preference in college housing if all students cannot be accommodated. Sexes segregated in coed dormitories by floor. There are 4 fraternities, 4 sororities on campus which about 14% of men, 15% of women join; they provide no residence facilities. About 10% of resident students leave campus on weekends.

Annual Costs. Tuition and fees, $8,612; room and board, $3,924; estimated $1,750 other, exclusive of travel. About 55% of students receive financial aid; average amount of assistance, $8,500. Assistance is typically divided 50% grant/scholarship, 40% loan, 16% work. College reports 30 scholarships awarded on the basis of academic merit alone; several awarded for special talents and need alone. *Meeting Costs:* college offers full year or term-length payment plans with low interest, participation in non-need based loan programs.

Elmira College

Elmira, New York 14901 (607) 734-1800

An independent, liberal arts college, Elmira became co-educational in 1969. The 38-acre main campus is located in a residential section of a city of 35,000, 90 miles southwest of Syracuse. Most convenient major airport: Elmira-Corning Regional Airport.

Founded: 1855
Affiliation: Independent
Total Enrollment: 440 M, 659 W (full-time)
Cost: $10K–$20K
% Receiving Financial Aid: 70%
Admission: Non-selective
Application Deadline: Rolling

Admission. Administration reports admission is based upon the combination of academic records, references, activities, and personal goals. About 72% of applicants accepted, 33% of these actually enroll; 42% of freshmen graduate in top fifth of high school class; 70% in top two-fifths. Average freshman scores: SAT, 461 M, 463 W verbal; 502 M, 494 W mathematical; ACT, 23 composite. *Required:* SAT or ACT, essay. Criteria considered in admissions, in order of importance: high school academic record, recommendations, extracurricular activities, writing sample, standardized test scores; other factors considered: special talents, alumni children, diverse student body. *Entrance programs:* early decision, midyear admission, deferred admission, advanced placement. About 21% of entering students from private, 14% from parochial schools. *Apply:* rolling admissions; January 15 for early decision. *Transfers* welcome; 115 accepted 1993–94.

Academic Environment. Administration reports 76% of courses required for graduation are elective; some distribution requirements; curriculum includes liberal studies core and communication skills program, 60 hours required community service for credit, 6 weeks of off-campus career-related field experience yearly. Degrees offered: bachelors. Average undergraduate class size: 18% under 20.

About 67% of students entering as freshmen graduate eventually; 88% of freshmen return for sophomore year. *Special programs:* 3-year degree, CLEP, honors, independent study, study abroad, undergraduate research, individualized majors, Washington Semester, United Nations Semester, government internships, Bahamas Program, self-instruction in critical languages, junior year at other U.S. colleges, internship required of all students. *Calendar:* 3 terms (12–12–6), summer school.

Undergraduate degrees conferred (249). 28% were in Business and Management, 22% were in Education, 8% were in Psychology, 8% were in Health Sciences, 6% were in Public Affairs, 6% were in Liberal/General Studies, 5% were in Social Sciences, 3% were in Mathematics, 3% were in Letters, 3% were in Protective Services, remainder in 4 other fields.

Graduates Career Data. Advanced studies pursued by 50% of students; 33% enter graduate school; 10% enter business school; 5% enter law school; 1% each enter medical and dental schools. Law schools typically enrolling largest numbers of graduates include Dickinson, NYU; business schools include Syracuse, Penn State. About 98% of 1993–94 graduates (not attending post-graduate program) employed. Fields typically hiring largest numbers of graduates include education, management, marketing, accounting. Career Development Services include career workshops related to resume writing, job search strategies, interviewing, etc.; career counseling, interest inventories, software programs ("Discover"), graduate school information, monthly newsletters.

Faculty. About 98% of faculty hold PhD or equivalent. About 66% of undergraduate classes taught by tenured faculty. About 36% of teaching faculty are female; 4% minority.

Student Body. About 48%% of students from in state, 60% Middle Atlantic, 25% New England, 5% Midwest, 1% each South, West, Northwest, 7% Foreign. An estimated 2% of students reported as Black, 3% Hispanic, 3% Asian, 1% Native American.

Varsity Sports. Men (Div.III): Basketball, Golf, Ice Hockey, Lacrosse, Soccer, Tennis. Women (Div.III): Basketball, Soccer, Softball, Tennis, Volleyball.

Campus Life. Students report many college-sponsored events, clubs, and intramural sports on-campus. One student recommends "Get involved RIGHT away! People are very busy here with clubs and organizations and that's the best way to fit in!" Administration source adds that the area is noted for the outdoor activities that are available. Intervisitation permitted within scheduled hours. Residence in dormitories required for all non-commuting students. Cars permitted. About 15% of students live in traditional dormitories; 80% of men, 70% of women in coed dormitories; rest commute. There are no fraternities or sororities on campus. About 20% of resident students leave campus on weekends.

Annual Costs. Tuition and fees, $13,900; room and board, $4,550; estimated $1,000 other, exclusive of travel. About 70% of students receive financial aid; average amount of assistance, $11,300. Assistance is typically divided 55% scholarship, 15% grant, 25% loan, 5% work. College reports 416 scholarships awarded on the basis of academic merit alone; 600 for need alone. *Meeting Costs:* college offers Parents Loan Program with no income restrictions.

Elon College

Elon College, North Carolina 27244 **(800) 334-8448 or (910) 584-2370**

A church-related college, located in a town of 3,500, 17 miles east of Greensboro. Most convenient major airport: Greensboro.

Founded: 1889
Affiliation: United Church of Christ
UG Enrollment: 1,295 M, 1,638 W (full-time); 89 M, 119 W (part-time)
Total Enrollment: 3,141
Cost: < $10K
% Receiving Financial Aid: 54%
Admission: Non-selective
Application Deadline: Rolling

Admission. Graduates of accredited high schools with minimum 2.0 GPA in 16 units of academic subjects eligible; others admitted conditionally; 77% of applicants accepted, 35% of these actually enroll. About 25% of freshmen graduate in top fifth of high school class, 53% in top two-fifths. Average freshman scores: SAT, 432 M, 444 W verbal; 486 M, 473 W mathematical. *Required:* SAT or ACT; interview recommended. Criteria considered in admissions, in order of importance: high school academic record, standardized test scores, extracurricular activities and leadership, recommendations; other factors considered: special talents, diverse student body, alumni children, leadership ability. About 15% of entering students from private schools. *Entrance programs:* early decision, midyear admission, deferred admission, advanced placement. *Apply:* rolling admissions. *Transfers* welcome; 125 enrolled 1993–94.

Academic Environment. Degrees offered: bachelors, masters. Graduation requirements include courses in English, math, fine arts, science, history, social sciences, physical education. *Majors offered* include broadcast and corporate communications, sports medicine, theatre arts, music theatre. Average undergraduate class size: 36% under 20, 62% 20–40.

About 45% of students entering as freshmen graduate within four years, 57% within 6 years; 80% of freshmen return for sophomore year. *Special programs:* development program, CLEP, advanced placement, independent study, study abroad, honors, undergraduate research, cross registration with consortium schools, 3–2 in engineering, N.C. Teaching Fellows Program. *Calendar:* 4–1–4, summer school.

Undergraduate degrees conferred (627). 34% were in Business and Management, 17% were in Social Sciences, 9% were in Psychology, 9% were in Education, 8% were in Communications, 5% were in Communications Technologies, 5% were in Public Affairs, 3% were in Letters, remainder in 9 other fields.

Graduates Career Data. Advanced studies pursued by 24% of graduates; 6% enter graduate school, 6% enter business school; 2% enter law school; 1% enter medical school. Business schools typically enrolling largest numbers of graduates include U. of Virginia, U. of North Carolina, North Carolina State. About 70% of 1992–93 graduates employed. Employers typically hiring largest numbers of graduates include Burlington Industries, IBM, Wachovia Bank, APCOM Telecommunications, Perdue Farms, Ernst & Young.

Faculty. About 75% of faculty hold PhD or equivalent. About 34% of undergraduate classes taught by tenured faculty. About 36% of teaching faculty are female; 3% Black, 1% Hispanic, 6% other minority.

Student Body. About 40% of students from in state; 48% South, 41% Middle Atlantic; 8% New England, 1% Midwest, 2% foreign. An estimated 52% of students reported as Protestant, 24% Catholic, 1% Jewish, 23% unaffiliated or other; 3% Black, 1% each Hispanic, Asian, 1% other minority.

Religious Orientation. Elon is a church-related institution; 28% of students affiliated with the church; no courses in religion required; participation in religious activities encouraged.

Varsity Sports. Men (Div.II): Baseball, Basketball, Cross Country, Football, Golf, Soccer, Tennis, Track. Women (Div.II): Basketball, Cross Country, Soccer, Softball, Tennis, Volleyball.

Campus Life. Students report "lots of exciting programs and entertainers", "over 90 different organizations and activities", "strong volunteers program", and access to city night life in Burlington and other more distant cities.

About 36% of men, 48% of women live in traditional dormitories; 4% of men, 6% of women live in off-campus housing; 58% of men, 44% of women commute. Limited intervisitation in men's and women's dormitory rooms. There are 11 fraternities, 9 sororities on campus which about 23% of men, 29% of women join; 2% of men live in fraternities, 3% of women live in sororities.

Annual Costs. Tuition and fees, $8,630; room and board, $3,660; estimated $1,575 other, exclusive of travel. About 54% of students receive financial aid; average amount of assistance, $6,815. College reports 307 scholarships awarded on the basis of academic merit alone; 276 for special talents alone; 141 for need alone; 272 for leadership scholarships. *Meeting Costs:* college offers 10-month payment plan, VISA/Mastercard accepted.

Embry-Riddle Aeronautical University

Daytona Beach, Florida 32114 (800) 222-ERAU

An independent, specialized school, offering 2- and 6-year programs in aviation fields; located at the regional airport in Daytona Beach (pop. 45,300). A second campus is located in Prescott, Arizona. Most convenient major airport: Daytona Beach.

Founded: 1926
Affiliation: Independent
UG Enrollment: 3,102 M, 401 W (full-time); 599 M, 76 W (part-time)
Total Enrollment: 4,357
Cost: < $10K
% Receiving Financial Aid: 75%
Admission: Non-selective
Application Deadline: 30 days before semester

Admission. Graduates of accredited high schools eligible; others given individual consideration; 81% of applicants accepted, 43% of these actually enroll; 31% of freshman graduate in the top fifth of their high school class; 59% in the top two fifths. Average freshman scores: SAT, 449 M, 446 W verbal; 517 M, 532 W mathematical; 28% score above 500 on verbal; 66% score above 500 on mathematical, 25% above 600, 3% above 700; ACT, 22.9 M, 23 W composite. *Required:* SAT or ACT. Criteria considered in admissions, in order of importance: high school academic record, standardized test scores, class rank, extracurricular activities, writing sample, recommendations. About 20% of entering students from private schools. *Entrance programs:* midyear admission, rolling admission. *Apply* 30 days prior to beginning of semester. *Transfers* welcome; 297 enrolled 1993–94.

Academic Environment. Degrees offered: associates, bachelors, masters. About 40% of general education requirements for graduation are elective; distribution requirements fairly numerous. *Majors offered* include aerospace studies. Average undergraduate class size: 24% under 20, 70% 20–40. *Special programs:* independent study, 3-year degree, 3–2 program with Georgia Tech, extensive cooperative education program, Miami Education Consortium with Barry College. *Calendar:* trimester, summer school.

Undergraduate degrees conferred (1773). 42% were in Engineering and Engineering Related Technology, 39% were in Transportation and Material Moving, 10% were in Business and Management, 8% were in Engineering, remainder in Computer and Engineering Related Technology.

Graduates Career Data. About 95% of 1992–93 graduates employed. Corporations typically hiring largest numbers of graduates include ERAU, US Air Force, US Army, Naval Air Warfare Center.

Student Body. About 23% of students from in state, 24% South, 34% Middle Atlantic, 15% Midwest, 11% New England, 2% Northwest, 7% foreign. An estimated 5% of students reported as Black, 6% Hispanic, 5% Asian, 6% other minority. Average age of undergraduate student: 22.

Varsity Sports. Men: Baseball, Basketball, Golf, Soccer, Tennis.

Campus Life. About 18% men, 25% women live in coed dormitories; 5% live in off-campus college-related housing; rest commute. Freshmen given preference in college housing if all students cannot be accommodated. Intervisitation in men's and women's dormitory rooms limited. There are 7 fraternities, 2 sororities on campus; 5% men, 2% women join; 2% of men live in fraternities. About 20% of students leave campus on weekends.

Annual Costs. Tuition and fees, $7,430; room and board, $3,400; estimated $1,740 other, exclusive of travel. About 75% of students receive financial aid; assistance is typically divided 10% scholarship, 15% grant, 70% loan, 5% work. College reports 45 scholarships awarded on the basis of academic merit alone; 30 for special talents alone.

Emerson College

Boston, Massachusetts 02116 (617) 578-8600

An independent, co-educational college, specializing in communication and performing arts, located in the Back Bay area of Boston. Most convenient major airport: Logan (Boston).

Founded: 1880
Affiliation: Independent
UG Enrollment: 742 M, 1,170 W (full-time); 136 M, 189 W (part-time)
Total Enrollment: 2,547
Cost: $10K–$20K
% Receiving Financial Aid: 50%
Admission: Non-selective
Application Deadline: Rolling

Admission. High school graduates with 10 units in college preparatory subjects eligible; 72% of applicants accepted, 34% of these actually enroll. About 31% of freshmen graduate in top fifth of high school class, 66% in top two-fifths. *Required:* SAT (ACT acceptable), essay. *Non-academic factors* considered in admissions: special talents, alumni children, diverse student body. *Entrance programs:* early admission, midyear admission, deferred admission, advanced placement. *Apply:* rolling admissions. *Transfers* welcome.

Academic Environment. In addition to requirements for a major, all students must fulfill 60 credits of All-College Requirements consisting of liberal arts and communication courses. The majority of All-College Requirements are completed in the first two years in addition to prerequisite and introductory courses in the major areas of concentration. *Degrees:* BA, BS, BS (in speech), BFA, BLI. New programs include: American Culture and Communications, European studies.

About 55% of students entering as freshmen graduate eventually; 30% of freshmen do not return for sophomore year. *Special programs:* CLEP, honors, independent study, summer study abroad, undergraduate research, individualized majors, cross-registration with nearby Suffolk U., Mass. College of Art, Boston Conservatory of Music, Boston Architectural Center, and School of the Museum of Fine Arts, BM program with Longy School of Music, mass communication seminar in Hollywood (CA). Calender: semester, 2 summer sessions.

Undergraduate degrees conferred (459). 59% were in Communications, 20% were in Visual and Performing Arts, 13% were in Letters, 4% were in Multi/Interdisciplinary Studies, remainder in 2 other fields.

Graduates Career Data. According to most recent data available, full-time graduate or professional study pursued immediately after graduation by 10% of students. *Careers in business and industry* pursued by 88% of graduates. Corporations typically hiring largest numbers of graduates include Paramount, ABC, WZLX.

Faculty. About 72% of faculty hold PhD or equivalent.

Student Body. According to most recent data available, 45% of students from Massachusetts; 63% New England, 25% Middle Atlantic. An estimated 3% of students reported as Black, 2% Hispanic, 1% Asian, 1% Native American, 1% other minority.

Varsity Sports. Men (NCAA Div. III): Baseball, Basketball, Golf, Hockey, Soccer, Tennis, Wrestling. Women (NCAA Div. III): Basketball, Soccer, Softball, Tennis, Volleyball.

Campus Life. College makes extensive use of Boston facilities and opportunities to enhance curriculum. Only freshmen required to live in residence halls.

According to most recent data available, about 8% of women live in traditional dormitories; 13% of men, 31% of women live in coed dormitories; rest commute. Freshmen given preference in college housing if all students cannot be accommodated. Intervisitation in men's and women's dormitory rooms unlimited. Sexes segregated in coed dormitories either by floor or room. There are 6 fraternities, 3 sororities, which about 12% of men, 7% of women join, they provide no residence facilities. About 25% of resident students leave campus on weekends.

Annual Costs. Tuition and fees, $14,831; room and board, $7,662. About 50% of students receive financial aid; assistance is typically divided 50% scholarship, 30% loan, 20% work. College reports all scholarships awarded on the basis of need. *Meeting Costs:* college offers alternative financing programs, monthly payment plans.

Emmanuel College

Boston, Massachusetts 02115 (617) 735-9715 (800) TRY-EMMA

A church-related college, conducted by the Sisters of Notre Dame of Namur, Emmanuel was the first Catholic liberal arts college for women established in New England. Although college maintains its relationship to the church, it is not under church control. The 16-acre campus is located in metropolitan Boston. Most convenient major airport: Logan International.

Founded: 1919
Affiliation: Independent (Roman Catholic)
Total Enrollment: 911 M, W (full-time)
Cost: $10K–$20K
% Receiving Financial Aid: 75%
Admission: Non-selective
Application Deadline: Rolling

Admission. High school graduates with 16 units eligible. Admission is based on academic record, application and essays, recommendations, extracurricular activities, interview, SAT or ACT scores. *Entrance programs:* early decision, rolling admission. *Apply:* rolling admissions. *Transfers* welcome.
Academic Environment. The academic plan permits student to develop individual program in consultation with faculty adviser. Degrees offered: bachelors, masters. *Majors offered* include career-oriented and pre-professional programs. Average undergraduate class size: 13. *Special programs:* independent study, individualized majors, cooperative programs, 3–2 engineering, internships. *Calendar:* semester.
Undergraduate degrees conferred (178). 19% were in Social Sciences, 15% were in Education, 15% were in Psychology, 13% were in Health Sciences, 11% were in Business and Management, 6% were in Life Sciences, 6% were in Letters, 4% were in Visual and Performing Arts, 4% were in Foreign Languages, 3% were in Allied Health, remainder in 4 other fields.
Faculty. About 75% of faculty hold PhD or equivalent.
Graduates Career Data. Career Development Services include interest testing, career counseling, mentorships, resume development, professional seminars, internships, partnerships, and alumni network.
Student Body. College reports students from "throughout the U.S. and more than 60 countries."
Religious Orientation. Emmanuel is an independent institution with a Roman Catholic orientation.
Varsity Sports. Women (NCAA Div.III): Basketball, Softball, Tennis, Volleyball.
Campus Life. About 51% of students live on campus.
Annual Costs. Tuition and fees, $11,973; room and board, $5,800. About 75% of students receive financial aid. College "is committed to meeting 100% of students' demonstrated financial need." Meeting Costs: college offers information sessions, subsidized loans, low-interest loans, payment plans.

Emory and Henry College

Emory, Virginia 24327-0947 (703) 944-4121

A church-related, liberal arts college, located in a village in southwest Virginia near Abingdon (pop. 10,500) and 130 miles west of Roanoke. Most convenient major airport: Tri-Cities.

Founded: 1836
Affiliation: United Methodist
Total Enrollment: 407 M, 402 W (full-time)
Cost: < $10K
Admission: Non-selective
Application Deadline: Rolling

Admission. High school graduates (preferably with 14 academic units) eligible; about 84% of applicants accepted, 35% of these actually enroll; 44% of freshmen graduate in top fifth of high school class, 77% in top two-fifths. Average freshman scores: SAT, 434 M, 452 verbal, 498 M, 473 W mathematical; ACT, 22.4 M, 23.1 W composite. *Required:* SAT or ACT, essay; interview recommended. Criteria considered in admissions, in order of importance: high school academic record and essay considered most important; standardized test scores, recommendations, extracurricular activities, and special talents also considered. *Apply:* rolling admissions. *Transfers* welcome; 77 enrolled 1993–94.
Academic Environment. Degrees offered: bachelors. General studies requirements of liberal arts curriculum include Western Tradition seminar, Great Books seminar, Value Inquiry, religion, global studies, mathematics or language. *Majors offered* include usual arts and sciences, computer science, land use planning, international studies, interdisciplinary majors including elementary education, geography, mass communication, medical technology, environmental studies. Students report small classes promote student participation and individual attention.

According to most recent data available, about 71% of students entering as freshmen graduate eventually; 24% of freshmen do not return for sophomore year. *Special programs:* CLEP, independent study, study abroad, honors, internships, student teaching, individualized majors, student-directed seminars, 3–2 programs in engineering, medical technology, forestry. *Calendar:* semester, summer school.
Undergraduate degrees conferred (179). 25% were in Business and Management, 18% were in Social Sciences, 9% were in Psychology, 8% were in Multi/Interdisciplinary Studies, 8% were in Communications, 7% were in Letters, 6% were in Education, 4% were in Computer and Engineering Related Technology, 3% were in Philosophy and Religion, 3% were in Mathematics, 3% were in Foreign Languages, remainder in 4 other fields.
Graduates Career Data. According to most recent data available, full-time graduate or professional study pursued immediately after graduation by 23% of students. Graduate and professional schools enrolling largest numbers of graduate include U. of Virginia, Medical College of Virginia, U. of Tennessee, Washington & Lee, Virginia Tech., Emory, Duke. *Careers in business and industry* pursued by 37% of graduates.
Faculty. About 90% of faculty hold PhD or equivalent. About 17% of teaching faculty are female; 6% ethnic minorities.
Student Body. According to most recent data available, 84% of students from in state; 96% South. An estimated 75% of students reported as Protestant, 7% Catholic, 16% unaffiliated, 2% other; 2% as Black, 1% Asian.
Religious Orientation. Emory and Henry is a church-related institution; 1 course in religion required; attendance at religious services (included in convocation program series) voluntary. Religious clubs on campus include College Church Class, Church Vocations Club, independent Bible study groups.
Varsity Sports. Men (Div.III): Baseball, Basketball, Cross Country, Football, Soccer, Tennis, Track. Women (Div.III): Basketball, Cross Country, Tennis, Track, Volleyball.
Campus Life. Students have voting member on Board of Governors and are "encouraged to form special-interest clubs on political, professional, or recreational themes." Students regulate their own hours. Intervisitation limited to 45 hours per week. Alcohol prohibited on campus or at college functions. Cars allowed for all students. Students report that the majority of students go home on weekends, but there has been an attempt to schedule more campus activities on weekends.

About 77% of men, 68% of women live in traditional dormitories; no coed dormitories; rest commute. Freshmen given preference in college housing if all students cannot be accommodated. There are 7 fraternities, 6 sororities on campus which about 14% of men, 17% of women join; they provide no residence facilities. About 40% of resident students leave campus on weekends.
Annual Costs. Tuition and fees, $9,200; room and board, $4,408; estimated $1,500 other, exclusive of travel. Financial aid assistance typically attempts to avoid heavy debt burden and therefore higher percentage scholarship and work, lower percentage loans. College reports some scholarships awarded on the basis of academic merit alone. *Meeting Costs:* college offers AMS and payment plans.

Emory University

Atlanta, Georgia 30322 (800) 727-6036

Long one of the leading universities in the South, Emory is rapidly expanding its student body, faculty and facilities. One of the most heavily endowed institutions in the country, Emory is seeking to become a major national university. More than 50% of its students come from outside the South. Although affiliated with the United Methodist Church, the university accepts students without reservation as to race, religion, sex, age, handicap, or national origin. The 600-acre main campus is located in a residential area, 5 miles from the center of Atlanta, the major business and cultural center of the region.

The 9 major divisions of the university are Emory College, professional schools of law, medicine, nursing, business administration, and theology, a graduate school of arts and sciences, the division of Public Health, and the 2-year undergraduate Oxford College, located some 40 miles away. Emory College, the university's undergraduate school of arts and sciences, is the oldest division of the university. Most convenient major airport: Hartsfield International.

Founded: 1836
Affiliation: United Methodist
UG Enrollment: 2,250 M, 2,750 W (full-time)
Total Enrollment: 10,367
Cost: $10K–$20K
% Receiving Financial Aid: 55%
Admission: Very (+) Selective
Application Deadline: February 1

Admission is very (+) selective for Emory College. About 48% of applicants accepted, 28% of these actually enroll; 60% of freshman graduate in top tenth of high school class, 85% in top quarter. Average freshman scores: SAT, 570 verbal, 650 mathematical; ACT, 28 composite. *Required:* SAT or ACT; essay, B average, campus visit recommended. Criteria considered in admissions, in order of importance: high school academic record, standardized test scores, recommendations, writing sample, extracurricular activities; other factors considered: alumni children, diverse student body, special talents. About 35% of entering students from private or parochial schools. *Entrance programs:* early decision, early admission, deferred admission, advanced placement. *Apply* by February 1. *Transfers* welcome; 100 enrolled 1993–94.

Academic Environment. Strong liberal arts program as well as pre-professional and pre-graduate emphasis. Students encouraged to plan a curriculum to match their own interests and goals, but also one which introduces them to the broad areas of inquiry in the liberal arts. Graduation requirements include 2 years of broad liberal arts study. A substantial number of endowed Woodruff Scholarships and Fellowships are attracting "outstanding students" outside the South. Freshman support program, pre-professional and pre-graduate advisors for medicine, nursing, law, business, and graduate school. Some student influence in determining curriculum. Students serve as voting members on most university standing committees. A few departments have given students some voice in faculty tenure decisions. Degrees offered: associates, bachelors, masters, doctoral. Average undergraduate class size: 30.

About 85% of students entering as freshmen graduate eventually; 92% of freshmen return for sophomore year. *Special programs:* independent study, study abroad (scholarship available), honors, undergraduate research, individualized majors, 4-year bachelors/masters programs in 9 departments, professional internships, Washington Semester, special humanities seminars, Stipe Society Scholars, Oak Ridge program, exchange programs with Agnes Scott, Morehouse, Spelman, Atlanta School of Art, 3–2 in engineering. *Library:* outstanding special collections in Reformation, English religious history, African religion, Southern history, Georgia politics, Southern literature, W.B. Yeats. *Calendar:* semester, summer school.

Undergraduate degrees conferred (1438). 32% were in Social Sciences, 14% were in Psychology, 13% were in Life Sciences, 10% were in Business and Management, 7% were in Letters, 6% were in Philosophy and Religion, 4% were in Visual and Performing Arts, 3% were in Health Sciences, 3% were in Foreign Languages, remainder in 8 other fields.

Doctoral degrees: Biological Sciences 11, Letters 7, Theology 20, Social Sciences 5, Psychology 7, Physical Sciences 15, Liberal/General Studies 16, Philosophy and Religion 14, Education 1.

Graduates Career Data. Advanced studies pursued by 65–70% of graduates. Career Development Services include interview preparation, internships, on-campus interviewing, recruitment, alumni network.

Faculty. About 98% of faculty hold PhD or equivalent. About 85% of undergraduate classes taught by tenured faculty.

Student Body. About 20% of students from in state; 45% South, 25% Middle Atlantic, 10.5% West and Southwest, 10% Midwest, 9% New England. An estimated 30% of students reported to be Protestant, 13% Catholic, 29% Jewish, 37% other; 10% Asian, 9% Black, 3% Hispanic, 1% other minority. *Minority group students:* special financial and social provisions including "Black House" through the Black Student Alliance.

Varsity Sports. Men (NCAA Div.III): Baseball, Basketball, Cross Country, Diving, Golf, Soccer, Swimming, Tennis, Track. Women (NCAA Div.III): Basketball, Cross Country, Diving, Soccer, Swimming, Tennis, Track, Volleyball.

Campus Life. Student reports over 170 student-run organizations, "very" popular intramural sports and Greek system "is still strong and running smoothly." Wide range of cultural and recreational opportunities available to students on campus and in Atlanta—the major cultural center in the South. Cars allowed, parking permit required. Smoking restricted to specific, designated areas only. Single freshmen expected to live in university residences. Residents of each dormitory now determine intervisitation and other dormitory regulations.

About 70% of students live in university housing; rest commute. Freshmen given preference in college housing if all students cannot be accommodated. Sexes segregated in coed dormitories by floor or room. There are 15 fraternities, 10 sororities on campus which about 33% of each join. About 5% of resident students leave campus on weekends.

Annual Costs. Tuition and fees, $16,820; room and board, $5,110; estimated $1,500 other, exclusive of travel. About 55% of freshmen receive financial aid; average amount of assistance, $14,000. Assistance is typically divided 71% grant, 19% loan, 10% work. University reports number of scholarships awarded on the basis of academic merit alone varies yearly; some awarded for special talents alone (music and debate). *Meeting Costs:* university offers university loan program.

Emporia State University

Emporia, Kansas 66801-5087 (316) 343-5465

A state-supported university, located in a city of 23,300, 55 miles south of Topeka. Institution offers special facilities and a program of rehabilitation for the physically handicapped. Most convenient major airports: Kansas City, Wichita.

Founded: 1863
Affiliation: State
UG Enrollment: 1,692 M, 2,139 W (full-time); 246 M, 371 W (part-time)
Total Enrollment: 5,088
Cost: < $10K
% Receiving Financial Aid: 70%
Admission: Non-selective
Application Deadline: Rolling

Admission. Graduates of accredited Kansas high schools eligible; graduates of unaccredited schools may be admitted provisionally; all applicants accepted, 35% of these actually enroll. Average freshman ACT scores, according to most recent data available: 18.3 M, 17.6 W composite, 18 M, 16.0 W mathematical. *Required:* ACT. *Out-of-state* freshman applicants: university seeks students from out of state. State does not limit out-of-state enrollment; requirements for out-of-state students slightly higher than for in-state. *Apply*; rolling admissions. *Transfers* welcome.

Academic Environment. *Degrees:* AB, BS, BFA, BGS, BM, BMEd, BSB, BSEd, BSN. About 20% of general education requirements for graduation are elective; distribution requirements fairly numerous. About 30% of freshmen do not return for sophomore year. *Special programs:* 3–2 programs in agriculture, dental, engineering, journalism, law, medical, nursing, optometry, osteopathic medicine, pharmacy, physical therapy, social work, veterinary medicine, dual degree programs, cooperative degree programs. *Calendar:* semesters, summer school.

Undergraduate degrees conferred (650). 26% were in Education, 26% were in Business and Management, 12% were in Social Sciences, 9% were in Psychology, 5% were in Life Sciences, 4% were in Computer and Engineering Related Technology, 3% were in Communications, 3% were in Liberal/General Studies, 3% were in Mathematics, remainder in 7 other fields.

Graduates Career Data. According to most recent data available, full-time graduate or professional study pursued immediately after graduation by 14% of students. *Careers in business and industry* pursued by 57% of graduates.

Faculty. About 68% of teaching faculty hold PhD or equivalent.

Varsity Sports. Men (NAIA Div.I): Baseball, Basketball, Cross Country, Football, Golf, Tennis, Track. Women (NAIA Div.I): Basketball, Cross Country, Softball, Tennis, Track, Volleyball.
Student Body. According to most recent data available, 86% of students from Kansas. An estimated 49% of students reported as Protestant, 45% Catholic, 2% unaffiliated, 4% other; 2% Black, 1% Hispanic, 14% other minority.
Campus Life. According to most recent data available, about 3% of men, 5% of women live in traditional residence halls; 22% of men, 25% of women in coed residence halls; 58% of men, 55% of women live in off-campus college-related housing; 8% of men, 9% of women commute. Freshmen given preference in college housing if all students cannot be accommodated. Intervisitation in men's and women's dormitory rooms limited. Sexes segregated in coed dormitories either by wing or floor. There are 8 fraternities, 4 sororities on campus which about 21% of men, 12% of women join; 9% of men, 6% of women live in fraternities and sororities.
Annual Costs. Tuition and fees, $1,584 (out-of-state, $4,464); room and board, $2,790; about 70% of students receive financial aid. University reports some scholarships awarded on the basis of academic merit alone.

Erskine College

Due West, South Carolina 29639 **(803) 379-2131**

A small, church-related, liberal arts college, located in a village of 1,400, 40 miles southwest of Greenville. Most convenient major airport: Greenville-Spartanburg Jetport.

Founded: 1839
Affiliation: Presbyterian
Total Enrollment: 228 M, 304 W (full-time)
Cost: $10K–$20K
% Receiving Financial Aid: 97%
Admission: Non-selective
Application Deadline: Aug. 15

Admission. High school graduates with 14 units in college preparatory subjects and rank in top half of class eligible; 84% of applicants accepted, 30% of these actually enroll; 47% of freshman graduated in the top tenth of high school class; 74% in top quarter. Average freshman scores: SAT, 467 M, 495 W verbal; 537 M, 533 W mathematical; 43% score above 500 on verbal, 15% above 600; 62% score above 500 on mathematical, 23% above 600. *Required:* SAT (ACT acceptable). Criteria considered in admissions, in order of importance: high school academic record (grades from college prep courses weighted twice as heavily as SAT scores), standardized test scores, recommendations, extracurricular activities. About 8% of entering students from private schools. *Entrance programs:* early admission, mid-year admission, rolling admission. *Apply* by: August 15. *Transfers* welcome; 18 enrolled 1993–94.
Academic Environment. Degrees offered: bachelors, masters, doctoral. About 50% of general education requirements for graduation are elective; some distribution requirements. Unusual majors offered include: sports management. Average undergraduate class size: 76% under 20, 22% 20–40. About 66% of students entering as freshmen graduate within four years, 69% eventually; 80% of freshmen return for sophomore year. *Special programs:* CLEP, Interim (on-campus and off-campus opportunities), study abroad, independent study, honors, 3-year degree, individualized majors, Erskine Scholars, 3–2 programs in engineering and medical technology. *Calendar:* 4–1–4, summer school.
Undergraduate degrees conferred (104). 26% were in Business and Management, 17% were in Education, 14% were in Social Sciences, 12% were in Physical Sciences, 11% were in Psychology, 7% were in Life Sciences, 7% were in Letters, 4% were in Mathematics, remainder in 2 other fields.
Graduates Career Data. Advanced studies pursued by 25% of graduates.
Faculty. About 80% of faculty hold PhD or equivalent. About 28% of teaching faculty are female; 2% minority.
Student Body. About 78% of students from in state, 97% South, 1% Middle Atlantic, 1% Midwest, 1% Foreign. An estimated 84% of students reported as Protestant, 5% Catholic, 10% unaffiliated; 4% Black, 2% other minority.
Religious Orientation. Erskine is a church-related institution, and seeks "to provide a liberal arts education in a Christian environment"; 22% of students affiliated with the church; 2 courses in religious studies required.
Varsity Sports. Men (NCAA): Baseball, Basketball, Golf, Soccer, Tennis. Women (NCAA): Basketball, Soccer, Tennis, Volleyball.
Campus Life. Students report "the small town atmosphere is very relaxing", however, "There is not much to do in town so students get to become more active in dorm and church activities."

About 95% of students live in traditional dormitories; rest commute. Intervisitation in men's and women's dormitory rooms limited. There are 3 fraternities and 3 sororities on campus of which 40% of men, 40% of women join. About 50% of resident students leave campus on weekends.
Annual Costs. Tuition and fees, $10,630; room and board, $3,680; estimated $1,201 other, exclusive of travel. About 97% of students receive financial aid; average amount of assistance, $9,600. Assistance is typically divided 40% scholarship, 30% grant, 20% loan, 10% work. College reports 200 scholarships awarded on the basis of academic merit alone; 125 for special talents alone. *Meeting Costs:* college offers ten month payment plan.

Eugene Bible College

Eugene, Oregon 97405

A small Bible college offering a "preview to ministry" with certificate and baccalaureate degree programs. College prepares students for Christian ministries or church vocations through a program of Biblical, general, and professional studies.

Founded: 1925 **Affiliation:** Open Bible Churches

Eureka College

Eureka, Illinois 61530 **(309) 467-6350 (Illinois, 800-322-3756)**

A church-related, liberal arts college, affiliated with the Christian Church (Disciples of Christ), located in a community of 5,000, 20 miles east of Peoria. Most convenient major airport: Greater Peoria.

Founded: 1855
Affiliation: Disciples of Christ
Total Enrollment: 246 M, 238 W (full-time)
Cost: $10K–$20K
% Receiving Financial Aid: 93%
Admission: Non-selective
Application Deadline: Rolling

Admission. High school graduates, preferably with 12 units in college preparatory subjects, eligible; 82% of applicants accepted, 25% of these actually enroll. About 42% of freshmen graduate in top fifth of high school class, 73% in top two-fifths. Average freshman scores: 22 composite. *Required:* ACT; interview recommended. Criteria considered in admissions, in order of importance: high school academic record, standardized test scores, recommendations, extracurricular activities. *Entrance programs:* mid-year admission, deferred admission, advanced placement. *Apply:* rolling admissions. *Transfers* welcome; 35 enrolled 1993–94.
Academic Environment. Degrees offered: bachelors. About 47% of general education requirements for graduation are elective; distribution requirements fairly numerous. About 50% of students entering as freshmen graduate eventually; 70% of freshmen return for sophomore year. *Majors offered* include economics and finance, biology/occupational therapy. Special programs: CLEP, independent study, honors, optional May term, 3-year degree, individualized majors, 3–2 engineering. *Calendar:* 4 8½-week terms between September and June, summer school.
Undergraduate degrees conferred (70). 26% were in Business and Management, 23% were in Education, 14% were in Letters, 6% were in Physical Sciences, 6% were in Mathematics, 6% were in Communications, 4% were in Social Sciences, 4% were in Psychology, 4% were in Life Sciences, 3% were in Visual and Performing Arts, remainder in 3 other fields.
Graduates Career Data. Advanced studies pursued by 15% of graduates. About 85% of 1992–93 graduates employed. Corporations typically hiring largest numbers of graduates include State Farm Insurance. Career Development Services include career planning, interview skills, resume writing, alumni network.
Faculty. About 85% of faculty hold PhD or equivalent. About 40% of teaching faculty are female; 3% minority.

Student Body. About 92% of students from in state; 97% Midwest. An estimated 4% of students reported as Black, 2% Hispanic, 1% Asian, 5% other minority.
Religious Orientation. Eureka is a church-related institution; 15% of students affiliated with the church; attendance at chapel services voluntary.
Varsity Sports. Men (NCAA Div.III, NAIA II): Basketball, Diving, Football, Golf, Swimming, Tennis, Track. Women (NCAA Div.III, NAIA II): Basketball, Diving, Golf, Softball, Tennis, Track, Volleyball.
Campus Life. About half of students live on-campus; rest commute. Intervisitation in men's and women's dormitory rooms limited. There are 3 fraternities, 3 sororities on campus which 35% of men, 40% of women join; about 13% of each live in fraternities and sororities.
Annual Costs. Tuition and fees, $11,105; room and board, $3,450; estimated $500 other, exclusive of travel. About 93% of students receive financial aid, average amount of assistance, $7,600. College reports, 33 scholarships available on the basis of academic merit alone. *Meeting Costs:* college offers four different payment plans.

Evangel College

Springfield, Missouri 65802 (417) 865-2811

A church-related, liberal arts college, located in a city of 120,100. Most convenient major airports: Springfield, Kansas City, St. Louis.

Founded: 1955
Affiliation: Assemblies of God
Total Enrollment: 1,388 M, W (full-time)
Cost: < $10K
Admission: Non-selective
Application Deadline: August 15

Admission. Graduates of accredited high schools with 15 units and C average eligible; 69% of applicants accepted, 87% of these actually enroll. *Required:* ACT; acceptance of college code (prohibits tobacco, alcohol, drugs, dancing, and requires "modesty in dress," regular attendance at daily chapel, regular church attendance). *Apply* by August 15. *Transfers* welcome.
Academic Environment. *Degrees:* AB, BS, BBA, BM. About 36–42% of general education requirements for graduation are elective; distribution requirements fairly numerous. *Special programs:* 3–2 engineering with Washington U.. *Calendar:* semester, January term, summer school.
Undergraduate degrees conferred (342). 26% were in Education, 16% were in Business and Management, 14% were in Communications, 9% were in Social Sciences, 9% were in Psychology, 6% were in Theology, 5% were in Letters, 4% were in Life Sciences, 3% were in Visual and Performing Arts, 3% were in Foreign Languages, remainder in 4 other fields.
Varsity Sports. Men (NAIA, Div.II): Baseball, Basketball, Football, Track. Women (NAIA, Div.II): Basketball, Softball, Track, Volleyball.
Student Body. According to most recent data available, 28% of students from Missouri; 64% of students from North Central, 9% Middle Atlantic, 15% South. All students reported as Protestant; 2% Black, 1% Hispanic, 1% other minority.
Religious Orientation. Evangel is a church-related institution with "emphasis on conduct compatible with a Christian witness"; 16 credits in Biblical studies and philosophy, attendance at daily chapel and Sunday morning and evening church services required of all students.
Campus Life. According to most recent data available, about 21% of men, 12% of women live in traditional dormitories; 12% of men, 35% of women in coed dormitories; rest live in off-campus housing or commute. Freshmen given preference in college housing if all students cannot be accommodated. No intervisitation in men's or women's dormitory rooms. There are no fraternities or sororities. About 10% of students leave campus on weekends.
Annual Costs. Tuition and fees, $6,730; room and board, $3,090.

University of Evansville

Evansville, Indiana 47722 (812) 479-2451

A church-related university, located in a residential area of a city of nearly 150,000. Most convenient major airport: Evansville Regional.

Founded: 1854
Affiliation: United Methodist
UG Enrollment: 1,132 M, 1,520 W (full-time); 131 M, 226 W (part-time)
Total Enrollment: 3,009
Cost: $10K–$20K
% Receiving Financial Aid: 87%
Admission: Selective
Application Deadline: Feb. 15

Admission is selective. About 78% of applicants accepted, 43% of these actually enroll. About 58% of freshmen graduate in top fifth of high school class, 86% in top two-fifths. Average freshman scores: SAT 494 M, 502 W verbal; 546 M, 531 W mathematical; 51% score above 500 on verbal, 15% above 600; 70% score above 500 on mathematical, 27% above 600; ACT, 25 composite. *Required:* SAT or ACT; essay. Criteria considered in admissions, in order of importance: high school academic record, standardized test scores, class rank, writing sample, recommendations, extracurricular activities; other factors considered: special talents, alumni children, religious affiliation and/or commitment, diverse student body. About 30% of entering students from private and parochial schools. *Entrance programs:* early admission, mid-year admission. *Apply* by February 15. *Transfers* welcome; 192 enrolled 1993–94.
Academic Environment. Undergraduate programs offered in Arts and Sciences, Fine Arts, Business Administration, Education, Engineering, Nursing. Graduation requirements include 9 hours in World Cultures, 6 in humanities/fine arts, 7 in natural sciences, 6 in social sciences, 3 in math, 6 in foreign languages, 3 in senior seminar. Degrees offered: associates, bachelors, masters.

About 60% of students entering as freshmen graduate within four years, 65% eventually; 83% of freshmen return for sophomore year. *Special programs:* CLEP, independent study, advanced placement, study abroad, honors, individualized majors, business internship, co-op engineering. Adult programs: Bachelor of Liberal Studies. *Calendar:* quarter, summer school.
Undergraduate degrees conferred (519). 17% were in Business and Management, 14% were in Engineering, 10% were in Education, 8% were in Health Sciences, 8% were in Communications, 6% were in Allied Health, 6% were in Liberal/General Studies, 5% were in Visual and Performing Arts, 5% were in Life Sciences, 4% were in Social Sciences, 3% were in Protective Services, 3% were in Psychology, 3% were in Multi/Interdisciplinary Studies, remainder in 7 other fields.
Graduates Career Data. Advanced studies pursued by 20% of graduates. Professional schools typically enrolling largest numbers of graduates include Indiana U. Corporations typically hiring largest numbers of graduates include Bristol Myers, Eli Lilly, Whirlpool. Career Development Services include career counseling, interest and aptitude testing, placement assistance, job market preparation workshop, credential file service, national placement database, placement newsletter, resource library, co-op education.
Faculty. About 81% of faculty hold PhD or equivalent. About 66% of undergraduate classes taught by tenured faculty. About 28% of teaching faculty are female; 2% Black, 2% Hispanic, 4% other.
Student Body. About 56% of students from in state; 73% Midwest, 13% South, 7% West, 2% Middle Atlantic, 5% Foreign. An estimated 36% of students reported as Protestant, 19% Catholic, 44 unknown 3% Black, 7% other minority.
Religious Orientation. University is a church-related institution, but makes no religious demands on students; 15% of students affiliated with the church.
Varsity Sports. Men (Div.I): Baseball, Basketball, Cross Country, Football (Div.II), Golf, Soccer, Swimming, Tennis. Women (Div.I): Basketball, Cross Country, Soccer, Softball, Swimming, Tennis, Volleyball.
Campus Life. Students report campus is in a safe, residential neighborhood, accessible to shopping, movies, etc. Students attend on-campus theater productions and athletic events, as well as fraternity parties ("not necessarily to drink").

About 42% of men, 53% of women live in traditional and coed dormitories; 8% men, 19% women live in off-campus college-related housing; 41% of men, 28% of women commute. Freshmen given preference in college housing if all students cannot be accommodated. Intervisitation options exist between open visitation and regulated visitation. Sexes segregated in coed dormitories by wing. There are 5 fraternities, 4 sororities on campus which about 18% of men, 17% of women join; 8% of men live in fraternities, 19% of women live in sororities.
Annual Costs. Tuition and fees, $11,330; room and board, $4,170; estimated $600 other, exclusive of travel. About 87% of students

receive financial aid; average amount of assistance, $9,032. Assistance is typically divided 26% scholarship, 38% grant, 29% loan, 7% work. University reports 1,179 scholarships awarded on the basis of academic merit alone; 322 for talents alone; 188 for need alone. *Meeting Costs:* university offers alternative loans.

Evergreen State College

Olympia, Washington 98505 (206) 866-6824

A highly innovative college located in a town of 26,000, Evergreen has charted new approaches to higher education as a state-supported institution. Most convenient major airport: Sea-Tac.

Founded: 1967
Affiliation: State
Total Enrollment: 3,377 M, W (full-time)
Cost: < $10K
% Receiving Financial Aid: 49%
Admission: Selective
Application Deadline: March 1

Admission is selective. High school graduates who rank in top half of class eligible (others given individual consideration); 43% of applicants accepted, 56% of these actually enroll. *Required:* Washington Uniform Application, rank in class, Washington Pre-College Test, SAT or ACT. Average freshman scores, according to most recent data available: SAT, 532 M, 520 W verbal, 539 M, 505 W mathematical; 60% of freshman score above 500 on verbal, 27% above 600, 5% above 700; 62% score above 500 on mathematical, 24% above 600, 5% above 700. *Out-of-state* freshman applicants: college does not seek, but welcomes, students from out of state. No special requirements for out-of-state applicants. *Apply* by March 1. *Transfers* welcome.

Academic Environment. All studies are interdisciplinary. Students enroll each quarter in a single comprehensive program, called Coordinated Studies, that brings a group of students and faculty together in intensive study of a single topic from a variety of perspectives. No required courses, but freshmen and transfers are strongly advised to take one of the year-long Core programs to develop skills in writing and independent research. *Degrees:* BA, BS. About 25% of freshmen do not return for sophomore year. *Special programs:* CLEP, independent study, study abroad, undergraduate research, 3-year degree, external credit, 3–2 programs in engineering, agriculture. *Calendar:* quarter, summer school.

Undergraduate degrees conferred (693). 100% were in Liberal/General Studies.

Graduates Career Data. According to most recent data available, full-time graduate or professional study pursued by 16% of students immediately after graduation. *Careers in business and industry* pursued by 80% of graduates. Employers typically hiring largest numbers of graduates include Microsoft, Boeing, state government.

Faculty. About 76% of faculty hold PhD or equivalent.

Varsity Sports. Men (NAIA): Soccer, Swimming & Diving. Women (NAIA): Soccer, Swimming & Diving.

Student Body. According to most recent data available, 80% of students from Washington. An estimated 4% of students reported as Black, 2% Hispanic, 4% Asian.

Campus Life. According to most recent data available, about 33% of men, 33% of women live in coed dormitories; rest live in off-campus housing or commute. Sexes segregated in coed dormitories by room. There are no fraternities or sororities. About 60% of resident students leave campus on weekends.

Annual Costs. Tuition and fees, $1,971 (out-of-state, $6,948). About 49% of students receive financial aid; assistance is typically divided 42% scholarship, 38% loan, 20% work. College reports some scholarships awarded on the basis of academic merit alone.

Fairfield University

Fairfield, Connecticut 06430-7524 (203) 254-4000

Founded by the Jesuits as a school for men, Fairfield has become an independent, fully co-educational institution while maintaining ties with its Roman Catholic origins. The 200-acre campus is located in a town of 56,500, 5 miles west of Bridgeport and 50 miles east of New York City. Most convenient major airport: LaGuardia, JFK.

Founded: 1942
Affiliation: Independent (Roman Catholic)
UG Enrollment: 1,310 M, 1,607 W (full-time); 382 M, 722 W (part-time)
Total Enrollment: 4,777
Cost: $10K–$20K
% Receiving Financial Aid: 66%
Admission: Very Selective
Application Deadline: March 1

Admission is very selective. About 68% of applicants accepted, 25% of these actually enroll; 57% of freshmen graduate in top fifth of high school class, 89% in top two-fifths. Average freshman scores: SAT, 501 M, 497 W verbal; 571 M, 548 W mathematical; 53% of freshmen score above 500 on verbal, 8% above 600, 1% above 700; 82% score above 500 on mathematical, 33% above 600, 4% above 700. *Required:* SAT or ACT; 3 ACH including English and mathematics (language for liberal arts, chemistry for premed, physics for engineering), interview recommended, required for nursing. Criteria considered in admissions, in order of importance: high school academic record, extracurricular activities, standardized test scores, recommendations; other factors considered: special talents, alumni children, diverse student body. *Entrance programs:* early decision, early admission, advanced placement. About 50% of entering students from private and parochial schools. *Apply* by March 1. *Transfers* welcome; 40 enrolled 1993–94.

Academic Environment. Both administration and student sources report that the economics, sciences, finance and accounting programs are the strongest academically, the School of nursing is also considered very strong. Overwhelming proportion of students reported to be primarily concerned with occupational/professional goals. Graduation requirements include 2 semesters each mathematics, natural sciences, history, social sciences, philosophy, religious studies, 1 additional course in either religious studies or philosophy, 3 semesters English, 2 semesters fine arts, 2 semesters (at least to the intermediate level) of a classical or modern language. *Undergraduate studies* offered by College of Arts and Sciences, School of Nursing and School of Business. Degrees offered: bachelors, masters. *Majors offered* include: international business, women's studies minor. Average undergraduate class size: 25.

About 84% of students entering as freshmen graduate within four years, 86% eventually; 89% of freshmen return for sophomore year. *Special programs:* CLEP, January Term offers Writing Center, internships, study abroad, honors, 3–2 engineering with U. of Connecticut, 3–3 dental program with NYU, cross-registration with U. of Bridgeport and Sacred Heart U., freshman year seminar series, writing center. Adult programs: School of Continuing Education. *Calendar:* semester, summer school.

Undergraduate degrees conferred (823). 23% were in Social Sciences, 23% were in Business and Management, 14% were in Letters, 10% were in Marketing and Distribution, 6% were in Life Sciences, 6% were in Psychology, 4% were in Mathematics, 4% were in Communications, 3% were in Health Sciences, remainder in 8 other fields.

Graduates Career Data. Advanced studies pursued by 18% of graduates; 5% enter law school; 4% enter medical school; 3% enter dental school; 3% enter business schools. Medical schools typically enrolling largest numbers of graduates include U. of Connecticut, Georgetown; dental schools include U. of Connecticut, Tufts; law schools include U. of Connecticut, St. John's, Fordham; business schools include U. of Connecticut, Boston U. About 70–75% of 1992–93 graduates employed. Employers typically hiring largest numbers of graduates include "Big 8" accounting firms, AETNA, Chase Manhattan Bank. Career Development Services include resume writing, interview preparation, on-campus interviewing, alumni referral service.

Faculty. About 90% of faculty hold PhD or equivalent. About 75% of undergraduate classes taught by tenured faculty. About 35% of teaching faculty are female; 3% minority.

Student Body. About 32% of students from in state; 49% New England, 45% Middle Atlantic; 3% Midwest, 1% each South, West, Northwest, 1% foreign. An estimated 92% of students reported as Catholic, 7% Protestant,1% other; 2% as Black, 4% Hispanic, 4% Asian. *Minority group students:* minority counselor available on full-time basis.

Religious Orientation. University is an independent institution, affiliated with the Catholic Church; 92% of students affiliated with

the church; 2 courses in religious studies required as part of the core curriculum.
Varsity Sports. Men (Div.I): Baseball, Basketball, Cross Country, Diving, Golf, Ice Hockey, Lacrosse, Soccer, Swimming, Tennis. Women (Div. I): Basketball, Cross Country, Diving, Golf, Ice Hockey, Lacrosse, Soccer, Softball, Swimming, Tennis.
Campus Life. Administration reports that intervisitation policy established by each residence hall; drinking permitted in accordance with state law (legal age, 21); all non-residential buildings are "smoke-free". Juniors and seniors may live off campus. High interest is reported in both intramural sports (most popular: football, basketball, softball) and varsity athletics (most popular: basketball, baseball, ice hockey, tennis).

About 82% of students live in coed dormitories; 10% of students live in on-campus housing; rest commute. Freshmen given preference in college housing if all students cannot be accommodated. Sexes segregated in coed dormitories by floor. There are no fraternities or sororities on campus. About 20% of resident students leave campus on weekends.
Annual Costs. Tuition and fees, $14,560; room and board, $5,900; estimated $1,100 other, exclusive of travel. About 66% of students receive financial aid; average amount of assistance, $7,913. Assistance is typically divided 5% scholarship, 64% grant, 30% loan, 2% work. University reports 374 scholarships awarded on the basis of academic merit alone; 88 for special talents alone; 1,189 for need alone. *Meeting Costs:* university offers participation with outside tuition plan company, discount to families with 2 or more siblings, scholarships for qualified students with a mentally handicapped sibling.

Fairleigh Dickinson University

Rutherford, New Jersey 07070-2299 (201) 460-5267

An independent university with 3 major centers in residential suburbs of northern New Jersey—the Rutherford (pop. 20,800) campus, a predominantly residential campus at Madison (pop. 16,700), and a campus at Teaneck, which has the largest enrollment. The university operates overseas campuses: in Wroxton Abbey, England, for English literature and in the Virgin Islands for marine sciences.

Founded: 1942
Affiliation: Independent
Total Enrollment: 11,644 M, W (full-time)
Cost: $10K–$20K
% Receiving Financial Aid: 70%
Admission: Non-selective
Application Deadline: Rolling

Admission. Graduates of accredited high schools with 16 units eligible. For all campuses, 85% of applicants accepted, 31% of these actually enroll. About 27% of entering freshmen graduate in top fifth of high school class, 55% in top two-fifths. *Required:* SAT; interview recommended. *Non-academic factors* considered in admissions: special talents, diverse student body. *Entrance programs:* early decision, early admission, midyear admission, advanced placement. *Apply:* rolling admissions. *Transfers* welcome.
Academic Environment. Administration reports percent of general education courses required for graduation varies on all campuses from one college and program to another. Distribution requirements fairly numerous on all campuses: 9 credits each in social sciences, humanities, 12 in natural sciences, 31 in arts and letters. *Undergraduate studies* offered by colleges of Arts and Sciences, Liberal Arts (Teaneck–Hackensack), Business Administration, Education, Science and Engineering, Leonard Dreyfuss College (Florham–Madison); some specialized programs not available at all campuses, e.g. engineering at Teaneck only. *Majors offered* include more than 70 programs in arts and sciences and professional/vocational fields (including arts and sciences programs in international studies, marine biology, dental hygiene, nursing).

Special programs: CLEP, independent study, study abroad, honors, undergraduate research, optional intersession, 3-year degree. *Calendar:* 4–1–4, summer school.
Undergraduate degrees conferred (1080). 48% were in Business and Management, 7% were in Psychology, 7% were in Engineering, 7% were in Social Sciences, 7% were in Letters, 5% were in Life Sciences, 5% were in Engineering and Engineering Related Technology, 4% were in Health Sciences, 4% were in Communications, remainder in 8 other fields.
Faculty. About 71% of faculty hold PhD or equivalent.
Student Body. According to most recent data available, 78% of students from in state, 92% Middle Atlantic. An estimated 11% of students reported as Black, 5% Hispanic, 3% Asian, 15% other minority.
Varsity Sports. For Rutherford & Teaneck, Men (Div.I): Baseball, Basketball, Cross Country, Equestrian, Golf, Lacrosse, Soccer, Tennis, Track (Indoor), Wrestling; (Div. III): Baseball, Basketball, Football, Golf, Lacrosse, Soccer, Tennis. Women (Div.I): Basketball, Cross Country, Equestrian, Fencing, Golf, Softball, Tennis, Track (Indoor). For Madison, Men (Div.III): Baseball, Basketball, Football, Golf, Lacrosse, Soccer, Tennis, Track, Volleyball. Women (Div.III): Basketball, Golf, Field Hockey, Softball, Tennis, Volleyball.
Campus Life. Multicampus structure of university permits, to some extent, small-college environment at each campus. Community governance less of an issue with initiation of broad-based University Senate; each campus includes representatives of all groups on Campus Council. Alcohol generally prohibited on campus, except at student functions conforming to specified regulations; cars allowed.

According to most recent data available, about 50% of students at Florham–Madison live in coed and traditional dormitories, 38% at Teaneck–Hackensack, 61% at Rutherford. For all campuses, intervisitation in men's and women's dormitory rooms unlimited. Sexes segregated in coed dormitories either by room or floor.
Annual Costs. Tuition and fees, $10,295(varies slightly between campuses); room and board, $5,336. About 70% of students receive financial aid. University reports some scholarships awarded on the basis of academic merit alone. *Meeting Costs:* university offers Family Plan Grants, and PLUS/HELP.

Fairmont State College

Fairmont, West Virginia 26554 (304) 367-4000

A state-supported college, located in a community of 27,000, 90 miles south of Pittsburgh. Most convenient major airport: Pittsburgh.

Founded: 1865
Affiliation: State
Total Enrollment: 1,982 M, 2,422 W (full-time); 866 M, 1,059 W (part-time)
Cost: < $10K
% Receiving Financial Aid: 60%
Admission: Non-selective
Application Deadline: June 15

Admission. Graduates of approved high schools with 2.5 GPA eligible; 95% of applicants accepted, 76% of these actually enroll. About 5% of entering freshman graduate in top fifth of high school class, 20% in top two-fifths. Average freshman scores: ACT, 18.1 M, 18.3 W composite. *Required:* ACT. Criteria considered in admissions, in order of importance: high school academic record, standardized test scores. *Out-of-state* freshman applicants: college seeks students from out-of-state. State does not limit out-of-state enrollment. No special requirements for out-of-state applicants. About 84% of out-of-state applicants accepted, 60% of these actually enroll. States from which most out-of-state students are drawn: Maryland, Pennsylvania, Virginia, Ohio. *Entrance programs:* early decision, rolling admission. *Apply* by June 15. *Transfers* welcome; 479 enrolled 1992–93.
Academic Environment. Degrees offered: associates, bachelors. About 30% of general education requirements for graduation are elective; distribution requirements fairly numerous. Average undergraduate class size: 5% under 20, 67% 20–40. About 35% of students entering as freshmen graduate within four years, 45% eventually; 70% of freshmen return for sophomore year. *Special programs:* CLEP, independent study, honors, undergraduate research. *Calendar:* semester, summer school.
Undergraduate degrees conferred (541). 31% were in Business and Management, 24% were in Education, 12% were in Engineering and Engineering Related Technology, 9% were in Protective Services, 8% were in Multi/Interdisciplinary Studies, 5%

were in Psychology, 3% were in Social Sciences, remainder in 8 other fields.
Graduates Career Data. Full-time advanced studies pursued by 22% of students immediately after graduation.
Faculty. About 37% of faculty hold PhD or equivalent. About 50% of undergraduate classes taught by tenured faculty.
Student Body. About of 95% of students from in state. Average age of undergraduate student: 24.
Varsity Sports. Men (NAIA): Baseball, Basketball, Cross Country, Football, Golf, Swimming, Tennis. Women (NAIA): Basketball, Cross Country, Golf, Swimming, Tennis, Volleyball.
Campus Life. About 2% of men, 4% of women live in traditional dormitories; rest commute. Intervisitation in men's and women's dormitory rooms limited. There are 4 fraternities, 3 sororities on campus which about 10% of men, 15% of women join; they provide no residence facilities. About 50% of resident students leave campus on weekends.
Annual Costs. Tuition and fees, $1,800 (out-of-state, $4,400); estimated $700 other, exclusive of room and board, and travel. About 60% of students receive financial aid; average amount of assistance, $1,700. Assistance is typically divided 25% scholarship, 40% grant, 25% loan, 10% work. College reports 250 scholarships awarded on the basis of academic merit alone; 80 for special talents alone.

Fayetteville State University

Fayetteville, North Carolina 28301 (919) 486-1371

A state-supported university, located in a city of 53,100; founded as a college for Negroes and still serving a predominantly Black student body. Most convenient major airport: Grannis Field (Fayetteville).

Founded: 1867
Affiliation: State
UG Enrollment: 766 M, 1,296 W (full-time); 136 M, 305 W (part-time)
Total Enrollment: 3,736
Cost: < $10K
% Receiving Financial Aid: 65%
Admission: Non-selective
Application Deadline: Aug. 15

Admission. Graduates of accredited high schools with 16 units who with overall GPA of 2.0 eligible; 82% of applicants accepted, 38% of these actually enroll. About 10% of freshmen graduate in top fifth of high school class, 33% in top two-fifths. *Required:* SAT. *Out-of-state* freshman applicants: university welcomes out-of-state students. State limits out-of-state students to 10% of student body. About 65% of applicants accepted, 35% enroll. *Non-academic factors* considered in admissions: special talents. *Apply* by August 15. *Transfers* welcome.
Academic Environment. *Degrees:* AB, BS. About 90% of general education requirements for graduation are elective; distribution requirements fairly numerous. About 15% of entering students graduate within four years. *Special programs:* CLEP, independent study, undergraduate research, credit by examination, variety of 3–2 programs with North Carolina State U.. *Calendar:* semester, summer school.
Undergraduate degrees conferred (255). 29% were in Business and Management, 22% were in Education, 14% were in Social Sciences, 12% were in Protective Services, 8% were in Psychology, 5% were in Mathematics, 3% were in Visual and Performing Arts, 3% were in Life Sciences, 3% were in Letters, remainder in 2 other fields.
Student Body. About 92% of students from North Carolina. An estimated 70% of students reported as Black, 1% Hispanic, 1% Asian, 1% Native American, according to most recent data available.
Varsity Sports. Men (CIAA): Basketball, Cheerleaders, Cross Country, Golf, Football, Tennis, Track. Women (CIAA): Basketball, Cheerleading, Cross Country, Golf, Softball, Tennis, Track, Volleyball.
Campus Life. According to most recent data available, about 44% of men, 33% of women live in traditional dormitories; rest commute. No intervisitation in men's or women's dormitory rooms. There are 4 fraternities, 4 sororities on campus which 8% of men, 5% of women join; they provide no residence facilities.
Annual Costs. Tuition and fees, $1,246 (out-of-state, $6,918); room and board, $2,250. About 65% of students receive financial aid.

Federal City College

(See University of the District of Columbia)

Felician College

Lodi, New Jersey 07644 (201) 778-1029

A Catholic college for women conducted by the Felician Sisters, Felician offers a liberal arts education while preparing students for a career. Campus is located in a community of 25,000. Most convenient major airport: Newark, LaGuardia, JFK.

Founded: 1942
Affiliation: Roman Catholic
Total Enrollment: 70 M, 435 W (full-time); 85 M, 555 W (part-time)
Cost: < $10K
% Receiving Financial Aid: 36%
Admission: Non-selective
Application Deadline: Rolling

Admission. High school graduates with 16 credits in academic subjects eligible; 71% of applicants accepted, 60% of these actually enroll. About 20% of freshmen graduate in top fifth of high school class; 45% in top two-fifths. Average freshman scores: 450 M, 450 W verbal, 450 M, 450 W mathematical. *Required:* SAT. Criteria considered in admissions, in order of importance: high school academic record, interview, standardized test scores, extracurricular activities, recommendations, writing sample. *Entrance programs:* mid-year admission, advanced placement. *Apply:* rolling admissions. *Transfers* welcome; 170 enrolled 1993–94.
Academic Environment. Degrees offered: associates, bachelors. Graduation requirements include 42 credit liberal arts core curriculum. *Majors offered* include elementary education, special education, art, computer science, business, nursing, sciences. Average undergraduate class size: 80% under 20; 20% 20–40. About 87% of freshmen return for sophomore year. Special programs include internships. Adult programs: Weekend College program allows adults to complete Bachelor's in 4 1/2 years. *Calendar:* semester.
Undergraduate degrees conferred (47). 34% were in Health Sciences, 15% were in Life Sciences, 13% were in Psychology, 13% were in Education, 6% were in Visual and Performing Arts, 6% were in Multi/Interdisciplinary Studies, 4% were in Letters, remainder in 4 other fields.
Faculty. About 75% of faculty hold PhD or equivalent.
Student Body. About 99% of students from in state; 99% Middle Atlantic. Average age of undergraduate student: 24.
Religious Orientation. Felician is a church-related institution; 2 courses in religious studies required of all Catholic students, recommended to others.
Campus Life. No on campus housing; all women commute. There is 1 fraternity, 2 sororities on campus; which about 20% of men, 25% of women join.
Annual Costs. Tuition and fees, $7,900; estimated $500 other, exclusive of travel. About 36% of students receive financial aid; average amount of assistance, $1,500. College reports 15 scholarships awarded on the basis of academic merit alone. *Meeting Costs:* college offers deferred payment plan.

Ferris State College

Big Rapids, Michigan 49307 (616) 592-2100

A state-supported college, located in a town of 15,000, 55 miles north of Grand Rapids, Ferris State emphasizes "practical, vocational and technical education." Most convenient major airport: Grand Rapids.

Founded: 1884
Affiliation: State
UG Enrollment: 5,457 M, 3,539 W (full-time); 967 M, 934 W (part-time)
Total Enrollment: 11,165
Cost: < $10K
% Receiving Financial Aid: 68%
Admission: Non-selective
Application Deadline: Rolling

Admission. High school graduates with GPA of 2.0 or equivalent eligible. About 96% of applicants accepted, 76% of these actually enroll. Average freshman scores: ACT, 18.4 composite. *Required:* ACT. Criteria considered in admissions, in order of importance: high school academic record, standardized test scores, recommendations. *Out-of-state* freshman applicants: college welcomes out-of-state students. State does not limit out-of-state enrollment; 432 enrolled for 1993–94. States from which most out-of-state students are drawn: Indiana. *Entrance programs:* early decision, rolling admission. *Apply:* rolling admissions. *Transfers* welcome.
Academic Environment. Degrees offered: associates, bachelors, masters, doctoral. General education requirements for graduation vary with school; distribution requirements fairly numerous. About 46% of freshmen return for sophomore year. Notable majors offered include professional tennis management. *Special programs:* CLEP, individualized majors. *Calendar:* quarter, summer school.
Undergraduate degrees conferred (1662). 35% were in Business and Management, 13% were in Health Sciences, 12% were in Engineering and Engineering Related Technology, 10% were in Marketing and Distribution, 6% were in Protective Services, 5% were in Communications, 5% were in Education, 3% were in Public Affairs, 3% were in Computer and Engineering Related Technology, remainder in 7 other fields.
Graduate Career Data. About 89% of 1992–93 graduates employed. Fields typically hiring largest numbers of graduates include professional golf management, pharmacy, management.
Faculty. About 37% of faculty hold PhD or equivalent.
Student Body. About 91% of students from in state, 3% foreign.
Varsity Sports. Men (NCAA Div.II): Baseball, Basketball, Cross Country, Football, Golf, Hockey (Div. I), Swimming, Tennis, Track, Wrestling. Women (Div.II): Basketball, Cross Country, Golf, Softball, Swimming, Tennis, Track, Volleyball.
Campus Life. About 22% of men, 13% of women live in coed dormitories; apartments on campus for married students. Intervisitation in men's and women's dormitory rooms limited. There are 12 fraternities, 7 sororities on campus, which about 5% of men, 6% of women join.
Annual Costs. Tuition and fees, $3,222 (out-of-state, $6,526); room and board, $3,923. About 68% of students receive financial aid; average amount of assistance, $5,200. Assistance is typically divided 5% scholarship, 35% grant, 35% loan, 25% work. College reports 135 scholarships awarded on the basis of academic merit alone; 516 for special talents alone.

Ferrum College

Ferrum, Virginia 24088 **(800) 868-9797**

Founded as a 2-year college, Ferrum has been offering 4-year degree programs since 1974. The campus is located in the foothills of the Blue Ridge Mountains in southwestern Virginia. Most convenient major airport: Roanoke Regional.

Founded: 1913
Affiliation: United Methodist
Total Enrollment: 680 M, 463 W (full-time)
Cost: < $10K
% Receiving Financial Aid: 94%
Admission: Non-selective
Application Deadline: Aug. 1

Admission. Graduates of accredited high school or equivalent eligible; 74% of applicants accepted, 37% of these actually enroll. Average freshman SAT scores, according to most recent data available: 416 M, 363 W verbal, 430 M, 383 W mathematical. *Required:* SAT or ACT; interview recommended. *Apply* by August 1; rolling admissions. *Transfers* welcome.
Academic Environment. *Degrees:* BA, BS, BSW. College offers baccalaureate programs in child development, educational theatre, fine arts, foreign languages, international studies, language resources for management, liberal studies, medical technology, philosophy, psychology, recreation and leisure, religion, social work, environmental studies, general agriculture, business enterprise, professional music, biology.
Undergraduate degrees conferred (133). 29% were in Business and Management, 16% were in Psychology, 13% were in Life Sciences, 6% were in Visual and Performing Arts, 6% were in Social Sciences, 6% were in Public Affairs, 5% were in Letters, 4% were in Liberal/General Studies, 4% were in Computer and Engineering Related Technology, 4% were in Agribusiness and Agricultural Production, 3% were in Philosophy and Religion, remainder in 3 other fields.
Varsity Sports. Men (Div. III): Baseball, Basketball, Equitation, Football, Golf, Tennis, Track, Wrestling. Women (Div. III): Basketball, Equitation, Soccer, Softball, Tennis, Track, Volleyball.
Student Body. According to most recent data available, about 91% of students from Virginia. An estimated 8% of students reported as Black, 2% Hispanic.
Religious Orientation. Ferrum is a church-related college, but welcomes students of all denominations. Makes no religious demands on students.
Campus Life. According to most recent data available, all students not living at home required to live on campus. Cars allowed. About 60% of men, 70% of women live in traditional dormitories; 35% of men, 25% of women live in coed dormitories; rest commute.
Annual Costs. Tuition and fees, $8,800; room and board, $4,000. About 94% of students receive financial aid; assistance is typically divided 63% scholarship, 30% loan, 7% work. College reports some scholarships awarded on the basis of academic merit alone.

The University of Findlay

Findlay, Ohio 45840 **(800) 548-0932**

Affiliated with the Churches of God in North America, Findlay is located in a city of 40,000, 50 miles south of Toledo. Most convenient major airports: Toledo or Detroit.

Founded: 1882
Affiliation: Churches of God
Total Enrollment: 2,178 (full-time)
Cost: < $10K
% Receiving Financial Aid: 75%
Admission: Non-selective
Application Deadline: Aug. 1

Admission. Graduates of accredited high schools with 16 units in academic subjects, GPA of 2.9 in college preparatory subjects eligible; exceptions made on individual basis. About 82% of applicants accepted, 23% of these actually enroll; 10% of entering freshman graduate in top fifth of high school class, 67% in top two-fifths. Average freshman scores: SAT, 408 M, 451 W verbal, 469 M, 475 W mathematical; ACT, 20.2 composite. *Required:* ACT or SAT; interview recommended. Criteria considered in admissions, in order of importance: high school academic record, standardized test scores, recommendations; other factors considered: alumni children. About 12% of entering students from private or parochial schools. *Entrance programs:* mid-year admission, rolling admission. *Apply* by August 1. *Transfers* welcome; 85 enrolled 1993–94.
Academic Environment. Degrees offered: associates, bachelors, masters. *Majors offered* include environmental hazardous materials management, equestrian studies, technical writing, bilingual business education, criminal justice emphasis, gerontology. About 91% of freshmen return for sophomore year. *Special programs:* CLEP, independent study, study abroad, honors, undergraduate research, 3-year degree, individualized majors, internships in elementary education, business, 3–2 engineering, accounting cooperative. Adult programs: Weekend College. *Calendar:* 3–3, summer school.
Undergraduate degrees conferred (228). 29% were in Business and Management, 17% were in Education, 9% were in Social Sciences, 9% were in Computer and Engineering Related Technology, 5% were in Marketing and Distribution, 4% were in Engineering and Engineering Related Technology, 4% were in Communications, 4% were in Psychology, 4% were in Letters, 4% were in Health Sciences, 3% were in Life Sciences, 3% were in Agricultural Sciences, remainder in 8 other fields.
Graduates Career Data. About 90% of 1992–93 graduates employed.
Faculty. About 45% of faculty hold PhD or equivalent.
Student Body. About 85% of students from in state; 88% Midwest, 6% foreign. An estimated 66% of students reported as Protestant, 33% Catholic; 6% Black, 2% Hispanic, 2% Asian.
Religious Orientation. Findlay is a church-related institution, "considers the religious life of the students one of its primary concerns."
Varsity Sports. Men (NAIA Div.II): Basketball, Cross Country, Football, Golf, Soccer, Swimming, Tennis, Track, Wrestling. Women (NCAA): Basketball, Cross Country, Soccer, Softball, Swimming, Tennis, Track, Volleyball.

Campus Life. About 75% of students live in traditional dormitories; 15% of students commute. Intervisitation in men's and women's dormitory rooms limited. There are 4 fraternities, 2 sororities on campus which about 10% of men, 8% of women join. About 50% of resident students leave campus on weekends.
Annual Costs. Tuition and fees, $10,920; room and board, $4,780; estimated $1,000 other, exclusive of travel. About 75% of students receive financial aid; average amount of assistance, $5,500. Assistance is typically divided 60% scholarship/grant, 30% loan, 10% work. College reports scholarships awarded on the basis of academic merit alone varies. *Meeting Costs:* University offers prepayment plan.

Fisk University

Nashville, Tennessee 37203 (615) 329-8665

An independent university, located in the state capital, Fisk serves a predominantly black student body. The university participates in a student exchange program with leading institutions throughout the country.

Founded: 1865
Affiliation: Independent
Total Enrollment: 838 M, W (full-time)
Cost: < $10K
Admission: Non-selective
Application Deadline: June 15

Admission. Graduates of accredited high schools with 15 units, preferably ranking in top third of class, eligible; 76% of applicants accepted, 36% of these actually enroll. About 44% of freshmen graduate in top fifth of high school class, 66% in top two-fifths. *Required:* SAT or ACT recommended but not required. *Entrance programs:* early admission, midyear admission. *Apply* by June 15 (April 1 for financial aid). *Transfers* welcome.
Academic Environment. *Degrees:* AB, BS, BM. About 50% of general education requirements for graduation are elective; 36 hour core curriculum required in first 2 years. About 75% of students entering as freshmen graduate eventually. *Calendar:* semester.
Undergraduate degrees conferred (134). 20% were in Social Sciences, 19% were in Business and Management, 18% were in Psychology, 12% were in Physical Sciences, 12% were in Life Sciences, 11% were in Letters, 4% were in Visual and Performing Arts, remainder in 3 other fields.
Student Body. According to most recent data available, 36% of students from South, 24% Middle Atlantic, 29% North Central, 17% West/Northwest.
Varsity Sports. Men (SIAC): Baseball, Basketball, Cross Country, Football, Tennis, Track. Women (SIAC): Basketball, Tennis, Track, Volleyball.
Campus Life. According to most recent data available, about 74% of men, 87% of women live in traditional dormitories; rest live in off-campus housing or commute. Intervisitation for sophomores, juniors and seniors; sexes segregated in coed dormitories by floor. About 15% of students leave campus on weekends.
Annual Costs. Tuition and fees, $6,305; room and board, $3,690.

Fitchburg State College

Fitchburg, Massachusetts 01420 (508) 345-2151

A state-supported, liberal arts and teachers college, located in a city of 43,300, 45 miles west of Boston. Most convenient major airports: Logan (Boston), Worcester Municipal.

Founded: 1894
Affiliation: State
UG Enrollment: 1,223 M, 1,656 W (full-time); 713 M, 699 W (part-time)
Total Enrollment: 5,208
Cost: < $10K
% Receiving Financial Aid: 55%
Admission: Non-selective
Application Deadline: March 1

Admission. High school graduates with 16 units, preferably in college preparatory subjects, eligible; 70% of applicants accepted, 23% of these actually enroll. About 18% of freshmen graduate in top fifth of high school class; 49% in top two-fifths. Average freshman scores: SAT, 423 verbal, 465 mathematical. *Required:* SAT. Criteria considered in admissions, in order of importance: high school academic record, standardized test scores, recommendations, extracurricular activities, writing sample; other factors considered: special talents, alumni children, diverse student body. *Out-of-state* freshman applicants: college welcomes students from out-of-state. State does not limit out-of-state enrollment. No special requirements for out-of-state applicants. About 50% of entering students from private or parochial schools. *Entrance programs:* mid-year admission, deferred admission, advanced placement, rolling admission. *Apply* by March 1. *Transfers* welcome; 345 enrolled 1993–94.
Academic Environment. Graduation requirements include 3 writing courses, Health and Fitness, courses in quantitative/scientific, ideas/events, BEHA. Degrees offered: bachelors, masters. *Majors offered* include environmental science, exercise science, middle school education. Average undergraduate class size: 25% under 20, 70% 20–40. About 55% of entering students graduate eventually; 80% of freshman return for sophomore year. *Special programs:* CLEP, CAPS, independent study, honors, undergraduate research, study abroad. *Calendar:* semester.
Undergraduate degrees conferred (825). 25% were in Education, 21% were in Business and Management, 11% were in Communications, 8% were in Social Sciences, 8% were in Health Sciences, 7% were in Engineering and Engineering Related Technology, 5% were in Letters, 4% were in Psychology, 4% were in Allied Health, 3% were in Computer and Engineering Related Technology, 3% were in Life Sciences, remainder in 2 other fields.
Graduate Career Data. Fields typically hiring largest numbers of graduates include school systems, hospitals, television-film companies.
Faculty. About 61% of faculty hold PhD or equivalent. About 75% of undergraduate classes taught by tenured faculty. About 44% of teaching faculty are female; 9% Black, 1% Hispanic, 8% Asian, 1% American Indian.
Student Body. About 93% of students from in state; 99% from New England, 1% foreign. An estimated 73% of students reported as Catholic, 20% Protestant, 2% Jewish; 4% Black, 2% Hispanic, 1% Asian, 7% other minority.
Varsity Sports. Men (Div.III): Baseball, Basketball, Cross Country, Football, Ice Hockey, Soccer, Track. Women (Div.III): Basketball, Cross Country, Field Hockey, Soccer, Softball, Track, Volleyball.
Campus Life. About 30% of women live in traditional dormitories; 50% of men, 20% of women in coed dormitories; 20% of each in college-related off-campus housing; rest commute. Intervisitation in men's and women's dormitory rooms limited. There are 5 fraternities, 5 sororities, which about 6% of men, 10% of women join; they provide no residence facilities. About 50% of resident students leave campus on weekends.
Annual Costs. Tuition and fees, $3,234 (out-of-state, $7,368); room and board, $3,728; estimated $1,000 other, exclusive of travel. About 55% of students receive financial aid; average amount of assistance, $3,900. Assistance is typically divided 20% scholarship, 20% grant, 40% loan, 20% work. *Meeting Costs:* college offers AMS Payment Plan.

Five Towns College

Dix Hills, New York 11746

An independent, specialized music school offering associate and baccalaureate degree programs in music and related areas. Five Towns was the first college in New York State to offer a degree in Jazz/Commercial Music. Other unusual degree programs include music business, audio recording technology, video arts.

Founded: 1972
Affiliation: Independent

Flagler College

St. Augustine, Florida 32084 (904) 829-6481

A small, independent liberal arts college located in a community of 15,000, midway between Jacksonville and Daytona Beach. Most convenient major airport: Jacksonville International.

Founded: 1968	**Cost:** < $10K
Affiliation: Independent	**% Receiving Financial Aid:** 79%
Total Enrollment: 1,238 M, W (full-time)	**Admission:** Non-selective
	Application Deadline: March 1

Admission. Graduates of recognized high schools with 16 units (13 in academic subjects) eligible; 33% of applicants accepted, 49% of these actually enroll. About 45% of freshmen graduate in top fifth of high school class, 78% in top two-fifths. Average freshman scores, according to most recent data available: SAT, 465 M, 481 W verbal, 518 M, 500 W mathematical; 32% of freshman score above 500 on verbal, 5% above 600; 55% score above 500 on mathematical, 13% above 600, 1% above 700; ACT (enhanced), 22 M, 21 W composite, 21 M, 20 W mathematical. *Required:* SAT or ACT. About 18% of entering students from private or parochial schools. *Entrance programs:* early admission, midyear admission, deferred admission, advanced placement. *Non-academic factors* considered in admissions: special talents, alumni children. *Apply* by March 1. *Transfers* welcome.

Academic Environment. *Degree:* AB. About 80% of general education requirements for graduation are elective; distribution requirements fairly numerous. About 48% of students entering as freshmen graduate eventually; 28% of freshmen do not return for sophomore year. *Special programs:* CLEP, independent study, study abroad, individualized majors. *Calendar:* semester.

Undergraduate degrees conferred (260). 33% were in Business and Management, 15% were in Education, 10% were in Communications, 9% were in Visual and Performing Arts, 8% were in Social Sciences, 8% were in Letters, 8% were in Psychology, 4% were in Foreign Languages, remainder in 4 other fields.

Faculty. About 50% of faculty hold PhD or equivalent.

Graduates Career Data. According to most recent data available, full-time graduate or professional study pursued by 15–25% of students immediately after graduation. *Careers in business and industry* pursued by 50% of graduates.

Student Body. According to most recent data available, 56% of students from Florida; 62% from South, 21% Middle Atlantic; 10 foreign students 1990–91. An estimated 62% of students reported as Protestant, 35% Catholic, 1% Jewish, 2% other; 1% Black, 2% Hispanic, 1% other minority.

Varsity Sports. Men (NAIA): Baseball, Basketball, Cross Country, Golf, Soccer, Tennis. Women (NAIA): Basketball, Cross Country, Tennis, Volleyball.

Campus Life. According to most recent data available, about 53% of men, 59% of women live in traditional dormitories; no coed dormitories; 35% of men, 31% of women live in off-campus housing; 12% of men, 10% of women commute. No intervisitation in men's or women's dormitory rooms. There are no fraternities or sororities.

Annual Costs. Tuition and fees, $4,920; room and board, $3,070. About 79% of students receive financial aid; assistance is typically divided 60% scholarship, 33% loan, 7% work. College reports some scholarships awarded on the basis of academic merit alone. *Meeting Costs:* college offers Knight Tuition Plan.

Florida Agricultural and Mechanical University

Tallahassee, Florida 32307 (904) 599-3000

A state-supported, land-grant university, located in the state capital (pop. 121,000); founded as a college for Negroes and still serving a predominantly Black student body.

Founded: 1887	**Total Enrollment:** 9,871
Affiliation: State	**Cost:** < $10K
UG Enrollment: 3,281 M, 4,524 W (full-time); 605 M, 813 W (part-time)	**Admission:** Non-selective
	Application Deadline: July 15

Admission. Graduates of accredited high schools with 16 units eligible; 60% of applicants accepted, 47% of these actually enroll.

About 36% of entering freshmen graduate in top fifth of high school class, 63% in top two-fifths. *Required:* SAT or ACT. Criteria considered in admissions, in order of importance: high school academic record, standardized test scores, recommendations, class rank, writing sample. *Out-of-state* freshman applicants: university welcomes out-of-state students. State does not limit out-of-state enrollment. *Entrance programs:* early decision, early admission. *Apply* by July 15. *Transfers* welcome; 509 enrolled 1993–94.

Academic Environment. About 6% of general education requirements for graduation are elective; distribution requirements fairly numerous. Degrees offered: associates, bachelors, masters, doctoral. About 62% of students entering as freshmen graduate eventually; 18% of freshmen return for sophomore year. *Special programs:* CLEP, independent study, honors, 3-year degree, cross-registration with Florida State U. *Calendar:* semester, summer school.

Undergraduate degrees conferred (586). 14% were in Education, 14% were in Business and Management, 12% were in Social Sciences, 11% were in Health Sciences, 8% were in Architecture and Environmental Design, 7% were in Protective Services, 5% were in Allied Health, 5% were in Computer and Engineering Related Technology, 4% were in Psychology, 3% were in Engineering and Engineering Related Technology, 3% were in Communications, 3% were in Public Affairs, 3% were in Visual and Performing Arts, remainder in 7 other fields.

Graduates Career Data. Corporations typically hiring largest numbers of graduates include Sears, General Motors, Honeywell.

Faculty. About 42% of teaching faculty are female.

Varsity Sports. Men (Div.I): Baseball, Basketball, Football (IAA), Golf, Swimming, Tennis, Track. Women (Div.I): Basketball, Swimming, Tennis, Volleyball.

Campus Life. About 14% of men, 18% of women live in traditional dormitories; rest live in off-campus housing or commute. Freshmen given preference in college housing if all students cannot be accommodated. No intervisitation in men's or women's dormitory rooms. There are 4 fraternities, 4 sororities on campus which about 4% each of men, women join. They provide no residence facilities.

Annual Costs. Tuition and fees, $1,749 (out-of-state, $6,651); room and board, $2,822; estimated $1,500 other, exclusive of travel. *Meeting Costs:* university offers federal, state, private and institutional grants, scholarships, loans and work study programs.

Florida Baptist Theological College

(See Baptist Bible Institute)

Florida Bible College

Kissimmee, Florida 34758

A non-denominational Bible college offering associates and baccalaureate degree programs. The 35-acre campus is located in a rural area, near Walt Disney World.

Affiliation: Independent

Florida Christian College

Kissimmee, Florida 34744

A small Bible college offering associate and baccalaureate degree programs. The campus is located in a suburban area, near Orlando.

Founded: 1975	**Affiliation:** Christian Churches, Churches of Christ

Florida Institute of Technology

Melbourne, Florida 32901-6988 (407) 768-8000

An independent, co-educational institution, specializing in engineering and science programs, Florida Institute of Technology attracts more than one-third its students from the Northeast. The

Institute is located on a 146-acre campus in a community of 55,000, south of the Kennedy Space Center. Most convenient major airport: Melbourne Regional.

Founded: 1958
Affiliation: Independent
UG Enrollment: 1,342 M, 521 W (full-time); 168 M, 65 W (part-time)
Total Enrollment: 4,982
Cost: $10K–$20K
% Receiving Financial Aid: 70%
Admission: Selective (+)
Application Deadline: Rolling

Admission is selective (+). About 83% of applicants accepted; 68% of freshmen graduate in top fifth of high school class, 89% in top two-fifths. Average freshman scores: SAT, 470 M, 499 W verbal, 582 M, 563 W mathematical. *Required:* SAT. Criteria considered in admissions, in order of importance: high school academic record, standardized test scores, recommendations. *Entrance programs:* advanced placement, rolling admission. About 20% of entering students from private or parochial schools. *Apply:* rolling admission. *Transfers* welcome; 120 enrolled 1993–94.
Academic Environment. Administration reports percentage of elective courses required for graduation depends on program. Degree programs highly structured; minimum 21 quarter hours in humanities scheduled for each. Overwhelming majority of students reported to be primarily concerned with occupational/professional goals. Degrees offered: bachelors, masters, doctoral. *Majors offered* include hospitality management, aquaculture, aerospace engineering.

About 25% of students entering as freshmen graduate within four years, 58% eventually; 75% of freshmen return for sophomore year. *Special programs:* APP, undergraduate research, cooperative work/study program, credit by examination. *Calendar:* quarter, summer school.
Undergraduate degrees conferred (546). 35% were in Transportation and Material Moving, 28% were in Engineering, 12% were in Business and Management, 8% were in Life Sciences, 4% were in Physical Sciences, 4% were in Computer and Engineering Related Technology, 3% were in Psychology, remainder in 7 other fields.
Graduates Career Data. Advanced studies pursued by 16% of graduates. About 80% of 1992–93 graduates employed. Employers typically hiring largest numbers of graduates include Harris Corporation, NASA, Lockheed, MacDonald Douglas. Career Development Services include workshops, career days, employer days, resume assistance, resource library.
Faculty. About 85% of faculty hold PhD or equivalent. About 15% of teaching faculty are female; 10% minority.
Student Body. About 38% of students from in state; 39% South, 20% New England, 20% Middle Atlantic, 4% Midwest, 2% West, 3% West/Northwest, 14% Foreign. Average age of undergraduate student: 22.
Varsity Sports. Men (Div.II): Baseball, Basketball, Crew, Cross Country, Soccer, Tennis. Women (Div.II): Basketball, Crew, Cross Country, Softball, Volleyball.
Campus Life. Students play significant role in determining policies governing campus life. No regulations limiting car ownership, smoking, alcoholic beverages; 24-hour intervisitation. Administration representative and student leader differ on whether parking space is adequate. High interest reported in both varsity sports (most popular: basketball and crew) and intramurals (most popular: football, basketball, softball, soccer).

About 50% of men, 50% of women live in coed dormitories; 45% of men, 47% of women commute. Freshmen given preference in college housing if all students cannot be accommodated. There are 7 fraternities, 3 sororities on campus; which about 5% of men, 3% of women join; 5% of men live in fraternities, 3% of women live in sororities. About 50% of resident students leave campus on weekends.
Annual Costs. Tuition and fees, $13,035; room and board, $3,900; estimated $1,500 other, exclusive of travel. About 70% of students receive financial aid. Assistance is typically divided 39% scholarship/grant, 47% loan, 14% work. *Minority group students:* special financial provisions. *Meeting Costs:* institute offers parent loans, payment plans.

Florida Memorial College

Miami, Florida 33054 (305) 625-4141

A church-related college, located in a city of 334,900; founded as a college for Negroes and still serving a predominantly Black student body.

Founded: 1892
Affiliation: American Baptist
Total Enrollment: 1,715 M, W (full-time)
Cost: < $10K
Admission: Non-selective

Admission. Graduates of approved high schools with 15 units (8 in academic subjects) eligible; 81% of applicants accepted, 40% of these actually enroll. *Required:* ACT, 3 letters of recommendation. *Apply:* no specific deadline. *Transfers* welcome.
Academic Environment. *Degrees:* BA, BS. About 5% of general education requirements for graduation are elective; distribution requirements fairly numerous. About 50% of students entering as freshmen graduate eventually; about 30% of freshmen do not return for sophomore year. Special program: independent study. *Calendar:* semester, summer school.
Undergraduate degrees conferred (160). 28% were in Business and Management, 22% were in Education, 13% were in Protective Services, 9% were in Life Sciences, 7% were in Psychology, 5% were in Transportation and Material Moving, 5% were in Public Affairs, 3% were in Social Sciences, 3% were in Business (Administrative Support), remainder in 5 other fields.
Student Body. According to most recent data available, 90% of students from South. An estimated 90% of students reported as Protestant, 8% Catholic, 2% unaffiliated; 65% Black, 33% Hispanic.
Varsity Sports. Men (NAIA): Baseball, Basketball, Track. Women (NAIA): Basketball, Track, Volleyball.
Campus Life. According to most recent data available, about 14% of men, 21% of women live in traditional dormitories; no coed dormitories; rest live in off-campus housing or commute. No intervisitation in men's and women's dormitory rooms. There are 5 fraternities, 4 sororities on campus which about 6% of men, 5% of women join; they provide no residence facilities.
Annual Costs. Tuition and fees, $4,750; room and board, $2,950.

Florida Southern College

Lakeland, Florida 33801 (800) 274-4131

A church-related, liberal arts college, located in a city of 50,000, 35 miles east of Tampa. Most convenient major airport: Tampa International.

Founded: 1885
Affiliation: United Methodist
Total Enrollment: 1,970 M, W (full-time)
Cost: < $10K
Admission: Non-selective
Application Deadline: August 1

Admission. High school graduates with C average in college preparatory courses with GPA of 2.5, SAT of 950 or ACT of 19 eligible; 65% of applicants accepted, 55% of those accepted actually enroll. *Required:* SAT or ACT; interview recommended. *Apply* by August 1. *Transfers* welcome.
Academic Environment. Students on all major committees and Board of Trustees. *Degrees:* AB, BS. *Majors offered* include usual arts and sciences, accounting, business, citrus studies, education, journalism, sports management, music management.

About 75% of students entering as freshmen graduate eventually. *Special programs:* CLEP, independent study, study abroad, May Option, Washington Semester, United Nations Semester, 3–2 engineering with Washington U.. *Calendar:* semester, summer school.
Undergraduate degrees conferred (507). 45% were in Business and Management, 16% were in Education, 7% were in Health Sciences, 7% were in Communications, 4% were in Social Sciences, 3% were in Psychology, 3% were in Life Sciences, 3% were in Mathematics, remainder in 10 other fields.
Graduates Career Data. According to most recent data available, full-time graduate or professional study pursued by 20% of students immediately after graduation. *Careers in business and industry* pursued by 35% of graduates.
Student Body. According to most recent data available, 75% of students from Florida; 76% South, 20% New England. An estimated 38% of students reported as Protestant, 40% Catholic, 2% Jewish, 20% unaffiliated; 1% as Black, less than 3% other minority.
Religious Orientation. Florida Southern is a church-related institution; 6 semester hours of religion required of all students; attendance

at weekly chapel and convocation services "encouraged." Religious clubs on campus include Methodist, Baptist, Lutheran, Christian Science, Canterbury. Catholic Mass once a week on campus; other places of worship available in immediate community for major faiths.
Varsity Sports. Men (NCAA II): Baseball, Basketball, Cross Country, Golf, Soccer. Women (NCAA II): Basketball, Cross Country, Softball, Tennis, Volleyball.
Campus Life. Drinking or possession of alcohol on or off campus by enrolled students contrary to college policy. Curfew hours for all women. About 50% of men, 48% of women live in traditional dormitories; no coed dormitories; 15% of men, 12% of women commute. No intervisitation in men's or women's dormitory rooms. There are 7 fraternities, 6 sororities on campus; 35% of men, 40% of women live in fraternities and sororities. About 20% of students leave campus on weekends.
Annual Costs. Tuition and fees, $7,610; room and board, $4,600. According to most recent data available, about 82% of students receive financial aid; assistance is typically divided 40% scholarship, 45% loan, 15% work. College reports some scholarships awarded on the basis of academic merit alone.

Florida State University

Tallahassee, Florida 32306 (904) 644-2525

One of the major institutions in the state system, this state-supported university is located on a 347-acre main campus near downtown Tallahassee (pop. 150,000), the state capital. Most convenient major airport: Tallahassee Municipal.

Founded: 1851
Affiliation: State
UG Enrollment: 8,588 M, 10,281 W (full-time); 1,171 M, 1,278 W (part-time)
Total Enrollment: 28,669
Cost: < $10K
% Receiving Financial Aid: 48%
Admission: Selective (+)
Application Deadline: March 1

Admission is selective. About 75% of applicants accepted, 35% of these actually enroll. Average freshman scores: SAT, middle 50% range, 460–560 verbal, 510–630 mathematical; ACT, 23–27 composite. *Required:* SAT or ACT. Criteria considered in admissions: high school academic record and standardized test scores, auditions/portfolios for BFA programs; other factors considered: special talents, alumni children, diverse student body. *Out-of-state* freshman applicants: university welcomes students from out of state. State limits out-of-state enrollment. Requirements for out-of-state students slightly higher than for Florida residents. *Entrance programs:* early admission, advanced placement. *Apply* by March 1. *Transfers* welcome.
Academic Environment. Degrees offered: bachelors, masters, doctoral. Administration reports 45% of general education courses required for graduation are elective; distribution requirements fairly numerous; include 12 credits each in social sciences, humanities, 13 in natural sciences, 9 in history, 13 in communications. *Undergraduate studies* offered by colleges of Arts and Sciences, Business, Communication, Education, Engineering, Social Sciences, schools of Criminology, Home Economics, Music, Nursing, Social Work, Theatre, Visual Arts. Division of Undergraduate Studies administers academic program of entering students (except for students of nursing and music). *Majors offered* in Arts and Sciences in addition to usual studies include Asian studies, computer science, fashions, Inter-American studies, medical technology, Slavic and East European studies, theater, nutrition and fitness, industrial engineering. Average undergraduate class size: 49% of classes under 20, 35% between 20–40, 16% over 40.

About 29% of entering students graduate within four years, 55% eventually; 15% of freshmen do not return for sophomore year. *Special programs:* CLEP, study abroad (including centers in Florence and London), honors, 3-year degree, cross-registration with Florida A & M. Adult programs: administration reports that average age of student body is 24, therefore, most programs are designed for "adult students." *Library:* 1,829,826 volumes, 25,059 periodicals, 3,103,577 microforms; other materials include Claude Pepper Collection; open-stack privileges. *Calendar:* semester, summer school.
Undergraduate degrees conferred (4842). 26% were in Business and Management, 17% were in Social Sciences, 12% were in Education, 7% were in Communications, 7% were in Protective Services, 5% were in Psychology, 4% were in Letters, 4% were in Home Economics, 3% were in Visual and Performing Arts, 3% were in Engineering, remainder in 13 other fields.
Graduates Career Data. Advanced studies pursued by 35% of students; 25% enter business school; 4% enter law school. Fields typically hiring the largest number of graduates include business/industry, education, state/federal government. Career Development Services provide assistance in "determining career goals and realizing them."
Faculty. About 90% of faculty hold PhD or equivalent. About 53% of undergraduate classes taught by regular faculty. About 20% of teaching faculty are female.
Student Body. University seeks a national student body; 80% of students from Florida; 88% from South, 3% Middle Atlantic; 5% foreign. An estimated 9% of students reported as Black, 5% Hispanic, 2% Asian, 3% other minority. *Minority group students:* special scholarships, other financial aid; entrance requirements waivers, tutorial programs, counseling program; ethnic, racial centers and organizations.
Varsity Sports. Men (Div.I): Baseball, Basketball, Football, Golf, Swimming, Tennis, Track. Women (Div.I): Basketball, Golf, Softball, Swimming, Tennis, Track, Volleyball.
Campus Life. Campus affected to some extent by rural location. No issues relating to campus life of particular concern to students. Students given intervisitation options in dormitories ranging from no intervisitation to 24-hour. A special fund provides for cooperative living houses "for academically gifted" students of limited financial means.

About 17% of students live in traditional or coed dormitories; 10% in fraternities or sororities; 5% live in off-campus college-related housing; majority of students live in off-campus apartments or commute. Freshmen given preference in college housing if all students cannot be accommodated. Sexes segregated in coed dormitories either by wing or floor. There are 25 fraternities, 19 sororities on campus which about 20% of men, 20% of women join.
Annual Costs. Tuition and fees, $1,780 (out-of-state, $6,680); room and board, $4,060; estimated $600 other, exclusive of travel. About 48% of undergraduate students receive financial aid; average amount of assistance, $2,000. University reports some scholarships awarded on the basis of academic merit alone. *Meeting Costs:* university offers prepayment plan.

Florida Technological University

(See University of Central Florida)

University of Florida

Gainesville, Florida 32611 (904) 392-1365

A state-supported, land-grant university, located in a city of 85,000, 72 miles southwest of Jacksonville, the University of Florida has 20 colleges and schools on a single campus. Gainesville is in effect a "university city." Most convenient major airport: Gainesville Regional.

Founded: 1853
Affiliation: State
UG Enrollment: 12,851 M, 11,235 W (full-time); 1,807 M, 1,580 W (part-time)
Total Enrollment: 35,978
Cost: < $10K
% Receiving Financial Aid: 64%
Admission: Very Selective
Application Deadline: Feb. 1

Admission is very selective. About 71% of applicants accepted, 41% of these actually enroll. Average freshman SAT scores, middle fifty percent range: 480–590 verbal, 560–680 mathematical; 52% of freshman score above 500 on verbal, 14% above 600, 1% above 700; 83% score above 500 on mathematical, 45% above 600, 8% above 700; ACT, 24–28 composite. *Required:* SAT or ACT. Criteria considered in admissions, in order of importance: high school academic record, standardized test scores, recommendations; other factors considered: diverse student body, special talents, alumni children, extracurricular activities. *Out-of-state* freshman applicants: university welcomes students from out of state, but residents are given priority. *Out-of-state* enrollment limited to 10% of student body. No special requirements for out-of-state applicants. *Entrance programs:* early decision, early admission, midyear admission, advanced placement. *Apply* by February 1; rolling admissions. *Transfers* welcome; 1,761 enrolled 1993–94.

Academic Environment. Degrees offered: associates, bachelors, masters, doctoral. Students have representation on 39 university committees and appear to have influence on all areas of college life, including curriculum and selection and promotion of faculty. Distribution requirements for Liberal Arts and Sciences include 6 hours credit each in composition, literature and the arts, historical and philosophical studies, international studies and diversity, social and behavioral sciences, physical and biological sciences, mathematics. *Undergraduate studies* offered by colleges of Liberal Arts and Sciences, Agriculture, Architecture, Fine Arts, Business Administration, Education, Engineering, Health Related Professions, Journalism and Communications, Nursing, Pharmacy, Physical Education, Health, and Recreation, and Schools of Forest Resources and Conservation, Accounting and Building Construction. University of Florida curriculum is one of the three most diverse in North American higher education, with offerings in virtually every academic subject area. *Majors offered* in addition to usual arts and sciences include anthropology, Asian studies, computer and information science, geography, statistics, criminal justice, Jewish Studies.

About 31% of entering students graduate within four years, 64% within six years; 12% of freshmen do not return for sophomore year. *Special programs:* CLEP, independent study, study abroad, honors, undergraduate research, individualized majors, 3-year master's program, area studies (Latin American, Soviet and East European, African, Afro-American), cooperative work/study programs, 3–2 programs in engineering. Adult programs: SOTA (Students Over Traditional Age) meets weekly for social activities. *Library:* more than 3,000,000 titles, 32,000 periodicals, special collections include Latin American, Florida history, Isser & Rae Price Library of Judaica, Delknap Collection (performing arts); open-stack privileges. *Calendar:* quarter, summer school.

Undergraduate degrees conferred (5498). 19% were in Business and Management, 11% were in Social Sciences, 11% were in Communications, 11% were in Engineering, 9% were in Education, 6% were in Letters, 5% were in Psychology, 4% were in Health Sciences, 3% were in Life Sciences, 3% were in Architecture and Environmental Design, remainder in 16 other fields.

Graduates Career Data. According to most recent data available, full-time graduate or professional study pursued immediately after graduation by 23% of students. *Careers in business and industry* pursued by 54% of graduates. Corporations typically hiring largest numbers of graduates include General Electric, Deloitte & Touche, NCNB, Toys R Us. *Career Counseling Program* offers computerized career exploration and information system, seminars cooperative education program, on-campus interviewing, placement services, career days.

Faculty. About 93% of faculty hold PhD or equivalent. About 18% of full-time undergraduate faculty are female; 3% Black, 8% other ethnic minorities.

Student Body. About 92% of students from in state; 1.4% foreign students 1993–94. An estimated 6% of students reported as Black, 7% Hispanic, 5% Asian. *Minority group students:* financial, academic, and/or social provisions through Office for Minority Affairs, Student Special Services; Institute for Black Culture; Afro-American studies program. Ten percent of beginning freshman spaces are held open for academically unqualified students with evidence of strong motivation and ability, who are offered scholastic help.

Varsity Sports. Men (Div. I): Baseball, Basketball, Cross Country, Football, Golf, Swimming/Diving, Tennis, Track. Women (Div. I): Basketball, Cross Country, Golf, Gymnastics, Swimming/Diving, Tennis, Track, Volleyball.

Campus Life. Student interest reported high in varsity sports (most popular: football, basketball, women's gymnastics) and intramurals (most popular: softball, weight lifting, club sports) as well as in fraternities/sororities. Intervisitation determined by university policies and student preference; some restrictions on cars, parking described as "inadequate"; alcohol regulated by state law (legal age: 21).

About 18% of students live in campus housing; single-sex and coed dormitories are available, as well as school owned/operated apartments, and married student housing. Freshmen given preference in college housing if all students cannot be accommodated. Sexes segregated in dormitories either by wing, room, or floor. There are 28 fraternities, 18 sororities on campus which about 15% of men, 15% of women join.

Annual Costs. Tuition and fees, 1,770; (out-of-state, $6,890); room and board, $4,080. About 64% of students receive financial aid; average amount of assistance, $1,800. Assistance is typically divided 26% scholarship, 20% grant, 46% loan, 8% work. University reports some scholarships awarded on the basis of academic merit alone, about 224 athletic scholarships awarded.

Fontbonne College

St. Louis, Missouri 63105 **(314) 889-1400**

A church-related, co-educational liberal arts college, founded by the Sisters of St. Joseph of Carondelet and now governed by a predominantly lay board of trustees, Fontbonne is located in a residential suburb of St. Louis.

Founded: 1917
Affiliation: Independent (Roman Catholic)
UG Enrollment: 213 M, 542 W (full-time); 503 M, 272 W (part-time)
Total Enrollment: 1,984
Cost: < $10K
% Receiving Financial Aid: 85%
Admission: Non-selective
Application Deadline: August 1

Admission. Graduates of accredited high schools with 16 units (12 in academic subjects) eligible; 84% of applicants accepted, 51% of these actually enroll. About 38% of freshmen graduate in top fifth of high school class, 72% in top two-fifths. Average freshman scores: ACT, 21. *Required:* SAT or ACT, essay; interview encouraged. Criteria considered in admissions, in order of importance: high school academic record, standardized test scores, recommendations, writing sample, extracurricular activities. About 65% of entering students from private schools. *Entrance programs:* early admission, midyear admission, advanced placement, rolling admission. *Apply* by August 1. *Transfers* welcome; 132 enrolled 1993–94.

Academic Environment. Degrees offered: bachelors, masters. Graduation requirements include 44 hours of general education courses. *Majors offered* include deaf education, speech pathology, dietetics, early childhood-special education. Small classes and "personable," "knowledgeable" faculty cited by students as strengths of the academic program. Both faculty and student sources report extensive practicum/internship opportunities in the area. About 65% of students entering as freshmen graduate eventually. *Special programs:* CLEP, individualized majors, cooperative programs with 5 other institutions in St. Louis area, 3–2 social work with Washington U.. Adult program: Options Program for students over 24. *Calendar:* semester, summer school.

Undergraduate degrees conferred (202). 46% were in Business and Management, 12% were in Education, 9% were in Visual and Performing Arts, 6% were in Liberal/General Studies, 6% were in Home Economics, 6% were in Communications, 4% were in Life Sciences, 3% were in Computer and Engineering Related Technology, remainder in 4 other fields.

Graduate Career Data. About 95% of 1992–93 graduates employed. Corporations typically hiring largest numbers of graduates include Coca-Cola, Anheuser Busch. Career Development Services include resume writing and interview classes, on-campus interviews, job search, job fairs.

Faculty. About 55% of faculty hold PhD or equivalent. About 50% of undergraduate classes taught by tenured faculty. About 54% of teaching faculty are female.

Student Body. About 85% of students from in state, 19% Midwest, 3% Foreign. An estimated 55% of students reported as Catholic, 23% as Protestant; 18% Black, 1% Hispanic, 1% Asian. Average age of undergraduate student: 23.

Religious Orientation. "Fontbonne is a Catholic college"; 50% of students affiliated with the church; one course in religious studies included in general education requirements.

Varsity Sports. Men (Div.III): Baseball, Basketball, Cross Country, Golf, Soccer. Women (Div.III): Basketball, Cross Country, Soccer, Softball, Volleyball.

Campus Life. Students report "there is always something going on in the surrounding community." Campus is close to museums, shopping, St. Louis Zoo, and other attractions.

About 33% of men and 33% women live in coed dormitories; rest commute. Intervisitation in women's dormitory rooms limited. There is 1 fraternity and no sororities on campus. About 30% of resident students leave campus on weekends.

Annual Costs. Tuition and fees, $8,090; room and board, $4,000; estimated $1,100 other, exclusive of travel. About 85% of students receive financial aid; average amount of assistance, $7,300. Assistance is typically divided 43% scholarship/grant, 36% loan, 22% work. College reports all scholarships awarded on the basis of academic merit alone. *Meeting Costs:* college offers institutional loan program, work/study-Fontbonne grants.

Fordham University

Bronx, New York 10458 (718) 817-4000

Founded by the Jesuit fathers, Fordham now is an independent university in the Jesuit tradition. Fordham recognizes "the importance of religion and of religious values in the life of mankind and in the life of its students." Fordham's 85-acre Rose Hill campus is located in the Bronx. Rose Hill houses Fordham College, the liberal arts division, and the College of Business Administration. A midtown campus is located in the Lincoln Center cultural complex which includes the Law School and the Leon Lowenstein Center, which contains the coeducational College at Lincoln Center and graduate schools of Education, Social Service, and Business Administration. Most convenient major airport: LaGuardia.

Founded: 1841
Affiliation: Independent (Roman Catholic)
UG Enrollment: 2,322 M, 2,418 W (full-time); 528 M, 1,118 W (part-time)
Total Enrollment: 14,611
Cost: $10K–$20K
% Receiving Financial Aid: 90%
Admission: Very Selective
Application Deadline: February 15

Admission is very selective for Fordham College, selective (+) for College of Business Administration and College at Lincoln Center. About 68% of applicants accepted, 33% of these actually enroll; 49% of freshmen graduate in top fifth of high school class, 77% in top two-fifths. Average freshman SAT scores: 506 verbal, 535 mathematical; 40% of freshmen score over 550 on verbal; 52% score over 550 on mathematical. *Required:* SAT or ACT, essay. Criteria considered in admissions, in order of importance: high school academic record, standardized test scores, recommendations, writing sample, extracurricular activities; other factors considered: diverse student body, alumni children, special talents, community service. About 15% of entering students are from private schools, 49% from parochial schools. *Entrance programs:* early decision, early admission, deferred admission, advanced placement. *Apply* by February 1. *Transfers* welcome; 137 enrolled 1993–94.

Academic Environment. Academic competition is somewhat more rigorous at Fordham College than at the other undergraduate schools. Administration source characterizes student body as about equally concerned with scholarly/intellectual interests and occupational/professional goals. Graduation requirements include core curriculum classes in English, history, philosophy, theology, sciences, mathematics, life sciences, and physical sciences. Degrees offered: bachelors, masters, doctoral. *Majors offered* include Russian studies, interdisciplinary majors in Afro-American studies, chemical physics, medieval studies, urban studies; Puerto Rican studies, theater and drama at Lincoln Center, bilingual-bicultural studies, peace and justice studies, international business(GLOBE). Average undergraduate class size: 49% under 20, 41% 20–40, 10% over 40.

About 77% of entering students graduate within four years, 82% eventually; 92% of freshmen return for sophomore year. *Special programs:* independent study, study abroad, honors, undergraduate research, January interterm (optional program offered at Lincoln Center only), 3–2 engineering with Columbia or Case Western Reserve, 3–4 dental with Columbia, internships with over 2,000 companies. Adult programs: Ignatius College Evening Program. *Calendar:* semester, summer school.

Undergraduate degrees conferred (1371). 28% were in Social Sciences, 23% were in Business and Management, 9% were in Psychology, 9% were in Letters, 9% were in Communications, 4% were in Philosophy and Religion, 3% were in Computer and Engineering Related Technology, 3% were in Visual and Performing Arts, 3% were in Life Sciences, 3% were in Area and Ethnic Studies, remainder in 5 other fields.

Graduates Career Data. Advanced studies pursued by 29% of students immediately after graduation; 13% enter graduate school; 10% enter law school; 5% enter business school; 1% enter medical school. Medical schools enrolling largest numbers of graduates include Albany Medical, Columbia; law schools include NYU, Pace, Georgetown, Harvard; business schools include Wharton, NYU. About 91% of 1992–93 graduates hired in their major within 2 years. Corporations typically hiring largest numbers of graduates include Waterhouse, J.P. Morgan, Aetna, Xerox. Career Development Services include career counseling, resume writing, tutoring, and internship preparation.

Faculty. About 97% of faculty hold PhD or equivalent. About 60% of undergraduate classes taught by tenured faculty. About 3% of teaching faculty are Black, 8% Hispanic, 2% other minority.

Student Body. About 67% of students from in state; 20% New England, 5% Middle Atlantic, 2% each from South, Midwest, West, 2% foreign. An estimated 80% of students reported as Catholic, 5% Protestant, 1% Jewish, 14% other; 6% as Black, 15% Hispanic, 5% Asian, 3% other minority.

Religious Orientation. Founded and for many years conducted by the Society for Jesus, Fordham remains essentially a Catholic campus, although it is now independent. Two courses in religious studies are part of the core requirements. University states there are no other required religious practices.

Varsity Sports. Men (Patriots League; Div.IAA): Baseball, Basketball, Cross Country, Diving, Football, Golf, Soccer, Swimming, Tennis, Track. Women (Div.IAA): Basketball, Cross Country, Diving, Soccer, Softball, Swimming, Tennis, Track.

Campus Life. The Rose Hill campus offers students the "luxury of country life with complete access to the city"; while the Lincoln Center campus puts students in the middle of New York City's limitless entertainment, educational, and cultural opportunities. Students agree "There are as many clubs as you can think of", as well as campus sponsored entertainment, discussions, movies, and athletic events. As at virtually any urban institution, security is strict, but geared towards safety; other than that, few regulations govern student social life; 24-hour intervisitation; NYC regulations limit smoking; drinking permitted those over 21; drugs prohibited, counseling provided.

About 70% of men, 70% of women in coed dormitories; rest commute. Housing guaranteed for all four years. There are no fraternities or sororities on campus. About 25% of resident students leave campus on weekends.

Annual Costs. Tuition and fees, $13,200; room and board, $6,600; estimated $600 other, exclusive of travel. About 90% of students receive financial aid; average amount of assistance, $10,000. Assistance is typically divided 10% scholarship, 60% grant, 90% loan, 40% work. University reports 400 scholarships awarded on the basis of academic merit alone. *Meeting Costs:* university offers tuition stabilization plan, budget plan, Education Credit Corporation.

Fort Hays State University

Hays, Kansas 67601-4099 (913) 628-4222

A state-assisted university, located in a city of 16,648 midway between Kansas City and Denver. Most convenient major airports: Hays, Wichita

Founded: 1902
Affiliation: State
Total Enrollment: 4,518 M, W (full-time)
Cost: < $10K
% Receiving Financial Aid: 71%
Admission: Non-selective
Application Deadline: 15 days before term

Admission. Kansas graduates of accredited high schools admitted by diploma; all applicants accepted, 46% of these actually enroll. *Required:* ACT. *Out-of-state* freshman applicants: university welcomes students from out of state. State does not limit out-of-state enrollment. Requirement for out-of-state applicants: C average; 97% of applicants accepted, 76% enroll. *Apply* by 15 days before term. *Transfers* welcome.

Academic Environment. Degrees offered: AB, BS, BFA, BGS, BM. About 93% of general education requirements for graduation are elective; distribution requirements fairly numerous. About 40% of students entering as freshmen graduate eventually; 34% of freshmen do not return for sophomore year. *Special programs:* CLEP, independent study, study abroad, undergraduate research, individualized majors. *Calendar:* semester, summer school.

Undergraduate degrees conferred (642). 27% were in Education, 17% were in Business and Management, 9% were in Social Sciences, 9% were in Health Sciences, 7% were in Communications, 6% were in Visual and Performing Arts, 4% were in Psychology, 3% were in Letters, remainder in 12 other fields.

Varsity Sports. Men (NCAA, Div. II): Baseball, Basketball, Cross Country, Football, Golf, Track, Wrestling. Women (NCAA, Div. II): Basketball, Cross Country, Gymnastics, Track, Volleyball.

Campus Life. University seeks a national student body; 94% of students from Kansas; 95% North Central. An estimated 21% of students reported as Protestant, 23% Catholic, 53% unaffiliated, 4% other; 1% Black, 1% Hispanic, 1% Asian, 7% other minority, according to most recent data available.

About 19% of men, 17% of women live in traditional dormitories; 2% of men, 2% of women in coed dormitory; 72% of students live in off-campus housing or commute. Intervisitation in men's and women's dormitory rooms limited. Sexes segregated in coed dormitory by wing. There are 5 fraternities, 3 sororities on campus which about 7% of men, 4% of women join; 1% of men, 1% of women live in fraternities and sororities. About 40% of resident students leave campus on weekends.

Annual Costs. Tuition and fees, $1,711 (out-of-state, $4,763); room and board, $2,941. About 71% of students receive financial aid. University reports some scholarships awarded on the basis of academic merit alone.

Fort Lewis College

Durango, Colorado 81301 **(303) 247-7184**

A state-supported, liberal arts college, located on a mesa surrounded by the Rocky Mountains, in a town of 13,000. Most convenient major airport: La Plata (Durango).

Founded: 1910
Affiliation: State
Total Enrollment: 2,082 M, 1,711 W (full-time)
Cost: < $10K
% Receiving Financial Aid: 75%
Admission: Non-selective
Application Deadline: June 30

Admission. High school graduates with high school GPA of 2.0 eligible; 80% of applicants accepted, 45% of these actually enroll. About 20% of freshmen graduate in top fifth of high school class, 65% in top two-fifths. Average freshman ACT scores: 21.0 composite. *Required:* SAT or ACT, Colorado Commission on Higher Education index. Criteria considered in admissions, in order of importance: high school academic record, standardized test scores; recommendations and extracurricular activities; other factors considered: special talents. *Out-of-state* freshmen applicants: college seeks students from out of state. State limits out-of-state enrollment. No special requirements for out-of-state applicants. *Apply* by June 30; rolling admissions. *Transfers* welcome; 360 enrolled 1993–94.

Academic Environment. Degrees offered: associates (only in agriculture), bachelors. General education requirements for graduation include 2 courses in composition, 3 in language and arts, 3 in quantitative and natural sciences, 2 in foundations of culture, 2 in behavioral sciences, 1 in non-Western culture, 2 in physical education. Unusual majors include Southwest studies. Average undergraduate class size: 27.

About 20% of entering students graduate within four years, 50% eventually; 33% of freshmen do not return for sophomore year. *Special programs:* CLEP, independent study, study abroad, honors, individualized majors, intercultural program for bilingual students (especially American Indians and Chicanos), 3–2 program in engineering. *Calendar:* trimester (third trimester includes 5-week spring term, 3 5-week summer terms).

Undergraduate degrees conferred (532). 29% were in Business and Management, 17% were in Multi/Interdisciplinary Studies, 14% were in Social Sciences, 12% were in Letters, 7% were in Psychology, 5% were in Physical Sciences, 4% were in Life Sciences, 3% were in Visual and Performing Arts, 3% were in Education, remainder in 4 other fields.

Graduates Career Data. Advanced studies pursued by 35% of graduates; 10% enter business school; 3% enter law school; 2–3% enter medical or dental school. Most students attending graduate or professional programs "stay in the region". Career Development Services include counseling, interview workshops, career fairs.

Varsity Sports. Men (NAIA Div.II): Basketball, Cross Country, Football, Golf, Soccer, Tennis, Wrestling. Women (NAIA Div.II): Basketball, Cross Country, Soccer, Softball, Tennis, Volleyball. Popular club sports include alpine skiing, lacrosse.

Student Body. College seeks a national student body; 70% of students from in state; largest percentages of out-of-state students are from West, Midwest. An estimated 1% of students reported as Black, 5% Hispanic, 1% Asian, 15% Native American or other minority.

Campus Life. About 9% of men, 10% of women live in traditional dormitories; 13% of men, 15% of women in coed dormitories; 13% of men, 15% of women live in campus apartments; rest commute. Freshmen given preference in college housing if all students cannot be accommodated. There are no fraternities or sororities. About 25% of resident students leave campus on weekends.

Annual Costs. Tuition and fees, $1,777 (out-of-state, $6,525); room and board, $3,480; estimated $1,400 other, exclusive of travel. About 75% of students receive financial aid; average amount of assistance, $3,500. Assistance is typically divided 10% scholarship, 15% grant, 60% loan, 15% work. College reports some scholarships awarded on the basis of academic merit alone. *Meeting Costs:* college offers Tuition Payment Plan.

Fort Valley State College

Fort Valley, Georgia 31030-3298 **(912) 825-7307**

A state-supported land-grant college, located in a community of 10,500, 100 miles south of Atlanta; founded as a college for black students, Fort Valley now serves a diverse student body. Most convenient major airport: Lewis B. Wilson.

Founded: 1895
Affiliation: State
Total Enrollment: 2,528 M, W (full-time)
Cost: < $10K
% Receiving Financial Aid: 93%
Admission: Non-selective
Application Deadline: 10 days before registration

Admission. Graduates of accredited high schools with 16 units (11 in academic subjects) and 1.8 GPA, SAT score of 750 combined eligible; 65% of applicants accepted. *Required:* SAT. *Apply* by 10 days before registration. *Transfers* welcome.

Academic Environment. Degrees offered: AB, BS, BBA, BSAg, BSEd, BSHEc, BSMEd. *Majors offered* in addition to usual studies include veterinary technology, ornamental horticulture, commercial design. *Calendar:* quarter, summer school.

Undergraduate degrees conferred (175). 26% were in Business and Management, 16% were in Protective Services, 15% were in Education, 6% were in Psychology, 5% were in Computer and Engineering Related Technology, 4% were in Engineering and Engineering Related Technology, 4% were in Agribusiness and Agricultural Production, 3% were in Public Affairs, 3% were in Letters, 3% were in Communications, 3% were in Social Sciences, 3% were in Agricultural Sciences, remainder in 6 other fields.

Varsity Sports. Men (NCAA, Div.II): Basketball, Football, Tennis, Track. Women (Div.II): Basketball, Tennis, Track, Volleyball.

Student Body. College does not seek a national student body; 90% of students from Georgia; 97% South. An estimated 95% of students reported as Protestant, 2% Catholic; 94% Black, 1% other minority, according to most recent data available.

Campus Life. About 57% of men, 49% of women live in traditional dormitories; no coed dormitories; rest live in off-campus housing or commute. Freshmen given preference in college housing if all students cannot be accommodated. No intervisitation in women's dormitory rooms; limited in men's dormitory rooms. There are 4 fraternities, 4 sororities on campus, which about 7% of men, 5% of women join; they provide no residence facilities. About 50% of resident students leave campus on weekends.

Annual Costs. Tuition and fees, $1,779 (out-of-state, $3,159); room and board, $2,460. About 93% of students receive financial aid. College reports all scholarships awarded on the basis of need. *Meeting Costs:* college offers Parent PLUS Loans.

Framingham State College

Framingham, Massachusetts 01701 (617) 620-1220

A state-supported college, located in a suburban community of 70,000, 20 miles from Boston.

Founded: 1839
Affiliation: State
Total Enrollment: 3,882 M, W (full-time)
Cost: < $10K
Admission: Non-selective
Application Deadline: March 1

Admission. About 69% of applicants accepted, 36% of these actually enroll. *Required:* SAT. *Out-of-state* freshman applicants: college welcomes students from out of state. State does not limit out-of-state enrollment. Requirement for out-of-state applicants: "must be superior in terms of academic requirements." *Apply* by March 1. *Transfers* welcome.
Academic Environment. Students required to take 12 general education courses including 1 in government, 3 each in humanities, social sciences, 2 in natural sciences, math, or computer science. Degrees offered: BA, BS, BSEd, BSMT. *Majors offered* include arts and sciences, education, home economics, medical technology, food science, computer science. About 60% of students entering as freshmen graduate eventually; 25% of freshmen do not return for sophomore year. *Special programs:* CLEP, independent study, honors, undergraduate research, individualized majors. *Calendar:* semester.
Undergraduate degrees conferred (703). 17% were in Education, 17% were in Social Sciences, 12% were in Psychology, 12% were in Home Economics, 11% were in Business and Management, 8% were in Letters, 5% were in Visual and Performing Arts, 4% were in Communications, 3% were in Life Sciences, remainder in 9 other fields.
Varsity Sports. Men (Div.III): Baseball, Basketball, Cross Country, Football, Hockey, Soccer, Tennis. Women (Div. III): Basketball, Field Hockey, Soccer, Softball, Tennis, Volleyball. Coed (Div. III): Equestrian.
Campus Life. College does not seek a national student body; almost all students from New England.

About 34% of women live in traditional dormitories; 29% of men, 36% of women in coed dormitories; rest live in off-campus housing or commute. Sexes segregated in coed dormitories by wing. There are no fraternities or sororities. About 35% of resident students leave campus on weekends.
Annual Costs. Tuition and fees, $3,017 (out-of-state, $6,881); room and board, $3,466. College reports some scholarships awarded on the basis of academic merit alone.

Francis Marion College

Florence, South Carolina 29501 (803) 661-1231

A state-supported college located 7 miles east of a town of 32,000. Most convenient major airport: Florence Regional.

Founded: 1970
Affiliation: State
UG Enrollment: 1,463 M, 1,758 W (full-time); 191 M, 248 W (part-time)
Total Enrollment: 4,103
Cost: < $10K
% Receiving Financial Aid: 51%
Admission: Non-selective
Application Deadline: Rolling

Admission. High school graduates eligible; 92% of applicants accepted, 45% of these actually enroll. About 30% of freshmen graduate in top fifth of high school class, 57% in top two-fifths. Average freshman SAT scores: 397 M, 395 W verbal; 454 M, 431 W mathematical. *Required:* SAT. Criteria considered in admissions, in order of importance: standardized test scores, high school academic record. *Out-of-state* freshman applicants: no special requirements for out-of-state students. About 15% of entering students from private schools. *Apply*: rolling admissions. *Transfers* welcome.
Academic Environment. Degrees offered: bachelors, masters. Graduation requirements include 15 credit hours in humanities, 12 in science, 6 in English, 6 in mathematics, 9 in social sciences; internships required in health physics, and communications programs. Average undergraduate class size: 24. No teaching assistants, small classes, and "lots of individual attention" from faculty seen by students as strengths of the academic program. *Special programs:* CLEP, independent study, honors, study abroad, 3-year degree, Special Semester, cooperative fourth-year programs in art, geography, theatre, 3–2 engineering with Clemson U.. *Calendar:* semester, summer school.
Undergraduate degrees conferred (474). 26% were in Business and Management, 22% were in Social Sciences, 17% were in Education, 8% were in Life Sciences, 8% were in Letters, 5% were in Psychology, 3% were in Mathematics, 3% were in Liberal/General Studies, remainder in 6 other fields.
Graduates Career Data. Office of Guidance and Placement's services include job locator, career recruitment day.
Faculty. About 79% of faculty hold PhD or equivalent. About 26% of teaching faculty are female.
Student Body. About 95% of students from in state. An estimated 22% of students are reported as Black, 1% other minority. Average age of undergraduate student: 22.
Varsity Sports. Men (NCAA Div. II): Baseball, Basketball, Cross Country, Golf, Soccer, Tennis, Track. Women (NCAA Div. II): Basketball, Cross Country, Softball, Tennis, Volleyball.
Campus Life. Campus is secluded but not isolated, with easy access to town, according to students. Clubs, campus organizations, and intramurals reported popular. Approximately 75% of students commute; high percentage work, according to student source, who notes that this affects student participation and attendance at extracurricular events. There are 8 fraternities, 6 sororities on campus which about 13% of men, 9% of women join; fraternities and sororities provide no residence facilities.
Annual Costs. Tuition and fees, $2,800 (out-of-state, $5,600); room and board, $3,078; estimated $400 other, exclusive of travel. About 51% of students receive financial aid; average amount of assistance, $3,350. *Meeting Costs:* college offers federal loan programs.

Franciscan University of Steubenville

Steubenville, Ohio 43952 (614) 283-6226

A church-related university, conducted by the Franciscan Friars of the Third Order Regular, located in a community of 25,000, 42 miles west of Pittsburgh. Formerly known as University of Steubenville. Most convenient major airport: Pittsburgh International.

Founded: 1946
Affiliation: Roman Catholic
UG Enrollment: 534 M, 767 W (full-time); 85 M, 157 W (part-time)
Total Enrollment: 1,901
Cost: < $10K
% Receiving Financial Aid: 80%
Admission: Selective
Application Deadline: July 31

Admission is selective. About 82% of applicants accepted, 50% of these actually enroll; 43% of freshmen graduate in top fifth of high school class, 65% in top two-fifths. Average freshman scores: SAT, 488 verbal, 516 mathematical; 49% score above 500 on verbal, 15% above 600, 2% above 700; 56% score above 500 on mathematical, 22% above 600, 1% above 700; ACT, 23.5 composite. *Required:* SAT or ACT; interview recommended. Criteria considered in admissions, in order of importance: standardized test scores, high school academic record, recommendations, extracurricular activities, writing sample. About 44% of entering students from private schools. *Entrance programs:* rolling admission. *Apply* by July 31. *Transfers* welcome; 209 enrolled 1993–94.
Academic Environment. Degrees offered: associates, bachelors, masters. About 30% of general education requirements for graduation are elective; distribution requirements fairly numerous. University operates a campus in Austria where all students spend a semester studying humanities. About 57% of students entering as freshmen graduate within four years, 68% eventually. *Special programs:* CLEP, advanced placement, study abroad. Adult program: Older Student Association. *Calendar:* early semester, summer school.
Undergraduate degrees conferred (256). 26% were in Business and Management, 14% were in Education, 11% were in Theology, 9% were in Allied Health, 8% were in Health Sciences, 5% were in Letters, 5% were in Social Sciences, 4% were in Psychology,

4% were in Philosophy and Religion, 4% were in Communications, remainder in 8 other fields.

Faculty. About 64% of faculty hold PhD or equivalent. About 41% of teaching faculty are female.

Student Body. About 37% of students from in state. An estimated 93% of students reported as Catholic, 7% other; 1% Black, 4% Hispanic, 3% Asian, 8% other minority.

Religious Orientation. Steubenville is a church-related institution; 90% of students affiliated with the church; no religious studies required; attendance at Mass voluntary.

Campus Life. Student reports campus is far enough from town to focus most activities on campus; students spend time "studying, socializing, exercising, going to talks, dances, mass, and in prayer." She also asserts "we do not worry about crime, it's a safe campus."

About 59% of men and women live in traditional dormitories; rest commute. No intervisitation in men's or women's dormitory rooms. There are 2 fraternities, 2 sororities on campus, which about 2% each men, women join and live in. About 5% of resident students leave campus on weekends.

Annual Costs. Tuition and fees, $9,200, room and board, $4,200; estimated $600 other, exclusive of travel. About 80% of students receive financial aid; average amount of assistance, $6,000. Assistance is typically divided 25% scholarship, 11% grant, 44% loan, 20% work. *Meeting Costs:* University offers deferred payment plans, university loans.

Franklin and Marshall College

Lancaster, Pennsylvania 17604-3003 (717) 291-3951

One of the nation's oldest liberal arts colleges, Franklin and Marshall celebrated its bicentennial in 1987. College was founded under the auspices of the Lutheran and German Reformed churches, but is now independent. The college has long emphasized strong preparation for medicine, law, business, accounting, science and earth science. The college attracts students from 40 states and 47 foreign countries. The 125-acre main campus is located in a city of 60,000, 60 miles west of Philadelphia. Most convenient major airports: Harrisburg International or Philadelphia.

Founded: 1787
Affiliation: Independent
Total Enrollment: 972 M, 836 W (full-time)
Cost: > $20K
% Receiving Financial Aid: 60%
Admission: Highly Selective
Application Deadline: Feb. 1

Admission is highly selective. About 65% of applicants accepted, 24% of these actually enroll; 70% of freshmen graduate in top fifth of high school class, 93% in top two-fifths. Average freshman scores: SAT, 77% of freshmen score above 500 on verbal, 26% above 600; 94% score above 500 on mathematical, 58% above 600, 14% above 700; ACT, 26 composite. *Required:* SAT or ACT (SAT preferred), ACH in English Composition; interview recommended. Criteria considered in admissions, in order of importance: high school academic record, recommendations, extracurricular activities, standardized test scores, writing sample; other factors considered: diverse student body, special talents, alumni children. About 44% of entering students from non-public schools. *Entrance programs:* early decision, deferred admission, advanced placement. *Apply* by February 1. *Transfers* welcome; 10 enrolled 1993–94.

Academic Environment. Student body is academically able, intellectually energetic. As at other competitive institutions, there is some student concern voiced about the "stress" and "intensity" of some programs. Overall, however, students report that the breadth and the rigor of the academic program prepares them well for the "changing world in which we live." Many opportunities for independent study, student research, and faculty/student collaboration available. Academic requirements include 11 college studies (general education) electives that cover scientific inquiry, social analysis, arts, foreign cultures, historical studies, language studies, literature, and systems of knowledge and belief. Strongest academic offerings reported to be biology, business, chemistry, geology, physics, psychology, government, drama, anthropology, English. Degree offered: bachelors. *Majors offered* include Asian studies, women's studies, environmental studies. Average undergraduate class size: 56% under 20, 42% 20–40, 2% over 40.

About 80% of students entering as freshmen graduate within four years, 84% eventually; 95% of freshmen return for sophomore year. *Special programs:* CLEP, independent study, freshmen seminars, internships, study abroad programs (semester, year, and summer), undergraduate research, individualized majors, Washington semester, semester at School of Visual Arts in NYC, junior year at Institute for Architecture and Urban Studies in New York City, 3–2 forestry/environmental studies, 3–2 engineering, cross registration with Millersville U., Lancaster Theological Seminary, Gettysburg, Dickinson, 7-week Japanese Studies summer program, member of Central Pennsylvania Consortium with Dickinson and Gettysburg. *Calendar:* semester, summer school.

Undergraduate degrees conferred (431). 35% were in Social Sciences, 15% were in Business and Management, 14% were in Letters, 7% were in Life Sciences, 5% were in Visual and Performing Arts, 5% were in Physical Sciences, 4% were in Psychology, 3% were in Mathematics, 3% were in Foreign Languages, 3% were in Area and Ethnic Studies, remainder in 2 other fields.

Graduates Career Data. Advanced studies pursued by 33% of graduates; 14% enter graduate school; 6% enter medical school; less than 1% enter dental school; 5% enter law school; 2% enter business school. Medical schools typically enrolling graduates include Pennsylvania, Temple, Cornell; law schools include New York Law, Villanova, Temple, Pittsburgh; business schools include American Graduate School of International Management, Pennsylvania. About 51% of 1992–93 graduates employed. Fields typically hiring largest numbers of graduates include financial services, law, medicine, industry. Career Development Services available to students and alumni include self-assessment, search techniques, graduate school application process, initial employment searches, and career changes on individual and group levels. Alumni as well as parents of students reported to be involved in both career guidance and job placement.

Faculty. About 96% of faculty hold PhD or equivalent. About 41% of undergraduate classes taught by tenured faculty. About 41% of teaching faculty are female; 9% minority.

Student Body. About 33% of students from in state; 35% Middle Atlantic, 11% New England, 3% Midwest, 4% South, 5% West/Northwest, 8% foreign. An estimated 30% of students reported as Protestant, 30% Catholic, 11% Jewish; 4% as Black, 3% Hispanic, 6% Asian, 6% other minority.

Varsity Sports. Men (Div.III): Baseball, Basketball, Cross Country, Football, Golf, Lacrosse, Soccer, Squash, Swimming, Tennis, Track, Wrestling (I). Women (Div.III): Basketball, Cross Country, Field Hockey, Golf, Lacrosse, Soccer, Softball, Swimming, Tennis, Track, Volleyball, Squash.

Campus Life. Lancaster is a small city (pop. 350,000) located in the Pennsylvania Dutch country. Students report that, despite the cultural and historical learning opportunities of the area, most students stay on campus, except when they "wish to take advantage of the incredible restaurants located throughout Lancaster." Many cultural and intellectual activities on campus, supplemented by resources of Philadelphia and Baltimore, 60 and 75 miles respectively from campus. Regulations governing student conduct emphasize students' responsibility to institution and its regulations. Use of alcohol and drugs governed by state law; smoking restricted to designated areas. Cars allowed for all students. Freshmen and sophomores required to live in college residences; others given permission to live off campus as long as dormitories are filled to capacity. High interest reported in intramural sports (most popular: basketball, softball, touch football), as well as varsity sports.

About 74% of students live in coed residence halls; 4% in other college-related housing; rest live in off-campus housing or commute. Freshmen given preference in college housing if all students cannot be accommodated. Sexes segregated in coed dormitories by wing, floor or room. There are 9 off-campus fraternities, 3 off-campus sororities, which about 40% of men, 30% of women join. There are no fraternities or sororities on campus. About 20% of resident students leave campus on weekends.

Annual Costs. Comprehensive fee (includes tuition, fees, room and board), $23,655; estimated $1,500 other, exclusive of travel. About 60% of students receive financial aid (42% receive need-based grant money); average amount of assistance, $15,165 (all forms). Assistance is typically divided 70% grant, 23% loans, 7% work. College awards 118 scholarships on the basis of academic merit alone.

Franklin College of Indiana

Franklin, Indiana 46131 (317) 736-8441

A small, independent, liberal arts college, located in a town of 15,000, 20 miles south of Indianapolis. Most convenient major airport: Indianapolis International.

Founded: 1834
Affiliation: Independent (American Baptist)
Total Enrollment: 864 M, W (full-time)
Cost: $10K–$20K
% Receiving Financial Aid: 92%
Admission: Non-selective
Application Deadline: August 1

Admission. High school graduates with 16 units in academic subjects eligible; 75% of applicants accepted, 43% of these actually enroll. About 42% of freshmen graduate in top fifth of high school class, 68% in top two-fifths. *Required:* SAT or ACT; interview preferred. *Non-academic factors* considered in admissions: special talents, alumni children. *Apply* by August 1. *Transfers* welcome.
Academic Environment. *Degree:* AB. About 39% of general education requirements for graduation are elective; distribution requirements fairly numerous. About 50% of students entering as freshmen graduate eventually; 17% of freshmen do not return for sophomore year. *Special programs:* CLEP, independent study, study abroad, honors, undergraduate research, 3-year degree, individualized majors, Washington Semester, college-in-escrow program for high school students, 3–2 programs in engineering, occupational therapy. *Calendar:* 4–1–4, summer school.
Undergraduate degrees conferred (145). 21% were in Social Sciences, 18% were in Business and Management, 14% were in Life Sciences, 12% were in Education, 12% were in Communications, 4% were in Philosophy and Religion, 4% were in Foreign Languages, 3% were in Mathematics, 3% were in Visual and Performing Arts, 3% were in Psychology, remainder in 3 other fields.
Graduates Career Data. According to most recent data available, full-time graduate or professional study pursued immediately after graduation by 16% of students.
Varsity Sports. Men (NAIA II): Baseball, Basketball, Cross Country, Football (also NCAA), Golf, Soccer, Tennis, Track. Women (NAIA): Basketball, Field Hockey, Golf, Softball, Tennis, Track, Volleyball.
Student Body. According to most recent data available, 90% of students from in state; 97% Middle Atlantic. An estimated 55% of students reported as Protestant, 20% Catholic, 23% unaffiliated, 2% other; 2% Black, 2% other minority.
Campus Life. According to most recent data available, about 32% of men, 58% of women live in traditional dormitories; 28% of men, 20% of women live in coed dormitories; 11% of men, 22% of women live in off-campus housing or commute. Freshmen given preference in college housing if all students cannot be accommodated. Intervisitation in men's and women's dormitory rooms limited. There are 5 fraternities, 4 sororities on campus which about 49% of men, 39% of women join; 29% of men live in fraternities; sororities provide no residence facilities. About 30% of resident students leave campus on weekends.
Annual Costs. Tuition and fees, $10,090; room and board, $3,870. About 92% of students receive financial aid, according to most recent data available. College reports some scholarships awarded on the basis of academic merit alone. *Meeting Costs:* college offers institutional deferred payment plan.

Franklin Pierce College

Rindge, New Hampshire 03461 (603) 899-5111

An independent, liberal arts college, located in a town of 2,200, 18 miles southeast of Keene and 70 miles west of Boston.

Founded: 1962
Affiliation: Independent
Total Enrollment: 2,765 M, W (full-time)
Cost: $10K–$20K
Admission: Non-selective
Application Deadline: Rolling

Admission. Graduates of accredited high schools with 16 units (12 in college preparatory subjects) eligible; others admitted conditionally. *Required:* SAT or ACT; interview recommended. *Apply:* rolling admissions. *Transfers* welcome.
Academic Environment. *Degree:* AB. *Special programs:* CLEP, independent study, study abroad, honors, 3-year degree, individualized majors, cooperative programs through NHCUC. *Calendar:* 4–1–4, summer school.
Undergraduate degrees conferred (626). 49% were in Business and Management, 16% were in Computer and Engineering Related Technology, 8% were in Visual and Performing Arts, 6% were in Liberal/General Studies, 6% were in Marketing and Distribution, 5% were in Communications, 4% were in Social Sciences, remainder in 6 other fields.
Campus Life. According to most recent data available, about 52% of women live in traditional dormitories; 72% of men, 32% of women in coed dormitories; rest live in off-campus housing or commute.
Annual Costs. Tuition and fees, $13,105; room and board, $4,450.

Franklin University

Columbus, Ohio 43215 (614) 224-6237

A co-educational institution located in Ohio's capital city, Franklin admits students to each trimester; 40% of "new" students are transfers and university attracts substantial numbers of part-time, adult learners. Most convenient major airport: Port Columbus International.

Affiliation: Independent
Total Enrollment: 2,634 M, W
Cost: < $10K
Admission: Non-selective
Application Deadline: Rolling

Admission. Open admissions; high school graduates or equivalent eligible; all applicants accepted. *Apply:* rolling admissions. *Transfers* welcome.
Academic Environment. *Degree:* BS. University offers 4-year programs in business, banking, data processing, accounting, computer science, management science, real estate, public administration, and in engineering technology. *Calendar:* trimester, summer school.
Undergraduate degrees conferred (748). 76% were in Business and Management, 7% were in Computer and Engineering Related Technology, 6% were in Engineering and Engineering Related Technology, 4% were in Psychology, 4% were in Health Sciences, 3% were in Communications, remainder in Public Affairs.
Student Body. About 99% of students from in state. An estimated 14% of students reported as Black, 2% other minority. No residential facilities; all commute.
Annual Costs. Tuition and fees, $4,110. University reports all scholarships awarded on the basis of need.

State University College at Fredonia

(See State University of New York)

Freed-Hardeman College

Henderson, Tennessee 38340 (800) 342-7837 or (901) 989-6651)

Established in 1869 and for 50 years a junior college, Freed-Hardeman has been a 4-year institution since 1974. The campus is located in a west Tennessee community of 4,633.

Founded: 1869
Affiliation: Independent (Church of Christ)
Total Enrollment: 551 M, 623 W (full-time)
Cost: < $10K
% Receiving Financial Aid: 82%
Admission: Non-selective
Application Deadline: September 1

Admission. High school graduates or equivalent with minimum 2.5 GPA eligible. About 61% of applicants accepted, 57% of these actually enroll. Average freshman scores: SAT, 418 M, 456 W verbal, 499 M, 490 W mathematical; ACT, 19.7 M, 20.2 W composite, 18.5 M,

18.4 W mathematical according to most recent data available. *Required:* ACT, "sincere interest in a Christian education." Criteria considered in admissions, in order of importance: high school academic record, standardized test scores, recommendations, extracurricular activities; other factors considered: diverse student body. *Entrance programs:* early admission, deferred admission, advanced placement, rolling admission. *Apply* by September 1. *Transfers* welcome; 134 enrolled 1993–94.

Academic Environment. Graduation requirements include courses in Introduction to Universal Studies, Bible, speech communication, English Composition, physical education, literature, humanities, math or computer science, lab science, history or political science, fine arts, Values in Human Thought and Action. *Degrees:* bachelors, masters. *Majors offered* include graphic design, family studies. Average undergraduate class size: 52% under 20, 42% 20–40, 6% over 40. About 33% of entering students graduate within four years, 46% eventually; 70% of freshmen return for sophomore year. *Special programs:* 3–2 engineering, honors, study abroad, independent study, cross-registration with Lambuth College, Union U., 2 two-week short term courses in May.

Undergraduate degrees conferred (197). 28% were in Business and Management, 24% were in Education, 10% were in Theology, 8% were in Multi/Interdisciplinary Studies, 7% were in Communications, 6% were in Life Sciences, 5% were in Public Affairs, remainder in 12 other fields.

Graduates Career Data. Full-time advanced studies pursued by 40% of students immediately after graduation.

Faculty. About 55% of faculty hold PhD or equivalent. About 50% of undergraduate classes taught by tenured faculty. About 30% of teaching faculty are female.

Student Body. About 45% of students from in state; 81% South, 10% Midwest, 3% Middle Atlantic, 1% each West, Northwest, 3% foreign. An estimated 98% of students reported as Protestant; 5% Black, 1% other minority.

Religious Orientation. Freed-Hardeman is a Christian college; 1 courses of Bible study required each semester student is in residence.

Varsity Sports. Men (NAIA): Baseball, Basketball, Golf, Tennis. Women (NAIA): Basketball, Softball, Tennis, Volleyball.

Campus Life. About 75% of men, 73% of women live in traditional dormitories; rest live in married student housing or commute. There are 6 fraternities, 6 sororities on campus, which about 67% of men, 74% of women join. About 20% of resident students leave campus on weekends.

Annual Costs. Tuition and fees, $5,940; room and board, $3,020; estimated $1,575 other, exclusive of travel. About 82% of students receive financial aid; average amount of assistance, $3,500. Assistance is typically divided 30% scholarship, 22% grant, 30% loan, 8% work. College reports 780 scholarships awarded on the basis of academic merit alone, 145 for special talents alone, 289 for need and merit combination.

Fresno Pacific College

Fresno, California 93702 **(209) 453-2000**

A church-related liberal arts college, located in a city of 200,000, 165 miles southeast of San Francisco.

Founded: 1944
Affiliation: Mennonite Brethren
UG Enrollment: 291 M, 426 W (full-time)
Total Enrollment: 1,583
Cost: < $10K
% Receiving Financial Aid: 95%
Admission: Non-selective
Application Deadline: Rolling

Admission. High school graduates with 15 units (9 in college preparatory subjects) and GPA of 3.1 eligible; 79% of applicants accepted, 53% of these actually enroll. *Required:* SAT(accepted) or ACT(preferred), essay. Criteria considered in admissions, in order of importance: high school academic record, standardized test scores, writing sample, recommendations, extracurricular activities. *Apply:* rolling admissions. *Transfers* welcome; 114 enrolled 1993–94.

Academic Environment. Degrees offered: associates, bachelors, masters. General education requirements amount to 58–61 out of 124 total units for graduation. About 30% of students entering as freshmen graduate within four years, 42% eventually; about 89% of freshmen return for sophomore year. Average undergraduate class size: 69% of classes under 20, 24% between 20–40, 7% over 40. *Special programs:* CLEP, independent study, study abroad, individualized majors, internships in teacher education and social work, Small Business Institute, cross registration with San Joaquin College of Law, MB Biblical Seminary. *Calendar:* semester, summer school.

Undergraduate degrees conferred (103). 49% were in Education, 13% were in Theology, 11% were in Business and Management, 7% were in Social Sciences, 7% were in Public Affairs, 6% were in Psychology, 4% were in Letters, remainder in 4 other fields.

Faculty. About 55% of faculty hold PhD or equivalent. About 25% of teaching faculty are female; 4% ethnic minorities.

Varsity Sports. Men (NAIA): Basketball, Cross Country, Soccer, Track. Women (NAIA): Basketball, Cross Country, Track, Volleyball.

Student Body. About 96% of students from California; 1% foreign. An estimated 59% of students reported as Protestant, 14% Catholic, 8% unaffiliated, 19% other; 3% Black, 15% Hispanic, 4% Asian, 6% other ethnic minorities.

Religious Orientation. Pacific is a church-related institution; 4 courses in religion required of all students; attendance at convocations "expected."

Campus Life. About 65% of men, 65% of women live in traditional dormitories; rest live in off-campus college-related housing or commute. Freshmen given preference in college housing if all students cannot be accommodated. Intervisitation in men's and women's dormitory rooms limited. There are no fraternities or sororities. About 65% of resident students leave campus on weekends.

Annual Costs. Tuition and fees, $9,900; room and board, $3,670; about $1,278 estimated other, exclusive of travel. About 95% of students receive financial aid; average amount of assistance, $6,050. Assistance is typically divided 20% scholarship, 27% grant, 49% loan, 4% work. College reports 369 scholarships awarded on the basis of academic merit alone, 189 for special talents, 242 for need.

Fresno State College

(See California State University/Fresno)

Friends University

Wichita, Kansas 67213 **(316) 261-5842**

A small, private institution, located in a city of 280,000. Most convenient major airport: Wichita Mid-Continent.

Founded: 1898
Affiliation: Friends
Total Enrollment: 1,488 M, W (full-time)
Cost: < $10K
% Receiving Financial Aid: 78%
Admission: Non-selective
Application Deadline: July 1

Admission. Graduates of accredited high schools or equivalent with C average eligible; others given individual consideration; 86% of applicants accepted, 79% of these actually enroll. *Required:* ACT; interview encouraged. *Apply* by July 1. *Transfers* welcome.

Academic Environment. *Degrees:* BA, BFA, BS, BM. About 55% of general education requirements for graduation are elective; distribution requirements fairly numerous. Majors in addition to usual studies include art/business, ballet, health management, international business, music/business, sports communication, New College. Students report small classes allow opportunities for individualized attention. About 48% of students entering as freshmen graduate eventually; 35% of freshmen do not return for sophomore year. *Special programs:* CLEP, independent study, internships, cooperative program with Kansas Newman. *Calendar:* semester, summer school.

Undergraduate degrees conferred (316). 67% were in Business and Management, 14% were in Education, 6% were in Allied Health, 3% were in Visual and Performing Arts, remainder in 11 other fields.

Graduates Career Data. According to most recent data available, full-time graduate or professional study pursued by 18% of students immediately after graduation; 8% enter business school. *Careers in business and industry* pursued by 39% of graduates.

Varsity Sports. Men (NAIA Div.II): Baseball, Basketball, Cross Country, Football, Soccer, Tennis. Women (NAIA Div.II): Basketball, Cross Country, Softball, Tennis, Volleyball.
Student Body. About 92% of students from in state. An estimated 86% of students reported as Protestant, 10% Catholic, 4% other; 5% Black, 1% Hispanic, 1% Asian, according to most recent data available.
Religious Orientation. Friends is a church-related institution; 2 courses from division of religion and philosophy required of all students; attendance at weekly chapel services voluntary.
Campus Life. According to most recent data available, about 21% of men, 21% of women live in traditional dormitories; no coed dormitories; rest live in off-campus housing or commute. There are 2 fraternities, 2 sororities on campus which about 13% of men, 11% of women join. About 50% of resident students leave campus on weekends.
Annual Costs. Tuition and fees, $8,230; room and board, $2,890. According to most recent data available, about 78% of students receive financial aid; assistance is typically divided 43% scholarship, 55% loan, 2% work. College reports some scholarships awarded on the basis of academic merit alone. *Meeting Costs:* college offers Parent PLUS Loans.

Frostburg State College

Frostburg, Maryland 21532 (301) 689-4201

A state-supported college, located in a community of 7,500, 100 miles southeast of Pittsburgh and 150 miles west of both Baltimore and Washington, D.C.

Founded: 1898
Affiliation: State
Total Enrollment: 2,161 M, 2,380 W (full-time)
Cost: < $10K
% Receiving Financial Aid: 60%
Admission: Non-selective
Application Deadline: Rolling

Admission. High school graduates with a minimum GPA in a college preparatory program eligible; 65% of applicants accepted. Average freshman scores: SAT, 930 combined; ACT, 23 composite. *Required:* SAT. Criteria considered in admissions, in order of importance: high school academic record, standardized test scores, recommendations, extracurricular activities, writing sample; other factors considered: diverse student body. *Out-of-state* freshman applicants: college seeks students from out-of-state. State does not limit out-of-state enrollment. No special requirements for out-of-state applicants. States from which most out-of-state applicants are drawn: Virginia, Pennsylvania, New Jersey, West Virginia, Delaware. *Entrance programs:* advanced placement. *Apply:* rolling admissions. *Transfers* welcome; 399 enrolled 1993–94.
Academic Environment. Graduation requirements include freshman composition, advanced composition, mathematics, computer science, speech, and personalized health fitness, 2 lab sciences, 2 social sciences, 2 humanities, and 2 arts. *Degrees:* bachelors, masters. *Majors offered* include: wildlife fisheries, education, pre-law. About 80% of freshmen return for sophomore year. *Special programs:* CLEP, honors, internships, cooperative education, independent study, 2–2 engineering. *Calendar:* semester, summer school.
Undergraduate degrees conferred (733). 30% were in Business and Management, 18% were in Social Sciences, 18% were in Education, 8% were in Psychology, 4% were in Letters, 3% were in Computer and Engineering Related Technology, 3% were in Life Sciences, remainder in 11 other fields.
Graduates Career Data. Career Development Services include credential service, positions listings, newsletters, resume writing and interview seminars, on-campus interviews, career options.
Faculty. About 70% of faculty hold PhD or equivalent. All undergraduate classes taught by tenured faculty.
Student Body. About 85% of students from in state.
Varsity Sports. Men (Div.III): Baseball, Basketball, Cross Country, Diving, Football, Soccer, Swimming, Tennis, Track. Women (Div.III): Basketball, Cross Country, Diving, Soccer, Swimming, Tennis, Track, Volleyball.
Campus Life. About 45% of students live on campus; rest live in off-campus housing or commute. Freshmen given preference in college housing if all students cannot be accommodated. Intervisitation in men's and women's dormitory rooms unlimited. Sexes segregated in coed dormitories by wing. There are 11 fraternities, 9 sororities on campus which about 15% of men, 15% of women join; they provide no residence facilities. About 30% of resident students leave campus on weekends.
Annual Costs. Tuition and fees, $2,700 (out-of-state, $5,200); room and board, $4,150; estimated $950 other, exclusive of travel. About 60% of students receive financial aid; average amount of assistance, $3,000. *Meeting Costs:* college offers deferred payment plan.

Furman University

Greenville, South Carolina 29613 (803) 294-2000

Founded by the South Carolina Baptist Convention, Furman is now independent. Despite its designation as a university and its small graduate enrollment, Furman is essentially a liberal arts college, with a predominantly Southern student body. The 750-acre campus is located 5 miles north of Greenville (pop. 61,200). Most convenient major airport: Greenville/Spartanburg.

Founded: 1826
Affiliation: Independent
Total Enrollment: 1,078 M, 1,293 W (full-time)
Cost: $10K–$20K
% Receiving Financial Aid: 70%
Admission: Very (+) Selective
Application Deadline: Feb. 1

Admission is very (+) selective. About 90% of applicants accepted, 35% of these actually enroll; 76% of freshmen graduate in top fifth of high school class, 93% in top two-fifths. Average freshman scores: SAT, middle 50% range, 470–580 verbal; middle 50% range, 520–640 mathematical; 61% of freshmen score above 500 on verbal, 23% above 600, 4% above 700; 84% score above 500 on mathematical, 44% above 600, 11% above 700; ACT middle 50% range, 23–27 composite. *Required:* SAT or ACT; essay. Criteria considered in admissions, in order of importance: high school academic record, standardized test scores; extracurricular activities and writing sample considered equally; other factors considered: alumni children, diverse student body, special talents. *Entrance programs:* early decision, advanced placement. About 25% of entering students from private schools. *Apply* by February 1. *Transfers* welcome; 43 enrolled 1993–94.
Academic Environment. University offers a cooperative work/study program which a student leader termed "outstanding." Special program allowing individualized curriculum open to any student by formal application to a faculty committee; may include a major or may be interdisciplinary. Most popular programs reported to be natural sciences, psychology, history, music, English, premed, pre-law, and foreign study. Graduation requirements include 2 courses each in English, natural sciences, 3 courses in history/religion, 1 course each in fine arts, mathematics; proficiency in language, physical education. *Degrees:* bachelors, masters. *Majors offered* include Asian-African studies, individualized curriculum program. Average undergraduate class size: 57% under 20, 41% 20–40, 2% over 40.

About 82% of students entering as freshmen graduate within four years, 84% eventually; 92% of freshmen return for sophomore year. *Special programs:* independent study, study abroad, honors, undergraduate research, credit by examination, 3-year degree, individualized majors, 3–2 in engineering, forestry and environmental studies. Adult programs: Bachelor of General Studies degree. *Calendar:* 3 terms (12-week fall and spring terms, 8-week winter term), summer school.
Undergraduate degrees conferred (607). 31% were in Social Sciences, 15% were in Business and Management, 11% were in Education, 7% were in Life Sciences, 6% were in Letters, 6% were in Psychology, 6% were in Visual and Performing Arts, 5% were in Physical Sciences, 4% were in Foreign Languages, 3% were in Philosophy and Religion, remainder in 4 other fields.
Graduates Career Data. Advanced studies pursued by 40% of graduates; 23% enter graduate school; 4% enter medical and dental school; 5% enter law school; 3% enter business school. Medical schools typically enrolling largest numbers of graduates include Medical U. of South Carolina, U. of Georgia; dental schools include Medical U. of South Carolina; law schools include U. of South Carolina, Stetson U., Georgia State U.; business schools include Georgia State U., U. of South Carolina, U. of Georgia. About 40% of 1992–93 graduates employed. Office of Career Services offers career

counseling, vocational testing, computer-assisted decision-making program, internship and cooperative education opportunities, and job placement.

Faculty. About 91% of faculty hold PhD or equivalent. About 70% of undergraduate classes taught by tenured faculty. About 28% of teaching faculty are female; less than 2% are Black, 2% Hispanic, 2% other minority.

Student Body. About 33% of students from in state, 84% South, 6% Middle Atlantic, 5% Midwest, 3% New England, 2% foreign. An estimated 81% of students reported as Protestant, 11% Catholic, 8% other or unaffiliated; 3% as Black, 1% other minority.

Religious Orientation. Furman is an independent institution; course in religion required as part of the general education program.

Varsity Sports. Men (Div.I): Baseball, Basketball, Cross Country, Football, Golf, Soccer, Tennis, Track. Women (Div.I): Basketball, Cross Country, Golf, Soccer, Softball, Tennis, Track, Volleyball.

Campus Life. Despite the severance of official ties with the Baptist Church, students report a conservative, Christian atmosphere on campus. About 80–90% of students reported involved in various religious, service, and volunteer organizations. Regulations governing intervisitation determined by administration with student participation; hours limited to set times, primarily on weekends. Use of alcohol and drugs forbidden on campus; smoking prohibited in the stadium and all campus buildings with the exception of students' rooms. Cars permitted. Freshmen and sophomores not living at home or with immediate family required to live in residence halls and to take meals in university dining hall. High interest reported in varsity sports (most popular: football, basketball) and intramurals (most popular duplicate varsity sports plus volleyball).

About 45% of men, 47% of women live in traditional dormitories; 6% of men, 5% of women in coed dormitories; rest commute. There are 8 fraternities, 7 sororities on campus which about 30% of men, 30% of women join; they provide no residence facilities. About 25% of resident students leave campus on weekends.

Annual Costs. Tuition and fees, $12,605; room and board, $3,952; estimated $1,350 other, exclusive of travel. About 70% of students receive financial aid; average amount of assistance, $8,500. Assistance is typically divided 75% grants/scholarship, 25% loan and work. University reports 100 scholarships awarded on the basis of academic merit alone, 208 for special talents alone. *Minority group students:* special financial and academic provisions. *Meeting Costs:* university offers tuition payment plans.

Gallaudet College

Washington, D.C. 20002 **(202) 651-5114**

An independent, liberal arts college for the deaf, Gallaudet is the only institution of its kind in the world. The 92-acre campus is located in the northeastern section of the nation's capital. Most convenient major airport: National (Washington D.C.).

Founded: 1856
Affiliation: Independent
Total Enrollment: 2,175 M, W (full-time)
Cost: < $10K
Admission: Non-selective
Application Deadline: March 1

Admission. High school graduates, preferably with college preparatory curriculum, who have sufficient hearing loss to warrant consideration eligible; 65% of applicants accepted, 66% of these actually enroll. *Required:* written essay, in-house test, audiogram. *Entrance programs:* early admission, deferred admission. About 58% of entering students from residential schools, 38% from mainstreamed schools. *Apply* by March 1. *Transfers* welcome.

Academic Environment. College also provides graduate programs for prospective teachers and interpreters of the hearing-impaired and a 1-year preparatory course for those requiring additional precollege work. *Degrees:* AB, BS. About 33% of general education requirements for graduation are elective; distribution requirements fairly numerous. About 87% of students entering as freshmen graduate eventually; 30% of freshmen do not return for sophomore year. *Special programs:* CLEP, honors, study abroad, independent study, Consortium of Universities, Gallaudet–Oberlin Exchange, Western Maryland Exchange, entrepreneurial studies. *Library:* more than 250,000 volumes, 1,400 periodicals, largest collection on deafness-related subjects in the world. *Calendar:* semester, summer school.

Undergraduate degrees conferred (204). 24% were in Business and Management, 16% were in Psychology, 9% were in Education, 7% were in Visual and Performing Arts, 7% were in Social Sciences, 5% were in Vocational Home Economics, 4% were in Mathematics, 4% were in Letters, 4% were in Computer and Engineering Related Technology, 3% were in Public Affairs, 3% were in Parks and Recreation, 3% were in Communications, remainder in 5 other fields.

Graduates Career Data. According to most recent data available, full-time graduate or professional study pursued by 40% of students immediately after graduation. *Careers in business and industry* pursued by 25% of graduates.

Varsity Sports. Men (Div.III): Baseball, Basketball, Cross Country, Football, Soccer, Softball, Swimming, Tennis, Track, Volleyball, Wrestling. Women (Div.III): Basketball, Field Hockey, Softball, Swimming, Tennis, Track, Volleyball.

Student Body. About 26% of students from New England, 19% North Central, 16% South, 15% West, 12% Northwest, 12% Middle Atlantic. An estimated 9% of students reported as Black, 5% Hispanic, 2% Asian, 1% Native American, according to most recent data available.

Campus Life. According to most recent data available, about 48% of men, 45% of women live in traditional dormitories; 50% of men, 50% of women in coed dormitories; rest commute. Freshmen given preference in college housing if all students cannot be accommodated. Intervisitation in men's and women's coed dormitory rooms unlimited; limited in others. There are 3 fraternities, 3 sororities on campus, which about 15% of men, 20% of women join. About 7% of students leave campus on weekends.

Annual Costs. Tuition and fees, $4,570; room and board, $5,110. About 85% of students receive financial aid; assistance is typically divided 33% scholarship, 33% loan, 33% work. University reports some scholarships awarded on the basis of academic merit alone. *Meeting Costs:* many hearing impaired students receive VR and SSD support which usually covers all of student need.

Gannon University

Erie, Pennsylvania 16541 **(800) 426-6668**

A Catholic liberal arts university, conducted by the Diocese of Erie, Gannon is located near Lake Erie in a county of 275,500, 100 miles from Buffalo and Cleveland.

Founded: 1925
Affiliation: Roman Catholic
UG Enrollment: 1,299 M, 1,394 W (full-time); 275 M, 416 W (part-time)
Total Enrollment: 3,981
Cost: $10K–$20K
% Receiving Financial Aid: 92%
Admission: Non-selective
Application Deadline: Rolling

Admission. About 77% of applicants accepted, 36% of these actually enroll; 44% of freshmen graduate in top fifth of high school class, 77% in top two-fifths. Average freshman scores: SAT, 466 M, 461 W verbal, 534 M, 502 W mathematical; ACT, 22 M, 23 W composite. *Required:* SAT or ACT; interview recommended. Criteria considered in admissions, in order of importance: high school academic record, standardized test scores, recommendations, extracurricular activities. About 20% of entering students from private and parochial schools. *Entrance programs:* early admission, mid-year admission. *Apply:* rolling admissions. *Transfers* welcome; 141 enrolled 1993–94.

Academic Environment. Graduation requirements include a liberal arts core consisting of college composition, Western Consciousness, Philosophy of Human Nature, Sacred Scriptures, and other science, social science, philosophy, religion, and fine arts courses. Degrees offered: associates, bachelors, masters. Average undergraduate class size: 67% under 20, 29% 20–40, 4% over 40.

About 63% of students entering as freshmen graduate eventually; 81% of freshmen return for sophomore year. *Special programs:* CLEP, independent study, study abroad, undergraduate research, optional May interterm, cross-registration with Mercyhurst, 3–2 program in chemical engineering, BS/MD with Hahnemann U.. Adult program: Weekend College Program. *Calendar:* semester, summer school.

Undergraduate degrees conferred (543). 21% were in Business and Management, 10% were in Engineering, 8% were in Health Sciences, 7% were in Life Sciences, 7% were in Education, 6%

were in Allied Health, 6% were in Engineering and Engineering Related Technology, 5% were in Physical Sciences, 4% were in Social Sciences, 3% were in Multi/Interdisciplinary Studies, 3% were in Communications, 3% were in Business (Administrative Support), 3% were in Protective Services, 3% were in Psychology, remainder in 12 other fields.

Graduates Career Data. Advanced studies pursued by 22% of graduates.

Faculty. About 51% of faculty hold PhD or equivalent. About 38% of teaching faculty are female; 4% minority.

Student Body. About 82% of students from in state; 92% Middle Atlantic, 6% Midwest, 2% foreign. An estimated 63% of students reported as Catholic, 25% Protestant, 13% other; 4% Black, 1% Hispanic, 2% Asian, 2% other minority. *Minority group students:* Office of Minority Affairs.

Religious Orientation. Gannon is a church-related institution; 61% of students affiliated with the church; 2 semesters of theology required of all students.

Varsity Sports. Men (Div.II): Baseball, Basketball, Cross Country, Diving, Football, Golf, Soccer, Swimming, Tennis, Wrestling. Women (Div.II): Basketball, Cross Country, Diving, Soccer, Softball, Swimming, Tennis, Volleyball.

Campus Life. Campus is located in downtown Erie, near government offices, museums, theaters, and other attractions. Student reports location "limits use of cars, but there are enough things to do in walking distance." There are plentiful activities on-campus, as well. Cars allowed. Smoking not allowed in classrooms. Regulations governing drugs reported as "very strict; students possessing or using illegal substances may be expelled." Sports, both varsity and intramural, as well as religious and cultural activities are very popular.

About 27% of men, 25% of women live in dormitories or other college-related housing; rest commute. Freshmen given preference in college housing if all students cannot be accommodated. There are 7 fraternities, 5 sororities on campus. About 10% of resident students leave campus on weekends.

Annual Costs. Tuition and fees, $10,332 for engineering and health sciences; $9,842 for other undergraduate schools; room and board, $4,540; estimated $1,450 other, exclusive of travel. About 92% of students receive financial aid; average amount of assistance, $6,936. Assistance is typically divided 57% scholarship/grant, 38% loan, 5% work. University reports 510 scholarships awarded on the basis of academic merit alone; 181 for special talents alone; 1,410 for need alone. *Meeting Costs:* university offers monthly payment plan and prepayment plan.

Gardner-Webb College

(See Gardner-Webb University)

Gardner-Webb University

Boiling Springs, North Carolina 28017 **(704) 434-4498**

A church-related, liberal arts university, Gardner-Webb states that its purpose is "to develop quality Christian students who think for themselves, and who will dedicate themselves to the Christian way of life." Most convenient major airport: Charlotte (NC) /Greenville/Spartanburg (SC).

Founded: 1928
Affiliation: Southern Baptist
Total Enrollment: 703 M, 807 W (full-time); 97 M, 290 W (part-time)
Cost: < $10K
% Receiving Financial Aid: 70%
Admission: Non-selective
Application Deadline: Rolling

Admission. Graduates of accredited high schools with 16 units eligible; others admitted by examination; 66% of applicants accepted, 66% of these actually enroll; 29% of freshmen graduate in top fifth of high school class, 50% in top two-fifths. Average freshman SAT scores: 400 verbal, 445 mathematical. *Required:* SAT or ACT. *Nonacademic factors* considered in admissions: special talents, diverse student body. *Apply:* rolling admissions. *Transfers* welcome; 1,348 enrolled 1993–94.

Academic Environment. Degrees offered: bachelors. About 40% of general education requirements for graduation are elective; distribution requirements fairly numerous. About 65% of students entering as freshmen graduate eventually; 70% of freshmen return for sophomore year. *Special programs:* study abroad, 3–2 engineering with Auburn U.. *Calendar:* semester, summer school.

Undergraduate degrees conferred (429). 44% were in Business and Management, 21% were in Education, 11% were in Social Sciences, 7% were in Health Sciences, 5% were in Philosophy and Religion, 4% were in Psychology, remainder in 8 other fields.

Graduates Career Data. *Careers in business and industry* pursued by 70% of graduates. Corporations typically hiring largest numbers of graduates include Burlington Industries, Electronic Data Systems, Doran Mills (Textiles).

Faculty. About 72% of faculty hold PhD or equivalent.

Student Body. About 81% of students from in state, 95% from South, 4% foreign.

Religious Orientation. Gardner-Webb is a church-related institution; 6 hours of religion, attendance at weekly convocation required of all students.

Varsity Sports. Men (NCAA Div.II): Baseball, Basketball, Cross Country, Football, Golf, Soccer, Tennis, Track, Wrestling. Women (NAIA): Basketball, Cross Country, Soccer, Softball, Tennis, Volleyball.

Campus Life. About 52% of men, 29% of women live in traditional dormitories; no coed dormitories; rest live in off-campus housing or commute. Freshmen given preference in college housing if all students can not be accommodated. No intervisitation in men's or women's dormitory rooms. There are no fraternities or sororities on campus. About 50% of resident students leave campus on weekends.

Annual Costs. Tuition and fees, $7,650; room and board, $4,130; estimated $700 other, exclusive of travel. About 72% of students receive financial aid.

General Motors Institute

(See GMI)

State University College at Geneseo

(See State University of New York)

Geneva College

Beaver Falls, Pennsylvania 15010 **(412) 847-5100**

A "church-controlled" college, with a "serious Christian commitment," located in a town of 16,000, 30 miles northwest of Pittsburgh. Most convenient major airport: Pittsburgh.

Founded: 1848
Affiliation: Reformed Presbyterian
Cost: < $10K
% Receiving Financial Aid: 95%
Admission: Non-selective
Application Deadline: Rolling

Admission. Graduates of accredited high schools with 16 units eligible; 80% of applicants accepted, 44% of these actually enroll. About 34% of freshmen graduate in top fifth of high school class, 62% in top two-fifths. Average freshman scores: SAT, 457 verbal, 525 M, 472 W mathematical; ACT, 22 composite. *Required:* SAT or ACT, essay; interview recommended. Criteria considered in admissions, in order of importance: high school academic record, standardized test scores, writing sample, recommendations, extracurricular activities. About 25% of entering students from private schools. *Entrance programs:* early admission, mid-year admission, deferred admission, advanced placement. *Apply:* rolling admissions. *Transfers* welcome; 113 enrolled 1993–94.

Academic Environment. Degrees offered: associates, bachelors, masters. Graduation requirements include Freshman Experience, 9 hours of biblical studies, 6 hours communications, 12 hours humanities, 8–10 hours natural sciences, 2 hours physical education, 9 hours social science. About 46% of students entering as freshmen graduate within four years, 64% eventually; 70% of freshmen return for sophomore year. *Special programs:* CLEP, honors, independent study, study abroad, undergraduate research, individualized majors, 3–2 in nursing, cross registration with Penn State U., 3-week "experimester" following graduation. Adult programs: degree completion program for working adults. *Calendar:* semester, summer school.

Undergraduate degrees conferred (347). 44% were in Business and Management, 10% were in Education, 8% were in Engineering, 5% were in Life Sciences, 5% were in Social Sciences, 5% were in Psychology, 4% were in Letters, 3% were in Physical Sciences, 3% were in Computer and Engineering Related Technology, remainder in 9 other fields.

Graduates Career Data. Advanced studies pursued by 20% of graduates. Career Development Services include counseling, resume referrals, graduate school guidance.

Faculty. About 66% of faculty hold PhD or equivalent. About 24% of teaching faculty are female; 3% are Black.

Student Body. About 77% of students from in state, 7% Midwest, 6% Middle Atlantic, 6% New England, 1% each South, West, 3% foreign. An estimated 80% of students reported as Protestant, 20% Catholic.

Religious Orientation. Geneva is "a Christian institution," controlled by the Reformed Presbyterian Church of North America; 9 hours of Bible, attendance at 1 chapel service per week required of all students.

Varsity Sports. Men (NAIA, Div.II): Baseball, Basketball, Cross Country, Football, Soccer, Tennis, Track, Volleyball. Women (NAIA, Div.II): Basketball, Cross Country, Soccer, Softball, Tennis, Track, Volleyball.

Campus Life. Use of alcohol or narcotics grounds for dismissal; use of tobacco, profanity, and gambling prohibited on campus. About 50% of students live in traditional dormitories; no coed dormitories; rest commute. Freshmen given preference in college housing if all students cannot be accommodated. No intervisitation in men's or women's dormitory rooms. There are no fraternities or sororities on campus. About 10–15% of resident students leave campus on weekends according to most recent data available.

Annual Costs. Tuition and fees, $8,810; room and board, $4,220; estimated $1,100 other, exclusive of travel. About 95% of students receive financial aid (including state grants); average amount of assistance, $6,108. Assistance is typically divided 56% scholarship/grant, 37% loan, 7% work. College reports 352 scholarships awarded on the basis of academic merit alone, 465 for special talents alone, 803 for need alone. *Meeting Costs:* college offers payment plan.

George Fox College

Newberg, Oregon 97132 **(503) 538-8383**

A "Christian, liberal arts" college, located in a town of 13,000, 23 miles southwest of Portland, George Fox is affiliated with Evangelical Friends (Quakers). Most convenient major airport: Portland International (50 minutes away).

Founded: 1891
Affiliation: Quaker
Total Enrollment: 1,217 M, W (full-time)
Cost: $10K–$20K
% Receiving Financial Aid: 92%
Admission: Non-selective
Application Deadline: Aug. 1

Admission. Graduates of accredited high schools or equivalent with minimum GPA of 2.5 eligible; 83% of applicants accepted, 54% of these actually enroll. About 30% of freshmen graduate in top fifth of high school class, 68% in top two-fifths. *Required:* SAT, WPCT, or ACT; "willingness to profit from the Christian environment," acceptance of ban on "use or possession of alcoholic beverages, illegal drugs, tobacco, and participation in gambling." *Apply by* August 1. *Transfers* welcome.

Academic Environment. *Degrees:* AB, BS. *Majors offered* in addition to usual studies include telecommunications, home economics, engineering, biblical studies. About 40% of students entering as freshmen graduate eventually; 30% of freshmen do not return for sophomore year. *Special programs:* CLEP, independent study, honors, individualized majors, American Studies in Washington, D.C., Latin America studies program, 1 semester visit to a Christian College Consortium school, May term abroad, 3–2 engineering. *Calendar:* semester.

Undergraduate degrees conferred (249). 61% were in Business and Management, 14% were in Education, 6% were in Communications, 6% were in Social Sciences, 3% were in Psychology, remainder in 10 other fields.

Graduates Career Data. According to most recent data available, full-time graduate or professional study pursued by 34% of students immediately after graduation. *Careers in business and industry* pursued by 66% of graduates.

Varsity Sports. Men (NAIA): Baseball, Basketball, Cross Country, Soccer, Track. Women (NAIA): Basketball, Cross Country, Softball, Track, Volleyball.

Student Body. About 52% of students from Oregon; 80% Northwest, 10% West. An estimated 89% of students reported as Protestant, 6% Catholic, 4% unaffiliated, 1% other; 2% Black, 4% Hispanic, 2% Asian, 1% Native American, according to most recent data available.

Religious Orientation. George Fox is a church-related institution; 10 hours of religion, attendance at twice-weekly chapel services required of all students.

Campus Life. According to most recent data available, about 82% of men, 85% of women live in traditional dormitories; rest live in off-campus housing or commute. Freshmen given preference in college housing if all students cannot be accommodated. There are no fraternities or sororities. About 25% of students leave campus on weekends.

Annual Costs. Tuition and fees, $11,740; room and board, $3,890. About 92% of students receive financial aid; assistance is typically divided 39% scholarship, 44% loan, 17% work. College reports some scholarships awarded on the basis of academic merit alone. *Meeting Costs:* college offers monthly budget plan (no interest).

George Mason University

Fairfax, Virginia 22030 **(703) 993-2400**

Originally a college of the University of Virginia, George Mason was established as an independent institution in 1972. It offers daytime, evening, and off-campus courses. The 585-acre campus is located in a suburban area just 16 miles from downtown Washington, D.C. Most convenient major airport: Dulles International.

Founded: 1956
Affiliation: State
Enrollment: 9,528 (full-time); 3,823 (part-time)
Total Enrollment: 20,620
Cost: < $10K
% Receiving Financial Aid: 25%
Admission: Selective (+)
Application Deadline: February 1

Admission is selective (+). About 81% of applicants accepted, 31% of these actually enroll. About 27% of entering freshmen graduate in top fifth of high school class; 61% in top two-fifths. Average freshman SAT scores, according to most recent data available: 507 M, 499 W verbal, 581 M, 541 W mathematical; 49% of freshmen score above 500 on verbal, 11% above 600, 1% above 700; 82% score above 500 on mathematical, 28% above 600, 4% above 700. *Required:* SAT, ACH in English, Math and Science. *Out-of-state* freshman applicants: university welcomes students from out-of-state. State does not limit out-of-state enrollment. No special requirements for out-of-state students. *Entrance programs:* early decision, early admission. *Apply* by February 1. *Transfers* welcome; 1,782 enrolled 1993–94.

Academic Environment. Nature of academic experience is strongly influenced by rapid growth of both student body and course offerings. Student leader notes that "we are growing very fast and trying to adapt along the way." *Degrees:* associates, bachelors. About 40–45% of students entering as freshmen graduate eventually; 78% of freshmen return for sophomore year. *Special programs:* honors, study abroad, independent study, individualized majors, Plan for Alternative General Education (PAGE), cooperative education, honors, credit by examination. Adult programs: Bachelor of Individualized Study, an interdisciplinary, individualized program. *Calendar:* early semester, summer school.

Undergraduate degrees conferred (2455). 22% were in Social Sciences, 17% were in Business and Management, 13% were in Letters, 8% were in Psychology, 7% were in Health Sciences, 6%

were in Education, 4% were in Engineering, 4% were in Life Sciences, 3% were in Public Affairs, 3% were in Computer and Engineering Related Technology, 3% were in Visual and Performing Arts, remainder in 9 other fields.

Graduates Career Data. Full-time advanced studies pursued immediately after graduation by 21% of students. Corporations typically hiring largest numbers of graduates include American Management Systems, AT&T, Hughes Aircraft.

Faculty. About 86% of faculty hold PhD or equivalent.

Student Body. About 89% of students from in state.

An estimated 5% of students reported as Black, 3% Hispanic, 8% Asian according to most recent data available.

Varsity Sports. Men (Div.I): Baseball, Basketball, Cross Country, Golf, Soccer, Tennis, Track, Volleyball, Wrestling. Women (Div.I): Basketball, Cross Country, Soccer, Softball, Tennis, Track, Volleyball.

Campus Life. Large commuter population has strong influence on campus life; student leader reports "empty campus on weekends." About 20% of men, 20% of women live in coed dormitories; rest live in off-campus housing or commute. Freshmen given preference in college housing if all students cannot be accommodated. There are 17 fraternities, 8 sororities on campus which about 5% of men, 5% of women join.

Annual Costs. Tuition and fees, $3,888 (out-of-state, $10,056); room and board, $4,840; estimated $1,400 other, exclusive of travel. University reports some scholarships awarded on the basis of academic merit alone. *Meeting Costs:* university offers payment plans.

George Peabody College for Teachers

(See Vanderbilt University)

George Washington University

Washington, D.C. 20052 (202) 994-6000

A relatively large, urban university, George Washington comprises a number of graduate and professional schools which enroll more than half of the total student body. University attracts a substantial number of foreign students because of its location in the nation's capital, just four blocks from the White House. Most convenient major airport: Washington National.

Founded: 1821
Affiliation: Independent
UG Enrollment: 2,528 M, 2,782 W (full-time); 298 M, 292 W (part-time)
Total Enrollment: 14,853
Cost: $10K–$20K
% Receiving Financial Aid: 70%
Admission: Highly Selective
Application Deadline: Dec. 1

Admission is highly selective for school of Engineering and Applied Science, very (+) selective for school of Business and Public Management, Elliott School of International Affairs, Columbian College of Arts and Sciences, selective (+) for school of Education. For all schools, 64% of applicants accepted, 30% of these actually enroll; 61% of freshmen graduate in top fifth of high school class, 89% in top two-fifths. Average freshman scores: SAT, 490–600 middle 50% range on verbal, 530–650 middle 50% range on mathematical; 73% of freshmen score above 500 on verbal, 28% above 600, 3% above 700; 89% score above 500 on mathematical, 39% above 600, 11% above 700; ACT, 24–29 middle 50% range composite.

For Columbian College of Arts & Sciences (1,362 M, 1,876 W), 64% of applicants accepted, 28% of these actually enroll; 60% of freshman graduate in top fifth of high school class, 90% in top two-fifths. Middle 50% range of freshman SAT scores: 490–600 verbal, 540–650 mathematical; 74% of freshman score above 500 on verbal, 28% above 600, 3% above 700; 90% score above 500 on mathematical, 50% above 600, 11% above 700.

For College of Engineering & Applied Science (394 M, 106 W), 62% of applicants accepted, 27% of these actually enroll; 71% of freshman graduate in top fifth of high school class, 91% in top two-fifths. Middle 50% range of freshman SAT scores: 470–595 verbal, 580–680 mathematical; 65% of freshman score above 500 on verbal, 24% above 600, 3% above 700; 93% score above 500 on mathematical, 71% above 600, 17% above 700.

For College of Business & Public Management (534 M, 385 W), 62% of applicants accepted, 29% of these actually enroll; 54% of freshman graduate in top fifth of high school class, 86% in top two-fifths. Middle 50% range of freshman SAT scores: 460–555 verbal, 530–630 mathematical; 62% of freshman score above 500 on verbal, 12% above 600; 87% score above 500 on mathematical, 50% above 600, 7% above 700.

For College of Education & Human Development (27 M, 57 W), 39% of applicants accepted, 23% of these actually enroll; 57% of freshman graduate in top fifth of high school class, 71% in top two-fifths. Middle 50% range of freshman SAT scores: 430–500 verbal, 520–610 mathematical; 27% of freshmen score above 500 on verbal, 9% above 600; 99% score above 500 on mathematical, 27% above 600.

For Elliott School of International Affairs (439 M, 548 W), 73% of applicants accepted, 41% of these actually enroll; 65% of freshman graduate in top fifth of high school class, 90% in top two-fifths. Middle 50% range of freshman SAT scores: 510–620 verbal, 520–640 mathematical; 82% of freshman score above 500 on verbal, 38% above 600, 4% above 700, 87% score above 500 on mathematical, 45% above 600, 11% above 700.

Required: SAT or ACT, ACH (English composition and mathematics). Criteria considered in admissions, in order of importance: high school academic record, "strength of courses taken", writing sample, standardized test scores, recommendations, extracurricular activities; other factors considered: special talents, alumni children. *Entrance programs:* early decision, early admission, advanced placement, deferred admission. About 20% of entering students from private schools. *Apply* by December 1. *Transfers* welcome; 346 enrolled 1993–94.

Academic Environment. College-wide requirements include prescribed curricula in liberal arts and proficiency in English composition. Language proficiency may be required (or recommended) by individual departments. Requirements for students in Columbian College of Arts and Sciences include a general curriculum of course work in 8 categories. Administration reports in liberal arts 60% of courses needed for graduation are required, in pre-professional fields as much as 75% may be. Ninety-hour degree program permits student with honor grades in 45 hours of course work to graduate in 3 normal academic years. Substantial number of graduates go on to George Washington's own law and medical schools. Majority of student body reported by both administration and student leader to be oriented toward occupational/professional goals. *Undergraduate studies* offered by Columbian College of Arts and Sciences, schools of Engineering and Applied Science, Education and Human Development, Business and Public Management, Medicine and Health Sciences, Elliott School of International Affairs. Degrees offered: associates, bachelors, masters, doctoral. Average undergraduate class size: 64% under 20, 28% 20–40, 8% over 40.

An estimated 64% of students entering as freshmen graduate within four years, 71% eventually; 87% of freshman return for sophomore year. *Special programs:* CLEP, independent study, study abroad, 3-year degree, individualized majors, work/study courses, interschool study program, cross-registration through Washington Consortium, combined program with School of Medicine, waiver of required courses by examination. Adult program: selected undergraduate and graduate courses scheduled in evening to accommodate part-time students. *Calendar:* semester, summer school.

Undergraduate degrees conferred (1447). 26% were in Social Sciences, 23% were in Business and Management, 8% were in Engineering, 7% were in Psychology, 6% were in Letters, 5% were in Life Sciences, 4% were in Allied Health, 4% were in Visual and Performing Arts, 3% were in Education, 3% were in Communications, remainder in 12 other fields.

Graduates Career Data. Advanced studies pursued by 48% of graduates; 8% enter graduate school; 12% enter law school; 9% enter medical school. Medical schools typically enrolling largest numbers of graduates include George Washington U.; law schools include NYU, George Washington U.; business schools include George Washington U.. About 56% of 1992–93 graduates employed. Career Development Services include workshops, consulting sessions, and numerous resource materials on career development.

Faculty. About 93% of faculty hold PhD or equivalent. About 38% of undergraduate classes taught by tenured faculty. About 30% of teaching faculty are female; 3% are Black, 2% Hispanic, 7% other minority.

Student Body. About 2% of students from in district; 48% Middle Atlantic, 16% South, 10% New England, 7% Midwest, 5% West, 1% Northwest, 11% foreign. An estimated 20% of students reported as Catholic, 11% Protestant, 10% Jewish; 8% Black, 5% Hispanic, 11% Asian, 11% other minority. *Minority group students:* Educational Opportunity Program for District of Columbia residents provides financial aid, special tutoring, and "opportunity for social interaction."

Varsity Sports. Men (Div.I): Baseball, Basketball, Crew, Cross Country, Diving, Golf, Soccer, Swimming, Tennis. Women (Div.I): Baseball, Basketball, Crew, Cross Country, Diving, Gymnastics, Soccer, Swimming, Tennis, Volleyball.

Campus Life. This is an urban campus in the middle of the nation's capital; in the words of one recent student, "Social life at GW is like any other University...but multiplied. Like other schools we play softball...on the national mall. We go to the theater...at the Kennedy Center. We find quiet corners to study...on the back of the Lincoln Memorial." "GW is truly a part of the city, and the city is a part of the lives of every GW student." On-campus activities are also plentiful: "over 300 speakers yearly, films weekly, and theater productions often." No limitations on cars except those arising from chronic parking problems. Smoking restricted to certain areas, not allowed in classrooms. University reports "appropriate sanctions against possession, use, and selling" of illegal drugs.

About 4% of women live in traditional dormitories; 56% of men, 58% of women live in coed dormitories; 2% each live in off-campus college-related housing; rest commute. Freshmen given preference in college housing if all students cannot be accommodated. Sexes segregated by room in coed dormitories. There are 12 fraternities, 8 sororities on campus which about 15% of men, 14% of women join; 12% of men live in fraternities; sororities provide no residence facilities.

Annual Costs. Tuition and fees, $16,988; room and board, $5,480; estimated $1,550 other, exclusive of travel. About 70% of students receive financial aid; average amount of assistance, $13,616. Assistance is typically divided 37% scholarship, 34% grant, 25% loan, 4% work. University reports some scholarships awarded on the basis of academic merit alone. *Meeting Costs:* university offers installment payment plan.

Georgetown College

Georgetown, Kentucky 40324 (502) 863-8009

A church-related, liberal arts college, located in a town of 12,000, 70 miles south of Cincinnati and 12 miles north of Lexington. Most convenient major airport: Blue Grass Field (Lexington).

Founded: 1829
Affiliation: Southern Baptist
Total Enrollment: 499 M, 564 W (full-time)
Cost: < $10K
% Receiving Financial Aid: 92%
Admission: Non-selective
Application Deadline: Aug. 1

Admission. High school graduates with C average who rank in top half of class eligible; 87% of applicants accepted, 41% of these actually enroll. About 49% of freshmen graduate in top fifth of high school class, 79% in top two-fifths. *Required:* ACT (SAT acceptable), essay; interview encouraged. Criteria considered in admissions, in order of importance: high school academic record, extracurricular activities, standardized test scores, writing sample, recommendations. *Entrance programs:* rolling admissions. *Apply* by August 1. *Transfers* welcome; 29 enrolled 1993–94.

Academic Environment. *Degrees:* bachelors, masters. About 50% of general education requirements for graduation are elective; distribution requirements fairly numerous. Average undergraduate class size: 59% under 20, 41% 20–40. About 33% of students entering as freshmen graduate within four years, 48% eventually; 73% of freshmen return for sophomore year. *Special programs:* CLEP, honors, study abroad, undergraduate research, area majors, 3–2 nursing, engineering, internships with Lex Mark, Toyota Motor Manufacturing. *Calendar:* early semester, summer school.

Undergraduate degrees conferred (152). 34% were in Business and Management, 12% were in Life Sciences, 11% were in Visual and Performing Arts, 7% were in Psychology, 7% were in Education, 6% were in Letters, 4% were in Social Sciences, 4% were in Physical Sciences, 3% were in Mathematics, 3% were in Philosophy and Religion, 3% were in Foreign Languages, remainder in 5 other fields.

Faculty. About 72% of faculty hold PhD or equivalent. About 63% of undergraduate classes taught by tenured faculty. About 41% of teaching faculty are female.

Student Body. About 79% of students from in state; 14% Midwest, 3% South, 3% foreign. An estimated 84% of students reported as Protestant, 8% Catholic, 7% unaffiliated, 6% other; 3% Black, less than 1% other minority.

Religious Orientation. Georgetown is a church-related institution; 55% of students affiliated with the church; 2 courses of religion/philosophy required of all students.

Varsity Sports. Men (NAIA, Div.I): Baseball, Basketball, Cross Country, Football, Golf, Soccer, Tennis. Women (NAIA, Div.I): Basketball, Cross Country, Softball, Tennis, Volleyball.

Campus Life. Campus is located in a small town, some distance from the distractions of urban life. Students report they spend time studying, participating in Greek life and other campus activities, as well as in local service and religious organizations. Cars permitted on campus. Under no circumstances are students allowed to possess or use alcoholic beverages.

About 49% of men, 62% of women live in traditional dormitories; no coed dormitories; 19% of men, 19% of women commute. Freshmen given preference in college housing if all students cannot be accommodated. Intervisitation in men's and women's dormitory rooms limited. There are 5 fraternities, 3 sororities on campus which about 40% of men, 30% of women join; 32% of men, 19% of women live in fraternities and sororities. About 30% of resident students leave campus on weekends.

Annual Costs. Tuition and fees, $7,390 (out-of-state, $7,490); room and board, $3,600; estimated $1,100 other, exclusive of travel. About 92% of students receive financial aid; average amount of assistance, $7,290. Assistance is typically divided 16% scholarship, 44% grant, 34% loan, 6% work. College reports 320 scholarships awarded on the basis of academic merit alone, 424 for special talents alone. *Meeting Costs:* college offers deferred payment plan.

Georgetown University

Washington, D.C. 20057 (202) 687-3600

Georgetown University, a Jesuit institution originally founded for men, is now a co-educational university. In many ways it is the most prestigious of Catholic undergraduate institutions in the country because of its location and its influential graduate and professional schools. All undergraduate students must fulfill requirements in theology and philosophy. The 110-acre campus is located in the nation's capital, a 10-minute drive from downtown Washington. Most convenient major airports: Washington National, Dulles International.

Founded: 1789
Affiliation: Roman Catholic
UG Enrollment: 2,841 M, 3,040 W (full-time); 130 M, 276 W (part-time)
Total Enrollment: 12,321
Cost: $10K–$20K
% Receiving Financial Aid: 55%
Admission: Most Selective
Application Deadline: Jan. 10

Admission is among the most selective in the country for Arts and Sciences, Foreign Service, highly (+) selective for Languages and Linguistics, Business Administration, very selective for Nursing. For all schools, 26% of applicants accepted, 48% of these actually enroll; 71% of freshmen graduate in top tenth of high school class, 87% in top fifth. Middle 50% of freshman scores: SAT, 540–650 verbal, 590–690 mathematical; 91% of freshmen score above 500 on verbal, 80% above 600, 26% above 700; 91% score above 500 on mathematical, 80% above 600, 26% above 700; ACT, 26–31 composite.

For Arts and Sciences (1,212 M, 1,083 W), 19% of applicants accepted, 40% of these actually enroll; 71% of freshmen graduate in top tenth of high school class, 87% in top fifth. Middle 50% of freshman scores: SAT, 540–660 verbal, 600–690 mathematical; 92% of freshmen score above 500 on verbal, 59% above 600, 9% above 700; 96% score above 500 on mathematical, 82% above 600, 27% above 700; ACT, 26–30 composite.

For Business Administration (687 M, 409 W), 33% of applicants accepted, 55% of these actually enroll; 69% of freshmen graduate in top tenth of high school class, 88% in top fifth. Middle 50% of freshman scores: SAT, 520–620 verbal, 610–700 mathematical; 85% of freshmen score above 500 on verbal, 41% above 600, 3% above 700; 98% score above 500 on mathematical, 84% above 600, 29% above 700; ACT, 26–30 composite.

For Walsh School of Foreign Service (606 M, 621 W), 30% of applicants accepted, 52% of these actually enroll; 85% of freshmen graduate in top tenth of high school class, 93% in top fifth. Middle 50% of freshman scores: SAT, 590–680 verbal, 610–710 mathematical; 96% of freshmen score above 500 verbal, 76% above 600, 17% above 700; 98% score above 500 on mathematical, 85% above 600, 34% above 700; ACT, 28–31 composite.

For Languages and Linguistics (226 M, 512 W), 46% of applicants accepted, 58% of these actually enroll; 64% of freshmen graduate in top tenth of high school class, 86% in top fifth. Middle 50% of freshman scores: SAT, 540–640 verbal, 580–660 mathematical; 93% of freshmen score above 500 on mathematical, 70% above 600, 12% above 700; ACT, 24–30 composite.

For Nursing (5 M, 196 W), 63% of applicants accepted, 59% of these actually enroll; 29% of freshmen graduate in top tenth of high school class, 58% in top fifth. Middle 50% of freshman scores: SAT, 490–580 verbal, 540–630 mathematical; 75% of freshmen score above 500 on verbal, 17% above 600; 93% score above 500 on mathematical, 46% above 600, 4% above 700; ACT, 24–26 composite.

Required: SAT or ACT, interview with alumnus; ACH strongly recommended, required in modern foreign language for Foreign Service, Language and Linguistics. *Non-academic factors* considered in admissions: essays, extracurricular activities, recommendations, alumni relatives, special talents, athletics, geographic diversity. About 34% of entering students from private schools, 24% from parochial schools. *Entrance programs:* early action, advanced placement, deferred admission. About 60% of entering students from private and parochial schools. *Apply* by January 10. *Transfers* welcome; 250 enrolled 1993–94.

Academic Environment. Administration source and student leader agree that student body is primarily oriented to occupational/professional goals, with substantial interest in scholarly/intellectual pursuits. Academically motivated, career oriented students said to feel most at home on campus; "math-major type" least at home. Some student influence on curriculum decision making, but student leader doubts that it has much effect. Pressures for academic achievement likely to be most intense in School of Foreign Service, College of Arts and Sciences, and School of Language and Linguistics; primarily because of the composition of their respective student bodies. Graduation requirements: administration reports percentage of required courses "varies greatly among the various schools, with the College having the least"; all students must take 2 semesters each in English, philosophy, and theology; students in arts and sciences must also take 2 semesters each in social science, mathematics/science, and history, as well as intermediate mastery of a foreign language. *Degrees:* bachelors, masters, doctoral. *Majors offered* include Arabic, Chinese, foreign management, foreign trade, international affairs, international economics, international transportation, Japanese, Portuguese, women's studies. Average undergraduate class size: 51% under 20, 29% 20–40, 20% over 40.

About 87% of students entering as freshmen graduate within four years, 92% eventually; 95% of freshmen return for sophomore year. *Special programs:* independent study, undergraduate research, study abroad, honors, accounting internship, interpretation and translation programs, international projects, cross-registration through Washington Consortium, freshman liberal arts seminars, interdisciplinary business/law program. Adult programs: Bachelor of Liberal Studies. *Calendar:* semester, summer school.

Undergraduate degrees conferred (1438). 40% were in Social Sciences, 17% were in Business and Management, 11% were in Letters, 11% were in Foreign Languages, 5% were in Psychology, 4% were in Life Sciences, 3% were in Area and Ethnic Studies, 3% were in Health Sciences, remainder in 7 other fields.

Graduates Career Data. Advanced studies pursued by 25% of graduates; 11% enter graduate school; 4% enter medical school; 8% enter law school; 1% enter business school. Medical schools typically enrolling largest numbers of graduates include Johns Hopkins, Duke; law schools include Georgetown, Duke, UVA, Harvard, Columbia, U. of Chicago; business schools include Georgetown, Penn, Harvard, Northwestern.

Faculty. About 90% of faculty hold PhD or equivalent. About 70% of undergraduate classes taught by tenured faculty. About 31% of teaching faculty are female; 6% Black, 4% Hispanic, 3% other minority.

Student Body. About 3% of students from in district; 38% of students from Middle Atlantic, 12% each Northwest, New England, 11% each Midwest, South, 19% foreign. An estimated 54% of students reported as Catholic, 20% Protestant, 4% Jewish, 2% Muslim, 9% unaffiliated, 11% other; 7% as Black, 6% Hispanic, 7% Asian, 12% other minority.

Religious Orientation. Georgetown is a Jesuit institution; 54% of students affiliated with the church; all students must take 2 semesters of theology, but "not Catholic theology."

Varsity Sports. Men (Div.I): Baseball, Basketball, Crew, Cross Country, Football (III), Golf, Lacrosse, Sailing, Soccer, Swimming, Tennis, Track. Women (Div.I): Basketball, Crew, Cross Country, Field Hockey, Lacrosse, Soccer,Sailing, Swimming, Tennis, Track, Volleyball.

Campus Life. Strong interest reported in both men's and women's varsity sports (most popular: basketball, football, women's basketball) and intramural sports (most popular: basketball, football, softball, women's basketball, soccer, tennis). Students appear to have achieved substantial degree of control over significant aspects of campus life, including dormitory rules. Campus located in Georgetown, the combined Greenwich Village and haut monde of Washington. Rich cultural and intellectual facilities of the city easily accessible to students. Student leader comments that "we have such a wide variety [LBRK]of students[RBRK] that anyone can feel at home." Cars limited to off-campus and commuting students; parking a problem. All out-of-town freshmen live in residence halls. Freshmen "encouraged to keep reasonable hours."

About 80% of students live in coed dormitories; 20% of students live in off-campus housing (including university-owned townhouses and apartment complex) or commute. Freshmen guaranteed college housing. Intervisitation in men's and women's dormitory rooms limited for first-term freshmen only; unlimited for others; sexes segregated by floor. There are no fraternities or sororities on campus.

Annual Costs. Tuition and fees, $17,586; room and board, $6,824; $2,300 other expenses, exclusive of travel. About 55% of students receive financial aid; average amount of assistance, $16,176. Assistance is typically divided 70% grant, 16% loan, 14% work. *Minority group students:* special financial aid provided. *Meeting Costs:* university offers parents' loan program, SHARE, CONCERN, monthly payment plan.

Georgia College

Milledgeville, Georgia 31061 (912) 453-5004

A state-supported college, located in the antebellum capital of Georgia, a town of 18,000, 100 miles southeast of Atlanta. Most convenient major airports: Atlanta or Macon Municipal.

Founded: 1889
Affiliation: State
UG Enrollment: 1,273 M, 2,194 W (full-time); 486 M, 681 W (part-time)
Total Enrollment: 5,668
Cost: < $10K
Admission: Non-selective
Application Deadline: 2 weeks before quarter

Admission. Graduates of accredited high schools with minimum SAT scores of 250 verbal, 280 mathematical eligible; 96% of applicants accepted, 50% of these actually enroll. Average freshman SAT scores: 433 verbal, 483 mathematical. *Required:* SAT or ACT. Criteria considered in admissions, in order of importance: high school academic record, standardized test scores. *Out-of-state* freshman applicants: State does not limit out-of-state enrollment. No special requirements for out-of-state applicants. *Entrance programs:* early admission, midyear admission, advanced placement, rolling admissions. *Apply* by 2 weeks prior to quarter of entry. *Transfers* welcome; 850 enrolled 1993–94.

Academic Environment. Degrees offered: bachelors, masters. Core requirements include 20 quarter hours each of humanities, mathematics and science, social sciences, and 6 quarter hours of wellness. *Majors offered* in addition to usual studies include nursing, logistics systems, logistics management, early childhood education, pre-law. About 58% of students entering as freshmen graduate within four years, 75% eventually; 17% of freshmen do not return for sophomore year. Average undergraduate class size: 10% of classes under 20, 80% between 20–40, 10% over 40. *Special programs:* CLEP, study abroad, honors, independent study, undergraduate research, pre-professional programs, cooperative education, internships, 2–2 and 3–2 programs in engineering with Georgia Inst. of Tech. Adult programs: Non-traditional advisors in both Macon and Milledgeville; night courses designed for working/adult students. *Calendar:* quarter, 2 summer sessions.

Undergraduate degrees conferred (690). 35% were in Business and Management, 24% were in Education, 12% were in Health Sciences, 8% were in Psychology, 6% were in Computer and Engineering Related Technology, 4% were in Social Sciences, remainder in 12 other fields.

Faculty. About 70% of faculty hold PhD or equivalent.

Varsity Sports. Men (NCAA, Div. II): Baseball, Basketball, Cross Country, Golf, Tennis. Women (NCAAN, Div. II): Basketball, Gymnastics, Softball, Tennis.

Student Body. About 95% of students from Georgia; 2% foreign students. An estimated 17% of students reported as Black, 1% Hispanic, 1% Asian, 1% other minority.

Campus Life. About 7% of men, 13% of women live in traditional dormitories; no coed dormitories; 92% of men, 86% of women commute. Intervisitation in men's and women's dormitory rooms limited. There are 8 fraternities, 5 sororities on campus which about 20% of men, 20% of women join; about 1% of students live in fraternities and sororities. About 85% of resident students leave campus on weekends.

Annual Costs. Tuition and fees, $1,694 (out-of-state, $4,457); room and board, $2,616. Average amount of financial aid package, $3,500. Assistance is typically divided 10% scholarship, 25% grant, 50% loan, 15% work. College reports some scholarships awarded on the basis of academic merit alone.

Georgia Institute of Technology

Atlanta, Georgia 30332 (404) 894-2000

Georgia Tech has long been one of the most prestigious engineering schools, perhaps the most eminent of its kind in the South. Institute enrolls more black students than any other engineering school through direct enrollment and closely coordinated dual degree programs with the Atlanta University Colleges. The 280-acre campus is located in the heart of Atlanta (pop. 2,600,000). Most convenient major airport: Hartsfield.

Founded: 1885
Affiliation: State
UG Enrollment: 6,334 M, 2,194 W (full-time); 488 M, 166 W (part-time)
Total Enrollment: 12,846
Cost: < $10K
% Receiving Financial Aid: 69%
Admission: Highly Selective
Application Deadline: Feb. 1

Admission is highly selective. About 51% of applicants accepted, 41% of these actually enroll; 89% of freshmen graduate in top fifth of high school class, 99% in top two-fifths. Average freshman SAT scores: 559 verbal, 673 mathematical; 80% of freshmen score above 500 on verbal, 30% above 600, 4% above 700; 99% score above 500 on mathematical, 87% above 600, 39% above 700. *Required:* SAT or ACT. Criteria considered in admissions, in order of importance: high school academic record, standardized test scores. *Out-of-state* freshman applicants: Institute seeks students from out-of-state. State does not limit out-of-state enrollment. Requirements for out-of-state applicants are somewhat higher than for residents. About 53% of applicants accepted, 15% enroll. About 14% of entering students from private schools. *Entrance programs:* early decision, early admission, advanced placement. *Apply* by February 1. *Transfers* welcome; 337 enrolled 1993–94.

Academic Environment. *Undergraduate studies* offered by colleges of Architecture, Computing, Engineering, Sciences, and the Ivan Allen College (management and economics). Student notes the fast pace set by the quarter system, "It teaches you to work hard and manage your time. Excellent preparation for the real world." Continuing student concern reported about class-size which sometimes makes relations with faculty difficult. Graduate and undergraduate divisions cooperate in research activities, which are considered important elements within the institution. Cooperative education program that alternates quarters of study and work also available to students (33% participate) —degree earned in 5 years. Graduation requirements: all curricula include 36 credit hours of humanities and social sciences, 10–12 hours of sciences, 15 hours of math, 2 hours of physical education. *Majors offered* in 33 fields. Degrees offered: bachelors, masters, doctoral. Undergraduate class size: 39% under 20, 39% 20–40, 21% over 40.

About 30% of students entering as freshmen graduate within four years, 69% within six years; 83% of freshmen return for sophomore year. *Special programs:* honors, undergraduate research, study abroad, individualized majors, cross registration with University Center in Georgia. *Calendar:* quarter, summer school.

Undergraduate degrees conferred (1829). 62% were in Engineering, 20% were in Business and Management, 6% were in Architecture and Environmental Design, 5% were in Computer and Engineering Related Technology, 4% were in Physical Sciences, remainder in 5 other fields.

Graduates Career Data. About 65% of 1992–93 graduates are employed, in graduate school, or in the military. Employers typically hiring largest numbers of graduates include GE, Milliken, Northern Telecom/BNR, Anderson Consulting. Career Development Services include aptitude testing, counseling, resume/interview workshops, internships, on-campus recruitment, library resources.

Faculty. About 91% of faculty hold PhD or equivalent. About 11% of teaching faculty are female; 3% Black, 11% other minority.

Student Body. About 66% of students from in state; 22% South; 9% Black, 3% Hispanic, 9% Asian. *Minority group students:* individual counseling, special assistance upon request.

Varsity Sports. Men (Div.I): Baseball, Basketball, Cross Country, Diving, Football, Golf, Swimming, Tennis, Track. Women (Div.I): Basketball, Cross Country, Softball, Tennis, Track, Volleyball.

Campus Life. Interest in fraternities and sororities, as well as in varsity and intramural sports reported; another student agrees and adds "studying, partying, NOT sleeping." No women's dorm hours, but intervisitation hours limited. Atlanta's extensive cultural and recreational opportunities offer strong supplement to campus offerings ("If you have the time to." says one student). Students must register cars and pay fee. Administration source reports parking facilities as "adequate"; but adds wryly "students wouldn't agree", student leader confirms this insight. Smoking not allowed in classrooms.

About 24% of men, 23% of women live in traditional dormitories, 10% of men, 16% of women live in coed dormitories; 4% of students live family housing units; rest commute. Freshmen given preference in college housing if all students cannot be accommodated. There are 31 fraternities, 8 sororities on campus which about 30% of men, 24% of women join.

Annual Costs. Tuition and fees, $2,265 (out-of-state, $6,765); room and board, $4,404; estimated $1,970 other, exclusive of travel. About 69% of students receive financial aid; average amount of assistance, $2,290. Assistance is typically divided 55% scholarship/grant, 44% loan, 1% work. Institute reports 2,014 scholarships awarded on the basis of academic merit alone, 185 for special talents alone, 352 for need alone. *Meeting Costs:* institute offers short term loan program.

Georgia Southern College

Statesboro, Georgia 30460 (912) 681-5531

A state-supported college, located in a town of 17,500, 50 miles west of Savannah. Most convenient major airport: Savannah International.

Founded: 1908
Affiliation: State
UG Enrollment: 4,896 M, 5,173 W (full-time); 419 M, 530 W (part-time)
Total Enrollment: 12,857
Cost: < $10K
% Receiving Financial Aid: 39%
Admission: Non-selective
Application Deadline: Sept. 1

Admission. Graduates of approved high schools with 18 units in academic subjects, GPA of 2.0, minimum SAT score of 750 combined eligible; 59% of applicants accepted, 62% of these actually enroll. Average freshman SAT scores, according to most recent data available: 405 M, 402 W verbal, 460 M, 431 W mathematical. *Required:* SAT. *Out-of-state* freshman applicants: college seeks students from out of state. State does not limit out-of-state enrollment. No special requirements for out-of-state applicants. *Apply* by September 1. *Transfers* welcome.

Academic Environment. Degrees offered: AB, BS, BBA, BM, BSCrim, BSEd, BSEc, BSHEc, BSMT, BSOA, BSR, BST. About 20% of general education requirements for graduation are elective; distribution requirements fairly numerous. About 32% of students entering as freshmen graduate eventually; 36% of freshmen do not return for sophomore year. *Majors offered* in addition to usual studies include anthropology, computer science, criminal justice, medical technology, recreation, printing management, sport management. New programs include: apparel design, apparel manufacturing, exercise science, restaurant, hotel and institutional administration. *Special programs:* CLEP, independent study, study abroad, honors, individualized majors, 3–2 programs in engineering, English as a Second Language, enrichment program. *Calendar:* quarter, summer school.

Undergraduate degrees conferred (1327). 32% were in Business and Management, 20% were in Education, 10% were in Engineering and Engineering Related Technology, 6% were in Communications, 5% were in Social Sciences, 4% were in Parks and Recreation, 3% were in Protective Services, 3% were in Psychology, 3% were in Computer and Engineering Related Technology, 3% were in Health Sciences, remainder in 7 other fields.

Faculty. About 63% of faculty hold PhD or equivalent.

Varsity Sports. Men (Div.I): Baseball, Basketball, Cross Country, Football, Golf, Soccer, Swimming, Tennis. Women (Div.I): Basketball, Cross Country, Softball, Swimming, Tennis, Volleyball.

Student Body. About 88% of students from Georgia. An estimated 13% of students reported as Black, 1% Asian, according to most recent data available.

Campus Life. About 9% of men, 11% of women live in traditional dormitories; less than 1% each of men, women live in coed dormitories; 89% of men, 91% of women live in off-campus housing or commute. Intervisitation in men's and women's dormitory rooms limited in designated halls. There are 13 fraternities, 10 sororities on campus which about 16% of men, 10% of women join; 3% of men, 1% of women live in fraternities and sororities. About 30% of resident students leave campus on weekends.

Annual Costs. Tuition and fees, $1,827 (out-of-state, $3,207); room and board, $2,700. About 39% of students receive financial aid. College reports some scholarships awarded on the basis of academic merit alone.

Georgia Southwestern College

Americus, Georgia 31709 **(912) 928-1273**

A state-supported institution, located in a town of 17,000, 75 miles southwest of Macon. Most convenient major airports: Columbus, Albany, Macon, Atlanta.

Founded: 1906
Affiliation: State
UG Enrollment: 859 M, 1,696 W (full-time)
Total Enrollment: 2,555
Cost: < $10K
% Receiving Financial Aid: 89%
Admission: Non-selective
Application Deadline: 20 days before quarter

Admission. Graduates of accredited high schools with 16 units (13 in academic subjects) eligible; 93% of applicants accepted, 65% of these actually enroll. Average freshman scores: SAT, 403 verbal, 439 mathematical; ACT, 18 composite. *Required:* SAT or ACT. *Out-of-state* freshman applicants: college seeks students from out-of-state. State does not limit out-of-state enrollment. No special requirements for out-of-state applicants. States from which most out-of-state students are drawn: Florida. About 30% of entering students from private schools. *Entrance programs:* early admission, rolling admission. *Apply* by 20 days prior to beginning of quarter. *Transfers* welcome; 198 enrolled 1993–94.

Academic Environment. Degrees offered: associates, bachelors, masters. Graduation requirements include 20 hours each in humanities, math and science, and social science. About 24% of entering freshmen graduate within four years. *Special programs:* CLEP, study abroad, 3–2 engineering. Adult programs: complete evening program offered in business. *Calendar:* quarter, summer school.

Undergraduate degrees conferred (315). 37% were in Education, 30% were in Business and Management, 8% were in Social Sciences, 4% were in Psychology, 4% were in Physical Sciences, 3% were in Life Sciences, 3% were in Health Sciences, remainder in 6 other fields.

Faculty. About 70% of faculty hold PhD or equivalent. About 66% of undergraduate classes taught by tenured faculty. About 34% of teaching faculty are female.

Student Body. About 95% of students from in state, 69% South; 1% foreign. An estimated 20% of students reported as Black, 1% Asian, 1% other minority. Average age of undergraduate student: 23.

Varsity Sports. Men (NAIA): Baseball, Basketball, Cross Country, Golf, Volleyball. Women (NAIA): Basketball, Cross Country, Volleyball.

Campus Life. About 60% of students live in traditional dormitories; no coed dormitories; rest commute. There are 7 fraternities, 6 sororities on campus; 10% of men, 10% of women join. About 98% of resident students leave campus on weekends.

Annual Costs. Tuition and fees, $1,747 (out-of-state, $4,144); room and board, $2,610; estimated $2,000 other, exclusive of travel. About 89% of students receive financial aid; average amount of assistance, $3,048. Assistance is typically divided 15% scholarship, 50% grant, 25% loan, 10% work. College reports 3 scholarships awarded on the basis of academic merit alone, 20 for special talents alone.

Georgia State University

Atlanta, Georgia 30303 **(404) 651-2365**

A state-supported, urban university for commuters, located in a city of 2,000,000. Most convenient major airport: Hartsfield International.

Founded: 1913
Affiliation: State
UG Enrollment: 5,000 M, 6,406 W (full-time); 3,816 M, 5,238 W (part-time)
Total Enrollment: 23,395
Cost: < $10K
Admission: Selective
Application Deadline: July 15

Admission is selective. About 71% of applicants accepted, 82% of these actually enroll. Average freshman scores: SAT, 19% of freshmen score above 500 on verbal, 3% above 600, 41% score above 500 on mathematical, 8% above 600. *Required:* SAT or ACT, essay. *Out-of-state* freshmen applicants: State does not limit out-of-state enrollment. No special requirements for out-of-state applicants; 50% of applicants accepted, 36% enroll. Criteria considered in admissions, in order of importance: standardized test scores, high school academic record, writing sample, extracurricular activities, recommendations. *Entrance programs:* early admission, midyear admission, advanced placement. About 10% of students from private or parochial schools. *Apply* by July 15. *Transfers* welcome; 3,392 accepted 1993–94.

Academic Environment. Degrees offered: associates, bachelors, masters, doctoral. *Undergraduate studies* offered by colleges of Arts and Sciences, Health Sciences, Business Administration, Education, Public and Urban Affairs. About 35% of general education requirements for graduation are elective; distribution requirements fairly numerous. About 50% of students entering as freshmen graduate eventually (high enrollment of non-traditional students who "stop-out" but return to complete degree); 28% of freshmen do not return for sophomore year. *Majors offered* in addition to usual studies include actuarial science, commercial music-recording, computer science, hotel, restaurant, & travel administration, urban studies. New programs include film and video, human resources. *Special programs:* CLEP, study abroad, independent study, honors, co-op education and work study programs, Summer Scholars Program (for high school juniors and seniors). Average undergraduate class size: 48% of classes under 20, 42% 20–40, 10% over 40. *Calendar:* quarter, summer school.

Undergraduate degrees conferred (2332). 45% were in Business and Management, 8% were in Social Sciences, 7% were in Education, 5% were in Psychology, 4% were in Communications, 4% were in Visual and Performing Arts, 4% were in Computer and Engineering Related Technology, 3% were in Letters, 3% were in Health Sciences, 3% were in Allied Health, remainder in 12 other fields.

Graduates Career Data. Advanced studies pursued by 50% of students. Career Development Services include assistance in resume writing, interview skills, on-campus recruitment.

Faculty. About 82% of faculty hold PhD or equivalent. About 59% of undergraduate classes taught by tenured faculty. About 32% of teaching faculty are female; 5% Black, 3% Hispanic, 2% other minorities.

Varsity Sports. Men (Div.IAAA): Baseball, Basketball, Cross Country, Golf, Soccer, Swimming, Tennis, Wrestling. Women

(Div.IAAA): Baseball, Basketball, Cross Country, Golf, Soccer, Swimming, Tennis, Volleyball.
Student Body. About 92% of students from Georgia; almost all from South. An estimated 20% of students reported as Black, 2% Hispanic, 6% Asian. Average age of undergraduate student is 26.
Campus Life. About 5% of students live in coed dormitories. There are 10 fraternities, 9 sororities on campus which about 35% of men, 40% of women join; they provide no residence facilities.
Annual Costs. Tuition and fees, $2,019 (out-of-state, $6,451); 2,655 room and board; estimated $500 per quarter other, exclusive of travel. Average amount of financial aid, $750; assistance is typically divided 5% scholarship, 25% grant, 60% loan, 10% work. University reports 10 scholarships awarded on the basis of academic merit alone, about 200 for special talents.

University of Georgia

Athens, Georgia 30602-1661 (404) 542-3000

The first state-chartered university in America, the University of Georgia consists of 13 schools and colleges at the undergraduate and graduate levels. The 1,500-acre main campus is divided between the South and North campuses; the latter is located in the heart of Athens (pop. 44,300), 65 miles east of Atlanta. Most convenient major airport: Atlanta.

Founded: 1785
Affiliation: State
UG Enrollment: 9,184 M, 10,369 W (full-time); 1,464 M, 1,284 W (part-time)
Total Enrollment: 28,753
Cost: < $10K
% Receiving Financial Aid: 50%
Admission: Selective (+)
Application Deadline: Feb. 1

Admission is selective (+). About 68% of applicants accepted, 42% of these actually enroll. About 43% of freshmen graduated in top tenth of high school class, 79% in top quarter. Average freshman SAT scores: 521 M, 509 W verbal, 595 M, 552 W mathematical; 56% of freshman score above 500 on verbal, 14% above 600, 2% above 700; 84% score above 500 on mathematical, 29% above 600, 8% above 700. *Required:* SAT or ACT. Criteria considered in admissions: high school academic record, standardized test scores, special talents, diverse student body. *Out-of-state* freshman applicants: university does not seek students from out of state. State does not limit out-of-state enrollment. Requirements for out-of-state applicants: "slightly better records and SAT scores than in-state students." About 66% of applicants accepted, 31% enroll. *Entrance programs:* early admission, midyear admission, deferred admission, advanced placement. About 13% of entering students from private or parochial schools. *Apply* by February 1; rolling admissions. *Transfers* welcome; 1,928 accepted 1993–94.
Academic Environment. Degrees offered: associates, bachelors, masters, doctoral. Pressures for academic achievement vary among the different colleges from slight to strong. Undergraduate studies offered to freshmen by Franklin College of Arts and Sciences, colleges of Agriculture, Business and Administration, Education, schools of Forest Resources, Home Economics, Henry W. Grady School of Journalism; 5-year degree program available through schools of Environmental Design, Pharmacy (juniors admitted to latter). *Majors offered* in addition to usual range of studies include anthropology, broadcasting, computer science, drama and theater, medical technology, medieval studies, microbiology, music therapy, dietetics, biological engineering, agribusiness, exercise and sports science, consumer economics and science.

About 61% of students entering as freshmen graduate eventually; 14% of freshmen do not return for sophomore year. *Special programs:* CLEP, independent study, undergraduate research, study abroad, honors, 3-year degree, individualized majors, 3-year master's degree program, combined degree programs in medicine, dentistry, veterinary medicine, engineering, and nursing, (with Medical College of Georgia, U. of Georgia, Georgia Tech), internships, cooperative work/study program, academic remediation, LD student services. Average undergraduate class size: 44% of classes under 20, 44% 20–40, 12% over 40. *Calendar:* quarter, summer school.
Undergraduate degrees conferred (4329). 23% were in Business and Management, 13% were in Education, 11% were in Social Sciences, 8% were in Communications, 7% were in Letters, 5% were in Psychology, 4% were in Visual and Performing Arts, 4% were in Life Sciences, 4% were in Health Sciences, 3% were in Home Economics, remainder in 19 other fields.
Graduates Career Data. Graduate and professional schools typically enrolling largest numbers of graduates include Medical College of Georgia, Emory, Duke, U. of Georgia, U. of North Carolina. *Careers in business and industry* pursued by 70% of graduates. Corporations typically hiring largest numbers of graduates include National Cash Register, Baxter Health Care, Black & Decker, Milliken. *Career Counseling Program* offers career planning and development, co-op programs, internships, student employment, on-campus recruitment, job listings, career days, job search workshops. Student assessment of program reported as fair for career guidance, good for job placement. Alumni reported by administration source as active in career guidance and job placement.
Faculty. About 94% of faculty hold PhD or equivalent. About 46% of undergraduate credit hours produced by tenured faculty. About 23% of teaching faculty are female; 3% Black, 4% other minorities.
Student Body. Approximately 84% of students from in state; 93% South, 2% Middle Atlantic, 2% foreign. An estimated 43% of students reported as Protestant, 10% Catholic, 2% Jewish, 42% unaffiliated, 3% other; 6% Black, 1% Hispanic, 2% Asian. *Minority group students:* special admissions counseling, "some flexibility in SAT score requirements."
Varsity Sports. Men (Div.I): Baseball, Basketball, Football(IA), Golf, Swimming, Tennis, Track. Women (Div.I): Basketball, Golf, Gymnastics, Swimming, Tennis, Track.
Campus Life. Administration and student representatives agree that interest in fraternities/sororities is high, varsity athletics and intramurals is high, most popular varsity sports: football, basketball; intramurals: softball, flag football. Intervisitation and dorm hours set by residents. Cars allowed, but parking is inadequate, "horrendous" around student housing according to recent student leader. Campus transit system operates 7 bus routes at regular intervals during the week. Sophomores, juniors and seniors may live off campus.

About 3% of men, 13% of women live in traditional dormitories; 15% of men, 10% of women live in coed dormitories; 65% of men, 59% of women live in off-campus college-related housing; 20% of men, 20% of women commute. Intervisitation in men's and women's dormitory rooms limited. There are 24 fraternities, 22 sororities on campus which about 19% of men, 23% of women join; 3% of men, 7% of women live in fraternities and sororities.
Annual Costs. Tuition and fees, $2,250 (out-of-state, $5,940); room and board, $3,405; estimated $1,845 other, exclusive of travel. About 50% of all students receive financial aid; assistance is typically divided 20% grants/scholarship, 45% loan, 35% work. University reports 2,900 scholarships awarded on the basis of academic merit alone.

Georgian Court College

Lakewood, New Jersey 08701 (908) 367-4440

A church-related, liberal arts college for women, Georgian Court also accepts men in evening division and graduate levels. Conducted by the Sisters of Mercy, the college is located on a 170-acre campus in a community of 43,000, 33 miles southeast of Trenton. Most convenient major airport: Newark or Philadelphia.

Founded: 1908
Affiliation: Roman Catholic
UG Enrollment: 47 M, 901 W (full-time); 108 M, 616 W (part-time)
Total Enrollment: 2,490
Cost: < $10K
% Receiving Financial Aid: 42%
Admission: Non-selective
Application Deadline: Aug. 1

Admission. High school graduates with 16 academic units and rank in top half of high school class eligible; 89% of applicants accepted, 54% of these actually enroll; 35% of freshmen graduate in top fifth of high school class, 71% in top two-fifths. Average freshman SAT scores, according to most recent data available: 380 M, 420 W verbal, 565 M, 458 W mathematical. *Required:* SAT, interview. *Apply* by August 1; rolling admissions. *Transfers* welcome.
Academic Environment. Administration reports 44–49% of courses required for graduation are elective; curriculum allows student freedom in fulfilling general education requirements. Degrees offered: AB, BS, BSW. *Majors offered* include usual arts and sciences, elementary education, special education, accounting.

About 58% of students entering as freshmen graduate eventually; 23% of freshmen do not return for sophomore year. *Special programs:* independent study, study abroad, undergraduate research, women's studies, 3–2 engineering. Adult programs: Evening Division. *Calendar:* semester, summer school.

Undergraduate degrees conferred (326). 31% were in Business and Management, 16% were in Psychology, 12% were in Multi/Interdisciplinary Studies, 10% were in Social Sciences, 8% were in Letters, 6% were in Education, 5% were in Visual and Performing Arts, 4% were in Life Sciences, 3% were in Public Affairs, 3% were in Mathematics, remainder in 3 other fields.

Graduates Career Data. According to most recent data available, full-time graduate or professional study pursued by 28% of students immediately after graduation; 14% attend business schools. *Careers in business and industry* pursued by 76% of graduates.

Faculty. About 50% of faculty hold PhD or equivalent.

Varsity Sports. Women (NAIA/CACC): Basketball, Cross Country, Karate (ECKA), Soccer, Softball.

Student Body. According to most recent data available, about 99% of students from New Jersey. An estimated 6% of students reported as Black, 4% Hispanic, 2% Asian, 1% Native American. *Minority group students:* special financial, academic, and social provisions available.

Religious Orientation. Georgian Court is a church-related institution; 1 semester each in religious studies, philosophy required of all students. Daily Mass available. Places of worship available on campus for Catholics, in immediate community for Protestants and Jews.

Campus Life. According to most recent data available, about 26% of eligible women live in dormitories (dormitory accommodations are provided only for day division women); rest in off-campus housing or commute. There are no sororities.

Annual Costs. Tuition and fees, $8,750; room and board, $3,850. According to most recent data available, about 42% of students receive financial aid; assistance is typically divided 50% scholarship/grant, 40% loan, 10% work. College reports some scholarships awarded on the basis of academic merit alone.

Gettysburg College

Gettysburg, Pennsylvania 17325 (717) 337-6100

A co-educational college that emphasizes the liberal arts as a preparation for graduate and professional study, and teaching, Gettysburg cherishes its distinction as the oldest Lutheran Church-related college in the U.S. However, the college seeks to increase social, cultural, and religious diversity and attracts a cosmopolitan student body from many regions of the country. The 200-acre campus is located in historic Gettysburg, still a small semirural town of 7,300, 36 miles south of Harrisburg.

Founded: 1832
Affiliation: Independent (Lutheran)
Total Enrollment: 2,152 M, W (full-time)
Cost: $10K–$20K
Admission: Very Selective
Application Deadline: February 15

Admission is very selective. About 59% of applicants accepted, 31% of these actually enroll; 57% of freshmen graduate in top fifth of high school class, 97% in top two-fifths. *Required:* SAT; ACH recommended. *Non-academic factors* considered in admissions: special talents, alumni children, diverse student body, Lutheran affiliation. *Entrance programs:* early decision, early admission, midyear admission, advanced placement, deferred admission. About 24% of entering students from private schools. *Apply* by February 15. *Transfers* welcome.

Academic Environment. Student body appears to be increasingly career oriented, but insistent upon retaining the liberal arts character of the curriculum, avoiding an overly vocational emphasis. Pressures for academic achievement are rated by students as "moderate to high." Special advisory committees assist students in planning for legal and health-related fields. Administration reports one-third of courses required for graduation are elective; distribution requirements fairly numerous; 1 or more courses each in foreign language, arts, history/philosophy, literature, natural sciences (or lab science), religion, social science, non-Western culture; 3 terms physical education. *Degrees:* AB, BSMEd. *Majors offered* include usual arts and science, business administration.

About 80% of students entering as freshmen graduate eventually; 9% of freshmen do not return for sophomore year. *Special programs:* honors, independent study, study abroad, undergraduate research, individualized majors, Washington Semester, Asian studies at U. of Pennsylvania, 3–2 forestry with Duke, engineering with Penn State and RPI, credit by examination, programs of Central Pennsylvania Consortium. *Calendar:* 4–1–4, summer school.

Undergraduate degrees conferred (481). 31% were in Social Sciences, 24% were in Business and Management, 10% were in Psychology, 7% were in Letters, 6% were in Life Sciences, 4% were in Foreign Languages, 4% were in Visual and Performing Arts, 4% were in Philosophy and Religion, 3% were in Multi/Interdisciplinary Studies, remainder in 4 other fields.

Graduates Career Data. According to most recent data available, full-time graduate or professional study pursued immediately after graduation by 25% of students. *Careers in business and industry* pursued by 43% of graduates. *Career Counseling Program:* Student assessment of program reported as good for both career guidance and job placement. Alumni reported as active in both career guidance and job placement.

Faculty. About 90% of faculty hold doctorate or equivalent.

Student Body. College recruits principally in the Northeast; according to most recent data available, 30% of students from Pennsylvania; 70% Middle Atlantic, 15% New England, 11% South. An estimated 60% of students reported as Protestant, 35% Catholic, 2% Jewish, 10% unaffiliated, 3% other; 2% as Black, 1% Hispanic, 1% Asian.

Religious Orientation. Gettysburg is "related to, but not controlled or owned by, the Lutheran Church in America"; attendance at Sunday chapel, twice-weekly evening services voluntary. Chapel Council sponsors community tutorial program, social service activities, seminars.

Varsity Sports. Men (Div.III): Baseball, Basketball, Cross Country, Football, Golf, Lacrosse, Soccer, Swimming, Tennis, Track, Wrestling. Women (Div.III): Basketball, Cross Country, Field Hockey, Golf, Lacrosse, Softball, Swimming, Tennis, Track, Volleyball.

Campus Life. Most women and all freshmen and sophomores normally live on campus. Students may choose among 3 residential options, including 24-hour intervisitation. Alcoholic beverages permitted in residential facilities. Gettysburg is a quiet, rural campus within easy driving distance of Harrisburg, Baltimore, and Washington.

About 5% of men, 35% of women live in traditional dormitories; 61% of men, 53% of women in coed dormitories; 16% of men, 12% of women live in off-campus housing. Sexes segregated in coed dormitories by wing or floor. There are 11 fraternities, 7 sororities on campus which about 60% of men, 56% of women join; 18% of men live in fraternities; sororities provide no residence facilities. About 5% of resident students leave campus on weekends.

Annual Costs. Tuition and fees, $18,870; room and board, $4,090. College reports some scholarships awarded on the basis of academic merit alone. *Meeting Costs:* college offers college-sponsored parent loans for maximum of half-tuition.

Glassboro State College

(See Rowan College of New Jersey)

Glenville State College

Glenville, West Virginia 26351 (304) 462-7361

A state-supported college, located in a town of 2,200, 50 miles south of Clarksburg. Most convenient major airport: Charleston (WV) (90 miles away).

Founded: 1872
Affiliation: State
Total Enrollment: 832 M, 891 W (full-time); 169 M, 402 W (part-time)
Cost: < $10K
Admission: Non-selective

Admission. Graduates of approved high schools with 17 units with minimum GPA of 2.0 or ACT of 17 eligible, almost all applicants accepted, 46% of these actually enroll; 32% of freshmen graduate in top fifth of high school class, 68% in top two-fifths. Average freshman ACT scores: 18.3 M, 18.1 W composite. *Required:* ACT or SAT. Criteria considered in admissions, in order of importance: high school academic record, standardized test scores. *Out-of-state* freshmen applicants: State does not limit out-of-state enrollment. Required for out of state students: top half of high school class; almost all applicants accepted, 86% enroll. *Apply* by no specific deadline. *Transfers* welcome; 84 enrolled 1993–94.

Academic Environment. Degrees offered: bachelors. Core requirements include 44 hours of general studies. Average undergraduate class size: 60% under 20, 30% 20–40, 10% over 40. *Special programs:* CLEP, independent study, honors. About 42% of entering students graduate eventually; 42% of freshmen do not return for sophomore year. *Calendar:* semester, summer school.

Undergraduate degrees conferred (274). 46% were in Education, 28% were in Business and Management, 11% were in Multi/Interdisciplinary Studies, 4% were in Life Sciences, 3% were in Social Sciences, 3% were in Liberal/General Studies, remainder in 3 other fields.

Faculty. About 42% of faculty hold PhD or equivalent. About 80% of undergraduate classes taught by tenured faculty. About 1% of teaching faculty minorities.

Student Body. About 91% of students from in state; 95% Middle Atlantic, 3% South. An estimated 90% of students reported as Protestant, 10% Catholic; 2% Black, 1% Hispanic, 1% Asian. Average age of undergraduate student: 26.

Varsity Sports. Men (NAIA): Basketball, Cross Country, Football, Golf, Track. Women (WV. Conference): Basketball, Cross Country, Track, Volleyball.

Campus Life. About 25% of men, 31% of women live in traditional dormitories; 25% of men, 21% of women live in off-campus college-related housing; 50% of men, 50% of women commute. There are 2 fraternities, 2 sororities on campus which about 3% each of men, women join. About 90% of resident students leave campus on weekends.

Annual Costs. Tuition and fees, $1,730 (out-of-state, $3,944); room and board, $2,980; estimated $1,000 other, exclusive of travel. About 70% of students receive financial aid; average amount of assistance, $2,600. Assistance is typically divided 4% scholarship, 64% grant, 30% loan, 2% work. College reports 121 scholarships awarded on the basis of academic merit alone, 46 for special talents, 20 based on need.

GMI Engineering and Management Institute

Flint, Michigan 48504-4898 (313) 762-9500 or (800) 955-4464

An independent college of engineering and management, with all students enrolled sponsored by companies in the United States and overseas; located near the Flint River in a city of 200,000. Most convenient major airport: Detroit Metropolitan.

Founded: 1919
Affiliation: Independent
UG Enrollment: 1,963 M, 542 W (full-time)
Total Enrollment: 3,204
Cost: $10K–$20K
% Receiving Financial Aid: 57%
Admission: Very Selective
Application Deadline: Rolling

Admission is very selective. About 78% of applicants accepted, 44% of these actually enroll. About 90% of freshmen graduate in top fifth of high school class, 10% in top two-fifths. Average freshman scores, SAT, 56% of freshmen score above 500 on verbal, 14% above 600, 1% above 700; 95% score above 500 on mathematical, 69% above 600, 19% above 700; ACT, 26 composite. *Required:* SAT or ACT, minimum high school GPA 3.0. Criteria considered in admissions, in order of importance: high school academic record, standardized test scores, extracurricular activities, recommendations, writing sample; other factors considered: special talents. About 15% of entering students from private schools, 5% parochial. *Apply:* rolling admissions; recommended by February 1. *Transfers* welcome.

Academic Environment. All students participate in 5-year cooperative work/study program in one of the five curricula offered. Students are assisted in getting placed with employers "who become partners in the education of the student." Administration source reports, "two separate student bodies; 90% engineers, 10% management." Degrees offered: bachelors, masters. Core requirements include liberal arts minor. *Computer Science* courses offered; some required for all students; minors offered. Facilities reported as adequate to meet student demand; 24-hour access 7 days/week to mainframe, CAD, and microcomputers; terminals in computer center, microprocessors in classrooms and labs. About 75% of entering students graduate eventually; 25% of freshmen do not return for sophomore year. Average undergraduate class size: 20% under 20, 75% 20–40, 5% over 40. *Calendar:* semester.

Undergraduate degrees conferred (529). 90% were in Engineering, 10% were in Business and Management.

Graduates Career Data. Advanced studies pursued by 41% of students; 20% enter business school; 20% engineering. Graduate schools typically enrolling largest numbers of graduates include Harvard, Stanford, Northwestern, MIT. About 90% of 1992–93 graduates employed. Fields typically hiring largest numbers of graduates include engineering, management.

Faculty. About 62% of faculty hold PhD or equivalent. About 100% of undergraduate classes taught by tenured faculty.

Student Body. About 49% of students from Michigan; 79% Midwest, 10% New England, 6% Middle Atlantic, 3% South, 2% West. An estimated 38% of students reported as Protestant, 36% Catholic, 1% Jewish, 17% unaffiliated; 6% Black, 2% Hispanic, 7% Asian, 1% Native American.

Campus Life. About 30% of students live in coed residence halls; 15% live in off-campus housing; 5% commute. There are 14 fraternities, 6 sororities on campus; 50% of students live in fraternities and sororities. About 50% of resident students leave campus on weekends.

Annual Costs. Tuition and fees, $10,910; room and board, $3,158; other costs, $590. About 57% of students receive financial aid; average amount of assistance, $5,200. Assistance is typically divided 35% scholarship, 55% loan, 10% work. Institute reports some scholarships awarded on the basis of academic merit alone. *Meeting Costs:* through cooperative employment students earn $35,000–$75,000 (average: $56,000) over the five years.

Goddard College

Plainfield, Vermont 05667 (802) 454-8311

Goddard is a small, actively experimental, co-educational college whose program is based on the liberal arts. Much of the educational program is concerned directly with contemporary social and political issues. The main campus, 2 adjoining clusters of small buildings on hilly Vermont farmland, is located in a village of 1,400, 10 miles northeast of Montpelier.

Founded: 1938
Affiliation: Independent
Total Enrollment: 443 M, W (full-time)
Cost: $10K–$20K
% Receiving Financial Aid: 66%
Admission: Non-selective
Application Deadline: April 15

Admission. About 67% of applicants accepted, 48% of these actually enroll. *Required:* written personal statement, interview. *Non-academic factors* considered of major importance in admissions: special talents, diverse student body, "demonstration of responsibility" as shown in "use of time in and out of school," student's "image of himself"; "self-reliance and perseverance, creativity." Entrance programs: midyear admission, advanced placement, deferred admission. *Apply* by April 15. *Transfers* welcome.

Academic Environment. No particular courses are required at Goddard—each student defines his own education interests and needs. "Self-motivation is the keystone of the Goddard philosophy." The college is thus a very difficult school for some students because it places great responsibility on its students and faculty to achieve a genuine education for each person. The faculty operates without tenure, distinctions of rank, or departmental assignment. In contrast to traditional college catalogs, course lists "evolve from faculty-student needs, and are published before each semester." Small living/learning centers (with 16–24 students) "are the heart of the residential campus." Each student must complete 8 semesters for the degree, of which 2 must be, and 3 may be, done in nonresident work or study. Work of senior year culminates in independent project. No examinations or grades. *Degree:* AB.

Majors offered: college reports about one-third of studies undertaken are in the 3 broad fields of psychology, education, and literature—including creative writing; another third are in visual or performing arts; many students also work in natural sciences and social sciences.

About 90% of students entering as freshmen graduate eventually; 2% of freshmen do not return for sophomore year, according to most recent data available. *Special programs:* CLEP, independent study, study abroad, undergraduate research, 3-year degree, individualized majors, field service, subsidized nonresident study, architecture, social ecology, mental hospital and medical health internships. Adult programs: off-campus (low residency) programs, leading to BA, MA and MFA degrees. *Calendar:* semester, summer school.

Undergraduate degrees conferred (65). 22% were in Visual and Performing Arts, 18% were in Education, 15% were in Psychology, 11% were in Letters, 9% were in Multi/Interdisciplinary Studies, 6% were in Life Sciences, 6% were in Business and Management, 5% were in Philosophy and Religion, 3% were in Social Sciences, 3% were in Home Economics, remainder in Allied Health.

Graduates Career Data. *Full-time graduate or professional study* pursued immediately after graduation by 60% of students, according to most recent data available.

Student Body. College does not seek a national student body; 21% of students from in state, 56% New England, 30% Middle Atlantic, 12% West/Northwest, according to most recent data available.

Religious Orientation. Founded by Universalists, Goddard has long been an independent institution, makes no religious demands on students. No religious clubs on campus. Places of worship available in immediate community for 3 major faiths, Friends.

Campus Life. Students at Goddard have always been free of arbitrary adult control. The college is governed by a number of joint student/faculty/staff committees. Relatively isolated, Goddard students rely on the wide variety of cultural offerings brought to the campus. Students "expected to be truly resident" when on campus; only married students live off-campus. College reminds students that state laws limit alcohol and use, sale, and possession of drugs. Cars allowed but college reserves right to revoke registration; cars "not necessary for study at Goddard."

About 33% of women live in traditional dormitories; 99% of men, 66% of women in coed dormitories; 1% each in off-campus housing. Sexes segregated in dormitories by room. There are no fraternities or sororities.

Annual Costs. Tuition and fee, $13,400; room and board, $4,520. About 66% of students receive financial aid; assistance is typically divided 53% scholarship, 38% loan, 9% work. College reports some scholarships are awarded on the basis of academic merit alone. *Meeting Costs:* college offers Academic Management Service, 12-month payment plan.

Golden Gate University

San Francisco, California 94105 (415) 442-7000

An independent, nonresidential institution, located in San Francisco, providing class schedules "especially geared to the self-supporting student"; concentrating on "professional training for business, government, and law." Most convenient major airport: San Francisco International.

Founded: 1853
Affiliation: Independent
UG Enrollment: 235 M, 318 W (full-time); 1,474 (part-time)
Total Enrollment: 7,489
Cost: < $10K
% Receiving Financial Aid: 15%
Admission: Non-selective
Application Deadline: July 1

Admission. Graduates of approved high schools with 3.0 GPA eligible; 73% of applicants accepted, 32% of these actually enroll. *Entrance programs:* mid-year admission. *Apply* by: July 1 recommended; rolling admissions. *Transfers* welcome; 266 enrolled 1992–93.

Academic Environment. Degrees offered: associates, bachelors, masters, doctoral. *Majors offered* in addition to usual studies include business and humanities, aviation and operations management; new program offering Bachelor of Business Administration. General Education Foundation requirements include basic proficiency in writing, speech and quantitative reasoning, as well as a liberal studies core to provide an "introduction to the fundamental areas of human knowledge." About 60% of entering students graduate within five years; 13% of freshmen do not return for sophomore year. Average undergraduate class size: 20. *Special programs:* internships, cooperative education program which allows students to alternate semesters of full time work & full time study. *Calendar:* trimester, full summer semester.

Undergraduate degrees conferred (310). 85% were in Business and Management, 4% were in Computer and Engineering Related Technology, 4% were in Multi/Interdisciplinary Studies, remainder in 5 other fields.

Faculty. About 62% of faculty hold PhD. About 25% of teaching faculty are female; 9% are Hispanic, 6% are black.

Student Body. About 80% of students from California, 19% foreign. An estimated 11% of students reported as Black, 6% Hispanic, 16% Asian.

Campus Life. No dormitories on campus.

Annual Costs. Tuition and fees, $5,596; room and board (off-campus), $8,199; estimated $3,240 other, exclusive of travel. About 15% of students receive financial aid; average amount of assistance, $4,840. Assistance is typically divided 20% scholarship, 20% grant, 58% loan, 2% work. University reports 227 scholarships awarded on the basis of academic merit alone, 100 for need, 51 full tuition scholarships per year to transferring students, 15 full tuition scholarships per year for under-represented minorities.

Goldey Beacom College

Wilmington, Delaware 19808 (800) 833-4877

Formerly a two-year college conferring associate degrees, Goldey Beacom is now accredited as a four-year institution. Campus is located in the center of a community of 80,000. Most convenient major airport: Philadelphia International.

Founded: 1886
Affiliation: Independent
Total Enrollment: 1,852 M, W (full-time)
Cost: < $10K
% Receiving Financial Aid: 42%
Admission: Non-selective
Application Deadline: Rolling

Admission. High school graduates or the equivalent eligible, preferably in the top three-fifths of high school class; 13% of freshmen graduate in top fifth of high school class, 33% in top two-fifths. *Required:* SAT or Placement Test; 2.5 GPA. *Apply:* rolling admissions. *Transfers* welcome.

Academic Environment. Program focused exclusively on business and management. *Degree:* BS. *Majors offered* in addition to usual studies include management information systems, international business management. About 42% of freshmen do not return for sophomore year, according to most recent data available.

Undergraduate degrees conferred (201). 70% were in Business and Management, 15% were in Business (Administrative Support), 14% were in Computer and Engineering Related Technology, remainder in Education.

Graduates Career Data. *Careers in business and industry* pursued by 96% of graduates, according to most recent data available.

Varsity Sports. Men (NAIA): Soccer. Women (NAIA): Softball.

Campus Life. This is largely a commuter school; about 50% of students from Delaware; 95% from Middle Atlantic. An estimated 13% of students reported as Black, 1% Asian, according to most recent data available. About 13% of students live in coed dormitories; rest live in off-campus housing or commute. There are 2 fraternities, 2 sororities on campus which about 4% of students join.

Annual Costs. Tuition and fees, $5,820. About 42% of students receive financial aid; assistance is typically divided 15% scholarship, 56% loan, 3% work. College reports some scholarships awarded on the basis of academic merit alone. *Meeting Costs:* college offers monthly payment plan.

Gonzaga University

Spokane, Washington 99258-0001 (509) 328-4220

A church-related, urban university, conducted by the Society of Jesus, offering both undergraduate and graduate study, Gonzaga is located in the heart of a city of 185,000. Most convenient major airport: Spokane International.

Founded: 1887	**Total Enrollment:** 4,399
Affiliation: Roman Catholic	**Cost:** $10K–$20K
UG Enrollment: 1,225 M, 1,298 W (full-time); 89 M, 207 W (part-time)	**% Receiving Financial Aid:** 75%
	Admission: Selective
	Application Deadline: April 1

Admission is selective. About 81% of applicants accepted, 35% of these actually enroll; 59% of freshmen graduate in top fifth of high school class, 83% in top two-fifths. Average freshman scores: SAT, 499 M, 499 W verbal, 569 M, 527 W mathematical; 48% of freshmen score above 500 on verbal, 10% above 600, 1% above 700; 73% score above 500 on mathematical, 22% above 600, 6% above 700; ACT, 25 M, 25 W composite. *Required:* SAT or ACT, essay. Criteria considered in admissions, in order of importance: high school academic record, standardized test scores, writing sample, extracurricular activities, recommendations; other factors considered: special talents, alumni children, diverse student body, community service. *Entrance programs:* midyear admission, advanced placement, deferred admission. About 32% of entering students from private or parochial schools. *Apply* by April 1; rolling admissions. *Transfers* welcome; 345 enrolled 1993–94.

Academic Environment. Degrees offered: bachelors, masters, doctoral. University primarily oriented to students concerned with occupational/professional goals. Core curriculum includes English composition, critical thinking, speech, mathematics, literature, philosophy, and religious studies, in addition to the requirements of the specific program. *Undergraduate studies* offered by College of Arts and Sciences, schools of Business Administration, Education, Engineering, and Professional Studies. *Majors offered* in addition to usual studies include communications, computer science, Italian studies, medical technology, BEd in Native Indian Leadership.

About 54% of students entering as freshmen graduate within four years; 57% eventually; 16% of freshmen do not return for sophomore year. Average undergraduate class size: 37% under 20, 59% 20–40, 4% over 40. *Special programs:* CLEP, study abroad (including Gonzaga-in-Florence, -in-Paris, London program, Chongqing U. exchange), honors, undergraduate research, individualized majors. Adult programs: Bachelor of General Studies degree, part-time degree study, adult continuing education. *Calendar:* early semester, summer school.

Undergraduate degrees conferred (494). 25% were in Business and Management, 14% were in Social Sciences, 14% were in Engineering, 10% were in Communications, 5% were in Letters, 5% were in Liberal/General Studies, 5% were in Education, 5% were in Psychology, 3% were in Philosophy and Religion, 3% were in Mathematics, 3% were in Health Sciences, remainder in 7 other fields.

Graduates Career Data. Advanced studies pursued by 27% of students. Medical schools typically enrolling largest numbers of graduates include U. of Washington, Creighton; law schools include Gonzaga, U. of Washington; business schools include U. of Washington, Northwestern, Case Western. *Careers in business and industry* pursued by 74% of graduates. Corporations typically hiring largest numbers of graduates include Boeing, Arthur Andersen, Microsoft, Kaiser, according to most recent data available. *Career Counseling Program:* Alumni reported as active in job placement, and career guidance.

Faculty. About 88% of faculty hold PhD or equivalent. About 29% of teaching faculty are female; 7% minorities.

Student Body. About 51% of students from Washington; 90% West/Northwest, 5% North Central. An estimated 62% of students reported as Catholic, 13% Protestant, 1% Jewish; 1% Black, 4% Hispanic, 5% Asian, 11% other minority.

Religious Orientation. Gonzaga is a church-related institution; 3 courses of religious studies required of all students. Places of worship available on campus for Catholics, in immediate community for Protestants, Jews, and Moslems.

Varsity Sports. Men (NCAA Div.I): Baseball, Basketball, Cross Country, Golf; (WCC): Crew, Soccer, Tennis. Women (NCAA Div. I): Cross Country, Golf; (WCC): Crew, Soccer, Tennis, Volleyball.

Campus Life. Intervisitation permitted within scheduled hours. Alcohol and smoking allowed in rooms only with doors shut (legal drinking age is 21); no drugs allowed. Cars allowed; parking a problem for commuting students. "All full-time, out-of-town, freshman and sophomore students under the age of 21 are required to live and dine in university residences."

About 17% of men, 15% of women live in traditional dormitories; 25% of men, 27% of women in coed dormitories; 5% each of men, women live in off-campus college-related housing; rest commute. Sexes segregated in coed dormitories either by wing or floor. There are no fraternities or sororities, however a student leader notes that many dorms are small and larger ones are divided into areas with about 40 people so that dorm life "is very active socially." About 15% of students leave campus on weekends.

Annual Costs. Tuition and fees, $12,200; room and board, $4,150; estimated $700 other, exclusive of travel. About 75% of students receive financial aid; average amount of assistance, $11,435. Assistance is typically divided 25% scholarship, 25% grant, 40% loan, 10% work. University reports 635 scholarships awarded on the basis of academic merit alone, 120 for special talents.

Gordon College

Wenham, Massachusetts 01984 (508) 927-2300

An independent, Protestant-oriented, liberal arts college, Gordon seeks to admit students of Christian commitment. College merged with Barrington College on Gordon campus in September, 1985. The 730-acre campus is located on Cape Ann in a suburban community of 4,100, 26 miles northeast of Boston. Most convenient major airport: Logan International (Boston).

Founded: 1889	**Cost:** $10K–$20K
Affiliation: Independent	**% Receiving Financial Aid:** 85%
Total Enrollment: 1,165 M, W (full-time)	**Admission:** Selective
	Application Deadline: July 15

Admission is selective. About 82% of applicants accepted; 41% of freshmen graduate in top fifth of high school class, 72% in top two-fifths. Average freshman SAT scores, according to most recent data available: 482 M, 479 W verbal, 561 M, 502 W mathematical. *Required:* SAT or ACT; ACH in foreign language recommended (if continuing study), interview "if possible." Non-academic factors considered in admissions: Christian commitment, diverse student body, special talents, affirmative action. *Entrance programs:* early decision, early admission, midyear admission, advanced placement, deferred admission. About 20% of entering students from private schools, 5% from parochial schools. *Apply* by July 15; rolling admissions. *Transfers* welcome.

Academic Environment. Pressures for academic achievement appear moderate. Administration reports 10% of courses required for graduation are elective; numerous distribution requirements. *Degrees:* AB, BS, BM, BME. *Majors offered* include usual arts and sciences, computer science, education, youth ministries, social work, marine biology, accounting. Strongest programs reported to be psychology, biology, Biblical studies, business. Students report that the classes are small and the faculty is "very accessible".

About 60% of students entering as freshmen graduate eventually; 14% of freshmen do not return for sophomore year. *Special programs:* CLEP, study abroad, honors, independent study, undergraduate research, 3–2 engineering. *Calendar:* 3 11-week quarters.

Undergraduate degrees conferred (241). 17% were in Social Sciences, 14% were in Education, 13% were in Business and Management, 12% were in Letters, 9% were in Theology, 8% were in Psychology, 7% were in Public Affairs, 6% were in Life Sciences, 4% were in Computer and Engineering Related Technology, 3% were in Allied Health, remainder in 5 other fields.

Graduates Career Data. According to most recent data available, full-time graduate or professional study pursued immediately after graduation by 18% of students. *Careers in business and industry* pursued by 37% of graduates. Corporations typically hiring largest numbers of graduates include Raytheon, Digital, computer software companies.

Faculty. About 80% of faculty hold PhD or equivalent.

Student Body. According to most recent data available, 34% of students from in state; 60% New England, 22% Middle Atlantic. An estimated 89% of students reported as Protestant, 3% Catholic; 1% Black, 2% Hispanic, 2% Asian.

Religious Orientation. Gordon is a non-denominational Christian college; 2 semester courses in Biblical studies, attendance at twice-weekly chapels and periodic convocations required of all students; limited number of absences permitted each term. Religious clubs on campus include Foreign Mission Fellowship. Places of worship available on campus for Protestants, in immediate community for Catholics and Protestants.

Varsity Sports. Men (NCAA Div.III): Baseball, Basketball, Cross Country, Soccer, Tennis. Women (NCAA Div.III): Basketball, Cross Country, Field Hockey, Softball, Tennis, Volleyball.

Campus Life. As an evangelical Christian college, Gordon does not permit use of alcohol or tobacco on campus, nor is social dancing allowed. Campus is within walking distance to the Ocean, and only one-half hour from Boston. Limited intervisitation. Cars allowed.

About 90% of men, 90% of women live in traditional dormitories; rest commute. Freshmen given preference in college housing if all students cannot be accommodated. Sexes segregated in coed dormitories by wing. There are no fraternities or sororities. About 60% of students leave campus on weekends.

Annual Costs. Tuition and fees, $12,720; room and board, $4,070. About 85% of students receive financial aid.

Goshen College

Goshen, Indiana 46526 **(219) 535-7535**

A church-related college, located in a town of 25,000, 110 miles east of Chicago; "strong emphasis on Christian discipleship, peace, international education, and service-oriented goals." Most convenient major airport: South Bend.

Founded: 1894
Affiliation: Mennonite
Total Enrollment: 416 M, 540 W (full-time); 58 M, 108 W (part-time)
Cost: < $10K
% Receiving Financial Aid: 90%
Admission: Selective
Application Deadline: August 15

Admission is selective. About 84% of applicants accepted, 51% of these actually enroll. Average freshman SAT scores: 503 M, 471 W verbal, 553 M, 485 W mathematical; 45% of freshman score above 500 on verbal, 15% above 600; 54% score above 500 on mathematical, 23% above 600, 7% above 700. *Required:* SAT or ACT, minimum high school GPA of 2.0, commitment to "Standards of Life Together" based on Christian commitment and prohibiting on-campus smoking, use of alcoholic beverages; interview recommended. Criteria considered in admissions, in order of importance: high school academic record, standardized test scores, recommendations, extracurricular activities; other factors considered: diverse student body, special talents, alumni children. About 23% of entering students from private schools, 77% from public schools. *Apply* by August 15, rolling admissions; May 1 priority date for aid and services. *Transfers* welcome; 50 accepted 1993–94.

Academic Environment. Degrees offered: bachelors. Core requirements include 8–9 hours of religion, 8 hours of English, 8 of science, 6 of social science, 13 of international education, 1 of fitness. Average undergraduate class size: 26. About 62% of entering students graduate eventually; 10% of freshmen do not return for sophomore year. *Special programs:* CLEP, study abroad, 3–2 programs in pre-engineering, 3-year degree, individualized majors, study/service in Germany, Ivory coast, Costa Rica, Dominican Republic, and Indonesia, study and work program with nearby business and industry. Adult programs include: degree completion programs for students over 25. *Calendar:* semester, summer school.

Undergraduate degrees conferred (246). 22% were in Business and Management, 11% were in Visual and Performing Arts, 11% were in Education, 10% were in Health Sciences, 7% were in Communications, 6% were in Social Sciences, 6% were in Life Sciences, 4% were in Public Affairs, 4% were in Psychology, 4% were in Multi/Interdisciplinary Studies, 4% were in Physical Sciences, 3% were in Letters, remainder in 5 other fields.

Graduates Career Data. Full-time graduate study pursued immediately after graduation by 20% of students; 4% enter medical school. Medical schools typically enrolling largest numbers of graduates include Indiana U, Penn State, Ohio State. *Career Counseling Program* designed specifically for liberal arts students. Student assessment of program reported as fair for both career guidance and job placement. Liberal arts majors urged to seek interviews with business/industry representatives who visit campus. Help provided in preparation for interviews. Alumni reported as "sometimes" helpful in job placement and career counseling. Data from 1990–91

Faculty. About 65% of faculty hold PhD or equivalent. All undergraduate classes taught by tenured faculty. About 40% of teaching faculty are female; 2% black, 2% Hispanic, 1% other.

Student Body. About 40% of students from in state; 60% Midwest, 10% Middle Atlantic, 10% South, 10% foreign, 5% Northwest, 4% West, 1% New England. An estimated 97% of students reported as Protestant, 3% Catholic; 5% Black, 6% Hispanic, 2% Asian, 1% other.

Religious Orientation. Goshen is a church-related institution; 9 hours of religion and 3 religious courses required, attendance at any 2 of 3 chapels and convocations weekly required of all students; attendance at worship services encouraged.

Varsity Sports. Men (NAIA, MCCC): Baseball, Basketball, Cross Country, Golf, Soccer, Tennis, Track. Women (NAIA, HCW): Basketball, Cross Country, Soccer, Softball, Tennis, Track, Volleyball.

Campus Life. Goshen is a Christian community that believes smoking, and drinking should not be allowed "in the vicinity of" the campus. Student leader reports parietal regulations have "eased some." High interest in intramural sports, most popular: basketball, soccer, softball. Cars allowed; intervisitation limited.

About 60% each of men, women live in coed dormitories; rest commute. Freshmen given preference in college housing if all students cannot be accommodated. There are no fraternities or sororities. About 15% of resident students leave campus on weekends.

Annual Costs. Tuition and fees, $8,770; room and board, $3,590; estimated $560 other, exclusive of travel. About 90% of students receive financial aid; average amount of assistance, $7,000. Assistance is typically divided 61% scholarship, 32% loan, 6% work, according to most recent data available. College reports 450–500 scholarships awarded on the basis of academic merit alone, 25–30 for special talents.

Goucher College

Baltimore, Maryland 21204 **(410) 337-6000**

In a period when many single-sex schools were going coed, Goucher remained a women's college, but it admitted its first coed class in the fall of 1987. A strong cooperative program with Johns Hopkins and several other area colleges has continued to give variety to campus life. Somewhat more women than men on the faculty. The college has been located since 1950 on a 287-acre campus, 8 miles north of the center of Baltimore. Most convenient major airport: Baltimore-Washington International.

Founded: 1885
Affiliation: Independent
UG Enrollment: 266 M, 584 W (full-time)
Total Enrollment: 1,001 M, W
Cost: $10K–$20K
% Receiving Financial Aid: 65%
Admission: Very Selective
Application Deadline: February 1

Admission is very selective. About 70% of applicants accepted, 30% of these actually enroll. About 52% of freshmen graduated in top fifth of high school class, 85% in the top two fifths. Average freshman scores: SAT, 539 M and W verbal, 572 M and W mathematical; 52% of freshmen score above 500, 19% above 600 verbal; 68% score above 500, 27% above 600 mathematical. *Required:* SAT or ACT, essay, 14 academic units. Criteria considered in admissions, in order of importance: high school academic record, standardized test scores, recommendations, extracurricular activities, leadership record, writing sample; other factors considered: special talents. *Entrance programs:* early decision, early admission, deferred admission. *Apply* by February 1. *Transfers* welcome; 47 accepted 1993–94.

Academic Environment. Faculty meeting (with 30% student representation) exercises power in areas traditionally covered by faculty, except faculty appointment, promotion, and tenure. College offers strong liberal arts curriculum; campus atmosphere both intellectual and scholarly. Honors program for all levels recently introduced. Goucher also opened in fall, 1988, the International Technology and Media Center, which utilizes computers, satellite technology, and audio and video tapes in the teaching of modern languages. Opportunities for independent study now begin second semester of freshman year; upper-class students may write senior thesis in place of some course work. Required is one off-campus experience. All may take courses at other area universities, including Johns Hopkins, and have access to libraries. Shuttle bus available to Hopkins. Administration reports 57% of courses required for graduation are elective (but notes variation according to major); eight element distribution requirement. *Degrees:* bachelors, masters. Administration reports academic programs considered to be strongest include Math, science, English and the Arts. Strong emphasis on political science makes use of the opportunities offered by Washington, D.C. and the Federal government for internships and study within easy access. Extensive computer and technological resources; students able to explore areas ranging from artificial intelligence to computer music; international networking.

About 75% of students entering as freshmen graduate eventually; 11% of freshmen do not return for sophomore year. Average undergraduate class size: 83% under 20, 15% 20–40, 2% over 40. *Special programs:* independent study, study abroad, honors, undergraduate research, individualized majors, exchange programs with Johns Hopkins, Towson State, Morgan State, Maryland Art Institute, Loyola (all in Baltimore). Adult programs: Goucher Center for Continuing Studies includes programs in fund raising, technical writing, public relations management; Goucher II Scholars program for men and women with less than 2 years of previous college work; Postbaccalaureate Premedical Program offers intensive one year program. *Calendar:* 4–4, some summer courses.

Undergraduate degrees conferred (209). 22% were in Social Sciences, 11% were in Letters, 11% were in Visual and Performing Arts, 10% were in Communications, 9% were in Psychology, 8% were in Life Sciences, 7% were in Education, 4% were in Foreign Languages, 4% were in Business and Management, 3% were in Multi/Interdisciplinary Studies, 3% were in Mathematics, remainder in 4 other fields.

Graduates Career Data. Advanced studies pursued immediately after graduation by 80% of students; 32% enter graduate school; 5% enter medical school; 7% enter law school; 1% enter dental school; 9% enter business school. Medical schools typically enrolling largest numbers of graduates include U. of Maryland, George Washington U., Tulane; law schools include Georgetown U., Emory U., George Washington U.; business schools include Wharton, U. of Pennsylvania, U. of Chicago. About 62% of 1992–93 graduates employed. Fields typically employing largest numbers of graduates include business, education, government agencies.

Faculty. About 85% of faculty hold PhD or equivalent. About 75% of undergraduate classes taught by tenured faculty. About 60% of teaching faculty are female; 4% minority.

Student Body. About 49% of students from in state; 80% Middle Atlantic, 6% South, 5% New England, 3% Midwest, 3% West, 2% foreign, 1% Northwest. An estimated 25% of students reported to be Protestant, 40% Catholic, 15% Jewish; 4% Black, 3% Hispanic, 5% Asian, 2% other minority, according to most recent data available. *Minority group students:* special grants available.

Religious Orientation. Goucher is an independent institution, makes no religious demands on students. College "offers ample opportunity for religious worship and active service." Chapel services conducted by representatives of major faiths; counselors representing 3 main faiths "available each week for conferences with individual students." College also has chaplain-in-residence, and Chaplain's Advisory Board composed of students, staff and faculty.

Varsity Sports. Women (Div.III): Basketball, Cross Country, Field Hockey, Lacrosse, Soccer, Swimming, Tennis, Volleyball. Men (Div. III): Basketball, Cross Country, Tennis, Soccer, Swimming. (Developmental varsity teams in men's Crew and Lacrosse. Riding club.).

Campus Life. The introduction of men on a 100-year-old campus has brought changes, but not as dramatic as they would have been without the long-term association with Johns Hopkins. The Goucher student body has also changed significantly in recent years reflecting contemporary student concerns. Relatively few rules governing student conduct: cars allowed for all but freshmen (must be registered); consumption of alcohol limited by state law; 24-hour visitation permitted.

About 73% of men, 71% of women live in coed dormitories; rest commute. Freshmen are required to live on campus unless they commute from home. There are no fraternities or sororities.

Annual Costs. Tuition and fees, $14,400; room and board, $5,995; estimated $1,800 other, exclusive of travel. About 65% of students receive financial aid; average amount of assistance, $13,000. Assistance is typically divided 67% scholarship, 24% loan, 9% work; according to most recent data available. College reports 35–40 scholarships awarded on the basis of academic merit alone.

Grace College

Winona Lake, Indiana 46590 **(219) 372-5100**

Grace is an undergraduate liberal arts institution "that is committed to Christ." The 150-acre campus is located in a small community 40 miles west of Fort Wayne. Most convenient major airport: Fort Wayne Baer Field.

Founded: 1948
Affiliation: Grace Brethren
Total Enrollment: 276 M, 342 W (full-time); 64 M, 49 W (part-time)
Cost: < $10K
% Receiving Financial Aid: 84%
Admission: Non-selective
Application Deadline: August 1

Admission. High school graduates ranking in upper half of class eligible; 78% of applicants accepted, 44% of these actually enroll. About 35% of freshmen graduate in top fifth of their high school class, 61% in top two-fifths. *Required:* SAT or ACT, minimum high school GPA of 2.0, references from a pastor and guidance counselor. Average freshman scores: SAT 450 verbal, 492 mathematical; ACT, 22 composite. Criteria considered in admissions, in order of importance: high school academic record, recommendations, standardized test scores, extracurricular activities; other factors considered: religious affiliation and/or commitment, those "with any record of divorce should not apply." Entrance programs available: midyear admission, deferred admission, advanced placement. *Apply* by August 1, rolling admissions. *Transfers* welcome; 44 accepted 1993–94.

Academic Environment. Degrees offered: associates, bachelors. "The Christian liberal arts philosophy of Grace College pervades each of its programs of study and recognizes the need for a broad common core of general education." About 39% of entering freshmen graduate within four years, 47% eventually. Approximately 18% of freshmen do not return for sophomore year. Average undergraduate class size: 40% under 20, 55% 20–40, 5% over 40.Special programs: January term, study abroad.

Undergraduate degrees conferred (135). 31% were in Education, 21% were in Psychology, 18% were in Business and Management, 7% were in Visual and Performing Arts, 6% were in Social Sciences, 5% were in Communications, 3% were in Theology, 3% were in Life Scie'nces, remainder in 5 other fields.

Graduates Career Data. Advanced studies pursued immediately after graduation by 15% of students; 15% enter graduate school; 5% enter medical school; 2% enter business school. Medical schools typically enrolling largest number of graduates include: Ohio State, Indiana U., Medical College of Ohio; business schools include: Purdue, American Graduate School of International Management; others: Grace Theological Seminary, Colorado State. About 75% of 1992–93 graduates employed. Fields typically hiring largest number of graduates include education, business/management, medical, social services.

Faculty. About 43% of faculty hold PhD or equivalent. About 85% of undergraduate classes taught by tenured faculty. About 25% of teaching faculty are female.

Student Body. About 41% of students from in state, 71% Midwest, 12% Middle Atlantic, 6% South, 4% West, 3% Northwest and foreign, 1% New England. Almost all students reported as Protestant; 1% Black, 1% Hispanic.

Religious Orientation. Grace College is a church-related institution; four courses of religious study required of all students.

Varsity Sports. Men (NAIA, Div. II): Baseball, Basketball, Golf, Soccer, Tennis, Track. Women (AIAW, Div. II): Basketball, Softball, Track, Volleyball.

Campus Life Faculty, staff, and students expected to refrain from the use of alcoholic beverages, illegal drugs, and tobacco and avoid gambling and social dancing. About 90% each of men, women live in traditional dormitories; remainder live at home or commute. Freshmen given preference in college housing if all students cannot be accommodated. There are no fraternities or sororities. About 31% of resident students leave campus on weekends.

Annual Costs. Tuition and fees, $8,450; room and board, $3,670; estimated $1,100 other, exclusive of travel. About 84% of students receive financial aid; average amount of assistance, $7,800. Assistance is typically divided 22% scholarship, 23% grant, 45% loan, 10% work. College reports 90 scholarships awarded on the basis of academic merit alone, 115 for special talents, 300 for need. *Meeting Costs:* college offers AMS payment plan, institutional loans.

Grace Bible College

Grand Rapids, Michigan 49509

A small Bible college offering associates and bachelor's degree programs. About 19% of graduates pursue advanced theological studies.

Founded: 1939
Affiliation: Grace Gospel Fellowship

Graceland College

Lamoni, Iowa 50140 **(515) 784-5000**

A church-related college seeking "to maintain a Christian atmosphere," located in a rural community of 2,500, 3 miles north of the Iowa–Missouri border. Substantial enrollment of non-traditional, off-campus students. Most convenient major airports: Des Moines (IA), Kansas City (MO).

Founded: 1895
Affiliation: Reorganized Latter-Day Saints
Total Enrollment: 483 M, 513 W (full-time); 23 M, 86 W (part-time)
Cost: < $10K
% Receiving Financial Aid: 90%
Admission: Non-selective
Application Deadline: August 15

Admission. High school graduates with C average who rank in top half of class eligible; nongraduates with 15 units may be admitted; 75% of applicants accepted, 59% of these actually enroll. About 14% of freshmen graduate in top tenth of high school class, 41% in top one-fourth. Average freshman scores: SAT, 453 M, 451 W verbal, 513 M, 500 W mathematical, 32% score above 500, 18% above 600 mathematical; ACT, 21.6 M, 21.6 W composite. *Required:* SAT or ACT, GPA in upper half of high school class or minimum of 2.0, interview, "willingness to live by" standards of college. Criteria considered in admissions, in order of importance: standardized test scores, high school academic record, extracurricular activities, recommendations, writing sample; other factors considered: special talents. *Entrance programs:* midyear admission. *Apply* by August 15, rolling admission. *Transfers* welcome; 127 accepted 1993–94.
Academic Environment. Degree offered: bachelors. About 20% of general education requirements for graduation are elective; distribution requirements fairly numerous. About 29% of students entering as freshmen graduate within four years, 40% eventually; 78% of freshmen do not return for sophomore year. *Majors offered* in addition to usual studies include outreach nursing and addiction studies leading to BSN or BS (home study with on-campus residencies required). *Special programs:* CLEP, January term, independent study, study abroad, honors, individualized majors. Adult programs: Older Adult Student Information Service. Average undergraduate class size: 67% under 20, 25% 20–40, 8% over 40. *Calendar:* semester, January interterm, summer school.
Undergraduate degrees conferred (176). 24% were in Health Sciences, 21% were in Business and Management, 18% were in Education, 7% were in Social Sciences, 6% were in Life Sciences, 5% were in Visual and Performing Arts, 5% were in Letters, 3% were in Computer and Engineering Related Technology, 3% were in Psychology, 3% were in Liberal/General Studies, remainder in 4 other fields.
Graduates Career Data. Advanced studies pursued by 17% of students. About 74% of 1992–93 graduates employed. Fields or employers typically hiring largest number of graduates include hospitals, financial organizations, school districts, EDS, DST Systems.
Faculty. About 63% of faculty hold PhD or equivalent. About 54% of undergraduate classes taught by tenured faculty. About 33% of teaching faculty are female.
Student Body. About 31% of students from in state; 69% Midwest, 10% foreign, 9% West/Northwest, 7% South, 4% New England/Middle Atlantic. An estimated 81% of students reported as Protestant, 9% Catholic, 7% other, 3% unaffiliated; 4% Black, 2% Hispanic, 1% Asian, 7% other minority.
Religious Orientation. Graceland is a church-related institution; many opportunities for worship on campus.
Varsity Sports. Men (NAIA, Div. II): Basketball, Baseball, Cross Country, Football, Soccer, Tennis, Track, Volleyball (MVIC). Women (NAIA, Div. II): Basketball, Cross Country, Soccer, Softball, Tennis, Track, Volleyball.
Campus Life. About 65% of men, 63% of women live in traditional dormitories; no coed dormitories; rest commute. Freshmen given preference in college housing if all students cannot be accommodated. Intervisitation in men's and women's dormitory rooms limited. There are no fraternities or sororities. About 40% of students leave campus on weekends.
Annual Costs. Tuition and fees, $8,680; room and board, $2,920; estimated $1,430 other, exclusive of travel. About 90% of students receive financial aid; average amount of assistance, $9,271. Assistance is typically divided 64% scholarship and grant, 27% loan, 9% work. College reports 409 scholarships awarded on the basis of academic merit alone, 657 for special talents, 330 for need.

Grambling State University

Grambling, Louisiana 71245 **(318) 274-2456**

A state-supported university, located in a village of 5,513, 60 miles east of Shreveport; founded as a college for Negroes and still serving a predominantly Black student body. Most convenient major airport: Monroe Regional.

Founded: 1901
Affiliation: State
UG Enrollment: 2,268 M, 3,299 W (full-time); 144 M, 185 W (part-time)
Total Enrollment: 6,729
Cost: < $10K
% Receiving Financial Aid: 87%
Admission: Non-selective
Application Deadline: July 15

Admission. Louisiana graduates of accredited high schools eligible. About 67% of applicants accepted, 59% of these actually enroll. About 7% of entering freshmen graduate in top fifth of their high school class, 24% in top two-fifths. *Out-of-state* freshman applicants: university welcomes out-of-state students. State does not limit out-of-state enrollment. Requirements for out-of-state students: minimum 2.0 GPA. *Required:* ACT or SAT. *Apply* by July 15. *Transfers* welcome.
Academic Environment. *Degrees:* BA, BS. About 67% of entering students graduate eventually; 50% of freshmen do not return for sophomore year. *Special programs:* Eight College Consortium, cooperative program with Louisiana Tech., study abroad. *Calendar:* semester, summer school.
Undergraduate degrees conferred (576). 23% were in Business and Management, 16% were in Computer and Engineering Related Technology, 14% were in Protective Services, 6% were in Health Sciences, 6% were in Social Sciences, 5% were in Education, 5% were in Communications, 5% were in Psychology, 4% were in Engineering and Engineering Related Technology, 3% were in Public Affairs, 3% were in Allied Health, remainder in 8 other fields.
Graduates Career Data. According to most recent data available, full-time graduate or professional study pursued immediately after graduation by 25% of students.
Faculty. About 50% of faculty hold PhD or equivalent.
Varsity Sports. Men (Div.IA): Baseball, Basketball, Football, Golf, Tennis, Track. Women (Div.I): Basketball, Softball, Tennis, Track.
Campus Life. Grambling is a state institution, makes no religious demands on students. About 57% of students from in state; 71% from South.

About 45% of men, 53% of women live in traditional dormitories; rest live in off-campus housing or commute. Freshmen given preference in college housing if all students cannot be accommodated. There are 4 fraternities, 5 sororities, which about 1% of men, 2% of women join.
Annual Costs. Tuition and fees, $2,088 (out-of-state, $3,738); room and board, $2,612. About 87% of students receive financial aid; assistance is typically divided 5% scholarship, 82% loan, 15% work. University reports some scholarships awarded on the basis of academic merit alone. *Meeting Costs:* university offers PLUS Loans.

Grand Canyon University

Phoenix, Arizona 85061 **(602) 249-3300**

A church-related, liberal arts and teachers college "with a Christian perspective," located in the state capital (pop. 800,000). Most convenient major airport: Sky Harbor International.

Founded: 1949
Affiliation: Southern Baptist
UG Enrollment: 523 M, 895 W (full-time); 126 M, 293 W (part-time)
Total Enrollment: 1,963
Cost: < $10K
% Receiving Financial Aid: 76%
Admission: Non-selective
Application Deadline: Aug. 1

Admission. Graduates of accredited high schools with 16 units who rank in top half of class or score in top 50th percentile on ACT or SAT eligible; others admitted on probation; 80% of applicants accepted, 62% of these actually enroll. *Required:* ACT, "evidence of good moral character"; interview recommended. Criteria considered in admissions, in order of importance: high school academic record, standardized test scores, recommendations, writing sample, extracurricular activities; other factors considered: special talents. *Apply* by August 1; rolling admissions. *Transfers* welcome; 493 enrolled 1993–94.
Academic Environment. Degrees offered: bachelors, masters. General education requirements vary with program, but include history, English, science, fine arts, social sciences, mathematics, physical education/health, and Bible. About 70% of students entering as freshmen graduate within four years; 25% of freshmen do not return for sophomore year. Average undergraduate class size: 45% of classes under 20, 50% between 20–40, 5% over 40. *Special programs:* CLEP, independent study, study abroad, internships in most majors, individualized majors, 3–2 programs in physical therapy, occupational therapy. *Calendar:* 4–1–4, summer school.
Undergraduate degrees conferred (326). 31% were in Education, 18% were in Business and Management, 8% were in Psychology, 8% were in Health Sciences, 6% were in Social Sciences, 5% were in Communications, 5% were in Theology, 4% were in Visual and Performing Arts, 3% were in Life Sciences, 3% were in Protective Services, remainder in 7 other fields.
Faculty. About 51% of faculty hold PhD or equivalent. About 32% of undergraduate classes taught by tenured faculty. About 55% of teaching faculty are female; 4% minorities.
Varsity Sports. Men (NCAA, Div.II): Baseball(I), Basketball, Cross Country, Golf, Soccer. Women (NCAA, Div.II): Basketball, Cross Country, Tennis, Volleyball.
Student Body. College seeks a national student body; 84% of students from Arizona; 86% from West.
Religious Orientation. Grand Canyon is a church-related institution; 6 hours of religion, attendance at chapel services required of all students.
Campus Life. About 5% of men, 8% of women live in traditional dormitories; no coed dormitories; rest live in off-campus housing or commute. No intervisitation in men's or women's dormitory rooms. There are no fraternities or sororities.
Annual Costs. Tuition and fees, $6,730; room and board, $2,950; estimated $1,725 other, exclusive of travel. About 76% of students receive financial aid; average amount of assistance, $6,432. Assistance is typically divided 30% scholarship, 15% grant, 50% loan, 5% work. College reports 385 scholarships awarded on the basis of academic merit alone, 409 for special talents. *Meeting Costs:* university offers PLUS Loans.

Grand Rapids Baptist College

Grand Rapids, Michigan 49505 (616) 949-5300

A church-related institution, Grand Rapids Baptist seeks students "who wish to have a Christian education that is characterized by high academic standards and Christian commitment." The 127-acre campus is 4 miles from downtown Grand Rapids. Most convenient major airport: Kent County International.

Founded: 1963
Affiliation: Baptist
Total Enrollment: 823 M, W (full-time); 52 M, 44 W (part-time)
Cost: < $10K
% Receiving Financial Aid: 79%
Admission: Non-selective
Application Deadline: August 15

Admission. High school graduates with an average of C or above eligible; 95% of applicants accepted, 71% of these actually enroll. Average freshman ACT score, according to most recent data available: 20.1 composite. *Required:* ACT, pastor's recommendation. *Apply* by August 15. *Transfers* welcome.
Academic Environment. *Degrees:* BA, BM, BREd. *Majors offered* in basic arts and sciences, Bible, religion and ministries, music, speech, sociology, business administration, church music, pre-law, social work. About 41% of students entering as freshmen graduate eventually; 39% of freshmen do not return for sophomore year. *Special programs:* study abroad (Peru).
Undergraduate degrees conferred (117). 26% were in Business and Management, 19% were in Letters, 15% were in Education, 12% were in Theology, 8% were in Psychology, 7% were in Visual and Performing Arts, 7% were in Life Sciences, 4% were in Social Sciences, remainder in 2 other fields.
Varsity Sports. Men (NAIA, NCCAA): Baseball, Basketball, Cross Country, Golf, Soccer, Tennis. Women (NAIA, NCCAA): Basketball, Cross Country, Softball, Volleyball.
Campus Life. All students, except first semester freshmen, required to have one Christian service assignment each semester. Faithful attendance at church required. Alcohol, tobacco, gambling and possession of playing cards prohibited. About 88% of students from in state. All students reported as Protestant; 1% Black, less than 1% other minority, according to most recent data available.

About 62% of students live in traditional dormitories; rest commute. Freshmen given preference in college housing if all students cannot be accommodated.
Annual Costs. Tuition and fees, $5,920; room and board, $3,738. About 79% of students receive financial aid; assistance is typically divided 56% scholarship/grant, 33% loan, 11% work. College reports some scholarships awarded on the basis of academic merit alone. *Meeting Costs:* college offers Easy Pay Plan.

Grand Valley State University

Allendale, Michigan 49401 (616) 895-2025

A state-supported, liberal arts and professional institution, located 12 miles west of Grand Rapids. Most convenient major airport: Grand Rapids.

Founded: 1960
Affiliation: State
UG Enrollment: 3,454 M, 4,780 W (full-time); 1,075 M, 1,544 W (part-time)
Total Enrollment: 13,384
Cost: < $10K
% Receiving Financial Aid: 70%
Admission: Non-selective
Application Deadline: Feb. 1

Admission. High school graduates with minimum GPA of 2.7 in college preparatory program eligible; 75% of applicants accepted, 40% of these actually enroll; 22% of freshmen graduate in top fifth of high school class, 42% in top two-fifths. Average freshman ACT scores: 23.3 composite. *Required:* ACT (minimum of 19). Criteria considered in admissions, in order of importance: high school academic record, standardized test scores. *Out-of-state* freshman applicants: college welcomes students from out of state. State does not limit out-of-state enrollment. *Entrance programs:* early admission, mid-year admission. *Apply* by February 1 to be considered for scholarships; rolling admissions. Applications must be received by the end of July. *Transfers* welcome; 1,454 accepted 1993–94.
Academic Environment. *Degrees:* bachelors, masters. Distribution requirements for graduation include 3 courses each from natural sciences, social science, humanities/arts; all students must demonstrate proficiency in mathematics and English composition. *Special programs:* CLEP, independent study, study abroad, honors, 3-year degree, individualized majors, internships. *Calendar:* semester, summer school.
Undergraduate degrees conferred (1208). 23% were in Business and Management, 10% were in Health Sciences, 10% were in Psychology, 8% were in Communications, 7% were in Multi/Interdisciplinary Studies, 5% were in Letters, 5% were in Social Sciences, 4% were in Visual and Performing Arts, 4% were in Public Affairs, 4% were in Protective Services, 3% were in Computer and Engineering Related Technology, 3% were in Allied Health, 3% were in Life Sciences, 3% were in Engineering and Engineering Related Technology, 3% were in Education, remainder in 9 other fields.
Graduates Career Data. According to most recent data available, full-time graduate or professional study pursued by 9% of students immediately after graduation; 1% enter medical school; 1% enter law school; 1% enter business school. *Careers in business and*

industry pursued by 23% of graduates. Career counseling and placement services available.
Faculty. About 71% of faculty hold PhD or equivalent. About 87% of undergraduate classes taught by tenured faculty.
Student Body. About 98% of students from Michigan. About 5% of students are Black, 2% Hispanic, 2% Asian, 3% other. Average age of undergraduate student is 23.
Varsity Sports. Men (Div.II): Baseball, Basketball, Cross Country, Football, Swimming, Track, Wrestling. Women (Div.II): Basketball, Softball, Swimming, Track, Volleyball.
Campus Life. About 25% of students live in coed dormitories; rest commute. Freshmen given preference in college housing if all students cannot be accommodated. Sexes segregated in coed dormitories by wing. There are 4 fraternities, 5 sororities on campus which 5% of men, 5% of women join. About 30% of students leave campus on weekends.
Annual Costs. Tuition and fees, $2,890 (out-of-state, $6,100); room and board, $3,930; estimated $1,100 other, exclusive of travel. About 70% of students receive financial aid. Assistance is typically divided 56% scholarship and grant, 30% loan, 14% work. College reports most scholarships awarded on the basis of academic merit alone.

Grand View College

Des Moines, Iowa 50316 (515) 263-2800

A Lutheran liberal arts college, Grand View is located in northeast Des Moines, capital city of Iowa. Most convenient major airport: Des Moines International.

Founded: 1896
Affiliation: Evangelical Lutheran Church in America
Total Enrollment: 365 M, 653 W (full-time); 142 M, 223 W (part-time)
Cost: < $10K
% Receiving Financial Aid: 90%
Admission: Non-selective
Application Deadline: August 15

Admission. About 94% of applicants accepted, 46% of these actually enrolled. Average freshman ACT scores: 20 composite. *Required:* ACT. Criteria considered in admissions, in order of importance: high school academic record, standardized test scores. *Apply* by August 15. *Transfers* welcome.
Academic Environment. Degrees offered: associates, bachelors. Majors include nursing, education, communications, commercial art. New programs include biology, criminal justice, religion. *Special programs:* study abroad, cross-enrollment with Drake U., Des Moines Area Community College. Adult programs: orientation and service programs, adult support group.
Undergraduate degrees conferred (162). 19% were in Business and Management, 18% were in Health Sciences, 18% were in Education, 12% were in Communications, 9% were in Precision Production, 8% were in Public Affairs, 6% were in Social Sciences, 3% were in Visual and Performing Arts, 3% were in Life Sciences, 3% were in Computer and Engineering Related Technology, remainder in 2 other fields.
Graduates Career Data. Advanced studies pursued by 8% of students. *Careers in business and industry* pursued by 63% of graduates.
Faculty. About 35% of faculty hold PhD or equivalent. About 56% of undergraduate classes taught by tenured faculty. About 49% of teaching faculty are female.
Student Body. About 97% of students from in state; 99% Midwest; 18 foreign students 1993–94. An estimated 25% of students reported as Protestant, 20% Catholic, 37% unaffiliated, 17% other; 5% Black, 1% Hispanic, 2% Asian, 1% other. Average age of undergraduate student is 25.
Varsity Sports. Men (NAIA): Baseball, Basketball, Cross Country, Golf, Soccer, Tennis. Women (NAIA): Basketball, Cross Country, Softball, Tennis, Volleyball.
Campus Life. About 13% of men, 14% of women live in traditional dormitories; rest commute. There are no fraternities or sororities. About 75% of resident students leave campus on weekends.
Annual Costs. Tuition and fees, $9,820; room and board, $3,360. About 90% of students receive financial aid; average amount of assistance, $7,000. College reports some scholarships awarded on the basis of academic merit alone.

Grantham College of Engineering

Slidell, Louisiana 70469-5700

A private engineering college offering associates and bachelors degrees through independent study for students "planning career advancement in electronics or computers." Over 90% of students have prior college experience. Applicants for admission must have a high school diploma or GED and practical experience in electronics or computers at the technician level. The degree requirements include independent coursework, work experience, and laboratory proficiency (electronics).

Founded: 1951 **Affiliation:** Independent

Gratz College

Philadelphia, Pennsylvania 19141

Gratz, the oldest non-denominational college of Jewish studies in the U.S., offers bachelors, masters, diploma and certificate programs in Jewish, Hebrew and Middle East studies, Jewish education and Jewish music. New offerings include an English language Jewish teachers diploma, M.A. in Jewish education and Jewish Studies and certificates in Judaica librarianship, Jewish Chaplaincy, Sephardic Studies.

Founded: 1895 **Affiliation:** Jewish

Undergraduate degrees conferred (5). 80% were in Area and Ethnic Studies, 20% were in Foreign Languages.

College of Great Falls

Great Falls, Montana 59405 (406) 761-8210

A small, church-related college, conducted by the Sisters of Providence, located in a city of 55,100. Most convenient major airport: Great Falls International.

Founded: 1932
Affiliation: Roman Catholic
Total Enrollment: 283 M, 528 W (full-time); 210 M, 416 W (part-time)
Cost: < $10K
% Receiving Financial Aid: 70%
Admission: Non-selective

Admission. Graduates of accredited high schools, preferably with 11 units in academic subjects and rank in top half of class, eligible; open admission policy; all applicants accepted, 63% of these actually enroll. *Apply* by: no specific deadline. *Transfers* welcome; 327 admitted 1993–94.
Academic Environment. Degrees offered: associates, bachelors, masters. *Majors offered* include education, criminal justice, music, health care administration, paralegal studies, gerontology. General education requirements for graduation include philosophy and/or religious studies, writing, speech, mathematics and/or natural sciences, literature, fine arts, and social sciences. Average undergraduate class size: 80% under 20, 18% 20–40, 2% over 40. Students report that small classes and the student learning center, which provides free tutoring, are strengths of the academic program. *Special programs:* CLEP, independent study, credit by examination, internships, cross registration with Central Michigan U.. Adult programs: courses offered evenings and weekends; day care available on campus. *Calendar:* semester, summer school.
Undergraduate degrees conferred (114). 22% were in Education, 22% were in Business and Management, 14% were in Protective Services, 12% were in Law, 10% were in Social Sciences, 4% were in Mathematics, 4% were in Life Sciences, 4% were in Computer and Engineering Related Technology, 4% were in Communications, remainder in 2 other fields.
Graduates Career Data. Advanced studies pursued by 14% of graduates; 5% enter law school, 2% enter business school. Professional schools typically enrolling largest numbers of graduates

include U. of Montana. Employers typically hiring largest numbers of graduates include public school systems, State of Montana. Career Development Services include individual counseling, for-credit courses in Job Search and Career Planning, assessment, full and part-time job listings.
Faculty. About 46% of faculty hold PhD or equivalent. About 37% of classes taught by tenured faculty. About 41% of teaching faculty are female.
Student Body. About 89% of students from in state; 95% Northwest, 8% foreign. An estimated 27% of students reported as Protestant, 35% Catholic, 27% other, 12% unaffiliated; 1% Black, 2% Asian, 7% other minority. Average age of undergraduate student is 31.
Religious Orientation. College is a church-related institution; 1 course in religious studies required of all students.
Campus Life. Great Falls has large percentage of adult students and many activities on campus include families of students. About 3% of men, 3% of women live in off-campus college-related housing; rest commute. Freshmen given preference in college housing if all students cannot be accommodated. Intervisitation in men's and women's dormitory rooms limited. Sexes segregated in dormitory by floor. There are no fraternities or sororities.
Annual Costs. Tuition and fees, $5,240; room only, $990; estimated $5,210 other, exclusive of travel. About 70% of students receive financial aid; average amount of assistance, $5,600. Assistance is typically divided 10% scholarship, 25% grant, 55% loan, 10% work. College reports 20 scholarships awarded on basis of academic merit alone.

Great Lakes Christian College

Lansing, Michigan 48837

A small church-related, liberal arts college offering associates and bachelor degree programs.

Founded: 1949 **Affiliation:** Church of Christ

Green Mountain College

Poultney, Vermont 05764 (802) 287-9313

Green Mountain is an accredited four-year, co-educational institution. The 155-acre campus is located in a historic village of 1,900, 25 miles southwest of Rutland. Most convenient major airport: Albany (NY) (commuter flights to Rutland, VT).

Founded: 1834
Affiliation: Independent
Total Enrollment: 753 M, W (full-time)
Cost: $10K–$20K
% Receiving Financial Aid: 52%
Admission: Non-selective
Application Deadline: June 1

Admission. Graduates of accredited high schools or equivalent eligible; 75% of applicants accepted, 40% of these actually enroll. Average freshman SAT scores: 440 M, 450 W verbal, 450 M, 450 W mathematical; ACT, 20 composite. *Required:* SAT or ACT, essay, recommendation; interview highly recommended. Criteria considered in admissions, in order of importance: high school academic record, standardized test scores, writing sample, recommendations, extracurricular activities, interview; other factors considered: special talents. About 28% of entering students from private schools, 12% from parochial schools. Entrance programs available: early decision, early admission, midyear admission, deferred admission, advanced placement. *Apply* by June 1, rolling admissions. *Transfers* welcome; 25 enrolled 1993–94.
Academic Environment. Degree offered: bachelors. Academic program largely oriented to career-oriented studies; business and management most popular; also offered: fine arts, gerontology, liberal studies, therapeutic recreation, leisure resource facilities management. All majors offer externships. Core requirements include English, history, mathematics, sciences, health and well-being. About 65% of students entering as freshman graduate eventually; 15% of freshmen do not return for sophomore year. *Special programs:* January term, study abroad. Average undergraduate class size: 80% under 20, 20% 20–40. Students find small classes allow for individual attention from the faculty.
Undergraduate degrees conferred (66). 24% were in Parks and Recreation, 18% were in Education, 18% were in Business and Manage-ment, 12% were in Social Sciences, 8% were in Visual and Performing Arts, 8% were in Liberal/General Studies, 6% were in Marketing and Distribution, 3% were in Letters, 3% were in Allied Health.
Graduates Career Data. Advanced studies pursued by about 28% of students; 10% enter business school. About 70% of 1992–93 graduates employed. Fields typically hiring largest numbers of graduates include recreation, education, business/industry. Career Development Services offered by the school include resume writing, career counseling, interview techniques, job fair.
Faculty. About 85% of faculty hold PhD or equivalent. About 85% of undergraduate classes taught by tenured faculty. About 35% of teaching faculty are female; 1% ethnic minorities.
Varsity Sports. Men (NAIA): Basketball, Lacrosse, Skiing, Soccer. Women (NAIA): Basketball, Skiing, Soccer, Softball, Volleyball.
Campus Life. Students report that the "small school atmosphere is very friendly"; popular activities include hiking, camping, skiing. About 90% each of men, women live in traditional and coed dormitories; rest commute. All students are guaranteed housing. About 20% of resident students leave campus on weekends.
Annual Costs. Tuition and fees, $10,900; room and board, $2,880; estimated $600 other, exclusive of travel. About 52% of students receive financial aid; average amount of assistance, $9,500. Assistance is typically divided 20% scholarship, 20% grant, 40% loan, 20% work. College reports 40 scholarships awarded on basis of academic merit alone, 45 for special talents, 75 for need. *Meeting Costs:* college offers payment plans from outside lenders.

Greensboro College

Greensboro, North Carolina 27401-1875 (800) 346-8226

A small, church-related, liberal arts college, located in a city of 156,000, 80 miles northwest of Raleigh. Most convenient major airport: Piedmont Triad International.

Founded: 1838
Affiliation: United Methodist
Total Enrollment: 847 M, W (full-time); 265 M, W (part-time)
Cost: < $10K
% Receiving Financial Aid: 47%
Admission: Non-selective
Application Deadline: Rolling

Admission. Graduates of accredited high schools with 16 units, preferably all in college preparatory subjects, eligible; 79% of applicants accepted, 37% of these actually enroll. About 17% of freshmen graduate in the top fifth of their high school class; 34% in top two-fifths. Average freshman scores, according to most recent data available: SAT, 421 M, 410 W verbal, 454 M, 431 W mathematical; ACT, 17 composite. *Required:* SAT or ACT; interview recommended. *Apply:* rolling admissions, prefer by March 1. *Transfers* welcome.
Academic Environment. *Degrees:* AB, BS, BM, BMEd, BFA. *Majors offered* include usual arts and sciences, education. About 50% of general education requirements for graduation are elective; distribution requirements fairly numerous. About 40% of students entering as freshmen graduate eventually; 35% of freshmen do not return for sophomore year. *Special programs:* CLEP, independent study, study abroad, honors, 3-year degree, individualized majors, Greensboro Regional Consortium for Higher Education, combined programs with North Carolina hospitals (for medical technology, medical record library science, radiological technology). *Calendar:* semester, summer school.
Undergraduate degrees conferred (138). 38% were in Business and Management, 15% were in Education, 12% were in Social Sciences, 10% were in Life Sciences, 6% were in Psychology, 6% were in Liberal/General Studies, 6% were in Letters, 4% were in Visual and Performing Arts, 4% were in Philosophy and Religion, remainder in Parks and Recreation.
Graduates Career Data. According to most recent data available, full-time graduate or professional study pursued by 10–12% of students immediately after graduation. *Careers in business and industry* pursued by 55% of graduates.
Faculty. About 80% of faculty hold PhD or equivalent.

Student Body. College seeks a national student body; 50% of students from in state; 72% South, 23% Middle Atlantic; according to most recent data available. An estimated 50% of students reported as Protestant, 22% Catholic, 3% Jewish, 25% unaffiliated or other; 11% Black, 1% Hispanic, 1% Asian, 1% Native American.
Religious Orientation. Greensboro is a church-related institution; 6 hours of Bible studies required of all students; attendance at chapel services voluntary. Religious clubs on campus include student Christian Fellowship, Christian Education Club. Places of worship available on campus and in immediate community for major faiths.
Varsity Sports. Men (Div.III): Basketball, Golf, Lacrosse, Soccer, Tennis. Women (Div.III): Basketball, Soccer, Softball, Tennis, Volleyball.
Campus Life. Limited intervisitation; alcohol permitted in residence halls only; cars allowed. About 80% of men, 80% of women live in traditional dormitories; no coed dormitories; rest live in off-campus housing or commute. Freshmen given preference in college housing if all students cannot be accommodated. There are no fraternities or sororities. About 30% of resident students leave campus on weekends.
Annual Costs. Tuition and fees, $7,816; room and board, $3,680. About 47% of students receive financial aid; assistance is typically divided 59% grant/scholarship, 31% loan, 10% work. College reports some scholarships awarded on basis of academic merit alone. *Meeting Costs:* college offers monthly payment plan.

Greenville College

Greenville, Illinois 62246 (618) 664-2800

A church-related college, governed by an independent board of trustees, Greenville welcomes "students of any faith who seek a liberal education taught and interpreted within the context of an evangelical Christian persuasion"; located in a village of 5,000, 50 miles east of St. Louis. Most convenient major airport: St. Louis (MO).

Founded: 1855
Affiliation: Independent (Free Methodist)
Total Enrollment: 379 M, 399 W (full-time)
Cost: < $10K
% Receiving Financial Aid: 90%
Admission: Non-selective
Application Deadline: August 1

Admission. High school graduates who rank in top half of class with 2.0 GPA eligible; 64% of applicants accepted; 6% of freshmen graduate in top fifth of high school class, 50% in top two-fifths. Average freshman ACT scores: 21.3 composite. *Required:* SAT (minimum combined score of 700) or ACT (minimum 18), reference from counselor, acceptance of the "Christian Liberal Arts Mission of the college and its life style which precludes the use of harmful drugs, tobacco, and alcohol." Criteria considered in admissions, in order of importance: high school academic record, standardized test scores, recommendations, class rank, writing sample, extracurricular activities; other factors considered: special talents, alumni children, diverse student body. *Apply* by August 1. *Transfers* welcome; 104 enrolled 1993–94.
Academic Environment. Degrees offered: bachelors. Core requirements for graduation include 3 courses in science/mathematics, 2 in English, 3 in social sciences, 2 in fine arts, 2 in religion, 4 in physical education. Majors include: contemporary Christian music, management information systems, pastoral ministries. About 45% of students entering as freshmen graduate within four years, 52% eventually; 26–38% of freshmen do not return for sophomore year. *Special programs:* CLEP, independent study, study abroad, honors, 3-year degree, interterm, individualized majors, internships, 3–2 programs in nursing, engineering, medicine. Average undergraduate class size: 50% of classes under 20, 40% between 20–40, 10% over 40. *Calendar:* 4–1–4, summer school.
Undergraduate degrees conferred (162). 31% were in Education, 20% were in Business and Management, 10% were in Life Sciences, 7% were in Visual and Performing Arts, 6% were in Psychology, 5% were in Social Sciences, 4% were in Philosophy and Religion, 3% were in Parks and Recreation, remainder in 8 other fields.
Graduates Career Data. Advanced studies pursued by 15% of students; 1% enter law school, 2% enter medical school, 2% enter business school. Fields typically hiring the largest number of graduates include churches, retail business, education. Career Development Services include planning career resources, workshops, on-campus interviewing, cooperative education, placement services.
Faculty. More than 50% of faculty hold PhD or equivalent. All classes are taught by tenured faculty. About 15% of faculty are female; 2% Black, 3% Hispanic.
Varsity Sports. Men (NAIA): Baseball, Basketball, Cross Country, Football, Golf, Soccer, Tennis, Track. Women (NAIA): Basketball, Cross Country, Softball, Tennis, Track, Volleyball.
Student Body. College seeks a national student body; 56% of students from in state; 65% from Midwest, 20% Middle Atlantic, 6% West, 5% South, 3% foreign. An estimated 96% of students reported as Protestant, 4% Catholic; 7% as Black, 5% Hispanic, 2% Asian, 2% other minority.
Religious Orientation. Greenville is "church-affiliated, but not church-controlled"; 2 courses in religion, attendance at chapel services 3 times weekly, student vespers, Sunday church service required of all students. College "is dedicated to a clearly Christian set of values for dealing with contemporary issues."
Campus Life. About 53% of men, 47% of women live in traditional dormitories; no coed dormitories; rest live in off-campus housing or commute. No intervisitation in men's or women's dormitory rooms. There are no fraternities or sororities. About 30–40% of resident students leave campus on weekends.
Annual Costs. Tuition and fees, $9,910; room and board, $4,360; estimated $1,500 other, exclusive of travel. About 90% of students receive financial aid; average amount of assistance, $7,900. Assistance is typically divided 10% scholarship, 40% grant, 40% loan, 10% work. College reports 6–10 scholarships awarded on the basis of academic merit alone, 15–20 for leadership, more than 500 for need. Meeting costs: College offers PLUS Loans.

Grinnell College

Grinnell, Iowa 50112 (515) 269-3600

A small, widely respected, Midwestern, liberal arts college, Grinnell has, in recent decades, been attracting an increasingly cosmopolitan student body from all parts of the country as well as substantial numbers of foreign students. The college places major emphasis on academic goals, together with a commitment to a rich social and cultural environment. The 90-acre campus is located in a town of 8,900, 55 miles east of Des Moines. Most convenient major airport: Des Moines (IA).

Founded: 1846
Affiliation: Independent
Total Enrollment: 1,305 M, W (full-time)
Cost: $10K–$20K
% Receiving Financial Aid: 69%
Admission: Highly (+) Selective
Application Deadline: Feb. 1

Admission is highly (+) selective. About 69% of applicants accepted, 31% of these actually enroll; 79% of freshmen graduate in top fifth of high school class, 95% in top two-fifths. Average freshman SAT scores, according to most recent data available: 597 M, 608 W verbal, 651 M, 615 W mathematical; 87% of freshmen score above 500 on verbal, 48% above 600, 11% above 700; 94% score above 500 on mathematical, 70% above 600, 24% above 700; ACT scores: 29 M, 28 W composite, 29 M, 27 W mathematical. *Required:* SAT or ACT, interview recommended (on- or off-campus). *Non-academic factors* considered in admissions: diverse student body, special talents, geographical distribution, alumni children. *Entrance programs:* early decision, early admission, deferred admission, advanced placement. *Apply* by February 1. *Transfers* welcome.
Academic Environment. Unhampered by any core or distribution requirements, students are expected, with maximum accessibility to faculty for guidance, to construct their own courses of study. Grinnell assumes that "students who qualify for admission have the ability to direct their own studies and their own lives in a supportive campus environment." Classes are small (10:1 student/faculty ratio) and opportunities for independent study are available to students throughout their college careers. Both administration and student sources agree that students who feel "most at home" on campus are "self directed, independent, academically motivated." *Degree:* BA. *Majors offered* include usual arts and sciences, Chinese studies, education, theater, interdisciplinary major in general science.

About 79% of students entering as freshmen graduate eventually; 4% of freshmen do not return for sophomore year. *Special programs:* freshman tutorials, independent study, study abroad (48 programs in 20 countries, 4 Grinnell-sponsored programs), Alternate Language Study Option, January term, honors, undergraduate research, 3-year degree, individualized majors, Washington Semester, semester with Eugene O'Neill Memorial Theater in Connecticut, programs of Associated Colleges of the Midwest, 3–2 engineering with Caltech, Columbia, Rensselaer, Washington U., 3–4 architecture with Washington U., 3–3 law with Columbia, cooperative programs with Rush in dentistry, medicine, nursing, early-entry MBA with U. of Chicago. *Calendar:* semester.

Undergraduate degrees conferred (280). 33% were in Social Sciences, 11% were in Life Sciences, 11% were in Foreign Languages, 9% were in Physical Sciences, 9% were in Letters, 6% were in Psychology, 6% were in Mathematics, 5% were in Visual and Performing Arts, 4% were in Philosophy and Religion, 4% were in Area and Ethnic Studies, remainder in 2 other fields.

Graduates Career Data. Graduate and professional schools typically enrolling largest numbers of graduates include U. of Iowa, Minnesota, Illinois, Yale.

Faculty. About 85% of faculty hold doctorate or equivalent.

Student Body. College seeks a national student body; 17% of students from in state; 37% North Central, 11% West, 13% Middle Atlantic, 7% New England, 4% South, 3% Northwest. An estimated 5% of students reported as Black, 4% Asian, 1% Hispanic, according to most recent data available.

Varsity Sports. Men (Div.III):. Baseball, Basketball, Cross Country, Football, Golf, Soccer, Swimming/Diving, Tennis, Track. Women (Div.III): Basketball, Cross Country, Soccer, Softball, Swimming/Diving, Tennis, Track, Volleyball.

Campus Life. Student leader asserts: "Although we cater to the academic crowd, we know how to have fun at the appropriate times." Students enjoy considerable freedom in setting standards for individual behavior. The same student leader also states that "We like to think that, in general, the rules here are that there are no rules [LBRK]but[RBRK] the ones we do have, academic rules, plagiarism, etc., are enforced rigorously." There are few security problems on campus, a benefit of Grinnell's small town location. Cars allowed for all students. Drinking permitted only in college owned student halls and houses; smoking restricted in classes; drug distributors subject to disciplinary action. Juniors and seniors may live off campus. No limitations on dorm or visitation hours.

Administration reports "Billboard Magazine has twice commended Grinnell for the "quality of its concerts and public events programs,' and "major national theater, music and dance companies are regularly featured at the college.'[THINSPACE]" The "Grinnell Experience" assumes that these activities are vital adjuncts to the academic life.

About 80% of men, 77% of women live in coed dormitories; 8% of men, 8% of women in off-campus college-related housing; rest commute. Freshmen given preference in college housing if all students cannot be accommodated. Sexes segregated in coed dormitories by floor or room. There are no fraternities or sororities. About 2–3% students leave campus on weekends.

Annual Costs. Tuition and fees, $15,404; room and board, $4,386. About 69% of students receive financial aid; assistance is typically divided 77% scholarship, 19% loan, 4% work. College reports some scholarships awarded on the basis of academic merit alone. *Meeting Costs:* college offers monthly installment plan, parent loan programs.

Grove City College

Grove City, Pennsylvania 16127-2104 (412) 458-2100

A church-related, liberal arts college at which students "are expected to observe Christian moral standards. The 150-acre campus is located in a town of 8,000, 60 miles north of Pittsburgh. Most convenient major airport: Pittsburgh International.

Founded: 1876
Affiliation: United Presbyterian
Total Enrollment: 1,123 M, 1,090 W (full-time)
Cost: < $10K
% Receiving Financial Aid: 50%
Admission: Very Selective
Application Deadline: February 15

Admission is very selective. About 45% of applicants accepted, 52% of these actually enroll; 57% of freshmen graduate in top fifth of high school class, 82% in top two-fifths. Average freshman SAT scores: 533 M, 541 W verbal, 623 M, 591 W mathematical; 72% of freshmen score above 500 on verbal, 18% above 600, 2% above 700; 92% score above 500 on mathematical, 44% above 600, 13% above 700; ACT, 27 M, W composite. *Required:* SAT or ACT, essay; interview recommended. Criteria considered in admissions, in order of importance: high school academic record, standardized test scores, extracurricular activities, recommendations, writing sample; other factors considered: special talents, alumni children, diverse student body. *Entrance programs:* early decision, early admission, midyear admission, deferred admission, advanced placement. About 10% of entering students from private or parochial schools. *Apply* by February 15: rolling admissions. *Transfers* welcome; 36 accepted 1993–94.

Academic Environment. Pressures for academic achievement appear moderately strong. Students report that "classes are tough, and the amount of homework can be exhausting", but they find the professors easily accessible in most departments. Administration reports 38–50 hour core curriculum with emphasis in the humanities, social sciences, quantitative and logical reasoning, natural sciences, and foreign languages. Degree offered: bachelors. Average undergraduate class size: 43% of classes under 20, 38% between 20–40, 19% over 40.

About 74% of students entering as freshmen graduate within four years, 79% eventually; 12% of freshmen do not return for sophomore year. *Special programs:* CLEP, independent study, junior year abroad, honors, internships, 3-year degree, individualized majors, professional option (student enters professional school after 3 years and then transfer back credits for BA/BS). *Calendar:* semester.

Undergraduate degrees conferred (468). 33% were in Business and Management, 20% were in Education, 9% were in Social Sciences, 9% were in Engineering, 7% were in Computer and Engineering Related Technology, 6% were in Life Sciences, 6% were in Communications, 3% were in Psychology, remainder in 8 other fields.

Graduates Career Data. Advanced studies pursued after graduation by 14% of students; 2% enter medical school; 2% enter law school; 1% enter business school. Medical schools typically enrolling largest numbers of graduates include Med. C. of Ohio, Hahnemann Med. C., Jefferson; law schools include Case Western Reserve, Dickinson, Cooley; business schools include Georgetown, U. of Pittsburgh, Pennsylvania St., WVU, Hofstra. About 35% of 1993–94 graduates employed. Fields typically hiring largest numbers of graduates include teaching, accounting, engineering, sales. Career Development Services include resource library, video tapes, networking directories, career connection service with alumni, job and graduate school fairs, seminars, on-campus interviewing, resume assistance, internships.

Faculty. About 66% of faculty hold PhD or equivalent. About 25% of teaching faculty are female.

Student Body. Approximately 64% of students from in state; 74% Middle Atlantic, 18% Midwest, 3% South, 2% West, 2% New England, 1% foreign students 1993–94. An estimated 77% of students reported as Protestant, 19% Catholic, 4% unaffiliated; 3% minorities.

Religious Orientation. Grove City is a church-related institution; makes no religious demands on students. Places of worship available on campus for Protestants, in immediate community for Catholics and Protestants.

Varsity Sports. Men (Div.III): Baseball, Basketball, Cross Country, Diving, Football, Golf, Soccer, Swimming, Tennis, Track. Women (Div.III): Basketball, Cross Country, Diving, Golf, Soccer, Softball, Swimming, Tennis, Track, Volleyball.

Campus Life. Campus includes a Physical Learning Center which houses 2 swimming pools, handball/racquetball courts, tennis courts, volleyball courts, intramural room, running track, weight room and an 8 lane bowling alley. Interest in fraternities/sororities, intramural sports and religious activities is quite strong. Cars discouraged for resident freshmen. Drinking, use or possession of drugs prohibited. Smoking permitted if roommate agrees. Freshman curfew; self-regulated hours after first freshman semester. Intervisitation Friday and Saturday nights, Saturday and Sunday afternoons. All noncommuters required to live in residence halls.

About 90% each of men, women live in traditional dormitories; no coed dormitories; rest commute. There are 6 fraternities, 9 sororities on campus which about 28% of men, 50% of women join; they provide no residence facilities. About 10% of students leave campus on weekends.

Annual Costs. Tuition and fees, $4,976; room and board, $2,894; estimated $800 other, exclusive of travel. About 50% of students receive financial aid; average amount of assistance, $4,236. Assistance is typically divided 28% scholarship, 11% grant, 61% loan. College reports 50 scholarships awarded on the basis of academic merit alone, 12% for special talents.

Guilford College

Greensboro, North Carolina 27410 **(910) 316-2000 or (800) 992-7759**

A church-related, liberal arts college, Guilford is located on a 300-acre campus, 6 miles west of downtown Greensboro (pop.190,000), 80 miles northwest of Raleigh. Most convenient major airport: Greensboro.

Founded: 1837
Affiliation: Friends
Total Enrollment: 580 M, 628 W (full-time)
Cost: $10K–$20K
% Receiving Financial Aid: 49%
Admission: Selective (+)
Application Deadline: March 1

Admission is selective (+). About 80% of applicants accepted, 31% of these actually enroll; 38% of freshmen graduate in top fifth of high school class, 71% in top two-fifths. Average freshman SAT scores: 45% above 500 on verbal, 12% above 600, 2% above 700; 70% above 500 mathematical, 21% above 600, 4% above 700. *Required:* SAT or ACT, essay; interview recommended. Criteria considered in admissions, in order of importance: high school academic record, writing sample, standardized tests, recommendations, extracurricular activities; other factors considered: diverse student body, alumni children, special talents. *Entrance programs:* early decision, early admission, midyear admission, deferred admission, advanced placement. About 35% of entering students from private schools. *Apply* by March 1. *Transfers* welcome; 58 accepted 1993–94.

Academic Environment. All freshmen take an interdisciplinary problem-oriented course. Core requirements include Freshman Seminar; 2 semesters of English; intercultural course; 2 courses from religion/literature/philosophy; history; 2 courses in science (including lab); 2 social sciences; 1 year of foreign language; and senior interdisciplinary seminar. According to student leader, "Excellent academics are available, but must be sought. [ELLIPSE] People who know how to take advantage of its (Guilford's) qualities love it." Degree offered: bachelors. *Majors offered* include accounting, justice and policy studies, management, sports medicine, education, humanistic studies, BFA in art. New programs include interdisciplinary international studies, and education studies which requires double major. Average undergraduate class sizes: 59% under 20, 39% 20–40, 2% above 40.

About 52% of students entering as freshmen graduate within four years, 62% eventually; 16% of freshmen do not return for sophomore year. Special programs include: study abroad, honors, internships in all majors, individualized majors, interdisciplinary minors and concentrations, Washington Semester; cross-registration with Greensboro, Salem; 3–2 programs in physics, forestry. Adult programs: full evening program offers degree programs in management, accounting, justice and policy studies; some requirements are dropped. *Library:* 200,000 titles, 1,046 periodicals, other materials include Friend's Historical Collection, Poetry Collection, Boles Collection, Women's Studies Collection, Science Fiction collection. *Calendar:* semester, summer school.

Undergraduate degrees conferred (319). 30% were in Business and Management, 18% were in Social Sciences, 13% were in Letters, 6% were in Psychology, 5% were in Visual and Performing Arts, 5% were in Life Sciences, 4% were in Protective Services, 4% were in Education, 4% were in Health Sciences, 3% were in Physical Sciences, 3% were in Philosophy and Religion, 3% were in Foreign Languages, remainder in 2 other fields.

Graduates Career Data. Advanced studies pursued after graduation by 17% of students; 3% enter medical school; 2% enter law school; 1% enter business school. Medical schools typically enrolling largest numbers of graduates include Wake Forest, West Virginia U., Tulane; law schools include Campbell, Wake Forest, Dickinson; business schools include Wake Forest, UNC Greensboro and Chapel Hill. About 25% of 1992–93 graduates employed. Fields typically hiring largest numbers of graduates include accounting/management, teaching, banking, non-profit administrators. Career Development Services offered by college include alumni panels, job fairs for careers, career library, career planning course for credit. Alumni and parents reported as active in both career guidance and job placement.

Faculty. About 88% of faculty hold PhD or equivalent. About 48% of classes taught by tenured faculty. About 33% of teaching faculty are female; 5% Black, 1% Hispanic, 1% Asian.

Student Body. Approximately 29% of students from in state; 50% Middle Atlantic, 26% South, 9% New England, 7% Midwest, 1% West, 7% foreign 1993–94. An estimated 48% of students reported as Protestant, 11% Catholic, 2% Jewish, 39% unaffiliated or other; 7% as Black, 2% Hispanic, 1% Asian, 1% other minority.

Religious Orientation. Guilford is a church-related institution; 1 course of religious study required. Places of worship available on campus for Protestants, in immediate community for other major faiths.

Varsity Sports. Men (NCAA, III, ODAC): Baseball, Basketball, Football, Golf, Lacrosse, Soccer, Tennis. Women (NCAA, III, ODAC): Basketball, Lacrosse, Soccer, Tennis, Volleyball.

Campus Life. Rules governing campus life have been significantly relaxed to encourage personal responsibility. Daily intervisitation during scheduled hours (9 am–1 am). Students report that there is plenty to keep them busy, such as intramural sports, extracurricular clubs, school sponsored events (many speakers, films, lectures). Alcohol permitted in dormitory rooms. Cars allowed for all students.

About 5% of men, 10% of women live in traditional residence halls; 75% of men, 70% of women in coed residence halls; rest commute. Freshmen given preference in college housing if all students cannot be accommodated. There are no fraternities or sororities. About 50% of resident students leave campus on weekends.

Annual Costs. Tuition and fees, $12,610; room and board, $5,070; estimated $1,290 other, exclusive of travel. About 49% of students receive financial aid; average amount of assistance, $13,243. Assistance is typically divided 50% scholarship, 10% grant, 30% loan, 10% work. College reports 273 scholarships awarded on the basis of academic merit alone, 45 for special talents, 658 for need. *Meeting Costs:* college offers Alden Plan, TERI Loan, EXCEL Loan.

Gulf-Coast Bible College

(See Mid-America Bible College)

Gustavus Adolphus College

St. Peter, Minnesota 56082 **(507) 933-7676**

A liberal arts college, located in a town of 9,000, 65 miles southeast of Minneapolis. Gustavus Adolphus is a college of the Evangelical Lutheran Church in America. Most convenient major airport: Minneapolis-St. Paul.

Founded: 1862
Affiliation: Evangelical Lutheran Church in America
Total Enrollment: 1,028 M, 1,253 W (full-time)
Cost: $10K–$20K
% Receiving Financial Aid: 65%
Admission: Very (+) Selective
Application Deadline: April 15

Admission is very (+) selective. About 79% of applicants accepted, 49% of these actually enroll; 62% of freshmen graduate in top fifth of high school class, 88% in top two-fifths. Average freshman scores: SAT, 540 M, 510 W verbal, 620 M, 550 W mathematical; 58% of freshmen score above 500 on verbal, 25% above 600, 3% above 700; 79% score above 500 on mathematical, 33% above 600, 15% above 700; ACT, 26 M, 25 W composite. *Required:* SAT or ACT, essay; interview recommended. Criteria considered in admissions, in order of importance: high school academic record, writing sample, standardized tests, recommendations, extracurricular activities; other factors considered: special talents, alumni children, religious affiliation, diverse student body. *Entrance programs:* early decision, early admission, midyear admission, advanced placement, deferred admission. About 3% of entering students from private schools, 5% from parochial schools. *Apply* by April 15; rolling admissions. *Transfers* welcome; 44 enrolled 1993–94.

Academic Environment. Degree offered: bachelors. Pressures for academic achievement appear moderate. Students are members of all committees except for Faculty Senate and Faculty Personnel committee. They are also part of the tenure review process and interview candidates for faculty positions. Student body reported to be equally concerned with occupational/professional goals and scholarly/intellectual interests. Strongest academic programs said to be physics, music, languages, psychology, political science, writing program. New major in biochemistry. Undergraduate research has become increasingly important on the Gustavus Adolphus campus. Curriculum emphasizes liberal arts core, increased writing requirements. Alternative Curriculum II focuses on Western Heritage; courses are designed for a four-year sequence and include a foreign language requirement; enrollment is limited to 240 students.

Average undergraduate class size: 35% under 20, 50% 20–40, 15% over 40. Students report that the faculty is "very accessible" outside of class. About 82% of students entering as freshmen graduate eventually; 9% of freshmen do not return for sophomore year. *Special programs:* January term, internships, independent study, study abroad (in numerous international programs), honors, undergraduate research, credit by examination, Washington Semester, education programs (5-month internship in elementary and secondary teaching), combined programs in engineering, medical technology, physical therapy. *Calendar:* 4–1–4, summer school.

Undergraduate degrees conferred (699). 19% were in Social Sciences, 16% were in Business and Management, 11% were in Education, 11% were in Psychology, 8% were in Communications, 5% were in Life Sciences, 5% were in Visual and Performing Arts, 4% were in Physical Sciences, 4% were in Letters, 3% were in Mathematics, 3% were in Allied Health, remainder in 6 other fields.

Graduates Career Data. Advanced studies pursued by 35% of graduates; 3% enter medical school; 2% enter dental school; 5% enter law school; 4% enter business school. Medical, dental, law and business schools typically enrolling largest numbers of graduates include U. of Minnesota. About 60% of 1992 graduates employed, many enter teaching. Corporations typically hiring largest numbers of graduates include: Andersen Consulting, IBM, Ernst & Young. Career Development Services offered by college include career interest days, co-op education internships, job fair, career and interest testing. Alumni involved in January career exploration as well as career interest days.

Faculty. About 83% of faculty hold PhD or equivalent. About 65% of undergraduate classes taught by tenured faculty. About 27% of teaching faculty are female; 2% Black, 1% Hispanic, 4% Asian.

Student Body. Approximately 73% of students from in state; 88% Midwest, 6% West, 2% South, 2% foreign. An estimated 75% of students reported as Protestant, 17% Catholic, 6% unaffiliated, 2% other; 2% as Black, 3% Asian. *Minority group students:* special financial, academic, and social provisions.

Religious Orientation. Gustavus Adolphus is a church-related institution; 1 course in religion required of all students; voluntary daily chapel. Places of worship available on campus for Protestants and Catholics, in Minneapolis suburbs for Jews.

Varsity Sports. Men (NCAA Div.III): Baseball, Basketball, Cross Country, Diving, Football, Golf, Ice Hockey, Soccer, Swimming, Tennis, Track. Women (NCAA Div.III): Basketball, Cross Country, Diving, Golf, Gymnastics, Soccer, Softball, Swimming, Tennis, Track, Volleyball.

Campus Life. High student interest reported in intramurals (most popular: broomball, basketball, softball), cultural and religious activities. Intervisitation may be set by each residence unit within limits. Alcohol allowed in residence halls, subject to state laws; smoking restricted, all public facilities smoke-free; no tobacco sold on campus; drugs are forbidden. Students required to live in residence halls unless special permission obtained from dean. Student leader reports that the small size of the college "gives you a chance to be someone and develop your potential."

About 90% of men, 90% of women live in coed dormitories; 10% of men, 10% of women live in off-campus college-related housing. Sexes segregated in coed dormitories by wing, floor, or "section." There are 3 fraternities and 5 sororities on campus in which 20% of men, 25% of women join. About 15% of resident students leave campus on weekends.

Annual Costs. Tuition and fees, $13,400; room and board $3,500, estimated $1,000 other, exclusive of travel. About 65% of students receive financial aid; average amount of assistance, $12,300. Assistance is typically divided 60% scholarship/grant, 25% loan, 15% work. College reports 40 scholarships per class awarded on the basis of academic merit alone, the rest for need. *Meeting Costs:* college offers a Guaranteed Cost Plan which limits tuition increase to 2.5% per year.

Gwynedd-Mercy College

Gwynedd Valley, Pennsylvania 19437 (215) 646-7300

A church-related co-educational college, sponsored by the Sisters of Mercy, located in a suburban community, 20 miles from the center of Philadelphia. Most convenient major airport: Philadelphia.

Founded: 1948
Affiliation: Independent (Roman Catholic)
UG Enrollment: 136 M, 580 W (full-time); 215 M, 893 W (part-time)

Total Enrollment: 1,986
Cost: $10K–$20K
% Receiving Financial Aid: 75%
Admission: Non-selective
Application Deadline: Rolling

Admission. High school graduates with 16 units eligible; 48% of applicants accepted, 45% of these actually enroll. About 48% of freshmen graduate in top fifth of high school class, 81% in top two-fifths. Average freshman scores: SAT; 485 M, 451 W verbal, 495 M, 475 W mathematical; 31% of students score above 500 on verbal, 43% score above 500 mathematical. *Required:* SAT or ACT, letter of recommendation, high school transcripts; interview for allied health fields. Criteria considered in admissions, in order of importance: high school academic record, standardized tests, recommendations, course selection; other factors considered: alumni children. Entrance programs available: midyear admission, deferred admission, advanced placement. *Apply:* rolling admissions. About 17% of freshmen from private schools, 38% from parochial schools. *Transfers* welcome; 431 enrolled 1993–94.

Academic Environment. Degrees offered: associates, bachelors, masters. General education requirements vary with program, but all include language, literature, fine arts; humanities, behavioral and social sciences; natural sciences. Nursing program allows students to sit for RN exam in 2 years. Unusual programs include BS in Business Administration with Health Administration Concentration. Opportunities for clinical internships are required for some programs, encouraged for others. Average undergraduate class size: 73% under 20, 24% 20–40, 3% over 40. About 84% of students entering as freshmen graduate eventually; 15% of freshmen do not return for sophomore year. *Special programs:* CLEP, independent study, study abroad, cooperative work-study programs. *Calendar:* semester.

Undergraduate degrees conferred (275). 32% were in Health Sciences, 27% were in Business and Management, 19% were in Education, 7% were in Letters, 5% were in Computer and Engineering Related Technology, 3% were in Psychology, 3% were in Life Sciences, remainder in 4 other fields.

Graduates Career Data. Career Development Services include career counseling, resource center workshops, resume/cover letter critique service, job search skills, SIGI Plus computerized career guidance system, graduate school information.

Faculty. About 29% of faculty hold PhD or equivalent. About 77% of teaching faculty are female; 4% minority.

Student Body. Approximately 94% of students from Pennsylvania; almost all from Middle Atlantic; 3% foreign 1993–94. An estimated 59% of students reported as Catholic, 22% Protestant, 2% Jewish, 16% unaffiliated or other; 4% Black, 2% Hispanic, 5% Asian. Average age of undergraduate student is 29.

Religious Orientation. Gwynedd-Mercy is a church-related institution; 2 courses in religious study required of all baccalaureate degree students, 3 hours each of religion and philosophy required of all associate degree students.

Varsity Sports. Men (NAIA, Div.III): Basketball, Golf, Soccer, Tennis. Women (NAIA,Div. III): Basketball, Field Hockey, Lacrosse, Tennis, Softball, Volleyball.

Campus Life. About 8% of students live in coed dormitories; rest live in off-campus housing or commute. Intervisitation in women's dormitory rooms limited. There are no fraternities or sororities. About 80% of resident students leave campus on weekends.

Annual Costs. Tuition and fees, $10,200 (nursing and allied health, $10,960); room and board, $5,250. About 75% of students receive financial aid; average amount of assistance, $9,075. Aid is typically divided 65% scholarship, 10% grant, 20% loan, 5% work. College reports 33 scholarships awarded on the basis of academic merit alone, 10 for special talents, 431 for need.

Hahnemann University School of Health Sciences and Humanities

Philadelphia, Pennsylvania 19122

Hahnemann is a private, non-profit, progressive academic health sciences center in Center City, Philadelphia that includes the Graduate School, School of Medicine, School of Health Sciences and Humanities, and a 636-bed Hahnemann University Hospital. More than 2,400 students are enrolled in degree programs annually. In addition, postgraduate and continuing education programs are offered for physicians, health scientists, and other health professionals. Hahnemann confers associates, baccalaureate and graduate degrees. Bachelor degrees offered in cardiovascular perfusion technology, emergency medical services, health sciences and society, humanities and social sciences, laboratory sciences, mental health technology, nursing, physician assistant, occupational and environmental health.

Founded: 1848 **Affiliation:** Independent

Hamilton College

Clinton, New York 13323 **(315) 859-4421 or Financial Aid, 859-4434**

Hamilton is a small, high quality, co-educational, liberal arts college. For 166 years a men's college, it became a co-educational institution in 1978 by combining with Kirkland College, a coordinate women's college that had been established 10 years earlier under Hamilton's auspices. The 350-acre campus is located 1 mile from a village of 2,300, 9 miles from Utica. Most convenient major airports: Oneida County (15 minutes), Syracuse (50 minutes).

Founded: 1793
Affiliation: Independent
Total Enrollment: 904 M, 742 W (full-time)
Cost: $10K–$20K
% Receiving Financial Aid: 45%
Admission: Highly Selective
Application Deadline: Jan. 15

Admission is highly selective. About 57% of applicants accepted, 25% of these actually enroll; 73% of freshmen graduate in top fifth of high school class, 95% in top two-fifths. Average freshman SAT scores: 72% of freshmen score above 500 on verbal, 20% above 600, 1% above 700; 92% score above 500 on mathematical, 48% above 600, 10% above 700. *Required:* SAT or ACT. *Non-academic factors* considered in admissions: geographical distribution, alumni children, diverse student body, special talents. *Entrance programs:* early decision, early admission, advanced placement, deferred admission. About 58% of entering students from private schools, 3% from parochial schools. *Apply* by January 15. *Transfers* welcome.

Academic Environment. Hamilton students characterized as primarily concerned with occupational/professional goals combined with a lively interest in social activities. Students are counseled by faculty members of the Board of Advisers in the first 2 years, and by departmental advisers in the last 2. Interdisciplinary work and programs in the arts which Kirkland emphasized continue to be an integral part of the Hamilton curriculum. Pressures for academic achievement appear fairly intense. Classes generally small; instruction in freshman composition largely individual. There is strong emphasis on effective writing and oral skills. Administration reports graduation requirements include completion of a concentration, the Senior Program (may take the form of independent research culminating in a paper or presentation, comprehensive exams, a major aural or visual creation, etc.) completion of or exemption from Writing 100, and demonstrated proficiency in physical education skills. In addition, distribution requirements include 2 courses from each of the following areas: natural sciences and mathematics/computer science; humanities; social sciences; and the arts. Degree offered: bachelors. *Majors offered* include usual arts and sciences, American studies, ancient Mediterranean civilization, Asian studies, African-American studies, biochemistry/molecular biology, computer science, international and comparative political studies, linguistics, psychobiology, public policy, theater and dance.

About 87% of students entering as freshmen graduate within four years, 89% eventually; 4% of freshmen do not return for sophomore year. *Special programs:* honors, independent study, study abroad, undergraduate research, senior fellowships, Washington Semester, acceleration, credit by examination, Williams College/Mystic Seaport program, 3–2 engineering, early assurance program in medicine (allows for more broadly based course of study in junior and senior years than usual pre-med). Adult programs: Hamilton Horizons Program for student who have been away from formal collegiate education for more than five years, students take regular Hamilton courses. *Calendar:* semester, optional 2-week interterm.

Undergraduate degrees conferred (74). 51% were in Allied Health, 46% were in Health Sciences, 3% were in Multi/Interdisciplinary Studies.

Graduates Career Data. *Full-time graduate or professional study* pursued immediately after graduation by 20% of students; 3% enter medical school; less than 1% enter dental school; 5% enter law school; 1% enter business school. Medical schools typically enrolling largest numbers of graduates include SUNY (Upstate, Buffalo, Syracuse); law schools include Harvard, Yale, Columbia; business schools include U. of Chicago, NYU, U. of Rochester. *Careers in business and industry* pursued by 69% of graduates. Career Fields typically pursued by largest numbers of graduates include investment banking, accounting/financial management, paralegal, teaching, publishing/journalism. *Career Counseling Program:* Student assessment of program reported as good for both career guidance and job placement. Students urged to seek interviews with business/industry representatives who visit campus. Help provided in preparing for interviews. Alumni reported as active in both career guidance and job placement.

Faculty. About 96% of faculty hold doctorate or appropriate terminal degree. About 36% of teaching faculty are female; 4% Black, 2% Hispanic, 5% Asian.

Student Body. College seeks a national student body; 46% of students from in state; 58% Middle Atlantic, 21% New England, 5% South, 6% North Central. An estimated 31% of students reported as Protestant, 34% Catholic, 10% Jewish, 16% unaffiliated, 8% other; 3% as Black, 3% Hispanic, 3% Asian, less than 1% Native American. *Minority group students:* scholarship aid available; special tutoring assistance; summer college readiness program. Black and Latin student union provides focus for social life and programs.

Varsity Sports. Men (Div.III): Baseball, Basketball, Cross Country, Diving, Football, Golf, Ice Hockey, Lacrosse, Soccer, Squash, Swimming, Tennis, Track. Women (Div.III): Basketball, Cross Country, Diving, Field Hockey, Lacrosse, Soccer, Softball, Squash, Swimming, Tennis, Track, Volleyball.

Campus Life. Students have virtually total control over campus social life—revolving around a wide variety of living situations including coed dormitories, a cooperative, and fraternities. The recently completed Walter Beinecke Student Activities Village includes a diner, post office, coffee house and common areas for social interaction including the Student Events Barn. The strong fraternity system coexists with independents. Student leader reports students likely to feel most at home on campus are those who want a small community campus life. Those least at home want an urban, "fast-paced" campus life. Interest in men's and women's intercollegiate and intramural athletics remains moderate. All-weather track and field, and intramural field have been added, as well as 37-meter swimming and diving pool. Variety of cultural and intellectual activities on campus; Emerson Art Gallery offers exhibitions in visual arts; center for music and performing arts recently completed. On-campus offerings supplemented by those in Utica, 9 miles away and Syracuse, 1 hour distant. Motor vehicles not allowed for freshmen.

About 79% of men, 95% of women in coed dormitories; 19% of men, 3% of women live in private societies; 2% of men, 2% of women live in off-campus college-related housing. Freshmen given preference in college housing if all students cannot be accommodated. Sexes segregated in coed dormitories by floor or room. There

are 8 fraternities, 1 coed society, 2 sororities on campus which about 30% of students join. About 5–10% of students leave campus on weekends.
Annual Costs. Tuition and fees, $18,650; room and board, $4,850; estimated $1,200 other, exclusive of travel. About 45% of students receive financial aid; average amount of assistance, $4,697. College reports scholarships awarded only on the basis of need.

Hamline University

Saint Paul, Minnesota 55104 **(612) 641-2207**

Hamline is a church-related university with an undergraduate, liberal arts college and a school of law. Located on a 44-acre campus midway between Saint Paul and Minneapolis, the University emphasizes liberal arts in a context of practical application. Individually designed interdisciplinary programs possible. Most convenient major airport: Minneapolis/Saint Paul International.

Founded: 1854
Affiliation: United Methodist
UG Enrollment: 642 M, 822 W (full-time); 43 M, 46 W (part-time)
Total Enrollment: 2,562
Cost: $10K–$20K
% Receiving Financial Aid: 75%
Admission: Very Selective
Application Deadline: Rolling

Admission is very selective. About 80% of applicants accepted, 40% of these actually enroll; 57% of freshmen graduate in top fifth of high school class, 89% in top two-fifths. Average freshman scores: SAT, middle 50% range, 460–610 verbal, 520–620 mathematical; 64% of freshmen score above 500 on verbal, 20% above 600, 8% above 700; 87% score above 500 on mathematical, 32% above 600, 8% above 700; ACT, 22–28 composite. *Required:* SAT or ACT. Criteria considered in admissions, in order of importance: high school academic record, recommendations, writing sample, extracurricular activities, standardized test scores; other factors considered: alumni children, diverse student body, special talents. *Entrance programs:* early action, early admission, midyear admission, advanced placement, deferred admission. About 18% of entering students from private schools, 6% from parochial schools. *Apply:* rolling admissions. *Transfers* welcome; 124 enrolled 1993–94.
Academic Environment. Students appear to play significant part in college governance, interview all candidates for faculty positions, are voting members of almost all faculty committees. Pressures for academic achievement appear moderately strong. Student leader characterizes student body as primarily concerned with vocational/professional goals. Another student finds, "The strengths of the academic program begin with a tough curriculum that challenges all the students. It is backed up with dedicated and helpful professors that work hard so their students are successful." For graduation students required to complete 32 courses spread over 4 academic divisions of college and to demonstrate proficiency in written English, oral communications, and computer literacy. *Majors offered* include anthropology, international relations, Latin American studies, East Asian studies, medical technology, theater, interdisciplinary environmental studies.

About 70% of students entering as freshmen graduate eventually; 18% of freshmen do not return for sophomore year. *Special programs:* CLEP, independent study, study abroad (sites in over fifty countries), honors, undergraduate research, credit by examination, Washington Semester, United Nations Semester, extensive programs of cooperation with Twin Cities area colleges (including cross-registration with Augsburg, Macalester, St. Catherine, St. Thomas), 3–2 and 4–2 programs in engineering, 3–3 BA/JD, 3–2 Occupational Therapy with Washington U., New York art semester, internships. Adult programs: continuing education (non-degree) programs for teachers, MA programs. *Calendar:* 4–1–4.
Undergraduate degrees conferred (391). 23% were in Social Sciences, 16% were in Psychology, 13% were in Business and Management, 12% were in Letters, 6% were in Physical Sciences, 5% were in Law, 4% were in Mathematics, 3% were in Philosophy and Religion, 3% were in Communications, 3% were in Life Sciences, 3% were in Education, 3% were in Foreign Languages, remainder in 4 other fields.
Graduates Career Data. Advanced studies pursued by 27% of graduates; 2% enter medical school; 6% enter law school; 2% enter business school. Medical schools typically enrolling largest numbers of graduates include U. of Minnesota; law schools include U. of Minnesota, William Mitchell, Hamline U.; business schools include U. of Minnesota. *Careers in business and industry* pursued by 49% of graduates. Career Development Services: Student assessment of program reported as fair to good for career guidance and fair for job placement. Alumni reported to be "very active" in career guidance and job placement.
Faculty. About 93% of faculty hold PhD or equivalent.
Student Body. Approximately 73% of students from in state; 85% Midwest, 9% Northwest, 1% New England, 1% Middle Atlantic, 1% West; 53 foreign students 1993–94. An estimated 55% of students reported as Protestant, 24% Catholic, 3% Jewish, 2% Muslim, 12% unaffiliated, 4% other; 3% as Black, 4% Asian, 4% other minority. *Minority group students:* coordinator of special programs for minority students; minority student advisor; Pride House.
Religious Orientation. Although Hamline is a church-related institution, it is nonsectarian in its educational program; makes no religious demands on students. University charter has always banned discrimination based on race, religion, or sex. Places of worship available in immediate community for all major faiths.
Varsity Sports. Men (Div.III): Baseball, Basketball, Cross Country, Diving, Football, Ice Hockey, Soccer, Swimming, Tennis, Track. Women (Div.III): Basketball, Cross Country, Gymnastics, Soccer, Diving, Softball, Swimming, Tennis, Track, Volleyball.
Campus Life. Dormitories self-governing; each unit makes its own rules on such matters as intervisitation. No restrictions on use of cars.

About 46% of men, 44% of women live in coed dormitories; 48% of men, 48% of women live in nearby off-campus housing; 4% of men, 6% of women commute. Freshmen given preference in college housing if all students cannot be accommodated. Sexes segregated in coed dormitories by wing. There are 2 fraternities, 2 sororities on campus which about 4% of men, 5% of women join; 2% of men, 2% of women live in fraternities and sororities. About 10–20% of resident students leave campus on weekends.
Annual Costs. Tuition and fees, $13,022; room and board, $4,100; estimated $1,100 other, exclusive of travel. About 75% of students receive financial aid; average amount of assistance, $12,000. Assistance is typically divided 60% scholarship, 22% loan, 18% work. University reports some scholarships awarded on the basis of academic merit alone. *Meeting Costs:* university offers early payment discount, budget payment plans, PLUS, SELF Loans.

Hampden-Sydney College

Hampden-Sydney, Virginia 23943 **(804) 223-6120 or (800) 755-0733**

A small, church-related, liberal arts college for men, Hampden-Sydney dates from Revolutionary War days, when it counted Patrick Henry and James Madison among the members of its first board of directors. It has a notable record of producing leading professional men for the region and the nation. The 820-acre campus is located in a rural setting 7 miles south of Farmville (pop. 5,674) and 70 miles southwest of Richmond. Most convenient major airport: Richmond, Virginia.

Founded: 1776
Affiliation: Presbyterian Church (USA)
Total Enrollment: 945 M (full-time)
Cost: $10K–$20K
% Receiving Financial Aid: 74%
Admission: Selective (+)
Application Deadline: March 1

Admission is selective (+). About 79% of applicants accepted, 48% of these actually enroll; 32% of freshmen graduate in top fifth of high school class, 65% in top two-fifths. Average freshman scores: SAT, 517 verbal, 564 mathematical; 58% score above 500 verbal, 16% above 600, 1% above 700, 92% score above 500 mathematical, 27% above 600, 8% score above 700. *Required:* SAT or ACT; ACH strongly recommended, essay; interview recommended. Criteria considered in admissions, in order of importance: high school academic record, writing sample, standardized test scores, recommendations, extracurricular activities; other factors considered: diverse student body, alumni children, special talents, religious affiliation and/or commitment. Entrance programs: early decision, early admission, midyear admission, advanced placement. About 42% of entering students from private and parochial schools. *Apply* by March 1. *Transfers* welcome; 20 enrolled 1993–94.

Academic Environment. Degree offered: bachelors. Student body characterized by administration source as primarily concerned with occupational/professional goals. Academic programs considered to be strongest include foreign languages, chemistry, rhetoric/writing, managerial economics, history, micro-computer labs, Fuqua International Communications Center, pre-med and pre-law programs. "Very effective" student-run honor code reported by both student leader and administration source. One student reports, "...academic program is rigorous, yet fair." Several students support the core curriculum general education requirements, and one advises that Hampden-Sydney is "not in the process of educating specialists. You don't come here to be something; you come here to be someone." Average undergraduate class size 62% under 20, 36% 20–40, 2% over 40.

About 61% of students entering as freshmen graduate within four years, 67% eventually; 15% of freshmen do not return for sophomore year. *Special programs:* independent study, study abroad, honors, undergraduate research, 3-year degree, individualized majors, internships, Washington Semester, 3–2 engineering with Georgia Tech and Virginia Tech, Eight College Exchange Program, cross-registration with nearby Longwood College. *Calendar:* early semester.

Undergraduate degrees conferred (233). 61% were in Social Sciences, 10% were in Life Sciences, 9% were in Letters, 6% were in Psychology, 6% were in Physical Sciences, 3% were in Philosophy and Religion, 3% were in Liberal/General Studies, remainder in 2 other fields.

Graduates Career Data. Advanced studies pursued by 11% of students immediately after graduation; 3% enter medical school; 2% enter law school. Medical schools typically enrolling largest numbers of graduates include Medical College of Virginia, Eastern Medical School; law schools include U. of Richmond, Wake Forest, William & Mary. About 70% of 1992–93 graduates employed. Employers typically hiring largest numbers of graduates include Wachovia Bank, Ferguson Enterprises, Sovran Bank. Career Development Services include interview techniques, career counseling, resume writing workshops, on-campus interviewing, career days. Alumni reported as active in both career guidance and job placement.

Faculty. About 87% of faculty hold PhD or equivalent. About 60% of undergraduate classes taught by tenured faculty. About 18% of teaching faculty are female; 2% ethnic minorities.

Student Body. Approximately 53% of students from in state; 90% South, 6% Middle Atlantic, 1% New England, 1% West, 1% Midwest, 1% foreign students 1993–94. An estimated 77% of students reported as Protestant, 14% Catholic, 1% Jewish, 8% unaffiliated; 3% as Black, 1% Hispanic, 1% Asian, 1% other minority.

Religious Orientation. Hampden-Sydney is a church-related institution, but makes no religious demands on students. Places of worship available on campus for Presbyterians, 7 miles away for Catholics and other Protestant denominations, 70 miles away for Jews.

Varsity Sports. Men (Div.III): Baseball, Basketball, Cross Country, Football, Golf, Lacrosse, Soccer, Tennis.

Campus Life. As one administrator notes, "for a church college, one would consider us very progressive on rules of conduct." Students set own hours. Fraternity system very strong, about half of students join. A recent student writes, "I wish I had known the intensity of the all-male atmosphere. With our honor code and general sense of fraternity, Hampden Sydney men bond in ways that go well beyond a passing wave or handshake. We earn each other's respect, and that respect builds deeper friendships." High interest in both varsity and intramural athletics reported. Most popular varsity sports: football, lacrosse, basketball; intramurals: football, basketball, soccer, softball, ultimate frisbee. Hampden-Sydney has been described as "an outdoorman's paradise" - hunting, fishing, hiking, canoeing, skeet-shooting are popular activities. Small, somewhat isolated campus mitigated by both sponsored activities and student initiated events; four women's colleges within driving distance add to social life. Alcohol permitted those over 21; no smoking in classrooms; illegal drugs not permitted. Cars allowed.

About 82% of men live in dormitories; 5% live in off-campus housing. Freshmen given preference in college housing if all students cannot be accommodated. There are 12 fraternities on campus which about 50% of men join; 13% of men live in fraternities. About 15–40% leave campus on weekends, "depending on the weekend."

Annual Costs. Tuition and fees, $12,974; room and board, $4,398; estimated $500 other, exclusive of travel. About 74% of students receive financial aid; average amount of assistance, $12,800. Assistance typically divided 60% scholarship, 40% loan and work. College reports 95 scholarships awarded on the basis of academic merit alone, 408 for need.

Hampshire College

Amherst, Massachusetts 01002 **(413) 549-4600**

Hampshire is a liberal arts college developed under the aegis of its sister institutions in the Five College Consortium (Amherst, Mount Holyoke, Smith, and University of Massachusetts). The college includes many innovations in academic structure, governance, courses of study, and social arrangements. Hampshire is located on the outskirts of Amherst (pop. 18,000) on 800 acres of high land overlooking the Connecticut River Valley, within a 7-mile radius of its sister institutions. Most convenient major airport: Bradley International.

Founded: 1965
Affiliation: Independent
Total Enrollment: 456 M, 623 W (full-time)
Cost: > $20K
% Receiving Financial Aid: 56%
Admission: Very Selective
Application Deadline: Feb. 1

Admission is very selective. About 75% of applicants accepted, 31% of these actually enroll; 48% of entering students graduate in top fifth of high school class, 80% in top two-fifths. *Required:* interview, personal statement/essay or example of creative work, detailed description of interests/activities; SAT optional. Criteria considered in admissions, in order of importance: high school academic record, writing sample, extracurricular activities, recommendations, interview evaluation, standardized test scores; other factors considered: special talents, community service, self-reliance, ability to initiate academic work. *Entrance programs:* early decision, early action, early entrance, midyear admission, deferred admission. About 23% of entering students from private schools, 9% from parochial schools. *Apply* by February 1 (March 15 for transfers). *Transfers* welcome; 39 enrolled 1993–94.

Academic Environment. Hampshire continues to value its insistence on students assuming major responsibility for structuring their own academic and social life. Students who, for one reason or another, are neither ready nor willing to assume so active and responsible a role for their academic experience may encounter difficulties at Hampshire. Studies offered by schools of Humanities and Arts, Communications and Cognitive Science, Natural Science, and Social Science. Special interdisciplinary programs offered in American studies, business and society, civil liberties and public policy, computer studies, cultural studies, educational studies, feminist studies, law program, Luce Program in food, resources and international policy, population and development, public service and social change, third world studies; the Lemelson Program in Invention, Innovation and Creativity supports students who collaborate to solve problems or create new approaches in and field. All students follow 3 consecutive Divisions of Study. A general core program, based on seminars, constitutes Division I during the first 2 years—may be completed in less than 2 years. The second division requires concentration in one or more areas. The final division is devoted primarily to a thesis or project. Students are encouraged to progress at their own pace—may graduate in 3, 4, or 5 years. Progress from one division to the next based on completion of course work and projects in each area of study. All students are expected to consider some aspect of their work from a non-Western perspective. Students must include volunteer service to the surrounding community. Normally 3 courses taken each semester. Students may take courses not offered at Hampshire at the 4 sister institutions—regular bus service provided, most students take some courses off-campus. Degree offered: bachelors. *Majors offered* in each school are individually designed by student in consultation with faculty. Average undergraduate class size: 75% under 20, 24% 20–40, 1% over 40.

About 68% of students entering as freshmen graduate eventually; 14% of freshmen do not return for sophomore year. *Special programs:* honors, independent study, undergraduate research, 3-year degree, individualized majors, nonresident first-year studies, study abroad, cross registration with sister institutions; the Lemelson Program in Invention, Innovation, and Creativity. *Calendar:* 4–1–4.

Undergraduate degrees conferred (211). 56% were in Multi/Interdisciplinary Studies, 44% were in Social Sciences.
Graduates Career Data. Advanced studies pursued by 56% of graduates. Medical schools typically enrolling largest numbers of graduates include New York Medical College, NYU, U. of Massachusetts; law schools include Georgetown, Columbia, Boston U., Rutgers, NYU; business schools include Columbia, Chicago, NYU. Career Options Resources Center provides resources and assistance. Alumni reported as active in both career guidance and job placement.
Faculty. About 81% of faculty hold PhD or equivalent; no tenure system. About 44% of teaching faculty are female; 12% Black, 3% Hispanic, 6% other ethnic minority.
Student Body. About 15% of students from in state; 36% New England, 29% Middle Atlantic, 9% Midwest, 8% West, 8% South, 5% Northwest, 3% foreign 1993–94. An estimated 3% of students reported as Black, 4% Hispanic, 3% Asian, 5% other. *Minority group students:* special financial, academic, and social provisions available; full-time counselor for Third World students plus Third World Organization, Advising Center, and Third World admissions staff member.
Campus Life. Students live in co-educational residential academic clusters called Houses in which the sexes are segregated by room. Most rooms are single and soundproofed. Students have "option of living in residences where small groups cook and eat together." Substance free housing available. Houses are substantially self-governing. Drinking restricted to those of legal age; smoking prohibited at all meetings, some residence halls non-smoking. Cultural and intellectual activities at all of the Five Colleges are open to Hampshire students. Outdoors Program emphasizing sports and activities that can be pursued throughout an individual's lifetime (many of them coed) replaces physical education and conventional athletics. No varsity sports. Most popular intramurals: softball, volleyball, basketball, ultimate frisbee. Motor vehicles permitted; college discourages use because of concern for environmental quality and expense of providing parking.

About 96% of students live in coed dormitories; 4% live off-campus. Freshmen given preference in college housing if all students cannot be accommodated. There are no fraternities or sororities. Small number of students leave campus on weekends, usually to enjoy recreational opportunities in immediate vicinity.
Annual Costs. Tuition and fees, $20,160; room and board, $5,160; estimated $825 other, exclusive of travel. About 56% of students receive financial aid; average amount of assistance, $18,235. Assistance is typically divided 72% grant, 20% loan, 8% work. College reports 25 scholarships awarded on the basis of academic merit alone. Hampshire will match, dollar-for-dollar, National Service Scholarships.

Hampton University

Hampton, Virginia 23668 **(804) 727-5328**

A co-educational non-sectarian institution of higher education, founded as a college for Negroes, now interracial and intercultural in both student body and faculty. Campus is located on the Virginia peninsula, a region intimately associated with early American history. Formerly known as Hampton Institute. Most convenient major airport: Norfolk International.

Founded: 1868
Affiliation: Independent
Total Enrollment: 5,276 M, W (full-time, graduate and undergraduate); 177 M, 141 W (part-time)
Cost: < $10K
Admission: Non-selective
Application Deadline: February 15

Admission. Graduates of accredited high schools with C average or better and rank in top half of class eligible; others admitted by examination; 49% of applicants accepted, 41% of these actually enroll; 10% of freshmen graduate in top fifth of high school class, 30% in top two-fifths. *Required:* SAT (minimum combined of 800 "desirable") or ACT; interview recommended. *Non-academic factors* considered in admissions: special talents. *Apply* by February 15. *Transfers* welcome.
Academic Environment. *Degrees:* AB, BS, BArch. About 60% of general education requirements for graduation are elective; distribution requirements fairly numerous. About 65% of students entering as freshmen graduate within four years; 17% of freshmen do not return for sophomore year. *Special programs:* CLEP, independent study, honors, cooperative work/study program in business and engineering, University Humanities Consortium, external program in emergency medical systems management. *Calendar:* 4–1–4, summer school.
Undergraduate degrees conferred (848). 37% were in Business and Management, 10% were in Social Sciences, 8% were in Life Sciences, 7% were in Communications, 7% were in Psychology, 5% were in Letters, 5% were in Health Sciences, 4% were in Education, 3% were in Mathematics, remainder in 10 other fields.
Graduates Career Data. According to most recent data available, full-time graduate study pursued immediately after graduation by 18% of students. *Careers in business and industry* and government service pursued by 80% of graduates. Corporations typically hiring largest numbers of graduates include Dow, AT&T, Johnson & Johnson.
Faculty. About 45% of faculty hold PhD or equivalent.
Varsity Sports. Men (Div.II): Basketball, Football, Golf, Track. Women (Div.II): Basketball, Track, Softball, Volleyball.
Campus Life. University seeks a national student body; 39% of students from in state; 50% South, 42% Middle Atlantic. An estimated 65% of students reported as Protestant, 15% Catholic, 20% unaffiliated or other; 89% reported as Black, 2% other minority, according to most recent data available. Hampton is an independent institution, makes no religious demands on students.

About 56% of men, 54% of women live in traditional dormitories; rest commute. Freshmen given preference in college housing if all students cannot be accommodated. Intervisitation in men's and women's dormitory rooms limited. Sexes segregated in coed dormitories by floor. There are 3 fraternities, 3 sororities on campus; they provide no residence facilities. About 8% of students leave campus on weekends.
Annual Costs. Tuition and fees, $7,356; room and board, $3,350. About 75% of students receive financial aid; assistance is typically divided 30% scholarship, 40% loan, 30% work. College reports some scholarships awarded on basis of academic merit alone. *Meeting Costs:* university offers deferred payment plan.

Hannibal–Lagrange College

Hannibal, Missouri 63401 **(314) 221-3113**

A church-related liberal arts college, Hannibal–LaGrange was formerly a branch campus of Missouri Baptist College. Most convenient major airport: St. Louis, Missouri.

Founded: 1858
Affiliation: Southern Baptist
Total Enrollment: 189 M, 304 W (full-time); 135 M, 247 W (full-time)
Cost: < $10K
Admission: Non-selective
Application Deadline: First day of classes

Admission. Graduates of accredited high schools eligible; 85% of applicants accepted. Average freshman ACT scores: 20.4 composite. *Required:* SAT or ACT. Criteria considered in admissions, in order of importance: standardized test scores, high school academic record, recommendations, extracurricular activities, writing sample. *Apply* by first day of classes. *Transfers* welcome; 90 enrolled 1993–94.
Academic Environment. Degrees offered: associates, bachelors. Administration reports 20% of courses required for graduation are elective. Special program: study abroad. *Calendar:* semester, May Miniterm.
Undergraduate degrees conferred (87). 34% were in Education, 17% were in Allied Health, 16% were in Business and Management, 11% were in Theology, 8% were in Public Affairs, 7% were in Liberal/General Studies, 3% were in Computer and Engineering Related Technology, remainder in 2 other fields.
Faculty. About 37% of faculty hold PhD or equivalent.
Student Body. About 88% of students from in state. Average age of freshman student is 22.
Religious Orientation. Hannibal-LaGrange is a church related institution; 2 courses of religious study required of all students.
Varsity Sports. Men (NAIA): Baseball, Basketball.Women (NAIA): Softball, Volleyball.

Campus Life. Largely a commuting school, 31% of students live in dormitories; rest commute. Freshmen given preference in college housing if all students cannot be accommodated.
Annual Costs. Tuition and fees, $6,000; room and board, $2,400. College reports some scholarships awarded on basis of academic merit alone.

Hanover College

Hanover, Indiana 47243 **(812) 866-7021**

Hanover is one of a number of small, Midwestern liberal arts colleges which have provided quality education for generations. The college maintains some ties with the United Presbyterian Church. The 650-acre campus is located in a town of 3,600, adjacent to Madison (pop. 13,100) and 40 miles northeast of Louisville, Kentucky. Most convenient major airport: Louisville (KY).

Founded: 1827
Affiliation: Independent (Presbyterian Church (USA))
Total Enrollment: 457 M, 587 W (full-time)
Cost: < $10K
% Receiving Financial Aid: 65%
Admission: Selective (+)
Application Deadline: March 15

Admission is selective (+). About 80% of applicants accepted, 42% of these actually enroll; 57% of freshmen graduate in top fifth of high school class, 81% in top two-fifths. Average freshman scores: SAT, 488 M, 510 W verbal, 550 M, 538 W mathematical; ACT, 24 M, 25 W composite. *Required:* SAT or ACT, essay; interview strongly encouraged. Criteria considered in admissions, in order of importance: high school academic record, standardized test scores, writing sample, extracurricular activities, recommendations; other factors considered: special talents, alumni children, diverse student body. *Entrance programs:* midyear admission, deferred admission. About 10% of entering students from private schools, 10% from parochial schools. *Apply* by March 15; rolling admissions. *Transfers* welcome; 28 enrolled 1993–94.
Academic Environment. Students have some influence on academic policy making through voting membership in all faculty/administration committees. The Hanover Plan divides the academic year into 3 terms; 2 13½ week terms and 1 4-week term. The student takes 4 courses during each of the 13½-week terms, 1 during the 4-week spring term. Graduation requirements ensure that every student is introduced in some depth to each of the broad areas of human knowledge. Seniors pursue independent study and take comprehensive exam in major field. Distribution requirements fairly numerous: 2 courses each in social science, humanities, natural sciences, one course each in history, non-Western studies, philosophy, theology, world literature, writing; proficiency in fine arts, foreign language, mathematics, speech, physical education. Degree offered: bachelors. *Majors offered* include usual arts and sciences, business administration, speech, drama, computer science. Psychology, pre-med, pre-law, and teacher education reported to be strong programs. Average undergraduate class size: 20% under 20, 75% 20–40, 5% over 40. Several recent students find the small classes and "friendly student-faculty interaction" to be the greatest strengths of Hanover.

About 65% students entering as freshmen graduate eventually; 10% of freshmen do not return for sophomore year. *Special programs:* honors, independent study, study abroad, undergraduate research, Washington Semester, off-campus study during 4-week spring term, exchange agreement through Spring Term Consortium, 3–2 engineering with Washington U. *Calendar:* 3 terms.
Undergraduate degrees conferred (214). 26% were in Business and Management, 21% were in Social Sciences, 12% were in Communications, 11% were in Education, 7% were in Life Sciences, 6% were in Psychology, 5% were in Letters, 5% were in Visual and Performing Arts, 3% were in Physical Sciences, 3% were in Mathematics, remainder in 3 other fields.
Graduates Career Data. Advanced studies pursued by 45% of graduates; 5% enter medical school; 3% enter dental school; 5% enter law school; 25% enter business school. Medical, dental, and law schools typically enrolling largest numbers of graduates include Indiana U; business schools include Duke, U. of Kentucky, Indiana U.. About 35% of 1992–93 graduates are employed. Corporations typically hiring largest numbers of graduates include Eli Lilly, Fifth Third Bank, Procter & Gamble, insurance companies. *Career Counseling Program* offers workshops and job fairs. The "Hanover Connection" brings industry representatives to campus. Student assessment of program reported as fair for career guidance and poor for job placement. Alumni reported by administration source as active in both career guidance and job placement, student leader disagrees.
Faculty. About 85% of faculty hold PhD or equivalent. About 90% of classes taught by tenured faculty. About 25% of teaching faculty are female; 1% Black, 1% Hispanic, 5% other ethnic minorities.
Student Body. Approximately 60% of students from in state; 77% Midwest, 5% South, 5% Middle Atlantic, 5% New England, 3% foreign 1993–94. An estimated 30% of students reported as Protestant, 30% Catholic, 2% Jewish, 2% unaffiliated, 36% other; 2% as Black, 2% Hispanic, 2% Asian, 2% other ethnic minorities.
Religious Orientation. Hanover is an independent institution with a continuing relationship to the United Presbyterian Church; 1 course in theological studies required of all students. Nondenominational Campus Fellowship coordinates religious activities on campus. Places of worship available in immediate community for Protestants, 5 miles away for Catholics.
Varsity Sports. Men (NCAA III): Baseball, Basketball, Cross Country, Football, Golf, Soccer, Tennis, Track. Women (NCAA III): Basketball, Cross Country, Field Hockey, Golf, Softball, Tennis, Track, Volleyball.
Campus Life. Students and administrative sources describe the political philosophy of the campus as conservative. Student interest in fraternities/sororities reported very high. About two-thirds of both men and women live in Greek houses. Variety of cultural and social activities available on campus; nearest metropolitan centers are Louisville and Cincinnati, 40 and 65 miles from campus, respectively. Cars allowed. Use or possession of alcohol on campus or at college functions cause for dismissal. Students expected to live in college housing. Intervisitation limited. Students informed that "minimal dress expectations are in keeping with the philosophy of the college."

About 36% of men, 36% of women live in traditional dormitories; no coed dormitories; 2% each men, women commute. There are 5 fraternities, 4 sororities on campus which about 62% of men, 62% of women join; 62% of men, 62% of women live in fraternities and sororities. About 40% of resident students leave campus on weekends.
Annual Costs. Tuition and fees, $7,750; room and board, $3,200; estimated $1,200 other, exclusive of travel. About 65% of students receive financial aid; average amount of assistance, $4,000. Assistance is typically divided 35% scholarship/grant, 32% loan, 33% work. College reports 23 major scholarships awarded per year on the basis of academic merit alone, 60 minor scholarships, 650 for need.

Harding University

Searcy, Arkansas 72149 **(501) 279-4000**

A church-related university, seeking "provide academic excellence in a Christian environment." Harding is located in a town of 15,000, 40 miles northeast of Little Rock, in the foothills of the Ozark Mountains. Most convenient major airport: Little Rock.

Founded: 1919
Affiliation: Church of Christ
UG Enrollment: 1,458 M, 1,558 W (full-time); 92 M, 118 W (part-time)
Total Enrollment: 3,552
Cost: < $10K
% Receiving Financial Aid: 80%
Admission: Selective
Application Deadline: May 1

Admission is selective. About 61% of applicants accepted, 93% of these actually enroll; 65% of freshmen graduate in top fifth of high school class, 90% in top two-fifths. Average freshmen scores: SAT, 1050 total; ACT, 24 composite. *Required:* SAT or ACT; interview required. Criteria considered in admissions, in order of importance: high school academic record, standardized test scores, recommendations, extracurricular activities; other factors considered: special talents, diverse student body. About 25% of entering students from private schools. *Entrance programs:* early decision, early admission, midyear admission, deferred admission, advanced placement. *Apply* by May 1; rolling admissions. *Transfers* welcome; 150 enrolled 1993–94.

Academic Environment. Degrees offered: bachelors, masters. Graduation requirements include four 9-hour courses: Communication and Critical Thinking, Social Environment, The Natural World, Religion, a 7-hour course: The Creative Spirit, and two 6-hour courses: The Historical Perspective, and Global Literacy. Average undergraduate class size: 70% under 20, 20% 20–40, 10% over 40.

About 60% of entering freshmen graduate within four years; 65% eventually; 80% of freshmen return for sophomore year. *Special programs:* CLEP, independent study, study abroad (college-owned campus in Florence, programs in Athens and London), individualized majors, American Studies program. *Calendar:* semester, summer school.

Undergraduate degrees conferred (523). 23% were in Business and Management, 22% were in Education, 8% were in Psychology, 8% were in Health Sciences, 7% were in Communications, 4% were in Theology, 4% were in Life Sciences, 3% were in Social Sciences, 3% were in Computer and Engineering Related Technology, 3% were in Visual and Performing Arts, 3% were in Home Economics, remainder in 10 other fields.

Graduates Career Data. Advanced studies pursued by 36% of graduates; 26% enter graduate school; 4% enter medical school; 2% enter law school; 2% enter business school; 1% enter dental school. Medical schools typically enrolling largest numbers of graduates include U. of Arkansas, Johns Hopkins, U. of Missouri; dental schools include U. of Tennessee; law schools include U.of Arkansas, U. of Texas; business schools include U. of Arkansas, Duke, Harvard. About 99% of 1992–93 graduates employed. Fields typically hiring largest numbers of graduates include accounting, management, education, health. Career Development Services range from career exploration to final interviews.

Faculty. About 70% of faculty hold PhD or equivalent. About 90% of undergraduate classes taught by tenured faculty. About 30% of teaching faculty are female; 2% Black.

Student Body. About 25% of students from in state; 40% South, 25% Midwest, 15% West, 10% Middle Atlantic, 3% New England, 2% Northwest, 5% foreign. An estimated 95% of students reported as Protestant, 3% Catholic; 5% Black, 2% Hispanic, 1% Asian.

Religious Orientation. Harding is controlled by trustees who are members of the Church of Christ; students take religious classes all four years; daily chapel required of all students; attendance at Sunday morning and evening church services encouraged.

Varsity Sports. Men (NAIA): Baseball, Basketball, Cross Country, Football (AIC), Golf, Tennis, Track. Women (NAIA): Cross Country, Track, Volleyball.

Campus Life. College maintains a 1,200-acre camp in the Ozarks for student use, including horseback riding, hiking, backpacking, etc. About 70% of students live in traditional residence halls; 5% of men, 15% of women live in off-campus college-related housing; rest commute. No intervisitation in men's or women's dormitory rooms. There are no fraternities or sororities on campus. About 10% of resident students leave campus on weekends.

Annual Costs. Tuition and fees, $5,800; room and board, $3,800; estimated $1,000 other, exclusive of travel. About 80% of students receive financial aid; average amount of assistance, $4,000. Assistance is typically divided 20% scholarship, 20% grant, 40% loan, 20% work. University reports 1200 scholarships awarded on basis of academic merit alone, 100 for special talents alone, 200 for need alone. *Meeting Costs:* university offers payment plan.

Hardin-Simmons University

Abilene, Texas 79698 **(915) 670-1000**

A small, church-related university, located in a city of 100,000, 146 miles west of Fort Worth. Most convenient major airport: Abilene Municipal.

Founded: 1891
Affiliation: Southern Baptist
UG Enrollment: 649 M, 716 W (full-time); 133 M, 201 W (part-time)
Total Enrollment: 1,699
Cost: < $10K
% Receiving Financial Aid: 88%
Admission: Non-selective
Application Deadline: Rolling

Admission. Graduates of accredited high schools with 16 units (3 in vocational subjects allowed) eligible; 91% of applicants actually enroll; 39% of freshmen graduate in top fifth of high school class, 65% in top two-fifths. Average freshman scores: SAT, 470 verbal, 510 mathematical; 35% of freshmen score above 500 on verbal, 10% above 600, 1% above 700; 53% score above 500 on mathematical, 21% above 600, 2% above 700; ACT, 22 composite. *Required:* ACT or SAT. Criteria considered in admissions, in order of importance: standardized test scores, high school academic record. *Entrance programs:* early decision, early admission, midyear admission, deferred admission, advanced placement. *Apply:* rolling admissions. *Transfers* welcome; 148 enrolled 1993–94.

Academic Environment. Graduation requirements include 49 hours of basic core courses: English, social sciences, natural sciences, bible, humanities, math, oral communication, physical education, computer sciences; English proficiency required. Degrees offered: associates, bachelors, masters. Average undergraduate class size: 84% under 20, 14% 20–40, 2% over 40. About 33% of students entering as freshmen graduate eventually; 59% of freshmen return for sophomore year. *Special programs:* study abroad, cross registration with Abilene Christian, McMurry. *Calendar:* semester, summer school.

Undergraduate degrees conferred (253). 29% were in Education, 20% were in Business and Management, 8% were in Health Sciences, 5% were in Theology, 5% were in Public Affairs, 5% were in Protective Services, 5% were in Psychology, 4% were in Visual and Performing Arts, 4% were in Life Sciences, 3% were in Communications, 3% were in Letters, remainder in 7 other fields.

Faculty. About 76% of faculty hold PhD or equivalent. About 54% of undergraduate classes taught by tenured faculty. About 34% of teaching faculty are female.

Student Body. About 93% of students from in state; 4% West, 1% South, less than 1% foreign. An estimated 73% of students reported as Protestant, 7% Catholic, 15% unaffiliated, 5% other; 5% Black, 8% Hispanic, 1% Asian, 2% other minority. Average age of undergraduate student: 25.

Religious Orientation. Hardin-Simmons is a church-related institution; 58% of students affiliated with the church; 6 hours of religion, attendance at weekly chapel and assembly required of all students; attendance at Sunday school and church services encouraged.

Varsity Sports. Men: Baseball, Basketball, Football, Golf, Soccer, Tennis. Women: Basketball, Golf, Soccer, Tennis, Volleyball.

Campus Life. About 51% of men, 45% of women live in traditional dormitories; rest commute. No intervisitation in men's or women's dormitory rooms. There are 4 fraternities, 4 sororities which about 11% of men, 10% of women join.

Annual Costs. Tuition and fees, $6,780; room and board, $3,000; estimated $2,000 other, exclusive of travel. About 88% of students receive financial aid; average amount of assistance, $7,000. Assistance is typically divided 20% scholarship, 2% grant, 50% loan, 10% work. University reports 500 scholarships awarded on the basis of academic merit alone, 220 for special talents alone. *Meeting Costs:* college offers variety of payment plans and outside loan services.

Harpur College

(See State University of New York at Binghamton)

Harris-Stowe State College

St. Louis, Missouri 63103 **(314) 533-3000**

A municipal college for commuters, located in a metropolitan area of two million, Harris-Stowe prepares teachers and urban education professionals. Most convenient major airport: St. Louis.

Founded: 1857
Affiliation: City
Total Enrollment: 889 M, W (full-time)
Cost: < $10K
Admission: Non-selective
Application Deadline: August 20

Admission. Missouri graduates of accredited high schools with 11 units in academic subjects and C average eligible; about 90% of applicants accepted, 64% of those accepted actually enroll. *Required:* college's own examination, SAT or ACT, interview. *Non-academic factors* considered in admissions: diverse student body. *Apply* by August 20. *Transfers* welcome.

Academic Environment. *Degree:* BSEd, BSUrEd. About 10% of general education requirements for graduation are elective; distribution requirements fairly numerous. *Special programs:* CLEP, independent study, honors. *Calendar:* semester, summer school.
Undergraduate degrees conferred (62). 100% were in Education.
Student Body. About 97% of students from in state.
Varsity Sports. Men (NAIA): Baseball, Basketball, Soccer. Women (NAIA): Basketball, Softball, Volleyball.
Campus Life. No dormitories on campus. There are no sororities or fraternities on campus.
Annual Costs. Tuition and fees, $1,635 (out-of-state, $3,207). About 75% of students receive financial aid; assistance is typically divided 68% scholarship, 18% loan, 14% work. College reports some scholarships awarded on the basis of academic merit alone.

University of Hartford

West Hartford, Connecticut 06117 (203) 768-4296

An independent institution, the University of Hartford offers study for the associate, baccalaureate and master's degrees in 9 schools and colleges. The 320-acre main campus is located in a residential section of a suburban community of 68,000, adjoining Hartford. Most convenient major airport: Bradley International.

Founded: 1877
Affiliation: Independent
UG Enrollment: 1,933 M, 1,835 W (full-time); 748 M, 938 W (part-time)
Total Enrollment: 7,530
Cost: $10K–$20K
Admission: Non-selective
Application Deadline: Rolling

Admission. About 78% of applicants accepted, 29% of these actually enroll; 31% of freshmen graduate in top fifth of high school class. Average freshman SAT scores: 27% score above 500 on verbal, 5% above 600; 50% score above 500 on mathematical, 15% above 600. *Required:* SAT or ACT; interview recommended. Criteria considered in admissions, in order of importance: high school academic record, standardized test scores, recommendations, extracurricular activities. About 26% of entering students from private schools. *Entrance programs:* early admission, midyear admission, deferred admission, advanced placement. *Apply:* rolling admissions. *Transfers* welcome; 379 enrolled 1992–93.
Academic Environment. *Undergraduate studies* offered by colleges of Arts and Sciences, Education, Engineering, Hillyer College, Hartford College for Women, School of Business and Public Administration, Hartt School (music), Hartford Art School, Ward Technical College. Degrees offered: associates, bachelors, masters, doctoral. *Majors offered* include mechanical engineering technology, audio engineering technology, actuarial science, dance, medical technology, respiratory therapy, illustration, interdisciplinary student-designed "contract majors". Average undergraduate class size: "most" between 20 and 30.

About 47% of students entering as freshmen graduate within four years; 75% of freshmen return for sophomore year. *Special programs:* CLEP, independent study, honors, individualized majors, programs of Greater Hartford Consortium for Higher Education, Washington internship, study abroad, 5-year combined BS/MBA, cooperative work/study program in all schools; University Scholar Program; on-campus summer programs for elementary and high school students. *Calendar:* semester, summer school.
Undergraduate degrees conferred (1114). 20% were in Business and Management, 15% were in Communications, 12% were in Visual and Performing Arts, 12% were in Engineering, 8% were in Social Sciences, 8% were in Marketing and Distribution, 5% were in Education, 5% were in Psychology, 4% were in Engineering and Engineering Related Technology, 4% were in Letters, remainder in 10 other fields.
Graduate Career Data. About 85% of 1992–93 graduates employed. Career Development Services: "students are encouraged to seek help starting in freshman year; resume assistance, interest inventories, etc., are available."
Faculty. About 77% of faculty hold PhD or equivalent. About 29% of teaching faculty are female.
Student Body. About 33% of students from in state; 92% Northeast. An estimated 30% of students reported as Protestant, 40% Catholic, 25% Jewish; 7% as Black, 4% Hispanic, 2% Asian. *Minority group students:* special financial, academic (including special reading program for foreign students), writing, reading and mathematics labs, tutorial services, social provisions; African-American Student Association, International Student Association.
Varsity Sports. Men (Div.I): Baseball, Basketball, Cross Country, Golf, Lacrosse, Soccer, Tennis. Women (Div.I): Basketball, Cross Country, Soccer, Tennis, Track, Volleyball.
Campus Life. Campus is close to ski areas, beaches; accessible to Boston and NYC. Alcohol allowed in designated areas for those of legal age. Cars and motorbikes unrestricted except for parking.

About 70% of students live in apartment-style university housing, including a condominium; 2% live in traditional dormitories; rest commute. There are 8 fraternities, 5 sororities on campus, which about 12% of men, 12% of women join; they provide no residence facilities. About 15% of resident students leave campus on weekends.
Annual Costs. Tuition and fees, $14,260; room and board, $5,598; estimated $1,200 other, exclusive of travel. About 40% of students receive financial aid; average amount of assistance, $11,018. Assistance is typically divided 66% grant, 25% loan, 9% work. College reports academic scholarships awarded on the basis of class rank and SAT scores; talent scholarships awarded in art, music, and sports. *Meeting Costs:* college offers 10-month installment plan, long term educational loans.

Hartwick College

Oneonta, New York 13820-4020 (607) 431-4200

A private, liberal arts college, Hartwick was founded by Lutherans and maintained affiliation with the church until 1968 when it became independent. The college places special emphasis on its pre-professional and professional/vocational programs. It is located on a 375-acre campus in a town of 14,000, 23 miles south of Cooperstown, N.Y. The 1,100-acre Pine Lake campus, located 5 miles outside of Oneonta, is used for workshops in the arts, science studies, and recreation; major portion of campus designated an ecological preserve. Oneonta is also home of the SUNY College at Oneonta. Most convenient major airport: Albany.

Founded: 1797
Affiliation: Independent
Total Enrollment: 673 M, 783 W (full-time)
Cost: $10K–$20K
% Receiving Financial Aid: 85%
Admission: Selective
Application Deadline: Feb. 15

Admission is selective. About 82% of applicants accepted, 25% of these actually enroll; 41% of freshmen graduate in top fifth of high school class, 69% in top two-fifths. Average freshmen scores: SAT, 477 M, 479 W verbal, 531 M, 517 W mathematical; ACT, 23 composite. *Required:* SAT or ACT, audition for music; interview strongly recommended (on or off-campus). Criteria considered in admissions, in order of importance: high school academic record, standardized test scores, recommendations, extracurricular activities, writing sample; other factors considered: special talents, diverse student body. About 25% of freshmen from private schools. *Entrance programs:* early decision, early notification, midyear admission, deferred admission, advanced placement. *Apply* by February 15; rolling admissions. *Transfers* welcome; 53 enrolled 1993–94.
Academic Environment. Students may select one of 26 major areas of study or develop his or her own major with the advice of a faculty committee. Liberal arts curriculum (Curriculum XXI), includes foreign language, writing competency, one computer, logic, or math course, freshman seminar, baccalaureate thesis. Off-campus study programs, independent and directed study options encouraged; exchange program with Chaing Mai University (Thailand) recently introduced. Degrees offered: bachelors. *Majors offered* include science, management, ecology, and environmental studies, accounting. Small classes, accessible faculty, and friendly student body reported as strengths. Average undergraduate class size: 60% under 20, 37% 20–40, 3% over 40.

About 70–75%% of students entering as freshmen graduate eventually. About 82% of freshmen return for sophomore year. Starting in 1993, every first year student will receive a notebook sized computer, with modem and printer, and access to the on-campus network. *Special programs:* January Term, CLEP, honors, undergraduate research, internships, independent study, study abroad, outward bound, individualized majors, Washington Semester, United Nations Semester, cooperative programs of CCFL, 3–2 engineering with Columbia and Clarkson, cross-registration with SUNY Oneonta. Adult programs: R.N. Mobility Program. *Calendar:* 4–1–4.

Undergraduate degrees conferred (384). 29% were in Social Sciences, 21% were in Business and Management, 12% were in Letters, 8% were in Psychology, 7% were in Visual and Performing Arts, 5% were in Life Sciences, 4% were in Health Sciences, 3% were in Liberal/General Studies, 3% were in Physical Sciences, remainder in 5 other fields.

Graduates Career Data. Advanced studies pursued by 20% of graduates; 6% enter graduate school; 2% enter medical school; 2% enter law school; 6% enter business school. Medical schools typically enrolling largest numbers of graduates include Albany Medical, Upstate Medical Center, SUNY Buffalo; dental schools include Tufts, U. of Pennsylvania; law schools include Syracuse, Albany Law, American, Georgetown, Cornell, Suffolk. About 70% of 1992–93 graduates employed. Fields typically hiring largest numbers of graduates include human services, financial, management, education. Trustee Center for Professional Development provides career exploration, mentor program, and other career development services.

Faculty. About 87% of faculty hold PhD or equivalent. About 73% of undergraduate classes taught by tenured faculty. About 34% of teaching faculty are female; 1% Black, 2% Hispanic, 3% other minority.

Student Body. About 63% of students from in state; 73% Middle Atlantic, 24% New England; 1% each Midwest, South, 1% foreign. An estimated 45% of students reported as Catholic, 27% Protestant, 3% Jewish, 11% other or unaffiliated; 3% as Black, 2% Hispanic, 2% Asian.

Varsity Sports. Men (Div.III): Baseball, Basketball, Cross Country, Diving, Football, Golf, Lacrosse, Soccer (I), Swimming, Tennis, Track. Women (Div.III): Basketball, Cross Country, Diving, Golf, Field Hockey, Lacrosse, Soccer, Softball, Swimming, Tennis, Track, Volleyball.

Campus Life. Rural location, in the Catskill Mountain foothills, provides opportunities for outdoor recreation; skiing reported "very big." Sporting events, especially soccer, reported popular. "Main Street is very accessible"; and students also report wide range of cultural and social activities on campus; Albany and Binghamton are an hour away. Cars permitted for all students; but parking reported to be a problem. Intervisitation hours determined by each residence hall; rules enforced "judiciously." Off-campus living privileges for juniors and seniors.

About 71% of students live in coed dormitories; 21% live in off-campus college-related housing; rest commute. There are 4 fraternities, 4 sororities on campus which about 23% of men, 26% of women join; 7% live in fraternities and sororities. About 10% of resident students leave campus on weekends.

Annual Costs. Tuition and fees, $16,400; room and board, $4,550; estimated $1,000 other, exclusive of travel. About 85% of students receive financial aid; average amount of assistance, $12,907. Assistance is typically divided 53% scholarship/grant, 41% loan, 6% work. College reports 152 scholarships awarded on the basis of academic merit alone, 99 for special talents alone, 278 for need alone. *Meeting Costs:* college offers Parent Aid Loan, installment plan.

Harvard University

Cambridge, Massachusetts 02138

Harvard is perhaps best described in the words of former President Charles W. Eliot as "the oldest, the richest, and the freest" American university. The 2 major undergraduate divisions, amid a galaxy of famous graduate and professional schools, are Harvard College for men and Radcliffe College for women. They have a joint admissions office, all classes are co-educational, and students receive a Harvard degree. The main campus is located just across the Charles River from Boston in a city of 100,400.

Total Enrollment: 18,437 total graduate and undergraduate

Admission is among the most selective in the country. About 15% of applicants accepted, 73% of these actually enroll; 95% of freshmen graduate in top fifth of high school class, 100% in top two-fifths. Average freshman SAT scores: Harvard and Radcliffe Colleges modestly report SAT scores ranging from 500–800. Average scores are "not released." However, on those rare occasions when average SAT scores do become public they are in the mid- to upper 600's to low 700's. Yet the reported range of all scores is correct. For many years Harvard has admitted some students whose scores are far below the university's average (though they must demonstrate ability to do "Harvard level" work) who have demonstrated truly extraordinary talent and accomplishment in one or more fields. In other words, Harvard leavens its mass of bright, well-rounded students with a limited number of oddballs.

Required: SAT, 3 ACH including English Composition, interview. *Non-academic factors* considered in admissions: diverse student body, special talents, alumni children, athletics. *Entrance programs:* early action, deferred admission. About 36% of entering students from private schools. *Apply* by January 1. *Transfers* welcome.

Undergraduate degrees conferred (1733). 46% were in Social Sciences, 10% were in Letters, 8% were in Life Sciences, 7% were in Liberal/General Studies, 5% were in Physical Sciences, 5% were in Psychology, 4% were in Foreign Languages, 4% were in Visual and Performing Arts, 3% were in Mathematics, 3% were in Philosophy and Religion, remainder in 3 other fields.

Doctoral degrees: Social Sciences 61, Education 68, Physical Sciences 42, Biological Sciences 24, Letters 14, Health Professions 51, Business and Management 9, Foreign Languages 21, Psychology 10, Fine and Applied Arts 12, Mathematics 13, Area Studies 8, Engineering 25, Theology 6, Architecture and Environmental Design 2, Law 9, Philosophy and Religion 7, Interdisciplinary Studies 3.

Faculty. About 99% of faculty hold PhD or equivalent; very high percentage hold doctorate earned at nation's leading graduate schools.

Religious Orientation. Historically, Harvard developed out of the New England Protestant tradition—has been nonsectarian for several generations.

Varsity Sports. Men (Div.I): Baseball, Basketball, Crew, Cross Country, Fencing, Football, Golf, Ice Hockey, Lacrosse, Sailing, Skiing (Alpine & Nordic), Squash, Soccer, Swimming, Tennis, Track, Volleyball, Water Polo, Wrestling. Women (Div.I): Basketball, Crew, Cross Country, Fencing, Field Hockey, Lacrosse, Ice Hockey, Sailing, Skiing (Alpine & Nordic), Soccer, Softball, Squash, Swimming, Tennis, Track, Volleyball, Water Polo.

Harvard College

(617) 495-1551

Admission to either Harvard or Radcliffe remains the ultimate in college choice for a vastly larger number of highly qualified students than can ever be accommodated.

Founded: 1636
Affiliation: Independent
Total Enrollment: 3,853 M (full-time)
Cost: $10K–$20K
% Receiving Financial Aid: 66%
Admission: Most Selective
Application Deadline: Jan. 1

Admission. (See Harvard University)

Academic Environment. Students have influence in curriculum matters through Committee on Undergraduate Education, a student-faculty committee, which also publishes a guide to courses. Graduation requirements include a modified general education curriculum with firm requirements. Pressures for academic achievement are rigorous. In the words of one student "Someone said, 'The hardest thing about Harvard is getting in'—NOT TRUE!" College environment likely to be extraordinarily gratifying to the scholar, the intellectual, "and the highly motivated student of more modest academic aptitude who has serious interests in a wide range of extracurricular activities from Athletics to Zen." But it can overwhelm the unprepared. There is "a strong cultural and intellectual life outside the classroom." Graduate School of Arts and Sciences shares faculty and facilities with college—this is reason college is called a "University College"; capable undergraduates may take graduate courses. With very high proportion of students anticipating entrance to highly selective graduate and professional schools, college seeks to preserve integrity of liberal education in undergraduate years from pressures for early specialization, but it is difficult to buck the nationwide tide. *Degree:* AB. *Majors offered* include wide range of arts and sciences in 40 fields, including Afro-American studies, anthropology, applied mathematics, astronomy, biochemical sciences, computer science, engineering, East Asian languages, Sanskrit and Indian studies, Scandinavian, statistics, visual and environmental studies, women's studies, as well as combined and interdisciplinary majors.

About 78% of students entering as freshmen graduate within four years, 97% eventually; 98% of freshmen return for sophomore year. *Special programs:* independent study, study abroad, honors, undergraduate research, 3-year degree, individualized majors, post-baccalaureate engineering program leading to BS, freshman seminars, cross-registration with all Harvard graduate schools and MIT. *Calendar:* semester, summer school.

Graduates Career Data. According to most recent data, full-time graduate or professional study pursued immediately after graduation by 31% of students (86% eventually); 10% (14% eventually) enter medical school; 6% (15% eventually) enter law school; 1% (14% eventually) enter business school. Medical, dental, law, and business schools typically enrolling largest numbers of graduates include Harvard, Columbia, Einstein, NYU. *Careers in business and industry* pursued by 19% of graduates.

Student Body. About 18% of students from in state; 33% Middle Atlantic, 23% New England, 24% West/Northwest, 13% South, 3% North Central. An estimated 50% of students reported as Protestant, 20% each Catholic, Jewish, 10% unaffiliated; 6% as Black, 5% Asian, 17% other minority, according to most recent data available. *Minority group students:* financial aid available; black and other minority graduate students are members of the staff of the residential houses serving as resident tutors and proctors.

Campus Life. Harvard and Radcliffe students live in residence "houses" on both campuses—all are coed. The House system is the norm, providing intellectual, social, and recreational opportunities. One recent student observes "Living on campus is crucial towards enhancing extracurriculars and social life." Harvard Square, the cultural center of student life, offers "clubs, bars, restaurants, movies. It's all around us." Cultural and intellectual activities on campus and in adjacent Boston are diverse enough to satisfy any taste. The Cambridge/Boston area is still the student Mecca of the U.S. Cars permitted on campus. Smoking not prohibited, but there are "no cigarette machines on campus."

About 96% of men live in coed dormitories; rest live in off-campus housing. Sexes segregated in coed dormitories by room. There are no fraternities on campus.

Annual Costs. Tuition and fees, $18,745; room and board, $6,135. About 66% of students receive financial aid; assistance is typically divided 67% scholarship, 24% loan, 9% work. College reports scholarships awarded only on the basis of need. *Meeting Costs:* university offers monthly and installment payment plans, pre-payment option, PLUS, Parent Loan Plan.

Radcliffe College

(617) 495-1551

"Radcliffe is an integral part of Harvard University. Radcliffe retains her independent corporate status and programs such as the Radcliffe Seminars, the Radcliffe Institute Fellowship Program and the Schlesinger Library on the History of Women in America. All Radcliffe and Harvard Houses are co-residential and students of both colleges share classes under Harvard's Faculty of Arts and Sciences and receive Harvard degrees." Since 1975–76 a joint Harvard-Radcliffe Admissions office selects undergraduates through an "equal access" process in which the same criteria apply to both women and men. As in all other areas of campus life women are treated no differently than men.

Founded: 1879
Affiliation: Independent
Total Enrollment: 2,692 W (full-time)
Cost: $10K–$20K
% Receiving Financial Aid: 66%
Admission: Most Selective
Application Deadline: Jan. 1

Admission. (See Harvard University)

Academic Environment. Judging solely by several reasonably objective measures of academic capacity, Radcliffe women have no trouble competing with Harvard men. Both student bodies are among the most academically capable in the country. As at Harvard College, all students take core curriculum with firm general education requirements. *Degree:* AB. *Majors offered* include wide range of arts and sciences in 40 fields, including Afro-American studies, anthropology, applied mathematics, astronomy, biochemical sciences, computer science, engineering, East Asian languages, Sanskrit and Indian studies, Scandinavian, statistics, visual and environmental studies, women's studies, as well as combined and interdisciplinary majors.

About 78% of students entering as freshmen graduate within four years; 97% eventually; 98% of freshmen return for sophomore year for academic reasons. *Special programs:* independent study, study abroad, honors, undergraduate research, individualized majors, freshman seminars, 3-year degree. *Calendar:* semester, summer school.

Undergraduate degrees conferred (643). 34% were in Social Sciences, 16% were in Letters, 10% were in Life Sciences, 9% were in Multi/Interdisciplinary Studies, 8% were in Psychology, 6% were in Foreign Languages, 6% were in Visual and Performing Arts, 4% were in Physical Sciences, 3% were in Area and Ethnic Studies, remainder in 5 other fields.

Graduates Career Data. According to most recent data available, full-time graduate or professional study pursued immediately after graduation by 31% of students (86% eventually); 10% (14% eventually) enter medical school; 6% (15% eventually) enter law school; 1% (14% eventually) enter business school. Medical, dental, law, and business schools typically enrolling largest numbers of graduates include Harvard, Columbia, Einstein, NYU. *Careers in business and industry* pursued by 19% of graduates.

Student Body. About 18% of students from in state; 33% Middle Atlantic, 23% New England, 24% West/Northwest, 13% South, 3% North Central. An estimated 50% of students reported as Protestant, 20% each Catholic, Jewish, 10% unaffiliated; 6% Black, 5% Asian, 17% other minority, according to most recent data available. *Minority group students:* financial aid available; black and other minority graduate students are members of the staff of the residential Houses, serving as resident tutors and proctors.

Campus Life. Character of campus life significantly affected by coed living. No parietals or limitation of freshman hours. Although there are more men on campus than women, the number of women is high enough to make undergraduate life genuinely co-educational. About 95% of women live in coed dormitories; rest live in off-campus housing. All freshmen offered housing. There are no sororities on campus.

Annual Costs. Tuition and fees, $18,745; room and board, $6,135. About 66% of students receive financial aid; assistance typically divided 67% scholarship, 24% loan, 9% work. College reports scholarships awarded only on the basis of need. *Meeting Costs:* university offers monthly and installment payment plans, pre-payment option, PLUS, Parent Loan Plan.

Harvey Mudd College

Claremont, California 91711 (909) 621-8011

Founded to produce annually a small crop of highly educated engineers and scientists who have devoted at least one-third of their study to the humanities and social sciences, Harvey Mudd has become one of the most selective colleges in the country. No student need fail to apply because of lack of funds, since the college is able to aid nearly all qualified applicants. Most convenient major airport: Ontario International.

Founded: 1955
Affiliation: Independent
Total Enrollment: 505 M, 149 W (full-time)
Cost: $10K–$20K
% Receiving Financial Aid: 50%
Admission: Most Selective
Application Deadline: Feb. 1

Admission is among the most selective in the country (see also The Claremont Colleges.) About 42% of applicants accepted, 31% of these actually enroll; 90% of freshmen graduate in top tenth of high school class, 100% graduate in top two-tenths. Average freshman scores: SAT, 630 M, 630 W verbal, 740 M, 710 W mathematical; 98% score above 500 on verbal, 75% above 600, 21% above 700; all score above 600 on mathematical, 85% above 700. *Required:* SAT, 3 ACH (including mathematics II and English Composition), essay; interview strongly recommended. Criteria considered in admissions, in order of importance: high school academic record, standardized test scores, extracurricular activities, recommendations, writing sample.

Entrance programs: early decision, deferred admission. *Apply* by February 1. *Transfers* welcome; 7 enrolled 1993–94.
Academic Environment. Pressures for academic achievement are very intense. Only students with strong aptitude and background in mathematics and physical sciences feel at home. Verbal ability of students also greater than usual among science and engineering students. Recent student observes "It is difficult for students who did so well in high school to deal with the rigorous curriculum—they are used to doing well with little effort." Science programs offer strong preparation for graduate study; engineering has design emphasis. Nearly all students are involved in research as engineers in an Engineering Clinic which undertakes to solve real problems brought to the

college by industry and other agencies. One student leader observed that an entering freshman "should be sure that he or she wants to be a chemist, physicist, mathematician, or engineer." (Administration source adds biologist and computer scientist, to the list.) Relatively heavy emphasis, nevertheless, on humanities and social sciences; 32% of courses must be in these two areas, 33% in technical requirements, 35% in major and electives. Faculty reported to be primarily oriented toward teaching; classes reported to be small. College has an honor code. Student leader notes "intensity of work load," while administration calls academic program "rigorous, competitive, time consuming." Relations with faculty are said to be "personal and informal." Degrees offered: bachelors, masters. *Majors offered* include chemistry, engineering, mathematics, physics; individual program of studies may also be designed.

About 75% of students entering as freshmen graduate eventually; 89% of freshmen return for sophomore year. *Special programs:* independent study, individualized majors, directed reading, 5-year BS/ME, Bates Aeronautics Program, 3–2 engineering management with Claremont McKenna, cross registration with other Claremont Colleges, exchange programs with Rensselaer and Swarthmore.

Calendar: semester.
Undergraduate degrees conferred (121). 49% were in Engineering, 35% were in Physical Sciences, 12% were in Mathematics, remainder in 3 other fields.
Graduates Career Data. Advanced studies pursued by 53% of graduates. Graduate schools typically enrolling largest numbers of graduates include: UC Berkeley, UC San Diego, Cal Tech, Stanford. About 37% of 1992–93 graduates employed. Corporations typically hiring largest numbers of graduates include Andersen Consulting, Hewlett-Packard, Microsoft, Teradyne Inc. Career Development Services include skills development workshops, career fair, individual counseling, interest/skills assessment tools, graduate school programing.
Faculty. All faculty hold PhD or equivalent. About 60% of undergraduate classes taught by tenured faculty. About 18% of teaching faculty are female; 3% Black, 3% Hispanic, 8% other minority..
Student Body. About 49% from in state; 71% West, 16% Northwest, 14% Midwest, 6% Middle Atlantic, 4% South, 2% New England, 2% foreign. An estimated 22% of students reported as Asian, 4% Hispanic, 2% Black.
Varsity Sports. Men (Div.III): Baseball, Basketball, Cross Country, Diving, Football, Golf, Lacrosse, Soccer, Swimming, Tennis, Track. Women (Div.III): Basketball, Cross Country, Diving, Golf, Soccer, Softball, Swimming, Tennis, Track, Volleyball.
Campus Life. Proximity to the other Claremont colleges expands extracurricular opportunities: "Activities on our campus and others abound." Much of the time outside of classes "IS spent studying, but other than that students participate in intramural sports, varsity sports, music, student government, theater groups, and many, many other things." Cars allowed but are not to be used for commuting among the Claremont colleges.

About 98% of men, 80% of women live in coed dormitories; rest commute. Intervisitation in men's and women's dormitory rooms unlimited. There are no fraternities or sororities on campus. About 10% of resident students leave campus on weekends.
Annual Costs. Tuition and fees, $16,876; room and board, $6,440; estimated $1,500 other, exclusive of travel. About 50% of students receive financial aid; average amount of assistance, $15,604. Assistance is typically divided 70% scholarship, 23% loan, 7% work. College reports 321 scholarships awarded on the basis of need alone. *Minority group students:* financial aid based on need. *Meeting Costs:* college offers 10-month payment plan, outside financing plans.

Hastings College

Hastings, Nebraska 68902 **(402) 461-7315 or (800) 532-7642**

A church-related, liberal arts college, located in a town of 23,600, 150 miles west of Omaha. Most convenient major airport: Lincoln (NE).

Founded: 1882
Affiliation: Presbyterian Church (USA)
Total Enrollment: 458 M, 477 W (full-time)
Cost: < $10K
% Receiving Financial Aid: 95%
Admission: Selective
Application Deadline: July 15

Admission is selective. About 87% of applicants accepted, 37% of these actually enroll; 45% of freshmen graduate in top fifth of high school class, 70% in top two-fifths. Average freshman ACT scores: 23 composite. *Required:* ACT or SAT. Criteria considered in admissions, in order of importance: high school academic record, standardized test scores, recommendations, extracurricular activities, writing sample; other factors considered: special talents, diverse student body, alumni children, religious affiliation/commitment. *Entrance programs:* early admission, midyear admission. *Apply* by July 15. *Transfers* welcome; 37 enrolled 1993–94.
Academic Environment. Degrees offered: bachelors, masters. Graduation requirements include 6 hours each social science, fine arts, physical education, 2 hours science, 18 hours humanities, 1 course in religious studies. Recent student applauds the "non-threatening atmosphere" for learning and the faculty focus on teaching. Average undergraduate class size: 50% under 20, 50% 20–40.

About 50% of students entering as freshmen graduate eventually; 74% of freshmen return for sophomore year. *Special programs:* CLEP, independent study, directed study, internships, personalized program, 3–2 engineering, 3–2 occupational therapy, ATLAS (Action Toward Learning Academic Success). Adult programs: 22 PLUS Program, one-half scholarship for first 60 hours of credit. *Calendar:* 4–1–4.
Undergraduate degrees conferred (172). 17% were in Education, 14% were in Business and Management, 12% were in Social Sciences, 10% were in Psychology, 9% were in Multi/Interdisciplinary Studies, 8% were in Life Sciences, 8% were in Letters, 6% were in Physical Sciences, 6% were in Communications, 5% were in Visual and Performing Arts, 3% were in Mathematics, remainder in 2 other fields.
Graduates Career Data. Advanced studies pursued by 24% of graduates; 17% enter graduate school; 3% enter law school; 2% enter medical school; 1% enter dental school. Medical schools typically enrolling largest numbers of graduates include U. of Nebraska Medical Center; dental schools include U. of Nebraska; law schools include Creighton U., U. of Nebraska; business schools include U. of Texas at Austin. About 98% of 1992–93 graduates employed. Fields and corporations typically hiring largest numbers of graduates include accounting, Coopers & Lybrand, Country General, FDIC. Career Development Services include career counseling, interest and personality testing, Career Alumni Network, resume, interview, and letter writing assistance, career seminars.
Faculty. About 63% of faculty hold PhD or equivalent. About 54% of undergraduate classes taught by tenured faculty. About 25% of teaching faculty are female.
Student Body. About 78% of students from in state; 89% from Midwest, 10% West, 1% foreign. An estimated 68% of students reported as Protestant, 20% Catholic, 11% other; 3% Black, 2% Hispanic. Average age of undergraduate student: 22.
Religious Orientation. Hastings is a church-related institution; course in Christian religion required of all students. Weekly chapel optional. Religious activities on campus coordinated by Religious Programs Committee.
Varsity Sports. Men (NAIA): Baseball, Basketball, Cross Country, Football, Golf, Tennis, Track. Women (NAIA): Basketball, Cross Country, Golf, Softball, Tennis, Track, Volleyball.
Campus Life. Student reports "Campus organizations include a local greek system, a strong Christian outreach program, and an athletic intramural program." Intervisitation permitted during scheduled open hours. Possession or use of alcohol forbidden on campus or at any college-related activity. Cars allowed. Students required to live in college housing if space available.

About 41% of men, 39% of women live in traditional dormitories; 9% of men, 18% of women in coed dormitories; rest live in off-campus housing or commute. Freshmen given preference in college housing if all students cannot be accommodated. There are 4 fraternities, 4 sororities on campus which about 31% of men, 43% of women join; they provide no residence facilities. About 50% of resident students leave campus on weekends.

Annual Costs. Tuition and fees, $8,920; room and board, $3,130; estimated $2,000 other, exclusive of travel. About 95% of students receive financial aid; average amount of assistance, $7,994. Assistance is typically divided 51% scholarship, 8% grant, 74% loan, 42% work. *Minority group students:* special financial provisions. College reports 619 scholarships awarded on the basis of academic merit alone, 646 for need alone. *Meeting Costs:* college offers 9, 10, and 12-month payment plans.

Haverford College

Haverford, Pennsylvania 19041-1392 (610) 896-1000

One of the smallest major academic institutions in the country, and overshadowed by its better-known Quaker neighbors, Swarthmore and Bryn Mawr, Haverford nevertheless holds its own in the acquisition of academic honors for its graduates. The college has long had a quasi-coordinate relationship with Bryn Mawr, just a mile away. Despite the fact that Haverford went coed in 1980, relations between the two schools remain extremely close; students live, eat, take courses and major at either campus. The 216-acre campus is located in a Main Line suburb, 10 miles west of the center of Philadelphia. Most convenient major airport: Philadelphia.

Founded: 1833
Affiliation: Independent (Friends)
Total Enrollment: 563 M, 521 W (full-time)
Cost: $10K–$20K
% Receiving Financial Aid: 45%
Admission: Most Selective
Application Deadline: January 15

Admission is among the most selective in the country. About 44% of applicants accepted, 32% of these actually enroll; 97% of freshmen graduate in top fifth of high school class, all in top two-fifths. Freshman SAT scores, middle 50% range; 580–660 verbal, 620–720 mathematical; 95% score above 500 on verbal, 71% above 600, 14% above 14, 97% score above 500 on mathematical, 86% above 600, 39% above 700. *Required:* SAT, 3 ACH including English Composition, interview if student lives within 150 miles of school, recommendation. Criteria considered in admissions, in order of importance: high school academic record, standardized test scores, recommendations, extracurricular activities, writing sample; other factors considered: diverse student body, special talents, alumni children. *Entrance programs:* early decision, early admission, deferred admission, advanced placement. About 40% of entering students from private or parochial schools. *Apply* by January 15. *Transfers* welcome; 2 enrolled 1993–94.

Academic Environment. As a result of the complete cooperative arrangement with Bryn Mawr, some departments are federated and most plan curriculum jointly to avoid duplication. There are more than 3,500 cross-registrations annually. Cooperative programs with Swarthmore and U. of Pennsylvania also expand opportunities. Students permitted to take 1- or 2-semester leave from college to work or study elsewhere. Graduation requirements include 3 courses in each of the 3 academic divisions of the College: Humanities, Natural Sciences, and Social Sciences. One of the 9 courses must fulfill the quantitative reasoning requirement. Freshman writing, 1 year of foreign language, and 1 course meeting the social justice requirement must also be part of a student's program. The academic program at Haverford is described as "rigorous and demanding," but administration source asserts that "there is very little competition among students for grades." Students concur: "The academic atmosphere at Haverford is by far its best attribute. We do a highly competitive level of work, without letting it affect our ability to be relaxed, cooperative, and get the most out of classes by truly enjoying them." Classes are small, seminar-style, emphasis is on the individual; many opportunities for independent study. Strong honor system governs both academic and social affairs; students allowed to schedule their exams at their own convenience during exam period, and take them without supervision. Degrees offered: bachelors. *Majors offered* include astronomy, comparative literature, East Asian studies, biochemistry, biophysics. Average undergraduate class size: 72% under 20, 20% 20–40, 8% over 40.

About 84% of students entering as freshmen graduate within four years; 92% eventually; 98% of freshmen return for sophomore year. *Special programs:* independent study, study abroad (46 programs in 24 countries), undergraduate research, 3-year degree, individualized majors, freshman seminars, Princeton Critical Languages Program, courses for double credit, African studies, 3–2 engineering with U. of Pennsylvania, cross registration with Bryn Mawr, Swarthmore, U. of Pennsylvania, dual majors, self-designed majors. *Calendar:* semester.

Undergraduate degrees conferred (301). 36% were in Social Sciences, 17% were in Letters, 12% were in Philosophy and Religion, 11% were in Life Sciences, 10% were in Physical Sciences, 5% were in Foreign Languages, 4% were in Psychology, 3% were in Visual and Performing Arts, remainder in 3 other fields.

Graduates Career Data. Advanced studies pursued within 5 years of graduation by 60% of graduates. Immediately following graduation: 16% enter graduate school; 7% enter medical or dental school; 5% enter law school; 1% enter business school. Medical schools typically enrolling largest numbers of graduates include: Columbia, Cornell, Jefferson; law schools include: American, Duke, Georgetown; business schools include Duke, Harvard, MIT. About 58% of 1991–92 graduates employed. Career Development Services include assistance in investigating career interests, developing search methods, internship database, alumni network, active recruiting program, resume referral service, participation in graduate and professional school forum.

Faculty. About 99% of tenure-track faculty hold PhD or equivalent. About 60% of classes taught by tenured faculty. About 40% of teaching faculty are female; 6% Black, 6% Hispanic, 6% other minority.

Student Body. About 16% of students from in state; 42% Middle Atlantic, 20% South, 17% New England, 7% Midwest, 7% Pacific, 3% West, 4% foreign. An estimated 5% of students reported as Black, 4% Hispanic, 9% Asian.

Religious Orientation. A school founded by Quakers, Haverford retains some of the flavor of its origins. Every Tuesday the period from 10–11 am is reserved for "Collection," a speaker's series. No compulsory religious activities; attendance at weekly Fifth Day Meeting voluntary.

Varsity Sports. Men (Div.III): Baseball, Basketball, Cricket, Cross Country, Fencing (Coed), Lacrosse, Soccer, Squash, Tennis, Track, Wrestling. Women (Div.III): Basketball, Cross Country, Fencing, Field Hockey, Lacrosse, Soccer, Softball, Squash, Tennis, Track, Volleyball.

Campus Life. Students have virtually complete control over their own social life. Haverford and Bryn Mawr student governments coordinate the many activities open to students of both colleges. Socializing with professors and administrators outside of their official capacity is common. Approximately three-fourths of faculty live on campus which fosters close ties between faculty and students. Social regulations covered by student-created and -administered Honor Code. Elected student representatives on Board of Managers (trustees) and students serve on almost all faculty and administrative committees, all of which operate by consensus. Expanded coed living with Bryn Mawr; bus runs regularly between 2 campuses. Cars permitted for all except freshmen.

About 31% of men, 28% of women live in traditional dormitories; 66% of men, 69% of women in coed dormitories; 3% live in off-campus housing. Freshmen given preference in college housing if all students cannot be accommodated. Sexes segregated in coed dormitories either by floor or room. There are no fraternities or sororities on campus. About 10% of resident students leave campus on weekends.

Annual Costs. Tuition and fees, $18,000; room and board, $5,950; estimated $1,575 other, exclusive of travel. About 45% of students receive financial aid; average amount of assistance for freshmen receiving grants, $16,197. Assistance is typically divided 71% grant, 13% loan, 8% work, 8% other (Pell, SEOG, outside scholarships). College reports scholarships awarded only on the basis of need. *Meeting Costs:* college offers monthly payment plan.

Hawaii Pacific College

(See Hawaii Pacific University)

Hawaii Pacific University

Honolulu, Hawaii 96813 **(808) 544-0200**

Hawaii Pacific university has an urban, downtown campus and a residential, suburban campus, eight miles apart, linked by shuttle. Most convenient major airport: Honolulu International.

Founded: 1965
Affiliation: Independent
UG Enrollment: 2,163 M, 2,181 W (full-time); 1,373 M, 897 W (part-time)
Total Enrollment: 7,526
Cost: < $10K
% Receiving Financial Aid: 25%
Admission: Non-selective
Application Deadline: Rolling

Admission. High school graduates eligible; 78% of applicants accepted, 79% of these actually enroll; 10% of freshmen graduate in top fifth of high school class, 30% in top two-fifths. Average freshman scores: SAT, 478 verbal, 525 mathematical. *Required:* SAT, interview. Criteria considered in admissions, in order of importance: high school academic record, standardized test scores, recommendations, extracurricular activities, writing sample. *Entrance programs:* early decision, midyear admission, deferred admission, advanced placement. *Apply:* rolling admissions. *Transfers* welcome; 700 enrolled 1993–94.

Academic Environment. Degrees offered: associates, bachelors, masters. Graduation requirements include lower and upper division courses in communication skills, research/epistemology, global systems, world cultures, values and choices. *Majors offered* include travel management, credit management, entrepreneurial studies, Pacific studies, marine science, nursing, international studies. Average undergraduate class size: 15% under 20, 80% 20–40, 5% over 40.

About 65% of students entering as freshmen graduate within four years; 70% of freshmen return for sophomore year. *Special programs:* study abroad, 3–2 in engineering. Adult programs: Adult & Continuing Education Program offers evening, weekend and late afternoon courses, special counseling; primary majors are human services, and human resource development. *Calendar:* semester, accelerated sessions, summer school.

Undergraduate degrees conferred (439). 61% were in Business and Management, 19% were in Computer and Engineering Related Technology, 10% were in Marketing and Distribution, 4% were in Public Affairs, 3% were in Education, remainder in 4 other fields.

Graduates Career Data. Advanced studies pursued by 65% of graduates. About 80% of 1992–93 graduates employed. Fields typically hiring largest numbers of graduates include travel industry, business, technical (computers), not-for-profit organizations.

Faculty. About 77% of faculty hold PhD or equivalent. About 75% of undergraduate classes taught by tenured faculty.

Student Body. About 44% of students from in state; 50% West, 10% Northwest, 5% South, 3% New England, 3% Middle Atlantic, 2% Midwest, 27% foreign. Average age of undergraduate student: 25.

Varsity Sports. Men (NAIA): Baseball, Basketball, Cross Country, Golf, Soccer, Tennis. Women (NAIA): Cross Country, Softball, Tennis, Volleyball.

Campus Life. About 2% of students live in traditional dormitories; 5% live in off-campus college-related housing; rest commute. There are no fraternities or sororities on campus.

Annual Costs. Tuition and fees, $5,900; room and board, $6,400; estimated $1,300 other, exclusive of travel. About 25% of students receive financial aid; average amount of assistance, $3,500. Assistance is typically divided 10% scholarship, 15% grant, 50% loan, 25% work. College reports 100 scholarships awarded on the basis of academic merit alone, 225 for special talents alone, 600 for need alone.

University of Hawaii at Manoa

Honolulu, Hawaii 96822 **(808) 956-8975**

A multiracial student body, an unusually attractive location, and the East-West Center, which is on campus, make the University of Hawaii unique among the nation's state universities. The 300-acre campus is located in the Manoa Valley, 3 miles from the center of Honolulu. A 4-year branch campus is located in Hilo on the island of Hawaii, about 200 miles southeast of Honolulu. A community college system was established in 1965 with a 2-year transfer program from all 7 campuses. Most convenient major airport: Honolulu International.

Founded: 1907
Affiliation: State
UG Enrollment: 4,980 M, 5,996 W (full-time); 1,154 M, 1,221 W (part-time)
Total Enrollment: 20,037
Cost: < $10K
% Receiving Financial Aid: 42%
Admission: Non-selective
Application Deadline: May 1

Admission. Requirements vary slightly among the undergraduate schools and programs; standard college preparatory course and demonstrated ability to do college-level work covers most prerequisites; 64% of applicants accepted, 40% of these actually enroll. Average freshman scores: SAT, 441 verbal, 601 mathematical. *Required:* SAT. *Out-of-state* freshman applicants: university does not actively seek students from out of state. State limits out-of-state enrollment to 20% of entering class. Requirement for out-of-state applicants: minimum SAT 960 combined, 3.2 GPA. Criteria considered in admissions, in order of importance: high school academic record, standardized test scores, recommendations, extracurricular activities. *Entrance programs:* early admission, advanced placement. *Apply* by May 1; rolling admissions. *Transfers* welcome; 1,759 enrolled 1993–94.

Academic Environment. Hawaii offers exceptional opportunities for study in several areas, notably oceanography, marine biology, sociology, and Asian and Pacific studies. All undergraduates take core program consisting of 3 semesters each in arts and humanities, natural sciences, social sciences, 2 semesters in world civilization, 1 semester each expository writing and math/logic, and 4 semesters of foreign language or Hawaiian; in addition, 5 courses must be writing intensive. The East-West Center, set up by act of Congress, adds a unique dimension to both academic and social life. The Center concentrates on coordinating programs "seeking solutions to problems of mutual concern to East and West." Projects involve communications, population, food, a program in cross-cultural understanding and technological development. The East-West Center does not offer formal academic instruction; most of its grantees attend U. of Hawaii, which offers special facilities, including intensive instruction in English as a second language. Fellowships available for American students interested in Asian studies, overseas operations, or Pacific Islands studies offered by university. *Undergraduate studies* offered by colleges of Arts and Sciences, Business Administration, Engineering, Tropical Agriculture, School of Hawaiian, Asian and Pacific Studies; juniors may enter College of Education, School of Nursing. Degrees offered: bachelors, masters, doctoral. *Majors offered* include Hawaiian language, Hawaiian studies.

About 51% of students entering as freshmen graduate eventually. *Special programs:* CLEP, honors, individualized majors, liberal studies, study abroad non-major degree program, freshmen seminars, ethnic studies, National Student Exchange. Adult program: College of Continuing Education and Community Services; Center for Adults Returning to Education. *Calendar:* semester, summer school.

Undergraduate degrees conferred (2362). 26% were in Business and Management, 13% were in Social Sciences, 7% were in Education, 7% were in Engineering, 6% were in Communications, 6% were in Psychology, 5% were in Letters, 5% were in Health Sciences, 5% were in Visual and Performing Arts, 4% were in Life Sciences, remainder in 14 other fields.

Faculty. About 77% of faculty hold PhD or equivalent.

Student Body. About 84% of students from in state. An estimated 56% of students reported as Asian, 1% Black, 1% Hispanic, 17% other minority. Age of average undergraduate student: 22.5.

Varsity Sports. Men (Div.I): Baseball, Basketball, Football, Golf, Sailing, Swimming & Diving, Tennis, Volleyball. Women (Div.I): Basketball, Cross Country, Golf, Sailing, Softball, Swimming & Diving, Tennis, Volleyball.

Campus Life. About 32% of men, 43% of women live in traditional or coed dormitories; rest live in off-campus housing or commute. Freshmen given preference in college housing if all students cannot be accommodated. There are 8 fraternities, 7 sororities on campus, which about 10% of each join. About 25% of resident students leave campus on weekends. Sexes segregated in coed dormitories either by floor or room.
Annual Costs. Tuition and fees, $1,400 (out-of-state, $4,260); room and board, $4,129; estimated $1,968 other, exclusive of travel. About 42% of students receive financial aid. Assistance is typically divided 11% scholarship, 20% grant, 54% loan, 15% work. College reports 634 scholarships awarded on basis of need alone.

University of Hawaii at Hilo

Hilo, Hawaii 96720-4091 **(808) 933-3414**

The Hilo campus of the University of Hawaii includes the colleges of Arts and Sciences, Agriculture, and Continuing Education and several research centers. The 115-acre campus is in a city of 40,000 on the largest of the Hawaiian Islands. Most convenient major airport: Hilo International.

Founded: 1970
Affiliation: State
UG Enrollment: 833 M, 1,249 W (full-time); 348 M, 523 W (part-time)
Total Enrollment: 2,953
Cost: < $10K
% Receiving Financial Aid: 41%
Admission: Non-selective
Application Deadline: June 30

Admission. High school graduates with a 2.5 GPA and combined 800 SAT eligible; 58% of applicants accepted, 54% of these actually enroll. Average freshman SAT scores: 401 verbal, 473 mathematical. *Required:* SAT. Criteria considered in admissions, in order of importance: high school academic record, standardized test scores, recommendations, writing sample, extracurricular activities. *Out-of-state* students: state limits out-of-state enrollment. About 50% of out-of-state students accepted, 58% of these actually enroll. No special requirements for out-of-state students. About 19% of entering students from private schools. *Entrance programs:* advanced placement. *Apply* by June 30; rolling admissions. *Transfers* welcome; 446 enrolled 1993–94.
Academic Environment. Emphasis of UH-Hilo is on liberal arts and sciences, "particularly those with special relevance to Hawaii." College of Agriculture stresses production techniques and basic management programs in the field. Graduation requirements include 6 hours each communication, world culture, quantitative, 10 hours natural science, 12 hours each humanities, and social sciences. Degrees offered: bachelors. *Majors offered* include marine science. Average undergraduate class size: 77% under 20, 19% 20–40, 4% over 40. About 71% of freshmen return for sophomore year. *Special programs:* study abroad, cross registration with Hawaii Community College, internship. Calendar: semester, summer school.
Undergraduate degrees conferred (210). 18% were in Business and Management, 16% were in Social Sciences, 13% were in Psychology, 11% were in Letters, 10% were in Agricultural Sciences, 6% were in Mathematics, 6% were in Area and Ethnic Studies, 5% were in Visual and Performing Arts, 5% were in Liberal/General Studies, 3% were in Life Sciences, 3% were in Computer and Engineering Related Technology, 3% were in Physical Sciences, remainder in Philosophy and Religion.
Faculty. About 87% of faculty hold PhD or equivalent.
Student Body. About 89% of students from in state; 5% West, 6% foreign. Average age of undergraduate student: 27.
Varsity Sports. Men (NAIA): Baseball, Basketball, Cross Country, Golf, Tennis. Women (NAIA): Cross Country, Softball, Tennis, Volleyball.
Campus Life. Number of older, non-traditional students doubtless affect student life. Plenty of activities, on- and off-campus are available, though: "Beach-going, sight-seeing, there are several acting groups in the area and there are constantly art showings."

About 12% of students live in coed dormitories; rest live in off-campus college-related housing or commute. There are no fraternities or sororities on campus. About 10% of resident students leave campus on weekends.
Annual Costs. Tuition and fees, $480 (out-of-state, $3,000); room and board $2,400; estimated $1,300 other, exclusive of travel. About 41% of students receive financial aid; average amount of assistance, $1,277. College reports 80 scholarships awarded on the basis of special talents alone.

Hebrew College

Brookline, Massachusetts 02146

An independent, liberal arts and teacher training institution, Hebrew College specializes in Hebrew culture and prepares men and women for careers in Jewish education and scholarship. It serves its community with a library of 75,000 volumes of Hebraica and Judaica.

Founded: 1921 **Affiliation:** Independent

Undergraduate degrees conferred (3). 67% were in Education, 33% were in Area and Ethnic Studies.

Heidelberg College

Tiffin, Ohio 44883 **(419) 448-2330**

A church-related, liberal arts college, located in a town of 21,600, 52 miles southeast of Toledo. Through its Junior Year Abroad program, Heidelberg maintains ties with its famous German namesake. Most convenient major airports: Cleveland Hopkins International.

Founded: 1850
Affiliation: United Church of Christ
Total Enrollment: 493 M, 425 W (full-time); 88 M, 124 W (part-time)
Cost: $10K–$20K
% Receiving Financial Aid: 82%
Admission: Non-selective
Application Deadline: July 1

Admission. About 79% of applicants accepted, 31% of these actually enroll; 34% of entering students graduate in top fifth of high school class, 61% in top two-fifths. Average freshman scores: SAT, 408 M, 422 W verbal, 458 M, 454 W mathematical; ACT, 20 M, 21.4 W composite. *Required:* SAT or ACT; interview "strongly recommended." Criteria considered in admissions, in order of importance: high school academic record, writing sample, standardized test scores, recommendations, extracurricular activities; other factors considered: special talents, diverse student body. About 35% of entering students from private and parochial schools. *Entrance programs:* early decision, early admission, midyear admission, deferred admission, advanced placement. *Apply* by July 1; rolling admissions. *Transfers* welcome; 49 enrolled 1993–94.
Academic Environment. High-ability students may design their own graduation requirements; others must take 40 credits in traditional liberal arts core. Degrees offered: bachelors, masters. *Majors offered* include music merchandising, sports medicine, water resource management, environmental biology, pre-med sequences, special education. Average undergraduate class size: 76% under 20, 23% 20–40, 1% over 40.

About 72% of students entering as freshmen graduate eventually; 83% of freshmen return for sophomore year. *Special programs:* CLEP, independent study, credit by examination, study abroad (junior year at U. of Heidelberg), honors, undergraduate research, Washington Semester, innovative College Studies Program with seminars on interdisciplinary or special topics, study at Argonne National Laboratories, 3–2 in forestry, medical technology, engineering, nursing. Adult programs: Lifelong Learning Program for adult students over 24.

Calendar: semester, summer school.
Undergraduate degrees conferred (195). 30% were in Business and Management, 14% were in Education, 10% were in Social Sciences, 9% were in Communications, 7% were in Life Sciences, 7% were in Psychology, 7% were in Letters, 4% were in Mathematics, 3% were in Visual and Performing Arts, 3% were in Parks and Recreation, remainder in 6 other fields.
Graduate Career Data. Advanced studies pursued by 36% of graduates; 19% enter graduate school; 12% enter medical school; 2% enter dental school; 2% enter business school; 1% enter law. About

95% of 1992–93 graduates employed. Fields typically hiring largest numbers of graduates include business, counseling, education, research. Career Development Services include career planning beginning in freshman year, students working with staff in identifying majors, internships, job or graduate school placement.

Faculty. About 78% of faculty hold PhD or equivalent. About 90% of undergraduate classes taught by tenured faculty. About 41% of teaching faculty are female; 4% minority.

Student Body. About 78% of students from in state; 81% from Midwest, each New England, Middle Atlantic, 12% foreign. An estimated 54% of students reported as Protestant, 42% Catholic; 3% Black, 3% Hispanic, 10% Asian, 2% other minority. *Minority group students:* special guidance for students needing extra help and tutoring sponsored by College Council; Black Student Union.

Religious Orientation. Heidelberg is a church-related institution; 1 required course in religion; attendance at regular chapel services voluntary.

Varsity Sports. Men (Div.III): Baseball, Basketball, Cross Country, Football, Golf, Soccer, Tennis, Track, Wrestling. Women (Div.III): Basketball, Cross Country, Soccer, Softball, Tennis, Track, Volleyball.

Campus Life. Current student reports, "Many students participate in sports, intramurals, and are involved with clubs." Students are voting members of faculty committees and of College Council which sets social regulations. All students allowed cars; smoking permitted only in specified areas; alcohol use limited to those over 21; illegal drugs prohibited. All except seniors required to live in college residences; selected seniors may live off campus if residence halls are fully occupied.

About 16% of men, 13% of women live in traditional dormitories; 80% of men, 75% of women live in coed dormitories; rest commute. Freshmen given preference in college housing if all students cannot be accommodated. Intervisitation in men's and women's dormitory rooms limited. There are 4 fraternities, 5 sororities on campus which about 14% of men, 12% of women join; they provide no residence facilities. About 5% of resident students leave campus on weekends.

Annual Costs. Tuition and fees, $13,000; room and board, $4,100; estimated $1000 other, exclusive of travel. About 82% of students receive financial aid; average amount of assistance, $10,600. Assistance is typically divided 40% scholarship, 18% grant, 36% loan, 6% work. College reports some scholarships awarded on the basis of academic merit alone. *Meeting Costs:* college offers 10-month interest-free payment plan.

Hellenic College

Brookline, Massachusetts 02146 **(617) 731-3500**

The only Orthodox Christian institution of higher learning in the Western Hemisphere, Hellenic College offers "undergraduate programs leading to careers in selected professions and the church." It also serves as "a center for study of Orthodox Christianity, Hellenism and the Greek-American Experience." The 52-acre campus bridges the Boston/Brookline boundary.

Founded: 1937
Affiliation: Greek Orthodox
Total Enrollment: 141 M, W (full-time)
Cost: < $10K
Admission: Non-selective
Application Deadline: May 1

Admission. High school graduates with 11 units in academic subjects eligible; 84% of applicants accepted, 75% of these actually enroll. *Required:* SAT or ACT, ACH in English; interview preferred. *Apply* by May 1. *Transfers* welcome.

Academic Environment. *Degree:* AB. About 96% of students entering as freshmen graduate eventually.

Undergraduate degrees conferred (9). 100% were in Theology.

Student Body. College welcomes students of all races, faiths, and nationalities.

Religious Orientation. Hellenic is a church-related institution; 6 hours of religion, attendance at daily worship services required of all students of Greek Orthodox faith.

Campus Life. About 85% of men, 95% of women live in traditional dormitories; no coed dormitories; rest commute. Intervisitation in men's and women's dormitory rooms limited.

Annual Costs. Tuition and fees, $7,135; room and board, $4,920.

Henderson State University

Arkadelphia, Arkansas 71923 **(501) 246-5511**

A state-supported University, located in a city of 10,000, 70 miles southwest of Little Rock.

Founded: 1890
Affiliation: State
Total Enrollment: 3,195 M, W (full-time)
Cost: < $10K
Admission: Non-selective

Admission. Arkansas graduates of accredited high schools with 15 units admitted by certificate; Arkansas non-graduates with 15 units also admitted; almost all applicants accepted, 80% of these actually enroll. *Required:* ACT. *Out-of-state* freshman applicants: university does not seek students from out of state. Requirement for out-of-state students: C average or rank in top half of class. *Apply* by registration. *Transfers* welcome.

Academic Environment. *Degrees:* AB, BS, BM, BMEd, BSEd, BSBA. About 50% of students entering as freshmen graduate eventually; 70% of freshmen return for sophomore year. *Special programs:* CLEP, honors, 3-year degree. *Calendar:* semester, summer school.

Undergraduate degrees conferred (418). 40% were in Education, 19% were in Business and Management, 6% were in Social Sciences, 6% were in Health Sciences, 5% were in Public Affairs, 4% were in Psychology, 4% were in Life Sciences, 3% were in Transportation and Material Moving, 3% were in Parks and Recreation, 3% were in Visual and Performing Arts, remainder in 8 other fields.

Varsity Sports. Men (NAIA): Baseball, Basketball, Cross Country, Football, Golf, Swimming, Tennis, Track. Women (NAIA): Basketball, Swimming, Tennis, Volleyball.

Campus Life. About 43% of men, 50% of women live in traditional dormitories; no coed dormitories; rest live in off-campus housing or commute. Limited intervisitation in men's and women's dormitory rooms. There are 6 fraternities, 6 sororities; they provide no residence facilities.

Annual Costs. Tuition and fees, $1,660 (out-of-state, $3,220); room and board, $2,490.

Hendrix College

Conway, Arkansas 72032 **(501) 450-1362**

A church-related, liberal arts college, located in a town of 23,000 and in the foothills of the Ozark Mountains, 25 miles northwest of Little Rock. Most convenient major airport: Little Rock, Arkansas.

Founded: 1876
Affiliation: United Methodist
Total Enrollment: 418 M, 535 W (full-time)
Cost: < $10K
% Receiving Financial Aid: 74%
Admission: Very Selective
Application Deadline: Rolling

Admission is very selective. About 86% of applicants accepted, 38% of these actually enroll; 30% of freshmen graduate in top fifth of high school class, 51% in top two-fifths. Average freshman scores: SAT, 32% of freshmen score above 500 on verbal, 11% above 600, 1% above 700; 42% score above 500 on mathematical, 10% above 600; ACT, 25.7 composite. *Required:* SAT or ACT, essay; interview not required, but college "reserves the right to interview." Criteria considered in admissions, in order of importance: high school academic record, standardized test scores, writing sample, extracurricular activities, recommendations; other factors considered: special talents, diverse student body. About 26% of entering students from private and parochial schools. *Entrance programs:* early admission, midyear admission. *Apply:* rolling admissions. *Transfers* welcome; 20 enrolled 1993–94.

Academic Environment. Core requirements for graduation include 2-course sequence in Western Intellectual Tradition and 2 courses in other Cultural or Linguistic Traditions; distribution requirements include 3 courses each in humanities, natural science, social science. In addition all students must demonstrate "an acceptable level of skill in written communication" before admittance to senior class. Students enjoy the accessibility of faculty outside the classroom and the challenge of small classes with in-depth discussions. Degrees offered: bachelors. *Majors offered* include Integrative Studies (student-designed, inter-disciplinary majors). Average undergraduate class size: 58% under 20, 40% 20–40, 2% over 40.

About 82% of students entering as freshmen graduate within four years, 88% eventually; 87% of freshmen return for sophomore year. *Special programs:* CLEP, independent study, study abroad, honors, undergraduate research, 3–2 engineering. *Calendar:* 3–3.

Undergraduate degrees conferred (228). 18% were in Business and Management, 16% were in Life Sciences, 14% were in Social Sciences, 13% were in Psychology, 11% were in Letters, 7% were in Physical Sciences, 5% were in Education, 5% were in Visual and Performing Arts, 4% were in Philosophy and Religion, 3% were in Mathematics, remainder in 2 other fields.

Graduates Career Data. Advanced studies pursued by 65% of graduates. Medical schools typically enrolling largest numbers of graduates include Vanderbilt, U. of Arkansas, Emory; dental schools include U. of Tennessee; law schools include U. of Arkansas, Vanderbilt, SMU; business schools include U. of Arkansas, SMU, Wharton. Fields typically hiring largest numbers of graduates include "Big 6" accounting firms, banking, pharmaceutical. Career Development Services include work on resumes and interviewing skills starting freshman year for summer work and internships.

Faculty. About 97% of faculty hold PhD or equivalent. All undergraduate classes taught by tenured faculty. About 23% of teaching faculty are female.

Student Body. About 75% of students from in state; 15% South, 6% West, 2% Midwest, 2% Northwest, 1% Middle Atlantic, 2% foreign. An estimated 65% of students reported as Protestant, 12% Catholic, 20% unaffiliated; 6% as Black, 2% Hispanic, 2% Asian, 2% other minority.

Religious Orientation. Hendrix is affiliated with the Methodist Church in Arkansas, makes no religious demands on students.

Varsity Sports. Men (NAIA): Baseball, Basketball, Cross Country, Diving, Golf, Soccer, Swimming, Tennis, Track. Women (AIC): Basketball, Cross Country, Diving, Soccer, Swimming, Tennis, Track, Volleyball.

Campus Life. Student reports indicate most social life revolves around the campus: "The college brings in an impressive amount of entertainment: dances, movies, comedians, speakers, musicians." Another student asserts students spend their time "studying, hanging-out, working out, having FUN!" A former student leader reports "rules are lenient, but leave the students with a great deal of responsibility in holding them up." Cars allowed for all students, must be registered with college. Alcohol permitted in residence hall rooms for students 21 and over; counseling required for abusers. Smoking restricted to designated areas; drugs "not tolerated."

About 85% of students live in traditional and coed dormitories; rest live in off-campus housing or commute. Freshmen given preference in college housing if all students cannot be accommodated. Sexes segregated in coed dormitories by floor. There are no fraternities or sororities on campus. About 15% of resident students leave campus on weekends.

Annual Costs. Tuition and fees, $8,607; room and board, $3,060; estimated $800 other, exclusive of travel. About 74% of students receive financial aid; average amount of assistance, $9,298. Assistance is typically divided 38% grant, 51% loan, 11% work. College reports 37% scholarships awarded on the basis of academic merit alone, 16% for special talents alone. Meeting costs: installment payment plan.

Herbert H. Lehman College

(See City University of New York)

Heritage College

Toppenish, Washington 98948

A private, independent liberal arts college, Heritage is the successor to Fort Wright College of the Holy Names. Most convenient major airport: Yakima.

UG Enrollment: 51 M, 177 W (full-time); 25 M, 110 W (part-time)	**Total Enrollment:** 1,041 **Admission:** Non-selective **Application Deadline:** Rolling

Admission. High school graduates or equivalent eligible. *Apply:* rolling admissions. *Transfers* welcome.

Academic Environment. *Majors offered* include computer science, bilingual education, mathematics, psychology, public administration, Spanish. *Degrees:* AA, BA, BS, BAEd, MAEd.

Undergraduate degrees conferred (51). 71% were in Education, 18% were in Business and Management, 10% were in Computer and Engineering Related Technology, remainder in Psychology.

Student Body. Nearly all students from within state. Average age of undergraduate student: 36.

Campus Life. College provides no residence facilities.

Annual Costs. Tuition and fees, $5,490. College reports some scholarships awarded on the basis of academic merit alone.

High Point College

High Point, North Carolina 27261

In-state (800) 422-4644 or out-of-state (800) 345-6993

A church-related, liberal arts college, located in a residential area of a city of 75,000, 15 miles southwest of Greensboro. Most convenient major airport: Piedmont Triad International.

Founded: 1924	**Cost:** < $10K
Affiliation: United Methodist	**% Receiving Financial Aid:** 70%
Total Enrollment: 2,146 M, W (full-time)	**Admission:** Non-selective **Application Deadline:** Rolling

Admission. High school graduates with 16 units (10 in academic subjects) eligible; 84% of applicants accepted, 30% of these actually enroll; 20% of freshmen graduate in top fifth of high school class, 40% in top two-fifths. Average freshman SAT scores, according to most recent data available: 419 M, W verbal, 459 M, W mathematical. *Required:* SAT or ACT (not always necessary); interview helpful. *Apply:* rolling admissions. *Transfers* welcome.

Academic Environment. Contract program permits selected students to plan individualized curriculum. General education requirements include courses in writing techniques, religion and physical education, proficiency in foreign language; distribution requirements include minimum of 6 semester hours to be taken from 4 broad academic "areas." *Degrees:* BA, BS. *Majors offered* include usual arts and sciences, communications, human relations ("undergraduate background for professional leadership in youth serving agencies"), medical technology, sports medicine, home furnishings marketing, chemistry-business.

About 90% of students entering as freshmen graduate eventually; 90% of freshmen return for sophomore year. *Special programs:* honors, undergraduate research, study abroad, independent study, credit by examination, Greensboro Regional Consortium for Higher Education. Adult programs: Evening Degree Program. *Calendar:* semester, summer school.

Undergraduate degrees conferred (403). 47% were in Business and Management, 9% were in Letters, 7% were in Social Sciences, 7% were in Computer and Engineering Related Technology, 6% were in Education, 5% were in Marketing and Distribution, 5% were in Psychology, 3% were in Life Sciences, remainder in 9 other fields.

Graduates Career Data. According to most recent data available, full-time graduate or professional study pursued immediately after graduation by 16% of students. *Careers in business and industry* pursued by 68% of graduates.

Student Body. About 68% of students from in state; 79% South, 17% Middle Atlantic. An estimated 60% of students reported as Protestant, 25% Catholic, 4% Jewish; 9% Black, 2% other minority, according to most recent data available.

Religious Orientation. High Point is a church-related institution; 3 hours of religion required of all students.

Varsity Sports. Men (NAIA): Baseball, Basketball, Cross Country, Golf, Soccer, Tennis, Track. Women (NAIA): Basketball, Cross Country, Field Hockey, Tennis, Volleyball.

Campus Life. Cars allowed for dormitory students with C average. About 34% of men, 26% of women live in traditional dormitories; 22% of men, 24% of women in coed dormitories; 15% of men, 15% of women live in off-campus college-related housing; 24% of men, 24% of women commute. Intervisitation in men's and women's dormitory rooms limited. Sexes segregated in coed dormitories by floor. There are 4 fraternities, 4 sororities on campus which about 40% of men, 40% of women join. About 25% of resident students leave campus on weekends.
Annual Costs. Tuition and fees, $7,760; room and board, $3,700. About 70% of students receive financial aid; assistance is typically divided 45% scholarship, 45% loan, 10% work. College reports some scholarships awarded on basis of academic merit alone.

Hillsdale College

Hillsdale, Michigan 49242 **(517) 437-7341**

Hillsdale is an independent, liberal arts college, located on a 155-acre campus in a community of about 10,000, midway between Cleveland and Chicago. Most convenient major airports: Detroit Metro, Toledo (OH).

Founded: 1844
Affiliation: Independent
Total Enrollment: 529 M, 562 W (full-time)
Cost: $10K–$20K
% Receiving Financial Aid: 70%
Admission: Selective (+)
Application Deadline: July 15

Admission is selective (+). About 79% of applicants accepted, 47% of these actually enroll; 55% of freshmen graduate in top fifth of high school class, 90% in top two-fifths. Average freshman scores: SAT, 520 verbal, 570 M, 530 W mathematical; 58% of freshman score above 500 on verbal, 18% above 600, 3% above 700; 74% score above 500 on mathematical, 24% above 600, 6% above 700; ACT, 24 composite. *Required:* SAT or ACT, essay. Criteria considered in admissions, in order of importance: high school academic record, standardized test scores, writing sample, extracurricular activities, recommendations; other factors considered: alumni children. *Entrance programs:* early decision, midyear admission. About 24% of entering students from private or parochial schools. *Apply* by July 15; rolling admissions. *Transfers* welcome; 45 enrolled 1993–94.
Academic Environment. Graduation requirements include 2 course English series, 1 course American history, 3 courses in humanities, 2 courses in math and science, and 2 courses in social sciences. Students agree that small and challenging classes are a plus: "I have a German class which has two students. Every day we must be prepared and be able to discuss our ideas in German. The situation is the same in all my classes—preparation and defense of one's ideas is demanded." Degrees offered: bachelors. *Majors offered* include speech and theater arts, political economy, international business, American studies. Average undergraduate class size: 39% under 20, 61% 20–40, less than 1% over 40.

About 68% of students entering as freshmen graduate within four years, 75% eventually; 90% of freshmen return for sophomore year. *Special programs:* CLEP, independent study, study abroad, honors, undergraduate research, credit by examination, acceleration, individualized majors, on-campus preschool laboratory for early childhood education, January Term Family Business Institute, visiting professor program, 3–2 engineering, Washington-Hillsdale intern program. *Calendar:* semester, summer school.
Undergraduate degrees conferred (221). 45% were in Business and Management, 19% were in Social Sciences, 12% were in Education, 9% were in Letters, 6% were in Psychology, 4% were in Life Sciences, remainder in 6 other fields.
Graduates Career Data. Advanced studies pursued by 25% of graduates; 10% enter graduate school; 7% enter law school; 5% enter medical school; 3% enter business school. Medical schools typically enrolling largest numbers of graduates include U. of Michigan, Wayne State, Michigan State; dental schools include U. of Michigan; law schools include Wake Forest, U. of Toledo, Valparaiso; business schools include Notre Dame, U. of Arizona. About 93% of 1992–93 graduates employed. Fields typically hiring largest number of graduates include accounting, sales, education, management. Career Development Services include on-campus recruiting, resume and interview workshops, interest inventories, alumni career development programs.
Faculty. About 85% of faculty have PhD or equivalent. About 95% of undergraduate classes taught by tenured faculty.
Student Body. About 56% of students from in state; 25% Midwest, 7% each West, South, 2% Northwest, 1% each New England, Middle Atlantic, 1% foreign.
Varsity Sports. Men (Div.I): Baseball, Basketball, Cross Country, Football, Golf, Tennis, Track. Women (Div.I): Basketball, Cross Country, Diving, Softball, Swimming, Tennis, Track, Volleyball.
Campus Life. Social life focused on campus activities: "numerous clubs and school-sponsored activities, as well as Greek life and on-campus employment." Students and administration agree that campus is conservative; some student concern about rules, but also appreciation of their intent and effect. Atmosphere termed "personal", "wonderful", but "School is serious at Hillsdale. People 'dress-up' to go to class and are almost always prepared." Intervisitation permitted on weekends. Cars allowed for all students.

About 83% of men, 80% of women live in traditional dormitories; no coed dormitories; 7% of men, 8% of women live in off-campus college-related housing or commute. Freshmen given preference in college housing if all students cannot be accommodated. There are 5 fraternities, 4 sororities on campus which about 50% of men, 50% of women join; 10% of men, 12% of women live in fraternities and sororities. About 15% of resident students leave campus on weekends.
Annual Costs. Tuition and fees, $10,460; room and board, $4,440; estimated $750 other, exclusive of travel. About 70% of students receive financial aid; average amount of assistance, $6,500. Assistance is typically divided 40% scholarship, 40% grant, 10% loan, 10% work. College reports 45 scholarships awarded on the basis of academic merit alone, 45 for special talents alone, 100 for need alone.

Hiram College

Hiram, Ohio 44234 **(800) 362-5280 or (216) 569-5169**

An independent, liberal arts college, Hiram was founded by members of the Christian Church (Disciples of Christ). The 110-acre main campus is located in a rural community (pop. 1,500), about 35 miles from Cleveland, Akron, and Youngstown. Most convenient major airport: Cleveland Hopkins.

Founded: 1850
Affiliation: Independent (Disciples of Christ)
Total Enrollment: 408 M, 432 W (full-time)
Cost: $10K–$20K
% Receiving Financial Aid: 90%
Admission: Selective (+)
Application Deadline: April 15

Admission is selective (+). About 79% of applicants accepted, 33% of these actually enroll; 44% of freshmen graduate in top fifth of high school class; 66% in top two-fifths. Average freshman scores: SAT, 510 verbal, 540 mathematical; 52% of freshmen score above 500 on verbal, 14% above 600; 64% score above 500 on mathematical, 24% above 600; ACT, 25 composite. *Required:* SAT or ACT; essay, teacher recommendation. Criteria considered in admissions, in order of importance: high school academic record, standardized test scores, recommendations, interview, writing sample, extracurricular activities; factors considered in admissions: special talents, diverse student body, alumni children. *Entrance programs:* deferred admission. *Apply* by April 15. *Transfers* welcome; 34 enrolled 1993–94.
Academic Environment. Freshman curriculum begins with 1-week institute for small-group training in communication skills. Core curriculum required of all students includes English Composition, and selections from divisions of fine arts, humanities, social sciences, and physical sciences, also required are 2 courses in writing and public speaking, and 2 courses in computer science, foreign language, reasoning and analysis, or the arts. Accessible, "student-oriented" faculty termed "incredible." Degrees offered: bachelors. *Majors offered* include theater arts and speech, psycho-biology, individually designed areas of concentration.

About 98% of students entering as freshmen graduate eventually; 88% of freshmen return for sophomore year. *Special programs:* CLEP, independent study, study abroad, Interterm, individually designed internships, individualized majors, science field stations, affiliation with John Cabot International College, Washington Semester. Adult programs: Weekend College. *Calendar:* 3 terms, summer school.

Undergraduate degrees conferred (312). 29% were in Business and Management, 14% were in Social Sciences, 14% were in Life Sciences, 9% were in Education, 8% were in Communications, 5% were in Visual and Performing Arts, 4% were in Psychology, 4% were in Physical Sciences, 3% were in Letters, 3% were in Mathematics, 3% were in Allied Health, remainder in 3 other fields.
Graduates Career Data. Advanced studies pursued by 20% of graduates within one year, 64% within five years. About 70% of 1992–93 graduates employed. Career Development Services include aptitude testing, resume/interview workshops, individual counseling, on-campus recruitment, alumni career network, library, career interest software program.
Faculty. About 92% of faculty hold PhD or equivalent. About 37% of teaching faculty are female.
Student Body. About 80% of students from in state. *Minority group students:* Alliance for Black Consciousness.
Religious Orientation. Hiram is affiliated with the Christian Church (Disciples of Christ), but is not church-controlled.
Varsity Sports. Men (Div.III): Baseball, Basketball, Cross Country, Football, Soccer, Swimming & Diving, Tennis, Track. Women (Div.III): Basketball, Cross Country, Soccer, Softball, Swimming & Diving, Tennis, Track, Volleyball.
Campus Life. Very rural location (nearest town is 3 miles away) fosters "an incredible sense of community." Most professors live in the village and attend events on campus. Student reports that the Student Programing Board "does an exceptional job of planning activities for students." Lecturers, comedians, bands, magicians, etc., perform on-campus 3–4 times a week.

About 93% of students live in coed dormitories; rest live in off-campus housing or commute. Sexes segregated in coed dormitories by floor or room. There are no fraternities or sororities on campus.
Annual Costs. Tuition and fees, $13,825; room and board, $4,515; estimated $800 other, exclusive of travel. About 90% of students receive financial aid; average amount of assistance, $12,533. Assistance is typically divided 73% scholarship, 18% loan, 9% work. *Meeting Costs:* college offers installment plans with institution and with outside agencies.

Hobart and William Smith Colleges

Geneva, New York 14456 **(Hobart) (800) 852-2256 or (Wm. Smith) (800) 245-0100**

Hobart is a private liberal arts college for men; historically related to the Episcopal Church, the college is now independent and nonsectarian. William Smith, the coordinate college for women, has never had any church relationship. The two colleges share faculty, curriculum, and college administration, but have separate deans, student governments, and athletic administration. Together they comprise a liberal arts institution located on a 170-acre campus in a community of 16,800 at the north end of Seneca Lake, largest of the Finger Lakes, in central New York. Most convenient major airports: Syracuse, Rochester.

Founded: 1822, 1908
Affiliation: Independent
Total Enrollment: 953 M, 839 W (full time)
Cost: $10K–$20K
% Receiving Financial Aid: 57%
Admission: Very (+) Selective
Application Deadline: Feb. 15

Admission is very (+) selective. About 77% of applicants accepted, 24% of these actually enroll; 43% of freshmen graduate in top fifth of high school class, 67% in top two-fifths. Average freshman SAT scores: 48% score above 500 on verbal, 8% above 600, 75% score above 500 on mathematical, 24% above 600, 4% above 700. *Required:* SAT or ACT; essay. Criteria considered in admissions, in order of importance: high school academic record, standardized test scores, writing sample, extracurricular activities, recommendations; other factors considered: special talents, alumni children, diverse student body. *Entrance programs:* early decision, early admission, advanced placement, deferred admission. About 42% of entering students from private and parochial schools. *Apply* by February 15. *Transfers* welcome; 58 enrolled 1993–94.
Academic Environment. General education requirements seek to introduce students to the breadth and depth of the liberal arts curriculum, while developing skills and interests in a variety of fields and increasing competence in reading, writing, speaking and listening. All first-year students participate in a seminar in the fall term, exploring a topic in-depth. The professor serves as the students' academic advisor until they chose a major. In the sophomore year, each student takes a bi-disciplinary course taught by two faculty members from different departments. In addition, during the first two years students fulfill general distribution requirements of two courses each in humanities (including fine arts), social sciences, natural sciences (including a lab science). In the junior year, in addition to work on their major, students fulfill their "Third Tier" requirement: a bi-disciplinary course, an interdisciplinary independent study, or a term off-campus or abroad. There is strong encouragement to study abroad, 60–65% of students do so. Many majors require a senior seminar. Senior years honors program also available. Degrees offered: bachelors. *Majors offered* include environmental science, fine and applied arts, dance, architectural studies, self-designed individual majors, creative writing, natural sciences. Average undergraduate class size: 69% under 20, 26% 20–40, 5% over 40.

About 78% of students entering as freshmen graduate within four years, 80% within five years; 93% of freshmen return for sophomore year. *Special programs:* CLEP, independent study, study abroad, honors, undergraduate research, 3-year degree, individualized majors, Washington Semester, credit by examination, visiting students program, Third World studies, American studies, women's studies, United Nations Semester, bi-disciplinary courses, 3–2 engineering with Columbia, U. of Rochester, RPI, Dartmouth, 4–1 MBA with Clarkson, cooperative programs through Rochester Area Colleges Consortium, 7 year architecture, cross registration with Rochester area colleges. Adult programs: Life-Long Learner Program. *Calendar:* 3–3–3.
Undergraduate degrees conferred (468). 44% were in Social Sciences, 21% were in Letters, 7% were in Psychology, 6% were in Liberal/General Studies, 4% were in Visual and Performing Arts, 4% were in Life Sciences, 4% were in Foreign Languages, 3% were in Area and Ethnic Studies, 3% were in Philosophy and Religion, 3% were in Physical Sciences, remainder in 2 other fields.
Graduates Career Data. Advanced studies pursued by 41% of graduates; 25% enter graduate school; 7% enter law school; 5% enter business school; 4% enter medical and dental school. Medical schools typically enrolling largest numbers of graduates include SUNY Buffalo, Health Science Center at Syracuse U.; dental schools include Tufts, SUNY Buffalo, U. of Pennsylvania; law schools include Cornell, Georgetown, Case Western Reserve; business schools include Columbia, Dartmouth, NYU. About 76% of 1992–93 graduates employed. Fields typically hiring largest numbers of graduates include education, business, government/law, communications. Career Development Services include counseling, interest inventories, wide variety of workshops, internships, externships, recruitment program, career fairs and panels, alumni/alumnae/parent career contact program, peer counselor program.
Faculty. About 98% of faculty hold PhD or equivalent. About 57% of undergraduate classes taught by tenured faculty.
Student Body. About 41% of students from in state; 24% New England, 22% Middle Atlantic, 4% Midwest, 3% West, 2% South, 1% Northwest, 3% foreign. An estimated 30% of students reported as Protestant, 30% Catholic, 15% Jewish, 20% unaffiliated; 5% Black, 4% Hispanic, 2% Asian. *Minority group students:* scholarship aid; cultural center and special administrator.
Varsity Sports. Men (Div.III): Baseball, Basketball, Diving, Football, Golf, Ice Hockey, Lacrosse, Soccer, Swimming, Tennis. Women (Div.III): Basketball, Crew, Cross Country, Diving, Field Hockey, Lacrosse, Soccer, Swimming, Tennis.
Campus Life. Student reports majority of socializing occurs on-campus. Most students reported to spend their time "studying, athletics, jobs, community service, etc. Socializing, of course." Social regulations under jurisdiction of student government. Smoking prohibited; alcohol restricted by state and local laws (age 21), and by college regulations; drugs prohibited, penalties include counseling, disciplinary action, or referral to federal/state/local authorities. Cars allowed; some parking regulations. Unlimited intervisitation.

About 46% of men, 50% of women live in traditional dormitories; 20% men, 30% women live in coed dormitories; 13% of men, 20% of women live in off-campus college-related housing; 1% of men commute. Freshmen given preference in college housing if all students cannot be accommodated. There are 7 fraternities on campus which about 30% of men join; there are no sororities. About 5–10% of the resident students leave campus on weekends.
Annual Costs. Tuition and fees, $18,309; room and board, $5,616; estimated $1,400 other, exclusive of travel. About 57% of students

receive financial aid; average amount of assistance, $13,400. Assistance is typically divided 65% scholarship, 10% grant, 19% loan, 6% work. College reports 5 scholarships awarded on the basis of academic merit alone, 979 for need alone. *Meeting Costs:* various institutional and outside payment options available.

Hobe Sound Bible College

Hobe Sound, Florida 33475

A small, interdenominational Bible college, offering associates and bachelors degrees; all degree programs are a double major one of which is Bible.

Founded: 1960 **Affiliation:** Independent

Hofstra University

Hempstead, New York 11550 **(516) 463-6700**

A private, independent university, Hofstra was founded as a commuter institution, but now half of its students live on campus and a substantial fraction of its students come from other states and abroad. The 238-acre main campus, located 25 miles east of Manhattan, includes Hofstra College of Liberal Arts and Sciences, New College of Hofstra, School of Business, School of Education, University College, School of Law, University Without Walls, and Alumni College. Most convenient major airport: JFK International.

Founded: 1935
Affiliation: Independent
UG Enrollment: 3,113 M, 3,664 W (full-time); 641 M, 752 W (part-time)
Total Enrollment: 11,998
Cost: $10K–$20K
% Receiving Financial Aid: 75%
Admission: Selective (+)
Application Deadline: Rolling

Admission is selective (+). For all schools, 79% of applicants accepted, 26% of these actually enroll; 60% of freshmen graduate in top fifth of high school class, 97% in top two-fifths. Average freshman scores: SAT, 480 verbal, 545 mathematical; 56% score above 500 on verbal, 11% score above 600, 75% score above 500 on mathematical, 28% above 600, 4% above 700; ACT, 25 composite. *Required:* SAT or ACT; interview recommended. Criteria considered in admissions, in order of importance: high school academic record, standardized test scores, recommendations, writing sample, extracurricular activities; other factors considered: special talents. About 35% of entering students from private and parochial schools. Entrance program: early decision, early admission, midyear admission, deferred admission, advanced placement. *Apply:* rolling admissions. *Transfers* welcome; 805 enrolled 1993–94.

Academic Environment. Students have some influence on academic decision making through representation on student/faculty committees and All University Senate. Administration source reports liberal arts and pre-professional programs are considered strong, also communications programs including TV Institute. New College, a self-contained "academic community" within the university, offers superior students opportunity for concentrated programs (4 terms of 10 weeks each) leading to baccalaureate degree in 3–4 years; individually designed programs contain relatively few distribution requirements. Graduation requirements for 4-year AB: 9 credits from social sciences, humanities, natural sciences, English 1 and 2, foreign language. Degrees offered: associates, bachelors, masters, doctoral. *Majors offered* include anthropology, dance, economics/business, elementary education, engineering sciences, fine arts, geography, Hebrew, Judaica, speech arts and therapy, theater arts. Average undergraduate class size: 5% under 20, 90% 20–40, 5% over 40.

About 58% of entering freshmen graduate eventually; 90% of freshmen return for sophomore year. *Special programs:* CLEP, independent study, study abroad, honors, undergraduate research, individualized majors, 3–2 engineering with Columbia, marine biology lab in Jamaica. *Calendar:* semester, January session, summer school.

Undergraduate degrees conferred (1771). 46% were in Business and Management, 11% were in Social Sciences, 9% were in Psychology, 7% were in Communications, 5% were in Letters, 4% were in Liberal/General Studies, 4% were in Computer and Engineering Related Technology, 3% were in Engineering, 3% were in Education, 3% were in Life Sciences, remainder in 8 other fields.

Graduates Career Data. Advanced studies pursued by 35% of graduates; 4% enter graduate school; 3% enter medical and dental school; 6% enter law school; 20% enter business school. Fields typically hiring largest numbers of graduates include accounting, education, and communications. Career Development Services include interview and resume skills, on-campus recruitment.

Faculty. About 90% of faculty hold PhD or equivalent. About 90% of undergraduate classes taught by tenured faculty. About 40% of teaching faculty are female.

Student Body. About 65% of students from in state; 73% Middle Atlantic, 12% New England, 4% each Midwest, South, 3% West, 1% Northwest, 3% foreign. An estimated 45% of students reported as Catholic, 30% Protestant, 18% Jewish; 7% Black, 4% Hispanic, 4% Asian, 4% other minority. Average age of undergraduate student: 22. *Minority group students:* New Opportunities at Hofstra (NOAH) program for special tutoring and academic aid.

Varsity Sports. Men (Div.I): Baseball, Basketball, Cross Country, Football (IAA), Golf, Lacrosse, Soccer, Tennis, Wrestling. Women (Div.I): Basketball, Cross Country, Field Hockey, Lacrosse, Soccer, Softball, Tennis, Volleyball.

Campus Life. Regulations governing student social life relaxed. Campus provides wide variety of cultural and social activities which are supplemented by the many resources of New York City, just 25 miles to the west. Cars allowed; adequate parking. Drinking permitted in accordance with state law (age 21); alcohol may be served at some student functions. County restricts smoking in public places. Intervisitation permitted.

About 58% of men, 58% of women live in traditional or coed residence halls; 2% live in off-campus college-related housing; rest commute. Sexes segregated in coed dormitories by floor or room. There are 16 fraternities, 10 sororities on campus which about 14% of men, 12% of women join. About 10% of resident students leave campus on weekends.

Annual Costs. Tuition and fees, $11.080; room and board, $5,500; estimated $1,000 other, exclusive of travel. About 75% of students receive financial aid; average amount of assistance, $6,000. Assistance is typically divided 47% scholarship/grant, 36% loan, 17% work. University reports some scholarships awarded on the basis of academic merit alone. *Meeting Costs:* university offers Middle Income Plan of grants and scholarships.

Hollins College

Hollins College, Virginia 24020 **(800) 456-9595 or (703) 362-6401**

Long a prestigious women's college, Hollins emphasizes both academic achievement in a liberal arts curriculum and career goals. College attracts significant numbers of students from all parts of the country. The college's 475-acre campus is located 2 miles north of Roanoke (area pop. 225,000) in southwestern Virginia and close to recreation opportunities in the Blue Ridge Mountains. Most convenient major airport: Roanoke Regional.

Founded: 1842
Affiliation: Independent
UG Enrollment: 779 W (full-time); 63 W (part-time)
Total Enrollment: 1,030
Cost: $10K–$20K
% Receiving Financial Aid: 60%
Admission: Selective (+)
Application Deadline: February 15

Admission is selective (+). About 83% of applicants accepted, 43% of these actually enroll; 50% of freshmen graduate in top fifth of high school class, 76% in top two-fifths. Average freshman scores: SAT, 505 W verbal, 502 W mathematical; middle 50% range, 450–560 verbal, 440–550 mathematical; 50% score above 500 on verbal, 16% score above 600, 50% score above 500 on mathematical, 13% above 600; ACT, 23 composite. *Required:* SAT or ACT; recommendations, essay, interview strongly recommended, ACH recommended. Criteria considered in admissions, in order of importance: high school academic record, standardized test scores, recommendations, extracurricular activities, writing sample; other factors considered: diverse student body, special talents, alumni children. *Entrance programs:* early decision, early admission, deferred admission, advanced placement. About 27% of entering students from private and parochial schools. *Apply*: February 15. *Transfers* welcome; 22 enrolled 1993–94.

Academic Environment. Students have significant degree of influence over curriculum. They serve as members of most committees and as departmental and divisional representatives, and their participation has been solicited in the selection of new administrative officers. Students are proud of the highly-regarded creative writing program and enjoy Hollins' small classes and accessible faculty. Graduation requirements mandate minimum of 8 credits in each of 4 divisions: humanities, social sciences, natural sciences and mathematics, and fine arts; physical education or participation in a varsity sport. Degrees offered: bachelors, masters. *Majors offered* include American studies, computational studies, communication studies, international relations, Latin studies, theater arts, self-designed majors. Average undergraduate class size: 78% under 20, 20% 20–40, 2% over 40 (college reports: 93% under 30, none over 59).

About 68% of students entering as freshmen graduate eventually; 82% of freshmen return for sophomore year. *Special programs:* honors, undergraduate research, individualized majors, creative writing sequence, interdisciplinary programs, January Short Term, Seven College Exchange Program, Washington Semester, United Nations Semester, Christie's Program (through the auction house), summer reading for credit, program in film, study abroad programs in Kobe, Japan, Paris, London, U. of Dublin, Goethe Institutes (West Germany), exchange program with Mills, 3–2 engineering, 3–2 architecture. Adult programs: Horizon Program offers full and part-time programs with flexible scheduling and re-entry courses for women over 25. *Calendar:* 4–1–4.

Undergraduate degrees conferred (199). 34% were in Social Sciences, 14% were in Letters, 13% were in Psychology, 12% were in Visual and Performing Arts, 8% were in Communications, 6% were in Foreign Languages, 5% were in Area and Ethnic Studies, 4% were in Life Sciences, remainder in 5 other fields.

Graduates Career Data. Advanced studies pursued by 36% of graduates; 22% enter graduate school; 5% enter law school; 3% each enter dental and business school. Medical schools typically enrolling largest numbers of graduates include Georgetown, Cornell, John Hopkins; dental schools include Medical College of Virginia; law schools include Washington & Lee, Yale, William & Mary; business schools include College of Charleston, U. of Richmond, Virginia Commonwealth. About 57% of 1992–93 graduates employed. Employers typically hiring largest numbers of graduates include U.S. Government (Capitol Hill), Time Warner/Time Life Books, First Union Bank, Smithsonian Institute, Sothebys. Career Development Services include a Career Assistance Network, counseling, resource library, computer software, resume referral program.

Faculty. About 91% of faculty hold PhD or equivalent. About 47% of undergraduate classes taught by tenured faculty. About 45% of teaching faculty are female; 12% minority.

Student Body. About 32% of students from in state; 32% South, 10% Middle Atlantic, 8% each Midwest, Southwest; 5% New England, 3% West, 2% foreign. An estimated 46% of students reported as Protestant, 17% Catholic, 2% Jewish, 35% unaffiliated or unknown; 3% Black, 2% Hispanic, 1% Asian, 3% other minority.

Religious Orientation. "Hollins was founded as a Christian College but has never had denominational connections." All students belong to Religious Life Association, which sponsors religious and service activities.

Varsity Sports. Women (Div.III): Basketball, Equestrian, Fencing, Field Hockey, Lacrosse, Riding, Soccer, Swimming & Diving, Tennis, Volleyball.

Campus Life. Guidelines and regulations concerning student conduct determined by student government association. Wide range of activities available, on-campus and off; several other campuses in vicinity supplement offerings. As one student observes: "We are within a 100 mile radius of over 30,000 undergraduate students which means that Roanoke is a great location." In cooperation with nearby men's colleges, student organizations plan social functions during year; concerts, films, educational programs and athletic events are also presented. In addition, students are encouraged to plan and present their own programs within residence halls. Most students live in college housing: 35 apartments, 3 houses, 5 traditional residence halls.

About 98% of women live in traditional residence halls. There are no sororities on campus. About 23% of resident students leave campus on weekends.

Annual Costs. Tuition and fees, $13,184; room and board $5,300; estimated $1,050 other, exclusive of travel. About 60% of students receive financial aid; average amount of assistance, $13,765. Assistance is typically divided 59% scholarship/grant, 29% loan, 12% work. College reports 138 scholarships awarded on the basis of academic merit alone, 110 for special talents, 17 for need alone. *Meeting Costs:* college offers budget payment plan, guaranteed tuition plan, and outside payment plans.

Holy Apostles College

Cromwell, Connecticut 06416

An accredited 4-year college for men, Holy Apostles offers programs in the liberal arts leading to a baccalaureate degree.

Affiliation: Roman Catholic
Total Enrollment: 171 M (full-time)
Cost: < $10K
Admission: Non-selective

Undergraduate degrees conferred (15). 93% were in Philosophy and Religion, 7% were in Multi/Interdisciplinary Studies.

College of the Holy Cross

Worcester, Massachusetts 01610 (508) 793-2443

Holy Cross, a Jesuit institution, draws its students from every region of the country. Backed by very strong alumni support, the college continues to prepare students for the learned professions (medicine and law) and for careers in business. The 174-acre campus is located 2 miles from the center of Worcester, a city of 176,000, 40 miles from Boston. Most convenient major airport: Logan International (Boston).

Founded: 1843
Affiliation: Roman Catholic
Total Enrollment: 1,281 M, 1,394 W (full-time)
Cost: $10K–$20K
% Receiving Financial Aid: 55%
Admission: Highly Selective
Application Deadline: Feb. 1

Admission is highly selective. About 56% of applicants accepted, 39% of these actually enroll; 89% of freshmen graduate in top fifth of high school class, 99% in top two-fifths. Average freshman SAT scores: 573 verbal, 627 mathematical; 92% of freshmen score above 500 on verbal, 39% above 600; 97% score above 500 on mathematical, 69% above 600. *Required:* SAT, 3 ACH including English Composition; interview recommended (on- or off-campus). Criteria considered in admissions, in order of importance: high school academic record, standardized test scores, writing sample, recommendations, extracurricular activities; other factors considered: special talents, diverse student body, alumni children. *Entrance programs:* early decision, early admission, midyear admission, advanced placement, deferred admission. About 15% of entering students from private schools, 35% from parochial schools. *Apply* by February 1. *Transfers* welcome; 14 enrolled 1993–94.

Academic Environment. In contrast to recent trends in higher education, Holy Cross continues to place primary emphasis on the liberal arts. Students appear to be involved in all areas of decision making, including selection and promotion of faculty—rare in all but a very few institutions. From 1–3 students are members of almost all faculty committees and student members have a vote in faculty meetings. Graduation requirements include 10 distribution requirements: 1 course each in the arts, language or literature, history, religious studies, philosophy, cross-cultural studies, 2 courses in math and natural sciences; students must also demonstrate competence in a classical or foreign language. College characterized as "student centered" and oriented "very much toward developing the college as an academic institution." Students report liberal arts program as "strong" and "challenging". Degrees offered: bachelors. *Majors offered* include economics/accounting, fine arts, Chinese language, international studies with emphasis on Asia, Latin America, Middle East, or Russia, student-devised multi-disciplinary major, peace and conflict studies, psychobiology. Average undergraduate class size: 61% under 20, 36% 20–40, 2% over 40.

About 98% of students entering as freshmen graduate within four

years; 98% of freshmen return for sophomore year. *Special programs:* CLEP, independent study, study abroad, honors, internships, undergraduate research, 3-year degree, individualized majors, academic internships through Center for Experimental Studies, gerontology studies, freshman studies and seminars, 3–2 engineering, cross registration with colleges and universities in Worcester Consortium. Music Library: 3,000 volumes, 12,000 recordings, 4,000 scores. *Calendar:* semester.

Undergraduate degrees conferred (613). 47% were in Social Sciences, 20% were in Letters, 12% were in Psychology, 5% were in Life Sciences, 4% were in Mathematics, 4% were in Physical Sciences, 3% were in Philosophy and Religion, 3% were in Foreign Languages, remainder in 2 other fields.

Graduates Career Data. Advanced studies pursued by 33% of graduates; 18% enter graduate school; 6% enter medical school; 7% enter law school; 5% enter dental school; 2% enter business school. Medical schools typically enrolling largest numbers of graduates include Dartmouth, Georgetown, Tufts; dental schools include U. of Connecticut, U. of Pennsylvania; law schools include Boston College, Georgetown, Harvard; business schools include Babson, Boston College, Northwestern. About 60% of 1992–93 graduates employed. Career Development Services provides career advising through all stages of career planning; also offered: assistance with internship opportunities, and "extensive" alumni networking system.

Faculty. About 96% of faculty hold PhD or equivalent. About 72% of undergraduate classes taught by tenured faculty. About 33% of teaching faculty are female; 2% Black, 3% Hispanic, 3% other minority.

Student Body. About 39% of students from in state; 57% New England, 31% Middle Atlantic, 5% Midwest, 3% South, 2% each West, Northwest, 1% foreign. An estimated 95% of students reported as Catholic, 4% Protestant, 1% other; 4% Black, 2% Hispanic, 2% Asian, according to most recent data available. *Minority group students:* tutoring available to all students; support for Black Student Union (in part to carry on social program).

Religious Orientation. "As a Roman Catholic institution, in the Jesuit tradition, Holy Cross encourages voluntary expression of students' religious life and practices; 1 course in religion required of all students."

Varsity Sports. Men (Div.I): Baseball, Basketball, Crew, Cross Country, Diving, Football (IAA), Golf, Ice Hockey (III), Lacrosse, Soccer, Swimming, Tennis, Track. Women (Div.I): Basketball, Crew, Cross Country, Diving, Golf, Field Hockey, Lacrosse, Soccer, Softball, Swimming, Tennis, Track, Volleyball.

Campus Life. Students enjoy large amount of freedom in controlling own social life. College considers as "unacceptable" behavior which violates rights of others or is inconsistent with educational and religious commitments of the college. High interest reported in both varsity sports (most popular: football, basketball, lacrosse) and intramurals (most popular: football, softball for men; basketball, volleyball for men and women). Drinking rules conform to state law; drugs prohibited by state and federal laws. Smoking restricted in public buildings; students may request non-smoking roommate. Parking for residents reported as "inadequate" (only junior and senior residents allowed to park on-campus); situation for commuters is better.

About 87% of students live in coed dormitories; rest live in off-campus college-related housing or commute. Freshmen are given preference in college housing if all students cannot be accommodated. Intervisitation in men's and women's dormitory rooms unlimited. Sexes segregated in coed dormitories by floor; some floors impose intervisitation limits. There are no fraternities or sororities on campus. About 5% of resident students leave campus on weekends.

Annual Costs. Tuition and fees, $17,550; room and board, $6,300; estimated $1,300 other, exclusive of travel. About 55% of students receive financial aid; average amount of assistance, $14,500. Assistance is typically divided 66% scholarship/grant, 24% loan, 10% work. College reports 2 scholarships awarded on the basis of academic merit alone. *Meeting Costs:* university offers tuition prepayment plan.

Holy Family College

Philadelphia, Pennsylvania 19114 **(215) 637-7700**

A co-educational, liberal arts college for commuters, conducted by the Sisters of the Holy Family of Nazareth, Holy Family is located in a suburban section of Philadelphia. Most convenient major airport: Philadelphia International.

Founded: 1954
Affiliation: Roman Catholic
Total Enrollment: 282 M, 863 W (full-time); 292 M, 856 W (part-time)
Cost: < $10K
% Receiving Financial Aid: 87%
Admission: Non-selective
Application Deadline: June 1

Admission. Graduates of accredited high schools or equivalent with 16 units (12 in academic subjects) eligible; 57% of applicants accepted, 48% of these actually enroll; 26% of freshmen graduate in top fifth of high school class, 61% in top two-fifths. Average freshman SAT scores: 423–481 verbal, 444–512 mathematical. *Required:* SAT or ACT; interview recommended. Criteria considered in admissions, in order of importance: high school academic record, standardized test scores, extracurricular activities, recommendations; other factors considered: special talents, alumni children, diverse student body. About 10% of entering students from private schools, 69% from parochial schools. *Apply* by June 1. *Transfers* welcome.

Academic Environment. Graduation requirements include work in communications, quantification, religious studies, philosophy, humanities, social sciences, natural sciences, and ethics. Each department holds weekly seminar for its majors. All seniors take comprehensive examination. Degrees offered: associates, bachelors masters. *Majors offered* include usual arts and sciences, accounting, computer science, criminal justice, education, fire science administration, management, marketing, medical technology, nursing, psychobiology, psychology for business.

About 52% of students entering as freshmen graduate within four years, 65% within five years; 99% of first-time, full-time freshmen return for sophomore year. *Special programs:* CLEP, internships/work-study, independent study, undergraduate research, individualized majors. *Calendar:* semester, summer school.

Undergraduate degrees conferred (260). 24% were in Business and Management, 23% were in Education, 22% were in Health Sciences, 6% were in Protective Services, 6% were in Psychology, 3% were in Multi/Interdisciplinary Studies, 3% were in Letters, 3% were in Social Sciences, 3% were in Life Sciences, remainder in 6 other fields.

Graduates Career Data. Advanced studies pursued by 10% of graduates. About 84% of 1992 graduates employed. Fields typically hiring largest numbers of graduates include nursing, education, accounting, and marketing/business.

Student Body. About 94% of students from in state; 99% from Middle Atlantic, 1% foreign. An estimated 75% of students reported as Catholic, 10% Protestant, 3% Jewish, 12% other or unaffiliated; 2% Black, 1% Hispanic, 2% other minority.

Religious Orientation. Holy Family is a church-related institution; 9 credits of Religious Studies required of Catholic students; all students take 9 credits of philosophy.

Varsity Sports. Men: (NAIAW) Basketball, Soccer. Women: (NAIA, KAC, PAIAW, II), Basketball, Softball (IV).

Campus Life. Holy Family is a commuter college; no residence facilities; cars allowed for all. Students prohibited from using and possessing alcohol. Smoking allowed in designated area.

Annual Costs. Tuition and fees, $6,500. About 87% of students receive financial aid; average amount of assistance, $2,930. Assistance is typically divided 15% scholarship, 20% grant, 64% loan, 6% work. College reports 30% of scholarships awarded on the basis of academic merit alone, 30% for need alone. *Meeting Costs:* college offers deferred tuition payment plan.

Holy Names College

Oakland, California 94619 **(510) 436-1000**

A liberal arts institution, founded by the Sisters of the Holy Names, the college is independent but has a strong Roman Catholic heritage. Most convenient major airport: Oakland International.

Founded: 1868
Affiliation: Independent (Roman Catholic)
UG Enrollment: 98 M, 185 W (full-time); 44 M, 264 W (part-time)
Total Enrollment: 966
Cost: $10K–$20K
% Receiving Financial Aid: 71%
Admission: Non-selective
Application Deadline: August 1

Admission. High school graduates with B average in college preparatory program or GED average of at least 50 eligible; 63% of applicants accepted, 40% of these actually enroll. Average freshman SAT scores: 448 verbal, 450 mathematical. *Required:* SAT or ACT, essay. Criteria considered in admissions, in order of importance: high school academic record, standardized test scores, writing sample, recommendations, extracurricular activities. Entrance programs: midyear admission, deferred admission, advanced placement. About 27% of entering students from parochial or private schools. *Apply* by August 1; rolling admissions. *Transfers* welcome; 31 enrolled 1993–94.

Academic Environment. Graduation requirements include written and oral communication, foreign language, math, computer competency, American Institutions, humanistic studies, and 4 disciplinary courses. Degrees offered: bachelors, masters. *Majors offered* include business administration/economics, computer science/applied mathematics, nursing, individualized programs.

About 40% of entering freshmen graduate within four years; 78% of freshman return for sophomore year. *Special programs:* CLEP, independent study, internships, honors, study abroad, undergraduate research, 3–2 engineering, credit by examination, cross-registration with 8 neighboring colleges. Adult program: Weekend College offers bachelors and masters degree on weekends for adults over 24 years of age. *Calendar:* semester, summer session.

Undergraduate degrees conferred (69). 20% were in Health Sciences, 19% were in Business and Management, 13% were in Liberal/General Studies, 10% were in Social Sciences, 10% were in Multi/Interdisciplinary Studies, 10% were in Letters, 6% were in Psychology, 4% were in Philosophy and Religion, 3% were in Visual and Performing Arts, 3% were in Life Sciences, remainder in Foreign Languages.

Graduates Career Data. Advanced studies pursued by 25% of graduates.

Faculty. About 75% of faculty hold PhD or equivalent. About 67% of teaching faculty are female; 1% Black, 3% Hispanic, 5% Asian, 1% Native-American.

Student Body. An estimated 65% of students reported as Catholic; 22% as Black, 7% Hispanic, 6% Asian, 27% other minority.

Varsity Sports. Men (BAIAA): Basketball. Women (BAIAA): Basketball, Volleyball.

Campus Life. This is primarily a commuter institution; about 20% of men, 15% of women of students live in coed dormitories; rest commute. There are no fraternities or sororities on campus. About 50% of resident students leave campus on weekends.

Annual Costs. Tuition and fees, $10,784; room and board, $4,876; estimated $2,160 other, exclusive of travel. About 71% of students receive financial aid. Assistance is typically divided 5% scholarship, 35% grant, 55% loan, 5% work. College reports 51 scholarships awarded on the basis of academic merit alone, 30 for special talents alone, 70 for need alone. *Meeting Costs:* college offers deferred payment plan.

Hood College

Frederick, Maryland 21701-8575 **(301) 663-3400 or (800) 922-1599**

Hood is an independent college for women, historically affiliated with the United Church of Christ, which offers career-oriented programs as well as traditional liberal arts and sciences. College admits non-resident men to its undergraduate programs; graduate programs are non-residential and co-educational. The 50-acre campus is located in Frederick, a community of 30,000, 45 miles west of Baltimore and Washington, D.C. Most convenient major airports: Baltimore-Washington International, Dulles, National.

Founded: 1893
Affiliation: Independent
UG Enrollment: 38 M, 672 W (full-time); 109 M, 290 W (part-time)
Total Enrollment: 2,080
Cost: $10K–$20K
% Receiving Financial Aid: 60%
Admission: Selective
Application Deadline: Mar. 31

Admission is selective. About 80% of applicants accepted, 31% of these actually enroll; 55% of freshmen graduate in top fifth of high school class, 77% in top two-fifths. Average freshman scores: SAT, 493 verbal, 521 mathematical; middle 50% range: 430–540 verbal, 440–580 mathematical. *Required:* SAT or ACT, essay. Criteria considered in admissions, in order of importance: high school academic record, writing sample, standardized test scores, extracurricular activities, recommendations; other factors considered: special talents. *Entrance programs:* early decision, midyear admission, deferred admission, advanced placement. About 20% of entering students from private or parochial schools. *Apply* by March 31. *Transfers* welcome; 39 enrolled 1993–94.

Academic Environment. Since its founding Hood has been a liberal arts college committed to preparing women for the world of work and, over the years, has adapted its curriculum to the changing professional opportunities for women. Many students continue to choose majors in the arts and sciences, but increasing numbers choose business and management, computer and informational sciences, biology, education, communication arts, also humanities and social sciences. Graduation requirements include core curriculum: Foundation section has courses in English, computation, and physical education; Methods of Inquiry section includes one course in literature, and one in art, music, film, or another appropriate field of "Aesthetic Appreciation", 2 semesters of science, including a lab science, and at least one course in "Historical Analysis", "Social and Behavioral Analysis", and "Philosophical Inquiry"; Civilization section covers important periods of Western Civilization, including American society, at least one non-Western culture, and the impact of science and technology on the modern world. College honor code, enforced by students, allows for self-scheduling of final exams. Degrees offered: bachelors, masters. *Majors offered* include molecular biology, marine biology, environmental studies, management, humanities, social work, political science, sociology, philosophy, psychobiology, dietetics and nutrition, law and society, Latin American studies, special education, medical technology. Average undergraduate class size: 83% under 20, 17% 20–40, none over 40.

About 65% of students entering as freshmen graduate within four years, 65% eventually; 80% of freshmen return for sophomore year. *Special programs:* internships, Washington Semester, field work, CLEP, independent study, study abroad, honors, Duke U. Marine Sciences Education Consortium Member, 2–2 engineering, individualized majors, cross registration with Frederick, Hagerstown, Montgomery Community College, semester at American U. Adult programs: Upper division program in BBA and BS in Computer Science offered in evening programs. *Calendar:* semester.

Undergraduate degrees conferred (271). 20% were in Business and Management, 11% were in Social Sciences, 10% were in Education, 10% were in Home Economics, 8% were in Psychology, 8% were in Life Sciences, 6% were in Law, 6% were in Communications, 4% were in Public Affairs, 4% were in Letters, 3% were in Computer and Engineering Related Technology, 3% were in Mathematics, 3% were in Foreign Languages, remainder in 4 other fields.

Graduates Career Data. Advanced studies pursued by 30% of graduates; 12% enter business school; 7% enter graduate school; 5% enter social work; 3% enter medical school; 3% enter law school. Medical schools enrolling largest numbers of graduates include Cornell, U. of Rochester, U. of Maryland at Baltimore; law schools include Georgetown, Catholic U.; business schools include Loyola. About 80% of 1992–93 graduates employed. Fields typically hiring largest numbers of graduates include public school systems, banks, computer companies. Career Development Services include career and graduate school advising from freshman year, access to national job listing databases, workshops, alumnae networks.

Faculty. About 91% of faculty hold PhD or equivalent. About 46% of undergraduate classes taught by tenured faculty. About 58% of teaching faculty are female; 5% Black, 2% Hispanic, 2% other minority.

Student Body. About 58% of students from in state; 76% Middle Atlantic, 10% New England, 4% South, 2% Midwest, 1% West, 7% foreign. An estimated 41% of students reported as Protestant, 13% Catholic, 1% Jewish; 17% as Black, 3% Hispanic, 2% Asian.

Varsity Sports. Women (NCAA, Div. III): Field Hockey, Lacrosse, Swimming, Tennis, Volleyball.

Campus Life. Both student leaders and administration source consider social life good, but cite the need for a student center, which is reported to be in the planning stages. Student-planned activities and active student government are also praised. Both sources feel the student who would be "least at home on campus" would be a "party animal." Students have significant voice in changing regulations governing campus social life through numerous committees consisting of students, faculty, and administration. College attracts a substantial number of adult learners; about one third of undergraduates are 23 or older, all commute, many attend part-time. Cars allowed for all students; drinking in residence halls permitted for those over 21; dormitory option of 24-hour male weekend guests. Fairly wide variety of cultural and social activities on campus, supplemented by resources of Washington and Baltimore, 45 miles away. Daily college shuttle service to Washington metro rail.

About 73% of traditional-age women live in dormitories; all men, rest of women commute. Freshmen given preference in college housing if all students cannot be accommodated. There are no fraternities or sororities on campus. About 25% of resident students leave campus on weekends.

Annual Costs. Tuition and fees, $13,258; room and board, $5,752; estimated $1,090 other, exclusive of travel. About 60% of students receive financial aid; average amount of assistance, $11,000. Assistance is typically divided 20% scholarship, 40% grant, 27% loan, 13% work. College reports 50 scholarships awarded on the basis of academic merit alone. *Meeting Costs:* college offers prepayment plan, long-term low-interest loans, family tuition plan for second student from one family.

Hope College

Holland, Michigan 49423 **(616) 394-7850**

A liberal arts college, Hope is affiliated with the Reformed Church in America, and is independent of church control. The campus is located near Lake Michigan in a city of 28,000, 25 miles southwest of Grand Rapids. Most convenient major airport: Grand Rapids.

Founded: 1851
Affiliation: Independent (Reformed Church)
Total Enrollment: 1,082 M, 1,423 W (full-time); 94 M, 114 W (part-time)
Cost: $10K–$20K
% Receiving Financial Aid: 56%
Admission: Selective
Application Deadline: Rolling

Admission is selective. About 87% of applicants accepted, 43% of these actually enroll; 62% of freshmen graduate in top fifth of high school class, 88% in top two-fifths. Average freshman scores, middle 50% range: SAT, 950–1210 combined verbal, mathematical; ACT, 22–28 composite. *Required:* SAT or ACT. *Apply:* rolling admissions. *Transfers* welcome; 105 enrolled 1993–94.

Academic Environment. President states that students "included in just about every policy matter." According to student leader, academic program extends to "student/staff participation in living/learning experiences." Core curriculum requires completion of 57 hours of general education courses distributed among 8 different subject groups. Degrees offered: bachelors. *Majors offered* include biochemistry, physics, engineering, chemistry, physics, biology, computer science. Average undergraduate class size: 61% under 20, 34% 20–40, 5% over 40.

About 58% of students entering as freshmen graduate within four years, 73% eventually; 90% of freshmen return for sophomore year. *Special programs:* CLEP, independent study, study abroad, undergraduate research, 3-year degree, individualized majors, optional May term, June term, programs of GLCA, Washington Semester, Community Semester (work/study program in business, social agencies, industry in Western Michigan area), electronic piano laboratory, "hundreds" of local internships, 3–2 engineering. *Calendar:* semester, summer school.

Undergraduate degrees conferred (516). 19% were in Business and Management, 10% were in Social Sciences, 9% were in Letters, 8% were in Life Sciences, 7% were in Multi/Interdisciplinary Studies, 7% were in Psychology, 6% were in Education, 6% were in Visual and Performing Arts, 5% were in Physical Sciences, 5% were in Public Affairs, 4% were in Communications, 3% were in Health Sciences, 3% were in Philosophy and Religion, 3% were in Foreign Languages, 3% were in Engineering, remainder in 2 other fields.

Graduates Career Data. Advanced studies pursued by 27% of graduates; 4% enter medical school; 1% enter dental school; 3% enter law school; 1% enter business school. *Careers in business and industry* pursued by 42% of graduates.

Faculty. About 79% of faculty hold PhD or equivalent. About 70% of undergraduate classes taught by tenured faculty. About 33% of teaching faculty are female.

Student Body. About 77% of students from in state; 90% Midwest, 4% Middle Atlantic, 1% each South, West, New England, 3% foreign. An estimated 69% of students reported as Protestant, 13% Catholic, 18% unaffiliated; 1% as Black, 2% Hispanic, 2% Asian, 3% other minority. *Minority group students:* special financial provisions, academic advising.

Religious Orientation. Hope is an independent institution with ties to the Reformed Church in America; 2 courses in religion required of all students; attendance at tri-weekly chapel optional.

Varsity Sports. Men (Div.III): Baseball, Basketball, Cross Country, Diving, Football, Golf, Soccer, Swimming, Tennis, Track. Women (Div.III): Basketball, Cross Country, Diving, Golf, Soccer, Softball, Swimming, Tennis, Track, Volleyball.

Campus Life. Regulations governing campus life relaxed. Intervisitation allowed. Alcohol use restricted on campus and at college functions to licensed establishments. Students expected to live in college housing; exemptions available for juniors and seniors.

About 21% of men, 35% of women live in traditional dormitories; 32% of students live in coed dormitories; 23% of men, 14% of women live in off-campus college-related housing; 11% of men, 19% of women commute. Freshmen given preference in college housing if all students cannot be accommodated. Sexes segregated in coed dormitories either by wing or floor. There are 5 fraternities, 6 sororities on campus which about 12% of men, 8% of women join; 13% of men, 2% of women live in fraternities and sororities.

Annual Costs. Tuition and fees, $11,542; room and board, $4,156; estimated $1,135 other, exclusive of travel. About 56% of students receive financial aid; average amount of assistance, $8,605. Assistance is typically divided 55% scholarship, 32% loan, 13% work. College reports 30 scholarships awarded for special talent in the arts. *Meeting Costs:* college offers monthly payment plan.

Houghton College

Houghton, New York 14744 **(716) 567-9353 or (800) 777-2556**

A church-related college, offering "a liberal arts education from the evangelical Christian perspective," Houghton's 1,300 acre campus is located in a village of 1,600, 65 miles southeast of Buffalo. College also has branch campus in Buffalo. Most convenient major airports: Buffalo, Rochester.

Founded: 1883
Affiliation: Wesleyan
Total Enrollment: 483 M, 727 W (full-time)
Cost: < $10K
% Receiving Financial Aid: 91%
Admission: Very Selective
Application Deadline: Rolling

Admission is very selective. About 83% of applicants accepted, 40% of these actually enroll; 56% of freshmen graduate in top fifth of high school class, 85% in top two-fifths. Average freshman scores: SAT, 500 verbal, 535 mathematical; 51% of freshmen score above 500 on verbal, 22% above 600, 3% above 700; 69% score above 500 on mathematical, 26% above 600, 6% above 700; ACT, 24 composite. *Required:* SAT or ACT, pastor's recommendation, essay; interview recommended. Criteria considered in admissions, in order of importance: high school academic record, Christian commitment, standardized test scores, recommendations, writing sample, extracurricular activities; other factors considered: special talents. *Entrance programs:* midyear admission, deferred admission. About 20% of entering class are from private schools, 80% from public schools. *Apply:* rolling admissions. *Transfers* welcome; 78 enrolled 1993–94.

Academic Environment. Degrees offered: associates, bachelors. Student body characterized as strongly oriented toward occupational/professional goals. Pressures for academic achievement appear moderate. Core requirements include coursework in English composition and research, natural sciences, mathematics, social sciences, fine arts, religion/philosophy, physical education, and foreign language. College includes a 300-acre equestrian center, as well as the Buffalo Suburban Campus which offers student teaching opportunities, business and psychology internships, and the adult degree completion program. Average undergraduate class size: 37% under 20, 60% between 20–40, 3% over 40.

About 63% of students entering as freshmen graduate within four years, 66% eventually; 87% of freshmen return for sophomore year. *Special programs:* CLEP, independent study, study abroad, honors, undergraduate research, 3-year degree, cross registration through Christian College Consortium, 3–2 engineering, combined nursing programs (with Columbia, Cornell, Rochester, Case Western Reserve), medical technology programs with many hospitals, Religion-Salvation Army School for Officers Training; internship in business, psychology. Adult programs: 15 month degree program in organizational studies for those 25 years or older and with 62 acceptable credits. *Calendar:* semester, May term, summer school.

Undergraduate degrees conferred (213). 29% were in Education, 12% were in Business and Management, 9% were in Philosophy and Religion, 8% were in Psychology, 8% were in Social Sciences, 8% were in Letters, 6% were in Life Sciences, 5% were in Communications, 4% were in Mathematics, 3% were in Physical Sciences, 3% were in Visual and Performing Arts, 3% were in Multi/Interdisciplinary Studies, remainder in 2 other fields.

Graduates Career Data. Advanced studies pursued by 21% of students; 3% enter medical school; 1% enter dental school; 2% enter law school; 6% enter business school; 5% education schools; 1% enter seminary. Business schools typically enrolling largest number of students include RIT. Fields typically hiring largest numbers of graduates include education, business, Christian service, scientific/technical. Career Development Services include identifying career options, preparing placement files/resumes, developing interviewing skills, helping to initiate contact with employers.

Faculty. About 85% of faculty hold PhD or equivalent. About 80% of undergraduate classes taught by tenured faculty. About 24% of teaching faculty are female; 2% Black.

Student Body. College seeks a national student body; 60% from Middle Atlantic, 12% New England, 10% Midwest, 2% West, 2% Northwest, 12% New England, 5% Foreign. An estimated 97% of students reported as Protestant, 3% Catholic; 2% as Black, 1% Hispanic, 2% Asian, 1% other minority. *Minority group students:* special financial provisions.

Religious Orientation. Houghton is a church-related institution; 4 hours of Biblical literature, 3 hours of religion or philosophy elective, attendance at chapel services Tuesday through Friday required of all students. Places of worship available on campus for Protestants.

Varsity Sports. Men (NAIA): Basketball, Cross Country, Soccer, Track. Women (NAIA): Basketball, Cross Country, Field Hockey, Soccer, Track, Volleyball.

Campus Life. Student leader notes that campus life is influenced by college's "country setting" and Christian principles. Students sign a statement of community responsibilities prohibiting social dancing, drugs, alcohol, smoking, chewing tobacco, drinking, and premarital sex. Faculty and administration similarly restricted. Intervisitation scheduled once a week. All freshman and sophomores live in the college dormitories. Juniors and seniors may choose college dormitories or community-owned housing approved for dormitory use. Freshmen given preference in college housing if all students cannot be accommodated.

According to most recent data available about 59% of men, 66% of women live in traditional dormitories; no coed dormitories; rest live in off-campus housing or commute. There are no fraternities or sororities. About 10–15% of resident students leave campus on weekends.

Annual Costs. Tuition and fees, $9,720; room and board, $3,400; estimated $1,200 other, exclusive of travel. About 91% of students receive financial aid; average amount of assistance, $9,000. Assistance is typically divided 20% scholarship, 25% grant, 40% loan, 15% work. College reports 150 scholarships awarded for academic merit alone, 40 for special talents.

Houston Baptist University

Houston, Texas 77074-3298 **(713) 774-3210 or (800) 969-3210**

A church-related, liberal arts institution, located in Houston.

Founded: 1960	**Cost:** < $10K
Affiliation: Southern Baptist	**Admission:** Non-selective
Total Enrollment: 592 M, 1,111 W (full-time)	**Application Deadline:** 15 days before registration

Admission. Graduates of accredited high schools with college preparatory program eligible; 59% of applicants accepted; 98% of these actually enroll. *Required:* SAT or ACT, essay; interview recommended. Criteria considered in admissions, in order of importance: standardized test scores, high school academic record, recommendations. *Apply* by 15 days before registration. *Transfers* welcome.

Academic Environment. Degrees offered: associates (in nursing), bachelors, masters. About 40% of general education requirements for graduation are elective; distribution requirements fairly numerous. *Special programs:* CLEP, January term, independent study, study abroad, honors, undergraduate research, cross-registration with U. of Houston. *Calendar:* quarter, summer school.

Undergraduate degrees conferred (514). 27% were in Business and Management, 13% were in Education, 8% were in Health Sciences, 8% were in Psychology, 7% were in Social Sciences, 6% were in Life Sciences, 5% were in Physical Sciences, 5% were in Computer and Engineering Related Technology, 5% were in Communications, 4% were in Public Affairs, 4% were in Visual and Performing Arts, 3% were in Letters, 3% were in Foreign Languages, remainder in 2 other fields.

Faculty. About 71% of faculty hold PhD or equivalent. About 43% of teaching faculty are female.

Student Body. University seeks a national student body; 97% of students from in state; 1% foreign.

Religious Orientation. Houston Baptist is a church-related institution; 3 courses in Christianity, "regular attendance at all convocations, student assemblies, and chapel services" required of all students.

Campus Life. About 11% of men, 10% of women live in traditional dormitories; no coed dormitories; rest live in off-campus housing or commute. No intervisitation in men's or women's dormitory rooms. There are 4 fraternities, 2 sororities on campus which about 13% of men, 8% of women join; they provide no residence facilities.

Annual Costs. Tuition and fees, $6,500; room and board, $2,340. University reports some scholarships awarded for academic merit alone, some for music, some for athletics; federal aid awarded on the basis of need.

University of Houston

Houston, Texas 77204-2161 **(713) 743-1000**

A state-supported institution, the University of Houston is located on a 540-acre campus, 3 miles from downtown Houston. Most convenient major airport: Hobby.

Founded: 1927	**Total Enrollment:** 32,124
Affiliation: State	**Cost:** < $10K
UG Enrollment: 14,999 M, W (full-time); 7,387 M, W (part-time)	**Admission:** Selective
	Application Deadline: June 15

Admission is very selective for College of Engineering; selective for colleges of Humanities and Fine Arts, Architecture, Business Administration, Natural Sciences and Mathematics, Social Sciences and Technology, and Hilton School of Hotel and Restaurant Management. For all schools, 60% of applicants accepted, 60% of these actually enroll.

For Humanities and Fine Arts (658 M, 877 W, f-t; 291 M, 544 W, p-t), 41% of freshmen graduate in top fifth of high school class, 83% in top two-fifths. Average freshman scores: SAT, 499 M, 498 W verbal, 519 M, 483 W mathematical; ACT, 22 M, 22 W composite, 19 M, 18 W mathematical, according to most recent data available.

For Architecture (259 M, 73 W, f-t; 68 M, 28 W, p-t), 48% of freshmen graduate in top fifth of high school class, 84% in top two-fifths. Average freshman scores: SAT, 448 M, 446 W verbal, 523 M, 478 W mathematical; ACT, 25 M, 17 W composite, 27 M, 17 W mathematical, according to most recent data available.

For Business Administration (851 M, 911 W, f-t; 404 M, 637 W, p-t), 56% of freshmen graduate in top fifth of high school class, 96% in top two-fifths. Average freshman scores: SAT, 490 M, 475 W verbal, 562 M, 523 W mathematical; ACT, 24 M, 24 W composite, 24 M, 24 W mathematical, according to most recent data available.

For Education (146 M, 431 W, f-t; 59 M, 272 W, p-t), 29% of freshmen graduate in top fifth of high school class, 75% in top two-fifths. Average freshman scores: SAT, 416 M, 403 W verbal, 457 M, 431 W mathematical; ACT, 16 M, 19 W composite, 15 M, 19 W mathematical, according to most recent data available.

For Engineering (971 M, 181 W, f-t; 412 M, 72 W, p-t), 72% of freshmen graduate in top fifth of high school class, all in top two-fifths. Average freshman scores: SAT, 530 M, 495 W verbal, 627 M, 560 W mathematical; 57% score above 500 on verbal, 22% above 600, 4% above 700; 88% score above 500 on mathematical, 53% above 600, 19% above 700; ACT, 26 M, 24 W composite, 27 M, 24 W mathematical, according to most recent data available.

For Hotel and Restaurant Management (312 M, 276 W, f-t; 90 M, 71 W, p-t), 41% of freshmen graduate in top fifth of high school class, 76% in top two-fifths. Average freshman scores: SAT, 484 M, 487 W verbal, 529 M, 494 W mathematical; ACT, 22 M, 22 W composite, 21 M, 21 W mathematical, according to most recent data available.

For Natural Science and Mathematics (909 M, 701 W, f-t; 493 M, 425 W, p-t), 60% of freshmen graduate in top fifth of high school class, 94% in top two-fifths. Average freshman scores: SAT, 499 M, 466 W verbal, 574 M, 511 W mathematical; 38% score above 500 on verbal, 13% above 600, 2% above 700; 62% score above 500 on mathematical, 31% above 600, 6% above 700; ACT, 25 M, 23 W composite, 26 M, 23 W mathematical, according to most recent data available.

For Social Science (603 M, 798 W, f-t; 225 M, 453 W, p-t), 50% of freshmen graduate in top fifth of high school class, 85% in top two-fifths. Average freshman scores: SAT, 516 M, 467 W verbal, 541 M, 455 W mathematical; ACT, 24 M, 19 W composite, 23 M, 18 W mathematical, according to most recent data available.

For Technology (560 M, 99 W, f-t; 558 M, 146 W, p-t), 61% of freshmen graduate in top fifth of high school class, 78% in top two-fifths. Average freshman scores: SAT, 460 M, 464 W verbal, 494 M, 482 W mathematical; ACT, 21 M composite, 22 M mathematical, according to most recent data available.

Required: SAT or ACT. Criteria considered in admissions, in order of importance: high school academic record, standardized test scores, extracurricular activities; other factors considered: special talents. *Out-of-state* freshman applicants: university welcomes students from out of state. State does not limit out-of-state enrollment. No special requirements for out-of-state applicants. States from which most out-of-state students are drawn include Louisiana, California, New York. *Entrance programs:* advanced placement. *Apply* by June 15; April 1 for financial aid. *Transfers* welcome; 3,000 enrolled 1993–94.

Academic Environment. Administration reports core curriculum required of all students. *Undergraduate studies* offered to freshmen by colleges listed above; upperclassmen may enter colleges of Optometry, Pharmacy. Core curriculum requires 12 hours of English and writing, algebra and 3 additional hours in mathematics or computer science, 6 hours physical or life science, and 6 hours American history, government, cultural heritage and social or behavioral sciences. *Majors offered* in 120 fields including usual arts and sciences, architecture, biophysical sciences, drama, computer science, engineering, finance, journalism, Latin American studies, management systems and strategies, radio and television, speech pathology and audiology. Numerous programs have received national recognition, including business administration, chemical engineering, creative writing, and hotel and restaurant management. In addition, the affiliated Law Center is highly rated as well as the School of Optometry.

Special programs: CLEP, independent study, study abroad, honors, undergraduate research, Washington Semester, London Semester, cooperative work/study program (offered in arts and sciences, hotel and restaurant management, engineering, technology, education). *Calendar:* semester, summer school.

Undergraduate degrees conferred (3125). 31% were in Business and Management, 10% were in Social Sciences, 10% were in Education, 9% were in Psychology, 6% were in Health Sciences, 6% were in Engineering, 5% were in Communications, 3% were in Life Sciences, 3% were in Engineering and Engineering Related Technology, 3% were in Architecture and Environmental Design, remainder in 13 other fields.

Graduates Career Data. According to most recent data available, full-time graduate or professional study pursued immediately after graduation by 23% of students; 2% enter medical school; 2% enter dental school; 3% enter law school; 8% enter business school. Medical, dental, law, and business schools typically enrolling largest numbers of graduates include U. of Texas, Baylor, U. of Houston. *Careers in business and industry* pursued by 75% of graduates. Corporations typically hiring the largest number of graduates include Arthur Andersen, HISD, Peat Marwick & Mitchell, DeLoitte Haskins & Sells. *Career Counseling Program* assists students in defining career goals and job placement during college and after graduation. Student assessment of program reported as good for both career guidance and job placement. Alumni reported as active in job placement, but not in career guidance.

Faculty. About 80% of faculty hold PhD or equivalent. About 30% of teaching faculty are female.

Student Body. About 90% of students from in state; 4% foreign. An estimated 9% of students reported as Black, 13% Hispanic, 13% Asian, 1% other minority. *Minority group students:* special financial, academic, and social provisions available including Basic Educational Grant Program, Afro-American and Mexican American studies, tutorial projects, Black Student Union, Mexican American Youth Organization.

Varsity Sports. Men (Div.IA): Baseball, Basketball, Cross Country, Football, Golf, Track. Women (Div.IA): Basketball, Cross Country, Swimming, Tennis, Track, Volleyball.

Campus Life. University still serves a largely commuter student body; however, a substantial number of students live on campus allowing for a wide range of student organizations and activities. Intervisitation regulated by residents of each dormitory. Cars allowed for all.

About 9% of students live in dormitories on campus; rest live in off-campus housing or commute. There are 17 fraternities, 10 sororities on campus; they provide no residence facilities.

Annual Costs. Tuition and fees, $1,015 (out-of-state, $4,007); room and board, $4,200. About 39% of students receive financial aid. University reports some scholarships awarded on the basis of academic merit alone. *Meeting Costs:* university offers installment plan.

Howard Payne University

Brownwood, Texas 76801 **(915) 646-2502**

A church-related university, located in a town of 23,000, 80 miles southeast of Abilene. Most convenient major airport: Dallas-Fort Worth.

Founded: 1889
Affiliation: Southern Baptist
Total Enrollment: 649 M, 561 W (full-time); 138 M, 119 W (part-time)
Cost: < $10K
% Receiving Financial Aid: 85%
Admission: Non-selective
Application Deadline: August 15

Admission. Graduates of accredited high schools who rank in top half of class admitted; others admitted conditionally or by examination; 88% of applicants accepted; 71% actually enroll. About 28% of freshmen graduate in top fifth of high school class, 62% in top two-fifths. Average freshman scores: SAT, 405 verbal, 458 mathematical; ACT, 20 composite. *Required:* SAT or ACT. Criteria considered in admissions, in order of importance: standardized test scores, high school academic record, recommendations, extracurricular activities; other factors considered: special talents, religious affiliation and/or commitment. *Entrance programs:* early decision, early admission, midyear admission, advanced placement. *Apply* by August 15; rolling admission. *Transfers* welcome; 106 enrolled 1993–94.

Academic Environment. Degrees offered: bachelors. Core requirements include courses in Bible, computer science, English, fine arts, natural sciences, mathematics, social sciences, oral communication, and physical education activity. Douglas MacArthur Academy of Freedom Program offers an interdisciplinary honors program. Average undergraduate class size: 70% under 20, 21% between 20–40, 9% over 40. About 20% of students entering as freshmen graduate within four years, 30% eventually; 66% of freshmen return for sophomore year. *Special programs:* CLEP, independent study, study abroad, honors, cross registration with nearby schools. *Calendar:* semester, summer school.

Undergraduate degrees conferred (186). 22% were in Business and Management, 14% were in Letters, 14% were in Education, 12% were in Social Sciences, 9% were in Theology, 6% were in Life Sciences, 5% were in Psychology, 4% were in Public

Affairs, 4% were in Liberal/General Studies, 4% were in Mathematics, 3% were in Visual and Performing Arts, remainder in 4 other fields.

Graduates Career Data. Advanced studies pursued by 25% of students. About 78% of 1992–93 graduates employed. Fields typically hiring largest number of graduates include education, business, church-affiliated. Career Development Services include aptitude testing, placement services, resume/interview workshops, on-campus recruitment, internships, placement video library, monthly placement bulletin.

Faculty. About 59% of faculty hold PhD or equivalent. About 16% of undergraduate classes taught by tenured faculty. About 28% of teaching faculty are female.

Student Body. University does not seek a national student body; 97% of students from Texas, 3% other southwestern states. An estimated 83% of students reported as Protestant, 1% Catholic, 16% unaffiliated. Average age of undergraduate student: 24.

Religious Orientation. Howard Payne is a church-related institution; 6 semester hours of religion, attendance at chapel service or assembly 3 times weekly required of all students. About 76% of students are affiliated with Baptist church.

Varsity Sports. Men (NAIA, Div.II): Baseball, Basketball, Cross Country, Football, Golf, Tennis, Track. Women (NAIA, Div.II): Basketball, Cross Country, Tennis, Track, Volleyball.

Campus Life. About 44% of students live in traditional dormitories; no coed dormitories; rest commute. No intervisitation in men's or women's dormitory rooms. There are 8 fraternities, 4 sororities, and 4 honorary societies on campus, which about 12% of men, 18% of women join. About 50% of resident students leave campus on weekends.

Annual Costs. Tuition and fees, $5,070; room and board, $2,982. About 85% of students receive financial aid; average amount of assistance, $6,000. Assistance is typically divided 17% scholarship, 33% grant, 43% loan, 7% work. College reports some scholarships awarded on the basis of academic merit alone.

Howard University

Washington, D.C. 20059 (202) 636-6200

A national institution, established primarily to give the American Negro opportunities for higher education, Howard University was chartered by Congress and receives support annually from the Federal Government. It is now interracial, with an international student body and faculty. The 72-acre campus is located in the heart of the nation's capital. Most convenient major airport: National.

Founded: 1867
Affiliation: National and Independent
UG Enrollment: 2,579 M, 4,144 W (full-time); 431 M, 586 W (part-time)
Total Enrollment: 10,868
Cost: < $10K
% Receiving Financial Aid: 65%
Admission: Non-selective
Application Deadline: April 1

Admission. Requirements vary between schools; for most schools high school graduates with minimum combined SAT of 700 and rank in top half of high school class eligible; 56% of applicants accepted, 31% of these actually enroll. Average freshman scores: SAT, 420 verbal, 450 mathematical; ACT, 20 composite. *Required:* SAT or ACT; ACH for some majors. Criteria considered in admissions, in order of importance: standardized test scores, high school academic record, recommendations; other factors considered: special talents for some programs. *Entrance programs:* early decision, early admission, advanced placement. About 25% of entering students from private or parochial schools. *Apply* by April 1. *Transfers* welcome.

Academic Environment. Degrees offered: bachelors, masters, doctoral. Effort made to adapt curriculum to individual needs of students. While size of university makes this difficult, the number of students who go on to graduate and professional schools suggests an impressive degree of success. University has many celebrated faculty members, teaching either full- or part-time, who provide unusual opportunities for more able students. Uneven preparation of many students does, however, create situation where some students are doing advanced independent study while others are receiving remedial instruction. Administration reports 75% of courses needed for graduation are required; distribution requirements fairly numerous. *Undergraduate studies* offered by colleges of Liberal Arts, Allied Health Sciences, Fine Arts, schools of Architecture Planning, Business and Communications, Education, Engineering, Human Ecology, Nursing. *Majors offered* in Liberal Arts in addition to usual studies include African studies, Afro-American studies, computer science, home economics, aerospace studies. Average undergraduate class size: 65% of classes under 20, 23% between 20–40, 12% over 40.

About 21% of entering freshmen graduate in four years, 50% eventually; 47% of freshmen do not return for sophomore year. *Special programs:* independent study, undergraduate research, study abroad, honors, cross-registration with other Washington universities, 3–3 combined law program, cooperative work-study program. *Calendar:* semester, summer school.

Undergraduate degrees conferred (1384). 20% were in Business and Management, 14% were in Communications, 10% were in Social Sciences, 8% were in Engineering, 6% were in Psychology, 6% were in Health Sciences, 5% were in Life Sciences, 5% were in Allied Health, 5% were in Home Economics, 3% were in Letters, 3% were in Computer and Engineering Related Technology, 3% were in Physical Sciences, 3% were in Architecture and Environmental Design, remainder in 9 other fields.

Graduates Career Data. Advanced studies pursued by about 65% of graduates; 5% enter law school; 3% enter medical school; 4% enter dental school; 6% enter business school. Medical, dental, law, business schools typically enrolling largest numbers of students include Howard U, U. of Maryland, U. of Pennsylvania. About 60% of 1992–93 graduates are employed. Fields typically employing largest numbers of graduates include business, engineering, communications, education.

Faculty. About 89% of full-time faculty hold PhD or equivalent. About 34% of teaching faculty are female; 65% Black, 15% other ethnic minorities.

Student Body. University seeks a national student body; 13% of students from in city; 39% South, 5% Midwest, 12% West, 9% foreign. An estimated 40% of students reported as Protestant, 15% Catholic, 40% unaffiliated, 5% other; 85% as Black, 2% white, 2% Asian, 11% other minorities.

Religious Orientation. University makes no religious demands on students. Religious clubs on campus include YM-YWCA, Bahai, Canterbury, Christian Science, Newman Society of Ecumenical Dialogue, United Christian Fellowship, United Pentecostal Association, Walter Brooks, Wesley. Churches and other places of worship available in immediate community for major faiths; nondenominational chapel on campus.

Varsity Sports. Men (Div.I): Baseball, Basketball, Cross Country, Football, Soccer, Tennis, Track, Volleyball, Wrestling. Women (Div.I): Basketball, Track, Volleyball.

Campus Life. Freshmen are given preference in college housing if all students cannot be accommodated.

About 30% of students live in traditional dormitories; 15% of students in coed dormitories; rest live in off-campus housing or commute. Intervisitation in men's and women's dormitory rooms unlimited. Sexes segregated in coed dormitories by floor. There are 2 fraternities, 4 sororities on campus; they provide no residence facilities. An estimated 3% of resident students leave campus on weekends.

Annual Costs. Tuition and fees, $7,535; room and board, $4,145. About 65% of students receive financial aid; average amount of assistance, $6,770. Assistance is typically divided 70% scholarship, grant and loan, 8% work. University reports 1,293 scholarships awarded on the basis of academic merit alone, 565 for special talents, 1,945 for need.

Humphreys College

Stockton, California 95207

An independent college of business, offering associates, bachelors and doctoral degrees, Humphreys College is affiliated with the Humphreys College of Law. All programs can be scheduled with evening attendance only; average age of undergraduate student is 27. Admissions are open.

Founded: 1896 **Affiliation:** Independent

College for Human Services
(see Audrey Cohen College)

Humboldt State University
(See California State University/Humboldt State University)

Hunter College
(See City University of New York)

Huntingdon College
Montgomery, Alabama 36106 (205) 834-3300

An independent college, maintaining ties with the United Methodist Church, Huntingdon is located in the state capital (pop. 133,400). Most convenient major airport: Dannelly Field (Montgomery).

Founded: 1854
Affiliation: Independent (United Methodist)
Total Enrollment: 282 M, 382 W (full-time); 32 M, 94 W (part-time)
Cost: < $10K
% Receiving Financial Aid: 89%
Admission: Non-selective
Application Deadline: June 1

Admission. Graduates of accredited high schools, preferably with 15 units, eligible; 85% of applicants accepted, 32% of these actually enroll; according to most recent data available 20% of freshmen graduate in top fifth of high school class, 34% in top two-fifths. Average freshman scores: ACT: 23 composite. *Required:* SAT or ACT; minimum HS GPA. Criteria considered in admissions, in order of importance: high school academic record, standardized test scores, extracurricular activities, recommendations; other factors considered: special talents. *Entrance programs:* early admission. *Apply* by June 1; rolling admission. About 83% of freshmen come from public schools, 17% private schools. *Transfers* welcome; 47 enrolled 1993–94.

Academic Environment. Degrees offered: associates, bachelors. About 60% of general education requirements for graduation are elective; no distribution requirements. Students cite small classes and faculty accessibility as strengths of the program. Average undergraduate class size: 95% under 20, 5% between 20–40. About 42% of students entering as freshmen graduate within four years, 48% eventually; 68% of freshmen return for sophomore year. *Special programs:* CLEP, independent study, honors, individualized majors, study abroad, 2-week January Term, 3–2 engineering. *Calendar:* semester, January interterm, summer school.

Undergraduate degrees conferred (138). 28% were in Business and Management, 13% were in Education, 12% were in Letters, 11% were in Visual and Performing Arts, 9% were in Physical Sciences, 8% were in Psychology, 7% were in Social Sciences, 5% were in Computer and Engineering Related Technology, 4% were in Philosophy and Religion, remainder in 3 other fields.

Graduates Career Data. Advanced studies pursued by 37% of 1992 graduates. Career Development Services include career counseling, internships, resume preparation, intervention techniques.

Faculty. About 70% of faculty hold PhD or equivalent. About 20% of teaching faculty are female.

Student Body. About 90% of students from South, 4% Foreign. An estimated 77% of students reported as Protestant, 10% Catholic; 8% as Black, 1% Hispanic, 1% Asian.

Religious Orientation. Huntingdon is an independent institution with ties to the United Methodist Church; about 33% of students are affiliated with the Methodist church; 6 hours of Biblical heritage required of all freshmen. Student religious activities are coordinated by Campus Ministries Association Council.

Varsity Sports. Men (NAIA): Baseball, Golf, Soccer, Tennis. Women (NAIA): Soccer, Softball, Tennis, Volleyball.

Campus Life. Students report that the location allows easy access to cultural, recreational and social activities in Montgomery, Atlanta, New Orleans and the Gulf of Mexico. About 51% of men, 44% of women live in traditional dormitories; no coed dormitories; rest commute, according to most recent data available. Intervisitation in men's and women's dormitory rooms limited. There are 2 fraternities, 2 sororities on campus which about 25% of men, 25% of women join, they provide no residence facilities. About 40% of resident students leave campus on weekends.

Annual Costs. Tuition and fees, $7,640; room and board, $3,760. About 89% of students receive financial aid. Assistance is typically divided 72% scholarship, 6% loan, 7% work, according to most recent data available. College reports some scholarships awarded on the basis of academic merit alone.

Huntington College
Huntington, Indiana 46750 (219) 359-6000 or (800) 642-6493

A church-related college, located in a community of 18,000, 25 miles west of Fort Wayne.

Founded: 1897
Affiliation: United Brethren
Total Enrollment: 254 M, 277 W (full-time)
Cost: < $10K
% Receiving Financial Aid: 92%
Admission: Non-selective
Application Deadline: Aug. 1

Admission. High school graduates with C+ average in college preparatory program eligible; others may enter special summer and remedial programs; 80% of applicants accepted, 30% of these actually enroll; 30% of freshmen graduate in top fifth of high school class, 65% in top two-fifths. Average freshmen scores: SAT, 480 verbal, 420 mathematical; ACT, 21 M, 21 W composite. *Required:* SAT or ACT, interview, essay. Criteria considered in admissions, in order of importance: high school academic record, standardized test scores, extracurricular activities, recommendations, writing sample; other factors considered: diverse student body, special talents, alumni children, religious affiliation and/or commitment. *Entrance programs:* early decision, early admission, midyear admission, deferred admission. About 25% of freshmen come from private schools, 5% parochial schools. *Apply* by August 1; rolling admissions. *Transfers* welcome; 16 enrolled 1993–94.

Academic Environment. Degrees offered: associates, bachelors, masters. Core requirements include courses in English, Bible, psychology, science, mathematics, history, and fitness. Unusual majors offered include theatre, recreation management, exercise science, graphic design. Average undergraduate class size: 55% under 20, 45% between 20–40; student-faculty ratio of 13:1. About 60% of students entering as freshmen graduate within four years, 70% eventually; 80% of freshmen return for sophomore year. *Special programs:* January term, CLEP, independent study, study abroad, undergraduate research. Adult programs: EXCEL-degree completion program, cross registration through Christian College Consortium. *Calendar:* 4–1–4.

Undergraduate degrees conferred (90). 30% were in Education, 18% were in Business and Management, 16% were in Theology, 10% were in Social Sciences, 7% were in Communications, 6% were in Parks and Recreation, 4% were in Life Sciences, 3% were in Psychology, remainder in 4 other fields.

Graduates Career Data. Advanced studies pursued by 20% of graduates.

Faculty. About 78% of faculty hold PhD or equivalent. All undergraduate classes taught by tenured faculty. About 50% of teaching faculty are female; 2% Hispanic.

Student Body. About 69% of students from in state; 90% Midwest, 2% Middle Atlantic, 1% West, 7% Foreign. About 90% of students reported as Protestant, 5% Catholic, 5% unaffiliated; 3% Black, 1% Hispanic, 2% Asian.

Varsity Sports. Men (NAIA): Baseball, Basketball, Cross Country, Golf, Soccer, Tennis, Track. Women (NAIA): Basketball, Cross Country, Softball, Tennis, Track, Volleyball.

Religious Orientation. Huntington is a church-related institution; 2 courses in Bible and religion, attendance at 2 chapel and convocation services weekly required of all students.
Campus Life. About 75% of men, 75% of women live in traditional dormitories; no coed dormitories; 5% live in off-campus housing; rest commute. No intervisitation in men's or women's dormitory rooms. There is 1 fraternity, 1 sorority on campus which about 2% of men, 3% of women join; they provide no residence facilities. About 25% of resident students leave campus on weekends.
Annual Costs. Tuition and fees, $9,490; room and board, $3,370; estimated $900 other, exclusive of travel. About 92% of students receive financial aid; average amount of assistance, $7,800. Assistance is typically divided 25% scholarship, 20% grant, 35% loan, 20% work. College reports 150 scholarships awarded for academic merit, 180 for special talents, 220 for need. *Meeting Costs:* college offers tuition freeze plan, and installment payment option.

Huron University

Huron, South Dakota 57350 (605) 352-8721

An independent, liberal arts college offering career-oriented programs. Huron is located in a community of 14,000, 125 miles northwest of Sioux Falls. About 54% of student body is "non-traditional." Most convenient major airport: Sioux Falls.

Founded: 1883
Affiliation: Independent (Presbyterian Church (USA))
Total Enrollment: 207 M, 192 W (full-time); 36 M, 51 W (part-time)
Cost: < $10K
% Receiving Financial Aid: 96%
Admission: Non-selective
Application Deadline: Rolling

Admission. Graduates of accredited high schools eligible; 80% of applicants accepted, 15% of these actually enroll. Average freshmen ACT scores: 18 M, 18 W composite. *Required:* ACT. Criteria considered in admissions, in order of importance: high school academic record, standardized test scores, extracurricular activities, recommendations, writing sample; other factors considered: special talents, alumni children. *Entrance programs:* early admission, deferred admission. *Apply:* no specific deadline, rolling admission. *Transfers* welcome; 77 enrolled 1993–94.
Academic Environment. Degrees offered: associates, bachelors, masters. Forty-eight general education credits are required for graduation; distribution requirements limited. Program in hotel and restaurant management recently added. About 66% of students entering as freshmen graduate eventually; 43% of freshmen return for sophomore year. *Special programs:* CLEP, credit for experiential learning, January term, study abroad. *Calendar:* semester, 2 summer sessions.
Undergraduate degrees conferred (44). 45% were in Education, 32% were in Business and Management, 14% were in Protective Services, 7% were in Allied Health, remainder in Life Sciences.
Faculty. About 20% of faculty hold PhD or equivalent.
Student Body. About 50% of students from South Dakota; 80% from Midwest. Average age of undergraduate student: 22.
Varsity Sports. Men (NAIA Div.II): Baseball, Basketball, Football, Track. Women (NAIA Div.II): Basketball, Softball, Track, Volleyball.
Campus Life. Location is described as "great for outdoor recreational opportunities." About 30% of men, 30% of women live in coed dormitories; 60% live in off-campus housing; rest commute. Freshmen given preference in college housing if all students cannot be accommodated. Intervisitation in men's and women's dormitory rooms limited. There are no fraternities or sororities. About 15% of resident students leave campus on weekends.
Annual Costs. Tuition and fees, $6,850; room and board, $2,900; estimated $1,440 other, exclusive of travel. About 96% of students receive financial aid; average amount of assistance, $8,000. Assistance is typically divided 40% scholarship, 50% loan, 10% work, according to most recent data available. College reports 150 scholarships awarded for special talents, 200 for need.

Husson College

Bangor, Maine 04401

A private business college offering over thirty undergraduate programs in business, education, health and professional studies, as well as a master's program in business. Unusual programs offered include court and conference reporting, sports management.

Founded: 1898
Affiliation: Independent

Undergraduate degrees conferred (182). 80% were in Business and Management, 8% were in Health Sciences, 8% were in Business (Administrative Support), 4% were in Education.

Huston-Tillotson College

Austin, Texas 78731 (512) 505-3000

A church-related college, located in a city of 251,800; founded as a college for Blacks, now serving a much more diverse student body. Most convenient major airport: Robert Mueller (Austin).

Founded: 1876
Affiliation: United Methodist, United Church of Christ
Total Enrollment: 213 M, 242 W (full-time); 36 M, 48 W (part-time)
Cost: < $10K
% Receiving Financial Aid: 82%
Admission: Non-selective
Application Deadline: March 1

Admission. Graduates of accredited high schools with 15 units or GED average of 45 eligible; 90% of applicants accepted, 75% of these actually enroll. Average freshman scores: SAT, 786 combined verbal, mathematical; ACT, 16 composite. *Required:* SAT or ACT. Criteria considered in admissions, in order of importance: standardized test scores, high school academic record, recommendations, extracurricular activities, writing sample; other factors considered: special talents, alumni children. *Entrance programs:* early admission. About 99% of freshmen come from public schools. *Apply* by March 1. *Transfers* welcome; 52 enrolled 1993–94.
Academic Environment. Degrees offered: bachelors. Required core curriculum of 60 credit hours, mastery of 9 core competencies required by end of second year. About 5% of general education requirements for graduation are elective; distribution requirements fairly numerous; 3 hours of computer science required of all students. Faculty-student ratio of 1:13 allows for small classes and "good family and learning atmosphere." About 70% of students entering as freshmen graduate eventually; 24% of freshmen do not return for sophomore year, according to most recent data available. *Special programs:* independent study, undergraduate research, 3–2 programs in science and engineering. *Calendar:* semester, summer school.
Undergraduate degrees conferred (54). 57% were in Business and Management, 9% were in Social Sciences, 9% were in Education, 9% were in Communications, 6% were in Computer and Engineering Related Technology, 4% were in Life Sciences, 4% were in Letters, remainder in Physical Sciences.
Graduates Career Data. Advanced studies pursued by 18% of students; 1% enter law school. About 11% of 1992–93 graduates employed. Fields typically hiring the largest number of graduates include business, education. Career Development Services include helping students in sharpening their interviewing skills, developing effective resumes, identifying career options, selecting and gaining admission to graduate and professional schools, locating employment.
Faculty. About 43% of faculty hold PhD or equivalent. About 47% of teaching faculty are female; 49% Black, 10% Hispanic, 10% other.
Student Body. College seeks a national student body; 74% of students from in state, 12% South, 14% Foreign. An estimated 63% of students are Protestant, 10% Catholic, 6% Muslim, 5% unaffiliated, 17% other; 78% Black, 7% Hispanic, 6% Asian, 8% other minority.
Varsity Sports. Men (NAIA): Baseball, Basketball. Women (NAIA): Basketball, Volleyball.
Campus Life. About 36% of men, 37% of women live in traditional dormitories; rest commute. Intervisitation in men's and women's dor-

mitory rooms limited. There are 4 fraternities, 4 sororities on campus which about 25–30% of men, 25–30% of women join; they provide no residence facilities. About 20–30% of resident students leave campus on weekends.
Annual Costs. Tuition and fees, $5,040; room and board, $3,450; estimated $600 other, exclusive of travel. About 82% of students receive financial aid; average amount of assistance, $6,216. Assistance is typically divided 30% scholarship, 40% grant, 15% loan, 15% work. College reports 208 scholarships awarded on the basis of academic merit alone.

College of Idaho

(see Albertson College)

Idaho State University

Pocatello, Idaho 83209 **(208) 236-2475**

A state-supported university, located in a town of 50,000 about 150 miles north of Salt Lake City. Most convenient major airports: Pocatello, Salt Lake City.

Founded: 1901
Affiliation: State
UG Enrollment: 3,116 M, 3,431 W (full-time); 1,059 M, 1,405 W (part-time)
Total Enrollment: 10,779
Cost: < $10K
% Receiving Financial Aid: 70%
Admission: Non-selective
Application Deadline: Registration

Admission. Idaho graduates of accredited high schools units eligible; 73% of applicants accepted, 71% of these actually enroll. Average freshman ACT scores: 20.8 composite. *Required:* ACT. Criteria considered in admissions, in order of importance: high school academic record, standardized test scores. State does not limit out-of-state enrollment. Requirement for out-of-state applicants: minimum ACT composite score 22 or 948 combined SAT, others must submit high school transcript. States from which most out-of-state students are drawn include California, Utah. *Entrance programs:* early decision, early admission, midyear admission, advanced placement. *Apply* by: any time up to registration. *Transfers* welcome; 1,183 enrolled 1993–94.
Academic Environment. Degrees offered: associates, bachelors, masters, doctoral. *Undergraduate studies* offered by colleges of Liberal Arts, Business, Education, Engineering, Pharmacy, Medical Arts. University operates School of Vocational-Technical Education as vocational adjunct. *Majors offered* in addition to usual studies include health care administration, corporate training, education of hearing impaired. Core requirements include 6 credits in English, 2 in Speech, 7–9 in mathematics, 4 in each of biological and physical sciences, 3 in each of fine arts, literature, philosophy, U.S. history/culture, political science, 8 in foreign language. About 20% of students entering as freshmen graduate eventually; 30% of freshmen do not return for sophomore year, according to most recent data available. *Special programs:* CLEP, cross registration with U. of Idaho. *Calendar:* semester, summer school.
Undergraduate degrees conferred (719). 30% were in Education, 19% were in Business and Management, 10% were in Health Sciences, 6% were in Life Sciences, 5% were in Social Sciences, 5% were in Psychology, 5% were in Allied Health, 3% were in Computer and Engineering Related Technology, 3% were in Public Affairs, 3% were in Communications, remainder in 11 other fields.
Faculty. About 88% of faculty hold PhD or equivalent. About 29% of teaching faculty are female.
Student Body. University seeks a national student body; 92% of students from Idaho, 5% West, 2% Foreign. College offers a "strong, comprehensive Wilderness Program for disabled, as well as able-bodied, students." Average age of undergraduate student: 27.
Varsity Sports. Men (Div.IAA): Basketball, Cross Country, Football, Tennis, Track. Women (Div.IAA): Basketball, Cross Country, Tennis, Track, Volleyball.
Campus Life. According to most recent data available, about 5% each of men, women live in traditional dormitories; no coed dormitories; rest commute. No intervisitation in men's dormitory rooms; limited in women's dormitory rooms. There is 1 fraternity on campus which about 5% of men join. About 25% of students leave campus on weekends.
Annual Costs. Tuition and fees, $1,602 (out-of-state, $5,216); room and board, $2,840. About 70% of students receive financial aid. University reports some scholarships are awarded on academic merit alone.

University of Idaho

Moscow, Idaho 83844-4140 **(208) 885-6326**

Established as a land-grant institution before Idaho became a state, the University of Idaho is located on a 1,200-acre campus in a community of 18,000, 30 miles north of Lewiston. Most convenient major airport: Pullman (WA) or Spokane (WA).

Founded: 1889
Affiliation: State
UG Enrollment: 4,298 M, 2,944 W (full-time); 837 M, 594 W (part-time)
Total Enrollment: 11,543
Cost: < $10K
% Receiving Financial Aid: 60%
Admission: Selective
Application Deadline: Feb. 15

Admission is selective, varies somewhat among the schools. For all schools: 89% of applicants accepted, 48% of those actually enroll; 40% of freshmen graduate in top fifth of high school class, 69% in top two-fifths. Average freshman scores: SAT, 462 verbal, 516 mathematical; 36% of freshman score above 500 on verbal, 9% above 600; 56% score above 500 on mathematical, 23% above 600; ACT, 22.9 composite. *Required:* for all applicants: SAT or ACT, high school record (college preparatory program); some colleges have additional requirements. Criteria considered in admissions, in order of importance: high school academic record, standardized test score. *Out-of-state* freshman applicants: university welcomes students from out of state. Board of Regents limits out-of-state enrollment to 30% of entering class. Requirement for out-of-state students: rank in upper 3/4, C average; about 95% of applicants accepted, 47% enroll. *Entrance programs:* advanced placement. About 2% of entering students from private schools, 10% from parochial schools. *Apply* by February 15; rolling admissions. *Transfers* welcome.
Academic Environment. Degrees offered: bachelors, masters, doctoral. *Undergraduate studies* offered by colleges of Letters and Science, Agriculture, Art and Architecture, Business and Economics, Education, Engineering, Forestry, General Studies, Mines and Earth Resources. General education requirements include two semesters of English composition, fall semester courses in four out of the five core areas: communication, natural and applied science, mathematics, humanities, and social sciences. Other requirements vary widely with major. Strong programs reported in agriculture, engineering, business, and architecture. *Majors offered* in addition to usual studies include anthropology, architecture, bacteriology, child development, drama, geography, home economics, interior design, journalism, landscape architecture, Latin American studies, naval science, radio-television, computer engineering, computer science/foreign language combined major, international studies. Average undergraduate class size: 30% under 20, 55% between 30–40, 15% over 40.

About 11% of students entering as freshmen graduate within four years, 50% eventually; 76% of freshmen return for sophomore year. *Special programs:* CLEP, study abroad, honors, January interterm, individualized majors, work/study program with Bureau of Mines, combined 6-year program in Letters and Science or Business and Economics with College of Law, cross registration with Washington State U.. *Calendar:* semester, summer school.
Undergraduate degrees conferred (1040). 17% were in Business and Management, 15% were in Education, 15% were in Engineering, 9% were in Communications, 6% were in Social Sciences, 5% were in Renewable Natural Resources, 5% were in Architecture and Environmental Design, 3% were in Visual and Performing Arts, 3% were in Liberal/General Studies, 3% were in Letters, 3% were in Physical Sciences, 3% were in Home Economics, 3% were in Agricultural Sciences, remainder in 13 other fields.
Graduate Career Data. According to most recent data available, full-time graduate or professional study pursued immediately after graduation by 26% of students; 2% enter medical school; 1% enter dental school; 4% enter law school; 2% enter business school.

Careers in business and industry pursued by 25% of graduates. Career Development Services include career counseling, testing, job interviews, interview and resume workshops.
Faculty. About 83% of faculty hold PhD or equivalent. About 5% of teaching faculty reported as ethnic minorities.
Student Body. University seeks a national student body; 67% of students from in state; 89% of students from West/Northwest, 5% Foreign. An estimated 1% of students reported as Black, 3% Hispanic, 2% Asian, 6% other minority. Average age of undergraduate student: 23.
Varsity Sports. Men (Div.I): Basketball, Cross Country, Football (IAA), Golf, Tennis, Track. Women (Div.I): Basketball, Cross Country, Golf, Tennis, Track, Volleyball.
Campus Life. About 20% of students live in traditional dormitories; 10% of students live in off-campus college-related student housing; rest commute. There are 18 fraternities, 8 sororities on campus which about 28% of men, 21% of women join; about 20% of students live in fraternities and sororities.
Annual Costs. Tuition and fees, $1,426 (out-of-state, $5,326); room and board, $3,404; estimated $2,546 other, exclusive of travel. About 60% of students receive financial aid; average amount of assistance, $4,200. Assistance is typically divided 22% scholarship, 19% grant, 55% loan, 4% work. College reports 2,000 scholarships awarded for academic merit, 550 for special talents, 1,000 for need.

Illinois Benedictine College

Lisle, Illinois 60532 **(708) 960-1500**

A church-related, liberal arts college, founded and aided by the Benedictine monks of St. Procopius Abbey, Illinois Benedictine is located on a 100-acre campus in a town of 15,000, 25 miles west of Chicago. Most convenient major airport: O'Hare International (Chicago).

Founded: 1887
Affiliation: Roman Catholic
Total Enrollment: 614 M, 614 W (full-time); 171 M, 294 W (part-time)
Cost: $10K–$20K
% Receiving Financial Aid: 94%
Admission: Selective
Application Deadline: Rolling

Admission is selective. About 84% of applicants accepted, 67% of these actually enroll; 41% of freshmen graduate in top fifth of high school class, 70% in top two-fifths. Average freshman scores: ACT, 22.7 composite. *Required:* SAT or ACT. Criteria considered in admissions, in order of importance: high school academic record, standardized test scores, recommendations, writing sample, extracurricular activities; other factors considered: diverse student body. About 50% of entering students from private or parochial schools. *Apply:* rolling admissions. *Transfers* welcome; 240 enrolled 1993–94.
Academic Environment. Degrees offered: bachelors, masters. Graduation requirements include basic skills courses in written and oral communication, quantitative skills, and linguistics and logic; distribution requirements include 18 hours from arts and humanities (including 6 hours in religion and 3 in philosophy), 9 hours in science, 12 hours in social sciences. *Majors offered* include some arts and sciences, accounting, biochemistry, business economics, computer science, jazz studies, international business, nuclear medicine, nutrition, special education, finance, marketing management, Spanish. Average undergraduate class size: 20% of classes under 20, 70% between 20–40, 10% over 40.

Special programs: CLEP, honors, independent study, study abroad, undergraduate research, internships in some areas, 3–2 engineering, 4–1 Nutrition, Exercise/Physiology, International Institute for Marketing, cross registration through consortium of nearby colleges. *Calendar:* semester, summer school.
Undergraduate degrees conferred (287). 33% were in Business and Management, 11% were in Education, 10% were in Life Sciences, 8% were in Health Sciences, 7% were in Psychology, 7% were in Social Sciences, 7% were in Computer and Engineering Related Technology, 6% were in Letters, 3% were in Mathematics, remainder in 7 other fields.
Graduates Career Data. According to most recent data available, full-time graduate or professional study pursued immediately after graduation by 21% of students; 12% enter medical school; 2% enter law school; 2% enter business school. Medical schools typically enrolling largest numbers of graduates include Chicago College of Osteopathies, Loyola; business schools include Northwestern. *Careers in business and industry* pursued by 91% of graduates. Career Development Services include SIGI Plus computer assisted career guidance system, individual and group counseling, alumni career guidance network, mock interview workshops, career information shadowing opportunities.
Faculty. About 82% of faculty hold PhD or equivalent. About 68% of undergraduate classes taught by tenured faculty. About 36% of teaching faculty are female.
Student Body. College seeks a national student body; 90% of students from Illinois. An estimated 68% of students reported as Catholic, 12% Protestant; 6% Black, 8% Asian, 3% Hispanic, 4% other minority. *Minority group students:* special financial, academic, and social provisions; Minority Student Association.
Religious Orientation. Illinois Benedictine is a church-related institution; 6 hours of religious studies required of all students. Places of worship available on campus for Catholics, in immediate community for Protestants.
Varsity Sports. Men (Div.III): Baseball, Basketball, Cross Country, Football, Golf, Soccer, Swimming/Diving, Tennis, Track. Women (Div.III): Basketball, Cross Country, Golf, Softball, Swimming/Diving, Tennis, Track, Volleyball.
Campus Life. Student body reported to be concerned with occupational/professional goals. Active interest in social life endures, however. Alcohol permitted in conformity with state law; cars allowed.

About 24% of men, 22% of women live in traditional dormitories; 10% of men, 10% of women live in coed dormitories; 66% of men 68% of women live in off-campus housing or commute. Freshmen given preference in college housing if all students cannot be accommodated. There are no fraternities or sororities. About 40% of resident students leave campus on weekends.
Annual Costs. Tuition and fees, $10,080; room and board, $4,067. About 94% of students receive financial aid; average amount of assistance, $7,761. College reports 30 scholarships awarded on the basis of academic merit alone, 55% are for need. *Meeting Costs:* college offers payment plans.

Illinois College

Jacksonville, Illinois 62650 **(217) 245-3000**

A church-related, liberal arts college, Illinois is located on a 62-acre campus in a community of 25,000, 35 miles west of Springfield. Most convenient major airport: Lambert Field (St. Louis).

Founded: 1829
Affiliation: Independent (Presbyterian, United Church of Christ)
Total Enrollment: 432 M, 477 W (full-time)
Cost: < $10K
% Receiving Financial Aid: 93%
Admission: Selective
Application Deadline: August 15

Admission is selective. About 88% of applicants accepted, 33% of these actually enroll; 50% of freshmen graduate in top fifth of high school class, 73% in top two-fifths. Average freshman scores: SAT, 440 M, 507 W verbal, 528 M, 563 W mathematical; ACT, 23 M, 23 W composite. *Required:* SAT or ACT. Criteria considered in admissions, in order of importance: high school academic record, standardized test scores, recommendations. *Entrance programs:* midyear admission, advanced placement. *Apply* by August 15; rolling admissions. *Transfers* accepted; 57 enrolled 1993–94.
Academic Environment. Degrees offered: bachelors. All freshmen required to take interdisciplinary year course, "Man in Change." Distribution requirements include 2 courses in each of social science, literature, laboratory science, religion, history/political science; 1 course in fine arts, composition, speech, additional science; intermediate level modern language. Majors offered in addition to usual studies include computer science, international studies, fine arts, cytotechnology, art management, information systems, interdisciplinary studies. Programs considered to be strongest academically include history, political science, business administration, English. Average undergraduate class size: 64% of classes under 20, 32% between 20–40, 4% over 40.

About 45% of students entering as freshmen graduate within four

years, 50% eventually; 20% of freshmen do not return for sophomore year. *Special programs:* CLEP, independent study, study abroad, individualized majors, internships is some majors, Brethren Colleges abroad program, cross-registration with MacMurray, work/study program at local schools for handicapped (involving 5% of students), summer reading programs for credit, 3–2 programs in engineering, nursing, medical technology, occupational therapy, cytotechnology. *Calendar:* semester.

Undergraduate degrees conferred (157). 25% were in Business and Management, 19% were in Social Sciences, 17% were in Education, 10% were in Visual and Performing Arts, 6% were in Life Sciences, 6% were in Letters, 5% were in Psychology, 3% were in Mathematics, 3% were in Computer and Engineering Related Technology, remainder in 6 other fields.

Graduates Career Data. Advanced studies pursued by 19% of students. Graduate and professional schools typically enrolling largest numbers of graduates include Southern Illinois U., U. of Illinois. Career Development Services include seminars, job search, workshops, on-campus interviewing, career/internship fair, graduate school fair, resource library. Alumni reported as helpful in both career guidance and job placement.

Faculty. About 70% of faculty hold PhD or equivalent. About 36% of undergraduate classes taught by tenured faculty. About 35% of teaching faculty are female; 7% minorities.

Student Body. About 92% of students from in state; 97% from Midwest, 2% foreign. An estimated 86% of students reported as Protestant, 13% Catholic, 1% other; 2% Black, 2% Asian.

Religious Orientation. Illinois is a church-related institution; 2 semester courses in religion required of all students; attendance at weekly chapel services voluntary. Religious clubs on campus include Campus Christian Fellowship, Newman. Places of worship available in immediate community for Catholics and Protestants, 30 miles away for Jews.

Varsity Sports. Men (Div.III): Baseball, Basketball, Cross Country, Football, Golf, Soccer, Tennis, Track, Wrestling. Women (Div.III): Basketball, Cross Country, Soccer, Softball, Tennis, Track, Volleyball.

Campus Life. Cars allowed for all students. Campus literary societies (4 for men, 3 for women) provide social programs for their members.

About 41% of men, 49% of women live in traditional dormitories; 29% of men, 25% of women live in coed dormitories; rest commute. Freshmen are given preference in college housing if all students cannot be accommodated. There are no fraternities or sororities. About 30% of resident students leave campus on weekends.

Annual Costs. Tuition and fees, $7,550; room and board, $3,650; estimated $1,150 other, exclusive of travel. About 93% of students receive financial aid; average amount of assistance, $6,540. Assistance is typically divided 33% scholarship, 36% grant, 40% loan, 1% work. College reports 595 scholarships awarded on the basis of academic merit alone, 25 for special talents, 488 for need. *Meeting Costs:* college offers PLUS Loans, deferred payment plan.

Illinois Institute of Technology

Chicago, Illinois 60616 **(312) 567-3025**

The Illinois Institute of Technology is a co-educational institution offering both undergraduate and graduate programs through 6 separate schools and colleges: Armour College of Engineering; Lewis College of Sciences and Letters; the College of Architecture, Planning and Design; Stuart School of Management and Finance; Chicago-Kent College of Law; and the School of Advanced Studies. The 120-acre city campus is located 3 miles south of downtown Chicago. It also maintains a Downtown Center which houses Chicago-Kent College of Law and day and evening courses offered by the other colleges of the Institute. Most convenient major airport: O'Hare or Midway (Chicago).

Founded: 1892
Affiliation: Independent
UG Enrollment: 1,419 M, 375 W (full-time); 552 M, 111 W (part-time)

Total Enrollment: 4,402
Cost: $10K–$20K
% Receiving Financial Aid: 85%
Admission: Very Selective
Application Deadline: Rolling

Admission is very selective. For all schools: about 80% of applicants accepted, 40% of these actually enroll. Average freshman scores, middle fifty percent range: SAT, 1000–1200 combined verbal, mathematical; ACT, 22–28 composite.

For Architecture and Planning and Design (292 M, 87 W): about 76% of applicants accepted, 35% of these actually enroll; 44% of freshmen graduate in top fifth of high school class, 86% in top two-fifths. Average freshman scores, according to most recent data available: ACT, 25 M, 26 W composite, 24 M, 26 W mathematical.

For Engineering (869 M, 182 W): about 82% of applicants accepted, 42% of these actually enroll; 66% of freshmen graduate in top fifth of high school class, 92% in top two-fifths. Average freshman scores, according to most recent data available: ACT, 24 M, 24 W composite, 26 M, 24 W mathematical.

For Science and Letters (144 M, 58 W): about 78% of applicants accepted, 41% of these actually enroll; 55% of freshmen graduate in top fifth of high school class, 70% in top two-fifths. Average freshman ACT scores, according to most recent data available: 25 M, 20 W composite, 27 M, 24 W mathematical.

For Management and Finance (81 M, 45 W): about 71% of applicants accepted, 30% of these actually enroll; 25% of freshmen graduate in top fifth of high school class, 50% in top two-fifths. Average freshman ACT scores, according to most recent data available: 21 M, 21 W composite, 25 M, 20 W mathematical.

Required: SAT or ACT; interview recommended. *Non-academic factors* considered in admissions: special talents, alumni children, diverse student body. *Entrance programs:* early admission, advanced placement, deferred admission, midyear admission (except for architecture majors). *Apply:* rolling admissions. *Transfers* welcome.

Academic Environment. Students represented on all committees, including admissions and curriculum. Administration reports most courses needed for graduation in Architecture are required, 80% in Engineering, and 40% in Liberal Arts; distribution requirements in general education for all curricula include 3 courses each in mathematics and information sciences, natural science and engineering, 4 courses each in humanities, social sciences, year physical education. *Undergraduate studies* offered by colleges of Engineering, Sciences and Letters, Architecture Planning and Design, Stuart School of Management and Finance. *Degrees:* BA, BS, BArch. *Majors offered* in respectable range of arts and sciences (including business, history, psychology, management), applied solid state physics, artificial intelligence, computer science, energy technology, environmental design, medical technology, technical communications; 7-year honors program in engineering and medicine, 6-year honors program in law. Architecture curriculum based on tutorial model.

About 56% of students entering as freshmen graduate eventually; 20% of freshmen do not return for sophomore year. *Special programs:* independent study, study abroad, honors, undergraduate research, 3-year degree, individualized majors, cooperative work/study program in almost all curricula, cooperative program with Rush College of Nursing and Allied Health Sciences. *Calendar:* semester, summer school.

Undergraduate degrees conferred (360). 64% were in Engineering, 11% were in Architecture and Environmental Design, 10% were in Business and Management, 6% were in Computer and Engineering Related Technology, remainder in 8 other fields.

Graduates Career Data. According to most recent data available, careers in business and industry pursued by 94% of graduates. Corporations typically hiring largest numbers of graduates include General Motors, Motorola, Consolidated Edison, Amoco.

Faculty. About 90% of faculty hold doctorate or equivalent.

Student Body. Institute seeks a national student body; 77% of students from in state. An estimated 12% of students reported as Black, 8% Hispanic, 16% Asian, 6% other minority, according to most recent data available.

Religious Orientation. IIT is an independent institution, makes no religious demands on students. Religious clubs on campus include Newman, Intervarsity, Christian Science. Places of worship available on campus.

Varsity Sports. Men (NAIA): Baseball, Basketball, Bowling, Golf, Soccer, Swimming, Tennis. Women (NAIA): Bowling, Tennis, Volleyball.

Campus Life. Substantial numbers of students now live on campus although majority still live off campus or at home. Hermann Union Building is a center for student programs, especially for commuters. Student leader characterizes regulations governing student conduct as "strict," but enforced leniently. Institute restrictions on use of alcohol conform with city and state laws. Cars allowed; parking space is ample.

About 30% of men, 54% of women in traditional dormitories; 1% of men, 4% of women in coed dormitories; 39% of men, 29% of women live in off-campus housing or commute. Freshmen given preference in college housing if all students cannot be accommodated. Intervisitation in men's and women's dormitory rooms limited. There are 10 fraternities, 2 sororities on campus which about 30% of men, 13% of women join; 30% of men, 13% of women live in fraternities or sororities.

Annual Costs. Tuition and fees, $13,750; room and board, $4,540. About 85% of students receive financial aid; assistance is typically divided 58% scholarship, 30% loan, 12% work. College reports some scholarships awarded on the basis of academic merit alone.

Illinois State University

Normal, Illinois 61790 **(309) 438-2181 or (800) 366-2478**

A state-supported university, located near the center of Illinois, in the twin cities of Bloomington–Normal (pop. 80,000), Illinois State expanded from a teachers college into a multipurpose liberal arts and professional/vocational institution. Campus is 1 mile from Illinois Wesleyan University in Bloomington. Most convenient major airport: O'Hare International (Chicago).

Founded: 1857
Affiliation: State
UG Enrollment: 7,040 M, 8,623 W (full-time); 814 M, 927 W (part-time)
Total Enrollment: 20,067
Cost: < $10K
% Receiving Financial Aid: 49%
Admission: Non-selective
Application Deadline: March 1

Admission. Graduates of accredited high schools, who demonstrate competence in English composition and math, eligible; 77% of applicants accepted, 36% of these actually enroll; 26% of freshmen graduate in top fifth of high school class, 64% in top two-fifths. Average freshman ACT scores: 22 M, 22 W composite. *Required:* ACT or SAT. Criteria considered in admissions: high school academic record, standardized test scores, special talents. *Out-of-state* freshman applicants: university seeks students from out of state. State does not limit out-of-state enrollment. No special requirements for out-of-state students. *Entrance programs:* early admission, midyear admission, advanced placement. *Apply* by March; rolling admissions. *Transfers* welcome; 1,992 enrolled 1993–94.

Academic Environment. Degrees offered: bachelors, masters, doctoral. Students have option of satisfying general education requirements through the standard University Studies program or Individual University Studies which allows for a completely individualized program. Core requirements include coursework in communications, humanities, natural sciences, quantitative and logical studies, social sciences and psychological studies, contemporary life, aesthetics, and non-Western cultures and traditions. *Undergraduate studies* offered by colleges of Arts and Sciences, Applied Science and Technology, Business, Education, Fine Arts.

About 22% of students entering as freshmen graduate within four years, 57% eventually; 74% of freshmen return for sophomore year. Average undergraduate class size: 48. *Special programs:* CLEP, independent study, study abroad, honors, undergraduate research, internship and cooperative education programs, 3–2 physics and engineering, summer opportunity for freshmen, national student exchange. Adult programs: Adult Learner Program. *Calendar:* semester, summer school.

Undergraduate degrees conferred (3984). 21% were in Business and Management, 16% were in Education, 14% were in Social Sciences, 7% were in Communications, 6% were in Visual and Performing Arts, 4% were in Letters, 4% were in Psychology, 4% were in Engineering and Engineering Related Technology, 4% were in Protective Services, 3% were in Home Economics, remainder in 14 other fields.

Graduates Career Data. Career Development Services include offices of Career Planning, which provides assessment and exploration services, Professional Practice, which coordinates internships and cooperative education programs, and Placement, which offers counseling, credential services, computerized referral, vacancy listings, and on-campus recruitment.

Faculty. About 83% of faculty hold PhD or equivalent. About 34% of teaching faculty are female.

Student Body. University seeks a national student body; 99% of students from Illinois. An estimated 7% of students reported as Black, 2% Asian, 2% Hispanic, 2% other minority.

Varsity Sports. Men (Div. I): Baseball, Basketball, Cross Country, Football (IAA), Golf, Soccer, Tennis, Track, Wrestling. Women (Div.I): Basketball, Cross Country, Golf, Gymnastics, Softball, Swimming, Tennis, Track, Volleyball.

Campus Life. All single full-time students must reside in university-operated residence halls for first 4 semesters in residence. Alcoholic beverages forbidden students under legal age; cars allowed. About 36% of students live in traditional or coed dormitories; rest live in off-campus housing or commute. There are 26 fraternities, 17 sororities on campus; which about 7% men, 5% women join. About 30% of resident students leave campus on weekends.

Annual Costs. Tuition and fees, $3,253 (out-of-state, $8,203); room and board, $3,160; and according to most recent data an estimated $2,194 other, exclusive of travel. According to most recent data available about 49% of students receive financial aid. Assistance is typically divided 47% scholarship, 34% loan, 19% work. University reports some scholarships awarded on academic merit alone.

University of Illinois at Urbana–Champaign

Champaign, Illinois 61820 **(217) 333-0302**

Total enrollment of the 2 campuses of the University of Illinois (61,606) makes it one of the largest collegiate institutions in the U.S. Its eminence does not, however, depend on size alone. Its graduate school is rated as one of the most productive in the country, and is being supported by a student body that is among the more academically capable in major state universities. The main campus of 705 acres is located in the twin cities of Urbana–Champaign (pop. 100,000), 128 miles south of Chicago. The University of Illinois at Chicago, a 4-year commuter institution, is located in Chicago proper (see below). Most convenient major airport: Willard.

Founded: 1867
Affiliation: State
UG Enrollment: 14,204 M, 11,218 W (full-time); 531 M, 380 W (part-time)
Total Enrollment: 36,436
Cost: < $10K
% Receiving Financial Aid: 80%
Admission: Most Selective
Application Deadline: Jan. 1

Admission is among the most selective in the country for Engineering, Commerce and Business Administration, very (+) selective for Liberal Arts and Sciences, very selective for Agriculture, Applied Life Studies, Aviation, Education, Fine and Applied Arts. For all schools, 78% of applicants accepted, 49% of these actually enroll; 82% of freshmen graduate in top fifth of high school class, 96% in top two-fifths. Average freshman scores: SAT, 521 verbal, 616 mathematical; ACT middle 50% range, 25–30 M, 24–28 W composite. Criteria considered in admissions, in order of importance: high school academic record, standardized test scores, college preparatory courses; other factors considered: special talents, diverse student body, extracurricular activities, optional Supplemental Background Statement.

For Liberal Arts and Sciences (6,076 M, 5,974 W), 78% of applicants accepted, 45% of these actually enroll; 82% of freshmen graduate in top fifth of high school class, 96% in top two-fifths. Median freshman ACT scores: 26 composite.

For Engineering (4,213 M, 734 W), 82% of applicants accepted, 50% of these actually enroll; 92% of freshmen graduate in top fifth of high school class, 99% in top two-fifths. Median freshman ACT scores: 29 composite.

For Commerce and Business Administration (1,678 M, 1,324 W), 80% of applicants accepted, 52% of these actually enroll; 87% of freshmen graduate in top fifth of high school class, 99% in top two-fifths. Median freshman ACT scores: 27 composite.

For Fine and Applied Arts (964 M, 971 W), 73% of applicants accepted, 55% of these actually enroll; 59% of freshmen graduate in top fifth of high school class, 94% in top two-fifths. Median freshman ACT scores: 25 composite.

For Aviation (173 M, 37 W), 70% of applicants accepted, 50% of these actually enroll; 55% of freshmen graduate in top fifth of high school class, 96% in top two-fifths. Median freshman ACT scores: 25 composite.

For Agriculture (927 M, 1,007 W), 73% of applicants accepted, 65% of these actually enroll; 45% of freshmen graduate in top fifth of high school class, 86% in top two-fifths. Median freshman ACT scores: 24 composite.

For Education (195 M, 698 W), 74% of applicants accepted, 48% of these actually enroll; 83% of freshmen graduate in top fifth of high school class, all in top two-fifths. Median freshman ACT scores: 26 composite.

For College of Applied Life Studies (357 M, 546 W), 76% of applicants accepted, 60% of these actually enroll; 64% of freshmen graduate in top fifth of high school class, 97% in top two-fifths. Median freshman ACT scores: 24 composite.

Required: ACT or SAT; other requirements for certain specialized programs. *Out-of-state* freshman applicants: university welcomes students from out of state. State does not limit out-of-state enrollment. *Out-of-state* applicants admitted, if space available, on the same basis as residents. About 72% of out-of-state students accepted, 22% of these actually enroll. States from which most out-of-state students are drawn include Missouri, New York, Ohio, New Jersey, California, Florida, Pennsylvania. Entrance programs: early admission, midyear admission, deferred admission, advanced placement. About 13% of students come from private schools, 9% parochial schools. *Apply* by January 1. *Transfers* welcome; 1,155 enrolled 1993–94.

Academic Environment. Degrees offered: bachelors, masters, doctoral. Student leader reports students "tend to be conservative. They want an education. They want a job, one that's well paying. They will go into... engineering or business to get those jobs. Students at Illinois are very practical." Yet Illinois graduates a substantial number of students who enroll in the university's first rate graduate and professional schools. Pressures for academic achievement appear moderately strong at university as a whole, but vary substantially among the undergraduate schools and colleges. As in other major state universities with graduate schools of national repute, young teacher/scholars, newly graduated from the very top graduate schools, are a source of guidance and instruction for the large undergraduate student body. In a university of this size such instructional talent is a welcome addition, but several students still report that large survey courses and emphasis on research limit faculty-student interaction. Courses required for graduation include some distribution requirements: minimum of 6 hours each in humanities, social sciences, natural sciences, proficiency in English. *Undergraduate studies* offered to freshmen in 7 colleges listed above and Institute of Aviation; juniors may enter colleges of Veterinary Medicine, Communications, Social Work. *Majors offered* in Liberal Arts and Sciences in addition to wide range of studies include anthropology, astronomy, computer science, entomology, geography, microbiology, physiology, Portuguese, rhetoric and composition, Russian studies, statistics. Average class size: lecture, 125; lab, 18; regular class, 29.

About 52% of students entering as freshmen graduate within four years, 79% eventually; 91% of freshmen return for sophomore year. *Special programs:* independent study, study abroad, honors, undergraduate research, combined 5-year engineering/liberal arts and sciences, cooperative work/study program in industrial education and engineering, various other combined programs (some by special arrangements), 3–2 in engineering, credit by examination, intersession. *Calendar:* semester, summer school.

Undergraduate degrees conferred (6068). 19% were in Engineering, 14% were in Business and Management, 13% were in Social Sciences, 8% were in Letters, 7% were in Education, 7% were in Life Sciences, 6% were in Psychology, 4% were in Communications, 3% were in Architecture and Environmental Design, 3% were in Visual and Performing Arts, remainder in 14 other fields.

Graduates Career Data. Full-time advanced studies pursued by 31% of students (1991 graduates); of these, 9% enter medical school; 8% enter law school; 1% enter dental school. Law schools typical enrolling the largest number of graduates include U. of Illinois, Chicago Kent C. of Law, DePaul. About 76% of 1991 graduates employed. Corporations typically hiring largest numbers of graduates include IBM, Procter & Gamble, Motorola, Arthur Andersen. Career Development Services include resume help, practice interviews, professional career counseling, SIGI-Plus individualized career guidance computer program.

Faculty. About 93% of faculty hold PhD or equivalent. About 20% of teaching faculty are female; 2% Black, 2% Hispanic, 12% other minority.

Student Body. University welcomes a national student body; 93% of students from in state; 96% from the Midwest. An estimated 7% of students reported as Black, 5% Hispanic, 12% Asian, 2% other minority. *Minority group students:* provisions made for financial, academic, and social aid; Special Education Opportunity Program offers well-developed program.

Varsity Sports. Men (Div.I): Baseball, Basketball, Cross Country, Fencing, Football, Golf, Gymnastics, Tennis, Track, Wrestling. Women (Div.I): Basketball, Cross Country, Diving, Golf, Gymnastics, Swimming, Tennis, Track, Volleyball.

Campus Life. Size of the university alone ensures a wide variety of cultural and intellectual activities; students of every taste will find activities of interest and value. Prospective students should consider fact that any institution of this size has high degree of impersonality and survival requires equally high degree of maturity; university reports, however, active effort to provide counseling and other services. Student leader reports "administration believes very much in "in loco parentis'" and "in most cases the students don't care." "Greek life here is big—very big. If you're not Greek you're not going to be invited to many of the big social events.... Independents are far from being as organized as the Greeks." A campus ombudsman is available to students. Cars permitted, but parking remains a problem for both residential and commuting students. Intervisitation permitted with some exceptions. Married students and those over 21 or who have completed 30 semester hours "may live where they please"; others expected to reside in approved housing.

About 6% of men, 9% of women live in traditional residence halls; 11% of men, 6% of women in coed residence halls; 76% of men, 80% of women in off-campus college-related housing; rest commute. Freshmen are given preference in college housing if all students cannot be accommodated. Sexes segregated in coed dormitories by wing, floor or suite. There are 56 fraternities, 28 sororities on campus which about 22% of men, 26% of women join; 7% of men, 5% of women live in fraternities and sororities.

Annual Costs. Tuition and fees, $2,486; (out-of-state, $6,738); room and board, $4,358; estimated $1,500 other, exclusive of travel. About 80% of students receive financial aid. Assistance is typically divided 43% scholarship, 22% loan, 35% work, according to most recent data available. University reports some scholarships awarded on the basis of academic merit alone, 293 for athletics.

University of Illinois at Chicago

Chicago, Illinois 60680 (312) 996-4350

A large university, serving a primarily commuting student body, Illinois at Chicago is the largest public, comprehensive, degree-granting university (baccalaureate, masters, doctorate) in the city of Chicago. Most convenient major airport: O'Hare International (Chicago).

Founded: 1946
Affiliation: State
UG Enrollment: 6,563 M, 6,954 W (full-time); 1,473 M, 1,442 W (part-time)
Total Enrollment: 25,170
Cost: < $10K
% Receiving Financial Aid: 64%
Admission: Non-selective
Application Deadline: June 15

Admission. Graduates of accredited high schools with 16 units (completion of specified college-preparatory program) or satisfactory GED test and satisfactory ACT or SAT eligible. About 69% of applicants accepted, 47% of these actually enroll; 40% of freshmen graduate in top fifth of high school class, 73% in top two-fifths. Average freshman ACT scores: 21.7 M, 20.4 W composite, 22.0 M, 20.0 W mathematical. *Required:* ACT (SAT accepted). *Out-of-state* freshman applicants: university welcomes students from out of state. State does not limit out-of-state enrollment. *Out-of-state* applicants admitted on same basis as residents, except in engineering. Criteria considered in admissions, in order of importance: high school academic record, standardized test scores; other factors considered: special talents, diverse student body. *Entrance programs:* early decision, early admission, midyear admission, advanced placement, rolling admissions. About 65% of entering students from public schools, 35% from parochial schools. *Apply* by June 15; February 28 recommended. *Transfers* welcome; 2,159 enrolled 1993–94.

Academic Environment. Degrees offered: bachelors masters, doctoral. *Undergraduate studies* offered in Engineering, Liberal Arts and Sciences, Nursing, Social Work, Architecture, Art and Performing Arts, Pharmacy, Business Administration, Education, Honors College, and Kinesiology. *Majors offered* in a wide range of studies including administration of criminal justice, anthropology, geography, Slavic languages and literatures, athletic training, physical therapy, occupational therapy, performing arts. Core requirements include 5 hours English composition, 9 in humanities, 9 in social sciences, 15 in natural sciences, 3–5 in quantitative reasoning, 3 in world culture, and 4 semesters foreign language. Free computer facilities open to all students 24 hours daily. Average undergraduate class size: 31.

About 20% of students entering as freshmen graduate within four years, 40% eventually; 70% of freshmen return for sophomore year. *Special programs:* independent study, study abroad, honors, undergraduate research, credit by examination, cooperative work/study programs, various combined programs (some by special arrangements), various teacher training programs. *Calendar:* semester.

Undergraduate degrees conferred (2891). 19% were in Business and Management, 12% were in Engineering, 10% were in Health Sciences, 9% were in Social Sciences, 7% were in Psychology, 7% were in Education, 5% were in Life Sciences, 5% were in Visual and Performing Arts, 5% were in Communications, 4% were in Protective Services, 3% were in Allied Health, 3% were in Mathematics, 3% were in Letters, remainder in 8 other fields.

Graduates Career Data. Advanced studies pursued and completed by 19.6% of 1988 graduates surveyed in 1993; 4% entered medical school, 1% entered dental school, 10% entered law school, 24% entered business school. About 68% of 1991–92 graduates employed within 6–8 months of graduation. Fields typically hiring largest numbers of graduates include business, engineering and computer science, health care, and public and social services. Career Development Services include a 3-hour career preparation seminar on resumes, networking, interview workshops, skills assessment; video-taped mock interviews; on-campus recruitment; individual counseling; resume referral; library resources.

Faculty. About 80% of faculty hold PhD or equivalent. About 25% of teaching faculty are female; 3% Black, 3% Hispanic, 11% other minority.

Student Body. University seeks a national student body; 95% of students from Illinois; 97% from Midwest, 2% Foreign. An estimated 10% of students reported as Black, 14% Hispanic, 17% Asian, 5% other minority. *Minority group students:* provisions made for financial, academic, and social aid; Education Assistance Program offers well-developed program. Average age of undergraduate student: 23.

Varsity Sports. Men (Div.I): Baseball, Basketball, Cross Country, Diving, Gymnastics, Ice Hockey, Soccer, Swimming, Tennis. Women (Div.I): Basketball, Cross Country, Diving, Gymnastics, Softball, Swimming, Tennis, Volleyball.

Campus Life. Chicago's many cultural and intellectual opportunities are easily available to students. Illinois at Chicago is primarily a commuter campus but has residence halls that accommodate 2,100 students. About 11% of men, 9% of women live in coed dormitories; rest commute. There are 8 fraternities, 5 sororities, 1 coed fraternity on campus which about 2% of men, 2% of women join; they provide no residence facilities. About 30% of resident students leave campus on weekends.

Annual Costs. Average tuition and fees, $3,445; (out-of-state, $7,898); room and board, $4,988; estimated $3,100 other, exclusive of travel. About 64% of students receive financial aid; average amount of assistance, $4,900 (1992–93). Assistance is typically divided 40% gift assistance, 36% loan, 24% work. University reports some scholarships awarded for academic merit alone.

Illinois Wesleyan University

Bloomington, Illinois 61702 **(309) 556-3031**

An independent, Methodist-related institution, Illinois Wesleyan combines professional schools of music, art, drama, and nursing with a traditional liberal arts program. The 60-acre campus is located in a residential area of a city of 100,000, 130 miles southwest of Chicago. Most convenient major airport: o'hare International (Chicago).

Founded: 1850
Affiliation: Independent (United Methodist)
Total Enrollment: 847 M, 971 W (full-time)
Cost: $10K–$20K
% Receiving Financial Aid: 86%
Admission: Very (+) Selective
Application Deadline: March 1

Admission is very (+) selective. For all schools, 44% of applicants accepted, 35% of these actually enroll; 78% of freshmen graduate in top fifth of high school class, 99% in top two-fifths. Average freshman scores: SAT, 587 M, 532 W verbal, 631 M, 605 W mathematical; 66% of freshman score above 500 on verbal, 29% above 600, 2% above 700; 92% score above 500 on mathematical, 60% above 600, 20% above 700; ACT, 27.6 M, 27.6 W composite. *Required:* ACT or SAT; interview for nursing, auditions for music, drama; portfolio for art; essay. Criteria considered in admissions, in order of importance: high school academic record, standardized test scores, writing sample, extracurricular activities, recommendations; other factors considered: diverse student body, special talents, alumni children. *Entrance programs:* early admission, midyear admission, advanced placement, deferred admission. About 5% of entering students from private schools, 12% from parochial schools. *Apply* by March 1; rolling admissions. *Transfers* welcome; 9 enrolled 1993–94.

Academic Environment. Student body characterized as primarily oriented towards scholarly/intellectual interests with a majority also concerned with occupational/professional goals. Administration reports 30% of courses required for graduation are elective; distribution requirements include: 6 courses from natural sciences and social sciences, 4 courses humanities (including minimum of 1 course in religion), proficiency in reading and writing English, foreign language, 1 year physical education. *Undergraduate studies* by colleges of Liberal Arts, Fine Arts, School of Nursing. Degrees offered: bachelors. *Majors offered* include international studies, international business, Russian, Japanese, Black studies, drama, risk management, nursing, dual majors available in liberal arts and fine arts. Average undergraduate class size: 54% under 20, 44% between 20–40, 2% over 40.

About 78% of students entering as freshmen graduate within four years; 95% of freshmen return for sophomore year. *Special programs:* CLEP, January term, study with the Institute of European Studies, independent study, study abroad, honors, 3-year degree, individualized majors, undergraduate research, Washington Semester, United Nations Semester, summer independent study program, internships (available in industry, insurance, journalism, nursing, social work, teaching), 3–2 engineering, 2–2 with U. of Illinois, combined program with Duke School of Forestry, summer music camp, programs with GLCA and ACM. *Calendar:* 4–1–4.

Undergraduate degrees conferred (390). 30% were in Business and Management, 14% were in Social Sciences, 12% were in Life Sciences, 10% were in Visual and Performing Arts, 8% were in Health Sciences, 7% were in Education, 6% were in Psychology, 4% were in Letters, 3% were in Physical Sciences, 3% were in Foreign Languages, remainder in 3 other fields.

Graduates Career Data. Advanced studies pursued by 29% of students; 4% enter medical school; 1% enter dental school; 6% enter law school; 1% enter business school. Medical schools typically enrolling largest numbers of graduates include Southern Illinois; dental schools include Southern Illinois; law schools include DePaul, Chicago; business schools include Baylor, Chicago. About 60% of 1992–93 graduates employed. Corporations typically hiring largest numbers of graduates include State Farm Insurance; Price Waterhouse; Crone, Chick & Co.; J.P. Morgan. *Career Counseling Program* designed specifically for liberal arts students. Liberal arts majors urged to seek interviews with business/industry representatives who visit campus. Help provided in preparing for interviews. Alumni reported as helpful in both career guidance and job placement.

Faculty. About 86% of faculty hold PhD or equivalent. About 63% of undergraduate classes taught by tenured faculty. About 41% of teaching faculty are female; 8% ethnic minorities.

Student Body. University seeks a national student body; 82% of students from in state; 99% Midwest; 5% Foreign. An estimated 65% of students reported as Protestant, 27% Catholic, 1% Jewish, 1% Muslim, 4% unaffiliated, 2% other; 3% as Black, 1% Hispanic, 4% Asian, 5% other minority. *Minority group students:* Afro-American Culture Center; Black studies.

Religious Orientation. Illinois Wesleyan is an independent institution with ties to the United Methodist Church; 1 course in religion required of all students; attendance at student-sponsored weekly chapel programs voluntary.

Varsity Sports. Men (Div.III): Baseball, Basketball, Cross Country, Diving, Football, Golf, Soccer, Swimming, Tennis, Track. Women (Div.III): Basketball, Cross Country, Diving, Softball, Swimming, Tennis, Track, Volleyball.

Campus Life. Several students report that IWU students are kept busy with studying and the wide selection of college sponsored activities. Notable variety of student attitudes and interests reported by one student leader, due to substantial numbers of students majoring in diverse fields of business, nursing, and fine arts, as well as liberal arts. Cars allowed. Alcohol prohibited on campus. Limited intervisitation. Students over 21 may live off campus.

About 38% of men, 52% of women live in traditional dormitories; 23% of men, 11% of women in coed dormitories; rest commute. Sexes segregated in coed dormitories by wing or room. There are 6 fraternities, 5 sororities on campus which about 25% of men, 30% of women join; 24% of men, 25% of women live in fraternities and sororities. About 20% of resident students leave campus on weekends.

Annual Costs. Tuition and fees, $13,395; room and board, $3,985; estimated $1,050 other, exclusive of travel. About 86.4% of students receive financial aid; average amount of assistance, $12,019. Assistance is typically divided 20% scholarship, 50% grant, 20% loan, 10% work. University reports 408 scholarships awarded for academic merit alone, 67 for special talents, 1,162 for need.

Immaculata College

Immaculata, Pennsylvania 19345 (215) 296-9067

A church-related, liberal arts college for women, conducted by the Sisters Servants of the Immaculate Heart of Mary, located on the Main Line in a Philadelphia suburb, 20 miles west of the city. Evening Division is co-educational. Most convenient major airport: Philadelphia International.

Founded: 1920
Affiliation: Roman Catholic
UG Enrollment: 13 M, 549 W (full-time); 204 M, 1,269 W (part-time)
Total Enrollment: 2,345
Cost: < $10K
% Receiving Financial Aid: 29%
Admission: Non-selective
Application Deadline: June 1

Admission. Graduates of accredited high schools or equivalent with 2.5 GPA in college prep courses, eligible; 78% of applicants accepted, 67% of these actually enroll; 44% of freshmen graduate in top fifth of high school class, 72% in top two-fifths. Average freshman SAT scores, according to most recent data available: 460 M, 460 W verbal, 490 M, 470 W mathematical. *Required:* SAT or ACT; interview preferred. *Non-academic factors* considered in admissions: special talents, diverse student body, activities. About 16% of entering students from private schools, 42% from parochial schools. *Apply* by June 1; rolling admissions. *Transfers* welcome.

Academic Environment. Curriculum includes independent study programs, tutorials, individually designed honors programs. College is committed to a strong liberal arts core. Administration reports 40% of general education courses required for graduation are elective; distribution requirements, though numerous, have options within the various areas. *Degrees:* AB, BS, BM, BSN. *Majors offered* in addition to usual studies include business, accounting, dietetics, fashion merchandising.

About 70% of students entering as freshmen graduate eventually; 20–25% of freshmen do not return for sophomore year. *Special programs:* CLEP, CLEO, independent study, study abroad, honors, undergraduate research, optional January interterm, joint majors. *Calendar:* semester.

Undergraduate degrees conferred (203). 21% were in Social Sciences, 20% were in Health Sciences, 12% were in Psychology, 10% were in Letters, 8% were in Business and Management, 4% were in Home Economics, 3% were in Multi/Interdisciplinary Studies, 3% were in Marketing and Distribution, 3% were in Theology, 3% were in Life Sciences, remainder in 8 other fields.

Graduates Career Data. *Full-time graduate or professional study* pursued immediately after graduation by 18% of students; 5% enter medical school. Medical schools typically enrolling largest numbers of graduates include Hahnemann. *Careers in business and industry* pursued by 75% of graduates. Corporations typically hiring largest numbers of graduates include Chester County Hospital, Federal Government, Unisys.

Student Body. College does not seek a national student body; 90% of students from in state; 98% Middle Atlantic. An estimated 65% of students reported as Catholic, 28% Protestant, 1% Jewish, 2% unaffiliated, 4% other; 2% as Black, 1% Hispanic, 1% Asian, according to most recent data available. *Minority group students:* Academic Development Program to recruit and retain minority students.

Religious Orientation. Immaculata is a church-related institution, but college states "that all faiths are welcome—there is no religious discrimination." No religious demands on students.

Varsity Sports. Women (Div.II): Basketball, (Div. III): Field Hockey, Softball, Tennis, Volleyball.

Campus Life. Changes in recent years have emphasized student role in responsibility and governance, and involvement in curriculum and organization of cultural and social events. No visitation hours. Alcohol prohibited on campus and at almost all college dances or parties.

About 20% of women live in dormitories; rest commute. There are no sororities. About 25–30% of students leave campus on weekends.

Annual Costs. Tuition and fees, $9,600; room and board, $5,110. About 29% of students receive financial aid; assistance is typically divided 17% scholarship, 38% loan, 27% work. College reports some scholarships awarded on the basis of academic merit alone. *Meeting Costs:* university offers budget payment plan.

Incarnate Word College

San Antonio, Texas 78209 (512) 829-6005

A church-related college, conducted by the Sisters of Charity of the Incarnate Word, located in a residential section of a city of 1,000,000. Most convenient major airport: San Antonio International.

Founded: 1881
Affiliation: Roman Catholic
UG Enrollment: 574 M, 1,576 (full and part-time)
Total Enrollment: 2,142
Cost: < $10K
% Receiving Financial Aid: 59%
Admission: Non-selective
Application Deadline: Rolling

Admission. High school graduates with 16 units (12 in academic subjects) eligible; 76% of applicants accepted, 49% of these actually enroll; 67% of freshmen graduate in top fifth of high school class, 86% in top two-fifths. Average freshman scores, according to most recent data available: SAT, 450 verbal, 480 mathematical; ACT, 18.6 composite. *Required:* ACT or SAT; interview recommended. *Non-academic factors* considered in admissions: special talents. *Apply:* rolling admissions. *Transfers* welcome.

Academic Environment. *Degrees:* AB, BS, BBA, BSN. General education requirements for graduation vary with major; distribution requirements fairly numerous. About 55% of students entering as freshmen graduate eventually; 20% of freshmen do not return for sophomore year. *Special programs:* CLEP, honors, independent study, study abroad, undergraduate research, 3-year degree, PREP 88, training teachers of mentally retarded and emotionally disturbed, 3–2 programs in hotel/restaurant management, nursing, and banking. *Library:* 183,628 volumes, 675 periodicals; Texana Collection, rare books, audio-visuals. *Calendar:* semester, summer school.

Undergraduate degrees conferred (321). 33% were in Business and Management, 14% were in Education, 13% were in Health Sciences, 7% were in Social Sciences, 6% were in Psychology, 5% were in Communications, 5% were in Visual and Performing Arts, 4% were in Architecture and Environmental Design, 3% were in Life Sciences, remainder in 8 other fields.

Varsity Sports. Men (NAIA,III): Basketball, Baseball, Cross Country, Soccer, Tennis, Track. Women (NAIA, III): Basketball, Cross Country, Soccer, Softball, Tennis, Volleyball.

Student Body. College seeks a national student body; 95% of students from Texas; 96% South. An estimated 41% of students reported as Protestant, 55% Catholic, 3% unaffiliated; 8% Black, 46% Hispanic, 4% Asian.

Religious Orientation. Incarnate Word is a church-related institution; 9 hours of theology or philosophy required of all students.

Campus Life. About 15% of men, 15% of women live in traditional residence halls; 5% of each men, women live in coed residence halls; rest commute. Freshmen given preference in college housing if all students cannot be accommodated. There are 2 fraternities (one coed), 1 sorority on campus. About 50% of resident students leave campus on weekends.

Annual Costs. Tuition and fees, $8,325; room and board, $4,060. About 59% of students receive financial aid. College reports some scholarships awarded on the basis of academic merit alone. *Meeting Costs:* college offers PLUS Loans.

Indiana Central University

(See University of Indianapolis)

Indiana Institute of Technology

Fort Wayne, Indiana 46803 (219) 422-5561

An independent, co-educational institution located in a city of 195,000, offering degree programs in engineering (civil, mechanical, and electrical), computer science, accounting, business administration and data processing. Most convenient major airport: Baer Field, Fort Wayne.

Founded: 1930
Affiliation: Independent
Total Enrollment: 650 M, W (full-time, day program)
Cost: < $10K
Admission: Non-selective
Application Deadline: 1 week before term

Admission. High school graduates with "a good high school record" eligible; 10% of freshmen graduate in top fifth of high school class, 50% in top two-fifths. *Required:* interview. *Apply* by 1 week before term. *Transfers* welcome.
Academic Environment. Degrees offered: associates, bachelors. Programs include engineering, business, technical communications, recreation management, therapeutic recreation, human services management. Special program: CLEP. Adult programs: evening program available. *Calendar:* semester, summer school.
Undergraduate degrees conferred (45). 67% were in Business and Management, 27% were in Computer and Engineering Related Technology, 4% were in Engineering, remainder in Communications.
Graduates Career Data. According to most recent data available, full-time graduate or professional study pursued by 30% of students immediately after graduation. *Careers in business and industry* pursued by 70% of graduates. Corporations typically hiring largest numbers of graduates include General Electric, General Motors, IBM.
Varsity Sports. Men (NAIA): Basketball. Women (NAIA): Basketball.
Student Body. Institute seeks a national student body; 30% of students from in state; 50% North Central, 35% Middle Atlantic, 15% New England.
Campus Life. About 70% of men, 90% of women in traditional dormitories; 20% of men, 10% of women live in off-campus housing or commute. Freshmen given preference in college housing if all students cannot be accommodated. Intervisitation in men's and women's dormitory rooms limited. Sexes segregated in coed dormitory by floor. There are 3 fraternities on campus which about 18% of men join; no sororities; 10% of men live in fraternities. About 25% of students leave campus on weekends.
Annual Costs. Tuition and fees, $4,060; room and board, $3,790. Institute reports some scholarships awarded on the basis of academic merit alone.

Indiana Wesleyan University

Marion, Indiana 46953 (317) 677-2138

A church-sponsored liberal arts institution, located in the Marion/Grant County area (pop. 80,000), 65 miles northeast of Indianapolis. Formerly known as Marion College.

Founded: 1920
Affiliation: Wesleyan
UG Enrollment: 300 M, 550 W (full-time)
Total Enrollment: 2,490
Cost: < $10K
% Receiving Financial Aid: 86%
Admission: Non-selective
Application Deadline: September 1

Admission. Graduates of approved high schools with 10 units in college-preparatory subjects and C average eligible. About 74% of applicants accepted, 69% of these actually enroll; 33% of freshmen graduate in top fifth of high school class, 56% in top two-fifths. *Required:* SAT or ACT, compliance with college's ban on use of alcohol, tobacco, playing cards, dancing. *Apply* by September 1. *Transfers* welcome.
Academic Environment. *Degrees:* BA, BS. *Majors offered* include usual arts and sciences, elementary education, nursing. General education requirements for graduation fairly specified. About 28% of students entering as freshmen graduate within 4 years; 39% of freshmen do not return for sophomore year. *Calendar:* semester, January term, summer sessions.
Undergraduate degrees conferred (174). 33% were in Health Sciences, 17% were in Education, 14% were in Business and Management, 9% were in Theology, 4% were in Social Sciences, 4% were in Protective Services, 4% were in Letters, 3% were in Computer and Information Sciences, 3% were in Public Affairs, remainder in 5 other fields.
Varsity Sports. Men (NCCAA, NAIA, Div. I): Baseball, Basketball, Cross Country, Golf, Soccer, Tennis, Track. Women (Div. I): Basketball, Field Hockey, Track, Volleyball.
Student Body. About 75% of students from Indiana. An estimated 67% of students reported as Protestant, 4% Catholic, 29% unaffiliated or other; 5% Black, 1% other minority, according to most recent data available.
Religious Orientation. Indiana Wesleyan is a church-related institution; 3 courses in Biblical literature and religion required of all students; attendance at chapel expected. Religious clubs on campus include Fellowship of Christian Athletes, Student Ministerial Association, Student Missionary Fellowship, Volunteer Student Outreach.
Campus Life. About 36% of students live in dormitories. There are no fraternities or sororities.
Annual Costs. Tuition and fees, $8,660; room and board, $3,672. About 86% of students receive financial aid. Assistance is typically divided 50% scholarship, 25% loan, 25% work, according to most recent data available. College reports some scholarships awarded on the basis of academic merit alone. *Meeting Costs:* college offers AMA, PLUS Loans.

Indiana State University

Terre Haute, Indiana 47809 (812) 237-2121

A state-supported university, located in a city of 70,300, 74 miles southwest of Indianapolis. Most convenient major airport: Hulman Regional.

Founded: 1865
Affiliation: State
Total Enrollment: 9,700 M, W (full-time); 786 M, 1,041 W (part-time)
Cost: < $10K
% Receiving Financial Aid: 58%
Admission: Non-selective
Application Deadline: August 1

Admission. Indiana graduates of commissioned high schools who rank in top half of class admitted; other Indiana graduates accepted on probation; 85% of applicants accepted; 47% of these actually enroll; 21% of freshmen graduate in top fifth of high school class, 46% in top two-fifths. Average freshman SAT scores, according to most recent data available, middle fifty percent range: 330–440 verbal, 350–490 mathematical. *Required:* SAT or ACT. *Out-of-state* freshman applicants: university seeks students from out of state. State does not limit out-of-state enrollment. Requirements for out-of-state applicants: same as for residents; 96% of applicants accepted, 64% enroll. *Apply* by August 1; rolling admissions. *Transfers* welcome.
Academic Environment. *Undergraduate studies* offered by College of Arts and Sciences, schools of Business, Education, Nursing, Technology, Health, Physical Education, and Recreation. About 8% of general education requirements for graduation are elective; distribution requirements fairly numerous. *Majors offered* in addition to usual studies include computer integrated manufacturing technology, computer science, insurance, management information systems, sports studies, speech/language pathology, music with merchandising or business administration concentration. About 40% of students entering as freshmen graduate eventually; 35% of freshmen do not return for sophomore year. *Special programs:* CLEP, independent study, honors, Learning Skills Program, 3-year degree.

Undergraduate degrees conferred (1392). 20% were in Business and Management, 18% were in Education, 16% were in Engineering and Engineering Related Technology, 14% were in Social Sciences, 7% were in Health Sciences, 4% were in Home Economics, 4% were in Communications, 4% were in Letters, 3% were in Computer and Engineering Related Technology, remainder in 11 other fields.

Graduates Career Data. According to most recent data available. careers in business and industry pursued by 76% of graduates. Employers typically hiring largest numbers of graduates include EDS, State Farm Insurance, Hyster, Frito-Lay.

Faculty. About 65% of full-time faculty hold PhD or equivalent.

Varsity Sports. Men (Div.I): Baseball, Basketball, Cross Country, Football (IAA), Tennis, Track. Women (Div.I): Basketball, Bowling, Cross Country, Softball, Tennis, Track, Volleyball.

Student Body. University seeks a national student body; 88% of students from in state; 93% North Central. An estimated 7% of students reported as Black, 2% other minority, according to most recent data available.

Campus Life. About 13% of men, 16% of women live in traditional dormitories; 16% of men, 17% of women in coed dormitories; 5% of men, 2% of women live in off-campus housing; 62% of men, 65% of women commute. Intervisitation in men's and women's dormitory rooms unlimited. Sexes segregated in coed dormitories by floor. There are 20 fraternities, 13 sororities on campus which about 19% of men, 12% of women join; 4% of men live in fraternities, sororities provide no residence facilities. About 46% of resident students leave campus on weekends.

Annual Costs. Tuition and fees, $2,452 (out-of-state, $5,960); room and board, $3,468. About 58% of students receive financial aid; assistance is typically divided 51% scholarship, 45% loan, 5% work. University reports some scholarships awarded on academic merit alone. Meeting Costs. university offers PLUS.

Indiana University System

Bloomington, Indiana 47401

The 8 campuses comprising Indiana U. include: the main residential campus at Bloomington, the oldest and largest campus with undergraduate, professional, and graduate programs; 6 commuter campuses located at Fort Wayne (shared with Purdue U.), Gary, Kokomo, New Albany, Richmond, and South Bend. The Indianapolis campus, also shared with Purdue offers 4-year degree courses and professional programs in medicine, dentistry, nursing, law, and social service.

Admission. Graduates of Indiana commissioned or accredited high schools with 16 units in academic subjects and minimum GPA of 2.0 eligible; others may be admitted on probationary basis; some programs have additional requirements. *Required:* SAT or ACT. *Out-of-state* freshman enrollment is not limited by the state. Requirements for out-of-state applicants: rank and test scores in top third of high school seniors. Specific admissions policies vary significantly with the individual campuses.

Indiana University Bloomington

Bloomington, Indiana 47405 (812) 855-0661

One of the largest universities in the United States, Indiana also includes one of the nation's major graduate schools. The 1,800-acre wooded main campus has been described as one of the most beautiful in the country, with its hilly gardens and an arboretum boasting more than 450 trees and shrubs and hundreds of varieties of plants. It is located in a community of 52,000, 50 miles southwest of Indianapolis, site of the IU Medical Center. Most convenient major airport: Indianapolis International.

Founded: 1820
Affiliation: State
UG Enrollment: 12,115 M, 14,128 W (full-time); 1,176 M, 1,500 W (part-time)
Total Enrollment: 35,551
Cost: < $10K
% Receiving Financial Aid: 60%
Admission: Selective
Application Deadline: Feb. 15

Admission is selective. (See also Indiana University System.) While the overwhelming majority of admitted students completed an average of 19 year-long academic courses and rank in the upper third of their high school class, there are always exceptions, including students from schools that do not provide rank. Each application is personally reviewed with attention focused primarily upon the number of strong, college-preparatory courses, their level of difficulty, the student's willingness to accept challenge, and grade trends. Test scores for any application are rarely a factor.

About 80% of applicants accepted, 44% of these actually enroll; 50% of freshmen graduate in top fifth of high school class, 88% in top two-fifths. Average freshman scores: SAT, 466 verbal, 530 mathematical; 37% above 500 verbal, 8% above 600, 66% above 500 mathematical, 27% above 600, 5% above 700; ACT, 24 composite. *Required:* SAT or ACT; interview recommended; audition required for music. *Out-of-state* freshman applicants: university actively seeks students from out-of-state. State does not limit out-of-state enrollment. Required of out-of-state students: more rigorous number of academic units, rank, and senior year. About 80% of out-of-state students accepted, 26% of these actually enroll. States from which most out-of-state students are drawn include Illinois, Ohio, New York, New Jersey, Missouri. *Apply* by February 15; rolling admissions. *Transfers* welcome; 677 enrolled 1993–94.

Academic Environment. Degrees offered: associates, bachelors, masters, doctoral. *Undergraduate studies* offered by College of Arts and Sciences, schools of Business, Education, Music, Health, Physical Education, and Recreation, Public and Environmental Affairs, Continuing Education. All freshmen enroll in University Division for first year. Intensive Freshman Seminar offers small-group intensive study of selected topics for 3 weeks in August before start of fall semester. Administration reports that new COAS requirements encourage a well-rounded education. Distribution courses for freshmen and sophomores include small classes that stress writing and other active learning skills. In addition to completing requirements for a major, all students complete courses in arts and humanities, social and behavioral sciences, natural and mathematical sciences, English and writing skills, and, in many majors, foreign language. Independent Learning Program, however, frees selected students from all requirements of standard BA program. *Majors offered* in Arts and Sciences in a wide range of studies including computer science, folklore, geology, journalism, speech communication, speech and hearing sciences, telecommunications, theatre/drama, public health, audio recording. Pressures for academic achievement appear moderate, but vary considerably among the various schools and colleges of the university. Academically capable students can devise a first rate educational experience because of the wide range of academic opportunities available. Average undergraduate class size: 54% under 20, 30% between 20–40, 16% over 40.

About 47% of students entering as freshman graduate within 4 years, 66% within 6 years; 87% return for sophomore year. *Special programs:* CLEP, independent study, honors, undergraduate research, January term, 3–3 in optometry, residence centers, study abroad, cooperative education. Adult programs: Returning Women Students Program, Evening Class Program, Continuing Education for Professionals, Elderhostel. *Calendar:* semester, summer school.

Undergraduate degrees conferred (5123). 22% were in Business and Management, 14% were in Social Sciences, 10% were in Education, 8% were in Communications, 6% were in Psychology, 6% were in Letters, 5% were in Visual and Performing Arts, 5% were in Public Affairs, 4% were in Life Sciences, 3% were in Protective Services, 3% were in Foreign Languages, 3% were in Liberal/General Studies, 3% were in Home Economics, remainder in 9 other fields.

Faculty. About 87% of faculty hold PhD or equivalent. About 80% of undergraduate classes taught by tenured faculty. About 24% of teaching faculty are female; 3% Black, 6% other minority.

Student Body. About 73% of students from Indiana; 82% Midwest, 7% foreign. An estimated 4% of students reported as Black, 2% Hispanic, 3% Asian, 3% other minority.

Varsity Sports. Men (Div.I): Baseball, Basketball, Cross Country, Diving, Football, Golf, Soccer, Swimming, Tennis, Track, Wrestling. Women (Div.I): Basketball, Cross Country, Diving, Golf, Soccer, Softball, Swimming, Tennis, Track, Volleyball.

Campus Life. Students enjoy considerable freedom in their personal and social activities within the fairly broad regulations of the college. Students may request assignment to living unit where intervisitation is open, limited or closed. University forbids use of alcohol in university-related residences or on campus. IU has adopted a proactive policy to combat racism, sexual harassment, and assault, and offers workshops and classes in all dormitories to publicize incidents and to encourage students to adopt appropriate, prudent behavior.

About 38% of students live in coed and traditional dormitories; 36% in off-campus college-related housing; rest commute. Freshmen given preference in college housing if all students cannot be accommodated, but all requests are generally accommodated. Sexes segregated in coed dormitories by wing or floor. There are 33 fraternities, 27 sororities on campus which about 12% of men, 11% of women join; 23% of students live in fraternities and sororities.

Annual Costs. Tuition and fees, $2,782 (out-of-state, $8,962); room and board, $3,733; estimated $2,000 other, exclusive of travel. About 60% of freshmen, 52% of continuing students, receive financial aid; average amount of assistance, $4,704. Assistance is typically divided 39% scholarship/grant, 53% loan, 8% work. University reports scholarships awarded for academic merit, special talents, and need.

Indiana University at Fort Wayne

(See Indiana University–Purdue University at Fort Wayne)

Indiana University East

Richmond, Indiana 47374-1289 (317) 973-8200

A commuter campus located in a city of 41,000.

Founded: 1971
Affiliation: State
Total Enrollment: 315 M, 675 W (full-time); 415 M, 939 W (part-time)
Cost: < $10K
Application Deadline: August 11

Admission. (See also Indiana University System.) About 94% of applicants accepted, 74% of those actually enroll; 18% of freshmen graduate in top fifth of high school class, 39% in top two-fifths. Average freshman SAT scores: 374 verbal, 411 mathematical; ACT, 19 composite. *Out-of-state* applicants welcome; no limit, no special requirements. *Apply* by August 11; rolling admissions. *Transfers* welcome; 78 enrolled 1993–94.

Academic Environment. Degrees offered: associates, bachelors. About 45% of students entering as freshmen do not return for sophomore year (some enroll at other I.U. campuses). *Special programs:* January term, cross registration with Earlham, IU Tech. Calendar: semester, summer school.

Faculty. About 66% of full-time faculty hold PhD or equivalent. About 31% of undergraduate classes taught by tenured faculty. About 53% of teaching faculty are female; 3% Black, 1% Hispanic, 7% other ethnic minorities.

Student Body. About 98% of students from in state. An estimated 3% of students reported as Black, 1% Hispanic, 1% Asian.

Annual Costs. Tuition and fees, $1,918 (out-of-state, $4,927); an estimated $126 other, exclusive of travel. About 65% of students receive financial aid; assistance is typically divided 4% scholarship, 54% grant, 35% loan, 1% work. University reports 123 scholarships awarded on academic merit alone.

Indiana University at Kokomo

Kokomo, Indiana 46902 (317) 453-2000

A commuter campus, located in a city of 67,000. Most convenient major airport: Dayton (OH).

Founded: 1945
Affiliation: State
UG Enrollment: 279 M, 709 W (full-time); 531 M, 1,356 W (part-time)
Total Enrollment: 3,115
Cost: < $10K
Application Deadline: Rolling

Admission. (See also Indiana University System.) Almost all applicants accepted. *Out-of-state* freshman applicants: about 80% accepted, 50% enroll. *Apply:* rolling admissions. *Transfers* welcome.

Academic Environment. *Degrees:* AB (Liberal Studies), BSEIEd, BSMT. About 25% of general education credits for graduation are required; distribution requirements fairly numerous. About 45% of freshmen do not return for sophomore year (some enroll at other I.U. campuses). *Special programs:* CLEP, independent study, individualized majors, study abroad. *Calendar:* semester, summer school.

Undergraduate degrees conferred (142). 27% were in Education, 25% were in Business and Management, 15% were in Health Sciences, 13% were in Social Sciences, 11% were in Liberal/General Studies, 4% were in Multi/Interdisciplinary Studies, 3% were in Letters, remainder in 3 other fields.

Campus Life. University does not seek a national student body; almost all students from Indiana. An estimated 2% of students reported as Black, 1% Hispanic, 1% other minority according to most recent data available. No dormitories on campus.

Annual Costs. Tuition and fees, $2,255 (out-of-state, $5,450).

Indiana University Northwest

Gary, Indiana 46408 (219) 980-6991

A commuter institution, located on a 240-acre main campus in a city of 175,400. Most convenient major airport: O'Hare or Midway (Chicago).

Founded: 1959
Affiliation: State
UG Enrollment: 945 M, 1,754 W (full-time); 758 M, 1,408 W (part-time)
Total Enrollment: 5,910
Cost: < $10K
% Receiving Financial Aid: 62%
Application Deadline: July 15

Admission. (See also Indiana University System.) About 80% of applicants accepted, 70% of these actually enroll. Average freshman scores: SAT, 375 M, 364 W verbal, 430 M, 388 W mathematical, according to most recent data available. *Required:* SAT, minimum H.S. GPA of 2.0. Criteria considered in admissions, in order of importance: high school academic record, standardized test scores, recommendations. *Out-of-state* applicants: no special requirements; no limitations on out-of-state enrollment. States from which most out-of-state students are drawn include Illinois. *Entrance programs:* early admission, midyear admission. *Apply* by July 15; rolling admissions. *Transfers* welcome.

Academic Environment. Degrees offered: associates, bachelors, masters. General requirements for graduation vary with program; core requirements include English composition, foreign language, mathematics, Western Civilization, and 30 credit hours in two of three broad areas: humanities; math, physical and life sciences; and social-behavioral sciences. About 16% of entering freshmen graduate within 4 years, 32% within 6 years. *Special programs:* CLEP, independent study, study abroad, honors, undergraduate research. Adult programs: General Studies Degree. *Calendar:* semester, summer school.

Undergraduate degrees conferred (333). 31% were in Business and Management, 14% were in Education, 10% were in Health Sciences, 7% were in Liberal/General Studies, 7% were in Protective Services, 5% were in Life Sciences, 4% were in Psychology, 4% were in Communications, 4% were in Social Sciences, 3% were in Visual and Performing Arts, 3% were in Physical Sciences, 3% were in Computer and Engineering Related Technology, remainder in 6 other fields.

Graduates Career Data. Advanced studies pursued by 14% of students. Fields typically employing largest numbers of graduates include accounting, nursing, business.

Faculty. About 63% of faculty hold PhD or equivalent.

Student Body. University does not seek a national student body; almost all students from Indiana. An estimated 21% of students reported as Black, 8% Hispanic, 1% Asian. Average undergraduate age: 27.

Campus Life. This is a commuter institution, provides no residential facilities. Students report lack of parking spaces is something of a problem.

Annual Costs. Tuition and fees, $2,310 (out-of-state, $5,781). About 62% of students receive financial aid; average amount of assistance, $4,500. University reports more than 100 scholarships awarded for academic merit alone. Meeting costs: university offers Indiana Guaranteed tuition certificates.

Indiana University at South Bend

South Bend, Indiana 46634 **(219) 237-4455**

A commuter campus serving an approximately 25-mile radius; located in a city of 125,600. Most convenient major airports: Michiana Regional (South Bend), O'Hare International (Chicago).

Founded: 1940
Affiliation: State
UG Enrollment: 862 M, 1,405 W (full-time); 1,088 M, 1,960 W (part-time)
Total Enrollment: 4,162
Cost: < $10K
Application Deadline: June 1

Admission. (See also Indiana University System.) About 93% of applicants accepted, 44% of those actually enroll; 21% of freshmen graduate in top fifth of high school class, 53% in top two-fifths. *Out-of-state* applicants: 97% accepted, 48% enroll. *Apply* by June 1 for priority. *Transfers* welcome.
Academic Environment. *Undergraduate studies* offered by divisions of Arts and Sciences, Business and Economics, Education, Music, Nursing, Public and Environmental Affairs; program in dental assisting available as well as joint offering of Purdue's freshman engineering curriculum. About 40% of general education requirements for graduation are elective; distribution requirements fairly numerous. About 49% of students entering as freshmen do not return for sophomore year (some enroll at other I.U. campuses). *Special programs:* CLEP, independent study, study abroad. *Calendar:* semester, summer school.
Undergraduate degrees conferred (479). 30% were in Business and Management, 20% were in Education, 18% were in Liberal/General Studies, 6% were in Health Sciences, 5% were in Social Sciences, 4% were in Psychology, 4% were in Protective Services, 4% were in Public Affairs, 3% were in Computer and Engineering Related Technology, remainder in 7 other fields.
Faculty. About 80% of full-time faculty hold PhD or equivalent.
Campus Life. University does not seek a national student body; 98% of students from in state; 99% North Central. An estimated 4% of students reported as Black, 1% His panic, 1% other minority, according to most recent data available. No dormitories on campus.
Annual Costs. Tuition and fees, $2,255 (out-of-state, $5,450). About 30% of students receive financial aid; assistance is typically divided 62% scholarship/grant, 28% loan, 10% work. University reports some scholarships awarded on academic merit alone. *Meeting Costs:* university offers PLUS program.

Indiana University Southeast

New Albany, Indiana 47150 **(812) 941-2212**

A commuter institution, located on a 180-acre campus near New Albany (pop. 38,400). Most convenient major airport: Standiford Field (Louisville, KY).

Founded: 1941
Affiliation: State
UG Enrollment: 972 M, 1,640 W (full-time); 1,040 M, 1,752 W (part-time)
Total Enrollment: 5,642
Cost: < $10K
% Receiving Financial Aid: 45%
Admission: Non-selective
Application Deadline: July 15

Admission. (See also Indiana University System.) Almost all applicants accepted. Average freshman scores, according to most recent data available: SAT, 396 verbal, 425 mathematical. *Out-of-state* applicants: 97% accepted, 54% enroll. *Apply* by July 15. *Transfers* welcome.
Academic Environment. *Degrees:* BA, BSBA, BSEd, BSMT, BSN. About 50% of general education requirements for graduation are elective; distribution requirements fairly numerous. About 55% of students entering as freshmen graduate eventually; 40% of freshmen do not return for sophomore year. About 45% of freshmen do not return for sophomore year (some enroll at other I.U. campuses). *Special programs:* CLEP, independent study, study abroad, 3-year degree. Adult programs: Adult Student Center. *Calendar:* semester, summer school.
Undergraduate degrees conferred (388). 32% were in Education, 25% were in Business and Management, 11% were in Liberal/General Studies, 10% were in Health Sciences, 5% were in Social Sciences, 4% were in Psychology, 4% were in Communications, 3% were in Letters, remainder in 5 other fields.
Varsity Sports. Men (NAIA): Baseball, Basketball. Women (NAIA): Basketball, Volleyball.
Campus Life. University does not seek a national student body; 98% of students from Indiana. An estimated 2% of students reported as Black, 1% other minority. No dormitories on campus.
Annual Costs. Tuition and fees, $1,509 (out-of-state, $3,600). About 45% of students receive financial aid. Assistance is typically divided 60% scholarship, 35% loan, 5% work. University reports some scholarships awarded on the basis of academic merit alone. *Meeting Costs:* university offers guaranteed tuition certificates.

Indiana University–Purdue University at Fort Wayne

Fort Wayne, Indiana 46805 **(219) 481-6812**

Sharing a 412-acre campus and facilities since 1964, Indiana and Purdue took further steps in 1974 to integrate the 2 universities on the Fort Wayne campus. The commuter institution is located in a city of 177,700. Most convenient major airport: Fort Wayne.

Founded: 1964
Affiliation: State
UG Enrollment: 2,147 M, 2,376 W (full-time); 2,957 M, 3,642 W (part-time)
Total Enrollment: 11,701
Cost: < $10K
% Receiving Financial Aid: 90%
Admission: Non-selective
Application Deadline: Rolling

Admission is handled by university responsible for applicant's study area. (See also Indiana University System and Purdue U.) About 96% of applicants accepted, 70% of those accepted actually enroll; 20% of freshmen graduate in top fifth of high school class, 53% in top fifth. *Required:* SAT or ACT; audition for music. Criteria considered in admissions, in order of importance: high school academic record, standardized test scores, recommendations. Out-of state applicants: university actively seeks students from out-of-state. State does not limit out-of-state enrollment. States from which most out-of-state students are drawn include Ohio, Michigan. *Entrance programs:* advanced placement. *Apply:* rolling admission. *Transfers* welcome.
Academic Environment. Each university assumes responsibility for instruction in a specific discipline; degree awarded accordingly by either Indiana or Purdue. *Degrees:* AB, BS, BSB, BSE, BSEd, BM, BMEd, BSM. About 50% of general education requirements for graduation are elective; distribution requirements fairly numerous. About 60% of students entering as freshmen graduate eventually; 30% of freshmen do not return for sophomore year, according to most recent data available. *Special programs:* CLEP, study abroad, honors, individualized majors. *Calendar:* semester, 2 summer sessions.
Undergraduate degrees conferred (690). 29% were in Business and Management, 15% were in Education, 12% were in Engineering and Engineering Related Technology, 8% were in Liberal/General Studies, 7% were in Psychology, 4% were in Communications, 3% were in Computer and Engineering Related Technology, 3% were in Visual and Performing Arts, 3% were in Protective Services, 3% were in Social Sciences, remainder in 8 other fields.
Student Body. University does not seek a national student body; 95% of students from Indiana. An estimated 3% of students are Black, 1% Hispanic. Average age of undergraduate student: 27.
Varsity Sports. Men (NCAA, Div.II): Baseball, Basketball, Cross Country, Golf, Soccer, Tennis, Volleyball. Women (NCAA, Div.II): Basketball, Softball, Tennis, Volleyball.
Campus Life. College provides no residence facilities; a small group of students live in residence facility of nearby seminary. There are 2 fraternities, 2 sororities on campus which about 1% of men, 1% of women join; they provide no residence facilities.

Annual Costs. Tuition and fees, $2,300 (out-of-state, $4,200); estimated $1,200 other, exclusive of travel. About 90% of students receive financial aid; average amount of assistance, $1,500. University reports some scholarships awarded on the basis of academic merit alone. *Meeting Costs:* university offers Indiana University Guaranteed Tuition Certificates.

Indiana University–Purdue University at Indianapolis

Indianapolis, Indiana 46202 (317) 274-4591

Combining programs of 2 Big Ten universities in an urban context, instruction at Indianapolis has been jointly supervised by Indiana and Purdue since 1969. Complex also includes Medical Center (encompassing schools of Dentistry, Medicine, Nursing), Herron School of Art, as well as graduate and professional schools. Most convenient major airport: Indianapolis International.

Founded: 1969
Affiliation: State
UG Enrollment: 3,800 M, 5,416 W (full-time); 4,475 M, 6,701 W (part-time)
Total Enrollment: 27,552
Cost: < $10K
% Receiving Financial Aid: 44%
Admission: Non-selective
Application Deadline: June 1

Admission is handled by campus responsible for applicant's study area. (See also Indiana University System and Purdue U.) About 80% of applicants accepted, 63% of these actually enroll; 14% of freshmen graduate in top fifth of high school class, 36% in top two-fifths. Average freshman scores: SAT, 396 M, 382 W verbal, 453 M, 407 W mathematical; ACT, 19 M, 18 W, composite. *Required:* SAT or ACT; portfolio for art applicants. Criteria considered in admissions, in order of importance: high school academic record, standardized test scores, recommendations. *Out-of-state* applicants: state does not limit out-of-state enrollment. Required for out-of-state students: must rank in top third of H.S. class. States from which most out-of-state students are drawn include Midwestern states. *Entrance programs:* midyear admission, advanced placement. *Apply* by June 1; rolling admissions. *Transfers* welcome; 1,196 enrolled 1993–94.

Academic Environment. Each university assumes responsibility for instruction in a specific discipline; degree awarded accordingly by either Indiana or Purdue. Degrees offered: associates, bachelors, masters, doctoral. About 5% of freshmen graduate in 4 years; 51% return for sophomore year (some enroll at other I.U. campuses). *Special programs:* honors, undergraduate research, study abroad, January term, independent study, cross registration with Butler, Franklin, Marian, U. of Indianapolis. *Calendar:* semester, summer school. Adult programs: Adult Education Orientation.

Undergraduate degrees conferred (1767). 21% were in Business and Management, 15% were in Health Sciences, 11% were in Education, 8% were in Liberal/General Studies, 7% were in Public Affairs, 6% were in Allied Health, 5% were in Engineering and Engineering Related Technology, 4% were in Engineering, 4% were in Social Sciences, 4% were in Letters, 3% were in Psychology, 3% were in Computer and Engineering Related Technology, remainder in 8 other fields.

Faculty. About 89% of faculty hold PhD or equivalent. About 27% of teaching faculty are female: 4% Black, 10% other minority.

Student Body. About 97% of students from in state; 2% Foreign. An estimated 7% of students reported as Black, 1% Hispanic, 2% Asian, 2% other minority, according to most recent data available. Average age of undergraduate student: 27.

Varsity Sports. Men (NAIA/NCAA,Div.II): Baseball, Basketball, Soccer, Tennis. Women (NAIA/NCAA,Div.II): Basketball, Softball, Volleyball.

Campus Life. About 1% men, 1% women live in traditional dormitories; rest commute. There are 2 fraternities, 2 sororities on campus, which about 1% of men, 1% of women join. They provide no residence facilities.

Annual Costs. Tuition and fees, $2,662 (out-of-state, $7,938); room and board, $3,000. About 44% of students receive financial aid. Assistance is typically divided 48% scholarship/grant, 47% loan, 5% work. University reports some scholarships awarded on the basis of academic merit alone.

Indiana University of Pennsylvania

Indiana, Pennsylvania 15705 (412) 357-2230

A state-supported university, located in a town of 25,000, 50 miles northeast of Pittsburgh. University maintains 2-year branch campuses at Punxsutawney and Kittanning.

Founded: 1871
Affiliation: State
UG Enrollment: 5,041 M, 6,334 W (full-time); 488 M, 644 W (part-time)
Total Enrollment: 14,062
Cost: < $10K
% Receiving Financial Aid: 85%
Admission: Selective
Application Deadline: Rolling

Admission is selective. About 51% of applicants accepted, 50% of these actually enroll. Average freshmen scores: SAT, 495 verbal, 444 mathematical. *Required:* SAT or ACT. Criteria considered in admissions, in order of importance: high school academic record, standardized test scores, extracurricular activities, recommendations, writing sample; other factors considered: special talents, diverse student body. *Out-of-state* freshman applicants: no special requirements for out-of-state applicants, state limits out-of-state enrollment. *Entrance programs:* early decision, early admission, midyear admission, advanced placement. *Apply:* rolling admissions; December 31 recommended. *Transfers* welcome.

Academic Environment. Degrees offered: associates, bachelors, masters, doctoral. Administration reports 42% of courses needed for graduation are required. *Undergraduate studies* offered by schools of Humanities and Social Sciences, Business, Education, Fine Arts, Health Sciences, Home Economics, Natural Sciences and Mathematics. *Majors offered* in Arts and Sciences, in addition to usual studies, include criminology, geography, geology, journalism, international studies; interdisciplinary studies, e.g. premed, urban and regional planning, also available. Students report small class sizes and emphasis on practical applications of courses as strengths of the academic program.

About 70% of students entering as freshmen graduate within 4 years, 81% of freshmen return for sophomore year, according to most recent data available. *Special programs:* CLEP, study abroad, honors, 3-year degree, individualized majors. *Calendar:* semester, summer school.

Undergraduate degrees conferred (2157). 27% were in Business and Management, 23% were in Education, 14% were in Social Sciences, 6% were in Communications, 4% were in Health Sciences, 3% were in Home Economics, 3% were in Psychology, 3% were in Life Sciences, 3% were in Computer and Engineering Related Technology, remainder in 13 other fields.

Graduates Career Data. Advanced studies pursued by 14% of students. Medical schools typically enrolling largest numbers of graduates include Jefferson; dental schools include U. of Pittsburgh; laws schools include Dickinson, U. of Pittsburgh; business schools include Indiana U. of Pennsylvania, Penn State. About 63% of 1992–93 graduates employed. Career Development Services include career exploration lab - SIGI Plus computerized career guidance system, career planning and placement activities through Office of Career Services.

Faculty. About 76% of faculty hold PhD or equivalent.

Student Body. University does not seek a national student body; 96% of students from Pennsylvania; 3% Foreign. An estimated 5% of students reported as Black, 1% Hispanic, 1% Asian, 3% other minority. *Minority group students:* Economic Opportunity Program; International Student Organization; Black Student League.

Varsity Sports. Men (Div.II): Baseball, Basketball, Cross Country, Football, Golf, Swimming, Track. Women (Div.II): Basketball, Cross Country, Gymnastics, Softball, Swimming, Tennis, Track, Volleyball.

Campus Life. Student leader reports "healthy social life, but little sponsored by university." Student-initiated activities considered strong, as are Greek life and campus organizations. Parking is evidently a problem, students who live on campus with the exception of University Towers are not issued parking permits.

According to most recent data available, about 1% of men, 1% of women live in traditional residence halls; 11% of men, 17% of women in coed residence halls; 67% of men, 51% of women in off-campus housing; 20% of men, 28% of women commute. Freshmen given preference in college housing if all students cannot be accommodated. There are 17 fraternities, 13 sororities on campus which about 21% of men, 15% of women join; 2% of men, less than 1% of women live in fraternities or sororities. About 15% of students leave campus on weekends.

Annual Costs. Tuition and fees, $3,539 (out-of-state, $7,937); room and board, $2,906; estimated $500 other, exclusive of travel. About 85% of students receive financial aid; average amount of assistance, $2,000. Assistance is typically divided 25% scholarship, 60% loan, 15% work. University reports some scholarships awarded on the basis of academic merit alone.

University of Indianapolis

Indianapolis, Indiana 46227 **(317) 788-3216 or (800) 232-8634**

A church-related, liberal arts university, located in suburban Indianapolis. University is committed to a philosophy of "education for service." Formerly known as Indiana Central University. Most convenient major airport: Indianapolis.

Founded: 1902
Affiliation: United Methodist
UG Enrollment: 548 M, 870 W (full-time); 362 M, 1,280 W (part-time)
Total Enrollment: 3,767
Cost: $10K–$20K
% Receiving Financial Aid: 82%
Admission: Non-selective
Application Deadline: Aug. 15

Admission. High school graduates with 24 academic units who rank in top half of class eligible; others may be admitted on basis of test scores and level of motivation; 85% of applicants accepted, 33% of these actually enroll; 43% of freshmen graduate in top fifth of high school class, 71% in top two-fifths. Average freshman scores: SAT, 432 verbal, 487 mathematical. *Required:* SAT or ACT, minimum H.S. GPA of 2.0; interview suggested. Criteria considered in admissions, in order of importance: high school academic record, extracurricular activities, recommendations, writing sample, standardized test scores. *Apply* by August 15; rolling admissions. *Transfers* welcome.

Academic Environment. Degrees offered: associates, bachelors, masters. *Majors offered* in addition to usual studies include management information systems, sports information, sports management, travel and tourism, hotel management, cultural anthropology, physical therapy. Average undergraduate class size: 58% under 20, 40% between 20–40, 2% over 40. About 52% of entering freshmen graduate within four years, 54% eventually; 75% return for sophomore year. *Special programs:* CLEP, independent study, study abroad, honors, undergraduate research, graduation in 3 years by attending all 3 terms each year, cross registration with 6 area colleges, 3–2 programs in physical and occupational therapy, medical technology with Methodist Hospital, cooperative programs with Indiana U. schools of Medicine, Dentistry, Spring Term Consortium. *Calendar:* semester, "fleximester" (varying from 4 to 14 weeks), summer school.

Undergraduate degrees conferred (277). 32% were in Business and Management, 18% were in Education, 8% were in Health Sciences, 7% were in Life Sciences, 5% were in Communications, 5% were in Social Sciences, 4% were in Psychology, 4% were in Visual and Performing Arts, 4% were in Computer and Engineering Related Technology, 3% were in Protective Services, 3% were in Letters, remainder in 7 other fields.

Faculty. About 53% of faculty hold PhD or equivalent.

Student Body. University seeks a national student body; 89% of students from in state. An estimated 70% of students reported as Protestant, 25% Catholic, 5% other; 7% Black, 7% other minority.

Varsity Sports. Men (Div.II): Baseball, Basketball, Cross Country, Diving, Football, Golf, Soccer, Swimming, Tennis, Track, Wrestling. Women (Div.II): Basketball, Cross Country, Diving, Golf, Soccer, Softball, Swimming, Tennis, Track, Volleyball.

Religious Orientation. Indianapolis is a church-related institution; about 25% of students affiliated with Methodist Church; attendance at convocation programs twice weekly required of all students during 4 of 8 semesters. One religious course required of all students.

Campus Life. About 45% of students live in traditional or coed dormitories; rest commute. Freshmen are given preference in college housing if all students cannot be accommodated. Intervisitation in men's and women's dormitory rooms limited. There are no fraternities or sororities.

Annual Costs. Tuition and fees, $10,590; room and board, $3,920. About 82% of students receive financial aid; average amount of assistance, $9,800. Assistance is typically divided 69% scholarship, 28% loan, 3% work, according to most recent data available. University reports some scholarships awarded on the basis of academic merit alone.

College of Insurance

New York, New York 10038 **(800) 356-5146**

An independent, professional school, supported by insurance firms and offering a 5-year work/study degree program; located in the heart of New York's financial district. Most convenient major airport: JFK International.

Founded: 1962
Affiliation: Independent
UG Enrollment: 80 M, 45 W (full-time); 388 M, 50 W (part-time)
Total Enrollment: 672
Cost: $10K–$20K
Admission: Non-selective
Application Deadline: December 1

Admission. Graduates of approved high schools with 16 academic units and satisfactory scores on college's entrance examinations eligible; 73% of applicants accepted, 55% of those accepted actually enroll. *Required:* SAT or ACT, interview. *Entrance programs:* early decision, midyear admission, deferred admission. *Apply* by December 1. *Transfers* welcome.

Academic Environment. Curriculum about 50% liberal arts; remainder evenly divided between business administration and insurance. *Degrees:* BS, BBA. About 25% of general education requirements for graduation are elective; distribution requirements fairly numerous. *Special programs:* CLEP, independent study. *Calendar:* trimester, summer school.

Undergraduate degrees conferred (34). 76% were in Business and Management, 24% were in Mathematics.

Campus Life. About 84% of students from Middle Atlantic. College is an independent institution, makes no religious demands on students. About 65% of students live in dormitories, rest commute.

Annual Costs. Tuition and fees, $10,500; room and board, $6,888. College reports some scholarships awarded on the basis of academic merit alone.

Inter American University of Puerto Rico

Hato Rey, Puerto Rico 00919 **(809) 250-1912**

An independent institution, founded under the auspices of the United Presbyterian Church, but "ecumenical in concept." The university has two major campuses at San Germán and San Juan, seven 2-year regional campuses, and a law school.

Founded: 1912
Affiliation: Independent (Presbyterian Church (USA))
Total Enrollment: 39,163 M, W (full-time)
Cost: < $10K
Admission: Non-selective
Application Deadline: May 1

Admission. Graduates of accredited high schools with C average eligible; 89% of applicants accepted, 76% of these actually enroll. *Required:* SAT (English or Spanish); interview when necessary. *Apply* by May 1. *Transfers* welcome.

Academic Environment. *Degrees:* AB, BS. About 24% of general education requirements for graduation are elective; distribution requirements fairly numerous. *Special programs:* CLEP, independent study. *Calendar:* semester, summer school.

Undergraduate degrees conferred (827). 26% were in Business and Management, 21% were in Education, 12% were in Health Sciences, 9% were in Life Sciences, 7% were in Business and Office, 7% were in Public Affairs, 5% were in Psychology, 5% were in Social Sciences, remainder in 8 other fields.

Campus Life. University does not seek a national student body; 100% of students from Puerto Rico. No residence facilities at San Juan or regional campuses. There are no fraternities or sororities.

Annual Costs. Tuition and fees, $3,154.

International Academy of Merchandising and Design

Chicago, Illinois 60602

An independent career college offering associates and bachelors degrees in fashion design, interior design, advertising design and communications, and merchandising management.

Affiliation: Independent

Iona College

New Rochelle, New York 10801 **(914) 633-2502**

An independent, liberal arts college for commuters, Iona, though Catholic in its tradition, is now a non-sectarian institution governed by an independent board of trustees. The 55-acre campus is located in a suburban city of 75,400, 16 miles northeast of New York City. Most convenient major airport: LaGuardia.

Founded: 1940
Affiliation: Independent
UG Enrollment: 1,652 M, 1,763 W (full-time); 526 M, 877 W (part-time)
Total Enrollment: 5,983
Cost: < $10K
% Receiving Financial Aid: 89%
Admission: Non-selective
Application Deadline: Rolling

Admission. High school graduates with 16 units eligible; 66% of applicants accepted, 37% of these actually enroll; 24% of freshmen graduate in top fifth of high school class, 52% in top two-fifths. Average freshman SAT scores, according to most recent data available: 409 M, 399 W verbal, 463 M, 431 W mathematical. *Required:* SAT or ACT, interview. *Apply:* rolling admissions. *Transfers* welcome.

Academic Environment. Joint course registration with College of New Rochelle; bus makes hourly trips between campuses. *Degrees:* BA, BS, BBA. *Majors offered* include usual arts and sciences, accounting, finance, marketing and management, international business, area studies.

About 60% of students entering as freshmen graduate eventually; 20% of freshmen do not return for sophomore year. *Special programs:* Winter intersession, CLEP, independent study, study abroad, honors, cooperative cross-registration programs with nearby College of New Rochelle and Concordia College, medical technology degree program, environmental sciences, combined programs with NY College of Podiatric Medicine, NY Chiropractic College, NYU College of Dentistry. Adult programs: The School of General Studies is exclusively designed for adult students. *Calendar:* semester, summer school.

Undergraduate degrees conferred (866). 50% were in Business and Management, 11% were in Communications, 8% were in Social Sciences, 7% were in Computer and Engineering Related Technology, 5% were in Psychology, 4% were in Education, 3% were in Letters, 3% were in Protective Services, remainder in 9 other fields.

Graduates Career Data. According to most recent data available, full-time graduate or professional study pursued by 10% of students immediately after graduation. *Careers in business and industry* pursued by 70% of graduates. Corporations typically hiring largest numbers of graduates include Arthur Andersen, Peat Marwick, Ernst & Young, Coopers & Lybrand, Shearson Lehman & Hutton.

Faculty. About 61% of faculty hold PhD or equivalent.

Student Body. College does not seek a national student body; 93% of students from New York; 97% Middle Atlantic. An estimated 15% of students reported as Black, 8% Hispanic, 2% Asian, according to most recent data available. *Minority group students:* financial and academic assistance through Community Leadership program; social activities through student-run clubs.

Religious Orientation. Iona has a Catholic heritage; 6 credits of religious studies in Western and non-Western religious traditions required of all students as part of general education curriculum. No required religious practices. Places of worship available on campus for Catholics, in immediate community for major faiths.

Varsity Sports. Men (Div.I): Baseball, Basketball, Soccer, Tennis, Track, Water Polo. (Div.III): Crew, Football, Golf, Hockey, Swimming. Women (Div.I): Basketball. (Div.III): Crew, Softball, Tennis, Volleyball.

Campus Life. College is primarily for commuters. About 6% of men, 8% of women live in traditional dormitories; 8% of men, 10% of women live in coed dormitories; rest live off campus or commute. Freshmen given preference in college housing if all students cannot be accommodated. There are 10 fraternities, 8 sororities on campus; they provide no residence facilities. About 30% of resident students leave campus on weekends.

Annual Costs. Tuition and fees, $9,540; room and board, $6,000. About 89% of students receive financial aid; assistance is typically divided 50% scholarship, 30% loan, 20% work. College reports some scholarships awarded on the basis of academic ability alone. *Meeting Costs:* college offers payment plan.

Iowa State University

Ames, Iowa 50011-2010 **(515) 294-5836 or (800) 262-3810**

Iowa State is a major state university with undergraduate and graduate programs in a wide variety of fields. Traditionally, it has been known for particular emphasis in the areas of science, engineering, and agriculture, but today the College of Liberal Arts and Sciences has the greatest enrollment of the nine colleges. The 1,000-acre campus is located in a city of approximately 45,000, about 30 miles north of Des Moines. Most convenient major airport: Des Moines International.

Founded: 1858
Affiliation: State
UG Enrollment: 11,175 M, 7,867 W (full-time); 856 M, 731 W (part-time)
Total Enrollment: 25,112
Cost: < $10K
% Receiving Financial Aid: 75%
Admission: Selective (+)
Application Deadline: Aug. 19

Admission is selective (+). About 88% of applicants accepted, 46% of these actually enroll; 49% of freshmen graduate in top fifth of high school class, 81% in top two-fifths. Average freshman scores: SAT, middle 50% range, 380–460 verbal, 530–640 mathematical; ACT, 22–27 composite.

For Engineering (3,524 M, 491 W), 92% of applicants accepted, 49% of these actually enroll; 65% of freshmen graduate in top fifth of high school class, 94% in top two-fifths. Average freshman ACT scores: 26.6 composite.

For Liberal Arts and Sciences (3,705 M, 3,460 W), 86% of applicants accepted, 42% of these actually enroll; 45% of freshmen graduate in top fifth of high school class, 80% in top two-fifths. Average freshman ACT scores: 23.9 composite.

For Agriculture (1,407 M, 511 W), 90% of applicants accepted, 63% of these actually enroll; 44% of freshmen graduate in top fifth of high school class, 82% in top two-fifths. Average freshman ACT scores: 24.0 composite.

For Design (1,081 M, 814 W), 89% of applicants accepted, 55% of these actually enroll; 39% of freshmen graduate in top fifth of high school class, 80% in top two-fifths. Average freshman ACT scores: 23.7 composite.

For Education (584 M, 1,139 W), 84% of applicants accepted, 55% of these actually enroll; 33% of freshmen graduate in top fifth of high school class, 77% in top two-fifths. Average freshman ACT scores: 21.5 composite.

For Family and Consumer Sciences (191 M, 1,029 W), 82% of applicants accepted, 54% of these actually enroll; 45% of freshmen graduate in top fifth of high school class, 82% in top two-fifths. Average freshman ACT scores: 22.2 composite.

Required: ACT or SAT, class rank. Criteria considered in admissions, in order of importance: high school academic record, standardized test scores, specified high school courses. *Out-of-state* freshman applicants: state does not limit out-of-state enrollment. Requirement for out-of-state applicants: applicants "may be held to higher standard"; 85% of applicants accepted, 29% enroll. *Entrance programs:* deferred admission, advanced placement. About 8% of entering students from private schools. *Apply* by August 19; rolling admissions. *Transfers* welcome; 1,672 enrolled 1993–94.

Academic Environment. Degrees offered: bachelors, masters, doctoral. The presence of a number of distinguished graduate departments encourages a substantial number of students to pursue scholarly and intellectual interests. However, majority of students major in occupational/professional areas. Core requirements include English, speech, arts and humanities, natural and mathematical sciences, social sciences, foreign language, and library instruction. *Undergraduate studies* offered by colleges of Agriculture, Design, Education, Engineering, Family and Consumer Sciences, Liberal Arts and Sciences; upperclassmen admitted to Business Administration and Veterinary Medicine. *Majors offered* in more than 100 areas of studies; in including accounting, agricultural studies-farm operation, biological/premedical illustration, community and regional planning, entomology, finance, fisheries and wildlife biology, landscape architecture, management, marketing, metallurgy, occupational safety, pre-professional health programs, transportation and logistics, management information systems, early childhood education, general undergraduate studies, pre-landscape architecture, international studies, neurosciences, disabilities in young children, African American studies, ecology and evolutionary biology, foreign study. Average undergraduate class size: 36% of classes under 20, 46% between 20–40, 18% over 40.

About 63% of students entering as freshmen graduate eventually; 17% of freshmen do not return for sophomore year. *Special programs:* CLEP, study abroad, honors, undergraduate research, broad range of courses in environmental studies, cross registration-Regents' Exchange with U. of Iowa and U. of Northern Iowa, internships in many areas. Adult programs: Bachelor of Liberal Studies (adult external degree program). *Calendar:* semester, summer school.

Undergraduate degrees conferred (3906). 22% were in Business and Management, 18% were in Engineering, 11% were in Education, 6% were in Social Sciences, 4% were in Letters, 4% were in Agribusiness and Agricultural Production, 4% were in Architecture and Environmental Design, 4% were in Communications, 4% were in Visual and Performing Arts, 3% were in Psychology, 3% were in Agricultural Sciences, 3% were in Home Economics, remainder in 16 other fields.

Graduates Career Data. Advanced studies pursued by 18% of students; 1% enter medical school; 1% enter dental school; 1% enter law school; 2% enter business school; 2% enter veterinary school. About 93% of 1992–93 graduates employed. Fields typically hiring the largest number of graduates include engineering, business, agriculture, veterinary medicine. Career Development Services include seven college-based career planning and placement offices offering courses, workshops, individual counseling, assistance in preparing resumes and interviewing skills, on-campus recruitment is reported to be extensive. Alumni reported as active in both career guidance and job placement. Extern program available.

Faculty. About 88% of faculty hold PhD or equivalent. About 62% of undergraduate classes taught by tenured faculty. About 24% of teaching faculty are female; 9% minorities.

Student Body. University seeks a diverse student body; 76% of students from in state; 91% Midwest, 3% other U.S. regions, 6% foreign. An estimated 3% of students reported as Black, 1% Hispanic, 2% Asian, 6% other ethnic minorities. *Minority group students:* special financial, academic, and social provisions available through office of minority programs.

Varsity Sports. Men (Div.IA): Baseball, Basketball, Cross Country, Football, Golf, Gymnastics, Swimming, Tennis, Track, Wrestling. Women (Div.I): Basketball, Cross Country, Golf, Gymnastics, Softball, Swimming, Tennis, Track, Volleyball.

Campus Life. Administration source reports sports (both varsity and intramural), cultural activities, and fraternities/sororities popular on campus. Most popular sports include football and basketball. Relations between Greeks and independents include "good-natured snowball fights." More than 500 student organizations, 60 intramural sports, and multitude of arts and recreational activities offer students plenty to keep them busy. Students have significant role in determining rules governing campus social life; residents of each house determine hours. Minimum drinking age of 21; smoking not permitted except in designated areas, in public facilities, including bathrooms.

About 21% of men, 14% of women live in traditional dormitories; 2% of men, 2% of women live in coed dormitories; 30% of men, 23% of women live in off-campus college-related housing; 5% of men, 3% of women live in fraternities and sororities; rest commute. Sexes segregated in coed dormitories by wing, floor or room. There are 32 fraternities, 15 sororities on campus which about 17% of men, 16% of women join.

Annual Costs. Tuition and fees, $2,192 (out-of-state, $7,226); room and board, $3,104; estimated $640 other, exclusive of travel. About 75% of students receive financial aid; average amount of assistance, $5,482. University reports 2,766 scholarships awarded on the basis of academic merit or special talents, 2,563 for need. *Meeting Costs:* university offers no-cost installment fee payment plans.

University of Iowa

Iowa City, Iowa 52242 — **(319) 335-3847 or (800) 553-4692**

The University of Iowa ranks among the foremost research institutions in the country. The campus houses the major professional schools of law, medicine, and dentistry, and provides strong liberal arts and sciences at both the graduate and undergraduate levels. A sister institution, Iowa State located in Ames, is also one of the nation's more eminent universities. Most convenient major airport: Cedar Rapids.

Founded: 1847
Affiliation: State
UG Enrollment: 7,482 M, 7,930 W (full-time); 1,315 M, 1,563 W (part-time)
Total Enrollment: 27,051
Cost: < $10K
% Receiving Financial Aid: 75%
Admission: Very (+) Selective
Application Deadline: May 15

Admission is very (+) selective. For all schools, 87% of applicants accepted, 41% of these actually enroll; 43% of freshmen graduate in top fifth of high school class, 76% in top two-fifths. Average freshman ACT scores, middle 50% range: 22–27 composite. *Required:* SAT or ACT; must complete specific set of high school courses; admission determined by class rank or combination of class rank and ACT or SAT. Criteria considered in admissions, in order of importance: high school academic record, standardized test scores, recommendations; other factors considered: special talents, alumni children, diverse student body. *Out-of-state* freshman applicants: university actively seeks students from out-of-state. State does not limit out-of-state enrollment. Requirement for out-of-state applicants: top 30% of high school class or acceptable admission of combination of rank and ACT or SAT. About 85% of applicants accepted, 28% enroll. States from which most out-of-state students are drawn include Illinois. *Entrance programs:* early admission, midyear admission, deferred admission, advanced placement. *Apply* by May 15; rolling admissions. *Transfers* welcome; 1,342 enrolled 1993–94.

Academic Environment. Competition for academic achievement varies among the different colleges and from department to department, as at other large and complex institutions. Recent student reports increased emphasis on undergraduate education, though he feels the graduate schools still receive more attention and money. Graduation requirements vary with college and program; basic core requirements of liberal arts program comprise one third of students' time and include quantitative or formal reasoning, natural and social sciences, humanities and historical perspectives, foreign civilization and culture, plus proficiency in foreign language, rhetoric, and physical education. *Undergraduate studies* offered by College of Liberal Arts with divisions of Fine Arts and Mathematical Sciences, schools of Art, Journalism, Letters, Library Science, Music, Religion, Social Work, College of Engineering; colleges of Business Administration, Education, Nursing, Pharmacy, Medicine, Dentistry, and Law all require previous work. Degrees offered: bachelors, masters, doctoral. *Majors offered* in wide range of studies include anthropology, astronomy, Chinese, computer science, dance, East European and Eurasian studies, Japanese, journalism, linguistics, medical technology, microbiology, music, Russian, social work, theater, Philosophies and Ethics of Politics, economics.

About 29% of students entering as freshmen graduate within four years, 60% within six years; 89% of freshmen return for sophomore year. *Special programs:* CLEP, independent study, study abroad, honors, undergraduate research, credit for military experience, student-designed majors, pass/non pass options, combined liberal arts programs (with engineering, dental hygiene, dentistry, medicine, law, medical technology, nuclear medical technology), cross registration, internships/cooperative education, certificate programs, unified program. Adult programs: Saturday and Evening Class program offers courses for non-traditional students. *Calendar:* semester, summer school.

Undergraduate degrees conferred (3627). 19% were in Business and Management, 14% were in Social Sciences, 10% were in Communications, 9% were in Education, 7% were in Health Sciences, 6% were in Engineering, 6% were in Letters, 5% were in Psychology, 4% were in Visual and Performing Arts, 4% were in Liberal/General Studies, 3% were in Life Sciences, remainder in 11 other fields.

Graduates Career Data. Career Development Services include business and liberal arts placement office, on-campus recruitment, active alumni reported in both career guidance and job placement.

Faculty. About 98% of full-time faculty hold PhD or equivalent. About 21% of teaching faculty are female; 2% Black, 2% Hispanic, 7% other minority.

Student Body. About 70% of students from in state; less than 1% foreign. An estimated 2% of students reported as Black, 3% Asian, 2% Hispanic, 3% other minority. *Minority group students:* financial, academic, and social assistance provided for "economically disadvantaged students" by Special Support Services.

Varsity Sports. Men (Div.I): Baseball, Basketball, Cross Country, Football, Golf, Gymnastics, Swimming & Diving, Tennis, Track, Wrestling. Women (Div.I): Basketball, Crew, Cross Country, Field Hockey, Golf, Gymnastics, Softball, Swimming & Diving, Tennis, Track, Volleyball.

Campus Life. Student leader reports "loose, free atmosphere . . . an excess of other things to do besides academics." University provides cultural and intellectual activities; very full schedule of artists and lecturers brought to the campus. Another recent student comments "For such a big school, it has a small town effect, everybody is really nice." Both residence halls and Greek houses available; apartments for married students. Cars permitted, but university encourages use of free shuttle bus serving all parts of campus.

About 26% of men, 29% of women in coed dormitories; 66% of men, 64% of women in off-campus housing or commute. Freshmen who apply early given preference in college housing if all students cannot be accommodated. There are 23 fraternities, 20 sororities on campus which about 15% of men, 16% of women join; 8% men, 7% women live in fraternities and sororities.

Annual Costs. Tuition and fees, $2,352 (out-of-state, $7,740); room and board, $3,306; estimated $2,464 other, exclusive of travel. About 75% of students receive financial aid, average amount of assistance, $2,132. *Meeting Costs:* university offers tuition management systems.

Iowa Wesleyan College

Mount Pleasant, Iowa 52641 (319) 385-6231

A church-related, liberal arts college, located in a community of 8,000, 70 miles south of Cedar Rapids and 28 miles west of the Mississippi River. Most convenient major airport: Cedar Rapids or Burlington.

Founded: 1842
Affiliation: United Methodist
Total Enrollment: 699 M, W (full-time)
Cost: < $10K
% Receiving Financial Aid: 95%
Admission: Non-selective
Application Deadline: Rolling

Admission. High school graduates with 15 units in academic subjects, preferably ranking in top half of class or with C average, eligible; 72% of applicants accepted, 27% of these actually enroll. Average freshman ACT score, according to most recent data available: 18.7 composite. *Required:* SAT or ACT. *Apply:* rolling admissions. *Transfers* welcome.

Academic Environment. *Degrees:* BA, BS, BMEd, BSN, BGS. About 75% of general education requirements for graduation are elective; liberal arts core curriculum (includes Freshman Experience course to ease transition to college life and course in microcomputer applications) required of all students. About 54% of students entering as freshmen graduate within four years; 80% of freshmen return for sophomore year. *Special programs:* CLEP, independent study, study abroad, individualized majors, computer center, required student service project (for 6 hours academic credit), 3–2 in forestry, medical technology, physical therapy, MBA prep program. *Library:* archives of Iowa Wesleyan and local district of United Methodist Church. *Calendar:* 4–1–4, summer school.

Undergraduate degrees conferred (143). 29% were in Business and Management, 27% were in Education, 8% were in Health Sciences, 6% were in Life Sciences, 5% were in Psychology, 5% were in Letters, 4% were in Social Sciences, 4% were in Protective Services, 4% were in Communications, 3% were in Computer and Engineering Related Technology, remainder in 4 other fields.

Graduates Career Data. According to most recent data available, full-time graduate or professional study pursued by 9% of students immediately after graduation.

Faculty. About 42% of faculty hold PhD or equivalent.

Student Body. About 68% of students from Iowa; 4% foreign. An estimated 2% of students reported as Protestant, 10% Catholic, 45% unaffiliated, 43% other; 9% Black, 1% Hispanic, 1% Asian, 1% other minority, according to most recent data available.

Religious Orientation. Iowa Wesleyan is a church-related institution.

Campus Life. About 62% of men, 62% of women live in traditional dormitories; no coed dormitories; rest commute. Freshmen given preference in college housing if all students cannot be accommodated. Intervisitation in men's and women's dormitory rooms limited. There is 1 fraternity, 2 sororities on campus which about 9% of men, 14% of women join; they provide no residence facilities.

Annual Costs. Tuition and fees, $9,850; room and board, $3,400. About 95% of students receive financial aid; all need is met. Assistance is typically divided 74% scholarship, 13% loan, 13% work. College reports scholarships awarded only on the basis of need. *Meeting Costs:* college offers deferred payment plan.

Ithaca College

Ithaca, New York 14850 (607) 274-3124

An independent, liberal arts, and professional college, Ithaca is located in a town of 26,200, 45 miles south of Syracuse. The 400-acre campus overlooks Cayuga Lake in New York's Finger Lake region.

Founded: 1892
Affiliation: Independent
Total Enrollment: 2,718 M, 3,400 W (full-time)
Cost: $10K–$20K
Admission: Selective
Application Deadline: March 1

Admission is selective. Both academic and non-academic factors considered in admission. Most entering freshmen high school graduates, but college urges those from non-traditional schools and those who wish to enter college early to write for information. About 59% of applicants accepted, 34% of these actually enroll; 50% of freshmen graduate in top fifth of high school class, 80% in top two-fifths. *Required:* SAT or ACT; audition for music and drama, portfolio for art. *Non-academic factors* considered in admissions: diverse student body, alumni children, special talents. *Entrance programs:* early decision, early admission, midyear admission, deferred admission, advanced placement. About 20% of entering students from private and parochial schools. *Apply* by March 1. *Transfers* welcome.

Academic Environment. *Undergraduate studies* offered by schools of Health Sciences and Human Performance; Humanities and Sciences, Music; Business; Communications. Each school determines requirements for graduation; some schools have distribution requirements. *Majors offered* include international business, art history, film photography and visual arts, clinical science, athletic training/exercise science, fitness and cardiac rehab/exercise science, 5-year BS/MS in physical therapy, music-Jazz studies.

About 64% of students entering as freshmen graduate eventually; 83% of freshmen return for sophomore year. *Special programs:* CLEP, independent study, study abroad, honors, undergraduate research, individualized majors, 3–2 engineering, exchange program with Cornell. *Calendar:* semester, summer school.

Undergraduate degrees conferred (1347). 19% were in Business and Management, 16% were in Social Sciences, 13% were in Communications, 11% were in Visual and Performing Arts, 9% were in Letters, 8% were in Allied Health, 7% were in Psychology, 7% were in Education, remainder in 9 other fields.

Student Body. About 50% of students from in state; 73% Middle Atlantic, 18% New England. An estimated 24% of students reported as Protestant, 21% Jewish, 34% Catholic, 20% unaffiliated, 2% other; 2% Black, 1% Hispanic, 1% other minority, according to most recent data available.

Varsity Sports. Men (Div.III): Baseball, Basketball, Crew, Cross Country, Football, Golf, Lacrosse, Soccer, Swimming, Tennis, Track, Wrestling. Women (Div.III): Basketball, Crew, Cross Country, Field Hockey, Gymnastics, Lacrosse, Soccer, Softball, Swimming, Tennis, Track, Volleyball.
Campus Life. Variety of living units available, including coed dorms; sexes segregated by wing, floor or room. Cars allowed for all. Freshmen required to live on campus.

About 8% of women live in traditional dormitories; 71% of men, 55% of women in coed dormitories; 28% of men, 36% of women live in off-campus housing. Freshmen given preference in college housing if all students cannot be accommodated. There are 2 fraternities, 3 sororities. About 10% of resident students leave campus on weekends.
Annual Costs. Tuition and fees, $13,642; room and board, $5,842. College reports scholarships awarded primarily on the basis of need. *Meeting Costs:* college offers monthly payment plans.

Jackson College

(See Tufts University)

Jackson State University

Jackson, Mississippi 39217 (601) 968-2121

A state-supported university, located in a city of 180,000; founded as a college for Negroes and still serving a predominantly Black student body. Most convenient major airport: Jackson Municipal.

Founded: 1877
Affiliation: State
UG Enrollment: 2,122 M, 2,664 W (full-time); 229 M, 440 W (part-time)
Total Enrollment: 6,346
Cost: < $10K
% Receiving Financial Aid: 94%
Admission: Non-selective
Application Deadline: 20 days before registration

Admission. Graduates of approved high schools with 10 units and C average eligible; others admitted by examination; 68% of applicants accepted, 55% of these actually enroll; 35% of entering students graduate in top quarter of high school class, 69% in top-half. Average freshman ACT scores: 17 composite. *Required:* ACT. Criteria considered in admissions, in order of importance: standardized test scores, high school academic record; other factors considered: special talents, diverse student body, alumni children, extracurricular activities. *Out-of-state* freshman applicants: university actively seeks students from out-of-state. State does not limit out-of-state enrollment. Special requirements for out-of-state applicants: minimum ACT composite score of 16. States from which most out-of-state students are drawn are Illinois, Michigan, Missouri. *Entrance programs:* early decision, early admission. *Apply* by 20 days prior to scheduled registration date; rolling admissions. *Transfers* welcome; 271 enrolled 1993–94.
Academic Environment. Degrees offered: bachelors, masters, doctoral. Graduation requirements include 15–21 semester hours in communications, 12 hours of social and behavioral sciences, 9–12 hours of natural sciences, 9 hours of humanities, 2–3 hours of health and physical education, 2 hours of guidance. *Majors offered* include meteorology, computer science. Jackson State is nationally recognized for graduating the largest number of African-American computer science majors.

About 39% of entering freshmen graduate eventually; 76% of freshmen return for sophomore year. *Special programs:* independent study, honors, weekend college, cooperative education, visiting/exchange student program. Adult program: Meteorology, Public Policy and Administration. *Calendar:* quarter, summer school.
Undergraduate degrees conferred (551). 38% were in Business and Management, 8% were in Protective Services, 7% were in Social Sciences, 6% were in Computer and Engineering Related Technology, 5% were in Life Sciences, 5% were in Engineering and Engineering Related Technology, 5% were in Education, 5% were in Business (Administrative Support), 5% were in Letters, 4% were in Communications, 3% were in Psychology, 3% were in Public Affairs, remainder in 4 other fields.
Graduate Career Data. Fields typically hiring largest numbers of graduates include computer science, accounting, business administration, education.
Faculty. About 70% of faculty hold PhD or equivalent.

About 38% of teaching faculty are women; 62% Black, 1% Hispanic, 13% other minority.
Student Body. About 62% of students from in state; 86% South. An estimated 94% of students reported as Black, 1% Hispanic, 1% Asian. Average age of undergraduate student: 22.
Varsity Sports. Men (Div.IA): Baseball, Basketball, Football, Golf, Swimming, Tennis, Track, Volleyball. Women (Div.IA): Basketball.
Campus Life. About 46% of men, 54% of women live in traditional dormitories; no coed dormitories; rest commute. Freshmen given preference in college housing if all students cannot be accommodated. Limited intervisitation in men's and women's dormitory rooms. There are 4 fraternities and 4 sororities on campus which about 1% each men, women join.
Annual Costs. Tuition and fees, $2,230 (out-of-state, $4,464); room and board, $2,766; estimated $1,000 other, exclusive of travel. About 94% of students receive financial aid; average amount of assistance, $1,900.

Jacksonville State University

Jacksonville, Alabama 36265-9982 (205) 782-5400

A state-supported institution, located in a town of 7,700, in the foothills of the Appalachian Mountains, 60 miles northeast of Birmingham. Most convenient major airport: Birmingham.

Founded: 1883
Affiliation: State
UG Enrollment: 2,390 M, 2,770 W (full-time); 769 M, 706 W (part-time)
Total Enrollment: 6,635
Cost: < $10K
Admission: Non-selective
Application Deadline: Rolling

Admission. Graduates of accredited high schools with 15 units; 87% of applicants accepted, 63% of these actually enroll. Average freshman ACT scores: 20 composite. *Required:* SAT or ACT. Criteria considered in admissions, in order of importance: standardized test scores, high school academic record. *Out-of-state* freshman applicants: university actively seeks students from out-of-state. State does not limit out-of-state enrollment. No special requirements for out-of-state students. States from which most out-of-state students are drawn include Georgia. *Entrance programs:* early admission, midyear admission, deferred admission, advanced placement. *Apply:* rolling admissions. *Transfers* welcome; 665 enrolled 1993–94.
Academic Environment. Degrees offered: bachelors, masters. *Special programs:* CLEP, cooperative education. *Calendar:* 4–4–1, summer school.
Undergraduate degrees conferred (1041). 31% were in Business and Management, 31% were in Education, 6% were in Protective Services, 5% were in Social Sciences, 5% were in Health Sciences, 4% were in Engineering and Engineering Related Technology, 3% were in Psychology, remainder in 12 other fields.
Graduate Career Data. Advanced studies pursued by 40% of graduates; 1% enter medical school; 1% enter dental school; 1% enter law school; 40% enter business school. About 65–75% of 1992–93 graduates employed. Fields typically hiring largest numbers of graduates include educational, retail sales, management. Career Development and Counseling Services offer self-assessment and testing, a career information library, employability skill workshops.
Faculty. About 65% of faculty hold PhD or equivalent. About 39% of teaching faculty are female; 5% ethnic minority.
Student Body. About 80% from in state; less than 1% foreign. Average age of undergraduate students: 23.
Varsity Sports. Men: Baseball, Basketball, Football, Golf, Riflery, Tennis. Women: Basketball, Riflery, Softball, Tennis, Volleyball.
Campus Life. About 25% of men, 25% of women live in traditional dormitories; no coed dormitories; rest live in off-campus housing or commute, according to most recent data available. There are 10 fraternities, 9 sororities on campus, which about 5% of men, women join.
Annual Costs. Tuition, $1,680 (out-of-state, $2,520); room and board, $2,600; estimated $570 other, exclusive of travel. About 42% of students receive financial aid; average amount of assistance, $2,100, according to most recent data available. Assistance is typically divided 52% scholarship, 38% loan, 10% work.

Jacksonville University

Jacksonville, Florida 32211 (904) 745-7000

An independent university, located in a suburban area in a city of 528,900, on a 260-acre riverfront campus.

Founded: 1934
Affiliation: Independent
UG Enrollment: 841 M, 723 W (full-time); 224 M, 285 W (part-time)
Total Enrollment: 2,407
Cost: $10K–$20K
% Receiving Financial Aid: 83%
Admission: Non-selective
Application Deadline: Aug. 1

Admission. Graduates of accredited high schools with 14 units in academic subjects who rank in top half of class eligible; 83% of applicants accepted, 27% of these actually enroll. *Required:* SAT or ACT. *Apply* by August 1. *Transfers* welcome; 166 enrolled 1993–94.

Academic Environment. Degrees offered: bachelors, masters. Graduation requirements include courses in humanities, fine arts, science and math, social sciences, economics, and physical education. Faculty seen as very accessible: "one of the most positive aspects of JU." Majors offered include entrepreneurship, aviation management, finance, geography, international business, theater arts.

About 67% of entering freshman graduate eventually, according to most recent data available. *Special programs:* CLEP, independent study, honors, study abroad, undergraduate research, individualized majors, credit by examination, internships/practica in all disciplines, co-op program in art, 3–2 engineering. *Calendar:* year-round calendar (2 semesters followed by 8-week spring and summer sessions).

Undergraduate degrees conferred (365). 32% were in Business and Management, 12% were in Communications, 9% were in Social Sciences, 8% were in Education, 6% were in Life Sciences, 5% were in Visual and Performing Arts, 4% were in Physical Sciences, 4% were in Mathematics, 3% were in Health Sciences, 3% were in Psychology, 3% were in Precision Production, remainder in 9 other fields.

Graduate Career Data. Career Development Services include career interest/personality testing, interview training, computerized self-assessment, video interviewing, Career Day, Career Expos, Career Fairs with other universities.

Faculty. About 70% of faculty hold PhD or equivalent. About 33% of teaching faculty are female; 2% Black, 4% other minority.

Student Body. About 64% of students from in state; 75% South, 10% Middle Atlantic, 5% New England, 3% Midwest, 2% West, 7% foreign. An estimated 18% of students reported as Catholic, 3% Protestant, 2% Jewish, 47% unaffiliated, 30% other; 8% as Black, 5% Hispanic, 2% Asian, 4% other minority. Average age of undergraduate student: 23.

Varsity Sports. Men (Div.I): Baseball, Basketball, Crew, Cross Country, Golf, Rifle, Soccer, Tennis. Women (Div.I): Crew, Cross Country, Golf, Rifle, Tennis, Track, Volleyball.

Campus Life. Sports and other extracurricular activities reported popular. Cars permitted for all. Students expected to live in university housing. About 44% of men, 42% of women live in traditional dormitories; no coed dormitories; rest commute. Freshmen given preference in college housing if all students cannot be accommodated. There are 7 fraternities, 5 sororities on campus which about 30% of men, 23% of women join; they provide no residence facilities. About 25%-30% of students leave campus on weekends, according to most recent data available.

Annual Costs. Tuition and fees, $10,080; room and board, $4,250; estimated $1,500 other, exclusive of travel. *Meeting Costs:* university offers tuition prepayment plan.

James Madison University

Harrisonburg, Virginia 22807 (703) 568-6830

A state-supported, liberal arts, and teachers university, located in a community of 30,000, in the Shenandoah Valley, 125 miles southwest of Washington, D.C. Most convenient major airport: Dulles International (Washington, D.C.).

Founded: 1908
Affiliation: State
UG Enrollment: 4,243 M, 5,302 W (full-time); 224 M, 158 W (part-time)
Total Enrollment: 10,738
Cost: < $10K
% Receiving Financial Aid: 49%
Admission: Very Selective
Application Deadline: Jan. 15

Admission is very selective. About 47% of applicants accepted, 39% of these actually enroll; 63% of freshmen graduate in top fifth of high school class, 87% in top two-fifths. Average freshman SAT scores: 518 M, 523 W verbal, 600 M, 575 W mathematical; 59% of freshmen score above 500 on verbal, 12% above 600, 1% above 700; 87% of freshmen score above 500 on mathematical, 43% above 600, 5% above 700. *Required:* SAT, essay. Criteria considered in admissions, in order of importance: high school academic record, standardized test scores, extracurricular activities, writing sample, counselor recommendation form; other factors considered: special talents, alumni children, diverse student body. *Out-of-state* freshman applicants: university actively seeks students from out-of-state. State limits out-of-state enrollment to 40% of entering class. No special requirements for out-of-state applicants. About 43% of out-of-state students accepted, 32% of these actually enroll. States from which most out-of-state students are drawn include Maryland, Pennsylvania, New Jersey, New York, Connecticut, Delaware, Massachusetts, North Carolina. *Entrance programs:* early action, advanced placement. *Apply* by January 15. *Transfers* welcome; 467 enrolled 1993–94.

Academic Environment. Graduation requirements include The Freshman Seminar, English reading and composition, and courses in fine arts and aesthetics, history and civilization, literature, mathematics, natural sciences, oral communication, philosophy/religion, physical education/dance, social sciences, and U.S. and global culture. Degrees offered: bachelors, masters. *Majors offered* include usual arts and sciences, accounting, business administration, computer science, education, library science, Russian studies, speech pathology and audiology, human communications, international affairs, mass communications, office systems management, integrated science and technology, financial engineering.

About 58% of students entering as freshmen graduate within four years, 81% eventually; 91% of freshmen return for sophomore year. *Special programs:* CLEP, independent study, study abroad, honors, acceleration, internships/cooperative work study, combined programs in medical technology. *Calendar:* early semester, summer school.

Undergraduate degrees conferred (2256). 29% were in Business and Management, 16% were in Social Sciences, 9% were in Education, 8% were in Psychology, 8% were in Communications, 6% were in Computer and Engineering Related Technology, 4% were in Visual and Performing Arts, 4% were in Letters, 3% were in Health Sciences, remainder in 11 other fields.

Graduates Career Data. Advanced studies pursued by 20% of graduates; 16% enter graduate school; 2% enter law school; 2% enter business school. Law schools typically enrolling largest numbers of graduates include College of William and Mary, U. of Virginia; business schools include James Madison, William and Mary. Corporations typically hiring largest numbers of graduates include Arthur Andersen, Electronic Data Systems, Marriott. Career Development Services include career library, career decisions program including workshops on career assessment, values, interests, abilities and career information, on-campus interviews, job vacancy postings, biweekly job vacancy newsletter, credential files, exploration and job search assistance.

Faculty. About 81% of faculty hold PhD or equivalent. About 32% of teaching faculty are female; 3% Black, 1% Hispanic, 3% other minority.

Student Body. About 77% of students from in state; 22% Middle Atlantic, 1% foreign. An estimated 38% of students reported as Protestant, 28% Catholic, 2% Jewish, 19% unaffiliated, 13% other; 7% Black, 1% Hispanic, 3% Asian, 2% other minority.

Varsity Sports. Men (Div.I): Archery, Baseball, Basketball, Cross Country, Football (I-AA), Golf, Gymnastics, Soccer, Swimming & Diving, Tennis, Track, Wrestling. Women (Div.I): Archery, Basketball, Cross Country, Fencing, Field Hockey, Golf, Gymnastics, Lacrosse, Soccer, Swimming & Diving, Tennis, Track, Volleyball.

Campus Life. Students have role in determining policy in academic matters as well as student life through Student Government and participation in University Council. "Considerable autonomy" allowed each residence hall in developing individual life styles.

Alcoholic beverages permitted in individual dormitory rooms (legal age: 21). Cars not allowed for freshmen.

About 7% of men, 13% of women live in traditional dormitories; 36% of men, 33% of women live in coed dormitories; 52% of men, 50% of women commute. Freshmen given preference in college housing if all students cannot be accommodated. Intervisitation limited and unlimited by dorm. Sexes segregated in coed dormitories either by wing or floor. There are 17 fraternities, 12 sororities on campus which about 16% of men, 20% of women join; 5% of men, 4% of women live in fraternities and sororities.

Annual Costs. Tuition and fees, $3,798 (out-of-state, $7,650); room and board, $4,400; estimated $1,234 other, exclusive of travel. About 49% of students receive financial aid; average amount of assistance, $3,500. Assistance is typically divided 12% scholarship, 30% grant, 54% loan, 4% work. University reports 50 scholarships awarded on the basis of academic merit alone, 480 for special talents alone, 993 for need alone. *Meeting Costs:* university offers various payment plans.

Jamestown College

Jamestown, North Dakota 58401 (701) 252-3467

A church-related college, located in a city of 15,400, 90 miles west of Fargo. Most convenient major airport: Fargo.

Founded: 1883
Affiliation: Presbyterian Church (USA)
Total Enrollment: 486 M, 509 W (full-time)
Cost: < $10K
% Receiving Financial Aid: 97%
Admission: Non-selective
Application Deadline: August 1

Admission. High school graduates with minimum ACT composite of 15 or GPA of 2.5 and rank in top half of class admitted without restriction, others reviewed by committee; 87% of applicants accepted, 64% of these actually enroll; 30% of entering students graduate in top fifth of high school class, 56% in top two-fifths. Average freshman ACT scores: 21.3 M, 21.8 W composite. *Required:* ACT. Criteria considered in admission, in order of importance; high school academic record, recommendations, standardized test scores, extracurricular activities; other factors considered include special talents. *Entrance programs:* early admission, midyear admission, deferred admission. *Apply* by August 1; rolling admissions. *Transfers* welcome; 55 enrolled 1993–94.

Academic Environment. Degrees offered: bachelors. About 41–46% of general education credits for graduation are required; distribution requirements limited. *Majors offered* include accounting, actuarial science, information management science, radiology technology. About 50% of students entering as freshmen graduate eventually; 72% of freshmen return for sophomore year. Average undergraduate class size: 10% under 20, 75% 20–40, 15% over 40. *Special programs:* CLEP, independent study, internships, undergraduate research, honors.

Undergraduate degrees conferred (104). 20% were in Health Sciences, 20% were in Education, 18% were in Business and Management, 12% were in Social Sciences, 8% were in Psychology, 6% were in Life Sciences, 5% were in Mathematics, 5% were in Computer and Engineering Related Technology, 3% were in Philosophy and Religion, 3% were in Letters, remainder in Physical Sciences.

Graduate Career Data. Advanced studies pursued by 15% of graduates. Medical schools typically enrolling largest numbers of graduates include U. of North Dakota; law schools include U. of North Dakota. Fields typically hiring largest numbers of graduates include medical, computer firms, education. Career Resource Center offers classes and placement services to current students and alumni.

Faculty. About 55% of faculty hold PhD or equivalent. About 32% of teaching faculty are female.

Student Body. About 56% of students from in state; 90% Midwest, 1% each West, Northwest, 8% foreign.

Religious Orientation. Jamestown is a church-related institution; 1 course each in religion, philosophy required of all students.

Varsity Sports. Men (NAIA, Div.II): Baseball, Basketball, Cross Country, Football, Golf, Track, Wrestling. Women (NAIA, Div.II): Basketball, Cross Country, Softball, Track, Volleyball.

Campus Life. Administration reports low crime, no traffic problems, peaceful location, and variety of recreational activities as special advantages.

About 39% of men, 33% of women live in coed dormitories; rest commute. Freshmen given preference in college housing if all students cannot be accommodated. Intervisitation in men's and women's dormitory rooms limited. There are no fraternities or sororities on campus. About 25% of resident students leave campus on weekends.

Annual Costs. Tuition and fees, $7,270; room and board, $2,980, an estimated $1,000 on expenses, exclusive of travel. About 97% of students receive financial aid; average amount of assistance, $7,000. Assistance is typically divided 50% scholarship, 20% grant, 20% loan, 10% work.

Jarvis Christian College

Hawkins, Texas 75765 (214) 769-2174

A church-related, liberal arts college, affiliated with the Christian Church (Disciples of Christ), located in a community of 1,000, 100 miles southeast of Dallas; founded as a college for Negroes and still serving a predominantly black student body.

Founded: 1912
Affiliation: Disciples of Christ
Total Enrollment: 542 M, W (full-time)
Cost: < $10K
Admission: Non-selective
Application Deadline: July 25

Admission. Graduates of accredited high schools with 16 units accepted; others admitted conditionally; all applicants accepted, 65% of these actually enroll; 4% of freshmen graduate in top fifth of high school class, 10% in top two-fifths. *Required:* ACT. *Apply* by July 25. *Transfers* welcome.

Academic Environment. *Degrees:* AB, BS, BSEd. *Special programs:* independent study, undergraduate research, individualized majors, Eight College Consortium Program, Brookhaven Semester. *Calendar:* semester, summer school.

Undergraduate degrees conferred (78). 29% were in Business and Management, 22% were in Social Sciences, 14% were in Mathematics, 10% were in Life Sciences, 10% were in Education, 5% were in Letters, 4% were in Physical Sciences, 3% were in Philosophy and Religion, 3% were in Computer and Engineering Related Technology.

Student Body. About 61% of students from in state; 78% South, 14% Midwest. An estimated 78% of students reported as Protestant, 3% Catholic, 18% unaffiliated; 98% Black, 1% Hispanic, according to most recent data available.

Religious Orientation. Jarvis Christian is a church-related institution; 6 hours of religion required of all students.

Varsity Sports. Men (NAIA): Baseball, Basketball, Volleyball. Women (NAIA): Basketball, Volleyball.

Campus Life. About 76% of men, 80% of women live in traditional dormitories; no coed dormitories; rest live in off-campus housing or commute. Intervisitation in men's and women's dormitory rooms limited. There are 4 fraternities, 3 sororities on campus which about 16% of men, 14% of women join; they provide no residence facilities.

Annual Costs. Tuition and fees, $4,015; room and board, $2,999.

Jersey City State College

Jersey City, New Jersey 07305 (800) 441-5272

A state-supported, urban institution, located in a city of 250,500. Most convenient major airport: Newark International.

Founded: 1927
Affiliation: State
UG Enrollment: 1,765 M, 2,052 W (full-time); 720 M, 1,074 W (part-time)
Total Enrollment: 6,845
Cost: < $10K
% Receiving Financial Aid: 49%
Admission: Non-selective
Application Deadline: May 1

Admission. Graduates of approved high schools with 16 units (14 in college preparatory subjects) eligible; 60% of applicants accepted, 45% of these actually enroll; 21% of freshmen graduate in top fifth of high school class, 53% in top two-fifths. Average freshman SAT scores: 400 verbal, 430 mathematical. *Required:* SAT; interview optional. *Out-of-state* freshman applicants: state limits out-of-state enrollment to 7% of entering class. No special requirements for out-of-state applicants; 52% accepted, 19% enroll. *Non-academic factors* considered in admissions: special talents, diverse student body. *Apply* by May 1; rolling admissions. *Transfers* welcome; 976 enrolled 1993–94.

Academic Environment. Degrees offered: bachelors. About 80% of students entering as freshmen graduate eventually; 70% of freshman return for sophomore year. Small class size and attentive faculty seen as strengths by students. *Special programs:* CLEP, independent study, study abroad, honors, undergraduate research, 3–2 in biology/chemistry with UMDNJ. Adult programs: Continuing Education and Occupational Education Programs. *Calendar:* semester, summer school.

Undergraduate degrees conferred (626). 30% were in Business and Management, 11% were in Social Sciences, 9% were in Protective Services, 9% were in Education, 9% were in Health Sciences, 8% were in Computer and Engineering Related Technology, 5% were in Visual and Performing Arts, 4% were in Psychology, 4% were in Letters, 4% were in Communications, remainder in 4 other fields.

Graduates Career Data. Advanced studies pursued by 35% of graduates.

Student Body. About 95% of students from in state; less than 1% foreign. An estimated 18% of students reported as Black, 19% Hispanic, 8% Asian.

Varsity Sports. Men (NCAA, Div.III): Baseball, Basketball, Football, Soccer, Tennis, Volleyball. Women (NCAA, Div.III): Basketball, Cross Country, Softball, Volleyball.

Campus Life. Recent students report "friendly" and "supportive" atmosphere on campus. Both agree, however, that long lines at registration are a problem. About 2% of men, 3% of women live in coed dormitories; rest live in off-campus housing or commute. Freshmen given preference in college housing if all students cannot be accommodated. There are 4 fraternities, 2 sororities, 2 "fororities."

Annual Costs. Tuition and fees, $2,797 (out-of-state, $3,945); room and board, $5,000; estimated $1,450 other, exclusive of travel. About 49% of students receive financial aid; average amount of assistance, $5,614. Assistance is typically divided 74% scholarship, 14% loan, 12% work. College offers cooperative education paid internships in all majors.

Jewish Theological Seminary of America

New York, New York 10027

List College, the undergraduate divisions of JTS, is a private, coeducational, liberal arts college specializing in all aspects of Jewish studies. College offers BA/BS programs with Barnard and Columbia colleges, its close neighbors. Students live in modern dormitories and have access to all social, athletic, and cultural activities at the Seminary as well as at Columbia and Barnard.

Founded: 1886
Affiliation: Conservative Jewish
Total Enrollment: 435 M, W (full-time)
Cost: < $10K

Undergraduate degrees conferred (32). 88% were in Social Sciences, 13% were in Visual and Performing Arts.

John B. Stetson University

(See Stetson University)

John Brown University

Siloam Springs, Arkansas 72761 (800) 634-6969

An independent, evangelical Christian institution, located in a community of 8,000 in the Ozarks, 90 miles east of Tulsa, Oklahoma, John Brown combines a liberal arts curriculum with pre-professional training in several fields. Most convenient major airport: Fayetteville, AR.

Founded: 1919
Affiliation: Independent
Total Enrollment: 477 M, 484 W (full-time)
Cost: < $10K
% Receiving Financial Aid: 82%
Admission: Non-selective
Application Deadline: June 1

Admission. Graduates of standard high schools with 15 units who place above 25th percentile on a college aptitude test and GPA of 2.5 eligible; others may be admitted on probation; 70% of applicants accepted, 63% of these actually enroll; 46% of freshmen graduate in top fifth of high school class, 66% in top two-fifths. Average freshman scores: SAT, 510 verbal, 485 mathematical; 48% of freshmen score above 500 on verbal, 22% above 600, 5% above 700, 58% score above 500 on mathematical, 35% above 600, 8% above 700; ACT, 23 composite. *Required:* ACT or SAT;, essay, two references, acceptance of standards of conduct that prohibit use of alcohol and tobacco, strongly discourage gambling, dancing, "indiscriminate attendance at movies." Criteria considered in admission, in order of importance; high school academic record, standardized test scores, recommendations, writing sample, extracurricular activities; other factors considered include alumni children, diverse student body. About 35% of entering students from private schools. *Entrance programs:* midyear admission, advanced placement. *Apply* by June 1; rolling admissions. *Transfers* welcome; 65 enrolled 1993–94.

Academic Environment. Degrees offered: associates, bachelors. Graduation requirements include courses in Intro to Higher Education, English I and II, contemporary math, Western Civilization, biology, physical science, Wellness I and II, psychology, political thought, economics, technology, philosophy, literature, American Studies, Old Testament, New Testament, Bible Doctrines, Christian Life. *Majors offered* include construction management, corporate/community wellness management, family studies, graphic arts, engineering, broadcasting, sports medicine, teacher education, pre-med, intercultural studies. Average undergraduate class size: 70% under 20, 24% 20–40, 6% over 40.

About 53% of entering freshmen graduate eventually; 78% of students entering as freshmen return for sophomore year. *Special programs:* CLEP, honors, Mayterm trip to Israel. Adult program: advance degree completion program, night classes. *Calendar:* semester.

Undergraduate degrees conferred (160). 30% were in Business and Management, 23% were in Education, 13% were in Communications, 9% were in Psychology, 6% were in Engineering and Engineering Related Technology, 4% were in Engineering, 4% were in Theology, 3% were in Business (Administrative Support), remainder in 7 other fields.

Graduates Career Data. Advanced studies pursued by 15% of graduates; 14% enter graduate school; 1% enter medical school; 1% enter dental school; 2% enter law school; 5% enter business school. Law and business schools typically enrolling largest numbers of graduates include U. of Arkansas. About 85% of 1992–93 graduates employed. Career Development Services include resume writing workshops, interview skills development and career fairs.

Faculty. About 67% of faculty hold PhD or equivalent. About 75% of undergraduate classes taught by tenured faculty. About 15% of teaching faculty are female.

Student Body. About 25% of students from in state; 40% South, 20% Midwest, 15% West, 7% Middle Atlantic, 3% each New England, Northwest, 12% foreign. An estimated 83% of students reported as Protestant, 3% Catholic, 14% unaffiliated.

Religious Orientation. John Brown is an independent Christian institution, makes some religious demands on students; 12 semester hours in Bible and Christian education, attendance at chapel services required of all students.

Varsity Sports. Men (NAIA): Basketball, Soccer, Swimming, Tennis, Track. Women (NAIA): Basketball, Swimming, Tennis, Track, Volleyball.

Campus Life. About 73% of men, 72% of women live in traditional dormitories; rest commute. No intervisitation in men's or women's dormitory rooms. There are no fraternities or sororities on campus. About 15% of resident students leave campus on weekends.

Annual Costs. Tuition and fees, $6,520; room and board, $3,360; estimated $1,200 other, exclusive of travel. About 82% of students receive financial aid; average amount of assistance, $5,809. Assistance is typically divided 28% scholarship, 8% grant, 50% loan, 21% work. University reports 300 scholarships awarded on the basis of academic merit alone, 100 for special talents alone, 300 for need alone. *Meeting Costs:* university offers monthly payment plan.

John Carroll University

University Heights, Ohio 44118 **(216) 397-4294**

A church-related university, conducted by the Society of Jesus, the 60-acre campus is located in University Heights, a suburb of Cleveland (pop. 750,900). Most convenient major airport: Cleveland Hopkins International.

Founded: 1886
Affiliation: Roman Catholic
UG Enrollment: 1,587 M, 1,583 W (full-time); 162 M, 218 W (part-time)
Total Enrollment: 4,430
Cost: $10K–$20K
% Receiving Financial Aid: 85%
Admission: Selective
Application Deadline: June 1

Admission is selective. About 87% of applicants accepted, 39% of these actually enroll; 58% of freshmen graduate in top fifth of high school class, 86% in top two-fifths; average high school GPA, 3.2. Average freshman scores: SAT, 489 M, 518 W verbal, 573 M, 548 W mathematical; 53% of freshman score above 500 on verbal, 15% above 600, 1% above 700; 78% score above 500 on mathematical, 36% above 600, 6% above 700; ACT, 23, M, 22.5 W composite. *Required:* SAT or ACT; essay and interview recommended. Criteria considered in admission, in order of importance: quality of high school curriculum, high school academic record, standardized test scores, extracurricular activities, recommendations, writing sample (optional), interview on campus (optional); other factors considered include special talents, alumni children, diverse student body. About 1% of entering students from private schools, 50% from parochial schools. *Entrance programs:* deferred admission, advanced placement. *Apply* by June 1; rolling admissions. *Transfers* welcome; 144 enrolled 1993–94.

Academic Environment. Graduation requirements include a specific number of courses (usually with three or more credits) in each of 6 designated area: written and oral communication, humanities, social sciences, natural science and math, philosophy, and religious studies. *Undergraduate studies* offered by College of Arts and Sciences, School of Business. Degrees offered: bachelors, masters. Strong programs reported to be pre-dentistry, pre-engineering, pre-law, pre-medicine, interdisciplinary concentrations. Average undergraduate class size: 42% under 20, 55% 20–40, 3% over 40.

About 72% of students entering as freshmen graduate within five years; 88% of freshmen return for sophomore year. *Special programs:* CLEP, independent study, study abroad, honors, undergraduate research, 3–2 engineering, 3–2 nursing, cross registration with Consortium of Higher Education and 16 colleges throughout Cleveland area. Adult programs: adult attendance on part-time basis attending day or evening classes, with special pre-admission counseling, extensive academic advising and other services to meet student needs. *Calendar:* semester, summer school.

Undergraduate degrees conferred (692). 27% were in Business and Management, 15% were in Social Sciences, 14% were in Communications, 11% were in Letters, 8% were in Education, 8% were in Psychology, 5% were in Physical Sciences, 3% were in Life Sciences, remainder in 6 other fields.

Graduates Career Data. Advanced studies pursued by 27% of graduates; 20% enter graduate school; 2% of students enter medical school; 1% enter dental school; 5% enter law school; 1% enter business school. About 67% of 1992–93 graduates employed. Corporations typically hiring largest numbers of graduates include Ernst & Young, Cleveland Clinic, National City Bank, Sherwin Williams. Office of Student Career Development provides a campus interview program, job referral service, career nights, cooperative education and part-time placement.

Faculty. About 89% of faculty hold PhD or equivalent. About 55% of undergraduate classes taught by tenured faculty. About 31% of teaching faculty are female; 2% Black, 2% Hispanic, 4% other minority.

Student Body. About 65% of students from in state; 79% Midwest, 13% Middle Atlantic, 6% New England, 1% foreign. An estimated 70% of students reported as Catholic, 11% Protestant, 9% unaffiliated, 7% other; 5% as Black, 1% Hispanic, 2% Asian, 3% other minority. *Minority group students:* special financial and social provisions including Afro-American Society.

Religious Orientation. John Carroll is a Catholic, Jesuit institution, 2 courses in religious studies required of all students as part of core curriculum; attendance at religious services voluntary.

Varsity Sports. Men (Div.III): Baseball, Basketball, Cross Country, Diving, Football, Golf, Soccer, Swimming, Tennis, Track, Wrestling. Women (Div.III): Basketball, Cross Country, Diving, Soccer, Softball, Swimming, Tennis, Volleyball.

Campus Life. Current student reports "Cleveland is very accessible. There is a lot to do in the area." Cars permitted for upperclassmen and commuters; parking for commuters reported as a problem.

About 9% of men, 21% of women live in traditional residence halls; 49% of men, 40% of women live in coed dormitories; rest live in off-campus college-related housing or commute. There are 12 fraternities, 7 sororities which about 32% of men, 35% of women join; they provide no residence facilities. About 15% of resident students leave campus on weekends.

Annual Costs. Tuition and fees, $11,060; room and board, $5,450; estimated $600 other, exclusive of travel. About 85% of students receive financial aid; average amount of assistance, $9,435. Assistance is typically divided 54% scholarship/grant, 40% loan, 6% work. University reports 350 scholarships awarded on the basis of academic merit alone, 10 for volunteer service scholarships, 4 for math and science scholarships, over 500 for need and merit. *Meeting Costs:* university offers monthly payment plan.

John F. Kennedy University

Orinda, California 94563

Founded as one of the first institutions dedicated solely to adult education, JFKU offers undergraduate degrees in liberal studies and business administration. Graduate studies are offered in the graduate schools of Professional Psychology, Holistic Studies, and Management, as well as in the School of Liberal Arts. Classes meet in the late afternoon, evenings and weekends. Average age of undergraduate students is 37.

Founded: 1964 **Affiliation:** Independent

John Jay College of Criminal Justice

(See City University of New York)

John Wesley College

High Point, North Carolina 27265

A non-denominational Bible college, offering associates and bachelors degrees in a "Biblically based education." Majors offered include pastoral ministries, Christian ministries, elementary education, Christian counseling, Bible/theology, and management and ethics.

Founded: 1932 **Affiliation:** Independent

The Johns Hopkins University

Baltimore, Maryland 21218 **(410) 516-8171**

Johns Hopkins offers a broad range of undergraduate programs in arts and sciences and engineering fields, all of which are co-educational. The university was founded as a graduate institution in the European tradition and the strong emphasis on graduate education and research persists. The 140-acre Homewood campus is located in a residential area of Baltimore. Most convenient major airport: Baltimore-Washington International.

Founded: 1876
Affiliation: Independent
UG Enrollment: 2,092 M, 1,244 W (full-time)
Total Enrollment: 4,659
Cost: $10K–$20K
% Receiving Financial Aid: 55%
Admission: Most Selective
Application Deadline: January 1

Admission is among the most selective in the country. About 40% of applicants accepted, 27% of these actually enroll; 92% of freshmen graduate in top fifth of high school class, 99% in top two-fifths. Average freshman scores: SAT, 606 verbal, 686 mathematical; 95% score above 500 on verbal, 70% above 600, 15% above 700; all score above 500 on mathematical, 90% above 600, 49% above 700; ACT, 31 composite. *Required:* SAT, 3 ACH, including English Composition, academic recommendation; essay recommended. Criteria considered in admissions, in order of importance; high school academic record, standardized test scores, extracurricular activities, writing sample, recommendations; other factors considered include special talents, alumni children, diverse student body. *Entrance programs:* early decision, early admission, advanced placement, deferred admission, midyear admission. About 33% of students from private schools, 8% from parochial schools. *Apply* by January 1. *Transfers* welcome; 42 enrolled 1993–94.

Academic Environment. Recent student observes "We learn things from the people who discovered them. The large amount of research that goes on here fosters a very intellectual environment." She also notes, however, that "Many of the people discovering things are not the best teachers." Long famed for its eminence in science and engineering, the university also offers strong programs in the humanities and social sciences. The level of competition is high and, according to one recent student, "much of the academic training is in preparation for graduate school." Data on percent of students pursuing advanced degrees bears this out. Arts program offered through cooperative arrangement with Goucher College and the Maryland Institute's College of Arts. Peabody Conservatory of Music is an autonomous division of the university. University also offers a 7-year AB/MD program with Johns Hopkins Medical School, a 5-year AB/MA program with the School of Advanced International Studies and a 5-year AB/MPH program in cooperation with JHU School of Hygiene and Public Health; flexible medical program offered at JHU Medical School. Approximately 59% of the students are enrolled in science and engineering fields and 41% in the social sciences and humanities. Depending on area of study 50–60% of courses required for graduation are elective; distribution requirements specified for each major; area distribution requirements outside major field may now be taken *Pass/fail.* Degrees offered: bachelors, masters, doctoral. *Majors offered* include geography and environmental engineering, international studies, Near Eastern studies, political economy, writing seminars; area majors in natural sciences, social and behavioral sciences and humanities, music, minor in multicultural studies. Average undergraduate class size: 15% under 20, 35% 20–40, 50% over 40.

About 88% of students entering as freshmen graduate eventually; 94% of freshmen return for sophomore year. *Special programs:* honors, independent study, study abroad, undergraduate research, internships, "unstructured" January interterm, 3-year degree, individualized majors, cooperative work/study programs, cooperative arrangements with nearby institutions, cross registration with all local colleges. Adult programs: School of Continuing Studies. *Calendar:* 4–1–4, summer school.

Undergraduate degrees conferred (765). 27% were in Social Sciences, 22% were in Engineering, 16% were in Life Sciences, 7% were in Multi/Interdisciplinary Studies, 6% were in Letters, 6% were in Health Sciences, 4% were in Psychology, 3% were in Mathematics, 3% were in Physical Sciences, remainder in 7 other fields.

Graduates Career Data. Advanced studies pursued by 66% of graduates; 20% enter graduate school; 25% enter medical school; 10% enter law school; 7% enter business school. Medical schools typically enrolling largest numbers of graduates include Johns Hopkins, Harvard, Stanford. About 44% of 1992–93 graduates employed. Corporations typically hiring largest numbers of graduates include AT&T, Andersen Consulting, Westinghouse, General Electric. Career Development Services include a full range of testing, workshops, mock interviews, employer recruitment activities.

Faculty. About 99% of faculty hold PhD or equivalent. About 95% of undergraduate classes taught by tenured faculty.

Student Body. About 14% of students from in state; 51% Middle Atlantic, 16% West/Northwest, 10% New England, 11% South, 8% Midwest, 4% foreign. An estimated 30% of students reported as Protestant, 25% Catholic, 15% Jewish, 5% other; 6% Black, 2% Hispanic, 23% Asian, 4% other minority.

Varsity Sports. Men (Div. III): Baseball, Basketball, Cross Country, Football, Lacrosse (I), Soccer, Swimming, Tennis, Track, Water Polo, Wrestling. Women (Div.III): Basketball, Cross Country, Lacrosse, Soccer, Swimming, Tennis, Track, Volleyball, Water Polo.

Campus Life. Student leader reports "the people at Hopkins are really very decent; no cliques, and people are accepted for what they are; little peer pressure re: social status." Another student applauds the "many opportunities for students who are actively interested in academics and extracurricular activities. The administration encourages individuality and involvement outside the classroom for 'real-life' experiences." Freshman men and women required to live on campus unless living at home. Freshmen may not have vehicles; upperclassmen must live more than 3/4 of a mile from campus to register and park a car.

About 81% of students live in traditional dormitories; 10% of men, 10% of each live in off-campus college-related housing; 3% each commute. Freshmen are given preference in college housing if all students cannot be accommodated. Intervisitation in men's and women's dormitory rooms unlimited. Sexes segregated in coed dormitories by "section." There are 13 fraternities, 8 sororities which about 30% of men, 25% of women join; 6% of each live in fraternities or sororities.

Annual Costs. Tuition and fees, $17,900; room and board, $6,460. About 55% of students receive financial aid; average amount of assistance, $15,700. Assistance is typically divided 70% scholarship, 20% loan, 10% work. University reports 70 scholarships are awarded on the basis of academic merit alone, 12 for special talents alone. *Meeting Costs:* university offers tuition stabilization, long-term financing and monthly payment plans.

Johnson Bible College

Knoxville, Tennessee 37998 **(615) 573-4517**

A small Bible college providing training primarily for church-related professions.

Founded: 1893
Affiliation: Christian Church
Total Enrollment: 233 M, 172 W (full-time)
Cost: < $10K
% Receiving Financial Aid: 98%
Admission: Non-selective
Application Deadline: Aug. 1

Admission. High school graduates eligible; 82% of applicants accepted, 77% of these actually enroll; 23% of entering freshman graduate in top fifth of high school class, 49% in top two-fifths. Average freshman ACT scores: 21 composite. *Required:* ACT, three character references. Criteria considered in admission, in order of importance; standardized test scores, high school academic record, recommendations; other factors considered include religious affiliation and/or commitment. *Entrance programs:* midyear admission, deferred admission. *Apply* by August 1; rolling admission. *Transfers* welcome; 37 enrolled 1993–94.

Academic Environment. Degrees offered: associates, bachelors, masters. All students major in Bible and minor in church-related areas: preaching, youth ministry, missions, deaf missions, Christian education, counseling, telecommunications, microcomputer skills, nursing. About 75% of entering freshmen return for sophomore year. Average class size: 30.

Undergraduate degrees conferred (50). 80% were in Theology, 20% were in Education.

Graduate Career Data. Seminary studies pursued by 15% of graduates. Career Development provides limited placement services.

Faculty. About 50% of faculty hold PhD or equivalent. About 12% of teaching faculty are female.

Student Body. About 18% of students from in state.

An estimated 99% of students reported as Protestant, 1% unaffiliated.

Varsity Sports. Men (Div. II): Baseball, Basketball. Women (Div. II): Basketball, Volleyball.

Campus Life. About 92% of men, 95% of women live in traditional dormitories; rest commute.

Annual Costs. Tuition and fees, $3,800; room and board, $3,030; estimated $1,000 other, exclusive of travel. About 98% of students receive financial aid. *Meeting Costs:* college offers Parent PLUS Loans.

Johnson C. Smith University

Charlotte, North Carolina 28216 (704) 378-1010

Johnson C. Smith University was founded as a college for Negroes and still serves a predominantly Black student body, but accepts applicants without regard to race, creed, or color. University is located in a city of 300,000. Most convenient major airport: Charlotte-Douglass.

Founded: 1867
Affiliation: Independent
Total Enrollment: 1,239 M, W (full-time)
Cost: < $10K
% Receiving Financial Aid: 85%
Admission: Non-selective
Application Deadline: Aug. 15

Admission. Graduates of accredited high schools with 15 units eligible; 52% of applicants accepted, 31% of these actually enroll. *Required:* SAT or ACT. *Apply* by August 15; rolling admissions. *Transfers* welcome.
Academic Environment. *Degrees:* AB, BS. About 35% of students entering as freshmen graduate eventually; 70% of freshmen return for sophomore year. *Special programs:* independent study, honors, undergraduate research, 3-year degree, 3–2 in engineering. Adult programs: continuing education program. *Calendar:* semester.
Undergraduate degrees conferred (144). 37% were in Business and Management, 19% were in Communications, 13% were in Social Sciences, 8% were in Computer and Engineering Related Technology, 7% were in Education, 4% were in Psychology, 3% were in Public Affairs, 3% were in Letters, remainder in 3 other fields.
Graduates Career Data. According to most recent data available, full-time graduate or professional study pursued by 27% of students immediately after graduation. *Careers in business and industry* pursued by 70% of graduates.
Faculty. About 61% of faculty hold PhD or equivalent.
Student Body. About 30% of students from in state. An estimated 60% of students reported as Baptist; 100% Black, according to most recent data available.
Religious Orientation. Johnson C. Smith is an independent institution with ties to the Presbyterian Church (USA); 6 hours of religion and/or philosophy required of all students.
Varsity Sports. Men (CIAA): Basketball, Football, Golf, Tennis, Track. Women (CIAA): Basketball, Softball, Track, Volleyball.
Campus Life. About 72% of men, 77% of women live in traditional dormitories; no coed dormitories; rest commute. Freshmen given preference in college housing if all students cannot be accommodated. No intervisitation in men's or women's dormitory rooms. There are 4 fraternities, 4 sororities which about 20% of men, 20% of women join; they provide no residence facilities.
Annual Costs. Tuition and fees, $6,338; room and board, $2,438. About 85% of students receive financial aid. Assistance is typically divided 20% scholarship, 60% loan, 20% work. College reports some scholarships awarded on the basis of academic merit alone.

Johnson State College

Johnson, Vermont 05656 (802) 635-2356

A state-supported institution, located in a village of 1,300, in the Green Mountains, 40 miles northeast of Burlington.

Founded: 1828
Affiliation: State
Total Enrollment: 639 M, 587 W (full-time); 137 M, 259 W (part-time)
Cost: < $10K
% Receiving Financial Aid: 67%
Admission: Non-selective
Application Deadline: Rolling

Admission. High school graduates with 16 units (12 in academic subjects) eligible; 89% of applicants accepted, 48% of these actually enroll; 6% of freshmen graduate in top fifth of high school class, 31% in top two-fifths. *Required:* SAT or ACT; interview recommended. Criteria considered in admission, considered of equal importance: high school academic record, writing sample, recommendations, extracurricular activities. *Out-of-state* freshman applicants: college actively seeks students from out-of-state. State does not limit out-of-state enrollment. No special requirements for out-of-state applicants. About 90% of out-of-state students accepted, 30% actually enroll. *Apply:* rolling admissions. *Transfers* welcome.
Academic Environment. Graduation requirements include a 37 hour general education program. Degrees offered: associates, bachelors, masters. Students report the faculty, small classes, and work-study experiences as significant strengths of the academic program. About 40% of students entering as freshmen graduate eventually; 60% of freshmen return for sophomore year. *Special programs:* CLEP, independent study, study abroad, individualized majors. Adult program: External Degree Program, continuing education. *Calendar:* semester, summer school.
Undergraduate degrees conferred (234). 29% were in Multi/Interdisciplinary Studies, 19% were in Business and Management, 16% were in Education, 10% were in Psychology, 9% were in Life Sciences, 6% were in Social Sciences, 5% were in Visual and Performing Arts, 3% were in Letters, 3% were in Health Sciences, remainder in Mathematics.
Faculty. About 80% of faculty hold PhD or equivalent; all undergraduate classes taught by tenured faculty. About 34% of teaching faculty are female.
Student Body. About 87% of students from New England, 12% Middle Atlantic, 2% foreign.
Varsity Sports. Men (Div.III): Baseball, Basketball, Cross Country, Skiing (Div.I), Soccer, Tennis. Women (NAIA): Baseball, Basketball, Cross Country, Skiing (Div.I), Soccer, Softball, Tennis.
Campus Life. Students report that campus is quite isolated (with a "spectacular view"), but "there are a lot of things to do." Skiing, skating, and indoor intramurals are reported popular. About 50% of students live in coed dormitories; rest live in off-campus housing or commute. Intervisitation in men's and women's dormitory rooms unlimited; sexes segregated either by wing or floor. There are no fraternities or sororities on campus.
Annual Costs. Tuition and fees, $3,753 (out-of-state, $7,905); room and board, $4,040; estimated $1,000 other, exclusive of travel. About 67% of students receive financial aid. *Meeting Costs:* university offers PLUS Loans.

University of Judaism

Los Angeles, California 90077 (310) 476-9777

The University of Judaism is a fully accredited institution offering undergraduate liberal arts degree programs through its Lee College and graduate degree programs in business, education, and rabbinics. The university also serves the community through two policy institutes and a broad range of adult education and cultural arts programs. The university was founded in 1947 and is dedicated to the study and advancement of Jewish life.

Founded: 1947
Affiliation: Conservative Jewish
Cost: < $10K
% Receiving Financial Aid: 75%
Admission: Non-selective
Application Deadline: January 31

Admission. About 75% of applicants accepted, 47% of these actually enroll; 40% of freshmen graduate in top fifth of high school class, 60% in top two-fifths. *Required:* SAT or ACT; minimum 3.2 high school GPA, essay recommended. Criteria considered in admission, in order of importance; high school academic record, writing samples, recommendations, standardized test scores, extracurricular activities. *Entrance programs:* early decision, midyear admission, deferred admission. *Apply* by January 31; rolling admissions. *Transfers* welcome; 18 enrolled 1993–94.
Academic Environment. Graduation requirements include 67 credits in liberal arts core courses. Degrees offered: bachelors, masters. *Majors offered* include joint bioethics with Mount St. Mary's. About 92% of students entering as freshmen graduate eventually; 92% of freshmen return for sophomore year. *Special programs:* study abroad, cross registration with Mount St. Mary's, internships, 3–2 arts.

Undergraduate degrees conferred (15). 40% were in Psychology, 33% were in Area and Ethnic Studies, 20% were in Letters, 7% were in Business and Management.
Graduates Career Data. Advanced studies pursued by 85% of graduates. All 1992–93 graduates employed. Career Development Services include aptitude testing, resume/interview workshops, internships, library resources, and individual counseling.
Faculty. About 88% of faculty hold PhD or equivalent. About 34% of undergraduate classes taught by tenured faculty. About 25% of teaching faculty are female.
Student Body. About 35% of students from in state: 65% West, 10% Midwest, 6% Middle Atlantic, 5% Northwest, 4% each South, New England, 6% foreign. An estimated 95% of students are Jewish, 4% Protestant, 1% Catholic; 1% Black, 3% Hispanic, 1% Asian. Average age of undergraduate student: 23.
Campus Life. About 70% of students live in coed dormitories; rest live in off-campus housing or commute. There are no fraternities or sororities on campus.
Annual Costs. Tuition and fees, $9,710; room and board, $5,890; estimated $3,110 other, exclusive of travel. About 75% of students receive financial aid; average amount of assistance, $5,326. Assistance is typically divided 45% scholarship, 13% grant, 20% loan, 12% work. University reports 10 scholarships awarded on basis of academic merit alone, 10 for "leadership", more than 150 for need alone.

Judson College

Marion, Alabama 36756 (205) 683-6161

A church-related college for women, located in a town of 4,139, 75 miles southwest of Birmingham.

Founded: 1838
Affiliation: Southern Baptist
Total Enrollment: 263 W (full-time); 168 W (part-time)
Cost: < $10K
% Receiving Financial Aid: 94%
Admission: Non-selective
Application Deadline: Aug. 1

Admission. Graduates of accredited high schools with 15 units (12 in academic subjects) eligible; others admitted by examination; 74% of applicants accepted, 50% of these actually enroll; 41% of entering students graduate in top fifth of high school class, 51% in top two-fifths. Average freshman ACT score: 21.6 composite. *Required:* ACT or SAT. Criteria considered in admission, in order of importance; high school academic record, standardized test scores, recommendations, extracurricular activities, writing sample. *Apply* by August 1; rolling admissions. *Transfers* welcome; 5 enrolled 1993–94.
Academic Environment. Graduation requirements include freshman English, 3 hours computer science, 4 hours health and physical education, 6 hours fine arts, 2 courses in religious studies, upper-level English, history, and social science. Degrees offered: bachelors. *Majors offered* include equine science. Average undergraduate class size: 80% under 20, 20% 20–40. *Special programs:* CLEP, independent study, study abroad, honors, undergraduate research, optional May-June short term, 3-year degree, cooperative programs with nearby Marion Institute (2-year military college). About 43% of students entering as freshmen graduate eventually; 55% of freshmen return for sophomore year. *Calendar:* 2 full terms.
Undergraduate degrees conferred (46). 17% were in Social Sciences, 17% were in Business and Management, 13% were in Education, 11% were in Psychology, 11% were in Home Economics, 7% were in Mathematics, 7% were in Life Sciences, 7% were in Computer and Engineering Related Technology, 4% were in Visual and Performing Arts, remainder in 3 other fields.
Graduate Career Data. Advanced studies pursued by 34% of graduates; 4% enter medical school; 2% enter law school; 2% enter business school. Medical schools typically enrolling largest numbers of graduates include U. of South Alabama; law schools include U. of Alabama Law School; business schools include U. of Alabama. About 59% of 1992–93 graduates employed.
Faculty. About 59% of faculty hold PhD or equivalent. About 43% of teaching faculty are female.
Student Body. About 75% of students from in state; 97% South, 3% foreign. An estimated 95% of students reported as Protestant; 5% Black, 1% Asian, 2% other minority.
Religious Orientation. Judson is a church-related institution; 65% of students affiliated with the church; 6 semester hours of religion, attendance at weekly chapel services required of all students.
Varsity Sports. Women: Basketball, Equestrian, Golf, Tennis.
Campus Life. Campus life focused on school organizations; student reports "There are many leadership positions available." Sports and intramural also popular. About 85% of women live in traditional dormitories; rest commute. No intervisitation in women's dormitory rooms. There are no sororities on campus. About 75% of resident students leave campus on weekends.
Annual Costs. Tuition and fees, $5,560; room and board, $3,470; estimated $1,000 other, exclusive of travel. About 94% of students receive financial aid; average amount of assistance, $7,245. Assistance is typically divided 50% scholarship, 30% loan, 15% work.

Judson College

Elgin, Illinois 60123 (708) 695-2500

A church-related, liberal arts college located in a city of 61,000, 40 miles northwest of Chicago. Most convenient major airport: O'Hare International (Chicago).

Founded: 1913
Affiliation: American Baptist
Total Enrollment: 220 M, 291 W (full-time)
Cost: < $10K
% Receiving Financial Aid: 92%
Admission: Non-selective
Application Deadline: Aug. 1

Admission. High school graduates with 15 academic units eligible; 73% of applicants accepted, 59% of these actually enroll; 22% of freshmen graduate in top fifth of high school class, 48% in top two-fifths. Average ACT scores: 20.9 composite. *Required:* SAT or ACT; minimum high school GPA. Criteria considered in admissions, in order of importance: standardized test scores, high school academic record, writing sample, recommendations, extracurricular activities; other factors considered: special talents, alumni children, diverse student body, religious affiliation and/or commitment. *Entrance programs:* deferred admission. *Apply* by August 1; rolling admissions. *Transfers* welcome; 90 enrolled 1993–94.
Academic Environment. Degrees offered: bachelors. *Majors offered* include accounting, graphic design, international business, youth leadership. Average undergraduate class size: 40% under 20, 39% 20–40, 1% over 40. About 38% of students entering as freshmen graduate within four years; 43% eventually; 93% of freshmen return for sophomore year. *Special programs:* independent study, honors, January interterm, study abroad, cross registration with Christian College Coalition schools, internships/cooperative work study in business, biology, chemistry, art. Adult programs: accelerated degree completion program for bachelors in business, can be completed in as little as 66 months. *Calendar:* trimester.
Undergraduate degrees conferred (118). 22% were in Psychology, 21% were in Education, 12% were in Business and Management, 8% were in Visual and Performing Arts, 7% were in Computer and Engineering Related Technology, 7% were in Communications, 6% were in Philosophy and Religion, 6% were in Multi/Interdisciplinary Studies, 4% were in Letters, 3% were in Social Sciences, 3% were in Theology, remainder in 3 other fields.
Graduates Career Data. Advanced studies pursued by 20% of graduates. Fields typically hiring largest numbers of graduates include teaching, business, social services. Career Development Services include testing and alumni counseling, workshops in placement, classes in career development.
Faculty. About 54% of faculty hold PhD or equivalent. About 1% of teaching faculty are female.
Student Body. About 73% of students from in state; 91% Midwest, 1% each New England, Middle Atlantic, South, Northwest, 2% foreign. An estimated 89% of students reported as Protestant, 4% Catholic, 4% unaffiliated, 4% other; 7% Black, 5% Hispanic, 1% Asian, 2% other minority.
Religious Orientation. Judson is a church-related institution; 20% of students affiliated with the church; 7 hours of Christian Religion, attendance at 3 weekly chapel services required of all students.
Varsity Sports. Men (NAIA): Baseball, Basketball, Soccer, Tennis. Women (NAIA): Basketball, Softball, Tennis, Volleyball.
Campus Life. About 58% of students live in traditional dormitories; rest commute. Freshmen given preference in college housing if all

students cannot be accommodated. There are no fraternities or sororities on campus. About 75% of resident students leave campus on weekends.
Annual Costs. Tuition and fees, $9,284; room and board, $4,422; estimated $1,450 other, exclusive of travel. About 92% of students receive financial aid; assistance is typically divided 67% scholarships/grants, 26% loan, 7% work. College reports 157 scholarships awarded on the basis of academic merit alone, 272 for special talents alone, 270 for need alone.

Juilliard School

New York, New York 10023

An independent, professional school, Juilliard is primarily concerned with the training of gifted students as performers in the musical arts, dance, and theater.

Founded: 1905 **Affiliation:** Independent

Undergraduate degrees conferred (85). 100% were in Visual and Performing Arts.

Juniata College

Huntingdon, Pennsylvania 16652 **(814) 643-4310**

Founded by the Church of the Brethren, Juniata is today a small liberal arts institution governed by an independent board of trustees. The 100-acre campus is located in a town of 9,000 in central Pennsylvania. Most convenient major airport: Blair County, or State College.

Founded: 1876
Affiliation: Independent
Total Enrollment: 504 M, 546 W (full-time)
Cost: $10K–$20K
% Receiving Financial Aid: 80%
Admission: Selective (+)
Application Deadline: March 1

Admission is selective (+). About 80% of applicants accepted, 37% of these actually enroll; 55% of freshmen graduate in top fifth of high school class, 96% in top two-fifths. Average freshman SAT scores: 53% score above 500 on verbal, 15% above 600, 1% above 700; 82% score above 500 on mathematical, 29% above 600, 3% above 700; ACT, 26 composite. *Required:* SAT or ACT, minimum 2.8 high school GPA, essay. Criteria considered in admission, in order of importance; high school academic record, standardized test scores, writing sample, recommendations, extracurricular activities; other factors considered include special talents, alumni children, diverse student body. *Entrance programs:* early decision, early admission, midyear admission, deferred admission, advanced placement. About 25% of students entering from private and parochial schools. *Apply* by March 1. *Transfers* welcome; 30 enrolled 1993–94.
Academic Environment. Academic program requires each student to design a personal "Program of Emphasis" to meet individual goals rather than follow an established major. This flexibility is applauded by students, one of whom has pursued interests in "foreign languages, natural sciences, and music simultaneously." College's commitment to education outside the classroom, through internships and field work, is also appreciated. Graduation requirements include liberal arts core: fine arts, international studies, social science, humanities, natural sciences. Degrees offered: bachelors. *Majors offered* include peace and conflict studies, international studies, self designed majors. Average undergraduate class size: 60% under 20, 35% 20–40, 5% over 40.

About 78% of students entering as freshmen graduate eventually; 97% of freshmen return for sophomore year. *Special programs:* independent study, study abroad, undergraduate research, private tutorial, Washington Semester, United Nations Semester, Urban Semester, various special internships, private tutorial, credit by examination, 3–2 engineering, allied health. *Calendar:* semester, summer sessions.
Undergraduate degrees conferred (248). 25% were in Business and Management, 12% were in Education, 10% were in Social Sciences, 10% were in Life Sciences, 7% were in Health Sciences, 6% were in Psychology, 4% were in Physical Sciences, 4% were in Communications, 4% were in Public Affairs, 4% were in Letters, 3% were in Allied Health, 3% were in Computer and Engineering Related Technology, remainder in 6 other fields.
Graduates Career Data. Advanced studies pursued by 40% of graduates; 14% enter graduate school; 14% of these enter medical school; 6% enter dental school; 3% enter law school; 2% enter business school. Medical schools typically enrolling largest numbers of graduates include Hershey, Temple; dental schools include U. of Pittsburgh, Temple; law schools include Dickinson. About 97% of 1992–93 graduates employed. Career Development Services include computer-aided surveys, interviewing techniques, resume writing and publication, and reference portfolio for all students.
Faculty. About 92% of faculty hold PhD or equivalent. About 95% of undergraduate classes taught by tenured faculty. About 40% of teaching faculty are female.
Student Body. About 75% of students from in state; 87% Middle Atlantic, 5% each South,New England, 3% foreign. An estimated 60% of students reported as Protestant, 20% as Catholic, 2% Jewish, 5% unaffiliated; 1% each Black, Asian.
Religious Orientation. Juniata is an independent institution, with historical ties to Church of the Brethren; 8% of students affiliated with the church; diversity of religious faiths on campus.
Varsity Sports. Men (Div.III): Baseball, Basketball, Cross Country, Football, Golf, Skiing, Soccer, Swimming, Tennis, Track, Volleyball (Div.I), Wrestling. Women (Div.III): Baseball, Basketball, Cross Country, Field Hockey, Skiing, Softball, Swimming, Tennis, Track, Volleyball.
Campus Life. Campus location may, in the words of one student, "cut down on some of the cultural/social activities, but it's rural location more than makes up for it in outdoor activities." Campus described as "friendly" and "close." Rules for individual dorms range from 24-hour visitation to no visitation during weekdays—students may choose dormitory according to personal taste. Cars allowed. Alcohol permitted on campus for those of age, within certain restrictions. Use of tobacco discouraged; prohibited in class.

About 5% of women live in traditional dormitories; 98% of men, 93% of women in coed dormitories; rest live in off-campus housing or commute. Freshmen given preference in college housing if all students cannot be accommodated. Sexes segregated in coed dormitories by wing, floor or room. There are no fraternities or sororities on campus. About 30% of resident students leave campus on weekends.
Annual Costs. Tuition and fees, $14,150; room and board, $4,240; estimated $500 other, exclusive of travel. About 80% of students received financial aid; average amount of assistance, $12,000. Assistance is typically divided 40% scholarship, 50% grant, 8% loan, 2% work. College reports 140 scholarships awarded on the basis of academic merit alone. *Meeting Costs:* college offers reduced costs for local residents, institutional loan program, deferred payment plan.

Kalamazoo College

Kalamazoo, Michigan 49007 **(616) 337-7166 or (800) 253-3602**

Kalamazoo is a small, Midwestern college of liberal arts and sciences. Campus life strongly influenced by the subsidized foreign study program which involves 90% of all students and by the career development internship program which involves 85% of students. The 52-acre campus is located in a metropolitan area of 200,000, 3 hours from both Chicago and Detroit. Most convenient major airport: Kalamazoo/Battle Creek.

Founded: 1833
Affiliation: Independent (American Baptist)
Total Enrollment: 543 M, 675 W (full-time)
Cost: $10K–$20K
% Receiving Financial Aid: 85%
Admission: Very (+) Selective
Application Deadline: February 1

Admission is very (+) selective. About 90% of applicants accepted, 31% of these actually enroll; 75% of freshmen graduate in top fifth of high school class, 97% graduate in top two-fifths. Average freshman SAT scores: 85% score above 500 on verbal, 44% above 600, 5% above 700, 93% score above 500 on mathematical, 69% score above 600, 23% score above 700. *Required:* SAT or ACT, essay, teacher and counselor recommendations. Criteria considered in admission, in order of importance; high school academic record, standardized test scores, recommendations, extracurricular activities, writing sample; other factors considered include special talents, diverse student body. About 20% of entering students from private schools. *Entrance programs:* advanced placement, deferred admission. *Apply* by February 15; rolling admissions. *Transfers* welcome; 14 enrolled 1993–94.

Academic Environment. College operates on year-round quarter system; students are "on" and "off" campus at different times for regular classroom work, study abroad, and career development internships. The system is, in the words of one student, "Just another Kalamazoo challenge. The real purpose of the 'K' plan. It's not to look good on a resume. It's to apply what you learn about life and in class to the real world." Graduation requirements include 4 courses in social sciences, 3 in math/computer science/natural science, 2 each in literature, and in religion and/or philosophy, 1 course in fine arts, freshman writing seminar, proficiency in foreign language, 6 quarters non-credit physical education. All seniors take departmental examination. Degrees offered: bachelors. *Majors offered* include international and area studies, human development and social relations, 9 languages taught. Average undergraduate class size: 65% under 20, 33% 20–40, 2% over 40.

About 72% of students entering as freshmen graduate eventually; 86% of freshmen return for sophomore year. *Special programs:* independent study, internships, study abroad (centers in France, Germany, Spain, Sierra Leone, Kenya, Japan, China, Ecuador, Senegal, Swaziland), undergraduate research, individualized majors, programs of GLCA, consortium with Western Michigan, neglected languages program, 3–2 in engineering, cross registration with Western Michigan U. *Calendar:* quarter.

Undergraduate degrees conferred (255). 39% were in Social Sciences, 11% were in Visual and Performing Arts, 11% were in Letters, 10% were in Physical Sciences, 9% were in Life Sciences, 7% were in Psychology, 5% were in Mathematics, 3% were in Foreign Languages, remainder in 3 other fields.

Graduate Career Data. Advanced studies pursued by 33% of graduates; 18% enter graduate school; 6% enter medical school; 4% enter law school. Medical schools typically enrolling largest numbers of graduates include Northwestern U., U. of Michigan, John Hopkins; dental schools include U. of Detroit, Northwestern U., Harvard; law schools include U.of Notre Dame, U. of Michigan, Yale. About 60% of 1991–92 graduates employed. Fields typically hiring largest numbers of graduates include education, science research, non-profit/social services, finance/insurance. Career Development Center provides cooperative education and internship programs, counseling, job listings, job fairs and forums, on-campus interviews, workshops, resume critique service, career exploration through media resources, newsletter publication, and alumni contact in both career guidance and job placement.

Faculty. About 86% of faculty hold PhD or equivalent. About 95% of undergraduate classes taught by tenured faculty. About 33% of teaching faculty are female; 2% Black, 3% Hispanic, 3% other minority.

Student Body. About 70% of students from in state; 85% Midwest, 3% each Middle Atlantic, New England, 2% Northwest, 5% foreign. An estimated 35% of students reported as Protestant, 30% Catholic, 5% Jewish, 1% Muslim, 25% unaffiliated, 4% other minority; 2% Black, 1% Hispanic, 7% Asian, 5% other minority. *Minority group students:* financial aid provided according to need; tutoring available when necessary; Black Student Organization.

Religious Orientation. Kalamazoo, which maintains its historic connection with the American Baptist Convention, is nonsectarian in practice. Each student must complete 2 quarter courses in philosophy and/or religion as part of general education requirements.

Varsity Sports. Men (Div.III): Baseball, Basketball, Cross Country, Diving, Football, Golf, Soccer, Swimming, Tennis. Women (Div.III): Basketball, Cross Country, Diving, Golf, Soccer, Softball, Swimming, Tennis, Volleyball.

Campus Life. Current student reports "On weekdays we study. Weekends we have parties, dorm-sponsored activities. We usually have some big event every quarter." Western Michigan University is nearby, "so we interact with those students." Cars not allowed for freshmen. Smoking permitted in designated areas. College Forum sponsors a series of lectures, concerts, films, etc. High interest reported in intramural sports (most popular: basketball, volleyball, softball) and sponsored social activities. Increasing interest in varsity sports noted (most popular: tennis, swimming, basketball, soccer).

About 98% of students live in coed dormitories; rest commute. Freshmen are given preference in college housing if all students cannot be accommodated. Sexes segregated in coed dormitories by wing, floor or room. There are no fraternities or sororities on campus. About 20% of resident students leave campus on weekends.

Annual Costs. Tuition and fees, $15,135; room and board, $4,839; estimated $1,175 other, exclusive of travel. About 85% of students receive need-based financial aid; average amount of assistance, $11,200. Assistance is typically divided 40% scholarship, 20% grant, 30% loan, 10% work. College reports 250 scholarships awarded on the basis of academic merit alone, 9 for fine arts. *Meeting Costs:* college offers MI Loans, PLUS Loans.

Kansas City Art Institute

Kansas City, Missouri 64111

An independent college offering a BFA in sculpture, painting/printmaking, design, ceramics, fiber, and photography.

Founded: 1885 **Affiliation:** Independent

Undergraduate degrees conferred (111). 100% were in Visual and Performing Arts.

Kansas Newman College

Wichita, Kansas 67213 (800) 736-7585

A church-related, liberal arts college, conducted by the Congregation of the Adorers of the Blood of Christ, located in a city of 276,600. Most convenient major airport: Wichita.

Founded: 1933
Affiliation: Roman Catholic
Total Enrollment: 759 M, W (full-time)
Cost: < $10K
% Receiving Financial Aid: 70%
Admission: Non-selective
Application Deadline: Rolling

Admission. Graduates of accredited high schools eligible; 95% of applicants accepted, 45% of these actually enroll; 1% of freshmen graduate in top fifth of high school class, 6% in top two-fifths. Average freshman ACT scores, according to most recent data available: 19 M, 21 W composite. *Required:* SAT or ACT. *Entrance programs:* early admission, deferred admission, advanced placement. *Apply:* rolling admissions. *Transfers* welcome.

Academic Environment. *Degrees:* AB, BS. About 25% of students entering as freshmen graduate within four years; 60% of freshmen return for sophomore year. *Special programs:* CLEP, independent study, honors, undergraduate research, cooperative program with Friends U., cooperative program in occupational therapy with Washington U.. *Calendar:* semester, summer school.

Undergraduate degrees conferred (184). 64% were in Business and Management, 17% were in Education, 5% were in Health Sciences, 4% were in Social Sciences, 3% were in Life Sciences, remainder in 6 other fields.

Student Body. About 80% of students from in state; 82% Midwest. An estimated 50% of students reported as Catholic, 38% Protestant, 10% unaffiliated; 2% as Black, 4% Hispanic, 13% Asian, 1% Native American, according to most recent data available.

Religious Orientation. Kansas Newman is a church-related institution; makes no religious demands on students.

Varsity Sports. Men (NAIA): Baseball, Golf, Soccer. Women (NAIA): Basketball, Soccer, Volleyball.

Campus Life. About 12% of men, 11% of women live in coed dormitories; rest commute. Freshmen given preference in college housing if all students cannot be accommodated. Intervisitation in men's and women's dormitory rooms limited; sexes segregated either by wing or floor. There are no fraternities or sororities on campus. About 15% of resident students leave campus on weekends.

Annual Costs. Tuition and fees, $7,380; room and board, $3,486; estimated $1,800 other, exclusive of travel. About 70% of students receive financial aid; assistance is typically divided 25% scholarship, 50% loan, 25% work. College reports some scholarships awarded on the basis of academic merit alone.

Kansas State University

Manhattan, Kansas 66506 (913) 532-6250

A land-grant institution, Kansas State offers more than 200 undergraduate programs and options, 60 master's degree programs, and 42 doctoral programs. It is located in a city of 27,600, 120 miles west of Kansas City. University draws students from every state in the nation. Most convenient major airport: Kansas City International.

Founded: 1863	**Total Enrollment:** 20,775
Affiliation: State	**Cost:** < $10K
UG Enrollment: 8,083 M, 6,831 W (full-time); 1,127 M, 1,119 W (part-time)	**% Receiving Financial Aid:** 70%
	Admission: Selective
	Application Deadline: Rolling

Admission is selective. About 69% of applicants accepted, 69% of these actually enroll; 46% of freshmen graduate in top fifth of high school class, 75% in top two-fifths. Average freshman ACT scores: 22 composite. *Required:* ACT. Criteria considered equally in admissions: high school academic record, standardized test scores. *Out-of-state* freshman applicants: university welcomes students from out-of-state. Special requirements for out-of-state students: rank in top 50% of high school graduation class, 2.5 GPA. *Entrance programs:* midyear admission. *Apply:* rolling admissions. *Transfers* welcome; 2,176 enrolled 1993–94.

Academic Environment. *Undergraduate studies* offered by colleges of Agriculture, Architecture and Design, Arts and Sciences, Business Administration, Education, Engineering, Human Ecology; Veterinary Medicine admits juniors. Distribution requirements vary with major. All students have an academic advisor who, according to student report, "personally works with the student to choose the best courses." Administration reports 8 Rhodes Scholars since 1974, 4 Marshall Scholars in the '90's, 17 Truman Scholars, and 27 Fulbright Scholars since 1975. Degrees offered: associates, bachelors, masters, doctoral. *Majors offered* include milling science and management, horticulture therapy, hotel and restaurant management, nutrition and exercise science, electrical and computer engineering, feed science, bakery science.

About 45% of students entering as freshmen graduate eventually; 75% of freshmen return for sophomore year. *Special programs:* CLEP, independent study, study abroad, honors, undergraduate research, 3–2 in engineering, cooperative work/study program in engineering. Adult programs: adult student services. *Calendar:* semester, summer school.

Undergraduate degrees conferred (2685). 20% were in Business and Management, 14% were in Education, 11% were in Engineering, 9% were in Social Sciences, 6% were in Home Economics, 6% were in Communications, 5% were in Agricultural Sciences, 5% were in Architecture and Environmental Design, 4% were in Agribusiness and Agricultural Production, 4% were in Life Sciences, remainder in 14 other fields.

Graduates Career Data. University reports that "over 95% of K-State's pre-law students are accepted into law school, 80% of it's pre-medical students into medical school, and all of it's nursing students into nursing school." Career Development Services include aptitude testing, on-campus recruitment, individual services, internships/cooperative education, library resources, counseling, placement services and resume interview workshops. Student reports "Great advising programs for choosing careers are available."

Faculty. About 77% of faculty hold PhD or equivalent. About 22% of teaching faculty are female; 9% minority.

Student Body. About 87% of students from in state; 96% Midwest, 3% each New England, Northwest, 2% West, 1% South, 4% foreign. An estimated 50% of students reported as Protestant, 25% Catholic, 1% Jewish, 22% unaffiliated; 3% Black, 2% Hispanic, 2% Asian, 6% other minority.

Varsity Sports. Men (Big 8, Div. I): Baseball, Basketball, Crew, Cross Country, Football, Golf, Track. Women (Big 8, Div. I): Basketball, Crew, Cross Country, Golf, Tennis, Track, Volleyball.

Campus Life. Student reports "a lot of opportunities" for extracurricular activities, on- and off-campus; administration reports more than 300 student organizations are available and 78% of students participate in recreational activities.

About 20% of students live in traditional or coed dormitories; 65% live in off-campus housing or commute. Dormitories self-regulated; parking reported to be a problem for commuters. Sexes segregated in coed dormitories by wing or floor. There are 26 fraternities, 12 sororities on campus; which about 20% of men, 21% of women join.

Annual Costs. Tuition and fees, $1,980 (out-of-state, $7,390; room and board, $3,120; estimated $2,750 other, with transportation. About 70% of students receive financial aid.

University of Kansas-Lawrence

Lawrence, Kansas 66045 (913) 864-2700

A large and diverse state institution, the University of Kansas-Lawrence includes 10 schools and colleges. The 1,000-acre campus is located in a community of 60,000, 40 miles west of Kansas City, site of the schools of Nursing, Allied Health, and Medicine. Most convenient major airport: Kansas City International (50 miles).

Founded: 1866	**Total Enrollment:** 26,020
Affiliation: State	**Cost:** < $10K
UG Enrollment: 8,970 M, 8,910 W (full-time); 841 M, 832 W (part-time)	**% Receiving Financial Aid:** 33%
	Admission: Selective
	Application Deadline: Feb. 1

Admission is selective. About 65% of applicants accepted, 46% of these actually enroll; 35% of freshmen graduate in top fifth of high school class, 65% in top two-fifths. Average freshman ACT scores: 23.6 M, 23 W composite. *Required:* SAT or ACT, minimum high school GPA. Criteria considered in admissions, with equal importance: high school academic record, standardized test scores; other factors considered: special talents in fine arts and music. *Out-of-state* freshman applicants: university actively seeks students from out-of-state. State does not limit out-of-state enrollment. Required for out-of-state applicants: minimum 2.0 high school GPA (higher for some programs). About 55% of out-of-state applicants accepted, 50% of these actually enroll. States from which most out-of-state students are drawn include Missouri, Illinois, Nebraska, Oklahoma. *Entrance programs:* deferred admission, midyear admission, advanced placement. *Apply* by April 1 (February 1 for out-of-state); rolling admissions. *Transfers* welcome; 1,408 enrolled 1993–94.

Academic Environment. Graduation requirements include 3 units in English, 1 in oral communication, 2 in math, 2 in Western civilization, 1 in non-Western culture, 1 in laboratory science, proficiency in a foreign language, 3 units in humanities, 3 in natural sciences, and 3 in social sciences. *Undergraduate studies* offered to freshmen in College of Liberal Arts and Sciences, schools of Architecture and Urban Design, Engineering, Fine Arts, Physical Education; upperclassmen admitted to schools of Business, Education, Journalism, Pharmacy, Social Welfare. While students consider the faculty overall to be "really good" and "high class", there is also concern that some intro level classes are too large and are taught by graduate teaching assistants with too little experience. Degrees offered: bachelors, masters, doctoral. *Majors offered* in Liberal Arts and Sciences in addition to wide range of studies include classical archaeology, computer science, computer engineering, environmental studies, East Asian studies, geography, geophysics, Latin American studies, linguistics, microbiology, radiation biophysics, Slavic and Soviet studies, systematics and ecology, theater. Average undergraduate class size: 46% under 20, 40% 20–40, 14% over 40.

About 25% of students entering as freshmen graduate within four years, 55% eventually; 80% of freshmen return for sophomore year. *Special programs:* independent study, study abroad, honors, Washington Semester, undergraduate research, credit by examination, combined 2-degree programs, combined undergraduate/graduate enrollment in last semester of senior year. *Calendar:* semester, summer school.

Undergraduate degrees conferred (3395). 18% were in Communications, 13% were in Business and Management, 12% were in Social Sciences, 8% were in Psychology, 8% were in Engineering, 7% were in Visual and Performing Arts, 7% were in Education, 5% were in Life Sciences, 4% were in Letters, 3% were in Health Sciences, remainder in 11 other fields.

Graduates Career Data. Professional schools typically enrolling largest numbers of graduates include U. of Kansas. Career Development Services include resume preparation, assistance with job search and interview preparation, placement center offers career internships and summer employment fairs.

Faculty. About 96% of faculty hold PhD or equivalent. About 64% of undergraduate classes taught by tenured faculty. About 26% of teaching faculty are female; 2% Black, 1% Hispanic, 6% other minority.
Student Body. About 69% of students from in state; 22% Midwest, 2% South, 1% each Middle Atlantic, West, 5% foreign. An estimated 3% students reported as Black, 2% Hispanic, 3% Asian, 9% other minority. *Minority group students:* Supportive Educational Services Program provides financial, academic, and social counseling to minority group students; engineering program; Black Student Union. Average age of undergraduate student: 22.
Varsity Sports. Men (Div.I): Baseball, Basketball, Cross Country, Football, Golf, Swimming & Diving, Tennis, Track. Women (Div.I): Basketball, Cross Country, Golf, Softball, Swimming & Diving, Tennis, Track, Volleyball.
Campus Life. Student describes the campus as "Awesome, close to the city, but far enough to enjoy the peace and quiet of small town life." Another says "safe" and "homey", and adds, "KU attracts people from across the nation. I enjoy the activeness of our international student groups." Variety of housing arrangements possible including single-sex or coed units with intervisitation policies decided by each floor of the residence hall. Use of alcohol prohibited on campus or premises of student living group. Motor vehicles allowed, but limited parking facilities on campus.

About 14% of men, 18% of women live in traditional or coed dormitories; 6% of each men, women live in other on-campus housing; 60% of men, 50% of women live in off-campus housing; 10% of each commute. All students contracting for college housing must be accommodated. There are 28 fraternities, 18 sororities on campus which about 20% of men, 25% of women join; 11% of men, 16% of women live in fraternities and sororities.
Annual Costs. Tuition and fees, $1,920 (out-of-state, $6,538); room and board, $3,280; estimated $2,300 other, exclusive of travel. About 33% of students receive financial aid; average amount of assistance, $3,280. Assistance is typically divided 23% scholarship/grant, 54% loan, 23% work. University reports 3,640 scholarships awarded on the basis of academic merit alone, 322 for special talents alone, 2,474 for need alone. *Meeting Costs:* university offers Parent Loan Program.

Kansas Wesleyan University

Salina, Kansas 67401 (913) 827-5541

A church-related, liberal arts college, located in a city of 43,000, 90 miles north of Wichita.

Founded: 1885
Affiliation: United Methodist
Total Enrollment: 606 M, W (full-time)
Cost: < $10K
Admission: Non-selective
Application Deadline: Rolling

Admission. Graduates of accredited high schools with GPA of 2.5 or higher eligible; others admitted on basis of test scores; 58% of applicants accepted, 84% of these actually enroll; 50% of freshmen graduate in top fifth of high school class, 70% in top two-fifths. *Required:* ACT or SAT. *Apply:* rolling admissions. *Transfers* welcome.
Academic Environment. *Degree:* AB. About 40% of general education credits for graduation are required; distribution requirements fairly numerous. About 62% of students entering as freshmen graduate eventually; 62% of freshmen return for sophomore year. *Special programs:* CLEP, independent study, study abroad, undergraduate research, individualized majors, environmental studies, interdisciplinary major in survival studies, summer in Mexico or Austria, Washington Semester, United Nations Semester, 3–2 engineering, cooperative programs through ACCK. *Calendar:* 4–1–4.
Undergraduate degrees conferred (48). 29% were in Business and Management, 23% were in Education, 8% were in Psychology, 8% were in Computer and Engineering Related Technology, 6% were in Life Sciences, 4% were in Visual and Performing Arts, 4% were in Engineering, 4% were in Communications, remainder in 6 other fields.
Student Body. About 65% of students from in state.
Religious Orientation. Kansas Wesleyan is a church-related institution; 1 course in religion required of all students.
Varsity Sports. Men (NAIA): Baseball, Basketball, Cross Country, Football, Track. Women (NAIA): Basketball, Cross Country, Softball, Track, Volleyball.
Campus Life. About 41% of students live in traditional dormitories; rest commute. Intervisitation in men's and women's dormitory rooms limited. There is 1 fraternity, 1 sorority on campus; they provide no residence facilities.
Annual Costs. Tuition and fees, $8,020; room and board, $3,200.

Kean College of New Jersey

Union, New Jersey 07083 (201) 527-2195

A state-supported institution, located in a community of 58,500, Kean College offers programs in the liberal arts, teacher training, and applied disciplines. Most convenient major airport: Newark International.

Founded: 1855
Affiliation: State
UG Enrollment: 6,374 M, W (full-time); 4,897 (part-time)
Total Enrollment: 11,692
Cost: < $10K
% Receiving Financial Aid: 36%
Admission: Non-selective
Application Deadline: June 1

Admission. Graduates of approved high schools with 16 units who rank in top half of class eligible; 51% of applicants accepted, 42% of these actually enroll; 18% of freshmen graduate in top fifth of high school class, 52% in top two-fifths. Average freshman scores, according to most recent data available: SAT, 466 verbal, 423 mathematical. *Required:* SAT, interview in some fields including music. *Out-of-state* freshman applicants: college welcomes students from out-of-state. No special requirements for out-of-state applicants. *Apply* by June 1; rolling admissions. *Transfers* welcome.
Academic Environment. *Degrees:* AB, BS. *Majors offered* include usual arts and sciences, fine arts, social welfare, wide variety of teaching fields, management science, computer science, philosophy and religion, study of the future, medical technology and other technology areas. About 53% of students entering as freshmen graduate eventually; 77% of freshmen return for sophomore year. *Special programs:* CLEP, independent study, study abroad, honors, undergraduate research, optional Mid-Year Study Program, 3-year degree, individualized majors. Adult programs: EPIC (Entry Program Into College) facilitates reentry for mature students. *Calendar:* semester, summer school.
Undergraduate degrees conferred (1397). 35% were in Business and Management, 19% were in Education, 6% were in Social Sciences, 6% were in Visual and Performing Arts, 5% were in Computer and Engineering Related Technology, 4% were in Psychology, 4% were in Allied Health, 4% were in Public Affairs, 3% were in Communications, 3% were in Letters, 3% were in Health Sciences, remainder in 7 other fields.
Student Body. Almost all students from Middle Atlantic. An estimated 22% of students reported as Black, 19% Hispanic, 7% Asian, 14% other minority, according to most recent data available.
Campus Life. About 10% each of men, women live in coed dormitories; rest live in off-campus housing or commute. Intervisitation in men's and women's dormitory rooms unlimited; sexes segregated by room. There are 10 fraternities, 23 sororities on campus which about 2% of men, 2% of women join; they provide no residence facilities.
Annual Costs. Tuition and fees, $2,613 (out-of-state, $3,413); room and board, $3,690. About 36% of students receive financial aid; assistance is typically divided 81% grant/scholarship, 19% loan. College reports some scholarships awarded on the basis of academic merit alone.

Kearney State College

(See University of Nebraska at Kearney)

Keene State College

Keene, New Hampshire 03431 (603) 352-1909

A state-supported college, located in a city of 20,000, 85 miles northwest of Boston, Keene State is a division of the University System of New Hampshire. Most convenient major airport: Bradley International (Windsor Locks, CT).

Founded: 1909
Affiliation: State
UG Enrollment: 1,521 M, 1,959 W (full-time); 371 M, 554 W (part-time)
Total Enrollment: 4,839
Cost: < $10K
Admission: Non-selective
Application Deadline: April 1

Admission. High school graduates with C average or better in college preparatory course eligible; 78% of applicants accepted, 34% of these actually enroll; 14% of freshmen graduate in top fifth of high school class, 41% in top two-fifths. Average freshman SAT scores, according to most recent data available: 434 M, 418 W verbal, 486 M, 449 W mathematical. *Required:* SAT; interview recommended, essay. Criteria considered in admissions, in order of importance: high school academic record, class rank, standardized test scores, recommendations, writing sample; other factors considered: special talents, alumni children, diverse student body. *Out-of-state* freshman applicants: college welcomes students from out-of-state; 77% of applicants accepted, 29% enroll. States from which most out-of-state students are drawn are Connecticut, Massachusetts, New York, Vermont. About 20% of entering freshman from private schools. *Entrance programs:* midyear admission, deferred admission, advanced placement. *Apply* by April 1; rolling admissions. *Transfers* welcome; 314 enrolled 1993–94.
Academic Environment. Degrees offered: associates, bachelors, masters. Graduation requirements include English composition, literature, history, 1 course in fine arts, 2 courses in arts and humanities, 4 courses in social sciences, biology, 2 courses in science/math, 1 course in physical education. *Majors offered* include safety, sports medicine. Average undergraduate class size: 63% under 20, 32% 20–40, 5% over 40.

About 53% of students entering as freshmen graduate eventually; 72% of freshmen return for sophomore year. *Special programs:* CLEP, independent study, study abroad, honors, undergraduate research, 3-year degree, contract course-work, cooperative programs through NHCUC, 3–2 engineering. Adult programs: Adult Learner Services. *Calendar:* semester, summer school.
Undergraduate degrees conferred (502). 26% were in Education, 22% were in Business and Management, 11% were in Social Sciences, 9% were in Psychology, 7% were in Engineering and Engineering Related Technology, 5% were in Communications, 5% were in Home Economics, 4% were in Visual and Performing Arts, 4% were in Letters, remainder in 6 other fields.
Graduate Career Data. Advanced studies pursued by 33% of graduates; 24% enter graduate school; 2% enter law school; 3% enter business school. Law schools typically enrolling largest numbers of graduates include New England School of Law; business schools include New Hampshire College. About 46% of 1992–93 graduates employed. Corporations typically hiring largest numbers of graduates include J.C. Penney, Keene State College, PC Connection. Career Development Services include advising for cooperative education, career placement and career decision making, job fairs, resume writing assistance, and job listings.
Faculty. About 75% of faculty hold PhD or equivalent. About 44% of undergraduate classes taught by tenured faculty. About 42% of teaching faculty are female.
Student Body. About 62% of students from in state; 96% New England, less than 1% foreign. An estimated 48% of students reported as Catholic, 20% Protestant, 2% Jewish, 21% unaffiliated, 10% other minority.
Varsity Sports. Men (Div.II): Baseball, Basketball, Cross Country, Diving, Skiing, Soccer, Swimming, Track. Women (Div.II): Basketball, Cross Country, Diving, Skiing, Soccer, Softball, Swimming, Volleyball.
Campus Life. Student reports indicate significant Greek influence on campus social life. Parties, special events, movies/concerts, and pick-up sports all vie with trips to Boston (2 hours away) and other cities for student attention. Small size of campus considered a plus.

About 49% of men, 62% of women live in traditional and coed dormitories; rest commute. Intervisitation in men's and women's dormitory rooms limited. Sexes segregated in coed dormitories either by wing or floor. There are 6 fraternities, 6 sororities, which about 21% of men, 14% of women join.
Annual Costs. Tuition and fees, $3,120 (out-of-state, $7,960); room and board, $3,961; estimated $1,300 other, exclusive of travel. About 63% of students receive financial aid; average amount of assistance, $6,022. Assistance is typically divided 42% scholarship/grant, 50% loan, 8% work. College reports 17 scholarships awarded on basis of academic merit alone, 63 for special talents alone, 867 for need alone. *Meeting Costs:* college offers Parent PLUS Loans, ALPS Loans, TERI Loans, AMS Payment Plan.

Kendall College

Evanston, Illinois 60201 **(312) 866-1304**

For many years a co-educational 2-year college, Kendall is now accredited as a 4-year liberal arts institution. Most convenient major airports: O'Hare International, Midway.

Founded: 1934
Affiliation: Methodist
Total Enrollment: 285 M, 218 W (full-time)
Cost: < $10K
% Receiving Financial Aid: 85%
Admission: Non-selective
Application Deadline: Oct. 9

Admission. Graduates of accredited high schools with GPA of 2.5 and ACT composite score of 18 eligible; 89% of applicants accepted, 69% of these actually enroll; 15% of freshmen graduate in top fifth of high school class, 40% in top two-fifths. *Required:* ACT, essay, 2 letters of recommendation, interview. Criteria considered in admissions, in order of importance: high school academic record, class rank, standardized test scores, recommendations, writing sample, extracurricular activities; other factors considered: special talents. *Entrance programs:* early admission, midyear admission. *Apply* by October 9; rolling admissions. *Transfers* welcome.
Academic Environment. Degrees offered: associates, bachelors. Graduation requirements include courses in English, math, humanities, social science. *Majors offered* include hospitality management, communications, concepts & careers, independent scholar. Average undergraduate class size: 50% under 20, 50% 20–40. About 55% of students entering as freshmen graduate within four years; 60% of freshmen return for sophomore year. *Special programs:* independent study, January term, study abroad. *Calendar:* semester.
Undergraduate degrees conferred (26). 62% were in Business and Management, 23% were in Public Affairs, 8% were in Social Sciences, 8% were in Education.
Graduate Career Data. Career Development Services offers aid with job seeking, resume writing, interview process, and help with following up on job leads and contacts.
Faculty. About 50% of faculty hold PhD or equivalent.
Student Body. About 85% of students from in state; 75% Midwest. An estimated About 88% of students from Illinois; 96% Midwest, 2% West. An estimated 60% of students reported as Protestant, 20% Catholic, 15% Jewish, 5% unaffiliated, according to most recent data available; 23% Black, 1% Hispanic, 1% Asian, 2% other minority. Average age of undergraduate student: 22.
Campus Life. About 30% each of men, women live in dormitories; rest commute. There are no fraternities or sororities on campus. About 90% of resident students leave campus on weekends.
Annual Costs. Tuition and fees, $7,800; room and board $4,851; estimated $600 other, exclusive of travel. About 85% of students receive financial aid. Assistance is typically divided 46% scholarship/grant, 38% loan, 16% work. *Meeting Costs:* college offers payment plan.

Kendall College of Art and Design

Grand Rapids, Michigan 49503

A private, independent, co-educational school of art and design, offering baccalaureate degrees. Bachelor degrees conferred in interior, industrial, furniture design, and illustration, as well as visual communication and fine arts.
Undergraduate degrees conferred (116). 75% were in Visual and Performing Arts, 25% were in Architecture and Environmental Design.

Kennesaw State College

Marietta, Georgia 30061 **(404) 423-6300**

Primarily a commuter college offering traditional liberal arts as well as business and education programs. Kennesaw enrolls a large number of employed and older students.

Founded: 1963
Affiliation: State
UG Enrollment: 1,580 M, 2,304 W (full-time)
Total Enrollment: 8,641
Cost: < $10K
% Receiving Financial Aid: 17%
Admission: Non-selective
Application Deadline: 20 days before registration

Admission. High school graduates with 2.0 GPA or higher, SAT combined of 650, or ACT composite of 13 eligible; 63% of applicants accepted, 78% of these actually enroll. *Required:* SAT or ACT. *Out-of-state* freshman applicants: college welcomes out-of-state students. State does not limit out-of-state enrollment. *Apply* by 20 days prior to registration. *Transfers* welcome.
Academic Environment. *Degrees:* BA, BS, BBA, BSN. *Majors offered* in addition to liberal arts include business administration, computer science, education (elementary, secondary), nursing, pre-professional programs. About 60% of students entering as freshmen graduate eventually. *Special programs:* study abroad.
Undergraduate degrees conferred (848). 33% were in Business and Management, 17% were in Marketing and Distribution, 13% were in Education, 7% were in Psychology, 6% were in Communications, 4% were in Social Sciences, 4% were in Public Affairs, 4% were in Health Sciences, 4% were in Computer and Engineering Related Technology, 3% were in Life Sciences, remainder in 5 other fields.
Varsity Sports. Men (NAIA): Baseball, Basketball. Women (NAIA): Basketball, Softball.
Campus Life. All students commute. There are 2 fraternities, 2 sororities on campus which about 10% of men, 11% of women join.
Annual Costs. Tuition and fees, $1,560 (out-of-state, $2,940). About 17% of students receive financial aid; assistance is typically divided 45% scholarship, 45% loan, 10% work. College reports some scholarships awarded on the basis of academic merit alone.

Kent State University

Kent, Ohio 44242-0001 (216) 672-2444

A state-supported university, located in a town of 31,980, 33 miles south of Cleveland, Kent State maintains regional campuses at 7 localities in northeastern Ohio. Most convenient major airport: Akron/Canton.

Founded: 1910
Affiliation: State
UG Enrollment: 9,552 M, 13,148 W (full-time)
Total Enrollment: 22,700
Cost: < $10K
% Receiving Financial Aid: 70%
Admission: Non-selective
Application Deadline: March 15

Admission. Ohio residents who are graduates of accredited high schools with 12 academic credits and 800–1050 minimum SAT eligible; those with 870 SAT admitted unconditionally, those with less than C average admitted "with warning"; 86% of applicants accepted, 37% of these actually enroll; 7% of freshmen graduate in top fifth of high school class. Criteria considered in admissions, in order of importance: high school academic record, standardized test scores; other factors considered: consideration for members of unrepresented groups.

For College of Arts and Sciences (2,706 M, 3,047 W), 98% of applicants accepted, 37% of these actually enroll; 22% of freshmen graduate in top fifth of high school class, 50% in top two-fifths. Average freshman scores, according to most recent data available: SAT, 415 M, 419 W verbal, 474 M, 438 W mathematical; ACT, 19.5 M, 19.4 W composite, 18.7 M, 17.7 W mathematical

For College of Business Administration (1,522 M, 1,123 W), 73% of applicants accepted, 42% of these actually enroll; 29% of freshmen graduate in top fifth of high school class, 62% in top two-fifths. Average freshman scores, according to most recent data available: SAT, 410 M, 403 W verbal, 493 M, 463 W mathematical; ACT, 21.1 M, 20.3 W composite, 21.1 M, 19.7 W mathematical.

For College of Education (389 M, 1,524 W), 71% of applicants accepted, 41% of these actually enroll; 38% of freshmen graduate in top fifth of high school class, 82% in top two-fifths. Average freshman scores, according to most recent data available: SAT, 459 M, 426 W verbal, 529 M, 473 W mathematical; ACT, 19.8 M, 19.6 W composite, 19.2 M, 18.8 W mathematical.

For College of Fine and Professional Arts (2,262 M, 2,871 W), 91% of applicants accepted, 46% of these actually enroll; 31% of freshmen graduate in top fifth of high school class, 62% in top two-fifths. Average freshman scores, according to most recent data available: SAT, 442 M, 447 W verbal, 511 M, 464 W mathematical; ACT, 20.7 M, 20.1 W composite, 19.8 M, 18.5 W mathematical.

Required: SAT or ACT; audition or other more selective criteria for some fields. *Out-of-state* freshman applicants: university seeks students from out- of-state. State does not limit out-of-state enrollment. Requirements for out-of-state applicants: minimum high school GPA of 2.5, 900 SAT or 21 ACT composite, rank in upper half of class. States from which most out-of-state students are drawn include Pennsylvania. *Entrance programs:* early admission, deferred admission, advanced placement. *Apply* by March 15; rolling admissions. *Transfers* welcome; 815 enrolled 1993–94.
Academic Environment. Degrees offered: bachelors, masters, doctoral. Graduation requirements include 6 hours English Composition, 6 hours math/foreign language, 12 hours humanities/fine arts, 9 hours social sciences, 6 hours basic sciences. *Majors offered* include anthropology, cytotechnology, geography, government service, hospitality food service management, international relations, journalism and mass communication, law enforcement administration, nursing, social work, aerospace flight technology. Honors and Experimental College offers 4-year program of innovative experiences for selected students concurrently enrolled in undergraduate college.

About 40% of students entering as freshmen graduate eventually; 77% of freshmen return for sophomore year. *Special programs:* CLEP, independent study, study abroad, student and faculty exchange programs, honors, undergraduate research, individualized majors, credit by examination, area studies, Washington Semester. *Calendar:* quarter, summer school.
Undergraduate degrees conferred (2812). 23% were in Business and Management, 18% were in Education, 7% were in Health Sciences, 5% were in Social Sciences, 5% were in Letters, 4% were in Visual and Performing Arts, 4% were in Home Economics, 4% were in Architecture and Environmental Design, 4% were in Psychology, 4% were in Engineering, 3% were in Liberal/General Studies, 3% were in Communications, 3% were in Communications Technologies, 3% were in Protective Services, remainder in 12 other fields.
Graduate Career Data. Career Planning and Placement Center offers career library, career counseling, exploration courses and workshops addressing resume writing, interviewing and job hunting skills.
Faculty. About 77% of faculty hold PhD or equivalent.
Student Body. About 80% of students from in state. An estimated 6% of students reported as Black, less than 1% Hispanic, 1% Asian, 2% other minority. *Minority group students:* minority or disadvantaged student scholarships, reading and developmental services. Average age of undergraduate student: 23.
Varsity Sports. Men (Div.I): Baseball, Basketball, Cross Country, Football, Golf, Gymnastics, Ice Hockey, Track, Wrestling. Women (Div.I): Basketball, Cross Country, Field Hockey, Gymnastics, Softball, Track, Volleyball.
Campus Life. All nonresident, single students entering as freshmen must live in on-campus housing for first six quarters.

About 14% of men, 22% of women live in traditional dormitories; 24% of men, 34% of women live in coed dormitories; 50% of men, 34% of women live in off-campus housing or commute. Intervisitation in men's and women's dormitory rooms limited. There are 20 fraternities, 11 sororities on campus which about 9% of men, 8% of women join; 3% of men, 4% of women live in fraternities and sororities. About 60% of resident students leave campus on weekends.
Annual Costs. Tuition and fees, $3,740 (out-of-state, $7,480); room and board, $3,534; estimated $2,000 other, exclusive of travel. About 70% of students receive financial aid. Assistance is typically divided 5% scholarship, 30% grant, 49% loan, 16% work. *Meeting Costs:* university offers Ohio Tuition Bond Program, Ohio Tuition Trust.

Kentucky State University

Frankfort, Kentucky 40601 (502) 227-6813

A small state-assisted university, located in the state capital of 28,000. Founded as a college for Negroes, the university now serves a diverse student body. Most convenient major airport: Bluegrass (Lexington).

Founded: 1886
Affiliation: State
UG Enrollment: 656 M, 779 W (full-time); 341 M, 649 W (part-time)
Total Enrollment: 1,984
Cost: < $10K
% Receiving Financial Aid: 85%
Admission: Non-selective
Application Deadline: Rolling

Admission. Kentucky graduates of accredited high schools with minimum ACT composite score of 16, or SAT equivalent, or rank in top 40% of class, or GPA of 2.75 eligible; 61% of applicants accepted, 35% of these actually enroll. Average freshman ACT scores, according to most recent data available: 14.5 composite. *Required:* ACT or SAT. *Out-of-state* freshman applicants: university actively seeks students from out-of-state. Requirement for out-of-state applicants: score at 50th percentile and 2.5 GPA, or above 18 on ACT (or SAT equivalent); 46% of applicants accepted, 81% enroll. *Apply:* rolling admissions. *Transfers* welcome.

Academic Environment. *Degrees:* BA, BS, BME, BM. About 26% of students entering as freshmen graduate eventually; 59% of freshmen return for sophomore year. *Majors offered* include computer science, integrative fine arts, Great Books-based liberal studies. *Special programs:* CLEP, undergraduate research, honors, 3–2 engineering, 3–1 in medical technology, study abroad, pre-professional programs. *Calendar:* 4–1–4, summer school.

Undergraduate degrees conferred (149). 27% were in Business and Management, 11% were in Computer and Engineering Related Technology, 10% were in Public Affairs, 9% were in Education, 7% were in Letters, 7% were in Social Sciences, 7% were in Protective Services, 5% were in Psychology, 3% were in Mathematics, 3% were in Home Economics, 3% were in Life Sciences, 3% were in Engineering, remainder in 4 other fields.

Graduates Career Data. According to most recent data available, full-time graduate or professional study pursued immediately after graduation by about 25% of students; 6% enter law school. *Careers in business and industry* pursued by 70% of graduates.

Student Body. About 77% of students from in state; 85% South.

Varsity Sports. Men (Div.II): Baseball, Basketball, Cross Country, Football, Golf, Tennis, Track. Women (Div.II): Basketball, Softball, Tennis, Track, Volleyball.

Campus Life. About 35% of men, 25% of women live in traditional dormitories; rest commute. Freshmen are given preference in college housing if all students cannot be accommodated. Intervisitation in men's and women's dormitory rooms limited.

Annual Costs. Tuition and fees, $1,600 (out-of-state, $4,600); room and board, $2,682. About 85% of students receive financial aid. University reports some scholarships awarded on the basis of academic merit alone.

University of Kentucky

Lexington, Kentucky 40506 **(606) 257-2000**

Kentucky's land-grant college and state university, the University of Kentucky offers instruction through 13 undergraduate colleges, 3 professional colleges, the Graduate School, and 14 2-year community colleges. The 625-acre central campus is located in a city of 220,000, 89 miles south of Cincinnati. Most convenient major airport: Bluegrass Field (Lexington).

Founded: 1865
Affiliation: State
UG Enrollment: 6,922 M, 7,140 W (full-time)
Total Enrollment: 19,219
Cost: < $10K
% Receiving Financial Aid: 50%
Admission: Non-selective
Application Deadline: February 15

Admission. Kentucky residents who are graduates of accredited high schools eligible; 65% of applicants accepted, 28% of these actually enroll. *Required:* SAT or ACT. *Out-of-state* freshman applicants: university seeks students from out of state. State does not limit out-of-state enrollment. No special requirements for out-of-state applicants. *Non-academic factors* considered in admission: special talents, diverse student body. *Entrance programs:* advanced placement. *Apply* by February 15. *Transfers* welcome.

Academic Environment. Administration reports general education requirements for graduation "vary depending upon individual college"; distribution requirements fairly numerous: include 39–42 hours of "university studies" core curriculum. Honors program offers 4-year special academic track for superior students. *Undergraduate studies* offered to freshmen by colleges of Arts and Sciences, Agriculture, Allied Health Professions, Business and Economics, Communications, Education, Engineering, Fine Arts, Home Economics, Nursing, Social Professions; Architecture and Pharmacy both offering 5-year degree programs, require 4 and 2 years of college general work respectively. *Majors offered* in addition to wide range of liberal arts studies include anthropology, astronomy, biological sciences, computer science, diplomacy and international commerce, geography, history, linguistics, physician's assistant, political science, psychology, sociology, statistics, agricultural biotechnology.

About 75% of freshmen return for sophomore year. *Special programs:* CLEP, independent study, study abroad, honors, experiential education, individualized majors, combined programs (liberal arts with medicine, law, or dentistry). *Calendar:* semester, 4-week spring intersession, summer school.

Undergraduate degrees conferred (2635). 22% were in Business and Management, 8% were in Health Sciences, 8% were in Education, 8% were in Communications, 8% were in Social Sciences, 8% were in Engineering, 5% were in Home Economics, 5% were in Psychology, 4% were in Life Sciences, 3% were in Letters, 3% were in Allied Health, 3% were in Public Affairs, remainder in 15 other fields.

Faculty. About 98% of faculty hold PhD or equivalent.

Student Body. About 84% of students from in state.

Varsity Sports. Men (Div.I): Baseball, Basketball, Football, Golf, Rifle (coed), Swimming, Tennis, Track. Women (Div.I): Basketball, Golf, Gymnastics, Rifle (coed), Swimming, Tennis, Track, Volleyball.

Campus Life. About 25% of men, 29% of women live in traditional dormitories; 13% men, 10% women in coed dormitory; rest live in off-campus housing or commute. Intervisitation in men's and women's dormitory rooms limited. Sexes segregated in coed dormitory by floor. There are 23 fraternities, 15 sororities on campus which about 17% of men, 17% of women join; 5% of men, 5% of women live in fraternities and sororities.

Annual Costs. Tuition and fees, $2,290 (out-of-state, $6,210); room and board, $4,190. About 50% of students receive financial aid; assistance is typically divided 50% scholarship, 25% loan, 25% work. University reports some scholarships awarded on the basis of academic merit alone. *Meeting Costs:* university offers PLUS Loans.

Kentucky Wesleyan College

Owensboro, Kentucky 42301-1039 **(502) 926-3111**

A church-related college, located in a city of 60,000, 110 miles west of Louisville. Most convenient major airport: Owensboro Regional.

Founded: 1858
Affiliation: United Methodist
Total Enrollment: 313 M, 349 W (full-time); 19 M, 102 W (part-time)
Cost: < $10K
% Receiving Financial Aid: 90%
Admission: Non-selective
Application Deadline: Rolling

Admission. Graduates of accredited high schools with 12 units in academic subjects, minimum 2.25 GPA and 800 SAT or 19 ACT test scores eligible; 85% of applicants accepted, 35% of these actually enroll; 40% of freshmen graduate in top fifth of high school class, 72% in top two-fifths. Average freshman scores: SAT, 406 M, 448 W verbal, 459 M, 466 W mathematical; ACT 20.3 M, 23 W; 22.1 composite. *Required:* SAT or ACT. Criteria considered in admissions, in order of importance: high school academic record, standardized test scores, extracurricular activities, recommendations, writing sample; other factors considered: special talents, alumni children, diverse student body, religious affiliation and/or commitment. *Entrance programs:* early admission, midyear admission, deferred admission, advanced placement. *Apply:* rolling admissions. *Transfers* welcome; 74 enrolled 1993–94.

Academic Environment. Degrees offered: associates, bachelors. Graduation requirements include 8 hours science, 9 hours social science, 6 hours history, 3 hours religion, 3 hours each in multicultural studies and integrated studies, 2 hours physical education, 9 hours humanities, all students must also demonstrate proficiency in math, communication, and foreign language. *Majors offered* include criminal justice, mass communications, nursing, human resources management. Average undergraduate class size: 83% under 20, 16% 20–40, 1% over 40. About 50% of students entering as freshmen graduate eventually; 60% of freshmen return for sophomore year. *Special programs:* honors, study abroad, 3–2 engineering, Washington Semester. *Calendar:* semester, January mini semester, summer school.

Undergraduate degrees conferred (110). 24% were in Business and Management, 18% were in Education, 12% were in Protective Services, 10% were in Psychology, 8% were in Social Sciences, 6% were in Communications, 4% were in Visual and Performing Arts, 4% were in Physical Sciences, 4% were in Letters, 3% were in Computer and Engineering Related Technology, remainder in 7 other fields.

Graduates Career Data. Advanced studies pursued by 50% of graduates; 24% enter graduate school; 4% enter medical school; 3% enter law school; 8% enter business school; 1% enter veterinary school. Medical schools typically enrolling largest numbers of graduates include U. of Louisville, U. of Kentucky, Ohio State; law schools include Southern Methodist U., Salmon P. Chase, U. of Louisville; business schools include Murray State U., Vanderbilt. About 29% of 1992–93 graduates employed. Fields typically hiring largest numbers of graduates include hospitals, business administration. Career Development Services include reference library, interest inventories, resume service, career counseling and interview seminars.

Faculty. About 70% of faculty hold PhD or equivalent. About 42% of undergraduate classes taught by tenured faculty. About 44% of teaching faculty are female; 1% Black, 4% other minority.

Student Body. About 77% of students from in state; 84% South; 13% Midwest, 1% Middle Atlantic, 1% foreign. An estimated 50% of students reported as Protestant, 23% Catholic, 13% unaffiliated, 13% other; 3% Black.

Religious Orientation. Kentucky Wesleyan is a church-related institution; 17% of students affiliated with the church; 1 course in religion required of all students; attendance at chapel services voluntary.

Varsity Sports. Men (Div.II): Baseball, Basketball, Football, Golf, Soccer, Tennis. Women (Div.II): Basketball, Golf, Soccer, Softball, Tennis.

Campus Life. About 55% of men, 7% of women live in traditional dormitories and coed dormitories; rest commute. Freshmen given preference in college housing if all students cannot be accommodated. Intervisitation in men's and women's dormitory rooms limited. There are 3 fraternities, 2 sororities on campus which about 22% of men, 23% of women join. About 25% of resident students leave campus on weekends.

Annual Costs. Tuition and fees, $7,600; room and board, $3,900; estimated $1,200 other, exclusive of travel. About 90% of students receive financial aid; average amount of assistance, $8,100. Assistance is typically divided 36% scholarship, 22% grant, 32% loan, 10% work. College reports 256 scholarships awarded on the basis of academic merit alone, 141 for special talents, 35 for need.

Kenyon College

Gambier, Ohio 43022-9623 (800) 848-2468

Long a prestigious liberal arts college for men, Kenyon has been co-educational since 1969. The Kenyon Review, a distinguished literary journal is published on campus, as is The Psychological Record. The 800-acre campus is located in a village of 2,000 (including students), 5 miles from Mount Vernon (pop. 14,500) and 50 miles northeast of Columbus. Most convenient major airport: Columbus, Ohio.

Founded: 1824
Affiliation: Episcopal
Total Enrollment: 685 M, 760 W (full-time)
Cost: $10K–$20K
% Receiving Financial Aid: 50%
Admission: Highly Selective
Application Deadline: Feb. 15

Admission is highly selective. About 69% of applicants accepted, 27% of these actually enroll; 69% of freshmen graduate in top fifth of high school class, 94% in top two-fifths. Average freshman scores: SAT, 570 verbal, 593 mathematical; middle fifty percent range: 520–630 verbal, 550–640 mathematical; average ACT, 27 composite. *Required:* SAT or ACT, essay. Criteria considered in admissions, in order of importance: high school academic record, standardized test scores, recommendations, writing sample, extracurricular activities; other factors considered: special talents, alumni children, diverse student body, "interest in learning". *Entrance programs:* early decision, deferred admission, advanced placement. About 37% of students from private schools. *Apply* by February 15. *Transfers* welcome; 17 enrolled 1993–94.

Academic Environment. Student leader reports "Kenyon is clearly oriented towards academics and most students, I believe, while at Kenyon concentrate on academics and worry about jobs senior year." College has strong tradition of excellence in history and English that reportedly continues to flourish together with the 3–2 engineering program and the interdisciplinary program in humane studies. Kenyon has no required general education courses, although there are modest requirements for major and distribution—each student works out his program individually with his adviser, and students are involved in academic decision making. Students expected to be enrolled in at least 2 departments at all times and in at least 5 departments in 4 years. The student body is superior; clear stress on developing student's intellectual powers. Administration reports "strong commitment to the liberal arts" and "Great emphasis placed on close faculty/student relationships, inside and outside classroom." Vigorous honors program for more able students. Seniors take comprehensive exercise in major subject. Degrees offered: bachelors. *Majors offered* include neurosciences, environmental studies, creative writing, drama, international studies. Average undergraduate class size: 64% under 20, 32% 20–40, 4% over 40.

About 86% of students entering as freshmen graduate within four years, 87% eventually; 94% of freshmen return for sophomore year. *Special programs:* independent study, study abroad and domestic off-campus study, honors, undergraduate research, individualized majors, programs of GLCA, 5-year AB/MA in teacher education with Columbia Teachers College or Bank Street College of Education or Tufts U., 3–2 in engineering. *Calendar:* early semester.

Undergraduate degrees conferred (418). 31% were in Social Sciences, 23% were in Letters, 12% were in Psychology, 9% were in Visual and Performing Arts, 6% were in Philosophy and Religion, 4% were in Foreign Languages, 4% were in Physical Sciences, 4% were in Multi/Interdisciplinary Studies, 4% were in Life Sciences, remainder in Mathematics.

Graduates Career Data. Advanced studies pursued by 75% of graduates. Career Development Services include counseling, workshops, interviews with corporate and government recruiters, externships, and job placement services.

Faculty. About 96% of faculty hold PhD or equivalent. About 60% of undergraduate classes taught by tenured faculty. About 35% of teaching faculty are female; 3% Black, 2% Hispanic, 3% other.

Student Body. About 24% of students from in state; 42% Midwest, 25% Middle Atlantic, 12% South, 10% New England, 3% foreign. An estimated 34% of students reported as Protestant, 19% Catholic, 7% Jewish, 31% unaffiliated, 8% other; 3% as Black, 5% Asian, 3% Hispanic, 1% other minority.

Religious Orientation. Kenyon is a church-related institution, makes no religious demands on students.

Varsity Sports. Men (Div.III): Baseball, Basketball, Cross Country, Diving, Football, Golf, Lacrosse, Soccer, Swimming, Tennis, Track. Women (Div.III): Basketball, Cross Country, Diving, Field Hockey, Golf, Lacrosse, Soccer, Swimming, Tennis, Track, Volleyball.

Campus Life. Very small size of community is a significant factor in student life. In the words of one recent student "Kenyon IS located in the middle of corn fields, so students who are happy here tend to be 'doers.' If you want to go to school to be entertained, Kenyon isn't for you. If a student is willing to run for office, lead a group—or start a new one, or organize his or her own friends to have a party, Kenyon offers excellent opportunities." Immediate area offers rails-to-trails bike path and "good options in restaurants, deli, pub." Mt. Vernon, 2 miles away, offers more extensive shopping and entertainment. Kenyon itself offers many extracurricular and cultural activities. More than 100 student organizations, many with programs that foster student/faculty activities, in residences and on campus. Cars permitted, but not encouraged.

About 8% of men, 11% of women live in traditional dormitories; 92% of men, 89% of women in coed dormitories. Freshmen are given preference in college housing if all students cannot be accommodated. Sexes segregated in coed dormitories by wing, floor or room. There are 9 fraternities, 1 sorority on campus which about 25% of men, 2% of women join. About 5% of resident students leave campus on weekends.

Annual Costs. Tuition and fees, $18,730; room and board, $3,700; estimated $800 other, exclusive of travel. About 50% of students receive financial aid; average amount of assistance $10,020. College reports 135 scholarships awarded on the basis of need alone. *Meeting Costs:* college offers monthly payment plans, and School Chex.

Keuka College

Keuka Park, New York 14478 (800) 54-KEUKA

An independent college offering programs in the liberal arts, business, education, and nursing. The 173-acre campus is located in a small village near Penn Yan (pop. 5,200), 50 miles southeast of Rochester. Most convenient major airport: Rochester International.

Founded: 1890
Affiliation: Independent
Total Enrollment: 204 M, 523 W (full-time); 13 M, 108 W (part-time)
Cost: < $10K
% Receiving Financial Aid: 97%
Admission: Non-selective
Application Deadline: Rolling

Admission. High school graduates with 15 academic units eligible; 83% of applicants accepted, 45% of these actually enroll; 26% of freshmen graduate in top fifth of high school class, 51% in top two-fifths. Average freshman SAT scores: 24% score above 500 on verbal, 3% above 600; 50% score above 500 on mathematical, 10% above 600, 1% above 700. *Required:* SAT or ACT, essay. Criteria considered in admissions, in order of importance: high school academic record, standardized test scores, writing sample, recommendations, extracurricular activities. *Entrance programs:* early decision, early admission, advanced placement. *Apply:* rolling admissions. *Transfers* welcome; 91 enrolled 1993–94.

Academic Environment. All students participate in work/study projects, during Field Period in January. Degrees offered: bachelors. *Majors offered* include criminal justice, occupational therapy, nursing, food, hotel and resort management. About 54% of students entering freshmen graduate within four years; 71% of freshmen return for sophomore year. Average undergraduate class size: 51% under 20, 44% 20–40, 5% over 40. *Special programs:* CLEP, independent study, undergraduate research, study abroad, honors, individualized majors, cross registration with Rochester Area Colleges Consortium, credit by examination, Washington Semester, 3–2 engineering, internship. *Calendar:* 4–1–4.

Undergraduate degrees conferred (103). 27% were in Allied Health, 26% were in Education, 14% were in Business and Management, 10% were in Social Sciences, 10% were in Public Affairs, 4% were in Life Sciences, 3% were in Psychology, 3% were in Health Sciences, remainder in 3 other fields.

Graduates Career Data. Advanced studies pursued by 18% of graduates; 16% enter graduate school; 1% enter medical school; 1% enter business school. Fields typically hiring largest numbers of graduates include occupational therapy, nursing, business, education. Career Development Services include information on perspective employers, resume writing and interviewing seminars, listings of job openings, job fairs.

Faculty. About 86% of faculty hold PhD or equivalent. About 86% of teaching faculty are female.

Student Body. About 94% of students from in state; 3% New England, 1% South, 1% foreign. An estimated 60% of students reported as Catholic, 30% Protestant, 2% Jewish; 5% Black, 1% Hispanic, 1% Asian. Average age of undergraduate student: 23.

Varsity Sports. Men (Div.III): Basketball, Cross Country, Lacrosse, Soccer. Women (Div.III): Basketball, Cross Country, Soccer, Softball, Tennis, Volleyball.

Campus Life. Student leader reports that "there are plenty of males floating around campus both during the week and on weekends." Curfews for freshmen women. Alcohol permitted in dormitory rooms, in the Barn, and at social events. College bus available for daily trips to Penn Yan.

About 25% of women live in traditional dormitories; 94% of men, 58% women live in coed dormitories; rest commute. Freshmen are given preference in college housing if all students cannot be accommodated. Intervisitation in women's dormitory rooms limited, unlimited depending on lifestyle of dormitory. There are no fraternities or sororities on campus. About 25% of resident students leave campus on weekends.

Annual Costs. Tuition and fees, $9,310; room and board, $4,350; estimated $1,100 other, exclusive of travel. About 97% of students receive financial aid; average amount of assistance, $9,400. Assistance is typically divided 64% scholarship/grant, 26% loan, 10% work. College reports 36 scholarships awarded on the basis of academic merit alone, 684 for need alone.

King College

Bristol, Tennessee 37620 (615) 652-4861

A small, church-related, liberal arts college, King is located on a 135-acre campus in a community of 24,000 in northeastern Tennessee, in the foothills of the Appalachians. Most convenient major airport: Tri City.

Founded: 1867
Affiliation: Presbyterian Church (USA)
Total Enrollment: 233 M, 276 W (full-time)
Cost: < $10K
% Receiving Financial Aid: 90%
Admission: Selective
Application Deadline: Rolling

Admission is selective. About 85% of applicants accepted, 47% of these actually enroll; 57% of freshmen graduate in top fifth of high school class, 83% in top two-fifths. Average freshman scores: SAT, 476 M, 469 W verbal, 538 M, 503 W mathematical; ACT, 24.1 M, 23.3 W composite. *Required:* SAT or ACT; 2.4 minimum high school GPA, essay recommended. Criteria considered in admission, in order of importance: high school academic record, standardized test scores, writing sample, extracurricular activities; other factors considered: special talents, diverse student body. About 22% of entering students from private and parochial schools. Entrance program: midyear admission. *Apply:* rolling admissions. *Transfers* welcome; 42 enrolled 1993–94.

Academic Environment. To graduate, students are expected to complete a minimum core of 65 semester hours in specified subjects such as English, mathematics, history, Bible and religion, foreign language, natural science, social science, humanities. In addition, all students take a comprehensive exam in their major area of concentration. Degrees offered: bachelors. New majors offered include Spanish. Average undergraduate class size: 79% under 20, 20% 20–40, 1% over 40.

About 85% of students entering as freshmen graduate within four years, 93% eventually; 85% of freshmen return for sophomore year. *Special programs:* CLEP, independent study, study abroad, honors, undergraduate research, internships, cooperative education, cooperative programs with Virginia Intermont, 3–2 engineering and medical technology, cross registration with Virginia Intermont College. *Calendar:* 4–4–1.

Undergraduate degrees conferred (110). 42% were in Social Sciences, 11% were in Letters, 10% were in Psychology, 10% were in Education, 6% were in Life Sciences, 5% were in Philosophy and Religion, 4% were in Visual and Performing Arts, 4% were in Physical Sciences, 4% were in Mathematics, 3% were in Foreign Languages, remainder in Liberal/General Studies.

Graduates Career Data. Advanced studies pursued by 7% of graduates; 3% enter graduate school; 2% enter medical school; 1% enter law school; 1% enter business school. Medical schools typically enrolling largest numbers of graduates include Vanderbilt, U. of Tennessee, U. of Virginia; law schools include U. of Virginia, U. of Tennessee; business schools include U. of Virginia, U. of Tennessee. About 50% of 1992–93 graduates employed. Career Development Services assist students in making transition to work world by providing career resources, resume writing and interviewing skill resources.

Faculty. About 65% of faculty hold PhD or equivalent. About 29% of teaching faculty are female; 1% Hispanic.

Student Body. About 38% of students from in state; 52% South, 39% Middle Atlantic, 1% New England, 6% foreign. An estimated 97% of students reported as Protestant, 2% Catholic, 1% other.

Religious Orientation. King is a church-related institution; 21% of students affiliated with the church; 6 courses in religious study

required; attendance at weekly chapel and convocation, required of all students; other religious services voluntary.
Varsity Sports. Men (NAIA): Baseball, Basketball, Golf, Soccer, Tennis. Women (NAIA): Basketball, Softball, Tennis, Volleyball.
Campus Life. Administration reports rules governing campus life "reflect college mission and encourage responsible freedom." Drinking and smoking prohibited on campus. Students may live in college residences or off-campus. Intervisitation limited.

About 75% of students live in traditional dormitories; no coed dormitories; rest commute. Freshmen are given preference in college housing if all students cannot be accommodated. Intervisitation in men's and women's dormitory rooms limited to 33 hours per week. There are no fraternities or sororities on campus. About 40% of students leave campus on weekends.
Annual Costs. Tuition and fees, $8,250; room and board, $3,250; estimated $500 other, exclusive of travel. About 90% of students receive financial aid; average amount of assistance, $7,032. Assistance is typically divided 26% scholarship, 32% grant, 36% loan, 6% work. College reports 230 scholarships awarded on the basis of academic merit alone, 91 for special talents alone, 287 for need alone. *Meeting Costs:* 10-month payment plan.

King's College

Briarcliff Manor, New York 10510 (914) 944-5650

An independent, liberal arts college, with an "evangelical philosophy of education," located in a Westchester suburb, 30 miles north of Manhattan. Most convenient major airports: Kennedy, LaGuardia, or Newark.

Founded: 1938	**Cost:** < $10K
Affiliation: Independent	**% Receiving Financial Aid:** 90%
UG Enrollment: 80 M, 141 W (full-time)	**Admission:** Non-selective
Total Enrollment: 246	**Application Deadline:** August 1

Admission. High school graduates with minimum GPA of "B" eligible; 65% of applicants accepted, 31% of these actually enroll; 8% of freshmen graduate in top fifth of high school class, 24% in top two-fifths. Average freshman scores: SAT, 431 M, 444 W verbal, 506 M, 443 W mathematical. *Required:* SAT or ACT. College requires abstinence from alcohol, tobacco, gambling, playing cards, social dancing, attendance at motion pictures and theater. Criteria considered in admissions, in order of importance: high school academic record, standardized test scores, extracurricular activities, recommendations, writing sample; other factors considered: special talents, alumni children, religious affiliation and/or commitment. About 60% of entering students from private schools. *Entrance programs:* early admission, mid-year admission, deferred admission. *Apply* by August 1; rolling admissions. *Transfers* welcome; 17 enrolled 1993–94.
Academic Environment. Graduation requirements include courses in English, Bible, ethics, physical education, culture, science, history. Degrees offered: associates, bachelors. *Majors offered* include: accounting, nursing with Pace University. About 45% of students entering as freshmen graduate within four years; 70% of freshmen return for sophomore year. *Special programs:* CLEP, independent study, study abroad, cross registration with Pace U. *Calendar:* semester, summer school.
Undergraduate degrees conferred (106). 39% were in Education, 16% were in Business and Management, 13% were in Social Sciences, 13% were in Letters, 6% were in Life Sciences, 4% were in Psychology, 4% were in Mathematics, remainder in 4 other fields.
Faculty. About 46% of faculty hold PhD or equivalent. About 80% of undergraduate classes taught by tenured faculty. About 78% of teaching faculty are female; 1% Black.
Student Body. About 45% of students from in state; 49% from New England. An estimated 95% of students reported as Protestant, 1% Catholic, 2% unaffiliated; 6% Black, 5% Hispanic, 3% Asian, according to most recent data available.
Religious Orientation. King's is a non-denominational Christian institution in the evangelical Protestant tradition; 4 courses in religious studies and attendance at daily chapel required of all students.
Varsity Sports. Men (NAIA): Basketball, Cross Country, Soccer; Women (NAIA): Basketball, Cross Country, Soccer, Softball.
Campus Life. About 97% of men, 97% of women live in traditional dormitories; no coed dormitories; rest commute. No intervisitation in men's or women's dormitory rooms. There are no fraternities or sororities on campus. About 50% of resident students leave campus on weekends.
Annual Costs. Tuition and fees, $8,440; room and board, $3,920; estimated $1,000 other, exclusive of travel. About 90% of students receive financial aid; average amount of assistance, $9,115. Assistance is typically divided 51% scholarship, 29% loan, 20% work. College reports some scholarships awarded on the basis of academic merit alone. *Meeting Costs:* college offers Parent Loans, payment plans.

King's College

Wilkes-Barre, Pennsylvania 18711 (717) 826-5900

A church-related, liberal arts college, conducted by the Holy Cross fathers, located in a city of 58,900, 120 miles north of Philadelphia. Most convenient major airport: Wilkes Barre/Scranton.

Founded: 1946	**Cost:** $10K–$20K
Affiliation: Roman Catholic	**% Receiving Financial Aid:** 82%
Total Enrollment: 916 M, 855 W (full-time); 184 M, 316 W (part-time)	**Admission:** Non-selective
	Application Deadline: August 15

Admission. High school graduates with 15 units academic subjects and 2.5 GPA (3.0 for science majors) eligible; 72% of applicants accepted, 36% of these actually enroll; 40% of freshmen graduate in top fifth of high school class, 73% in top two-fifths. Average freshman scores: SAT, 466 verbal, 512 mathematical. *Required:* SAT or ACT. Criteria considered in admissions, in order of importance: high school academic record, standardized test scores, recommendations, writing sample, extracurricular activities; other factors considered: alumni children, diverse student body, religious affiliation and/or commitment. About 37% of freshmen from parochial and private schools. *Entrance programs:* early decision, early admission, midyear admission, deferred admission, advanced placement. *Apply* by August 15; rolling admissions. *Transfers* welcome; 135 enrolled 1993–94.
Academic Environment. Graduation requirements include 51 credits in critical thinking, effective writing, effective oral communication, library and information literacy, computer competence, creative thinking and problem solving, quantitative reasoning, and moral reasoning. Degrees offered: associates, bachelors, masters. *Majors offered* include elementary education. Average undergraduate class size: 51% under 20, 49% between 20–40, less than 1% over 40.

About 66% of students entering as freshmen graduate within four years, 70% eventually; 85% of freshmen return for sophomore year. *Special programs:* study abroad, independent study, honors, individualized majors, co-operative education, internships, career planning programs, 3–2 engineering, cross registration with College Misericordia, Wilkes U. *Calendar:* semester, summer school.
Undergraduate degrees conferred (459). 37% were in Business and Management, 9% were in Communications, 8% were in Social Sciences, 7% were in Psychology, 6% were in Protective Services, 5% were in Letters, 5% were in Education, 5% were in Marketing and Distribution, 4% were in Computer and Engineering Related Technology, 3% were in Allied Health, 3% were in Life Sciences, remainder in 6 other fields.
Graduates Career Data. Advanced studies pursued by 13% of graduates; 8% enter graduate school; 2% medical school; 2% business school; 1% law school. Medical schools typically enrolling largest numbers of graduates include Thomas Jefferson; law schools include Seton Hall; business schools include King's, SUNY. About 82% of 1992–93 graduates employed. Fields typically hiring largest numbers of graduates include Big 6 accounting, financial services, computer-related, health care. Career Development Services include on-campus recruitment, career counseling, resume development, career resource center, career classes, computerized career guidance programs, graduate and professional school exploration.
Faculty. About 68% of faculty hold PhD or equivalent. About 23% of teaching faculty are female; 3% minority.

Student Body. About 72% of students from in state; 96% Middle Atlantic, 2% New England, less than 1% foreign. An estimated 75% of students reported as Catholic, 15% Protestant, 10% other; 2% Black, 1% Asian, 2% other minority.

Religious Orientation. King's is a Roman Catholic institution; 2 courses in theology required of all students.

Varsity Sports. Men (Div.III): Baseball, Basketball, Cross Country, Football, Golf, Soccer, Swimming, Tennis, Wrestling. Women (Div.III): Basketball, Cross Country, Hockey (field), Soccer, Softball, Swimming, Tennis, Volleyball. Coed (Div. III): Cross Country, Rifle, Swimming.

Campus Life. Campus is located within walking distance of the center of Wilkes-Barre and close to restaurants, shopping, entertainment, including the Kirby Center for the Performing Arts, and the Lackawanna Baseball Stadium.

About 41% of men, 37% of women live in traditional dormitories; 23% of men, 21% of women live off-campus; 36% of men, 42% of women commute. Freshmen are given preference in college housing if all students cannot be accommodated. Intervisitation in men's and women's dormitory rooms allowed during specified hours. There are no fraternities or sororities on campus. About 30% of resident students leave campus on weekends.

Annual Costs. Tuition and fees, $10,600; room and board, $4,820; estimated $2,300 other, exclusive of travel. About 82% of students receive financial aid; average amount of assistance $8,440. Assistance is typically divided 16% scholarship, 41% grant, 9% loan, 4% work. College reports 470 scholarships awarded on the basis of academic merit and need alone.

Kirkland College

(See Hamilton College)

Knox College

Galesburg, Illinois 61401 (309) 343-0112

A small, venerable, midwestern liberal arts college, Knox sends substantial numbers of its graduates on to professional schools as well as to careers in business. The 70-acre campus is located in the center of a city of 32,500, 180 miles southwest of Chicago. Most convenient major airports: Moline or Peoria.

Founded: 1837
Affiliation: Independent
Total Enrollment: 461 M, 506 W (full-time)
Cost: $10K–$20K
% Receiving Financial Aid: 88%
Admission: Very Selective
Application Deadline: Feb. 15

Admission is very selective. About 81% of applicants accepted, 34% of these actually enroll; 69% of freshmen graduate in top fifth of high school class, 92% in top two-fifths. Average freshman scores, middle 50% range: SAT, 470–600 verbal, 570–650 mathematical; 69% of freshmen score above 500 on verbal, 26% above 600, 4% above 700; 77% of freshmen score above 500 on mathematical, 49% above 600, 12% above 700; ACT, 23–28 composite. *Required:* SAT or ACT, essay, recommendations; interview encouraged. Criteria considered in admissions, in order of importance: high school academic record, writing sample, recommendations, extracurricular activities, standardized test scores; other factors considered: special talents, alumni children, diverse student body. *Entrance programs:* early admission, midyear admission, deferred admission, advanced placement. *Apply* by February 15. *Transfers* welcome; 31 enrolled 1993–94.

Academic Environment. Student leader reports almost all students "are concerned primarily with academics, but this interest reflects their post-graduate goals." Independent study available to all students and honors program available to superior students. Classes mostly small; senior professors teach substantial number of beginning courses. Students are full voting members on joint student/faculty committees. Graduation requirements include 2 courses each in humanities, social sciences, science/mathematics, 1 freshman preceptorial, 1 advanced preceptorial, proficiency in mathematics and foreign language. Degrees offered: bachelors. *Majors offered* include usual arts and sciences, biochemistry, anthropology, creative writing, education, international relations, American studies, German area studies, Russian area studies, Japanese, theater, independent majors, interdisciplinary majors.

About 75% of students entering as freshmen graduate eventually; 86% of freshmen return for sophomore year. Average undergraduate class size: 95% under 20. *Special programs:* January miniterm, CLEP, independent study, study abroad, honors, undergraduate research, programs of ACM, group interest courses, Washington Semester, 3–2 engineering, 3–2 forestry, 3–2 nursing, 3–2 business administration, 3–2 law, 2–2 medical education. *Calendar:* 3–3.

Undergraduate degrees conferred (222). 39% were in Social Sciences, 10% were in Psychology, 9% were in Life Sciences, 9% were in Letters, 8% were in Physical Sciences, 6% were in Computer and Engineering Related Technology, 5% were in Education, 4% were in Foreign Languages, 3% were in Visual and Performing Arts, 3% were in Philosophy and Religion, remainder in 2 other fields.

Graduates Career Data. Advanced studies pursued by 65% of graduates (eventually); more immediately: 16% enter graduate school; 5% enter medical school; 3% enter law school; 3% enter business school. Medical schools typically enrolling largest numbers of graduates include U. of Illinois, Rush, Northwestern; law schools include U. of Illinois; business schools include U. of Chicago, Washington U., U. of Iowa. About 50% of 1992–93 graduates employed. Employers typically hiring largest numbers of graduates include Arthur Andersen. Career Development Services include student assessment for career guidance and job placement, on-campus interviews, interview guidance and preparation, alumni assistance.

Faculty. About 90% of faculty hold PhD or equivalent. About 65% of undergraduate classes taught by tenured faculty. About 32% of teaching faculty are female; 2% Black, 6% Hispanic, 3% other minority.

Student Body. About 52% of students from in state; 83% Midwest, 3% each South, West, 1% each New England, Middle Atlantic, Northwest, 8% foreign. An estimated 28% of students reported as Protestant, 17% Catholic, 1% Jewish, 2% Muslim, 50% unaffiliated, 3% other; 6% Black, 5% Asian, 2% Hispanic, 8% other. *Minority group students:* financial aid available; Educational Development Program "designed for students whose cultural and academic backgrounds differ somewhat from those of most Knox students."

Varsity Sports. Men (Div.III): Baseball, Basketball, Cross Country, Football, Golf, Soccer, Swimming, Tennis, Track, Wrestling. Women (Div.III): Basketball, Cross Country, Golf, Soccer, Softball, Swimming, Tennis, Track, Volleyball.

Campus Life. Students appear to have significant role in decisions concerning campus life. Daily intervisitation available; student leader asserts "intervisitation is not an issue." Intervisitation in men's and women's dormitory rooms limited from noon to midnight weekdays; noon to 1:30 am weekends. Use of alcoholic beverages, including beer, restricted; larger parties must be registered with Dean's office. Cars permitted, parking reported as inadequate. Dominant tone of campus set by large numbers of students from Midwest, some from small towns. Fraternities and sororities have maintained influence on social life. Relative isolation of the campus makes students largely dependent on Knox for cultural and intellectual opportunities; college provides full schedule of events. Student leader says average student is involved in 5 extracurricular activities as a part of their education.

About 13% of men, 30% of women live in traditional dormitories; 45% of men, 66% of women live in coed dormitories; 4% of men, 4% of women live in off-campus college-related housing or commute. Sexes segregated in coed dormitories either by floor or room. There are 5 fraternities, 2 sororities on campus which about 30% of men, 15% of women join; 20% of men live in fraternities; sororities provide no residence facilities. About 10% of resident students leave campus on weekends.

Annual Costs. Tuition and fees, $15,132; room and board, $3,858; estimated $950 other, exclusive of travel. About 88% of students receive financial aid; average amount of assistance, $14,735. Assistance is typically divided 68% scholarship and grant, 22% loan, 10% work. College reports 140 scholarships awarded on the basis of academic merit alone, 30 for special talents alone. *Meeting Costs:* college offers Campus Parent-Loan Program, installment payment plan.

Knoxville College

Knoxville, Tennessee 37921 (615) 524-6500

A church-related college, Knoxville was one of the first Negro colleges admitted to membership in the Southern Association of Colleges and Secondary Schools. Faculty is multiracial; mixed student body is predominantly Black. College is located in a city of 174,600.

Founded: 1875
Affiliation: Presbyterian Church (USA)
Total Enrollment: 1,207 M, W (full-time)
Cost: < $10K
Admission: Non-selective
Application Deadline: March 31

Admission. Graduates of accredited high schools with 15 academic units with C+ average eligible. *Required:* SAT or ACT. *Apply* by March 31. *Transfers* welcome.
Academic Environment. *Degrees:* AB, BS, BSCom, BSEd, BSMEd. About 38% of general education requirements for graduation are elective; distribution requirements fairly numerous. About 40% of students entering as freshmen graduate eventually; 85% of freshmen return for sophomore year. Special Programs: cooperative programs and 3–2 engineering. *Calendar:* 3 10-week terms, 4-week interim.
Undergraduate degrees conferred (30). 37% were in Business and Management, 17% were in Social Sciences, 10% were in Communications Technologies, 7% were in Visual and Performing Arts, 7% were in Psychology, 7% were in Life Sciences, 7% were in Education, 3% were in Parks and Recreation, 3% were in Mathematics, 3% were in Computer and Engineering Related Technology.
Student Body. About 87% of students from in state; 11% Midwest, according to most recent data available.
Campus Life. About 85% of men, 90% of women live in traditional dormitories; rest live in off-campus housing or commute. Intervisitation in men's and women's dormitory rooms limited. Sexes segregated in coed dormitories by wing. There are 4 fraternities, 4 sororities on campus which about 45% men, 40% women join; they provide no residence facilities.
Annual Costs. Tuition and fees, $5,470; room and board, $2,850; estimated $150 other, exclusive of travel.

Kutztown University

Kutztown, Pennsylvania 19530 (215) 683-4060

A state-supported university, Kutztown State offers undergraduate programs in arts and sciences, business, education, and visual and performing arts. Campus is located on 325 acres in a town of 6,000, midway between Reading and Allentown, 90 miles north of Philadelphia. Most convenient major airport: Allentown-Bethlehem-Easton.

Founded: 1866
Affiliation: State
UG Enrollment: 2,594 M, 3,367 W (full-time); 275 M, 621 W (part-time)
Total Enrollment: 7,764
Cost: < $10K
% Receiving Financial Aid: 75%
Admission: Non-selective
Application Deadline: Aug. 15

Admission. About 60% of applicants accepted, 40% of these actually enroll; 22% of freshmen graduate in top fifth of high school class, 58% in top two-fifths. Average freshman SAT scores: 450 verbal, 480 mathematical. *Required:* SAT or ACT, minimum 2.0 high school GPA. Criteria considered in admissions, in order of importance: advanced placement or honors courses, special talents, leadership record, recommendations, extracurricular activities, personality and "intangible qualities", alumni children, diverse student body. *Out-of-state* freshman applicants: university actively seeks students from out-of-state. State does not limit out-of-state enrollment. About 78% of out-of-state applicants accepted, 34% of these actually enroll. *Entrance programs:* early admissions, deferred admissions. *Apply* by August 15; rolling admissions. *Transfers* welcome; 573 enrolled 1993–94.
Academic Environment. Graduation requirements: general education requirements vary by program, but all students must take speech, English composition, physical education or introduction to dance; distribution requirements include courses in humanities, social sciences, natural sciences, and mathematics; students in Liberal Arts and Sciences must take a comprehensive exam. Degrees offered: bachelors, masters. *Majors offered* include communication design, library science, medical laboratory technologies, nursing, international business and finance.

About 25% of students entering as freshmen graduate within four years, 50% within five years; 77% of freshmen return for sophomore year. *Special programs:* independent study, honors, study abroad, undergraduate research, midyear term, credit by examination, 3–2 engineering, internships including Harrisburg Internship Program, Washington semester, internships, International Business, school nursing certification. *Calendar:* semester, summer school.
Undergraduate degrees conferred (1071). 30% were in Education, 21% were in Business and Management, 11% were in Visual and Performing Arts, 8% were in Communications, 6% were in Letters, 4% were in Social Sciences, 4% were in Psychology, 3% were in Protective Services, remainder in 12 other fields.
Faculty. About 50% of faculty hold PhD or equivalent. About 73% of undergraduate classes taught by tenured faculty. About 33% of teaching faculty are female.
Student Body. About 86% of students from in state; 96% Northeast. An estimated 3% of students reported as Black, 2% Hispanic, 1% Asian, 1% Native American. *Minority group students:* special grants; "strong tutoring and counseling program."
Varsity Sports. Men (Div.II): Baseball, Basketball, Cross Country, Football, Golf, Lacrosse (Div.III), Soccer, Swimming, Tennis, Track, Wrestling (Div.I). Women (Div.II): Basketball, Cross Country, Field Hockey (Div. III), Lacrosse, Soccer, Softball, Swimming, Tennis, Track, Volleyball.
Campus Life. Alcohol prohibited. No cars allowed for most resident freshmen and sophomores, or some students receiving student aid.

About 50% of undergraduates live on campus; rest live in off-campus housing or commute. Sexes segregated in coed residence halls either by wing or floor. There are 8 fraternities, 6 sororities on campus which 4% each of men, 4% of women join; they provide no residence facilities. About 40% of resident students leave campus on weekends.
Annual Costs. Tuition and fees, $3,558 (out-of-state, $8,286); room and board, $2,970; estimated $1,000 other, exclusive of travel. About 75% of freshmen receive financial aid, 80% of continuing students; average amount of assistance; $4,000. Assistance is typically divided 26% scholarship, 56% loan, 13% work, according to most recent data available. College reports 50% scholarships awarded on the basis of academic merit alone. *Meeting Costs:* university offers parents' loans, tuition plans.

Laboratory Institute of Merchandising

New York, New York, 10022 (212) 752-1530

A small, private institution offering programs in the business of the fashion industry.

Founded: 1939
Affiliation: Independent
Total Enrollment: 9 M, 161 W (full-time)
Cost: < $10K
% Receiving Financial Aid: 65%
Admission: Non-selective
Application Deadline: Rolling

Admission. High school graduates with C+/B- average or higher eligible; 75% of applicants accepted, 63% of these actually enroll. *Required:* SAT or ACT, interview, essay. Criteria considered in admissions, in order of importance: high school academic record, interview, standardized test scores, writing sample, recommendations, extracurricular activities; other factors considered: special talents, alumni children. *Entrance programs:* midyear admission, deferred admission. *Apply:* rolling admissions. *Transfers* welcome; 35 accepted 1993–94.
Academic Environment. Curriculum includes mandatory work projects for which students receive academic credit. Degrees offered: associates, bachelors. Average undergraduate class size: 100% under 20. Most students graduate within four years; 69% of freshmen

return for sophomore year. *Special programs:* cooperative work study, internships (including foreign opportunities), study abroad, cross registration with Fordham U. and Marymount Manhattan College. Adult programs: one year ACCESS program for students with bachelor's degree or 30 transfer credits; after one academic year students receive an associates degree.

Undergraduate degrees conferred (33). 100% were in Business and Management.

Graduate Career Data. About 97% of 1992–93 graduates employed. Corporations typically hiring largest numbers of graduates include Bloomingdales, Saks Fifth Avenue, Abraham and Strauss. Career Development Services include work study and career guidance, conferences, placement interviews, career option counseling.

Faculty. About 15% of faculty hold PhD or equivalent.

Student Body. About 45% of students from in state; 93% Middle Atlantic. An estimated 9% of students reported as Black, 10% Hispanic, 2% Asian, according to most recent data available.

Campus Life. All students commute.

Annual Costs. Tuition and fees, $9,950, estimated book expenses, $300. About 65% of students receive financial aid. Institute reports 11 scholarships awarded on basis of academic merit alone.

Lafayette College

Easton, Pennsylvania 18042 **(215) 250-5000**

Lafayette is a small liberal arts college with a strong engineering–technical program. Traditionally the college has prepared substantial numbers of students for careers in law, medicine, business, and engineering. The 110-acre main campus is located in a city of 30,000 at the fork of the Delaware and Lehigh rivers, about 55 miles north of Philadelphia and about 80 miles west of New York City. Most convenient major airport: Allentown-Bethlehem-Easton.

Founded: 1826
Affiliation: Presbyterian Church (USA)
Total Enrollment: 1,116 M, 902 W (full-time); 176 M, 50 W (part-time)
Cost: $10K–$20K
% Receiving Financial Aid: 43%
Admission: Highly Selective
Application Deadline: January 15

Admission is highly selective. About 59% of applicants accepted, 57% of these actually enroll; 59% of freshmen graduate in top fifth of high school class, 94% in top two-fifths. Average freshman SAT scores, middle 50% range: 470–570 verbal; 560–670 mathematical. *Required:* SAT or ACT, recommendation, essay. Criteria considered in admissions, in order of importance: high school academic record, standardized test scores; extracurricular activities, recommendations, and writing sample rank with equal importance; other factors considered: special talents, alumni children, diverse student body. *Entrance programs:* early decision, early admission, advanced placement, deferred admission. About 30% from private and parochial schools. *Apply* by January 15. *Transfers* welcome; 14 enrolled 1993–94.

Academic Environment. Graduation requirements for liberal arts program includes first year seminar and VAST (Value and Science/Technology) seminar: interdisciplinary liberal arts seminars; 4 courses in arts and humanities/social sciences, 4 in natural sciences (1 math, 2 lab sciences); Knowledge of Foreign Culture. Student leader characterizes student body as primarily oriented toward occupational/professional career goals. Degrees offered: bachelors. *Majors offered* include: anthropology, biochemistry, computer science, engineering, interdisciplinary majors in American civilization, international affairs, joint degree in math/economics. Average undergraduate class size: 18% under 20; 60% between 20–40.

About 88% of students entering as freshmen graduate within four years, 92% eventually; 96% of freshmen return for sophomore year. *Special programs:* internships, independent study, study abroad, honors, undergraduate research, individualized majors, optional January term, Scholars Program, 5-year combined programs, cooperative programs including cross-registration through 6 members of Lehigh Valley Association. *Calendar:* semester, summer school.

Undergraduate degrees conferred (530). 41% were in Social Sciences, 19% were in Engineering, 9% were in Letters, 9% were in Life Sciences, 7% were in Psychology, 3% were in Area and Ethnic Studies, 3% were in Physical Sciences, remainder in 6 other fields.

Graduates Career Data. Advanced studies pursued by 27% of graduates; 16% enter graduate school; 5% enter medical school; 6% enter law school. Medical schools typically enrolling largest number of graduates include Hahnemann, Temple; law schools include Pennsylvania, Boston U., American. About 60% of 1991–92 graduates employed. Employers and fields typically hiring largest numbers of graduates include Arthur Andersen & Co., banking, engineering, scientific research. Career Development Services seminars on resume writing and choosing a major, career fair, alumni contact, internships, on-campus interviews.

Faculty. About 96% of faculty hold PhD or equivalent. About 26% of teaching faculty are female; 3% Black, 1% Hispanic, 3% other minority.

Student Body. About 25% of students from in state; 60% from Middle Atlantic, 17% New England, 5% South, 5% West, 4% Midwest, 8% foreign. An estimated 30% of students reported as Protestant, 36% Catholic, 10% Jewish, 17% unaffiliated, 7% other; 4% as Black, 3% Asian, 2% Hispanic, 8% other. *Minority group students:* financial aid according to need; Black Cultural Center provides recreational and social areas.

Religious Orientation. Lafayette is a church-related institution, but makes no religious demands on students; attendance at religious services and programs voluntary; 7% of students affiliated with the church.

Varsity Sports. Men (Div.I): Baseball, Basketball, Cross Country, Diving, Fencing, Football, Golf, Lacrosse, Soccer, Softball, Swimming, Tennis, Track. Women (Div.I): Basketball, Cross Country, Diving, Fencing, Field Hockey, Lacrosse, Soccer, Softball, Swimming, Tennis, Track, Volleyball.

Campus Life. Since college is some distance from a major metropolitan center (Philadelphia—55 miles, NYC—70 miles) students look to many extracurricular activities on campus on weekends. "Everyone is involved in a sport or activity outside their academic life, according to current student. The Williams Center provides facilities for the departments of art, music and the drama programs as well as for "an extensive variety of touring cultural programs." Students are reported to "work hard and play hard." Greek influence is very strong. Cars not allowed for freshmen, sophomores, except under certain conditions. Lafayette enforces state's drinking age law; "severe" penalties for underage drinking. Smoking prohibited in classrooms.

About 20% of men, 20% of women live in traditional dormitories; 59% of men, 69% of women live in coed dormitories; 3% of each men, women live in off-campus college-related housing or commute. All students are guaranteed housing for 4 years. There are 12 fraternities, 6 sororities on campus which about 50% of men, 70% of women join; 19% of men, 10% of women live in fraternities and sororities. About 5% of resident students leave campus on weekends.

Annual Costs. Tuition and fees, $17,950; room and board, $5,500; estimated $1,450 other, exclusive of travel. About 43% of students receive financial aid. Assistance is typically divided 75% grant, 20% loan, 5% work. College reports all scholarships awarded on the basis of need. *Meeting Costs:* college offers Higher Education Loan to Parents (HELP), fixed tuition and fees program.

Lagrange College

LaGrange, Georgia 30240 **(706) 882-2911**

A church-related, liberal arts college, located in a town of 25,000, 70 miles southwest of Atlanta. Most convenient major airport: Atlanta (62 miles).

Founded: 1831
Affiliation: United Methodist
UG Enrollment: 295 M, 390 W (full-time)
Total Enrollment: 1,023
Cost: < $10K
% Receiving Financial Aid: 78%
Admission: Non-selective
Application Deadline: August 15

Admission. Graduates of accredited high schools in college preparatory program eligible; 58% of applicants accepted, 73% of these actually enroll. Average freshman scores: SAT, 410 verbal, 370 mathematical; ACT, 21 composite. *Required:* SAT or ACT, minimum high school GPA. Criteria considered in admissions, in order of importance: high school academic record, standardized test scores, extracurricular activities; other factors considered: special talents. *Entrance programs:* early admission, deferred admission. *Apply* by August 15; rolling admissions. *Transfers* welcome; 105 enrolled 1993–94.

Academic Environment. Graduation requirements include general education curriculum consisting of 40 hours in common core courses and 55 hours in electives. Degrees offered: associates, bachelors, masters. *Majors offered* include creative music technologies, international business, early childhood education. About 75% of students entering as freshmen graduate eventually, 89% of freshmen return for sophomore year. *Special programs:* CLEP, independent study, honors, undergraduate research, study abroad, credit by examination, social work field placement, 3–2 engineering, internships. Adult programs: Evening Studies Program. *Calendar:* quarter, summer school; no classes in December.

Undergraduate degrees conferred (135). 30% were in Business and Management, 18% were in Education, 10% were in Psychology, 10% were in Public Affairs, 8% were in Visual and Performing Arts, 4% were in Social Sciences, 4% were in Mathematics, 4% were in Physical Sciences, 4% were in Life Sciences, 3% were in Letters, remainder in 3 other fields.

Graduates Career Data. Advanced studies pursued by 20% of graduates. Employers and fields typically hiring most graduates include Milliken, business, nursing/health. Career Development Services include resume writing services, assistance with part-time employment, seasonal employment, internship opportunities, on-campus recruitment.

Faculty. About 83% of faculty hold PhD or equivalent. About 65% of undergraduate classes taught by tenured faculty. About 30% of teaching faculty are female.

Student Body. About 85% of students from in state; 92% South, 1% New England, 0.5% Midwest. An estimated 72% of students reported as Protestant, 8% Catholic, 2% Jewish, 16% unaffiliated, 7% other; 11% as Black, 2% Hispanic, 6% other minority. Average age of undergraduate students: 22.

Religious Orientation. LaGrange is a church-related institution; 21% of students affiliated with the church; 1 course in religious studies required; attendance at assemblies and convocations optional.

Varsity Sports. Men (NAIA): Baseball, Basketball, Golf, Soccer, Tennis. Women (NAIA): Soccer, Softball, Tennis, Volleyball.

Campus Life. About 45% of students live in traditional dormitories; 55% live in off-campus housing or commute. Freshmen are given preference in college housing if all students cannot be accommodated. There are 3 fraternities, 3 sororities on campus which about 25% of students join; they provide no residence facilities. About 40% of resident students leave campus on weekends.

Annual Costs. Tuition and fees, $7,197; room and board, $3,405; estimated $210 other, exclusive of travel. About 78% of students receive financial aid; average amount of assistance, $6,891. Assistance is typically divided 32% scholarship and grant, 39% loan, 11% work. College reports some scholarships awarded on the basis of academic merit alone. *Meeting Costs:* college offers budget planning.

Lake Erie College

Painesville, Ohio 44077 (216) 352-3361

A small, 4-year co-educational liberal arts residential college. College offers both traditional liberal arts and career oriented programs. Juniors may choose to spend the winter term abroad at one of the college's study centers in 6 European countries, Australia, and Mexico. The 57-acre campus is located in the residential section of a town of 20,000, 2 miles from Lake Erie and 29 miles northeast of Cleveland. The college-owned 300-acre Morley Farm, 5 miles south of campus, is the site of an equestrian center.

Founded: 1856
Affiliation: Independent
Total Enrollment: 82 M, 236 W (full-time); 61 M, 148 W (part-time)
Cost: < $10K
% Receiving Financial Aid: 68%
Admission: Non-selective
Application Deadline: August 15

Admission. About 52% of applicants actually enroll. Average freshmen scores: SAT, 50% of freshmen score above 500 on verbal, 12% above 600, 66% score above 500 on mathematical, 16% score above 600, 4% score above 700; ACT, 22.1 composite. *Required:* SAT or ACT, minimum high school GPA, interview recommended, essay, recommendations. Criteria considered in admissions, in order of importance: high school academic record, standardized test scores, recommendations, writing sample, extracurricular activities, equestrian video; other factors considered: special talents, alumni children, diverse student body. *Entrance programs:* midyear admission, deferred admission, advanced placement. *Apply* by August 15; rolling admissions. *Transfers* welcome.

Academic Environment. Curriculum places considerable emphasis on the study of languages; all entering students expected to have better than average skills in writing, reading, and speaking English. Graduation requirements include 20 semester credits in basic proficiencies: math English, computers, foreign language or advanced computers and math, 24–25 credits in core requirements: courses involving critical thinking, scientific inquiry, cultures and aesthetic form, and social process. Degrees offered: bachelors, masters. *Majors offered* include usual arts and sciences, accounting, computer information systems, education, environmental management, fine arts, legal studies, theater, equestrian studies, international business, business administration. Average undergraduate class size: 80% under 20, 20% 20–40.

About 76% of freshmen students return for sophomore year. *Special programs:* CLEP, independent study, study abroad, undergraduate research, individualized majors, internships, cross registration with Cleveland Commission on Higher Education. Adult programs: LEAD allows students to pursue degrees through individualized instruction working with faculty on individual basis. *Calendar:* semester summer school, weekend college.

Undergraduate degrees conferred (133). 50% were in Business and Management, 17% were in Education, 5% were in Social Sciences, 5% were in Life Sciences, 4% were in Psychology, 4% were in Health Sciences, 4% were in Foreign Languages, 4% were in Agribusiness and Agricultural Production, 3% were in Communications, remainder in 3 other fields.

Graduates Career Data. Career Development Services include career guidance, resume assistance, networking assistance, placement.

Faculty. About 83% of faculty hold PhD or equivalent. About 12% of teaching faculty are female; 1% Hispanic, 2% other minority.

Student Body. About 82% of students from in state; 5% each Midwest, South, West, Northwest, 4% New England, 1% foreign. An estimated 65% of students reported as Protestant, 30% Catholic, 5% Jewish; 5% as Black, 2% Asian, according to most recent data available. Average age of undergraduate student: 29.

Varsity Sports. Men (Div. III): Basketball, Equestrian, Golf, Soccer, Tennis. Women (Div.III): Basketball, Equestrian, Golf, Soccer, Softball, Tennis, Volleyball.

Campus Life. Rich cultural and social resources of Cleveland, just 29 miles from campus, supplement numerous on-campus activities. Cars allowed. Use of alcohol subject to state law; legal age, 21. Students not from immediate area required to live in residence halls.

About 30% of men, 36% of women live in traditional or coed dormitories; rest commute. Intervisitation in dormitory rooms limited. There are no fraternities or sororities on campus. About 10% of resident students leave campus on weekends.

Annual Costs. Tuition and fees, $9,600; room and board, $4,250; estimated $1,900 other, exclusive of travel. About 68% of students receive financial aid; average amount of assistance, $7,362. Assistance is typically divided 13% scholarship, 31% grant, 45% loan, 2% work. College reports 20 scholarships awarded on the basis of academic merit alone, 6 for special talents alone, 7 for need alone. *Meeting Costs:* college offers tuition payment plan.

Lake Forest College

Lake Forest, Illinois 60045 (708) 234-3100

Lake Forest is a small, Midwestern liberal arts college that attracts a national student body of great diversity and considerable capability. The 107-acre campus near Lake Michigan is located in a town of 18,000, 25 miles north of Chicago. Most convenient major airport: O'Hare International (Chicago).

Founded: 1857
Affiliation: Independent (Presbyterian Church (USA))
Total Enrollment: 458 M, 511 W (full-time)
Cost: $10K–$20K
% Receiving Financial Aid: 67%
Admission: Very Selective
Application Deadline: March 1

Admission is very selective. About 70% of applicants accepted, 39% of these actually enroll; 53% of freshmen graduate in top fifth of high school class, 87% in top two-fifths. Average freshman scores, middle 50% range: SAT, 440–560 verbal, 480–600 mathematical; ACT, 22–27 composite. *Required:* SAT or ACT, essay. Criteria considered in admissions, in order of importance: high school academic record, recommendations, extracurricular activities, writing sample, standardized tests; other factors considered: special talents, alumni children, diverse student body. *Entrance programs:* early decision, early admission, midyear admission, advanced placement, deferred admission. About 22% of entering students from private schools, 12% from parochial schools. *Apply* by March 1. *Transfers* welcome; 62 enrolled 1993–94.

Academic Environment. Graduation requirements include freshman studies course, freshman writing (or another course that requires a substantial amount of writing), 3 courses in natural sciences and mathematics/computer science, 1 course each in humanities and social sciences, 2 courses in cultural diversity, and senior studies (such as senior seminar or senior thesis) in the major. Students are enthusiastic about the "brilliant and challenging" faculty, "leaders in their fields". Undergraduate research is possible; overall, students report the curriculum is "flexible", offering more study opportunities than exist in the formal curriculum. Students report computer facilities are adequate for those "who begin their research/assignments on time", not so for "procrastinators". System has been recently upgraded. Degrees offered: bachelors. *Majors offered* include Asian studies, international relations, environmental studies, Japanese, self-designed majors. Average undergraduate class size: 75% under 20, 23% between 20–40, 2% over 40.

About 78% of entering freshman class graduate eventually; 83% of freshmen return for sophomore year. *Special programs:* cross registration with Barat College, internships, independent study, tutorials, study abroad, undergraduate research, credit by examination, group study programs, senior thesis, undergraduate institute, 3–2 engineering, 2–2 cooperative programs in nursing, medical technology. 3–2 BA/MA programs in public policy studies, social services administration. *Calendar:* 4–4 with divisible semester, summer school.

Undergraduate degrees conferred (257). 35% were in Social Sciences, 13% were in Psychology, 12% were in Visual and Performing Arts, 10% were in Letters, 9% were in Business and Management, 7% were in Foreign Languages, 4% were in Philosophy and Religion, 4% were in Life Sciences, 3% were in Physical Sciences, remainder in 3 other fields.

Graduates Career Data. Advanced studies pursued by 20% of students within six months of graduation, 45–50% within five years. Medical schools typically enrolling largest numbers of graduates include U. of Illinois; dental schools include Loyola, Northwestern, U. of Illinois; law schools include Loyola, Northwestern, U. of Illinois; business schools include U. of Chicago, Northwestern, DePaul. Employers typically hiring largest numbers of graduates include Abbot Labs, Baxter Health Care, Arthur Anderson, Hewitt Associates. Career Development Services include national database of alumni contacts, Alumni Mentor Program, extensive employer and student database matching student career interests to employment and internship possibilities.

Faculty. About 96% of faculty hold PhD or equivalent. About 44% of undergraduate classes taught by tenured faculty. About 42% of teaching faculty are female; 5% Black, 3% Hispanic, 3% Asian.

Student Body. About 38% of students from in state; 55% Midwest, 12% New England, 7% Middle Atlantic, 12% West, 5% South, 3% Northwest, 6% foreign. An estimated 7% of students reported as Black, 1% Hispanic, 4% Asian, according to most recent data available. *Minority group students:* minority student organizations provide support system; Black studies program.

Religious Orientation. Lake Forest was founded by Presbyterians; "there is a relationship based on heritage."

Varsity Sports. Men (Div.III): Basketball, Cross Country, Diving, Football, Hockey, Soccer, Swimming, Tennis. Women (Div.III): Basketball, Cross Country, Diving, Soccer, Softball, Swimming, Tennis, Volleyball.

Campus Life. Campus is located in a suburb of Chicago, allowing for a quiet environment with access to downtown for "a taste of the nightlife." Social life focuses on campus organizations; student reports "this is a GREAT school for getting involved. People get involved with the Greek system, join clubs and organizations, join the paper or the yearbook, and play sports." Cars not allowed for freshmen. All-freshman dormitory houses 54% of class; several dorms have "purpose units"—groups of students with common interests who chose to live together.

About 20% of women live in traditional dormitories; 83% of men, 61% of women in coed dormitories; 17% of men, 19% of women commute. Freshmen guaranteed college housing. Sexes segregated in coed dormitories by wing or floor. There are 4 fraternities, 3 sororities on campus which about 21% of men, 22% of women join; they provide no residence facilities. About 10% of resident students leave campus on weekends.

Annual Costs. Tuition and fees, $16,175; room and board, $3,785; estimated $950 other, exclusive of travel. About 67% of students receive financial aid; average amount of assistance, $15,300; assistance is typically divided 80% scholarship and grant, 20% loan and work. College reports 9 scholarships awarded on the basis of academic merit alone, varies for need alone. *Meeting Costs:* college offers 10 month payment plan.

Lake Superior State University

Sault Ste. Marie, Michigan 49774 (906) 635-2231

A small, state-supported college, located in a city of 15,000 at the Canadian border. Most convenient major airport: Sault Ste. Marie, Ontario.

Founded: 1946	**Cost:** < $10K
Affiliation: State	**% Receiving Financial Aid:** 70%
Total Enrollment: 2,852 M, W (full-time)	**Admission:** Non-selective
	Application Deadline: Aug. 16

Admission. Graduates of accredited high schools with 15 units (13 in academic subjects) with GPA of 2.0 in academic subjects and "above-average standing in their class" eligible; 79% of applicants accepted, 42% of these actually enroll. *Required:* ACT (for placement only). *Out-of-state* freshman applicants: college welcomes students from out of state. State does not limit out-of-state enrollment. No special requirements for out-of-state applicants. Non-academic factor considered in admissions: geographical distribution. *Apply* by August 16. *Transfers* welcome.

Academic Environment. *Degree:* BS. About 59% of general education requirements for graduation are elective; distribution requirements fairly numerous. About 53% of freshmen return for sophomore year. *Majors offered* include automated systems engineering technology, computer science, legal assistant, business administration, hospitality management. *Special programs:* CLEP, honors, transfer programs. *Calendar:* quarter, summer school.

Undergraduate degrees conferred (381). 19% were in Business and Management, 18% were in Engineering and Engineering Related Technology, 10% were in Protective Services, 10% were in Health Sciences, 7% were in Social Sciences, 6% were in Public Affairs, 5% were in Marketing and Distribution, 4% were in Psychology, 4% were in Multi/Interdisciplinary Studies, 4% were in Life Sciences, 3% were in Allied Health, 3% were in Parks and Recreation, remainder in 6 other fields.

Student Body. About 74% of students from in state; 79% Midwest; many Canadian students from twin city across the border and other contiguous areas of Ontario. An estimated 1% of students reported as Black, 4% Native American, 1% other minority, according to most recent data available.

Varsity Sports. Men (Div.II): Basketball, Cross Country, Golf, Hockey (I), Tennis, Wrestling. Women (Div.II): Basketball, Cross Country, Softball, Tennis, Volleyball.

Campus Life. About 16% each of men, women live in traditional dormitories; 19% men, 11% of women in coed dormitories; rest live in off-campus housing or commute. Freshmen are given preference in college housing if all students cannot be accommodated. Intervisitation in men's and women's dormitory rooms somewhat limited. There are 4 fraternities, 4 sororities on campus. About 40–50% of resident students leave campus on weekends.

Annual Costs. Tuition and fees, $2,880 (out-of-state, $5,610); room and board, $4,080; estimated $420 other, exclusive of travel. About 70% of students receive financial aid; assistance is typically divided 56% grant/scholarship, 29% loan, 15% work. College reports some scholarships awarded on the basis of academic merit alone.

Lakeland College

Sheboygan, Wisconsin 53082 **(414) 565-1217**

A church-related college, located in a rural area, 12 miles northwest of a city of 50,000, and 60 miles north of Milwaukee. Most convenient major airport: Milwaukee.

Founded: 1862
Affiliation: United Church of Christ
Total Enrollment: 1,439 M, W (full-time)
Cost: < $10K
% Receiving Financial Aid: 90%
Admission: Non-selective
Application Deadline: August 15

Admission. Graduates of accredited high schools, with rank in upper half of class, minimum GPA of 2.0, ACT composite of 16, or combined SAT of 840 eligible; others may interview to demonstrate motivation; 66% applicants accepted, 41% of these actually enroll; 19% of freshmen graduate in top fifth of high school class, 52% in top two-fifths. Average freshman ACT scores, according to most recent data available: 19 M, 19 W composite. *Required:* SAT or ACT. *Apply* by August 15; rolling admissions. *Transfers* welcome.
Academic Environment. *Degree:* BA. Curriculum emphasizes 4 components: basic skills; literacy in the fields of humanities, social and natural sciences; interdisciplinary studies; honors for superior students. *Majors offered* include computer science, marketing and management, international business, physical fitness and health, specialized administration. About 45% of students entering as freshmen graduate eventually; 55% of freshmen return for sophomore year. *Special programs:* CLEP, independent study, internships, honors, study abroad, 3–2 engineering. Adult programs: Lifelong Learning Evening Degree Program in business, accounting, computer science. *Calendar:* 4–1–4, summer school.
Undergraduate degrees conferred (308). 82% were in Business and Management, 5% were in Computer and Engineering Related Technology, 3% were in Letters, 3% were in Education, remainder in 8 other fields.
Graduates Career Data. According to most recent data available, full-time graduate or professional study pursued by 17% of students immediately after graduation. *Careers in business and industry* pursued by 72% of graduates.
Faculty. About 74% of faculty hold PhD or equivalent.
Student Body. About 89% of students from in state; 99% Midwest. An estimated 10% of students reported as Protestant, 7% Catholic, 81% unaffiliated, 2% other; 5% as Black, 1% Hispanic, 1% Asian, according to most recent data available.
Religious Orientation. Lakeland is a church-related institution; makes no religious demands on students; attendance at chapel services and religious classes voluntary.
Varsity Sports. Men (NAIA Div.II): Baseball, Basketball, Cross Country, Football, Golf, Soccer, Tennis, Track. Women (NAIA Div.II): Basketball, Cross Country, Softball, Tennis, Track, Volleyball.
Campus Life. About 40% of men, 40% of women live in traditional dormitories; 25% of men, 25% of women in coed dormitories; rest commute. Freshmen are given preference in college housing if all students cannot be accommodated. Intervisitation in men's and women's dormitory rooms limited. Sexes segregated in coed dormitories by floor or room. There are 3 fraternities, 2 sororities on campus which about 11% of men, 9% of women join; they provide no residence facilities. About 30% of resident students leave campus on weekends.
Annual Costs. Tuition and fees, $9,145; room and board, $3,700; estimated $1,200 other, exclusive of travel. About 90% of students receive financial aid; assistance is typically divided 60% scholarship/grant, 23% loan, 17% work. College reports some scholarships awarded on the basis of academic merit alone. *Meeting Costs:* college offers interest free 12-month payment plan.

Lamar University

Beaumont, Texas 77710 **(800) 458-7558**

A state-supported university, located in a city of 120,000, 87 miles northeast of Houston. Most convenient major airport: Houston.

Founded: 1923
Affiliation: State
UG Enrollment: 2,331 M, 2,661 W (full-time); 1,554 M, 2,278 W (part-time)
Total Enrollment: 8,824
Cost: < $10K
Admission: Non-selective
Application Deadline: August 10

Admission. Graduates of accredited high schools eligible; 70% of applicants accepted, 64% of these actually enroll; 40% of freshmen graduate in top fifth of high school class, 65% in top two-fifths. Average freshman SAT scores: 413 verbal, 459 mathematical. *Required:* SAT or ACT, minimum high school GPA. Criteria considered in admissions, in order of importance: standardized test scores, high school academic record, writing sample. *Out-of-state* freshman applicants: university actively seeks students from out-of-state; state does not limit out-of-state enrollment. *Entrance programs:* early admission, advanced placement. *Apply* by August 10; rolling admissions. *Transfers* welcome; 1,486 enrolled 1993–94.
Academic Environment. Graduation requirements include courses in Philosophy of Knowledge, English, sciences (math, social, and political). Degrees offered: bachelors, masters, doctoral. Average undergraduate class size: 24% between 20–40, 24% over 40. About 35% of students entering as freshmen graduate eventually, 65% return for sophomore year. *Special programs:* CLEP, study abroad. Adult programs: adult learner program, applied arts and sciences degree. *Calendar:* semester, summer school.
Undergraduate degrees conferred (1214). 31% were in Education, 17% were in Business and Management, 8% were in Engineering, 5% were in Social Sciences, 5% were in Protective Services, 5% were in Multi/Interdisciplinary Studies, 4% were in Health Sciences, 3% were in Letters, 3% were in Computer and Engineering Related Technology, 3% were in Communications, remainder in 15 other fields.
Faculty. About 75% of faculty hold PhD or equivalent. About 65% of undergraduate classes taught by tenured faculty. About 30% of teaching faculty are female; 12% Black, 3% Hispanic, 15% other minority.
Student Body. About 95% of students from in state; 3% New England, 2% foreign. Average age of undergraduate student: 25.
Varsity Sports. Men (Div.I): Baseball, Basketball, Golf, Tennis, Track, Volleyball. Women (Div.I): Baseball, Tennis, Track, Volleyball.
Campus Life. About 5% of men, 7% of women live in traditional dormitories; no coed dormitories; rest of men, and women live in off-campus housing or commute. Intervisitation in men's and women's dormitory rooms limited. There are 11 fraternities, 7 sororities on campus which about 5% of men, 5% women join; 2% of men, 4% of women live in fraternities and sororities. About 90% of resident students leave campus on weekends.
Annual Costs. Tuition and fees, $1,080 (out-of-state, $4,320); room and board, $2,500; estimated $500 other, exclusive of travel. Average amount of assistance, $3,427; assistance is typically divided 30% scholarship, 40% loan, 30% work. *Meeting Costs:* university offers PLUS, ALAS loans to parents.

Lambuth College

Jackson, Tennessee 38301 **(901) 417-1500**

A church-related college, offering a "liberal arts program in a Christian environment," located in a city of 40,000, 80 miles east of Memphis.

Founded: 1843
Affiliation: United Methodist
Total Enrollment: 860 M, W (full-time)
Cost: < $10K
Admission: Non-selective
Application Deadline: Rolling

Admission. Graduates of accredited high schools with 16 units eligible; others admitted by special action; 96% of applicants accepted, 59% of these actually enroll; 42% of freshmen graduate in top fifth of high school class, 64% in top two-fifths. *Apply:* rolling admissions. *Transfers* welcome.
Academic Environment. *Degrees:* BA, BS, BBA, BM. About 50% of students entering as freshmen graduate eventually; 75% of freshmen return for sophomore year. *Special programs:* CLEP, independent study, study abroad, honors. *Calendar:* 4–1–4, summer school.

Undergraduate degrees conferred (136). 25% were in Education, 23% were in Business and Management, 8% were in Social Sciences, 8% were in Letters, 7% were in Psychology, 4% were in Mathematics, 4% were in Communications, 4% were in Liberal/General Studies, 4% were in Architecture and Environmental Design, 3% were in Visual and Performing Arts, 3% were in Physical Sciences, 3% were in Computer and Engineering Related Technology, remainder in 2 other fields.
Student Body. About 89% of students from in state; 95% South, according to most recent data available.
Religious Orientation. Lambuth is a church-related institution; 1 course in religion required of all students; attendance at Sunday chapel "encouraged.
Varsity Sports. Men (NAIA): Baseball, Basketball, Tennis. Women (NAIA): Basketball, Tennis, Volleyball.
Campus Life. About 47% of men, 52% of women live in traditional dormitories; no coed dormitories; rest commute. No intervisitation in men's or women's dormitory rooms. There are 3 fraternities, 4 sororities on campus which about 26% of men, 30% of women join; 2% of men live in fraternities. About 50% of resident students leave campus on weekends.
Annual Costs. Tuition and fees, $4,834; room and board, $3,160; estimated $1,500 other, exclusive of travel.

Lancaster Bible College

Lancaster, Pennsylvania 17601 **(717) 560-8271**

A small, non-denominational Bible college which "exists to educate Christian men and women to live according to a biblical world view and to serve through professional Christian ministries." Most convenient major airport: Harrisburg.

Founded: 1933
Affiliation: Independent
Total Enrollment: 165 M, 180 W (full-time); 81 M, 81 W (part-time)
Cost: < $10K
% Receiving Financial Aid: 88%
Admission: Non-selective
Application Deadline: August 15

Admission. High school graduates eligible. About 87% of applicants accepted, 74% of these actually enroll; 20% of freshmen graduate in top fifth of high school class, 40% in top two-fifths. Average freshman ACT scores: 20.5 M, 19.8 W composite. *Required:* minimum 2.0 high school GPA, essay, references; ACT recommended. Criteria considered in admissions, in order of importance: Christian testimony, high school academic record, recommendations, extracurricular activities, writing sample, standardized test scores. About 40% of freshmen from private schools. *Entrance programs:* early decision, early admission, midyear admission, deferred admission, advanced placement. *Apply* by August 15; rolling admissions. *Transfers* welcome; 90 enrolled 1993–94.
Academic Environment. Degrees offered: associates, bachelors. Average undergraduate class size: 61% under 20, 25% between 20–40, 14% over 40. About 56% of entering students graduate eventually; 64% of freshmen return for sophomore year. *Special programs:* study abroad, January term, Israel Institute of the Holy Land Studies, independent study. *Calendar:* semester, summer school.
Undergraduate degrees conferred (49). 100% were in Theology.
Graduate Career Data. About 85% of 1992–93 graduates employed. Employers typically hiring largest numbers of graduates include churches, Christian schools, parachurch ministries. Career Development Services include published bulletin, resume writing and interview workshops.
Student Body. About 74% of students from in state; 14% Middle Atlantic, 4% New England, 3% South, 4% foreign. All students reported as Protestant; 3% Black, 1% Hispanic, 3% Asian, 1% other minority. Average age of undergraduate student: 25.
Religious Orientation. Lancaster is a non-denominational church-related institution; 40% of the curriculum is religious courses.
Varsity Sports. Men (NCCAA, Div.II): Baseball, Basketball, Soccer. Women (NCCAA, Div.II): Basketball, Softball, Volleyball.
Campus Life. About 34% of men, 42% of women live in traditional dormitories; rest commute.
Annual Costs. Tuition and fees, $7,410; room and board, $3,300; an estimated $1,850 other, exclusive of travel. About 88% of students receive financial aid; average amount of assistance, $4,000. Assistance is typically divided 23% scholarship, 29% grant, 34% loan, 14% work. College reports 60 scholarships awarded on the basis of academic merit alone, 2 for special talents alone, 2 for need alone. Meeting Costs: college offers deferred payment plan.

Lander College

(See Lander University)

Lander University

Greenwood, South Carolina 29646 **(803) 229-8307**

A state-supported, liberal arts institution located in a town of 24,650, 75 miles west of Columbia. Formerly known as Lander College.

Founded: 1872
Affiliation: State
Total Enrollment: 735 M, 1,339 W (full-time); 108 M, 233 W (part-time)
Cost: < $10K
Admission: Non-selective
Application Deadline: Rolling

Admission. High school graduates eligible. About 87% of applicants accepted, 44% of these actually enroll. About 34% of freshmen graduate in top fourth of high school class, 68% in top half. *Required:* SAT or ACT. Criteria considered in admissions, in order of importance: high school academic record, standardized test scores, recommendations. *Out-of-state* freshman applicants: university actively seeks out-of-state students. State does not limit out-of-state enrollment. Requirement for out-of-state applicants: rank in top half of class. *Entrance programs:* midyear admission, deferred admission. *Apply:* rolling admissions. *Transfers* welcome; 244 enrolled 1993–94.
Academic Environment. Degrees offered: bachelors, masters. About 50% of general education requirements for graduation are elective; distribution requirements fairly numerous. About 45% of entering students graduate eventually. *Special programs:* study abroad, tutorial laboratories, 3–2 engineering, internship. *Calendar:* semester, summer school.
Undergraduate degrees conferred (299). 30% were in Business and Management, 20% were in Education, 12% were in Social Sciences, 7% were in Health Sciences, 5% were in Visual and Performing Arts, 5% were in Psychology, 5% were in Letters, 4% were in Multi/Interdisciplinary Studies, 4% were in Mathematics, 4% were in Computer and Engineering Related Technology, 3% were in Life Sciences, remainder in Foreign Languages.
Student Body. About 96% of students from in state; 98% South. Average age of undergraduate students: 22.
Varsity Sports. Men (Div.II): Basketball, Cross Country, Soccer, Tennis. Women (Div.II): Basketball, Cross Country, Softball, Tennis.
Campus Life. About 37% of men, 42% of women live in traditional dormitories; rest commute. Intervisitation in men's and women's dormitory rooms limited. There are 6 fraternities, 6 sororities on campus which about 12% of men, 7% of women join. About 65% of resident students leave campus on weekends.
Annual Costs. Tuition and fees, $3,270 (out-of-state, $4,648); room and board, $2,960; estimated $600 other, exclusive of travel. University reports some scholarships awarded on the basis of academic merit alone. *Meeting Costs:* college offers Tuition Plan, Inc., supplemental loans for parents.

Lane College

Jackson, Tennessee 38301 **(901) 424-4600**

A church-related college, located in a city of 40,000; founded as a college for Negroes and still serving a predominantly Black student body.

Founded: 1882
Affiliation: Christian Methodist Episcopal
Total Enrollment: 561 M, W (full-time)
Cost: < $10K
Admission: Non-selective
Application Deadline: 30 days before registration

Admission. Graduates of approved high schools with 15 units, 10 in academic subjects, eligible. About 10% of freshmen graduate in top fifth of high school class, 30% in top two-fifths. *Required:* ACT or SAT. *Apply* by 30 days before registration. *Transfers* welcome.
Academic Environment. *Degrees:* AB, BS. *Special programs:* undergraduate research, individualized majors. *Calendar:* semester, summer school.
Undergraduate degrees conferred (48). 40% were in Business and Management, 19% were in Social Sciences, 13% were in Education, 10% were in Life Sciences, 6% were in Physical Sciences, 6% were in Communications, 4% were in Computer and Engineering Related Technology, remainder in Letters.
Student Body. About 58% of students from in state; 72% South, 25% Midwest.
Religious Orientation. Lane is a church-related institution; 4 semester hours of religion required of all students.
Varsity Sports. Men (Div.III): Baseball, Basketball, Cross Country, Football, Tennis. Women (Div.III): Basketball, Cross Country, Tennis.
Campus Life. About 78% of men, 79% of women live in traditional dormitories; no coed dormitories; rest live in off-campus housing or commute. No intervisitation in men's or women's dormitory rooms. There are 4 fraternities, 4 sororities on campus which about 18% of men, 15% of women join; they provide no residence facilities.
Annual Costs. Tuition and fees, $4,766; room and board, $2,862; estimated $1,500 other, exclusive of travel.

Langston University

Langston, Oklahoma 73050 (405) 466-2231

A state-supported, land-grant university, located in a village of 500, 38 miles north of Oklahoma City; founded as a college for Negroes and still serving a predominantly Black student body.

Founded: 1897
Affiliation: State
Total Enrollment: 2,294 M, W (full-time)
Cost: < $10K
Admission: Non-selective

Admission. Oklahoma graduates of accredited high schools with C average, rank in top three-quarters of class, or score in top three-quarters on ACT eligible; others admitted on probation during summer session; 98% of applicants accepted, 54% of these actually enroll. *Required:* ACT. *Out-of-state* freshman applicants: state does not limit out-of-state enrollment. Requirement for out-of-state applicants: rank in top half of class or score in top half on ACT. *Apply* by no specific deadline. *Transfers* welcome.
Academic Environment. *Degrees:* AB, BS, BAEd, BSEd. About 60% of students entering as freshmen graduate eventually; 65% of freshmen return for sophomore year. *Special programs:* Urban Clinical Center, internships. *Calendar:* semester, summer school.
Undergraduate degrees conferred (368). 27% were in Business and Management, 16% were in Education, 11% were in Health Sciences, 8% were in Protective Services, 8% were in Psychology, 7% were in Allied Health, 7% were in Social Sciences, 7% were in Computer and Engineering Related Technology, remainder in 8 other fields.
Student Body. About 75% of students from Midwest; 12% West, 5% South.
Varsity Sports. Men (NAIA): Basketball, Football, Track. Women (NAIA): Basketball, Track.
Campus Life. About 75% of men, 50% of women live in traditional dormitories; no coed dormitories; rest live in off-campus housing or commute. Intervisitation permitted in men's and women's dormitory rooms. There are 4 fraternities, 4 sororities on campus which about 1% of men, 2% of women join; they provide no residence facilities.
Annual Costs. Tuition and fees, $1,561 (out-of-state, $3,793); room and board, $2,499; estimated $1,331 other, exclusive of travel.

La Roche College

Pittsburgh, Pennsylvania 15237 (412) 367-9241

A small, private, liberal arts college, founded by the Sisters of Divine Providence; located 12 miles from the center of metropolitan Pittsburgh. Most convenient major airport: Pittsburgh International.

Founded: 1963
Affiliation: Roman Catholic
UG Enrollment: 258 M, 392 W (full-time); 196 M, 623 W (part-time)
Total Enrollment: 1,813
Cost: < $10K
% Receiving Financial Aid: 74%
Admission: Non-selective
Application Deadline: Rolling

Admission. High school graduates eligible; 97% of applicants accepted, 53% of these actually enroll; 19% of freshmen graduate in top fifth of high school class, 40% in top two-fifths. Average freshman SAT scores: 370 M, 390 W on verbal; 410 M, 410 W on mathematical. *Required:* SAT, minimum 2.0 high school GPA. Criteria considered in admissions, in order of importance: high school academic record, standardized test scores, recommendations, extracurricular activities; other factors considered: special talents. *Entrance programs:* early admission, midyear admission, deferred admission, advanced placement. *Apply:* rolling admissions. *Transfers* welcome; 102 enrolled 1993–94.
Academic Environment. Graduation requirements include 42–43 credits in Basic Skills, Natural World, Aesthetics/Reality, Global World. Degrees offered: bachelors, masters. *Majors offered* include chemistry management, graphic and interior design, science education. Average undergraduate class size: 57% under 20, 42% 20–40, 1% over 40. About 77% of freshmen return for sophomore year. *Special programs:* CLEP, independent study, honors, undergraduate research, Washington Center, internships, study abroad, individualized majors, cross registration with U. of Pittsburgh, Carlow, Chatham. *Calendar:* semester.
Undergraduate degrees conferred (287). 29% were in Health Sciences, 28% were in Business and Management, 10% were in Psychology, 7% were in Visual and Performing Arts, 5% were in Architecture and Environmental Design, 5% were in Social Sciences, 4% were in Life Sciences, 4% were in Allied Health, 3% were in Communications, remainder in 5 other fields.
Graduate Career Data. Advanced studies pursued by 32% of graduates. Career Development Services include a four-year comprehensive program with career counseling, workshops, seminars, career library, job fair, on-campus interviews.
Faculty. About 70% of faculty hold PhD or equivalent. About 50% of teaching faculty are female; 2% minority.
Student Body. About 93% of students from in state; almost all Middle Atlantic. An estimated 56% of students reported as Catholic; 27% Protestant, 3% Black, 1% Hispanic, 1% Asian, 2% other minority. Average age of undergraduate student: 29.
Religious Orientation. University is a church-related institution; makes no religious demands on students.
Varsity Sports. Men (Div.III): Baseball, Basketball, Soccer. Women (Div.III): Basketball, Softball, Volleyball.
Campus Life. About 46% of students live in coed dormitories; rest commute. Freshmen given preference in college housing if all students cannot be accommodated. Intervisitation in men's and women's dormitory rooms limited. There is 1 sorority on campus which about 10% of women join. About 25% of resident students leave campus on weekends.
Annual Costs. Tuition and fees, $8,422; room and board, $4,555; estimated $1,200 other, exclusive of travel. About 74% of students receive financial aid; average amount of assistance, $5,200. College reports 60 scholarships awarded on the basis of academic merit alone. *Meeting Costs:* college offers tuition payment plan, estimating service.

La Salle University

Philadelphia, Pennsylvania 19141 (215) 951-1500

Founded as a college for men, La Salle is now co-educational and governed by a predominantly lay board of trustees. A liberal arts institution conducted by the Christian Brothers, La Salle is located in the Germantown section of Philadelphia. Most convenient major airport: Philadelphia International.

Founded: 1863
Affiliation: Independent (Roman Catholic)
UG Enrollment: 1,540 M, 1,529 W (full-time); 480 M, 1,158 W (part-time)
Total Enrollment: 5,993
Cost: $10K–$20K
% Receiving Financial Aid: 85%
Admission: Selective (+)
Application Deadline: Rolling

Admission is selective (+). About 62% of applicants accepted; 47% of freshmen graduate in top fifth of high school class, 77% in top two-fifths. Average freshman scores: SAT, 500 M, 510 W verbal, 570 M, 530 W mathematical; 60% of freshmen score above 500 on verbal, 19% above 600, 9% above 700; 85% score above 500 on mathematical, 35% above 600, 15% above 700. *Required:* SAT, essay. Criteria considered in admissions, in order of importance: high school academic record, extracurricular activities, standardized test scores, recommendations, writing sample; other factors considered: special talents, alumni children, diverse student body. About 30% of entering students from private schools, 35% from parochial schools. *Apply*: rolling admissions. *Transfers* welcome; 258 enrolled 1993–94.
Academic Environment. Administration reports 25% of general education courses required for graduation are elective; numerous distribution requirements. *Undergraduate studies* offered by schools of Arts and Sciences, Business Administration. Small classes, individual attention from faculty cited, by students, as strengths of the academic program. Degrees offered: associates, bachelors, masters. *Majors offered* include nursing, earth science, combination elementary education/special education. Average undergraduate class size: 90% under 20, 10% between 20–40.

About 87% of students entering as freshmen graduate eventually; 91% of freshmen return for sophomore year. *Special programs:* CLEP, independent study, study abroad, honors, individualized majors, cross-registration with Chestnut Hill, dual majors, cooperative program in business, American College Program of the U. of Fribourg. *Calendar:* semester, summer school.
Undergraduate degrees conferred (986). 45% were in Business and Management, 9% were in Health Sciences, 7% were in Communications, 7% were in Letters, 6% were in Education, 5% were in Social Sciences, 5% were in Life Sciences, 4% were in Computer and Engineering Related Technology, 4% were in Psychology, 3% were in Protective Services, remainder in 6 other fields.
Graduates Career Data. Advanced studies pursued by 20% of graduates; 9% enter graduate school; 4% enter medical school; 4% law school; 2% business school; 1% enter dental school. About 73% of 1992–93 graduates employed. Fields typically hiring largest numbers of graduates include accounting, nursing, communication, computer science. Career Development Services include career planning and placement for all students starting in the freshman year.
Faculty. About 87% of faculty hold PhD or equivalent. About 75% of undergraduate classes taught by tenured faculty. About 26% of teaching faculty are female; 2% Black, 1% Hispanic, 1% other minority.
Student Body. About 64% of students from within the state; 27% Middle Atlantic; 5% New England; 4% South. An estimated 70% of students reported as Catholic, 25% Protestant, 5% Jewish; 4% as Black, 3% Hispanic, 3% Asian. *Minority group students:* special financial, academic, and social provisions.
Religious Orientation. La Salle is a church-related institution with a majority of laymen on its board of trustees; 2 courses in religious studies required of all students.
Varsity Sports. Men (Div.I): Baseball, Basketball, Crew, Cross Country, Diving, Golf, Soccer, Softball, Swimming, Tennis, Track, Volleyball, Wrestling. Women (Div.I): Basketball, Crew, Cross Country, Diving, Golf, Field Hockey, Soccer, Softball, Swimming, Tennis, Track, Volleyball.
Campus Life. Location allows easy access to city for entertainment or internships/co-op opportunities. Possession or use of alcohol by students under 21 not permitted; alcohol not allowed in common rooms of residence halls. No rules limiting ownership of cars; parking reported to be a problem. Some student dissatisfaction with regulations governing student conduct, one student characterizes them as "very strict."

About 20% of men, 21% of women live in traditional dormitories; 48% of men, 52% of women live in coed dormitories; rest commute. Intervisitation in men's and women's dormitory rooms. Sexes segregated in coed dormitories by floor. There are 8 fraternities, 7 sororities on campus which about 13% of men, 12% of women join. About 18% of resident students leave campus on weekends.
Annual Costs. Tuition and fees, $11,510; room and board, $5,430; estimated $500 other, exclusive of travel. About 85% of students receive financial aid; average amount of assistance, $9,500. Assistance is typically divided 30% scholarship, 30% grant, 20% loan, 20% work. University reports 50 scholarships awarded on the basis of academic merit alone, 5 for special talents alone. *Meeting Costs:* university offers deferred payment plan.

University of La Verne

La Verne, California 91750 (714) 593-3511

A small, independent college, with historical ties to the Church of the Brethren, located in a community of 18,000, 30 miles east of Los Angeles.

Founded: 1891
Affiliation: Independent
UG Enrollment: 475 M, 598 W (full-time); 120 M, 154 W (part-time)
Total Enrollment: 2,456
Cost: $10K–$20K
% Receiving Financial Aid: 78%
Admission: Non-selective
Application Deadline: March 1

Admission. High school graduates with "B" average and minimum SAT combined score of 800 eligible, others accepted provisionally; 67% of applicants accepted, 31% of these actually enroll; 15% of freshmen graduate in top fifth of high school class, 45% in top two-fifths. Average freshman scores: SAT, 400 M, 410 W verbal, 464 M, 458 W mathematical. *Required:* SAT, minimum 2.5 high school GPA, essay, interview recommended. Criteria considered in admissions, in order of importance: high school academic record, recommendations, standardized test scores, extracurricular activities, writing sample; other factors considered: special talents, alumni children, diverse student body, religious affiliation/commitment. *Entrance programs:* early decision, early admission, midyear admission, deferred admission. About 26% of entering students from parochial schools, 8% from private schools. *Apply* preferably by March 1. *Transfers* welcome; 247 enrolled 1993–94.
Academic Environment. Degrees offered: associates, bachelors, masters. About 65% of general education requirements for graduation are elective; some distribution requirements. *Majors offered* include environmental management, environmental biology. About 34% of students entering as freshmen graduate within four years, 36% eventually; 85% of freshmen return for sophomore year. Average undergraduate class size: 70% under 20, 28% 20–40, 2% over 40. *Special programs:* CLEP, internship with College of Osteopathic Medicine of the Pacific, independent study, study abroad, honors, 3-year degree, individualized majors. Adult programs: accelerated program. *Calendar:* 4–1–4, summer school.
Undergraduate degrees conferred (608). 100% were in Unknown.
Graduates Career Data. Advanced studies pursued by 25% of students. Career Development Services works with students and offers special programs.
Faculty. About 72% of faculty hold PhD or equivalent. About 76% of undergraduate classes taught by tenured faculty. About 32% of teaching faculty are female; 3% Black, 1% Hispanic, 7% other minority.
Student Body. About 96% of students from in state; 3% foreign. An estimate 40% of students reported as Catholic, 30% Protestant, 2% Jewish, less than 1% Muslim, 25% unaffiliated, 2% other; 8% Black, 30% Hispanic, 10% Asian, 9% other minority.
Religious Orientation. La Verne is now an independent institution; "Christian emphasis at La Verne College takes many forms.
Varsity Sports. Men (Div.III): Baseball, Basketball, Cross Country, Football, Tennis, Track, Volleyball. Women (Div.III): Basketball, Cross Country, Softball, Tennis, Track, Volleyball.
Campus Life. About 36% of men, 39% of women live in traditional dormitories; 10% of men, 21% of women live in coed dormitories; rest live in off-campus housing or commute. Freshmen given preference in college housing if all students cannot be accommodated. Intervisitation in men's and women's dormitory rooms limited. There are 3 fraternities, 3 sororities, about 12% of men, 8% of women join. Sororities provide no residence facilities. About 30% of resident students leave campus on weekends.

Annual Costs. Tuition and fees, $12,900; room and board, $4,500; estimated $5,000 other, exclusive of travel. About 78% of students receive financial aid; average amount of assistance, $7,500. *Meeting Costs:* university offers loan programs.

Lawrence Technological University

Southfield, Michigan 48075 **(313) 356-0200**

An independent, co-educational institution, primarily for commuters, with schools of architecture, engineering, business and industrial management, and arts and science; located in a Detroit suburb of 69,300.

Founded: 1932
Affiliation: Independent
Total Enrollment: 1,670 M, 506 W (full-time); 1,612 M, 451 W (part-time)
Cost: < $10K
% Receiving Financial Aid: 60%
Admission: Non-selective
Application Deadline: August 1

Admission. High school graduates with 16 units eligible; 80% of applicants accepted, 36% of those accepted actually enroll. Average freshman ACT scores: 22 composite. *Required:* ACT, minimum GPA, interview. *Apply* by August 1. *Transfers* welcome; 538 enrolled 1993–94.
Academic Environment. Degrees offered: associates, bachelors, masters. Distribution requirements vary with school. About 32% of students entering as freshmen graduate within four years, 50% eventually; 73% of freshmen return for sophomore year. Average undergraduate class size: 55% under 20, 40% 20–40, 5% over 40. *Special programs:* CLEP, undergraduate research, individualized majors. *Calendar:* quarter, summer school.
Undergraduate degrees conferred (752). 57% were in Engineering, 28% were in Business and Management, 11% were in Architecture and Environmental Design, 3% were in Mathematics, remainder in 2 other fields.
Graduate Career Data. Fields typically hiring largest numbers of graduates include engineering, business, architecture.
Student Body. Majority of students from Midwest states. Average age of undergraduate students: 24.
Varsity Sports. Men: Golf, Hockey, Soccer.
Campus Life. About 8% each of men, women live in co-ed apartments on campus.
Annual Costs. Tuition and fees, $7,380; room and board, $2,412. About 60% of students receive financial aid; average amount of assistance: $2,500.

Lawrence University

Appleton, Wisconsin 54912 **(414) 832-7000**

Lawrence University, a widely known midwestern liberal arts institution, also includes a Conservatory of Music. The 37-acre main campus is located in a community of 60,000, 100 miles north of Milwaukee. Most convenient major airport: Outagamie County.

Founded: 1847
Affiliation: Independent
Total Enrollment: 567 M, 644 W (full-time)
Cost: $10K–$20K
% Receiving Financial Aid: 84%
Admission: Very (+) Selective
Application Deadline: Feb. 1

Admission is very (+) selective. About 76% of applicants accepted, 34% of these actually enroll; 70% of freshmen graduate in top fifth of high school class, 91% in top two-fifths. Average freshman scores, middle 50% range: SAT, 500–640 verbal, 560–700 mathematical; 71% of freshmen score above 500 on verbal, 35% above 600, 4% above 700; 84% of freshmen score above 500 on mathematical, 54% above 600, 17% above 700; ACT, 25–31 composite. *Required:* SAT or ACT, essay, audition for conservatory applicants. Criteria considered in admissions, in order of importance: high school academic record, standardized test scores, extracurricular activities, recommendations, writing sample; other factors considered: special talents, alumni children, diverse student body; for Conservatory applicants the audition is of first importance. *Entrance programs:* early decision, early admission, midyear admission, advanced placement, deferred admission, common application. About 10% of entering students from private schools, 10% from parochial schools. *Apply* by February 1. *Transfers* welcome; 18 enrolled 1993–94.
Academic Environment. University has 4 divisions: fine arts, humanities, social sciences, and natural sciences. Graduation requirements include 2 courses in freshman studies, 5 in Logic and Observation (social and natural sciences), and 5 in Language and Civilization (fine and performing arts, and humanities). Conservatory offers a professional music program and all students may participate in performance groups and classes. Academic demands are substantial. Student leader reports that "all scholastic areas are strong academically", and points particularly at "independent study and tutorial programs." Faculty reported to be "very approachable and more than willing to individually help students" (at both the remedial and the advanced levels). Both the introspective academics and pre-professional types reported to feel at home on campus. Degrees offered: bachelors. *Majors offered* include Chinese, East Asian Languages and Cultures, Russian and Slavic studies; interdisciplinary areas include computer studies, environmental studies, gender studies, linguistics, international studies, neuroscience, public policy analysis, social thought. Wide variety of off-campus programs offered through study abroad and at other institutions in the U.S. Average undergraduate class size: 16; 86% under 20, 11% 20–40, 3% over 40.

About 78% of students entering as freshmen graduate eventually; 87% of freshmen return for sophomore year. *Special programs:* independent study, tutorials, study abroad, honors, undergraduate research, Scholar of the University program, self-designed majors, programs of ACM, study at Classical Center in Rome, Paris Seminar, German Seminar, Spanish Seminar (in Spain or Mexico), overseas campus in London, Washington Semester, Bahamas marine term, geology field term, Eastern Europe and Soviet Union summer tour, 5-year BA/BMus., 3–2 nursing, 3–2 engineering, 3–2 social services administration, 3–2 forestry and environmental studies. *Calendar:* 3–3.
Undergraduate degrees conferred (296). 25% were in Social Sciences, 12% were in Visual and Performing Arts, 11% were in Life Sciences, 11% were in Letters, 11% were in Physical Sciences, 11% were in Foreign Languages, 7% were in Psychology, 4% were in Education, 3% were in Philosophy and Religion, remainder in 2 other fields.
Graduates Career Data. Advanced studies pursued by 25%-30% of students immediately after graduation, 66% eventually. About 70% of 1992–93 graduates employed. Career Development Services include individual career counseling, assistance with resume writing, interviewing and job search strategies, career development workshops, SIGI-PLUS computerized guidance system, Myers-Briggs Type Indicator, and Campbell Interest and Skill Survey.
Faculty. About 92% of faculty hold PhD or equivalent. All undergraduate classes taught by faculty, no teaching assistants. About 27% of teaching faculty are female; 1% Black, 2% Hispanic, 3% other minority.
Student Body. About 44% of students from in state; 73% Midwest, 3% New England, 2% Middle Atlantic, 2% South, 8% West, 10% foreign. An estimated 2% of students reported as Black, 3% Asian, 2% Hispanic, 11% other minority. *Minority group students:* strong financial aid program; College Methods Lab and special services program; Black Organization of Students, Multicultural Affairs Committee.
Religious Orientation. While Lawrence was founded under the auspices of the Methodist Church and Milwaukee-Downer had Congregational and Baptist connections, the university today is nonsectarian.
Varsity Sports. Men (Div.III): Baseball, Basketball, Cross Country, Diving, Fencing, Football, Golf, Hockey, Soccer, Swimming, Tennis, Track, Wrestling. Women (Div.III): Basketball, Cross Country, Diving, Fencing, Soccer, Softball, Swimming, Tennis, Track, Volleyball.
Campus Life. College reports a strong effort to provide a full and varied calendar of campus activities; in addition, student leader notes an "abundance of student-initiated activities." Another student observes: "Everyone is hardworking and eager to learn." Students 21 or over allowed to drink alcoholic beverages in their rooms. Cars not permitted for those receiving financial aid. No restrictions on intervisitation.

About 86% of men, 96% of women live in coed dormitories; 4% of each men, women live in off-campus college-related housing or

commute. Sexes segregated in coed dormitories either by floor or room. There are 5 fraternities, 3 sororities on campus which about 42% of men, 24% of women join; 10% of men live in fraternities, sororities provide no residence facilities. About 5% of resident students leave campus on weekends.
Annual Costs. Tuition and fees, $16,431; room and board, $3,555; estimated $1,500 other, exclusive of travel. About 84% of students receive financial aid; average amount of assistance, $13,687. Assistance is typically divided 21% scholarship, 51% grant, 22% loan, 6% work. University reports 343 scholarships awarded on the basis of academic merit alone, 94 for special talents alone.

Lebanon Valley College

Annville, Pennsylvania 17003 **(800) 445-6181**

A church-related, liberal arts college, Lebanon Valley is located in the Pennsylvania Dutch region of the state. The college draws its students largely from Pennsylvania and surrounding states. The 200-acre campus is located in a village of 5,000, 20 miles east of Harrisburg. Most convenient major airport: Harrisburg International.

Founded: 1866
Affiliation: United Methodist
UG Enrollment: 498 M, 467 W (full-time); 158 M, 344 W (part-time)
Total Enrollment: 1,680
Cost: $10K–$20K
% Receiving Financial Aid: 81%
Admission: Selective
Application Deadline: June 1

Admission is selective. About 75% of applicants accepted, 32% of these actually enroll; 52% of freshmen graduate in top fifth of high school class, 79% in top two-fifths. Average freshman SAT scores: 461 M, 472 W verbal, 537 M, 509 W mathematical; 35% of freshman score above 500 on verbal, 7% above 600; 58% score above 500 on mathematical, 19% above 600, 4% above 700. *Required:* SAT or ACT, audition for music majors. Criteria considered in admissions, in order of importance: high school academic record; other factors considered: special talents, alumni children, diverse student body, religious affiliation/commitment, extracurricular activities. *Entrance programs:* early decision, early admission, midyear admission, advanced placement, deferred admission. About 15% of entering students from private schools. *Apply* by June 1. *Transfers* welcome; 50 enrolled 1993–94.
Academic Environment. Administration source describes student body as concerned with both academic pursuits and occupational/professional goals. Students serve on several faculty committees dealing with such matters as curriculum, chapel/convocation program, academic policies. Graduation requirements include study in communications, history, social sciences, math, natural sciences, humanities, and foreign language. Degrees offered: associates, bachelors, masters. *Majors offered* include sound recording technology, actuarial science, psycho-biology, sacred music, American studies. Average undergraduate class size: 71% under 20, 28% between 20–40, 1% over 40.

About 68% of students entering as freshmen graduate eventually; 80% of freshmen return for sophomore year. *Special programs:* independent study, study abroad, honors, undergraduate research, 3–2 engineering, 3–2 forestry 2–2 and 3–2 programs in allied health professions, marine biology program, Germantown Semester, Washington Semester. Adult programs: Weekend College, MBA program for part-time students. *Calendar:* semester, summer school.
Undergraduate degrees conferred (202). 25% were in Business and Management, 17% were in Education, 10% were in Psychology, 8% were in Letters, 6% were in Social Sciences, 6% were in Mathematics, 6% were in Life Sciences, 5% were in Public Affairs, 4% were in Physical Sciences, remainder in 8 other fields.
Faculty. About 80% of faculty hold PhD or equivalent. About 75% of undergraduate classes taught by tenured faculty. About 23% of teaching faculty is female; 1% Black, 1% Hispanic, 1% other minority.
Student Body. About 82% of students from in state; 98% Middle Atlantic, 1% New England, 1% foreign. An estimated 74% of students reported as Protestant, 23% Catholic, 1% Jewish; 1% Black, 1% Hispanic, 1% Asian, 3% other minority. *Minority group students:* special financial provisions.
Religious Orientation. Lebanon Valley is a church-related institution; 19% of students affiliated with the church; no religious studies courses required.
Varsity Sports. Men (Div. III): Baseball, Basketball, Cross Country, Football, Golf, Soccer, Swimming, Tennis, Track, Volleyball, Wrestling. Women (Div. III): Basketball, Cross Country, Field Hockey, Softball, Swimming, Tennis, Track, Volleyball.
Campus Life. Campus location, within easy traveling distance of other colleges, enhances social opportunities. Very active music and drama productions reported. Possession or use of alcohol prohibited on campus; opportunity to live off campus may be given to seniors and students over 21 who are not on academic or social probation.

About 59% of men, 57% of women live in traditional dormitories; 23% men, 25% women live in coed dormitories; rest commute. There are 4 fraternities, 3 sororities on campus which about 18% of men, 17% of women join. About 40% of resident students leave campus on weekends.
Annual Costs. Tuition and fees, $13,700; room and board, $4,600; estimated $1,125 other, exclusive of travel. About 81% of students receive financial aid; average amount of assistance, $11,454. Assistance is typically divided 24% scholarship, 32% grant, 34% loan, 10% work. College reports 321 scholarships awarded on the basis of academic merit alone, 57 for need alone. *Meeting Costs:* college offers deferred payment plans.

Lee College

Cleveland, Tennessee 37311 **(615) 472-2111**

A church-related, liberal arts college, located in a city of 20,700 in the lower region of the Appalachian Mountains; offers education within framework of "conservative, evangelical, Pentecostal religious position of its sponsoring denomination."

Founded: 1918
Affiliation: Church of God
Total Enrollment: 2,011 M, W (full-time)
Cost: < $10K
% Receiving Financial Aid: 91%
Admission: Non-selective

Admission. Graduates of approved high schools with C average or ACT composite score of 17 eligible; 87% of applicants accepted, 85% of these actually enroll; 19% of freshmen graduate in top fifth of high school class, 51% in top two-fifths. Average freshmen scores: SAT, 916 verbal and mathematical; ACT, 21.3 composite. *Required:* SAT or ACT. *Apply:* no specific deadline. *Transfers* welcome; 209 enrolled 1993–94.
Academic Environment. Degrees offered: associates, bachelors. About 59% of general education requirements for graduation are elective; distribution requirements fairly numerous. Average undergraduate class size: 17. *Special programs:* CLEP, independent study, study abroad, honors. *Calendar:* semester, summer school.
Undergraduate degrees conferred (258). 24% were in Business and Management, 18% were in Education, 17% were in Theology, 9% were in Social Sciences, 8% were in Psychology, 7% were in Communications, 6% were in Life Sciences, 5% were in Visual and Performing Arts, 3% were in Mathematics, remainder in 2 other fields.
Faculty. About 44% of faculty hold PhD or equivalent. About 45% of undergraduate classes taught by tenured faculty. About 30% of teaching faculty are female.
Student Body. About 39% of students from in state; 12% New England, 8% Middle Atlantic.
Religious Orientation. Lee is a church-related institution; 4 courses in religion, attendance at 3 weekly chapel services, Sunday school and morning worship, all assemblies and convocations required of all students.
Campus Life. About 53% of men, 61% of women live in traditional dormitories; no coed dormitories; rest live in off-campus housing or commute. No intervisitation in men's or women's dormitory rooms. There are no fraternities or sororities on campus. About 10% of resident students leave campus on weekends.
Annual Costs. Tuition and fees, $4,692; room and board, $2,912; estimated $1,490 other, exclusive of travel. About 91% of students receive financial aid.

Lehigh University

Bethlehem, Pennsylvania 18015 (215) 758-3100

Lehigh is a small university based on a well-known undergraduate engineering college of substantial quality. It has expanded its graduate and professional offerings in recent years. Originally an institution for men, it has been co-educational since 1971. The 1,600-acre campus is located in an industrial city of 72,700, 60 miles north of Philadelphia and 90 miles west of New York City. Most convenient major airport: Allentown-Bethlehem-Easton.

Founded: 1865
Affiliation: Independent
UG Enrollment: 2,749 M, 1,549 W (full-time); 104 M, 81 W (part-time)
Total Enrollment: 6,476
Cost: $10K–$20K
% Receiving Financial Aid: 52%
Admission: Highly Selective
Application Deadline: Feb. 15

Admission is highly selective. For all schools, 69% of applicants accepted, 25% of these actually enroll; 67% of freshmen graduate in top fifth of high school class, 90% in top two-fifths. Average freshman SAT scores: 70% of freshmen score above 500 on verbal, 16% above 600, 1% above 700; 96% score above 500 on mathematical, 73% above 600, 20% above 700, according to most recent data available.

For Arts and Science (946 M, 1,022 W), 69% of applicants accepted, 30% of these actually enroll. Average freshman SAT scores, middle 50% range: 480–580 verbal, 570–660 mathematical, according to most recent data available.

For Engineering and Applied Sciences (1,280 M, 260 W), 73% of applicants accepted, 32% of these actually enroll. Average freshman SAT scores, middle 50% range: 480–580 verbal, 620–710 mathematical, according to most recent data available.

For Business and Economics (638 M, 377 W), 59% of applicants accepted, 35% of these actually enroll. Average freshman SAT scores, middle 50% range: 480–570 verbal, 590–680 mathematical, according to most recent data available.

Required: SAT or ACT. Criteria considered in admissions, in order of importance: high school academic record, extracurricular activities, standardized test scores, recommendations, writing sample; other factors considered: special talents, alumni children, diverse student body. *Entrance programs:* early decision, early admission, deferred admission, advanced placement. About 30% of entering students from private schools. *Apply* by February 15. *Transfers* welcome; 68 enrolled 1993–94 fall semester.

Academic Environment. Lehigh has a University Forum, composed of 60 students, 60 faculty, and 5 administrators, which makes policy in many areas of institutional life. Faculty still retains primary responsibility in academic matters, however. Pressures for academic achievement appear intense. Curriculum is considered very "rigorous" especially for engineering students. Although Lehigh takes pride in its non-engineering studies and its graduates in these areas, it is the College of Engineering, with the many specialties it offers, that is still the heart of the university's program. However, as a result of the presence on campus of the College of Arts and Science and the College of Business and Economics, engineering graduates are likely to be more broadly educated than graduates of purely technical schools. College of Business and Economics places its graduates in a very wide range of business enterprises and has been especially successful in preparing students for employment in major national accounting firms. Graduation requirements: 50% of courses required for graduation are elective, distribution requirements in Arts and Science and Engineering fairly numerous: 12 semester hours each in humanities, natural sciences and mathematics, social sciences (2 groups must be represented in each of the 3 areas), year English, 1 semester mathematics or logic, foreign language proficiency, year physical education. Degrees offered: bachelors, masters, doctoral. *Majors offered* include environmental sciences, foreign careers, international relations, journalism/science writing, material resources, Russian, science, technology & society.

About 75% of students entering as freshmen graduate within four years, 88% eventually; 92% of freshmen return for sophomore year. *Special programs:* independent study, study abroad, honors, undergraduate research, freshman seminars, Washington Semester, Philadelphia Urban Semester, 5-year combined arts/engineering program, cooperative programs including cross-registration with 5 other Lehigh Valley colleges, cooperative work/study program in engineering, 2–4 pre-med program, 3–4 pre-dental. Adult programs: continuing education programs. *Library:* 25,000 rare books. *Calendar:* semester, summer school.

Undergraduate degrees conferred (1153). 33% were in Engineering, 31% were in Business and Management, 11% were in Social Sciences, 5% were in Multi/Interdisciplinary Studies, 4% were in Psychology, 3% were in Letters, 3% were in Life Sciences, remainder in 10 other fields.

Graduates Career Data. Advanced studies pursued by 22% of graduates. About 58% of 1992 graduates employed. Employers typically hiring largest numbers of graduates include General Electric, IBM, Price Waterhouse, Arthur Andersen. Career Development Services include on-campus employer interviewing, employment listings, alumni biweekly publication distributed on campus.

Faculty. About 98% of faculty hold PhD or equivalent. About 80% of undergraduate classes taught by tenured faculty. About 19% of teaching faculty are female; 2% Black, 2% Hispanic, 9% other minority.

Student Body. About 34% of students from in state; 79% Middle Atlantic, 5% New England, 4% Midwest, 7% South, 2% West, 3% foreign. An estimated 20% of students reported as Protestant, 30% Catholic, 13% Jewish, 2% unaffiliated, 35% other; 2% Black, 2% Hispanic, 4% Asian, 2% other minority, according to most recent data available. *Minority group students:* special tutorial programs, recruiting efforts, facilities for social activities.

Varsity Sports. Men (Div.I): Baseball, Basketball, Cross Country, Diving, Football (IAA), Golf, Lacrosse, Soccer, Swimming, Tennis, Track, Wrestling. Women (Div.I): Basketball, Cross Country, Diving, Field Hockey, Lacrosse, Soccer, Softball, Swimming, Tennis, Track, Volleyball.

Campus Life. Students most likely to feel at home on campus are "conservative, upper middle class," according to administration source. Strong fraternity system dominates social life at Lehigh and relations between independents and fraternity men sometimes show strain. However, fraternity residences are a vital necessity to university because dormitory space has not expanded as rapidly as enrollment. Variety of cultural and intellectual events provided by university. Nearest major cultural center, Philadelphia, is 60 miles from campus, sufficient distance to make its cultural facilities available on a limited basis. Motor vehicles prohibited for all freshmen, financial aid recipients, and sophomores in poor standing academically or in trouble with Discipline Committee. Use of alcohol subject to state law; permitted in residential buildings for those over 21.

About 38% of men, 41% of women live in coed dormitories; 26% of men, 22% of women live in off-campus college-related housing; 2% of men, 3% of women commute. Freshmen are guaranteed college housing if all students cannot be accommodated. Intervisitation in men's and women's dormitory rooms unlimited. Sexes segregated in coed dormitories either by wing or floor. There are 28 fraternities, 8 sororities on campus which about 48% of men, 45% of women join; 34% of men, 34% of women live in fraternities and sororities.

Annual Costs. Tuition and fees, $17,500; room and board, $5,500; estimated $1,750 other, exclusive of travel. About 52% of students receive financial aid; average amount of assistance, $16,400. Assistance is typically divided 79% scholarship and grant, 15% loan, 6% work. University reports 8 scholarships awarded on the basis of athletic talents (wrestling) alone, 1,926 for need alone. *Meeting Costs:* university offers prepayment plan.

Le Moyne College

Syracuse, New York 13214-1399 (315) 445-4100

A private, liberal arts institution, in the Jesuit tradition. Le Moyne is located on a 150-acre campus in a city of 198,200. Most convenient major airport: Hancock International (Syracuse).

Founded: 1946
Affiliation: Roman Catholic
UG Enrollment: 831 M, 1,011 W (full-time); 227 M, 333 W (part-time)
Total Enrollment: 2,542
Cost: $10K–$20K
% Receiving Financial Aid: 94%
Admission: Very Selective
Application Deadline: Mar. 15

Admission is very selective. About 82% of applicants accepted, 35% of these actually enroll; 46% of freshmen graduate in top fifth of high school class, 77% in top two-fifths. Average freshman scores, middle 50% range: SAT, 420–510 verbal, 480–590 mathematical; 34% of freshmen score above 500 on verbal, 8% above 600; 69% of freshmen score above 500 on mathematical, 23% above 600, 3% above 700; ACT, 23–27 composite. *Required:* SAT or ACT, essay; interview recommended. Criteria considered in admissions: high school academic record ranks as most important; standardized test scores, extracurricular activities, recommendations and writing sample rank equally; other factors considered: special talents, alumni children, diverse student body. *Entrance programs:* early decision, early admission, midyear admission, advanced placement, deferred admission. About 38% of entering students from private or parochial schools. *Apply* by March 15. *Transfers* welcome; 132 enrolled 1993–94.

Academic Environment. Graduation requirements include 12 course humanities core curriculum: English, history, religious studies, natural science, social sciences, and philosophy. Degrees offered: bachelors, masters. *Majors offered* include usual arts and sciences, business administration, math concentrations in operations research, actuarial sciences, industrial relations and human resources management. Average undergraduate class size: 50% under 20, 47% 20–40, 3% over 40.

About 76% of students entering as freshmen graduate eventually; 92% of freshmen return for sophomore year. *Special programs:* CLEP, independent study, study abroad, honors, undergraduate research, 3-year degree, graduate credit at Syracuse for some upper-division courses at Le Moyne, pre-engineering with Clarkson, Detroit and Manhattan, pre-environmental science and forestry with SUNY-Environmental Science and Forestry, early assurance programs with SUNY Buffalo (Dental Medicine, Medical degree), SUNY Health Science Center Syracuse (Medical degree), pre-optometry with Pennsylvania College of Optometry, 3–2 in engineering, environmental studies internships. *Calendar:* semester, summer school.

Undergraduate degrees conferred (497). 52% were in Business and Management, 16% were in Letters, 12% were in Social Sciences, 7% were in Life Sciences, 6% were in Psychology, remainder in 5 other fields.

Graduates Career Data. Advanced studies pursued by 29% of students; 14% enter graduate school; 5% enter law school; 4% enter business school; 3% enter medical/dental school; 5% other. Medical schools typically enrolling largest numbers of graduates include SUNY Health Science Center; dental schools include SUNY Buffalo; law schools include Albany Law, Cornell, Notre Dame; business schools include RIT, LeMoyne, SUNY Buffalo. About 64% of 1992–93 graduates employed. Fields typically hiring largest numbers of graduates include accounting, education, business management, communications. Career Development Services include career information, career planning, job search assistance, on-campus recruiting, employer fair, individual and group advising.

Faculty. About 93% of faculty hold PhD or equivalent. About 36% of teaching faculty are female; 2% Black, 2% Hispanic, 6% other minority.

Student Body. About 92% of students from in state; 98% Middle Atlantic, 2% New England, less than 1% foreign. An estimated 85% of students reported as Catholic, 14% Protestant; 4% as Black, 3% Hispanic, 2% Asian, 1% Native American, 2% other minority. *Minority group students:* special financial, academic (including summer remedial services program, supportive service during school year), social provisions available.

Religious Orientation. Le Moyne is a church-related institution; 2 semesters of nondenominational religious studies required of all students.

Varsity Sports. Men (Div.II): Baseball (I), Basketball, Cross Country, Diving, Golf, Lacrosse, Soccer, Swimming, Tennis. Women (Div.II): Basketball, Cross Country, Diving, Lacrosse, Soccer, Softball, Swimming, Tennis, Volleyball.

Campus Life. College provides a relatively wide range of cultural and social activities on campus, supplemented by the resources of Syracuse. Student leader describes student body as primarily interested in social affairs. Cars allowed for all. Drinking permitted for those over 21 at "recognized social events" and in residence halls. All out-of-town students expected to live in dormitories or college-approved housing.

About 25% of men, 22% of women live in traditional dormitories; 50% of men, 50% of women live in coed dormitories; rest live in off-campus housing or commute. Freshmen given preference in college housing if all students cannot be accommodated. Intervisitation in men's and women's dormitory rooms limited. There are no fraternities or sororities on campus. About 20% of resident students leave campus on weekends.

Annual Costs. Tuition and fees, $10,640; room and board, $4,540; estimated $1,250 other, exclusive of travel. About 94% of students receive financial aid; average amount of assistance, $10,450. Assistance is typically divided 54% scholarship, 35% loan, 10% work. College reports 258 scholarships awarded on the basis of academic merit alone, 94 for special talents alone, 1,006 for need alone. *Meeting Costs:* college offers loan programs, monthly payment plan.

Lemoyne-Owen College

Memphis, Tennessee 38126 **(901) 942-7302**

A church-related college, primarily for commuters, located in a city of 623,500; founded as a college for Negroes and still serving a predominantly Black student body.

Founded: 1870
Affiliation: United Church of Christ, Baptist
Total Enrollment: 1,013 M, W (full-time)
Cost: < $10K
% Receiving Financial Aid: 95%
Admission: Non-selective
Application Deadline: June 15

Admission. Graduates of accredited high schools with 16 units eligible; 92% of applicants accepted, 79% of these actually enroll. About 3% of freshmen graduate in top fifth of high school class, 13% in top two-fifths. *Required:* SAT or ACT. *Apply* by June 15. *Transfers* welcome.

Academic Environment. *Degrees:* AB, BS. About 29% of general education credits for graduation are required; distribution requirements fairly numerous. About 26% of students entering as freshmen graduate within four years; 95% of freshmen return for sophomore year. *Special programs:* Greater Memphis Consortium, exchange program with Grinnell, Washington Semester, 3–2 engineering, Eight College Consortium. *Calendar:* trimester, summer school).

Undergraduate degrees conferred (100). 100% were in Unknown.

Student Body. About 98% of students from in state; 99% South.

Religious Orientation. LeMoyne-Owen is a church-related institution; makes no religious demands on students; attendance at convocation/chapel services voluntary.

Varsity Sports. Men (Div.III): Baseball, Basketball, Cross Country, Track. Women (Div.III): Basketball, Cross Country, Track, Volleyball.

Campus Life. No dormitories on campus. There are 4 fraternities on campus, 4 sororities which about 2% of men, 3% of women join; they provide no residence facilities.

Annual Costs. Tuition and fees, $3,750; estimated $1,500 other, exclusive of travel. About 95% of students receive financial aid. Assistance is typically divided 2% scholarship, 18% loan, 80% work. College reports some scholarships awarded on the basis of academic merit alone.

Lenoir Rhyne College

Hickory, North Carolina 28601 **(704) 328-7300**

A church-related college, located in a town of 25,000, 55 miles northwest of Charlotte.

Founded: 1891
Affiliation: Evangelical Lutheran Church in America
UG Enrollment: 477 M, 696 W (full-time); 59 M, 107 W (part-time)
Total Enrollment: 1,425
Cost: $10K–$20K
% Receiving Financial Aid: 65%
Admission: Non-selective
Application Deadline: Rolling

Admission. High school graduates with 11 units in academic subjects eligible; 78% of applicants accepted, 38% of these actually enroll; 39% of freshmen graduate in top fifth of high school class, 68% in top two-fifths. Average freshman scores: SAT, 447 M, 453 W verbal, 500 M, 491 W mathematical; 31% of freshmen score above 500 on verbal, 7% above 600, 1% above 700; 50% of freshmen score above 500, 15% above 600, 2% above 700 mathematical; ACT, 22 composite. *Required:* SAT or ACT, essay, minimum high school GPA 2.5. Criteria considered in admissions, in order of importance: high school academic record, extracurricular activities, standardized test scores, recommendations, writing sample. *Entrance programs:* early admission, midyear admission, deferred admission. About 17% of freshmen from private schools. *Apply:* rolling admissions. *Transfers* welcome.

Academic Environment. Graduation requirements include 53 semester hours of basic core requirements. Degrees offered: bachelors, masters. Average undergraduate class size: 90% under 20, 10% 20–40. About 65% of students entering as freshmen graduate eventually; 88% of freshmen return for sophomore year. *Special programs:* CLEP, independent study, study abroad, honors, undergraduate research, 3-year degree, individualized majors, 3–2 engineering, 3–2 environmental science, 3–2 physical therapy, internships. *Calendar:* semester, summer school.

Undergraduate degrees conferred (325). 30% were in Business and Management, 20% were in Education, 10% were in Social Sciences, 8% were in Psychology, 6% were in Letters, 4% were in Parks and Recreation, 4% were in Health Sciences, 3% were in Life Sciences, 3% were in Foreign Languages, remainder in 7 other fields.

Graduate Career Data. Advanced studies pursued by 40% of graduates. About 50% of 1992–93 graduates employed. Fields typically hiring most graduates include education, business, sciences. Career Development Services available.

Faculty. About 70% of faculty hold PhD or equivalent. About 70% of undergraduate classes taught by tenured faculty. About 36% of teaching faculty are female; 1% Black.

Student Body. About 45% of students from in state; 33% South, 56% Middle Atlantic, 7% New England, 1% each Midwest, West, Northwest, 1% foreign. Approximately 63% of students reported as Protestant, 14% Catholic, 23% other; 5% Black, 1% Hispanic.

Religious Orientation. Lenoir Rhyne is a church-related institution, owned and operated by the North Carolina Synod of the Lutheran Church in America; 33% of students affiliated with the church; 2 religious courses, attendance at monthly convocations required of all students; attendance at weekly chapel services "strongly encouraged."

Varsity Sports. Men (Div.II): Baseball, Basketball, Cross Country, Football, Golf, Soccer, Tennis, Track. Women (Div.II): Basketball, Cross Country, Soccer, Softball, Tennis, Volleyball.

Campus Life. About 70% of students live in traditional dormitories; no coed dormitories; rest commute. There are 4 fraternities, 4 sororities on campus which 30% of men, 35% of women join; they provide no residence facilities. About 30% of resident students leave campus on weekends.

Annual Costs. Tuition and fees, $10,220; room and board, $3,848; estimated $1,400 other, exclusive of travel. About 65% of students receive financial aid, average amount of assistance, $2,000. Assistance is typically divided 30% scholarship, 30% grant, 30% loan, 10% work. College reports 200 scholarships awarded on the basis of academic merit alone, 120 for athletic talents alone, 500 for need alone. *Meeting Costs:* college offers monthly payment plan.

Lesley College

Cambridge, Massachusetts 02138 **(617) 349-8500**

A specialized college for women, Lesley offers training in day care, early childhood, elementary, and special education. The urban campus is located in metropolitan Boston area, near Harvard. Most convenient major airport: Logan International (Boston).

Founded: 1909
Affiliation: Independent
Total Enrollment: 477 W (full-time)
Cost: $10K–$20K
% Receiving Financial Aid: 65%
Admission: Non-selective
Application Deadline: April 1

Admission. Graduates of accredited high schools with 15 units in college preparatory course who achieve "college recommending grades" eligible; 81% of applicants accepted, 41% of these actually enroll. About 16% of freshmen graduate in top fifth of high school class, 32% in top two-fifths. Average freshman SAT scores: 410 verbal, 410 mathematical. *Required:* SAT or ACT, writing sample. Criteria considered in admissions, in order of importance: high school academic record, recommendations, writing sample, extracurricular activities, standardized test scores; other factors considered: special talents, diverse student body. *Entrance programs:* early decision, midyear admission, deferred admission, advanced placement. *Apply* by April 1; rolling admissions (after January 15). *Transfers* welcome; 46 enrolled 1993–94.

Academic Environment. Lesley provides 4 laboratory schools for its teacher education programs: a day-care center, a nursery and kindergarten for normal and gifted students, a school for emotionally disturbed children, and one for mentally retarded children. Graduation requirements include cross-cultural components in writing, critical and quantitative reasoning, multi-cultural and global perspectives, and leadership and ethics, 52 credits of distribution requirements. Degrees offered: associates, bachelors, masters, doctoral. About 55% of students entering as freshmen graduate within four years, 85 eventually; 75% of freshmen return for sophomore year. *Special programs:* CLEP, independent study, study abroad, cross registration with Harvard Extension, 3–2 in counseling psychology, internships, child and community degree. Adult programs: bachelor's degree programs offered in several disciplines. *Calendar:* 4–1–4, summer school.

Undergraduate degrees conferred (458). 44% were in Business and Management, 34% were in Education, 22% were in Allied Health.

Graduates Career Data. About 90% of 1991–92 graduates employed. Career Development Services include comprehensive career planning and job search services, job bulletin and monthly newsletter, career resource library, on-campus interviewing, human services job fair, credentials service, alumni contact network.

Faculty. About 60% of faculty hold PhD or equivalent. About 70% of teaching faculty are female.

Student Body. About 60% of students from in state; 91% New England. An estimated 7% of students reported as Black, 5% Hispanic, 5% Asian, 6% other minority.

Varsity Sports. Women: Crew, Cross Country, Soccer, Softball, Tennis.

Campus Life. About 70% of women live in traditional dormitories; rest commute. Intervisitation in women's dormitory rooms limited. There are no sororities on campus. About 30% of resident students leave campus on weekends.

Annual Costs. Tuition and fees, $11,700; room and board, $5,300; estimated $1,145 other, exclusive of travel. About 65% of students receive financial aid; average amount of assistance, $10,062. Assistance is typically divided 57% scholarship, 29% loan, 14% work. College reports 315 scholarships awarded on the basis of academic merit alone, 42 for non-need. *Meeting Costs:* college offers extended monthly payment plans.

Letourneau University

Longview, Texas 75607 **(800) 759-8811**

An independent, Christian university with programs in arts, sciences, engineering, and technology; located in a city of 60,000 in east Texas. Student body largely composed of "those who have made a profession of faith in Jesus Christ." Most convenient major airport: Shreveport (LA).

Founded: 1946
Affiliation: Independent
Total Enrollment: 983 M, W (full-time)
Cost: < $10K
% Receiving Financial Aid: 72%
Admission: Non-selective
Application Deadline: Rolling

Admission. Graduates of approved high schools who rank in top 50% of their class, with GPA of 2.0, and minimal SAT/ACT scores of 800/18 eligible; 85% of applicants accepted, 77% of these actually enroll. Average freshman scores, according to most recent data available: SAT, 486 verbal, 545 mathematical; ACT, 22.9 composite. *Required:* ACT, pastor's recommendation. *Non-academic factors* considered in admissions: special talents, "character." About 40% of entering students from private schools. *Apply:* rolling admissions. *Transfers* welcome.

Academic Environment. *Degrees:* BA, BS. About 40% of general education requirements for graduation are elective; no distribution requirements. *Majors offered* include welding engineering, aviation technology, teacher certification. About 55% of students entering as freshmen graduate eventually; 78% of freshmen return for sophomore year. *Special programs:* CLEP, independent study. Adult programs: 43-hour business management degree for adults with 80 credit hours toward degree. *Calendar:* semester, summer school.

Undergraduate degrees conferred (126). 45% were in Engineering and Engineering Related Technology, 28% were in

Business and Management, 21% were in Engineering, remainder in 4 other fields.

Graduates Career Data. *Careers in business and industry* pursued by 95% of graduates. Corporations typically hiring largest numbers of graduated include Cardone, Conoco, Delta Airlines, Micronyx.

Faculty. About 25% of students from in state; 20% Midwest, 20% Middle Atlantic, 25% West/Northwest, 5% South. An estimated 99% of students reported as Protestant, 1% Catholic, according to most recent data available.

Religious Orientation. LeTourneau is a "Christ-centered" institution; 3–4 courses in Bible as well as attendance at chapel 4 times weekly and Sunday services required of all students.

Varsity Sports. Men (NAIA): Baseball, Basketball, Cross Country, Soccer. Women (NAIA): Volleyball.

Campus Life. About 65% of men, 54% of women live in traditional dormitories; no coed dormitories; rest live in off-campus housing or commute. Freshmen given preference in college housing if all students cannot be accommodated. No intervisitation in men's or women's dormitory rooms. About 10% of resident students leave campus on weekends.

Annual Costs. Tuition and fees, $7,940; room and board, $3,860; estimated $700 other, exclusive of travel. About 72% of students receive financial aid; assistance is typically divided 50% scholarship, 30% loan, 20% work. College reports some scholarships awarded on basis of academic merit alone. *Meeting Costs:* college offers monthly payment plan with no interest.

Lewis and Clark College

Portland, Oregon 97219 **(503) 768-7040 or (800) 444-4111**

A liberal arts college emphasizing the arts and sciences, with an international focus, and also offering pre-professional studies in medicine, dentistry and law, as well as graduate and professional studies in education, music, law, public administration, counseling, teacher training of the deaf. Lewis and Clark was founded by Presbyterian pioneers. The 130-acre campus is located in the metropolitan Portland area (pop. 1.5 million), about 6 miles from the center of the city. Most convenient major airport: Portland International.

Founded: 1867
Affiliation: Independent (Presbyterian Church (USA))
UG Enrollment: 778 M, 961 W (full-time)
Total Enrollment: 3,216
Cost: $10K–$20K
% Receiving Financial Aid: 70%
Admission: Selective (+)
Application Deadline: Feb 1

Admission is selective (+). About 75% of applicants accepted, 23% of these actually enroll; 56% of freshmen graduate in top tenth of high school class, 81% in top two-fifths. Average freshman scores, middle 50% range: SAT, 490–590 verbal, 520–640 mathematical; 71% of freshmen score above 500 on verbal, 21% above 600, 4% above 700; 85% score above 500 on mathematical, 40% above 600, 9% above 700; ACT, 24–28 composite. *Required:* SAT or ACT, recommendations, essay; interview recommended. Criteria considered in admissions, in order of importance: high school academic record, standardized test scores, writing sample, recommendations, extracurricular activities; other factors considered: special talents, alumni children, diverse student body, geographic diversity. Alternative admissions procedure, Portfolio Path, allows students to create a portfolio of materials that they feel best demonstrates the breadth and strength of their academic program; these students have the option of not submitting standardized test scores. *Entrance programs:* early decision, early admission, midyear admission, deferred admission, advanced placement. About 26% of entering students from private or parochial schools. *Apply* by February 1; rolling admissions. *Transfers* welcome; 92 enrolled 1993–94.

Academic Environment. Graduation requirements include year-long common syllabus course for freshmen; 3 semesters (or equivalent) of foreign language, 2 courses in international studies, 2 in natural sciences, 1 each in creative arts, quantitative reasoning, physical education. About 53% of students study abroad during their 4 years at LC. Degrees offered: bachelors, masters. *Majors offered* include: international affairs, English, biology, psychology, journalism, biochemistry, sociology/anthropology. Average undergraduate class size: 55% under 20, 41% 20–40, 4% over 40.

About 66% of students entering as freshmen graduate within four years; 77% of freshmen return for sophomore year. *Special programs:* independent study, study abroad, honors, undergraduate research, individualized majors, training teachers of the deaf, study at Merrill-Palmer Institute, 3–2 engineering, English as a Second Language through Institute for the study of American Language and Culture. *Calendar:* 3–3, summer school.

Undergraduate degrees conferred (486). 29% were in Social Sciences, 13% were in Business and Management, 11% were in Letters, 9% were in Psychology, 8% were in Communications, 7% were in Visual and Performing Arts, 5% were in Foreign Languages, 5% were in Life Sciences, 4% were in Physical Sciences, 3% were in Philosophy and Religion, remainder in 5 other fields.

Graduates Career Data. Advanced studies pursued by 57% of graduates. Medical schools typically enrolling largest numbers of graduates include Oregon Health Sciences U.; law schools include Northwestern, Wilamette; business schools include Keller, Emerson. About 75% of 1992–93 graduates employed. Career Development Services include aptitude testing, counseling, placement, resume/interview workshops, on-campus recruitment, library resources, internships.

Faculty. About 96% of faculty hold PhD or equivalent. About 79% of undergraduate classes taught by tenured faculty. About 30% of teaching faculty are female, 1% Black, 2% Hispanic, 4% other minority.

Student Body. About 32% of students from in state; 31% Northwest/West, 15% East/Midwest, 8% South, 6% foreign. An estimated 20% of students reported as Protestant, 10% Catholic, 5% Jewish, 3% other; 2% Black, 2% Hispanic, 10% Asian, 7% other minority. *Minority group students:* Moslem Student Group.

Religious Orientation. Lewis and Clark is historically related to the United Presbyterian Church; makes no religious demands on students.

Varsity Sports. Men (NAIA Div.II): Baseball, Basketball, Cross Country, Football, Golf, Swimming, Tennis, Track. Women (NAIA Div.II): Basketball, Cross Country, Softball, Swimming, Tennis, Track, Volleyball.

Campus Life. "Rules and campus policy are established through the peer group system in which students are delegated areas in which they establish policy and are held responsible for the decisions." Substantial number of cultural and social activities on campus, which are supplemented by the resources of Portland, 6 miles away. Cars permitted except for resident freshmen. Possession or use of alcoholic beverages conforms with state law—allowed for students over 21 in private areas only. Freshmen not living at home required to live on campus for 2 years; 7 coed residence halls, 1 women's residence hall. Intervisitation regulations established by student-run dorm councils; most dorms choose to prohibit smoking.

About 3% of women live in traditional dormitories; 23% of men, 25% of women in coed dormitories; 51% of men, 51% of women live in off-campus housing or commute. Freshmen given preference in college housing if all students cannot be accommodated. Sexes segregated in coed dormitories either by floor or suite. There is 1 fraternity on campus which about 1% of men join; no sororities. About 1% of men live in fraternities. About 2% of resident students leave campus on weekends.

Annual Costs. Tuition and fees, $15,051; room and board, $4,929; estimated $1,125 other, exclusive of travel. About 70% of students receive financial aid; average amount of assistance, $13,864. Assistance is typically divided 67% scholarship/grant, 23% loan, 10% work. College reports 30 scholarships awarded on the basis of academic merit alone, some for special talents alone, some for need alone. *Meeting Costs:* college offers 10-month payment plan, alternative loans.

Lewis-Clark State College

Lewiston, Idaho 83501 **(208) 799-2210**

A state-supported college located in a community of 40,000. Most convenient major airport: Nez Perce County.

Founded: 1893
Affiliation: State
Total Enrollment: 2,816 M, W (full-time)
Cost: < $10K
% Receiving Financial Aid: 65%
Admission: Non-selective
Application Deadline: Rolling

Admission. Graduates of accredited high schools with 15 units eligible; almost all applicants accepted, 89% actually enroll. *Required:* ACT; interview for nursing and vocational students. *Out-of-state* freshman applicants: college seeks students from out of state. State does not limit out-of-state enrollment. No special requirements for out-of-state applicants; all applicants accepted, 67% enroll. *Apply:* rolling admissions. *Transfers* welcome.
Academic Environment. *Degree:* BS. About 33% of general education requirements for graduation are elective; distribution requirements fairly numerous. About 25% of students entering as freshmen graduate eventually; 50% of freshmen return for sophomore year. *Special programs:* independent study, honors. *Calendar:* semester.
Undergraduate degrees conferred (197). 30% were in Business and Management, 21% were in Education, 18% were in Liberal/General Studies, 9% were in Health Sciences, 5% were in Social Sciences, 5% were in Protective Services, 4% were in Mathematics, 3% were in Letters, 3% were in Communications, remainder in 2 other fields.
Student Body. About 98% of students from Northwest.
Varsity Sports. Men (NAIA): Baseball, Basketball, Tennis. Women (NAIA): Basketball, Tennis, Volleyball.
Campus Life. About 8% of men, 5% of women live in traditional dormitories; no coed dormitories; rest live in off-campus housing or commute. Intervisitation in men's and women's dormitory rooms limited.
Annual Costs. Tuition and fees, $1,320 (out-of-state, $4,240); room and board, $3,026; estimated $1,305 for books and supplies. About 65% of students receive financial aid. College reports some scholarships awarded on the basis of academic merit alone.

Lewis University

Romeoville, Illinois 60441 (815) 838-0500

A co-educational, career-oriented university affiliated with the Christian Brothers which includes colleges of Arts and Sciences, Business, and Nursing. The campus is located in a town of 10,000, 30 miles southwest of Chicago. Most convenient major airport: O'Hare (Chicago).

Founded: 1874
Affiliation: Roman Catholic
Total Enrollment: 2,606
Cost: $10K–$20K
% Receiving Financial Aid: 75%
Admission: Non-selective
Application Deadline: August 26

Admission. Graduates of approved high schools with 15 units and C average who rank in top half of class eligible; 84% of applicants accepted, 42% of these actually enroll; 24% of freshmen graduate in top fifth of high school class, 53% in top two-fifths. Average freshman ACT scores, according to most recent data available: 22.0 composite. *Required:* ACT. About 31% of entering students from parochial schools. *Apply* by August 26. *Transfers* welcome.
Academic Environment. *Degrees:* BA, BS, BSN. *Majors offered* include arts and sciences, accounting, aviation maintenance, aviation administration, military science, avionics, non-destructive evaluation, business administration, computer science, management science, marketing, medical technology, nursing, social justice. Administration reports graduation requirements include completion of university core, major core, and major requirements. About 42% of students entering as freshmen graduate eventually; 63% of freshmen return for sophomore year. *Special programs:* CLEP, independent study, honors, internships. Adult programs: accelerated degree program for working adults in business administration. *Calendar:* semester, summer school.
Undergraduate degrees conferred (463). 35% were in Business and Management, 14% were in Health Sciences, 12% were in Protective Services, 7% were in Transportation and Material Moving, 5% were in Public Affairs, 4% were in Education, 4% were in Communications, 3% were in Psychology, 3% were in Liberal/General Studies, remainder in 10 other fields.
Graduates Career Data. According to most recent data available, graduate or professional study pursued immediately after graduation by 23% of students.
Faculty. About 58% of faculty hold PhD or equivalent.
Student Body. About 99% of students from in state. An estimated 60% of students reported as Catholic, 40% other; 30% as minority, according to most recent data available. *Minority group students:* special studies skill program.
Religious Orientation. Lewis is a church-related institution; course in Religious Dimension of Man required of all students.
Varsity Sports. Men (Div.II): Baseball, Basketball, Cross Country, Golf, Soccer, Tennis, Track. Women (Div.II): Basketball, Cross Country, Golf, Soccer, Softball, Tennis, Track.
Campus Life. Administration reports regulations governing curfew for women and intervisitation enforced "judiciously." Alcohol allowed on campus by those of legal age "only within confines of their residence room"; cars permitted. About 16% of men, 12% of women live in traditional or coed dormitories; rest live in off-campus housing or commute. Intervisitation in men's and women's dormitory rooms limited. Sexes segregated in coed dormitories either by wing or floor. There are 9 fraternities, 4 sororities on campus which 20% of men, 20% of women join. Fraternities and sororities provide no residence facilities. About 60% of resident students leave campus on weekends.
Annual Costs. Tuition and fees, $10,112; room and board, $4,340; estimated $1,600 other, exclusive of travel. About 75% of students receive financial aid; assistance is typically divided 69% scholarship, 21% loan, 10% work. University reports some scholarships awarded on the basis of academic merit alone. *Meeting Costs:* college offers monthly payment plan.

Liberty University

Lynchburg, Virginia 24506 (804) 582-2270

A church-related liberal arts college, Liberty is located in a small city in central Virginia.

Founded: 1971
Affiliation: Baptist
Total Enrollment: 10,549 M, W (full-time)
Cost: < $10K
% Receiving Financial Aid: 70%
Admission: Non-selective
Application Deadline: Aug. 1

Admission. High school graduates or the equivalent eligible; 92% of applicants accepted. *Required:* SAT or ACT, 3 references, "personal salvation experience with Jesus Christ." Apply by August 1. *Transfers* welcome.
Academic Environment. *Degree:* AB. About 50% of entering students graduate eventually.
Undergraduate degrees conferred (1067). 29% were in Business and Management, 13% were in Psychology, 11% were in Education, 10% were in Philosophy and Religion, 8% were in Liberal/General Studies, 6% were in Social Sciences, 6% were in Communications, 4% were in Health Sciences, 3% were in Home Economics, remainder in 9 other fields.
Student Body. About 33% of students from in state; 54% South, 23% Middle Atlantic, 8% each New England, Midwest, according to most recent data available.
Religious Orientation. All students reported as Protestant; 6% as minority.
Varsity Sports. Men (Div.II): Baseball (I), Basketball, Cross Country, Football, Golf, Soccer, Tennis, Track, Wrestling. Women (Div.II): Basketball, Cross Country, Track, Volleyball.
Campus Life. About 45% of men, 53% of women live in traditional dormitories; rest commute. Freshmen given preference in college housing if all students cannot be accommodated.
Annual Costs. Tuition and fees, $6,600; room and board, $4,380; estimated $600 other, exclusive of travel. About 70% of students receive financial aid. University reports some scholarships awarded on the basis of academic merit alone.

Life College

Marietta, Georgia 30060

An independent liberal arts college, affiliated with the Life Chiropractic College; most students are studying to meet prerequisites for the chiropractic college.

Founded: 1975
Affiliation: Independent

College for Lifelong Learning

Durham, New Hampshire 03824 **(603) 862-1692**

A unit of the University System of New Hampshire, the College for Lifelong Learning offers associate and baccalaureate programs for adult students.

Founded: 1972
Affiliation: State
Total Enrollment: 79 M, 153 W (full-time); 341 M, 1,183 W (part-time)
Cost: < $10K
% Receiving Financial Aid: 25%
Admission: Non-selective
Application Deadline: Rolling

Admissions. Criteria considered in admissions: writing sample, admissions interview. *Apply:* rolling admissions.
Academic Environment. Degrees offered: associates, bachelors. *Special programs:* January interterm, internships. Adult programs: all institutional programs designed for adult population.

Undergraduate degrees conferred (142): 63% were in Business and Management, 31% were in Multi/Interdisciplinary Studies, 6% were in Liberal/General Studies.
Graduates Career Data. Advanced studies pursued by 25% of graduates; 24% enter graduate school; 1% enter law school. About 90% of 1992–93 graduates employed. Career Development Services available.
Student Body. About 92% of students from in state; all from New England. Average age of undergraduate student: 36.
Annual Costs. Tuition and fees, $2,838; estimated book expenses, $450. About 25% of students receive financial aid. Assistance is typically divided 10% scholarship, 40% grant, 40% loan.

Limestone College

Gaffney, South Carolina 29340 **(803) 489-7151**

An independent college, located in a town of 19,000, 50 miles southwest of Charlotte, North Carolina. Most convenient major airport: Spartanburg/Greenville.

Founded: 1845
Affiliation: Independent
Total Enrollment: 324 M, W (full-time)
Cost: < $10K
% Receiving Financial Aid: 98%
Admission: Non-selective
Application Deadline: Rolling

Admission. Graduates of accredited high schools with 12–16 academic units eligible; 74% of applicants accepted, 43% of these actually enroll. Average freshman SAT scores: 420 verbal, 380 mathematical. *Required:* SAT or ACT, minimum high school GPA. Criteria considered in admissions, in order of importance: high school academic record and standardized test scores rank with equal importance, recommendations, extracurricular activities; other factors considered: special talents, alumni children, diverse student body, religious affiliation/commitment. *Apply:* rolling admissions. *Transfers* welcome; 32 enrolled 1993–94.
Academic Environment. Degrees offered: associates, bachelors. All general education requirements for graduation are elective; no distribution requirements. Average undergraduate class size: 80% under 20, 15% 20–40, 5% over 40. About 35% of students entering as freshmen graduate eventually. *Special programs:* Limestone Adventure Program (involves physical activity out-of-doors and classroom theory), KANTO (brings 40 Japanese students and their teachers to campus twice annually for 2 months). Adult programs: The Block Program: classes meet Monday, Tuesday, Thursday evenings for 11 sessions, students take one course per block. *Calendar:* semester, summer school.
Undergraduate degrees conferred (119). 51% were in Multi/Interdisciplinary Studies, 49% were in Business and Management.
Faculty. About 63% of faculty hold PhD or equivalent.
Student Body. About 87% of students from in state. An estimated 80% of students reported as Protestant, 11% Catholic, 6% Jewish, 2% unaffiliated, 1% other; 25% Black, 2% Hispanic, 1% Asian, 2% other minority, according to most recent data available.
Varsity Sports. Men (Div.I): Baseball, Basketball, Golf, Lacrosse, Soccer, Tennis. Women (Div.I): Basketball, Soccer, Softball, Tennis, Volleyball.
Campus Life. About 62% of men, 38% of women live in traditional dormitories; no coed dormitories; rest commute. Intervisitation in men's and women's dormitory rooms limited. There are 2 fraternities, 2 sororities on campus which about 12% of men, 23% of women join; they provide no residence facilities.
Annual Costs. Tuition and fees, $7,200; room and board, $3,600; estimated $1,427 other, exclusive of travel. About 98% of students receive financial aid; average amount of assistance, $8,000. Assistance is typically divided 33% scholarship, 33% loan, 33% work. College reports 80 scholarships awarded on the basis of academic merit alone, 115 for special talents alone, 40 for need alone. *Meeting Costs:* college offers AMS, Tuition Payment Plan.

Lincoln Memorial University

Harrogate, Tennessee 37752 **(615) 869-3611**

An independent institution, located in a small town a few miles south of Middlesboro, Kentucky (pop. 15,000), and 50 miles north of Knoxville. The university's Lincoln Museum houses the world's largest collection of Lincolniana. Most convenient major airport: McGhee-Tyson (Knoxville).

Founded: 1897
Affiliation: Independent
UG Enrollment: 382 M, 543 W (full-time); 120 M, 485 W (part-time)
Total Enrollment: 1,904
Cost: < $10K
% Receiving Financial Aid: 60%
Admission: Non-selective
Application Deadline: Aug. 1

Admission. Graduates of accredited or approved high schools eligible; 71% of applicants accepted, 65% of these actually enroll; 41% of freshmen graduate in top fifth of high school class, 68% in top two-fifths. Average freshman ACT scores: 22.4 M, 21.8 W composite. *Required:* SAT or ACT, minimum high school GPA. Criteria considered in admissions, in order of importance: high school academic record, standardized test scores, recommendations, extracurricular activities; other factors considered: special talents. *Entrance programs:* early decision, early admission, midyear admission, advanced placement. *Apply* by August 1; rolling admissions. *Transfers* welcome; 163 enrolled 1993–94.
Academic Environment. Degrees offered: associates, bachelors, masters. Graduation requirements include 12 semester hours of English or oral communication, 6 each of science and math, 9 of humanities or fine arts, 6 of behavioral science, 3 of U.S. history. *Majors offered* include communications, computer science, veterinary technology, wildlife management. Average undergraduate class size: 77% under 20, 18% 20–40, 5% over 40. About 56% of entering students graduate eventually; 84% of freshmen return for sophomore year. *Calendar:* quarter, summer school.
Undergraduate degrees conferred (170). 38% were in Education, 30% were in Business and Management, 5% were in Life Sciences, 4% were in Letters, 4% were in Communications, 3% were in Renewable Natural Resources, remainder in 11 other fields.
Graduates Career Data. Advanced studies pursued by 30% of students; 7% enter business school; 2% enter law school; 2% enter medical school; 1% enter dental school. About 70% of 1992–93 graduates employed.
Faculty. About 68% of faculty hold PhD or equivalent. About 51% of teaching faculty are female.
Student Body. About 57% of students from in state; 91% from South, 1% each New England, Middle Atlantic, West, 4% foreign. An estimated 2% of students reported as Black, 1% Hispanic, 1% Asian, 4% other minority. Average age of undergraduate student: 23.
Varsity Sports. Men (NCAA Div.II): Baseball, Basketball, Cross Country, Golf, Soccer, Tennis. Women (NCAA Div.II): Basketball, Cross Country, Softball, Tennis, Volleyball.
Campus Life. Campus is located in a rural area, students note "There are a few spots of entertainment, but mainly just shopping centers." However, they also report "an active student life", with sports, dances, and the Campus Center.

About 40% of men, 25% of women live in traditional dormitories; 10% each in coed dormitories; rest commute. Freshmen given preference in college housing if all students cannot be accommodated.

No intervisitation in men's or women's dormitory rooms. There are 3 fraternities, 3 sororities on campus which about 5% of men, 15% of women join; they provide no residence facilities. About 40% of resident students leave campus on weekends.
Annual Costs. Tuition and fees, $5,510; room and board, $2,708; estimated $1,500 other, exclusive of travel. About 60% of students receive financial aid; average amount of assistance, $5,500. Assistance is typically divided 25% scholarship, 40% grant, 20% loan, 15% work. University reports 100 scholarships awarded on the basis of academic merit alone, 50 for special talents alone, 150 for need alone.

Lincoln University

Jefferson City, Missouri 65102 (314) 681-5000

A state-supported university, located in the state capital (pop. 32,400), 125 miles west of St. Louis; founded as a college for Negroes but now serving a fully integrated student body with a majority of white students. Most convenient major airports: St. Louis, Kansas City.

Founded: 1866
Affiliation: State
Total Enrollment: 913 M, 1,106 W (full-time); 430 M, 851 W (part-time)
Cost: < $10K
% Receiving Financial Aid: 63%
Admission: Non-selective
Application Deadline: July 15

Admission. Graduates of accredited high schools eligible; 99% of applicants accepted, 49% of these actually enroll. About 12% of freshmen graduate in top fifth of high school class, 27% in top two-fifths. Average freshman ACT scores: 18 M, 19 W composite. *Required:* ACT. *Out-of-state* freshman applicants: state does not limit out-of-state enrollment. Requirement for out-of-state applicants: open admissions. About 99% of out-of-state students accepted, 33% of these actually enroll. States from which most out-of-state students are drawn: Illinois, Kansas, Nebraska, Michigan, Indiana, California. *Apply* by July 15; rolling admissions. *Transfers* welcome; 223 enrolled 1993–94.
Academic Environment. About 57% of general education credits for graduation are required; distribution requirements fairly numerous. Degrees offered: associates, bachelors, masters. Average undergraduate class size: 50% under 20, 42% 20–40, 8% over 40. About 49% of freshmen return for sophomore year. *Special programs:* CLEP, independent study, honors, cross-registration with U.of Missouri-Columbia, Westminster, William Woods, Columbia College, study abroad, internships, cooperative work-study programs. Adult programs: several programs designed for non-traditional students. *Calendar:* semester, summer school.
Undergraduate degrees conferred (209). 30% were in Business and Management, 29% were in Education, 7% were in Protective Services, 6% were in Social Sciences, 6% were in Engineering and Engineering Related Technology, 5% were in Marketing and Distribution, 4% were in Psychology, 3% were in Agricultural Sciences, remainder in 10 other fields.
Graduates Career Data. Advanced studies pursued by 60% of graduates, according to most recent data available.
Faculty. About 53% of faculty hold PhD or equivalent. About 46% of undergraduate classes taught by tenured faculty. About 21% of teaching faculty are Black, 7% other minority.
Student Body. About 80% of students from in state. An estimated 27% of students reported as Black, 4% other minority. Average age of undergraduate students: 25.
Varsity Sports. Men (Div.II): Baseball, Basketball, Golf, Soccer, Track. Women (Div.II): Basketball, Softball, Tennis, Track.
Campus Life. About 7% of men, 8% of women live in traditional dormitories; no coed dormitories; rest commute. Intervisitation in men's and women's dormitory rooms limited. There are 4 fraternities, 4 sororities on campus.
Annual Costs. Tuition and fees, $1,800 (out-of-state, $3,600); room and board, $2,728; estimated $1,975 other, exclusive of travel. About 63% of students receive financial aid; average amount of assistance, $3,086. Assistance is typically divided 18% scholarship, 29% grant, 42% loan, 11% work. University reports 187 scholarships awarded on the basis of academic merit alone, 386 for special talents alone.

Lincoln University of Pennsylvania

Lincoln University, Pennsylvania 19352 (215) 932-8300

A state-related institution, located in a small village, 45 miles southwest of Philadelphia, Lincoln was founded as a college for Negroes, is now interracial and international in character. An extensive compensatory program is offered for talented but disadvantaged students. Most convenient major airport: Philadelphia International.

Founded: 1854
Affiliation: Independent/State
Total Enrollment: 1,458 M, W (full-time)
Cost: < $10K
% Receiving Financial Aid: 72%
Admission: Non-selective
Application Deadline: January 1

Admission. Graduates of accredited high schools with 15 units eligible; 85% of applicants accepted, 33% of these actually enroll; 20% of freshmen graduate in top fifth of high school class, 44% in top two-fifths. Average freshman scores, according to most recent data available: SAT, 352 M, 355 W verbal, 384 M, 373 W mathematical. *Required:* SAT or ACT, interview. *Apply* by January 1; rolling admissions. *Transfers* welcome
Academic Environment. *Degree:* AB. About 58% of students entering as freshmen graduate eventually; 75% of freshmen return for sophomore year. *Majors offered* include criminal justice, sociology. *Special programs:* CLEP, study abroad, honors, undergraduate research, 3–2 engineering, pre-nursing. *Calendar:* early semester, January term.
Undergraduate degrees conferred (208). 26% were in Business and Management, 17% were in Social Sciences, 12% were in Physical Sciences, 8% were in Protective Services, 7% were in Public Affairs, 6% were in Life Sciences, 6% were in Education, 5% were in Letters, 4% were in Psychology, 3% were in Computer and Engineering Related Technology, remainder in 5 other fields.
Faculty. About 67% of faculty hold PhD or equivalent.
Student Body. About 95% of students from Middle Atlantic. An estimated 90% of students reported as Protestant, 3% Catholic, 3% unaffiliated, 4% other; 95% Black, 2% other minority, according to most recent data available.
Varsity Sports. Men (NCAA, ECAC, NAIA, IC4A): Baseball, Basketball, Cross Country, Soccer, Swimming, Track, Wrestling. Women (NCAA, ECAC, NAIA, IC4A): Basketball, Cross Country, Swimming, Track, Volleyball.
Campus Life. About 95% of men, 92% of women live in traditional dormitories; 3% of men, 7% of women live in coed dormitories; rest live in off-campus housing or commute. Intervisitation in men's and women's dormitory rooms unlimited. There are 4 fraternities, 3 sororities on campus which about 11% of men, 7% of women join.
Annual Costs. Tuition and fees, $3,140 (out-of-state, $4,650); room and board, $3,000; estimated $500 other, exclusive of travel. About 72% of students receive financial aid; assistance is typically divided 61% grant/scholarship, 26% loan, 13% work. College reports some scholarships awarded on the basis of academic merit alone.

Lindenwood College

St. Charles, Missouri 63301 (314) 949-4949

Lindenwood College is located on a 100-acre campus in a suburban community of 50,000, 20 miles northwest of downtown St. Louis. Most convenient major airport: Lambert International (St. Louis).

Founded: 1827
Affiliation: Independent (Presbyterian Church (USA))
UG Enrollment: 907 M, 1,248 W (full-time)
Total Enrollment: 3,137
Cost: < $10K
% Receiving Financial Aid: 80%
Admission: Non-selective
Application Deadline: Rolling

Admission. Graduates of accredited high schools with 16 units, an minimum high school GPA of 2.0 eligible; 50% of applicants accepted, 75% of these actually enroll; 21% of freshmen graduate in top fifth of high school class, 56% in top two-fifths. Average freshman ACT scores: 22 M, 22 W composite. *Required:* SAT or ACT. Criteria considered in admissions, in order of importance: standardized test scores, high school academic record, extracurricular activities, recommendations, writing sample; other factors considered: special talents, diverse student body, alumni children. *Entrance programs:* early decision, early admission, midyear admission. About 15% of entering students from private schools, 45% from parochial schools. *Apply:* rolling admissions. *Transfers* welcome; 374 enrolled 1993–94.

Academic Environment. Degrees offered: bachelors, masters. *Majors offered* include usual arts and sciences, fashion marketing, valuation science, communication arts (broadcasting, creative writing, film), a number of health related and pre-professional programs, human service management, studio art, music, theatre. Core requirements include 6 hours English composition, 9 hours humanities, 3 hours fine arts, 9 hours cross-cultural civilization, 9 hours social science, 13 hours natural sciences and mathematics. Internships and cooperative work-study programs are available in all areas, students are also strongly encouraged to complete at least one semester of community work service. Average undergraduate class size: 60% under 20, 37% 20–40, 3% over 40.

About 44% of students entering as freshmen graduate within four years; 44% of freshmen return for sophomore year. *Special programs:* CLEP, independent study, study abroad, undergraduate research, individualized majors, Washington Semester, internships, cross-registration with Greater St. Louis colleges (Fontbonne, Maryville, Webster), special program in business, 3–2 programs in engineering and social work. *Calendar:* semester, summer school.

Undergraduate degrees conferred (264). 63% were in Business and Management, 14% were in Communications, 7% were in Education, 4% were in Social Sciences, 3% were in Visual and Performing Arts, 3% were in Psychology, remainder in 6 other fields.

Graduates Career Data. Advanced studies pursued by 13% of students; 6% enter business school; 1% enter medical school. Business schools typically enrolling largest number of graduates include Lindenwood College. About 85% of 1992–93 graduates employed. Fields typically hiring largest number of graduates include management, government. Career Development Services include assessment, community work service and interviewing workshop, all graduates complete a "talent transcript" which is included in "LIONETWORK" catalog and distributed to potential employers.

Faculty. About 68% of faculty hold PhD or equivalent. About 98% of undergraduate classes taught by full-time faculty.

Student Body. College seeks a national student body; 89% of students from in state; 95% Midwest, 3% South, 2% Middle Atlantic, 1% West, 1% Northwest. An estimated 40% of students reported as Protestant, 49% Catholic, 1% Jewish, 10% unaffiliated; 8% Black, 1% Hispanic, 1% Asian, 6% other minority. Average age of undergraduate student: 22.

Religious Orientation. Lindenwood is an independent institution with covenanta relationship with the Presbyterian Church; makes no religious demands on students. Places of worship available in immediate community for major faiths.

Varsity Sports. Men (NAIA): Baseball, Basketball, Cross Country, Football, Golf, Soccer, Track, Wrestling. Women (NAIA): Basketball, Cross Country, Golf, Soccer, Softball, Tennis, Track, Volleyball.

Campus Life. Students participate with faculty and administration on committees; dormitories are self-governed; intervisitation during designated periods. About 45% of men, 40% of women live in traditional dormitories; 10% of men live in dormitory fraternities; 10% of men, 2% of women live in off-campus college-related housing; rest commute. Freshmen given preference in college housing if all students cannot be accommodated. There are 3 fraternities, 2 sororities on campus, which about 20% men, 8% women join. About 40% of resident students leave campus on weekends.

Annual Costs. Tuition and fees, $8,880; room and board, $4,600; estimated $1,500 other, exclusive of travel. About 80% of students receive financial aid; average amount of assistance, $10,000. Assistance is typically divided 50% scholarship/grant, 35% loan, 15% work. College reports 600 scholarships awarded on the basis of academic merit alone, 400 for special talents, 1,200 for need.

Linfield College

McMinnville, Oregon 97128 **(503) 434-2213**

An independent, liberal arts college with an "American Baptist heritage," located only forty minutes from the Pacific Coast, one hour from downtown Portland or skiing at Mt. Hood, in a community of 18,000, 25 miles northwest of Salem. Most convenient major airport: Portland International.

Founded: 1849
Affiliation: Independent (American Baptist)
Total Enrollment: 675 M, 886 W (full-time)
Cost: $10K–$20K
% Receiving Financial Aid: 95%
Admission: Selective
Application Deadline: February 15

Admission is selective. High school graduates considered on own merits in terms of past achievement and future promise; 75% of applicants accepted, 35% of these actually enroll; 61% of freshmen graduate in top fifth of high school class, 86% in top two-fifths. Average freshman SAT scores: 495 verbal, 556 mathematical; 45% score above 500 on verbal, 15% above 600, 4% above 700; 76% score above 500 on mathematical, 33% above 600, 7% above 700. *Required:* SAT or ACT, essay; interview recommended. Criteria considered in admissions, in order of importance: high school academic record, standardized test scores, recommendations, extracurricular activities, writing sample; other factors considered: special talents, diverse student body, alumni children. *Entrance programs:* early decision, early admission, mid-year admission, deferred admission, advanced placement. *Apply* by February 15. *Transfers* welcome; 55 enrolled 1993–94.

Academic Environment. Under Linfield College Plan, students may attend fall and spring semesters, with the summer off, or may opt for continuous enrollment for 12 months and then work for as long as 6 months before returning to the campus. Degrees offered: bachelors, masters (education only). Linfield is one of only five sites in the world to host Nobel Prize winners as part of the Oregon Nobel Laureate Symposium, where speakers not only lecture to large audiences but also spend time in classrooms and special sessions with students. Linfield also offers international programs in Japan, Costa Rica, Austria, England, and Korea, all transportation costs for study abroad programs are provided by the college. Students list small classes and personal interaction with professors as strengths of the academic program. *Special programs:* CLEP, independent study, January term, study abroad, honors program, nursing, undergraduate research, 3-year degree, individualized, self-designed, and cross-disciplinary majors, 3–2 programs in engineering, environmental studies, forestry, internship and cooperative work-study programs. Average undergraduate class size: 22. About 58% of entering freshman graduate within four years, 62% eventually; 78% of freshman return for sophomore year. Adult programs: Division of Continuing Education caters entire program to adult learners. *Calendar:* semester, 5-week "winter block," summer school.

Undergraduate degrees conferred (515). 38% were in Business and Management, 17% were in Health Sciences, 11% were in Liberal/General Studies, 10% were in Education, 6% were in Social Sciences, 4% were in Psychology, 3% were in Visual and Performing Arts, 3% were in Communications, remainder in 10 other fields.

Graduates Career Data. Advanced studies pursued by 33% of students. About 87% of 1992–93 graduates employed. Fields typically hiring largest numbers of graduates include education, retail, banking and finance, technical, scientific.

Faculty. About 92% of faculty hold PhD or equivalent. About 39% of teaching faculty are female; 3% ethnic minority.

Student Body. College seeks a national student body; 63% of students from in state; 75% Northwest, 13% West, 5% foreign. An estimated 47% of students reported as Protestant, 23% Catholic, 2% Jewish, 2% Muslim, 17% unaffiliated, 9% other.

Religious Orientation. Linfield is an independent, nonsectarian institution which "affirms its historic relationship with the American Baptist Church." General education core curriculum includes course in either Western religious heritage or living issues in philosophy. Attendance at chapel services voluntary.

Varsity Sports. Men (NAIA II): Baseball, Basketball, Cross Country, Football, Golf, Soccer, Swimming, Tennis, Track. Women (NAIA II): Baseball, Basketball, Cross Country, Soccer, Softball, Swimming, Tennis, Track, Volleyball.

Campus Life. About 26% of men, 40% of women live in traditional dormitories; 39% of men, 40% of women live in coed dormitories; 13% of men, 20% of women live in off-campus housing or commute. Intervisitation in men's and women's dormitory rooms limited. There are 4 fraternities, 3 sororities on campus which about 25% of men, 30% of women join; 22% of men live in fraternities; sororities provide no residence facilities. About 20% of resident students leave campus on weekends.

Annual Costs. Tuition and fees, $12,510; room and board, $3,970; estimated $1,800 other, exclusive of travel. About 95% of students receive financial aid; average amount of assistance, $9,579. Assistance is typically divided 57% scholarship, 37% loan, 6% work. College reports 375 scholarships awarded on the basis of academic merit alone, 127 for special talent (special music achievement scholarships for a select few), 898 for need.

Livingston College (N.J.)

(See Rutgers—The State University of New Jersey)

Livingston University

Livingston, Alabama 35470 (205) 652-9661

A state-supported institution, located in a town of 3,400, 116 miles southwest of Birmingham. Most convenient major airport: Birmingham.

Founded: 1835
Affiliation: State
UG Enrollment: 801 M, 958 W (full-time)
Total Enrollment: 1,985
Cost: < $10K
% Receiving Financial Aid: 75%
Admission: Non-selective
Application Deadline: Rolling

Admission. Graduates of accredited high schools with C average or better eligible; 83% of applicants accepted, 46% of these actually enroll. Average freshman ACT scores: 18.6 M, 18.9 W composite. *Required:* ACT. Criteria considered in admissions, in order of importance: high school academic record, standardized test scores. *Out-of-state* freshman applicants: state does not limit out-of-state enrollment; no limit; no special requirements. States from which most out-of-state students are drawn: Mississippi, Florida. *Entrance programs:* early decision, early admission, mid-year admission, deferred admission, advanced placement. *Apply:* rolling admission. *Transfers* welcome; 250 enrolled 1993–94.
Academic Environment. *Undergraduate studies* offered by colleges of General Studies, Business and Commerce, Education. Degrees offered: associates, bachelors, masters. About 33% of general education requirements for graduation are elective; distribution requirements fairly numerous. *Majors offered* in addition to usual studies include environmental science, marine biology, industrial management, athletic training, technology. Average undergraduate class size: 18. About 25% of entering freshman graduate within four years, 34% eventually; 55% of freshmen return for sophomore year. *Special programs:* CLEP, honors, independent study, 3–2 programs in engineering and textile chemistry, January term. *Calendar:* quarter, summer school.
Undergraduate degrees conferred (211). 46% were in Education, 22% were in Business and Management, 10% were in Social Sciences, 6% were in Life Sciences, 5% were in Multi/Interdisciplinary Studies, 3% were in Computer and Engineering Related Technology, 3% were in Letters, remainder in 4 other fields.
Faculty. About 60% of faculty hold PhD or equivalent. About 75% of undergraduate classes taught by tenured faculty.
Student Body. University seeks a national student body; 70% of students from in state; 95% South. An estimated 80% of students reported as Protestant; 27% as Black, 3% other minority, according to most recent data available.
Varsity Sports. Men (Div.II): Baseball, Basketball, Football, Tennis. Women (Div.II): Basketball, Softball, Tennis, Volleyball.
Campus Life. About 40% of men, 40% of women live in traditional dormitories; 10% of men, 10% of women live in fraternities or sororities; 20% of men, 20% of women live in off-campus college-related housing; rest commute. There are 6 fraternities, 4 sororities on campus which about 10% of men, 10% of women join. About 75% of resident students leave campus on weekends.
Annual Costs. Tuition and fees, $1,800; room and board, $2,400; estimated $750 other, exclusive of travel. About 80% of students receive financial aid; average amount of assistance, $3,000. University reports 300 scholarships awarded on the basis of special talent alone.

Livingstone College

Salisbury, North Carolina 28144 (704) 638-5502

A church-related institution, located in a city of 22,515, 45 miles northeast of Charlotte; founded as a college for Negroes and still serving a predominantly Black student body. Most convenient major airport: Douglas International (Charlotte).

Founded: 1879
Affiliation: African Methodist Episcopal Zion
Total Enrollment: 666 M, W (full-time)
Cost: < $10K
% Receiving Financial Aid: 96%
Admission: Non-selective
Application Deadline: 1 month before term

Admission. Graduates of approved high schools with 16 units or GED and recommendations eligible; 75% of applicants accepted, 44% of these actually enroll. *Required:* SAT or ACT; interview "desirable." Non-academic factors considered in admissions: special talents, alumni children, religious affiliation and/or commitment. *Apply* by 1 month prior to term. *Transfers* welcome.
Academic Environment. *Degrees:* AB, BS. About 42% of general education requirements for graduation are elective; distribution requirements fairly numerous. About 45% of students entering as freshmen graduate within four years; 20% of freshmen do not return for sophomore year. *Special programs:* dual-degree programs in engineering and pharmacy. *Calendar:* semester, summer school.
Undergraduate degrees conferred (77). 38% were in Business and Management, 21% were in Education, 10% were in Computer and Engineering Related Technology, 8% were in Social Sciences, 8% were in Psychology, 6% were in Public Affairs, 4% were in Letters, 3% were in Life Sciences, remainder in 2 other fields.
Varsity Sports. Men (Div.II): Basketball, Football, Golf, Tennis, Track, Wrestling. Women (Div.II): Basketball, Track, Volleyball.
Student Body. College seeks a national student body; 44% of students from in state; 64% South, 7% New England, 7% North Central. An estimated 55% of students reported as Protestant, 1% Catholic, 36% unaffiliated, 8% other; 98% Black, 1% other minority, according to most recent data available.
Religious Orientation. Livingstone is a church-related institution; 4 hours of religion, attendance at weekly assembly (for credit) and monthly vespers required of all students.
Campus Life. About 75% of men, 97% of women live in traditional dormitories; no coed dormitories; rest commute. No intervisitation in men's or women's dormitory rooms. There are 4 fraternities, 3 sororities which about 10% of men, 10% of women join, they provide no residence facilities. About 90% of resident students leave campus on weekends.
Annual Costs. Tuition and fees, $5,200; room and board, $3,400. About 96% of students receive financial aid; assistance is typically divided 50% scholarship, 25% loan, 25% work. College reports some scholarships awarded on the basis of academic merit alone. *Meeting Costs:* college offers PLUS Loans.

Lock Haven University of Pennsylvania

Lock Haven, Pennsylvania 17745 (717) 893-2027

A state-supported university, located in a town of 9,600, 25 miles southwest of Williamsport. Most convenient major airport: Williamsport, Harrisburg.

Founded: 1870
Affiliation: State
Total Enrollment: 3,712 M, W (full-time)
Cost: < $10K
% Receiving Financial Aid: 80%
Admission: Non-selective
Application Deadline: Rolling

Admission. Graduates of approved high schools with college preparatory course who rank in top two-fifths of class eligible; 53% of applicants accepted; 36% of these actually enroll. About 45% of freshmen graduate in top fifth of high school class, 83% in top two-fifths. Average freshman SAT scores, according to most recent data available: 463 M, 468 W verbal, 542 M, 506 W mathematical.

Required: SAT or ACT. *Out-of-state* freshman applicants: no special requirements for out-of-state applicants. *Apply:* rolling admissions. *Transfers* welcome.
Academic Environment. *Degrees:* AB, BS, BSEd, BFA. About 25% of general education requirements for graduation are elective; distribution requirements fairly numerous. About 50% of students entering as freshmen graduate eventually; 30% of freshmen do not return for sophomore year. *Special programs:* independent study, study abroad, undergraduate research, internships, 3–2 engineering with Penn State. *Calendar:* semester, summer school.
Undergraduate degrees conferred (527). 35% were in Education, 12% were in Business and Management, 8% were in Communications, 7% were in Health Sciences, 7% were in Parks and Recreation, 5% were in Social Sciences, 5% were in Psychology, 5% were in Multi/Interdisciplinary Studies, 3% were in Public Affairs, 3% were in Life Sciences, remainder in 10 other fields.
Faculty. More than 50% of faculty hold PhD or equivalent.
Varsity Sports. Men (Div.II): Baseball, Basketball, Cross Country, Football, Golf, Soccer, Tennis, Track, Wrestling (I). Women (Div.II): Basketball, Cross Country, Field Hockey, Gymnastics, Lacrosse, Softball, Swimming, Tennis, Track.
Student Body. University welcomes a national student body; 78% of students from in state; 91% Middle Atlantic. An estimated 3% of students reported as Black, 1% Asian.
Campus Life. About 12% of students live in traditional dormitories; 37% of students in coed dormitories; rest live in off-campus housing or commute. There are 8 fraternities, 4 sororities which about 15% of students join. Intervisitation in men's and women's dormitory rooms limited. Sexes segregated in coed dormitories by floor. About 25–30% of resident students leave campus on weekends.
Annual Costs. Tuition and fees, $3,260 (out-of-state, $6,654); room and board, $3,524. About 80% of students receive financial aid. University reports some scholarships awarded on the basis of academic merit alone. *Meeting Costs:* university offers deferred payment plan.

Loma Linda University

Riverside, California 92505 (714) 785-2176

A church-related institution, Loma Linda offers instruction on 2 main campuses in the Los Angeles area; "provides a distinctly religious setting for education." The university's campus in Riverside (pop. 145,000) includes the College of Arts and Sciences and School of Education. On the original campus in Loma Linda (pop. 10,000) are professional schools offering programs in dental hygiene, dentistry, dietetics, medical record administration, medical technology, medicine, nursing, occupational and physical therapy, public health, radiological technology. Most convenient major airport: Ontario.

Founded: 1905
Affiliation: Seventh-day Adventist
UG Enrollment: 443 M, 546 W (full-time); 64 M, 76 W (part-time)
Total Enrollment: 2,263
Cost: < $10K
% Receiving Financial Aid: 80%
Admission: Non-selective
Application Deadline: August 15

Admission. Graduates of accredited high schools with C average eligible; 65% of applicants accepted, 40% of these actually enroll; 32% of freshmen graduate in top fifth of high school class. Average freshman scores, according to most recent data available: SAT, 460 M, 440 W verbal, 500 M, 480 W mathematical; ACT, 20.3 M, 19.5 W composite. *Required:* SAT or ACT. About 70% of entering students from parochial schools. *Apply* by August 15. *Transfers* welcome.
Academic Environment. *Degrees:* AB, BS, BM. *Special programs:* CLEP, independent study. Adult programs: Center for Lifelong Learning offers evening programs for associate, bachelors, and masters degrees. *Calendar:* quarter, summer school.
Undergraduate degrees conferred (268). 63% were in Allied Health, 26% were in Health Sciences, 6% were in Life Sciences, 4% were in Home Economics.
Faculty. About 70% of faculty hold PhD or equivalent.
Student Body. Most of students from West/Northwest. An estimated 76% of students reported as Protestant, 5% Catholic, 8% unaffiliated; 8% Black, 15% Hispanic, 36% Asian, 2% Native American, according to most recent data available.
Religious Orientation. University is a church-related institution; course each year in religion, attendance at chapel and religious services required of all students.
Campus Life. About 17% of men, 21% of women live in traditional dormitories; no coed dormitories. No intervisitation in men's or women's dormitory rooms. About 66% of students leave campus on weekends.
Annual Costs. Tuition and fees, $9,435; room and board, $3,246; estimated $2,052 other, exclusive of travel. About 80% of students receive financial aid. College reports some scholarships awarded on the basis of academic merit alone.

Long Island University

University Center, Brookville, New York 11548

A university of arts and sciences, with professional schools and programs, offering associate, baccalaureate, masters and doctoral degrees as well as certificate programs. University comprises Brooklyn Campus, C. W. Post College, (Greenvale, L.I.), Southampton Campus, Brentwood Campus (Suffolk County, L.I.), Rockland Campus and Westchester Campus. The nonsectarian co-educational institution offers undergraduate, graduate and professional programs (days, evenings, weekends) on its various campuses.

LIU–Brooklyn Campus

University Plaza, Brooklyn, New York 11201 (718) 403-1011

Oldest unit of the university, the Brooklyn Campus offers undergraduate instruction through the Richard L. Conolly College of Liberal Arts and Sciences, the School of Business, Public Administration and Information Sciences, the School of Communications, Visual and Performing Arts, The School of Health Professions, and the Arnold and Marie Schwartz College of Pharmacy and Health Sciences. The 22-acre campus is located in downtown Brooklyn, "in the midst of many cultural, business and governmental institutions." Most convenient major airport: LaGuardia.

Founded: 1926
Affiliation: Independent
Total Enrollment: 980 M, 1,718 W (full-time)
Cost: $10K–$20K
% Receiving Financial Aid: 84%
Admission: Non-selective
Application Deadline: Rolling

Admission. High school graduates with 16 academic units and B-average or better eligible; 79% of applicants accepted, 49% of these actually enroll. *Required:* minimum SAT of 800 combined. *Apply:* rolling admissions. *Transfers* welcome.
Academic Environment. *Degrees:* BA, BS. *Majors offered* include usual arts and sciences, accounting, business, computer science, education, journalism, marketing, nursing, pharmacy, pharmacy administration and other health sciences. *Special programs:* CLEP, independent study, United Nations Semester, honors, undergraduate research, facilities for disabled students. *Calendar:* semester, summer school.
Undergraduate degrees conferred (470). 50% were in Health Sciences, 11% were in Business and Management, 10% were in Allied Health, 5% were in Multi/Interdisciplinary Studies, 4% were in Social Sciences, 4% were in Psychology, 4% were in Communications, 3% were in Education, 3% were in Life Sciences, remainder in 6 other fields.
Graduates Career Data. According to most recent data available, full-time graduate or professional study pursued immediately after graduation by 65% of students; 10% enter medical school; 4% enter dental school; 6% enter law school; 21% enter business school. *Careers in business and industry* pursued by 40% of graduates. Corporations typically hiring largest numbers of graduates include Con Edison, IBM.
Varsity Sports. Men (Div.I): Baseball, Basketball, Cross Country, Golf, Soccer, Tennis, Track. Women (Div. I): Basketball, Cross Country, Golf, Softball, Tennis, Track.
Student Body. LIU–Brooklyn does not seek a national student body; 95% of students from New York State. An estimated 47% of

students reported as Black, 13% Hispanic, 7% Asian, 13% unknown, according to most recent data available.

Campus Life. About 10% of students live in coed dormitory; rest live in off-campus housing or commute. Intervisitation in men's and women's dormitory rooms limited. Sexes segregated in coed dormitory by floor.

Annual Costs. Tuition and fees, $10,805; room and board, $5,790. About 84% of students receive financial aid; assistance is typically divided 53% scholarship, 40% loan, 7% work. College reports some scholarships awarded on the basis of academic merit alone.

LIU–C. W. Post College

Brookville, New York 11548 (516) 299-2413

Primarily a liberal arts institution offering a variety of professional/vocational studies, C. W. Post also includes School of Business Administration and Graduate School. The 350-acre campus is located in a rural suburban area of Long Island, 25 miles east of Manhattan.

Founded: 1954
Affiliation: Independent
UG Enrollment: 1,652 M, 2,038 W (full-time); 362 M, 705 W (part-time)
Total Enrollment: 8,110
Cost: $10K–$20K
% Receiving Financial Aid: 75%
Admission: Non-selective
Application Deadline: Rolling

Admission. Graduates of accredited high schools, preferably with rank in top half of class, eligible; 79% of applicants accepted, 29% of these actually enroll. Average freshman SAT scores: 479 verbal, 547 mathematical; 41% of entering freshman score above 500 on verbal, 10% above 600; 68% score above 500 on mathematical, 27% above 600. *Required:* SAT or ACT, minimum high school academic average of 75; audition or portfolio for art, music, theater; interview recommended. Criteria considered in admissions, in order of importance: high school academic record, standardized test scores, recommendations, writing sample. *Entrance programs:* early admission, midyear admission, deferred admission, academic remediation. About 29% of entering students from private schools. *Apply:* rolling admissions. *Transfers* welcome; 743 enrolled 1993–94.

Academic Environment. Degrees offered: associates, bachelors, masters, doctoral. *Majors offered* within areas of arts and sciences, accounting, business, public service, health professions, education, visual and performing arts. Core requirements include 8 credits lab science, 9 credits history and philosophy, 6 credits each in language and literature, arts, social sciences, 3 credits in mathematics. Average undergraduate class size: 12. About 63% of students entering as freshmen graduate within four years; 69% of freshmen return for sophomore year. *Special programs:* CLEP, honors, undergraduate research, study abroad, optional January and May mini-semesters, branch campus at Brentwood jointly sponsored with St. Joseph's College of Brooklyn, Weekend College, 3–2 pre-engineering. Adult programs: office of adult student services, return to learning seminars, on-campus child care services. *Calendar:* semester, summer school.

Undergraduate degrees conferred (962). 36% were in Business and Management, 13% were in Education, 12% were in Social Sciences, 7% were in Communications, 6% were in Visual and Performing Arts, 6% were in Protective Services, 5% were in Psychology, 3% were in Letters, 3% were in Life Sciences, remainder in 9 other fields.

Faculty. About 87% of faculty hold PhD or equivalent.

Student Body. College seeks a national student body; 66% of students from in state; 71% Middle Atlantic, 25% New England, 4% foreign.

Varsity Sports. Men (Div.II): Baseball(I), Basketball, Cross Country, Football, Lacrosse, Soccer, Track. Women (Div.II): Basketball, Cross Country, Field Hockey, Softball, Track, Volleyball.

Campus Life. Students describe the suburban Long Island campus as beautiful and appreciate the proximity of New York City. The Commuter Service Association addresses the needs of the many nonresidential students. About 33% of students live in dormitories; rest commute. Intervisitation in men's and women's dormitory rooms unlimited. Sexes segregated in coed dormitories either by wing or floor. There are 10 fraternities, 10 sororities on campus, which about 6% men, 4% women join; they provide no residence facilities. About 30% of resident students leave campus on weekends.

Annual Costs. Tuition and fees, $11,590; room and board, $5,280; estimated $1,000 other, exclusive of travel. About 75% of students receive financial aid. University reports some scholarships awarded on the basis of academic merit alone.

LIU–Southampton College

Southampton, New York 11968 (516) 283-4000

Youngest of the university's campuses, Southampton is a liberal arts college, located near a rural resort community of 5,200 in Suffolk County, at the eastern end of Long Island, 90 miles from New York City. Most convenient major airport: Long Island MacArthur.

Founded: 1963
Affiliation: Independent
UG Enrollment: 462 M, 693 W (full-time)
Total Enrollment: 1,269
Cost: $10K–$20K
% Receiving Financial Aid: 85%
Admission: Non-selective
Application Deadline: Rolling

Admission. High school graduates who rank in top two-thirds of high school class eligible; 88% of applicants accepted, 30% of these actually enroll; 20% of freshmen graduate in top fifth of high school class, 60% in top two-fifths. Average freshman SAT scores: 478 verbal, 506 mathematical. *Required:* SAT. Criteria considered in admissions, in order of importance: high school academic record, standardized test scores, recommendations, extracurricular activities, writing sample. *Entrance programs:* midyear admission, deferred admission, advanced placement. *Apply:* rolling admissions. *Transfers* welcome; 158 enrolled 1993–94.

Academic Environment. Degrees offered: bachelors, masters. *Majors offered* include marine science, environmental science, English/writing. Oceanside location of school provides unique opportunities for marine science studies. Core requirements include 3 fundamental English courses, 2 courses from each of humanities, social sciences, natural sciences, 1 course from fine arts. Students report that classes are small and personal, the faculty is accessible, and computer and library facilities are more than adequate, college has 12:1 ratio of students to computers, and all dorm rooms have hook-ups. Average undergraduate class size: 90% under 20, 10% 20–40. *Special programs:* optional intersession, LIU Plan, CLEP, independent study, co-operative education, undergraduate research, honors, 3-year degree, Seamester Travel Term (9 weeks at sea in the Caribbean), tropical marine biology, study abroad, January term, Higher Education Opportunity Program. About 94% of entering freshman graduate within 4 years, 6% graduate eventually. *Library:* 139,000 volumes, 625 periodicals, national depository for government documents; hours until 11 PM (earlier on weekends). *Calendar:* semester.

Undergraduate degrees conferred (216). 24% were in Business and Management, 18% were in Life Sciences, 14% were in Education, 9% were in Psychology, 9% were in Visual and Performing Arts, 7% were in Multi/Interdisciplinary Studies, 7% were in Social Sciences, 6% were in Letters, 4% were in Communications, remainder in 2 other fields.

Graduates Career Data. Advanced studies pursued by 55% of students; of these, 5% enter law school; 10% enter business school; 2% enter medical school. About 81% of 1992–93 graduates employed. Fields typically hiring largest number of graduates include marine science, environmental science, business, education.

Faculty. About 88% of faculty hold PhD or equivalent. About 85% of undergraduate classes taught by tenured faculty. About 25% of teaching faculty are female; 3% Hispanic, 6% other minority.

Student Body. College seeks a national student body; 67% of students from in state; 73% Middle Atlantic, 22% New England, 4% South, 2% West, 17 foreign students 1993–94. An estimated 8% of students reported as Black, 4% Hispanic, 1% Asian, 1% other minority.

Varsity Sports. Men (Div.II): Basketball, Lacrosse (III), Soccer, Volleyball. Women (Div.II): Basketball, Soccer, Softball, Volleyball.

Campus Life. College "encourages students to participate in the development of the life of the college community," including residence hall policy making. Students report that outside of classes they enjoy the movies, clubs, shops of Southampton, and, most of all, the "BEACH." About 4% of women live in traditional dormitories; 51% of men, 57% of women live in coed dormitories; rest commute. On-campus housing is guaranteed. Intervisitation in men's and women's dormitory rooms unlimited. Sexes segregated in coed dormitories by suite. There are no fraternities or sororities. About 15% of resident students leave campus on weekends.

Annual Costs. Tuition and fees, $11,800; room and board, $5,500; estimated $400 other, exclusive of travel. About 85% of students receive financial aid. Assistance is typically divided 70% scholarship, 15% grant, 10% loan, 5% work. University reports some scholarships awarded on the basis of academic merit alone.

Longwood College

Farmville, Virginia 23909 (800) 281-4677

A state-supported, co-educational comprehensive and teachers college, located in a town of 7,500, 50 miles east of Lynchburg and 65 miles west of Richmond.

Founded: 1839
Affiliation: State
UG Enrollment: 941 M, 1,933 W (full-time)
Total Enrollment: 3,360
Cost: < $10K
% Receiving Financial Aid: 60%
Admission: Non-selective
Application Deadline: November 15

Admission. Graduates of accredited high schools with 8 units in academic subjects who rank in top half of class eligible; 68% of applicants accepted, 39% of these actually enroll; 32% of freshmen graduate in top fifth of high school class, 73% in top two-fifths. Freshman SAT scores: 455 verbal, 497 mathematical; 28% score above 500 on verbal, 2% above 600; 50% score above 500 on mathematical, 7% above 600, 2% above 700. *Required:* SAT or ACT, essay, minimum GPA; interview recommended. Criteria considered in admissions, in order of importance: high school academic record, standardized test scores, extracurricular activities, writing sample, recommendations; other factors considered: special talents, alumni children, diverse student body. *Out-of-state* freshman applicants: college actively seeks students from out-of-state. State does not limit out-of-state enrollment. About 157 out-of-state students accepted, 28 of these actually enrolled. States from which most out-of-state students are drawn: New York, New Jersey, Maryland, Delaware. *Entrance programs:* early action, early admission, midyear admission. *Apply* by November 15 for early action, February 15 (priority); rolling admissions. *Transfers* welcome; 208 enrolled 1993–94.

Academic Environment. Degrees offered: bachelors, masters. *Majors offered* in addition to usual arts and sciences include therapeutic recreation, drama therapy, liberal studies for elementary education. General education requirements for graduation include 33 semester hours of courses which promote "development if disciplined, informed and creative minds." The administration reports that Longwood places emphasis on quality teaching and individualized attention. Average undergraduate class size: 48% under 20, 43% 20–40, 9% over 40; "nearly all classes have fewer than 30 students." About 45% of students entering as freshmen graduate within 4 years, 55% graduate eventually; 80% of freshmen return for sophomore year. *Special programs:* CLEP, study abroad, honors, 3-year degree, cross-registration with Hampden-Sydney, 3–2, 2–2 engineering, pre-professional medical, 3–1 speech pathology and audiology, combined degree programs in nursing, medical technology. *Calendar:* semester, summer school.

Undergraduate degrees conferred (599). 30% were in Business and Management, 24% were in Education, 14% were in Social Sciences, 8% were in Psychology, 5% were in Physical Sciences, 5% were in Life Sciences, 4% were in Visual and Performing Arts, 4% were in Letters, remainder in 5 other fields.

Graduates Career Data. Advanced studies pursued by 14% of students; 1% enter law school; 3% enter business school; 2% enter medical school. Law schools typically enrolling largest numbers of graduates include George Mason; medical schools include U. of Virginia. About 95% of 1992–93 graduates employed. Fields typically hiring largest numbers of graduates include education, business, state government. Career Development Services include resource library for career exploration, computerized career guidance systems.

Faculty. About 59% of faculty hold PhD or equivalent. About 59% of undergraduate classes taught by tenured faculty. About 33% of teaching faculty are female; 4% Black; 1% other minority.

Student Body. College seeks a national student body; 90% of students from in state; 99% Middle Atlantic, 1% foreign. An estimated 8% of students reported as Black, 1% Asian, 1% Hispanic, 1% other minority.

Varsity Sports. Men (Div.II): Baseball, Basketball, Golf, Soccer, Tennis, Wrestling. Women (Div.II): Basketball, Field Hockey, Golf, Lacrosse, Softball, Tennis.

Campus Life. Student and administration representatives agree that "school spirit still exists here." Cars allowed, but parking is difficult.

About 21% of women live in traditional dormitories; 78% of men, 62% of women live in coed dormitories; 8% of women live in sororities; rest either live in off-campus college-related housing or commute. Freshmen given preference in college housing if all students cannot be accommodated. Intervisitation in women's dormitory rooms allowed. There are 8 fraternities, 10 sororities on campus which about 27% of men, 22% of women join. About 20% of resident students leave campus on weekends.

Annual Costs. Tuition and fees, $4,106 (out-of-state, $9,190); room and board, $3,694; estimated $1,000 other, exclusive of travel. About 60% of students receive financial aid; average amount of assistance, $6,220. College reports 255 scholarships awarded on the basis of academic merit alone, 84 for special talents, 151 for need alone.

Loras College

Dubuque, Iowa 52004 (319) 588-7236

A church-related, liberal arts college conducted by the Archdiocese of Dubuque. Located on a 60-acre campus in a city of 62,300, Loras carries on cooperative programs with Clarke College and the University of Dubuque. Most convenient major airport: Dubuque Regional.

Founded: 1839
Affiliation: Roman Catholic
Total Enrollment: 1,644 M, W (full-time)
Cost: $10K–$20K
% Receiving Financial Aid: 75%
Admission: Selective
Application Deadline: April 1

Admission is selective. About 45% of applicants accepted, 82% of these actually enroll; 27% of freshmen graduate in top fifth of high school class, 65% in top two-fifths. Average freshman ACT scores, according to most recent data available: 21.5 composite. *Required:* ACT or SAT. *Non-academic factors* considered in admissions: religious affiliation and/or commitment, extra-curricular activities. *Entrance programs:* midyear admission, advanced placement. About 1% of entering students from private schools, 36% from parochial schools. *Apply* by April 1. *Transfers* welcome.

Academic Environment. Administration reports 20% of courses needed for graduation are required; some distribution requirements. *Degrees:* AB, BS, BM. *Majors offered* include usual arts and sciences, accounting, business, computer science, medical technology, public relations, international studies, human resources.

About 57% of entering students graduate eventually; 20% of freshmen do not return for sophomore year. *Special programs:* honors, credit by examination, individualized majors, independent study, 3–1 medical technology, 2–2 nursing, 3–2 engineering. *Calendar:* semester, summer school.

Undergraduate degrees conferred (277). 47% were in Business and Management, 12% were in Social Sciences, 10% were in Communications, 8% were in Education, 6% were in Letters, 6% were in Psychology, 4% were in Life Sciences, remainder in 6 other fields.

Graduates Career Data. According to most recent data available, full-time graduate or professional study pursued immediately after graduation by 15% of students. *Careers in business and industry:* Corporations typically hiring largest numbers of graduates include William C. Brown Publisher, Cottingham & Butler, Arthur Andersen, Osco Drug Co. *Career Counseling Program:* Student assessment of program reported as good for career guidance and fair for job placement. Alumni reported as active in both career guidance and job placement.

Faculty. About 59% of faculty hold PhD or equivalent.

Student Body. College seeks a national student body; 59% of students from in state; 95% North Central, 3% foreign. An estimated 80% of students reported as Catholic, 15% Protestant, 5% unaffiliated; 2% as Black, 1% other minority, according to most recent data available.

Religious Orientation. Loras is a Catholic institution; Loras Parish Council coordinates and plans liturgical and religious activities on

campus. Religious clubs on campus include St. Vincent de Paul; daily Mass. Places of worship available on campus for Catholics, in immediate community for major faiths.
Varsity Sports. Men (Div.III): Baseball, Basketball, Cross Country, Football, Golf, Soccer, Swimming, Tennis, Track, Wrestling. Women (Div.III): Basketball, Cross Country, Golf, Softball, Swimming, Tennis, Track, Volleyball.
Campus Life. About 27% of men, 18% of women live in traditional dormitories; 19% of men, 38% of women in coed dormitories; rest live in off-campus housing or commute. Freshmen given preference in college housing if all students cannot be accommodated. Sexes segregated in coed dormitories by wing or floor. There are 3 fraternities, 5 sororities; they provide no residence facilities. About 40% of resident students leave campus on weekends.
Annual Costs. Tuition and fees, $10,580; room and board, $3,660. About 75% of students receive financial aid; assistance is typically divided 68% scholarship, 25% loan, 7% work. College reports some scholarships awarded on the basis of academic merit alone. *Meeting Costs:* college offers loan programs, Alumni Grant for children of alumni.

Louise Salinger Academy of Fashion

San Francisco, California 94105

An independent college of fashion design and fashion merchandising offering associates and bachelors degrees. Programs include associates degree in millinery, minor in theater costume design. Criteria considered in admissions, in order of importance: school administered aptitude test, recommendations, portfolio. Graduates typically hired by fashion design companies, manufacturers, retail stores, theatrical costumers.

Affiliation: Independent

Louisiana College

Pineville, Louisiana 71360 **(318) 487-7386**

A church-related college, located in a community of 9,000, near Alexandria. Most convenient major airport: Baton Rouge.

Founded: 1906
Affiliation: Southern Baptist
Total Enrollment: 992 M, W (full-time)
Cost: < $10K
% Receiving Financial Aid: 77%
Admission: Non-selective
Application Deadline: Rolling

Admission. Graduates of accredited high schools with 17 units who rank in top half of class, C average, or ACT composite of 18 eligible; 64% of applicants accepted, 39% of these actually enroll. Average freshman ACT scores, according to most recent data available: 19.8 composite. *Required:* ACT. *Apply:* rolling admissions. *Transfers* welcome.
Academic Environment. *Degrees:* BA, BS, BM. About 51% of general education requirements for graduation are elective; distribution requirements fairly numerous. *Special programs:* CLEP, independent study, study abroad, honors, undergraduate research, 3-year degree, individualized majors, interdisciplinary studies. Adult programs: Continuing Education. *Calendar:* semester, summer school.
Undergraduate degrees conferred (178). 26% were in Education, 15% were in Business and Management, 11% were in Health Sciences, 7% were in Public Affairs, 6% were in Life Sciences, 5% were in Psychology, 4% were in Visual and Performing Arts, 4% were in Theology, 4% were in Liberal/General Studies, 3% were in Letters, 3% were in Law, remainder in 10 other fields.
Faculty. About 64% of faculty hold PhD or equivalent.
Varsity Sports. Men (NAIA): Baseball, Basketball. Women (NAIA): Basketball.
Student Body. College does not seek a national student body; 95% of students from in state.
Religious Orientation. Louisiana is a church-related institution; 6 hours of religion, attendance at chapel services required of all students.

Campus Life. About 48% of men, 38% of women live in traditional dormitories or on-campus apartments; rest live in off-campus housing or commute. No intervisitation in men's or women's dormitory rooms. There are 2 fraternities, 3 sororities on campus which about 8% of men, 11% of women join; they provide no residence facilities.
Annual Costs. Tuition and fees, $4,770; room and board, $2,984. About 77% of students receive financial aid; assistance is typically divided 40% scholarship, 53% loan, 7% work. College reports some scholarships awarded on the basis of academic merit alone. *Meeting Costs:* college offers AMS Loans.

Louisiana State University and Agricultural and Mechanical College System

Baton Rouge, Louisiana 70802

The LSU System, composed of 8 institutions on 10 campuses, was established by the Louisiana legislature in 1965. Louisiana State University and Agricultural College, the oldest and largest institution in the LSU System, is an influential factor in the state through its instruction, research, and service. Other components of the system are the LSU Agricultural Center in Baton Rouge which includes the Louisiana Agricultural Experiment Station and the Louisiana Cooperative Extension Service; the Paul M. Herbert Law Center, also in Baton Rouge; the LSU Medical Center, with 2 campuses in New Orleans, 1 in Shreveport, includes the schools of Allied Health Professions, Medicine, Dentistry, Nursing, and a Graduate School; the University of New Orleans and LSU in Shreveport are both 4-year institutions; LSU at Alexandria and Eunice are both 2-year institutions.

Louisiana State University and Agricultural and Mechanical College

Baton Rouge, Louisiana 70803 **(504) 388-1175**

The oldest and largest campus of the LSU system is located on a 1,944-acre tract on the southern edge of the state capital. Most convenient major airport: Baton Rouge.

Founded: 1860
Affiliation: State
UG Enrollment: 8,725 M, 8,731 W (full-time); 1,344 M, 1,922 W (part-time)
Total Enrollment: 25,667
Cost: < $10K
Admission: Non-selective
Application Deadline: Rolling

Admission. Qualified Louisiana residents who are graduates of state-approved high schools admitted; others considered on basis of test scores; 77% of applicants accepted, 62% of these actually enroll. Average freshman scores, according to most recent data available: ACT, 23.0 M, 22.0 W composite. *Required:* ACT. *Out-of-state* freshman applicants: state does not limit out-of-state enrollment. No special requirements for out-of-state applicants. *Apply:* rolling admissions. *Transfers* welcome.
Academic Environment. Specific course and distribution requirements vary with major. All freshmen enroll in Junior Division for 1 year. *Undergraduate studies* offered by colleges of Arts and Sciences (including schools of Geoscience, Journalism), Agriculture (including schools of Forestry and Wildlife Management, Home Economics, Vocational Education), Business Administration, Chemistry and Physics, Education, Engineering, schools of Environmental Design, Music. *Majors offered* in 128 fields; majors in Arts and Sciences, in addition to usual studies, include anthropology, astronomy, family and community living (for women), geography, journalism, law enforcement, microbiology, Portuguese.

Special programs: CLEP, independent study, study abroad, honors, undergraduate research, cross-registration with Southern U., cooperative work/study program in engineering, combined programs in arts/medicine or law, business administration/law, engineering/business administration. Adult programs: Program for Adult Special Students (PASS) for individuals who have been out of school for three years or more. *Calendar:* semester, summer school.

Undergraduate degrees conferred (3057). 19% were in Business and Management, 12% were in Liberal/General Studies, 10% were in Education, 10% were in Social Sciences, 8% were in Engineering, 6% were in Psychology, 6% were in Communications, 5% were in Letters, 4% were in Architecture and Environmental Design, 4% were in Home Economics, 3% were in Life Sciences, 3% were in Visual and Performing Arts, remainder in 15 other fields.

Student Body. University seeks a national student body; 92% of students from Louisiana; 97% from South.

Campus Life. Campus offers a program of "differential housing" under which students may choose from a wide variety of dormitory living conditions, ranging from traditional to liberal. Alcoholic beverages may be consumed at registered social functions and in some dormitories under "differential housing." Cars permitted. Students with under 30 semester hours expected to live on campus.

About 13% of men, 18% of women live in traditional dormitories; no coed dormitories; 2% of men, 1% of women live in off-campus housing married student apartments; 80% of men, 77% of women commute. There are 24 fraternities, 15 sororities on campus which about 12% of men, 15% of women join; 5% of men, 4% of women live in fraternities and sororities.

Annual Costs. Tuition and fees, $2,170 (out-of-state, $5,243); room and board, $2,710. Financial assistance is typically divided 33% scholarship, 33% loan, 33% work. College reports some scholarships awarded on the basis of academic merit alone. *Meeting Costs:* college offers payment plans, Parent PLUS Loans, CONCERN Loans.

Medical Center at New Orleans

New Orleans, Louisiana 70112

LSU Medical Center offers degrees from the associates level through the doctoral in health related fields. Programs offered include dental laboratory technology, medical technology, nursing, occupational therapy, physical therapy, respiratory therapy, speech pathology and audiology.

Undergraduate degrees conferred (268). 71% were in Allied Health, 29% were in Health Sciences.

Louisiana State University in Shreveport

Shreveport, Louisiana 71115 (318) 797-5000

Formerly a 2-year commuter college, LSU in Shreveport was given baccalaureate degree-granting status in 1972. Located in a city of 234,004, the institution offers undergraduate studies in 5 colleges as well as graduate studies in secondary education. Most convenient major airport: Shreveport Regional.

Founded: 1965	**Cost:** < $10K
Affiliation: State	**% Receiving Financial Aid:** 30%
Total Enrollment: 1066 M, 1,347 W (full-time); 561 M, 916 W (part-time)	**Admission:** Non-selective
	Application Deadline: August 5

Admission. Louisiana graduates of approved high schools eligible; almost all applicants accepted; 71% of these actually enroll. Average freshman ACT composite scores: 20.1. *Required:* ACT (for placement). Criteria considered in admissions: high school academic record (GPA), standardized test scores. *Out-of-state* freshman applicants: State does not limit out-of-state enrollment. Requirement for out-of-state applicants: rank in top half of class. State from which most out-of-state students are drawn: Texas. *Entrance programs:* midyear admission, advanced placement. *Apply* by August 5; rolling admissions. *Transfers* welcome; 462 enrolled 1993–94.

Academic Environment. Degrees offered: bachelors, masters. General education requirements for graduation vary with college; core requirements in liberal arts include 9 semester hours of written and oral communications, 9 hours social and behavioral sciences, 15 hours science and mathematics, 12 hours humanities and fine arts. *Majors offered* include environmental science, biochemical science, international studies. About 20% of students entering as freshmen graduate eventually; 50% of freshmen return for sophomore year. Average undergraduate class size: 22% under 20, 72% 20–40, 6% over 40. *Special programs:* CLEP, independent study, study abroad, honors, undergraduate research, 3–2 programs in engineering. *Calendar:* semester, summer school.

Undergraduate degrees conferred (408). 30% were in Business and Management, 20% were in Education, 9% were in Psychology, 7% were in Liberal/General Studies, 7% were in Social Sciences, 7% were in Computer and Engineering Related Technology, 6% were in Life Sciences, 4% were in Protective Services, 4% were in Communications, remainder in 6 other fields.

Graduates Career Data. Advanced studies pursued by 8% of students. Career Development Services include interest inventory and assessment, resume assistance, on-campus interviews.

Faculty. About 80% of faculty hold PhD or equivalent. About 60% of undergraduate classes taught by tenured faculty. About 34% of teaching faculty are female; 6% Black, 3% other minority.

Student Body. University does not seek a national student body; 98% of students from in state; 2% South. An estimated 14% of students reported as Black, 1% Hispanic, 2% Asian, 3% other minority. Average age of undergraduate student: 27.

Varsity Sports. Men: Baseball, Basketball, Soccer. Women: Basketball.

Campus Life. No dormitories. There are 2 fraternities, 3 sororities on campus which about 1% of men, 2% of women join; they provide no residence facilities.

Annual Costs. Tuition and fees, $2,060 (out-of-state, $4,990); estimated $1,620 other, exclusive of room and board and travel. About 30% of students receive financial aid. University reports 170 scholarships awarded on the basis of academic merit alone, 2 for need alone.

University of New Orleans

New Orleans, Louisiana 70148 (504) 286-6000

A part of the state university system, UNO offers undergraduate studies in 4 colleges. There are also graduate, junior, and evening divisions. Most convenient major airport: New Orleans International.

Founded: 1958	**Cost:** < $10K
Affiliation: State	**% Receiving Financial Aid:** 43%
Total Enrollment: 3,761 M, 4,397 W (full-time); 1,535 M, W (part-time)	**Admission:** Non-selective
	Application Deadline: August 15

Admission. Louisiana graduates of approved high schools eligible; 89% of applicants accepted, 62% of these actually enroll. Average freshman ACT scores: 21 M, 20 W composite. *Required:* minimum ACT score of 20 or SAT combined score of 810 or 2.0 GPA in 17 units high school core subjects. Criteria considered in admissions, in order of importance: standardized test scores, high school academic record, recommendations. *Out-of-state* freshman applicants: state does not limit out-of-state enrollment. No special requirements for out-of-state applicants. About 251 out-of-state students accepted, 106 of these actually enrolled. States from which most of out-of-state students are drawn: Mississippi, Alabama, Texas, Florida. *Entrance programs:* early admission, midyear admission, advanced placement. About 34% of entering students from private or parochial schools. *Apply* by August 15; rolling admissions. *Transfers* welcome; 1,051 enrolled 1993–94.

Academic Environment. All freshmen enter Junior Division for first year, then select one of the university's colleges in which to complete undergraduate study. Degrees offered: associates, bachelors, masters, doctoral. *Undergraduate studies* offered by colleges of Business Administration, Education, Engineering, Liberal Arts, Sciences; degree programs in medical technology, nursing. About 10% of general education requirements for graduation are elective; no distribution requirements. Average undergraduate class size: 38% under 20, 45% 20–40, 17% over 40. About 10% of students entering as freshmen graduate within 4 years, 25% graduate eventually; 62% of freshmen return for sophomore year. *Special programs:* independent study, honors, international summer school in Munich, combined program for School of Medicine, 3–2 in engineering. Adult programs: Golden Agers Program, free tuition for those over 65. *Calendar:* semester, summer school.

Undergraduate degrees conferred (1237). 33% were in Business and Management, 13% were in Social Sciences, 13% were in Education, 8% were in Engineering, 7% were in Communications, 6% were in Liberal/General Studies, 5% were in Psychology, 4% were in Letters, 3% were in Visual and Performing Arts, remainder in 10 other fields.

Faculty. About 76% of faculty hold PhD or equivalent. About 33% of teaching faculty are female; 5% Black, 2% Hispanic, 6% other minority.

Student Body. University seeks a national student body; 94% of students from in state; 96% South, 1% Middle Atlantic, 1% Midwest, 2% foreign. An estimated 55% of students reported as Protestant, 42% Catholic; 12% Black, 5% Hispanic, 3% Asian, 3% other minority, according to most recent data available. Average age of undergraduate student: 25.

Varsity Sports. Men: Baseball, Basketball, Cross Country, Gold, Swimming, Tennis, Track. Women: Basketball, Cross Country, Swimming, Tennis, Track, Volleyball.

Campus Life. About 5% of men, 5% of women live in coed dormitories; rest commute. Intervisitation in men's and women's dormitory rooms limited. There are 9 fraternities, 7 sororities on campus which about 2% of men, 2% of women join; they provide no residence facilities. About 50% of resident students leave campus on weekends.

Annual Costs. Tuition and fees, $2,362 (out-of-state, $5,154); room, $3,106; estimated $2,590 other, exclusive of travel. About 43% of students receive financial aid; average amount of assistance, $4,700. Assistance is typically divided 11% scholarship, 18% grant, 52% loan, 19% work. College reports 778 scholarships awarded on the basis of academic merit alone.

Louisiana Tech University

Ruston, Louisiana 71272 (318) 257-2238

A state university, located in a suburban town of 17,400, 69 miles east of Shreveport, Louisiana Tech offers programs in the liberal arts, fine arts, and professional fields. Most convenient major airport: Monroe.

Founded: 1894
Affiliation: State
UG Enrollment: 3,736 M, 2,984 W (full-time); 816 M, 1,006 W (part-time)
Total Enrollment: 10,100
Cost: < $10K
% Receiving Financial Aid: 77%
Admission: Non-selective
Application Deadline: Aug. 15

Admission. Open admissions for graduates of Louisiana and adjacent states high schools; others must have ACT composite of 20. About 89% of applicants accepted, 71% actually enroll; 36% of freshman graduate in top fifth of high school class, 64% in top two fifths. Average freshman ACT scores: 22 composite. Criteria considered in admissions, in order of importance: high school academic record, class rank, standardized test scores; other factors considered: special talents. *Required:* ACT. *Out-of-state* freshman applicants: state does not limit out-of-state enrollment. States from which most out-of-state students are drawn: Arkansas, Texas, Mississippi. Entrance program: early admission. About 20% of entering students from private schools. *Apply* by August 15. *Transfers* welcome; 562 enrolled 1993–94.

Academic Environment. Degrees offered: associates, bachelors, masters, doctoral. *Undergraduate studies* offered by colleges of Administration and Business, Arts and Sciences, Education, Engineering, Home Economics, Life Sciences. About 15% of general education requirements for graduation are elective; distribution requirements vary with college. About 20% of students entering as freshmen graduate within 4 years, 33% graduate eventually; 70% of freshmen return for sophomore year. Average undergraduate class size: 10% under 20, 75% 20–40, 15% over 40. *Special programs:* CLEP, study abroad, Inter-Institutional Cooperative Program with Grambling. *Calendar:* quarter, summer school.

Undergraduate degrees conferred (1165). 26% were in Business and Management, 13% were in Education, 12% were in Liberal/General Studies, 9% were in Engineering, 6% were in Transportation and Material Moving, 4% were in Social Sciences, 4% were in Home Economics, remainder in 19 other fields.

Graduates Career Data. Employers typically hiring largest number of graduates include Arthur Andersen, Chevron, International Paper. Career Development Services provided for current students and alumni.

Faculty. About 74% of faculty hold PhD or equivalent. About 90% of undergraduate classes taught by tenured faculty. About 30% of teaching faculty are female; 19% Black, 5% other minority.

Student Body. University does not seek a national student body; 83% of students from in state; 97% South, 1% New England, 1% Midwest, 1% West, 4% foreign. An estimated 65% of students reported as Protestant, 13% Catholic, 22% other; 13% Black, 1% Hispanic, 1% Asian, 6% other minority.

Varsity Sports. Men (Div.IA): Baseball, Basketball, Football (IAA), Golf, Track. Women (Div.IA): Basketball, Softball, Tennis, Track, Volleyball.

Campus Life. About 36% men, 35% women live in traditional dormitories; no coed dormitories; 3% men live in fraternities; 23% men, 19% women live in off-campus college-related housing; 38% men, 46% women commute. Freshmen given preference in college housing if all students cannot be accommodated. Intervisitation in men's and women's dormitory rooms limited. There are 11 fraternities, 5 sororities on campus which about 9% of men, 12% of women join.

Annual Costs. Tuition and fees, $2,169 (out-of-state, $3,624); room and board, $2,325; estimated $1,695 other, exclusive of travel. About 77% of students receive financial aid; average amount of assistance, $1,500. Assistance is typically divided 15% scholarship, 20% grant, 45% loan, 20% work. University reports 1,671 scholarships awarded on the basis of academic merit alone, 652 for special talents alone, 53 for need alone.

University of Louisville

Louisville, Kentucky 40292 (502) 852-5155

The first municipal university in the U.S., the University of Louisville became a state institution in 1970. The university counts among its alumni a major portion of Kentucky's physicians and a majority of the state's dentists. Most undergraduate schools are located on the university's Belknap Campus, 3 miles south of downtown Louisville. Most convenient major airport: Standiford (Louisville).

Founded: 1798
Affiliation: State
UG Enrollment: 4,768 M, 5,076 W (full-time); 2,830 M, 3,415 W (part-time)
Total Enrollment: 21,826
Cost: < $10K
% Receiving Financial Aid: 50%
Admission: Non-selective
Application Deadline: 6 weeks before term

Admission criteria vary between different schools. For all schools, 65% of applicants accepted, 52% of these actually enroll. Average freshman ACT scores: 21.4 M, 20.5 W composite.

For Speed Scientific School (890 M, 227 W full-time): 60% of applicants accepted, 63% of these actually enroll; 69% of freshmen graduate in top fifth of high school class, 92% in top two-fifths. Average freshman enhanced ACT scores: 23.0 composite, 23.0 mathematical. *Required:* minimum ACT score of 16, GPA 2.25. Criteria considered in admissions, in order of importance: high school academic record, standardized test scores. *Out-of-state* freshman applicants: university welcomes students from out of state. State limits out-of-state enrollment to 10% of entering class for professional schools. No special requirements for out-of-state applicants. *Entrance programs:* early decision, early admission, deferred admission, advanced placement. *Apply:* six weeks prior to start of term. *Transfers* welcome; 1,015 enrolled 1993–94.

Academic Environment. Degrees offered: associates, bachelors, masters, doctoral. Administration reports all students take similar program for first 2 years with choices permitted within fields; general education courses required for graduation include written and oral communication, quantitative and logical reasoning, natural sciences, arts and humanities, social and cultural studies; specific courses vary with program. *Undergraduate studies* offered by College of Arts and Sciences, School of Music, Speed Scientific School; School of Nursing, School of Business, School of Education, College of Urban & Public Affairs Division of Allied Health. *Majors offered* in Arts and Sciences in addition to usual studies include anthropology, dramatic arts, recreation. Average undergraduate class size: 32% of classes under 20, 53% between 20–40, 15% over 40.

About 35% of students entering as freshmen graduate eventually; 30% of freshmen do not return for sophomore year. *Special programs:* CLEP, independent study, study abroad, honors, credit by examination, internships, credit for intersession study, cross-registration with other Louisville area colleges, combined programs including nursing and medical technology with university's schools of Dentistry, Medicine. Adult programs: Continuing Studies Program. *Calendar:* semester, summer school.

Undergraduate degrees conferred (1859). 26% were in Business and Management, 16% were in Education, 11% were in Engineering, 11% were in Social Sciences, 5% were in Communications, 5% were in Health Sciences, 4% were in Life Sciences, 3% were in Letters, 3% were in Psychology, 3% were in Visual and Performing Arts, 3% were in Protective Services, remainder in 11 other fields.

Graduates Career Data. *Career Counseling Program* includes cooperative education programs and junior year preparation programs, on-campus interviewing. Alumni reported as not active in either career guidance or job placement.

Faculty. About 88% of faculty hold PhD or equivalent. About 34% of teaching faculty are female; 5% Black, 9% other ethnic minorities.

Student Body. University seeks a national student body; 93% of students from in state; 96% South; 1% foreign. An estimated 10% of students reported as Black, 1% Hispanic, 3% Asian, 3% other minority. *Minority group students:* special scholarship program; funding for social affairs.

Varsity Sports. Men (Div.I): Baseball, Basketball, Cross Country, Football, Golf, Soccer, Swimming, Tennis, Track. Women (Div.I): Basketball, Cross Country, Field Hockey, Soccer, Swimming, Tennis, Track, Volleyball.

Campus Life. Campus life influenced by large percentage of commuters. Student leader characterizes regulations governing student conduct as "very free," enforced "judiciously." Cars allowed. About 2% of men, 2% of women live in coed dormitories; rest live in off-campus housing or commute. Sexes segregated in coed dormitories by wing or floor. There are 15 fraternities, 10 sororities on campus; about 2% of men, 2% of women join; less than 1% live in fraternities and sororities.

Annual Costs. Tuition and fees, $2,170 (out-of-state, $6,090); room and board, $3,468; estimated $2,300 other, exclusive of travel. About 50% of students receive financial aid; average amount of assistance, $1,600. Assistance is typically divided 45% scholarship/grant, 50% loan, 5% work. University reports some scholarships awarded on the basis of academic merit alone. *Meeting Costs:* university offers PLUS loan program.

Lourdes College

Sylvania, Ohio 43560 **(419) 885-3211**

A small, Roman Catholic, liberal arts institution, founded by the Sisters of St. Francis, Lourdes confers both associate and baccalaureate degrees and offers programs for adult students. Most convenient major airport: Toledo.

Founded: 1958
Affiliation: Roman Catholic
Total Enrollment: 74 M, 356 W (full-time); 162 M, 1,013 W (part-time)
Cost: < $10K
% Receiving Financial Aid: 33%
Admission: Non-selective
Application Deadline: August 10

Admission. About 96% of applicants are accepted, 58% of these actually enroll; 41% of freshman graduate in top fifth of high school class, 63% in top two-fifths. Average freshman ACT scores: 24 M, 20 W composite. *Required:* SAT or ACT, minimum HS GPA. Criteria considered in admissions, in order of importance: high school academic record, standardized test scores, writing sample, recommendations, extracurricular activities, placement tests. *Entrance programs:* early admission, midyear admission, deferred admission, advanced placement. About 23% of entering students from parochial schools. *Apply* by August 10; rolling admissions. *Transfers* welcome; 342 enrolled 1993–94.

Academic Environment. Degrees offered: associates, bachelors. *Majors offered* include Bachelor of Individualized Studies, a flexible degree for non-traditional students. Core requirements include 55 semester hours distributed over language and literature, religious studies, philosophy, art or music, natural science and mathematics, history, social sciences, physical education or health. Average undergraduate class size: 80% under 20, 20% 20–40. Adult programs: Weekend College, prior learning assessment, Bachelor of Individualized Studies. About 83% of entering freshman graduate within four years; 80% of freshman return for sophomore year.

Undergraduate degrees conferred (84). 30% were in Business and Management, 24% were in Health Sciences, 20% were in Multi/Interdisciplinary Studies, 7% were in Public Affairs, 6% were in Social Sciences, 6% were in Psychology, 4% were in Visual and Performing Arts, 4% were in Philosophy and Religion.

Faculty. About 18% of faculty hold PhD or equivalent. About 73% of teaching faculty are female.

Student Body. About 90% of students from in state; almost all from the Midwest. An estimated 38% of students reported as Protestant, 60% Catholic, 1% Jewish, 1% other. Average age of undergraduate student: 32.

Religious Orientation. Lourdes is a church-related institution; 2 religious courses are required of all students.

Campus Life. All students commute. There is 1 sorority on campus, which about 2% of women join.

Annual Costs. Tuition and fees, $6,410. About 33% of students receive financial aid; average amount of assistance, $3,400. Assistance is typically divided 40% scholarship/grants, 58% loan, 2% work.

Loyola College

Baltimore, Maryland 21210 **(410) 617-2252**

Loyola, long a Jesuit college for men, has been coeducational since 1971. The college occupies the 37-acre Loyola campus located in the northern suburbs of Baltimore. Most convenient major airport: Baltimore/Washington International.

Founded: 1852
Affiliation: Roman Catholic
UG Enrollment: 1,286 M, 1,724 W (full-time)
Total Enrollment: 6,000
Cost: $10K–$20K
% Receiving Financial Aid: 60%
Admission: Very Selective
Application Deadline: February 1

Admission is very selective. About 77% of applicants accepted, 24% of these actually enroll; 44% of fresh men graduate in top fifth of high school class, 75% in top two-fifths. Average freshman SAT scores: 507 verbal, 563 mathematical. *Required:* SAT, essay; HS GPA 3.0 is recommended. Criteria considered in admissions, in order of importance: high school academic record, standardized test scores, class rank, writing sample, recommendations, extracurricular activities; other factors considered: special talents, alumni children, diverse student body. *Entrance programs:* early admission, midyear admission, deferred admission, advanced placement, early acceptance. About 44% of entering students from private or parochial schools, according to most recent data available. *Apply* by February 1. *Transfers* welcome.

Academic Environment. Degrees offered: bachelors, masters, doctoral. *Majors offered* include 5 year bachelors and masters program in psychology. Most popular majors are business, communications, and biology. Student body reported as overwhelmingly concerned with occupational/professional goals. Liberal arts core required of all students regardless of major; core includes 2 years of foreign language, 1 year of each history, theology, philosophy, English, social science, 1 semester of ethics, 3 semesters of mathematics/science. Recent student reports that Loyola has a "very demanding program. However, because of small class sizes, the teachers are able to give individual attention."

About 71% of students entering as freshmen graduate eventually; 91% of freshmen return for sophomore year. *Special programs:* CLEP, independent study, study abroad, cooperative programs, cross registration with numerous schools. Adult programs: a variety of graduate programs as well as professional development courses offered. *Calendar:* semester, summer school.

Undergraduate degrees conferred (767). 36% were in Business and Management, 14% were in Social Sciences, 10% were in Psychology, 10% were in Communications, 9% were in Letters, 4% were in Education, 4% were in Health Sciences, 3% were in Life Sciences, remainder in 7 other fields.

Graduates Career Data. Full-time advanced studies pursued by 59% of students; 10% enter medical school; 14% enter law school; 15% enter business school, according to most recent data available. Medical schools typically enrolling largest numbers of graduates include U. of Maryland, Georgetown, John Hopkins; law schools include U. of Baltimore, Georgetown, Emory; business schools include U. of Pennsylvania. Fields typically hiring largest numbers of graduates include accounting, business, law firms. Career Development Services include advisement on resumes and interview techniques, arrangement of interviews and career fairs.

Faculty. About 87% of faculty hold PhD or equivalent.

Student Body. About 35% of students from in state. An estimated 3% of students reported as Black, 2% Hispanic, 3% Asian.

Religious Orientation. Loyola is a church-related institution; 2 semester courses in theology required of all students.

Varsity Sports. Men (Div.I): Basketball, Cross Country, Diving, Golf, Lacrosse, Soccer, Swimming, Tennis. Women (Div.I): Basketball, Cross Country, Diving, Lacrosse, Soccer, Swimming, Tennis, Volleyball. Many club sports also available.

Campus Life. Many students are involved in athletics, student activities or community service. Baltimore offers recreational and cultural opportunities. Students who do not live in Baltimore metropolitan area required to live on campus. About 12% of men, 9% of women live in traditional dormitories; 51% of men, 63% of women live in coed dormitories; rest live in off-campus housing or commute. There are no fraternities or sororities. About 25% of resident students leave campus on weekends.

Annual Costs. Tuition and fees, $11,975; room and board, $6,000–$6,200. About 60% of students receive financial aid. Assistance is typically divided 40% grant/scholarship, 45% loan, 15% work. College reports some scholarships awarded on the basis of academic merit alone. *Meeting Costs:* college offers family tuition reduction grants, prepayment plan.

Loyola Marymount University

Los Angeles, California 90045-2699 (310) 338-2750

A Catholic university which combines the educational traditions of the Jesuits, the Religious of the Sacred Heart of Mary and the Sisters of St. Joseph of Orange. The 100-acre Westchester campus is located in the southwest section of Los Angeles, on a mesa overlooking Marina Del Rey and the Pacific Ocean, midway between Santa Monica and Palos Verdes. Most convenient major airport: Los Angeles International.

Founded: 1914
Affiliation: Independent (Roman Catholic)
UG Enrollment: 1,571 M, 1,974 W (full-time)
Total Enrollment: 4,994
Cost: $10K–$20K
% Receiving Financial Aid: 78%
Admission: Selective
Application Deadline: Feb. 1

Admission is selective. For all schools, 74% of applicants accepted, 28% of these actually enroll. Average freshman SAT scores: 481 M, 467 W verbal, 556 M, 519 W mathematical; 38% of entering freshman score above 500 on verbal, 9% above 600; 69% score above 500 on mathematical, 22% above 600.

For Liberal Arts (454 M, 923 W), average freshman SAT scores: 486 verbal, 525 mathematical; 44% of freshman score above 500 on verbal, 10% above 600, 2% above 700; 62% score above 500 on mathematical, 18% above 600, 3% above 700.

For Science and Engineering (396 M, 335 W), average freshman SAT scores: 477 verbal, 564 mathematical; 35% of freshman score above 500 on verbal, 12% above 600; 83% score above 500 on mathematical, 33% above 600, 8% above 700.

For Communications and Fine Arts (304 M, 374 W), average freshman SAT scores: 472 verbal, 516 mathematical; 41% of freshman score above 500 on verbal, 8% above 600, 1% above 700; 59% score above 500 on mathematical, 15% above 600, 2% above 700.

For Business Administration (534 M, 504 W), average freshman SAT scores: 449 verbal, 532 mathematical; 25% of freshman score above 500 on verbal, 3% above 600; 66% score above 500 on mathematical, 20% above 600.

Required: SAT or ACT; essay; on-campus interview encouraged. Criteria considered in admissions, in order of importance: high school academic record, standardized test scores, writing sample, recommendations, interview, extracurricular activities; other factors considered: diverse student body, special talents, alumni children, disadvantaged students, under-represented minorities, first in family to attend college. *Entrance programs:* early admission, advanced placement, deferred admission, midyear admission, honors at entrance. About 3% of entering students from private schools, 48% from parochial schools. *Apply* by February 1. *Transfers* welcome; 379 enrolled Fall 1993.

Academic Environment. A liberal arts core curriculum is required of all undergraduate students for graduation; specific requirements differ for each of the 4 colleges. Degrees offered: bachelors, masters. *Undergraduate studies* offered to freshmen by colleges of Liberal Arts, Business Administration, Communications and Fine Arts, and Science and Engineering. *Majors offered* include Latin, Greek, television and film production and recording arts. Computer facilities include terminals to mainframes and microcomputers are decentralized; all residence halls are wired to provide students access to campus-wide network; but students still report that during finals week facilities are overburdened.

About 56% of students entering as freshmen graduate within 4 years, 71% eventually; 87% of freshmen return for sophomore year. *Special programs:* CLEP, independent study, study abroad, honors, Washington Semester, credit by examination, coordinate major in business/chemistry, individualized majors. Adult programs: ENCORE—a pre-admission program for adults over 30 who have completed high school. *Calendar:* semester, summer school.

Undergraduate degrees conferred (929). 33% were in Business and Management, 16% were in Communications, 15% were in Social Sciences, 9% were in Psychology, 6% were in Letters, 5% were in Life Sciences, 5% were in Visual and Performing Arts, 3% were in Engineering, 3% were in Liberal/General Studies, remainder in 8 other fields.

Graduates Career Data. Medical schools typically enrolling largest numbers of graduates include USC, UCLA; dental schools include USC; law schools include Loyola Marymount, UCLA, Southwestern. Career Development Services include work-skill development, job recruitment and referrals, internship program, and work/study program. Student assessment of program reported as good for both career guidance and job placement. Alumni reported as actively helpful in both career guidance and job placement.

Faculty. About 81% of faculty hold PhD or equivalent. About 12% of the faculty are members of a religious community, primarily the Society of Jesus. About 26% of teaching faculty are female; 4% Black, 3% Hispanic, 5% Asian.

Student Body. University seeks a "diversified" student body; 81% of undergraduate students from within state; 88% West, 2% Midwest, 2% South, 2% Northwest, 1% New England, 5% foreign. An estimated 62% of students reported as Catholic, 11% Protestant, 1% Jewish, 26% other or unaffiliated; 6% as Black, 18% Hispanic, 15% Asian, 6% other minority. *Minority group students:* special programs of counseling and peer support are provided.

Religious Orientation. Loyola Marymount is a Catholic university; 2 term courses (1 lower and 1 upper division) in religious studies required of all students; participation in religious activities completely voluntary. Active campus ministry provides religious experiences for all faiths. Places of worship available on campus for Catholics, in nearby community for those of other beliefs.

Varsity Sports. Men (Div.I): Baseball, Basketball, Crew, Cross Country, Golf, Soccer, Tennis, Volleyball, Water Polo. Women (Div.I): Basketball, Crew, Cross Country, Soccer, Softball, Swimming, Tennis, Volleyball.

Campus Life. Students enjoy considerable freedom in their personal and social activities within the fairly broad range of university regulations. Students sit on all committees of the university and hold full voting rights. Campus life is active with a variety of cultural, recreational, and social opportunities; service organizations are very popular.

About 21% of men, 16% of women live in traditional dormitories; 23% of men, 28% of women live in coed dormitories; 3% of men, 4% of women live in on-campus apartments; 4% of men, 7% of women live in off-campus college-related housing; rest commute. Freshmen given preference in college housing if all students cannot be accommodated. There are 6 fraternities, 3 sororities on campus, about 10–15% of students join.

Annual Costs. Tuition and fees, $13,060; room and board, $5,500–$6,100; estimated $1,900 other, exclusive of travel. About 78% of students receive financial aid. Assistance is typically divided

58% scholarship, 26% loan, 15% work, according to most recent data available. University reports some scholarships awarded on the basis of academic merit alone.

Loyola University, New Orleans

New Orleans, Louisiana 70118 (504) 865-3240

A church-related university, conducted by Jesuits, located on a 19-acre campus in a residential section of New Orleans. Most convenient major airport: New Orleans International.

Founded: 1912
Affiliation: Roman Catholic
UG Enrollment: 1,141 M, 1,599 W (full-time); 217 M, 544 W (part-time)
Total Enrollment: 4,888
Cost: $10K–$20K
% Receiving Financial Aid: 65%
Admission: Selective
Application Deadline: Aug. 1

Admission is selective. For all schools about 89% of applicants accepted, 42% of these actually enroll; 42% of freshman graduate in top fifth of high school class, 44% in top two-fifths. Average freshman scores: SAT, 510 verbal, 520 mathematical; ACT, 25 composite.

For Arts and Sciences (772 M, 1,225 W), 54% of applicants accepted, 35% of these actually enroll.

For Music (95 M, 107 W), 59% of applicants accepted, 55% of these actually enroll.

For Business Administration (339 M, 370 W), 52% of applicants accepted, 32% of these actually enroll.

Required: SAT or ACT, essay. Criteria considered in admissions, in order of importance: standardized test scores, high school academic record, recommendations; other factors considered: special talents, diverse student body, extracurricular activities. *Entrance programs:* early admission, advanced placement. *Apply* by August 1. *Transfers* welcome; 327 enrolled 1993–94.

Academic Environment. Degrees offered: bachelors, masters. Loyola's Common Curriculum "complements the major and adjunct courses by providing a broad humanistic dimension to every undergraduate student's chosen program of study." Second language competency requirement and Writing Across the Curriculum program included. Students characterized as primarily concerned with occupational/professional goals, minority pursue primarily scholarly/intellectual interests. *Undergraduate studies* offered to freshmen by 3 colleges listed above. *Majors offered* include communications, religious studies, business administration, guidance and counseling, music, law, drama, education, journalism, radiologic technologies. Average undergraduate class size: 70% under 20, 30% 20–40.

About 70% of students entering as freshmen graduate eventually; 78% of freshmen return for sophomore year. *Special programs:* independent study, study abroad (including summer sessions in London, Eastern Europe, Japan and Mexico City), honors, undergraduate research, individualized majors, consortium with St. Mary's Dominican and Xavier U., limited cross-registration with Tulane, 3–2 engineering. Adult programs: City College is a separate division specifically for working adults, classes held evenings and weekends. *Library:* materials include special collections of rare Spanish and French colonial archival documents, Jesuitica holdings; open-stack privileges. *Calendar:* semester, summer school.

Undergraduate degrees conferred (617). 24% were in Communications, 24% were in Business and Management, 16% were in Social Sciences, 8% were in Psychology, 5% were in Education, 5% were in Visual and Performing Arts, 4% were in Letters, 4% were in Health Sciences, remainder in 9 other fields.

Graduates Career Data. Full-time graduate study pursued immediately after graduation by 20% of students. Medical schools typically enrolling largest numbers of graduates include Tulane, Louisiana State; dental schools include Louisiana State; law schools include Loyola. *Career Counseling Program:* Student assessment of program reported as good for both career guidance and job placement.

Faculty. About 86% of faculty hold PhD or equivalent. About 30% of teaching faculty are female.

Student Body. University seeks a national student body; 80% of students from South. An estimated 66% of students reported as Catholic, 13% Protestant, 1% Jewish, 24% other or unaffiliated; 12% as Black, 9% Hispanic, 3% Asian, 4% other minority. *Minority group students:* Minority Student Affairs committee "studies special problems and makes appropriate recommendations."

Religious Orientation. Loyola is a church-related institution; 2 religious courses are required of all students. Places of worship available on campus for Catholics; Protestants may attend services at Tulane or at nearby churches.

Campus Life. Alcoholic beverages available to those of legal age; beer for sale at campus pub. Cars allowed, parking available on campus. Smoking prohibited in classrooms and hallways, restricted in dining areas. Illegal drugs "strictly prohibited." Limited intervisitation (88 hours per week) allowed; students reportedly would like more.

About 6% of men, 12% of women live in traditional dormitories; 1% of men, 2% of women live in coed dormitories; rest commute. Freshmen given preference in college housing if all students cannot be accommodated. There are 12 fraternities, 10 sororities, which about 16% of men, 31% of women join; they provide no residence facilities. About 5% of resident students leave campus on weekends.

Annual Costs. Tuition and fees, $10,560; room and board, $5,100. About 65% of students receive financial aid. Assistance is typically divided 36% scholarship, 55% loan, 9% work. University reports some scholarships awarded on the basis of academic merit alone.

Loyola University of Chicago

Chicago, Illinois 60611 (312) 915-6500

A church-related private university dedicated to the Jesuit ideals of education, Loyola is a complex urban institution in an urban setting, comprised of three campuses. Undergraduate students normally choose between the Lake Shore Campus, at which over half live in dormitories, and the Water Tower Campus, which is commuter-oriented and is located in the heart of Chicago's Magnificent Mile. A third campus, in suburban Maywood, houses the medical and dental schools and a research and teaching hospital. Most convenient major airport: O'Hare International (Chicago).

Founded: 1870
Affiliation: Roman Catholic
UG Enrollment: 2,079 M, 3,165 W (full-time); 1,228 M, 2,189 W (part-time)
Total Enrollment: 14,361
Cost: $10K–$20K
% Receiving Financial Aid: 75%
Admission: Selective
Application Deadline: July 14

Admission is selective, though varies somewhat among the different programs. For all schools, 83% of applicants accepted, 29% of these actually enroll; 43% of freshmen graduate in top fifth of high school class, 77% in top two-fifths. Average freshman SAT scores: 45% of freshman score above 500 on verbal, 12% above 600, 1% above 700; 63% score above 500 on mathematical, 23% above 600, 4% above 700.

Required: SAT or ACT; some programs may have additional requirements. Criteria considered in admissions, in order of importance: high school academic record, standardized test scores, recommendations, extracurricular activities. *Entrance programs:* midyear admission, advanced placement. About 60% of entering students from private schools. *Apply* by July 14. *Transfers* welcome; 440 enrolled 1993–94.

Academic Environment. Degrees offered: bachelors, masters, doctoral. In the College of Arts and Sciences the liberal arts core consists of 54 hours and includes philosophy, theology, natural science, literature, history, social science, math, and expressive arts. Core requirements in the schools of Business Administration, Education, and Nursing vary to some degree. All colleges require 2 writing courses in addition to the core. The above 4 colleges are essentially full-time. In addition, the Mundelien College offers a full baccalaureate degree program in conjunction with the other colleges. The program is pursued part-time and on weekends at the Water Tower campus. Mundelien College has an open enrollment policy, but after a period of successful study, the student must apply for and be accepted into degree candidacy. *Majors offered* include anthropology, communications, dental hygiene, fine arts, theater, criminal justice, social work.

About 38% of students entering as freshmen graduate within four years, 70% eventually; 81% of freshmen return for sophomore year. *Special programs:* CLEP, internships, study abroad (including year at university's Rome center), honors, credit by examination, individualized majors, 3–2 engineering, 3–3 law. *Calendar:* semester, summer school.

Undergraduate degrees conferred (1478). 29% were in Business and Management, 12% were in Social Sciences, 11% were in Psychology, 11% were in Communications, 8% were in Life Sciences, 5% were in Letters, 5% were in Health Sciences, 4% were in Protective Services, 3% were in Education, remainder in 8 other fields.

Graduates Career Data. Full-time graduate study pursued by 29% of students immediately after graduation, according to most recent data available. Medical schools typically enrolling largest numbers of graduates include Loyola, U. of Illinois; dental schools include Loyola, U. of Illinois, DePaul; law schools include Loyola, Northwestern, DePaul; business schools include Loyola, DePaul. *Careers in business and industry* pursued by 61% of graduates. Corporations typically hiring largest numbers of graduates include Peat Marwick, Arthur Andersen, American Can Corp., Continental Bank. *Career Counseling Program* includes both career guidance and job placement. Alumni are involved informally in career guidance and job placement.

Faculty. About 93% of faculty hold PhD or equivalent. About 35% of teaching faculty are female.

Student Body. University seeks a diverse student body; 83% of students from in state; 93% North Central. An estimated 62% of students reported as Catholic, 11% Protestant, 2% Jewish; 8% Black, 6% Hispanic, 10% Asian, 3% other minority.

Religious Orientation. Loyola is a church-related institution, makes no religious demands on students. Places of worship available on campus for Catholics, in immediate community for major faiths.

Varsity Sports. Men (NCAA, Div.I): Basketball, Cross Country, Soccer, Swimming, Track. Women (Div.I): Basketball, Cross Country, Soccer, Softball, Track, Volleyball. Golf (Div.I).

Campus Life. Wide variety of activities available to students both on campus and in Chicago. Substantial number of students live on campus. Cars allowed, but parking is limited. Undergraduates are not allowed to drink on campus. Residents may choose among variety of housing options.

About 32% of men, 32% of women in coed dormitories. Sexes segregated in coed dormitories by wing, floor or room. There are 6 fraternities, 9 sororities which about 8% of men, 7% of women join. About 30% of resident students leave campus on weekends.

Annual Costs. Tuition and fees, $10,470; room and board, $5,310. About 75% of students receive financial aid. Assistance is typically divided 35% scholarship, 60% loan, 5% work. University reports some scholarships awarded on the basis of academic merit alone.

Lubbock Christian University

Lubbock, Texas 79407 (806) 796-8800

A church-related, liberal arts institution, Lubbock Christian "strives for academic quality within a Christian environment"; located in a city of 156,000. Most convenient major airport: Lubbock International.

Founded: 1957
Affiliation: Church of Christ
Total Enrollment: 948 M, W (full-time)
Cost: < $10K
% Receiving Financial Aid: 85%
Admission: Non-selective
Application Deadline: Aug. 15

Admission. Graduates of accredited high schools eligible; others admitted by examination; 99% of applicants accepted. Average freshman scores, according to most recent data available: SAT, 380 M, 390 W verbal, 490 M, 490 W mathematical; ACT, 20 M, 21 W composite. *Required:* SAT or ACT. *Non-academic factors* considered in admissions: "willing to be part of Christian environment." *Apply* by August 15. *Transfers* welcome.

Academic Environment. *Degrees:* BA, BS, BSEd. About 20% of general education requirements for graduation are elective; distribution requirements fairly numerous. About 20% of students entering as freshmen graduate within four years; 48% of freshmen do not return for sophomore year. *Calendar:* semester, summer school.

Undergraduate degrees conferred (168). 46% were in Education, 15% were in Liberal/General Studies, 9% were in Business and Management, 7% were in Psychology, 7% were in Business (Administrative Support), 4% were in Public Affairs, remainder in 9 other fields.

Varsity Sports. Men (NAIA): Baseball, Basketball, Cross Country, Track. Women (NAIA): Basketball, Cross Country, Track, Volleyball.

Student Body. College seeks national student body; 72% of students from in state; 74% South. An estimated 76% of students reported as Protestant, 3% Catholic, 16% unaffiliated; 3% Black, 6% Hispanic, 1% Asian, 1% other minority, according to most recent data available.

Religious Orientation. Lubbock Christian is a church-related institution; 14 semester hours of Biblical studies, attendance at daily chapel services required of all students.

Campus Life. About 32% of men, 45% of women live in traditional dormitories; no coed dormitories; rest live in off-campus housing or commute. Freshmen given preference in college housing if all students cannot be accommodated. No intervisitation in men's or women's dormitory rooms. There are 5 fraternities, 5 sororities on campus which about 35% of men, 32% of women join; they provide no residence facilities.

Annual Costs. Tuition and fees, $6,450; room and board, $2,600. About 85% of students receive financial aid; assistance is typically divided 33% scholarship, 40% loan, 27% work. College reports some scholarships awarded on the basis of academic merit alone. *Meeting Costs:* college offers parent loans, payment plans.

Luther College

Decorah, Iowa 52101 (319) 387-1287

A church-related, liberal arts college, Luther is located on an 800-acre rural campus in a community of 8,000, 70 miles south of Rochester, Minnesota. Most convenient major airport: Rochester (MN).

Founded: 1861
Affiliation: Evangelical Lutheran Church in America
Total Enrollment: 946 M, 1,408 W (full- and part-time)
Cost: $10K–$20K
% Receiving Financial Aid: 80%
Admission: Very Selective
Application Deadline: March 1

Admission is very selective. About 90% of applicants accepted, 42% of these actually enroll; 72% of freshmen graduate in top quarter of high school class, 95% in top half. Average freshman scores: SAT, 470–580 M, 460–570 W verbal, 570–680 M, 510–610 W mathematical; 62% of entering freshman score above 500 on verbal, 21% above 600, 3% above 700; 87% score above 500 on mathematical, 50% above 600, 12% above 700; ACT, 22–28 M, 23–28 W composite. *Required:* ACT or SAT, essay. Criteria considered in admissions, in order of importance: high school academic record, standardized test scores, recommendations, writing sample, extracurricular activities. *Entrance programs:* early admission, midyear admission, deferred admission, advanced placement. *Apply* by March 1 for priority; rolling admissions. *Transfers* welcome; 72 enrolled 1993–94.

Academic Environment. Degrees offered: bachelors. Pressures for academic achievement appear challenging, but not intense. Administration reports requirements for graduation include a 3 course integrated program for all students, 3 units in religion/philosophy, 3 units social sciences, 3 units foreign language, 2 units mathematics/science, and 2 semester hours physical education. Senior research paper required in field of concentration. Student body reported to be primarily concerned with occupational/professional goals, though a substantial minority pursues scholarly/intellectual interests. *Majors offered* include African-American studies, arts management, international management, Latin American studies, management information systems, museum studies, psychobiology, Scandinavian studies, sports management. Average undergraduate class size: 45% under 20, 48% 20–40, 7% over 40.

About 67% of students entering as freshmen graduate within four years; 74% within five years; 88% of freshmen return for sophomore year. *Special programs:* January term, CLEP, independent study, study abroad, honors, internships, undergraduate research, Washington Semester, credit by examination, social sciences field experience programs, 3–2 engineering, 3–2 forestry, nursing internship at Mayo Clinic. *Calendar:* 4–1–4, summer school.

Undergraduate degrees conferred (498). 16% were in Business and Management, 13% were in Social Sciences, 12% were in Life Sciences, 10% were in Education, 9% were in Visual and Performing Arts, 8% were in Letters, 7% were in Psychology, 4%

were in Health Sciences, 4% were in Communications, 4% were in Public Affairs, 3% were in Foreign Languages, 3% were in Philosophy and Religion, remainder in 3 other fields.

Graduates Career Data. Advanced studies pursued by 21% of students; 5% enter medical school; 2% enter law school; 2% enter business school; 1% dental school. Medical, dental, law and business schools typically enrolling largest numbers of graduates include U. of Iowa, U. of Minnesota, U. of Wisconsin, Mayo, Drake, William Mitchell. About 70% of 1992–93 graduates employed. Employers typically hiring largest numbers of graduates include Lutheran Brotherhood, Mayo Clinic, Carlson Companies, Principal Financial Group. *Career Counseling Program*: Student assessment of program reported as good for both career guidance and job placement. Alumni reported as active in both career guidance and job placement.

Faculty. About 85% of faculty hold PhD or equivalent. About 37% of teaching faculty are female; 4% Black, 3% Hispanic.

Student Body. College seeks a national student body; 39% of students from in state; 89% Midwest. An estimated 71% of students reported as Protestant, 13% as Catholic. *Minority group students:* foreign student and Black student advisers.

Religious Orientation. Luther is a church-related institution; religion/philosophy requirement of 9 credits; attendance at daily chapel services voluntary. Student body congregation carries on a student-directed program of worship and activity. Places of worship available on campus for Catholics and Protestants, 70 miles away for Jews.

Varsity Sports. Men (NCAA Div.III): Baseball, Basketball, Cross Country, Diving, Football, Golf, Soccer, Swimming, Tennis, Track, Wrestling. Women (NCAA Div.III): Basketball, Cross Country, Diving, Golf, Soccer, Softball, Swimming, Tennis, Track, Volleyball.

Campus Life. High percentage of students said to be involved in college community life and activities. Students have significant role in policy making through Community Assembly (19 students, 11 faculty and administration). "No hours" privilege for all residents. Intervisitation may be scheduled by each residence unit within college-wide regulations of 9:30 am to 1 am daily, 2 am on weekends. Alcohol permitted in student rooms only; legal age, 21. Smoking restricted to designated areas. Drugs prohibited.

About 85% each of men, women live in dormitories; rest live in off-campus housing or commute. Freshmen given preference in college housing if all students cannot be accommodated. There are 5 fraternities, 6 sororities on campus, which about 7% of men, 9% of women join. About 85% of students leave campus on weekends.

Annual Costs Tuition and fees, $12,375; room and board, $3,525; estimated $1,000 other, exclusive of travel. About 80% of students receive financial aid; average amount of assistance, $8,228. Assistance is typically divided 65% grant, 25% loan, 10% work. College reports 1,080 scholarships awarded on the basis of academic merit alone, 343 for special talents. *Meeting Costs:* college offers guaranteed cost plan, monthly payment plan with no interest.

Lycoming College

Williamsport, Pennsylvania 17701 (800) 345-3920

A church-related, liberal arts college, Lycoming is located on a 35-acre campus in a city of 37,900, 90 miles north of Harrisburg. Most convenient major airports: Harrisburg, or Avoca (near Wilkes Barre).

Founded: 1812
Affiliation: United Methodist
Total Enrollment: 642 M, 721 W (full-time)
Cost: $10K–$20K
% Receiving Financial Aid: 84%
Admission: Non-selective
Application Deadline: April 1

Admission. Graduates of approved high schools with 16 academic units eligible; 78% of applicants accepted, 36% of these actually enroll; 28% of freshman graduate in top fifth of high school class, 59% in top two-fifths. Average freshman SAT scores: 450 M, 455 W verbal, 511 M, 480 W mathematical; 28% score above 500 on verbal, 6% above 600; 48% score above 500 on mathematical, 13% above 600. *Required:* SAT, 2 essays; interview recommended. Criteria considered in admissions, in order of importance: high school academic record, standardized test scores, recommendations, writing sample, extracurricular activities; other factors considered: diverse student body, special talents, alumni children. *Entrance programs:* early admission, midyear admission. About 15% of entering students from parochial schools, 10% from private schools. *Apply* by April 1; rolling admissions. *Transfers* welcome; 64 enrolled 1993–94.

Academic Environment. Degree offered: bachelors. Administration reports 40–45% of courses required for graduation are distribution requirements; remainder are major requirements and electives. Individualized curriculum possible for all students. Internship program with possibility of full semester of credit in supervised work experience. *Majors offered* in addition to usual arts and sciences include accounting, astronomy, business administration, computer science, BFA in sculpture, nursing, theater, photography, creative writing, criminal justice; interdisciplinary majors include Near East culture and archaeology, accounting-mathematics, literature. Most popular majors are business, psychology, biology. Average undergraduate class size: 62% under 20, 34% 20–40, 4% over 40.

About 52% of students entering as freshmen graduate within four year, 59% eventually; 82% of freshmen return for sophomore year. *Special programs:* CLEP, independent study, study abroad, honors, undergraduate research, 3-year degree, individualized majors, optional May term, London Semester, seminar study, Washington Semester, United Nations Semester, 3–2 engineering, 3–2 forestry, cooperative program with American Academy of Dramatic Arts, internship program, cross registration with Pennsylvania College of Technology. Calendar: 4–4–1, summer school.

Undergraduate degrees conferred (202). 23% were in Business and Management, 20% were in Social Sciences, 15% were in Psychology, 10% were in Protective Services, 7% were in Communications, 5% were in Health Sciences, 5% were in Letters, 4% were in Visual and Performing Arts, 3% were in Physical Sciences, remainder in 4 other fields.

Graduates Career Data. Advanced studies pursued by 15% of students; 4% enter law school; 2% enter medical school; 3% enter dental school. About 90% of 1992–93 graduates employed. Fields typically hiring largest number of graduates include business, non-profit organizations, education, medical. Career Development Services include resources for career exploration, SIGI Plus computerized career guidance system, mock interviews, resume typing service, job shadowing program.

Faculty. About 80% of faculty hold PhD or equivalent. About 64% of undergraduate classes taught by tenured faculty. About 30% of teaching faculty are female.

Student Body. College seeks a national student body; 77% of students from in state; 96% of students from Middle Atlantic, 2% foreign students. An estimated 49% of students reported as Protestant, 31% Catholic, 2% Jewish; 4% ethnic minorities. Average age of undergraduate student: 22.

Religious Orientation. Lycoming is a church-related institution; distribution requirements include 2 courses in either philosophy or religion for all students.

Varsity Sports. Men (Div.III): Basketball, Cross Country, Football, Golf, Soccer, Swimming, Tennis, Track, Wrestling. Women (Div.III): Basketball, Cross Country, Field Hockey, Soccer, Softball, Swimming, Tennis, Track, Volleyball.

Campus Life. All freshmen (and their parents) participate in Summer Orientation Program. Eighty percent of college's programs are accessible to mobility-impaired students. Security curfew on all dorms (11 PM Sunday-Thursday, 2 am weekends); intervisitation is limited. Cars allowed; smoking restricted; those 21 and older may have alcohol on campus; drugs prohibited.

About 23% of men, 42% of women live in traditional dormitories; 48% of men, 19% of women live in coed dormitories; 18% of men, 26% of women commute. Freshmen given preference in college housing if all students cannot be accommodated. Sexes segregated in coed dormitories either by wing or floor. There are 5 fraternities, 4 sororities on campus which about 31% men, 27% women join; 11% of men, 13% of women live in fraternities and sororities. More than 20% of resident students leave campus on weekends.

Annual Costs. Tuition and fees, $13,000; room and board, $4,200; estimated $1,300 other, exclusive of travel. About 84% of students receive financial aid; average amount of assistance, $11,267. Assistance is typically divided 7% scholarship, 60% grant, 29% loan, 4% work. College reports 5 scholarships awarded on the basis of academic merit alone, 3 for special talents.

Lynchburg College

Lynchburg, Virginia 24501 (804) 522-8300

An independent college, historically related to the Christian Church (Disciples of Christ), located in a city of 155,000, 120 miles west of Richmond. Most convenient major airport: Lynchburg.

Founded: 1903
Affiliation: Independent (Disciples of Christ)
UG Enrollment: 581 M, 943 W (full-time); 98 M, 182 W (part-time)
Total Enrollment: 2,244
Cost: $10K–$20K
% Receiving Financial Aid: 70%
Admission: Non-selective
Application Deadline: Rolling

Admission. Graduates of approved high schools with 15 units eligible; 74% of applicants accepted, 23% of these actually enroll. Average freshman SAT scores, middle fifty percent range: 800–1,000 combined verbal, mathematical. *Required:* SAT or ACT, 3 ACH including English plus preferably language and mathematics (for placement); interview recommended. Criteria considered in admissions, in order of importance: high school academic record, standardized test scores, extracurricular activities, writing sample, recommendations, leadership qualities; other factors considered: special talents, alumni children, diverse student body, leadership, volunteer work, "distinctive characteristics", religious affiliation and/or commitment. *Entrance programs:* early decision, early admission, midyear admission, deferred admission, advanced placement. About 24% of entering students from private or parochial schools. *Apply:* rolling admissions. *Transfers* welcome; 98 enrolled 1993–94.
Academic Environment. Degrees offered: bachelors, masters. General education requirements account for about half of total program. About 55% of students entering as freshmen graduate within four years, 65% eventually; 25% of freshmen do not return for sophomore year. Average undergraduate class size: 52% of classes under 20, 47% between 20–40, 1% over 40. *Special programs:* CLEP, honors, Black Incentive Program, independent study, study abroad, internships, cross-registration with Sweet Briar and Randolph-Macon Women's colleges, 3–2 BA/MBA, 3–2 engineering, medical technology program with Duke. *Calendar:* semester, summer school.
Undergraduate degrees conferred (423). 27% were in Business and Management, 17% were in Social Sciences, 14% were in Communications, 13% were in Education, 6% were in Letters, 5% were in Psychology, 4% were in Visual and Performing Arts, 4% were in Health Sciences, 3% were in Life Sciences, remainder in 6 other fields.
Graduates Career Data. Advanced studies pursued by 27% of students. Graduate and professional schools typically enrolling largest numbers of graduates include U. of Virginia, U. of Richmond, Washington & Lee. About 65% of 1992–93 graduates employed. Fields typically hiring the largest number of graduates include education, accounting, communications, marketing.
Faculty. About 66% of faculty hold PhD or equivalent. About 60% of undergraduate classes taught by tenured faculty. About 36% of teaching faculty are female; 5% minorities.
Student Body. College seeks a national student body; 40% of students from in state; 74% Middle Atlantic, 17% New England, 5% South, 2% foreign. An estimated 47% of students reported as Protestant, 30% Catholic, 2% Jewish, 20% unaffiliated, 1% other; 7% as Black, 1% Hispanic, 1% Asian.
Religious Orientation. Lynchburg is independent, and historically related to the Christian Church (Disciples of Christ). Religious Activities Committee plans and supervises religious program of campus. Ecumenical service and Mass held in chapel building each Sunday.
Varsity Sports. Men (Div.III): Baseball, Basketball, Cross Country, Equestrian, Golf, Lacrosse, Soccer, Tennis, Track. Women (Div.III): Basketball, Cross Country, Equestrian, Field Hockey, Lacrosse, Soccer, Softball, Tennis, Track, Volleyball.
Campus Life. About 20% of men, 20% of women live in traditional dormitories; 70% of men, 70% of women live in coed dormitories; rest live in off-campus housing or commute. Freshmen given preference in college housing if all students cannot be accommodated. Intervisitation hours in men's and women's dormitory rooms determined by each dorm. There are 6 fraternities, 3 sororities, which about 25% of men, 14% of women join. About 10% of resident students leave campus on weekends.
Annual Costs. Tuition and fees, $11,600; room and board, $5,400; estimated $300 other, exclusive of travel. About 70% of students receive financial aid; average amount of assistance, $10,000. Assistance is typically divided 40% scholarship, 20% grant, 20% loan, 20% work. College reports some scholarships awarded on the basis of academic merit alone. *Meeting Costs:* college offers deferred payment and prepayment plans.

Lyndon State College

Lyndonville, Vermont 05851 (802) 626-9371

A state-supported college, located in a community of 3,500, 45 miles northeast of Montpelier. Most convenient major airport: Burlington.

Founded: 1911
Affiliation: State
Total Enrollment: 1,152 M, W (full-time)
Cost: < $10K
% Receiving Financial Aid: 60%
Admission: Non-selective
Application Deadline: Rolling

Admission. High school graduates with 16 units eligible; 88% of applicants accepted, 49% of these actually enroll. Average freshman scores, according to most recent data available: SAT, 440 M, 410 W verbal, 400 M, 390 W mathematical. *Required:* SAT or ACT; interview recommended. *Out-of-state* freshman applicants: state does not limit out-of-state enrollment. No special requirements for out-of-state applicants; 82% accepted, 61% enroll. *Apply:* rolling admissions. *Transfers* welcome.
Academic Environment. *Degrees:* AB, BS. About 97% of general education requirements for graduation are elective; distribution requirements limited. About 45% of students entering as freshmen graduate eventually; 35% of freshmen do not return for sophomore year. *Special programs:* CLEP, independent study, undergraduate research, study abroad, 3-year degree. *Calendar:* semester, summer school.
Undergraduate degrees conferred (152). 26% were in Education, 17% were in Business and Management, 15% were in Psychology, 9% were in Physical Sciences, 9% were in Communications, 7% were in Letters, 6% were in Communications Technologies, 4% were in Social Sciences, remainder in 6 other fields.
Student Body. College seeks a national student body; 61% of students from in state; 94% New England, 3% Middle Atlantic.
Campus Life. About 60% of men, 40% of women live in coed dormitories; rest live in off-campus housing or commute. Intervisitation in men's and women's dormitory rooms "permitted"; sexes segregated either by wing or floor. About 80% of students leave campus on weekends.
Annual Costs. Tuition and fees, $3,753 (out-of-state, $7,905); room and board, $4,640. About 60% of students receive financial aid; assistance is typically divided 49% scholarship, 41% loan, 10% work. College reports some scholarships awarded on the basis of academic merit alone.

Macalester College

St. Paul, Minnesota 55105 (612) 696-6357

One of a small number of colleges in the upper North Central region that attract an able student body from all parts of the country. The 50-acre campus is located in a residential area of St. Paul. Most convenient major airport: Minneapolis/St. Paul.

Founded: 1885
Affiliation: Presbyterian Church (USA)
Total Enrollment: 760 M, 963 W (full-time)
Cost: $10K–$20K
% Receiving Financial Aid: 75%
Admission: Very (+) Selective
Application Deadline: January 15

Admission is very (+) selective. About 57% of applicants accepted, 30% of these actually enroll; 79% of freshmen graduate in top fifth of high school class, 98% in top two-fifths. Average freshman scores, middle fifty percent range: SAT, 550–660 verbal, 580–690 mathematical; 92% of students score above 500 on verbal, 58% above 600, 9%

above 700; 95% score above 500 on mathematical, 66% above 600, 23% above 700; ACT, 27–31 composite. *Required:* SAT or ACT, essay, teacher and secondary school counselor recommendations; interview recommended. Criteria considered in admissions, in order of importance: high school academic record, extracurricular activities, standardized test scores, recommendations, writing sample; other factors considered: diverse student body, special talents, alumni children, "commitment to ethical concerns (service, international awareness, political awareness, etc.)." *Entrance programs:* early decision, early admission, deferred admission. About 32% of entering students from private or parochial schools. *Apply* by January 15. *Transfers* welcome; 41 enrolled 1993–94.

Academic Environment. Degree offered: bachelors. Students are members of major faculty and trustee committees. Macalester is nationally known for its academic excellence. Outstanding faculty, small classes, honors and research projects and a learning environment that stresses participation and one-on-one work with professors provide the basis for this challenging academic experience. Distribution requirements mandate 2 courses each in social sciences, natural sciences and mathematics, 3 courses in humanities, 1 in fine arts, 1 course in international diversity; proficiency in foreign language and First Year Seminar and Senior Year Capstone project also required; interim term (courses or projects) recommended. Students reported to be strongly oriented toward scholarly/intellectual pursuits, but also with some concern for occupational/professional goals. *Majors offered* include usual arts and sciences, computer science, environmental studies, geography, Japan Studies, women's studies; 4 types of majors possible: departmental major, core concentration (2 related sets of 6 courses each), interdepartmental major, student-designed interdepartmental major. Average undergraduate class size: 25.

About 65% of students entering as freshmen graduate within four years, 75% eventually; 9% of freshmen do not return for sophomore year. *Special programs:* January Term, independent study, study abroad, honors, undergraduate research, individualized majors, double majors, programs of ACM, cross-registration with 4 other Twin Cities colleges, exchanges with Japan, Germany, Costa Rica, 3–2 programs in engineering and architecture. *Calendar:* 4–1–4, summer school. *Miscellaneous:* Phi Beta Kappa.

Undergraduate degrees conferred (398). 42% were in Social Sciences, 9% were in Letters, 8% were in Psychology, 7% were in Philosophy and Religion, 6% were in Multi/Interdisciplinary Studies, 6% were in Visual and Performing Arts, 6% were in Foreign Languages, 5% were in Life Sciences, 5% were in Physical Sciences, 4% were in Mathematics, remainder in 3 other fields.

Graduates Career Data. Advanced studies pursued by 25% of students within 6 months of graduation; 3% enter medical school; 3% enter law school. About 63% of 1992–93 graduates are employed. Career Development Services provided for students and alumni; include career advising program, job listings, graduate school advising, Discover program, on-campus recruiting, testing, alumni network, mentor program, credential service, workshops, internships. Alumni reported as active in both career guidance and job placement.

Faculty. About 91% of faculty hold PhD or equivalent. About 65% of undergraduate classes taught by tenured faculty. About 42% of teaching faculty are female; 4% African American, 6% Hispanic-American, 6% Asian-American, 1% Native American.

Student Body. College seeks a national student body; 24% of students from in state; 51% Midwest, 11% Middle Atlantic, 9% New England, 7% West, 7% Northwest, 4% South, 11% international. An estimated 5% of students reported as African American, 5% Hispanic American, 5% Asian American, 1% Native American.

Religious Orientation. Macalester is a church-related institution, but makes no religious demands on students. Ecumenical chapel on campus offers Protestant and Catholic services, and a Hebrew House. Places of worship available in immediate community for 3 major faiths.

Varsity Sports. Men (Div.III): Baseball, Basketball, Cross Country, Diving, Football, Golf, Soccer, Swimming, Tennis, Track. Women (Div.III): Basketball, Cross Country, Diving, Golf, Soccer, Swimming, Tennis, Track, Volleyball.

Campus Life. Students have "integral" role in setting regulations governing student life. All on-campus residences coed, varying by floor, or adjacent rooms. Cars allowed; smoking restricted to posted areas; alcohol allowed for those 21 and older; drugs prohibited. Centers of St. Paul and Minneapolis 3–5 miles from campus; college provides free shuttle bus service on regular schedule to libraries, cultural events, and other area campuses, including U. of Minnesota.

About 19% of men, 16% of women live in traditional dormitories; 45% of men, 49% of women live in coed dormitories; 35% of men, 35% of women live in off-campus housing or commute. There are no fraternities or sororities. Less than 5% of students leave campus on weekends.

Annual Costs. Tuition and fees, $15,704; room and board, $4,502; estimated $1,200 other, exclusive of travel. About 75% of students receive financial aid; average amount of assistance, $11,915. Assistance is typically divided 76% scholarship/grant, 15% loan, 9% work. College reports 99 scholarships awarded on the basis of academic merit alone, 1,197 for need. *Meeting Costs:* college offers 8-installment payment plan, interest-subsidized PLUS loans, Minnesota SELF Loans, EXCEL Loans.

MacMurray College

Jacksonville, Illinois 62650 (217) 479-7000

A church-related, co-educational liberal arts college, MacMurray welcomes students of all races and creeds. The campus is located in a community of 25,000, 35 miles west of Springfield and 80 miles north of St. Louis. Most convenient major airport: Springfield.

Founded: 1846
Affiliation: Independent (United Methodist)
Total Enrollment: 272 M, 356 W (full-time); 27 M, 36 W (part-time)
Cost: < $10K
% Receiving Financial Aid: 90%
Admission: Non-selective
Application Deadline: July 15

Admission. About 75% of applicants accepted, 32% of these actually enroll; 24% of freshman graduate in top fifth of high school class, 46% in top two-fifths. Average freshman ACT scores: 20.7 composite. *Required:* SAT or ACT, essay; interview strongly recommended. Criteria considered in admissions, in order of importance: high school academic record, writing sample, recommendations, standardized test scores, extracurricular activities; other factors considered: diverse student body, special talents, alumni children religious affiliation and/or commitment. *Entrance programs:* early admission, midyear admission, deferred admission, advanced placement. *Apply* by July 15; rolling admissions. *Transfers* welcome; 49 enrolled 1993–94.

Academic Environment. Degrees offered: associates, bachelors. General education requirements include 3-course rhetoric sequence, 5-course history of ideas sequence, 4-course distribution sequence, math and composition competency exams. *Majors offered* include elementary education, special education, nursing, criminal justice, Russian and East European studies, theater arts, administration of justice, sports management, education of the hearing impaired. Nearby facilities for deaf and visually impaired, State Developmental Center, and medium security prison offer unusual opportunities for practical experience for many popular majors. Average undergraduate class size: 20% under 20, 75% 20–40, 5% over 40.

About 41% of students entering as freshmen graduate within four year, 47% graduate eventually; 85% of freshmen return for sophomore year. *Special programs:* CLEP, independent study, honors, undergraduate research (in physical sciences), January Term (included in full-time tuition), study abroad, urban semester in St. Louis, Washington, United Nations Semester, programs of CSCA, 3–2 programs in engineering, occupational therapy, 3–1 premed, 3–1 pre-veterinary, cross-registration with Illinois College, credit by examination. *Library:* government depository; open stack privileges. *Calendar:* 4–1–4, summer school.

Undergraduate degrees conferred (91). 31% were in Education, 12% were in Business and Management, 11% were in Health Sciences, 8% were in Psychology, 5% were in Visual and Performing Arts, 5% were in Life Sciences, 4% were in Social Sciences, 4% were in Public Affairs, 4% were in Protective Services, 4% were in Liberal/General Studies, 3% were in Letters, remainder in 4 other fields.

Graduates Career Data. Full-time advanced studies pursued immediately after graduation (1993) by 12% of students; 4% enter law school; 2% enter business school; 2% enter medical school. Law schools typically enrolling largest number of graduates include U. of Illinois, Loyola, Washington U.; business schools include U. Of Illinois, IN University; medical schools include U. Of Illinois, Southern Illinois U., IN University, Washington U. About 85% of 1992–93 graduates employed in major field. Fields typically hiring largest number of graduates include nursing, special education, criminal justice. *Career Counseling Program* includes career guidance, field experience opportunities, alumni mentor network, and job placement. Alumni reported as active in both career guidance and job placement.

Faculty. About 50% of faculty hold PhD or equivalent. About 48% of undergraduate classes taught by tenured faculty. About 35% of teaching faculty are female; 5% Black, 3% other minority.

Student Body. College seeks a national student body; 80% of students from in state; 90% Midwest, 4% South, 3% West, 1% New England, 1% foreign. An estimated 48% of students reported as Protestant, 26% Catholic, 26% unaffiliated; 5% Black, 2% Hispanic, 1% Asian, 1% other minority.

Religious Orientation. MacMurray is a church-related institution; all juniors required to complete 4 hours in philosophy or religion; attendance at chapel services and convocations voluntary. Places of worship available in immediate community for Catholics and Protestants, 35 miles away for Jews.

Varsity Sports. Men (Div.III): Baseball, Basketball, Football, Golf, Soccer, Tennis, Wrestling. Women (Div.III): Basketball, Golf, Soccer, Softball, Tennis, Volleyball.

Campus Life. Limited intervisitation in freshmen halls; about 100 hours per week in upper-class halls. Campus relatively isolated; students depend in large part on variety of college-sponsored cultural and social events. St. Louis, 80 miles away, is nearest major metropolitan center. Cars allowed for all. Alcohol (beer and wine) is permitted in upper-class halls, not allowed at campus functions.

About 19% of men, 35% women live in traditional dormitories; 51% men, 27% women in coed dormitories; 30% men, 38% women commute. Sexes segregated in coed dormitories by floor or room. There is 1 fraternity which 9% of men join. About 40% of resident students leave campus on weekends.

Annual Costs. Tuition and fees, $9,160; room and board, $3,640; estimated $1,050 other, exclusive of travel. About 90% of students receive financial aid; average amount of assistance, $8,200. Assistance is typically divided 58% scholarship/grant, 36% loan, 6% work. College reports 62 major and unlimited minor scholarships awarded on the basis of academic merit alone, 10 for special talents alone, unlimited awarded for need.

Madison College

(See James Madison University)

Madonna University

Livonia, Michigan 48150-1173 (313) 591-5052

A church-related college, conducted by the Felician Sisters, located in a Detroit suburb of 115,000. Most convenient major airport: Detroit Metro.

Founded: 1947
Affiliation: Roman Catholic
UG Enrollment: 299 M, 1,118 W (full-time); 584 M, 1,851 W (part-time)
Total Enrollment: 4,311
Cost: < $10K
% Receiving Financial Aid: 31%
Admission: Non-selective
Application Deadline: Oct. 1

Admission. Graduates of accredited high schools eligible; 63% of applicants accepted, 87% of these actually enroll. Average freshman ACT scores: 21 composite. *Required:* ACT, minimum HS GPA 2.5; interview recommended. Criteria considered in admissions, in order of importance: high school academic record, standardized test scores, extracurricular activities, writing sample, recommendations; other factors considered: special talents, alumni children, diverse student body. Entrance program: advanced placement. About 23% of entering students from parochial schools. *Apply* by October 1; rolling admissions. *Transfers* welcome.

Academic Environment. Degrees offered: associates, bachelors, masters. About 40% of general education requirements for graduation are elective; distribution requirements fairly numerous. About 47% of students entering as freshmen graduate within four years, 52% eventually; 70% of freshmen return for sophomore year. Average undergraduate class size: 59% under 20, 37% 20–40, 4% over 40. *Special programs:* Interpreters for Deaf Program, CLEP, study abroad, 3-year degree, individualized majors, home study program, cooperative education program, consortium with Marygrove, Mercy, U. of Detroit, Sacred Heart, Michigan Bell Program (undergraduate business administration), gerentology, Japanese studies. Adult programs: "All programs give due consideration to the adult learner." Calendar: semester, post-term following spring semester.

Undergraduate degrees conferred (562). 23% were in Business and Management, 16% were in Health Sciences, 8% were in Protective Services, 6% were in Social Sciences, 6% were in Public Affairs, 6% were in Law, 5% were in Allied Health, 4% were in Home Economics, 4% were in Psychology, 4% were in Vocational Home Economics, 3% were in Education, 3% were in Letters, remainder in 15 other fields.

Graduates Career Data. Advanced studies pursued by 19% of students. About 89% of 1992–93 graduates employed. Fields typically hiring largest numbers of graduates include accounting, business, legal assistant, management, nursing. Career Development Services include career counseling, job listings, resume referral, training in job search techniques.

Faculty. About 50% of faculty hold PhD or equivalent. No tenure system; about 53% of teaching faculty are female; 3% Black, 10% other minority.

Student Body. College does not seek a national student body; 99% of students from in state. An estimated 31% of students reported as Protestant, 51% Catholic, 1% Jewish, 18% unaffiliated; 9% as Black, 2% Hispanic, 3% Asian, 2% other minority. Average age of undergraduate student: 31.

Religious Orientation. Madonna is a Catholic institution; 8 hours of theology required of all students.

Varsity Sports. Men: Baseball, Basketball, Softball. Women: Basketball, Volleyball.

Campus Life. About 3% of men, 4% of women live in traditional dormitories; rest commute. Freshmen given preference in college housing if all students cannot be accommodated. Intervisitation in women's dormitory rooms limited. There are no fraternities or sororities.

Annual Costs. Tuition and fees, $4,790; room and board, $3,676 (semi/21 meals); estimated $1,050 other, exclusive of travel. About 31% of students receive financial aid; average amount of assistance, $1,948. Assistance is typically divided 2% scholarship, 50% grant, 43% loan, 5% work. College reports 12 scholarships awarded on the basis of academic merit alone, 4 for special talents alone.

Maharishi International University

Fairfield, Iowa 52556

An accredited 4-year institution, Maharishi International offers baccalaureate programs in letters, business and management, biological sciences, fine and applied arts, physical sciences, psychology, and the science of creative intelligence. University also offers masters and doctoral programs. Significant number of undergraduate foreign students.

Affiliation: Independent

Undergraduate degrees conferred (61). 30% were in Multi/Interdisciplinary Studies, 21% were in Visual and Performing Arts, 16% were in Business and Management, 8% were in Letters, 8% were in Computer and Engineering Related Technology, 7% were in Life Sciences, 3% were in Public Affairs, remainder in 4 other fields.

Maine College of Art

Portland, Maine 04101

One of the nation's more venerable schools of art which offers a variety of programs in fine and applied arts. Formerly known as Portland School of Art.

Affiliation: Independent

Maine Maritime Academy

Castine, Maine 04421 **(207) 326-4311**

A state institution designed primarily to train students to become officers in the merchant marine.

Founded: 1941
Affiliation: State
Total Enrollment: 645 M, 45 W (full-time)
Cost: < $10K
Admission: Non-selective
Application Deadline: July 1

Admission. High school graduates or equivalent who are U.S. citizens eligible; 70% of applicants accepted, 45% of these actually enroll. *Required:* SAT or ACT; interview recommended. Criteria considered in admissions, in order of importance: high school academic record, recommendations, standardized test scores, interview, extracurricular activities, writing sample; other factors considered: special talents, alumni children, diverse student body. *Out-of-state* freshman applicants: academy actively seeks students from out-of-state. State does not limit out-of-state enrollment. States from which most out-of-state students are drawn: Connecticut, New Hampshire. Entrance program: deferred admission. *Apply* by July 1; rolling admission.

Academic Environment. Degrees offered: associates, bachelors, masters. About 30% of general education requirements for graduation are elective; no distribution requirements. Annual training cruise required of all students. About 70% of entering freshman graduate within four years, 75% eventually; 70% of freshman return for sophomore year. *Special programs:* Navy ROTC. *Calendar:* semester, 2-month training cruise.

Undergraduate degrees conferred (81). 100% were in Engineering.

Graduate Career Data. About 95% of 1992–93 graduates are employed. Employers typically hiring largest numbers of graduates include shipping companies, shipyards, engineering firms.

Faculty. About 50% of faculty hold PhD or equivalent. About 15% of teaching faculty are female.

Student Body. Academy seeks a national student body; 60% of students from in state; 25% of students from New England, 50% Middle Atlantic, 3% foreign.

Varsity Sports. Men (Div.III): Basketball, Cross Country, Football, Lacrosse, Soccer, Sailing (N.E. ISA). Women (Div.III): Cross Country, Sailing.

Campus Life. About 80% men, 90% women live in coed dormitories; rest commute. No intervisitation in men's or women's dormitory rooms. There is 1 fraternity which about 6% of men join. About 75% of resident students leave campus on weekends.

Annual Costs. Tuition and fees, $3,940; room and board, $4,396. Academy reports 100 scholarships awarded on the basis of need alone.

University of Maine System

Bangor, Maine 04401

The University of Maine System, created by statute in 1968, encompasses the State's seven public universities - the University of Maine in Orono, Maine's land- and sea-grant institution; the University of Southern Maine, a comprehensive urban university; four regional baccalaureate institutions: University of Maine at Farmington, at Fort Kent, at Machias, and at Presque Isle; and a community college, the University of Maine at Augusta.

University of Maine at Orono

Orono, Maine 04469 **(207) 581-1110**

The parent campus of the university, Orono is not only the oldest but also the largest within the system. The 300-acre campus is located in a town of 10,000, 8 miles north of Bangor. Most convenient major airport: Bangor International.

Founded: 1865
Affiliation: State
UG Enrollment: 3,938 M, 3,428 W (full-time)
Total Enrollment: 11,343
Cost: < $10K
% Receiving Financial Aid: 57%
Admission: Selective
Application Deadline: February 1

Admission is selective. For all schools, 87% of applicants accepted, 33% of these actually enroll; 44% of freshmen graduate in top fifth of high school class, 73% in top two-fifths. Average freshman SAT scores: 453 verbal, 501 mathematical. *Required:* SAT or ACT, interview (off-campus can be arranged). Criteria considered in admissions, in order of importance: high school academic record, standardized test scores, recommendations, extracurricular activities, writing sample; other factors considered: special talents. *Out-of-state* freshman applicants: state does not limit out-of-state enrollment. No special requirements for out-of-state applicants; 72% accepted, 37% enroll. *Entrance programs:* early decision, early admission, advanced placement. *Apply* by February 1. *Transfers* welcome; 554 enrolled 1993–94.

Academic Environment. Degrees offered: associates, bachelors, masters, doctoral. Administration reports that student interests are primarily focused on occupational/professional goals, but with some interest in scholarly/intellectual pursuits, and social activities. Administration reports 50% of courses required for graduation are elective; distribution requirements for AB, however, fairly numerous: 4 courses in social sciences, 2 years in natural sciences and mathematics, 2 semesters in 1 field of humanities, public-speaking course, foreign language proficiency (except for nursing), year physical education. English proficiency placement exam required of all entering freshmen. *Undergraduate studies* offered by colleges of Arts and Sciences, Business Administration, Education, Engineering and Science, Life Sciences and Agriculture, School of Engineering Technology, Technical Divisions of Life Sciences and Agriculture, University College, and Forest Resources. *Majors offered* in addition to usual studies include anthropology, broadcasting/film, international affairs, medical technology, nursing, public management, theater, surveying engineering, computer engineering, landscape horticulture, molecular and cellular biology, food science. Programs generally considered to be strongest academically include: engineering, forest resources, international affairs, Canadian studies, German, art.

About 29% of students entering as freshmen graduate within four years, 55% eventually; 23% of freshmen do not return for sophomore year. *Special programs:* CLEP, independent study, study abroad, honors, internships, individualized majors, Center for Environmental Studies, Onwards Program, credit by examination. *Calendar:* semester, summer school.

Undergraduate degrees conferred (1464). 15% were in Business and Management, 12% were in Social Sciences, 12% were in Education, 10% were in Engineering, 7% were in Letters, 5% were in Renewable Natural Resources, 5% were in Home Economics, 5% were in Psychology, 5% were in Communications, 4% were in Engineering and Engineering Related Technology, 4% were in Public Affairs, 3% were in Life Sciences, 3% were in Health Sciences, remainder in 12 other fields.

Graduates Career Data. According to most recent data available, full-time graduate or professional study pursued by 24% of students immediately after graduation. Employers typically hiring largest numbers of graduates include Ball Iron Works, UNUM, Digital Equipment, Maine Yankee. *Career Counseling Program:* Alumni reported as active in both career guidance and job placement.

Faculty. About 81% of faculty hold PhD or equivalent. About 40% of teaching faculty are female.

Student Body. About 81% of students from in state; 96% New England, 1% Middle Atlantic, 1% Midwest, 2% foreign. An estimated 2% of students reported as Black, 3% other ethnic minorities. *Minority group students:* special financial, academic, and social provisions.

Varsity Sports. Men (Div.I): Baseball, Basketball, Cross Country, Football (IAA), Golf, Hockey, Soccer, Swimming & Diving, Tennis, Track. Women (Div.I): Basketball, Cross Country, Field Hockey, Golf, Soccer, Softball, Swimming & Diving, Tennis, Track.

Campus Life. Student interest in sororities/fraternities and intercollegiate athletics reported high. Students have influence on regulations governing campus social life. Campus is located in "a semi-rural setting with access to the great Maine woods." Student leader reports that "atmosphere of our campus is warm," with close faculty/student relationships, and adds that it "is an ideal spot for the outdoor enthusiast as well as scholar." Administration source adds that those least likely to feel at home on campus would be "city folk." Nearest major cultural center is Boston, 200 miles away. Cars allowed; limited campus parking facilities.

About 23% of men, 19% of women live in traditional dormitories; 1% of men, 1% of women in coed dormitories; 64% of men, 79% of women live in off-campus housing or commute. Freshmen given preference in college housing if all students cannot be accommodated. Sexes segregated in coed dormitories either by wing or floor. There are 13 fraternities, 7 sororities on campus which about 18% of men, 11% of women join; 12% of men, less than 1% of women live in fraternities and sororities.

Annual Costs. Tuition and fees, $3,085 (out-of-state, $7,975); room and board, $4,355. About 57% of students receive financial aid; average amount of assistance, $6,414. Assistance is typically divided 38% scholarship/grant, 45% loan, 17% work. University reports some scholarships awarded on the basis of academic merit alone. *Meeting Costs:* university offers budget payment plan.

University of Maine at Farmington

Farmington, Maine 04938 (207) 778-7065

A campus of the University of Maine, located in a town of 5,600, 30 miles northwest of Augusta. Most convenient major airport: Portland.

Founded: 1863
Affiliation: State
Total Enrollment: 606 M, 1,300 W (full-time); 87 M, 257 W (part-time)
Cost: < $10K
% Receiving Financial Aid: 70%
Admission: Non-selective
Application Deadline: April 15

Admission. Graduates of approved high schools with 16–18 units in college preparatory program preferably in top half of class eligible; 66% of applicants accepted, 55% of these actually enroll; 45% of freshmen graduate in top quarter of high school class, 83% in top half. Average freshman scores: SAT, 452 M, 430 W verbal, 504 M, 462 W mathematical. *Required:* essay, college preparatory courses, top half of graduating class, counselor recommendation; interview recommended. Criteria considered in admissions, in order of importance: high school academic record, recommendations, extracurricular activities; writing sample for creative writing applicants; other factors considered: leadership roles in high school, for older students most weight is placed on current motivation. *Out-of-state* freshman applicants: university actively seeks students from out-of-state. State does not limit out-of-state enrollment. About 73 out-of-state students enrolled. States from which most out-of-state students are drawn: Massachusetts, Vermont, Rhode Island, Connecticut, New Hampshire. Students from other New England states can apply through New England Regional Student Program and are given consideration over other out-of-state students and reduced tuition for certain programs not offered by their home state university. Entrance program: early action exemplary achievement. *Apply* by April 15; modified rolling admission. *Transfers* welcome; 121 enrolled 1993–94.

Academic Environment. Degrees offered: bachelors. Core requirements include English composition, mathematics, natural sciences, humanities, social and behavioral sciences, and health and fitness. Majors offered include: ski industries, environmental sciences, theater arts, visual arts/performing arts, creative writing, international studies, early childhood special education. *Special programs:* CLEP, honors, independent study, study abroad, undergraduate research, individualized majors, Program of Basic Studies, internships in health and rehabilitation, French immersion. Average undergraduate class size: 61% under 20, 38% 20–40, 1% over 40. About 30% of entering freshman graduate within four years, 68% eventually; 71% of freshman return for sophomore year. *Calendar:* semester, summer school.

Undergraduate degrees conferred (333). 60% were in Education, 16% were in Multi/Interdisciplinary Studies, 7% were in Public Affairs, 4% were in Psychology, 4% were in Liberal/General Studies, remainder in 5 other fields.

Graduates Career Data. Advanced studies pursued by 16% of students. About 87% of 1992–93 graduates employed. Fields typically hiring largest numbers of graduates include education, social service agencies, insurance, retail, technical. Career Development Services include resources for career exploration, job listings, alumni networking, training in job search techniques, newsletter.

Faculty. About 74% of faculty hold PhD or equivalent. About 31% of teaching faculty are female; 4% other minority.

Student Body. University does not seek a national student body; 89% of students from in state; 89% from New England, 1% foreign. Average age of undergraduate student: 24.

Varsity Sports. Men (NAIA Div.II): Baseball, Basketball, Golf, Soccer. Women (NAIA, Div.II): Basketball, Field Hockey, Soccer, Softball, Volleyball.

Campus Life. About 11% of women live in traditional dormitories; 40% of men, 35% of women live in coed dormitories; rest commute. All students are assured of on-campus housing, none are required to live on campus. Intervisitation in men's and women's dormitory rooms limited. Sexes segregated in coed dormitories either by wing or floor. There are no fraternities or sororities on campus. About 50% of resident students leave campus on weekends.

Annual Costs. Tuition and fees, $2,910 (out-of-state, $6,750); room and board, $3,890; estimated $450 for books and supplies. About 70% of students receive financial aid. University reports 70 scholarships awarded on the basis of academic merit alone, 5 for special talents, 8 for need alone.

University of Maine at Fort Kent

Fort Kent, Maine 04743 (207) 834-3162

The university of Maine's northernmost campus is located on the Canadian border in Fort Kent, a town of 4,600, 57 miles north of Presque Isle. The location offers unique opportunities for the environmental studies and forest technology programs.

Founded: 1878
Affiliation: State
Total Enrollment: 207 M, 248 W (full-time); 58 M, 116 W (par-time)
Cost: < $10K
% Receiving Financial Aid: 90%
Admission: Non-selective
Application Deadline: August 15

Admission. Graduates of approved high schools or equivalent with 12 units in academic subjects and rank in top half of class eligible; 72% of applicants accepted, 64% of these actually enroll. About 22% of freshmen graduate in top quarter of high school class, 55% in top half. Average freshmen SAT scores: 430 verbal, 390 mathematical. *Required:* SAT or ACT; interview recommended; placement exams. Criteria considered in admissions, in order of importance: high school academic record, standardized test scores, recommendations, writing sample, extracurricular activities; other factors considered: special talents. *Out-of-state* freshman applicants: university actively seeks students from out-of-state. State does not limit out-of-state enrollment. About 74% of out-of-state students accepted, 32% of these actually enroll. Most out-of-state students are drawn from New England. *Entrance programs:* early decision, early admission, midyear admission, deferred admission, advanced placement. *Apply* by August 15; rolling admissions. *Transfers* welcome; 101 enrolled 1993–94.

Academic Environment. Degrees offered: associates, bachelors. General education requirements for graduation vary with degree; distribution requirements include 12 hours of "competency courses", 6 hours of civilization, 7 hours of natural sciences, 6 hours of human/social sciences, 6 hours of arts, 6 hours of foreign language. *Majors offered* include environmental studies, forest technology, bilingual/multicultural studies, nursing, education. Average undergraduate class size: 38% under 20, 58% between 20-40, 5% over 40. About 31% of students entering as freshmen graduate in 4 years, 69% eventually; 60% of freshmen return for sophomore year. *Special programs:* CLEP, January term, study abroad, independent study, honors, individualized majors, cross registration with Saint Louis Maillet. *Calendar:* semester, summer school.

Undergraduate degrees conferred (58). 24% were in Social Sciences, 19% were in Health Sciences, 14% were in Liberal/General Studies, 12% were in Letters, 10% were in Education, 7% were in Business and Management, 5% were in Multi/Interdisciplinary Studies, 3% were in Foreign Languages, 3% were in Computer and Engineering Related Technology, remainder in Life Sciences.

Graduates Career Data. Advanced studies pursued by 75% of students; 5% enter medical school; 5% enter law school; 10% business school. About 68% of 1992–93 graduates employed. Fields typically hiring largest number of graduates include education, nursing. Career Development Services include career guidance programs, various career planning workshops, graduate school information.

Faculty. About 53% of faculty hold PhD or equivalent. About 50% of undergraduate classes taught by tenured faculty. About 44% of teaching faculty are female.
Student Body. University seeks a national student body; 76% of students from in state; 9% of students from New England, 4% Foreign. Average age of undergraduate student: 23.
Varsity Sports. Men (NSCAA): Basketball, Soccer. Women (NSCAA): Basketball, Soccer.
Campus Life. About 18% of students live in coed dormitories; rest commute. Intervisitation in men's and women's dormitory rooms limited. There are 2 fraternities and 2 sororities on campus, which about 10% men, 10% women join; neither provides residence facilities. About 5% of resident students leave campus on weekends.
Annual Costs. Tuition and fees, $2,685 (out-of-state, $6,435); room and board, $3,600; estimated $655 other, exclusive of travel. About 90% of students receive financial aid; average amount of assistance, $2,570. Assistance is typically divided 57% scholarship/grant, 43% work.

University of Maine at Machias

Machias, Maine 04654 (207) 255-3313

An institution for the preparation of teachers, with programs also in business administration and environmental studies, with additional 2-year programs in liberal arts and business technology, Maine's Machias campus is located in a town of 2,500, on the Atlantic coast.

Founded: 1909
Affiliation: State
Total Enrollment: 183 M, 339 W (full-time)
Cost: < $10K
Admission: Non-selective

Admission. High school graduates preferably with college preparatory program eligible; 58% of applicants accepted, 88% of these actually enroll. About 30% of freshmen graduate in top fifth of high school class, 60% in top two-fifths. *Required:* SAT. *Out-of-state* freshman applicants: state does not limit out-of-state enrollment. No special requirements for out-of-state applicants. *Apply* by no specific deadline. *Transfers* welcome.
Academic Environment. *Degree:* BS. *Majors offered* in 4 teacher education programs (early childhood, elementary, junior high, secondary business). About 60% of students entering as freshmen graduate eventually; 25% of freshmen do not return for sophomore year. *Special programs:* CLEP, independent study, Summer School of the Arts. *Calendar:* semester.
Undergraduate degrees conferred (66). 33% were in Education, 33% were in Business and Management, 11% were in Social Sciences, 11% were in Letters, 6% were in Life Sciences, 5% were in Parks and Recreation, remainder in Allied Health.
Campus Life. University seeks a national student body; 99% of students from New England. UMM is a state institution, makes no religious demands on students. About 39% of men, 40% of women live in traditional dormitories; 10% of men, 11% of women live in one coed dormitory; rest live in off-campus housing or commute. Intervisitation limited "by vote of the residents in the hall." There are 3 fraternities, 3 sororities on campus which about 26% of men, 22% of women join; they provide no residence facilities. About 25% of students leave campus on weekends.
Annual Costs. Tuition and fees, $2,577 (out-of-state, $6,472); room and board, $3,530.

University of Maine at Portland–Gorham

(See University of Southern Maine)

University of Maine at Presque Isle

Presque Isle, Maine 04769 (207) 764-0311

A state university offering both liberal arts and a variety of career-oriented programs, located in a rural community of 12,000, 160 miles north of Bangor. Most convenient major airport: Presque Isle.

Founded: 1903
Affiliation: State
Total Enrollment: 430 M, 544 W (full-time); 231 M, 272 W (part-time)
Cost: < $10K
% Receiving Financial Aid: 75%
Admission: Non-selective
Application Deadline: August 14

Admission. High school graduates with 16 units in college preparatory program and minimum combined SAT score of 800 eligible, others admitted on conditional basis; 77% of applicants accepted, 61% of these actually enroll. Average freshman SAT scores: 381 M, 394 W verbal, 452 M, 413 W mathematical. *Required:* SAT, minimum HS GPA, essay. Criteria considered in admissions, in order of importance: high school academic record, standardized test scores, recommendations, writing sample, extracurricular activities; other factors considered: special talents, diverse student body. *Out-of-state* freshman applicants: state limits out-of-state enrollment. No special requirements for out-of-state applicants. Students from other New England states can apply through New England Regional Student Program, which offers reduced tuition for certain programs not offered by their home state university. *Apply* by August 14; rolling admissions. *Transfers* welcome; 214 enrolled 1993–94.
Academic Environment. Degrees offered: associates, bachelors. General education requirements vary with program. *Majors offered* in addition to usual arts and sciences include nursing, social work, recreation/leisure, health education. Average undergraduate class size: 60% of classes under 20, 40% between 20-40. About 40% of students entering as freshmen graduate eventually; 45% of freshmen do not return for sophomore year, according to most recent data available. *Library:* 59,239 titles, 586 periodicals, other materials include Aroostook County Historical Collection. *Calendar:* semester, summer school.
Undergraduate degrees conferred (132). 30% were in Education, 22% were in Business and Management, 15% were in Multi/Interdisciplinary Studies, 9% were in Social Sciences, 8% were in Liberal/General Studies, 6% were in Parks and Recreation, 5% were in Letters, remainder in 4 other fields.
Graduates Career Data. Advanced studies pursued by 10% of graduates.
Faculty. About 57% of undergraduate classes taught by tenured faculty. About 36% of teaching faculty are female.
Varsity Sports. Men (Div.III): Baseball, Basketball, Cross Country, Soccer. Women (Div.III): Basketball, Cross Country, Soccer, Softball.
Student Body. About 80% of students from Maine; 97% of students from New England.
Campus Life. About 35% of men, 35% of women live in dormitories; 5% of each live in off-campus college related housing; rest commute. Freshmen given preference in college housing if all students cannot be accommodated. Intervisitation limited or unlimited depending on dormitory. There are 3 fraternities, 3 sororities on campus; they provide no residence facilities. About 40% of resident students leave campus on weekends, depending on scheduled activities.
Annual Costs. Tuition and fees, $2,610 (out-of-state, $6,360; room and board, $3,494. About 75% of students receive financial aid. University reports some scholarships awarded on the basis of academic merit alone. *Meeting Costs:* university offers payment plans.

Malone College

Canton, Ohio 44709 (216) 471-8100

A church-related college, the 78-acre campus is located in a city of 125,000, 50 miles south of Cleveland. Most convenient major airport: Akron-Canton.

Founded: 1892
Affiliation: Evangelical Friends Church
Total Enrollment: 680 M, 925 W (full-time); 59 M, 151 W (part-time)
Cost: < $10K
% Receiving Financial Aid: 77%
Admission: Non-selective
Application Deadline: Rolling

Admission. High school graduates with minimum GPA of 2.5 or ACT of 18 eligible; others granted conditional admission; 87% of applicants accepted, 57% of these actually enroll. About 36% of entering freshmen graduate in top fifth of high school class; 62% in top two-fifths. Average freshman scores: SAT, 419 M, 450 W verbal, 488 M, 467 W mathematical; ACT, 21 M, 22 W composite. *Required:* ACT or SAT, acceptance of college standard prohibiting alcohol, tobacco, social dancing; essay, interview strongly recommended (required in some cases). Criteria considered in admissions, in order of importance: high school academic record, standardized test scores, writing sample. *Entrance programs:* midyear admission, advanced placement. *Apply:* rolling admissions. *Transfers* welcome; 86 enrolled 1993–94.

Academic Environment. Degrees offered: associates, bachelors, masters. *Majors offered* in addition to usual studies include commercial music technology. General education requirements include 60-62 hours focused on the theme of stewardship: Stewardship and Skills, Stewardship under God, Stewardship and the Sciences, Stewardship and Society. Average undergraduate class size: 24; 44% of classes under 20, 43% between 20-40, 13% over 40. About 29% of students entering as freshmen graduate in four years, 45% eventually; 69% of freshmen return for sophomore year. *Special programs:* study abroad in Kenya, Hong Kong, Guatemala, Costa Rica, Latin America, Russia; cross registration with Stark Technical. Adult programs: degree completion program in management, and BSN for RN's. *Calendar:* semester, summer school.

Undergraduate degrees conferred (300). 49% were in Business and Management, 18% were in Education, 5% were in Public Affairs, 4% were in Mathematics, 4% were in Health Sciences, 4% were in Philosophy and Religion, 3% were in Psychology, 3% were in Communications, remainder in 7 other fields.

Graduates Career Data. Advanced studies pursued by 7% of students. About 93% of 1992–93 graduates employed. Fields typically hiring the largest number of graduates include education, nursing, business. Career Development Services include individual and group counseling, computerized career guidance, career-related courses, resume assistance and service, job vacancy listings, career newsletter, annual job fair, assistance with co-op experiences, interviewing techniques.

Faculty. About 45% of faculty hold PhD or equivalent. About 30% of undergraduate classes taught by tenured faculty. About 31% of teaching faculty are female, 3% minority.

Student Body. College does not seek a national student body; 95% of students from Ohio; less than 1% Foreign. An estimated 81% of students reported as Protestant, 10% Catholic, 9% unaffiliated; 5% Black, 2% other minority. Average age of undergraduate student: 23.

Religious Orientation. "Malone's heritage is conservative, evangelical"; 9 hours of Bible courses, attendance at chapel services required of all students; chapel-convocation program is an integral part of the campus community.

Varsity Sports. Men (NAIA): Baseball, Basketball, Cross Country, Football, Golf, Soccer, Tennis, Track. Women (NAIA): Basketball, Cross Country, Softball, Tennis, Track, Volleyball.

Campus Life. About 49% of men, 48% of women live in traditional dormitories; no coed dormitories; rest live in off-campus housing or commute. Freshmen given preference in college housing if all students cannot be accommodated. No intervisitation in men's and women's dormitory rooms. There are no fraternities or sororities. About 75% of resident students leave campus on weekends.

Annual Costs. Tuition and fees, $9,172; room and board, $3,400; estimated $1,250 other, exclusive of travel. About 77% of students receive financial aid; average amount of assistance, $7,511. Assistance is typically divided 55% scholarship/grant, 39% loan, 6% work. College reports 3 scholarships awarded for academic merit, 74 for special talents, 6 for need.

Manchester College

North Manchester, Indiana 46962 **(219) 982-2141**

A church-related, liberal arts college, Manchester also offers professional preparation for teaching, business, and other fields. The 120-acre campus is located in a town of 6,000, 35 miles southwest of Fort Wayne. Most convenient major airport: Fort Wayne.

Founded: 1889
Affiliation: Church of the Brethren
Total Enrollment: 1,102 M, W (full-time)
Cost: < $10K
% Receiving Financial Aid: 88%
Admission: Non-selective
Application Deadline: August 1

Admission. Graduates of accredited high schools with 16 units (10 in academic subjects) eligible; 71% of applicants accepted, 43% of these actually enroll; 45% of freshmen graduate in top fifth of high school class, 77% in top two-fifths. *Required:* SAT or ACT. *Non-academic factors* considered in admissions: special talents, diverse student body, religious affiliation and/or commitment. *Apply* by August 1. *Transfers* welcome.

Academic Environment. *Degrees:* AB, BS. *Majors offered* include usual arts and sciences, business, accounting, computer science, elementary and secondary education, environmental studies, home economics, peace studies, communication and drama. About 55% of students entering as freshmen graduate eventually; 15% of freshmen do not return for sophomore year. *Special programs:* CLEP, independent study, interdisciplinary majors, study abroad, honors, undergraduate research, semester or January term exchange program. *Calendar:* 4–1–4, summer school.

Undergraduate degrees conferred (188). 28% were in Education, 27% were in Business and Management, 7% were in Psychology, 7% were in Health Sciences, 5% were in Public Affairs, 5% were in Life Sciences, 4% were in Social Sciences, 4% were in Letters, 3% were in Multi/Interdisciplinary Studies, 3% were in Allied Health, remainder in 8 other fields.

Varsity Sports. Men (NAIA, Div. II): Baseball, Basketball, Cross Country, Football, Golf, Soccer, Tennis, Track, Wrestling. Women (NAIA, Div. II): Basketball, Cross Country, Softball, Tennis, Track, Volleyball.

Student Body. College does not seek a national student body; 81% of students from Indiana; 98% from North Central. An estimated 80% of students reported as Protestant, 13% Catholic, 7% unaffiliated; 2% as Black, 2% Hispanic, 1% Asian, according to most recent data available.

Religious Orientation. Manchester is a Christian institution; attendance at Convocation–Fine Arts series required of all students.

Campus Life. About 80% of men, 75% of women live in traditional dormitories; rest commute. Freshmen given preference in college housing if all students cannot be accommodated, currently there is no shortage on campus. Intervisitation in men's and women's dormitory rooms limited. Sexes segregated in coed dormitories by wing. There are no fraternities or sororities. About 40% of resident students leave campus on weekends.

Annual Costs. Tuition and fees, $9,600; room and board, $3,640. About 88% of students receive financial aid; assistance is typically divided 67% scholarship, 26% loan, 7% work. College reports some scholarships awarded on the basis of academic merit alone. *Meeting Costs:* college offers tuition installment plan.

Manhattan College

Riverdale, New York 10471 **(718) 920-0200**

A private, liberal arts college, sponsored by the Brothers of the Christian Schools, Manhattan is now under the control of an independent board of trustees. The college maintains a cooperative program with the nearby College of Mount Saint Vincent. The campus is located in the Riverdale section of New York City. Most convenient major airports: LaGuardia, Newark.

Founded: 1853
Affiliation: Independent (Roman Catholic)
UG Enrollment: 1,492 M, 1,088 (full-time); 147 M, 107 W (part-time)
Total Enrollment: 3,495
Cost: $10K–$20K
% Receiving Financial Aid: 84%
Admission: Selective
Application Deadline: March 1

Admission is selective. About 69% of applicants accepted, 33% of these actually enroll; 39% of freshmen graduate in top fifth of high school class, 63% in top two-fifths. Average freshman SAT scores: 467 verbal, 539 mathematical; 25% of freshmen score above 500 on verbal, 1% above 600; 62% score above 500 on mathematical, 21% above 600, 1% above 700. *Required:* SAT or ACT, essay, minimum H.S. GPA. College reports that the admissions process is "highly personalized" and takes into account the high school, sequence of courses studied, high school average in academic subjects, rank in class, recommendations, test scores, interview, and essay. *Non-academic factors* considered in admissions: special talents, alumni children, diverse student body, extracurricular activities. *Entrance pro-*

grams: early decision, early admission, midyear admission, deferred admission, advanced placement. About 2% of entering students from private schools, 62% from parochial schools. *Apply* by March 1. *Transfers* welcome; 195 enrolled 1993–94.

Academic Environment. Degrees offered: associates, bachelors, masters. Student body is reported to be primarily concerned with the acquisition of marketable skills, although a broad liberal arts core curriculum is required of all students. A College Senate, composed of representatives of faculty, administration, students, and alumni, is designed to give students some voice in curriculum matters. *Undergraduate studies* offered by schools of Arts and Sciences, Business, Engineering, Education and Human Resources. *Majors offered* include managerial sciences, sports medicine, exercise physiology, environmental engineering, international business studies, peace studies, Russian and East Central European area studies, urban affairs, health education (cooperative program with College of Mount St. Vincent), nuclear medicine technology, radiological and health sciences. Requirements for graduation include courses in Western Civilization (history, literature, art/music), and science. Average undergraduate class size: 40% under 20, 59% between 20-40, 1% over 40.

About 53% of students entering as freshmen graduate within four years, 72% eventually; 86% of freshmen return for sophomore year. *Special programs:* CLEP, independent study, study abroad, honors, undergraduate research, 3-year degree, cross registration with College of Mt. St. Vincent, open admissions for veterans, tutorial program for the disadvantaged, environmental studies, business internship, 3-2 in engineering. *Calendar:* semester, summer school.

Undergraduate degrees conferred (682). 33% were in Business and Management, 29% were in Engineering, 6% were in Education, 5% were in Social Sciences, 5% were in Computer and Engineering Related Technology, 5% were in Letters, 4% were in Life Sciences, 3% were in Communications Technologies, remainder in 7 other fields.

Graduates Career Data. Advanced studies pursued by 25% of students; 4% enter medical school; 2% enter law school, 4% business school. About 75% of 1992–93 graduates employed. Fields typically hiring largest numbers of graduates include engineering, education, accounting, computers. In recent studies, Manhattan has ranked high for number of graduates pursuing doctoral studies, and for number of graduates who are corporate leaders. Career Development Services include co-op placement seminars, career fairs, on-campus job interviews, workshops and testing.

Faculty. About 89% of faculty hold PhD or equivalent. About 72% of undergraduate classes taught by tenured faculty. About 23% of teaching faculty are female; 10% minority.

Student Body. College seeks a national student body; 82% of students from in state; 12% Middle Atlantic; 2% Foreign. An estimated 80% of students reported as Catholic, 6% Protestant, 1% Jewish, 5% Muslim, 8% unaffiliated; 5% as Black, 12% Hispanic, 7% Asian. *Minority group students:* financial aid, special programs for "educationally deprived."

Religious Orientation. For many years a Roman Catholic institution, Manhattan is now governed by a predominantly secular board of trustees; 9 hours (including 6 elective hours) of religious studies required of all students. Variety of religious programs available; counselors include clergymen of several different faiths. The Campus Ministry Center provides a range of religious and social activities. Places of worship available on campus for Catholics, in immediate community for all faiths.

Varsity Sports. Men (Div.I): Baseball, Basketball, Cross Country, Golf, Soccer, Tennis, Track, Wrestling. Women (Div.I): Basketball, Cross Country, Soccer, Softball, Swimming, Track, Volleyball.

Campus Life. Large number of commuting students influences campus life, but "active social life, including weekends," reported. Intervisitation unlimited. Location of campus makes cultural and social resources of New York City easily available to students, but still, according to recent student, "makes you feel as if you are in small town." Cars permitted, but parking for commuting students is reported to be a problem. Use of alcohol limited to those over 21; use of illegal drugs can result in suspension or expulsion.

About 44% of men, 52% of women live in coed dormitories; 1% men live in off-campus college-related housing; rest live in off-campus housing or commute. Freshmen given preference in college housing if all students cannot be accommodated. Sexes segregated in coed dormitories by apartment. There are 4 fraternities, 4 sororities on campus, which less than 1% of students join; they provide no residence facilities. About 20% of resident students leave campus on weekends.

Annual Costs. Tuition and fees, $12,500; room and board, $6,500; estimated $1,000 other, exclusive of travel. About 84% of students receive financial aid; average amount of assistance, $13,250. Assistance is typically divided 25% grant, 20% scholarship, 25% loan, 15% work. College reports 150 scholarships awarded for academic merit, 25 for special talents, 200 for need.

Manhattan Christian College

Manhattan, Kansas 66502

A small Christian college offering associates and bachelors degrees; students can earn a dual degree through an agreement with nearby Kansas State University.

Founded: 1927
Affiliation: Independent Christian Church

Manhattan School of Music

New York, New York 10027

A private conservatory of music with major fields of study in performance and composition; offering the BM, MM, DMA degrees and diploma.

Founded: 1917
Affiliation: Independent

Undergraduate degrees conferred (66). 100% were in Visual and Performing Arts.

Manhattanville College

Purchase, New York 10577 **(914) 694-2200**

Originally a Roman Catholic college for women, Manhattanville has been nonsectarian and co-educational for many years. Located on a 220-acre campus 25 miles north of midtown Manhattan, the college has a strong attraction to those students who prefer both a rural setting and proximity to the career and cultural advantages of New York City. Most convenient major airports: Westchester County, LaGuardia.

Founded: 1841
Affiliation: Independent
UG Enrollment: 361 M, 643 W (full-time); 60 M, 184 W (part-time)
Total Enrollment: 1,499
Cost: $10K–$20K
% Receiving Financial Aid: 65%
Admission: Very Selective
Application Deadline: March 1

Admission is very selective. About 77% of applicants accepted, 31% of these actually enroll; 35% of freshmen graduate in top fifth of high school class, 66% in top two-fifths. Average freshman SAT scores, according to most recent data available: 508 M, 498 W verbal, 563 M, 532 W mathematical; 42% of freshmen score above 500 on verbal, 7% above 600; 66% score above 500 on mathematical, 14% above 600, 2% above 700. *Required:* SAT or ACT; Plan II, English and math ACH, and major research/term paper; interview recommended. *Non-academic factors* considered in admissions: special talents, alumni children, diverse student body, leadership qualities. *Entrance programs:* early decision, early admission, midyear admission, advanced placement, deferred admission. About 28% of entering freshmen from private schools, 19% from parochial schools. *Apply* by March 1. *Transfers* welcome.

Academic Environment. Student leader describes college as hospitable to "a bright, career oriented student that wants a fine education without a lot of pressures." A faculty committee reviews the contents of student "Portfolios" to determine whether academic requirements for a degree have been satisfied. Program offers substantial flexibility within a traditional curriculum that offers instruction in 24 fields and 9 languages. *Degrees:* BA, BFA, BMus. *Majors offered* include usual arts and sciences, area studies (Asian, American, Russian), dance/drama, music management, international studies. New programs include: majors in classical studies, international studies, dance and theater.

About 75% of students entering as freshmen graduate eventually; 10% of freshmen do not return for sophomore year. *Special programs:* CLEP, independent study, study abroad, undergraduate research, 3-year degree, individualized majors, summer archaeology and art study in Greece, Oxford Semester, semester exchange with Mills (CA), dual-degree programs in law, business administration, BA/DDS with Georgetown Dental School, BA/RN with Columbia School of Nursing, 3-2 engineering with Clarkson. Adult programs: paralegal program, corporate seminars, certificate credit programs, and "Mornings at Manhattanville" series of non-credit courses. *Calendar:* semester, summer school.

Undergraduate degrees conferred (219). 23% were in Social Sciences, 23% were in Business and Management, 13% were in Visual and Performing Arts, 13% were in Psychology, 8% were in Area and Ethnic Studies, 7% were in Letters, 3% were in Philosophy and Religion, 3% were in Computer and Engineering Related Technology, 3% were in Life Sciences, remainder in 4 other fields.

Graduates Career Data. According to most recent data available, full-time graduate or professional study pursued immediately after graduation by 35% of students; 7% enter medical school; 1% enter dental school; 8% enter law school; 14% enter business school. Medical schools typically enrolling largest numbers of graduates include Columbia, Tufts, NJ College of Medicine and Dentistry; dental schools include Buffalo, Georgetown, U. of Connecticut; law schools include SUNY Buffalo, Harvard, American; business schools include Fletcher, NYU, Columbia. Corporations typically hiring largest numbers of graduates include Chemical Bank, Chubb Insurance, Simon & Schuster, Merrill, Lynch, Pierce, Fenner & Smith. *Career Counseling Program* offers workshops, seminars, etc. Alumni reported as active in both career guidance and job placement.

Faculty. About 95% of faculty hold doctorate or equivalent.

Student Body. College seeks a national student body; 51% of students from in state; 60% Middle Atlantic, 29% New England. An estimated 50% of students reported as Catholic, 25% Protestant, 4% Jewish, 15% unaffiliated, 5% other; 7% as Black, 8% Hispanic, 4% Asian, 5% other minority. *Minority group students:* full financial aid when needed.

Religious Orientation. Manhattanville, a former Roman Catholic college, is now an independent institution, makes no religious demands on students.

Varsity Sports. Men (Div.III): Baseball, Basketball, Lacrosse, Soccer, Tennis. Women (Div.III): Basketball, Soccer, Softball, Swimming, Tennis, Volleyball.

Campus Life. Students reported as equally concerned with scholarly/intellectual interests, occupational/professional goals, and social activities. Students have the opportunity and responsibility to participate in the life of the college. Student Government, the College Judiciary and the Student Programming Board are major campus organizations; residence and commuter councils serve as resources for their constituents. School is characterized by student leader as "very friendly, diversified." Students have option of a variety of dormitory arrangements ranging from limited to 24 hour intervisitation.

About 90% of men, 90% of women live in coed dormitories; rest commute. Freshmen given preference in college housing if all students cannot be accommodated. Sexes segregated in dormitories by floor or room. There are no fraternities or sororities. About 25% of resident students leave campus on weekends.

Annual Costs. Tuition and fees, $14,290; room and board, $6,250. About 65% of students receive financial aid; assistance is typically divided 68% scholarship, 26% loan, 6% work. College reports some scholarships awarded on the basis of academic merit alone. *Meeting Costs:* college offers budget payment plan.

Mankato State University

Mankato, Minnesota 56002-8400 (507) 389-1822

A state-supported college, located in a small city of 45,000, 85 miles southwest of Minneapolis. Most convenient major airport: Twin Cities International.

Founded: 1868
Affiliation: State
UG Enrollment: 4,766 M, 4,883 W (full-time); 825 M, 967 W (part-time)
Total Enrollment: 13,003
Cost: < $10K
% Receiving Financial Aid: 75%
Admission: Non-selective

Admission. Minnesota graduates of accredited high schools (or hold GED) who rank in top two-thirds of class or score in upper two-thirds on ACT composite eligible; 23% of freshmen graduate in top fifth of high school class, 53% in top two-fifths. Average freshman ACT scores: 21.3 M, 20.7 W composite. *Required:* ACT. Criteria considered in admissions, in order of importance: high school academic record, standardized test scores. *Out-of-state* freshman applicants: state does not limit out-of-state enrollment. Requirements for out-of-state applicants: normally same as for residents; when space is limited: ACT score of 19, SAT composite score of 800, or rank in top half of class. *Apply* by no specific deadline. *Transfers* welcome; 903 enrolled 1993–94.

Academic Environment. Degrees offered: bachelors, masters. About 90% of general education requirements for graduation are elective; distribution requirements fairly numerous. Average undergraduate class size: 44% of classes under 20, 45% between 20–40, 11% over 40. About 21% of entering students graduate within four years, 50% eventually; 27% of freshmen do not return for sophomore year. *Special programs:* study abroad. *Calendar:* quarter, summer school.

Undergraduate degrees conferred (2059). 35% were in Business and Management, 20% were in Education, 5% were in Protective Services, 5% were in Computer and Engineering Related Technology, 4% were in Social Sciences, 4% were in Health Sciences, 3% were in Psychology, 3% were in Public Affairs, remainder in 17 other fields.

Graduates Career Data. Advanced studies pursued by 8% of graduates. About 72% OF 1992–93 graduates are employed. Fields typically employing largest numbers of graduates include government, business, industry, education. Career Development Services are available.

Faculty. About 60% of faculty hold PhD or equivalent. About 35% of teaching faculty are female; 7% ethnic minorities.

Varsity Sports. Men (Div.II): Baseball, Basketball, Cross Country, Football, Golf, Hockey, Swimming, Tennis, Track, Wrestling. Women (Div.II): Basketball, Cross Country, Golf, Softball, Swimming, Tennis, Track, Volleyball.

Student Body. College does not seek a national student body; 85% of students from in state; 96% North Central. About 1% of students reported as Black, 2% Asian, 3% other minority.

Campus Life. About 25% of students live in coed dormitories; rest live in off-campus housing or commute. Intervisitation in men's and women's dormitory rooms unlimited. There are 9 fraternities, 5 sororities on campus.

Annual Costs. Tuition and fees, $2,176 (out-of-state, $4,041); room and board, $2,535. About 75% of students receive financial aid; average amount of assistance, $3,000. University reports some scholarships awarded on the basis of academic merit alone.

Mansfield University of Pennsylvania

Mansfield, Pennsylvania 16933 (717) 662-4243

A state-supported university, located in a rural community of 4,000, 50 miles north of Williamsport. Most convenient major airport: Elmira-Corning.

Founded: 1857
Affiliation: State
Total Enrollment: 3,371 M, W (full-time)
Cost: < $10K
% Receiving Financial Aid: 89%
Admission: Non-selective
Application Deadline: July 15

Admission. Graduates of approved high schools who rank in upper half of high school class eligible. About 73% of applicants accepted, 46% of these actually enroll; 16% of freshmen graduate in top fifth of high school class, 42% in top two-fifths. *Required:* SAT or ACT. *Out-of-state* freshman applicants: state does not limit out-of-state enrollment. No special requirements for out-of-state applicants; 68% accepted, 37% enroll. *Apply* by July 15. *Transfers* welcome.

Academic Environment. *Degrees:* AB, BM, BSEd, BSGS, BSN. About 54% of general education/liberal arts requirements for graduation are elective; distribution requirements fairly numerous. *Majors offered* in addition to usual studies include computer science, music therapy, fisheries, travel/tourism. About 45% of entering students graduate within four years; 25% of freshmen do not return for sophomore year. eventually. *Special programs:* CLEP, independent

study, study abroad, internships, 3–2 programs in physics, engineering. *Calendar:* semester, summer school.
Undergraduate degrees conferred (431). 26% were in Education, 12% were in Protective Services, 12% were in Business and Management, 7% were in Psychology, 6% were in Social Sciences, 6% were in Communications, 5% were in Computer and Engineering Related Technology, 4% were in Health Sciences, 3% were in Marketing and Distribution, 3% were in Life Sciences, 3% were in Home Economics, remainder in 8 other fields.
Graduates Career Data. According to most recent data available, full-time graduate or professional study pursued by 14% of students immediately after graduation. *Careers in business and industry* pursued by 67% of graduates. Employers typically hiring largest numbers of graduates include AT&T, FBI, Youth Services, Hyatt Regency, GTE.
Varsity Sports. Men (Div.II): Baseball, Basketball, Cross Country, Football, Track, Wrestling. Women (Div.II): Basketball, Field Hockey, Softball, Swimming, Tennis.
Student Body. University welcomes out-of-state students; 75% of students from in state; 99% Middle Atlantic. An estimated 4% of students reported as Black, 1% Asian, 1% other minority according to most recent data available.
Campus Life. About 16% of men, 25% of women live in traditional dormitories; 36% of men, 35% of women in coed dormitories; 42% of men, 33% of women live in off-campus housing or commute. Freshmen given preference in college housing if all students cannot be accommodated. There are 3 fraternities, 4 sororities on campus; 6% of men, 7% of women live in fraternities and sororities.
Annual Costs. Tuition and fees, $3,304 (out-of-state, $8,128); room and board, $2,988. About 89% of students receive financial aid; assistance is typically divided 32% scholarship, 63% loan, 5% work. University reports some scholarships awarded on the basis of academic merit alone. Meeting costs: university offers AIMS.

Marian College

Indianapolis, Indiana 46222 **(317) 929-0321**

A church-related, liberal arts college, conducted by the Sisters of St. Francis, located on a 114-acre campus in the state capital (pop. 744,600). Most convenient major airport: Indianapolis International.

Founded: 1851
Affiliation: Roman Catholic
Total Enrollment: 312 M, 611 W (full-time); 67 M, 360 W (part-time)
Cost: < $10K
% Receiving Financial Aid: 94%
Admission: Non-selective
Application Deadline: Rolling

Admission. High school graduates with 16 units eligible; 70% of applicants accepted, 48% of these actually enroll; 38% of freshmen graduate in top fifth of high school class, 76% in top two-fifths. Average freshman scores: SAT, 423 M, 419 W verbal, 460 M, 475 W mathematical. *Required:* SAT or ACT. Criteria considered in admissions, in order of importance: standardized test scores, high school academic record, recommendations; other factors considered: special talents, service to community. *Entrance programs:* midyear admission. About 30% of entering students from private and parochial schools. *Apply:* rolling admissions. *Transfers* welcome; 90 enrolled 1993–94.
Academic Environment. Degrees offered: associates, bachelors. About 50% of students entering as freshmen graduate within 4 years, 60% eventually; 75% of freshmen return for sophomore year. *Majors offered* include "Career Ladder" nursing programs, athletic training, speech communication. Distribution and core requirements include English composition, speech, philosophy and theology, humanities, sciences, languages, and social studies. Average undergraduate class size: 65% under 20, 30% between 20–40, 5% over 40. *Special programs:* CLEP, study abroad, honors, 2–2 engineering, combined medical and dental programs with Indiana, Marquette, Loyola, St. Louis U; cross registration with Butler, U. of Indianapolis, Indiana U.. Adult programs: BSN completion program, LPN to AN nursing program, evening bachelors degree. *Calendar:* semester, summer school.
Undergraduate degrees conferred (141). 21% were in Education, 21% were in Business and Management, 11% were in Health Sciences, 8% were in Visual and Performing Arts, 6% were in Social Sciences, 6% were in Life Sciences, 6% were in Letters, 5% were in Psychology, 5% were in Allied Health, 3% were in Mathematics, remainder in 4 other fields.
Faculty. About 38% of faculty hold PhD or equivalent. About 50% of undergraduate classes taught by tenured faculty. About 70% of teaching faculty are female; 1% Black.
Student Body. College does not seek a national student body; 94% of students from in state; 97% Midwest; 1% Foreign. An estimated 50% of students reported as Protestant, 42% Catholic, 1% Jewish, 1% Muslim; 12% Black, 1% Hispanic, 1% Asian, 1% other minority. Average age of undergraduate student: 25.9.
Religious Orientation. Marian is a church-related institution; 6 hours of theology required of all students.
Varsity Sports. Men (NAIA): Baseball, Basketball, Cross Country, Cycling, Golf, Soccer, Tennis, Track. Women (NAIA): Basketball, Cross Country, Cycling, Golf, Softball, Tennis, Volleyball.
Campus Life. About 20% of men, 20% women live in traditional dormitories; 40% of men, 20% of women in coed dormitories; rest live in off-campus housing or commute. Freshmen given preference in college housing if all students cannot be accommodated. Intervisitation in men's and women's dormitory rooms limited. There are no fraternities or sororities. About 40% of resident students leave campus on weekends, according to most recent data available.
Annual Costs. Tuition and fees, $9,200; room and board, $3,616; estimated $1,000 other, exclusive of travel. About 94% of students receive financial aid; average amount of assistance, $8,807. Assistance is typically divided 66% scholarship, 30% loan, 4% work. College reports some scholarships awarded on the basis of academic merit alone.

Marian College of Fond Du Lac

Fond du Lac, Wisconsin 54935 **(414) 923-7650**

A church-related, liberal arts college, sponsored by the Sisters of the Congregation of St. Agnes, located in a city of 36,000, 60 miles northwest of Milwaukee. Most convenient major airport: Wittman Field (OshKosh), Milwaukee.

Founded: 1936
Affiliation: Roman Catholic
UG Enrollment: 422 M, 744 W (full-time); 273 M, 390 W (part-time)
Total Enrollment: 2,404
Cost: < $10K
% Receiving Financial Aid: 85%
Admission: Non-selective
Application Deadline: Aug. 15

Admission. Graduates of accredited high schools with 16 units eligible; 81% of applicants accepted, 49% of these actually enroll; about 15% of freshmen graduate in top fifth of high school class, 38% in top two-fifths. Average freshman ACT scores: 20 composite. *Required:* ACT; interview highly recommended, minimum H.S. GPA of 2.0. Criteria considered in admissions, in order of importance: high school academic record, standardized test scores, recommendations, extracurricular activities; other factors considered: diverse student body, special talents, alumni children. *Entrance programs:* early admission, midyear admission, deferred admission, advanced placement. About 20% of freshmen students come from private schools. *Apply* by August 15; rolling admissions. *Transfers* welcome; 130 enrolled 1993–94.
Academic Environment. Degrees offered: bachelors, masters. *Majors offered* in addition to usual studies include operation management, retail management, administration of justice, communication, fashion merchandising, sports management, marketing education, athletic coaching. Core requirements include courses from four divisions. Average undergraduate class size: 14. About 60% of students entering as freshmen graduate within four years; 73% of freshmen return for sophomore year. *Special programs:* CLEP, study abroad, 3–2 program in cytotechnology, 2–2 in radiologic technology, 3–1 medical technology, independent study, individualized majors. Adult programs: Bachelor of Business Administration, Operations Management, BS Nursing Completion Program, Radiologic Technology Completion Program. *Calendar:* semester, summer school.
Undergraduate degrees conferred (202). 48% were in Business and Management, 37% were in Health Sciences, 6% were in Education, 3% were in Psychology, remainder in 8 other fields.

Graduates Career Data. Advanced studies pursued by 13% of students. About 98.5% of 1992–93 graduates employed. Fields typically hiring the largest number of students include nursing, business, education. Career Development Services include student support center, co-op education, community service.
Faculty. About 43% of faculty hold PhD or equivalent. About 60% of undergraduate classes taught by tenured faculty. About 60% of teaching faculty are female; 3% minority.
Student Body. College seeks a national student body; 80% of students from Wisconsin; 97% Midwest; 1% Foreign. An estimated 49% of students reported as Protestant, 48% Catholic, 1% Jewish, 1% unaffiliated, 1% other; 2% Black, 1% Hispanic, 2% Asian, 1% other.
Religious Orientation. Marian Fond du Lac is a church-related institution; 6 hours of religion and philosophy required of all students.
Varsity Sports. Men (NAIA): Baseball, Basketball, Cross Country, Golf, Ice Hockey, Soccer, Tennis. Women (NAIA): Basketball, Cross Country, Soccer, Softball, Tennis, Volleyball.
Campus Life. Wide variety of college housing options available, including 3-bedroom suites, apartments, and townhouse villages with cooking facilities. About 60% of men and women live in coed dormitories; rest live in off-campus housing or commute. Intervisitation in men's and women's dormitory rooms limited. There is 1 fraternity, 1 sorority on campus, which 1% men, 1% women join; 1% of men and women live in fraternity and sorority. About 20% of resident students leave campus on weekends.
Annual Costs. Tuition and fees, $8,650; room and board, $3,700; estimated $800 other, exclusive of travel. About 85% of students receive financial aid; average amount of assistance from college, $1,700. College reports 210 scholarships awarded for academic merit alone.

Marietta College

Marietta, Ohio 45750 **(614) 374-4600**

An independent, liberal arts college, Marietta is located on a 120-acre campus on the Ohio River in an historic town of 17,000, 114 miles southeast of Columbus. Most convenient major airport: Wood County (Parkersburg, WV).

Founded: 1797
Affiliation: Independent
Total Enrollment: 750 M, 529 W (full-time)
Cost: $10K–$20K
% Receiving Financial Aid: 82%
Admission: Selective
Application Deadline: Rolling

Admission is selective. About 60% of applicants accepted, 38% of these actually enroll; according to most recent data available 39% of freshmen graduate in top fifth of high school class, 70% in top two-fifths. Average ACT scores: 24 composite. *Required:* SAT or ACT; interview recommended. Criteria considered in admissions, in order of importance: high school academic record, standardized test scores, recommendations and writing sample, extracurricular activities; other factors considered: alumni children, diverse student body, special talents. *Entrance programs:* advanced placement. About 30% of entering students from private schools, according to most recent data available. *Apply:* rolling admissions. *Transfers* welcome; 27 enrolled 1993–94.
Academic Environment. Administration reports distribution requirements include sequential core program of 12 credits in humanities, 8 in lab sciences, 6 in fine arts, 6 in social sciences. Degrees offered: bachelors, masters. *Majors offered* in addition to usual studies include mass media/communications, sports medicine, petroleum engineering.

About 72% of students entering as freshmen graduate in four years; 68% of freshmen return for sophomore year. *Special programs:* CLEP, independent study, study abroad, honors, undergraduate research, Washington internship, individualized majors; 3–2 in forestry, nursing, natural resources, mechanical and electrical engineering. *Calendar:* semester, summer school.
Undergraduate degrees conferred (222). 34% were in Business and Management, 11% were in Communications, 9% were in Education, 8% were in Social Sciences, 6% were in Letters, 5% were in Engineering, 5% were in Health Sciences, 5% were in Life Sciences, 4% were in Psychology, 4% were in Visual and Performing Arts, 4% were in Physical Sciences, remainder in 4 other fields.

Graduates Career Data. According to most recent data available, full-time graduate or professional study pursued immediately after graduation by 28% of students; 15% enter medical school; 1% enter dental school; 4% enter law school; 8% enter business school. Career Development Services include variety of workshops, career fairs, and seminars beginning as early as the freshman year. Alumni reported as active in job placement.
Faculty. About 65% of faculty hold PhD or equivalent. About 75% of undergraduate classes taught by tenured faculty. About 40% of teaching faculty are female; 2% Black.
Student Body. College seeks a national student body; 50% of students from in state; 25% New England, 35% Middle Atlantic, 25% Midwest, 5% South, 5% West, 5% Northwest; 5% Foreign.
Varsity Sports. Men (Div.III): Baseball, Basketball, Crew, Football, Golf. Women (Div.III): Basketball, Crew, Softball, Soccer, Tennis, Volleyball.
Campus Life. Student-sponsored and -initiated activities reported strong; intramural sports also popular. Drinking permitted, individual and private only, no public events or consumption. Intervisitation may be scheduled by vote of residence unit up to 24 hours, limited for freshmen women only. Cars allowed for all.

About 25% of men, 25% of women live in traditional dormitories; 65% of men, 65% of women in coed dormitories. Freshmen given preference in college housing if all students cannot be accommodated. Sexes segregated in coed dormitories by room. There are 7 fraternities, 4 sororities on campus which about 25% of men, 15% of women join according to most recent data available; 10% of men, 10% of women live in fraternities and sororities. About 10% of resident students leave campus on weekends.
Annual Costs. Tuition and fees, $13,170; room and board, $3,770; estimated $200 other, exclusive of travel. About 82% of students receive financial aid; average amount of assistance, $5,200. College reports 3 scholarships awarded for academic merit, 1 for special talents.

Marion College

(See Indiana Wesleyan University)

Marist College

Poughkeepsie, New York 12601 **(914) 471-3240**

A liberal arts college, founded for men by the Marist Brothers, Marist is now under independent control. The 120-acre riverside campus is located 1 mile north of a community of 40,000, midway between New York City and Albany. Most convenient major airport: Dutchess County (Poughkeepsie).

Founded: 1929
Affiliation: Independent
Total Enrollment: 1,440 M, 1,550 W (full-time)
Cost: $10K–$20K
% Receiving Financial Aid: 66%
Admission: Non-selective
Application Deadline: March 1

Admission. Graduates of accredited high schools with 16 units (14 in academic subjects) eligible; 78% of applicants accepted, 31% of these actually enroll. About 20% of freshmen graduate in top fifth of high school class, 53% in top two-fifths. *Required:* SAT or ACT; interview strongly recommended. *Non-academic factors* considered in admissions: special talents, alumni children, diverse student body. *Entrance programs:* early decision, early admission, midyear admission, deferred admission, advanced placement. About 26% of entering students from private schools. *Apply* preferably by March 1. *Transfers* welcome.
Academic Environment. Members of administration and student body concur that students have significant influence on policy making. Administration reports some required liberal arts (CORE) courses for all students. *Degrees:* BA, BS, BPS. *Majors offered* include usual arts and sciences, business, computer science, computer information systems, communications, environmental science, fashion design. Computer facilities reported as adequate to meet student demand.

About 78% of students entering as freshmen graduate eventually;

10% of freshmen do not return for sophomore year. *Special programs:* independent study, individualized study abroad program, intersession travel options, cross-registration with neighboring institutions in mid-Hudson area, internships (in all 24 major fields), cooperative education in 14 majors, visiting students program for New York State colleges, Franklin D. Roosevelt studies, Washington Semester, New York Botanical Gardens Institute of Ecosystems internship. *Calendar:* semester, summer school.

Undergraduate degrees conferred (742). 35% were in Business and Management, 28% were in Communications, 6% were in Computer and Engineering Related Technology, 6% were in Social Sciences, 5% were in Psychology, 4% were in Protective Services, 4% were in Letters, 3% were in Education, 3% were in Visual and Performing Arts, remainder in 7 other fields.

Faculty. About 80% of faculty hold PhD or equivalent.

Student Body. College seeks a national student body; 65% of students from New York; 75% from Middle Atlantic, 20% New England. An estimated 65% of students reported as Catholic, 10% Protestant, 5% Jewish, 20% unreported; 6% Black, 3% Hispanic, 1% Asian, 1% other minority, according to most recent data available. *Minority group students:* financial aid incentives for minority students.

Religious Orientation. Marist is an independent institution with a Catholic heritage, but makes no religious demands on students. Campus Ministry staff includes Catholic, Jewish and Protestant chaplains; religious counseling available for students of all faiths.

Varsity Sports. Men (Div. I): Basketball, Crew, Cross Country, Football (III), Lacrosse, Soccer, Swimming & Diving, Tennis. Women (Div.I): Basketball, Crew, Cross Country, Swimming & Diving, Tennis, Volleyball.

Campus Life. Cars discouraged for freshmen. Housing options include freshmen residences, townhouses, and garden apartment complex for upper-class students.

About 70% of students live in coed dormitories; 10% live in off-campus housing; rest commute. Freshmen given preference in college housing if all students cannot be accommodated. Sexes segregated in coed dormitories either by wing or floor. There is 1 fraternity, no sororities; about 1% of men live in off-campus college-related fraternity.

Annual Costs. Tuition and fees, $10,545; room and board, $5,817. About 66% of students receive financial aid; assistance is typically divided 65% scholarship, 25% loan, 10% work. College reports some scholarships awarded on the basis of academic merit alone. *Meeting Costs:* college offers SHELF Loans, tuition payment plans.

State University of New York Maritime College

(See State University of New York)

Marlboro College

Marlboro, Vermont 05344 (802) 257-4333

Marlboro is a small, independent, non-traditional college that combines a "closely knit residential community with a traditional liberal arts curriculum." The college is governed by a College Town Meeting "composed of students, teachers, and permanent members of the staff, including spouses." The 300-acre Green Mountain campus is located just west of Brattleboro (pop. 12,200). Most convenient major airports: Logan International (Boston), Bradley (Hartford).

Founded: 1946	**Cost:** $10K–$20K
Affiliation: Independent	**% Receiving Financial Aid:** 65%
Total Enrollment: 130 M, 135 W (full-time)	**Admission:** Very Selective
	Application Deadline: Aug. 1

Admission is very selective. About 66% of applicants accepted, 59% of these actually enroll. Average freshman SAT scores, according to most recent data available: 560 verbal, 530 mathematical. *Required:* SAT or ACT, writing sample, autobiographical statement, recommendation, interview. *Non-academic factors* are considered in admissions. *Entrance programs:* early decision, early admission, midyear admission, advanced placement, deferred admission. About 35% of entering students from private schools. *Apply* by August 1; rolling admissions; recommend by March 15. *Transfers* welcome.

Academic Environment. Students have considerable influence on all aspects of college life, including the budget. English requirement, but no distribution requirements. During upper-class years, each student pursues an individually tailored Plan of Concentration. Recent student leader characterizes student body as primarily concerned with scholarly and intellectual interests. Artistic interests and concern with marketable skills attract a minority of students. Degrees offered: bachelors, masters. *Majors offered* include usual arts and sciences, computer science, theater, writing, World Studies. Computer literacy "strongly recommended." Facilities reported to meet student demand, "Absolutely. Ten students: one terminal."

About 40% of students entering as freshmen graduate within 4 years; 18% of freshmen do not return for sophomore year. *Special programs:* plan of concentration, independent study, World Studies Program allows internships while traveling, undergraduate research, individualized majors, tutorials, intensified courses. *Calendar:* semester.

Undergraduate degrees conferred (54). 19% were in Multi/Interdisciplinary Studies, 17% were in Letters, 13% were in Area and Ethnic Studies, 11% were in Social Sciences, 9% were in Visual and Performing Arts, 9% were in Life Sciences, 6% were in Physical Sciences, 6% were in Philosophy and Religion, 6% were in Foreign Languages, 4% were in Psychology, remainder in Liberal/General Studies.

Graduates Career Data. According to most recent data available, full-time graduate or professional study pursued within five years of graduation by 60% of students. Graduate schools typically enrolling largest numbers of graduates include U. Mass., Antioch, Yale, Harvard, New School for Social Research, Columbia.

Faculty. About 65% of faculty hold PhD or equivalent.

Student Body. College seeks a national student body; 30% of students from in state; 50% New England, 20% Middle Atlantic, 10% each North Central, Northwest, 5% each West, South. An estimated 1% of students reported as Black, 1% Hispanic, 2% Asian.

Religious Orientation. Marlboro is an independent institution, makes no religious demands on students. Places of worship available 10 miles away for Protestants and Catholics, 30 miles away for Jews.

Campus Life. Students accorded a large degree of freedom within the small college community. Social and recreational activities largely under the direction of the community. Students expected to take leadership in initiating activities of interest to them—they are also expected to participate in the college work program, which includes one week of dining hall duty and one week of dormitory maintenance each term. Nearest major cultural center, Boston, is 100 miles from campus—which may explain, in part, the high percentage of students leaving the campus on weekends. First term freshmen are required to live on campus. Cars permitted. Recreation is informal and noncompetitive: cross country skiing, bicycling, volleyball, jogging, etc.

About 15% each of men, women live in traditional dormitories; 60% each of men, women live in coed dormitories; rest live in off-campus housing. Sexes segregated in coed dormitories by room. There are no fraternities or sororities. About 20% of students leave campus on weekends.

Annual Costs. Tuition and fees, $17,615; room and board, $5,680. About 65% of students receive financial aid, assistance is typically divided 74% grant, 1% scholarship, 23% loan, 2% work/study and summer job. College reports scholarships awarded only on the basis of need. *Meeting Costs:* college offers tuition payment plan through TERI, PLUS Loans.

Marquette University

Milwaukee, Wisconsin 53233 (414) 288-7302 or (800) 222-6544

A church-related, urban university, conducted under the auspices of the Society of Jesus, Marquette's 80-acre campus is located adjacent to downtown Milwaukee and one mile west of Lake Michigan lakefront. The university offers 50 undergraduate majors, 29 master's degrees and 13 doctorates through its 12 colleges, programs and schools. Most convenient major airport: General Mitchell International.

Founded: 1881	**Total Enrollment:** 10,764
Affiliation: Roman Catholic	**Cost:** $10K–$20K
UG Enrollment: 3,409 M, 3,620 W (full-time); 410 M, 381 W (part-time)	**% Receiving Financial Aid:** 80%
	Admission: Very Selective
	Application Deadline: Rolling

Admission is very selective for colleges of Arts and Sciences, Engineering, Physical Therapy, selective (+) for colleges of Business Administration; Communication, Journalism and Performing Arts; Nursing, selective for Medical Technology, Dental Hygiene. For all schools, 89% of applicants accepted, 37% of these actually enroll; 60% of freshmen graduate in top fifth of high school class, 89% in top two-fifths. Average freshman scores: SAT, 490 M, 495 W verbal, 576 M, 544 W mathematical; 51% of freshmen score above 500 on verbal, 13 above 600, 1% above 700; 77% score above 500 on mathematical, 35% above 600, 8% above 700; ACT, 25 M, 25 W composite.

For Arts and Sciences, 91% of applicants accepted, 33.7% of these actually enroll; 61% of freshmen graduate in top fifth of high school class, 89% in top two-fifths. Average freshman scores: SAT, 501 M, 508 W verbal, 567 M, 547 W mathematical; 55% above 500 on verbal, 17% above 600, 1% above 700, 83% above 500 on mathematical, 32% above 600, 5% above 700; ACT, 26 M, 26 W composite.

For Business Administration, 85% of applicants accepted, 37% of these actually enroll; 46% of freshmen graduate in top fifth of high school class, 84% in top two-fifths. Average freshman scores: SAT, 466 M, 453 W verbal, 548 M, 546 W mathematical; 29% above 500 on verbal, 5% above 600, 74% above 500 on mathematical, 28% above 600; ACT, 24 M, 24 W composite.

For College of Communication, Journalism, and Performing Arts, 85% of applicants accepted, 44% of these actually enroll; 58% of freshmen graduate in top fifth of high school class, 86% in top two-fifths. Average freshman scores: SAT, 495 M, 505 W verbal, 550 M, 520 W mathematical; 49% above 500 on verbal, 12% above 600, 1% above 700, 67% above 500 on mathematical, 21% above 600, 4% above 700; ACT, 25 M, 25 W composite.

For Dental Hygiene, 78% of applicants accepted, 56% of these actually enroll; 46% of freshmen graduate in top fifth of high school class, 85% in top two-fifths. Average freshman scores: SAT, 370 M, 420 W verbal, 505 M, 470 W mathematical; ACT, 21 M, 21 W composite.

For Engineering, 92% of applicants accepted, 36% of these actually enroll; 63% of freshmen graduate in top fifth of high school class, 94% in top two-fifths. Average freshman scores: SAT, 486 M, 513 W verbal, 617 M, 605 W mathematical; 46% above 500 on verbal, 10% above 600, 1% above 700, 94% above 500 on mathematical, 56% above 600, 19% above 700; ACT, 26 M, 26 W composite.

For Nursing, 87% of applicants accepted, 49% of these actually enroll; 64% of freshmen graduate in top fifth of high school class, 90% in top two-fifths. Average freshman scores: SAT, 527 M, 451 W verbal, 580 M, 481 W mathematical; 34% above 500 on verbal, 2% above 600, 50% above 500 on mathematical, 10% above 600, 2% above 700; ACT, 27 M, 24 W composite.

For Medical Technology, 74% of applicants accepted, 60% of these actually enroll; 77% of freshmen graduate in top fifth of high school class, 95% in top two-fifths. Average freshman scores: SAT, 410 M, 429 W verbal, 480 M, 574 W mathematical; 22% above 500 on verbal, 66% above 500 on mathematical, 22% above 600, 11% above 700; ACT, 24 M, 25 W composite.

For Physical Therapy, 25% of applicants accepted, 59% of these actually enroll; 90% of freshmen graduate in top fifth of high school class, 98% in top two-fifths. Average freshman scores: SAT, 510 M, 526 W verbal, 603 M, 591 W mathematical; 72% above 500 on verbal, 19% above 600, 86% above 500 on mathematical, 53% above 600, 11% above 700; ACT, 26 M, 27 W composite.

Required: SAT or ACT. Criteria considered in admissions, in order of importance: standardized test scores, high school academic record. About 43% of entering students from private or parochial schools. *Entrance programs:* advanced placement, midyear admission. *Apply:* rolling admissions. *Transfers* welcome; 280 enrolled 1993–94.

Academic Environment. Degrees offered: bachelors, masters, doctoral. *Undergraduate studies* offered by 8 schools listed above; 4-year curricula available in dental hygiene, medical technology, physical therapy. *Majors offered* in addition to usual studies include: Bio-mechanics as an option in the Biomedical Engineering Program, international business, M.P.T. in physical therapy - 6 years. Freshman Frontier Program offers special training for students who do not meet standard admission criteria but show sufficient promise for "successful college career." Administration reports requirements for graduation varies among colleges; distribution requirements encourage a "well-rounded curriculum with emphasis on the liberal arts, Christian ideals and humanistic concern for others." Student leader reports "Marquette students are known for working hard (academically) and playing hard (socially)." The student body appears to be oriented toward both scholarly/intellectual interests and occupational/professional goals.

About 57% of students entering as freshmen graduate within four years, 75% eventually; 85% of freshmen return for sophomore year. *Special programs:* CLEP, independent study, study abroad, honors, undergraduate research, cooperative work/study program in engineering, internships in business, Freshman Frontier Program, Educational Opportunity Program. Adult Programs: The Part-Time Studies Division has been established for students, primarily adults, for enrichment as well as degree programs. *Calendar:* semester, summer school.

Undergraduate degrees conferred (1799). 24% were in Business and Management, 17% were in Engineering, 15% were in Communications, 11% were in Social Sciences, 6% were in Health Sciences, 5% were in Allied Health, 5% were in Psychology, 4% were in Letters, 3% were in Life Sciences, remainder in 10 other fields.

Graduates Career Data. Advanced studies pursued by 21% of students; 2% enter medical school; 1% enter dental school; 5% enter law school; 1% enter business school. About 67% of 1992–93 graduates employed. Career Development Services include individual and group career counseling/planning, job placement, on-campus recruitment, resume preparation and referral to employers.

Faculty. About 94% of faculty hold PhD or equivalent. About 28% of teaching faculty are female.

Student Body. University seeks a national student body; 53% of students from the state; 5% Foreign. An estimated 63% of students reported as Catholic, 19% Protestant, 1% Jewish, 17% other; 5% as Black, 4% Hispanic, 6% Asian, 1% other minority.

Varsity Sports. Men (Div.I): Basketball, Cross Country, Golf, Soccer, Tennis, Track, Wrestling. Women (Div.I): Basketball, Cross Country, Soccer, Tennis, Track.

Campus Life. A recently implemented Touchtone Voice Response Advance Registration System has eliminated long lines for registration and is popular with both students and faculty. Location of the university permits easy access to city entertainment. Student leader asserts the student most likely to feel at home on campus would be "An open, wild conservative"; least at home: "A wild liberal." Strong enthusiasm for intramural sports (volleyball, basketball, and soccer) and varsity sports (basketball, soccer), and religious activities reported. Increasing interest in cultural activities reported. Marquette is an urban, central city school with both the advantages and disadvantages of such a location.

According to most recent data available, about 5% of men, 7% of women live in traditional residence halls; 28% of men, 30% of women in coed dormitories; 30% of men, 33% of women live in off-campus college-related housing; 30% of each men, women commute. Freshmen given preference in college housing if all students cannot be accommodated. Sexes segregated in coed dormitories by floor. There are 10 fraternities, 8 sororities on campus which about 7% of men, 7% of women join. About 7% of men live in fraternities, sororities provide no residence facilities.

Annual Costs. Tuition and fees, $10,884; room and board, $5,230; estimated $2,100 other, exclusive of travel. About 80% of freshmen received financial aid; average amount of assistance, $11,050. Assistance is typically divided 48% grant/scholarship, 36% loan, 16% work. University reports unlimited number of scholarships awarded for academic merit, 144 for special talents.

Mars Hill College

Mars Hill, North Carolina 28754 (800) 543-1514

A church-related, liberal arts college, located on a 180-acre campus in the heart of the Blue Ridge mountains, in a town of 1,600, 19 miles north of Asheville.

Founded: 1856	**Cost:** < $10K
Affiliation: Southern Baptist	**% Receiving Financial Aid:** 80%
Total Enrollment: 486 M, 517 W (full-time)	**Admission:** Non-selective
	Application Deadline: Rolling

Admission. Graduates of accredited high schools with 18 units and C average in college preparatory subjects eligible, conditional admission for limited number of students who do not meet these requirements; 82% of applicants accepted, 36% of these actually enroll; 34% of entering freshmen graduate in top fifth of high school class, 59% in top second fifth. Average freshmen SAT scores: 406 verbal, 442 mathematical. *Required:* SAT or ACT, interview. Criteria considered in admissions, in order of importance: high school academic record, standardized test scores, recommendations, extracurricular activities; other factors considered: special talents, alumni children, diverse student body. *Apply:* rolling admissions. *Transfers* welcome; 66 enrolled 1993–94.

Academic Environment. Degrees offered; bachelors. *Majors offered* in addition to usual studies include zoology, sports medicine. Most majors require or encourage internships. Recent student finds that small classes allow her to get to know her professors. Average undergraduate class size: 75% under 20, 25% between 20–40. About 49% of entering students graduate within four years, 75% eventually; 73% of freshmen return for sophomore year. *Special programs:* CLEP, independent study, study abroad, freshman seminars as part of core curriculum, experimental courses in January, cross-registration with U. of North Carolina at Asheville, physician assistant program, internships, double majors, interdisciplinary programs. Adult programs: strong continuing education program for older students. *Calendar:* semester, summer school.

Undergraduate degrees conferred (201). 27% were in Education, 23% were in Business and Management, 7% were in Communications, 6% were in Social Sciences, 6% were in Public Affairs, 4% were in Philosophy and Religion, 4% were in Marketing and Distribution, 3% were in Parks and Recreation, 3% were in Life Sciences, remainder in 10 other fields.

Graduates Career Data. Advanced studies pursued by 28% of students. Career Development Services include career counseling, career resource library, on-campus interviews.

Faculty. About 70% of faculty hold PhD or equivalent. About 42% of teaching faculty are female.

Student Body. College seeks a regional student body; 60% of students from in state; 97% South; 1% Foreign. An estimated 81% of students reported as Protestant, 4% Catholic, 1% Jewish, 1% other; 7% Black, 1% Hispanic, 1% Asian.

Religious Orientation. Mars Hill is a church-related institution; one course in religion required of all students.

Varsity Sports. Men (Div.II): Baseball, Basketball, Cross Country, Football, Golf, Soccer, Tennis. Women (Div.II): Basketball, Cross Country, Soccer, Softball, Tennis, Volleyball.

Campus Life. About 85% of men, 85% of women live in traditional dormitories; no coed dormitories; rest live in off-campus housing or commute. Intervisitation limited to "open house" events in men's or women's dormitory rooms. There are 5 fraternities, 5 sororities on campus which about 30% of men, 30% of women join; they provide no residence facilities. About 50% of resident students leave campus on weekends.

Annual Costs. Tuition and fees, $7,500; room and board, $3,550. About 80% of students receive financial aid; average amount of assistance, $7,000. Assistance is typically divided 35% scholarship, 23% grant, 28% loan, 14% work. College reports some scholarships awarded on basis of academic merit alone.

Marshall University

Huntington, West Virginia 25755 **(304) 696-3160**

A state-supported university, located in a city of 60,000. Most convenient major airport: Tri-State.

Founded: 1837	**Total Enrollment:** 12,717
Affiliation: State	**Cost:** < $10K
UG Enrollment: 3,581 M, 4,122 W (full-time); 1,121 M, 1,218 W (part-time)	**% Receiving Financial Aid:** 55%
	Admission: Non-selective
	Application Deadline: Aug. 15

Admission. West Virginia graduates of approved high schools with 17 units in college preparatory curriculum; 99% of applicants accepted, 53% of these actually enroll. Median freshmen scores: SAT, 480 verbal, 450 mathematical; ACT, 21 composite. *Required:* ACT. Criteria considered in admissions, in order of importance: high school academic record, standardized test scores. *Out-of-state* freshman applicants: state does not limit out-of-state enrollment. No special requirements for out-of-state applicants. About 97% of out-of-state applicants accepted, 47% of these actually enroll. *Apply* by August 15. *Transfers* welcome; 549 enrolled 1993–94.

Academic Environment. *Undergraduate studies* offered by colleges of Liberal Arts, Fine Arts, Science, Business, Education, and Community College. General education core requirements for graduation include English, foreign language, communications, literature, fine arts, classics/philosophy. Degrees offered: associates, bachelors, masters, doctoral. *Majors offered* in addition to usual studies include computer science, finance and business law, marketing, safety technology, music, nursing, rehabilitation education, sports management and marketing, theatre/dance. Average undergraduate class size: 5% of classes under 20, 90% between 20–40, 5% over 40. About 37% of freshmen do not return for sophomore year. *Library:* 395,458 titles, 2,769 periodicals, 980,154 other materials; students report that library facilities are adequate, but computer facilities do get over-crowded at times. *Special programs:* CLEP, independent study, study abroad, honors, Yeager Scholar's Program, cooperative programs in accounting, general business, library media technology, banking, RBA, Academic Common Market, 3–2 program in forestry with Duke. Adult programs: Returning Students Program, credit for life experience. *Calendar:* semester, summer school.

Undergraduate degrees conferred (1132). 28% were in Business and Management, 20% were in Education, 8% were in Multi/Interdisciplinary Studies, 7% were in Health Sciences, 5% were in Protective Services, 5% were in Letters, 5% were in Social Sciences, 4% were in Psychology, 4% were in Communications, 4% were in Life Sciences, 3% were in Allied Health, remainder in 7 other fields.

Faculty. About 73% of faculty hold PhD or equivalent. About 36% of teaching faculty are female.

Varsity Sports. Men (Div.IA): Baseball, Basketball, Cross Country, Football (IAA), Golf, Soccer, Track. Women (Div.IA): Basketball, Cross Country, Softball, Tennis, Track, Volleyball.

Student Body. University does not seek a national student body; 87% of students from in state; 94% from North Central. An estimated 65% of students reported as Protestant, 9% Catholic, 9% unaffiliated, 17% other; 4% Black, 1% Asian, 1% other minority.

Campus Life. About 7% of men, 8% of women live in traditional dormitories; 3% of men, 2% of women live in coed dormitories; 41% of men, 35% of women live in off-campus college-related housing; 47% of men, 54% of women commute. Freshmen given preference in college housing if all students cannot be accommodated. Intervisitation in men's and women's dormitory rooms limited. There are 8 fraternities, 5 sororities on campus which about 3% of men, 3% of women join; 3% of men, 3% of women live in fraternities and sororities.

Annual Costs. Tuition and fees, $1,882 (out-of-state, $5,146; metro fee for 6 bordering counties in Kentucky and Ohio, $3.450); room and board, $3,800. About 55% of students receive financial aid; average amount of assistance, $3,250. Assistance is typically divided 10% scholarship, 50% loan, 7% work. University reports some scholarships awarded on the basis of academic merit alone.

Martin University

Indianapolis, Indiana 46218

An independent liberal arts college offering bachelors and masters degrees. College states "Our mission is to the adult, the poor, and the minority student." Average student is described as "a 40-year old, poor, African-American."

Founded: 1977	**Affiliation:** Independent

Mary Baldwin College

Staunton, Virginia 24401 (703) 887-7019

Mary Baldwin alumnae have staunchly supported the college through many changes. The formerly traditional institution now includes an adult degree program. The campus is located in a community of 28,000, in the Shenandoah Valley, 150 miles southwest of Washington, D.C. Most convenient major airport: Shenandoah Valley.

Founded: 1842
Affiliation: Presbyterian Church (USA)
Total Enrollment: 52 M, 774 W (full-time); 28 M, 316 W (part-time)
Cost: $10K–$20K
% Receiving Financial Aid: 75%
Admission: Non-selective
Application Deadline: April 15

Admission. High school graduates with 16 units in academic subjects eligible; 92% of applicants accepted, 42% of these actually enroll; 24% of freshmen graduate in top fifth of high school class, 48% in top two-fifths. Average freshman scores: SAT, 454 W verbal, 461 W mathematical; ACT, 21 W composite. *Required:* SAT or ACT; interview suggested. Criteria considered in admissions, in order of importance: high school academic record, standardized test scores, recommendations, extracurricular activities, writing sample; other factors considered: special talents, diverse student body, alumni children, motivation, maturity level. *Entrance programs:* early decision, early admission, midyear admission, deferred admission, advanced placement. About 30% of freshmen students come from private schools. *Apply* by April 15; rolling admissions. *Transfers* welcome; 53 enrolled 1993–94.

Academic Environment. Degrees offered: bachelors, masters. *Majors offered* in addition to usual studies include dramatic arts, Japanese, medical technology, health care administration, philosophy, preparation for ministry. Both students and administration report close student/faculty relationships and significant student influence not only on curriculum, but on selection and promotion of faculty. Laboratory nursery school on campus. General education requirements include demonstrated competency in mathematics and writing; central curriculum including 3 courses in each of 4 broad areas, Arts, Humanities, Social Sciences and Natural Sciences; 2 courses in international education; 1 course in experiential education; 1 course in women's studies. All students take experiential learning courses and complete externships. Average undergraduate class size: 75% under 20, 25% between 20–40.

About 75% of students graduate in 4 years, 80% eventually; 70% of freshmen return for sophomore year. *Special programs:* CLEP, independent study, study abroad, honors, undergraduate research, 3-year degree, individualized majors, freshman studies program, Seven College Exchange Program, social work studies, May term. Adult programs: Adult Degree Program is a nonresidential, individualized baccalaureate program designed to meet the needs of mature women. It offers credit for college level learning acquired prior to admission. *Calendar:* 4–4–1.

Undergraduate degrees conferred (265). 23% were in Business and Management, 22% were in Social Sciences, 14% were in Multi/Interdisciplinary Studies, 11% were in Psychology, 7% were in Visual and Performing Arts, 5% were in Communications, 5% were in Letters, 3% were in Health Sciences, 3% were in Foreign Languages, 3% were in Life Sciences, remainder in 3 other fields.

Graduates Career Data. Advanced studies pursued by 40% of students. Graduate and professional schools typically enrolling largest numbers of graduates include U. of Virginia, Virginia Tech, Duke.

Faculty. About 75% of faculty hold PhD or equivalent.

Student Body. College seeks a national student body; 54% of students from Virginia; 69% South, 23% Middle Atlantic, 3% New England, 1% Midwest, 1% West; 3% Foreign. An estimated 60% of students reported as Protestant, 15% Catholic, 1% Jewish, 18% unaffiliated, 6% other; 2% as Black, 2% Hispanic, 5% Asian.

Religious Orientation. Mary Baldwin is a church-related institution. Nonsectarian Campus Religious Life Council coordinates religious activities; weekly chapel services planned by chaplain.

Varsity Sports. Women (Div.III): Basketball, Diving, Field Hockey, Lacrosse, Soccer, Swimming, Tennis, Volleyball.

Campus Life. Students influence regulations governing social life. "Moderately strict" rules governing student behavior are said, by student leaders, to be enforced "rigorously." Relative isolation of campus mitigated by proximity of Washington and Lee, Virginia Military Institute, U. of Virginia. Cars allowed; drinking now permitted on campus. Curfew for freshmen only during first 2 months of freshman year. No visitation except during scheduled hours.

About 90% of women live in dormitories or on-campus apartments; 5% live in off-campus college-related housing, 5% commute. Freshmen given preference in college housing if all students cannot be accommodated. There are no sororities. About 25–30% of resident students leave campus on weekends.

Annual Costs. Tuition and fees, $10,654; room and board, $7,046; estimated other, $1,000, exclusive of travel. About 75% of students receive financial aid; average amount of assistance, $7,500. Assistance is typically divided 60% scholarship/grant, 40% loan/work. College reports many scholarships awarded for academic merit.

University of Mary

Bismarck, North Dakota 58504 (701) 255-7500

A church-related institution, sponsored by the Benedictine Sisters, located 7 miles south of the state capital (pop. 45,000). Formerly known as Mary College. Most convenient major airport: Bismarck Municipal.

Founded: 1959
Affiliation: Roman Catholic
Total Enrollment: 538 M, 938 W (full-time); 86 M, 196 W (part-time)
Cost: < $10K
Admission: Non-selective
Application Deadline: August 25

Admission. Graduates of accredited high schools with minimum ACT composite score of 17 eligible; about 97% of applicants accepted, 54% of these actually enroll. Average freshman ACT scores: 21 composite. *Required:* SAT or ACT, minimum H.S. GPA; interview recommended. Criteria considered in admissions, in order of importance: standardized test scores, high school academic record, recommendations, writing sample, extracurricular activities; other factors considered: diverse student body, special talents, alumni children, religious affiliation and/or commitment. *Entrance programs:* early decision, early admission, midyear admission, deferred admission, advanced placement. *Apply* by August 25; rolling admissions. *Transfers* welcome; 209 enrolled 1993–94.

Academic Environment. Degrees offered: associates, bachelors, masters. Distribution requirements include 3 courses from each of four broad areas: humanities, mathematics/science, philosophy/religion, social sciences. *Majors offered* in addition to usual studies include athletic training, nursing. Students report that small classes and low student:teacher ratio encourage faculty to treat each student as an individual; free tutoring is available. About 40% of students entering as freshmen graduate in four years; 71% return for sophomore year. *Special programs:* CLEP, study abroad, independent study, internships in most areas. *Calendar:* 4–4–1, summer school.

Undergraduate degrees conferred (283). 35% were in Business and Management, 19% were in Health Sciences, 16% were in Education, 11% were in Public Affairs, 4% were in Communications, 3% were in Science Technologies, 3% were in Allied Health, remainder in 8 other fields.

Faculty. All of undergraduate classes taught by tenured faculty. About 54% of teaching faculty are female; 2% minority.

Student Body. University does not seek universal student body; 83% of students from in state; 90% North Central, according to most recent data available. An estimated 40% of students reported as Protestant, 50% Catholic, 5% unaffiliated, 5% other; 1% Black, 1% Hispanic, 1% Asian, 1% other minority. Average age of undergraduate student: 22.

Religious Orientation. Mary is a church-related institution; 3 courses in philosophy and theology required of all students.

Varsity Sports. Men (NAIA, Div.II): Basketball, Cross Country, Football, Tennis, Track, Wrestling. Women (NAIA): Basketball, Cross Country, Softball, Tennis, Track, Volleyball.

Campus Life. One recent student finds that U. of Mary is "small, friendly campus". Distance from town encourages students to "stay around campus". Parking is reported to be a problem. About 54% of men, 28% of women live in traditional dormitories; no coed dormitories; rest live in off-campus housing or commute, according to most recent data available. Intervisitation in men's and women's dormitory rooms limited. There are no fraternities or sororities. About 20% of resident students leave campus on weekends.

Annual Costs. Tuition and fees, $6,640; room and board, $2,620; estimated $1,800 other, exclusive of travel. University reports some scholarships awarded on the basis of academic merit alone.

University of Mary Hardin-Baylor

Belton, Texas 76513 **(817) 939-4514**

A church-related university, located in a community of 8,700, 130 miles south of Dallas. Most convenient major airport: Austin.

Founded: 1845
Affiliation: Southern Baptist
Total Enrollment: 1,557 M, W (full-time)
Cost: < $10K
% Receiving Financial Aid: 75%
Admission: Non-selective

Admission. High school graduates with 15 units who rank in top half of class, have a minimum ACT composite score of 15 or minimum combined SAT score of 700, and a minimum GPA of 2.0 eligible; 99% of applicants accepted. About 25% of freshmen graduate in top fourth of high school class, 78% in top half. *Apply* by no specific deadline. *Transfers* welcome.

Academic Environment. Degrees offered: bachelors, masters. General education requirements include 6 semester hours in each of the following areas; English, religion, social sciences, and mathematics, lab. science or foreign language; and 3 semester hours in humanities/fine arts. About 65% of students entering as freshmen graduate within 4 years; 10% of freshmen do not return for sophomore year. *Special programs:* CLEP, independent study, honors. *Library:* 8,000 volumes, 11,000 periodicals, 21,000 other materials. *Calendar:* semester, summer school.

Undergraduate degrees conferred (303). 29% were in Education, 15% were in Health Sciences, 14% were in Business and Management, 9% were in Liberal/General Studies, 7% were in Social Sciences, 3% were in Psychology, 3% were in Letters, 3% were in Life Sciences, 3% were in Home Economics, 3% were in Computer and Engineering Related Technology, remainder in 8 other fields.

Varsity Sports. Men (NAIA): Baseball, Basketball, Golf, Soccer, Tennis. Women (NAIA): Basketball, Softball, Tennis, Volleyball.

Student Body. University does not seek a national student body; 94% of students from Texas. An estimated 72% of students reported as Protestant, 14% Catholic, 1% Jewish, 14% unaffiliated; 7% Black, 2% Asian, 9% Hispanic, 6% other minority, according to most recent data available.

Religious Orientation. Mary Hardin-Baylor is a church-related institution; 6 hours of religion, 4 semesters of chapel required of all students.

Campus Life. About 27% of men, 20% of women live in traditional dormitories; no coed dormitories; rest commute. Freshmen given preference in college housing if all students cannot be accommodated. No intervisitation in men's or women's dormitory rooms. There are no fraternities or sororities. About 60% of residential students leave campus on weekends.

Annual Costs. Tuition and fees, $5,250; room and board $3,106. About 80% of students receive financial aid; assistance is typically divided 50% scholarship, 25% loan, 25% work. University reports some scholarships awarded on the basis of academic merit alone. Meeting costs: university offers college-funded work program.

Mary Washington College

Fredericksburg, Virginia 22401-5358 **(703) 899-4681**

Mary Washington is a state-supported, co-educational, liberal arts college. The 381-acre campus is located in an historic town of 19,000, midway between Richmond and Washington. Most convenient major airports: National (Washington, D.C.), Richmond International.

Founded: 1908
Affiliation: State
Total Enrollment: 1,069 M, 1,928 W (full-time); 221 M, 515 W (part-time)
Cost: < $10K
% Receiving Financial Aid: 53%
Admission: Very Selective
Application Deadline: February 1

Admission is very selective. About 50% of applicants accepted, 35% of these actually enroll; 70% of freshmen graduate in top fifth of high school class, 94% in top two-fifths. Average freshman SAT scores: 69% of freshman score above 500 on verbal; 18% above 600, 5% above 700; 95% score above 500 on mathematical, 37% above 600, 10% above 700. *Required:* SAT; ACH strongly recommended; essay. Criteria considered in admissions, in order of importance: high school academic record, standardized test scores, writing sample, extracurricular activities, recommendations; other factors considered: diverse student body, special talents. *Out-of-state* freshman applicants: college seeks students from out of state. State does not limit out-of-state enrollment, but preference given to in-state students. About 52% of applicants accepted, 31% of these enroll. States from which most out-of-state students are drawn include New York, Maryland, New Jersey, Pennsylvania. *Entrance programs:* early decision, early admission. About 17% of entering students from private schools or parochial schools. *Apply* by February 1. *Transfers* welcome; 256 enrolled 1993–94.

Academic Environment. Degrees offered: bachelors, masters. Students have some influence on curriculum decisions as well as choice of faculty. Pressures for academic achievement appear moderately intense. Mary Washington traditionally has emphasized the liberal arts; but administration source reports business classes "fill up fast." An internship program offers opportunities for off-campus instruction and career exploration. Graduation requirements include competency in English composition as well as five writing intensive courses, proficiency in foreign language, and distribution requirements of courses from five broad areas: the natural world and laboratory experience, the human world, abstract thought, intellectual frameworks, and modes of creativity. *Majors offered* in addition to usual studies include historic preservation, geology, geography, international affairs, American studies, classical civilization. Programs in historic preservation and political science/international affairs have received national recognition. Students report that classes are small and challenging, and the faculty is very accessible. The library and computer facilities are reported to be more than adequate, although the computer network can be overtaxed during midterms and finals. Average undergraduate class size: 35% under 20, 61% between 20–40, 4% over 40.

About 65% of students entering as freshmen graduate within four years, 75% in five years; 92% of freshmen return for sophomore year. *Special programs:* CLEP, independent study, study abroad, honors, undergraduate research, 3-year degree, individualized majors, credit by examination, Servicemen's Opportunity College. Adult programs: Bachelor of Liberal Studies Program designed for students 24 or over. *Calendar:* semester, summer school.

Undergraduate degrees conferred (756). 26% were in Social Sciences, 17% were in Liberal/General Studies, 17% were in Business and Management, 9% were in Letters, 8% were in Psychology, 6% were in Life Sciences, 4% were in Physical Sciences, 4% were in Visual and Performing Arts, 3% were in Foreign Languages, remainder in 4 other fields.

Graduates Career Data. Advanced studies pursued by 20% of students within one year of graduation. About 78% of 1992–93 graduates employed. Career Development Services include career counseling, resume writing workshops, interviewing skills workshops, Career Day, Occupational Fair, internship program, graduate school information.

Faculty. About 85% of faculty hold PhD or equivalent. About 70% of undergraduate classes taught by tenured faculty. About 33% of teaching faculty are female.

Student Body. College seeks a national student body; 75% of students from in state; 79% Middle Atlantic, 7% New England, 3% Midwest, 5% South, 2% West, 2% Northwest; 2% Foreign. An estimated 4% of students reported as Black, 2% Hispanic, 3% Asian, 1% other minority.

Varsity Sports. Men (Div.III): Baseball, Basketball, Cross Country, Equestrian, Lacrosse, Soccer, Swimming, Tennis, Track. Women (Div.III): Basketball, Cross Country, Equestrian, Field Hockey, Lacrosse, Soccer, Softball, Swimming, Tennis, Track, Volleyball.

Campus Life. Regulations governing campus social life relatively free. Alcohol allowed in student rooms and designated areas for those over 21; as at many campuses, non-drinking activities are gaining popularity. Dorms segregated by floor; choice of 3 types of intervisitation; students may live off campus. Wide variety of cultural activities on campus, supplemented by the resources of Richmond and Washington, each about 50 miles away. Cars allowed.

About 21% of students live in traditional dormitories; 78% live in coed dormitories, according to most recent data available. Sexes segregated in coed dorms by floor There are no fraternities or sororities. About 10–15% of resident students leave campus on weekends.

Annual Costs. Tuition and fees, $3,066 (out-of-state, $7,136); room and board, $4,844. About 53% of students receive financial aid; average amount of assistance, $4,700. Assistance is typically divided 7% merit- based grant, 9% need-based grant, 65% loan, 19% work. College reports some scholarships awarded on the basis of academic merit alone.

Marycrest College

(See Teikyo Marycrest College)

Marygrove College

Detroit, Michigan 48221-2599 (313) 862-5200

Founded by the Sisters Servants of the Immaculate Heart of Mary, Marygrove is now governed by an independent board of trustees. The college is located on a 68-acre campus in northwest Detroit.

Founded: 1910
Affiliation: Independent (Roman Catholic)
Total Enrollment: 96 M, 504 W (full-time); 490 (part-time)
Cost: < $10K
% Receiving Financial Aid: 90%
Admission: Non-selective
Application Deadline: August 15

Admission. Graduates of accredited high schools with 9–11 units in college preparatory program and rank in top third of class eligible; 61% of applicants accepted, 44% of these actually enroll. About 39% of freshmen graduate in top fifth of high school class, 68% in top two-fifths, according to most recent data available. *Required:* SAT or ACT; interview and campus visit recommended. *Apply* by August 15. *Transfers* welcome.

Academic Environment. Degrees offered: associates, bachelors, masters. *Majors offered* include human ecology, journalism, social work, special education, dance therapy, art therapy. About 51–69% of general education requirements for graduation are elective; distribution requirements fairly numerous. About 65% of students entering as freshmen graduate eventually; 18% of freshmen do not return for sophomore year, according to most recent data available. *Special programs:* CLEP, independent study, study abroad, undergraduate research, credit by examination, cross-registration with U. of Detroit, Madonna, Mercy, dual-degree program with Georgia Tech. *Calendar:* semester, summer school.

Undergraduate degrees conferred (121). 23% were in Business and Management, 15% were in Public Affairs, 12% were in Computer and Engineering Related Technology, 11% were in Letters, 9% were in Visual and Performing Arts, 7% were in Social Sciences, 5% were in Home Economics, 4% were in Psychology, 4% were in Education, 3% were in Vocational Home Economics, remainder in 6 other fields.

Student Body. College does not seek a national student body; majority of students from North Central. An estimated 64% are Protestant, 20% Catholic, 1% Jewish, 6% unaffiliated, 1% other, according to most recent data available; 80% Black, 1% Hispanic, 11% other minority.

Religious Orientation. Marygrove is an independent institution with a Catholic orientation; course in phenomenology of religious experience strongly recommended for all students; "no required chapel or religious assemblies.."

Campus Life. Community government of college involves students "in all college affairs that affect them." Cars allowed. Almost all students commute. There are no fraternities or sororities.

Annual Costs. Tuition and fees, $7,554; room and board, $3,840; estimated $50 other, exclusive of travel. About 90% of students receive financial aid; average amount of assistance, $1,300 loan, $1,600 scholarship/grant. Some scholarships are awarded on basis of academic merit alone.

Maryland Institute, College of Art

Baltimore, Maryland 21217

An independent, professional institution, the college provides training leading to the BFA and MFA in fine arts, art education, graphic design and illustration, photography, painting, sculpture and printmaking, interior design, craft design, ceramics. New program offers 5-year dual degree in Bachelor of Fine Arts/Master of Art in Teaching.

Founded: 1826
Affiliation: Independent

Undergraduate degrees conferred (176). 90% were in Visual and Performing Arts, 6% were in Architecture and Environmental Design, 4% were in Education.

Maryland State College

(See University of Maryland, Eastern Shore)

University of Maryland

College Park, Maryland 20742 (301) 314-8385

A major state university and land-grant institution, the University of Maryland includes a wide variety of undergraduate, graduate, and professional schools as well as specialized research programs. Campus consists of 11 colleges and School of Architecture. The 500-acre College Park campus is located in a town of 26,200, 9 miles northeast of Washington, D.C. Most convenient major airports: Baltimore/Washington International, Washington National.

Founded: 1807
Affiliation: State
UG Enrollment: 11,121 M, 10,422 W (full-time); 2,194 M, 1,934 W (part-time)
Total Enrollment: 34,837
Cost: < $10K
% Receiving Financial Aid: 50%
Admission: Selective (+)
Application Deadline: April 30

Admission is selective (+). For all schools, 61% of applicants accepted, 35% of these actually enroll. Average freshman SAT scores: 509 M, 499 W verbal, 608 M, 554 W mathematical; 53% of freshmen score above 500 on verbal, 14% above 600, 4% above 700; 84% score above 500 on mathematical, 48% above 600, 10% above 700.

For Arts and Humanities (1,083 M, 1,580 M), 52% of applicants accepted, 34% of these actually enroll. Average freshman SAT scores: 528 M, 511 W verbal, 581 M, 517 W mathematical; 46% of freshmen score above 500 on verbal, 18% above 600, 4% above 700; 45% score above 500 on mathematical, 28% above 600, 4% above 700, according to most recent data available.

For Agriculture (246 M, 196 W), 61% of applicants accepted, 50% of these actually enroll. Average freshman SAT scores: 391 M, 511 W verbal, 426 M, 520 W mathematical, according to most recent data available.

For Architecture (88 M, 39 W), 97% of applicants accepted, 39% of these actually enroll. Average freshman SAT scores: 565 M, 580 W verbal, 693 M, 615 W mathematical, according to most recent data available.

For Behavioral and Social Sciences (2,038 M, 1,943 W), 52% of applicants accepted, 41% of these actually enroll. Average freshman SAT scores: 506 M, 490 W verbal, 552 M, 508 W mathematical, according to most recent data available.

For Business and Management (1,020 M, 824 W), all of applicants accepted, 36% of these actually enroll. Average freshman SAT scores: 592 M, 563 W verbal, 658 M, 634 W mathematical, according to most recent data available.

For Mathematics and Physical Sciences and Engineering (676 M, 276 W), 80% of applicants accepted, 41% of these actually enroll. Average freshman SAT scores: 537 M, 514 W verbal, 635 M, 611 W mathematical, according to most recent data available.

For Education (166 M, 484 W), 81% of applicants accepted, 28% of these actually enroll. Average freshman SAT scores: 440 M, 545 W verbal, 580 M, 575 W mathematical, according to most recent data available.

For Engineering (2,238 M, 485 W), almost all of applicants accepted, 40% of these actually enroll. Average freshman SAT scores: 539 M, 529 W verbal, 660 M, 636 W mathematical, according to most recent data available.

For Human Ecology (256 M, 641 W), 27% of applicants accepted, 36% of these actually enroll. Average freshman SAT scores: 449 M, 471 W verbal, 470 M, 497 W mathematical, according to most recent data available.

For Journalism (128 M, 396 W), 98% of applicants accepted, 31% of these actually enroll. Average freshman SAT scores: 650 M, 637 W verbal, 645 M, 618 W mathematical, according to most recent data available.

For Life Sciences (611 M, 643 W), 71% of applicants accepted, 39% of these actually enroll. Average freshman SAT scores: 506 M, 496 W verbal, 575 M, 547 W mathematical, according to most recent data available.

For Physical Education, Health and Recreation (127 M, 183 W), 32% of applicants accepted, 79% of these actually enroll. Average freshman SAT scores: 530 M, 410 W verbal, 610 M, 400 W mathematical, according to most recent data available.

For Undergraduate Studies (958 M, 1,175 W), 49% of applicants accepted, 42% of these actually enroll. Average freshman SAT scores: 462 M, 460 W verbal, 536 M, 506 W mathematical, according to most recent data available.

For Pre-Selectives (2,711 M, 2,322 W), 47% of applicants accepted, 41% of these actually enroll. Average freshman SAT scores: 466 M, 458 W verbal, 555 M, 505 W mathematical, according to most recent data available.

Required: SAT. *Out-of-state* freshman applicants: university welcomes students from out of state. *Out-of-state* enrollment is limited. About 52% of applicants accepted, 26% enroll. Requirement for out-of-state applicants: "higher than average SAT scores and high school grades." Non-academic factors considered in admissions: special talents, alumni children, diverse student body. *Entrance programs:* midyear admission, advanced placement. *Apply* by April 30. *Transfers* welcome.

Academic Environment. Students are reported to be almost equally oriented toward vocational/professional goals and scholarly/intellectual interests. Administration reports about 30% of general education courses needed for graduation are required (varies with curriculum): distribution requirements fairly numerous. *Majors offered* in Arts and Humanities in addition to wide range of studies include anthropology, astronomy, dance, dramatic art, geography, microbiology, radio and television, Russian studies, speech and hearing, Italian.

About 59% of students entering as freshmen graduate eventually; 55% of freshmen do not return for sophomore year. *Special programs:* CLEP, honors, 3-year degree, individualized majors, credit by examination, cooperative work/study program in engineering, study abroad. *Calendar:* semester, summer school.

Undergraduate degrees conferred (5514). 17% were in Social Sciences, 15% were in Business and Management, 12% were in Engineering, 7% were in Education, 7% were in Letters, 6% were in Communications, 5% were in Life Sciences, 5% were in Psychology, 5% were in Home Economics, 4% were in Visual and Performing Arts, 4% were in Protective Services, remainder in 15 other fields.

Graduates Career Data. According to most recent data available, full-time graduate or professional study pursued immediately after graduation by 33% of students. *Careers in business and industry* pursued by 49% of graduates. Corporations typically hiring largest numbers of graduates include IBM, General Electric, Ernst & Whinney.

Faculty. About 77% of faculty hold PhD or equivalent.

Student Body. University seeks a national student body; 73% of students from in state. An estimated 11% of students reported as Black, 3% Hispanic, 10% Asian, 3% other minority.

Varsity Sports. Men (Div.I): Baseball, Basketball, Cross Country, Football, Golf, Lacrosse, Soccer, Swimming, Tennis, Track, Wrestling. Women (Div.I): Basketball, Cross Country, Field Hockey, Gymnastics, Lacrosse, Soccer, Swimming, Tennis, Track, Volleyball.

Campus Life. College Park is a large, complex campus influenced by a substantial commuter population. Those who reside on campus, according to one student leader, have no complaints about regulations governing campus. Daily intervisitation schedule subject to approval of each residence hall. Rules for drinking conform to state law; prohibited for those under 21. Cars allowed for upperclassmen; weekend privileges for others; but parking is a serious problem.

About 31% of men, 37% of women live in traditional dormitories; 69% of men, 63% of women live in coed dormitories. Sexes segregated in coed dormitories either by wing or floor. There are 29 fraternities, 23 sororities on campus which about 15% of men, 15% of women join; 8% of men, 10% of women live in fraternities or sororities.

Annual Costs. Tuition and fees, $3,179 (out-of-state, $8,783); room and board, $5,003. About 50% of students receive financial aid; assistance is typically divided 43% scholarship, 34% loan, 23% work. University reports some scholarships awarded on the basis of academic merit alone.

University of Maryland Baltimore County

Baltimore, Maryland 21228 **(410) 455-2291**

The University of Maryland Baltimore County, established in 1963 and located in suburban Baltimore, offers programs in the traditional arts and sciences and in a growing number of professional and health-related fields. Most convenient major airport: Baltimore/Washington International.

Founded: 1963
Affiliation: State
UG Enrollment: 3,303 M, 3,173 W (full-time); 1,216 M, 1,376 W (part-time)
Total Enrollment: 10,667
Cost: < $10K
% Receiving Financial Aid: 38%
Admission: Non-selective
Application Deadline: May 1

Admission. Graduates of accredited high schools with appropriate courses eligible; admission based on combination of SAT scores and GPA. About 61% of applicants accepted, 38% of these actually enroll; 50% of entering freshmen graduate in top fifth of high school class, 79% in top two fifths. Average freshman scores: SAT, 506 M, 504 W verbal, 598 M, 550 W mathematical; 49% above 500 verbal, 18% above 600, 2% above 700, 84% above 500 mathematical, 42% above 600, 10% above 700; ACT 24 M, 22 W composite. *Required:* SAT or ACT. Criteria considered in admissions, in order of importance: high school academic record, standardized test scores, recommendations, writing sample, extracurricular activities; other factors considered: diverse student body, special talents. *Out-of-state* freshman applicants: university welcomes students from out of state. State limits out-of-state enrollment to 30%. About 53% of out-of-state students accepted, 22% of these actually enroll. States from which most out-of-state students are drawn include Pennsylvania, New Jersey, New York. *Entrance programs:* early admission, midyear admission, advanced placement. About 15% of freshmen from private schools. *Apply* by May 1. *Transfers* welcome; 1,383 enrolled 1993–94.

Academic Environment. Degrees offered: bachelors, masters, doctoral. *Majors offered* include information systems, emergency health services, health science and policy, biochemistry and molecular biology, modern languages and linguistics, visual arts, theatre. The administration boasts the largest co-operative education program in Maryland. General education requirements include courses in four areas: arts/humanities, social science, mathematics/science, and language/culture. Average undergraduate class size: 41% under 20, 40% between 20–40, 19% over 40.

About 18% of students entering as freshmen graduate in four years, 50% eventually; 83% of freshmen return for sophomore year. *Special programs:* CLEP, independent study, honors, study abroad, undergraduate research, 3-year degree, individualized majors, January term, cross registration with all other UMS institutions, six 5-year BA/MA programs, cooperative education, cooperative program with state colleges in Baltimore area. *Calendar:* 4–1–4, summer school.

Undergraduate degrees conferred (1499). 21% were in Social Sciences, 19% were in Computer and Engineering Related Technology, 12% were in Psychology, 11% were in Health Sciences,

6% were in Visual and Performing Arts, 6% were in Life Sciences, 5% were in Public Affairs, 4% were in Engineering, 4% were in Letters, remainder in 7 other fields.

Graduates Career Data. Advanced studies pursued by 32% of students; 2% enter medical school; 1% enter law school; 3% business school; 1.5% other professional schools. About 87.2% of 1991 graduates employed. Fields typically hiring the largest number of graduates include computer programmer/analyst, health professional, manager/executive, statistician/science researcher. Career Development Services include individual career advisement, a computerized career guidance system, career exploration workshops, a short-term employment program and job referral service, on-campus recruitment program.

Faculty. About 85% of faculty hold PhD or equivalent. About 29% of undergraduate classes taught by tenured faculty. About 36% of teaching faculty are female; 5% Black, 1% Hispanic, 11% other minority.

Student Body. University seeks a national student body; 94% of students from in state; 2% Foreign. An estimated 13% of students reported as Black, 9% Asian, 1% Hispanic, 1% other minority, according to most recent data available. Average age of undergraduate student: 22.

Varsity Sports. Men (Div.I): Baseball, Basketball, Cross Country, Diving, Golf, Lacrosse, Soccer, Swimming, Tennis, Track. Women (Div.I): Basketball, Cross Country, Diving, Lacrosse, Soccer, Softball, Swimming, Tennis, Track, Volleyball.

Campus Life. About 22% of men, 23% of women live in coed dormitories; rest commute. Freshmen given preference in college housing if all students cannot be accommodated. Intervisitation in men's and women's dormitory rooms limited, unlimited depending on student choice of dormitory; sexes segregated by room. There are 12 fraternities, 8 sororities on campus which about 6% of men, 6% of women join; they provide no residence facilities. About 25% of resident students leave campus on weekends.

Annual Costs. Tuition and fees, $2,338 (out-of-state, $8,594); room and board, $4,306; estimated $1,000 other, exclusive of travel. About 38% of students receive financial aid; average amount of assistance, $2,879. Assistance is typically divided 20% scholarship, 25% grant, 35% loan, 20% work. University reports 537 scholarships awarded for academic merit, 173 for special talents, 598 for need.

University of Maryland, Eastern Shore

Princess Anne, Maryland 21853 **(410) 651-6410**

A state-supported, land-grant college, located in a town of 2,000; founded as a college for Negroes, college now seeks a multiracial student body. Most convenient major airport: Baltimore/ Washington International.

Founded: 1886
Affiliation: State
UG Enrollment: 1,076 M, 1,166 W (full-time); 214 M, 261 W (part-time)
Total Enrollment: 2,717
Cost: < $10K
% Receiving Financial Aid: 90%
Admission: Non-selective
Application Deadline: Rolling

Admission. Graduates of accredited high schools with 16 units, C average in academic subjects, and rank in top half of class eligible; others admitted to summer session. About 86% of applicants accepted, 45% of these actually enroll. Average freshman scores: SAT, 368 verbal, 400 mathematical. *Required:* SAT or ACT; minimum H.S. GPA of 2.5. Criteria considered in admissions, in order of importance: high school academic record, standardized test scores, extracurricular activities, recommendations, writing sample; other factors considered: special talents, alumni children, diverse student body. *Out-of-state* freshman applicants: university welcomes students from out of state. State limits out-of-state enrollment to 15% of entering class. Requirement for out-of-state applicants: B average in academic subjects (those with C average "considered, based on space"). States from which most out-of-state students are drawn include Pennsylvania, New York, New Jersey, Virginia, Washington D.C. *Entrance programs:* early decision, early admission, midyear admission, advanced placement. About 5% of freshmen from private schools, 5% parochial schools. *Apply:* rolling admissions. *Transfers* welcome; 163 enrolled 1993–94.

Academic Environment. Degrees offered: bachelors, masters, doctoral. General education requirements for graduation vary with program; distribution requirements fairly numerous. *Majors offered* include airway science, hotel and restaurant management, physical therapy. Average undergraduate class size: 25. About 21% of students entering as freshman graduate in four years, 40% eventually; 70% of freshmen return for sophomore year. *Special programs:* CLEP, Eight College Consortium, January term, cross registration with Salisbury State U. Adult programs: General Studies degree. *Calendar:* semester, summer school.

Undergraduate degrees conferred (159). 31% were in Business and Management, 16% were in Allied Health, 11% were in Education, 8% were in Social Sciences, 7% were in Multi/Interdisciplinary Studies, 7% were in Computer and Engineering Related Technology, 6% were in Life Sciences, 4% were in Engineering and Engineering Related Technology, 4% were in Letters, 3% were in Agricultural Sciences, remainder in 3 other fields.

Graduates Career Data. Advanced studies pursued by 20% of students.

Faculty. About 75% of faculty hold PhD or equivalent. About 80% of undergraduate classes taught by tenured faculty. About 45% of teaching faculty are female; 55% Black, 15% other minority.

Student Body. UMES seeks a national student body; 72% of students from in state; 75% Middle Atlantic, 2% West, 4% South, 2% Midwest, 3% New England, 2% Northwest; 9% Foreign. An estimated 90% of students are Protestant, 2% Catholic, 8% other; 71% Black, 1% Hispanic, 3% Asian.

Varsity Sports. Men (Div.I): Baseball, Basketball, Cross Country, Soccer, Tennis, Track. Women (Div.I): Basketball, Cross Country, Softball, Tennis, Track, Volleyball.

Campus Life. About 45% of men and 55% of women live in traditional dormitories; 10% of men, 15% of women in coed dormitories; rest commute. Intervisitation in men's and women's dormitory rooms; controlled access. There are 4 fraternities, 3 sororities on campus which about 7% of men, 6% of women join; they provide no residence facilities. About 45% of resident students leave campus on weekends.

Annual Costs. Tuition and fees, $2,674 (out-of-state, $7,401) room and board, $3,580; estimated $1,500 other, exclusive of travel. About 90% of students receive financial aid; average amount of assistance, $3,500. University reports 15 scholarships awarded for academic merit, 20 for special talents.

Marylhurst College for Lifelong Learning

Marylhurst, Oregon 97036 **(503) 636-8141**

A non-traditional liberal arts college with open admissions and a predominantly part-time student body that ranges in age from 18 to 70 years, Marylhurst places special emphasis on life-long learning for adults. Most convenient major airport: Portland International.

Affiliation: Roman Catholic
UG Enrollment: 40 M, 135 W (full-time); 202 M, 493 W (part-time)
Total Enrollment: 1,005
Cost: < $10K
% Receiving Financial Aid: 52%
Admission: Non-selective
Application Deadline: Rolling

Admission. Graduates of accredited high schools or equivalent eligible; open admissions policy. *Apply:* rolling admissions. *Transfers* welcome; make up majority of student body.

Academic Environment. *Degrees:* BA, BS, BFA, BM. College offers baccalaureate degree programs in usual arts and sciences, business management, fine and applied arts, interdisciplinary studies. *Library:* 100,000 volumes, 300 periodicals, other materials include special collections, audio-visuals.

Undergraduate degrees conferred (160). 28% were in Multi/Interdisciplinary Studies, 26% were in Business and Management, 17% were in Social Sciences, 14% were in Communications, 12% were in Visual and Performing Arts, 4% were in Philosophy and Religion, remainder in Life Sciences.

Campus Life. About 99% of students from in state. Most students hold full-time jobs, all commute.

Annual Costs. Tuition and fees, $7,644; estimated $1,600 other, exclusive of travel. About 52% of all students receive financial aid; assistance is typically divided 10% scholarship, 80% loan, 10% work. College reports all scholarships awarded on the basis of need.

Marymount College

Tarrytown, New York 10591-3796 (914) 631-3200

A Catholic, liberal arts college for women, founded by the Religious of the Sacred Heart of Mary, the college is now controlled by an independent board of trustees. The 60-acre campus overlooking the Hudson River is located in a Westchester County village of 11,100, 30 miles north of New York. Most convenient major airport: LaGuardia.

Founded: 1907
Affiliation: Independent (Roman Catholic)
Total Enrollment: 40 M, 691 W (full-time); 67 M, 303 W (part-time)
Cost: $10K–$20K
% Receiving Financial Aid: 75%
Admission: Non-selective
Application Deadline: April 1

Admission. About 68% of applicants accepted, 36% of these actually apply; 23% graduate in the top fifth of high school class, 51% in top two fifths. Average freshman SAT scores: 460 W verbal, 456 W mathematical. *Required:* SAT or ACT, essay, graded writing sample, guidance counselor recommendation, minimum H.S. GPA; ACH optional, interview recommended. *Non-academic factors* considered in admissions: special talents, alumni children, diverse student body, extracurricular activities, leadership. *Entrance programs:* early admission, midyear admission, deferred admission, advanced placement. About 29% of entering students from private and parochial schools, according to most recent data available. *Apply* by April 1; rolling admissions. *Transfers* welcome; 87 enrolled 1993–94.

Academic Environment. Administration source reports students are equally concerned with occupational/professional goals and scholarly/intellectual pursuits. Students reported to take an active role in all aspects of academic decision making, including curriculum and hiring and promotion of faculty. Open curriculum "requires the student to structure her own program of studies." Student may make program choices "from a wide variety of courses, teaching styles, and areas of concentration," including independent study, tutorials, colloquia. Distribution requirements mandate studies in verbal, analytical, and mathematical skills. Teaching internships allow seniors to gain experience as seminar discussion leaders, tutors, and laboratory assistants. Evaluations as well as letter grades in major field. Degrees offered: bachelors. *Majors offered* include drama, environmental studies, human ecology, foods for business and industry, international business. Average undergraduate class size: 85% under 20, 15% between 20–40.

About 55% of students entering as freshmen graduate in four years, 58% eventually; 85% of freshmen return for sophomore year. *Special programs:* HEOP, CLEP, independent study, study abroad, honors, undergraduate research, 3–2 in physical therapy, occupational therapy, speech language pathology, audiology, internships, tutorials, programs through Westchester Consortium. Adult programs: weekend college for working adults. *Calendar:* semester, summer school.

Undergraduate degrees conferred (224). 45% were in Business and Management, 12% were in Social Sciences, 10% were in Visual and Performing Arts, 9% were in Psychology, 9% were in Letters, 5% were in Education, 3% were in Home Economics, remainder in 6 other fields.

Graduates Career Data. Advanced studies pursued by 27% of students. About 79% of 1992–93 graduates employed. Fields typically hiring largest number of graduates include business, fashion, education. Career Development Services include a credential file service; placement for full-time, part-time, and internships; recruitment interviews for seniors; individual and group counseling; workshops on resume writing, job search, career planning.

Faculty. About 86% of full-time faculty hold PhD or equivalent. About 59% of full-time teaching faculty are female; 4% Black, 2% Hispanic, 5% other minority.

Student Body. College seeks a national student body; 97% Northeast. An estimated 16% of students reported as Black, 14% Hispanic, 10% other minority.

Religious Orientation. Formerly a Catholic institution, Marymount is now controlled by a lay board of trustees; students must take one of eight religious courses; attendance at religious services voluntary. Places of worship available on campus for Catholics, within walking distance for major faiths.

Varsity Sports. Women: Basketball, Softball, Tennis, Volleyball.

Campus Life. Campus is just 30 miles north of New York City; some effort made to bring cultural and intellectual activities to campus. Cars allowed for all, but parking "sometimes a problem." Drinking permitted in designated areas for students and guests 21 and older. Curfew hours for first semester freshmen. Guidelines for guests in the residence halls are determined by the residence staff. About 65% of traditional-age women live in dormitories; rest commute. There are no sororities. About 20% of resident students leave campus on weekends, according to most recent data available.

Annual Costs. Tuition and fees, $11,150, room and board, $6,200; estimated $1,155 other, exclusive of travel. About 75% of students receive financial aid. College reports 3 scholarships awarded for academic merit, 2 for special talents.

Marymount College of Virginia

(See Marymount University)

Marymount University

Arlington, Virginia 22207 (703) 522-5600

Marymount offers undergraduate and graduate programs in the liberal arts and professional fields. Founded as a college for women, all undergraduate programs became co-educational in 1987. The campus is located two miles from Washington, D.C. in a residential area of Arlington. Formerly known as Marymount College of Virginia. Most convenient major airports: National, Dulles International.

Founded: 1950
Affiliation: Roman Catholic
UG Enrollment: 309 M, 938 W (full-time); 198 M, 653 W (part-time)
Total Enrollment: 3,965
Cost: $10K–$20K
% Receiving Financial Aid: 80%
Admission: Non-selective
Application Deadline: Rolling

Admission. Graduates of accredited high schools eligible; 75% of applicants accepted, 27% of these actually enroll. Average freshman scores: SAT, 429 M, 445 W verbal, 478 M, 463 W mathematical. *Required:* ACT or SAT, minimum high school GPA of 2.0. Criteria considered in admissions, in order of importance: high school academic record and standardized test scores, recommendations, writing sample and extracurricular activities. About 38% of entering students come from private or parochial schools. *Apply:* rolling admissions. *Transfers* welcome; 468 enrolled 1993–94.

Academic Environment. Degrees offered: associates, bachelors, masters. Degree programs offered by schools of Arts and Sciences, Business Administration, Education and Human Services, Nursing. Core requirements include 9 credits in written communication, 18 credits in humanities, 10 credits in mathematics/sciences, 9 credits in social sciences, 1 in credit physical education; computer literacy required of all students. Internships required of all students during junior or senior year. Several students cite the small classes and individualized attention from faculty as strengths of the academic program. Average undergraduate class size: 17. About 38% of students entering as freshmen graduate within four years, 47% within six years; 72% of entering freshman return for sophomore year. *Special programs:* 3-year degree, internships in Washington in government and area corporate settings. Adult programs: most programs provide full range of course offerings in evening and weekend programs encouraging adult student enrollment. Special MEd program catering to current military personnel changing careers. *Calendar:* semester, summer school.

Undergraduate degrees conferred (358). 33% were in Business and Management, 9% were in Marketing and Distribution, 8% were in Liberal/General Studies, 8% were in Psychology, 8% were in Architecture and Environmental Design, 7% were in

Communications, 6% were in Health Sciences, 4% were in Visual and Performing Arts, 3% were in Social Sciences, remainder in 9 other fields.

Graduates Career Data. Career Development Services include library resources, individual and group counseling, resume/interview workshops, placement office, on-campus recruitment.

Faculty. About 82% of faculty hold PhD or equivalent. About 61% of teaching faculty are female.

Varsity Sports. Men (Div.III): Basketball, Golf, Lacrosse, Soccer, Swimming, Tennis. Women (Div.III): Basketball, Soccer, Swimming, Tennis, Volleyball.

Student Body. College seeks a national student body; 69% of students from in state; 87% Middle Atlantic, 2% New England, 11% foreign. An estimated 13% of students reported as Protestant, 42% Catholic, 1% Jewish, 22% unaffiliated, 19% other; 12% Black, 5% Hispanic, 6% Asian.

Religious Orientation. Marymount is a church related institution; makes no religious demands on students.

Campus Life. Free shuttle to Washington D.C. allows students to take advantage of educational, cultural and recreational opportunities of the city. Students cite the small school, friendly atmosphere as one of their favorite things about Marymount, but several lament the lack of school spirit for athletics and other campus activities. About 30% of full-time undergraduate women live in traditional dormitories; 48% of men, 12% of women live in coed dormitories; rest commute. Freshmen given preference in college housing if all students cannot be accommodated.

Annual Costs. Tuition and fees, $10,804; room and board, $5,126; estimated $1,000 other, exclusive of travel. About 80% of full-time undergraduate students receive financial aid; average amount of assistance, $11,296. Assistance typically divided 77% scholarship/grant, 13% loan, 10% work. University reports 170 scholarships awarded on the basis of academic merit alone, 14 for special talents. *Meeting Costs:* university offers deferred payment plan, family discount, prepayment plan, monthly budgeting plan.

Marymount Manhattan College

New York, New York 10021 (212) 517-0555

Marymount Manhattan College is a private, independent, liberal arts college for women founded by the Religious of the Sacred Heart of Mary. College offers "substantial pre-professional preparation in addition to liberal studies." The campus is located on the Upper East Side of Manhattan and affords easy access to the city's many cultural and recreational facilities. Most convenient major airports: LaGuardia, JFK, or Newark.

Founded: 1936
Affiliation: Independent
Total Enrollment: 50 M, 480 W (full-time); 43 M, 742 W (part-time)
Cost: < $10K
% Receiving Financial Aid: 75%
Admission: Non-selective
Application Deadline: July 1

Admission. Graduates of accredited high schools with 16 units eligible; 67% of applicants accepted, 20% of these actually enroll; 19% of freshmen graduate in top fifth of high school class; 31% in upper two-fifths. *Required:* SAT; interview, auditions for some majors. *Non-academic factors* considered in admissions: extracurricular activities, special talents, alumni children, diverse student body. About 13% of entering students from private schools, 29% from parochial schools. *Apply* by July 1. *Transfers* welcome.

Academic Environment. Students have some voice in curriculum and long range planning decisions through joint student/faculty committees. Strong effort made to employ the resources of the city to enrich many dimensions of academic life. College has cooperative programs with New York School of Interior Design, Laboratory Institute of Merchandising, Mannes College of Music. Internships arranged with law firms, Congressional offices, theater groups. No major in education, but requisite studies for city and state certification offered. *Degrees:* AB, BS, BFA. *Majors offered* include usual arts and sciences, business management, communication arts, dance, speech pathology, theatre.

About 33% of students entering as freshmen graduate eventually; 17% of freshmen do not return for sophomore year. *Special programs:* honors, independent study, study abroad, Life Experience program, Community leadership program. *Calendar:* 4–1–4, 2 summer sessions.

Undergraduate degrees conferred (148). 28% were in Business and Management, 17% were in Psychology, 14% were in Visual and Performing Arts, 14% were in Social Sciences, 8% were in Letters, 7% were in Communications, 3% were in Liberal/General Studies, 3% were in Health Sciences, 3% were in Life Sciences, remainder in 3 other fields.

Faculty. About 57% of faculty hold PhD or equivalent.

Student Body. About 76% of students from in state; 84% from Middle Atlantic. An estimated 15% of students reported as Black, 10% Hispanic, 2% Asian, 4% other minority, according to most recent data available.

Religious Orientation. For many years a Roman Catholic institution, Marymount Manhattan is now governed by an independent board of trustees, makes no religious demands on students.

Campus Life. Location of college makes all the cultural, intellectual, and social resources of New York City immediately available. Marymount is designed to serve commuter students from the New York metropolitan area. About 3% of women live in dormitories and off-campus college-related housing, rest commute. Freshmen given preference in college housing if all students cannot be accommodated. There is 1 sorority which about 1% of women join.

Annual Costs. Tuition and fees, $9,820. About 75% of eligible students receive financial aid; assistance is typically divided 53% scholarship, 45% loan, 2% work. College reports some scholarships awarded on the basis of academic merit alone. *Meeting Costs:* college offers loan program, financial planning.

Maryville University—St. Louis

St. Louis, Missouri 63141-7299 (314) 576-9350

An independent university with bachelor's and master's degree programs in professional and liberal arts disciplines, founded by the Religious of the Sacred Heart, Maryville is governed by a board of trustees. University is located in a suburban setting in a city of 622,200. Most convenient major airport: Lambert Field.

Founded: 1872
Affiliation: Independent (Roman Catholic)
UG Enrollment: 460 M, 883 W (full-time); 500 M, 1,251 W (part-time)
Total Enrollment: 3,7648
Cost: < $10K
% Receiving Financial Aid: 27%
Admission: Non-selective
Application Deadline: Rolling

Admission. Graduates of accredited high schools with 16 units eligible; minimum ACT of 25 for actuarial science, 21 for physical therapy; 38% of applicants accepted, 82% of these actually enroll. About 44% of freshmen graduate in top fifth of high school class, 72% in top two-fifths. Average freshman ACT scores: 24 composite. *Required:* ACT or SAT, minimum H.S. GPA, interview and volunteer experience for physical therapy, portfolio for art. About 26% of freshmen students from parochial schools. *Apply:* rolling admissions. *Transfers* welcome; 204 enrolled 1993–94.

Academic Environment. Degrees offered: bachelors, masters. *Majors offered* in addition to usual studies include actuarial science, music therapy, nursing, occupational therapy, accounting, marketing. Maryville strives to integrate liberal arts with professional education by providing innovative and interactive programs with and for the business, education, health care, cultural and arts communities it serves. This commitment is demonstrated by the campus location as the anchor of the Maryville Centre, a one-of-a-kind academic, corporate, professional and residential development in suburban St. Louis. About 48% of students entering as freshmen graduate eventually; 75% of freshmen return for sophomore year. *Special programs:* CLEP, independent study, Prior Learning Assessment, cooperative education, internships, cooperative programs with Missouri Baptist, Fontbonne, Lindenwood, Webster, 3–2 programs in pre-engineering, occupational therapy, graduate bridge program in MSW. Adult programs: Week-End College which meets alternate weekends offers degree completion programs in 10 different majors. *Calendar:* 4–1–4.

Undergraduate degrees conferred (466). 38% were in Business and Management, 10% were in Computer and Engineering Related Technology, 9% were in Health Sciences, 8% were in

Marketing and Distribution, 7% were in Communications, 7% were in Psychology, 6% were in Allied Health, 3% were in Mathematics, 3% were in Education, remainder in 8 other fields.
Graduates Career Data. About 95% of 1992 graduates employed. Fields typically employing the largest numbers of graduates include management, education, marketing, health care professions.
Faculty. About 60% of faculty hold PhD or equivalent. About 41% of undergraduate classes taught by tenured faculty. About 60% of teaching faculty are female; 3% ethnic minorities.
Student Body. University seeks a national student body; 90% of students from Missouri; 8% Foreign. An estimated 4% of students reported as Black, 1% Asian, 10% other minority.
Varsity Sports. Men (Div.III): Baseball, Basketball, Cross Country, Golf, Soccer, Tennis. Women (Div.III): Basketball, Cross Country, Soccer, Softball, Tennis, Volleyball.
Campus Life. About 25% of students live in coed dormitories; rest live in off-campus housing or commute. Sexes segregated in coed dormitory by floor. There are no fraternities or sororities. About 65% of resident students leave campus on weekends.
Annual Costs. Tuition and fees, $8,700; room and board, $4,200; estimated $780 other, exclusive of travel. About 27% of students receive financial aid; average amount of assistance, $6,942. Assistance is typically divided 28% scholarship, 26% grant, 42% loan, 4% work. University reports 475 scholarships awarded for academic merit, 23 for special talents, 364 for need.

Maryville College

Maryville, Tennessee 37801 **(615) 981-8092 or (800) 597-2687**

A church-related, liberal arts college, located in a community of 13,800, 15 miles south of Knoxville. Unusual All College Council, consisting of 6 representatives each of students, faculty, administration and staff, is the "top legislative body on all matters" of concern to the campus community.

Founded: 1819
Affiliation: Independent (Presbyterian)
Total Enrollment: 313 M, 310 W (full-time); 43 M, 86 W (part-time)
Cost: $10K–$20K
% Receiving Financial Aid: 85%
Admission: Non-selective
Application Deadline: Rolling

Admission. High school graduates with 15 academic units eligible; 54% of applicants accepted, 20% of these actually enroll; 65% of freshmen graduate in top fifth of high school class. Average freshman scores: SAT, 439 M, 465 W verbal, 512 M, 493 W mathematical; 28% above 500 verbal, 4% above 600, 47% above 500, 16% above 600; ACT, 22 M, 23 W composite. Required: SAT or ACT, minimum H.S. GPA. Criteria considered in admissions, in order of importance: high school academic record, standardized test scores, recommendations, writing sample, extracurricular activities, interview; other factors considered: special talents, alumni children, diverse student body. *Entrance programs:* deferred admission, advanced placement. About 5% of freshmen students from private schools. *Apply:* rolling admissions. *Transfers* welcome; 46 enrolled 1993–94.
Academic Environment. Students take 14–15 credit hours in each of the semesters and 3 credit hours during an Interim period. Degrees offered: bachelors. *Majors offered* in addition to usual studies include medical technology, sign language/ interpreting for deaf, physical therapy, Physics for Teacher Licensure.

About 34% of students entering as freshmen graduate in four years; 62% of freshmen return for sophomore year. *Special programs:* CLEP, independent study, study abroad, January term, 3–2 in engineering, undergraduate research, individualized majors, internships and practica, Washington Experience. Adult programs: Management offered with special scheduling and course requirements designed for adult students. *Calendar:* 2 15-week terms, January 3-week interim, 2 3-week summer sessions.
Undergraduate degrees conferred (103). 37% were in Business and Management, 11% were in Education, 10% were in Health Sciences, 9% were in Psychology, 8% were in Allied Health, 7% were in Social Sciences, 6% were in Physical Sciences, 5% were in Life Sciences, 4% were in Letters, remainder in 4 other fields.

Graduates Career Data. Advanced studies pursued by 26% of students; 6% enter medical school; 1% enter law school; 2% enter business school; 16% enter other schools.
Faculty. About 92% of faculty hold PhD or equivalent. About 40% of undergraduate classes taught by tenured faculty. About 44% of teaching faculty are female; 3% Black, 3% Hispanic, 3% other minority.
Student Body. College does not seek a national student body; 60% of students from in state; 84% South, 4% Midwest; 7% Foreign. An estimated 69% of students reported as Protestant, 9% Catholic, 22% unaffiliated; 5% Black, 1% Hispanic, 7.5% other minority.
Religious Orientation. Maryville is a church-related institution; 1 course each in philosophy and religion required of all students.
Varsity Sports. Men (NCAA,Div.III): Baseball, Basketball, Football, Soccer. Women (Div.III): Basketball, Soccer, Softball, Volleyball.
Campus Life. Cars allowed; college discourages use of alcohol; drinking permitted in residence hall rooms and designated areas. Single students expected to live in residence halls. Daily open-house hours; key system for upper-class women (for freshmen on weekends).

About 29% of men, 21% of women live in traditional dormitories; 38% of men, 44% of women in coed dormitories; rest commute. Sexes segregated in coed dormitories by floor. There are no fraternities or sororities on campus. About 50% of resident students leave campus on weekends.
Annual Costs. Tuition and fees, $10,278; room and board, $4,046; estimated $1,500 other, exclusive of travel. About 85% of students receive financial aid; average amount of assistance, $10,647. Assistance is typically divided 58% scholarship/grant, 37% loan, 5% work. College reports 271 scholarships awarded for academic merit, 51 for special talents, 394 for need.

Marywood College

Scranton, Pennsylvania 18509 **(717) 348-6234 or (800) 346-5014**

A church-related, liberal arts college, conducted by the Sisters Servants of the Immaculate Heart of Mary, Marywood is located in a city of 101,000. Most convenient major airport: Avoca (PA).

Founded: 1915
Affiliation: Independent (Roman Catholic)
UG Enrollment: 404 M, 1,450 W (full-time); 117 M, 285 W (part-time)
Total Enrollment: 3,017
Cost: $10K–$20K
% Receiving Financial Aid: 80%
Admission: Non-selective
Application Deadline: May 1

Admission. Graduates of accredited high schools with 16 units (12 in academic subjects) eligible; others given individual consideration; 78% of applicants accepted, 39% of these actually enroll; 27% of freshmen graduate in top fifth of high school class, 53% in top two-fifths. Average freshman SAT scores: 448 M, 450 W verbal, 500 M, 463 W mathematical. *Required:* SAT or ACT; minimum scores and/or GPA required for some programs; interview recommended. Criteria considered in admissions, in order of importance: high school academic record, class rank, standardized test scores, recommendations, writing sample, extracurricular activities; other factors considered: diverse student body, special talents. *Entrance programs:* early decision, early admission, midyear admission, deferred admission, advanced placement. About 18% of freshmen students come from private schools. *Apply* by May 1; rolling admissions. *Transfers* welcome; 180 enrolled 1993–94.
Academic Environment. Degrees offered: associates, bachelors, masters. Liberal arts core requirements include courses in religious studies, philosophy, mathematics, science, psychology, history, social science, world literature, foreign language, and fine arts; additional requirements include speech, writing, and physical education. *Majors offered* in addition to usual studies include communication disorders, international business, advertising, legal assistants program. Average undergraduate class size: 66% under 20, 33% between 20–40, 1% over 40.

About 38% of students entering as freshmen graduate in four years; 76% of freshmen return for sophomore year. *Special programs:* CLEP, independent study, study abroad, honors, undergraduate research, 3-year degree, individualized majors, internships in most areas, program in retailing/fashion merchandising with Fashion

Institute of Technology. Adult programs: School of continuing Education. *Calendar:* semester, summer school

Undergraduate degrees conferred (362). 19% were in Business and Management, 18% were in Education, 10% were in Health Sciences, 10% were in Visual and Performing Arts, 8% were in Marketing and Distribution, 6% were in Communications, 4% were in Psychology, 4% were in Letters, 4% were in Home Economics, 3% were in Public Affairs, 3% were in Law, remainder in 9 other fields.

Graduates Career Data. Advanced studies pursued by 17% of students. About 78% of 1992–93 graduates employed. Employers typically hiring the largest number of graduates include IBM, KMart, Emery Worldwide, schools, health related facilities. Career Development Services include job announcement service, credential file service, resume development, interview assistance, career counseling, computer career exploration, employment fairs, employer information.

Faculty. About 79% of faculty hold PhD or equivalent. About 40% of undergraduate classes taught by tenured faculty. About 50% of teaching faculty are female; 8% minority.

Student Body. About 75% of students from in state; 96% Middle Atlantic; less than 1% Foreign. An estimated 72% of students reported as Catholic, 12% Protestant, 6% unaffiliated, 10% other; 1% Black, 2% Hispanic, 1% Asian, 1% other. Average age of undergraduate student: 22.

Religious Orientation. Marywood is a church-oriented institution; 3 courses in religion/philosophy required of all students.

Varsity Sports. Men (Div. III): Basketball, Tennis. Women (Div.III): Basketball, Field Hockey, Softball, Tennis, Volleyball.

Campus Life. According to most recent data available about 5% of men, 27% of women live in dormitories; all men, rest of women commute. Freshmen given preference in college housing if all students cannot be accommodated. About 45–50% of resident students leave campus on weekends.

Annual Costs. Tuition and fees, $10,590; room and board, $4,300; estimated $1,200 other, exclusive of travel. About 80% of students receive financial aid; average amount of assistance, $9,000. Assistance typically divided 35% scholarship, 30% grant, 25% loan, 10% work. College reports 256 scholarships awarded for academic merit, 43 for special talents, 850 for need and academic achievement.

Massachusetts College of Art

Boston, Massachusetts 02215-5882

The only free-standing state-supported college of visual art in the country, the college specializes in the training of professionals in design, fine and applied arts, teacher education, and media. Specific programs include architectural, fashion, graphics, industrial design, illustration, ceramics, fibers, glass, metals, sculpture, painting, printmaking, film making, and photography. Dormitory is designed specifically for art students.

Founded: 1873 **Affiliation:** State

Undergraduate degrees conferred (121). 92% were in Visual and Performing Arts, 8% were in Education.

Massachusetts Institute of Technology

Cambridge, Massachusetts 02139 (617) 253-4791

MIT, the renowned Cambridge institution of engineering and science includes the schools of Architecture and Planning, Engineering, Humanities and Social Science, Management, and Science. The Institute is joining increasingly with neighboring institutions such as Harvard, Wellesley, the Woods Hole Oceanographic Institution, and the Whitehead Institute in cooperative programs, including reciprocal opportunities for study at the other institutions. The 130-acre campus is located on the Charles River, facing the city of Boston. Most convenient major airport: Logan International (Boston).

Founded: 1861
Affiliation: Independent
UG Enrollment: 2,962 M, 1,519 W (full-time)
Total Enrollment: 9,790
Cost: $10K–$20K
% Receiving Financial Aid: 55%
Admission: Most Selective
Application Deadline: January 1

Admission is among the most selective in the country. About 33% of applicants accepted, 51% of these actually enroll; 99% of freshmen graduate in top fifth of high school class, all in top two-fifths. Average freshman scores, middle 50% range: SAT, 570–690 verbal, 720–780 mathematical; 94% of freshmen score above 500 on verbal, 70% above 600, 21% above 700; all score above 500 on mathematical, 99% above 600, 84% above 700; ACT, 29–33. *Required:* SAT or ACT, 3 ACH (English or history, chemistry, physics or biology, mathematics I or II), interview, essay. Criteria considered in admissions, in order of importance: high school academic record, standardized test scores, recommendations and extracurricular activities rank with equal importance, writing sample, interview; other factors considered: special talents, alumni children. *Entrance programs:* early action, advanced placement, deferred admission. *Apply* by January 1; November 1 for international students. *Transfers* welcome; 28 enrolled 1993–94.

Academic Environment. Schools of Engineering and Science traditionally have enrolled largest numbers of students. Despite this emphasis, MIT has been unusually successful in preparing premedical students for entrance into some of the nation's top medical schools. Greater stress now being placed on participation of student in developing his-her own course of study. Pressures for academic achievement are intense; likely to be overwhelming for all but very able or highly motivated. Freshman year is on a pass/no credit basis in order to allow students to adjust to the pace at MIT. About half of students enroll with credit toward their degree already earned through the Advanced Placement Program or the Institute's own Advanced Standing Examinations. About 80% of courses required for graduation are elective; all programs require about 20% of undergraduate work in humanities, completion of science requirement (chemistry/biology, physics, and calculus, additional work in science areas outside major department, laboratory subjects); writing proficiency and physical education requirements for all students. Undergraduate programs offered by School of Architecture and Planning include architecture, art and design, and urban studies; School of Engineering offers programs in chemical, civil, electrical engineering and computer science, naval architecture and ocean engineering, mechanical engineering, materials science and engineering, aeronautics and astronautics, and nuclear engineering; School of Science offers programs in chemistry, earth and planetary sciences, mathematics, physics, life sciences, plus the option of an individually developed program in interdisciplinary science; School of Humanities and Social Science offers programs in economics, humanities and engineering, humanities and science, philosophy, and political science; School of Management offers 4 undergraduate degree options. New program in visual arts recently added. An important aspect of the MIT program for undergraduates is the Undergraduate Research Opportunities Program (UROP) which fosters and supports research and collaboration between undergraduates and faculty members of the many prestigious research institutes affiliated with MIT. Students may receive either academic credit or a stipend for their work. This UROP has served as a model for innovation in education. Degrees offered: bachelors, masters, doctoral, engineering. *Majors offered* include visual arts, engineering.

About 90% of students entering as freshmen graduate eventually; 97% of freshmen return for sophomore year. *Special programs:* independent study, study abroad, undergraduate research, individualized majors, interdepartmental majors, interdisciplinary majors, January interterm, study abroad, special freshman programs, cross-registration with Wellesley, Harvard, Wood's Hole, Oceanographic Institute, engineering internship program, undergraduate seminars, special summer program for disadvantaged students, 5-year combined program for baccalaureate and master's, and program for 2 bachelor's degrees. *Calendar:* 4–1–4, summer school.

Undergraduate degrees conferred (1107). 48% were in Engineering, 9% were in Life Sciences, 9% were in Physical Sciences, 9% were in Computer and Engineering Related Technology, 6% were in Mathematics, 6% were in Social Sciences, 4% were in Business and Management, 4% were in Architecture and Environmental Design, remainder in 4 other fields.

Graduates Career Data. Advanced studies pursued by 55% of graduates; 45% enter graduate school; 6% enter medical school; 2% enter law school; 2% enter business school. Medical schools typically enrolling largest numbers of graduates include Harvard, Tufts, U. of Massachusetts, NYU, Stanford; law schools include Columbia, Harvard, Boston College, Yale, U. of Virginia; business schools include Harvard, Stanford, Wharton. About 45% of 1992–93 graduates employed. Fields typically hiring largest numbers of graduates include engineering, finance, consulting. Career Development Services include comprehensive career services for undergraduates through alumni.
Faculty. About 99% of faculty hold PhD or equivalent. MIT's faculty is distinguished; many of its scholars, scientists, and engineers have worldwide reputations. About 74% of undergraduate classes taught by tenured faculty.
Student Body. About 8% of students from in state; 24% Middle Atlantic, 22% South, 12% New England, 15% Midwest, 17% West; 8% foreign. An estimated 6% of students reported as Black, 9% Hispanic, 27% Asian.
Varsity Sports. Men (Div.III): Baseball, Basketball, Crew (I), Cross Country, Diving, Fencing, Football, Golf, Gymnastics, Hockey, Lacrosse, Rifle, Skiing, Soccer, Squash, Swimming, Tennis, Track, Volleyball, Water Polo (Div.I & III), Wrestling. Women (Div.III): Basketball, Crew (Div.I), Cross Country, Diving, Fencing, Field Hockey, Gymnastics, Lacrosse, Riflery, Skiing, Soccer, Softball, Swimming, Tennis, Track, Volleyball.
Campus Life. Students enjoy considerable personal freedom in their campus social life. Both Boston and Cambridge are easily accessible for extracurricular activities. Over 120 recognized campus organizations, as well as many more informal groups, represent the wide range of student activities. A sampling of organizations includes: bridge, chess, flying, folk dance, and outing clubs; debate and film societies; foreign students' clubs and associations; several musical and theater groups; religious groups, and other political, public interest, and social service organizations. Students are also active in student government and campus media and serve on many faculty committees dealing with educational policy, academic performance, judicial system and student environment. MIT offers a wide program of intercollegiate sports. Intramural sports and informal recreational activities attract the greatest number of students. Typically, three-fourths of the students are actively involved in the intramural program, administered largely by students.

Cambridge is a student mecca with both MIT and Harvard located there. Harvard Square serves as a meeting place for students from Harvard, MIT and the numerous colleges and universities in the Boston/Cambridge area. Off-campus housing is available in the Cambridge area, but rents are likely to be high. Cars are allowed, although parking at MIT is very tight.

About 63% of students live in coed dormitories; 7% commute. Freshmen given preference in college housing if all students cannot be accommodated. All unmarried freshmen except those living at home are required to live in Institute housing, either in fraternities or dormitories. There are 30 fraternities, 5 sororities, which about 46% of men, 30% of women join; 30% of students live in fraternities and sororities.
Annual Costs. Tuition and fees, $19,000; room and board, $5,800; estimated $2,250 other, exclusive of travel. About 55% of students receive financial aid; average amount of assistance, $18,770. Assistance is typically divided 64% grant, 28% loan, 8% work. Institute reports scholarships awarded only on the basis of need. *Meeting Costs:* Institute offers PLUS parent loan program, installment payment plan.

Massachusetts Maritime Academy

Buzzards Bay, Massachusetts 02532 (508) 830-5000

A state maritime academy and professional college offering undergraduate programs in marine engineering and marine transportation. All students become members of the Cadet Regiment. Campus is located on the Cape Cod Canal entrance to Buzzards Bay.

Founded: 1891
Affiliation: State
Total Enrollment: 600 M, 55 W (full-time)
Cost: < $10K
Admission: Non-selective
Application Deadline: March 1

Admission. Graduates of accredited high schools with 15 units; candidates must be U.S. citizens; 68% applicants accepted, 64% of these actually enroll. *Required:* SAT, essay. Criteria considered in admissions, in order of importance: high school academic record, standardized test scores, recommendations, writing sample, extracurricular activities; other factors considered: diverse student body. *Out-of-state* freshman applicants: academy actively seeks students from out-of-state; state limits out-of-state enrollment to 10% of entering class. States from which most out-of-state students are drawn include New England states. *Entrance programs:* early decision. *Apply* by March 1; rolling admissions. *Transfers* welcome.
Academic Environment. Degree offered: bachelors. About 18% of general education requirements for graduation are elective; distribution requirements fairly numerous. About 68% of students entering as freshmen graduate eventually. *Majors offered* include marine safety and environmental protection. Special program: CLEP, Sea Term-winter training course. *Calendar:* semester, summer sea term.
Undergraduate degrees conferred (119). 100% were in Military Sciences.
Graduate Career Data. About 90% of 1992–93 graduates employed. Fields typically hiring largest number of graduates include private shipping, power plants, environmental companies. Career Development Services include assistance with resume preparation, interviewing, on-campus recruiting.
Faculty. About 70% of faculty hold PhD or equivalent.
Student Body. About 85% of students from in state; 90% from New England, 10% Middle Atlantic.
Varsity Sports. Men (Div.III): Baseball, Cross Country, Football, Lacrosse, Sailing, Soccer, Tennis, Wrestling. Women (Div.III) Sailing, Softball, Volleyball.
Campus Life. About 60% of cadets live in traditional dormitories; 40% of cadets live in co-ed dormitories. There are no fraternities or sororities on campus. About 60% of resident students leave campus on weekends.
Annual Costs. Tuition and fees, $3,500 (out-of-state, $8,600); room and board, $4,000; estimated $925 other, including travel.

University of Massachusetts/Amherst

Amherst, Massachusetts 01003 (413) 545-0222

A state-supported university and land-grant college, the University of Massachusetts shares with its neighboring colleges—Amherst, Hampshire, Mount Holyoke, and Smith—in the Five College Cooperative Program, which expands academic resources and opportunities. The campus is located in a town of 18,000, 90 miles west of Boston. The university is part of a five campus system with other campuses in Boston, Lowell, Dartmouth, and the Medical School in Worcester. Most convenient major airport: Bradley International (Hartford, CT).

Founded: 1863
Affiliation: State
UG Enrollment: 8,307 M, 7,691 W (full-time)
Total Enrollment: 22,765
Cost: < $10K
% Receiving Financial Aid: 50%
Admission: Selective
Application Deadline: February 15

Admission is selective. About 86% of applicants accepted, 31% of these actually enroll; 29% of freshmen graduate in top fifth of high school class, 64% in top two-fifths. Average freshman SAT scores: 410–520 M, 410–520 W verbal, 490–610 M, 440–560 W mathematical; 34% of freshmen score above 500 on verbal, 7% above 600; 64% score above 500 on mathematical, 24% above 600, 4% above 700. *Required:* SAT, essay. Criteria considered in admissions, in order of importance: high school academic record, standardized test scores, recommendations, writing sample, extracurricular activities; other factors considered: special talents, alumni children, diverse student body. *Out-of-state* freshman applicants: university actively seeks students from out of state. Board of Trustees limits out-of-state enrollment to a floating cap of 25% of total enrollment. Admissions for out-of-state applicants: somewhat more selective; 88% accepted, 24% enroll. About 20% of entering freshmen from private schools. *Entrance programs:* early admission, midyear admission, advanced placement, deferred admission. *Apply* by February 15; rolling admissions. *Transfers* encouraged; 1,269 enrolled 1993–94.

Academic Environment. *Undergraduate studies* offered by colleges and schools of Humanities and Fine Arts, Education, Engineering, Food and Natural Resources, Management, Natural Sciences and Mathematics, Public Health and Health Sciences. Pressures for academic achievement appear moderately strong, but vary somewhat among different colleges and schools. Graduation requirements include 2 courses in writing, 8 in Social World, 3 in Biological and Physical World, 1 in basic math skills, and 1 in analytic reasoning. Most competitive academic programs reported to be business, engineering, computer science. Student reports "many majors" and the "opportunity to create your own [major]" as strengths of the academic program; she wasn't as happy with the "bureaucracy that is slow to get things done." Degrees offered: associates, bachelors, masters, doctoral. Individualized degree program possible. Average undergraduate class size: 44% under 20, 38% 20–40, 18% over 40.

About 45% of students entering as freshmen graduate within four years, 66% eventually; 76% of freshmen return for sophomore year. *Special programs:* independent study, undergraduate research, study abroad, honors, January term, credit by examination, cross-registration with Five College Cooperative, cooperative education, United Asia Learning Resource Center, Learning Center, internships, Stockbridge School of Agriculture, ESL, National Student Exchange Program, Inquiry Program, field experience programs in every major. Adult programs: University Without Walls offers BA and BS with 45 credit required residency. *Calendar:* 4–1–4, summer school.

Undergraduate degrees conferred (4378). 19% were in Social Sciences, 18% were in Business and Management, 8% were in Engineering, 7% were in Communications, 6% were in Letters, 6% were in Psychology, 5% were in Education, 5% were in Life Sciences, 4% were in Multi/Interdisciplinary Studies, 4% were in Visual and Performing Arts, remainder in 16 other fields.

Graduate Career Data. Advanced studies pursued by 41% of graduates; 7% enter business school; 5% enter law school; 4% enter graduate school in arts and sciences; 2% enter medical school; 23% enter other postgraduate school. The Mather Career Center offers individual career counseling and job placement, employer recruitment on campus, resume preparation, job fairs and a careers library.

Faculty. About 92% of faculty hold PhD or equivalent. About 23% of teaching faculty are female; 3% Black, 3% Hispanic, 9% other minority.

Student Body. About 78% of students from in state; 83% New England, 10% Middle Atlantic, 1% each Midwest, South, West; 4% foreign. An estimated 25% of students reported as Catholic, 6% Protestant, 5% Jewish, 1% Muslim, 4% other (58% of undergraduate students did not report religious affiliation); 3% Black, 4% Hispanic, 5% Asian, 6% other minority or unknown. *Minority group students:* tutoring and financial aid through Committee for Collegiate Education of Black and Other Minority Students; Bilingual Collegiate Program assists Spanish-speaking and other bilingual students.

Varsity Sports. Men (Div.I): Baseball, Basketball, Cross Country, Diving, Equestrian, Football (I-A), Gymnastics, Hockey, Lacrosse, Skiing, Soccer, Swimming, Tennis, Track, Water Polo. Women (Div.I): Basketball, Crew, Cross Country, Diving, Equestrian, Field Hockey, Gymnastics, Lacrosse, Skiing, Soccer, Softball, Swimming, Tennis, Track, Volleyball.

Campus Life. Wide variety of living styles, and academic and social opportunities possible. Student reports "Amherst is a great town with lots to do" and "there's always someone to have a great conversation with." Strong women's athletic programs reported. Students may select between traditional and coed dorms. Intervisitation policies determined by vote of each residence unit. Cars allowed; use of alcohol permitted in residence halls subject to state law. Juniors, seniors, married students and veterans may live off campus.

About 57% of men, 59% of women live in traditional or coed dormitories; 37% of men, 35% of women commute. Freshmen given preference in college housing if all students cannot be accommodated. Sexes segregated in coed dormitories by wing, floor, or room. There are 21 fraternities, 13 sororities on campus which about 7% of men, 5% of women join; 3% of men, 3% of women live in fraternities or sororities.

Annual Costs. Tuition and fees, $5,467 (out-of-state, $11,813); room and board, $3,897; estimated $1,900 other, exclusive of travel. About 50% of students receive financial aid; average amount of assistance, $6,400. Assistance is typically divided $2,400 grant, $2,500 loan, $1,500 work. University reports 200 scholarships awarded on the basis of academic merit alone, 250 for special talents alone, 50 for need alone. *Meeting Costs:* university offers budget payment plan and parent loans.

University of Massachusetts—Boston

Boston, Massachusetts 02125-3393 (617) 287-6000

Located in its Harbor campus in Dorchester by the sea, the University of Massachusetts-Boston offers undergraduate programs in the colleges of Arts and Sciences, Management, Nursing, and Public and Community. Most convenient major airport: Logan International (Boston).

Founded: 1964
Affiliation: State
UG Enrollment: 2,905 M, 3,090 W (full-time); 1,702 M, 2,111 W (part-time)
Total Enrollment: 12,136
Cost: < $10K
% Receiving Financial Aid: 52%
Admission: Non-selective
Application Deadline: June 15

Admission. About 60% of applicants accepted, 54% of these actually enroll; 22% of freshmen graduate in top fifth of high school class, 52% in top two-fifths. Average freshman scores: SAT, 425 M, 430 W verbal, 474 M, 461 W mathematical. *Required:* SAT or ACT, minimum 2.0 high school GPA. Criteria considered in admissions, in order of importance: high school academic record, standardized test scores, recommendations, writing sample; other factors considered: special talents. *Out-of-state* freshman applicants: state does not limit out-of-state enrollment. About 74% of out-of-state applicants accepted, 28% enroll. States from which most out-of-state students are drawn include New England, New York, New Jersey, Pennsylvania. Competition among out-of-state candidates "always extremely keen." Entrance programs: midyear admission, deferred admission, advanced placement. *Apply* by June 15; rolling admissions. *Transfers* welcome; 1,666 enrolled 1993–94.

Academic Environment. Degrees offered: bachelors, masters, doctoral. About 20% of general education credits for graduation are required; distribution requirements limited. Average undergraduate class size: 34% under 20, 55% 20–40, 11% over 40. About 14% of students entering as freshmen graduate within four years, 45% eventually; 71% of freshmen return for sophomore year. *Special programs:* honors, undergraduate research, study abroad, cross registration with Massachusetts College of Art, Bunker Hill and Roxbury community colleges, Hebrew College, January term, individualized majors, 2–2 in engineering, internships. *Calendar:* semester.

Undergraduate degrees conferred (1629). 22% were in Social Sciences, 18% were in Business and Management, 10% were in Letters, 10% were in Health Sciences, 9% were in Education, 9% were in Psychology, 4% were in Public Affairs, 4% were in Visual and Performing Arts, remainder in 11 other fields.

Graduates Career Data. Advanced studies pursued by 22% of students within six months of graduation. Career Development Services include aptitude testing, group and individual counseling, resume and interview workshops, placement service, cooperative education, internships, on-campus recruitment, and library resources.

Faculty. About 88% of faculty hold PhD or equivalent. About 36% of teaching faculty are female; 7% Black, 3% Hispanic, 7% other minority.

Student Body. About 96% of students from in state; 2% foreign. An estimated 14% of students are Black, 8% Hispanic, 8% Asian, 2% other minority. Average age of undergraduate students: 28.

Varsity Sports. Men (Div.III): Baseball, Basketball, Cross Country, Diving, Football, Hockey, Lacrosse, Soccer, Swimming, Tennis, Wrestling. Women (Div.III): Basketball, Cross Country, Diving, Softball, Swimming, Volleyball.

Campus Life. There are no dormitories on campus; all students commute. There are no fraternities or sororities on campus.

Annual Costs. Tuition and fees, $4,253 (out-of-state, $10,601); room and board allowance, $4,501; estimated $890 other, exclusive of travel. About 52% of students receive financial aid; average amount of assistance, $6,620. Assistance is typically divided 44% scholarship/grant, 48% loan, 8% work. College reports 5 scholarships awarded on the basis of academic merit alone.

University of Massachusetts—Dartmouth

North Dartmouth, Massachusetts 02747 (508) 999-8605

A state-supported institution, primarily for commuters, located in a town of 18,800, 50 miles south of Boston. Formerly known as Southeastern Massachusetts University. Most convenient major airport: Logan International (Boston).

Founded: 1895
Affiliation: State
UG Enrollment: 2,349 M, 2,280 W (full-time); 265 M, 329 W (part-time)
Total Enrollment: 5,623
Cost: < $10K
% Receiving Financial Aid: 52%
Admission: Non-selective
Application Deadline: Rolling

Admission. About 74% of applicants accepted, 43% of these actually enroll; 24% of freshmen graduate in top fifth of high school class, 62% in top two-fifths. Average freshman SAT scores: 423 verbal, 482 mathematical. *Required:* SAT or ACT, essay, class rank; portfolio for Fine and Applied Arts. Criteria considered in admissions, in order of importance: high school academic record, standardized test scores, writing sample, recommendations, extracurricular activities; other factors considered: special talents. *Out-of-state* freshman applicants: state actively seeks out-of-state students. State does not limit out-of-state enrollment. No special requirements for out-of-state students. States from which most out-of-state students are drawn include New York, Rhode Island, Connecticut. *Entrance programs:* early decision, early admission, midyear admission, deferred admission, advanced placement, alternative admissions programs. About 15% of entering students from private or parochial schools. *Apply:* rolling admissions. *Transfers* welcome; 568 enrolled 1993–94.

Academic Environment. Student leader assesses student interests as overwhelmingly social, with strong supplementary concern for artistic activities and acquisition of marketable skills. Administration source, on the other hand, sees students primarily concerned with occupational/professional goals and only minimally interested in social activities. Different perceptions probably reflect different interests of residential and commuting students. *Undergraduate studies* offered by colleges of Arts and Sciences, Business and Industry, Engineering, Visual and Performing Arts, Nursing. Graduation requirements include 2 classes in critical writing and reading, 2 in literature, 3 classes in natural sciences, 3 in humanities, and 4 in social sciences. Degrees offered: bachelors, masters. Average undergraduate class size: 25.

About 35% of students entering as freshmen graduate within four years; 76% of freshmen return for sophomore year. *Special programs:* CLEP, independent study, January interterm, honors, individualized majors, undergraduate research, study abroad, internships, experiential learning credit, interdisciplinary studies, cross registration with Bridgewater State, Bristol Community College, Cape Cod Community College, Dear Junior College, Massachusetts Maritime, Stonehill College, Wheaton College. *Calendar:* semester, summer school.

Undergraduate degrees conferred (1034). 29% were in Business and Management, 13% were in Engineering, 10% were in Social Sciences, 9% were in Visual and Performing Arts, 8% were in Multi/Interdisciplinary Studies, 6% were in Health Sciences, 5% were in Psychology, 5% were in Letters, 4% were in Engineering and Engineering Related Technology, 3% were in Life Sciences, remainder in 6 other fields.

Graduates Career Data. About 90% of 1992–93 graduates employed. Career Development Services include career counseling/assessment, life planning sessions, group workshops, career forums, career expositions, job fairs.

Faculty. About 90% of faculty hold PhD or equivalent.

Student Body. About 94% of students from in state; 2% foreign. An estimated 4% of students are Black, 1% Hispanic, 2% Asian, 5% other minority.

Varsity Sports. Men (Div.III): Baseball, Basketball, Cross Country, Diving, Football, Golf, Ice Hockey, Soccer, Swimming, Tennis, Track. Women (Div.III): Field Hockey, Soccer, Softball, Swimming, Tennis, Track, Volleyball.

Campus Life. About 38% of students live in coed dormitories; rest commute. Freshmen given preference in college housing if all students cannot be accommodated. Sexes segregated by suite. There are no fraternities or sororities on campus.

Annual Costs. Tuition and fees, $3,568 (out-of-state, $9,025); room and board $4,500; estimated $500 other, exclusive of travel. About 52% of students receive financial aid.

University of Massachusetts—Lowell

Lowell, Massachusetts 01854 (508) 934-4000

A state-supported institution, the university is located in a city of 94,200, 25 miles north of Boston. Formerly known as University of Lowell. Most convenient major airport: Logan International (Boston).

Founded: 1894
Affiliation: State
UG Enrollment: 3,616 M, 2,124 W (full-time); 2,715 M, 1,467 W (part-time)
Total Enrollment: 12,485
Cost: < $10K
% Receiving Financial Aid: 64%
Admission: Non-selective
Application Deadline: April 1

Admission. About 76% of applicants accepted, 36% of these actually enroll; 23% of freshmen graduate in top fifth of high school class, 53% in top two-fifths. Average freshman scores: SAT, 449 M, 444 W *Required:* SAT, minimum high school GPA. Criteria considered in admissions, in order of importance: high school academic record, standardized test scores, class rank, recommendations. *Out-of-state* freshman applicants: university actively seeks students from out-of-state. No limitations or special requirements for out-of-state students. About 69% of out-of-state applicants accepted, 26% of these actually enroll. States from which most out-of-state students are drawn include New York, New Jersey, Pennsylvania, New Hampshire, Connecticut. *Entrance programs:* midyear admission, deferred admission, advanced placement. *Apply* by April 1; rolling admissions. *Transfers* welcome; 720 enrolled 1993–94.

Academic Environment. Degrees offered: associates, bachelors, masters, doctoral. Administration reports 10–50% of courses required for graduation are elective (depending on major); distribution requirements fairly numerous. *Majors offered* in 17 fields of engineering, biological sciences, management, physical and environmental sciences, 12 fields of liberal arts, 5 fields in health, 2 in education and 4 in music. About 20% of students entering as freshmen graduate within four years; 67% of freshmen return for sophomore year. *Special programs:* 3–2 engineering, internships, cooperative work/study. Adult programs: ENCORE program as part-time studies. *Calendar:* semester.

Undergraduate degrees conferred (1585). 27% were in Business and Management, 21% were in Engineering, 8% were in Engineering and Engineering Related Technology, 7% were in Protective Services, 6% were in Psychology, 5% were in Social Sciences, 4% were in Computer and Engineering Related Technology, 3% were in Visual and Performing Arts, 3% were in Allied Health, 3% were in Health Sciences, 3% were in Physical Sciences, 3% were in Education, 3% were in Letters, remainder in 6 other fields.

Graduates Career Data. Career Development Services available to all students.

Faculty. About 82% of faculty hold PhD or equivalent.

Student Body. About 93% of students from in state; 4% New England, 2% foreign. An estimated 2% of students are Black, 2% Hispanic, 5% Asian, 14% other minority. Average age of undergraduate students: 22.

Varsity Sports. Men (Div.II): Baseball, Basketball, Bowling, Crew, Cross Country, Football (III), Golf, Ice Hockey (I), Lacrosse (III), Skiing, Soccer, Swimming, Tennis, Track, Wrestling. Women (Div.II): Basketball, Bowling, Crew, Cross Country, Field Hockey, Skiing, Softball, Tennis, Track, Volleyball.

Campus Life. Quality of campus life influenced by large percentage of commuters. About 24% of students live in traditional or coed dormitories; rest commute. There are no fraternities or sororities on campus.

Annual Costs. Tuition and fees, $4,602 (out-of-state, $9,746); room and board, $4,165; estimated $1,500 other, exclusive of travel. About 64% of students receive financial aid; average amount of assistance, $4,892. Assistance is typically divided 42% scholarship, 39% loan, 19% work. College reports 2,900 scholarships awarded on the basis of need alone.

Mayville State College

(See Mayville State University)

Mayville State University

Mayville, North Dakota 58257-1299 (701) 786-4873

A state-supported, teachers college, located in a community of 3,500, 60 miles north of Fargo. Formerly known as Mayville State College.

Founded: 1889
Affiliation: State
Total Enrollment: 351 M, 307 W (full-time)
Cost: < $10K
% Receiving Financial Aid: 75%
Admission: Non-selective
Application Deadline: Rolling

Admission. Graduates of accredited North Dakota high schools with 15 units accepted; graduates of non-accredited schools admitted by examination; all applicants accepted, 66% of these actually enroll; 12% of freshmen graduate in top fifth of high school class, 32% in top two-fifths. Average freshmen ACT scores: 19.6 composite. *Required:* ACT. Criteria considered in admissions, in order of importance: high school academic record, standardized test scores. *Out-of-state* freshman applicants: university actively seeks students from out-of-state. State does not limit out-of-state enrollment. States from which most out-of-state students are drawn: Minnesota, Manitoba (Canada). *Entrance programs:* early decision, advanced placement. *Apply:* rolling admissions. *Transfers* welcome; 73 enrolled 1993–94.

Academic Environment. Graduation requirements include 3 semester hours each in CIS, physical education, math, and speech, 6 in English, 7 in humanities, 8 in science, and 9 in social sciences. Degrees offered: associates, bachelors. About 50% of students entering as freshmen graduate eventually; 70% of freshmen return for sophomore year. Average undergraduate class size: 20; 58% under 20, 40% 20–40, 3% over 40. *Special programs:* cooperative education. *Calendar:* quarter, summer school.

Undergraduate degrees conferred (122). 56% were in Education, 31% were in Business and Management, 3% were in Social Sciences, 3% were in Life Sciences, remainder in 4 other fields.

Student Body. About 74% of students from in state; 93% from Midwest, 1% Northwest, 6% foreign. An estimated 75% of students reported as Protestant, 25% Catholic.

Varsity Sports. Men (NDCAC): Baseball, Basketball, Football, Golf. Women (WACND): Basketball, Golf, Softball, Volleyball.

Campus Life. About 27% of men, 23% of women live in traditional or co-ed dormitories; rest commute. There is 1 fraternity and 1 sorority on campus which about 2% of men, 2% of women join. About 65% of resident students leave campus on weekends.

Annual Costs. Tuition and fees, $1,831 (contiguous states, $2,231; out-of-state, $4,511); room and board, $2,444; estimated $2,400 other, inclusive of travel. About 75% receive financial aid; average amount of assistance, $2,400. University reports 3 scholarships awarded on the basis of academic merit alone, 24 for special talents alone, 47 for need alone.

McKendree College

Lebanon, Illinois 62254 (618) 537-4481 or (800) BEARCAT

A church-related, liberal arts institution, located in a community of 3,600, 23 miles east of St. Louis. Most convenient major airport: St. Louis International.

Founded: 1828
Affiliation: United Methodist
Total Enrollment: 348 M, 488 W (full-time); 252 M, 432 W (part-time)
Cost: < $10K
% Receiving Financial Aid: 85%
Admission: Non-selective
Application Deadline: Rolling

Admission. Graduates of approved high schools with C average who rank in top half of class eligible; others given individual consideration; 65% of applicants accepted, 11% of these actually enroll; 8% of freshmen graduate in top fifth of high school class, 23% in top two-fifths. Average freshman scores: ACT 20.9 composite. *Required:* ACT. Criteria considered in admissions, in order of importance: high school academic record, standardized test scores, recommendations, writing sample, extracurricular activities. *Entrance programs:* early admission, midyear admission, deferred admission, advanced placement. *Apply:* rolling admissions. *Transfers* welcome; 126 enrolled 1993–94.

Academic Environment. Degrees offered: bachelors. About 50% of general education requirements for graduation are elective; distribution requirements fairly numerous. Average undergraduate class size: 90% under 20, 10% 20–40. About 75% of freshmen return for sophomore year. *Special programs:* CLEP, January interterm, study abroad, 3–2 in occupational therapy, internships, cooperative work/study, independent study, honors, 3-year degree, individualized majors, combined liberal arts–engineering, combined medical technology. Adult programs: night school. *Calendar:* 4–1–4, summer school.

Undergraduate degrees conferred (294). 52% were in Business and Management, 10% were in Computer and Engineering Related Technology, 8% were in Social Sciences, 7% were in Health Sciences, 6% were in Education, 4% were in Life Sciences, 4% were in Psychology, 3% were in Protective Services, remainder in 7 other fields.

Faculty. About 72% of faculty hold PhD or equivalent. About 60% of undergraduate classes taught by tenured faculty. About 43% of teaching faculty are female.

Student Body. About 90% of students from in state; 97% Midwest, 1% each South, West, 2% foreign. An estimated 15% of students reported as Black. Average age of undergraduate student: 25.

Religious Orientation. McKendree is a church-related institution; 15% of students affiliated with the church; 1 course in philosophy or religion required of all students as part of general education requirements; attendance at weekly chapel services voluntary.

Varsity Sports. Men (NAIA): Baseball, Basketball, Golf, Soccer. Women (NAIA): Basketball, Golf, Soccer, Softball.

Campus Life. About 25% of students live in traditional or coed dormitories, 75% commute. Intervisitation in men's and women's dormitory rooms limited. Sexes segregated in coed dormitory by floor. There are 4 fraternities, 4 sororities on campus which about 15% of men, 18% of women join. About 80% of resident students leave campus on weekends.

Annual Costs. Tuition and fees, $7,200; room and board, $3,440; estimated $500 other, exclusive of travel. About 85% of students receive financial aid; assistance is typically divided 33% grant, waivers, scholarship, 33% loan, 33% work. College reports some scholarships awarded on the basis of academic merit alone.

McMurry College

Abilene, Texas 79697 (915) 691-6402

A church-related college, located in a city of 90,000, 150 miles west of Fort Worth. Students may take courses at nearby Abilene Christian and Hardin-Simmons. Most convenient major airport: Abilene Regional.

Founded: 1920
Affiliation: United Methodist
Total Enrollment: 1,189 M, W (full-time)
Cost: < $10K
% Receiving Financial Aid: 80%
Admission: Non-selective
Application Deadline: Rolling

Admission. Graduates of accredited high schools who rank in top half of class and score above 19 ACT composite or 780 SAT combined eligible; others given individual consideration; 83% of applicants accepted, 54% of these actually enroll; 31% of freshmen graduate in top quarter of high school class, 60% in top two-fifths. Average freshman scores, according to most recent data available: SAT, 399 M, 437 W verbal, 455 M, 485 W mathematical; ACT, 20 M, 21 W composite. *Required:* SAT or ACT. *Apply:* rolling admissions. *Transfers* welcome.

Academic Environment. *Degrees:* BA, BS, BBA, BM, BMEd. About 35% of students entering as freshmen graduate eventually; 53% of freshmen return for sophomore year. *Special programs:*

CLEP, independent study, honors, 3-year degree, individualized majors, study abroad, 3-2 medical technology, physical therapy, human services, engineering, optional May term. *Calendar:* semester, summer school.

Undergraduate degrees conferred (179). 33% were in Education, 16% were in Business and Management, 8% were in Public Affairs, 6% were in Business (Administrative Support), 5% were in Health Sciences, 4% were in Psychology, 4% were in Visual and Performing Arts, 4% were in Marketing and Distribution, 3% were in Life Sciences, 3% were in Allied Health, 3% were in Computer and Engineering Related Technology, 3% were in Communications, remainder in 6 other fields.

Student Body. About 93% of students from in state; 94% South, 5% West. An estimated 80% of students reported as Protestant, 10% Catholic, 10% unaffiliated; 8% Black, 8% Hispanic, 1% Asian, 2% other minority, according to most recent data available.

Religious Orientation. McMurry is a church-related institution; 6 semester hours of religion, attendance at 8 College Series Programs each semester required of all students.

Varsity Sports. Men (NAIA): Basketball, Football, Golf, Tennis, Track. Women (NAIA): Basketball, Golf, Tennis, Track, Volleyball.

Campus Life. About 49% of men, 47% of women live in traditional dormitories; no coed dormitories; rest live in off-campus housing or commute. No intervisitation in men's or women's dormitory rooms. There are 6 fraternities, 5 sororities on campus which about 28% of men, 27% of women join; they provide no residence facilities. About 15% of resident students leave campus on weekends.

Annual Costs. Tuition and fees, $7,040; room and board, $3,100. About 80% of students receive financial aid; assistance is typically divided 50% scholarship, 40% loan, 10% work. College reports some scholarships awarded on the basis of academic merit alone. *Meeting Costs:* college offers extended payment plans.

McNeese State University

Lake Charles, Louisiana 70609 (318) 475-5000

A state-supported university, located in a city of over 100,000, between Houston, Texas and New Orleans, Louisiana. Most convenient major airport: Houston.

Founded: 1939
Affiliation: State
UG Enrollment: 2,654 M, 3,367 W (full-time); 546 M, 780 W (part-time)
Total Enrollment: 8,403
Cost: < $10K
% Receiving Financial Aid: 55%
Admission: Non-selective
Application Deadline: 30 days before registration

Admission. Graduates of approved Louisiana high schools eligible; other Louisiana high school graduates admitted by examination; 99% of applicants accepted, 70% of these actually enroll. Average freshman ACT scores: 18.9 M, 19.1 W composite. *Required:* ACT. Criteria considered in admissions, in order of importance: high school academic record, standardized test scores. *Out-of-state* freshman applicants: university actively seeks students from out-of-state. State does not limit out-of-state enrollment. Requirement for out-of-state applicants: rank in top half of class; others given individual consideration. About 98% of out-of-state students accepted, 51% of these actually enroll. States from which most out-of-state students are drawn include Texas. *Entrance programs:* early admission, midyear admission, advanced placement. *Apply* by 30 days before registration; rolling admissions. *Transfers* welcome; 424 enrolled 1993–94.

Academic Environment. Graduation requirements include work in freshman English, natural sciences, mathematics, computer literacy, arts, humanities, and social sciences. Degrees offered: associates, bachelors, masters. *Majors offered* include wildlife management. Average undergraduate class size: 49% under 20, 34% 20-40, 17% over 40. About 10% of students entering as freshmen graduate within four years, 40% eventually; 55% of freshmen return for sophomore year. Special program: honors, January term, internships. Adult programs: EASE program (Emphasis on Adult Special Entry). *Calendar:* semester, summer school.

Undergraduate degrees conferred (734). 31% were in Education, 19% were in Business and Management, 10% were in Health Sciences, 4% were in Psychology, 4% were in Protective Services, 4% were in Home Economics, 3% were in Engineering and Engineering Related Technology, 3% were in Communications, 3% were in Engineering, remainder in 13 other fields.

Graduate Career Data. About 80% of 1992–93 graduates employed. Fields typically hiring largest numbers of graduates include education, nursing, business, engineering.

Faculty. About 56% of faculty hold PhD or equivalent. About 76% of undergraduate classes taught by tenured faculty. About 37% of teaching faculty are female; 1% Black, 1% other minority.

Student Body. About 94% of students from in state; 80% from South. An estimated 14% of students reported as Black, 3% other minority. Average age of undergraduate student: 25.

Varsity Sports. Men (Div.I): Baseball, Basketball, Cross Country, Football, Golf, Track. Women (Div.I): Basketball, Cross Country, Softball, Tennis, Track, Volleyball.

Campus Life. About 61% of men, 48% of women live in traditional dormitories; 39% men, 52% women live in coed dormitories; rest commute. There are 8 fraternities, 6 sororities on campus which about 5% of men, 5% of women join; 1% of men live in fraternities; sororities provide no residence facilities. About 50% of resident students leave campus on weekends.

Annual Costs. Tuition and fees, $1,951 (out-of-state, $3,501); room and board, $2,620; estimated $1,770 other, exclusive of travel. About 55% of students receive financial aid; average amount of assistance, $3,126. Assistance is typically divided 17% scholarship, 31% grant, 34% loan, 8% work. University reports 1,592 scholarships awarded on the basis of academic merit alone, 642 on special talents alone. *Meeting Costs:* university offers payment plan students.

McPherson College

McPherson, Kansas 67460 (316) 241-0731

A church-related college, located in a town of 12,000, 50 miles north of Wichita.

Founded: 1887
Affiliation: Brethren
Total Enrollment: 406 M, W (full-time)
Cost: < $10K
% Receiving Financial Aid: 96%
Admission: Non-selective
Application Deadline: Rolling

Admission. Graduates of approved high schools with GPA of 2.0, rank in top half of graduating class, and minimum ACT composite score of 15 eligible; 72% of applicants accepted, 42% of these actually enroll; 14% of freshmen graduate in top tenth of high school class, 35% in top quarter. Average freshman ACT scores, according to most recent data available: 20.9 composite. *Required:* ACT, acceptance of college's standards; interview recommended. *Apply:* rolling admissions. *Transfers* welcome.

Academic Environment. *Degree:* AB. About 45-50% of students entering as freshmen graduate within four years; 70% of freshmen return for sophomore year. *Special programs:* CLEP, independent study, study abroad, undergraduate research, individualized majors,"broad program in international and intercultural experiences" during interterm, 3-2 in medical technology. Adult programs: 2+2 program in Business Administration for non-traditional students; Continuing Education programs in California and Wisconsin for teachers. *Calendar:* 4–1–4, summer school.

Undergraduate degrees conferred (68). 38% were in Business and Management, 22% were in Education, 9% were in Social Sciences, 6% were in Psychology, 3% were in Visual and Performing Arts, 3% were in Physical Sciences, 3% were in Multi/Interdisciplinary Studies, 3% were in Life Sciences, 3% were in Engineering and Engineering Related Technology, 3% were in Agricultural Sciences, remainder in 5 other fields.

Faculty. About 54% of faculty hold PhD or equivalent.

Student Body. About 61% of students from in state; 87% Midwest. An estimated 66% of students reported as Protestant, 9% Catholic, 20% unaffiliated, 5% other; 3% Black, 3% other minority, according to most recent data available.

Religious Orientation. McPherson is a church-related institution; attendance at 7 convocations each semester required of all students; chapel attendance voluntary; "worship is considered personal, but highly important."

Varsity Sports. Men (NAIA): Basketball, Cross Country, Football, Golf, Tennis, Track. Women (NAIA): Basketball, Cross Country, Golf, Tennis, Track, Volleyball.

Campus Life. About 60% of men, 60% of women live in traditional dormitories; rest live in off-campus housing or commute. Freshmen given preference in college housing if all students cannot be accommodated. Intervisitation in men's and women's dormitory rooms limited. There are no fraternities or sororities on campus. About 10%-15% of resident students leave campus on weekends.
Annual Costs. Tuition and fees, $7,810; room and board, $3,550. About 96% of students receive financial aid; assistance is typically is divided 57% scholarship, 35% loan, 8% work. College reports some scholarships awarded on the basis of academic merit alone. *Meeting Costs:* college offers Plus loans, Academic Management Service, The Tuition Plan.

Medaille College

Buffalo, New York 14214 (716) 884-3281

An independent, urban, liberal arts college, Medaille offers 15 career-oriented programs in a variety of fields. College also offers associates degrees and a masters program. Campus is adjacent to Delaware Park and the Buffalo Zoological Gardens. Most convenient major airport: Greater Buffalo International.

Founded: 1875
Affiliation: Independent
UG Enrollment: 399 M, 511 W (full-time); 55 M, 181 W (part-time)
Total Enrollment: 1,146
Cost: < $10K
% Receiving Financial Aid: 91%
Admission: Non-selective
Application Deadline: May 15

Admission. Graduates of approved high schools or GED eligible; 60% of applicants accepted, 60% of these actually enroll. About 16% of freshmen graduate in top fifth of high school class, 38% in top two-fifths. Average freshman scores: SAT, 356 M, 332 W verbal, 402 M, 370 W mathematical, according to most recent data available. *Required:* essay, interview, recommendation. Criteria considered in admissions, in order of importance: high school academic record, recommendations, writing sample, extracurricular activities, standardized test scores; other factors considered: alumni children, diverse student body. *Entrance programs:* midyear admission, deferred admission. *Apply* by May 15; rolling admissions. *Transfers* welcome; 235 enrolled 1993–94.
Academic Environment. Graduation requirements include Theme I: Self and Others (3 credits), Theme II: Global Perspectives (9 credits), Theme III: Creative Expression (3 credits), Theme IV: Science, Technology and Environment (3 credits), Theme V: Communication (9 credits), and 3 credits each in math and computers; in addition, internships are required for all degree programs. Degrees offered: associates, bachelors. About 40% of students entering as freshmen graduate eventually; 28% of freshmen return for sophomore year. Average undergraduate class size: 99% under 20, 1% 20-40. *Special programs:* CLEP, independent study, honors, cross-registration with 18 West New York consortium schools, internships. Adult programs: evening module, Saturday program. *Calendar:* semester, summer school.
Undergraduate degrees conferred (167). 32% were in Liberal/General Studies, 22% were in Business and Management, 18% were in Education, 13% were in Public Affairs, 8% were in Computer and Engineering Related Technology, 5% were in Communications Technologies, remainder in 2 other fields.
Graduates Career Data. Advanced studies pursued by 16% of graduates; all enter graduate school. Career Development Services include career planning, career library, job listings, group workshops, interest inventories, placement folders, personal counseling.
Faculty. About 65% of faculty hold PhD or equivalent.
Student Body. About 99% of students from in state. An estimated 22% of the students are Black, 2% Hispanic, 1% Asian.
Campus Life. About 1% each of men, women live in traditional dormitories, rest commute; dormitory space available at nearby colleges. There are no fraternities or sororities on campus.
Annual Costs. Tuition and fees, $8,350; room and board, $4,300; estimated $1,000 other, exclusive of and travel. About 91% of students receive financial aid; average amount of assistance, $6,170. Assistance is typically divided 47% scholarship, 47% loan, 6% work. College reports 1 scholarship awarded on the basis of academic merit alone. Meeting costs: college offers Academic Management Service, and institutional interest-free payment plan.

Medgar Evers College

(See City University of New York)

Medical College of Georgia

Augusta, Georgia 30912 (404) 721-2725

The Medical College of Georgia is that state's primary institution of higher education for training health professionals. Today the college includes the School of Medicine and the Schools of Graduate Studies, Nursing, Allied Health Sciences, and Dentistry. Undergraduate studies are offered by the Schools of Nursing and Allied Health Professions. Most convenient major airport: Bush Field.

Founded: 1828
Affiliation: State
UG Enrollment: 119 M, 605 W (full-time)
Total Enrollment: 1,905
Cost: <$5,000
% Receiving Financial Aid: 69%

Undergraduate degrees conferred (316). 54% were in Health Sciences, 46% were in Allied Health.
Annual Costs. Tuition and fees, $2,085 (out-of-state, $3,930); room and board, $3,807. About 69% of students receive financial aid.

Memphis College of Art

Memphis, Tennessee 38112

An independent, professional college, the school offers degree programs leading to the BFA in painting, advertising design, clay, decorative design, fiber, metal arts, sculpture, printmaking, photography, and visual information design.

Founded: 1936
Affiliation: Independent

Undergraduate degrees conferred (19). 100% were in Visual and Performing Arts.

Memphis State University

Memphis, Tennessee 38152 (901) 678-2101

A state-supported university, located in a city of 700,000. Most convenient major airport: Memphis International.

Founded: 1912
Affiliation: State
UG Enrollment: 5,258 M, 5,838 W (full-time); 2,143 M, 2,968 W (part-time)
Total Enrollment: 16,138
Cost: < $10K
% Receiving Financial Aid: 50%
Admission: Non-selective
Application Deadline: Aug. 1

Admission. Graduates of approved or accredited high schools with GPA of 3.0 or minimum ACT composite score of 18 eligible; others admitted by examination; 68% of applicants accepted, 63% of these actually enroll. Average freshman ACT scores, according to most recent data available: 23.0 M, 21.7 W composite. *Required:* ACT. *Out-of-state* freshman applicants: university welcomes students from out of state. State limits out-of-state enrollment to 15% of entering class. No special requirements for out-of-state applicants; 51% accepted, 36% enroll. *Apply* by August 1. *Transfers* welcome.
Academic Environment. *Undergraduate studies* offered by colleges of Arts and Sciences, Business Administration, Communications and Fine Arts, Education, Engineering, School of Nursing and the University College; freshmen and sophomores enroll in General Advising Center. About 35% of students entering as freshmen graduate eventually; 77% of freshmen return for sophomore year. *Special programs:* independent study, study abroad, honors, internships with State Legislature. *Calendar:* semester, summer school.

Undergraduate degrees conferred (1858). 31% were in Business and Management, 9% were in Education, 7% were in Visual and Performing Arts, 7% were in Engineering, 6% were in Social Sciences, 5% were in Psychology, 4% were in Engineering and Engineering Related Technology, 4% were in Marketing and Distribution, 4% were in Communications, 4% were in Computer and Engineering Related Technology, 3% were in Multi/Interdisciplinary Studies, 3% were in Home Economics, remainder in 12 other fields.
Faculty. About 72% of faculty hold PhD or equivalent.
Student Body. About 88% of students from in state; 94% South. An estimated 18% of students reported as Black, 2% Asian, according to most recent data available.
Varsity Sports. Men (Div.I): Baseball, Basketball, Cross Country, Football, Golf, Gymnastics, Tennis, Track. Women (Div.I): Basketball, Golf, Gymnastics, Tennis, Volleyball.
Campus Life. About 10% of men, 10% of women live in traditional dormitories; no coed dormitories; rest commute. Intervisitation in men's and women's dormitory rooms limited. There are 15 fraternities, 11 sororities on campus which about 9% of men, 6% of women join; 1% of men live in fraternities, sororities provide no residence facilities. About 85% of resident students leave campus on weekends.
Annual Costs. Tuition and fees, $1,828 (out-of-state, $5,610); room an board, $3,220. About 50% of students receive financial aid; assistance is typically is divided 16% scholarship, 70% loan, 14% work. University reports some scholarships awarded on the basis of academic merit alone.

Menlo College

Atherton, California 94027 (415) 688-3753

An independent, co-educational college offering 2- and 4-year programs in business and liberal studies. The 62-acre campus is located in a Peninsula community of 28,500, 30 miles south of San Francisco.

Founded: 1927
Affiliation: Independent
Total Enrollment: 364 M, 196 W (full-time)
Cost: $10K–$20K
% Receiving Financial Aid: 47%
Admission: Non-selective
Application Deadline: Rolling

Admission. High school graduates with minimum 2.0 GPA and satisfactory SAT scores eligible; 87% of applicants accepted, 42% of these actually enroll. *Required:* SAT or ACT, essay. Criteria considered in admissions, in order of importance: high school academic record, standardized test scores, writing sample, extracurricular activities, recommendations. *Out-of-state* freshmen applicants: college actively seeks students from out-of-state. State does not limit out-of-state enrollment. States from which most out-of-state students are drawn include Hawaii, Texas, Oregon. *Entrance programs:* early decision, early admission, midyear admission, deferred admission, advanced placement. About 70% of freshmen from private schools. *Apply:* rolling admissions. *Transfers* welcome; 89 enrolled 1993–94.
Academic Environment. Students report small classes and accessible faculty as strengths of the academic program; "The professors are really cool and they do a lot of unusual things that makes class very interesting." Graduation requirements include courses in Western Culture, English, math, computer competency, critical thinking, American Institutions, social sciences, lab science, humanities, physical education. Degrees offered: associates, bachelors. New majors offered include advertising, broadcast communications, finance, history, human resource management, international business, journalism, marketing, media studies, philosophy, pre-professional biological science. Average undergraduate class size: 75% under 20, 23% 20-40, 2% over 40. About 36% of entering freshmen graduate within four years, 57% eventually; 80% of freshmen return for sophomore year. *Special programs:* internships. *Calendar:* 4–1–4, summer study skills courses.
Undergraduate degrees conferred (92). 50% were in Business and Management, 26% were in Communications, 13% were in Liberal/General Studies, 5% were in Computer and Engineering Related Technology, 3% were in Life Sciences, remainder in Psychology.
Graduates Career Data. About 90% of 1992–93 graduates employed. Fields typically hiring largest numbers of graduates include business, communications, biotechnology. Career Development Services include career assessment, placement, resource library.
Faculty. About 30% of faculty hold PhD or equivalent.
Student Body. About 60% of students from in state; 99% West/Northwest.
Varsity Sports. Men (Div. III): Baseball, Basketball, Cross Country, Football, Golf, Soccer, Tennis, Track. Women (Div. III): Cross Country, Softball, Tennis, Track, Volleyball.
Campus Life. Campus located near Stanford University and is accessible to shopping and entertainment. Students report interest in campus clubs and organizations.

About 19% of men, 6% of women live in traditional dormitories; 22% of men, 15% of women live in coed dormitories; rest commute. Freshmen given preference in college housing if all students cannot be accommodated. There are 2 fraternities on campus, which about 7% of men join. About 20% of resident students leave campus on weekends.
Annual Costs. Tuition and fees, $14,125; room and board, $6,200; estimated $2,275 other, exclusive of travel. About 42% of students receive financial aid; average amount of assistance, $10,100. College reports 3 scholarships awarded on the basis of academic merit alone, 1 for need alone.

Mercer University

Macon, Georgia 31207 (912) 744-2650

A church-related institution, Mercer includes the College of Liberal Arts and School of Law on the 75-acre main campus in Macon (pop. 144,000); a second campus including the School of Pharmacy and located in Atlanta, 95 miles to the north, is known as Mercer University in Atlanta. Most convenient major airport: Atlanta.

Founded: 1833
Affiliation: Southern Baptist
UG Enrollment: 1,309 M, 1,634 W (full-time); 685 M, 575 W (part-time)
Total Enrollment: 6,729
Cost: $10K–$20K
% Receiving Financial Aid: 93%
Admission: Non-selective
Application Deadline: Rolling

Admission. About 83% of applicants accepted, 30% of these actually enroll. Average freshmen scores: SAT, 445 M, 440 W verbal; 518 M, 477 W mathematical; ACT, 23 M, 24 W composite. *Required:* SAT or ACT, essay, minimum 2.5 high school GPA; interview recommended. Criteria considered in admissions: high school academic record ranks with highest importance, standardized test scores, recommendations and writing sample rank with equal importance, recommendations rank third; other factors considered: special talents, alumni children, diverse student body, religious affiliation/commitment. *Entrance programs:* early decision, early admission. *Apply:* rolling admissions. *Transfers* welcome; 232 enrolled 1993–94.
Academic Environment. Graduation requirements include work in writing and speech, math, heritage, literature and fine arts, lab science, foreign language, contemporary society, and senior capstone. Degrees offered: masters, doctoral. Average undergraduate class size: 12-1 ratio. About 71% of students entering as freshmen graduate within four years; 81% of freshmen return for sophomore year. *Special programs:* independent study, study abroad, undergraduate research, combined arts/law or pharmacy programs, 3-2 in forestry, internships. Adult programs: university college for non-traditional students. *Calendar:* quarter, summer school.
Undergraduate degrees conferred (269). 25% were in Business and Management, 16% were in Social Sciences, 11% were in Education, 10% were in Psychology, 8% were in Communications, 8% were in Letters, 6% were in Life Sciences, 5% were in Philosophy and Religion, 4% were in Visual and Performing Arts, 3% were in Physical Sciences, 3% were in Public Affairs, remainder in 5 other fields.
Graduate Career Data. Advanced studies pursued by 29% of liberal arts graduates, 10% of engineering graduates, 17% of business graduates. About 42% of liberal arts graduates are employed, 51% of engineering graduates, 17% of business graduates. Career Development Services include counseling, testing, placement service, resume and interview workshops, on-campus recruiting, cooperative education.
Faculty. About 93% of faculty hold PhD or equivalent. About 58% of undergraduate classes taught by tenured faculty. About 31% of teaching faculty are female.

Student Body. About 63% of students from in state; 24% from South, 2% Northwest, New England, 2% Midwest, 4% foreign. An estimated 66% of students reported as Protestant, 7% Catholic, 1% Jewish, 5% unaffiliated, 7% other; 13% Black, 2% Hispanic, 2% Asian, 4% other minority.
Religious Orientation. Mercer is a church-related institution; 33% of students affiliated with the church; 1 course in Christianity required of all students; attendance at university worship services voluntary.
Varsity Sports. Men (Div.I): Baseball, Basketball, Cross Country, Golf, Soccer, Tennis. Women (Div.I): Basketball, Cross Country, Soccer, Softball, Tennis, Volleyball.
Campus Life. About 7% of men, 14% of women live in traditional dormitories; 31% each live in coed dormitories; rest commute. Freshmen given preference in college housing if all students cannot be accommodated. There are 9 fraternities, 6 sororities which about 35% each of men, women join; 2% of women live in sororities, fraternities provide no residence facilities.
Annual Costs. Tuition and fees, $11,160; room and board, $3,963. About 93% of students receive financial aid; average amount of assistance, $10,725. Assistance is typically divided 50% scholarship, 25% loan, 25% work. College reports 164 scholarships awarded on the basis of special talents alone.

Mercer University Atlanta

Atlanta, Georgia 30341 (404) 458-5904

A small, church-related, liberal arts, commuter institution located 12 miles from downtown Atlanta.

Founded: 1964
Affiliation: Southern Baptist
Total Enrollment: 391 M, 377 W (full-time)
Cost: < $10K
Admission: Non-selective

Admission. High school graduates with 16 units (13 in academic subjects) eligible; 69% of applicants accepted, 65% of these actually enroll. *Required:* SAT, interview. *Apply* by no specific deadline. *Transfers* welcome.
Academic Environment. *Degrees:* AB, BS, BBA, BM. *Special programs:* CLEP, independent study, study abroad, undergraduate research. *Calendar:* quarter, summer school.
Undergraduate degrees conferred (641). 28% were in Business and Management, 18% were in Education, 14% were in Social Sciences, 7% were in Engineering, 5% were in Communications, 5% were in Life Sciences, 5% were in Letters, 4% were in Psychology, 4% were in Visual and Performing Arts, remainder in 8 other fields.
Student Body. All students from the South.
Religious Orientation. Mercer Atlanta is a church-related institution; attendance at university worship services is "completely voluntary.
Campus Life. No dormitories on campus. There are no fraternities or sororities on campus.
Annual Costs. Tuition and fees, $5,895. University reports some scholarships awarded on the basis of academic merit alone.

Mercy College

Dobbs Ferry, New York 10522 (914) 693-7600

An independent, co-educational, nonsectarian college with major programs in liberal arts and sciences, education, and business administration. Primarily serving commuters, the campus is located in a Westchester suburb of 10,400, 20 miles from New York, with branch campuses in Yorktown Heights, Peekskill, White Plains, and the Bronx. Mercy also offers 2-year degree programs. Most convenient major airports: JFK International, LaGuardia, Newark.

Founded: 1961
Affiliation: Independent
UG Enrollment: 1,257 M, 1,669 W (full-time); 550 M, 1,312 W (part-time)
Total Enrollment: 3,103
Cost: < $10K
Admission: Non-selective
Application Deadline: Rolling

Admission. About 90% of applicants accepted, 66% of these actually enroll. Open admissions policy. *Apply:* rolling admissions. *Transfers* welcome.
Academic Environment. Mercy is a commuter college with a broad career oriented program. *Degrees:* AB, BS. *Majors offered* include arts and sciences, speech pathology, music, business administration, interdisciplinary studies, social work, accounting, journalism and media. About 35% of students entering as freshmen graduate eventually; 55% of freshmen return for sophomore year. *Special programs:* CLEP, independent study, study abroad, honors, 3-year degree, individualized majors, law enforcement education program, combined programs (medical technology, nursing, pharmacy, chiropractic), music major with Westchester Conservatory of Music, certification in education (secondary program in cooperation with neighboring colleges). Adult programs: Currently about 60% of students attending Mercy are over 25 years of age, the college models its programs, schedules its classes, and located the extension campuses with this in mind. *Calendar:* 5–1–5, summer school.
Undergraduate degrees conferred (754). 38% were in Business and Management, 16% were in Social Sciences, 13% were in Psychology, 7% were in Protective Services, 6% were in Computer and Engineering Related Technology, 4% were in Letters, 3% were in Foreign Languages, 3% were in Health Sciences, 3% were in Public Affairs, remainder in 6 other fields.
Graduates Career Data. According to most recent data available, full-time graduate or professional study pursued immediately after graduation by 11% of students. *Careers in business and industry* pursued by 83% of graduates.
Student Life. Almost all students from in state. *Minority group students:* financial and academic help; Black Students Union.
Varsity Sports. Men (Div.II): Baseball, Basketball, Cross Country, Golf, Soccer, Tennis. Women (Div.II): Basketball, Cross Country, Softball, Tennis, Volleyball.
Campus Life. College is a commuter institution; administration reports 116 students living in dorms or off-campus college-related residences, rest live in other off-campus housing or commute. There are no fraternities or sororities on campus.
Annual Costs. Tuition and fees, $7,200; room and board, $6,380. College reports some scholarships awarded on the basis of academic merit alone.

Mercy College of Detroit

(See University of Detroit Mercy)

Mercyhurst College

Erie, Pennsylvania 16546 (814) 825-2202

An independent, co-educational, liberal arts college, founded by the Sisters of Mercy, Mercyhurst is located in a city of 129,200, midway between Buffalo and Cleveland. Most convenient major airport: Erie International.

Founded: 1926
Affiliation: Independent (Roman Catholic)
UG Enrollment: 764 M, 1,066 W (full-time); 171 M, 237 W (part-time)
Total Enrollment: 2,317
Cost: < $10K
% Receiving Financial Aid: 87%
Admission: Non-selective
Application Deadline: Rolling

Admission. High school graduates with 16 units eligible; 68% of applicants accepted, 38% of these actually enroll; 41% of freshmen graduate in top fifth of high school class, 73% in top two-fifths. Average freshman scores: SAT, 461 M, 453 W verbal, 513 M, 501 W mathematical; 28% of freshmen score above 500 on verbal, 4% above 600; 55% of freshmen score above 500 on mathematical, 11% above 600, 1% above 700; ACT, 20 M, 20 W composite. *Required:* SAT or ACT, essay, minimum 2.5 high school GPA, interview encouraged. Criteria considered in admissions, in order of importance: high school academic record, standardized test scores, extracurricular activities, recommendations, writing sample; other factors considered: special talents, alumni children, diverse student body. About 2% of entering students from private schools, 29% from parochial schools. *Entrance programs:* early admission, midyear admission, deferred admission, advanced placement. *Apply:* rolling admissions. *Transfers* welcome; 124 enrolled 1993–94.

Academic Environment. Graduation requirements include work in English/language, math, science, philosophy, history, social sciences, arts, religion, human studies, and senior seminars. Degrees offered: associates, bachelors, masters. *Majors offered* include arts and sciences, accounting, art, business, computer management, risk management/insurance, research intelligence analyst, archaeology/anthropology, interior design/fashion merchandising, business/chemistry, earth/space science education, philosophy. Average undergraduate class size: 27% under 20, 65% 20-40, 8% over 40.

About 55% of students entering as freshmen graduate within four years, 65% eventually; 75% of freshmen return for sophomore year. *Special programs:* CLEP, independent study, study abroad, honors, undergraduate research, cadet teacher program, cross-registration with Gannon College, 3-2 engineering, internship/work-study. Adult programs: weekend college, accelerated degree completion program. *Calendar:* 4–3–3, summer school.

Undergraduate degrees conferred (300). 40% were in Business and Management, 12% were in Protective Services, 11% were in Education, 6% were in Health Sciences, 4% were in Visual and Performing Arts, 4% were in Home Economics, 4% were in Communications, 4% were in Architecture and Environmental Design, 3% were in Psychology, remainder in 9 other fields.

Graduates Career Data. Advanced studies pursued by 17% of graduates; 9% enter graduate school; 2% each enter medical, dental, law, and business schools. Medical schools typically enrolling largest numbers of graduates include Hahnemann; law schools include U. of Pittsburgh; business schools include Case Western Reserve. About 85% of 1992–93 graduates employed. Fields typically hiring largest numbers of graduates include business, education, hospitality. Career Development Services include resume preparation, career counseling, on-campus job interviews, job placement center.

Faculty. About 63% of faculty hold PhD or equivalent. About 55% of undergraduate classes taught by tenured faculty.

Student Body. About 64% of students from in state; 74% from Middle Atlantic, 11% Midwest, 4% New England, 2% West, 1% each South, Northwest, 7% foreign. An estimated 64% of students reported as Catholic, 23% Protestant, 13% other; 8% as Black, 2% Hispanic, 1% other minority. Average age of undergraduate student: 25.

Religious Orientation. Mercyhurst is a Roman Catholic institution; 1 course in religious studies required.

Varsity Sports. Men (Div.II): Baseball, Basketball, Crew, Cross Country, Football, Golf, Ice Hockey, Soccer, Tennis. Women (Div.II): Basketball, Crew, Cross Country, Golf, Soccer, Softball, Tennis, Volleyball.

Campus Life. Administration describes campus as "safe, secure, beautiful suburban setting, with easy access to four major cities (Pittsburgh, Buffalo, Cleveland, and Toronto)." Students note that it is "sometimes hard to get off-campus if you don't have a car", "limited transportation". But they also agree that "It is nice and small, everyone knows everyone, and the teachers are always available."

About 83% of men and women live in traditional dormitories; rest commute. Freshmen given preference in college housing if all students cannot be accommodated. Intervisitation in men's and women's dormitory rooms limited. There are no fraternities or sororities on campus. About 31% of resident students leave campus on weekends.

Annual Costs. Tuition and fees, $9,883; room and board, $3,650; estimated $1,500 other, exclusive of travel. About 87% of students receive financial aid; average amount of assistance, $6,500. Assistance typically divided 30% scholarship, 30% grant, 20% loan, 20% work. College reports some scholarships awarded on the basis of academic merit alone.

Meredith College

Raleigh, North Carolina 27607-5298 (919) 829-8581

A church-related, liberal arts college for women, Meredith is located on a 225-acre campus in a city of 200,000. Most convenient major airport: Raleigh-Durham.

Founded: 1891
Affiliation: Southern Baptist
UG Enrollment: 1,741 W (full-time); 297 W (part-time)
Total Enrollment: 2,321
Cost: < $10K
% Receiving Financial Aid: 32%
Admission: Non-selective
Application Deadline: February 15

Admission. About 76% of applicants accepted, 37% of these actually enroll; 55% of freshmen graduate in top fifth of high school class, 84% in top two-fifths. Average freshman SAT scores, according to most recent data available: 446 verbal, 486 mathematical. *Required:* SAT or ACT; interview recommended. *Apply* by February 15. *Transfers* welcome.

Academic Environment. Student leader characterizes academic program as "providing quality Christian education for the women who will be mothers, teachers, lawyers, doctors, and community leaders in the future." *Degrees:* AB, BS, BM. *Majors offered* include arts and sciences, business, home economics, non-Western civilizations, dance, fashion merchandising, interior design, child development, food management and nutrition.

About 65% of students entering as freshmen graduate eventually; 89% of freshmen return for sophomore year. *Special programs:* independent study, study abroad, undergraduate research, 3-year degree, inter-institutional program with cooperating Raleigh Colleges consortium, United Nations Semester, Washington Semester, New York Semester, Capital City Semester. *Calendar:* early semester, summer school.

Undergraduate degrees conferred (390). 25% were in Business and Management, 12% were in Vocational Home Economics, 10% were in Social Sciences, 8% were in Psychology, 7% were in Visual and Performing Arts, 7% were in Life Sciences, 7% were in Architecture and Environmental Design, 5% were in Home Economics, 4% were in Marketing and Distribution, 4% were in Public Affairs, 3% were in Letters, remainder in 8 other fields.

Graduates Career Data. According to most recent data available, full-time graduate or professional study pursued by 23% of students immediately after graduation. *Careers in business and industry* pursued by 50% of graduates.

Faculty. About 86% of faculty hold PhD or equivalent.

Student Body. About 88% of students from in state. An estimated 75% of students reported as Protestant, 7% Catholic, 9% other; 3% Black, 1% other minority, according to most recent data available. *Minority group students:* financial aid provided for most members of minority groups.

Religious Orientation. Meredith is a Baptist institution; 2 courses in religion required of all students; attendance at Wednesday morning services voluntary.

Varsity Sports. Women (NCAA, Div.III): Basketball, Golf, Softball, Tennis, Volleyball.

Campus Life. Student Life Committee, composed of students, faculty, and administrators, directs campus life. Students serve on most college committees. Seniors and juniors and sophomores have "self-determining hours." Student leader reports that "as a Baptist woman's college we have no male visitation policy." Alcohol not allowed on campus or at college functions; cars allowed for all except freshmen and sophomores. Campus culture likely to be congenial for those who "fit"; does not offer variety of life styles. About 64% of women live in dormitories; rest commute. Freshmen from outside Raleigh area are required to live on campus.

Annual Costs. Tuition and fees, $6,340; room and board, $3,100. About 32% of students receive financial aid; assistance is typically divided 63% scholarship, 29% loan, 8% work. College reports some scholarships awarded on the basis of academic merit alone.

Merrimack College

North Andover, Massachusetts 01845 (508) 837-5100

A church-related, comprehensive college, conducted by the Augustinian Fathers, Merrimack is located on a 220-acre campus in a town of 25,000, 25 miles north of Boston. Most convenient major airport: Logan International (Boston).

Founded: 1947
Affiliation: Roman Catholic
Total Enrollment: 1,069 M, 931 W (full-time); 448 M, 573 W (part-time)
Cost: $10K–$20K
% Receiving Financial Aid: 82%
Admission: Non-selective
Application Deadline: March 1

Admission. Graduates of accredited high schools with 16 units eligible; 79% of applicants accepted, 32% of these actually enroll; 22% of freshmen graduate in top fifth of high school class, 48% in top two-fifths. Average freshman SAT scores: 470 verbal, 490 mathematical. *Required:* SAT, minimum 2.0 high school GPA, essay, 4 years of math and physics for engineering students. Criteria considered in admissions, in order of importance: high school academic record, standardized test scores, writing sample, recommendations, extracurricular activities; other factors considered: alumni children, diverse student body. *Entrance programs:* early decision, early admission, midyear admission, deferred admission, advanced placement. *Apply* by March 1. *Transfers* welcome; 135 enrolled 1993–94.

Academic Environment. Degrees offered: associates, bachelors. *Majors offered* include: chemistry/biology, civil and electrical engineering, medical technology, religious studies. Average undergraduate class size: cap on freshman class is 25; 15:1 student to faculty ratio. About 72% of students entering as freshmen graduate eventually; 85% of freshmen return for sophomore year. *Special programs:* study abroad, cooperative work/study programs in business administration, civil and electrical engineering, Urban Institute, internships, international business. *Calendar:* 4–1–4, summer school.

Undergraduate degrees conferred (580). 55% were in Business and Management, 16% were in Social Sciences, 8% were in Psychology, 6% were in Engineering, 5% were in Letters, 4% were in Computer and Engineering Related Technology, remainder in 6 other fields.

Graduates Career Data. Advanced studies pursued by 70% of graduates. Career Development Services available.

Faculty. About 67% of faculty hold PhD or equivalent. About 69% of undergraduate classes taught by tenured faculty. About 28% of teaching faculty are female.

Student Body. About 74% of students from in state; 91% New England, 5% Middle Atlantic. An estimated 75% of students reported as Catholic, 15% Protestant, 10% other; 5% as minority. *Minority group students:* limited financial aid; special academic scheduling and counseling.

Religious Orientation. Merrimack is a Roman Catholic institution; 2 courses in Religious Studies and 2 courses in philosophy required as part of all degree programs.

Varsity Sports. Men (Div.II): Baseball, Basketball, Cross Country, Golf, Hockey (I), Lacrosse, Soccer, Tennis. Women (Div.II): Basketball, Cross Country, Golf, Hockey (Field), Soccer, Softball, Tennis.

Campus Life. Nearly half of students are commuters. Cars allowed. About 51% of men, 52% of women live in coed dormitories; no traditional dormitories; 49% of men, 48% of women live in off-campus housing or commute. Freshmen given preference in college housing if all students cannot be accommodated. There are 6 fraternities, 3 sororities on campus which about 15% of men 7% of women join; they provide no residence facilities. About 50% of resident students leave campus on weekends.

Annual Costs. Tuition and fees, $11,825; room and board, $6,200; estimated $750 other, exclusive of travel. About 82% of students receive financial aid; average amount of assistance, $10,100. Assistance is typically divided 75% scholarship/grant, 15% loan, 10% work. College reports some scholarships awarded on the basis of academic merit alone. *Meeting Costs:* college offers parent loans, monthly payment plans.

Mesa State College

Grand Junction, Colorado 81502 (303) 248-1020

Mesa offers both 2-year and baccalaureate programs; the campus is located in a Rocky Mountain West community of 25,000. Most convenient major airport: Walker Field (Grand Junction).

Founded: 1925
Affiliation: State
UG Enrollment: 1,585 M, 1,869 W (full-time); 414 M, 732 W (part-time)
Total Enrollment: 4,600
Cost: < $10K
% Receiving Financial Aid: 74%
Admission: Non-selective
Application Deadline: Aug. 1

Admission. Colorado high school graduates with 15 units eligible; all applicants accepted, 59% of these actually enroll. Average freshman ACT scores: 19 M, 19 W composite. *Required:* SAT or ACT, minimum high school GPA. Criteria considered in admissions, in order of importance: high school academic record, recommendations, extracurricular activities, standardized test scores, writing sample; other factors considered: special talents, diverse student body. *Out-of-state* freshman applicants: college actively seeks students from out-of-state. State does not limit out-of-state enrollment. About 75% of out-of-state students accepted, 51% of these actually enroll. States from which most out-of-state students are drawn: Arizona, California, New Mexico, Utah. *Entrance programs:* midyear admission, deferred admission, advanced placement. *Apply* preferably by August 1. *Transfers* welcome; 692 enrolled 1993–94.

Academic Environment. Students agree that small classes and "very skilled" and "quality" faculty are particular strengths of the academic program. Degrees offered: associates, bachelors. *Majors offered* include environmental restoration and waste management. Average undergraduate class size: 56% under 20, 31% 20–40, 13% over 40. About 20% of students entering as freshmen graduate eventually; 58% of freshmen return for sophomore year. *Special programs:* CLEP, independent study, 3-year degree, individualized majors, intensive English program designed for international students. *Library:* materials include USGS map sheets, 135,000 volumes on natural resources and sciences; U.S. government depository. *Calendar:* semester, summer school.

Undergraduate degrees conferred (274). 56% were in Multi/Interdisciplinary Studies, 25% were in Social Sciences, 14% were in Health Sciences, 5% were in Parks and Recreation.

Faculty. About 50% of faculty hold PhD or equivalent. About 31% of undergraduate classes taught by tenured faculty. About 6% of the teaching faculty are minority.

Student Body. About 91% of students from in state; 94% from West. An estimated 6% of students reported as Hispanic, 1% Black, 1% Asian, 7% other minority. Average age of undergraduate student: 26.

Varsity Sports. Men (NAIA, Div.II): Baseball, Basketball, Football. Women (NAIA, Div.II): Basketball, Softball.

Campus Life. About 8% of men, 8% of women live in co-ed dormitories; rest commute. Freshmen given preference in college housing if all students cannot be accommodated. Intervisitation in men's and women's dormitory rooms limited. There are no fraternities or sororities on campus. About 50% of resident students leave campus on weekends.

Annual Costs. Tuition and fees, $1,728 (out-of-state, $4,922); room and board, $3,624; estimated $1,000 other, exclusive of travel. About 74% of students receive financial aid; assistance is typically divided 48% scholarship, 40% loan, 12% work. *Meeting Costs:* college offers PLUS Loans.

Messiah College

Grantham, Pennsylvania 17027-0800 (717) 766-2511

A church-related college, offering a "liberal arts education within the context of the Christian world view," Messiah is located in a small community, 11 miles southwest of Harrisburg (pop. 68,100). College maintains an urban center in Philadelphia for juniors and seniors who may take courses at Temple University and complete degree programs not available on main campus. Most convenient major airport: Harrisburg.

Founded: 1909
Affiliation: Brethren in Christ
Total Enrollment: 911 M, 1,347 W (full-time)
Cost: < $10K
% Receiving Financial Aid: 86%
Admission: Selective (+)
Application Deadline: March 1

Admission is selective (+). About 79% of applicants accepted, 44% of these actually enroll; 58% of freshmen graduate in top fifth of high school class, 88% in top two-fifths. Average freshman scores: SAT, 511 M, 507 W verbal, 588 M, 535 W mathematical; 51% of freshmen score above 500 on verbal, 14% above 600, 1% above 700; 70% score above 500 on mathematical, 28% above 600, 1% above 700. *Required:* SAT or ACT, essay, minimum 2.5 high school GPA. Criteria considered in admissions, in order of importance: high school academic record, standardized test scores, writing sample, recommendations, extracurricular activities; other factors considered: special talents, alumni children, diverse student body, religious affiliation/commitment. About 24% of entering freshmen students from private schools. *Apply* by March 1; rolling admissions. *Transfers* welcome; 97 enrolled 1993–94.

Academic Environment. Degrees offered: bachelors. *Majors offered* include sports medicine, computer science, international business, Christian education. About 70% of students entering as freshmen graduate 70% eventually; 86% of freshmen return for sophomore year. Average undergraduate class size: 5% under 20, 90% 20–40, 5% over 40. *Special programs:* CLEP, January interterm, cross registration, honors, study abroad, independent study, internship in all areas. Adult programs: degree completion program for nursing and business. *Calendar:* 4–1–4, summer school.

Undergraduate degrees conferred (466). 22% were in Business and Management, 19% were in Education, 7% were in Social Sciences, 7% were in Health Sciences, 6% were in Communications, 6% were in Multi/Interdisciplinary Studies, 6% were in Letters, 5% were in Life Sciences, 4% were in Psychology, 4% were in Home Economics, 3% were in Mathematics, 3% were in Engineering, remainder in 6 other fields.

Graduates Career Data. Advanced studies pursued by 30% of graduates; 16% enter graduate school; 10% enter business school; 2% enter law school; 2% enter medical school. Medical schools typically enrolling largest numbers of graduates include Temple; law schools include Georgetown; business schools include Temple, Penn State. Fields typically hiring largest numbers of graduates include business, education, health care, social services. Career Development staff begin working with students the freshman year, program is designed to "meet the needs of students to and beyond graduation."

Faculty. About 66% of faculty hold PhD or equivalent. About 22% of teaching faculty are female.

Student Body. About 49% of students from in state; 71% from Middle Atlantic, 15% from New England, 5% Midwest, 4% Northwest, 2% South; 2% foreign. An estimated 98% are reported as Protestant, 2% Catholic; 3% as Black, 3% Hispanic, 2% Asian, 2% other minority.

Religious Orientation. Messiah is a church-related institution, "committed to the basic doctrines of historic Christianity"; 5% of students affiliated with the church; 27 hours of integrated studies required of all students constitute core curriculum showing "interrelationship of man-discovered truth and God-revealed truth." Attendance at chapel expected.

Varsity Sports. Men (NCAA, Div. III): Baseball, Basketball, Cross Country, Golf, Soccer, Tennis, Track, Wrestling. Women (NCAA, Div. III): Basketball, Cross Country, Field Hockey, Soccer, Softball, Tennis, Track, Volleyball.

Campus Life. About 90% of men, 90% of women live in traditional dormitories or college-owned apartments; no coed dormitories; rest commute. Freshmen given preference college housing if all students cannot be accommodated. Intervisitation in men's and women's dormitory rooms limited. There are no fraternities or sororities on campus. About 30% of resident students leave campus on weekends.

Annual Costs. Tuition and fees, $9,720; room and board, $4,860; estimated $550 other, exclusive of travel. About 86% of students receive financial aid; average amount of assistance, $7,500. Assistance is typically divided 25% scholarship, 25% grant, 40% loan, 10% work. College reports 1,250 scholarships awarded on the basis of academic merit alone, 275 for special talents alone, 1,150 for need alone.

Methodist College

Fayetteville, North Carolina 28311-1499 (919) 630-7127

A church-related college, located in a city of 250,000. Most convenient major airport: Fayetteville.

Founded: 1956
Affiliation: United Methodist
Total Enrollment: 591 M, 518 W (full-time); 230 M, 367 W (part-time)
Cost: < $10K
% Receiving Financial Aid: 85%
Admission: Non-selective
Application Deadline: Rolling

Admission. Graduates of accredited high schools with 16 units and "seriousness of purpose" eligible; 71% of applicants accepted, 49% of these actually enroll; 12% of freshmen graduate in top fifth of high school class, 28% in top two-fifths. *Required:* SAT, minimum 2.0 high school GPA, essay. Criteria considered in admissions, in order of importance: high school academic record, standardized test scores, writing sample, recommendations, extracurricular activities. *Apply*: rolling admissions. *Transfers* welcome; 157 enrolled 1993–94.

Academic Environment. Graduation requirements include 62 credit hours in humanities, communications, sciences and math, history, literature. Degrees offered: associates, bachelors. *Majors offered* include equine management, golf management, tennis management, health care administration. About 60% of freshmen return for sophomore year. Average undergraduate class size: 85% under 20, 12% 20–40, 3% over 40. *Special programs:* CLEP, independent study, 3-year degree, January Term, internships. *Calendar:* semester, summer school.

Undergraduate degrees conferred (216). 44% were in Business and Management, 21% were in Social Sciences, 13% were in Education, 6% were in Multi/Interdisciplinary Studies, 5% were in Visual and Performing Arts, 3% were in Psychology, 3% were in Communications, remainder in 7 other fields.

Student Body. About 47% of students from in state; 20% from South, 13% Middle Atlantic, 10% New England, 5% Midwest, 2% West, 1% Northwest, 2% foreign. An estimated 44% of students reported as Protestant, 36% Catholic, 1% Jewish, 7% unaffiliated, 1% other; 14% as Black, 6% Hispanic, 4% Asian, 2% other minority.

Religious Orientation. Methodist is a church-related institution; 28% of students affiliated with the church; 2 religious courses required of all students.

Varsity Sports. Men (Div.III): Baseball, Basketball, Cross Country, Football, Golf, Soccer, Tennis, Track. Women (Div.III): Basketball, Cross Country, Golf, Soccer, Softball, Tennis, Track, Volleyball.

Campus Life. About 29% of men, 28% of women live in traditional dormitories; 30% of men, 17% of women live in coed dormitories; rest commute. Freshmen given preference in college housing if all students cannot be accommodated. Intervisitation in men's and women's dormitory rooms limited. There are no fraternities or sororities on campus. About 25% of students leave campus on weekends.

Annual Costs. Tuition and fees, $8,850; room and board, $3,550; estimated $1,100 other, exclusive of travel. About 85% of students receive financial aid; average amount of assistance, $6,400. Assistance is typically divided 15% scholarship, 15% grant, 50% loan, 20% work. College reports 110 scholarships awarded on the basis of academic merit alone.

Metropolitan State College

Denver, Colorado 80217-3362 (303) 556-3058

A state-supported, commuter college, located adjacent to Denver's downtown business area. Most convenient major airport: Stapleton International.

Founded: 1963
Affiliation: State
Total Enrollment: 4,608 M, 4,877 W (full-time); 3,616 M, 4,419 W (part-time)
Cost: < $10K
% Receiving Financial Aid: 75%
Admission: Non-selective
Application Deadline: August 1

Admission. High school graduates with 2 of 3: minimum ACT/SAT scores of 19/810, 2.5 GPA, rank in upper two-thirds of class, eligible; others considered on individual basis; 86% of applicants accepted, 56% of these actually enroll; 17% of freshmen graduating in top fifth of class, 47% in top two-fifths. Average freshman ACT scores: 20 M, 19.4 W composite. *Required:* SAT or ACT. Criteria considered in admissions, in order of importance: standardized test scores, high school academic record, recommendations, extracurricular activities, writing sample. *Entrance programs:* early decision, early admission, midyear admission, advanced placement. *Apply* by August 1. *Transfers* welcome; 2,061 enrolled 1993–94.

Academic Environment. Degrees offered: bachelors. *Majors offered* include fire services administration, human performance and sport, leisure studies. Average undergraduate class size: 46% under 20, 43% 20–40, 11% over 40. About 4% of students entering as freshman graduate within four years, 17% within 7 years; 56% of freshmen return for sophomore year. *Special programs:* CLEP, honors, study abroad independent study, International Language Center, cross-registration with U.of Colorado, Community College of Colorado, internship programs in business and communications. Adult programs: assistance re-entering education system. *Calendar:* semester, summer school.

Undergraduate degrees conferred (1928). 22% were in Business and Management, 10% were in Social Sciences, 9% were in Education, 7% were in Protective Services, 7% were in Computer and Engineering Related Technology, 6% were in Transportation and Material Moving, 5% were in Public Affairs, 5% were in Communications, 4% were in Psychology, 4% were in Multi/Interdisciplinary Studies, 4% were in Engineering and Engineering Related Technology, 3% were in Health Sciences, 3% were in Letters, 3% were in Visual and Performing Arts, 3% were in Mathematics, remainder in 6 other fields.

Graduate Career Data. Career Development Services include testing (interest, personality, values), resume workshops, job strategies, interviewing skills, mock interviews, critiquing, career library, job listings, COCIS computerized guidance system, resume referral service, career counseling, walk-in counseling, student employment service, on-campus interviewing, career assessment inventories.

Faculty. About 75% of faculty hold PhD or equivalent. About 40% of teaching faculty are female.

Student Body. About 97% of students from in state; almost all from West. An estimated 10% of students reported as Hispanic, 5% Black, 4% Asian, 2% other minority. Average age of undergraduate student: 27.

Varsity Sports. Men (NCAA, Div.II): Baseball, Basketball, Soccer, Swimming, Tennis. Women (NCAA, Div.II): Basketball, Soccer, Swimming, Tennis, Volleyball.

Campus Life. No dormitories on campus. All students commute.

Annual Costs. Tuition and fees, $1,751 (out-of-state, $6,047); $4,620 room and board; estimated $1,578 other, exclusive of travel. About 75% of students who apply receive financial aid; assistance typically divided 30% grant/scholarship, 50% loan, 20% work.

Miami University

Oxford, Ohio 45056 **(513) 529-1809**

Miami University is one of Ohio's network of state institutions, though it seeks to draw students from other states as well. Out-of-state enrollment is no longer limited and is currently about 27% of the student body—a significant number, given the size of the student body. The 1,000-acre main campus is located in a community of 9,000, 35 miles north of Cincinnati and 46 miles south of Dayton. The university operates 2-year commuter campuses at Hamilton and Middletown. Most convenient major airport: Cincinnati.

Founded: 1809
Affiliation: State
UG Enrollment: 6,353 M, 7,265 W (full-time); 363 M, 428 W (part-time)
Total Enrollment: 16,202
Cost: < $10K
% Receiving Financial Aid: 30%
Admission: Selective (+)
Application Deadline: Jan. 31

Admission is selective (+). About 84% of applicants accepted, 42% of these actually enroll; 64% of freshmen graduate in top fifth of high school class, 93% in top two-fifths. Average freshman scores: SAT, middle 50% range: 470–560 verbal, 540–640 mathematical; 59% of freshmen score above 500 on verbal, 13% above 600, 1% above 700; 90% score above 500 on mathematical, 47% above 600, 9% above 700; ACT, middle 50% range: 23–27 composite. *Required:* SAT or ACT, high school transcript. Criteria considered in admissions, in order of importance: standardized test scores rank with most importance, high school academic record, extracurricular activities, recommendations and writing sample rank with equal importance; other factors considered: special talents, alumni children, diverse student body. *Out-of-state* freshman applicants: university actively seeks students from out-of-state. State does not limit out-of-state enrollment. About 85% accepted, 35% of these actually enroll. States from which most out-of-state students are drawn: Indiana, Illinois, Michigan, Pennsylvania. *Entrance programs:* early decision, midyear admission, advanced placement. *Apply* by January 31. *Transfers* welcome; 387 enrolled 1993–94.

Academic Environment. Students call the academic program "demanding" and "competitive"; small classes very much a "plus", but can make registration difficult since many classes fill early. "Hands-on" experiences, available in many programs, reported by student to be "intense" and beneficial. Graduation requirements: all student take Foundation Requirement including 6 semester hours each in English composition, humanities, 3 hours in fine arts, 3 hours in social sciences and world cultures, 3 hours in biological and physical sciences, and 3 hours in either mathematics, formal reasoning, or technology. In addition, all students must take 9 hours of thematic and sequential study in depth outside the major, and 3 hours of senior year capstone experiences. *Undergraduate studies* offered by College of Arts and Science, schools of Applied Science, Business Administration, Education and Allied Professions, Fine Arts, Western College (Interdisciplinary Studies). Degrees offered: bachelors, masters, doctoral. *Majors offered* include anthropology, Black studies, diplomacy and foreign affairs, gerontological studies, international studies, paper and science engineering, public administration, speech and hearing therapy, interdisciplinary studies. Average undergraduate class size: 38% under 20, 49% 20–40, 13% over 40.

About 83% of students entering as freshmen graduate eventually; 97% of freshmen return for sophomore year. *Special programs:* independent study, study abroad, honors, undergraduate research, 3-year degree, 3–2 engineering, 3–2 forestry, 3–1 and 4–1 medical technology, cross-registration with the Greater Cincinnati Consortium, internship through the School of Applied Science. Miami University/Wilmington College offers graduate programs for educators, Hamilton and Middletown campuses offer evening programs, Elderhostel summer program. Adult programs: evening programs offered. *Calendar:* semester, summer school.

Undergraduate degrees conferred (3393). 31% were in Business and Management, 17% were in Social Sciences, 10% were in Education, 7% were in Letters, 6% were in Psychology, 5% were in Life Sciences, 4% were in Communications, remainder in 16 other fields.

Graduates Career Data. Advanced studies pursued by 52% of graduates; 19% enter graduate school; 12% enter law school; 9% enter business school; 8% enter medical school. Medical schools typically enrolling largest numbers of graduates include Ohio State, U. of Cincinnati; law schools include Ohio State, U. of Cincinnati, Case Western Reserve; business schools include Miami, Northwestern. Employers typically hiring largest numbers of graduates include Procter and Gamble, Ernst and Young, Fifth Third Bank, Deloitte Touche. Career Planning and Placement Office "assists students in making transition from academic pursuits to career goals." Career Assistance Center offers SIGI-Plus and DISCOVER computer programs, self-assessment, career counseling, vocational interest testing and interpretation, career decision making workshops and outreach.

Student Body. About 73% of students from in state; 87% from Midwest, 7% Middle Atlantic, 4% South, 2% foreign. An estimated 3% of students reported as Black, 2% Asian, 1% Hispanic. *Minority group students:* Educational Opportunity Program sponsors recruitment, financial aid, academic support services including free tutoring for students needing financial aid.

Varsity Sports. Men (Div.I): Baseball, Basketball, Cross Country, Diving, Football, Golf, Hockey, Soccer, Swimming, Tennis, Track, Wrestling. Women (Div.I): Basketball, Cross Country, Diving, Field Hockey, Soccer, Softball, Swimming, Tennis, Track, Volleyball.

Campus Life. Regulations governing student social life remain somewhat more stringent than at many other institutions, but students do not seem concerned. No curfews, but dorms locked at dusk, students have keys. Students report "The campus is basically the only thing in Oxford. Therefore, student life is very strong." "There are TONS of extracurricular activities to become involved with." "I've loved the independence and responsibility placed on me since I've been a student." Nearest major cultural center, Cincinnati, is 35 miles away. Students of legal age permitted alcoholic beverages in designated areas; smoking not allowed in buildings; illegal drugs prohibited. Fraternities/sororities, intramural athletics, and sponsored social events reported by administration as strong interests on campus.

About 20% of men, 40% of women live in traditional dormitories; 80% of men, 60% of women in coed dormitories. There are 28 fraternities, 22 sororities on campus which about 33% of men, 39% of women join; 16% of men live in fraternities; sororities have suites in residence halls. About 5–10% of resident students leave campus on weekends.

Annual Costs. Tuition and fees, $4,226 (out-of-state, $9,098); room and board, $3,840; estimated $1,900 other, exclusive of travel. About 30% of students receive financial aid; average amount of assistance, $5,100. Assistance is typically divided 7% scholarship, 30% grant, 58% loan, 5% work. University reports 1,224 scholarships awarded on the basis of academic merit alone, 340 for special talents alone. *Meeting Costs:* university offers a 10-month installment payment plan.

University of Miami

Coral Gables, Florida 33124 (305) 284-4323

An independent university that encompasses a wide range of student ability, academic opportunity, and recreational facilities, the University of Miami has worked actively to raise admission standards and the level of academic achievement demanded of students, strengthen the faculty and curriculum, and expand graduate and research facilities. Special opportunities offered in a number of areas such as tropical ecological studies at the undergraduate level and the Rosenstiel School of Marine and Atmospheric Science, Institute of Molecular and Cellular Evolution, the Graduate School of Advanced International Studies, and the Center for Theoretical Studies. The 260-acre main campus is located in a Miami suburb of 45,000. Most convenient major airport: Miami International.

Founded: 1925
Affiliation: Independent
UG Enrollment: 4,017 M, 3,625 W (full-time); 291 M, 419 (part-time)
Total Enrollment: 13,558
Cost: $10K–$20K
% Receiving Financial Aid: 75%
Admission: Selective (+)
Application Deadline: March 1

Admission is selective (+). For all schools, 76% of applicants accepted, 31% of these actually enroll; 61% of freshmen graduate in top fifth of high school class, 84% in top two-fifths. Average freshman SAT scores: 46% of freshmen score above 500 on verbal, 14% above 600, 2% above 700; 72% score above 500 on mathematical, 38% above 600, 9% above 700. *Required:* SAT or ACT, essay, recommendations, audition for School of Music; ACH for some programs; interview recommended. Criteria considered in admissions, in order of importance: standardized test scores, high school academic record, recommendations, extracurricular activities, writing sample; other factors considered: special talents, alumni children, diverse student body. *Entrance programs:* early decision, early admission, early action, midyear admission, deferred admission, advanced placement. *Apply:* March 1 (January 15 for scholarship consideration). *Transfers* welcome; 618 enrolled 1993–94.

Academic Environment. Degrees offered: bachelors, masters, doctoral. The honors curriculum features small, seminar-style, classes taught by the University's most distinguished professors. The privileged studies program allows a limited number of honors students to participate in a wholly elective degree program in which all specific course requirements are waived. *Undergraduate studies* offered to freshmen in schools of Arts and Science, Architecture, Business Administration, Communications, Engineering, Music, and Nursing. *Majors offered* include advertising communication, aerospace engineering, American Studies, Judaic Studies, Latin American studies, audio engineering, environmental engineering and science, entrepreneurship, health sciences, meteorology, music engineering technology, marine science, psychobiology, international comparative studies. Average undergraduate class size: 75% have 26 or fewer students.

Special programs: CLEP, privileged study, honors programs (medicine, law, marine and atmospheric science, international business, and engineering/medicine), study abroad (22 countries, 53 schools), undergraduate research, 3-year degree, cooperative work/study program in engineering and business fields, senior internship in communications. Adult programs: Bachelor of Continuing Studies, General Studies. *Calendar:* early semester, summer school.

Undergraduate degrees conferred (1820). 22% were in Business and Management, 11% were in Engineering, 11% were in Communications, 10% were in Visual and Performing Arts, 7% were in Psychology, 7% were in Social Sciences, 7% were in Life Sciences, 4% were in Letters, 4% were in Health Sciences, 4% were in Marketing and Distribution, 3% were in Physical Sciences, 3% were in Architecture and Environmental Design, 3% were in Computer and Engineering Related Technology, remainder in 9 other fields.

Graduates Career Data. Advanced studies pursued by 41% of graduates. Medical and law schools typically enrolling largest numbers of graduates include U. of Miami, U. of Florida. About 56% of 1991–92 graduates employed. Career Development Services include placement services, resume writing/interview workshops, on-campus recruitment, library resources, job development services, career mentor program, computerized career information system.

Faculty. About 95% of faculty hold PhD or equivalent. About 56% of undergraduate classes taught by tenured faculty. About 29% of teaching faculty are female; 13% Hispanic, 3% Black, 8% other minority.

Student Body. About 52% of students from in state; 59% South, 16% Middle Atlantic, 6% New England, 6% Midwest, 6% Northwest, 4% West, 10% foreign. An estimated 19% of students reported as Protestant, 34% Catholic, 11% Jewish, 2% Muslim, 31% unaffiliated, 3% other; 9% as Black, 24% Hispanic, 4% Asian, 11% other minority. *Minority group students:* special financial, academic, and social provisions; United Black Students organization, Black fraternities/sororities.

Varsity Sports. Men (Div.IA): Baseball, Basketball, Crew, Cross Country, Diving, Football, Golf, Swimming, Tennis, Track. Women (Div.IA): Basketball, Crew, Cross Country, Diving, Golf, Swimming, Tennis, Track.

Campus Life. Student disciplinary code guarantees counsel for students at judicial hearings and attempts to expedite procedure. Council of Ombudsmen available to students. Both administration and student leader report a number of different life/living styles available. Motor vehicles allowed; parking remains a problem. Drinking permitted at Rathskeller, other campus locations and in residence facilities in accordance with state laws and University policies. Freshmen expected to live in university residences.

About 53% of men, 55% of women live in coed residential colleges; rest commute. Sexes segregated in coed residences either by wing, floor, room or apartment. There are 15 fraternities, 11 sororities on campus which about 16% of men, 18% of women join; 2% of men live in fraternities.

Annual Costs. Tuition and fees, $15,880; room and board, $6,227; estimated $1,525 other, exclusive of travel. About 75% of students receive financial aid; average amount of assistance, $14,392. Assistance is typically divided 34% scholarship, 40% grant, 20% loan, 6% work. University reports 3,156 scholarships awarded on the basis of academic merit alone, 413 for special talents alone, 164 for need alone.

Michigan Christian College

Rochester Hills, Michigan 48307 (313) 651-5800

A former 2-year college, affiliated with the Church of Christ, now offering baccalaureate degrees.

Founded: 1959
Affiliation: Church of Christ
Total Enrollment: 151 M, 160 W (full-time); 30 M, 33 W (part-time)
Cost: < $10K
Admission: Non-selective
Application Deadline: Rolling

Admission. About 68% of applicants accepted, 74% of these actually enroll. *Required:* ACT. Criteria considered in admissions, in order of importance: high school academic record, standardized test scores. *Entrance programs:* early decision, early admission, midyear admission, deferred admission, advanced placement. *Apply:* rolling admissions. *Transfers* welcome; 24 enrolled 1993–94.

Academic Environment. Graduation requirements include "standard liberal arts plus Bible." Degrees offered: associates, bachelors. *Majors offered* include psychology, sociology, social work, business administration, management, human resources management. Special Programs: January interterm, cross registration with Oakland U. and Oakland Community College, internships.

Undergraduate degrees conferred (3). 100% were in Theology.

Faculty. About 18% of faculty hold PhD or equivalent. About 30% of teaching faculty are female.

Student Body. About 74% of students from in state; 92% from Midwest, 5% foreign. An estimated 96% of students reported as Protestant, 4% Catholic; 13% Black, 1% Hispanic, 1% Asian, 4% other minority. Average age of undergraduate student: 23.

Religious Orientation. Michigan Christian College is a church-related institution; 71% of students affiliated with the church; 1 religious course per semester is required of all students.

Varsity Sports. Men: Baseball, Basketball, Cross Country, Soccer, Track. Women: Basketball, Cross Country, Softball, Track, Volleyball.

Campus Life. Student reports she likes best the college's "emphasis on Christianity, it's spirituality, the close friendships, the friendliness of faculty and the opportunity for involvement."

About 72% of men, 74% of women live in traditional dormitories, rest commute. There are no fraternities or sororities on campus. About 75% of resident students leave campus on weekends.

Annual Costs. Tuition and fees, $4,944; room and board, $3,070.

Michigan State University

East Lansing, Michigan 48824 (517) 355-8332

One of the nation's premier land-grant universities, Michigan State has become, in recent decades, a major research and teaching university. The University attracts a very capable student body including substantial numbers from out-of-state. MSU, a residential school with a 2,000-acre campus, is located in a community of 40,000, midway between Detroit and Grand Rapids; an additional 3,760 acres in the East Lansing area are devoted to experimental farms and research installations. Most convenient major airport: Capital City.

Founded: 1855
Affiliation: State
UG Enrollment: 26,935 (full-time); 3,825 (part-time)
Total Enrollment: 39,743
Cost: < $10K
% Receiving Financial Aid: 44%
Admission: Selective
Application Deadline: July 30

Admission is selective—somewhat more so for out-of-state students than Michigan residents. About 83% of applicants accepted, 41% of these actually enroll; 44% of freshmen graduate in top fifth of high school class, 82% in top two-fifths. Average freshman scores: SAT, 458 verbal, 524 mathematical; 33% of freshmen score above 500 on verbal, 9% above 600, 1% above 700; 60% score above 500 on mathematical, 24% above 600, 5% above 700; ACT, 23 composite. *Required:* SAT or ACT, minimum high school GPA. Criteria considered in admissions, in order of importance: high school academic record, standardized test scores, class rank, recommendations, extracurricular activities; other factors considered: special talents, diverse student body. *Out-of-state* freshman applicants: university actively seeks students from out-of-state. State does not limit out-of-state enrollment. About 78% of out-of-state applicants accepted, 27% actually enrolled. States from which most out-of-state students are drawn: Illinois, Ohio, New York. *Entrance programs:* early decision, early admission, deferred admission, advanced placement. *Apply:* July 30; rolling admissions. *Transfers* welcome; 1,931 enrolled 1993–94.

Academic Environment. Graduation requirements include 4 credit writing course, 8 credits in arts and humanities, 7 in general science, 8 in social, behavioral, and economic sciences, 3 in a transcollegiate course; also demonstrated knowledge in mathematics equal to 4 years of college preparatory math at the high school level (2 years of algebra, 1 of geometry, and 1 from topics of probability, trigonometry, or calculus). Some student concern reported over difficulty in enrolling in over-subscribed programs such as engineering and business, also about availability of required courses. Through housing arrangements, university attempts to emphasize the advantages of its great size and minimize the problems created by great numbers. Honors College for students with superior high school records and test scores waives usual graduation requirements and allows student and adviser to develop individual programs. Highly motivated students with well-defined goals are likely to do best at Michigan State. The number of distractions on the busy, varied campus can be academically fatal to others. *Undergraduate studies* offered by colleges of Arts and Letters, Agriculture and Natural Resources, Business, Communication Arts and Sciences, Education, Engineering, Human Ecology, Human Medicine, Natural Science, Nursing, Osteopathic Medicine, Social Science, and Veterinary Medicine. Degrees offered: bachelors, masters, doctoral. *Majors offered* in nearly 200 fields of study in arts and sciences and professional/vocational areas. Average undergraduate class size: 35% under 21, 39% 20–35, 26% over 35.

About 31% of students entering as freshmen graduate within four years, 67% eventually; 86% of freshmen return for sophomore year. *Special programs:* January interterm, cross-registration with Big Ten and Chicago area colleges, CLEP, independent study, study abroad, honors, individualized majors, credit by examination, 5-year BM program for school music and music therapy, study at Merrill-Palmer Institute. *Calendar:* semester, summer school.

Undergraduate degrees conferred (7210). 18% were in Business and Management, 13% were in Communications, 11% were in Social Sciences, 9% were in Engineering, 6% were in Agribusiness and Agricultural Production, 5% were in Psychology, 4% were in Home Economics, 4% were in Education, 4% were in Letters, 3% were in Protective Services, remainder in 17 other fields.

Graduates Career Data. Advanced studies pursued by 21% of graduates; 14% enter graduate school; 3% enter medical school; 2% enter law school; 2% enter business school. Medical schools typically enrolling largest numbers of graduates include MSU, Wayne State; law schools include Detroit College of Law, Wayne State, U. of Detroit; business schools include MSU, Walsh, Wayne State. About 62% of 1992–93 graduates employed. Employers typically hiring largest numbers of graduates include General Motors, IBM, Amway, and Ford. Career Development Services include individual advising and workshops on job strategies, resume writing, interviewing, minority student career program and preplanning workshops, annual career programs, teacher placement fair, government and international career fairs, international placement program, on-campus interviewing.

Faculty. About 95% of faculty hold PhD or equivalent. About 65% of undergraduate classes taught by tenured faculty.

Student Body. About 90% of undergraduate students from in state; 95% Midwest, 2% Middle Atlantic; 2% foreign. An estimated 35% of students reported as Catholic, 40% Protestant, 3% Jewish, 12% unaffiliated, 10% other; 7% as Black, 3% Asian, 2% Hispanic, 2% other minority. *Minority group students:* special financial and academic provisions.

Varsity Sports. Men (Div. IA): Baseball, Basketball, Cross Country, Diving, Fencing, Football, Golf, Gymnastics, Hockey, Lacrosse, Soccer, Swimming, Tennis, Track, Wrestling. Women (Div. IA): Basketball, Cross Country, Diving, Field Hockey, Golf, Gymnastics, Soccer, Softball, Swimming, Tennis, Track, Volleyball.

Campus Life. Students enjoy considerable freedom in their personal and social activities within the fairly broad regulations of the university. Ombudsman available to students with grievances involving faculty and administration. All traditional-aged freshmen required to live in university residence halls. Liberal and varied (including limited) provisions for intervisitation. Both co-educational and sex-segregated housing available. Undergraduate University Division has 3 advisement centers in coed dorms. Most residence halls feature classrooms, faculty offices, dining rooms, recreational areas and living areas. Cars not allowed for freshmen; campus bus system provides regular service.

About 1% of women live in traditional dormitories; 37% each of men, women live in coed dormitories; 9% each of men, women live in on-campus apartments; 52% of men, 50% of women live in off-campus housing or commute. Freshmen given preference in college housing if all students cannot be accommodated. Sexes segregated in coed dormitories by wing or floor. There are 35 fraternities, 19 sororities which about 8% each of men, women join; 3% of men, 4% of women live in off-campus fraternities and sororities.

Annual Costs. Tuition and fees, $4,504 (out-of-state, $10,838); room and board, $3,675; estimated $1,650 other, exclusive of travel. About 44% of students receive financial aid; average amount of assistance, $6,284. Assistance is typically divided 16% scholarship, 26% grant, 28% loan, 30% work. University reports some scholarships awarded on the basis of academic merit alone.

Michigan Technological University

Houghton, Michigan 49931 (906) 487-1885

A state-supported university, Michigan Tech is located in a town of 6,067, 10 miles from Lake Superior and 421 miles north of Chicago. Administration reports that its engineering graduates in minerals and metallurgy are widely sought after. University welcomes out-of-state students and enrolls a substantial number. Most convenient major airport: Houghton County Memorial.

Founded: 1885
Affiliation: State
UG Enrollment: 4,157 M, 1,367 W (full-time)
Total Enrollment: 6,603
Cost: < $10K
% Receiving Financial Aid: 71%
Admission: Very Selective
Application Deadline: August 1

Admission is very selective. About 85% of applicants accepted, 47% of these actually enroll; 72% of freshmen graduate in top fifth of high school class, 95% in top two-fifths. Average freshman scores: SAT, 509 M, 526 W verbal, 621 M, 622 W mathematical; 60% of freshmen score above 500 on verbal, 22% above 600, 2% above 700; 92% score above 500 on mathematical, 63% above 600, 20% above 700; ACT, 26.1 M, 25.5 W composite. *Required:* rank in top half of class (engineering students in top third); SAT or ACT "strongly" recommended, used for placement only. Criteria considered in admissions, in order of importance: high school academic record, standardized test scores. *Out-of-state* freshman applicants: university actively seeks students from out-of-state. State does not limit out-of-state enrollment. States from which most out-of-state students are drawn: Wisconsin, Minnesota, Illinois. *Entrance programs:* midyear admission, deferred admission, advanced placement. *Apply:* August 1; rolling admissions. *Transfers* welcome; 302 enrolled 1993–94.
Academic Environment. Graduation requirements include 9 credits each in communications, science, humanities, and social sciences, 12 credits in mathematics, 4 in physical education, and 9 in upper-division thematic studies. Student body overwhelmingly oriented toward occupational/professional goals. Degrees offered: associates, bachelors, masters, doctoral. *Majors offered* include 8 fields of engineering, 7 fields of sciences; manufacturing, environmental engineering, wood science, secondary science teacher education, scientific and technical communication, and surveying. Average undergraduate class size: 45% under 20, 38% 20–40, 17% over 40.

About 60% of all students graduate eventually; 67% of engineering students; 85% of freshmen return for sophomore year. *Special programs:* study abroad, CLEP, honors, undergraduate research, individualized majors, cooperative work/study program, 3–2 engineering, 3–2 forestry. *Calendar:* quarter, summer school.
Undergraduate degrees conferred (998). 69% were in Engineering, 8% were in Business and Management, 6% were in Computer and Engineering Related Technology, 4% were in Mathematics, 4% were in Communications, 3% were in Physical Sciences, 3% were in Life Sciences, remainder in 4 other fields.
Graduates Career Data. Advanced studies pursued by 15% of graduates. About 90% of 1992–93 graduates employed. Fields typically hiring largest numbers of graduates include civil engineering, electrical engineering, and mechanical engineering. Career Development Services include job fairs, on-campus job interviews, resume assistance, cooperative education, summer employment, alumni placement assistance.
Faculty. About 78% of faculty hold PhD or equivalent. About 52% of undergraduate classes taught by tenured faculty. About 17% of teaching faculty are female; 1% Black, 1% Hispanic, 17% other minority.
Student Body. About 77% of students from in state; 4% foreign. An estimated 2% of students reported as Black, 2% Asian, 1% Hispanic, 5% other minority.
Varsity Sports. Men (Div.II): Basketball, Cheerleading, Cross Country, Football, Ice Hockey (I), Skiing (Nordic), Tennis, Track. Women (Div.II): Basketball, Cheerleading, Cross Country, Skiing (Nordic), Tennis, Track, Volleyball.
Campus Life. Administration source reports that "conventional, hard working, intelligent, outdoor types" will feel most at home on campus, those who "like a metropolitan area and hate snow" likely to feel least at home. Student notes nearest "big" city is four hours away; she agrees that the weather can be a problem. High interest reported in intramural sports (most popular: hockey, basketball, skiing); increasing interest in fraternities/sororities, varsity sports. University owns and operates a downhill ski area and an 18-hole golf course. Residence halls set visitation hours, up to 24-hour available. For students age 21 or over alcohol permitted in student rooms, but prohibited at university functions; cars permitted. University requires all first-year students to live in residence halls.

About 36% of men, 36% of women live in coed dormitories and apartment housing; 60% of men, 64% of women commute. Freshmen are given preference in college housing if all students cannot be accommodated. Sexes segregated in dormitories by floor. There are 16 fraternities, 8 sororities on campus which about 13% of men, 16% of women join; 4% of men, 4% of women live in fraternities and sororities. About 20% of resident students leave campus on weekends.
Annual Costs. Tuition and fees, \$3,441 (out-of-state, \$7,785); room and board, \$3,842; estimated \$1,350 other, exclusive of travel. About 71% of students receive financial aid; average amount of assistance, \$4,638. Assistance is typically divided 28% scholarship, 21% grant, 33% loan, 18% work. University reports 230 scholarships awarded on the basis of academic merit alone, 35 for special talents alone.

University of Michigan

Ann Arbor, Michigan 48109 **(313) 764-7433**

One of the very few giant universities that has achieved both quantity and quality education, the University of Michigan has often been called the "Mother of State Universities." Its student body has for years been cosmopolitan, geographically and otherwise. It has 17 schools and colleges, including numerous professional schools—many of the first rank—and one of the nation's top-ranked graduate schools. The main campus consists of 2,117 acres, located in a city of 100,000, 35 miles west of Detroit. The university also offers 4-year undergraduate programs at Dearborn and Flint (see below). Most convenient major airport: Detroit Metropolitan.

Founded: 1817
Affiliation: State
UG Enrollment: 11,595 M, 10,216 W (full-time)
Total Enrollment: 34,232
Cost: < \$10K
% Receiving Financial Aid: 36%
Admission: Highly (+) Selective
Application Deadline: February 15

Admission is highly (+) selective for Engineering; highly selective for Literature, Science, and the Arts; very (+) selective for Natural Resources; very selective for Art, Music; selective (+) for Nursing, selective for Kinesiology. For all schools, 60% of applicants accepted, 46% of these actually enroll; 89% of freshmen graduate in top fifth of high school class, 99% in top two-fifths. Average freshman scores, according to most recent data available: SAT, 72% of freshmen score above 500 on verbal, 29% above 600, 4% above 700; 92% score above 500 on mathematical, 69% above 600, 25% above 700; ACT, middle 50% range, 24–30 composite.

Literature, Science, and the Arts (7,117 M, 7,543), 59% of applicants accepted, 42% of these actually enroll; 90% of freshmen graduate in top fifth of high school class, 99% in top two-fifths. Average freshman scores, according to most recent data available: SAT, 75% of freshmen score above 500 on verbal, 32% above 600, 4% above 700; 92% score above 500 on mathematical, 69% above 600, 23% above 700; ACT, middle 50% range, 26–30 composite.

Engineering (3,146 M, 870 W), 62% of applicants accepted, 47% of these actually enroll; 95% of freshmen graduate in top fifth of high school class, all in top two-fifths. Freshman scores, according to most recent data available: SAT, 73% of freshmen score above 500 on verbal, 26% above 600, 4% above 700; 98% score above 500 on mathematical, 82% above 600, 37% above 700; ACT, middle 50% range, 27–31 composite.

Natural Resources (138 M, 166 W), 68% of applicants accepted, 51% of these actually enroll; 77% of freshmen graduate in top fifth of high school class, all in top two-fifths. Freshman scores, according to most recent data available: SAT, 68% of freshmen score above 500 on verbal, 19% above 600; 94% score above 500 on mathematical, 63% above 600, 10% above 700; ACT, middle 50% range, 25–29 composite.

Art (151 M, 320 W), 48% of applicants accepted, 63% of these actually enroll; 72% of freshmen graduate in top fifth of high school class, 99% in top two-fifths. Freshman scores, according to most recent data available: SAT, 58% of freshmen score above 500 on verbal, 21% above 600; 84% score above 500 on mathematical, 37% above 600, 5% above 700; ACT, middle 50% range, 23–28 composite.

Music (201 M, 237 W), 50% of applicants accepted, 48% of these actually enroll; 76% of freshmen graduate in top fifth of high school class, all in top two-fifths. Freshman scores, according to most recent data available: SAT, 74% of freshmen score above 500 on verbal, 27% above 600, 1% above 700; 82% score above 500 on mathematical, 51% above 600, 15% above 700; ACT, middle 50% range, 24–30 composite.

Nursing (29 M, 396 W), 78% of applicants accepted, 59% of these actually enroll; 68% of freshmen graduate in top fifth of high school class, all in top two-fifths. Freshman scores, according to most recent data available: SAT, 38% of freshmen score above 500 on verbal, 3% above 600; 69% score above 500 on mathematical, 28% above 600, 3% above 700; ACT, middle 50% range, 22–26 composite.

Kinesiology (245 M, 149 W), 57% of applicants accepted, 65% of these actually enroll; 38% of freshmen graduate in top fifth of high school class, 72% in top two-fifths. Freshman scores, according to most recent data available: SAT, 20% score above 500 on verbal, 2% above 600; 50% score above 500 on mathematical, 19% above 600, 2% above 700; ACT, middle 50% range, 21–24 composite.

Required: SAT or ACT. *Out-of-state* freshman applicants: university welcomes students from out of state. *Out-of-state* enrollment informally limited to 30% of student body. Requirement for out-of-state applicants: "competitive level higher academically for admission." Some preference given to qualified out-of-state applicants who are alumni children. About 42% of applicants accepted, 33% enroll. *Non-academic factors* considered in admissions: special talents, alumni children, diverse student body, "unique or special achievements." Entrance program: deferred admission, advanced placement. About 11% of entering students from private schools, 9% from parochial schools. *Apply* by February 15 (for equal consideration); rolling admissions. *Transfers* welcome.

Academic Environment. Students are reported as equally concerned with occupational/professional goals and scholarly/intellectual pursuits. Pressures for academic achievement appear moderately intense for university as a whole, intense for colleges of Literature, Science, and the Arts, and Engineering. The university for years has been a favorite with eastern students, and competition for admission from certain areas—New York City, for instance—is great, particularly for the 4-year Residential College of about 600 students. The Residential College provides a small-college atmosphere within the larger College of Literature, Science, and the Arts; all students take a specially designed core curriculum. Administration reports 40% of general education courses required for graduation are elective; distribution requirements fairly numerous for most curricula in Literature, Science, and the Arts: include 1 term English composition, 3 terms each natural sciences, social sciences, humanities; foreign language requirement may be met by 4 years high school study of single language. *Undergraduate studies* offered to freshmen by colleges of Literature, Science, and the Arts, Engineering, schools of Art, Music, Natural Resources, Nursing; upperclassmen admitted to schools of Architecture and Urban Planning, Business Administration, Education, Pharmacy. *Majors offered* in Literature, Science, and the Arts in addition to wide range of studies including anthropology, astronomy, Chinese, classical archaeology, computer and communications sciences, geography, journalism, linguistics, statistics; area programs (Far Eastern, Near Eastern and North African, Russian); interdepartmental programs in Afro-American studies, biophysics, cellular biology, microbiology, psychology/speech/hearing science, romance linguistics, social anthropology, religion.

About 81% of students entering as freshmen graduate eventually; 94% of freshmen return for sophomore year. *Special programs:* CLEP, independent study, study abroad, honors, 3-year degree, individualized majors, freshman and sophomore seminars, double majors, Washington Semester, internships, cooperative education, liberal arts/2-degree programs in arts/engineering, forestry, health sciences, architecture, natural resources, combined professional programs in arts/medicine or dentistry, journalism, MPP, preferred admission programs to several UM graduate and professional schools, cross-registration with Big Ten institutions and U. of Chicago, Weekend College (public Health only). *Calendar:* trimester, summer school.

Undergraduate degrees conferred (5477). 19% were in Social Sciences, 14% were in Engineering, 10% were in Letters, 9% were in Psychology, 6% were in Business and Management, 5% were in Life Sciences, 5% were in Communications, 5% were in Visual and Performing Arts, 5% were in Liberal/General Studies, 4% were in Health Sciences, 3% were in Multi/Interdisciplinary Studies, remainder in 10 other fields.

Graduates Career Data. Career Development Services include career guidance and job placement, on-campus recruitment, assistance with interview preparation, alumni assistance.

Faculty. About 93% of faculty hold PhD or equivalent.

Student Body. About 70% of students from in state; 80% North Central, 13% Middle Atlantic, 3% South, 2% New England. An estimated 7% of students reported as Black, 8% Asian, 3% Hispanic, 2% other minority, according to most recent data available.

Varsity Sports. Men (Div.I): Baseball, Basketball, Cross Country, Football, Golf, Gymnastics, Hockey, Swimming & Diving, Tennis, Track, Wrestling. Women (Div.I): Basketball, Cross Country, Field Hockey, Golf, Gymnastics, Softball, Swimming & Diving, Tennis, Track, Volleyball.

Campus Life. Student leader asserts those likely to feel most at home at Michigan are the "extremely career oriented" who "aspire to be the future yuppies of America," least at home: those who want a "party" school. Students have considerable freedom in determining parietal rules and other standards governing campus social life. Great variety of cultural and intellectual activities on campus. Problem for student is one of selection. Strong interest reported in fraternities/sororities, varsity sports (especially football) and social activism. Free bus service connects main campus and north campus; bicycles popular with students. Alcohol policy conforms to state and local regulations.

About 5% of women live in traditional dormitories; 40% of men, 35% of women in coed dormitories; 1% of men, 1% of women live in off-campus co-ops and family housing; rest live in other off-campus housing or commute. Freshmen given preference in college housing if all students cannot be accommodated. There are 51 fraternities, 28 sororities on campus which about 15% of men, 15% of women join; 14% of men, 11% of women live in fraternities and sororities. About 10% of resident students leave campus on weekends.

Annual Costs. Tuition and fees, $4,365 (out-of-state, $14,069); room and board, $4,285. About 36% of students receive financial aid; assistance is typically divided 42% scholarship, 54% loan, 5% work. University reports limited number of scholarships awarded on the basis of academic merit alone. *Meeting Costs:* university offers installment payment plan.

University of Michigan—Dearborn

Dearborn, Michigan 48128 **(313) 593-5100**

One of three campuses of the University of Michigan, Dearborn is a commuter institution, serving students in the immediate area. The 212-acre campus is located on the former estate of Henry Ford. Most convenient major airport: Detroit Metropolitan.

Founded: 1959
Affiliation: State
UG Enrollment: 1,700 M, 1,812 W (full-time); 1,396 M, 1,829 W (part-time)
Total Enrollment: 5,253
Cost: < $10K
Admission: Selective
Application Deadline: Rolling

Admission is selective. About 71% of applicants accepted, 59% of these actually enroll; 50% of freshmen graduate in top fifth of high school class. Average freshman scores, according to most recent data available: ACT, 23.5 M, 21.4 W composite. *Required:* SAT or ACT, ACH. *Out-of-state* freshman applicants: university welcomes students from out-of-state. No special requirements for out-of-state applicants. *Entrance programs:* early decision, early admission, midyear admission, advanced placement. *Apply:* rolling admissions. *Transfers* welcome.

Academic Environment. College has 2+2 programs with all local community colleges. *Degrees:* AB, BS, BBA, BGS, BSA, BSE. About 25% of general education requirements for graduation are elective; distribution requirements fairly numerous. *Special programs:* CLEP, honors, independent study, 3-year degree, individualized majors, study abroad, political internships. Adult programs: offered through Schools of Education, Design and Development, Professional and Continuing Education. *Calendar:* trimester.

Undergraduate degrees conferred (932). 20% were in Business and Management, 18% were in Engineering, 14% were in Social Sciences, 11% were in Psychology, 10% were in Liberal/General Studies, 7% were in Computer and Information Sciences, 5% were in Life Sciences, 4% were in Education, 3% were in Letters, remainder in 9 other fields.

Faculty. About 84% of faculty hold PhD or equivalent.

Student Body. About 99% of students from in state. An estimated 6% of students reported as Black, 3% Asian, 2% Hispanic, less than 1% Native American, according to most recent data available.

Varsity Sports. Men (NAIA): Basketball, Football, Ice Hockey, Tennis, Volleyball, Weightlifting. Women (NAIA): Basketball, Volleyball.

Campus Life. All students commute. There are 7 fraternities, 4 sororities on campus which about 4% of men, 7% of women join; they provide no residence facilities.

Annual Costs. Tuition and fees, $2,954 (out-of-state, $9,302). University reports some scholarships awarded on the basis of academic merit alone. *Meeting Costs:* university offers deferred tuition payment plan.

University of Michigan—Flint

Flint, Michigan 48502 (313) 762-3300

One of the University of Michigan's two campuses outside Ann Arbor, Flint offers undergraduate programs in liberal arts, management, nursing, fine arts, health sciences and teacher certification; located in a city of 193,300. Most convenient major airport: Bishop International.

Founded: 1956
Affiliation: State
Total Enrollment: 1,216 M, 1,872 W (full-time); 1,037 M, 1,901 W (part-time)
Cost: < $10K
% Receiving Financial Aid: 35%
Admission: Non-selective
Application Deadline: August 20

Admission. High school graduates with 15 units in academic subjects eligible. About 90% of freshman applicants accepted, 63% of these actually enroll; 48% of freshmen graduate in top fifth of high school class, 84% in top two-fifths. Average freshman ACT scores, middle 50% range: 19–24 composite. *Required:* SAT or ACT, minimum high school GPA. Criteria considered in admissions, in order of importance: high school academic record, standardized test scores, recommendations, writing sample, extracurricular activities; other factors considered: special talents, diverse student body. *Out-of-state* freshman applicants: State does not limit out-of-state enrollment. *Entrance programs:* advanced placement. *Apply* by August 20; rolling admissions. *Transfers* welcome; 753 enrolled 1993–94.
Academic Environment. Graduation requirements include work in English composition, fine arts, humanities, lab science, and social sciences. Degrees offered: bachelors, masters. *Majors offered* include nursing and environmental health. About 49% of entering freshmen graduate within four years, 49% eventually; 83% of freshmen return for sophomore year. *Special programs:* independent study, study abroad, individualized majors, internship/work-study. Adult programs: Adult Resource Center (advisors). *Calendar:* semester.
Undergraduate degrees conferred (788) 26% were in Business and Management, 10% were in Social Sciences, 10% were in Computer and Information Sciences, 9% were in Health Sciences, 7% were in Psychology, 7% were in Education, 6% were in Allied Health, 6% were in Life Sciences, 5% were in Multi/Interdisciplinary Studies, 3% were in Letters, remainder in 8 other fields.
Graduate Career Data. Career Development Services include resume assistance, interviewing, job search workshops.
Faculty. About 85% of faculty hold PhD or equivalent. About 33% of teaching faculty are female; 5% Black, 3% Hispanic, 9% other minority.
Varsity Sports. Men (UIBC). Bowling.
Student Body. About 99% of students from in state. An estimated 10% of students reported as Black, 2% Hispanic, 1% Asian, 1% other minority. Average age of undergraduate student: 28.
Campus Life. All students commute. There are no fraternities or sororities on campus.
Annual Costs. Tuition and fees, $2,916 (out-of-state, $9,534); estimated $800 other, exclusive of housing and travel. About 35% of students receive financial aid. University reports 40 scholarships awarded on the basis of academic merit alone, 10 for special talents alone. *Meeting Costs:* college offers Parent PLUS Loans, CONCERN Loans.

Mid-America Bible College

Oklahoma City, Oklahoma 73170 (405) 691-3800

A private, independent Bible college located about 9 miles from downtown Oklahoma City. Most convenient major airport: Oklahoma City.

Founded: 1953
Affiliation: Independent
Total Enrollment: 182 M, W (full-time)
Cost: < $10K
% Receiving Financial Aid: 75%
Admission: Open

Admission. Open admissions policy; all applicants accepted, 64% of these actually enroll; 31% of freshmen graduate in top fifth of high school class, 42% in top two-fifths. *Required:* ACT, GPA, high school record. Non-academic factor considered in admissions: religious affiliation and/or commitment.
Academic Environment. *Degrees:* AA, BA, BS. Graduation requirements include 50 hours of general studies, 30 hours of Bible/theology, and a major. About 29% of students entering as freshmen graduate within four years, 90% of freshmen return for sophomore year.
Religious Orientation. College is a church-related institution, 30 hours of Bible/Theology required for graduation.
Student Body. About 30% of students from in state; 70% from South, 10% North Central, 7% West. All students reported as Protestant; 15% Black, 5% Hispanic, 5% Asian, 5% Native American, according to most recent data available.
Campus Life. About 80% of students live in traditional dormitories; no coed dormitories; rest commute.
Annual Costs. Tuition and fees, $4,712; room and board, $3,920; estimated $1,000 other, exclusive of travel. About 75% of students receive financial aid.

Mid-America Nazarene College

Olathe, Kansas 66061 (913) 782-3750

A church-related institution located in a community of 43,000, 15 miles from Kansas City, Missouri.

Founded: 1964
Affiliation: Nazarene
Total Enrollment: 1,191 M, W (full-time)
Cost: < $10K
Admission: Non-selective
Application Deadline: August 15

Admission. High school graduates who rank in top three-quarters of class with ACT composite score of 15 eligible; others "accepted with some qualifications"; all applicants accepted, 65% of these actually enroll. About 25% of freshmen graduate in top fifth of high school class, 45% in top two-fifths. *Required:* ACT. *Apply* by August 15. *Transfers* welcome.
Academic Environment. *Degree:* BA, BSN. About 82% of general education requirements for graduation are elective; distribution requirements fairly numerous. About 40% of students entering as freshmen graduate eventually; 64% of freshmen return for sophomore year. *Special programs:* CLEP, independent study, 3-year degree, individualized majors. *Calendar:* 4–1–4.
Undergraduate degrees conferred (256). 57% were in Business and Management, 14% were in Theology, 8% were in Education, 6% were in Health Sciences, 5% were in Psychology, remainder in 8 other fields.
Religious Orientation. Mid-America Nazarene is a church-related institution; 4 courses of religion and philosophy, attendance at biweekly chapel services required of all students; attendance at Sunday and mid-week church services expected. Drinking, smoking, and gambling prohibited.
Student Body. About 50% of students from in state; 80% Midwest, according to most recent data available.
Varsity Sports. Men (NAIA): Baseball, Basketball, Football, Soccer, Track. Women (NAIA): Basketball, Softball, Track, Volleyball.
Campus Life. About 70% of men, 70% of women live in traditional dormitories; no coed dormitories; rest live in off-campus housing or commute. No intervisitation in men's or women's dormitory rooms.
Annual Costs. Tuition and fees, $6,656; room and board, $3,614. College reports some scholarships awarded on the basis of academic merit alone.

Middle Tennessee State University

Murfreesboro, Tennessee 37132 (615) 898-2111

A state-supported university, located in a small city of 30,000, 30 miles southeast of Nashville. Most convenient major airport: Nashville (TN).

Founded: 1909
Affiliation: State
UG Enrollment: 5,048 M, 5,543 W (full-time); 938 M, 986 W (part-time)
Total Enrollment: 15,090
Cost: < $10K
% Receiving Financial Aid: 50%
Admission: Non-selective
Application Deadline: July 1

Admission. Graduates of approved or accredited high schools with 14 units in specified academic courses with a 2.0 overall average or ACT composite score of 16 eligible; others admitted on probation; 76% of applicants accepted, 78% of these actually enroll; 23% of freshmen graduate in top fifth of their high school class; 51% in top two-fifths. *Required:* ACT, GPA. *Out-of-state* freshman applicants: university welcomes students from out of state. State limits out-of-state enrollment to 15% of enrollment. Requirements for out-of-state applicants: minimum ACT composite score of 17 or SAT combined score of 825. *Apply:* July 1 recommended, rolling admissions. *Transfers* welcome.

Academic Environment. *Degrees:* BA, BS, BBA, BFA, BM, BSN, BUS, BSW. About 20% of general education requirements for graduation are elective; distribution requirements fairly numerous. *Majors offered* include recording industry management, aerospace, historic preservation, animal science. About 62% of students entering as freshmen graduate eventually; 60% of freshmen return for sophomore year. *Special programs:* CLEP, honors, Academic Common Market. *Calendar:* early semester, May intersession, summer school.

Undergraduate degrees conferred (1703). 22% were in Business and Management, 17% were in Education, 13% were in Communications, 6% were in Transportation and Material Moving, 5% were in Social Sciences, 5% were in Psychology, 4% were in Visual and Performing Arts, 3% were in Life Sciences, 3% were in Protective Services, 3% were in Computer and Engineering Related Technology, remainder in 17 other fields.

Student Body. About 96% of students from in state, according to most recent data available.

Varsity Sports. Men (OVC): Baseball, Basketball, Cross Country, Football, Golf, Tennis. Women (NCAA): Basketball, Cross Country, Tennis, Track, Volleyball.

Campus Life. About 28% of students live in traditional dormitories; no coed dormitories; rest live in off-campus housing or commute. Intervisitation in men's and women's dormitory rooms limited. There are 14 fraternities, 6 sororities on campus which about 1% of men, 1% of women join.

Annual Costs. Tuition and fees, $1,668 (out-of-state, $5,450); room and board, $2,600. About 50% of students receive financial aid. University reports some scholarships awarded on the basis of academic merit alone.

Middlebury College

Middlebury, Vermont 05753 (802) 388-3711

Middlebury is a liberal arts college with a student body primarily from New England and the Middle Atlantic states, but with representatives from every part of the United States—as many students are enrolled from California as from Vermont. In addition to its strong academic programs in languages, literature, and sciences, the school has a very active outdoor orientation with skiing and mountain climbing in season. The 250-acre campus is located in a town of 6,500, 40 miles south of Burlington and 2 hours by car from Montreal. Most convenient major airport: Burlington (VT).

Founded: 1800
Affiliation: Independent
Total Enrollment: 950 M, 950 W (full-time)
Cost: > $20K
% Receiving Financial Aid: 37%
Admission: Highly Selective
Application Deadline: Jan. 15

Admission is highly selective. About 40% of applicants accepted, 36% of these actually enroll; 86% of freshmen graduate in top fifth of high school class, 97% in top two-fifths. *Required:* SAT and 3 ACH including English Composition, or 5 ACH in different areas including English Composition with or without essay, or ACT; interview recommended. *Non-academic factors* considered in admissions: special talents, alumni children, diverse student body. *Entrance programs:* early decision, advanced placement, deferred admission. About 44% of entering students from private and parochial schools. *Apply* by January 15. *Transfers* welcome.

Academic Environment. Pressures for academic achievement continue strong at Middlebury, but do not appear to be overwhelming. Administration source reports most popular academic departments are history, English, biology, economics, and political science. Graduation requirements include: a major of at least 10 semester courses, a concentration of 4 or more courses in a different field of study, foundations courses in 3 of the 4 academic divisions, freshman writing course, physical education. Students are consulted on decisions concerning curriculum and faculty tenure; student evaluation of faculty reported to be a consideration in retention and promotion. Administration source reports "environment and relative isolation promotes an intense academic atmosphere." Students reported to be concerned with scholarly/intellectual pursuits as well as vocational/professional goals. As one student leader phrased it: "All are concerned with jobs, but few are here to learn a marketable skill." *Degree:* AB. *Majors offered* include arts and sciences, computer science, drama, geography; interdisciplinary environmental studies major, American studies, international politics and economics, teacher education, Northern studies, Russian, Soviet area studies, Japanese, women's studies, molecular biology, biochemistry.

About 92% of students entering as freshmen graduate eventually; 98% of freshmen return for sophomore year. *Special programs:* independent study, study abroad, honors, undergraduate research, 3-year degree (with proper acceleration), Departmental Scholar, Winter Term internships and student-led courses, Washington Semester, combined professional school plan for medicine, dentistry, engineering, dual degree, extended major, exchange programs, semester at Mystic Seaport, schools abroad in France, Italy, Germany, Spain, and USSR, summer language programs in Arabic, Chinese, French, German, Italian, Japanese, Russian, and Spanish; Independent Scholar Program allows qualified students to pursue nonstandard programs. *Calendar:* 4–1–4; summer school.

Undergraduate degrees conferred (494). 34% were in Social Sciences, 17% were in Letters, 11% were in Foreign Languages, 8% were in Life Sciences, 7% were in Visual and Performing Arts, 6% were in Area and Ethnic Studies, 4% were in Psychology, 4% were in Physical Sciences, 3% were in Multi/Interdisciplinary Studies, 3% were in Mathematics, remainder in Philosophy and Religion.

Graduates Career Data. Career Development Services include career guidance and job placement assistance, on campus recruitment, assistance with resume preparation, alumni networking.

Faculty. About 90% of faculty hold PhD or equivalent.

Student Body. About 41% of students from New England, 30% Middle Atlantic, 9% West, 7% Midwest. An estimated 50% of students reported as Protestant, 23% Catholic, 10% Jewish, 16% unaffiliated, 1% other; 4% Black, 3% Hispanic, 5% Asian, 2% other minority, according to most recent data available. *Minority group students:* special academic provisions.

Varsity Sports. Men (Div.III): Baseball, Basketball, Cross Country, Football, Golf, Hockey(II), Lacrosse, Alpine and Nordic Skiing(I), Soccer, Swimming, Tennis, Track. Women (Div.III): Basketball, Cross Country, Field Hockey, Hockey, Lacrosse, Alpine and Nordic Skiing(I), Soccer, Squash, Swimming, Tennis, Track.

Campus Life. Middlebury students tend to be active in winter recreational activities—largest organization on campus is the Mountain Club whose activities range from hiking to ice climbing. Relative isolation of college makes campus the focus of student activities—active schedule of visual and performing arts events, lectures, movies, and student social activities. Strong interest reported in fraternities, varsity sports (most popular: soccer, skiing, lacrosse, hockey, basketball) and intramurals (most popular: softball, basketball, hockey). Although there are 5 fraternities on campus, most social events are reported to be non-Greek. Few rules governing student conduct and students have a significant degree of freedom in controlling their own social lives. All students eligible for cars. Variety of dormitory arrangements available; no regulations on dorm or visitation hours. Students expected to live in residence halls or fraternities.

About 98% of students live on campus; there is one all women's dormitory, rest are coed. Sexes segregated in coed dormitories by wing, floor or room. Less than 5% of resident students leave campus on weekends.

Annual Costs. Comprehensive fee, $24,570. About 37% of students receive financial aid. College reports all scholarships awarded on the basis of need. *Meeting Costs:* college offers several parent loan programs and payment options.

Midland Lutheran College

Fremont, Nebraska 68025 (402) 721-5480

A church-related college, located in a community of 24,000, 35 miles northwest of Omaha. Most convenient major airport: Eppley Airfield, Omaha.

Founded: 1883
Affiliation: Evangelical Lutheran Church in America
Total Enrollment: 943 M, W (full-time); 20 M, 91 W (part-time)
Cost: < $10K
% Receiving Financial Aid: 93%
Admission: Non-selective
Application Deadline: Rolling

Admission. Graduates of accredited high schools with 15 units who rank in top half of class eligible; others given consideration; 95% of applicants accepted, 47% of these actually enroll; about 37% of freshmen graduate in top fifth of high school class, 68% in top two-fifths. Average freshman ACT scores, according to most recent data available: 22.1 composite. *Required:* ACT; interview recommended. *Apply:* rolling admissions. *Transfers* welcome.
Academic Environment. *Degree:* BA, BS, BSBA, BSN. About 92% of general education requirements for graduation are elective; distribution requirements fairly numerous. About 43% of students entering as freshmen graduate within four years; 80% of freshmen return for sophomore year. *Special programs:* CLEP, independent study, study abroad, undergraduate research, 3-year degree, individualized majors, 3–2 occupational therapy. Adult programs: BSN degree completion program. *Calendar:* 4–1–4, summer school.
Undergraduate degrees conferred (130). 32% were in Business and Management, 18% were in Education, 15% were in Health Sciences, 9% were in Social Sciences, 5% were in Psychology, 5% were in Communications, 4% were in Parks and Recreation, remainder in 8 other fields.
Graduates Career Data. According to most recent data available, full-time graduate or professional study pursued by 15% of students immediately after graduation.
Faculty. About 46% of faculty hold PhD or equivalent.
Student Body. About 80% of students from in state; 97% from Midwest. An estimated 70% of students reported as Protestant, 20% Catholic, 9% unaffiliated, 1% other; 3% Black, 2% other minority, according to most recent data available.
Religious Orientation. Midland Lutheran is a church-related institution; 6 hours of religion required of all students; attendance at chapel services voluntary.
Varsity Sports. Men (NAIA): Baseball, Basketball, Cross Country, Football, Golf, Tennis, Track. Women (NAIA): Basketball, Cross Country, Golf, Softball, Tennis, Track, Volleyball.
Campus Life. About 25% of men, 53% of women live in traditional dormitories; 38% of men, 10% of women in coed dormitories; rest commute. Freshmen given preference in college housing if all students cannot be accommodated. Intervisitation in men's and women's dormitory rooms limited. There are 4 fraternities, 4 sororities on campus which about 36% of men, 30% of women join; they provide no residence facilities. About 50% of resident students leave campus on weekends.
Annual Costs. Tuition and fees, $8,800; room and board, $2,700. About 93% of students receive financial aid; assistance is typically divided 35% scholarship/grant, 40% loan, 10% work. College reports some scholarships awarded on the basis of academic merit alone. *Meeting Costs:* college offers monthly payment plan.

Mid-South Bible College

(See Crichton College)

Midwestern State University

Wichita Falls, Texas 76308 (817) 689-4000

A state-supported university, located in a city of 103,000. Most convenient major airport: Dallas/Fort Worth.

Founded: 1922
Affiliation: State
Total Enrollment: 1,568 M, 1,836 W (full-time)
Cost: < $10K
% Receiving Financial Aid: 54%
Admission: Non-selective
Application Deadline: Aug. 7

Admission. Graduates of accredited high schools with 15 units and ACT composite score of 18 or combined SAT score of 800 or rank in top three-quarters of class eligible; others admitted by examination or considered for advised admission; 70% of applicants accepted, 47% of these actually enroll. *Required:* ACT or SAT. Criteria considered in admissions, in order of importance: high school academic record, standardized test scores, recommendations. *Out-of-state* freshman applicants: state does not limit out-of-state enrollment. No special requirements for out-of-state applicants. *Apply* by August 7. *Transfers* welcome; 561 enrolled 1993–94.
Academic Environment. *Undergraduate studies* offered by schools of Business Administration, Education, Humanities and Social Sciences, Sciences and Mathematics. Average undergraduate class size: 30% of classes under 20, 69% between 20–40, 1% over 40. About 30% of students entering as freshmen graduate eventually; 70% of freshmen return for sophomore year. *Special programs:* CLEP, honors, undergraduate research, 3-year degree, study abroad, independent study. *Calendar:* semester, summer school.
Undergraduate degrees conferred (566). 27% were in Education, 20% were in Business and Management, 8% were in Social Sciences, 7% were in Multi/Interdisciplinary Studies, 5% were in Psychology, 4% were in Protective Services, 4% were in Health Sciences, 4% were in Allied Health, 3% were in Life Sciences, 3% were in Communications, 3% were in Public Affairs, 3% were in Letters, remainder in 6 other fields.
Faculty. About 67% of faculty hold PhD or equivalent. About 49% of undergraduate classes taught by tenured faculty. About 33% of teaching faculty are female; 5% ethnic minorities.
Student Body. About 93% of students from in state.
Varsity Sports. Men (NAIA, Div.I): Basketball, Football (II), Golf, Soccer, Tennis. Women (NAIA, Div.I): Basketball, Tennis, Volleyball.
Campus Life. About 7% of men, 4% of women live in traditional dormitories, 3% of men, 2% of women live in coed dormitories; rest live in off-campus housing or commute. Intervisitation in men's and women's dormitory rooms limited. There are 6 fraternities, 4 sororities on campus which about 13% of men, 10% of women join. About 80% of resident students leave campus on weekends.
Annual Costs. Tuition and fees, $1,422 (out-of-state, $5,562); room and board, $3,120. About 54% of students receive financial aid; assistance is typically divided 24% scholarship, 29% grants, 47% loan, less than 1% work. College reports some scholarships awarded on the basis of academic merit alone.

Miles College

Birmingham, Alabama 35208 (205) 923-2771

A church-related, liberal arts college, located in a suburban area of metropolitan Birmingham; founded as a college for Negroes and still serving a predominantly Black student body.

Founded: 1907
Affiliation: Christian Methodist Episcopal
Total Enrollment: 255 M, 287 W (full-time)
Cost: < $10K
Admission: Non-selective
Application Deadline: Rolling

Admission. High school graduates with 15 acceptable units eligible; others given individual consideration. *Required:* college's own testing program (for placement purposes). *Apply:* no specific deadline. *Transfers* welcome.
Academic Environment. Degrees offered: associates, bachelors. All general education credits for graduation are required; distribution requirements fairly numerous. *Special programs:* honors, cross-registration with U. of Alabama in Birmingham. *Calendar:* semester, summer school.
Undergraduate degrees conferred (62). 45% were in Business and Management, 23% were in Social Sciences, 15% were in Education, 8% were in Communications, 5% were in Mathematics, 3% were in Visual and Performing Arts, remainder in Letters.
Religious Orientation. Miles is a church-related institution; 6 hours of religion required of all students.
Campus Life. About 30% of students live in traditional dormitories; no coed dormitories; rest live in off-campus housing or commute. No intervisitation in men's or women's dormitory rooms.
Annual Costs. Tuition and fees, $4,150; room and board, $2,400.

Annual Costs. Tuition and fees, $3,488 (out-of-state, $6,882); room and board, $3,620. About 68% of students receive financial aid; assistance is typically divided 38% scholarship, 46% loan, 16% work. University reports some scholarships awarded on the basis of academic achievement alone. *Meeting Costs:* university offers tuition installment payment plan.

Millersville University of Pennsylvania

Millersville, Pennsylvania 17551 (717) 872-3371

Pennsylvania's oldest state college, Millersville is located on a 225-acre campus in a community of 6,400, 3 miles from Lancaster.Most convenient major airport: Harrisburg International.

Founded: 1854
Affiliation: State
UG Enrollment: 2,111 M, 3,156 W (full-time); 498 M, 1,231 W (part-time)
Total Enrollment: 7,805
Cost: < $10K
% Receiving Financial Aid: 68%
Admission: Selective
Application Deadline: Rolling

Admission is selective. About 48% of applicants accepted, 36% of these actually enroll; 46% of freshmen graduate in top fifth of high school class, 81% in top two-fifths. Average freshman SAT scores, according to most recent data available: 476 verbal, 529 mathematical. *Required:* SAT. *Out-of-state* freshmen applicants: college welcomes students from out-of-state. State does not limit out-of-state enrollment. No special requirements for out-of-state applicants. *Non-academic factors* considered in admissions: special talents, diverse student body. *Entrance programs:* early admission, midyear admission, deferred admission, advanced placement. *Apply:* rolling admissions. *Transfers* welcome.

Academic Environment. Administration source reports that student body is relatively traditional and conservative in values. Student leader reports overwhelming concern among students is the acquisition of occupational/professional skills. Administration reports 79% of courses required for graduation are elective; numerous distribution requirements, however. *Degrees:* BA, BS, BSN, BFA, BSEd. *Majors offered* include arts and sciences, business administration, computer science, wide variety of majors in education fields, medical technology, meteorology, nuclear medicine technology, oceanography, respiratory therapy, nursing, occupational safety and hygiene management, speech communications, social work, geology, Greek and Russian, anthropology, industrial technology, international studies.

About 66% of students entering as freshmen graduate eventually; 85% of freshmen return for sophomore year. *Special programs:* cooperative education, CLEP, double majors, exchange agreements with local colleges, independent study, individualized instruction, Scholars program, honors, undergraduate research, study abroad, 3–2 and 4–1 programs in physics and chemistry. *Calendar:* 4-1-4, summer school.

Undergraduate degrees conferred (1,166). 30% were in Education, 18% were in Business and Management, 7% were in Social Sciences, 6% were in Psychology, 6% were in Life Sciences, 4% were in Letters, 4% were in Engineering and Engineering Related Technology, 4% were in Health Sciences, 4% were in Computer and Engineering Related Technology, 3% were in Communications, 3% were in Physical Sciences, 3% were in Mathematics, 3% were in Visual and Performing Arts, remainder in 4 other fields.

Faculty. About 65% of faculty hold PhD or equivalent.

Student Body. About 93% of students from in state; almost all from Middle Atlantic. An estimated 5% of students reported as Black, 2% Hispanic, 2% Asian, according to most recent data available. *Minority group students:* special financial provisions; Black Student's Union, Vietnamese Students Association, Omega Psi Phi, Alpha Kappa Kappa.

Varsity Sports. Men (Div.II): Baseball, Basketball, Cross Country, Football, Golf, Soccer, Tennis, Track, Wrestling (I). Women (Div.II): Basketball, Cross Country, Field Hockey (III), Lacrosse, Softball, Swimming, Tennis, Track, Volleyball.

Campus Life. Cars permitted for juniors and seniors; alcohol prohibited on campus or at college events. Freshmen required to live on campus.

About 25% of men, 37% of women live in traditional dormitories; 25% of men, 18% of women in coed dormitories; the rest live in off-campus housing or commute. Freshmen given preference in college housing if all students cannot be accommodated. There are 12 fraternities, 12 sororities on campus which about 3% of men and 5% of women join; they provide no residence facilities. About 30–40% of resident students leave campus on weekends.

Milligan College

Milligan College, Tennessee 37682 (615) 461-8730

A small college in a suburban setting, 5 miles east of Johnson City (pop. 50,000), Milligan maintains an active relationship to a religious movement committed to the restoration of New Testament Christianity. "It is a distinguishing characteristic of Milligan College that Biblical data (LBRK)are(RBRK) introduced into the content of each course taught."Most convenient major airport: Tri-Cities

Founded: 1866
Affiliation: Independent
UG Enrollment: 292 M, 416 W (full-time); 20 M, 48 W (part-time)
Total Enrollment: 828
Cost: < $10K
% Receiving Financial Aid: 90%
Admission: Non-selective
Application Deadline: July 1

Admission. High school graduates with 16 units and score of 16 on ACT composite eligible; 76% of applicants accepted, 45% of these actually enroll; 80% of freshmen graduate in top fifth of high school class, 100% in top two-fifths. Average freshman scores: SAT, 450 verbal, 450 mathematical; ACT, 22.5 M, 23 W composite. *Required:* ACT or SAT; minimum high school GPA, church and school references. Criteria considered in admission, in order of importance: high school academic record, standardized test scores, recommendations, writing samples, extracurricular activities; other factors considered: religious affiliation and/or commitment. About 20% of entering students from private schools. *Apply* by July 1; rolling admissions. *Transfers* welcome.

Academic Environment. *Degrees:* associates, bachelors, masters. Small classes and personal attention cited as strengths of the academic program; "the professors are always eager to help". Average undergraduate class size: 60% under 20, 30% 20–40, 10% over 40. About 50% of students entering as freshmen graduate within four years; 71% of freshmen return for sophomore year. *Special programs:* study abroad, 3–2 in engineering. Adult program: business administration degree completion program. *Calendar:* semester, summer school.

Undergraduate degrees conferred (177). 50% were in Business and Management, 10% were in Education, 9% were in Communications, 8% were in Psychology, 5% were in Life Sciences, 5% were in Theology, 5% were in Computer and Engineering Related Technology, remainder in 8 other fields.

Faculty. About 72% of faculty hold PhD or equivalent. About 60% of undergraduate classes taught by tenured faculty. About 40% of teaching faculty are female.

Student Body. About 35% of students from in state; 57% South, 25% Midwest, 8% West, 6% Middle Atlantic, 2% each New England, Northwest, 2% foreign. An estimated 94% students reported to be Protestant, 1% Catholic, 5% unaffiliated; 4% Black, 4% Hispanic, 4% Asian. Average age of undergraduate student: 23.

Religious Orientation. Milligan is a nondenominational institution; "Bible is central in the curriculum"; 3 courses in Bible, attendance at twice weekly convocation required of all students.

Varsity Sports. Men (NAIA): Baseball, Basketball, Golf, Soccer, Tennis. Women (NAIA): Basketball, Softball, Tennis, Volleyball.

Campus Life. Students report rural location provides ample outdoor activities (hiking, skiing, camping), but also means "a car is almost a necessity." Students like the Christian atmosphere and values, and one adds "Milligan is awesome!"

About 80% of each men, women live in traditional dormitories; no coed dormitories; rest live in off-campus housing or commute. No intervisitation in men's or women's dormitory rooms.

Annual Costs. Tuition and fees, $7,500; room and board, $3,100; estimated $1,000 other, exclusive of travel. About 90% of students receive financial aid; average amount of assistance, $2,500. *Meeting Costs:* university offers time payment plan.

Millikin University

Decatur, Illinois 62522 (217) 424-6210

A church-related institution, located on a 50-acre campus in a city of 85,000, 170 miles south of Chicago and 130 miles northeast of St. Louis. University includes Colleges of Arts and Sciences, and Fine Arts, Schools of Business, and Nursing. Most convenient major airport: Decatur (IL)

Founded: 1901
Affiliation: Presbyterian Church (USA)
Total Enrollment: 767 M, 1,021 W (full-time)
Cost: $10K–$20K
% Receiving Financial Aid: 90%
Admission: Selective
Application Deadline: Rolling

Admission is selective (+). About 88% of applicants accepted, 36% of these actually enroll; 53% of freshmen graduate in top fifth of high school class, 80% in top two-fifths. Average freshman scores: SAT, 511 verbal, 541 mathematical; 56% of freshmen score above 500 on verbal, 16% above 600; 73% score above 500 on mathematical, 24% above 600, 5% above 700; ACT, 24 composite. *Required:* SAT or ACT. Criteria considered in admission, in order of importance; high school academic record, standardized test scores, recommendations, extracurricular activities; other factors considered: special talents, alumni children, diverse student body. *Apply:* rolling admissions. *Transfers* welcome; 100 enrolled 1993–94.

Academic Environment. Flexible university-wide general education requirements substitute broad area requirements for specific courses: communication skills, humanities, fine arts, natural science, social sciences, library research, modern language. *Degrees:* bachelors. *Majors offered* include athletic training, commercial music, computer science, nursing, international business, computer art graphics, writing. Average undergraduate class size: 55% under 20, 43% 20–40, 2% over 40.

About 64% of students entering as freshmen graduate eventually; 80% of freshmen return for sophomore year. *Special programs:* independent study, study abroad, honors, undergraduate research, internships, individualized majors, credit by examination, Washington Semester, United Nations Semester, combined programs leading to BS (medical technology, physical therapy), American Studies, Environmental Studies, Humanities Seminar, Urban Studies, Continental European Studies, 3–2 engineering with Washington U., 3–2 in architecture, SCORE (Service Corps of Retired Executives) provides work and teams with students to provide counseling assistance to small businesses. *Calendar:* semester, summer school.

Undergraduate degrees conferred (398). 32% were in Business and Management, 15% were in Education, 13% were in Visual and Performing Arts, 10% were in Health Sciences, 6% were in Life Sciences, 5% were in Communications, 4% were in Letters, 3% were in Social Sciences, 3% were in Public Affairs, 3% were in Psychology, 3% were in Mathematics, remainder in 5 other fields.

Graduates Career Data. Advanced studies pursued by 22% of graduates. About 98% of 1992–93 graduates employed. Fields typically hiring largest numbers of graduates include retail sales, hospitals, social service agencies. Career Development Services include personal career counseling and SIGI Plus.

Faculty. About 76% of faculty hold PhD or equivalent. About 61% of undergraduate classes taught by tenured faculty. About 32% of teaching faculty are female.

Student Body. About 87% of students from in state; 97% Midwest, less than 1% foreign. An estimated 56% of students reported as Protestant, 27% Catholic, 11% unaffiliated, 6% other; 3% as Black, 1% Hispanic, 2% Asian. *Minority group students:* Black cultural house.

Religious Orientation. Millikin is a church-related institution; course in religion or philosophy optional under general education program. Religious Life Committee "coordinates and encourages activities of individual religious groups.

Varsity Sports. Men (Div.III): Baseball, Basketball, Cross Country, Diving, Football, Golf, Soccer, Swimming, Tennis, Track, Wrestling. Women (Div.III): Basketball, Cross Country, Diving, Softball, Swimming, Tennis, Track, Volleyball.

Campus Life. Wide diversity of campus culture and interests. Student activities varied and provide ample opportunity for involvement. Cooperation and participation in university decision making is encouraged of all members of academic community. Cars forbidden for freshmen and sophomores because of parking problems. Drinking allowed in student rooms for those over 21; students have requested a non-alcoholic bar on campus. Visitation in residence halls limited to noon to 1 am; students, reportedly, would like more. "Students expected to live in college housing if space permits."

About 27% of men, 33% of women live in traditional dormitories; 22% of men, 18% of women in coed dormitories; 43% of men, 35% of women live in off-campus housing or commute. Freshmen given preference in college housing if all students cannot be accommodated. Intervisitation in men's and women's dormitory rooms limited. There are 5 fraternities, 4 sororities on campus which about 29% of men, 24% of women join; 8% of men, 14% of women live in fraternities and sororities. About 25% of resident students leave campus on weekends.

Annual Costs. Tuition and fees, $11,331; room and board, $4,168; estimated $800 other, exclusive of travel. About 90% of students receive financial aid; average amount of assistance, $10,000. Assistance is typically divided 60–70% scholarship/grant, 20% loan, 10–20% work. University reports 5 scholarships awarded on the basis of academic merit alone. *Meeting Costs:* university offers monthly payment plans, long term loans.

Mills College

Oakland, California 94613 (415) 430-2135

For years Mills has been one of the few West Coast women's colleges that have attracted students from other parts of the country and abroad. Today it has an extremely diverse student body, 21% of whom are American minorities, and 8% come from abroad. The 135-acre campus is located in a city of 361,600, across the bay from San Francisco. Mills has affirmed its intention to remain a college for women, but will continue to be co-educational at the graduate level. Most convenient major airport: Oakland International.

Founded: 1852
Affiliation: Independent
UG Enrollment: 749 W (full-time); 25 W (part-time)
Total Enrollment: 1,044
Cost: $10K–$20K
% Receiving Financial Aid: 67%
Admission: Very Selective
Application Deadline: August 1

Admission is very selective. About 85% of applicants accepted, 31% of these actually enroll. Average freshman SAT scores, according to most recent data available: 530 verbal, 520 mathematical. *Required:* SAT or ACT; interview recommended. *Non-academic factors* considered in admissions: diverse student body, special talents, activities, work experience. *Entrance programs:* early decision, early admission, midyear admission, deferred admission. About 25% of entering students from private and parochial schools. *Apply* by August 1. *Transfers* welcome.

Academic Environment. Very high proportion of classes are said to have fewer than 20 students, 58% reported to have 12 or fewer. Mills has been a pioneer in the development of career preparation based upon foundation of the liberal arts. The first women's college to institute a computer science major, Mills inaugurated a Women in Science program in 1972 which encourages women to acquire the quantitative skills needed in science and technology. To ensure breadth students must complete at least 2 courses in each of the College's four divisions: Fine Arts, Letters, Natural Sciences, and Social Sciences. Degrees offered: bachelors, masters. *Majors offered* include arts and sciences, administration and legal processes, business economics, computer science, dance, dramatic arts, ethnic studies, political, legal, and economic analysis, women's studies; several interdisciplinary majors.

About 68% of students entering as freshmen graduate within four years; 75% of freshmen return for sophomore year. *Special programs:* independent study, study abroad (including Wales, Ireland, Scotland, England, Germany, France, Austria, Spain, Italy, Israel, and Japan), undergraduate research, self-scheduled examination, credit by examination, exchange with Agnes Scott, Manhattanville, Wheaton (Mass.), Mt. Holyoke, Fisk, Spelman, Swarthmore, Howard, Wellesley, Simmons, 3–2 engineering, 3–2 computer science, freshman seminars. *Library:* 11,000 rare books, 10,000 manuscripts, 7,196 reels of microfilm, and 12,000 music scores. *Calendar:* semester.

Undergraduate degrees conferred (219). 16% were in Multi/Interdisciplinary Studies, 14% were in Social Sciences, 14% were in Letters, 13% were in Visual and Performing Arts, 10% were in Communications, 8% were in Life Sciences, 7% were in Psychology, 4% were in Liberal/General Studies, 4% were in Foreign Languages, 3% were in Computer and Engineering Related Technology, remainder in 6 other fields.
Faculty. About 79% of faculty hold PhD or equivalent.
Student Body. About 66% of students from in state; 82% West/Northwest. An estimated 30% of students reported as Protestant, 13% Catholic, 2% Jewish, 43% unaffiliated, 13% other; 8% Black, 6% Hispanic, 7% Asian, 1% Native American, according to most recent data available. *Minority group students:* academic and social aid available through Black Women's Collective, Mecha, Asian Alliance, ethnic studies program.
Varsity Sports. Women: Basketball, Crew, Cross Country, Tennis, Volleyball.
Campus Life. Mills is essentially a residential college where housing regulations are based more on security "and promotion of community spirit" than on an effort to regulate student social life. San Francisco, just across the bay, is a storied city, offering unparalleled cultural and social resources, where students may be found on most weekends. UC Berkeley graduate men and women are housed in one residence hall on campus. Alcohol permitted at social events and in the residences for those over 21. Students under 21 expected to live on campus; special facilities provided for commuters.

About 73% of undergraduate women live in dormitories; rest commute. Freshmen given preference in college housing if all students cannot be accommodated. There are no sororities on campus. About 15% of resident students leave campus on weekends.
Annual Costs. Tuition and fees, $14,100; room and board, $6,000. About 67% of students receive financial aid; assistance is typically divided 89% scholarship, 10% work. College reports some scholarships awarded on the basis of academic merit alone.

Millsaps College

Jackson, Mississippi 39210 (601) 974-1050

A small, church-related, institution, Millsaps not only offers a strong liberal arts program, but also pre-professional and professional studies. The 100-acre campus is located in the state capitol (pop. 350,000). Most convenient major airport: Allen C. Thompson Field (Jackson)

Founded: 1890
Affiliation: United Methodist
UG Enrollment: 596 M, 538 W (full-time); 51 M, 104 W (part-time)
Total Enrollment: 1,410
Cost: $10K–$20K
% Receiving Financial Aid: 64%
Admission: Very Selective
Application Deadline: Rolling

Admission is very selective. About 84% of applicants accepted, 41% of these actually enroll; 54% of freshmen graduate in top fifth of high school class, 86% in top two-fifths. Average freshman scores, according to most recent data available: SAT, 490 verbal, 560 mathematical; ACT, 25.2 composite. *Required:* ACT or SAT, interview recommended. *Entrance programs:* early admission, midyear admission, advanced placement, deferred admission. About 35% of entering students from private schools, 10% from parochial schools. *Apply:* rolling admissions. *Transfers* welcome.
Academic Environment. Pressures for academic achievement appear moderate. Administration reports 50% of courses required for graduation are elective. Interdisciplinary Heritage Program for freshmen offers alternative to numerous distribution requirements. Interdisciplinary Science for sophomores includes study of biology, chemistry, geology, and physics. *Degrees:* AB, BS, BSEd, BLS, BM, BBA. *Majors offered* include arts and sciences, accounting, business administration, classics, women's studies.

About 64% of students entering as freshmen graduate eventually; 83% of freshmen return for sophomore year. *Special programs:* independent study, study abroad, honors, undergraduate research, Washington Semester, United Nations Semester, London Semester, Oak Ridge Semester, combined programs (engineering with Auburn, Columbia, Vanderbilt, Georgia Tech. and Washington U., medical technology with Vanderbilt), internships (in accounting, business, economics, legislative process), summer program at Gulf Coast Research Laboratory. Adult programs: BLS Degree Program. *Calendar:* semester, summer school.
Undergraduate degrees conferred (246). 27% were in Business and Management, 17% were in Letters, 16% were in Social Sciences, 8% were in Life Sciences, 7% were in Education, 6% were in Psychology, 5% were in Physical Sciences, 5% were in Philosophy and Religion, 4% were in Visual and Performing Arts, remainder in 3 other fields.
Graduates Career Data. According to most recent data available, full-time graduate or professional study pursued immediately after graduation by 56% of students; 4% enter medical school; 1% enter dental school; 6% enter law school; 10% enter business school. Medical schools typically enrolling largest numbers of graduates include U. of Mississippi, U. of Alabama, Vanderbilt; law schools include Tulane, U. of Mississippi, Emory, Vanderbilt; business schools include Millsaps, Tulane, Emory, Vanderbilt. *Careers in business and industry* pursued by 46% of graduates. Corporations typically hiring largest numbers of graduates include EDS, Peat Marwick Main, AC3, United Financial Corp. Career Development Services include testing, advising, counseling, seminars, internships, externships, and on-campus interviewing, assistance with interview preparation, alumni active in both career counseling and job placement.
Faculty. About 84% of faculty hold PhD or equivalent.
Student Body. About 50% of students from in state; 63% South; 30% West. An estimated 56% of students reported as Protestant, 13% Catholic, 1% Jewish, 27% unknown, 3% other; 4% Black, 2% Asian, 1% other minority, according to most recent data available.
Religious Orientation. Millsaps is a church-related institution; 3 hours of religion required of all students.
Varsity Sports. Men (CAC, Div.III): Baseball, Basketball, Cross Country, Football, Golf, Soccer, Tennis. Women (CAC, Div.III): Basketball, Cross Country, Soccer, Tennis.
Campus Life. Fraternities/sororities provide an active social life for the campus, almost two-thirds of students join. About 70% of students involved in intramural sports (most popular: basketball). Interest increasing in varsity sports, cultural and religious activities. No curfew; intervisitation noon to midnight Sunday-Thursday, noon-1 am weekends; first semester freshmen: limited to weekends.

About 46% of men, 71% of women live in traditional dormitories; about 5% each of men and women live in coed dormitories; 33% of men, 24% of women commute. Freshmen given preference in college housing if all students cannot be accommodated. There are 6 fraternities, 5 sororities on campus which about 70% of men, 70% of women join; 16% of men live in fraternities; sororities provide no residence facilities. About 25% of resident students leave campus on weekends.
Annual Costs. Tuition and fees, $11,236; room and board, $4,250. About 64% of students receive financial aid; assistance is typically divided 60% scholarship, 5% loan, 35% work. College reports some scholarships awarded on the basis of academic merit alone. *Meeting Costs:* college offers deferred payment plan.

Milwaukee School of Engineering

Milwaukee, Wisconsin 53201 (800) 332-6763

An independent, co-educational college, located in downtown Milwaukee, 6 blocks from Lake Michigan. Most convenient major airport: General Mitchell International.

Founded: 1903
Affiliation: Independent
UG Enrollment: 1,669 M, 249 W (full-time); 878 M, W (part-time)
Total Enrollment: 2,925
Cost: $10K–$20K
% Receiving Financial Aid: 85%
Admission: Non-selective
Application Deadline: Rolling

Admission. ; 57% of freshmen graduate in top fifth of high school class; 85% in top two-fifths. Average freshman scores, according to most recent data available: SAT, 455 M, 497 W verbal, 565 M, 593 W mathematical; ACT, 24.4 M, 23.7 W composite. *Required:* ACT preferred; SAT accepted. *Apply:* rolling admissions. *Transfers* welcome.
Academic Environment. *Degrees:* BS. *Majors offered* include architectural and building construction engineering, business and management systems, computer science and engineering, technical communications. About 50% of students entering as freshmen graduate eventually; 74% of freshmen return for sophomore year. *Calendar:* quarter, summer quarter optional for most programs.

Undergraduate degrees conferred (312). 58% were in Engineering, 33% were in Engineering and Engineering Related Technology, 9% were in Business and Management.
Graduates Career Data. According to most recent data available, careers in business and industry pursued by 96% of graduates. Corporations typically hiring largest numbers of graduates include Texas Instruments, Compaq, Allen Bradley, Commonwealth Edison.
Student Body. About 75% of students from within state; 92% Midwest, 3% Middle Atlantic. An estimated 3% of students reported as Black, 2% Hispanic, 3% Asian, according to most recent data available.
Varsity Sports. Men (NAIA): Baseball, Basketball, Cross Country, Golf, Ice Hockey, Soccer, Wrestling. Women (NAIA): Basketball, Cross Country, Softball, Volleyball.
Campus Life. About 36% of men, 38% of women live in coed dormitories; rest live in off-campus housing or commute. Freshmen given preference in college housing if all students cannot be accommodated. There are 6 fraternities, 2 sororities which 10% of men, 15% of women join. Intervisitation in men's and women's dormitory rooms unlimited. About 20% of resident students leave campus on weekends.
Annual Costs. Tuition and fees, $10,800; room and board $3,480. About 85% of students receive financial aid. College reports some scholarships awarded on the basis of academic merit alone.

Minneapolis College of Art and Design

Minneapolis, Minnesota 55404

An independent, professional college of visual arts which provides an interdisciplinary program of studio and liberal arts courses, leading to the BFA. Major areas of specialization include painting, sculpture, printmaking, graphic design, intermedia, photography, film, video, and various areas of design.

Founded: 1886 **Affiliation:** Independent

Undergraduate degrees conferred (113). 100% were in Visual and Performing Arts.

University of Minnesota

Minneapolis, Minnesota 55455 **(612) 625-5000**

One of the nation's largest and most famous land-grant colleges and state universities, the University of Minnesota enrolls a substantial number of out-of-state students. A 4-year liberal arts program is offered at the University of Minnesota, Morris; a more extensive program, plus some graduate and professional studies are offered at the university's Duluth campus. Two-year programs are offered at the technical colleges in Crookston and Waseca. Most convenient major airport: Minneapolis/St. Paul International.

Founded: 1851
Affiliation: State
UG Enrollment: 12,250 M, 11,629 W
Total Enrollment: 37,548
Cost: < $10K
% Receiving Financial Aid: 50%
Admission: Selective (+)
Application Deadline: Rolling

Admission is selective (+). For all schools, 58% of applicants accepted, 55% of these actually enroll; 46% of freshmen graduate in top fifth of high school class, 74% in top two-fifths. Average freshman scores: SAT, 487 M, 480 W verbal, 598 M, 530 W mathematical; 45% of freshmen score above 500 on verbal, 13% above 600, 1% above 700; 76% score above 500 on mathematical, 45% above 600, 13% above 700; ACT, 24 M, 23 W composite. *Required:* SAT or ACT. Criteria considered in admission, in order of importance; high school academic record, standardized test scores. *Out-of-state* freshman applicants: university actively seeks students from out-of-state. State does not limit out-of-state enrollment. About 49% of out-of-state students accepted, 47% of these actually enroll. States from which most out-of-state students are drawn include Wisconsin. *Entrance programs:* midyear admission. *Apply:* rolling admissions. *Transfers* welcome; 2,083 enrolled 1993–94.

Academic Environment. Pressures for academic achievement moderately strong for Technology, less so for Liberal Arts. Administration reports proportion of required courses needed for graduation "varies tremendously", includes a diversified core with major societal themes. University College has no fixed curriculum, admits juniors seeking inter-college programs, sponsors Living/Learning Center for development of off-campus field study projects. *Undergraduate studies* offered to freshmen in schools of Liberal Arts, Agriculture, Forestry, Home Economics, Technology; colleges of Biological Sciences, Pharmacy, schools of Business Administration, Nursing require previous college work. Degrees offered: bachelors, masters, doctoral. *Majors offered* include Black studies, American Indian studies, applied business, biometry, Chicano studies, East Asian languages, geophysics, information networking, international relations, journalism and mass communications, microbiology, Middle Eastern languages, physiology, Scandinavian languages and literature, social welfare, South Asian languages and literature, statistics, theater; individually designed interdepartmental majors also possible.

About 12% of students entering as freshmen graduate within four years, 52% eventually; 81% of freshmen return for sophomore year. *Special programs:* CLEP, independent study, study abroad, honors, undergraduate research, individualized majors, credit by examination, combined 7-year programs in arts/dentistry or medicine, "informal" 3-year degree. Adult programs: evening MBA, and "one of the largest continuing education/extension programs in the nation." Calendar: quarter, summer school.
Undergraduate degrees conferred (5,561). 16% were in Social Sciences, 13% were in Engineering, 9% were in Business and Management, 6% were in Psychology, 6% were in Letters, 5% were in Multi/Interdisciplinary Studies, 5% were in Education, 5% were in Visual and Performing Arts, 4% were in Communications, 4% were in Life Sciences, 4% were in Health Sciences, remainder in 18 other fields.
Graduate Career Data. Career Development Services: each individual college of the university system offers "a vast array of counseling, placement and interviewing services."
Faculty. About 91% of faculty hold PhD or equivalent.
Student Body. Almost all students from Midwest. *Minority group students:* special coordination of recruiting, financial aid, tutoring, counseling through Martin Luther King program, grants-in-aid for American Indians. Average age of undergraduate student: 22.
Varsity Sports. Men (Div.I): Baseball, Basketball, Cross Country, Diving, Football (Div.1A), Golf, Gymnastics, Ice Hockey, Swimming, Tennis, Track, Wrestling. Women (Div.I): Basketball, Cross Country, Diving, Golf, Gymnastics, Soccer, Softball, Swimming, Tennis, Track, Volleyball.
Campus Life. Recent student leader describes typical student as "commuter, slightly older than average." Residents of dorms allowed to determine whether intervisitation hours will be limited or unlimited. "Limited" permission for alcohol on campus. Another student leader reports large classes on "very large Minneapolis campus. St. Paul (Ag.) campus small and beautiful." Cars allowed, but parking a severe problem. Limited on-campus housing; university assists students in locating private housing.

About 12% of students live in coed dormitories; 85% live in off-campus housing or commute. There are 27 fraternities, 15 sororities on campus which about 3% of men, 3% of women join; 3% of students live in fraternities and sororities.
Annual Costs. Tuition and fees, $3,266 (out-of-state, $8,854); room and board, $3,564. Approximately 50% of students receive financial aid; average amount of assistance, $4,500. *Meeting Costs:* university offers deferred payment plan, PLUS Loans.

University of Minnesota—Duluth

Duluth, Minnesota 55812 **(218) 726-7171**

A state-supported institution, Minnesota's Duluth campus offers 2- and 4-year programs; located in a city of 100,600. Most convenient major airport: Duluth International.

Founded: 1902
Affiliation: State
UG Enrollment: 3,888 M, 3,350 W (full-time); 1,298 M, W (part-time)
Cost: < $10K
Admission: Non-selective
Application Deadline: June 15

Admission. High school graduates in top 50% of class automatically admitted; 30% of freshmen graduate in top fifth of high school class, 63% in top two-fifths. *Required:* ACT. *Out-of-state* freshman applicants: state does not limit out-of-state enrollment. Requirements for out-of-state applicants: rank in top half of class. Non-academic factor considered in admissions: diverse student body. *Apply* by June 15. *Transfers* welcome.
Academic Environment. *Degrees:* BA, BS, BApA, BApS, BBA, BFA, BM. About 65% of students entering as freshmen graduate eventually; 80% of freshmen return for sophomore year. *Special programs:* CLEP, independent study, study abroad, honors, undergraduate research, individualized majors, cooperative programs through LSACU, American Indian Learning and Resource Center. *Calendar:* quarter, summer school.
Undergraduate degrees conferred (1,049). 23% were in Business and Management, 14% were in Social Sciences, 13% were in Education, 10% were in Communications, 7% were in Psychology, 6% were in Engineering, 5% were in Life Sciences, 5% were in Visual and Performing Arts, 3% were in Letters, 3% were in Engineering and Engineering Related Technology, 3% were in Physical Sciences, 3% were in Computer and Engineering Related Technology, remainder in 8 other fields.
Student Body. About 89% of students from in state; 95% Midwest. An estimated 1% of students reported as Native American, 9% other minority, according to most recent data available.
Varsity Sports. Men (NCAA,Div.II): Baseball, Basketball (NAIA), Cross Country, Football, Golf, Hockey (Div. I), Tennis, Track. Women (NCAA, Div.II): Basketball, Cross Country, Softball, Tennis, Track, Volleyball.
Campus Life. About 2% of men, 3% of women live in traditional dormitories; 19% of men, 20% of women in coed dormitories; rest commute. Intervisitation in men's and women's dormitory rooms unlimited if agreed upon by three-quarters of dormitory residents. There are 5 fraternities, 4 sororities on campus which 2% of men, 2% of women join; they provide no residence facilities.
Annual Costs. Tuition and fees, $3,061 (out-of-state, $8,479); room and board, $3,213. College reports some scholarships awarded on the basis of academic merit alone.

University of Minnesota—Morris

Morris, Minnesota 56267 **(800) 992-8863**

The University of Minnesota's Morris campus offers undergraduate liberal arts studies in a rural setting in a community of 5,400, 150 miles northwest of the Twin Cities. Most convenient major airport: Minneapolis International.

Founded: 1959
Affiliation: State
Total Enrollment: 857 M, 1,076 W (full-time)
Cost: < $10K
% Receiving Financial Aid: 87%
Admission: Very Selective
Application Deadline: Mar. 15

Admission is very selective. About 60% of applicants accepted, 67% of these actually enroll; 54% of freshmen graduate in top fifth of their high school class, 76% in top two-fifths. Average freshman scores: SAT, 65% of freshmen score above 500 on verbal, 27% above 600, 5% above 700; 68% score above 500 on mathematical, 50% above 600, 18% above 700; ACT, 26 composite. *Required:* ACT. Criteria considered in admission, in order of importance: high school academic record and standardized test scores rank equally, recommendations and extracurricular activities rank equally, writing sample: other factors considered: special talents, alumni children. *Out-of-state* freshman applicants: state actively seeks students from out-of-state. State does not limit out-of-state enrollment. No special requirements for out-of-state applicants. States from which most out-of-state students are drawn include South Dakota. *Entrance programs:* early decision, deferred admission, advanced placement. *Apply* by March 15. *Transfers* welcome; 81 enrolled 1993–94.
Academic Environment. *Degrees:* bachelors. About 63% of general education requirements for graduation are elective; distribution requirements fairly numerous. Emphasis on liberal arts; vast majority of transfers are seeking professional programs on Twin Cities campus. Student describes academic program as "Challenging!!" Average undergraduate class size: 35% under 20, 55% 20–40, 10% over 40.
About 46% of students entering as freshmen graduate within four years; 76% eventually. *Special programs:* CLEP, honors, independent study, study abroad, undergraduate research, individualized majors, 3–2 engineering, cross registration with U. of Minnesota TC, undergraduate opportunities program. *Calendar:* quarter, summer school.
Undergraduate degrees conferred (366). 17% were in Social Sciences, 15% were in Business and Management, 14% were in Letters, 11% were in Education, 10% were in Liberal/General Studies, 8% were in Physical Sciences, 5% were in Psychology, 5% were in Life Sciences, 5% were in Mathematics, 3% were in Foreign Languages, 3% were in Visual and Performing Arts, remainder in 2 other fields.
Graduates Career Data. Advanced studies pursued by 27% of graduates; 14% enter graduate school; 4% enter medical school; 1% enter dental school; 4% enter law school; 4% enter business school. Professional schools typically enrolling largest numbers of graduates include U. of Minnesota. About 84% of 1992–93 graduates employed. Employers typically hiring largest numbers of graduates include Honeywell, financial companies. Career Development Services include help with interview preparation, resume writing, counseling and on campus recruitment.
Faculty. About 83% of faculty hold PhD or equivalent. About 85% of undergraduate classes taught by tenured faculty. About 35% of teaching faculty are female; 1% Black, 3% Hispanic, 26% other minority.
Student Body. About 79%% of students from in state. An estimated 4% of students reported as Black, 1% Hispanic, 4% Asian, 3% Native American, 1% International.
Varsity Sports. Men (Div.II): Baseball, Basketball, Football, Golf, Tennis, Track, Wrestling. Women (NAIA, Div.I): Basketball, Golf, Softball, Tennis, Track, Volleyball.
Campus Life. Student leader comments that campus is so intimate that "no one gets lost in the shuffle." Another student feels "there's not much to do off-campus, but it's easier to get involved in campus activities because there's not a lot of competition with such a small campus." Sports, intramural and varsity, movies, and campus performances reported popular.
About 64% of men, 74% of women live in coed dormitories; 35% of men, 25% of women live in off-campus housing; rest commute. Intervisitation in men's and women's dormitory rooms unlimited; sexes segregated by wing or floor. There are 2 fraternities, 1 sorority on campus which about 1% each of men and women join. Fraternities or sororities provide no residence facilities. About 35% of resident students leave campus on weekends.
Annual Costs. Tuition and fees, $3,645 (out-of-state, $10,158); room and board, $3,180 estimated $600 other, exclusive of travel. About 87% of students receive financial aid; average amount of assistance, $3,480. Assistance is typically divided 52% scholarship/grant, 38% loan, 10% work. University reports 473 scholarships awarded on the basis of academic merit alone. *Meeting Costs:* university offers supplemental loans for parents.

Minnesota Bible College

Rochester, Minnesota 55902

A small Bible college offering associates and bachelors degrees. All bachelors degree candidates major in biblical studies, they may also chose a second major in pastoral leadership or Christian education.

Founded: 1913
Affiliation: Christian Churches/ Churches of Christ

Minot State University

Minot, North Dakota 58701 **(701) 857-3000**

A state-supported university, located in a community of 35,000. Formerly known as Dakota Northwestern University.

Founded: 1913
Affiliation: State
UG Enrollment: 1,354 M, 1,945 W (full-time)
Total Enrollment: 4,026
Cost: < $10K
% Receiving Financial Aid: 66%
Admission: Non-selective
Application Deadline: Rolling

Admission. North Dakota high school graduates with 17 units eligible; almost all applicants accepted, 96% of these actually enroll. Criteria considered in admission, in order of importance: high school academic record, standardized test scores. *Out-of-state* freshman applicants: university actively seeks students from out-of-state. State does not limit out-of-state enrollment. Most out-of-state students are drawn from Saskatchewan, Canada. *Transfers* welcome; 458 enrolled 1993–94.
Academic Environment. *Degrees:* associates, bachelors, masters. Graduation requirements include core studies in seven areas: communications, history, humanities, leisure time, math, science, social science. About 40% of students entering as freshmen graduate eventually; 85% of freshmen return for sophomore year. *Special programs:* CLEP, independent study. *Calendar:* quarter, summer school.
Undergraduate degrees conferred (498). 27% were in Education, 21% were in Business and Management, 11% were in Health Sciences, 8% were in Protective Services, 7% were in Business (Administrative Support), 7% were in Public Affairs, 5% were in Allied Health, 4% were in Social Sciences, remainder in 9 other fields.
Faculty. About 36% of faculty hold PhD or equivalent. About 40% of undergraduate classes taught by tenured faculty. About 45% of teaching faculty are female, 1% Black, 4% other minority.
Student Body. About 78% of students from in state; 16% Canadian.
Varsity Sports. Men (NAIA): Baseball, Basketball, Cross Country, Football, Golf, Tennis, Track & Field, Wrestling. Women (NAIA): Basketball, Gymnastics, Softball, Track & Field, Volleyball.
Campus Life. About 9% of men, 14% of women live in traditional dormitories or other on-campus housing; rest commute. Housing available on campus for married students. Intervisitation in men's and women's dormitory rooms limited.
Annual Costs. Tuition and fees, $1,836 (out-of-state, $4,642); room and board, $2,571; estimated $1,993 other, exclusive of travel. About 66% of students receive financial aid; average amount of assistance, $4,321. Assistance is typically divided 7% scholarship, 24% grant, 67% loan, 2% work. University reports 486 scholarships awarded on the basis of academic merit alone, 101 for special talents alone, 100 for need alone. *Meeting Costs:* university offers PLUS.

College Misericordia

Dallas, Pennsylvania 18612 **(717) 675-4449**

A Christian liberal arts college conducted by the Religious Sisters of Mercy of the Union. The campus is located in a suburban community of 2,900, 9 miles west of Wilkes-Barre. Most convenient major airport: Scranton-Wilkes Barre International.

Founded: 1924
Affiliation: Roman Catholic
UG Enrollment: 214 M, 626 W (full-time); 106 M, 305 W (part-time)
Cost: $10K–$20K
% Receiving Financial Aid: 92%
Admission: Non-selective
Application Deadline: Rolling

Admission. Graduates of accredited high schools with 16 units with "acceptable record" eligible; 82% of applicants accepted, 37% of these actually enroll; 24% of freshmen graduate in top fifth of high school class, 48% in top two-fifths. Average freshman scores, according to most recent data available: SAT, 405 M, 400 W verbal, 410 M, 420 W mathematical. *Required:* SAT or ACT. *Apply:* rolling admissions. *Transfers* welcome.
Academic Environment. *Degrees:* AB, BS, BM, BSN. *Majors offered* include physical therapy, psychology, secondary education. About 80% of students entering as freshmen graduate eventually; 90% of freshmen return for sophomore year. *Special programs:* CLEP, independent study, study abroad, undergraduate research, cross-registration with King's College, cooperative graduate and 5-year AB/MA programs with U. of Scranton. Adult programs: occupational therapy assistant certification completion program. *Calendar:* semester, summer session.
Undergraduate degrees conferred (206). 34% were in Allied Health, 16% were in Education, 14% were in Business and Management, 14% were in Health Sciences, 9% were in Liberal/General Studies, 4% were in Public Affairs, 3% were in Social Sciences, remainder in 3 other fields.
Student Body. About 80% of students are from in state; 97% of students from Middle Atlantic.
Religious Orientation. Misericordia is a church-related institution "in the Catholic tradition."
Campus Life. About 55% of women, 55% of men live in traditional dormitories; no coed dormitories; rest commute. No intervisitation in women's dormitory rooms.
Annual Costs. Tuition and fees, $10,460; room and board, $5,360. About 92% of students receive financial aid; assistance is typically divided 42% scholarship, 54% loan, 4% work. College reports some scholarships awarded on the basis of academic merit alone. *Meeting Costs:* college offers AMS deferred payment plan.

Mississippi College

Clinton, Mississippi 39058 **(601) 925-3240**

A church-related college, located in a town of 12,000, 5 miles west of Jackson, the state capital.Most convenient major airport: Jackson Municipal.

Founded: 1826
Affiliation: Southern Baptist
UG Enrollment: 764 M, 933 W (full-time); 159 M, 484 W (part-time)
Total Enrollment: 3,157
Cost: < $10K
% Receiving Financial Aid: 61%
Admission: Non-selective
Application Deadline: Rolling

Admission. Graduates of accredited high schools with standard ACT composite score of 15, or combined SAT of 700, and GPA of 2.0 eligible; those with lower score must offer evidence of ability; graduates of nonaccredited schools admitted by examination; 80% of applicants accepted, 94% of these actually enroll. *Required:* ACT or SAT. *Apply:* rolling admissions. *Transfers* welcome.
Academic Environment. *Degrees:* BA, BS, BM, BMEd, BSEd, BSN, BSBA. About 50% of general education requirements for graduation are elective; distribution requirements fairly numerous. *Special programs:* CLEP, study abroad, honors, 3-year degree, 3–2 engineering. *Calendar:* early semester, summer school.
Undergraduate degrees conferred (492). 34% were in Business and Management, 14% were in Education, 10% were in Health Sciences, 5% were in Social Sciences, 5% were in Psychology, 4% were in Philosophy and Religion, 3% were in Life Sciences, 3% were in Mathematics, 3% were in Letters, 3% were in Visual and Performing Arts, remainder in 12 other fields.
Student Body. About 76% of students from in state. An estimated 92% of students reported as Protestant, 5% Catholic, 3% other; 12% Black, 2% other minority, according to most recent data available.
Religious Orientation. Mississippi is a church-related institution; 6 semester hours of Bible, attendance at twice-weekly chapel services required of all students.
Varsity Sports. Men (Div.II): Baseball, Basketball, Cross Country, Football, Golf. Women (Div.II): Basketball (I), Softball, Tennis, Volleyball.
Campus Life. About 30% of men, 19% of women live in traditional dormitories; no coed dormitories; rest live in off-campus housing or commute. Freshmen given preference in college housing if all students cannot be accommodated. No intervisitation in men's or women's dormitory rooms. There are no fraternities or sororities on campus. About 50% of resident students leave campus on weekends.
Annual Costs. Tuition and fees, $5,618; room and board, $2,730. About 61% of students receive financial aid; assistance is typically divided 20% scholarship, 66% loan, 4% work. College reports some scholarships awarded on the basis of academic merit alone. *Meeting Costs:* college offers deferred and monthly payment plans.

Mississippi State University

Starkville, Mississippi 39762 **(601) 325-3920**

A state-supported, land-grant institution, located in Starkville (pop. 11,400), 130 miles northeast of Jackson. Most convenient major airport: Jackson.

Founded: 1862
Affiliation: State
UG Enrollment: 5,904 M, 3,995 W (full-time); 847 M, 516 W (part-time)
Total Enrollment: 13,651
Cost: < $10K
% Receiving Financial Aid: 75%
Admission: Non-selective
Application Deadline: Rolling

Admission. Mississippi graduates of approved high schools with 15 units, and minimum ACT composite score of 15 or SAT combined score of 720 eligible; others admitted provisionally; 77% of applicants accepted, 38% of these actually enroll. Average freshman ACT scores: 22.8 M, 22.1 W composite. *Required:* ACT. Criteria considered in admission, in order of importance: standardized test scores, high school academic record. *Out-of-state* freshman applicants: university actively seeks out-of-state students. State does not limit out-of-state enrollment. No special requirements for out-of-state applicants. States from which most out-of-state students are drawn include Alabama. *Entrance programs:* early admission, midyear admission, advanced placement. *Apply* ; rolling admissions. *Transfers* welcome; 1,302 enrolled 1993–94.

Academic Environment. *Undergraduate studies* offered by colleges of Agriculture, Architecture, Arts and Sciences, Business and Industry, Education, Engineering, School of Forest Resources, Veterinary Medicine. Graduation requirements include 6 hours English Composition, 15 hours math, 9 hours humanities/fine arts, 6 hours social/behavioral sciences, 3 hours public speaking, 3 hours writing, 3 hours computer literacy, 12 hours upper division courses. Students feel curriculum is challenging, faculty supportive; they are also enthusiastic about the co-operative education program. *Degrees:* associates, bachelors, masters, doctoral. Average undergraduate class size: 31.

About 51% of students entering as freshmen graduate within 6 years; 78% of freshmen return for sophomore year. *Special programs:* CLEP, study abroad, cooperative work/study program, 3–2 engineering, cross registration with Academic Common Market, accelerated degree programs in pre-veterinary and pre-medicine, independent study available in all schools. *Calendar:* semester, summer school.

Undergraduate degrees conferred (1,964). 31% were in Business and Management, 19% were in Education, 16% were in Engineering, 4% were in Communications, 3% were in Home Economics, 3% were in Social Sciences, 3% were in Agricultural Sciences, 3% were in Agribusiness and Agricultural Production, remainder in 17 other fields.

Graduate Career Data. Career Development Services include aptitude testing, counseling groups, placement services, resume and interview workshops, on-campus recruitment, and cooperative education programs.

Faculty. About 77% of faculty hold PhD or equivalent. About 49% of undergraduate classes taught by tenured faculty. About 23% of teaching faculty are female; 4% Black, 1% Hispanic, 4% other minority.

Student Body. About 75% of students from in state; 87% South, 2% West, 6% foreign. Average age of undergraduate student: 23.

Varsity Sports. Men (NCAA, Southeastern Conf. Div.I): Baseball, Basketball, Cross Country, Football, Golf, Tennis, Track. Women (NCAA, Southeastern Conf. Div.I): Basketball, Cross Country, Golf, Tennis, Track, Volleyball.

Campus Life. On-campus activities attract large numbers of participants, according to students. Clubs, intramural sports, and student government reported popular.

About 15% of men, 13% of women live in traditional dormitories; 1% each live in coed dormitories; 71% of men, 51% of women live in off-campus college-related housing; 10% of men, 33% of women commute. No intervisitation in men's or women's dormitory rooms. There are 18 fraternities, 11 sororities on campus which about 17% of men, 20% of women join; about 3% of each live in fraternities and sororities.

Annual Costs. Tuition and fees, $2,474 (out-of-state, $4,933); room and board, $3,130; estimated $2,348 other, exclusive of travel. About 75% of students receive financial aid; average amount of assistance, $3,863. Assistance is typically divided 33% scholarship, 42% loan, 25% work. University reports 52% of scholarships awarded based on need alone.

University of Mississippi

Oxford, Mississippi 38677 **(601) 232-7226**

A state-supported institution, the University of Mississippi has a 3-square-mile main campus in Oxford (pop. 11,200), in north central Mississippi. The university's schools of Dentistry, Medicine, Nursing, and Health Related Professions are located in Jackson. Most convenient major airport: Memphis, TN.

Founded: 1844
Affiliation: State
UG Enrollment: 3,792 M, 3,736 W (full-time); 268 M, 361 W (part-time)
Total Enrollment: 10,369
Cost: < $10K
% Receiving Financial Aid: 66%
Admission: Non-selective
Application Deadline: Aug. 1

Admission. Mississippi graduates of high schools with 15 acceptable units and ACT composite standard score of 18 or SAT combined score of 720 eligible; 88% of applicants accepted, 49% of these actually enrolled. Average freshman ACT scores, middle 50% range: 20–25 composite. *Required:* SAT or ACT. Criteria considered in admission, in order of importance: standardized test scores, high school academic record. *Out-of-state* freshman applicants: university seeks students from out-of-state. State does not limit out-of-state enrollment. No special requirements for out-of-state applicants. States from which most out-of-state students are drawn include Tennessee, Louisiana, Texas. *Entrance programs:* early admission, deferred admission. *Apply* by August 1; rolling admissions. *Transfers* welcome; 754 enrolled 1993–94.

Academic Environment. *Undergraduate studies* offered by College of Liberal Arts, schools of Business Administration, Education, Accountancy, Engineering, Pharmacy. *Degrees:* bachelors, masters, doctoral. *Majors offered* include court reporting, Southern Studies. About 52% of students entering as freshmen graduate eventually; 80% of freshmen return for sophomore year. *Special programs:* CLEP, study abroad, honors, independent study scholars program, combined business/law and arts/medicine or dentistry programs, internships in journalism. Adult program: Adult Learners Orientation Conference specifically geared to help older adults return to college. *Calendar:* semester, summer school.

Undergraduate degrees conferred (1,475). 37% were in Business and Management, 10% were in Education, 7% were in Health Sciences, 6% were in Social Sciences, 6% were in Life Sciences, 5% were in Psychology, 5% were in Letters, 4% were in Visual and Performing Arts, 3% were in Communications, 3% were in Public Affairs, 3% were in Engineering, 3% were in Home Economics, remainder in 11 other fields.

Graduate Career Data. Career Development Services include career planning, resume and interview workshops, on-campus recruitment, aptitude testing, counseling; placement services include mock interviews and resume writing instruction.

Faculty. About 84% of faculty hold PhD or equivalent. About 30% of teaching faculty are female.

Student Body. About 51% of students from in state; 6% foreign.

Varsity Sports. Men (Div.I): Baseball, Basketball, Cross Country, Football, Golf, Tennis, Track. Women (Div.I): Basketball, Cross Country, Golf, Tennis, Track, Volleyball.

Campus Life. Fraternities and sororities play a "positive" role in campus social life; opportunities for independents reported to be "very good." Cars permitted for all students. About 48% of students live in on-campus housing; rest live in off-campus college-related housing or commute. Freshmen given preference in college housing if all students cannot be accommodated. There are 19 fraternities, 14 sororities on campus which about 35% of men, 40% of women join.

Annual Costs. Tuition and fees, $2,456 (out-of-state, $4,916); room and board $3,300; estimated $2,500 other, exclusive of travel. About 66% of students receive financial aid; average amount of assistance, $6,044. Assistance is typically divided 23% scholarship/grant, 66% loan, 10% work. *Meeting Costs:* university offers The Tuition Plan.

Mississippi University for Women

Columbus, Mississippi 39701 **(601) 328-5891**

A state-supported university, located in a community of 40,000, 150 miles northeast of Jackson.

Founded: 1884
Affiliation: State
UG Enrollment: 275 M, 1,308 W (full-time); 290 M, 814 W (part-time)
Total Enrollment: 2,864
Cost: < $10K
% Receiving Financial Aid: 81%
Admission: Non-selective
Application Deadline: Aug. 15

Admission. Graduates of accredited high schools with 15 units (10 in academic subjects) who rank in top half of class eligible; others admitted on basis of SAT or ACT scores; 88% of applicants accepted;

51% of these actually enroll. About 60% of freshmen graduate in top fifth of high school class, 96% in top two-fifths. Average freshmen ACT scores: 20 M, 22 W composite. *Required:* ACT. Criteria considered in admissions, in order of importance: standardized test scores, high school academic record, extracurricular activities, recommendations; other factors considered: alumni children, diverse student body. *Out-of-state* freshman applicants: state actively recruits out-of-state students. State does not limit out-of-state enrollment. No special requirements for out-of-state applicants. About 92% of out-of-state students accepted, 42% of these actually enroll. States from which most out-of-state students are drawn include Alabama, Louisiana, Tennessee. *Entrance programs:* early admission, deferred admission. *Apply* by August 15. *Transfers* welcome; 363 enrolled 1993–94.

Academic Environment. *Degrees:* associates, bachelors, masters. About 95% of general education requirements for graduation are elective; distribution requirements fairly numerous. Average undergraduate class size: 53% under 20, 37% 20–40, 10% over 40. About 30% of students entering as freshmen graduate within four years; 57% of freshmen return for sophomore year. *Special programs:* CLEP, independent study, honors, study abroad, cross registration with Mississippi State U., 3–2 in engineering, internships, cooperative work/study. *Calendar:* semester, summer school.

Undergraduate degrees conferred (298). 23% were in Business and Management, 19% were in Health Sciences, 12% were in Education, 11% were in Law, 6% were in Life Sciences, 5% were in Home Economics, 5% were in Communications, 4% were in Physical Sciences, 4% were in Visual and Performing Arts, 4% were in Mathematics, 3% were in Letters, remainder in Social Sciences.

Faculty. About 53% of faculty hold PhD or equivalent. About 36% of undergraduate classes taught by tenured faculty. About 63% of teaching faculty are female; 3% Black, 2% Hispanic, 2% other minority.

Student Body. About 91% of students from in state; 99% South. An estimated 20% of students reported as Black; 1% Hispanic, 1% Asian, 1% other minority. Average age of undergraduate student: 26.5.

Varsity Sports. Women: Basketball, Softball, Tennis, Volleyball.

Campus Life. About 6% of men, 22% of women live in dormitories; rest commute. No intervisitation in women's dormitory rooms. There are 3 fraternities, 2 sororities on campus, which about 18% of men, 22% of women join. About 58% of resident students leave campus on weekends.

Annual Costs. Tuition and fees, $2,239 (out-of-state, $4,381); room and board, $2,217; estimated $500 other, exclusive of travel.

About 81% of students receive financial aid; average amount of assistance, $2,950. Assistance is typically divided 1,250 scholarship, 1,250 grant, 1,980 loan, 1,200 work.

Mississippi Valley State University

Itta Bena, Mississippi 38941-1900 (601) 254-9041

A state university offering teacher education and technical programs, Mississippi Valley State is located in a town of 2,500, 43 miles east of Greenville; founded as a college for Negroes and still serving a predominantly Black student body.

Founded: 1946
Affiliation: State
UG Enrollment: 980 M, 1,153 W (full-time); 96 M, 100 W (part-time)
Total Enrollment: 2,329
Cost: < $10K
% Receiving Financial Aid: 95%
Admission: Non-selective
Application Deadline: Rolling

Admission. Graduates of accredited high schools with 16 units eligible; 30% of applicants accepted, 56% of these actually enroll; 10% of freshmen graduate in top fifth of high school class, 35% in top two-fifths. Average freshman ACT scores: 16.1 M, 17 W composite. *Required:* ACT. Criteria considered in admission, in order of importance: standardized test scores, high school academic record, recommendations, extracurricular activities; other factors considered: special talents, alumni children, diverse student body. *Out-of-state* freshman applicants: state actively seeks students from out-of-state. No special requirements for out-of-state applicants. State does not limit out-of-state enrollment; 313 enrolled. States from which most out-of-state students are drawn include Illinois, Tennessee, Alabama, Louisiana. *Entrance programs:* early decision, early admission, deferred admission, advanced placement. *Apply* by 20 days before registration. *Transfers* welcome; 250 enrolled 1993–94.

Academic Environment. *Degrees:* bachelors, masters. Graduation requirements include 12 hours of English, 3 of fine arts, 6 of social studies, 3 of speech, 3 of health education, 3 of general psychology, 2 of physical education or ROTC, 6 of science with lab, 3 of algebra. Average undergraduate class size: 25; 15% under 20, 80% 20–40, 5% over 40. About 35% of students entering as freshmen graduate within four years, 40% eventually; 75% of freshmen return for sophomore year. *Special programs:* study abroad, honors, undergraduate research. *Calendar:* semester, summer school.

Undergraduate degrees conferred (184). 28% were in Education, 15% were in Protective Services, 14% were in Business and Management, 11% were in Public Affairs, 9% were in Social Sciences, 8% were in Engineering and Engineering Related Technology, 5% were in Computer and Engineering Related Technology, 5% were in Life Sciences, 3% were in Letters, remainder in 3 other fields.

Graduate Career Data. Advanced studies pursued by 14% of graduates; 10% enter graduate school; 1% enter medical school; 2% enter law school. Medical schools typically enrolling largest numbers of graduates include U. of Mississippi, Meharry Medical; dental and law schools include U. of Mississippi. About 65% of 1992–93 graduates employed. Fields typically hiring largest numbers of graduates include public schools, corrections department, human services. Career Development Services designed to aid students and graduates to identify individual capabilities, interests and skills.

Faculty. About 40% of faculty hold PhD or equivalent. About 60% of undergraduate classes taught by tenured faculty. About 33% of teaching faculty are female; 75% Black, 1% Hispanic, 14% other minority.

Student Body. About 85% of students from in state; 90% South, 5% Midwest, 2% New England, 1% each West, Northwest, Middle Atlantic. An estimated 87% of students are reported as Protestant, 5% Catholic, 2% Muslim, 1% unaffiliated, 5% other; 97% Black, 1% Hispanic, 1% Asian.

Varsity Sports. Men: Baseball, Basketball, Cross Country, Football, Golf, Gymnastics, Softball, Swimming, Tennis, Track, Volleyball. Women: Basketball, Cross Country, Golf, Gymnastics, Softball, Swimming, Tennis, Track, Volleyball.

Campus Life. About 65% of men, 70% of women live in traditional dormitories; rest commute. No intervisitation in men's or women's dormitory rooms. There are 4 fraternities, 3 sororities on campus which about 8% of men, 9% of women join; they provide no residence facilities. About 60% of resident students leave campus on weekends.

Annual Costs. Tuition and fees, $2,164 (out-of-state, $4,306); room and board, $1,900; estimated $200 other, exclusive of travel.

About 95% of students receive financial aid; average amount of assistance, $4,400. Assistance is typically divided 12% scholarship, 45% grant, 37% loan, 6% work. University reports 118 scholarships awarded on basis of academic merit alone, 285 for special talents alone.

Missouri Baptist College

St. Louis, Missouri 63141 (314) 434-1115

"A Christian liberal arts college," Missouri Baptist is sponsored by the Missouri Baptist Convention. The 84-acre campus is located in the suburban community of Creve Coeur, 20 miles west of downtown St. Louis. Most convenient major airport: St. Louis International.

Founded: 1964
Affiliation: Southern Baptist
UG Enrollment: 654 M, 1,094 W (full-time)
Cost: < $10K
% Receiving Financial Aid: 90%
Admission: Non-selective
Application Deadline: Rolling

Admission. Graduates of accredited high schools with 15 credits who rank in the top 50% of their high school class eligible. About 80% of applicants accepted, 75% of these actually enroll; 28% of entering students graduate in top fifth of high school class; 75% in top two-fifths. Average freshman ACT scores: ACT, 17.9 composite, according to most recent data available. *Required:* ACT. Criteria considered in admission, in order of importance: standardized test scores, high school academic record. *Entrance programs:* early decision, early admission, midyear admission. *Apply:* rolling admissions. *Transfers* welcome; 211 enrolled 1993–94.

Academic Environment. *Degrees:* associates, bachelors. Administration reports 10% of courses required for graduation are elective. Average undergraduate class size: 80% under 20. About 21% of entering freshmen graduate within four years; 64% of freshmen return for sophomore year. *Special programs:* January term, study abroad, cross registration with Harlexton U., Oxford, England, pre-law, 3–2 engineering. Adult programs: bachelors in nursing and evening business program for adult students. *Calendar:* semester, Winterterm, May Term.

Undergraduate degrees conferred (101). 31% were in Education, 25% were in Business and Management, 7% were in Social Sciences, 6% were in Philosophy and Religion, 5% were in Psychology, 5% were in Health Sciences, 4% were in Mathematics, 4% were in Communications, 3% were in Letters, 3% were in Computer and Engineering Related Technology, remainder in 4 other fields.

Graduate Career Data. Career Development Services include computerized system to aid students in career choice, internships.

Faculty. About 55% of faculty hold PhD or equivalent.

Student Body. High proportion of students live in the St. Louis area; 92% of students from in state. An estimated 87% of students reported as Protestant, 10% Catholic; 14% Black, 5% other minority.

Religious Orientation. Missouri Baptist is a church-related institution; 50% of students affiliated with the church; 2 courses in religious studies required; chapel-convocation programs held twice weekly; attendance required for full-time students.

Varsity Sports. Men (NAIA): Baseball, Basketball, Golf, Soccer. Women (NAIA): Baseball, Basketball, Soccer, Softball.

Campus Life. About 6% of men, 12% of women live in traditional dormitories; rest commute. There are no fraternities or sororities on campus. About 80% of students leave campus on weekends.

Annual Costs. Tuition and fees, $6,800; room and board, $2,900; estimated $600 other, exclusive of travel. About 90% of students receive financial aid. Assistance is typically divided 63% scholarship, 34% loan, 3% work. *Meeting Costs:* college offers institutional and outside aid sources.

Missouri Southern State College

Joplin, Missouri 64801-1595 (417) 625-9300

A state-supported institution, offering 2- and 4-year programs, located in a city of 45,000, near the Kansas, Arkansas, and Oklahoma borders. Most convenient major airport: Tulsa.

Founded: 1937
Affiliation: State
UG Enrollment: 1,638 M, 2,012 W (full-time); 823 M, 1,193 W (part-time)
Cost: < $10K
% Receiving Financial Aid: 78%
Admission: Non-selective
Application Deadline: August 13

Admission. Graduates of accredited Missouri high schools admitted; 96% of applicants accepted, 58% actually enroll; 18% of freshmen graduate in top fifth of high school class, 80% in top two-fifths. Average freshman ACT scores: 21.3 M, 21.3 W composite. *Required:* ACT, will accept SAT and GED. Criteria considered in admission, in order of importance: high school academic record, standardized test scores. *Out-of-state* freshman applicants: state actively seeks out-of-state students. State does not limit out-of-state enrollment. No special requirements for out-of-state applicants. About 99% of out-of-state students accepted, 71% of these actually enroll. States from which most out-of-state students are drawn include Kansas. *Entrance programs:* early decision, early admission, midyear admission, deferred admission, advanced placement, service admissions. *Apply* by August 13. *Transfers* welcome; 600 enrolled 1993–94.

Academic Environment. *Degrees:* associates, bachelors. About 25% of general education requirements for graduation are elective; distribution requirements fairly numerous. Average undergraduate class size: 40% under 20, 60% 20–40. About 78% of students entering as freshmen graduate eventually; 60% of freshmen return for sophomore year. *Special programs:* CLEP, honors, study abroad, internships, independent study. Adult programs: 60+ program, several continuing education courses. *Calendar:* semester, summer school.

Undergraduate degrees conferred (519). 30% were in Business and Management, 28% were in Education, 8% were in Social Sciences, 7% were in Protective Services, 4% were in Life Sciences, 4% were in Computer and Engineering Related Technology, 4% were in Communications, 3% were in Psychology, 3% were in Health Sciences, remainder in 6 other fields.

Graduate Career Data. Advanced studies pursued by 15% of graduates; 5% enter graduate school; 1% enter medical school; 1% dental school; 2% enter law school; 5% business school. Medical schools typically enrolling largest numbers of graduates include U. of Missouri; dental schools include U.of Kansas City; law schools include U. of Missouri; business schools include U. of Missouri. Fields typically hiring largest numbers of graduates include education, local business, State of Missouri, private business. Career Development Services available.

Faculty. About 62% of faculty hold PhD or equivalent. All undergraduate classes taught by tenured faculty. About 54% of teaching faculty are female; 2% Black, 2% Hispanic, 2% other minority.

Student Body. About 78% of students from in state; 90% Midwest, 8% West, 1% South. An estimated 50% of students reported as Protestant, 33% Catholic, 1% Jewish, 16% unaffiliated; 10% Black, 3% Hispanic, 1% Asian, 2% Native American. Average age of undergraduate student: 24.

Varsity Sports. Men (NAIA): Baseball, Basketball, Cross Country, Football, Golf, Soccer, Track. Women (NAIA): Basketball, Cross Country, Softball, Tennis, Volleyball.

Campus Life. About 50% of men, 50% of women live in traditional dormitories; rest commute. Freshmen given preference in college housing if all students cannot be accommodated. No intervisitation in men's or women's dormitory rooms. There are 2 fraternities, 2 sororities on campus which about 1% of each join. About 50% of resident students leave campus on weekends.

Annual Costs. Tuition and fees, $1,754 (out-of-state, $3,508); room and board, $2,700; estimated $2,600 other, exclusive of travel. About 78% of students receive financial aid; average amount of assistance, $2,000. Assistance is typically divided 10% scholarship, 20% grant, 50% loan, 20% work. College reports 20 scholarships awarded on the basis of academic merit alone, 75 for special talents alone, 5 for need alone. *Meeting Costs:* college offers AMS monthly payment plan.

University of Missouri

A large, comprehensive, land-grant, state university, the University of Missouri has 4 campuses: Columbia, Kansas City, Rolla, and St. Louis. Columbia, the original campus founded in 1839, has the broadest course of study, the largest enrollment, and a number of professional schools. Kansas City, which was a large, comprehensive, independent university, became part of the university in 1963. Rolla, founded in 1870, as the university's former School of Mines and Metallurgy, offers science, engineering, mines and metallurgy, and other programs. St. Louis, founded as an entirely new campus in 1963, offers arts, sciences, business, education, nursing and optometry programs.

Admission granted to applicants presenting evidence indicating reasonable probability of success. Selection of freshmen based on secondary school course requirements and combination of high school class rank and SAT or ACT score.

University of Missouri—Columbia

Columbia, Missouri 65211 (314) 882-2456

The first state university west of the Mississippi, the University of Missouri's Columbia campus is located in a community of 65,500, 125 miles west of St. Louis. Most convenient major airports: Columbia Regional.

Founded: 1839
Affiliation: State
UG Enrollment: 7,375 M, 7,407 W (full-time); 758 M, 825 W (part-time)
Total Enrollment: 23,000
Cost: < $10K
% Receiving Financial Aid: 72%
Admission: Selective (+)
Application Deadline: May 15

Admission is selective (+). (See also University of Missouri.) About 71% of applicants accepted, 63% of these actually enroll; 54% of freshmen graduate in top fifth of high school class, 84% in top two-fifths.

Average freshmen ACT scores: 24.7 M, 23.8 W composite, 23.9 M, 22.3 W mathematical, according to most recent data available. *Required:* ACT. Criteria considered in admissions: a combination of ACT, high school rank and college preparatory curriculum used in admission decision. *Out-of-state* applicants: university actively seeks students from out-of-state. State does not limit out-of-state enrollment. No special requirements for out-of-state applicants. States from which most out-of-state students are drawn include Illinois, Kansas, Texas, California. *Apply* by May 15; rolling admissions. *Transfers* welcome.

Academic Environment. Wide range of academic and professional programs. Honors College open to freshmen who graduate in top 10% of class. *Undergraduate studies* offered to freshmen by colleges of Arts and Sciences, Agriculture, Education, Engineering, Home Economics, School of Forestry, Fisheries, and Wildlife; upperclassmen may enroll in College of Business and Public Administration, schools of Health-Related Professions, Nursing, and Journalism. Students agree that a diverse selection of degree programs (over 250) is MU's "greatest asset." Graduation requirements include 2 writing intensive classes, math beyond algebra, 2 9-hour "cluster courses" in areas outside the major, and 1 seminar in the first 60 hours of study. *Degrees:* bachelors, masters, doctoral. Average undergraduate class size: 44% under 20, 42% 20–40, 14% over 40.

About 30% of students entering as freshmen graduate within four years, 56% within six years; 82% of freshmen return for sophomore year. *Special programs:* CLEP, independent study, study abroad, honors, individualized majors, cooperative education, internships, cross-registration with Mid-Missouri Associated Colleges. *Calendar:* early semester, summer school.

Undergraduate degrees conferred (3,466). 19% were in Business and Management, 12% were in Engineering, 10% were in Education, 10% were in Social Sciences, 8% were in Communications, 5% were in Home Economics, 5% were in Letters, 4% were in Psychology, 3% were in Life Sciences, 3% were in Health Sciences, 3% were in Agricultural Sciences, 3% were in Multi/Interdisciplinary Studies, 3% were in Allied Health, remainder in 13 other fields.

Faculty. About 87% of faculty hold PhD or equivalent. About 40% of undergraduate classes taught by tenured faculty. About 23% of teaching faculty are female; 3% Black, 2% Hispanic, 8% other minority.

Student Body. About 88% of students from in state. An estimated 4% of students reported as Black, 1% Hispanic, 2% Asian, 7% other minorities. *Minority group students:* coordinator for minority group programs (providing financial and academic help); special cultural programming; Black Culture House.

Varsity Sports. Men (Div. I): Baseball, Basketball, Football, Golf, Swimming, Tennis, Track, Wrestling. Women (Div. I): Basketball, Golf, Gymnastics, Softball, Swimming, Track, Volleyball.

Campus Life. Campus is located next to downtown area, walking distance to restaurants, movie theaters, and dance clubs. Many campus organizations and activities also keep students busy. One honors student worries that her peers are "so involved and not studying enough", but another student puts studying at the top of his list. Cars allowed for all, including freshmen; parking situation reportedly "improving." Drinking prohibited on campus or in university housing. College has 20-sport intramural program.

About 12% of men, 23% of women live in traditional dormitories; 65% of each live in coed dormitories; rest commute. Intervisitation limited. There are 32 fraternities, 19 sororities on campus which about 25% of each join.

Annual Costs. Tuition and fees, $2,934 (out-of-state, $8,010); room and board, $3,320; estimated $1,700 other, exclusive of travel. About 72% of students receive financial aid; average amount of assistance, $5,660. Assistance is typically divided 30% scholarship, 10% grant, 37% loan, 23% work. University reports some scholarships awarded on the basis of academic merit alone. *Meeting Costs:* university offers deferred installment payment plan, pre-payment plan, "Meal Deal" (free meals in exchange for 12 hours per week work in dining hall).

University of Missouri—Kansas City

Kansas City, Missouri 64110 **(816) 235-1000**

An urban campus, Missouri at Kansas City serves a largely commuter population and is located on 85 acres in the heart of a city of 513,800, close to other cultural and intellectual centers. Most convenient major airport: Kansas City International.

Founded: 1929
Affiliation: State
UG Enrollment: 1,614 M, 1,802 W (full-time); 932 M, 1,052 W (part-time)
Total Enrollment: 9,858
Cost: < $10K
% Receiving Financial Aid: 77%
Admission: Selective (+)
Application Deadline: Rolling

Admission is selective (+). (See also University of Missouri.) About 70% of applicants accepted, 49% of these actually enroll; 56% of freshmen graduate in top fifth of high school class, 76% in top two-fifths. Average freshman ACT scores: 24.2 composite. *Required:* ACT. Criteria considered in admissions, in order of importance: standardized test scores, high school academic record. *Out-of-state* freshman applicants: university actively seeks out-of-state students. State does not limit out-of-state enrollment. No special requirements for out-of-state students. States from which most out-of-state students are drawn include Kansas. *Entrance programs:* early admission, midyear admission, deferred admission. *Apply:* rolling admissions. *Transfers* welcome; 1,068 enrolled Fall 1993.

Academic Environment. Administration source reports that students are primarily concerned with occupational/professional goals; far less interested in scholarly/intellectual pursuits. *Undergraduate studies* offered by College of Arts and Sciences, Conservatory of Music, schools of Administration, Dentistry (for dental hygiene), Education, Pharmacy. Degrees offered: bachelors, masters, doctoral. *Majors offered* include communication studies, computer science, geosciences, medical technology, theater; area studies and interdepartmental majors also possible.

About 16% of students entering as freshmen graduate within four years, 43% graduate eventually; 64% of freshmen return for sophomore year. *Special programs:* CLEP, independent study, honors, study abroad, undergraduate research, credit by examination, cross registration with schools in Kansas City Regional Council for Higher Education. Adult programs: PACE, Program for Adult College Education on weekends. *Calendar:* semester, summer school.

Undergraduate degrees conferred (1,104). 24% were in Business and Management, 17% were in Education, 10% were in Life Sciences, 8% were in Social Sciences, 7% were in Liberal/General Studies, 6% were in Health Sciences, 6% were in Psychology, 6% were in Visual and Performing Arts, 4% were in Communications, 3% were in Letters, 3% were in Computer and Engineering Related Technology, 3% were in Allied Health, remainder in 6 other fields.

Faculty. About 92% of faculty hold PhD or equivalent. bout 26% of teaching faculty are female; 3% Black, 1% Hispanic, 4% other minority.

Student Body. About 80% of students from in state; 93% Midwest, 1% each South, West, 4% foreign. An estimated 8% of students reported to be Black, 3% Hispanic, 5% Asian, 11% other minority. Average age of undergraduate student: 26.5.

Varsity Sports. Men (NCAA, Div.I): Basketball, Cross Country, Golf, Riflery, Soccer, Tennis, Track. Women (NCAA, Div.I): Basketball, Cross Country, Golf, Riflery, Softball, Tennis, Track, Volleyball.

Campus Life. Overwhelming proportion of commuters on campus affects quality of student life. About 2% of men, 2% of women live in coed dormitories; rest commute. Freshmen given preference in college housing if all students cannot be accommodated. There are 4 fraternities, 4 sororities on campus which about 2% men, 2% women join.

Annual Costs. Tuition and fees, $3,152 (out-of-state, $8,582); room and board, $3,525. About 77% of students receive financial aid; average amount of assistance, $5,255. Assistance is typically divided 31% scholarship, 17% grant, 49% loan, 3% work. College reports 440 scholarships awarded on the basis of academic merit alone, 240 for special talents alone, 164 for need alone. *Meeting Costs:* college offers PLUS Loans, short-term installment loans.

University of Missouri—Rolla

Rolla, Missouri 65401 **(314) 341-4114**

A technological institution, the university's Rolla campus offers specialized curricula in engineering, mines and metallurgy, as well as in arts and science fields; located in a town of 15,000, 100 miles southwest of St. Louis. Most convenient major airport: St. Louis.

Founded: 1870
Affiliation: State
UG Enrollment: 3,036 M, 890 W (full-time); 373 M, 188 W (part-time)
Total Enrollment: 5,681
Cost: < $10K
% Receiving Financial Aid: 66%
Admission: Very Selective
Application Deadline: Rolling

Admission is very selective. (See also University of Missouri.) About 94% of applicants accepted, 50% of these actually enroll; 69% of freshmen graduate in top fifth of high school class, 92% in top two-fifths. Average freshman scores: SAT, 547 verbal, 655 mathematical; 66% score above 500 on verbal, 23% above 600, 2% above 700; 93% score above 500 on mathematical, 70% above 600, 27% above 700; ACT; 27 composite. *Required:* ACT or SAT; high school rank. Criteria considered in admission, in order of importance: standardized test scores, high school academic record; other factors considered include alumni children. *Out-of-state* freshman applicants: university welcomes out-of-state students. State does not limit out-of-state enrollment. About 96% of out-of-state students accepted, 31% of these actually enroll. *Apply* by July 1; rolling admissions. *Transfers* welcome; 375 enrolled 1993–94.

Academic Environment. Eighty percent of student body majors in engineering and sciences. Student notes "It's competitive! but you don't compete against anyone but yourself. Students help out other students." Graduation requirements include 12 hours each in sciences, humanities, and social sciences. Students are involved in selection and promotion of faculty as well as in curriculum decisions, according to administration. *Undergraduate studies* offered by College of Arts and Sciences, Schools of Engineering, Mines and Metallurgy. *Degrees:* bachelors, masters, doctoral. *Majors offered* in 13 fields of engineering, 6 fields of science, and 5 liberal arts disciplines. Average undergraduate class size: 24.

About 10% of students entering as freshmen graduate within four years, 50% eventually; 79% of freshmen return for sophomore year. *Special programs:* independent study, honors, individualized majors, study abroad, combined 2-degree engineering program, pre-professional program, intercampus BSEd with Columbia. *Calendar:* semester, summer school.

Undergraduate degrees conferred (702). 85% were in Engineering, 6% were in Computer and Engineering Related Technology, 3% were in Social Sciences, remainder in 5 other fields.

Graduates Career Data. Advanced studies pursued by 19% of graduates. Corporations typically hiring largest numbers of graduates include McDonnell Douglas, Missouri Highway Transportation, Ford, Black & Beach. Career Development Services include individual counseling, student resource centers, and interest instruments to assess skills, personality and values.

Faculty. About 91% of faculty hold PhD or equivalent. About 6% of teaching faculty are female; 3% Black, 1% Hispanic, 12% other minority.

Student Body. About 78% of students from in state; 62% Midwest. An estimated 40% of students reported as Protestant, 25% Catholic, 1% Jewish, 30% unaffiliated, 4% other; 4% Black, 1% Hispanic, 3% Asian, 11% other minority. Average age of undergraduate student: 22. *Minority group students:* special financial, academic, and social provisions including minority engineering program; Black fraternities.

Varsity Sports. Men (Div.II): Baseball, Basketball, Cross Country, Diving, Football, Golf, Rifle, Soccer, Swimming, Tennis, Track. Women (Div.II): Basketball, Cross Country, Soccer, Softball, Swimming, Track.

Campus Life. "We do a lot of studying during the week" says one student, another agrees, but she also finds time for various workshops, professional societies, and use of the recreational facilities on campus.

About 24% of men, 6% of women in coed dormitories; 53% of men, 77% of women live in off-campus housing or commute. Freshmen given preference in college housing if all students cannot be accommodated. There are 22 fraternities, 5 sororities on campus which about 28% of men, 20% of women join; 23% of men, 17% of women live in fraternities and sororities.

Annual Costs. Tuition and fees, $3,254 (out-of-state, $8,693); room and board, $3,475; estimated $600 other, exclusive of travel. About 66% of students receive financial aid; average amount of assistance, $5,649. Assistance is typically divided 29% scholarship, 24% grant, 24% loan, 23% work. University reports 2,019 scholarships awarded on the basis of academic merit alone, 162 for special talents alone. *Meeting Costs:* university offers installment plan.

University of Missouri—St. Louis

St. Louis, Missouri 63121-4499 (314) 553-5000

The St. Louis campus of the university is a commuter institution serving the state's largest population center. Most convenient major airport: St. Louis.

Founded: 1963
Affiliation: State
UG Enrollment: 2,238 M, 2,555 W (full-time); 2,150 M, 2,547 W (part-time)
Total Enrollment: 11,868
Cost: < $10K
% Receiving Financial Aid: 53%
Admission: Non-selective
Application Deadline: Rolling

Admission. (See also University of Missouri.) Graduates of accredited high schools with 15 units in academic subjects eligible; non-graduates admitted by examination; others admitted to summer session; 650% of applicants accepted, 54% of these actually enroll; 36% of freshmen graduate in top fifth of high school class, 64% in top two-fifths. Average freshman ACT scores: 22.1 composite. *Required:* SAT or ACT, high school record and rank. Criteria considered in admissions, in order of importance: high school academic record and standardized test scores rank with equal importance, recommendations. *Out-of-state* freshman applicants: university actively seeks out-of-state students. State does not limit out-of-state enrollment. States from which most out-of-state students are drawn include Illinois. *Entrance programs:* early admission, midyear admission, advanced placement, visiting students. *Apply* by July 1; rolling admissions. *Transfers* welcome; 1,675 enrolled 1993–94.

Academic Environment. Degrees offered: bachelors, masters, doctoral. *Undergraduate studies* offered by College of Arts and Sciences, Schools of Business Administration, Education. Graduation requirements include 42 hours in humanities/natural sciences and mathematics/social sciences, 3 hours in non-Euro-American studies, 3 hours in American history or government, 3 hours in writing; math proficiency. Average undergraduate class size: 48% under 20, 42% 20–40, 10% over 40. About 60% of freshmen return for sophomore year. *Special programs:* CLEP, independent study, honors, study abroad, undergraduate research, individualized majors, cross registration with Washington U., St. Lodi U., Southern Illinois U., Edwardsville, 3–4 architecture. Adult programs: evening college providing bachelors of general studies along with 28 other undergraduate degree programs, 17 minors and 2 certificate programs. *Calendar:* semester, summer school.

Undergraduate degrees conferred (1,657). 41% were in Business and Management, 18% were in Education, 8% were in Letters, 6% were in Social Sciences, 5% were in Psychology, 5% were in Health Sciences, 4% were in Protective Services, 4% were in Liberal/General Studies, 3% were in Public Affairs, remainder in 7 other fields.

Graduates Career Data. About 83% of 1992–93 graduates employed. Fields typically hiring largest numbers of graduates include industry, public utility, education. Career Development Services include job counseling and assistance with job placement, SIGI computerized program.

Faculty. About 57% of faculty hold PhD or equivalent. About 26% of undergraduate classes taught by tenured faculty. About 39% of teaching faculty are female; 5% Black, 3% Hispanic, 5% other minority.

Student Body. About 97% of students from in state; 98% Midwest. An estimated 12% of students reported as Black, 1% Hispanic, 3% Asian, 1% other minority.

Varsity Sports. Men (Div.II): Baseball, Basketball, Golf, Soccer, Swimming, Tennis. Women (Div.II): Basketball, Soccer, Softball, Swimming, Tennis, Volleyball.

Campus Life. Primarily a commuter institution; 1% of each men, women live in coed dormitories; 99% of each men, women live in off-campus housing or commute. There are 3 fraternities and 3 sororities on campus which about 5% of men and 3% of women join; less than 1% each of men, women live in fraternities or sororities. About 35% of resident students leave campus on weekends.

Annual Costs. Tuition and fees, $2,500 (out-of-state, $6,851); room and board, $3,878; estimated $1,615 other, exclusive of travel. About 53% of students receive financial aid; average amount of assistance, $3,540. Assistance is typically divided 9% scholarship, 14% grant, 54% loan, 8% work. University reports 932 scholarships awarded on the basis of academic merit alone, 103 for special talents alone.

Missouri Valley College

Marshall, Missouri 65340 (816) 886-6924

A church-related college, located in a town of 15,000, 80 miles east of Kansas City.

Founded: 1889
Affiliation: Presbyterian Church (USA)
UG Enrollment: 1,103 M, W (full-time)
Cost: < $10K
% Receiving Financial Aid: 99%
Admission: Non-selective
Application Deadline: September 1

Admission. Graduates of accredited high schools with "satisfactory academic records" eligible; others admitted by examination; 65% of applicants accepted, 36% of these actually enroll. About 35% of freshmen graduate in top fifth of high school class, 70% in top two-fifths. Average freshman scores: SAT, 380 verbal, 380 mathematical; ACT, 18 composite. *Required:* SAT or ACT; minimum high school GPA, interview required. Criteria considered in admission, in order of importance: recommendations, high school academic record, extracurricular activities, standardized test scores; other factors considered: special talents, alumni children, diverse student body. *Entrance programs:* early admission, midyear admission. *Apply* by September 1; rolling admissions. *Transfers* welcome; 185.

Academic Environment. Degrees offered: bachelors. Specific courses and distribution requirements vary with department. About 35% of students entering as freshmen graduate eventually, 60% of freshmen return for sophomore year. *Special programs:* CLEP, internships, January Term, independent study, honors, 3-year degree. *Calendar:* semester, summer school.

Undergraduate degrees conferred (112). 40% were in Business and Management, 17% were in Education, 10% were in Allied Health, 6% were in Psychology, 5% were in Communications, 4% were in Computer and Engineering Related Technology, 4% were in Visual and Performing Arts, 4% were in Social Sciences, 4% were in Mathematics, 3% were in Life Sciences, remainder in 3 other fields.

Faculty. About 35% of faculty hold PhD or equivalent. About 40% of teaching faculty are female; 1% Black, 1% Hispanic, 5% other minority.

Student Body. About 65% of students from in state; 90% Midwest, 5% South, 2% Middle Atlantic, 1% each New England, West, 1% foreign. An estimated 15% of students are reported as Black, 5% Hispanic, 2% Asian, 8% other minority.

Religious Orientation. Missouri Valley is a church-related institution; 1% of students affiliated with the church; no religious course study required.

Varsity Sports. Men (NAIA Div.II): Baseball, Basketball, Cross Country, Football, Soccer, Track, Volleyball, Wrestling. Women (NAIA Div.II): Basketball, Cross Country, Soccer, Softball, Track, Volleyball.

Campus Life. About 50% of men, 59% of women live in traditional dormitories; no coed dormitories; 30% of men, 21% of women live in off-campus housing or commute. Intervisitation in men's and women's dormitory rooms limited. There are 3 fraternities, 3 sororities on campus which about 20% of men, 2% of women join; 20% of each live in fraternities and sororities. About 25% of resident students leave campus on weekends.

Annual Costs. Tuition and fees, $9,100: room and board, $4,950; estimated $1,500 other, exclusive of travel. About 99% of students receive financial aid; average amount of assistance, $4,000. University reports 500 scholarships awarded on the basis of academic merit alone, 500 for special talents alone, 500 for need alone.

Missouri Western State College

St. Joseph, Missouri 64507 (816) 271-4200

A state-supported institution, Missouri Western is located in a city of 77,888. Most convenient major airport: Kansas City International.

Founded: 1915
Affiliation: State/District
UG Enrollment: 1,488 M, 2,127 W (full-time); 540 M, 966 W (part-time)
Cost: < $10K
% Receiving Financial Aid: 75%
Admission: Non-selective
Application Deadline: August 1

Admission. Graduates of accredited Missouri high schools admitted; 99% of applicants accepted, 79% of these actually enroll; 20% of freshmen graduate in top fifth of high school class. Average freshman ACT scores: 19 composite. *Required:* ACT. *Out-of-state* freshman applicants: college actively seeks students from out-of-state. State does not limit out-of-state enrollment. No special requirements for out-of-state applicants. States from which most out-of-state students are drawn include Iowa, Kansas, Nebraska, Illinois, California, Florida. *Entrance programs:* midyear admission, advanced placement. *Apply* by August 1. *Transfers* welcome; 358 enrolled 1993–94.

Academic Environment. Degrees offered: associates, bachelors. Graduation requirements include 4 credit hours in physical education, 8–10 in natural sciences, 9–10 in humanities, 9 in social sciences, 6 in English composition, 3 in algebra, 3 in speech communications. About 40% of students entering as freshmen graduate eventually, 55% of freshmen return for sophomore year. *Special programs:* CLEP, intersession, independent study, study abroad, honors, internships, 3–2 in engineering. *Calendar:* semester, summer school.

Undergraduate degrees conferred (477). 22% were in Education, 21% were in Business and Management, 10% were in Health Sciences, 8% were in Protective Services, 7% were in Psychology, 6% were in Social Sciences, 4% were in Parks and Recreation, 3% were in Life Sciences, 3% were in Letters, remainder in 11 other fields.

Graduates Career Data. Advanced studies pursued by 22% of graduates; 7% enter graduate school; 4% enter business school; 1% enter medical school; 1% enter law school. About 90% of 1992–93 graduates employed. Fields typically hiring largest numbers of graduates include law enforcement, public schools, hospitals. Career Development Services available.

Faculty. About 65% of faculty hold PhD or equivalent. About 75% of undergraduate classes taught by tenured faculty. About 33% of teaching faculty are female; 1% Black, 1% Hispanic, 5% other minority.

Student Body. About 91% of students from in state; 95% Midwest, 1% each Middle Atlantic, South, West. An estimated 6% of students reported as Black, 1% Hispanic, 1% Asian, 2% other minority. Average age of undergraduate student: 26.

Varsity Sports. Men (Div.II): Baseball, Basketball, Football, Golf. Women (Div.II): Basketball, Soccer, Volleyball.

Campus Life. About 17% of each live in traditional and coed dormitories; rest commute. Intervisitation in men's and women's dormitory rooms not limited; sexes segregated by suites. There are 4 fraternities, 3 sororities on campus, which about 4% of men, 2% of women join; fraternities and sororities provide no residence facilities. About 50% of resident students leave campus on weekends.

Annual Costs. Tuition and fees, $1,930 (out-of-state, $3,676); room and board, $2,454; estimated $2,000 other, exclusive of travel. About 75% of students receive financial aid.

Mobile College

(See University of Mobile)

University of Mobile

Mobile, Alabama 36663-0220(205) 675-5990

A church-related, liberal arts college, located near a city of 210,000. Most convenient major airport: Mobile.

Founded: 1963
Affiliation: Southern Baptist
UG Enrollment: 560 M, 866 W (full-time); 73 M, 228 W (part-time)
Total Enrollment: 1,879
Cost: < $10K
% Receiving Financial Aid: 96%
Admission: Non-selective
Application Deadline: Aug. 30

Admission. Graduates of accredited high schools, with minimum 2.0 GPA in 13 units of academic subjects, eligible; 73% of applicants accepted, 81% of these actually enroll; 25% of entering freshmen graduate in top fifth of high school class, 73% in top two-fifths. Average freshmen ACT scores: 20 composite. *Required:* SAT or ACT; interview recommended. Criteria considered in admission, in order of importance: standardized test scores, high school academic record, extracurricular activities; other factors considered: special talents, alumni children, diverse student body, religious affiliation and/or commitment. *Entrance programs:* early admission, midyear admission, advanced placement. *Apply* by August 30. *Transfers* welcome; 265 enrolled 1993–94.

Academic Environment. Graduation requirements include 60 hours in general liberal arts curriculum. Degrees offered: associates, bachelors, masters. New and unusual majors offered include religion/concentration in youth ministry, foreign languages, environmental technology. Small classes, accessible faculty cited as strengths of the academic program; schools of Nursing, Education, Music, and computer science program considered strong. Learning Center offers free tutoring in math, English, and foreign languages. Average undergraduate class size: 63% under 20, 31% 20–40, 6% over 40. About 70% of students entering as freshmen graduate within four years; 75% eventually. *Special programs:* CLEP, independent study, individualized majors, 3–2 engineering, pharmacy, law, and allied health. Adult programs: Degree Completion Program for persons over 25 with at least two years completed college work. *Calendar:* semester, summer school.

Undergraduate degrees conferred (134). 19% were in Health Sciences, 17% were in Education, 16% were in Business and Management, 8% were in Philosophy and Religion, 7% were in Communications, 6% were in Social Sciences, 4% were in Letters, 4% were in Computer and Engineering Related Technology, 4% were in Visual and Performing Arts, 4% were in Physical Sciences, 3% were in Mathematics, remainder in 6 other fields.

Graduates Career Data. Advanced studies pursued by 28% of graduates; 10% enter graduate school; 4% enter medical school; 4% enter business school; 1% enter law school. Fields typically hiring largest numbers of graduates include health related education, computer, business. Career Development Services include seminars, job fairs, testing, counseling, resume writing, library with written materials and films.

Faculty. About 65% of faculty hold PhD or equivalent. About 21% of undergraduate classes taught by tenured faculty. About 62% of teaching faculty are female; 2% Black, 4% Hispanic, 1% other minority.

Student Body. About 85% of students from within state; 91% South, 1% each New England, Middle Atlantic, Midwest, West, 4% foreign. An estimated 82% of students reported as Protestant, 8% Catholic, 1% unaffiliated, 8% other; 12% Black, 1% Hispanic, Asian, 1% other minority. Average age of undergraduate student: 27.

Religious Orientation. Mobile is a church-related institution; 59% of students affiliated with the church; 2 courses in religion required of all students.

Varsity Sports. Men (NAIA): Baseball, Basketball, Cross Country, Golf, Soccer, Tennis. Women (NAIA): Basketball, Cross Country, Golf, Soccer, Softball, Tennis.

Campus Life. Campus is located 10 miles from Mobile (pop. 210,000), in a residential area; most social life focused on campus activities; many students reported involved with local churches.

About 22% of men, 24% of women live in traditional dormitories; no coed dormitories; rest commute. No intervisitation in men's or women's dormitory rooms. There are no fraternities or sororities on campus. About 50% of resident students leave campus on weekends.

Annual Costs. Tuition and fees, $5,920; room and board, $3,480; estimated $1,600 other, exclusive of travel. About 96% of students receive financial aid; average amount of assistance, $2,500. Assistance is typically divided 36% scholarship, 35% grants, 25% loan, 4% work. College reports 3 scholarships awarded on the basis of academic merit alone, 13 for special talents alone.

Molloy College

Rockville Centre, New York 11560 (516) 678-5000

A Catholic, co-educational college, conducted by the Dominican Sisters, Molloy is located in a Long Island suburb, 29 miles from Manhattan. Most convenient major airports: JFK International or LaGuardia.

Founded: 1955
Affiliation: Roman Catholic
UG Enrollment: 248 M, 1,154 W (full-time); 88 M, 491 W (part-time)
Total Enrollment: 2,075
Cost: < $10K
% Receiving Financial Aid: 65%
Admission: Non-selective
Application Deadline: Rolling

Admission. High school graduates with minimum B- average eligible; 83% of applicants accepted, 46% of these actually enroll; 13% of freshmen graduate in top fifth of high school class, 48% in top two fifths. Average freshman scores: SAT, 442 M, 392 W verbal, 483 M, 423 W mathematical. *Required:* SAT or ACT, essay; interview optional. Criteria considered in admission, in order of importance: high school academic record, standardized test scores, recommendations, writing sample, extracurricular activities; other factors considered include special talents. *Entrance programs:* early decision, early admission, deferred admission, advanced placement. *Apply:* rolling admissions. *Transfers* welcome.

Academic Environment. Graduation requirements include 62 credits in liberal arts and science courses. Degrees offered: associates, bachelors, masters. *Majors offered* include accounting, cardiorespiratory sciences, computer science, gerontology, speech, social work, music therapy, education, nursing, international peace and justice. About 80% of students entering as freshmen graduate eventually; 96% of freshmen return for sophomore year. *Special programs:* CLEP, independent study, January interterm, cross-registration through LIRACHE, HEOP, remediation, internships, accelerated programs, freshman orientation course. Adult programs: social work, cardio-respiratory sciences. *Calendar:* 4–1–4, summer school.

Undergraduate degrees conferred (253). 28% were in Health Sciences, 13% were in Business and Management, 10% were in Letters, 10% were in Psychology, 9% were in Social Sciences, 8% were in Public Affairs, 5% were in Visual and Performing Arts, 4% were in Life Sciences, 4% were in Education, 3% were in Liberal/General Studies, 3% were in Allied Health, remainder in 4 other fields.

Graduates Career Data. Advanced studies pursued by 51% of graduates; 40% enter graduate school; 6% enter law school; 5% enter medical school. Fields typically hiring largest numbers of graduates include health, education, business. Career Development Services include career seminars, networking with alumni, Act Discover computer program, and individual career counseling.

Faculty. About 30% of faculty hold PhD or equivalent. About 70% of undergraduate classes taught by tenured faculty. About 76% of teaching faculty are female; 3% Black, 6% Hispanic, 2% other minority.

Student Body. About 98% students from in state. An estimated 66% of students reported as Catholic, 7% Protestant, 22% Jewish, 1% unaffiliated, 4% other, according to most recent data available. *Minority group students:* Higher Education Opportunity Program; corps of tutors. Average age of undergraduate student: 27.

Religious Orientation. Molloy is a Catholic institution; 9 credits in theology required of all students; no required religious services.

Varsity Sports. Men (Div.II): Baseball, Basketball, Cross Country, Equestrian, Golf. Women (Div.II): Basketball, Cross Country, Equestrian, Soccer, Softball, Tennis, Volleyball.

Campus Life. No housing facilities on campus; local housing available for noncommuting students. There are no fraternities or sororities on campus.

Annual Costs. Tuition and fees, $8,200; estimated $800 other, exclusive of travel. About 65% of students receive financial aid; average amount of assistance, $5,662. Assistance is typically divided 48% scholarship, 25% loan, 2% work. *Meeting Costs:* college offers New Hampshire Tuition Plan.

Monmouth College

Monmouth, Illinois 61462 (309) 457-2131

A church-related, liberal arts college, Monmouth is located in a community of 11,000, 180 miles southwest of Chicago. Most convenient major airports: Moline (IL) or Galesburg (IL).

Founded: 1853
Affiliation: Presbyterian Church (USA)
UG Enrollment: 325 M, 343 W (full-time)
Cost: $10K–$20K
% Receiving Financial Aid: 95%
Admission: Selective
Application Deadline: August 1

Admission is selective. About 82% of applicants accepted, 44% of these actually enroll; 25% of freshmen graduate in top tenth of high school class, 50% in top quarter. Average freshman ACT scores: 23 composite. *Required:* ACT, minimum 2.5 high school GPA, interview on- or off-campus. Criteria considered in admissions, in order of importance: high school academic record, standardized test scores, recommendations, writing sample, extracurricular activities. *Entrance programs:* early admission, midyear admission, advanced placement. About 5% of entering students from private schools, 10% from parochial schools. *Apply* by August 1; rolling admissions. *Transfers* welcome; 57 enrolled 1993–94.

Academic Environment. Administration reports a "carefully structured four-year curriculum, stressing coherence and purpose." Graduation requirements include completion of five components of the general education program: Language, The Physical Universe and its Life Forms, Beauty and Meaning in Works of Art, Human Societies, and Systems of Thought and Belief. Degrees offered: bachelors. *Majors offered* include business administration, computer science, education; nursing, medical technology with Rush Medical School, Chicago. Average undergraduate class size: 60% under 20, 40% 20–40, 2% over 40.

About 47% of students entering as freshmen graduate within four years, 53% eventually; 77% of freshmen return for sophomore year. *Special programs:* CLEP, independent study, study abroad, honors, undergraduate research, programs of ACM, geology in the Rocky Mountains, business internships, India studies, Washington Semester, urban studies, credit by examination. *Calendar:* 3–3, summer school.

Undergraduate degrees conferred (137). 20% were in Business and Management, 15% were in Letters, 10% were in Social Sciences, 10% were in Education, 9% were in Visual and Performing Arts, 7% were in Physical Sciences, 7% were in Life Sciences, 6% were in Foreign Languages, 5% were in Mathematics, 4% were in Psychology, 3% were in Liberal/General Studies, remainder in 2 other fields.

Graduates Career Data. Advanced studies pursued by 40% of graduates; 24% enter graduate school; 6% enter law school; 5% enter business school; 4% enter medical school; 1% enter dental school. Medical schools typically enrolling largest numbers of graduates include U. of Iowa; law schools include U. of Illinois; business schools include U. of Illinois; dental schools include Northwestern. About 50% of 1992–93 graduates employed. Fields typically hiring largest numbers of graduates include education, banks, investment, environmental. Career Development Services include workshops, career education course, DISCOVER program, individual career counseling.

Faculty. About 74% of faculty hold PhD or equivalent. About 60% of undergraduate classes taught by tenured faculty. About 32% of teaching faculty are female.

Student Body. About 81% of students from in state; 10% Midwest, 5% West, 3% South, 2% foreign. An estimated 3% of students reported as Black, 2% Hispanic, 5% Asian. *Minority group students:* Black Action and Affairs Council.

Religious Orientation. Monmouth is a church-related institution; religious studies optional under humanities and fine arts requirement.

Varsity Sports. Men (Div.III): Baseball, Basketball, Cross Country, Football, Soccer, Track, Wrestling. Women (Div.III): Basketball, Cross Country, Soccer, Softball, Volleyball.

Campus Life. Dormitories cater to variety of life styles; key system available to all students with consent of parents. Alcohol allowed in selected residential areas. All students, except commuters living at home or married students, required to live in college residence halls.

About 60% of men, 85% of women live in traditional dormitories; 10% of each men, women live in coed dormitories; 5% of each men, women commute. Sexes segregated in coed dormitories by room. There are 3 fraternities, 3 sororities on campus which about 40% of men, 40% of women join; 25% of men live in fraternities; sororities provide no residence facilities. About 15% of resident students leave campus on weekends.

Annual Costs. Tuition and fees, $13,000; room and board, $3,800; estimated $550 other, exclusive of travel. About 95% of students receive financial aid; average amount of assistance, $12,440. Assistance is typically divided 30% scholarship, 52% grant, 15% loan, 3% work. College reports 250 scholarships awarded on the basis of academic merit alone, 40 for special talents alone, 500 for need alone. *Meeting Costs:* college offers monthly payment plans, PLUS Loans.

Monmouth College

West Long Branch,
New Jersey 07764-1898 **(908) 571-3456**

A private, liberal arts and professional college, offering 45 graduate and undergraduate programs and concentrations, Monmouth is located on a 125-acre campus, in a town of 7,500. College is an hour and a half drive from both New York City and Philadelphia. Most convenient major airport: Newark International.

Founded: 1933	**Total Enrollment:** 4,197
Affiliation: Independent	**Cost:** $10K–$20K
UG Enrollment: 845 M, 1,082 W (full-time); 420 M, 616 W (part-time)	**% Receiving Financial Aid:** 60%
	Admission: Non-selective
	Application Deadline: March 1

Admission. Graduates of accredited high schools with 16 units eligible; 81% of applicants accepted, 27% of these actually enroll. About 18% of freshmen graduate in top fifth of high school class, 39% in top two-fifths. Average freshman SAT scores, according to most recent data available: 442 M, 433 W verbal, 499 M, 467 W mathematical. *Required:* SAT or ACT; interview recommended. *Non-academic factors* considered in admissions: special talents, diverse student body, alumni children, outside activities, community service. *Apply* by March 1. *Transfers* welcome.

Academic Environment. *Degrees:* BA, BS, BSN. *Majors offered* include business administration, computer science, software engineering, criminal justice, communications, electronic engineering, fine arts, medical technology, social work, education. *Special programs:* CLEP, honors, independent study, individualized majors, study abroad, January internships, Washington D.C. internship, combined BS/MBA program. Adult programs: Weekend College, large number of evening courses at undergraduate and graduate levels. *Calendar:* early semester, summer school, intersession.

Undergraduate degrees conferred (518). 44% were in Business and Management, 12% were in Communications, 8% were in Psychology, 6% were in Social Sciences, 5% were in Engineering, 4% were in Protective Services, 4% were in Computer and Engineering Related Technology, 3% were in Health Sciences, 3% were in Education, 3% were in Letters, remainder in 7 other fields.

Graduates Career Data. According to most recent data available, careers in business and industry pursued by 75–85% of graduates. Corporations typically hiring largest numbers of graduates include Coopers & Lybrand, Concurrent Computer, AT&T.

Faculty. About 70% of faculty hold PhD or equivalent.

Student Body. About 90% of students from within state. An estimated 4% of students reported as Black, 3% Hispanic, 2% Asian, 4% other minority, according to most recent data available.

Varsity Sports. Men (NCAA,Div.I): Baseball, Basketball, Cross Country, Golf, Soccer, Tennis, Track. Women (NCAA,Div.I): Basketball, Cross Country, Soccer, Softball, Tennis, Track.

Campus Life. Limited intervisitation. Rules on alcohol conform to state law; cars permitted. Freshmen under 21 must live in college residence halls.

About 23% of men, 26% of women live in traditional dormitories; 23% of men, 25% of women live in coed dormitories; rest live in off-campus housing or commute. Freshmen given preference in college housing if all students cannot be accommodated. Intervisitation in men's and women's dormitory rooms limited; determined by residents in coed dormitories. There are 5 fraternities, 5 sororities on campus which about 16% of men, 16% of women join.

Annual Costs. Tuition and fees, $11,820; room and board, $5,160. About 60% of students receive financial aid; assistance is typically divided 61% scholarship, 33% loan, 6% work. College reports some scholarships awarded on the basis of academic merit alone. *Meeting Costs:* college offers payment plans, institutional work-study.

Montana College of Mineral Science and Technology

Butte, Montana 59701-8997 **(406) 496-4178**

A state-supported college offering programs in the main branches of mineral industry, engineering science, business and computer science; located in a community of 40,000.Most convenient major airport: Bert Mooney Airport.

Founded: 1895
Affiliation: State
UG Enrollment: 953 M, 517 W (full-time); 184 M, 232 W (part-time)
Total Enrollment: 1,992
Cost: < $10K
% Receiving Financial Aid: 54%
Admission: Non-selective
Application Deadline: August 2

Admission. Graduates of accredited high schools with minimum GPA in college preparatory curriculum eligible; 95% of applicants accepted, 59% of these actually enroll; 41% of freshmen graduate in the top fifth of their high school class, 68% in top two-fifths. Average freshman scores: SAT, 467 M, 431 W verbal, 573 M, 510 W mathematical; ACT, 23 M, 21 W composite. *Required:* ACT or SAT; minimum high school GPA. Criteria considered in admission, in order of importance: standardized test scores, high school academic record, class size and rank, recommendations. *Out-of-state* freshman applicants: university actively seeks out-of-state students. State does not limit out-of-state enrollment. About 84% of out-of-state applicants accepted, 62% of these actually enroll. States from which most out-of-state students are drawn include Wyoming, Idaho, Washington, Nevada. *Entrance programs:* early admission, advanced placement. *Apply* by August 2; rolling admissions. *Transfers* welcome; 136 enrolled 1993–94.

Academic Environment. Degrees offered: bachelors, masters. Graduation requirements include 6 hours each of communications, humanities, physical and life sciences, social sciences, 5 hours of mathematical sciences. Administration source notes that campus is surrounded by mineral deposits which "creates a real life laboratory for many of our students in the minerals, energy, and materials processing areas." She also notes "we have a great occupational safety and health program." Average undergraduate class size: 62% under 20, 24% 20–40, 14% over 40. About 40% of students entering as freshmen graduate within four years; 66% of freshmen return for sophomore year. *Special programs:* CLEP, independent study, internships, co-operative education. *Calendar:* early semester, summer field work.

Undergraduate degrees conferred (158). 55% were in Engineering, 15% were in Computer and Engineering Related Technology, 13% were in Multi/Interdisciplinary Studies, 7% were in Engineering and Engineering Related Technology, 6% were in Business and Management, 3% were in Mathematics, remainder in Physical Sciences.

Graduates Career Data. About 95% of 1992–93 graduates employed. Fields typically hiring largest numbers of graduates include petroleum engineering, environmental engineering, occupational safety and health, industrial hygiene, and mining engineering. Career Development Services include career counseling and testing, job search preparation and training, job announcement mailings, job opportunities.

Faculty. About 69% of faculty hold PhD or equivalent. About 75% of undergraduate classes taught by tenured faculty. About 14% of teaching faculty are female; 7% minority.

Student Body. About 81% of students from in state. An estimated 93% of students reported as Catholic, 6% Protestant; 1% each as Black, Hispanic, Asian. Average age of undergraduate student: 25.

Varsity Sports. Men (NAIA Div.I): Basketball, Football. Women (NAIA Div.I): Basketball, Volleyball.

Campus Life. Student reports "Being in the mountains, Tech is very social considering the climate. There is a lot of snow and cold here during the winter." Socializing and intramural sports occupy leisure time on campus; hiking, fishing, skiing, and other outdoor activities take students off campus; religious groups, church, movies and bowling also enjoyed.

About 85% of students live in coed dormitories; 13% live in off-campus college-related housing; 2% commute. Freshmen given preference in college housing if all students cannot be accommodated. Sexes segregated in coed dormitories by floor. There are no fraternities or sororities on campus.

Annual Costs. Tuition and fees, $1,767 (out-of-state, $5,743); room and board, $3,210; estimated $1,500 other, exclusive of travel. About 54% of students receive financial aid; average amount of assistance, $3,339. Assistance is typically divided 22% scholarship, 28% grant, 40% loan, 10% work. College reports 88 scholarships awarded on the basis of academic merit alone, 5 for special talents alone.

Montana State University

Bozeman, Montana 59717 (406) 994-4390

A state-supported, land-grant university, Montana State is located in a town of 35,000 (including students), 135 miles west of Billings. Most convenient major airport: Gallatin Field (8 miles away).

Founded: 1893
Affiliation: State
UG Enrollment: 4,896 M, 3,864 W (full-time); 573 M, 581 W (part-time)
Total Enrollment: 10,798
Cost: < $10K
% Receiving Financial Aid: 70%
Admission: Non-selective
Application Deadline: July 1

Admission. Graduates of accredited high schools who meet college prep requirements and rank in top half of class or have a minimum GPA of 2.5 or minimum ACT of 22 are admitted to regular standing; 81% of applicants accepted, 51% of these actually enroll; 34% of freshmen graduate in top fifth of high school class, 65% in top two-fifths. Average freshmen scores: SAT, 451 M, 451 W verbal, 535 M, 500 W mathematical; ACT 23.4 M, 22.2 W composite. *Required:* SAT or ACT. Criteria considered in admission, in order of importance: high school academic record, standardized test scores, recommendations, extracurricular activities; other factors considered: special talents, diverse student body. *Out-of-state* freshman applicants: university actively seeks out-of-state students. State does not limit out-of-state enrollment. About 65% of out-of-state applicants accepted, 37% of these actually enroll. States from which most out-of-state students are drawn include Wyoming, Minnesota, Colorado, North Dakota, Washington, Alaska, California. *Entrance programs:* deferred admission, advanced placement. *Apply* by July 1; rolling admissions. *Transfers* welcome; 893 enrolled 1993–94.

Academic Environment. Many university programs "attuned to the region." Administration reports percent of courses required for graduation that are elective varies with major. *Undergraduate studies* offered by colleges of Letters and Science, Agriculture, Art and Architecture, Business, Education, Health & Human Development, Engineering, Nursing. Degrees offered: bachelors, masters, doctoral. *Majors offered* include anthropology, communication, computer science, environmental health, fish and wildlife management, geography, geophysics, medical technology, microbiology, social justice, abused land management, watershed management. Average undergraduate class size: 39% under 20, 36% 20–40, 25% over 40.

About 69% of freshmen return for sophomore year. *Special programs:* CLEP, honors, interdisciplinary majors, independent study, study abroad, undergraduate research, domestic student exchange with 19 other institutions, Washington Semester, Latin American studies, Asian studies, American Indian Research Opportunities, WAMI (medical education). *Calendar:* semester.

Undergraduate degrees conferred (1,480). 15% were in Education, 13% were in Business and Management, 13% were in Engineering, 7% were in Engineering and Engineering Related Technology, 6% were in Health Sciences, 6% were in Visual and Performing Arts, 5% were in Social Sciences, 4% were in Letters, 4% were in Home Economics, 4% were in Life Sciences, 4% were in Agribusiness and Agricultural Production, 3% were in Agricultural Sciences, 3% were in Protective Services, remainder in 10 other fields.

Graduates Career Data. About 53% of 1992–93 graduates employed. Career Development Services available.

Faculty. About 73% of faculty hold PhD or equivalent. About 58% of undergraduate classes taught by tenured and tenure track faculty. About 31% of teaching faculty are female; 3% minority.

Student Body. About 64% of students from in state; 20% Northwest, 12% West, 1% Midwest, 3% foreign. Average age of undergraduate student: 23. *Minority group students:* special advisers work directly with American Indians and foreign students; Center for Native American Studies, Women's Resource Center on campus.

Varsity Sports. Men (Div.I): Basketball, Cross Country, Football, Tennis, Indoor Track, Outdoor Track. Women (Div.I): Basketball, Cross Country, Golf, Skiing, Tennis, Indoor Track, Outdoor Track, Volleyball.

Campus Life. Student leader, speaking of "disarming openness" of people on campus, reports visitor "can expect a greeting and a smile from at least 50% of students here." Student body reported to be "somewhat conservative" and oriented to outdoor activities such as skiing, camping, rafting.

About 28% of men, 23% of women live in traditional or coed dormitories; 64% of men, 72% of women live in off-campus housing or commute. Freshmen are required to live in dormitories. There are 10 fraternities, 5 sororities on campus in which about 8% men, 5% women join; 8% of men, 5% of women live in fraternities and sororities.
Annual Costs. Tuition and fees, $2,002 (out-of-state $5,978); room and board, $3,532; estimated $1,900 other, exclusive of travel. About 70% of students receive financial aid; average amount of assistance, $4,465. Assistance is typically divided 5% scholarship, 15% grant, 70% loan, 10% work. University reports 600 scholarships awarded on the basis of academic merit alone, 300 for special talents alone, 250 for need alone.

University of Montana

Missoula, Montana 59812 (406) 243-6266

A state-supported university, Montana is located on a 116-acre campus in a town of 50,000, 110 miles west of Helena. Most convenient major airport: Missoula.

Founded: 1893
Affiliation: State
UG Enrollment: 3,324 M, 3,455 W (full-time); 428 M, 548 W (part-time)
Total Enrollment: 10,788
Cost: < $10K
% Receiving Financial Aid: 80%
Admission: Non-selective
Application Deadline: Rolling

Admission. Montana graduates of accredited high schools eligible; 93% of applicants accepted, 67% of these actually enroll. *Required:* ACT or SAT. *Out-of-state* freshman applicants: university seeks students from out of state. State does not limit out-of-state enrollment. Requirement for out-of-state applicants: GPA of 2.5 or rank in top half of class or equivalent level of competence on ACT or SAT. Non-academic factor considered in admissions: alumni children. *Apply* one month prior to registration. *Transfers* welcome.
Academic Environment. *Undergraduate studies* offered by College of Arts and Sciences, schools of Business Administration, Education, Fine Arts, Forestry, Journalism, Pharmacy. *Majors offered* include anthropology, computer science, geography, medical technology, microbiology, physical therapy, recreation, speech pathology and audiology, social work, wildlife biology. University has eliminated mandatory physical education. Language study made a departmental option. About 20% of students entering as freshmen graduate within four years. *Special programs:* CLEP, honors, independent study, study abroad, credit by examination. *Calendar:* quarter, summer school.
Undergraduate degrees conferred (1,067). 27% were in Business and Management, 13% were in Social Sciences, 12% were in Education, 8% were in Letters, 5% were in Renewable Natural Resources, 5% were in Psychology, 4% were in Public Affairs, 4% were in Life Sciences, 4% were in Communications, 3% were in Visual and Performing Arts, remainder in 10 other fields.
Faculty. About 80% of faculty hold PhD or equivalent.
Student Body. About 81% of students from in state. An estimated 2% of students reported as Native American, 1% other minority, according to most recent data available.
Varsity Sports. Men (Div.I): Basketball, Cross Country, Football (IAA), Tennis, Track. Women (Div.I): Basketball, Cross Country, Tennis, Track, Volleyball.
Campus Life. Students may opt for a specific hall with acceptance of hall's living option. Intervisitation in men's and women's traditional dormitory rooms limited, unlimited depending on dormitory. Alcohol forbidden on campus except in dormitory rooms; cars allowed.

About 20% of men, 19% of women live in traditional or coed dormitories; 5% of men, 6% of women live in off-campus housing; 70% of men, 72% of women commute. Sexes segregated in coed dormitories by floor. There are 8 fraternities, 5 sororities on campus which about 5% of men, 3% of women join; 5% of men, 3% of women live in fraternities and sororities.
Annual Costs. Tuition and fees, $1,962 (out-of-state, $5,854); room and board, $3,600. About 80% of students receive financial aid; assistance is typically divided 38% scholarship, 38% loan, 24% work. University reports that some scholarships awarded on the basis of academic merit alone.

Montclair State College

(See Montclair State University)

Montclair State University

Upper Montclair, New Jersey 07043 (201) 655-4000

A state-supported, liberal arts, and teacher education institution, located in a town of 44,000, 15 miles west of New York City. Most convenient major airport: Newark International.

Founded: 1908
Affiliation: State
UG Enrollment: 2,587 M, 3,818 W (full-time); 1,048 M, 2,135 W (part-time)
Total Enrollment: 13,203
Cost: < $10K
% Receiving Financial Aid: 60%
Admission: Selective
Application Deadline: March 1

Admission is selective. About 41% of applicants accepted, 41% of these actually enroll; 47% of freshmen graduate in top fifth of high school class, 90% in top two-fifths. Average freshman SAT scores: 30% of freshmen score above 500 on verbal, 3% above 600; 68% score above 500 on mathematical, 13% above 600, 1% above 700. *Required:* SAT. Criteria considered in admissions, in order of importance: high school academic record, standardized test scores, recommendations, extracurricular activities, writing sample; other factors considered: special talents. *Out-of-state* freshman applicants: college actively seeks students from out-of-state. State does not limit out-of-state enrollment. No special requirements for out-of-state applicants. States from which most out-of-state students are drawn include New York, Pennsylvania. *Entrance programs:* midyear admission, advanced placement. *Apply* by March 1; rolling admissions. *Transfers* welcome; 560 enrolled 1993–94.
Academic Environment. Student body is characterized as being overwhelmingly concerned with vocational/professional goals. Graduation requirements include 40 semester hours in communication, contemporary issues, fine and performing arts, foreign language, humanities, mathematics, natural and physical sciences, and physical education. Degrees offered: bachelors, masters. *Majors offered* include interdisciplinary transcultural studies; extensive teacher education curricula; biochemistry, molecular biology. Average undergraduate class size: 30% under 20, 30% 20–40, 40% over 40.

About 23% of students entering as freshmen graduate within four years, 55% eventually; 84% of freshmen return for sophomore year. *Special programs:* CLEP, January interterm, study abroad, honors, urban studies program, internships/cooperative work/study. Adult programs: The Second Careers Program offers full- and part-time programs to adults over 25. *Calendar:* 4–1–4, summer school.
Undergraduate degrees conferred (1,488). 30% were in Business and Management, 14% were in Social Sciences, 10% were in Visual and Performing Arts, 10% were in Psychology, 9% were in Letters, 7% were in Home Economics, 7% were in Education, 3% were in Life Sciences, remainder in 9 other fields.
Graduate Career Data. Career Development Services include assisting students with all phases of career development from choosing a major, finding part-time work, planning long-range career goals, and obtaining full-time work upon graduation.
Faculty. About 85% of faculty hold PhD or equivalent. About 38% of teaching faculty are female; 7% Black, 5% Hispanic, 7% other minority.
Student Body. About 97% of students from in state; 1% Middle Atlantic, 2% foreign. An estimated 9% of students reported as Black, 12% Hispanic, 3% Asian, 9% other minority. *Minority group students:* financial, academic, and social help available. Average age of undergraduate student: 24.
Varsity Sports. Men (Div.III): Baseball, Basketball, Cross Country, Football, Golf, Lacrosse, Soccer, Swimming/Diving, Tennis, Track, Wrestling. Women (Div.III): Basketball, Field Hockey, Soccer, Softball, Swimming/Diving, Tennis, Track, Volleyball.
Campus Life. Leave of absence for 1 or 2 semesters, with guaranteed readmission, available to students in good academic standing. Alcohol permitted in accordance with state law. Campus life influ-

enced by high percentage of commuters. Nearest major cultural center is New York, 15 miles from campus. Cars allowed.

About 5% each of men, women live in traditional dormitories; 5% each live in coed dormitories; rest commute. Freshmen given preference in college housing if all students cannot be accommodated. Sexes segregated in coed dormitories by wing or suite. There are 13 fraternities, 13 sororities which about 7% of men, 4% of women join; they provide no residence facilities.

Annual Costs. Tuition and fees, $2,845 (out-of-state, $4,016); room and board, $4,694; estimated $1,650 other, exclusive of travel. About 60% of students receive financial aid; average amount of assistance, $4,000. Assistance is typically divided 54% grants, 2% scholarship, 42% loan, 2% work. College reports 180 scholarships awarded on the basis of academic merit alone.

University of Montevallo

Montevallo, Alabama 35115 **(205) 665-6030**

A state-supported university, located in a town of 4,000, 32 miles south of Birmingham.

Founded: 1896
Affiliation: State
UG Enrollment: 777 M, 1,610 W (full-time); 119 M, 212 W (part-time)
Total Enrollment: 3,315
Cost: < $10K
% Receiving Financial Aid: 60%
Admission: Non-selective
Application Deadline: July 31

Admission. Graduates of accredited high schools with 15 units (11 in academic subjects) and minimum high school GPA of 2.0 eligible; 66% of applicants accepted, 55% of these actually enroll; 35% of freshmen graduate in top fifth of high school class, 80% in top two-fifths. Average freshmen ACT: 21.8 M, 21.4 W. *Required:* ACT or SAT. Criteria considered in admission, in order of importance: high school academic record, standardized test scores, extracurricular activities, recommendations; other factors considered: special talents, alumni children, diverse student body. *Out-of-state* freshman applicants: university actively seeks students from out-of-state. State does not limit out-of-state enrollment. No special requirements for out-of-state applicants. *Entrance programs:* early decision, early admission, midyear admission, deferred admission, advanced placement. *Apply* by July 31; rolling admissions. *Transfers* welcome; 294 enrolled 1993–94.

Academic Environment. Degrees offered: bachelors, masters. Graduation requirements include 6 hours in composition, 3 in speech, 6 in world literature, 6 in world civilization, 3 in fine arts, 1–3 in computer science, 7 in science, 3 in math, 6 in Institutions and Issues, 3 in Human Behavior Inquiry, 12 in writing reinforcement, and 4 in health and physical education. Average undergraduate class size: 10% under 20, 80% 20–40, 10% over 40.

About 42% of students entering as freshmen graduate eventually; 70% of freshmen return for sophomore year. *Special programs:* CLEP, study abroad, honors, undergraduate research, independent study, 3–2 engineering, mathematics. *Calendar:* semester, summer session.

Undergraduate degrees conferred (401). 27% were in Education, 20% were in Business and Management, 12% were in Social Sciences, 8% were in Letters, 6% were in Visual and Performing Arts, 5% were in Health Sciences, 5% were in Communications Technologies, 5% were in Psychology, 5% were in Home Economics, remainder in 6 other fields.

Graduate Career Data. Advanced studies pursued by 21% of graduates; 18% enter graduate school; less than 1% enter medical school, law school, business school. About 20% of 1992–93 graduates employed. Fields typically hiring largest numbers of graduates include business, education, speech pathology. Career Development Services include career assessment inventories, resource center, job seeking skills training and on campus interviews.

Faculty. About 71% of faculty hold PhD or equivalent. About 48% of teaching faculty are female; 6% Black, 6% other minority.

Student Body. About 95% of students from in state; all from South. An estimated 10% of students reported as Black, 1% other minority.

Varsity Sports. Men: Baseball, Basketball, Golf. Women: Basketball, Volleyball.

Campus Life. About 38% of men, 41% of women live in traditional dormitories; rest commute. Freshmen given preference in college housing if all students cannot be accommodated. Intervisitation in men's and women's dormitory rooms limited. There are 7 fraternities, 7 sororities on campus which about 23% of men, 23% of women join; they provide no residence facilities. About 75% of resident students leave campus on weekends.

Annual Costs. Tuition and fees, $2,280 (out-of-state, $4,480); room and board, $3,000; estimated $1,000 other, exclusive of travel. About 50% of students receive financial aid; average amount of assistance, $3,200. Assistance is typically divided 10% scholarship, 22% grant, 50% loan, 18% work. University reports 300 scholarships awarded on the basis of academic merit alone, 70 for special talents alone, 100 for need alone.

Moody Bible Institute

Chicago, Illinois 60610

A non-denominational Bible college, offering associates, bachelors and masters degrees in Christian ministry.

Founded: 1886 **Affiliation:** Independent

Moore College of Art

Philadelphia, Pennsylvania 19103

The only women's art college in the U.S., Moore offers a BFA in 12 fields of fine and applied arts and a certification program in art teacher education.

Founded: 1844 **Affiliation:** Independent

Undergraduate degrees conferred (152). 72% were in Visual and Performing Arts, 14% were in Architecture and Environmental Design, 11% were in Home Economics, 3% were in Multi/Interdisciplinary Studies.

Moorhead State University

Moorhead, Minnesota 56563 **(218) 236-2161**

A state-supported college, located in a city of 29,700, adjoining Fargo, North Dakota. University participates in cooperative study program with North Dakota State University and nearby Concordia College. Most convenient major airport: Hector International (Fargo, ND).

Founded: 1885
Affiliation: State
UG Enrollment: 2,440 M, 3,812 W (full-time); 233 M, 420 W (part-time)
Total Enrollment: 7,552
Cost: < $10K
% Receiving Financial Aid: 69%
Admission: Selective
Application Deadline: Aug. 15

Admission is selective. About 95% of applicants accepted, 60% of these actually enroll; 32% of freshmen graduate in top fifth of high school class, 69% in top two-fifths. Average freshman ACT scores: 22.1 M, 21.5 W composite. *Required:* ACT; rank in top 50% of class. Criteria considered in admission, in order of importance: high school academic record, standardized test scores, recommendations; other factors considered: diverse student body. *Out-of-state* freshman applicants: university actively seeks out-of-state students. State does not limit out-of-state enrollment. No special admissions requirements for out-of-state applicants. States from which most out-of-state students are drawn include North Dakota, South Dakota. *Entrance programs:* early decision, early admission, midyear admission, deferred admission, advanced placement. *Apply* by August 15; rolling admissions. *Transfers* welcome; 936 enrolled 1993–94.

Academic Environment. Degrees offered: bachelors, masters. Graduation requirements include 2 courses in English composition and literature, 3 in natural sciences, 3 in social sciences, 3 in humanities, 3 in communication and symbolic process, 2 in cultural diversity. In addition to its baccalaureate programs, University offers master's degree programs in Business Administration, Liberal Arts or

Science, and a master's or specialist degree in Educational Administration with North Dakota State/Concordia College. *Majors offered* include computer science, cytotechnology, music industry, energy management, dual major in English and Speech Communication/Theater Arts. Average undergraduate class size: 5% under 20, 65% 20–40, 30% over 40.

About 48% of students entering as freshmen graduate eventually; 77% of freshmen return for sophomore year. *Special programs:* CLEP, independent study, study abroad, honors, undergraduate research, individualized majors, cross registration with North Dakota State U. and Concordia, National Student Exchange, campus in Akita, Japan. Adult programs: external studies program provides night and weekend courses for students. *Calendar:* quarter, summer school.

Undergraduate degrees conferred (1,457). 27% were in Education, 27% were in Business and Management, 6% were in Communications, 5% were in Public Affairs, 4% were in Social Sciences, 4% were in Protective Services, 3% were in Visual and Performing Arts, 3% were in Letters, 3% were in Psychology, 3% were in Health Sciences, remainder in 13 other fields.

Graduates Career Data. Career Development Services include counseling, resume workshops, interview skills, on campus recruitment and placement information.

Faculty. About 66% of faculty hold PhD or equivalent. About 32% of teaching faculty are female; 4% Black, 1% Hispanic, 7% other minority.

Student Body. About 66% of students from in state; 98% Midwest, 1% each West, foreign. An estimated 4% of students reported as minorities. Average age of undergraduate student: 24.

Varsity Sports. Men (Div.II): Basketball, Cross Country, Football, Golf, Tennis, Track, Wrestling. Women (Div.II): Basketball, Cross Country, Golf, Softball, Tennis, Track, Volleyball.

Campus Life. About 40% of men, 45% of women live in traditional and coed dormitories; 59% of men, 54% of women commute. Intervisitation in men's and women's dormitory rooms limited. Sexes segregated in coed dormitories by floor. There is 1 fraternity and 2 sororities on campus which about 1% each of men, women join and live. About 40% of resident students leave campus on weekends.

Annual Costs. Tuition and fees, $2,400 (out-of-state, $4,700); room and board, $2,664; estimated $1,200 other, exclusive of travel. About 69% of students receive financial aid; average amount of assistance, $2,700. Assistance is typically divided 37% grant, 50% loan, 13% work. University reports 193 scholarships awarded on the basis of academic merit alone, 169 for special talents alone.

Moravian College

Bethlehem, Pennsylvania 18018 **(215) 861-1320**

A church-related, liberal arts college, located in a city of 75,000, 55 miles north of Philadelphia and 90 miles west of New York City. Most convenient major airport: Allentown-Bethlehem-Easton.

Founded: 1742
Affiliation: Moravian
UG Enrollment: 576 M, 595 W (full-time)
Cost: $10K–$20K
% Receiving Financial Aid: 82%
Admission: Selective
Application Deadline: March 1

Admission is selective. About 76% of applicants accepted, 32% of these actually enroll; 46% of freshmen graduate in top fifth of high school class, 83% in top two-fifths. Average freshman scores: SAT, 38% score above 500 on verbal, 8% above 600; 64% score above 500 on mathematical, 20% above 600, 2% above 700; ACT, 25 composite. *Required:* SAT, essay; interview recommended. Criteria considered in admission, in order of importance: high school academic record, recommendations, standardized test scores, extracurricular activities, writing sample; other factors considered: special talents, alumni children, diverse student body. *Entrance programs:* early decision, early admission, midyear admission, deferred admission, advanced placement. About 15% of entering students from private schools, 25% from parochial schools. *Apply* by March 1. *Transfers* welcome; 83 enrolled 1993–94.

Academic Environment. Effort made to balance liberal learning with preparation for careers. Student representatives are voting members of college committees and serve on board of trustees. Concerned faculty, challenging courses, and diversity of majors cited as strengths of academic program. Graduation requirements: students have the option of 3 liberal arts programs: Core Curriculum, Guidelines for Liberal Studies, Add-Venture. *Degrees:* bachelors, masters. *Majors offered* include computer science, criminal justice, management, accounting, journalism, graphic and advertising design, elementary and secondary education, and several optional tracks in music, psychology, and international management. Average undergraduate class size: 40% under 20, 55% 20–40, 5% over 40.

About 70% of students entering as freshmen graduate within four years, 75% eventually; 88% of students entering as freshmen return for sophomore year. *Special programs:* CLEP, independent study, study abroad, honors, undergraduate research, January interterm (2 terms required), 3-year degree, individualized majors, field study, Washington Semester, cooperative programs including cross-registration through 6 colleges of Lehigh Valley Association, 3–2 engineering, 3–2 natural resources management, 3–2 allied health. *Library:* extensive music collection, map room. *Calendar:* 4–1–4, summer school.

Undergraduate degrees conferred (355). 27% were in Business and Management, 14% were in Social Sciences, 10% were in Education, 10% were in Psychology, 8% were in Letters, 7% were in Visual and Performing Arts, 6% were in Life Sciences, 6% were in Protective Services, 3% were in Mathematics, 3% were in Foreign Languages, remainder in 7 other fields.

Graduates Career Data. About 80% of 1992–93 graduates employed. Corporations typically hiring largest numbers of graduates include Merck, Air Products, AT&T, Bethlehem Steel. Career Development Services include counseling, resume writing assistance, mock interviews, seminars, on campus recruitment, job bank USA, SIGI Plus, and graduate and professional school fairs.

Faculty. About 92% of faculty hold PhD or equivalent. About 75% of undergraduate classes taught by tenured faculty. About 25% of teaching faculty are female; 1% Hispanic, 1% other minority.

Student Body. About 50% of students from in state; 87% Middle Atlantic, 8% New England, 2% South, 1% Midwest, 2% foreign. An estimated 46% of students reported as Catholic, 31% Protestant, 2% Jewish, 2% other; 1% Black, 2% Hispanic, 1% Asian. *Minority group students:* financial aid; counseling available.

Religious Orientation. Moravian is a church-related institution; 3% of students affiliated with the church; no religious course study required.

Varsity Sports. Men (NCAA Div.III): Baseball, Basketball, Cross Country, Football, Golf, Soccer, Tennis, Track, Wrestling. Women (NCAA Div.III): Basketball, Cross Country, Softball, Tennis, Track, Volleyball.

Campus Life. Variety of cultural and social activities available on campus and in Bethlehem and Allentown. Nearest major cultural centers are Philadelphia and New York, 55 and 90 miles, respectively, from campus. Dorms locked at midnight, but residents have keys; intervisitation limited: midnight on weeknights, 2 am on weekends. Use of alcohol restricted to those over 21; social hosts required to participate in workshop before holding social events. Cars allowed for all students, but parking reported as inadequate. Students expected to live in college residences, unless they live at home, but a limited number of upperclassmen may live off-campus.

About 2% of men, 12% of women live in traditional dormitories; 82% of men, 72% of women in coed dormitories; 2% each live in off-campus college-related housing; 10% each commute. Freshmen given preference in college housing if all students cannot be accommodated. There are 3 fraternities, 3 sororities on campus which about 25% of each, men and women join; 4% of each, men and women live in fraternities and sororities. About 20% of resident students leave campus on weekends.

Annual Costs. Tuition and fees, $14,490; room and board, $4,470; estimated $1,415 other, exclusive of travel. About 82% of students receive financial aid; average amount of assistance, $9,000. Assistance is typically divided 80% scholarship, 15% loan, 5% work. College reports some scholarships awarded on the basis of academic merit alone and need alone. *Meeting Costs:* college offers various payment plans.

Morehead State University

Morehead, Kentucky 40351 **(606) 783-2022**

A state-supported university, located in a community of 10,000, midway between Lexington and Ashland. Most convenient major airport: Lexington Bluegrass.

Founded: 1922
Affiliation: State
UG Enrollment: 2,832 M, 3,678 W (full-time); 261 M, 761 W (part-time)
Total Enrollment: 9,169
Cost: < $10K
% Receiving Financial Aid: 70%
Admission: Non-selective
Application Deadline: Rolling

Admission. Graduates of accredited Kentucky high schools who have completed the minimum educational preparation eligible; 88% of applicants accepted, 52% of these actually enroll. Average freshman ACT scores: 19.8 composite. *Required:* SAT or ACT. Criteria considered in admissions, in order of importance: standardized test scores, high school academic record. *Out-of-state* freshman applicants: university actively seeks students from out of state; no limits; no special requirements. States from which most out-of-state students are drawn: Ohio, Indiana, West Virginia. Entrance program: midyear admission. *Apply:* rolling admission. *Transfers* welcome.
Academic Environment. Degrees offered: associates, bachelors, masters. *Majors offered* include nursing, Spanish, veterinary technology. About 34% of students entering as freshmen graduate within five years; 64% of freshmen return for sophomore year. *Special programs:* cooperative education, television courses, correspondence courses, CLEP, study abroad, honors, individualized majors, pre-engineering, pre-optometry. *Calendar:* semester, summer school.
Undergraduate degrees conferred (843). 23% were in Education, 17% were in Business and Management, 10% were in Social Sciences, 8% were in Communications, 6% were in Engineering and Engineering Related Technology, 4% were in Health Sciences, 4% were in Liberal/General Studies, 4% were in Public Affairs, 3% were in Life Sciences, 3% were in Law, 3% were in Home Economics, 3% were in Visual and Performing Arts, 3% were in Letters, remainder in 10 other fields.
Faculty. About 59% of full-time faculty hold PhD. About 35% of full-time faculty are female.
Student Body. University seeks a national student body; 86% of students from in state. An estimated 3% of students reported as Black, 2% other ethnic minorities.
Varsity Sports. Men (Div.I): Baseball, Basketball, Cross Country, Football (I-AA), Golf, Soccer, Swimming, Tennis, Track. Women (Div.I): Basketball, Cross Country, Golf, Swimming, Tennis, Track, Volleyball.
Campus Life. About 45% of undergraduate students live in traditional or coed dormitories; rest commute. There are 14 fraternities, 7 sororities on campus, which about 20% of men, 20% of women join; they provide no residence facilities.
Annual Costs. Tuition and fees, $1,800 (out-of-state, $4,800); room and board, $2,800; estimated $1,350 other, exclusive of travel. About 70% of students receive financial aid. Assistance is typically divided 22% scholarship, 41% grant, 25% loan, 8% work. University reports some scholarships awarded on the basis of academic merit alone. *Meeting Costs:* university offers PLUS Loans, 10-month payment plan.

Morehouse College

Atlanta, Georgia 30314 (404) 681-2800

An independent college for men, Morehouse is located on a 30-acre campus near the center of a city of over a million. Affiliated with the Atlanta University Center, Morehouse was founded as a college for Negroes and still serves a predominantly Black student body. (See also Atlanta University Center.) Most convenient major airport: Atlanta International.

Founded: 1867
Affiliation: Independent
UG Enrollment: 2,983 M (full-time)
Cost: < $10K
Admission: Non-selective
Application Deadline: March 15

Admission. Graduates of approved high schools with 2.5 GPA and 12 units in specified academic courses eligible; 47% of applicants accepted, 57% of these actually enroll; 19% of freshmen graduate in top fifth of high school class, 88% in top two-fifths. *Required:* SAT or ACT. *Non-academic factors* considered in admissions: special talents, alumni children. *Apply* by March 15. *Transfers* welcome.
Academic Environment. *Degrees:* AB, BS. About 22% of general education requirements for graduation are elective; distribution requirements fairly numerous. About 50% of students entering as freshmen graduate eventually; 80% of freshmen return for sophomore year. *Special programs:* CLEP, independent study, study abroad, honors, individualized majors, dual degree programs in engineering with Georgia Tech., in law with Columbia. *Calendar:* early semester, summer school.
Undergraduate degrees conferred (339). 47% were in Business and Management, 11% were in Multi/Interdisciplinary Studies, 11% were in Social Sciences, 9% were in Psychology, 9% were in Computer and Engineering Related Technology, 4% were in Physical Sciences, 4% were in Letters, 3% were in Mathematics, remainder in 4 other fields.
Graduates Career Data. According to most recent data available, full-time graduate or professional study pursued by 40% of students immediately after graduation. *Careers in business and industry* pursued by 30% of graduates, according to most recent data available.
Student Body. College seeks a national student body; 30% of students from in state; 50% South, 28% Middle Atlantic, 13% North Central. An estimated 88% of students reported as Protestant, 10% Catholic, 2% unaffiliated; 100% Black, according to most recent data available.
Religious Orientation. Morehouse, now independent, was long affiliated with American Baptist Convention; 1 course in religion required of all students.
Varsity Sports. Men (Div.II): Basketball, Football, Tennis, Track.
Campus Life. About 50% of men live in dormitories; 50% of men live in off-campus housing or commute. Freshmen given preference in college housing if all students cannot be accommodated. No intervisitation in men's dormitory rooms. There are 4 fraternities on campus which 10% of men join.
Annual Costs. Tuition and fees, $8,000; room and board, $5,224. College reports some scholarships awarded on the basis of academic merit alone. *Meeting Costs:* college offers Financial Planning Loan, counseling and debt management.

Morgan State University

Baltimore, Maryland 21239 (410) 319-3000

A state-supported urban institution, located in a residential section of Baltimore, 40 miles from Washington, D.C.; founded as a college for Negroes and still serving a predominantly African American student body.Most convenient major airport: Baltimore/Washington International.

Founded: 1867
Affiliation: State
UG Enrollment: 1,900 M, 2,100 W (full-time); 500 M, 400 W (part-time)
Total Enrollment: 5,800
Cost: < $10K
% Receiving Financial Aid: 75–80%
Admission: Non-selective
Application Deadline: April 15

Admission. Graduates of Maryland high schools with GPA of 2.0 and combined SAT score of 750 eligible; 51% of applicants accepted, 46% of these actually enroll. Average freshman SAT scores: 405 verbal, 441 mathematical. *Required:* SAT or ACT, minimum high school GPA of 2.5. Criteria considered in admissions, in order of importance: standardized test scores, high school academic record, recommendations, extracurricular activities. *Out-of-state* freshman applicants: university actively seeks students from out of state. State limits out-of-state enrollment to 20% of entering class. About 45% of out-of-state applicants accepted, 40% enroll. States from which most out-of-state students are drawn: Pennsylvania, New York, New Jersey. *Entrance programs:* early decision, early admission, midyear admission. *Apply* by April 15; rolling admissions. Transfers welcome; 300 enrolled 1993–94.
Academic Environment. Degrees offered: bachelors, masters, doctoral. Core requirements include 46 hours of general education courses including English composition, humanities, social sciences, mathematics. About 40% of students entering as freshmen graduate eventually; 75% of freshman return for sophomore year. Average undergraduate class size: 18. *Special programs:* CLEP, independent study, study abroad, honors, undergraduate research, optional January interterm, cooperative education program with Coppin, Towson, U. of Maryland, Baltimore County, cross-registration with

Goucher, Loyola, Towson, dual engineering with U. of Pennsylvania, U. of Rochester, U. of Maryland, 3–3 pharmacy and 3–4 dentistry, medicine with U. of Maryland. *Calendar:* semester, summer school.

Undergraduate degrees conferred (497). 32% were in Business and Management, 11% were in Social Sciences, 10% were in Engineering, 8% were in Communications, 7% were in Public Affairs, 7% were in Psychology, 5% were in Education, 4% were in Computer and Engineering Related Technology, 3% were in Life Sciences, remainder in 10 other fields.

Graduates Career Data. Advanced studies pursued by 25% of students, according to most recent data available.

Faculty. About 80% of faculty hold PhD or equivalent. About 35% of teaching faculty are female; 70% Black, 5% other ethnic minorities.

Student Body. University seeks a national student body; 90% from Middle Atlantic, 5% South, 3% New England, 2% foreign. An estimated 93% of students reported as Black, 2% Hispanic, 1% Asian, 3% other ethnic minorities.

Varsity Sports. Men (Div.I): Basketball, Cross Country, Football, Tennis, Track, Wrestling. Women (Div.I): Basketball, Cross Country, Tennis, Track, Volleyball.

Campus Life. About 30% of men, 30% of women live in traditional dormitories; 5% of men, 5% of women live in coed dormitories; 5% of men, 5% of women live in off-campus college-related housing; rest commute. Intervisitation in men's and women's dormitory rooms limited. There are 4 fraternities, 4 sororities on campus. They provide no residence facilities. About 60% of resident students leave campus on weekends.

Annual Costs. Tuition and fees, $2,526 (out-of-state, $5,062); room and board, $4,840; estimated $300–$500 other, exclusive of travel. About 75–80% of students receive financial aid. University reports some scholarships awarded on the basis of academic merit alone. *Meeting Costs:* University offers deferred payment plan.

Morningside College

Sioux City, Iowa 51106-1751 **(712) 274-5000**

A church-related college, located in a residential section of a city of 85,900. Most convenient major airport: Sioux Gateway.

Founded: 1894
Affiliation: United Methodist
UG Enrollment: 405 M, 547 W (full-time); 78 M, 150 W (part-time)
Cost: $10K–$20K
% Receiving Financial Aid: 97%
Admission: Selective
Application Deadline: August 1

Admission is selective. About 90% of applicants accepted, 45% of these actually enroll. About 32% of freshmen graduate in top fifth of high school class, 59% in top two-fifths. Average freshman ACT scores: 22 composite. *Required:* SAT or ACT; interview (on- or off-campus) recommended. Criteria considered in admissions, in order of importance: standardized test scores and high school academic record, extracurricular activities, recommendations, writing sample; other factors considered: special talents, diverse student body, alumni children. *Entrance programs:* midyear admission, advanced placement. *Apply* by August 15; rolling admissions. *Transfers* welcome; 87 enrolled 1993–94.

Academic Environment. Degrees offered: associates, bachelors, masters. General education requirements include 44 credits distributed in the humanities, natural sciences and mathematics, social sciences, fine arts, physical education, and an interdisciplinary seminar; computer literacy required of all students. Campus Electronic Communication Interface Loop provides every dorm room with a computer and access to campus wide network. *Majors offered* in addition to usual studies include Indian Studies, tribal management, agri-business, behavioral disorders, multicategorical disabilities, engineering physics. Average undergraduate class size: 73% under 20, 25% 20–40, 2% over 40. About 40% of entering freshmen graduate within four years, 55% eventually; 69% of freshman return for sophomore year. *Special programs:* CLEP, independent study, interdepartmental honors program, undergraduate research, individualized majors, study abroad, combined programs (3–2 engineering, fashion merchandising and hotel/motel management with Iowa State, Washington Semester, United Nations Semester, internship/cooperative work-study programs. Adult programs: ACCEL, CLEP, non-traditional student orientation, non-traditional study room, Phi Beta (non-traditional student organization), column in student newspaper, non-traditional handbook. *Calendar:* semester, May interim, summer school.

Undergraduate degrees conferred (197). 23% were in Education, 23% were in Business and Management, 10% were in Visual and Performing Arts, 9% were in Health Sciences, 7% were in Life Sciences, 6% were in Psychology, 5% were in Parks and Recreation, 4% were in Social Sciences, 4% were in Communications, remainder in 8 other fields.

Graduate Career Data. Advanced studies pursued by 18% of students; 5% enter medical school; 1% enter law school; 5% enter business school. Corporations typically hiring largest numbers of graduates include IBP, Great West Casualty, Direct Transit, Payless Cashways, Gateway 2000. Career Development Services include help with job search skills, preparation of resumes, letters of application, interview skills, on-campus interviewing, career services newsletter.

Faculty. About 64% of faculty hold PhD or equivalent. About 22% of teaching faculty are female; 5% ethnic minorities.

Student Body. College seeks a national student body; 78% of students from in state; 90% Midwest, 4% West, 1% South, 1% New England, 4% foreign. An estimated 59% of students reported as Protestant, 23% Catholic, 18% unaffiliated; 3% Black, 3% Asian, 1% Native American, 4% other ethnic minorities.

Religious Orientation. Morningside is a church-related institution; one course in religion is required of all students.

Varsity Sports. Men (NCAA Div.II): Baseball, Basketball, Cross Country, Football, Track. Women (NCAA Div.II): Basketball, Cross Country, Softball, Track, Volleyball.

Campus Life. About 67% of men, 61% of women live in coed dormitories; rest commute. Intervisitation in men's and women's dormitory rooms limited. There are 1 fraternity, 2 sororities on campus which about 3% of men, 5% of women join. About 30% of resident students leave campus on weekends.

Annual Costs. Tuition and fees, $10,376; room and board, $3,520; estimated $500 other, exclusive of travel. About 97% of students receive financial aid; average amount of assistance, $9,442. Assistance is typically divided 67% gift aid, 29% loan, 4% work. College reports some scholarships awarded on the basis of academic merit alone. *Meeting Costs:* college offers open credit account system.

Morris Brown College

Atlanta, Georgia 30314 **(404) 525-7831**

A church-related college, located in a city of 497,000. Affiliated with Atlanta University Center, Morris Brown was founded as a college for Negroes and still serves a predominantly Black student body. (See also Atlanta University Center.).

Founded: 1881
Affiliation: African Methodist Episcopal
UG Enrollment: 2,015 M, W (full-time)
Cost: < $10K
Admission: Non-selective
Application Deadline: June 30

Admission. Graduates of approved high schools with 15 units (12 in academic subjects) who rank in top half of class eligible; 60% of applicants accepted, 52% of these actually enroll. About 10% of freshmen graduate in top fifth of high school class, 15% in top two-fifths. *Required:* SAT. *Apply* by June 30. *Transfers* welcome.

Academic Environment. *Degrees:* AB, BS. About 25% of general education requirements for graduation are elective; distribution requirements fairly numerous. About 55% of students entering as freshmen graduate eventually; 65% of freshmen return for sophomore year. *Special programs:* CLEP, honors. *Calendar:* semester, summer school.

Undergraduate degrees conferred (145). 34% were in Business and Management, 19% were in Health Sciences, 10% were in Education, 8% were in Social Sciences, 6% were in Life Sciences, 3% were in Mathematics, 3% were in Computer and Engineering Related Technology, 3% were in Business (Administrative Support), 3% were in Protective Services, 3% were in Physical Sciences, remainder in 6 other fields.

Student Body College seeks a national student body; 88% of students from South, 10% Northwest.

Religious Orientation. Morris Brown is a church-related institution; 1 course in religion required of all students.
Campus Life. About 19% of men, 57% of women live in traditional dormitories; no coed dormitories; rest commute. No intervisitation in men's or women's dormitory rooms. There are 6 fraternities, 5 sororities on campus which about 4% of men, 5% of women join; they provide no residence facilities.
Annual Costs. Tuition and fees, $7,796; room and board, $4,438.

Morris College

Sumter, South Carolina 29150 (803) 775-9371

Founded as a college "for the Christian and intellectual education of Negro youth," Morris opened its doors to all ethnic groups in 1961. The 44-acre campus is located on the north side of the city of Sumter. Most convenient major airport: Columbia (SC).

Founded: 1908	**Cost:** < $10K
Affiliation: Baptist	**% Receiving Financial Aid:** 93%
UG Enrollment: 329 M, 597 W (full-time)	**Admission:** Non-selective
	Application Deadline: Rolling

Admission. Graduates of accredited high schools with 18 credits eligible; open admissions policy. About 83% of applicants accepted, 45% of these actually enroll. About 6% of freshmen graduate in top fifth of high school class; 27% in top two-fifths. SAT or ACT recommended. *Entrance programs:* midyear admission, deferred admission. *Apply:* rolling admissions. *Transfers* welcome; 63 enrolled 1993–94.
Academic Environment. Degree offered: bachelors. Degree programs offered by Divisions of Education, General Studies, Humanities, Natural Sciences and Mathematics, Social Sciences and Business. Administration reports core curriculum includes English, fine arts, general studies, health education, mathematics, natural science, philosophy, social science, and speech; developmental studies may be required. Students report that professors are very accessible and willing to provide one-on-one help when needed. Average undergraduate class size: 52% under 20, 38% 20–40, 20% over 40. *Special programs:* work-study, internships, cooperative education. About 30% of entering students graduate within four years, 38–40% eventually; 57% of freshmen return for sophomore year. *Calendar:* semester, summer school.
Undergraduate degrees conferred (109). 37% were in Business and Management, 27% were in Social Sciences, 10% were in Education, 7% were in Visual and Performing Arts, 6% were in Mathematics, 6% were in Liberal/General Studies, 4% were in Life Sciences, 4% were in Letters, remainder in Parks and Recreation.
Graduates Career Data. Advanced studies pursued by 10% of students. Graduate and professional schools typically enrolling largest numbers of graduates include Ohio State U., USC-Columbia, SC, Bowling Green State U., Atlanta U. About 36% 1992–93 graduates employed. Fields typically employing largest numbers of graduates include sales, education, human services, management. Career Development Services offered to students and alumni include opportunities for the student to develop "awareness, exploration, experience and choice."
Faculty. About 42% of faculty hold PhD or equivalent. About 5% of undergraduate classes taught by tenured faculty. About 39% of teaching faculty are female; 53% Black, 12% other ethnic minorities.
Student Body. About 91% of students from in state; 94% South, 4% Middle Atlantic. All students reported as Protestant; almost all Black.
Religious Orientation. Morris is a church-related institution; two courses in religion are required of all students.
Varsity Sports. Men (NAIA): Baseball, Basketball, Track. Women (NAIA): Basketball, Softball, Track.
Campus Life. About 69% of men, 76% of women live in traditional dormitories; 5% of men live in off-campus college-related housing; rest commute. Freshmen given preference in college housing if all students cannot be accommodated. There are 4 fraternities, 4 sororities on campus, which about 5% of men, 5% of women join; they provide no residence facilities. About 50% of resident students leave campus on weekends.
Annual Costs. Tuition and fees, $4,405; room and board, $2,475; estimated $1,050 other, exclusive of travel. About 93% of students receive financial aid; average amount of assistance, $6,500. Assistance is typically divided 58% grant, 30% loan, 12% work. College reports 1 scholarships awarded on the basis of academic merit alone, 2 for special talents.

Morrison College

Reno, Nevada 95207

An independent college of business, offering associates and bachelors degrees. Year round calendar allows accelerated programs. All programs designed for working adults; day and evening classes offered.

Founded: 1902	**Affiliation:** Independent

Mount Angel Seminary

St. Benedict, Oregon 97373

A church-related, liberal arts college and graduate school of theology, conducted by a staff of Benedictine Monks, diocesan priests, and lay professors, that trains students for priesthood in dioceses and religious communities; it also provides programs for those who wish to pursue theological studies.

Founded: 1889	**UG Enrollment:** 149
Affiliation: Roman Catholic	

Undergraduate degrees conferred (20). 100% were in Philosophy and Religion.

Mount Holyoke College

South Hadley, Massachusetts 01075 (413) 538-2023

Mount Holyoke characterizes itself as "the forerunner of women's colleges in the U.S." College remains small by design to make for a viable college community. Along with Amherst, Hampshire, the University of Massachusetts, and Smith, it participates in the Five College cooperative program which enriches resources and opportunities. A regularly scheduled, free bus service links the campuses with which Mount Holyoke shares some courses, faculty, and facilities. The large 800-acre campus is located in South Hadley (pop. 17,000), 12 miles north of Springfield. Most convenient major airport: Bradley International.

Founded: 1837	**Cost:** $10K–$20K
Affiliation: Independent	**% Receiving Financial Aid:** 60%
UG Enrollment: 1,891 W (full-time)	**Admission:** Highly Selective
	Application Deadline: Feb. 1

Admission is highly selective. About 73% of applicants accepted, 40% of these actually enroll; 24% of freshmen graduate in top fifth of high school class; 48% in top two-fifths. Average freshman scores: SAT, 549 W verbal, 571 W mathematical; 94% of freshmen score above 450 on verbal, 62% above 550, 13% above 650; 95% score above 450 on mathematical, 62% above 550, 19% above 650; ACT, 26 W composite. *Required:* SAT plus 3 ACH including English (other ACH must be in 2 different fields), or ACT, essay; interview recommended (on campus or with alumnae representative). Criteria considered in admissions, in order of importance: high school academic record, writing sample, standardized test scores, recommendations, extra curricular activities; other factors considered: diverse student body, alumni children, special talents. *Entrance programs:* early decision, early admission, advanced placement, deferred admission. About 20% of entering students from private schools, 7% from parochial schools. *Apply* by February 1. *Transfers* welcome; 45 enrolled 1993–94.
Academic Environment. Students appear to have significant, though still limited, influence on curriculum through membership on joint student/faculty committees, membership of recent graduate on board of trustees. Influence on selection and promotion of faculty varies with department. Faculty is rated privately on quality of their teaching, and is reported to be very concerned about student judgments. Five College courses freely available to all but first-semester

freshmen. Over one fifth of Mount Holyoke students take courses at the other colleges each semester. Roughly comparable numbers of other Five College students take courses at Mount Holyoke. College continues to offer substantial degree of academic flexibility to students: no freshman English requirement, no failures on transcript of grades, no cumulative averages or ranking in class, freedom to schedule own examinations, exemption from some course requirements for qualified students, credit for independent study beginning in freshman year. Washington and international internships, as well as those related to the program on the Administration of Complex Organizations. Core requirements include 3 courses in humanities, 2 courses natural sciences/mathematics, 2 courses in social sciences. Requirements for graduation include completion of 4-credit course devoted primarily to some aspect of third world countries. Degrees offered: bachelors, masters. *Majors offered* include usual arts and sciences, geography, theater arts, environmental science; interdepartmental majors in biochemistry, black studies, Latin American studies; Five College majors in astronomy, dance; interdisciplinary majors. Interdisciplinary courses offered in humanities, mathematics, social science. Student to faculty ratio of 10:1.

More than 80% of students entering as freshmen graduate within four years; 96% of freshmen return for sophomore year. *Special programs:* independent study, study abroad (in 27 countries, almost half Third World), honors, undergraduate research, individualized majors, Twelve College Exchange, political internships in Washington and abroad, interdisciplinary seminars for freshmen, dual degree engineering, January term, cross registration with U. of Massachusetts, Amherst, Smith, Hampshire. *Library:* 576,000 titles, 1,800 periodicals, 14,121 microforms; separate art and music collections; resources of all Five College libraries available to students. *Calendar:* semester, winter term (2 required for graduation).

Undergraduate degrees conferred (526). 33% were in Social Sciences, 13% were in Letters, 11% were in Life Sciences, 8% were in Visual and Performing Arts, 7% were in Psychology, 7% were in Area and Ethnic Studies, 7% were in Foreign Languages, 4% were in Philosophy and Religion, 3% were in Physical Sciences, 3% were in Multi/Interdisciplinary Studies, remainder in 2 other fields.

Graduates Career Data. According to most recent data available, full-time graduate and professional study pursued immediately after graduation by 20% of students; 3% enter medical school, 3% enter law school. Medical schools typically enrolling largest numbers of graduates include Tufts, U. of Massachusetts, Harvard, Boston U.; law schools include Cornell, Boston U.; business schools include Columbia, NYU, Northwestern. *Careers in business and industry* pursued by 44% of graduates. Corporations typically hiring largest numbers of graduates include Aetna, Citicorp, Travelers, National Westminster Bank.

Faculty. About 93% of faculty hold PhD or equivalent.

Student Body. College seeks a national student body; 22% of students from in state; 32% New England, 16% Middle Atlantic, 10% Midwest, 11% South, 14% West, 16% foreign. An estimated 26% of students reported as Catholic, 23% Protestant, 4% Jewish, 12% other (Moslem/Eastern), 51% unreported or unaffiliated; 3% Black, 3% Hispanic, 6% Asian, according to most recent data available. *Minority group students:* special scholarship aid available; academic advising/tutoring, black studies department; black cultural and social center, Asian Group, La Unidad.

Religious Orientation. Mount Holyoke is an independent institution, makes no religious demands on students; religion is treated as personal matter. College conducts its own Sunday services for Protestants and Catholics; facilities also available in immediate community for major faiths.

Varsity Sports. Women (NCAA Div.III): Basketball, Crew, Cross Country, Diving, Equestrian, Field Hockey, Golf, Lacrosse, Soccer, Softball, Squash, Swimming/Diving, Tennis, Track, Volleyball.

Campus Life. All students have keys to residence halls; intervisitation hours established by student government. Drinking regulations according to state law; cars allowed for all. New Campus Center and Art Museum. Full and varied calendar of cultural and intellectual activities on campus and in the surrounding Five College campuses; Boston and New York City, 90 and 150 miles from college, respectively; regular bus service available. Students expected to live in residence halls. "The total community experience is geared toward helping women to realize potential." A recent student adds that the all women's college "harbors strong feelings of camaraderie and sisterhood." About 99% of women live in traditional dormitories; 1% commute. All students are expected to live in on campus housing for all four years, unless living at home with their parents. There are no sororities.

Annual Costs. Tuition and fees, $18,110; room and board, $5,520; estimated $1,400 other, exclusive of travel. About 60% of students receive financial aid, average amount of assistance from all sources, $18,111. Assistance is typically divided 70% scholarship, 20% loan, 10% work. College reports scholarships awarded only on the basis of need. *Meeting Costs:* college offers 10-month payment plan, insured tuition payment plan, repayment option; several parent loan plans.

Mount Marty College

Yankton, South Dakota 57078 **(800) 658-4552**

A church-related, liberal arts college, conducted by the Benedictine Sisters, Mount Marty is located in a town of 15,000, 65 miles northwest of Sioux City. Most convenient major airports: Sioux City (IA), Sioux Falls (SD).

Founded: 1936
Affiliation: Roman Catholic
UG Enrollment: 137 M, 310 W (full-time); 70 M, 149 W (part-time)
Total Enrollment: 792
Cost: < $10K
% Receiving Financial Aid: 97%
Admission: Non-selective
Application Deadline: Rolling

Admission. Graduates of approved high schools with minimum GPA of 2.5 and minimum ACT composite score of 16 eligible; 90% of applicants accepted, 52% of these actually enroll; about 27% of entering freshmen graduate in top fifth of their high school class, 45% in top two-fifths. *Required:* SAT or ACT; interview highly desirable. *Non-academic factors* considered in admissions: special talents, diverse student body, alumni children, religious affiliation and/or commitment. About 19% of entering students from parochial schools. *Apply* by March 1 for financial aid; rolling admissions. *Transfers* welcome.

Academic Environment. *Degrees:* AB, BS. About 33% of general education requirements for graduation are elective; distribution requirements fairly numerous. About 65% of students entering as freshmen graduate within four years; 88% of freshmen return for sophomore year. *Special programs:* January Interim, CLEP, credit for prior learning, independent study, study abroad, undergraduate research, individualized majors, dual degree in engineering with Georgia Inst. of Technology. *Calendar:* 4–1–4, summer school.

Undergraduate degrees conferred (81). 30% were in Health Sciences, 22% were in Business and Management, 14% were in Social Sciences, 14% were in Education, 4% were in Visual and Performing Arts, 4% were in Life Sciences, 4% were in Allied Health, remainder in 5 other fields.

Graduates Career Data. According to most recent data available, full-time graduate or professional study pursued by 10% of students immediately after graduation.

Faculty. About 45% of faculty hold PhD or equivalent.

Student Body. College does not seek a national student body; 70% of students from in state, 3 foreign. An estimated 75% of students reported as Catholic; 1% Black, 1% other minority, according to most recent data available.

Religious Orientation. Mount Marty is a Roman Catholic institution; 2 courses in religion and philosophy required of all students.

Varsity Sports. Men (NAIA): Baseball, Basketball, Golf. Women (NAIA): Basketball, Golf, Softball, Volleyball.

Campus Life. About 70% of men, 70% of women live in traditional dormitories; rest live in off-campus housing or commute. Intervisitation in men's and women's dormitory rooms limited. There are no fraternities or sororities. About 50% of resident students leave campus on weekends.

Annual Costs. Tuition and fees, $7,470; room and board, $2,980. About 97% of students receive financial aid; assistance is typically divided 9% scholarship, 40% loan, 6% work. College reports all scholarships awarded on the basis of academic merit alone. *Meeting Costs:* college offers monthly payment plan with no interest.

Mount Mary College

Milwaukee, Wisconsin 53222 **(414) 259-9220**

An independent college for women, conducted by the School Sisters of Notre Dame, located on an 80-acre campus in a city of 717,100. Most convenient major airport: Mitchell International.

Founded: 1913
Affiliation: Independent (Roman Catholic)
UG Enrollment: 932 W (full-time); 14 M, 487 W (part-time)
Cost: < $10K
% Receiving Financial Aid: 78%
Admission: Non-selective
Application Deadline: Rolling

Admission. Graduates of accredited high schools with 15 units (11 in academic subjects) who rank in top half of class, with minimum high school GPA 2.3 eligible; 90% of applicants accepted, 65% of these actually enroll; majority of freshmen graduate in top two-fifths of their high school class. Average freshman ACT scores: 20 composite. *Required:* SAT or ACT. *Entrance programs:* early admission, midyear admission, advanced placement. About 23% of entering freshman from parochial schools. *Apply* by August 15; rolling admissions. *Transfers* welcome; 211 enrolled 1993–94.

Academic Environment. Degree offered: bachelors. About 33% of general education credits for graduation are required; distribution requirements fairly numerous. About 50% of students entering as freshmen graduate within four years; 80% of freshmen return for sophomore year. *Majors offered* in addition to usual studies include art therapy, dietetics, fashion merchandising, fashion patternmaking, biology/food and water technology, hotel and restaurant management, interior design, occupational therapy. Average undergraduate class size: 18–20. *Special programs:* CLEP, independent study, honors, study abroad, undergraduate research, 3-year degree, individualized majors, 3–3 in biology, 3–2 in dentistry. *Calendar:* semester, summer school.

Undergraduate degrees conferred (235). 25% were in Allied Health, 18% were in Business and Management, 12% were in Education, 8% were in Home Economics, 7% were in Social Sciences, 6% were in Visual and Performing Arts, 6% were in Architecture and Environmental Design, 6% were in Marketing and Distribution, 4% were in Communications, 4% were in Public Affairs, remainder in 5 other fields.

Graduates Career Data. Advanced studies pursued by 6% of students. About 91% of 1991–92 graduates employed. Fields typically hiring largest numbers of graduates include health fields, education, small business, non-profit organizations. Career Development Services include individual career guidance, testing, resume and job preparation, career planning class, career workshops, internship development.

Faculty. About 50% of faculty hold PhD or equivalent. About 80% of teaching faculty are female.

Student Body. College does not seek a national student body; 96% of students from in state; 96% Midwest. An estimated 61% of students reported as Catholic, 34% Protestant, 1% Jewish; 6% Black, 2% Asian, 2% Hispanic. Average age of undergraduate student: 23.

Religious Orientation. Mount Mary is a Catholic institution; 2 courses in religion required of all students.

Varsity Sports. Women (NCAA III): Cross Country running, Indoor Track, Soccer, Softball, Tennis, Volleyball.

Campus Life. About 32% of women live in traditional dormitories; 68% commute. Intervisitation in women's dormitory rooms limited. There are no sororities. About 50% of resident students leave campus on weekends.

Annual Costs. Tuition and fees, $8,100; room and board, $2,868; estimated $1,625 other, exclusive of travel. About 78% of students receive financial aid; average amount of assistance, $8,400. Assistance is typically divided 12% scholarship, 30% grant, 47% loan, 11% work. College reports 146 scholarships awarded on the basis of academic merit alone, 550 for need alone. *Meeting Costs:* college offers Academic Management Services, EFI Fund Management.

Mount Mercy College

Cedar Rapids, Iowa 52402 **(319) 363-8213 or (800) 248-45042**

A church-related college, founded by the Sisters of Mercy, Mount Mercy is located on a 30-acre campus in a city of 150,000, 130 miles east of Des Moines.

Founded: 1928
Affiliation: Roman Catholic
UG Enrollment: 206 M, 600 W (full-time); 208 M, 335 W (part-time)
Cost: < $10K
% Receiving Financial Aid: 85%
Admission: Non-selective
Application Deadline: Rolling

Admission. Graduates of accredited high schools with 16 units who rank in top half of class with minimum high school GPA of 2.5 eligible; 86% of applicants accepted, 50% of these actually enroll; 39% of freshmen graduate in top fifth of high school class, 73% in top two-fifths. Average freshman ACT scores: 22.6 M, 21.7 W composite. *Required:* ACT or SAT, essay, second party recommendation; interview encouraged. Criteria considered in admissions, in order of importance: high school academic record, recommendations, writing sample, extracurricular activities, standardized test scores; other factor considered: diverse student body. *Entrance programs:* midyear admission, deferred admission, advanced placement. *Apply* by August 15; rolling admissions. *Transfers* welcome; 189 enrolled 1993–94.

Academic Environment. Degree offered: bachelors. *Majors offered* include arts and sciences, art, accounting, business, criminal justice administration, education, medical technology, music, nursing, piano pedagogy, social work, speech/drama, public relations. General education requirements for graduation include 12 courses from the following areas: English, fine arts, history, mathematics, science, multicultural studies, philosophy, religion, social sciences, and speech. Average undergraduate class size: 35% under 20, 65% 20–40. Several students report that low faculty to student ratio allows for individualized attention and "the teachers actually know who you are!" About 49% of students entering as freshmen graduate within four years, 56% eventually; 78% of freshmen return for sophomore year. Special programs: January term, study abroad, semester long internships with job shadowing, cross registration with Coe College. *Calendar:* 4–1–4, 2 5-week summer sessions.

Undergraduate degrees conferred (322). 42% were in Business and Management, 11% were in Education, 9% were in Health Sciences, 7% were in Protective Services, 5% were in Social Sciences, 5% were in Public Affairs, 4% were in Computer and Engineering Related Technology, 4% were in Communications, 3% were in Psychology, 3% were in Mathematics, remainder in 6 other fields.

Graduates Career Data. Advanced studies pursued by 6% of students. Graduate and professional schools typically enrolling largest number of graduates include U. of Iowa. About 98% of 1992–93 graduates employed. Fields typically employing largest number of graduates include business, education, nursing, human services. Career Development Services include resume workshops, skills inventory, personal counseling.

Faculty. About 49% of faculty hold PhD or equivalent. About 69% of teaching faculty are female; 7% ethnic minorities.

Student Body. College seeks a national student body; 97% of students from in state; 98% Midwest, 1% South. An estimated 40% of students reported as Protestant, 50% Catholic, 2% Jewish, 1% Muslim, 7% unaffiliated or other; 3% ethnic minorities. Average age of undergraduate student: 24.

Religious Orientation. Mount Mercy is a Catholic institution but makes no religious demands on students. General education requirements include one course in philosophy; attendance at religious exercises voluntary.

Varsity Sports. Men (NAIA Div.II): Baseball, Basketball, Cross Country, Golf, Soccer, Track. Women (Div. III): Basketball, Cross Country, Golf, Softball, Track, Volleyball.

Campus Life. Large number of commuters and percentage of students going home on weekends tends to leave campus pretty empty on weekends. Several students report that there isn't much to do off-campus within walking distance and so "a car is needed to go places." The campus is within 4 or 5 hours of many major cities (Chicago, Omaha, St. Louis, Minneapolis/St. Paul).

About 16% of men, 23% of women live in coed residence halls; 9% men, 11% women live in off-campus college-related housing; rest commute. Intervisitation in men's and women's dormitory rooms limited. There are no fraternities or sororities. About 40% of resident students leave campus on weekends.

Annual Costs. Tuition and fees, $9,900; room and board, $3,300; estimated $1,000 other, exclusive of travel. About 85% of students receive financial aid; average amount of assistance, $9,500.

Assistance is typically divided 34% scholarship, 28% grant, 32% loan, 6% work. College reports 988 scholarships awarded on the basis of academic merit alone, 20 for special talents.

Mount Olive College

Mt. Olive, North Carolina 28365 **(919) 658-2502**

A church-related, liberal arts college, located in a small town of 4,000, 20 miles from Goldsboro, N.C. (pop. 20,000) and 70 miles from Raleigh (pop. 100,000). Most convenient major airport: Raleigh-Durham.

Founded: 1951
Affiliation: Original Free Will Baptist
UG Enrollment: 210 M, 218 W (full-time); 244 M, 191 W (part-time)
Cost: < $10K
% Receiving Financial Aid: 95%
Admission: Non-selective
Application Deadline: Rolling

Admission. High school graduates eligible; 82% of applicants accepted, 41% of these actually enroll. About 20% of freshmen graduate in top fifth of high school class, 49% in top two-fifths. Average freshman scores: SAT, 378 M, 384 W verbal, 448 M, 428 W mathematical; ACT, 17 M, 16 W composite. *Required:* SAT or ACT. Criteria considered in admissions, in order of importance: high school academic record, standardized test scores, recommendations, extracurricular activities; other factors considered: religious affiliation and/or commitment. *Apply*: rolling admissions. *Transfers* welcome; 58 enrolled 1993–94.
Academic Environment. Degrees offered: associates, bachelors. General education requirements include 27 semester hours in humanities, 21 in science and mathematics, 12 in social sciences, 3 in computer awareness. Unusual majors offered include BS in management and organizational development, which is a degree completion program designed specifically for the adult learner delivered in 10 modules totaling 55 weeks. About 30% of students entering as freshmen graduate eventually; 60% of freshmen return for sophomore year. *Special programs:* study abroad, internship and cooperative work-study programs available in all programs, management and organizational development, human recourse development. Adult programs: Adult Scholars Program offers 1 course free. *Calendar:* semester.
Undergraduate degrees conferred (115). 63% were in Business and Management, 16% were in Psychology, 12% were in Liberal/General Studies, 6% were in Parks and Recreation, 3% were in Theology.
Graduates Career Data. Advanced studies pursued by 7% of students; 4% enter business school. Business schools typically enrolling largest number of graduates include East Carolina U. About 50% of 1992–93 graduates employed. Career Development Services include job listings, career and job fair, workshops on resume writing, mock and actual interviews, graduate schools, career resource library, career talks featuring employed speakers, self-assessment instruments.
Faculty. About 35% of faculty hold PhD or equivalent. About 44% of teaching faculty are female; 4% ethnic minorities.
Student Body. About 94% of students from in state. An estimated 95% of students reported as Protestant; 18% Black, 2% other ethnic minorities, according to most recent data available. Average age of undergraduate student: 27.
Religious Orientation. Mount Olive is church-related institution; two courses in religion are required of all students.
Varsity Sports. Men (NAIA and NCAA Div. II): Baseball, Basketball, Golf, Soccer, Tennis. Women (NAIA and NCAA Div. II): Basketball, Softball, Tennis, Volleyball.
Campus Life. About 40% of students live in traditional dormitories; 9% in coed dormitories; rest commute. There are no fraternities or sororities.
Annual Costs. Tuition and fees, $7,100; room and board, $2,550; estimated $800 other, exclusive of travel. About 95% of students receive financial aid; average amount of assistance, $5,800. Assistance is typically divided 20% scholarship, 32% grant, 40% loan, 8% work. College reports some scholarships awarded on the basis of academic merit alone. *Meeting Costs:* college offers PLUS Loans.

Mount Saint Clare College

Clinton, Iowa 52732 **(319) 242-4023**

Mount Saint Clare is a liberal arts, pre-professional college which awards associate degrees and baccalaureate degrees. Most convenient major airport: Moline (IL).

Founded: 1895
Affiliation: Roman Catholic
UG Enrollment: 247 M, W (full-time)
Cost: < $10K
% Receiving Financial Aid: 95%
Admission: Non-selective
Application Deadline: Aug. 15

Admission. High school graduates with minimum Act of 18 and GPA of 2.0 eligible; other must have letters of recommendation; 85% of applicants accepted, 54% of these actually enroll. *Required:* ACT. *Apply* by August 15. *Transfers* welcome.
Academic Environment. Baccalaureate programs offered in business administration, accounting, computer information systems, liberal arts and office administration. About 51% of students entering as freshmen graduate eventually; 68% of freshmen return for sophomore year. *Special programs:* 3–1 cytotechnology with U. of Wisconsin.
Undergraduate degrees conferred (51). 67% were in Business and Management, 20% were in Liberal/General Studies, 10% were in Computer and Engineering Related Technology, remainder in 2 other fields.
Student Body. About 66% of students from in state; 98% North Central.
Varsity Sports. Men (NAIA): Basketball. Women (NAIA): Basketball, Volleyball.
Campus Life. About 6% of men, 22% of women live in coed dormitories (segregated by floor); rest live in off-campus housing or commute.
Annual Costs. Tuition and fees, $9,280; room and board $3,600. About 95% of students receive financial aid; assistance is typically divided 57% scholarship, 15% loan, 28% work. College reports some scholarships awarded on the basis of academic merit alone.

College of Mount St. Joseph

Cincinnati, Ohio 45233 **(513) 244-4531**

A liberal arts college for women, founded by the Sisters of Charity, the 75-acre campus is located in suburban Delhi Hills, 7 miles southwest of downtown Cincinnati. Most convenient major airport: Greater Cincinnati.

Founded: 1920
Affiliation: Independent (Roman Catholic)
UG Enrollment: 369 M, 797 W (full-time); 251 M, 1,031 W (part-time)
Cost: < $10K
% Receiving Financial Aid: 80%
Admission: Non-selective
Application Deadline: Rolling

Admission. High school graduates with 16 academic units who rank in top half of senior class with minimum high school GPA 2.25 eligible; 78% of applicants accepted, 42% of these actually enroll; 30% of freshmen graduate in top fifth of high school class, 58% in top two-fifths. Average freshman SAT scores: 420 verbal, 460 mathematical; ACT, 21.6 composite. *Required:* SAT or ACT; interview recommended. Criteria considered in admissions, in order of importance: high school academic record, standardized test scores, recommendations, extracurricular activities, writing sample; other factors considered: special talents, alumni children, diverse student body, leadership ability. *Entrance programs:* early admission, midyear admission, advanced placement. About 10% of entering students from private schools, 30% from parochial. *Apply* by August 15; rolling admissions. *Transfers* welcome; 53 enrolled 1993–94.
Academic Environment. Administration reports general education requirements for graduation include 48 semester hours within six broad areas. Degrees offered: associates, bachelors, masters. *Majors offered* include usual arts and sciences, business, communication arts, dietetics, elementary and special education, gerontological studies, home economics, interior design, medical technology, music therapy, nursing, management of nursing services, physical therapy. Average undergraduate class size: 25.

About 66% of students entering as freshmen graduate within four years, 74% eventually; 88% of freshmen return for sophomore year. *Special programs:* CLEP, honors, independent study, undergraduate research, study abroad, 3-year degree, Seton College Exchange, cooperative program with Edgecliff and Thomas More, and other Greater Cincinnati Consortium Colleges, cross registration. Adult programs: about 50% of college enrollment is through continuing education programs which offer day, evening and weekend courses. *Calendar:* early semester.

Undergraduate degrees conferred (320). 22% were in Health Sciences, 20% were in Business and Management, 15% were in Education, 10% were in Visual and Performing Arts, 9% were in Liberal/General Studies, 5% were in Social Sciences, 5% were in Computer and Engineering Related Technology, 4% were in Communications, 3% were in Law, 3% were in Public Affairs, remainder in 7 other fields.

Graduates Career Data. Advanced studies pursued by 10% of students; 2% enter medical school; 2% enter law school; 2% enter business school. About 88% of 1992–93 graduates are employed. Fields typically employing largest numbers of graduates include education, nursing, business, science related. Career Development Services include professional development courses, career guidance, mock and actual interviews.

Faculty. About 55% of full-time faculty hold PhD or equivalent.

Student Body. College seeks a national student body; 90% of students from in state; 96% Midwest, 4% foreign. An estimated 62% of students reported as Catholic, 35% Protestant, 3% unaffiliated or other; 6% as Black, 3% other ethnic minorities. *Minority group students:* financial help available. Average age of undergraduate student: 23.

Religious Orientation. Mount St. Joseph is a church-related institution; one course in religion required of all students; attendance at worship services voluntary. Places of worship available on campus for Catholics, in immediate community for major faiths.

Varsity Sports. Men (NAIA Div. II): Baseball, Football, Tennis, Wrestling. Women (NAIA Div. II): Basketball, Softball, Tennis, Volleyball.

Campus Life. College Council and all administrative committees include student representatives. About 30% of men, 35% of women live in dormitories; rest commute. There are no fraternities or sororities. About 70% of resident students leave campus on weekends.

Annual Costs. Tuition and fees, $9,180; room and board, $4,242; estimated $400 other, exclusive of travel. About 80% of students receive financial aid; average amount of assistance, $7,600. Assistance is typically divided 50% scholarship, 50% loan/work, according to most recent data available. College reports 335 scholarships awarded on the basis of academic merit alone, 10 for special talents. *Meeting Costs:* college offers Equiline, First-Line, Extra-Credit.

Mount Saint Mary College

Newburgh, New York 12550 (914) 569-3248

Mount Saint Mary is an independent, co-educational liberal arts college founded by the Dominican Sisters of Newburgh. The 44-acre campus is located in a city of 26,200, 58 miles north of New York City. Most convenient major airport: Stewart International.

Founded: 1959
Affiliation: Independent
Total Enrollment: 1,706
Cost: < $10K
% Receiving Financial Aid: 80%
Admission: Non-selective
Application Deadline: Rolling

Admission. Graduates of approved high schools with 16 units eligible; 68% of applicants accepted, 25% of these actually enroll; 10% of freshmen graduate in top fifth of high school class, 70% in top two-fifths. Average freshman scores: SAT, 440 M, 442 W verbal, 455 M, 452 W mathematical; ACT, 20 M, 19 W composite. *Required:* SAT or ACT; interview and essay recommended. Criteria considered in admissions, in order of importance: high school academic record, standardized test scores, recommendations, extracurricular activities, writing sample; other factors considered: special talents, alumni children. *Entrance programs:* early decision, early admission, midyear admission, deferred admission, advanced placement. About 30% of entering freshman from private schools, 28% from parochial schools. *Apply:* rolling admissions. *Transfers* welcome; 163 enrolled 1993–94.

Academic Environment. Degrees offered: bachelors, masters. *Majors offered* in addition to usual arts and sciences include accounting, business management, elementary, secondary and special education, media studies, medical technology, public relations, nursing, and theater arts. Average undergraduate class size: 25; 49% of classes under 20, 50% between 20–40, 1% over 40. About 62% of students entering as freshmen graduate within four years, 73% eventually; 84% of freshmen return for sophomore year. *Special programs:* CLEP, independent study, study abroad, honors, undergraduate research, 3-year degree, individualized majors, on-campus elementary school, visiting students program for New York State colleges, January term, internship/cooperative work-study programs. Adult programs: accelerated degree - adults can finish a 4 year degree in 2 1/2 years. *Calendar:* 4–1–4, summer school.

Undergraduate degrees conferred (229). 25% were in Business and Management, 15% were in Health Sciences, 12% were in Social Sciences, 10% were in Computer and Engineering Related Technology, 9% were in Letters, 8% were in Communications, 7% were in Psychology, 5% were in Education, 4% were in Liberal/General Studies, remainder in 5 other fields.

Graduates Career Data. Advanced studies pursued by 75% of students; of these, 25% enter business school; 5% enter law school; 5% enter medical school; 3% enter dental school. About 92% of 1992–93 graduates employed. Fields typically hiring largest numbers of graduates include education, nursing, accounting, communications. Career Development Services include interviews on campus, resume, cover letter writing, interview skills, preparation for graduate school exams, help with graduate school research.

Faculty. About 90% of faculty hold PhD or equivalent. About 92% of undergraduate classes taught by tenured faculty. About 50% of teaching faculty are female; 10% Black, 3% other ethnic minorities.

Student Body. About 70% of students from in state; 78% Middle Atlantic, 16% New England, 2% South, 1% West, 1% Midwest. An estimated 44% of students reported as Protestant, 50% Catholic, 3% Jewish, 3% unaffiliated or other; 10% Black, 4% Hispanic, 2% Asian, 1% other ethnic minorities. *Minority group students:* Higher Education Opportunity Program provides finances, tutoring, counseling, lighter course load; college's special scholarship program for "local disadvantaged men and women."

Varsity Sports. Men (NCAA Div.III): Baseball, Basketball, Soccer, Tennis. Women (NCAA Div.III): Basketball, Soccer, Softball, Tennis, Volleyball.

Campus Life. College offers various resident living plans ranging from regulated residence halls to independent housing. Curfew and limited intervisitation hours for freshmen. Campus is located within easy access to New York City (about 1 hour away) for expanded cultural, recreational and educational resources. About 80% of men, 80% of women live in traditional dormitories; no coed dormitories; rest commute. There are no fraternities or sororities. About 10% of resident students leave campus on weekends.

Annual Costs. Tuition and fees, $8,000; room and board, $4,800; estimated $2,000 other, exclusive of travel. About 80% of students receive financial aid; average amount of assistance, $5,000. Assistance is typically divided 20% scholarship, 30% grant, 47% loan, 3% work. College reports 70 scholarships awarded on the basis of academic merit alone, 15 for need alone. *Meeting Costs:* college offers Academic Management Services, The Tuition Plan.

Mount St. Mary's College

Los Angeles, California 90049 (310) 471-9516

A church-related college, Mount St. Mary's was founded by the Sisters of St. Joseph of Carondelet. Primarily a college for women, the college admits men to nursing and music curricula and all graduate programs. Mount St. Mary's offers baccalaureate programs on its main campus located in the hills above Santa Monica. A second campus on a former private estate in downtown Los Angeles offers 2-year and master's degree programs. Most convenient major airport: Los Angeles International.

Founded: 1925
Affiliation: Independent (Roman Catholic)
UG Enrollment: 18 M, 940 W (full-time); 22 M, 176 W (part-time)
Total Enrollment: 1,491
Cost: $10K–$20K
% Receiving Financial Aid: 86%
Admission: Non-selective
Application Deadline: Rolling

Admission. Graduates of accredited high schools with B average in college preparatory program eligible; 70% of applicants accepted, 32% of these actually enroll; 70% of freshmen graduate in top fifth of high school class, 90% in top two-fifths. Average freshman scores: SAT, middle fifty percent range 860–1060 combined verbal, mathematical; 36% of freshman score above 500 verbal, 10% above 600, 1% above 700; 53% score above 500, 14% above 600, 4% above 700; ACT, 21 composite. *Required:* SAT or ACT, essay; interview recommended. Criteria considered in admissions, in order of importance: standardized test scores and high school academic record, writing sample, recommendations and extracurricular activities; other factors considered: special talents, alumni children. About 24% of entering freshman from private schools. *Apply* by March 1; rolling admissions. *Transfers* welcome; 116 enrolled 1993–94.

Academic Environment. Degrees offered: associates, bachelors, masters. *Majors offered* include usual arts and sciences, home economics, nursing, business and organizational management. Distribution requirements account for 59 out of 129 total units. About 67% of students entering as freshmen graduate eventually; 86% of freshmen return for sophomore year. Average undergraduate class size: 17. *Special programs:* independent study, study abroad, honors, undergraduate research, individualized majors, credit by examination, cross registration with UCLA, internship/cooperative work-study programs within the business department. *Calendar:* 2 14-week semesters, 1-month interterm.

Undergraduate degrees conferred (200). 22% were in Health Sciences, 20% were in Psychology, 19% were in Allied Health, 17% were in Business and Management, 7% were in Social Sciences, 7% were in Education, 5% were in Life Sciences, remainder in 4 other fields.

Graduates Career Data. About 92% of 1992–93 graduates employed.

Faculty. About 79% of faculty hold PhD or equivalent. About 52% of undergraduate classes taught by tenured faculty. About 75% of teaching faculty are female.

Student Body. College seeks a national student body; 86% of students from in state. An estimated 7% of students reported as Protestant, 60% Catholic, 1% Jewish, 4% other; 9% Black, 35% Hispanic, 16% Asian. *Minority group students:* special financial, academic, social provisions.

Religious Orientation. Mount St. Mary's is an independent institution with a Catholic orientation; 9 units of religious studies or theology required of all students. Religious Affairs Committee sponsors retreats, speakers, and other religious activities. Places of worship available on campus for Catholics, in immediate community for all faiths.

Varsity Sports. Women (NAIA): Cross Country, Tennis, Volleyball.

Campus Life. One recent student finds "the serenity and beauty" of the campus to be one of the things she likes best about Mount St. Mary's. Location in Los Angeles area permits access to full range of cultural and recreational events in addition to campus activities and events. Dorm hours set by student and parent. Intervisitation limited. No on-campus residence facilities for men. About 50% of women live in traditional dormitories; all men, remainder of women commute. Freshmen given preference in college housing if all students cannot be accommodated. There is 1 sorority on campus, which about 6% of women join; it provides no residence facilities; no fraternities. About 50% of resident students leave campus on weekends.

Annual Costs. Tuition and fees, $11,340; room and board, $4,600; estimated $500 other, exclusive of travel. About 86% of students receive financial aid; average amount of assistance, $8,000. Assistance is typically divided 70% scholarship/grant, 15% loan, 15% work. College reports 30 scholarships awarded on the basis of academic merit alone.

Mount Saint Mary's College

Emmitsburg, Maryland 21727 **(800) 448-4347**

The second oldest Catholic college in the U.S., Mount Saint Mary's is a liberal arts institution, located in a village of 1,800, 50 miles west of Baltimore. Most convenient major airport: Baltimore/Washington International or Dulles.

Founded: 1808
Affiliation: Roman Catholic
UG Enrollment: 588 M, 655 W (full-time)
Total Enrollment: 1,737

Cost: $10K–$20K
% Receiving Financial Aid: 76%
Admission: Selective
Application Deadline: March 1

Admission is selective. About 88% of applicants accepted, 28% of these actually enroll. About 31% of freshmen graduate in top fifth of high school class, 58% in top two-fifths. Average freshman SAT scores: 460 M, 460 W verbal, 520 M, 495 W mathematical; 31% of entering freshman score above 500 verbal, 8% above 600; 56% score above 500 mathematical, 15% above 600, 3% above 700. *Required:* SAT or ACT, essay; interview recommended. Criteria considered in admissions, in order of importance: high school academic record, standardized test scores, recommendations, extracurricular activities, writing sample; other factors considered: special talents, alumni children, diverse student body. *Entrance programs:* early admission, midyear admission, deferred admission, advanced placement. About 3% of entering students from private schools, 52% from parochial schools. *Apply* by March 1. *Transfers* welcome; 42 enrolled 1993–94.

Academic Environment. Degrees offered: bachelors, masters. Widely-acclaimed core curriculum includes 6-credit freshman seminar in critical thinking and communications skills, comprehensive freshman year program features year-long "cluster courses" in Western Civilization and American experience, 4-year, 61-credit vertical core curriculum. Thirty majors offered in the liberal arts and sciences including biochemistry, international studies. Stronger students have options for Freshman and College Honors programs. Average undergraduate class size: 19; 54% of classes under 20, 45% 20–40, 1% over 40. Faculty to student ratio of 1:14 assures students of strong, one-on-one faculty mentoring, advising, and teaching.

About 71% of students entering as freshmen graduate within four years, 77% eventually; 82% of freshmen return for sophomore year. *Special programs:* CLEP, independent study, study abroad, honors, undergraduate research, 3-year degree, inter-departmental and individualized majors, 3–2 programs in computer science, engineering and nursing, cross registration with Frederick Community College, summer school. *Calendar:* semester.

Undergraduate degrees conferred (318). 45% were in Business and Management, 24% were in Social Sciences, 6% were in Psychology, 6% were in Education, 4% were in Visual and Performing Arts, 4% were in Letters, 3% were in Life Sciences, 3% were in Multi/Interdisciplinary Studies, remainder in 4 other fields.

Graduates Career Data. Advanced studies pursued by 20% of students; 3% enter medical or dental schools; 3% enter law schools; 8% enter business schools. Medical schools typically enrolling largest numbers of students include Georgetown, George Washington, Maryland; law schools include Maryland, U. of Baltimore, Catholic U., Dickinson; business schools include Mount St. Mary's. About 90% of 1992–93 graduates employed. Fields typically employing largest numbers of graduates include finance, education, government. Career Development Services include a four year career access plan, internship opportunities, job placement services "to discover, evaluate and implement career plans."

Faculty. About 84% of faculty hold PhD or equivalent. About 38% of undergraduate classes taught by tenured faculty. About 29% of teaching faculty are female; 5% ethnic minorities.

Student Body. College seeks a national student body; 46% of students from in state; 91% Middle Atlantic, 2% New England, 1% West, 2% Midwest, 2% South, 1% foreign. An estimated 83% of students reported as Catholic, 8% Protestant, 1% Jewish, 4% unaffiliated, 4% other; 6% Black, 2% Hispanic, 2% Asian.

Religious Orientation. Mount Saint Mary's is a church-related institution; 2 courses in theology required of all students.

Varsity Sports. Men (Div.I): Baseball, Basketball, Cross Country, Golf, Lacrosse, Soccer, Tennis, Track. Women (Div.I): Basketball, Cross Country, Golf, Soccer, Softball, Tennis, Track.

Campus Life. The 1,400-acre campus is set in a rural, mountainside area which offers a wide array of recreational activities, but, only an hour away from the many cultural and educational resources of Washington, D.C. and Baltimore. Strong intramural and recreational athletics program involves two-thirds of all students. About 85% of students live in coed dormitories; rest commute. Freshmen given preference in college housing if all students cannot be accommodated. Intervisitation in men's and women's dormitory rooms limited. Sexes segregated in coed dormitories by floor. There

are no fraternities or sororities. About 15% of resident students leave campus on weekends.
Annual Costs. Tuition and fees, $11,725; room and board, $6,100; estimated $1,275 other, exclusive of travel. About 76% of students (1992–93) received financial aid; average amount of assistance, $7,595. Assistance is typically divided 53% scholarship, 16% grant, 27% loan, 4% work. College reports 340 scholarships awarded on the basis of academic merit alone, 125 for special talents, 330 for need alone. *Meeting Costs:* college offers cost stabilization plan.

College of Mount Saint Vincent

Riverdale, New York 10471 (718) 405-3200

A liberal arts college founded by the Sisters of Charity of New York, Mount Saint Vincent has developed an interinstitutional program with nearby Manhattan College for men. The cooperative program expands resources through sharing of facilities, programs of study, and faculties. The 70-acre campus is located in the Riverdale section of New York City. Most convenient major airports: JFK International, LaGuardia.

Founded: 1847
Affiliation: Independent
UG Enrollment: 144 M, 563 W (full-time); 50 M, 382 W (part-time)
Cost: $10K–$20K
% Receiving Financial Aid: 86%
Admission: Non-selective
Application Deadline: Rolling

Admission. About 61% of applicants accepted, 26% of these actually enroll; about 22% of entering freshmen graduate in top fifth of their high school class, 38% in top two-fifths. Average freshman scores: SAT 454 verbal, 474 mathematical; 22% of entering freshman score above 500 verbal, 4% above 600, 1% above 700; 37% score above 500 mathematical, 8% above 600, 1% above 700; ACT, 24 M, 24 W composite. *Required:* SAT or ACT, minimum high school grade average of C+, high school official transcript, two letters of recommendation; interview suggested, essay recommended. Criteria considered in admissions, in order of importance: high school academic record, recommendations, standardized test scores, extracurricular activities, writing sample (essay); other factors considered: special talents, alumni children. *Entrance programs:* early decision, early admission, midyear admission, deferred admission. About 62% of entering students from private schools. *Apply:* rolling admissions. *Transfers* welcome; 30 enrolled 1993–94.
Academic Environment. Administration reports 54 credits of core curriculum are required for graduation, distributed among the humanities, social sciences, and mathematics/natural science; computer literacy required of all students. Degrees offered: associates, bachelors, masters. *Majors offered* include usual arts and sciences, aquatic biology, business administration, economics, communications, environmental studies, nursing; interdepartmental majors in Latin American studies; through Manhattan College: urban area studies, physical education, peace studies; chemistry and physics (Manhattan campus), biology and psychology (Mount campus) are integrated departments.

About 64% of students entering as freshmen graduate eventually; 74% of freshmen return for sophomore year. *Special programs:* CLEP, independent study, study abroad, January term, undergraduate research, 3-year degree, individualized majors, Seton College's Exchange, credit by examination, independent study of foreign languages, 3–2 engineering, cross registration with Manhattan College, internship/cooperative work-study programs. *Calendar:* semester, mini-sessions in January and May, summer school.
Undergraduate degrees conferred (150). 33% were in Health Sciences, 15% were in Communications Technologies, 13% were in Business and Management, 9% were in Life Sciences, 7% were in Psychology, 6% were in Social Sciences, 5% were in Education, 5% were in Letters, 3% were in Liberal/General Studies, remainder in 3 other fields.
Graduates Career Data. Advanced studies pursued by 18% of students; 7% enter business school; 3% enter law school; 2% enter medical school; 1% enter dental school. Business schools typically enrolling largest number of graduates include St. John's U., Fordham U., Pace U.; law schools include Pace U., CUNY; medical schools include SUNY; dental schools include NYU. About 85% of 1992–93 graduates employed. Fields typically hiring largest numbers of graduates include business, communications, nursing, education. Career Development Services include career counseling, graduate school advisement, job search techniques, resume preparation and interviewing skills, business etiquette, establishing credential files, internship placements, career/interest inventories, career library, job listings for full-time, part-time, and summer jobs.
Faculty. About 77% of faculty hold PhD or equivalent. About 67% of teaching faculty are female; 4% Hispanic, 4% other ethnic minorities.
Student Body. College seeks a national student body; 92% of students from in state; 4% Middle Atlantic, 1% New England, 1% foreign. An estimated 3% of students reported as Protestant, 73% Catholic, 2% Jewish, 13% unaffiliated, 9% other; 13% Black, 14% Hispanic, 4% Asian, 10% other ethnic minorities. *Minority group students:* special financial and academic provisions. Average age of undergraduate student: 25.
Religious Orientation. Mount Saint Vincent is an independent institution "in the Catholic tradition"; 3 credits of religious studies required of all students as part of core curriculum; attendance at religious services voluntary. Administration reports no religious clubs on campus; campus ministry team plans liturgy and religious activities. Places of worship available on campus for Catholics, in immediate community for all faiths.
Varsity Sports. Men (Div.III): Basketball, Cross Country, Soccer, Tennis, Volleyball. Women (Div.III): Basketball, Cheerleading, Cross Country, Soccer, Softball, Tennis, Volleyball.
Campus Life. Students reported to have some influence over policies governing campus social life. Cooperative program with Manhattan, according to student leaders, is successful both academically and socially. Intercampus travel facilitated by college bus. Curfew and ban on cars for freshmen. Alcohol normally forbidden on campus; dean may give permission for special occasions. About 29% of women live in traditional dormitories; 62% of men, 28% of women in coed dormitories; rest commute. There are no fraternities or sororities. About 20% of resident students leave campus on weekends, 20–40% on "off" weekends.
Annual Costs. Tuition and fees, $11,130; room and board, $5,600; estimated $1,350 other, exclusive of travel. About 86% of students receive financial aid; average amount of assistance, $10,238. Assistance is typically divided 18% scholarship, 37% grant, 43% loan, 2% work. College reports 171 scholarships awarded on the basis of academic merit alone. *Meeting Costs:* college offers deferred payment plans, monthly budget plans.

Mount Senario College

Ladysmith, Wisconsin 54848 (715) 532-5511

A small liberal arts college offering BA and BS degrees in the arts and sciences, Mount Senario places strong emphasis on teacher education. Most convenient major airport: Eau Claire (65 miles).

Founded: 1962
Affiliation: Independent
UG Enrollment: 254 M, 208 W (full-time); 489 M, 211 W (part-time)
Cost: < $10K
% Receiving Financial Aid: 92%
Admission: Non-selective
Application Deadline: Rolling

Admission. About 71% of applicants accepted, 47% of these actually enroll; 20% of freshmen graduate in top fifth of high school class, 60% in top two-fifths. *Required:* ACT, minimum high school average "C", essay, two letters of recommendation; interview recommended (on- or off-campus). Criteria considered in admissions, in order of importance: high school academic record, standardized test scores, recommendations, extracurricular activities, writing sample; other factor considered: special talents. *Entrance programs:* early admission, midyear admission, deferred admission, advanced placement. *Apply:* rolling admissions. *Transfers* welcome; 51 enrolled 1993–94.
Academic Environment. Degrees offered: associates, bachelors. *Majors offered* include usual arts and sciences, business and management, criminal justice, education, engineering, interdisciplinary studies, social work, public administration. Average undergraduate class size: 25. About 7% of entering freshman graduate within four years, 21% eventually; 60% of freshmen return for sophomore year. *Special programs:* study abroad, 3–2 programs in

engineering and forestry, internship/cooperative work-study programs. Adult programs: OUTREACH program, degree completion in criminal justice, business and public administration, night classes. *Calendar:* semester.

Undergraduate degrees conferred (124). 31% were in Protective Services, 23% were in Business and Management, 23% were in Health Sciences, 9% were in Education, 4% were in Multi/Interdisciplinary Studies, remainder in 5 other fields.

Faculty. About 35% of faculty hold PhD or equivalent. About 30% of teaching faculty are female; 2% ethnic minorities.

Student Body. About 78% of students from in state; 95% Midwest, 2% from South, 3% foreign. An estimated 4% Black, 3% Asian, 20% ethnic minorities. Average age of undergraduate student: 24.

Varsity Sports. Men (NLCAA): Baseball, Basketball, Football. Women (NLCAA): Basketball, Softball, Volleyball.

Campus Life. About 40% of men, 40% of women live in coed dormitories, remainder live in off-campus housing or commute, according to most recent data available. Freshmen given preference in college housing if all students cannot be accommodated. There are no fraternities or sororities. About 15% of resident students leave campus on weekends, according to most recent data available.

Annual Costs. Tuition and fees, $7,720; room and board, $3,250; estimated $1,800 other, exclusive of travel. About 92% of students receive financial aid; average amount of assistance, $6,886. Assistance is typically divided 42% grant, 49% loan, 9% work. College reports 99 scholarships awarded on the basis of academic merit alone, 342 for need alone.

Mount Union College

Alliance, Ohio 44601 **(216) 823-5320**

A church-related, liberal arts college, Mount Union is located in a town of 24,000, 60 miles southeast of Cleveland. Most convenient major airports: Akron, Canton.

Founded: 1846
Affiliation: United Methodist
UG Enrollment: 711 M, 642 W (full-time)
Cost: $10K–$20K
% Receiving Financial Aid: 94%
Admission: Non-selective
Application Deadline: Rolling

Admission. Graduates of accredited high schools with a minimum of 15 units eligible. About 82% of applicants accepted; 24% of these actually enroll; 47% of freshmen graduate in top fifth of high school class, 73% in top two-fifths. Average freshman scores: SAT, 48% of entering freshman score above 500 verbal, 15% above 600, 1% above 700; 71% score above 500 mathematical, 37% above 600, 8% above 700; ACT, 23 composite. *Required:* SAT or ACT, essay, high school transcript, recommendation form. Criteria considered in admissions, in order of importance: high school academic record and course selection, standardized test scores, writing sample, recommendations, extracurricular activities; other factors considered: special talents, alumni children, diverse student body. *Entrance programs:* early admission, midyear admission, advanced placement. About 12% of entering students from parochial schools. *Apply:* rolling admissions. *Transfers* welcome; 43 enrolled 1993–94.

Academic Environment. Degree offered: bachelors. *Majors offered* include usual arts and sciences, astronomy, business administration, education, non-Western studies, sports medicine, sports management, cytotechnology. Core requirements include 49 semester hours in 10 different disciplines. Average undergraduate class size: 8% under 20, 90% 20–40, 2% over 40.

About 68% of students entering as freshmen graduate eventually; 85% of freshmen return for sophomore year. *Special programs:* CLEP, independent study, study abroad, honors, undergraduate research, individualized majors, self-designed interdisciplinary majors, acceleration for superior students, combined program in medical technology, 3–2 engineering, internship/cooperative work-study programs in all areas of study. Adult programs: Non-traditional students provided individualized tutorials, evening adult-study program. *Calendar:* 3–3, summer school.

Undergraduate degrees conferred (294). 36% were in Business and Management, 14% were in Social Sciences, 13% were in Education, 5% were in Health Sciences, 5% were in Letters, 4% were in Computer and Engineering Related Technology, 4% were in Psychology, 4% were in Life Sciences, 4% were in Communications, 3% were in Visual and Performing Arts, 3% were in Mathematics, 3% were in Foreign Languages, remainder in 2 other fields.

Graduates Career Data. Advanced studies pursued by 24% of students; 4% enter medical school; 5% enter law school; 4% enter business school; 1% enter dental school. Medical schools typically enrolling largest numbers of graduates include Ohio State, John Carroll; law schools include Ohio Northern, Ohio State. About 94% of 1992–93 graduates employed. Corporations typically hiring largest numbers of graduates include Ernest & Young, Arthur Andersen. Career Development Services include referral service, resume workshops, interviews, graduate school investigations.

Faculty. About 75% of faculty hold PhD or equivalent. About 80% of undergraduate classes taught by tenured faculty. About 23% of teaching faculty are female; 3% Black.

Student Body. College seeks a national student body; 84% of students from in state; 86% Midwest, 9% Middle Atlantic, 4% foreign. An estimated 50% of students reported as Protestant, 29% Catholic, 19% unaffiliated, 2% other; 5% as Black, 2% Hispanic, 2% Asian, 6% other ethnic minorities. *Minority group students:* "extensive" financial aid; Black Cultural Center.

Religious Orientation. Mount Union is a church-related institution; one course in religion required of all students; attendance at chapel-convocation services voluntary. Places of worship available in immediate community for Protestants and Catholics, 20 miles away for Jews.

Varsity Sports. Men (NCAA,Div.III): Baseball, Basketball, Cross Country, Football, Golf, Soccer, Swimming, Tennis, Track, Wrestling. Women (NCAA,Div.III): Basketball, Cross Country, Soccer, Softball, Swimming, Tennis, Track, Volleyball.

Campus Life. No hours for students in residence halls; intervisitation permitted 4 PM–11 PM Monday-Thursday, noon–2 am Friday and Saturday, until 11 PM Sunday. Cars allowed; alcohol not sold on-campus; beer permitted in student's rooms.

About 50% of men, 71% of women live in traditional dormitories; no coed dorms; 15% of men, 4% of women live in off-campus college-related housing; 18% of men, 15% of women commute. There are 5 fraternities, 5 sororities on campus which about 40% of each men and women join; 17% of men live in fraternities; sororities provide no residence facilities. About 30% of resident students leave campus on weekends.

Annual Costs. Tuition and fees, $12,320; room and board, $3,530; estimated $1,000 other, exclusive of travel. About 94% of students receive financial aid; average amount of assistance, $9,600. Assistance is typically divided 6% scholarship, 25% loan, 87% work. College reports 8 scholarships awarded on the basis of academic merit alone, 5 for special talents, 1 for need alone. *Meeting Costs:* college offers various payment plans and pre-payment plan.

Mount Vernon College

Washington, D.C. 20007 **(202) 331-3444**

An independent, liberal arts college for women located in the northwest residential section of the nation's capital. Mount Vernon offers 10 baccalaureate degree programs in addition to its 2-year associate degree programs and is a member of the Consortium of Universities of the Washington Metropolitan Area.

Founded: 1875
Affiliation: Independent
UG Enrollment: 412 W (full-time)
Cost: $10K–$20K
Admission: Non-selective
Application Deadline: Rolling

Admission. High school graduates with 16 academic units eligible; 88% of applicants accepted, 40% of these actually enroll; 10% of freshmen graduate in top fifth of high school class, 30% in top two-fifths. *Required:* SAT or ACT; interview recommended. *Apply:* rolling admissions. *Transfers* welcome.

Academic Environment. *Degree:* AB. The curriculum emphasizes interdisciplinary courses in the liberal arts and develops practical skills for career development. About 60% of students entering as freshmen graduate eventually; 64% of freshmen return for sophomore year. *Majors offered* include usual arts and sciences, business administration, communications, computer science, human development, childhood education, interior design, health science, international studies, U.S. policy and politics, urban and comparative cul-

tures. *Special programs:* CLEP, independent study, study abroad, individualized majors, individualized internships, cross-registration in the Washington Consortium. *Calendar:* term (3 10-week terms).
Undergraduate degrees conferred (109). 22% were in Architecture and Environmental Design, 19% were in Business and Management, 18% were in Psychology, 18% were in Communications, 10% were in Multi/Interdisciplinary Studies, 5% were in Social Sciences, 4% were in Health Sciences, remainder in 4 other fields.
Student Body. College seeks a national student body; 20% of students from in state; 50% Middle Atlantic, 20% New England, 10% South. An estimated 45% of students reported as Protestant, 30% Catholic, 12% Jewish, 12% unaffiliated, 1% other; 10% Black, 2% Hispanic, 5% Asian, 3% other minority, according to most recent data available.
Varsity Sports. Women (Ind): Field Hockey, Tennis, Volleyball.
Campus Life. About 50% of women live in traditional dormitories; rest live in off-campus housing or commute. Intervisitation in women's dormitory rooms limited. There are no sororities. About 10% of resident students leave campus on weekends.
Annual Costs. Tuition and fees, $13,250; room and board, $6,918. College reports some scholarships awarded on the basis of academic merit alone. *Meeting Costs:* college offers deferred payment plan, CONCERN Loan Program.

Mount Vernon Nazarene College

Mount Vernon, Ohio 43050 (614) 397-1244

A church-related institution located in a community of 15,000, 40 miles from Columbus. Most convenient major airport: Columbus.

Founded: 1964
Affiliation: Church of the Nazarene
UG Enrollment: 479 M, 635 W (full-time); 55 M, 39 W (part-time)
Cost: < $10K
% Receiving Financial Aid: 89%
Admission: Non-selective
Application Deadline: Rolling

Admission. Graduates of accredited high schools with 15 academic units who rank in top two-thirds of class with ACT composite score of 15 eligible; 95% of applicants accepted, 69% of these actually enroll. Average freshman ACT scores: 21.5 composite. *Required:* ACT, essay, two references, all transcripts for transfers; interview, acceptance of policies of the Church of the Nazarene (ban on use of alcohol, tobacco, social dancing, attendance at motion picture theaters). Criteria considered in admissions, in order of importance: standardized test scores, high school academic record, recommendations, writing sample, extracurricular activities. *Entrance programs:* deferred admission, advanced placement. New Enrollment Services Division eases process of enrollment, financial planning and registration. *Apply* by August 15; rolling admissions. *Transfers* welcome; 74 enrolled 1993–94.
Academic Environment. Degrees offered: associates, bachelors, masters. Graduation requirements include 9–14 hours of general courses (English, writing, physical education, Senior Colloquium), and distribution requirements of 18–19 hours of humanities, 6 hours social sciences, 7–8 hours natural sciences. Average undergraduate class size: 23. About 76% of freshmen return for sophomore year. *Special programs:* CLEP, independent study, study abroad, January term, cross registration for Spanish majors with U. of Costa Rica, double majors, internships, biology field experiences at Padre Island, Texas, inner-city work in Washington, D.C. and New York City. Adult programs: bachelor of business administration for adult students who have completed 60 hours of college level work, EXCELL (Executive Center for Lifelong Learning). *Calendar:* 4–1–4, 2 summer sessions.
Undergraduate degrees conferred (177). 23% were in Business and Management, 19% were in Education, 10% were in Social Sciences, 8% were in Psychology, 8% were in Philosophy and Religion, 6% were in Communications, 5% were in Mathematics, 4% were in Home Economics, 4% were in Business (Administrative Support), 3% were in Life Sciences, 3% were in Theology, remainder in 5 other fields.
Graduates Career Data. Advanced studies pursued by 22% of students. About 90% of 1991–92 graduates employed. Fields typically employing largest numbers of graduates include education, business, religion, pastors. Career Development Services include resume writing, on-campus interviewing, job listings.
Faculty. About 56% of faculty hold PhD or equivalent. About 100% of undergraduate classes taught by tenured faculty. About 22% of teaching faculty are female.
Student Body. About 82% of students from in state; 95% Midwest, 1% South, 3% New England, 1% Middle Atlantic, 1% foreign. An estimated 73% of students reported as Protestant, 2% Catholic, 4% unaffiliated; 4% minorities.
Religious Orientation. Mount Vernon Nazarene is a church-related institution; 10 hours of religion and philosophy required of all students; attendance at triweekly chapel services and Sunday services expected.
Varsity Sports. Men (NAIA): Baseball, Basketball, Golf, Soccer. Women (NAIA): Basketball, Softball, Volleyball.
Campus Life. A recent student reports that, "we really support our athletic teams," she also adds that, "the spiritual aspect of our school is one of community..most students are involved in some kind of ministry." About 68% of students live in traditional dormitories; no coed dormitories; rest commute. No intervisitation in men's or women's dormitory rooms. There are no fraternities or sororities. About 40% of resident students leave campus on weekends.
Annual Costs. Tuition and fees, $7,190; room and board, $3,200; estimated $1,000 other, exclusive of travel. About 89% of students receive financial aid; average amount of assistance, $6,668. College reports 355 scholarships awarded on the basis of academic merit alone. *Meeting Costs:* college offers payment plans.

Muhlenberg College

Allentown, Pennsylvania 18104 (215) 821-3200

A church-related, co-educational, liberal arts college, Muhlenberg is located on a 75-acre campus in a city of 110,000, 50 miles north of Philadelphia and about 90 miles west of New York City. The college's proximity to major population centers has helped to ensure substantial registration of students from New Jersey, New York, and other Middle Atlantic states. Student body is remarkably diverse religiously despite college's church affiliation. Most convenient major airport: Allentown-Bethlehem-Easton.

Founded: 1848
Affiliation: Evangelical Lutheran Church in America
UG Enrollment: 736 M, 918 W (full-time)
Cost: $10K–$20K
% Receiving Financial Aid: 60%
Admission: Very Selective
Application Deadline: February 15

Admission is very selective. About 73% of applicants accepted, 25% of these actually enroll; 54% of freshmen graduate in top fifth of high school class, 81% in top two-fifths. Average freshman scores: SAT, 501 M, 514 W verbal, 582 M, 556 W mathematical; 54% of freshmen score above 500 on verbal, 13% above 600, 1% above 700; 84% score above 500 on mathematical, 34% above 600, 4% above 700; ACT, 26 M, 24 W composite. *Required:* SAT or ACT, ACH in mathematics and English, essay; interview highly recommended. Criteria considered in admissions, in order of importance: high school academic record, standardized test scores, extracurricular activities, writing sample, recommendations, interview; other factors considered: alumni children, special talents, diverse student body. *Entrance programs:* early decision, early admission, midyear admission, advanced placement, deferred admission. About 18% of entering students from private schools, 12% from parochial. *Apply* by February 15. *Transfers* welcome; 27 enrolled 1993–94.
Academic Environment. Degree offered: bachelors. Pressures for academic achievement continue to be quite strong. Muhlenberg has a good record in preparing students for medicine, law, dentistry and related professions. Most popular majors: business and management, accounting, biological and physical sciences. Administration reports 50% of general education courses needed for graduation are required; distribution requirements numerous: 4 courses each in humanities, natural sciences/mathematics, 5 courses in social sciences, 2 semesters religion, foreign language proficiency, 4 quarters physical education. One student describes the academic program by saying, "In a classroom of fifteen students and a professor who chooses to be at a small, challenging, liberal arts college, how can

the experience be anything but intense and engaging? The workload is tremendous, and the curriculum excellent..Muhlenberg is devoted to teaching and learning." Majors offered include usual arts and sciences, information science, international studies, Russian studies, political economy, human resource administration, philosophy/political thought, individualized majors, international studies, entrepreneurial studies. Average undergraduate class size: 56% under 20, 42% 20–40, 2% over 40.

About 79% of students entering as freshmen graduate within four years, 82% eventually; 94% of freshmen return for sophomore year. *Special programs:* CLEP, independent study, study abroad, self-designed major, internships, cooperative programs (including cross-registration with members of Lehigh Valley Association), combined programs (forestry/wildlife management with Duke, engineering with Columbia, Washington U., nursing with Columbia), Scholars Program, 4–4 dual admission program with Hahnemann U., 3–4 accelerated dental program with U. of Pennsylvania. Adult programs: Evening College. *Calendar:* semester, summer school.

Undergraduate degrees conferred (395). 24% were in Social Sciences, 23% were in Business and Management, 14% were in Psychology, 9% were in Life Sciences, 9% were in Letters, 4% were in Visual and Performing Arts, 4% were in Communications, 3% were in Physical Sciences, 3% were in Multi/Interdisciplinary Studies, remainder in 6 other fields.

Graduates Career Data. Advanced studies pursued immediately after graduation by 30% of students; 6% enter medical school; 2% enter dental school; 6% enter law school; 1% enter business school. Medical schools typically enrolling largest numbers of graduates include Jefferson, Penn State, Hahnemann, Temple, NJ Medical.; dental schools include Temple, Pennsylvania, Tufts, NJ Medical; law schools include Seton Hall, Syracuse, Temple, Rutgers-Camden; business schools include Lehigh, St. John's, Colorado. About 65% of 1992–93 graduates employed. Corporations typically hiring largest numbers of graduates include Deloitte & Touche, Air Products, Dun & Bradstreet, Sony. *Career Counseling Program* includes non-credit seminars, mock interviews, resume reviews, career coaches and faculty career liaisons, extensive career library, SIGI computerized system for career guidance and graduate school exploration. Student assessment of program reported as good for both career guidance and for job placement. Alumni reported as active in both career guidance and job placement.

Faculty. About 87% of faculty hold PhD or equivalent. About 59% of undergraduate classes taught by tenured faculty. About 35% of faculty are female; 5% ethnic minorities.

Student Body. College seeks a national student body; 32% of students from in state; 76% Middle Atlantic, 14% New England; 2% Midwest, 3% South, 3% West, 2% foreign. An estimated 36% of students reported as Protestant, 30% Catholic, 22% Jewish, 1% Muslim, 11% unaffiliated; 3% Black, 2% Hispanic, 4% Asian. *Minority group students:* financial aid and academic counseling provided.

Religious Orientation. Muhlenberg is a church-related institution; 1 course in religion required as part of liberal arts studies; attendance at chapel services voluntary. Places of worship available on campus for Protestants and Catholics, in immediate community for Jews.

Varsity Sports. Men (Div.III): Baseball, Basketball, Cross Country, Football, Golf, Soccer, Tennis, Track, Wrestling. Women (Div.III): Basketball, Cross Country, Field Hockey, Lacrosse, Soccer, Softball, Tennis, Track, Volleyball.

Campus Life. Students have considerable freedom in determining their own life styles. Visitation hours in student's rooms unlimited. Quiet hours in residence halls voted by residents of the floor or wing. Smoking permitted only in specified areas; alcohol use limited to those over 21; illegal drugs prohibited. Despite reports of strong academic competition, a "very cordial atmosphere" and a "strong social life" on campus are said to prevail. Students are actively involved in close to 100 student-run and -financed clubs and organizations. Intramural sports reported as very popular. Intercollegiate club competition in ice hockey, rugby and lacrosse (men) and swimming (coed). Substantial number of cultural and intellectual activities offered on campus; Philadelphia and New York are 50 and 90 miles away, respectively. Cars allowed, freshmen must have special permission.

About 22% of women live in traditional dormitories; 74% of men, 63% of women in coed dormitories; 3% of men, 3% of women live in off-campus housing; rest commute. All students are guaranteed on-campus housing for all four years. Sexes segregated in coed dormitories by wing, floor, or room. There are 6 fraternities, 4 sororities on campus, which about 55% of men, 45% of women join; 22% of men live in fraternities; 8% of women live in sororities. About 15% of resident students leave campus on weekends.

Annual Costs. Tuition and fees, $16,385; room and board, $4,410; estimated $1,355 other, exclusive of travel. About 60% of students receive financial aid, average amount of financial aid, $11,200. Assistance is typically divided 66% scholarship/grant, 24% loan, 10% work. College reports 328 scholarships awarded on the basis of academic merit alone, 7 for special talents, 769 for need alone. *Meeting Costs:* college offers insured monthly payment plan.

Mundelein College

(Merged with Loyola University of Chicago)

Murray State University

Murray, Kentucky 42071 **(502) 762-3741**

A state-supported university, located in a town of 19,000, 45 miles south of Paducah. Most convenient major airport: Nashville (TN).

Founded: 1922
Affiliation: State
UG Enrollment: 3,000 M, 3,364 W (full-time); 660 M, 1,166 W (part-time)
Total Enrollment: 8,190
Cost: < $10K
% Receiving Financial Aid: 60%
Admission: Non-selective
Application Deadline: Rolling

Admission. Graduates of accredited Kentucky high schools with pre-college curriculum and minimum ACT composite score of 18 or rank in upper half of class eligible, others may be admitted to preparatory status; 86% of applicants accepted, 65% of these actually enroll. Average freshman ACT scores: 22 M, 22 W composite. *Required:* ACT, interview. Criteria considered in admissions, in order of importance: high school academic record, standardized test scores, recommendations; other factors considered: special talents, alumni children, diverse student body. *Out-of-state* freshman applicants: university actively seeks students from out of state. Requirement for out-of-state applicants: pre-college curriculum and minimum ACT composite score of 22, and rank in top one-third of class; 75% of applicants accepted, 82% enroll. States from which most out-of-state students are drawn: Tennessee, Illinois, Indiana, Missouri. *Entrance programs:* early admission, midyear admission, deferred admission, advanced placement. *Apply* by August 1; rolling admissions. *Transfers* welcome; 470 M, 505 W enrolled 1993–94.

Academic Environment. Degrees offered: associates, bachelors, masters. *Majors offered* in usual arts and sciences, wide variety of professional/vocational fields including majors in rehabilitation, occupational safety and health, engineering technology, urban and regional planning, government affairs and public administration, organizational communication. Average undergraduate class size: 30. About 43% of students entering as freshmen graduate within four years. *Special programs:* CLEP, independent study, study abroad, honors, 3-year degree, internship programs. Adult programs: Bachelor of Independent Studies Program offers adult students correspondence, television, experiential credit and contract learning. *Calendar:* semester, summer school.

Undergraduate degrees conferred (949). 21% were in Business and Management, 16% were in Education, 11% were in Engineering and Engineering Related Technology, 10% were in Communications, 5% were in Life Sciences, 5% were in Health Sciences, 4% were in Home Economics, 3% were in Social Sciences, 3% were in Allied Health, 3% were in Psychology, remainder in 16 other fields.

Graduates Career Data. *Full-time graduate or professional study* pursued by 27% of students immediately after graduation. *Careers in business and industry* pursued by 53% of graduates.

Faculty. About 80% of faculty hold PhD or equivalent. About 85% of undergraduate classes taught by tenured faculty.

Student Body. University seeks a national student body; 76% of students from in state; 90% South, 7% Midwest, 2% foreign.

Varsity Sports. Men (Div.I): Baseball, Basketball, Cross Country, Football(IAA), Golf, Horsemanship, Riflery, Rodeo(NIRA), Tennis,

Track. Women (Div.I): Basketball, Cross Country, Horsemanship, Riflery, Rodeo, Tennis, Track, Volleyball.

Campus Life. About 41% of men, 43% of women live in traditional dormitories; 15% of men, 12% of women in coed dormitories; 49% of men, 51% of women live in off-campus housing or commute. Intervisitation in men's and women's dormitory rooms. There are 13 fraternities, 7 sororities on campus which about 19% of men, 13% of women join; 2% of men, 1% of women live in fraternities/sororities.

Annual Costs. Tuition and fees, $1,780 (out-of-state, $4,780); room and board, $2,922; estimated $1,100 other, exclusive of travel. About 60% of students receive financial aid; average amount of assistance, $3,000. Assistance is typically divided 52% scholarship, 30% loan, 18% work. University reports some scholarships awarded on the basis of academic merit alone. *Meeting Costs:* university offers deferred payment plan, and monthly payment plan.

Museum Art School

(See Pacific Northwest College of Art)

Muskingum College

New Concord, Ohio 43762 (614) 826-8137

A church-related, liberal arts college, Muskingum is located on a 215-acre campus in a village of 2,300, 70 miles east of Columbus and 115 miles west of Pittsburgh. Most convenient major airport: Columbus (OH).

Founded: 1837
Affiliation: Presbyterian Church USA
UG Enrollment: 572 M, 542 W (full-time)
Cost: $10K–$20K
% Receiving Financial Aid: 90%
Admission: Non-selective
Application Deadline: Rolling

Admission. About 83% of applicants accepted, 41% of these actually enroll; 38% of freshmen graduate in top fifth of high school class, 65% in top two-fifths. Average freshman scores: SAT, 405 M, 468 W verbal, 468 M, 513 W mathematical; 27% score above 500 on verbal, 5% above 600, 2% above 700; 52% score above 500 on mathematical, 15% above 600, 1% above 700; ACT, 21 M, 22 W composite. *Required:* SAT or ACT; interview strongly recommended. Criteria considered in admissions, in order of importance: high school academic record, standardized test scores, recommendations, extracurricular activities, writing sample; other factor considered: leadership qualities. *Apply* by August 1; rolling admissions. *Transfers* welcome; 43 enrolled 1993–94.

Academic Environment. Degrees offered: bachelors, masters. *Majors offered* include usual arts and sciences, accounting and business, education, geography, theater, communications, public and international affairs, interdisciplinary majors, self-designed majors. Average undergraduate class size: 50% under 20, 50% 20–40.

About 60% of freshmen graduate within four years, 63% eventually; 78% of freshmen return for sophomore year. *Special programs:* CLEP, independent study, study abroad, undergraduate research, individualized majors, Washington Semester, United Nations Semester, study at Merrill-Palmer Institute, Princeton Critical Languages Program, internships, liberal arts/nursing with Western Reserve U., liberal arts/medical technology with Southwest General Hospital, 3–2 engineering. *Calendar:* 4 8-week terms.

Undergraduate degrees conferred (236). 26% were in Business and Management, 22% were in Education, 19% were in Social Sciences, 12% were in Letters, 5% were in Psychology, 5% were in Mathematics, 3% were in Physical Sciences, remainder in 6 other fields.

Graduates Career Data. Advanced studies pursued by 12% of students; 2% enter law school. Professional schools typically enrolling largest numbers of graduates include Ohio State, Ohio U., Wright State, Akron, Toledo, Capital. About 78% of 1992–93 graduates employed. Fields typically hiring largest numbers of graduates include small business, school systems, retail, banking. *Career Counseling Program* offers counseling, workshops, resource library, alumni and parent career advisory program. Student assessment of program reported as fair for career guidance and good for job placement. Alumni reported as active in both career guidance and job placement.

Faculty. About 72% of faculty hold PhD or equivalent. About 60% of undergraduate classes taught by tenured faculty. About 31% of teaching faculty are female; 4% ethnic minorities.

Student Body. College seeks a national student body; 86% of students from in state; 94% Midwest, 2% foreign students. An estimated 60% of students reported as Protestant, 25% Catholic, 1% Jewish, 4% unaffiliated, 10% other; 2% Black, 2% Asian, 1% Hispanic.

Religious Orientation. Muskingum is a church-related institution; 2 courses in religion required of all students; attendance at vespers services voluntary. Places of worship available on campus for Protestants and Catholics, in vicinity for Jews.

Varsity Sports. Men (NCAA Div.III): Baseball, Basketball, Cross Country, Football, Golf, Soccer, Tennis, Track, Wrestling. Women (NCAA Div.III): Basketball, Cross Country, Soccer, Softball, Tennis, Track, Volleyball.

Campus Life. General student regulations are quite liberal, including intervisitation policy (88 hours per week). Alcohol permitted in students' dormitory rooms. Cars permitted.

About 20% of men, 25% of women live in traditional dormitories; 45% of men, 55% of women live in coed dormitories; 5% each men, women commute. Freshmen given preference in college housing if all students cannot be accommodated. There are 4 fraternities, 4 sororities on campus which about 53% of men, 56% of women join; 30% of men, 15% of women live in fraternities and sororities. About 15% of resident students leave campus on weekends.

Annual Costs. Tuition and fees, $13,010; room and board, $3,740; estimated $1,200 other, exclusive of travel. About 90% of students receive financial aid; average amount of assistance, $12,000. Assistance is typically divided 20% scholarship, 45% grant, 30% loan, 5% work. College reports 380 scholarships awarded on the basis of academic merit alone, 150 for special talents, 870 for need alone. *Meeting Costs:* college offers low-interest payment plans.

National College of Education

(See National Louis University)

National University

San Diego, California 92108 (619) 563-7100

National University is a liberal arts and professional institution with a program designed specifically for the convenience and educational needs of working adults. In addition to the main campus, branch campuses are located throughout the greater San Diego area.

Founded: 1971
Affiliation: Independent
UG Enrollment: 2,132 M, 1,567 W (full-time); 2,089 M, 1,333 W (part-time)
Total Enrollment: 7,469
Cost: < $10K
% Receiving Financial Aid: 45%
Admission: Non-selective
Application Deadline: Rolling

Admission is "based on evidence of a student's ability to benefit from the educational program." Five years recent work history a major factor. Students admitted each month. Very few freshmen; most students have advanced standing or are transfers.

Academic Environment. Baccalaureate degrees offered in business administration, behavioral science, criminal justice administration, occupational safety and health, airway science, industrial technology logistics, technical education, interdisciplinary studies. About 95% of classes meet at night. Students enroll in 1 course at a time which lasts for a month. Many graduates continue graduate or professional studies.

Undergraduate degrees conferred (1,444). 55% were in Business and Management, 12% were in Computer and Engineering Related Technology, 11% were in Multi/Interdisciplinary Studies, 10% were in Psychology, 4% were in Protective Services, 3% were in Engineering and Engineering Related Technology, remainder in 4 other fields.

Annual Costs. Tuition and fees, $5,985. About 45% of students receive financial aid. Assistance is typically divided 15% scholarship, 80% loan/grant, 5% work. College reports some scholarships awarded on the basis of academic merit alone.

National Louis University

Evanston, Illinois 60201 **(708) 475-1100**

An independent institution, located in a Chicago suburb of 80,000, the National Louis University has long prepared teachers for elementary classrooms in every state. Urban Campus in Chicago focuses on education in city schools; a third campus in Lombard, Illinois offers upper division studies only. Formerly known as National College of Education.

Founded: 1886
Affiliation: Independent
UG Enrollment: 961 M, 1,861 W (full-time); 103 M, 391 W (part-time)
Total Enrollment: 7,400
Cost: < $10K
% Receiving Financial Aid: 84%
Admission: Non-selective
Application Deadline: Rolling

Admission. Graduates of accredited high schools eligible; 54% of applicants accepted, 51% of these actually enroll. About 42% of freshmen graduate in top fifth of high school class, 67% in top two fifths. Average freshman ACT scores: 17.1 M, 16.3 W composite. *Required:* SAT or ACT, 2 recommendations; interview recommended. Criteria considered in admissions, in order of importance: high school academic record, standardized test scores, extra curricular activities, interview, recommendations. *Entrance programs:* early decisions, early admission, midyear admission, deferred admission, advanced placement. *Apply* by September 1; rolling admission. *Transfers* welcome; 426 enrolled 1993–94.
Academic Environment. College has on-campus demonstration school from junior nursery through eighth grade; programs in human services and allied health also offered. University also maintains Academic Centers in Virginia, Florida, Georgia, Missouri, Wisconsin and Germany. Degrees offered: bachelors, masters, doctoral. All programs are scheduled for adults as well as traditional students; about 77% of the student body is over 25. About one-third of courses required for graduation are general education core requirements. Average undergraduate class size: 90% of classes under 20, 10% 20–40. About 25% of students entering as freshmen graduate within four years, 45% eventually. *Special programs:* CLEP, independent study. *Calendar:* quarter, summer school.
Undergraduate degrees conferred (348). 56% were in Psychology, 27% were in Education, 15% were in Allied Health, remainder in 3 other fields.
Graduates Career Data. Advanced studies pursued by 30% of students; 5% enter business school. Career Development Services include career counseling, credential files, resume development, job fairs.
Faculty. About 65% of faculty hold PhD or equivalent. About 50% of undergraduate classes taught by tenured faculty.
Student Body. College seeks a national student body; 83% of students from in state; 6% from Middle Atlantic, 4% South. An estimated 20% of students reported as Black, 9% Hispanic, 5% Asian. Average age of undergraduate student: 32.
Campus Life. About 1% of men, 2% of women live in coed dormitories; rest commute. Intervisitation in men's and women's dormitory rooms limited. There are no fraternities or sororities. About 65% of resident students leave campus on weekends, according to most recent data available.
Annual Costs. Tuition and fees, $9,090; room and board, $4,128. About 84% of students receive financial aid; average amount of assistance, $2,400. College reports some scholarships awarded on the basis of academic merit alone.

Nazareth College of Rochester

Rochester, New York 14618 **(716) 586-2525**

Founded by the Sisters of St. Joseph, Nazareth is now a co-educational independent, liberal arts college. College has cooperative program with nearby St. John Fisher College and other area colleges. The 75-acre campus is located in the residential suburb of Pittsford, 7 miles from downtown Rochester (pop. 296,200). Most convenient major airport: Rochester/Monroe County.

Founded: 1924
Affiliation: Independent (Roman Catholic)
UG Enrollment: 350 M, 1,012 W (full-time); 105 M, 435 W (part-time)
Cost: $10K–$20K
% Receiving Financial Aid: 81%
Admission: Non-selective
Application Deadline: Rolling

Academic Environment. Degree offered: bachelors. *Majors offered* include usual arts and sciences, anthropology, business, speech pathology, theater arts, gerontology, music therapy, social work, nursing, management science, business, economics, international studies. Strongest programs reported to be in education and human services. Average undergraduate class size, (major courses): 18; student/faculty ratio: 14:1.

About 49% of students entering as freshmen graduate within four years, 57% in five years; 85% of freshmen return for sophomore year. *Special programs:* CLEP, independent study, study abroad, honors, undergraduate research, individualized majors, cooperative programs through Rochester Area Colleges consortium, internships and field placements. *Calendar:* semester, summer school.
Undergraduate degrees conferred (410). 26% were in Business and Management, 14% were in Psychology, 12% were in Education, 11% were in Social Sciences, 11% were in Letters, 7% were in Visual and Performing Arts, 6% were in Foreign Languages, 5% were in Public Affairs, remainder in 5 other fields.
Graduates Career Data. Full-time graduate study pursued immediately after graduation by 30% of students, 65% eventually. *Careers in business and industry* pursued by 45% of graduates; 35% pursue careers in education and human services. Career Development Services include computerized resource on professional opportunities and graduate schools, decision-making workshops, individual and peer counseling, career resource room, on-campus interviewing, job vacancy newsletter.
Faculty. About 92% of faculty hold PhD or equivalent.
Student Body. College seeks a national student body; 96% of students from in state; 98% Middle Atlantic, 12 foreign students. An estimated 4% of students reported as Black, 2% Hispanic, 1% Asian.
Religious Orientation. Nazareth is an independent institution with a Roman Catholic heritage; makes no religious demands on students.
Varsity Sports. Men (NCAA, Div.III): Basketball, Golf, Lacrosse, Soccer, Swimming, Tennis. Women (NCAA, Div.III): Basketball, Golf, Lacrosse, Soccer, Swimming, Tennis, Volleyball.
Campus Life. College provides some cultural activities on campus, supplemented by extensive opportunities of Rochester, including programs of Eastman School of Music and Rochester Philharmonic. About 50% of students belong to an academic club or organization, 25% participate in intramural sports, 83% participate in community/volunteer service. No curfews; alcohol allowed in students' rooms; visitation limited; cars allowed.

About 63% of men, 55% of women live in coed dormitories; rest commute. There are no fraternities or sororities. About 25% of resident students leave campus on weekends.
Annual Costs. Tuition and fees, $10,240; room and board, $4,880; estimated $1,200 other, exclusive of travel. About 80% of students receive financial aid; average amount of assistance, $8,108. Assistance is typically divided 53% scholarship, 38% loan, 9% work. College reports some scholarships awarded on the basis of academic merit alone. *Meeting Costs:* college offers Academic Management Services.

University of Nebraska—Lincoln

Lincoln, Nebraska 68588 **(402) 472-7211**

A land-grant college and state university, the University of Nebraska-Lincoln is located on the main City Campus in Lincoln (pop, 171,932) as well as the nearby East Campus, site of the colleges of Agriculture, Home Economics, Dentistry, and Law. Most convenient major airport: Lincoln Regional.

Founded: 1869
Affiliation: State
UG Enrollment: 9,019 M, 7,611 W (full-time); 1,650 M, 1,549 W (part-time)
Total Enrollment: 24,695
Cost: < $10K
% Receiving Financial Aid: 61%
Admission: Selective
Application Deadline: Rolling

Admission is selective for all schools. About 96% of applicants accepted, 54% of these actually enroll; 33% of freshmen graduate in top one fifth of high school class, 63% in two-fifths. Average freshman scores: SAT, 447 verbal, 513 mathematical; 36% score above 500 verbal, 10% above 600, 3% above 700; 60% score above 500 mathematical, 27% above 600, 8% above 700; ACT, 22.4 composite. *Required:* SAT or ACT. Criteria considered in admissions, in order of importance: standardized test scores, high school academic record. *Out-of-state* freshman applicants: university actively seeks students from out of state; no limits; no requirements. State from which most out-of-state students are drawn: South Dakota. Entrance program: midyear admission. *Apply* by July 15; rolling admissions. *Transfers* welcome; 1,257 enrolled 1993–94.

Academic Environment. Degrees offered: associates, bachelors, masters, doctoral. Administration reports percentage of elective courses varies by college and major; distribution requirements for Arts and Sciences fairly numerous. Strongest academic programs reported to be agriculture, engineering, sciences, journalism. *Undergraduate studies* offered to freshmen in colleges of Arts and Sciences, Architecture, Agriculture, Business Administration, Home Economics, Engineering, Journalism and Teachers College. *Majors offered* in Arts and Sciences in addition to usual studies include agribusiness, anthropology, dance, geography, Latin American studies, microbiology, Slavic and East European studies, social welfare, speech pathology and audiology, theater arts, women's studies, actuarial science, biochemistry, hospitality management, natural resources with majors in fisheries and wildlife, range science, soil science, and water science.

About 16% of students entering as freshmen graduate within four years, 54% eventually; 77% of freshmen return for sophomore year. *Special programs:* internships, independent study, study abroad, January Term with study abroad options, honors, undergraduate research, credit by examination, co-operative education in College of Engineering and Technology, combined and pre-professional programs in medicine, dentistry, law, or pharmacy. Adult programs: The Division of Continuing Studies' evening program serves adult students and offers degree programs in business and five areas in arts and sciences. *Calendar:* semester, summer school.

Undergraduate degrees conferred (2,766). 20% were in Business and Management, 14% were in Education, 10% were in Communications, 8% were in Home Economics, 7% were in Social Sciences, 7% were in Engineering, 6% were in Psychology, 4% were in Agribusiness and Agricultural Production, 4% were in Letters, 3% were in Life Sciences, 3% were in Engineering and Engineering Related Technology, remainder in 16 other fields.

Graduates Career Data. Career Development Services include career counseling, resume and interview preparation, information regarding employers, credential files maintenance, arrangement of interviews, job listings.

Faculty. About 71% of faculty hold PhD or equivalent. About 26% of teaching faculty are female; 9% ethnic minorities.

Student Body. University seeks a national student body; 89% of students from in state; 92% Midwest, 5% foreign. An estimated 2% of students reported as Black, 2% Hispanic, 5% Asian, 1% other ethnic minorities. *Minority group students:* financial help, special staff, tutoring programs. Average age of undergraduate student: 23.

Varsity Sports. Men (Div.I): Baseball, Basketball, Cross Country, Football, Golf, Gymnastics, Swimming, Tennis, Track, Wrestling. Women (Div.I): Basketball, Golf, Gymnastics, Soccer, Swimming, Tennis, Track, Volleyball.

Campus Life. Rules governing campus life liberalized in recent years. Provision for intervisitation hours. Cars allowed. Freshmen required to live on campus. Much of campus social life reported to revolve around athletic events and Greek system.

About 19% of men and women live in traditional or coed dormitories; 73% of men and women commute. Sexes segregated in coed dormitories either by wing or floor. There are 28 fraternities, 17 sororities on campus which about 15% of men and women join; 8% of men and women live in fraternities and sororities.

Annual Costs. Tuition and fees, $2,283 (out-of-state, $5,628); room and board, $2,995; estimated $500 other, exclusive of travel. About 61% of students receive financial aid; average amount of assistance, $3,463. Assistance is typically divided 18% scholarship, 33% grant, 46% loan, 3% work. University reports 664 scholarships awarded on the basis of academic merit alone, 405 for special talents, 399 for need alone.

University of Nebraska—Kearney

Kearney, Nebraska 68849 **(308) 234-8526**

A state-supported university, located in a small city of 19,200. Previously known as Kearney State College. Most convenient major airport: Lincoln.

Founded: 1905
Affiliation: State
UG Enrollment: 2,820 M, 3,248 W (full-time); 528 M, 862 W (part-time)
Total Enrollment: 6,773
Cost: < $10K
% Receiving Financial Aid: 65%
Admission: Non-selective
Application Deadline: Rolling

Admission. Graduates of accredited high schools with 15 units eligible; almost all applicants accepted, 60% of these actually enroll. Average freshman ACT scores, according to most recent data available: 20.6 M, 21.1 W composite. *Required:* SAT or ACT. *Out-of-state* freshman applicants: state does not limit out-of-state enrollment. No special requirements for out-of-state applicants. *Apply* by four weeks prior to start of term. *Transfers* welcome.

Academic Environment. *Degrees:* AB, BS, BAEd, BSEd, BFA. About 75% of general education requirements for graduation are elective; distribution requirements fairly numerous. *Majors offered* in addition to usual studies include travel/tourism and actuarial science. About 40% of students entering as freshmen graduate eventually; 38% of freshmen do not return for sophomore year. *Special programs:* CLEP, independent study, honors, individualized majors, study abroad. *Calendar:* semester, summer school.

Undergraduate degrees conferred (1,064). 38% were in Business and Management, 19% were in Education, 6% were in Social Sciences, 5% were in Protective Services, 4% were in Health Sciences, 4% were in Letters, 4% were in Communications, 3% were in Visual and Performing Arts, 3% were in Life Sciences, 3% were in Psychology, 3% were in Computer and Engineering Related Technology, 3% were in Home Economics, remainder in 5 other fields.

Faculty. About 55% of faculty hold PhD or equivalent.

Student Body. College seeks a national student body; 97% of students from Nebraska.

Varsity Sports. Men (NAIA I): Baseball, Basketball, Cross Country, Football, Golf, Tennis, Track, Wrestling. Women (NAIA I): Basketball, Cross Country, Golf, Softball, Swimming & Diving, Tennis, Track, Volleyball.

Campus Life. About 3% of men, 9% of women live in traditional dormitories; 16% of men, 15% of women in coed dormitories; rest live in off-campus housing or commute. Freshmen are given preference in college housing if all students cannot be accommodated. Intervisitation in men's and women's dormitory rooms limited. Sexes segregated in coed dormitories by wing. There are 7 fraternities, 4 sororities; about 13% of men, 9% of women join.

Annual Costs. Tuition and fees, $1,721 (out-of-state, $2,771); room and board, $2,400. About 65% of students receive financial aid; assistance is typically divided 46% scholarship, 48% loan, 6% work. College reports some scholarships awarded for academic merit alone.

University of Nebraska at Omaha

Omaha, Nebraska 68182 **(402) 554-2393**

A state-supported, commuter institution, located in a city of 347,300. Most convenient major airport: Eppley Airfield.

Founded: 1908
Affiliation: State
UG Enrollment: 7,641 M, W (full-time); 6,537 M, W (part-time)
Total Enrollment: 11,739
Cost: < $10K
% Receiving Financial Aid: 50%
Admission: Non-selective
Application Deadline: Aug. 1

Admission. Graduates of accredited high schools eligible; others may be admitted provisionally; about 92% of applicants accepted, 71% of these actually enroll. Average freshman ACT scores, according to most recent data available: 19.7 M, 18.1 W composite. *Required:* ACT or SAT. *Out-of-state* freshman applicants: university does not seek students from out of state. Requirement for out-of-state applicants: "some demonstration of" rank in top half of class. *Apply* by August 1. *Transfers* welcome.

Academic Environment. *Undergraduate studies* offered by colleges of Arts and Sciences, Business Administration, Education, Engineering and Technology, Home Economics, Public Affairs and Community Service, School of Fine Arts. *Majors offered* in addition to usual studies include aviation. About 40% of students entering as freshmen graduate eventually; 50% of freshmen return for sophomore year. *Special programs:* CLEP, independent study, study abroad, undergraduate research, 3-year degree, individualized majors. Adult programs: College of Continuing Studies. *Calendar:* semester, summer school.

Undergraduate degrees conferred (1,333). 26% were in Business and Management, 16% were in Education, 12% were in Protective Services, 8% were in Social Sciences, 7% were in Multi/Interdisciplinary Studies, 5% were in Communications, 5% were in Psychology, 4% were in Computer and Engineering Related Technology, 4% were in Public Affairs, 3% were in Life Sciences, 3% were in Letters, remainder in 8 other fields.

Graduates Career Data. According to most recent data available, careers in business and industry pursued by 65% of graduates. Corporations typically hiring largest numbers of graduates include Mutual of Omaha.

Student Body. University does not seek a national student body; 90% of students from in state; 98% from North Central. An estimated 5% of students reported as Black, 1% Hispanic, 1% Asian, according to most recent data available.

Varsity Sports. Men (Div.II): Baseball, Basketball, Cross Country, Football, Wrestling. Women (Div.II): Basketball, Cross Country, Softball, Volleyball.

Campus Life. No dormitories on campus. There are 9 fraternities, 7 sororities on campus; they provide no residence facilities.

Annual Costs. Tuition and fees, $1,805 (out-of-state, $4,678). About 50% of students receive financial aid. Assistance is typically divided 10% scholarship, 50% loan, 10% work, 30% grant. University reports some scholarships awarded on the basis of academic merit alone.

Nebraska Wesleyan University

Lincoln, Nebraska 68504-2794 (402) 465-2237

An independent institution with ties to the United Methodist Church, located in the state capital (pop. 185,000). Most convenient major airport: Lincoln Municipal.

Founded: 1887
Affiliation: Independent (United Methodist)
UG Enrollment: 653 M, 790 W (full-time); 55 M, 205 W (part-time)
Cost: < $10K
% Receiving Financial Aid: 93%
Admission: Selective (+)
Application Deadline: March 15

Admission is selective (+). About 79% of applicants accepted, 50% of these actually enroll; 26% of freshmen graduate in top decile of high school class, 49% in top second decile. Average freshman ACT scores: 23.6 M, 23.1 W composite. *Required:* ACT or SAT. Criteria considered in admissions, in order of importance: high school academic record, standardized test scores, writing sample, extracurricular activities, recommendations; other factors considered: special talents, diverse student body. Entrance program: early decision (requires essay, resume; interview recommended). *Apply* by March 15, November 15 (early decision). *Transfers* welcome; 63 enrolled 1993–94.

Academic Environment. Degree offered: bachelors. *Majors offered* include usual arts and sciences, business, information systems, education, global studies, theater, nursing. Core requirements include 14 hours communication and symbolic thought, 2 hours healthy lifestyles, 9 hours humanistic studies, 5 hours fine arts, 7 hours physical and biological sciences, 9 hours social aspects of American culture, 8 hours cultural perspectives, 3 hours attitudes and values seminar.

About 50% of students entering as freshmen graduate within four years, 70% eventually; 82% of freshmen return for sophomore year. *Special programs:* CLEP, independent study, study abroad, honors, undergraduate research, optional January interterm, 3–2 engineering, 3–2 physical therapy, Exchange program with American U., Washington Semester, United Nations Semester. Adult programs: evening degree programs. *Calendar:* semester, summer school.

Undergraduate degrees conferred (324). 24% were in Business and Management, 13% were in Social Sciences, 11% were in Life Sciences, 10% were in Psychology, 10% were in Education, 5% were in Communications, 4% were in Visual and Performing Arts, 4% were in Letters, 4% were in Mathematics, 4% were in Health Sciences, 3% were in Foreign Languages, remainder in 4 other fields.

Graduates Career Data. Professional schools typically enrolling largest numbers of graduates include U. of Nebraska. *Career Counseling Program* offers assessment, assistance with choosing a major, career alternatives, on-campus interviewing. Alumni network reported as helpful in both career guidance and job placement.

Faculty. About 80% of faculty hold PhD or equivalent.

Student Body. University seeks a national student body; 93% of students from in state. An estimated 65% of students reported as Protestant, 21% Catholic, 6% unaffiliated, 5% other; 2% Black, 2% Hispanic, 1% Asian.

Varsity Sports. Men (NCAA, Div.III, NAIA, Div. II): Baseball, Basketball, Cross Country, Football, Golf, Soccer, Tennis, Track. Women (NCAA Div.III, NAIA Div.II): Basketball, Cross Country, Golf, Soccer, Softball, Tennis, Track, Volleyball.

Campus Life. About 24% of men, 22% of women live in traditional dormitories; 15% of men, 19% of women in coed dormitories; rest commute. Freshmen given preference in college housing if all students cannot be accommodated. Unlimited intervisitation; sexes segregated in coed dormitories by wing. There are 4 fraternities, 3 sororities on campus which about 38% of men, 32% of women join.

Annual Costs. Tuition and fees, $9,186; room and board, $3,200; estimated $1,900 other, exclusive of travel. About 93% of students receive financial aid; average amount of assistance, $6,300. Assistance is typically divided 52% scholarship/grant, 44% loan, 4% work. University reports 1,326 scholarships awarded on the basis of academic merit alone, 75 for special talents, 1,186 for need alone. *Meeting Costs:* university offers monthly payment plan.

Neumann College

Aston, Pennsylvania 19014 (215) 558-5616

A small church-related college primarily for women, Neumann is a commuter institution. Most convenient major airport: Philadelphia International.

Founded: 1965
Affiliation: Roman Catholic
UG Enrollment: 130 M, 375 W (full-time); 156 M, 545 W (part-time)
Total Enrollment: 1,248
Cost: < $10K
% Receiving Financial Aid: 62%
Admission: Non-selective
Application Deadline: No specific

Admission. Graduates of approved high schools with 16 units in academic subjects "with satisfactory grades" eligible; 72% of applicants accepted; 47% of these actually enroll. About 18% of freshmen graduate in top fifth of high school class, 51% in top two-fifths. Average freshman SAT scores, according to most recent data available: 415 M, 409 W verbal, 465 M, 437 W mathematical. *Required:* SAT or ACT; interview recommended. *Apply* by no specific deadline. *Transfers* welcome.

Academic Environment. *Degrees:* AB, BS. About 85% of freshmen return for sophomore year. *Special programs:* independent study, optional January term, study abroad, individualized majors, cooperative arrangement with St. Joseph's College for certification in elementary and/or secondary education. *Calendar:* semester, summer school.

Undergraduate degrees conferred (173). 39% were in Liberal/General Studies, 28% were in Health Sciences, 13% were in Education, 6% were in Psychology, 5% were in Business and Management, remainder in 6 other fields.

Faculty. About 48% of faculty hold PhD or equivalent.

Student Body. College does not seek a national student body; 80% of students from Pennsylvania; virtually all from Middle Atlantic. An estimated 5% of students reported as Black, 1% Asian, 1% Hispanic, 1% other minority, according to most recent data available.

Religious Orientation. Neumann is a church-related institution; 6 hours of theology required of all students.
Varsity Sports. Men (NAIA): Baseball, Basketball, Cross Country, Tennis. Women (NAIA): Basketball, Cross Country, Softball, Tennis, Volleyball.
Campus Life. All students live in off campus housing or commute.
Annual Costs. Tuition and fees, $9,406. About 62% of students receive financial aid; assistance is typically divided 33% scholarship, 66% loan, 1% work. College reports some scholarships awarded on the basis of academic merit alone. *Meeting Costs:* college offers 10-month and 12-month payment plans, deferred payment plan.

University of Nevada—Las Vegas

Las Vegas, Nevada 89154 (702) 739-3443

The University of Nevada, Las Vegas, is an autonomous division of the University of Nevada System, governed by the state's Board of Regents. The 300-acre campus is located in metropolitan Las Vegas (pop. 550,000). Most convenient major airport: McCarran.

Founded: 1955
Affiliation: State
UG Enrollment: 4,192 M, 4,325 W (full-time); 2,439 M, 2,875 W (part-time)
Total Enrollment: 19,504
Cost: < $10K
% Receiving Financial Aid: 55%
Admission: Non-selective
Application Deadline: 20 working days before start of classes

Admission. Nevada graduates of accredited high schools with 2.3 average eligible. *Required:* ACT or SAT (for placement only). *Out-of-state* freshman applicants: university welcomes students from out of state. State does not limit out-of-state enrollment. Requirement for out-of-state applicants: 2.3 minimum GPA. *Apply* by 20 working days before start of classes. *Transfers* welcome.
Academic Environment. Academic Advising and Resources Center gives special attention to interdisciplinary programs for freshmen. *Degrees:* BA, BS, BFA, BLA. About 58% of freshmen return for sophomore year. *Special programs:* CLEP, honors, independent study, study abroad. *Calendar:* semester, summer school.
Undergraduate degrees conferred (1,268). 46% were in Business and Management, 15% were in Education, 5% were in Social Sciences, 5% were in Communications, 5% were in Protective Services, 3% were in Public Affairs, 3% were in Health Sciences, 3% were in Psychology, 3% were in Engineering, 3% were in Visual and Performing Arts, remainder in 10 other fields.
Student Body. University seeks a national student body; 86% of students from in state.
Varsity Sports. Men (Div.I): Baseball, Basketball, Football, Golf, Soccer, Swimming & Diving, Tennis. Women (Div.I): Basketball, Cross Country, Softball, Swimming & Diving, Tennis, Track.
Campus Life. About 6% of men, 5% of women live in coed dormitories; 93% of men, 94% of women live in off-campus housing or commute. There are 10 fraternities, 6 sororities on campus which about 11% of men, 4% of women join; about 1% each men, women live in fraternities and sororities.
Annual Costs. Tuition and fees, $1,665 (out-of-state, $5,965). About 55% of students receive financial aid; assistance is typically divided 47% scholarship, 33% loan, 20% work. University reports some scholarships awarded on the basis of academic merit alone. *Meeting Costs:* university offers PLUS Loans.

University of Nevada—Reno

Reno, Nevada 89557 (702) 784-6865

A state-supported, land-grant institution and one of the 4 components of the University of Nevada System; located in a city of 100,000, 200 miles northeast of San Francisco.

Founded: 1874
Affiliation: State
UG Enrollment: 4,233 M, 4,378 W (full-time); 1,148 M, 1,336 W (part-time)
Total Enrollment: 12,137
Cost: < $10K
Admission: Non-selective
Application Deadline: Rolling

Admission. Graduates of accredited or approved high schools with 2.3 average or score 19 on ACT composite eligible; Nevada residents with 2.0 average admitted on probation; 84% of applicants accepted, 59% of these actually enroll. Average freshman scores: SAT, 432 verbal, 488 mathematical; 35% of entering freshman score above 500, 9% above 600, 1% above 700; 63% score above 500, 25% above 600, 5% above 700; ACT, 22 composite. *Required:* ACT or SAT. Criteria considered in admissions: high school academic record. *Out-of-state* freshman applicants: university actively seeks out-of-state students; no limits; no special requirements. State from which most out-of-state students are drawn: California. *Apply* by July 1; rolling admissions. *Transfers* welcome; 10% enrolled 1993–94.
Academic Environment. Degrees offered: bachelors, masters, doctoral. *Undergraduate studies* offered by colleges of Arts and Science, Agriculture, Business Administration, Education, Engineering, schools of Home Economics, Medical Sciences, Mines, Nursing. *Majors offered* in Arts and Science in addition to usual studies include anthropology, biochemistry, cellular molecular biology, journalism, social services and corrections, speech and theater. Core requirements include 3–6 credits writing, 3 credits mathematics, 6 credits natural sciences, 3 credits social science, 3 credits fine arts, 9 credits Western traditions, 6 credits capstone, other requirements vary with program. Recent student finds the strengths of the academic program to include small classes, free tutoring, excellent library facility. About 70% of freshman return for sophomore year.

Special programs: credit by examination, independent study, study abroad, honors, National Student Exchange Program, affiliation with Institute of European Studies. *Calendar:* semester, summer school.
Undergraduate degrees conferred (1,079). 16% were in Business and Management, 14% were in Education, 10% were in Social Sciences, 10% were in Health Sciences, 8% were in Liberal/General Studies, 8% were in Engineering, 5% were in Psychology, 4% were in Communications, 4% were in Life Sciences, 4% were in Public Affairs, 4% were in Home Economics, 3% were in Computer and Engineering Related Technology, remainder in 10 other fields.
Graduates Career Data. According to most recent data available, full-time graduate or professional study pursued by 15–20% of students immediately after graduation. Fields typically hiring largest numbers of graduates include engineering, business management, accounting.
Faculty. About 77% of faculty hold PhD or equivalent. About 28% of teaching faculty are female; 1% Black, 3% Hispanic, 6% other.
Student Body. University seeks a national student body; 80% of students from in state; 12% West, 6% foreign. An estimated 2% of students reported as Black, 4% Hispanic, 5% Asian. Average age of undergraduate student: 24.
Varsity Sports. Men (Div.I): Baseball, Basketball, Cross Country, Football (I-AA), Golf, Skiing, Tennis, Track. Women (Div.I): Basketball, Cross Country, Skiing, Swimming, Tennis, Volleyball.
Campus Life. About 10% of men, 10% of women live in coed dormitories; rest live in off-campus housing or commute. Students may choose between limited and unlimited intervisitation. Sexes segregated in coed dormitories by floor or suite. There are 10 fraternities, 4 sororities on campus. About 25% of resident students leave campus on weekends.
Annual Costs. Tuition and fees, $1,665 (out-of-state, $5,965); room and board, $4,952; about $2,400 (on campus), excluding travel. University reports some scholarships awarded on the basis of academic merit alone.

New College

(See University of South Florida)

New College of California

San Francisco, California. 94102 (415) 241-1381

A small liberal arts commuter college offering some career oriented and preprofessional programs. The college includes a law school and graduate programs in psychology.

Founded: 1972
Affiliation: Independent
Total Enrollment: 1,200
Cost: < $10K
% Receiving Financial Aid: 90%
Admission: Non-selective
Application Deadline: Rolling

Admission. About 99% of applicants accepted, 70% of these actually enroll. *Required:* interview, essay. *Entrance programs:* early decision, early admission, midyear admission. *Apply:* rolling admissions. *Transfers* welcome; 120 enrolled 1993–94.
Academic Environment. Degrees offered: associates, bachelors, masters. *Majors offered* include self-designed emphasis areas. Average undergraduate class size: 95% under 20. *Special programs:* January term, study abroad, internship/cooperative work-study programs. About 50% of students entering as freshmen graduate within four years, 80% eventually; 90% of freshmen return for sophomore year. Adult program: weekend completion program. *Calendar:* semester.
Undergraduate degrees conferred (92). 100% were in Liberal/General Studies.
Faculty. About 70% of faculty hold PhD or equivalent. About 70% of undergraduate classes taught by tenured faculty. About 60% of teaching faculty are female; 5% Black, 5% Hispanic.
Student Body. About 90% of students from in state. An estimated 2% of students reported as Black, 7% Hispanic, 1% Asian, 3% other minorities. Average age of undergraduate student: 24.
Annual Costs. Tuition and fees, $7,000; estimated $5,000 other, exclusive of travel. About 90% of students receive financial aid; average amount of assistance, $14,000. Assistance is typically divided 2% scholarship, 30% grant, 60% loan, 8% work. College reports 80% of scholarships awarded on the basis of need alone.

New England College

Henniker, New Hampshire 03242 (603) 428-2223

An independent, liberal arts college, located in a village of 3,000, 16 miles west of Concord. College has established a 4-year branch campus in Arundel, England. Most convenient major airport: Manchester.

Founded: 1946
Affiliation: Independent
UG Enrollment: 480 M, 320 W (full-time)
Cost: $10K–$20K
% Receiving Financial Aid: 38%
Admission: Non-selective
Application Deadline: Rolling

Admission. High school graduates with 12 units in college-preparatory subjects eligible; 82% of applicants accepted. Average freshman SAT scores: 400 M, 400 W verbal, 430 M, 400 W mathematical, according to most recent data available. About 16% of entering freshman graduate in top fifth of high school class, 43% in top two-fifths. *Required:* essay, recommendations, class rank, minimum HS GPA 2.0. Criteria considered in admissions, in order of importance: high school academic record, writing sample, recommendations, extracurricular activities, class rank; other factors considered: special talents, alumni children. *Entrance programs:* midyear admission, deferred admission, advanced placement. About 40% of entering students from private schools. *Apply:* rolling admissions. *Transfers* welcome; 50 enrolled 1992–93.
Academic Environment. Degree offered: bachelors. All general education requirements for graduation are elective; distribution requirements limited. About 47% of students entering as freshmen graduate eventually; 25% of freshmen do not return for sophomore year, according to most recent data available. *Majors offered* include social and economic development. *Special programs:* CLEP, honors, undergraduate research, independent study, study abroad at British Campus, individualized majors, internships, touring theater, PIONEERS, cooperative programs through NHCUC, cross registration with other NH schools. Average undergraduate class size: 90% under 20, 10% 20–40. *Calendar:* 4–1–4.
Undergraduate degrees conferred (239). 23% were in Business and Management, 18% were in Psychology, 17% were in Communications, 10% were in Education, 9% were in Visual and Performing Arts, 9% were in Social Sciences, 4% were in Letters, 4% were in Engineering, remainder in 5 other fields.
Graduates Career Data. Advanced studies pursued by 40% of students within three years after graduation. About 75% of graduates employed in their fields within two years after graduation.
Faculty. About 65% of faculty hold PhD or equivalent.
Student Body. College seeks a national student body; 15% of students from in state; 65% New England, 20% Middle Atlantic, 8% foreign. An estimated 30% of students reported as Protestant, 30% Catholic, 30% Jewish.
Varsity Sports. Men (Div. III): Baseball, Basketball, Ice Hockey, Lacrosse, Skiing (Div.II), Soccer. Women (Div. III): Basketball, Field Hockey, Lacrosse, Skiing (Div.II), Soccer, Softball.
Campus Life. About 60% of men, 60% of women live in coed dormitories; 35% of men, 40% of women live in off-campus housing; 5% of men commute. Freshmen given preference in college housing if all students cannot be accommodated. Intervisitation in men's and women's dormitory rooms unlimited. Sexes segregated in coed dormitories either by wing or floor. There are 3 fraternities, 3 sororities on campus, which about 15% of each men and women join. About 15% of resident students leave campus on weekends.
Annual Costs. Tuition and fees, $12,690; room and board, $5,180; estimated $1,000 other, exclusive of travel. About 38% of students receive financial aid. Assistance is typically divided 45% scholarship, 55% loan and work, according to most recent data available. College reports 100% of scholarships awarded on the basis of need.

New England Conservatory of Music

Boston, Massachusetts 02115

An independent, professional, and teacher education institution, the conservatory is a college of music and offers undergraduate and graduate degrees in vocal and instrumental music, jazz studies, third stream studies, early music performance, music education, composition, conducting, music history, and music theory.

Founded: 1867
Affiliation: Independent

Undergraduate degrees conferred (77). 97% were in Visual and Performing Arts, 3% were in Education.

University of New England

Biddeford, Maine 04005 (207) 283-0171

An independent, liberal arts university founded by the Franciscan Fathers. The 125-acre campus is located on the banks of the Saco River and the shore of the Atlantic Ocean in a community of 20,000, 16 miles southeast of Portland. Most convenient major airport: Portland International.

Founded: 1953
Affiliation: Independent
UG Enrollment: 229 M, 569 W (full-time)
Total Enrollment: 1,371
Cost: $10K–$20K
% Receiving Financial Aid: 88%
Admission: Non-selective
Application Deadline: Rolling

Admission. High school graduates with 8 units in academic subjects eligible; 62% of applicants accepted, 41% of these actually enroll. About 47% of freshmen graduate in top fifth of high school class, 78% in top two-fifths, according to most recent data available. Average freshman SAT scores: 440 M, 420 W verbal, 500 M, 460 W mathematical. *Required:* SAT, essay, 2 letters of recommendation, "exposure" (for pt & ot); interview recommended. Criteria considered in admissions: high school academic record, standardized test scores, recommendations, extra curricular activities, writing sample. *Entrance programs:* early decision, midyear admission, deferred admission. *Apply:* rolling admission; first week of March for physical therapy. *Transfers* welcome; 43 enrolled 1993–94.
Academic Environment. Degrees offered: associates, bachelors, masters. *Majors offered* in addition to usual studies include laddered BSN program. Core requirements include English, mathematics, computer science, psychology, sociology, political science, life science, humanities. About 55% of students entering as freshmen graduate eventually; 90% of freshmen return for sophomore year. Average undergraduate class size: 55% of classes under 20, 37% 20–40, 8% over 40. *Special programs:* CLEP, 3-week interterm,

January term, independent study, study abroad, 3-year degree, individualized majors, 2–3 program in prepharmacy with Massachusetts College of Pharmacy and Allied Health, 3–4 in pre-med/osteopathic medical school, cross registration with St. Joseph's College, USM Westbrook College, ME College of Art, South ME Tech. College. *Calendar:* 4–1–4.

Undergraduate degrees conferred (102). 68% were in Allied Health, 16% were in Life Sciences, 6% were in Psychology, 5% were in Liberal/General Studies, 4% were in Education, remainder in Business and Management.

Graduates Career Data. *Full-time graduate or professional study* pursued by 9% of students immediately after graduation, according to most recent data available. Fields typically employing largest numbers of graduates include physical and occupational therapy, nursing, social work. Career Development Services include career counseling, career related workshops, resume writing, job hunting assistance, resource room for graduate schools, career opportunities and other related materials.

Faculty. About 90% of faculty hold PhD or equivalent, according to most recent data available.

Student Body. University does not seek a national student body; 58% of students from in state; 89% New England, 7% Middle Atlantic, 1% foreign. An estimated 20% of students reported as Protestant, 40% Catholic, 10% Jewish, 10% unaffiliated, 20% other; 2% Black, 2% Hispanic, 2% Asian, 2% Native American, 2% other minority, according to most recent data available. Average age of undergraduate student: 23.

Varsity Sports. Men (Div.III): Basketball, Cross Country, Lacrosse, Soccer. Women (Div.III): Basketball, Cross Country, Soccer, Softball, Volleyball.

Campus Life. About 8% of women live in traditional dormitories; 22% of men, 14% of women in coed dormitories; 1% of men, 2% of women live in off-campus housing; rest commute. Intervisitation in men's and women's dormitory rooms unlimited. There are no fraternities or sororities. About 40% of resident students leave campus on weekends.

Annual Costs. Tuition and fees, $11,195; room and board, $4,875. About 88% of students receive financial aid; average amount of assistance, $11,000. Assistance is typically divided 10% scholarship, 20% grant, 60% loan, 10% work. College reports 8 scholarships awarded on the basis of academic merit alone, 2 for special talents, 1 for need alone. *Meeting Costs:* college offers AMS, TMS, Knight Repayment Plan, deferred payment plan.

New Hampshire College

Manchester, New Hampshire 03106 (603) 645-9611

An independent, professional college offering programs in business, liberal arts, and hospitality administration, located in a city of 100,000, 50 miles from Boston. Most convenient major airports: Manchester or Logan (Boston).

Founded: 1932
Affiliation: Independent
UG Enrollment: 622 M, 409 W (full-time, day program); 34 M, 28 W (part-time)
Total Enrollment: 2,793
Cost: $10K–$20K
% Receiving Financial Aid: 75%
Admission: Non-selective
Application Deadline: Rolling

Admission. Graduates of approved high schools eligible; 85% of applicants accepted, 23% of these actually enroll. About 6% of freshmen graduate in top fifth of high school class, 28% in top two-fifths. Average freshman SAT scores: 405 M, 405 W verbal, 455 M, 455 W mathematical. *Required:* SAT, minimum H.S. GPA of 2.0, essay, guidance counselor recommendation; interview recommended. Criteria considered in admissions, in order of importance: high school academic record, recommendations, writing sample, standardized tests, extracurricular activities, class rank; other factors considered: special talents, diverse student body, alumni children. *Entrance programs:* early admission, midyear admission, deferred admission. About 20% of freshmen from private schools. *Apply:* rolling admissions. *Transfers* welcome; 94 enrolled 1993–94.

Academic Environment. Degrees offered: associates, bachelors, masters. Core requirements include 18 credits in English, 6 in history, 3 in psychology, 3 in sociology, 3 in government, 6 in economics, 6 in humanities, 3 in computer, 1 course mathematics, 1 course in sciences. *Majors offered* include hotel/restaurant management, culinary arts, sports management, international business. Liberal arts programs recently added in English, humanities, social science, teacher education (secondary), communications. Average undergraduate class size: 10% under 20, 90% between 20–40. Students report that the Learning Center and faculty provide extra help when needed. About 60% of students entering as freshmen graduate within five years; 75% of freshmen return for sophomore year, according to most recent data available. *Special programs:* CLEP, January session, independent study, study abroad, foreign and domestic internships, cross registration with other New Hampshire schools. Adult programs: Continuing Education division with classes in the evenings and weekends. *Calendar:* semester, summer school.

Undergraduate degrees conferred (824). 91% were in Business and Management, 4% were in Computer and Engineering Related Technology, remainder in 5 other fields.

Graduates Career Data. About 91% of 1992–93 graduates employed. Fields typically employing the largest number of graduates include technical, hospitality, communications, finance. Career Development Services include on-campus recruiting, resume writing workshops, mock interviews, assistance with co-ops, individual career counseling, computerized employer data bank, off-campus recruiting assistance.

Faculty. About 70% of faculty hold PhD or equivalent. About 25% of teaching faculty are female; 1% minority.

Student Body. College does not seek a national student body; 30% of students from in state; 80% New England; 15% Foreign. An estimated 20% of students reported as Protestant, 55% Catholic, 9% Jewish, 13% Muslim, 3% other; 1% Black, 1% Hispanic, 3% Asian, 14% other minority.

Varsity Sports. Men (Div.II): Baseball, Basketball, Ice Hockey, Lacrosse, Soccer. Women (Div.II): Basketball, Soccer, Softball, Volleyball.

Campus Life. A recent student reports, "Great location, close to skiing, close to Boston, only 5–10 minutes to shopping malls and center of Manchester." Another student finds plenty of organized activities on campus. On-campus housing options include residence halls, apartments, and townhouses. Culinary arts students run the dining room which is open to the public 2 days a week. About 60% men, 40% women live in coed dormitories; rest live in off-campus housing or commute. There are 4 fraternities, 4 sororities on campus, which about 10% of students join; 1% of women live in sororities. About 20% of resident students leave campus on weekends.

Annual Costs. Tuition and fees, $10,464; room and board, $4,634; estimated other, $1,400, exclusive of travel. About 75% of students receive financial aid; average amount of assistance, $7,500. Assistance is typically divided 5% scholarship, 35% grant, 45% loan, 15% work. College reports 125 scholarships awarded for academic merit, 512 for need. *Meeting Costs:* college offers several payment plans.

University of New Hampshire

Durham, New Hampshire 03824 (603) 862-1360

A medium-sized state university, New Hampshire is more selective than most state institutions. This is one of the factors that makes the university attractive to out-of-state students. The 200-acre Durham campus is located in a town of 5,500, about 65 miles north of Boston, "an equal distance from the White Mountains, and 20 minutes from the beaches and rocky coasts of New Hampshire and Maine." Most convenient major airport: Manchester, Logan (Boston, MA).

Founded: 1866
Affiliation: State
UG Enrollment: 4,791 M, 6,040 W (full-time)
Total Enrollment: 12,397
Cost: $10K–$20K
% Receiving Financial Aid: 63%
Admission: Selective (+)
Application Deadline: February 1

Admission is selective (+). About 78% of applicants accepted, 33% of these actually enroll; 48% of freshmen graduate in top fifth of high school class, 89% in top two-fifths. Average freshman SAT scores: 476 M, 475 W verbal, 536 M, 518 W mathematical; 39% above 500 verbal, 6% above 600; 68% above 500 mathematical, 25% above 600, 3% above 700. *Required:* SAT; B average; essay; portfolio for art students, audition for music students; interview recommended. Criteria considered in admissions, in order of importance: high school academic record, recommendations, extracurricular activities, writing sample, standardized test scores; other factors considered: special talents, alumni children, diverse student body. *Out-of-state* freshman applicants: university actively seeks out-of-state students; "competitive, selective admission to individual colleges" for out-of-state applicants. *Out-of-state* enrollment limited to 40% of student body. About 75% of applicants accepted, 24% of these actually enroll. *Entrance programs:* early admission, deferred admission, advanced placement. *Apply* by February 1. *Transfers* welcome; 586 enrolled 1993–94.

Academic Environment. While many schools have been trying to cut costs recently, UNH has been expanding and improving many academic and residential campus facilities within the past few years. Students have representation with faculty on Unicameral University Senate, which gives them some influence over most areas of university life, including curriculum and faculty affairs. Pressures for academic achievement vary somewhat among different colleges and schools. Administration reports General Education Program provides a solid liberal arts background to all students, requirements include 10 courses spread out over 8 areas: writing skills; quantitative reasoning; biological, physical or technological sciences; historical perspectives; foreign culture; fine arts; social sciences; and works of literature, philosophy and ideas. Degrees offered: associates, bachelors, masters, doctoral. *Undergraduate studies* offered by colleges of Liberal Arts, Life Sciences and Agriculture, Engineering and Physical Sciences, Whittemore School of Business and Economics (including degree program in hotel administration), School of Health Studies, 2-year Thompson School of Applied Science. *Majors offered* in addition to usual studies include dairy management, women's studies, communications, journalism, social work, theater. Variety of new departments and programs recently introduced include: Center for the Humanities, Institute for the Study of Earth, Oceans and Space, Institute for Marine Science and Ocean/Engineering, Center for the Biological Sciences, Institute for Policy and Social Science Research, equine science, agronomy, and a variety of interdisciplinary programs ranging from technology, society and values to gerontology. Average undergraduate class size: 56% under 20, 32% between 20–40, 12% over 40; faculty to student ratio, 1:18. Several recent students list the faculty as the greatest academic strength at UNH, a current senior describes the faculty as "enthusiastic and always available and willing to help." Students also find the library and computer facilities to be adequate, but warn that, "if you put things off to the last minute you may have to wait."

About 51% of students entering as freshmen graduate within four years, 80% eventually; 87% of freshmen return for sophomore year. *Special programs:* CLEP, independent study, study abroad, undergraduate research, student-designed majors, 5-year 2-degree programs, cooperative programs through NHCUC, honors program, Program in International Perspectives, New England/Quebec Student Exchange Program, UNH/USA Exchange Program, Field Experience Program. Adult programs: AA degree program offered. *Calendar:* semester, summer school.

Undergraduate degrees conferred (2,225). 17% were in Social Sciences, 14% were in Business and Management, 11% were in Letters, 8% were in Communications, 6% were in Engineering, 6% were in Psychology, 5% were in Life Sciences, 5% were in Health Sciences, 3% were in Visual and Performing Arts, 3% were in Allied Health, 3% were in Renewable Natural Resources, 3% were in Home Economics, remainder in 12 other fields.

Faculty. About 85% of faculty hold PhD or equivalent. About 45% of undergraduate classes are taught by tenured faculty. About 35% of teaching faculty are female; 5% ethnic minority.

Graduates Career Data. According to most recent data available, advanced studies pursued by 15% of students immediately after graduation. Fields typically employing largest numbers of graduates include business, engineering, health. Career Development Services "aid students in each facet of the job search, from resume writing to interviewing."

Student Body. About 60% of students from in state; 88% New England, 9% Middle Atlantic; less than 1% Foreign. An estimated 9% of students reported as minorities.

Varsity Sports. Men (Div.I): Baseball, Basketball, Cross Country, Diving, Football(IAA), Golf, Ice Hockey, Lacrosse, Skiing, Soccer, Swimming, Tennis, Track. Women (Div. I): Basketball, Crew, Cross Country, Diving, Field Hockey, Golf, Gymnastics, Ice Hockey, Lacrosse, Skiing, Soccer, Swimming, Tennis, Track.

Campus Life. Regulations governing campus social life relatively relaxed. Daily intervisitation may be voted by each residence unit. Alcohol permitted for those 21 and over in university-related housing; large parties and public drinking prohibited. Cars allowed for upper-class students. UNH students enjoy an active campus, with many speakers, musicians, artists and comedians coming to perform, as well as abundant athletic activities. Off-campus cultural and recreational opportunities are easily accessible in nearby Boston, the White Mountains, and beaches.

About 52% of students live in traditional or coed dormitories; 28% of men, 28% of women live in off-campus college-related housing; rest commute. Freshmen given preference in college housing if all students cannot be accommodated. There are 10 fraternities, 6 sororities on campus, which 10% of men, 10% of women join; 10% of men, 10% of women live in fraternities and sororities. The majority of resident students leave campus on weekends, according to most recent data available.

Annual Costs. Tuition and fees, $4,380 (out-of-state, $12,010); room and board, $3,862; estimated $2,800 other, exclusive of travel. About 63% of students receive financial aid; average amount of assistance, $5,238. University reports scholarships awarded for academic merit, special talents, and need.

University of New Haven

West Haven, Connecticut 06516 (203) 932-7319

An independent institution, offering programs in the liberal arts, business administration, criminal justice and public safety, hotel/restaurant/tourism administration, and engineering; located in a New Haven suburb of 53,000. Most convenient major airport: Tweed (New Haven).

Founded: 1920
Affiliation: Independent
UG Enrollment: 1,488 M, W (full-time); 1,931 M, W (part-time)
Total Enrollment: 5,931
Cost: $10K–$20K
% Receiving Financial Aid: 70%
Admission: Non-selective
Application Deadline: Rolling

Admission. Graduates of accredited high schools with 15 units eligible; others given individual consideration; 86% applicants accepted, 24% of these actually enroll; 13% of entering freshmen graduate in top fifth of high school class, 31% in top two-fifths. Average freshman SAT scores: 434 verbal, 495 mathematical. *Required:* SAT or ACT, or university's own tests; interview recommended. Criteria considered in admissions, in order of importance: high school academic record, extracurricular activities, standardized test scores; other factors considered: special talents, diverse student body. *Entrance programs:* midyear admission, deferred admission, advanced placement. About 21% of entering students from private or parochial schools. *Apply* by September 1; rolling admissions. *Transfers* welcome; 248 enrolled 1993–94.

Academic Environment. Degrees offered: associates, bachelors, masters, doctoral. Students take 34 credits from the Core Curriculum which includes English composition, literature, mathematics/computer science, the scientific method, lab science, history, social science, and fine arts. *Majors offered* include air transportation management, aviation, music and sound recording, forensic science, arson investigation, fire science administration and technology, fire protection engineering, criminal justice, management of sports industries, dental hygiene, medical technology, music industry, environmental science. About 40% of students entering as freshmen graduate within four years; 75% of freshmen return for sophomore year. *Special programs:* CLEP, honors, cooperative education, internship, January term, cross registration with Albertus Magnus. *Calendar:* 4–1–4.

Undergraduate degrees conferred (432). 40% were in Business and Management, 22% were in Engineering, 12% were in Protective Services, 5% were in Computer and Engineering Related Technology, 5% were in Visual and Performing Arts, 3% were in Communications, 3% were in Architecture and Environmental Design, remainder in 10 other fields.

Faculty. About 90% of faculty hold PhD or equivalent; there are no teaching assistants.

Graduate Career Data. Advanced studies pursued by 15% of students within six months of graduation. About 93% of 1991–92 graduates employed. Fields typically employing the largest number

of graduates include criminal justice, business, engineering. Career Development Services include career counseling, resume/interview workshops, career fairs, on-campus recruitment, internships/cooperative education, library resources, alumni networking.
Student Body. About 65% of students from Connecticut. An estimated 12% of students reported as Black, 6% Hispanic, 2% Asian, 5% other minority.
Varsity Sports. Men (Div.II): Baseball, Basketball, Cross Country, Football, Lacrosse, Soccer, Track. Women (Div.II): Basketball, Soccer, Softball, Tennis, Volleyball.
Campus Life. About 42% of students live in coed dormitories; rest live in off-campus housing or commute. Freshmen given preference in college housing if all students cannot be accommodated. Intervisitation in men's and women's dormitory rooms unlimited. Sexes segregated in coed dormitories by suite. There are 5 fraternities, 3 sororities on campus, which about 8% of men, 8% of women join. About 50% of resident students leave campus on weekends.
Annual Costs. Tuition and fees, $10,180; room and board, $4,750; estimated $500 other, exclusive of travel. About 70% of students receive financial aid; average amount of assistance offered to freshmen; $9,699. University reports 5% scholarships awarded for academic merit, 95% for special talents and need. *Meeting Costs:* university offers revolving credit plan through an area bank with university subsidized interest.

New Jersey Institute of Technology

Newark, New Jersey 07102 (201) 596-3300

Originally an engineering institution, New Jersey Institute of Technology offers degrees in computer science, architecture, engineering, management, applied sciences, technology, and an interdisciplinary degree program. Most convenient major airport: Newark International.

Founded: 1881
Affiliation: State/City
UG Enrollment: 2,784 M, 527 W (full-time); 1,369 M, 277 W (part-time)
Total Enrollment: 7,551
Cost: < $10K
% Receiving Financial Aid: 60%
Admission: Very Selective
Application Deadline: Rolling

Admission is very selective. About 65% of applicants accepted, 40% of these actually enroll; 50% of freshmen graduate in top fifth of high school class, 81% in top two-fifths. Average freshman SAT scores: 463 M, 482 W verbal, 601 M, 592 W mathematical; 35% of freshmen score above 500 on verbal, 7% above 600; 96% score above 500 on mathematical, 49% above 600, 10% above. *Required:* SAT, ACH in mathematics I or II for all applicants, portfolio for architecture students. Criteria considered in admissions, in order of importance: high school academic record, standardized test scores, recommendations, extracurricular activities; other factors considered: special talents. *Out-of-state* freshman applicants: institute actively seeks students from out-of-state. State does not limit out-of-state enrollment. About 54% of out-of-state students accepted, 25% of these actually enroll. States from which most out-of-state students come include New York, Pennsylvania, Connecticut. *Entrance programs:* early decision, early admission, midyear admission, advanced placement. About 20% of entering students from private and parochial schools. *Apply* by April 1 (March 1 for Architecture); rolling admissions. *Transfers* welcome; 442 enrolled 1993–94.
Academic Environment. Administration reports percent of courses required for graduation that are elective varies widely among different programs; general university core curriculum is required. Most popular undergraduate programs reported to be mechanical, civil, and environmental engineering, architecture. Degrees offered: bachelors, masters, doctoral. *Majors offered* in 19 different areas including 7 fields of engineering; engineering science curriculum includes options in biomedical/engineering, environmental sciences, pre-medical/pre-dental. NJIT is a highly specialized professional institution. Only liberal arts major offered is Science, Technology and Society. New program in materials science and engineering. *Computer Science:* all full-time freshmen receive their own personal computer to use during their undergraduate years, including software and hardware enhancements. Upon graduation, students may purchase the computer and software package for a nominal fee. Facilities reported as continually being upgraded to meet student demand; they include access to artificial intelligence equipment; link with New Jersey's supercomputer based at John Von Neumann Advanced Scientific Computer Center. Average undergraduate class size: 24% under 20, 67% between 20–40, 9% over 40.

About 40% of students entering as freshmen graduate in four years, 75% eventually; many students take more than four years to participate in co-op program, or to work part-time, or to complete 5-year architecture program; 80% of freshmen return for sophomore year. *Special programs:* CLEP, honors, 3-year degree, 3–2 in engineering and liberal arts, extensive co-operative education program, cross-registration with Rutgers/Newark and Essex County College, College of Medicine & Dentistry of New Jersey. Adult programs: special support services for women over 25. *Calendar:* semester, summer school.
Undergraduate degrees conferred (622). 54% were in Engineering, 20% were in Engineering and Engineering Related Technology, 12% were in Architecture and Environmental Design, 7% were in Computer and Engineering Related Technology, 6% were in Business and Management, remainder in 3 other fields.
Graduates Career Data. Advanced studies pursued by 10% of students, immediately after graduation. About 85% of 1992–93 graduates employed. Corporations typically hiring largest numbers of graduates include AT&T Bell Labs, AT&T, General Electric, Public Service Electric & Gas. Career Development Services include on-campus interviews, resume writing assistance, career planning workshops, individual career planning/counseling sessions, career resource library and career materials, job posting/job listing service.
Faculty. About 98% of faculty hold PhD or equivalent. About 50% of undergraduate classes taught by tenured faculty; 84% of classes taught by full-time faculty. About 11% of teaching faculty are female; 2% Black, 17% other minority.
Student Body. Institute does not seek a national student body; 93% of students from in state; 4% Foreign. An estimated 19% of students reported as Protestant, 48% Catholic, 1% Jewish, 4% Muslim, 14% unaffiliated, 14% other; 13% Black, 13% Hispanic, 17% Asian, 4% other minority. Average age of undergraduate student: 22.
Varsity Sports. Men (Div.III): Baseball, Basketball, Cross Country, Fencing, Golf, Judo, Soccer, Tennis, Volleyball. Women (Div.III): Basketball, Fencing, Judo, Softball, Tennis, Volleyball.
Campus Life. This is an urban institution very close to New York City. About 25% men, 26% women live in coed dormitories; rest commute. There are 18 fraternities, 7 sororities on campus, which about 18% men, 19% women join. Fraternities own or rent houses in the vicinity of the campus; NJIT neither regulates nor supervises them. About 40% of resident students leave campus on weekends. Freshmen given preference in college housing if all students cannot be accommodated.
Annual Costs. Tuition and fees, $4,790 (out-of-state, $9,134); room and board, $5,175; estimated $1,000 other, exclusive of travel. About 60% of students receive financial aid; average amount of assistance, $5,466. Assistance is typically divided 9% scholarship, 39% grant, 27% loan, 25% work. Institute reports 300 scholarships awarded for academic merit, 300 for need and merit.

New Mexico Highlands University

Las Vegas, New Mexico 87701 (505) 425-7511

A state-supported university, located in a town of 16,000, 70 miles northeast of Santa Fe. Most convenient major airport: Albuquerque.

Founded: 1893
Affiliation: State
UG Enrollment: 664 M, 780 W (full-time); 103 M, 218 W (part-time)
Cost: < $10K
% Receiving Financial Aid: 85%
Admission: Non-selective
Application Deadline: Rolling

Admission. Graduates of accredited high schools with 15 units (9 in academic subjects) and C average eligible; others admitted probationally; 82% of accepted applicants actually enroll. *Required:* ACT (for placement only). *Out-of-state* freshman applicants: university welcomes students from out of state. State does not limit out-of-state enrollment. No special requirements for out-of-state applicants. *Apply:* rolling admissions. *Transfers* welcome.

Academic Environment. *Degrees:* BA, BS. About 25% of general education requirements for graduation are elective; distribution requirements fairly numerous. About 60% of students entering as freshmen graduate eventually; 30% of freshmen do not return for sophomore year. *Special programs:* AP, CLEP, cooperative education, career counseling and placement, independent study, honors, undergraduate research. *Calendar:* semester, summer school.

Undergraduate degrees conferred (163). 29% were in Education, 25% were in Business and Management, 9% were in Public Affairs, 8% were in Social Sciences, 6% were in Visual and Performing Arts, 6% were in Psychology, 3% were in Communications, remainder in 12 other fields.

Varsity Sports. Men (RMAC, NAIA): Baseball, Basketball, Cross Country, Football. Women (RMAC, AIAW): Basketball, Softball, Volleyball.

Student Body. University does not seek a national student body; about 84% of students from New Mexico. An estimated 68% of students reported as Hispanic, 4% other minority, according to most recent data available.

Campus Life. About 28% of students live in traditional dormitories; no coed dormitories; rest live in off-campus housing or commute. Freshmen given preference in college housing if all students cannot be accommodated. No intervisitation in men's dormitory rooms; limited in women's. About 50% of students leave campus on weekends.

Annual Costs. Tuition and fees, $1,480 (out-of-state, $5,234); room and board, $2,780. About 85% of students receive financial aid, according to most recent data available. University reports some scholarships awarded on the basis of academic merit alone. *Meeting Costs:* university offers deferred payment plan.

New Mexico Institute of Mining and Technology

Socorro, New Mexico 87801 **(505) 835-5424 (Toll-free, 800-428-TECH)**

A state-supported college of technology and science, New Mexico Tech is located in a town of 9,000, 75 miles south of Albuquerque. Most convenient major airport: Albuquerque International.

Founded: 1889
Affiliation: State
UG Enrollment: 690 M, 327 W (full-time); 166 M, 245 W (part-time)
Total Enrollment: 1,726
Cost: < $10K
% Receiving Financial Aid: 92%
Admission: Very (+) Selective
Application Deadline: Rolling

Admission is very (+) selective. About 76% of applicants accepted, 39% of these actually enroll; 64% of freshmen graduate in top fifth of their high school class, 73% in top two-fifths. Average freshman scores: SAT: 507 M, 502 W verbal, 603 M, 568 W mathematical; 56% above 500 verbal, 22% above 600, 3% above 700, 81% above 500 mathematical, 53% above 600, 18% above 700; ACT: 26.3 M, 25.4 W composite. *Required:* SAT or ACT, minimum H.S. GPA; interview recommended. Criteria considered in admissions, in order of importance: high school academic record, standardized test scores, recommendations, extracurricular activates; other factors considered: special talents. *Out-of-state* freshman applicants: institute actively seeks students from out-of-state. State does not limit out-of-state enrollment. About 77% of applicants accepted, 26% enroll. States from which most out-of-state students are drawn include Texas, California, Colorado, Florida, New York. *Entrance programs:* early admission, deferred admission, advanced placement. *Apply* by August 1; rolling admissions. *Transfers* welcome; 80 enrolled 1993–94.

Academic Environment. Students serve on faculty committees and attend faculty meetings, and are involved in the decision making process. Nearly two-thirds of students employed on campus, many in academic activities, including large research division. Student leader touts Tech as "The ideal place for earth science engineering." Administration source and student leader agree that strongest programs are geoscience, astrophysics, computer science, technical communications, environmental engineering. Administration reports 25% of courses required for graduation are elective; distribution requirements fairly numerous: for BS, 6 hours in humanities and 9 hours in social sciences, 6 science courses, and 2 in mathematics (Calculus). Degrees offered: associates, bachelors, masters, doctoral. *Majors offered* include environmental engineering, physics with astrophysics option, petroleum engineering, materials engineering. Current students find the faculty friendly and accessible. Average undergraduate class size: 30% under 20, 50% between 20–40, 20% over 40.

About 38% of students entering as freshmen graduate in four years, 55% eventually; 71% of freshmen return for sophomore year. *Special programs:* CLEP, undergraduate research, cooperative work/study programs, credit by examination, industrial cooperative program, dual degrees in computer science and electrical engineering, M.S. in hydrology. *Calendar:* semester, summer school.

Undergraduate degrees conferred (113). 32% were in Engineering, 29% were in Physical Sciences, 12% were in Computer and Engineering Related Technology, 8% were in Mathematics, 7% were in Letters, 4% were in Life Sciences, 4% were in Liberal/General Studies, 4% were in Psychology.

Graduates Career Data. Advanced studies pursued by 36% of 1992–93 graduates; 4% enter medical school; 1% enter veterinary school. About 22% of 1992–93 graduates employed. Corporations typically hiring largest numbers of graduates include Hewlett Packard, Westinghouse Hanford, ASARCO, Intel. Career Development Services include coordinating on-campus interviews; advisement on job search procedures for permanent/summer/cooperative education; resource area of employer and other job related information.

Faculty. About 95% of faculty hold PhD or equivalent. About 90% of undergraduate classes taught by tenured faculty. About 17% of teaching faculty are female; 18% minority.

Student Body. Institute seeks a national student body; 75% of students from New Mexico; 4.4% Foreign. An estimated 1% of students reported as Black, 16% Hispanic, 2% Asian, 12% other minority. Average age of undergraduate student: 23.

Campus Life. New Mexico Tech has no intercollegiate sports; emphasis on intramurals, most popular: soccer, rugby, racquetball, volleyball, cycling. Recent student leader notes "a lot of student-motivated and initiated activities." Minimal rules govern campus life; intervisitation limited only by vote of residence unit. State law bans alcohol on campus. Cars allowed. Socorro is a small town and offers little to supplement campus cultural and recreational offerings. But student leader extols the countryside: "mountains (with mountain lions), many abandoned mines, ghost towns . . . a bird refuge with whooping cranes. . . excellent mineral collecting, superb fossil collecting, backpacking, skiing, and only 9,000 people." Administration source reports "Tech is a bargain!"; student leader agrees: [costs] "couldn't be better!—except free!"

About 15% of men, 15% of women live in traditional dormitories; 18% of men, 5% of women in coed dormitories; rest live in off-campus housing or commute. Freshmen given preference in college housing if all students cannot be accommodated. Sexes segregated in coed dormitories by floor. There are no fraternities or sororities. About 50% of resident students leave campus on weekends, according to most recent data available.

Annual Costs. Tuition and fees, $1,784 (out-of-state, $5,6464,842); room and board, $3,426; estimated $1,734 other, exclusive of travel. About 92% of students receive financial aid; average amount of assistance, $5,150. Assistance is typically divided 18% scholarship, 21% grant, 36% loan, 25% work. Institute reports 480 scholarships awarded for academic merit. *Meeting Costs:* institute offers deferred payment plan.

New Mexico State University

Las Cruces, New Mexico 88003 **(505) 646-2035**

A state-supported, land-grant institution, located in a city of 37,900, 40 miles north of El Paso. The university is closely affiliated with NASA and interservice missile test ranges nearby, making for significant influence on college curriculum.

Founded: 1888
Affiliation: State
UG Enrollment: 5,003 M, 4,670 W (full-time); 1,550 M, 1,931 W (part-time)
Total Enrollment: 15,788
Cost: < $10K
% Receiving Financial Aid: 68%
Admission: Non-selective
Application Deadline: 1 month before registration

Admission. Graduates of accredited or approved high schools with 15 units and C average or ACT composite standard score of 19 eligible; 78% of applicants accepted, 52% of these actually enroll. Average freshman ACT score: 21.9 composite. *Required:* ACT, minimum HS GPA. Criteria considered in admissions: high school academic record, standardized test scores, high school curriculum. *Apply* by 1 month before registration. *Transfers* welcome; 650 enrolled 1993–94.

Academic Environment. Degrees offered: associates, bachelors, masters, doctoral. *Undergraduate studies* offered by colleges of Arts and Sciences, Agriculture and Home Economics, Business Administration and Economics, Education, Engineering. About 60% of general education requirements for graduation are elective; distribution requirements fairly numerous. About 38% of students entering as freshmen graduate within six years; 27% of freshmen do not return for sophomore year. *Special programs:* CLEP, independent study, honors, individualized majors, cooperative work/study program (academic credit possible in engineering), courses on environmental matters, emphasis on field experience in introductory courses. *Calendar:* 4–1–4, summer school.

Undergraduate degrees conferred (1,705). 24% were in Business and Management, 15% were in Engineering, 12% were in Education, 6% were in Social Sciences, 4% were in Communications, 4% were in Psychology, 4% were in Engineering and Engineering Related Technology, 3% were in Public Affairs, 3% were in Life Sciences, 3% were in Home Economics, 3% were in Agricultural Sciences, 3% were in Protective Services, 3% were in Agribusiness and Agricultural Production, remainder in 11 other fields.

Faculty. About 80% of faculty hold PhD or equivalent. About 26% of teaching faculty are female; 8% Hispanic, 6% other ethnic minorities.

Varsity Sports. Men (Div.IA): Baseball, Basketball, Cross Country, Football, Golf, Swimming, Tennis, Track. Women (Div.IA): Basketball, Cross Country, Golf, Softball, Swimming, Tennis, Track.

Student Body. University seeks a national student body; more than 87% of students from North Central. An estimated 30% of students reported as Hispanic, 2% Black, 4% other ethnic minorities.

Campus Life. About 2% of men, 10% of women live in traditional dormitories; 19% of men, 13% of women in coed dormitories; rest live in off-campus housing or commute. Limited intervisitation in men's or women's dormitory rooms. There are 11 fraternities, 5 sororities on campus which about 7% of men, 3% of women join; 2% each men, women live in fraternities and sororities.

Annual Costs. Tuition and fees, $1,824 (out-of-state, $6,082); room and board, $2,972. About 70% of students receive financial aid; average amount of assistance, $3,300. Assistance is typically divided 23% grant/scholarship, 51% loan, 25% work.

University of New Mexico

Albuquerque, New Mexico 87131 (505) 277-2446

Because of its location and climate, the University of New Mexico has long attracted students and faculty from all parts of the country, although as a state university a high proportion of students come from within the state. The 640-acre campus is located in a city of 375,000, 60 miles south of Santa Fe. Most convenient major airport: Albuquerque International.

Founded: 1889
Affiliation: State
UG Enrollment: 5,867 M, 6,441 W (full-time); 1,547 M, 2,139 W (part-time)
Total Enrollment: 18,208
Cost: < $10K
% Receiving Financial Aid: 54%
Admission: Non-selective
Application Deadline: one month prior to start of classes

Admission. Graduates of accredited high schools with 13 units and C average eligible; 76% of applicants accepted, 64% of these actually enroll; about 46% of entering freshmen graduate in top fifth of high school class, 72% in top two-fifths. Average freshman ACT scores, according to most recent data available: 21.9 composite. *Required:* ACT (preferred) or SAT. *Out-of-state* freshman applicants: university welcomes students from out of state. State does not limit out-of-state enrollment. No special requirements for out-of-state applicants. *Entrance programs:* early admission, mid-year admission, deferred admission, advanced placement. *Apply* by one month prior to start of classes. *Transfers* welcome.

Academic Environment. All freshmen enroll in the University College for first year and most then proceed to one of the undergraduate degree-granting divisions: Architecture, Arts and Sciences, Education, Engineering, Fine Arts, Management, Nursing, Pharmacy. In addition, the University College administers a completely unstructured degree program, the Bachelor of University Studies. *Majors offered* in addition to usual studies include anthropology, astrophysics, computer science, geography, journalism, Latin American Studies, medical technology, Russian studies, Asian studies, entrepreneurial studies.

About 33% of students entering as freshmen graduate eventually; 28% of freshmen do not return for sophomore year. *Special programs:* independent study, study abroad, honors, Latin American studies, 5-year combined degree program in Arts and Sciences and Engineering, 3–2 MBA program in Arts and Sciences and Management. *Calendar:* semester, summer school.

Undergraduate degrees conferred (2,252). 15% were in Business and Management, 12% were in Social Sciences, 11% were in Liberal/General Studies, 10% were in Engineering, 9% were in Education, 8% were in Health Sciences, 7% were in Letters, 5% were in Psychology, 4% were in Visual and Performing Arts, 4% were in Life Sciences, 3% were in Protective Services, remainder in 11 other fields.

Faculty. About 82% of faculty hold PhD or equivalent.

Student Body. University does not seek a national student body; 87% of students from in state. An estimated 21% of students reported as Hispanic, 3% Native American, 2% Black, 2% Asian, 3% other minority, according to most recent data available.

Varsity Sports. Men (NCAA,Div.I, WAC): Baseball, Basketball, Cross Country, Football, Golf, Gymnastics, Skiing (RMISA), Soccer (RMISL), Swimming, Tennis, Track, Wrestling. Women (HCAC): Cross Country, Golf, Gymnastics, Skiing (RMISA), Softball, Swimming, Tennis, Track, Volleyball.

Campus Life. Cars allowed. About 3% of men, 2% of women live in traditional dormitories; 5% of men, 4% of women live in coed dormitories; 89% of men, 91% of women live in off-campus housing or commute. Intervisitation hours in men's and women's dormitory rooms vary with choice of dormitory. Sexes segregated in coed dormitories by wing, floor, or room. There are 11 fraternities, 5 sororities on campus which about 4% of men, 3% of women join; 4% of men, 3% of women live in fraternities and sororities.

Annual Costs. Tuition and fees, $1,788 (out-of-state, $6,468); room and board, $4,726. About 54% of students receive financial aid; assistance is typically divided 20% scholarship, 40% loan, 40% work. University reports some scholarships awarded on the basis of academic merit alone.

State University College at New Paltz

(See State University of New York)

College of New Rochelle

New Rochelle, New York 10805-2308 (914) 654-5452

The College of New Rochelle, founded by the Ursulines, is now independent. The School of Arts and Sciences continues to enroll only women, while the other schools are coeducational. The College includes schools of Arts and Sciences, Nursing, School of New Resources (for older students), and the Graduate School. The 30-acre campus is located in a suburban city of 75,400, 16 miles north of New York City.

Founded: 1904
Affiliation: Independent (Roman Catholic)
UG Enrollment: 10 M, 671 W (full-time); 7 M, 287 W (part-time)
Total Enrollment: 2,358
Cost: $10K–$20K
% Receiving Financial Aid: 90%
Admission: Non-selective
Application Deadline: August 15

Admission. About 63% of applicants accepted, 36% of these actually enroll; 30% of freshmen graduate in top fifth of high school class, 51% in top two-fifths. Average freshmen SAT scores: 420 W verbal, 424 W mathematical. *Required:* SAT, essay; interview recommended. Criteria considered in admissions, in order of importance: high school academic record, standardized tests and recommendations, writing sample; other factors considered: alumni children. *Entrance programs:* early decision, early admission, midyear admission, advanced placement. About 30% of entering students from private schools. *Apply* by August 15; rolling admissions. *Transfers* welcome; 61 enrolled 1993–94.

Academic Environment. Degrees offered: bachelors, masters. Administration source reports students primarily concerned with occupational/professional goals, somewhat less interested in scholarly/intellectual pursuits and social activities. Core requirements for the School of Arts and Sciences include about 40 credits in an interdisciplinary program which exposes students to, "a broad spectrum of human cultural achievements enabling them to develop their writing, critical thinking, quantitative and analytical skills." Average undergraduate class size: 71% of classes under 20, 27% between 20–40, 2% over 40.

About 54% of students entering as freshmen graduate in four years, 58% eventually; 84% of freshmen return for sophomore year. *Special programs:* CLEP, independent study, study abroad, honors, undergraduate research, 3-year degree, individualized majors, visiting students program for New York State colleges, interdepartmental seminars, cooperative program with nearby Iona, field work for credit, child study center on campus. Adult programs: New Resources Program offers curriculum leading to BA for adult men and women. *Calendar:* semester, June session, summer school.

Undergraduate degrees conferred (575). 76% were in Liberal/General Studies, 9% were in Health Sciences, 3% were in Communications, 3% were in Business and Management, remainder in 10 other fields.

Graduates Career Data. Advanced studies pursued by 22% of students. *Careers in business and industry* pursued by 70% of graduates, according to most recent data available. Career Development Services imclude individual and group counseling; resume, interview, job search workshops; internships and coop education; career program; credential file service; library resources; computerized career guidance program.

Faculty. About 74% of full-time faculty, 16% of part-time faculty hold PhD or equivalent. About 76% of undergraduate classes taught by tenured faculty. About 64% of teaching faculty are female; 6% Hispanic, 6% Asian.

Student Body. College seeks a national student body; 90% of students from in state; 97% Middle Atlantic, 2% New England; 1% Foreign. An estimated 34% of students reported as Black, 12% Hispanic, 4% Asian.

Varsity Sports. Women (Div.III): Basketball, Softball, Swimming, Tennis, Volleyball.

Campus Life. Residential students live in four residence halls in a variety of room arrangements. Student members of the Hall Councils cooperate with residence staff in "establishing and maintaining policies that ensure a safe and congenial environment, supportive of the academic aims of the college." Student clubs offer opportunities in performing arts, cultural and political, and service organizations. Cultural and social resources of New York City, just 16 miles from campus, are relatively accessible to students.

About 66% of women live in traditional dormitories; rest live in off-campus housing or commute. Freshmen given preference in college housing if all students cannot be accommodated. There are no sororities. About 50% of resident students leave campus on weekends.

Annual Costs. Tuition and fees, $10,680; room and board, $4,760; estimated $550 other, exclusive of travel. About 90% of students receive financial aid; average amount of assistance, $11,996. Assistance is typically divided 30% scholarship, 30% grant, 30% loan, 8% work, 2% other. College reports 80 scholarships awarded for academic merit. *Meeting Costs:* college offers SHELF, PLUS, TSP, PASS.

Eugene Lang College of the New School for Social Research

New York, New York 10011 (212) 229-5665

Founded as the first university for adults by a group of the most eminent figures in American higher education, the New School has long enjoyed a unique reputation for its graduate and adult education divisions. More recently emphasis has been placed on the rapidly growing undergraduate division, the Eugene Lang College, a four-year liberal arts institution featuring seminar-style classes. All students design their own academic programs in consultation with faculty advisors. The urban campus is located on the northern edge of Greenwich Village in the heart of Manhattan. Most convenient major airports: JFK International, LaGuardia, or Newark.

Founded: 1985
Affiliation: Independent
UG Enrollment: 175 M, 225 W (Eugene Lang)
Total Enrollment: 6,800
Cost: $10K–$20K
Admission: Very Selective
Application Deadline: Feb. 1

Admission is very selective. About 75% of applicants accepted, 77% of these actually enroll. Average freshman SAT scores: 540 verbal, 520 mathematical; 74% of freshmen score above 500 on verbal, 30% above 600, 2% above 700; 69% score above 500 on mathematical, 26% above 600, 3% above 700. *Required:* SAT, teacher recommendation, essay, on-campus or phone interview. Criteria considered in admissions, in order of importance: high school academic record, recommendations, standardized test scores, writing sample, extracurricular activities, interview; other factors considered: special talents, diverse student body. *Entrance programs:* early decision, early admission, midyear admission, deferred admission, advanced placement, transfer admission. *Apply* by February 1 for freshmen, July 1 for transfers. *Transfers* welcome.

Academic Environment. Degrees offered: bachelors. Eugene Lang features small classes, no more than 15 students in a seminar, and an innovative curriculum. Freshmen chose from a selection of broad-based seminars before choosing a concentration for their sophomore and junior years. Some of the concentrations are in conventional disciplines, other are cross-disciplinary groups of courses. The concentrations are: literature, writing and the arts; social and historical inquiry; mind, nature and value; cultural studies; urban studies. Students may also design their own course of study in consultation with a faculty advisor. All freshmen take a writing course, otherwise programs are flexible and interdisciplinary. A new senior seminar allows students to gain a broad perspective on the more specialized work of their middle years.

About 85% of students entering as freshmen graduate in four years. *Special programs:* study abroad; cross-registration with Cooper Union, Brooklyn Polytechnic; 3–2 in teaching; combined BA/BFA dual degree programs with Parsons School of Design, Mannes School of Music; Adult Media Studies Program; Graduate Faculty in Political Science, Graduate School of Management and Urban Professions. *Calendar:* semester.

Undergraduate degrees conferred (687). 50% were in Visual and Performing Arts, 23% were in Multi/Interdisciplinary Studies, 15% were in Public Affairs, 6% were in Health Sciences, 5% were in Architecture and Environmental Design.

Graduates Career Data. Full-time graduate study pursued immediately after graduation by 43% of students; 2% enter law school, according to most recent data available. Fields typically hiring largest number of graduates include law, teaching, social service. Career Development Services include resume writing workshops, job file/postings, meetings with alumni, active internship program as part of Lang curriculum.

Faculty. About 95% of faculty hold PhD or equivalent. No tenured faculty.

Student Body. College seeks a national student body; 49% of students from in state; 65% Middle Atlantic, 16% New England, 6% South, 5% each West, Northwest, Midwest; 3% Foreign. An estimated 6% of students reported as Black, 6% Hispanic, 3% Asian, according to most recent data available.

Campus Life. Beyond the varied resources of Greenwich Village the almost limitless resources of New York City are easily accessible. Intramural and recreational athletic program offered in cooperation with Cooper Union. New dormitory under construction.

About 30% of students live in coed dormitories; rest live in off-campus housing or commute. Freshmen given preference in college housing if all students cannot be accommodated. No restrictions on off-campus housing. There are no fraternities or sororities on campus.

Annual Costs. Tuition and fees, $13,760; room and board, $7,310; an estimated $1,730 other, exclusive of travel. College reports all scholarships awarded for need. *Meeting Costs:* college offers 12-month payment plan.

New School for Social Research/ Parsons School of Design

New York, New York 10011

A highly regarded professional school of art and design that attracts students from every part of the country and abroad, Parsons is administratively affiliated with the New School. Program offers instruction in an unusually wide range of fields including: fine arts, interior, fashion design, illustration, communication design, product design, photography, environmental design, and design marketing.

Founded: 1896
Affiliation: Independent
UG Enrollment: 650 M, 1,150 W

Undergraduate degrees conferred (91). 74% were in Visual and Performing Arts, 15% were in Home Economics, 5% were in Communications Technologies, 5% were in Architecture and Environmental Design.

The New School of Music

(See Temple University)

New York City Technical College

(See City University of New York)

New York Institute of Technology

Old Westbury, New York 11568 (516) 686-7520

An independent, professional institution offering programs in science, related technologies, education, business and management, architecture, communication fields, and fine and applied arts at its Metropolitan Center in Manhattan as well as the 750-acre Old Westbury Campus, and the Commack College Center.

Founded: 1910
Affiliation: Independent
UG Enrollment: 2,723 M, 1,089 W (full-time); 1,645 M, W (part-time)
Total Enrollment: 12,000
Cost: < $10K
Admission: Non-selective
Application Deadline: Rolling

Admission. Graduates of approved high schools with 16 units eligible; others given individual consideration; 62% of applicants accepted; 54% of these actually enroll. About 16% of freshmen graduate in top fifth of high school class, 39% in top two-fifths. *Required:* SAT or ACT; interview optional. *Apply:* rolling admissions. *Transfers* welcome.

Academic Environment. *Degrees:* BS, BArch, BFA, BT. About 30% of general education credits for graduation are required; distribution requirements vary with major. Computer facilities reported as adequate to meet student demand. *Special programs:* honors, study abroad, independent study, Corporate College Program. *Calendar:* 4–1–4, summer school.

Undergraduate degrees conferred (1,012). 28% were in Business and Management, 16% were in Engineering, 14% were in Architecture and Environmental Design, 11% were in Communications, 6% were in Liberal/General Studies, 6% were in Engineering and Engineering Related Technology, 5% were in Visual and Performing Arts, 5% were in Social Sciences, 4% were in Computer and Engineering Related Technology, remainder in 4 other fields.

Varsity Sports. Men (Div.II): Baseball(I), Basketball, Cross Country, Golf, Soccer, Tennis, Track. Women (Div.II): Basketball, Golf, Softball, Track, Volleyball(I).

Student Body. About 87% of students from in state; 90% Middle Atlantic. An estimated 14% of students reported as Protestant, 69% Catholic, 7% Jewish, 4% unaffiliated, 6% other; 6% Black, 3% Hispanic, 2% Asian, according to most recent data available.

Campus Life. About 5% of students live in dormitories; rest live in off-campus housing or commute. There are no fraternities or sororities.

Annual Costs. Tuition and fees, $8,225; room and board, $5,480. Institute reports some scholarships awarded on the basis of academic merit alone. *Meeting Costs:* institute offers extended payment loan program.

State University of New York

Albany, New York 12246

The State University of New York (SUNY) was established in 1948 to provide coordination among the state's varied institutions of higher learning and access to higher education opportunities for residents in every region of the state. Today the university comprises 64 colleges and centers, including 4 university centers (at Albany, Binghamton, Buffalo, and Stony Brook), 5 colleges and centers for the health sciences, 13 colleges of arts and science, 3 specialized colleges, 6 agricultural and technical colleges, 5 statutory colleges, and 30 locally sponsored community colleges. The arts and science campuses are at Brockport, Buffalo, Cortland, Fredonia, Geneseo, New Paltz, Old Westbury, Oneonta, Oswego, Plattsburgh, Potsdam, Purchase, and the non-traditional Empire State College, which has a network of nine regional centers and more than 40 learning centers and units located throughout the state. Although their activities are coordinated by the university, each of the colleges and centers functions, in large part, as an autonomous institution. Full- and part-time enrollment on the 64 campuses is about 380,000. The nation's youngest state university, SUNY has also become its largest.

Admission. Admission to all "institutions of the State University of New York is based on academic qualifications without regard to sex, race, color, creed, national origin, disability, or handicap of applicant." SUNY campuses offer a broad range of undergraduate admissions opportunities from very selective to open admissions. Student must have a high school diploma, be in satisfactory academic standing, or have qualifications which the admitting authorities may deem equivalent. Previous academic achievement is generally regarded as the most significant factor in admissions decisions, with scores on Regents Scholarship Examination, the Scholastic Aptitude Test, or the American College Test serving as additional factors. *Out-of-state* freshman enrollment not limited by state. No special requirements for out-of-state applicants. In some cases where test scores are given for institutions (see below) they represent SAT equivalents of state examinations computed by the individual institutions.

State University of New York at Albany

Albany, New York 12222 (518) 442-5435

One of four University Centers in the SUNY system, Albany offers programs for undergraduate and graduate students in the traditional arts and sciences and in 6 professional areas. The main campus, 3 miles from the State Capitol, was designed by Edward Durell Stone and completed in 1968. Four of the six professional schools are located on the recently modernized downtown campus. Most convenient major airport: Albany County.

Founded: 1844
Affiliation: State
UG Enrollment: 5,600 M, 5,298 W (full-time); 724 M, 8 W (part-time)
Total Enrollment: 16,976
Cost: < $10K
% Receiving Financial Aid: 74%
Admission: Very (+) Selective
Application Deadline: Mar. 15

Admission is very (+) selective. (See also State University of New York.) About 60% of applicants accepted, 25% of these actually enroll; 60% of freshmen graduate in top fifth of high school class, 95% in top two-fifths. Average freshman SAT scores, according to most recent data available: 518 verbal, 607 mathematical; 59% of freshmen score above 500 on verbal, 14% above 600, 1% above 700; 97% score above 500 on mathematical, 50% above 600, 9% above 700. *Required:* SAT or ACT. *Out-of-state* freshman applicants: university welcomes out-of-state students. State does not limit out-of-state enrollment. *Non-academic factors* considered in admissions: special talents, diverse student body, "extenuating circumstances." *Entrance programs:* early admission, midyear admission, advanced placement, deferred admission. *Apply* by March 15. *Transfers* welcome.

Academic Environment. Students are involved in all levels of academic decision making, including curriculum matters. General education requirements consist of 6 credits in each of 6 areas: literature/fine arts, natural science, social science, symbolics (language, math), values, and world cultures. Enrollment has been stabilized at current levels with undergraduate offerings in 43 fields. *Undergraduate studies* offered by colleges of Humanities and Fine Arts, Science and Mathematics, Social and Behavioral Sciences, schools of Business, Education, Public Affairs, Social Welfare. Most freshmen do not choose a major until their sophomore year. *Majors offered* in addition to usual arts and sciences include African and Afro-American studies, anthropology, atmospheric science, communications, criminal justice, geography, Inter-American language and area studies, Japanese, medical technology, music, theater, Judaic studies; interdisciplinary majors in Asian studies, Chinese studies, computer science and applied mathematics, Inter-American studies, linguistics, Russian and East European studies, women's studies.

About 70% of students entering as freshmen graduate eventually; 11% of freshmen do not return for sophomore year. *Special programs:* CLEP, CPE, independent study, study abroad, honors, undergraduate research, individualized majors, internships with many state agencies and the Legislature, selected seniors may take graduate courses for credit, Visiting Student Program, 3–2 program in law with Albany Law School, 3–2 engineering with Rensselaer. *Library:* 1,300,000 volumes, 7,000 periodicals, 2,400,000 other materials; open-stack privileges. *Calendar:* semester, summer school.

Undergraduate degrees conferred (2,534). 27% were in Social Sciences, 18% were in Letters, 16% were in Business and Management, 15% were in Psychology, 5% were in Life Sciences, 3% were in Foreign Languages, remainder in 11 other fields.

Graduates Career Data. According to most recent data available, full-time graduate or professional study pursued immediately after graduation by 40% of students. Medical schools typically admitting largest numbers of graduates include SUNY-Downstate, SUNY-Upstate; dental schools include SUNY at Buffalo, Georgetown; law schools include Albany Law School, SUNY at Buffalo, Boston U. *Careers in business and industry* pursued by 35% of graduates. Largest numbers find employment in school systems, government agencies, accounting firms, businesses, and banking.

Faculty. About 98% of faculty hold PhD or equivalent.

Student Body. University does not seek a national student body; 97% of students from New York; 98% Middle Atlantic; about 150 handicapped students (modified residence, library, physical education, classroom, and laboratory facilities). An estimated 7% of students reported as Black, 4% Hispanic, 3% Asian, 1% Native American, according to most recent data available. *Minority group students:* full Educational Opportunity Program—special admissions personnel and criteria; remedial programs; reduced course loads; financial assistance; some separate social and recreational programs.

Varsity Sports. Men (Div.III): Baseball, Basketball, Crew, Cross Country, Football, Lacrosse, Soccer, Swimming & Diving, Tennis, Track, Wrestling. Women (Div.III): Baseball, Basketball, Cross Country, Soccer, Swimming & Diving, Tennis, Track, Volleyball.

Campus Life. Student leader reports "SUNY Albany is a moderate and informal place—most students aren't involved," and adds that their tastes do not run to "organized demonstrations or fraternities or proms." Intervisitation, up to 24 hours, determined by residents of each hall. Cars allowed; parking reported as adequate for residents, but not adequate for commuters. Smoking restricted to designated areas; alcohol limited to those over 21.

About 60% of full-time undergraduate students live in coed dormitories; rest live in off-campus housing or commute. Freshmen given preference in college housing if all students cannot be accommodated. Sexes segregated in coed dormitories by suite. There are 26 fraternities, 13 sororities on campus which about 15% of men, 10% of women join; they provide no residence facilities.

Annual Costs. Tuition and fees, $2,877 (out-of-state, $6,777); room and board, $3,666. About 74% of students receive financial aid; assistance is typically divided 51% scholarship, 42% loan, 7% work. University reports some scholarships awarded on the basis of academic merit alone. *Meeting Costs:* university offers installment payment plan.

State University of New York at Binghamton

Binghamton, New York 13902-6000 (607) 777-2171

The State University of New York at Binghamton started with the prestigious liberal arts institution, Harpur College, and has now grown to include 4 other degree-granting undergraduate schools, the School of Management, the Decker School of Nursing, the School of Education and Human Development, and the Thomas J. Watson School of Engineering and Applied Science. The campus is located in the town of Vestal, 1 mile west of Binghamton (metropolitan population of 260,000), 45 miles southeast of Ithaca and 75 miles south of Syracuse. New York City and Philadelphia are approximately 200 miles from Binghamton. Most convenient major airport: Binghamton.

Founded: 1946
Affiliation: State
UG Enrollment: 3,875 M, 4,669 W (full-time); 322 M, 349 W (part-time)
Total Enrollment: 11,997
Cost: < $10K
% Receiving Financial Aid: 56%
Admission: Very (+) Selective
Application Deadline: Jan. 15

Admission is very (+) selective. (See also State University of New York.) About 43% of applicants accepted, 29% of these actually enroll; 91% of freshmen graduate in top fifth of high school class, all in top two-fifths. Average freshman SAT scores: 538 M, 528 W verbal, 642 M, 594 W mathematical; according to most recent data available 66% of freshman score above 500 on verbal, 20% above 600, 1% above 700; 93% score above 500 on mathematical, 61% above 600, 15% above 700. *Required:* SAT or ACT, essay,(see also State University of New York) for Talented Student Program: audition, portfolio review, or other consideration by an academic department. Criteria considered in admissions, in order of importance: high school academic record, writing sample and extracurricular activities, standardized test scores; other criteria considered: special talents, diverse student body. *Out-of-state* freshmen applicants: university actively seeks students from out-of-state. State does not limit out-of-state enrollment. States from which most out-of-state students are drawn include New Jersey, Connecticut, Pennsylvania, Maryland, Massachusetts. *Entrance programs:* early decision, early admission, midyear admission (rarely), deferred admission, advanced placement, special admissions program for disadvantaged (academically and financially) students. *Apply* preferably by January 15. *Transfers* welcome; 811 enrolled 1993–94.

Academic Environment. The five undergraduate schools are competitive academically, and the liberal arts tradition of Harpur College continues to influence the academic offerings of each of them. All five "emphasize the acquisition of academic breadth as well as depth of specialization." Degrees offered: bachelors, masters, doctoral. *Majors offered* in Harpur include Afro-American studies, anthropology, interdepartmental studies, biochemistry, cinema, environmental studies, geography, geophysics, Latin American and Caribbean studies, psychobiology, studio arts, theater. Average undergraduate class size: 45% under 20, 39% between 20–40, 16% over 40. Recent students find the greatest academic strength to be the excellent faculty, but they lament the large, lecture-style classes for introductory level courses which don't allow for much interaction.

About 67% of students entering as freshmen graduate within four years, 78% within six years; 92% of freshmen return for sophomore year. *Special programs:* CLEP, independent study, student-designed majors, honors, undergraduate research, credit by examination, medieval studies, women's studies, area studies, internships, veteran's programs, programs for the handicapped, various overseas programs, 3–2 BA/MBA with School of Management, 3–4 optometry with SUNY-Optometry, 3–2 and 3–3 engineering, 3–2 with SUNY Environmental Science and Forestry. *Calendar:* semester, summer school.

Undergraduate degrees conferred (2,274). 27% were in Social Sciences, 13% were in Business and Management, 11% were in Letters, 10% were in Psychology, 8% were in Life Sciences, 5% were in Engineering and Engineering Related Technology, 4% were in Computer and Engineering Related Technology, 4% were in Visual and Performing Arts, 3% were in Foreign Languages, 3% were in Health Sciences, 3% were in Engineering, remainder in 7 other fields.

Graduates Career Data. Advanced studies pursued immediately after graduation by 39% of students; 4% enter medical school; 1% enter dental school; 7% enter law school; 5% enter business school. Medical schools typically enrolling largest numbers of graduates include SUNY-HSC at Brooklyn, Syracuse and Stony Brook; dental schools include SUNY-Buffalo, NYU; law schools include Albany, Brooklyn, Hofstra; business schools include Binghamton, NYU, Baruch. *Careers in business and industry* pursued by 61% of graduates. Corporations typically hiring largest numbers of graduates include "Big Six" accounting firms, May Company, American Management Systems. Career Development Center publishes reference guides and provides reviews, workshops and counseling, on-campus interviewing. Alumni reported as helpful in both career guidance and job placement.

Faculty. About 84% of faculty hold PhD or equivalent. About 26% of teaching faculty are female; 3% Black, 3% Hispanic, 7% Asian/Pacific Islander.

Student Body. University seeks a diverse student body; 94% of students from within state; 97% Middle Atlantic; 2% Foreign. An estimated 6% of students reported as Black, 11% Asian, 5% Hispanic, 2% other minority.

Varsity Sports. Men (Div.III): Baseball, Basketball, Cross Country, Diving, Golf, Soccer, Swimming, Tennis, Track, Wrestling. Women (Div.III): Basketball, Cross Country, Diving, Soccer, Softball, Swimming, Tennis, Track, Volleyball.

Campus Life. High interest reported in intramural sports (most popular basketball, softball, floor hockey, football), and in sororities and fraternities. Students have almost total control over their own social affairs. Freshmen must live on campus. University now divided into 4 residential colleges, which house approximately 1,000 members each, and an off campus college for students living off campus. Drinking permitted on campus, legal age, 21; but university "follows a strict program of code enforcement and education regarding alcohol abuse." Cars allowed. Fairly wide variety of cultural and social activities available on campus, supplemented by substantial resources of the Triple Cities area.

About 41% of men, 45% of women live in coed dormitories; 47% of men, 44% of women live in off-campus college-related housing; rest commute. Freshmen are given preference in college housing if all students cannot be accommodated. Sexes segregated in dormitories either by floor or room. There are 17 fraternities, 11 sororities, which about 19% of men, 14% of women join. About 5% of resident students leave campus on weekends.

Annual Costs. Tuition and fees, $2,961 (out-of-state, $6,861); room and board, $4,960; estimated $1,100 other, exclusive of travel. About 56% of students receive financial aid; average amount of assistance, $4,120. Assistance is typically divided 1% scholarship, 63% grant, 21% loan, 15% work. University reports 25 scholarships awarded for academic merit, 3 for special talents, 37 for need. *Meeting Costs:* university offers federal loan program for parents.

State University of New York at Buffalo

Buffalo, New York 14260 **(716) 645-6900**

The State University of New York at Buffalo (UB), is the largest, most comprehensive university in the SUNY system. The University's North campus is located on 1,200 acres of land in suburban Amherst. The older South campus, on the northeast edge of Buffalo, is the primary site for the University's health science schools. In addition to its regular day schedule of undergraduate, graduate and professional programs, the University, through Millard Fillmore College, offers adults the opportunity to earn a baccalaureate or master's degree or to enroll in courses of interest during the evening hours. Most convenient major airport: Buffalo International.

Founded: 1846
Affiliation: State
UG Enrollment: 8,066 M, 5,897 W (full-time); 1,516 M, 1,608 W (part-time)
Total Enrollment: 25,635
Cost: < $10K
% Receiving Financial Aid: 60%
Admission: Very Selective
Application Deadline: Jan. 5

Admission is very selective. (See also University of New York.) About 64% of applicants accepted, 32% of these actually enroll; 50% of freshmen graduate in top fifth of high school class, 91% in top two-fifths. Average freshman SAT scores: 506 verbal, 599 mathematical, according to most recent data available; 41% of freshmen score above 500 on verbal, 8% above 600, 1% above 700; 83% score above 500 on mathematical, 39% above 600, 8% above 700. *Required:* SAT or ACT. Criteria considered in admissions, in order of importance: high school academic record and standardized tests; then recommendations, extracurricular activities, and writing sample; other factors considered: special talents, diverse student body. *Out-of-state* freshmen applicants: university has limited recruitment of out-of-state students. State does not limit out-of-state enrollment. States from which most out-of-state students are drawn include New Jersey, Pennsylvania, Connecticut. *Entrance programs:* early admission, midyear admission, advanced placement. *Apply* by January 5. *Transfers* welcome; 1,957 enrolled 1993–94.

Academic Environment. Most students attend classes on the new Amherst campus where the majority of non-health-related departments are located. General education requirements emphasize demonstrable mathematics and writing skills combined with a broad based education. Competition is moderate, but varies somewhat among different schools and curricula. Degrees offered: associates, bachelors, masters, doctoral. All undergraduates are part of the Division of Undergraduate Education, the baccalaureate degree-granting body. *Majors offered* include African-American studies, anthropology, architecture, environmental design, linguistics, management, speech pathology and audiology, sports and exercise studies, statistics, and theater.

About 28% of students entering as freshmen graduate in four years, 55% eventually; 88% of freshmen return for sophomore year. *Special programs:* CLEP, independent study, study abroad, honors, individualized majors, freshman seminars, Center for Critical Languages, 3–2 in engineering, visiting students program for New York State colleges, cross-registration with SUNY College at Buffalo and other Buffalo area colleges, joint and double majors, double degrees, Early Medical School Assurance Program, Shortened degree programs in BA/JD and BA/MBA. Adult programs: Millard Fillmore College offers full- and part-time evening programs. *Calendar:* semester, summer school.

Undergraduate degrees conferred (3,205). 16% were in Social Sciences, 15% were in Engineering, 15% were in Business and Management, 10% were in Multi/Interdisciplinary Studies, 7% were in Psychology, 7% were in Health Sciences, 6% were in Communications, 5% were in Letters, 5% were in Allied Health, 4% were in Life Sciences, 3% were in Computer and Engineering Related Technology, 3% were in Architecture and Environmental Design, remainder in 7 other fields.

Graduates Career Data. Career Development Services include workshops, resume referral, interest inventories, and counseling.

Faculty. About 97% of faculty hold PhD or equivalent. About 23% of teaching faculty are female.

Student Body. University seeks a national student body; 97% of students from in state; 2% Foreign. An estimated 7% of students reported as Black, 9% Asian, 4% Hispanic, 2% other minority. Average age of undergraduate student: 22.

Varsity Sports. Men (Div.I): Basketball, Cross Country, Diving, Football(Div.IAA), Soccer, Swimming, Tennis, Track, Wrestling. Women (Div.I): Basketball, Cross Country, Diving, Soccer, Swimming, Tennis, Volleyball.

Campus Life. Students have considerable voice in determining rules governing campus social life and significant degree of freedom in defining their own life styles. As on many campuses currently, students are reported to be more career-oriented. However, one student leader reports that Buffalo still "has a cosmopolitan atmosphere, and is a stimulating, diverse institution." There are no dormitory hours; each residence unit decides on intervisitation hours. Cars allowed.

About 20% of students live in coed dormitories; 80% of students commute. Freshmen are given preference in college housing if all

students cannot be accommodated. Sexes segregated in dormitories either by wing, floor, or room. There are 22 fraternities, 9 sororities which about 8% of men, 4% of women join.
Annual Costs. Tuition and fees, $3,074 (out-of-state, $6,974); room and board, $4,822; estimated $1,448 other, exclusive of travel. About 60% of undergraduate students receive financial aid; average amount of assistance, $4,440. Assistance is typically divided 2% scholarships, 28% grant, 59% loan, 11% work. University reports 10 scholarships awarded for academic merit, 5 for special talents, 25 for need.

State University of New York at Stony Brook

Stony Brook, New York 11794 (516) 632-6868

One of four University Centers of the State University of New York, Stony Brook was mandated to develop strong academic programs in the basic liberal arts as well as in the sciences and engineering. Now thirty years old, it has grown into a major public university center. Located on Long Island's North Shore, the campus includes a large research library, a Fine Arts Center, and a Health Sciences Center including a 540-bed University Hospital. Most convenient major airport: Islip MacArthur.

Founded: 1957
Affiliation: State
UG Enrollment: 4,875 M, 4,869 W (full-time); 600 M, 751 W (part-time)
Total Enrollment: 17,205
Cost: < $10K
% Receiving Financial Aid: 70%
Admission: Very Selective
Application Deadline: July 15

Admission is very selective. About 57% of applicants accepted, 25% of these actually enroll; 57% of entering freshmen graduate in top fifth of high school class, 88% in top two-fifths. Average freshman SAT scores: 473 verbal, 547 mathematical; 37% of freshman score above 500 on verbal, 6% above 600; 72% score above 500 on mathematical, 27% above 600, 5% above 700. *Required:* SAT. Criteria considered in admissions, in order of importance: high school academic record, standardized tests, recommendations, extracurricular activities, writing sample; other factors considered: special talents. *Out-of-state* freshmen applicants: university actively seeks students from out-of-state. State does not limit out-of-state enrollment. States from which most out-of-state students are drawn include New Jersey, Connecticut, Massachusetts, Pennsylvania, California, Florida. *Entrance programs:* advanced placement, early decision. About 3% of freshmen from private schools, 12% from parochial schools. *Apply* by July 15 for freshmen; rolling admissions. *Transfers* welcome; 1,323 enrolled 1993–94.
Academic Environment. Competition strong in preprofessional programs and the sciences. Engineering curriculum more flexible than traditional engineering programs. Science departments offer courses for non-majors. General Education requirements include 13 courses covering writing and quantitative reasoning, literary and philosophic analysis, exposure to the arts, disciplinary diversity (distribution among natural sciences, social sciences, and humanities), the interrelationship of science and society, and 3 culminating multicultural requirements; baccalaureate candidates in Arts and Sciences are also required to meet proficiency standards in a foreign language. Federated Learning Communities Program joins small groups of undergraduates and senior faculty "master learners" in interdisciplinary learning experiences around a common theme. Many opportunities available for undergraduate research and internships. Degrees offered: bachelors, masters, doctoral. *Majors offered* include African studies, applied math and statistics, biochemistry, electrical engineering, physical therapy, physician's assistant. Programs with strong regional or national reputations include physical sciences, biological sciences, health sciences, computer science, and electrical engineering.

About 53% of entering students graduate in 6 years, 56% eventually; 83% of freshmen return for sophomore year. *Special programs:* Visiting Student Program, honors, Undergraduate Research and Creative Activities Program (URECA), independent study, study abroad, individualized majors, 5-year BE/MS program, 5-year BA/MS offered in policy analysis and public management.
Undergraduate degrees conferred (2,164). 25% were in Social Sciences, 12% were in Liberal/General Studies, 11% were in Psychology, 10% were in Life Sciences, 8% were in Engineering, 6% were in Letters, 5% were in Mathematics, 5% were in Health Sciences, 4% were in Allied Health, 3% were in Physical Sciences, 3% were in Computer and Engineering Related Technology, remainder in 7 other fields.
Graduates Career Data. Advanced studies pursued immediately after graduation by 55% of students. Career Development Services include two computerized guidance services, job fairs, SUNY/Kinexus computerized job matching system, career development resource library.
Faculty. About 95% of faculty hold PhD or equivalent. About 41% of teaching faculty are female; 3% Black, 2% Hispanic, 8% other minority.
Student Body. About 95% of students from New York State; 3% Foreign. An estimated 14% of freshmen students reported as Protestant, 43% Catholic, 9% Jewish; 9% Black, 7% Hispanic, 17% Asian, 16% other or unknown.
Varsity Sports. Men (Div.III): Baseball, Basketball, Cross Country, Diving, Football, Lacrosse (I), Soccer, Swimming, Tennis, Track. Women (Div.III): Basketball, Cross Country, Diving, Soccer (I), Softball, Swimming, Tennis, Track, Volleyball.
Campus Life. Students are generally treated as responsible adults; there are no curfews, dorm visitation is open. Beer is sold at campus bars and liquor is permitted in the rooms for students who are of legal age. Cars allowed for juniors and seniors. Students are in charge of many of the extracurricular activities. Residence halls sponsor a wide range of programs and activities. Several current students find the diversity of the student body and the many activities, clubs and organizations contribute to campus life.

According to most recent data available, about 49% of students live in coed dormitories; rest commute. Sexes segregated in dormitories by floor, section or suite. There are 12 fraternities and 11 sororities on campus. About 45% of resident students leave campus on weekends.
Annual Costs. Tuition and fees, $2,945.50 (out-of-state, $6,845.50); room and board, $4,712. About 70% of students receive financial aid; average amount of assistance, $5,000 -$6,000 for freshmen, $2,000–$3,000 for others. University reports some scholarships awarded for academic merit. *Meeting Costs:* university offers The Tuition Assistance Program.

State University College at Brockport

Brockport, New York 14420-2915 (716) 395-2751

The SUNY campus at Brockport is located in a village of 9,800, 16 miles west of Rochester. About 45% of students are sophomore and junior transfers. Most convenient major airport: Rochester/Monroe County International.

Founded: 1836
Affiliation: State
UG Enrollment: 2,685 M, 3,073 W (full-time); 545 M, 818 W (part-time)
Total Enrollment: 9,006
Cost: < $10K
% Receiving Financial Aid: 85%
Admission: Non-selective
Application Deadline: Rolling

Admission. (See also State University of New York.) About 49% of applicants accepted, 28% of these actually enroll; 26% of freshmen graduate in top fifth of high school class, 75% in top two-fifths. Average freshman scores: SAT, 448 M, 444 W verbal, 530 M, 490 W mathematical; 21% of freshmen score above 500 verbal, 1% above 600, 56% score above 500 mathematical, 11% above 600, 1% above 700; ACT, 22.7 M, 21.8 W composite. *Required:* ACT or SAT, Supplemental Information Form; interview recommended. Criteria considered in admissions, in order of importance: high school academic record, standardized test scores, extracurricular activities, recommendations, writing sample, campus visit; other factors considered: special talents, alumni children, diverse student body. *Out-of-state* freshmen applicants: university actively seeks students from out-of-state. State does not limit out-of-state enrollment. About 66% of out-of-state students accepted, 7% of these actually enroll. States from which most out-of-state students are drawn include New Jersey, Massachusetts, Vermont. *Entrance programs:* early decision, early admission, midyear admission, advanced placement, deferred admission. *Apply* by February 15 (recommended); rolling admissions. *Transfers* welcome; 1,188 enrolled 1993–94.

Academic Environment. Distribution requirements include liberal arts core which includes composition; quantitative skills; humanities; social sciences; fine arts; natural sciences; and contemporary issues, comparative literature, and perspectives on women. Degrees offered: bachelors, masters. *Majors offered* include anthropology, computer science, dance, education, medical technology, nursing, theater, recreation and leisure, sociology, criminal justice, sports management, American studies, African and Afro-American studies, Arts for Children, international business, physical education, accounting, water resources. Average undergraduate class size: 45% under 20, 43% between 20–40, 12% over 40.

About 32% of entering freshmen graduate in four years, 53% eventually; 75% of freshmen return for sophomore year. *Special programs:* CLEP, independent study, study abroad, honors, undergraduate research, 3-year degree, individualized majors, January term, political science semester in Washington and Albany, internships, African studies, Latin American studies, cooperative registration program through Rochester Area Colleges Consortium, 3–2 programs in engineering. Adult programs: Bachelor in Liberal Studies; many evening programs available. *Calendar:* semester, summer school.

Undergraduate degrees conferred (1,498). 20% were in Business and Management, 10% were in Psychology, 10% were in Protective Services, 9% were in Communications, 8% were in Social Sciences, 8% were in Health Sciences, 8% were in Education, 5% were in Letters, 3% were in Public Affairs, 3% were in Visual and Performing Arts, 3% were in Mathematics, 3% were in Computer and Engineering Related Technology, 3% were in Life Sciences, 3% were in Physical Sciences, remainder in 4 other fields.

Graduates Career Data. Advanced studies pursued by 25% of students; 1% enter medical school; 1% enter law school; 6% enter business school; 17% enter other schools. Business schools typically enrolling largest number of graduates include St. John Fisher, U. of Rochester. *Careers in business and industry* pursued by 73% of graduates, according to most recent data available. Fields typically hiring largest number of graduates include business, education, health related areas, criminal justice agencies. Career Development Services include placement services, resume and interviewing workshops, individual advisement, co-op community service and part-time employment, computerized guidance information system, computerized employee data base for employers.

Faculty. About 78% of faculty hold PhD or equivalent. About 75% of undergraduate classes taught by tenured faculty. About 38% of teaching faculty are female; 6% Black, 1% Hispanic, 5% other minority.

Student Body. College does not seek a national student body; 98% of students from in state; 99% Middle Atlantic; 1% Foreign. An estimated 46% of students reported as Catholic, 27% Protestant, 4% Jewish, 1% Muslim, 18% unaffiliated, 4% other; 6% Black, 2% Hispanic, 1% Asian, 1% other minority. Average age of undergraduate student: 23.

Varsity Sports. Men (Div.III): Baseball, Basketball, Cross Country, Diving, Football, Ice Hockey, Soccer, Swimming, Track, Wrestling. Women (Div.III): Basketball, Cross Country, Diving, Field Hockey, Gymnastics, Soccer, Softball, Swimming, Tennis, Track, Volleyball.

Campus Life. Unusual special living options include the First Year Experience, Traditional, PEARL (Progressive Environmental and Academic Residence Hall Living), Transfer Student, and Wellness programs; also single sex and 24-hour quiet options. All facilities are co-educational. Alcohol permitted for those 21 and over.

About 15% of men, 13% of women live in coed dormitories; rest live in off-campus housing or commute. Freshmen are given preference in college housing if all students cannot be accommodated; no tripling. Sexes segregated in coed dormitories by floor or suite. There are 9 fraternities, 7 sororities which about 4% men, 4% women join; 2% of men, 2% of women live in fraternities and sororities. About 23% of resident students leave campus on weekends.

Annual Costs. Tuition and fees, $2,940 (out-of-state, $6,840); room and board, $4,360; estimated $1,230 other, exclusive of travel. About 85% of students receive financial aid; average amount of assistance, $5,109. Assistance is typically divided 1% scholarship, 31% grant, 56% loan, 12% work. College reports 15 scholarships awarded for academic merit, 10 for need. *Meeting Costs:* university offers installment payment plan.

State University College at Buffalo

Buffalo, New York 14222 **(716) 878-4017**

The largest unit among the SUNY colleges, Buffalo is located in a city of 462,800, home also of the State University Center. The two institutions cooperate in a program of cross-registration. Most convenient major airport: Buffalo International.

Founded: 1867
Affiliation: State
UG Enrollment: 3,132 M, 4,889 W (full-time)
Total Enrollment: 12,718
Cost: < $10K
% Receiving Financial Aid: 85%
Admission: Non-selective
Application Deadline: August 1

Admission. (See also State University of New York.) About 56% of applicants accepted, 40% of these actually enroll. *Required:* high school record; SAT tests not required. Non-academic factor considered in admissions: special talents. *Entrance programs:* early admission, midyear admission, deferred admission, advanced placement. *Apply* by August 1. *Transfers* welcome.

Academic Environment. *Degrees:* BA, BS, BSEd, BFA, BTech. *Majors offered* include usual arts and sciences, anthropology, art, criminal justice, engineering, geography, food systems management, industrial technology, information systems management, journalism, speech, theater, variety of education programs, social work. Distribution requirements total 60 hours; students may choose a variety of courses from specific categories. About 55% of entering freshmen graduate eventually; 33% of freshmen do not return for sophomore year. *Special programs:* CLEP, independent study, honors, undergraduate research, study abroad, individualized degree program, National Student Exchange, Western New York Consortium, 3–2 programs in engineering. *Calendar:* semester, summer school.

Undergraduate degrees conferred (1,776). 30% were in Education, 18% were in Multi/Interdisciplinary Studies, 9% were in Social Sciences, 7% were in Engineering and Engineering Related Technology, 6% were in Public Affairs, 6% were in Communications, 6% were in Visual and Performing Arts, 5% were in Protective Services, 3% were in Computer and Engineering Related Technology, 3% were in Home Economics, remainder in 8 other fields.

Graduates Career Data. *Career Counseling Program:* Student assessment of program reported as good for both career guidance and job placement.

Faculty. About 88% of full-time faculty hold PhD or equivalent.

Varsity Sports. Men (Div.III): Basketball, Cross Country, Football, Golf, Hockey, Soccer, Swimming & Diving, Tennis, Track. Women (Div.III): Basketball, Cross Country, Soccer, Softball, Swimming & Diving, Tennis, Track, Volleyball.

Campus Life. College does not seek a national student body; 98% of students from New York. An estimated 8% of students reported as Black, 2% Hispanic, 1% Asian, 1% Native American. State College at Buffalo makes no religious demands on students. Religious clubs on campus include Newman, Hillel, Campus/Church Coalition of Western New York. Places of worship available in immediate community for major faiths. About 18% of students live in coed dormitories; rest live in off-campus housing or commute. There are 8 fraternities, 7 sororities on campus. Intervisitation in men's and women's dormitory rooms unlimited.

Annual Costs. Tuition and fees, $3,074 (out-of-state, $6,974); room and board, $4,731. About 85% of students receive financial aid. Assistance is typically divided 57% scholarship, 40% loan, 3% work. College reports some scholarships awarded on the basis of academic merit alone. *Meeting Costs:* university offers various payment plans.

State University College at Cortland

Cortland, New York 13045 **(607) 753-4711**

Located in a city of 25,000, 35 miles south of Syracuse, Cortland is a liberal arts and teachers college, one of a dozen colleges and universities situated within a 50-miles radius in central New York. Most convenient major airport: Ithaca.

Founded: 1868
Affiliation: State
UG Enrollment: 2,286 M, 2,909 W (full-time)
Cost: < $10K
Admission: Non-selective
Application Deadline: February 1

Admission. (See also State University of New York.) About 46% of applicants accepted, 29% of these actually enroll; 26% of entering freshmen graduate in top fifth of high school class, 75% in top two-fifths. Average freshman SAT scores: 461 M, 459 W verbal, 538 M, 513 W mathematical; 61% of score above 500 mathematical, 9% above 600; ACT, 23 M, 23 W composite. *Required:* SAT or ACT, essay, recommendation. Criteria considered in admissions, in order of importance: high school academic record, standardized test scores, writing sample, extracurricular activities, recommendations; other factors considered: special talents, alumni children, diverse student body. *Out-of-state* freshmen applicants: state does not limit out-of-state enrollment. About 50% of out-of-state students accepted, 26% of these actually enroll. States from which most out-of-state students are drawn include New Jersey, Connecticut, Massachusetts, Vermont, Pennsylvania. *Entrance programs:* early decision, early admission, midyear admission, deferred admission, advanced placement. About 1% of freshmen from private schools, 8% from parochial schools. *Apply* by February 1. *Transfers* welcome; 809 enrolled 1993–94.

Academic Environment. Degrees offered: bachelors, masters. Cortland has been designated a Center for Environmental Education by the International Alliance for Environmental Education. Additionally, Cortland is a national headquarters for the Coalition for Education in the Outdoors. Three adjunct campuses enhance on-campus instruction, including the Outdoor Education Center situated in the Adirondacks, the Brauer Field Station located south of Albany, and the college's nature preserve, Hoxie Gorge, just 15 minutes from the campus. Cortland also claims the largest enrolled undergraduate physical education program in the United states, and graduates more teachers, of any sort, than any other New York State school. General education requirements include courses in 10 different categories; total of 34 hours. *Majors offered* include international studies, recreation and leisure studies, outdoor and environmental education, physical education. Average undergraduate class size: 39% under 20, 51% between 20–40, 10% over 40.

About 40% of students entering as freshmen graduate in four years, 53% eventually; 75% of freshmen return for sophomore year. *Special programs:* CLEP, January term, extensive study abroad program, independent study, honors, undergraduate research, Washington Semester, field experience for credit (may be graded satisfactory/unsatisfactory), 3–2 programs in engineering. *Calendar:* semester, summer school.

Undergraduate degrees conferred (1,145). 59% were in Education, 19% were in Social Sciences, 7% were in Communications, 3% were in Health Sciences, 3% were in Psychology, remainder in 8 other fields.

Graduates Career Data. *Full-time graduate or professional study* pursued by 18% of students immediately after graduation.

Faculty. About 82% of faculty hold PhD or equivalent. About 43% of teaching faculty are female; 8% minority.

Student Body. About 96% of students from in state; 98% from New England.

Varsity Sports. Men (Div.III): Baseball, Basketball, Cross Country, Diving, Football, Gymnastics, Ice Hockey, Lacrosse, Soccer, Swimming, Track, Wrestling. Women (Div.III): Basketball, Cross Country, Diving, Field Hockey, Gymnastics, Lacrosse, Soccer, Softball, Swimming, Tennis, Track, Volleyball.

Campus Life. No curfew; 24-hour intervisitation option. Alcohol permitted on campus; freshmen are not allowed to have cars on campus; parking for both residents and commuters described as "unsatisfactory." About 60% of students live in traditional or coed dormitories; 35% live in off-campus college-related housing; rest commute. All students are guaranteed on-campus housing. Sexes segregated in coed dormitories by wing or floor. There are 6 fraternities, 4 sororities on campus which about 10% of men, 10% of women join. About 5% of resident students leave campus on weekends.

Annual Costs. Tuition and fees, $2,926 (out-of-state, $6,826); room and board, $4,400; estimated $1,200 other, exclusive of travel. College reports some scholarships awarded on the basis of academic merit alone.

SUNY—Empire State College

Saratoga Springs, N.Y. 12866 (518) 587-2100

Empire State College is an unusual institution of higher learning whose students do not reside on a campus or meet in a classroom. Instead, the institution operates Regional Centers and Units located throughout New York State where students may meet with faculty and utilize the facilities.

Founded: 1971
Affiliation: State
UG Enrollment: 421 M, 656 W (full-time); 2,685 M, 1,826 W (part-time)
Total Enrollment: 6,322
Cost: < $10K
Admission: Non-selective
Application Deadline: Rolling

Admission. High school graduates or equivalent or those who have demonstrated ability to do college level work eligible. Admission also dependent on "ability of learning location" to meet applicant's educational needs and objectives. About 94% of applicants accepted, 98% of these actually enroll. *Apply:* rolling admissions; students admitted monthly. *Transfers* welcome; about 75% of entering students are transfers.

Academic Environment. Degree programs draw on diverse resources; internships, study at other colleges, independent study, correspondence work, media-related instruction, tutorials, etc. In cooperation with faculty mentors, students design a degree program within the framework of both ESC and personal goals. This may be a traditional discipline, problem area, or interdisciplinary study. Credit is also granted for prior college-level learning from both formal and informal educational experience. Graduate studies may be undertaken in Business and Policy Studies, Labor and Policy Studies, or Culture and Policy Studies. *Degrees:* AA, AS, BA, BS, BPS, MA. *Special programs:* study abroad, independent study. *Library:* instructional materials and reference materials only; not open to students. Students use existing libraries at other SUNY campuses.

Undergraduate degrees conferred (941). 29% were in Business and Management, 19% were in Public Affairs, 11% were in Multi/Interdisciplinary Studies, 8% were in Physical Sciences, 7% were in Visual and Performing Arts, 7% were in Education, 7% were in Letters, 6% were in Psychology, 4% were in Social Sciences.

Graduates Career Data. Full- and part-time graduate or professional study pursued by 60% of students immediately after graduation. *Careers in business and industry* pursued by 35% of graduates.

Campus Life. About 99% of students from in state. An estimated 10% of students reported as Black, 5% Hispanic, 1% Asian, according to most recent data available. College reports students range in age from 18 to 78 (average age, 36); 65% of students employed full-time.

Annual Costs. Tuition and fees, $2,887 (out-of-state, $6,787. About 35% of students receive financial aid.

SUNY—Fashion Institute of Technology

New York City, New York 10001-5992 (212) 760-7675

A State University of New York college for design and business professions, FIT was founded to serve the needs of the fashion and related industries. It is accredited to confer associate, baccalaureate, and masters degrees. The college is located in the Chelsea area of Manhattan, at the north edge of Greenwich Village, close to the heart of the fashion industry. But the campus effectively includes all of N.Y. City with its many museums, libraries, galleries, theaters, and cultural activities. Most convenient major airports: LaGuardia, JFK International, or Newark.

Founded: 1944
Affiliation: State
UG Enrollment: 742 M, 3,701 W (full-time); 1,702 M, 6,566 W (part-time)
Total Enrollment: 12,120
Cost: < $10K
% Receiving Financial Aid: 49%
Admission: Non-selective
Application Deadline: Mar. 15

Admission. About 38% of applicant accepted, 83% of these actually enroll; 21% of students graduate in the top fifth of high school class, 51% in top two fifths. *Required:* SAT or ACT, essay; portfolio for art and design. *Entrance programs:* midyear admission, advanced placement. *Apply* by March 15. *Transfers* welcome.
Academic Environment. FIT's programs in art and design, business and technology provide training for careers in advertising, production, packaging and merchandising. Unusual majors offered in restoration, applied art, toy design. *Computer Science:* computer literacy not required for all students. Construction of new Academic Computing Center is in progress. About 75% of entering freshmen graduate eventually. *Special programs:* study abroad, internships, cooperative education, 2+2 program with City College leads to vocational Teacher Education BA.
Undergraduate degrees conferred (425). 73% were in Marketing and Distribution, 12% were in Visual and Performing Arts, 8% were in Engineering and Engineering Related Technology, 4% were in Home Economics, 3% were in Education.
Graduates Career Data. *Full-time graduate or professional study* pursued immediately after graduation by 33% of students. *Careers in business and industry* pursued by 46% of graduates (90% of those available for work). Corporations typically hiring largest numbers of graduates include Liz Claiborne, The Limited, The Gap.
Campus Life. About 79% of students from in-state; 91% Middle Atlantic. An estimated 11% of students reported as Black, 12% Hispanic, 18% Asian, 1% Native American (67% of students reported ethnicity). About 20% of women, 24% of men live in coed college housing; rest commute. Freshmen given preference in college housing if all students cannot be accommodated.
Annual Costs. Tuition and fees, $2,210 (out-of-state, $4,860); room, $4,655. About 49% of students receive financial aid; assistance is typically divided 61% scholarship, 34% loan, 5% work. College reports some scholarships awarded on the basis of academic merit alone. *Meeting Costs:* institute offers installment payment plan, parent loan program.

State University College at Fredonia

Fredonia, New York 14063 (716) 673-3251

A liberal arts college, Fredonia is located in a village of 10,300, 45 miles southwest of Buffalo. Most convenient major airport: Greater Buffalo International.

Founded: 1866
Affiliation: State
UG Enrollment: 1,857 M, 2,267 W (full-time); 107 M, 191 W (part-time)
Total Enrollment: 4,838
Cost: < $10K
% Receiving Financial Aid: 61%
Admission: Selective (+)
Application Deadline: March 1

Admission is selective (+). (See also State University of New York.) About 57% of applicants accepted, 31% of these actually enroll; 37% of freshmen graduate in top fifth of high school class, 84% in top two-fifths. Average freshman scores: SAT, 477 M, 468 W verbal, 547 M, 508 W mathematical. *Required:* SAT or ACT; audition or portfolio for fine and performing arts; interview recommended. *Non-academic factors* considered in admissions: diverse student body, special talents, alumni children. *Entrance programs:* early admission, midyear admission, advanced placement, deferred admission. *Apply* by March 1; rolling admissions after January 15. *Transfers* welcome; 458 enrolled 1993–94.
Academic Environment. Administration reports percent of general education courses required for graduation that are elective varies with program; distribution requirements fairly numerous. Degrees offered: bachelors, masters. *Majors offered* include environmental studies, law and justice, industrial management, sound recording technology, recombinant gene technology, medical technology, theater arts, teacher preparatory fields including speech pathology and audiology, sound recording technology and music, health services administration.

About 60% of students entering as freshmen graduate eventually; 14% of students do not return for sophomore year. *Special programs:* CLEP, independent study, honors, study abroad, undergraduate research, 3-year degree, individualized majors, internships, credit by examination, Lake Erie Environmental Studies Program, cooperative engineering programs with numerous schools. *Calendar:* semester, summer school.
Undergraduate degrees conferred (991). 26% were in Education, 21% were in Business and Management, 12% were in Social Sciences, 8% were in Communications, 8% were in Visual and Performing Arts, 5% were in Psychology, 5% were in Letters, 3% were in Physical Sciences, remainder in 9 other fields.
Graduates Career Data. Advanced studies pursued immediately after graduation by 26% of students. *Careers in business and industry* pursued by 38% of graduates. Corporations typically hiring largest numbers of graduates include IBM, EDS, Marine Midland Bank, Eastman Kodak. *Career Counseling Program:* Alumni reported as helpful in career guidance and in job placement.
Faculty. About 90% of faculty hold PhD or equivalent.
Student Body. College seeks a national student body; 98% of students from in state; 15 foreign students 1993–94. An estimated 3% of students reported as Black, 3% other minority.
Varsity Sports. Men (Div.III): Baseball, Basketball, Cross Country, Hockey, Soccer, Tennis, Track. Women (Div.III): Basketball, Cross Country, Soccer, Tennis, Track, Volleyball.
Campus Life. Freshmen and sophomores required to live in dormitories. Intervisitation limited or unlimited depending on dormitory. Cars allowed.

About 20% of men, 29% of women live in traditional dormitories; 31% of men, 28% of women live in coed dormitories; 22% of men, 16% of women in off-campus college-related housing; rest commute. Sexes segregated in coed dormitories by wing or floor. There are 5 fraternities or sororities.
Annual Costs. Tuition and fees, $2,959 (out-of-state, $6,859); room and board, $4,200, maximum plan; estimated $1,100 other, exclusive of travel. About 67% of freshmen students, 61% of continuing students receive financial aid; average amount of assistance, $4,302. Assistance is typically divided 10% scholarship, 60% loan, 30% work. College reports some scholarships awarded for academic merit alone. *Meeting Costs:* college offers monthly payment plans; parent's loans, accepts credit cards.

State University College at Geneseo

Geneseo, New York 14454 (716) 245-5571

A liberal arts college with professional programs in accounting, business, computer science, teacher education, special education, and speech pathology and audiology. The college is located in a village of 5,700, 30 miles south of Rochester. Most convenient major airport: Monroe County, Rochester.

Founded: 1867
Affiliation: State
UG Enrollment: 1,796 M, 3,260 W (full-time)
Total Enrollment: 5,630
Cost: < $10K
% Receiving Financial Aid: 70%
Admission: Very Selective
Application Deadline: January 15

Admission is very selective. (See also State University of New York.) About 53% of applicants accepted, 25% of these actually enroll; 89% of freshmen graduate in top fifth of high school class, 99% in top two-fifths. Average freshman SAT scores: 541 verbal, 608 mathematical; 73% of freshmen score above 500 on verbal, 20% above 600, 1% above 700; 97% of freshmen score above 500 on mathematical, 59% above 600, 11% above 700; ACT, 25 composite. *Required:* SAT or ACT, essay. Criteria considered in admissions, in order of importance: rigor of high school program, high school academic record, standardized test scores; of equal importance: recommendations, extracurricular activities, writing sample; other factors considered: special talents, diverse student body. *Out-of-state* freshman applicants: university does not actively seek students from out of state. State does not limit out-of-state enrollment. About 45% of out-of-state students accepted, 18% of these actually enroll. States from which most out-of-state students are drawn include New Jersey, Pennsylvania, Connecticut. *Entrance programs:* early decision, early admission, midyear admission, advanced placement, deferred admission. About 2% of entering freshmen are from private schools, 15% from parochial schools. *Apply* by January 15; rolling admissions after February 15. *Transfers* welcome; 336 enrolled 1993–94.

Academic Environment. Students describe the academic programs at Geneseo as "rigorous" and "challenging". Flexible general education common core required for all students. Degrees offered: bachelors, masters. *Majors offered* in addition to usual studies include anthropology, biophysics, black studies, dramatic arts, medical technology, pre-med, speech pathology and audiology, variety of teacher training programs, biochemistry, geochemistry, geophysics. Very strong programs include business, English, history, biology, and education. Undergraduate Research Grants program allows many students to engage in research each year. A recent senior reports that "academic departments are constantly working to improve their curriculum and expand their programs." He also finds the faculty to be "very accessible." Average undergraduate class size: 35% under 20, 50% between 20–40, 15% over 40.

About 59% of students entering as freshmen graduate in four years, 74% eventually; 92% of freshmen return for sophomore year. *Special programs:* CLEP, January intersession, study abroad, undergraduate research, 3–2 and 4–1 engineering, 3–2 MBA, 2–2 Pre-Forestry with SUNY College of Environmental Science and Forestry, Washington Semester, credit by examination, visiting student program for New York State colleges, cooperative programs through Rochester Area Colleges Consortium. *Calendar:* semester, summer school.

Undergraduate degrees conferred (1,153). 26% were in Education, 16% were in Business and Management, 15% were in Social Sciences, 15% were in Letters, 11% were in Psychology, 4% were in Life Sciences, 4% were in Health Sciences, 3% were in Visual and Performing Arts, remainder in 5 other fields.

Graduates Career Data. Advanced studies pursued by 26% of students. About 62% of 1991–92 graduates employed. Fields typically hiring largest numbers of graduates include business, education, health clinics. Career Development Services include career planning and placement, graduate school nights, resume preparation.

Faculty. About 87% of faculty hold PhD or equivalent. About 62% of undergraduate classes taught by tenured faculty. About 30% of teaching faculty are female; 8% minority.

Student Body. College does not seek a national student body; 98% of students from in state; less than 1% Foreign. An estimated 53% of students reported to be Catholic, 29% Protestant, 3% Jewish, 12% unaffiliated, 3% other; 2% as Black, 2% Hispanic, 2% Asian, 1% Native American, according to most recent data available.

Varsity Sports. Men (Div.III): Basketball, Cross Country, Diving, Hockey, Lacrosse, Soccer, Swimming, Track. Women (Div.III): Basketball, Cross Country, Diving, Soccer, Softball, Swimming, Track, Volleyball.

Campus Life. Geneseo, like many other colleges in SUNY system, has adopted intervisitation regulations that combine wishes of dormitory residents within some limits set by administration. Alcohol not permitted in dormitory rooms. Cars are allowed. Freshmen required to live on campus. Recent student reports that the small campus is an aid "to very good relations" with faculty.

About 58% of men, 61% of women live in coed dormitories; 34% of men, 28% of women live in off-campus housing or commute. Freshmen are given preference in college housing if all students cannot be accommodated. Sexes segregated in coed dormitories by floor or room. There are 4 fraternities, 10 sororities on campus which about 7% of men, 15% of women join; 6% of men, 10% of women live in fraternities and sororities. About 30% of resident students leave campus on weekends.

Annual Costs. Tuition and fees, $2,955 (out-of-state, $6,855); room and board, $3,994; estimated $1,250 other, exclusive of travel. About 70% of students receive financial aid; average amount of assistance, $2,830. Assistance is typically divided 3% scholarship, 27% grant, 60% loan, 10% work. College reports 250 scholarships awarded for academic merit. *Meeting Costs:* college offers Academic Management Services, PLUS Loans.

State University of New York Maritime College

Fort Schuyler, Bronx, New York 10465 (212) 409-7220

SUNY's Maritime College is the oldest U.S. Coast Guard-approved nautical science college in the United States. Cadets earn bachelor's degrees in various fields of engineering, science, business, and humanities, while concurrently preparing for the U.S. Merchant Marine officer license of third mate or third assistant engineer. The curriculum includes an annual Summer Sea Term training cruise to European ports. The college is located at the Throgs Neck Bridge in the Bronx, where the East River meets Long Island Sound. Most convenient major airport: LaGuardia.

Founded: 1874
Affiliation: State
UG Enrollment: 617 M, 65 W (full-time)
Total Enrollment: 910
Cost: < $10K
% Receiving Financial Aid: 60%
Admission: Selective
Application Deadline: Rolling

Admission is selective. (See also State University of New York.) Graduates of accredited high schools with 16 units in academic subjects, GPA of 2.5, and minimum combined SAT score of 1050 eligible; 53% of applicants accepted, 28% of these actually enroll. About 27% of freshmen graduate in top fifth of high school class. Average freshman scores: SAT, 32% of freshmen score above 500 verbal, 10% above 600; 68% above 500 mathematical, 22% above 600, 2% above 700. *Required:* SAT; interview recommended. Criteria considered in admissions, in order of importance: high school record, standardized test scores, recommendations, extracurricular activities; other factors considered: special talents. *Out-of-state* freshmen applicants: college actively seeks students from out-of-state. State does not limit out-of-state enrollment. States from which most out-of-state students are drawn include New Jersey, Connecticut, Maryland. *Entrance programs:* early decision, early admission, midyear admission (transfers only), deferred admission, advanced placement. About 5% of freshmen from private schools, 41% from parochial schools.Apply: rolling admissions. *Transfers* welcome; 40 enrolled 1993–94.

Academic Environment. Degrees offered: bachelors, masters. *Majors offered* include naval architecture, marine engineering, oceanography/meteorology, marine transportation. Core requirements include 4 semesters of English composition/literature. An important part of all Maritime College curricula is the Annual Summer Sea Term aboard the 565-foot training ship, The Empire State. The Summer Term provides a leadership laboratory in which cadets assume responsibility for the operation of the ship under the supervision of licensed officers and staff. The Empire State normally calls on three European ports on each cruise. During the academic year, cadets also have the opportunities for training in inland waterways aboard the college's 110-foot tugboat, and a 171-foot coastal training tanker. Average undergraduate class size: 18% under 20, 80% between 20–40, 2% over 40. About 69% of students entering as freshmen graduate eventually; 88% of freshmen return for sophomore year. Special program: CLEP, internships. *Calendar:* semester, required Summer Sea Term. *Miscellaneous:* N ROTC.

Undergraduate degrees conferred (144). 50% were in Engineering, 33% were in Business and Management, 8% were in Physical Sciences, 8% were in Computer and Engineering Related Technology.

Graduates Career Data. Advanced studies pursued by 14% of students; 2% enter law schools, 4% enter business schools, 8% enter engineering programs. About 96% of 1992–1993 graduates employed. Employers typically hiring largest numbers of graduates include General Electric, Sealand. Career Development Services include seminars, mock interviews, long range career planning, on-campus interviews with prospective employers.

Faculty. About 49% of faculty hold PhD or equivalent. About 37% of undergraduate classes taught by tenured faculty.

Varsity Sports. Men (Div.III): Baseball, Basketball, Crew, Cross Country, Lacrosse, Sailing, Swimming, Tennis. Women (Div.III): Baseball, Basketball, Crew, Cross Country, Sailing, Swimming, Tennis.

Student Body. About 72% of students from New York; 85% Middle Atlantic, 8% New England, 5% foreign. An estimated 5% of students reported as Black, 7% Hispanic, 5% Asian.

Campus Life. About 88% of students live in coed dormitories; rest commute. Intervisitation in men's and women's dormitory rooms limited. There are no fraternities or sororities.

Annual Costs. Tuition and fees, $2,650 (out-of-state, $6,550); room and board, $4,600; estimated $2,000 other including required uniforms and clothing, but excluding travel. About 60% of students receive financial aid; average amount of assistance, $7,950. Assistance is typically divided 5% scholarship, 35% grant, 50% loan, 10% work. College reports 40 scholarships awarded for academic merit. *Meeting Costs:* college offers Academic Management Services.

State University College at New Paltz

New Paltz, New York, 12561-2499 (914) 257-3200

Located in the historic village of New Paltz (pop. 6,058), midway between Albany and New York City in the mid-Hudson region of New York, the College at New Paltz offers a variety of academic programs in liberal arts and sciences, fine and performing arts and education. In response to the growth of high technology related industries in the mid-Hudson Valley, the College has developed programs in business, computer science and engineering to help sustain and encourage this regional growth. Most convenient major airport: Stewart International, (Newburgh, NY).

Founded: 1828
Affiliation: State
UG Enrollment: 1,985 M, 2,761 W (full-time); 541 M, 888 W (part-time)
Total Enrollment: 7,941
Cost: < $10K
% Receiving Financial Aid: 75%
Admission: Selective
Application Deadline: May 1

Admission is selective (See also State University of New York.) About 43% of applicants accepted, 22% of these actually enroll; 41% of freshmen graduate in top fifth of high school class, 84% in top two-fifths. Average freshmen scores: SAT, 479 verbal, 537 mathematical; 38% of freshmen score above 550 on verbal, 7% above 600, 1% above 700; 70% of freshmen score above 500 on mathematical, 22% above 600, 2% above 700; ACT, 24 composite. *Required:* SAT or ACT, minimum H.S. GPA, portfolio for art applicants, audition for music and theater applicants. Criteria considered in admissions, in order of importance: high school academic record, standardized test scores, recommendations and extracurricular activities; other factors considered: special talents. *Out-of-state* freshmen applicants: college actively seeks students from out-of-state. State does not limit out-of-state enrollment. About 58% of out-of-state students accepted, 17% of these actually enroll. States from which most out-of-state students are drawn include New Jersey, Connecticut, Massachusetts, Pennsylvania. *Entrance programs:* early decision, early admission, midyear admission, deferred admission, advanced placement. *Apply* by May 1; rolling admissions. *Transfers* welcome; 850 enrolled 1993–94.

Academic Environment. Degrees offered: bachelors, masters. Undergraduate majors offered in 104 areas including anthropology, Black studies, electrical engineering, jazz studies, international relations, music therapy, nursing, speech and hearing, theater arts, fine arts, scenography, elementary and secondary education. All students must complete General Education Program which consists of a total of 45 credits in 9 areas of the arts, sciences and humanities. The College houses the Haggerty Institute for English as a Second Language, and the nationally recognized Language Immersion Institute. Academic programs are enhanced by on-campus art gallery, 3 theaters, a radio station, a T.V. station, an electron microscope facility, a robotics laboratory, and a "clean room"(electrical engineering facility). Average undergraduate class size: 21; 48% of classes under 20, 42% between 20–40, 10% over 40.

About 26% of students entering as freshmen graduate in four years, 51% eventually; 78% of freshmen return for sophomore year. *Special programs:* internships, honors, undergraduate research, study abroad, independent study, cooperative education, study abroad, "Legislative Gazette" internship, U.N. semester, London Theatre Winterim, "Lively Arts in NYC" semester, foreign language immersion program, computer immersion program, 3–2 engineering, 3–2 geological engineering, 2–2 environmental science and forestry, 2–2 physical therapy, 3–1 pre-optometry, cross registration with Mid-Hudson Consortium of Colleges. *Calendar:* semester, 2 summer sessions.

Undergraduate degrees conferred (1,213). 18% were in Education, 15% were in Letters, 14% were in Business and Management, 12% were in Social Sciences, 11% were in Psychology, 9% were in Visual and Performing Arts, 3% were in Health Sciences, 3% were in Liberal/General Studies, remainder in 11 other fields.

Graduates Career Data. Career Development Services include workshops, special programs, counseling, career resource library, credentials service, campus recruitment program, interactive computerized career guidance system.

Faculty. About 78% of faculty hold PhD or equivalent. About 34% of teaching faculty are female; 11% ethnic minorities.

Student Body. College seeks a national student body; 91% of students from New York; 450 foreign students. An estimated 39% of students reported as Catholic, 16% Jewish, 13% Protestant, 21% unaffiliated, 11% other; 10% as Black, 9% as Hispanic, 4% Asian, 4% other. Average age of undergraduate student: 23; average age of first-year freshman: 18.

Varsity Sports. Men (Div.III): Baseball, Basketball, Cross Country, Diving, Golf, Soccer, Swimming, Tennis, Volleyball. Women (Div.III): Cross Country, Diving, Soccer, Softball, Swimming, Tennis, Volleyball.

Campus Life. High interest reported in intramural sports; club sports include ice hockey, rugby, lacrosse. Eleven coed residence halls coordinate a variety of educational, cultural and social activities through the Office of Residence Life and the Residence Hall Student Association. Student Association, through student activity fees, coordinates and oversees more than 150 different organizations and groups.

About 45% of students live in coed dormitories; 21% live in off-campus non-college-related housing, rest commute. Freshmen are given preference in college housing if all students cannot be accommodated. There are 15 fraternities, 8 sororities on campus, which about 3% of men, 3% of women join. About 15% of residential students leave campus on weekends.

Annual Costs. Tuition and fees, $2,965 (out-of-state, $6,865); room and board, $4,460); estimated $900 other, exclusive of travel. About 75% of students receive financial aid; average amount of assistance, $2,862. Assistance is typically divided 2% scholarship, 28% grant, 60% loan, 10% work. College reports 46 scholarships awarded for academic merit, 14 for special talents.

State University College at Old Westbury

Old Westbury, New York 11568 (516) 876-3000

Founded as an experimental school, Old Westbury attracts substantial numbers of non-traditional students, most of whom do not enter directly from high school. Most convenient major airport: LaGuardia.

Founded: 1965
Affiliation: State
UG Enrollment: 1,273 M, 1,575 W (full-time); 470 M, 629 W (part-time)
Cost: < $10K
Admission: Non-selective
Application Deadline: March 15

Admission. Requirements very flexible; motivation and previous experience important; about 80% of applicants accepted, 37% of these actually enroll. Criteria considered in admissions, in order of importance: high school academic record, recommendations, extracurricular activities, writing sample. *Apply* by March 15. *Transfers* welcome; 767 enrolled 1993–94.

Academic Environment. *Degree:* AB. College offers wide range of programs in the arts and sciences, including health and society, criminology, language and literature, management information systems, media and communications, philosophy and religion, world cultures; few specific requirements. About 26% of students entering as freshmen graduate eventually. Special programs for minority and low-income students. *Calendar:* semester, summer school.

Undergraduate degrees conferred (720). 41% were in Business and Management, 23% were in Education, 7% were in Social Sciences, 7% were in Computer and Engineering Related Technology, 7% were in Psychology, 4% were in Life Sciences, 3% were in Area and Ethnic Studies, remainder in 5 other fields.

Graduates Career Data. Advanced studies pursued by 52% of students; 6% enter professional schools. About 87% of 1992–93 graduates employed. Fields typically hiring the largest number of graduates include accounting, education, social services. Career Development Services include individual and group counseling, placement services, on-campus recruitment.

Faculty. About 75% of faculty hold PhD or equivalent. About 48% of teaching faculty are female; 21% Black, 11% hispanic, 12% other minorities.

Varsity Sports. Men (Div.III): Baseball, Basketball, Soccer, Tennis, Volleyball. Women (Div.III): Basketball, Softball, Tennis, Volleyball.
Student Body. About 98% of students from New York.
Campus Life. About 19% of men, 21% of women live in coed dormitories; rest commute. There are 5 fraternities, 2 sororities on campus which about 3% of men, 1% of women join. About 75% of resident students leave campus on weekends.
Annual Costs. Tuition and fees, $2,928 (out-of-state, $6,828; room and board, $4,200; estimated $1,000 other, exclusive of travel. About 68% of students receive financial aid. College reports all scholarships awarded on the basis of need. *Meeting Costs:* college offers Parent PLUS Loans.

State University College at Oneonta

Oneonta, New York 13820-4015 (607) 436-2524

A state-supported, liberal arts, and teachers college, located in a town of 15,000, 175 miles northwest of New York City. Most convenient major airport: Broome County (Binghamton).

Founded: 1889
Affiliation: State
UG Enrollment: 1,851 M, 2,776 W (full-time); 161 M, 322 W (part-time)
Total Enrollment: 5,665
Cost: < $10K
% Receiving Financial Aid: 70%
Admission: Selective
Application Deadline: May 1

Admission is selective. (See also State University of New York.) About 58% of applicants accepted, 20% of these actually enroll. Average freshman SAT scores: 463 verbal, 509 mathematical. *Required:* SAT or ACT. *Non-academic factors* considered in admissions: special talents, alumni children, diverse student body, extracurricular activities, non-traditional student. *Out-of-state* freshmen applicants: university actively seeks out-of-state students. State does not limit out-of-state enrollment. States from which most out-of-state students are drawn include New Jersey, Massachusetts, Connecticut. *Entrance programs:* midyear admission, early admission, advanced placement, deferred admission. *Apply* by May 1; rolling admissions. *Transfers* welcome; 678 enrolled 1993–94.
Academic Environment. Degrees offered: bachelors, masters. *Majors offered* include accounting, international studies, child development and family studies, adulthood and aging studies, mineralogy, theater, home economics fields, music industry.

About 45% of students entering as freshmen graduate in four years, 54% eventually; 80% of freshmen do not return for sophomore year. *Special programs:* January term, independent study, undergraduate research, study abroad, alternative studies; program in Black-Hispanic studies; 3–2 in engineering, accounting, management, physical therapy; 3–1 programs in studio art/fashion, business economics/fashion, home economics-clothing and textiles/fashion with FIT; Washington Semester, New York State Legislative Intern Program; cross registration with Hartwick. *Calendar:* semester, summer school.
Undergraduate degrees conferred (1,152). 29% were in Education, 28% were in Business and Management, 9% were in Letters, 8% were in Psychology, 8% were in Home Economics, 8% were in Social Sciences, 3% were in Visual and Performing Arts, remainder in 9 other fields.
Graduates Career Data. According to most recent data available, full-time graduate or professional study pursued immediately after graduation by 17% of students. *Careers in business and industry* pursued by 68% of graduates. Fields typically hiring the largest number of graduates include business, education. Career Development Services include career counseling, career classes, interest inventory, on-campus job interviews, resume assistance.
Faculty. More than 70% of faculty hold PhD or equivalent.
Student Body. College does not seek a national student body; 98% of students from in state; 99% Middle Atlantic; 21 foreign students 1993–94. An estimated 2% of students reported as Black, 3% Hispanic, 1% Asian, 1% other minority.
Varsity Sports. Men (Div.III): Baseball, Basketball, Cross Country, Lacrosse, Soccer (I), Tennis, Wrestling. Women (AIAW III): Basketball, Cross Country, Field Hockey, Lacrosse, Soccer, Softball, Swimming, Tennis, Volleyball.
Campus Life. Campus ombudsman available to students. High interest reported in intramural sports (most popular: softball, basketball, floor hockey, volleyball, racquetball). All dormitories self-regulating. Provisions for intervisitation hours daily. Special interest housing available. Alcoholic beverages prohibited in residential housing; cars not permitted for freshmen and sophomores. College recommends that new students live on campus.

About 6% of women live in traditional dormitories; 55% of men, 49% of women in coed dormitories; 45% of men, 45% of women live in off-campus housing or commute. Freshmen given preference in college housing if all students cannot be accommodated. Sexes segregated in coed dormitories either by floor or room. There are 13 fraternities, 8 sororities on campus.
Annual Costs. Tuition and fees, $2,926 (out-of-state, $6,826); room and board, $4,952; estimated $1,800 other, exclusive of travel. About 70% of students receive financial aid (including state and federal programs); average amount of assistance, $2,625. College reports some scholarships awarded on the basis of academic merit alone. *Meeting Costs:* College offers Academic Management Services 10-month payment plan.

State University College at Oswego

Oswego, New York 13126 (315) 341-2250

A liberal arts college that produces substantial numbers of business and management, and teacher education majors. Oswego is located in a city of 23,800, on the shores of Lake Ontario, 35 miles from Syracuse and 65 miles east of Rochester. Most convenient major airport: Hancock International (Syracuse).

Founded: 1861
Affiliation: State
UG Enrollment: 3,000 M, 3,600 W (full-time); 468 M, 537 W (part-time)
Total Enrollment: 7,605
Cost: < $10K
% Receiving Financial Aid: 78%
Admission: Selective
Application Deadline: Jan. 15

Admission is selective. (See also State University of New York.) About 57% of applicants accepted, 32% of these actually enroll; 65% of freshmen graduate in top fifth of high school class, 96% in top two-fifths. Average freshman SAT scores: 54% of freshmen score above 500 on verbal, 22% above 600, 79% score above 500 on mathematical, 24% above 600, 1% above 700; ACT: 24 composite. *Required:* SAT or ACT. Criteria considered in admissions, in order of importance: high school academic record, standardized test scores, class rank, writing sample, recommendations, extracurricular activities; other factors considered: special talents, alumni children. *Out-of-state* freshmen applicants: university actively seeks students from out-of-state. State does not limit out-of-state enrollment. About 33% of out-of-state students accepted, 50% of these actually enroll. States from which most out-of-state students are drawn include New Jersey, Pennsylvania, Connecticut. *Entrance programs:* early admission, deferred admission. *Apply* by January 15. *Transfers* welcome; 850 enrolled 1993–94.
Academic Environment. Degrees offered: bachelors, masters. *Majors offered* include anthropology, business administration, public justice, information science, meteorology, linguistics, zoology, education fields including technology education, industrial arts; accounting/management bachelors and masters in five years. Core requirements include 6 credits in English, 6 in mathematics, 9 in social sciences, humanities, and natural sciences, 6 in cultural heritage. Academic environment enhanced by "beautiful lakeside environment and a biological field station." Several recent students report that computer and library facilities are adequate to meet student demand. Average undergraduate class size: 28.

About 54% of students entering as freshmen graduate in four years, 63% eventually; 88% of freshmen return for sophomore year. *Special programs:* CLEP, independent study, study abroad, honors, undergraduate research, field internships, area studies programs (Asian, Latin American, Middle East/African), visiting student program for New York State Colleges, 3–2 engineering. Adult programs: social and support network for non-traditionals. *Calendar:* semester, summer school.
Undergraduate degrees conferred (1,598). 27% were in Education, 22% were in Business and Management, 11% were in Social Sciences, 8% were in Psychology, 8% were in

Communications, 5% were in Letters, 4% were in Protective Services, 4% were in Visual and Performing Arts, 3% were in Life Sciences, 3% were in Computer and Engineering Related Technology, remainder in 6 other fields.

Graduates Career Data. Advanced studies pursued immediately after graduation by 31% of students, 40% within five years; 1% enter medical school; 2% enter law school; 1% enter dental school; 8% enter business school; 8% enter other schools. About 97% of 1992–93 graduates employed or in graduate school. Employers typically hiring the largest number of graduates include IBM, Marine Midland, Xerox, Ford Motor Co.

Faculty. About 72% of faculty hold PhD or equivalent. About 70% of undergraduate classes taught by tenured faculty. About 13% of teaching faculty are Black, 16% other minority.

Student Body. About 95% of students from in state; 98% from Middle Atlantic. An estimated 4% of students reported as Black, 3% Hispanic, 2% Asian, 1% other

Varsity Sports. Men (Div.III): Baseball, Basketball, Cross Country, Diving, Golf, Ice Hockey, Lacrosse, Soccer, Swimming, Tennis, Wrestling. Women (Div.III): Basketball, Cross Country, Diving, Field Hockey, Lacrosse, Soccer, Softball, Swimming, Tennis, Volleyball.

Campus Life. Rules for intervisitation set by residents of each dormitory. Alcohol permitted under special circumstances; cars allowed. Upper-class students under 21 who have parental consent may petition to live off campus. Students and administration report that Oswego offers a friendly, comfortable, and safe environment.

About 5% of students live in traditional dormitories; 60% of students live in coed dormitories; 20% of students live in off-campus college-related housing; rest commute. Freshmen are given preference in college housing if all students cannot be accommodated. Sexes segregated in coed dormitories either by wing or suite. There are 11 fraternities, 12 sororities on campus which about 12% of men, 12% of women join; 5% each live in fraternities and sororities. About 10–15% of resident students leave campus on weekends.

Annual Costs. Tuition and fees, $2,930 (out-of-state, $6,830); room and board, $4,400; estimated $425 other, exclusive of travel. About 78% of students receive financial aid. College reports 15 scholarships awarded for academic merit, 10 for need.

State University College at Plattsburgh

Plattsburgh, New York 12901 **(518) 564-2040**

Plattsburgh State University College is a four-year, co-educational college offering a wide range of baccalaureate programs and a limited number of master's programs in the liberal arts and professional studies. The 300-acre campus is located in New York's historic Champlain Valley in a community of less than 40,000, two and a half hours by car north of Albany, an hour south of Montreal, and an hour from Lake Placid and Burlington, Vermont. Most convenient major airports: Burlington, VT or Montreal, Canada.

Founded: 1889
Affiliation: State
UG Enrollment: 2,219 M, 2,852 W (full-time); 188 M, 276 W (part-time)
Total Enrollment: 6,253
Cost: < $10K
% Receiving Financial Aid: 50%
Admission: Selective
Application Deadline: May 1

Admission is selective. (See also State University of New York.) About 65% of applicants accepted, 24% of these actually enroll; 29% of freshmen graduate in top fifth of high school class, 67% in top two-fifths. Average freshman SAT scores: 450 M, 440 W verbal, 530 M, 490 W mathematical; 24% of freshmen score above 500 on verbal, 2% above 600, 59% score above 500 on mathematical, 13% above 600, 1% above 700; ACT, 22 M, 22 W composite. *Required:* SAT or ACT, minimum H.S. GPA; interview recommended. Criteria considered in admissions, in order of importance: high school academic record, standardized test scores, recommendations, writing sample, extracurricular activities; other factors considered: special talents, alumni children, diverse student body. *Out-of-state* freshmen applicants: university actively seeks students from out-of-state. State does not limit out-of-state enrollment. About 78% of out-of-state students accepted, 23% of these actually enroll. States from which most out-of-state students are drawn include Vermont, New Jersey. *Entrance programs:* early decision, early admission, midyear admission, deferred admission, advanced placement. *Apply* by May 1; rolling admissions. *Transfers* welcome; 789 enrolled 1993–94.

Academic Environment. Degrees offered: bachelors, masters. *Majors offered* include biotechnology and in-vitro cell biology, communication, Canadian studies, environmental science, hearing and speech science, medical technology, hotel/restaurant management, social work, international business, special education. Core requirements include 41–43 credits including courses in English, mathematics, natural sciences, social sciences, history, fine arts, and foreign culture/language. Current students report computer and library facilities are adequate to meet student demand. Average undergraduate class size: 40% under 20, 44% between 20–40, 16% over 40.

About 37% of students entering as freshmen graduate in four years, 60% eventually; 78% of freshmen return for sophomore year. *Special programs:* CLEP, independent study, honors individualized studies, study abroad, undergraduate research, cross registration with Clinton Community College,Canadian and Latin American studies, credit by examination, cooperative education, internships, women's studies; 3–2 engineering, international policy studies. Adult programs: individualized studies program. *Calendar:* semester, summer school.

Undergraduate degrees conferred (1,203). 21% were in Business and Management, 20% were in Education, 9% were in Social Sciences, 8% were in Psychology, 7% were in Letters, 5% were in Health Sciences, 5% were in Communications, 4% were in Public Affairs, 4% were in Protective Services, 3% were in Renewable Natural Resources, 3% were in Home Economics, remainder in 10 other fields.

Graduates Career Data. Advanced studies pursued by 35% of students; 1% enter medical school; 1% enter law school; 3% enter business school; 7% enter other schools. About 94% of 1992–93 graduates employed. Fields typically hiring the largest number of graduates include education, business and industry, health care, government. Career Development Services include career counseling, part-time and summer employment services, internship and cooperative education, employment referral for graduates.

Faculty. About 90% of faculty hold PhD or equivalent. About 68% of undergraduate classes taught by tenured faculty. About 29% of teaching faculty are female; 9% minority.

Student Body. College does not seek a national student body; 96% of students from New York State; 99% North West; 1% Foreign. An estimated 3% of students reported as Black, 2% Hispanic, 2% Asian, 11% other minority. Average age of undergraduate student: 22.

Varsity Sports. Men (Div.III): Basketball, Cross Country, Diving, Ice Hockey, Soccer, Swimming, Track. Women (Div.III): Basketball, Cross Country, Diving, Soccer, Swimming, Tennis, Track, Volleyball.

Campus Life. Current students report recreational opportunities include skiing, hiking, and snowboarding in the nearby Adirondack Mountains, trips to nearby Montreal and Burlington, as well as diverse on-campus programs. Freshmen and sophomores expected to live on campus, unless married or living at home. About 49% of students live in coed dormitories; 36% of students live off-campus college-related housing; rest commute. Sexes segregated in coed dormitories by floor. There are 9 fraternities, 9 sororities, which about 10% of men, 10% of women join; 3% of students live in fraternities and sororities. About 15% of resident students leave campus on weekends.

Annual Costs. Tuition and fees, $2,925 (out-of-state, $6,825); room and board, $3,812; estimated $1,000 other, exclusive of travel. About 50% of students receive financial aid; average amount of assistance, $6,000. Assistance is typically divided 5% scholarship, 37% grant, 55% loan, 3% work. College reports 100 scholarships awarded for academic merit, 25 for special talents, 300 for need. *Meeting Costs:* college offers Academic Management Services, monthly payment plan, central job referral, job location and development.

State University College at Potsdam

Potsdam, New York 13676 **(315) 267-2180**

A liberal arts college with a teacher certification program, Potsdam is located in a community of 10,000, 90 miles south of Ottawa, also the home of Clarkson University. College includes Crane School of Music. Most convenient major airport: Syracuse.

Founded: 1816
Affiliation: State
UG Enrollment: 1,447 M, 2,151 W (full-time); 87 M, 147 W (part-time)
Total Enrollment: 4,403
Cost: < $10K
% Receiving Financial Aid: 80%
Admission: Selective
Application Deadline: Dec. 1

Admission is selective +. (See also State University of New York.) About 73% of applicants accepted, 28% of these actually enroll; 16% of freshmen graduate in top tenth of high school class, 53% in top quarter. Average freshman SAT scores: 480 verbal, 520 mathematical; 32% of freshmen score above 500 on verbal, 4% above 600, 65% score above 500 on mathematical, 14% above 600, 2% above 700; ACT: 23 composite. *Required:* SAT or ACT, minimum H.S. GPA of 80, audition for music; a portfolio is suggested for art. Criteria considered in admissions, in order of importance: high school academic record, standardized tests, class rank, recommendations, extracurricular activities; other factors considered: special talents, diverse student body. Entrance program: early decision, advanced placement, early admission, mid-year admission, deferred admission. About 20% of freshmen come from private schools. *Apply* by December 1 (recommended): rolling admissions. *Transfers* welcome; 408 enrolled 1993–94.

Academic Environment. Degrees offered: bachelors, masters. *Majors offered* in addition to usual studies include anthropology, drama, painting, pottery, sculpture. Programs receiving national recognition include Crane School of Music, and mathematics. Most popular programs reported to be computer science, mathematics, psychology, music, teacher education. Library facilities include on-line cataloging and search service. Extensive computer network and 24-hour computer lab available for student use.

About 30% of entering freshmen graduate in four years, 50% eventually; 84% of freshmen return for sophomore year. *Special programs:* honors, study abroad, career experience, independent study, undergraduate research, exemption from requirements, internship with state government in Albany, inter-college courses in 4 college consortium, BA/MA in mathematics, 4–1 MBA at Clarkson, 3–4 SUNY College of optometry, 3–2 programs in accounting, management, engineering; cross registration with Clarkson U., St. Lawrence U., Canton College of Technology. *Calendar:* semester, summer school.

Undergraduate degrees conferred (667). 31% were in Education, 19% were in Social Sciences, 10% were in Psychology, 9% were in Letters, 6% were in Visual and Performing Arts, 6% were in Mathematics, 4% were in Life Sciences, 4% were in Business and Management, 4% were in Computer and Engineering Related Technology, 3% were in Physical Sciences, remainder in 3 other fields.

Graduates Career Data. Advanced studies pursued by 26% of students; 1% enter medical school; 1% enter law school; 3% enter business school; 22% other schools. Fields typically hiring largest number of graduates include education. Career Development Services include aptitude testing, counseling group, placement service, resume/interview workshops, on-campus recruitment, internships, library resources, Potsdam Interview Network.

Faculty. About 68% of faculty hold PhD or equivalent. About 60% of faculty are tenured, all teach undergraduate classes. About 33% of teaching faculty are female; 11% minority.

Student Body. College does not seek a national student body; 97% of students from New York State; 1% from New England, 1% Middle Atlantic; 1% Foreign. Average age of undergraduate student: 22.

Varsity Sports. Men (Div.III): Basketball, Diving, Ice Hockey, Lacrosse, Soccer, Swimming. Women (Div.III): Basketball, Diving, Equestrian, Soccer, Swimming, Tennis, Volleyball.

Campus Life. According to administration, students have great freedom in determining rules governing their activities—they are student-regulated, subject only to conformity with state law. No dorm hours; 24-hour intervisitation subject to specific residence hall regulations. Smoking permitted in specific areas. Alcohol and illegal drugs regulated by NY State law and college policies. Potsdam is a "great school with a friendly atmosphere and a "laid back attitude.'" Both interest in social activities and in scholarly/intellectual pursuits reported as very high.

About 9% of men, 18% of women live in traditional dormitories; 73% of students live in coed dormitories; rest commute. Freshmen are given preference in college housing if all students cannot be accommodated. There are 6 social fraternities, 8 social sororities, which about 10% each of men, 15% of women join.

Annual Costs. Tuition and fees, $2,800 (out-of-state, $6,700) room and board, $4,200; estimated $600 other, exclusive of travel. About 80% of students receive financial aid; average amount of assistance, $5,500. Assistance is typically divided 50% scholarship/ grant, 50% loan/work. College reports some scholarships awarded on the basis of academic merit alone. *Meeting Costs:* college offers PLUS Loans, Budget Management Services, Tuition Payment Plan.

Suny College at Purchase

Purchase, New York 10577-1400 (914) 251-6300

Among the newest of the State University of New York colleges, Purchase was conceived as a college which offered both a liberal arts curriculum and fine arts training in the visual and performing arts. In addition to meeting general admissions standards, fine arts students are admitted on the basis of portfolio or audition. The 500-acre campus is located in a suburban setting about 30 miles north of New York City. Most convenient major airport: Westchester County.

Founded: 1967
Affiliation: State
UG Enrollment: 1,126 M, 1,354 W (full-time); 949 M, 498 W (part-time)
Cost: < $10K
% Receiving Financial Aid: 68%
Admission: Selective (+)
Application Deadline: January 1

Admission is selective (+). (See also State University of New York.)
For School of Letters and Science. About 60% of applicants accepted, 31% of these actually enroll; 16% of students graduate in top fifth of high school class; 36% in top two fifths. Average freshman SAT scores: 40% of freshmen score above 500 on verbal, 9% above 600, 1% above 700; 49% score above 500 on mathematical, 13% above 600, 1% above 700. *Required:* SAT. Criteria considered in admissions, in order of importance: high school academic record, standardized test scores, recommendations, writing sample; other factors considered: diverse student body.

For School of the Arts. About 41% of applicants accepted, 47% of these actually enroll. *Required:* audition, portfolio or interview. Criteria considered in admissions, in order of importance: talent, high school academic record, writing sample, recommendations, standardized test scores; other factors considered: diverse student body.

Out-of-state freshmen applicants: university actively seeks students from out-of-state. State does not limit out-of-state enrollment. States from which most out-of-state students are drawn include Connecticut, New Jersey, Texas, Florida, California, Illinois. *Entrance programs:* mid-year admission, deferred admission, advanced placement. *Apply* by July 1 for School of Letters and Science, January 1 for Acting, Film, Design Tech; rolling admissions. *Transfers* welcome; 476 enrolled 1993–94.

Academic Environment. Degrees offered: bachelors, masters. General education core curriculum and senior thesis required for students in Letters and Science. *Majors offered* include conservatory programs in acting, dance, theater design/technology, film, music, and visual arts. About 21% of students entering as freshmen graduate in four years; 73% of freshmen return for their sophomore year. *Special programs:* undergraduate research, freshmen seminars, study abroad, independent study, cross registration with Manhattanville College, internships. Adult programs: Evening degree programs available in Liberal Studies.

Undergraduate degrees conferred (489). 40% were in Visual and Performing Arts, 15% were in Liberal/General Studies, 14% were in Letters, 12% were in Social Sciences, 8% were in Psychology, remainder in 6 other fields.

Graduates Career Data. Career Development Services include internships, resume writing, interview skills, job fairs, listings of career opportunities, letters of recommendations.

Faculty. About 35% of faculty hold PhD or equivalent, according to most recent data available. About 6% of faculty are minority.

Student Body. About 84% of students from in state; 2% Foreign. An estimated 8% of students reported as Black, 8% Hispanic, 3% Asian, 3% other. Average age of undergraduate student: 23.5.

Varsity Sports. Men (Div.III): Basketball, Fencing, Soccer, Tennis. Women (Div.III): Tennis, Volleyball.

Campus Life. About 54% of men, 54% of women live in coed dormitories (sexes segregated by floor or room), according to most recent data available; rest commute. There are no fraternities or sororities. About 70% of students leave campus on weekends.

Annual Costs. Tuition and fees, $3,030 (out-of-state, $6,930); room and board $4,294; estimated $1,000–$1,500 other, exclusive of travel. About 68% of students receive financial aid; average amount of assistance $1,100. College reports 175 scholarships awarded for academic merit. Meeting Costs: college offers installment payment plan.

New York University

New York, New York 10011 (212) 998-4500

One of the largest private universities in the country, NYU has 7 undergraduate colleges on an urban campus at the foot of Fifth Avenue, in the heart of Manhattan: College of Arts and Science, Stern School of Business, School of Education, Health, Nursing and Arts Professions, and the Tisch School of the Arts, which offers professional training in the theater, films, and TV, School of Social Work, Gallatin Division, which offers innovative and interdivisional programs, and School of Continuing Education. The university also has 7 other major divisions on the main campus and at other locations in the city. Despite the scope of the university, individual undergraduate divisions are modest in size with entering freshman classes of about 200 each in the professional schools and about 900 in the liberal arts college. A high percentage of students are in graduate and professional studies, and nearly 11,000 noncredit students are not included in enrollment totals above. Once primarily a commuter campus, the university has increasingly become residential. Most convenient major airports: JFK International, LaGuardia, or Newark, NJ.

Founded: 1831
Affiliation: Independent
UG Enrollment: 6,437 M, 8,788 W (full-time and part-time)
Total Enrollment: 30,469
Cost: $10K–$20K
% Receiving Financial Aid: 66%
Admission: Very (+) Selective
Application Deadline: Feb. 1

Admission is very selective. For all schools; about 53% of applicants accepted, 35% of these actually enroll; according to most recent data available 80% of freshmen graduate in top fifth of high school class, 99% in top two-fifths. Average freshman scores: 77% of freshman score above 500 on verbal, 29% above 600, 4% above 700; 88% score above 500 on mathematical, 53% above 600, 13% above 700.

Required: SAT or ACT; interview recommended; 3 ACH including English and essay for BA/MD program; audition or portfolio for theater program of School of the Arts. Criteria considered for admissions, in order of importance: high school academic record, standardized test scores, extracurricular activities, recommendations, writing sample; other factors considered: special talents, alumni children, diverse student body. *Entrance programs:* early decision, early admission, midyear admission, deferred admission, advanced placement. *Apply* by February 1. *Transfers* welcome; 1,746 enrolled 1993–94.

Academic Environment. The campus, set in the very heart of Greenwich Village, is the epitome of the urban campus. Presence of graduate schools on campus makes undergraduate instruction by major NYU faculty luminaries a fairly common practice. Students must be quite mature, since they have to function in a very large and heterogeneous campus culture, encompassing great numbers of full-time and part-time, day and evening studies, with a minimum of faculty guidance and direction. However, for the more mature student who wants to make use of a university with some offerings of the first rank and wishes to combine this academic experience with the varied educational opportunities of New York, there could be few more satisfactory choices. Degrees offered: associates, bachelors, masters, doctoral. More than 160 majors offered including anthropology, Black studies, drama, fine arts, journalism, medical technology, Near Eastern languages and literature, meteorology and oceanography, psychobiology, engineering, women's studies, pre-med, pre-dental, pre-law. Average undergraduate class size: 25–30; although many introductory courses are large lectures, advanced classes tend to be small.

About 70% of students entering as freshmen graduate within five years; 85% of freshmen return for sophomore year. *Special programs:* January term, study abroad, 3–2 engineering, 8-year BA/MD, 5-year BA/MBA, BA/MPA, BA/DDS. Adult programs: BA degrees through School of Continuing Education, non-degree/non-credit courses also. *Calendar:* semester, summer session.

Undergraduate degrees conferred (2,675). 23% were in Visual and Performing Arts, 19% were in Business and Management, 18% were in Social Sciences, 5% were in Liberal/General Studies, 5% were in Psychology, 5% were in Communications, 4% were in Letters, 4% were in Computer and Engineering Related Technology, 3% were in Life Sciences, 3% were in Foreign Languages, remainder in 11 other fields.

Graduates Career Data. Advanced studies pursued by 85% of students; 14% enter medical school; 13% enter law school; 8% enter business school. Medical schools enrolling largest numbers of graduates include Columbia, Down State, NYU, Cornell; law schools include NYU, Fordham, Harvard; business schools include NYU, Columbia, Harvard, Wharton, Chicago. About 90% of 1992–93 graduates employed. Corporations typically hiring largest numbers of graduates include IBM, Chemical Bank, Citicorp. Career Development Services include resume writing, interview techniques, career planning and placement.

Faculty. About 95% of faculty hold PhD or equivalent.

Student Body. About 60% of students come from New York; 6% New England, 73% Middle Atlantic, 4% Midwest, 4% South, 5% West, 2% Northwest; 6% Foreign.

Varsity Sports. Men (NCAA,Div.III): Cross Country, Diving, Fencing, Golf, Soccer, Swimming, Tennis, Track, Volleyball, Wrestling. Women (NCAA,Div.III): Cross Country, Diving, Fencing, Swimming, Tennis, Track, Volleyball.

Campus Life. Major factor in campus social life is the accessibility of the cultural and social resources of the city. One student leader reports that a student "had better enjoy city life before considering NYU." Provision for 24-hour intervisitation; residence halls are coed and self-governing. Cars allowed; difficult parking situation. The Office of Student Life, Protection, and Residence Halls offers a variety of workshops on safety and programs such as NYU Trolley and Escort Van Service to promote security.

About 60% of freshmen, 48% of all students, live in wide variety of residence halls; rest commute. University guarantees four years of housing to all freshmen. Sexes segregated in coed dormitories by room. There are 12 fraternities, 9 sororities on campus which about 7% of students join.

Annual Costs. Tuition and fees, $17,640; room and board, $7,065; estimated $1,000 other, exclusive of travel. About 66% of freshmen, 70% of all undergraduate students receive financial aid; average amount of assistance awarded to 1993 freshmen, $11,300. The University admits students on a "need-blind" basis. University reports 300 scholarships awarded to freshmen for academic merit, no athletic scholarships. *Meeting Costs:* University offers installment plans, deferred payment plan, tuition stabilization plan and subsidized loan programs.

Newberry College

Newberry, South Carolina 29108 (803) 321-5127 (800) 845-4955

A church-related college, located in a town of 10,000, 43 miles northwest of Columbia. Most convenient major airport: Columbia.

Founded: 1856
Affiliation: Lutheran
UG Enrollment: 315 M, 300 W (full-time)
Cost: < $10K
% Receiving Financial Aid: 92%
Admission: Non-selective
Application Deadline: preferably by spring

Admission. Graduates of approved high schools with 16 units in college-preparatory program eligible; 67% of applicants accepted, 25% of these actually enroll; 34% of freshmen graduate in top fifth of high school class, 65% in top two-fifths. Average freshman scores: SAT, 396 M, 414 W verbal, 450 M, 435 W mathematical, according to most recent data available. *Required:* SAT; interview recommended. *Apply* preferably by spring. *Transfers* welcome.

Academic Environment. Degrees offered: bachelors. About 60% of general education requirements for graduation are elective; distribution requirements fairly numerous. Average undergraduate class size: 85% under 20, 19% 20–40, 6% over 40. About 41% of students entering as freshmen graduate within four years; 65% of freshmen return for sophomore year. *Special programs:* CLEP, independent study, study abroad, undergraduate research, 3-year degree, 3–2 programs in engineering and forestry. Adult program: evening and weekend programs for adults. *Calendar:* semester, summer school.

Undergraduate degrees conferred (129). 38% were in Business and Management, 22% were in Social Sciences, 11% were in Education, 8% were in Visual and Performing Arts, 7% were in Letters, 6% were in Life Sciences, 5% were in Mathematics, remainder in 3 other fields.

Faculty. About 68% of faculty hold PhD or equivalent. All of undergraduate classes taught by tenured faculty. About 17% of teaching faculty are female.

Student Body. About 82% of students from in state; 99% South, 1% Middle Atlantic. An estimated 72% of students reported as Protestant, 10% Catholic, 1% Jewish, 12% unaffiliated, 5% other; 17% Black, 1% Hispanic.

Religious Orientation. Newberry is a church-related institution; 30% of students affiliated with the church; 1 course in religious studies required of all students; attendance at weekly chapel services, bimonthly assemblies voluntary.

Varsity Sports. Men (NCAA): Baseball, Basketball, Football, Golf, Tennis. Women (NCAA): Basketball, Softball, Volleyball.

Campus Life. About 72% of men, 71% of women live in traditional dormitories; rest live in off-campus housing or commute. Intervisitation in men's and women's dormitory rooms limited. There are 5 fraternities, 2 sororities on campus which about 29% of men, 36% of women join. About 60% of students leave campus on weekends.

Annual Costs. Tuition and fees, $8,894; room and board, $3,100; estimated $1,450 other, exclusive of travel. About 92% of students receive financial aid; average amount of assistance, $6,741. Assistance is typically divided 50% scholarship, 48% loan, 2% work. *Meeting Costs:* college offers 10-month payment plan.

Newcomb College

(See Tulane University)

Niagara University

Niagara University, New York 14109 (716) 286-8700

Founded by the Vincentian Community, Niagara is an independent, co-educational institution. The 160-acre campus is located near Niagara Falls, overlooking the Niagra River gorge, 30 minutes from Buffalo and 90 minutes from Toronto, in a suburban section of a city of 61,840. Most convenient major airport: Buffalo International.

Founded: 1856
Affiliation: Independent
UG Enrollment: 767 M, 1,152 W (full-time); 99 M, 235 W (part-time)
Total Enrollment: 2,836
Cost: $10K–$20K
% Receiving Financial Aid: 95%
Admission: Non-selective
Application Deadline: Rolling

Admission. About 81% of applicants accepted, 26% of these actually enroll; 32% of freshmen graduate in top fifth of high school class, 65% in top two-fifths. Average freshman scores: SAT, 450 verbal, 478 mathematical; ACT, 21.5 composite. *Required:* SAT or ACT; minimum 3.0 HS GPA, 16 academic units and top 50% of high school class. Criteria considered in admission, in order of importance: high school academic record, class rank, standardized test scores, recommendations, extracurricular activities; other factors considered: special talents, alumni relations, diverse student body. *Entrance programs:* early decision, early admission, mid-year admission, deferred admission, advanced placement. About 25% of entering students from private and parochial schools. *Apply* by August 1; rolling admissions. *Transfers* welcome; 213 enrolled 1993–94.

Academic Environment. *Undergraduate studies* offered by colleges of Arts and Sciences, Business Administration, Education, Nursing, Institute of Travel, Hotel and Restaurant Administration, and Division of General Academic Studies. All students take a common liberal arts core curriculum that is divided between required subjects (English, history, University Studies, religion, philosophy, and Freshman Seminar) and elective areas. Administration reports that the percentage of elective courses required for graduation varies with the academic major. Degrees offered: associates, bachelors, masters. *Majors offered* in 50 academic, career-oriented, and pre-professional programs, elementary education, communication studies, travel, hotel and restaurant administration, criminal justice, theater, nursing, and accounting. Average undergraduate class size: 22.

About 47% of students entering as freshmen graduate within four years, 58% eventually, 75% of freshmen return for sophomore year. *Special programs:* CLEP, credit by examination, independent study, study abroad, undergraduate research, honors, 3-year degree, 2–3 engineering with Detroit, visiting students program, cross registration with Western New York Consortium. Adult program: evening accelerated program. *Calendar:* semester, summer school.

Undergraduate degrees conferred (445). 39% were in Business and Management, 11% were in Social Sciences, 9% were in Health Sciences, 9% were in Marketing and Distribution, 6% were in Communications, 5% were in Life Sciences, 4% were in Protective Services, 4% were in Psychology, 3% were in Public Affairs, 3% were in Letters, remainder in 7 other fields.

Graduates Career Data. Advanced studies pursued by 11% of graduates; 2% enter medical school; 1% enter law school; 2% enter business school; 3% enter graduate education program. Career Development Services include interviewing and resume writing workshops, employment networks, cooperative education, career fairs, job placement, on-campus recruitment, career counseling, summer and temporary job location.

Faculty. About 85% of faculty hold PhD or equivalent. About 77% of undergraduate classes taught by tenured faculty. About 37% of teaching faculty are female.

Student Body. About 91% of students from in state; 97% Northeast/New England, 1% foreign. An estimated 62% of students reported as Catholic, 19% other; 5% Black, 2% Hispanic, 1% Asian, 1% other minority. *Minority group students:* special financial aid; tutoring; Black student and foreign student organizations.

Religious Orientation. Niagara maintains a Vincentian tradition. Some general religious studies courses are required in all degree programs.

Varsity Sports. Men (Div.I): Baseball, Basketball, Cross Country, Diving, Golf, Soccer, Swimming, Tennis. Women (Div.I): Basketball, Cross Country, Diving, Soccer, Softball, Swimming, Tennis, Volleyball.

Campus Life. Niagara provides a wide range of social, cultural, and athletic activities. Limited intervisitation; cars allowed for all students. Freshmen and sophomores required to live in residence halls; upperclassmen may request off-campus housing.

About 1% of men, 3% of women live in traditional dormitories; 24% of men, 37% of women live in coed dormitories; rest live in off-campus housing or commute. There are 2 fraternities on campus which about 2% men, women join. About 25% of resident students leave campus on weekends.

Annual Costs. Tuition and fees, $10,070; room and board, $4,482; estimated $1,210 other, exclusive of travel. About 95% of students who apply for it receive financial aid; average amount of assistance, $8,800. Assistance is typically divided 63% grant, 32% loan, 5% work. *Meeting Costs:* university offers deferred and monthly payment plans.

Nicholls State University

Thibodaux, Louisiana 70301 (504) 448-4507

A state-supported university, located in a city of 15,000, 60 miles southwest of New Orleans. Most convenient major airport: New Orleans International.

Founded: 1948
Affiliation: State
UG Enrollment: 2,060 M, 2,861 W (full-time); 458 M, 880 W (part-time)
Total Enrollment: 7,076
Cost: < $10K
% Receiving Financial Aid: 68%
Admission: Non-selective
Application Deadline: Rolling

Admission. All graduates of accredited high schools admitted without examination. About 97% of applicants accepted, 68% of these actually enroll. Average freshman ACT scores: 18.6 M, 18.8 W composite. *Required:* ACT. Criteria considered in admissions, in order of importance: high school academic record, standardized test scores. *Out-of-state* freshman applicants: university actively seeks students from out-of-state. State does not limit out-of-state enrollment. No special requirements for out-of-state applicants. States from which most out-of-state students are drawn include Florida, California, Texas, Mississippi. *Entrance programs:* early decision, early admission, mid-year admission, deferred admission, advanced placement. *Apply* by August 15; rolling admissions. *Transfers* welcome; 340 enrolled 1993–94.

Academic Environment. Degrees offered: associates, bachelors, masters. Graduation requirements include 10 hours of natural sciences, 6 of social sciences, 3 of art, 1 of English, 6 of math, 9 of humanities. Average undergraduate class size: 24; 60% under 20, 40% 20–40. About 42% of students entering as freshmen graduate eventually, 62% of freshmen return for sophomore year. *Special programs:* CLEP, independent study, honors, study abroad, program for oil field workers: 7 days in/7 days out. *Calendar:* semester, summer school.

Undergraduate degrees conferred (558). 27% were in Business and Management, 22% were in Education, 14% were in Liberal/General Studies, 10% were in Health Sciences, 5% were in Home Economics, 3% were in Engineering and Engineering Related Technology, 3% were in Social Sciences, 3% were in Communications, 3% were in Psychology, remainder in 11 other fields.

Faculty. About 54% of faculty hold PhD or equivalent. About 65% of undergraduate classes taught by tenured faculty. About 41% of teaching faculty are female; 4% Black, 1% Hispanic, 3% other minority.

Student Body. About 98% of students from in state; 99% South, less than 1% foreign. An estimated 12% of students reported as Black, 2% Hispanic, 1% Asian, 1% other minority. Average age of undergraduate student: 25.

Varsity Sports. Men (Div.I): Baseball, Basketball, Cross Country, Football(IAA), Golf, Track & Field. Women (Div.I): Basketball, Cross Country, Softball, Tennis, Track & Field, Volleyball.

Campus Life. About 6% of men, 7% of women live in traditional and coed dormitories; 94% of men, 93% of women commute. Intervisitation in men's and women's dormitory rooms limited. Sexes segregated in coed dormitories by floor. There are 10 fraternities, 6 sororities on campus which about 9% of men, 4% of women join; they provide no residence facilities. About 50% of resident students leave campus on weekends.

Annual Costs. Tuition and fees, $1,980 (out-of-state, $4,572); room and board, $2,550; estimated $600 other, exclusive of travel. About 68% of students receive financial aid; average amount of assistance, $3,500. Assistance is typically divided 20% scholarship, 8% loan, 20% work. College reports 230 scholarships awarded on the basis of academic merit alone, 260 for special talents alone.

Nichols College

Dudley, Massachusetts 01571 **(508) 943-2055**

An independent, professional school located on a 200-acre campus in a town of 7,400, south of Worcester and near the Connecticut state line. Most convenient major airports: Worcester, Logan (Boston), or Bradley (Hartford, CT).

Founded: 1815
Affiliation: Independent
UG Enrollment: 454 M, 243 W (full-time); 240 M, 397 W (part-time)
Total Enrollment: 1,713
Cost: < $10K
% Receiving Financial Aid: 70%
Admission: Non-selective
Application Deadline: Rolling

Admission. High school graduates with 16 units in academic subjects eligible; others given individual consideration; 90% of applicants accepted, 33% of these actually enroll; 11% of entering freshmen graduate in top fifth of high school class. *Required:* SAT or ACT; interview encouraged. Criteria considered in admission, in order of importance: high school academic record, standardized test scores, recommendations, extracurricular activities, writing sample; other factors considered: special talents. *Entrance programs:* early decision, early admission, mid-year admission, deferred admission. *Apply:* rolling admissions. *Transfers* welcome; 31 enrolled 1993–94.

Academic Environment. Degrees offered: associates, bachelors, masters. About 85% of general education credits for graduation are required; distribution requirements fairly numerous. *Majors offered* in accounting, economics, finance, marketing, management information systems, general business management, finance/real estate, psychology/industrial international business. Accessible, supportive faculty and small classes cited by students as primary strengths of academic program. Average undergraduate class size: all between 20–40. About 55% of students entering as freshmen graduate within four years, 58% eventually, 85% of freshmen return for sophomore year. *Special programs:* CLEP, study abroad, internships. *Calendar:* semester, summer school.

Undergraduate degrees conferred (215). 89% were in Business and Management, 7% were in Engineering, remainder in 4 other fields.

Graduates Career Data. Advanced studies pursued by 5% of graduates; all enter business school. About 95% of 1992–93 graduates employed. Career Development Services include help with interviewing and resume writing, career and placement library, counseling, workshops, and "Discover" software.

Faculty. About 72% of faculty hold PhD or equivalent. About 18% of teaching faculty are female; 1% Hispanic.

Student Body. About 78% of students from in state; 90% New England, 5% Middle Atlantic, 1% foreign. An estimated 65% of students reported as Catholic.

Varsity Sports. Men (Div.III): Baseball, Basketball, Cross Country, Football, Golf, Ice Hockey, Lacrosse, Soccer, Tennis, Track. Women (Div.III): Basketball, Field Hockey, Soccer, Softball, Tennis, Track.

Campus Life. Campus is located in a rural and scenic area. Students suggest a car is "helpful", but on-campus activities (clubs, sports, and on-campus work) are strong and varied.

About 80% of men, women live in traditional dormitories; rest commute. Intervisitation in men's and women's dormitory rooms limited. There are no fraternities or sororities on campus. About 50% of resident students leave campus on weekends.

Annual Costs. Tuition and fees, $9,040; room and board, $5,160; estimated $1,000 other, exclusive of travel. About 70% of students receive financial aid; average amount of assistance, $8,500. Assistance is typically divided 40% scholarship, 55% loan, 15% work. College reports 85 scholarships awarded on the basis of academic merit alone, 100 for special talents alone, 350 for need alone. *Meeting Costs:* college offers Freshman Guaranteed Tuition Plan, Massachusetts Family Loan Program.

Norfolk State University

Norfolk, Virginia 23504 **(804) 623-8600**

A state-supported, liberal arts and teachers university, located in a city of 308,000; founded as a college for Negroes and still serving a predominantly black student body.

Founded: 1935
Affiliation: State
UG Enrollment: 7,701 M, W (full-time)
Cost: < $10K
Admission: Non-selective
Application Deadline: July 15

Admission. Graduates of accredited high schools with 16 units eligible; others admitted by examination or on condition; 83% of applicants accepted, 69% of these actually enroll; 19% of freshmen graduate in top fifth of high school class, 43% in top two-fifths. *Required:* SAT. *Out-of-state* freshman applicants: university seeks students from out of state. State does not limit out-of-state enrollment. No special requirements for out-of-state applicants. *Apply* by July 15. *Transfers* welcome.

Academic Environment. *Degrees:* AB, BS. About 15% of general education requirements for graduation are elective; no distribution requirements. About 72% of students entering as freshmen graduate eventually; 63% of freshmen return for sophomore year. *Special programs:* CLEP, independent study, study abroad, honors, undergraduate research. *Calendar:* semester, intersession, summer school.

Undergraduate degrees conferred (536). 18% were in Education, 15% were in Business and Management, 10% were in Communications, 9% were in Social Sciences, 8% were in Engineering and Engineering Related Technology, 8% were in Health Sciences, 7% were in Multi/Interdisciplinary Studies, 4% were in Psychology, 4% were in Home Economics, 3% were in Public Affairs, 3% were in Life Sciences, 3% were in Visual and Performing Arts, remainder in 7 other fields.

Student Body. About 90% of students from South, 5% Middle Atlantic.
Campus Life. About 6% of men, 11% of women live in traditional dormitories; no coed dormitories; rest live in off-campus housing or commute. Scheduled visitation in men's and women's dormitory rooms. There are 11 fraternities, 8 sororities on campus which about 5% of men, 11% of women join; they provide no residence facilities.
Annual Costs. Tuition and fees, $2,725 (out-of-state, $6,025); room and board, $3,600.

North Adams State College

North Adams, Massachusetts 01247 (413) 664-4511

A state-supported college, located in a community of 15,000, 130 miles west of Boston. Most convenient major airport: Albany (NY).

Founded: 1894
Affiliation: State
UG Enrollment: 683 M, 697 W (full-time); 53 M, 83 W (part-time)
Total Enrollment: 1,516
Cost: < $10K
% Receiving Financial Aid: 60%
Admission: Non-selective
Application Deadline: Rolling

Admission. High school graduates with 2.0 minimum GPA eligible; 64% of applicants accepted, 24% of these actually enroll; 11% of entering freshmen graduate in top fifth of high school class, 43% in top two-fifths. Average freshman SAT scores: 427 verbal, 470 mathematical. *Required:* SAT or ACT; interview recommended, essay. Criteria considered in admission, in order of importance: high school academic record, standardized test scores, writing sample, recommendations, extracurricular activities; other factors considered: special talents, alumni children, diverse student body. *Out-of-state* freshman applicants: college actively seeks students from out-of-state. No special requirements for out-of-state applicants. About 71% of out-of-state applicants accepted, 32% actually enroll. States from which most out-of-state students are drawn include New York, New Jersey, Connecticut, Vermont, Rhode Island. About 20% of entering students from private schools. *Entrance programs:* early admission, mid-year admission, deferred admission. *Apply* by June 1; rolling admissions. *Transfers* welcome; 186 enrolled 1993–945.
Academic Environment. Degrees offered: bachelors, masters. Graduation requirements include a distribution of liberal arts courses spanning science, math, fine arts, literature, etc. *Majors offered* include secondary school teacher education, fine and performing arts, crime and delinquency concentration, allied health, cyrotechnology. Average undergraduate class size: 80% under 20, 15% 20–40, 5% over 40. About 45% of students entering as freshmen graduate within four years, 58% eventually, 82% of freshmen return for sophomore year. *Special programs:* CLEP, independent study, study abroad, Canadian Area Studies, exchange program with Southern U. in New Orleans, cross registration with Bennington and Williams, internships. *Calendar:* 4–1–4, summer school.
Undergraduate degrees conferred (439). 38% were in Business and Management, 15% were in Education, 15% were in Social Sciences, 15% were in Letters, 8% were in Psychology, remainder in 7 other fields.
Graduates Career Data. Career Development Services include counseling, resume workshops and mock interview workshops.
Faculty. About 60% of faculty hold PhD or equivalent. All undergraduate classes taught by tenured faculty. About 31% of teaching faculty are female.
Student Body. About 92% of students from in state; 97% New England. An estimated 80% of students are reported as Catholic; 4% Black, 1% each Hispanic, Asian. Average age of undergraduate student: 23.
Varsity Sports. Men (Div.III): Baseball, Basketball, Cross Country, Ice Hockey, Soccer. Women (Div.III): Basketball, Cross Country, Soccer, Softball, Tennis.
Campus Life. Campus is located in rural area. Administration source notes wealth of opportunities for outdoor activities (skiing, hiking, boating); student source mentions "many concerts, movies and guest speakers", but she says many of her classmates spend their time partying, instead.

About 47% of men, 44% of women live in coed dormitories; 45% of each live in off-campus housing or commute. Freshmen are given preference in college housing if all students cannot be accommodated. Sexes segregated in coed dormitories by wing, floor or room. There are 4 fraternities, 5 sororities on campus which about 5% of men, 10% of women join; 13% of each men, women live in fraternities and sororities. About 20% of resident students leave campus on weekends.
Annual Costs. Tuition and fees, $3,493 (out-of-state, $7,629); room and board, $4,212; estimated $700 other, exclusive of travel. About 60% of students receive financial aid; average amount of assistance, $4,315. Assistance is typically divided 30% grant, 50% loan, 20% work. College reports 15 scholarships awarded only on the basis of academic merit alone, 11 for need alone. *Meeting Costs:* college offers budget service for tuition payment.

University of North Alabama

Florence, Alabama 35632-0001 (205) 760-4318

A state-supported institution, located in a city of 34,000, 135 miles northwest of Birmingham. Most convenient major airport: Huntsville.

Founded: 1830
Affiliation: State
UG Enrollment: 1,780 M, 2,325 W (full-time); 372 M, 529 W (part-time)
Total Enrollment: 5,797
Cost: < $10K
% Receiving Financial Aid: 55%
Admission: Non-selective
Application Deadline: 2 weeks prior to term

Admission. Graduates of accredited high schools eligible; almost all of applicants accepted, 69% of these actually enroll. *Required:* ACT or SAT. *Out-of-state* freshman applicants: university welcomes out-of-state students. State does not limit out-of-state enrollment. No special requirements for out-of-state applicants. *Apply* by . *Transfers* welcome.
Academic Environment. *Degrees:* AB, BS. About 10–50% of general education requirements for graduation are elective; distribution requirements fairly numerous; 3 semester hours of computer instruction required for all students. About 30% of students entering as freshmen graduate within five years; 27% of freshmen do not return for sophomore year. *Special programs:* CLEP, independent study, honors, Marine Environmental Sciences Consortium. *Calendar:* semester, summer school.
Undergraduate degrees conferred (722). 32% were in Business and Management, 23% were in Education, 6% were in Health Sciences, 6% were in Public Affairs, 4% were in Social Sciences, 4% were in Communications, 4% were in Physical Sciences, 3% were in Life Sciences, remainder in 14 other fields.
Faculty. About 58% of faculty hold PhD or equivalent.
Student Body. About 75% of students from in state. An estimated 8% of students reported as Black, 1% other minority, according to most recent data available.
Varsity Sports. Men (Div.II): Baseball, Basketball, Cross Country, Football, Golf, Riflery, Tennis. Women (Div.II): Basketball, Cross Country, Softball, Tennis, Volleyball.
Campus Life. About 16% of men, 14% of women live in traditional dormitories; no coed dormitories; 82% of men, 84% of women live in off-campus housing or commute. Intervisitation in men's and women's dormitory rooms limited. There are 8 fraternities, 6 sororities on campus which about 6% of men, 4% of women join; 2% of each men, women live in fraternities and sororities.
Annual Costs. Tuition and fees, $1,368 (out-of-state, $1,968); room and board, $2,580. About 55% of students receive financial aid; assistance is typically divided 15% scholarship, 50% loan, 35% work. University reports some scholarships awarded on the basis of academic merit alone.

North Carolina Agricultural and Technical State University

Greensboro, North Carolina 27411 (919) 334-7946

A state-supported university, located in a city of 155,000, 78 miles west of Raleigh, the state capital. North Carolina A&T was founded as a college for Negroes and still serves a predominantly black student body. Most convenient major airport: Piedmont Triad International.

Founded: 1891
Affiliation: State
UG Enrollment: 2,985 M, 3,177 W (full-time); 451 M, 420 W (part-time)
Total Enrollment: 7,973
Cost: < $10K
% Receiving Financial Aid: 61%
Admission: Non-selective
Application Deadline: June 1

Admission. High school graduates with 16 acceptable units eligible; 64% of applicants accepted, 47% of these actually enroll. About 25% of freshmen graduate in top fifth of high school class, 50% in top two-fifths. *Required:* SAT; minimum high school GPA. Criteria considered in admissions, in order of importance: standardized test scores, high school academic record, extracurricular activities; other factors considered: diverse student body, alumni children. *Out-of-state* applicants: university actively seeks students from out-of-state. State does limits out-of-state enrollment to 16% of entering class. Required for out-of-state applicants: higher GPA, class rank, and SAT scores. About 45% of out-of-state students accepted, 25% of these actually enroll. States from which most out-of-state students are drawn: Virginia, Maryland, South Carolina. *Entrance programs:* early decision, deferred admission, advanced placement, rolling admission. *Apply* by June 1. *Transfers* welcome; 433 enrolled 1993–94.
Academic Environment. Degrees offered: bachelors, masters. Graduation requirements include a minimum of 6 hours each of English, social sciences, natural sciences, humanities, mathematics, and health or physical education. Unusual, new, or notable majors include architectural engineering, laboratory animal science, math-based computer science, civil engineering. About 42% of students entering as freshmen graduate eventually; 97% of freshmen return for sophomore year. *Special programs:* CLEP, Greensboro Regional Consortium for Higher Education, cross-registration with UNC at Greensboro, High Point U., Gilford, and Bennett colleges, internships. Adult programs: continuing education division. *Calendar:* semester, summer school.
Undergraduate degrees conferred (750). 27% were in Business and Management, 19% were in Education, 19% were in Engineering, 6% were in Communications, 5% were in Computer and Engineering Related Technology, 5% were in Social Sciences, 3% were in Health Sciences, 3% were in Agricultural Sciences, remainder in 12 other fields.
Graduates Career Data. Advanced studies pursued by 10% of graduates (1990–91). About 30% of 1990–91 graduates employed. Fields typically hiring largest numbers of graduates include business management, accounting, engineering, computer science. Career Development Services provides help in finding short and long term employment for students and alumni.
Faculty. About 59% of faculty hold PhD or equivalent. About 39% of teaching faculty are female; 57% Black, 1% Hispanic, 12% other minority.
Student Body. About 73% of students from in state; 90% South, 6% Middle Atlantic, 2% foreign students. An estimated 85% of students reported as Black, 4% other minority according to most recent data available.
Varsity Sports. Men (Div.I): Baseball, Basketball, Cross Country, Football, Soccer, Track, Wrestling. Women (Div.I): Basketball, Cross Country, Gymnastics, Softball, Track, Volleyball.
Campus Life. About 35% of men, 43% of women live in traditional dormitories; no coed dormitories; rest live in off-campus housing or commute. Freshmen are given preference in college housing if all students cannot be accommodated. Intervisitation in men's and women's dormitory rooms limited. There are 4 fraternities, 4 sororities on campus which 1% of men, 1% of women join; they provide no residence facilities. About 75% of resident students leave campus on weekends.
Annual Costs. Tuition and fees, $1,367 (out-of-state, $7,433); room and board, $3,110; estimated $3,650 other, exclusive of travel. About 61% of students receive financial aid; average amount of assistance, $2,900. Assistance is typically divided 38% scholarship, 30% grant, 2% loan, 3% work. University reports 2,046 scholarships awarded on the basis of academic merit alone; 196 on special talents alone; 3,228 on need alone. *Meeting Costs:* university offers deferred payment plan, employee children assistance programs offered by General Motors and Ford Motors, Emergency Student Assistance Program.

North Carolina Central University

Durham, North Carolina 27707 (919) 560-6298

A state-supported university, located in a city of 102,000. Institution was founded as a college for Negroes and still serves a predominantly Black student body. Most convenient major airport: Raleigh-Durham.

Founded: 1910
Affiliation: State
UG Enrollment: 1,248 M, 2,107 W (full-time); 290 M, 482 W (part-time)
Total Enrollment: 4,585
Cost: < $10K
% Receiving Financial Aid: 66%
Admission: Non-selective
Application Deadline: July 1

Admission. Graduates of accredited North Carolina high schools who meet the minimum UNC-System course requirements eligible; 71% of applicants accepted, 54% of these actually enroll. About 13% of freshmen graduate in top fifth of high school class, 32% in top two-fifths. *Required:* SAT or ACT. *Out-of-state* freshman applicants: university seeks students from out of state. State limits out-of-state enrollment to 18% of entering class. No special requirements for out-of-state applicants. *Apply* by July 1. *Transfers* welcome.
Academic Environment. *Degrees:* AB, BS, BBA, BSHEc, BSN. About 90% of general education requirements for graduation are elective; distribution requirements fairly numerous. About 36% of students entering as freshmen graduate eventually; 25% of freshmen do not return for sophomore year. *Special programs:* CLEP, independent study, honors, undergraduate research. *Calendar:* semester, summer school.
Undergraduate degrees conferred (506). 26% were in Social Sciences, 20% were in Business and Management, 11% were in Education, 10% were in Protective Services, 6% were in Health Sciences, 5% were in Visual and Performing Arts, 4% were in Letters, 4% were in Home Economics, 4% were in Life Sciences, 3% were in Mathematics, remainder in 4 other fields.
Graduates Career Data. According to most recent data available, full-time graduate or professional study pursued by 22% of students immediately after graduation. *Careers in business and industry* pursued by 36% of graduates.
Student Body. About 83% of students from in state; 88% South, 10% Middle Atlantic. An estimated 83% of students reported as Black, 4% other minority, according to most recent data available.
Varsity Sports. Men (Div.II): Basketball, Cross Country, Football, Tennis, Track. Women (Div.II): Basketball, Softball, Tennis, Volleyball.
Campus Life. About 31% of men, 35% of women live in traditional dormitories; 2% of men, 5% of women live in coed dormitories; rest live in off-campus housing or commute. Freshmen given preference in college housing if all students cannot be accommodated. Intervisitation in men's and women's dormitory rooms limited. There are 6 fraternities, 7 sororities on campus, which about 10% each men, women join. About 50% of resident students leave campus on weekends.
Annual Costs. Tuition and fees, $1,211 (out-of-state, $6,883); room and board, $2,894. About 66% of students receive financial aid; assistance is typically divided 50% scholarship/grant, 43% loan, 7% work. University reports some scholarships awarded on the basis of academic merit alone.

North Carolina School of the Arts

Winston-Salem, North Carolina 27117-2189

A constituent institution of the 16-campus University of North Carolina, the North Carolina School of the Arts trains students at the college and high school levels for professional careers in the performing arts. About 85% of students are employed in the performing arts directly after graduation. Students are admitted by audition to the programs of the schools of Dance, Design and Production, Drama, and Music. A liberal arts program, is provided along with supplementary programs and services to assist students in their personal development. The arts and academic curricula lead to a high school diploma with arts concentration in dance, music, and visual arts, the Bachelor of Fine Arts degree in dance, design and production, and drama, and the Bachelor of Music. A Master of Fine Arts is also offered in the School of Design and Production.

Founded: 1965	**UG Enrollment:** 470 M, W (full-time)
Affiliation: State	

Undergraduate degrees conferred (67). 100% were in Visual and Performing Arts.

North Carolina State University

(See University of North Carolina)

University of North Carolina

Chapel Hill, North Carolina 27514

The University of North Carolina includes the nation's oldest state university, Chapel Hill, as well as North Carolina State University at Raleigh and 4 additional campuses—at Asheville, Charlotte, Greensboro, and Wilmington. The other 10 state-supported senior institutions were merged into the University in 1972 without changing their names and are listed in alphabetical order. Each of the 16 constituent institutions has a local board of trustees. The other institutions now part of the university are: Appalachian State University, East Carolina University, Elizabeth City State University, Fayetteville State University, North Carolina Central University, North Carolina School of the Arts, Pembroke State University, Western Carolina University, Winston-Salem State University, and North Carolina Agricultural and Technical State University.

University of North Carolina at Chapel Hill

Chapel Hill, North Carolina 27599 (919) 962-1500

The nation's first state university, Chapel Hill has long been one of America's distinguished institutions of higher learning. The university includes 14 schools and colleges on its 500-acre campus, located in a town of 25,500, about 25 miles northwest of Raleigh and near the Research Triangle Park. Most convenient major airport: Raleigh-Durham.

Founded: 1789	**Total Enrollment:** 24,299
Affiliation: State	**Cost:** < $10K
UG Enrollment: 5,907 M, 8,997 W (full-time); 313 M, 457 W (part-time)	**% Receiving Financial Aid:** 38%
	Admission: Very (+) Selective
	Application Deadline: Jan. 15

Admission is very (+) selective. About 40% of applicants accepted, 56% of these actually enroll; 92% of freshmen graduate in top fifth of high school class, 98% in top two-fifths. Average freshman SAT scores: 527 verbal, 594 mathematical. *Required:* SAT or ACT. Criteria considered in admissions, in order of importance: high school academic record and degree of difficulty of course work, standardized test scores, extracurricular activities; other factors considered: special talents, alumni children. *Out-of-state* freshman applicants: university actively seeks students from out-of-state. State limits out-of-state enrollment to 18% of entering class. No special requirements for out-of-state applicants; 20% of out-of-state applicants accepted, 38% actually enroll. States from which most out-of-state students are drawn include Georgia, Virginia, Florida, New Jersey, New York. *Entrance programs:* advanced placement. *Apply* by January 15. *Transfers* welcome; 960 enrolled 1993–94.

Academic Environment. General College curriculum, program of freshman seminars, establishment of Office of Experimental Studies part of "vigorous recommitment of the University's resources to the education of beginning students." Administration reports 57% of general education courses needed for AB are elective; distribution requirements fairly numerous, requirements include foreign language, history, philosophy. Most freshmen enroll in General College for 2 years' academic work to complete general education requirements: 3 courses each in social sciences, humanities/fine arts, 2 courses in natural sciences, choice of foreign language or mathematics, proficiency in English composition, 2 semesters physical education. Dental hygiene students enroll directly in professional program. Administration source recommends Chapel Hill to those students "seeking a well rounded liberal arts education in a large institution." It is not for those "seeking technical skill training." Undergraduate studies offered by College of Arts and Sciences, schools of Business Administration, Education, Journalism, Nursing, Pharmacy. Degrees offered: bachelors, masters, doctoral. *Majors offered* in Arts and Sciences, in addition to usual studies include Afro-American studies, African studies, Latin American studies, criminal justice, dramatic arts, industrial relations, international studies, medical technology.

About 65% of students entering as freshmen graduate within four years, 82% eventually, 95% of freshmen return for sophomore year. *Special programs:* independent study, study abroad, honors (including summer independent honors study), undergraduate research, 3-year degree, individualized majors, credit by examination, advanced sections, interdisciplinary curricula, 3–2 in pre-law, pre-dental, premedical, pre-law, business, accounting. *Calendar:* semester, summer school.

Undergraduate degrees conferred (3,538). 22% were in Social Sciences, 14% were in Business and Management, 11% were in Letters, 11% were in Communications, 9% were in Health Sciences, 8% were in Psychology, 6% were in Life Sciences, 4% were in Education, 3% were in Area and Ethnic Studies, 3% were in Physical Sciences, remainder in 9 other fields.

Graduates Career Data. Advanced studies pursued by 19% of graduates. About 64% of 1992–93 graduates employed.

Faculty. About 94% of faculty hold PhD or equivalent. About 27% of teaching faculty are female; 4% Black, 2% Hispanic, 3% other minority.

Student Body. About 83% of students from in state; 1% foreign. An estimated 9% of students reported as Black, 1% Hispanic, 4% Asian, less than 1% Native American, 4% other minority. *Minority group students:* special financial, academic, and social provisions.

Varsity Sports. Men (ACC Div.IA): Baseball, Basketball, Cross Country, Diving, Fencing, Football, Golf, Lacrosse, Soccer, Swimming, Tennis, Track, Wrestling. Women (ACC Div.IA): Basketball, Cross Country, Diving, Fencing, Field Hockey, Golf, Gymnastics, Soccer, Softball, Swimming, Tennis, Track, Volleyball.

Campus Life. One student observes Chapel Hill is "a beautiful city that is totally student oriented." Another enthuses "I love the Chapel Hill experience. The academics, the athletics, social life, community all blend together to make this the greatest time of my life." Full calendar of cultural and intellectual events sponsored by university. Events in Charlotte and Greensboro supplement campus offerings. Student conduct regulated by elected courts, based on honor system. Each residence unit establishes intervisitation schedule within specific guidelines and restrictions. Smoking restricted; students may request non-smoking roommate. University's rules on alcohol conform to state law. Freshmen required to live in university housing. Cars permitted except for freshmen; campus bus system operates daily. Parking is said to be a problem.

About 26% of students live in traditional dormitories; no coed dormitories; 56% live in off-campus college-related housing; 6% commute. There are 29 fraternities, 15 sororities on campus which about 25% of students join; 5% of men, 7% of women live in fraternities and sororities.

Annual Costs. Tuition and fees, $1,419 (out-of-state, $8,461); room and board, $4,050; estimated $2,650 other, exclusive of travel. About 38% of students receive financial aid; average amount of assistance, $2,000.

North Carolina State University

Raleigh, North Carolina 27695-7103 (919) 515-2434

A land-grant, state-supported university, North Carolina State is a major scientific and technological university, with the College of Engineering accounting for 28% of total enrollment. But Humanities and Social Sciences attracts the second largest number of students, about 21% of total enrollment. The university also offers liberal arts and teacher education programs. The 600-acre main campus is located in a city of 217,200 in the central part of the state. Most convenient major airport: Raleigh-Durham.

Founded: 1887	**Total Enrollment:** 27,170
Affiliation: State	**Cost:** < $10K
UG Enrollment: 11,649 M, 6,995 W (full-time); 1,511 M, 1,253 W (part-time)	**Admission:** Very (+) Selective
	Application Deadline: February 1

Admission is very (+) selective for School of Design, College of Engineering; selective (+) for Physical and Mathematical Sciences; selective for colleges of Forest Resources, Humanities and Social Sciences, Agriculture and Life Sciences, Education. For all colleges and schools, 67% of applicants accepted, 30% of these actually enroll; 68% of students graduate in top fifth of high school class, 96% in top two fifths. Average freshman SAT scores: 495 M, 489 W verbal, 597 M, 551 W mathematical; 45% of freshmen score above 500 on verbal, 11% above 600, 1% above 700; 84% score above 500 on mathematical, 40% above 600, 10% above 700.

Required: SAT, interview for School of Design; ACH for placement only. Criteria considered in admissions, in order of importance: high school academic record, class rank, standardized test scores, extracurricular activities, writing sample, recommendations; other factors considered: diverse student body. *Out-of-state* freshman applicants: university actively seeks students from out-of-state. State limits out-of-state enrollment to 18% of entering class. About 58% of out-of-state freshman applicants accepted, 23% actually enroll. States from which most out-of-state students are drawn include Virginia, Maryland, New Jersey. *Entrance programs:* mid-year admission, advanced placement. *Apply* by February 1, January 1 for School of Design. *Transfers* welcome; 1,206 enrolled 1993–94.

Academic Environment. General education distribution requirements compose 42 out of 124–139 credit hours required for graduation; number of free electives determined by major requirements. *Undergraduate studies* offered by colleges of Humanities and Social Sciences, Engineering, Agriculture and Life Sciences, Education, Forest Resources, and Physical and Mathematical Sciences, and School of Design. Degrees offered: associates, bachelors, masters, doctoral. *Majors offered* in about 81 fields of study, business administration and management, electrical electronics and communications engineering, mechanical engineering, environmental engineering. Average undergraduate class size: 30.

About 28% of students entering as freshmen graduate within four years, 80% eventually, 93% of freshmen return for sophomore year. *Special programs:* CLEP, internships, independent study, honors, individualized majors, credit by examination, co-operative education in engineering, and physical and mathematical sciences, inter-institutional registration with University of North Carolina at Chapel Hill, and Greensboro, and Duke, cross-registration with Cooperating Raleigh Colleges consortium, living/learning program for selected freshmen. Adult programs: Adult Services Office as part of a Lifelong Education Program. *Library:* special collections in entomology, music, architecture and design, and U.S. patents. *Calendar:* semester, summer school.

Undergraduate degrees conferred (3,406). 28% were in Engineering, 18% were in Business and Management, 9% were in Letters, 9% were in Social Sciences, 5% were in Life Sciences, 4% were in Education, 4% were in Agricultural Sciences, 3% were in Computer and Engineering Related Technology, 3% were in Physical Sciences, 3% were in Architecture and Environmental Design, remainder in 11 other fields.

Graduates Career Data. Advanced studies pursued by 25% of graduates. Professional schools typically enrolling largest numbers of graduates include UNC-Chapel Hill, Duke. Employers typically hiring largest numbers of graduates include IBM, DuPont, General Electric, Proctor & Gamble. Career Development Services include job search folders, scheduled interviews, campus database for recruiters.

Faculty. About 88% of faculty hold PhD or equivalent. About 22% of teaching faculty are female; 5% Black, 1% Hispanic, 14% other minority.

Student Body. About 86% of students from in state; 98% South, 3% Middle Atlantic, 1% Midwest, 1% foreign. An estimated 48% of students reported as Protestant, 9% Catholic, 1% Jewish, 11% unaffiliated, 35% other; 9% as Black, 3% Asian, 1% Hispanic, less than 1% Native American, 4% other minority. *Minority group students:* Pan African Weekend, Black Students Cultural Center, Society of Afro-American Culture. Average age of undergraduate student: 22.

Varsity Sports. Men (Div.I): Baseball, Basketball, Cross Country, Diving, Fencing, Football, Golf, Rifle, Soccer, Swimming, Tennis, Track, Wrestling. Women (Div.I): Basketball, Cross Country, Diving, Fencing, Gymnastics, Rifle, Soccer, Swimming, Tennis, Track, Volleyball.

Campus Life. Both the school itself and Raleigh offer wide range of cultural activities. Recent student observes, "students can be involved strictly on campus or get involved in the community." Time outside of classes reported spent on "cultural events, greek parties, hall-sponsored programs or activities, clubs and organizational meetings." Cars allowed; parking is a "significant" problem, according to students. Smoking prohibited in classrooms; alcohol limited to those over 21; users and sellers of illegal drugs subject to suspension or expulsion. Intervisitation limited.

About 17% of men, 12% of women live in traditional dormitories; 16% of men, 23% of women live in coed dormitories; 4% of men, 7% of women live in off-campus college-related housing; 58% of men, 56% of women commute. Freshmen are assured college housing if they wish it. Sexes segregated in coed dorms by floor. There are 24 fraternities, 10 sororities on campus which about 15% of men, 15% of women join; 5% of men, 2% of women live in fraternities, sororities. About 10% of resident students leave campus on weekends.

Annual Costs. Tuition and fees, $1,584 (out-of-state, $8,498); room and board, $3,400; estimated $1,650 other, exclusive of travel. About 42% of students receive financial aid; average amount of assistance, $4,837. University reports 300 scholarships awarded on the basis of academic merit alone, 525 for special talents alone, 2,857 for need alone.

University of North Carolina at Asheville

Asheville, North Carolina 28804-3299 (704) 251-6619

The university's Asheville campus is a liberal arts institution, located in the Blue Ridge and Great Smoky Mountains near a city of 60,000. Most convenient major airport: Asheville Regional.

Founded: 1927	**Total Enrollment:** 3,165
Affiliation: State	**Cost:** < $10K
UG Enrollment: 958 M, 1,075 W (full-time); 446 M, 632 W (part-time)	**% Receiving Financial Aid:** 40%
	Admission: Selective
	Application Deadline: April 1

Admission is selective. About 56% of applicants accepted, 41% of these actually enroll. About 64% of freshmen graduate in top fifth of high school class, 95% in top two-fifths. Average freshman scores: SAT, 508 M, 501 W verbal, 570 M, 535 W mathematical; 53% of freshmen score above 500 on verbal, 17% above 600, 2% above 700; 75% score above 500 on mathematical, 29% above 600, 4% above 700; ACT, 24 M, 23 W composite. *Required:* SAT or ACT. Criteria considered in admissions, in order of importance: high school academic record, standardized test scores, extracurricular activities, recommendations, writing sample; other factors considered: special talents, alumni children, diverse student body. *Out-of-state* freshman applicants: university actively seeks students from out-of-state. State limits out-of-state enrollment to 18% of entering class. No special requirements for out-of-state applicants. About 52% of out-of-state students accepted, 28% actually enroll. States from which most out-of-state students are drawn include Florida, Georgia, Virginia, South Carolina, Tennessee. *Entrance programs:* early decision, early admission, mid-year admission, deferred admission, advanced placement. About 15% of entering students from private schools. *Apply* by April 1; rolling admissions. *Transfers* welcome; 301 enrolled 1993–94.

Academic Environment. Degrees offered: bachelors, masters. Graduation requirements include 4 hours in arts, 16 in humanities, 3–6 in English, 1 in library research, 2 in health/fitness, 4 in math, 3–6 in foreign language, 8 in natural science, including lab, 6 in social science. *Majors offered* include recording arts, atmospheric science, environmental studies. Average undergraduate class size: 50% under 20, 46% 20–40, 4% over 40. About 34% of students entering as freshmen graduate within four years, 77% of freshmen return for sophomore year. *Special programs:* honors, undergraduate research, independent study, study abroad, individualized majors, cross registration with Mars Hill, health promotions, Environmental Quality Institute, 3–2 engineering, pre-law, pre-med, cross registration with Mars Hill, Warren Wilson. *Calendar:* 4 8-week terms, summer school.

Undergraduate degrees conferred (354). 28% were in Business and Management, 21% were in Social Sciences, 11% were in Psychology, 7% were in Visual and Performing Arts, 6% were in Computer and Engineering Related Technology, 5% were in Life Sciences, 5% were in Communications, 5% were in Physical Sciences, 3% were in Letters, 3% were in Mathematics, remainder in 3 other fields.

Faculty. About 84% of faculty hold PhD or equivalent. About 52% of undergraduate classes taught by tenured faculty. About 32% of teaching faculty are female; 3% Black, 1% Hispanic, 2% other minority.

Student Body. About 90% of students from in state; 95% South, 2% Middle Atlantic, 1% each New England, West, 1% foreign. An estimated 4% of students reported as Black, 1% each Hispanic, Asian, 1% other minority. Average age of undergraduate student: 26.

Varsity Sports. Men (NCAA, Div.I): Baseball, Basketball, Cross Country, Golf, Soccer, Tennis. Women (NCAA, Div.I): Basketball, Cross Country, Soccer, Softball, Tennis, Track, Volleyball.

Campus Life. About 26% of men, 25% of women live in traditional and coed dormitories; rest commute. There are 2 fraternities, 3 sororities on campus which about 6% of men, 6% of women join.

Annual Costs. Tuition and fees, $1,470 (out-of-state, $6,840); room and board, $3,310; estimated $650 other, exclusive of travel. About 40% of students receive financial aid; average amount of assistance, $2,164. Assistance is typically divided 4% scholarship, 52% grant, 42% loan, 2% work. University reports 435 scholarships awarded on the basis of academic merit alone, 123 for special talents alone, 1,324 for need alone. *Meeting Costs:* university offers grants and scholarships, loans, college assigned jobs, work study.

University of North Carolina at Charlotte

Charlotte, North Carolina 28223 **(704) 547-2000**

A state-supported institution, the Charlotte campus of the University of North Carolina is located 8 miles from the center of a city of 400,000. Most convenient major airport: Charlotte-Douglas International.

Founded: 1946
Affiliation: State
UG Enrollment: 5,100 M, 4,999 W (full-time); 1,559 M, 1,558 W (part-time)
Total Enrollment: 15,645
Cost: < $10K
% Receiving Financial Aid: 43%
Admission: Non-selective
Application Deadline: July 1

Admission. Graduates of accredited high schools with 16 units (14 in academic subjects) eligible; 77% of applicants accepted, 39% of these actually enroll. About 47% of freshmen graduate in top fifth of high school class, 90% in top two-fifths. Average freshman SAT scores: 443 M, 426 W verbal, 520 M, 463 W mathematical. *Required:* SAT or ACT; interview recommended for Architecture, Performing Arts and Visual Arts. Criteria considered in admission, in order of importance: high school academic record, standardized test scores, recommendations, extracurricular activities; other factors considered: diverse student body. *Out-of-state* freshman applicants: university actively seeks students from out-of-state. State limits out-of-state enrollment to 18% of entering class. No special requirements for out-of-state applicants. About 71% of out-of-state students accepted, 24% actually enroll. States from which most out-of-state students are drawn include New York, New Jersey, South Carolina, Virginia, Pennsylvania, Florida, Maryland. *Entrance programs:* early admission, mid-year admission, deferred admission, advanced placement. *Apply* by July 1; rolling admissions. *Transfers* welcome; 1,645 enrolled 1993–94.

Academic Environment. Graduation requirements include completion of approved courses in communication and problem solving, and in 4 areas of understanding: understanding values, science and technology, the arts, literature and ideas, and the individual, society and culture. Degrees offered: bachelors, masters, doctoral. Average undergraduate class size: 32% under 20. About 25% of entering freshmen graduate within four years, 53% within seven years, 80% of freshmen return for sophomore year. *Special programs:* Charlotte Area Educational Consortium, Exchange Programs, cooperative education and experiential learning, CLEP, cross registration through Charlotte Area Educational Consortium, study abroad, National Student Exchange, honors, undergraduate research, independent study. *Calendar:* semester, summer school.

Undergraduate degrees conferred (1,928). 23% were in Business and Management, 15% were in Social Sciences, 8% were in Education, 7% were in Engineering, 7% were in Psychology, 7% were in Protective Services, 6% were in Letters, 6% were in Engineering and Engineering Related Technology, 5% were in Health Sciences, 3% were in Life Sciences, remainder in 10 other fields.

Graduate Career Data. Employers typically hiring largest numbers of graduates include Duke Power, Underwriters Lab, Nations Bank, Hoechst Celanese. Career Development Services include information guidance and advising students in identifying their career objectives and plans; internships and cooperative education opportunities; and placement assistance to obtain career positions. The Center also teaches career management processes and skills.

Faculty. About 91% of faculty hold PhD or equivalent. About 56% of undergraduate classes taught by tenured faculty. About 32% of teaching faculty are female; 4% Black, 1% Hispanic, 6% other minority.

Student Body. About 88% of students from in state; 91% South, 4% Middle Atlantic, 2% Midwest, 1% New England, 3% foreign. An estimated 44% of students reported as Protestant, 9% Catholic, 1% Jewish, 46% other; 13% Black, 1% Hispanic, 3% Asian, 4% other minority. Average age of undergraduate student: 23.

Varsity Sports. Men (Div.I): Baseball, Basketball, Cross Country, Diving, Golf, Soccer, Swimming, Tennis, Track. Women (Div.I): Basketball, Cross Country, Diving, Softball, Swimming, Tennis, Track, Volleyball.

Campus Life. About 24% of men, 23% of women live in coed dormitories; 75% of men, 77% of women commute. Intervisitation in men's and women's dormitory rooms limited. Sexes segregated in coed dormitories by floor. There are 12 fraternities, 8 sororities which about 11% of men, 9% of women join; 1% of men live in fraternities, sororities provide no housing facilities. About 60% of resident students leave campus on weekends.

Annual Costs. Tuition and fees, $1,385 (out-of-state, $7,451); room and board, $3,212; estimated $1,500 other, exclusive of travel. About 43% of students receive financial aid; average amount of assistance, $4,100. Assistance is typically divided 5% scholarship, 20% grant, 74% loan, 1% work. University reports 420 scholarships awarded on the basis of academic merit alone, 200 for special talents alone, 140 for need alone. *Meeting Costs:* university offers deferred payment plan for room and board.

University of North Carolina at Greensboro

Greensboro, North Carolina 27412 **(919) 334-5243**

Originally the women's coordinate college within the University of North Carolina, UNC-Greensboro has been co-educational since 1963. Although number of men enrolled has been increasing, there are still significantly more women than men on campus. The campus is located in a city of 173,000, 80 miles west of Raleigh. Most convenient major airport: Piedmont Triad International.

Founded: 1891
Affiliation: State
UG Enrollment: 2,683 M, 4,849 W (full-time); 735 M, 1,112 W (part-time)
Total Enrollment: 12,114
Cost: < $10K
% Receiving Financial Aid: 50%
Admission: Non-selective
Application Deadline: Aug. 1

Admission. About 80% of applicants accepted, 37% of these actually enroll; 35% of freshmen graduate in top fifth of high school class, 66% in top two-fifths. Average freshman SAT scores: 956 combined; 28% of freshmen score above 500 on verbal, 7% above 600; 49% score above 500 on mathematical, 11% above 600, 2% above 700. *Required:* SAT or ACT. Criteria considered in admission, in order of importance: high school academic record, standardized test scores. *Out-of-state* freshman applicants: university actively seeks students from out-of-state. State limits out-of-state enrollment to 18% of entering class. No special requirements for out-of-state applicants. About 79% of out-of-state applicants accepted, 21% actually enroll. States from which most out-of-state students are drawn include Virginia, New Jersey, New York, Maryland, Connecticut, Florida. *Entrance programs:* deferred admission, mid-year admission, advanced placement. *Apply* by August 1. *Transfers* welcome; 959 enrolled 1993–94.

Academic Environment. Graduation requirements include 3 semester hours each in analytic and evaluative studies, British or American Literature, fine arts, historical perspectives on Western culture, mathematics, non-Western studies, world literature, 6 hours each in reasoning and discourse, social and behavioral studies, and 6 additional hours either in a foreign language or from any of the areas specified above. Strongest programs reported to be human environmental sciences, liberal arts. *Undergraduate studies* offered by College of Arts and Sciences, schools of Business and Economics, Education, Health, Physical Education, Recreation, Dance, Home Economics, Music, Nursing. Degrees offered: bachelors, masters, doctoral. *Majors offered* include usual arts and sciences, anthropology, dance, drama, geography, social welfare, social work, speech pathology, international studies, Asian studies, Latin American studies, women's studies, banking and finance, inter-departmental student-designed majors. The Residential College is an unusual 2-year living/learning program, primarily for freshmen and sophomores, in which students live and have classes in a coed, residential hall. Faculty also have offices in the hall.

About 58% of students entering as freshmen graduate eventually, 75% of freshmen return for sophomore year. *Special programs:* CLEP, independent study, study abroad, honors, individualized majors, undergraduate research, Greensboro Regional Consortium for Higher Education, inter-institutional registration with Chapel Hill, Duke, North Carolina State, co-op programs in most majors, accelerated master's degrees. Adult programs: (ACES) Adult Continuing and Evening Student program. *Calendar:* semester, summer school.

Undergraduate degrees conferred (1,635). 20% were in Business and Management, 14% were in Education, 13% were in Letters, 11% were in Social Sciences, 10% were in Home Economics, 7% were in Health Sciences, 5% were in Visual and Performing Arts, 5% were in Psychology, 4% were in Business (Administrative Support), 3% were in Life Sciences, remainder in 7 other fields.

Faculty. About 71% of faculty hold PhD or equivalent.

Student Body. About 87% of students from in state; 90% South. Average age of undergraduate student: 23. *Minority group students:* Special Services Project provides tutorial, personal, vocational counseling; special admission standards; Director of Minority Affairs coordinates programs; Neo-Black Society; Office of International Affairs provides personal counseling and appropriate student referrals.

Varsity Sports. Men (Div.II): Baseball, Basketball, Cross Country, Golf, Soccer. Women (Div.II): Basketball, Cross Country, Golf, Soccer, Softball, Volleyball.

Campus Life. Flexible dorm and intervisitation hours determined by residents of each hall; no 24-hour intervisitation. Alcohol allowed in dormitory rooms for those over 21. Cars allowed; on-campus parking limited to commuters and resident juniors and seniors; parking for commuters reported as inadequate.

About 45% of men, 46% of women live in traditional dormitories; 14% of men, 6% of women in coed dormitories; rest live in off-campus housing or commute. Freshmen are given preference in college housing if all students cannot be accommodated. Sexes segregated in coed dormitories either by wing or floor. There are 6 fraternities, 8 sororities which about 15% each of men and women join.

Annual Costs. Tuition and fees, $1,717 (out-of-state, $8,759); room and board, $3,475; estimated $1,100 other, exclusive of travel. *Meeting Costs:* university offers Richard C. Knight, The Tuition Plan.

University of North Carolina at Wilmington

Wilmington, North Carolina 28403-3297 (919) 395-3000

The university's Wilmington campus is a liberal arts institution, located in a city of 57,300 in southeastern North Carolina. Most convenient major airport: New Hanover County.

Founded: 1947
Affiliation: State
UG Enrollment: 2,750 M, 3,885 W (full-time); 468 M, 677 W (part-time)
Total Enrollment: 8,157
Cost: < $10K
% Receiving Financial Aid: 41%
Admission: Non-selective
Application Deadline: Rolling

Admission. Graduates of accredited high schools with C average and satisfactory SAT or ACT score eligible; others considered individually; 64% of applicants accepted, 38% of these actually enroll; 42% of freshmen graduate in top fifth of high school class, 79% in top two-fifths. Average freshman scores: SAT, 43% of freshmen score above 500 on mathematical, 2% above 600, 1% above 700; ACT, 23 M, 21 W composite. *Required:* SAT or ACT. Criteria considered in admission, in order of importance: standardized test scores, high school academic record. *Out-of-state* freshman applicants: university actively seeks students from out-of-state. State limits out-of-state enrollment to 18% of entering class. No special requirements for out-of-state applicants; 62% of out-of-state students accepted, 27% actually enroll. States from which most out-of-state students are drawn include New Jersey. *Entrance programs:* early admission, mid-year admission. *Apply:* rolling admissions. *Transfers* welcome; 843 enrolled 1993–94.

Academic Environment. Degrees offered: bachelors, masters. About 26% of general education requirements for graduation are elective; distribution requirements fairly numerous. *Majors offered* in addition to usual studies include anthropology, computer science, marine biology, music education, social work, criminal justice. About 20% of students entering as freshmen graduate within four years, 46% eventually. *Special programs:* CLEP, independent study, honors, Near Eastern Archaeological Seminar. *Calendar:* semester, summer school.

Undergraduate degrees conferred (1,099). 31% were in Business and Management, 17% were in Education, 11% were in Letters, 9% were in Social Sciences, 8% were in Life Sciences, 7% were in Psychology, 3% were in Health Sciences, 3% were in Parks and Recreation, remainder in 9 other fields.

Faculty. About 74% of faculty hold PhD or equivalent. About 38% of teaching faculty are female; 2% Black, 5% other minority.

Student Body. About 87% of students from in state; 90% South, 17% each New England, Midwest, 6% Middle Atlantic, 1% West, 1% foreign; 6% Black, 1% Hispanic, 1% Asian. Average age of undergraduate student: 22.

Varsity Sports. Men (NCAA,Div.I): Baseball, Basketball, Cross Country, Diving, Golf, Soccer, Swimming, Tennis, Track, Volleyball. Women (NCAA,Div.I): Basketball, Cross Country, Diving, Golf, Softball, Swimming, Tennis, Track, Volleyball.

Campus Life. About 23% of men, 24% of women live in coed dormitories; rest commute. Freshmen are given preference in college housing if all students cannot be accommodated. Intervisitation in men's and women's dormitory rooms limited. Sexes segregated in coed dormitories by floor. There are 13 fraternities, 11 sororities on campus which about 14% of men, 9% of women join. About 50% of resident students leave campus on weekends.

Annual Costs. Tuition and fees, $1,492 (out-of-state, $7,558); room and board, $3,680; estimated $1,590 other, exclusive of travel. About 41% of students receive financial aid; average amount of assistance, $2,751. Assistance is typically divided 45% scholarships/grants, 48% loans, 10% work. University reports 516 scholarships awarded on the basis of academic merit alone, 132 for athletic talents alone. *Meeting Costs:* university offers PLUS.

North Carolina Wesleyan College

Rocky Mount, North Carolina 27804 (919) 985-5100

A church-related college, located in a community of 40,000, 50 miles east of Raleigh. Most convenient major airport: Raleigh-Durham.

Founded: 1956
Affiliation: United Methodist
UG Enrollment: 309 M, 337 W (full-time); 33 M, 51 W (part-time)
Cost: < $10K
% Receiving Financial Aid: 70%
Admission: Non-selective
Application Deadline: July 15

Admission. Graduates of recognized high schools with 16 units, preferably all in academic subjects, minimum combined SAT score of 800, and 2.0 GPA eligible; 85% of applicants accepted, 28% of these actually enroll; 13% of freshmen graduate in top fifth of high school class, 29% in top two-fifths. Average freshman SAT scores: 13% score above 500 on verbal, 2% above 600; 17% score above 500 on mathematical, 4% above 600. *Required:* SAT or ACT. Criteria considered in admission, in order of importance: high school academic record, standardized test scores, recommendations, extracurricular activities, writing sample; other factors considered: special talents. About 70% of entering students from private schools. *Apply* by July 15; rolling admissions. *Transfers* welcome; 96 enrolled 1993–94.

Academic Environment. Degrees offered: bachelors. Graduation requirements include 50 semester hours in 5 areas of interdisciplinary requirements, sciences courses, social science courses, humanities, and other graduation requirements. About 25% of students entering as freshmen graduate within four years, 35% eventually, 55% of freshmen return for sophomore year. *Majors offered* include usual arts and sciences, business administration, accounting, computer information systems, food service and hotel management, criminal justice, justice and public policy, various education programs. Average undergraduate class size: 60% under 20, 40% 20–40. *Special programs:* developmental studies, CLEP, independent study, study abroad, undergraduate research, cooperative education, internships, individualized majors. Adult programs: Adult Degree Program offers evening and extension program. *Calendar:* semester, summer school.

Undergraduate degrees conferred (224). 52% were in Business and Management, 14% were in Computer and Engineering Related Technology, 14% were in Protective Services, 8% were in Education, 4% were in Social Sciences, 3% were in Psychology, remainder in 5 other fields.

Graduates Career Data. Advanced studies pursued by 25% of graduates; 8% enter graduate school; 2% enter law school; 10% enter business school. About 93% of 1992–93 graduates employed. Career Development Services include "Discover" computer inventory, individualized counseling, and career library.

Faculty. About 68% of faculty hold PhD or equivalent. About 65% of undergraduate classes taught by tenured faculty. About 32% of teaching faculty are female.

Student Body. About 49% of students from in state. An estimated 70% of students reported as Protestant, 16% Catholic; 18% Black, 2% Hispanic, 1% Asian, 1% other minority.

Religious Orientation. North Carolina Wesleyan is a church-related institution; no required courses in religious studies.

Varsity Sports. Men (Div.III): Baseball, Basketball, Golf, Soccer. Women (Div.III): Golf, Soccer, Softball, Volleyball.

Campus Life. About 32% of men, 27% of women live in traditional and coed dormitories; rest commute. Freshmen given preference in college housing if all students cannot be accommodated. Intervisitation in men's and women's dormitory rooms limited. There are 3 fraternities, 2 sororities on campus which about 5% of men, 5% of women join; they provide no residence facilities. About 40% of resident students leave campus on weekends.

Annual Costs. Tuition and fees, $8,350; room and board, $4,130. About 70% of students receive financial aid. Assistance is typically divided 24% scholarship, 27% grant, 46% loan, 3% work. *Meeting Costs:* college offers tuition payment plan.

North Central College

Naperville, Illinois 60566-7063 **(708) 420-3414**

A church-related, liberal arts college, North Central is located in a town of 75,000, 28 miles west of Chicago. Most convenient major airport: O'Hare International (Chicago).

Founded: 1861
Affiliation: United Methodist
UG Enrollment: 602 M, 708 W (full-time); 331 M, 435 W (part-time)
Total Enrollment: 2,453
Cost: $10K–$20K
% Receiving Financial Aid: 83%
Admission: Selective (+)
Application Deadline: Rolling

Admission is selective (+). About 79% of applicants accepted, 26% of these actually enroll; 80% of freshmen graduate in top fifth of high school class, 92% in top two-fifths. Average freshman scores: ACT, 24.5 composite. *Required:* SAT or ACT; rank in top half of high school class. Criteria considered in admission, in order of importance: high school academic record, standardized test scores, recommendations, extracurricular activities, writing sample; other factors considered: special talents, alumni children. *Apply:* rolling admissions. *Transfers* welcome; 200 enrolled 1993–94.

Academic Environment. General curriculum consists of 36-course degree program with foundation, exploration, concentration objectives, each constituting about one-third of program. Student leader reports "ample opportunity for involvement in a large variety of activities." Another student adds "great teachers" and "active, seminar-type learning" as strengths of the academic program. Degrees offered: bachelors, masters. *Majors offered* include usual arts and sciences, anthropology, classics, computer science, elementary education; cross-disciplinary programs possible in such areas as environmental studies, psychobiology, Asian studies, management informational systems, journalism, broadcasting, Japanese. Average undergraduate class size: 16.

About 60% of students entering as freshmen graduate within four years, 74% of freshmen return for sophomore year. *Special programs:* CLEP, independent study, study abroad, honors, undergraduate research, December interterm, 3-year degree, individualized majors, cross registration with Illinois Benedictine College, Washington Semester, United Nations Semester, cooperative work/study program, 3–2 engineering, 2–2 in Nursing and medical technology with Rush, Council of West Suburban Colleges, Richter Fellowship funds self-designed independent study projects of unusual scope or merit. Adult programs: Weekend and night programs offered, non-traditional student organization. *Calendar:* 3–3, summer school.

Undergraduate degrees conferred (468). 44% were in Business and Management, 17% were in Computer and Engineering Related Technology, 8% were in Letters, 6% were in Education, 6% were in Social Sciences, 6% were in Psychology, 4% were in Communications, 3% were in Life Sciences, remainder in 6 other fields.

Graduates Career Data. Advanced studies pursued by 15–20% of graduates.

Faculty. Over 70% of faculty hold PhD or equivalent. About 30% of undergraduate classes taught by tenured faculty. About 35% of teaching faculty are female; 3% Black, 1% Hispanic, 7% Asian.

Student Body. About 75% of students from in state; 45% South, 15% Midwest, 4% Northwest, 1% each West, New England. An estimated 35% of students reported as Catholic, 22% Protestant, 1% Jewish, 9% other minority; 5% Black, 3% Hispanic, 2% Asian. *Minority group students:* Black Student Association, Minority Student Organization.

Religious Orientation. North Central is a church-related institution; 9% of students affiliated with the church; no required religious studies.

Varsity Sports. Men (Div.III): Baseball, Basketball, Cross Country, Football, Golf, Soccer, Swimming, Tennis, Track, Wrestling. Women (Div.III): Basketball, Cross Country, Softball, Swimming, Tennis, Track, Volleyball.

Campus Life. Access to Chicago, 28 miles away, considered "a great asset socially and culturally." Campus activities and sports (intramural and varsity) reported as popular. Student finds the "balance between academic and social" a strength. Cars permitted for all students. Any student who wishes to live off campus "may do so."

About 32% of men, 31% of women live in traditional and coed dormitories; rest live in off-campus housing or commute. Freshmen are given preference in college housing if all students cannot be accommodated. Sexes segregated in coed dormitories by floor. There are no fraternities or sororities on campus. About 10% of resident students leave campus on weekends.

Annual Costs. Tuition and fees, $11,266; room and board, $4,212; estimated $1,500 other, exclusive of travel. About 83% of students receive financial aid; average amount of assistance, $8,000. Assistance is typically divided 68% scholarship, 27% loan, 5% work. College reports over 100 scholarships awarded on the basis of academic merit alone. *Meeting Costs:* college offers loan program.

North Central Bible College

Minneapolis, Minnesota 55404

A specialized liberal arts college offering associates and bachelors degrees in ministry training.

Founded: 1930 **Affiliation:** Assemblies of God

North Dakota State University

Fargo, North Dakota 58105-5454 (701) 237-8643

A state-supported, land-grant university, located in the twin cities of Fargo-Moorhead (pop. 120,000). Most convenient major airport: Hector International (Fargo).

Founded: 1890
Affiliation: State
UG Enrollment: 4,434 M, 2,989 W (full-time); 582 M, 491 W (part-time)
Total Enrollment: 8,496
Cost: < $10K
% Receiving Financial Aid: 55%
Admission: Non-selective
Application Deadline: Rolling

Admission. North Dakota high school graduates with 17 units in academic subjects eligible; open admissions in most programs; University reports selection more rigorous for architecture, engineering, nursing, third-year pharmacy, and animal health technology; 75% of applicants accepted. About 54% of freshmen graduate in top fifth of high school class, 59% in top two-fifths. Average freshman scores: SAT, 482 M, 468 W verbal, 597 M, 519 W mathematical; ACT, 23.1 M, 22.2 W composite. *Required:* ACT or SAT (will accept PSAT for open admissions). Criteria considered in admission, in order of importance: high school academic record, standardized test scores, recommendations. *Out-of-state* freshman applicants: university actively seeks students from out-of-state. State does not limit out-of-state enrollment. No special requirements for out-of-state applicants. States from which most out-of-state students are drawn include Minnesota, South Dakota. *Entrance programs:* early admission, deferred admission. *Apply:* rolling admissions. *Transfers* welcome; 868 enrolled 1993–94.

Academic Environment. *Undergraduate studies* offered by colleges of Humanities and Social Sciences, Agriculture, Business Administration, Engineering and Architecture, Home Economics, Pharmacy, Science and Mathematics, University Studies, School of Education. Graduation requirements include 6 credits in written/oral communication, 12 in humanities/social and behavioral sciences, 6 in math/science (1 course must be math, statistics, or computer science), and 2 in physical education. Degrees offered: bachelors, masters, doctoral. *Majors offered* include aero-manufacturing engineering technology.

About 55% of students entering as freshmen graduate eventually, 67% of freshmen return for sophomore year. *Special programs:* CLEP, independent study, honors, undergraduate research, 3-year degree, individualized majors, cross registration with Moorhead State and Concordia, Student Opportunity Program (for academic assistance), internships. *Calendar:* quarter, summer school.

Undergraduate degrees conferred (1,310). 25% were in Engineering, 13% were in Business and Management, 9% were in Architecture and Environmental Design, 8% were in Health Sciences, 7% were in Home Economics, 5% were in Life Sciences, 5% were in Education, 4% were in Agribusiness and Agricultural Production, 4% were in Agricultural Sciences, 4% were in Social Sciences, 4% were in Multi/Interdisciplinary Studies, 3% were in Allied Health, 3% were in Communications, remainder in 8 other fields.

Graduates Career Data. Fields typically hiring largest numbers of graduates include engineering. Career Development Services available to all students.

Faculty. About 87% of faculty hold PhD or equivalent.

Student Body. About 60% of students from in state. An estimated 61% of students reported as Protestant, 32% Catholic, 6% unaffiliated; 1% other minority. Average age of undergraduate student: 23.

Varsity Sports. Men (Div.II): Baseball, Basketball, Cross Country, Football, Golf, Swimming/Diving, Tennis, Track, Wrestling. Women (Div.II): Basketball, Cross Country, Softball, Track, Volleyball.

Campus Life. Freshmen under 19 required to live in university-related housing. About 16% of men, 11% of women live in traditional and coed dormitories; rest live in off-campus housing or commute. Intervisitation in men's and women's dormitory rooms limited. Sexes segregated in coed dormitories by floor. There are 8 fraternities, 5 sororities on campus which about 10–15% of men, 10–15% of women join. About 60% of resident students leave campus on weekends.

Annual Costs. Tuition and fees, $2,184 (out-of-state, $5,300); room and board, $2,590; estimated $600 other, exclusive of travel. About 55% of students receive financial aid; average amount of assistance, $4,000. Assistance is typically divided 4% scholarship, 28% grant, 65% loan, 3% work. University reports 1,100 scholarships awarded on the basis of academic merit alone, 250 for special talents alone, 100 for need alone.

University of North Dakota

Grand Forks, North Dakota 58202 (701) 777-3304

Established as a "Territorial University" before North Dakota became a state, the University of North Dakota is located in a city of 42,600 in the middle of the Red River Valley. Most convenient major airport: Mark Andrews International (Grand Forks).

Founded: 1883
Affiliation: State
UG Enrollment: 4,466 M, 3,868 W (full-time); 630 M, 773 W (part-time)
Total Enrollment: 12,029
Cost: < $10K
Admission: Non-selective
Application Deadline: July 1

Admission. Graduates of accredited or approved high schools with 13 units in English, math (algebra I and above), lab science, and social studies eligible (advanced algebra and a foreign language "strongly recommended); others given individual consideration; 77% of applicants accepted, 66% of these actually enroll. Average freshman scores: most recent data available, SAT, 438 M, 464 W verbal, 525 M, 505 W mathematical; ACT, 23 M, 21 W composite, 23 M, 20 W mathematical. *Required:* SAT or ACT. *Out-of-state* freshman applicants: university seeks students from out of state. State does not limit out-of-state enrollment. No special requirements for out-of-state applicants. *Apply* by July 1. *Transfers* welcome; 762 enrolled 1993–94.

Academic Environment. *Undergraduate studies* offered by colleges of Arts and Sciences, Business and Public Administration, Engineering and Mines, Fine Arts, Human Resources Development, Nursing, Center for Teaching and Learning. Students in medical technology, physical therapy enroll in School of Medicine after freshman year. All freshmen enter University College for a year of basic general education. About 66% of general education requirements for graduation are elective; distribution requirements fairly numerous. Degrees offered: bachelors, masters, doctoral. *Majors offered* in addition to usual studies include anthropology, communications, computer science, geography, home economics, journalism, library science, Indian Studies, Scandinavian languages, social work, communication disorders, airway science, aerospace sciences, space studies, secondary education/special education, peace studies, environmental studies.

About 50% of students entering as freshmen graduate within five years; 80% of freshmen return for sophomore year, according to most recent data available. *Special programs:* CLEP, honors, individualized majors, study abroad. Adult programs: Weekend and Evening College, classes offered at malls.

Undergraduate degrees conferred (1,655). 19% were in Business and Management, 12% were in Transportation and Material Moving, 9% were in Education, 7% were in Social Sciences, 7% were in Health Sciences, 6% were in Engineering, 5% were in Communications, 5% were in Allied Health, 4% were in Psychology, 3% were in Public Affairs, 3% were in Protective Services, 3% were in Physical Sciences, remainder in 14 other fields.

Faculty. About 69% of faculty hold PhD or equivalent.

Student Body. Administration reports students are from all 50 states and 44 countries; 476 international students. Average age of undergraduate student: 22.

Varsity Sports. Men (NCAA,Div.II): Baseball, Basketball, Cross Country, Diving, Football, Golf, Gymnastics, Ice Hockey (Div.I), Swimming, Track, Volleyball, Wrestling. Women (NCAA,Div.II): Basketball, Cross Country, Diving, Golf, Gymnastics, Softball, Swimming, Track, Volleyball.

Campus Life. City bus route runs through campus; "everything is at your fingertips" according to student reports. Students free to choose housing "according to their individual needs and desires." Intervisitation in men's and women's dormitory rooms regulated by residents. Sexes segregated in coed dormitories by suite.

About 23% of men, women each live in traditional and coed dormitories; 65% commute. There are 13 fraternities, 7 sororities on campus which about 10% of men, 8% of women join; 5% of men, 5% of women live in fraternities and sororities.

Annual Costs. Tuition and fees, $2,298 (out-of-state, $5,612); room and board, $2,604. About 50% of students receive financial aid; average amount of assistance, $5,000.

North Georgia College

Dahlonega, Georgia 30597 **(404) 864-1800**

A state-supported college that is both a co-educational and military college, located in a village of 2,700, 75 miles northeast of Atlanta; designated as an essentially military college by the Department of the Army. Most convenient major airport: Atlanta.

Founded: 1873
Affiliation: State
UG Enrollment: 835 M, 1,275 W (full-time); 138 M, 291 W (part-time)
Total Enrollment: 2,898
Cost: < $10K
% Receiving Financial Aid: 70%
Admission: Non-selective
Application Deadline: Sept. 1

Admission. Graduates of accredited or approved high schools with 16 units eligible; 73% of applicants accepted, 53% of these actually enroll. *Required:* SAT or ACT. Criteria considered in admission, in order of importance: high school academic record, standardized test scores. *Out-of-state* freshman applicants: university actively seeks out-of-state students. State does not limit out-of-state enrollment. No special requirements for out-of-state students. States from which most out-of-state students are drawn include Florida, South Carolina, Alabama, Virginia. *Entrance programs:* early decision, early admission, mid-year admission, deferred admission. About 20% of entering students from private schools. *Apply* by September 1. *Transfers* welcome; 279 enrolled 1993–94.

Academic Environment. Degrees offered: associates, bachelors, masters. Graduation requirements include 60 quarter hours in math, science, and social science. Average undergraduate class size: 5% under 20, 85% 20–40, 10% over 40. About 40% of students entering as freshmen graduate within four years, 43% eventually, 85% of freshmen return for sophomore year. *Special programs:* CLEP, dual-degree programs in chemistry and physics with Georgia Tech, 3–2 in engineering. *Calendar:* quarter, summer school.

Undergraduate degrees conferred (410). 31% were in Business and Management, 29% were in Education, 9% were in Protective Services, 7% were in Life Sciences, 6% were in Psychology, 5% were in Social Sciences, 3% were in Physical Sciences, remainder in 8 other fields.

Graduate Career Data. Advanced studies pursued by 30% of graduates; 3% enter medical school; 1% enter dental school; 3% enter law school; 10% enter business school. Medical schools typically enrolling largest numbers of graduates include Emory; dental schools include Medical College of Georgia; law schools include Emory, U. of Georgia; business schools include Georgia State, U. of Georgia. About 80% of 1992–93 graduates employed. Fields typically hiring largest numbers of graduates include public school systems, U.S. Army, business and management, nursing. Career Development Services include assistance with resume preparation, interview techniques, job interviewing and career fairs.

Faculty. About 55% of faculty hold PhD or equivalent. About 90% of undergraduate classes taught by tenured faculty. About 45% of teaching faculty are female; 1% Black.

Student Body. About 97% of students from in state; 97% South. An estimated 2% of students reported as Black, less than 1% each Hispanic, Asian, other minority. Average age of undergraduate student: 23.

Varsity Sports. Men (NAIA): Basketball, Cross Country, Soccer, Tennis. Women (NAIA): Basketball, Cross Country, Softball.

Campus Life. Large number of commuting students and significant percentage of students who leave on weekends affects student life. Those who remain spend their time "playing sports, exercising, socializing."

About 39% of men, 38% of women live in dormitories; rest commute. No intervisitation in men's dormitory rooms; limited in women's dormitory lobbies. There are 6 fraternities, 4 sororities on campus; they provide no residence facilities. About 40% of resident students leave campus on weekends.

Annual Costs. Tuition and fees, $1,660 (out-of-state, $4,424); room and board, $2,460; estimated $2,000 other, exclusive of travel. About 70% of students receive financial aid; average amount of assistance, $3,732. College reports 110 scholarships awarded on the basis of academic merit alone, 20 for special talents alone.

North Park College

Chicago, Illinois 60625 **(312) 583-2700**

A church-related, liberal arts college, North Park shares its metropolitan Chicago campus with a theological seminary. Most convenient major airport: O'Hare International (Chicago).

Founded: 1891
Affiliation: Evangelical Covenant
UG Enrollment: 376 M, 574 W (full-time)
Total Enrollment: 1,014
Cost: $10K–$20K
% Receiving Financial Aid: 75%
Admission: Non-selective
Application Deadline: Rolling

Admission. About 63% of applicants accepted, 68% of these actually enroll; 30% of freshmen graduate in top fifth of high school class. *Required:* SAT or ACT. *Non-academic factors* considered in admissions: alumni children, special talents. *Entrance programs:* early admission, midyear admission, advanced placement. *Apply:* rolling admissions. *Transfers* welcome.

Academic Environment. Administration reports 50% of general education courses required for graduation are elective; distribution requirements fairly numerous. *Degrees:* AB, BS, BM, BSMT. *Majors offered* include usual arts and sciences, accounting, business administration, computer science, medical technology, nursing, youth ministries.

About 48% of students entering as freshmen graduate within four years; 71% of freshmen return for sophomore year. *Special programs:* CLEP, independent study, study abroad, honors, undergraduate research, 3-year degree, individualized majors, credit by examination, 3–2 programs in engineering. *Calendar:* 3 terms, summer school.

Undergraduate degrees conferred (185). 18% were in Business and Management, 17% were in Letters, 14% were in Education, 11% were in Psychology, 9% were in Life Sciences, 6% were in Philosophy and Religion, 6% were in Health Sciences, 4% were in Visual and Performing Arts, 4% were in Social Sciences, 4% were in Mathematics, 3% were in Physical Sciences, 3% were in Foreign Languages, remainder in 2 other fields.

Graduates Career Data. According to most recent data available, full-time graduate or professional study pursued by 25–30% of students immediately after graduation. Career Development Services include help in preparing for interviews, career guidance, and job placement.

Student Body. About 64% of students from in state; 85% Midwest, 7% New England. An estimated 62% of students reported as Protestant, 16% Catholic, 1% Jewish, 22% unaffiliated; 6% as Black, 13% Hispanic, 4% Asian, 2% other minority, according to most recent data available. *Minority group students:* Black Students Association.

Religious Orientation. North Park is a church-related institution; 2 courses in religion required of all students; attendance at chapel services voluntary.

Varsity Sports. Men (Div.III): Baseball, Basketball, Cross Country, Football, Golf, Soccer, Tennis, Track. Women (Div.III): Basketball, Cross Country, Soccer, Softball, Swimming, Tennis, Track, Volleyball.

Campus Life. Student leader reports "a great deal of participation in student-sponsored activities" and notes, that with downtown Chicago only 20 minutes away, "we feel we have a lot to offer." Those most at home on campus described as "a Christian student who is dedicated to his/her studies and faith." Intervisitation limited to specified hours on weekend. Use or possession of alcohol prohibited on campus and at college events. Cars permitted. Smoking is not permitted in campus buildings, including residence halls. Students not living at home required to live in college residence halls. Student leader, however, reports that "we have a relatively unrestricted environment," and expresses no student concern over social regulations.

About 54% of men, 45% women live in traditional dormitories; no coed dormitories; rest commute. There are no fraternities or sororities.

Annual Costs. Tuition and fees, $11,990; room and board, $4,290. About 75% of students receive financial aid; assistance is typically divided 60% scholarship, 25% loan, 20% work. College reports some scholarships awarded on the basis of academic merit alone. *Meeting Costs:* college offers tuition pre-payment plans.

University of North Texas

Denton, Texas 76203-3797 **(817) 565-2681**

A state-supported university, located in a city of 62,750, 38 miles north of Dallas and Fort Worth. Formerly known as North Texas State University. Most convenient major airport: Dallas-Fort Worth International.

Founded: 1890
Affiliation: State
UG Enrollment: 6,827, 7,220 W (full-time); 2,634 M, 2,500 W (part-time)
Total Enrollment: 25,759
Cost: < $10K
% Receiving Financial Aid: 32%
Admission: Non-selective
Application Deadline: June 15

Admission. Graduates of accredited high schools with 16 units and minimum combination of SAT or ACT scores and high school class rank eligible; others admitted by examination; 62% of applicants accepted, 73% of these actually enroll; 37% of freshmen graduate in top fifth of high school class; 71% of freshmen in top two-fifths. Average freshman scores: SAT, 467 verbal, 526 mathematical; ACT, 23 composite. *Required:* SAT or ACT, interview, essay. Criteria considered in admission, in order of importance: high school academic record, standardized test scores. *Out-of-state* freshman applicants: university actively seeks students from out-of-state. State does not limit out-of-state enrollment. No special requirements for out-of-state applicants. States from which most out-of-state students are drawn include Oklahoma. *Entrance programs:* early admission, mid-year admission, advanced placement. *Apply* by June 15; rolling admissions. *Transfers* welcome; 2,581 enrolled 1993–94.

Academic Environment. *Undergraduate studies* offered by colleges of Arts and Sciences, Business Administration, Education, schools of Human Resource Management, Library and Information Sciences, Music, and Community Service. *Degrees:* bachelors, masters, doctoral. Students praise the "quality professors who care about education", but have reservations about "too many teaching fellows who don't seem 'into' teaching." Library and computer facilities reported as "excellent". Graduation requirements include The Basic Literacies in math, computer science, and writing; The Liberal Arts: courses in foreign language, humanities, natural/life sciences, physical sciences, social sciences; and distribution requirements in fine arts, non-Western societies, and oral communication. Unusual majors offered include emergency management.

About 33% of entering freshmen graduate within four years, 61% of freshmen return for sophomore year. *Special programs:* Winter Institute, Summer Institute, CLEP, honors, study abroad, 3-year degree, 3–2 programs available through Federation program with TWU, ETSU, NTU in wide variety of fields, cooperative education. *Calendar:* semester, summer school.

Undergraduate degrees conferred (3,026). 33% were in Business and Management, 21% were in Education, 5% were in Communications, 5% were in Visual and Performing Arts, 4% were in Psychology, 3% were in Letters, 3% were in Home Economics, 3% were in Precision Production, 3% were in Social Sciences, remainder in 19 other fields.

Graduate Career Data. Fields typically hiring largest numbers of graduates include business and education. Career Development Services include career planning and placement to all students and alumni.

Faculty. About 81% of faculty hold PhD or equivalent. About 60% of undergraduate classes taught by tenured faculty. About 27% of teaching faculty are female; 3% Black, 7% other minority.

Student Body. About 90% of students from in state; 7% foreign. An estimated 7% of students reported as Black, 5% Hispanic, 2% Asian, 5% other minority. Average age of undergraduate student: 27.

Varsity Sports. Men (Div.IA): Basketball, Cross Country, Football, Golf, Soccer, Tennis, Track. Women (Div.IA): Basketball, Cross Country, Golf, Soccer, Tennis, Track, Volleyball.

Campus Life. About 6% of men, 8% of women live in traditional and coed dormitories; rest live in off-campus housing or commute. Intervisitation in men's and women's dormitory rooms limited. Sexes segregated in coed dormitories by floor. There are 16 fraternities, 10 sororities which about 5% of each men, women join; 3% each of men, women live in fraternities and sororities.

Annual Costs. Tuition and fees, $1,274 (out-of-state, $4,538); room and board, $3,579; estimated $1,450 other, exclusive of travel. About 32% of students receive financial aid. Assistance is typically divided 2% scholarship, 26% grant, 70% loan, 2% work. University reports 460 scholarships awarded on the basis of academic merit alone. *Meeting Costs:* university offers PLUS Loans.

Northeast Louisiana University

Monroe, Louisiana 71209 **(318) 342-1000**

A state-supported university, located in a city of 56,400, 100 miles east of Shreveport. Most convenient major airport: Monroe Regional.

Founded: 1931
Affiliation: State
UG Enrollment: 3,733 M, 4,985 W (full-time); 644 M, 1,063 (part-time)
Total Enrollment: 11,571
Cost: < $10K
% Receiving Financial Aid: 60%
Admission: Non-selective
Application Deadline: Rolling

Admission. Graduates of accredited high schools eligible; others admitted by examination; all applicants accepted, 63% actually enroll. Average freshman ACT scores: 18 M, 19 W composite. *Required:* ACT. *Out-of-state* applicants: university actively seeks students from out-of-state. State does not limit out-of-state enrollment. States from which most out-of-state students are drawn: Mississippi, Arkansas, Texas. *Entrance programs:* midyear admission, advanced placement. *Apply:* rolling admission. *Transfers* welcome; 810 enrolled 1993–94.

Academic Environment. Degrees offered: associates, bachelors, masters, doctoral. Unusual, new, or notable majors include computer science, toxicology, atmospheric sciences, communication disorders, journalism, radio/television/film, speech communication and theater. Average undergraduate class size: 46% under 20, 41% 20–40, 13% over 40. About 8% of the entering class graduate within four years, 35% eventually; 59% of freshmen return for sophomore year. *Special programs:* CLEP, study abroad, undergraduate research, 3-year degree. *Calendar:* semester, summer session.

Undergraduate degrees conferred (1,128). 22% were in Health Sciences, 18% were in Business and Management, 14% were in Education, 8% were in Liberal/General Studies, 7% were in Allied Health, 4% were in Communications, 4% were in Psychology, 3% were in Protective Services, remainder in 16 other fields.

Faculty. About 53% of faculty hold PhD or equivalent. About 40% of teaching faculty are female; 3% Black, 3% other minority.

Student Body. About 93% of students from in state; 96% from South, 2% Midwest; 1% foreign. An estimated 55% of students reported as Protestant, 15% Catholic, 30% other; 19% Black, 2% Asian, 2% other minority. Average age of undergraduate student: 23.

Varsity Sports. Men (Div.I): Baseball, Basketball, Cross Country, Football, Golf, Swimming, Tennis, Track. Women (Div.I): Basketball, Cross Country, Softball, Swimming, Tennis, Track, Volleyball.

Campus Life. About 28% of men, 28% of women live in traditional dormitories; 72% of men, 72% of women commute. Freshmen given preference in college housing if all students cannot be accommodated. Intervisitation in men's and women's dormitory rooms limited. There are 7 fraternities, 8 sororities on campus which about 3% of men, 2% of women join.

Annual Costs. Tuition and fees, $1,925 (out-of-state, $3,773); room and board, $1,980; estimated $1,766 other, exclusive of travel. About 60% of students receive financial aid; average amount of assistance, $423. Assistance is typically divided 17% scholarship, 28% grant, 52% loan, 3% work. University reports 675 scholarships awarded on the basis of academic merit alone; 1,560 on special talents alone. *Meeting Costs:* university offers federal and state education assistance programs.

Northeast Missouri State University

Kirksville, Missouri 63501 **(816) 785-4114**

A state-supported institution, located in a town of 18,000, 200 miles northwest of St. Louis and 150 miles south of Des Moines, Iowa. Most convenient major airports: Kansas City or St. Louis.

Founded: 1867
Affiliation: State
UG Enrollment: 2,485 M, 3,155 W (full-time); 111 M, 155 W (part-time)
Total Enrollment: 6,153
Cost: < $10K
% Receiving Financial Aid: 76%
Admission: Selective
Application Deadline: Nov. 15

Admission is selective. About 76% of applicants accepted, 35% of these actually enroll; 64% of freshmen graduate in top fifth of high school class, 91% in top two-fifths. Average freshman scores: ACT, 26.2 M, 25.5 W composite, according to most recent data available. *Required:* ACT (SAT accepted), essay. Criteria considered in admission, in order of importance: high school curriculum, high school academic record, standardized test scores, extracurricular activities, writing sample; other factors considered: special talents, diverse student body. *Out-of-state* freshman applicants: university welcomes actively seeks students from out-of-state. State limits out-of-state enrollment to 35% of freshman class. States from which most out-of-state students are drawn include Illinois, Iowa, Kansas, Nebraska. *Entrance programs:* early admission, mid-year admission, deferred admission. About 20% of entering students from private and parochial schools. *Apply* by for early admission (recommended); rolling admissions. *Transfers* welcome; 199 enrolled 1993–94.

Academic Environment. *Degrees:* bachelors, masters. Graduation requirements include liberal arts and sciences core of 49–50 semester hours, 10–11 hours of discipline directed requirements, and 12–14 hours of BS degree required science courses or BA degree required foreign language courses. Students praise the "well-developed" core classes, but also grumble that thc curriculum is "not extremely flexible" and that it is "hard to graduate in four years, unless you're pretty well decided on a major." New majors offered include art history, Russian. Average undergraduate class size: 45% under 20, 46% 20–40, 9% over 40.

About 55% of students entering as freshmen graduate within four years, 61% within six years, 83% of freshmen return for sophomore year. *Special programs:* CLEP, January term, honors, study abroad, independent study, undergraduate research, MA in education, residential colleges, 3–2 engineering, Missouri legislative internship, NMSU public relations. *Calendar:* semester, summer school.

Undergraduate degrees conferred (956). 28% were in Business and Management, 12% were in Letters, 9% were in Social Sciences, 7% were in Psychology, 6% were in Health Sciences, 6% were in Life Sciences, 4% were in Engineering and Engineering Related Technology, 4% were in Home Economics, 4% were in Protective Services, 3% were in Education, 3% were in Visual and Performing Arts, 3% were in Communications, 3% were in Computer and Engineering Related Technology, remainder in 6 other fields.

Graduates Career Data. Advanced studies pursued by 40% of graduates; 3% enter medical school; 1% enter dental school; 3% enter law school; 5% enter business school. Medical schools typically enrolling largest numbers of graduates include Kirksville College of Osteopathic Medicine, Southern Illinois, U. of Illinois; dental schools include U. of Oklahoma, U. of Missouri-Kansas City, U. of Iowa; law schools include U. of Missouri-Columbia, Drake U., Loyola U.; business schools include U. of Missouri-Columbia, Southern Illinois, St. Louis U. About 47% of 1992–93 graduates employed. Fields typically hiring largest numbers of graduates include business, accounting, communications, nursing. Career Placement Center offers a full range of services, including career counseling, mock interviewing, and graduate school placement.

Faculty. About 72% of faculty hold PhD or equivalent. About 95% of undergraduate classes taught by tenured or tenure-track faculty. About 31% of teaching faculty are female; 2% Black, 2% Hispanic, 4% other minority.

Student Body. About 66% of students from in state; 90% Midwest, 2% each Middle Atlantic, South, 1% each New England, West, Northwest, 3% foreign. An estimated 50% of students reported as Protestant, 34% Catholic, 1% Jewish, 15% other or unknown; 3% Black, 1% Hispanic, 2% Asian, 4% other minority.

Varsity Sports. Men (Div.II): Baseball, Basketball, Cross Country, Football, Golf, Rifle, Soccer, Swimming, Tennis, Track, Wrestling. Women (Div.II): Basketball, Cross Country, Golf, Rifle, Soccer, Softball, Swimming, Tennis, Track, Volleyball.

Campus Life. College is located in a small, rural town. Administration source feels setting is "conducive to study", with "water sports and other outdoor recreational activities" nearby; one student agrees and adds that university sponsored activities are plentiful; another student notes that students from urban areas may feel "bored and out-of-touch," but adds that the "town and campus are very safe and the rural setting is peaceful."

About 14% of men, 23% of women live in traditional dormitories; 26% of men, 32% of women live in coed dormitories; rest commute. Freshmen given preference in college housing if all students cannot be accommodated. There are 16 fraternities, 7 sororities on campus which about 30% of men, 19% of women join; they provide no residence facilities.

Annual Costs. Tuition and fees, $2,456 (out-of-state, $4,336); room and board, $3,080; estimated $400 for books. About 76% of students receive financial aid; average amount of assistance, $3,558. Assistance is typically divided 36% scholarship, 13% grant, 39% loan, 12% work. University reports 2,170 scholarships awarded on the basis of academic merit alone, 387 for special talents alone.

Northeastern Bible College

Essex Fells, New Jersey 07021

An interdenominational college that prepares students for professional full-time Christian service including the ministry, mission field, sacred music, Christian education, teaching at the elementary level, and music teaching.

Founded: 1950
Affiliation: Independent

Northeastern Illinois University

Chicago, Illinois 60625 **(312) 794-3059**

A state-supported, commuter institution, located in Chicago. University operates a center for inner-city studies which "focuses on minority group problems and inner-city teacher training." Most convenient major airport: O'Hare International (Chicago).

Founded: 1867
Affiliation: State
UG Enrollment: 1,704 M, 2,352 W (full-time); 1,409 M, 2,084 W (part-time)
Total Enrollment: 7,549
Cost: < $10K
% Receiving Financial Aid: 54%
Admission: Non-selective
Application Deadline: July 1

Admission. Graduates of accredited high schools who rank in top half of class or have a minimum ACT composite score of 17 eligible; others given consideration; 72% of applicants accepted, 42% of these actually enroll; 23% of freshmen graduate in top fifth of high school class, 50% in top two-fifths. Average freshman ACT scores: 17.9 M, 16.8 W composite. *Required:* ACT. Criteria considered in admission, in order of importance: high school academic record and standardized test scores rank equally, recommendations. Entrance program: advanced placement. *Apply* by July 1; rolling admissions. *Transfers* welcome; 766 enrolled 1993–94.

Academic Environment. *Degrees:* bachelors, masters. General education requirements for graduation consist of 42 credits distributed among the following five areas: fine arts, humanities, behavioral/social sciences, natural sciences, interdisciplinary/professional studies. About 70% of entering freshmen return for sophomore year. *Special programs:* CLEP, independent study, 3-year degree, individualized majors, Board of Governors Degree, Chicago Consortium of Colleges and Universities, National Student Exchange, Minority Mentoring Program, Summer Transition Program for at-risk entering freshmen. Adult programs: University Without Walls Program offers self-paced degree program which incorporates on-campus and off-campus learning experiences; Board of Governors/Bachelor of Arts is an alternative and self-paced program combining traditional course work and credit for life experience. *Calendar:* trimester.

Undergraduate degrees conferred (982). 25% were in Business and Management, 20% were in Multi/Interdisciplinary Studies, 17% were in Education, 9% were in Computer and Engineering Related Technology, 8% were in Social Sciences, 4% were in Letters, 4% were in Psychology, 3% were in Protective Services, remainder in 8 other fields.
Graduate Career Data. About 15% of graduates enter graduate school; 1% enter law school; 9% enter business school. About 90% of 1992–93 graduates employed. Fields typically hiring largest numbers of graduates include business, industry, education. Career Development Services include job listings, job referrals, resume and interview assistance, and job fairs.
Faculty. About 80% of faculty hold PhD or equivalent.
Student Body. About 98% of students from in state; 99% Midwest, 1% foreign. An estimated 12% of students reported as Black, 19% Hispanic, 19% Asian, 11% other minority. Average age of undergraduate student: 27.
Varsity Sports. Men (NCAA, Div. I): Baseball, Basketball, Cross Country, Football, Golf, Swimming, Tennis. Women (NCAA, Div. I): Basketball, Cross Country, Golf, Softball, Swimming, Tennis, Volleyball.
Campus Life. Northeastern Illinois is a commuter institution; no dormitories on campus.
Annual Costs. Tuition and fees, $2,062 (out-of-state, $5,758); estimated $2,706 other, exclusive of travel. About 54% of students receive financial aid; average amount of assistance, $2,830. Assistance is typically divided 13% scholarship, 59% grant, 12% loan, 16% work. University reports 99 scholarships awarded on the basis of academic merit alone, 154 for special talents alone, 104 for need alone.

Northeastern State University

Tahlequah, Oklahoma 74464 **(918) 456-5511**

A state-supported university, located in a town of 14,200; founded as an institution for Cherokees. University includes a School of Optometry and a Weekend College. Formerly known as Northeastern Oklahoma State University. Most convenient major airport: Tulsa International.

Founded: 1909
Affiliation: State
UG Enrollment: 2,303 M, 3,145 W (full-time); 578 M, 1,006 W (part-time)
Total Enrollment: 9,299
Cost: < $10K
% Receiving Financial Aid: 50%
Admission: Non-selective
Application Deadline: Aug. 1

Admission. Graduates of accredited Oklahoma high schools who have 2.7 GPA or rank in top half of class or score above 18 on ACT composite eligible; 80% of applicants accepted, 74% of these actually enroll. Average freshman ACT scores: 20 composite. *Required:* SAT or ACT. Criteria considered in admissions, in order of importance: high school academic record, standardized test scores, extracurricular activities, recommendations; other factors considered: special talents. *Out-of-state* freshman applicants: university actively seeks students from out-of-state. No special requirements for out-of-state applicants. States from which most out-of-state students are drawn include Arkansas. *Entrance programs:* early admission, mid-year admission, advanced placement. *Apply* by August 1. *Transfers* welcome.
Academic Environment. *Degrees:* bachelors, masters, doctoral. About 20% of general education requirements for graduation are elective; distribution requirements fairly numerous. *Majors offered* in addition to usual studies include baccalaureate degree in nursing for those already licensed, tourism management, environmental management. About 40% of students entering as freshmen graduate eventually, 62% of freshmen return for sophomore year. *Special programs:* CLEP, honors. Adult programs: Weekend College.
Undergraduate degrees conferred (1,156). 39% were in Education, 18% were in Business and Management, 6% were in Marketing and Distribution, 6% were in Engineering and Engineering Related Technology, 4% were in Psychology, 4% were in Health Sciences, 3% were in Public Affairs, 3% were in Protective Services, 3% were in Mathematics, remainder in 13 other fields.
Faculty. About 67% of faculty hold PhD or equivalent.
Student Body. About 99% of students from in state. An estimated 17% of students reported as Native American, 4% Black, 2% other minority, according to most recent data available. Average age of undergraduate student: 24.
Varsity Sports. Men (NAIA): Baseball, Basketball, Football, Golf, Soccer, Tennis, Track. Women (NAIA): Basketball, Softball, Tennis.
Campus Life. About 19% of men, 14% of women live in traditional and dormitories; rest live in off-campus housing or commute. Sexes segregated in coed dormitories by room. There are 5 fraternities, 3 sororities on campus which about 7% men, 4% of women join (according to most recent data available).
Annual Costs. Tuition and fees, $1,190 (out-of-state, $2,946); room and board, $2,112. About 50% of students receive financial aid. Assistance is typically divided 25% scholarship, 53% loan, 22% work. College reports some scholarships awarded on the basis of academic merit alone.

Northeastern University

Boston, Massachusetts 02115 **(617) 437-2000**

The university has long been a recognized leader in cooperative education which integrates classroom study and related work experience. Northeastern is located in the Back Bay section of Boston. Most convenient major airport: Logan International (Boston).

Founded: 1898
Affiliation: Independent
UG Enrollment: 6,686 M, 4,605 W (full-time); 4,746 M, 5,344 (part-time)
Total Enrollment: 26,552
Cost: $10K–$20K
% Receiving Financial Aid: 60%
Admission: Non-selective
Application Deadline: March 1

Admission. For all schools, 71% of applicants accepted, 30% of these actually enroll; 27% of freshmen graduate in top fifth of high school class, 52% in top two-fifths. Average freshman scores: SAT, 467 M, 466 W verbal, 550 M, 503 W mathematical; 34% of freshman score above 500 on verbal, 8% above 600, 1% above 700; 66% score above 500 on mathematical, 26% above 600, 6% above 700; ACT, 22 M, 23 W composite. *Required:* SAT or ACT; essay and personal statement. Criteria used in admission, in order of importance: high school academic record, standardized test scores, recommendations, extracurricular activities, writing sample; other factors considered: special talents, alumni children, diverse student body. *Entrance programs:* early admission, mid-year admission, deferred admission, advanced placement. *Apply* by March 1; rolling admissions. *Transfers* welcome; 578 enrolled 1993–94.
Academic Environment. *Undergraduate studies* offered to freshmen in schools of Arts and Sciences, Business Administration, Criminal Justice, Education, Engineering, Lincoln College, College of Nursing, Bouve College of Pharmacy and Allied Health Sciences. *Degrees:* associates, bachelors, masters, doctoral. Most undergraduate programs include an experiential learning component and integrate work experience with classroom-based study. Typical cooperative work/study program calls for a freshman year (3 12-week quarters) of full-time study followed by 4 upper-class years of study and on-the-job work—slightly different patterns for Pharmacy and Nursing; 90% of students participate in work/study programs after freshman year. Most off-campus experience involves paid positions in business and industry arranged through the University's program. Graduation requirements: each of the seven undergraduate programs sets its own core requirements; all students must complete freshman English, and a "middler" year writing requirement. Strong programs reported in engineering, nursing, business administration, arts and science. Majors offered include anthropology, art and architecture, computer science, drama, English as a second language, journalism, African-American studies, international business. Average undergraduate class size: 19% under 20, 39% 20–40, 42% over 40.

About 38% of students entering as freshmen graduate within four years, 43% within five years; 71% of freshmen return for sophomore year. *Special programs:* CLEP, independent study, study abroad, honors, 3-year degree, individualized majors, 3–2 in business, cooperative education, self-paced programs. *Calendar:* quarter, summer school.
Undergraduate degrees conferred (3,020). 34% were in Business and Management, 14% were in Engineering, 8% were in Social Sciences, 6% were in Health Sciences, 6% were in Engineering and Engineering Related Technology, 6% were in Protective

Services, 6% were in Communications, 5% were in Allied Health, remainder in 13 other fields.

Graduate Career Data. Advanced studies pursued by 12% of graduates; 5% enter graduate school; 2% enter law school. About 82% of 1992–93 graduates employed. Department of Career Services offers career guidance, counseling, and placement assistance to students and alumnae. Career Resource Center offers occupational information, resume and interviewing resources, job search guides, directories of employers and graduate schools, Job Bank of current, local and international job opportunities and internships, career related seminars, on-campus recruitment, and resume matching service.

Faculty. About 80% of faculty hold PhD or equivalent. About 31% of teaching faculty are female; 4% Black, 15 Hispanic, 4% Asian, 7% foreign.

Student Body. About 57% of students from in state; 71% New England, 17% Middle Atlantic, 2% South, 1% each West, Midwest, 8% foreign. An estimated 8% of students reported as Black, 3% Hispanic, 5% Asian, 9% other minority. *Minority group students:* financial aid including Martin Luther King scholarship; special extended freshman year; African American Center.

Varsity Sports. Men (Div. I): Baseball, Basketball, Crew, Cross Country, Diving, Football, Golf, Ice Hockey, Soccer, Swimming, Track. Women (Div. I): Basketball, Crew, Cross Country, Diving, Field Hockey, Gymnastics, Ice Hockey, Swimming, Track, Volleyball.

Campus Life. No dorm or visitation regulations. No smoking or alcoholic beverages allowed in any university facilities. Cars permitted for all students except resident freshmen.

About 1% of women live in traditional dormitories; 17% of men 16% of women live in coed dormitories; rest commute. Sexes segregated in coed dormitories by wing or floor. There are 18 fraternities, 8 sororities on campus which about 9% of men, 5% of women join; fraternities, sororities provide no residence facilities.

Annual Costs. Tuition and fees, $12,771; room and board, $6,375; estimated $1,500 other, exclusive of travel. About 60% of students receive financial aid; average amount of assistance, $9,152. Assistance is typically divided 67% scholarship/grant, 18% loan, 15% work. University reports 100 scholarships awarded on the basis of academic merit alone, 300 for athletic talents alone.

Northern Arizona University

Flagstaff, Arizona 86011-4132 (602) 523-5511

A state-supported university, located in a community of 40,000, 140 miles north of Phoenix. Most convenient major airport: Pulliam (Flagstaff).

Founded: 1899
Affiliation: State
UG Enrollment: 5,315 M, 5,934 W (full-time); 1,099 M, 1,583 W (part-time)
Total Enrollment: 18,817
Cost: < $10K
% Receiving Financial Aid: 60%
Admission: Non-selective
Application Deadline: April 1

Admission. Graduates of accredited Arizona high schools with 16 units who rank in top half of class, have a GPA of 2.5, or ACT composite score of 22 (24 for out-of-state applicants), or SAT combined score of 930 (1010 for out-of-state) eligible. About 84% of applicants accepted, 33% of these actually enroll. Average freshman ACT scores: 22 M, 21.1 W composite. *Required:* SAT or ACT. Criteria considered in admission, in order of importance: high school academic record, standardized test scores. *Out-of-state* freshman applicants: university actively seeks out-of-state students. State does not limit out-of-state enrollment. About 83% of out-of-state applicants accepted, 28% of these actually enroll. States from which most out-of-state students are drawn include California, Colorado, New Mexico. *Apply* by April 1; rolling admissions. *Transfers* welcome; 1,847 enrolled 1993–94.

Academic Environment. *Undergraduate studies* offered by colleges of Arts and Sciences, Business Administration, Creative and Communication Arts, Education, Engineering and Technology, Forestry, Hotel/Restaurant Management, Health Professions, Social and Behavioral Sciences. University divided into North and South Centers in effort to maintain virtues of smaller campuses within an expanding institution. About 44% of liberal studies are required for graduation. *Degrees:* bachelors, masters, doctoral. *Majors offered* in addition to usual studies include forestry, hotel and restaurant management, international affairs, environmental engineering, social work, speech pathology and audiology. Average undergraduate class size: 31.

About 35% of student entering as freshmen graduate within four years; 69% of freshmen return for sophomore year. *Special programs:* CLEP, independent study, study abroad, honors, undergraduate research. *Calendar:* semester, summer school.

Undergraduate degrees conferred (2,106). 22% were in Business and Management, 19% were in Education, 10% were in Multi/Interdisciplinary Studies, 7% were in Communications, 6% were in Social Sciences, 4% were in Letters, 3% were in Psychology, 3% were in Engineering, 3% were in Visual and Performing Arts, 3% were in Protective Services, 3% were in Computer and Engineering Related Technology, 3% were in Life Sciences, remainder in 13 other fields.

Faculty. About 80% of faculty hold PhD or equivalent. About 80% of undergraduate classes taught by tenured faculty.

Student Body. About 84% of students from in state. An estimated 1% of students reported as Black, 8% Hispanic, 2% Asian, 3% International, 6% Native American.

Varsity Sports. Men (Div.I): Basketball, Cross Country, Diving, Football (IAA), Swimming, Tennis, Track. Women (Div.I): Basketball, Cross Country, Diving, Swimming, Tennis, Track, Volleyball.

Campus Life. About 26% of men, 35% of women live in traditional dormitories; 19% of men, 21% of women in coed dormitories; rest commute. Freshmen given preference in college housing if all students cannot be accommodated. There are 8 fraternities, 5 sororities, which about 4% of men, 5% of women join; 6% of each men, women live in fraternities and sororities. About 10–20% of resident students leave campus on weekends.

Annual Costs. Tuition and fees, $1,844 (out-of-state, $6,596); room and board, $3,000; estimated $1,200 other, exclusive of travel. About 60% of students receive financial aid, average amount of assistance, $3,000. Assistance is typically divided 25% scholarship, 25% grant, rest loan/work.

University of Northern Colorado

Greeley, Colorado 80639 (303) 351-2881

A state-supported university, located in a community of 65,000, 52 miles north of Denver. Most convenient major airport: Denver.

Founded: 1890
Affiliation: State
UG Enrollment: 3,374 M, 4,651 W (full-time); 325 M, 436 W (part-time)
Total Enrollment: 10,458
Cost: < $10K
% Receiving Financial Aid: 63%
Admission: Non-selective
Application Deadline: Rolling

Admission. Graduates of accredited high schools with 15 units eligible; 72% of applicants accepted, 43% of these actually enroll; 29% of freshmen graduate in top fifth of high school class, 63% in top two-fifths. Average freshman scores: SAT, 440 M, 433 W verbal, 506 M, 464 W mathematical; ACT, 21.8 composite. *Required:* ACT or SAT. Criteria considered in admission, in order of importance: high school academic record, standardized test scores, recommendations; other factors considered: special talents, diverse student body. *Out-of-state* freshman applicants: university actively seeks students from out-of-state. State limits out-of-state enrollment. No special requirements for out-of-state applicants; 74% of applicants accepted, 28% of these actually enroll. States from which most out-of-state students are drawn include Hawaii, California, Wyoming, Nebraska. *Entrance programs:* early decision, early admission, mid-year admission, deferred admission. *Apply:* rolling admissions. *Transfers* welcome; 995 enrolled 1993–94.

Academic Environment. Degrees offered: bachelors, masters, doctoral. Graduation requirements: about one-third of courses required for graduation are general education requirements; also required: English essay exam. Interdisciplinary programs encouraged. Average undergraduate class size: 46% under 20, 35% 20–40, 19% over 40. About 16% of students entering as freshmen graduate within four years, 45% eventually, 65% of freshmen return for sophomore year. *Special programs:* CLEP, independent study, study abroad, honors, undergraduate research, individualized majors. *Calendar:* quarter, summer school.

Undergraduate degrees conferred (1,291). 21% were in Education, 18% were in Business and Management, 14% were in Social Sciences, 9% were in Health Sciences, 8% were in Communications, 6% were in Psychology, 5% were in Visual and Performing Arts, 4% were in Letters, 3% were in Parks and Recreation, 3% were in Mathematics, remainder in 8 other fields.
Graduates Career Data. Advanced studies pursued by 9% of graduates. About 85% of 1991–92 graduates employed.
Faculty. About 68% of faculty hold PhD or equivalent. About 57% of undergraduate classes taught by tenured faculty. About 38% of teaching faculty are female; 2% Black, 4% Hispanic, 5% other minority.
Student Body. About 89% of students from in state. An estimated 2% of students reported as Black, 7% Hispanic, 2% Asian, 4% other minority. Average age of undergraduate student: 22.
Varsity Sports. Men (Div.II): Baseball, Basketball, Football, Golf, Tennis, Track, Wrestling. Women (Div.II): Basketball, Cross Country, Soccer, Swimming, Tennis, Track, Volleyball.
Campus Life. Students reported to spend on-campus leisure time with clubs/organizations, parties, dances, school-sponsored entertainment; off-campus: bowling, work, sports, and games.

About 29% of men, 31% of women live in coed dormitories; 70% of men, 68% of women commute. Freshmen given preference in college housing if all students cannot be accommodated. Intervisitation in men's and women's dormitory rooms unlimited. Sexes segregated in coed dormitories either by floor or room. There are 9 fraternities, 5 sororities on campus which about 9% of men, 6% of women join; 1% of each men, women live in fraternities and sororities.
Annual Costs. Tuition and fees, $2,114 (out-of-state, $7,400); room and board, $3,894; estimated $2,380 other, exclusive of travel. About 63% of students receive financial aid; average amount of assistance, $3,748. Assistance is typically divided 17% scholarship, 19% grant, 46% loan, 18% work.

Northern Illinois University

DeKalb, Illinois 60115 **(815) 753-0446 (in-state, (800) 892-3050)**

A state-supported university, Northern Illinois is located in a town of 32,900, about 65 miles west of Chicago. Most convenient major airport: O'Hare International (Chicago).

Founded: 1895
Affiliation: State
UG Enrollment: 6,910 M, 7,916 W (full-time); 886 M, 1,093 W (part-time)
Total Enrollment: 23,177
Cost: < $10K
% Receiving Financial Aid: 54%
Admission: Non-selective
Application Deadline: Aug. 1

Admission. About 67% of applicants accepted, 33% of these actually enroll; 28% of freshmen graduate in top fifth of high school class, 67% in top two fifths. Average freshman ACT scores: 22 composite. *Required:* ACT. Criteria considered in admission, in order of importance: standardized test scores, high school academic record. *Out-of-state* freshman applicants: state does not actively seek out-of-state students. State does not limit out-of-state. *Apply* by August 1; rolling admissions. *Transfers* welcome; 2,208 enrolled 1993–94.
Academic Environment. Innovative living and learning program includes courses from 13 departments taught in part in residence halls. University ombudsman active on behalf of students. Administration reports 25% of courses required for graduation are elective; distribution requirements fairly numerous. *Undergraduate studies* offered by colleges of Liberal Arts and Sciences, Business, Education, Visual and Performing Arts, and Professional Studies. Degrees offered: bachelors, masters, doctoral. *Majors offered* in addition to usual studies include anthropology, geography, geology, journalism, speech communication.

About 23% of entering freshmen graduate within four years, 54% eventually, 77% of freshmen return for sophomore year. *Special programs:* CLEP, independent study, study abroad, honors, undergraduate research, May interterm, individualized majors, combined programs, 3–2 engineering, Southeast Asian studies, urban studies, Latin American studies. *Calendar:* 4–1–4, summer school.
Undergraduate degrees conferred (3,709). 23% were in Business and Management, 14% were in Social Sciences, 14% were in Education, 11% were in Letters, 6% were in Health Sciences, 6% were in Visual and Performing Arts, 4% were in Home Economics, 4% were in Computer and Engineering Related Technology, 3% were in Liberal/General Studies, remainder in 11 other fields.
Graduates Career Data. Advanced studies pursued by 9% of graduates. About 66% of 1991–92 graduates employed full-time, 11% part-time; 83% of employed graduates reported their employment was related to their major. Fields typically hiring largest numbers of graduates include sales, management training, programmer, computer science, customer service. Career Resource Center provides students with career information tapes through the CAREER system; tapes provide information about each major, related careers, availability of jobs, salary ranges, and job market projections.
Student Body. About 96% of students from in state. An estimated 8% of students reported as Black, 5% Hispanic, 5% Asian. *Minority group students:* CHANCE program gives special consideration for admission to inner-city minority group students; special counseling, tutoring, and financial assistance. Average age of undergraduate student: 22.
Varsity Sports. Men (Div.I): Baseball, Basketball, Diving, Football, Golf, Soccer, Swimming, Tennis, Wrestling. Women (Div.I): Basketball, Diving, Golf, Gymnastics, Soccer, Softball, Swimming, Tennis, Volleyball.
Campus Life. A variety of living styles available to students; no curfew; coed dorms; unlimited intervisitation; regulations governing social life determined jointly by students/administration. Student leader reports "great recreation/performing arts facility."

About 30% of students live in coed dormitories; 36% commute. Freshmen given preference in college housing if all students cannot be accommodated. Sexes segregated in coed dormitories by room. There are 22 fraternities, 15 sororities on campus; 16% of men, 13% of women live in fraternities and sororities.
Annual Costs. Tuition and fees, $3,343 (out-of-state, $8,292); room and board, $3,066; estimated $2,000 other, exclusive of travel. About 54% of students receive financial aid; average amount of assistance, $3,666. Assistance is typically divided 48% scholarship/grant, 40% loan, 12% work.

University of Northern Iowa

Cedar Falls, Iowa 50614-0030 **(319) 273-2281**

A state-supported university, located in a town of 35,000, 100 miles northeast of Des Moines. Most convenient major airport: Waterloo-Cedar Falls.

Founded: 1876
Affiliation: State
UG Enrollment: 4,448 M, 5,697 W (full-time); 548 M, 774 W (part-time)
Total Enrollment: 12,717
Cost: < $10K
% Receiving Financial Aid: 81%
Admission: Selective
Application Deadline: Rolling

Admission is selective. About 89% of applicants accepted, 55% of these actually enroll; 41% of freshmen graduate in top fifth of high school class, 81% in top two-fifths. Average freshman ACT scores: 23 composite. *Required:* ACT, rank in top 50% of high school graduating class. Criteria considered in admission, in order of importance: high school academic record, standardized test scores, recommendations, extracurricular activities; other factors considered include special talents, diverse student body. *Out-of-state* freshman applicants: university actively seeks students from out-of-state. State does not limit out-of-state enrollment. No special requirements for out-of-state applicants. About 74% of out-of-state applicants accepted, 41% of these actually enroll. States from which most out-of-state students are drawn include Illinois, Minnesota, Wisconsin. *Entrance programs:* early decision, midyear admission, advanced placement. *Apply* by ten days before beginning of term; rolling admissions. *Transfers* welcome; 917 enrolled 1993–94.
Academic Environment. Graduation requirements include 47 hours in six categories: civilization and cultures; fine arts, literature, philosophy, and religion; natural science and technology; social science; communication essentials; and personal wellness. Student body characterized as interested in career-oriented programs. Degrees offered: bachelors, masters, doctoral. *Majors offered* include usual arts and sciences, business, computer science, education, geography, home economics, industrial arts and technology, speech pathology, bio-technology, natural history interpretation, construc-

tion technology, graphic communication, criminology, finance, management information systems. Average undergraduate class size: 58% under 25, 33% 25–50, 9% over 50.

About 33% of students entering as freshmen graduate within four years, 64% within six years, 80% of freshmen return for sophomore year. *Special programs:* CLEP, independent study, study abroad, honors, undergraduate research, 3-year degree, individualized majors, workshops and study tours for credit, National Student Exchange Program, credit by examination, 3–2 in hospital & health administration, 3–2 in physical therapy, internships, Iowa Regents' Universities Student Exchange, National Student Exchange. *Calendar:* semester, summer school.

Undergraduate degrees conferred (2,027). 24% were in Business and Management, 23% were in Education, 7% were in Liberal/General Studies, 6% were in Social Sciences, 5% were in Communications, 4% were in Visual and Performing Arts, 4% were in Public Affairs, 3% were in Psychology, 3% were in Home Economics, 3% were in Engineering and Engineering Related Technology, 3% were in Letters, remainder in 13 other fields.

Graduates Career Data. Advanced studies pursued by 13% of graduates. About 67% of 1992–93 graduates employed. Corporations typically hiring largest numbers of graduates include Maytag, Principal Financial Group, McGladrey and Pullen. Career Development Services include aptitude testing, counseling, placement services, resume and interview workshops, on campus recruitment, internships and cooperative education, library resources, interview coaching, computerized job listings and employer referrals, mainframe electronic bulletin board, career fairs, career decision-making classes for elective credit.

Faculty. About 62% of faculty hold PhD or equivalent. About 73% of undergraduate classes taught by tenured faculty. About 39% of teaching faculty are female; 3% Black, 2% Hispanic, 5% other minority.

Student Body. About 96% of students from in state; 98% Midwest, 1% foreign. An estimated 60% of students reported as Protestant, 33% Catholic, 4% unaffiliated, 3% other; 2% Black, less than 1% other minority, according to most recent data available. *Minority group students:* Center for Academic Achievement, Ethnic Minority Cultural and Educational Center. Average age of undergraduate student: 22.

Varsity Sports. Men (Div.I): Baseball, Basketball, Cross Country, Diving, Football, Golf, Swimming, Tennis, Track, Wrestling. Women (Div.I): Basketball, Cross Country, Diving, Golf, Softball, Swimming, Tennis, Track, Volleyball.

Campus Life. Student reports on-campus leisure time is spent "studying, playing catch (football, baseball, etc.), skating, walking, lying around." Shopping, movies, and bowling are also nearby. Cars permitted; parking reported to be a problem for students living off-campus. Sexes segregated in coed dormitories by floor; 24-hour visitation in 6 residence halls, limited in 3 halls.

About 18% of students live in traditional dormitories; 17% live in coed dormitories; 4% live in on-campus, married student housing; 61% commute. Freshmen given preference in college housing if all students cannot be accommodated. There are 7 fraternities, 4 sororities on campus which about 6% of men, 4% of women join. About 70% of resident students leave campus on weekends.

Annual Costs. Tuition and fees, $2,192 (out-of-state, $5,834); room and board, $2,628; estimated $2,365 other, exclusive of travel. About 81% of students receive financial aid; average amount of assistance, $3,800. Assistance is typically divided 12% scholarship, 21% grant, 62% loan, 5% work.

Northern Kentucky University

Highland Heights, Kentucky 41076 (606) 572-5220

A state-supported, commuter institution located on its new 300-acre campus in an urban area 8 miles from Cincinnati, Ohio. Most convenient major airport: Greater Cincinnati International.

Founded: 1968
Affiliation: State
UG Enrollment: 3,173 M, 3,939 W (full-time); 1,658 M, 2,174 W (part-time)
Total Enrollment: 11,578
Cost: < $10K
% Receiving Financial Aid: 46%
Admission: Non-selective
Application Deadline: May 1

Admission is open. *Required:* ACT. *Out-of-state* applicants: university actively seeks students from out-of-state. State does not limit out-of-state enrollment. States from which most out-of-state students are drawn: Ohio, Indiana. *Entrance programs:* early admission, advanced placement, rolling admission. *Apply* by May 1 (priority date). *Transfers* welcome; 531 enrolled 1993–94.

Academic Environment. Degrees offered: associates, bachelors, doctoral. About 53% of general education requirements for graduation are elective; distribution requirements fairly numerous. Average undergraduate class size: 38% under 20, 50% 20–40, 12% over 40. About 19% of students entering as freshmen graduate within four years, 46% eventually; 73% of freshmen return for sophomore year. *Special programs:* CLEP, honors, study abroad, independent study, internship, 3-year degree, individualized majors, portfolio credit. *Library:* Kentuckiana Special Collection. *Calendar:* semester, summer school.

Undergraduate degrees conferred (771). 27% were in Business and Management, 15% were in Education, 11% were in Social Sciences, 7% were in Communications, 6% were in Psychology, 5% were in Letters, 5% were in Visual and Performing Arts, 5% were in Public Affairs, 4% were in Computer and Engineering Related Technology, 3% were in Life Sciences, remainder in 7 other fields.

Graduates Career Data. Advanced studies pursued by 9% of graduates; 5% enter graduate school; 4% enter law school. About 90% of 1990–91 graduates employed.

Faculty. About 66% of faculty hold PhD or equivalent. About 44% of teaching faculty are female; 5% minority.

Student Body. About 78% of students from in state. An estimated 2% of students reported as Black, 2% as other minority. Average age of undergraduate student: 26.

Varsity Sports. Men (Div.II): Baseball, Basketball, Cross Country, Golf, Soccer, Tennis. Women (Div.II): Basketball, Cross Country, Softball, Tennis, Volleyball.

Campus Life. About 4% of men, 5% of women live in traditional dormitories; rest commute. Freshmen given preference in college housing if all students cannot be accommodated. There are 6 fraternities, 3 sororities on campus which about 2% each of men, women join; they provide no residence facilities.

Annual Costs. Tuition and fees, $1,720 (out-of-state, $4,720); room and board, $3,095; estimated $1,300 other, exclusive of travel. About 46% of students receive financial aid; average amount of assistance, $2,500. Assistance is typically divided 19% scholarship, 30% grant, 41% loan, 10% work. University reports 15 scholarships awarded on the basis of academic merit alone; 2 on special talents alone. *Meeting Costs:* University offers installment plan.

Northern Michigan University

Marquette, Michigan 49855 (906) 227-2650

A multipurpose, state-supported university, located in a town of 25,000, on the shores of Lake Superior, 300 miles north of Milwaukee. Most convenient major airport: Marquette County.

Founded: 1899
Affiliation: State
Total Enrollment: 6,579
Cost: < $10K
% Receiving Financial Aid: 63%
Admission: Non-selective
Application Deadline: August 1

Admission. High school graduates with strong college preparatory program eligible; recomputed GPA of 2.0 and ACT composite of 16 or SAT of 685 admit a student in good standing; 85% of applicants accepted, 28% of these actually enroll. Average freshman ACT scores, according to most recent data available: 18.5 composite, 16.5 mathematical. *Required:* SAT or ACT; interview "desired." Out-of-state freshman applicants: university welcomes students from out of state. State does not limit out-of-state enrollment. No special requirements for out-of-state applicants; 66% accepted, 32% enroll. *Non-academic factors* considered in admissions: special talents. *Apply* by August 1. *Transfers* welcome.

Academic Environment. *Undergraduate studies* offered by schools of Arts and Science, Business, Behavior Science and Human Services, Nursing and Allied Health Sciences. About 42% of general education requirements for graduation are elective; distribution requirements fairly numerous. New program include: international

studies, public relations. About 45% of students entering as freshmen graduate eventually; 69% of freshmen return for sophomore year. *Special programs:* CLEP, honors, individualized majors. *Calendar:* semester, May interterm, summer school.
Undergraduate degrees conferred (839). 16% were in Business and Management, 10% were in Education, 8% were in Health Sciences, 8% were in Social Sciences, 8% were in Protective Services, 7% were in Liberal/General Studies, 6% were in Communications, 5% were in Letters, 5% were in Visual and Performing Arts, 4% were in Psychology, 4% were in Public Affairs, 4% were in Business (Administrative Support), 4% were in Life Sciences, remainder in 14 other fields.
Faculty. About 64% of faculty hold PhD or equivalent.
Student Body. About 90% of students from in state; 92% from Midwest. An estimated 2% of students reported as Black, 2% Native American, 1% other minority, according to most recent data available.
Varsity Sports. Men (Div.II): Basketball, Cross Country, Football, Ice Hockey (I), Nordic Skiing, Track, Wrestling. Women (Div.II): Basketball, Cross Country, Swimming & Diving, Nordic Skiing, Track, Volleyball.
Campus Life. About 3% of women live in traditional dormitories; 13% of men, 10% of women in coed dormitories; 86% of men, 87% of women live in off-campus housing or commute. Freshmen given preference in college housing if all students cannot be accommodated. Sexes segregated in coed dormitories by wing, floor, or suite. There are 5 fraternities and 4 sororities on campus which about 1% of men, 1% of women join; 1% of men live in fraternities, sororities provide no residence facilities.
Annual Costs. Tuition and fees, $2,528 (out-of-state, $4,639); room and board, $3,811. About 63% of students receive financial aid; assistance is typically divided 55% scholarship, 10% loan, 35% work. University reports some scholarships awarded on the basis of academic merit alone. *Meeting Costs:* university offers parent loan program through the State of Michigan, and payment plans.

Northern Montana College

Havre, Montana 59501 (406) 265-3700

A state-supported college, located in a town of 12,000, 30 miles south of the Canadian border. Most convenient major airport: Great Falls International.

Founded: 1913
Affiliation: State
UG Enrollment: 647 M, 498 W (full-time); 121 M, 30 W (part-time)
Total Enrollment: 1,973
Cost: < $10K
Admission: Non-selective
Application Deadline: September 24

Admission. Graduates of accredited high schools with 16 units eligible; 74% of applicants accepted, all of these enrolled. *Required:* ACT. *Out-of-state* freshman applicants: college seeks students from out of state. State does not limit out-of-state enrollment, but "priority given to state students if and when there is a need." Requirement for out-of-state applicants: rank in top half of class or ACT. *Apply* by . *Transfers* welcome.
Academic Environment. *Degrees:* AB, BS, BSN. About 25% of general education requirements for graduation are elective; distribution requirements vary with program. About 27% of students entering as freshmen graduate eventually; 50% of freshmen do not return for sophomore year. *Special programs:* honors. *Calendar:* quarter, summer school.
Undergraduate degrees conferred (150). 45% were in Education, 26% were in Engineering and Engineering Related Technology, 23% were in Business and Management, 4% were in Multi/Interdisciplinary Studies, remainder in Health Sciences.
Student Body. About 89% of students from in state; 97% Northwest. An estimated 11% of students reported as Native American, 1% other minority, according to most recent data available.
Varsity Sports. Men (NAIA): Basketball, Wrestling. Women (NAIA): Basketball, Volleyball.
Campus Life. About 15% of students live in traditional dormitories; no coed dormitories; rest live in off-campus housing or commute. Freshmen given preference in college housing if all students cannot be accommodated. Intervisitation in men's and women's dormitory rooms limited. There are no fraternities or sororities. About 90% of resident students leave campus on weekends.
Annual Costs. Tuition and fees, $1,802 (out-of-state, $5,358); room and board, $3,216. About 60% of students receive financial aid.

Northern State College

Aberdeen, South Dakota 57401 (605) 622-2544

A state-supported college, located in a city of 27,000. Most convenient major airport: Aberdeen Municipal.

Founded: 1901
Affiliation: State
UG Enrollment: 893 M, 1,220 W (full-time); 233 M, 440 W (part-time)
Total Enrollment: 2,286
Cost: < $10K
% Receiving Financial Aid: 73%
Admission: Non-selective
Application Deadline: Aug. 15

Admission. Graduates of approved South Dakota high schools with "C" average in academic courses, or score 18 or above on ACT composite, or rank in top two-thirds of graduating class eligible; almost all applicants accepted, 74% of these actually enroll. *Required:* ACT; interview recommended. *Out-of-state* freshman applicants: college welcomes students from out of state. Requirement for out-of-state applicants: rank in top half of class or score in top half on ACT. *Apply* by August 15. *Transfers* welcome.
Academic Environment. *Degrees:* AB, BS, BSEd. About 30% of general education requirements for graduation are elective; distribution requirements fairly numerous. About 54% of students entering as freshmen graduate eventually; 70% of freshmen return for sophomore year. *Special programs:* CLEP, honors, National Student Exchange, undergraduate research, independent study, 3-year degree, optional spring interim. *Calendar:* early semester, summer school.
Undergraduate degrees conferred (344). 40% were in Business and Management, 31% were in Education, 8% were in Social Sciences, 7% were in Psychology, remainder in 11 other fields.
Graduates Career Data. According to most recent data available, careers in business and industry pursued by 50% of graduates. State of South Dakota typically hires large numbers of graduates.
Faculty. About 75% of faculty hold PhD or equivalent.
Student Body. About 95% of students from in state; 99% Midwest. An estimated 2% of students reported as Native American, 1% other minority, according to most recent data available.
Varsity Sports. Men (NAIA): Baseball, Basketball, Cross Country, Football, Golf, Tennis, Track, Wrestling. Women (Div.II): Basketball, Cross Country, Golf, Softball, Tennis, Track, Volleyball.
Campus Life. About 10% of men, 13% of women live in traditional dormitories; 18% of men, 13% of women in coed dormitories; 73% of men, 74% of women live in off-campus housing or commute. Intervisitation in men's and women's dormitory rooms limited. Sexes segregated in coed dormitories by wing. There are no fraternities or sororities. About 85% of resident students leave campus on weekends.
Annual Costs. Tuition and fees, $2,006 (out-of-state, $3,574); room and board, $2,399. About 73% of students receive financial aid; assistance is typically divided 45% grant/scholarship, 49% loan, 6% work. College reports some scholarships awarded on the basis of academic merit alone. *Meeting Costs:* college offers Academic Management Services budget payment plan, PLUS Loans.

Northland College

Ashland, Wisconsin 54806 (715) 682-4531

An independent college, maintaining "a cooperative, nonsubordinate relationship to its successor organization, the United Church of Christ"; located in a northern Wisconsin town of 10,000, 75 miles east of Duluth, Minnesota.

Founded: 1892
Affiliation: Independent (United Church of Christ)
UG Enrollment: 752 M, W (full-time)
Cost: < $10K
Admission: Non-selective
Application Deadline: no deadline

Admission. High school graduates with 16 units (12 in academic subjects) eligible; 57% of applicants accepted, 33% of these actually enroll. About 37% of freshmen graduate in top fifth of high school class, 70% in top two-fifths. *Required:* SAT or ACT. *Apply:* no deadline. *Transfers* welcome.
Academic Environment. Environmental studies program includes fisheries and wildlife management. *Degree:* AB. About 80% of general education requirements for graduation are elective; distribution requirements limited; 42 credits in general studies program. *Special programs:* CLEP, independent study, study abroad, honors, exchange agreement through Spring Term Consortium, cooperative program. *Calendar:* 4–4–1.
Undergraduate degrees conferred (107). 32% were in Life Sciences, 29% were in Education, 17% were in Business and Management, 7% were in Multi/Interdisciplinary Studies, 5% were in Social Sciences, 5% were in Physical Sciences, remainder in 5 other fields.
Student Body. About 65% of students from Midwest.
Campus Life. About 20% each of men, women live in traditional dormitories; 40% each of men, women in coed dormitories; rest live in off-campus housing or commute. Intervisitation in men's and women's dormitory rooms limited. Sexes segregated in coed dormitories by room. There are 3 fraternities, 2 sororities on campus which about 10% of men, 15% of women join; they provide no residence facilities. About 20% of resident students leave campus on weekends.
Annual Costs. Tuition and fees, $9,800; room and board, $3,750. College reports some scholarships awarded on the basis of academic merit alone. *Meeting Costs:* college guarantees every student a campus job.

Northwest Christian College

Eugene, Oregon 97401 (503) 343-1641

A small, church-related institution, Northwest Christian is now an accredited liberal arts college; the majority of degrees are conferred in business related fields.

Founded: 1895	**Total Enrollment:** 351
Affiliation: Churches of Christ/Disciples of Christ	**Cost:** < $10K
UG Enrollment: 178 M, 173 W; 42 M, 32 W (part-time)	**% Receiving Financial Aid:** 80%
	Admission: Non-selective
	Application Deadline: March 1

Admission. About 60% of applicants accepted, 66% of these actually enroll. Average freshman SAT scores: 439 verbal, 481 mathematical. *Required:* SAT or ACT, essay, minimum high school GPA. Criteria considered in admissions, in order of importance: standardized test scores, high school academic record, recommendations, writing sample. *Entrance programs:* early decision, early admission, midyear admission, deferred admission. *Apply* by March 1. *Transfers* welcome; 32 enrolled 1993–94.
Academic Environment. Graduation requirements include courses in math, science, language, and Bible study. Degrees offered: associates, bachelors, masters. *Special programs:* study abroad, cross registration with U. of Oregon. Adult program: degree completion program in managerial leadership for working adults.
Undergraduate degrees conferred (51). 49% were in Business and Management, 24% were in Theology, 12% were in Multi/Interdisciplinary Studies, 8% were in Communications, 4% were in Social Sciences, remainder in 2 other fields.
Graduates Career Data. Advanced studies pursued by 60% of graduates; 53% enter graduate school; less than 1% enter medical school; 6% enter law school. Career Development Services available to students in partnership with U. of Oregon.
Faculty. About 74% of faculty hold PhD or equivalent. About 30% of teaching faculty are female.
Student Body. About 54% of students from in state; 92% West, 2% Midwest, 6% foreign. An estimated 76% of students are reported as Protestant, less than 1% Catholic, 23% unaffiliated; 1% Black, 1% Hispanic, 4% Asian.
Religious Orientation. College is a church-related institution; 10% of students affiliated with the church; 3 classes in religious studies required.
Varsity Sports. Men (NAIT): Basketball.
Campus Life. About 15% of each men, women live in traditional dormitories; rest live in off-campus housing or commute.
Annual Costs. Tuition and fees, $7,200; room and board, $3,800; estimated $1,000 other, exclusive of travel. About 80% of students receive financial aid; average amount of assistance, $2,500. Assistance is typically divided 10% scholarship, 10% grant, 50% loan, 30% work. University reports 80% of scholarships awarded on the basis of academic merit alone.

Northwest College of the Assemblies of God

(See Northwest College)

Northwest College

Kirkland, Washington 98083 (206) 822-7266

A church-related institution, "devoted to preparing students for service and leadership." Largest majors are teacher education, church ministries, behavioral science, and business management/administration. Formerly known as Northwest College of the Assemblies of God.

Founded: 1934	**Cost:** < $10K
Affiliation: Assemblies of God	**% Receiving Financial Aid:** 79%
UG Enrollment: 339 M, 365 W; 26 M, 27 W (part-time)	**Admission:** Non-selective
	Application Deadline: Aug. 1

Admission. About 66% of applicants accepted, 82% of these actually enroll. Average freshman scores: SAT, 910 combined; ACT, 21 composite. *Required:* SAT or ACT, minimum GPA, essay, references. Criteria considered in admissions, in order of importance: recommendations, high school academic record, standardized test scores, writing sample, extracurricular activities; other factors considered: religious commitment. *Entrance programs:* early decision, midyear admission, deferred admission, advanced placement. *Apply* by August 1; rolling admissions. *Transfers* welcome; 137 enrolled 1993–94.
Academic Environment. Graduation requirements include 17 semester credits in humanities, 12 in social sciences, 10 in math/science, 10 in religion. Degrees offered: associates, bachelors. New majors include business management and administration, secondary education, health sciences. Average undergraduate class size: 30% under 20, 50% 20–40, 20 over 40. About 60% of students entering as freshmen graduate eventually; 65% of freshmen return for sophomore year. *Special programs:* study abroad.
Undergraduate degrees conferred (88). 52% were in Theology, 26% were in Education, 16% were in Psychology, 6% were in Philosophy and Religion.
Graduates Career Data. Fields typically hiring largest numbers of graduates include education, churches, counseling, business.
Faculty. About 50% of faculty hold PhD or equivalent. About 60% of undergraduate classes taught by tenured faculty. About 30% of teaching faculty are female.
Student Body. About 71% of students from in state; 91% Northwest, 3% foreign. An estimated 99% of students are reported as Protestant; 1% Black, 3% Hispanic, 4% Asian, 2% other minority. Average age of undergraduate student: 23.
Religious Orientation. University is a church-related institution; 70% of students affiliated with the church; 18 semester hours of religious courses required.
Varsity Sports. Men (NCCAA Div.I): Basketball, Soccer. Women (NCCAA Div.I): Basketball, Volleyball.
Campus Life. About 54% of men, 62% women live in traditional dormitories; rest live in off-campus housing or commute. About 20% of resident students leave campus on weekends.
Annual Costs. Tuition and fees, $6,600; room and board, $3,300; estimated $1,000 other, exclusive of travel. About 79% of students receive financial aid, average amount of assistance, $6,540. Assistance is typically divided 38% scholarship/grant, 59% loan, 3% work. University reports 108 scholarships awarded on the basis of academic merit alone, 37 for special talents alone.

Northwest Missouri State University

Maryville, Missouri 64468 **(800) 633-1175**

A state-supported college, located in a town of 10,000, 100 miles north of Kansas City. Most convenient major airport: Kansas City.

Founded: 1905
Affiliation: State
UG Enrollment: 2,159 M, 2,582 W (full-time); 170 M, 229 W (part-time)
Total Enrollment: 5,802
Cost: < $10K
% Receiving Financial Aid: 64%
Admission: Non-selective
Application Deadline: Rolling

Admission. Graduates of approved Missouri high schools eligible; 92% of applicants accepted, 49% of these actually enroll; 15% of entering students graduate in top fifth of high school class, 44% in top two fifths. Average freshmen ACT scores: 21 composite. *Required:* ACT, minimum 2.0 GPA. Criteria considered in admissions, in order of importance: high school academic record, standardized test scores, recommendations. *Out-of-state* freshman applicants: university actively seeks out-of-state students. State does not limit out-of-state enrollment. Special requirements for out-of-state students: higher rank and ACT scores. States from which most out-of-state students are drawn include Iowa. *Entrance programs:* early admission, midyear admission, advanced placement. *Apply:* rolling admissions. *Transfers* welcome; 407 enrolled 1993–94.
Academic Environment. Degrees offered: bachelors, masters. About 30% of general education requirements for graduation are elective; distribution requirements fairly numerous. Average undergraduate class size: 27. About 44% of students entering as freshmen graduate within four years; 83% of freshmen return for sophomore year. *Special programs:* CLEP, honors, individualized majors, 3–2 in engineering, study abroad, cross registration with Missouri Western State, internships. *Library:* rare book collection of Missouriana. *Calendar:* semester, summer school.
Undergraduate degrees conferred (748). 26% were in Education, 20% were in Business and Management, 9% were in Communications, 8% were in Social Sciences, 5% were in Psychology, 4% were in Home Economics, 4% were in Agricultural Sciences, 4% were in Agribusiness and Agricultural Production, 3% were in Engineering and Engineering Related Technology, 3% were in Computer and Engineering Related Technology, 3% were in Visual and Performing Arts, remainder in 9 other fields.
Graduates Career Data. Advanced studies pursued by 20% of graduates. Career Development Services include counseling, summer internship and cooperative education opportunities, career resource library, SIGI Plus, credential files, resume assistance, employer computerized referral service, company and school district files, career fairs, teacher placement days, in campus interviews and annual reports.
Faculty. About 71% of faculty hold PhD or equivalent.
Student Body. About 58% of students from in state; 3% foreign. An estimated 2% of students reported as Black, 1% Hispanic, 1% Asian, 3% other minority.
Varsity Sports. Men (NCAA, Div.II): Baseball, Basketball, Cross Country, Football, Tennis, Track. Women (NCAA, Div.II): Basketball, Cross Country, Softball, Tennis, Track, Volleyball.
Campus Life. About 17% of men, 22% of women live in traditional and coed dormitories; rest live in off-campus housing or commute. Freshmen given preference in college housing if all students cannot be accommodated. Intervisitation in men's and women's dormitory rooms limited. There are 9 fraternities, 5 sororities; which 20% of men, 14% of women join; 6% of men live in fraternities. About 40% of resident students leave campus on weekends.
Annual Costs. Tuition and fees, $2,010 (out-of-state, $3,570); room and board, $3,000. About 64% of students receive financial aid; assistance is typically divided 1% scholarship, 37% grant, 57% loan, 5% work. *Meeting Costs:* university offers installment payment plan.

Northwest Nazarene College

Nampa, Idaho 83686 **(208) 467-8496** **(800) NNC-4-YOU**

A church-related college, located in a small city of 29,000, Northwest Nazarene emphasizes its "basic religious suppositions and serious spiritual commitment."

Founded: 1913
Affiliation: Nazarene
UG Enrollment: 1,489 M, W (full-time)
Cost: < $10K
% Receiving Financial Aid: 80%
Admission: Non-selective
Application Deadline: no specific deadline

Admission. Graduates of accredited high schools with C average eligible; others admitted provisionally; virtually all applicants accepted, 71% of these actually enroll. *Required:* ACT, acceptance of campus code forbidding drinking, smoking, and drug-taking. *Apply:* no specific deadline. *Transfers* welcome.
Academic Environment. *Degree:* AB. General education requirements for graduation are the same for all majors; distribution requirements fairly numerous. *Special programs:* CLEP, undergraduate research, study abroad, 3–2 engineering, cooperative program with Fashion Institute of Technology. *Calendar:* quarter, summer school.
Undergraduate degrees conferred (150). 29% were in Education, 10% were in Philosophy and Religion, 10% were in Letters, 8% were in Business and Management, 7% were in Public Affairs, 5% were in Life Sciences, 4% were in Psychology, 4% were in Physical Sciences, 4% were in Liberal/General Studies, 3% were in Visual and Performing Arts, 3% were in Social Sciences, 3% were in Theology, 3% were in Computer and Engineering Related Technology, remainder in 6 other fields.
Faculty. About 53% of faculty hold PhD or equivalent.
Student Body. About 39% of students from in state; 90% from West/Northwest. An estimated 96% of students reported as Protestant, 2% Catholic, 2% unaffiliated; 1% Hispanic, 1% Asian, 2% other minority, according to most recent data available.
Religious Orientation. Northwest Nazarene is a church-related institution; 16 quarter credits in philosophy and religion courses, attendance at regular church and triweekly chapel services required of all students.
Campus Life. About 61% of men, 68% of women live in traditional or coed dormitories; 8% of men, 3% of women live in off-campus college-related housing; rest commute. No intervisitation in men's or women's dormitory rooms. There are no fraternities or sororities on campus. About 32% of resident students leave campus on weekends.
Annual Costs. Tuition and fees, $9,105; room and board, $2,645. About 80% of students receive financial aid; assistance is typically divided 55% scholarship/grant, 45% loan, work. College reports some scholarships awarded on the basis of academic merit alone.

Northwestern College of Iowa

Orange City, Iowa 51041 **(712) 737-7000**

A church-related college, located in a village of 5,000, 40 miles north of Sioux City, "committed to an evangelical Christian liberal arts philosophy." Most convenient major airports: Sioux City (IA), Sioux Falls (SD).

Founded: 1882
Affiliation: Reformed Church
UG Enrollment: 452 M, 588 W (full-time); 14 M 38 W (part-time)
Total Enrollment: 1,100
Cost: < $10K
% Receiving Financial Aid: 98%
Admission: Non-selective
Application Deadline: Aug. 15

Admission. About 91% of applicants accepted, 47% of these actually enroll; 36% of freshmen graduate in top fifth of high school class, 68% in top two-fifths. Average freshman ACT scores: 22.5 composite. *Required:* ACT, minimum GPA. Criteria considered in admissions, in order of importance: high school academic record, standardized test scores, recommendations, "legacy", writing sample, extracurricular activities; other factors considered: alumni children, diverse student body, religious affiliation and/or commitment. *Entrance programs:* deferred admission. *Apply* by August 15; rolling admissions. *Transfers* welcome; 52 enrolled 1993–94.
Academic Environment. Degrees offered: associates, bachelors, masters. Administration source characterizes student body as primarily concerned with religious activities. Graduation requirements include 8 credits in Biblical studies, 6 in history, 4 each in fine arts, social sciences, natural sciences, philosophy, senior seminar, literature, 8 in cross-cultural/language, 2 in physical education; writing

competency, math competency. Average undergraduate class size: 30% under 20, 50% 20–40, 20% over 40.

About 60% of students entering as freshmen graduate eventually; 88% of freshmen return for sophomore year. *Special programs:* CLEP, independent study, study abroad, undergraduate research, cross registration with Christian College Coalition, 3–2 in engineering, internships in Washington D.C., American Studies Program, Chicago Metro summer, Summer Institute for international students. *Calendar:* semester, summer school.

Undergraduate degrees conferred (194). 34% were in Education, 23% were in Business and Management, 11% were in Social Sciences, 7% were in Life Sciences, 6% were in Public Affairs, remainder in 11 other fields.

Graduates Career Data. Advanced studies pursued by 15% of graduates; 5% enter graduate school; 2% enter medical school; less than 1% each enter dental, law or business school. Professional schools typically enrolling largest numbers of graduates include U. of Iowa. Fields typically hiring largest numbers of graduates include education, business, accounting, social services. Career Development Services include credential files and career counseling.

Faculty. About 72% of faculty hold PhD or equivalent. About 80% of undergraduate classes taught by tenured faculty. About 35% of teaching faculty are female.

Student Body. About 70% of students from in state; 81% Middle Atlantic, 8% Midwest, 2% each West, Northwest, 1% South, 6% foreign. An estimated 89% of students reported as Protestant, 5% Catholic, 6% unaffiliated; 2% as Black, 1% Hispanic, 8% Asian.

Religious Orientation. Northwestern is a church-related institution; 35% of students affiliated with the church; 8 semester hours of religious study required; attendance at chapel services 3 times weekly required of all students.

Varsity Sports. Men (NAIA, Div.II): Baseball, Basketball, Cross Country, Football, Golf, Soccer, Tennis, Track, Wrestling. Women (NAIA): Basketball, Cross Country, Golf, Soccer, Tennis, Track, Volleyball.

Campus Life. Current student describes the campus location as: "a small rural town, full of friendly people and a great Christian atmosphere. The quietness and tranquility provide a great atmosphere for Christian study and learning."

About 70% of men, 65% of women live in traditional dormitories; no coed dormitories; rest live in off-campus housing or commute. Freshmen given preference in college housing if all students cannot be accommodated. Intervisitation in men's and women's dormitory rooms limited. There are no fraternities or sororities on campus. About 25% of resident students leave campus on weekends.

Annual Costs. Tuition and fees, $9,000; room and board, $2,050; estimated $700 other, exclusive of travel. About 98% of students receive financial aid; average amount of assistance, $8,000. Assistance is typically divided 20% scholarship, 25% grant, 45% loan, 10% work. College reports unlimited scholarships awarded on the basis of academic merit alone, 400 for special talents alone, 50 for need alone. *Meeting Costs:* college offers institutional loans.

Northwestern College

Roseville, Minnesota 55113 (612) 631-5111

An interdenominational, Christian liberal arts college, all degrees include an emphasis on Bible along with the academic major. The 95-acre lake-shore campus is located in suburban St. Paul. Most convenient major airport: Minneapolis/St. Paul.

Founded: 1902
Affiliation: Independent
UG Enrollment: 521 M, 691 W (full-time); 16 M, 14 W (part-time)
Cost: $10K–$20K
% Receiving Financial Aid: 92%
Admission: Non-selective
Application Deadline: August 1

Admission. About 99% of applicants accepted, 58% of those actually enroll. Average freshman scores: SAT, 453 verbal, 489 mathematical; ACT, 21.8 composite. *Required:* SAT or ACT, essay, "evidence of the new birth in Christ, a vibrant Christian faith and walk and a willingness to subscribe to the ideals and patterns of life and conduct of the college." Criteria considered in admissions, in order of importance: Christian commitment, recommendations, high school academic record, standardized test scores, writing sample, extracurricular activities. *Entrance programs:* early decision, midyear admission. About 25% of entering students from Christian parochial schools. *Apply* by August 1; rolling admissions. *Transfers* welcome; 124 enrolled 1993–94.

Academic Environment. Graduation requirements include 6–9 credits in English, 4 in speech, 12 in humanities, 16 in social sciences, 1–4 in computer, 3 in physical education, 12 in math/science. Degrees offered: associates, bachelors. *Majors offered* include international business with Japanese emphasis, children's ministry. About 40% of entering students graduate within four years; 71% of freshmen return for sophomore year. *Special programs:* study abroad, January Term: Holy Land Studies Tour of Israel, Christian College Coalition, American Studies program in Washington D.C., Latin American Studies program in Honduras. Adult programs: Focus 15 is adult degree completion program.

Undergraduate degrees conferred (167). 28% were in Education, 11% were in Theology, 11% were in Psychology, 10% were in Communications, 10% were in Business and Management, 8% were in Marketing and Distribution, 7% were in Visual and Performing Arts, 5% were in Social Sciences, 4% were in Business (Administrative Support), remainder in 4 other fields.

Graduates Career Data. About 82% of 1992–93 graduates employed. Fields typically hiring largest numbers of graduates include education, services industries, non-profit social service, banking, finance, insurance. Career Development Services include career assessment, placement services, career development skills and seminars.

Faculty. About 45% of faculty hold PhD or equivalent. About 12% of teaching faculty are female; 1% minority.

Student Body. About 67% of students from in state; 25% Midwest, 2% Northwest, 1% each New England, South, West, 3% foreign. An estimated 98% of students reported as Protestant, 2% Catholic.

Religious Orientation. College is a non-denominational Christian institution; 42 denominations represented; 45 quarter credits of religious study required.

Varsity Sports. Men (Div.I): Baseball, Basketball, Cross Country, Football, Golf, Soccer, Tennis, Track. Women (Div.I): Basketball, Cross Country, Soft ball, Track, Volleyball.

Campus Life. About 58% of men, 74% of women live in traditional dormitories; rest commute. There are no fraternities or sororities on campus. About 40% of resident students leave campus on weekends.

Annual Costs. Tuition and fees, $10,554; room and board, $2,895; estimated $1,500 other. About 92% of students receive financial aid; average amount of assistance, $6,900. Assistance is typically divided 70% scholarship, 28% grant, 2% loan. College reports 25–30 scholarships awarded on the basis of music talents alone.

Northwestern Oklahoma State University

Alva, Oklahoma 73717 (405) 327-1700

A state-supported college, located in a town of 8,000, 170 miles northwest of Oklahoma City.

Founded: 1897
Affiliation: State
UG Enrollment: 541 M, 632 W (full-time); 185 M, 266 W (part-time)
Total Enrollment: 1,896
Cost: < $10K
% Receiving Financial Aid: 75%
Admission: Non-selective
Application Deadline: two weeks prior to beginning of semester

Admission. Graduates of accredited high schools eligible; 94% of applicants accepted, 88% of those actually enroll. *Required:* SAT or ACT. Criteria considered in admission: high school academic record and standardized test scores. *Out-of-state* freshman applicants: university actively seeks students from out-of-state. No special requirements for out-of-state applicants. States from which most out-of-state students are drawn include Kansas. *Apply* at least two weeks prior to beginning of semester. *Transfers* welcome; 157 enrolled 1993–94.

Academic Environment. Degrees offered: bachelors, masters. Graduation requirements include 19 hours in communications and humanities, 15 hours in social and behavioral sciences, 11 hours in math and natural sciences, 9 hours in practical arts. Average undergraduate class size: 51% under 20, 38% 20–40, 11% over 40.

About 26% of entering students graduate eventually; 58% of freshmen return for sophomore year. *Special programs:* 3–2 in physical therapy, occupational therapy. *Calendar:* semester, summer school.

Undergraduate degrees conferred (218). 25% were in Education, 21% were in Business and Management, 8% were in Health Sciences, 8% were in Protective Services, 6% were in Social Sciences, 6% were in Psychology, 6% were in Agribusiness and Agricultural Production, 3% were in Public Affairs, 3% were in Communications, 3% were in Life Sciences, 3% were in Letters, remainder in 8 other fields.

Graduates Career Data. About 62% of registered 1992–93 graduates employed. Fields typically hiring largest numbers of graduates include education, accounting, business administration, computers. Career Development Services offers job search skills, seminars, and career education classes.

Faculty. About 42% of faculty hold PhD or equivalent. About 23% of undergraduate classes taught by tenured faculty. About 39% of teaching faculty are female.

Student Body. About 86% of students from in state. An estimated 3% of students are reported as Black, 2% Hispanic, 3% Native American. Average age of undergraduate student: 25.

Varsity Sports. Men: Baseball, Basketball, Football, Rodeo, Tennis, Track. Women: Basketball, Rodeo, Tennis, Track.

Campus Life. About 41% of men, 25% of women live in traditional dormitories; no coed dormitories; rest live in off-campus housing or commute. No intervisitation in men's or women's dormitory rooms. There is 1 fraternity, 1 sorority on campus.

Annual Costs. Tuition and fees, $1,468 (out-of-state, $3,668); room and board, $1,956; estimated $1,000 other, exclusive of travel.

About 75% of students receive financial aid; average amount of assistance, $4,800. Assistance is typically divided 5% scholarship, 35% grant, 45% loan, 15% work.

Northwestern State University of Louisiana

Natchitoches, Louisiana 71497 **(318) 357-4503**

A state-supported university, located in a town of 17,000, 75 miles southeast of Shreveport.

Founded: 1884
Affiliation: State
UG Enrollment: 2,294 M, 3,450 W (full-time); 681 M, 1,286 W (part-time)
Total Enrollment: 8,552
Cost: < $10K
Admission: Non-selective
Application Deadline: August 1

Admission. Graduates of approved high schools eligible; others admitted by examination; 99% of applicants accepted, 62% of those actually enroll. Average freshman ACT scores: 19.7 M, 19.2 W composite. *Required:* ACT. Criteria considered in admissions: high school diploma; open-admissions by state law. *Out-of-state* freshman applicants: university actively seeks out-of-state students. State does not limit out-of-state enrollment. No special requirements for out-of-state students; 488 out-of-state students enrolled 1993–94. States from which most out-of-state students are drawn include Texas, Arkansas, Florida, Mississippi. *Entrance programs:* early admission, midyear admission. *Apply* by August 1; rolling admissions. *Transfers* welcome; 804 enrolled 1993–94.

Academic Environment. Graduation requirements include 12 semester hours in communication, 6 in mathematics, 9 in social sciences, including 3 in American history, 9 in natural sciences, 6 in fine arts, 4 in personal fitness. Degrees offered: associates, bachelors, masters. The Louisiana Scholar's College offers academically talented students a selective admissions liberal arts school within the university. Average undergraduate class size: 11% under 20, 52% 20–40, 37% over 40. Special program: CLEP, study abroad, 3–2 in business, 3–2 in psychology. *Doctoral degrees:* Education 5. *Calendar:* semester, summer school.

Undergraduate degrees conferred (605). 22% were in Business and Management, 19% were in Health Sciences, 15% were in Education, 7% were in Liberal/General Studies, 5% were in Social Sciences, 4% were in Communications, 3% were in Public Affairs, 3% were in Computer and Engineering Related Technology, 3% were in Engineering and Engineering Related Technology, 3% were in Psychology, remainder in 11 other fields.

Graduates Career Data. Advanced studies pursued by 18% of graduates. Medical schools typically enrolling largest numbers of graduates include LSU; dental schools include LSU, U. of Texas; law schools include LSU; Loyola, Tulane; business schools include LSU, Louisiana, Tulane. About 81% of 1992–93 graduates employed. Fields typically hiring largest numbers of graduates include hospitals, school systems, IBM.

Faculty. About 71% of faculty hold PhD or equivalent. About 63% of undergraduate classes taught by tenured faculty.

Student Body. About 94% of students from in state; 96% South, 1% each West, Midwest, Middle Atlantic, less than 1% foreign. Average age of undergraduate student: 25.

Varsity Sports. Men (Div.I): Baseball, Basketball, Cross Country, Football, Golf, Track. Women (Div.I): Basketball, Cross Country, Softball, Tennis, Track, Volleyball.

Campus Life. About 32% of men, 39% of women live in traditional dormitories; 62% each commute. There are 6 fraternities, 6 sororities on campus, which about 21% of men, 26% of women join; 6% of men live in fraternities. About 85% of resident students leave campus on weekends.

Annual Costs. Tuition and fees, $2,071 (out-of-state, $4,081); room and board, estimated $1,350 other, exclusive of travel. University reports 1,329 scholarships awarded on basis of academic merit alone, 632 for special talents alone, 745 for need alone. *Meeting Costs:* university offers Academic Management Service.

Northwestern University

Evanston, Illinois 60208 **(708) 491-7271**

Northwestern is one of two outstanding national universities in the Chicago area (the other is the University of Chicago). Most of the university is located on a 180-acre campus on the shores of Lake Michigan. The Evanston campus houses the university's 6 undergraduate schools, the graduate school, and the Graduate School of Management. Other graduate professional schools are located on the 14-acre Chicago campus. The university's main campus is about 12 miles north of Chicago. Most convenient major airport: O'Hare International (Chicago).

Founded: 1851
Affiliation: Independent
Total Enrollment: 14,764
Cost: $10K–$20K
% Receiving Financial Aid: 60%
Admission: Highly (+) Selective
Application Deadline: January 1

Admission is highly (+) selective for College of Arts and Sciences, Technological Institute, Medill School of Journalism, highly selective for schools of Music, Speech, very selective for School of Education. For all schools, 46% of applicants accepted, 35% of these actually enroll; 94% of freshmen graduate in top fifth of high school class, 99% in top two-fifths. Average freshman scores, according to most recent data available: SAT, middle 50% range, 530–640 verbal, 610–710 mathematical; 88% of freshmen score above 500 on verbal, 43% above 600, 6% above 700; 96% score above 500 on mathematical, 77% above 600, 32% above 700; ACT, 27–31 composite.

For Arts and Sciences (2,016 M, 2,023 W), 47% of applicants accepted, 30% of these actually enroll; 97% of freshmen graduate in top fifth of high school class, 99% in top two-fifths. Average freshman scores, according to most recent data available: SAT, 510–640 verbal, 610–720 mathematical; 95% of freshmen score above 500 on verbal, 64% above 600, 15% above 700; 99% score above 500 on mathematical, 89% above 600, 78% above 700; ACT, 27–31 composite.

For Journalism (175 M, 417 W), 42% of applicants accepted, 48% of these actually enroll; 98% of freshmen graduate in top fifth of high school class, all in top two-fifths. Average freshman scores, according to most recent data available: SAT, 520–660 verbal, 570–690 mathematical; 99% of freshmen score above 500 on verbal, 74% above 600, 23% above 700; 97% score above 500 on mathematical, 80% above 600, 38% above 700; ACT, 27–31 composite.

For Music (170 M, 170 W), 54% of applicants accepted, 51% of these actually enroll; 28% of freshmen graduate in top fifth of high school class, 50% in top two-fifths, according to most recent data available.

For Speech (403 M, 614 W), 40% of applicants accepted, 57% of these actually enroll; 32% of freshmen graduate in top fifth of high school class, 53% in top two-fifths, according to most recent data available.

For Technological Institute (816 M, 284 W), 61% of applicants accepted, 31% of these actually enroll; 51% of freshmen graduate in top fifth of high school class, 71% in top two-fifths, according to most recent data available.

For Education (106 M, 149 W), 32% of applicants accepted, 58% of these actually enroll; 28% of freshmen graduate in top fifth of high school class, 52% in top two-fifths, according to most recent data available.

Required: SAT or ACT; 3 ACH recommended for all candidates, required for honors programs; interview recommended; audition for music. *Non-academic factors* considered in admissions: diverse student body, special talents, alumni children. *Entrance programs:* early action, deferred admission, advanced placement. About 15% of entering students from private schools, 10% from parochial schools. *Apply* by January 1. *Transfers* welcome.

Academic Environment. Students participate in decision making and program of course and teacher evaluation. Student academic capability varies somewhat among the 6 undergraduate colleges, as does the pressure for academic achievement. The pressures appear to be greatest at the Medill School of Journalism, the Technical Institute, and in Arts and Sciences. *Undergraduate studies* offered by 6 schools listed above. *Majors offered* include African-American studies, American culture, anthropology, Asian studies, astronomy, communication sciences and disorders, computers in the Arts & Sciences, geography, international studies, Jewish studies, journalism, linguistics, radio/TV/film, theatre, urban studies; student designed majors, an interdisciplinary program in integrated arts.

About 86% of students entering as freshmen graduate eventually; 94% of freshmen return for sophomore year. *Special programs:* independent study, study abroad, honors, undergraduate research, 3-year degree, individualized majors, urban studies, cooperative work/study program in engineering, student-organized seminar, integrated science program, BA/BM in liberal arts/music, 5-year BM/BS in music/electrical engineering or computer science, 3–2 in management, 7-year honors program in medicine, BS/DDS for biomedical engineers, 5-year BS/Master of Urban and Regional Planning, other combined degree programs in variety of disciplines, BS/MM with Kellogg Graduate School, BS/PHD in research, Junior Tutorial Program. *Calendar:* quarter, summer school.

Undergraduate degrees conferred (2,068). 29% were in Social Sciences, 12% were in Engineering, 12% were in Letters, 10% were in Communications, 9% were in Visual and Performing Arts, 4% were in Allied Health, 4% were in Psychology, 3% were in Life Sciences, 3% were in Public Affairs, remainder in 11 other fields.

Graduates Career Data. According to most recent data available, full-time graduate or professional study pursued after graduation by 75% of students. Medical schools typically enrolling largest numbers of graduates include Northwestern, U. of Chicago, Washington U., U. of Illinois; law schools include Harvard, U. of Michigan, Northwestern, Georgetown. *Careers in business and industry* pursued by 60% of graduates. Corporations typically hiring largest numbers of graduates include IBM, Arthur Andersen, General Motors, Dow.

Faculty. All faculty hold PhD or equivalent.

Student Body. About 29% of students from in state; 64% Midwest, 15% Middle Atlantic, 5% West, 9% South, 4% New England. An estimated 36% of students reported as Protestant, 26% Catholic, 11% Jewish, 18% unaffiliated, 9% other; 8% as Black, 2% Hispanic, 12% Asian, according to most recent data available. *Minority group students:* "special counseling for students as regards academic, social, and financial aspects of Northwestern attendance.

Varsity Sports. Men (Div.I): Baseball, Basketball, Fencing, Football(IA), Golf, Soccer, Swimming/Diving, Tennis, Wrestling. Women (Div.I): Basketball, Fencing, Field Hockey, Lacrosse, Softball, Swimming/Diving, Tennis, Volleyball.

Campus Life. Students report that the proximity to Chicago provides "a wide variety of activities to chose from." They also note that Evanston "is very quiet" and "not very conducive to student life." While the usual student theatre productions, sporting events, and fraternity/sorority interests are reported as popular, on the whole, students agree that the campus social life is quiet, and geared towards small groups of friends. In addition, however, they also agree that "The administration is wonderful, the faculty is top-notch, the campus is beautiful, and the overall experience at Northwestern is fabulous!" Freshmen not allowed cars and are required to live in university residences. Beer and wine for those over 21 allowed in dormitory rooms and at approved campus functions.

About 54% of men, 58% of women live in traditional or coed dormitories; 26% of men, 26% of women live in off-campus housing or commute. Freshmen given preference in college housing if all students cannot be accommodated. Sexes segregated in coed dormitories either by wing, floor, or room. There are 24 fraternities, 12 sororities on campus which about 39% of men, 39% of women join; 20% of men, 16% of women live in fraternities and sororities. About 3–5% of resident students leave campus on weekends.

Annual Costs. Tuition and fees, $15,804; room and board, $5,289. About 60% of students receive financial aid; assistance is typically divided 73% grant/scholarship, 20% loan, 7% work. University reports scholarships awarded only on the basis of need. *Meeting Costs:* university offers Parent/Student Loan Program.

Northwood Institute—Midland Campus

Midland, Michigan 48640

(517) 837-4273
(800) 457-7878

An independent, professional institution, specializing in business administration and management, located in a city of 40,000, 140 miles from Detroit. Most convenient major airport: Tri-City (Freeland, MI).

Founded: 1959
Affiliation: Independent
UG Enrollment: 970 M, 800 W (full-time)
Cost: < $10K
% Receiving Financial Aid: 70%
Admission: Non-selective
Application Deadline: Rolling

Admission. High school graduates with C average or SAT of 450 verbal, 450 mathematical or ACT of 18 composite eligible; 96% of applicants accepted, 42% of these actually enroll. Average freshman scores, according to most recent data available: ACT, 17 M, 19 W composite, 15 M, 17 W mathematical. *Required:* SAT or ACT. *Apply:* rolling admissions. *Transfers* welcome.

Academic Environment. Graduation requirements include general education courses totalling 40% of the first two years of study. Degrees offered: associates, bachelors, masters. *Majors offered* include advertising, automotive marketing, computer information management, fashion marketing and merchandising, hotel and restaurant management, management marketing. Average undergraduate class size: 26. About 50% of entering students graduate eventually; 70% of freshmen return for sophomore year. *Special programs:* CLEP, independent study, study abroad. Adult programs: degree program for mature working adults. *Calendar:* quarter, summer school.

Undergraduate degrees conferred (209). 100% were in Business and Management.

Graduates Career Data. According to most recent data available, careers in business and industry pursued by 94% of graduates. Corporations typically hiring largest numbers of graduates include Tenneco, JC Penney, EDS.

Faculty. About 90% of faculty hold PhD or equivalent.

Student Body. About 60% of students from in state; 6% foreign.

Varsity Sports. Men (NAIA Div.I): Baseball, Basketball, Cross Country, Football, Golf, Lacrosse, Tennis, Outdoor Track & Field. Women (NAIA Div.I): Basketball, Cross Country, Softball, Tennis, Track & Field, Volleyball.

Campus Life. About 65% of students live on campus; rest live in off-campus housing or commute. Freshmen given preference in college housing if all students cannot be accommodated. Intervisitation in men's and women's dormitory rooms limited. There are 9 fraternities, 3 sororities on campus which about 25% of students join. About 65% of resident students leave campus on weekends.

Annual Costs. Tuition and fees, $9,113; room and board, $4,272. About 70% of students receive financial aid; assistance is typically divided 70% scholarship, 27% loan, 3% work. Institute reports some scholarships awarded on the basis of academic merit alone.

Norwich University

Northfield, Vermont 05663 (802) 485-2001

Norwich University consists of two student bodies and operates from two campuses. Members of the Corps of Cadets are enrolled in The Military College of Vermont, the first private military college in the U.S., located in Northfield, Vermont. All other University students are members of the Vermont College student body on the campus in Montpelier. Members of either student body may enroll in any academic program on either campus. Men and women in the Corps of Cadets are required to enroll in ROTC course work for four years.

The University also offers undergraduate and graduate programs for adult learners requiring limited or no residency on campus. Most convenient major airport: Burlington International.

Founded: 1819
Affiliation: Independent
Total Enrollment: 2,484
Cost: $10K–$20K
Admission: Non-selective
Application Deadline: July 1

Admission. Graduates of recognized high schools eligible; 86% of applicants accepted, 32% of these actually enroll; 23% of freshmen graduate in top fifth of high school class, 46% in top two-fifths. *Required:* SAT or ACT. *Non-academic factors* considered in admissions: special talents, alumni children, diverse student body, leadership potential. *Entrance programs:* early decision, early admission, midyear admission, deferred admission, advanced placement. About 14% of entering students from private schools, 13% from parochial schools. *Apply* by July 1. *Transfers* welcome.

Academic Environment. Administration reports 90% of general education courses required for AB are elective; distribution requirements fairly numerous. *Degrees:* AB, BS, BET. *Majors offered* business administration, computer science, education, engineering, hotel administration, peace war and diplomacy studies, nursing.

About 64% of students entering as freshmen graduate eventually; 82% of freshmen return for sophomore year. *Special programs:* CLEP, independent study, area studies, 5-year AB/BS program, Peace Corps preparatory program. *Calendar:* semester, summer school.

Undergraduate degrees conferred (403). 18% were in Liberal/General Studies, 13% were in Social Sciences, 12% were in Engineering, 12% were in Business and Management, 10% were in Protective Services, 9% were in Communications, 9% were in Health Sciences, 7% were in Education, remainder in 11 other fields.

Faculty. About 70% of faculty hold PhD or equivalent.

Student Body. About 20% of students from in state; 65% New England, 22% from Middle Atlantic, according to most recent data available.

Varsity Sports. Men (NCAA,Div.II): Baseball, Basketball, Cross Country, Football, Hockey, Lacrosse, Skiing, Soccer, Swimming, Rifle, Track, Wrestling. Women (NCAA,Div.II): Basketball, Cross Country, Soccer, Swimming, Track.

Campus Life. Men and women enrolled in The Military College are members of the self-governing Cadet Corps and wear military uniforms until after the evening meal. Vermont College students participate in a separate Student Government Association. All cadets live in dormitories.

For both campuses, 36% of men, live in traditional dormitories; 60% of men, 36% of women live in coed dormitories; rest commute. Freshmen given preference in college housing if all students cannot be accommodated. There are no fraternities or sororities on campus. About 30% of resident students leave campus on weekends.

Annual Costs. Tuition and fees, $13,460; room and board, $5,270. University reports some scholarships awarded on the basis of academic merit alone. *Meeting Costs:* university offers Norwich Parent Loan, pre-payment plan, payment plan.

Notre Dame College

Manchester, New Hampshire 03104 (603) 669-4298

An independent, Catholic, liberal arts college, conducted by the Sisters of Holy Cross. Notre Dame, formerly a college for women, is now co-educational. College is located in the northern residential section of a city of 100,000. Most convenient major airports: Manchester, or Logan International (Boston).

Founded: 1950
Affiliation: Independent (Roman Catholic)
UG Enrollment: 102 M, 325 W (full-time); 85 M, 360 W (part-time)
Total Enrollment: 1,300
Cost: < $10K
% Receiving Financial Aid: 85%
Admission: Non-selective
Application Deadline: Rolling

Admission. High schools graduates with 16 academic units eligible; 85% of applicants accepted, 37% of these actually enroll. About 15% of freshmen graduate in top fifth of high school class, 40% in top two-fifths. Average freshman SAT scores: 440 verbal, 442 mathematical. *Required:* SAT, essay, one recommendation. Criteria considered in admission, in order of importance: high school academic record, standardized test scores, recommendations, extracurricular activities, writing sample. About 15% of entering students from private schools, 20% from parochial schools. *Entrance programs:* midyear admission, deferred admission, advanced placement. *Apply:* rolling admission. *Transfers* welcome; 60 enrolled 1993–94.

Academic Environment. Graduation requirements include 3 semesters of English, 2 each of science, foreign language, and history, 1 each of math, music, art, philosophy, and 2 of religious studies. Degrees offered: associates, bachelors, masters. *Majors offered* in addition to usual studies include commercial art, communications, early childhood education, learning disabilities, teaching English as a second language. Average undergraduate class size: 58% under 20, 40% 20–40, 2% over 40.

About 55% of entering students graduate eventually, 75% of freshmen return for sophomore year. *Special programs:* CLEP, independent study, study abroad, cross registration with New Hampshire Consortium, 3–2 in pre-pharmacy with Massachusetts College of Pharmacy, cooperative programs through NHCUC. Adult programs: Department of Continuing Education offers evening courses on 8-week terms. *Calendar:* semester, summer school.

Undergraduate degrees conferred (87). 48% were in Education, 14% were in Business and Management, 13% were in Psychology, 8% were in Precision Production, 7% were in Law, 3% were in Visual and Performing Arts, remainder in 4 other fields.

Graduates Career Data. Advanced studies pursued by 20% of graduates; 10% enter graduate school; 10% enter law school. About 90% of 1992–93 graduates employed. Fields typically hiring largest numbers of graduates include school systems, law firms. Career Development Services include SIGI Plus, workshops, resume writing and interviewing techniques, and on campus recruitment.

Faculty. About 40% of faculty hold PhD or equivalent. About 60% of teaching faculty are female; 2% Black, 3% other minority.

Student Body. About 60% of students from in state; 95% New England, 2% Middle Atlantic, 1% each Midwest, South, 1% foreign. An estimated 80% of students reported as Catholic, 16% Protestant, 2% Jewish, 2% other; 3% Black, 2% Hispanic, 1% Asian. Average age of undergraduate student: 23.

Religious Orientation. Notre Dame is an independent institution with a Catholic heritage; 80% of students affiliated with the church; 2 courses in philosophy and religious studies required of all students; daily religious exercises voluntary.

Varsity Sports. Men (NAIA): Basketball, Soccer. Women (NAIA): Basketball, Soccer.

Campus Life. About 30% of each men, women live in traditional dormitories; 10% each in coed dormitories; rest commute. Freshmen given preference in college housing if all students cannot be accommodated. Intervisitation in women's dormitory rooms limited. There are no fraternities or sororities on campus. About 15% of resident students leave campus on weekends.

Annual Costs. Tuition and fees, $9,320; room and board, $4,900; estimated $600 other, exclusive of travel. About 85% of students receive financial aid; average amount of assistance, $7,200. Assistance is typically divided 30% scholarship, 15% grant, 35% loan, 20% work. College reports 60 scholarships awarded on the basis of academic merit alone, 36 for athletic talents alone, varies for need alone. *Meeting Costs:* college offers monthly payment plan, discounts available for family members enrolled simultaneously, family of clergy.

Notre Dame College of Ohio

Cleveland, Ohio 44121 (216) 382-1680

A church-related, liberal arts college, Notre Dame College of Ohio is "committed to the specific educational needs of women and assists in the development of their individual gifts and talents." A Master of Education program is also open to men. College is located in a city of 750,900. Most convenient major airport: Cleveland.

Founded: 1922
Affiliation: Roman Catholic
UG Enrollment: 377 W (full-time); 373 W (part-time)
Total Enrollment: 794
Cost: < $10K
% Receiving Financial Aid: 83%
Admission: Non-selective
Application Deadline: Rolling

Admission. High school graduates with 15 units (11 in academic subjects) eligible; 78% of applicants accepted, 39% of these actually enroll; 20% of freshmen graduate in top fifth of high school class, 55% in top two-fifths. Average freshman scores: SAT, 443 verbal, 418 mathematical; ACT, 19 composite. *Required:* SAT or ACT, minimum high school GPA; interview recommended. Criteria considered in admission, in order of importance: high school academic record, writing sample, standardized test scores, extracurricular activities, recommendations; other factors considered: special talents, diverse student body. *Entrance programs:* early admission, midyear admission, advanced placement. About 36% of entering students from parochial schools. *Apply* by December 15, April 30; rolling admissions. *Transfers* welcome; 16 enrolled 1993–94.

Academic Environment. Graduation requirements include courses in written and oral communication, computer literacy, literature, fine arts, modern languages, health education/physical education, mathematics, science, world civilization, economics/history/psychology/sociology, philosophy, theology, and a senior seminar. Degrees offered: associates, bachelors, masters. Average undergraduate class size: 65% under 20, 25% 20–40, 10% over 40.

About 40% of students entering as freshmen graduate within four years, 65% of freshmen return for sophomore year. *Special programs:* study abroad, cross registration with John Carroll U., Cleveland State U., Ursuline, and colleges associated with Cleveland Commission on Higher Education, 3–2 in engineering. Adult programs: WECO (Weekend College) Earn a degree in four years by attending classes every other weekend. *Calendar:* semester.

Undergraduate degrees conferred (110). 67% were in Business and Management, 6% were in Psychology, 5% were in Home Economics, 4% were in Life Sciences, 4% were in Foreign Languages, 3% were in Visual and Performing Arts, 3% were in Letters, 3% were in Education, 3% were in Communications, remainder in 2 other fields.

Graduates Career Data. Advanced studies pursued by 15% of graduates; 6% enter graduate school; 2% enter medical school; 1% enter law school; 2% enter business school. About 42% of 1992–93 graduates employed. Fields typically hiring largest numbers of graduates include business, education, health field, sciences. Career Development Services include career counseling, career/life planning, career and job market awareness, reality testing and decision making, workshops, for-credit Career Development course, career day, on campus recruitment.

Faculty. About 61% of full-time faculty hold PhD or equivalent. About 59% of teaching faculty are female; 3% Black, 3% other minority.

Student Body. About 98% of students from in state; 99% Midwest, less than 1% foreign. An estimated 48% of students reported as Catholic, 17% Protestant, 4% Jewish, 14% "not stated"; 27% Black, 2% Hispanic, 1% Asian, 1% other minority.

Religious Orientation. Notre Dame is a church-related institution; 3 theology courses required of students. Strong Campus Ministry program on campus.

Varsity Sports. Women (NAIA): Basketball, Softball, Volleyball.

Campus Life. About 55% of 18–22 year-old women live in dormitories; rest commute. No intervisitation in women's dormitory rooms. There are no sororities on campus.

Annual Costs. Tuition, $240 per undergraduate credit; room and board, $3,690; estimated $1,350 other, exclusive of travel. About 83% of students receive financial aid; average amount of assistance, $6,731. Assistance is typically divided 20% scholarship, 20% grant, 49% loan, 1% work. College reports 5 scholarships awarded on the basis of academic merit alone, 1 for special talents alone, 42 for need alone.

College of Notre Dame

Belmont, California 94002 (415) 508-3607

Notre Dame, an independent, co-educational, liberal arts college, aims "to assist the student to acquire a deeper understanding of Christianity in its Catholic interpretation." The 65-acre campus is located in a residential suburb of 23,700, 25 miles south of San Francisco. Most convenient major airport: San Francisco International.

Founded: 1851
Affiliation: Independent (Catholic)
UG Enrollment: 151 M, 349 W (full-time); 85 M, 246 W (part-time)
Total Enrollment: 1,641
Cost: $10K–$20K
% Receiving Financial Aid: 67%
Admission: Non-selective
Application Deadline: June 1

Admission. High school graduates with 13 academic units and GPA of 2.0 or higher eligible; about 76% of applicants accepted, 97% of these actually enroll. About 23% of freshmen graduate in top fifth of high school class, 62% in top two-fifths. Average freshman scores, middle 50% range: SAT, 380–470 verbal, 370–510 mathematical; ACT, 21 composite. *Required:* SAT or ACT, essay. Criteria considered in admissions, in order of importance: high school academic record, standardized test scores, recommendations, extracurricular activities, writing sample; other factors considered: special talents, alumni children. *Entrance programs:* deferred admission. About 39% of entering students from private or parochial schools. *Apply* by June 1; rolling admissions. *Transfers* welcome; 90 enrolled 1993–94.

Academic Environment. Students have voting representation at department meetings and on curriculum committee. Graduation requirements include 6 units each of English, Western Civilization, foreign language/foreign culture, religious studies, and 3 units each of behavioral science, natural sciences, mathematics, computer science, art/music/theater, and philosophy. Career Development requirement mandated for all students seeking baccalaureate degree. Students report small classes and individual attention from faculty are strengths of the academic program. Degrees offered: bachelors, masters. *Majors offered* include business administration, environmental studies, interior design, human services/human services administration, computer science, education, home economics, theater arts, liberal studies, humanities, communication. Average undergraduate class size: 10–15.

About 50% of students entering as freshmen graduate within four years; 80% of freshmen return for sophomore year. *Special programs:* CLEP, independent study, study abroad, undergraduate research (for biology), optional January interterm, cross registration with sister colleges Emmanuel (Boston, MA) and Trinity (Washington D.C.), 3–2 engineering, work internships in environmental science, psychology, social welfare. Adult Program: intensive adult evening degree programs. *Calendar:* semester, summer school.

Undergraduate degrees conferred (132). 37% were in Business and Management, 10% were in Social Sciences, 10% were in Liberal/General Studies, 9% were in Visual and Performing Arts, 7% were in Psychology, 6% were in Letters, 5% were in Communications, 4% were in Multi/Interdisciplinary Studies, 4% were in Life Sciences, 3% were in Computer and Engineering Related Technology, remainder in 5 other fields.

Graduates Career Data. According to most recent data available, full-time graduate or professional study pursued immediately after graduation by 39% of students; 6% enter law school. *Careers in business and industry* pursued by 41% of graduates.

Faculty. About 85% of faculty hold PhD or equivalent. About 62% of teaching faculty are female.

Student Body. About 75% of students from in state; 15% foreign. An estimated 50% of students reported as Catholic; 6% as Black, 12% Hispanic, 17% Asian. *Minority group students:* special financial and academic provisions. Average age of undergraduate student: 24.

Religious Orientation. Notre Dame is an independent institution with ties to the Catholic Church; 2 courses in religious studies required but may be "nondenominational, Christian, non-Christian, or Roman Catholic.

Varsity Sports. Men (Div.II): Basketball, Cross Country, Soccer, Tennis, Track. Women (Div.II): Basketball, Cross Country, Softball, Tennis, Track, Volleyball.

Campus Life. Cars allowed; alcohol policies conform to state law. Coed dorms, limited intervisitation. Large commuter population is considerable influence on campus community. Student leader reports that social activities are limited on the small campus; those who desire more "must go out and create their own." About 37% of students live on campus; rest commute. Freshmen given preference in college housing if all students cannot be accommodated. Sexes segregated in coed dormitories by floor. There are no fraternities or sororities on campus. About 50% of resident students leave campus on weekends.

Annual Costs. Tuition and fees, $11,750; room and board $5,600. About 67% of students receive financial aid; assistance is typically divided 40% scholarship, 49% loan, 11% work. College reports 56 scholarships awarded on the basis of academic merit alone. *Meeting Costs:* college offers payment plan.

College of Notre Dame of Maryland

Baltimore, Maryland 21210 (301) 532-5332

The first Catholic college for women in the U.S., Notre Dame of Maryland is now a private, liberal arts college under the auspices of the School Sisters of Notre Dame. The 62-acre campus is located in the northern suburbs of Baltimore. Most convenient major airport: Baltimore-Washington International.

Founded: 1848
Affiliation: Roman Catholic
Total Enrollment: 2,647
Cost: $10K–$20K
% Receiving Financial Aid: 65%
Admission: Non-selective
Application Deadline: February 15

Admission. About 79% of applicants accepted, 48% of these actually enroll. Average freshman scores, according to most recent data available: SAT, 473 verbal, 495 mathematical. *Required:* SAT or ACT, interview. *Entrance programs:* early decision, midyear admission, deferred admission, advanced placement. About 3% of entering students from private schools, 29% from parochial schools. *Apply* by February 15. *Transfers* welcome.

Academic Environment. Proximity to Johns Hopkins, Loyola, and other area colleges enables Notre Dame to arrange cooperative exchange programs. Administration reports 42% of courses required for graduation are elective; distribution requirements fairly numerous. *Degree:* AB. *Majors offered* include business, computer science, education, communications arts; interdisciplinary majors available; speech pathology and nursing through cooperative programs.

About 77% of students entering as freshmen return for sophomore year. *Special programs:* CLEP (continuing education students only), independent study, internships, study abroad, honors, 3-year degree, individualized majors, interdisciplinary program in art, English, and consumer studies, pre-professional programs in law, medicine, nursing, and pharmacy, 3–2 engineering, cooperative arrangements with 5 nearby institutions. Adult programs: Weekend College, Continuing Education Program. *Calendar:* 4–1–4.

Undergraduate degrees conferred (308). 25% were in Business and Management, 9% were in Health Sciences, 9% were in Communications, 9% were in Public Affairs, 8% were in Multi/Interdisciplinary Studies, 6% were in Psychology, 6% were in Social Sciences, 5% were in Life Sciences, 5% were in Visual and Performing Arts, 5% were in Education, 4% were in Letters, 3% were in Computer and Engineering Related Technology, remainder in 4 other fields.

Graduates Career Data. According to most recent data available, full-time graduate or professional study pursued immediately after graduation by 16% of students; 1% enter medical school; 2% enter law school; 2% enter business school. Medical schools typically enrolling largest numbers of graduates include U. of Maryland; law schools include U. of Maryland, U. of Baltimore; business schools include Johns Hopkins, U. of Baltimore. *Careers in business and industry* pursued by 40% of graduates. Corporations typically hiring largest numbers of graduates include MCI, USF&G, Maryland banks.

Faculty. About 55% of faculty hold PhD or equivalent.

Student Body. About 70% of students from in state; 95% Middle Atlantic. An estimated 12% of students reported as Black, 4% Hispanic, 3% Asian. *Minority group students:* scholarship aid.

Religious Orientation. Notre Dame of Maryland is a church-related institution; 2 courses in theology required of all Catholic students.

Varsity Sports. Women (Div.II): Basketball, Field Hockey, Lacrosse, Soccer, Swimming, Tennis, Volleyball.

Campus Life. Students have some influence on decisions governing campus social life. No curfew, alcoholic beverages permitted those over 21. Limited intervisitation on weekend afternoons and evenings.

About 66% of women live in dormitories; rest commute. Freshmen given preference in college housing if all students cannot be accommodated. There are no sororities on campus. About 35% of resident students leave campus on weekends.

Annual Costs. Tuition and fees, $10,650; room and board, $5,400. About 65% of students receive financial aid. College reports some scholarships awarded on the basis of academic merit alone.

University of Notre Dame

Notre Dame, Indiana 46556-5602 (219) 631-7505

Notre Dame, a nationally known university with Roman Catholic sponsorship, has been coed since 1972. Its founding order, the Congregation of the Holy Cross, is still a strong factor in governance of the university, although lay members of the board of trustees, alumni, and students share increasingly in decision making. The 1,250-acre campus is located just north of South Bend (pop. 125,600), 90 miles east of Chicago. Most convenient major airport: Michiana Regional (South Bend).

Founded: 1842
Affiliation: Independent (Roman Catholic)
UG Enrollment: 4,500 M, 3,100 W (full-time)
Total Enrollment: 9,900
Cost: $10K–$20K
% Receiving Financial Aid: 65%
Admission: Highly Selective
Application Deadline: Jan. 6

Admission is highly selective. About 48% of applicants accepted, 51% of these actually enroll; 94% of freshmen graduate in top fifth of high school class, 98% in top two-fifths. Average freshman SAT scores: 87% of freshmen score above 500 on verbal, 39% above 600, 5% above 700; 97% score above 500 on mathematical, 78% above 600, 30% above 700. *Required:* SAT or ACT, essay, "strong high school curriculum". Criteria considered in admission: high school academic record ranks as most important, standardized test scores, writing sample, and recommendations rank equally as second most important criteria; other factors considered: extracurricular activities, special talents, alumni children, diverse student body. *Entrance programs:* early action, deferred admission, advanced placement. About 7% of entering students from private schools, 38% from parochial schools. *Apply* by January 6. *Transfers* welcome; 150 enrolled 1993–94.

Academic Environment. Degrees offered: bachelors, masters, doctoral. Pressures for academic achievement are strong but not overwhelming. All freshmen take a common course of study, with slight variations, and choose the particular college they will attend at the beginning of their sophomore year. (These are colleges of Arts and Letters, School of Architecture, Business Administration, Engineering, Science.) Graduation requirements include courses in English, mathematics, science, social science, philosophy, theology. Notre Dame offers excellent opportunities for scholarship for capable students. The university is determined to raise the quality and status of Catholic higher education in the U.S. To this end Notre Dame has created and filled more than four dozen endowed chairs as the beginning of a plan to fill some four dozen chairs. *Majors offered* in colleges of Arts and Letters and Science in addition to usual studies include communication arts, drama, liberal studies (Great Books), 3-year interdisciplinary general program; American studies/Black studies, area studies, urban studies may be carried as second major, accounting, international relations, pre-med, English, chemical engineering, Institute for International Peace Studies. Average undergraduate class size: 40% under 20, 30% 20–40, 30% over 40.

About 94% of students entering as freshmen graduate eventually; 97% of freshmen return for sophomore year. *Special programs:* independent study, study abroad, honors, undergraduate research, January Term, 3-year degree, 3–2 in engineering, 3–2 in arts and letters, cross registration with St. Mary's, internships, area programs (Soviet and East European, Latin American, West European, African), interdisciplinary Collegiate Seminar Program. *Calendar:* semester, summer school.

Undergraduate degrees conferred (1,908). 24% were in Business and Management, 20% were in Social Sciences, 12% were in Engineering, 7% were in Letters, 7% were in Health Sciences, 6% were in Area and Ethnic Studies, 5% were in Psychology, 4% were in Life Sciences, 3% were in Mathematics, 3% were in Liberal/General Studies, remainder in 6 other fields.

Graduates Career Data. Advanced studies pursued by 32% of graduates; 14% enter graduate school; 8% enter medical school; 9% enter law school; 1% enter business school. Medical schools typically enrolling largest numbers of graduates include Loyola, Northwestern, Georgetown; law schools include Notre Dame, Loyola U., Northwestern; business schools include Notre Dame, American U., Carnegie Mellon. Fields typically hiring significant numbers of graduates include accounting, engineering, business, community and military service. Career Development Services include career counseling available to all students.

Faculty. About 95% of faculty hold PhD or equivalent. About 66% of undergraduate classes taught by tenured faculty. About 15% of teaching faculty are female; 1% Black, 4% Hispanic, 7% other minority.

Student Body. About 9% of students from in state; 42% Midwest, 27% Northeast, 11% West, 10% South, 8% Southwest, 2% foreign. An estimated 85% of students reported as Catholic, 10% Protestant, 1% each Jewish, Muslim, unaffiliated, other; 4% Black, 6% Hispanic, 4% Asian, 3% other minority.

Religious Orientation. Notre Dame is an institution with a strong Catholic heritage, but governed by a predominantly lay board of trustees; 86% of students affiliated with the church; 6 hours of theology required of all students; religious services offered, but attendance not demanded.

Varsity Sports. Men (Div.I): Baseball, Basketball, Cross Country, Diving, Fencing, Football, Golf, Ice Hockey, Lacrosse, Soccer, Swimming, Tennis, Track. Women (Div.I): Basketball, Cross Country, Diving, Fencing, Soccer, Softball, Swimming, Tennis, Track, Volleyball.

Campus Life. Students have some influence on determining rules governing campus social life; however some student concern voiced about need for "more social space." Football remains a major interest on campus, but students concerned also with campus reform and wider social issues. Cars are permitted for all but freshmen. Visitation hours permitted 11 am to midnight Sunday–Thursday, to 2 am Friday and Saturday. Alcohol permitted for those over 21, however, intoxication is prohibited and no alcohol allowed on campus grounds. Possession, sale or use of illegal drugs will result in suspension or dismissal. Smoking not officially regulated. Permission to live off campus given after freshman year; Housing Office provides list of university-approved housing.

About 80% of men, 86% of women live in traditional dormitories; no coed dormitories; 20% of men, 14% of women live in off-campus housing. Freshmen given preference in college housing if all students cannot be accommodated. There are no fraternities or sororities on campus. About 10–15% of resident students leave campus on weekends.

Annual Costs. Tuition and fees, $16,000; room and board, $4,150; estimated $1,400 other, exclusive of travel. About 65% of students receive financial aid, average amount of assistance $9,000. Assistance is typically divided 35% scholarship, 32% loan, 32% work. University reports 50 scholarships awarded on the basis of special talents alone, varies for need alone. *Meeting Costs:* university offers tuition budget payment plans.

Nova University

Fort Lauderdale, Florida 33314 **(305) 475-7300**

A university offering career-oriented bachelors, masters, and doctoral degrees. The campus is located in a suburb of Fort Lauderdale. Most convenient major airport: Fort Lauderdale-Hollywood International.

Affiliation: Independent
UG Enrollment: 801 M, 1,236 W (full-time); 510 M, 931 W (part-time)
Total Enrollment: 12,109
Cost: < $10K
% Receiving Financial Aid: 90%
Admission: Non-selective
Application Deadline: Rolling

Admission. About 75% of freshman applicants accepted, 40% of these actually enroll. Average freshman SAT scores: 416 M, 438 W verbal, 486 M, 469 W mathematical. *Required:* SAT or ACT,. minimum 2.0 high school GPA. *Apply:* rolling admissions "year round". *Transfers* welcome; 494 enrolled 1993–94.

Academic Environment. Degrees offered: bachelors, masters, doctoral. Graduation requirements vary with student's major. Average undergraduate class size: 75% under 20, 24% 20–40, 1% over 40. About 50% of students entering as freshmen graduate eventually; 75% of freshmen return for sophomore year. *Special programs:* study abroad. Adult program: extensive career development program designed for working adults.

Undergraduate degrees conferred (828). 60% were in Business and Management, 30% were in Education, 5% were in Psychology, 3% were in Law, remainder in 4 other fields.

Graduates Career Data. Advanced studies pursued by 50% of graduates. Professional schools typically enrolling largest numbers of graduates include Nova U. Career Development Services include multi-service job placement and career counseling programs for all students.

Faculty. About 85% of faculty hold PhD or equivalent. About 29% of teaching faculty are female; 5% Black, 5% Hispanic, 2% other minority.

Student Body. About 87% of students from South, 3% Middle Atlantic, 1% each New England, Midwest, West, 7% foreign. An estimated 18% of students reported as Black, 18% Hispanic, 2% Asian, 3% other minority. Average age of undergraduate student: 22 in day programs; 33 in evening programs.

Varsity Sports. Men (NAIA): Baseball, Basketball, Cross Country, Soccer. Women (NAIA): Cross Country, Tennis, Volleyball.

Campus Life. About 5% of men, 3% of women live in coed dormitories; rest commute. There are 3 fraternities, 2 sororities on campus, which about 11% of each men, women join. About 95% of resident students leave campus on weekends.

Annual Costs. Tuition and fees, $8,100; room and board, $4,740; estimated $2,800 other, exclusive of travel. About 90% of students receive financial aid. Assistance is typically divided 2% scholarship, 17% grant, 80% loan, 1% work. University reports 115 scholarships awarded on basis of academic merit alone.

Nyack College

Nyack, New York 10960

A church-related institution, the college offers degree programs in the liberal arts, business, education, music, and professional religious vocations.

Founded: 1882
Affiliation: Christian and Missionary Alliance

Oakland City College

Oakland City, Indiana 47660

A private, liberal arts institution offering baccalaureate degrees in business and management, education, theology, biological sciences, fine and applied arts, physical sciences, interdisciplinary studies.

Affiliation: Baptist

Undergraduate degrees conferred (98). 23% were in Education, 19% were in Psychology, 14% were in Philosophy and Religion, 13% were in Social Sciences, 12% were in Letters, 8% were in Theology, 5% were in Liberal/General Studies, remainder in 2 other fields.

Oakland University

Rochester, Michigan 48309-4401 (313) 370-3360

Oakland University is an undergraduate institution with a substantial masters degree program in education and other fields. The university is located in a suburban community of 80,000, 25 miles north of Detroit. Most convenient major airport: Detroit Metropolitan.

Founded: 1957
Affiliation: State
UG Enrollment: 2,360 M, 4,081 W (full-time); 1,368 M, 2,614 W (part-time)
Total Enrollment: 12,895
Cost: < $10K
% Receiving Financial Aid: 35%
Admission: Non-selective
Application Deadline: July 1

Admission. High school graduates with minimum GPA of 2.5 eligible; 85% of applicants accepted, 45% of these actually enroll; 48% of entering freshmen graduate in top fifth of high school class, 89% in top two-fifths. Average freshman ACT scores: 23.8 M, 22.7 W composite. *Required:* ACT, minimum high school average. Criteria considered in admissions, in order of importance: high school academic record, standardized test scores, recommendations, extracurricular activities. *Out-of-state* freshman applicants: university actively seeks students from out-of-state. State does not limit out-of-state enrollment; 178 enrolled. States from which most out-of-state students are drawn include Ohio, California. About 16% of entering students from private and parochial schools. *Entrance programs:* advanced placement. *Apply* by July 1; rolling admissions. *Transfers* welcome; 1,150 enrolled 1993–94.

Academic Environment. Students select general education studies from an approved list of particular courses. *Undergraduate studies* offered by College of Arts and Sciences, schools of Education and Human Services, Business Administration, Engineering and Computer Science, Health Sciences and Nursing. Degrees offered: bachelors, masters, doctoral. *Majors offered* include anthropology, Chinese, computer science, education, Latin American studies. Average undergraduate class size: 42% under 20, 35% 20–40, 23% over 40.

About 67% of freshmen return for sophomore year. *Special programs:* CLEP, honors, independent study, study abroad, undergraduate research, individualized majors, student-organized courses. *Calendar:* modified trimester, Fall-Winter semesters, with split Spring-Summer sessions (each a half semester).

Undergraduate degrees conferred (1,628). 21% were in Business and Management, 12% were in Liberal/General Studies, 11% were in Health Sciences, 9% were in Communications, 8% were in Education, 8% were in Engineering, 7% were in Social Sciences, 6% were in Psychology, 5% were in Public Affairs, 4% were in Letters, 3% were in Life Sciences, remainder in 8 other fields.

Graduates Career Data. About 87% of 1992–93 graduates employed. Fields typically hiring largest numbers of graduates include business, engineering, computer industry, health institutions, education.

Faculty. About 87% of faculty hold PhD or equivalent. About 65% of undergraduate classes taught by tenured faculty. About 30% of teaching faculty are female; 6% Black, 2% Hispanic, 11% other minority.

Student Body. About 99% of students from in state; less than 1% foreign. An estimated 6% of students reported as Black, 1% Hispanic, 3% Asian, 5% other minority. *Minority group students:* special financial, academic, and social provisions. Average age of undergraduate student: 25.

Varsity Sports. Men (Div.II): Baseball, Basketball, Cross Country, Diving, Golf, Soccer, Swimming. Women (Div.II): Basketball, Cross Country, Diving, Golf, Swimming, Tennis, Volleyball.

Campus Life. A University Congress, of which students are the only voting members, has virtually complete control over campus social life. Regulations quite relaxed: no women's curfew, students determine their own intervisitation by floor or by hall ("most choose 24-hour open for 7 days/week"). Alcohol permitted in dormitory rooms; cars allowed.

About 10% of men, 11% of women live in coed dormitories; rest commute. Freshmen given preference in college housing if all students cannot be accommodated. There are 7 fraternities, 8 sororities on campus, which about 3% of men, 4% of women join. About 45% of resident students leave campus on weekends.

Annual Costs. Tuition and fees, $3,029 (out-of-state, $8,598); room and board, $3,890; estimated $650 other, exclusive of travel. About 35% of students receive financial aid; average amount of assistance, $3,000. Assistance is typically divided 5% scholarship, 52% grant, 39% loan, 4% work. University reports 110 scholarships awarded on the basis of special talents alone. *Meeting Costs:* university offers payment plans for room and board.

Oakwood College

Huntsville, Alabama 35896 (205) 726-7000

A church-related college, located in a city of 160,000; founded as a college for Negroes and still serving a predominantly Black student body.

Founded: 1896
Affiliation: Seventh-day Adventist
UG Enrollment: 547 M, 769 W (full-time); 66 M, 69 W (part-time)
Cost: < $10K
% Receiving Financial Aid: 60%
Admission: Non-selective
Application Deadline: Rolling

Admission. High school graduates (or nongraduates with 18 units from approved schools) with C average eligible; others given individual consideration; 64% of applicants accepted, 64% of these actually enroll. Average freshmen scores: SAT, 325 M, 331 W verbal; 352 M, 363 W mathematical; ACT, 16 M, 18 W composite. *Required:* SAT or ACT; minimum 2.0 high school GPA, recommendations. Criteria considered in admissions, in order of importance: high school academic record, recommendations, standardized test scores. About 46% of entering students from private school. *Entrance programs:* early decision. *Apply:* rolling admissions. *Transfers* welcome; 90 enrolled 1993–94.

Academic Environment. Degrees offered: associates, bachelors. About 39% of general education requirements for graduation are elective; distribution requirements fairly numerous. *Majors offered* include nursing, physical education, music performance. Average undergraduate class size: 68% under 20, 22% 20–40, 10% over 40. About 63% of freshmen return for sophomore year. *Special programs:* CLEP, study abroad, 2–3 in engineering, 3–2 in medical technology. *Calendar:* quarter, summer school.

Undergraduate degrees conferred (143). 22% were in Business and Management, 17% were in Life Sciences, 10% were in Theology, 8% were in Psychology, 5% were in Visual and Performing Arts, 5% were in Letters, 5% were in Education, 5% were in Communications, 4% were in Public Affairs, 3% were in Physical Sciences, 3% were in Multi/Interdisciplinary Studies, 3% were in Mathematics, 3% were in Home Economics, remainder in 5 other fields.

Faculty. About 52% of faculty hold PhD or equivalent. About 28% of undergraduate classes taught by tenured faculty. About 47% of teaching faculty are female; 86% Black, 5% other minority.

Student Body. About 18% of students from in state; 42% South, 21% Middle Atlantic, 11% Midwest, 9% West, 2% New England, 1% Northwest, 12% foreign. An estimated 88% of students reported as Black, 11% other minority.

Religious Orientation. Oakwood is a church-related institution; 16–22 hours of religion; attendance at five evening or morning worships per week expected of all residential students.

Campus Life. About 59% of men, 71% of women live in traditional dormitories; no coed dormitories; rest live in off-campus housing or commute. No intervisitation in men's or women's dormitory rooms. There are no fraternities or sororities on campus.

Annual Costs. Tuition and fees, $6,384; room and board, $3,846; estimated $1,800 other, exclusive of travel. About 60% of students receive financial aid. Assistance is typically divided 31% scholarship, 47% loan, 22% work. *Meeting Costs:* college offers The Tuition Plan, American Management Services.

Oberlin College

Oberlin, Ohio 44074 (800) 622-6243 (216) 775-8411

One of the nation's most esteemed, co-educational, liberal arts colleges, Oberlin is unique among its peers because in addition to a superior academic program it boasts a conservatory that is one of the most prestigious schools of music in the country. The first college in the country to admit women, Oberlin also was an early leader in the education of blacks. Abolitionists played a major role in Oberlin's early history, and students at Oberlin, which was once a stop on the Underground Railroad, retain a concern for social justice. The campus is located in the heart of a small community (pop. 8,000), 35 miles southwest of Cleveland. Most convenient major airport: Cleveland Hopkins.

Founded: 1833	**Cost:** $10K–$20K
Affiliation: Independent	**% Receiving Financial Aid:** 70%
UG Enrollment: 1,114 M, 1,469 W (full-time); 48 M, 38 W (part-time)	**Admission:** Highly (+) Selective
	Application Deadline: January 15

Admission is highly (+) selective for Arts & Sciences, highly selective for Conservatory. For both schools, 63% of applicants accepted, 25% of these actually enroll; 79% of entering freshmen graduate in top fifth of high school class; 99% in top two-fifths. Average freshman scores: SAT, 603 M, 596 W verbal; 650 M, 609 W mathematical; 90% of freshmen score above 500 on verbal, 53% above 600, 10% above 700; 95% score above 500 on mathematical, 65% above 600, 21% above 700; ACT, 28 composite.

For Arts and Sciences (1,068 M, 1,174 W f-t, 35 M, 30 W p-t): 54% of applicants accepted, 30% of these actually enroll; about 66% of freshmen graduate in top tenth of high school class, 88% in top fifth. Average freshman scores: SAT, 611 M, 611 W verbal, 658 M, 621 W mathematical; 90% of freshmen score above 500 on verbal, 57% above 600, 10% above 700; 93% score above 500 on mathematical, 72% above 600, 21% above 700. Required for Arts & Sciences: SAT or ACT, 3 ACH, interview strongly recommended.

For Conservatory (254 M, 273 W f-t, 7 M, 5 W p-t): 36% of applicants accepted, 44% of these actually enroll. College emphasizes that Conservatory students submit SATs, but "admission is based almost solely on a personal (or taped) audition on one's instrument for members of the faculty."

Required for Arts and Sciences: SAT or ACT, essay. Criteria considered in admissions, in order of importance: high school academic record, standardized test scores, recommendations, extracurricular activities, writing sample; other factors considered include special talents, alumni children, diverse student body. *Entrance programs:* early decision, early admission, midyear admission, advanced placement, deferred admission. About 33% of entering students from private and parochial schools. *Apply* by January 15. *Transfers* welcome; 56 enrolled 1993–94.

Academic Environment. High academic standards have led to international reputation for extraordinary number of graduates who have made significant contributions to teaching, sciences and research, the arts, the professions, and public life. Grading system offers students option of either A+ to C-/no entry or credit/no entry. Graduation requirements for Arts and Sciences students include certified completion of both writing and quantitative proficiency, and the requirements for major, 27 hours of distribution requirements, and a total of 112 credits. Conservatory students must complete the individual requirements for their major and earn 124 credit hours, of which 76 must be Conservatory courses and 24 Arts and Sciences courses. In addition, all students participate in three January winter terms, during which they pursue individual projects—traditional or unique—on or off-campus. All students share access to the curriculum, housing and dining accommodations, and social life. Students in either division may take courses in the other division, and many do. All students are advised by faculty member in department of major. Degrees offered: bachelors. About one-third of Conservatory students enroll in double-degree program, which requires admission to both Arts & Sciences and the Conservatory of Music. *Majors offered* in College of Arts & Sciences include anthropology, astronomy, black studies, classics, Chinese language and literature, creative writing, East Asian studies, environmental studies, Judaic and Near Eastern studies, neuroscience and biopsychology, and women's studies; interdisciplinary majors are offered in archaeological studies, comparative literature, Latin American studies, law and society, Soviet studies, and third world studies. Average undergraduate class size: 25–30.

About 84% of entering freshmen graduate eventually; 94% of freshmen return for sophomore year. *Special programs:* independent study, study abroad, honors, undergraduate research, individualized majors, archaeological summer field study, 3–2 in engineering, student run experimental college (EXCO) offers nontraditional courses taught by students, faculty, and townspeople with a particular expertise. Oberlin sponsors 5 study abroad programs and students have access to 20 programs sponsored by other institutions in 21 countries, plus numerous domestic off-campus programs. About 50% of each class spends at least one semester studying off-campus. *Calendar:* 4–1–4.

Undergraduate degrees conferred (764). 23% were in Social Sciences, 19% were in Visual and Performing Arts, 17% were in Letters, 11% were in Life Sciences, 6% were in Area and Ethnic Studies, 5% were in Physical Sciences, 4% were in Philosophy and Religion, 4% were in Foreign Languages, 3% were in Psychology, 3% were in Multi/Interdisciplinary Studies, remainder in 4 other fields.

Graduates Career Data. Advanced studies pursued by 33% of graduates. About 66% of 1992–93 graduates employed. Career Development Services include counseling, interviewing and internships.

Faculty. About 95% of faculty hold PhD or equivalent. About 72% of undergraduate classes taught by tenured faculty. About 30% of teaching faculty are female; 6% Black, 4% Hispanic, 7% Asian.

Student Body. About 10% of students from in state; 34% Middle Atlantic, 13% New England, 12% each West, Midwest, 11% South, 4% Northwest, 6% foreign. An estimated 8% of students reported as Black, 4% Hispanic, 9% Asian, 1% other minority. *Minority group students:* financial aid available; black studies, East Asian Studies, third world studies, Latin American studies; Afrikan Heritage House, Asia House, Third World House; various ethnic-related extracurricular activities.

Religious Orientation. An independent college, founded by Congregationalists, Oberlin has a Judeo-Christian tradition, but is nonsectarian and welcomes students of all faiths; makes no religious demands on students. Protestant, Catholic and Jewish chaplains on campus.

Varsity Sports. Men (Div.III): Baseball, Basketball, Cross Country, Diving, Football, Lacrosse, Soccer, Swimming, Tennis, Track. Women (Div.III): Basketball, Cross Country, Diving, Field Hockey, Lacrosse, Soccer, Swimming, Tennis, Track, Volleyball.

Campus Life. Administration characterizes student body as predominantly concerned with academic and artistic pursuits. No curfew; daily intervisitation hours specified by each living unit. Alcohol regulations conform to state law. Policy on drugs and alcohol stresses prevention of abuse through counseling. Smoking restricted to limited areas. Freshmen permitted to have cars only for critical medical reasons; other students must register vehicles with security department. Student-run co-ops for living and dining available. College provides an extraordinarily wide range of cultural, intellectual, and recreational activities. Music is a vital part of campus life and over 350 concerts take place on campus annually. Arts and Sciences students have numerous opportunities to participate in performances. Cleveland, 35 miles from campus, offers full range of cultural events.

About 90% of each men, women live in traditional dormitories; rest live in off-campus housing. Freshmen given preference in college housing if all students cannot be accommodated. Sexes segregated in coed dormitories by wing, floor, or room. There are no fraternities or sororities on campus. About 5–10% of resident students leave campus on weekends.

Annual Costs. Tuition and fees, $18,949; room and board, $5,620; estimated $1,000 other, exclusive of travel. About 70% of students receive financial aid; average amount of assistance, $17,250. Assistance is typically divided 69% grant, 23% loan, 8% work. College reports 100 scholarships awarded on basis of need alone. *Meeting Costs:* college offers Parent Loan Program, and deferred payment plan.

Occidental College

Los Angeles, California 90041 **(213) 259-2500**

A small, high-quality college of liberal arts and sciences, located in a major metropolitan area, Occidental affords students the luxury of a 120-acre college campus near the cultural resources of the city. Established by Presbyterians, it is now independent and nonsectarian. The campus is located in the residential northeast section of Los Angeles. Most convenient major airport: Burbank/Los Angeles International.

Founded: 1887
Affiliation: Independent
UG Enrollment: 729 M, 857 W (full-time); 18 M, 17 W (part-time)
Total Enrollment: 1,661
Cost: $10K–$20K
% Receiving Financial Aid: 70%
Admission: Highly Selective
Application Deadline: Jan. 15

Admission is highly selective. About 66% of applicants accepted, 24% of these actually enroll; 80% of freshmen graduate in top fifth of high school class, 94% in top two-fifths. Average freshman SAT scores: middle 50% range, 1,000–1,210 combined. *Required:* SAT or ACT, essay. About 32% of entering students from private and parochial schools. *Entrance programs:* early decision, early admission, advanced placement. *Apply* by January 15. *Transfers* welcome; 770 enrolled 1993–94.

Academic Environment. Administration and student sources report a mix of academic and career oriented goals among students. This "is a rigorous academic climate. Students study hard and play hard." Strongest academic programs reported to be pre-med (biology, chemistry), economics, diplomacy and world affairs, political science, history and theater. Approach to general education allows students a high degree of flexibility in creating individual curricular programs. All qualified students encouraged to do independent study in areas not covered by formal courses. Graduation requirements include 2 years of core classes in American, European, and World cultures. Degrees offered: bachelors, masters. *Majors offered* include anthropology, biochemistry, urban studies; interdepartmental majors in diplomacy and world affairs, geochemistry, cognitive science, public policy. Average undergraduate class size: 64% under 20, 28% 20–40, 8% over 40.

About 90% of freshmen return for sophomore year. *Special programs:* independent study, study abroad (term and year programs available), honors, undergraduate research, individualized majors, 3–2 in engineering, credit by examination, area studies (Asian, Hispanic, Latin American), marine biology, courses at CalTech. *Calendar:* 3–3, summer school.

Undergraduate degrees conferred (393). 37% were in Social Sciences, 11% were in Letters, 10% were in Life Sciences, 8% were in Psychology, 8% were in Visual and Performing Arts, 6% were in Physical Sciences, 5% were in Mathematics, 5% were in Philosophy and Religion, 3% were in Public Affairs, 3% were in Multi/Interdisciplinary Studies, 3% were in Foreign Languages, remainder in Area and Ethnic Studies.

Graduate Career Data. Advanced studies pursued by 22% of graduates; 13% enter graduate school; 4% enter medical school; less than 1% enter dental school; 4% enter law school. About 74% of 1992–93 graduates employed. Career Development Services available.

Faculty. About 93% of faculty hold PhD or equivalent. About 60% of undergraduate classes taught by tenured faculty. About 39% of teaching faculty are female; 5% Black, 7% Hispanic, 6% other minority.

Student Body. About 58% of students from in state; 3% foreign. An estimated 6% of students reported as 5% Black, 18% Hispanic, 17% Asian, 6% other minority. *Minority group students:* "recruitment and financing of minorities a college policy."

Varsity Sports. Men (Div.III): Baseball, Basketball, Cross Country, Diving, Football, Golf, Soccer, Swimming, Tennis, Track. Women (Div.III): Basketball, Cross Country, Diving, Golf, Soccer, Softball, Swimming, Tennis, Track, Volleyball.

Campus Life. Strongest element of student life appears to be residence hall system. All dormitories are coed with no restrictions on visitation. Freshmen required to live in college residence hall. Recent student leader reports "we have a lot of diverse interests among students and there is an underlying 'community' feeling." Cars allowed. College offers numerous opportunities for cultural and recreational activities both on campus and in surrounding communities. Downtown Los Angeles, 6 miles from campus, offers full range of cultural activities. Student body owns 2 vans to provide transportation for students on request.

About 71% each of men, women live in coed dormitories. Freshmen given preference in college housing if all students cannot be accommodated. Sexes segregated in coed dormitories by wing, floor or suite. There are 4 fraternities, 3 sororities on campus; 20% of each men, women join; 5% of each men, women live in fraternities and sororities.

Annual Costs. Tuition and fees, $16,182; room and board, $5,325; estimated $1,710 other, exclusive of travel. About 70% of students receive financial aid. Assistance is typically divided 60% scholarship, 25% loan, 15% work. *Meeting Costs:* college offers long term financing through Knight Insurance Company, and monthly payment plans.

Oglethorpe University

Atlanta, Georgia 30319
(404) 364-8307
(800) 428-4484

Oglethorpe is a small liberal arts college most of whose students come from the South, but it also draws substantial numbers from the Middle Atlantic states and North Central region. The campus is located in a metropolitan area of 3,000,000. Most convenient major airport: Hartsfield International (Atlanta).

Founded: 1835
Affiliation: Independent
UG Enrollment: 314 M, 446 W (full-time); 103 M, 285 W (part-time)
Total Enrollment: 1,215
Cost: $10K–$20K
% Receiving Financial Aid: 89%
Admission: Very Selective
Application Deadline: Aug. 1

Admission is very selective. About 82% of applicants accepted, 29% of these actually enroll; 77% of freshmen graduate in top fifth of high school class, 93% in top two-fifths. Average freshman scores: SAT, 549 verbal, 570 mathematical; 72% of freshmen score above 500 on verbal, 26% above 600, 1% above 700; 82% score above 500 on mathematical, 38% above 600, 7% above 700; ACT, 27 composite. *Required:* SAT or ACT. Criteria considered in admissions, in order of importance: high school academic record, standardized test scores, recommendations, extracurricular activities, special talents, writing sample. *Entrance programs:* early decision, early admission, midyear admission, deferred admission, advanced placement. About 17% of entering students from private schools, 8% from parochial schools. *Apply* by August 1; rolling admissions. *Transfers* welcome; 57 enrolled 1993–94.

Academic Environment. College has been working actively in recent years to attract students of greater academic capability, and its efforts have been successful. Increased academic competition is likely to be a consequence. Graduation requirements include courses that "examine ways of knowing" in writing, history, philosophy, interdisciplinary social sciences, psychology, fine arts, literature, mathematical or computer science problem solving, and physical and biological sciences. Degrees offered: bachelors, masters. *Majors offered* include business, education, medical technology, accounting, writing, pre-medicine. Average undergraduate class size: 70% under 20, 30% 20–40.

About 73% of students entering as freshmen graduate eventually; 83% of freshmen return for sophomore year. *Special programs:* CLEP, honors, undergraduate research, independent study, study abroad, individualized majors, 3–2 in engineering, 3–2 in art, cross registration with 17 schools in Atlanta area. Adult programs: Credit and non-credit programs offered nights and weekends in accounting, business administration, communications and liberal arts. *Calendar:* semester, summer school.

Undergraduate degrees conferred (197). 33% were in Business and Management, 18% were in Liberal/General Studies, 12% were in Social Sciences, 10% were in Psychology, 7% were in Letters, 7% were in Life Sciences, 6% were in Area and Ethnic Studies, 3% were in Philosophy and Religion, 3% were in Mathematics, 3% were in Education.

Graduates Career Data. Advanced studies pursued by 30% of graduates; 18% enter graduate school; 5% enter medical school; 2% enter dental school; 3% enter law school; 2% enter business school. Medical schools typically enrolling largest numbers of graduates include Emory U., Medical College of Georgia; dental schools include Emory U., Medical College of Georgia; law schools include Emory U., Georgia State, U. of Georgia; business schools include Georgia State U. About 60% of 1992–93 graduates employed. Fields typically hiring largest numbers of graduates include accounting firms, business, education. Career Development Services include resources for career exploration and career decision making.

Faculty. About 95% of faculty hold PhD or equivalent. About 64% of undergraduate classes taught by tenured faculty. About 30% of teaching faculty are female; 2% Black, 5% other minority.

Student Body. About 63% of students from in state; 24% South, 4% Middle Atlantic, 1% each New England, West, Northwest, 4% for-

eign. An estimated 43% of students reported as Protestant, 14% Catholic, 3% Jewish, 26% unaffiliated, 6% other; 7% Black, 2% Hispanic, 4% Asian, 6% other minority.
Varsity Sports. Men (Div.III): Baseball, Basketball, Cross Country, Golf, Soccer, Tennis, Track. Women (Div. III): Basketball, Cross Country, Soccer, Tennis, Track, Volleyball.
Campus Life. Student most likely to feel at home on campus, according to student leader, is "Yuppie oriented conservative." Administration source phrases it differently: "Academically qualified, involved in extracurricular activities, moderately affluent." High interest reported in both varsity and intramurals (most popular: basketball and volleyball). Basketball and soccer rated as most popular varsity sports. Another student reports "The Atlanta area provides and inexhaustible supply of options: everything from restaurants and clubs to museums, shopping, malls and amusement parks."

About 48% of men, 61% of women live in traditional and coed dormitories; 11% of men, 17% of women commute. Freshmen given preference in college housing if all students cannot be accommodated. Intervisitation in student rooms, Sunday–Thursday, 9 am–midnight; 9 am–2 am Friday, Saturday. There are 4 fraternities, 2 sororities on campus which about 41% of men, 22% of women join; 41% of men, 22% of women live in fraternities and sororities. About 50% of resident students leave campus on weekends.
Annual Costs. Tuition and fees, $11,990; room and board, $4,330; estimated $2,990 other, exclusive of travel. About 89% of students receive financial aid; average amount of assistance, $12,256. Assistance is typically divided 39% scholarship, 25% grant, 31% loan, 5% work. University reports 471 scholarships awarded on the basis of academic merit alone. *Meeting Costs:* university offers several financing options.

Ohio Dominican College

Columbus, Ohio 43219 **(614) 251-4500**

A church-related, liberal arts college, conducted by the Dominican Sisters, located in a city of 605,200. Most convenient major airport: Port Columbus.

Founded: 1911
Affiliation: Roman Catholic
UG Enrollment: 438 M, 626 W (full-time); 130 M, 400 W (part-time)
Cost: < $10K
% Receiving Financial Aid: 85%
Admission: Non-selective
Application Deadline: August 1

Admission. Graduates of accredited high schools with 16 units in academic subjects with GPA of 2.0 or better eligible; 20% of entering freshmen actually enroll. *Required:* SAT or ACT, interview for in-state students, minimum 2.0 high school GPA, essay. Criteria considered in admissions, in order of importance: high school academic record, standardized test scores, "curriculum and school", writing sample, extracurricular activities, recommendations. *Entrance programs:* midyear admission, deferred admission, advanced placement. *Apply* by August 1; rolling admissions. *Transfers* welcome; 173 enrolled 1993–94.
Academic Environment. Degrees offered: associates, bachelors. *Majors offered* include business administration, computer science, education, health administration, public relations, social welfare, criminal justice, special education. About 46% of general education requirements for graduation are elective; distribution requirements fairly numerous. Average undergraduate class size: 54% under 20, 46% 20–40, 1% over 40. About 46% of students entering as freshmen graduate eventually. *Special programs:* CLEP, independent study, internships, study abroad, honors, cross registration with Higher Education Council of Columbus. Adult programs: Weekend College. *Calendar:* semester.
Undergraduate degrees conferred (204). 23% were in Education, 21% were in Business and Management, 9% were in Social Sciences, 9% were in Liberal/General Studies, 8% were in Communications, 6% were in Psychology, 4% were in Protective Services, 4% were in Library and Archival Sciences, 4% were in Letters, 3% were in Life Sciences, 3% were in Public Affairs, remainder in 6 other fields.
Faculty. About 50% of faculty hold PhD or equivalent. About 56% of teaching faculty are female.
Student Body. About 83% of students from in state; 1% each New England, Middle Atlantic, Midwest, West, 2% U.S. Possessions, 11% foreign. An estimated 45% of students reported as Catholic, 30% Protestant, 1% each Jewish, Muslim, 27% other; 13% Black, 2% Hispanic, 1% Asian, 11% other minority. Average age of undergraduate student: 26.
Religious Orientation. Ohio Dominican is a church-related institution; 3 courses in religious studies and philosophy required of all students; attendance at all religious services voluntary.
Varsity Sports. Men (NAIA): Baseball, Basketball, Soccer. Women (NAIA): Basketball, Softball, Volleyball.
Campus Life. About 25% of students live in traditional and coed dormitories; rest commute. Intervisitation in men's and women's dormitory rooms limited. Sexes segregated in coed dormitories by floor. There are no fraternities or sororities on campus. About 10% of resident students leave campus on weekends.
Annual Costs. Tuition and fees, $7,730; room and board, $4,090; estimated $600 other, exclusive of travel. About 85% of students receive financial aid. College reports some scholarships awarded on the basis of academic merit alone. *Meeting Costs:* college offers payment plans.

Ohio Northern University

Ada, Ohio 45810 **(419) 772-2000**

A church-related university, located in a town of 5,300, 75 miles southwest of Toledo and 15 miles east of Lima, Ohio Northern offers programs in colleges of arts and sciences, business administration, engineering, pharmacy, and law. Most convenient major airport: Dayton.

Founded: 1871
Affiliation: United Methodist
UG Enrollment: 1,387 M, 1,182 W (full-time); 35 M, 31 W (part-time)
Total Enrollment: 2,964
Cost: $10K–$20K
% Receiving Financial Aid: 87%
Admission: Selective
Application Deadline: May 1

Admission is selective. About 84% of applicants accepted, 27% of these actually enroll; about 63% of freshmen graduate in top fifth of high school class, 85% in top two-fifths. Average freshman ACT scores: 23.4 composite. *Required:* SAT or ACT, interview recommended. Criteria considered in admissions, in order of importance: high school academic record, standardized test scores, extracurricular activities, recommendations; other factors considered include alumni children, diverse student body. *Apply* preferably by May 1; rolling admissions. *Transfers* welcome; 84 enrolled 1993–94.
Academic Environment. According to administration source students who are career-oriented, conservative, and comfortable with close faculty contact will find a congenial campus atmosphere. *Undergraduate studies* offered by colleges of Arts and Sciences, Business Administration, Engineering, Pharmacy. Graduation requirements include study in English, speech, literature, Western civilization, economics, philosophy, religion, foreign language. Degrees offered: bachelors, doctoral. *Majors offered* include computer science, sports management, industrial technology, international studies, biochemistry, criminal justice, environmental studies. Average undergraduate class size: 24% under 20.

About 58% of students entering as freshmen graduate within four years; 78% of freshmen return for sophomore year. *Special programs:* inter-college majors, internships, independent study, study abroad, undergraduate research. Admission at ONU College of Law guaranteed for Ohio Northern graduates meeting academic requirements. *Calendar:* quarter, summer school.
Undergraduate degrees conferred (420). 29% were in Health Sciences, 21% were in Business and Management, 15% were in Engineering, 7% were in Life Sciences, 5% were in Social Sciences, 4% were in Education, 3% were in Engineering and Engineering Related Technology, 3% were in Communications, remainder in 8 other fields.
Graduates Career Data. Advanced studies pursued by 24% of graduates; 12% enter graduate school; 4% enter medical school; 4% enter law school; 3% enter business school. Medical schools typically enrolling largest numbers of graduates include Ohio State U., Medical College of Ohio; law schools include Ohio Northern U., Ohio State U., U. of Cincinnati; business schools include Miami. About 63% of 1992–93 graduates employed. Fields typically hiring largest numbers of graduates include retail pharmacy, civil engineer-

ing, mechanical engineering, retail marketing firms. Career Development Center include group consultations, workshops, job fairs, bi-weekly listings of job opportunities, credential service, resume and cover letter critiquing, and on campus recruitment.

Faculty. About 82% of faculty hold PhD or equivalent. About 47% of teaching faculty are female.

Student Body. About 77% of students from in state. An estimated 35% of students reported as Protestant, 22% Catholic, 31% unaffiliated, 12% other; 3% Black, 1% Asian, 5% other minority.

Religious Orientation. Ohio Northern is a church-related institution; 19% of students affiliated with the church; 1 course in religion required of undergraduates.

Varsity Sports. Men (Div.III): Baseball, Basketball, Cross Country, Diving, Football, Golf, Soccer, Swimming, Tennis, Track, Wrestling. Women (Div.III): Basketball, Cross Country, Diving, Soccer, Softball, Swimming, Tennis, Track, Volleyball.

Campus Life. Students report campus is located in a "friendly" and "safe" small town which focuses student life towards on-campus activities. "Excellent" Student Planning Committee brings entertainers to campus and promotes other activities.

About 45% of men, 30% of women live in traditional dormitories; 12% of men, 33% of women in coed dormitories; 30% of men, 32% of women live in off-campus housing or commute. Freshmen given preference in college housing if all students cannot be accommodated. Intervisitation limited in residence halls. There are 8 fraternities, 4 sororities on campus which about 26% of men, 24% of women join; 14% of men live in fraternities; 5% of women live in sororities.

Annual Costs. Tuition and fees, $13,815; room and board, $3,885; estimated $1,425 other, exclusive of travel. About 87% of students receive financial aid; average amount of assistance, $12,500. Assistance is typically divided 20% scholarship, 40% grant, 35% loan, 5% work. University reports 1,400 scholarships awarded on the basis of academic merit alone, 100 for special talents alone, 1,200 for need alone. *Meeting Costs:* college offers monthly payment plan, PLUS Loans, CONCERN Loans.

Ohio State University

Columbus, Ohio 43210-1200 (614) 292-3980

The largest of Ohio's state universities, OSU is also the state's land-grant institution. It is increasingly becoming one of the nation's major graduate centers; its undergraduate student body is one of the largest in the country. The 3,255-acre main campus, supplemented by a variety of other facilities and 4 regional campuses (see below), is located in the state's capital (pop. 591,200). Most convenient major airport: Port Columbus (Columbus).

Founded: 1870
Affiliation: State
UG Enrollment: 16,418 M, 14,621 W (full-time); 3,234 M, 2,771 W (part-time)
Total Enrollment: 50,623
Cost: < $10K
% Receiving Financial Aid: 65%
Admission: Selective
Application Deadline: Feb. 15

Admission is selective. About 85% of applicants accepted, 42% of these actually enroll; 44% of freshmen graduate in top fifth of high school class, 73% in top two-fifths. Average freshman scores: SAT, 400–530 verbal, 450–610 mathematical; 62% score above 500 on mathematical, 29% above 600, 8% above 700; ACT, 23 composite.

Required: ACT or SAT. Criteria considered in admissions, in order of importance: high school academic record and curriculum, standardized test scores, recommendations, extracurricular activities; other factors considered include special talents, diverse student body, leadership. *Out-of-state* freshman applicants: university actively seeks students from out-of-state. State does not limit out-of-state enrollment. No special requirements for out-of-state students. About 88% of out-of-state students accepted, 19% enrolled. States from which most out-of-state students are drawn include Illinois, New Jersey, New York, Pennsylvania, Virginia, Michigan. *Entrance programs:* midyear admission, advanced placement. *Apply* by February 15; rolling admissions. *Transfers* welcome; 1,987 enrolled for Fall, 1993.

Academic Environment. Curriculum in the 5 Arts and Sciences colleges provides wide range of majors. Personalized Study Program permits students to plan own degree programs including interdisciplinary majors. All freshmen enroll in University College for at least 1, but not more than 2 years and then transfer to one of the undergraduate degree-granting colleges: Arts and Sciences (including colleges of the Arts, Biological Sciences, Humanities, Mathematical and Physical Sciences, Social and Behavioral Sciences—latter includes School of Journalism), Administrative Science, Agriculture and Home Economics (including schools of Home Economics, Natural Resources), Education, Engineering (including School of Architecture), and Social Work; preprofessional work required before admission to baccalaureate programs in schools of Allied Medical Professions, Nursing, Division of Dental Hygiene, College of Pharmacy. Degrees offered: bachelors, masters, doctoral. *Majors offered* in about 211 programs of study in broad range of arts and sciences and professional/vocational fields; also individualized majors. Average undergraduate class size: 87% under 50, 6% 50–99, 7% over 100.

About 57% of students entering as freshmen graduate within six years; 82% of freshmen return for sophomore year. *Special programs:* independent study, study abroad, honors, individualized majors, Freshman Scholar Program, cross registration with other central Ohio schools. Adult program: Bridge Program for adult students assists them with reentry issues relating to work, school and family priorities. *Calendar:* quarter, summer school.

Undergraduate degrees conferred (6,844). 15% were in Business and Management, 11% were in Education, 9% were in Social Sciences, 9% were in Communications, 8% were in Engineering, 6% were in Marketing and Distribution, 4% were in Psychology, 4% were in Health Sciences, 4% were in Home Economics, 4% were in Allied Health, 3% were in Visual and Performing Arts, 3% were in Letters, 3% were in Life Sciences, remainder in 16 other fields.

Graduates Career Data. Advanced studies pursued by 25% of graduates. About 38% of 1992–93 graduates employed. Career Development Services are decentralized in college offices and include on-campus interviews, referrals, and resume writing workshops.

Faculty. About 95% of faculty hold PhD or equivalent. About 27% of teaching faculty are female; 4% Black, 2% Hispanic, 7% other minority.

Student Body. About 91% of students from in state; 3% foreign. An estimated 7% of students reported as Black, 2% Hispanic, 4% Asian, 4% other minority. *Minority group students:* special financial, academic, and social help available.

Varsity Sports. Men (Div.I): Baseball, Basketball, Football, Golf, Gymnastics, Ice Hockey, Swimming, Tennis, Track, Volleyball, Wrestling. Women (Div.I): Baseball, Basketball, Field Hockey, Golf, Gymnastics, Softball, Swimming, Tennis, Track, Volleyball.

Campus Life. As members of University Senate and many committees, students are involved in governance. Code of Student Rights and Responsibilities has established guidelines for university disciplinary procedures, and contains statement of student rights. Guest hours in most dormitories are student-regulated although some restrictions are made. Alcohol permitted for students 21 and over; some university regulations also apply. Cars allowed but student parking generally restricted to perimeter of main campus. New students who have not been out of high school at least 1 year are required to live in university residence halls. Freshmen may live in living/learning or experimental units providing counseling and academic assistance.

About 19% of each men, women live in traditional dormitories; 81% of each men, women live in off-campus housing. Freshmen given preference in college housing if all students cannot be accommodated. There are 41 fraternities, 23 sororities on campus which about 10% of men, 11% of women join.

Annual Costs. Tuition and fees, $2,940 (out-of-state, $8,871); room and board, $4,278; estimated $1,108 other, exclusive of travel. About 65% of students receive financial aid. *Meeting Costs:* university offers The Tuition Plan.

Ohio State University—Lima Campus

Lima, Ohio 45804

Founded: 1960
Affiliation: State
UG Enrollment: 412 M, 544 W (full-time); 326 M, W (part-time)

Ohio State University—Mansfield Campus

Mansfield, Ohio 44906

Founded: 1958
Affiliation: State
UG Enrollment: 369 M, 503 W (full-time); 154 M, 280 W (part-time)

Ohio State University—Marion Campus

Marion, Ohio 43302

Founded: 1957
Affiliation: State
UG Enrollment: 335 M, 425 W (full-time); 325 M, W (part-time)

Ohio State University—Newark Campus

Newark, Ohio 43055

Ohio State University's regional campuses are commuter institutions serving students in their immediate areas.

Founded: 1957
Affiliation: State
UG Enrollment: 654 M, 933 W (full-time); 1,675 total graduate and undergraduate

Admission. Ohio graduates of accredited high schools or equivalent eligible; others given individual consideration; almost all applicants accepted. *Required:* ACT or SAT (for placement only). *Entrance programs:* midyear admission, advanced placement. *Apply:* through first day of classes. *Transfers* welcome.
Academic Environment. *Degree:* BSEd. General education requirements for graduation vary with program; distribution requirements limited. *Special programs:* honors, study abroad, individualized majors. *Calendar:* quarter, summer school.
Student Body. About 95–99% of students from in state.
Campus Life. All students commute.
Annual Costs. Tuition and fees, $2,700 (out-of-state, $10,893).

Ohio University

Athens, Ohio 45701 **(614) 593-1000**

A state university of substantial size, located in a college town of 20,000, 70 miles southeast of Columbus, Ohio University—the oldest institution of higher learning in the historic Northwest Territory—has changed rapidly in recent years. Branch campuses with 2-year programs are located in Chillicothe, Zanesville, Lancaster, Belmont County, and Ironton. Most convenient major airport: Port Columbus (Columbus).

Founded: 1804
Affiliation: State
UG Enrollment: 6,831 M, 7,972 W (full-time); 325 M, 468 W (part-time)
Total Enrollment: 18,484
Cost: < $10K
% Receiving Financial Aid: 67%
Admission: Selective
Application Deadline: March 1

Admission is selective. About 75% of applicants accepted, 38% of these actually enroll; 42% of freshmen graduate in top fifth of high school class. Average freshmen scores: SAT, 473 verbal, 522 mathematical; 60% score above 500 on mathematical, 19% above 600, 2% above 700; ACT, 23.5 composite. *Required:* SAT or ACT. Criteria considered in admissions, in order of importance: high school academic record, class rank, standardized test scores, recommendations, extracurricular activities; other factors considered include special talents, diverse student body. *Out-of-state* freshman applicants: university actively seeks students from out-of-state. State does not limit out-of-state enrollment. No special requirements for out-of-state applicants. States from which most out-of-state students are drawn include Pennsylvania, New York. *Entrance programs:* early admission, midyear admission, deferred admission, advanced placement. *Apply* by March 1; rolling admissions. *Transfers* welcome; 528 enrolled 1993–94.
Academic Environment. *Undergraduate studies* are offered through colleges of Arts and Sciences, Business Administration, Communication (including schools of Journalism, Telecommunications, Interpersonal Communication, Communication Systems Management, and Visual Communication), Education, Engineering and Technology, Fine Arts (including schools of Art, Comparative Arts, Dance, Film, Music, and Theater), Health and Human Services (including schools of Health and Sport Sciences, Hearing and Speech Sciences, Nursing, Home Economics, and Physical Therapy), Honors Tutorial College, and University College. Master's degrees are offered in approximately 50 areas; PhD programs in 20 areas; and the D.O. degree is offered through the College of Osteopathic Medicine. Freshmen may seek direct entry to a major, or may enroll in University College as exploratory students if they are undecided. Those entering University College may remain there where they can earn the associate degree or self-structured baccalaureate degree in general studies. All students take 30 hours of general education courses. All freshmen must take composition course and follow it up with advanced composition when juniors. Degrees offered: associates, bachelors, masters, doctoral. *Majors offered* include athletic training, geography, international business, social work, physical therapy, airways science. Average undergraduate class size: 22.

About 66% of students entering as freshmen graduate within four years; 86% of freshmen return for sophomore year. *Special programs:* CLEP, independent study, study abroad, Honors, Tutorial College, undergraduate research, individualized majors, early admission to graduate college, 3–2 in forestry, 3–2 in natural resources, internship in engineering, journalism. *Calendar:* quarter, summer school.
Undergraduate degrees conferred (3,243). 20% were in Education, 15% were in Business and Management, 14% were in Communications, 11% were in Letters, 7% were in Social Sciences, 6% were in Liberal/General Studies, 5% were in Engineering, 4% were in Visual and Performing Arts, 4% were in Life Sciences, 4% were in Psychology, 3% were in Health Sciences, 3% were in Home Economics, remainder in 9 other fields.
Graduates Career Data. Advanced studies pursued by 28% of graduates; 25% enter graduate school; 3% enter medical school; 1% enter dental school; 3% enter law school; 5% enter business school. About 85% of 1992–93 graduates employed. Career Development Services include aptitude testing, on campus recruitment, placement services, career counseling, resume and interview workshops and library resources.
Faculty. About 87% of faculty hold PhD or equivalent. About 28% of teaching faculty are female.
Student Body. About 87% of students from in state; 90% Midwest. An estimated 56% of students reported as Protestant, 38% Catholic, 2% Jewish, 4% other; 4% Black, 1% Hispanic, 1% Asian. *Minority group students:* special financial aid; degree program in Black studies.
Varsity Sports. Men (Div.I): Baseball, Basketball, Cross Country, Diving, Football, Golf, Swimming, Track, Wrestling. Women (Div.I): Basketball, Cross Country, Diving, Field Hockey, Softball, Swimming, Track, Volleyball.
Campus Life. A student leader reports that the university "does have its share of excellent cultural affairs, excellent publications, and young (and stimulating) professors." Students can choose from unlimited to variously limited visitation zones in residence halls. Policy on alcohol conforms to state law. Motor vehicles allowed for all. University now requires virtually all freshmen and sophomores to live in dormitories to guarantee sufficient income to retire bonds financing dorm construction.

About 45% of students live in traditional and coed dormitories; rest live in off-campus housing or commute. Returning upperclassmen and freshmen given preference in college housing if all students cannot be accommodated. Sexes segregated in coed dormitories either by wing or floor. There are 20 fraternities, 14 sororities on campus which about 18% of men, 21% of women join. About 15% of resident students leave campus on weekends.

Annual Costs. Tuition and fees, $3,384 (out-of-state, $7,266); room and board, $3,957; estimated $2,850 other, exclusive of travel. About 68% of students receive financial aid; average amount of assistance, $3,292. Assistance is typically divided 9% scholarship, 41% loan, 13% work, according to most recent data available. *Meeting Costs:* university offers alternative loan programs, on and off-campus employment programs.

Ohio Wesleyan University

Delaware, Ohio 43015 (614) 368-3020

Founded by Methodists, Ohio Wesleyan is today an independent, liberal arts college. Original charter of the university provided, however, that it "is forever to be conducted on the most liberal principles, accessible to all religious denominations and designed for the benefit of our citizens in general." The 200-acre campus is located in a town of 20,000, 20 miles north of Columbus. Most convenient major airport: Columbus (27 miles).

Founded: 1842
Affiliation: Independent (United Methodist)
UG Enrollment: 871 M, 909 W (full-time); 15 M, 34 W (part-time)
Cost: $10K–$20K
% Receiving Financial Aid: 68%
Admission: Selective (+)
Application Deadline: March 1

Admission is selective (+). About 77% of applicants accepted, 27% of these actually enroll; 54% of freshmen graduate in top fifth of high school class, 75% in top two-fifths. Average freshman scores: SAT, 530 verbal, 580 mathematical; 64% of freshmen score above 500 on verbal, 26% above 600, 2% above 700; 86% score above 500 on mathematical, 46% above 600, 12% above 700; ACT, 25 M, 26 W composite. *Required:* SAT or ACT. Criteria considered in admissions, in order of importance: high school academic record, extracurricular activities, recommendations, standardized test scores, writing sample, campus interview; other factors considered include special talents, alumni children, diverse student body. *Entrance programs:* early admission, deferred admission. About 17% of entering students from private schools, 13% from parochial schools. *Apply* by March 1; rolling admissions. *Transfers* welcome; 32 enrolled 1993–94.

Academic Environment. The National Colloquium, is an effort "to integrate the liberal arts with civic arts through year long guest lectures, seminars, and a spring symposium." Each colloquium focuses on a single major national issue. The Center for Economics and Business develops programs of special interest to students in economics, management, and international business. Honors program, a 4-year integrated program for outstanding students, includes team-taught seminars, tutorials, independent study, and a senior comprehensive exam in the major. Top entering students named Achievement Scholars and leading upperclassmen named University Scholars as mark of distinction in honors program, which includes priority in financial aid awards if needed. College has made a determined effort to involve students in all levels of decision making except faculty promotion and tenure, and even in this area student boards submit evaluations of faculty. Students are deeply involved in all decisions in some departments, less so in others. Natural and social sciences reported to be among strongest programs. General education requirements include 3 courses each in English/humanities, math/science, social sciences. Degrees offered: bachelors. *Majors offered* include bacteriology, education, fine arts, geography, journalism, music, nursing; student-designed interdisciplinary majors. Average undergraduate class size: 60% under 20, 28% 20–40, 12% over 40.

About 75% of students entering as freshmen graduate eventually; 84% of freshmen return for sophomore year. *Special programs:* independent study, study abroad, honors, undergraduate research, National Colloquium, 3-year degree, individualized majors, extensive off-campus apprenticeships including Washington Semester, programs of GLCA in New York (arts), Philadelphia (urban studies), Chicago (humanities), Oak Ridge National Laboratory (sciences), English Language Program for foreign students, combined 3–2 in engineering. *Calendar:* 4–4 early semester, 2 summer sessions.

Undergraduate degrees conferred (406). 31% were in Social Sciences, 20% were in Business and Management, 10% were in Visual and Performing Arts, 7% were in Psychology, 6% were in Letters, 6% were in Education, 5% were in Foreign Languages, 4% were in Life Sciences, 3% were in Communications, 3% were in Health Sciences, remainder in 6 other fields.

Graduates Career Data. Advanced studies pursued by 55% of graduates within 10 years of graduation; 20% enter graduate school; 8% enter medical school; 1% enter dental school; 10% enter law school; 16% enter business school. Medical schools typically enrolling largest numbers of graduates include Ohio State, Case Western, John Hopkins; dental schools include Ohio State; law schools include Ohio State, Duke, Vanderbilt; business schools include U. of Pennsylvania, Harvard, Ohio State. About 90% of 1992–93 graduates employed. Corporations and fields typically hiring largest numbers of graduates include Nationwide Insurance, Kidder Peabody, Proctor & Gamble, education, federal government. Career Development Services include counseling, training, career awareness and on campus interviews.

Faculty. About 94% of faculty hold PhD or equivalent. About 70% of undergraduate classes taught by tenured faculty. About 38% of teaching faculty are female; 3% Black, 2% Hispanic, 4% other minority.

Student Body. About 48% of students from in state; 54% Midwest, 17% Middle Atlantic, 12% New England, 4% South, West, 8% foreign. An estimated 42% of students reported as Protestant, 26% Catholic, 7% Jewish, 5% Muslim, 15% unaffiliated, 5% other; 5% Black, 1% Hispanic, 2% Asian, 9% other minority. *Minority group students:* special financial, advising, and social provisions.

Varsity Sports. Men (Div.III): Baseball, Basketball, Cross Country, Diving, Equestrian, Football, Golf, Lacrosse, Soccer, Swimming, Tennis, Track. Women (Div.III): Basketball, Cross Country, Diving, Equestrian, Field Hockey, Lacrosse, Soccer, Swimming, Tennis, Track, Volleyball.

Campus Life. Joint student/faculty/administration council makes policy in Non-academic areas. Dormitories set own intervisitation hours. Freshmen and parents select residence with unlimited, limited, or no visitation. Alcohol permitted in residence halls; cars not allowed. Special interest houses include foreign languages, fine arts, international living, Black Culture, and women's issues. All freshmen required to live in residence halls. Campus highly residential with active weekend social life.

About 20% of women live in traditional dormitories; 50% of men, 70% of women in coed dormitories; 5% of men, 7% of women live in off-campus housing; 5% of men, 3% of women commute. Freshmen given preference in college housing if all students cannot be accommodated. Sexes segregated in coed dormitories either by wing, floor or room. There are 11 fraternities, 7 sororities on campus which about 45% of men, 35% of women join; 40% of men live in fraternities; sororities provide no residence facilities. About 7% of resident students leave campus on weekends.

Annual Costs. Tuition and fees, $15,726; room and board, $5,382; estimated $900 other, exclusive of travel. About 68% of students receive financial aid; average amount of assistance, $15,000. Assistance is typically divided 30% scholarship, 37% grant, 25% loan, 8% work. University reports 514 scholarships awarded on the basis of academic merit alone, 30 for arts alone, 930 for need alone. *Meeting Costs:* university offers monthly payment plans.

Oklahoma Baptist University

Shawnee, Oklahoma 74801 (405) 878-2033

A church-related institution, located in a community of 25,100, 40 miles southeast of Oklahoma City. Most convenient major airport: Will Rogers (Oklahoma City).

Founded: 1906
Affiliation: Southern Baptist
UG Enrollment: 734 M, 989 W (full-time); 422 M, 287 W (part-time)
Total Enrollment: 2,432
Cost: < $10K
% Receiving Financial Aid: 85%
Admission: Non-selective
Application Deadline: Aug. 1

Admission. Graduates of accredited high schools with 16 units and C average and SAT combined score of 720, or ACT composite score of 20 eligible; others admitted on probation on recommendation of Admissions Committee; 92% of applicants accepted, 70% of these actually enroll. Average freshman ACT scores: 23.8 composite. *Required:* ACT or SAT. Criteria considered in admissions, in order of importance: high school academic record, standardized test scores, recommendations, writing sample, extracurricular activities; other factors considered include special talents, diverse student body. *Apply* by August 1; rolling admissions. *Transfers* welcome; 150 enrolled 1993–94.

Academic Environment. *Undergraduate studies* offered by College of Arts and Sciences, Warren M. Angell College of Fine Arts, schools of Business Administration, Christian Service, and Nursing. Graduation requirements include 12 hours of English composition/literature, 6 of Bible, 6 of language, 6 of history, 3 of fine arts, 6 of social sciences, 3 of math, 2 of speech, and 2 of philosophy. Degrees offered: bachelors, masters. *Majors offered* include telecommunications, international business. Average undergraduate class size: 40% under 20, 50% 20–40, 10% over 40.

About 44% of students entering as freshmen graduate eventually; 78% of freshmen return for sophomore year. *Special programs:* CLEP, independent study, study abroad, honors, 3-year degree, undergraduate research, individualized majors, cross registration with St. Gregory's. *Calendar:* 4–1–4, summer school.

Undergraduate degrees conferred (302). 24% were in Education, 12% were in Business and Management, 12% were in Theology, 9% were in Visual and Performing Arts, 8% were in Health Sciences, 6% were in Communications, 5% were in Social Sciences, 4% were in Marketing and Distribution, 4% were in Psychology, 3% were in Philosophy and Religion, 3% were in Letters, remainder in 9 other fields.

Graduates Career Data. Advanced studies pursued by 45% of graduates. Medical schools typically enrolling largest numbers of graduates include U. of Oklahoma School of Medicine; dental schools include U. of Oklahoma School of Dentistry; law schools include U. of Oklahoma School of Law, Oklahoma City U., Baylor. Fields typically hiring largest numbers of graduates include health fields, education, and business. Career Development Services include resume writing workshops, on-campus interviews and testing for job placement.

Faculty. About 64% of faculty hold PhD or equivalent.

Student Body. About 72% of students from in state; 12% South, 7% Midwest, 6% West, 2% Northwest, 2% foreign. An estimated 94% of students reported as Protestant, 1% Catholic, 2% unaffiliated; 4% Black, 1% Hispanic, less than 1% Asian, 6% Native American.

Religious Orientation. Oklahoma Baptist is a church-related institution; 88% of students affiliated with the church; 2 courses in religion, attendance at 70% of weekly chapel services/assembly programs required of all students.

Varsity Sports. Men (NAIA): Baseball, Basketball, Tennis, Track. Women (NAIA): Basketball, Softball.

Campus Life. About 50% of men, 60% of women live in traditional dormitories; no coed dormitories; rest commute. Freshmen given preference in college housing if all students cannot be accommodated. No intervisitation in men's or women's dormitory rooms. There are 5 fraternities, 5 sororities on campus. About 65% of resident students leave campus on weekends.

Annual Costs. Tuition and fees, $5,436; room and board, $3,050; estimated $2,000 other, exclusive of travel. About 85% of students receive financial aid; average amount of assistance, $4,200.

Oklahoma Christian University of Science and Arts

Oklahoma City, Oklahoma 73136-1100 (405) 425-5200

An independent college, "related to individual members of the Church of Christ," located in a city of 382,000. Formerly known as Oklahoma Christian College. Most convenient major airport: Will Rogers (Oklahoma City).

Founded: 1950
Affiliation: Independent (Church of Christ)
UG Enrollment: 733 M, 686 W (full-time); 110 M, 118 W (part-time)
Total Enrollment: 1,676
Cost: < $10K
% Receiving Financial Aid: 83%
Admission: Non-selective
Application Deadline: Rolling

Admission. Graduates of accredited high schools with 15 units or minimum ACT composite score of 17, and "good moral character" eligible; 98% of applicants accepted, 46% of these actually enroll. *Required:* SAT or ACT. *Entrance programs:* early admission, midyear admission. *Apply:* rolling admissions. *Transfers* welcome; 170 enrolled 1993–94.

Academic Environment. Degrees offered: bachelors, masters. Graduation requirements include 60 hours of general education curriculum. *Majors offered* include mechanical and electrical engineering, liberal studies, finance, organizational communications, ad design. About 70% of freshmen return for sophomore year. *Special programs:* CLEP, independent study, study abroad, cross registration with U. of Central Oklahoma. *Calendar:* trimester, including spring short session, summer school.

Undergraduate degrees conferred (262). 15% were in Education, 15% were in Business and Management, 9% were in Communications, 9% were in Theology, 8% were in Engineering, 6% were in Marketing and Distribution, 5% were in Visual and Performing Arts, 5% were in Computer and Engineering Related Technology, 5% were in Social Sciences, 5% were in Psychology, 5% were in Life Sciences, 3% were in Letters, 3% were in Mathematics, remainder in 6 other fields.

Graduates Career Data. Career Development Services offer career planning/testing, resource center, workshops, and on campus interviews.

Faculty. About 59% of faculty hold PhD or equivalent. About 50% of undergraduate classes taught by tenured faculty. About 24% of teaching faculty are female; 2% Black, 1% other minority.

Student Body. About 44% of students from in state; 64% Midwest, 18% South, 6% Middle Atlantic, 3% West, 2% Northwest, 1% New England, 5% foreign. An estimated 5% of students reported as Black, 2% Hispanic, 4% Asian, 2% other minority.

Religious Orientation. Oklahoma Christian is a church-related institution; 81% of students affiliated with the church; 16 hours in Bible, attendance at daily chapel services required of all students.

Varsity Sports. Men (NAIA): Baseball, Basketball, Cross Country, Soccer, Tennis, Track. Women (NAIA): Basketball, Cross Country, Soccer, Track (indoor & outdoor).

Campus Life. About 32% of men, 33% of women live in traditional dormitories or apartments; no coed dormitories; 6% live in on-campus married housing; 29% commute. Freshmen given preference in college housing if all students cannot be accommodated. No intervisitation in men's or women's dormitory rooms. There are no fraternities or sororities on campus.

Annual Costs. Tuition and fees, $5,810; room and board, $2,980; estimated $1,350 other, exclusive of travel. About 83% of students receive financial aid; average amount of assistance, $5,180. Assistance is typically divided 29% scholarship, 14% grant, 52% loan, 5% work. College reports 496 scholarships awarded on the basis of academic merit alone, 240 for special talents alone, 390 for need alone. *Meeting Costs:* college offers prepayment plan.

Oklahoma City Southwestern College

(See Southwestern College of Christian Ministries)

Oklahoma City University

Oklahoma City, Oklahoma 73106 (800) 633-7242

A church-related university, located in a city of 900,000. Most convenient major airport: Will Rogers (Oklahoma City).

Founded: 1904
Affiliation: United Methodist
Total Enrollment: 3,485
Cost: < $10K
% Receiving Financial Aid: 82%
Admission: Non-selective
Application Deadline: Rolling

Admission. About 83% of applicants accepted, 35% of these actually enroll. About 37% of freshmen graduate in top fifth of high school class, 58% in top two-fifths. Average freshman scores, according to most recent data available: SAT, 452 M, 453 W verbal, 538 M, 457 W mathematical; ACT, 22.3 M, 21.7 W composite. *Required:* ACT or SAT; interview recommended. *Entrance programs:* early decision, early admission, midyear admission, deferred admission, advanced placement. *Apply:* rolling admissions. *Transfers* welcome.

Academic Environment. *Undergraduate studies* offered by College of Arts and Sciences, schools of Management and Business Science,

Music and Performing Arts, Religion, and Nursing. Oklahoma City has developed an impressive academic specialization in Pacific Basin studies. The University's Asian studies program is an extension of this specialization. Faculty members and students teach, study and conduct research in the Far East through a variety of programs and institutional affiliations. *Special programs:* CLEP, independent study, study abroad, honors, 3-year degree, individualized majors, United Nations Semester, Washington Semester, Mid-Year Institute. Adult programs: Competency Based Degree Program is designed to meet the needs of working adults. *Calendar:* semester, 2 summer sessions.

Undergraduate degrees conferred (248). 20% were in Business and Management, 14% were in Liberal/General Studies, 10% were in Visual and Performing Arts, 9% were in Computer and Engineering Related Technology, 9% were in Communications, 8% were in Education, 6% were in Marketing and Distribution, 4% were in Psychology, 3% were in Social Sciences, 3% were in Physical Sciences, 3% were in Protective Services, 3% were in Letters, remainder in 7 other fields.

Graduates Career Data. According to most recent data available, full-time graduate or professional study pursued by 34% of students immediately after graduation. *Careers in business and industry* pursued by 78% of graduates. Career Development Services include career guidance assistance and job placement, on-campus interviewing, interview preparation assistance, active alumni guidance.

Faculty. About 62% of faculty hold PhD or equivalent.

Student Body. About 60% of students from in state. An estimated 5% of students reported as Black, 2% Hispanic, 25% Asian, 3% Native American, 5% other minority, according to most recent data available.

Varsity Sports. Men (NAIA): Baseball, Basketball, Golf, Soccer, Tennis. Women (NAIA): Basketball, Softball, Tennis.

Campus Life. About 12% of men, 17% of women live in traditional dormitories; no coed dormitories; 86% of men, 83% of women live in off-campus housing or commute. Freshmen given preference in college housing if all students cannot be accommodated. No intervisitation in men's or women's dormitory rooms. There are 3 fraternities, 3 sororities on campus which about 5% of men, 8% of women join; 2% of men live in fraternities; sororities provide no residence facilities. About 20% of resident students leave campus on weekends.

Annual Costs. Tuition and fees, $6,185; room and board, $3,420. About 82% of students receive financial aid; assistance is typically divided 40% scholarship, 56% loan, 4% work. University reports some scholarships awarded on the basis of academic merit alone. *Meeting Costs:* university offers payment plans, PLUS Loans.

Oklahoma Panhandle State University

Goodwell, Oklahoma 73939 (405) 349-2611

A state-supported university, located in a village of 1,500, 120 miles north of Amarillo. Most convenient major airport: Amarillo, TX (120 miles).

Founded: 1909
Affiliation: State
UG Enrollment: 1,027 M, W (full-time)
Cost: < $10K
Admission: Non-selective
Application Deadline: August 23

Admission. Oklahoma graduates of accredited high schools eligible; almost all applicants accepted, 84% of these actually enroll. About 21% of freshmen graduate in top fifth of high school class, 43% in top two-fifths. *Required:* SAT or ACT. *Out-of-state* freshman applicants: university welcomes students from out-of-state. State does not limit out-of-state enrollment. Requirement for out-of-state applicants: rank in top half of class or score in top half on ACT. *Non-academic factors* considered in admissions: special talents. *Apply* by August 23. *Transfers* welcome.

Academic Environment. *Degrees:* AB, BS. About 40% of general education requirements for graduation are elective; distribution requirements fairly numerous. About 61% of students entering as freshmen graduate eventually; 70% of freshmen return for sophomore year. *Special programs:* CLEP, independent study. *Calendar:* semester, summer session.

Undergraduate degrees conferred (117). 38% were in Education, 13% were in Business and Management, 10% were in Agricultural Sciences, 10% were in Agribusiness and Agricultural Production, 5% were in Computer and Engineering Related Technology, 4% were in Letters, 3% were in Psychology, 3% were in Home Economics, 3% were in Social Sciences, 3% were in Mathematics, remainder in 5 other fields.

Student Body. About 99% of students from in state. An estimated 13% of students reported as minority.

Varsity Sports. Men (NAIA Div.II): Basketball, Football, Track. Women (NAIA Div.II): Basketball, Track.

Campus Life. About 47% of students live in traditional dormitories; 50% of students live in off-campus housing or commute. Freshmen given preference in college housing if all students cannot be accommodated. There are no fraternities or sororities on campus. About 60% of resident students leave campus on weekends.

Annual Costs. Tuition and fees, $1,261 (out-of-state, $3,018); room and board, $2,744. About 50% of students receive financial aid. University reports some scholarships awarded on the basis of academic merit alone.

Oklahoma State University

Stillwater, Oklahoma 74078 (405) 744-5000

A state-supported, land-grant university, located on a 415-acre main campus in a community of 31,100, 50 miles northeast of Oklahoma City. Most convenient major airports: Tulsa or Oklahoma City.

Founded: 1890
Affiliation: State
UG Enrollment: 6,981 M, 5,849 W (full-time); 855 M, 803 W (part-time)
Total Enrollment: 18,729
Cost: < $10K
% Receiving Financial Aid: 60%
Admission: Non-selective
Application Deadline: Rolling

Admission. Graduates of accredited high schools with 11 specific units eligible; others admitted provisionally; 86% of applicants accepted, 56% of these actually enroll; 48% of freshmen graduate in top fifth of high school class, 76% in top two-fifths. Average freshman ACT scores: 23.9 M, 23.3 W composite. *Required:* SAT or ACT, minimum high school GPA, 11 units: 4 years English, 3 math, 2 history, 2 science. Criteria considered in admissions, in order of importance: high school academic record, standardized test scores, curricular requirements from high school; other factors considered include special talents, diverse student body. *Out-of-state* freshman applicants: university actively seeks out-of-state students. State does not limit out-of-state enrollment. No special requirements for out-of-state applicants. About 72% of out-of-state students accepted, 42% of these actually enroll. States from which most out-of-state students are drawn include Texas, Kansas, Missouri, Arkansas. *Entrance programs:* early decision, early admission, midyear admission, advanced placement. *Apply* by Friday before classes begin; rolling admissions. *Transfers* welcome; 1,561 enrolled 1993–94.

Academic Environment. *Undergraduate studies* offered by colleges of Arts and Sciences, Agriculture, Business Administration, Education, Engineering, Home Economics, School of Hotel and Restaurant Administration, Technical Education. Graduation requirements include 6 hours of English composition, 6 of American History and U.S. Government, 8 of natural sciences, 6 of humanities, 6 of social and behavioral sciences. Degrees offered: bachelors, masters, doctoral. *Majors offered* in addition to usual studies include geography, journalism, medical technology, microbiology, public administration, physiology and pharmacology, secondary school teaching, speech pathology and audiology, management information systems, aviation science, manufacturing systems engineering, Russian language. Average undergraduate class size: 36% under 20, 39% 20–40, 24% over 40.

About 17% of students entering as freshmen graduate within four years, 46% within six years, 75% of freshmen return for sophomore year. *Special programs:* study abroad, 3–2 in accounting. Adult programs: program available to adults over 21 who do not meet normal requirements for freshmen admission and have no previous college experience. *Calendar:* semester, summer school.

Undergraduate degrees conferred (2,665). 31% were in Business and Management, 16% were in Education, 8% were in Engineering, 6% were in Social Sciences, 5% were in Home Economics, 5% were in Agricultural Sciences, 4% were in Engineering and Engineering Related Technology, 4% were in Life Sciences, 4%

were in Communications, 3% were in Psychology, 3% were in Agribusiness and Agricultural Production, remainder in 15 other fields.
Graduates Career Data. About 75% of 1992–93 graduates employed. Fields typically hiring largest numbers of graduates include accounting, marketing, engineering, education.
Faculty. About 88% of faculty hold PhD or equivalent. About 48% of undergraduate classes taught by tenured faculty. About 20% of teaching faculty are female; 2% Black, 1% Hispanic, 7% other minority.
Student Body. About 88% of students from in state; 3% South, 2% West, 1% Midwest, 6% foreign. An estimated 3% of students reported as Black, 2% Asian, 4% Native American, 1% Hispanic, according to most recent data available. *Minority group students:* special grants and scholarships; annual Black heritage week and other Black programs. Average age of undergraduate student: 22.
Varsity Sports. Men (Div.IA): Baseball, Basketball, Cross Country, Football, Golf, Tennis, Track, Wrestling. Women (Div.I): Basketball, Cross Country, Golf, Softball, Tennis, Track.
Campus Life. Campus is an hour away from Tulsa and Oklahoma City. Alcohol not allowed on campus or in fraternity/sorority houses or university properties. Cars allowed but parking spaces on campus are limited.

About 9% each men, women live in traditional and coed dormitories; 2% of men, 1% of women live in on campus apartments; 68% of men, 71% of women live in off-campus college-related housing; 15% of students commute. Freshmen given preference in college housing if all students cannot be accommodated. There are 25 fraternities and 14 sororities; 18% of men, 16% of women join; 6% of men, 4% of women live in fraternities and sororities. About 30% of resident students leave campus on weekends.
Annual Costs. Tuition and fees, $1,760 (out-of-state, $4,980); room and board, $3,150. About 60% of students receive financial aid; average amount of assistance, $6,546. Assistance is typically divided 30% scholarship, 16% grant, 51% loan, 3% work. University reports 1,249 scholarships awarded on the basis of special talents alone, 1,193 for need alone.

University of Oklahoma

Norman, Oklahoma 73019 (405) 325-2251

One of the major state universities in the West, the University of Oklahoma offers a variety of undergraduate, graduate, and professional studies. The main campus of 3,000 acres is located in Norman, a community of 80,000, about 20 miles south of Oklahoma City. The Health Sciences Center, a 200-acre educational complex in Oklahoma City, enrolls an additional 2,400 students. Most convenient major airport: Will Rogers (Oklahoma City).

Founded: 1890	**Total Enrollment:** 19,680
Affiliation: State	**Cost:** < $10K
UG Enrollment: 6,753 M, 5,571 W (full-time); 1,348 M, 1,160 W (part-time)	**% Receiving Financial Aid:** 63%
	Admission: Non-selective
	Application Deadline: Rolling

Admission. Graduates of accredited high schools with 3.0 average and rank in top third of class or a minimum ACT composite score of 21 (990 combined SAT) eligible; 84% of applicants accepted, 56% of these actually enroll; 53% of freshmen graduate in top fifth of high school class; 82% in top two-fifths. Average freshman scores: SAT, 1,042 combined; ACT, 23.9 composite. *Required:* ACT or SAT. Criteria considered in admissions, in order of importance: high school academic record, standardized test scores, writing sample, recommendations; other factors considered include special talents, diverse student body. *Out-of-state* freshman applicants: university actively seeks students from out-of-state. Requirements for out-of-state students include 2.0 GPA on all transfer work; 550 TOEFL score for foreign students. About 77% of out-of-state students accepted, 43% of these actually enroll. *Entrance programs:* early admission, midyear admission, advanced placement. *Apply:* rolling admissions. *Transfers* welcome; 1,800 enrolled 1993–94.
Academic Environment. All freshmen enroll in University College for at least 1 year before transferring to degree-granting colleges. General education requirements for graduation vary with program; distribution requirements fairly numerous. *Undergraduate studies* offered by colleges of Architecture, Arts and Sciences, Business Administration, Education, Engineering, Fine Arts, Geosciences, Liberal Studies, Nursing, Pharmacy, Dentistry, and Medicine. Degrees offered: bachelors, masters, doctoral, first professional. *Majors offered* in addition to usual arts and sciences include anthropology, Asian studies, astronomy, astrophysics, citizenship and public affairs, computer science, European studies, human development, journalism, laboratory technology, Latin American studies, law enforcement administration, logistics and materials management, medical technology, microbiology, petroleum land management, physical therapy, public affairs and administration, Russian studies, social work, Bachelor of Musical Arts, geography, and geosciences. Average undergraduate class size: 54% under 25, 29% 26–50, 17% over 50.

About 47% of students entering as freshmen graduate eventually, 75% of freshmen return for sophomore year. *Special programs:* study abroad, cross registration with Oklahoma State U., Langston U., U. Center of Tulsa, Northeastern State U., Rose State College and Oklahoma City Community College, individually planned majors, honors, advanced placement, learning disabilities program, English as second language. Adult program: part-time degree study available to adults through daytime, evening, weekend and summer courses. *Calendar:* semester, summer school.
Undergraduate degrees conferred (2,407). 16% were in Business and Management, 12% were in Engineering, 12% were in Communications, 9% were in Social Sciences, 8% were in Education, 5% were in Marketing and Distribution, 4% were in Letters, 4% were in Psychology, 4% were in Architecture and Environmental Design, 4% were in Public Affairs, 3% were in Visual and Performing Arts, 3% were in Life Sciences, 3% were in Communications Technologies, 3% were in Physical Sciences, remainder in 10 other fields.
Graduates Career Data. Fields typically hiring largest numbers of graduates include accounting firms and major energy companies. Career Development Services include individual career counseling and planning, job placement, on campus recruitment, job bank, job fairs, job interview workshops, career library, resume preparation and workshops and career classes.
Faculty. About 82% of faculty hold PhD or equivalent. About 27% of teaching faculty are female; 3% Black, 2% Hispanic, 10% other minority.
Student Body. About 80% of students from in state; 83% Midwest, 8% South, 1% each New England, Middle Atlantic, West, 6% foreign. An estimated 5% of students reported as Black, 2% Hispanic, 3% Asian, 3% Native American, 7% other minority, according to most recent data available. Average age of undergraduate student: 22.
Varsity Sports. Men (Div.I): Baseball, Basketball, Cross Country, Football, Golf, Gymnastics, Tennis, Track, Wrestling. Women (Div.I): Basketball, Cross Country, Golf, Gymnastics, Softball, Tennis, Track, Volleyball.
Campus Life. Representatives of administration and student government agree that undergraduates have a significant role in policy making on campus. Alcohol forbidden on campus or at university events; cars allowed.

About 14% of students live in coed dormitories; 7% live in off-campus college-related housing; 58% commute. Freshmen given preference in college housing if all students cannot be accommodated. Sexes segregated in coed dormitories by wing, floor or room. There are 23 fraternities, 15 sororities on campus which about 19% of men, 17% of women join; 21% of students live in fraternities and sororities. About 50% of resident students leave campus on weekends.
Annual Costs. Tuition and fees, $2,066 (out-of-state, $5,513); room and board, $3,526; estimated $3,000 other, exclusive of travel. About 63% of students receive financial aid; average amount of assistance, $3,526. Assistance is typically divided 36% scholarship, 13% grant, 53% loan, 2% work. University reports 4,633 scholarships awarded on the basis of academic merit alone, 508 for special talents alone, 4,271 for need alone. *Meeting Costs:* university offers parental PLUS Loans.

University of Science and Arts of Oklahoma

Chickasha, Oklahoma 73018-0001 (405) 224-3140

A small, state-supported university, located in a city of 17,000, 47 miles southwest of Oklahoma City. Most convenient major airport: Will Rogers International (Oklahoma City).

Founded: 1908
Affiliation: State
UG Enrollment: 395 M, 745 W (full-time); 158 M, 315 W (part-time)
Cost: < $10K
% Receiving Financial Aid: 73%
Admission: Non-selective
Application Deadline: August 20

Admission. Graduates of accredited high schools who rank in top half of class or with score of 12 or higher on ACT or with C average eligible; 91% of applicants accepted, 52% of these actually enroll. About 20% of freshmen graduate in top fifth of high school class, 47% in top two-fifths. Average freshman ACT scores: 20.6 M, 19.1 W composite. *Required:* SAT or ACT. *Out-of-state* freshman applicants: university actively seeks students from out of state; no limits; no special requirements; 63 students enrolled 1993–94. States from which most out-of-state students are drawn: Texas, Illinois. *Apply* by August 20. *Transfers* welcome; 191 enrolled 1993–94.
Academic Environment. Degree offered: bachelors. *Majors offered* in addition to usual studies include deaf education, speech pathology. Core requirements are fulfilled by a unique 52 hour team-taught interdisciplinary studies program. About 25% of students entering as freshmen graduate within four years, 35% eventually; 62% of freshmen return for sophomore year. Average undergraduate class size: 59% under 20, 30% 20–40, 11% over 40. *Special programs:* CLEP, independent study sessions in April and May, study abroad, honors, 3-year degree, Tutorial Scholars Program. Adult programs: Adult and Continuing Education Programs. *Calendar:* year-round trimester with third period including 5-week independent study term and summer school.
Undergraduate degrees conferred (161). 29% were in Education, 29% were in Business and Management, 9% were in Social Sciences, 6% were in Visual and Performing Arts, 5% were in Letters, 4% were in Psychology, 4% were in Computer and Engineering Related Technology, 4% were in Mathematics, 3% were in Communications, remainder in 7 other fields.
Graduates Career Data. Advanced studies pursued by 14% of students. About 51% of 1992–93 graduates are employed.
Faculty. About 78% of faculty hold PhD or equivalent. About 55% of undergraduate classes taught by tenured faculty. About 41% of teaching faculty are female; 2% Black, 6% Hispanic.
Student Body. University seeks a national student body; 96% of students from in state; 98% from North Central, 2% foreign. An estimated 3% of students reported as Black, 1% Hispanic, 12% other ethnic minorities. Average age of undergraduate student: 29.
Varsity Sports. Men: Basketball, Golf, Tennis. Women: Basketball, Tennis.
Campus Life. About 18% of men, 13% of women live in traditional dormitories; no coed dormitories; rest live in off-campus housing or commute. No intervisitation in men's or women's dormitory rooms. There are no fraternities or sororities on campus. About 80% of resident students leave campus on weekends.
Annual Costs. Tuition and fees, $1,385 (out-of-state, $3,447); room and board, $960. About 73% of students receive financial aid. Assistance is typically divided 11% scholarship, 43% federal grants, 39% loan, 7% work, according to most recent data available. College reports some scholarships awarded on the basis of academic merit alone.

Old Dominion University

Norfolk, Virginia 23529-0050 **(804) 683-3637; (800) 348-7926**

A state-supported university, serving primarily Virginia. Most convenient major airport: Norfolk International.

Founded: 1930
Affiliation: State
UG Enrollment: 4,820 M, 4,805 W (full-time); 999 M, 1,000 W (part-time)
Total Enrollment: 16,799
Cost: < $10K
% Receiving Financial Aid: 65%
Admission: Non-selective
Application Deadline: May 1

Admission. High school graduates with 16 academic units, B/C average, minimum combined SAT score of 850, and rank in upper half of high school class eligible. About 78% of applicants accepted, 37% of these actually enroll; 35% of freshman graduate in top fifth of high school class, 70% in top two-fifths. Average freshman SAT scores: 440 verbal, 494 mathematical. *Required:* SAT(preferred) or ACT. Criteria considered in admissions, in order of importance: high school academic record, standardized test scores, recommendations, writing sample, extracurricular activities. *Out-of-state* freshman applicants: university actively seeks students from out of state; no limit; no special requirements. States from which most out-of-state students are drawn: New Jersey, New York, Pennsylvania, Maryland. *Entrance programs:* early admission, midyear admission, advanced placement. *Apply* by May 1. *Transfers* welcome; 1,104 enrolled 1993–94.
Academic Environment. Degrees offered: bachelors, masters, doctoral. *Undergraduate studies* offered by schools of Arts and Letters, Business and Public Administration, Education, Engineering and Technology, Sciences, and Health Sciences. *Majors offered* in addition to usual studies include nuclear medicine technology, environmental engineering, graphic arts, sports medicine. General education requirements include composition, literature, mathematics, foreign language, fine arts, philosophy, history, natural science, social science. Average freshman class size: 35.

About 40% of students entering as freshmen graduate within four years, 45% eventually; 75% of freshman return for sophomore year. *Special programs:* CLEP, independent study, study abroad, honors, undergraduate research, individualized majors, articulation agreements with area community colleges, joint BS/MD program with Eastern Virginia Medical School, extensive internship/cooperative work-study programs, cross registration with William & Mary, Norfolk State. *Calendar:* semester, summer school.
Undergraduate degrees conferred (1,819). 20% were in Business and Management, 18% were in Education, 11% were in Social Sciences, 9% were in Engineering, 7% were in Letters, 7% were in Engineering and Engineering Related Technology, 6% were in Psychology, 5% were in Health Sciences, 5% were in Life Sciences, 4% were in Allied Health, 3% were in Visual and Performing Arts, remainder in 7 other fields.
Graduates Career Data. Career Development Services provided. *Careers in business and industry* pursued by 70% of graduates, according to most recent data available. Fields typically hiring largest numbers of graduates include engineering, banking, accounting, public school systems, medical.
Faculty. About 86% of faculty hold PhD or equivalent. About 85% of undergraduate classes taught by tenured faculty. About 37% of teaching faculty are female.
Student Body. About 86% of students from in state; 99% from Middle Atlantic. An estimated 11% of students reported as Black, 5% Asian, 2% Hispanic. Average age of undergraduate student: 23.
Varsity Sports. Men (Div.I): Baseball, Basketball, Diving, Golf, Soccer, Swimming, Tennis, Wrestling. Women (Div.I): Basketball, Cross Country, Diving, Field Hockey, Lacrosse, Soccer, Swimming, Tennis.
Campus Life. Current students report over 200 student organizations and intramural sports offer opportunities for extracurricular activities and recreation, and, of course, "the beach!". About 20% of men, 20% of women live in coed dormitories; 70% of men, 70% women commute. Freshmen given preference in college housing if all students cannot be accommodated. Intervisitation in men's and women's dormitory rooms limited; sexes segregated by suite. There are 15 fraternities, 9 sororities on campus, which about 9% of men, 9% of women join; 10% of men, 10% of women live in fraternities and sororities.
Annual Costs. Tuition and fees, $3,817 (out-of-state, $9,427); room and board, $4,500; estimated $500 other, exclusive of travel. About 65% of students receive financial aid; average amount of assistance, $4,487. University reports scholarships awarded on the basis of merit alone.

Olivet College

Olivet, Michigan 49076 **(800) 456-7189**

An independent college, affiliated with the United Church of Christ and the Congregational Church, located in a village of 1,200, 22 miles northeast of Battle Creek, and 30 miles south of Lansing. Most convenient major airport: Lansing, MI.

Founded: 1844
Affiliation: Independent (United Church of Christ, Congregational Church)
UG Enrollment: 673 M, W (full-time)
Cost: $10K–$20K
Admission: Non-selective
Application Deadline: July 1

Admission. About 92% of applicants accepted, 47% of these actually enroll. About 14% of freshmen graduate in top fifth of high school class, 44% in top two-fifths. *Required:* SAT or ACT; interview in some cases. *Non-academic factors* considered in admissions: special talents. *Apply* by July 1. *Transfers* welcome.

Academic Environment. *Degrees:* BA, BM, BMEd. About 50% of general education requirements for graduation are elective; distribution requirements fairly numerous. The CORE Curriculum requires students to become involved in a 6-semester experience during which they learn about their social, cultural, historical, political, economic, and scientific backgrounds. Facilities reported as adequate to meet student demand.

About 38% of students entering as freshmen graduate eventually; 67% of freshmen return for sophomore year. *Special programs:* CLEP, independent study, study abroad, honors, undergraduate research, professional semester, personalized majors. *Calendar:* semester, summer school.

Undergraduate degrees conferred (152). 24% were in Business and Management, 20% were in Social Sciences, 20% were in Education, 10% were in Life Sciences, 9% were in Psychology, 7% were in Visual and Performing Arts, 3% were in Communications, 3% were in Letters, remainder in 4 other fields.

Graduates Career Data. According to most recent data available, full-time graduate or professional study pursued immediately after graduation by 9% of students. *Careers in business and industry* pursued by 41% of graduates.

Student Body. College seeks a national student body; 99% of students from North Central. An estimated 52% of students reported as Protestant, 26% Catholic, 20% unaffiliated, 2% other; 9% Black, 1% Hispanic, 1% other minority, according to most recent data available.

Varsity Sports. Men (NCAA,Div.III): Baseball, Basketball, Cross Country, Football, Golf, Soccer, Tennis, Track, Wrestling. Women (NCAA,Div.III): Basketball, Softball, Swimming, Tennis, Volleyball.

Campus Life. About 27% of men, 28% of women live in traditional dormitories; 44% of men, 22% of women in coed dormitories; 23% of men, 41% of women live in off-campus housing or commute. Freshmen given preference in college housing if all students cannot be accommodated. Sexes segregated in coed dormitories by wing. There are 2 fraternities, 3 sororities, 1 coed society on campus which about 15% each of men, women join; 6% of men, 9% of women live in fraternities and sororities. About 65% of students leave campus on weekends.

Annual Costs. Tuition and fees, $10,500; room and board, $3,500. About 80% of students receive financial aid. College reports some scholarships awarded on the basis of academic merit alone. *Meeting Costs:* college offers auxiliary loan program, monthly payment plan.

Olivet Nazarene College

Kankakee, Illinois 60901 **(815) 939-5011**

An evangelical liberal arts institution, located in a tri-city area (pop. 60,000), 60 miles south of Chicago. Most convenient major airport: O'Hare or Midway (Chicago).

Founded: 1907
Affiliation: Church of the Nazarene
UG Enrollment: 968 M, 1,226 W (full and part-time)
Total Enrollment: 2,194
Cost: < $10K
% Receiving Financial Aid: 80%
Admission: Non-selective
Application Deadline: Aug. 31

Admission. Graduates of accredited high schools with 15 units and C average eligible; others admitted by examination. Average freshman ACT scores, according to most recent data available: 20.7 composite. *Required:* ACT (for placement only), acceptance of "moral standards" which forbid use of tobacco and alcohol, immoral conduct. *Apply* by August 31. *Transfers* welcome.

Academic Environment. Degrees offered: associates, bachelors, masters. General education requirements for bachelors degree include 53–64 hours (out of 128 total). Olivet fosters "education with a Christian purpose". *Majors offered* in addition to usual studies include Biblical literature, Christian education, environmental science, medical technology, nursing, social justice, social work, interdisciplinary general studies. About 45% of entering students graduate eventually. *Special programs:* CLEP, independent study, honors, undergraduate research, 3-year degree, individualized majors. Adult programs: Adult Degree Completion Program. *Calendar:* semester, summer school.

Undergraduate degrees conferred (258). 17% were in Education, 12% were in Business and Management, 9% were in Psychology, 9% were in Public Affairs, 7% were in Health Sciences, 6% were in Marketing and Distribution, 5% were in Philosophy and Religion, 5% were in Home Economics, 4% were in Social Sciences, 4% were in Life Sciences, 4% were in Physical Sciences, 3% were in Protective Services, 3% were in Letters, 3% were in Communications, remainder in 8 other fields.

Graduates Career Data. According to most recent data available, full-time graduate or professional study pursued immediately after graduation by 24% of students.

Faculty. More than half of faculty hold PhD or equivalent.

Student Body. College does not seek a national student body; about 50% of students from Illinois; 70% from North Central. An estimated 4% of students reported as Black, 1% Hispanic, 2% Asian, 1% other minority, according to most recent data available.

Religious Orientation. Olivet Nazarene is a church-related institution; 12 hours in Biblical literature and theology, attendance at chapel services 2 times weekly required of all students. "Students and faculty are expected to practice a lifestyle consistent with a Christian commitment to the ethical standards of the Bible and the sponsoring denomination."

Varsity Sports. Men (NAIA, NCCAA): Baseball, Basketball, Cross Country, Football, Golf, Soccer, Tennis, Track. Women (NAIA, NCCAA): Basketball, Softball, Tennis, Volleyball.

Campus Life. About 80% of men, 80% of women live in traditional dormitories; no coed dormitories; rest live in off-campus housing or commute. No intervisitation in men's or women's dormitory rooms. There are no fraternities or sororities. About 20% of resident students leave campus on weekends.

Annual Costs. Tuition and fees, $7,836; room and board, $4,140. About 90% of students receive financial aid. University reports some scholarships awarded on the basis of academic merit alone.

State University College at Oneonta

(See State University of New York)

Oral Roberts University

Tulsa, Oklahoma 74171 **(918) 495-6518**

An interdenominational, Christian institution, located on a 500-acre campus in the Tulsa metropolitan area of 724,000. Most convenient major airport: Tulsa International.

Founded: 1963
Affiliation: Independent
UG Enrollment: 1,431 M, 1,709 W (full-time)
Total Enrollment: 3,905
Cost: < $10K
% Receiving Financial Aid: 82%
Admission: Selective (+)
Application Deadline: Rolling

Admission is selective (+). Applicants are expected to demonstrate "compatibility with the spiritual and intellectual philosophy." About 60% of applicants accepted, 53% of these actually enroll. About 25% of freshmen graduate in top fifth of high school class, 70% in top two-fifths. Average freshman scores: SAT, 524 verbal, 589 mathematical; ACT, 22 M, 26 W composite. *Required:* SAT or ACT, pastor's recommendation, essay; interview recommended. Criteria considered in admissions, in order of importance: standardized test scores, high school academic record, writing sample, recommendations, extracurricular activities; other factor considered: special talents. About 23% of entering freshman from private schools. *Apply:* rolling admissions. *Transfers* welcome; 247 enrolled 1993–94.

Academic Environment. Degrees offered: bachelors, masters. General education requirements for graduation include 70 hours of core courses. Students report that small classes allow for a challenging program and individualized attention. Undergraduate class size: 82% of classes under 20, 17% 20–40, 1% over 40. About 49% of entering freshman graduate within four years, 63% eventually; 85% of freshman return for sophomore year. *Special programs:* CLEP, independent study, honors, undergraduate research, 3-year degree. Adult programs: Center for Lifelong Education offers credit and noncredit courses. *Calendar:* semester, summer school.

Undergraduate degrees conferred (508). 26% were in Business and Management, 18% were in Education, 9% were in Theology, 8% were in Communications Technologies, 6% were in Visual and Performing Arts, 6% were in Life Sciences, 4% were in Psychology, 4% were in Communications, 3% were in Public Affairs, 3% were in Social Sciences, 3% were in Health Sciences, 3% were in Letters, remainder in 6 other fields.
Graduates Career Data. Advanced studies pursued by 63% of students; 14% enter law school; 21% enter business school; 11% enter medical school; 6% enter dental school. Student assessment of Career Counseling Program reported as good for both career guidance and job placement. Alumni reported as active in career guidance, but there is not a large enough network to be helpful in job placement yet.
Faculty. About 79% of faculty hold PhD or equivalent. About 34% of undergraduate classes taught by tenured faculty. About 36% of teaching faculty are female; 10% Black, 2% Hispanic.
Student Body. University seeks a national student body; 23% of students from in state; 14% New England, 10% Midwest, 17% South, 18% West, 10% Northeast, 7% foreign. An estimated 98% of students reported as Protestant, 2% Catholic; 19% Black, 3% Hispanic.
Religious Orientations. Oral Roberts is a "Christian-centered" institution; makes some religious demands on students; 12 hours of theology, attendance at 2 chapel services each week, Sunday worship off-campus required of all students.
Varsity Sports. Men (NCAA, Div.I): Baseball, Basketball, Golf, Soccer, Tennis, Track. Women (NCAA, Div.I): Basketball, Soccer, Tennis, Volleyball.
Campus Life. About 70% of men, 70% of women live in traditional dormitories; no coed dormitories; 20% of men, 20% of women live in off-campus college-related housing; rest commute, according to most recent data available. Freshmen given preference in college housing if all students cannot be accommodated. Intervisitation in men's and women's dormitory rooms limited. There are no fraternities or sororities. About 10% of students leave campus on weekends, according to most recent data available.
Annual Costs. Tuition and fees, $7,369; room and board, $3,724; estimated $1,000 other, exclusive of travel. About 82% of students receive financial aid; average amount of assistance, $8,000. Assistance is typically divided 15% scholarship, 25% grant, 40% loan, 20% work. University reports 754 scholarships awarded on the basis of academic merit alone, 319 for special talents, 1,214 for need alone. Meeting Cost: University offers tuition installment plan.

Oregon College of Education

(See Western Oregon State College)

Oregon Health Sciences University

Portland, Oregon 97201

A state institution offering associate, baccalaureate, and professional degrees in the health sciences.

Undergraduate degrees conferred (161). 76% were in Health Sciences, 24% were in Allied Health.

Oregon Institute of Technology

Klamath Falls, Oregon 97601-8801 (503) 885-1151

Oregon Institute of Technology is the polytechnic college of the Oregon State System of Higher Education; the 173-acre campus is located at the northern edge of a city of 17,600. Most convenient major airport: Klamath Falls.

Founded: 1946
Affiliation: State
UG Enrollment: 1,000 M, 800 W (full-time); 400 M, 300 W (part-time)
Cost: < $10K
% Receiving Financial Aid: 78%
Admission: Non-selective
Application Deadline: July 1

Admission. Graduates of accredited high schools with 14 units in college preparatory courses with 2.5 GPA, or with minimum combined SAT score of 890 or ACT composite of 20 eligible; 92% of applicants accepted, 60% actually enroll; 10% of freshman graduate in top fifth of high school class, 30% in top two-fifths. Average freshman SAT scores: 421 M, 412 W verbal, 517 M, 465 W mathematical. *Required:* SAT. Criteria considered in admissions, in order of importance: high school academic record, standardized test scores. *Out-of-state* freshman applicants: institute actively seeks students from out of state; no limit; no special requirements. States from which most out-of-state students are drawn: Washington, California. *Entrance programs:* early decision, midyear admission, advanced placement. *Apply* by July 1; rolling admissions. *Transfers* welcome; 220 enrolled 1993–94.
Academic Environment. Degrees offered: associates, bachelors. About 20% of general education requirements for graduation are elective; distribution requirements limited. *Majors offered* in addition to usual studies include laser electro-optics technology, vascular technology option in medical imaging, diesel power technology. About 39% of students entering as freshmen graduate within four years, 63% eventually; 70% of freshmen return for sophomore year. Average undergraduate class size: 55% under 20, 35% 20–40, 10% over 40. *Special programs:* CLEP, independent study, work experience externships, internship/cooperative work-study programs in engineering. *Calendar:* quarter, summer school.
Undergraduate degrees conferred (357). 64% were in Engineering and Engineering Related Technology, 13% were in Business and Management, 13% were in Allied Health, 7% were in Health Sciences, 3% were in Business (Administrative Support).
Graduates Career Data. About 92% of 1992–93 graduates employed. Employers typically hiring largest numbers of graduates include Boeing, Intel, Hewlett-Packard, Microsoft. Career Development Services include classes and seminars in interviewing, resume writing and job-search. On-Campus interviewing is extensive.
Faculty. About 20% of faculty hold PhD or equivalent. About 40% of undergraduate classes taught by tenured faculty.
Student Body. Institute seeks a national student body; 70% of students from in state; 8% West, 20% Northwest, 2% foreign. An estimated 3% of students reported as Black, 4% Hispanic, 4% Asian, 2% other ethnic minorities. Average age of undergraduate student: 25.
Varsity Sports. Men: Basketball. Women: Softball.
Campus Life. About 10% of men, 10% of women live in coed dormitories; rest commute. Intervisitation in men's and women's dormitory rooms limited; sexes segregated by wing. There are 2 fraternities, 1 sorority; about 1% of men, 1% of women join; they provide no on-campus residence facilities. About 40% of resident students leave campus on weekends.
Annual Costs. Tuition and fees, $2,742 (out-of-state, $7,600); room and board, $3,500; estimated $1,350 other, exclusive of travel. About 78% of students receive financial aid; average amount of assistance, $2,100. Assistance is typically divided 10% scholarship, 50% grant, 20% loan, 20% work. Institute reports 13% of scholarships awarded on the basis of academic merit, 2% for special talents, 85% for need alone. *Meeting Costs:* institute offers deferred tuition plan and payment by credit card.

Oregon State University

Corvallis, Oregon 97331 (503) 737-4411

A land-grant and sea-grant institution, Oregon State offers studies in the liberal arts, as well as in the sciences, technology, and professional/vocational fields. The 400-acre campus is located in a community of 42,000, 80 miles south of Portland. Most convenient major airports: Portland or Eugene.

Founded: 1858
Affiliation: State
UG Enrollment: 6,964 M, 5,417 W (full-time); 424 M, 436 W (part-time)
Total Enrollment: 16,024
Cost: < $10K
% Receiving Financial Aid: 55%
Admission: Non-selective
Application Deadline: March 1

Admission. Oregon graduates of standard high schools with 14 units and 2.75 average eligible; 78% of applicants accepted, 50% of these actually enroll. Average freshman scores, according to most recent data available: SAT, 452 M, 438 W verbal, 542 M, 485 W mathematical; ACT, 21.7 M, 19.8 W composite, 23.0 M, 19.7 W mathematical. *Required:* SAT or ACT. *Out-of-state* freshman applicants:

university welcomes students from out of state. Requirements for out-of-state applicants: GPA of 3.0, 14 high school academic units. State does not limit out-of-state enrollment. *Entrance programs:* early admission, advanced placement. *Apply* by March 1. *Transfers* welcome.

Academic Environment. *Undergraduate studies* offered by colleges of Liberal Arts, Science, Agriculture, Business, Education, Engineering, Forestry, Home Economics, Pharmacy (5-year), Health and Physical Education. *Majors offered* include usual arts and sciences, anthropology, geography, medical technology, microbiology, technical journalism, physical activity for the older adult, hotel, restaurant and tourism management, health promotion and education, environmental health and safety, certificate in science, technology and society; departments of Geoscience, and Crop and Soil Science. General education requirements for graduation include 9 hours in English, 15 hours in natural sciences and/or mathematics, 12 hours in humanities and/or arts, 12 hours in social sciences.

About 50–55% of students entering as freshmen graduate eventually; 76% of freshmen return for sophomore year. *Special programs:* CLEP, independent study, study abroad, honors, marine science center at Newport, 3–2 program in engineering, 2–2 program in food science and technology, 3–1 programs in nursing, dental hygiene, 3–1 program in occupational therapy, joint programs in education, geological, metallurgical, mining engineering. Adult programs: Continuing Higher Education Programs; Evening/Weekend College. *Calendar:* quarter, summer school.

Undergraduate degrees conferred (2,917). 18% were in Business and Management, 11% were in Engineering, 10% were in Education, 9% were in Social Sciences, 7% were in Letters, 6% were in Home Economics, 4% were in Liberal/General Studies, 4% were in Life Sciences, 4% were in Health Sciences, 4% were in Computer and Engineering Related Technology, 3% were in Multi/Interdisciplinary Studies, 3% were in Psychology, 3% were in Renewable Natural Resources, 3% were in Agribusiness and Agricultural Production, remainder in 10 other fields.

Graduate Career Data. According to most recent data available, full-time graduate or professional study pursued immediately after graduation by 35% of students. Graduate and professional schools enrolling largest numbers of graduates include U. of Oregon, U. of Washington, U. of California Davis, Oregon Health Sciences. *Careers in business and industry:* Corporations typically hiring largest numbers of graduates include Westinghouse Electric, U.S. Forest Service, Boeing, Microsoft.

Faculty. About 80% of faculty hold PhD or equivalent.

Student Body. University seeks a national student body; 82% of students from Oregon; 1,541 foreign. An estimated 1% of students reported as Black, 2% Hispanic, 6% Asian, 2% Native American, 4% other minority, according to most recent data available.

Varsity Sports. Men (NCAA Div.I): Baseball, Basketball, Crew, Football, Golf, Soccer, Wrestling. Women (NCAA Div.I): Basketball, Crew, Golf, Gymnastics, Soccer, Softball, Swimming, Volleyball.

Campus Life. Cars allowed. Alcohol prohibited in any recognized student living unit (except for married student housing) and at all university functions attended by minors.

About 17% of men, 22% of women live in traditional dormitories; 1% of men, 3% of women live in coed dormitories; 3% of men, 2% of women live in off-campus college-related housing; 64% of men, 63% of women commute. Intervisitation in men's and women's dormitory rooms limited. There are 28 fraternities, 15 sororities on campus which about 22% of men, 20% of women join; 15% of men live in fraternities and 11% of women live in sororities.

Annual Costs. Tuition and fees, $2,691 (out-of-state, $6,972); room and board, $3,177. About 55% of students receive financial aid; assistance is typically divided 46% scholarship, 52% loan, 2% work. University reports some scholarships awarded on the basis of academic merit alone. *Meeting Costs:* University offers alternative loan programs, PLUS Loans.

University of Oregon

Eugene, Oregon 97403 **(503) 346-1279**

A state-supported university, located in a city of 106,000, 110 miles south of Portland, site of the schools of Medicine, Dentistry, and Nursing. Most convenient major airports: Eugene, or Portland.

Founded: 1876
Affiliation: State
UG Enrollment: 5,378 M, 5,736 W (full-time); 923 M, 847 W (part-time)

Cost: $10K–$20K
% Receiving Financial Aid: 55%
Admission: Selective
Application Deadline: March 1

Admission is selective. About 80% of applicants accepted, 38% of these actually enroll. Average freshman scores: SAT, 40% of freshman score above 500 on verbal, 11% above 600, 1% above 700; 67% score above 500 on mathematical, 26% above 600, 5% above 700. *Required:* SAT or ACT. Criteria considered in admissions, in order of importance: high school academic record, standardized test scores, recommendations. *Out-of-state* freshman applicants: university actively seeks students from out of state; no limits. Required for out-of-state students: transfer GPA 2.50; 79% accepted, 28% enroll. States from which most out-of-state students are drawn: California, Hawaii, Washington. Entrance program: advanced placement. *Apply* by March 1; rolling admissions. *Transfers* welcome; 1,560 enrolled 1993–94.

Academic Environment. Degrees offered: bachelors, masters, doctoral. Administration source characterizes student body as primarily interested in occupational/professional goals, and reports student concern about the relationship of the academic program to future careers. Student concern also reported about access to high demand programs such as business, computer science. *Undergraduate studies* offered by colleges of Arts and Sciences, Business Administration, Education, schools of Architecture and Allied Arts, Community Service and Public Affairs, Journalism, Music, School of Health, Physical Education, Recreation. *Majors offered* in Arts and Sciences in addition to usual studies include area studies (African, Asian, Latin American, Russian and East European), Chinese, classical civilizations, geography, Japanese, linguistics, theater.

About 32% of students entering as freshmen graduate within four years, 53% eventually; 84% of freshmen return for sophomore year. *Special programs:* CLEP, independent study, study abroad, 4-year honors college, undergraduate research, individualized majors, credit by examination, combined programs physics/engineering, 3–2 programs with Oregon State, cross registration with Oregon State. *Library:* 1,804,926 volumes, 21,081 periodicals, other materials include extensive collections of manuscripts, slides, photos, maps, media, government documents; open-stack privileges. *Calendar:* 3 12-week terms, summer school.

Undergraduate degrees conferred (2,656). 21% were in Social Sciences, 15% were in Business and Management, 12% were in Letters, 11% were in Psychology, 9% were in Communications, 6% were in Education, 6% were in Visual and Performing Arts, 4% were in Architecture and Environmental Design, 3% were in Foreign Languages, remainder in 11 other fields.

Graduates Career Data. Advanced studies pursued by 16% of students. About 83% of 1992–93 graduates employed, (75% full-time). Career Development Services include courses plus assistance with interviews, resume writing, as well as placement services.

Faculty. About 81% of faculty hold PhD or equivalent. About 35% of teaching faculty are female; 2% Black, 3% Hispanic, 4% other ethnic minorities.

Student Body. University seeks a national student body; 55% of students from in state; 62% Northwest, 2% Middle Atlantic, 4% Midwest, 2% South, 21% West, 10% foreign. An estimated 1% of students reported as Black, 2% Hispanic, 5% Asian, less than 1% Native American, according to most recent data available. *Minority group students:* majority of minority students given financial and academic help through special programs. Average age of undergraduate student: 22.

Varsity Sports. Men (Div.I): Basketball, Cross Country, Football, Golf, Tennis, Track, Wrestling. Women (Div.I): Basketball, Cross Country, Golf, Softball, Tennis, Track, Volleyball.

Campus Life. Students reported to be very much "'oriented to environmental concerns, the outdoors, and track/jogging." All students may select place of residence from variety of options, including fraternity/sorority houses, cooperative houses, dormitories (choice of with or without closing hours open to all students), private housing. Cars allowed.

About 14% of men, 16% of women live in coed dormitories; 76% of men, 72% of women live in off-campus college-related housing; 3% of men, 3% of women commute. Freshmen given preference in college housing if all students cannot be accommodated. Sexes segregated in coed dorms by wing, floor, suite. There are 16 fraternities, 11 sororities on campus; about 7% of men, 9% of women live in fraternities and sororities. About 20% of resident students leave campus on weekends.

Annual Costs. Estimated for 1994–95: tuition and fees, $3,027 (out-of-state, $10,590); room and board, $3,800; estimated $2,200 other, exclusive of travel. About 55% of students receive financial aid. University reports over $2,000,000 in scholarships awarded on the basis of academic merit, (some require demonstrated need).

State University College at Oswego

(See State University of New York)

Ottawa University

Ottawa, Kansas 66067 (913) 242-5200

A small, church-related, liberal arts institution, located in a town of 12,000, 50 miles southwest of Kansas City.

Founded: 1865
Affiliation: American Baptist
UG Enrollment: 299 M, 241 W (full-time)
Cost: < $10K
% Receiving Financial Aid: 90%
Admission: Non-selective
Application Deadline: Rolling

Admission. Graduates of accredited high schools, preferably with college preparatory curriculum, eligible; others admitted on basis of testing and recommendation; 64% of applicants accepted, 39% of these actually enroll; 27% of freshmen graduate in top fifth of high school class, 51% in top two-fifths. Average freshman ACT score: 21 composite. *Required:* SAT or ACT; interview recommended. Criteria considered in admissions, in order of importance: high school academic record, standardized test scores, recommendations (alumni), extracurricular activities; other factors considered: special talents, alumni children, religious affiliation and/or commitment. *Apply:* no specific deadline; rolling admissions. *Transfers* welcome; 113 enrolled 1993–94.

Academic Environment. Educational program includes 3 required interdisciplinary seminars (one for freshmen and transfers, and one for seniors), and general education distribution requirements. Independent and directed study is an option. Degree offered: bachelors. About 36% of students entering as freshmen graduate eventually; 72% of freshmen return for sophomore year. Students report that small classes allow for a great deal of interaction between students and faculty. Average undergraduate class size: 34. *Special programs:* CLEP, independent study, study abroad, honors, undergraduate research, 3-year degree, individualized majors. *Calendar:* 2 15-week semesters each including 15-week and 7½ week courses, summer session.

Undergraduate degrees conferred (100). 25% were in Business and Management, 24% were in Education, 9% were in Communications, 8% were in Computer and Engineering Related Technology, 7% were in Public Affairs, 6% were in Psychology, 5% were in Visual and Performing Arts, 5% were in Social Sciences, 5% were in Letters, 4% were in Life Sciences, remainder in Mathematics.

Graduate Career Data. Advanced studies pursued by 23% of students. About 95% of 1992–93 graduates employed. Career Development Services include resume writing techniques, interview skills, networking skills, vacancy bulletins, career counseling, career fairs and interview days.

Faculty. About 42% of faculty hold PhD or equivalent. About 40% of teaching faculty are female.

Student Body. University seeks a national student body; 55% of students from in state; 83% from Midwest. An estimated 61% of students reported as Protestant, 11% Catholic; 7% Black, 2% Hispanic, 2% Native American, 1% Asian.

Religious Orientation. Ottawa is a church-related institution; attendance at cultural or religious events each semester and one course in religion required of all students. Places of worship available in immediate community for Catholics and Protestants, 40 miles away for Jews.

Varsity Sports. Men (NAIA): Baseball, Basketball, Cross Country, Football, Soccer, Track. Women (NAIA): Basketball, Cross Country, Track, Volleyball.

Campus Life. About 59% of students live in traditional dormitories; rest commute. Intervisitation in men's and women's dormitory rooms limited. There are no fraternities or sororities. About 35% of resident students leave campus on weekends.

Annual Costs. Tuition and fees, $7,245; room and board, $3,245; estimated $1,780 other, exclusive of travel. About 90% of students receive financial aid; average amount of assistance $8,500. Assistance is typically divided 50% scholarship/grant, 38% loan, 12% work. University reports 230 scholarships awarded on the basis of academic merit alone, 250 for special talents. *Meeting Costs:* monthly payment plan.

Otterbein College

Westerville, Ohio 43081 (800) 488-8144

An independent, liberal arts college with a strong association with the United Methodist Church, Otterbein is located on a 70-acre campus in a community of 22,000, 10 miles north of Columbus. Most convenient major airport: Columbus.

Founded: 1847
Affiliation: Independent (United Methodist)
UG Enrollment: 649 M, 1,041 W (full-time); 208 M, 567 W (part-time)
Cost: $10K–$20K
% Receiving Financial Aid: 90%
Admission: Selective
Application Deadline: April 20

Admission is selective. About 79% of applicants accepted, 33% of these actually enroll; 26% of freshmen graduate in top tenth of high school class, 57% in top quarter. Average freshman scores: SAT, 453 verbal, 504 mathematical; 31% of freshman score above 500 on verbal, 8% above 600; 46% score above 500 on mathematical, 9% above 600; ACT, 22 composite. *Required:* SAT or ACT, minimum HS GPA 2.5; interview recommended. Criteria considered in admissions, in order of importance: high school academic record, standardized test scores, recommendations, extracurricular activities; other factor considered: special talents. *Entrance programs:* deferred admission, advanced placement. *Apply* by April 20; rolling admissions. *Transfers* welcome; 93 enrolled 1993–94.

Academic Environment. Degrees offered: bachelors, masters. Students characterized by administration spokesman as primarily concerned with occupational/professional goals, but with strong social interests as well. College governance system gives equal representation to students and faculty. Core requirements include 10 courses in "integrative studies" which include fine arts, literature, religion/philosophy, natural and social sciences. Otterbein has developed an unusual BA in equine science and stable management and has added a BFA in theater/musical theater. *Majors offered* include usual arts and sciences, business administration, business/organization communications, international studies, elementary education, home economics, dual degree engineering.

About 74% of entering students graduate within four years; 82% of freshmen return for sophomore year. Average undergraduate class size: 25. *Special programs:* CLEP, independent study, study abroad (including semester at sea), honors, Washington Semester, Philadelphia Semester, teaching experience in New Mexico, individualized degree program, nursing program with St. Ann's Hospital, credit by examination, 3–2 program in engineering, cross registration with Columbus State Community College. Adult programs: Weekend College and Graduate Education Program. *Calendar:* quarters, summer school.

Undergraduate degrees conferred (380). 23% were in Business and Management, 15% were in Communications, 13% were in Education, 8% were in Psychology, 7% were in Health Sciences, 7% were in Social Sciences, 6% were in Life Sciences, 4% were in Visual and Performing Arts, 4% were in Letters, 3% were in Physical Sciences, 3% were in Agribusiness and Agricultural Production, remainder in 6 other fields.

Graduates Career Data. Advanced studies pursued immediately after graduation by 13% of students; 3% enter medical school; 2% enter law school; 2% enter business school. Medical schools typically enrolling largest numbers of graduates include Ohio State U.;

law schools include U. of Toledo, Ohio State U. Career Development Services include resume writing, interviewing techniques, interview preparation, on-campus interviews. Alumni reported as active in both career guidance and job placement.

Faculty. About 64% of faculty hold PhD or equivalent. About 61% of teaching faculty are female; 3% Black, 1% Hispanic, 7% other ethnic minority.

Student Body. About 89% of students from in state. An estimated 40% of students reported as Protestant, 20% Catholic, 2% other; 4% as Black, 1% Hispanic, 1% Asian, 2% other ethnic minority. *Minority group students:* special financial and academic provisions.

Religious Orientation. Otterbein is an independent institution with ties to the United Methodist Church, 1 course in philosophy or non-Western religion, 2 religious courses required of all students. All religious activities on campus interdenominational in nature; coordinated by Religious Activities Council. Places of worship available in immediate community for Protestants and Catholics, 15 miles away for Jews.

Varsity Sports. Men (Div.III): Baseball, Basketball, Cross Country, Football, Golf, Soccer, Tennis, Track. Women (Div.III): Basketball, Cross Country, Soccer, Softball, Tennis, Track, Volleyball.

Campus Life. Student leader describes college as "a quiet campus in a peaceful village." High interest reported in fraternities/sororities, varsity sports (most popular football, basketball), and intramurals (most popular men's football, basketball, coed volleyball). Limited intervisitation in suite rooms (available only to upper-class students). Alcohol prohibited on campus in any college-related housing or at college functions. Seniors, selected juniors, commuters and students 22 or over may live off campus. Other students must live in residence halls or fraternity and sorority houses.

About 45% of men, 55% of women live in traditional dormitories; 24% of men, 22% of women live in off-campus college-related housing; 19% of men, 17% of women commute, according to most recent data available. Freshmen given preference in college housing if all students cannot be accommodated. There are 7 local social fraternities, 6 sororities, which about 50% of men, 50% of women join; 12% of men, 6% of women live in fraternities and sororities, according to most recent data available. About 50% of resident students leave campus on weekends.

Annual Costs. Tuition and fees, $12,888; room and board, $4,440; estimated $500 other, exclusive of travel. About 90% of students receive financial aid. Assistance is typically divided 25% scholarship, 25% loan, 15% work, according to most recent data available. College reports some scholarships awarded on basis of academic merit alone. *Meeting Costs:* college offers payment plan, PLUS Loans.

Ouachita Baptist University

Arkadelphia, Arkansas 71998-0001 (501) 245-5000

A church-related university, located in a community of 10,100, 70 miles southwest of Little Rock. Most convenient major airport: Little Rock.

Founded: 1885
Affiliation: Southern Baptist
UG Enrollment: 646 M, 659 W (full-time)
Cost: < $10K
% Receiving Financial Aid: 93%
Admission: Non-selective
Application Deadline: Aug. 15

Admission. High school graduates with 15 units and minimum HS GPA 2.5 eligible; others admitted conditionally; 85% of applicants accepted, 75% of these actually enroll. Average freshmen ACT scores: 23.8 composite. *Required:* ACT score of 19 or equivalent on SAT. Criteria considered in admissions, in order of importance: high school academic record, standardized test scores, recommendations, writing sample. Entrance program: advanced placement. *Apply* by August 15; rolling admissions. *Transfers* welcome; 53 enrolled 1993–94.

Academic Environment. Degree offered: bachelors. *Majors offered* in addition to usual studies include environmental analysis, cross cultural studies major in religion, finance, management, marketing. The burgeoning international studies program provides opportunities for students to study in six nations; in addition the honors program offers a competitive scholarship component in which students may apply for University funds to travel anywhere in the world for research for a senior thesis. A new translation service provides businesses and institutions help in translation in seventeen languages. About 32% of students entering as freshmen graduate within four years, 60% eventually; 75% of freshmen return for sophomore year. Average undergraduate class size: 58% under 20, 37% 20–40, 5% over 40. *Special programs:* January term offering limited number of special courses, CLEP, independent study, study abroad, honors, undergraduate research, individualized majors, 3–2 programs in engineering, medical technology, religion, cross registration with Henderson State U., internships, shadowing program as part of placement. *Calendar:* semester, summer school.

Undergraduate degrees conferred (211). 24% were in Education, 20% were in Business and Management, 12% were in Social Sciences, 9% were in Theology, 6% were in Communications, 5% were in Psychology, 4% were in Visual and Performing Arts, 4% were in Physical Sciences, 4% were in Life Sciences, 4% were in Home Economics, remainder in 6 other fields.

Graduates Career Data. Advanced studies pursued by 33% of students. Fields typically hiring largest numbers of graduates include education, business, public service, medical professions. Career Development Services include seminars in resume development, interview skills, job fairs, services of a certified counselor to help students identify career interests and opportunities.

Faculty. About 65% of faculty hold PhD or equivalent. About 60% of undergraduate classes taught by tenured faculty. About 26% of teaching faculty are female.

Student Body. University seeks a national student body; 80% of students from in state; 8% Midwest, 5% South, 3% West, 5% foreign. An estimated 88% of students reported as Protestant, 2% Catholic, 3% unaffiliated, 7% other; 5% Black, 1% Hispanic, 6% other ethnic minority.

Religious Orientation. Ouachita Baptist is a church-related institution; 2 courses in religion, attendance at chapel services required of all students.

Varsity Sports. Men (NAIA): Baseball, Basketball, Cross Country, Diving, Football, Golf, Soccer, Swimming, Tennis, Track. Women (NAIA): Basketball, Soccer, Swimming, Tennis, Volleyball.

Campus Life. Students enjoy intramural sports, nearby State and National Parks, and occasional trips to Little Rock and Hot Springs for recreation, when not studying. About 70% of students live in traditional dormitories; 8% live in off-campus college related housing; rest commute. No intervisitation in men's or women's dormitory rooms. There are 4 fraternities, 4 sororities. About 35–40% of students leave campus on weekends, according to most recent data available.

Annual Costs. Tuition and fees, $6,230; room and board, $2,760; estimated $500 other, exclusive of travel. About 93% of students receive financial aid; average amount of assistance, $4,954. Assistance is typically divided 59% scholarship, 13% grants, 14% loan, 14% work. College reports 400 scholarships awarded on the basis of academic merit alone, 400 for special talents, 20 for need alone.

Our Lady of Angels College

(See Neumann College)

College of Our Lady of the Elms

Chicopee, Massachusetts 01013 (413) 592-3189

A church-related college for women, which now accepts some men into special programs, conducted by the Sisters of St. Joseph, located in a city of 66,700. Previously listed as Elm College. Most convenient major airport: Bradley International.

Founded: 1928
Affiliation: Roman Catholic
UG Enrollment: 8 M, 538 W (full-time); 32 M, 388 W (part-time)
Total Enrollment: 955
Cost: < $10K
% Receiving Financial Aid: 80%
Admission: Non-selective
Application Deadline: Rolling

Admission. Graduates of accredited high schools with 16 units in academic subjects eligible; 91% of applicants accepted, 41% of these actually enroll. About 35% of freshmen graduate in top fifth of high school class, 80% in top two-fifths. Average freshman SAT scores, according to most recent data available: 470 verbal, 460 mathematical. *Required:* SAT or ACT; interview highly recommended. *Nonacademic factors* considered in admissions: diverse student body, alumni children. *Entrance programs:* early decision, early admission, midyear admission, deferred admission, advanced placement. About 5% of entering students from private schools, 40% from parochial schools. *Apply:* rolling admissions. *Transfers* welcome.

Academic Environment. *Degrees:* AB, BSMT. About 22% of general education requirements for graduation are elective; distribution requirements fairly numerous. About 75% of freshmen return for sophomore year. *Majors offered* in addition to usual studies include communication disorders, arts management. *Special programs:* independent study, study abroad, undergraduate research, individualized majors, 3–2 social work with Boston C. Adult programs: Weekend College, Continuing Education (part-time). *Calendar:* semester.

Undergraduate degrees conferred (142). 33% were in Health Professions, 15% were in Education, 11% were in Business and Management, 9% were in Public Affairs and Services, 8% were in Letters, 7% were in Social Sciences, 4% were in Biological Sciences, 3% each in Foreign Languages, Physical Sciences, remainder in 4 other fields.

Faculty. About 55% of faculty hold PhD or equivalent.

Student Body. College seeks a national student body; 50% of students from in state; 80% New England, 10% Middle Atlantic; 31 foreign. An estimated 80% of students reported as Catholic, 15% Protestant, 5% other; 8% Black, 5% Hispanic, 2% Asian, according to most recent data available.

Religious Orientation. The College of Our Lady of the Elms is a church-related institution; 1 course each in religion and philosophy required of all freshmen. Places of worship available on campus for Catholics, in immediate community for Protestants, 5 miles away for Jews.

Varsity Sports. Women (Div.III): Basketball, Field Hockey, Equestrian, Lacrosse, Soccer, Softball.

Campus Life. About 58% of women live in dormitories; rest commute. Freshmen given preference in college housing if all students cannot be accommodated. No intervisitation in women's dormitory rooms. There are no sororities. About 35% of resident students leave campus on weekends.

Annual Costs. Tuition and fees, $9,190; room and board, $4,400. About 80% of students receive financial aid; assistance is typically divided 61% scholarship, 34% loan, 5% work. College reports some scholarships awarded on the basis of academic merit alone. *Meeting Costs:* college offers deferred payment plan.

Our Lady of Holy Cross College

New Orleans, Louisiana 70131 (504) 394-7744

A small, co-educational, church-related college, Our Lady of Holy Cross aims to serve both college-age students and adults who have not previously completed a degree program. Most convenient major airport: New Orleans.

Founded: 1916
Affiliation: Roman Catholic
UG Enrollment: 155 M, 519 W (full-time); 118 M, 354 W (part-time)
Total Enrollment: 1,279
Cost: < $10K
% Receiving Financial Aid: 70%
Admission: Non-selective
Application Deadline: Rolling

Admission. High school graduates with 16 units who rank in top half of class eligible; 95% of applicants accepted, 51% of these actually enroll. *Required:* ACT. Criteria considered in admissions, in order of importance: high school academic record, recommendations, standardized test scores, extracurricular activities. *Apply* before registration; rolling admissions. *Transfers* welcome; 804 enrolled 1993–94.

Academic Environment. Degrees offered: associates, bachelors, masters. In spite of expanding enrollment, students still report that professors "know you by name and offer personal attention, even the President of the College knows students by name!" About 10% of students entering as freshmen graduate within four years, 60% eventually; 30% of freshmen return for sophomore year. Average undergraduate class size: 10% under 20, 90% 20–40. *Special programs:* CLEP, independent study, study abroad. *Calendar:* semester, summer school.

Undergraduate degrees conferred (106). 32% were in Education, 29% were in Health Sciences, 16% were in Psychology, 16% were in Business and Management, 5% were in Social Sciences, remainder in 2 other fields.

Faculty. About 30% of faculty hold PhD or equivalent. About 59% of teaching faculty are female; 2% Black, 2% Hispanic, 1% other ethnic minority.

Student Body. College does not seek a national student body; 98% of student from in state; 2% West. An estimated 16% of students reported as Protestant, 70% Catholic, 9% unaffiliated, 5% other; 14% Black, 5% Hispanic, 2% Asian, 2% other ethnic minority. Average age of undergraduate student: 28.

Religious Orientation. Our Lady of Holy Cross is a church-related institution that "embraces the philosophy of the Roman Catholic Church"; 6 hours each of theology and philosophy required of all students.

Campus Life. A commuter institution, college provides no residence facilities.

Annual Costs. Tuition and fees, $4,600. About 70% of students receive financial aid; average amount of assistance, $7,000. *Meeting Costs:* college offers ALAS/PLUS.

Our Lady of the Lake University of San Antonio

San Antonio, Texas 78207-4689 (210) 434-6711

A church-related, liberal arts university, owned by the Sisters of Divine Providence, Our Lady of the Lake is located in a city of 1,000,000. University participates in cooperative program with other Catholic colleges in San Antonio, including Incarnate Word and St. Mary's University. Most convenient major airport: San Antonio.

Founded: 1895
Affiliation: Roman Catholic
UG Enrollment: 290 M, 912 W (full-time); 247 M, 695 W (part-time)
Total Enrollment: 3,103
Cost: < $10K
% Receiving Financial Aid: 75%
Admission: Non-selective
Application Deadline: Rolling

Admission. High school graduates with 16 acceptable units eligible; others admitted on conditional basis; 58% of applicants accepted, 22% of these actually enroll. Average freshman SAT scores: 407 verbal, 434 mathematical. *Required:* SAT or ACT. Criteria considered in admissions, in order of importance: high school academic record, standardized test scores. *Apply:* no specific deadline. *Transfers* welcome; 176 enrolled 1993–94.

Academic Environment. Degrees offered: bachelors, masters, doctoral. *Majors offered* include usual arts and sciences, business, education, home economics, medical technology, public administration, social work, speech pathology and audiology. Curriculum emphasis on multidisciplinary studies. A current student reports, "This is a small school where you can really get to know your instructors", but she adds, "some programs get better facilities than others." Adult programs: extensive Weekend College program has been in operation for 15 years.

About 14% of students entering as freshmen graduate within four years, 30% eventually; 60% of freshmen return for sophomore year. *Special programs:* CLEP, independent study, undergraduate research, optional May interterm, study abroad, credit by examination, 3–2 programs in engineering, student-organized seminars. Adult program: extensive weekend program. *Calendar:* semester, summer school.

Undergraduate degrees conferred (246). 36% were in Business and Management, 15% were in Liberal/General Studies, 9% were in Public Affairs, 8% were in Education, 7% were in Computer and Engineering Related Technology, 6% were in Social Sciences, 5% were in Psychology, remainder in 11 other fields.

Faculty. About 58% of faculty hold PhD or equivalent. About 48% of teaching faculty are female.

Student Body. University seeks a national student body; 98% from South; 1% Midwest, 1% foreign. An estimated 57% of students reported as Catholic; 6% as Black, 49% Hispanic, 1% Asian, 4% other minority. *Minority group students:* special program designed to interest students in becoming bilingual teachers; special services program includes tutoring, counseling. Average age of undergraduate student: 29.

Religious Orientation. Our Lady of the Lake is a church-related institution in the Catholic tradition. Places of worship available on campus for Catholics, in immediate community for major faiths.
Campus Life. About 11% of men, 16% of women live in traditional dormitories; no coed dormitories; rest live in off-campus housing or commute, according to most recent data available. Intervisitation in men's and women's dormitory rooms limited. There are no fraternities or sororities. About 5% of resident students leave campus on weekends, according to most recent data available.
Annual Costs. Tuition and fees, $8,180; room and board, $3,756; estimated $1,141 other, exclusive of travel. About 75% of students receive financial aid. Assistance is typically divided 18% scholarship, 46% loan, 8% work. College reports some scholarships awarded on the basis of academic merit alone.

College of the Ozarks

Point Lookout, Missouri 65726 **(417) 334-6411**

An independent college located near a small town (Branson), 40 miles south of Springfield. Scholarship Work Program eliminates tuition in exchange for 560 work-hours per year on one of 78 campus jobs or industries. College accepts mainly those students who are financially unable to attend another institution. Formerly known as School of the Ozarks. Most convenient major airport: Springfield, MO.

Founded: 1906
Affiliation: Independent
UG Enrollment: 590 M, 687 W (full-time); 83 M, 112 W (part-time)
Cost: < $10K
% Receiving Financial Aid: 100%
Admission: Non-selective
Application Deadline: Rolling

Admission. High school graduates or GED certificate holders eligible; 13% of applicants accepted, 97% of these actually enroll. About 50% of freshmen graduate in top fifth of high school class, 80% in top two-fifths. Average freshman ACT scores: 21 composite. *Required:* SAT or ACT, financial reports (90% of those accepted must show financial need). Criteria considered in admissions, in order of importance: financial need, standardized test scores, recommendations, high school academic tests; other factors considered: special talents, alumni children. *Apply:* rolling admissions. *Transfers* welcome; 92 enrolled 1993–94.
Academic Environment. Degree offered: bachelors. Academic load 15–18 semester hours, no summer school. Core curriculum includes 6 hours of religion, 6 hours history/political science, 3 hours each mathematics, public speaking, physical education, 6 hours composition. About 70% of students entering as freshmen graduate eventually; 80% of freshman return for sophomore year. Average undergraduate class size: 58% under 20, 37% 20–40, 5% over 40. *Majors offered* in addition to usual studies include hotel/restaurant management, aviation science, dietetics, graphic arts, theatre. *Special programs:* CLEP, study abroad, independent study, undergraduate research, 3–2 and 2–2 engineering, Ozark studies. *Calendar:* semester.
Undergraduate degrees conferred (147). 38% were in Business and Management, 27% were in Education, 6% were in Liberal/General Studies, 5% were in Life Sciences, 5% were in Communications, 4% were in Multi/Interdisciplinary Studies, 3% were in Mathematics, 3% were in Physical Sciences, remainder in 6 other fields.
Graduates Career Data. Advanced studies pursued by 12% of students; 2% enter medical school; 1% enter business school. About 86% of 1992–93 graduates employed. Career Development Services include training in resume, cover letter, job skills and interview skills. Assistance information of career goals is provided through testing services, the career resource library and individual counseling.
Faculty. About 53% of faculty hold PhD or equivalent. About 62% of undergraduate classes taught by tenured faculty. About 30% of teaching faculty are female.
Student Body. School does not actively seek a national student body; 67% of students from in state; rest from Midwest. An estimated 55% of students reported as Protestant, 10% Catholic, 31% unaffiliated, 4% other; 1% Black, 1% Hispanic, 3% other ethnic minority.
Religious Orientation. Ozarks is a church-related institution; 6 hours (2 courses) are required of all students.
Varsity Sports. Men (NAIA Div. II): Baseball, Basketball. Women (NAIA Div. II): Basketball, Volleyball.
Campus Life. About 70% of students live in traditional dormitories; no coed dormitories; rest commute. Freshmen given preference in college housing if all students cannot be accommodated. No intervisitation in men's or women's dormitory rooms. There are no fraternities or sororities. About 20% of resident students leave campus on weekends.
Annual Costs. Fees, $100; room and board, $1,900; estimated $1,800 other, exclusive of travel. All students receive financial aid. Assistance is typically divided 73% scholarship, 27% work. *Meeting Costs:* all full-time students work 15 hours per week to pay for total tuition costs.

University of the Ozarks

Clarksville, Arkansas 72201 **(501) 754-3839**

A church-related college, located in a town of 5,500, 100 miles northwest of Little Rock. Most convenient major airport: Little Rock.

Founded: 1834
Affiliation: Presbyterian Church (USA)
UG Enrollment: 292 M, 324 W (full-time); 31 M, 73 W (part-time)
Total Enrollment: 615
Cost: < $10K
% Receiving Financial Aid: 74%
Admission: Non-selective
Application Deadline: August 24

Admission. Graduates of accredited high schools with either C average or 15 units and acceptable ACT scores eligible; others admitted by evaluation; 65% of applicants accepted, 74% of these actually enroll. Average freshman ACT scores, according to most recent data available: 18.9 M, 19.3 W composite. *Required:* ACT or SAT. *Apply* by August 24. *Transfers* welcome.
Academic Environment. *Degrees:* BA, BS, BGS. About 50% of general education requirements for graduation are elective; distribution requirements fairly numerous. About 57% of students entering as freshmen graduate within four years; 65% of freshmen return for sophomore year. *Majors offered* in addition to usual studies include entrepreneurship, communications, music business. *Special programs:* CLEP, independent study, dual degree programs in engineering, Christian education, special learning center for specific learning disabilities. *Calendar:* 4–1–4.
Undergraduate degrees conferred (212). 18% were in Education, 18% were in Business and Management, 11% were in Visual and Performing Arts, 9% were in Psychology, 8% were in Protective Services, 6% were in Engineering and Engineering Related Technology, 6% were in Social Sciences, 5% were in Agribusiness and Agricultural Production, 4% were in Home Economics, 4% were in Communications, 3% were in Mathematics, remainder in 5 other fields.
Graduates Career Data. According to most recent data available, full-time graduate or professional study pursued immediately after graduation by 30% of students; 1% enter medical school; 5% enter law school; 23% enter business school. Professional schools typically enrolling largest numbers of graduates include U. of Arkansas, U. of Central Arkansas. *Careers in business and industry* pursued by 59% of graduates. Employers typically hiring largest numbers of graduates include Wal Mart, public schools, financial institutions.
Faculty. About 45% of faculty hold PhD or equivalent.
Student Body. College seeks a national student body; 72% of students from Arkansas; 99 foreign. An estimated 60% of students reported as Protestant, 10% Catholic, 20% unaffiliated; 3% Black, 14% other minority or not reported, according to most recent data available.
Religious Orientation. University of the Ozarks is a church-related institution; 3 hours in religion required of all students.
Varsity Sports. Men (NAIA): Basketball, Cross Country, Golf, Track. Women (NAIA): Basketball, Cross Country, Tennis, Track.
Campus Life. About 45% of students live in traditional dormitories; no coed dormitories; rest live in off-campus housing or commute. Intervisitation in men's and women's dormitory rooms limited. There are no fraternities or sororities.
Annual Costs. Tuition and fees, $4,920; room and board, $2,850. About 74% of students receive financial aid; assistance is

typically divided 66% grant/scholarship, 16% loan, 18% work. University reports some scholarships awarded on the basis of academic merit alone.

Pace University

New York, New York 10038 **(212) 346-1323**

An independent university, Pace is located in downtown New York City across from City Hall. Most convenient major airports: JFK, LaGuardia, Newark.

Founded: 1906
Affiliation: Independent
UG Enrollment: 1,257 M, 1,593 W (full-time); 1,227 M, 2,071 W (part-time)
Total Enrollment: 7,644
Cost: $10K–$20K
% Receiving Financial Aid: 76%
Admission: Non-selective
Application Deadline: Aug. 15

Admission. High school graduates with 16 units eligible; 69% of applicants accepted, 39% of these actually enroll. About 54% of freshmen graduate in top fifth of high school class; 80% in top two-fifths. Average freshman SAT scores, according to most recent data available: 432 M, 426 W verbal, 520 M, 497 W mathematical. *Required:* SAT; interview recommended. *Non-academic factors* considered in admissions: special talents, alumni children. *Entrance programs:* early decision, early admission, midyear admission, deferred admission, advanced placement. *Apply* by August 15; rolling admissions. *Transfers* welcome.
Academic Environment. Degrees offered: associates, bachelors, masters, doctoral. *Undergraduate studies* offered by Dyson College of Arts and Sciences, School of Education and Lubin School of Business Administration. *Majors offered* include usual arts and sciences, dramatic arts, human relations, medical technology, speech pathology; extensive programs in business, education.

About 55% of students entering as freshmen graduate within four years; 81% of freshmen return for sophomore year. *Special programs:* CLEP, independent study, study abroad, honors, undergraduate research, Cooperative Education Program, 3–2 programs in engineering. Adult programs: variety of degree and enrichment programs offered for adult students. *Calendar:* semester, summer school.
Undergraduate degrees conferred (787). 61% were in Business and Management, 13% were in Computer and Engineering Related Technology, 6% were in Health Sciences, 5% were in Letters, 5% were in Psychology, 3% were in Liberal/General Studies, 3% were in Social Sciences, remainder in 6 other fields.
Faculty. About 70% of faculty hold PhD or equivalent.
Student Body. University does not seek a national student body; 86% of students from in state.
Campus Life. About 10% of students live in coed dormitories; rest commute. Intervisitation in men's and women's dormitory rooms unlimited. There are 5 fraternities, 5 sororities on campus, which about 5% of students join.
Annual Costs. Tuition and fees, $10,780; room and board, $4,760. About 76% of students receive financial aid. College reports some scholarships awarded on the basis of academic merit alone.

Pace University Westchester

Pleasantville, New York 10570 **(914) 773-3746**

A sister institution of Pace University New York, the Westchester campus provides a dramatically different environment. Credits earned at either campus are interchangeable. Most convenient major airport: Westchester or LaGuardia.

Founded: 1963
Affiliation: Independent
UG Enrollment: 1,340 M, 1,566 W (full-time); 378 M, 653 W (part-time)
Cost: $10K–$20K
% Receiving Financial Aid: 58%
Admission: Non-selective
Application Deadline: August 15

Admission. (See also NYC campus above) High school graduates with 16 units eligible; 74% of applicants accepted; about 30% of freshmen graduate in top fifth of high school class, 55% in top two-fifths. Average freshman SAT scores, according to most recent data available: 432 M, 426 W verbal, 520 M, 497 W mathematical. *Required:* SAT or ACT; interview recommended. *Apply* by August 15; rolling admissions. *Transfers* welcome.
Academic Environment. Degrees offered: associates, bachelors, masters. *Special programs:* CLEP, independent study, study abroad, individualized majors, nursing programs, cross-registration with neighboring institutions in mid-Hudson area and Westchester County, intersession in the Caribbean, 3–2 programs in engineering. Adult programs: variety of degree and enrichment programs offered for adult students. *Calendar:* semester, summer school.
Undergraduate degrees conferred (783). 62% were in Business and Management, 7% were in Computer and Engineering Related Technology, 6% were in Health Sciences, 6% were in Letters, 5% were in Social Sciences, 4% were in Protective Services, 3% were in Liberal/General Studies, remainder in 6 other fields.
Faculty. About 70% of faculty hold PhD or equivalent.
Student Body. University seeks a national student body.
Campus Life. About 52% of students live in coed dormitories; rest live in off-campus housing or commute. Intervisitation in men's and women's dormitory rooms limited, unlimited depending on floor. There are 4 fraternities, 4 sororities which about 10% of students join; they provide no residence facilities. About 40% of resident students leave campus on weekends.
Annual Costs. Tuition and fees, $10,780; room and board, $4,760. About 58% of students receive financial aid.

The College of White Plains of Pace University

White Plains, New York 10603 **(914) 422-4070**

The College of White Plains is an independent, co-educational undergraduate school within Pace University. Students may take courses on other campuses of university without extra charge. The 32-acre campus is located in a Westchester suburb of 50,200, 25 miles north of New York City. Most convenient major airports: Westchester or LaGuardia.

Founded: 1923
Affiliation: Independent
UG Enrollment: 305 M, 493 W (full-time); 200 M, 433 W (part-time)
Cost: $10K–$20K
% Receiving Financial Aid: 61%
Admission: Non-selective
Application Deadline: August 15

Admission. (See also NYC campus above) High school graduates with 16 academic units eligible; 76% of applicants accepted, 28% of these actually enroll; 30% of freshmen graduate in top fifth of high school class, 56% in top two-fifths. Average freshman SAT scores, according to most recent data available: 442 M, 432 W verbal, 505 M, 475 W mathematical. *Required:* SAT or ACT optional; interview recommended. *Non-academic factors* considered in admissions: special talents, alumni children. *Entrance programs:* early decision, early admission, midyear admission, deferred admission, advanced placement. *Apply* by August 15; rolling admissions. *Transfers* welcome.
Academic Environment. Core curriculum (66 credits of 96 required for graduation) allows wide elective choice; although distribution requirements remain fairly numerous, many options available to students. *Majors offered* include some arts and sciences, business and business education, elementary education, journalism.

About 53% of students entering as freshmen graduate within four years; 77% of freshmen return for sophomore year. *Special programs:* CLEP, independent study, study abroad, honors, undergraduate research, 3-year degree, individualized majors, tutorials, intern programs for seniors, 3–2 programs in engineering. Adult programs: variety of degree and enrichment programs offered for adult students. *Calendar:* semester, summer school.
Undergraduate degrees conferred (214). 49% were in Business and Management, 12% were in Liberal/General Studies, 11% were in Education, 10% were in Computer and Engineering Related Technology, 5% were in Letters, 4% were in Social Sciences, 4% were in Multi/Interdisciplinary Studies, remainder in 6 other fields.
Faculty. About 70% of faculty hold PhD or equivalent.
Student Body. College does not seek a national student body; 68% of students from in state.

Campus Life. About 31% of students live in coed dormitories; rest commute. There are no fraternities or sororities. About 50% of resident students leave campus on weekends.
Annual Costs. Tuition and fees, $10,780; room and board, $4,760. About 61% of students receive financial aid.

Pacific Christian College

Fullerton, California 92631

Pacific Christian College offers the BA and MA degrees in church-related ministries, management, education, humanities, psychology, and music.

Founded: 1928
Affiliation: Christian Churches, Churches of Christ

Undergraduate degrees conferred (804). 24% were in Business and Management, 16% were in Education, 13% were in Health Sciences, 7% were in Social Sciences, 6% were in Communications, 5% were in Life Sciences, 5% were in Psychology, 4% were in Visual and Performing Arts, 4% were in Computer and Information Sciences, 3% were in Letters, remainder in 8 other fields.

Pacific College

(See Fresno Pacific College)

Pacific Lutheran University

Tacoma, Washington 98447 (206) 535-7151

A church-related institution, Pacific Lutheran is located on a 130-acre suburban campus, 7 miles south of the center of Tacoma. Most convenient major airport: Seattle-Tacoma International.

Founded: 1890
Affiliation: Independent (Lutheran)
UG Enrollment: 1,177 M, 1,592 W (full-time); 135 M, 229 W (part-time)
Total Enrollment: 3,571
Cost: $10K–$20K
% Receiving Financial Aid: 70%
Admission: Selective (+)
Application Deadline: May 1

Admission is selective (+). About 80% of applicants accepted, 34% of these actually enroll; 68% of freshmen graduate in top fifth of high school class, 93% in top two-fifths. Average freshman SAT scores, according to most recent data available: 460–580 verbal, 480–630 mathematical. *Required:* SAT or ACT or WPCT for state residents. *Non-academic factors* considered in admissions: diverse student body, special talents. *Entrance programs:* early decision, early admission, midyear admission, deferred admission, advanced placement. About 3% of entering students from private schools. *Apply* by May 1 (March 1 for priority). *Transfers* welcome.
Academic Environment. Administration reports 62% of general education courses required for graduation are elective; distribution requirements, however, fairly numerous for College of Arts and Sciences. *Undergraduate studies* offered by College of Arts and Sciences, schools of Business Administration, Education, Fine Arts, Nursing, Physical Education. *Majors offered* in Arts and Sciences in addition to usual studies include communication arts, global studies, computer engineering.

About 58% of students entering as freshmen graduate eventually; 81% of freshmen return for sophomore year. *Special programs:* CLEP, independent study, honors, undergraduate research, study abroad, 3–2 engineering, Washington universities, and regional state universities. Adult programs: AURA (accelerated undergraduate reentry for adults) one year program including classes and assessment of life experiences. *Library:* 213,276 titles, 75,461 periodicals, Scandinavian Immigrant Experience Collection. *Calendar:* 4–1–4, summer school.
Undergraduate degrees conferred (837). 23% were in Business and Management, 17% were in Education, 11% were in Social Sciences, 8% were in Life Sciences, 7% were in Communications, 6% were in Health Sciences, 5% were in Visual and Performing Arts, 5% were in Psychology, 4% were in Letters, 3% were in Public Affairs, 3% were in Computer and Engineering Related Technology, remainder in 8 other fields.
Graduate Career Data. *Career Counseling Program:* Student assessment of program reported as good for career guidance and fair for job placement. Alumni reported by administration source as active in both career guidance and job placement.
Faculty. About 76% of faculty hold PhD or equivalent.
Student Body. University seeks a national student body; 67% of students from in state; 87% Northwest; 86 foreign. An estimated 61% of students reported as Protestant, 9% Catholic, 29% unaffiliated, 2% other; 1% Black, 1% Hispanic, 4% Asian, 8% other minority, according to most recent data available. *Minority group students:* scholarship and book fund program; Office for Minority, International, Commuter, Adult Services; Black Student Organization.
Religious Orientation. Pacific Lutheran is a church-related institution; 2 courses in religion required of all students; attendance at tri-weekly chapel services voluntary. Places of worship available on campus for major faiths.
Varsity Sports. Men (NAIA): Baseball, Basketball, Crew, Cross Country, Football, Golf, Skiing (USCSA), Soccer, Swimming, Tennis, Track, Wrestling. Women (Div.II): Basketball, Crew, Cross Country, Golf, Skiing (USCSA), Soccer, Softball, Swimming, Tennis, Track, Volleyball.
Campus Life. High interest reported in varsity sports (most popular: football, basketball, soccer), and intramurals (most popular: flag football, softball, volleyball). Most dormitories are coed by wing; intervisitation hours allowed 8 am–2 am. No curfew. Use of cars discouraged; interior of campus limited to service vehicles; parking permitted in assigned areas. Smoking prohibited in public buildings; permitted in designated areas. Alcohol and drugs prohibited on campus.

About 6% of men, 7% of women live in traditional dormitories; 37% of men, 32% of women in coed dormitories; rest live in off-campus housing or commute. Sexes segregated in coed dormitories by wing or floor. There are no fraternities or sororities.
Annual Costs. Tuition and fees, $12,672; room and board, $4,272. About 70% of students receive financial aid; assistance is typically divided 50% scholarship, 40% loan, 10% work. University reports some scholarships awarded on the basis of academic merit alone. *Meeting Costs:* university offers long term loans.

Pacific Northwest College of Art

Portland, Oregon 97205

An independent college of visual art offering bachelors degrees and 5-year BA/BFA with Reed College.

Founded: 1909
Affiliation: Independent

Pacific Union College

Angwin, California 94508 (707) 965-6336

A church-related college, located in a village of 2,700, 70 miles north of San Francisco. Most convenient major airport: San Francisco International.

Founded: 1882
Affiliation: Seventh-day Adventist
UG Enrollment: 380 M, 464 W (full-time); 11 M, 11 W (part-time)
Total Enrollment: 1,469
Cost: $10K–$20K
% Receiving Financial Aid: 70%
Admission: Non-selective
Application Deadline: Rolling

Admission. Graduates of accredited high schools with C average eligible; others admitted by examination; 84% of applicants accepted. *Required:* ACT. *Apply:* no specific deadline. *Transfers* welcome.
Academic Environment. *Degrees:* BA, BS, BMus, BBA, BSMT, BSW. New program in Liberal Studies recently added. *Special pro-*

grams: CLEP, study abroad (Spain, France, Austria, Russia), honors, undergraduate research, individualized majors, American Life Program, Korean English Program, ESL. Adult programs: Adult Education Program offered. *Calendar:* quarter, summer school.
Undergraduate degrees conferred (214). 25% were in Business and Management, 19% were in Health Sciences, 12% were in Life Sciences, 8% were in Theology, 7% were in Psychology, 6% were in Communications, 6% were in Public Affairs, 3% were in Social Sciences, 3% were in Letters, remainder in 12 other fields.
Faculty. About 33% of faculty hold PhD or equivalent.
Student Body. College does not seek a national student body; 86% of students from in state; 110 foreign. An estimated 3% of students reported as Black, 8% Hispanic, 17% Asian, 6% other minority, according to most recent data available.
Religious Orientation. Pacific Union is a church-related institution; 18 hours of religion required of all students; attendance at daily worship services, chapels and Sabbath services expected.
Campus Life. Some students travel to San Francisco for weekend cultural and recreational events. Most popular intramural sports include football, softball, volleyball. Popular and accessible outdoor recreational activities include skiing, surfing, water skiing, motor biking. About 75% of men, 72% of women live in traditional dormitories; no coed dormitories; rest live in off-campus housing or commute. Limited intervisitation. There are no fraternities or sororities. About 60% of resident students leave campus on weekends.
Annual Costs. Tuition and fees, $11,400; room and board, $3,675. About 70% of students receive financial aid. University reports some scholarships available for academic merit alone.

Pacific University

Forest Grove, Oregon 97116 (800) 635-0561

An independent institution maintaining "strong ties with the Congregational Church through the United Church of Christ Council for Higher Education"; located in a community of 11,500, 25 miles west of Portland. Most convenient major airport: Portland.

Founded: 1849
Affiliation: Independent (United Church of Christ)
UG Enrollment: 409 M, 464 W (full-time); 10 M, 17 W (part-time)
Total Enrollment: 1,596
Cost: $10K–$20K
% Receiving Financial Aid: 89%
Admission: Non-selective
Application Deadline: Rolling

Admission. Graduates of accredited high schools eligible; 89% of applicants accepted, 35% of these actually enroll. Average SAT scores, according to most recent data available: 479 verbal, 523 mathematical; ACT, 23 composite. *Required:* SAT or ACT, interview (on-campus preferred, off-campus possible). *Non-academic factors* considered in admissions: special talents. *Apply:* rolling admissions. *Transfers* welcome.
Academic Environment. Pacific's educational program has been "characterized as a liberal arts education with a career focus." The attempt is to provide students with a liberal education and at the same time develop practical skills. Several options are offered for the student's senior year: experiential learning as a student career intern, study abroad, independent study, or a traditional academic program. *Undergraduate studies* offered by College of Arts and Sciences. *Majors offered* in addition to usual studies include communications, education, speech correction, theater.

About 31% of students entering as freshmen graduate eventually. *Special programs:* honors, undergraduate research, individualized majors, credit by examination, study abroad, business internships, 3–1 medical technology with U. of Oregon Medical School, 3–2 engineering, 3–2 programs in electronic science and computer science, 3–2 medical technology, 5-year occupational therapy program. *Calendar:* 7–3–7 (7-week fall and spring terms, 3-week winter term), summer school.
Undergraduate degrees conferred (242). 15% were in Business and Management, 13% were in Psychology, 12% were in Health Sciences, 10% were in Education, 9% were in Allied Health, 7% were in Life Sciences, 7% were in Letters, 6% were in Public Affairs, 5% were in Social Sciences, 5% were in Communications, 3% were in Foreign Languages, remainder in 6 other fields.
Faculty. About 78% of faculty hold PhD or equivalent.
Student Body. University seeks a national student body; 54% of students from in state; 72% Northwest, 23% West; 32 foreign, according to most recent data available.
Varsity Sports. Men (NAIA): Baseball, Basketball, Cross Country, Football, Golf, Soccer, Swimming, Tennis, Wrestling. Women (NAIA): Basketball, Cross Country, Golf, Softball, Soccer, Swimming, Tennis, Volleyball.
Campus Life. All freshmen and sophomores under 21 are required to live on campus. No curfews. Students have choice of lifestyles: General floors (follow traditional university policy); Study Support Floors have extended quiet hours and other study-oriented policies; Intensive Study Floors also participate in extended study hours during exams and major paper-writing periods. Alcohol allowed only in dormitory rooms of students 21 and over.

About 62% of men, 62% of women live in coed dormitories; rest live in off-campus housing or commute. There are 3 fraternities, 3 sororities on campus which about 32% of men, 35% of women join; they provide no residence facilities.
Annual Costs. Tuition and fees, $13,490; room and board, $3,815. About 80% of students receive financial aid; assistance is typically divided 64% scholarship, 20% loan, 16% work. College reports some scholarships awarded on the basis of academic merit alone. *Meeting Costs:* university offers Tuition Contract, limiting tuition increases to Consumer Price Index after student enrolls.

University of the Pacific

Stockton, California 95211 (800) 959-2867

The university is located on a very beautiful 175-acre campus in a city of 215,000, 90 miles east of San Francisco. The university also operates the McGeorge School of Law in Sacramento, and School of Dentistry in San Francisco. Most convenient major airport: Stockton.

Founded: 1851
Affiliation: Independent
UG Enrollment: 1,601 M, 1,957 W (full-time)
Total Enrollment: 4,140
Cost: $10K–$20K
% Receiving Financial Aid: 65%
Admission: Selective
Application Deadline: March 1

Admission is selective. For all schools, 78% of applicants accepted, 30% of these actually enroll; 50% of freshmen graduate in top fifth of high school class, 76% in top two-fifths. Average freshman SAT scores: 444 verbal, 531 mathematical. *Required:* SAT or ACT, essay; letter of recommendation, interview recommended. Criteria considered in admissions, in order of importance: high school academic record, standardized test scores, recommendation, writing sample, extracurricular activities; other factors considered: diverse student body, special talents, co-curricular activities. *Entrance programs:* early action, early admission, midyear admission, advanced placement, deferred admission. About 18% of entering students from private school, 2% parochial. *Apply* by March 1; rolling admissions. *Transfers* welcome; 496 enrolled 1993–94.
Academic Environment. Pressures for academic achievement vary at the different colleges from modest to moderate. Recent student leader characterizes student body as equally interested in scholarly/intellectual pursuits and social activities. All undergraduates must complete a general education program which includes the interdisciplinary liberal learning program and the fundamental learning skills classes, as well as a series of seminars; all selected in consultation with faculty advisor. Degrees offered: bachelors, masters, doctoral. *Majors offered* include usual arts and sciences, Black studies, business administration, chemistry-biology, medical chemistry, drama, geophysics, international relations, speech therapy, sports medicine, music management, entertainment management. The strongest programs are reported to be in engineering, pharmacy and business, music education, mathematics and the sciences. Average undergraduate class size: 25; 20% of classes under 10, 75% under 30.

About 63% of students entering as freshmen graduate within four years; 84% of freshmen return for sophomore year. *Special programs:* CLEP, independent study, study abroad, January term, United Nations Semester, cooperative work/study program in engineering, undergraduate research, government internships, extensive co-op and internship program, individualized majors, University without Walls, 2–3 programs available in Pharmacy and Dentistry. Adult pro-

grams: re-entry division, self-designed programs. *Calendar:* semester (trimester for Pharmacy School), summer school.
Undergraduate degrees conferred (757). 23% were in Business and Management, 13% were in Engineering, 11% were in Liberal/General Studies, 10% were in Communications, 6% were in Visual and Performing Arts, 6% were in Social Sciences, 5% were in Health Sciences, 4% were in Psychology, 4% were in Letters, 4% were in Education, 4% were in Area and Ethnic Studies, 3% were in Life Sciences, remainder in 8 other fields.
Graduates Career Data. Advanced studies pursued by 30% of students immediately after graduation, 50% eventually. About 70% of 1992–93 graduates employed. Fields typically hiring largest numbers of graduates include business, education, professions. *Career Counseling Program* begins as early as the freshman year. Student assessment of program reported as good for both career guidance and job placement. Alumni reported as actively helpful in both career guidance and job placement.
Faculty. About 84% of faculty hold PhD or equivalent. About 25% of teaching faculty are female.
Student Body. University seeks a national student body; 80% of students from in state. An estimated 4% of students reported as Black, 9% Hispanic, 23% Asian, 5% other ethnic minority. *Minority group students:* community involvement program grants 100 full scholarships to minority students from county; special tutoring available.
Varsity Sports. Men (Div.IA): Baseball, Basketball, Football, Golf, Swimming, Tennis, Volleyball, Water Polo. Women (Div.IA): Basketball, Cross Country, Field Hockey, Soccer, Softball, Swimming, Tennis, Volleyball.
Campus Life. A current student describes the campus as, "Gorgeous. We have perfectly manicured green lawns all year, beautiful roses, palm trees, volleyball sand-courts, and wonderful brick buildings." Another student rates rules governing student conduct as "relatively free," and adds that they are enforced "judiciously." No curfews. Students of legal age may have beer or wine in their dormitory room; cars allowed. Freshmen and sophomores must live in campus housing. Students report weekend road trips to San Francisco, Lake Tahoe, Reno, Sacramento, and Yosemite supplement the many on-campus activities.

About 50% of undergraduate students live on campus in residence halls, Greek houses and apartments. Freshman and Sophomores are required to live on campus. Sexes segregated in coed dormitories by floor or room. There are 5 fraternities, 4 sororities on campus which about 17% of men, and 18% of women join.
Annual Costs. Tuition and fees, $15,800; room and board, $5,300; estimated $1,600 other, exclusive of travel. About 65% of students receive financial aid; average amount of assistance, $16,000. Assistance is typically divided 60% scholarship/grant, 30% loan, 10% work. University reports 150 scholarships awarded on the basis of academic merit alone, 300 for special talents, 1,800 for need alone. *Meeting Costs:* University offers institutional family loan plan.

Paine College

Augusta, Georgia 30910-3182 (404) 821-8319

A church-related college, located in a city of 59,900; founded as a college for Negroes and still serving a predominantly Black student body; college reports increased efforts to recruit non-Blacks. Most convenient major airport: Bush Field (Augusta).

Founded: 1882
Affiliation: United Methodist, Christian Methodist Episcopal
UG Enrollment: 186 M, 444 W (full-time); 38 M, 55 W (part-time)
Cost: < $10K
% Receiving Financial Aid: 90%
Admission: Non-selective
Application Deadline: August 1

Admission. High school graduates with 15 units and C average eligible; others admitted by examination; 49% of applicants accepted, 33% of these actually enroll. Average freshman scores: ACT, 17 composite. *Required:* SAT or ACT, essay. Criteria considered in admissions, in order of importance: high school academic record, standardized test scores, writing sample, recommendations, extracurricular activities; other factors considered: special talents, alumni children. *Entrance programs:* early decision, early admission, midyear admission, deferred admission. *Apply* by August 1; rolling admission. *Transfers* welcome; 21 enrolled 1993–94.
Academic Environment. Degree offered: bachelors. Common Core Curriculum consists of 55–57 hours out of 124 required for graduation. About 9% of students entering as freshmen graduate within four years, 20% eventually; 55% of freshmen return for sophomore year. *Special programs:* independent study, undergraduate research, honors, study abroad, 3–2 programs in engineering, mass communications, biomedical science, chemistry, cross registration with Clark Atlanta U. and Augusta College, internship/cooperative work-study programs. *Calendar:* quarter, summer school.
Undergraduate degrees conferred (63). 33% were in Business and Management, 24% were in Social Sciences, 11% were in Life Sciences, 11% were in Education, 10% were in Psychology, 5% were in Mathematics, 3% were in Letters, remainder in 2 other fields.
Graduates Career Data. Advanced studies pursued by 28% of students; 10% enter medical school. Medical schools enrolling largest numbers of graduates include Medical College of Georgia. About 29% of 1992–93 graduates employed. Career Development Services include a centrally located center on campus which coordinates activities for students and alumni seeking employment counseling and guidance.
Faculty. About 47% of faculty hold PhD or equivalent. About 47% of teaching faculty are female; 49% Black, 2% Hispanic, 16% other ethnic minority.
Student Body. About 77% of students from in state; 86% South, 4% Middle Atlantic, 4% Midwest, 2% West, 3% foreign. An estimated 98% of students reported as Protestant, 2% Catholic; 98% Black. Average age of undergraduate student: 23.
Religious Orientation. Paine is a church-related institution; one course in religion required of all students.
Varsity Sports. Men (Div.II): Baseball, Basketball, Cross Country, Track. Women (Div.II): Basketball, Cross Country, Softball, Track, Volleyball.
Campus Life. About 63% of students live in traditional dormitories; no coed dormitories; rest live in off-campus housing or commute. Intervisitation in men's dormitory rooms limited; no intervisitation in women's dormitory rooms. There are 4 fraternities, 4 sororities on campus which about 10% of men, 10% of women join; they provide no residence facilities. Over 50% of resident students leave campus on weekends.
Annual Costs. Tuition and fees, $8,207; room and board, $2,814; estimated $2,200 other, exclusive of travel. About 90% of students receive financial aid. College reports some scholarships awarded on the basis of academic merit alone. *Meeting Costs:* College offers sibling grants, and grants for specified groups.

Palm Beach Atlantic College

West Palm Beach, Florida 33416-4700 (407) 835-4339

A Christian liberal arts college located near the downtown section of a city of 150,000, 60 miles north of Miami. Most convenient major airport: Palm Beach International.

Founded: 1968
Affiliation: Southern Baptist
UG Enrollment: 616 M, 814 W (full-time); 156 M, 169 W (part-time)
Cost: < $10K
% Receiving Financial Aid: 90%
Admission: Non-selective
Application Deadline: Rolling

Admission. Graduates of accredited high schools with 18 academic units eligible; 86% of applicants accepted, 56% of these actually enroll; 21% of freshman graduate in top fifth of high school class, 42% in top two-fifths. Average freshman scores: SAT, 450 M, 452 W verbal, 516 M, 480 W mathematical; ACT, 22 M, 21 W composite. *Required:* ACT or SAT, essay; interview. Criteria considered in admissions, in order of importance: high school academic record, standardized test scores, writing sample, recommendations, extracurricular activities; other factors considered: special talents, religious affiliation and/or commitment. *Entrance programs:* early admission, midyear admission, deferred admission, advanced placement. *Apply:* rolling admissions. *Transfers* welcome; 226 enrolled 1993–94.
Academic Environment. Degrees offered: bachelors, masters. *Majors offered* in addition to usual studies include marine biology,

theatre arts. Strongest programs reported to be in business, music, and sciences. Core curriculum includes work in literature, composition, mathematics and computing, humanities, social sciences, natural science (with lab), communication, physical education, religion, and American free enterprise. About 27% of students entering as freshman graduate within four years, 40% eventually; 60% of freshman return for sophomore year. Average undergraduate class size: 5% under 20, 90% 20–40, 5% over 40. *Special programs:* CLEP, independent study, 4-week January mini-term, London semester. Adult programs: numerous evening programs offering credit and non-credit courses, and the Bachelor of Human Resource Management degree-completion program offered for adult learners. *Calendar:* 4–1–4, summer school.

Undergraduate degrees conferred (244). 48% were in Business and Management, 22% were in Psychology, 11% were in Education, 5% were in Life Sciences, 4% were in Letters, 4% were in Social Sciences, 3% were in Philosophy and Religion, remainder in 3 other fields.

Graduates Career Data. Advanced studies pursued by 20% of students. Career Development services offered.

Faculty. About 73% of faculty hold PhD or equivalent. About 17% of teaching faculty are female.

Student Body. College seeks a national student body; 63% of students from in state. An estimated 80% of students reported as Protestant, 17% Catholic, 1% Jewish, 2% unaffiliated or other; 5% Black, 4% Hispanic, 1% Asian, 6% ethnic minority.

Religious Orientation. Palm Beach Atlantic is a church-related institution; 2 courses in religion required of all students; attendance at weekly chapel programs required. Churches and other places of worship available in immediate community for major faiths.

Varsity Sports. Men (NAIA): Baseball, Basketball, Golf, Soccer, Tennis. Women (NAIA): Golf, Tennis, Volleyball.

Campus Life. Palm Beach Atlantic is only 5 minutes away from the Atlantic Ocean, and, of course, students report beach-related activities provide for outside recreation. About 36% of men, 40% of women live in traditional dormitories; no coed dormitories; rest commute. No intervisitation in men's or women's dormitory rooms. There are no fraternities or sororities.

Annual Costs. Tuition and fees, $7,500; room and board, $3,220. About 90% of students receive financial aid; average amount of assistance, $5,075. Assistance is approximately divided 57% scholarship/grant, 20% loan, 20% work.

Pan American University

(See University of Texas-Pan American)

Park College

Parkville, Missouri 64152 (816) 741-2000

A church-related college, located in a community of 1,300, 9 miles north of downtown Kansas City. Most convenient major airport: Kansas City International.

Founded: 1875
Affiliation: Reorganized Latter Day Saints
UG Enrollment: 350 M, 350 W (full-time); 70 M, 70 W (part-time)
Cost: < $10K
% Receiving Financial Aid: 80%
Admission: Non-selective
Application Deadline: August 1

Admission. Graduates of accredited high schools eligible; 80% of applicants accepted, 40% of these actually enroll; 26% of freshman graduate in top fifth of high school class, 61% in top two-fifths. Average freshman ACT scores: 19.6 M, 21.3 W composite. *Required:* ACT, essay, class rank; interview "if possible." Criteria considered in admissions, in order of importance: high school academic record, standardized test scores, writing sample, recommendations, extracurricular activities. *Entrance programs:* midyear admissions, deferred admission. About 20% of entering freshman from parochial schools, 5% private school. *Apply* by August 1; rolling admissions. *Transfers* welcome; 183 enrolled 1993–94.

Academic Environment. Degrees offered: associates, bachelors, masters. Major offered in addition to usual studies: equine studies. About 30% of entering freshman graduate within four years, 33% eventually; 66% of freshman return for sophomore year. Average undergraduate class size: 65% under 20, 35% 20–40. *Special programs:* CLEP, independent study, honors, study abroad, undergraduate research, individualized majors, cross registration with several schools through Kansas City Regional Council of Higher Education. Adult programs: weekend and evening programs available. *Calendar:* semester, summer school.

Undergraduate degrees conferred (1,307). 60% were in Business and Management, 15% were in Computer and Engineering Related Technology, 10% were in Psychology, 4% were in Protective Services, 3% were in Health Sciences, remainder in 12 other fields.

Graduate Career Data. Advanced studies pursued by 28% of students (1991); 5% enter law school; 6% enter business school; 3% enter medical school; 1% enter dental school. Law schools typically enrolling largest numbers of graduates include U. of Missouri, U. of Kansas, U. of Nebraska; business school include Rockhurst, U. of Missouri; medical and dental schools include U. of Missouri. About 80% of 1992–93 graduates employed. Fields typically hiring largest numbers of graduates include sales, health care, teaching, criminal justice, marketing and accounting.

Faculty. About 70% of faculty hold PhD or equivalent. About 50% of undergraduate classes taught by tenured faculty. About 25% of teaching faculty are female; 4% Black, 2% Hispanic, 4% other ethnic minority.

Student Body. College seeks a national student body; about 50% of students from in state; 18% Midwest, 4% Middle Atlantic, 10% South, 6% West, 1% New England, 1% Northwest, 10% foreign. An estimated 65% of students reported as Protestant, 20% Catholic; 25% Black, 10% Hispanic, 5% Asian. Average age of undergraduate student: 24.

Religious Orientation. Park is a church-related institution; 4 religious courses required of all students.

Varsity Sports. Men (NAIA): Basketball, Cross Country, Soccer, Track, Volleyball. Women (NAIA): Basketball, Cross Country, Soccer, Softball, Track, Volleyball.

Campus Life. About 10% of men, 15% of women live in traditional dormitories; 20% of men, 25% of women live in coed dormitories; rest commute. Freshmen given preference in college housing if all students cannot be accommodated. There are no fraternities or sororities. About 50% of resident students leave campus on weekends.

Annual Costs. Tuition and fees, $3,540; room and board, $3,780; an estimated $1,100 other, exclusive of travel. About 80% of students receive financial aid; average amount of assistance, $6,500. Assistance is typically divided 25% scholarship, 25% grant, 25% loan, 25% work. College reports 100 scholarships awarded on the basis of academic merit alone, 140 for special talents. *Meeting Costs:* college offers PLUS Loans, Academic Management Services.

Parks College of St. Louis University

Cahokia, Illinois 62206 (618) 337-7500

The oldest certified school of aeronautics in the country, Parks is an independently accredited college of St. Louis University. The campus is located in a small community directly across the Mississippi from St. Louis. Most convenient major airport: Lambert-St. Louis International.

Founded: 1927
Affiliation: Roman Catholic
UG Enrollment: 900 M, 110 W (full-time)
Cost: < $10K
% Receiving Financial Aid: 85%
Admission: Non-selective
Application Deadline: August 1

Admission. Graduates of accredited high schools or the equivalent eligible; 80% of applicants accepted, 40% of these actually enroll. About 35% of freshmen graduate in top fifth of high school class, 90% in top two-fifths. Average freshman scores: SAT, 480 verbal, 580 mathematical; ACT, 24 composite. *Required:* SAT or ACT. Criteria considered in admissions, in order of importance: high school academic record, standardized test scores, recommendations, extracurricular activities. *Entrance programs:* midyear admission, advanced

placement. *Apply* by August 1; rolling admissions. *Transfers* welcome; 70 enrolled 1993–94.
Academic Environment. Degrees offered: associates, bachelors, masters. *Majors offered* include aerospace engineering, aircraft maintenance engineering and management, avionics, aviation science/professional pilot, logistics, travel and tourism, meteorology, aviation management, airway science, computer software engineering, applied computer science. College maintains a flightline hangar and fleet of 28 aircraft at the airport 1 mile away from campus. Affiliation with Saint Louis University allows cross registration, as well as use of their facilities such as library. Every department offers internships and co-op programs. Average undergraduate class size: 20% of classes under 20, 70% between 20–40, 10% over 40. About 65% of students entering as freshmen graduate within four years. *Calendar:* trimester.
Undergraduate degrees conferred (266). 49% were in Engineering, 36% were in Transportation and Material Moving, 8% were in Business and Management, 6% were in Mechanics and Repairers, remainder in Physical Sciences.
Faculty. About 90% of faculty hold PhD or other terminal degree. All undergraduate classes taught by tenured faculty. About 10% of teaching faculty are female; 5% Black, 20% other ethnic minorities.
Graduates Career Data. Advanced studies pursued by 21% of students; 5% enter law school; 5% enter business school. About 75% of 1992–93 graduates employed. Fields typically hiring the largest number of graduates include electrical engineering, aerospace engineering, aviation, military. Career Development Services include on-campus recruitment, resume service, company profiles, career specialist.
Varsity Sports. Men (NCAA,Div.III): Baseball, Basketball, Cross Country, Soccer, Tennis.
Student Body. About 30% of students from in state; 70% Midwest, 15% New England, 10% West/Northwest, 10% Middle Atlantic, 5% South, 20% foreign. An estimated 40% of students reported as Protestant, 35% Catholic, 5% Jewish, 15% Muslim; 8% Black, 4% Hispanic, 6% Asian, 4% other ethnic minorities.
Campus Life. About 55% of men, 65% of women live in traditional dormitories, 10% of men, 6% of women live in coed dormitories; remainder live in off-campus housing or commute. Freshmen given preference in college housing if all students cannot be accommodated. There are 5 fraternities, 2 sororities on campus, which about 25% of men, 30% of women join.
Annual Costs. Tuition and fees, $8,460; room and board, $3,900; estimated $1,000 other, exclusive of travel. About 85% of students receive financial aid; average amount of assistance, $8,500. Assistance is typically divided 20% scholarship, 40% grant, 40% loan. College reports 40% scholarships awarded on the basis of academic merit alone, 15 for special talents. *Meeting Costs:* college offers The Tuition Plan.

Parsons School of Design

(See New School for Social Research)

Patten College

Oakland, California 94601

A small, co-educational and multi-ethnic college of Christian Ministries which focuses on biblical and career education in a spiritual environment. In the BA program the Biblical Studies major is balanced by general education and a second major—in Christian Education, Pastoral Studies, or Sacred Music—or by a pre-professional option in Pre-seminary or Liberal Studies. A fifth-year Multiple Subject Teaching Credential program is also offered. Opportunities for practical Christian experience and service help to define and develop students talents and ministries.

Founded: 1944 **Affiliation:** Independent

Undergraduate degrees conferred (4). 100% were in Theology.

Paul Quinn College

Waco, Texas 76704 **(817) 753-6415**

A private, church-related institution, Paul Quinn has always welcomed students of any race or faith; located in a city of 150,000 in the center of the state. Most convenient major airports: Dallas-Fort Worth or Austin.

Founded: 1872
Affiliation: African Methodist Episcopal
UG Enrollment: 229 M, 234 W (full-time)
Total Enrollment: 1,009
Cost: < $10K
% Receiving Financial Aid: 86%
Admission: Non-selective
Application Deadline: Rolling

Admission. Graduates of accredited high schools with 15 units eligible; others given individual consideration; 81% of applicants accepted, 74% of these actually enroll. *Required:* SAT or ACT. *Apply:* no specific deadline. *Transfers* welcome.
Academic Environment. Degrees offered: bachelors. *Majors offered* in addition to usual studies include social work, education. About 5% of general education requirements for graduation are elective; distribution requirements fairly numerous. About 70% of students entering as freshmen graduate eventually; 95% of freshmen return for sophomore year. *Special programs:* CLEP, honors, independent study. *Calendar:* semester, summer school.
Undergraduate degrees conferred (58). 100% were in Unknown.
Student Body. College seeks a national student body; 80% of students from in state; 86% South. An estimated 90% of students reported as Protestant, 3% Catholic, 4% unaffiliated, 3% other; 94% Black, 1% Hispanic, 1% other minority, according to most recent data available.
Religious Orientation. Paul Quinn is a church-related institution; 4 hours of religion required of all students; participation in religious services on campus generally expected.
Varsity Sports. Men (NAIA): Baseball, Basketball, Track, Volleyball(IAC). Women (NAIA): Basketball, Softball, Track, Volleyball.
Campus Life. About 60% of men, 60% of women live in traditional dormitories; no coed dormitories; rest live in off-campus housing or commute. Freshmen given preference in college housing if all students cannot be accommodated. Intervisitation in men's and women's dormitory rooms limited. There are 4 fraternities, 4 sororities on campus which about 6% of men, 5% of women join. About 65% of resident students leave campus on weekends.
Annual Costs. Tuition and fees, $3,635; room and board, $2,975. About 86% of students receive financial aid; assistance is typically divided 5% scholarship, 52% loan, 24% work. College reports some scholarships awarded on the basis of academic merit alone. *Meeting Costs:* college offers payment plan.

The Peabody Conservatory of the Johns Hopkins University

(See Johns Hopkins University)

Pembroke State University

Pembroke, North Carolina 28372 **(910) 521-6000**

A state-supported university, located in a village of 2,000, 80 miles south of Raleigh. Most convenient major airport: Fayetteville, NC.

Founded: 1887
Affiliation: State
UG Enrollment: 980 M, 1,194 W (full-time); 168 M, 361 W (part-time)
Total Enrollment: 3,045
Cost: < $10K
Admission: Non-selective
Application Deadline: July 15

Admission. Graduates of accredited high schools with minimum combined SAT score of 750 eligible; 82% of applicants accepted, 57% of these actually enroll. About 30% of freshmen graduate in top fifth of high school class, 55% in top two-fifths. *Required:* SAT, interview. Criteria considered in admissions, in order of importance: high school academic record, standardized test scores, recommendations, writing sample, extracurricular activities, class rank. *Out-of-state* freshman applicants: university actively seeks students from out-of-state. State limits out-of-state enrollment to 18% of enrollment. *Entrance programs:* deferred admission, advanced placement. *Apply* by July 15; rolling admission. *Transfers* welcome; 303 enrolled 1993–94.

Academic Environment. Degrees offered: bachelors, masters. *Majors offered* in addition to usual studies include American Indian Studies, science education, social work, broadcasting. Core requirements include 1 hour orientation, 6 hours basic skills, 2 hours health/physical education, 18 hours humanities, 12 hours social sciences, 12 hours natural sciences. Broadcasting program is enriched by a student run studio; internships offered in some departments. About 42% of entering students graduate eventually; 64% of freshmen return for sophomore year, according to most recent data available. Adult programs: freshman requirements waived for students over 21. *Calendar:* semester, summer school.

Undergraduate degrees conferred (411). 31% were in Education, 18% were in Business and Management, 16% were in Social Sciences, 8% were in Letters, 5% were in Public Affairs, 5% were in Psychology, 5% were in Life Sciences, 4% were in Mathematics, remainder in 6 other fields.

Graduates Career Data. Career Development Services include a library of resources related to careers, employers, salary trends, the job market, graduate and professional schools, part-time and full-time employment, opportunities, internships and co-ops.

Faculty. About 77% of faculty hold PhD or equivalent. About 26% of teaching faculty are female; 6% Black, 1% Hispanic, 42% other ethnic minority.

Student Body. About 97% of students from in state. An estimated 12% of students reported as Black, 1% Hispanic, 1% Asian, 24% other ethnic minority. Average age of undergraduate student: 24.

Varsity Sports. Men (Div.II): Baseball, Basketball, Cross Country, Golf, Soccer, Tennis, Track, Wrestling. Women (Div.II): Basketball, Cross Country, Softball, Tennis, Volleyball.

Campus Life. About 23% of students live in traditional dormitories; no coed dormitories; rest commute. Freshmen given preference in college housing if all students cannot be accommodated. Intervisitation in men's and women's dormitory rooms limited. There are 8 fraternities, 6 sororities on campus which about 2% each of men, women join.

Annual Costs. Tuition and fees, $1,078 (out-of-state, $6,442); room and board, $2,460; estimated $450 other, exclusive of travel. About 33% of student receive financial aid; average amount of assistance, $2,969. Assistance is typically divided 20% scholarship, 50% grant, 22% loan, 8% work. University reports 174 scholarships awarded on the basis of academic merit alone, 141 for special talents, 2,265 for need alone.

Pennsylvania State University

University Park, Pennsylvania 16802 (814) 865-7641

Penn State is Pennsylvania's land-grant institution. Its main campus is supplemented by 2 graduate centers and by 17 Commonwealth campuses which provide the first 2 years of study toward a baccalaureate degree as well as 2-year terminal programs, the Harrisburg Capitol Campus in Middletown offering upper-division programs and graduate studies, and Erie Behrend College offering both baccalaureate and graduate programs. The 390-acre main academic campus is part of more than 4,592 acres—much of which is devoted to agricultural experiments—located near the geographic center of the state. Most convenient major airport: Harrisburg International.

Founded: 1855
Affiliation: State
UG Enrollment: 16,253 M, 12,685 W (full-time)
Total Enrollment: 37,658
Cost: < $10K
% Receiving Financial Aid: 76%
Admission: Highly Selective
Application Deadline: Rolling

Admission is highly selective for schools of Science, Engineering, very (+) selective for school of Earth and Mineral Sciences, very selective for schools of Liberal Arts and Business Administration, Communication, selective (+) for schools of Agriculture, Arts and Architecture, and Education, selective for school of Health and Human Development. For all schools about 53% of applicants accepted, 33% of these actually enroll; 78% of freshmen graduate in top fifth of high school class, 96% in top two-fifths. Average freshman SAT scores: 507 M, 505 W verbal, 613 M, 569 W mathematical; 37% of freshmen score above 500 on verbal, 10% above 600, 1% above 700; 58% score above 500 on mathematical, 33% above 600, 8% above 700.

Required: SAT or ACT. Criteria considered in admissions: standardized test scores and high school academic record; other factors considered: special talents, alumni children, diverse student body. *Out-of-state* freshman applicants: university actively seeks students from out of state. State does not limit out-of-state enrollment. No special requirements for out-of-state applicants. States from which most out-of-state students are drawn: New Jersey, New York, Maryland. *Entrance programs:* midyear admission, advanced placement. *Apply* by November 30 for priority consideration; rolling admissions. *Transfers* welcome; 462 enrolled 1993–94.

Academic Environment. Degrees offered: associates, bachelors, masters, doctoral. Pressures for academic achievement vary widely among the different programs of study from moderate to moderately intense; likely to be most rigorous in schools of Engineering, Science, and Earth and Mineral Sciences. Penn State encompasses both the professional/vocational training and service function usually offered by land-grant institutions as well as liberal education in the arts and sciences. Student body reported to be oriented toward occupational/professional career goals. Some student concern reported over large classes taught by teaching assistants. Considerable interest continues in non-credit, out-of-class instructional experiences in a wide variety of subject areas. Administration reports requirements vary widely with individual programs; distribution requirements for AB include 9 credits in speaking and writing skills, 18 credits in science/mathematics (with at least 3 credits in each of 4 divisions), 27 credits in humanities/social sciences (with at least 6 credits each in arts and humanities, 9 credits in social sciences), 4 credits in physical education. *Undergraduate studies* offered by colleges of Liberal Arts, Agricultural Science, Arts and Architecture, Business Administration, Earth and Mineral Sciences, Education, Engineering, Science, Health and Human Development, and the School of Communications. *Majors offered* in tremendously wide range of areas, from usual liberal arts and sciences to unusual interdisciplinary degree programs such as agricultural business management, agricultural engineering, and a dual degree program in earth and mineral science and liberal arts. Penn State is known for very strong programs in the agricultural fields, the scientific and technical fields, engineering, architecture, communications, journalism, and business. Relatively new programs include landscape architecture, marketing and international business, women's studies, and musical arts.

About 33% of students entering as freshmen graduate within four years, 61% eventually; 84% of freshmen return for sophomore year. *Special programs:* CLEP, independent study, abroad, honors, undergraduate research, credit by examination, 5-year BS/MD program with Jefferson Medical College of Philadelphia, self-instructional critical languages program, combined liberal arts/earth and mineral sciences or engineering, area studies (Asian, Middle East, Russian and East European), 3–2 programs in nursing with Lincoln U. *Calendar:* 2 15-week semesters and summer sessions.

Undergraduate degrees conferred (8,293). 23% were in Business and Management, 14% were in Engineering, 8% were in Education, 6% were in Social Sciences, 5% were in Health Sciences, 5% were in Communications, 5% were in Letters, 4% were in Liberal/General Studies, 3% were in Life Sciences, 3% were in Protective Services, 3% were in Psychology, remainder in 16 other fields.

Graduates Career Data. Employers typically hiring largest numbers of graduates include IBM, Westinghouse, Proctor & Gamble. Career Development Services include individual and group counseling; computer assisted career guidance; career planning courses; outreach programming and seminars on resume writing, interviewing skills, etc.; career information center; interview training center; placement services include on-campus interviewing, job listings, specialized education career services.

Faculty. About 88% of faculty hold PhD or equivalent. About 24% of teaching faculty are female; 2% Black, 1% Hispanic, 8% ethnic minority.

Student Body. University does not seek a national student body but welcomes out-of-state students; 88% of students from in state; less than 1% foreign. An estimated 3% of students reported as Black, 2% Hispanic, 5% Asian. *Minority group students:* special financial, academic, and social provisions including Educational Opportunities Program.
Varsity Sports. Men (Div. I): Baseball, Basketball, Cross Country, Fencing, Football(IA), Golf, Gymnastics, Lacrosse, Soccer, Swimming, Tennis, Track, Volleyball, Wrestling. Women (Div.I): Basketball, Cross Country, Fencing, Field Hockey, Golf, Gymnastics, Lacrosse, Softball, Swimming, Tennis, Track, Volleyball.
Campus Life. University provides many types of cultural activities, is the cultural center of central Pennsylvania; guest artists attract largest audiences. The very popular varsity sports program is supplemented by a wide range of intramural sports offered, also very popular. The campus is located 45 miles from Altoona, 90 miles from Harrisburg, 140 miles from Pittsburgh. Students are voting members of the University Council, the Faculty Senate, and departmental committees. One student, appointed by the governor, serves on the Board of Trustees. Intervisitation hours voted by each residence unit under an intricate system of regulations. Drinking prohibited on campus. Cars permitted for commuters only; parking is a problem. Students under 21 expected to live in university housing for freshman year.

About 30% of men, 41% of women live in traditional dormitories; no coed dormitories; rest live in off-campus housing or commute. Freshmen given preference in college housing if all students cannot be accommodated. There are 54 fraternities, 23 sororities on campus which about 15% of men, 17% of women join.
Annual Costs. Tuition and fees, $4,822 (out-of-state, $10,170); room and board, $3,930 (cost varies depending on meal plan); estimated $2,501 other, exclusive of travel. About 76% of undergraduate students (1992–93) received financial aid; average amount of assistance $5,100. Assistance is typically divided 14% scholarship, 30% grant, 47% loan, 9% work. University reports 1,500 scholarships awarded on the basis of academic merit alone, 410 for athletics, 4,300 for need alone.

University of Pennsylvania

Philadelphia, Pennsylvania 19104 (215) 898-7507

A major research institution and a member of the Ivy League, the university was founded by Benjamin Franklin, who valued a more practical education than was offered by the classical New England schools of his time. The university now combines four undergraduate schools as well as twelve prestigious graduate and professional schools on a 260-acre tree-shaded campus located in University City, just outside the center of Philadelphia. Undergraduates apply for admission to one of the four undergraduate schools, the College of Arts and Sciences, the School of Engineering and Applied Science, the School of Nursing, and the Wharton School, or to one of the dual degree programs. Most convenient major airport: Philadelphia International.

Founded: 1740
Affiliation: Independent/State
UG Enrollment: 5,313 M, 4,125 W (full-time)
Total Enrollment: 22,469
Cost: $10K–$20K
Admission: Most Selective
Application Deadline: January 1

Admission is among the most selective in the country (varies somewhat among the different schools). For all schools, 42% of applicants accepted, 47% of these actually enroll; 94% of freshmen graduate in top fifth of high school class, 99% in top two-fifths. Average freshman scores: SAT, 599 verbal, 670 mathematical; 89% of freshman score above 500 on verbal, 55% above 600, 8% above 700; 98% score above 500 on mathematical, 87% above 600, 47% above 700; ACT, 28 composite.

Required: SAT or ACT, 3 ACH including English Composition or English with writing sample (mathematics for Wharton and Engineering). Criteria considered in admissions, in order of importance: high school academic record, standardized test scores, recommendations, extracurricular activities, writing sample; other factors considered: special talents, alumni children, diverse student body, leadership skills, personality. *Entrance programs:* early decision, deferred admission. About 32% of entering students from private schools, 7% from parochial schools. *Apply* by January 1, November 1 (early). *Transfers* welcome; 199 enrolled 1993–94.
Academic Environment. Students represented on all policy-making committees except tenure and promotion. University has developed a number of special programs that provide substantial autonomy for highly competent and motivated students in the design of their academic experiences. All students, including those enrolled in undergraduate professional schools, take liberal arts courses under the general education requirements which vary somewhat between programs, but assure "the benefit of a comprehensive and well-rounded academic curriculum", including proficiency in one of forty-five foreign languages. Students are reported to be concerned with scholarly/intellectual interests as well as with occupational/professional goals. Degrees offered: associates, bachelors, masters, doctoral. *Majors offered* in addition to usual liberal arts include anthropology, architecture and fine arts, astronomy, biochemistry, design of environment, elementary education, environmental studies, history and sociology of science, cognitive science, international relations, linguistics, Oriental studies, South Asia regional studies, urban studies, individualized and interdisciplinary majors; many dual degree programs offered. Most popular majors: business and finance, English, accounting, economics. Undergraduate class size: varies widely, but large introductory lectures are supplemented by small sections taught by teaching assistants.

About 88% of students entering as freshmen graduate within four years, 90% eventually; 97% of freshmen return for sophomore year. *Special programs:* independent study, study abroad, honors, undergraduate research, individualized majors, freshman seminars, University Scholars Program, Benjamin Franklin Scholars Program, Joseph Wharton Scholars program, combined programs (3–2 with engineering schools, 7-year programs in veterinary medicine or dentistry, accelerated programs with Graduate School of Fine Arts in architecture, landscape architecture, studio art), submatriculation (early entry) for selected undergraduates in graduate programs, Hahnemann Medical College and Hospital 1–1 College Accelerated Program, internship/cooperative work-study programs. Adult programs: Wharton Executive MBA and Executive Engineering programs designed for working adults. *Calendar:* semester, summer school.
Undergraduate degrees conferred (2,803). 27% were in Social Sciences, 25% were in Business and Management, 8% were in Engineering, 8% were in Letters, 7% were in Psychology, 4% were in Life Sciences, 4% were in Communications, remainder in 13 other fields.
Graduates Career Data. Advanced studies pursued by 45% of graduates; 7% enter medical school; 10% enter law school; 1% enter business school; 1% enter dental. Employers typically hiring largest numbers of graduates include Merrill Lynch, Goldman Sachs, Hospital of U. of Penn., Children's Hospital, General Electric, Procter and Gamble. Extensive Career Counseling Program. Alumni reported as active in both career guidance and job placement.
Faculty. About 99% of faculty hold PhD or equivalent.
Student Body. University seeks a national student body; 22% of students from in state; 53% from Middle Atlantic, 10% New England, 7% South, 10% North Central, 12% West, according to most recent data available. An estimated 7% of students reported as Black, 3% Hispanic, 15% Asian, 9% other ethnic minority. *Minority group students:* academic and social counseling for students with "unusual credentials"; Black Students League; experimental residential centers devoted to Black culture and remedial counseling and teaching.
Varsity Sports. Men (Div.I; Ivy): Baseball, Basketball, Crew, Cross Country, Diving, Fencing, Football(AA), Golf, Lacrosse, Soccer, Swimming, Tennis, Track, Wrestling. Women (Ivy): Basketball, Crew, Cross Country, Diving, Fencing, Field Hockey, Gymnastics, Lacrosse, Soccer, Softball, Swimming, Tennis, Track, Volleyball.
Campus Life. This is an urban campus located in the midst of an area that has undergone substantial reconstruction which has made the university a large enclave in the inner city. Students are able to use the nearby cultural facilities with ease and freedom. Students, who have virtually total control over their own social and cultural lives, will find many lifestyles available to them, both on campus and off. No curfews; intervisitation unlimited; alcohol permitted for those over 21. Students at Penn balance their demanding academic programs with active social lives and great school spirit. University has its own museums, theaters, and other cultural activities. Resources of the city are within walking distance of the campus.

About 58% of each men, women live in coed dormitories; 23% of each men, women live in off-campus housing; 1% each men and women commute. Freshmen given preference in college housing if all students cannot be accommodated. Sexes segregated in dormitories by room. There are 29 fraternities, 14 sororities on campus which about 33% of men, 32% of women join; 7% men, 2% women live in fraternities and sororities. About 10% of resident students leave campus on weekends.

Annual Costs. Tuition and fees, $17,838; room and board, $6,800; estimated $1,742 other, exclusive of travel. About 44% of students receive financial aid; average amount of assistance, $12,930. Assistance is typically divided 68% scholarship/grant, 21% loan, 10% work. University reports scholarships awarded only on the basis of need. *Meeting Costs:* university offers several long-term financing options with state and federal supplements.

Pepperdine University

Malibu, California 90263 **(310) 456-4392**

A Christian, liberal arts institution, maintaining ties with the Church of Christ. The main campus is located in Malibu which houses the undergraduate Liberal Arts school, Seaver College and the School of Law. The Graduate School of Education and Psychology and the School of Business and Management are administered from the Pepperdine University Plaza in West Los Angeles. Most convenient major airport: Los Angeles International.

Founded: 1937
Affiliation: Independent (Church of Christ)
UG Enrollment: 1,296 M, 1,404 W (full-time)
Total Enrollment: 7,000
Cost: $10K–$20K
% Receiving Financial Aid: 65%
Admission: Selective (+)
Application Deadline: Feb. 1

Admission is selective (+). About 57% of applicants accepted, 36% of these actually enroll; 95% of freshmen graduate in top fifth of high school class, 96% in top two-fifths. Average freshman scores: SAT, 498 M, 490 W verbal, 583 M, 543 W mathematical; 57% of freshmen score above 500 on verbal, 12% above 600, 2% above 700; 50% of freshmen score above 500 on mathematical, 20% above 600, 2% above 700; ACT, 25 M, 24 W composite. *Required:* SAT or ACT, essay, high school transcripts, recommendations. Criteria considered in admissions, in order of importance: high school academic record, standardized test scores, recommendations, writing sample, extracurricular activities; other factors considered: special talents, alumni children, diverse student body, religious affiliation/commitment. About 55% of entering students from private schools, 24% from parochial schools. *Entrance programs:* early action. *Apply* by February 1. Limited number of transfers welcome; 107 enrolled 1993–94.

Academic Environment. Graduation requirements include 2 semesters of English, 3 of Western Heritage, 2 of American Heritage, 1 of non-Western Heritage, 1 semester each of behavioral science, foreign language, lab science, math, and speech, 3 semesters of religion, 4 of physical education. Administration source says Pepperdine is "dedicated to the development of the 'whole' student", student concurs and adds "It is a well rounded academic program." Degrees offered: bachelors, masters, doctoral. *Majors offered* include sports medicine, computer science, contract majors.

About 65% of students entering as freshmen graduate within four years; 85% of freshmen return for sophomore year. *Special programs:* CLEP, January, Term, independent study, study abroad (including programs in Germany, Italy, England, Japan, Spain, France, and Australia), honors, undergraduate research, 3–2 engineering, internships, individualized majors. *Calendar:* year-round trimester, summer school.

Undergraduate degrees conferred (734). 42% were in Business and Management, 19% were in Communications, 12% were in Social Sciences, 5% were in Liberal/General Studies, 4% were in Multi/Interdisciplinary Studies, 3% were in Psychology, 3% were in Health Sciences, 3% were in Visual and Performing Arts, remainder in 8 other fields.

Graduates Career Data. Advanced studies pursued by 60% of graduates. Career Development Services include internships, on-campus interviews, assistance with job seeking process, counseling, assistance with interview preparation, alumni active in both career guidance and job placement.

Faculty. About 99% of faculty hold PhD or equivalent. About 73% of undergraduate classes taught by tenured faculty. About 20% of teaching faculty are female.

Student Body. About 50% of students from in state; 60% from West, 8% New England, 8% Northwest, 7% Midwest, 7% South, 10% foreign. An estimated 21% of students reported as Catholic, 6% Protestant, 1% Jewish, 1% Muslim, 7% unaffiliated, 4% other; 3% Black, 7% Hispanic, 6% Asian. *Minority group students:* special financial and academic provisions.

Religious Orientation. Pepperdine "wishes to be known as a Christian college emphasizing the standards and concerns of the Christian faith." Members of Church of Christ direct religion courses and conduct devotional services on campus; 12% of students affiliated with the church; 3 religious courses, attendance at weekly chapel required of all students.

Varsity Sports. Men (Div.I): Baseball, Basketball, Cross Country, Golf, Tennis, Volleyball, Water Polo. Women (Div.I): Basketball, Cross Country, Diving, Golf, Soccer, Swimming, Tennis, Volleyball.

Campus Life. Campus overlooks the Pacific. Student extols the "serene surroundings of Malibu" which "help student life with its inspiring beauty." Another student reports "There are many things to do on campus". She mentions sports, clubs, Bible studies, residence hall activities, and "great facilities." No curfew; limited intervisitation.

About 66% of men, 66% of women live in traditional dormitories; no coed dormitories; rest live in off-campus housing or commute. Freshmen given preference in college housing if all students cannot be accommodated. There are 6 fraternities, 7 sororities on campus which about 15% each of men, 17% of women join; they provide no residence facilities. About 50% of resident students leave campus on weekends.

Annual Costs. Tuition and fees, $17,200; room and board, $6,530; estimated $800 other, exclusive of travel. About 65% of students receive financial aid; average amount of assistance, $17,000. Assistance is typically divided 59% scholarship, 34% loan, 7% work. University reports some scholarships awarded on the basis of academic merit alone.

Peru State College

Peru, Nebraska 68421 **(402) 872-3815**

A state-supported college, located in a village of 1,380, 62 miles south of Omaha.

Founded: 1867
Affiliation: State
UG Enrollment: 321 M, 526 W (full-time)
Total Enrollment: 1,703
Cost: < $10K
% Receiving Financial Aid: 65%
Admission: Non-selective
Application Deadline: Rolling

Admission. Graduates of Nebraska high schools eligible. About 78% of applicants accepted, 93% of these actually enroll; 10% of freshmen graduate in top fifth of high school class. *Required:* SAT or ACT, interview. Criteria considered in admissions, in order of importance: high school academic record, standardized test scores. *Out-of-state* freshman applicants: college actively seeks students from out-of-state. State does not limit out-of-state enrollment. Required for out-of-state students: minimum high school GPA 2.0, higher test scores. About 79% of out-of-state applicants accepted, 88% of these actually enroll. States from which most out-of-state students are drawn include Missouri, Iowa. *Entrance programs:* early admission, midyear admission, deferred admission, advanced placement. *Apply:* rolling admission. *Transfers* welcome.

Academic Environment. Graduation requirements include a "wide range of courses." Degrees offered: associates, bachelors, doctoral. Average undergraduate class size: 16; 60% under 20.

About 51% of students entering as freshmen graduate within four years, 57% graduate eventually; 63% of freshmen return for sophomore year. *Special programs:* CLEP, independent study, study abroad, honors, internships (all majors), undergraduate research, 3-year degree. Adult programs: Bachelors of Technology for students with an Associates of Applied Science. *Calendar:* semester, summer school.

Undergraduate degrees conferred (206). 36% were in Education, 34% were in Business and Management, 21% were in

Social Sciences, 5% were in Visual and Performing Arts, remainder in 3 other fields.
Graduates Career Data. About 91% of 1992–93 graduates employed. Career Development Services available.
Faculty. About 67% of faculty hold PhD or equivalent.
Student Body. About 87% of students from in state; 96% Midwest, 1% South, 1% Northwest, 2% foreign. Average age of undergraduate student: 27.
Varsity Sports. Men (NAIA, Div.II): Baseball, Basketball, Football. Women (NAIA, Div.II): Basketball, Softball, Volleyball.
Campus Life. About 13% of men, 13% of women live in traditional dormitories; 14% men, 9% women live in coed dormitories; rest live in off-campus housing or commute. There is 1 fraternity and 1 sorority on campus. About 50% of resident students leave campus on weekends.
Annual Costs. Tuition and fees, $1,687 (out-of-state, $2,834); room and board, $2,625; estimated $1,700 other, exclusive of travel. About 65% of students receive financial aid. College reports some scholarships awarded on the basis of academic merit alone.

Pfeiffer College

Misenheimer, North Carolina 28109 (704) 463-1360

A church-related, liberal arts college, located in a small village, 40 miles northeast of Charlotte (pop. 241,200). Most convenient major airport: Charlotte, NC.

Founded: 1885
Affiliation: United Methodist
UG Enrollment: 320 M, 334 W (full-time); 65 M, 97 W (part-time)
Total Enrollment: 1,005
Cost: < $10K
% Receiving Financial Aid: 90%
Admission: Non-selective
Application Deadline: Rolling

Admission. High school graduates with 800 combined SAT score, GPA of 2.0 and rank in upper 50% of class eligible, others considered by committee review; 78% of applicants accepted, 24% of these actually enroll; 17% of freshmen graduate in top fifth of high school class, 44% in top two-fifths. Average freshman SAT score: 392 M, 387 W verbal, 449 M, 432 W mathematical. *Required:* SAT or ACT (for placement only). Criteria considered in admissions, in order of importance: high school academic record, standardized test scores, recommendations, extracurricular activities. *Entrance programs:* early decision, early admission, midyear admission. *Apply:* rolling admission. *Transfers* welcome, 132 enrolled 1993–94.
Academic Environment. Graduation requirements include work in writing, oral communication, language and literature, history, music/art/theater, natural sciences, mathematics, economics/psychology/sociology, religion. Student reports "great student-teacher relationships. Good sports medicine program." Degrees offered: bachelors, masters. *Majors offered* include communications, sports medicine, Christian education. Average undergraduate class size: 70% under 20, 27% 20–40, 3% over 40.

About 22% of students entering as freshmen graduate within four years, 42% eventually; 63% of freshmen return for sophomore year. *Special programs:* CLEP, independent study, honors, study abroad, undergraduate research, 3–2 engineering, internships, optional 3-week January interterm for independent study, 3-year degree. *Calendar:* semester, summer school.
Undergraduate degrees conferred (132). 30% were in Business and Management, 15% were in Education, 12% were in Protective Services, 11% were in Social Sciences, 8% were in Letters, 4% were in Psychology, 4% were in Physical Sciences, 4% were in Allied Health, 3% were in Visual and Performing Arts, 3% were in Mathematics, remainder in 4 other fields.
Graduates Career Data. Career Development Services include on-campus interviewing, resume and interviewing workshops, resume mailing service.
Student Body. About 66% of students from in state; 80% from South, 15% Middle Atlantic, 2% New England, 1% Midwest, 2% foreign. An estimated 59% of students reported as Protestant, 13% Catholic, 1% Jewish, 10% unaffiliated, 17% other; 10% Black, 1% Hispanic, 1% Asian, 3% other minority. Average age of undergraduate student: 23.
Religious Orientation. Pfeiffer is a church-related institution; 22% of students affiliated with the church; 2 courses in religion required of all students.
Varsity Sports. Men (NAIA; NCAA Div. II): Baseball, Basketball, Cross Country, Golf, Lacrosse, Soccer, Tennis. Women (NAIA; NCAA Div. II): Basketball, Cross Country, Soccer, Softball, Swimming, Tennis, Volleyball.
Campus Life. Campus is located in a rural area. Student reports student life focuses on campus activities. About 58% of men, 60% of women live in traditional dormitories; no coed dormitories; rest live in off-campus housing or commute. Freshmen given preference in college housing if all students cannot be accommodated. Intervisitation in men's and women's dormitory rooms limited. There are no fraternities or sororities on campus. About 50% of resident students leave campus on weekends.
Annual Costs. Tuition and fees, $8,190; room and board, $3,480. About 90% of students receive financial aid; assistance is typically divided 50% scholarship, 25% loan, 25% work. College reports some scholarships awarded on the basis of academic merit alone.

Philadelphia College of Art

(See University of the Arts)

Philadelphia College of Bible

Langhorne, Pennsylvania 19047-2990 (800) 366-0049

A non-denominational, conservative, evangelical college that prepares students for service in church-related vocations.

Founded: 1913
Affiliation: Independent
Total Enrollment: 986
Cost: < $10K
% Receiving Financial Aid: 85%
Admission: Non-selective
Application Deadline: Rolling

Admission. About 68% of freshmen applicants accepted; 43% of these actually enroll; 32% of freshmen graduate in top fifth of high school class, 56% in top two-fifths. Average freshman scores: SAT, 461 verbal, 448 mathematical; ACT, 22 composite. *Required:* SAT or ACT, minimum high school GPA, essay, Pastor's reference. Criteria considered in admissions, in order of importance: writing sample, high school academic record, standardized test scores, recommendations, extracurricular activities; other factors considered: special talents, alumni children, diverse student body, religious affiliation/commitment. *Entrance programs:* early decision, early admission, midyear admission, deferred admission, advanced placement. About 20% of entering students from parochial schools, 4% private schools. *Apply:* rolling admissions. *Transfers* welcome; 118 enrolled 1993–94.
Academic Environment. Degrees offered: associates, bachelors, masters. *Majors offered* include counseling, Christian education, communications, missions, pastoral studies, youth ministries. *Special programs:* January Term, study abroad, internships.
Undergraduate degrees conferred (115). 68% were in Philosophy and Religion, 18% were in Education, 8% were in Public Affairs, 6% were in Visual and Performing Arts.
Student Body. About 90% of students from Middle Atlantic, 1% New England, 9% foreign. An estimated 98% of students reported as Protestant, 1% Catholic, 1% Jewish.
Religious Orientation. College is a church-related institution; 50 hours of Bible and related subjects required of all students.
Varsity Sports. Men (NCAAA): Baseball, Basketball, Cross Country, Soccer. Women (PAIAW): Basketball, Cross Country, Field Hockey, Softball.
Campus Life. About 17% of men, 18% of women live in traditional dormitories; there are no co-ed dormitories; rest commute. There are no fraternities or sororities on campus. About 75% of resident students leave campus on weekends.
Annual Costs. Tuition and fees, $7,140; room and board, $4,130; estimated $1,420 other, exclusive of travel. About 85% of students receive financial aid; average amount of assistance, $4,650. Assistance is typically divided 32% scholarship, 28% grant, 34% loan, 6% work. College reports 5 scholarships awarded on the basis of academic merit alone, 6 for special talents alone, 1 for need alone.

Philadelphia College of Performing Arts

(See University of the Arts)

Philadelphia College of Pharmacy and Science

Philadelphia, Pennsylvania 19104 (215) 596-8800

An independent, professional institution, located in metropolitan Philadelphia. Philadelphia College of Pharmacy and Science was the first school of pharmacy in the country.

Founded: 1821
Affiliation: Independent
UG Enrollment: 671 M, 1,046 W (full-time)
Total Enrollment: 1,870
Cost: $10K–$20K
% Receiving Financial Aid: 75%
Admission: Selective (+)
Application Deadline: Rolling

Admission is selective (+). About 61% of applicants accepted, 47% of these actually enroll; 59% of freshmen graduate in top fifth of high school class, 85% in top two-fifths. Average freshman SAT scores: 474 verbal, 545 mathematical. *Required:* SAT, essay, interview for physical therapy only. Criteria considered in admissions, in order of importance: high school academic record, standardized test scores, writing sample, recommendations, extracurricular activities; other factors considered: special talents, alumni children, diverse student body. About 27% of entering students from private schools, 4% parochial schools. *Apply:* rolling admissions; January 15 for transfers. *Transfers* welcome; 75 enrolled 1993–94.
Academic Environment. Degrees offered: bachelors, masters, doctoral. About 80% of entering students graduate within five years; 91% of freshmen return for sophomore year. *Special programs:* undergraduate research. *Calendar:* semester, summer school.
Undergraduate degrees conferred (270). 89% were in Health Sciences, 10% were in Life Sciences, remainder in 2 other fields.
Graduates Career Data. About 90% of 1992–93 graduates employed.
Faculty. About 66% of faculty hold PhD or equivalent. About 60% of undergraduate classes taught by tenured faculty. About 34% of teaching faculty are female; 1% Black, 9% Asian.
Student Body. About 70% of students from in state; 95% from Middle Atlantic. An estimated 50% of students reported as Catholic, 28% Protestant, 5% Jewish, 1% Muslim, 9% other; 4% Black, 1% Hispanic, 18% Asian.
Varsity Sports. Men (NAIA): Baseball, Basketball, Cross Country, Rifle, Tennis. Women (PAIAW): Basketball, Cross Country, Softball, Rifle, Tennis, Volleyball.
Campus Life. About 37% of students live in coed dormitories; 58% of students live in off-campus housing or commute. Freshmen given preference in college housing if all students cannot be accommodated. Intervisitation in men's and women's dormitory rooms limited; sexes segregated by floor. There are 7 coed fraternities; 5% of students live in fraternities.
Annual Costs. Tuition and fees, $10,600; room and board, $4,166; estimated $1,300 other, exclusive of travel. About 75% of students receive financial aid, average amount of assistance, $3,000. Assistance is typically divided 25% scholarship, 25% grant, 50% loan/work. College reports 150 scholarships awarded on the basis of academic merit alone, 25 for special talents alone. *Meeting Costs:* college offers PLUS Loans.

Philadelphia College of Textiles and Science

Philadelphia, Pennsylvania 19144 (215) 951-2800

An independent, professional institution, specializing in textile management and offering programs in related fields; located 15 minutes from center city Philadelphia. Most convenient major airport: Philadelphia International.

Founded: 1884
Affiliation: Independent
UG Enrollment: 587 M, 1,087 W (full-time); 326 M, 716 W (part-time)
Total Enrollment: 2,706
Cost: $10K–$20K
% Receiving Financial Aid: 78%
Admission: Non-selective
Application Deadline: Rolling

Admission. High school graduates eligible; 82% of applicants accepted, 31% of these actually enroll; 24% of entering freshmen graduate in top fifth of high school class, 52% in top two-fifths. Average freshman scores: SAT, 480 verbal, 500 mathematical; 26% of freshmen score above 500 on verbal, 3% above 600; 43% score above 500 on mathematical, 9% above 600, 1% above 700. *Required:* SAT or ACT; interview recommended. Criteria considered in admissions, in order of importance: high school academic record, standardized test scores, extracurricular activities, writing sample, recommendations; other factors considered: special talents, diverse student body. *Entrance programs:* early admission, deferred admission. *Apply:* rolling admissions. *Transfers* welcome; 316 enrolled 1993–94.
Academic Environment. Degrees offered: associates, bachelors, masters. *Majors offered* include 5-year architecture, computer science and information systems, fashion, design, textiles. Average undergraduate class size: all under 20. About 55% of entering students graduate within four years, 59% within six years; 64% of freshmen return for sophomore year. *Special programs:* study abroad, co-op education. Adult programs: BS for registered nurses. *Calendar:* semester, summer school.
Undergraduate degrees conferred (486). 44% were in Business and Management, 18% were in Marketing and Distribution, 12% were in Home Economics, 8% were in Architecture and Environmental Design, 6% were in Health Sciences, 5% were in Computer and Engineering Related Technology, 3% were in Visual and Performing Arts, remainder in 4 other fields.
Graduates Career Data. About 94% of 1993–94 graduates employed. Fields typically hiring largest numbers of graduates include marketing, merchandising, other business related areas. Career Development Services include workshops, special events, extensive on-campus recruiting program, published resume book and annual report.
Faculty. About 52% of faculty hold PhD or equivalent. All undergraduate classes taught by tenured faculty. About 30% of teaching faculty are female; 1% Black, 1% Hispanic, 1% other minority.
Student Body. About 72% of students from in state; 87% New England, 7% foreign. An estimated 9% of students reported as Black, 2% Hispanic, 4% Asian, 7% other minority.
Varsity Sports. Men (Div.II): Baseball, Basketball, Golf, Soccer(I), Tennis. Women (Div.II): Basketball, Field Hockey, Lacrosse, Soccer, Softball, Tennis.
Campus Life. About 36% of men, 30% of women live in coed dormitory; 28% of men, 19% of women live in college-related off-campus housing; rest commute. There are 2 fraternities, 3 sororities. About 50% of resident students leave campus on weekends.
Annual Costs. Tuition and fees, $10,914–11,690, depending on program; room and board, $5,062; estimated $2,270 other, exclusive of travel. About 78% of students receive financial aid; average amount of assistance, $9,000. Assistance is typically divided 14% scholarship, 44% grant, 36% loan, 6% work. College reports some scholarships awarded on the basis of academic merit alone.

Philander Smith College

Little Rock, Arkansas 72202 (501) 370-5219

A church-related college, located in a city of 132,500; founded as a college for Negroes and still serving a predominantly Black student body. Most convenient major airport: Little Rock Municipal.

Founded: 1877
Affiliation: United Methodist
UG Enrollment: 326 M, 393 W (full-time); 86 M, 110 W (part-time)
Total Enrollment: 915
Cost: < $10K
% Receiving Financial Aid: 90%
Admission: Non-selective
Application Deadline: Aug. 1

Admission. High school graduates with 16 units (12 in academic subjects) and C average eligible; 99% of applicants accepted, 63% of these actually enroll; 25% of freshmen graduate in top fifth of high school class, 60% in top two-fifths. *Required:* ACT. *Entrance programs:* early admission. *Apply* by August 1. *Transfers* welcome; 53 enrolled 1993–94.
Academic Environment. *Degrees:* bachelors. Unusual, new, or notable majors include organizational management. Average undergraduate class size: 50% under 20, 50% 20–40. About 95% of freshmen return for sophomore year. *Special programs:* CLEP, independent study, study abroad, undergraduate research, individualized majors, 3–2 programs. *Calendar:* semester, summer school.
Undergraduate degrees conferred (62). 47% were in Business and Management, 29% were in Education, 15% were in Social Sciences, 3% were in Life Sciences, 3% were in Home Economics, remainder in 2 other fields.
Graduates Career Data. Advanced studies pursued by 46% of graduates. About 50% of 1992–93 graduates employed.
Faculty. About 45% of faculty hold PhD or equivalent. About 50% of undergraduate classes taught by tenured faculty. About 34% of teaching faculty are female; 74% Black, 6% other minority.
Student Body. About 82% of students from in state; 86% Midwest, 4% South, 8% foreign students. An estimated 91% of students reported as Protestant, 1% Catholic, 8% other; 87% Black, 7% Asian, 1% other minority.
Religious Orientation. Philander Smith is a church-related institution; 15% of students affiliated with the church; 3 hours in religion required of all students; attendance at Sunday vespers, weekday convocations "encouraged.
Varsity Sports. Men: Baseball, Basketball, Volleyball. Women: Volleyball.
Campus Life. About 17% of men, 13% of women live in traditional dormitories; rest live in off-campus housing or commute. No intervisitation in men's or women's dormitory rooms. There are 4 fraternities, 4 sororities on campus which 1% of men, 1% of women join. About 5–10% of resident students leave campus on weekends.
Annual Costs. Tuition and fees, $5,520; room and board, $2,415; estimated $800 other, exclusive of travel. About 90% of students receive financial aid. Assistance is typically divided 21% scholarship, 53% grant, 18% loan, 10% work. College reports 202 scholarships awarded on the basis of academic merit alone; 30 on special talents alone.

Phillips University

Enid, Oklahoma 73701 **(800) 238-1185**

A church-related institution, affiliated with the Christian Church (Disciples of Christ), located in a community of 45,000, 85 miles northwest of Oklahoma City.

Founded: 1906
Affiliation: Disciples of Christ
UG Enrollment: 292 M, 361 W (full-time); 30 M, 47 W (part-time)
Total Enrollment: 774
Cost: < $10K
% Receiving Financial Aid: 80%
Admission: Non-selective
Application Deadline: Aug. 1

Admission. Graduates of accredited high schools with C average eligible; 83% of applicants accepted, 25% of these actually enroll. Average freshman scores: SAT, 430 verbal, 470 mathematical; 21 composite. *Required:* ACT or SAT, minimum high school GPA of 2.75. Criteria considered in admissions, in order of importance: high school academic record and standardized test scores rank equally, recommendations, extracurricular activities; other factors considered: special talents, alumni children, diverse student body, religious affiliation/commitment. *Entrance programs:* early decision, early admission, midyear admission. *Apply* by August 1; rolling admissions. *Transfers* welcome; 52 enrolled 1993–94.
Academic Environment. Graduation requirements include study in English, religion or philosophy, U.S. history and government, economics, psychology or sociology, mathematics, science, and music or art. Degrees offered: associates, bachelors, masters, doctoral. Average undergraduate class size: all under 20. *Special programs:* individualized majors, study abroad (Phillips U. in Sweden), cross-registration. *Calendar:* semester, 3 1-month summer modules.
Undergraduate degrees conferred (107). 27% were in Business and Management, 21% were in Education, 12% were in Social Sciences, 8% were in Psychology, 7% were in Visual and Performing Arts, 6% were in Life Sciences, 5% were in Liberal/General Studies, 4% were in Area and Ethnic Studies, 3% were in Communications, remainder in 6 other fields.
Graduates Career Data. Career Development Services include placement service, credentials service, on-campus recruitment.
Faculty. About 70% of faculty hold PhD or equivalent. About 47% of undergraduate classes taught by tenured faculty. About 26% of teaching faculty are female.
Student Body. About 55% of students from in state; 26% from Midwest. An estimated 20% of students reported as Protestant, 13% Catholic, 67% other; 6% as Black, 4% Hispanic, 2% Asian, 13% other minority.
Religious Orientation. Phillips is a church-related institution; 23% of students affiliated with the church; 6 courses in religion required of all students.
Varsity Sports. Men (NAIA): Basketball, Golf, Soccer, Tennis. Women (NAIA): Basketball.
Campus Life. Campus is located in a rural area. Students report they are "very involved" with campus organizations, as well as in the community.

About 30% each of men, women live in traditional dormitories; 20% each live in coed dormitories; rest commute. Freshmen given preference in college housing if all students cannot be accommodated. Intervisitation in men's and women's dormitory rooms limited. About 20% of resident students leave campus on weekends.
Annual Costs. Tuition and fees, $9,310; room and board, $3,004; estimated $1,560 other, exclusive of travel. About 80% of students receive financial aid; average amount of assistance, $9,270. Assistance is typically divided 52% scholarship, 15% grant, 28% loan, 5% work. University reports 277 scholarships awarded on the basis of academic merit alone, 99 for special talents alone, 173 for need alone. *Meeting Costs:* university offers program for middle income families.

Piedmont College

Demorest, Georgia 30535 **(706) 778-8500 or (800) 277-7020**

A church-related college, located in a village of 1,100, 85 miles northeast of Atlanta. Most convenient major airport: Atlanta.

Founded: 1897
Affiliation: Congregational Christian Churches
UG Enrollment: 268 M, 373 W (full-time); 21 M, 42 W (part-time)
Total Enrollment: 704
Cost: < $10K
% Receiving Financial Aid: 95%
Admission: Non-selective
Application Deadline: July 1

Admission. Graduates of approved high schools with 16 units eligible; students from non accredited schools admitted on probation; 85% of applicants accepted, 47% of these actually enroll. About 20% of freshmen graduate in the top fifth of high school class, 60% in top two-fifths. Average freshman SAT scores: 452 verbal, 499 mathematical. *Required:* SAT or ACT, minimum high school GPA. Criteria considered in admissions, in order of importance: standardized test scores, high school academic record, recommendations, extracurricular activities. *Entrance programs:* early admission. *Apply* by: July 1; rolling admissions. *Transfers* welcome; 86 enrolled 1993–94.
Academic Environment. Graduation requirements include 52 semester hours and Piedmont Studies. Degrees offered: bachelors, masters. Average undergraduate class size: 63% under 20, 37% 20–40. About 24% of entering students graduate within four years, 67% of freshmen return for sophomore year. *Special programs:* 3–2 nursing, internship programs (teacher education, psychology, and sociology; business and art management). Adult programs: night program for students over 25 years old. *Calendar:* quarter, summer school.
Undergraduate degrees conferred (107). 37% were in Business and Management, 18% were in Education, 16% were in Social Sciences, 8% were in Psychology, 6% were in Computer and Engineering Related Technology, 5% were in Life Sciences, 4% were in Mathematics, 4% were in Letters, 3% were in Physical Sciences.
Graduates Career Data. According to most recent data available, advanced studies pursued by 40% of graduates. About 70% of

graduates employed. Career Development Services include career planning and placement office providing career guidance, job placement and graduate school admissions assistance.

Faculty. About 79% of faculty hold PhD or equivalent. About 35% of undergraduate classes taught by tenured faculty. About 36% of teaching faculty are female; 3% Black, 3% Hispanic, 5% other minority.

Student Body. About 85% of students from in state; 72% South, 6% Midwest, 6% New England; 1% foreign. An estimated 5% of students reported as Black, 1% Hispanic, 1% Asian, 1% other minority. Average age of undergraduate student: 26.

Religious Orientation. Piedmont is a church-related institution; 2% of students affiliated with the church; attendance at Sunday vespers and weekly chapel services required of all students.

Varsity Sports. Men (NAIA): Baseball, Basketball, Golf, Cross Country, Soccer, Tennis. Women (NAIA): Basketball, Cross Country, Golf, Soccer, Softball, Tennis.

Campus Life. Campus is located in a rural area. Students report social life is focused on campus activities, organizations and sports. Some interest in outdoor activities also reported.

About 56% of men, 40% of women live in traditional dormitories; rest commute. Freshmen given preference in college housing if all students cannot be accommodated. There is 1 fraternity and 1 sorority on campus which 5% of men, 5% of women join. About 50% of resident students leave campus on weekends.

Annual Costs. Tuition and fees, $4,920; room and board, $3,620; estimated $1,400 other, exclusive of travel. About 95% of students receive financial aid; average amount of assistance, $4,350. Assistance is typically divided 17% scholarship, 36% grant, 41% loan, 6% work. College reports some scholarships awarded on the basis of academic merit alone. Meeting costs: college offers deferred payment plan.

Pikeville College

Pikeville, Kentucky 41501 (606) 432-9200

A church-related college, located in a town of 5,000, 143 miles southeast of Lexington.

Founded: 1889
Affiliation: Presbyterian Church (USA)
UG Enrollment: 241 M, 560 W (full-time); 24 M, 72 W (part-time)
Cost: < $10K
% Receiving Financial Aid: 90%
Admission: Non-selective
Application Deadline: April 1

Admission. Open admissions; all freshmen applicants are accepted, 50% actually enroll. Average freshmen ACT scores: 20 composite. *Required:* ACT, interview. *Entrance programs:* early decision, early admission, midyear admission, deferred admission, advanced placement. *Apply* by April 1. *Transfers* welcome; 110 enrolled 1993–94.

Academic Environment. Graduation requirements include 1 course in computer science, 2 in English, 1 in math, 1 in speech, 2 in religion, 1 lab science for BS, 2 for BA, and 2 years of a foreign language. Degrees offered: associates, bachelors. About 40% of entering class graduate within four years, 50% eventually; 70% of freshmen return for sophomore year. Average undergraduate class size: 20% under 20, 80% 20–40. *Special programs:* CLEP, credit by examination. *Calendar:* 4–1–4, 2 summer sessions.

Undergraduate degrees conferred (120). 43% were in Education, 20% were in Business and Management, 8% were in Multi/Interdisciplinary Studies, 6% were in Mathematics, 4% were in Life Sciences, 3% were in Social Sciences, 3% were in Psychology, 3% were in Letters, 3% were in Allied Health, remainder in 4 other fields.

Graduates Career Data. Advanced studies pursued by 20% of graduates; 15% enter graduate school; 1% enter business school; 1% enter dental school; 1% enter law school; 1% enter medical school. Medical, dental and law schools typically enrolling largest numbers of graduates include Kentucky, U. of Louisville; business schools include Kentucky, Marshall. Career Development Services include resume assistance, job fairs.

Faculty. About 55% of faculty hold PhD or equivalent. About 65% of undergraduate classes taught by tenured faculty. About 30% of teaching faculty are female.

Student Body. About 90% of students from the state; 95% South, 4% Midwest. An estimated 85% students are reported Protestant, 14% Catholic, 1% other or unaffiliated; 2% Black, 1% Hispanic and Asian.

Religious Orientation. Pikeville is a "nonsectarian institution, affiliated with the Presbyterian Church (USA) "; 12% of students affiliated with the church; 2 religious courses required of all students, attendance at church of student's choice "encouraged."

Varsity Sports. Men: Baseball, Basketball, Tennis. Women: Basketball, Softball, Tennis.

Campus Life. About 50% of men, 25% of women live in traditional dormitories; no coed dormitories; rest commute. Intervisitation in men's and women's dormitory rooms limited. About 90% of resident students leave campus on weekends.

Annual Costs. Tuition and fees, $5,500, room and board, $3,000; estimated $500 other, exclusive of travel. About 90% of students receive financial aid, average amount received, $2,000. Assistance is typically divided 10% scholarship, 40% grant, 40% loan, 10% work. University reports 5 scholarships awarded on the basis of special talents alone, 95 for need alone.

Pine Manor College

Chestnut Hill, Massachusetts 02167 (617) 731-7104

A four-year liberal arts college for women, Pine Manor attracts students from throughout the United States and abroad to its 75-acre suburban campus, just 5 miles from Boston. The College offers an internship program designed for career exploration, as well as options to study for the AA, AS or BA degree. Most convenient major airport: Logan International (Boston).

Founded: 1911
Affiliation: Independent
UG Enrollment: 370 W (full-time); 30 W (part-time)
Cost: $10K–$20K
% Receiving Financial Aid: 32%
Admission: Non-selective
Application Deadline: July 1

Admission. High school graduates with a minimum GPA of 2.0 eligible; 91% of applicants accepted, 39% of those actually enroll; 30% of freshmen graduate in the top half of their high school class. Average freshman SAT scores: 391 verbal, 373 mathematical. *Required:* SAT; interview recommended. Criteria considered in admissions, in order of importance: standardized test scores, high school academic record, recommendations, extracurricular activities, writing sample; other factors considered: alumni children. *Entrance programs:* early decision, midyear admission, deferred admission. About 41% of entering students from private schools, 9% from parochial schools. *Apply* by July 1. *Transfers* welcome; 26 enrolled 1993–94.

Academic Environment. Graduation requirements include 2 semesters college composition, 1–2 semesters math, 36 credits equally divided between humanities, social sciences, natural and behavioral sciences, and arts and communication; internships required for degree programs. Degrees offered: associates, bachelors, masters. *Majors offered* include advertising, biology, marketing, sociology, international business, international relations, American studies, communications. Average undergraduate class size: 88% under 20, 12% 20–40.

About 45% of entering students graduate within four years, 51% eventually, 72% of freshmen return for sophomore year. *Special programs:* cross-registration with Babson College, Boston College, marine studies consortium, study abroad, honors, undergraduate research, independent study, individualized degree, internship required for degree programs. Adult programs: continuing education programs offered with part-time day and evening classes (including teacher certification). *Calendar:* semester.

Undergraduate degrees conferred (115). 23% were in Business and Management, 22% were in Visual and Performing Arts, 19% were in Communications, 18% were in Psychology, 6% were in Letters, 3% were in Foreign Languages, 3% were in Education, 3% were in Area and Ethnic Studies, remainder in 2 other fields.

Faculty. About 60% of faculty hold PhD or equivalent.

Student Body. About 33% of students from in state; 46% New England, 11% Middle Atlantic, 7% Midwest, 10% South, 4% West, 20% foreign. An estimated 7% of students reported as Black, 8% Hispanic, 15% Asian, 5% other minority.

Varsity Sports. Women (Div.III): Basketball, Cross Country, Field Hockey, Lacrosse, Soccer, Tennis.

Campus Life. About 85% of students live on campus; housing guaranteed. There are no sororities on campus. About 10–15% of resident students leave campus on weekends.

Annual Costs. Tuition and fees, $15,865; room and board, $6,460. About 32% of students receive financial aid; assistance is typically divided 65% scholarship, 25% loan, 10% work. College reports scholarships awarded only on the basis of need.

Pittsburg State University

Pittsburg, Kansas 66762 **(316) 231-7000**

A state-supported university, located in a town of 20,200, 125 miles south of Kansas City. Most convenient major airport: Springfield, MO.

Founded: 1903
Affiliation: State
UG Enrollment: 2,080 M, 1,863 W (full-time); 266 M, 254 W (part-time)
Total Enrollment: 5,806
Cost: < $10K
% Receiving Financial Aid: 56%
Admission: Non-selective
Application Deadline: Rolling

Admission. Graduates of accredited Kansas high schools accepted; 93% of applicants accepted, 62% of these actually enroll. Average freshman ACT scores: 20.6 M, 20.7 W composite. *Required:* ACT. Criteria considered in admissions, in order of importance: standardized test scores, high school academic record. *Out-of-state* freshman applicants: college actively seeks students from out of state. State does not limit out-of-state enrollment. Requirements for out-of state applicants: rank in top half of high school class; foreign students, minimum TOEFL of 520. States from which most out-of-state students are drawn include Missouri, Oklahoma. *Apply*: rolling admissions. *Transfers* welcome; 739 accepted 1993–94.

Academic Environment. Graduation requirements include new interdisciplinary general education requirements starting Fall, 1994. Degrees offered: bachelors, masters. Average undergraduate class size: 15% under 20, 75% 20–40, 10% over 40. About 40% of students entering as freshmen graduate within four years, 69% eventually; 86% of freshmen return for sophomore year. *Special programs:* CLEP, independent study, study abroad, honors, undergraduate research, individualized majors, 3–2 in engineering. *Calendar*: semester, summer school.

Undergraduate degrees conferred (850). 26% were in Business and Management, 18% were in Education, 11% were in Engineering and Engineering Related Technology, 8% were in Health Sciences, 6% were in Psychology, 5% were in Life Sciences, 5% were in Social Sciences, 4% were in Communications, 3% were in Public Affairs, 3% were in Liberal/General Studies, 3% were in Visual and Performing Arts, remainder in 7 other fields.

Faculty. About 75% of faculty hold PhD or equivalent. About 90% of undergraduate classes taught by tenured faculty. About 30% of teaching faculty are female.

Student Body. About 83% of students from in state; 85% Midwest, 9% foreign. Average age of undergraduate student: 27.

Varsity Sports. Men (NAIA, Div.II): Baseball, Basketball, Cross Country, Football, Golf, Track. Women (NAIA, Div.II): Basketball, Cross Country, Softball, Track, Volleyball.

Campus Life. About 10% of students live in traditional dormitories; 5% live in coed dormitories, 20% live in off-campus housing; 59% commute. Freshmen given preference in college housing if all students cannot be accommodated. Intervisitation in men's and women's dormitory rooms limited, unlimited depending on student choice of dormitory. Sexes segregated in coed dormitory by floor. There are 6 fraternities, 6 sororities on campus which about 6% of men, 6% of women join, 6% of men, 6% of women live in fraternities and sororities. About 50% of resident students leave campus on weekends.

Annual Costs. Tuition and fees, $1,664 (out-of-state, $4,798); room and board, $2,814. About 56% of students receive financial aid. University reports some scholarships awarded on the basis of academic merit alone. *Meeting Costs:* university offers low interest loans.

University of Pittsburgh

Pittsburgh, Pennsylvania 15260 **(412) 624-PITT**

The University of Pittsburgh is a co-educational, state-related, research university, offering a wide range of undergraduate and graduate programs on the 132-acre Pittsburgh campus located in the cultural center of the city. The University also operates regional campuses in Johnstown, Bradford, and Greensburg which offer four-year baccalaureate programs, and in Titusville which has primarily lower-division programs. Most convenient major airport: Pittsburgh International.

Founded: 1787
Affiliation: State-related
UG Enrollment: 6,714 M, 6,557 W (full-time); 2,113 M, 2,176 W (part-time)
Total Enrollment: 27,528
Cost: < $10K
% Receiving Financial Aid: 60%
Admission: Very Selective
Application Deadline: Rolling

Admission is very selective for School of Engineering, selective for College of Arts and Sciences. For all schools, 76% of applicants accepted, 36% of these actually enroll; 45% of freshmen graduate in top fifth of high school class, 80% in top two-fifths. Median freshman SAT scores: 470 verbal, 530 mathematical.

For College of Arts and Science (4,306 M, 4,628 W f-t, 444 M, 468 W p-t): 76% of applicants accepted, 36% of these actually enroll; 42% of freshmen graduate in top fifth of high school class, 79% in top two-fifths. Median freshmen SAT scores: 470 verbal, 520 mathematical; 32% of freshmen score above 500 on verbal, 6% above 600; 64% score above 500 on mathematical, 20% above 600, 2% above 700.

For School of Engineering (1,125 M, 247 W f-t, 104 M, 17 W p-t): 81% of applicants accepted, 36% of these actually enroll; 63% of freshmen graduate in top fifth of high school class, 89% in top two-fifths. Median freshmen SAT scores: 490 verbal, 600 mathematical; 43% of freshmen score above 500 on verbal, 9% above 600; 88% score above 500 on mathematical, 47% above 600, 9% above 700.

For School of Nursing (60 M, 415 W f-t, 13 M, 74 W p-t): 58% of applicants accepted, 47% of these actually enroll; 67% of freshmen graduate in top fifth of high school class, 87% in top two-fifths. Median freshmen SAT scores: 460 verbal, 510 mathematical.

Required: SAT or ACT; interview recommended; other requirements vary by school. Criteria considered in admissions: high school academic record, standardized test scores; other factors considered: alumni children, diverse student body, interview, school and community activities, essay, recommendations, and minority status. *Out-of-state* applicants: university actively seeks students from out-of-state. State does not limit out-of-state enrollment. About 70% of out-of-state applicants accepted, 17% of these actually enroll. States from which most out-of-state students are drawn: New York, New Jersey, Ohio, Pennsylvania. *Entrance programs:* early admission, midyear admission, advanced placement, deferred admission (freshmen only). *Apply*: rolling admissions. *Transfers* welcome; 650 enrolled 1993–94.

Academic Environment. Graduation requirements in Arts and Sciences include 4 units of English, 3 units of mathematics, 3 units of laboratory science, 1 unit of social studies, 4 units of academic electives, of which it is recommended that 3 be of a single foreign language. Requirements for other schools and programs may vary. Students have option of selecting letter-grade system or satisfactory/audit open for many courses. *Undergraduate studies* offered to freshmen in colleges of Arts and Sciences and General Studies (which offers mostly night classes) and schools of Engineering, Nursing; juniors admitted to schools of Education, Health and Rehabilitation Sciences, Social Work, and Library and Information Science; sophomores to Pharmacy.

Degrees offered: associates, bachelors, masters, doctoral. *Majors offered* in a wide range of liberal arts, as well as Africana studies, Chinese, earth and planetary sciences, history of art and architecture, health related technologies, theater arts, urban studies, self-designed major programs available. Average undergraduate class size: 42% under 20, 45% 20–40, 13% over 40.

About 39% of students entering as freshmen graduate within four years, 58% within five years; 86% of freshmen return for sophomore year. *Special programs:* Freshman Seminars, January Term, independent study, study abroad, Semester at Sea, Honors College, 3–2 engineering, 3–2 arts and sciences, undergraduate research, credit by examination, joint and combined degree programs, cross-registration with 10 other Pittsburgh colleges and universities, graduate courses for credit, University Honors College, external studies. Adult programs: College for the Over 60, University External Studies, Saturday College, Day-Class Program. *Calendar*: three 15-week terms, 2 summer sessions.

Undergraduate degrees conferred (3,005). 13% were in Social Sciences, 12% were in Letters, 11% were in Engineering, 10% were in Business and Management, 10% were in Health Sciences, 9% were in Psychology, 5% were in Liberal/General Studies, 4% were in Computer and Engineering Related Technology, 4% were in Life Sciences, 4% were in Allied Health, 3% were in Physical Sciences, remainder in 12 other fields.

Graduates Career Data. Advanced studies pursued by 39% of graduates; 6% enter graduate school; 8% enter business school; 3% enter dental school; 3% enter law school. Employers typically hiring largest numbers of graduates include Westinghouse, Rite-Aid, Thrift Drug. Career Development Services include on campus interviews, preparation assistance with resumes and placement services; alumni reported helpful with career and job placement.

Faculty. About 90% of faculty hold PhD or equivalent. About 61% of undergraduate classes taught by full-time faculty. About 28% of full-time faculty are female; 4% Black, 2% Hispanic, 8% other minority.

Student Body. About 92% of students from in state, 1% foreign students. Average age of undergraduate student: 23. *Minority group students:* 3 programs offer academic assistance: Pitt Engineering Impact Program, University-Challenge for Excellence Program, special nursing minority program; Africana Studies department; Black Action Society; black fraternities and sororities, Minority Premedical Organization; Black American Law Student Association.

Varsity Sports. Men (Div.I): Baseball, Basketball, Cross Country, Football, Gymnastics, Soccer, Swimming and Diving, Tennis, Track, Wrestling. Women (Div.I): Basketball, Cross Country, Gymnastics, Swimming and Diving, Tennis, Track, Volleyball.

Campus Life. University provides wide range of cultural and intellectual events which are supplemented by those on other campuses in the city and by its location in a major cultural area of Pittsburgh. No regulations governing student hours. Limited intervisitation hours Sunday through Thursday; open visitation policy for weekends. Alcoholic beverages are permitted only for those over 21; cars allowed.

About 38% of students live in dormitories; rest live in off-campus housing or commute. Freshmen given preference in college housing. Sexes segregated in coed dormitories by floor. There are 22 fraternities, 14 sororities on campus which about 11% of men, 9% of women join; 2% of students live in off-campus chapter houses.

Annual Costs. Tuition and fees for Arts and Sciences, other schools and/or programs may vary, $5,186 (out-of-state, $10,708); room and board, $4,286; estimated $1,300 other, exclusive of travel. About 60% of students receive financial aid; average amount of assistance, $5,000. Assistance is typically divided 5% scholarship, 41% grant, 50% loan, 4% work. University reports 700 scholarships awarded on the basis of academic merit alone, 250 for special talents alone. *Meeting Costs:* university offers installment payment plan.

University of Pittsburgh, Bradford Campus

Bradford, Pennsylvania 16701 **(800) 872-1787**

A state-related liberal arts college located in a rural area of northeastern Pennsylvania. Bradford is part of the University of Pittsburgh.

Founded: 1963
Affiliation: State-related
UG Enrollment: 372 M, 464 W (full-time); 178 M, 247 W (part-time)
Cost: < $10K
% Receiving Financial Aid: 98%
Admission: Non-selective
Application Deadline: July 1

Admission. About 90% of applicants accepted; 57% of these actually enroll; 34% of freshmen graduate in top fifth of high school class, 60% in top two-fifths. Average freshman SAT scores: 440 verbal, 487 mathematical. *Required:* SAT or ACT, minimum high school GPA of 2.0, essay; interview recommended. Criteria considered in admissions, in order of importance: high school academic record, standardized test scores, writing sample, campus visit, recommendations, extracurricular activities; other factors considered: alumni children, diverse student body. *Out-of-state* applicants: university actively seeks students from out-of-state. State does not limit out-of-state enrollment. No special requirements for out of state students. States from which most out-of-state students are drawn include New York. *Entrance programs:* early decision, early admission, midyear admission, deferred admission, advanced placement. *Apply* by July 1; rolling admissions. *Transfers* welcome; 98 enrolled 1993–94.

Academic Environment. Graduation requirements include 7 credits in English, 12 credits each in natural sciences, social sciences, and humanities core, 3 credits in math. Degrees offered: associates, bachelors. *Majors offered* include nursing, writing, public relations. Average undergraduate class size: 80% under 20, 20% 20–40. About 50% of entering class graduate within four years, 77% eventually; 80% of freshman class return for sophomore year. *Special programs:* January Term, study abroad, cross-registration with all Pittsburgh campuses, 3–2 optometry, 3–2 pharmacology, 3–2 engineering, 3–2 occupational therapy, internships, cooperative work-study. Adult programs: courses taught at regional sites and night classes offered.

Graduates Career Data. Professional schools typically enrolling largest numbers of graduates include U. of Pittsburgh. Career Development Services include workshops, resume assistance and job fairs.

Faculty. About 80% of faculty hold PhD or equivalent. About 40% of teaching faculty are female.

Student Body. About 90% of students from in state. An estimated 8% of students reported as Black, 2% Hispanic, 1% Asian, 1% other minority.

Varsity Sports. Men (NAIA Div.): Basketball, Cross Country, Golf, Soccer. Women (NAIA Div): Basketball, Cross Country, Golf, Soccer, Softball, Volleyball.

Campus Life. About 55% of men, 55% of women live in coed dormitories; 40% of each men, women commute. There are no fraternities or sororities on campus. About 70% of resident students leave campus on weekends.

Annual Costs. Tuition and fees, $5,150, (out-of-state, $10,672); room and board, $3,000; estimated $700 other, exclusive of travel. About 98% of students receive financial aid; average amount of assistance, $4,700. Assistance is typically divided 48% scholarship/grant, 49% loan, 3% work. University reports 3 scholarship programs awarded on the basis of academic merit alone, one program for need alone.

Pitzer College

Claremont, California 91711 **(909) 621-8129**
(See also The Claremont Colleges)

Pitzer, newest of the Claremont Colleges, was founded as a college for women, but has long since been co-educational. The college, which emphasizes the social and behavioral sciences, has a Community Government, comprising students, faculty, administration, and trustees. It is a full member of the Claremont group, and shares the advantages that accrue from that membership. Most convenient major airport: Ontario International.

Founded: 1963
Affiliation: Independent
UG Enrollment: 360 M, 390 M (full-time)
Cost: $10K–$20K
% Receiving Financial Aid: 50%
Admission: Highly Selective
Application Deadline: Feb. 1

Admission is highly selective. About 50% of applicants accepted, 38% of these actually enroll; 65% of freshmen graduate in top fifth of high school class, 96% in top two-fifths. Average freshman scores: SAT, 560 M, 560 W verbal, 590 M, 580 W mathematical; ACT, 27 M, 26 W composite. *Required:* SAT or ACT, essay. Criteria considered in admissions, in order of importance: high school academic record, standardized test scores, recommendations, writing sample, extracurricular activities; other factors considered: special talents, alumni children, diverse student body. *Entrance programs:* early admission, deferred admission. About 45% of entering students from private or parochial schools. *Apply* by February 1. *Transfers* welcome; 35 enrolled 1993–94.

Academic Environment. Students comprise one-fourth of the votes at faculty meetings, one-half of the membership of committees on curriculum, academic standards, and campus regulations, and have minority representation on committee dealing with appointment and promotion of faculty. Flexibility offered in freshman seminars, interdisciplinary colloquia, independent study, internship programs, external studies which take students off campus, and individually designed majors, including interdisciplinary major program in environmental studies. Administration spokesman reports that students seem to reflect a "growing concern about academic achievement and relevance for future occupational choices." Pitzer has the advantage of access to facilities shared with the other Claremont colleges, exchange of students, and some jointly appointed faculty. Graduation requirements include 2 courses each in humanities, sciences, arts and social sciences. Degrees offered: bachelors. *Majors offered* include Asian studies, environmental studies, international relations, Latin American studies, linguistics, folklore, psychobiology. Average undergraduate class size: 15; 85% under 20, 18% 20–40, 2% over 40.

About 75% of students entering as freshmen graduate within four years, 80% eventually; 95% of freshmen return for sophomore year. *Special programs:* independent study, study abroad, undergraduate research, individualized majors, special field work and work/study programs, Washington Semester, summer independent study for credit, participation in Claremont's Human Resources Institute (programs in Black, Chicano studies; urban affairs), 3–2 management/engineering. Adult programs: new resource program for students over 25. *Calendar:* semester.

Undergraduate degrees conferred (200). 37% were in Social Sciences, 23% were in Psychology, 14% were in Letters, 7% were in Visual and Performing Arts, 5% were in Area and Ethnic Studies, 4% were in Life Sciences, 3% were in Renewable Natural Resources, remainder in 8 other fields.

Graduates Career Data. Advanced studies pursued by 75% of graduates; 40% enter graduate school; 10% enter medical school; 2% enter dental school; 10% enter law school; 10% enter business school. Medical schools typically enrolling largest numbers of graduates include Harvard, Johns Hopkins, UCLA; law schools include Stanford, Berkeley, Harvard; business schools include UCLA, Harvard, USC. About 35% of 1992–93 graduates employed. Employers typically hiring largest numbers of graduates include business, education, entertainment. Career Development Services include on-campus interviews, preparation assistance with resumes and placement services; alumni reported helpful with career and job placement.

Faculty. All faculty hold PhD or equivalent. About 90% of undergraduate classes taught by tenured faculty. About 40% of teaching faculty are female; 10% Hispanic, 4% Black, 1% other minority.

Student Body. About 50% of students from in state; 60% West, 9% Northwest, 10% New England, 5% Middle Atlantic, 5% Midwest, 2% South, 5% foreign. An estimated 15% of students reported as Protestant, 10% Catholic, 30% Jewish, 35% unaffiliated, 5% other; 7% as Black, 12% Hispanic, 7% Asian, 6% other minority. *Minority group students:* financial aid available; tutoring and other help offered to all students with academic deficiencies; centers for Black and Chicano studies.

Varsity Sports. Men (Div.III; SCAC): Baseball, Basketball, Cross Country, Diving, Football, Golf, Hockey (field), Lacrosse, Skiing, Soccer, Softball, Swimming, Tennis, Track. Women (Div.III; SCAC): Baseball, Basketball, Cross Country, Diving, Golf, Hockey (field), Lacrosse, Skiing, Soccer, Softball, Swimming, Tennis, Track, Volleyball.

Campus Life. Policies governing campus social life are determined by students—with the sole exception of regulations concerning use of cars and motorbikes. Wide variety of cultural and social activities available on the Claremont campuses. Resources of Los Angeles, 30 miles away, supplement campus offerings. Cars allowed. State laws govern use of alcohol; drinking not permitted in public areas. Provisions for daily intervisitation. Students may petition to live off campus if space filled in residence halls.

About 92% of men, 92% of women live in coed dormitories; rest live in off-campus housing or commute. Freshmen given preference in college housing if all students cannot be accommodated. Sexes segregated in dormitories by room. There are no fraternities or sororities. About 23% of resident students leave campus on weekends.

Annual Costs. Tuition and fees, $18,198; room and board, $5,582; estimated $1,200 other, exclusive of travel. About 50% of students receive financial aid; average amount of assistance, $16,900. Assistance is typically divided 70% scholarship/grant, 15% loan, 15% work. College reports all scholarships awarded on the basis of need alone.

State University College at Plattsburgh

(See State University of New York)

Plymouth State College

Plymouth, New Hampshire 03264 (603) 535-2237

A state-supported college, located in a community of 3,500, 120 miles north of Boston, Plymouth State is a division of the University System of New Hampshire. College is located 20 minutes away from 5 major ski areas. Most convenient major airport: Manchester.

Founded: 1871
Affiliation: State
UG Enrollment: 1,750 M, 1,750 W (full-time); 250 M, 250 W (part-time)
Total Enrollment: 4,200
Cost: < $10K
% Receiving Financial Aid: 70%
Admission: Non-selective
Application Deadline: April 1

Admission. About 68% of applicants accepted, 30% of these actually enroll; 20% of freshmen graduate in top fifth of high school class, 50% in top two-fifths. Average freshman SAT scores: 405 verbal, 449 mathematical. *Required:* SAT, minimum high school GPA C+/B-. Criteria considered in admissions, in order of importance: high school academic record, extracurricular activities, recommendations, writing sample, standardized test scores. *Out-of-state* freshman applicants: college actively seeks students from out of state. State does not limit out-of-state enrollment. *Apply* by April 1; rolling admissions. *Transfers* welcome.

Academic Environment. Degrees offered: associates, bachelors, masters. *Majors offered* include meteorology, medieval studies, graphic design, interdisciplinary majors. About 60% of students entering as freshmen graduate within four years, 75% eventually; 85% of freshmen return for sophomore year. *Special programs:* CLEP, January Term, study abroad, cross-registration (with Keene State), independent study, honors, undergraduate research, interdisciplinary majors, cooperative programs through NHCUC, including Marine Science Program. Adult programs: evening courses offered. *Calendar:* 4–1–4, summer school.

Undergraduate degrees conferred (587). 27% were in Education, 22% were in Business and Management, 10% were in Social Sciences, 7% were in Multi/Interdisciplinary Studies, 7% were in Marketing and Distribution, 6% were in Business (Administrative Support), 5% were in Psychology, 4% were in Visual and Performing Arts, 3% were in Letters, 3% were in Computer and Engineering Related Technology, remainder in 7 other fields.

Faculty. About 88% of faculty hold PhD or equivalent. About 31% of teaching faculty are female.

Student Body. About 60% of students from in state.

Varsity Sports. Men (Div.III): Baseball, Basketball, Football, Hockey (Ice), Lacrosse, Skiing, Soccer, Tennis, Wrestling. Women (Div.III): Basketball, Diving, Hockey (field), Lacrosse, Skiing, Soccer, Softball, Swimming, Tennis.

Campus Life. About 70% each of men, women live in traditional dormitories; rest live in off-campus housing or commute. Freshmen given preference in college housing if all students cannot be accommodated. Intervisitation in men's and women's dormitory rooms limited. There are 7 fraternities, 5 sororities on campus. About 30% of resident students leave campus on weekends.

Annual Costs. Tuition and fees, $2,926 (out-of-state, $7,406); room and board, $3,756; estimated $1,350 other, exclusive of travel. About 70% of students receive financial aid; assistance is typically divided 41% scholarship, 47% loan, 12% work. College reports some scholarships awarded on the basis of academic merit alone.

Point Loma Nazarene College

San Diego, California 92106 (619) 221-2273

A church-related liberal arts college, located in a city of over 1,000,000. Most convenient major airport: Lindbergh Field (San Diego).

Founded: 1902
Affiliation: Nazarene
UG Enrollment: 802 M, 1328 W (full-time); 133 M, 221 W (part-time)
Cost: < $10K
% Receiving Financial Aid: 75%
Admission: Non-selective
Application Deadline: Rolling

Admission. Graduates of accredited high schools with B average in 6 units of academic subjects eligible; others admitted on provisional basis; 85% of applicants accepted, 62% of these actually enroll; 20% of freshmen graduate in top tenth of high school class, 43% in top quarter. Average freshman scores: SAT, 425 verbal, 472 mathematical; ACT, 21 composite. *Required:* SAT, English placement test. *Apply:* rolling admissions. *Transfers* welcome; 273 enrolled 1993–94.
Academic Environment. Degrees offered: bachelors. About 35% of general education requirements for graduation are elective; distribution requirements fairly numerous. About 35% of students entering as freshmen graduate eventually; 75% of freshmen return for sophomore year. *Special programs:* independent study, education workshops during summer for teacher certification. *Calendar:* semester, summer school.
Undergraduate degrees conferred (295). 28% were in Business and Management, 11% were in Health Sciences, 10% were in Liberal/General Studies, 7% were in Social Sciences, 7% were in Letters, 5% were in Communications, 5% were in Psychology, 4% were in Visual and Performing Arts, 4% were in Vocational Home Economics, 4% were in Life Sciences, 3% were in Philosophy and Religion, remainder in 9 other fields.
Faculty. About 60% of faculty hold PhD or equivalent.
Student Body. About 86% of students from in state; 91% West/Northwest. An estimated 80% of students reported as Protestant, 12% Catholic, 8% unaffiliated; 3% Black, 7% Hispanic, 4% Asian, 1% Native American, 5% other minority.
Religious Orientation. Point Loma is a church-related institution; 8 units in religion, 3 units in philosophy, attendance at chapel services required of all students.
Varsity Sports. Men (NAIA): Baseball, Basketball, Tennis, Track, Soccer. Women (NAIA): Baseball, Softball, Track, Tennis, Volleyball.
Campus Life. About 60% of men, 58% of women live in traditional dormitories; no coed dormitories; rest commute. Freshmen given preference in college housing if all students cannot be accommodated. Intervisitation in men's and women's dormitory rooms limited. There are 6 fraternities, 2 sororities on campus, which about 15% of men, 8% of women join. About 20% of residential students leave campus on weekends.
Annual Costs. Tuition and fees, $9408; room and board, $3,990; estimated $2,052 other, exclusive of travel. About 75% of students receive financial aid; average amount of assistance, $2,200. Assistance is typically divided 50% scholarship, 30% loan, 20% work. College reports some scholarships awarded on the basis of academic merit alone. *Meeting Costs:* college offers various payment plans, Insured Tuition Plan.

Point Park College

Pittsburgh, Pennsylvania 15222 (412) 391-4100

An independent, urban college, offering 2- and 4-year programs, located in downtown Pittsburgh. Most convenient major airport: Pittsburgh International.

Founded: 1960
Affiliation: Independent
UG Enrollment: 494 M, 679 W (full-time); 779 M, 623 W (part-time)
Total Enrollment: 2,669
Cost: < $10K
% Receiving Financial Aid: 80%
Admission: Non-selective
Application Deadline: Rolling

Admission. High school graduates with 15 units eligible; 85% of applicants accepted, 28% of these actually enroll; 25% of freshmen graduate in top fifth of high school class, 49% in top two-fifths. Average freshman scores: SAT, 418 verbal, 424 mathematical; ACT, 21 composite. *Required:* SAT or ACT; audition for theater and dance; interview recommended. Criteria considered in admissions, in order of importance: high school academic record, standardized test scores, extracurricular activities, recommendations, writing sample; other factors considered: special talents. *Entrance programs:* early admission, advanced placement. *Apply:* rolling admissions. *Transfers* welcome; 376 enrolled 1993–94.
Academic Environment. Graduation requirements include 30 credits in liberal arts and sciences, minimum 12 credits in English and humanities, 6 credits each in human, natural and social sciences. Degrees offered: associates, bachelors, masters. *Majors offered* in usual arts and sciences, applied arts, business administration, dance, education, funeral service, respiratory therapy, journalism and communications, capstones in health services, legal studies, theater arts, film production, arts management, performance arts. Average undergraduate class size: 25; introductory lecture: 40; laboratories: 12.

About 55% of students entering as freshmen graduate eventually; 28% of freshmen return for sophomore year. *Special programs:* CLEP, honors, individualized majors, double majors, College Plus, cross-registration with other Pittsburgh colleges and universities, three-year degree, internships/co-op work study. Adult programs: part-time studies, off-campus programs at numerous locations. *Calendar:* semester, summer school.
Undergraduate degrees conferred (470). 24% were in Engineering and Engineering Related Technology, 21% were in Business and Management, 13% were in Visual and Performing Arts, 9% were in Communications, 7% were in Computer and Engineering Related Technology, 5% were in Education, 4% were in Public Affairs, 4% were in Law, 4% were in Health Sciences, 3% were in Psychology, remainder in 9 other fields.
Graduates Career Data. Advanced studies pursued by 15% of 1991 graduates; 8% enter graduate schools; 4% enter business schools; 3% enter law schools. *Careers in business and industry* pursued by 91% of 1991 graduates. Fields typically hiring largest number of graduates include business, engineering, journalism and communication, fine and applied arts. Career Development Services include resource room, job postings, individual counseling, workshops, on-campus interviews, DISCOVER computer system.
Faculty. About 44% of faculty hold PhD or equivalent. About 86% of all classes taught by tenured faculty. About 36% of teaching faculty are female.
Student Body. About 88% of students from in state; 5% foreign. An estimated 10% of students reported as Black, 1% Hispanic. Average age of undergraduate student: 23.
Varsity Sports. Men (NAIA): Baseball, Basketball, Soccer. Women (NAIA): Basketball, Softball, Volleyball.
Campus Life. About 27% of men, 36% of women live in coed dormitories; rest live in off-campus housing or commute. Intervisitation in dorms unlimited; sexes segregated by room. There are 2 fraternities, 4 sororities which about 2% of men, 2% of women join. About 60% of resident students leave campus on weekends.
Annual Costs. Tuition and fees, $9,312; room and board, $4,610; estimated $850 other, exclusive of travel. About 80% of students receive financial aid; average amount of assistance, $7,500. Assistance is typically divided 60% scholarship, 30% loan, 10% work. College reports some scholarships awarded on the basis of academic merit alone. *Meeting Costs:* college offers time payment options.

Polytechnic Institute of New York

(See Polytechnic University)

Polytechnic University

Brooklyn, New York 11201 (718) 260-3100; (800) POLYTEC

An independent, technological institution, located in metropolitan New York, Polytechnic was formed in 1973 by merger of the NYU School of Engineering and Science and the Polytechnic Institute of Brooklyn. The urban campus is designed primarily to serve—and to benefit from—its diverse environment. An undergraduate, graduate and research campus is located in suburban Farmingdale on Long Island. Formerly known as Polytechnic Institute of New York. Most convenient major airports: JFK or LaGuardia.

Founded: 1854
Affiliation: Independent
UG Enrollment: 1,186 M, 193 W (full-time); 190 M, 24 W (full-time)
Total Enrollment: 3,637
Cost: $10K–$20K
% Receiving Financial Aid: 83%
Admission: Selective (+)
Application Deadline: Feb. 1

Admission is selective (+). About 75% of applicants accepted, 36% of these actually enroll; 70% of freshmen graduate in top fifth of high school class, 93% in top two-fifths. Average freshman SAT scores: 36% of freshmen score above 500 on verbal; 9% above 600; 97% score above 500 on mathematical, 66% above 600, 19% above 700. *Required:* SAT or ACT, 2 recommendations. Criteria considered in admissions, in order of importance: high school academic record, standardized test scores, recommendations, extracurricular activities; other factors considered: diverse student body. *Entrance programs:* early admission, midyear admission, deferred admission, advanced placement. About 12% of entering students from parochial schools, 4% from private. *Apply* by February 1 (preferred); rolling admissions. *Transfers* welcome; 134 enrolled 1993–94.

Academic Environment. Students have some influence on curriculum policy and other academic matters through membership on joint student/faculty committees. Program of study prescribed in each field of concentration; distribution requirements include at least 24 credits in humanities and social sciences. *Degree:* bachelors, masters, doctoral. *Majors offered* in 10 fields of engineering, environmental science, environmental engineering, computer science, mathematics, physics, premedicine, social sciences, humanities, computer engineering, information management. Average undergraduate class size: 30.

About 28% of students entering as freshmen graduate within four years, 66% eventually; 75% of freshmen return for sophomore year. *Special programs:* honors, internships with area companies, credit by examination, graduate work for selected seniors. *Calendar:* semester, summer school.

Undergraduate degrees conferred (332). 89% were in Engineering, 7% were in Computer and Engineering Related Technology, remainder in 3 other fields.

Graduates Career Data. About 84% of 1992–93 graduates employed. Employers typically hiring largest numbers of graduates include IBM, Bell Labs, Grumann, LILCO. Career Development Services include counseling on placement issues, resume and interview workshops, placement services, on-campus recruitment, internships, cooperative education, resource library.

Faculty. About 90% of faculty hold PhD or equivalent. About 70% of undergraduate classes taught by tenured faculty.

Student Body. About 93% of students from in state; 5% foreign. An estimated 11% of students reported as Black, 8% Hispanic, 33% Asian, 7% other minority. *Minority group students:* special scholarship funds; special Higher Education Opportunity Program.

Varsity Sports. Men (Div.III): Baseball, Basketball, Cross Country, Golf, Lacrosse, Soccer, Tennis, Wrestling. Women (Div.III): Cross Country, Tennis, Volleyball.

Campus Life. Located just 6 miles from mid-Manhattan, students can easily supplement campus activities with the endless cultural and social resources of New York City. Nature of student life influenced by large percentage of commuters.

About 25% of students live in coed dormitories; 74% commute. Sexes segregated in dormitories by room. There are 4 fraternities on campus; 20% of men, 18% of women join co-ed fraternities; 1% of students live in fraternities. About 2% of resident students leave campus on weekends.

Annual Costs. Tuition and fees, $15,580; room and board, $3,620; estimated $1,200 other, exclusive of travel. About 83% of students receive financial aid; average amount of assistance, $11,758. Institute reports 737 scholarships awarded on the basis of academic merit alone, 505 for need alone. *Meeting Costs:* Institute offers deferred payment, institutional loans.

Pomona College

Claremont, California 91711 **(909) 621-8134**
(See also The Claremont Colleges)

One of the best known of the West Coast colleges, Pomona is oldest of the Claremont Colleges and the founder of that unique complex. The 130-acre campus is located in a community of 35,000, 35 miles from Los Angeles. Most convenient major airport: Ontario International.

Founded: 1887
Affiliation: Independent
UG Enrollment: 726 M, 621 W (full-time)
Cost: $10K–$20K
% Receiving Financial Aid: 54%
Admission: Most Selective
Application Deadline: Jan. 15

Admission is among the most selective in the country. About 32% of applicants accepted, 38% of these actually enroll; 92% of freshmen graduate in top fifth of high school class. Average freshman scores: SAT, 640 verbal, 700 mathematical; 94% of freshmen score above 500 on verbal, 72% above 600, 13% above 700; 97% score above 500 on mathematical, 89% above 600, 51% above 700; ACT, 31 composite. *Required:* SAT or ACT, essay; ACH and interview recommended; "submission of extra materials encouraged". Criteria considered in admissions, in order of importance: high school academic record, standardized test scores, writing sample, recommendations, extracurricular activities; other factors considered: alumni children, diverse student body. *Entrance programs:* early decision, early admission, advanced placement, deferred admission. About 23% of entering students from private schools. *Apply* by January 15; rolling admissions. *Transfers* welcome; 19 enrolled 1993–94.

Academic Environment. While all majors are in the liberal arts, administration source notes a strong pragmatic orientation to the student body. Students are very capable and are encouraged to make many academic decisions on their own. Those unaccustomed to academic self-reliance may have trouble. Students call the faculty the "driving force behind the academics"; professors are accessible, helpful, and "tops in their fields". Graduation requirements: all general education courses needed for graduation are elective; distribution requirements include 3 courses in each of 3 broad divisions (Humanities, Social and Natural Sciences), foreign language proficiency, and 2 writing intensive courses, 1 physical education course. Strongest academic programs reported to be physical and biological sciences, economics, public policy, music, and international relations (although a student asserts: "There are no weak academic departments."). Degrees offered: bachelors. *Majors offered* include usual arts and sciences, American studies, Asian studies, astronomy, Chinese, classics, international relations, public policy analysis, technology. Average undergraduate class size: 14.

About 85% of students entering as freshmen graduate within four years, 90% eventually; 98% of freshmen return for sophomore year. *Special programs:* independent study, study abroad (50% of Pomona students go abroad), undergraduate research, cross registration with Claremont Colleges, individualized majors, exchange with Colby, CalTech, Spelman, Fiske, Smith and Swarthmore, Washington Semester, joint program with Claremont Graduate School for teaching credentials or MAT, summer reading/research for credit, 3–2 engineering. *Calendar:* semester.

Undergraduate degrees conferred (367). 35% were in Social Sciences, 13% were in Letters, 9% were in Psychology, 7% were in Liberal/General Studies, 7% were in Life Sciences, 7% were in Philosophy and Religion, 5% were in Area and Ethnic Studies, 5% were in Foreign Languages, 5% were in Visual and Performing Arts, 4% were in Mathematics, 3% were in Physical Sciences, remainder in Computer and Engineering Related Technology.

Graduates Career Data. Advanced studies pursued by 28% of graduates; 14% enter graduate schools; 4% enter law schools; 4% enter business schools; 4% enter medical schools. Medical schools typically enrolling largest numbers of graduates include UCLA, UC-San Diego; law schools include UC-Berkeley, Pepperdine, UC-Davis; business schools include Columbia, U. of Chicago; veterinary schools include Cornell. About 60% of 1992 graduates employed. Fields typically hiring largest numbers of graduates include business, teaching, science, non-profit organizations. Career Development Services include counseling and information about graduate study and post graduate employment.

Faculty. All faculty members hold PhD or equivalent. All undergraduate classes taught by tenured-track faculty. About 33% of teaching faculty are female.

Student Body. About 44% of students from in state; 50% West, 11% Northwest, 6% New England, 9% Midwest, 3% South, 2% Middle Atlantic; 2% foreign. An estimated 4% of students reported as Black, 11% Hispanic, 21% Asian, 9% other minority. *Minority group students:* major financial aid program includes minority students; Black Studies Center, Chicano Studies Center common to all Claremont colleges.

Varsity Sports. Men (Div.III): Baseball, Basketball, Cross Country, Football, Golf, Soccer, Swimming, Tennis, Track. Women (Div.III): Basketball, Cross Country, Golf, Soccer, Softball, Swimming, Tennis, Track, Volleyball.
Campus Life. Most student activities occur on-campus: "Pomona, as well as the other colleges, keep activities going strong and constantly." Substantial opportunities for faculty/student interaction outside of classroom. Informal relations of students and faculty said to be "one of the college's greatest strengths." Facilities of the Oldenborg Center for Modern Languages and International Education offer an unusual residential living/learning program for men and women. Pomona shares the cultural and social resources of all the Claremont Colleges. Los Angeles, 35 miles from campus, offers wide variety of activities; college provides transportation to concerts, plays and clubs, but students assert: "People don't go every night". Interest in intramural sports reported high. Intervisitation hours determined by residents of each living unit. Smoking prohibited in "common" spaces. Use of alcohol governed by state law; drinking prohibited on campus in public places and at public events. Strict prohibitions against illegal drugs. Rules about cars related only to campus parking area. Students need special permission to live off campus.

About 95% of men, 95% of women live in coed dormitories; rest live in off-campus housing. Sexes segregated in coed dormitories by wing, floor, or room. There are 7 fraternities on campus (4 are coed) which about 15% of men, 8% of women join; they provide no residence facilities.
Annual Costs. Tuition and fees, $16,900; room and board, $6,920; estimated $1,750 other exclusive of travel. About 54% of students receive financial aid; average amount of assistance, $18,360. College assistance is typically divided 70% scholarship/grant, 15% loan, 10% work. College reports 1 scholarship is awarded on the basis of academic merit alone. *Meeting Costs:* college offers Pomona Parent Loan Program, S.H.A.R.E., payment plans.

Pontifical Catholic University of Puerto Rico

Ponce, Puerto Rico 00732 (809) 841-2000

A church-related institution, sponsored by the Catholic Hierarchy of Puerto Rico, located on a 92-acre campus in the city of Ponce. The university is officially bilingual but most courses are taught in Spanish. Most convenient major airport: Mercedita Airport, Ponce.

Founded: 1948
Affiliation: Roman Catholic
UG Enrollment: 3,123 M, 5,838 W (full-time)
Total Enrollment: 12,251
Cost: < $10K
% Receiving Financial Aid: 90%
Admission: Non-selective
Application Deadline: July 15

Admission. Graduates of accredited high schools with 16 units (14 in academic subjects) or with 12 units and C average eligible; 81% of applicants accepted, 76% of these actually enroll. Average freshman scores: SAT, 453 verbal, 490 mathematical. *Required:* SAT; ACH (for placement only) in English, Spanish, mathematics, minimum HS GPA 2.0. Criteria considered in admission, in order of importance: standardized test scores, high school academic record, recommendations, extracurricular activities, writing sample; other factors considered: special talents. *Entrance programs:* advanced placement. *Apply* by July 15. *Transfers* welcome; 245 enrolled 1993–94.
Academic Environment. About 30% of general education requirements for graduation are elective; distribution requirements limited. *Undergraduate studies* offered by colleges of Arts and Humanities, Business Administration, Education, Science. Degrees offered: associates, bachelors, masters. Unusual, new, or notable majors include: communications, computer science, medical technology, gerontology. About 84% of freshman return for the sophomore year. *Special programs:* CLEP, independent study, honors, undergraduate research, 3–2 programs in engineering, and pharmacy, cross registration with Seton Hall. Adult programs: extension and continuing education. *Calendar:* semester, summer school.
Undergraduate degrees conferred (943). 43% were in Business and Management, 23% were in Education, 15% were in Health Sciences, 8% were in Business (Administrative Support), 5% were in Social Sciences, remainder in 7 other fields.

Faculty. About 16% of faculty hold PhD or equivalent. About 26% of undergraduate classes taught by tenured faculty. About 49% of teaching faculty are female; 99% Hispanic.
Student Body. About 99% of students from Puerto Rico. An estimated 99% of students reported as Catholic; 99% Hispanic.
Religious Orientation. University is a church-related institution; students are required to take 4 religious courses; attendance at daily Mass encouraged; one Protestant and 3 Catholic chaplains on campus.
Varsity Sports. Men: Baseball, Basketball, Cross Country, Judo, Soccer, Softball, Swimming, Tennis, Track, Volleyball, Water Polo, Weight Lifting, Wrestling. Women: Basketball, Cross Country, Judo, Softball, Swimming, Tennis, Track, Volleyball.
Campus Life. About 20% of men, 30% of women live in traditional dormitories; rest live in off-campus housing or commute. Out-of-town women may apply directly to 3 residences affiliated with the university but operated by religious congregations. Freshmen given preference in college housing if all students cannot be accommodated. No intervisitation in men's or women's dormitory rooms. There are 12 fraternities, 10 sororities on campus which about 12% of men, 10% of women join; they provide no residence facilities. About 4% of resident students leave campus on weekends.
Annual Costs. Tuition and fees, $3,129; room and board, $2,678; estimated $1,950 other, exclusive of travel. About 90% of students receive PELL Grant, 68% receive other aid. University reports 90% scholarships awarded on the basis of academic need alone.

The Pontifical College of Josephinum

Columbus, Ohio 43085

The only seminary in the Western Hemisphere under the immediate direction of the Vatican; chancellor is Apostolic Pro-Nuncio to the U.S. Primary purpose is to offer preparation for the priesthood.

Affiliation: Roman Catholic **UG Enrollment:** 110 M (full-time)

Undergraduate degrees conferred (10). 50% were in Philosophy and Religion, 20% were in Psychology, 20% were in Area and Ethnic Studies, 10% were in Social Sciences.

Portland School of Art

(See Maine College of Art)

Portland State University

Portland, Oregon 97207 (503) 725-3000

A state-supported, urban university, primarily for commuters, located in a city of 420,000. Most convenient major airport: Portland International.

Founded: 1946
Affiliation: State
UG Enrollment: 2,889 M, 2,879 W (full-time); 2,115 M, 2,394 W (part-time)
Total Enrollment: 14,486
Cost: < $10K
% Receiving Financial Aid: 50%
Admission: Non-selective
Application Deadline: July 1

Admission. About 97% of applicants accepted, 50% of these actually enroll; freshmen had a median high school GPA of 3.1. Average freshman scores: SAT, 426 M, 409 W verbal, 508 M, 454 W mathematical; ACT, 23 M, 21 W composite. *Required:* SAT or ACT. Criteria considered in admissions, in order of importance: high school academic record, standardized test scores; a limited number of students admitted through special action. *Out-of-state* freshman applicants: university actively seeks out-of-state students. State does not limit out-of-state enrollment. States from which most out-of-state students are drawn include Washington, California. *Entrance programs:* early admission, midyear admission, deferred admission, advanced placement. *Apply* by July 1; rolling admissions. *Transfers* welcome; 1,417 enrolled 1993–94.

Academic Environment. Graduation requirements include 3 5-credit Freshman Inquiry courses, 3 4-credit courses from different approved programs or clusters, 4 3-credit courses from 1 program or cluster, 6- credit senior "capstone" experience. Degrees offered: bachelors, masters, doctoral. *Undergraduate studies* offered by College of Liberal Arts and Sciences, schools of Business Administration, Education, Engineering and Applied Science, Health and Physical Education, Fine and Performing Arts, and Urban and Public Affairs. Average undergraduate class size: 33% under 20, 40% 20–40, 27% over 40.

About 5% of students entering as freshmen graduate within four years, 35% eventually; 66% of freshmen return for sophomore year. *Special programs:* study abroad, cross-registration with all Oregon State System of Higher Education schools, internships, School of Extended Studies, extensive foreign language program (more than 20 languages offered each year), statewide MBA program via video. Adult programs: continuing education, afternoon and evening offerings. *Calendar:* 4 terms including summer school.

Undergraduate degrees conferred (1,893). 24% were in Business and Management, 22% were in Social Sciences, 9% were in Multi/Interdisciplinary Studies, 8% were in Psychology, 7% were in Letters, 7% were in Engineering, 5% were in Education, 4% were in Visual and Performing Arts, 3% were in Computer and Engineering Related Technology, remainder in 7 other fields.

Graduates Career Data. About 89% of 1992–93 graduates employed. Fields typically hiring largest numbers of students include business, industry, education, governmental agencies. Career Development Services include career and job search counseling and seminars, on-campus recruiting, extensive resource library, computerized guidance and information system.

Faculty. About 85% of faculty hold PhD or equivalent. About 48% of undergraduate classes taught by tenured faculty. About 34% of teaching faculty are female; 1% Black, 1% Hispanic, 28% other minority.

Student Body. About 84% of students from in state; 3% foreign. An estimated 3% of students are reported as Black, 2% Hispanic, 8% Asian, 17% other minority. Average age of undergraduate student: 27.

Varsity Sports. Men (Div.II): Baseball(I), Cross Country, Football, Golf, Soccer, Track, Wrestling. Women (Div.II): Basketball, Cross Country, Soccer, Softball, Tennis, Track, Volleyball.

Campus Life. About 10% of men, women live in college-related apartments on- and off-campus; 1% of men, women live in fraternities and sororities; rest commute. There are 5 fraternities and 3 sororities on campus which 2% each of men, women join.

Annual Costs. Tuition and fees, $2,826 (out-of-state, $7,923); room and board, $4,365; estimated $1,850 other, exclusive of travel. About 50% of students receive financial aid; average amount of assistance, $7,694. Assistance is typically divided 4% scholarship, 21% grant, 69% loan, 6% work. University reports some scholarships awarded on the basis of academic merit alone. *Meeting Costs:* college offers credit card payment, deferred payment plan.

University of Portland

Portland, Oregon 97203 **(503) 283-7147**

An independent institution, founded by Congregation of Holy Cross, located in a city of 400,000. Most convenient major airport: Portland International.

Founded: 1901
Affiliation: Independent (Roman Catholic)
UG Enrollment: 904 M, 1,137 W (full-time)
Total Enrollment: 2,700
Cost: $10K–$20K
% Receiving Financial Aid: 74%
Admission: Non-selective
Application Deadline: Aug. 15

Admission. High school graduates eligible; 84% of applicants accepted, 29% of these actually enroll; 46% of freshmen graduate in top fifth of high school class, 75% in top two-fifths. Average freshman SAT scores: 470 verbal, 530 mathematical; 34% of freshmen score above 500 on verbal, 8% above 600; 62% score above 500 on mathematical, 18% above 600, 3% above 700; ACT, 25 composite. *Required:* SAT or ACT, 2 essays, high school counselor rating. Criteria considered in admissions, in order of importance: high school academic record, standardized test scores, recommendations, writing sample, extracurricular activities. *Entrance programs:* midyear admission, deferred admission, advanced placement. About 30% of entering students from private schools. *Apply* by August 15; rolling admissions. *Transfers* welcome; 193 enrolled 1993–94.

Academic Environment. Graduation requirements include 3 semester hours each in fine arts, history, literature, mathematics, 6 semester hours each in science, social sciences, electives, 9 semester hours each in philosophy and theology. Degrees offered: bachelors, masters. *Undergraduate studies* offered by College of Arts and Sciences, schools of Nursing, Business Administration, Engineering, Education. Average undergraduate class size: 95% 20–40.

About 62% of students entering as freshmen graduate within five years; 75% of freshmen return for sophomore year. *Special programs:* CLEP, independent study, study abroad at overseas branches in Salzburg, Austria, honors, individualized majors, internships, freshman seminars. Adult programs: RN/BS/MS in nursing, several co-curricular programs. *Calendar:* semester, summer school.

Undergraduate degrees conferred (464). 21% were in Business and Management, 17% were in Engineering, 11% were in Health Sciences, 10% were in Education, 9% were in Communications, 6% were in Social Sciences, 4% were in Psychology, 4% were in Public Affairs, remainder in 11 other fields.

Graduates Career Data. Career Development Services include resume writing workshops, interviewing skills, job hunting assistance, resource center, job fairs, on-campus interviews.

Faculty. About 93% of faculty hold PhD or equivalent. About 47% of teaching faculty are female.

Student Body. About 58% of students from in state; 85% West/Northwest, 10% foreign. An estimated 34% of students reported as Protestant, 45% Catholic, 1% Jewish; 1% Black, 2% Hispanic, 6% Asian, 14% other minority. Average age of undergraduate student: 24.

Religious Orientation. Portland is a Catholic institution; 3 religious classes required of all students; non-Catholic theologians on faculty.

Varsity Sports. Men (NCAA, Div.I): Baseball, Basketball, Cross Country, Golf, Soccer, Tennis, Track. Women (NCAA, Div.I): Basketball, Cross Country, Soccer, Tennis, Track, Volleyball.

Campus Life. About 48% of men, women live in traditional dormitories and coed dormitories; rest live in off-campus housing or commute. Intervisitation in men's and women's dormitory rooms limited. There are no fraternities or sororities on campus. About 10% of resident students leave campus on weekends.

Annual Costs. Tuition and fees, $11,040; room and board, $4,060; estimated $600 other, exclusive of travel. About 74% of students receive financial aid; average amount of assistance, $8,432. Assistance is typically divided 22% scholarship, 31% grant, 38% loan, 9% work. University reports 516 scholarships awarded on the basis of academic merit alone, 730 for special talents alone, 1,170 for need alone. *Meeting Costs:* university offers payment plans, deferred tuition plan, Knight Monthly Payment Plan, EXCEL Loans.

Post College

(See Teikyo Post University)

State University College at Potsdam

(See State University of New York)

Prairie View Agricultural and Mechanical University

Prairie View, Texas 77446 **(409) 857-3348**

A state-supported, land-grant university, part of the Texas A&M University system, located in a community of 3,600, 46 miles northwest of Houston; founded as a college for Black citizens and still serving a predominantly Black student body. Most convenient major airport: Houston Intercontinental.

Founded: 1876
Affiliation: State
UG Enrollment: 2,262 M, 2,302 W (full-time)
Total Enrollment: 5,848
Cost: < $10K
Admission: Non-selective
Application Deadline: Aug. 1

Admission. About 72% of applicants accepted, 35% of these actually enroll. Average freshmen scores: SAT, 332 M, 333 W on verbal; 381 M, 373 W, on mathematical; ACT, 15 M, 17 W composite. *Required:* ACT or SAT, minimum 2.0 high school GPA, essay. Criteria considered in admissions, in order of importance: high school academic record and standardized test scores, recommendations, writing sample, extracurricular activities. *Out-of-state* freshman applicants: university actively seeks out-of-state students. State does not limit out-of-state enrollment. About 89% of out-of-state applicants accepted, 33% of these actually enroll. States from which most out-of-state students are drawn include Michigan, Illinois, Missouri. *Entrance programs:* early admission, deferred admission. *Apply* by August 1. *Transfers* welcome; 273 enrolled 1993–94.

Academic Environment. Graduation requirements include courses work in English, philosophy, history, literature, mathematics, physical and life sciences, political science, human performance activities, and visual and performing arts. Degrees offered: bachelors, masters. Average undergraduate class size: 46% under 20, 38% 20–40, 16% over 40. About 20% of students entering as freshmen graduate within four years, 80% eventually. *Special programs:* internships. *Library:* materials include Texas State Documents Collection, African-American Collection. *Calendar:* semester, summer school.

Undergraduate degrees conferred (528). 20% were in Engineering, 18% were in Business and Management, 12% were in Education, 7% were in Life Sciences, 7% were in Engineering and Engineering Related Technology, 6% were in Health Sciences, 4% were in Protective Services, 3% were in Communications, 3% were in Social Sciences, 3% were in Architecture and Environmental Design, remainder in 12 other fields.

Graduates Career Data. Advanced studies pursued by 25% of graduates; 8% enter business schools; 4% enter law schools; 3% enter medical schools. About 75% of 1992–93 graduates employed. Fields typically hiring largest numbers of graduates include engineering, business, education. Career Development Services include educational counseling, positive growth seminars, career exploration, cooperative education, job placement services.

Faculty. About 50% of faculty hold PhD or equivalent. About 52% of undergraduate classes taught by tenured faculty. About 47% of teaching faculty are female; 68% Black, 3% Hispanic, 16% other minority.

Student Body. About 73% of students from South. Average age of undergraduate student: 24.

Varsity Sports. Men (SWAC): Baseball, Basketball, Cross Country, Football, Golf, Tennis, Track. Women (SWAC): Basketball, Cross Country, Tennis, Track, Volleyball.

Campus Life. About 47% of men, 53% of women live in traditional dormitories; 50% of men, 45% of women live in off-campus housing; rest commute. Freshmen given preference in college housing if all students cannot be accommodated. There are 4 fraternities, 4 sororities on campus, which about 19% of men, 19% of women join. About 60% of resident students leave campus on weekends.

Annual Costs. Tuition and fees, $1,537 (out-of-state, $5,617); room and board, $3,740; estimated $533 other expenses, exclusive of travel. Average amount of financial assistance, $3,000. Assistance is typically divided 31% scholarship, 48% grant, 9% loan, 12% work. University reports some scholarships awarded on the basis of academic merit alone. *Meeting Costs:* university offers installment payment plan.

Pratt Institute

Brooklyn, New York 11205 **(718) 636-3669; (800) 331-3669**

An independent college, located on a 25-acre campus, 25 minutes from midtown Manhattan, Pratt offers a variety of highly specialized programs in two schools: Architecture, and Art and Design. Cooperative work/study program in art and design. Most convenient major airport: LaGuardia.

Founded: 1887
Affiliation: Independent
UG Enrollment: 1,050 M, 606 W (full-time); 123 M, 69 W (part-time)
Total Enrollment: 2,843
Cost: $10K–$20K
% Receiving Financial Aid: 80%
Admission: Selective
Application Deadline: Feb. 1

Admission is selective. For all schools, 77% of applicants accepted, 34% of these actually enroll; 40% of freshmen graduate in top fifth of high school class, 93% in top two-fifths. Average freshman scores: SAT, 430 verbal, 520 mathematical; ACT, 24.6 composite. *Required:* portfolio, SAT or ACT, essay, minimum high school GPA, interview. Criteria considered in admissions, in order of importance: portfolio, high school academic record, standardized test scores, recommendations, writing sample, extracurricular activities; other factors considered: special talents, alumni children, diverse student body. *Entrance programs:* early admission, midyear admission, deferred admission, advanced placement. About 8% of entering students from private schools, 11% parochial schools. *Apply* by February 1; rolling admissions. *Transfers* welcome; 220 enrolled 1993–94.

Academic Environment. Emphasis in all curricula on interdisciplinary programs. Liberal studies courses required of students in all disciplines; specific requirements vary among professional curricula. Degrees offered: associates, bachelors, masters. *Majors offered* include architecture, art history, construction management, art education, fashion merchandising, film, photography, fine arts, computer graphics, communication design, interior design, industrial design, fashion design, fashion merchandising. Average undergraduate class size: 95% under 20, 5% 20–40.

About 55% of students entering as freshmen graduate within four years; 90% of freshmen return for sophomore year. *Special programs:* HEOP, credit and non-credit travel-study tours, cooperative work/study program, internships. *Calendar:* 4–1–4, summer school.

Undergraduate degrees conferred (542). 29% were in Architecture and Environmental Design, 27% were in Visual and Performing Arts, 22% were in Engineering, 17% were in Communications, remainder in 3 other fields.

Graduates Career Data. About 88% of 1992–93 graduates employed. Fields typically hiring largest numbers of graduates include architectural firms and graphic design firms. Career Development Services include counseling and placement.

Faculty. About 83% of faculty hold PhD or equivalent. About 54% of undergraduate classes taught by tenured faculty. About 33% of teaching faculty are female; 5% Black, 2% Hispanic, 4% other minority.

Student Body. About 54% of students from in state; 67% Middle Atlantic, 6% New England, 5% South; 13% foreign. An estimated 10% of students reported as Black, 13% Asian, 9% Hispanic, 13% other minority. *Minority group students:* cooperative program in advertising (job and tuition); tutoring and remedial programs; number of ethnically oriented clubs.

Varsity Sports. Men (NCAA): Basketball, Cross-Country (Ind), Soccer, Tennis, Track, Volleyball. Women (NCAA): Basketball, Tennis, Track, Volleyball.

Campus Life. Nature of campus life affected by urban location in both positive and negative ways. Students mention crime as an issue, but also take full advantage of the city's many opportunities. Students have major control over campus social life: "Pratt is very creative and they create many festive events." Limited parking facilities available to students.

About 60% of students live in coed dormitories; rest live in off-campus housing or commute. Freshmen given preference in college housing if all students cannot be accommodated. Sexes segregated in coed dormitories by room. There are 4 fraternities, 1 sorority on campus which about 6% of men, 1% of women join.

Annual Costs. Tuition and fees, $13,298; room and board, $6,456; estimated $2,000 other, exclusive of travel. About 80% of students receive financial aid; average amount of assistance, $8,500. Assistance is typically divided 50% scholarship/grant, 38% loan, 12% work. Institute reports 810 scholarships awarded on the basis of academic merit alone. *Meeting Costs:* Institute offers prepaid and deferred payment plans, PLUS Loans.

Presbyterian College

Clinton, South Carolina 29325 **(800) 476-7272**

A church-related, liberal arts college, located in a town of 10,000, 64 miles northwest of Columbia. Most convenient major airport: Greenville/Spartanburg.

Founded: 1880
Affiliation: Presbyterian
UG Enrollment: 581 M, 582 W (full-time)
Cost: $10K–$20K
% Receiving Financial Aid: 75%
Admission: Selective (+)
Application Deadline: April 1

Admission is selective (+). About 76% of applicants accepted, 37% of these actually enroll; 68% of freshmen graduate in top fifth of high school class, 94% in top two-fifths. Average freshman SAT scores: 530 verbal, 570 mathematical; 70% of freshmen score above 500 on verbal, 22% above 600, 4% above 700; 91% score above 500 on mathematical, 33% above 600, 7% above 700; ACT, 27 composite. *Required:* SAT or ACT, essay; interview recommended. Criteria considered in admissions, in order of importance: high school academic record, standardized test scores, recommendations, writing sample, extracurricular activities; other factors considered: special talents, alumni children, diverse student body. About 27% of entering students from private schools. *Entrance programs:* early admission, midyear admission, deferred admission. *Apply* by April 1; rolling admissions. *Transfers* welcome; 22 enrolled 1993–94.

Academic Environment. Graduation requirements include English, mathematics, history, social sciences, laboratory science, foreign language, fine arts, religion, and physical education. Degrees offered: bachelors. Average undergraduate class size: 80% under 20, 17% 20–40, 3% over 40. About 79% of students entering as freshmen graduate within four years; 90% of freshmen return for sophomore year. *Special programs:* study abroad, summer program at Oxford (England), semester program at Abo Academy (Finland)), optional May interterm, international–intercultural studies, independent study, Washington Semester, 3–2 engineering and forestry, pre-pharmacy, cooperative program in Christian education, internships in all departments. *Calendar:* semester, summer school.

Undergraduate degrees conferred (230). 30% were in Business and Management, 20% were in Social Sciences, 12% were in Psychology, 11% were in Life Sciences, 10% were in Education, 5% were in Letters, 4% were in Philosophy and Religion, remainder in 4 other fields.

Graduates Career Data. Advanced studies pursued by 36% of graduates; 8% enter graduate school; 9% enter medical school; 3% enter dental school; 8% enter law school; 7% enter business school. Medical and dental schools typically enrolling largest numbers of graduates include Medical U. of South Carolina, Medical College of Georgia, Johns Hopkins; law schools include U. of South Carolina, U. of North Carolina; business schools include: U. of Pennsylvania, U. of North Carolina. About 64% of 1992–93 graduates employed. Fields typically employing largest numbers of graduates include banking, finance, marketing, industry. Career Development Services include career counseling, resume preparation, career testing, mock interviews, on-campus recruiting office, career fairs.

Faculty. About 90% of faculty hold PhD or equivalent. All of undergraduate classes taught by tenured faculty. About 20% of teaching faculty are female; 1% Black, 1% Hispanic.

Varsity Sports. Men (Div. II): Baseball, Basketball, Football, Golf, Riflery, Soccer, Tennis, Track. Women (Div. II): Basketball, Riflery, Tennis, Volleyball.

Student Body. About 46% of students from in state; 80% South, 12% Middle Atlantic, 5% New England; less than 1% foreign. An estimated 75% of students reported as Protestant, 10% Catholic, 15% unaffiliated or other; 5% Black, 2% Asian.

Religious Orientation. Presbyterian is a church-related institution; 32% of students affiliated with the church; 2 courses in religion required of all students.

Varsity Sports. Men (Div.II): Baseball, Basketball, Football, Golf, Soccer, Tennis, Track, Volleyball. Women (Div.II): Basketball, Soccer, Tennis, Track, Volleyball.

Campus Life. About 88% of men, 88% of women live in traditional dormitories; 2% of men, 1% of women live in fraternities and sororities; rest commute. Freshmen given preference in college housing if all students cannot be accommodated. There are 6 fraternities, 3 sororities on campus which about 44% of men, 41% of women join. About 20% of resident students leave campus on weekends.

Annual Costs. Tuition and fees, $11,984; room and board, $3,416, estimated $1,470 other, exclusive of travel. About 75% of students receive financial aid; average amount of assistance, $8,119. College reports 130 scholarships awarded on the basis of academic merit alone, 53 for special talents alone, some for need alone. *Meeting Costs:* college offers tuition gift certificate, 10-month payment plan.

Prescott College

Prescott, Arizona 86301 **(602) 776-5180**

A small, innovative liberal arts college with an environmental mission. The college is located in the mountains of central Arizona, in a city of 30,000.

Founded: 1966
Affiliation: Independent
UG Enrollment: 198 M, 158 W (full-time)
Cost: < $10K
% Receiving Financial Aid: 53%
Admission: Non-selective
Application Deadline: Rolling

Admission. About 70% of applicants accepted, 75% of these actually enroll. *Required:* 2 letters of reference, 4 essays, transcripts and high school diploma or GED. Criteria considered in admissions, all rank with equal importance: high school academic record, standardized test scores, extracurricular activities, recommendations, writing sample, "fit with the school's philosophy", community participation; other factors considered: special talents. About 35% of entering students from private schools. *Apply:* rolling admissions. *Transfers* welcome; 141 enrolled 1993–94.

Academic Environment. College program is designed for students interested in "alternative educational processes." The program stresses experiential learning and self-direction within an interdisciplinary curriculum. Degrees offered: bachelors, masters. Average undergraduate class size: all under 20.

About 53% of entering class graduate within four years, 80% eventually; 58% return for sophomore year. *Special programs:* undergraduate research, study abroad, independent study. Adult programs: independent, mentored study for returning adults; Center for Indian Bilingual Teacher Education.

Undergraduate degrees conferred (76). 39% were in Education, 21% were in Psychology, 8% were in Business and Management, 8% were in Renewable Natural Resources, 5% were in Visual and Performing Arts, 5% were in Parks and Recreation, 3% were in Social Sciences, 3% were in Life Sciences, 3% were in Liberal/General Studies, remainder in 4 other fields.

Graduates Career Date. Career Development Services include individual and group career counseling and planning, job bank, career library, resume workshops, resource listings.

Faculty. About 47% of faculty hold PhD or equivalent. About 56% of teaching faculty are female; 2% Black, 2% Hispanic, 5% other minority.

Student Body. About 2% of students from in state; 22% West, 4% Northwest, 45% New England, 17% Midwest, 9% Southeast, 3% foreign. About 5% of students are reported as Black, 1% Hispanic, 3% International. Average age of undergraduate student: 22.

Campus Life. All students commute.

Annual Costs. Tuition and fees, $9,775; estimated $1,160 other, exclusive of travel. About 53% of students receive financial aid; average amount of assistance, $7,125. Assistance is typically divided 35% grant, 37% loan, 28% work. All scholarships awarded on the basis of need alone.

Princeton University

Princeton, New Jersey 08544 **(609) 258-3060**

Princeton is probably the member of the Ivy League that still comes closest to the ideal of the "university college" where all senior faculty must teach or lecture undergraduates. The absence of prestigious professional schools of law or medicine also serves to emphasize the key role of undergraduate education. The 600-acre campus is located in a community of about 30,000, 50 miles southwest of New York City. Most convenient major airport: Newark International.

Founded: 1746	**Cost:** $10K–$20K
Affiliation: Independent	**% Receiving Financial Aid:** 40%
UG Enrollment: 2,676 M, 1,875 W (full-time)	**Admission:** Most Selective
Total Enrollment: 6,412	**Application Deadline:** January 2

Admission is among the most selective in the country. About 17% of applicants accepted, 55% of these actually enroll; 96% of freshmen graduate in top fifth of high school class, 99% in top two-fifths. Average freshman SAT scores, according to most recent data available: middle 50% range, 600–700 verbal, 660–750 mathematical. *Required:* SAT, 3 ACH (applicants to School of Engineering and Applied Science must offer ACH in physics or chemistry and mathematics I or II); interview strongly recommended. *Non-academic factors* considered in admissions: alumni children, diverse student body, American minorities, special talents (artistic or athletic). *Entrance programs:* early admission, deferred admission, advanced placement (in some departments). About 38% of entering students from private schools; 6% from parochial schools. *Apply* by January 2. *Transfers* welcome; "a handful are admitted each year."

Academic Environment. Princeton students influence the decision-making process in curriculum and related areas of university life other than faculty selection and promotion. University offers broad range of curricula in arts and sciences, engineering, architecture, and public and international affairs. Fairly numerous distribution requirements for AB include 2 term courses each in natural science, social science, arts and letters, history/philosophy/religion; proficiency in English and foreign language; physical education freshman year; most requirements can be met on *Pass/fail* or audited basis. *Degrees:* AB, BSE. *Majors offered* include relatively wide range of usual arts and sciences, anthropology, architecture and urban planning, area studies (Near Eastern, African-American, African, Latin American, East Asian, American, Russian), astrophysical sciences, biochemical sciences, computer science, variety of geosciences, engineering, history and philosophy of science, public and international affairs, freshman seminars, departments of molecular biology, computer science.

About 95% of students entering as freshmen graduate eventually; 98% of freshmen return for sophomore year. *Special programs:* CLEP (for entrance placement only), independent concentration, study abroad, undergraduate research, individualized majors, off-campus programs, graduation in 3 years, early concentration, interdepartmental concentration, admission to graduate courses, programs in science, human affairs, creative arts, University Scholars Program, student-initiated seminars, teacher preparation, senior thesis. Adult programs: access to regular courses for non-matriculated students. *Calendar:* semester.

Undergraduate degrees conferred (1,110). 32% were in Social Sciences, 15% were in Engineering, 13% were in Letters, 7% were in Life Sciences, 6% were in Public Affairs, 5% were in Philosophy and Religion, 5% were in Physical Sciences, 4% were in Visual and Performing Arts, 4% were in Psychology, 3% were in Foreign Languages, remainder in 4 other fields.

Graduates Career Data. According to most recent data available, full-time graduate or professional study pursued immediately after graduation by 30% of students; 16% enter professional schools. Medical schools enrolling largest numbers of graduates include NYU, Columbia, U. of Pennsylvania, law schools include Columbia, U. of Michigan, Harvard, Stanford; business schools include U. of Chicago, NYU. *Careers in business and industry* pursued by 54% of graduates.

Faculty. About 95% of faculty hold PhD or equivalent.

Student Body. About 15% of students from in state. An estimated 7% of students reported as Black, 4% Hispanic, 1% Native American, 9% Asian, 4% other minority, according to most recent data available. *Minority group students:* services for deaf, blind, and mobility-impaired students (60% of campus accessible to handicapped), foreign student advisors, Accíon Puertorriqueña, Asian American Student Association, Third World Center.

Religious Orientation. Founded by Presbyterians, Princeton has always been nonsectarian, makes no religious demands on students.

Varsity Sports. Men (Div.I): Baseball, Basketball, Crew, Cross Country, Fencing, Football(IAA), Golf, Hockey, Lacrosse, Soccer, Squash, Swimming/Diving, Tennis, Track, Volleyball, Water Polo, Wrestling. Women (Div.I): Basketball, Crew, Cross Country, Fencing, Field Hockey, Ice Hockey, Lacrosse, Soccer, Softball, Squash, Swimming/Diving, Tennis, Track, Volleyball.

Campus Life. Campus life at Princeton has gone through a period of drastic change. The "eating clubs," which for years dominated campus social life, now attract only some of any given class; interest in them remains high however, although juniors and seniors have a variety of social and dining options. Facilities include residential colleges for freshmen and sophomores, a Third World Center, an International Center, a Women's Center, and a Kosher dining hall. Students enjoy considerable freedom; virtually only specific university regulations forbid possession and use of illegal drugs. Parking reported as no problem. An unusually full and varied calendar of cultural and intellectual events is provided by the university; supplemented by many student groups. Nearest major cultural centers, New York City and Philadelphia, are both 50 miles away, but campus provides exceptional facilities.

About 96% of undergraduates live on-campus in traditional or coed dormitories; rest live off-campus. Sexes segregated in coed dormitories by floor or room. There are no fraternities or sororities on campus.

Annual Costs. Tuition and fees, $15,440; room and board, $5,058. About 40% of students receive financial aid. University reports scholarships awarded only on the basis of need.

Principia College

Elsah, Illinois 62028 **(618) 374-2131**

A co-educational college open to Christian Scientists, Principia is located in a small community, 40 miles northwest of St. Louis. All students must accept the premise of the college: "to serve the cause of Christian Science." Regular attendance at Christian Science services and a commitment to understand and practice the tenets of the religion is expected. College staff and faculty is entirely Christian Scientist. Most convenient major airport: Lambert Field (St. Louis).

Founded: 1898	**Cost:** $10K–$20K
Affiliation: Independent (Christian Science)	**% Receiving Financial Aid:** 74%
UG Enrollment: 236 M, 306 W (full-time)	**Admission:** Selective (+)
	Application Deadline: August 1

Admission is selective (+). About 87% of applicants accepted, 70% of these actually enroll; 26% of freshmen graduate in top fifth of high school class, 50% in top two-fifths. Average freshman scores: SAT, 489 M, 500 W verbal, 581 M, 526 W mathematical; 43% of freshmen score above 500 on verbal, 18% above 600, 1% above 700; 65% score above 500 on mathematical, 25% above 600, 5% above 700; ACT, 23 M, 23 W composite. *Required:* SAT or ACT, ACH in foreign language, minimum high school GPA of 2.5, essay, 3 references; interview highly recommended. Criteria considered in admissions, in order of importance: high school academic record, writing sample, recommendations, standardized test scores, extracurricular activities; other factors considered: special talents, alumni children, diverse student body, religious affiliation/commitment. *Entrance programs:* early decision, midyear admission, deferred admission, advanced placement. About 40% of entering students from private schools. *Apply* by August 1; rolling admissions. *Transfers* welcome; 36 enrolled 1993–94.

Academic Environment. Graduation requirements include foreign language, literature, history, arts, religion and philosophy, social sciences, laboratory science, math and computer science, natural sciences, and physical education. Degrees offered: bachelors. *Majors offered* include usual arts and sciences, computer science, drama, education, fine arts, engineering science, special majors and special studies program by petition, women's studies, environmental studies, world perspectives. Average undergraduate class size: 92% under 20, 8% 20–40.

About 65% of students entering as freshmen graduate within four years, 75% eventually; 89% of freshmen return for sophomore year. *Special programs:* honors, independent study, study abroad, undergraduate research, credit by examination, self-designed majors, internships, 3–2 program in engineering. *Calendar:* 3 quarters (no regular summer school).

Undergraduate degrees conferred (140). 19% were in Social Sciences, 18% were in Business and Management, 13% were in Visual and Performing Arts, 12% were in Letters, 9% were in Foreign Languages, 8% were in Communications, 6% were in Life Sciences, 4% were in Multi/Interdisciplinary Studies, 4% were in Mathematics, 4% were in Education, 3% were in Computer and Engineering Related Technology, remainder in Physical Sciences.
Graduates Career Data. Advanced studies pursued by 26% of graduates within five years. Fields typically hiring largest numbers of graduates include finance, sales/marketing, communications, education. Career Development Services include career counseling, job listings, resume and interview workshops, alumni contacts, job fairs, networking system.
Faculty. About 56% of faculty hold PhD or equivalent. About 55% of undergraduate classes taught by tenured faculty. About 35% of teaching faculty are female; 1% Black, 1% Hispanic.
Student Body. About 12% of students from in state; 22% Midwest, 41% West, 10% South, 12% New England, 4% Middle Atlantic, 10% Northwest, 2% foreign. All students are Christian Scientists; 3% are minority.
Religious Orientation. Principia is a private college for Christian Scientists. It is not formally affiliated with the Christian Science Church.
Varsity Sports. Men (NCAA Div.III): Baseball, Basketball, Cross Country, Diving, Football, Golf, Soccer, Swimming, Tennis, Track. Women (NCAA Div.III): Basketball, Cross Country, Diving, Golf, Soccer, Softball, Swimming, Tennis, Track, Volleyball.
Campus Life. All students are "expected to uphold the Basic Commitments and Community Moral Standards."

About 99% of men, 99% of women live in traditional dormitories; rest commute. There are no fraternities or sororities on campus. About 20% of resident students leave campus on weekends.
Annual Costs. Tuition and fees, $12,567; room and board, $5,232; estimated $1,125 other, exclusive of travel. About 74% of students receive financial aid; average amount of assistance, $8,220. Assistance is typically divided 60% grant, 26% loan, 6% work. College reports 55 scholarships awarded on the basis of academic merit alone. Meeting costs: college offers monthly payment plans.

Providence College

Providence, Rhode Island 02918 (401) 865-2535

A church-related, liberal arts college, conducted by the Dominican Fathers; the 93-acre campus is located in a city of 179,200. Most convenient major airport: T. F. Green State (Warwick).

Founded: 1917	**Total Enrollment:** 6,103
Affiliation: Roman Catholic	**Cost:** $10K–$20K
UG Enrollment: 1,648 M, 1,964 W (full-time); 569 M, 846 W (part-time)	**% Receiving Financial Aid:** 64%
	Admission: Selective (+)
	Application Deadline: Jan. 1

Admission is selective (+). About 64% of applicants accepted, 29% of these actually enroll; 46% of freshmen graduate in top fifth of high school class, 79% in top two-fifths. Average freshman scores: SAT, 495 M, 503 W verbal, 570 M, 549 W mathematical; 47% of freshmen score above 500 on verbal, 7% above 600; 75% of freshmen score above 500 on mathematical, 25% above 600, 2% above 700; ACT, 24 M, 25 W composite. *Required:* SAT or ACT, essay, recommendations, activities listing. Criteria considered in admissions, in order of importance: high school academic record, standardized test scores, extracurricular activities, writing sample, recommendations; other factors considered: special talents, alumni children, diverse student body. *Entrance programs:* early decision, early admission, advanced placement, deferred admission. About 8% of entering students from private schools, 31% from parochial schools. *Apply* by January 1 (part 1), February 1 (part 2). *Transfers* welcome; 76 enrolled 1993–94.
Academic Environment. Graduation requirements include 20 hours in Development of Western Civilization, 6 hours each in natural sciences, social sciences, philosophy, religion, 3 hours each in mathematics, fine arts; English proficiency, and 9 hours in electives outside of major. Students praise the liberal arts curriculum, especially the Western Civ. course. Opportunities for class participation and classes that are "challenging but not impossible" are also singled out as strengths. Degrees offered: bachelors, masters, doctoral. Students selection of majors strongly suggests a major concern with professional/occupational goals. Average undergraduate class size: 15% under 20, 80% 20–40, 5% over 40.

About 95% of students entering as freshmen graduate within 4 years, 96% eventually; 95% of freshmen return for sophomore year. *Special programs:* independent study, study abroad, cross registration with RISD, honors, individualized majors, internships in business, Latin American studies, American College Program at the U. of Fribourg, 3–2 nursing, 3–2 engineering. Adult programs: evening and Saturday classes. *Calendar:* semester, summer school.
Undergraduate degrees conferred (1,015). 33% were in Business and Management, 24% were in Social Sciences, 10% were in Multi/Interdisciplinary Studies, 8% were in Letters, 5% were in Liberal/General Studies, 4% were in Psychology, 4% were in Education, 4% were in Life Sciences, remainder in 9 other fields.
Graduates Career Data. Advanced studies pursued by 23% of graduates; 9% enter graduate school; 8% enter law school; 3% enter business school; 2% enter medical school; 1% enter dental school. Medical schools typically enrolling largest numbers of graduates include Brown; dental schools include Tufts; law schools include Suffolk, New England, Columbia; business schools include Northeastern, Cornell, Bryant. About 63% of 1992–93 graduates employed. Employers typically hiring largest numbers of graduates include Fleet National Bank, Coopers & Lybrand, Chase Manhattan, Big Six accounting firms. Career Development Services include individual and group sessions, job search, resume writing and interview skills, career resource library, computer assisted career planning program, on-campus recruitment, alumni network, job shadowing, internships.
Faculty. About 82% of faculty hold PhD or equivalent. About 73% of undergraduate classes taught by tenured faculty. About 29% of teaching faculty are female.
Student Body. About 14% of students from in state; 70% New England, 24% Mid Atlantic, 1% foreign. An estimated 85% of students reported as Catholic, 6% as Protestant, 1% Jewish, 8% other or unaffiliated; 4% as Black, 3% Hispanic, 2% Asian, 3% other minority.
Religious Orientation. Providence is a church-related institution; 2 courses of religious study required of all students.
Varsity Sports. Men (Div.I): Baseball, Basketball, Cross Country, Diving, Golf, Hockey (Ice), Lacrosse, Soccer, Swimming, Tennis, Track. Women (Div.I): Basketball, Cross Country, Diving, Hockey (Field), Hockey (Ice), Soccer, Softball, Swimming, Tennis, Track, Volleyball.
Campus Life. Campus is located in central Providence, within walking distance of "major necessities", as well as close to possible internships in business, social services, and the arts. Boston is an hour away, close enough for day trips. Students report strong involvement in student clubs and organizations (50% or more of students) and intramurals (85%); also many planned social activities. Limited intervisitation. Alcohol restricted to students of legal age; illegal drugs are forbidden; cars not allowed.

About 53% of men, 51% of women live in traditional dormitories; 8% of men, 14% of women live in coed apartments; rest live in off-campus housing or commute. Freshmen given preference in college housing if all students cannot be accommodated. There are no fraternities or sororities on campus. About 12% of resident students leave campus on weekends.
Annual Costs. Tuition and fees, $13,500, room and board, $5,900; estimated $1,100 other, exclusive of travel. About 64% of students receive financial aid; average amount of assistance, $9,900. Assistance is typically divided 20% scholarship, 40% grant, 31% loan, 9% work. College reports 40 scholarships awarded on the basis of academic merit alone, 160 for special talents alone, 2,100 for need alone. *Meeting Costs:* college offers 10-month tuition payment plan.

University of Puerto Rico

Rio Piedras, Puerto Rico 00931 (809) 764-7290

A publicly supported institution, with campuses and centers in different cities in Puerto Rico, the university has a bilingual student body. University campuses are located in Rio Piedras, Mayagüez, San Juan; university colleges at Cayey, Aguadilla, Carolina and

Humacao; Technological University Colleges at Bayamón, Arecibo; and 2-year regional colleges at Aguadilla, Carolina, Ponce, and "La Montaña at Utuado.".

Founded: 1900	**Cost:** < $10K
Affiliation: Commonwealth	**Admission:** Non-selective
Total Enrollment: 22,210	**Application Deadline:** Dec. 18

Admission. Graduates of accredited high schools with 2.0 average and 12 units in last 3 years of high school or 16 units in last 4 years eligible; 42% of applicants accepted, 83% of these actually enroll. *Required:* SAT (Spanish or English version acceptable). *Out-of-state* freshman applicants: state does not limit out-of-state enrollment. No special requirements for out-of-state applicants. *Apply* by December 18. *Transfers* welcome (limited).

Academic Environment. *Undergraduate studies* offered by colleges of Humanities, Social Sciences, Natural Sciences, General Studies, Education, Business Administration, Pharmacy, Engineering, school of Architecture. Specific course and distribution requirements vary with major. *Special programs:* study abroad, honors. *Calendar:* semester, summer school.

Undergraduate degrees conferred (2,612). 20% were in Business and Management, 13% were in Education, 12% were in Social Sciences, 11% were in Life Sciences, 6% were in Psychology, 5% were in Computer and Information Sciences, 4% were in Business and Office, 4% were in Multi/Interdisciplinary Studies, 4% were in Home Economics, 4% were in Foreign Languages, 3% were in Public Affairs, 3% were in Communications, 3% were in Physical Sciences, remainder in 8 other fields. *Doctoral degrees:* Physical Sciences 4, Letters 4.

Student Body. About 99% of students from Puerto Rico.

Varsity Sports. Men (PRSIC): Basketball, Decathlon, Judo, Soccer, Softball, Swimming, Tennis, Track, Volleyball, Weight Lifting. Women (PRSIC): Basketball, Decathlon, Soccer, Softball, Swimming, Tennis, Track, Volleyball.

Campus Life. Overwhelmingly a commuter institution, only 3% of students live on campus.

Annual Costs. Tuition and fees, $679 (varies by campus); out-of-state, $2,229; room and board, $2,890. University reports some scholarships awarded on the basis of academic merit alone.

University of Puget Sound

Tacoma, Washington 98416 (206) 756-3211

Puget Sound is a private institution offering programs in the liberal arts and sciences, business, law, music, and occupational therapy. The 90-acre main campus is located in a residential section of Tacoma (pop. 156,000). Most convenient major airport: Seattle-Tacoma International.

Founded: 1888	**Cost:** $10K–$20K
Affiliation: Independent	**% Receiving Financial Aid:** 75%
UG Enrollment: 1,132 M, 1,606 W (full-time)	**Admission:** Very Selective
Total Enrollment: 3,334	**Application Deadline:** March 1

Admission is very selective. About 70% of applicants accepted, 24% of these actually enroll; 75% of freshmen graduate in top fifth of high school class, 95% in top two-fifths. Average freshman SAT scores: 514 M, 524 W verbal, 600 M, 567 W mathematical; 60% of freshmen score above 500 on verbal, 19% above 600, 2% above 700; 84% score above 500 on mathematical, 45% above 600, 10% above 700; ACT, 25 M, 26 W composite. *Required:* SAT or ACT, essay, recommendation letters from teacher and counselor. Criteria considered in admissions: high school academic record ranks as most important; while standardized test scores, extracurricular activities, recommendations and writing sample rank with equal importance; other factors considered: special talents, alumni children, diverse student body. *Entrance programs:* early decision, early admission, midyear admission, advanced placement, deferred admission. About 17% of entering students from private schools. *Apply* by March 1; rolling admissions. *Transfers* welcome; 241 enrolled 1993–94.

Academic Environment. Majority of students are reported to be concerned with both scholarly/intellectual pursuits and professional/vocational goals. Graduation requirements include 2 units each of written and oral communication or 2 units of one foreign language, 1 unit of Mathematical Reasoning, 2 of Natural World, 1 each of International Studies, Science in Context, fine arts, Historical Perspective, Humanistic Perspective, Society, and Comparative Values. Student asserts "The choice of mandatory classes is enormous!" Degrees offered: bachelors, masters. *Majors offered* include usual arts and sciences, Asian studies, music business, occupational therapy, public administration, business leadership (combined business/liberal arts degree), interdisciplinary studies. Average undergraduate class size: 54% under 20, 40% 20–40, 6% over 40.

About 55% of students entering as freshmen graduate within four years, 62% eventually; 86% of freshmen return for sophomore year. *Special programs:* independent study, study abroad, honors, undergraduate research, cooperative education program, 3–2 in engineering. Center for Writing and Learning offers support for students with learning disabilities, as well as helping students "fine-tune" writing assignments. *Calendar:* early semester, summer school.

Undergraduate degrees conferred (725). 24% were in Business and Management, 17% were in Letters, 16% were in Social Sciences, 7% were in Multi/Interdisciplinary Studies, 7% were in Psychology, 6% were in Education, 5% were in Visual and Performing Arts, 4% were in Allied Health, 4% were in Life Sciences, 4% were in Physical Sciences, remainder in 5 other fields.

Graduates Career Data. Advanced studies pursued by 25% business school; 2% enter medical school. Medical schools typically enrolling largest numbers of graduates include U. of Washington, Duke; law schools include Puget Sound. About 64% of 1992–93 graduates employed. Fields typically hiring largest numbers of graduates include business, government, computer science. Career Development Services include individual sessions with a career counselor, interest assessments, career awareness class, career exploration, internships and cooperatives, graduate and professional school preparation, marketing strategies and job referral.

Faculty. About 86% of faculty hold PhD or equivalent. About 50% of undergraduate classes taught by tenured faculty. About 38% of teaching faculty are female; 2% Black, 1% Hispanic, 4% other minority.

Student Body. About 46% of students from in state; 54% Northwest, 35% West, 7% Midwest, 1% foreign. An estimated 36% of students reported as Protestant, 15% Catholic, 45% unaffiliated; 2% as Black, 2% Hispanic, 9% Asian, 9% other minority. *Minority group students:* minority student adviser; Black Student Union, Hui O Hawaii.

Religious Orientation. Puget Sound is an independent institution founded by the United Methodist Church, makes no religious demands on students.

Varsity Sports. Men (NAIA): Baseball, Basketball(NCAA I), Crew, Cross Country, Football (NCAA II), Golf, Skiing, Soccer, Swimming, Tennis, Track. Women (NAIA): Basketball (NCAA I), Crew, Cross Country, Skiing, Soccer, Softball, Swimming, Tennis, Track, Volleyball.

Campus Life. Campus is located in a suburban area, about 12 blocks from Puget Sound and its beaches and 60 miles from Mt. Ranier. Seattle and its big city lights are about 45 minutes away. Students report "plenty to do" locally and on-campus. Student-run organizations, theme houses, clubs, sports (varsity and intramural), outdoor activities and greek life compete with academic programs and studying for student attention. Alcohol permitted for those over 21, state and university permits required for student parties where alcohol is served; smoking prohibited in university buildings; cars allowed. Freshmen advised to live on campus, but not required to do so.

About 4% of women live in traditional dormitories; 45% each of men, women live in coed dormitories; 14% each of men, women live in fraternities and sororities, 22% each of men, women live in off-campus college-related housing; rest commute. Freshmen given preference in college housing if all students cannot be accommodated. Sexes segregated in coed dormitories by floor or room. There are 6 fraternities, 6 sororities on campus which about 33% of men, women join. About 30% of resident students leave campus on weekends.

Annual Costs. Tuition and fees, $15,220; room and board, $4,300; estimated $1,850 other, exclusive of travel. About 75% of students receive financial aid; average amount of assistance, $13,250. Assistance is typically divided 50% scholarship/grant, 40% loan, 10% work. University reports 1,055 scholarships awarded on the basis of academic merit alone, 440 for special talents alone, 1,456 for need alone. *Meeting Costs:* university offers loan programs and deferred payment plan.

Puget Sound Christian College

Edmonds, Washington 98020

A small undergraduate theological college offering associates and bachelors degrees leading to further study at seminary or a career in the church.

Founded: 1950

Affiliation: Independent Christian Church/ Churches of Christ

Purdue University

West Lafayette, Indiana 47907 (317) 494-4600

Purdue is Indiana's land-grant college which, since the 1950s, has increased its offers in the liberal arts, education, and scientific programs. It still excels in science, engineering and other technical areas, including agriculture. It is a very large institution both in terms of student body and campus area. The West Lafayette campus of 1,565 acres is located in a metropolitan area of 121,702, 60 miles northwest of Indianapolis. Four regional campuses are located in other parts of the state: Calumet (described below); Fort Wayne and Indianapolis, conducted jointly with Indiana University (see alphabetical listing under Indiana University—Purdue University); and North Central, offering 2-year degree programs and some 4-year programs. Most convenient major airport: Indianapolis International.

Founded: 1869
Affiliation: State
UG Enrollment: 14,838 M, 11,112 W (full-time); 1,251 M, 1,263 W (part-time)

Total Enrollment: 35,161
Cost: < $10K
% Receiving Financial Aid: 41%
Admission: Selective (+)
Application Deadline: Rolling

Admission is selective (+). For all schools, 86% of applicants accepted, 31% of these actually enroll; 54% of freshmen graduate in top fifth of high school class, 84% in top two-fifths. Average freshman scores: SAT, 457 M, 448 W verbal, 572 M, 513 W mathematical; 31% of freshmen score above 500 on verbal, 6% above 600; 69% score above 500 on mathematical, 25% above 600, 8% above 700; ACT, 25 M, 24 W composite. *Required:* SAT or ACT; ACH recommended for Schools of Engineering and Science only. Criteria considered in admissions, in order of importance: high school academic record, standardized test scores, recommendations; other factors considered: alumni children. *Out-of-state* freshman applicants: university actively seeks students from out of state. State does not limit out-of-state enrollment. Requirement for out-of-state applicants: "strong upper-half quality"; 88% of applicants accepted, 17% of these actually enroll. States from which most out-of-state students are drawn include Illinois, Michigan, Ohio. *Entrance programs:* midyear admission, advanced placement. *Apply* by one month before semester starts; rolling admissions. *Transfers* welcome; 863 enrolled 1993–94.

Academic Environment. Pressures for academic achievement vary among the different schools, highest for Engineering and Science. *Undergraduate studies* offered by schools of Agriculture, Consumer and Family Sciences, Engineering, Health Sciences, Humanities Social Science and Education, Management, Technology, Nursing; sophomores may enter 4-year School of Pharmacy and Pharmaceutical Sciences after year in School of Science in pre-pharmacy option. Graduation requirements include 1–2 courses in English composition, 1 in speech, 1–4 in foreign language, 1 each in math and statistics, 3 in social sciences, 5 in humanities, 2 in natural sciences, and 1 each in ethnic diversity, gender issues, and social ethics. Degrees offered: associates, bachelors, masters, doctoral. *Majors offered* include more than 200 areas of specialization in humanities, social science, and education; as well as wide range of programs in science, engineering, and professional/vocational fields. Average undergraduate class size: 41% under 20, 43% 20–40, 16% over 40.

About 30% of students entering as freshmen graduate within four years, 70% eventually; 84% of freshmen return for sophomore year. *Special programs:* CLEP, independent study, study abroad, honors, undergraduate research, 3-year degree, individualized majors, internships in many fields, cooperative work/study programs (engineering, management, and science), credit by examination, interdisciplinary programs in African-American studies, medieval studies. *Calendar:* semester, summer school.

Undergraduate degrees conferred (5,195). 25% were in Engineering, 14% were in Business and Management, 7% were in Engineering and Engineering-Related Technologies, 6% were in Home Economics, 6% were in Health Sciences, 6% were in Computer and Information Sciences, 5% were in Communications, 5% were in Social Sciences, 4% were in Education, 4% were in Agricultural Sciences, 3% were in Agribusiness and Agricultural Production, 3% were in Life Sciences, remainder in 11 other fields. *Doctoral degrees:* Engineering 111, Sciences 82, Veterinary Medicine 65, Humanities, Social Science, and Education 63, Consumer and Family Sciences 14, Agriculture 54, Management 19, Pharmacy, Nursing and Health Sciences 17, Technology 1.

Graduates Career Data. Advanced studies pursued by 20% of graduates. About 52% of 1992–93 graduates employed. Fields typically hiring largest numbers of graduates include engineering, technology, agriculture, health sciences. Career Development Services include on-campus recruitment, interview preparation; alumni reported as helpful in both career guidance and job placement.

Faculty. About 99% of faculty hold PhD or equivalent. About 13% of teaching faculty are female; 1% Black, 1% Hispanic, 7% other minority.

Student Body. About 73% of students from in state; 89% Midwest, 4% Middle Atlantic, 2% South, 2% West, 1% New England, 2% foreign. An estimated 26% of undergraduate students reported as Protestant, 19% Catholic, 52% unaffiliated, 2% other; 4% Black, 2% Hispanic, 4% Asian. *Minority group students:* financial aid available; Office of Special Academic Services provides special counseling.

Varsity Sports. Men (Div.I): Baseball, Basketball, Cross Country, Diving, Football, Golf, Swimming, Tennis, Track, Wrestling. Women (Div.I): Basketball, Cross Country, Diving, Golf, Softball, Swimming, Tennis, Track, Volleyball.

Campus Life. No curfews. Intervisitation permitted 10:30 am to 12:30 am Sunday to Thursday, to 2 am Friday and Saturday. Alcohol prohibited on campus; freshmen not allowed to have cars on campus. Students may apply for admission to cooperative residence houses (8 for men, 6 for women) which are operated by students themselves.

About 38% of men, 37% of women live in traditional and coed dormitories and cooperatives; 8% of men, women live in fraternities and sororities; 52% of men, 53% of women live in off-campus housing; 1% of men, 2% of women live in married student housing. Freshmen given preference in college housing if all students cannot be accommodated. Sexes segregated in coed dormitories by wing. There are 47 fraternities, 25 sororities on campus; which about 5% of men, 3% of women join. About 10% of resident students leave campus on weekends.

Annual Costs. Tuition and fees, $2,696 (out-of-state, $8,848); room and board, $3,940; estimated $1,700 other, exclusive of travel. About 41% of students receive financial aid; average amount of assistance, $7,740. Assistance is typically divided 14% scholarships, 27% grants, 56% loan, 3% work. University reports 1,700 scholarships awarded on the basis of academic merit alone, 315 for special talents alone. *Meeting Costs:* college offers 10-month interest free payment plan.

Purdue University/ Calumet Campus

Hammond, Indiana 46323 (219) 989-2213

A commuter campus, serving northwestern Indiana, located in a city of 107,800, a metropolitan area of 500,000. Most convenient major airports: Gary, IN or Chicago, IL.

Founded: 1951
Affiliation: State
UG Enrollment: 1,520 M, 1,586 W (full-time)

Cost: < $10K
% Receiving Financial Aid: 30%
Admission: Non-selective
Application Deadline: Rolling

Admission. Graduates of Indiana high schools with 15 units who rank in top half of class eligible; 98% of applicants accepted, 63% of these actually enroll; 27% of freshmen graduate in top fifth of high school class, 57% in top two-fifths. *Required:* SAT. *Out-of-state* freshman applicants: university seeks students from out of state. State does not limit out-of-state enrollment. No special requirements for out-of-state applicants; 97% accepted, 55% enroll. *Apply* by no specific deadline. *Transfers* welcome.
Academic Environment. *Degrees:* AB, BS, BSE. Specific course and distribution requirements vary with school. *Majors offered* include philosophy, biotechnology, criminal justice, manufacturing engineering technology. About 32% of students entering as freshmen graduate eventually; 57% of freshmen return for sophomore year. *Special programs:* CLEP, honors, undergraduate research, study abroad, independent study, cooperative education. *Calendar:* semester, summer school.
Undergraduate degrees conferred (581). 25% were in Business and Management, 16% were in Engineering and Engineering Related Technology, 11% were in Engineering, 8% were in Education, 8% were in Health Sciences, 6% were in Communications, 6% were in Social Sciences, 5% were in Psychology, 5% were in Computer and Engineering Related Technology, 4% were in Life Sciences, remainder in 4 other fields.
Student Body. About 89% of students are from in state; 95% Midwest.
Varsity Sports. Men (NAIA): Basketball. Women (NAIA): Basketball, Volleyball.
Campus Life. All students commute.
Annual Costs. Tuition and fees, $1,842 (out-of-state, 4,542). About 30% of students receive financial aid; assistance is typically divided 56% scholarship, 42% loan, 2% work. University reports some scholarships awarded on the basis of academic merit alone.

Purdue University/Fort Wayne

(See Indiana University—Purdue University at Fort Wayne)

Queens College (N.Y.)

(See City University of New York)

Queens College

Charlotte, North Carolina 28274 (704) 332-7121

A church-related, liberal arts college, Queens is located in a city of 328,607.

Founded: 1857
Affiliation: Presbyterian
UG Enrollment: 165 M, 465 W (full-time); 96 M, 453 W (part-time)
Total Enrollment: 1,549
Cost: $10K–$20K
% Receiving Financial Aid: 88%
Admission: Non-selective
Application Deadline: Rolling

Admission. High school graduates with 11 academic units eligible; 77% of applicants accepted, 40% of these actually enroll; 45% of freshmen graduate in top fifth of high school class, 70% in top two-fifths. Average freshman scores: SAT, 996 M, 1,007 W combined; 35% of entering freshman score above 500 on verbal; 11% above 600; 51% score above 500 on mathematical, 13% above 600; ACT, 26 composite. *Required:* SAT or ACT, interview recommended, essay. Criteria considered in admissions, in order of importance: high school academic record, recommendations, standardized test scores, extracurricular activities, writing sample, special talents. *Entrance programs:* midyear admission, deferred admission, advanced placement. About 18% of entering students from private schools. *Apply:* rolling admissions. *Transfers* welcome.
Academic Environment. Unusual International Experience Program is included in regular tuition; all students spend three weeks on study tours to European and Asian countries. Graduation requirements include a 6-course sequence of interdisciplinary classes, natural science, foreign language, 1 course each for mathematics proficiency and English composition, and physical education. Students praise the "talented" faculty, who bring "real world experience to the classroom" and the small classes which allow for individual attention. Degrees offered: bachelors, masters. *Majors offered* include usual arts and sciences, American studies, art, biochemistry, communications, music, music therapy, Latin American studies, business and economics, education, drama, journalism, nursing, public administration, psychology, religious education. Average undergraduate class size: 80% under 20, 20% 20–40.

About 51% of students entering as freshmen graduate within four years; 80% of freshmen return for sophomore year. *Special programs:* CLEP, undergraduate research, cross registration with Charlotte area consortium schools, 3–2 Christian education, independent study, professional and exploratory internships, study abroad, honors, 3-year degree, individualized majors, Washington Semester, double majors, summer program in marine biology, legislative internship in Raleigh, International Experience Program, junior-year exchange program with Davidson, women's leadership program. Adult programs: evening and Saturday classes; continuing education program offers wide variety of classes. *Calendar:* 4–1–4.
Undergraduate degrees conferred (140). 24% were in Business and Management, 14% were in Social Sciences, 11% were in Visual and Performing Arts, 11% were in Letters, 9% were in Communications, 8% were in Education, 6% were in Psychology, 6% were in Health Sciences, 3% were in Life Sciences, remainder in 4 other fields.
Graduates Career Data. Advanced studies pursued by 20% of graduates; 2% enter graduate school; 3% enter medical school; 1% enter dental school; 9% enter law school; 2% enter business school. Medical schools typically enrolling largest numbers of students include East Carolina U.; law schools include Emory U., UNC-Chapel Hill; business schools include U. of South Carolina. About 60% of 1992–93 graduates employed. Fields hiring largest numbers of students include education, health, banking, accounting. Career Development Services include career planning, experiential learning through academic internships, career placements, job referral, planning, career resource library.
Faculty. About 75% of faculty hold PhD or equivalent. About 35% of undergraduate classes taught by tenured faculty. About 48% of teaching faculty are female.
Student Body. About 55% of students from in state; 3% foreign. About 64% of students reported as Protestant, 11% Catholic; 10% Black, 3% Hispanic, 1% Asian, 3% other minority. *Minority group students:* special financial provisions.
Religious Orientation. Queens is a church-related institution, makes no religious demands on students; attendance at vespers and weekly chapel services voluntary.
Varsity Sports. Men (NCAA, Div.II): Basketball, Golf, Soccer, Tennis. Women (NCAA, Div II): Basketball, Soccer, Softball, Tennis, Volleyball.
Campus Life. Campus is located near uptown Charlotte. Students say city "has a lot to offer", but the school itself is set "away from the hustle and bustle" of the city. Urban location provides increased opportunities for jobs and internships. First-semester freshmen and all women under 21 without parental permission are subject to dorm hours; self-limiting hours "not meant to permit students to stay out all night." Open visitation on weekends. Drinking regulated in dormitories by state law and permitted elsewhere on campus "in specified areas." Cars allowed.

About 62% of men, 63% of women live in traditional dormitories; 11% of men, 9% of women live in coed dormitories; rest commute. There are 2 fraternities, 5 sororities on campus, which about 34% of men, 49% of women join; they provide no residence facilities. About 40% of resident students leave campus on weekends.
Annual Costs. Tuition and fees, $10,400; room and board, $4,550; estimated $1,500 other, exclusive of travel. About 88% of students receive financial aid; average amount of assistance, $12,250. Assistance is typically divided 34% scholarship, 31% grant, 25% loan, 10% work. College reports 250 scholarships awarded on the basis of academic merit alone, 92 for special talents alone, 308 for need alone. *Meeting Costs:* college offers deferred payment plans, several tuition budgeting programs.

Quincy College
(See Quincy University)

Quincy University
Quincy, Illinois 62301 (217) 222-8020

An independent, Catholic liberal arts university, conducted by the Franciscan Friars. Quincy is located on the bluffs of the Mississippi River in a residential section of a city of 50,000. Formerly known as Quincy College. Most convenient major airport: Quincy.

Founded: 1860
Affiliation: Independent, (Roman Catholic)
UG Enrollment: 540 M, 530 W (full-time)
Total Enrollment: 1,202
Cost: < $10K
% Receiving Financial Aid: 95%
Admission: Selective (+)
Application Deadline: Rolling

Admission is selective (+). About 69% of applicants accepted, 42% of these actually enroll; 47% of freshmen graduate in top fifth of high school class, 81% in top two-fifths. Average freshman scores: SAT, 465 M, 537 W verbal, 584 M, 555 W mathematical; 60% of freshmen score above 500 on verbal, 15% above 600, 1% above 700; 64% score above 500 on mathematical, 24% above 600, 4% above 700; ACT, 23 M, 23 W composite. Required ACT or SAT; minimum high school GPA. Criteria considered in admissions, in order of importance: standardized test scores, high school academic record, recommendations, extracurricular activities; other factors considered: special talents, diverse student body. *Entrance programs:* midyear admission, advanced placement. About 56% of entering students from private or parochial schools. *Apply:* rolling admissions. *Transfers* welcome; 78 enrolled 1993–94.

Academic Environment. Graduation requirements: 43 hour core curriculum includes rhetoric, humanities, social sciences, science, fine arts, theology, and physical education. Students report "a lot of student-teacher interaction", faculty are "very accessible" and even "call you when you're sick." Classes are "very challenging", but small classes and personal attention keep it from being a problem. Degrees offered: associates, bachelors, masters. *Majors offered* include athletic training, sports management, finance, art, arts management, music, music business, nuclear medicine technology. Preprofessional programs in engineering, dentistry, law, veterinary medicine and capstone program in nursing. Average undergraduate class size: 33% under 20, 60% 20–40, 7% over 40.

About 60% of students entering as freshmen graduate within four years, 65% eventually; 88% of freshmen return for sophomore year. *Special programs:* CLEP, independent study, study abroad, honors, student designed majors, internships, 3–2 engineering. *Calendar:* semester.

Undergraduate degrees conferred (198). 27% were in Business and Management, 18% were in Social Sciences, 12% were in Education, 7% were in Health Sciences, 7% were in Letters, 6% were in Public Affairs, 6% were in Life Sciences, 6% were in Communications, 5% were in Psychology, 4% were in Visual and Performing Arts, remainder in 4 other fields.

Graduates Career Data. Advanced studies pursued by 21% of graduates; 12% enter graduate school; 3% enter law school, 3% enter business school, 2% enter medical school, 1% enter dental school. Law schools typically enrolling largest numbers of graduates include St. Louis U.; business schools include Northern Illinois; medical schools include Northwestern; dental schools include U.of Iowa. About 78% of 1992–93 graduates employed. Employers typically hiring largest numbers of graduates include McDonnell Douglas, Arthur Andersen, Montsanto, Morris Broadcasting. Career Development Services include career counseling, resume and interview skills, job vacancy listings, placement assistance, on-campus interviews, alumni placement network.

Faculty. About 44% of faculty hold PhD or equivalent. About 44% of undergraduate classes taught by tenured faculty. About 30% of teaching faculty are female; 2% Black, 2% other minority.

Student Body. About 69% of students from in state; 94% Midwest, 1% foreign. An estimated 62% of students reported as Catholic, 27% Protestant, 2% other; 5% as Black, 4% other minority. Average age of undergraduate student: 22.

Religious Orientation. Quincy is a Catholic university with a strong Franciscan orientation; 2 courses in religious studies required of all students. A campus ministry program encourages the spiritual development of students. Friars are involved in all areas of the campus community, including teaching, administration, campus ministry, and student life.

Varsity Sports. Men (NCAA Div.II): Baseball, Basketball, Football, Soccer (I), Tennis, Volleyball. Women (NCAA Div.II): Basketball, Soccer, Softball, Tennis, Volleyball.

Campus Life. Students report campus is "close to everything we need", but most of the time students stay on campus. "The usual campus activities" occupy students: studying, socializing, athletics, on-campus entertainment. Campus housing options include single-sex and coed residence halls, apartments and houses. Alcohol allowed in private rooms for those of legal age. Students may request a non-smoking roommate. Intervisitation permitted noon to 11:30 PM weekdays, to 1:30 am Friday and Saturday. Cars allowed.

About 38% each of men, women live in traditional dormitories; 34% of men, 32% of women live in coed dormitories; rest commute. Freshmen given preference in university housing if all students cannot be accommodated. Intervisitation in men's and women's dormitory rooms limited. There are no fraternities or sororities on campus. About 15% of resident students leave campus on weekends.

Annual Costs. Tuition and fees, $9,742; room and board, $3,904; estimated $1,020 other, exclusive of travel. About 95% of students receive financial aid; average amount of assistance, $10,306. Assistance is typically divided 20% scholarship, 56% grant, 19% loan, 5% work. University reports 191 scholarships awarded on the basis of academic merit alone, 150 for special talents alone, 652 for need alone. *Meeting Costs:* university offers time payment plans, prepayment plan, unsubsidized loans.

Quinnipiac College
Hamden, Connecticut 06518 (203) 281-8600; (800) 462-19448

An independent institution, offering undergraduate programs in business, allied health, natural science fields, and liberal arts, as well as post baccalaureate programs through its School of Graduate and Continuing Education and the School of Law. College is located near New Haven and in the Northeast Corridor between New York and Boston.

Founded: 1929
Affiliation: Independent
UG Enrollment: 1,219 M, 1,489 W (full-time); 207 M, 491 W (part-time)
Total Enrollment: 4,634
Cost: $10K–$20K
% Receiving Financial Aid: 66%
Admission: Selective
Application Deadline: Dec. 1

Admission is selective. About 58% of applicants accepted, 31% of these actually enroll; 40% of freshmen graduate in top fifth of high school class, 75% in top two-fifths. Average freshman scores: SAT, 510 verbal, 535 mathematical; 56% of freshmen score above 500 on verbal, 18% above 600, 4% above 700; 65% of freshmen score above 500 on mathematical, 20% above 600, 6% above 700; ACT, 23 composite. *Required:* SAT, essay, minimum high school GPA, high school transcript. Criteria considered in admissions, in order of importance: high school academic record, standardized test scores, recommendations, extracurricular activities, writing sample; other factors considered: special talents, alumni children, diverse student body. *Entrance programs:* early admission, midyear admission, deferred admission, advanced placement. *Apply* by December 1 for Physical and Occupational Therapy; March 1 recommended for all others; rolling admissions. *Transfers* welcome; 193 enrolled 1993–94.

Academic Environment. Graduation requirements include 50 credits in English, history, humanities, social sciences, science, economics, management, math, and language arts. Degrees offered: bachelors, masters, doctoral (JD). *Majors offered* include legal studies, physical therapy, occupational therapy, physician assistant program, international business, mass communications, political science. Average undergraduate class size: 73% under 20, 23% 20–40, 4% over 40.

About 66% of students entering as freshmen graduate within five years, 70% within six years; 85% of freshmen return for sophomore year. *Special programs:* CLEP, study abroad, internships available in all majors-required for some, individualized majors. Adult programs: continuing education. *Calendar:* semester, summer school.

Undergraduate degrees conferred (481). 36% were in Business and Management, 25% were in Allied Health, 7% were in Psychology, 6% were in Law, 5% were in Health Sciences, 4% were in Computer and Engineering Related Technology, 4% were in Social Sciences, 4% were in Communications, 3% were in Liberal/General Studies, remainder in 6 other fields.

Graduates Career Data. Advanced studies pursued by 40% of graduates; 8% enter medical and dental school; 7% enter business school; 6% enter law school; 5% enter graduate school. Medical and dental schools typically enrolling largest numbers of graduates include U.of Connecticut; business schools include Quinnipiac; law schools include Quinnipiac. About 88% of 1992–93 graduates employed. Fields typically hiring largest numbers of graduates include corporations, non-profits, government agencies, medical. Career Development Services include job bank, job interviews, career library, resume referral, testing, career preparation workshops.

Student Body. About 45% of students from in state; 70% New England, 20% Middle Atlantic, 6% South, 2% foreign. An estimated 65% of students reported as Catholic, 20% Protestant, 12% Jewish, 3% unaffiliated; 5% Black, 3% Hispanic, 1% Asian, 2% other minority.

Varsity Sports. Men (Div.II): Baseball, Basketball, Cross Country, Golf, Hockey(Ice, III), Lacrosse (III), Soccer, Tennis. Women (Div.II): Basketball, Cross Country, Soccer, Softball, Tennis, Volleyball.

Campus Life. About 75% each of men, women live in traditional dormitories; rest commute. There are 4 fraternities, 3 sorority on campus, which 3% each of men, women join; they provide no residence facilities. About 25% of resident students leave campus on weekends.

Annual Costs. Tuition and fees, $11,810; room and board, $5,790; estimated $1,000 other, exclusive of travel. About 66% of students receive financial aid, average amount received, $6,600. Assistance is typically divided 12% scholarship, 40% grant, 43% loan, 5% work. University reports 363 scholarships awarded on the basis of academic merit alone. *Meeting Costs:* college offers deferred payment plan.

Radcliffe College

(See Harvard University)

Radford College

Radford, Virginia 24142 (703) 831-5182

A public college offering a variety of academic programs; campus is located in a town of 15,900, 45 miles southwest of Roanoke. Most convenient major airport: Roanoke.

Founded: 1910
Affiliation: State
UG Enrollment: 3,413 M, 4,697 W (full-time)
Total Enrollment: 9,380
Cost: < $10K
% Receiving Financial Aid: 33%
Admission: Non-selective
Application Deadline: April 1

Admission. About 85% of applicants accepted, 35% of these actually enroll; 14% of freshmen graduate in top fifth of high school class, 30% in top two-fifths. Average freshman scores: SAT, 462 verbal, 420 mathematical; ACT, 22 composite. *Required:* SAT, essay, minimum high school GPA 2.0. Criteria considered in admissions, in order of importance: high school academic record, standardized test scores, writing sample, extracurricular activities, recommendations; other factors considered: special talents. *Out-of-state* freshman applicants: college actively seeks students from out-of-state. State does not limit out-of-state enrollment. About 62% of out-of-state applicants accepted, 16% of these actually enroll. States from which most out-of-state students are drawn include Maryland, New York, New Jersey. *Apply* by April 1; rolling admissions. *Transfers* welcome; 839 enrolled 1993–94.

Academic Environment. Graduation requirements include English, history, psychology, health, laboratory science, mathematics/computer science, fine arts, and philosophy/religion. Degrees offered: bachelors, masters. Average undergraduate class size: 40% under 20. About 25% of students entering as freshmen graduate within four years, 52% eventually; 73% of freshmen return for sophomore year. *Special programs:* January Term, internships, independent study, study abroad, honors, 3-year degree, individualized majors. Adult programs: general studies degree. *Calendar:* semester, summer school.

Undergraduate degrees conferred (1,622). 26% were in Business and Management, 14% were in Education, 10% were in Social Sciences, 9% were in Visual and Performing Arts, 6% were in Psychology, 6% were in Letters, 5% were in Protective Services, 4% were in Health Sciences, 3% were in Communications, remainder in 13 other fields.

Graduates Career Data. Advanced studies pursued by 22% of graduates; 5% enter business school; 2% enter law school; 1% enter medical school. About 71% of 1992–93 graduates employed. Fields typically hiring largest numbers of graduates include school systems, government agencies, health care facilities, Auditor for Public Accounts. Career Services Center conducts mock interviews, career exploration day, resume writing seminars, on-campus recruitment.

Faculty. About 76% of faculty hold PhD or equivalent. About 56% of undergraduate classes taught by tenured faculty. About 41% of teaching faculty are female; 4% Black, 4% other minority.

Student Body. About 84% of students from in state; 4% foreign. An estimated 4% of students reported as Black, 1% Hispanic, 1% Asian, 3% other minority.

Varsity Sports. Men (Div.I): Baseball, Basketball, Cross Country, Golf, Gymnastics, Hockey (field), Lacrosse, Soccer, Tennis. Women (Div.I): Basketball, Cross Country, Hockey (field), Gymnastics, Soccer, Tennis, Volleyball.

Campus Life. About 36% of student live on-campus; 62% of students commute. Freshmen given preference in college housing if all students cannot be accommodated. Intervisitation in men's and women's dormitory rooms limited. There are 13 fraternities, 10 sororities on campus which about 18% of men, 19% of women join; 2% of students live in fraternities and sororities. About 20% of resident students leave campus on weekends.

Annual Costs. Tuition and fees, $2,924 (out-of-state, $6,684); room and board, $4,110; estimated $800 other, exclusive of travel. About 33% of students receive financial aid; assistance is typically divided 35% scholarship, 50% loan, 15% work. University reports 75 scholarships awarded on the basis of academic merit alone, 305 for special talents alone, 2,500 for need alone.

Ramapo College of New Jersey

Mahwah, New Jersey 07430 (201) 529-7600

A 4-year liberal arts college located in a suburban community about 35 miles from New York City. Most convenient major airport: Newark International.

Founded: 1969
Affiliation: State
UG Enrollment: 1,413 M, 1,332 W (full-time); 866 M, 1,072 W (part-time)
Cost: < $10K
% Receiving Financial Aid: 42%
Admission: Non-selective
Application Deadline: March 15

Admission. About 46% of applicants accepted, 39% of these actually enroll; 22% of freshmen graduate in top fifth of high school class, 63% in the top two-fifths. Average freshman SAT scores: 460 verbal, 510 mathematical; 27% of students score above 500 on verbal, 5% above 600; 55% score above 500 on mathematical, 18% above 600, 1% above 700. *Required:* SAT; essay; interview recommended. Criteria considered in admissions, in order of importance: high school academic record, standardized test scores, recommendations, extracurricular activities, writing sample; other factors considered: special talents, alumni children, diverse student body. *Out-of-state* freshman applicants: college actively seeks out-of-state students. State does not limit out-of-state enrollment. States from which most out-of-state students are drawn include New York, Connecticut, Pennsylvania. *Entrance programs:* midyear admission, deferred admission, advanced placement. *Apply* by March 15; rolling admissions. *Transfers* welcome; 667 enrolled 1993–94.

Academic Environment. Degrees offered: bachelors. College places considerable emphasis on social and behavioral sciences. *Majors offered* include international business, law and society. *Special programs:* honors, undergraduate research, study abroad, independent study. Adult programs: Adult Transition Program. *Calendar:* semester, summer school.
Undergraduate degrees conferred (511). 45% were in Business and Management, 12% were in Communications, 10% were in Social Sciences, 7% were in Psychology, 5% were in Letters, 4% were in Public Affairs, 3% were in Visual and Performing Arts, 3% were in Multi/Interdisciplinary Studies, remainder in 6 other fields.
Graduates Career Data. Advanced studies pursued by 33% of graduates. *Careers in business and industry* pursued by 74% of graduates.
Student Body. About 81% of students from in state; 96% Middle Atlantic, 4% foreign. Average age of undergraduate student: 26.
Varsity Sports. Men (Div.III): Baseball, Basketball, Cross Country, Golf, Soccer, Tennis, Volleyball. Women (Div.III): Basketball, Soccer, Softball, Tennis, Volleyball.
Campus Life. About 45% of students live in coed dormitories; rest commute. There are 8 fraternities and 4 sorority on campus; about 4% each of men, women join.
Annual Costs. Tuition and fees, $3,300 (out-of-state, $4,500); room and board, $1,500. About 42% of students receive financial aid, average amount of assistance, $5,150. Assistance is typically divided 7% scholarship, 48% grant, 42% loan, 3% work. University reports 50 scholarships awarded on the basis of academic merit alone.

Randolph-Macon College

Ashland, Virginia 23005 **(804) 752-7305 or (800) 888-1762**

Randolph-Macon is an independent, co-educational liberal arts college historically related to the United Methodist Church. The 111-acre campus is located in a town of 6,000, 15 miles north of Richmond. Most convenient major airport: Richmond International.

Founded: 1830
Affiliation: Independent (United Methodist)
UG Enrollment: 549 M, 543 W (full-time)
Cost: $10K–$20K
% Receiving Financial Aid: 76%
Admission: Selective (+)
Application Deadline: March 1

Admission is selective (+). About 75% of applicants accepted, 23% of these actually enroll; 36% of freshmen graduate in top fifth of high school class, 67% in top two-fifths. Average freshman SAT scores: middle 50% range: 430–520 W verbal, 480–580 mathematical; 35% of freshmen score above 500 on verbal, 10% above 600, 1% above 700; 66% score above 500 on mathematical, 20% above 600, 3% above 700. *Required:* SAT or ACT, essay; interview recommended. Criteria considered in admissions, in order of importance: high school academic record, standardized test scores, recommendations, writing sample, extracurricular activities; other factors considered: special talents, diverse student body, alumni children. *Entrance programs:* early decision, early admission, midyear admission, advanced placement, deferred admission. About 35% of entering students from private schools. *Apply* by March 1. *Transfers* welcome; 30 enrolled 1993–94.
Academic Environment. Core requirements include 2 courses each in English composition, mathematics, European history, lab sciences, literature, social sciences, philosophy/religion, oral communication, and physical education; 1 course each in computer proficiency, fine arts; and foreign language proficiency. Biology, political science, economics/business reported to be among strongest academic programs. Degrees offered: bachelors. *Majors offered* in 29 different areas including international relations, international studies, women's studies, environmental studies, arts management. Minors are available in most of the areas. Small classes offer the benefit of personal attention from faculty. Average undergraduate class size: 67% under 20, 33% between 20–40.

About 65% of students entering as freshmen graduate within four years, 76% eventually; 85% of freshmen return for sophomore year. *Special programs:* honors, independent study, January term, study abroad, undergraduate research, interdisciplinary majors, participation in college consortium with Washington and Lee, Hampden-Sydney, Mary Baldwin, Hollins, Sweet Briar, Randolph-Macon Woman's College, 3–2 programs in engineering and forestry, 4–1 program in accounting. *Calendar:* 4–1–4.
Undergraduate degrees conferred (269). 45% were in Social Sciences, 17% were in Psychology, 14% were in Letters, 6% were in Foreign Languages, 6% were in Life Sciences, 4% were in Philosophy and Religion, 3% were in Visual and Performing Arts, 3% were in Physical Sciences, remainder in 2 other fields.
Graduates Career Data. Advanced studies pursued immediately after graduation by 30% of students, 65% within five years; 3% enter medical school; 5% enter law school; 3% enter business school. Medical and dental schools typically enrolling largest numbers of graduates include Medical College of Virginia; law schools include U. of Virginia. About 95% of 1992–93 graduates employed within six months of graduation. Fields typically hiring the largest number of graduates include sales, education, banking and finance, business administration/management. Career Development Services include aptitude testing, internships, counseling group, placement services, resume/interview workshops, on-campus recruitment, library services, free resume design, mock interviews with video, SIGI- interest inventory.
Faculty. About 82% of faculty hold PhD or equivalent. About 38% of teaching faculty are female.
Student Body. College seeks a national student body; 55% of students from Virginia; 85% from Middle Atlantic. An estimated 56% of students reported as Protestant, 23% Catholic, 1% Jewish, 4% unaffiliated, 16 other or not specified; 4% as Black, 1% Hispanic, 2% Asian, 2% Foreign.
Religious Orientation. Randolph-Macon is an independent institution historically related to the United Methodist Church. Two courses in religion or philosophy required of all students. Kern Center Council, a student organization, plans and carries out all campus religious programs under the direction of the Director of Religious Life. Places of worship available on campus for Protestants, in immediate community for Protestants and Catholics, 15 miles away for Jewish students.
Varsity Sports. Men (Div.III): Baseball, Basketball, Cross Country, Football, Golf, Lacrosse, Soccer, Tennis. Women (Div.III): Basketball, Cross Country, Field Hockey, Lacrosse, Soccer, Tennis.
Campus Life. Students report that there are many on-campus activities to occupy their free time including active intramural as well as varsity sports, clubs and organizations, cultural and recreational events; high interest in fraternities and sororities. Off-campus trips to Richmond and fairly nearby mountains and beaches are also popular. Students may choose between single sex and coed dorms. No college restrictions on use of cars. College complies with state laws regarding alcohol consumption. Students expected to live in college housing.

About 74% of men, 83% of women live in traditional dormitories; 5% of men, 5% of women live in coed dormitories; rest commute. There are 7 fraternities, 4 sororities on campus which about 40% of men, 39% of women join; 9% of men live in fraternities, 3% of women live in sororities. About 35% of resident students leave campus on weekends.
Annual Costs. Tuition and fees, $12,230; room and board, $4,750; estimated $900 other, exclusive of travel. About 76% of students receive financial aid, 38% receive need-based financial aid; average amount of need-based assistance, $11,181. Assistance (need-based) is typically divided 59% scholarship/grant, 37% loan, 4% work. College reports 89 scholarships awarded for academic merit, 370 for need. *Meeting Costs:* college offers parent loan program, installment payment plan, half-tuition grant for second student attending concurrently with sibling, on-campus jobs.

Randolph-Macon Woman's College

Lynchburg, Virginia 24503 **(804) 947-8000**

Randolph-Macon has long been a college that attracts young women from both the North and the South. It is notable as the first women's college south of Washington, D.C. to receive a Phi Beta Kappa chapter and as the first Southern women's college to achieve regional accreditation. College emphasizes studies of particular interest to contemporary women. Affiliated with the United

Methodist Church, the college is nonsectarian. The 100-acre campus is located in a city of 70,000, in the foothills of the Blue Ridge Mountains, 110 miles west of Richmond. Most convenient major airport: Lynchburg.

Founded: 1891
Affiliation: Independent (United Methodist)
UG Enrollment: 653 W (full-time); 2 M, 54 W (part-time)
Cost: $10K–$20K
% Receiving Financial Aid: 50%
Admission: Selective (+)
Application Deadline: March 1

Admission is selective (+). About 88% of applicants accepted, 28% of these actually enroll; 58% of freshmen graduate in top fifth of high school class, 83% in top two-fifths. Average freshman scores: SAT, 502 verbal, 517 mathematical; 48% of freshman score above 500 on verbal, 17% above 600, 2% above 700; 62% score above 500 on mathematical, 17% above 600, 2% above 700; ACT 25 W, composite. *Required:* SAT or ACT; interview and campus visit recommended. Criteria considered in admissions, in order of importance: high school academic record, standardized test scores, recommendations, writing sample, extracurricular activities; other factors considered: special talents, diverse student body. *Entrance programs:* early decision, early admission, midyear admission, deferred admission, Prime Time (for women returning to complete degree after interruption in education). About 27% of entering students from private and parochial schools. *Apply* by March 1(for preferential consideration); rolling admissions. *Transfers* welcome; 34 W enrolled in 1993–94.

Academic Environment. Administration source characterizes student body as almost equally concerned with social activities and scholarly/intellectual pursuits. Core requirements include skills (English composition, mathematics, foreign language, and colloquium); distribution (literature or rhetoric, fine arts, history, philosophy or religion, social or behavioral sciences, and natural sciences); and dimension (study of women, cultural, intellectual or social tradition of U.S., European countries, and non-European countries); many courses satisfy more than one of the general education requirements. College prides itself on traditional symbols of academic excellence: small classes, low student-faculty ratio (10 to 1 in recent years), strong liberal arts sequences, and the like. Degrees offered: bachelors. *Majors offered* include museum studies, art history, studio art, dance, Russian studies, theater, interdepartmental majors in American studies, Asian studies, Classical Civilization, education/psychology, urban studies, international studies of Third World areas which includes funds for visiting scholars and for student and faculty research/travel/study abroad in Third World areas. Average undergraduate class size: 77% under 20, 21% between 20–40, 2% over 40.

About 64% of students entering as freshmen graduate in four years, 66% eventually; 78% of freshmen return for sophomore year. *Special programs:* CLEP, Experiential Learning (internships for academic credit), independent study, study abroad, honors, undergraduate research, 3-year degree, individualized majors, Seven College Exchange Program, cross-registration with Sweet Briar and Lynchburg, Washington Semester, United Nations Semester, self-scheduled examinations under honor study system, individual summer study projects for credit, Spring Semester American Culture Program, study at Classical center in Athens, Near Eastern archaeological seminar, junior year at U. of Reading, England, 3–2 cooperative programs in nursing, occupational therapy, public health, engineering. Adult programs: Prime Time Program is designed for women of non-traditional age, offering part and full-time programs. *Calendar:* semester.

Undergraduate degrees conferred (124). 32% were in Social Sciences, 17% were in Letters, 16% were in Visual and Performing Arts, 6% were in Communications, 6% were in Psychology, 5% were in Mathematics, 5% were in Life Sciences, 4% were in Education, 3% were in Physical Sciences, 3% were in Foreign Languages, remainder in Area and Ethnic Studies.

Graduates Career Data. Advanced studies pursued by 35% of students; 2% enter medical or dental school; 3% enter law school. About 50% of 1992–93 graduates employed. Fields typically hiring largest numbers of graduates include banking, law, government, medical/health services, education. Career Development Services include a comprehensive interest and career assessment, centralized credit-bearing internships program, graduate school application assistance, job search assistance, on-campus recruiting, job fairs, alumni networking.

Faculty. About 95% of full-time faculty hold PhD or equivalent. About 48% of teaching faculty are female; 3% minority.

Student Body. College seeks a national student body; 39% of students from Virginia; 5% New England, 65% South, 10% Middle Atlantic, 8% Midwest, 5% West, 2% South; 6% Foreign. An estimated 61% of students reported as Protestant, 18% Catholic, 1% Jewish, 1% Muslim, 1% other, 18% unaffiliated; 5% as Black, 3% Hispanic, 7% Asian, 1% other minority.

Varsity Sports. Women (Div.III): Basketball, Equestrian, Field Hockey, Soccer, Swimming, Tennis, Volleyball.

Campus Life. Full schedule of cultural activities provided by college. Campus includes The Maier Museum of Art, which houses an impressive collection of American art, the Thoresen Theatre, and 100-acre Riding Center. The campus is within an hour's drive of more than 28,000 college students at 6 schools in the surrounding area. Student leader characterized rules governing student conduct as very free. No curfew; limited visitation hours for freshwomen. Alcohol permitted for those of legal age. Smoking limited to designated areas. Cars allowed. Students required to live in college dormitories. About 83% of women live in traditional dormitories; rest commute. There are no sororities. "Many students leave the campus on weekends," according to a current student.

Annual Costs. Tuition and fees, $13,320; room and board, $5,780; estimated $940 other, exclusive of travel. About 50% of students receive need-based financial aid; average amount of assistance, $14,013. Assistance is typically divided 60% scholarship/grant, 28% loan, 12% work. College reports 25 scholarships awarded for academic merit for Fall 1993 freshmen. *Meeting Costs:* college offers various loan and budget payment plans.

University of Redlands

Redlands, California 92373-0999 (714) 793-2121

The University of Redlands characterizes itself as independent after a long history of association with the American Baptist Church. Its continuing concern with ethical values in education is demonstrated by the establishment of the Jameson Center for the Study of Religion and Ethics. The university includes the Johnston Center for Individualized Learning in which students construct their own majors. Founded in 1969 as Johnston College, an experimental college within the university, the Center is now a division of the university. The Alfred North Whitehead College of Liberal Arts and Career Studies serves a "new constituency of older students." Most convenient major airport: Ontario.

Founded: 1907
Affiliation: Independent
UG Enrollment: 610 M, 617 W (full-time); 37 M, W (part-time)
Total Enrollment: 3,583
Cost: $10K–$20K
Admission: Selective (+)
Application Deadline: February 1

Admission is selective (+). About 79% of applicants accepted, 38% of these actually enroll; 48% of freshmen graduate in top fifth of high school class, 69% in top two- fifths. Average freshman scores, according to most recent data available; SAT, 514 M, 509 W verbal, 560 M, 532 W mathematical; ACT, 24 M, 24 W composite. *Required:* SAT or ACT; interview recommended (on- or off-campus. *Non-academic factors* considered in admissions: special talents, alumni children, diverse student body, community service, high school leadership. *Entrance programs:* midyear admission, advanced placement, deferred admission, guest student/honors at entrance. About 20% of entering students from private schools, 13% from parochial schools. *Apply* by February 1. *Transfers* welcome.

Academic Environment. Students have a role in campus decision making and participate in faculty selection and evaluation. A core of required courses "emphasizes writing and quantitative skills and values exploration (personal commitment, social priorities, and the like)." Johnston Center offers opportunity for independent study of various kinds. *Degrees:* BA, BS, BM. *Majors offered* include usual arts and sciences, accounting, communicative disorders, computer science, engineering, international relations, group majors also possible. New programs added include Asian Studies, a variety of off-campus study programs.

About 61% of students entering as freshmen graduate eventually; 25% of freshmen do not return for sophomore year. *Special pro-*

grams: CLEP, independent study, study abroad, honors, undergraduate research, credit by examination, Washington Semester, exchange with foreign institutions, and with Eastern colleges, branch campus in Salzburg, Austria, Exploratory Studies program remains strong for freshmen who have not settled on career goals (taught by leading faculty), Johnston Center for Individualized Learning, Proudian Interdisciplinary Studies Program. *Calendar:* 4–1–4.

Undergraduate degrees conferred (742). 59% were in Business and Management, 9% were in Social Sciences, 5% were in Liberal/General Studies, 5% were in Education, 4% were in Visual and Performing Arts, 3% were in Psychology, 3% were in Letters, 3% were in Health Sciences, 3% were in Multi/Interdisciplinary Studies, remainder in 8 other fields.

Faculty. About 75% of faculty hold doctorate or equivalent.

Student Body. University seeks a national student body; 58% of students from California; 74% from West. An estimated 40% of students reported as Protestant, 25% Catholic, 3% Jewish, 30% unaffiliated, 1% other; 4% Black, 6% Hispanic, 9% Asian, 7% other minority or unknown, according to most recent data available. *Minority group students:* special financial, academic, and social provisions.

Religious Orientation. Redlands is an independent institution, makes no religious demands on students. Religious clubs on campus include Intervarsity, Newman, Mormon, Canterbury, Christian Science; religious activities coordinated by the Jameson Center for the Study of Religion and Ethics. Places of worship available in immediate community for Catholics and Protestants, 10 minutes away for Jews.

Varsity Sports. Men (Div.III): Baseball, Basketball, Cross Country, Diving, Football, Golf, Soccer, Swimming, Tennis, Track, Water Polo. Women (Div.III): Basketball, Cross Country, Diving, Golf, Soccer, Swimming, Tennis, Track, Volleyball.

Campus Life. Students reported to have virtually complete control over campus social life. Intervisitation hours set by each residence unit. Many lifestyles available in dormitory living. Student leader comments that "the two aspects students here appreciate most about Redlands are its small size and the personalized education. Faculty take a lot of time with students and are available to them outside of the classroom." Alcohol permitted for those over 21, in conformity with state law. Smoking not allowed in public areas. Cars allowed. Housing guaranteed for all who ask.

About 7% of men, 14% of women live in traditional dormitories; 80% of men, 80% of women live in coed dormitories; 12% of men, 6% of women live in off-campus housing or commute. Freshmen given preference in college housing if all students cannot be accommodated. Sexes segregated in coed dormitories either by wing, floor, or suite. There are 5 fraternities, 4 sororities on campus which about 8% of men, 8% of women join. About 20–25% of students leave campus on weekends.

Annual Costs. Tuition and fees, $15,760; room and board, $5,999. About 70% of students receive financial aid; assistance is typically divided 69% scholarship, 20% loan, 20% work. University reports some scholarships awarded on the basis of academic merit alone. *Meeting Costs:* university offers loans, referral services.

Reed College

Portland, Oregon 97202

(503) 777-7511 or (800) 547-4750

One of the national liberal arts colleges, widely reputed for its academic excellence and attracting students from every section of the country. Reed involved students in governance of the college community for many years before other institutions moved in that direction. The 100-acre campus is located in a residential area of Portland (pop. 382,600), 5 miles from the center of the city. Most convenient major airport: Portland International.

Founded: 1909
Affiliation: Independent
UG Enrollment: 594 M, 605 W (full-time)
Cost: $10K–$20K
% Receiving Financial Aid: 45%
Admission: Most Selective
Application Deadline: Feb. 1

Admission is among the most selective in the country. About 73% of applicants accepted, 23% of these actually enroll; 58% of freshmen graduate in top fifth of high school class, 83% in top two-fifths. Average freshman scores: SAT, 613 M, 594 W verbal, 666 M, 601 W mathematical; 90% of freshmen score above 500 on verbal, 60% above 600, 12% above 700; 94% score above 500 on mathematical, 69% above 600, 25% above 700; ACT, 28 composite. *Required:* SAT or ACT, personal essay, two teacher recommendations and one counselor recommendation; 3 ACH recommended; interview preferred. Criteria considered in admissions, in order of importance: high school academic record; standardized test scores, recommendations, writing sample; extracurricular activities; other factors considered: "proven ability, motivation and discipline"; special talents, diverse student body "considered occasionally for borderline cases." *Entrance programs:* early decision, early admission, midyear admission, deferred admission. About 24% of entering students from private schools, 9% from parochial schools, according to most recent data available. *Apply* by February 1. *Transfers* welcome; 65 enrolled 1993–94.

Academic Environment. "The humanities program is the foundation of Reed's traditional academic structure." Required freshman course focuses on the literature, philosophy and history of western civilization. Students can continue this program during their second and third years. Study at Reed "culminates with the senior thesis, based on the student's major field of study." The thesis is a required year-long project, with a depth unusual in undergraduate study. Classes are usually small, 5 to 20, in seminar form. Administration asserts that "although the academic environment is rigorous, it is not competitive. Reed de-emphasizes grades." The norm is hard work and serious study, "but also kinship and mutual support." Despite these supports Reed is a challenging academic environment, 42% of those who enroll graduate in four years, 69% eventually, some 90% return for sophomore year. Graduates are regularly accepted by the top graduate schools. The single largest post-graduate route . . . has been a career in the academic world. With drop in faculty recruitment, however, more Reed students are seeking other career routes. This accounts for some of the transfers to other institutions and for the interest in 3–2 programs in computer science, engineering, forestry/environmental studies, visual arts. Administration reports 55% of general education courses required for graduation are elective; distribution requirements fairly numerous: freshman course in introduction to humanities, year each in literature/philosophy/arts, history/social sciences, natural sciences, mathematics/foreign language/logic, and 3 semesters physical education; foreign language proficiency recommended, but required only in certain departments. Degrees offered: bachelors, masters. *Majors offered* include anthropology, theater linguistics; 12 interdisciplinary majors include chemistry/physics, international studies, American studies, medieval studies; special programs can also be designed. Average undergraduate class size: 91% under 25, 9% over 25.

Special programs: independent study, study abroad, undergraduate research, 3-year degree, January period for unstructured independent study, combined programs: forestry with Duke, joint course with Northwest School of Art, engineering with Caltech, Columbia, RPI, computer science with U. of Washington, applied physics with Oregon Graduate Center, business with U. of Chicago, interdisciplinary seminars. *Calendar:* semester.

Undergraduate degrees conferred (285). 20% were in Social Sciences, 16% were in Letters, 15% were in Life Sciences, 11% were in Physical Sciences, 8% were in Philosophy and Religion, 7% were in Multi/Interdisciplinary Studies, 6% were in Mathematics, 6% were in Psychology, 5% were in Foreign Languages, 4% were in Visual and Performing Arts, remainder in Area and Ethnic Studies.

Graduates Career Data. Advanced studies pursued immediately after graduation by 40% of students, 60% within 2 years after graduation; 5% enter medical school; 1% enter dental school; 5% enter law school; 5% enter business school. Medical schools typically enrolling largest numbers of graduates include Stanford; law schools include Harvard; business schools include U. of Chicago. About 40% of 1992–93 graduates employed. Fields typically hiring largest numbers of graduates include business, education. Career Development Services include individual and group career counseling, placement service, internships, resume/interview workshops, library resources.

Faculty. About 75% of faculty hold PhD or equivalent. About 31% of teaching faculty are female; 3% minority.

Student Body. College seeks a national student body; 20% of students from Northeast, 20% Northwest, 39% West, 13% Midwest, 4% South; 4% Foreign. An estimated 1% of students reported as Black, 4% Hispanic, 9% Asian, 10 other minority.

Campus Life. Student life at Reed has always been unstructured and student-directed. There is a unique sense of community on campus among those who have found this to be "their school." Student body is extremely diverse with representatives from every state and many foreign countries. Some students are critical of the rigorous academic emphasis which influences social life significantly. Others charge that Reed is only "an island of thought" without contact with the "real world outside." Some who nod in agreement are likely to be unhappy, but many others are more than willing to seek out the "island of thought" and the rich academic experience it offers. Prospective applicants are warned by student information bulletins to expect social life to be limited to campus for the most part. Seattle and San Francisco are the weekend retreats when studies allow. Intervisitation unlimited, determination of hours made by residents of dorm. Public drinking prohibited on campus. College permits any student, including freshmen, to live off campus.

About 5% of women live in traditional dormitories; 50% of men, 45% of women live in coed dormitories; rest live in off-campus housing or commute. Freshmen given preference in college housing if all students cannot be accommodated. Sexes segregated in coed dormitories either by floor or room. There are no fraternities or sororities. About 5% of resident students leave campus on weekends.

Annual Costs. Tuition and fees, $19,250; room and board, $5,230; estimated $950 other, exclusive of travel. About 45% of students receive need-based financial aid; average amount of assistance, $16,500. Assistance is typically divided 83% grant, 15% loan, 2% work. College reports scholarships awarded only on the basis of need.

Regis University

Denver, Colorado 80221-1099 **(303) 458-4900 or (800) 388-2366**

A church-related college of arts and sciences, conducted by the Society of Jesus, Regis is located in a residential area of Denver (pop. 1.5 million). Most convenient major airport: Stapleton International.

Founded: 1877
Affiliation: Roman Catholic
UG Enrollment: 493 M, 533 W (full-time)
Total Enrollment: 1,135
Cost: $10K–$20K
Admission: Non-selective
Application Deadline: Aug. 15

Admission. Graduates of approved high schools with 15 academic units eligible; 82% of applicants accepted, 34% of these actually enroll. Average freshman scores: SAT, 442 M, 442 W verbal, 497 M, 477 W mathematical; 24% of freshmen score above 500 verbal, 8% above 600, 2% above 700; 45% of freshmen score above 500 mathematical, 14% above 600, 3% above 700; ACT, 21 M, 22 W composite. *Required:* SAT or ACT, minimum H.S. GPA, essay, H.S. recommendations. Criteria considered in admissions, in order of importance: high school academic record and standardized test scores, recommendations and writing sample; other factors considered: special talents, diverse student body. About 43% of entering students from private schools. *Apply* by August 15; rolling admissions. *Transfers* welcome; 143 enrolled 1993–94.

Academic Environment. Degrees offered: bachelors, masters. *Majors offered* include administrative sciences, computer science, humanities, natural sciences, philosophy, religious studies, social sciences, nursing, dance. About 50% of general education requirements for graduation are elective; distribution requirements fairly numerous. About 50% of students entering as freshmen graduate eventually, according to most recent data available. Average undergraduate class size: 30. *Special programs:* CLEP, independent study, study abroad, honors, individualized majors, 3–2 engineering, internships, January term, cooperative program with 2 other nonpublic Denver institutions: Loretto Heights, Colorado Women's College, Freshman Success Program for high test scorers with low GPA. Adult programs: offered through the School for Professional Studies. *Calendar:* semester, summer school.

Undergraduate degrees conferred (903). 61% were in Business and Management, 14% were in Computer and Engineering Related Technology, 8% were in Health Sciences, 3% were in Social Sciences, 3% were in Communications, remainder in 16 other fields.

Faculty. About 90% of faculty hold PhD or equivalent. About 37% of teaching faculty are female.

Student Body. An estimated 4% of students reported as Black, 7% Hispanic, 2% Asian, 9% other minority. Average age of undergraduate student: 22.

Religious Orientation. Regis is a church-related institution; 9 hours of religious studies, 6 hours of philosophy required of all students. Places of worship available on campus for Catholics, in immediate community for Protestants and Jews.

Varsity Sports. Men (NAIA): Baseball, Basketball, Golf, Soccer, Tennis, Volleyball. Women (Div.II): Basketball, Golf, Soccer, Softball, Tennis, Volleyball.

Campus Life. About 50% of students live in coed dormitories; rest live in off-campus housing or commute. Freshmen given preference in college housing if all students cannot be accommodated. Intervisitation in men's and women's dormitory rooms limited. About 50% of resident students leave campus on weekends.

Annual Costs. Tuition and fees, $11,980; room and board, $5,500; estimated $1,900, exclusive of travel. *Meeting Costs:* college offers monthly payment plans.

Regis College

Weston, Massachusetts 02193 **(617) 893-1820**

A church-related, liberal arts college for women, conducted by the Sisters of St. Joseph, Regis is located in a town of 10,900, 12 miles west of Boston. Most convenient major airport: Logan International (Boston).

Founded: 1927
Affiliation: Independent (Roman Catholic)
UG Enrollment: 769 W (full-time); 376 W (part-time)
Cost: $10K–$20K
% Receiving Financial Aid: 66%
Admission: Non-selective
Application Deadline: Rolling

Admission. Graduates of accredited high schools with 12 academic units in college preparatory program eligible; others given consideration; 85% of applicants accepted, 47% of these actually enroll. About 27% of freshmen graduate in top fifth of high school class, 60% in top two-fifths. *Required:* SAT; interview recommended. *Non-academic factors* considered in admissions: special talents, diverse student body, alumni children, leadership and volunteer service. *Apply:* rolling admissions. *Transfers* welcome.

Academic Environment. College offers cross-registration with Babson, Bentley, and Boston colleges. Administration reports distribution requirements in natural and social sciences, fine arts, literature, philosophy or religious studies, writing, and foreign language. *Degree:* AB. *Majors offered* include usual arts and sciences. Students cite small classes, individualized attention, and the numerous opportunities for internships as the greatest strengths of the academic program.

About 74% of students entering as freshmen graduate eventually; 18% of freshmen do not return for sophomore year. *Special programs:* independent study, study abroad, undergraduate research, honors, individualized majors, field experiences in social work and psychology, Washington Semester, 2 upper-level seminars, interdisciplinary program on Africa, Asia, and Latin America, European studies (including colloquia, lecture programs, study trip abroad), 3–2 programs in science and engineering with Worcester Polytechnic Institute, Sisters of St. Joseph 12-college student exchange consortium. *Calendar:* 4–1–4.

Undergraduate degrees conferred (229). 22% were in Social Sciences, 19% were in Business and Management, 12% were in Communications, 7% were in Visual and Performing Arts, 7% were in Psychology, 7% were in Letters, 7% were in Life Sciences, 6% were in Foreign Languages, 4% were in Health Sciences, 3% were in Public Affairs, 3% were in Physical Sciences, remainder in 2 other fields.

Graduates Career Data. According to most recent data available, full-time graduate or professional study pursued immediately after graduation by 10% of students. *Careers in business and industry* pursued by 50% of graduates.

Faculty. About 83% of faculty hold PhD or equivalent.

Student Body. College seeks a national student body; 80% of students from in state; 89% of students from New England, 5% Middle Atlantic. An estimated 84% of students reported as Catholic, 9% Protestant, 1% Jewish, 3% unaffiliated; 2% Black, 8% Hispanic, 4%

Asian. *Minority group students:* financial, academic, social aid available; special faculty adviser.

Religious Orientation. Regis is a church-related institution. Administration reports no religious clubs on campus but notes that college is affiliated with Campus Ministry. Places of worship available on campus for Catholics, in immediate community for major faiths.

Varsity Sports. Women (Div.III): Basketball, Cross Country, Soccer, Softball, Swimming & Diving, Tennis, Volleyball.

Campus Life. A current student reports that, "location is great, close to all the advantages of Boston, but in a peaceful, quiet setting." Students have some voice in determining policies governing campus social life.

About 64% of women live in dormitories; rest commute. There are no sororities on campus.

Annual Costs. Tuition and fees, $11,850; room and board, $5,600. About 66% of students receive financial aid. *Meeting Costs:* college offers various prepayment and budget plans and loans.

Rensselaer Polytechnic Institute

Troy, New York 12180-3590 (518) 276-6216

The nation's oldest engineering and technological institution, RPI, a co-educational school throughout its long history, now enrolls significant numbers of women. The Institute offers more than 110 undergraduate and graduate degree programs in five schools— Architecture, Engineering, Humanities and Social Sciences, Management, and Sciences— as well as in several interdisciplinary areas. The 260-acre main campus is located on a plateau overlooking the city of Troy (pop. 62,900) and the Hudson River, 150 miles north of New York City. Most convenient major airport: Albany.

Founded: 1824
Affiliation: Independent
UG Enrollment: 3,427 M, 864 W (full-time)
Cost: $10K–$20K
% Receiving Financial Aid: 80%
Admission: Highly (+) Selective
Application Deadline: Jan. 15

Admission is highly (+) selective. For all schools, 83% of applicants accepted, 22% of these actually enroll; 53% of freshmen graduate in top tenth of high school class, 76% in top fifth. Average freshman scores: SAT, middle fifty percent range, 1,080–1,280 combined verbal-mathematical; ACT, middle fifty percent range, 26–30 composite; generally rank in top 3% on national tests of mathematical aptitude. *Required:* SAT or ACT; 3 ACH (English, mathematics I or II, chemistry or physics) recommended. Criteria considered in admissions, in order of importance: high school academic record, standardized test scores, extracurricular activities, recommendations, writing sample; other factors considered: special talents, diverse student body, alumni children. *Entrance programs:* early decision, midyear admission, advanced placement, deferred admission. About 20% of entering students from private schools, 15% from parochial schools, according to most recent data available. *Apply* by January 15. *Transfers* welcome.

Academic Environment. Quality of student body remains high and pressures for academic achievement intense. Some student concern for improvement of counseling and advising. Substantial number of course offerings in humanities and social sciences, supplemented by cross-registration with Union, Albany Medical College, Russell Sage, Skidmore, among others. Freshmen and sophomores in most curricula take 4 courses in mathematics, 6 courses in sciences, 9 credit hours in humanities and 9 in social sciences; all students take 3 semesters physical education or ROTC. A small but significant number of graduates enter medical and graduate business schools. Degrees offered: bachelors, masters, doctoral. *Majors offered* include nuclear science, computer science, 14 fields of engineering, architecture, building sciences, management. Six-year dual degree programs offered in medicine, dentistry and law.

About 70% of students entering as freshmen graduate within four years; 87% of freshmen return for sophomore year. *Special programs:* credit by examination, study abroad, dual degree programs, 3–2 in engineering, 6-year combined BS/MD program with Albany Medical College and BS/JD program with Albany Law School, BS/DMD with U. of Pennsylvania, affiliated program in engineering with liberal arts colleges, cooperative work/study program with industry (in engineering, management, science), RAMP (Rensselaer Accelerated Master's Program), programs of Hudson-Mohawk Consortium. Adult programs: executive MBA. *Calendar:* semester, summer school.

Undergraduate degrees conferred (963). 63% were in Engineering, 8% were in Business and Management, 7% were in Physical Sciences, 7% were in Computer and Engineering Related Technology, 5% were in Life Sciences, 5% were in Architecture and Environmental Design, remainder in 6 other fields.

Graduates Career Data. Advanced studies pursued by 18% of students. About 54% of 1992–93 graduates employed. Corporations typically hiring largest numbers of graduates include IBM, General Electric, Arthur Andersen, Northern Telecom. Career Development Services include individual counseling, career exploration seminars, job search technique presentations, on-campus recruitment by over 355 organizations from the public and private sectors.

Faculty. About 92% of faculty hold PhD or equivalent.

Student Body. Institute seeks a national student body; 40% of students from in state; 43% of students from Middle Atlantic, 24% New England, according to most recent data available. An estimated 4% of students reported as Black, 5% Hispanic, 14% Asian.

Varsity Sports. Men (Div.III): Baseball, Basketball, Cross Country, Diving, Football, Golf, Hockey(I), Lacrosse, Soccer, Swimming, Tennis, Track. Women (Div.III): Basketball, Cross Country, Diving, Field Hockey, Golf, Lacrosse, Soccer, Softball, Swimming, Tennis, Track.

Campus Life. Almost all areas of student life "now are handled by dormitory and fraternity self-government." Intervisitation hours decided by vote of residence hall or floor. Alcohol permitted in dormitories; smoking restricted; all students allowed cars. Social and cultural events on campus supplemented by active schedule sponsored by neighboring Russell Sage as well as by the tri-city community. Still some student concern reported about lack of diversity in student activities.

About two-thirds of undergraduate students live on campus; upperclass men and women may live in off-campus apartments. Freshmen given preference in college housing if all students cannot be accommodated. Sexes segregated in coed dormitories by floor or room. There are 30 fraternities, 5 sororities on campus which about 42% of men, 42% of women join; 18% of men, 2% of women live in fraternities and sororities. About 5% of resident students leave campus on weekends.

Annual Costs. Tuition and fees, $17,325; room and board, $5,742; estimated $1,183 other, exclusive of travel. About 80% of students receive financial aid; average amount of assistance, $13,000. Institute reports 100 scholarships awarded for academic merit, the rest for need. *Meeting Costs:* Institute offers monthly payment plan.

Research College of Nursing

Kansas City, Missouri 64110 (816) 926-4100

A church-related college of nursing offering the BSN degree in a joint program with Rockhurst College. Most convenient major airport: Kansas City International.

Founded: 1979
Affiliation: Roman Catholic
UG Enrollment: 24 M, 252 W (full-time)
Cost: < $10K
% Receiving Financial Aid: 90%
Admission: Non-selective
Application Deadline: Rolling

Admission. About 87% of applicants accepted, 54% of these actually enroll; 46% of freshmen graduate in top fifth of high school class, 75% in top two-fifths. Average freshman ACT scores: 22.6 composite. *Required:* SAT or ACT, high school courses in chemistry, algebra II. Criteria considered in admissions, in order of importance: high school academic record, standardized test scores, recommendations, extracurricular activities. About 45% of entering students from private schools. *Apply:* rolling admissions. *Transfers* welcome; 50 enrolled 1993–94.

Academic Environment. Graduation requirements include 69 hours in humanities, philosophy, theology, and social and natural sciences. Degrees offered: bachelors. Average undergraduate class size: 85% under 20, 10% 20–40, 5% over 40. *Special programs:* study abroad, accelerated degree for students with previous bachelors. *Calendar:* semester, summer school.

Graduates Career Data. All 1992–93 graduates are employed. Career Development Services offered.
Faculty. About 33% of faculty hold PhD or equivalent. About 90% of undergraduate classes taught by tenured faculty. About 98% of teaching faculty are female; less than 1% minority.
Student Body. About 90% of students from in state; all from Midwest. An estimated 50% of students reported as Protestant, 47% Catholic, 3% other; 4% Black, 5% Hispanic, 9% other minority.
Religious Orientation. Research College of Nursing is a Catholic institution; 4 courses in religious studies required.
Varsity Sports. Men (NAIA II): Baseball, Basketball, Cross Country, Soccer. Women (NAIA II): Basketball, Cross Country, Soccer, Volleyball.
Campus Life. About 60% of students live in traditional dormitories; no coed dormitories; rest commute. There are 4 fraternities and 2 sororities on campus. About 40% of resident students leave campus on weekends.
Annual Costs. Tuition and fees, $9,430; room and board, $4,020; estimated $1,500 other, exclusive of travel. About 90% of students receive financial aid; assistance is typically divided 50% scholarship/grant, 30% loan, 20% work.

Rhode Island College

Providence, Rhode Island 02908 (401) 456-8234

A state-supported, liberal arts, and teacher education institution, located in a city of 179,200. Most convenient major airport: Providence.

Founded: 1854
Affiliation: State
UG Enrollment: 1,725 M, 3,176 W (full-time); 920 M, 1,703 W (part-time)
Total Enrollment: 9,690
Cost: < $10K
% Receiving Financial Aid: 60%
Admission: Non-selective
Application Deadline: May 1

Admission. About 69% of applicants accepted, 59% of these actually enroll; 29% of freshmen graduate in top fifth of high school class, 65% in top two-fifths. *Required:* SAT, 18 college preparatory units. *Non-academic factors* considered in admissions: special talents, diverse student body. *Out-of-state* freshman applicants: college welcomes students from out of state. State does not limit out-of-state enrollment. Requirement for out-of-state applicants: must be equal in ability to average in-state students; 62% of applicants accepted, 44% enroll. *Apply* by May 1. *Transfers* welcome.
Academic Environment. Curriculum includes 2 options in 8-course general education requirement: (1) with colloquia and seminars, including special focus on 1 of 3 general areas, or (2) broad range of choices among traditional electives plus 1 colloquium. *Degrees:* AB, BS, BGS. *Majors offered* include usual arts and sciences, anthropology, education, medical technology, industrial technology, theater, justice studies. Center for Industrial Technology recently added.

About 50% of students entering as freshmen graduate eventually; 25% of freshmen do not return for sophomore year. *Special programs:* CLEP, undergraduate research, independent study, study abroad, honors, individualized majors, social service program, field study for credit. Adult programs: performance-based admissions for older, non-traditional students. *Calendar:* semester, summer school.
Undergraduate degrees conferred (981). 23% were in Education, 13% were in Letters, 12% were in Business and Management, 12% were in Psychology, 8% were in Social Sciences, 7% were in Health Sciences, 5% were in Visual and Performing Arts, 4% were in Computer and Engineering Related Technology, 3% were in Public Affairs, 3% were in Marketing and Distribution, 3% were in Engineering and Engineering Related Technology, remainder in 8 other fields.
Graduates Career Data. According to most recent data available, full-time graduate or professional study pursued immediately after graduation by 15% of students. *Careers in business and industry* pursued by 31% of graduates.
Faculty. About 71% of faculty hold PhD or equivalent.
Student Body. College does not seek a national student body; 94% of students from in state; 99% of students from New England. An estimated 70% of students reported as Catholic, 15% Protestant, 1% Jewish, 5% other, 9% unaffiliated; 2% as Black, 1% Hispanic, 2% Asian, according to most recent data available. *Minority group students:* special financial and academic provisions including Talent Search, Upward Bound, Student Development; Urban Educational Center located in Providence.
Varsity Sports. Men (Div.III): Baseball, Basketball, Cross Country, Soccer, Tennis, Track, Wrestling. Women (Div.III): Basketball, Cross Country, Fencing, Gymnastics, Softball, Tennis, Track, Volleyball.
Campus Life. Student leader observes that "RIC is a commuter campus and as such there is little community feeling here. In many ways RIC is a very good school. It offers its students a lot if they care to take the opportunity."

About 7% of women live in traditional dormitories; 8% of men, 4% of women live in coed dormitories; rest live in off-campus housing or commute. Freshmen given preference in college housing if all students cannot be accommodated. Sexes segregated in coed dormitories either by wing or room. There is 1 fraternity, 2 sororities on campus which about 2% of men, 2% of women join.
Annual Costs. Tuition and fees, $2,601 (out-of-state, $6,739); room and board, $5,210. About 60% of students (75% of financial aid applicants) receive financial aid; assistance is typically divided 50% grants, 25% loan, 25% work. College reports some scholarships awarded on the basis of academic merit alone.

Rhode Island School of Design

Providence, Rhode Island 02903 (401) 454-6305

An independent, professional school, located in a city of 179,200, offering 18 degree programs in a full range of fine arts, architecture, and design disciplines, as well as masters degrees in 11 areas. Most convenient major airports: T.F. Green (Warwick), or Logan (Boston, MA).

Founded: 1877
Affiliation: Independent
UG Enrollment: 840 M, 1,004 W (full-time)
Total Enrollment: 1,990
Cost: $10K–$20K
% Receiving Financial Aid: 63%
Admission: Very Selective
Application Deadline: February 15

Admission is very selective. About 46% of applicants accepted, 21% of these actually enroll. About 34% of freshmen graduate in top fifth of high school class, 64% in top two-fifths. Average freshman SAT scores: 513 M, 503 W verbal, 564 M, 541 W mathematical; 53% of freshmen score above 500 on verbal, 14% above 600, 2% score above 700; 72% score above 500 on mathematical, 33% above 600, 9% above 700. *Required:* SAT or ACT, essay, portfolio and drawing assignment. Criteria considered in admissions, in order of importance: high school academic record and portfolio, personal essay, standardized test scores, extracurricular activities, recommendations; other factors considered: special talents, alumni children. *Entrance programs:* early action, deferred admission. About 35% of entering students from private schools, 5% from parochial schools. *Apply* by February 15. *Transfers* welcome; 156 enrolled 1993–94.
Academic Environment. Degrees offered: bachelors, masters. Undergraduate degrees granted by divisions of Architectural Studies, Design, Fine Arts, and Illustration and Photographic Studies. General education requirements include 42 of the 126 credits required for graduation. Administration reports the reason students transfer elsewhere is that they "want more liberal arts."

About 85% of students entering as freshmen graduate in four years; 96% of freshmen return for sophomore year. *Special programs:* individualized majors, study abroad, cooperative arrangement with Brown, East Coast Consortium of Art Colleges, Mobility Program with 12 other U.S. art schools, international exchange programs. *Calendar:* semester, 6-week winter session, summer school.
Undergraduate degrees conferred (521). 60% were in Visual and Performing Arts, 32% were in Architecture and Environmental Design, 8% were in Home Economics.
Graduates Career Data. Advanced studies pursued by 5% of students. Corporations typically hiring largest numbers of graduates include design studios, publishing houses, corporate art departments. Career Development Services include weekly full-time and free lance job letter, monthly bulletin of internships, seminars addressing specific issues for art/design careers, on-campus recruitment, library resource of materials.

Faculty. About 70% of faculty hold PhD or equivalent. About 40% of teaching faculty are female; 5% minority.
Student Body. About 31% of students from Middle Atlantic, 22% New England, 12% South, 6% Midwest, 13% West/Northwest; 16% Foreign. An estimated 3% of students reported as Black, 3% Hispanic, 8% Asian, according to most recent data available. Average age of undergraduate student: 23.
Campus Life. Campus is 40 miles from Boston, near the ocean and Newport. Freshmen not allowed to have cars on-campus; no parking provided for students. No regulations concerning women's dorm hours, intervisitation. Smoking not allowed in classrooms and studios; alcohol not allowed on campus. No varsity sports, but high interest reported in intramurals, most popular: hockey, volleyball.

According to most recent data available about 30% each of men, women live in coed dormitories; rest live in off-campus housing or commute. Freshmen given preference in college housing if all students cannot be accommodated. Intervisitation in men's and women's dormitory rooms unlimited. There are no fraternities or sororities on campus. About 10% of resident students leave campus on weekends.
Annual Costs. Tuition and fees, $15,815; room and board, $6,415; estimated $1,000 other, exclusive of travel. About 63% of students receive financial aid. School reports some scholarships awarded on the basis of academic merit alone. *Meeting Costs:* college offers various payment plans.

University of Rhode Island

Kingston, Rhode Island 02881 **(401) 792-9800**

A state land- and sea-grant school, the University of Rhode Island is located on a 1,200-acre main campus in the village of Kingston, situated between Boston and New York in New England's hub of education and research. The University includes 3 other campuses in Providence, Narragansett, and West Greenwich. Most convenient major airport: Green (Warwick).

Founded: 1892
Affiliation: State
UG Enrollment: 4,232 M, 4,662 W (full-time); 1,012 M, 1,444 W (part-time)
Total Enrollment: 14,925
Cost: < $10K
% Receiving Financial Aid: 66%
Admission: Selective
Application Deadline: March 1

Admission is selective. About 75% of applicants accepted, 27% of these actually enroll; 30% of freshmen graduate in top fifth of high school class, 60% in top two-fifths. Average freshman scores: SAT, 456 M, 453 W verbal, 531 M, 495 W mathematical; ACT, 23 M, 23 W. *Required:* SAT or ACT; interview recommended. Criteria considered in admissions, in order of importance: high school academic record, standardized test scores, extracurricular activities, recommendations; other factors considered: alumni children, special talents, diverse student body. *Out-of-state* freshman applicants: university actively seeks students from out-of-state. About 80% of applicants accepted, 34% of these actually enroll. States from which most out-of-state students are drawn include New Jersey, Connecticut, Massachusetts, New York, Pennsylvania. *Entrance programs:* early admission, midyear admission, advanced placement. About 8% of freshmen come from private schools, 12% from parochial schools. *Apply* by March 1; rolling admissions. *Transfers* welcome; 690 enrolled 1993–94.
Academic Environment. Distribution requirements include English, communications, mathematics, fine arts and literature, foreign language or culture, letters (values), natural and social sciences. Administration reports academic areas with "best reputation" are business administration, engineering, pharmacy, nursing, resource development, and marine related disciplines. Degrees offered: bachelors, masters, doctoral. Undergraduate and graduate studies offered in the university's 8 colleges and 3 schools: the colleges of Arts and Sciences, Business Administration, Engineering, Human Science and Services, Nursing, Pharmacy, and Resource Development; the University College, in which all freshmen and sophomores are enrolled for the first 2 years; the Graduate School, Graduate School of Library and Information Sciences, and Graduate School of Oceanography. Two- and four-year programs in Dental Hygiene. *Majors offered* include marine affairs, international engineering, pharmacy, materials engineering, physics and physical oceanography, chemistry and chemical oceanography. Current students report that there are many student-support services including counseling, tutoring, and "very helpful advisors". Average undergraduate class size: 25% under 20, 55% between 20–40, 20% over 40.

About 50% of entering freshmen graduate in four years; about 77% return for sophomore year. *Special programs:* CLEP, study abroad, off-campus study, University Year for Action, honors, internships, independent study, undergraduate research. *Calendar:* semester, summer sessions.
Undergraduate degrees conferred (2,261). 16% were in Business and Management, 13% were in Social Sciences, 12% were in Home Economics, 8% were in Education, 8% were in Communications, 8% were in Health Sciences, 7% were in Psychology, 7% were in Engineering, 4% were in Letters, 4% were in Life Sciences, remainder in 14 other fields.
Graduates Career Data. *Career Counseling Program* designed specifically for liberal arts students. Student assessment of program reported as good for both career guidance and job placement. Liberal arts majors urged to seek interviews with business/industry representatives who visit campus. Help provided in preparing for interviews. Alumni reported as helpful in both career guidance and job placement.
Faculty. About 86% of faculty hold PhD or equivalent. About 56% of undergraduate classes taught by tenured faculty. About 25% of teaching faculty are female; 9% minority.
Student Body. University seeks a national student body; 69% of students from in state. An estimated 3% of students reported as Black, 2% Hispanic, 3% Asian, 13% other.
Varsity Sports. Men (Div.I): Baseball, Basketball, Cross Country, Diving, Field Hockey, Football(IAA), Golf, Soccer, Swimming, Tennis, Track. Women (Div.I): Basketball, Cross Country, Diving, Field Hockey, Gymnastics, Soccer, Softball, Swimming, Tennis, Track, Volleyball.
Campus Life. Campus is located 30 miles south of Providence, 25 minutes from Newport, 6 miles from Narragansett Bay, close to Rhode Island's famed beaches. Options of dormitory residence life and/or rentals along Rhode Island beaches or in nearby towns. Alcohol allowed for those 21 and over. Cars allowed. Students can combine advantages of scenic rural campus with accessibility of major centers, beaches. Student leader reports "dorms are becoming out-of-date"; waiting time for medical treatment "is rather long"; but relations with faculty are "very good."

About 1% of women live in traditional dormitories; 34% of men, 39% of women live in coed dormitories; rest live in off-campus housing or commute. Freshmen given preference in college housing if all students cannot be accommodated. Sexes segregated in coed dormitories by wing, floor or room. There are 17 fraternities and 8 sororities on campus which about 20% of men, 15% of women join; 13% of men, 8% of women live in fraternities and sororities. About 25% of resident students leave campus on weekends.
Annual Costs. Tuition and fees, $3,882 (out-of-state, $9,728); room and board, $5,323; estimated $1,600 other, exclusive of travel. About 66% of students receive financial aid; average amount of assistance, $3,750. Assistance is typically divided 20% scholarship/grant, 60% loan, 20% work. University reports 286 scholarships awarded for academic merit, many for need.

Rhodes College

Memphis, Tennessee 38112 **(901) 726-3700 or (800) 844-5969**

A small, high quality, liberal arts college, affiliated with the Presbyterian Church (USA), Rhodes draws most of its students from the South, but desires to attract more students from other parts of the country. The 100-acre campus, which has 13 of its buildings listed on the National Register of Historic Places, is located in a metropolitan area of about 1 million. Most convenient major airport: Memphis International.

Founded: 1848
Affiliation: Presbyterian
UG Enrollment: 605 M, 731 W (full-time)
Cost: $10K–$20K
% Receiving Financial Aid: 67%
Admission: Very (+) Selective
Application Deadline: Feb. 1

Admission is very (+) selective. About 79% of applicants accepted, 21% of these actually enroll; 77% of freshmen graduate in top fifth of high school class, 93% in top two-fifths. Average freshman scores:

SAT, 86% of freshmen score above 500 on verbal, 41% above 600, 7% above 700; 94% score above 500 on mathematical, 61% above 600, 18% above 700. *Required:* SAT or ACT, essay. Criteria considered in admissions, in order of importance: high school academic record, standardized test scores, recommendations, writing sample, extracurricular activities; other factors considered: geographical distribution, diverse student body, special talents, leadership traits, minorities, alumni children. *Entrance programs:* early decision, early admission, midyear admission, deferred admission, advanced placement. About 35% of entering students from private or parochial schools. *Apply* by February 1. *Transfers* welcome; 22 enrolled 1993–94.

Academic Environment. Strong student-led Honor System is at the heart of academic life at Rhodes. Students have some influence on curriculum decision-making through membership on faculty committees. Considerable freedom allowed students in designing their own majors with faculty assistance; may also initiate their own independent study projects. Distribution requirements fairly numerous: core curriculum in 4 broad areas, 1 term in writing unless exempted by English department, 1 term of a foreign language at the intermediate level unless exempted, and 12 hours of interdisciplinary course "Search for Values in the Light of Western History & Religion" or 12 hours of selected religion and philosophy courses. For BA, core curriculum also includes 3 courses in humanities, 3 courses each in social sciences, natural sciences, and 2 courses in fine arts. Degrees offered: bachelors, masters. *Majors offered* include anthropology, computer science (with math or business), theatre & media arts, international studies, interdisciplinary majors, American studies, women's studies, Asian studies. Average undergraduate class size: 66% under 20, 31% between 20–40, 3% over 40.

About 72% of students entering as freshmen graduate in four years, 75% eventually; 86% of freshmen return for sophomore year. *Special programs:* independent study, study abroad, honors, undergraduate research, directed inquiry, tutorials, non-Western studies, interdisciplinary courses, Washington semester, Oak Ridge Science Semester, Washington Semester, courses through Gulf Coast Research Laboratory, cross registration with Memphis College of Art. *Calendar:* semester.

Undergraduate degrees conferred (289). 32% were in Social Sciences, 17% were in Business and Management, 11% were in Life Sciences, 8% were in Philosophy and Religion, 8% were in Letters, 8% were in Physical Sciences, 7% were in Psychology, 4% were in Visual and Performing Arts, remainder in 3 other fields.

Graduates Career Data. Advanced studies pursued within a year of graduation by 36% of students; 8% enter medical school; 6% enter law school; 2% enter business school. Medical schools typically enrolling largest numbers of graduates include U. of Tennessee, Vanderbilt, U. of Alabama-Birmingham; law schools include Vanderbilt, Emory U., U. of Virginia, Yale. About 63% of 1992–93 graduates employed. National corporations typically hiring largest numbers of graduates include IBM, Federal Express, Merrill Lynch, Schering-Plough. Career Development Services include a career library (including SIGI Plus), on-campus recruitment, credentials service, career counseling, job search strategies, graduate school options.

Faculty. About 99% of tenured or tenurable faculty hold PhD or equivalent. About 50% of undergraduate classes taught by tenured faculty. About 36% of teaching faculty are female; 4% minority.

Student Body. College seeks a national student body; 36% of students from in state; 87% South, 7% Midwest; 2% Foreign. An estimated 77% of students reported as Protestant, 15% Catholic, 1% Jewish, 5% unaffiliated, 2% other; 5% as Black, 3% Asian, less than 1% Hispanic.

Religious Orientation. As a church-related institution, Rhodes emphasizes strengthening of personal values and religious commitment as "central to its educational mission." Four courses in religion and philosophy required. In addition to religious clubs on campus, places of worship for all faiths available in the community.

Varsity Sports. Men (Div.III): Baseball, Basketball, Cross Country, Football, Golf, Soccer, Tennis, Track. Women (Div.III): Basketball, Cross Country, Soccer, Tennis, Track, Volleyball.

Campus Life. Student body has responsibility for governing its social and moral conduct on campus through Social Regulations Council. Variety of cultural activities provided on campus; resources of Memphis also easily accessible. Intervisitation permitted in some dorms, restricted in others so students have choice. Drinking by those of legal age is permitted in some, not all, locations on campus. Cars permitted. Students report a strong sense of community on campus.

About 72% of men, 81% of women live in traditional dormitories; no coed dormitories; rest live in off-campus housing or commute. Freshmen given preference in college housing if all students cannot be accommodated. There are 6 fraternities, 7 sororities on campus which about 58% of men, 57% women join. About 5% of resident students leave campus on weekends.

Annual Costs. Tuition and fees, $14,916; room and board, $4,708; estimated $1,290 other, exclusive of travel. About 67% of students receive financial aid; average amount of need-based award, $13,752. Assistance is typically divided 76% scholarship/grant, 20% loan, 4% work. College reports 403 scholarships awarded for academic merit alone, 32 special talents, 165 for need and merit, 418 for need alone. *Meeting Costs:* College offers several alternative financing options.

Rice University

Houston, Texas 77251 (800) 527-6957

Rice is an unusual institution. Located in a region that has not thus far produced colleges and universities of the first rank, it is one of the most selective institutions in the country. Although it is known primarily for its science and engineering programs, Rice also provides very strong programs in the liberal arts. Shepherd School of Music provides training in performing arts and conducting. Expansion in the arts parallels Houston's "cultural explosion," and studies in premedicine, biochemistry, and biomedical engineering benefit from the cooperation of the nearby Texas Medical Center. The 300-acre campus is located about 3 miles from the center of Houston. Also known as William Marsh Rice University. Most convenient major airports: Hobby, or Intercontinental.

Founded: 1891
Affiliation: Independent
UG Enrollment: 1,666 M, 1,056 W (full-time)
Total Enrollment: 4,597
Cost: < $10K
% Receiving Financial Aid: 80%
Admission: Most Selective
Application Deadline: January 2

Admission is among the most selective in the country. About 25% of applicants accepted, 47% of these actually enroll; 75% of freshmen graduate in top fifth of high school class, 79% in top two-fifths (20% from schools that do not report rank). Average freshman SAT scores, according to most recent data available: middle fifty percent range, 570–690 M, 580–690 W verbal, 650–750 M, 620–730 W mathematical; 91% of freshmen score above 500 on verbal, 74% above 600, 25% above 700; 96% score above 500 on mathematical, 87% above 600, 60% above 700. *Required:* SAT, interview (on- or off-campus), 3 ACH including English (for science or engineering: mathematics I or II and chemistry or physics; for music: audition, music theory test). *Non-academic factors* considered in admissions: diverse student body, alumni children, special talents. *Entrance programs:* early decision, early admission, advanced placement, deferred admission, interim decision. About 25% of entering students from private and parochial schools. *Apply* by January 2. *Transfers* welcome.

Academic Environment. Students have some influence on faculty selection and tenure through an independent student evaluation. Student body reported to be almost equally concerned with scholarly/intellectual interests and pursuit of career goals. Pressures for academic achievement appear to be intense. Competition for admission and achievement appear to be strongest in Academics (Arts and Sciences), Engineering, and Science divisions; somewhat less intense in architecture and music. Professional degree in engineering requires 5 years—includes more work in non-science fields than is customary; also provides greater opportunity for advanced work in major field. Low student/faculty ratio tends to substantiate claim that "Rice may be the most personalized education in the U.S." Administration reports maximum of 50% of courses needed for graduation are required; distribution requirements fairly numerous: 4 courses each in literature/arts, history/social sciences, science or engineering/mathematics; and new "foundation courses." Degrees offered: bachelors, masters, doctoral. *Majors offered* include usual arts and sciences, accounting, anthropology, architecture, biochemistry, chemical physics, computer science, cognitive sciences, linguistics, legal studies, managerial studies, music, 5 fields of engineering; area majors also available.

About 90% of students entering as freshmen graduate eventually; 5% of freshmen do not return for sophomore year. *Special programs:* CLEP (chemistry and biology), study abroad, honors (in humanities, sciences, social sciences), undergraduate research, 3-year degree, individualized majors, 5-year combined AB/BArch program, semester exchange with Swarthmore, programs with Baylor College of Medicine, Columbia School of Law, and U. of Houston Law School, 3–2 programs in MBA, accounting, engineering. *Calendar:* semester.

Undergraduate degrees conferred (631). 23% were in Social Sciences, 19% were in Engineering, 9% were in Life Sciences, 9% were in Letters, 8% were in Visual and Performing Arts, 6% were in Business and Management, 5% were in Physical Sciences, 4% were in Psychology, 3% were in Foreign Languages, 3% were in Liberal/General Studies, 3% were in Education, 3% were in Architecture and Environmental Design, 3% were in Computer and Engineering Related Technology, remainder in 3 other fields.

Graduates Career Data. According to most recent data available, full-time graduate or professional study pursued immediately after graduation by 47% of students; 9% enter medical school; 10% enter law school; 3% enter business school. Medical schools typically enrolling largest numbers of graduates include Southwestern, Baylor College of Medicine; law schools include U. of Texas; business schools include U. of Texas. Corporations typically hiring largest numbers of graduates include Exxon, Arthur Andersen, Compaq Computer.

Faculty. About 95% of faculty hold doctorate or equivalent.

Student Body. University seeks a national student body; 50% of students from in state; 65% of students come from the South, 18% North Central, 8% Middle Atlantic, 5% West/Northwest, 3% New England; 2% foreign students 1990–91. It appears that Rice is beginning to attract larger numbers from the Eastern seaboard. An estimated 5% of students reported as Black, 6% Hispanic, 7% Asian, 2% other minority.

Varsity Sports. Men (Div.I): Baseball, Basketball, Cross Country, Football, Golf, Swimming, Tennis, Track. Women (Div.I): Basketball, Cross Country, Swimming, Tennis, Track, Volleyball.

Campus Life. Every student is a member of 1 of the 8 residential colleges (even when living off campus) "which are the real student governing bodies." Colleges form the basis for social, athletic, and cultural programs on campus. No curfew; intervisitation hours set by members of each residential college. Use of alcohol now extended to public rooms under certain circumstances. No restrictions on cars. Very high interest reported in intramurals and sponsored social activities such as the fall and winter formals. Student leader comments "We work hard, play hard and ignore the rest." He also notes "Rice is a bargain, and we know it."

About 62% of men, 65% of women live in coed dormitories; rest live in off-campus housing or commute. Freshmen given preference in college housing if all students cannot be accommodated. Sexes segregated in coed dormitories by wing or floor. There are no fraternities or sororities. "Few" students leave campus on weekends.

Annual Costs. Tuition and fees, $9,650; room and board, $5,460. About 80% of students receive financial aid. All students who receive financial aid, need-based or merit based, receive some scholarship funds; "self-help" (the maximum the student is expected to cover through loans and work) is limited to $1,950. University reports some scholarships awarded on the basis of academic merit alone. *Meeting Costs:* university offers installment payment plans.

University of Richmond

Richmond, Virginia 23173 (804) 289-8640

The university has a 350-acre campus located in the western suburbs of Richmond, a city of over 200,000. The university consists of three undergraduate programs: the School of Arts and Sciences, the Jepson School of Leadership Studies, and the E. Claiborne Robins School of Business, for juniors and seniors only. Other divisions include: T. C. Williams School of Law, Graduate School (arts and sciences), Richard S. Reynolds Graduate School (business administration), and University College, offering both evening and summer classes. Students are also members of one of two residential colleges: Richmond College (for men) and Westhampton College (for women). Most convenient major airport: Richmond International.

Founded: 1830
Affiliation: Baptist
UG Enrollment: 1,449 M, 1,427 W (full-time); 201 M, 388 W (part-time)
Total Enrollment: 4,327
Cost: $10K–$20K
% Receiving Financial Aid: 60%
Admission: Very (+) Selective
Application Deadline: Feb. 1

Admission is very (+) selective. About 46% of applicants accepted, 28% of these actually enroll; 72% of freshmen graduate in top fifth of high school class, 98% in top two-fifths. Average freshman scores, middle fifty percent range: SAT, 510–610 M, 530–630 W verbal, 600–700 M, 580–670 W mathematical; 86% of freshmen score above 500 verbal, 36% above 600, 4% above 700; 97% above 500 mathematical, 73% above 600, 20% above 700; ACT, 26–29 M, 27–30 W composite. *Required:* SAT and 3 ACH (including English Composition, mathematics I or II) or ACT; essay. Criteria considered in admissions, in order of importance: high school academic record; standardized test scores; recommendations, extracurricular activities, and writing sample; other factors considered: alumni children, special talents, diverse student body. *Entrance programs:* early decision, early admission, advanced placement, deferred admission. About 28% of entering freshmen are from private or parochial schools. *Apply* by February 1. *Transfers* welcome; 21 enrolled 1993–94.

Academic Environment. Administration reports 40% of the general education courses required for graduation are elective; some distribution requirements in 5 broad divisions, plus proficiency and basic knowledge requirements in English, foreign language, mathematics, and Western civilization. The Jepson School of Leadership offers the nation's first undergraduate degree program in leadership studies. Degrees offered: associates, bachelors, masters. *Majors offered* include creative writing, journalism, Third World studies, urban studies, women's studies, international business, leadership studies. Average undergraduate class size: 20; 58% of classes under 20, 36% between 20–40, 6% over 40.

About 79% of students entering as freshmen graduate within four years, 83% eventually; 92% of freshmen return for sophomore year. *Special programs:* CLEP, undergraduate research, independent study, study abroad, honors, 3-year degree, internships, guaranteed law school admission for qualified freshmen, 3–2 programs in forestry and environmental management, Women involved in Living and Learning (WILL). *Calendar:* semester, summer school.

Undergraduate degrees conferred (727). 27% were in Business and Management, 24% were in Social Sciences, 14% were in Letters, 6% were in Psychology, 6% were in Area and Ethnic Studies, 4% were in Education, 4% were in Life Sciences, 4% were in Physical Sciences, 3% were in Foreign Languages, remainder in 9 other fields.

Graduates Career Data. Advanced studies pursued immediately after graduation by 23% of students; 5% enter medical or dental school; 6% enter law school; 2% enter business school. Medical schools typically enrolling largest numbers of graduates include Medical College of Virginia; law schools include U. of Richmond. About 59% of 1992–93 graduates employed six months after graduation. Fields typically hiring largest numbers of graduates include management, marketing, education, communications. Career Development Services include on-campus recruiting, seminars, library resources, individual and group counseling, internship coordination, graduate school workshops, college/graduate school fairs.

Faculty. About 95% of faculty hold PhD or equivalent. About 60% of undergraduate classes taught by tenured faculty; no graduate assistants. About 32% of teaching faculty are female; 9% minority.

Student Body. University seeks a national student body; 20% of students from in state; 49% Middle Atlantic, 11% New England, 10% South; 2% Foreign. An estimated 55% of students reported as Protestant, 33% Catholic, 2% Jewish, 1% Muslim, 10% unaffiliated; 3% Black, 1% Hispanic, 3% Asian, 1% other minority.

Religious Orientation. Richmond is affiliated with the Virginia Baptist General Association; makes no religious demands on students.

Varsity Sports. Men (Div.I): Baseball, Basketball, Cross Country, Diving, Football, Golf, Soccer, Swimming, Tennis, Track, Water Polo. Women (Div.I): Basketball, Cross Country, Diving, Field Hockey, Lacrosse, Swimming, Synchronized Swimming, Tennis, Track.

Campus Life. The residential college system provides men and women single-gender extracurricular experiences within the framework of the coeducational university. Strong student interest reported in fraternities/sororities, varsity and intramural sports, and sponsored social activities. Students are also very much involved in community service; over 80% of the student body volunteered over 16,000 hours to service projects in 1992–93. Cars allowed; parking reported as adequate, but "somewhat inconvenient". No 24-hour intervisitation; intervisitation allowed 10 am to 2 am Sunday-Thursday, 10 am to 3 am Friday and Saturday. Drinking limited to designated areas by students of legal age; smoking not allowed in classrooms, students can request a non-smoking roommate.

About 65% of men, 67% of women live in traditional dormitories; 25% of students live in University apartments; 10% of men, 8% of women live in off- campus college-related housing; rest commute. Freshmen given preference in college housing if all students cannot be accommodated. There are 10 fraternities, 8 sororities on campus which about 50% of men, 60% of women join. Less than 10% of resident students leave campus on weekends.

Annual Costs. Tuition and fees, $15,660; room and board, $3,140; estimated $1,800 other, exclusive of travel. About 60% of students receive financial aid; average amount of assistance, $8,400. Assistance is typically divided 80% scholarship/grant, 17% loan, 3% work. University reports 360 scholarships awarded for academic merit, 200 for special talents, varied number for need. *Meeting Costs:* university offers Tuition Plan, Knight Plan.

Rider College

Lawrenceville, New Jersey 08648 **(609) 896-5042 or (800) 257-9026**

An independent college, located on a 340-acre suburban campus, 3 miles north of a city of 97,500. In 1992 Westminster Choir College merged with Rider, thus creating their new School of Music. Most convenient major airport: Newark.

Founded: 1865
Affiliation: Independent
UG Enrollment: 1,254 M, 1,522 W (full-time)
Cost: $10K–$20K
% Receiving Financial Aid: 70%
Admission: Non-selective
Application Deadline: Rolling

Admission. High school graduates with 2.0 GPA in 16 academic units and minimum combined SAT of 850 (950 for Business) eligible; 68% of applicants accepted, 28% of these actually enroll; 25% of freshmen graduate in top fifth of high school class, 50% in top two-fifths. Average freshmen SAT scores: 438 verbal, 500 mathematical. *Required:* SAT or ACT; interview "strongly recommended." Criteria considered in admissions, in order of importance: high school academic record, standardized test scores, extracurricular activities, recommendations, writing sample. *Apply:* rolling admissions. *Transfers* welcome; 210 enrolled 1993–94.

Academic Environment. *Undergraduate studies* offered by schools of Liberal Arts and Science, Business Administration, Education, Human Services, and the new School of Music. Internships and field study are available in most areas. Small, interactive classes appear to be the rule, although some introductory classes can be quite large. Degrees offered: bachelors, masters. *Majors offered* in addition to usual studies include advertising, computer science, fine arts, journalism, actuarial science, marine science.

About 60% of students entering as freshmen graduate within four years, 80% eventually; 85% of freshmen return for sophomore year. *Special programs:* CLEP, independent study, internships, study abroad, honors, 5-year BA/MBA. *Calendar:* semester, January interim study program (2 required), summer school.

Undergraduate degrees conferred (768). 61% were in Business and Management, 9% were in Education, 8% were in Social Sciences, 8% were in Communications, 4% were in Psychology, remainder in 8 other fields.

Undergraduate degrees conferred (Westminster Choir College) (45). 58% were in Education, 42% were in Visual and Performing Arts.

Graduates Career Data. Advanced studies pursued by 14% of students; 3% enter medical school; 1% enter dental school; 3% enter law school. About 96% of 1992–93 graduates employed or in graduate school. Corporations typically hiring largest numbers of graduates include Bloomberg Financial Markets, Merrill Lynch, AT&T, Bristol-Myers, Squibb. Career Development Services include resume writing workshops, mock interviews, career days.

Faculty. About 92% of faculty hold PhD or equivalent. About 78% of undergraduate classes taught by tenured faculty. About 38% of teaching faculty are female; 10% minority.

Student Body. College does not seek a national student body; 78% of students from New Jersey; 97% Middle Atlantic; 1% Foreign. An estimated 47% of students reported as Catholic, 13% Protestant, 6% Jewish, 7% unaffiliated, 2% other; 7% as Black, 4% Hispanic, 3% Asian, 7% other minority.

Varsity Sports. Men (Div.I): Baseball, Basketball, Cross Country, Diving, Golf, Soccer, Swimming, Tennis, Track, Wrestling. Women (Div.I): Basketball, Cross Country, Diving, Field Hockey, Softball, Swimming, Tennis, Track, Volleyball.

Campus Life. Although there are many academic and recreational organizations and activities, many students still leave campus on weekends. Intervisitation policies set by each living unit. Drinking allowed in dormitory rooms for those of legal age; no restrictions on cars. Students can apply for permission to live off campus; priority on basis of age and class standing. "Student Senate has the power to determine all social regulations subject to legal authority of the Board of Trustees."

About 10% of women live in traditional dormitories; 77% of students live in coed dormitories; rest live in off-campus housing or commute. Sexes segregated in coed dormitories by floor or wing. There are 6 fraternities, 6 sororities on campus which about 8% of men, 7% of women join; 13% of men and women live in fraternities and sororities. About 35% of resident students leave campus on weekends.

Annual Costs. Tuition and fees, $12,750; room and board, $5,210 (free laundry). About 70% of students receive financial aid; average amount of assistance, $11,000. Assistance is typically divided 24% scholarship, 39% grant, 29% loan, 9% work. College reports 131 scholarships awarded for academic merit, 35 for special talents. *Meeting Costs:* college offers The Tuition Plan, Academic Management Services.

Ringling School of Art

Sarasota, Florida 33580

A professional college of art, Ringling confers baccalaureate degrees in fine arts, graphic design, illustration and interior design/space planning.

Affiliation: Independent

Undergraduate degrees conferred (90). 76% were in Visual and Performing Arts, 24% were in Architecture and Environmental Design.

University of Rio Grande

Rio Grande, Ohio 45674-9989 **(614) 245-5353 or (800) 288-2746**

An interdenominational, liberal arts university, located on a 170-acre campus in a village of 800, 96 miles southeast of Columbus. In 1974, Rio Grande established a state-supported, 2-year college where community students can earn the private college degree and course credit at significantly reduced tuition. Formerly known as Rio Grande College.

Founded: 1876
Affiliation: Independent
UG Enrollment: 797 M, 1,007 W (full-time); 88 M, 145 W (part-time)
Cost: < $10K
% Receiving Financial Aid: 87%
Admission: Non-selective
Application Deadline: July 1

Admission. High school graduates eligible; others given consideration; almost all applicants accepted. Average freshmen ACT scores: 18.2. *Required:* ACT, minimum H.S. GPA. Criteria considered in admissions, in order of importance: high school academic record, standardized test scores, recommendations, extracurricular activities. *Entrance programs:* early admission, midyear admission, deferred admission. *Apply* by July 1(recommended); rolling admissions. *Transfers* welcome; 71 enrolled 1993–94.

Academic Environment. Degrees offered: associates, bachelors, masters. Unusual majors offered include Associate of Applied Science in Fine Woodworking. About 65% of students entering as freshmen graduate eventually; 25% of freshmen do not return for sophomore year, according to most recent data available. Average undergraduate class size: 15% under 20, 80% between 20–40, 5% over 40. *Special programs:* CLEP, independent study, 3-year degree, study abroad, individualized majors. Adult programs: evening courses in business; adult and continuing education. *Calendar:* quarter, summer school.

Undergraduate degrees conferred (153). 36% were in Education, 12% were in Mathematics, 10% were in Communications, 10% were in Business (Administrative Support), 10% were in Business and Management, 5% were in Social Sciences, 5% were in Letters, 3% were in Engineering and Engineering Related Technology, 3% were in Life Sciences, remainder in 5 other fields.

Graduates Career Data. *Careers in business and industry* pursued by 67% of graduates, according to most recent data available.

Faculty. About 52% of faculty hold PhD or equivalent. About 33% of teaching faculty are female; 4% minority.

Student Body. College does not seek a national student body; 88% of students from Ohio; 8% Foreign. Average age of undergraduate student: 24.

Varsity Sports. Men (Div.I): Baseball, Basketball, Cross Country, Soccer, Track. Women (Div.I): Cross Country, Softball, Track, Volleyball.

Campus Life. About 22% of men, 17% of women live in traditional dormitories; 17% of men, 2% of women live in coed dormitories; rest commute. Freshmen given preference in college housing if all students cannot be accommodated. Intervisitation in men's and women's dormitory rooms limited. There are 4 fraternities, 5 sororities on campus which about 3% of men, 3% of women join. About 45% of resident students leave campus on weekends.

Annual Costs. Tuition and fees, $2,400 for Ohio freshmen and sophomores (juniors, seniors and out-of-state, $6,000); room and board, $3,650; estimated $2,600 other, exclusive of travel. About 87% of students receive financial aid; average amount of assistance, $6,300. Assistance is typically divided 63% scholarship/grant, 35% loan, 2% work. College reports 468 scholarships awarded for academic merit, 126 for special talents.

Ripon College

Ripon, Wisconsin 54971 (414) 748-8102

A small, Midwestern liberal arts college, Ripon draws its students primarily from the North Central region. The 250-acre campus is located in a town of 7,500, 80 miles northwest of Milwaukee. Most convenient major airports: Oshkosh (20 miles), Appleton (40 miles), or Milwaukee (80 miles).

Founded: 1851
Affiliation: Independent
UG Enrollment: 395 M, 390 W (full-time)
Cost: $10K–$20K
% Receiving Financial Aid: 80%
Admission: Very Selective
Application Deadline: Mar. 15

Admission is very selective. About 86% of applicants accepted, 42% of these actually enroll; 43% of freshmen graduate in top fifth of high school class, 71% in top two-fifths. Average freshman scores: SAT, 513 verbal, 557 mathematical; 68% of freshmen score above 500 on verbal, 18% above 600, 3% above 700; 72% score above 500 on mathematical, 39% above 600, 6% above 700; ACT, 24 composite. *Required:* SAT or ACT, minimum H.S. GPA, essay; interview recommended. Criteria considered in admissions, in order of importance: high school academic record, standardized test scores, extracurricular activities, recommendations, writing sample; other factors considered: special talents, alumni children, diverse student body. *Entrance programs:* early decision, early admission, midyear admission, deferred admission. About 20% of entering students are from private schools, 20% from parochial schools. *Apply* by March 15. *Transfers* welcome; 22 enrolled 1993–94.

Academic Environment. Pressures for academic achievement vary from moderate to intense. Three-year degree option requires higher grade point average and semester course load of 18–19 hours. Student leader asserts that the small size of the college allows students "to create their own opportunities easily: self-designed majors, new clubs and sports, independent studies or research with faculty." Both student and administration sources note student desire for expansion of art department and some other programs. Degrees offered: bachelors. *Majors offered* include anthropology, computer science, Latin American studies, psychology, leadership studies, psychobiology, classical studies, religion. Average undergraduate class size: 80% of classes under 20, 18% between 20–40, 2% over 40.

About 70% of students entering as freshmen graduate in four years, 80% eventually, 91% of freshmen return for sophomore year. *Special programs:* independent study, semester or year programs in study abroad, undergraduate research, 3-year degree, individualized majors, programs of ACM, Princeton Semester, self-designed off-campus study for credit, guest-professor program, 3–2 engineering, environmental studies and forestry, nursing, cooperative programs in nursing and medical technology with Rush University Medical Center. *Calendar:* semester.

Undergraduate degrees conferred (138). 43% were in Social Sciences, 12% were in Life Sciences, 9% were in Letters, 9% were in Business and Management, 5% were in Physical Sciences, 5% were in Philosophy and Religion, 4% were in Visual and Performing Arts, 4% were in Mathematics, 4% were in Foreign Languages, remainder in 3 other fields.

Graduates Career Data. Advanced studies pursued by 33% of students; 5% enter medical school; 2% enter dental school; 3% enter law school; 3% enter business school. Medical schools typically enrolling largest numbers of graduates include Medical C. of Wisconsin. About 60% of 1992–93 graduates employed. Fields typically hiring largest numbers of graduates include history, English, Spanish, politics/government. Career Development Services include skills and interest assessment, numerous workshops for search skills, graduate school preparation, job fairs, alumni career network.

Faculty. About 91% of faculty hold PhD or equivalent. About 35% of teaching faculty are female.

Student Body. College seeks a national student body; 45% of students from in state; 60% of students from Midwest, 15% New England, 3% Middle Atlantic, 4% South, 10% West, 5% Northwest; 3% Foreign. An estimated 3% of students reported as Black, 3% Hispanic, 3% Asian, 1% other.

Varsity Sports. Men (Div.III): Baseball, Basketball, Cross Country, Diving, Football, Golf, Soccer, Swimming, Tennis, Track, Wrestling. Women (Div.III): Basketball, Cross Country, Diving, Soccer, Softball, Swimming, Tennis, Track, Volleyball.

Campus Life. Strong interest reported in fraternities/sororities, sponsored social activities, and intramural sports, most popular: basketball, football, flag football, soccer, volleyball. Students participate in governance of college by representation on major faculty committees and annual graduate elected by students to board of trustees. "Small student body adds to closeness and contact." Substantial numbers of students join fraternities and sororities, but they are housed in traditional dormitories. Up to 24-hour visitation determined by residents of each dormitory. Alcohol prohibited in common areas; legal age, 21. Motor vehicles permitted for all students.

About 20% of men, 57% of women live in traditional dormitories; 25% of men, 10% of women in coed dormitories; rest commute. Freshmen given preference in college housing if all students cannot be accommodated. There are 5 fraternities, 3 sororities on campus which about 55% of men, 33% of women join; about 55% of men, 33% of women live in fraternities and sororities. About 7% of resident students leave campus on weekends.

Annual Costs. Tuition and fees, $14,340; room and board, $3,810; estimated $1,000 other, exclusive of travel. About 80% of students receive financial aid; average amount of assistance, $12,986. Assistance is typically divided 65% grant, 20% loan, 15 work. College reports some scholarships awarded for academic merit. *Meeting Costs:* college offers various loan programs, Academic Management Services.

Rivier College

Nashua, New Hampshire 03060 (603) 888-1311

A private, independent college primarily for women, conducted by the Sisters of the Presentation of Mary, located on a 60-acre campus in a city of 80,000, 35 miles northwest of Boston. Most convenient major airport: Manchester.

Founded: 1933
Affiliation: Independent (Roman Catholic)
UG Enrollment: 82 M, 508 W (full-time); 198 M, 998 W (part-time)
Total Enrollment: 2,762
Cost: < $10K
% Receiving Financial Aid: 35%
Admission: Non-selective
Application Deadline: Rolling

Admission. Graduates of accredited high schools with 16 units eligible; 89% of applicants accepted; 16% of freshmen graduate in top fifth of high school class, 30% in top two-fifths. Average freshman SAT scores: 432 verbal, 447 mathematical, according to most recent data available. *Required:* SAT, essay, or GED; chemistry and algebra for nursing majors, portfolio for art. Criteria considered in admissions, in order of importance: high school academic record, recommendations, writing sample, standardized test scores, extracurricular activities; other factors considered: special talents, alumni children, diverse student body. *Entrance programs:* deferred admission, advanced placement. *Apply:* rolling admissions. *Transfers* welcome; 92 enrolled 1993–94.

Academic Environment. Degrees offered: associates, bachelors, masters. Core requirements include 1 course in English composition, 1 in mathematics, 1 in critical thinking, 1 in fine arts, 2 in English literature, 2 in natural sciences, 2 in social sciences, 2 in modern language, 2 in Western civilization, 3 in religion and 3 in philosophy. *Majors offered* include fashion merchandising, communications, information processing management, nursing. Average undergraduate class size: 79% under 20, 21% between 20–40, 1% over 40.

About 60% of students entering as freshmen graduate eventually, 34% of freshmen do not return for sophomore year, according to most recent data available. *Special programs:* CLEP, study abroad, cross registration with St. Anselm's, Daniel Webster, Notre Dame; cooperative programs through NHCUC. Adult programs: study skills for adults, a pass/fail course for adults for 1–3 credits, Undergraduate Evening School. *Calendar:* 5–5, summer school.

Undergraduate degrees conferred (157). 17% were in Education, 15% were in Business and Management, 9% were in Psychology, 9% were in Business (Administrative Support), 8% were in Law, 8% were in Communications, 6% were in Computer and Engineering Related Technology, 5% were in Life Sciences, 4% were in Visual and Performing Arts, 4% were in Allied Health, 3% were in Public Affairs, 3% were in Home Economics, 3% were in Liberal/General Studies, remainder in 6 other fields.

Graduates Career Data. Advanced studies pursued by 27% of students; 4% enter law school; 9% enter business school. About 88% of 1992–93 graduates employed. Career Development Services include self-assessment service, occupational exploration, plan of action service.

Faculty. About 44% of faculty hold PhD or equivalent. About 65% of teaching faculty are tenured. About 59% of teaching faculty are female.

Student Body. College does not seek a national student body; 78% of students from in state. An estimated 2% of students reported as Hispanic, 1% Asian. Average age of undergraduate student: 30.

Religious Orientation. Rivier College is an independent institution with a Catholic heritage: three courses in religion are required of all students.

Varsity Sports. Men (Div.III): Basketball, Cross Country, Golf, Soccer. Women (Div.III): Basketball, Cross Country, Field Hockey, Golf, Soccer, Volleyball.

Campus Life. About 40% of men, 40% women live in coed dormitories; rest commute. Freshmen given preference in college housing if all students cannot be accommodated. No intervisitation in women's dormitory rooms. There are no sororities.

Annual Costs. Tuition and fees, $9,870; room and board, $4,850; estimated $500 other, exclusive of travel. About 35% of students receive financial aid. Assistance is typically divided 40% grant, 50% loan, 10% work. College reports 13 scholarships awarded for academic merit. Meeting Costs: college offers deferred payment plan.

Roanoke College

Salem, Virginia 24153-3794 **(703) 375-2270 or 800) 388-2276**

An independent, liberal arts college, with continuing ties to the Lutheran Church, Roanoke is located in a city of 25,000, adjoining Roanoke (pop. 250,000). Most convenient major airport: Roanoke Regional.

Founded: 1842
Affiliation: Independent (Lutheran)
UG Enrollment: 579 M, 881 W (full-time); 108 M, 131 W (part-time)
Cost: $10K–$20K
% Receiving Financial Aid: 89%
Admission: Selective
Application Deadline: March 1

Admission is selective. About 79% of applicants accepted, 24% of these actually enroll; 48% of freshmen graduate in top fifth of high school class, 72% in top two-fifths. Average freshman SAT scores: 490 M, 485 W verbal, 552 M, 520 W mathematical; 43% of freshmen score above 500 verbal, 9% above 600; 69% score above 500 mathematical, 22% above 600, 3% above 700. *Required:* SAT. Criteria considered in admissions, in order of importance: high school academic record, standardized test scores, extracurricular activities, recommendations, writing sample; other factors considered: special talents, alumni children, diverse student body. *Entrance programs:* early decision, early admission, midyear admission, deferred admission, advanced placement. About 24% of entering freshmen from private schools. *Apply* by March 1. *Transfers* welcome; 83 enrolled 1993–94.

Academic Environment. Degrees offered: bachelors. *Majors offered* include business administration, computer information systems, fine arts, medical technology, interdisciplinary program in urban studies. Administration reports core requirements include: 2 units each of social science, writing, lab science, math, physical education, foreign language; 1 unit values seminar, 1 unit senior symposium. Four-year Honors Program for qualified students. Average undergraduate class size: 50% of classes under 20, 50% between 20–40.

About 52% of students entering as freshmen graduate in four years, 60% eventually; 75% of freshmen return for sophomore year. *Special programs:* independent study, honors, study abroad, May travel term, undergraduate research, credit by examination, acceleration, 3–2 in engineering, cross registration with Hollins C., The Learning Center (academic counseling & peer tutoring). Adult programs: Bachelor of Business Administration can be completed through evening classes. *Calendar:* semester, summer school.

Undergraduate degrees conferred (344). 31% were in Social Sciences, 21% were in Business and Management, 10% were in Visual and Performing Arts, 9% were in Education, 8% were in Psychology, 6% were in Letters, 5% were in Protective Services, 3% were in Life Sciences, 3% were in Foreign Languages, remainder in 4 other fields.

Graduates Career Data. Advanced studies pursued immediately after graduation by about 20% (1991–92) of students. About 83% of 1991–92 graduates employed. Career Development Services include help in preparing for interviews, computerized job matching, internships, on-campus interviews, alumni career network.

Faculty. About 89% of faculty hold PhD or equivalent. About 70% of undergraduate classes taught by tenured faculty. About 37% of teaching faculty are female; 2% minority.

Student Body. College seeks a national student body; 56% of students from in state; 76% Middle Atlantic, 13% Midwest, 7% South, 11% New England, 1% West, 1% Northwest; 1% Foreign. An estimated 65% of students reported as Protestant, 20% Catholic, 10% unaffiliated, 4% other; 2% as Black, 1% Hispanic, 1% Asian.

Varsity Sports. Men (Div.III): Basketball, Cross Country, Golf, Lacrosse, Soccer, Tennis, Track. Women (Div.III): Basketball, Cross Country, Field Hockey, Lacrosse, Soccer, Tennis, Volleyball.

Campus Life. Alcohol permitted in dormitory rooms in accordance with state and local laws. Intervisitation allowed 10 am to midnight (to 1 am on weekends) for freshmen; 10 am to 2 am for upperclassmen. Motor vehicles not allowed for first-term freshmen. All students, with certain exceptions, expected to live in campus housing. Administration reports "good opportunities for recreation in the Blue Ridge Mountains." Seven other colleges within an hour's drive of Roanoke.

About 11% of men, 31% of women live in traditional dormitories; 25% of men, 20% of women in coed dormitories; 45% of men, 43% of women commute. Freshmen given preference in college housing if all students cannot be accommodated. There are 4 fraternities, 3 sororities on campus, which about 30% of men, 30% of women join. About 19% of men live in fraternities, 6% of women live in sororities.

Annual Costs. Tuition and fees, $12,625; room and board, $4,350; estimated $1,050 other, exclusive of travel. About 89% of students receive financial aid; average amount of assistance, $7,700. Assistance is typically divided 60% scholarship/grant, 30% loan, 10% work. College reports all scholarships awarded for academic merit.

Assistance is typically divided 37% scholarship, 19% grant, 44% loan. College reports scholarships awarded for academic merit, special talents, and need. *Meeting Costs:* college offers tuition payment plan.

Robert Morris College

Coraopolis, Pennsylvania 15108-1189 (412) 262-8206

A co-educational institution that specializes in business administration with majors in many areas of business and management as well as business teacher education. The college operates two campuses: the Pittsburgh Center in the heart of the city's "Golden Triangle" and a 232-acre suburban campus located 17 miles from the city of Pittsburgh. Most convenient major airport: Greater Pittsburgh International.

Founded: 1921
Affiliation: Independent
UG Enrollment: 1,371 M, 1,250 W (full-time); 683 M, 1,125 W (part-time)
Total Enrollment: 5,345
Cost: < $10K
% Receiving Financial Aid: 82%
Admission: Non-selective
Application Deadline: Rolling

Admission. High school graduates or those with GED diploma eligible; 85% of applicants accepted, 50% of these actually enroll. About 24% of freshmen graduate in top fifth of high school class, 52% in top two-fifths. Average freshman SAT scores: 396 verbal, 451 mathematical. *Required:* minimum H.S. GPA, recommended SAT or ACT (for placement only); interview "on request." Criteria considered for admissions, in order of importance: high school academic record, recommendations, extracurricular activities, standardized test scores; other factors considered: special talents, alumni children, diverse student body. *Entrance programs:* early admission, deferred admission, advanced placement. *Apply:* rolling admissions. *Transfers* welcome; 506 enrolled 1993–94.

Academic Environment. Degrees offered: associates, bachelors, masters. Core requirements include English composition, speech, macro- and micro-economics, psychology, sociology, mathematics, history, science. *Majors offered* include aviation management, hospitality management, human resource management. About 32% of students entering as freshmen graduate in four years, 55% eventually; 82% of freshmen return for sophomore year. *Special programs:* CLEP, honors, January term, study abroad, non-degree study, dual majors, independent study, 3-year degree, individualized majors, cross-registration with 9 other Pittsburgh area colleges and universities. Adult programs: one-day-a-week college is a full-time degree program on Saturdays for all degrees. *Calendar:* semester, summer school.

Undergraduate degrees conferred (681). 80% were in Business and Management, 9% were in Computer and Engineering Related Technology, 6% were in Business (Administrative Support), 3% were in Education, remainder in 2 other fields.

Graduates Career Data. Fields typically hiring largest numbers of graduates include accounting, computer information systems. Career Development Services include aptitude testing, counseling groups, placement service, resume/interview workshops, on-campus recruiting, individual internships and co-op education, and library resources.

Faculty. About 58% of faculty hold PhD or equivalent. About 31% of teaching faculty are female.

Varsity Sports. Men (NCAA-Northeast): Basketball, Cross Country, Golf, Soccer, Tennis, Track. Women (NCAA-Northeast): Basketball, Cross Country, Softball, Tennis, Track, Volleyball.

Student Body. College does not seek a national student body; 94% of students from in state; 99% of students from Middle Atlantic; 1% Foreign. An estimated 5% of students reported as Black, 2% other minority. Average age of undergraduate student: 23.

Campus Life. About 8% of men, 8% of women live in traditional dormitories; 38% of men, 46% of women commute. Freshmen given preference in college housing if all students cannot be accommodated. Intervisitation in men's and women's dormitory rooms limited. There are 4 fraternities, 6 sororities on campus which about 15% of men, 5% of women join. About 75% of resident students leave campus on weekends.

Annual Costs. Tuition and fees, $6,300; room and board, $4,106; estimated $1,100 other, exclusive of travel. About 82% of students receive financial aid; average amount of assistance, $4,750.

Roberts Wesleyan College

Rochester, New York 14624-1997 (716) 594-6400; (800) 777-4RWC

A college in the Christian tradition located in suburban Rochester, 8 miles southwest of the city. Most convenient major airport: Rochester.

Founded: 1866
Affiliation: Free Methodist
UG Enrollment: 365 M, 567 W (full-time); 37 M, 70 W (part-time)
Cost: < $10K
% Receiving Financial Aid: 86%
Admission: Non-selective
Application Deadline: August 1

Admission. Graduates of approved high schools with 12 units in academic subjects who rank in top three-fifths of class eligible; 92% of applicants accepted, 50% of these actually enroll; according to most recent data available 37% of freshmen graduate in top fifth of high school class, 61% in top two-fifths. Average freshmen scores: SAT, 464 verbal, 503 mathematical; 31% of freshmen score above 500 verbal, 4% above 600; 53% score above 500 mathematical, 14% above 600, 1% above 700; ACT, 23 composite. *Required:* essay; "devotion to high moral and ethical standards"; SAT or ACT, interview recommended. Criteria considered in admissions, in order of importance: high school academic record, recommendations, standardized test scores, writing sample, extracurricular activities; other factors considered: special talents, alumni children, diverse student body, religious affiliation and/or commitment. *Entrance programs:* midyear admission. *Apply* by August 1; rolling admissions. *Transfers* welcome; 82 enrolled 1993–94.

Academic Environment. Degrees offered: associates, bachelors, masters. About 50% of general education requirements for graduation are elective; distribution requirements fairly numerous. About 57% of students entering as freshmen graduate eventually, according to most recent data available; 73% of freshmen return for sophomore year. Average undergraduate class size: 57% under 20, 35% between 20–40, 8% over 40. *Special programs:* CLEP, independent study, honors, January term, study abroad, cross-registration, Learning Center, internships, undergraduate research, 3–2 programs in engineering. Adult programs: Management of Human Resources Program. *Calendar:* 2 14-week semesters, January Experience, 2 summer sessions.

Undergraduate degrees conferred (236). 48% were in Business and Management, 13% were in Education, 7% were in Health Sciences, 4% were in Psychology, 4% were in Public Affairs, 4% were in Philosophy and Religion, 4% were in Communications, 3% were in Visual and Performing Arts, 3% were in Social Sciences, 3% were in Letters, remainder in 6 other fields.

Faculty. About 45% of faculty hold PhD or equivalent. About 48% of undergraduate classes taught by tenured faculty. About 46% of teaching faculty are female; 2% Hispanic, 2% Asian.

Student Body. College seeks a national student body; 90% of students from in state, 95% Middle Atlantic; 6% Foreign. An estimated 73% of students reported as Protestant, 12% Catholic, 14% unaffiliated; 8% Black, 1% Hispanic, 2% Asian.

Varsity Sports. Men (NAIA; NCCAA): Basketball, Cross Country, Soccer, Track. Women (NCCAA): Basketball, Cross Country, Soccer, Track.

Religious Orientation. Roberts Wesleyan is an institution in the Christian tradition; 2 courses in biblical literature, attendance at twice-weekly chapel services required of all students.

Campus Life. About 67% of men, 67% of women live in traditional dormitories; rest commute. Freshmen given preference in college housing if all students cannot be accommodated. There are no fraternities or sororities. About 50% of resident students leave campus on weekends.

Annual Costs. Tuition and fees, $9,951; room and board, $3,366. About 86% of students receive financial aid, average amount of assistance, $7,499. Assistance is typically divided 59% scholarship, 32% loan, 9% work. College reports some scholarships awarded on the basis of academic merit alone. *Meeting Costs:* college offers monthly payment plans.

Rochester Institute of Technology

Rochester, New York 14623 **(716) 475-6631**

An independent institution, specializing in a wide range of applied arts and sciences, Rochester Institute of Technology is located on a new 1,300-acre campus in suburban Rochester, N.Y., the state's third largest city. The institute offers special opportunities in science and engineering, art and photography, computer science, and management-related fields of study. Most convenient major airport: Rochester International.

Founded: 1855
Affiliation: Independent
UG Enrollment: 5,349 M, 2,408 W (full-time); 1,668 M, 910 W (part-time)
Total Enrollment: 12,637
Cost: $10K–$20K
% Receiving Financial Aid: 70%
Admission: Selective
Application Deadline: Rolling

Admission is selective. About 80% of applicants accepted, 38% of these actually enroll; 51% of entering students graduate in top fifth of high school class, 77% in top two-fifths. Average freshman SAT scores: 47% of freshmen score above 500 verbal, 13% above 600, 1% above 700; 79% score above 500 mathematical, 42% above 600, 10% above 700. *Required:* SAT or ACT, minimum H.S. GPA, essay, portfolio for art. Criteria considered in admissions, in order of importance: high school academic record, standardized test scores, recommendations, extracurricular activities, writing sample; other factors considered: special talents, alumni children, diverse student body. *Entrance programs:* early decision, early admission, midyear admission, deferred admission, advanced placement. About 5% of entering students from private schools, 5% from parochial schools. *Apply:* rolling admissions. *Transfers* welcome; 821 enrolled Fall 1993.

Academic Environment. All programs career oriented and students may begin work in major field in freshman year. RIT offers one of the largest cooperative education programs in the U.S. Through this program, students alternate periods of career-related work experience and periods of study on-campus. Cooperative education positions are full-time, salaried positions provided by over 1,200 participating firms in business, science, engineering, hotel management, computer science, engineering technology and printing. National Technical Institute for the Deaf provides technological education on campus for deaf students in fields of business, industry, government, and education. Core requirements total 54 quarter credit hours out of the total 180 required for BS or BFA degrees. Distribution requirements include humanities, social science, mathematics and science; liberal arts studies for technical and professional curricula provided by College of Liberal Arts. Degrees offered: associates, bachelors, masters, doctoral. *Undergraduate studies* offered by colleges of Business, Liberal Arts, Engineering (including Computer, Microelectronics, Electrical, Industrial, Mechanical Engineering departments), Imaging Arts & Sciences (including School of Art and Design, School for American Craftsmen), Liberal Arts, Photographic Arts and Sciences, Printing, Science (including Health Related Professions, Biology, Chemistry, Mathematics and Physics), Applied Science & Technology (including School of Engineering Technology, School of Computer Science and Technology, Department of Packaging Science. *Majors offered* include physician's assistance program, microelectronics engineering, biotechnology, imaging science, graphic arts, National Technical School for the Deaf. Average undergraduate class size: 65% under 20, 29% between 20–40, 6% over 40.

About 62% of students entering as freshmen graduate within seven years; 85% of freshmen return for sophomore year. *Special programs:* cooperative work/study, programs through Rochester Area Colleges Consortium, study abroad (England), co-ops, accelerated BS/MS programs in business, engineering, mathematics. Adult programs: executive MBA degree, executive hotel management degree, weekend college, Applied Arts & Sciences Program through College of Continuing Education. *Calendar:* quarter, summer session.

Undergraduate degrees conferred (1,857). 22% were in Business and Management, 18% were in Visual and Performing Arts, 16% were in Engineering and Engineering Related Technology, 13% were in Engineering, 6% were in Communications, 5% were in Computer and Engineering Related Technology, 4% were in Liberal/General Studies, 3% were in Life Sciences, 3% were in Allied Health, remainder in 10 other fields.

Graduates Career Data. Advanced studies pursued by 5% of students. About 95% of 1992–93 graduates employed. Corporations typically hiring largest numbers of graduates include Kodak, IBM, Xerox, Bausch & Lomb.

Faculty. About 78% of faculty hold PhD or equivalent. About 29% of teaching faculty are female; 9% minority.

Student Body. Institute seeks a national student body; 65% of students from in state; 73% from Middle Atlantic, 13% New England, 5% Midwest, 3% South; 4% Foreign. An estimated 5% of students reported as Black, 5% Asian, 3% Hispanic, 6% other minority.

Varsity Sports. Men (Div.III): Baseball, Basketball, Cross Country, Diving, Hockey, Lacrosse, Soccer, Swimming, Tennis, Track, Wrestling. Women (Div.III): Basketball, Diving, Hockey, Soccer, Softball, Swimming, Tennis, Track, Volleyball.

Campus Life. Students subject to very few rules controlling conduct on campus. Each house sets its own policies on hours and intervisitation. Cars allowed; rules against illegal parking "judiciously enforced." About 30% of full-time students live in coed residence halls; 30% live in off-campus college-related housing; rest live in other off-campus housing or commute. Freshmen given preference in college housing if all students cannot be accommodated. Sexes segregated by floor. There are 10 fraternities, 5 sororities on campus which 10% of men, 10% of women join; 10% of men, 10% of women live in fraternities and sororities.

Annual Costs. Tuition and fees, $13,515; room and board, $5,511; estimated $1,075 other, exclusive of travel. About 70% of students receive financial aid; average amount of assistance, $11,800. Assistance is typically divided 45% scholarship, 10% grant, 30% loan, 15% work. Institute reports 1,000 scholarships awarded for academic merit, 4,000 for need. *Meeting Costs:* institute offers interest-free monthly payment plan, tuition stabilization plan.

University of Rochester

Rochester, New York 14627 **(716) 275-3221**

Rochester is a moderate size university which includes a prestigious undergraduate college, the nationally known Eastman School of Music, a well-known graduate school and a major medical school. Eastman School and Memorial Art Gallery share a campus in downtown Rochester; the main River Campus is located at southwestern edge of Rochester (pop. 980,000). Most convenient major airport: Greater Rochester International.

Founded: 1850
Affiliation: Independent
UG Enrollment: 2,694 M, 2,382 W (full-time); 66 M, 128 W (part-time)
Total Enrollment: 8,401
Cost: $10K–$20K
% Receiving Financial Aid: 80%
Admission: Highly Selective
Application Deadline: Jan. 31

Admission is highly selective for College of Arts and Science. For all schools: 63% of applicants accepted, 23% of these actually enroll; 75% of freshmen graduate in top fifth of high school class, 92% in top two-fifths. Average freshman scores: SAT (middle 50% range), 470–590 verbal, 550–760 mathematical; 63% of freshmen score above 500 verbal, 22% above 600, 3% above 700; 88% score above 500 mathematical, 58% above 600, 16% above 700; ACT (middle 50% range), 23–29 composite.

For Arts and Science, 64% of applicants accepted, 23% of these actually enroll; 71% of freshmen graduate in top fifth of high school class, 91% in top two-fifths. Average freshman scores: SAT, 470–590 verbal, 550–660 mathematical; ACT, 24–29 composite, according to most recent data available.

For Engineering, 62% of applicants accepted, 24% of these actually enroll; 81% of freshmen graduate in top fifth of high school class, 97% in top two-fifths. Average freshman scores: SAT, 460–580 verbal, 610–700 mathematical; ACT, 27–31 composite, according to most recent data available.

For Eastman School of Music, 35% of applicants accepted, 56% of these actually enroll. SAT scores recommended but not required for Eastman applicants.

Required: SAT or ACT, essay, counselor recommendation. Criteria considered in admissions, in order of importance: high school academic record, extracurricular activities, standardized test scores and recommendations, writing sample; other factors considered: special talents, alumni children, diverse student body. *Entrance programs:*

deferred admission, early decision. *Apply* by January 31. *Transfers* welcome; 178 enrolled 1993–94.

Academic Environment. Pressures for academic achievement appear moderately intense. Competition strongest in pre-professional sequences. All students on the River Campus spend first 2 years in College of Arts and Science; after selection of major they may complete last 2 years in same college or in one of university's professional schools. A newly defined undergraduate College within the College of Arts and Science emphasizes the University's commitment to undergraduate education. The College features "a student-centered curriculum," interdisciplinary courses for freshmen, special interest housing, special orientation and convocation for incoming students, and a student-faculty advising system. Core requirements for all Arts and Science students include 2 courses in each of natural sciences, social sciences, and humanities; primary and upper-level writing courses; one semester of formal reasoning; and foreign language proficiency. No separate graduate faculty, and "name" professors are expected to teach undergraduate courses. This integration of undergraduate teaching and graduate research affords exceptional students an opportunity to move as far as their "abilities and knowledge can carry them." Much of Rochester's reputation has been built on programs in the sciences, but the majority of students are enrolled in programs that demand less intensity and offer more flexibility. *Undergraduate studies* offered by colleges of Arts and Science, Engineering and Applied Science, Eastman School of Music, School of Nursing. Degrees offered: bachelors, masters, doctoral. Majors offered include anthropology, cognitive science, health and society, microbiology, film studies, art history, studio arts, linguistics, optics, geomechanics, women's studies, statistics; interdisciplinary studies. Average undergraduate class size: 54% of classes under 20, 22% between 20–40, 24% over 40.

About 78% of students entering as freshmen graduate eventually; 10% of freshmen do not return for sophomore year, according to most recent data available. *Special programs:* independent study, study abroad, undergraduate research, individualized majors, Take Five—allows for tuition-free fifth year of courses to pursue broader academic interests, tuition-free courses leading to secondary school teacher certification for minority students, wide range of 3–2 programs offered within the university, collaborative biology-medicine program with medical school, Washington Semester program (including full-time work for members of Congress), freshman Ventures, freshman preceptorials (intensive small-group study under senior faculty member), Senior Scholars Program, interdisciplinary programs including certificate programs (International Relations, Management Studies, Russian Studies, Asian Studies, actuarial studies, biomedical engineering, biotechnology, secondary education), Rochester Plan (interdisciplinary programs to prepare students for careers in health professions), REMS, an 8-year BA/BS-MD program for exceptionally talented undergraduates with a guarantee of admission to University of Rochester Medical School, Biology-Geology Internship Program (selected undergraduates spend a semester at St. Croix, Virgin Islands); internships in U.S. and abroad, undergraduates may participate in work of unique Laboratory for Laser Energetics, cross registration through Rochester Area Colleges Consortium. Rochester possesses an extraordinary array of scientific laboratory facilities for a school of its size. Computer facilities are especially extensive with applications for fields as diverse as anthropology and education as well as the more conventional mathematics and engineering. *Calendar:* semester, summer school.

Undergraduate degrees conferred (1,135). 30% were in Social Sciences, 14% were in Engineering, 13% were in Psychology, 10% were in Life Sciences, 8% were in Visual and Performing Arts, 6% were in Letters, 4% were in Health Sciences, 3% were in Physical Sciences, remainder in 7 other fields.

Graduates Career Data. Advanced studies pursued by 35% of students; 8% enter medical school; 1% enter dental school; 6% enter law school; 1% enter business school. Medical schools typically enrolling largest numbers of graduates include U. of Rochester, Georgetown, SUNY-Buffalo; law schools include SUNY-Buffalo, Boston U. About 31% of 1992–93 graduates employed. Fields typically hiring largest numbers of graduates include manufacturing, banking/finance/insurance, education, technical consulting. Career Development Services include career library, counselor assistance, on-campus employment, on-campus recruitment, resume referral, resume and interview workshops, alumni networking, employer/job fairs, mock interviews, Summer Reach (a summer employment program).

Faculty. About 99% of faculty hold PhD or equivalent. About 17% of teaching faculty are female; 10% minority.

Student Body. University seeks a national student body; 43% of students from in state; 57% Middle Atlantic, 13% New England; 13% Foreign. An estimated 32% of students reported as Catholic, 27% Protestant, 17% Jewish, 14% unaffiliated, 10% other; 6% Black, 10% Asian, 4% Hispanic, 10% other minorities.

Varsity Sports. Men (Div.III): Baseball, Basketball, Cross Country, Football, Golf, Soccer, Swimming, Tennis, Track. Women (Div.III): Basketball, Cross Country, Field Hockey, Soccer, Swimming, Tennis, Track, Volleyball.

Campus Life. Competitive club sports (Alpine Skiing, Crew, Cycling, Lacrosse, Ice Hockey, Rugby, Volleyball, Nordic Skiing, Women's Softball) in addition to popular intramural and recreational sports programs. All dorms coed except for 1 women's and 1 men's. Intervisitation unlimited, at option of residents of each living unit. University has granted student request for "no-board" option; wide variety of lifestyles now possible on campus. Cars allowed, but parking is limited.

Full schedule of cultural, intellectual and social events provided by campus and community; abundance of musical programs presented at and by Eastman School; university's Memorial Art Gallery offers popular creative art workshop and exhibits; Medieval Studies Center and Drama House are living/learning centers which offer regular programs of lectures, concerts, related activities. The Eastman Theater, 3 miles from campus, regularly offers concerts, artist series, traveling and resident theater groups, art galleries. Wilson Commons, the Student Union, was designed by I. M. Pei; Zornow Center is a new athletic facility available to the large number of students interested in intramurals.

About 5% of men, 6% of women live in traditional dormitories; 72% of men, 71% of women live in coed dormitories; rest live in off-campus housing or commute. Housing guaranteed for all four years. Sexes segregated in coed dormitories either by wing, floor or room. There are 16 fraternities, 10 sororities on campus which about 24% of men, 19% of women join; 7% of men live in fraternities. About 10–15% of resident students leave campus on weekends.

Annual Costs. Tuition and fees, $17,355; room and board, $6,286; estimated $1,359 other, exclusive of travel. About 80% of students receive financial aid; average amount of assistance, $18,575. Assistance is typically divided 73% scholarship/grant, 19% loan, 8% work. University reports 92 scholarships awarded for academic merit, 904 for need. *Meeting Costs:* university offers SHARE, ABLE, and PLUS Loans, payment plans, long term loans(10–20 years), employment programs, seed-money for student business ventures, and paid internship experiences.

Rockford College

Rockford, Illinois 61108 **(815) 226-4050 or (800) 892-2984**

A small, independent, liberal arts college, Rockford draws a high percentage of its students from the North Central region. The campus is located in a city of 250,000, 85 miles west of Chicago. Most convenient major airports: Rockford or O'Hare International (Chicago).

Founded: 1847
Affiliation: Independent
UG Enrollment: 327 M, 571 W (full-time); 119 M, 245 W (part-time)
Total Enrollment: 1,610
Cost: $10K–$20K
% Receiving Financial Aid: 96%
Admission: Non-selective
Application Deadline: Rolling

Admission. About 86% of applicants accepted, 36% of these actually enroll; 23% of freshmen graduate in top fourth of high school class, 62% in top half. *Required:* SAT or ACT, minimum H.S. GPA of 2.5, top 50% of class; interview recommended. Criteria considered in admissions, in order of importance: standardized test scores, high school academic record, top 50% of class, recommendations, extracurricular activities, writing sample; other factors considered: special talents, alumni children, diverse student body. *Entrance programs:* early admission, midyear admission, deferred admission,advanced placement. About 21% of freshmen are from private. *Apply*: rolling admissions. *Transfers* welcome; 173 enrolled 1993–94.

Academic Environment. Administration source characterizes student body as evenly divided in its interests among scholarly/intellectual pursuits and occupational/professional goals. Students are encouraged to attend the London, England campus for a semester or year-long experience. Administration reports about 65% of courses required for graduation are elective; distribution requirements fairly numerous: 6 semester hours in English, 6 hours in arts, 8 hours in language and literature, 8 hours in science and mathematics, 12 hours in social studies, 12 hours in foreign language, 2 hours in physical education; Senior Project, Forum Series. BA candidates must demonstrate command of English by examination or completion of a course in writing or speaking. Interdisciplinary Honors Program offers qualified students an alternative core program. Degrees offered: bachelors, masters. *Majors offered* in addition to usual studies include child development, psychology, theater arts, physical education, nursing, business, urban studies. Average undergraduate class size: 80% under 20, 8% between 20–40, 2% over 40.

About 62% of freshmen return for sophomore year. *Special programs:* CLEP, independent study, study abroad, London Semester, honors, undergraduate research, individualized majors, Washington Semester, United Nations Semester, credit by examination, credit for Peace Corps service, 3–2 program in engineering. *Calendar:* semester, summer school.

Undergraduate degrees conferred (213). 26% were in Business and Management, 19% were in Home Economics, 11% were in Social Sciences, 8% were in Visual and Performing Arts, 8% were in Computer and Engineering Related Technology, 7% were in Letters, 7% were in Health Sciences, 5% were in Psychology, remainder in 8 other fields.

Graduates Career Data. Advanced studies pursued by 17% of students. About 74% of 1992–93 graduates were employed (at graduation time). Fields typically hiring the largest number of graduates include business, sales, education, non-profit agencies. Career Development Services include career counseling, placement activities, senior series, career fair, computerized inventories, interest and skills inventories.

Faculty. About 63% of faculty hold PhD or equivalent. About 54% of undergraduate classes taught by tenured faculty. About 30% of teaching faculty are female; 5% minority.

Student Body. College seeks a national student body; 89% of students from in state; 2% Foreign. An estimated 60% of students reported as Protestant, 30% Catholic, 2% Jewish, 3% Muslim, 5% other; 5% Black, 3% Hispanic, 4% Asian, 3% other minority. Average age of undergraduate student: 22.

Varsity Sports. Men (Div.III): Baseball, Basketball, Diving, Golf, Soccer, Tennis. Women (Div.III): Basketball, Soccer, Softball, Swimming, Tennis, Volleyball.

Campus Life. Students have some voice in determining regulations governing campus social life; regulations governing intervisitation and related policies set by Board of Trustees. Student leader reports availability of close student/faculty/administration relationship. Limited intervisitation. Alcohol may be consumed in dormitory rooms by students of legal age; cars allowed. Students expected to live in residence halls. High demand reported for single rooms.

About 12% of women live in traditional dormitories; 49% of men, 29% of women live in coed dormitories; rest commute. There are no fraternities or sororities. About 40% of resident students leave campus on weekends.

Annual Costs. Tuition and fees, $11,500; room and board, $3,800. About 96% of students receive financial aid; average amount of assistance, $3,913. Assistance is typically divided 20% scholarship, 29% grant, 35% loan, 16% work. College reports 43 scholarships awarded for academic merit. *Meeting Costs:* college offers institutional yearly time-payment plan, PLUS Loans.

Rockhurst College

Kansas City, Missouri 64110 (816) 926-4000

Founded by the Society of Jesus, Rockhurst is governed by a Jesuit and lay board of trustees. The urban campus is located in a city of 507,100. Most convenient major airport: Kansas City International.

Founded: 1910	**Total Enrollment:** 2,586
Affiliation: Independent (Roman Catholic)	**Cost:** < $10K
UG Enrollment: 501 M, 626 W (full-time); 242 M, 512 W (part-time)	**% Receiving Financial Aid:** 73%
	Admission: Selective (+)
	Application Deadline: Rolling

Admission is selective (+). About 92% of applicants accepted, 40% of these actually enroll. About 44% of freshmen graduate in top fifth of high school class, 69% in top two-fifths. Average freshman scores: ACT, 23.4 composite. *Required:* SAT or ACT; interview recommended (required for physical therapy). Criteria considered in admissions, in order of importance: high school academic record, standardized test scores, recommendations, extracurricular activities, writing sample; other factors considered: special talents, diverse student body, alumni children, school and community activities. *Entrance programs:* advanced placement. *Apply*: rolling admissions. *Transfers* welcome; 226 enrolled 1993–94.

Academic Environment. Degrees offered: bachelors, masters. *Majors offered* in usual arts and sciences and professional/vocational fields including administration of justice, industrial relations, medical technology, nursing, respiratory therapy, computer science, systems management, physical therapy (MS), and occupational therapy (MS), global studies. Core requirements include 9 hours communication, 12 hours humanities, 3 hours mathematics, 4–7 hours sciences, 3–6 hours social sciences, 15 hours religion/philosophy. Average undergraduate class size: 56% of classes under 20, 41% between 20–40, 3% over 40.

More than 60% of students entering as freshmen graduate eventually; 13% of freshmen do not return for sophomore year. *Special programs:* CLEP, junior year abroad, honors, independent study, study abroad, cooperative work/study program in all areas, 3–2 programs in engineering, premed scholar program, course exchange with 28 Kansas City area schools. Adult programs: special support services for adult students. *Calendar:* semester, summer school.

Undergraduate degrees conferred (291). 54% were in Business and Management, 10% were in Allied Health, 7% were in Communications, 7% were in Social Sciences, 4% were in Health Sciences, 3% were in Computer and Engineering Related Technology, 3% were in Psychology, 3% were in Life Sciences, remainder in 6 other fields.

Graduates Career Data. Advanced studies pursued by 11% of students. About 57% of 1992–93 graduates employed. Fields typically hiring the largest number of graduates include business, health services, non-profit organizations, education, media. Career Development Services include resume assistance, information services, cooperative education, graduate school information, placement services. Alumni reported as helpful in both career guidance and job placement.

Faculty. About 71% of faculty hold PhD or equivalent. About 33% of teaching faculty are female; 3% ethnic minorities.

Varsity Sports. Men (NAIA): Baseball, Basketball, Cross Country, Soccer, Tennis. Women (NAIA): Basketball, Cross Country, Soccer, Tennis, Volleyball.

Student Body. College seeks a national student body; 71% of students from in state; 98% of students from North Central; 1% foreign students. An estimated 57% of students reported as Catholic, 16% Protestant, 27% unaffiliated or not reported; 9% Black, 5% Hispanic, 2% Asian.

Religious Orientation. Rockhurst is an independent institution "in the Jesuit tradition"; 3 courses in theology or religious studies required of all students; daily Mass available, but not required. Places of worship available on campus for Catholics, in immediate community for 3 major faiths.

About 32% of women live in traditional dormitories; 50% of men, 20% of women in coed dormitories; rest live in off-campus housing or commute. Freshmen given preference in college housing if all students cannot be accommodated. Intervisitation in men's and women's dormitory rooms limited. Sexes segregated in coed dormitories by wing. There are 4 fraternities, 2 sororities on campus which about 18% of men, 16% of women join. About 15% of students leave campus on weekends.

Annual Costs. Tuition and fees, $9,130; room and board, $3,870; estimated $1,810 other, exclusive of travel. About 73% of undergraduate students receive financial aid; average amount of assistance, $8,251. Assistance is typically divided 27% grant, 27% scholarships, 43% loans, 4% work. College reports 310 scholarships awarded on the basis of academic merit alone, 141 for special talents, 616 for need. *Meeting Costs:* college offers family grants for more than one student from same family, alumni grants and scholarships.

Rocky Mountain College

Billings, Montana 59102 (800) 877-6259

A church-related, liberal arts college, located in a city of 130,000. Most convenient major airport: Billings Logan International.

Founded: 1878
Affiliation: Presbyterian, United Methodist, United Church of Christ
UG Enrollment: 298 M, 327 W (full-time); 41 M, 77 W (part-time)
Cost: < $10K
% Receiving Financial Aid: 80%
Admission: Non-selective
Application Deadline: Rolling

Admission. Graduates of accredited high schools with 16 units and C average in 11 academic subjects eligible; 70% of applicants accepted, 48% of these actually enroll. Average freshman ACT scores: 21 composite. *Required:* ACT or SAT, minimum high school GPA of 2.5, essay. Criteria considered in admissions, in order of importance: high school academic record, recommendations, writing sample, standardized test scores, extracurricular activities. *Apply:* rolling admissions. *Transfers* welcome; 84 enrolled 1993–94.
Academic Environment. Degrees offered: associates, bachelors. About 70% of students entering as freshmen graduate eventually; 17% of freshmen do not return for sophomore year. Core requirements include courses in writing, advanced writing, mathematics or foreign language, fine arts, social sciences, natural sciences. *Majors offered* in addition to usual studies include equestrian studies, aviation studies. Average undergraduate class size: 85% of classes under 20, 13% between 20–40, 2% over 40.

Special programs: CLEP, independent study, honors, study abroad, undergraduate research, 3-year degree, individualized majors, 3–2 engineering with Montana State U, 3–2 programs in occupational therapy and in engineering. Adult programs: degree completion program offered. *Calendar:* 4–4–1, summer school.
Undergraduate degrees conferred (100). 27% were in Business and Management, 16% were in Social Sciences, 12% were in Education, 11% were in Letters, 8% were in Transportation and Material Moving, 6% were in Psychology, 4% were in Visual and Performing Arts, 4% were in Life Sciences, 4% were in Allied Health, remainder in 5 other fields.
Graduates Career Data. Advanced studies pursued by 18% of students. About 97% of 1992–93 graduates employed. Fields typically hiring the largest number of graduates include business, education.
Varsity Sports. Men (NAIA, Div. I): Basketball, Football, Skiing (NCSA). Women (NAIA): Basketball, Volleyball, Skiing (NCSA).
Student Body. College seeks a national student body; 68% of students from in state; 83% West/Northwest, 7% foreign. An estimated 70% of students reported as Protestant, 25% Catholic, 5% other; 2% Black, 6% Native American, 1% Asian.
Religious Orientation. Rocky Mountain is a church-related institution, makes no religious demands on students.
Campus Life. About 36% of students live in coed dormitories; rest live in off-campus housing or commute. About 20% of resident students leave campus on weekends.
Annual Costs. Tuition and fees, $8,734; room and board, $3,362; estimated $1,250 other, exclusive of travel. About 80% of students receive financial aid; average amount of assistance, $9,623. Assistance is typically divided 9% scholarship, 23% grant, 42% loan, 3% work. College reports 355 scholarships awarded on the basis of academic merit alone, 228 for special talents, 198 for need. *Meeting Costs:* college offers monthly and quarterly payment plans.

Roger Williams College

Bristol, Rhode Island 02809 (401) 253-1040

Roger Williams is a co-educational college of liberal arts, business, engineering technology, architecture and sciences offering both associate and baccalaureate degrees. Most convenient major airport: Green (Warwick).

Founded: 1948
Affiliation: Independent
UG Enrollment: 1,175 M, 936 W (full-time); 1,011 M, 701 W (part-time)
Cost: $10K–$20K
% Receiving Financial Aid: 37%
Admission: Non-selective
Application Deadline: Rolling

Admission. High school graduates eligible; 86% of applicants accepted, 24% of these actually enroll. About 17% of freshmen graduate in top fifth of high school class, 39% in top two-fifths. Average freshman SAT scores, according to most recent data available: 409 M, 395 W verbal, 475 M, 424 W mathematical. *Required:* SAT; interview preferred. *Non-academic factors* considered in admissions: special talents, extra-curricular activities. *Apply:* rolling admissions. *Transfers* welcome.
Academic Environment. *Degrees:* BA, BArch, BFA, BS. About 42% of students entering as freshmen graduate eventually; 30% of freshmen do not return for sophomore year. *Majors offered* in addition to usual studies include historic preservation, marine biology, paralegal studies, creative writing, communications. *Special programs:* cooperative education programs, independent study, study abroad, honors, individualized majors, 2–2 program in natural sciences with SUNY College of Environmental Science and Forestry. Adult programs: Open Program in School of Continuing Education (an alternative external program). *Calendar:* semester, fall and spring intersessions, summer evening session.
Undergraduate degrees conferred (632). 25% were in Business and Management, 14% were in Protective Services, 11% were in Architecture and Environmental Design, 11% were in Engineering and Engineering Related Technology, 7% were in Psychology, 6% were in Visual and Performing Arts, 4% were in Health Sciences, 4% were in Communications, 4% were in Law, 3% were in Life Sciences, 3% were in Letters, remainder in 13 other fields.
Faculty. About 39% of faculty hold PhD or equivalent.
Varsity Sports. Men (Div.III): Baseball, Basketball, Hockey, Lacrosse, Soccer, Tennis, Volleyball. Women (Div.III): Basketball, Softball, Tennis, Volleyball. Coed (Div. III): Equestrian, Golf, Sailing.
Student Body. College seeks a national and international student body; 46% of students from in state; 87% from New England. An estimated 35% of students reported as Protestant, 60% Catholic, 5% Jewish; 1% Black, 2% Hispanic, 2% Asian.
Campus Life. About 60% of men, 65% of women live in coed dormitories; rest live in off-campus housing or commute. Freshmen given preference in college housing if all students cannot be accommodated. Intervisitation in men's and women's dormitory rooms unlimited; sexes segregated by floor. There are no fraternities or sororities on campus. About 30% of students leave campus on weekends.
Annual Costs. Tuition and fees, $12,070; room and board, $5,910. About 37% of students receive financial aid; assistance is typically divided 34% scholarship, 53% loan, 13% work. College reports some scholarships awarded on the basis of academic merit alone.

Rollins College

Winter Park, Florida 32789 (407) 646-2161

The first institution of higher learning in Florida, Rollins has long drawn a high percentage of students from outside the South. It is a small liberal arts institution, founded by Congregationalists, but now independent and nonsectarian. The 65-acre campus is located in a town of 30,000, adjacent to Orlando. Most convenient major airport: Orlando International.

Founded: 1885
Affiliation: Independent
UG Enrollment: 621 M, 791 W (full-time)
Total Enrollment: 2,066
Cost: $10K–$20K
% Receiving Financial Aid: 58%
Admission: Selective (+)
Application Deadline: February 15

Admission is selective (+). About 65% of applicants accepted, 34% of these actually enroll; 44% of freshmen graduate in top fifth of high school class, 68% in top two-fifths. Average freshman scores: SAT (mid 50% range); 500–550 verbal, 500–610 mathematical; ACT (mid 50% range); 23–27, composite. *Required:* SAT or ACT. Criteria considered in admissions, in order of importance: high school academic record, standardized test scores, extracurricular activities, recommendations; other factors considered: special talents, alumni children, diverse student body. *Entrance programs:* early decision, midyear admission. About 38% of freshmen are from private schools, 8% from parochial schools. *Apply* by February 15. *Transfers* welcome; 90 enrolled 1993–94.

Academic Environment. Student interest reported to be primarily career oriented, emphasizing vocational and professional preparation, and administration source points to "strong relationship between liberal arts and career preparation." Students have representatives on all major college committees and have some influence on decisions involving curriculum. The Rollins program "offers students the opportunity to combine a high-quality liberal arts education with a program designed specifically to ensure their post-graduate marketability." It consists of 5 structured components: professional development skills, computer competency, business basics, leadership development, and experiential learning. General Education Program includes courses in written communication, foreign language, mathematical reasoning; American and other cultures; science, arts and literature. Degrees offered: bachelors, masters. *Majors offered* include business administration, classical studies, elementary education, theater arts; interdisciplinary majors in behavioral science, environmental studies, international relations, Latin American and Caribbean Affairs, pre-engineering, pre-forestry, pre-medicine. Average undergraduate class size: 71% of classes under 20, 28% between 20–40, 1% over 40. Students and administration report emphasis on small, interactive classes, and very accessible faculty.

About 73% of students entering as freshmen graduate within four years, 75% eventually; 88% of freshmen return for sophomore year. *Special programs:* independent study, January term, study abroad, honors, undergraduate research, 3-year degree, individualized majors, study at Merrill-Palmer Institute, 3–2 in engineering. Adult programs: separate and distinct evening programs, one at main campus and one at branch location. *Calendar:* 4–1–4.

Undergraduate degrees conferred (561). 29% were in Social Sciences, 12% were in Business and Management, 11% were in Psychology, 10% were in Letters, 8% were in Multi/Interdisciplinary Studies, 7% were in Communications, 6% were in Visual and Performing Arts, 5% were in Computer and Engineering Related Technology, remainder in 8 other fields.

Graduates Career Data. Advanced studies pursued by 21% of students; 2% enter medical school; 3% enter law school; 2% enter business school. About 57% of 1992–93 graduates employed. Fields typically hiring largest numbers of graduates include sales & marketing, advertising/public relations, financial services. Career Development Services include individual assessment and counseling, group workshops, mock interviews, campus recruiting, career expo, graduate/professional school planning, pre-law advising, extensive career resource library.

Faculty. About 93% of faculty hold PhD or equivalent. About 72% of undergraduate classes taught by tenured faculty. About 32% of teaching faculty are female; 6% Hispanic, 5% other minority.

Student Body. College seeks a national student body; 40% of students from Florida; 15% South, 17% New England, 17% Middle Atlantic, 8% Midwest, 2% West; 4% Foreign. An estimated 58% of students reported as Protestant, 28% Catholic, 12% Jewish, 2% other; 3% Black, 6% Hispanic, 4% Asian, 2% other minority.

Varsity Sports. Men (Div.II): Baseball, Basketball, Crew, Cross Country, Golf, Sailing, Soccer, Tennis, Water Skiing. Women (Div.II): Basketball, Crew, Cross Country, Golf, Sailing, Soccer, Softball, Tennis, Volleyball, Water Skiing.

Campus Life. No regulations governing intervisitation; students may choose rooms where hours are restricted. Drinking permitted in approved areas; cars permitted, but freshmen may not park on campus. High interest reported in fraternities/sororities, varsity sports (most popular soccer, baseball, basketball, volleyball, football, tennis) and intramurals (most popular coed football, soccer, softball). Orlando, adjacent to campus, and Tampa, 90 miles away, offer wide variety of cultural activities.

About 17% of men, 27% of women live in coed dormitories; rest live in off-campus housing or commute. Freshmen are guaranteed college housing. Sexes segregated in coed dormitories by floor. There are 6 fraternities, 6 sororities on campus, which about 35% of men, 35% of women join; 18% of men, 18% of women live in fraternities and sororities. About 20% of resident students leave campus on weekends.

Annual Costs. Tuition and fees, $15,950, room and board, $4,925; estimated $950 other, exclusive of travel. About 58% of students receive financial aid; average amount of assistance, $13,856. Assistance is typically divided 28% scholarship, 32% grant, 30% loan, 10% work. College reports 245 scholarships awarded for academic merit, 59 for special talents, 20 for need.

Roosevelt University

Chicago, Illinois 60605 **(312) 341-3515**

An independent institution, primarily for commuters, located in metropolitan Chicago. The university has residential facilities for 350 students. Most convenient major airport: O'Hare International (Chicago).

Founded: 1945
Affiliation: Independent
UG Enrollment: 652 M, 668 W (full-time); 1,272 M, 1,520 W (part-time)
Total Enrollment: 6,130
Cost: < $10K
% Receiving Financial Aid: 66%
Admission: Non-selective
Application Deadline: Aug. 1

Admission. Graduates of accredited high schools with 15 units eligible; 54% of applicants accepted, 41% of these actually enroll. *Required:* SAT, ACT, or university's own entrance examination. *Apply* by August 1. *Transfers* welcome.

Academic Environment. *Undergraduate studies* offered by colleges of Arts and Sciences, Business Administration, Chicago Musical College, colleges of Education, Continuing Education. *Majors offered* in addition to usual studies include hospitality management, telecommunications, public administration for non-profit organizations, environmental studies. About 25% of freshmen do not return for sophomore year. *Special programs:* CLEP, independent study, honors, 3-year degree, individualized majors, Chicago Consortium of Colleges and Universities. Adult programs: Bachelor of General Studies for students over 25. *Calendar:* early semester, summer school.

Undergraduate degrees conferred (715). 100% were in Unknown.

Faculty. About 70% of faculty hold PhD or equivalent.

Varsity Sports. Men (NAIA): Basketball, Golf, Soccer, Tennis.

Student Body. University seeks a national student body; 95% of students from in state. An estimated 25% of students reported as Black, 3% Hispanic, 2% Asian, according to most recent data available.

Campus Life. Coed dormitories available on campus for 350 students; rest commute. Intervisitation in men's and women's dormitory rooms unlimited; sexes segregated by floor. There is 1 fraternity on campus which about 1% of men join; no sororities.

Annual Costs. Tuition and fees, $8,640; room and board, $4,950. About 66% of students receive financial aid; assistance is typically divided 56% gift aid, 44% self-help (loan, work). University reports scholarships awarded only on the basis of need.

Rosary College

River Forest, Illinois 60305 **(312) 366-2490**

A Catholic, liberal arts college, conducted by the Dominican Sisters of Sinsinawa, Wisconsin, Rosary is now co-educational. The 30-acre campus is located in a town of 13,400, 10 miles west of Chicago. Most convenient major airport: O'Hare International (Chicago).

Founded: 1901
Affiliation: Roman Catholic
UG Enrollment: 177 M, 614 W (full-time)
Total Enrollment: 1,207
Cost: $10K–$20K
% Receiving Financial Aid: 70%
Admission: Selective
Application Deadline: Rolling

Admission is selective. About 78% of applicants accepted, 52% of these actually enroll; 44% of freshmen graduate in top fifth of high school class, 71% in top two-fifths. *Required:* SAT or ACT; interview recommended. *Non-academic factors* considered in admissions: special talents. *Entrance programs:* midyear admission, advanced placement, deferred admission. About 49% of entering students from parochial schools. *Apply:* rolling admissions. *Transfers* welcome.

Academic Environment. Administration spokesman reports that students are equally concerned about scholarly/intellectual pursuits and career-oriented studies. Administration reports core curriculum of required courses plus freshman seminar. *Degree:* BA. *Majors offered* include usual arts and sciences, business administration, food service management, dietetics, fashion design and merchandising, international business, fine arts, home economics.

About 53% of students entering as freshmen graduate eventually; 11% of freshmen do not return for sophomore year. *Special programs:* CLEP, independent study, study abroad, honors, individualized majors, U. of Chicago program, cross-registration with Concordia, London Semester, junior-year program in Spain, honors at entrance, study at Argonne National Laboratory, 5-year BA/MBA. *Calendar:* semester, summer school.

Undergraduate degrees conferred (236). 35% were in Business and Management, 11% were in Psychology, 11% were in Letters, 8% were in Social Sciences, 8% were in Communications, 5% were in Home Economics, 5% were in Marketing and Distribution, 3% were in Life Sciences, 3% were in Foreign Languages, 3% were in Visual and Performing Arts, 3% were in Computer and Engineering Related Technology, remainder in 5 other fields.

Graduates Career Data. According to most recent data available, full-time graduate or professional study pursued immediately after graduation by 35–40% of students. *Careers in business and industry* pursued by 69% of graduates. Firms typically hiring largest numbers of graduates include banks, accounting firms.

Faculty. About 70% of full-time faculty hold PhD or equivalent.

Student Body. College seeks a national student body; 93% of students from in state; 99% of students from North Central. An estimated 73% of students reported as Catholic, 23% Protestant, 1% Jewish, 4% unaffiliated; 5% Black, 4% Hispanic, 1% Asian, 2% other minority, according to most recent data available. *Minority group students:* special admissions program "for students with potential but inadequate academic preparation."

Religious Orientation. Rosary is a Catholic institution offering a liberal education with a "religious dimension"; one course in religious studies required. Places of worship available in immediate community for major faiths.

Varsity Sports. Men (NAIA): Basketball, Soccer. Women (NAIA): Basketball, Tennis, Volleyball.

Campus Life. College responsive to student opinion; students represented on all administrative and trustee committees and on Board of Trustees. With the movement to full coeducation, nature of campus life has begun to change. Administration does not regulate women's hours; intervisitation allowed during specific hours; alcoholic beverages allowed in residence hall rooms for those of legal age (21 or older).

About 40% of students live in coed dormitories; rest commute. Freshmen given preference in college housing if all students cannot be accommodated. Sexes segregated in coed dormitories by floor. There are no fraternities or sororities.

Annual Costs. Tuition and fees, $10,550; room and board, $4,490. About 70% of students receive financial aid. Assistance is typically divided 75% scholarship, 15% loan, 10% work. College reports some scholarships awarded on the basis of academic merit alone. *Meeting Costs:* college offers monthly payment plans and family discounts.

Rose-Hulman Institute of Technology

Terre Haute, Indiana 47803 **(812) 877-1511**

Rose-Hulman, named after its founder, Chauncy Rose and a major benefactor, the Hulman Foundation, was formerly the Rose Polytechnic Institute. The school is primarily a science and engineering institution. Beginning in 1995, Rose-Hulman will be accepting women into its undergraduate program for the first time. The 130-acre campus is located in a city of 70,300. Most convenient major airport: Indianapolis.

Founded: 1874
Affiliation: Independent
UG Enrollment: 1,350 M (full-time)
Cost: $10K–$20K
% Receiving Financial Aid: 91%
Admission: Highly (+) Selective
Application Deadline: March 1

Admission is highly (+) selective. About 62% of applicants accepted, 21% of these actually enroll; 94% of freshmen graduate in top fifth of high school class, all in top two-fifths. Average freshman scores: SAT, 540 verbal, 670 mathematical; 69% of freshmen score above 500 on verbal, 22% above 600, 4% above 700; all score above 500 on mathematical, 81% above 600, 34% above 700; ACT, 31 composite. *Required:* SAT or ACT; interview recommended. Criteria considered in admissions, in order of importance: high school academic record, standardized tests, recommendations; other factors considered: special talents, alumni children, diverse student body. About 5% of entering students from private schools, 15% from parochial schools. Entrance program: advanced placement. *Apply* by March 1. *Transfers* welcome; 18 enrolled 1993–94.

Academic Environment. Academic competition at this highly respected engineering and science school is said to be "intense" and though some feel it is "too demanding," a recent chemical engineering student finds that "students help each other out in classes, and the faculty is very accessible". Enrollment is small, and scheduling conflicts sometimes result. Rose-Hulman is a traditional engineering college, which emphasizes teaching and laboratory opportunities, rather than research. Freshmen take common curriculum; degree programs all include 9 courses in humanities and social sciences; but administration also notes that "total emphasis [is] given to undergraduate degree programs for students in engineering and science." No liberal arts major is offered. Degrees offered: bachelors, masters. There are 11 degree programs in engineering, chemistry, mathematics, physics, computer engineering, and applied optics. Specialized equipment and facilities offer unusual opportunities to undergraduates in the scientific and technical fields. Average undergraduate class size: 20% of classes under 20, 75% 20–40, 5% over 40.

About 72% of students entering as freshmen graduate within four years; 75% eventually, 90% of freshmen return for sophomore year. *Special programs:* honors, study abroad, undergraduate research, freshman projects (in engineering and applied science problems), summer industrial internship program, Operation Catapult (3-week summer program for high school juniors), technical translators certificate program in Russian and German. *Calendar:* quarter, summer school.

Undergraduate degrees conferred (241). 78% were in Engineering, 15% were in Physical Sciences, 6% were in Computer and Engineering Related Technology, remainder in Mathematics.

Graduates Career Data. *Full-time graduate or professional study* pursued immediately after graduation by 24% of students (1990–91); 2% enter medical school; 2% enter law school; 5% enter business school. Medical, law and business schools typically enrolling largest numbers of graduates include Indiana U. *Careers in business and industry* pursued by 80% of graduates. More than 350 companies send representatives to the campus to interview graduating seniors. Corporations typically hiring largest numbers of graduates include General Motors, Eli Lilly, Ford, Dow. Career Development Services include a career fair held annually and career counseling is available.

Faculty. About 93% of faculty hold PhD or equivalent. About 95% of undergraduate classes taught by tenured faculty. About 10% of teaching faculty are female; 2% Black.

Student Body. Institute seeks a national student body; 60% of students from in state; 80% of students from Midwest, 10% South, 2% Middle Atlantic, 2% West, 4% Northwest, 2% New England. An estimated 65% of students reported as Protestant, 25% Catholic, 5% Jewish; 2% Black, 1% Hispanic, 2% Asian, according to most recent data available.

Varsity Sports. Men (Div.III): Baseball, Basketball, Cross Country, Football, Golf, Soccer, Swimming, Tennis, Track, Wrestling.

Campus Life. Like many other technologically oriented schools, this is not an activist campus. Rose-Hulman has been a men's school and Terre Haute offers only limited opportunities for social and cultural activity, but these drawbacks are somewhat mitigated by the proximity of Indiana State and Saint Mary-of-the-Woods. Students welcome the plans to go coed. Administration reports students feel need for additional housing to relieve overcrowding. No restrictions on smoking, but administration source notes "very few" students smoke. Alcoholic beverages allowed in dormitories for those over 21, in compliance with state law. Student leader reports no student concern about regulations. Cars allowed for all.

About 70% of men live in dormitories; 20% live in fraternities; 10% commute. There are 8 fraternities on campus which about 45% of men join.

Annual Costs. Tuition and fees, $13,400; room and board, $4,200; estimated $1,500 other, exclusive of travel. About 91% of students receive financial aid; average amount of assistance, $9,000. Assistance is typically divided 10% scholarship, 20% grant, 60% loan, 10% work. Institute reports some scholarships awarded on the basis of academic merit alone.

Rosemont College

Rosemont, Pennsylvania 19010 (215) 526-2966

Rosemont is a small, Catholic, liberal arts college for women, conducted by the Sisters of the Holy Child Jesus. The 56-acre campus is located in a Philadelphia suburb, 20 minutes from the center of the city. Most convenient major airport: Philadelphia.

Founded: 1921
Affiliation: Roman Catholic
UG Enrollment: 500 W (full-time); 125 W (part-time)
Cost: $10K–$20K
% Receiving Financial Aid: 65%
Admission: Non-selective
Application Deadline: Rolling

Admission. About 75% of applicants accepted, 45% of these actually enroll; 28% of freshmen graduate in top fifth of high school class, 50% in top two-fifths. Average freshman SAT scores: 505 verbal, 502 mathematical. *Required:* SAT, minimum HS GPA 2.0; interview recommended. Criteria considered in admissions, in order of importance: high school academic record, standardized tests, extra curricular activities, recommendations, writing sample; other factors considered: special talents, diverse student body. About 14% of entering students from private schools, 46% from parochial schools. *Entrance programs:* midyear admission, advanced placement, transfer. *Apply:* rolling admissions. *Transfers* welcome; 40 enrolled 1993–94.

Academic Environment. Degrees offered: bachelors, masters. *Majors offered* include usual arts and sciences, business administration, accounting, economics, education, humanities, American studies, Italian studies, individualized majors, interdisciplinary program in American Studies. Core requirements include 1 course in writing, 1 in fine arts, 2 each in religious studies, literature, foreign language, philosophy, history, social sciences, mathematics or natural sciences, and physical education; Freshman Colloquium also required. Student to faculty ratio of 12:1 ensures small classes.

About 68% of students entering as freshmen graduate within four years, 70% eventually; 88% of freshmen return for sophomore year. *Special programs:* CLEP, independent study, study abroad, honors, undergraduate research, individualized majors, cross-registration with Villanova, cooperative education option, joint medical school admissions program with Hahnemann Medical. Adult programs: REAP (Rosemont Educational Advancement Program), special support services, counseling for non-traditional age students, day care available. *Calendar:* semester.

Undergraduate degrees conferred (125). 22% were in Social Sciences, 19% were in Letters, 15% were in Psychology, 12% were in Visual and Performing Arts, 10% were in Business and Management, 6% were in Mathematics, 5% were in Foreign Languages, 3% were in Philosophy and Religion, 3% were in Life Sciences, remainder in 3 other fields.

Graduates Career Data. Advanced studies pursued by 30% of students. Career Development Services include planning, interviewing, computer programs, testing, resume service, career fairs, job bulletin.

Faculty. About 75% of faculty hold PhD or equivalent. About 55% of teaching faculty are female.

Student Body. College does not seek a national student body; 55% of students from in state; 89% of students from Middle Atlantic, 5% New England, 2% South, 1% Midwest, 1% West. An estimated 17% of students reported as Protestant, 60% Catholic, 3% Jewish, 2% Muslim, 16% unaffiliated, 2% other; 4% Black, 2% Hispanic, 4% Asia,.

Religious Orientation. Rosemont is a church-related institution; general education requirements include 2 religious courses studies. Religious activities on campus coordinated by Campus Ministry. Places of worship available on campus for Catholics, nearby for Protestants and Jews.

Varsity Sports. Women: Badminton, Basketball, Field Hockey, Softball, Tennis, Volleyball.

Campus Life. College provides variety of cultural opportunities on campus, supplemented by the resources of Philadelphia, 11 miles away, and other nearby colleges. A recent student find dormitory rules to be "stringent", but she says, "If I want to party, I go off campus; if I want to study, I stay there. It's the best of both worlds." Alcohol permitted in specified areas for students of legal age; cars allowed seniors, lower classmen with special permission of dean. About 85% of women live in dormitories; rest commute. Freshmen given preference in college housing if all students cannot be accommodated. There are no sororities. About 50% of resident students leave campus on weekends.

Annual Costs. Tuition and fees, $11,075; room and board, $5,700; estimated $1,400 other, exclusive of travel. About 65% of students receive financial aid; average amount of assistance, $8,934. Assistance is typically divided 20% scholarship, 40% grant, 30% loan, 10% work. College reports 16 scholarships awarded on the basis of academic merit alone, 12 for special talents, 76 for need alone. *Meeting Costs:* college offers monthly payment plans.

Rowan College of New Jersey

Glassboro, New Jersey 08028 (609) 863-5000

A state-supported college with programs in teacher preparation and the liberal arts, located in a town of 12,900, 20 miles southwest of Philadelphia. Formerly known as Glassboro State College.

Founded: 1923
Affiliation: State
UG Enrollment: 2,246 M, 3,144 W (full-time)
Total Enrollment: 9,803
Cost: < $10K
Admission: Non-selective
Application Deadline: Mar. 15

Admission. Graduates of accredited high schools with 2.8 average eligible; 58% of applicants accepted, 51% of these actually enroll; 27% of freshmen graduate in top fifth of high school class, 68% in top two-fifths. *Required:* SAT or ACT. *Out-of-state* freshman applicants: college seeks students from out of state. No special requirements for out-of-state applicants. *Apply* by March 15. *Transfers* welcome.

Academic Environment. Administration reports 15–30% of courses required for graduation are elective; numerous distribution requirements, however. Degrees offered: bachelors, masters. *Majors offered* in 9 areas of teacher education and 16 areas of arts and sciences including communications, music. About 70% of students entering as freshmen graduate eventually; 50% of freshmen do not return for sophomore year. *Special programs:* CLEP, independent study, study abroad, undergraduate research, 3-year degree, internships. *Calendar:* semester, summer school.

Undergraduate degrees conferred (1,313). 26% were in Education, 21% were in Business and Management, 16% were in Communications, 8% were in Social Sciences, 6% were in Protective Services, 5% were in Psychology, 4% were in Visual and Performing Arts, 3% were in Physical Sciences, 3% were in Letters, remainder in 6 other fields.

Faculty. About 46% of faculty hold doctorate.

Varsity Sports. Men (Div.III): Baseball, Basketball, Cross Country, Football, Golf, Gymnastics, Soccer, Swimming, Tennis, Track and Field. Women (Div.III): Basketball, Cross Country, Field Hockey, Gymnastics, Lacrosse, Softball, Swimming, Tennis, Track and Field, Volleyball.

Student Body. College does not seek a national student body; virtually all students from Middle Atlantic.

Campus Life. Relatively small proportion of students live on campus, about one-third live in off-campus housing and nearly one-half commute. Cars allowed on campus for commuters only. About 2% of men, 3% of women live in traditional dormitories; 12% of men, 12% of women in coed dormitories. Sexes segregated in coed dormitories either by wing or room. There are 8 fraternities, 9 sororities on campus which 2% of men, 2% of women join. About 85% of students leave campus on weekends.

Annual Costs. Tuition and fees, $2,703 (out-of-state, $3,753); room and board, $4,565; estimated $800 other, exclusive of travel.

Russell Sage College

Troy, New York 12180 (518) 270-2441; (800) 999-3RSC

A small, liberal arts college for women, Russell Sage also offers professional programs in nursing, medical technology, nutrition, physical therapy, economics and business, criminal science, public administration, physical education; and elementary, secondary, and special education, which more than half of students select as majors. The compact urban campus is small enough to make "contacts among students, faculty, and administration easy and frequent"; located in a city of 57,900, across the Hudson River from Albany. Most convenient major airport: Albany County.

Founded: 1916
Affiliation: Independent
UG Enrollment: 1,009 W (full-time); 119 W, (part-time)
Cost: $10K–$20K
% Receiving Financial Aid: 85%
Admission: Selective
Application Deadline: Aug. 1

Admission is selective. About 90% of applicants accepted, 34% of these actually enroll; 47% of freshman graduate in top fifth of high school class, 79% in top two-fifths. Average freshman SAT scores: 25% of freshman score above 500 verbal, 3% above 600; 48% score above 500 mathematical, 8% above 600. *Required:* SAT, essay, interview. Criteria considered in admissions, in order of importance: high school academic record, standardized tests, recommendations, pattern of academic performance through secondary level, writing sample, extra curricular activities; other factors considered: special talents, diverse student body. *Entrance programs:* early decision, early admission, midyear admission, deferred admission, advanced placement. About 10% of entering students are from parochial schools, 5% from private schools. *Apply* by August 1st. *Transfers* welcome; 160 enrolled 1993–94.

Academic Environment. Career-training orientation of college influences campus environment and should be attractive to contemporary, career-minded women. Programs place emphasis "on interdisciplinary work, international and intercultural sensitivity, and independent work." General education requirements for graduation include studies in the Humanities and Arts, the Natural and Social Sciences, Analytic and Quantitative Reasoning, Communications, and Values and Consequences. Degrees offered: bachelors, masters. *Majors offered* include usual arts and sciences, accounting, arts management, management, retailing, fine arts, nursing, physical therapy, computer information systems, creative arts in therapy (art, music, dance), occupational therapy. Over 75% of students participate in internships or cooperative work/study programs. Average undergraduate class size: 70% of classes under 20, 20% 20–40, 10% over 40.

About 60% of students entering as freshmen graduate within four years, 70% eventually; 81% of freshmen return for sophomore year. *Special programs:* independent study, study abroad, honors, undergraduate research, individualized majors, cross-registration through Hudson-Mohawk Association of Colleges and Universities (Higher Education Opportunity Program), 14 other members of local consortium include RPI, Union, Skidmore, all SUNY, 3–2 in engineering, 3–3 in law, accelerated undergraduate programs in pre-law, BA/MBA, BA/MPA, BS/MS in occupational therapy, internships for all majors, work/study program in merchandising, cooperative program with nearby museum for fine arts majors. *Calendar:* 4–1–4.

Undergraduate degrees conferred (330). 17% were in Allied Health, 16% were in Business and Management, 15% were in Health Sciences, 12% were in Psychology, 9% were in Social Sciences, 7% were in Life Sciences, 6% were in Education, 5% were in Visual and Performing Arts, 4% were in Protective Services, 4% were in Public Affairs, 3% were in Letters, remainder in 4 other fields.

Graduates Career Data. Advanced studies pursued by 12–15% of students; 1% enter medical school; 5% enter law school; 5% enter business school; 1% enter dental school. Law schools typically enrolling largest numbers of graduates include Albany; business schools include Sage Graduate School, St. Rose. About 70% of 1992–93 graduates employed. Fields typically hiring largest numbers of graduates include physical or occupational therapy, elementary/secondary education, nursing. Career Development Services include emphasis on identification of skills and interests through a comprehensive four year approach, coordination of very extensive internship/field experience program, networking through professionals (alumnae), traditional workshops on job preparation activity and placement services, weekly hotline and monthly newsletter on relevant topics.

Faculty. About 86% of faculty hold PhD or equivalent. About 95% of undergraduate classes taught by tenured faculty. About 58% of teaching faculty are female; 2% Black, 5% Hispanic.

Student Body. College seeks a national student body; 86% of students from in state; 96% from New England. An estimated 5% of students reported as Black, 4% Hispanic, 2% Asian, 6% undeclared. Average age of undergraduate student: 22.

Varsity Sports. Women (NCAA Div.III): Basketball, Soccer, Softball, Tennis, Volleyball.

Campus Life. Drinking allowed for those 21 and over, in accordance with state law. Permission required to park cars on campus. Expanded college schedule of cultural, intellectual, and social activities supplemented by presence of other colleges in Hudson-Mohawk Consortium. Nearest major cultural center is Albany, 10 miles from campus.

About 70% of women live in dormitories; 5% live in off-campus college-related housing; rest commute. Freshmen given preference in college housing if all students cannot be accommodated. There are no sororities. About 25% of resident students leave campus on weekends.

Annual Costs. Tuition and fees, $11,930; room and board, $4,860; estimated $1,500 other, exclusive of travel. About 85% of students receive financial aid; average amount of assistance, $11,500. Assistance is typically divided 10% scholarship, 50% grant, 30% loan, 10% work. College reports some scholarships awarded on the basis of academic merit or special talents alone, most awarded on the basis of need. *Meeting Costs:* college offers participates in private payment plans and long-term loans.

Rust College

Holly Springs, Mississippi 38635 (601) 252-4661

A church-related, liberal arts college, located in a town of 7,500, 50 miles southeast of Memphis; founded as a college for Negroes and still serving a predominantly black student body.

Founded: 1866
Affiliation: United Methodist
UG Enrollment: 1,075 M, W (full-time)
Cost: < $10K
Admission: Non-selective
Application Deadline: July 15

Admission. Graduates of approved high schools with 16 units (10 in academic subjects) and C average eligible; some admitted "as an academic risk"; 65% of applicants accepted, 53% of these actually enroll. *Required:* ACT. *Apply* by July 15. *Transfers* welcome.

Academic Environment. *Degrees:* AB, BS. About 62% of students entering as freshmen graduate eventually; 86% of freshmen return for sophomore year. *Special programs:* CLEP, independent study, study abroad, honors, undergraduate research. *Calendar:* semester, January intersession, summer school.

Undergraduate degrees conferred (123). 24% were in Business and Management, 20% were in Education, 13% were in Communications, 11% were in Public Affairs, 9% were in Social Sciences, 6% were in Life Sciences, 4% were in Letters, 4% were in Business (Administrative Support), 3% were in Physical Sciences, 3% were in Computer and Engineering Related Technology, remainder in 2 other fields.

Student Body. College seeks a national student body; 62% of students from in state.

Religious Orientation. Rust is a church-related institution; 4 semester hours of religion required of all students.

Varsity Sports. Men (Div.III): Baseball, Basketball, Cross Country, Tennis, Track. Women (Div.III): Basketball, Cross Country, Tennis, Track.

Campus Life. About 94% of men, 73% of women live in traditional dormitories; no coed dormitories; rest live in off-campus housing or commute. No intervisitation in men's or women's dormitory rooms. There are 5 fraternities, 4 sororities on campus which about 15% of men, 7% of women join. About 60% of resident students leave campus on weekends.

Annual Costs. Tuition and fees, $4,152; room and board, $1,948. College reports some scholarships awarded on the basis of academic merit alone. *Meeting Costs:* college offers extended payment plan.

Rutgers—The State University of New Jersey

New Brunswick, New Jersey 08903

Founded as a private college in 1766, Rutgers College provided the base on which the state, over the years, established a university. Rutgers became New Jersey's land-grant college in 1864 and was designated as the state university in 1917. In 1945 the legislature extended the name "The State University of New Jersey" to include all the colleges and divisions that made up the whole institution. The university comprises 28 degree-granting schools: 13 undergraduate, 12 graduate, and 3 schools which offer both undergraduate and graduate degrees on three separate campuses in New Brunswick, Newark, and Camden.

Founded: 1766
Affiliation: State
Total Enrollment: 47,899

Academic Environment. The University's central campus is located in New Brunswick, where undergraduate students enroll in one of 9 colleges located on both sides of the Raritan River and connected by a free, campus-wide bus system. Four are liberal arts colleges —Douglass College, Livingston College, Rutgers College, and University College — and five are professional schools — Cook College, Mason Gross School of the Arts, the College of Engineering, the upper division School of Business, and the College of Pharmacy. Each college sets its own admission standards and degree requirements and has its own special programs and mission. For example, Douglass is a liberal arts college for women; all of the other colleges are co-educational. Among the professional schools, Cook College specializes in agricultural, environmental, and life sciences, and other interdisciplinary programs related to those fields. Students attending Rutgers in New Brunswick can select from approximately 100 major fields of study. All major programs in the arts and sciences are offered to students at the four liberal arts colleges; some arts and sciences majors are also available to Cook students. In addition, numerous majors in professional subjects, ranging from agricultural engineering to urban studies, are available to students at the liberal arts colleges.

Newark College of Arts and Sciences and University College, the College of Nursing, Graduate School of Management, School of Law, and School of Criminal Justice share the Newark Campus. The Camden campus houses the Camden College of Arts and Sciences, University College, the upper division School of Business, and a separate School of Law.

Library: 4,846,337 bound volumes, 19,883 periodical subscriptions, 2,602,420 microforms; hours until 1 am (8 PM on Saturday).

Undergraduate degrees conferred (5,109). 27% were in Social Sciences, 9% were in Engineering, 9% were in Psychology, 8% were in Life Sciences, 8% were in Letters, 8% were in Business and Management, 7% were in Communications, 4% were in Visual and Performing Arts, 3% were in Health Sciences, 3% were in Foreign Languages, 3% were in Computer and Engineering Related Technology, remainder in 13 other fields.

Undergraduate degrees conferred, Camden campus, (614). 47% were in Business and Management, 11% were in Computer and Information Sciences, 9% were in Social Sciences, 6% were in Health Sciences, 6% were in Psychology, 4% were in Letters, 4% were in Visual and Performing Arts, 4% were in Physical Sciences, 3% were in Life Sciences, remainder in 4 other fields.

Undergraduate degrees conferred, Newark campus, (985). 44% were in Business and Management, 12% were in Social Sciences, 10% were in Life Sciences, 10% were in Health Sciences, 5% were in Letters, 4% were in Visual and Performing Arts, 4% were in Physical Sciences, 3% were in Psychology, remainder in 8 other fields.

Financial Aid. About 58% of entering students receive financial aid; average amount of assistance, $4,807. Assistance is typically divided 17% scholarship, 49% grant, 30% loan, 4% work. University reports 3,159 scholarships awarded university-wide on the basis of academic merit alone, 465 for special talents, 3,385 for need.

Rutgers College

New Brunswick, New Jersey 08903-2101 (908) 932-8789

The oldest division of the university, Rutgers College was a college for men from pre-revolutionary days until the early 1970s; it is now a co-educational, residential college. The 832-acre campus is located in a community of 42,000, 30 miles southwest of New York City. Most convenient major airport: Newark International.

Founded: 1766
Affiliation: State
UG Enrollment: 4,068 M, 4,162 W (full-time)
Cost: < $10K
% Receiving Financial Aid: 58%
Admission: Very (+) Selective
Application Deadline: Jan. 15

Admission is very (+) selective. About 46% of applicants accepted, 23% of these actually enroll; 75% of freshmen graduate in top fifth of high school class; 90% in top two-fifths. Average freshman SAT scores: 540 M, 530 W verbal, 630 M, 590 W mathematical; 68% of freshmen score above 500 on verbal, 25% above 600, 2% above 700; 91% score above 500 on mathematical, 58% above 600, 16% above 700. *Required:* SAT or ACT. Criteria considered in admissions, in order of importance: high school academic record, class rank, standardized tests, recommendations, extra curricular activities; other factors considered: special talents, diverse student body, leadership. *Entrance programs:* early admission, midyear admission (for transfers only), deferred admission, advanced placement. *Out-of-state* freshman applicants: college encourages qualified students from out of state. No special requirements for out-of-state applicants; 45% of applicants accepted, 13% of these actually enroll. *Apply* by January 15. *Transfers* welcome; 446 enrolled 1993–94.

Academic Environment. Pressures for academic achievement appear moderately strong. Degree offered: bachelors. The size of the school allows for diverse course offerings. *Majors offered* in liberal arts in addition to usual studies include African studies, anthropology, biochemistry, botany, chemistry, dance, dramatic art, foods and nutrition, geography, Greek and Latin, Hebraic studies, Latin American civilization, Middle Eastern language and area studies, Oriental language and area studies, Portuguese, physiology, Soviet and East European studies, women's studies, finance. Average undergraduate class size: 28% under 20, 45% 20–40, 27% over 40.

About 58% of entering freshmen graduate within four years, 77% within six years; 91% of freshmen return for sophomore year. *Special programs:* CLEP, independent study, study abroad, honors, undergraduate research, internships, individualized majors, double majors, National Student Exchange, combined 5-year liberal arts/engineering leading to both AB and BS, credit by examination, BA/MBA with Rutgers Graduate School of Management, 8-year BA/MD with U. of Medicine and Dentistry of NJ, 2–3 dual degree with College of Engineering. *Calendar:* semester.

Graduates Career Data. Advanced studies pursued by 43% of students (survey, May 1992); 5% enter medical school; 1% enter dental school; 8% enter law school; 4% enter business school, according to most recent data available. Medical schools typically enrolling largest numbers of graduates include UNM&D-NJ (both campuses), SUNY Downstate; dental schools include UNM&D-NJ, U. Penn., NYU; law schools include Rutgers, Seton Hall, NY Law; business schools include Rutgers, NYU, Columbia (1990–91). Corporations typically hiring largest numbers of graduates include Merck, Prudential, Deloitte & Touche, KPMG Peat Marwick. Career Development Services include Resource Bank, computerized career guidance system, on-campus recruiting, computerized resume and job banks, resume referral system, KiNexus, career days, workshops, resume assistance. Alumni reported as helpful in both career guidance and job placement. Approximately 60% of the 1992 graduating class rated career services from "good" to "excellent".

Faculty. About 95% of faculty of the New Brunswick campus hold PhD or equivalent. About 39% of undergraduate classes taught by tenured faculty. About 26% of teaching faculty are female; 4% Black, 3% Hispanic, 7% ethnic minority.

Student Body. College seeks a national student body; 89% of students from in state; 94% from Middle Atlantic, 2% New England, 1% South, 2% foreign. An estimated 8% of students reported as Black, 12% Hispanic, 15% Asian, 2% unknown. Educational Opportunity Program provides financial assistance and makes available special tutoring and developmental programs for academic assistance for New Jersey residents who are disadvantaged.

Varsity Sports. Men (Div.I): Baseball, Basketball, Crew, Cross Country, Diving, Fencing, Football (IA), Golf, Lacrosse, Soccer, Swimming, Tennis, Track, Wrestling. Women (Div.I): Basketball, Crew, Cross Country, Diving, Fencing, Field Hockey, Golf, Gymnastics, Lacrosse, Soccer, Softball, Swimming, Tennis, Track, Volleyball.

Campus Life. A current junior says, "..I need four more years here to explore all the clubs and options; my schedule is full, yet I've barely scratched the surface." Cultural and intellectual activities provided on campus are supplemented by the resources of New York City, just 30 miles away. Many different lifestyles available on campus. Most sections of residence halls have opted for 24-hour visitation. Students have a significant degree of control over decisions governing campus social life. All students (except freshmen) may have cars; parking is reported as inadequate for both residents and commuters.

About 46% of students live in coed dormitories; 11% of students live in school-owned/operated apartments; rest commute. Freshmen given preference in college housing if all students cannot be accommodated. Sexes segregated in coed dormitories either by floor, or room. There are 32 fraternities, 15 sororities on campus (open to all New Brunswick students); about 7% of men, 3% of women join fraternities and sororities.

Annual Costs. Tuition and fees, $4,387 (out-of-state, $7,942); room and board, $4,454. About 58% of students receive financial aid; average amount of assistance, $4,807. Assistance is typically divided 17% scholarship, 49% grant, 30% loan, 4% work.

Cook College

New Brunswick, New Jersey 08903 (908) 932-8789

Cook College places major emphasis on marine, life, and agricultural sciences. The college is appropriately named after the 19th-century geologist, George H. Cook. It shares many facilities with Douglass College on the eastern edge of New Brunswick. Most convenient major airport: Newark International.

Founded: 1972
Affiliation: State
UG Enrollment: 1,391 M, 1,183 W (full-time); 158 M, 199 W (part-time)
Cost: < $10K
% Receiving Financial Aid: 58%
Admission: Selective
Application Deadline: January 15

Admission is selective. About 56% of applicants accepted, 14% of these actually enroll; 64% of freshmen graduate in top fifth of high school class, 92% in top two-fifths. Average freshman SAT scores: 510 M, 510 W verbal, 600 M, 560 W mathematical; 58% of freshmen score above 500 on verbal, 11% above 600, 1% above 700; 89% score above 500 on mathematical, 45% above 600, 8% above 700. *Required:* SAT or ACT. Criteria considered in admissions, in order of importance: high school academic record, class rank, standardized tests, recommendations, extra curricular activities; other factors considered: special talents, diverse student body, leadership. *Out-of-state* freshman applicants: college encourages qualified students from out of state. No special requirements for out-of-state applicants; 59% of students accepted, 9% of these actually enroll. *Entrance programs:* early admission, midyear admission (for transfers only), advanced placement, deferred admission. *Apply* by January 15. *Transfers* welcome; 174 enrolled 1993–94.

Academic Environment. Cook attempts to apply the land-grant concept of teaching, research, and community outreach, which served the agricultural community so successfully in the past, "to a broader spectrum of society with special concern for the physical and social environments." Degree offered: bachelors. *Majors offered* include usual science-related fields as well as many of the programs formerly offered by the College of Agriculture and Environmental Science, chemistry, foods and nutrition, professional-occupational education, biotechnology. Average undergraduate class size: 28% of classes under 20, 45% 20–40, 27% over 40.

About 42% of entering students graduate within four years, 75% within six years; 93% of freshman return for sophomore year. *Special programs:* honors, undergraduate research, study abroad, independent study, cooperative education, individualized majors, 5-year agricultural engineering program leading to BA/BS, 8-year BA/MD with U. of Medicine and Dentistry of NJ, 2–3 with College of Engineering, cooperative work-study programs. *Calendar:* semester.

Graduates Career Data. Advanced studies pursued by 44% of students (survey, May 1992). Medical schools typically enrolling largest numbers of graduates include UNM&DNJ, NY Medical College, Hahnemann; dental schools include UNM&DNJ, NYU, Temple; law schools include Rutgers, Seton Hall, NY Law; business schools include Rutgers, NYU, Penn State, according to most recent data available. Corporations typically hiring largest numbers of graduates include Deloitte & Touche, Proctor & Gamble, Merck, KPMG Peat Marwick. Career Development Services include Resource Bank, computerized career guidance system, on-campus recruiting, computerized resume and job banks, resume referral system, KiNexus, career days, workshops, resume assistance. Alumni reported as helpful in both career guidance and job placement. Approximately 60% of the 1992 graduating class rated career services from "good" to "excellent".

Faculty. About 95% of faculty hold PhD or equivalent. About 39% of undergraduate classes taught by tenured faculty. About 21% of teaching faculty are female; 3% Black, 4% ethnic minority.

Student Body. About 91% of students from in state; 96% from Middle Atlantic, 2% New England, 1% foreign. An estimated 5% of students reported as Black, 6% Hispanic, 10% Asian, 2% unknown. Average age of undergraduate student: 22. Special financial and academic services for New Jersey students who are disadvantaged.

Varsity Sports. Men (Div.I): Baseball, Basketball, Crew, Cross Country, Diving, Fencing, Football (IA), Golf, Lacrosse, Soccer, Swimming, Tennis, Track, Wrestling. Women (Div.I): Basketball, Crew, Cross Country, Diving, Fencing, Field Hockey, Golf, Gymnastics, Lacrosse, Soccer, Softball, Swimming, Tennis, Track, Volleyball.

Campus Life. A current student reports that what he likes best about Cook is, "the faculty, the deans, and the close knit family of students." He also reports a "very competitive" intramural program, and "tons of activities" offered by the Student Center. Cultural activities are supplemented by the resources of New York City about 30 miles away. Students enjoy great freedom in determining their own lifestyles. All students (except freshmen) may have cars; parking is reported as inadequate for both residents and commuters.

About 2% of men live in traditional dormitories; 20% of students live in coed dormitories; 40% of students live in school-operated/owned apartments; rest commute. Freshmen given preference in college housing if all students cannot be accommodated. Sexes segregated in dormitories by floor. There are 32 fraternities, 15 sororities on campus, which about 7% men, 3% women join.

Annual Costs. Tuition and fees, $4,743 (out-of-state, $8,686); room and board, $4,454. About 58% of students receive financial aid; average amount of assistance, $4,807. Assistance is typically divided 17% scholarship, 49% grant, 30% loan, 4% work.

Douglass College

New Brunswick, New Jersey 08903 (908) 932-8789

Douglass College is a college for women offering a liberal education within a co-educational university setting. Most convenient major airport: Newark International.

Founded: 1918
Affiliation: State
UG Enrollment: 2,830 W (full-time)
Cost: < $10K
% Receiving Financial Aid: 58%
Admission: Selective (+)
Application Deadline: Jan. 15

Admission is selective (+). (See also Rutgers University). About 68% of applicants accepted, 17% of these actually enroll; 49% of freshmen graduate in top fifth of high school class, 90% in top two-fifths. Average freshman SAT scores: 500 verbal, 550 mathematical; 49% of freshman score above 500 on verbal, 12% above 600, 1% above 700; 76% score above 500 on mathematical, 23% above 600, 2% above 700. *Required:* SAT or ACT. Criteria considered in admissions, in order of importance: high school academic record, class rank, standardized test scores, recommendations, extracurricular activities; other factors considered: special talents, diverse student body, leadership. *Out-of-state* freshman applicants: university encourages qualified students from out-of-state. No special requirements for out-of-state students. About 70% of out-of-state students accepted, 12% of these actually enroll. *Entrance programs:* early admission, midyear admission (for transfers only), advanced placement, deferred admission. *Apply* by January 15. *Transfers* welcome; 166 enrolled 1993–94.

Academic Environment. Douglass's students are involved on committees that influence curriculum, admission, and scholarship. Access to courses at the other Rutgers in New Brunswick colleges adds variety to the college's own resources. Students must complete a major in addition to the distribution requirements of 24 credits across broad areas of social sciences, natural sciences, literature and the arts. Degree offered: bachelors. *Majors offered* include usual arts and sciences, African and Afro-American studies, American studies, classical civilization, medical technology, microbiology, dance, foods and nutrition, geography, Hebraic studies, home economics, Latin American studies, Russian studies, speech, theater arts; combined major also possible, finance, earth & atmosphere sciences. A recent student finds that professors are accessible, and many resources are available, but, "you have to search them out. In a school this size, you have to take responsibility for yourself."

About 64% of entering freshmen graduate within four years, 80% within six years; 91% of freshmen return for sophomore year. *Special programs:* CLEP, independent study, study abroad, honors, undergraduate research, individualized majors, double majors, 5-year BA/MBA in business, 5-year liberal arts/engineering leading to BA/BS, 8-year BA/MD, internships, Women's Studies, 5-year BA,BS/M.Ed. *Calendar:* semester.

Graduates Career Data. About 47% of graduates intend to pursue advanced studies (survey, May 1992). Corporations typically hiring largest numbers of graduates include Deloitte & Touche, Prudential, Bloomingdales, KPMG Peat Marwick. Career Development Services include Resource Bank, computerized career guidance system, on-campus recruiting, computerized resume and job banks, resume referral system, KiNexus, career days, workshops, resume assistance. Alumni reported as helpful in both career guidance and job placement. Approximately 70% of the 1992 graduating class rated career services from "good" to "excellent". Alumni reported as actively helpful in both career guidance and job placement.

Faculty. About 95% of faculty hold PhD or equivalent. About 39% of undergraduate classes taught by tenured faculty. About 26% of teaching faculty are female; 4% Black, 3% Hispanic, 7% ethnic minority.

Student Body. About 93% of students from in state; 96% from Middle Atlantic; 1% New England, 1% foreign. An estimated 10% of students reported as Black, 6% Hispanic, 13% Asian, 2% unknown. Special financial and academic services for New Jersey students who are disadvantaged.

Varsity Sports. Men (Div.I): Baseball, Basketball, Crew, Cross Country, Diving, Fencing, Football (IA), Golf, Lacrosse, Soccer, Swimming, Tennis, Track, Wrestling. Women (Div.I): Basketball, Crew, Cross Country, Diving, Fencing, Field Hockey, Golf, Gymnastics, Lacrosse, Soccer, Softball, Swimming, Tennis, Track, Volleyball.

Campus Life. Douglass is a fairly self-contained campus with a very diverse student body. Students are largely responsible for their own governance. Campus life is influenced by the small-unit housing plan. Cultural activities on campus are supplemented by activities at other colleges of the university and by the many resources of New York City, about 30 miles away. No curfew; hours for daily visitation set by each house. All students (except freshmen) may have cars; parking is reported as inadequate for both residents and commuters.

About 52% of women live in traditional dormitories; 9% live in school-owned/operated apartments; rest commute. Freshmen given preference in college housing if all students cannot be accommodated. There are 15 sororities on campus, which about 3% of women join.

Annual Costs. Tuition and fees, $4,341 (out-of-state, $7,896); room and board, $4,454. About 58% of students receive financial aid; average amount of assistance, $4,807. Assistance is typically divided 17% scholarship, 49% grant, 30% loan, 4% work.

Livingston College

New Brunswick, New Jersey 08903 (908) 932-8789

A co-educational unit of Rutgers, Livingston is located in Piscataway which is adjacent to New Brunswick. The college is "contemporary-minded" and offers degree programs in the humanities, social sciences, physical and natural sciences. Most convenient major airport: Newark International.

Founded: 1969
Affiliation: State
UG Enrollment: 2,073 M, 1,360 W (full-time)
Cost: < $10K
% Receiving Financial Aid: 58%
Admission: Selective
Application Deadline: Jan. 15

Admission is selective. About 60% of applicants accepted, 9% of these actually enroll; 39% of freshmen graduate in top fifth of high school class, 88% in top two-fifths. Average freshman SAT scores: 490 M, 470 W verbal, 570 M, 520 W mathematical; 44% of freshman score above 500 on verbal, 6% above 600, 1% above 700; 78% score above 500 on mathematical, 29% above 600, 3% above 700. *Required:* SAT or ACT. Criteria considered in admissions, in order of importance: high school academic record, class rank, standardized test scores, recommendations, extracurricular activities; other factors considered: special talents, diverse student body, leadership. No special requirements for out-of-state applicants. About 65% of out-of-state applicants accepted, 6% of these actually enroll. *Entrance programs:* early admission, midyear admission (for transfers only), deferred admission, advanced placement. *Apply* by January 15. *Transfers* welcome; 371 enrolled 1993–94.

Academic Environment. Livingston has a special commitment to students who have previously been denied educational opportunities. Degree offered: bachelors. *Majors offered* include usual arts and sciences, ethnic programs (African, Afro-American, Puerto Rican), anthropology, Chinese, labor studies, medical technology, urban studies, physician assistant, social work, finance. Average undergraduate class size: 28% under 20, 45% 20–40, 27% over 40. About 40% of entering students graduate within four years, 69% within six years; 87% of freshmen return for sophomore year.

Special programs: CLEP, independent study, study abroad, honors, undergraduate research, individualized majors, 5-year liberal arts engineering program leading to BA/BS, 8-year BA/MD, 5-year BA/MBA, 2–3 with College of Engineering. *Calendar:* semester.

Graduates Career Data. About 43% of graduates intend to pursue advanced studies (survey, May 1992). Corporations typically hiring largest numbers of graduates include Johnson & Johnson, Merck, Deloitte & Touche, Memorial Sloan Kettering Cancer Center. Career Development Services include Resource Bank, computerized career guidance system, on-campus recruiting, computerized resume and job banks, resume referral system, KiNexus, career days, workshops, resume assistance. Alumni reported as helpful in both career guidance and job placement. Approximately 60% of the 1992 graduating class rated career services from "good" to "excellent".

Faculty. About 95% of faculty hold PhD or equivalent. About 39% of undergraduate classes taught by tenured faculty. About 26% of teaching faculty are female; 4% Black, 3% Hispanic, 7% other ethnic minority.

Student Body. College seeks a national student body; 89% of students from in state; 94% from Middle Atlantic, 2% New England, 2% foreign. An estimated 14% of students reported as Black, 7% Hispanic, 12% Asian, 5% ethnic minority. Special financial and academic services for New Jersey students who are disadvantaged.

Varsity Sports. Men (Div. I): Baseball, Basketball, Crew, Cross Country, Diving, Fencing, Football (IA), Golf, Lacrosse, Soccer, Swimming, Tennis, Track, Wrestling. Women (Div.I): Basketball, Crew, Cross Country, Diving, Fencing, Field Hockey, Golf, Gymnastics, Lacrosse, Soccer, Softball, Swimming, Tennis, Track, Volleyball.

Campus Life. Cultural activities supplemented by the resources of New York City, about 30 miles away. All students (except freshmen) may have cars; parking is reported as inadequate for both residents and commuters.

About 42% of students live in coed dormitories; 2% live in school-owned/operated apartments; rest commute. Freshmen given preference in college housing if all students cannot be accommodated. Intervisitation in men's and women's dormitory rooms unlimited.

Sexes segregated in coed dormitories by floor. There are 32 fraternities, 15 sororities on campus, which 7% men, 3% women join.
Annual Costs. Tuition and fees, $4,423; (out-of-state, $7,978); room and board, $4,454. About 58% of students receive financial aid; average amount of assistance, $4,807. Assistance is typically divided 17% scholarship, 49% grant, 30% loan, 4% work.

Camden College of Arts and Sciences

Camden, New Jersey 08101 (908) 932-8789

Primarily a commuter campus of Rutgers University, Camden College of Arts and Sciences is designed to serve students from the Southern New Jersey area. Most convenient major airport: Philadelphia.

Founded: 1927
Affiliation: State
UG Enrollment: 885 M, 1,128 W (full-time); 236 M, 318 W (part-time)
Cost: < $10K
% Receiving Financial Aid: 58%
Admission: Selective
Application Deadline: May 1

Admission is selective. About 52% of applicants accepted, 13% of these actually enroll; 68% of freshmen graduate in top fifth of high school class; 90% in top two- fifths. Average freshman SAT scores: 490 M, 490 W verbal, 570 M, 520 W mathematical; 45% of freshman score above 500 on verbal, 8% above 600; 81% score above 500 on mathematical, 23% above 600, 2% above 700. *Required:* SAT or ACT. Criteria considered in admissions, in order of importance: high school academic record, class rank, standardized test scores, recommendations, extracurricular activities; other factors considered: special talents, diverse student body, leadership. *Out-of-state* freshman applicants: university actively seeks students from out-of-state students; no special requirements. About 60% of out-of-state students accepted, 1% of these actually enroll. *Entrance programs:* early admission, midyear admission, deferred admission, advanced placement. *Apply* by May 1. *Transfers* welcome; 464 enrolled 1993–94.
Academic Environment. Degree offered: bachelors. Average undergraduate class size: 36% of classes under 20, 43% 20–40, 21% over 40. About 20% of entering freshmen graduate within four years, 49% within six years; 79% of freshmen return for sophomore year. *Special programs:* individualized majors, honors, undergraduate research, study abroad, independent study, 2–2 and 2–3 programs in engineering and pharmacy, 8-year BA/MD program. *Calendar:* semester.
Undergraduate degrees conferred (641). 36% were in Business and Management, 21% were in Social Sciences, 8% were in Letters, 8% were in Psychology, 6% were in Computer and Engineering Related Technology, 5% were in Health Sciences, 4% were in Visual and Performing Arts, 3% were in Life Sciences, 3% were in Physical Sciences, 3% were in Mathematics, remainder in 5 other fields.
Graduates Career Data. About 43% of graduates intend to pursue advanced studies (survey, May 1992). Employers typically hiring largest numbers of graduates include CIGNA Corp, KPMG Peat Marwick, Federal Reserve Bank, Computer Services Corp. Career Development Services include computer career guidance, graduate test prep software, resume workstations, resume national referral services, internships, career classes, interest inventory, on-campus recruiting and interviews, individual job placement, group career counseling, placement services, alumni services.
Faculty. About 95% of faculty hold PhD or equivalent. About 33% of undergraduate classes taught by tenured faculty. About 35% of teaching faculty are female; 5% Black, 3% Hispanic, 10% ethnic minority.
Student Body. College does not seek a national student body; 98% of students from in state; 99% from Middle Atlantic. An estimated 13% of students reported as Black, 6% Hispanic, 4% Asian, 5% unknown. Average age of undergraduate student: 24.
Varsity Sports. Men (Div.III): Baseball, Basketball, Cross Country, Diving, Golf, Soccer, Swimming, Tennis, Track, Wrestling. Women (Div.III): Basketball, Cross Country, Diving, Softball, Swimming, Tennis, Track.
Campus Life. About 7% of students live in coed dormitories or school-owned/operated apartments; rest commute. Freshmen given preference in college housing if all students cannot be accommodated. There are 4 fraternities, 7 sororities which 6% of men, 6% of women join.
Annual Costs. Tuition and fees, $4,198 (out-of-state, $7,753); room and board, $4,454. About 58% of students receive financial aid; average amount of assistance, $4,807. Assistance is typically divided 17% scholarship, 49% grant, 30% loan, 4% work.

College of Engineering

New Brunswick, New Jersey 08903-2101 (908) 932-8789

A co-educational professional college which offers 4-year degree programs in 8 fields as well as 5-year programs with undergraduate colleges of the university. Most convenient major airport: Newark International.

Founded: 1864
Affiliation: State
UG Enrollment: 1,936 M, 412 W (full-time)
Cost: < $10K
% Receiving Financial Aid: 58%
Admission: Very Selective
Application Deadline: Jan. 15

Admission is very selective. About 70% of applicants accepted, 23% of these actually enroll; 63% of freshmen graduate in top fifth of their high school class, 86% in top two-fifths. Average freshman SAT scores: 510 M, 490 W verbal, 670 M, 650 W mathematical; 57% of freshman score above 500 on verbal, 18% above 600, 1% above 700; 99% score above 500 on mathematical, 86% above 600, 33% above 700. *Required:* SAT or ACT. Criteria considered in admissions, in order of importance: high school academic record, class rank, standardized test scores, recommendations, extracurricular activities; other factors considered: special talents, diverse student body, leadership. *Out-of-state* freshman applicants: university actively seeks students from out-of-state students. About 69% of out-of-state students accepted, 10% of these actually enroll. *Entrance programs:* early admission, midyear admission (for transfers only), advanced placement, deferred admission. *Apply* by January 15. *Transfers* welcome; 96 enrolled 1993–94.
Academic Environment. Degree offered: bachelors. College offers programs in agricultural, chemical, electrical, mechanical, ceramic, civil, and industrial engineering; applied sciences in engineering, bio-resource engineering. Average undergraduate class size: 28% under 20, 45% 20–40, 27% over 40. About 37% of entering freshman graduate within four years, 72% within six years; 89% of freshman return for sophomore year. *Special programs:* study abroad, dual degree programs with other Rutgers schools, 5-year BS/MBA, 8-year BS/MD in medicine and dentistry. *Calendar:* semester.
Graduates Career Data. About 37% of graduates intend to pursue advanced studies (survey, May 1992). Corporations typically hiring largest numbers of graduates include Exxon, Bellcore, Ingersoll & Rand, Merck. Career Development Services include Resource Bank, computerized career guidance system, on-campus recruiting, computerized resume and job banks, resume referral system, KiNexus, career days, workshops, resume assistance. Alumni reported as helpful in both career guidance and job placement. Approximately 70% of the 1992 graduating class rated career services from "good" to "excellent".
Faculty. About 95% of faculty hold PhD or equivalent. About 39% of undergraduate classes taught by tenured faculty. About 7% of teaching faculty are female; 4% Black, 2% Hispanic, 25% ethnic minority.
Student Body. About 87% of students from in state; 91% from Middle Atlantic; 1% New England, 6% foreign. An estimated 7% of students reported as Black, 6% Hispanic, 22% Asian, 8% ethnic minority. Special financial and academic services for New Jersey students who are disadvantaged.
Varsity Sports. Men (Div.I): Baseball, Basketball, Crew, Cross Country, Diving, Fencing, Football, Golf, Lacrosse, Soccer, Swimming, Tennis, Track, Wrestling. Women (Div.I): Basketball, Crew, Cross Country, Diving, Fencing, Field Hockey, Golf, Gymnastics, Lacrosse, Soccer, Softball, Swimming, Tennis, Track, Volleyball.
Campus Life. About 66% of students live in traditional or coed dormitories, and school-owned/operated apartments; rest commute. Freshmen given preference in college housing if all students cannot

be accommodated. Students share campus facilities and activities with Cook, Douglass, Livingston, and Rutgers colleges. There are 32 fraternities and 15 sororities on campus, which about 7% men, 3% women join. About 30% of resident students leave campus on weekends, according to most recent data available.
Annual Costs. Tuition, $3,810 (out-of-state, $7,753), fees vary with college of affiliation, $908–990; room and board, $4,454. About 58% of students receive financial aid; average amount of assistance, $4,807. Assistance is typically divided 17% scholarship, 49% grant, 30% loan, 4% work.

Mason Gross School of the Arts

New Brunswick, New Jersey 08903 (908) 932-8789

The newest undergraduate unit of the University, Mason Gross School of the Arts offers the BFA and the BMus. degrees. Most convenient major airport: Newark International.

Founded: 1976
Affiliation: State
UG Enrollment: 184 M, 214 W (full-time)
Cost: < $10K
% Receiving Financial Aid: 58%
Admission: Selective
Application Deadline: Jan. 15

Admission is selective. About 25% of applicants accepted, 44% of these actually enroll; 31% of freshmen graduate in top fifth of high school class; 57% in top two-fifths. Average freshman SAT scores: 490 M, 480 W verbal, 550 M, 510 W mathematical; 48% of freshman score above 500 on verbal, 9% above 600; 65% score above 500 on mathematical, 21% above 600, 3% above 700. *Required:* audition/portfolio, SAT or ACT. Criteria considered in admissions, in order of importance: talent assessment, high school academic record, class rank, standardized test scores, recommendations, extracurricular activities; other factors considered: special talents, diverse student body, leadership. *Out-of-state* freshman applicants: university actively seeks students from out-of-state; no special requirements. About 24% of out-of-state students accepted, 35% of these actually enroll. *Entrance programs:* early admission, midyear admission (for transfers only), deferred admission, advanced placement. *Apply* by January 15 for visual arts, February 15 for dance, music and theater arts. *Transfers* welcome; 27 enrolled 1993=94.
Academic Environment. Degrees offered: bachelors, masters, doctoral. Majors in dance, music, theater, and visual arts. Average undergraduate class size: 28% under 20, 45% 20–40, 27% over 40. About 41% of students entering as freshmen graduate within four years, 58% within six years; 76% of freshmen return for sophomore year. *Special programs:* honors, undergraduate research, study abroad, independent study. *Calendar:* semester.
Graduates Career Data. About 57% of graduates intend to pursue advanced studies (survey, May 1992). Corporations typically hiring largest numbers of graduates include Broadway theaters, popular film and television productions. Career Development Services include Resource Bank, computerized career guidance system, on-campus recruiting, computerized resume and job banks, resume referral system, KiNexus, career days, workshops, resume assistance. Alumni reported as helpful in both career guidance and job placement. Approximately 50% of the 1992 graduating class rated career services from "good" to "excellent".
Faculty. About 95% of faculty hold PhD or equivalent. About 39% of undergraduate classes taught by tenured faculty. About 31% of teaching faculty are female; 17% Black, 1% Hispanic, 1% other ethnic minority.
Student Body. About 86% of students from in state; 90% Middle Atlantic, 3% New England, 2% South, 1% Midwest, 2% foreign. An estimated 6% of students reported as Black, 7% Hispanic, 7% Asian, 2% unknown. Special financial and academic services for New Jersey students who are disadvantaged.
Varsity Sports. Men (Div.I): Baseball, Basketball, Crew, Cross Country, Diving, Fencing, Football (IA), Golf, Lacrosse, Soccer, Swimming, Tennis, Track, Wrestling. Women (Div.I): Basketball, Crew, Cross Country, Diving, Fencing, Field Hockey, Golf, Gymnastics, Lacrosse, Soccer, Softball, Swimming, Tennis, Track, Volleyball.
Campus Life. The Downtown Arts Center is located in New Brunswick. Students share facilities and activities with Douglass, Cook, Livingston, and Rutgers colleges.

About 50% of students live in coed dormitories, women's dormitories or school-owned/operated apartments; rest commute. Freshmen given preference in college housing if all students cannot be accommodated. There are 32 fraternities, 15 sororities on campus, which about 7% men, 3% women join.
Annual Costs. Tuition, $3,433 (out-of-state, $6,988), fees vary with program, $908–990; room and board $4,454. About 58% of students receive financial aid; average amount of assistance, $4,807. Assistance is typically divided 17% scholarship, 49% grant, 30% loan, 4% work. College reports some scholarships awarded on the basis of academic merit alone.

Newark College of Arts and Sciences

Newark, New Jersey 07102-1896 (908) 932-8789

Primarily a commuter campus of the university, Newark is designed to serve students from northern New Jersey. Most convenient major airport: Newark International.

Founded: 1910
Affiliation: State
UG Enrollment: 1,484 M, 1,638 W (full-time); 276 M, 245 W (part-time)
Cost: < $10K
% Receiving Financial Aid: 58%
Admission: Selective
Application Deadline: May 1

Admission is selective. About 52% of applicants accepted, 18% of these actually enroll; 43% of freshmen graduate in top fifth of high school class; 78% in top two-fifths. Average freshman SAT scores: 450 M, 460 W verbal, 550 M, 510 W mathematical; 26% of freshman score above 500 verbal, 5% above 600; 67% of freshman score above 500 mathematical, 19% score above 600, 2% score above 700. *Required:* SAT or ACT. Criteria considered in admissions, in order of importance: high school academic record, class rank, standardized test scores, recommendations, extracurricular activities; other factors considered: special talents, diverse student body, leadership. *Out-of-state* freshman applicants: college actively seeks students from out-of-state; no special requirements. About 62% of out-of-state students accepted, 3% of these actually enroll. *Entrance programs:* early admission, midyear admission, deferred admission, advanced placement. *Apply* by May 1. *Transfers* welcome; 422 enrolled 1993–94.
Academic Environment. Degree offered: bachelors. *Majors offered* include usual arts and sciences, Afro-American studies, accounting, business administration, Hebraic studies, journalism, medical technology, Russian and Slavic studies, applied mathematics, applied physics, science, technology and society, finance, laboratory sciences. Average undergraduate class size: 33% under 20, 41% 20–40, 26% over 40. About 27% of entering freshman graduate within four years, 56% within six years; 83% of freshman return for sophomore year.

Special programs: CLEP, honors, undergraduate research, study abroad, independent study, combined programs in pre-architecture, engineering, pharmacy, 5-year BA/MBA, BA/MA with School of Criminal Justice, 8-year BA/MD, 2–2 and 2–3 programs in engineering. *Calendar:* semester.
Undergraduate degrees conferred (1,062). 53% were in Business and Management, 12% were in Social Sciences, 9% were in Health Sciences, 6% were in Life Sciences, 5% were in Letters, 5% were in Psychology, 5% were in Computer and Engineering Related Technology, remainder in 8 other fields.
Graduates Career Data. About 38% of graduates intend to pursue advanced studies (survey, May 1992). Corporations typically hiring largest numbers of graduates include Big 6 Accounting firms, Merrill Lynch, K-Mart, AT&T, K-Mart. Career Development Services include on-campus interviews, resume assistance, alumni services, placement services, individual career counseling/placement, group career counseling, individual job placement, on-campus employer recruiting, career fairs, career conferences, vocational testing, internships, credentials file service, KINEXUS.
Faculty. About 95% of faculty hold PhD or equivalent. About 36% of undergraduate classes taught by tenured faculty. About 29% of teaching faculty are female; 8% Black, 3% Hispanic, 3% ethnic minority.
Student Body. About 94% of students from in state; 96% Middle Atlantic, 4% foreign. An estimated 18% of students reported as Black,

17% Hispanic, 14% Asian, 8% unknown. Average age of undergraduate student: 22. Special financial and academic services for New Jersey students who are disadvantaged.
Varsity Sports. Men (Div.III): Baseball, Basketball, Soccer, Tennis, Volleyball (I). Women (Div.III): Basketball, Softball, Tennis, Volleyball.
Campus Life. About 5% each of men, women live in coed dormitories, 1% reside in school-owned/operated apartments; rest commute. There are 5 fraternities, 7 sororities on campus.
Annual Costs. Tuition and fees, $4,191 (out-of-state, $7,746); room and board, $4,454. About 58% of students receive financial aid; average amount of assistance, $4,807. Assistance is typically divided 17% scholarship, 49% grant, 30% loan, 4% work.

College of Nursing

Newark, New Jersey 07102-1896 (908) 932-8789

The College of Nursing on the Rutgers in Newark campus is designed to serve men and women primarily from the north New Jersey area. Most convenient major airport: Newark.

Founded: 1951
Affiliation: State
UG Enrollment: 41 M, 347 W (full-time); 6 M, 34 W (part-time)
Cost: < $10K
% Receiving Financial Aid: 58%
Admission: Selective
Application Deadline: January 15

Admission is selective. About 17% of applicants accepted, 26% of these actually enroll; 70% of freshman graduate in top fifth of high school class, all in top two-fifths. Average freshman SAT scores: 470 M, 500 W verbal, 620 M, 550 W mathematical; 56% of freshman score above 500 verbal, 4% above 600; 82% score above 500 mathematical, 26% above 600, 4% above 700. *Required:* SAT or ACT. Criteria considered in admissions, in order of importance: high school academic record, class rank, standardized test scores, recommendations, extracurricular activities; other factors considered: special talents, diverse student body, leadership. *Out-of-state* freshman applicants: university actively seeks students from out-of-state; no special requirements. About 18% of out-of-state students accepted, 5% of these actually enroll. *Entrance programs:* early admission, deferred admission, advanced placement. *Apply* by January 15. *Transfers* and registered nurses welcome: 18 enrolled 1993–94.
Academic Environment. Degree offered: bachelors. A curriculum of unified liberal and professional studies leading to the degree of Bachelor of Science in Nursing. Classes are offered on the Newark and New Brunswick campuses and in northern and central New Jersey hospitals and health care agencies. Average undergraduate class size: 33% under 20, 41% 20–40, 26% over 40. About 42% of entering freshman graduate within four years, 54% within six years; 86% of freshman return for sophomore year.

Special programs: honors, undergraduate research, independent study. Adult programs: Self-paced program for RNs working toward BSN. *Calendar:* semester.
Graduates Career Data. About 71% of graduating seniors indicated plans to pursue advanced studies (survey, May 1992). About 98% of 1992–93 graduates employed. Employers typically hiring largest numbers of graduates include hospitals, health service organizations, community agencies. Career Development Services include career classes, resume assistance, alumni services, on-campus employer recruiting.
Faculty. About 95% of faculty hold PhD or equivalent. About 36% of undergraduate classes taught by tenured faculty. The teaching faculty are all female; 8% Black, 5% other ethnic minority.
Student Body. About 98% of students from in state; 99% Middle Atlantic, 1% foreign. An estimated 20% of students reported as Black, 10% Hispanic, 18% Asian, 4% unknown. Average age of undergraduate student: 24. Special financial and academic services for New Jersey students who are disadvantaged.
Varsity Sports. Men (Div.III): Baseball, Basketball, Soccer, Tennis, Volleyball (I). Women (Div.III): Basketball, Softball, Tennis, Volleyball.
Campus Life. About 30% of students live in coed dormitories; apartments are available for Nursing students in Newark; students may affiliate with Douglass or Rutgers College in New Brunswick. There are 5 fraternities, 7 sororities on campus.
Annual Costs. Tuition, $4,184 (out-of-state, $7,739), fees vary with college of affiliation; room and board, $4,454. About 58% of students receive financial aid; average amount of assistance, $4,807. Assistance is typically divided 17% scholarship, 49% grant, 30% loan, 4% work.

College of Pharmacy

New Brunswick, New Jersey 08903 (908) 932-8789

A co-educational professional college which offers the 5-year pharmacy program. Most convenient major airport: Newark.

Founded: 1892
Affiliation: State
UG Enrollment: 310 M, 556 W (full-time)
Cost: < $10K
% Receiving Financial Aid: 58%
Admission: Very Selective
Application Deadline: Jan. 15

Admission is very selective. About 35% of applicants are accepted, all enroll. About 97% of freshmen graduate in top fifth of high school class, 99% in top two-fifths. Average freshman SAT scores: 520 M, 530 W verbal, 670 M, 640 W mathematical; 66% of freshman score above 500 verbal, 19% above 600; 99% score above 500 mathematical, 83% above 600, 28% above 700. *Required:* SAT or ACT. Criteria considered in admissions, in order of importance: high school academic record, class rank, standardized test scores, recommendations, extracurricular activities; other factors considered: special talents, diverse student body, leadership. *Out-of-state* freshman applicants: college encourages qualified students from out-of-state; no special requirements. About 23% of our-of-state students accepted, 26% of these actually enroll. *Entrance programs:* early admission, deferred admission, advanced placement. *Apply* by January 15. *Transfers* welcome; 32 enrolled 1993–94.
Academic Environment. Degrees offered: bachelors, doctoral. Average undergraduate class size: 28% under 20, 45% 20–40, 27% over 40. About 68% of entering freshman graduate within five years, 81% within six years; 88% of freshman return for sophomore year. *Special programs:* honors, undergraduate research, study abroad, independent study, 6-year BS/Pharm.D. degree. *Calendar:* semester.
Graduates Career Data. About 52% of graduating seniors indicated plans to pursue advance studies (survey, May 1992). Corporations typically hiring largest numbers of graduates include Merck, Bristol-Myers Squibb, Hoffman LaRoche, Johnson & Johnson. Career Development Services include Resource Bank, computerized career guidance system, on-campus recruiting, computerized resume and job banks, resume referral system, KiNexus, career days, workshops, resume assistance. Alumni reported as helpful in both career guidance and job placement. Approximately 94% of the 1992 graduating class rated career services from "good" to "excellent".
Faculty. About 95% of faculty hold PhD or equivalent. About 39% of undergraduate classes taught by tenured faculty. About 36% of faculty are female; 6% Black, 2% Hispanic, 25% other ethnic minority.
Student Body. About 87% of students from in state; 95% Middle Atlantic, 1% New England, 2% foreign. An estimated 4% of students reported as Black, 8% Hispanic, 36% Asian, 2% unknown. Special financial and academic services for New Jersey students who are disadvantaged.
Varsity Sports. Men (Div I): Baseball, Basketball, Crew, Cross Country, Diving, Fencing, Football (IA), Golf, Lacrosse, Soccer, Swimming, Tennis, Track, Wrestling. Women (Div. I): Basketball, Crew, Cross Country, Diving, Fencing, Field Hockey, Golf, Gymnastics, LaCrosse, Soccer, Softball, Swimming, Tennis, Track, Volleyball.
Campus Life. About 63% of students live in coed dormitories or women's dormitories; rest live in off-campus housing or commute. Freshmen given preference in college housing if all students cannot be accommodated. Students share campus facilities and activities with Douglass, Livingston, and Rutgers colleges. There are 32 fraternities, 15 sororities on campus, which about 7% men, 3% women join.
Annual Costs. Tuition, $3,810 (out-of-state, $7,753), fees vary with college of affiliation, $908–990; room and board, $4,454. About 58% of students receive financial aid; average amount of assistance, $4,807. Assistance is typically divided 17% scholarship, 49% grant, 30% loan, 4% work.

University College

Camden, Newark, New Brunswick (908) 932-8789

University College is a part-time, evening, degree-granting division of Rutgers University with locations in Camden, Newark, and New Brunswick. All students commute.

Founded: 1934
Affiliation: State
Cost: < $10K
Admission: Non-selective
Application Deadline: Rolling

Admission. *Required:* SAT or ACT (except for transfers). Full credit for graduates of transfer curricula from New Jersey two-year colleges. *Apply:* rolling admissions. *Transfers* welcome.
Academic Environment. *Degrees:* BA, BS. *Majors offered* include: arts and sciences, accounting, computer science, criminal justice, labor studies, management, marketing, urban studies, vocational education. *Computer Science:* computer literacy not required of all students. *Special programs:* honors, undergraduate research, study abroad, independent study. Adult programs: evening and part-time degree programs offered.
Campus Life. About 98% of students from New Jersey; most employed during day. All students are commuters.
Annual Costs. Tuition $111 per credit hour (for out-of-state, $227 per credit hour), fees vary with campus, $89–98 per semester.

Sacramento State College

(See California State University/Sacramento)

University of Sacred Heart

San Juan, Puerto Rico 00914 (809) 728-1515

A co-educational liberal arts university founded by the Religious of the Sacred Heart, this bilingual institution includes a junior college and is located 10 minutes from downtown San Juan and Rio Piedras, home of the University of Puerto Rico. Most convenient major airport: Luis Munoz Marin International.

Founded: 1835
Affiliation: Independent (Roman Catholic)
UG Enrollment: 1,218 M, 2,391 W (full-time); 392 M, 691 W (part-time)
Cost: < $10K
Admission: Non-selective
Application Deadline: June 30

Admission. About 80% of applicants accepted, 72% of these actually enroll. Criteria considered in admissions: high school academic record, standardized test scores. *Required:* SAT (in English or Spanish). Entrance programs: early admission, midyear admission, deferred admission. *Apply* by June 30. *Transfers* welcome; 151 enrolled 1993–94.
Academic Environment. Degrees offered: associates, bachelors, masters. About 65% of students entering as freshmen graduate within four years; 78% of freshmen return for sophomore year. Average undergraduate class size: 12% of classes under 20, 88% 20–40. *Special programs:* honors. *Calendar:* semester, summer school.
Undergraduate degrees conferred (487). 24% were in Business and Management, 24% were in Communications, 11% were in Education, 9% were in Life Sciences, 8% were in Business and Office, 7% were in Psychology, 6% were in Computer and Information Sciences, remainder in 5 other fields.
Student Body. About 99% of students from Puerto Rico.
Religious Orientation. Sacred Heart is an independent institution with a Catholic heritage; 6 credits in theology required of all students.
Varsity Sports. Men: Basketball, Judo, Swimming, Tennis, Track, Volleyball, Weight. Women: Judo, Swimming, Tennis, Track, Volleyball, Weight.

Campus Life. About 2% of women live in traditional dormitories; rest live in off-campus housing or commute, according to most recent data available. Intervisitation in women's dormitory rooms limited.
Annual Costs. Tuition and fees, $3,245; room, $1,200. University reports some scholarships awarded on the basis of academic merit alone.

Sacred Heart Seminary

Detroit, Michigan 48206

A church-related institution, conducted by the archdiocese, the seminary admits candidates for the Roman Catholic priesthood. Seminary College also sponsors program for candidates for the Permanent Order of Deacon and the Institute for Pastoral Liturgical Ministries and offers an associate degree in lay pastoral ministry.

Founded: 1919
Affiliation: Roman Catholic

Undergraduate degrees conferred (1). 100% were in Social Sciences.

Sacred Heart University

Fairfield, Connecticut 06432 (203) 371-7880

A church-related, diocesan university for commuters, administered and staffed by laymen, located in a city of 156,500. Sacred Heart University is in the midst of a comprehensive expansion program which encompasses improvements and additions to academic, social and athletic facilities and offerings. Most convenient major airport: Sikorski.

Founded: 1963
Affiliation: Roman Catholic
UG Enrollment: 814 M, 893 W (full-time); 583 M, 1,306 W (part-time)
Total Enrollment: 5,118
Cost: $10K–$20K
% Receiving Financial Aid: 79%
Admission: Non-selective
Application Deadline: April 15

Admission. Graduates of approved high schools eligible; 82% of applicants accepted, 1% of these actually enroll; 43% of freshmen graduate in top fifth of high school class, 77% in top two-fifths. Average freshman SAT scores: 420 verbal, 480 mathematical. *Required:* SAT, essay; ACH (language for AB candidates, mathematics I for BS) recommended. Criteria considered in admissions, in order of importance: high school academic record, standardized test scores, extracurricular activities, recommendations, writing sample; other factors considered: special talents, alumni children, diverse student body. About 35% of entering students from private or parochial schools, according to most recent data available. *Entrance programs:* early decision, midyear admission, deferred admission, advanced placement. *Apply* by April 15: rolling admissions. *Transfers* welcome; 162 enrolled 1993–94.
Academic Environment. Degrees offered: associates, bachelors, masters. About 70% of students entering as freshmen graduate within four years, 73% eventually; 80% of freshmen return for sophomore year. *Majors offered* in addition to usual studies include social work, legal assistant program, baccalaureate program in nursing, global studies, sports management, international business and theatre studies, combined undergraduate/graduate programs in physical therapy and occupational therapy. Average undergraduate class size: 51% under 20, 44% 20–40, 5% over 40. *Special programs:* CLEP, independent study, study abroad, honors, undergraduates research, cross-registration with Fairfield U. and Bridgeport U., internship/cooperative work-study programs.
Undergraduate degrees conferred (371). 54% were in Business and Management, 10% were in Computer and Engineering Related Technology, 7% were in Psychology, 6% were in Social Sciences, 5% were in Health Sciences, 5% were in Letters, 3% were in Visual and Performing Arts, remainder in 8 other fields.
Graduates Career Data. *Full-time graduate or professional study* pursued by 22% of students immediately after graduation; of these, about 6% enter law school, 44% enter business school, 2% enter medical school. Law schools typically enrolling largest numbers of

students include U.of Connecticut; business schools include Sacred Heart U., U. of New Haven, Fairfield U.; medical schools include Boston U. About 51% of 1992–93 graduates employed. Fields typically hiring largest numbers of graduates include education systems, corporations, banks. Career Development Services include individual career counseling/planning, group counseling, individual job placement, on-campus recruitment, seminars, workshops, interest inventories.

Faculty. About 81% of faculty hold PhD or equivalent.

Student Body. University does not seek a national student body; 68% of students from in state; 80% from New England, 14% Middle Atlantic, 1% Midwest, 1% South, 4% foreign.

Religious Orientation. Sacred Heart is a church-related institution; 9 hours of philosophy or religious studies required of all students; attendance at chapel services voluntary.

Varsity Sports. Men (Div.II): Baseball, Basketball, Crew, Cross Country, Football, Golf, Ice Hockey, Lacrosse, Soccer, Tennis, Track, Volleyball. Women (Div.II): Basketball, Cross Country, Equestrian, Field Hockey, Golf, Lacrosse, Soccer, Softball, Tennis, Track, Volleyball.

Campus Life. About 25% of men, 25% of women live in coed dormitories; 6% of men, 6% of women live in off-campus college-related housing; rest commute. There are 3 sororities, 1 fraternity on campus, which about 5% of women, 2% of men join. About 25% of resident students leave campus on weekends.

Annual Costs. Tuition and fees, $10,500; room and board, $5,300; estimated $1,000 other, exclusive of travel. About 79% of students receive financial aid; average amount of assistance, $8,296. Assistance is typically divided 63% grant, 33% loan, 4% work. University reports 298 scholarships awarded on the basis of academic merit alone, 1,199 for need alone. *Meeting Costs:* university offers several payment plans.

Saginaw Valley State University

University Center, Michigan 48710 (517) 790-4200

A state-supported university offering bachelors and masters degree programs. Saginaw Valley is located in the tri-city area of Saginaw, Midland, and Bay City. Formerly known as Saginaw Valley State College. Most convenient major airport: Tri-City (Freeland).

Founded: 1965
Affiliation: State
UG Enrollment: 181 M, 459 W (full- and part-time)
Total Enrollment: 4,085
Cost: < $10K
% Receiving Financial Aid: 50%
Admission: Non-selective
Application Deadline: Rolling

Admission. Graduates of accredited high schools with 16 units (10 in academic subjects) and C average eligible; 84% of applicants accepted, 52% of these actually enroll. Average freshman ACT scores, according to most recent data available: 18.6 composite. *Required:* ACT (preferred) or SAT. *Out-of-state* freshman applicants: college welcomes students from out of state. State does not limit out-of-state enrollment. No special requirements for out-of-state applicants. *Apply:*rolling admissions. *Transfers* welcome.

Academic Environment. *Degrees:* BA, BS, BBA, BSN, BSW, BSEE, BSME. Program in computer information systems recently added. Facilities reported as adequate to meet student demand. *Special programs:* CLEP, independent study, study abroad, honors, undergraduate research, individualized majors. Adult programs: classes are scheduled to accommodate adult students. *Calendar:* semester, summer school.

Undergraduate degrees conferred (669). 24% were in Business and Management, 14% were in Education, 9% were in Public Affairs, 9% were in Protective Services, 7% were in Social Sciences, 6% were in Health Sciences, 5% were in Letters, 5% were in Engineering, 3% were in Computer and Engineering Related Technology, 3% were in Psychology, 3% were in Communications, remainder in 8 other fields.

Faculty. About 75% of faculty hold PhD or equivalent.

Student Body. University does "not at present" seek a national student body; about 98% of students from in state. An estimated 5% of students reported as Black, 3% Hispanic, 4% other minority, according to most recent data available.

Varsity Sports. Men (NCAA,Div.II): Baseball, Basketball, Bowling, Cross Country, Football, Golf, Hammer Throw, Javelin Throw, Track. Women (NCAA, Div.II): Basketball, Javelin Throw, Softball, Tennis, Track, Volleyball.

Campus Life. About 11% of men, 9% of women live in dormitories; rest live in off-campus housing or commute. Intervisitation in men's and women's dormitory rooms unlimited; sexes segregated by floor. There are 3 fraternities, 2 sororities on campus. About 55–65% of resident students leave campus on weekends.

Annual Costs. Tuition and fees, $2,883 (out-of-state, $5,709); room and board, $3,729. About 50% of students receive financial aid; assistance is typically divided 50% scholarship, 50% loan, work. College reports some scholarships awarded on the basis of academic merit alone.

St. Ambrose College

Davenport, Iowa 52803 (319) 383-8888

A church-related college, conducted by the Diocese of Davenport, located in a city of 100,000, 150 miles west of Chicago.

Founded: 1882
Affiliation: Roman Catholic
UG Enrollment: 1,862 M, W (full-time)
Cost: < $10K
Admission: Non-selective
Application Deadline: Rolling

Admission. About 88% of applicants accepted, 57% of these actually enroll. Almost all freshmen graduate in top two-fifths of high school class. *Required:* ACT, minimum composite score of 18, minimum high school GPA of 2.5. *Apply:* no specific deadline. *Transfers* welcome.

Academic Environment. *Degrees:* AB, BS. About 60% of students entering as freshmen graduate eventually; 80% of freshmen return for sophomore year. *Special programs:* CLEP, independent study, study abroad, individualized majors. *Calendar:* semester, summer school.

Undergraduate degrees conferred (320). 44% were in Business and Management, 12% were in Education, 10% were in Communications, 8% were in Psychology, 5% were in Engineering, 4% were in Social Sciences, 4% were in Protective Services, 3% were in Life Sciences, 3% were in Computer and Engineering Related Technology, 3% were in Visual and Performing Arts, 3% were in Multi/Interdisciplinary Studies, remainder in 5 other fields.

Student Body. College seeks a national student body; 68% of students from in state.

Religious Orientation. St. Ambrose is a church-related institution; 2 courses in philosophy and religion required of all students; no religious clubs on campus.

Varsity Sports. Men (NAIA II): Baseball, Basketball, Football, Golf, Tennis. Women (NAIA II): Basketball, Softball, Tennis, Volleyball.

Campus Life. About 30% of students live in traditional dormitories; no coed dormitories; rest live in off-campus housing or commute. Intervisitation in men's and women's dormitory rooms limited. There are no fraternities or sororities. About 30% of resident students leave campus on weekends.

Annual Costs. Tuition and fees, $9,850; room and board, $3,830. College reports some scholarships awarded on the basis of academic merit alone.

St. Andrews Presbyterian College

Laurinburg, North Carolina 28352 (919) 276-3652

A church-related, liberal arts college, located in a town of 15,000, 100 miles southwest of Raleigh. Most convenient major airport: Fayetteville Regional.

Founded: 1896
Affiliation: Presbyterian
UG Enrollment: 723 M, W (full-time)
Cost: < $10K
% Receiving Financial Aid: 85%
Admission: Non-selective
Application Deadline: Rolling

Admission. About 86% of applicants accepted, 38% of these actually enroll. Average freshman SAT score, according to most recent data available: 985 combined verbal, mathematical. *Required:* SAT. *Apply:* rolling admissions. *Transfers* welcome.

Academic Environment. *Degrees:* AB, BM, BSMT. *Majors offered* include usual arts and sciences, business administration, education, environmental studies, fine arts, computer information systems, mass communications, Asian studies.

About 65% of students entering as freshmen graduate eventually; 81% of freshmen return for sophomore year. *Special programs:* CLEP, independent study, study abroad, honors, undergraduate research, credit by examination, 3–2 programs in accounting, engineering; pre-law, premed, pre-veterinary medicine, pre-physical therapy, pre-ministerial. *Calendar:* 4–1–4, summer school.

Undergraduate degrees conferred (181). 21% were in Business and Management, 12% were in Life Sciences, 12% were in Letters, 10% were in Social Sciences, 10% were in Education, 9% were in Psychology, 7% were in Philosophy and Religion, 5% were in Communications, 4% were in Visual and Performing Arts, 3% were in Mathematics, remainder in 5 other fields.

Student Body. College seeks a national student body; 38% of students from in state. An estimated 7% of students reported as Black, 2% other minority, according to most recent data available. *Minority group students:* special academic counseling program; Black Student Union.

Religious Orientation. St. Andrews is a church-related institution; 3-year program in St. Andrews Studies required of all students; attendance at chapel services voluntary. Student Christian Council coordinates programs of various denominational groups on campus.

Varsity Sports. Men (NAIA): Baseball, Basketball, Cross Country, Golf, Soccer, Tennis, Track. Women (NAIA): Basketball, Softball, Tennis, Volleyball. Coed (IHSA, ANRC): Equitation, Hunt Seat and Stock Seat.

Campus Life. Students serve on all important college policy-making committees. Each suite of 12–16 students may determine intervisitation hours within limitations of college policy.

About 54% of men, 62% of women live in traditional dormitories; 46% of men, 38% of women in coed dormitories. Sexes segregated in coed dormitories by wing. There are no fraternities or sororities. About 20% of resident students leave campus on weekends.

Annual Costs. Tuition and fees, $9,880; room and board, $4,360. About 85% of students receive financial aid; assistance is typically divided 60% scholarship, 25% loan, 15% work. College reports some scholarships awarded on the basis of academic merit alone. *Meeting Costs:* college offers extended payment plan.

Saint Anselm College

Manchester, New Hampshire 03102-1310 (603) 641-7500

A church-related institution, conducted by the Order of St. Benedict. The campus is located on the outskirts of a city of 100,000, 50 miles north of Boston. Most convenient major airport: Logan International (Boston).

Founded: 1889
Affiliation: Roman Catholic
UG Enrollment: 823 M, 1,050 W (full-time)
Cost: $10K–$20K
% Receiving Financial Aid: 67%
Admission: Selective
Application Deadline: Mar. 15

Admission is selective. About 74% of applicants accepted, 33% of these actually enroll. About 30% of freshmen graduate in top fifth of high school class, 68% in top two-fifths. Average freshman SAT scores: 478 M, 482 W verbal, 518 M, 503 W mathematical; 46% of freshmen score above 500 on verbal, 4% above 600; 56% score above 500 on mathematical, 7% above 600. *Required:* SAT, interview, essay, 2 letters of recommendation. Criteria considered in admissions, in order of importance: high school academic record, standardized test scores, writing sample, recommendations, extracurricular activities; other factors considered: special talents, diverse student body, alumni children. *Entrance programs:* early decision, early admission, midyear admission, deferred admission, advanced placement. About 14% of entering students from private schools, 22% from parochial schools. *Apply* by March 15; rolling admissions. *Transfers* welcome; 41 enrolled 1993–94.

Academic Environment. Degrees offered: associates, bachelors. Core requirements include 2 semester courses in English composition and literature, 4 semester course in humanities, 2 semester courses beyond basic level in foreign language, 2 in laboratory science, 3 in philosophy, and 3 in Theology for Catholic students. A biology major reports that, "The student is constantly presented with challenges from both the course material and the faculty." A finance major found the humanities seminar to be one of her favorite classes, since it helped her strengthen public speaking and writing skills. About 74% of students entering as freshmen graduate within four years, 77% eventually; 86% of freshmen return for sophomore year. Students report that the newly renovated library is excellent, and computer center facilities are "very adequate, but it does get crowded during finals." Average undergraduate class size: 62% of classes under 20, 27% 20–40, 11% over 40. *Special programs:* CLEP, independent study, study abroad, cooperative programs through NHCUC, 3–2 programs in engineering, certificate programs in Soviet studies, classics, fine arts, French, Spanish, human work behavior, cross registration with New Hampshire Consortium, internships with Washington, D.C. *Calendar:* semester, summer school.

Undergraduate degrees conferred (400). 41% were in Social Sciences, 12% were in Protective Services, 11% were in Health Sciences, 10% were in Letters, 10% were in Psychology, 6% were in Life Sciences, 3% were in Foreign Languages, remainder in 8 other fields.

Graduates Career Data. Advanced studies pursued by 23% of students; 1% enter medical school; 2% enter dental school; 10% enter business school; 4% enter law school. Medical school typically enrolling largest numbers of graduates include Boston U., Tufts, Georgetown, Dartmouth, St. Louis U., U. of Massachusetts; dental schools include Tufts, U. of Connecticut, Boston U., U. of Pennsylvania; business schools include BC, U. of Massachusetts, Bentley, Catholic U.; law school include BC, BU, Georgetown, Catholic U., Suffolk U., Notre Dame, U.of Connecticut. *Careers in business and industry* pursued by 70% of graduates (1990–91). Corporations typically hiring largest numbers of graduates include Digital, American Express, IBM, AT&T, Kidder-Peabody. Career Development Services include career planning, coaching in resume writing and interviewing techniques, job trend analysis, comprehensive career counseling.

Faculty. About 84% of faculty hold PhD or equivalent. About 78% of undergraduate classes taught by tenured faculty. About 34% of teaching faculty are female.

Student Body. College does not seek a national student body; 20% of students from in state; 87% from New England, 10% Middle Atlantic. An estimated 87% of students reported as Catholic, 9% Protestant.

Religious Orientation. Saint Anselm is a church-related institution; 3 courses in theology required of all Roman Catholic students; attendance at Mass voluntary.

Varsity Sports. Men (Div.II): Baseball, Basketball, Cross Country, Golf, Ice Hockey, Lacrosse, Skiing, Soccer, Tennis. Women (Div.II): Basketball, Cross Country, Skiing, Soccer, Softball, Tennis, Volleyball.

Campus Life. Students find the setting to be ideal, "far enough away from the city to be quiet, but close enough to get there easily." Saint Anselm is just one hour away from Boston, and close to excellent skiing, but there are many activities and clubs on campus to keep students occupied. About 63% of men, 68% of women live in traditional dormitories; no coed dormitories; 25% of men, 19% of women live in off-campus housing; 12% of men, 13% of women commute. Intervisitation in men's and women's dormitory rooms limited. There are no fraternities or sororities. About 20% of resident students leave campus on weekends.

Annual Costs. Tuition and fees, $12,200; room and board, $5,200; estimated $1,450 other, exclusive of travel. About 67% of students receive financial aid; average amount of assistance, $9,000. Assistance is typically divided 60% scholarship, 25% loan, 15% work. College reports some scholarships available for special talents.

Saint Augustine's College

Raleigh, North Carolina 27610-2298 (919) 828-4451

A church-related college, located in a city of 144,000; founded as a college for Negroes and still serving a predominantly Black student body. Most convenient major airport: Raleigh-Durham.

Founded: 1867
Affiliation: Episcopal
UG Enrollment: 1,811 M, W (full-time)
Cost: < $10K
% Receiving Financial Aid: 90%
Admission: Non-selective
Application Deadline: Aug. 1

Admission. Graduates of accredited high schools with 16 units eligible; 73% of applicants accepted, 39% of these actually enroll. *Required:* SAT or ACT. *Apply* by August 1. *Transfers* welcome.

Academic Environment. *Degrees:* AB, BS. About 65% of students entering as freshmen graduate eventually; 80% of freshmen return for sophomore year. *Majors offered* in addition to usual studies include radio broadcast journalism, industrial hygiene, criminal justice, dual-degree program in engineering. *Special programs:* independent study, honors, cross-registration with Raleigh college consortium. *Calendar:* semester, summer school.

Undergraduate degrees conferred (188). 27% were in Business and Management, 26% were in Social Sciences, 14% were in Education, 9% were in Communications, 6% were in Psychology, 6% were in Computer and Engineering Related Technology, 4% were in Mathematics, 3% were in Letters, remainder in 6 other fields.

Graduates Career Data. According to most recent data available, full-time graduate or professional study pursued by 35% of students immediately after graduation; 5% enter business school. *Careers in business and industry* pursued by 15% of graduates. Corporations typically hiring largest numbers of graduates include IBM, Northern Telecom, Southern Bell.

Student Body. College seeks a national student body; 55% of students from in state. An estimated 85% of students reported as Protestant, 2% Catholic, 9% unaffiliated, 3% other; 97% Black, 1% Hispanic, 1% other minority, according to most recent data available.

Religious Orientation. Saint Augustine's is a church-related institution; 3 hours in Bible ethics, attendance at certain chapel services required of all students. Places of worship available on campus for all faiths.

Varsity Sports. Men (NCAA,II): Baseball, Basketball, Cross Country, Soccer, Tennis, Track. Women (NCAA,II): Basketball, Cross Country, Softball, Track, Volleyball.

Campus Life. About 64% of students live in traditional dormitories; no coed dormitories; rest live in off-campus housing or commute. Freshmen given preference in college housing if all students cannot be accommodated. No intervisitation in men's or women's dormitory rooms. There are 7 fraternities, 7 sororities on campus which about 10% of men, 10% of women join; they provide no residence facilities. About 33% of resident student leave campus on weekends.

Annual Costs. Tuition and fees, $5,700; room and board, $3,600. About 90% of students receive financial aid; assistance is typically divided 40% scholarship, 75% loan, 30% work. College reports some scholarships awarded on the basis of academic merit alone. *Meeting Costs:* university offers special arrangement with certain banks.

College of Saint Benedict

Saint Joseph, Minnesota 56374 **(612) 363-5308; (800) 544-1489**

The College of Saint Benedict is a Catholic, Benedictine, liberal arts college for women, sponsored by the Sisters of the Order of Saint Benedict. The College has a coordinate relationship with Saint John's University. The campus is located in a city of 3,500, 70 miles northwest of Minneapolis/St. Paul. Most convenient major airport: Hubert H. Humphrey (Minneapolis).

Founded: 1913
Affiliation: Independent (Roman Catholic)
UG Enrollment: 1,715 W (full-time)
Cost: $10K–$20K
% Receiving Financial Aid: 80%
Admission: Selective (+)
Application Deadline: June 1

Admission is selective (+). About 92% of applicants accepted, 59% of these actually enroll; 55% of freshmen graduate in top fifth of high school class, 82% in top two-fifths. Average freshmen scores: SAT, 484 verbal, 526 mathematical; 49% of freshman score above 500 verbal, 10% above 600, 1% above 700; 64% score above 500 mathematical, 31% above 600, 5% above 700; ACT, 23 composite, 20 mathematical. *Required:* SAT or ACT, minimum HS GPA 2.8, essay; interview recommended. Criteria considered in admissions, in order of importance: high school academic record, standardized test scores, extracurricular activities, writing sample, recommendations; other factors considered: special talents, alumni children, diverse student body. About 1% of entering students from private schools, 18% from parochial schools. *Apply* by June 1; rolling admissions. *Transfers* welcome; 69 enrolled 1993–94.

Academic Environment. Required core curriculum seeks to assist students in developing a common base of knowledge through the study of academic disciplines—humanities, mathematics, natural sciences, social sciences, and the fine arts. The partnership with Saint John's allows students access to all facilities and most extracurricular activities. Degree offered: bachelors. *Majors offered* include usual arts and sciences, accounting, business administration, theater, dietetics, elementary education, economics, medical technology, nursing, nutrition science, peace studies, physical therapy, theology; liberal studies major (with no particular emphasis on a specific discipline) also available. Students report small classes, no teaching assistants, and the faculty is "extremely accessible". Average undergraduate class size: 50% under 20, 50% 20–40.

About 60–65% of students entering as freshmen graduate within four years, 70–75% eventually; 80–85% of freshmen return for sophomore year. *Special programs:* CLEP, independent study, January term, study abroad, honors, undergraduate research, individualized majors, internships, cooperative work/study program, 3–2 programs in premed, pre-engineering, pre-pharmacy, physical therapy, occupational therapy, medical technology, pre-forestry, cross registration with St. Cloud State and St.John's U. Adult programs: Continuing Education and Extension Center programs available. *Calendar:* 4–1–4.

Undergraduate degrees conferred (461). 16% were in Education, 15% were in Business and Management, 10% were in Social Sciences, 9% were in Liberal/General Studies, 8% were in Psychology, 8% were in Health Sciences, 7% were in Letters, 6% were in Visual and Performing Arts, 4% were in Home Economics, 3% were in Life Sciences, 3% were in Foreign Languages, 3% were in Public Affairs, 3% were in Multi/Interdisciplinary Studies, remainder in 3 other fields.

Graduates Career Data. Advanced studies pursued by students immediately after graduation by 25% of students, 50% within five years; 5% enter law school; 5% enter business school; 5% enter medical or dental school. Graduate and professional schools enrolling largest numbers of graduates include U. of Minnesota, Mayo Medical, William Mitchell, Hamline, U. of St. Thomas. About 95% of 1992–93 graduates employed. Corporations and fields typically hiring largest numbers of graduates include Andersen Consulting, West Publishing, Minnesota Mutual, Deluxe, Chubb, Nursing, Accounting (Big 6). *Career Counseling Program* designed specifically for liberal arts students. Liberal arts majors urged to seek interviews with business/industry representatives who visit campus. Help provided in preparing for interviews. Alumni reported as helpful in both career guidance and job placement.

Faculty. About 73% of faculty hold PhD or equivalent. Over 50% of undergraduate classes taught by tenured faculty. About 59% of teaching faculty are female; 2% Black, 2% Hispanic, 2% ethnic minority.

Student Body. College seeks a national student body; 85% of students from in state; 90% of students from Midwest, 1% West, 6% Northwest, 2% foreign. An estimated 78% of students reported as Catholic, 17% Protestant, 3% other, 2% unaffiliated; 1% Black, 1% Hispanic, 2% Asian, 2% other minority.

Religious Orientation. Saint Benedict is Catholic Benedictine institution, Catholic and Lutheran chaplains available, as well as Episcopal Church House of Prayer; 2 religious courses are required of all students. Campus Ministry offers many opportunities to students.

Varsity Sports. Women (Div.III): Basketball, Cross Country, Diving, Golf, Soccer, Softball, Swimming, Tennis, Track, Volleyball.

Campus Life. College emphasizes importance of campus governance policy with decision making by committees of students, administrators, and faculty. Students enjoy a cooperative relationship with Saint John's in planning of co-educational social and educational events. Regular bus service to St. Cloud and the Twin Cities permits access to range of cultural and recreational activities. Outdoor activities are popular and, a current student reports, "student support for athletics is outstanding!" Intervisitation allowed noon to midnight Sunday-Thursday; to 2 am Friday and Saturday. Cars allowed; smoking restricted to designated areas; alcohol policy reflects state law; legal age, 21.

About 48% of women live in traditional dormitories; 29% live in off-campus college-related housing; 23% commute. There are no sororities. About 20–30% of resident students leave campus on weekends.

Annual Costs. Tuition and fees, $11,428; room and board, $4,040; estimated $1,000 other, exclusive of travel. About 80% of students receive financial aid; average amount of assistance, $11,200. Assistance is typically divided 60% scholarship/grant, 32% loan, 8% work. College reports 175 scholarships/grants awarded on the basis of academic merit alone, 60 for special talents, 1,050 for need alone. *Meeting Costs:* college offers monthly budget plan, tuition stabilization plan.

Saint John's University

Collegeville, Minnesota 56321 **(612) 363-2196; (800) 245-6467**

Saint John's is a Catholic Benedictine university for men, sponsored by the Benedictines of Saint John's Abbey. A coordinate relationship with neighboring College of Saint Benedict, 4 miles away, makes co-educational classes and extracurricular activities possible. The University is located on a 2,400-acre campus 80 miles northwest of the Twin Cities and 14 miles west of Saint Cloud (pop. 100,000). Most convenient major airport: Minneapolis/St. Paul.

Founded: 1857
Affiliation: Independent (Roman Catholic)
UG Enrollment: 1,689 M (full-time)
Cost: $10K–$20K
% Receiving Financial Aid: 75%
Admission: Selective (+)
Application Deadline: June 1

Admission is selective (+). About 86% of applicants accepted, 56% of these actually enroll; 37% of freshmen graduate in top fifth of high school class, 68% in top two-fifths. Average freshman scores: SAT, 465 verbal, 555 mathematical; 41% of freshman score above 500 verbal, 7% above 600, 1% above 700; 75% score above 500 mathematical, 34% above 600, 7% above 700; ACT, 24 composite. *Required:* PSAT, SAT or ACT, minimum HS GPA 2.8, essay; interview recommended. Criteria considered in admissions, in order of importance: high school academic record, standardized test scores, extracurricular activities, writing sample, recommendations; other factors considered: alumni sons, diverse student body, special talents. About 1% of entering students from private schools, 26% from parochial schools. *Apply* by June 1; rolling admissions. *Transfers* welcome; 82 enrolled 1993–94.

Academic Environment. Administration spokesman reports student body has equally strong interest in both scholarly/intellectual pursuits and occupational/professional goals, with a healthy secondary interest in college social life. Required core curriculum seeks to assist students in developing a common base of knowledge through the study of academic disciplines—humanities, mathematics, natural sciences, social sciences, and the fine arts. Coordinate relationship with the College of Saint Benedict, a nearby women's college, broadens facilities and programs available to students; one student finds "the advantages of two college campuses for the tuition of one" Degrees offered: bachelors, masters. *Majors offered* include usual arts and sciences, theater, communication, variety of pre-professional programs. Average undergraduate class size: 50% under 20, 50% 20–40.

About 60–65% of students entering as freshmen graduate within four years, 70–75% eventually; 80–85% of freshmen return for sophomore year. *Special programs:* independent study, study abroad, honors, January term, combined program in engineering with U. of Minnesota, Washington U., dual-degree programs in occupational therapy, internships, cooperative work-study programs, individualized majors, tutorial studies, undergraduate resource. Adult programs: continuing education, extension center. *Library:* 450,000 volumes, 2,100 periodicals; rare books, Hill Monastic Manuscript Library; open-stack privileges; hours until midnight. *Calendar:* 4–1–4, summer school.

Undergraduate degrees conferred (399). 36% were in Business and Management, 23% were in Social Sciences, 10% were in Letters, 7% were in Psychology, 6% were in Physical Sciences, 5% were in Multi/Interdisciplinary Studies, 5% were in Life Sciences, 3% were in Visual and Performing Arts, remainder in 5 other fields.

Graduates Career Data. Advanced studies pursued immediately after graduation by 25% of students, 50% within five years; 5% enter medical or dental schools; 5% enter law school; 5% enter business school. Graduate and professional schools typically enrolling largest numbers of graduates include U. of Minnesota, Mayo Medical, William Mitchell, Hamline, St. Thomas U. About 95% of 1992–93 graduates employed. Corporations and fields typically hiring largest numbers of graduates include Andersen Consulting, West Publishing, Minnesota Mutual, Deluxe, Chubb, accounting (Big 6). Career Development Services include four-phase career model (self-assessment, exploration of tentative career choices, experiential learning and preparation for career entry), individual and group counseling, workshops, class offerings.

Faculty. About 83% of faculty hold PhD or equivalent. About 50% of undergraduate classes taught by tenured faculty. About 27% of teaching faculty are female; 1% Black, 2% ethnic minority.

Student Body. University seeks a national student body; 76% of students from in state; 87% from Midwest, 1% South, 2% West, 7% Northwest, 2% foreign. An estimated 78% of students reported as Catholic, 17% Protestant, 3% unaffiliated, 3% other; 1% Black, 1% Hispanic, 2% Asian, 2% ethnic minority.

Religious Orientation. Saint John's is a Catholic Benedictine institution, Catholic and Lutheran chaplains available, as well as Episcopal Church House of Prayer; 2 religious courses are required of all students. Places of worship available on campus for Catholics, in immediate community for major faiths. Campus Ministry provides many opportunities for students.

Varsity Sports. Men (Div.III): Baseball, Basketball, Cross Country, Diving, Football, Golf, Ice Hockey, Soccer, Swimming, Tennis, Track, Wrestling.

Campus Life. Students enjoy a cooperative relationship with Saint Benedict's in planning of co-educational social and educational events. The peaceful, rural location offers abundant opportunities for fishing, hiking, cross country skiing, canoeing, and nature walks. Regular bus service to St. Cloud and the Twin Cities permits access to range of cultural and recreational activities. Intervisitation allowed noon to midnight Sunday-Thursday; to 2 am Friday and Saturday. Cars allowed; smoking restricted to designated areas; alcohol policy reflects state law; legal age, 21.

About 58% of men live in traditional dormitories; 17% of men live in other college-related housing; 25% commute. There are no fraternities on campus. About 20–30% of resident students leave campus on weekends.

Annual Costs. Tuition and fees, $11,428; room and board, $4,040; estimated $1,000 other, exclusive of travel. About 75% of students receive financial aid; average amount of assistance, $11,200. Assistance is typically divided 56% scholarship/grant, 33% loan, 11% work. University reports 115 scholarships awarded on the basis of academic merit alone, 20 for special talents, 900 scholarship and grants awarded for need alone. *Meeting Costs:* college offers tuition stabilization plan, monthly payment plan, AMS.

St. Bonaventure University

St. Bonaventure, New York 14778-2284 **(716) 375-2400**

A private, independent university, founded by the Franciscan Friars, St. Bonaventure is located near Olean (pop. 19,200), 70 miles southeast of Buffalo. Most convenient major airport: Buffalo.

Founded: 1858
Affiliation: Independent (Roman Catholic)
UG Enrollment: 877 M, 867 W (full-time)
Total Enrollment: 2,580
Cost: $10K–$20K
Admission: Selective
Application Deadline: Rolling

Admission is selective. About 85% of applicants accepted, 29% of these actually enroll; 40% of freshmen graduate in top fifth of high school class, 73% in top two-fifths. Average freshman scores: SAT, 469 M, 488 W verbal, 548 M, 524 W mathematical; 39% of freshman score above 500 verbal, 10% above 600; 71% score above 500 mathematical, 24% above 600; ACT, 25 M, 25 W composite. *Required:* SAT or ACT, minimum HS GPA 3.0; interview strongly recommended. Criteria considered in admissions, in order of importance: high school academic record, standardized test scores, recommendations, extracurricular activities, writing sample (optional); other factors considered: special talents, alumni children, diverse student body. *Entrance programs:* midyear admission, deferred admission. About 34% of entering students from independent schools. *Apply:* rolling admissions. *Transfers* welcome; 125 enrolled 1993–94.

Academic Environment. Administration reports percentage of elective courses required for graduation varies with majors; distribution requirements fairly numerous. All undergraduates must complete 9 hours of theology and philosophy. *Undergraduate studies* offered by schools of Arts and Sciences, Business Administration, Education. Degrees offered: bachelors, masters. Major offered in arts and sciences in addition to usual studies include journalism. Average undergraduate class size: 51% under 20, 48% 20–40, 1% over 40.

About 68% of students entering as freshmen graduate within four years, 72% eventually; 88% of freshmen return for sophomore year. *Special programs:* CLEP, independent study, January term, study abroad, honors, 3-year degree, combined engineering program with Detroit, credit by examination, internships in accounting, journalism, psychology; visiting student programs. *Calendar:* semester, summer school.

Undergraduate degrees conferred (532). 37% were in Business and Management, 14% were in Education, 11% were in Communications, 11% were in Social Sciences, 9% were in Letters, 7% were in Psychology, 3% were in Life Sciences, remainder in 7 other fields.

Graduates Career Data. According to most recent data available, full-time graduate or professional study pursued immediately after graduation by 22% of students. Employers typically hiring largest numbers of graduates include Deloitte Haskins & Sells, AT&T, Ernst & Young, KPMG Peat Marwick, according to most recent data available.

Faculty. About 90% of faculty hold PhD or equivalent. About 95% of undergraduate classes taught by tenured faculty. About 20% of teaching faculty are female; 1% Black, 6% other ethnic minority.

Student Body. University does not seek a national student body; 75% of students from in state; 87% from Middle Atlantic, 5% New England, 4% Midwest, 2% South, 1% West, 1% foreign. An estimated 65% of students reported as Catholic, 31% Protestant, 4% Jewish; 2% as Black, 1% Hispanic, according to most recent data available.

Religious Orientation. St. Bonaventure is a church-related institution; 9 hours of theology and philosophy required of all undergraduate students; attendance at chapel services voluntary. Campus Ministry team sponsors various programs throughout the year. Places of worship available on campus for Catholics, in immediate community for Protestants and Jews.

Varsity Sports. Men (Div.I): Baseball, Basketball, Cross Country, Golf, Soccer, Swimming, Tennis. Women (Div.I): Basketball, Cross Country, Soccer, Softball, Swimming, Tennis, Volleyball.

Campus Life. Students serve on all major committees of governance of university. Limited intervisitation. Drinking allowed in residence halls, "Rathskeller," and (with special permission) at social functions for those over 21. Cars allowed. Seniors and students over 21 may request permission to live off campus.

About 80% each of men, women live in coed dormitories; rest live in off-campus housing or commute, according to most recent data available. Freshmen given preference in college housing if all students cannot be accommodated. Sexes segregated in coed dormitories by floor. There are no fraternities or sororities. About 20% of resident students leave campus on weekends, according to most recent data available.

Annual Costs. Tuition and fees, $10,026; room and board, $4,736; estimated $600 other, exclusive of travel. About 75% of students receive financial aid; average amount of assistance, $8,559 (1990–91). Assistance is typically divided 56% scholarship, 35% loan, 9% work, according to most recent data available. University reports some scholarships awarded on the basis of academic merit alone. *Meeting Costs:* university offers AMS monthly payment plans.

College of St. Catherine

St. Paul, Minnesota 55105 (612) 690-6505

A church-related, liberal arts college for women, conducted by the Sisters of St. Joseph of Carondelet, St. Catherine is located on a 100-acre campus in a residential section midway between the centers of St. Paul and Minneapolis. Most convenient major airport: Minneapolis/St. Paul.

Founded: 1905
Affiliation: Roman Catholic
UG Enrollment: 1,584 W (full-time); 844 W (part-time)
Total Enrollment: 2,700
Cost: $10K–$20K
% Receiving Financial Aid: 90%
Admission: Selective
Application Deadline: August 1

Admission is selective. About 89% of applicants accepted, 50% of these actually enroll; 51% of freshmen graduate in top fifth of high school class, 74% in top two-fifths. Average freshman scores: SAT, 450 verbal, 485 mathematical; ACT, 21 composite, 20 mathematical. *Required:* SAT or ACT, interview. *Non-academic factors* considered in admissions: special talents, alumni children, diverse student body, leadership in school, church, or community. *Entrance programs:* early admission, midyear admission, advanced placement, deferred admission. *Apply:* by August 1; rolling admissions. *Transfers* welcome; 539 accepted 1990–91.

Academic Environment. Student leader observes that "The academic atmosphere is very sophisticated, the faculty is of very high caliber, and students are challenged academically." Five-college consortium enhances student opportunities. Administration reports that 10 of the 32 courses required for graduation are elective; distribution requirements fairly numerous. Degrees offered: associates, bachelors, masters. *Majors offered* include usual arts and sciences, business administration, home economics, information management, nursing, occupational therapy, social work, theater art; additional majors available through College of St. Thomas.

About 47% of students entering as freshmen graduate within four years; 24% of freshmen do not return for sophomore year. *Special programs:* CLEP, independent study, study abroad, honors, individualized majors, extensive program of cooperation with Twin Cities area colleges (including cross-registration with Hamline, Macalester, St. Thomas, Augsburg), courses in area studies. Adult programs: Weekend College; Re-entry Program for adult learners in day program. *Calendar:* 4–1–4, summer school.

Undergraduate degrees conferred (504). 18% were in Business and Management, 16% were in Education, 11% were in Health Sciences, 10% were in Allied Health, 7% were in Communications, 7% were in Letters, 7% were in Public Affairs, 4% were in Multi/Interdisciplinary Studies, 4% were in Social Sciences, 3% were in Psychology, 3% were in Home Economics, remainder in 9 other fields.

Graduates Career Data. *Full-time graduate or professional study* pursued by 35% of students. *Careers in business and industry* pursued by 50% of graduates; 30% enter health care fields; 13% enter education. *Career Counseling Program:* Student assessment of program reported as fair for both career guidance and job placement. Career mentoring programs and internships available.

Faculty. About 60% of faculty hold PhD or equivalent.

Student Body. College does not seek a national student body; 90% of students from in state; 97% North Central; 61 foreign students 1990–91. An estimated 60% of students reported as Catholic; 1% Black, 1% Asian, 1% Hispanic. *Minority group students:* financial aid available upon request.

Religious Orientation. St. Catherine is a church-related institution; 4 courses in philosophy and theology (at least 1 course in each field) required as part of core program; attendance at chapel services voluntary. Religious clubs on campus include Campus Ministry. Places of worship available on campus for Catholics, in immediate community for major faiths.

Varsity Sports. Women (MAIC): Cross Country, Softball, Swimming/Diving, Tennis (NCAA,III), Track, Volleyball.

Campus Life. Students represented on most administrative committees. Some student organizations coordinated with St. Thomas. No curfew. Rules for limited visitation enforced "judiciously." Students reported to be of "two minds" concerning regulations governing male guests—some would like to see them relaxed, others value their privacy and don't want it violated. Regulations on alcoholic beverages follow state law. Location of college permits full access to cultural and recreational opportunities of the Twin Cities area. About 34% of undergraduate day students live in dormitories; 66% commute. There are no sororities.

Annual Costs. Tuition and fees, $11,530; room and board, $4,210. About 90% of freshmen receive financial aid; assistance is typically divided 60% scholarship, 20% loan, 20% work. College reports some scholarships awarded on the basis of academic merit alone. *Meeting Costs:* college offers deferred payment plan.

Saint Charles Borromeo Seminary

Overbrook, Pennsylvania 19096

St. Charles, a private seminary for men, prepares students for the Roman Catholic priesthood. Programs for seminarians are offered in the College and Theology divisions at several levels: College, Pre-Theology, Spirituality Year, Theology. Undergraduate and graduate programs offered through the Religious Studies division are open to other persons interested in studying Catholic Theology, Sacred Scripture and related fields. For additional information, contact the Academic Dean of the appropriate division.

Founded: 1832 **Affiliation:** Roman Catholic

Undergraduate degrees conferred (20). 75% were in Philosophy and Religion, 25% were in Multi/Interdisciplinary Studies.

St. Cloud State University

St. Cloud, Minnesota 56301-4498 **(612) 255-0121**

A state-supported university, located in a city of 45,000, 70 miles northwest of Minneapolis. Most convenient major airport: Minneapolis/St. Paul.

Founded: 1869
Affiliation: State
UG Enrollment: 5,608 M, 5,732 W (full-time); 981 M, 1,275 W (part-time)
Total Enrollment: 16,300
Cost: < $10K
% Receiving Financial Aid: 85%
Admission: Non-selective
Application Deadline: Aug. 15

Admission. Graduates of accredited high schools who rank in the upper one-half of class or score 25 on ACT composite, combined score of 90 on PSAT, or combined score of 900 on SAT are eligible; 83% of applicants accepted, 58% of these actually enroll; 24% of students entering freshmen graduate in top fifth of high school class; 55% in top two-fifths. *Required:* SAT or ACT (for placement and registration purposes only). Criteria considered in admissions, in order of importance: high school academic record, standardized test, recommendations. *Out-of-state* freshman applicants: university actively seeks students from out of state; no limits; no special requirements. States from which most out-of-state students are drawn: Wisconsin, North Dakota, South Dakota, Iowa. *Apply* by August 15. *Transfers* welcome; 1,250 enrolled 1993–94.

Academic Environment. Degrees offered: associates, bachelors, masters. *Majors offered* in addition to usual studies include aviation, photographic engineering technology, earth science with meteorology emphasis, international business, electrical engineering. Core requirements include 70 credit interdisciplinary program. About 45% of students entering as freshmen graduate eventually; 76% of freshmen return for sophomore year. Average undergraduate class size: 5% of classes under 20, 65% 20–40, 30% over 40. *Special programs:* CLEP, independent study, study abroad, honors, undergraduate research, exchanges and cooperative programs, cross registration with St. John's and St. Benedict's. *Calendar:* quarter, summer school.

Undergraduate degrees conferred (2,382). 26% were in Education, 24% were in Business and Management, 7% were in Letters, 7% were in Social Sciences, 6% were in Psychology, 4% were in Communications, 4% were in Life Sciences, 3% were in Public Affairs, 3% were in Engineering and Engineering Related Technology, 3% were in Liberal/General Studies, 3% were in Visual and Performing Arts, 3% were in Protective Services, remainder in 11 other fields.

Faculty. About 70% of faculty hold PhD or equivalent. About 85% of undergraduate classes taught by tenured faculty. About 33% of teaching faculty are female; 5% Black, 3% Hispanic, 2% ethnic minority.

Student Body. University does not seek a national student body; 91% of students from in state. An estimated 1% of students reported as Black, 1% Hispanic, 1% Asian, 1% other ethnic minority. Average age of undergraduate student: 22.

Varsity Sports. Men (Div.II): Baseball, Basketball, Cross Country, Football, Golf, Ice Hockey, Swimming, Tennis, Track, Wrestling. Women (Div.II): Basketball, Cross Country, Golf, Softball, Swimming, Tennis, Track, Volleyball.

Campus Life. About 20% of men, 20% of women live in coed dormitories; 79% of men, 79% of women commute. Freshmen given preference in college housing if all students cannot be accommodated. Intervisitation in men's and women's dormitory rooms limited. Sexes segregated in coed dormitories by floor. There are 7 fraternities, 5 sororities on campus which about 1% of men, 1% of women join; 1% each live in fraternities and sororities. About 50% of resident students leave campus on weekends.

Annual Costs. Tuition and fees, $2,390; (out-of-state, $4,683); room and board, $2,625; estimated $1,450 other, exclusive of travel. About 85% of students receive financial aid; average amount of assistance, $3,700. University reports some scholarships awarded on the basis of academic merit alone. *Meeting Costs:* university offers payment plans.

St. Edward's University

Austin, Texas 78704 **(512) 448-8500**

An independent, liberal arts institution, founded by the Brothers of the Holy Cross and located in a city of 350,000. Most convenient major airport: Mueller (Austin).

Founded: 1885
Affiliation: Independent (Roman Catholic)
UG Enrollment: 730 M, 1,002 W (full-time); 398 M, 538 W (part-time)
Total Enrollment: 3,107
Cost: < $10K
% Receiving Financial Aid: 50%
Admission: Non-selective
Application Deadline: Rolling

Admission. Graduates of accredited high schools who rank in top half of class eligible; 78% of applicants accepted, 34% of these actually enroll; 45% of freshmen graduate in top quarter of high school class, 79% in top half. Average freshman scores: SAT, 446 M, 433 W verbal, 515 M, 462 W mathematical; ACT, 21.8 M, 21.6 W composite, 21.2 M, 20.4 W mathematical. *Required:* SAT or ACT. Criteria considered in admissions, in order of importance: high school academic record, standardized test scores, recommendations, extracurricular activities; other factor considered: alumni children. About 76% of entering students from private schools. *Apply*: rolling admissions. *Transfers* welcome; 383 enrolled 1993–94.

Academic Environment. Degrees offered: bachelors, masters. All general education requirements for graduation are elective; no distribution requirements; one computer course required of all students. About 17% of students entering as freshmen graduate within four years; 68% of freshmen return for sophomore year. Average undergraduate class size: 25. *Special programs:* CLEP, honors, independent study, study abroad, undergraduate research, internship/cooperative work-study programs. Adult programs: New College, offers assessment of prior learning, individualized study, flexible degree planning. *Calendar:* semester, summer school.

Undergraduate degrees conferred (424). 29% were in Liberal/General Studies, 17% were in Social Sciences, 15% were in Business and Management, 6% were in Letters, 5% were in Visual and Performing Arts, 5% were in Marketing and Distribution, 4% were in Computer and Engineering Related Technology, 4% were in Communications, 3% were in Life Sciences, 3% were in Education, remainder in 8 other fields.

Faculty. About 47% of faculty hold PhD or equivalent.

Student Body. University seeks a national student body; 91% of students from in state; 5% foreign. An estimated 60% of students reported as Roman Catholic, 30% Protestant, 1% Jewish, 4% unaffiliated; 4% Black, 26% Hispanic, 2% Asian, 6% other ethnic minority. Average age of undergraduate student: 23.

Religious Orientation. St. Edward's is an independent institution with a Roman Catholic heritage; 1 course in either philosophy or religious studies, 1 course in Ethnics; daily Mass on campus. Places of worship available on campus for Catholics, in immediate community for Protestants and Jews.

Varsity Sports. Men (NAIA): Baseball, Basketball, Golf, Soccer, Tennis. Women (NAIA): Basketball, Soccer, Softball, Tennis, Volleyball.

Campus Life. About 5% of men, 5% of women live in traditional dormitories; 3% of men, 7% of women live in coed dormitories; rest commute. Freshmen given preference in college housing if all students cannot be accommodated. Intervisitation in men's and women's dormitory rooms limited. There are no fraternities or sororities on campus. About 4% of resident students leave campus on weekends.

Annual Costs. Tuition and fees, $8,782; room and board, $3,610–$4,000. About 50% of students receive financial aid; assistance is typically divided 44% scholarship, 33% loan, 23% work, according to most recent data available. University reports some scholarships awarded on the basis of academic merit alone. *Meeting Costs:* college offers variety of loan programs.

College of Saint Elizabeth

Convent Station, New Jersey 07960-6989 (201) 292-6300

A church-related college for women, conducted by the Sisters of Charity of Saint Elizabeth, located in a village in northern New Jersey, 35 miles west of New York City. Most convenient major airport: Newark International.

Founded: 1899
Affiliation: Roman Catholic
UG Enrollment: 3 M, 490 W (full-time); 150 M, 818 W (part-time)
Cost: $10K–$20K
% Receiving Financial Aid: 90%
Admission: Non-selective
Application Deadline: August 15

Admission. Graduates of accredited high schools with 16 units of college preparatory work eligible; 81% of applicants accepted, 34% of these actually enroll; 47% of freshmen graduate in top fifth of high school class, 68% in top two-fifths; 34% of freshman score above 500 verbal, 8% above 600; 43% score above 500 mathematical, 13% above 600, 1% above 600. Average freshman SAT scores: 464 verbal, 486 mathematical. *Required:* SAT or ACT; interview strongly recommended. Criteria considered in admissions, in order of importance: high school academic record, standardized test scores, recommendations, extracurricular activities, writing sample. *Entrance programs:* early decision, early admission, midyear admission, deferred admission, advanced placement. About 11% of entering students from private schools, 25% from parochial schools. *Apply* by August 15; rolling admissions. *Transfers* welcome; 47 enrolled full-time 1993–94.

Academic Environment. Degrees offered: bachelors, masters. *Majors offered* include liberal arts and sciences, business administration, elementary education, home economics, upper level nursing. Core requirements include 6 courses in humanities, 3 in social/behavioral sciences, 3 in mathematics and science. About 51% of students entering as freshmen graduate within four years, 59% eventually; 77% of freshmen return for sophomore year. Average undergraduate class size: 77% under 20, 23% 20–40. *Special programs:* CLEP, independent study, study abroad, honors, undergraduate research, January Intersession, 3-year degree, Seton College Exchange, combined programs in medical technology and cytotechnology with U. of Medicine and Dentistry of NJ, internships, cross registration with Drew U. and Fairleigh Dickinson U. Adult programs: Continuing Education and Weekend College (coed), Tuesday College. *Calendar:* semester, summer school.

Undergraduate degrees conferred (161). 46% were in Business and Management, 14% were in Education, 11% were in Psychology, 8% were in Letters, 5% were in Social Sciences, 4% were in Home Economics, 3% were in Life Sciences, remainder in 6 other fields.

Graduates Career Data. Advanced studies pursued by 15% of students; 2% enter law school, 3% enter business school, 2% enter medical school. Law schools typically enrolling largest numbers of graduates include Rutgers, Indiana U.; business school include Montclair State, San Jose State U.; medical school include UMDNJ. About 59% of 1992–93 graduates employed. Corporations typically hiring largest numbers of graduates include AT&T, JCP&L, school districts. Career Development Services include counseling assistance for career/life planning issues, job placement information, part-time/full-time positions and summer job information, student internship, career field availability, potential employers and educational opportunity information available, resume writing, interviewing, career/life planning workshops.

Faculty. About 50% of faculty hold PhD or equivalent. About 67% of teaching faculty are female; 1% Black, 3% Hispanic, 2% other ethnic minorities.

Student Body. College seeks a national student body; 95% of students from in state; 96% Middle Atlantic, 3% foreign. An estimated 70% of students reported as Catholic, 10% Protestant, 4% unaffiliated, 16% other; 7% Black, 11% Hispanic, 3% Asian, 7% other ethnic minorities.

Religious Orientation. Saint Elizabeth is a church-related institution; 1 religious course is required of all students; Campus Ministry on campus. Places of worship available on campus for Catholics; nearby for other denominations.

Varsity Sports. Women (Div.III): Basketball, Equestrian, Softball, Swimming, Tennis, Volleyball.

Campus Life. About 62% of full-time women live in traditional dormitories; rest commute. There are no sororities. About 60% of resident students leave campus on weekends.

Annual Costs. Tuition and fees, $10,900; room and board, $5,000; estimated $1,030 other, exclusive of travel. About 90% of students receive financial aid; average amount of assistance, $4,000. Assistance is typically divided 36% scholarship, 39% grant, 20% loan, 5% work. College reports 123 scholarships awarded on the basis of academic merit alone, 229 for need alone. *Meeting Costs:* college offers AMS budget payment plan.

Saint Francis College

Fort Wayne, Indiana 46808 (219) 434-3100

A church-related liberal arts college, conducted by the Sisters of St. Francis of the Perpetual Adoration, located in a city of 177,700, 150 miles southeast of Chicago. Most convenient major airport: Fort Wayne (Baer Field).

Founded: 1890
Affiliation: Roman Catholic
UG Enrollment: 147 M, 366 W (full-time); 61 M, 186 W (part-time)
Total Enrollment: 961
Cost: < $10K
% Receiving Financial Aid: 97%
Admission: Non-selective
Application Deadline: Aug. 15

Admission. Graduates of accredited high schools who rank in top half of class or score above 800/19 combined on SAT/ACT eligible; 78% of applicants accepted, 60% of these actually enroll; 29% of freshmen graduate in top fifth of high school class, 55% in top two-fifths. Average freshman scores: SAT, 410 verbal, 450 mathematical; ACT, 21 composite. *Required:* SAT or ACT, essay. Criteria considered in admissions, in order of importance: high school academic record, standardized test scores, writing sample (essay), recommendations, extracurricular activities. Entrance program: deferred admission. *Apply* by August 15; rolling admissions. *Transfers* welcome.

Academic Environment. Degrees offered: associates, bachelors, masters. *Majors offered* in addition to usual studies include allied health, nursing, special education. Core requirements include courses in oral and written expression, humanities, social and behavioral sciences, natural and physical sciences, mathematics and computer science, religious studies, physical education. SFC sponsors "The Jesters", a drama troupe of physically and mentally challenged youth, providing practical experiences for special education students. Average undergraduate class size: 63% under 20, 34% 20–40, 3% over 40. *Special programs:* CLEP, independent study, study abroad through affiliations with other colleges, May term, internship required in some majors, optional in others. Adult programs: Adult Seminar, Adult Learner Office, New Horizons (adult support group), Liberal Studies Degree Program, credit for life experience. *Calendar:* semester, summer school.

Undergraduate degrees conferred (73). 26% were in Business and Management, 19% were in Education, 12% were in Visual and Performing Arts, 11% were in Health Sciences, 11% were in Business (Administrative Support), 5% were in Public Affairs, 4% were in Physical Sciences, 4% were in Communications, 3% were in Life Sciences, remainder in 3 other fields.

Graduates Career Data. *Full-time graduate or professional study* pursued by 6% of students immediately after graduation, 60% plan to pursue advanced studies eventually. About 1% of students enter law school; 1% enter business school. About 87% of 1992–93 graduates employed. Fields typically hiring largest numbers of graduates include business, education, health care. Career Development Services include comprehensive program for freshman through alumnae, career counseling/testing, resources, job board and

newsletter, employer information, credential files, recruiting events, job search, interview and resume assistance, computerized career planning, graduate school information, career course.
Faculty. About 60% of faculty hold PhD or equivalent. About 50% of undergraduate classes taught by tenured faculty. About 48% of teaching faculty are female; 7% ethnic minorities.
Student Body. College seeks a national student body; 83% of students from in state; 12% Midwest, 4% foreign. An estimated 54% of students reported as Protestant, 33% Catholic, 11% unaffiliated, 2% other; 3% Black, 2% Hispanic, 6% Asian, 4% other ethnic minorities. Average age of undergraduate student: 24.
Religious Orientation. Saint Francis is a church-related institution; attendance at Mass voluntary; 6 religious courses are required of all students.
Varsity Sports. Men (NAIA): Baseball, Basketball, Golf, Soccer. Women (NAIA): Basketball, Softball, Tennis, Volleyball.
Campus Life. About 35% of men, 65% of women live in traditional dormitories; no coed dormitories; rest commute. No intervisitation in men's or women's dormitory rooms. There are no sororities or fraternities on campus. About 80% of resident students leave campus on weekends.
Annual Costs. Tuition and fees, $4,150; room and board, $3,630; estimated $1,500 other, exclusive of travel. About 97% of students receive financial aid; average amount of assistance, $6,431. Assistance is typically divided 15% scholarship, 30% grant, 50% loan, 5% work. College reports 145 scholarships awarded on the basis of academic merit alone, 128 for special talents, 332 for need alone. *Meeting Costs:* college offers 10-month payment plan.

Saint Francis College
(See University of New England)

St. Francis College
Brooklyn, New York 11201 **(718) 522-2300**

An independent, liberal arts college for commuters, established by the co-educational Franciscan Brothers, located in the Brooklyn Heights section of New York City. Most convenient major airport: JFK International.

Founded: 1858
Affiliation: Independent
UG Enrollment: 661 M, 901 W (full-time); 280 M, 415 W (part-time)
Cost: < $10K
% Receiving Financial Aid: 83%
Admission: Non-selective
Application Deadline: Rolling

Admission. Graduates of approved high schools eligible; 90% of applicants accepted, 43% of these actually enroll. *Required:* SAT; interview strongly encouraged. Criteria considered in admissions, in order of importance: high school academic record, recommendations, class rank, standardized test scores, writing sample, extracurricular activities; other factors considered: special talents, alumni children. About 45% of entering students from private schools. *Apply:* rolling admissions. *Transfers* welcome; 239 enrolled 1993–94.
Academic Environment. Degrees offered: associates, bachelors. *Majors offered* include usual arts and sciences, accounting, aviation administration, aviation business studies, business management, education, medical technology, health-care management, health services administration, physical education, criminal justice, special education, international cultural studies. Core curriculum varies with major but all majors require courses in communications, English, fine arts, history, philosophy, sociology, and science or mathematics. St. Francis is committed to providing educational and cultural opportunities to its students and the surrounding community; the school presents a variety of programs focusing on local history and culture as well as current issues.

About 15% of students entering as freshmen graduate within four years, 30% within five years, 35% within six years; 75% of freshmen return for sophomore year. Average undergraduate class size: 36% under 20, 56% 20–40, 8% over 40. *Special programs:* CLEP, independent study, study abroad, honors, undergraduate research, January term, 3-year degree, Federal intern program, accounting internship, life experience credit, visiting students program for New York State colleges, 3–2 program in Podiatric Medicine, combined programs in nursing, occupational therapy, radiologic science with SUNY Health Center Brooklyn, NYC Transit Authority intern program, FAA co-op program for aviation students, dual majors, pass-fail options, credit for life experience. Adult programs: BS in Special Studies, BS in Health Care Management, experimental learning credit. *Calendar:* semester, summer school.
Undergraduate degrees conferred (249). 47% were in Business and Management, 12% were in Liberal/General Studies, 10% were in Health Sciences, 8% were in Social Sciences, 6% were in Psychology, 6% were in Communications, 5% were in Education, 3% were in Letters, remainder in 2 other fields.
Graduates Career Data. Advanced studies pursued by 50% of students; 2% enter law school; 40% enter business school; 1% enter medical school. *Careers in business and industry* pursued by 75% of graduates, according to most recent data available. Career Development Services include a career counseling center and alumni network for placement and counseling.
Faculty. About 40% of faculty hold PhD or equivalent. About 16% of faculty are tenured. About 34% of teaching faculty are female; 5% minorities.
Student Body. College does not seek a national student body; 99% of students from in state. An estimated 23% of students reported as Black, 15% Hispanic, 2% Asian, 6% other ethnic minority.
Religious Orientation. St. Francis is an independent institution "in the Franciscan tradition", makes no religious demands on students.
Varsity Sports. Men (Div.I): Baseball, Basketball, Cross Country, Soccer, Swimming, Tennis, Track. Women (Div.I): Basketball, Cross Country, Softball, Swimming, Tennis, Track, Volleyball.
Campus Life. College provides no residence facilities. There are 2 fraternities, 1 sorority on campus which about 5% of men, 2% of women join; they provide no residence facilities. While the school is conveniently located for public transportation, parking is extremely limited.
Annual Costs. Tuition and fees, $6,710; estimated $300 other, exclusive of travel. About 83% of students receive financial aid; average amount of assistance, $5,285. Assistance is typically divided 72% grant, 25% loan, 3% work. College reports 76 scholarships awarded on the basis of academic merit alone, 180 for special talents. *Meeting Costs:* college offers tuition payment plan.

Saint Francis College
Loretto, Pennsylvania 15940 **In state, (800) 457-6300; out-of-state, (800) 342-5732**

A church-related college, conducted by the Franciscan Fathers of the Third Order Regular, located in a village of 1,400, 15 miles west of Altoona and 85 miles east of Pittsburgh. Most convenient major airport: Pittsburgh.

Founded: 1847
Affiliation: Roman Catholic
UG Enrollment: 508 M, 493 W (full-time); 18 M, 25 W (part-time)
Total Enrollment: 1,853
Cost: $10K–$20K
% Receiving Financial Aid: 86%
Admission: Non-selective
Application Deadline: Aug. 1

Admission. Graduates of approved high schools with 16 units in academic subjects eligible; 80% of applicants accepted, 41% of these actually enroll; 20% of freshmen graduate in top fifth of high school class, 37% in top two-fifths. Average freshman scores, according to most recent data available: SAT, 480 verbal, 500 mathematical; ACT, 24 composite. *Required:* SAT or ACT, interview (on or off-campus. *Apply* by August 1. *Transfers* welcome.
Academic Environment. *Degrees:* AB, BS. *Majors offered* include usual arts and sciences, anthropology, art, business administration, commerce, elementary education, industrial relations, journalism, medical technology, modern language, pastoral ministry, physician's assistant, social work, pre-optometry, podiatric science. About 60% of students entering as freshmen graduate within four years; 24% of freshmen do not return for sophomore year. *Special programs:* CLEP, independent study, study abroad, undergraduate research, honors, 3-year degree, Washington Semester, Harrisburg Semester, double

and self-designed majors, 3–2 programs in engineering, forestry. *Calendar:* semester, summer school.

Undergraduate degrees conferred (198). 46% were in Business and Management, 11% were in Education, 9% were in Social Sciences, 7% were in Allied Health, 6% were in Life Sciences, 5% were in Public Affairs, 5% were in Health Sciences, 4% were in Psychology, 4% were in Letters, remainder in 4 other fields.

Graduates Career Data. According to most recent data available, full-time graduate or professional study pursued by 15% of students immediately after graduation. *Careers in business and industry* pursued by 52% of graduates.

Faculty. About 75% of faculty hold PhD or equivalent.

Varsity Sports. Men (Div.I): Basketball, Cross Country, Football(III), Golf, Rifle, Soccer, Tennis, Track, Volleyball. Women (Div.I): Basketball, Cross Country, Rifle, Soccer, Softball, Tennis, Track, Volleyball.

Student Body. College seeks a national student body; 67% of students from in state; 91% Middle Atlantic. An estimated 90% of students reported as Catholic, 6% Protestant, 4% unaffiliated; 2% Black, 1% Hispanic, 1% Asian, 1% other minority, according to most recent data available.

Religious Orientation. Saint Francis is a church-related institution; 6 credits in Biblical Studies required of all students.

Campus Life. About 67% of men, 64% of women live in traditional dormitories; no coed dormitories; 15% of men, 15% of women live in off-campus housing or commute. Intervisitation in men's and women's dormitory rooms limited. There are 4 fraternities, 3 sororities on campus which about 20% of men, 20% of women join. About 20% of students leave campus on weekends.

Annual Costs. Tuition and fees, $11,124; room and board, $4,720. About 86% of students receive financial aid. Assistance is typically divided 55% scholarship, 40% loan, 5% work. College reports some scholarships awarded on the basis of academic merit alone. *Meeting Costs:* college offers Tuition Payment Plan, Family Discount Plan.

College of St. Francis

Joliet, Illinois 60435 **(815) 740-3400**

A private, church-related college, founded by the Sisters of St. Francis of Mary Immaculate, located in a city of 80,400, 40 miles southwest of Chicago. Most convenient major airports: O'Hare or Midway.

Founded: 1920
Affiliation: Roman Catholic
UG Enrollment: 400 M, 430 W (full-time); 210 M, 250 W (part-time)
Cost: < $10K
% Receiving Financial Aid: 85%
Admission: Non-selective
Application Deadline: May 1

Admission. High school graduates who rank in top half of class and have minimum ACT composite score of 20 eligible, minimum HS GPA 2.5; 72% of applicants accepted, 52% of these actually enroll; 49% of freshmen graduate in top fifth of high school class, 78% in top two-fifths. Average freshman ACT scores: 23 M, 23 W composite. *Required:* ACT. Criteria considered in admissions, in order of importance: high school academic record, writing sample, recommendations, standardized test scores, extracurricular activities; other factor considered: diverse student body. About 40% of entering students from private schools. *Apply* by May 1. *Transfers* welcome; 120 enrolled 1993–94.

Academic Environment. Degrees offered: bachelors, masters. *Majors offered* in addition to usual studies include degree-completion course for nurses in Health Arts, nuclear medicine technology, commercial, recreation, actuarial science, public policy, environmental science, social work, biology, journalism. Core requirements include courses in writing, mathematics, philosophy, theology, literature, history, science, speech. Average undergraduate class size: 50% under 20, 50% 20–40. About 60% of students entering as freshmen graduate within four years, 65% eventually; 86% of freshmen return for sophomore year. *Special programs:* CLEP, independent study, study abroad, undergraduate research, individualized majors. Adult programs: Evening and Weekend College, programs available in health arts, health services administration, long-term care administration, special 2–2, applied organizational behavior. *Calendar:* semester, summer school.

Undergraduate degrees conferred (957). 74% were in Health Sciences, 9% were in Business and Management, 5% were in Education, remainder in 11 other fields.

Graduates Career Data. Advanced studies pursued by 15% of students; 2% enter law school; 6% enter business school; 3% enter medical school; 1% enter dental school. About 89% of 1992–93 graduates employed. Career Development Services include resume writing, interviewing technique, conducting a job search, dress for success. Part of a consortium of private colleges.

Faculty. About 55% of faculty hold PhD or equivalent. About 80% of undergraduate classes taught by tenured faculty. About 55% of teaching faculty are female; 3% Black.

Student Body. College does not seek a national student body; 90% of students from in state; 95 Midwest, 3% Middle Atlantic, 2% South, 5% West. An estimated 60% of students reported as Catholic, 38% Protestant, 2% Jewish; 6% Black, 3% Hispanic, 1% Asian. Average age of undergraduate student: 23.

Religious Orientation. St. Francis is a church-related institution; 2 courses in Religious Studies required of all students.

Varsity Sports. Men (Div.II): Baseball (I), Basketball, Football, Golf, Soccer, Tennis. Women (Div.II): Basketball, Cross Country, Softball, Tennis, Volleyball.

Campus Life. About 50% of students live in coed dormitories; rest commute. Freshmen given preference in college housing if all students cannot be accommodated. Intervisitation in men's and women's dormitory rooms limited; sexes segregated by wing or floor. There are no fraternities or sororities. About 25% of resident students leave campus on weekends.

Annual Costs. Tuition and fees, $9,100; room and board, $3,960; estimated $1,140 other, exclusive of travel. About 85% of students receive financial aid; average amount of assistance, $7,600. Assistance is typically divided 25% scholarship, 40% grant, 15% loan, 15% work. College reports 140 scholarships awarded on the basis of academic merit alone, 150 for special talents. *Meeting Costs:* college offers Tuition Payment Plan; college financial aid meets 100% of demonstrated financial need.

Saint Francis Seminary, School of Pastoral Ministry

Milwaukee, Wisconsin 53207

A private, professional institution sponsored by the Diocese of Milwaukee of the Roman Catholic Church, conferring both professional and graduate degrees.

Affiliation: Roman Catholic

St. Hyacinth College-Seminary

Granby, Massachusetts 01033

A church-related institution, conducted by the Order of Friars Minor Conventual, devoted to training Franciscan priests and brothers. Lay students (both men and women) are also admitted in limited numbers in some degree programs.

Founded: 1927 **Affiliation:** Roman Catholic

Undergraduate degrees conferred (7). 71% were in Philosophy and Religion, 29% were in Theology.

St. John Fisher College

Rochester, New York 14618 **(716) 385-8064**

Founded by the Basilian Fathers as a liberal arts college for men, St. John Fisher is now co-educational. The college participates in a consortium of 14 Rochester colleges which increases its academic resources through interinstitutional cooperation. The 125-acre campus is located in a residential area, 7 miles from downtown Rochester (pop. 296,200). Most convenient major airport: Rochester.

Founded: 1948
Affiliation: Independent (Roman Catholic)
UG Enrollment: 744 M, 943 W (full-time); 242 M, 435 W (part-time)
Total Enrollment: 2,644
Cost: $10K–$20K
% Receiving Financial Aid: 91%
Admission: Selective
Application Deadline: Rolling

Admission is selective. About 75% of applicants accepted, 33% of these actually enroll; 43% of freshmen graduate in top fifth of high school class, 74% in top two-fifths. Average freshman scores: SAT, 460 M, 470 W verbal, 550 M, 506 W mathematical; 30% of freshman score above 500 verbal, 5% above 600; 60% score above 500 mathematical, 20% above 600, 1% above 700; ACT, 23 M, 22 W composite. *Required:* SAT or ACT; interview recommended. Criteria considered in admissions, in order of importance: high school academic record, standardized test scores, recommendations, extracurricular activities, writing sample; other factors considered: special talents, alumni children, faculty children, diverse student body. *Entrance programs:* early admission, early admission, midyear admission, advanced placement, deferred admission. About 5% of entering students from private schools, 35% from parochial schools. *Apply:* rolling admissions. *Transfers* welcome; 211 enrolled 1993–94.

Academic Environment. Distribution requirements include 4 courses in each of social sciences, English literature/language, philosophy/religious studies, and mathematics/sciences. Degrees offered: bachelors, masters. *Majors offered* include usual arts and sciences, accounting, communication, management, biochemistry, nursing, pre-environmental science, international studies, optics concentration, African Studies concentration. Students can participate in collaborative research project with NASA Goddard Space Center and Marshal Space Center. Facilities include new computer and psychology labs; students report that even during finals computers are always available. Average undergraduate class size: 52% of classes under 20, 42% 20–40, 4% over 40; student to faculty ratio of 16:1. Faculty teach only 9 hours, instead of the typical 12, to allow more time for faculty-student interaction.

About 5% of students entering as freshmen graduate within four years, 57% eventually; 80% of freshmen return for sophomore year. *Special programs:* CLEP, honors, independent study, study abroad, undergraduate research, individualized majors, internships, Washington Semester, 3–2 international studies/MBA and management/MBA, 3–4 optometry program, 3–2 engineering with U. of Detroit, Manhattan, Columbia, Clarkson, SUNY Buffalo, 2–2 engineering with Detroit, Manhattan, 4–2 engineering with Columbia. Adult programs: Evening Division offers majors in accounting, communications, computer science, interdisciplinary studies, management, psychology, sociology. *Calendar:* semester, summer school.

Undergraduate degrees conferred (455). 43% were in Business and Management, 20% were in Social Sciences, 12% were in Communications, 9% were in Psychology, 5% were in Letters, 3% were in Computer and Engineering Related Technology, 3% were in Life Sciences, 3% were in Liberal/General Studies, remainder in 4 other fields.

Graduates Career Data. Advanced studies pursued by 13% of students; 5% enter business school; 2% enter law school; 1% enter medical school; 1% enter dental school. Business schools typically enrolling largest numbers of graduates include RIT, St. John Fisher, SUNY Buffalo, Syracuse, U. of Rochester; law schools include Harvard, Georgetown, SUNY Buffalo, Dayton, Syracuse; medical schools include U. of Rochester, Cornell, Marquette, Harvard, Georgetown; dental schools include Boston U., Tufts, SUNY Buffalo, Ohio State, Columbia. About 83% of 1992–93 graduates employed, (96% of graduates either in graduate school or employed). Corporations typically hiring largest numbers of graduates include Xerox, Paychex, Eastman Kodak, First Federal Bank, Wegmans, United Way Agencies. Career Development Services include comprehensive career planning, interview techniques, resume writing, alumni interviews, on-campus interviews, career exploration course, graduate school and career libraries, one-on-one counseling. Student assessment of program reported as good for both career guidance and job placement.

Faculty. About 86% of faculty hold PhD or equivalent. About 27% of teaching faculty are female; 2% Black, 2% Phillipino.

Student Body. College seeks a diverse student body; 97% of students from in state; 98% Middle Atlantic, 1% New England, 1% Midwest, 1% foreign. An estimated 30% of students reported as Protestant, 65% Catholic, 5% other; 5% Black, 2% Hispanic, 2% Asian, 6% other ethnic minority.

Religious Orientation. St. John Fisher is an independent institution, with a Basilian heritage; ethnically and religiously diverse board of trustees; 4 courses required of all students in philosophy and/or religious studies. Religious activities on campus coordinated by Campus Ministry. Places of worship available on campus for Catholics and Protestants, in immediate community for other major faiths.

Varsity Sports. Men (Div.III): Baseball, Basketball, Cross Country, Football, Golf, Soccer, Tennis. Women (Div.III): Basketball, Cross Country, Golf, Soccer, Softball, Tennis, Volleyball.

Campus Life. Students enjoy many on-campus activities— including varsity, intramural, and club sporting events, concerts, comedians, and lectures; the city of Rochester, only 10 minutes away also offers cultural and recreational opportunities. Dormitory visitation hours 12 PM-12 am Monday-Thursday, 3 PM-2 am Friday, noon-2 am Saturday, noon-12 am Sunday. Cars allowed. About 10% of women live in traditional residences; 55% of men, 40% of women live in coed dormitories, rest commute. Freshmen given preference in college housing if all students cannot be accommodated. There are no fraternities or sororities. About 30% of resident students leave campus on weekends, according to most recent data available.

Annual Costs. Tuition and fees, $10,275; room and board, $5,230; estimated $500 other, exclusive of travel. About 91% of students receive financial aid; average amount of assistance, $10,540. Assistance is typically divided 32% scholarship, 38% grant, 21% loan, 9% work. College reports 429 scholarships awarded on the basis of academic merit alone, 700 for need alone. *Meeting Costs:* college offers AMS monthly payment plan.

Saint John's College

Camarillo, California 93010

A church-related, liberal arts institution, conducted by the archdiocese, the college is devoted solely to the training of Roman Catholic priests.

Founded: 1927
Affiliation: Roman Catholic

Undergraduate degrees conferred (15). 100% were in Philosophy and Religion.

St. John's College

Annapolis, Maryland 21404 (410) 263-2371; (800) 727-9238

St. John's is a radically traditional, liberal arts college that believes its main function is to develop critical intelligence and understanding through direct confrontation between students and great books—"the original sources of our intellectual tradition." This unusual college experience attracts several types of students: those who remain to complete the 4 demanding and rewarding years; those who after 2 years have become enticed by a particular field and want to specialize—or merely want to move on to a more conventional academic environment; and finally, those few who leave early in the game because they may not have realized fully what the St. John's experience had in store for them. The college offers the same program on a second campus in Santa Fe, New Mexico. Applicants may indicate campus they wish to attend. The 36-acre Maryland campus is located in historic Annapolis (pop. 50,000) 26 miles from Baltimore and 30 miles from Washington, D.C. Most convenient major airport: Baltimore-Washington International.

Founded: 1696
Affiliation: Independent
UG Enrollment: 223 M, 170 W (full-time)
Total Enrollment: 495
Cost: $10K–$20K
% Receiving Financial Aid: 50%
Admission: Most Selective
Application Deadline: March 1

Admission is among the most selective in the country. About 86% of applicants accepted, 51% of these actually enroll; 44% of the 71% freshmen who reported rank graduate in top fifth of high school class, 75% in top two-fifths. Average freshman SAT scores, middle fifty percent range: 580–680 verbal, 530–660 mathematical; 90% of freshman score above 500 verbal, 70% score above 600, 18% above 700; 84% score above 500 mathematical, 52% score above 600, 14% above 700. *Required:* essay, written application; campus visit of 2 days to attend classes strongly recommended. (Admissions policy requests minimum of personal and academic information of student, and completion of lengthy written application which enables applicant to give "full account of himself.") Criteria considered in admissions, in order of importance: essay, high school academic record, recommendations, standardized test, extracurricular activities; other factors considered: special talents, alumni children, diverse student body. *Entrance programs:* early admission, midyear admission (for freshmen only with accelerated summer term), deferred admissions. About 60% of entering students from private schools, 10% from parochial schools. *Apply:* rolling admissions; March 1 suggested. *Transfers* must enroll as freshmen; 21 enrolled 1993–94.

Academic Environment. Pressures for academic achievement appear very intense, but they are of St. John's own unique variety. School continues to focus on its traditional mission and does not bend to contemporary student concern with professional/vocational training studies. All students must follow a common course of study throughout their 4 years (which explains why transfers are accepted only as freshmen, no matter how much college work they have completed), which is built around the great books of our culture, studied in roughly chronological order. Students' time is divided among seminars, tutorials (language and mathematics), laboratory periods, and weekly lecture. Twice a year tutors evaluate each student's intellectual development in his presence. Mathematics and science requirements (4 years of math, 3 years science) are demanding, and reading load is exceptionally heavy. Environment is almost wholly intellectual, but is remarkably rewarding for those attuned to it. College states explicitly that "the four years at St. John's do not purport to prepare a student for any future career. Nor do they prepare for any vocational school or any special kind of graduate work." Graduates, nevertheless, do enter both graduate and professional studies successfully. Law, mathematics, philosophy, education, and theology attract largest numbers. Smoking is banned in classrooms. Degrees offered: bachelors, masters. No majors; only program offered is the 4-year single course of study.

About 60% of students entering as freshmen graduate within four years, 70% eventually; 83% of freshmen return for sophomore year. Average undergraduate class size: under 20. *Calendar:* semester.

Undergraduate degrees conferred (74). 100% were in Liberal/General Studies.

Graduates Career Data. Advanced studies pursued by 70% of students; 7% enter law school; 3% enter business school; 6% enter medical school. A large number of graduates go on to work in law firms, education, political action groups, publishing. Career Development Services include information on career placement, fellowship and scholarships, internships, graduate school, resume writing and interviewing techniques, summer job opportunities, career changes and career counseling. Alumni reported as active in career counseling and job placement programs.

Faculty. About 60% of tutors hold PhD or equivalent. About 66% of undergraduate classes taught by tenured faculty. About 25% of teaching faculty are female; 1% Hispanic, 1% other ethnic minority.

Student Body. College seeks a national student body; 15% of students from in state; 38% Middle Atlantic, 12% Midwest, 20% South, 11% New England, 9% West/Northwest; 10% foreign. An estimated 3% of students reported Black, 2% Hispanic, 6% Asian, according to most recent data available.

Religious Orientation. A nonsectarian college, St. John's makes no religious demands on students. Informal religious groups on campus. Places of worship available in immediate community for 3 major faiths.

Campus Life. Virtually all of college program at St. John's is devoted to cultural and intellectual pursuits; extracurricular activities in large part extension of study program, but also include very active student government, film club, computer society, drama club, and political forum. There is also an extensive extracurricular arts program and an intramural sports program for both men and women. Washington, D.C., 30 miles from campus, offers all cultural events of a major city as well as the unique opportunity of attending the National Gallery and congressional committee meetings. Students and administration highly recommend that prospective students take advantage of the overnight visit program to get a true sense of the college community. Cars permitted; freshmen not allowed to use college parking lots. Students under 21 forbidden by state law from having alcoholic beverages in their possession. Informal dress requested for classes; more formal attire required at lectures, concerts, convocations, commencement exercises.

About 75% of students live in coed dormitories; rest in off-campus housing. Freshmen given preference in college housing if all students cannot be accommodated. Sexes segregated in coed dormitories by floor. There are no fraternities or sororities. About 5% of resident students leave campus on weekends.

Annual Costs. Tuition and fees, $16,150; room and board, $5,450; estimated $1,075 other, exclusive of travel. About 50% of students receive financial aid; average amount of assistance, $16,350. Assistance is typically divided 65% grant, 20% loan, 15% work. College reports scholarships awarded only on the basis of need. *Meeting Costs:* College offers PLUS, TERI, AMS, EXCEL.

St. John's College

Santa Fe, New Mexico 87501 **(505) 984-6060; (800) 331-5232**

St. John's at Santa Fe offers the same academic program as its sister institution in Annapolis in a significantly different setting which has a marked influence on student social life. Both institutions continue to test the applicability of a thoroughly traditional liberal education in the modern, specialized, technological world. The 250-acre campus is located within the city (pop. 62,000), over 2 miles from Santa Fe Plaza. Most convenient major airport: Albuquerque International.

Founded: 1964
Affiliation: Independent
UG Enrollment: 231 M, 180 W (full-time)
Cost: $10K–$20K
% Receiving Financial Aid: 65%
Admission: Highly Selective
Application Deadline: March 1

Admission is highly selective. About 85% of applicants accepted, 55% of these actually enroll; 47% of freshmen with reported class rank graduate in top fifth of high school class, 78% in top two-fifths. Average freshman SAT scores, middle fifty percent range: 550–650 verbal, 520–650 mathematical; 94% of freshman score above 500 verbal, 52% score above 600, 6% score above 700; 89% score above 500 mathematical, 46% score above 600, 8% above 700. *Required:* written application (admissions policy requests minimum of personal and academic information of student, and completion of lengthy written application which enables applicant to give "full account of himself"); test scores accepted but not required. Criteria considered in admissions, in order of importance: required admission essay, high school academic record, recommendations, standardized test scores, extracurricular activities; other factor considered: special talents. *Entrance programs:* early admission, midyear admission (students finish freshman year during summer), deferred admission. About 19% of entering students from private schools, 1% from parochial schools. *Apply:* rolling admissions; March 1 recommended. *Transfers* must enroll as freshmen; 25 enrolled 1993–94.

Academic Environment. School continues to focus on its traditional mission and does not bend to contemporary student concerns with professional/vocational training studies. All students follow common liberal arts curriculum centering on great books from Homer and Plato to Einstein and Tolstoy, combined with 4-year program of language, mathematics, and laboratory science, music and art. No required lectures, written examinations, textbooks, elective courses (except for 8 weeks during each of last 2 years), academic majors. Instruction by discussion among students and faculty (called tutors) in seminars; students take primary responsibility for their education, tutors guide students' discussion rather than lecture. Language study aims at development of student's linguistic skills through reading and translating great writings in their original language; mathematics inculcates skills of reasoning and demonstration as students gain insights into the nature and intention of mathematics; laboratories provide for student participation in processes of measurement, experimentation, and hypothesis and theory construction which are the foundation of the modern scientific tradition. Curriculum aims to interrelate the activities and subject matter of classes. Degrees offered: bachelors, masters. No majors; only program is the Great Books Program. Average undergraduate class size: 55% under 20, 37% 20–40, 8% over 40.

About 60% of students entering as freshmen graduate within four years, 70% eventually; 85% of freshmen return for sophomore year. *Calendar:* semester.

Undergraduate degrees conferred (103). 100% were in Liberal/General Studies.

Graduates Career Data. Advanced studies pursued by 75% of students. *Careers in business and industry* pursued by 20% of graduates (1990–91). Fields typically hiring largest numbers of graduates include computer industry, education, small business, journalism. Career Development Services include counseling, testing, resume preparation, off-campus recruiters, internships, graduate school application preparation.

Faculty. More than 60% of tutors hold PhD or equivalent. About 29% of teaching faculty are female.

Student Body. College seeks a national student body; 9% of students from in state; 36% West, 7% South, 16% Middle Atlantic, 15% Midwest, 7% Northwest, 9% New England, 1% foreign. An estimated 8% of students reported as Hispanic, 1% Native American.

Campus Life. Some indications that scholarly/intellectual interests are no less intense than at the sister institution in Annapolis, but somewhat more interest in social and outdoor activities (skiing, back-packing, search and rescue) —inspired, no doubt, by the environment. Those most likely to feel at home on campus are said to be "avid readers who enjoy the outdoors." Students currently have a student organization through which to influence college governance. Administration source reports informal, but effective, student influence on many matters, including faculty tenure and curriculum. Coed dorms have unlimited intervisitation; no curfew. State laws apply concerning alcohol. Cars allowed. Restrictions on pets, smoking in class, and similar matters remain. Freshmen and sophomores expected to live on campus.

About 80% each men, women live in coed dormitories; rest commute. Freshmen given preference in college housing if all students cannot be accommodated. Sexes segregated in coed dormitories by floor. There are no fraternities or sororities.

Annual Costs. Tuition and fees, $16,300; room and board, $5,450; estimated $1,000 other, exclusive of travel. About 65% of students receive financial aid; average amount of assistance, $13,101. Assistance is typically divided 73% grant, 15% loan, 12% work. College reports all scholarships awarded only on the basis of need. *Meeting Costs:* college offers tuition stabilization plan, 10-month interest-free payment plan, EXCEL and PAYMENT PLUS Loan programs.

Saint John's Seminary

Brighton, Massachusetts 02135

A church-related seminary and liberal arts college, maintained by the Archdiocese of Boston, for the training of Roman Catholic priests.

Founded: 1883	**Affiliation:** Roman Catholic

Undergraduate degrees conferred (12). 100% were in Unknown.

Saint John's University (Minnesota)

(See College of Saint Benedict/Saint John's University)

St. John's University

Jamaica, New York 11439 **(718) 990-6239**

Founded by the Vincentian Fathers, St. John's is an independent, urban institution for commuters, located in the borough of Queens. The university includes a second campus on Staten Island.

Founded: 1870	**Cost:** < $10K
Affiliation: Independent (Roman Catholic)	**% Receiving Financial Aid:** 80%
Total Enrollment: 19,037	**Admission:** Non-selective
	Application Deadline: Rolling

Admission. High school graduates with 16 units in academic subjects or equivalent eligible; 67% of applicants accepted, 62% of these actually enroll; 90% of freshmen graduate in top half of high school class. *Required:* SAT or ACT; portfolio for art. *Entrance programs:* early decision, early admission, advanced placement. About 15% of entering students from private schools. *Apply:* rolling admissions. *Transfers* welcome.

Academic Environment. Administration source characterizes student body as primarily concerned with the acquisition of marketable skills. Approximately 38% of courses needed for graduation are elective; numerous distribution requirements. *Undergraduate studies* offered by colleges of Liberal Arts and Sciences, Business Administration, Pharmacy and Allied Health Professions, St. Vincent's College, Notre Dame College, School of Education and Human Services, and the Evening Division and Weekend College. *Majors offered* in liberal arts and sciences in addition to usual studies include Asian studies, athletic administration, communication arts, court management, human services, legal assistants program, physician's assistant, and transportation.

Special programs: independent study, study abroad, honors, acceleration, combined BA or BS/MBA program, environmental studies program, various joint programs with other N.Y. schools. *Calendar:* semester, summer school.

Undergraduate degrees conferred (2,669). 43% were in Business and Management, 12% were in Health Sciences, 10% were in Social Sciences, 9% were in Communications, 6% were in Protective Services, 5% were in Education, 4% were in Psychology, 3% were in Computer and Engineering Related Technology, 3% were in Letters, remainder in 10 other fields.

Faculty. About 64% of full-time faculty hold PhD or equivalent.

Student Body. About 97% of students from New York State.

Religious Orientation. St. John's is an independent institution, with a Roman Catholic orientation; 9 hours of theology required of all students (requirements vary with each school).

Varsity Sports. Men (Div.I): Baseball, Basketball, Cross Country, Fencing, Football, Golf, Hockey, Lacrosse, Soccer, Swimming, Tennis, Track. Women (Div.I): Basketball, Cross Country, Fencing, Softball, Swimming, Tennis, Track. Coed (Div.I): Bowling, Riflery.

Campus Life. University provides no residence facilities. There are 11 fraternities, 11 sororities on campus.

Annual Costs. Tuition and fees, $9,100. University reports some scholarships awarded on the basis of academic merit alone. *Meeting Costs:* university offers PLUS, several commercial payment plans.

Saint Joseph College

West Hartford, Connecticut 06117 **(203) 232-4571**

Founded as a Roman Catholic institution by the Sisters of Mercy, Saint Joseph is governed by a predominantly lay board of trustees. A liberal arts college for women, co-educational at the graduate level, Saint Joseph is located in a Hartford suburb of 61,300. Most convenient major airport: Bradley Field (Hartford).

Founded: 1932	**Total Enrollment:** 2,022
Affiliation: Independent (Roman Catholic)	**Cost:** $10K–$20K
UG Enrollment: 543 W (full-time); 61 M, 651 W (part-time)	**% Receiving Financial Aid:** 51%
	Admission: Non-selective
	Application Deadline: May 1

Admission. About 83% of applicants accepted, 40% of these actually enroll; 35% of freshmen graduate in top fifth of high school class, 85% in top two-fifths. Average freshman SAT scores: 450 verbal, 430 mathematical. *Required:* SAT. *Non-academic factors* considered in admissions: special talents, diverse student body, extracurricular activities. *Entrance programs:* early decision, early admission, midyear admission. *Apply* by May 1; rolling admissions. *Transfers* welcome; 142 enrolled 1993–94.

Academic Environment. Administration source reports strongest academic programs include "well-known programs in nursing, medical technology, education, special education, and sociology/social work" within a liberal arts context. The career emphasis appears to predominate in student degree choices. Degrees offered: bachelors, masters. *Majors offered* include usual arts and sciences, American studies, child study, biology/chemistry, computer science, home economics. Average undergraduate class size: 15.

About 65% of students entering as freshmen graduate within four years, 70% eventually, 90% of freshmen return for sophomore year. *Special programs:* CLEP, independent study, study abroad, cross registration with U. of Hartford and Trinity College, internships in all majors, 3-year degree, individualized majors, programs of Greater Hartford Consortium for Higher Education. Adult programs: Weekend College offers 4 majors. *Calendar:* semester, summer school.

Undergraduate degrees conferred (177). 27% were in Education, 20% were in Health Sciences, 12% were in Social Sciences, 9% were in Business and Management, 6% were in Psychology, 6% were in Home Economics, 5% were in Public Affairs, 4% were in Letters, 3% were in Physical Sciences, remainder in 6 other fields.

Graduates Career Data. About 90% of 1992–93 graduates employed. Career Development Services include career counseling and computer search employment assistance.

Faculty. About 8% of faculty hold PhD or equivalent. About 50% of undergraduate classes taught by tenured faculty. About 70% of teaching faculty are female; 3% Black, 1% Hispanic, 1% other minority.

Student Body. Majority of students from New England. An estimated 8% of students reported as Black, 5% Hispanic, 2% Asian.

Religious Orientation. Saint Joseph is an independent institution with a Roman Catholic heritage; 6 credits of religious studies required of all students.

Campus Life. Students sit as voting members on 4 governance committees of faculty and on subcommittee of board of trustees. About 50% of women live in traditional dormitories; rest live in off-campus housing or commute. Freshmen given preference in college housing if all students cannot be accommodated. There are no sororities on campus.

Annual Costs. Tuition and fees, $11,600; room and board, $4,625, estimated $500 other, exclusive of travel. About 51% of students receive financial aid; average amount of assistance, $8,790. Assistance is typically divided 38% grant, 60% loan, 2% work. College reports some scholarships awarded on the basis of academic merit alone, majority awarded on basis of need.

Saint Joseph Seminary College

Saint Benedict, Louisiana 70457

A church-related, four-year liberal arts college conducted by the Benedictine Monks of Saint Joseph Abbey. The program provides the undergraduate preparation required for graduate study of theology.

Founded: 1891 **Affiliation:** Roman Catholic

Undergraduate degrees conferred (11). 100% were in Liberal/General Studies.

College of St. Joseph

Rutland, Vermont 05701 **(802) 773-5905**

The College of St. Joseph is an independent, co-educational college, located in a community of 20,000. Most convenient major airport: Burlington International.

Founded: 1954
Affiliation: Independent
UG Enrollment: 285 M, W (full-time)
Cost: < $10K
% Receiving Financial Aid: 60%
Admission: Non-selective
Application Deadline: Rolling

Admission. High school graduates with minimum GPA of C eligible; 94% of applicants accepted, 34% of these actually enroll; 10% of freshmen graduate in top fifth of high school class, 30% in top two-fifths. Average freshman scores, according to most recent data available: SAT, 370 M, 430 W verbal, 400 M, 440 W mathematical. *Required:* SAT or ACT; interview optional. About 20% of entering students from private schools, 40% from parochial schools. *Apply* by no specific deadline. *Transfers* welcome.

Academic Environment. *Degrees:* BA, BS. *Majors offered* include elementary, special and early childhood education, business, accounting, computer science, liberal studies, human services. About 78% of students entering as freshmen graduate within four years; 80% of freshmen return for sophomore year. *Special programs:* independent study. *Calendar:* semester.

Undergraduate degrees conferred (47). 40% were in Business and Management, 28% were in Education, 19% were in Allied Health, 6% were in Psychology, 4% were in Social Sciences, remainder in Liberal/General Studies.

Graduates Career Data. According to most recent data available, full-time graduate or professional study pursued by 10% of students immediately after graduation. *Careers in business and industry* pursued by 90% of graduates.

Student Body. About 40% of students from in state; 60% New England. An estimated 50% of students reported as Catholic, 20% Protestant, 10% unaffiliated, 20% other; 10% Black, 10% Hispanic, 10% Asian, according to most recent data available.

Varsity Sports. Men (NAIA III): Soccer. Women (NAIA III): Soccer, Softball.

Campus Life. About 50% of women live in traditional dormitories; 60% of men, 10% of women live in coed dormitories; rest live in off-campus housing or commute. There are no fraternities or sororities. About 10% of resident students leave campus on weekends.

Annual Costs. Tuition and fees, $8,000; room and board, $4,650. About 60% of students receive financial aid; assistance is typically divided 20% scholarship, 50% loan, 30% work. College reports some scholarships awarded on the basis of academic merit alone.

Saint Joseph's College

Rensselaer, Indiana 47978 **(219) 866-6170**

A church-related college, conducted by the Society of the Precious Blood, located in a community of 5,000, 73 miles southwest of Chicago. Most convenient major airport: Indianapolis or Chicago.

Founded: 1891
Affiliation: Roman Catholic
UG Enrollment: 411 M, 404 W (full-time); 28 M, 199 W (part-time)
Total Enrollment: 1,037
Cost: $10K–$20K
% Receiving Financial Aid: 81%
Admission: Non-selective
Application Deadline: Rolling

Admission. Graduates of approved high schools with 15 units and C average eligible; 85% of applicants accepted, 29% of these actually enroll; 37% of freshmen graduate in top fifth of high school class, 62% in top two-fifths. Average freshman scores: SAT, 416 M, 448 W verbal, 512 M, 487 W mathematical; ACT, 22 M, 23 W composite. *Required:* SAT or ACT. Criteria considered in admissions, in order of importance: high school academic record, standardized test scores, recommendations, extracurricular activities; other factors considered: alumni children, diverse student body. *Apply:* rolling admissions. *Transfers* welcome; 29 enrolled 1993–94.

Academic Environment. Graduation requirements include 45 credit hours of liberal arts core requirements. Core program and "well-rounded and diverse" faculty seen as strengths of the academic program. Degrees offered: associates, bachelors, masters. *Majors offered* include entrepreneurship, medical technology, music, radio/television. Average undergraduate class size: 80% under 20, 18% 20–40, 2% over 40.

About 60% of students entering as freshmen graduate eventually, 80% of freshmen return for sophomore year. *Special programs:* CLEP, independent study, study abroad, honors, undergraduate research, 3-year degree, 3–2 program in engineering, cross registration with St. Elizabeth's School of Nursing, nursing diploma and BSN completion program, internships, cooperative education. *Calendar:* semester, spring, summer sessions.

Undergraduate degrees conferred (202). 43% were in Business and Management, 15% were in Education, 10% were in Communications, 9% were in Social Sciences, 5% were in Health

Sciences, 5% were in Psychology, 4% were in Life Sciences, 3% were in Mathematics, 3% were in Computer and Engineering Related Technology, remainder in 3 other fields.

Graduates Career Data. About 75% of 1992–93 graduates employed. Fields typically hiring largest numbers of graduates include management, sales, education. Career Development Services include career counseling, job search assistance, alumni networking.

Faculty. About 73% of faculty hold PhD or equivalent. About 67% of undergraduate classes taught by tenured faculty. About 20% of teaching faculty are female; 1% Black, 1% other minority.

Student Body. About 72% of students from in state. An estimated 51% of students reported as Catholic, 5% Protestant, 6% unaffiliated, 14% other; 5% Black, 3% Hispanic. Average age of undergraduate student: 24.

Religious Orientation. Saint Joseph's is a church-related institution; attendance at annual retreat and daily Mass encouraged for Catholic students.

Varsity Sports. Men (Div.II): Baseball, Basketball, Cross Country, Football, Golf, Soccer, Tennis, Track. Women (Div.II): Basketball, Cross Country, Football, Golf, Soccer, Softball, Tennis, Track, Volleyball.

Campus Life. Students agree that "the people" are what they like best about their school: "Very interesting, nice. You won't get lost in the crowd here."

About 69% of each men, women live in traditional dormitories; no coed dormitories; rest commute. Freshmen given preference in college housing if all students cannot be accommodated. Intervisitation in men's and women's dormitory rooms limited. There are no fraternities or sororities on campus. About 30% of resident students leave campus on weekends.

Annual Costs. Tuition and fees, $10,380; room and board, $3,900; estimated $1,000 other, exclusive of travel. About 81% of students receive financial aid; average amount of assistance, $10,390. Assistance is typically divided 20% scholarship, 33% grant, 35% loan, 12% work. College reports 214 scholarships awarded on the basis of academic merit alone, 525 for special talents alone, 186 for need alone. *Meeting Costs:* college offers payment plans.

Saint Joseph's College

Windham, Maine 04062-1198 (207) 892-6766

A church-related, co-educational, liberal arts college, conducted by the Sisters of Mercy, located on the shores of Lake Sebago in the town of Windham (pop. 18,000), 16 miles northwest of Portland. Most convenient major airport: Portland.

Founded: 1912	**Cost:** < $10K
Affiliation: Roman Catholic	**% Receiving Financial Aid:** 72%
UG Enrollment: 265 M, 451 W (full-time); 64 M, 109 W (part-time)	**Admission:** Non-selective
	Application Deadline: April 1

Admission. High school graduates with 16 credits (10 in academic subjects) eligible, 77% of applicants accepted, 35% of these actually enroll; 27% of freshmen graduate in top fifths of high school class, 58% in top two-fifths. Average freshman SAT scores: 420 verbal, 460 mathematical. *Required:* SAT, minimum 2.0 GPA, essay. Criteria considered in admissions, in order of importance: high school academic record, class rank, standardized test scores, recommendations, writing sample, extracurricular activities; other factors considered: special talents, alumni children, diverse student body. About 3% of entering students from private schools, 12% from parochial schools. *Entrance programs:* early admission, midyear admission, deferred admission, advanced placement. *Apply* by April 1; rolling admissions. *Transfers* welcome; 58 enrolled 1993–94.

Academic Environment. Accessible faculty, small classes, and "family-like" atmosphere cited as strengths of the academic program. Graduation requirements include 12 semester hours of English, 2–3 of fine arts, 6 (to intermediate level) of foreign language, 6 of history, 3 of mathematics, 9 of philosophy, 6 of religious studies, 6–8 of science. Degrees offered: associates, bachelors. *Majors offered* in addition to usual studies include communications/broadcasting, radiologic technology completion program, business, pre-pharmacy, philosophy, psychology, physical education, religious studies. Average undergraduate class size: 60% under 20, 40% 20–40.

About 75% of students entering as freshmen graduate eventually, 89% of freshmen return for sophomore year. *Special programs:* study abroad, cross registration with South Maine Consortium, 2–3 pre-pharmacy with Massachusetts College of Pharmacy, internships. Adult programs: external degree program offers 3 bachelors and 1 masters degree; over 5,000 students enrolled. *Calendar:* term, summer term.

Undergraduate degrees conferred (483). 81% were in Health Sciences, 7% were in Business and Management, 4% were in Education, 3% were in Social Sciences, remainder in 5 other fields.

Graduates Career Data. Advanced studies pursued by 24% of graduates; 6% enter graduate school; 3% each enter medical, dental, and law schools; 4% enter business school. About 97% of 1992–93 graduates employed. Corporations typically hiring largest numbers of graduates include L.L. Bean, UNUM-Maine, Yale/New Haven Hospital, Barry, Dunn, McNeil & Parker. Career Development Services include counseling, workshops, resume preparation, on-campus career fairs, recruiting fairs, internships and reference service.

Faculty. About 96% of faculty hold PhD or equivalent. About 95% of undergraduate classes taught by tenured faculty. About 48% of teaching faculty are female.

Student Body. About 49% of students from in state; 95% New England, 2% Middle Atlantic, 1% each Midwest, South, 1% foreign. An estimated 65% of students reported as Catholic, 35% other; 2% Black, 1% Hispanic, 2% Asian.

Religious Orientation. Saint Joseph's is a church-related institution; 6 hours of religious studies required of all students.

Varsity Sports. Men (Div.III): Baseball, Basketball, Cross Country, Golf, Soccer. Women (Div.III): Basketball, Cross Country, Soccer, Softball, Volleyball.

Campus Life. Students reportedly spend their time with "socializing, studying, athletics." Campus is "close enough" to town; college owns beach front on Sebago Lake.

About 75% of each men, women live in traditional dormitories; no coed dormitories; rest commute. Freshmen given preference in college housing if all students cannot be accommodated. There are no fraternities or sororities on campus. About 35% of students leave campus on weekends.

Annual Costs. Tuition and fees, $9,785; room and board, $4,850; estimated $1,700 other, exclusive of travel. About 72% of students receive financial aid; average amount of assistance, $8,000. Assistance is typically divided 23% scholarship, 30% grant, 43% loan, 4% work. College reports 382 scholarships awarded on the basis of academic merit alone, 25 for need alone.

St. Joseph's College

Brooklyn, New York 11215 (718) 636-6868

St. Joseph's is a co-educational liberal arts college, governed by an independent board of trustees. The campus is located in Brooklyn, 25 minutes from mid-Manhattan.

Founded: 1916	**Cost:** < $10K
Affiliation: Independent	**% Receiving Financial Aid:** 85%
UG Enrollment: 85 M, 327 W (full-time)	**Admission:** Non-selective
	Application Deadline: Rolling

Admission. Graduates of accredited high schools with 16 units eligible; 61% of applicants accepted, 45% of these actually enroll; 23% of freshmen graduate in top fifth of high school class, 48% in top two-fifths. *Required:* SAT, minimum GPA. Criteria considered in admissions, in order of importance: high school academic record, standardized test scores, recommendations, extracurricular activities; other factors considered: special talents, alumni children. *Entrance programs:* early decision, early admission, midyear admission, deferred admission, advanced placement. About 25% of entering students from private schools. *Apply:* rolling admissions. *Transfers* welcome; 29 enrolled 1993–94.

Academic Environment. College governance system gives students influence on curriculum and other academic policy-making through representation on College Advisory Council. Graduation requirements include courses in humanities, social sciences, math/science, and English composition. Degrees offered: bachelors. *Majors offered* include usual arts and sciences, child study. Average undergraduate class size: 80% under 20, 20% 20–40.

About 72% of students entering as freshmen graduate within four years, 75% eventually, 80% of freshmen return for sophomore year. *Special programs:* CLEP, independent study, study abroad, undergraduate research, January interterm, individualized majors, affiliation with school for the deaf in Brooklyn, 3–2 in occupational therapy, 3–2 in podiatric medicine. Adult programs: degree and certificate programs for adult professionals in health, nursing, business and general studies; courses offered on weekdays, evenings, and Saturdays, both on campus and at extension sites. *Calendar:* 4–1–4, summer school.

Undergraduate degrees conferred (177). 31% were in Health Sciences, 18% were in Allied Health, 16% were in Education, 13% were in Business and Management, 5% were in Letters, 5% were in Social Sciences, 5% were in Liberal/General Studies, 3% were in Psychology, remainder in 4 other fields.

Graduates Career Data. Advanced studies pursued by 40% of graduates; 33% enter graduate school; 5% enter medical school; 5% enter law school; 4% enter business school. Medical schools typically enrolling largest numbers of graduates include Chicago Medical School, Syracuse; law schools include Buffalo Law School, St. John's; business schools include St. John's, Queens College. About 85% of 1992–93 graduates employed. Employers typically hiring largest numbers of graduates include New York Board of Education, U.S. Government, New York Police Department, Pfizer, Inc. Career Development Services include credit courses, Career Search I & II, career fair, senior placement files, resume and interviewing sessions, graduate school information, information on positions available, internships, scholarships and fellowships.

Faculty. About 50% of faculty hold PhD or equivalent. About 62% of teaching faculty are female; 20% Black, 3% Hispanic, 4% Asian.

Student Body. About 99% of students from in state; all from Middle Atlantic. An estimated 38% of students reported as Black, 8% Hispanic, 5% Asian.

Religious Orientation. St. Joseph's is now an independent institution; no religious demands on students.

Varsity Sports. Men (IC): Basketball. Women (HVWAC): Softball.

Campus Life. College provides no residence facilities. There is 1 fraternity and 1 sorority on campus, which about 15% of men, 10% of women join.

Annual Costs. Tuition and fees, $7,122; estimated $1,100 other, exclusive of travel. About 85% of students receive financial aid; average amount of assistance, $6,000. Assistance is typically divided 20% scholarship, 30% grant, 30% loan, 20% work. College reports number scholarships awarded on the basis of academic merit alone varies.

Saint Joseph's College Seminary

Mountain View, California 94042

A church-related, liberal arts institution, conducted by the diocese, for the training of Roman Catholic priests.

Founded: 1898 **Affiliation:** Roman Catholic

Undergraduate degrees conferred (12). 67% were in Multi/Interdisciplinary Studies, 33% were in Philosophy and Religion.

Saint Joseph's University

Philadelphia, Pennsylvania 19131 (619) 660-1000

A church-related, liberal arts university, conducted by the Society of Jesus, Saint Joseph's is located in metropolitan Philadelphia. Most convenient major airport: Philadelphia International.

Founded: 1851
Affiliation: Roman Catholic
UG Enrollment: 1,157 M, 1,306 W (full-time); 511 M, 812 W (part-time)
Total Enrollment: 6,915
Cost: $10K–$20K
% Receiving Financial Aid: 77%
Admission: Selective (+)
Application Deadline: Rolling

Admission is selective (+). About 80% of applicants accepted, 38% of these actually enroll; 56% of freshmen graduate in top fifth of high school class, 85% in top two-fifths. Average freshman SAT scores: 497 verbal, 544 mathematical. *Required:* SAT or ACT, essay. Criteria considered in admissions, in order of importance: high school academic record, standardized test scores, recommendations, writing sample, extracurricular activities. *Entrance programs:* midyear admission, advanced placement. About 30% of entering students from private, 45% from parochial schools. *Apply:* rolling admissions. *Transfers* welcome; 125 accepted 1993–94.

Academic Environment. Student leader reports students are concerned about "quality education with an eye to job placement." Graduation requirements include 5 common courses in English, philosophy, and history, and 14 courses distributed between foreign language, literature and fine arts, math, natural sciences, philosophy, social sciences, and theology. Degrees offered: associates, bachelors, masters. *Majors offered* include usual arts and sciences, accounting, American studies, computer science, criminal justice, Faith/Justice studies, finance and information systems, food marketing, health management, international relations, Latin American studies, management, marketing, medieval studies, public administration, physics, fine and performing arts. Average undergraduate class size: 43% under 20, 45% 20–40, 12% over 40.

About 72% of students entering as freshmen graduate within four years, 75% eventually; 83% of freshmen return for sophomore year. *Special programs:* independent study, study abroad, honors, undergraduate research, cooperative work/study programs, Washington Semester, Appalachian Semester, internships, 5-year BS/MS programs in international marketing and psychology. Adult programs: part-time day, evening and weekend programs. *Calendar:* semester, summer school.

Undergraduate degrees conferred (745). 57% were in Business and Management, 15% were in Social Sciences, 7% were in Letters, 5% were in Psychology, 5% were in Life Sciences, 4% were in Education, remainder in 8 other fields.

Graduates Career Data. Advanced studies pursued by 21% of graduates; 5% of students enter medical school; 5% enter law school; 6% enter business school. Professional schools typically enrolling largest numbers of graduates include Temple, Widener, St. Joseph's. About 69% of 1992–93 graduates employed. Fields typically hiring largest numbers of graduates include marketing, food marketing, accounting.

Faculty. About 90% of faculty hold PhD or equivalent. About 46% of undergraduate classes taught by tenured faculty. About 26% of teaching faculty are female; 5% minority.

Student Body. About 54% of students from in state. An estimated 85% of students reported as Catholic.

Religious Orientation. Saint Joseph's is a church-related institution; 3 courses in theology required of all students; campus ministry available.

Varsity Sports. Men (Div.IA): Baseball, Basketball, Crew, Cross Country, Golf, Lacrosse, Soccer, Tennis, Track. Women (Div.IA): Basketball, Crew, Cross Country, Field Hockey, Lacrosse, Softball, Tennis, Track.

Campus Life. Students have some voice in determining regulations governing campus life. Student leader reports intervisitation regulations are satisfactory. Cars allowed, freshmen residents not allowed to park cars on campus, parking facilities for commuters are described as inadequate.

About 10% of students live in traditional dormitories; 60% in coed dormitories; 15% live in off-campus housing; 15% commute. Freshmen given preference in college housing if all students cannot be accommodated. There are 4 fraternities, 3 sororities which about 25% of men, 25% of women join; they provide no residence facilities. About 40% of residential students leave campus on weekends.

Annual Costs. Tuition and fees, $12,000; room and board, $5,700; estimated $1,655 other, exclusive of travel. About 77% of students receive financial aid; average amount of assistance, $7,850. Assistance is typically divided 17% scholarship, 36% grant, 46% loan, 1% work. College reports 582 scholarships awarded on the basis of academic merit alone, 304 for special talents, 1,151 for need alone. *Meeting Costs:* university offers tuition installment plan, The Tuition Plan.

St. Lawrence University

Canton, New York 13617 (315) 379-5011

St. Lawrence University, despite its geographical location in upper New York State, has managed to attract a diverse student body from many parts of the United States as well as a substantial num-

ber of foreign students. The university welcomes transfer students, especially from 2-year colleges. The 1,000-acre campus is located in a village of 6,400, between the Adirondacks and the St. Lawrence River. Nearest major city is Ottawa, Canada, less than 2 hours away by car. Most convenient major airport: Ottawa, Ontario, Canada.

Founded: 1856	**Total Enrollment:** 2,068
Affiliation: Independent	**Cost:** $10K–$20K
UG Enrollment: 942 M, 987 W (full-time); 20 M, 29 W (part-time)	**% Receiving Financial Aid:** 60%
	Admission: Very Selective
	Application Deadline: Feb. 1

Admission is very selective. About 66% of applicants accepted, 28% of these actually enroll; 48% of freshmen graduate in top fifth of high school class, 74% in top two-fifths. Average freshman SAT scores: 515 verbal, 573 mathematical; 58% of freshmen score above 500 on verbal, 13% above 600; 89% score above 500 on mathematical, 35% above 600, 4% above 700. *Required:* SAT, essay, recommendations from teachers and counselors. Criteria considered in admissions, in order of importance: high school academic record, extracurricular activities, recommendations, writing sample, standardized test scores; other factors considered: special talents, diverse student body. About 30% of entering students from private schools, 7% from parochial schools. *Entrance programs:* early decision, midyear admission, advanced placement. *Apply* by February 1. *Transfers* welcome; 40 enrolled 1993–94.

Academic Environment. Student/faculty relations reported to be "excellent", although "faculty opposition to Greek System has created some strain in student/faculty relations outside classroom." The student body is reported to be almost equally devoted to scholarly/intellectual pursuits, occupational/professional goals, and social activities; substantial emphasis on liberal arts. Graduation requirements include 1 course each in lab science, humanities, non-Western culture, 2 courses in math, languages, or fine arts. Degrees offered: bachelors, masters. *Majors offered* include usual arts and sciences, biophysics, fine arts, geophysics, anthropology, Asian studies, Canadian studies, economics-mathematics combined major, mathematics-computer science combined major, environmental studies, international education and creative writing. Average undergraduate class size: "most" under 20, less than 1% over 40.

About 76% of students entering as freshmen graduate within four years, 81% eventually, 91% of freshmen return for sophomore year. *Special programs:* CLEP, honors, independent study, study abroad, undergraduate research, 3-year degree, individualized majors, credit by examination, 3–2 engineering, internships, practicums. *Calendar:* 4–1–4, summer school.

Undergraduate degrees conferred (512). 46% were in Social Sciences, 13% were in Letters, 12% were in Life Sciences, 8% were in Psychology, 6% were in Visual and Performing Arts, 4% were in Foreign Languages, 3% were in Liberal/General Studies, 3% were in Mathematics, remainder in 4 other fields.

Graduates Career Data. Advanced studies pursued by 27% of graduates. Medical schools typically enrolling largest numbers of graduates include Boston U., Georgetown, Tufts; dental schools include SUNY Buffalo, SUNY Stonybrook; law schools include Syracuse, U. of Chicago; business schools include Columbia, Cornell. About 67% of 1992–93 graduates employed. Fields typically hiring largest numbers of graduates include education, banking, marketing/advertising, environmental. Career Development Services include counseling, resume service, national data bank, job fairs and 2,500 member alumni network.

Faculty. About 95% of faculty hold PhD or equivalent. About 75% of undergraduate classes taught by tenured faculty. About 25% of teaching faculty are female.

Student Body. About 51% of students from in state; 3% foreign. An estimated 3% of students reported as Black, 1% Hispanic, 1% Asian, 1% Native American, according to most recent data available.

Varsity Sports. Men (Div.III): Baseball, Basketball, Cross Country, Diving, Equestrian (I),Football, Ice Hockey (I), Lacrosse, Skiing (I), Soccer, Swimming, Tennis, Track, Wrestling. Women (Div.III): Basketball, Cross Country, Diving, Equestrian (I), Field Hockey, Ice Hockey, Lacrosse, Riding, Skiing (I), Soccer, Swimming, Tennis, Track, Volleyball.

Campus Life. High interest reported in strong Greek System, varsity athletics (most popular: ice hockey, football), and intramurals (most popular: coed softball, soccer). Students have influence on campus decision-making through membership on faculty/student/administration Tri-Partite Committee and representation on Board of Trustees. St. Lawrence sponsors a relatively active schedule of cultural and intellectual activities. University remains somewhat isolated from any major cultural center, however, with Syracuse and Montreal 120 miles from campus, Ottawa 80 miles away. Visitation hours, up to 24 hours, set by individual residences. Cars discouraged but permitted; availability of parking is only restriction.

About 90% of students live in coed dormitories; 5% commute. Freshmen given preference in college housing if all students cannot be accommodated. Sexes segregated in coed dormitories by wing, floor or suite. There are 7 fraternities, 5 sororities on campus which about 35% of each men, women join; 5% of each men, women live in fraternities and sororities. About 70% of resident students leave campus on weekends.

Annual Costs. Tuition and fees, $17,890; room and board, $5,530; estimated $400 other, exclusive of travel. About 60% of students receive financial aid; average amount of assistance, $12,500. Assistance is provided mostly through grants. University reports 15 scholarships awarded on the basis of academic merit alone, most for need alone. *Meeting Costs:* university participates in payment plan options and long term loan programs.

Saint Leo College

Saint Leo, Florida 33574 (904) 588-8283

An independent, liberal arts college, founded by the Benedictine Monks, located in a rural area, 30 miles northeast of Tampa. Most convenient major airport: Tampa.

Founded: 1889	**Total Enrollment:** 1,179
Affiliation: Independent (Roman Catholic)	**Cost:** < $10K
	% Receiving Financial Aid: 75%
UG Enrollment: 500 M, 500 W (full-time); 90 M, 89 W (part-time)	**Admission:** Non-selective
	Application Deadline: August 1

Admission. High school graduates with 16 units eligible; 69% of applicants accepted, 45% of these actually enroll. Average freshman ACT scores: 21 composite. *Required:* SAT or ACT, minimum 2.5 high school GPA, essay. Criteria considered in admissions, in order of importance: high school academic record, recommendations, writing sample, extracurricular activities, standardized test scores; other factors considered: special talents, alumni children, diverse student body. *Entrance programs:* early admission, midyear admission, deferred admission, advanced placement. About 25% of entering students from private schools. *Apply* by August 1; rolling admissions. *Transfers* welcome; 150 enrolled 1993–94.

Academic Environment. Degrees offered: bachelors, masters. *Majors offered* in addition to usual studies include hotel/restaurant management, public administration, sports management. Average undergraduate class size: 90% under 20, 10% 20–40. About 43% of students entering as freshmen graduate within four years. *Special programs:* CLEP, independent study, study abroad, honors. *Calendar:* semester, 6 week summer session.

Undergraduate degrees conferred (1,183). 59% were in Business and Management, 18% were in Social Sciences, 9% were in Psychology, 4% were in Health Sciences, 3% were in Education, remainder in 8 other fields.

Graduates Career Data. Career Development Services include counseling, interview techniques, resume writing, career/job fair and candidate files.

Faculty. About 75% of faculty hold PhD or equivalent. About 55% of undergraduate classes taught by tenured faculty.

Student Body. About 60% of students from in state; 17% Middle Atlantic, 10% New England, 4% Midwest, 2% South, 1% West, 5% foreign. An estimated 75% of students reported as Catholic, 18% Protestant, 7% unaffiliated; 3% Black, 4% Hispanic, 1% Asian, 9% other minority.

Religious Orientation. Saint Leo is an independent institution with a strong Catholic orientation; 75% of students affiliated with the church.

Varsity Sports. Men (Div.II): Baseball, Basketball, Cross Country, Soccer, Tennis. Women (Div.II): Basketball, Cross Country, Softball, Tennis, Volleyball.
Campus Life. Campus is located in a small town, which students variously describe as "in the middle of nowhere" and "away from the hurley, burley of the city. It is scenic, small, and home-like." Clubs, sororities/fraternities, and campus entertainment occupy many students.

About 80% of each men, women live in traditional dormitories; rest commute. Intervisitation in men's and women's dormitory rooms limited. There are 7 fraternities, 5 sororities on campus which about 35% of men, 30% of women join; they provide no residence facilities. About 10% of resident students leave campus on weekends.
Annual Costs. Tuition and fees, $9,370; room and board, $4,200; estimated $900 other, exclusive of travel. About 75% of students receive financial aid; average amount of assistance, $8,000. College reports some scholarships awarded on the basis of academic merit alone. *Meeting Costs:* college offers Academic Management Services.

St. Louis College of Pharmacy

St. Louis, Missouri 63110 **(314) 367-8700**

A professional school, offering a 5- or 6-year degree program; located in a city of 622,200. Most convenient major airport: Lambert International.

Founded: 1864
Affiliation: Independent
UG Enrollment: 297 M, 488 W (full-time); 14 M, 12 W (part-time)
Total Enrollment: 820
Cost: < $10K
% Receiving Financial Aid: 84%
Admission: Very Selective
Application Deadline: Rolling

Admission is very selective. About 72% of applicants accepted, 64% of these actually enroll. About 60% of freshmen graduate in top fifth of high school class, 90% in top two-fifths. Average freshman ACT scores: 25 composite. *Required:* ACT, minimum GPA, interview, essay. Criteria considered in admissions, in order of importance: high school academic record, standardized test scores, writing sample, recommendations, extracurricular activities; other factors considered: alumni children. *Apply:* rolling admissions. *Transfers* welcome; 18 enrolled 1993–94.
Academic Environment. Degrees offered: bachelors, masters. All general education credits for graduation are required; distribution requirements fairly numerous. Average undergraduate class size: 30% under 20, 68% 20–40, 2% over 40. About 98% of entering students graduate within 5 years, 37% of freshmen return for sophomore year. Special program: CLEP. *Calendar:* semester, summer school.
Undergraduate degrees conferred (137). 100% were in Health Sciences.
Faculty. About 83% of faculty hold PhD or equivalent. About 44% of undergraduate classes taught by tenured faculty. About 46% of teaching faculty are female.
Student Body. About 39% of students from in state; 97% Midwest, 2% South, less than 1% each West, Middle Atlantic, foreign. An estimated 2% of students reported as Black, 6% Asian.
Varsity Sports. Men (NAIA Div.II): Basketball. Women (NAIA Div.II): Volleyball.
Campus Life. About 7% men, 10% of women live in coed dormitories; 90% of men, 89% of women commute. Freshmen given preference in college housing if all students cannot be accommodated. Intervisitation in men's and women's dormitory rooms limited. Sexes segregated in dormitory by wing or floor. There are 6 fraternities, 2 sororities on campus which about 7% of men, 12% of women join; 3% of men, 1% of women live in fraternities and sororities. About 40% of resident students leave campus on weekends.
Annual Costs. Tuition and fees, $8,850; room and board, $4,150; estimated $1,840 other, exclusive of travel. About 84% of students receive financial aid; average amount of assistance, $7,125. Assistance is typically divided 10% scholarship, 15% grant, 70% loan, 5% work. College reports 211 scholarships awarded on the basis of academic merit alone, 25 for special talents alone, 23 for need alone.

Saint Louis University

St. Louis, Missouri 63103 **(314) 658-2500 (in-state); (800) 325-6666 (out-of-state)**

Among the best known of the numerous Jesuit institutions of higher learning in the U.S., Saint Louis is one of the largest Catholic universities. It is an urban institution consisting of a complex of undergraduate, graduate, and professional schools and colleges. The main campus is located in a city of 380,000. Most convenient major airport: Lambert International (St. Louis).

Founded: 1818
Affiliation: Independent (Roman Catholic)
UG Enrollment: 3,103 M, 2,850 W (full-time); 440 M, 637 W (part-time)
Total Enrollment: 11,382
Cost: $10K–$20K
% Receiving Financial Aid: 80%
Admission: Selective (+)
Application Deadline: December 15

Admission is selective (+). For all schools, 85% of applicants accepted; 33% enroll; 52% of freshmen graduate in top fifth of high school class, 78% in top two-fifths. Average freshman scores: SAT, 940–1170 combined; 40% of freshmen score above 500 on verbal, 10% above 600; 62% score above 500 on mathematical; 24% above 600; ACT, 25 composite. *Required:* SAT or ACT. Criteria considered in admissions, in order of importance: high school college preparatory record, high school academic record, standardized test scores, recommendations, writing sample; other factors considered: special talents, alumni children, diverse student body, extracurricular activities. About 65% of entering students from private schools. *Entrance programs:* early admission, deferred admission, advanced placement. *Apply:* December 15 for Physical Therapy applicants; rolling admissions. *Transfers* welcome; 853 enrolled 1993–94.
Academic Environment. *Undergraduate studies* offered by College of Arts and Sciences, Parks College, schools of Allied Health Professions, Nursing, Business Administration, and Social Service. Strongest academic offerings reported to be premed, pre-law, business and allied health programs. Graduation requirements vary by program; core requirements include foundations of discourse, cultural diversity, foreign language, fine arts, literature, science, mathematics, world history, philosophy, theology, social science. Degrees offered: associates, bachelors, masters, doctoral. *Majors offered* in addition to usual studies include aerospace engineering, anthropology, communication disorders, computer science, criminal justice, geography, geophysics, management information systems, international business, meteorology, occupational therapy. Average undergraduate class size: 52% under 20, 40% 20–40, 8% over 40.

About 50% of students entering as freshmen graduate within four years, 70% eventually, 85% of freshmen return for sophomore year. *Special programs:* CLEP, independent study, study abroad, honors, undergraduate research, individualized majors, Latin American studies, Russian studies, 3–2 engineering, internships. Adult programs: Evening Division in College of Arts & Sciences. *Calendar:* semester, summer school.
Undergraduate degrees conferred (1,187). 39% were in Business and Management, 10% were in Health Sciences, 8% were in Allied Health, 8% were in Communications, 8% were in Social Sciences, 7% were in Psychology, 5% were in Life Sciences, 3% were in Education, remainder in 12 other fields.
Graduates Career Data. Advanced studies pursued by 19% of graduates; 7% enter graduate school; 4% enter medical school; 2% enter law school; 2% enter business school. Medical schools typically enrolling largest numbers of graduates include St. Louis U., Washington U.; law schools include St. Louis U., Washington U.; business schools include St. Louis U., U. of Missouri-St. Louis. About 69% of 1992–93 graduates employed. Corporations typically hiring largest numbers of graduates include McDonnell Douglas, Southwestern Bell, Monsanto, Ernst & Young. Career Center offers services related to choosing a major, internships/cooperative education, part-time employment on- and off-campus, and full-time professional employment for recent graduates and alumni.
Faculty. About 95% of faculty hold PhD or equivalent. About 47% of undergraduate classes taught by tenured faculty. About 28% of teaching faculty are female; 5% Black, 1% Hispanic, 6% other minority.
Student Body. About 61% of students from in state; 65% Midwest. An estimated 44% of students reported as Catholic, 19% Protestant,

1% Jewish, 36% other; 8% as Black, 5% Hispanic, 8% Asian, 8% other minority. Average age of undergraduate student: 23.

Religious Orientation. Saint Louis is a church-related institution; 9 semester hours of theology required of all students.

Varsity Sports. Men (NCAA Div.I): Baseball, Basketball, Cross Country, Diving, Golf, Riflery, Soccer, Swimming, Tennis. Women (NCAA Div.I): Basketball, Cross Country, Diving, Field Hockey, Softball, Swimming, Tennis, Volleyball.

Campus Life. Urban location strongly affects campus life; students note proximity to the many attractions and entertainment of the city. There are also many on-campus activities, from fraternities/sororities to volunteer organizations; sports are also popular. Intervisitation policy determined by residents of each dormitory, up to 24 hours. Alcohol prohibited for those under 21; cars allowed. Students may live off campus.

About 19% of men, 32% of women live in traditional and coed dormitories; rest live in off-campus housing or commute. Freshmen given preference in college housing if all students can not be accommodated. Sexes segregated in coed dormitories by wing, floor or room. There are 12 fraternities, 5 sororities on campus which about 17% of men, 8% of women join. About 25% of resident students leave campus on weekends.

Annual Costs. Tuition and fees, $10,900; room and board, $4,622; estimated $3,300 other, exclusive of travel. About 80% of students receive financial aid; average amount of assistance, $12,720. Assistance is typically divided 40% scholarship, 10% grant, 45% loan, 5% work. University reports 8 scholarships awarded on the basis of academic merit alone, 2 for special talents alone. *Meeting Costs:* university offers budget payment plan.

Saint Martin's College

Lacey, Washington 98503 (206) 491-4700

A church-related college, conducted by the Benedictine Order, located on a 160-acre campus, near the state capital (pop. 23,100). Most convenient major airport: Seattle-Tacoma.

Founded: 1895
Affiliation: Roman Catholic
UG Enrollment: 201 M, 288 W (full-time); 261 M, 321 W (part-time)
Total Enrollment: 1,359
Cost: $10K–$20K
% Receiving Financial Aid: 62%
Admission: Non-selective
Application Deadline: Rolling

Admission. Graduates of accredited high schools eligible; 87% of applicants accepted, 38% of these actually enroll; 20% of freshmen graduate in top fifth of high school class, 40% in top two-fifths. Average freshman scores: SAT, 460 verbal, 480 mathematical; ACT, 21 composite. *Required:* SAT or ACT, 2.5 minimum GPA, essay, recommendation from teacher or counselor. Criteria considered in admissions, in order of importance: high school academic record, recommendations, standardized test scores, extracurricular activities, writing sample. *Entrance programs:* early admission, midyear admission, advanced placement. About 30% of entering students from private schools. *Apply:* rolling admissions. *Transfers* welcome; 295 enrolled 1993–94.

Academic Environment. Graduation requirements include courses in English composition, literature, social sciences, history, religion, philosophy, physical education, computer, lab science. Degrees offered: associates, bachelors, masters. *Majors offered* in addition to usual studies include computer science, computers in education, finance. Average undergraduate class size: 80% under 20, 20% 20–40. About 22% of students entering as freshmen graduate within four years, 94% of freshmen return for sophomore year. *Special programs:* CLEP, independent study, honors, individualized majors. Adult program: nursing degree completion, extension programs. *Calendar:* semester, summer school.

Undergraduate degrees conferred (234). 29% were in Business and Management, 15% were in Education, 9% were in Psychology, 8% were in Protective Services, 7% were in Health Sciences, 6% were in Engineering, 6% were in Social Sciences, 6% were in Computer and Engineering Related Technology, 4% were in Public Affairs, 4% were in Life Sciences, remainder in 5 other fields.

Graduates Career Data. About 95% of 1992–93 graduates employed. Fields typically hiring largest numbers of graduates include state and community services. Career Development Services include support for interviewing, resume writing, aptitude testing, on-campus recruitment and job boards.

Faculty. About 66% of faculty hold PhD or equivalent. About 60% of undergraduate classes taught by tenured faculty. About 32% of teaching faculty are female.

Student Body. About 80% of students from in state; 95% Northwest, 2% West, 3% foreign. An estimated 50% of students reported as Catholic; 5% Black, 1% Hispanic, 4% Asian, 6% other minority. Average age of undergraduate student: 31.

Religious Orientation. Saint Martin's was founded by the Benedictine monks, who "believe in educating the whole individual, regardless of one's beliefs, philosophy, or background." While faculty, students and staff come from varied backgrounds, the Benedictine tradition forms the cornerstone of the college; 1 course in religious studies required.

Varsity Sports. Men (NAIA): Basketball, Golf. Women (NAIA): Basketball, Softball, Volleyball.

Campus Life. All full-time, out-of-town, undergraduate students under the age of 21 are required to live in college residences. Cars allowed. Administration source reports "The campus atmosphere encourages personal and social development."

About 15% each of men, women live on campus in coed dormitories; rest commute. There are 2 fraternities, 1 sorority on campus which about 2% of each join. About 85% of resident students leave campus on weekends.

Annual Costs. Tuition and fees, $10,905; room and board, $4,060. About 62% of students receive financial aid; average amount of assistance, $6,887. Assistance is typically divided 38% scholarship/grant, 38% loan, 24% work. College reports 18 scholarships awarded on the basis of academic merit alone. *Meeting Costs:* college offers institutional payment plan.

Saint Mary College

Leavenworth, Kansas 66048-5082 (913) 682-5151

A church-related, liberal arts college, conducted by the Sisters of Charity of Leavenworth, located in Leavenworth (pop. 31,000), 26 miles northwest of Kansas City. Most convenient major airport: Kansas City, MO.

Founded: 1923
Affiliation: Roman Catholic
UG Enrollment: 140 M, 299 W (full-time); 188 M, 227 W (part-time)
Total Enrollment: 875
Cost: < $10K
% Receiving Financial Aid: 80%
Admission: Non-selective
Application Deadline: Rolling

Admission. Graduates of accredited high schools with 16 units (11 in academic subjects) and minimum 2.0 GPA eligible; others admitted provisionally; 88% of applicants accepted, 29% of these actually enroll; 20% of freshmen graduate in top fifth of high school class, 80% in top two-fifths. Average freshman ACT scores: 21 composite. *Required:* SAT or ACT. Criteria considered in admissions, in order of importance: high school academic record and standardized test scores, leadership record, recommendations, extracurricular activities. Entrance program: advanced placement. *Apply:* rolling admissions. *Transfers* welcome; 250 enrolled 1993–94.

Academic Environment. Graduation requirements include freshman humanities core, fine arts core, humanities core, 2 courses each theology, philosophy, history, social/behavioral science, 3 courses in math/computer science/physical science, entry level language/literature course, 2 semesters each physical education, foreign language. Low student-faculty ratio and the liberal arts core curriculum cited by students as strengths of the academic program. Degrees offered: associates, bachelors, masters. Average undergraduate class size: 70% under 20, 30% 20–40.

About 49% of entering students graduate within four years. *Special programs:* CLEP, independent study, study abroad, undergraduate research, individualized majors, cooperative programs with U. of Kansas and 10 regional colleges. Adult programs: evening and weekend program on campus and at 3 metropolitan sites. *Calendar:* semester, summer school.

Undergraduate degrees conferred (100). 32% were in Business and Management, 22% were in Education, 16% were in Social Sciences, 8% were in Visual and Performing Arts, 6% were in

Psychology, 5% were in Letters, 3% were in Mathematics, remainder in 5 other fields.

Graduates Career Data. About 10% of students enter graduate school. About 75% of 1992–93 graduates employed. Fields typically hiring largest numbers of graduates include business, education, human services. Career Development Services include aptitude testing, counseling, placement service, internships and library resources.

Faculty. About 50% of faculty hold PhD or equivalent. About 52% of undergraduate classes taught by tenured faculty. About 65% of teaching faculty are female.

Student Body. About 51% of students from in state; 5% foreign. An estimated 46% of students reported as Protestant, 35% Catholic, 15% unaffiliated, 5% other; 18% Black, 5% Hispanic, 2% Asian, 4% other minority.

Religious Orientation. Saint Mary is a church-related institution; 35% of students affiliated with the church; 2 courses in religious studies required.

Varsity Sports. Men: Basketball, Soccer. Women: Basketball, Soccer, Softball, Volleyball.

Campus Life. Campus is described by students as "secluded in a small town" and "calm", but near enough to Kansas City, 25 miles away, for students to enjoy "urban bonuses".

About 20% of each men, women live in coed dormitories; rest live in off-campus housing or commute. Freshmen given preference in college housing if all students cannot be accommodated. No intervisitation in women's dormitory rooms. There are no fraternities or sororities on campus. About 20% of resident students leave campus on weekends.

Annual Costs. Tuition and fees, $7,550; room and board, $3,700; an estimated $925 other, exclusive of travel. About 80% of students receive financial aid; average amount of assistance, $6,627. Assistance is typically divided 30% scholarship, 10% grant, 45% loan, 15% work. College reports 55 scholarships awarded on the basis of academic merit alone, 100 for special talents, 5 for need alone. *Meeting Costs:* college offers 10-month payment plan.

College of Saint Mary

Omaha, Nebraska 68124 **(402) 399-2405**

An independent college primarily for women, College of Saint Mary still embodies the heritage and educational philosophy of its founder, the Sisters of Mercy. The college is located on a 45-acre campus in a city of 356,000. Most convenient major airport: Eppley Field.

Founded: 1923
Affiliation: Independent (Roman Catholic)
UG Enrollment: 859 M, W (full-time)
Cost: < $10K
% Receiving Financial Aid: 84%
Admission: Non-selective
Application Deadline: Rolling

Admission. High school graduates with minimum ACT score of 19 composite, GPA of 2.0 and rank in upper half of class eligible; 83% of applicants accepted, 64% of these actually enroll. *Required:* SAT or ACT. *Apply:* no specific deadline. *Transfers* welcome.

Academic Environment. *Degrees:* BA, BS. About 35% of students entering as freshmen graduate within four years, 56% of freshmen return for sophomore year. *Majors offered* in addition to usual studies include computer graphics, telecommunications systems management, health information management, paralegal studies, creative arts and communications. *Special programs:* CLEP, credit by examination, independent study, undergraduate research. Adult programs: Weekend College. *Calendar:* semester, summer school.

Undergraduate degrees conferred (122). 24% were in Business and Management, 15% were in Law, 15% were in Allied Health, 13% were in Health Sciences, 11% were in Education, 11% were in Computer and Engineering Related Technology, 4% were in Life Sciences, 3% were in Visual and Performing Arts, remainder in 3 other fields.

Graduates Career Data. According to most recent data available, full-time graduate or professional study pursued by 17% of students immediately after graduation. *Careers in business and industry* pursued by 41% of graduates.

Student Body. About 87% of students from in state. An estimated 3% of students reported as Black, 1% Hispanic, 1% Asian, 1% Native American, according to most recent data available.

Religious Orientation. College is a Christian-oriented institution; 6 hours of theology required of all students; campus religious services available.

Varsity Sports. Women (NAIA): Basketball, Softball, Volleyball.

Campus Life. About 20% of women live in traditional dormitories; no coed dormitories; rest live in off-campus housing or commute. Freshmen given preference in college housing if all students cannot be accommodated. There are no sororities.

Annual Costs. Tuition and fees, $9,300; room and board, $3,500. About 84% of students receive financial aid; assistance is typically divided 51% scholarship, 45% loan, 4% work. College reports all scholarships awarded only on the basis of need.

Saint Mary-of-the-Woods College

Saint Mary-of-the-Woods, Indiana 47876 **(812) 535-5106; (800) 926-SMWC**

A church-related, liberal arts college for women, conducted by the Congregation of Sisters of Providence, located 4 miles west of Terre Haute (pop. 80,500). Most convenient major airports: Indianapolis or Terre Haute.

Founded: 1840
Affiliation: Roman Catholic
UG Enrollment: 585 W (full-time); 622 W (part-time)
Cost: $10K–$20K
% Receiving Financial Aid: 87%
Admission: Non-selective
Application Deadline: Rolling

Admission. Graduates of approved high schools with 16 units eligible; 70% of applicants accepted, 83% of these actually enroll. About 15% of freshmen graduate in top fifth of high school class, 50% in top two-fifths. Average freshman scores, according to most recent data available: SAT, 400 verbal, 550 mathematical; ACT, 21 composite. *Required:* SAT or ACT, essay; interview encouraged. *Non-academic factors* considered in admissions: special talents, alumni children, diverse student body. *Entrance programs:* early decision, early admission, advanced placement. About 5% of entering students from private schools, 25% from parochial schools. *Apply:* rolling admissions. *Transfers* welcome.

Academic Environment. *Degrees:* AB, BS, BSHEd. *Majors offered* include usual arts and sciences, business administration, communications, computer science, drama, education, equine studies, food management/nutrition, medical technology, music therapy, paralegal, and political science. About 33% of general education requirements for graduation are elective; distribution requirements fairly numerous. "Computers Across the Curriculum" utilizes computers in all academic subjects.

About 70% of students entering as freshmen graduate within four years; 85% of freshmen return for sophomore year. *Special programs:* CLEP, independent study, study abroad, individualized majors, cooperative programs with Indiana State and Rose-Hulman Institute of Technology. Adult programs: Women's External Degree Program, Single Parent Program (opportunities for mothers with children to live on campus, day care available, extended support services). *Calendar:* semester.

Undergraduate degrees conferred (99). 32% were in Business and Management, 13% were in Education, 9% were in Psychology, 9% were in Communications, 5% were in Multi/Interdisciplinary Studies, 5% were in Foreign Languages, 4% were in Law, 3% were in Visual and Performing Arts, 3% were in Public Affairs, 3% were in Theology, 3% were in Life Sciences, 3% were in Home Economics, 3% were in Allied Health, remainder in 3 other fields.

Faculty. About 60% of faculty hold PhD or equivalent.

Student Body. College seeks a national student body; 46% of students from in state; 88% North Central, 7% South. An estimated 1% of students reported as Black, 1% Hispanic, 1% Asian, 1% other minority, according to most recent data available.

Religious Orientation. Saint Mary-of-the-Woods is a church-related institution; 6 hours of religion required of all students.

Varsity Sports. Women (NAIA Div.III): Basketball, Cross Country, Softball, Tennis, Volleyball; Equestrian.

Campus Life. Students represented equally with faculty on main governing body of college which also includes members of administration. Student leader reports students most likely to feel at home on campus are "interested in combining a Christian environment with an intellectual and pro-woman attitude."

Drinking prohibited on campus; cars allowed, but parking a problem.

About 63% of women live in dormitories; rest commute. Intervisitation in women's dormitory rooms limited. There are no sororities on campus. About 40% of resident students leave campus on weekends.

Annual Costs. Tuition and fees, $10,670; room and board, $4,130. About 87% of students receive financial aid; assistance is typically divided 60% scholarship/grant, 30% loan, 10% work. College reports some scholarships awarded on the basis of academic merit alone.

Saint Mary's College of California

Moraga, California 94575-3005 (510) 631-4224

A Catholic, co-educational, liberal arts college, conducted by the Christian Brothers (LaSalle Brothers worldwide); the 420-acre campus is located in a suburban community 10 miles east of Berkeley, and 30-minutes drive from San Francisco. Most convenient major airport: Oakland.

Founded: 1863
Affiliation: Roman Catholic
UG Enrollment: 1,065 M, 1,116 W (full-time)
Total Enrollment: 3,961
Cost: $10K–$20K
% Receiving Financial Aid: 65%
Admission: Selective
Application Deadline: March 1

Admission is selective. About 68% of applicants accepted, 30% of these actually enroll; 26% of freshmen graduate in top fifth of high school class, 84% in top two-fifths. Average freshman scores: SAT, 496 M, 493 W verbal, 536 M, 532 W mathematical; ACT, 23 composite. *Required:* SAT or ACT, essay, letter of recommendation. Criteria considered in admissions, in order of importance: high school academic record, standardized test scores, recommendations, extracurricular activities, writing sample; other factors considered: special talents, alumni children, diverse student body. *Entrance programs:* early admission, deferred admission, advanced placement. About 3% of entering students from private schools, 34% from parochial schools. *Apply* by March 1. *Transfers* welcome; 195 enrolled 1993–94.

Academic Environment. Administration reports student body slightly more inclined to career preparation than to scholarly/intellectual pursuits; majors of recent graduating classes appear to support that reading. Administration reports graduation requirements include 4 Collegiate Seminars, 2 courses in religious studies, and 6 "breadth requirements": 2 courses in humanities, 2 courses in mathematics/science, 2 courses in social sciences. Degrees offered: bachelors, masters. *Majors offered* in addition to usual arts and sciences include business administration, integral liberal arts, nursing, physics, anthropology/sociology, performing arts. Average undergraduate class size: 59% under 20, 40% 20–40, 1% over 40.

About 67% of entering students graduate eventually, 92% of freshmen return for sophomore year. *Special programs:* CLEP, advanced placement, independent study, study abroad, undergraduate research, individualized majors, internships, 3–2 programs in engineering, intercollegiate nursing program with Samuel Merritt College of Nursing. *Calendar:* 4–1–4.

Undergraduate degrees conferred (888). 52% were in Business and Management, 13% were in Health Sciences, 7% were in Multi/Interdisciplinary Studies, 6% were in Social Sciences, 6% were in Communications, 5% were in Psychology, 5% were in Letters, remainder in 7 other fields.

Graduates Career Data. Advanced studies pursued by 28% of graduates; 11% enter graduate school; 4% enter medical school; 1% enter dental school; 8% enter law school; 5% enter business school. Medical schools typically enrolling largest numbers of graduates include UCSF, Creighton, UCLA; dental schools include UCSF, UCLA; law schools include Hastings, McGeorge, UCLA; business schools include SMC, Santa Clara, UCLA. About 61% of 1992–93 graduates employed. Fields typically hiring largest numbers of graduates include marketing, management, sales, accounting. Career Development Services include job search preparation, placement services.

Faculty. About 93% of faculty hold PhD or equivalent. About 93% of undergraduate classes taught by tenured faculty. About 33% of teaching faculty are female.

Student Body. About 80% of students from in state; 80% West, 5% each New England, Middle Atlantic, Midwest, Northwest. An estimated 60% of students reported as Catholic, 20% Protestant, 1% Jewish, 3% Muslim, 4% unaffiliated, 12% other; 4% Black, 13% Hispanic, 11% Asian, 1% other minority. *Minority group students:* special financial, academic, and social provisions; administrators help to facilitate orientation of Third World students to campus life; Third World students' cultural center.

Religious Orientation. Saint Mary's College is a Catholic institution, but welcomes students of all faiths and beliefs; 2 courses in religious studies required. A Campus Ministry coordinates liturgy, preparation for baptism and confirmation, retreats, counseling, ecumenical outreach, and Christian service projects and programs.

Varsity Sports. Men (Div.I): Baseball, Basketball, Crew, Cross Country, Football, Golf, Lacrosse, Soccer, Tennis. Women (Div.I): Basketball, Cross Country, Soccer, Softball, Tennis, Volleyball.

Campus Life. Active social life is a joint effort of students, faculty, and staff. Student reports "there are athletic games (football, basketball, etc.), activities, and dances." She also exclaims over the "personal atmosphere of the campus." Intervisitation hours now 8 am to 2 am. Sexes segregated in coed dormitories either by floor or "integral apartment units." An adult residence hall staff of faculty and administration supervise residential living, and are assisted by a paraprofessional group of student Resident Assistants.

About 65% of men, 60% of women live in traditional and coed dormitories; rest commute. There are no fraternities or sororities on campus. About 20% of resident students leave campus on weekends.

Annual Costs. Tuition and fees, $12,638; room and board, $6,110; estimated $1,900 other, exclusive of travel. About 65% of students receive financial aid; average amount of assistance, $9,793. Assistance is typically divided 70% scholarship, 30% loan. College reports 25 scholarships awarded only on the basis of academic merit alone, 170 for special talents alone. *Meeting Costs:* college offers EXCEL Loan Program, Tuition Prepayment.

Saint Mary's College

Notre Dame, Indiana 46556 (219) 284-4587

A church-related, liberal arts college for women, sponsored by the Sisters of the Holy Cross, Saint Mary's has enjoyed a close and continuing relationship with the University of Notre Dame through an academic co-exchange program. The 275-acre campus is located along the Saint Joseph River, immediately north of South Bend (pop. 125,600), 90 miles east of Chicago. Most convenient major airports: Michiana (South Bend), or O'Hare and Midway (Chicago, IL).

Founded: 1844
Affiliation: Roman Catholic
UG Enrollment: 1,523 W (full-time); 3 M, 24 W (part-time)
Cost: $10K–$20K
% Receiving Financial Aid: 56%
Admission: Selective (+)
Application Deadline: March 1

Admission is selective (+). About 83% of applicants accepted, 54% of these actually enroll; 55% of freshmen graduate in top fifth of high school class, 89% in top two-fifths. Average freshman scores: SAT, 490 verbal, 538 mathematical; ACT, 25 composite. *Required:* SAT or ACT, essay; interview recommended. Criteria considered in admissions, in order of importance: high school academic record, class rank, recommendations, standardized test scores, writing sample, extracurricular activities; other factors considered: special talents, alumni children. *Entrance programs:* early decision, early admission, midyear admission, advanced placement, deferred admission. About 48% of entering students from parochial schools. *Apply* preferably by March 1; rolling admissions. *Transfers* welcome; 50 accepted 1993–94.

Academic Environment. "As a Catholic liberal arts college for women, St. Mary's is committed to a life of intellectual vigor, Christian faith and social responsibility." Degrees offered: bachelors. *Majors offered* include usual arts and sciences, business administration, cytotechnology, drama, elementary education, humanistic studies (interdisciplinary), medical technology, nursing. Average undergraduate class size: 19; 54% under 20, 43% 20–40, 3% over 40.

About 78–80% of students entering as freshmen graduate eventually; 93% of freshmen return for sophomore year. *Special programs:*

CLEP, independent study, study abroad (Italy, Ireland, India), undergraduate research, field internships, interdisciplinary programs, international studies, women's studies, 3–2 engineering. *Calendar:* semester.

Undergraduate degrees conferred (459). 20% were in Social Sciences, 16% were in Business and Management, 12% were in Communications, 10% were in Education, 8% were in Letters, 6% were in Psychology, 6% were in Life Sciences, 5% were in Visual and Performing Arts, 4% were in Health Sciences, 3% were in Mathematics, 3% were in Multi/Interdisciplinary Studies, remainder in 4 other fields.

Graduates Career Data. Advanced studies pursued by 21% of graduates; 3% enter medical school; 1% enter dental school; 5% enter law school; 3% enter business school. Medical schools enrolling largest numbers of graduates include Georgetown, Indiana U.; dental schools include Indiana U.; law schools include U. of Notre Dame, Ohio State; business schools include Northwestern, Notre Dame. About 79% of 1992–93 graduates employed. Corporations typically hiring largest numbers of graduates include Andersen Consulting, Cooper & Lybrand, Eastman Kodak, Peat Marwick. Career Development Services include help preparing for interviews, on-campus interviewing. Alumni reported as active in both career guidance and job placement.

Faculty. About 95% of faculty hold PhD or equivalent.

Student Body. About 18% of students from in state; 73% from Midwest, 8% Middle Atlantic, 8% South, 5% West, 1% foreign. An estimated 87% of students reported as Catholic, 6% Protestant, 4% unaffiliated, 3% other; 1% Black, 2% Hispanic, 1% Asian.

Religious Orientation. Saint Mary's is a church-related institution; 2 courses in religious studies required of all students; attendance at chapel voluntary.

Varsity Sports. Women (NCAA, Div. III): Basketball, Diving, Soccer, Softball, Swimming, Tennis, Track, Volleyball.

Campus Life. College provides the educational benefits of a women's college as well as the co-curricular opportunities associated with proximity to Notre Dame. High interest reported in religious as well as social activities and in varsity sports (most popular: tennis, soccer, volleyball, softball, basketball). Limited intervisitation. Rules for drinking conform to state law; legal age, 21. Cars allowed for all students.

About 89% of women live in dormitories; rest commute. Freshmen given preference in college housing if all students cannot be accommodated. There are no sororities. About 20% of students leave campus on weekends.

Annual Costs. Tuition and fees, $12,890; room and board, $4,252; estimated $1,750 other, exclusive of travel. About 56% of students receive financial aid; average amount of assistance, $10,435. Assistance is typically divided 9% scholarship, 50% grant, 35% loan, 6% work. College reports some scholarships awarded on the basis of academic merit alone; "majority" awarded only on the basis of need. *Meeting Costs:* college offers payment plans, loan programs.

St. Mary's College

Orchard Lake, Michigan 48324 (810) 683-0507

A small liberal arts college with a Polish Catholic tradition, the 120-acre campus is located in a community 27 miles northwest of Detroit. Most convenient major airport: Detroit Metropolitan.

Founded: 1885
Affiliation: Independent (Roman Catholic)
UG Enrollment: 61 M, 106 W (full-time); 43 M, 50 W (part-time)
Cost: < $10K
% Receiving Financial Aid: 55%
Admission: Non-selective
Application Deadline: August 15

Admission. About 94% of applicants accepted, 78% of these actually enroll; 25% of freshmen graduate in top fifth of high school class; 45% in top two-fifths. Average freshman ACT scores: 19 composite. *Required:* ACT, 2.5 minimum high school GPA, interview. Criteria considered in admissions, in order of importance: personal interview with admissions officer ranks first, high school academic record, standardized test scores, and recommendations together rank second, extracurricular activities and writing sample are third; other factors considered: special talents, alumni children, religious affiliation and/or commitment. *Entrance programs:* midyear admission, advanced placement. About 15% of entering freshmen from private schools, 15% from parochial schools. *Apply* by August 15; rolling admissions. *Transfers* welcome; 35 enrolled 1993–94.

Academic Environment. Graduation requirements include Communication, Ultimate Meaning and Value, Interpretation and Analysis of the Arts, Historical Consciousness, social science, natural science and mathematics. Degrees offered: associates, bachelors. *Majors offered* include humanities, philosophy, theology, religious education, social sciences, sociology, natural sciences, business administration, computer science and mathematics, teacher education, radiologic technology, Polish studies. Average undergraduate class size: 90% under 20, 10% over 40.

About 25% of students entering as freshmen graduate within four years, 55% eventually, 60% of freshmen return for sophomore year. *Special programs:* junior year in Poland, cross registration with Detroit area Catholic Consortium, 3–2 in radiologic technology. Adult programs: degree programs in human services and general studies. *Library:* special collections in Polish language and culture. *Calendar:* semester.

Undergraduate degrees conferred (33). 30% were in Multi/Interdisciplinary Studies, 30% were in Business and Management, 12% were in Theology, 9% were in Computer and Engineering Related Technology, 9% were in Communications, 3% were in Social Sciences, 3% were in Life Sciences, 3% were in Letters.

Graduates Career Data. Advanced studies pursued by 45% of graduates; 18% enter graduate school; 2% enter medical school; 2% enter law school; 14% enter business school. Medical schools typically enrolling largest numbers of graduates include Wayne State; law schools include Detroit College of Law; business schools include Wayne State U., Walsh College, U. of Detroit. Career Development Services available.

Faculty. About 95% of faculty hold PhD or equivalent. About 65% of teaching faculty are female.

Student Body. About 91% of students from in state; 91% Midwest, 2% Middle Atlantic, 1% each West, New England, 5% foreign. An estimated 60% of students reported as Catholic, 36% Protestant, 3% Muslim, 1% other minority; 12% Black, 1% Hispanic, 4% Asian.

Religious Orientation. College is a church-related institution; one course in religious studies required.

Campus Life. About 30% of men, 35% of women live in traditional dormitories; 55% of men, 55% of women commute. There are 2 fraternities, 1 sorority on campus, which about 15% of each men, women join; 15% of each men, women live in fraternities and sororities. About 50% of resident students leave campus on weekends.

Annual Costs. Tuition and fees, $5,250; room and board, $3,200; estimated $500 other, exclusive of travel. About 55% of students receive financial aid; average amount of assistance, $4,500. Assistance is typically divided 60% grant, 20% loan, 20% work. College reports 40% of scholarships awarded on the basis of academic merit alone, 60% for need alone.

Saint Mary's College

Winona, Minnesota 55987-1399 (507) 452-4430; (800) 635-5987

A liberal arts college, under the auspices of the Brothers of the Christian Schools, located in a community of 26,400, 120 miles southeast of Minneapolis–St. Paul. Most convenient major airport: LaCrosse, WI or Rochester, MN.

Founded: 1912
Affiliation: Roman Catholic
UG Enrollment: 660 M, 580 W (full-time)
Total Enrollment: 7,081
Cost: $10K–$20K
% Receiving Financial Aid: 70%
Admission: Non-selective
Application Deadline: Rolling

Admission. High school graduates eligible; 92% of applicants accepted, 46% of these actually enroll; 30% of freshmen graduate in top fifth of high school class, 47% in top two-fifths. Average freshman ACT scores: 21 M, 21.5 W composite. *Required:* ACT or SAT, minimum high school GPA, essay. Criteria considered in admissions, in order of importance: high school academic record, standardized test scores, writing sample, extracurricular activities, recommendations; other factors considered: special talents, alumni children, diverse student body. About 37% of entering students from private and parochial schools. *Entrance programs:* early admission, midyear admission, deferred admission, advanced placement. *Apply:* rolling admissions. *Transfers* welcome; 58 enrolled 1993–94.

Academic Environment. Graduation requirements include 23 credit core studies program and 24 credit area studies program. Students agree that the core program is a "great strength" of the academic program. Degrees offered: bachelors, masters. *Majors offered* include usual arts and sciences, business administration, communication arts, computer science, telecommunications, nuclear medicine technology, environmental biology, electronic publishing. Average undergraduate class size: 73% under 20, 26% 20–40, 1% over 40.

About 62% of students entering as freshmen graduate eventually, 75% of freshmen return for sophomore year. *Special programs:* CLEP, independent study, study abroad, student teaching abroad, cross registration with Winona State U., honors, undergraduate research, individualized majors, college cooperative program with Winona State U., professional semester in secondary education, internships, hydrobiology station, 3–2 programs in engineering. Adult programs: SNAP, a bachelors completion program designed for working adults. *Calendar:* semester, summer school.

Undergraduate degrees conferred (249). 29% were in Business and Management, 10% were in Life Sciences, 9% were in Communications, 7% were in Social Sciences, 7% were in Protective Services, 7% were in Psychology, 6% were in Education, 4% were in Philosophy and Religion, 3% were in Visual and Performing Arts, 3% were in Letters, 3% were in Theology, 3% were in Allied Health, remainder in 6 other fields.

Graduates Career Data. Advanced studies pursued by 18% of graduates; 13% enter graduate school; 1% enter medical school; 1% enter law school; 3% enter business school. About 65% of 1991–92 graduates employed. Career Development Services include counseling, resume workshops, on-campus recruitment and placement services.

Faculty. About 61% of faculty hold PhD or equivalent. About 61% of undergraduate classes taught by tenured faculty. About 21% of teaching faculty are female; 2% Asian-American.

Student Body. About 46% of students from in state; 90% Midwest, 1% each New England, Middle Atlantic, South, West, Northwest, 5% foreign. An estimated 85% of students reported as Catholic, 14% Protestant, 4% unaffiliated, 3% other; 1% Black, 6% Hispanic, 3% Asian, 1% other minority.

Religious Orientation. Saint Mary's is a Christian college with a Catholic view; 2 courses in religious studies required.

Varsity Sports. Men (NCAA Div.III): Baseball, Basketball, Cross Country, Golf, Ice Hockey, Skiing, Soccer, Tennis, Track (indoor). Women (NCAA Div.III): Basketball, Cross Country, Golf, Skiing, Soccer, Softball, Tennis, Track (indoor), Volleyball.

Campus Life. Students report that outside of class there are intramural sports, clubs/student groups, trails for hiking and cross country skiing, "and many other things to do."

About 13% of men, 27% of women live in traditional dormitories; 73% of men, 60% of women live in coed dormitories; rest commute. Freshmen given preference in college housing if all students cannot be accommodated. Intervisitation in men's and women's dormitory rooms limited; sexes segregated either by wing, floor or room. There are 2 fraternities, 3 sororities on campus, which about 4% of men, 4% of women join; they provide no residence facilities. About 25% of resident students leave campus on weekends.

Annual Costs. Tuition and fees, $10,380; room and board, $3,470; estimated $600 other, exclusive of travel. About 70% of students receive financial aid; average amount of assistance, $9,000. Assistance is typically divided 50% scholarship, 40% loan, 10% work. College reports 315 scholarships awarded on the basis of academic merit alone, 50 for special talents and need-based. *Meeting Costs:* college offers deferred payment plan, loan programs.

St. Mary's College of Maryland

St. Mary's City, Maryland 20686 **(301) 862-0274; (800) 492-7181**

A public liberal arts college, located in the state's historic colonial capital, 97 miles south of Baltimore, 68 miles south of Washington, D.C. Most convenient major airports: Washington, D.C., or Baltimore, MD.

Founded: 1840	**Cost:** < $10K
Affiliation: State	**% Receiving Financial Aid:** 54%
UG Enrollment: 601 M, 714 W (full-time); 80 M, 129 W (part-time)	**Admission:** Very Selective
	Application Deadline: January 15

Admission is very selective. About 52% of applicants accepted, 41% of these actually enroll; 64% of freshmen graduate in top fifth of high school class, 86% in top two-fifths. Average freshmen SAT scores: 579 M, 578 W verbal, 623 M, 608 W mathematical; 86% of freshmen score above 500 on verbal, 47% above 600, 5% above 700; 92% score above 500 on mathematical, 64% above 600, 12% above 700. *Required:* SAT, essay. Criteria considered in admissions, in order of importance: high school academic record, extracurricular activities, writing sample, recommendations, standardized test scores; other factors considered: special talents, diverse student body. *Out-of-state* freshman applicants: college actively seeks students from out-of-state. State does not limit out-of-state enrollment. No special requirements for out-of-state applicants. About 47% of out-of-state students accepted, 37% of these actually enroll. States from which most out-of-state students are drawn include Pennsylvania, New York, New Jersey, Virginia, Massachusetts. *Entrance programs:* early decision, midyear admission, advanced placement. About 5% of entering students from private schools, 16% from parochial schools. *Apply* by January 15. *Transfers* welcome; 66 enrolled 1993–94.

Academic Environment. Graduation requirements include general education courses in English, foreign language, history, sciences, and philosophy. Degrees offered: bachelors. *Majors offered* in addition to usual studies include chemistry, computer science, English, foreign language, individualized majors, philosophy, physics, psychology. Average undergraduate class size: 75% under 20, 21% 20–40, 4% over 40.

About 57% of entering students graduate within four years, 70% eventually, 90% of freshmen return for sophomore year. *Special programs:* CLEP, cross registration with John Hopkins U., Heidelberg U., honors, independent study, study abroad, undergraduate research, full semester internships, 3–2 in engineering and computer science. *Calendar:* semester, summer school.

Undergraduate degrees conferred (306). 44% were in Social Sciences, 15% were in Psychology, 10% were in Life Sciences, 10% were in Letters, 9% were in Education, 7% were in Visual and Performing Arts, remainder in 4 other fields.

Graduates Career Data. Advanced studies pursued by 39% of graduates; 33% enter graduate school; 2% enter law school; 4% enter business school. Law schools typically enrolling largest numbers of graduates include U. of Baltimore, Georgetown; business schools include Georgetown, Johns Hopkins. About 96% of 1992–93 graduates (of those not in graduate school) employed. Career Development Services include individual counseling, resume writing workshops, job search strategies, interview skills, career planning, career and graduate school information library.

Faculty. About 97% of faculty hold PhD or equivalent. About 43% of undergraduate classes taught by tenured faculty. About 38% of teaching faculty are female; 7% Black, 2% Hispanic, 7% other minority.

Student Body. About 84% of students from in state: 90% Middle Atlantic, 3% South, 2% each Midwest, New England, 1% West, 2% foreign. An estimated 37% of students reported as Protestant, 26% Catholic, 3% Jewish, 1% Muslim, 25% unaffiliated, 8% other; 9% Black, 2% Hispanic, 4% Asian, 1% other minority.

Varsity Sports. Men (Div.III): Baseball, Basketball, Diving, Lacrosse, Soccer, Swimming, Tennis. Women (Div.III): Basketball, Diving, Lacrosse, Soccer, Swimming, Tennis, Volleyball.

Campus Life. High interest reported in both varsity sports (most popular: soccer, lacrosse, basketball) and intramurals (most popular: men's basketball).

About 29% of men, 23% of women live in traditional dormitories; 39% of men, 46% of women live in coed dormitories; rest commute. Sexes segregated in coed dormitories either by wing or floor. There are no fraternities or sororities on campus. About 40% of resident students leave campus on weekends.

Annual Costs. Tuition and fees, $4,915 (out-of-state, $7,715); room and board, $4,730; estimated $1,250 other, exclusive of travel. About 54% of students receive financial aid; average amount of assistance, $3,286. Assistance is typically divided 23% scholarship, 20% grant, 52% loan, 5% work. College reports 149 scholarships awarded on the basis of academic merit alone, 48 for need alone.

St. Mary's Seminary and University

Baltimore, Maryland 21210

A seminary and university founded by the Society of St. Sulpice, St. Mary's offers bachelors and masters degrees.

Founded: 1791 **Affiliation:** Roman Catholic

St. Mary's University of San Antonio

San Antonio, Texas 78240 (512) 436-3126

A church-related university, conducted by the Society of Mary, located in a city of 900,000. Most convenient major airport: San Antonio International.

Founded: 1852
Affiliation: Roman Catholic
UG Enrollment: 4,055 M, W (full-time)
Cost: < $10K
% Receiving Financial Aid: 78%
Admission: Non-selective
Application Deadline: Aug. 15

Admission. Graduates of accredited high schools with 16 units (13 in academic subjects) who rank in upper half of class with SAT or ACT in upper 50th percentile eligible; others admitted by examination; 77% of applicants accepted, 45% of these actually enroll; 56% of freshmen graduate in top quarter of high school class, 83% in top half. *Required:* SAT or ACT. *Apply* by August 15. *Transfers* welcome.
Academic Environment. *Undergraduate studies* offered by schools of Humanities and Social Sciences, Business Administration, Science, Engineering and Technology. About 60% of students entering as freshmen graduate eventually; 82% of freshmen return for sophomore year. *Special programs:* CLEP, independent study, honors, undergraduate research, Washington Semester, 3-year degree, cooperative program with Incarnate Word and Our Lady of the Lake. *Calendar:* semester, 2 summer sessions.
Undergraduate degrees conferred (470). 34% were in Business and Management, 16% were in Social Sciences, 12% were in Life Sciences, 6% were in Education, 6% were in Communications, 6% were in Public Affairs, 5% were in Psychology, 3% were in Letters, 3% were in Multi/Interdisciplinary Studies, remainder in 8 other fields.
Faculty. About 73% of faculty hold PhD or equivalent.
Student Body. About 80% of students from Texas.
Religious Orientation. St. Mary's is a church-related institution; 6 hours of religion required of all students; attendance at Mass voluntary.
Varsity Sports. Men (NAIA): Baseball, Basketball, Golf, Soccer, Tennis. Women (NAIA): Basketball, Softball, Tennis, Volleyball.
Campus Life. About 40% of men, 54% of women live in traditional dormitories; 3% of men, 3% of women live in coed dormitories. Intervisitation in men's and women's dormitory rooms limited. There are 7 fraternities, 4 sororities on campus which about 25% of men, 20% of women join. About 20% of resident students leave campus on weekends.
Annual Costs. Tuition and fees, $8,536; room and board, $3,440. About 78% of students receive financial aid; assistance is typically divided 40% scholarship, 35% loan, 25% work. University reports some scholarships awarded on the basis of academic merit alone. *Meeting Costs:* university offers guaranteed tuition plan, monthly payment plans and deferred payment plan.
General Institutional Data. College newspaper: The Rattler. Percent of annual budget derived from tuition: 66%.

Saint Meinrad College

Saint Meinrad, Indiana 47577

A seminary conducted by Benedictine monks, Saint Meinrad is a liberal arts school for men who are considering the Roman Catholic priesthood as a vocational choice.

Founded: 1857 **Affiliation:** Roman Catholic

Undergraduate degrees conferred (24). 33% were in Philosophy and Religion, 21% were in Psychology, 21% were in Letters, 13% were in Social Sciences, 8% were in Multi/Interdisciplinary Studies, 4% were in Foreign Languages.

Saint Michael's College

Winooski Park, Vermont 05439 (800) 762-8000; (802) 654-2000

A Catholic, liberal arts college, founded by the Society of St. Edmund. Saint Michael's is located in Colchester (pop. 8,800), a suburb of Burlington. Most convenient major airport: Burlington International.

Founded: 1904
Affiliation: Roman Catholic
UG Enrollment: 795 M, 888 W (full-time)
Total Enrollment: 2,383
Cost: $10K–$20K
% Receiving Financial Aid: 65%
Admission: Selective
Application Deadline: February 15

Admission is selective. About 72% of applicants accepted, 34% of these actually enroll; 35% of freshmen graduate in top fifth of high school class, 82% in top two-fifths. Average freshman SAT scores: 950–1150 combined range; 31% of freshman score above 500 on verbal, 3% above 600; 58% score above 500 on mathematical, 14% above 600, 1% above 700. *Required:* SAT or ACT, essay. Criteria considered in admissions, in order of importance: high school academic record, recommendations, standardized test scores, writing sample, extracurricular activities, service, alumni relationship, diversity; other factors considered: special talents, alumni children, diverse student body. *Entrance programs:* early action, deferred admission, advanced placement. About 31% of entering students from private and parochial schools. *Apply* by February 15. *Transfers* welcome; 69 enrolled 1993–94.
Academic Environment. Administration source reports that student interests are overlapping with large majority devoted almost equally to social activities, occupational/professional goals, and scholarly/intellectual pursuits. Graduation requirements include 2 courses each in philosophy, religious studies, social sciences, communication skills, math/science. Degrees offered: bachelors, masters. *Majors offered* include usual arts and sciences, business administration, fine arts, biochemistry, environmental studies. Average undergraduate class size: 25.

About 75% of students entering as freshmen graduate within four years, 78% eventually, 87% of freshmen return for sophomore year. *Special programs:* CLEP, cross registration with Trinity College, independent study, study abroad, undergraduate research, honors, individualized majors, 3–2 in engineering, internships. *Calendar:* semester, summer school.
Undergraduate degrees conferred (482). 33% were in Business and Management, 20% were in Social Sciences, 11% were in Letters, 7% were in Psychology, 7% were in Education, 6% were in Communications, 4% were in Life Sciences, 3% were in Foreign Languages, remainder in 6 other fields.
Graduates Career Data. Advanced studies pursued immediately after graduation by 15% of students, 65% eventually. Career Development Services include interviewing skills, resume writing, career decision making, researching companies and employment fields.
Faculty. About 87% of faculty hold PhD or equivalent. About 70% of undergraduate classes taught by tenured faculty. About 29% of teaching faculty are female; 2% Black, 2% Hispanic, 3% other minority.
Student Body. About 18% of students from in state; 74% New England, 18% Middle Atlantic, 2% South, 1% each West, Midwest, 4% foreign. An estimated 82% of students reported as Catholic, 15% other; 3% Black, 1% Asian, 4% other minority.
Religious Orientation. St. Michael's is a church-related institution; 1 semester each in religious studies, philosophy required of all students, emphasis on peace and justice.
Varsity Sports. Men (Div.II): Baseball, Basketball, Cross Country, Diving, Golf, Ice Hockey (III), Field Hockey, Lacrosse, Skiing, Soccer, Swimming, Tennis. Women (Div.II): Basketball, Cross Country, Diving, Lacrosse, Skiing, Soccer, Softball, Swimming, Tennis, Volleyball.

Campus Life. Student exclaims "Burlington is a great place to be! There's something going on either downtown or on-campus every weekend"; other students agree. Cars allowed for all but first-semester freshmen. Alcoholic beverages allowed for students of legal age in designated areas.

About 83% of men, 90% of women live in traditional and coed dormitories; rest commute. Freshmen given preference in college housing if all students cannot be accommodated. There are no fraternities or sororities on campus. About 5–10% of students leave campus on weekends.

Annual Costs. Tuition and fees, $12,430; room and board, $5,600; estimated $1,000 other, exclusive of travel. About 65% of students receive financial aid; average amount of assistance, $11,345. Assistance is typically divided 54% scholarship, 34% loan, 12% work, according to most recent data available. College reports 20 partial scholarships awarded on the basis of academic merit alone, 20 for special talents alone. *Meeting Costs:* College offers tuition plan, extended payment plan, special loans.

St. Norbert College

DePere, Wisconsin 54115 **(414) 337-3005; (800) 236-4878**

Although St. Norbert is governed by a lay Board of Trustees and its administration, faculty, and student body represent all faiths, the college is a Roman Catholic institution. The college is located in a town of 16,000, 5 miles south of Green Bay. Most convenient major airport: Green Bay, WI.

Founded: 1898
Affiliation: Roman Catholic
UG Enrollment: 837 M, 1,109 W (full-time); 30 M, 65 W (part-time)
Total Enrollment: 2,059
Cost: $10K–$20K
% Receiving Financial Aid: 89%
Admission: Selective (+)
Application Deadline: Rolling

Admission is selective (+). About 90% of applicants accepted, 46% of these actually enroll; 48% of freshmen graduate in top fifth of high school class, 76% in top two-fifths. Average freshman scores: SAT, 553 verbal, 614 mathematical; ACT, 24 composite. *Required:* SAT or ACT, minimum 2.5 high school GPA, essay. Criteria considered in admissions, in order of importance: high school academic record, standardized test scores, recommendations, writing sample, extracurricular activities; other factors considered: special talents, alumni children, diverse student body. *Entrance programs:* midyear admission, deferred admission, advanced placement. About 5% of entering students from private schools, 35% from parochial schools. *Apply:* rolling admissions. *Transfers* welcome; 70 enrolled 1993–94.

Academic Environment. Graduation requirements include 2 courses in religious heritage, 1 each in human nature, human relationships, natural world, creative expression, American heritage, foreign heritage, quantitative skills, Western tradition, global society, and a senior colloquium. Students enjoy the small classes and easy access to teachers, and also "interesting and exciting teachers with challenging and fun programs." Degrees offered: bachelors, masters. *Majors offered* include visual arts and sciences, business administration, computer science, elementary education, environmental policy, international business and language area studies, international economic studies, medical technology, theater, Japanese and Russian. Average undergraduate class size: 25.

About 71% of students entering as freshmen graduate within four years, 84% of freshmen return for sophomore year. *Special programs:* CLEP, honors, independent study, study abroad, student teaching abroad, undergraduate research, individualized majors, 3–2 in engineering. *Calendar:* semester.

Undergraduate degrees conferred (425). 31% were in Business and Management, 18% were in Communications, 11% were in Social Sciences, 9% were in Education, 4% were in Mathematics, 4% were in Visual and Performing Arts, 4% were in Letters, 4% were in Psychology, 4% were in Life Sciences, 3% were in Physical Sciences, 3% were in Computer and Engineering Related Technology, remainder in 4 other fields.

Graduates Career Data. Advanced studies pursued by 19% of graduates; 14% enter graduate school; 2% enter medical school; 1% enter law school; 2% enter business school. Medical schools typically numbers of graduates include Medical College of Wisconsin; law schools include Marquette, DePaul. About 76% of 1992–93 graduates employed. Corporations typically hiring largest numbers of graduates include Firstar Bank, Heritage Insurance, Schneider National. Career Development Services include individual career assessment services.

Faculty. About 75% of faculty hold PhD or equivalent. About 30% of teaching faculty are female.

Student Body. About 71% of students from in state; 97% Midwest, 1% foreign. An estimated 88% of students reported as Catholic, 8% Protestant, 4% unaffiliated; 2% Asian, 2% Native American, 2% other minority.

Religious Orientation. St. Norbert is a church-related institution; 2 courses in religion and/or philosophy required of all students. Religious studies department presents an ecumenical approach, with Jewish and Protestant theologians included.

Varsity Sports. Men (NCAA Div.III, MCAC): Baseball, Basketball, Cross Country, Football, Golf, Ice Hockey, Soccer, Tennis, Track. Women (NCAA Div.III, MCAC): Basketball, Cross Country, Golf, Soccer, Softball, Tennis, Track, Volleyball.

Campus Life. Social life is centered around campus activities: movies, concerts, special events, athletics; "always social activities going on." Most town amenities are within walking distance. Students note "very friendly atmosphere" and that students are "want each other to succeed" and are "not cut-throat". Student leader notes that "in terms of willingness to experiment and to change, the college is fluid and active." Cars allowed. Students over 21 may live in approved off-campus housing. Intervisitation allowed 8 am-midnight on weekdays, to 2 am weekends.

About 85% of students live on campus; 15% commute. Intervisitation in men's and women's dormitory rooms limited. There are 6 fraternities, 4 sororities on campus which about 11% of men, 3% of women join. About 25% of resident students leave campus on weekends.

Annual Costs. Tuition and fees, $11,465; room and board, $4,245; estimated $1,175 other, exclusive of travel. About 89% of students receive financial aid; average amount of assistance, $9,649. Assistance is typically divided 57% scholarship/grant, 31% loan, 12% work. *Meeting Costs:* college offers several payment plans and loan options.

St. Olaf College

Northfield, Minnesota 55057 **(507) 646-3025**

St. Olaf is a church-related college that attempts to offer "a liberal arts education, rooted in the Christian gospel and incorporating a global perspective." It is the largest and best known college affiliated with the Evangelical Lutheran Church in America. The 350-acre campus overlooking the Cannon River in a town of 14,000, which is also the home of Carleton College, is located 40 miles south of Minneapolis–St. Paul. Most convenient major airport: Minneapolis/St. Paul.

Founded: 1874
Affiliation: Evangelical Lutheran Church in America
UG Enrollment: 1,299 M, 1,589 W (full-time); 47 M, 58 W (part-time)
Cost: $10K–$20K
% Receiving Financial Aid: 60%
Admission: Very (+) Selective
Application Deadline: Rolling

Admission is very (+) selective. About 74% of applicants accepted, 44% of these actually enroll; 62% of freshmen graduate in top fifth of high school class, 88% in top two-fifths. Average freshman scores: SAT, middle 50% range, 470–590 M, 460–590 W verbal, 530–670 M, 500–620 W mathematical; ACT, 26 composite. *Required:* SAT or ACT, PSAT for early decision applicants, essay. Criteria considered in admissions, in order of importance: high school academic record, standardized test scores, writing sample, recommendations, extracurricular activities; other factors considered: special talents, alumni children, diverse student body, religious affiliation and/or commitment. *Entrance programs:* early decision, early admission, midyear admission (limited), deferred admission. About 10% of entering students from private schools, 5% from parochial schools. *Apply* rolling admissions. *Transfers* welcome; 73 enrolled 1993–94.

Academic Environment. Administration reports college strong academically in chemistry, English, mathematics, music. Students generally concerned with occupational/professional goals, within strictly academic environment. Strong emphasis on premed, pre-law sequences. College has an abiding interest in Nordic culture, as well as studies in the history and culture of Latin America, Asia, and Africa. College-within-the-college emphasizes integrative and interdisciplinary studies. Graduation requirements include first year seminar, 3–4 semesters of a second language; mathematical reasoning, oral communication, historical studies, artistic and literary studies, natural sciences, human behavior and society, Biblical and theological studies, and multicultural studies. About 6% of students are currently in study abroad programs. Students praise strong academic programs ("a lot of studying"), "high-quality" faculty ("one of this school's best assets"), and the low student-faculty ratio. Degrees offered: bachelors. *Majors offered* include usual arts and sciences, Asian studies, dance, Norwegian, church music, family resources, nursing, women's studies. Average undergraduate class size: 21.

About 76% of students entering as freshmen graduate within four years, 85% eventually, 92% of freshmen return for sophomore year. *Special programs:* independent study, study abroad, Washington Semester, exchange with Fisk U., ACM programs, art semester in New York, individualized majors, internships, paracollege (an alternative program using tutorials and examinations), Great Conversation, 3–2 in engineering, cross registration with Carleton College. Adult programs: continuing education for non-degree seeking candidates. *Calendar:* 4–1–4, summer school.

Undergraduate degrees conferred (708). 21% were in Social Sciences, 12% were in Letters, 11% were in Visual and Performing Arts, 9% were in Life Sciences, 9% were in Physical Sciences, 8% were in Psychology, 8% were in Mathematics, 5% were in Multi/Interdisciplinary Studies, 4% were in Foreign Languages, 4% were in Area and Ethnic Studies, 3% were in Philosophy and Religion, 3% were in Education, remainder in 3 other fields.

Graduates Career Data. Advanced studies pursued by 29% of graduates. Medical schools typically enrolling largest numbers of graduates include U. of Minnesota, Mayo Medical; dental schools include U. of Minnesota; law schools include U. of Minnesota, Mitchell, Hamline U.; business schools include U. of Minnesota. Career Development Services include interest inventory tests, on campus interviews, job postings, alumni network, internship opportunities, graduate school information.

Faculty. About 60% of faculty hold PhD or equivalent. About 40% of teaching faculty are female.

Student Body. About 56% of students from in state; 3% foreign. An estimated 75% of students reported as Protestant, 15% Catholic, 6% unaffiliated, 4% other. *Minority group students:* special financial, academic, and social provisions including tutorial help, Black Cultural Union.

Religious Orientation. St. Olaf is a church-related institution; 2 courses in religion and 1 ethics course required of all students; chapel attendance encouraged.

Varsity Sports. Men (Div.III): Baseball, Basketball, Cross Country, Diving, Football, Golf, Hockey, Alpine/Nordic Skiing, Soccer, Swimming, Tennis, Track, Wrestling. Women (Div.III): Basketball, Cross Country, Diving, Golf, Alpine/Nordic Skiing, Soccer, Softball, Swimming, Tennis, Track, Volleyball.

Campus Life. Campus is within walking distance of Northfield and the Twin Cities of Minneapolis-St. Paul are "easily accessible" according to student source. On-campus activities varied and popular: dances, bands, intramural and varsity sports, volunteer services (Project Friendship, Habitat for Humanity), student government, and "many, many people belong to the numerous clubs." Annual concert series and fine arts festival sponsored by St. Olaf. Alcohol prohibited on campus, in off-campus housing, and at college functions; special permission needed to keep cars on campus (some student concern reported about car policy).

About 90% of men, 90% of women live in coed dormitories and off-campus college-related housing; rest commute. All students are guaranteed housing. Sexes segregated in coed dormitories by floor. There are no fraternities or sororities on campus. About 20% of resident students leave campus on weekends.

Annual Costs. Tuition and fees, $13,560; room and board, $3,640; estimated $1,000 other, exclusive of travel. About 60% of students receive financial aid; average amount of assistance, $11,900. Assistance is typically divided 64% scholarship/grant, 27% loan, 9% work. College reports 2 scholarships awarded on the basis of academic merit alone, 1 for music, many for need alone. *Meeting Costs:* college offers alternative financing options.

Saint Patrick's College

(See Saint Joseph's College)

Saint Paul's College

Lawrenceville, Virginia 23868 (804) 848-3111

A church-related college, located in a village of 1,600, 70 miles southwest of Richmond; founded as a college for Negroes and still serving a predominantly Black student body. Most convenient major airport: Richmond.

Founded: 1888
Affiliation: Episcopal
UG Enrollment: 236 M, 352 W (full-time)
Cost: < $10K
% Receiving Financial Aid: 90%
Admission: Non-selective
Application Deadline: Rolling

Admission. Graduates of accredited high schools with 16 units (10 in academic subjects) eligible; others admitted by examination; 86% of applicants accepted; 35% of these actually enroll; 16% of freshmen graduate in top fifth of high school class, 41% in top two-fifths. Average freshman SAT scores: 308 M, 305 W verbal, 347 M, 331 W mathematical. *Required:* SAT or ACT, minimum 2.0 high school GPA, references. Criteria considered in admissions, in order of importance: high school academic record, standardized test scores, recommendations. *Entrance programs:* early admission, midyear admission, deferred admission, advanced placement. *Apply:* rolling admissions. *Transfers* welcome.

Academic Environment. Graduation requirements include coursework in art, English, math, health, physical education, and science. Degrees offered: bachelors. About 88% of students entering as freshmen graduate within four years, 65% of freshmen return for sophomore year. *Special programs:* January term, study abroad, internships. Adult programs: Organizational Management Degree Program for students with at least two previous years of college work. *Calendar:* semester, summer school.

Undergraduate degrees conferred (83). 34% were in Social Sciences, 31% were in Business and Management, 22% were in Education, 6% were in Life Sciences, 5% were in Mathematics, remainder in Letters.

Graduates Career Data. Advanced studies pursued by 22% of graduates.

Student Body. About 65% of students from in state. An estimated 70% of freshmen reported as Protestant, 6% Catholic, 22% other; 95% Black, according to most recent data available.

Religious Orientation. Saint Paul's is a church-related institution; 1 course in religious studies required of all students.

Varsity Sports. Men (Div.II): Baseball, Basketball, Cross Country, Golf, Tennis, Track. Women (Div.II): Basketball, Cross Country, Softball, Tennis, Track, Volleyball.

Campus Life. About 65% of men, 85% of women live in traditional dormitories; no coed dormitories; rest live in off-campus college-related housing or commute. Freshmen given preference in college housing if all students cannot be accommodated. Intervisitation in men's and women's dormitory rooms limited. There are 4 fraternities, 4 sororities on campus which about 2% of men, 4% of women join; they provide no residence facilities.

Annual Costs. Tuition and fees, $5,521; room and board, $3,650; estimated $550 other, exclusive of travel. About 90% of students receive financial aid. Assistance typically divided 59% scholarship, 33% loan, 8% work.

Saint Peter's College

Jersey City, New Jersey 07306 (201) 915-9213

An independent, liberal arts college, sponsored by the Society of Jesus, Saint Peter's is located in a city of 228,537, just a few miles west of New York City. Saint Peter's also operates the Englewood Cliffs Campus, a branch campus in Bergen County. Most convenient major airport: Newark International.

Founded: 1872
Affiliation: Roman Catholic
UG Enrollment: 925 M, 1,056 W (full-time); 354 M, 854 W (part-time)
Total Enrollment: 3,567
Cost: < $10K
% Receiving Financial Aid: 75%
Admission: Non-selective
Application Deadline: April 1

Admission. High school graduates with 16 units, combined SAT scores of 800 minimum and rank in upper three-fifths of high school class eligible, others accepted under special program; 83% of applicants accepted, 55% of these actually enroll; 12% of freshmen graduate in top fifth of high school class, 29% in top two-fifths. Average freshmen SAT scores: 8% of freshmen score above 500 on verbal, less than 1% above 600; 15% score above 500 on mathematical, 4% above 600. *Required:* SAT or ACT, essay; interview strongly advised. Criteria considered in admissions, in order of importance: high school academic record, standardized test scores, writing sample, recommendations, extracurricular activities; other factors considered: special talents, alumni children. *Entrance programs:* early decision, early admission, midyear admission, advanced placement. *Apply* preferably by April 1. *Transfers* welcome.

Academic Environment. Graduation requirements include 3 credits each in communications, fine arts, 6 each in literature, modern language, history, social sciences, philosophy, theology, 6–8 in math, 9 in natural sciences, 12 in core electives, including course in ethical values. Degrees offered: associates, bachelors, masters. *Majors offered* in arts and sciences, computer science, accounting, education, marketing, management, health care management, urban studies, public policy, nursing, cytotechnology, medical technology, toxicology, math, economics. Average undergraduate class size: 13.

About 55% of students entering as freshmen graduate eventually, 81% of freshmen return for sophomore year. *Special programs:* CLEP, independent study, study abroad, honors, undergraduate research, internships, cooperative education, experiential learning credit, BS/DDS with NYU College of Dentistry, Washington Center Program, 3–2 in cytotechnology, medical technology and toxicology with UMDNJ. Adult programs: Englewood Cliffs campus is devoted to adult learners; Jersey City campus offers Evening/Saturday Session. *Calendar:* semester, trimester in evening division, summer school.

Undergraduate degrees conferred (435). 58% were in Business and Management, 11% were in Health Sciences, 7% were in Computer and Engineering Related Technology, 5% were in Education, 4% were in Social Sciences, 4% were in Psychology, remainder in 7 other fields.

Graduates Career Data. Advanced studies pursued by "at least" 35% of graduates; 25% enter graduate school; 2% enter medical school; 2% enter dental school; 5% enter law school. Medical schools typically enrolling largest numbers of graduates include UMDNJ; dental schools include NYU, Fairleigh Dickinson; law schools include Harvard, Fordham, Rutgers. Corporations typically hiring largest numbers of graduates include Deloitte & Touche, IRS, Arthur Anderson, AT&T. Career Development Center offers career counseling, career planning, self-assessment, career library, DISCOVER, annual career fair, St. Peter's Connection (alumni volunteers), on-campus recruitment, interviews with prospective employers, job listings, career skills workshops on resume writing, job searching strategies and interviewing skills.

Faculty. About 77% of faculty hold PhD or equivalent. About 90% of undergraduate classes taught by tenured faculty. About 23% of teaching faculty are female; 2% Black, 5% Hispanic, 1% other minority.

Student Body. About 86% of students from in state; 7% foreign. An estimated 76% of students reported as Catholic, 5% Protestant, 3% unaffiliated, 13% other; 11% Black, 19% Hispanic, 9% Asian.

Religious Orientation. Saint Peter's is a Jesuit sponsored institution; 6 credits in theology required of all students; courses in Protestant and Jewish theology and in other faiths available.

Varsity Sports. Men (Div.I): Baseball, Basketball, Bowling, Cross Country, Diving, Football, Golf, Soccer, Swimming, Tennis, Track. Women (Div.I): Basketball, Cross Country, Diving, Soccer, Swimming, Tennis, Track, Volleyball.

Campus Life. Cultural and intellectual activities on campus are supplemented by the proximity of resources of New York City. An extensive intercollegiate and intramural athletic program is available for both men and women; the Recreational Life Center offers modern facilities for athletic and recreational activities. Student life embraces more than 40 student clubs and organizations.

About 32% of students live in apartment-style coed dormitories; rest commute. Freshmen given preference in college housing if all students cannot be accommodated. There is 1 fraternity and no sororities on campus.

Annual Costs. Tuition and fees, $9,150; room and board, $5,330; an estimated $1,300, exclusive of travel. About 75% of students receive financial aid; average amount of assistance, $5,500. Assistance is typically divided 28% scholarship. *Meeting Costs:* college offers installment plan, accepts credit cards.

College of Saint Rose

Albany, New York 12203 **(518) 454-5150 or (800) 637-8556**

The College of Saint Rose is an independent co-educational, college of liberal arts and sciences, founded in 1920 by the Sisters of Saint Joseph of Carondelet. It is presently governed by a lay board of trustees. CSR is located in a residential section of the state capital (population 115,800). Most convenient major airport: Albany County.

Founded: 1920
Affiliation: Independent (Roman Catholic)
UG Enrollment: 429 M, 1,094 W (full-time); 255 M, 693 W (part-time)
Total Enrollment: 3,905
Cost: < $10K
% Receiving Financial Aid: 31%
Admission: Non-selective
Application Deadline: Rolling

Admission. About 68% of applicants accepted. Average freshman scores: SAT, 28% of freshmen score above 500 on verbal, 4% above 600; 49% score above 500 on mathematical, 11% above 600, 2% above 700; ACT, 23 composite. *Required:* SAT or ACT, essay, letter of recommendation, portfolio/audition for art/music. Criteria considered in admissions, in order of importance: high school academic record, recommendations, standardized test scores, writing sample, extracurricular activities; other factors considered: special talents, alumni children, diverse student body, portfolio, audition. *Entrance programs:* midyear admission, deferred admission, advanced placement. About 20% of entering students from private schools. *Apply:* rolling admissions. *Transfers* welcome; 454 enrolled 1993–94.

Academic Environment. Graduation requirements include 36 credit core program with courses in humanities, social sciences, natural sciences, fine arts, and writing and speech requirements. Degrees offered: bachelors, masters. *Majors offered* include usual arts and sciences, accounting, business, computer information systems, education, special education, advertising/design, studio art, music, medical technology, social sciences; interdisciplinary and special majors also possible.

About 52% of students entering as freshmen graduate eventually, 67% of freshmen return for sophomore year. *Special programs:* CLEP, independent study, internships, study abroad, cross registration with Hudson-Mohawk Consortium, 3–2 in engineering, 3–3 in law, JD/MBA program. Adult programs: interdepartmental studies and professional studies credit for Experiential Learning Program (EAP). *Calendar:* semester, summer school.

Undergraduate degrees conferred (460). 34% were in Education, 23% were in Business and Management, 8% were in Communications Technologies, 8% were in Health Sciences, 6% were in Social Sciences, 5% were in Visual and Performing Arts, 4% were in Liberal/General Studies, 3% were in Letters, remainder in 8 other fields.

Graduates Career Data. Advanced studies pursued by 32% of graduates. About 83% of 1991–92 graduates employed. Fields typically hiring largest numbers of graduates include education, business and industry, health and science, government. Career Development Services include job search, interviews, resume, career resource speakers, job listings, job hotline, on-campus interviews.

Faculty. About 70% of faculty hold PhD or equivalent. About 50% of teaching faculty are female.

Student Body. About 90% of students from in state; 10% New England, 3% foreign. An estimated 65% of students reported as Catholic; 7% minority. *Minority group students:* scholarship help, remedial classes. Average age of undergraduate student: 26.

Religious Orientation. Saint Rose is an independent institution with a Catholic heritage, makes no religious demands on students.

Varsity Sports. Men (NCAA, Div. II): Baseball, Basketball, Cross Country, Soccer, Swimming, Tennis, Track. Women (NCAA, Div. II): Basketball, Cross Country, Soccer, Softball, Swimming, Tennis, Track, Volleyball.
Campus Life. No curfews; cars permitted, but parking may be a problem; alcohol available on campus for those over 21; intervisitation allowed until 11 PM Sunday–Thursday, Friday and Saturday until 3 am. Three different styles of dormitories available: suites, high-rise, cottage and on-campus houses; some are coed.

About 25% of men, 64% of women live in traditional dormitories; 11% of students live in coed dormitories; rest commute. Freshmen given preference in college housing if all students cannot be accommodated. There are no fraternities or sororities on campus.
Annual Costs. Tuition and fees, $9,592; room and board, $5,428; estimated $800 other, exclusive of travel. About 31% of undergraduate students receive financial aid; average amount of assistance, $5,242. Assistance is typically divided 87% scholarship, 5% loan, 8% work. College reports all scholarships awarded only on the basis of need. *Meeting Costs:* college offers alternative loan programs.

College of St. Scholastica

Duluth, Minnesota 55811 (218) 723-6046

A church-related, co-educational college, under the auspices of the Sisters of St. Benedict, located in a city of 100,600. Most convenient major airport: Duluth International.

Founded: 1912
Affiliation: Roman Catholic
UG Enrollment: 380 M, 970 W (full-time); 79 M, 196 W (part-time)
Total Enrollment: 1,838
Cost: $10K–$20K
% Receiving Financial Aid: 92%
Admission: Non-selective
Application Deadline: Rolling

Admission. Graduates of accredited high schools eligible; 89% of applicants accepted, 47% of these actually enroll; 50% of freshmen graduate in top fifth of high school class, 81% in top two-fifths. Average freshman scores: SAT, 437 M, 445 W verbal, 545 M, 470 W, mathematical; ACT, 22 M, 23 W composite. *Required:* ACT, PSAT or SAT. Criteria considered in admissions, in order of importance: high school academic record and standardized test scores rank with equal importance, extracurricular activities, recommendations; other factors considered: special talents, diverse student body. *Entrance programs:* early admission, midyear admission, deferred admission, advanced placement. *Apply:* rolling admissions. *Transfers* welcome; 113 enrolled 1993–94.
Academic Environment. Graduation requirements include 72 credits in general education courses. Degrees offered: bachelors, masters. *Majors offered* include pastoral ministry, sports recreation management, health services management, physical therapy, occupational therapy. Average undergraduate class size: 68% under 20, 25% 20–40, 7% over 40.

About 38% of students entering as freshmen graduate within four years, 54% eventually, 76% of freshmen return for sophomore year. *Special programs:* CLEP, independent study, study abroad, undergraduate research, cooperative programs, cross registration with U. of Minnesota-Duluth and U. Wisconsin-Superior. Adult programs: separate admissions office and support programs. *Calendar:* quarter, summer school.
Undergraduate degrees conferred (276). 39% were in Health Sciences, 14% were in Business and Management, 7% were in Life Sciences, 7% were in Education, 5% were in Public Affairs, 5% were in Letters, 4% were in Psychology, 4% were in Multi/Interdisciplinary Studies, 4% were in Home Economics, 3% were in Allied Health, 3% were in Computer and Engineering Related Technology, remainder in 6 other fields.
Graduates Career Data. Advanced studies pursued by 20% of graduates. Fields typically hiring largest numbers of graduates include nursing, education, health science, management. Career Development Services include career counseling and assessment, resume development, job search strategies and interviewing skills, career resource library, job boards.
Faculty. About 75% of faculty hold PhD or equivalent. About 34% of undergraduate classes taught by tenured faculty. About 58% of teaching faculty are female.
Student Body. About 71% of students from in state; 98% Midwest, less than 1% foreign. An estimated 28% of students reported as Catholic, 25% Protestant, 47% other; 1% Black, 1% Hispanic, 1% Asian, 2% other minority.
Religious Orientation. St. Scholastica is a church-related institution, "open to, serves and counsels members of all faiths", attendance at Mass voluntary; 1 course in religious studies required of students.
Varsity Sports. Men (NCAA, NLCAA, UMCC, MCC Div. III): Baseball, Basketball, Cross Country, Golf, Ice Hockey, Soccer, Tennis. Women (NLCAA Div. III): Basketball, Cross Country, Golf, Soccer, Softball, Tennis, Volleyball.
Campus Life. Students reported involved in a variety of extracurricular activities, including volunteer programs, clubs and organizations, athletics. Outdoor recreation also available; skiing, hiking, mountain climbing, and biking reported popular.

About 31% of men, 46% of women live in coed dormitories or campus apartments; rest commute. Freshmen given preference in college housing if all students cannot be accommodated. Intervisitation in men's and women's dormitory rooms limited. There are no fraternities or sororities on campus.
Annual Costs. Tuition and fees, $11,280; room and board, $3,588; estimated $681 other, exclusive of travel. About 92% of students receive financial aid; average amount of assistance, $11,146. Assistance is typically divided 6% scholarship, 48% grant, 41% loan, 5% work. College reports 362 scholarships awarded on the basis of academic merit alone. *Meeting Costs:* College offers budget payment plans, installment plans.

St. Thomas Aquinas College

Sparkill, New York 19076 (914) 398-4000

An independent, co-educational institution, founded as a teacher training institution under the auspices of the Dominican Sisters of Sparkill.

Founded: 1952
Affiliation: Independent
UG Enrollment: 467 M, 650 W (full-time); 302 M, 513 W (part-time)
Total Enrollment: 2,090
Cost: < $10K
% Receiving Financial Aid: 75%
Admission: Non-selective
Application Deadline: Rolling

Admission. About 80% of applicants accepted, 45% of these actually enroll; 10% of freshmen graduate in top fifth of high school class, 35% in top two-fifths. *Required:* SAT (ACT acceptable), interview. Criteria considered in admissions, in order of importance: high school academic record, recommendations, standardized test scores, extracurricular activities; other factors considered: special talents. *Entrance programs:* early admission, mid-year admission. *Apply:* rolling admissions. *Transfers* welcome; 150 enrolled 1993–94.
Academic Environment. Student refers to the "close teacher/student relationship" as the "greatest advantage of the academic program". Degrees offered: associates, bachelors, masters. About 47% of students entering as freshmen graduate within four years, 75% eventually; 85% of freshmen return for sophomore year. *Special programs:* January Term, Program for College-Age Learning Disabled Students, HEOP, bilingual education, CLEP, independent study, study abroad, honors, 3–2 engineering, optional winter interim, 3-year degree, individualized majors. *Calendar:* 4–1–4, summer school.
Undergraduate degrees conferred (285). 38% were in Business and Management, 21% were in Education, 7% were in Communications, 6% were in Psychology, 6% were in Social Sciences, 4% were in Mathematics, 4% were in Visual and Performing Arts, 4% were in Protective Services, 3% were in Letters, remainder in 5 other fields.
Graduates Career Data. Advanced studies pursued by 35% of graduates. About 93% of 1992–93 graduates employed. Field typically hiring largest numbers of graduates include accounting, teaching.
Faculty. About 75% of faculty hold PhD or equivalent. About 41% of teaching faculty are female; 2% Black, 4% Hispanic, 2% other minority.
Student Body. About 65% of students from in state; almost all from Middle Atlantic.
Religious Orientation. St. Thomas Aquinas is an independent institution with a Catholic heritage; courses in religion may be selected as part of humanities requirements.

Varsity Sports. Men (NAIA): Baseball, Basketball, Cross Country, Golf, Tennis. Women (HVWAC/NAIA): Basketball, Cross Country, Golf, Soccer, Softball, Tennis, Volleyball.

Campus Life. The campus is located in a small suburban town about 20 miles from New York City's many offerings. Student reports "The area immediately around the school has a lot of history and beauty."

About 15% of students live in coed dormitories; rest live in off-campus housing or commute. Intervisitation in men's and women's dormitory rooms limited. There are no fraternities or sororities.

Annual Costs. Tuition and fees, $8,150; room and board, $5,400; estimated $1,000 other, exclusive of travel. About 75% of students receive financial aid.

University of St. Thomas

St. Paul, Minnesota 55105 **(612) 962-6150**

A church-related institution conducted by the Archdiocese of St. Paul–Minneapolis, the university is located on a suburban campus of 45 acres in a city of 310,000. St. Thomas participates in extensive cooperative programs with Twin Cities area colleges including cross-registration with the College of St. Catherine, Hamline, Macalester, and Augsburg. Most convenient major airport: Minneapolis/St. Paul.

Founded: 1885
Affiliation: Roman Catholic
UG Enrollment: 2,031 M, 2,075 W (full-time); 441 M, 541 W (part-time)
Total Enrollment: 10,245
Cost: $10K–$20K
% Receiving Financial Aid: 75%
Admission: Selective (+)
Application Deadline: Rolling

Admission is selective (+). About 88% of applicants accepted, 46% of these actually enroll; 46% of freshmen graduate in top fifth of high school class, 76% in top two-fifths. Average freshman scores: SAT, 457 M, 483 W verbal, 543 M, 527 W mathematical; 39% of freshmen score above 500 on verbal, 10% above 600; 67% score above 500 on mathematical, 25% above 600, 4% above 700; ACT, 23 M, 24 W composite. *Required:* SAT or ACT, essay. Criteria considered in admissions, in order of importance: high school academic record, standardized test scores, writing sample/essay, recommendations, extracurricular activities; other factors considered: special talents, alumni children, diverse student body, special circumstances. *Entrance programs:* advanced placement, deferred admission. *Apply* by no final date; rolling admissions. *Transfers* welcome; 354 enrolled 1993–94.

Academic Environment. Student body characterized as primarily concerned with vocational/professional goals. Students praise the accessible and "down-to-earth" faculty, and the "very structured" academic program, with its "well-defined majors" and "diverse yet applicable learning opportunities." Graduation requirements include 2 courses each in English, and philosophy, 1 each in history, fine arts, social sciences, and physical education, 3 courses in theology, 3 in foreign language (or high school equivalent), and 3 in natural sciences and mathematics including 1 lab science, 1 math, and 1 elective. Degrees offered: bachelors, masters, doctoral. *Majors offered* include usual arts and sciences, home economics, journalism, library science, nursing, physical education, quantitative methods, speech, theater. Average undergraduate class size: 45% under 20, 52% 20–40, 3% over 40.

About 46% of students entering as freshmen graduate within four years, 70% eventually; 81% of freshmen return for sophomore year. *Special programs:* CLEP, honors, independent study, study abroad, individualized majors, cross registration with Macalester, Augsburg, Hamline, and St. Catherine, 4–1 and 3–2 engineering programs. *Calendar:* 4–1–4, summer school.

Undergraduate degrees conferred (997). 51% were in Business and Management, 11% were in Social Sciences, 10% were in Communications, 5% were in Education, 4% were in Computer and Engineering Related Technology, 4% were in Psychology, 3% were in Letters, 3% were in Foreign Languages, remainder in 11 other fields.

Graduates Career Data. Advanced studies pursued by 19% of students within 1 year of graduation. Professional schools typically enrolling largest numbers of graduates include U. of Minnesota. About 96% of 1991–92 graduates employed. Employers typically hiring largest numbers of graduates include Carlson Companies, IDS Financial Services, 3-M, Big 6 accounting firms. Career Development Services include help preparing for interviews, on-campus interviewing. Alumni reported as active in both career guidance and job placement.

Faculty. About 62% of faculty hold PhD or equivalent. About 33% of teaching faculty are female; 5% minority.

Student Body. About 86% of students from Minnesota; 97% from Midwest, 1% foreign. An estimated 64% of students reported as Catholic, 21% Protestant, 1% Jewish, 5% unaffiliated, 9% other; 2% Black, 2% Hispanic, 3% Asian, 1% other minority.

Religious Orientation. College of St. Thomas is a church-related institution; 3 courses in theology required of all students; attendance at religious services voluntary.

Varsity Sports. Men (Div.III): Baseball, Basketball, Cross Country, Diving, Football, Golf, Ice Hockey, Soccer, Swimming, Tennis, Track, Wrestling. Women (Div.III): Basketball, Cross Country, Diving, Golf, Soccer, Softball, Swimming, Tennis, Track, Volleyball.

Campus Life. Campus is located in a residential area near the social, work, and internship opportunities of the Twin Cities. Student says campus is close to "shopping malls, movies and everything else that students do socially." Another student adds "There are many events and activities sponsored by the school. Intramural sports are a good release." Smoking restricted to a "very few smoking areas" on campus.

About 26% of men, 30% of women live in traditional dormitories; less than 1% live in off-campus college-related housing; rest commute. Freshmen given preference in college housing if all students cannot be accommodated. There are 2 fraternities and 3 sororities on campus which 2% each of men, women join; they provide no residence facilities. About 30% of resident students leave campus on weekends.

Annual Costs. Tuition and fees, $11,748; room and board, $4,037; estimated $1,300 other, exclusive of travel. About 75% of students receive financial aid; average amount of assistance, $10,287. Assistance is typically divided 47% scholarship/grant, 17% loan, 36% work. College reports 1,094 scholarships awarded on the basis of academic merit alone, 19 for special talents alone.

University of St. Thomas

Houston, Texas 77006-4696 **(713) 522-7911**

A church-related institution, founded by the Basilian Fathers, located in a city of 1,232,800. Most convenient major airport: William P. Hobby.

Founded: 1947
Affiliation: Roman Catholic
UG Enrollment: 339 M, 656 W (full-time); 161 M, 247 W (part-time)
Cost: < $10K
% Receiving Financial Aid: 75%
Admission: Selective
Application Deadline: April 1

Admission is selective. About 95% of applicants accepted, 58% of these actually enroll; 43% of freshmen graduate in top tenth of high school class, 54% in top quarter. Average freshman scores: SAT, 47% of freshman score above 500 on verbal, 11% above 600; 73% score above 500 on mathematical, 24% above 600, 2% above 700; ACT, 25 composite. *Required:* SAT or ACT; minimum high school GPA. Criteria considered in admissions, in order of importance: high school academic record, writing sample, standardized test scores, recommendations, extracurricular activities; other factors considered: special talents, diverse student body, religious affiliation/commitment. *Entrance programs:* early admission. *Apply:* rolling admissions; April 1 for priority. *Transfers* welcome; 240 enrolled 1993–94.

Academic Environment. Graduation requirements include 24 hours in philosophy/theology, 12 hours in English, 6–8 hours foreign language, 6 hours history/humanities, 6 hours social sciences, 8 hours lab sciences, and 3 hours math. *Degrees:* bachelors, masters, doctoral. Average undergraduate class size: 69% under 20, 29% 20–40, 2% over 40.

About 22% of students entering as freshmen graduate within four years, 50% eventually; 72% of freshmen return for sophomore year. Special program: study abroad, 3–2 engineering, cross registration with U.of Houston, TSU, Notre Dame, internships (mathematics, business administration), special event courses. *Calendar:* semester, summer school.

Undergraduate degrees conferred (206). 33% were in Business and Management, 9% were in Psychology, 8% were in Liberal/General Studies, 8% were in Social Sciences, 8% were in Communications, 7% were in Education, 5% were in Life Sciences, 5% were in Law, 4% were in Computer and Engineering Related Technology, 3% were in Visual and Performing Arts, 3% were in Mathematics, remainder in 5 other fields.

Student Body. About about 90% of students from in state. An estimated 57% of students reported as Catholic 26% Protestant, 2% Jewish, 6% unaffiliated; 6% Black, 17% Hispanic, 6% Asian, 8% other minority. Average age of undergraduate student: 25.

Religious Orientation. St. Thomas is a church-related institution; courses in theology and philosophy required as part of the core curriculum.

Faculty. About 75% of faculty hold PhD or equivalent. About 61% of undergraduate classes taught by tenured faculty. About 39% of teaching faculty are female.

Campus Life. About 6% of men, 10% of women live in co-ed dormitories; rest live in off-campus housing or commute. Intervisitation in men's and women's dormitory rooms allowed on weekends; sexes segregated by floor. There are no fraternities or sororities. About 32% of resident students leave campus on weekends.

Annual Costs. Tuition and fees, $8,046; room and board, $3,630; estimated $500 other, exclusive of travel. About 75% of students receive financial aid; average amount received, $7,350. Assistance is typically divided 41% scholarship/grant, 34% loan, 25% work. University reports some scholarships awarded on the basis of need. *Meeting Costs:* college offers installment plans, Parent PLUS Loans, alternate loan programs.

Saint Vincent College

Latrobe, Pennsylvania 15650 **(412) 537-4540**

A co-educational liberal arts college, sponsored by Benedictine monks, Saint Vincent is located in a community of 12,000, 35 miles east of Pittsburgh. Most convenient major airport: Pittsburgh with shuttle to Westmoreland County.

Founded: 1846
Affiliation: Roman Catholic
UG Enrollment: 533 M 502 W (full-time); 73 M, 109 W (part-time)
Cost: $10K–$20K
% Receiving Financial Aid: 80%
Admission: Selective
Application Deadline: May 1

Admission is selective. About 85% of applicants accepted, 47% of these actually enroll; 41% of freshmen graduate in top fifth of high school class, 69% in top two-fifths. Average freshman SAT scores, middle 50% range: 410–520 verbal, 430–560 mathematical. *Required:* SAT or ACT, minimum high school GPA. Criteria considered in admissions, in order of importance: high school academic record, standardized test scores, recommendations, writing sample, extracurricular activities; other factors considered: diverse student body. *Entrance programs:* early admission, midyear admission, deferred admission, advanced placement. About 1% of entering students from private schools, 31% from parochial schools. *Apply* by May 1; rolling admissions. *Transfers* welcome; 48 enrolled 1993–94.

Academic Environment. Academic exchange program with Seton Hill College. Graduation requirements include 9 credits each in history, philosophy, English, religious studies, 6 in foreign language, 12 in social sciences, 8 in natural sciences, and 3 in mathematics. Degrees offered: bachelors. *Majors offered* include usual arts and sciences, business administration, biochemistry, computing and information science, environmental science, environmental administration; additional majors through Seton Hill, including art, home economics, music, medical technology, social welfare, theater arts. Average undergraduate class size: 94% under 20, 6% 20–40.

About 65% of students entering as freshmen graduate eventually, 90% of freshmen return for sophomore year. *Special programs:* CLEP, internships, independent study, cooperative education, study abroad, undergraduate research, modified self-design interdisciplinary major, 3–2 engineering, cross registration with Seton Hill College. *Calendar:* semester, summer school.

Undergraduate degrees conferred (228). 24% were in Business and Management, 13% were in Social Sciences, 12% were in Psychology, 9% were in Life Sciences, 9% were in Liberal/General Studies, 7% were in Letters, 6% were in Physical Sciences, 6% were in Mathematics, 5% were in Communications, 4% were in Computer and Engineering Related Technology, remainder in 7 other fields.

Graduates Career Data. Advanced studies pursued by 25% of graduates; 12% enter graduate school; 4% enter medical school; 3% enter dental school; 2% law school; 2% enter business school. Medical schools typically enrolling largest numbers of graduates include U. of Pittsburgh, West Virginia Medical College; dental schools include U. of Pittsburgh; law schools include Duquesne. About 72% of 1992–93 graduates employed. Corporations typically hiring largest numbers of graduates include Kennametal, Peat Marwick, Mellon Bank, Pittsburgh National Bank. Career Development Services include career counseling, job placement, on campus recruitment, job banks, career fairs, resume preparation, internships, cooperatives.

Faculty. About 65% of faculty hold PhD or equivalent. About 65% of undergraduate classes taught by tenured faculty. About 25% of teaching faculty are female.

Student Body. About 89% of students from in state; 5% Middle Atlantic, 1% each New England, Midwest, South, West, Northwest, foreign. An estimated 72% of students reported as Catholic, 19% Protestant, 1% Jewish, 1% unaffiliated, 7% other; 1% as Black, 1% Hispanic, 1% Asian, 1% other minority.

Religious Orientation. Saint Vincent is a church-related institution; 9 credits in religious studies required of all students.

Varsity Sports. Men (NAIA): Baseball, Basketball, Cross Country, Lacrosse, Soccer, Tennis. Women (NAIA): Basketball, Cross Country, Soccer, Softball, Volleyball.

Campus Life. College reports no recent changes in rules governing student conduct. Visitation hours until midnight weekdays, 2 am weekends. Drinking in public places on campus and public display of alcoholic beverages prohibited. About 75% of students live in coed dormitories; rest commute. There are no fraternities or sororities on campus. About 10–15% of students leave campus on weekends.

Annual Costs. Tuition and fees, $10,318; room and board, $3,766; estimated $500 other, exclusive of travel. About 80% of students receive financial aid; average amount of assistance $8,368. Assistance is typically divided 15% scholarship, 46% grant, 29% loan, 10% work. College reports 150 scholarships awarded on the basis of academic merit alone, 78 for special talents alone, 750 for need alone. *Meeting Costs:* college offers deferred payment plan.

Saint Xavier University

Chicago, Illinois 60655 **(312) 298-3050**

A church-related, co-educational, liberal arts university, founded by the Sisters of Mercy, located in a suburban setting at the southwestern edge of Chicago. Formerly known as Saint Xavier College. Most convenient major airports: Midway or O'Hare (Chicago).

Founded: 1847
Affiliation: Roman Catholic
UG Enrollment: 641 M, 1,755 W (full-time); 4,100 total graduates and undergraduates
Cost: $10K–$20K
% Receiving Financial Aid: 85%
Admission: Non-selective
Application Deadline: Rolling

Admission. Graduates of accredited high schools with 16 units eligible; 82% of applicants accepted, 58% of these actually enroll; 30% of freshmen graduate in top fifth of high school class, 61% in top two-fifths. Average freshman ACT scores: 20.1 composite. *Required:* ACT, minimum 2.5 high school GPA. Criteria considered in admissions, in order of importance: high school academic record, standardized test scores, recommendations, writing sample, extracurricular activities; other factors considered: special talents, alumni children, diverse student body. About 38% of entering students from private schools, 6% from parochial schools. *Apply* rolling admissions. *Transfers* welcome; 341 enrolled 1993–94.

Academic Environment. Graduation requirements include 57 semester hours of general education courses. Degrees offered: bachelors, masters. *Majors offered* include usual arts and sciences, business and administration, criminal justice, education, international business, international business, nursing, speech therapy, voice/theater, mass communications, criminal justice. About 69% of students entering as freshmen graduate eventually, 90% of freshmen do not return for sophomore year. *Special programs:* CLEP, independent study, January interterm, individualized majors, study abroad, 2–2 in engineering. Adult programs: Weekend College. *Calendar:* 4–1–4, summer school.

Undergraduate degrees conferred (379). 28% were in Business and Management, 18% were in Education, 18% were in Health Sciences, 5% were in Psychology, 4% were in Protective Services, 4% were in Social Sciences, 4% were in Letters, 4% were in Allied Health, 3% were in Visual and Performing Arts, 3% were in Life Sciences, remainder in 8 other fields.

Graduates Career Data. Advanced studies pursued by 14% of graduates, "most" enter law or business school. About 85% of 1992–93 graduates employed. Fields typically hiring largest numbers of graduates include accounting, education, nursing. Career Development Center offers resume writing, resume referral, interviewing and job search skills, job fairs, resource library, cooperative.

Faculty. About 66% of faculty hold PhD or equivalent. About 55% of undergraduate classes taught by tenured faculty. About 59% of teaching faculty are female; 3% Black, 1% Hispanic, 7% other minority.

Student Body. About 98% of students from Midwest. An estimated 80% of students reported as Catholic. Average age of undergraduate student: 26.

Religious Orientation. Saint Xavier is a church-related institution, but seeks students from diverse religious backgrounds; 2 courses in religious studies required of students.

Varsity Sports. Men (NAIA): Baseball, Basketball, Football, Soccer. Women (NAIA): Cross Country, Softball, Volleyball.

Campus Life. About 2% each of men, women live in traditional dormitories; rest commute. Intervisitation in men's and women's dormitory rooms limited; sexes segregated by floor. There are no fraternities or sororities on campus. About 5% of resident students leave campus on weekends.

Annual Costs. Tuition and fees, $10,230; room and board, $4,360; estimated $779 other, exclusive of travel. About 85% of students receive financial aid; average amount of assistance $6,000. Assistance is typically divided 60% grant, 40% loan. College reports 199 scholarships awarded on the basis of academic merit alone, 249 for special talents alone. *Meeting Costs:* college offers a number of payment plans.

Salem College

Winston-Salem, North Carolina 27108 (919) 721-2621

A small, liberal arts college for women, Salem was founded by the Moravians more than 200 years ago. Today its primary emphasis is on liberal studies. The 56-acre campus is located less than a mile from the center of Winston-Salem (pop. 145,000), in the heart of the Old Salem Restoration. Most convenient major airport: Piedmont-Triad (Greensboro).

Founded: 1772
Affiliation: Moravian
UG Enrollment: 11 M, 523 W (full-time); 23 M, 193 W (part-time)
Total Enrollment: 862
Cost: < $10K
% Receiving Financial Aid: 60%
Admission: Selective
Application Deadline: Aug. 1

Admission is selective. About 87% of applicants accepted, 46% of these actually enroll; 24% of freshmen graduate in top fifth of high school class, 43% in top two-fifths. Average freshman SAT scores: 498 verbal, 511 mathematical; 47% of freshmen score above 500 on verbal, 13% above 600, 3% above 700; 87% score above 500 on mathematical, 40% above 600, 8% above 700. *Required:* SAT or ACT, essay. Criteria considered in admissions, in order of importance: high school academic record, standardized test scores, recommendations, writing sample, extracurricular activities; other factors considered: special talents, diverse student body. *Entrance programs:* midyear admission, deferred admission, advanced placement. *Apply* by August 1; rolling admissions. *Transfers* welcome; 22 enrolled 1993–94.

Academic Environment. Curriculum allows student great flexibility in course selection. Cross registration with Wake Forest University and medical technology program with Bowman Gray School of Medicine and Forsyth Memorial Hospital. Graduation requirements include 2 courses each in social sciences, English, and history, 3 in foreign language, 1 each in math, natural science, fine arts, and philosophy/religion, in addition 1 course in a choice of math, computer science, or science; junior year internship also required. Degrees offered: bachelors, masters. *Majors offered* include usual arts and sciences, medical technology, music education, environmental design, arts management, economics and management, international relations, interior design, management, environmental design, physician assistants program. Average undergraduate class size: 98% under 20, 2% 20–40.

About 58% of students entering as freshmen graduate eventually, 70% of freshmen return for sophomore year. *Special programs:* independent study, undergraduate research, study abroad, January term, honors, Washington Semester, cross registration with Ware Forest, 3–2 in engineering, interdisciplinary programs, on-campus special education clinic, learning disabilities certification, internships. Adult programs: continuing studies and evening division for adults over 23. *Calendar:* 4–1–4.

Undergraduate degrees conferred (127). 22% were in Communications, 13% were in Business and Management, 12% were in Social Sciences, 10% were in Visual and Performing Arts, 9% were in Architecture and Environmental Design, 9% were in Letters, 6% were in Psychology, 5% were in Life Sciences, 4% were in Foreign Languages, 4% were in Area and Ethnic Studies, 3% were in Philosophy and Religion, remainder in 2 other fields.

Graduates Career Data. Advanced studies pursued by 17% of graduates. About 77% of 1992–93 graduates employed. Fields typically hiring largest numbers of graduates include education, sales, research. Career Development Services offer counseling, on-campus recruitment, resume development, job placement.

Faculty. About 73% of faculty hold PhD or equivalent. About 50% of undergraduate classes taught by tenured faculty. About 41% of teaching faculty are female; 1% Black.

Student Body. About 65% of students from in state; 96% South, 2% Middle Atlantic; 2% foreign. An estimated 90% of students reported as Protestant, 5% Catholic, 5% other; 6% Black, 1% Asian, 8% other minority. *Minority group students:* financial aid available.

Religious Orientation. Salem is a church-related institution; 1 course in philosophy and/or religion (or demonstrated proficiency) required of all students as part of distribution requirements.

Varsity Sports. Men: Basketball, Cross Country, Equestrian, Soccer, Swimming, Tennis, Volleyball.

Campus Life. College provides a variety of cultural and intellectual activities that are supplemented by resources of the North Carolina School of the Arts, Winston-Salem, just a mile from campus, and Wake Forest U. Self-determined hours for all students. Administration reports increasing interest in student government and sponsored dances. Visitation hours limited: noon-midnight (2 am weekends). Alcohol permitted on campus (must be 21); cars permitted for all students. Student leader reports that students appear satisfied with present social regulations. Traditional age students (under 23) expected to live in dormitories.

About 88% of women live in dormitories; rest commute. There are no sororities on campus. About 35% of students leave campus on weekends.

Annual Costs. Tuition and fees, $9,825; room and board, $6,025; estimated $800 other, exclusive of travel. About 60% of students receive financial aid; average amount of assistance, $7,233. Assistance is typically divided 26% scholarship, 25% grant, 36% loan, 15% work. College reports scholarships awarded on the basis of academic merit alone vary. *Meeting Costs:* college offers 9-month payment plan.

Salem College, West Virginia

(See Salem Teikyo University)

Salem State College

Salem, Massachusetts 01970 (508) 741-6200

A state-supported college, located in a community of 40,600. Most convenient major airport: Logan (Boston).

Founded: 1854
Affiliation: State
UG Enrollment: 2,350 M, 3,100 W (full-time); 108 M, 183 W (part-time)
Total Enrollment: 8,000
Cost: < $10K
% Receiving Financial Aid: 50%
Admission: Non-selective
Application Deadline: Rolling

Admission. About 67% of applicants accepted, 39% of these actually enroll. About 10% of freshmen graduate in top fifth of high school class, 28% in top two-fifths. Average freshman SAT scores, according to most recent data available: 400 M, 399 W verbal, 454 M, 426 W mathematical. *Required:* SAT; interview may be required. *Out-of-state* freshman applicants: college seeks students from out of state. State does not limit out-of-state enrollment, preference for dormitories to in-state students. No special requirements for out-of-state applicants. *Apply:* rolling admissions. *Transfers* welcome.
Academic Environment. Graduation requirements include 6 credit hours in English composition, 3 in speech communication, 2 in personal and community health, and 2 in physical education; in addition, students must complete distribution requirements of 36–38 credit hours in Humanities, Natural Sciences, Mathematics; BA candidates must complete 12 credit hours in a foreign language. *Degrees:* AB, BS, BFA, BGS, BSBA, BSBEd, BSEd, BSW, BSN. *Majors offered* include usual arts and sciences, business administration, computer science, earth science, education, geography, nursing, theater, public services, social welfare. About 43% of students entering as freshmen graduate eventually. *Special programs:* CLEP, study abroad, honors, cross registration with 10 other college through Northeast Consortium of Colleges and Universities in Massachusetts. *Calendar:* semester, summer school.
Undergraduate degrees conferred (1,215). 27% were in Business and Management, 20% were in Education, 11% were in Social Sciences, 8% were in Health Sciences, 6% were in Psychology, 5% were in Protective Services, 5% were in Business (Administrative Support), 4% were in Letters, 3% were in Visual and Performing Arts, remainder in 8 other fields.
Faculty. About 70% of faculty hold PhD or equivalent.
Student Body. About 85% of students from Massachusetts; almost all from New England. An estimated 15% of students reported as Protestant, 75% Catholic, 5% Jewish, 5% unaffiliated; 4% Black, 2% Hispanic, 1% Asian, 1% Native American, 1% other minority, according to most recent data available.
Varsity Sports. Men (Div.III): Baseball, Basketball, Cross Country, Golf, Ice Hockey, Sailing, Soccer, Tennis, Track. Women (Div.III): Basketball, Cross Country, Field Hockey, Gymnastics, Soccer, Softball, Swimming, Tennis, Track, Volleyball.
Campus Life. About 4% of men, 8% of women live in traditional dormitories; 3% of men, 4% of women live in coed dormitories; rest live in off-campus housing or commute. Freshmen given preference in college housing if all students cannot be accommodated. Intervisitation in men's and women's dormitory rooms limited. Sexes segregated in coed dormitory by floor. There are no fraternities or sororities on campus.
Annual Costs. Tuition and fees, $2,980 (out-of-state, $6,844); room and board, $4,000; estimated $900 other, exclusive of travel. About 50% of students receive financial aid; assistance is typically divided 55% scholarship, 26% loan, 19% work. College reports some scholarships awarded on the basis of academic merit alone. *Meeting Costs:* college offers AMS tuition payment plan, and Massachusetts Education Loan Program.

Salem Teikyo University

Salem, West Virginia 26426 (304) 782-5336

Salem is an independent institution which emphasizes studies in occupational/professional fields as well as liberal arts; campus is located in a village of 2,600, 15 miles west of Clarksburg. Formerly known as Salem College. Most convenient major airport: Benedum (Clarksburg, WV).

Founded: 1888
Affiliation: Independent
UG Enrollment: 735 M, W (full-time)
Cost: < $10K
Admission: Non-selective
Application Deadline: Rolling

Admission. Graduates of accredited high schools with 16 units (11 in academic subjects) and minimum GPA of 2.5 with minimum SAT combined of 850 or ACT composite of 17 eligible; 72% of applicants accepted, 24% of these actually enroll; 15% of freshmen graduate in top fifth of high school class, 40% in top two-fifths. *Required:* SAT or ACT; interview recommended. *Apply:* rolling admissions. *Transfers* welcome.
Academic Environment. *Degrees:* AB, BS. About 30% of general education requirements for graduation are elective; distribution requirements fairly numerous. About 32% of students entering as freshmen graduate eventually; 60% of freshmen return for sophomore year. *Majors offered* in addition to usual studies include youth and human services, equestrian education, aviation. *Calendar:* semester, summer school.
Undergraduate degrees conferred (72). 29% were in Business and Management, 13% were in Education, 10% were in Life Sciences, 10% were in Health Sciences, 8% were in Transportation and Material Moving, 7% were in Communications, 6% were in Public Affairs, 6% were in Computer and Engineering Related Technology, 4% were in Protective Services, 3% were in Engineering and Engineering Related Technology, remainder in 4 other fields.
Student Body. About 51% of students from in state.
Varsity Sports. Men (NAIA): Baseball, Basketball, Football. Women (NAIA): Basketball, Softball, Volleyball.
Campus Life. About 50% of students live in traditional dormitories; 14% live in coed dormitories; rest live in off-campus housing or commute. There are 5 fraternities, 4 sororities on campus which about 20–25% of men, 30% of women join. About 50% of students leave campus on weekends.
Annual Costs. Tuition and fees, $9,233; room and board, $3,952; estimated $500 other, exclusive of travel. About 85% of students receive financial aid; assistance is typically divided 46% scholarship, 39% loan, 15% work. College reports some scholarships awarded on the basis of academic merit alone. *Meeting Costs:* college offers tuition payment plan.

Salisbury State University

Salisbury, Maryland 21801 (301) 543-6165

A state-supported college, located in a metropolitan area of 50,000. Most convenient major airport: Salisbury.

Founded: 1925
Affiliation: State
UG Enrollment: 1,689 M, 2,130 W (full-time); 400 M, 621 W (part-time)
Total Enrollment: 5,447
Cost: < $10K
% Receiving Financial Aid: 55%
Admission: Non-selective
Application Deadline: Aug. 1

Admission. High school graduates with 16 units (10 in academic subjects) and C average eligible; 45% of applicants accepted, 42% of these actually enroll. Average freshman scores: SAT, 484 M, 482 W verbal, 560 M, 538 W mathematical. *Required:* SAT. *Out-of-state* freshman applicants: college welcomes students from out of state. No special requirements for out-of-state applicants. *Apply* by August 1. *Transfers* welcome.
Academic Environment. *Degrees:* BA, BS, BSW. About 75% of general education requirements for graduation are elective; distribution requirements fairly numerous. Most popular majors include accounting, business administration, communication arts, biology, math, psychology, education. About 65% of students entering as freshmen graduate eventually; 20% of freshmen do not return for sophomore year. *Special programs:* CLEP, independent study, study abroad, honors, undergraduate research, individualized majors. *Calendar:* semester, summer school.
Undergraduate degrees conferred (915). 22% were in Business and Management, 14% were in Education, 14% were in Liberal/General Studies, 10% were in Social Sciences, 10% were in Communications, 5% were in Health Sciences, 4% were in Psychology, 4% were in Public Affairs, 3% were in Visual and Performing Arts, 3% were in Life Sciences, 3% were in Physical Sciences, remainder in 6 other fields.
Student Body. About 79% of students from in state, 23 foreign students 1993–94.
Varsity Sports. Men (Div.III): Baseball, Basketball, Cross Country, Football, Lacrosse, Soccer, Tennis, Track & Field. Women (Div.III):

Basketball, Cross Country, Field Hockey, Lacrosse, Swimming, Tennis, Track & Field, Volleyball.
Campus Life. About 5% of men, 7% of women live in traditional dormitories; 10% of men, 11% of women in coed dormitories; rest live in off-campus housing or commute. Intervisitation in men's and women's dormitory rooms unlimited. Sexes segregated in coed dormitories by room. There are 4 fraternities, 3 sororities. About 40% of students leave campus on weekends.
Annual Costs. Tuition and fees, $3,026 (out-of-state, $5,694); room and board, $4,490. About 55% of students receive financial aid; average amount of assistance, $1,200. Assistance is typically divided 35% scholarship, 45% loan, 20% work. College reports some scholarships awarded on the basis of academic merit alone.

Salve Regina, The Newport College

(See Salve Regina University)

Salve Regina University

Newport, Rhode Island 02840 (401) 847-6650

A co-educational Catholic university, located in a residential section of a city of 29,259, 30 miles southeast of Providence. Most convenient major airports: Green (Warwick), or Logan (Boston).

Founded: 1934
Affiliation: Roman Catholic
UG Enrollment: 468 M, 935 W (full-time); 75 M, 211 W (part-time)
Total Enrollment: 2,263
Cost: $10K–$20K
% Receiving Financial Aid: 61%
Admission: Non-selective
Application Deadline: Rolling

Admission. About 89% of applicants accepted, 30% of these actually enroll. *Required:* SAT or ACT, essay. Criteria considered in admissions, in order of importance: high school academic record, recommendations, writing sample, extracurricular activities, standardized test scores; other factors considered: special talents, diverse student body. *Apply:* rolling admissions. *Transfers* welcome; 90 accepted 1993–94.
Academic Environment. Graduation requirements include 3 credits each in visual and performing arts, economics or geography, history or politics, math, social sciences, logic, and philosophy, 6 each in language, and natural sciences, 9 in religious studies. Degrees offered: associates, bachelors, masters, doctoral. *Majors offered* include arts and sciences, computer science, management, medical technology, nursing, administration of justice, special education, social work. Average undergraduate class size: 20% under 20, 80% 20–40.

About 70% of students entering as freshmen graduate within four years, 79% eventually; 78% return for sophomore year. *Special programs:* CLEP, study abroad. *Calendar:* semester and trimester.
Undergraduate degrees conferred (407). 22% were in Business and Management, 14% were in Education, 13% were in Health Sciences, 12% were in Protective Services, 8% were in Social Sciences, 7% were in Letters, 5% were in Psychology, 4% were in Visual and Performing Arts, 4% were in Life Sciences, 4% were in Computer and Engineering Related Technology, remainder in 6 other fields.
Graduates Career Data. Advanced studies pursued by 56% of graduates. About 60% of 1992–93 graduates employed. Career Development Services include career exploration, resume writing, credential files, individual counseling, recruitment programs, career library, work-study positions.
Faculty. About 80% of faculty hold PhD or equivalent. About 77% of undergraduate classes taught by tenured faculty. About 49% of teaching faculty are female; 1% Hispanic.
Student Body. About 15% of students from Rhode Island; 78% from New England, 19% Middle Atlantic. An estimated 5% of students reported as minority.
Religious Orientation. Salve Regina is a Catholic institution; 9 semester hours of religious studies required of all students.
Varsity Sports. Men (Div.III): Baseball, Basketball, Cross Country, Football, Golf, Ice Hockey, Soccer, Tennis, Track. Women (Div.III): Basketball, Cross Country, Golf, Field Hockey, Soccer, Softball, Tennis, Track.
Campus Life. No curfew; limited intervisitation. About 44% of men, 55% of women live in traditional dormitories; no coed dormitories; 56% of men, 45% of women commute. Freshmen given preference in college housing if all students cannot be accommodated. There are no fraternities or sororities. About 50% of students leave campus on weekends.
Annual Costs. Tuition and fees, $13,800; room and board, $6,300; estimated $800 other, exclusive of travel. About 61% of students receive financial aid; assistance is typically divided 43% scholarship, 45% loan, 12% work. College reports some scholarships awarded on the basis of academic merit alone. *Meeting Costs:* college offers variety of loan programs.

Sam Houston State University

Huntsville, Texas 77341 (409) 294-1056

A state-supported college, located in a town of 28,000, 70 miles north of Houston. Most convenient major airport: Houston Intercontinental.

Founded: 1879
Affiliation: State
UG Enrollment: 4,423 M, 4,938 W (full-time); 975 M, 914 W (part-time)
Total Enrollment: 12,800
Cost: < $10K
% Receiving Financial Aid: 30%
Admission: Non-selective
Application Deadline: Rolling

Admission. Graduates of accredited high schools with minimum SAT combined score of 800, or ACT composite score of 18, or who graduate in top half of class eligible. About 73% of applicants accepted, 35% of these actually enroll. Average freshman scores: according to most recent data available, SAT, 820 combined verbal, mathematical; ACT, 19.1 composite. *Required:* SAT or ACT. Criteria considered in admissions, in order of importance: high school academic record, standardized test scores. *Out-of-state* freshman applicants: university actively seeks students from out-of-state. State does not limit out-of-state enrollments. *Entrance programs:* early admission, advanced placement. *Apply:* no specific deadline. *Transfers* welcome; 1,466 enrolled 1993–94.
Academic Environment. Degrees offered: bachelors, masters, doctoral. About 12% of general education requirements for graduation are elective; distribution requirements fairly numerous. *Special programs:* CLEP, honors, SOAR (Summer Orientation and Registration), study abroad, independent study. *Calendar:* semester, summer school.
Undergraduate degrees conferred (1,854). 26% were in Education, 24% were in Business and Management, 13% were in Social Sciences, 9% were in Protective Services, 5% were in Visual and Performing Arts, 5% were in Communications, 4% were in Psychology, 3% were in Letters, 3% were in Agribusiness and Agricultural Production, remainder in 12 other fields.
Faculty. About 64% of faculty hold PhD or equivalent. About 34% of teaching faculty are female; 1% Black, 2% Hispanic, 2% other minority.
Student Body. About 98% of students from in state; 98% Midwest. An estimated 11% of students reported as Black, 7% Hispanic, 2% Asian.
Varsity Sports. Men (Div.I): Baseball, Basketball, Cross Country, Football, Golf, Tennis, Track. Women (Div.I): Baseball, Basketball, Cross Country, Softball, Tennis, Track, Volleyball.
Campus Life. About 90% of men, 90% of women live in traditional dormitories; rest live in off-campus housing or commute. Freshmen given preference in college housing if all students cannot be accommodated. Intervisitation in men's and women's dormitory rooms limited. There are 14 fraternities, 5 sororities on campus; they provide no residence facilities.
Annual Costs. Tuition and fees, $1,536 (out-of-state, $5,616); room and board, $2,970. About 30% of students receive financial aid. University reports some scholarships awarded on the basis of academic merit alone. *Meeting Costs:* university offers Texas Parent Loan Program, College Access Loan Program.

Samford University

Birmingham, Alabama 35229 **(205) 870-2901**

A church-related university, located in a city of 300,900. Most convenient major airport: Birmingham.

Founded: 1841
Affiliation: Southern Baptist
UG Enrollment: 1,375 M, 1,664 W (full-time); 141 M, 322 W (part-time)
Total Enrollment: 4,443
Cost: < $10K
% Receiving Financial Aid: 80%
Admission: Non-selective
Application Deadline: Ma. 30

Admission. Graduates of approved high schools with 16 units (12 in academic subjects) eligible; 79% of applicants accepted, 50% of these actually enroll; 59% of freshmen graduate in top fifth of high school class, 85% in top two-fifths. Average freshman scores, middle 50% range: SAT, 920–1120; 42% of freshman score above 500 on verbal, 13% above 600, 1% above 700; 57% score above 500 on mathematical, 19% above 600, 2% above 700; ACT, middle 50% range, 22–26 composite. *Required:* SAT or ACT, 3.0 minimum high school GPA, essay, two references; interview recommended. Criteria considered in admissions, in order of importance: high school academic record, standardized test scores, recommendations, extracurricular activities, writing sample. Entrance program: early admission, midyear admission. *Apply* by March 30. *Transfers* welcome.

Academic Environment. *Undergraduate studies* offered by Howard College of Arts and Sciences, schools of Business, Education, Music, Nursing, Pharmacy. Graduation requirements include 6 semester hours each in English composition, literature, religion, and history, 4 hours in natural sciences and mathematics, 4 in fine arts and computer literacy, and 4 in physical activity. Degrees offered: associates, bachelors, masters, doctoral. Average undergraduate class size: 45% under 20, 46% 20–40, 9% over 40.

About 75% of students entering as freshmen graduate eventually, 80% of freshmen return for sophomore year. *Special programs:* January interterm, cross registration with Binghamton Southern & U. of Alabama-Binghamton independent study, study abroad, honors, undergraduate research, internships, cooperative programs (3–2 in engineering, 3–2 in forestry. Adult programs: Metro College offers classes on 9 week term leading to Bachelors of General Studies, Bachelors of Business Administration, Bachelors in Paralegal Studies, Associate of Science in Divinity, and Paralegal. *Calendar:* 4–1–4, summer school.

Undergraduate degrees conferred (652). 21% were in Business and Management, 17% were in Health Sciences, 11% were in Education, 9% were in Social Sciences, 5% were in Public Affairs, 5% were in Psychology, 4% were in Law, 4% were in Visual and Performing Arts, 3% were in Theology, 3% were in Mathematics, 3% were in Communications, 3% were in Philosophy and Religion, remainder in 12 other fields.

Graduates Career Data. Advanced studies pursued by 25% of graduates. Medical schools typically enrolling largest numbers of graduates include U. of Alabama-Birmingham, U. of Southern Alabama; dental schools include U. of Alabama-Birmingham; law schools include Samford, U. of Tennessee, Harvard; business schools include U. of Alabama-Birmingham, U.of Alabama-Tuscaloosa. About 43% of 1992–93 graduates employed. Fields typically hiring largest numbers of graduates include business, education, government. Career Development Services include career planning, resource center, job listings, resume referrals, presentation on various topics, resume critiquing, career interview days.

Faculty. About 75% of faculty hold PhD or equivalent. About 30% of undergraduate classes taught by tenured faculty. About 27% of teaching faculty are female.

Student Body. About 50% of students from in state; 77% South, 15% Middle Atlantic, 3% Northwest, 2% Midwest, 2% West, less than 1% foreign. An estimated 82% of students reported as Protestant, 3% Catholic, 4% unaffiliated; 7% Black, 1% other minority.

Religious Orientation. Samford is a church-related institution; 60% of students affiliated with the church; 6 hours of religion, attendance at weekly convocation required of all students.

Varsity Sports. Men (Div.I): Baseball, Basketball, Cross Country, Football(IAA), Golf, Tennis, Track. Women (Div.I): Cross Country, Golf, Softball, Tennis, Track, Volleyball.

Campus Life. About 56% of each men, women live in traditional dormitories; rest commute. Freshmen given preference in college housing if all students cannot be accommodated. No intervisitation in men's or women's dormitory rooms. There are 4 fraternities, 5 sororities on campus which about 30% of men, 30% of women join. About 50% of resident students leave campus on weekends.

Annual Costs. Tuition and fees, $7,770; room and board, $3,573; estimated $2,174 other, exclusive of travel. About 80% of students receive financial aid, average amount of assistance $8,438. Assistance is typically divided 45% scholarship, 10% grant, 43% loan, 2% work. University reports 100 scholarships awarded on the basis of academic merit alone, 273 for special talents alone, 316 for need alone.

Samuel Merritt College of Nursing

Oakland, California 94609

Samuel Merritt College in Oakland and Saint Mary's College in nearby Moraga offer a joint degree in nursing. The four-year program offers preparation for RN licensure and leads to the BSN degree. Entry options are designed for high school graduates, transfer students, college graduates, licensed vocational nurses and registered nurses interested in a bachelor's degree. Accelerated options include: FasTrack for RNs and college graduates.

San Diego State University

(See California State University)

University of San Diego

San Diego, California 92110-2492 **(619) 260-4600**

The University of San Diego is an independent, Catholic university. It includes the College of Arts and Sciences, and Schools of Business Administration, Education, Nursing and Law. The institution is situated on a 175-acre campus in a city of 900,000. Most convenient major airport: Lindbergh Field.

Founded: 1949
Affiliation: Independent (Roman Catholic)
UG Enrollment: 1,601 M, 2,097 W (full-time); 94 M, 123 W (part-time)
Total Enrollment: 6,202
Cost: $10K–$20K
% Receiving Financial Aid: 60%
Admission: Selective
Application Deadline: January 15

Admission is selective. About 71% of applicants accepted, 32% of these actually enroll; 53% of freshmen graduate in top fifth of high school class, 81% in top two-fifths. Average freshman SAT scores: 490 verbal, 548 mathematical; 44% of freshmen score above 500 on verbal, 13% above 600, 1% above 700; 70% score above 500 on mathematical, 26% above 600, 3% above 700. *Required:* SAT, essay, academic recommendation. Criteria considered in admissions, in order of importance: high school academic record, standardized test scores, recommendations, writing sample, extracurricular activities; other factors considered: special talents, diverse student body. *Entrance programs:* early admission, midyear admission. About 10% of entering students from private schools, 28% from parochial schools. *Apply* by January 15. *Transfers* welcome; 300 enrolled 1993–94.

Academic Environment. Graduation requirements: 40–50% of courses required for graduation are general education requirements; distribution requirements fairly numerous. Degrees offered: bachelors, masters, doctoral. *Majors offered* include usual arts and sciences, accounting, business administration, computer science, marine sciences, ocean studies, communication studies, electrical engineering, Hispanic studies, gender studies.

About 67% of students entering as freshmen graduate eventually, 84% of freshmen return for sophomore year. *Special programs:* CLEP, honors, independent study, study abroad, undergraduate research, optional January interterm, internships. *Calendar:* 4–1–4, summer school.

Undergraduate degrees conferred (614). 44% were in Business and Management, 20% were in Social Sciences, 6% were in Psychology, 6% were in Liberal/General Studies, 5% were in Letters, 4% were in Health Sciences, 4% were in Life Sciences, 3% were in Philosophy and Religion, remainder in 5 other fields.
Graduates Career Data. Advanced studies pursued by 40% of graduates. About 75% of 1992–93 graduates employed. Fields typically hiring largest numbers of graduates include business, education, social services, health services. Career Development Services include assessment of personal interests, values and skills, resume preparation, interviewing and job strategy workshops, on-campus recruitment, career days, employer information sessions.
Faculty. About 94% of faculty hold PhD or equivalent. About 60% of undergraduate classes taught by tenured faculty. About 38% of teaching faculty are female; 2% Black, 4% Hispanic, 8% other minority.
Student Body. About 70% of students from in state; 15% West, 5% Midwest, 4% New England, 2% South, 3% foreign. An estimated 65% of students reported as Catholic, 17% Protestant, 1% Jewish, 5% unaffiliated, 9% other; 2% Black, 14% Hispanic, 10% Asian, 5% other minority. *Minority group students:* special tutorial assistance through the Educational Opportunity Program.
Religious Orientation. San Diego is an independent, Catholic institution; 9 hours of religious studies required of all students; students may select any course in department.
Varsity Sports. Men (Div.I): Basketball, Cross Country, Football(III), Golf, Soccer, Tennis. Women (Div.I): Basketball, Cross Country, Swimming, Tennis, Volleyball.
Campus Life. Student representatives sit on many administrative committees. Majority of students live off campus or commute; students living on campus housed in separate residential areas. Intervisitation limited. Cars allowed. Smoking prohibited in public areas. Alcohol consumption restricted by legal age (21) and limited to certain residence areas, no parties are allowed.

About 39% of men, 44% of women live in traditional and coed dormitories; rest commute. There are 4 fraternities, 4 sororities on campus which about 20% of men, 20% of women join; they provide no residence facilities.
Annual Costs. Tuition and fees, $12,990; room and board, $6,400; estimated $2,160 other, exclusive of travel. About 60% of students receive financial aid; average amount of assistance, $13,000. Assistance is typically divided 22% scholarship, 27% grant, 34% loan, 17% work. University reports 327 scholarships awarded on the basis of academic merit alone, 116 for special talents alone, 417 for need alone. *Meeting Costs:* university offers monthly installment plan and discounts for prepayment.

San Francisco Art Institute

San Francisco, California 94133

An independent, professional institution that offers training in film making, painting, photography, printmaking, sculpture/ceramics, performance and video, supplemented by a humanities program, and grants the BFA and MFA degrees.

Founded: 1874 **Affiliation:** Independent

Undergraduate degrees conferred (105). 100% were in Visual and Performing Arts.

San Francisco Conservatory of Music

San Francisco, California 94122

An independent, professional institution, the conservatory offers the BM and MM in all orchestral instruments, keyboard instruments, classical guitar, voice, composition, and conducting. A major in Chamber Music is available on the MM level.

Founded: 1917 **Affiliation:** Independent

Undergraduate degrees conferred (29). 100% were in Visual and Performing Arts.

San Francisco State University

(See California State University)

University of San Francisco

San Francisco, California 94118 **(415) 666-6563**

A private, Catholic institution, founded by Jesuits, the University of San Francisco is located near Golden Gate Park on a hill overlooking the city. Most convenient major airport: San Francisco International.

Founded: 1855
Affiliation: Roman Catholic
UG Enrollment: 1,397 M, 1,394 W (full-time); 61 M, 98 W (part-time)
Total Enrollment: 6,253
Cost: $10K–$20K
% Receiving Financial Aid: 53%
Admission: Non-selective
Application Deadline: Rolling

Admission. Graduates of approved high schools with 17 units eligible; 75% of applicants accepted, 37% of these actually enroll; 33% of freshmen graduate in top fifth of high school class, 61% in top two-fifths. Average freshman scores, according to most recent data available: SAT, 28% of freshman score above 500 on verbal, 5% above 600; 50% score above 500 on mathematical, 19% above 600, 4% above 700; ACT, 23.8 M, 22.5 W composite. *Required:* SAT or ACT (for counseling and placement only). *Non-academic factors* considered in admissions: special talents, diverse student body, alumni children. About 10% of entering freshmen from private, 36% from parochial schools. *Entrance programs:* early admission, deferred admission, advanced placement. *Transfers* welcome.
Academic Environment. Administration reports 25% of courses required for graduation are elective; distribution requirements fairly numerous. *Undergraduate studies* offered by colleges of Arts and Sciences, Business Administration, School of Nursing and Education. *Majors offered* in addition to usual arts and sciences include computer engineering, hospitality management, electronic physics, mass media, psychological services, international business.

About 59% of students entering as freshmen graduate eventually. *Special programs:* Davies Forum, St. Ignatius Institute, study abroad, honors, undergraduate research, credit by examination, January interterm, combined arts/law program. Adult programs: College of Professional Studies requires 60 transferable units and work experience. *Calendar:* semester, intersession, summer school.
Undergraduate degrees conferred (1,069). 30% were in Multi/Interdisciplinary Studies, 20% were in Business and Management, 13% were in Computer and Engineering Related Technology, 9% were in Health Sciences, 7% were in Social Sciences, 4% were in Communications, 4% were in Letters, 3% were in Psychology, 3% were in Public Affairs, remainder in 12 other fields.
Graduates Career Data. According to most recent data available: full-time graduate or professional study pursued immediately after graduation by 60% of students; 7% enter law school; 5% enter business school. *Careers in business and industry* pursued by 82% of graduates.
Student Body. About 57% of students from California. An estimated 50% of students reported as Catholic, 17% Protestant, 1% Jewish, 11% unaffiliated, 20% other; 5% as Black, 7% Hispanic, 14% Asian, 15% other minority, according to most recent data available.
Religious Orientation. USF has a long standing association with the Jesuit order and is a Catholic university. Two religious studies courses required for graduation. Church attendance is not mandatory for any student.
Varsity Sports. Men (Div.I): Baseball, Basketball, Cross Country, Crew, Golf, Soccer, Rifle, Tennis. Women (Div.I): Basketball, Cross Country, Soccer, Rifle, Tennis, Volleyball.
Campus Life. Approximately 60% of undergraduate students live on campus; rest live in off-campus housing or commute. There are 2 fraternities, 2 sororities on campus which 5% of men, 5% of women join. About 25% of resident students leave campus on weekends.

Annual Costs. Tuition and fees, $12,578; room and board, $6,174. About 53% of students receive financial aid; assistance is typically divided 30% scholarship, 40% loan, 30% work. College reports some scholarships awarded on the basis of academic merit alone.

San Jose State University

(See California State University)

Santa Clara University

Santa Clara, California 95053 (408) 554-4700

An independent institution, founded by Jesuits, Santa Clara is located on a 103-acre campus in a city of 92,000, 45 miles south of San Francisco. The university's undergraduate divisions include College of Arts and Sciences, The Leavey School of Business Administration, and the School of Engineering. Most convenient major airport: San Jose International.

Founded: 1851
Affiliation: Independent (Roman Catholic)
UG Enrollment: 1,875 M, 2,016 W (full-time); 76 M, 52 W (part-time)
Total Enrollment: 7,678
Cost: $10K–$20K
% Receiving Financial Aid: 56%
Admission: Very Selective
Application Deadline: February 1

Admission is very selective. For all schools, 69% of applicants accepted, 32% of these actually enroll; 64% of freshmen graduate in top fifth of high school class, 86% in top two-fifths. Average freshman SAT scores: 47% of freshmen score above 500 on verbal, 11% above 600, 1% above 700; 84% score above 500 on mathematical, 42% above 600, 8% above 700. *Required:* SAT or ACT, essay, teacher or counselor recommendation. Criteria considered in admissions, in order of importance: high school academic record, standardized test scores, writing sample, recommendations, extracurricular activities, special talents; other factors considered: alumni children, diverse student body, religious commitment. About 7% of entering students from private schools, 37% from parochial schools. *Apply* by ; rolling admissions. *Transfers* welcome; 264 enrolled Fall 1993.

Academic Environment. University stresses development of moral as well as intellectual values in its educational programs. Graduation requirements include 3 courses each in English, Western culture, religious studies, 1 course in ethics; math, science, and foreign language also required. Degrees offered: bachelors, masters, doctoral. *Majors offered* in addition to usual studies include music performance, theater arts, engineering, physics, international business, dance, combined sciences, Real Estate Institute. Average undergraduate class size: 56% under 20, 31% 20–40, 13% over 40.

About 75% of students entering as freshmen graduate within four years, 80% eventually, 91% of freshmen return for sophomore year. *Special programs:* study abroad, honors, undergraduate research conferences, internships, interdisciplinary programs, independent study, engineering cooperatives, University Institutes, Retail Management, international business studies, ethnic studies program, women's studies. *Library:* U.S and California government documents, rare book collection, special California Fiction Collection. *Calendar:* quarter, summer sessions.

Undergraduate degrees conferred (915). 29% were in Business and Management, 18% were in Social Sciences, 14% were in Engineering, 8% were in Letters, 6% were in Communications, 5% were in Psychology, 4% were in Life Sciences, 3% were in Physical Sciences, 3% were in Visual and Performing Arts, 3% were in Foreign Languages, remainder in 4 other fields.

Graduates Career Data. Advanced studies pursued by 25% of graduates; 9% enter graduate school; 2% medical school, 1% enter dental school, 4% enter law school; 3% business school. Fields typically hiring largest numbers of graduates include engineering, accounting, banking, retail. Career Development Services include career planning services, on-campus recruitment, resume and interview workshops.

Faculty. About 91% of faculty hold PhD or equivalent. About 61% of undergraduate classes taught by tenured faculty. About 29% of teaching faculty are female; 2% Black, 4% Hispanic, 14% other minority.

Student Body. About 66% of students from in state; 79% West, 11% Northwest, 4% Midwest, 1% Middle Atlantic, 4% foreign. An estimated 55% of students reported as Catholic, 14% Protestant, 1% Jewish, 25% unaffiliated, 5% other; 3% as Black, 13% Hispanic, 16% Asian, 9% other minority. *Minority group students:* special university minority scholarship funds for California residents; special tutoring programs.

Religious Orientation. Santa Clara is an independent institution with a Roman Catholic orientation; 3 courses in religious studies required of all students.

Varsity Sports. Men (Div.I): Baseball, Basketball, Crew, Cross Country, Golf, Soccer, Tennis. Women (Div.I): Basketball, Crew, Cross Country, Golf, Soccer, Softball, Tennis, Volleyball.

Campus Life. Students have some voice in determining regulations governing campus life through participation in student government and committee system. High interest reported in community service, religious activities and intramural sports. Variety of cultural activities on campus supplemented by resources of San Francisco, 45 miles from campus. Cars permitted; students over 21 allowed to drink in their rooms. No curfews for students. Overnight guests of the opposite sex are not permitted in the residence halls.

About 50% of men, 52% of women live in coed dormitories; 48% of men, 46% of women live in off-campus housing or commute. Sexes segregated in coed dormitories either by wing or floor. There are 4 fraternities, 3 sororities which about 16% of men and 17% of women join; 2% of men, 2% of women live in fraternities and sororities.

Annual Costs. Tuition and fees, $12,879; room and board, $5,904; estimated $1,962 other, exclusive of travel. About 56% of students receive financial aid; average amount of assistance, $13,349. Assistance is typically divided 66% scholarship/grant, 23% loan, 11% work. University reports 7 scholarships awarded on the basis of academic merit alone, 20 for special talents alone. *Meeting Costs:* university offers 12-month budget plan, guaranteed tuition plan for prepayment up to four years; if three children from the same family attend simultaneously as undergraduates, the student furthest along with his/her studies attends tuition-free.

College of Santa Fe

Santa Fe, New Mexico 87501 (505) 473-6011

A church-related college, conducted by the Brothers of the Christian Schools, located in a city of 50,000. Most convenient major airport: Albuquerque.

Founded: 1874
Affiliation: Roman Catholic
UG Enrollment: 784 M, W(full-time)
Total Enrollment: 1,500
Cost: < $10K
% Receiving Financial Aid: 85%
Admission: Non-selective
Application Deadline: March 1

Admission. Graduates of approved high schools with 20 units and GPA of 2.0 or better eligible; 82% of applicants accepted, 43% of these actually enroll. Average freshman scores: SAT, 57% of freshmen score above 500 on verbal, 13% above 600, 2% above 700; 35% score above 500 on mathematical, 13% above 600, 1% above 700; ACT, 21 composite. *Required:* SAT or ACT (for students less than two years out of high school). Criteria considered in admissions, in order of importance: high school academic record, standardized test scores, writing samples, extracurricular activities, recommendations; other factors considered: special talents, alumni children, diverse student body, auditions and portfolio review for theater and visual art students respectively. *Entrance programs:* early admission, midyear admission, deferred admission, advanced placement. *Apply* by March 1; rolling admissions. *Transfers* welcome; 117 enrolled 1993–94.

Academic Environment. Graduation requirements include 45 credits in a combination of courses including humanities, physical science, communication, social sciences, physical education and health education. *Degrees:* associates, bachelors, masters. *Majors offered* include contemporary music, moving image arts, arts and entertainment management, environmental science. Average undergraduate class size: 40% under 20, 40% 20–40, 20% over 40.

About 55% of students entering as freshmen graduate within four years, 70% eventually; 62% of freshmen return for sophomore year. *Special programs:* CLEP, independent study, study abroad, internships, cross registration with Institute of American Indian Arts, semester in New York for performing arts and art students. Adult programs: The Graduate and External Programs offer weekend and evening courses at an accelerated pace as well as credit for life experience. *Calendar:* semester, summer school.

Undergraduate degrees conferred (173). 42% were in Business and Management, 21% were in Education, 12% were in Visual and Performing Arts, 10% were in Psychology, 3% were in Communications, 3% were in Multi/Interdisciplinary Studies, remainder in 8 other fields.

Graduates Career Data. Advanced studies pursued by 20% of graduates. About 98% of 1992–93 graduates employed. Career Development Services include aptitude testing, counseling, placement service, resume/interview workshops, on-campus recruitment, internships and library resources.

Faculty. About 75% of faculty hold PhD or equivalent. About 41% of undergraduate classes taught by tenured faculty. About 18% of teaching faculty are female.

Student Body. About 26% of students from in state; 49% West, 9% New England, 8% Northwest, 3% Midwest, 2% each Middle Atlantic, South, 1% foreign. An estimated 59% of students are Catholic, 5% Protestant, 2% Jewish, 30% unaffiliated, 4% other; 3% Black, 27% Hispanic, 2% Asian, 4% other minority. Average age of undergraduate student: 27.

Religious Orientation. Santa Fe is a church-related institution; 6 hours of theology required of all Catholic students; attendance at Mass voluntary.

Campus Life. About 49% each men, women live in coed dormitories; commute. Freshmen given preference in college housing if all students cannot be accommodated. Intervisitation in men's and women's dormitory rooms limited. There are no fraternities or sororities on campus. About 30% of resident students leave campus on weekends.

Annual Costs. Tuition and fees, $9,560; room and board, $4,108; estimated $3,000 other, exclusive of travel. About 85% of students receive financial aid; average amount of assistance, $7,650. Assistance is typically divided 10% scholarship, 10% grant, 23% loan, 26% work. *Meeting Costs:* college offers monthly payment plans.

Sarah Lawrence College

Bronxville, New York 10708 (914) 395-2510

For many years Sarah Lawrence has been one of the more distinctive liberal arts colleges with strong programs in the performing, creative, and visual arts, combined with a liberal education that includes offerings in the humanities, natural sciences, and the social sciences. The 35-acre campus is located in a wealthy New York suburb (pop. 6,700), 15 miles north of Manhattan. An extensive building program added additional library facilities, a Performing Arts Center, Rothschild Science Center, Early Childhood Center, and Center for Continuing Education. Most convenient major airport: LaGuardia or JFK.

Founded: 1926
Affiliation: Independent
UG Enrollment: 233 M, 699 W (full-time)
Total Enrollment: 1,242
Cost: $10K–$20K
% Receiving Financial Aid: 50%
Admission: Very Selective
Application Deadline: February 1

Admission is very selective. About 55% of applicants accepted, 34% of these actually enroll; 71% of freshmen graduate in top fifth of high school class, 89% in top two-fifths. Average freshman SAT scores: 590 verbal, 560 mathematical; 81% of freshmen score above 500 on verbal, 45% above 600, 7% above 700; 72% score above 500 on mathematical, 31% above 600, 4% above 700. *Required:* SAT or ACT or 3 ACH; interview strongly recommended, essay. Criteria considered in admissions, in order of importance: high school academic record, writing sample, recommendations, extracurricular activities, standardized test scores, special talents; other factors considered: alumni children, diverse student body. *Entrance programs:* early decision, early admission, midyear admission, advanced placement, deferred admission. About 30% of entering students from private schools, 10% from parochial schools. *Apply* by February 1. *Transfers* welcome; 59 enrolled 1993–94.

Academic Environment. Graduation requirements: all courses required for graduation are elective; first year studies include courses in 3 out of 4 academic areas. Students required to take 3 courses per year in combination with self-designed independent study planned with faculty in each course. Students meet biweekly in individual conference with their teachers; reports are in the form of written evaluations; grades used for purposes of transfer and application to graduate school. Student asserts "For a *motivated* and *focused* student I think the academic program is ideal." Faculty reported to be "incredibly" accessible outside the classroom. Strongest academic programs reported to be in theater, dance, women's studies, history, philosophy, religion; a current student reports film to be "weak". Degrees offered: bachelors, masters. *Majors offered* include science and society, public policy, American studies. Formal majors are not required, students may concentrate in any available field, or design their own concentration. Average undergraduate class size: 11.

About 80% of students entering as freshmen graduate eventually, 96% of freshmen return for sophomore year. *Special programs:* independent study, undergraduate research, study abroad, internships. Adult programs: Center for Continuing Education. *Calendar:* semester, summer school.

Undergraduate degrees conferred (247). 100% were in Liberal/General Studies.

Graduate Career Data. Advanced studies pursued by 70% of graduates; 7% enter medical school; 1% enter dental school; 14% enter law school. Professional schools typically enrolling largest numbers of graduates include NYU, Columbia, Berkeley. Career Development Services offer an "excellent" array of services, according to administration source.

Faculty. About 95% of faculty hold PhD or equivalent.

Student Body. About 23% of students from in state; 40% Middle Atlantic, 17% New England, 14% West, 11% South, 9% Midwest, 5% Northwest, 4% foreign. An estimated 6% of students reported as Black, 5% Hispanic, 5% Asian, 1% other minority. *Minority group students:* Minority Students Association.

Campus Life. Few rules governing campus social life—student body is self-governing. College provides wide range of lectures, concerts, exhibitions, and other presentations at its own performing arts center; much of the diverse talent available in New York City—and readily accessible there—is brought to the campus. Some student activities, though perhaps fewer than at colleges where regular attendance at professional plays and concerts and visits to major museums are not possible. Students free to select most congenial living arrangements from choice of cooperative houses, coed dormitories, apartments. No varsity sports. Some interest in intramurals, most popular coed soccer, women's volleyball.

About 90% of students live in coed dormitories; rest in off-campus housing or commute. Freshmen guaranteed college housing. Sexes segregated in coed dormitories either by wing or floor. There are no fraternities or sororities on campus. About 15% of resident students leave campus on weekends.

Annual Costs. Tuition and fees, $18,210; room and board, $6,515; estimated $1,200 other, exclusive of travel. About 50% of students receive financial aid; average amount of assistance, $16,400. College reports scholarships awarded only on the basis of need. *Meeting Costs:* college offers variety of loan programs.

Savannah College of Art and Design

Savannah, Georgia 31401

A widely respected school of art and design, Savannah offers BFA, MFA degrees in eight majors as well as a 5-year BArch. A fine arts degree program is combined with job training which includes internships, portfolio and resume preparation seminars, workshops with working artists, and an academic program stressing realistic problem solving.

Undergraduate degrees conferred (217). 79% were in Visual and Performing Arts, 21% were in Architecture and Environmental Design.

Savannah State College

Savannah, Georgia 31404 **(912) 356-2186**

A state-supported college, located in a city of 152,000; founded as a college for Negroes and still serving a predominantly Black student body. Most convenient major airport: Travis Field..

Founded: 1890
Affiliation: State
UG Enrollment: 1,217 M, 1,522 W (full-time); 196 M, 262 W (part-time)
Cost: < $10K
% Receiving Financial Aid: 62%
Admission: Non-selective
Application Deadline: September 1

Admission. Graduates of accredited high schools with 18 units (12 in academic subjects) and SAT combined score of 750 or above eligible. About 99% of applicants accepted, 46% of these actually enroll. Average freshman SAT scores: 332 M, 315 W verbal, 375 M, 350 W mathematical. *Required:* SAT or ACT, minimum high school GPA. Criteria considered in admissions, in order of importance: standardized test scores, high school academic record. *Out-of-state* freshman applicants: university actively seeks out-of-state students. State does not limit out-of-state enrollment. *Entrance programs:* early admission, midyear admission, advanced placement. *Apply* by September 1. *Transfers* welcome; 94 enrolled 1993–94.

Academic Environment. Graduation requirements include work in English, social sciences, mathematics, humanities, and physical education. Degrees offered: associates, bachelors. Average undergraduate class size: 30. About 40% of students entering as freshmen graduate eventually, 70% of freshmen return for sophomore year. *Special programs:* CLEP, honors, undergraduate research, study abroad, independent study. *Library:* extensive collection by and about Black Americans. *Calendar:* quarter, summer school.

Undergraduate degrees conferred (168). 43% were in Business and Management, 12% were in Engineering and Engineering Related Technology, 8% were in Protective Services, 7% were in Life Sciences, 7% were in Communications, 5% were in Public Affairs, 5% were in Mathematics, 4% were in Social Sciences, 3% were in Physical Sciences, remainder in 4 other fields.

Graduates Career Data. Career Development Services available.

Faculty. About 60% of faculty hold PhD or equivalent. About 60% of undergraduate classes taught by tenured faculty. About 33% of teaching faculty are female; 52% Black, 14% other minority.

Student Body. About 90% of students from in state. Average age of undergraduate student: 23.

Varsity Sports. Men (Div.II): Baseball, Basketball, Football, Track. Women (Div.II): Basketball, Cross Country, Tennis, Track, Volleyball.

Campus Life. About 45% of men, 45% of women live in traditional dormitories; commute. Freshmen given preference in college housing if all students cannot be accommodated. There are 6 fraternities, 4 sororities on campus.

Annual Costs. Tuition and fees, $1,742 (out-of-state, $4,505); room and board, $2,310; an estimated $1,225 other, exclusive of travel. About 62% of students receive financial aid.

Schreiner College

Kerrville, Texas 78028 **(800) 343-4919; (210) 846-5411**

A small, co-educational, church-related college, Schreiner offers degree programs in the arts and sciences and business and commerce. The 141-acre campus is located in a small community northeast of San Antonio. Most convenient major airport: San Antonio International.

Founded: 1923
Affiliation: Presbyterian
UG Enrollment: 255 M, 263 W (full-time)
Cost: < $10K
% Receiving Financial Aid: 71%
Admission: Non-selective
Application Deadline: July 15

Admission. Graduates of accredited high schools or holders of GED eligible; 77% of applicants accepted, 20% of these actually enroll; 31% of freshmen graduate in top fifth of high school class, 65% in top two-fifths. Average freshman scores: SAT, 410 verbal, 470 mathematical; ACT, 22 composite. *Required:* SAT or ACT, minimum high school, GPA. Criteria considered in admissions, in order of importance: high school academic record, standardized test scores, extracurricular activities, recommendations, writing sample. *Entrance programs:* early admission, advanced placement. *Apply* by July 15; rolling admissions. *Transfers* welcome.

Academic Environment. Graduation requirements include 12 hours in English,, 3 in speech, 6 in history, 3 in political science, 4 in natural sciences, 3 in mathematics, 3 in computing, and 3 in fine arts. Senior thesis for all BA students. Students consider small classes, college's "interdisciplinary approach" and accessible faculty to be strengths of the academic program. Degrees offered: associates, bachelors. *Majors offered* include biochemistry, real estate. Average undergraduate class size: 60% under 20, 40% 20–40.

About 60% of entering students graduate eventually, 75% of freshmen return for sophomore year, according to most recent data available. *Special programs:* January interterm, honors, undergraduate research, study abroad, independent study, 3–2 program in engineering, internships, learning disability students. *Calendar:* semester.

Undergraduate degrees conferred (53). 40% were in Business and Management, 15% were in Mathematics, 13% were in Psychology, 11% were in Letters, 11% were in Education, 4% were in Visual and Performing Arts, 4% were in Social Sciences, remainder in Life Sciences.

Graduate Career Data. Advanced studies pursued by 20% of graduates; 15% enter graduate school; 2% enter law school. Law schools typically enrolling largest numbers of graduates include Baylor U., St. Mary's U. About 66% of 1992–93 graduates employed. Fields typically hiring largest numbers of graduates include banking and finance, insurance, public schools, sales. Career Development Services include individual career counseling, interest testing, resource library, computerized guidance, interviewing and resume writing workshops, job search and employment referrals.

Faculty. About 68% of faculty hold PhD or equivalent.

Student Body. About 87% of students from in state; 2% Midwest, 1% each New England, South, West, Northwest, 7% foreign. An estimated 4% of students are Black, 16% Hispanic, 1% Asian, 8% other minority.

Religious Orientation. College is a church-related institution; 12% of students affiliated with the church; no religious study required of students.

Varsity Sports. Men (NAIA): Baseball, Basketball, Cross Country, Soccer, Tennis. Women (NAIA): Basketball, Cross Country, Soccer, Tennis, Volleyball.

Campus Life. College is located in the hill country of Texas. Administration reports "ideal climate"; students generally agree and report some interest in outdoor activities, but say social life mostly limited to campus activities.

About 65% of each men, women live in traditional dormitories; rest commute. There is 1 fraternity and 1 sorority on campus, which about 4% of each join. About 40% of resident students leave campus on weekends.

Annual Costs. Tuition and fees, $9,000; room and board, $5,900; an estimated $1,300 other, exclusive of travel. About 71% of students receive financial aid; assistance is typically divided 60% scholarship, 30% loan, 10% work. *Meeting Costs:* college offers various payment plans.

University of Scranton

Scranton, Pennsylvania 18510 **(717) 941-7540**

A church-related institution, conducted by the Jesuits, the University of Scranton is located in a city of 80,000. Most convenient major airport: Wilkes Barre/Scranton International.

Founded: 1888
Affiliation: Roman Catholic
UG Enrollment: 1,720 M, 1,954 W (full-time); 223 M, 270 W (part-time)
Total Enrollment: 4,917
Cost: $10K–$20K
% Receiving Financial Aid: 80%
Admission: Selective (+)
Application Deadline: March 1

Admission is selective (+). About 60% of applicants accepted, 33% of these actually enroll; 48% of freshmen graduate in top fifth of high school class, 75% in top two-fifths. Average freshman SAT scores: 503 M, 514 W verbal, 568 M, 556 W mathematical; 56% of freshmen score above 500 on verbal, 12% above 600, 1% above 700; 86% score above 500 on mathematical, 30% above 600, 4% above 700. *Required:* SAT. Criteria considered in admissions, in order of importance: high school academic record, standardized test scores, recommendations, extracurricular activities; other factors considered: alumni children. *Entrance programs:* early decision, early admission, midyear admission, advanced placement, deferred admission. About 49% of entering students from private and parochial schools. *Apply* by March 1. *Transfers* welcome.

Academic Environment. Graduation requirements include course work in five areas: quantitative studies/natural sciences, behavioral and social sciences, communications, humanities and theology/philosophy. Degrees offered associates, bachelors, masters. *Majors offered* include usual arts and sciences, accounting, biophysics, biochemistry, communications, computer science, Eastern Christian studies, electronics, environmental science, fine arts, health administration, human services, information systems, international language/business, medical technology, management, occupational therapy, secondary education, nursing, physical therapy, pre-med, pre-law, psychobiology. Average undergraduate class size: 25.

About 75% of students entering as freshmen graduate within four years, 85% eventually, 92% of freshman return for sophomore year. *Special programs:* CLEP, independent study, study abroad, honors, 3-year degree, individualized majors, faculty/student research program, 5-year master's program in English, business, biochemistry, chemistry and physics, internships, 3–2 in engineering, exchange program with 27 other Jesuit schools. *Calendar:* 4–1–4, summer school.

Undergraduate degrees conferred (888). 33% were in Business and Management, 11% were in Social Sciences, 10% were in Life Sciences, 6% were in Health Sciences, 6% were in Communications, 5% were in Allied Health, 5% were in Letters, 4% were in Psychology, 4% were in Education, 3% were in Protective Services, 3% were in Liberal/General Studies, remainder in 8 other fields.

Graduates Career Data. Advance studies pursued by 25% of graduates; 6% enter medical school; 1% enter dental school; 5% enter law school; 2% enter business school. Medical schools typically enrolling largest numbers of graduates include Georgetown, Pittsburgh, Temple; dental schools include Temple; law schools include Boston College, Columbia, Harvard. About 69% of 1992–93 graduates employed. Fields typically hiring largest numbers of graduates include accounting, physical therapy, financial services, nursing. Career Development Services include job location service, resume assistance, interview practice, on-campus job fair, assistance with application to graduate and professional schools.

Faculty. About 78% of faculty hold PhD or equivalent. About 27% of teaching faculty are female.

Student Body. About 48% of students from in state; 90% Middle Atlantic, 5% New England, 2% Midwest, 1% each South, West, 1% foreign. An estimated 83% of students reported as Catholic, 10% Protestant, 7% other; 1% Black, 1% Hispanic, 2% Asian, 1% other minority. *Minority group students:* financial and academic help available.

Religious Orientation. Scranton is a church-related institution; 4 courses of theology/philosophy required of all students.

Varsity Sports. Men (Div.III): Baseball, Basketball, Cross Country, Golf, Ice Hockey, Lacrosse, Soccer, Swimming, Tennis, Wrestling. Women (Div.III): Basketball, Cross Country, Field Hockey, Soccer, Softball, Swimming, Tennis, Volleyball.

Campus Life. Students agree that the location of the campus is "Perfect! Trees and parks and a city, so you get a little bit of everything!" They report a "friendly atmosphere" and "numerous student government activities every night, such as dances, comedians, game shows, etc." Drinking permitted in dormitory rooms by those 21 and over; cars allowed for all, resident freshmen not allowed to park on campus. Visitation hours limited to midnight on class days, 2 am on weekends.

About 60% of each men, women live in traditional and coed dormitories; rest live in off-campus housing or commute. Freshmen given preference in college housing if all students cannot be accommodated. There are no fraternities or sororities on campus. About 25% of resident students leave campus on weekends.

Annual Costs. Tuition and fees, $11,615; room and board, $5,456; estimated $1,000 other, exclusive of travel. About 80% of students receive financial aid; average amount of assistance, $9,275. Assistance is typically divided 21% scholarship, 42% grant, 32% loan, 5% work. *Meeting Costs:* college offers private payment plans.

Scripps College

Claremont, California 91711 **(714) 621-8149**
(See also The Claremont Colleges)

Scripps is a women's college and part of the Claremont Colleges, which include Pomona, Claremont McKenna, Harvey Mudd, Pitzer and Claremont Graduate School. It offers the many opportunities of a women's college as well as the social and extracurricular advantages of a co-educational setting. Scripps is one of two women's colleges on the West Coast. Most convenient major airport: Ontario International.

Founded: 1926
Affiliation: Independent
UG Enrollment: 629 W (full-time)
Cost: $10K–$20K
% Receiving Financial Aid: 45%
Admission: Very Selective
Application Deadline: Feb. 1

Admission is very selective. About 67% of applicants accepted, 30% of these actually enroll; 75% of freshmen graduate in top fifth of high school class, 95% in top two-fifths. Average freshman scores, according to most recent data available: SAT, 564 verbal, 590 mathematical; 77% of freshman score above 500 on verbal, 38% above 600, 4% above 700; 90% score above 500 on mathematical, 48% above 600, 7% above 700; ACT, 26 composite. *Required:* SAT or ACT, essay, graded English paper; interview strongly recommended. *Non-academic factors* considered in admissions: diverse student body, special talents, alumni children. *Entrance programs:* early decision, early admission, midyear admission, advanced placement, deferred admission. About 27% of entering students from private schools, 5% from parochial schools. *Apply* by February 1. *Transfers* welcome.

Academic Environment. Humanities Core is central feature of the curriculum; interdisciplinary humanities courses focus on major periods in western civilization and humanistic themes. Administration reports 32 courses required for graduation; including interdisciplinary humanities courses, four general education requirements, proficiency in science, a foreign language, and a writing course. Cross-registration with the Claremont Colleges allows students to take up to 1/3 of their programs through the other colleges and includes off-campus majors. Pressures for academic achievement can be quite strong; environment of a women's college encourages and supports achievement. Students have significant voice in curriculum and related academic matters. Internships available include "Corporate Training for Liberal Arts Women" and "The Humanities Internship Program" and "Career Education Development." *Degree:* BA. *Majors offered* in the areas of language and literature, the arts, social studies, philosophy and religion, sciences; area programs also available as concentrations (including American studies, Asian studies, Black studies, women's studies, European history and culture, Latin American or Mexican American studies). Other major fields offered through cross-registration at other Claremont colleges.

About 75% of students entering as freshmen graduate within four years; 15% of freshmen do not return for sophomore year. *Special programs:* honors, independent study, study abroad, 3-year degree, combined degrees in business and engineering, individualized majors, Washington Semester, reading courses, study at Classical Center in Rome, year in Paris, exchange program with Cal Tech., 3–2 programs in engineering. *Calendar:* semester.

Undergraduate degrees conferred (148). 29% were in Social Sciences, 18% were in Visual and Performing Arts, 16% were in Letters, 8% were in Psychology, 7% were in Area and Ethnic Studies, 6% were in Life Sciences, 5% were in Multi/Interdisciplinary Studies, 4% were in Business and Management, 3% were in Foreign Languages, remainder in 4 other fields.

Graduates Career Data. According to most recent data available: full-time graduate study pursued immediately after graduation by 33% of students; 2% enter medical school; 4% enter law school; 2% enter business school. Career Development Services include preparation for interviews, on-campus interviewing.

Faculty. About 94% of faculty hold doctorate or equivalent.
Student Body. College seeks a national student body; 53% of students from in state; 74% West/Northwest, 3% New England, 4% South, 4% Middle Atlantic, 16% North Central. An estimated 3% of students reported as Black, 8% Hispanic, 11% Asian, 3% other minority, according to most recent data available. *Minority group students:* Black Student Affairs Center, Chicano Student Affairs Center, International Place for foreign students.
Varsity Sports. Women (SCIA): Basketball, Cross Country, Golf, Swimming & Diving, Tennis, Track, Volleyball.
Campus Life. Students have substantial voice in determining policies governing campus social life. Scripps campus described as an especially beautiful one. Variety of cultural, intellectual, and social activities provided by the Claremont colleges. Students determine visitation policies for each dorm; up to 24-hour visitation possible. Use of alcohol restricted to dormitory facilities and social functions on campus.

About 82% of women live in dormitories; rest live in off-campus housing or commute. Freshmen given preference in college housing if all students cannot be accommodated. There are no sororities.
Annual Costs. Tuition and fees, $16,536 room and board, $7,077. About 45% of students receive financial aid; assistance is typically divided 74% scholarship, 18% loan, 8% work. College reports some scholarships awarded on the basis of academic merit alone. *Meeting Costs:* college offers monthly payment plan, low-interest loans.

Seattle Pacific University

Seattle, Washington 98119 **(206) 281-2000; (800) 482-INFO**

An evangelical Christian university whose primary purpose is "to serve the educational, social and spiritual needs of its students." Seattle Pacific is located in a city of 493,846. Most convenient major airport: Seattle-Tacoma International.

Founded: 1891
Affiliation: Free Methodist
UG Enrollment: 653 M, 1,244 W (full-time); 158 M, 217 W (part-time)
Total Enrollment: 3,437
Cost: $10K–$20K
% Receiving Financial Aid: 65%
Admission: Selective
Application Deadline: Sept. 1

Admission is selective. About 86% of applicants accepted, 40% of these actually enroll; 38% of freshmen graduate in top tenth of high school class, 78% in top quarter. Average freshman SAT scores: 479 verbal, 522 mathematical; 38% of freshmen score above 500 on verbal, 8% score above 600, 1% above 700; 50% of freshmen score above 500 on mathematical, 21% above 600, 4% above 700. *Required:* SAT or ACT or Washington Pre-College Test, recommendation from minister, youth leader, teacher, or employer. Criteria considered in admissions, in order of importance: high school academic record, standardized test scores, recommendations, writing sample, extracurricular activities; other factors considered: special talents, alumni children, diverse student body, religious affiliation and/or commitment. *Entrance programs:* early decision. *Apply* by September 1. *Transfers* welcome; 301 enrolled 1993–1994.
Academic Environment. Administration source reports that strongest student interests on campus are religious and social service; supplemented by significant concern for scholarly/intellectual pursuits and "social interaction among peers." Graduation requirements include 15 credits in Christian heritage, 56 credits in general education, up to 15 credits of foreign language. Degrees offered: bachelors, masters, doctoral. *Majors offered* include usual arts and sciences, computer science, electrical engineering, engineering science, home economics, nursing. Average undergraduate class size: 79% 20–40.

About 28% of students entering as freshmen graduate within four years, 41% eventually, 72% of freshmen return for sophomore year. *Special programs:* CLEP, independent study, study abroad, honors, undergraduate research, individualized majors, combined program in medical technology, cross registration with Christian College Consortium, internship with Fashion Institute of Technology in NY and LA, Washington semester. *Calendar:* quarter, summer school.
Undergraduate degrees conferred (446). 16% were in Business and Management, 15% were in Education, 11% were in Health Sciences, 8% were in Social Sciences, 7% were in Computer and Engineering Related Technology, 6% were in Psychology, 6% were in Letters, 4% were in Life Sciences, 4% were in Communications, 4% were in Home Economics, 3% were in Engineering, 3% were in Visual and Performing Arts, 3% were in Parks and Recreation, remainder in 8 other fields.
Graduates Career Data. About 84% of 1992–93 graduates employed. Fields typically hiring largest numbers of graduates include education, business, nursing, computer science. Career Development Services include career training and placement, job search assistance, resource library, alumni connection program.
Faculty. About 74% of faculty hold PhD or equivalent. About 85% of undergraduate classes taught by tenured faculty. About 38% of teaching faculty are female; 1% Black, 1% Hispanic.
Student Body. About 64% of students from in state; 76% Northwest, 11% West, 2% Midwest, 1% each New England, Middle Atlantic, 8% foreign. An estimated 59% of students reported as Protestant, 6% Catholic, 34% unaffiliated; 1% as Black, 1% Hispanic, 5% Asian, 1% Native American, 6% other minority. *Minority group students:* special financial and social provisions.
Religious Orientation. Seattle Pacific is "thoroughly committed to evangelical Christian doctrine and standards of conduct"; 5% of students affiliated with the church; 15 credits in Biblical literature and attendance at assembly/chapel services 3 times weekly required of all students.
Varsity Sports. Men (NAIA, NCAA Div.II): Basketball, Crew, Cross Country, Soccer, Track. Women (Div.II): Basketball, Crew, Cross Country, Gymnastics, Track, Volleyball.
Campus Life. Student government gives input to faculty and administration in governance of the university and maintenance of institution policies. University prohibits use of tobacco or alcohol and bans social dancing on campus or at any university-sponsored activity. Rules for women's dorm hours enforced "leniently," those for intervisitation "judiciously." Freshmen and sophomores required to live on campus.

About 40% of men, 41% of women live in coed dormitories; 60% of men, 59% of women live in college-related housing or commute. Students under the age of 22 given preference in college housing if all students cannot be accommodated. Sexes separated in coed dormitories by wing. There are no fraternities or sororities on campus. About 80% of resident students leave campus on weekends.
Annual Costs. Tuition and fees, $11,979; room and board, $4,524; estimated $600 other, exclusive of travel. About 65% of students receive financial aid; average amount of assistance, $12,457. University reports 564 scholarships awarded on the basis of academic merit alone, 169 for special talents alone. *Meeting Costs:* university offers extended payment plan.

Seattle University

Seattle, Washington 98122 **(206) 296-5800**

A church-related university, conducted by the Jesuits, located in a city of 530,800. Most convenient major airport: Sea-Tac International.

Founded: 1891
Affiliation: Roman Catholic
UG Enrollment: 921 M, 1,149 W (full-time); 456 M, 553 W (part-time)
Total Enrollment: 4,765
Cost: $10K–$20K
% Receiving Financial Aid: 55%
Admission: Selective
Application Deadline: May 1

Admission is selective. About 75% of applicants accepted, 36% of these actually enroll. Average freshman SAT scores, according to most recent data available: 471 M, 462 W verbal, 545 M, 503 W mathematical. *Required:* SAT, ACT, or Washington Pre-College Test. *Apply:* rolling admissions; May 1 preferred. *Transfers* welcome.
Academic Environment. *Undergraduate studies* offered by College of Arts and Sciences, schools of Business, Education, Nursing, Science and Engineering. About 20% of general education requirements for graduation are elective; distribution requirements fairly numerous. *Majors offered* in addition to usual arts and sciences include computer science, cytotechnology, diagnostic ultrasound, drama, journalism, nuclear medical technology, police science and administration, public affairs, rehabilitation, environmental engineering, international business, biochemistry, and international business.

Special programs: CLEP, independent study, study abroad, honors, undergraduate research, combined BE/MBA program, cooperative work/study program in engineering, Summer School Opportunity Program for under prepared students. *Calendar:* quarter, summer school.

Undergraduate degrees conferred (775). 29% were in Business and Management, 14% were in Engineering, 8% were in Health Sciences, 6% were in Social Sciences, 6% were in Psychology, 5% were in Letters, 5% were in Communications, 5% were in Multi/Interdisciplinary Studies, 4% were in Education, 3% were in Protective Services, 3% were in Liberal/General Studies, remainder in 9 other fields.

Faculty. About 78% of faculty hold PhD or equivalent.

Student Body. University seeks a national student body; almost all undergraduate students from Washington. An estimated 36% of students reported as Catholic, according to most recent data available.

Religious Orientation. Seattle is a church-related institution; 10 hours of theology required of all students.

Varsity Sports. Men (NAIA): Basketball, Soccer, Tennis. Women (NAIA): Basketball, Soccer, Tennis.

Campus Life. About 16% of men, 16% of women live in coed dormitories; rest live in off-campus housing or commute. Freshmen given preference in college housing if all students cannot be accommodated. Intervisitation in men's and women's dormitory rooms limited; some coed floors, some all male floors, some all female floors. There are no fraternities or sororities.

Annual Costs. Tuition and fees, $12,150; room and board, $4,680. About 55% of students receive financial aid; assistance is typically divided 30% scholarship, 40% loan, 30% work. University reports some scholarships awarded on the basis of academic merit alone. *Meeting Costs:* university offers tuition payment plan.

Seton Hall University

South Orange, New Jersey 07079 (201) 761-9332

A church-related university, under the auspices of the Archdiocese of Newark, located on a 58-acre campus in a suburban community of 17,000, 14 miles from New York City. Most convenient major airport: Newark.

Founded: 1856
Affiliation: Roman Catholic
UG Enrollment: 2,174 M, 2,224 W (full-time); 365 M, 555 W (part-time)
Total Enrollment: 9,938
Cost: $10K–$20K
% Receiving Financial Aid: 74%
Admission: Non-selective
Application Deadline: March 1

Admission. Graduates of accredited high schools with 16 units in a college preparatory program eligible; 76% of applicants accepted, 28% of these actually enroll; 35% of freshmen graduate in top fifth of high school class, 60% in top two-fifths. Average freshman SAT scores: 454 M, 456 W verbal, 525 M, 496 W mathematical; 24% of freshmen score above 500 on verbal, 5% above 600, 1% above 700, 48% score above 500 on mathematical, 14% above 600, 1% above 700. *Required:* SAT or ACT. Criteria considered in admissions, in order of importance: high school academic record, standardized test scores, extracurricular activities, writing sample, recommendations; other factors considered: special talents, alumni children, diverse student body. *Entrance programs:* midyear admission, advanced placement. About 5% of entering students from private schools, 35% from parochial schools. *Apply* by March 1. *Transfers* welcome; 258 enrolled 1993–94.

Academic Environment. Graduation requirements include study in English, oral communication, mathematics, natural sciences, behavioral sciences, culture and civilization, foreign language, civilizations, ethics, religion, and philosophy. Students praise the freshman studies program as "a tremendous help for 'lost and unsure' freshmen." Off-campus internships for degree credit in accounting, communications, sociology, psychology, and Black studies. *Undergraduate studies* offered to freshmen in colleges of Arts and Sciences, Nursing, and schools of Business Administration, Education. Degrees offered: bachelors, masters, doctoral. *Majors offered* in arts and sciences in addition to usual studies include American studies, Asian studies and non-Western civilization, African-American studies, communications, computer science, criminal justice. Average undergraduate class size: 53% under 20, 41% 20–40, 6% over 40.

About 63% of students entering as freshmen graduate within six years, 86% of freshmen return for sophomore year. *Special programs:* CLEP, independent study, study abroad, cross registration with NJIT, Stevens Institute of Technology, honors, undergraduate research, Russian area studies, internships, 3–2 in engineering, combined BA/MBA at Seton Hall. Adult programs: University College of Continuing Education. *Calendar:* semester, summer school.

Undergraduate degrees conferred (929). 40% were in Business and Management, 13% were in Communications, 10% were in Social Sciences, 6% were in Education, 6% were in Health Sciences, 6% were in Psychology, 4% were in Protective Services, 4% were in Letters, 3% were in Life Sciences, remainder in 11 other fields.

Graduates Career Data. Advanced studies pursued by 20% of graduates. Medical schools typically enrolling largest numbers of graduates include U. of Medicine and Dentistry of New Jersey, Tufts; dental schools include Stonybrook; law schools include Seton Hall, NYU, George Mason; business schools include Rutgers, NYU, Harvard. About 33% of 1992–93 graduates employed at time of graduation. Corporations typically hiring largest numbers of graduates include Coopers & Lybrand, AT&T, Ciba Geigy, Prudential. Career Development Services include a comprehensive four-year program of career development, cooperative education, graduate information, employment recruiting and training.

Faculty. About 66% of faculty hold PhD or equivalent. About 32% of teaching faculty are female; 5% Black, 5% Hispanic, 6% other minority.

Student Body. About 84% of students from in state; 93% Middle Atlantic, 2% New England, 1% South, 1% foreign. *Minority group students:* state's Economic Opportunity Program; tuition aid grants; lower admissions standards; Black Student League, Puerto Rican Institute.

Religious Orientation. Seton Hall is a church-related institution; 1–2 courses in religious studies required as part of general college requirements.

Varsity Sports. Men (Div.I): Baseball, Basketball, Cross Country, Golf, Soccer, Swimming, Tennis, Track, Wrestling. Women (Div.I): Basketball, Cross Country, Soccer, Softball, Swimming, Tennis, Track, Volleyball.

Campus Life. Campus is located 14 miles from New York City, an hour from the Pocono Mountains, and an hour from the Jersey Shore; students agree "There is lots to do and choose from." Public transportation reported "excellent." Athletics, student clubs and organizations, and work-study jobs all keep students busy. Limited intervisitation determined by students and administration jointly.

About 30% of men, 40% of women live in coed dormitories; rest live in off-campus housing or commute. Freshmen given preference in college housing if all students cannot be accommodated. There are 12 fraternities, 10 sororities on campus which about 25% each of men, women join; they provide no residence facilities. About 30% of resident students leave campus on weekends.

Annual Costs. Tuition and fees, $12,052; room and board, $6,254; estimated $600 other, exclusive of travel. About 74% of students receive financial aid; average amount of assistance, $8,400. Assistance is typically divided 63% scholarship/grant, 30% loan, 7% work. University reports 400 scholarships awarded on the basis of academic merit alone, 200 for special talents alone.

Seton Hill College

Greensburg, Pennsylvania 15601 (412) 834-2200

A church-related, liberal arts college primarily for women, conducted by the Sisters of Charity, Seton Hill is located in a town of 15,900, 30 miles east of Pittsburgh. Most convenient major airport: Pittsburgh.

Founded: 1883
Affiliation: Independent (Roman Catholic)
UG Enrollment: 47 M, 705 W (full-time); 23 M, 187 W (part-time)
Cost: $10K–$20K
% Receiving Financial Aid: 94%
Admission: Non-selective
Application Deadline: August 1

Admission. High school graduates with 15 academic units eligible; 70% of applicants accepted, 25% of these actually enroll; 47% of freshmen graduate in top fifth of high school class, 72% in top two-fifths. Average freshman SAT scores, middle 50% range: 400–520 verbal, 400–530 mathematical. *Required:* SAT or ACT. Criteria considered in admissions, in order of importance: high school academic record, recommendations, standardized test scores, extracurricular activities, writing sample; other factors considered: special talents, alumni children, diverse student body, high school class rank, GPA. About 2% of entering students from private schools, 19% from parochial schools. *Apply* by August 1; rolling admissions. *Transfers* welcome; 47 enrolled 1993–94.

Academic Environment. Graduation requirements include 40 credits in 10 areas; freshman and senior seminars, self-awareness, math/science, foreign language, Western culture, American studies, world cultures, artistic expression, theology, and philosophy. Students may, on approval, design own liberal arts curriculum. Degrees offered: bachelors. *Majors offered* include usual arts and sciences, computer science, home economics, family studies, social welfare, entrepreneurial studies, art therapy, actuary science; additional majors available through Saint Vincent. Average undergraduate class size: 25% under 20, 74% 20–40, 1% over 40.

About 55% of students entering as freshmen graduate within four years, 58% eventually, 72% of freshmen return for sophomore year. *Special programs:* CLEP, independent study, honors, undergraduate research, individualized majors, study abroad, 3–2 in engineering, 3–2 in medical technology, 2–2 in nursing, internships, cross registration with Saint Vincent College and U. of Pittsburgh at Greensburg. Adult programs: evening degree, Saturday and evening classes. *Calendar:* semester, summer school.

Undergraduate degrees conferred (127). 20% were in Business and Management, 15% were in Visual and Performing Arts, 14% were in Psychology, 9% were in Home Economics, 9% were in Letters, 8% were in Communications, 6% were in Social Sciences, 4% were in Public Affairs, remainder in 9 other fields.

Graduates Career Data. Advanced studies pursued by 22% of graduates; 12% enter graduate school; 1% enter medical school; 4% enter law school, 5% enter business school. Medical schools typically enrolling largest numbers of graduates include U. of Pennsylvania; law schools include Duquesne, U. of Pittsburgh; business school include Carnegie-Mellon, U. of Pittsburgh. About 81% of 1992–93 graduates employed. Fields typically hiring largest numbers of graduates include communication/public relations, retail, education. Career Development Services include career counseling, resume writing, internship/cooperative services, job fairs, and search services in senior year.

Faculty. About 67% of faculty hold PhD or equivalent. All undergraduate classes taught by tenured faculty. About 62% of teaching faculty are female; 2% Black, 2% Hispanic, 8% other minority.

Student Body. About 80% of students from in state; 91% Middle Atlantic, 3% New England, 2% Midwest, 1% South, 1% West, 2% foreign. An estimated 6% of students reported as Black, 5% Hispanic, 3% Asian, 1% other minority. *Minority group students:* special financial, academic, and social provisions.

Religious Orientation. Seton Hill is Catholic in philosophy; 6 hours of religious studies required of all students. Students who are not of the Catholic faith are required to take religious studies, but not specifically Catholic studies.

Varsity Sports. Women (NAIA): Basketball, Cross Country, Equestrian (IHSA), Soccer, Softball, Tennis, Volleyball.

Campus Life. Students report that campus location tends to focus social life towards on-campus activities. They mention watching movies, talking, reading, swimming, studying, dances and other planned activities as popular. They also report a "friendly" and "personable" atmosphere. Drinking regulations: "students may neither store nor consume alcoholic beverages"; cars and motorbikes permitted, but must be registered with college.

About 40% of men, 75% of women live in traditional and coed dormitories; rest commute. Freshmen given preference in college housing if all students cannot be accommodated. There are no fraternities or sororities on campus.

Annual Costs. Tuition and fees, $10,340; room and board, $3,980; estimated $1,500 other, exclusive of travel. About 94% of students receive financial aid; average amount of assistance, $9,260. Assistance is typically divided 15% scholarship, 50% grant, 25% loan, 10% work. College reports 10 scholarships awarded on the basis of academic merit alone, 9 for special talents alone, 40 for need alone. *Meeting Costs:* college offers installment payment plan.

Shaw University

Raleigh, North Carolina 27611 (919) 755-4800

A church-related college, located in downtown Raleigh (pop. 200,000), Shaw was founded to train ministers, but is now a liberal arts institution. Student body is predominantly black, but faculty is both interracial and polycultural.

Founded: 1865
Affiliation: American Baptist
UG Enrollment: 2,071 (full-time)
Cost: < $10K
Admission: Non-selective
Application Deadline: August 10

Admission. High school graduates with 15 units eligible; 99% of applicants accepted, 54% of these actually enroll. *Required:* SAT or ACT; interview in special cases. *Apply* by August 10. *Transfers* welcome.

Academic Environment. *Degrees:* AB, BS. About 11% of general education requirements for graduation are elective; distribution requirements fairly numerous. About 30% of students entering as freshmen graduate eventually; 65% of freshmen return for sophomore year. *Special programs:* CLEP, Center for Alternative Programs of Education, independent study, cooperative program in engineering and technology with North Carolina State, cross-registration with cooperating Raleigh colleges. *Calendar:* semester, summer school.

Undergraduate degrees conferred (230). 50% were in Business and Management, 17% were in Social Sciences, 10% were in Protective Services, 7% were in Public Affairs, 4% were in Computer and Engineering Related Technology, 3% were in Life Sciences, 3% were in Education, remainder in 8 other fields.

Student Body. About 73% of students from South, 18% Middle Atlantic, 3% North Central.

Religious Orientation. Shaw is a church-related institution.

Campus Life. About 67% of men, 76% of women live in traditional dormitories; no coed dormitories; rest live in off-campus housing or commute. There are 4 fraternities, 4 sororities on campus which about 2% of men, 6% of women join; they provide no residence facilities.

Annual Costs. Tuition and fees, $5,362; room and board, $3,374.

Sheldon Jackson College

Sitka, Alaska 99835 (907) 747-5221

Founded as a church-related 2-year college, Sheldon Jackson is now accredited as a 4-year institution of liberal arts, conferring both associate and baccalaureate degrees. Most convenient major airports: Sitka, Anchorage, Seattle (WA).

Founded: 1944
Affiliation: Presbyterian
UG Enrollment: 308 (full-time)
Cost: < $10K
% Receiving Financial Aid: 92%
Admission: Non-selective
Application Deadline: August 15

Admission. High school graduates or equivalent eligible; all applicants accepted, 51% of these actually enroll. *Apply* by August 15; rolling admissions. *Transfers* welcome.

Academic Environment. *Degrees:* BA, BS. Programs offered include liberal arts, aquatic resources, hatchery operations, business management, natural resource management and development. *Special programs:* 3-week interim offers special interest courses and travel courses.

Undergraduate degrees conferred (36). 47% were in Renewable Natural Resources, 28% were in Education, 14% were in Liberal/General Studies, 11% were in Business and Management.

Varsity Sports. Men (NAIA): Basketball. Women (NAIA): Basketball.

Student Body. About 47% of students from Alaska; 78% from Northwest. An estimated 3% of students reported as Black, 32% Native American, 2% Hispanic, 2% other minority, according to most recent data available.

Annual Costs. Tuition and fees, $9,116; room and board, $4,800. About 92% of students receive financial aid. College reports some scholarships awarded on the basis of academic merit alone.

Shenandoah College and Conservatory of Music

Winchester, Virginia 22601 **(703) 665-4581**

A church-related institution, offering undergraduate and graduate programs in music, performing arts, business administration, nursing and the liberal arts. Shenandoah is located in a town of 21,300 in the Shenandoah Valley, 70 miles west of Washington, D.C. Most convenient major airport: Washington D.C..

Founded: 1875
Affiliation: United Methodist
UG Enrollment: 260 M, 399 W (full-time); 57 M, 170 W (part-time)
Total Enrollment: 1,092
Cost: < $10K
% Receiving Financial Aid: 90%
Admission: Non-selective
Application Deadline: June 15

Admission. High school graduates, or equivalent, with C average or better eligible; 80% of applicants accepted, 51% of these actually enroll. *Required:* SAT or ACT; audition for Conservatory. *Non-academic factors* considered in admissions: special talents, diverse student body. *Entrance programs:* early decision, midyear admission, deferred admission, advanced placement, admission after junior year in high school. *Apply* by June 15. *Transfers* welcome.
Academic Environment. *Degrees:* BA, BS, BM. Specific course and distribution requirements vary with degree. *Majors offered* include accompanying arts, business administration, dance, communications, equestrian studies, music (braille, church, composition, education, jazz studies, performance, therapy, theater), nursing, pedagogy, piano technology, respiratory therapy, theater. About 75% of students entering as freshmen graduate eventually; 80% of freshmen return for sophomore year. *Special programs:* CLEP, independent study, study abroad. *Calendar:* semester, summer school.
Undergraduate degrees conferred (105). 28% were in Business and Management, 24% were in Visual and Performing Arts, 20% were in Education, 10% were in Health Sciences, 8% were in Allied Health, 6% were in Psychology, remainder in 4 other fields.
Student Body. About 70% of students from in state; 73% South, 23% Middle Atlantic.
Religious Orientation. Shenandoah is a church-related institution; 1 course in religion or philosophy required of all students.
Varsity Sports. Men (Div.III): Baseball, Basketball, Golf, Soccer, Tennis. Women (Div.III): Basketball, Softball, Tennis, Volleyball.
Campus Life. About 25% of women live in traditional dormitories; 50% of men, 25% of women in coed dormitories; rest live in off-campus housing or commute. Freshmen given preference in college housing if all students cannot be accommodated. Intervisitation in men's and women's dormitory rooms limited. Sexes segregated in coed dormitories by floor. There are 5 fraternities (academic), 4 sororities (academic), about 30% of men, 30% of women join; they provide no residence facilities. About 10% of resident students leave campus on weekends.
Annual Costs. Tuition and fees, $9,800; room and board, $4,400. About 90% of students receive financial aid; assistance is typically divided 60% scholarship, 30% loan, 10% work. College reports some scholarships awarded on the basis of academic merit alone. *Meeting Costs:* college offers Virginia Edvantage Loans.

Shepherd College

Shepherdstown, West Virginia 25443 **(304) 876-2511; (800) 344-5231**

A state-supported college, located in a community of 5,000, 65 miles northwest of Washington, D.C. Most convenient major airport: Washington Dulles (45 miles).

Founded: 1871
Affiliation: State
UG Enrollment: 1,431 M, 2,134 W (full-time)
Cost: < $10K
% Receiving Financial Aid: 39%
Admission: Very Selective
Application Deadline: Feb. 1

Admission is very selective. About 78% of applicants accepted, 52% of these actually enroll. About 30% of freshmen graduate in top fifth of high school class, 55% in top two-fifths. Average freshman scores: SAT, 550 verbal, 550 mathematical; ACT, 24 M, 24 W composite, 28 M, 26 W mathematical. *Required:* SAT or ACT, minimum high school GPA. Criteria considered in admissions, in order of importance: high school academic record, standardized test scores, recommendations, extracurricular activities; other factors considered: special talents, diverse student body. *Out-of-state* freshman applicants: college actively seeks students from out-of-state. State does not limit out-of-state enrollment. Requirements for out-of-state applicants: GPA of 2.5 and score 21 on ACT or 1000 on combined SAT. States from which most out-of-state students are drawn include Maryland, Virginia, Pennsylvania, New Jersey, Delaware. About 10% of entering students from private schools, 25% from parochial schools. *Apply* by February 1. *Transfers* welcome; 344 enrolled 1993–94.
Academic Environment. Graduation requirements include a 47 semester hour general studies core curriculum that is required for all bachelor degrees and provides liberal arts exposure. Administration reports opportunities for internships and co-ops in Washington, DC, as well as "extensive" research opportunities in the area. Degrees offered: associates, bachelors. *Majors offered* in addition to usual studies include fashion merchandising, photography, athletic training, therapeutic recreation. Average undergraduate class size: 15% under 20, 80% 20–40, 5% over 40.

About 78% of students entering as freshmen graduate eventually, 78% of freshmen return for sophomore year. *Special programs:* CLEP, independent study, undergraduate research, January interterm, internships, honors program, credit by examination. Adult programs: Regents BA degree program for older, non-traditional students. *Calendar:* early semester, summer school.
Undergraduate degrees conferred (386). 25% were in Business and Management, 19% were in Education, 13% were in Multi/Interdisciplinary Studies, 9% were in Social Sciences, 8% were in Psychology, 5% were in Computer and Engineering Related Technology, 4% were in Visual and Performing Arts, 4% were in Life Sciences, 3% were in Health Sciences, 3% were in Parks and Recreation, remainder in 6 other fields.
Graduates Career Data. Advanced studies pursued by 30% of graduates; 3% enter medical school; 5% enter law school; 20% enter business school. Medical, law, and business schools typically enrolling largest numbers of graduates include West Virginia U., U. of Virginia, U. of Maryland, George Washington U. About 45% of 1992–93 graduates employed. Corporations typically hiring largest numbers of graduates include Marriott, IBM, accounting firms, U.S. government agencies. Career Development Services include career guidance, interview preparation, job placement.
Faculty. About 70% of faculty hold PhD or equivalent. About 43% of undergraduate classes taught by tenured faculty. About 43% of teaching faculty are female; 5% Black, 3% Hispanic, 2% other minority.
Student Body. About 71% of students from in state. An estimated 61% of students reported as Protestant, 17% Catholic; 3% as Black, 1% other minority.
Varsity Sports. Men (NCAA, II, NAIA): Baseball, Basketball, Cross Country, Football, Golf, Soccer, Tennis. Women (NCAA, II, NAIA): Basketball, Cross Country, Golf, Softball, Tennis, Volleyball.
Campus Life. About 30% of men, 30% of women in coed dormitories; 46% of men, 46% of women live in off-campus college-related housing; rest commute. Intervisitation in men's and women's dormitory rooms. There are 5 fraternities, 5 sororities on campus which about 20% of men, 20% of women join; 18% of men live in fraternities; sororities provide no residence facilities. About 25% of students leave campus on weekends.
Annual Costs. Tuition and fees, $2,040 (out-of-state, $4,670); room and board, $3,500; estimated $2,000 other, exclusive of travel. About 39% of students receive financial aid; average amount of assistance, $2,500. Assistance is typically divided 52% scholarship, 37% loan, 11% work. College reports most scholarships awarded on the basis of academic merit alone. *Meeting Costs:* college offers AMS Tuition Payment Plan.

Shimer College

Waukegan, Illinois 60085 **(708) 623-8400**

An independent, liberal arts college, offering bachelor degree programs using a Great Books curriculum. Most convenient major airports: O'Hare (Chicago).

Founded: 1853
Affiliation: Independent
UG Enrollment: 58 M, 49 W (full-time)
Cost: $10K–$20K
% Receiving Financial Aid: 90%
Admission: Non-selective
Application Deadline: Rolling

Admission. About 97% of applicants accepted, 71% of these actually enroll; 40% of freshmen graduate in top fifth of high school class, 80% in top two-fifths. *Required:* interview, essay. Criteria considered in admissions, in order of importance: writing sample, interview, high school academic record, recommendations, extracurricular activities, standardized test scores; other factors considered: special talents, alumni children, diverse student body. *Entrance programs:* early admission, mid-year admission, advanced placement. *Apply:* rolling admissions. *Transfers* welcome; 10 enrolled 1993–94.
Academic Environment. Graduation requirements include 85 hours of humanities/social sciences/natural sciences, and 40 hours of electives. Degrees offered: bachelors. *Special programs:* study abroad, cross registration with Barat College, self-designed internship/cooperative work-study programs. Adult program: every third weekend program for working adults. *Calendar:* semester, summer session.
Undergraduate degrees conferred ().
Faculty. About 81% of faculty hold PhD or equivalent. About 28% of teaching faculty are female.
Student Body. About 67% of students from in state; 77% from Midwest, 5% each South, West, 4% Northwest, 3% each New England, Middle Atlantic, foreign. An estimated 14% of students reported as minority. Average age of undergraduate student: 23.
Campus Life. About 32% of men, 26% of women live in coed dormitories; 8% of men live in off-campus college-related housing; rest commute. There are no fraternities or sororities on campus. About 5% of resident students leave campus on weekends.
Annual Costs. Tuition and fees, $11,200; room and board, $1,650; estimated $1,550 other, exclusive of travel. About 90% of students receive financial aid; average amount of assistance, $8,500. Assistance is typically divided 9% scholarship, 38% grant, 50% loan, 2% work. College reports 3 scholarships awarded on the basis of academic merit alone, 98 for need alone.

Shippensburg University

Shippensburg, Pennsylvania 17257
(717) 532-9121; in-state, (800) 822-8028

A state-supported liberal arts institution which places considerable emphasis on vocational/professional studies in business and management, communications, public affairs and services, and education. The university is located in a town of 6,500, 40 miles southwest of Harrisburg. Most convenient major airport: Harrisburg International.

Founded: 1871
Affiliation: State
UG Enrollment: 2,462 M, 2,797 W (full-time); 137 M, 161 W (part-time)
Total Enrollment: 6,487
Cost: < $10K
% Receiving Financial Aid: 65%
Admission: Selective
Application Deadline: March 1

Admission is selective. About 56% of applicants accepted, 35% of these actually enroll; 38% of freshmen graduate in top fifth of high school class, 75% in top two-fifths. Average freshman SAT scores: 466 M, 470 W verbal, 547 M, 513 W mathematical. *Required:* SAT. Criteria considered in admissions, in order of importance: high school academic record, standardized test scores, recommendations, extracurricular activities; other factors considered: special talents, diverse student body. *Out-of-state* freshman applicants: university actively seeks out-of-state students. State limits out-of-state enrollment to 10% of total. No special requirements for out-of-state applicants. States from which most out-of-state students are drawn include Maryland, New Jersey, Virginia. About 50% of out-of-state students accepted, 24% of these actually enroll. *Entrance programs:* early admission, midyear admission, advanced placement. *Apply* by March 1; rolling admissions. *Transfers* welcome; 392 enrolled 1993–94.
Academic Environment. Graduation requirements include English composition, speech, mathematics competency, arts and literature, biological and physical sciences, social, political and geographical sciences. Student leader reports student body is overwhelmingly concerned with career-oriented goals. Degrees offered: bachelors, masters. *Majors offered* include arts and sciences, business administration, computer science, education, computer education, interdisciplinary arts. Average undergraduate class size: 24% under 20, 62% 20–40, 14% over 40.

About 48% of students entering as freshmen graduate within four years, 65% eventually, 83% of freshmen return for sophomore year. *Special programs:* CLEP, independent study, honors, individualized majors, study abroad, semester internship, cross registration with Wilson College, 3–2 programs in engineering. *Calendar:* semester, summer school.
Undergraduate degrees conferred (1,074). 23% were in Business and Management, 13% were in Education, 9% were in Social Sciences, 8% were in Communications, 7% were in Public Affairs, 7% were in Protective Services, 7% were in Psychology, 7% were in Letters, 5% were in Mathematics, 4% were in Computer and Engineering Related Technology, 3% were in Life Sciences, 3% were in Physical Sciences, remainder in 5 other fields.
Graduates Career Data. Fields typically hiring largest numbers of graduates include business, industry, education. Career Development Services include placement services, on-campus recruitment, individual and group counseling, resume and interviewing workshops, library resources.
Faculty. About 80% of faculty hold PhD or equivalent. About 27% of teaching faculty are female; 5% Black, less than 1% Hispanic, 3% other minority.
Student Body. About 91% of students from in state; 97% Middle Atlantic, 2% New England, less than 1% foreign. An estimated 3% of students reported as Black, 1% Hispanic, 1% Asian.
Varsity Sports. Men (Div.II): Baseball, Basketball, Cross Country, Football, Soccer, Swimming, Track, Wrestling (I). Women (Div.II): Basketball, Cross Country, Field Hockey, Lacrosse, Softball, Swimming, Tennis, Track, Volleyball.
Campus Life. Residents of each dormitory determine intervisitation hours including 24-hour if desired. Alcohol and drugs not permitted on campus; cars allowed for all students.

About 14% of men, 21% of women live in traditional dormitories; 24% of men, 23% of women live in coed dormitories; 40% of men, 30% of women live in off-campus college-related housing; rest commute. Freshmen given preference in college housing if all students cannot be accommodated. Sexes segregated in coed dormitories by floor. There are 13 fraternities, 11 sororities on campus which about 15% each of men, women join; they provide no residence facilities. About 50% of students leave campus on weekends.
Annual Costs. Tuition and fees, $3,710 (out-of-state, $8,108); room and board, $3,348; estimated $1,863 other, exclusive of travel. About 65% of students receive financial aid; average amount of assistance, $4,450. Assistance is typically divided 10% scholarship, 20% grant, 60% loan, 10% work. College reports 125 scholarships awarded on the basis of academic merit alone, 184 for special talents alone.

Shorter College

Rome, Georgia 30165-4298
(706) 291-2121; (800) 868-6980

A church-related college, located in a community of 55,000, 68 miles northwest of Atlanta. Adult degree completion programs offered at an urban campus in Atlanta. Most convenient major airport: Hartsfield Atlanta International.

Founded: 1873
Affiliation: Southern Baptist
UG Enrollment: 430 M, 685 W (full-time)
Cost: < $10K
% Receiving Financial Aid: 99%
Admission: Non-selective
Application Deadline: Rolling

Admission. Graduates of approved high schools with 16 units eligible; 82% of applicants accepted, 32% of these actually enroll; 60% of freshmen graduate in top fifth of high school class. Average freshman SAT scores, middle 50% range: 390–500 M, 380–532 W verbal, 430–580 M, 428–552 W mathematical; 33% of freshmen score above 500 on verbal, 6% above 600; 53% score above 500 on mathematical, 16% above 600. *Required:* SAT or ACT; essay. Criteria considered in admissions, in order of importance: high school academic record, standardized test scores, recommendations, special talents, writing sample, extracurricular activities; other factors considered: religious affiliation and/or commitment. *Entrance programs:* advanced placement. *Apply:* rolling admissions. *Transfers* welcome; 281 enrolled 1993–94.

Academic Environment. Graduation requirements include 42–43 hours in communications, English, mathematics, natural sciences, social sciences, fine arts, and religion. Degrees offered: bachelors. Average undergraduate class size: 77% under 20, 22% 20–40, 1% over 40.

About 31% of students entering as freshmen graduate within four years, 45% eventually. *Special programs:* CLEP, independent study, honors, individualized majors, study abroad, medical technology joint programs with GA Tech and Duke U. Adult programs: degree completion programs designed for working adults with at least 15 hours of prior college credit; bachelor degrees in business administration, and management. *Calendar:* semester, May Term, summer school.

Undergraduate degrees conferred (146). 27% were in Education, 22% were in Business and Management, 9% were in Parks and Recreation, 9% were in Multi/Interdisciplinary Studies, 7% were in Visual and Performing Arts, 5% were in Social Sciences, 3% were in Mathematics, 3% were in Liberal/General Studies, 3% were in Communications, 3% were in Psychology, 3% were in Letters, remainder in 4 other fields.

Graduates Career Data. Advanced studies pursued by 36% of graduates; 20% enter graduate school; 9% enter medical school; 1% enter law school; 3% enter business school. Fields typically hiring largest numbers of graduates include education, industry, government. Career Development Services offer DISCOVER and self-analysis packages.

Faculty. About 62% of faculty hold PhD or equivalent. About 40% of undergraduate classes taught by tenured faculty. About 25% of teaching faculty are female; 2% Black.

Student Body. About 94% of students from in state; 4% South, 1% West, 2% foreign. An estimated 78% of students reported as Protestant, 4% Catholic, 18% unaffiliated; 16% Black, 2% Hispanic, 1% Asian. Average age of undergraduate student: 23.

Religious Orientation. Shorter is a church-related institution; 63% of students affiliated with the church; 3 hours of religion required of all students.

Varsity Sports. Men (NAIA): Baseball, Basketball, Cross Country, Golf, Tennis, Track. Women (NAIA): Basketball, Softball, Tennis, Track.

Campus Life. About 53% of men, 48% of women live in traditional dormitories; no coed dormitories; rest live in off-campus housing or commute. No intervisitation in men's dormitory rooms, limited in women's dormitory rooms. There are 4 fraternities, 3 sororities on campus which about 35% of men, 32% of women join; they provide no residence facilities. About 43% of resident students leave campus on weekends.

Annual Costs. Tuition and fees, $6,670; room and board, $3,600; estimated $1,500 other, exclusive of travel. About 99% of students receive financial aid; average amount of assistance, $5,544. Assistance is typically divided 68% scholarship/grant, 31% loan, 1% work. College reports 2 types of scholarships awarded on the basis of academic merit alone, 12 for special talents alone, 1 for need alone. *Meeting Costs:* college offers prepayment and deferred payment plans.

Siena College

Loudonville, New York 12211 **(518) 783-2423; (800) 45-SIENA**

An independent, liberal arts college, founded by the Franciscans, Order of Friars Minor, Siena is located in a small community of 9,300, 5 miles north of Albany. Most convenient major airport: Albany County.

Founded: 1937
Affiliation: Independent
UG Enrollment: 1,247 M, 1,422 W (full-time); 372 M, 395 W (part-time)
Cost: $10K–$20K
% Receiving Financial Aid: 79%
Admission: Very Selective
Application Deadline: March 1

Admission is very selective. About 65% of applicants accepted, 33% of these actually enroll; 49% of freshmen graduate in top fifth of high school class, 82% in top two-fifths. Average freshman scores: SAT, 492 M, 489 W verbal, 574 M, 548 W mathematical; 43% of freshmen score above 500 on verbal, 7% above 600; 79% score above 500 on mathematical, 28% above 600, 3% above 700; ACT 24 composite. *Required:* SAT or ACT; ACH in language if continuing study, science and mathematics II for Science Division, essay; interview strongly recommended. Criteria considered in admissions, in order of importance: high school academic record, standardized test scores and recommendations rank second, extracurricular activities and writing sample rank equally; other factors considered: special talents, alumni children, diverse student body. *Entrance programs:* early decision, early admission, midyear admission, deferred admission, advanced placement. About 2% of entering students from private schools, 25% from parochial schools. *Apply* by March 1. *Transfers* welcome; 199 enrolled 1993–94.

Academic Environment. Administration reports 55% of general education courses required for graduation are elective; core curriculum includes 24 hours in humanities, 6 each in social sciences and mathematics/science. Degrees offered: bachelors. *Majors offered* include usual arts and sciences, accounting, computer science, finance, marketing, social work. Average undergraduate class size: 22.

About 82% of students entering as freshmen graduate eventually, 95% of freshmen return for sophomore year. *Special programs:* CLEP, honors, study abroad, independent study, cross-registration with 15 other colleges including RPI, Skidmore, Union, joint BA/MD program with Albany, 3–2 in engineering, 4–1 MBA, 2–2 in forestry. Adult programs: continuing professional education for CPA; non-credit workshops and seminars geared primarily to business community. *Calendar:* semester, summer session.

Undergraduate degrees conferred (788). 56% were in Business and Management, 15% were in Social Sciences, 7% were in Letters, 6% were in Psychology, 6% were in Life Sciences, 3% were in Computer and Engineering Related Technology, remainder in 6 other fields.

Graduates Career Data. Advanced studies pursued by 24% of graduates. Medical schools typically enrolling largest numbers of graduates include Albany Medical College; law schools include Albany Law, Western New England Law. About 74% of 1992–93 graduates employed. Career Development Services include career advisement, resume preparation assistance, career information, recruitment programs.

Faculty. About 79% of faculty hold PhD or equivalent. About 70% of undergraduate classes taught by tenured faculty. About 27% of teaching faculty are female.

Student Body. About 85% of students from in state; 89% Middle Atlantic, 10% New England, less than 1% foreign. An estimated 2% of students reported as Black, 2% Hispanic, 2% Asian. *Minority group students:* special financial, academic, and social provisions including Higher Education Opportunity Program.

Religious Orientation. Siena is an independent institution with a Roman Catholic orientation; 2 courses in religious studies required of all students.

Varsity Sports. Men (Div.I): Baseball, Basketball, Cross Country, Football (I-AA), Golf, Lacrosse, Soccer, Tennis, Track. Women (Div.I): Basketball, Cross Country, Field Hockey, Soccer, Softball, Tennis, Track, Volleyball.

Campus Life. Recent student leader characterizes regulations governing student conduct as "relatively free," enforced "judiciously." Alcohol permitted in residence halls and beer may be sold on campus; cars allowed except for freshmen.

About 52% of students live in coed dormitories; rest live in off-campus housing or commute. There are no fraternities or sororities on campus. About 10–15% of resident students leave campus on weekends.

Annual Costs. Tuition and fees, $10,505; room and board, $4,905; estimated $1,490 other, exclusive of travel. About 79% of students receive financial aid, average amount of assistance, $6,025. Assistance is typically divided 45% scholarship/grant, 41% loan, 13% work. College reports 203 scholarships awarded on the basis of academic merit alone, 35 for special talents, 1,843 for need alone. *Meeting Costs:* college offers interest-free budget plans and low-interest long term loans.

Siena Heights College

Adrian, Michigan 49221 **(517) 263-0731**

A church-related college, owned by the Dominican Sisters, located in a town of 22,000, 60 miles from Detroit. The college also operates three off-campus sites (Benton Harbor, Monroe, and Southfield-Michigan) primarily serving working adult students. Most convenient major airports: Detroit or Toledo, OH.

Founded: 1919
Affiliation: Roman Catholic
UG Enrollment: 272 M, 498 W (full-time); 101 M, 242 W (part-time)
Cost: < $10K
% Receiving Financial Aid: 81%
Admission: Non-selective
Application Deadline: August 30

Admission. Graduates of accredited high schools with 15 units (12 in academic subjects) and C average eligible; 86% of applicants accepted, 52% of these actually enroll. Average freshman ACT scores, according to most recent data available: 20 M, 19 W composite, 18 M, 18 W mathematical. *Required:* SAT or ACT; interview recommended. *Non-academic factors* considered in admissions: special talents, diverse student body, alumni children, religious affiliation and/or commitment, demonstrated leadership ability. *Apply* by August 30. *Transfers* welcome.
Academic Environment. *Degrees:* AB, BS, BApS, BFA. All general education requirements for graduation are elective; no distribution requirements. *Majors offered* in addition to usual studies include art, business, education, child development, computer science. About 40% of students entering as freshmen graduate eventually; 68% of freshmen return for sophomore year. *Special programs:* CLEP, contract degree, cooperative education, external degree program, off-campus study, study abroad (including semester trip to Italy with Art Dept), independent study, prior life experience, early entrance, 2–3 programs in engineering. Adult programs: special admissions and advising services, evening and weekend courses offered. *Calendar:* semester, summer school.
Undergraduate degrees conferred (393). 28% were in Business and Management, 15% were in Engineering and Engineering Related Technology, 13% were in Health Sciences, 11% were in Liberal/General Studies, 8% were in Allied Health, 4% were in Public Affairs, 4% were in Education, 3% were in Letters, 3% were in Visual and Performing Arts, remainder in 15 other fields.
Graduates Career Data. According to most recent data available: full-time graduate or professional study pursued by 12% of students immediately after graduation. *Careers in business and industry* pursued by 50% of graduates.
Faculty. About 60% of faculty hold PhD or equivalent.
Student Body. About 85% of students from Michigan. An estimated 5% of students reported as Black, 4% Hispanic, 3% other minority, according to most recent data available.
Religious Orientation. Siena Heights is a church-related institution, but makes no religious demands on students.
Varsity Sports. Men (NAIA): Baseball, Basketball, Cross Country, Soccer, Tennis, Track, Wrestling. Women (NAIA): Basketball, Soccer, Softball, Tennis, Track, Volleyball.
Campus Life. About 33% of students live in coed dormitories; rest live in off-campus housing or commute. Intervisitation in men's and women's dormitory rooms limited; sexes segregated by wing. There is 1 fraternity, 1 sorority on campus.
Annual Costs. Tuition and fees, $8,820; room and board, $3,700. About 81% of students receive financial aid; assistance is typically divided 65% scholarship, 32% loan, 3% work. College reports some scholarships awarded on the basis of academic merit alone. *Meeting Costs:* college offers deferred payment plan, family discounts.

Sierra Nevada College

Incline Village, Nevada 89450 **(702) 831-1314**

An accredited 4-year institution, Sierra Nevada is located in a small community in the western part of the state.

Founded: 1969
Affiliation: Independent
UG Enrollment: 1,503 (full-time)
Cost: < $10K
Admission: Non-selective
Application Deadline: September 1

Admission. About 90% of applicants accepted, 80% of these actually enroll. *Apply* by September. *Transfers* welcome.
Academic Environment. *Degrees:* AB, BS. General education course in research and writing required for graduation. About 25% of entering students graduate eventually.
Undergraduate degrees conferred (26). 38% were in Business and Management, 27% were in Visual and Performing Arts, 19% were in Liberal/General Studies, 8% were in Science Technologies, 8% were in Physical Sciences.
Campus Life. Sierra Nevada is a commuter school; no residential facilities.
Annual Costs. Tuition and fees, $7,500.

Silver Lake College of the Holy Family

Manitowoc, Wisconsin 54220 **(414) 684-6691**

A church-related, co-educational college, conducted by the Franciscan Sisters of Christian Charity. Primarily for commuters, the campus is located in a community of 33,400, 80 miles north of Milwaukee. Most convenient major airport: Green Bay.

Founded: 1869
Affiliation: Roman Catholic
UG Enrollment: 105 M, 284 W (full-time); 172 M, 268 W (part-time)
Total Enrollment: 948
Cost: < $10K
% Receiving Financial Aid: 56%
Admission: Non-selective
Application Deadline: Rolling

Admission. Graduates of accredited high schools with minimum GPA of 2.0 eligible; 75% of applicants accepted, 34% of these actually enroll; 18% of freshmen graduate in top fifth of high school class, 33% in top two-fifths. Average freshman ACT scores: 19 M, 21 W composite. *Required:* ACT. Criteria considered in admissions, in order of importance: high school academic record, standardized test scores, recommendations, writing sample, extracurricular activities. About 21% of entering students from private school. *Apply:* rolling admissions. *Transfers* welcome; 107 enrolled 1993–94.
Academic Environment. Graduation requirements include completion of a liberal arts core curriculum. Degrees offered: associates, bachelors, masters. *Majors offered* in addition to usual studies include nursing completion program, early childhood. Average undergraduate class size: 70% under 20, 30% 20–40.

About 60% of students entering as freshmen graduate eventually, 64% of freshmen return for sophomore year. *Special programs:* independent study, individualized majors. Adult programs: career directed programs, master's degree programs. *Calendar:* semester, summer school.
Undergraduate degrees conferred (111). 63% were in Business and Management, 14% were in Education, 5% were in Social Sciences, 5% were in Multi/Interdisciplinary Studies, 5% were in Health Sciences, 3% were in Life Sciences, remainder in 5 other fields.
Graduate Career Data. Advanced studies pursued by 20% of graduates. About 83% of 1992–93 graduates employed. Fields typically hiring largest numbers of graduates include management, education, human resources. Career Development Services include career counseling, job search strategy course, career fair, resume and teaching credential workshops.
Faculty. About 17% of faculty hold PhD or equivalent. About 62% of teaching faculty are female; 2% Hispanic.
Student Body. About 98% of students from in state; 99% Midwest, less than 1% foreign. An estimated 1% of students reported as Hispanic, 2% other minority.
Religious Orientation. Silver Lake is a church-related institution; 2–4 courses in religious studies required of all students as part of general/liberal curriculum.
Varsity Sports. Women (WICWAC): Basketball.
Campus Life. All students live in off-campus housing or commute. There are no fraternities or sororities on campus.

Annual Costs. Tuition and fees, $8,280; room and board, $3,414; estimated $1,472 other, exclusive of travel. About 56% of students receive financial aid; average amount of assistance, $7,782. Assistance is typically divided 57% scholarship/grant, 42% loan, 1% work. College reports 120 scholarships awarded on the basis of academic merit alone, 17 for special talents alone, 258 for need alone. *Meeting Costs:* college offers monthly payment plan.

Simmons College

Boston, Massachusetts 02115 **(800) 345-8468; (617) 521-2000**

Simmons was founded just before the turn of the century, to offer women professional/career training in combination with a liberal arts education. In keeping with its original function, the college opened a Career Resources Center and maintains a Career Planning and Counseling Center and student employment offices. The campus is located in the Back Bay section of Boston, in an area largely devoted to colleges, museums, parks, and hospitals. Most convenient major airport: Logan International (Boston).

Founded: 1899
Affiliation: Independent
UG Enrollment: 1,144 W (full-time); 160 W (part-time)
Total Enrollment: 3,334
Cost: $10K–$20K
% Receiving Financial Aid: 70%
Admission: Selective
Application Deadline: February 1

Admission is selective. About 78% of applicants accepted, 38% of these actually enroll; 46% of freshmen graduate in top fifth of high school class, 73% in top two-fifths. Average freshman scores: SAT, 39% of freshmen score above 500 on verbal, 8% above 600, 2% above 700; 46% score above 500 on mathematical, 9% above 600, 1% above 700; ACT, 24 composite. *Required:* SAT or ACT; minimum high school GPA, essay, interview strongly recommended. *Non-academic factors* considered in admissions: special talents, diverse student body. *Entrance programs:* early decision, deferred admission, advanced placement. About 22% of entering students from private schools. *Apply* by February 1. *Transfers* welcome; 55 enrolled 1993–94.

Academic Environment. Student reports the strengths of the academic program are the small class size, the all female undergraduate classes, and the accessibility of the faculty. Graduation requirements include 2 courses in freshman writing, proficiency in a foreign language, math comprehensive exam, independent learning, liberal arts and science distribution, field of concentration, designated writing course, and physical education. Students choose one of the more than 42 fields of concentration within three general areas: humanities, sciences and health sciences, and social science and professional sciences. Degrees offered: bachelors, masters, doctoral. Computer lab is described by student as "one of the best in the area." Average undergraduate class size: 16; 70% under 20, 20% 20–40, 10% over 40.

About 70% of entering students graduate within four years, 72% eventually, 80% of freshmen return for sophomore year. *Special programs:* independent study, undergraduate research, study abroad, individualized majors, freshman honors, internships and field work in several programs, Washington Semester at American U., inter-college registration with Emmanuel, Wheelock, Mass College of Pharmacy, Hebrew College, New England Conservatory of Music, Domestic exchange programs with Mills College, Spelman, and Frisk, joint degree programs with Mass College of Pharmacy. Adult programs: Scholars Program for women over 23 years old. *Calendar:* semester.

Undergraduate degrees conferred (381). 15% were in Social Sciences, 14% were in Communications, 14% were in Business and Management, 9% were in Allied Health, 7% were in Letters, 6% were in Public Affairs, 6% were in Psychology, 6% were in Education, 6% were in Marketing and Distribution, 4% were in Life Sciences, 3% were in Precision Production, remainder in 9 other fields.

Graduates Career Data. Advanced studies pursued by 30% of graduates; 18% enter graduate school; 1% enter medical school; 1% enter law school; 10% enter business school. Medical schools typically enrolling largest numbers of graduates include U. of Penn; law schools include Northeastern; business schools include Babson, Bentley. Fields typically hiring largest numbers of graduates include health care, education, business and management, law and government. Career Development Services include access to current job listings, job search support and career decision making support groups, credential services, workshops, video interviewing, extensive alumnae contact file, and extensive career resource library.

Faculty. About 78% of faculty hold PhD or equivalent. About 57% of undergraduate classes taught by tenured faculty.

Student Body. About 59% of students from in state; 80% New England, 8% Middle Atlantic, 2% each Midwest, South, West, 1% Northwest, 5% foreign. An estimated 30% of students reported as Catholic, 16% Protestant, 16% Jewish, 38% unaffiliated; 8% Black, 4% Hispanic, 7% Asian.

Varsity Sports. Women (Div.III): Basketball, Crew, Cross Country, Field Hockey, Sailing, Soccer, Swimming & Diving, Tennis, Track, Volleyball.

Campus Life. This is an urban campus; the many cultural, intellectual, and social resources of the Boston/Cambridge area are easily accessible. Because Simmons is within walking distance of ten or more other institutions, campus events—especially parties—are attended by students from other Boston colleges; co-sponsored events are common. Student observes that "although the undergraduate classes are single-sex, there are a lot of men on the residence campus due to housing students from another school in one dorm and the male graduate students." Administration reports a "very active Student Government and Activities Programming Board", as well as an organization for commuter students which holds parties and teas during the year.

About 70% of students live in traditional dormitories; rest commute. There are no sororities on campus. About 25% of resident students leave campus on weekends.

Annual Costs. Tuition and fees, $15,794; room and board, $6,740; estimated $1,400 other. About 70% of students receive financial aid; average amount of assistance, $16,650. Assistance is typically divided 3% scholarship, 72% grant, 16% loan, 9% work. College reports 2 scholarships awarded on the basis of academic merit alone, most for need alone. *Meeting Costs:* college offers various payment plans and supplementary parent loan programs.

Simon's Rock of Bard College

Great Barrington, Massachusetts 01230 **(413) 528-7312**

A most unusual college, Simon's Rock enrolls students who have successfully completed college preparatory studies through the 10th grade (as well as the 11th grade). Its policy is based on the conviction that many 16 year-olds are prepared to begin full-time college work. In 1979 Bard College took over the administration of Simon's Rock. The two institutions, however, retain their separate identities and the Simon's Rock early college admissions program continues. The campus is located in the Berkshires, equidistant from New York City and Boston. Most convenient major airports: Hartford, CT, or Albany, NY.

Founded: 1964
Affiliation: Independent
UG Enrollment: 151 M, 150 W (full-time)
Cost: $10K–$20K
% Receiving Financial Aid: 74%
Admission: Very Selective
Application Deadline: June 1

Admission is very selective. Early admission of students completing 10th and 11th grades distorts usual comparative data. About 66% of applicants accepted, 70% of these actually enroll. Average freshman SAT scores, according to most recent data available: 586 verbal, 589 mathematical; 85% of freshmen score above 500 on verbal, 47% above 600, 11% above 700; 92% score above 500 on mathematical, 48% above 600, 13% above 700. *Required:* SAT or ACT, interview, essay, parent statement. Criteria considered in admissions, in order of importance: high school academic record, interview, standardized test scores, recommendations, writing sample, extracurricular activities; other factors considered: special talents. About 20% of entering students from private schools. *Entrance programs:* early admission, midyear admission. *Apply* by June 1. *Transfers* welcome.

Academic Environment. Degrees offered: associates, bachelors. Students introduced immediately to college work. Strong advisory system. Administration source reports "small classes, seminar style, close relationship to teachers." All baccalaureate degree students must spend 4 years at the college whether entering after 10th, 11th, or 12th grade. College offers associate degree program as well as baccalaureate degree. Many students transfer after earning an AA degree to a larger institution. Average undergraduate class size: 11; 90% under 20, 10% 20–40. *Special programs:* undergraduate research, study abroad, independent study.

Undergraduate degrees conferred (26). 38% were in Visual and Performing Arts, 38% were in Social Sciences, 15% were in Letters, 8% were in Multi/Interdisciplinary Studies.

Graduates Career Data. Career Development Services available.

Faculty. About 92% of faculty hold PhD or equivalent. About 95% of undergraduate classes taught by tenured faculty. About 45% of teaching faculty are female; 5% Black.

Student Body. About 16% of students from in state; 43% Middle Atlantic, 36% New England, 11% from South, 4% West, 1% foreign, according to most recent data available. An estimated 8% of students reported as Black, 2% Hispanic, 4% Asian, according to most recent data available. Average age of undergraduate student: 16.7.

Campus Life. Students report location as "kind of isolated" but add "there are many activities planned". Small size and personal attention considered a plus; "You can be yourself. There are so many different kinds of people from all backgrounds."

About 70% of each men, women live in traditional dormitories; 20% in coed dormitories; rest live in off-campus housing. Freshmen given preference in college housing if all students cannot be accommodated. Intervisitation in dormitory rooms limited. Alcohol prohibited. There are no fraternities or sororities on campus. About 5% of resident students leave campus on weekends.

Annual Costs. Tuition and fees, $18,170; room and board, $5,620; estimated $1,200 other, exclusive of travel. About 74% of students receive financial aid; average amount of assistance, $9,000. College reports 20 scholarships awarded on the basis of academic merit alone.

Simpson College

San Francisco, California 94134

A church-related, liberal arts institution, the college prepares church workers, both lay and professional.

Founded: 1921

Affiliation: Christian and Missionary Alliance

Undergraduate degrees conferred (44). 61% were in Business and Management, 18% were in Theology, 9% were in Psychology, 5% were in Social Sciences, remainder in 3 other fields.

Simpson College

Indianola, Iowa 50125 **(800) 362-2454**

An independent, liberal arts college, historically related to the United Methodist Church, Simpson is located on a 63-acre campus in a suburban community of 12,500, 12 miles south of Des Moines. Most convenient major airport: Des Moines.

Founded: 1860
Affiliation: Independent (United Methodist)
UG Enrollment: 538 M, 578 W (full-time); 206 M, 396 W (part-time)
Cost: $10K–$20K
% Receiving Financial Aid: 95%
Admission: Selective
Application Deadline: Rolling

Admission is selective. About 86% of applicants accepted, 34% of these actually enroll; 49% of freshmen graduate in top fifth of high school class, 78% in top two-fifths. Average freshman ACT scores: 22–27 composite. *Required:* SAT or ACT; "strong high school curriculum". Criteria considered in admissions, in order of importance: high school academic record, standardized test scores, recommendations, extracurricular activities; other factors considered: special talents, alumni children, diverse student body. *Entrance programs:* early admission, midyear admission, deferred admission, advanced placement. *Apply:* rolling admissions. *Transfers* welcome; 63 enrolled 1993–94.

Academic Environment. Graduation requirements include 8 areas of cornerstone study for liberal arts education; also: writing, foreign language and math competency. Degrees offered: bachelors. *Majors offered* include usual arts and sciences, accounting, business administration, communications, computer science, criminal justice, corrections, education, engineering, medical technology, music performance, music education, nursing, theater arts, and sports administration. Average undergraduate class size: 60% under 20, 36% 20–40, 4% over 40.

About 49% of entering students graduate within four years, 63% within six years, 77% of freshmen return for sophomore year. *Special programs:* CLEP, May interterm, cross registration with American, Drew U., Union College, 3–2 in engineering, 3–2 in nursing, independent study, study abroad, honors, individualized majors, cooperative work/study program. Adult programs: Evening and weekend degree programs on-campus and in West Des Moines. *Calendar:* 4–4–1, summer school.

Undergraduate degrees conferred (274). 40% were in Business and Management, 17% were in Education, 9% were in Social Sciences, 5% were in Mathematics, 5% were in Communications, 5% were in Visual and Performing Arts, 4% were in Life Sciences, 4% were in Psychology, 3% were in Letters, 3% were in Protective Services, 3% were in Foreign Languages, remainder in 2 other fields.

Graduates Career Data. Advanced studies pursued by 15% of graduates; 8% enter graduate school; 2% enter medical school; 1% enter dental school; 2% enter law school; 2% enter business school. About 96% of 1992–93 graduates employed. Corporations typically hiring largest numbers of graduates include Principal Financial Group, Pete-Marwick, Ernst and Whinney. Career Development Services include internships, career observation, resume assistance, on-campus job interviews.

Faculty. About 73% of faculty hold PhD or equivalent. About 61% of undergraduate classes taught by tenured faculty. About 33% of teaching faculty are female.

Student Body. About 90% of students from in state; 10% Midwest, 2% foreign. An estimated 65% of students reported as Protestant, 19% Catholic, 16% unaffiliated; 1% as Black, 1% Hispanic, 1% Asian, less than 1% other minority.

Religious Orientation. Simpson is an independent institution with some ties to the United Methodist Church; 35% of students affiliated with the church; 1 course in religious studies required.

Varsity Sports. Men (Div.III): Baseball, Basketball, Cross Country, Football, Golf, Tennis, Track, Wrestling. Women (Div.III): Basketball, Cross Country, Golf, Softball, Tennis, Track, Volleyball.

Campus Life. Student praises the "sense of community" that exists on campus. Students participate on most faculty committees. Single students under 23 required to live in college-related residences. Regulations governing student life determined by majority of students in each dormitory within limits set by college.

About 8% of men, 18% of women live in traditional dormitories; 22% of each men, women live in coed dormitories; 6% of students live in off-campus housing; 20% commute. Freshmen given preference in college housing if all students cannot be accommodated. Intervisitation in men's and women's dormitory rooms unlimited. There are 4 fraternities, 4 sororities on campus which about 36% of each men, women join; 13% of men, 12% of women live in fraternities and sororities. About 15% of resident students leave campus on weekends.

Annual Costs. Tuition and fees, $10,825; room and board, $3,810; estimated $1,000 other, exclusive of travel. About 95% of students receive financial aid; average amount of assistance, $11,018. Assistance is typically divided 61% scholarship/grant, 30% loan, 5% work. College reports a total of 491 scholarships awarded on the basis of academic merit, special talents and need. Meeting costs: college offers two payment plans, and Simpson Loan Program.

Sinte Glesko University

Rosebud, South Dakota 57570

An independent liberal arts college offering associates, bachelors and masters degrees. Admissions are open.

Founded: 1970

Affiliation: Independent

Sioux Falls College

Sioux Falls, South Dakota 57105 (605) 331-5000

A church-related college, located in a community of 80,000. Most convenient major airport: Sioux Falls Municipal.

Founded: 1883
Affiliation: American Baptist
UG Enrollment: 271 M, 343 W (full-time); 104 M, 167 W (part-time)
Total Enrollment: 951
Cost: < $10K
% Receiving Financial Aid: 94%
Admission: Non-selective
Application Deadline: Rolling

Admission. Graduates of approved high schools who rank in top half of class or score 19 on ACT composite eligible; others evaluated on basis of individual recommendations; 92% of applicants accepted, 62% of these actually enroll; 44% of freshmen graduate in top fifth of high school class, 78% in top two-fifths. Average freshman ACT scores: 21 composite. *Required:* SAT or ACT; minimum high school GPA. Criteria considered in admissions, in order of importance: standardized test scores, high school academic record, recommendations, extracurricular activities. *Entrance programs:* early admission, advanced placement. *Apply*: rolling admissions. *Transfers* welcome; 72 enrolled 1993–94.
Academic Environment. Degrees offered: associates, bachelors, masters. About 30% of general education requirements for graduation are elective; distribution requirements fairly numerous. *Majors offered* include wellness program management and wellness fitness leadership.

About 44% of students entering as freshmen graduate eventually, 49% of freshmen return for sophomore year. Special program: January interterm, honors, study abroad, cross registration with Augustana College, North American Baptist Seminary, Dakota State U. Adult programs: Degree Completion Program for students with junior status and business major. *Calendar:* 4–1–4, summer school.
Undergraduate degrees conferred (150). 43% were in Business and Management, 13% were in Education, 8% were in Social Sciences, 7% were in Letters, 7% were in Psychology, 6% were in Communications, 4% were in Visual and Performing Arts, remainder in 8 other fields.
Graduates Career Data. Career Development Services include individual counseling, career resource center, information on interviewing, writing resumes and letters of application, and choosing academic majors.
Faculty. About 44% of faculty hold PhD or equivalent. About 22% of teaching faculty are female.
Student Body. About 72% of students from in state; 87% Midwest. An estimated 73% of students are reported as Protestant, 14% Catholic, 13% unaffiliated; 1% Black, 1% Asian, 1% other minority.
Religious Orientation. Sioux Falls is a church-related institution; 31% of students affiliated with the church; 2 courses in religion required of all students.
Varsity Sports. Men (NAIA): Basketball, Cross Country, Football, Tennis, Track. Women (NAIA): Basketball, Cross Country, Tennis, Track, Volleyball.
Campus Life. Student calls Sioux Falls "a great city with many opportunities for jobs and easy access to necessities and entertainment activities."

About 15% of men, 28% of women live in traditional dormitories; 5% of men, 10% of women live in coed dormitories; rest live in off-campus housing or commute. There are no fraternities or sororities on campus.
Annual Costs. Tuition and fees, $8,450; room and board, $3,090; estimated $800 other, exclusive of travel. About 94% of students receive financial aid; average amount of assistance, $7,950. Assistance is typically divided 43% scholarship, 50% loan, 7% work. *Meeting Costs:* college offers monthly payment plan.

Skidmore College

Saratoga Springs, New York 12866 (518) 587-7569

Skidmore offers a broad liberal arts curriculum with special strength in the fine and applied arts and pre-professional programs. The campus is located in a town of 28,000, about 35 miles north of Albany, within easy reach of the outdoor enticements of the Adirondacks. Most convenient major airport: Albany.

Founded: 1911
Affiliation: Independent
UG Enrollment: 2,645 (full-time)
Cost: $10K–$20K
% Receiving Financial Aid: 62%
Admission: Selective (+)
Application Deadline: Feb. 1

Admission is selective (+). About 43% of applicants accepted, 28% of these actually enroll. *Required:* SAT/ACT; strongly recommended: interview, 3 ACH including English, foreign language. *Non-academic factors* considered in admissions: special talents, alumni children, alternative learning experiences, geographical and ethnic diversity, extracurricular activities, leadership qualities. *Entrance programs:* early decision, early admission, midyear admission, advanced placement, deferred admission. About 45% of entering students from private schools. *Apply* by February 1. *Transfers* welcome.
Academic Environment. Curriculum features a core of required interdisciplinary liberal studies, foreign language and quantitative reasoning competencies, expository writing course and additional requirements in laboratory science, non-Western studies and a course in the visual or performing arts. Special emphasis also on "lived experience" provided by internships in business, museums, hospitals, service agencies and government. Internships "optional but highly recommended." *Degrees:* BA, BS. *Majors offered* include 21 BA programs in the humanities, social sciences and sciences, and 10 pre-professional programs in art, theater, dance, music, business, social work and education leading to the BS. In addition, college offers 22 interdepartmental majors as well as self-determined concentration options.

About 75% of students entering as freshmen graduate eventually; 91% of freshmen return for sophomore year. *Special programs:* HEOP, independent study, spring internship period, study abroad, undergraduate research, individualized majors, acceleration, Asian studies, Women's studies, cross-registration through the 14-college Hudson-Mohawk Consortium, BA/BS (engineering), BA/MBA, BA/JD (6-year). *Calendar:* semester.
Undergraduate degrees conferred (572). 22% were in Social Sciences, 16% were in Letters, 15% were in Business and Management, 14% were in Visual and Performing Arts, 10% were in Psychology, 6% were in Liberal/General Studies, 5% were in Life Sciences, 3% were in Education, remainder in 6 other fields.
Graduates Career Data. According to most recent data available: full-time graduate or professional study pursued immediately after graduation by 21% of students; 2% enter medical school; 4% enter law school; 2% enter business school. *Careers in business and industry* pursued by 40% of graduates.
Faculty. About 95% of liberal arts faculty hold doctorate.
Student Body. About 34% of students from in state; 41% Middle Atlantic, 45% New England, 6% North Central.
Varsity Sports. Men (Div.III): Baseball, Basketball, Golf, Hockey, Lacrosse, Skiing (II), Soccer, Tennis, Crew, Equestrian. Women (Div.III): Basketball, Field Hockey, Lacrosse, Skiing, Soccer (II), Softball, Swimming, Tennis, Volleyball, Crew, Equestrian.
Campus Life. The 650-acre campus is located at the edge of Saratoga Springs, the summer home of the Philadelphia Orchestra, New York City Ballet, and the country's oldest thoroughbred race track. The college offers about 80 clubs and organizations and "students participate regularly in the governance of the College."

About 66% of men, 74% of women live in coed dormitories; rest live in off-campus housing or commute. Sexes segregated in coed dormitories by room or floor. There are no fraternities or sororities. About 3% of students leave campus on weekends.
Annual Costs. Tuition and fees, $17,775; room and board, $5,455. About 62% of students receive college administered financial aid. College reports scholarships awarded only on the basis of need, with the exception of 16 Filene Music Competition Scholarships. *Meeting Costs:* college offers the Tuition Plan, Academic Management Services, tuition stabilization plan with prepayment of 2, 3 or 4 years.

Slippery Rock University

Slippery Rock, Pennsylvania 16057 (412) 738-2015

A state-owned university, located in a small town of 3,300, 50 miles north of Pittsburgh. Most convenient major airport: Pittsburgh International.

Founded: 1889	**Total Enrollment:** 7,844
Affiliation: State	**Cost:** < $10K
UG Enrollment: 2,780 M, 3,202 W (full-time); 181 M, 463 W (part-time)	**% Receiving Financial Aid:** 67%
	Admission: Non-selective
	Application Deadline: May 1

Admission. About 64% of applicants accepted, 48% of these actually enroll; 25% of freshmen graduate in top fifth of high school class, 60% in top two-fifths. *Required:* SAT or ACT. *Out-of-state* freshman applicants: university seeks students from out of state. State limits out-of-state enrollment to 10% of entering class. No special requirements for out-of-state applicants. *Entrance programs:* early decision, early admission, midyear admission, deferred admission, advanced placement. *Apply* by May 1. *Transfers* welcome.

Academic Environment. Administration reports 42% of general education courses required for graduation are elective; numerous distribution requirements. *Undergraduate studies* offered by schools of Education, Health, Physical Education, and Recreation, Natural Sciences and Mathematics, Social and Behavioral Sciences. *Majors offered* in addition to usual studies include community services for developmentally disabled, computer science, corrective therapy, geography, medical technology, music therapy, physical therapy, speech and theater, therapeutic recreation, dance, health services administration, travel and tourism; interdisciplinary concentration in environmental sciences.

About 46% of students entering as freshmen graduate eventually; 27% of freshmen do not return for sophomore year. *Special programs:* CLEP, honors, undergraduate research, independent study, study abroad, credit by examination, 3–2 programs in engineering. *Calendar:* semester, summer school.

Undergraduate degrees conferred (1,077). 35% were in Education, 19% were in Business and Management, 7% were in Communications, 7% were in Social Sciences, 6% were in Health Sciences, 4% were in Public Affairs, 3% were in Letters, 3% were in Parks and Recreation, 3% were in Computer and Engineering Related Technology, remainder in 12 other fields.

Graduates Career Data. According to most recent data available: full-time graduate study pursued immediately after graduation by 6% of students. *Careers in business and industry* pursued by 65% of graduates.

Faculty. About 60% of faculty hold PhD or equivalent.

Student Body. University seeks a national student body; 87% of students from Pennsylvania. An estimated 4% of students reported as Black, 3% other minority, according to most recent data available. *Minority group students:* Opportunity Program for Disadvantaged Students provides remedial programs and tutors at 6-week summer session and during year; Black Cultural Media Information Center.

Varsity Sports. Men (Div.II): Baseball, Basketball, Cross Country, Football, Golf, Judo, Soccer, Swimming, Tennis, Track, Wrestling (I). Women (Div.II): Basketball, Cross Country, Field Hockey (III), Golf, Judo, Lacrosse, Softball, Swimming, Tennis, Track, Volleyball.

Campus Life. University judicial process provides for student involvement in governance of college. Provisions for 24-hour visitation. Cars permitted, must be registered with university police.

About 9% of men, 13% of women live in traditional dormitories; 28% of men, 25% of women in coed dormitories; 60% of men, 60% of women live in off-campus housing or commute. Freshmen given preference in college housing if all students cannot be accommodated. Sexes segregated in coed dormitories by wing or floor. There are 12 fraternities, 9 sororities on campus which about 14% of men, 9% of women join; 14% of men, 9% of women live in fraternities and sororities.

Annual Costs. Tuition and fees, $3,510 (out-of-state, $8,240); room and board, $3,364. About 67% of students receive financial aid; assistance is typically divided 36% scholarship, 56% loan, 8% work. University reports some scholarships awarded on the basis of academic merit alone. *Meeting Costs:* university offers installment payment plan.

Smith College

Northampton, Massachusetts 01063 (413) 585-2500

Smith is the largest of the Five Sisters Colleges (Seven Sisters until Vassar went coed and Radcliffe was merged with Harvard), another member of which, Mount Holyoke, is a nearby neighbor and collaborator in the Five College Cooperative Program in the Connecticut River Valley (together with Amherst, Hampshire, and the University of Massachusetts). Smith decided "to remain a college for women" after considerable discussion whether to open its doors to male students. The 206-acre campus is located in a community of 29,700, 100 miles west of Boston. Most convenient major airport: Bradley International (Hartford, CT).

Founded: 1871	**Cost:** $10K–$20K
Affiliation: Independent	**% Receiving Financial Aid:** 48%
UG Enrollment: 2,418 W (full-time); 105 W (part-time)	**Admission:** Highly (+) Selective
Total Enrollment: 2,630	**Application Deadline:** January 15

Admission is highly (+) selective. About 55% of applicants accepted, 40% of these actually enroll; 81% of freshmen graduate in top fifth of high school class, 97% in top two-fifths. Average freshman scores, middle 50% range: SAT, 520–630 verbal, 550–650 mathematical; 83% of freshmen score above 500 on verbal, 44% above 600, 8% above 700; 91% score above 500 on mathematical, 52% above 600, 10% above 700; ACT, 25–30 composite. *Required:* SAT or ACT, 3 ACH including English, interview strongly recommended, essay. Criteria considered in admissions, in order of importance: high school academic record, standardized test scores, extracurricular activities, recommendations and writing sample; other factors considered: special talents, alumni children, diverse student body. *Entrance programs:* early decision, advanced placement, deferred admission. About 29% of entering students from private schools. *Apply* by January 15. *Transfers* welcome; 93 enrolled 1993–94.

Academic Environment. Smith has for years enjoyed a reputation for providing an educational program for women which combines an intellectual and scholarly emphasis with one attuned to the professional and occupational needs of its graduates. This program benefits from the additional resources available at the other Valley colleges—which are accessible through regular free bus service. Open curriculum; academic requirements include only the successful completion of a major field. Pressures for academic achievement appear very intense. Administration source comments that "you have to be academically oriented to survive at Smith." Student calls classes "very demanding" and adds "one spends a lot of time reading the material required". Another student exclaims: "GREAT professors, small classes, easy to get the classes you want." Degrees offered: bachelors, masters, doctoral. *Majors offered* include usual arts and sciences, Afro-American studies, anthropology, computer science, education and child study, Latin American studies, Medieval studies, Russian civilization, theater; interdepartmental majors include biochemistry; astronomy and dance through Five College Cooperative Program. Average undergraduate class size: 18.

About 86% of students entering as freshmen graduate within five years, 90% of freshmen return for sophomore year. *Special programs:* independent study, study abroad (including extensive junior year programs), honors, undergraduate research, internships, individualized majors, cross registration with Mt. Holyoke, Amherst, Hampshire and U. Mass., internships. Adult programs: Ada Comstock Scholars Program serves only adult students enrolled in credit bearing courses. *Calendar:* semester.

Undergraduate degrees conferred (741). 33% were in Social Sciences, 12% were in Visual and Performing Arts, 12% were in Letters, 9% were in Psychology, 7% were in Life Sciences, 5% were in Area and Ethnic Studies, 5% were in Foreign Languages, 3% were in Philosophy and Religion, 3% were in Multi/Interdisciplinary Studies, 3% were in Physical Sciences, 3% were in Mathematics, remainder in 4 other fields.

Graduates Career Data. Advanced studies pursued by 66% of graduates. Fields typically hiring largest numbers of graduates include business, education, human services, law. Career Development Office offers "lifetime" assistance with career and personal goals.

Faculty. About 90% of faculty hold PhD or equivalent. About 50% of teaching faculty are female; 3% Black, 7% other minority.

Student Body. About 19% of students from in state; 6% foreign. An estimated 4% of students reported as Black, 3% Hispanic, 13% Asian.

Varsity Sports. Women (Div.III): Basketball, Crew, Cross Country, Diving, Equestrian, Field Hockey, Lacrosse, Skiing, Soccer, Softball, Swimming, Tennis, Track, Volleyball.

Campus Life. Student describes campus as "quiet during the week/fun on weekends." All students have dormitory keys; intervisitation up to 24 hours decided by each house. Campus life influenced by strong house system which mixes students of varied geographic and cultural backgrounds as well as all ages. Alcoholic beverages subject to state minimum age of 21. Cars allowed but face "bad" parking problem, 160 parking places awarded by lottery to seniors each year; bicycles most frequent form of transportation. Free bus service to all points of interest, including other campuses. Northampton, 5 minutes walk from campus, is a major cultural and shopping center where Smith students can meet students from Amherst, Hampshire, and U. of Massachusetts.

About 98% of women live in college housing; 2% commute. There are no sororities on campus. "Most students stay on campus on weekends."

Annual Costs. Tuition and fees, $17,980; room and board, $6,100; estimated $1,100 other, exclusive of travel. About 48% of students receive financial aid; average amount of Smith College grant, $10,220. Assistance is typically divided 70% grant, 21% loan, 9% work. College reports all scholarships awarded only on the basis of need. *Meeting Costs:* college offers 10-month payment plan, and various loan programs.

Sojourner–Douglas College

Baltimore, Maryland 21205

An accredited institution, Sojourner–Douglas offers degree programs in applied social sciences.

Affiliation: Independent
UG Enrollment: 252 M, W (full-time)
Admission: Non-selective

Undergraduate degrees conferred (51). 75% were in Public Affairs, 25% were in Education.

Sonoma State College

(See California State University)

University of South Alabama

Mobile, Alabama 36688 (205) 460-6141

A state-supported university, located in a city of 190,000.

Founded: 1963
Affiliation: State
UG Enrollment: 12,276 (full-time)
Cost: < $10K
Admission: Non-selective
Application Deadline: September 10

Admission. Graduates of accredited high schools, preferably with 15 units, eligible. *Required:* ACT or SAT. *Out-of-state* freshman applicants: university seeks students from out of state. State does not limit out-of-state enrollment. No special requirements for out-of-state applicants. *Apply* by September 10. *Transfers* welcome.

Academic Environment. *Undergraduate studies* offered by colleges of Arts and Sciences, Business and Management Studies, Education, Engineering, Division of Allied Health Professions, School of Nursing, College of Medicine. About 50% of general education requirements for graduation are elective; distribution requirements vary with department. *Special programs:* CLEP, independent study, honors, undergraduate research, 3-year degree, cooperative education. *Calendar:* quarter, summer school.

Undergraduate degrees conferred (1,280). 21% were in Business and Management, 19% were in Education, 15% were in Health Sciences, 7% were in Engineering, 6% were in Social Sciences, 5% were in Communications, 4% were in Allied Health, 3% were in Psychology, 3% were in Computer and Engineering Related Technology, 3% were in Protective Services, 3% were in Liberal/General Studies, 3% were in Letters, remainder in 6 other fields.

Student Body. About 86% of students from in state; 95% South.

Varsity Sports. Men (Div.IA): Baseball, Basketball (IIA), Cross Country, Golf, Marksmanship, Soccer, Tennis, Track. Women (Div.IA): Basketball, Tennis, Volleyball.

Campus Life. About 20% of students live in coed dormitories; rest live in off-campus housing or commute. Intervisitation in men's and women's dormitory rooms limited. Sexes segregated in coed dormitories by floor. There are 13 fraternities, 6 sororities on campus which about 11% of men, 10% of women join; they provide no residence facilities.

Annual Costs. Tuition and fees, $2,349; (out-of-state, $3,249); room and board, $3,378.

South Carolina State College

Orangeburg, South Carolina 29115 (803) 536-7000

A state-supported college, located in a town of 13,300, 50 miles east of Columbia; founded as a college for Negroes and still serving a predominantly black student body.

Founded: 1895
Affiliation: State
UG Enrollment: 4,956 (full-time)
Cost: < $10K
Admission: Non-selective
Application Deadline: June 30

Admission. High school graduates with 16 units (10 in academic subjects) who rank in top half of class eligible. *Required:* SAT or ACT. *Apply* by June 30. *Transfers* accepted.

Academic Environment. *Undergraduate studies* offered by schools of Arts and Sciences, Agriculture, Education, Home Economics, Industrial Education and Engineering Technology. *Calendar:* semester, summer school.

Undergraduate degrees conferred (486). 17% were in Business and Management, 16% were in Marketing and Distribution, 12% were in Education, 8% were in Protective Services, 6% were in Engineering and Engineering Related Technology, 5% were in Psychology, 5% were in Computer and Engineering Related Technology, 5% were in Social Sciences, 4% were in Public Affairs, 4% were in Life Sciences, 4% were in Business (Administrative Support), 3% were in Home Economics, 3% were in Letters, 3% were in Agribusiness and Agricultural Production, remainder in 4 other fields.

Annual Costs. Tuition and fees, $2,200 (out-of-state, $4,380); room and board, $2,736.

University of South Carolina

Columbia, South Carolina 29208 (803) 777-7700

One of the oldest state universities in the country, South Carolina was the first to receive annual appropriations from the state government. In addition to the main campus, located in the state capital (pop. 322,880), the university includes 5 2-year and 2 4-year campuses throughout the state. Most convenient major airport: Columbia Metropolitan.

Founded: 1801
Affiliation: State
UG Enrollment: 5,950 M, 6,644 W (full-time); 1,652 M, 2,009 W (part-time)
Total Enrollment: 26,567
Cost: < $10K
% Receiving Financial Aid: 55%
Admission: Selective
Application Deadline: Rolling

Admission is selective for colleges of Engineering, Pharmacy, and Science and Mathematics. For all schools, 76% of applicants accepted, 40% of these actually enroll; 55% of freshmen graduate in top fifth of high school class, 89% in top two-fifths. Average freshman SAT scores: 475 M, 457 W verbal, 548 M, 499 W mathematical; ACT, 23 M, 22 W composite.

For Applied Professional Studies (748 M, 732 W full-time): 86% of applicants accepted, 41% of these actually enroll; 35% of freshmen graduate in top fifth of high school class, 78% in top two-fifths. Average freshman scores: SAT, 839 combined verbal, mathematical; ACT, 16 composite.

For Business Administration (1,474 M, 1,119 W full-time): 69% of applicants accepted, 42% of these actually enroll; 44% of freshmen graduate in top fifth of high school class, 86% in top two-fifths. Average freshman scores: SAT, 967 combined verbal, mathematical; ACT, 22 composite.

For Criminal Justice (242 M, 171 W full-time): 60% of applicants accepted, 45% of these actually enroll; 50% of freshmen graduate in top fifth of high school class, 87% in top two-fifths. Average freshman scores: SAT, 923 combined verbal, mathematical; ACT, 19 composite.

For Engineering (911 M, 227 W full-time): 83% of applicants accepted, 42% of these actually enroll; 65% of freshmen graduate in top fifth of high school class, 92% in top two-fifths. Average freshman scores: SAT, 1,022 combined verbal, mathematical; ACT, 23 composite.

For College of Public Health (71 M, 99 W full-time): 73% of applicants accepted, 44% of these actually enroll; 59% of freshmen graduate in top fifth of high school class, 88% in top two-fifths. Average freshman scores: SAT, 951 combined verbal, mathematical; ACT, 22 composite.

For Humanities and Social Sciences (1,792 M, 2,866 W full-time): 71% of applicants accepted, 40% of these actually enroll; 50% of freshmen graduate in top fifth of high school class, 88% in top two-fifths. Average freshman scores: SAT, 978 combined verbal, mathematical; ACT, 23 composite.

For Journalism and Mass Communication (240 M, 516 W full-time): 70% of applicants accepted, 44% of these actually enroll; 57% of freshmen graduate in top fifth of high school class, 87% in top two-fifths. Average freshman scores: SAT, 989 combined verbal, mathematical; ACT, 23 composite.

For Nursing (14 M, 285 W full-time): 71% of applicants accepted, 44% of these actually enroll; 53% of freshmen graduate in top fifth of high school class, 94% in top two-fifths. Average freshman scores: SAT, 878 combined verbal, mathematical; ACT, 20 composite.

For Pharmacy (127 M, 314 W full-time): 87% of applicants accepted, 48% of these actually enroll; 72% of freshmen graduate in top fifth of high school class, 93% in top two-fifths. Average freshman scores: SAT, 1,010 combined verbal, mathematical; ACT, 22 composite.

For Science and Mathematics (796 M, 675 W full-time): 81% of applicants accepted, 33% of these actually enroll; 65% of freshmen graduate in top fifth of high school class, 91% in top two-fifths. Average freshman scores: SAT, 1,029 combined verbal, mathematical; ACT, 24 composite.

For Education: 41% of applicants accepted, 43% of these actually enroll; 42% of freshmen graduate in top fifth of high school class, 75% in top two-fifths. Average freshman scores: SAT, 906 combined verbal, mathematical.

Required: SAT or ACT, minimum high school GPA, interview for nursing and pharmacy applicants. Non-academic factor considered of moderate importance in admissions: special talents. *Out-of-state* freshman applicants: university actively seeks students from out-of-state. State does not limit out-of-state enrollment. About 68% of out-of-state students accepted, 23% of these actually enroll. States from which most out-of-state students are drawn include Virginia, New Jersey, Pennsylvania, Georgia, New York, North Carolina. *Entrance programs:* advanced placement. *Apply* by Christmas for fall enrollment; rolling admissions. *Transfers* welcome; 944 enrolled 1993–94.

Academic Environment. Administration reports percent of general education courses required for graduation that are elective, as well as distribution requirements, vary among the different colleges and programs. Honors program for qualified students. Special programs for mature students (over 25 years of age) for whom freshman testing requirements are waived. *Undergraduate studies* offered by colleges of Humanities and Social Sciences, Applied Professional Sciences, Business Administration, Criminal Justice, Education, Engineering, Health, Journalism, Nursing, Science and Mathematics, and Pharmacy. Degrees offered: associates, bachelors, masters, doctoral.

About 80% of freshmen return for sophomore year. *Special programs:* independent study, study abroad, honors, undergraduate research, Opportunity Scholars, credit by examination. Adult programs: variety of credit courses and advisement services designed for adult students. *Calendar:* semester, summer school.

Undergraduate degrees conferred (3,049). 19% were in Business and Management, 13% were in Social Sciences, 11% were in Marketing and Distribution, 8% were in Liberal/General Studies, 7% were in Communications, 6% were in Psychology, 6% were in Engineering, 5% were in Health Sciences, 5% were in Letters, 4% were in Visual and Performing Arts, 4% were in Life Sciences, 3% were in Protective Services, remainder in 9 other fields.

Faculty. About 83% of faculty hold PhD or equivalent.

Student Body. About 80% of students from in state; 2% foreign. An estimated 14% of students reported as Black, 1% Hispanic, 2% Asian, 5% other minority. *Minority group students:* special financial, academic, and social provisions.

Varsity Sports. Men (SEC Div.I): Baseball, Basketball, Cross Country, Football (IA), Golf, Soccer, Swimming, Tennis, Track. Women (SEC Div. I): Basketball, Cross Country, Golf, Softball, Swimming, Tennis, Track, Volleyball.

Campus Life. Issues of particular concern to students reportedly include visitation, women's hours, coed housing. Present rules limit use of alcohol to dormitory rooms and other areas "approved by university." Housing program offers 3 options ranging from no intervisitation to 7-day with hours 12 noon to 11:30 PM during week, and 12 noon to 2 am on Friday and Saturday. Students under 21 must have parental approval for plans offering visitation. Campus has serious parking problems; cars discouraged for all and prohibited for freshmen. Freshmen and sophomores under 21 required to live on campus.

About 20% of men, 31% of women live in traditional dormitories; 13% of men, 10% of women in coed dormitories; 63% of men, 59% of women in off-campus housing or commute. Sexes segregated in coed dormitories by floor. There are 20 fraternities, 14 sororities on campus which about 14% of men, 14% of women join; 5% of men live in fraternities, sororities provide no residence facilities.

Annual Costs. Tuition and fees, $3,090 (out-of-state, $7,808); room and board, $3,522; estimated $3,400 other, exclusive of travel. About 55% of students receive financial aid; average amount of assistance, $5,695. Assistance is typically divided 10% scholarship, 15% grant, 60% loan, 15% work. College reports scholarships awarded on the basis of academic merit, special talents, and need.

University of South Carolina at Aiken

Aiken, South Carolina 29801 **(803) 648-6851**

One of South Carolina's regional campuses, USC-Aiken is a commuter institution serving primarily students in the immediate area. Student body is largely white, with fairly substantial numbers of Blacks and other minorities.

Founded: 1961
Affiliation: State
UG Enrollment: 759 M, 1,193 W (full-time); 423 M, 909 W (part-time)
Cost: < $10K
% Receiving Financial Aid: 44%
Admission: Non-selective
Application Deadline: Rolling

Admission About 66% of applicants accepted, 67% of these actually enroll. *Required:* SAT or ACT. Criteria considered in admissions, in order of importance: high school academic record, standardized test scores, recommendations, extracurricular activities, writing sample. *Out-of-state* freshman applicants: university actively seeks out-of-state students. State limits out-of-state enrollment to 20%. No special requirements for out-of-state students. States from which most out-of-state students are drawn include Georgia, New Jersey. *Apply:* rolling admissions.

Academic Environment. Degrees offered: associates, bachelors. *Special programs:* cross registration with system campuses, local cooperative education opportunities. Adult programs available.

Undergraduate degrees conferred (314). 42% were in Business and Management, 26% were in Education, 9% were in Liberal/General Studies, 8% were in Social Sciences, 4% were in Health Sciences, 4% were in Psychology, 3% were in Life Sciences, remainder in 3 other fields.

Graduate Career Data. Fields typically hiring largest numbers of graduates include business, education, nursing. Career Development Services include placements, resumes, testing, job shadowing, career days.

Faculty. About 68% of faculty hold PhD or equivalent. About 72% of undergraduate classes taught by tenured faculty.

Student Body. About 86% of students from in state; 97% South. Average age of undergraduate student: 24.
Varsity Sports. Men (Div.II): Baseball, Basketball, Cross Country, Golf, Soccer, Tennis. Women (Div.II): Basketball, Cross Country, Softball, Volleyball.
Annual Costs. Tuition and fees, $2,320 (out-of-state, $5,800); room and board, $3,066. About 44% of students receive financial aid; average amount of assistance, $3,000.

Coastal Carolina University

Conway, South Carolina 29526 (803) 347-3161

One of South Carolina's regional campuses, Coastal Carolina is primarily a commuter institution serving students in the immediate area. Campus is located 9 miles from Myrtle Beach. Formerly known as University of South Carolina at Coastal Carolina.

Founded: 1954
Affiliation: State
UG Enrollment: 1,513 M, 1,691 W (full-time); 307 M, 648 W (part-time)
Total Enrollment: 4,416
Cost: < $10K
% Receiving Financial Aid: 68%
Admission: Non-selective
Application Deadline: Aug. 15

Admission. About 75% of applicants accepted, 41% of these actually enroll; 22% of freshmen graduate in top fifth of high school class, 51% in top two-fifths. Average freshman scores: SAT, 415 M, 404 W verbal, 484 M, 443 W mathematical; ACT 20 composite. *Required:* SAT or ACT, minimum high school GPA. Criteria considered in admissions, in order of importance: high school academic record, standardized test scores, recommendations, class rank; other factors considered: special talents, alumni children. *Out-of-state* freshman applicants: university actively seeks out-of-state students. State does not limit out-of-state enrollment. No special requirements for out-of-state applicants. About 71% of out-of-state students accepted, 50% of these actually enroll. States from which most out-of-state students are drawn include New York, Virginia, New Jersey. *Entrance programs:* midyear admission, advanced placement. *Apply* by August 15; rolling admissions. *Transfers* welcome; 377 enrolled 1993–94.
Academic Environment. Graduation requirements include work in English, politics, foreign language, mathematics, science, humanities, literature, social sciences, history, and behavioral science. Degrees offered: bachelors, masters. *Majors offered* include marine science, business administration. Average undergraduate class size: 33% under 20, 67% 20–40. About 17% of students entering as freshmen graduate within four years, 40% eventually; 63% of freshmen return for sophomore year. *Special programs:* study abroad, internships.
Undergraduate degrees conferred (432). 28% were in Education, 23% were in Business and Management, 11% were in Social Sciences, 9% were in Marketing and Distribution, 8% were in Life Sciences, 8% were in Psychology, 4% were in Letters, 3% were in Liberal/General Studies, 3% were in Computer and Engineering Related Technology, remainder in 2 other fields.
Faculty. About 74% of faculty hold PhD or equivalent. About 51% of undergraduate classes taught by tenured faculty. About 35% of teaching faculty are female; 6% Black, 2% Hispanic.
Student Body. About 73% of students from in state; 75% South, 10% New England, 9% Middle Atlantic, 3% Midwest, 2% foreign. An estimated 7% of students reported as Black, 1% Hispanic, 1% Asian, 2% other minority.
Varsity Sports. Men: Baseball, Basketball, Cross Country, Golf, Soccer, Tennis, Track. Women: Basketball, Cross Country, Golf, Softball, Tennis, Track, Volleyball.
Campus Life. Administration reports excellent job opportunities in the area for students. About 12% of men, 12% of women live in coed dormitories; rest commute. There are 4 fraternities, 5 sororities on campus which about 7% of men, 6% of women join. About 15% of resident students leave campus on weekends.
Annual Costs. Tuition and fees, $2,470 (out-of-state, $6,280); room and board, $2,500; estimated $450 other, exclusive of travel. About 68% of students receive financial aid; average amount of assistance, $3,800. Assistance is typically divided 14% scholarship, 25% grant, 49% loan, 12% work. University reports 75 scholarships awarded on the basis of academic merit alone, 105 for special talents alone, 10 for need alone.

University of South Carolina at Spartanburg

Spartanburg, South Carolina 29303 (803) 599-2376

One of South Carolina's regional campuses, USC-Spartanburg is a commuter institutions serving primarily students in the immediate area. Campus is located near the foothills of the Blue Ridge Mountains, 65 miles from Charlotte, North Carolina and 30 miles from Greenville South Carolina.

Founded: 1967
Affiliation: State
UG Enrollment: 831 M, 1,376 W (full-time); 386 M, 672 W (part-time)
Cost: < $10K
% Receiving Financial Aid: 45%
Admission: Non-selective
Application Deadline: August 1

Admission. About 62% of applicants accepted, 69% of these actually enroll; 34% of freshmen graduate in top fifth of high school class, 65% in top two-fifths. Average freshman scores: SAT, 417 M, 408 W verbal, 473 M, 451 W mathematical; ACT, 19 composite. *Required:* SAT, minimum high school GPA. Criteria considered in admissions, in order of importance: standardized test scores, high school academic record. *Out-of-state* freshman applicants: university actively seeks out-of-state students. State does not limit out-of-state enrollment. States from which most out-of-state students are drawn include North Carolina. About 59% of out-of-state students accepted, 53% of these actually enroll. *Entrance programs:* midyear admission, deferred admission. *Apply* by August 1; rolling admissions. *Transfers* welcome; 408 enrolled 1993–94.
Academic Environment. Degrees offered: associates, bachelors. Average undergraduate class size: 47% under 20, 52% 20–40, 1% over 40. About 30% of students entering as freshmen graduate eventually, 66% of freshmen return for sophomore year. *Special programs:* study abroad, cross registration with Wofford College, Greenville Tech.
Undergraduate degrees conferred (476). 29% were in Business and Management, 21% were in Education, 13% were in Liberal/General Studies, 11% were in Health Sciences, 6% were in Psychology, 5% were in Social Sciences, 5% were in Letters, 4% were in Protective Services, 3% were in Computer and Engineering Related Technology, remainder in 3 other fields.
Faculty. About 42% of faculty hold PhD or equivalent. About 47% of undergraduate classes taught by tenured faculty. About 52% of teaching faculty are female; 5% Black, 1% Hispanic, 1% other minority.
Student Body. About 95% of students from in state; 96% South, 1% each New England, Middle Atlantic, Midwest, 1% foreign. An estimated 12% of students reported as Black, 1% Hispanic, 1% Asian, 1% other minority. Average age of undergraduate student: 23.
Varsity Sports. Men: Baseball, Basketball, Cross Country, Soccer, Tennis. Women: Basketball, Softball, Tennis, Volleyball.
Campus Life. There are 3 fraternities, 2 sororities on campus which about 4% of men, 5% of women join.
Annual Costs. Tuition and fees, $2,320 (out-of-state, $5,800); room and board, $2,000; estimated $1,500 other, exclusive of travel. About 45% of students receive financial aid. Assistance is typically divided 5% scholarship, 34% grant, 59% loan, 2% work.

South Dakota School of Mines and Technology

Rapid City, South Dakota 57701-3995 (605) 394-2400

A state-supported technological and professional institution, located in a community of 60,000 which is the eastern gateway to the Black Hills. Most convenient major airport: Rapid City Regional.

Founded: 1885
Affiliation: State
UG Enrollment: 1,241 M, 450 W (full-time); 241 M, 316 W (part-time)
Total Enrollment: 2,487
Cost: < $10K
% Receiving Financial Aid: 90%
Admission: Selective (+)
Application Deadline: Aug. 15

Admission is selective (+). About 75% of applicants accepted, 92% of these actually enroll; 44% of freshmen graduate in top fifth of high school class, 74% in top two-fifths. Average freshman ACT scores: 24 M, 25 W composite. *Required:* ACT, minimum high school GPA. Criteria considered in admissions, in order of importance: high school academic record, standardized test scores. *Out-of-state* freshman applicants: university actively seeks out-of-state students. State does not limit out-of-state enrollment. States from which most out-of-state students are drawn include Minnesota, Wyoming, Nebraska, North Dakota. About 12% of entering students from private schools, 10% from parochial schools. *Apply* by August 15. *Transfers* welcome; 284 enrolled 1993–94.

Academic Environment. Administration reports: "The primary objective of the South Dakota School of Mines & Technology is to offer high quality programs in engineering and science." Student body is characterized as overwhelmingly concerned with occupational/professional goals and with the academic preparation necessary to achieve them. "Very active student professional societies" reported. About 30% of general education requirements for graduation are elective; distribution requirements limited. Degrees offered: bachelors, masters, doctoral. *Majors offered* include 7 fields of engineering, chemistry, computer science, geology, mathematics, physics, interdisciplinary sciences. Average undergraduate class size: 80% under 20, 12% 20–40, 8% over 40.

About 50% of students entering as freshmen graduate within four years, 70% eventually; 70% of freshmen return for sophomore year. *Special programs:* CLEP, undergraduate research, independent study, credit by examination. *Calendar:* semester, summer school.

Undergraduate degrees conferred (226). 84% were in Engineering, 9% were in Computer and Engineering Related Technology, 5% were in Physical Sciences, remainder in Mathematics.

Graduates Career Data. About 86% of 1992–93 graduates employed.

Faculty. About 81% of faculty hold PhD or equivalent. About 95% of undergraduate classes taught by tenured faculty. About 10% of teaching faculty are female; 2% Black, 2% other minority.

Student Body. About 66% of students from in state; 5% foreign. An estimated 52% of students reported as Protestant, 22% Catholic, 1% Jewish, 25% other; 1% Black, 1% Hispanic, 1% Asian, 12% other minority. Average age of undergraduate student: 24.

Varsity Sports. Men (NAIA): Basketball, Cross Country, Football, Track. Women (NAIA): Basketball, Cross Country, Track, Volleyball.

Campus Life. Student interest in varsity athletics reported as still strong; regulations are enforced "judiciously." Drinking on campus prohibited. Parking facilities for both residential and commuting students described as "adequate" according to administration; students might disagree.

About 32% of men, 35% of women live in traditional dormitories; 48% of men, 45% of women commute. Freshmen given preference in college housing if all students cannot be accommodated. There are 4 fraternities, 2 sororities on campus which about 20% of men, 20% of women join; 20% of men, 20% of women live in fraternities and sororities.

Annual Costs. Tuition and fees, $2,391 (out-of-state, $4,200); room and board, $2,720; estimated $1,652 other, exclusive of travel. About 90% of students receive financial aid; average amount of assistance, $3,396. Assistance is typically divided 30% scholarship, 20% grant, 59% loan, 4% work. School reports 530 scholarships awarded on the basis of academic merit alone, 54 for special talents alone, 6 for need alone. *Meeting Costs:* school offers AMS, PLUS Loans.

South Dakota State University

Brookings, South Dakota 57006 (605) 688-4121

A land-grant university, located in a town of 15,000, near the Minnesota border. Most convenient major airport: Sioux Falls.

Founded: 1881
Affiliation: State
UG Enrollment: 3,708 M, 3,292 W (full-time); 356 M, 747 W (part-time)
Total Enrollment: 9,536
Cost: < $10K
% Receiving Financial Aid: 70%
Admission: Non-selective
Application Deadline: Rolling

Admission. South Dakota high school graduates with 13 units in specified areas eligible; others given consideration; 69% of applicants accepted, 59% of these actually enroll. Average freshman ACT scores: 23 composite. *Required:* ACT, minimum high school GPA. Criteria considered in admissions, in order of importance: high school academic record, standardized test scores, recommendations, extracurricular activities, writing sample. *Out-of-state* freshman applicants: university actively seeks students from out-of-state. State does not limit out-of-state enrollment. States from which most out-of-state students are drawn include Minnesota. *Apply:* rolling admissions. *Transfers* welcome; 637 enrolled 1993–94.

Academic Environment. Graduation requirements include 4 years of English, 3 years of social science, a half year each of fine arts, computer science, 2 years each of advanced math and lab science, with an additional year of either math or science. Degrees offered: associates, bachelors, masters, doctoral. *Undergraduate studies* offered by colleges of Agriculture and Biological Sciences, Arts and Science, Education, Engineering, General Registration, Home Economics, Nursing, Pharmacy. About 80% of freshmen return for sophomore year. *Special programs:* CLEP, independent study, honors, study abroad, internships. *Calendar:* semester, summer school.

Undergraduate degrees conferred (1,060). 17% were in Social Sciences, 16% were in Health Sciences, 14% were in Engineering, 7% were in Agricultural Sciences, 6% were in Home Economics, 6% were in Agribusiness and Agricultural Production, 5% were in Life Sciences, 5% were in Education, 4% were in Communications, 3% were in Psychology, 3% were in Letters, 3% were in Mathematics, 3% were in Engineering and Engineering Related Technology, remainder in 8 other fields.

Graduates Career Data. About 86% of 1992–93 graduates employed. Fields typically hiring largest numbers of graduates include medical. Career Development Services include resume writing classes, on-campus interviews, job service.

Faculty. About 75% of faculty hold PhD or equivalent. About 52% of undergraduate classes taught by tenured faculty. About 30% of teaching faculty are female.

Student Body. About 75% of students from in state; 20% Midwest, 1% foreign.

Varsity Sports. Men (Div.II): Baseball, Basketball, Cross Country, Diving, Football, Golf, Swimming, Tennis, Track. Women (Div.II): Basketball, Cross Country, Golf, Softball, Swimming, Track, Volleyball.

Campus Life. About 50% of students live in coed dormitories; 45% live in off-campus housing or commute. Freshmen given preference in college housing if all students cannot be accommodated. Intervisitation in men's and women's dormitory rooms limited. Sexes segregated in coed dormitories by wing. There are 5 fraternities, 3 sororities on campus, which about 4% of men, 3% of women join. About 35% of resident students leave campus on weekends.

Annual Costs. Tuition and fees, $2,250 (out-of-state, $4,212); room and board, $2,080. About 70% of students receive financial aid; average amount of assistance, $4,000. University reports 988 scholarships awarded on the basis of academic merit alone, 195 for special talents alone. *Meeting Costs:* college offers PLUS Loans.

University of South Dakota

Vermillion, South Dakota 57069 (605) 677-5434

A state-supported institution, located in a town of 10,000, 35 miles northwest of Sioux City, Iowa. Most convenient major airport: Sioux City (Iowa).

Founded: 1862
Affiliation: State
UG Enrollment: 2,317 M, 2,613 W (full-time); 215 M, 356 W (part-time)
Total Enrollment: 6,457
Cost: < $10K
% Receiving Financial Aid: 80%
Admission: Non-selective
Application Deadline: Rolling

Admission. Graduates of accredited South Dakota high schools with 16 units (12 in academic subjects) and either rank in top half of class or score 21 on ACT composite eligible; others admitted by examination; 89% of applicants accepted, 78% of these actually enroll. Average freshman ACT scores, according to most recent data available: 21.2 M, 19.5 W composite. *Required:* ACT. Requirement for out-of-state applicants: rank in top half of class or ACT composite score of 23. *Apply:* rolling admissions. *Transfers* welcome.

Academic Environment. *Undergraduate studies* offered by colleges of Arts Sciences, Fine Arts, schools of Business, Education,

Nursing, Medicine (for dental hygiene, medical technology). Specific course and distribution requirements vary by department. About 40% of students entering as freshmen graduate eventually. *Special programs:* CLEP, independent study, study abroad, honors, combined arts/medical program. *Calendar:* semester, summer school.

Undergraduate degrees conferred (737). 24% were in Business and Management, 22% were in Education, 7% were in Protective Services, 7% were in Letters, 7% were in Social Sciences, 7% were in Psychology, 5% were in Communications, 5% were in Health Sciences, 4% were in Life Sciences, 3% were in Public Affairs, remainder in 9 other fields.

Faculty. About 77% of faculty hold PhD or equivalent.

Student Body. About 70% of students from South Dakota; 94% Midwest. An estimated 60% of students reported as Protestant, 34% Catholic, 6% unaffiliated, 2% other; 2% Native American, 3% other minority, according to most recent data available.

Varsity Sports. Men (Div.II): Basketball, Cross Country, Football, Swimming, Tennis, Track. Women (Div.II): Basketball, Cross Country, Softball, Swimming, Tennis, Track, Volleyball.

Campus Life. About 4% of women live in traditional dormitories; 28% of men, 25% of women live in coed dormitories; 64% of men, 64% of women live in off-campus housing or commute. Freshmen given preference in college housing if all students cannot be accommodated. Intervisitation in men's and women's dormitory rooms limited. There are 9 fraternities, 5 sororities on campus; 14% of men, 12% of women join fraternities and sororities.

Annual Costs. Tuition and fees, $2,171 (out-of-state, $4,010); room and board, $2,538. About 80% of students receive financial aid. University reports some scholarships awarded on the basis of academic merit alone. *Meeting Costs:* university offers AMS tuition payment plan, PLUS Loans.

University of South Florida

Tampa, Florida 33620 (813) 974-3350

A state-supported institution, located 10 miles northeast of downtown Tampa (pop. 277,800). University also includes New College of South Florida, an honors college in Sarasota (see below), as well as upper division and graduate campuses at St. Petersburg, Fort Myers, and Lakeland.

Founded: 1956
Affiliation: State
UG Enrollment: 13,235 M, W(full-time); 8,435 M, W (part-time)
Total Enrollment: 34,776
Cost: < $10K
Admission: Non-selective
Application Deadline: June 1

Admission. About 62% of applicants accepted, 40% of these actually enroll. Average freshmen scores: SAT, 492 verbal, 553 mathematical; 47% of freshmen score above 500 on verbal, 14% above 600, 2% above 700; 75% score above 500 on mathematical, 32% above 600, 8% above 700; ACT, 23 composite. *Required:* SAT or ACT. Criteria considered in admissions, in order of importance: high school academic record, standardized test scores; other factors considered: special talents, diverse student body. *Out-of-state* freshman applicants: university actively seeks students from out-of-state. State limits out-of-state enrollment to 10% of total student body. No special requirements for out-of-state applicants. States from which most out-of-state students are drawn include New York, New Jersey, Pennsylvania, New England, Virginia, Maryland, Illinois. *Entrance programs:* early admission, midyear admission, advanced placement. *Apply* by June 1; rolling admissions. *Transfers* welcome; 3,743 enrolled 1993–94.

Academic Environment. *Undergraduate studies* offered by colleges of Business Administration, Education, Engineering, Fine Arts, Language and Literature, Natural Sciences, Nursing, Social and Behavioral Sciences. About 40% of general education requirements for graduation are elective; distribution requirements fairly numerous. Degrees offered: bachelors, masters, doctoral. *Majors offered* in over 100 fields, including usual arts and sciences, accounting, African-American studies, anthropology, business administration, dance, engineering, fine arts, geography, international relations, mass communications, microbiology, theater arts. Average undergraduate class size: 33% under 20, 48% 20–40, 19% over 40.

About 47% of students entering as freshmen graduate within four years. *Special programs:* CLEP, independent study, study abroad, honors, undergraduate research, 3-year degree, individualized majors, double major program, exchange with U. of Massachusetts, cooperative work/study program, area studies (non-Western, Latin American), off-campus term program. *Calendar:* semester, summer school.

Undergraduate degrees conferred (4,802). 25% were in Business and Management, 20% were in Education, 12% were in Social Sciences, 7% were in Engineering, 6% were in Letters, 5% were in Psychology, 4% were in Communications, 3% were in Life Sciences, 3% were in Protective Services, 3% were in Liberal/General Studies, remainder in 12 other fields.

Graduate Career Data. Career Development Services include aptitude testing, career counseling, placement services, resume and interviewing workshops, on-campus recruitment, job library, individual counseling services, internships and cooperative opportunities.

Faculty. About 70% of faculty hold PhD or equivalent.

Student Body. About 86% of students from in state. Average age of undergraduate school: 25.

Varsity Sports. Men (Div.I): Baseball, Basketball, Cross Country, Golf, Soccer, Tennis, Track. Women (Div.I): Basketball, Cross Country, Golf, Softball, Tennis, Track, Volleyball.

Campus Life. One student reports strong minority program. Another describes the campus as "young", with a "great" layout and "it meets a wide variety of needs." Administration reports: "There are no strictly coed or traditional dormitories. A residence hall may be traditional one quarter and coed the next depending on the space requirements of the university and the desires of the students." Cars allowed.

About 21% of men, 30% of women live in traditional and coed dormitories; rest live in off-campus housing or commute. Intervisitation in men's and women's dormitory rooms limited. Sexes segregated in coed dormitories by wing or floor. There are 21 fraternities, 11 sororities on campus which about 4% each of men, women join; they provide no residence facilities.

Annual Costs. Tuition and fees, $1,855 (out-of-state, $6,755); room and board, $3,620; estimated $500 other, exclusive of travel.

New College of the University of South Florida

Sarasota, Florida 34243-2197 (813) 359-4269

New College, founded in 1960 as a selective, private liberal arts college, became a separate honors-type college of the University of South Florida in 1975. The arrangement is a unique one in which public and private funding now support the institution. The campus is located on the north edge of Sarasota (pop. 80,000), fronting on Sarasota Bay. Most convenient major airport: Sarasota-Bradenton.

Founded: 1960
Affiliation: Independent/State
UG Enrollment: 260 M, 276 W (full-time)
Cost: < $10K
% Receiving Financial Aid: 60%
Admission: Highly (+) Selective
Application Deadline: May 1

Admission is highly (+) selective. About 35% of applicants accepted, 52% of these actually enroll; 89% of freshmen graduate in top fifth of high school class, 96% in top two-fifths. Average freshman SAT scores: 97% of freshmen score above 500 on verbal, 61% above 600, 15% above 700; 97% score above 500 on mathematical, 74% above 600, 27% above 700. *Required:* SAT or ACT, essay, interview required for students living within 100 mile radius, graded paper, transcripts, counselor and teacher recommendations. Criteria considered in admissions, in order of importance: course selection, high school academic record, writing sample, standardized test scores, recommendations, extracurricular activities; other factors considered: diverse student body in recruitment process. About 8% of entering students from private schools, 12% from parochial schools. *Apply* by May 1; rolling admissions. *Transfers* welcome; 49 enrolled 1993–94.

Academic Environment. Academic policies at New College are considered liberal in comparison with many traditional institutions. There are no specific required courses. Students allowed maximum flexibility in determining their own programs. Student body is very able academically and consequently members are expected to take more responsibility for their academic lives. Educational contracts are used to help students construct and follow up their individual programs. Course work is considered rigorous and most classes require considerable reading and research paper writing. A flexible calendar system permits students to complete their work in three years, or to opt for four or more years. Graduation requirements include 3 independent study projects, a senior thesis, and an oral defense of the thesis before a faculty panel. Pass/no grade grading system with written evaluations. Degrees offered: bachelors. *Majors offered* in usual arts and sciences as well as interdisciplinary or specialized fields. Average undergraduate class size: 18.

About 50% of students entering as freshmen graduate within four years, more than 60% eventually; 80% of freshmen return for sophomore year. *Special programs:* January interterm, honors, independent study, study abroad, undergraduate research, 3-year degree, individualized majors, National Student Exchange (82 member colleges). *Calendar:* semester, 4-week independent study period after fall term, off-campus summer independent study period.

Graduates Career Data. Advanced studies pursued by 32% of graduates, 85% eventually; 19% enter graduate school; 2% enter medical school; 8% enter law school; 3% enter business school. Fields typically hiring largest numbers of graduates include service industries. Career Development Services include graduate and professional school counseling, some on-campus recruitment.

Faculty. About 95% of faculty hold PhD or equivalent. All undergraduate classes taught by tenured faculty. About 35% of teaching faculty are female; 1% Black, 1% Hispanic, 1% other minority.

Student Body. About 60% of students from in state; 72% South, 10% Middle Atlantic, 7% Midwest, 4% New England, 3% West, 4% foreign. An estimated 1% of students reported as Black, 5% Hispanic, 6% Asian.

Campus Life. College operates with minimal regulations. "New College seeks students of strong motivation and unusual maturity." Restrictions on drinking according to state laws, not under 21. Cars allowed. Most "dormitories" are rooms or suites with outside entrances. Married student couples without children allowed to live on campus if space permits and nonstudent spouse pays rent. High interest reported in cultural activities and intramural sports (most popular: softball). No varsity sports.

About 60% of students live in coed dormitories; rest live off-campus. Freshmen given preference in college housing if all students cannot be accommodated. There are no fraternities or sororities on campus. "Not many" resident students leave campus on weekends.

Annual Costs. Tuition and fees, $2,030 (out-of-state $7,913); room and board; $3,667, estimated $3000–3500 other, exclusive of travel. About 60% of students receive financial aid. Assistance is typically divided 50% scholarship/grant, 30% loan, 20% work. *Meeting Costs:* State prepayment plan locks tuition in place.

University of the South

Sewanee, Tennessee 37383-1000 (615) 598-1238

Known popularly as Sewanee, the University of the South was for more than 100 years a college for men, offering a rigorous liberal arts and pre-professional program. Women were first admitted in 1969 and the college is now fully co-educational. The university is the home of the editorial offices of the famed Sewanee Review. The 10,000-acre campus is located on the Cumberland Plateau at an elevation of 2,000 feet. The town of Sewanee (pop. 1,500) is located within this domain, between Nashville and Chattanooga. Most convenient major airport: Nashville.

Founded: 1857
Affiliation: Episcopal
UG Enrollment: 577 M, 552 W (full-time)
Total Enrollment: 1,230
Cost: $10K–$20K
% Receiving Financial Aid: 45%
Admission: Highly Selective
Application Deadline: February 1

Admission is highly selective. About 67% of applicants accepted, 34% of these actually enroll; 75% of freshmen graduate in top fifth of high school class, 96% in top two-fifths. Average freshman SAT scores: 557 verbal, 601 mathematical; 76% of freshmen score above 500 on verbal, 31% above 600, 3% above 700; 96% score above 500 on mathematical, 50% above 600, 9% above 700; ACT scores; 27 composite. *Required:* SAT or ACT. Criteria considered in admissions, in order of importance: high school academic record, standardized test scores, recommendations, extracurricular activities, writing sample. *Entrance programs:* early decision, midyear admission, deferred admission. About 46% of entering students from private schools. *Apply* by February 1. *Transfers* welcome; 25 enrolled 1993–94.

Academic Environment. Pressures for academic achievement appear quite intense. Students call classes "difficult" and "challenging" and seem to enjoy every minute of them. Student/faculty ratio is 11:1 and students report close relations and "enduring friendships" with faculty. Classes generally are small and close supervision of student work is maintained. College has special strength in English, French, Spanish, and German literacy studies. Premed and pre-law programs notably successful (90% acceptance at medical school, 95% at law school). Honors seminars for superior students in all "major" departments; tutorials offered for seniors in major field; senior comprehensives required. Department of Natural Resources is the only vocationally oriented program on campus. College has a prestigious record in graduating future Rhodes Scholars. Graduation requirements include 3 courses (at least 1 each) in English, literature in a foreign language; 3 courses (at least 1 each) in experimental science, mathematics; 4 courses in the social sciences (anthropology, economics, history, political science) including 2 in history; 2 courses in religion and philosophy; 1 course in fine arts, music, or theater. Degrees offered: bachelors, masters, doctoral. *Majors offered* include usual arts and sciences, fine arts, forestry, German Studies, Third World Studies. Average undergraduate class size: 90% under 20, 9% 20–40, 1% over 40.

About 88% of students entering as freshmen graduate eventually; 98% of freshmen return for sophomore year. *Special programs:* honors, internships in economics and public affairs, natural resource program, independent study, study abroad, departmental and general honors, undergraduate research, individualized majors, 3–2 in engineering. *Calendar:* semester, summer school.

Undergraduate degrees conferred (255). 27% were in Social Sciences, 18% were in Letters, 13% were in Philosophy and Religion, 9% were in Visual and Performing Arts, 7% were in Foreign Languages, 5% were in Psychology, 5% were in Life Sciences, 5% were in Renewable Natural Resources, 4% were in Physical Sciences, 4% were in Area and Ethnic Studies, remainder in Mathematics.

Graduates Career Data. Advanced studies pursued by 70% of graduates; 35% enter graduate school; 12% enter medical school; 3% enter dental school; 8% enter law school; 6% enter business school. Medical schools enrolling largest numbers of graduates include U. of Tennessee, U. of Alabama; dental schools include U. of Alabama, U. of Tennessee; law schools include U. of Alabama, Vanderbilt; business schools include U. of Georgia, U. of Tennessee. About 62% of 1992–93 graduates employed. Fields typically hiring largest numbers of graduates include banking, retailing, finance, insurance. Career Development Services include courses, career library, employment counseling, career counseling, on-campus interviews, alumni networking, literature, alumni presentations on campus.

Faculty. About 93% of faculty hold PhD or equivalent. About 80% of undergraduate classes taught by tenured faculty. About 23% of teaching faculty are female; 1% Black, 1% Hispanic.

Student Body. About 20% of students from in state; 84% South, 8% Middle Atlantic, 2% each Midwest, West, 1% each New England, Northwest, 2% foreign. An estimated 78% of students reported as Protestant, 9% Catholic, 9% unaffiliated, 4% other; 3% Black, 4% other minority.

Religious Orientation. University is a church-owned institution; 42% of students affiliated with the church; no religious studies required of students; attendance at chapel services voluntary.

Varsity Sports. Men (Div.III): Baseball, Basketball, Cross Country, Diving, Football, Golf, Soccer, Swimming, Tennis, Track. Women (Div.III): Basketball, Cross Country, Diving, Field Hockey, Soccer, Softball, Swimming, Tennis, Track, Volleyball.

Campus Life. Regulations governing campus social life and dormitory rules are determined by administration/student committees. Dress tradition (maintained by students): coat and tie for men, skirts or dresses for women for class and performing arts series. Most fraternity and sorority parties open to nonmembers. Regulations governing alcohol educate students in use and abuse; party registration policy emphasizes social host responsibility, provision for non-alcoholic refreshments. Wide variety of social, recreational and cultural opportunities on campus, many student-sponsored. Campus activities are supplemented by resources of Chattanooga, 50 miles away;

Nashville also accessible, though more distant. Students report "Not many people leave campus during school." Intervisitation to midnight on weeknights, 1 am on weekends; quiet hours for study, weekday evenings. Cars allowed all students.

About 70% of men, 70% of women live in traditional dormitories; 26% of men, 27% of women live in coed dormitories; rest live in off-campus housing or commute. There are 11 fraternities, 7 sororities on campus which about 62% of men, 65% of women join; 2% of each men, women live in fraternities and sororities. About 5% of resident students leave campus on weekends.

Annual Costs. Tuition and fees, $14,910; room and board, $3,920; estimated $810 other, exclusive of travel. About 45% of students receive financial aid; average amount of assistance, $8,157. University reports 165 scholarships awarded on the basis of academic merit alone, 100% for demonstrated need. *Meeting Costs:* college offers installment payment plan, long-term loans.

Southampton Center

(See Long Island University)

Southeast Missouri State University

Cape Girardeau, Missouri 63701 (314) 651-2981

A state-supported university, located in a community of 35,000, 115 miles south of St. Louis. Most convenient major airport: St. Louis.

Founded: 1873
Affiliation: State
UG Enrollment: 2,936 M, 3,679 W (full-time); 479 M, 828 W (part-time)
Total Enrollment: 7,180
Cost: < $10K
% Receiving Financial Aid: 54%
Admission: Non-selective
Application Deadline: Aug. 1

Admission. Graduates of accredited Missouri high schools who rank in top two-thirds of high school class or above 33rd percentile on SCAT eligible for fall semester. About 86% of applicants accepted, 68% of these actually enroll; 29% of freshmen graduate in top fifth of high school class, 57% in top two-fifths. Average freshmen ACT score, according to most recent data available: 21 M, 20 W composite. *Required:* SCAT, SAT, or ACT. *Out-of-state* freshman applicants: university seeks students from out of state. State does not limit out-of-state enrollment. About 94% of out-of-state applicants accepted, 74% of these actually enroll. *Apply* by August 1. *Transfers* welcome.

Academic Environment. *Degrees:* AB, BS, BMEd, BSBA, BSEd, BSGS, BSN, BSVHEc. About 45% of general education requirements for graduation are elective; distribution requirements fairly numerous. *Majors offered* include historic preservation, health management. About 40% of students entering as freshmen graduate eventually; 65% of freshmen return for sophomore year. *Special programs:* CLEP, independent study, study abroad, honors, 3-year degree, individualized majors. *Calendar:* semester, summer school.

Undergraduate degrees conferred (1,142). 22% were in Education, 21% were in Business and Management, 8% were in Communications, 6% were in Liberal/General Studies, 6% were in Protective Services, 5% were in Home Economics, 4% were in Health Sciences, 4% were in Public Affairs, 4% were in Psychology, 3% were in Engineering and Engineering Related Technology, 3% were in Social Sciences, remainder in 15 other fields.

Student Body. About 90% of students from Missouri; 96% Midwest. An estimated 7% of students reported as Black, 3% Asian, 1% other minority, according to most recent data available.

Varsity Sports. Men (Div.II): Baseball, Basketball, Cross Country, Football, Soccer, Track. Women (Div.II): Basketball, Cross Country, Gymnastics, Softball, Track, Volleyball.

Campus Life. About 16% of men, 14% of women live in traditional dormitories; 21% of men, 35% of women live in coed-dormitories; rest live in off-campus housing or commute. Freshmen given preference in college housing if all students cannot be accommodated. No intervisitation in men's and women's dormitory rooms. There are 9 fraternities, 9 sororities on campus which provide housing for about 4% of men, 10% of women.

Annual Costs. Tuition and fees, $2,158 (out-of-state, $3,822); room and board, $3,085. About 54% of students receive financial aid. University reports some scholarships awarded on the basis of academic merit alone.

Southeastern College of the Assemblies of God

Lakeland, Florida 33801 (813) 665-4404

A Christian college of the Assemblies of God Church, Southeastern offers general education, teacher education, and specialized studies in ministry-related areas.

Affiliation: Assemblies of God
UG Enrollment: 550 M, 528 W (full-time)
Total Enrollment: 1,200
Cost: < $10K
% Receiving Financial Aid: 74%
Admission: Non-selective
Application Deadline: Rolling

Admission. About 80% of freshmen applicants accepted; 78% of these actually enroll. *Entrance programs:* early decision, early admission, midyear admission, deferred admission.

Academic Environment. College offers programs in education and psychology, as well as programs for missions and Christian ministry. Degrees offered: bachelors. About 31% of entering class graduate within four years; 69% of freshmen return for sophomore year. Average undergraduate class size: 53% under 20, 30% 20–40, 17% over 40.

Undergraduate degrees conferred (195). 48% were in Theology, 41% were in Education, 12% were in Psychology.

Graduates Career Data. Advanced studies pursued by 25% of 1993–94 graduates; all enter graduate school.

Faculty. About 55% of faculty hold PhD or equivalent. About 45% of undergraduate classes taught by tenured faculty. About 28% of teaching faculty are female; 3% Hispanic, 2% other minority.

Student Body. About 70% of students from South, 15% Middle Atlantic, 10% New England, 1% foreign. All students reported as Protestant; 8% Hispanic, 2% Black, 2% Asian, 1% Native American.

Religious Orientation. College is a church-related institution; 90% of students affiliated with the church; minimum of 30 semester hours of religious courses required of all students.

Varsity Sports. Men: Basketball, Soccer. Women: Basketball, Volleyball.

Campus Life. About 70% each of men, women live in traditional dormitories; rest commute. There are no fraternities or sororities on campus.

Annual Costs. Tuition and fees, $3,600; room and board, $2,860. About 74% of students receive financial aid. Assistance is typically divided 4% scholarship, 27% grant, 66% loan, 3% work.

Southeastern Bible College

Birmingham, Alabama 35243

An independent, non-denominational Bible college offering associates, bachelors, masters, and doctoral degrees.

Founded: 1935
Affiliation: Independent

Southeastern Louisiana University

Hammond, Louisiana 70402 (504) 549-2123

A state-supported university, located in a community of 15,000, 50 miles north of New Orleans. Most convenient major airport: New Orleans International.

Founded: 1925
Affiliation: State
UG Enrollment: 3,418 M, 4,373 W (full-time); 596 M, 1,024 W (part-time)
Total Enrollment: 10,454
Cost: < $10K
% Receiving Financial Aid: 41%
Admission: Non-selective
Application Deadline: July 15

Admission. Graduates of approved Louisiana high schools accepted, others admitted by examination; 99% of applicants accepted, 80% of these actually enroll. Average freshman ACT scores, according to most recent data available: 18.7 composite, 17.5 mathematical. *Required:* ACT. *Out-of-state* freshman applicants: university seeks students from out of state. State does not limit out-of-state enrollment. *Apply* by July 15. *Transfers* welcome.
Academic Environment. *Degrees:* AB, BS, BM, BMEd. About 8% of general education requirements for graduation are elective; distribution requirements fairly numerous. *Special programs:* CLEP, honors, "extensive remedial program." About 35% of students graduate eventually. *Calendar:* semester, summer school.
Undergraduate degrees conferred (781). 31% were in Business and Management, 26% were in Education, 10% were in Health Sciences, 4% were in Protective Services, 4% were in Engineering and Engineering Related Technology, 3% were in Liberal/General Studies, 3% were in Public Affairs, 3% were in Social Sciences, 3% were in Psychology, remainder in 14 other fields.
Faculty. About 59% of faculty hold PhD or equivalent.
Student Body. About 98% of students from in state. An estimated 7% of students reported as Black, 1% Hispanic, 1% other minority, according to most recent data available.
Varsity Sports. Men (Div.I): Baseball, Basketball, Football, Golf, Tennis. Women (Div.I): Basketball, Softball, Volleyball.
Campus Life. About 7% of men, 10% of women live in traditional dormitories; 3% of men, 2% of women live in coed dormitories; rest live in off-campus housing or commute. Freshmen given preference in college housing if all students cannot be accommodated. No intervisitation in men's or women's dormitory rooms. There are 8 fraternities, 5 sororities on campus; fraternities and sororities provide residence facilities.
Annual Costs. Tuition and fees, $1,615 (out-of-state, $3,415); room and board, $2,200. About 41% of students receive financial aid; assistance is typically divided 42% scholarship, 28% loan, 4% work. University reports some scholarships awarded on the basis of academic merit alone.

Southeastern Massachusetts University

(See University of Massachusetts Dartmouth)

Southeastern Oklahoma State University

Durant, Oklahoma 74701-0609 (405) 924-0121

A state-supported college, located in a town of 11,100, 120 miles southeast of Oklahoma City and 90 miles north of Dallas. Most convenient major airport: Dallas-Fort Worth, TX.

Founded: 1909
Affiliation: State
UG Enrollment: 1,420 M, 1,576 W (full-time); 263 M, 495 W (part-time)
Total Enrollment: 4,202
Cost: < $10K
% Receiving Financial Aid: 75%
Admission: Non-selective
Application Deadline: Aug. 5

Admission. Oklahoma graduates of accredited high schools with 2.8 average or rank in top two-thirds of class or score in top two-thirds on ACT composite eligible; 86% of applicants accepted, 80% of these actually enroll. Average freshmen scores: ACT, 19. *Required:* SAT or ACT. Criteria considered in admissions, in order of importance: standardized test scores, high school academic record, extracurricular activities; other factors considered: special talents. *Out-of-state* freshman applicants: university actively seeks students from out-of-state. State does not limit out-of-state enrollment. States from which most out-of-state students are drawn include Texas, Arkansas. Entrance program: advanced placement. *Apply* by August 5 for Fall admissions, January 5 for Spring admissions. *Transfers* welcome; 499 enrolled 1993–94.
Academic Environment. Degrees offered: bachelors, masters. About 40% of general education requirements for graduation are elective; distribution requirements fairly numerous. *Majors offered* include aviation, biomedical technology. Average undergraduate class size: 30% under 20, 66% 20–40, 4% over 40. About 37% of students entering as freshmen graduate eventually. *Special programs:* CLEP, independent study, undergraduate research, 3-year degree. *Calendar:* semester, summer school.
Undergraduate degrees conferred (537). 39% were in Education, 23% were in Business and Management, 6% were in Engineering and Engineering Related Technology, 4% were in Social Sciences, 4% were in Protective Services, 3% were in Physical Sciences, 3% were in Psychology, 3% were in Computer and Engineering Related Technology, remainder in 13 other fields.
Graduate Career Data. About 65% of 1992–93 graduates employed. Fields typically hiring largest numbers of graduates include education, business.
Faculty. About 57% of faculty hold PhD or equivalent. About 10% of undergraduate classes taught by tenured faculty. About 31% of teaching faculty are female; 1% Hispanic, 11% other minority.
Student Body. About 88% of students from in state; 2% foreign. An estimated 4% of students reported as Black, 1% Hispanic, 1% Asian, 33% other minority. Average age of undergraduate student: 25.
Varsity Sports. Men: Baseball, Basketball, Equestrian, Football, Golf, Tennis, Track. Women: Basketball, Equestrian, Tennis, Track.
Campus Life. About 7% of men, 6% of women live in traditional dormitories; rest commute. Intervisitation in men's and women's dormitory rooms limited. There are 5 fraternities, 2 sororities on campus which about 10% of men, 5% of women join; they provide no residence facilities. About 50% of resident students leave campus on weekends.
Annual Costs. Tuition and fees, $1,224 (out-of-state, $3,395); room and board, $2,088; estimated $1,470 other. About 75% of students receive financial aid; average amount of assistance, $4,000. Assistance is typically divided 10% scholarship, 45% grant, 30% loan, 15% work. University reports 330 scholarships awarded on basis of academic merit alone, 125 for special talents alone, 440 for need alone.

Southeastern University

Washington, D.C. 20024

A private university offering associates, baccalaureate, and master's level studies in business and management, computer science, public affairs and services, and social sciences.

Total Enrollment: 538
Cost: < $10K
Admission: Non-selective

Annual Costs. Tuition and fees, $8,250.
Undergraduate degrees conferred (82). 82% were in Business and Management, 15% were in Computer and Engineering Related Technology, remainder in 2 other fields.

Southern Arkansas University

Magnolia, Arkansas 71753 (501) 235-4000

A state-supported university, located in a community of 13,559, 60 miles east of Texarkana. Most convenient major airport: Shreveport, LA.

Founded: 1909
Affiliation: State
UG Enrollment: 965 M, 1,107 W (full-time)
Total Enrollment: 2,492
Cost: < $10K
% Receiving Financial Aid: 30%
Admission: Non-selective
Application Deadline: August 19

Admission. Graduates of accredited high schools with 15 units (10 in academic subjects) admitted; all applicants accepted, 63% of these actually enroll; 26% of freshmen graduate in top fifth of high school class, 53% in top two-fifths. Average freshman ACT scores, according to most recent data available: 17.9 M, 18.6 W composite. *Required:* ACT, minimum high school GPA. Criteria considered in admissions, in order of importance: standardized test scores, high school academic record, recommendations, writing sample, extracurricular activities. *Out-of-state* freshman applicants: university actively seeks students from out-of-state. State does not limit out-of-state enrollment. Required for out-of-state students: rank in top half of class. States from which most out-of-state students are drawn include Louisiana, Texas. Entrance program: early admission. *Apply* by August 19. *Transfers* welcome; 228 enrolled Fall, 1993.

Academic Environment. Degrees offered: associates, bachelors, masters. About 40% of general education requirements for graduation are elective; distribution requirements fairly numerous. About 31% of students entering as freshmen graduate eventually; 60% of freshmen return for sophomore year. *Special programs:* CLEP, 3-year degree, internships. *Calendar:* semester, summer school.

Undergraduate degrees conferred (224). 31% were in Business and Management, 29% were in Education, 8% were in Social Sciences, 7% were in Business (Administrative Support), 5% were in Psychology, 4% were in Life Sciences, 4% were in Agribusiness and Agricultural Production, 3% were in Communications, 3% were in Letters, remainder in 7 other fields.

Faculty. About 45% of faculty hold PhD or equivalent. About 45% of teaching faculty are female.

Student Body. About 78% of students from in state. An estimated 80% of students reported as Protestant, 15% Catholic, 4% unaffiliated; 18% Black, 3% other minority, according to most recent data available.

Varsity Sports. Men (NAIA): Baseball, Basketball, Cross Country, Football, Golf, Tennis, Track. Women (NAIA): Basketball, Cross Country, Tennis, Track, Volleyball.

Campus Life. About 39% of men, 21% of women live in traditional dormitories; no coed dormitories; rest commute. Intervisitation in men's and women's dormitory rooms limited. There are 7 fraternities, 7 sororities on campus which about 10% of men, 8% of women join; they provide no residence facilities. About 60% of resident students leave campus on weekends.

Annual Costs. Tuition and fees, $1,500 (out-of-state, $2,340); room and board, $2,240; estimated $800 other, exclusive of travel. About 30% of students receive financial aid; average amount of assistance, $700. Assistance is typically divided 15% scholarship, 25% loan, 60% work. University reports 214 scholarships awarded on the basis of academic merit alone, 223 for special talents alone. *Meeting Costs:* university offers PLUS loans.

Southern California College

Costa Mesa, California 92626 (714) 556-3610

A church-related college, located in a city of 77,200, 40 miles southeast of Los Angeles.

Founded: 1920	**Total Enrollment:** 965
Affiliation: Assemblies of God	**Cost:** < $10K
UG Enrollment: 384 M, 400 W (full-time); 57 M, 59 W (part-time)	**% Receiving Financial Aid:** 80%
	Admission: Non-selective
	Application Deadline: Rolling

Admission. Graduates of accredited high schools with 16 units and C average in college preparatory courses eligible; 98% of applicants accepted, 56% of these actually enroll; 50% of freshmen graduate in top fifth of high school class, 75% in top two-fifths. Average freshmen scores: SAT, 410 verbal, 460 mathematical; ACT, 22 composite. *Required:* SAT or ACT (for placement only), 2.5 minimum high school GPA, essay. Criteria considered in admissions, in order of importance: high school academic record, recommendations, standardized test scores, writing sample, extracurricular activities; other factors considered: religious affiliation and/or commitment. *Apply:* rolling admissions. *Transfers* welcome; 120 enrolled 1993–94.

Academic Environment. Graduation requirements include a minimum of 40 credits in upper level courses, 16 units in religion courses. Degrees offered: bachelors, masters. Average undergraduate class size: 30% under 20, 60% 20–40, 10% over 40. About 25% of students entering as freshmen graduate within four years; 85% of freshmen return for sophomore year. *Special programs:* CLEP, independent study, study abroad, internships, undergraduate research. *Calendar:* 4–1–4, summer school.

Undergraduate degrees conferred (141). 21% were in Business and Management, 20% were in Theology, 14% were in Education, 13% were in Social Sciences, 11% were in Psychology, 6% were in Communications, 5% were in Letters, 4% were in Life Sciences, 3% were in Visual and Performing Arts, remainder in 2 other fields.

Faculty. About 75% of faculty hold PhD or equivalent. About 97% of undergraduate classes taught by tenured faculty. About 23% of teaching faculty are female; 2% Black, 2% Latino.

Student Body. About 75% of students from in state and Northwest. An estimated 97% of students are reported as Protestant, 2% Catholic; 6% Black, 10% Hispanic, 7% Asian, 1% other minority.

Religious Orientation. Southern California is a church-related institution; 16 hours of religion, attendance at weekly chapel services required of all students; attendance at vespers, Sunday services expected.

Varsity Sports. Men: Baseball, Basketball, Cross Country, Soccer, Tennis, Track. Women: Basketball, Cross Country, Soccer, Softball, Tennis, Track, Volleyball.

Campus Life. About 41% of men, 59% of women live in traditional dormitories; no coed dormitories; rest commute. No intervisitation in men's or women's dormitory rooms. There are no fraternities or sororities on campus. About 60% of resident students leave campus on weekends.

Annual Costs. Tuition and fees, $8,686; room and board, $3,586; estimated $500 other, exclusive of travel. About 80% of students receive financial aid.

University of Southern California

Los Angeles, California 90089-0911 (213) 740-2311

A large, diverse, urban institution with 18 graduate and professional schools, USC is the second largest private research university in the country. The 165-acre campus is located 2 miles from downtown Los Angeles. Most convenient major airport: LAX International.

Founded: 1880	**Total Enrollment:** 27,000
Affiliation: Independent	**Cost:** $10K–$20K
UG Enrollment: 7,983 M, 6,618 W (full-time); 1,270 (part-time)	**% Receiving Financial Aid:** 61%
	Admission: Selective
	Application Deadline: Feb. 1

Admission is selective. About 69% of applicants accepted, 30% of these actually enroll; 65% of freshmen graduate in top fifth of high school class, 96% in top two-fifths. Average freshman SAT scores, middle 50% range: 980–1220 combined; ACT, 24–29 composite. *Required:* SAT or ACT, 3.0 minimum high school GPA, interview upon request, essay. Criteria considered in admissions, in order of importance: high school academic record, standardized test scores, writing sample, recommendations, extracurricular activities; other factors considered: special talents, alumni children, diverse student body. *Entrance programs:* early admission, midyear admission, deferred admission, advanced placement. About 20% of entering students from private schools, 15% from parochial schools. *Apply* by February 1; rolling admissions. *Transfers* welcome; 1,583 enrolled 1993–94.

Academic Environment. Pressures for academic achievement vary somewhat among the different schools and colleges. College of Letters, Arts and Sciences has largest enrollment and provides the general education core for the university; some professional schools on campus admit undergraduates. *Undergraduate studies* offered to freshmen by College of Letters, Arts, and Sciences, schools of Architecture and Fine Arts, Business, Engineering, Gerontology, Performing Arts (including School of Music), Social Work; juniors may enter schools of Education, Pharmacy, Public Administration; School of Dentistry offers upper-level program in dental hygiene. Graduation requirements include freshman writing, and general education core curriculum. Degrees offered: bachelors, masters, doctoral. *Majors offered* in over 400 major or major/minor fields; in addition to usual studies include anthropology, Asian studies, astronomy, cinema, drama, international relations, journalism, Latin American studies, Slavic studies, telecommunications, urban affairs, interdisciplinary major program, dental science, journalism/East Asian area studies, journalism/Spanish, music. Average undergraduate class size: 15% under 20, 70% 20–40, 15% over 40.

About 55% of students entering as freshmen graduate within four years, 69% eventually; 90% of freshmen return for sophomore year. *Special programs:* CLEP, JEP, study abroad, honors, individualized majors, internships, cross registration with Hebrew Union College, Howard U., 3–2 in engineering, thematic option, undergraduate research. *Calendar:* semester, summer school.

Undergraduate degrees conferred (3,181). 100% were in Unknown. *Doctoral degrees:* Education 140, Engineering 52, Public Affairs and Services 39, Biological Sciences 35, Social Sciences 38, Letters 14, Physical Sciences 22, Communications 14, Fine and Applied Arts 14, Psychology 15, Business and Management 17, Foreign Languages 5, Computer and Information Sciences 3, Library Science 4, Health Professions 1, Mathematics 4.

Graduate Career Data. Career Development Services provides students and alumni with the "knowledge and skills to systematically explore and select their career options."

Faculty. About 94% of faculty hold PhD or equivalent. About 69% of undergraduate classes taught by tenured faculty. About 21% of teaching faculty are female.

Student Body. About 64% of students from in state; 9% foreign. An estimated 42% of students reported as Protestant, 40% Catholic, 4% Jewish; 6% Black, 14% Hispanic, 23% Asian, 8% other minority. *Minority group students:* special financial provisions.

Varsity Sports. Men (Div.I): Baseball, Basketball, Crew, Cross Country, Diving, Football (IA), Golf, Swimming, Tennis, Track, Volleyball. Women (Div.I): Basketball, Crew, Cross Country, Diving, Golf, Soccer, Swimming, Tennis, Track, Volleyball.

Campus Life. Student interest in varsity athletics and fraternities continues high, according to reports. Students have considerable control over regulations governing campus social life. Active calendar of cultural and intellectual events, including visiting artists as well as student talent, is supplemented by the varied opportunities afforded by the Los Angeles area. Student leader comments that "our variety is so great, most all students feel at home on our campus, provided they are not liberal." No curfew; intervisitation unlimited. Alcohol prohibited on campus and in approved housing; cars allowed. University "encourages" new students to live on campus during first year.

About 4% of students live in traditional dormitories; 34% in coed dormitories; 9% live in off-campus college-related housing; 35% commute. Freshmen given preference in college housing if all students cannot be accommodated. Sexes segregated in coed dormitories by floor. There are 26 fraternities, 12 sororities on campus which about 18% of men, 18% of women join; 18% of students live in fraternities and sororities. About 45% of resident students leave campus on weekends.

Annual Costs. Tuition and fees, $16,810; room and board, $6,196; estimated $2,500 other, exclusive of travel. About 61% of students receive financial aid; average amount of assistance, $17,748. Assistance is typically divided 20% scholarship, 40% grant, 25% loan, 15% work. University reports 600–750 scholarships awarded on the basis of academic merit alone, $175 million for need alone. *Meeting Costs:* university offers a variety of loan programs and payment plans.

University of Southern Colorado

Pueblo, Colorado 81001 **(800) 872-4769**

A state-supported university, located in a city of 97,500. Most convenient major airport: Pueblo Memorial.

Founded: 1933
Affiliation: State
UG Enrollment: 1,820 M, 1,889 W (full-time); 397 M, 479 W (part-time)
Total Enrollment: 4,597
Cost: < $10K
% Receiving Financial Aid: 57%
Admission: Non-selective
Application Deadline: June 22

Admission. High schools graduates who rank in top two-thirds of class, have minimum ACT/SAT of 19/810 composite, or GPA of 2.5 eligible; up to 20% of class given individual consideration; 86% of applicants accepted, 40% of these actually enroll; 23% of students graduate in top fifth of high school class; 52% in top two-fifths. Average freshman ACT scores: 19.6 M, 19.8 composite. *Required:* ACT. Criteria considered in admissions, in order of importance: high school academic record, standardized test scores, recommendations, extracurricular activities, writing sample, interview (if necessary); other factors considered: special talents. *Out-of-state* freshman applicants: university actively seeks out-of-state students. State does not limit out-of-state enrollment. About 89% of out-of-state students accepted, 26% of these actually enroll. States from which most out-of-state students are drawn include New Mexico, Illinois, Texas, Kansas. *Entrance programs:* early decision, deferred admission, advanced placement. *Apply* by June 22; rolling admissions. *Transfers* welcome.

Academic Environment. Graduation requirements include English composition I and II, math requirements as determined by major, speech, computer science, and a 27-hour general education core. Degrees offered: bachelors, masters. *Majors offered* include automotive parts and service management, industrial engineering, industrial science/technology, sports medicine, sports psychology. Average undergraduate class size: 42% under 20, 39% 20–40, 19% over 40.

About 9% of students entering as freshmen graduate within four years, 33% eventually; 60% of freshmen return for sophomore year. *Special programs:* CLEP, study abroad, 3–2 in engineering, internships, undergraduate research, independent study, honors, individualized majors. *Calendar:* semester, summer school.

Undergraduate degrees conferred (571). 21% were in Business and Management, 18% were in Engineering and Engineering Related Technology, 13% were in Social Sciences, 6% were in Life Sciences, 6% were in Communications, 6% were in Psychology, 6% were in Letters, 5% were in Health Sciences, 5% were in Public Affairs, 4% were in Visual and Performing Arts, 3% were in Computer and Engineering Related Technology, 3% were in Education, remainder in 6 other fields.

Graduate Career Data. About 71% of 1992–93 graduates employed. Fields typically hiring largest numbers of graduates include education, government. Career Development Services available.

Faculty. About 81% of faculty hold PhD or equivalent. About 47% of undergraduate classes taught by tenured faculty. About 28% of teaching faculty are female; 2% Black, 11% Hispanic, 5% other minority.

Student Body. About 90% of students from within state; 2% Midwest, 3% foreign. Average age of undergraduate student: 24.

Varsity Sports. Men (NCAA, Div II): Baseball, Basketball, Golf, Soccer, Tennis, Wrestling. Women (NCAA, Div II): Basketball, Soccer, Softball, Tennis, Volleyball.

Campus Life. About 5% of men, 5% of women live in coed dormitories; 95% of men, 95% of women commute. Freshmen given preference in college housing if all students cannot be accommodated. Intervisitation in men's and women's dormitory rooms limited. There is 1 fraternity on campus, which about 1% of men join; less than 1% of men live in fraternity. There are no sororities on campus. About 40% of resident students leave campus on weekends.

Annual Costs. Tuition and fees, $1,878 (out-of-state, $6,768); room and board, $3,728; estimated $1,200–2,400 other, exclusive of travel. About 57% of students receive financial aid; average amount, $4,617. Assistance is typically divided 10% scholarship, 32% grant, 48% loan, 10% work. University reports 303 scholarships awarded on the basis of academic merit alone, 216 for special talents alone.

Southern Connecticut State University

New Haven, Connecticut 06515 **(203) 397-4000**

A state-supported, liberal arts, and teachers college, located in a city of 130,000. Most convenient major airports: JFK, LaGuardia (NY), or Bradley (Hartford).

Founded: 1893
Affiliation: State
UG Enrollment: 2,642 M, 3,250 W (full-time); 1,113 M, 1,365 W (part-time)
Total Enrollment: 12,144
Cost: < $10K
% Receiving Financial Aid: 53%
Admission: Non-selective
Application Deadline: May 1

Admission. Graduates of accredited high schools with 2.5 GPA in 16 units (13 in college preparatory work) and score of 800 on combined SAT eligible; 69% of applicants accepted, 39% of these actually enroll; 9% of freshmen graduate in top fifth of high school class, 26% in top two-fifths. Average freshman SAT scores: 397 M, 399 W verbal, 447 M, 415 W mathematical. *Required:* SAT, 2.5 minimum high school GPA, essay. Criteria considered in admissions, in order of importance: high school academic record, standardized test scores, recommendations, writing sample, extracurricular activities. *Out-of-state* freshman applicants: university actively seeks students from out-of-state. State does not limit out-of-state enrollment. No special requirements for out-of-state applicants. About 68% of out-of-state students accepted, 28% of these actually enroll. States from which most out-of-state students are drawn include New York, New Jersey. Entrance program: advanced placement. About 84% of entering students from public schools, 6% from private schools, 10% from parochial schools. *Apply* by May 1; rolling admissions. *Transfers* welcome; 823 enrolled 1993–94.

Academic Environment. Degrees offered: associates, bachelors, masters. Undergraduate programs offered by 5 schools: Arts and Sciences, Business Economics, Education, Library Science and Instructional Technology, and Professional Studies. *Majors offered* include usual arts and sciences, variety of programs in teacher preparation, corporate communications, earth sciences, geography, health sciences, journalism, library sciences, nursing, recreation, social work, theater. Average undergraduate class size: 26% under 20, 67% 20–40, 7% over 40.

About 20% of students entering as freshmen graduate within four years, 45% eventually; 75% of freshmen return for sophomore year. *Special programs:* January interterm, independent study, study abroad, honors, working internships, cooperative programs, undergraduate research, credit by examination. *Calendar:* semester, summer school.

Undergraduate degrees conferred (1,125). 23% were in Business and Management, 20% were in Education, 11% were in Communications, 8% were in Liberal/General Studies, 7% were in Social Sciences, 7% were in Health Sciences, 5% were in Psychology, 4% were in Public Affairs, 3% were in Computer and Engineering Related Technology, 3% were in Visual and Performing Arts, remainder in 8 other fields.

Graduates Career Data. Advanced studies pursued by 31% of graduates. About 86% of 1992–93 graduates employed. Employers typically hiring largest numbers of graduates include: business and industry, education, government, military. Career Development Services include assistance with resume writing, interviewing techniques and referral source.

Faculty. About 75% of faculty hold PhD or equivalent. About 69% of undergraduate classes taught by tenured faculty. About 36% of teaching faculty are female; 4% Black, 6% other minority.

Student Body. About 93% of students from in state; 1% foreign. An estimated 7% of students reported as Black, 3% Hispanic, 11% other minority. Average age of undergraduate student: 24. *Minority group students:* "intensive" recruitment effort; structured tutorial and supportive services programs available to all students.

Varsity Sports. Men (Div.II): Baseball, Basketball, Cross Country, Football, Gymnastics (Div. I), Soccer, Swimming, Track, Wrestling. Women (Div. II): Basketball, Cross Country, Gymnastics, Field Hockey, Softball, Swimming, Track, Volleyball.

Campus Life. Regulations concerning dorm hours and intervisitation enforced "rigorously." Cars allowed. About 18% of men, 14% of women live in coed dormitories; rest live in off-campus housing or commute. Intervisitation in men's and women's dormitory rooms limited. Sexes segregated in coed dormitories by floor. There are 4 fraternities, 3 sororities on campus which about 2% of men, 2% of women join; they provide no residence facilities. About 70% of resident students leave campus on weekends.

Annual Costs. Tuition and fees, $2,838 (out-of-state, $7,550); room and board, $4,452; estimated $1,500 other, exclusive of travel. About 53% of students receive financial aid; average amount of assistance, $4,500. Assistance is typically divided 1% scholarship, 34% grant, 55% loan, 10% work. University reports 82 scholarships awarded on the basis of academic merit alone.

Southern Illinois University at Carbondale

Carbondale, Illinois 62901 (618) 453-5351

A state-supported institution, located in a predominantly rural area, near a town of 27,000, 100 miles southeast of St. Louis. Most convenient major airport: Southern Illinois.

Founded: 1869
Affiliation: State
UG Enrollment: 10,157 M, 6,746 W (full-time); 1,484 M, 1,015 W (part-time)
Total Enrollment: 23,881
Cost: < $10K
% Receiving Financial Aid: 85%
Admission: Non-selective
Application Deadline: Rolling

Admission. Graduates of recognized high schools who rank in top half of class and score in upper two-thirds on ACT eligible; 61% of applicants accepted, 37% of these actually enroll; 4% of freshmen graduate in top fifth of high school class, 31% in top two-fifths. *Required:* ACT, class rank, GPA. Criteria considered in admissions, in order of importance: standardized test scores, class rank, high school academic record. *Out-of-state* freshman applicants: university actively seeks students from out-of-state. No special requirements for out-of-state applicants. Most most out-of-state students are international. *Apply:* rolling admissions. *Transfers* welcome; 6,218 enrolled 1993–94.

Academic Environment. *Undergraduate studies* offered by colleges of Business and Administration, Mass Communication and Media Arts, Education, Engineering, Liberal Arts, Science, Agriculture, Technical Careers. Graduation requirements include 9 semester hours each in science, social sciences, and humanities, 12 in communications, 4 in physical education, and an additional 3 in either science, social sciences, or humanities. Degrees offered: associates, bachelors, masters, doctoral. *Majors offered* in wide range of studies, including accounting, animal science, anthropology, aviation, computer science, engineering, environmental, equine science, foreign language/international trade, forensic/chemistry, forestry, geography, hotel, restaurant and travel administration, home economics, journalism, law enforcement, metalsmithing, microbiology, radio–television, speech pathology, theater; special concentrations also possible. Average undergraduate class size: 20% under 20.

About 19% of students entering as freshmen graduate within four years, 50% eventually; 68% of freshmen return for sophomore year. *Special programs:* January interterm, CLEP, independent study, study abroad, honors, 3-year degree, individualized majors, area studies (African, Asian, European, and Russian), internships, Scholar Program, credit for military experience. Adult programs: Continuing Education, Community Listener's Program, non-traditional student services, family housing, over-21 residence halls. *Calendar:* semester, summer school.

Undergraduate degrees conferred (4,586). 20% were in Education, 11% were in Engineering and Engineering Related Technology, 10% were in Business and Management, 6% were in Transportation and Material Moving, 4% were in Communications, 4% were in Social Sciences, 4% were in Protective Services, 4% were in Letters, 4% were in Multi/Interdisciplinary Studies, 4% were in Health Sciences, 3% were in Mechanics and Repairers, 3% were in Engineering, 3% were in Life Sciences, 3% were in Visual and Performing Arts, 3% were in Psychology, 3% were in Home Economics, remainder in 13 other fields.

Graduates Career Data. Advanced studies pursued by 19% of graduates. About 83% of 1992–93 graduates employed. Career Development Services include assistance with resume preparation, interview skill building, on-campus recruitment, placement services.

Faculty. About 69% of faculty hold PhD or equivalent. About 34% of teaching faculty are female; 3% Black, 1% Hispanic, 8% other minority.

Student Body. About 81% of students from in state; 82% Midwest, 4% South, 4% West, 1% Middle Atlantic, 8% foreign. An estimated 18% of students reported as Protestant, 10% Catholic, 64% other; 12% Black, 2% Asian, 2% Hispanic, 10% other minority. Average age of undergraduate student: 23.

Varsity Sports. Men (Div.I): Baseball, Basketball, Cross Country, Diving, Football (IAA), Golf, Swimming, Tennis, Track. Women (Div.I): Basketball, Cross Country, Diving, Golf, Softball, Swimming, Tennis, Track, Volleyball.

Campus Life. University serves a predominantly commuter student body, though increasing numbers of students live on campus. Campus van available to students. Administration source reports "excellent facilities for the handicapped."

About 24% of men, 21% of women live in traditional dormitories; 3% of men, 2% of women live in coed dormitories; rest live in off-campus housing or commute. Freshmen given preference in college housing if all students cannot be accommodated. Sexes segregated

in coed dormitories either by wing or floor. There are 17 fraternities, 8 sororities on campus which about 6% of men, 6% of women join.
Annual Costs. Tuition and fees, $3,052 (out-of-state, $7,552); room and board, $3,180. About 85% of students receive financial aid; average amount of assistance, $6,400. Assistance is typically divided 10% scholarship, 30% grant, 50% loan, 10% work. University reports 710 scholarships awarded on the basis of academic merit alone, 350 for special talents alone. *Meeting Costs:* college offers Student to Student Grant Program.

Southern Illinois University/Edwardsville

Edwardsville, Illinois 62026 **(618) 692-2720**

The Edwardsville campus of Southern Illinois, located near a town of 11,100, about 20 miles east of St. Louis, is primarily for commuters. Most convenient major airport: St. Louis Lambert International.

Founded: 1957
Affiliation: State
UG Enrollment: 2,759 M, 3,470 W (full-time); 1,057 M, 1,387 W (part-time)
Total Enrollment: 9,343
Cost: < $10K
Admission: Non-selective
Application Deadline: 30 days before registration

Admission. Graduates of accredited high schools who rank in top half of class or score 18 on ACT composite eligible; others admitted conditionally; 92% of applicants accepted, 45% of these actually enroll; 29% of freshmen graduate in top fifth of high school class, 60% in top two-fifths. *Required:* ACT. *Out-of-state* freshman applicants: university seeks students from out of state. State does not limit out-of-state enrollment. *Apply* by 30 days before registration. *Transfers* welcome.
Academic Environment. *Degrees:* AB, BS, BFA, BLS, BM, BSA, BSBA, BSE. *Majors offered* include usual arts and sciences, anthropology, business, computer science, elementary education, engineering, geography, human services, mass communications, nursing, sanitation technology, special education, speech pathology and audiology, theater, industrial engineering, construction. About 60% of general education requirements for graduation are elective; distribution requirements fairly numerous.

About 43% of students entering as freshmen graduate eventually; 57% of freshmen return for sophomore year. *Special programs:* CLEP, independent study, honors, individualized majors. *Calendar:* quarter, summer school.
Undergraduate degrees conferred (1,440). 28% were in Business and Management, 15% were in Education, 11% were in Health Sciences, 9% were in Engineering, 8% were in Social Sciences, 5% were in Communications, 4% were in Letters, 4% were in Psychology, 4% were in Visual and Performing Arts, 3% were in Life Sciences, remainder in 9 other fields.
Student Body. About 86% of students from Illinois. An estimated 11% of students reported as Black, 1% Asian, 1% Hispanic, 1% Native American, 2% other minority, according to most recent data available.
Varsity Sports. Men (Div.II): Baseball, Basketball, Cross Country, Golf, Soccer (I), Tennis, Track, Wrestling. Women (Div.II): Basketball, Soccer, Softball, Tennis, Track.
Campus Life. About 6% of men, 9% of women live in coed-dormitories; rest live in off-campus housing or commute. Intervisitation in men's and women's apartments unlimited. There are 9 fraternities, 7 sororities which about 4% of men, 5% of women join.
Annual Costs. Tuition and fees, $2,199 (out-of-state, $5,653), room and board, $3,300. University reports some scholarships awarded on the basis of academic merit alone. *Meeting Costs:* university offers six week tuition and fee deferment.

University of Southern Indiana

Evansville, Indiana 47712 **(812) 464-1765**

A state-supported institution located between Evansville (pop. 140,000) and Mt. Vernon metropolitan areas. Most convenient major airport: Evansville Dress Regional.

Founded: 1965
Affiliation: State
UG Enrollment: 1,689 M, 2,417 W (full-time); 936 M, 1,949 W (part-time)
Total Enrollment: 7,500
Cost: < $10K
% Receiving Financial Aid: 44%
Admission: Non-selective
Application Deadline: Aug. 15

Admission. Indiana graduates of commissioned high schools with C average eligible; others admitted conditionally; 96% of applicants accepted, 60% of these actually enroll; 11% of freshmen graduate in top fifth of high school class, 75% in top two-fifths. Average freshmen scores: ACT, 17 composite. *Required:* SAT or ACT. Criteria considered in admissions, in order of importance: high school academic record, standardized test scores, recommendations. *Out-of-state* freshman applicants: university seeks students from out-of-state. State does not limit out-of-state enrollment. About 85% of out-of-state students accepted, 64% of these actually enroll. States from which most out-of-state students are drawn include Kentucky, Illinois. *Entrance programs:* early decision, advanced placement. *Apply* by August 15. *Transfers* welcome; 510 enrolled 1993–94.
Academic Environment. Degrees offered: associates, bachelors, masters. Graduation requirements include Freshman English, English, Introduction to Speech, and physical education, also 9–15 hours in humanities and the arts, 10–15 hours in science and mathematics, and 9–15 hours in social and behavioral sciences. *Majors offered* include nursing, physical education, social work, and sports medicine. Average undergraduate class size: 10% under 20, 75% 20–40, 15% over 40. About 25% of students entering as freshmen graduate within five years; 64% of freshmen return for sophomore year. *Special programs:* CLEP, cross registration, internships. Adult programs: Student Mentor Program; adult orientation; adult recruitment and retention programs. *Calendar:* semester, summer school.
Undergraduate degrees conferred (516). 32% were in Business and Management, 25% were in Education, 8% were in Social Sciences, 8% were in Psychology, 8% were in Communications, 4% were in Engineering and Engineering Related Technology, 3% were in Public Affairs, remainder in 10 other fields.
Graduates Career Data. Advanced studies pursued by 19% of graduates, according to most recent data available. About 92% of 1991–92 graduates employed. Fields typically hiring largest number of graduates include business, health professions, engineering. Career Development Services include employment assistance for students and alumni.
Faculty. About 15% of faculty hold PhD or equivalent.
Student Body. About 95% of students from in state. An estimated 3% of students reported as Black, 1% Hispanic, 1% Asian.
Varsity Sports. Men (Div.II): Baseball, Basketball, Cross Country, Golf, Soccer, Tennis, Volleyball. Women (Div.II): Basketball, Softball, Tennis, Volleyball.
Campus Life. No dormitories on campus; 20% of students live in off-campus college-related apartments; rest commute. There are 5 fraternities, 3 sororities on campus, which about 50% of men, 40% of women join. They provide no residence facilities.
Annual Costs. Tuition and fees, $1,632 (out-of-state, $3,978), estimated $250 other, exclusive of travel. About 44% of students receive financial aid; average amount of assistance, $2,763. Assistance is typically divided 18% scholarship, 35% grant, 44% loan, 4% work. College reports 325 scholarships awarded on the basis of academic merit alone, 225 for special talents alone, 132 for need alone. *Meeting Costs:* college offers parental loan programs.

University of Southern Maine

Gorham, Maine 04038 **(207) 780-5670**

The University of Southern Maine offers degree programs in the Colleges of Arts and Sciences, and Education; schools of Business, Economics, and Management, Applied Science, and Nursing. University also includes the School of Law. Most convenient major airport: Portland.

Founded: 1878
Affiliation: State
UG Enrollment: 1,691 M, 1,965 W (full-time); 1,701 M, 2,456 W (part-time)
Total Enrollment: 9,522
Cost: < $10K
Admission: Selective
Application Deadline: July 15

Admission is selective. About 83% of applicants accepted, 47% of these actually enroll; 28% of freshmen graduate in top fifth of high school class, 65% in top two-fifths. Average freshman SAT scores: 449 verbal, 502 mathematical; 24% of freshmen score above 500 on verbal, 5% above 600, 1% above 700; 52% score above 500 on mathematical, 12% above 600, 1% above 700. *Required:* SAT or ACT. Criteria considered in admissions, in order of importance: high school academic record, standardized test scores, writing sample, recommendations, extracurricular activities; other factors considered: special talents. *Out-of-state* applicants: university actively seeks students from out-of-state. State does not limit out-of-state enrollment. About 75% of out-of-state students accepted, 26% of these actually enroll. Most out-of-state students are drawn from Northeastern states. *Entrance programs:* early admission, midyear admission, advanced placement. *Apply* by July 15; rolling admissions. *Transfers* welcome; 1,903 enrolled 1993–94.

Academic Environment. Graduation requirements include course work in English composition, quantitative decision making (mathematics), philosophy, fine arts, humanities, social sciences, natural sciences, and interdisciplinary studies. Administration reports that student interests, in declining order of importance, are academic, occupational/professional, and social. Degrees offered: associates, bachelors, masters. Unusual, new, or notable majors include environmental science, therapeutic recreation, nursing, electrical engineering.

About 64% of students entering as freshmen graduate eventually; 73% of freshmen return for sophomore year. *Special programs:* CLEP, January Term, cross registration with 5 schools in the greater Portland area, internship, independent study, study abroad, honors, self-designed majors. *Calendar:* semester, summer school.

Undergraduate degrees conferred (747). 24% were in Business and Management, 15% were in Social Sciences, 14% were in Education, 9% were in Health Sciences, 8% were in Communications, 6% were in Psychology, 5% were in Engineering and Engineering Related Technology, 3% were in Public Affairs, 3% were in Visual and Performing Arts, remainder in 11 other fields.

Graduates Career Data. Employers typically hiring largest numbers of graduates include business (retail and sales), banking and financial services, hospitals, education. Career Development Services include career counseling, placement service, resume/interview workshops, internships, co-op, on-campus recruitment, library resources.

Faculty. About 64% of faculty hold PhD or equivalent.

Student Body. About 94% of students from in state. An estimated 3% of students reported as minority. Average age of undergraduate student: 27. *Minority group students:* special financial and social provisions including International, Handicapped, and Native American Student Affairs.

Varsity Sports. Men (Div.III): Baseball, Basketball, Cross Country, Ice Hockey, Soccer, Tennis. Women (Div.III): Basketball, Cross Country, Field Hockey, Soccer, Softball, Volleyball.

Campus Life. Commuters are a strong majority. Students of legal age allowed to have alcohol in dormitory rooms and at special university functions. Student leader reports "we are given a very free hand in regulating student life." "Diverse Life Styles" plan for residence halls—students can select living style from 4 options ranging from unlimited intervisitation to none.

About 10% of men, 10% of women live in coed dormitories; 87% of men, 87% of women commute. Sexes segregated in coed dormitories by floor. There are 5 fraternities, 4 sororities on campus; 3% of men live in fraternities, women in sororities live in on-campus residence facilities. About 50% of students leave campus on weekends.

Annual Costs. Tuition and fees, $3,080 (out-of-state, $8,360); room and board, $4,219; estimated $1,533 other, exclusive of travel. About 60% of students receive financial aid; average amount received, $4,200. Assistance is typically divided 25% scholarship, 25% grant, 25% loan, 25% work. University reports 15 scholarships awarded on the basis of academic merit alone, 350 for need alone. *Meeting Costs:* university offers AMS Payment, loans.

Southern Methodist University

Dallas, Texas 75275 **(214) 692-2058**

A private, independent university that maintains ties with the United Methodist Church, Southern Methodist attracts a very diverse student body that includes all races, religions and economic levels and is drawn from every state and some 50 foreign countries. The 164-acre campus is located in a residential area, 5 miles from downtown Dallas. Most convenient major airports: Dallas Love Field, or Dallas-Fort Worth International.

Founded: 1911
Affiliation: Independent (United Methodist)
UG Enrollment: 2,356 M, 2,536 W (full-time); 144 M, 243 W (part-time)
Total Enrollment: 8,931
Cost: $10K–$20K
% Receiving Financial Aid: 66%
Admission: Very Selective
Application Deadline: January 15

Admission is selective. About 80% of applicants accepted, 34% of these actually enroll; 61% of freshmen graduate in top fifth of high school class, 85% in top two-fifths. Average freshman scores, middle 50% range: SAT, 940–1160; ACT, 22–27 composite. *Required:* SAT or ACT, interview optional, essay. Criteria considered "more important" in admissions: high school curriculum, GPA and pattern, class rank, standardized test scores, extracurricular activities, essay; "less important": counselor recommendation; other factors considered: special talents, diverse student body. *Entrance programs:* early action, deferred admission, advanced placement. About 32% of entering students from private and parochial schools. *Apply* by January 15; rolling admissions. *Transfers* welcome; 311 enrolled 1993–94.

Academic Environment. Students have some voice in curriculum matters through representation on various faculty committees. The university places a strong emphasis on the liberal arts, however, as with many urban universities, the campus climate is influenced by the high percentage of SMU's graduates who major in professional/vocational fields that offer immediately marketable skills. All freshmen enter Dedman College to take interdisciplinary liberal studies courses before transferring to a degree-granting school. *Undergraduate studies* offered by Dedman College, Ewin L. Cox School of Business, schools of Engineering and Applied Science, Meadows School of the Arts. Degrees offered: bachelors, masters, doctoral, professional. Average undergraduate class size: 75% under 25, 19% 25–49, 6% over 49.

About 68% of students entering as freshmen graduate within five years; 82% of freshmen return for sophomore year. *Special programs:* independent study, study abroad, honors, undergraduate research, 3–2 in business, cooperative programs available in engineering and applied science, 3-year degree, individualized majors, internships. Adult programs: Evening Degree Program - Bachelor of Humanities, Bachelor of Social Sciences. *Calendar:* semester, summer school.

Undergraduate degrees conferred (1,289). 24% were in Business and Management, 24% were in Social Sciences, 15% were in Communications, 8% were in Visual and Performing Arts, 6% were in Psychology, 5% were in Engineering, 4% were in Life Sciences, 3% were in Letters, remainder in 9 other fields.

Graduates Career Data. Advanced studies pursued by 20–30% of graduates; over past five years, the first-time application acceptance rate for medical school is 70–90%; for law school rate is 64–84%. Career Development Services include assessment, evaluation, information resources, contacts with potential employers, mock interviews, career-related seminars, computerized guidance programs, resume file for alumni.

Faculty. About 85% of faculty hold PhD or equivalent. All of undergraduate classes taught by tenured faculty. About 23% of teaching faculty are female; 2% Black, 3% Hispanic, 7% Asian.

Student Body. About 58% of students from in state; 63% Southwest, 14% South, 9% Midwest, 7% West, 3% Middle Atlantic, 2% New England, 3% foreign. An estimated 49% of students reported as Protestant, 23% Catholic, 2% Jewish, 1% Muslim, 4% unaffiliated, 21% other; 5% Black, 7% Hispanic, 5% Asian, 8% other minority. *Minority group students:* special funding programs available for members of minority groups. Special orientation and tutoring programs; residence projects, Inter-Cultural Affairs Office.

Religious Orientation. SMU is a church-related, non-sectarian institution; 20% of undergraduate students affiliated with the church; makes no religious demands on students. Most major, main-line religious traditions maintain some campus ministry on or near campus (Catholic, many Protestant denominations, Jewish, Muslim).

Varsity Sports. Men (Div.I): Basketball, Cross Country, Football, Golf, Soccer, Swimming& Diving, Tennis, Track. Women (Div.I): Basketball, Cross Country, Golf, Soccer, Swimming & Diving, Tennis, Track.

Campus Life. Student interest in athletics (both varsity and intramural) reported as high. Wide variety of cultural and intellectual activities provided on campus, supplemented by the extensive resources of Dallas. Women may choose to live in residence with no specific closing hour. Daily intervisitation possible within hours established by university. Alcohol may not be consumed in public places on campus; cars allowed. All freshmen, except those residing with parents required to live in university residence. Large percentage of students commute or live off campus.

About 40% of students and 70% of freshmen live on-campus; 8% live in off-campus college-related housing; rest commute. Sexes segregated in coed dormitories either by wing, floor, or apartment. There are 15 fraternities, 14 sororities on campus which about 44% of men, 51% of women join.

Annual Costs. Tuition and fees, $13,580; room and board, $4,941; estimated $1,100 other, exclusive of travel. About 66% of students receive financial aid; average amount of assistance, $12,041. Assistance is typically divided 20% scholarship, 40% grant, 36% loan, 4% work. University reports 2,068 scholarships awarded on the basis of academic merit alone, 295 for need alone. *Meeting Costs:* university offers payment plan.

Southern College of Seventh-Day Adventists

Collegedale, Tennessee 37315 (615) 238-2844

A church-related college, located in a village of 3,000, 18 miles east of Chattanooga. Formerly known as Southern Missionary College. Most convenient major airport: Chattanooga.

Founded: 1892
Affiliation: Seventh-day Adventist
UG Enrollment: 577 M, 691 W (full-time); 78 M, 181 W (part-time)
Cost: < $10K
% Receiving Financial Aid: 87%
Admission: Non-selective
Application Deadline: August 1

Admission. Graduates of approved high schools with C average and score of 15 on ACT composite eligible; others given individual consideration; 97% of applicants accepted, 51% of these actually enroll. Average freshmen ACT scores: 23 M, 22 W composite. *Required:* ACT, 2.0 minimum high school GPA, essay. Criteria considered in admissions, in order of importance: high school academic record, standardized test scores, recommendations, writing sample, extracurricular activities; other factors considered: special talents, religious affiliation/commitment. *Entrance programs:* early admission, midyear admission, advanced placement. About 6% of entering students from private schools, 75% from parochial schools. *Apply* by August 1. *Transfers* welcome; 124 enrolled 1993–94.

Academic Environment. Degrees offered: associates, bachelors. About 20% of general education requirements for graduation are elective; distribution requirements fairly numerous. *Special programs:* CLEP, honors, study abroad, internships. *Calendar:* semester, summer school.

Undergraduate degrees conferred (201). 35% were in Health Professions, 11% were in Education, 11% were in Business and Management, 7% each in Biological Sciences, Letters, Theology, 5% were in Physical Sciences, 3% each in Communications, Psychology, remainder in 7 other fields.

Graduate Career Data. Advanced studies pursued by 42% of graduates. Career Development Services available through the counseling office and directly by academic departments.

Faculty. About 42% of faculty hold PhD or equivalent. About 87% of undergraduate classes taught by tenured faculty. About 37% of teaching faculty are female; 3% Black.

Student Body. About 7% of students from in state; 63% South, 11% Middle Atlantic, 7% Midwest, 6% West, 5% New England, 1% Northwest, 7% foreign. An estimated 99% of students reported as Protestant; 6% Black, 8% Hispanic, 5% Asian, 1% other minority. Average age of undergraduate student: 22.

Religious Orientation. Southern is a church-related institution; 95% of students affiliated with the church; 12 hours of religion required of all students; chapel attendance expected.

Campus Life. About 85% of men, 90% of women live in traditional dormitories; no coed dormitories; rest live in off-campus housing or commute. No intervisitation in men's or women's dormitory rooms. There are no fraternities or sororities on campus. About 20% of resident students leave campus on weekends.

Annual Costs. Tuition and fees, $7,988; room and board, $3,360; estimated $900 other, exclusive of travel. About 87% of students receive financial aid; average amount of assistance, $1,200. Assistance is typically divided 20% scholarship, 50% loan, 30% work. *Meeting Costs:* college offers guaranteed tuition plan.

University of Southern Mississippi

Hattiesburg, Mississippi 39406-5167 (601) 266-4111

A state-supported institution, located in a community of 40,000, 85 miles southeast of Jackson. Most convenient major airport: Jackson Municipal.

Founded: 1910
Affiliation: State
UG Enrollment: 3,744 M, 4,675 W (full-time); 501 M, 685 W (part-time)
Total Enrollment: 11,487
Cost: < $10K
Admission: Non-selective
Application Deadline: August 15

Admission. Graduates of accredited high schools with 16 units (12 in academic subjects) and ACT composite score of 15 eligible; 72% of applicants accepted, 51% of these actually enroll. Average freshman ACT scores: 22 composite. *Required:* SAT or ACT. Criteria considered in admissions: high school academic record and standardized test scores rank with equal importance. *Out-of-state* freshman applicants: university actively seeks students from out-of-state. No special requirements for out-of-state applicants. States from which most out-of-state students are drawn include Louisiana, Alabama, Florida. *Entrance programs:* early decision, early admission, midyear admission, advanced placement. *Apply* by August 15; rolling admissions. *Transfers* welcome; 1,463 enrolled 1993–94.

Academic Environment. Degrees offered: bachelors, masters, doctoral. *Undergraduate studies* offered by colleges of Education and Psychology, Liberal Arts, Sciences, Business Administration, Fine Arts, Home Economics, Nursing, School of Health, Physical Education, and Recreation. About 25% of general education credits for graduation are required; no distribution requirements. About 42% of students entering as freshmen graduate eventually; 71% of freshmen return for sophomore year. *Special programs:* CLEP, study abroad, honors, undergraduate research, internships. Adult programs: The Institute for Learning in Retirement, students must be over 50 and partially retired. *Calendar:* semester, summer school.

Undergraduate degrees conferred (2,228). 23% were in Business and Management, 21% were in Education, 7% were in Psychology, 7% were in Health Sciences, 6% were in Communications, 5% were in Social Sciences, 4% were in Engineering and Engineering Related Technology, 3% were in Protective Services, 3% were in Letters, 3% were in Computer and Engineering Related Technology, 3% were in Mathematics, 3% were in Physical Sciences, 3% were in Home Economics, remainder in 12 other fields.

Graduates Career Data. Career Development Services include career counseling, individual vocational testing, career resource center, job finding skill development, computerized vocational guidance.

Faculty. About 94% of faculty hold PhD or equivalent. About 33% of teaching faculty are female; 4% Black.

Student Body. About 83% of students from in state; 95% South, 2% West, 1% Midwest, 2% foreign. An estimated 16% of students reported as Black, 1% Hispanic, 3% Asian.

Varsity Sports. Men (Div.IA): Baseball, Basketball, Cross Country, Equestrian, Fencing, Football, Golf, Tennis, Track. Women (Div.IA): Basketball, Cross Country, Golf, Tennis, Track, Volleyball.

Campus Life. Students report strong interest in intramural sports and "numerous" clubs and organizations. Road-trips to New Orleans (100 miles), the coast and other cities are also popular. Student notes "The campus is located in southern Mississippi. The summers are hot, the winters are mild. The air is always humid."

About 75% of men, 80% of women live in traditional dormitories; no coed dormitories; rest live in off-campus housing or commute.

Intervisitation in men's and women's dormitory rooms limited. There are 14 fraternities, 11 sororities on campus.
Annual Costs. Tuition and fees, $2,392 (out-of-state, $4,852); room and board, $2,276; estimated $500 other, exclusive of travel. *Meeting Costs:* university accepts offers deferred payment plan.

Southern Nazarene University

Bethany, Oklahoma 73008 **(405) 789-4610**

A church-related university, located in a city of over 20,000, near Oklahoma City, Southern Nazarene is maintained "for young people desiring a college education of excellence in Character and Culture through Christ." Formerly known as Bethany Nazarene College. Most convenient major airport: Oklahoma City.

Founded: 1899
Affiliation: Nazarene
UG Enrollment: 439 M, 562 W (full-time); 64 M, 94 W (part-time)
Total Enrollment: 1,311
Cost: < $10K
Admission: Non-selective
Application Deadline: August 15

Admission. Graduates of accredited high schools with C+ average, rank in top two-thirds of class, or score above 15 on ACT composite or 700 combined SAT eligible; others admitted on probationary status; all applicants accepted, 74% of these actually enroll. *Required:* SAT or ACT. *Apply* by August 15. *Transfers* welcome.
Academic Environment. *Degrees:* AB, BS, BMEd, BSN. About 80% of general education requirements for graduation are elective; distribution requirements fairly numerous. *Majors offered* in addition to usual studies include information systems, aviation. *Special programs:* CLEP, study abroad, individualized majors. *Calendar:* semester, summer school.
Undergraduate degrees conferred (329). 62% were in Business and Management, 7% were in Education, 5% were in Home Economics, 3% were in Health Sciences, 3% were in Letters, 3% were in Social Sciences, 3% were in Life Sciences, remainder in 13 other fields.
Graduates Career Data. According to most recent data available, full-time graduate or professional study pursued by 35% of students immediately after graduation.
Varsity Sports. Men (NAIA): Basketball, Soccer. Women (NAIA): Basketball, Volleyball.
Student Body. About 56% of students from in state; 93% Midwest. An estimated 92% of students reported as Protestant, 1% as Catholic, 6% as unaffiliated; 5% as Black, 1% Hispanic, 1% Asian, 5% other minority, according to most recent data available.
Religious Orientation. Southern Nazarene is a church-related institution; 3 courses in Bible and doctrine required of all students; attendance at chapel services required.
Campus Life. About 45% of men, 46% of women live in traditional dormitories; no coed dormitories; rest live in off-campus housing or commute. No intervisitation in men's or women's dormitory rooms.
Annual Costs. Tuition and fees, $6,176; room and board, $3,642. About 70% of students receive financial aid; university reports some scholarships awarded on the basis of academic merit alone. *Meeting Costs:* university offers prepayment plan, monthly payment plan.

Southern Oregon State College

Ashland, Oregon 97520 **(503) 552-6411**

A state-supported, liberal arts, business, professional, and teachers college, located in a town of 15,000, 285 miles south of Portland.

Founded: 1926
Affiliation: State
UG Enrollment: 1,637 M, 1,731 W (full-time); 418 M, 605 W (part-time)
Total Enrollment: 4,515
Cost: < $10K
% Receiving Financial Aid: 65%
Admission: Non-selective
Application Deadline: Rolling

Admission. High school graduates with 2.75 average in college preparatory program and minimum combined SAT score of 900 eligible; 84% of applicants accepted, 75% of these actually enroll. Average freshman scores: 438 M, 442 W verbal, 489 M, 458 W mathematical; ACT, 21 composite. *Required:* SAT. Criteria considered in admissions, in order of importance: high school academic record, standardized test scores, recommendations, writing sample, extracurricular activities; other factors considered: special talents. *Out-of-state* freshman applicants: college actively seeks students from out-of-state. State does not limit out-of-state enrollment. No special requirements for out-of-state applicants. About 84% of out-of-state students accepted, 63% of these actually enroll. States from which most out-of-state students are drawn include California, Washington, Alaska. *Entrance programs:* early admission, midyear admission. *Apply:* rolling admissions. *Transfers* welcome; 627 enrolled 1993–94.
Academic Environment. Graduation requirements include 60 units in core curriculum. Degrees offered: bachelors, masters. *Majors offered* include hotel, restaurant, and resort management, theater arts. Average undergraduate class size: 25. About 60% of freshmen return for sophomore year. *Special programs:* CLEP, honors, independent study, study abroad, undergraduate research with NASA, 3-year degree, combined programs with U. of Oregon schools of Medicine, Dentistry in medical technology, nursing, physical therapy, and with U. of Pacific in optometry, national student exchange. *Calendar:* quarter, summer school.
Undergraduate degrees conferred (659). 28% were in Business and Management, 12% were in Social Sciences, 10% were in Psychology, 10% were in Multi/Interdisciplinary Studies, 10% were in Education, 8% were in Letters, 6% were in Protective Services, 4% were in Visual and Performing Arts, 4% were in Health Sciences, remainder in 6 other fields.
Graduates Career Data. Career Development Services include "full career services and counseling."
Faculty. About 87% of faculty hold PhD or equivalent. About 75% of undergraduate classes taught by tenured faculty. About 35% of teaching faculty are female.
Student Body. About 90% of students from Northwest, 4% foreign. Average age of undergraduate student: 25.
Varsity Sports. Men (NAIA): Basketball, Cross Country, Football, Track, Wrestling. Women (NAIA): Basketball, Cross Country, Track, Volleyball.
Campus Life. About 25% each of men, women live in coed dormitories; rest live in off-campus housing or commute. Intervisitation in men's and women's dormitory rooms unlimited. Sexes segregated in coed dormitories by floor. There are no fraternities or sororities on campus. About 15% of resident students leave campus on weekends.
Annual Costs. Tuition and fees, $2,630 (out-of-state, $7,000); room and board, $3,500; estimated $2,500–$2,800 other, exclusive of travel. About 65% of students receive financial aid; average amount of assistance, $1,300. *Meeting Costs:* college offers deferred payment plan for tuition and housing.

Southern College of Seventh-Day Adventists

Collegedale, Tennessee 37315 **(615) 238-2844**

A church-related college, located in a village of 3,000, 18 miles east of Chattanooga. Formerly known as Southern Missionary College. Most convenient major airport: Chattanooga.

Founded: 1892
Affiliation: Seventh-day Adventist
UG Enrollment: 577 M, 691 W (full-time); 78 M, 181 W (part-time)
Cost: < $10K
% Receiving Financial Aid: 87%
Admission: Non-selective
Application Deadline: August 1

Admission. Graduates of approved high schools with C average and score of 15 on ACT composite eligible; others given individual consideration; 97% of applicants accepted, 51% of these actually enroll. Average freshmen ACT scores: 23 M, 22 W composite. *Required:* ACT, 2.0 minimum high school GPA, essay. Criteria considered in admissions, in order of importance: high school academic record, standardized test scores, recommendations, writing sample, extracurricular activities; other factors considered: special talents, religious affiliation/commitment. *Entrance programs:* early admission, midyear admission, advanced placement. About 6% of entering students from private schools, 75% from parochial schools. *Apply* by August 1. *Transfers* welcome; 124 enrolled 1993–94.

Academic Environment. Degrees offered: associates, bachelors. About 20% of general education requirements for graduation are elective; distribution requirements fairly numerous. *Special programs:* CLEP, honors, study abroad, internships. *Calendar:* semester, summer school.

Undergraduate degrees conferred (199). 22% were in Health Sciences, 19% were in Business and Management, 9% were in Life Sciences, 8% were in Education, 6% were in Theology, 6% were in Communications, 5% were in Social Sciences, 5% were in Public Affairs, 4% were in Letters, 4% were in Business (Administrative Support), 4% were in Philosophy and Religion, 3% were in Psychology, remainder in 7 other fields.

Graduates Career Data. Advanced studies pursued by 42% of graduates. Career Development Services available through the counseling office and directly by academic departments.

Faculty. About 42% of faculty hold PhD or equivalent. About 87% of undergraduate classes taught by tenured faculty. About 37% of teaching faculty are female; 3% Black.

Student Body. About 7% of students from in state; 63% South, 11% Middle Atlantic, 7% Midwest, 6% West, 5% New England, 1% Northwest, 7% foreign. An estimated 99% of students reported as Protestant; 6% Black, 8% Hispanic, 5% Asian, 1% other minority. Average age of undergraduate student: 22.

Religious Orientation. Southern is a church-related institution; 95% of students affiliated with the church; 12 hours of religion required of all students; chapel attendance expected.

Campus Life. About 85% of men, 90% of women live in traditional dormitories; no coed dormitories; rest live in off-campus housing or commute. No intervisitation in men's or women's dormitory rooms. There are no fraternities or sororities on campus. About 20% of resident students leave campus on weekends.

Annual Costs. Tuition and fees, $7,988; room and board, $3,360; estimated $900 other, exclusive of travel. About 87% of students receive financial aid; average amount of assistance, $1,200. Assistance is typically divided 20% scholarship, 50% loan, 30% work. *Meeting Costs:* college offers guaranteed tuition plan.

Southern State College

(See Southern Arkansas University)

Southern College of Technology

Marietta, Georgia 30060 (404) 424-7281

Southern Tech offers associate, baccalaureate and master's degrees in engineering technology and related technologies. Formerly known as Southern Technical Institute. Most convenient major airport: Atlanta.

Founded: 1948	**Total Enrollment:** 3,960
Affiliation: State	**Cost:** < $10K
UG Enrollment: 1,878 M, 352 W (full-time); 1,094 M, 195 W (part-time)	**% Receiving Financial Aid:** 33%
	Admission: Non-selective
	Application Deadline: Aug. 31

Admission. Graduates of accredited high schools with 9 specified units eligible; 57% of applicants accepted, 59% of these actually enroll. Average freshman SAT scores: 427 M, 432 W verbal, 515 M, 485 W mathematical; ACT, 22 composite. *Required:* SAT or ACT, minimum 2.0 high school GPA. Criteria considered in admissions, in order of importance: standardized test scores, high school academic record. *Out-of-state* freshman applicants: college actively seeks students from out-of-state. State does not limit out-of-state enrollment. No special requirements for out-of-state applicants. About 67% of out-of-state students accepted, 55% of these actually enroll. States from which most out-of-state students are drawn include New York, Illinois, Florida. *Apply* by August 31. *Transfers* welcome; 408 enrolled 1993–94.

Academic Environment. Graduation requirements include 20 hours of humanities, 10 of mathematics, 10 of lab science, 20 of social sciences. Degrees offered: associates, bachelors, masters. Average undergraduate class size: 40% under 20, 54% 20–40, 6% over 40. About 5% of students entering as freshmen graduate within four years, 35% eventually, 65% of freshmen return for sophomore year. *Special programs:* CLEP, cross registration with schools in the U. Center in Georgia, cooperative programs in all fields. *Calendar:* quarter, summer school.

Undergraduate degrees conferred (437). 91% were in Engineering and Engineering Related Technology, 9% were in Computer and Engineering Related Technology, remainder in Physical Sciences.

Graduates Career Data. Advanced studies pursued by 15% of graduates; 10% graduate school, 5% business school. Business schools typically enrolling largest numbers of graduates include Georgia State University, Southern College of Technology. About 70% of 1992–93 graduates employed. Fields typically hiring largest numbers of graduates include electrical, mechanical, and civil engineering technology, computer science. Career Development Services available to all students.

Faculty. About 50% of faculty hold PhD or equivalent. About 50% of undergraduate classes taught by tenured faculty. About 19% of teaching faculty are female; 5% Black, 2% Hispanic, 3% other minority.

Student Body. About 93% of students from in state; 96% South, 4% foreign. An estimated 17% of students reported as Black, 2% Hispanic, 5% Asian, 1% other minority. Average age of undergraduate student: 25.

Varsity Sports. Men (NAIA): Baseball, Basketball, Tennis.

Campus Life. About 4% of men live in traditional dormitories; 6% of men, 15% of women live in coed dormitories; rest live in off-campus housing or commute. Intervisitation in men's and women's dormitory rooms limited; sexes segregated by wing. There are 7 fraternities, 2 sororities on campus; of which 6% of each men, women join. They provide no residence facilities. About 80% of resident students leave campus on weekends.

Annual Costs. Tuition and fees, $1,649 (out-of-state, $4,412); room and board, $3,375; estimated $4,200 other, exclusive of travel. About 33% of students receive financial aid; average amount of assistance, $1,500. Assistance is typically divided 5% scholarship, 25% grant, 60% loan, 10% work. College reports 60 scholarships awarded on the basis of academic merit alone, 60 for special talents alone.

Southern University

Baton Rouge, Louisiana 70813 (504) 771-4500

A state-supported, land-grant institution, located in a city of 166,000; founded as a college for Negroes and still serving a predominantly Black student body. Southern has branch campuses in New Orleans and Shreveport.

Founded: 1880	**Total Enrollment:** 10,398
Affiliation: State	**Cost:** < $10K
UG Enrollment: 3,291 M, 4,243 W (full-time); 325 M, 450 W (part-time)	**% Receiving Financial Aid:** 90%
	Admission: Non-selective
	Application Deadline: July 1

Admission. Louisiana graduates of state approved high schools with 15 units eligible; 86% of applicants accepted, 71% of these actually enroll; 25% of freshmen graduate in top quarter of high school class, 64% in top-half. Average freshmen ACT scores, according to most recent data available: 16.5 M, 16.8 W composite. *Required:* SAT or ACT. Criteria considered in admissions: high school academic record, standardized test scores, immunization record all rank equally; other factors considered: alumni children. *Out-of-state* freshman applicants: university actively seeks students from out-of-state. State does not limit out-of-state enrollment. About 86% of out-of-state students accepted, 70% of these actually enroll. States from which most out-of-state students are drawn include California, Texas, Mississippi, Illinois. *Entrance programs:* early admission, advanced placement. *Apply* by July 1. *Transfers* welcome.

Academic Environment. Graduation requirements include specific courses in General Assembly, seminar, English, social sciences, math, science, health, reading, physical education, 60 hours of community service, African-American Experience. Degrees offered: associates, bachelors, masters. *Undergraduate studies* offered by colleges of Agriculture, Arts and Humanities, Business, Education, Engineering,

Home Economics, Sciences. Notable majors offered include urban forestry, jazz. Average undergraduate class size: 25% under 20, 60% 20–40, 15% over 40.

About 39% of students entering as freshmen graduate eventually; 67% of freshmen return for sophomore year. *Special programs:* honors, undergraduate research, cross registration with Louisiana State U. Adult programs: Continuing Education Program. *Calendar:* semester, summer school.

Undergraduate degrees conferred (784). 26% were in Business and Management, 13% were in Engineering, 11% were in Education, 9% were in Social Sciences, 7% were in Communications, 6% were in Psychology, 5% were in Computer and Engineering Related Technology, 4% were in Health Sciences, 4% were in Engineering and Engineering Related Technology, remainder in 13 other fields.

Graduates Career Data. Advanced studies pursued by 21% of graduates; 15% enter graduate school; 2% enter medical school; 1% enter dental school; 1% enter law school; 3% enter business school. About 61% of 1992–93 graduates employed. Fields typically hiring largest numbers of graduates include business, education, government. Career Development Services include employment assistance and help in entering graduate or professional schools.

Faculty. About 47% of faculty hold PhD or equivalent. About 52% of undergraduate classes taught by tenured faculty. About 47% of teaching faculty are female; 74% Black, 1% Hispanic, 13% other minority.

Student Body. About 76% of students from in state; 86% South, 10% New England, 7% Middle Atlantic, 5% West, 2% Midwest, 1% foreign. An estimated 78% of students reported as Protestant, 13% Catholic, 1% Muslim, 2% unaffiliated, 7% other; 92% Black, 3% other minority.

Varsity Sports. Men (Div.I): Baseball, Basketball, Football (IAA), Golf, Tennis. Women (Div.I): Basketball, Tennis.

Campus Life. About 29% of men, 24% of women live in traditional dormitories; no coed dormitories; rest commute. No intervisitation in men's or women's dormitory rooms. There are 4 fraternities, 4 sororities on campus which about 2% of men, 4% of women join; they provide no residence facilities. About 30% of resident students leave campus on weekends.

Annual Costs. Tuition and fees, $2,028 (out-of-state, $3,950); room and board, $2,866; other expenses, $1,305, exclusive of travel. About 90% of students receive financial aid; average amount of assistance, $5,800. *Meeting Costs:* university offers deferred payment plan, use of credit cards.

Southern University in New Orleans

New Orleans, Louisiana 70126 **(504) 282-4401**

A state-supported branch campus of Southern University, designated as a liberal arts, commuter institution; founded as a college for Negroes and still serving a predominantly Black student body in the greater New Orleans area.

Founded: 1956
Affiliation: State
UG Enrollment: 735 M, 1,705 W (full-time)
Total Enrollment: 3,793
Cost: < $10K
Admission: Non-selective
Application Deadline: July 1

Admission. Louisiana graduates of state-approved high schools eligible. *Required:* "open door policy." Out-of-state freshman applicants: university does not seek students from out of state. State does not limit out-of-state enrollment. No special requirements for out-of-state applicants. *Apply* by July 1. *Transfers* welcome.

Academic Environment. *Degrees:* AB, BS, BEd. About 84% of general education requirements for graduation are elective; distribution requirements fairly numerous. About 20% of students entering as freshmen graduate eventually; 42% of freshmen return for sophomore year. *Special programs:* exchange program with North Adams State, Eight College Consortium. *Calendar:* semester, summer school.

Undergraduate degrees conferred (303). 36% were in Business and Management, 16% were in Education, 11% were in Protective Services, 7% were in Public Affairs, 4% were in Psychology, 4% were in Business (Administrative Support), 4% were in Engineering and Engineering Related Technology, 3% were in Communications, 3% were in Physical Sciences, 3% were in Mathematics, 3% were in Allied Health, remainder in 5 other fields.

Student Body. Almost all students from South.

Campus Life. No dormitories on campus. There are 4 fraternities, 5 sororities on campus which about 1% of men, 2% of women join; they provide no residence facilities.

Annual Costs. Tuition and fees, $1,456 (out-of-state, $3,014); room and board, $3,793.

Southern Utah University

Cedar City, Utah 84720 **(801) 586-7740**

A state-supported institution, located in a community of 12,500, 265 miles south of Salt Lake City. Formerly known as Southern Utah State College.

Founded: 1897
Affiliation: State
UG Enrollment: 1,632 M, 1,979 W (full-time)
Total Enrollment: 4,293
Cost: < $10K
Admission: Non-selective
Application Deadline: 30 days before start of classes

Admission. Graduates of accredited high schools admitted; 85% of applicants accepted, 92% of these actually enroll; 14% of freshmen graduate in top fifth of high school class, 42% in top two-fifths. *Required:* ACT. *Out-of-state* freshman applicants: university seeks students from out of state. State does not limit out-of-state enrollment. *Apply* by 30 days before start of classes. *Transfers* welcome.

Academic Environment. *Degrees:* AB, BS. About 99% of general education requirements for graduation are elective; distribution requirements fairly numerous. About 70% of students entering as freshmen graduate within four years. *Special programs:* CLEP, independent study, undergraduate research. *Calendar:* quarter, summer school.

Undergraduate degrees conferred (527). 42% were in Education, 21% were in Business and Management, 8% were in Psychology, 6% were in Communications, 5% were in Social Sciences, 4% were in Life Sciences, 4% were in Visual and Performing Arts, remainder in 8 other fields.

Student Body. About 98% of students from Utah.

Varsity Sports. Men (Div.II; NAIA): Baseball, Basketball, Cross Country, Football, Golf, Track. Women (Div.II; NAIA): Basketball, Gymnastics, Softball, Track, Volleyball.

Campus Life. About 40% of students live in coed dormitories; rest live in off-campus housing or commute. Intervisitation in men's and women's dormitory rooms limited; sexes segregated by wing. About 15% of resident students leave campus on weekends.

Annual Costs. Tuition and fees, $1,599 (out-of-state, $4,760).

Southern Vermont College

Bennington, Vermont 05201 **(802) 442-5427**

A liberal arts college with a career orientation, Southern Vermont offers programs leading to both associate and baccalaureate degrees. Most convenient major airport: Albany (NY).

Founded: 1926
Affiliation: Independent
UG Enrollment: 267 M, 196 W (full-time); 65 M, 214 W (part-time)
Cost: < $10K
% Receiving Financial Aid: 65%
Admission: Non-selective
Application Deadline: Rolling

Admission. High school graduates eligible; 34% of applicants accepted, 84% of these actually enroll. *Required:* transcript, essay, 2 recommendations (English required); test scores optional; interview recommended. Criteria considered in admissions, in order of importance: high school academic record, recommendations, writing sample, extracurricular activities. *Entrance programs:* midyear admission, deferred admission. About 10% of entering students from private schools, 5% from parochial schools. *Apply:* rolling admissions. *Transfers* welcome; 68 enrolled 1993–94.

Academic Environment. Graduation requirements include economics, Effective Speaking, 2 courses in English composition, Living in the Environment, government history, 2 courses in cultural arts, college math, Intro to Computers, Biological World, Physical World, psychology, and sociology. *Degrees:* associates, bachelors. Unusual, new, or notable majors include resort management, gerontology management, child care management. Average undergraduate class size: 25.

About 41% of students entering as freshmen graduate within four years; 65% of freshmen return for sophomore year. *Special programs:* study abroad, internships, LD program. Adult programs: BS in management offered through weekend program.

Undergraduate degrees conferred (70). 40% were in Business and Management, 19% were in Protective Services, 9% were in Public Affairs, 9% were in Letters, 7% were in Business (Administrative Support), 6% were in Liberal/General Studies, 4% were in Life Sciences, 4% were in Communications, 3% were in Health Sciences.

Graduates Career Data. Advanced studies pursued by 8% of graduates; all entered graduate school. About 83% of 1992–93 graduates employed. Fields typically hiring largest numbers of graduates include professional, management.

Faculty. About 19% of faculty hold PhD or equivalent. About 54% of teaching faculty are female.

Student Body. About 40% of students from in state; 27% from New England, 30% Middle Atlantic, 2% South. An estimated 3% of students reported as Black, 2% other minority.

Varsity Sports. Men: Baseball, Basketball, Cross Country, Soccer. Women: Basketball, Cross country, Soccer, Softball.

Campus Life. About 33% of men, women live in coed dormitories; rest live in off-campus housing or commute. There are no fraternities or sororities on campus.

Annual Costs. Tuition and fees, $8,670; room and board, $4,304; estimated $1,050 other. About 65% of students receive financial aid; average amount of assistance, $7,520. Assistance is typically divided 48% scholarship, 42% loan, 10% work. College reports scholarships awarded only on the basis of need.

Southwest Baptist College

Bolivar, Missouri 65613 **(417) 326-1810**

A church-related college, located in a village of 7,000, 28 miles north of Springfield.

Founded: 1878
Affiliation: Southern Baptist
UG Enrollment: 755 M, 1,015 W (full-time); 215 M, 752 W (part-time)
Total Enrollment: 3,136
Cost: < $10K
Admission: Non-selective
Application Deadline: Rolling

Admission. Graduates of accredited high schools with C average or rank in top half of class eligible; 37% of applicants accepted, 96% of these actually enroll; 28% of freshmen graduate in top fifth of high school class, 58% in top two-fifths. Average freshman ACT scores: 22 M, 24 W composite. *Required:* SAT or ACT, minimum high school GPA. Criteria considered in admissions, in order of importance: high school academic record, standardized test scores, recommendations. *Entrance programs:* early decision, early admission, midyear admission, deferred admission, advanced placement. *Apply:* rolling admissions. *Transfers* welcome.

Academic Environment. Graduation requirements include 46–50 hours of core courses. Degrees offered: associates, bachelors, masters. Average undergraduate class size: 90% under 20, 8% 20–40, 2% over 40. About 58% of students entering as freshmen graduate eventually; 70% of freshmen return for sophomore year. *Special programs:* CLEP, January interterm, study abroad, 3–2 in engineering, independent study, undergraduate research. Adult programs: Associates of Applied Science, Bachelor of Applied Science. *Calendar:* 4–1–4, summer school.

Undergraduate degrees conferred (414). 18% were in Psychology, 17% were in Education, 14% were in Social Sciences, 12% were in Theology, 10% were in Business and Management, 4% were in Letters, 4% were in Communications, 4% were in Allied Health, 3% were in Life Sciences, 3% were in Mathematics, remainder in 7 other fields.

Faculty. About 55% of faculty hold PhD or equivalent. About 85% of undergraduate classes taught by tenured faculty. About 5% of teaching faculty are female.

Student Body. About 60% of students from Midwest. About 72% of students reported as Protestant, 25% unaffiliated. Average age of undergraduate student: 23.

Religious Orientation. Southwest Baptist is a church-related institution; 95% of students affiliated with the church; 8 hours of Biblical studies, attendance at two-thirds of triweekly convocation services required of all students.

Varsity Sports. Men (Div.II): Baseball, Basketball, Cross Country, Football, Golf, Soccer, Tennis. Women (Div.II): Basketball, Cross Country, Soccer, Softball, Tennis, Volleyball.

Campus Life. About 56% of men, 56% of women live in traditional dormitories; no coed dormitories; rest commute. No intervisitation in men's or women's dormitory rooms. There are no fraternities or sororities on campus. About 50% of resident students leave campus on weekends.

Annual Costs. Tuition and fees, $6,797; room and board, $2,395; estimated $500 other, exclusive of travel. *Meeting Costs:* college offers extended payment plan.

College of the Southwest

Hobbs, New Mexico 88240 **(505) 392-6561**

A small liberal arts college, Southwest awards a high percentage of degrees in professional areas.

Founded: 1962
Affiliation: Independent
UG Enrollment: 81 M, 146 W (full-time); 41 M, 102 W (part-time)
Cost: < $10K
% Receiving Financial Aid: 90%
Admission: Non-selective
Application Deadline: July 1

Admission. About 47% of applicants accepted, 27% of these actually enroll; 4% of freshmen graduate in top fifth of high school class, 17% in top two-fifths. Average freshmen ACT scores: ACT, 18.3 composite. *Required:* SAT or ACT, minimum 2.0 high school GPA. Criteria considered in admissions, in order of importance: high school academic record, standardized test scores, extracurricular activities. *Entrance programs:* early admission, advanced placement. *Apply* by July 1; rolling admissions. *Transfers* welcome; 86 enrolled 1993–94.

Academic Environment. Graduation requirements include 9 semester hours of humanities or fine arts, 12 of social sciences, 12 of math/science, 3 of economics, 9 of communications, 6 of religious studies. Degrees offered: bachelors. About 20% of students entering as freshmen graduate eventually, 33% of freshmen return for sophomore year.

Undergraduate degrees conferred (52). 50% were in Education, 23% were in Business and Management, 15% were in Multi/Interdisciplinary Studies, 12% were in Psychology.

Graduates Career Data. Advanced studies pursued by 40% of graduates.

Faculty. All faculty hold PhD or equivalent. About 51% of teaching faculty are female; 4% Hispanic.

Student Body. About 86% of students from in state; 96% Midwest, 2% Middle Atlantic, 2% West, 1% Northwest. An estimated 17% of students reported as Hispanic, 2% Black. Average age of undergraduate student: 28.

Varsity Sports. Men: Baseball. Women: Soccer, Volleyball.

Campus Life. About 21% of men, 3% of women live in apartment complex; rest commute.

Annual Costs. Tuition and fees, $4,100; room and board, $2,614; estimated $600 other, exclusive of travel. About 90% of students receive financial aid; average amount of assistance, $3,373. Assistance is typically divided 26% scholarship, 28% grant, 42% loan, 4% work. College reports 70% of scholarships awarded on basis of academic merit alone, 30% for special talents alone.

Southwest Missouri State University

Springfield, Missouri 65804 **(417) 836-5517**

A state-supported university, located in a city of 130,100, 220 miles southwest of St. Louis. Most convenient major airport: Springfield Municipal.

Founded: 1905
Affiliation: State
UG Enrollment: 6,192 M, 6,939 W (full-time); 1,534 M, 1,840 W (part-time)
Total Enrollment: 18,160
Cost: < $10K
Admission: Non-selective
Application Deadline: November 1

Admission. Missouri high school graduates eligible (admissions requirements based on sliding scale of class rank and ACT score); 81% of applicants accepted, 61% of these actually enroll; 28% of freshmen graduate in top fifth of high school class, 54% in top two-fifths. Average freshman ACT scores: 21.7 composite. *Required:* ACT. Criteria considered in admissions, in order of importance: standardized test scores, high school academic record. *Out-of-state* freshman applicants: university actively seeks students from out-of-state. Requirement for out-of-state applicants: minimum ACT composite score of 19. States from which most out-of-state students are drawn include Arkansas, Kansas, Oklahoma, Iowa, Texas. *Entrance programs:* advanced placement. *Apply* by November 1; rolling admissions. *Transfers* welcome; 953 enrolled 1993–94.
Academic Environment. Degrees offered: associates, bachelors, masters. About 25% of general education credits for graduation are required; distribution requirements fairly numerous. About 15% of students entering as freshmen graduate within four years; 69% of freshmen return for sophomore year. *Special programs:* honors, cooperative education, study abroad, 3–2 engineering. Adult programs: reentry seminars, adult orientation programs, scholarships, and evening college degree programs available to adults over 21 years. *Calendar:* semester, summer school.
Undergraduate degrees conferred (2,134). 28% were in Business and Management, 17% were in Education, 10% were in Communications, 7% were in Social Sciences, 5% were in Psychology, 4% were in Engineering and Engineering Related Technology, 3% were in Visual and Performing Arts, 3% were in Vocational Home Economics, 3% were in Home Economics, 3% were in Public Affairs, remainder in 17 other fields.
Graduates Career Data. Career Development Services available to all students.
Faculty. About 78% of faculty hold PhD or equivalent. About 60% of undergraduate classes taught by tenured faculty. About 30% of teaching faculty are female; 1% Black, 1% Hispanic, 6% other minority.
Student Body. About 94% of students from in state; 2% each Midwest, South, 1% foreign. An estimated 3% of students reported as Black, 1% Asian, 3% other minority. Average age of undergraduate student: 23.
Varsity Sports. Men (Div.I): Baseball, Basketball, Cross Country, Football (IAA), Soccer, Swimming, Tennis, Track, Wrestling. Women (Div.I): Basketball, Cross Country, Field Hockey, Golf, Softball, Tennis, Track, Volleyball.
Campus Life. About 3% of women live in traditional dormitories; 21% each of men, women live in coed dormitories; rest commute. Intervisitation in men's and women's dormitory rooms limited. There are 18 fraternities, 10 sororities on campus; 11% of men, 9% of women live in fraternities and sororities.
Annual Costs. Tuition and fees, $2,326 (out-of-state, $4,516); room and board, $2,630; estimated $2,760 other, exclusive of travel. About 50% of students receive financial aid; average amount of assistance, $3,200; assistance is typically divided 49% grant/scholarship, 46% loan, 5% work. College reports some scholarships awarded on the basis of academic merit alone.

Southwest State University

Marshall, Minnesota 56258 (507) 537-6286

A technical and liberal arts institution, Southwest State University is located in a community of about 12,000. The 216-acre campus was specially designed to accommodate handicapped students. Most convenient major airport: Minneapolis/St. Paul.

Founded: 1963
Affiliation: State
UG Enrollment: 993 M, 1,098 W (full-time); 211 M, 335 W (part-time)
Cost: < $10K
% Receiving Financial Aid: 84%
Admission: Non-selective
Application Deadline: 1 month prior to start of term

Admission. Minnesota high school graduates who rank in top half of high school class or score 21 on ACT composite (900 combined SAT) Åeligible; 88% of applicants accepted, 52% of these actually enroll. *Required:* SAT or ACT. *Out-of-state* freshman applicants: university seeks students from out-of-state. State does not limit out-of-state enrollment. *Apply* by 1 month prior to start of term. *Transfers* welcome; 181 enrolled 1992–93.
Academic Environment. Degrees offered: associates, bachelors. All students must take 68 credits in General/Rural Studies. *Majors offered* include social work, political science. About 65% of students entering as freshmen graduate eventually; 87% of freshmen return for sophomore year. *Special programs:* CLEP, independent study, study abroad, honors, undergraduate research, individualized majors, cross registration through Common Market (7 state universities). *Calendar:* quarter, summer school.
Undergraduate degrees conferred (362). 40% were in Business and Management, 19% were in Education, 9% were in Engineering and Engineering Related Technology, 8% were in Social Sciences, 4% were in Psychology, 3% were in Communications, 3% were in Multi/Interdisciplinary Studies, remainder in 8 other fields.
Faculty. About 77% of faculty hold PhD or equivalent.
Varsity Sports. Men (NAIA & NCAA Div.II): Baseball, Basketball, Cross Country, Football, Track, Wrestling. Women (NAIA & NCAA Div.II): Basketball, Softball, Tennis, Track, Volleyball.
Student Body. About 82% of students from in state; 95% Midwest, less than 1% foreign.
Campus Life. About 45% each of men, women live in traditional dormitories; 12% each in coed dormitories; rest live in off-campus housing or commute. Sexes segregated in coed dormitories by floor. About 50% of resident students leave campus on weekends.
Annual Costs. Tuition and fees, $2,650 (out-of-state, $4,650); room and board, $2,750; estimated $1,200 other, exclusive of travel. About 84% of students receive financial aid; average amount of assistance, $3,043. College reports some scholarships awarded on the basis of academic merit alone.

Southwest Texas State University

San Marcos, Texas 78666 (512) 245-2340

A state-supported university, located in a town of 22,000, 30 miles south of Austin. Most convenient major airports: Austin or San Antonio.

Founded: 1899
Affiliation: State
UG Enrollment: 6,857 M, 7,693 W (full-time); 1,949 M, 3,947 W (part-time)
Total Enrollment: 23,251
Cost: < $10K
% Receiving Financial Aid: 47%
Admission: Non-selective
Application Deadline: July 1

Admission. Graduates of accredited high schools with acceptable class rank/test score ratio eligible; 63% of applicants accepted, 45% of these actually enroll. Average freshman scores: SAT, 864 combined verbal, mathematical; ACT, 20.1 composite. *Required:* ACT or SAT, minimum 2.0 high school GPA. Criteria considered in admissions, in order of importance: high school academic record, standardized test scores, extracurricular activities; other factors considered: special talents. *Out-of-state* freshman applicants: university does not seek students from out of state. State does not limit out-of-state enrollment. No special requirements for out-of-state applicants. *Entrance programs:* midyear admission, deferred admission, advanced placement. *Apply* by July 1; rolling admissions. *Transfers* welcome; 1,634 enrolled 1993–94.
Academic Environment. Degrees offered: bachelors, masters. *Undergraduate studies* offered by schools of Fine Arts and Communication, Liberal Arts, Science, Allied Health Professions, Applied Arts and Technology, Business, Education. Average undergraduate class size: 10% under 20, 60% 20–40, 30% over 40. About 36% of students entering as freshmen graduate eventually; 71% of freshmen return for sophomore year. *Special programs:* CLEP, honors, undergraduate research, individualized majors. *Calendar:* semester, summer school.
Undergraduate degrees conferred (2,671). 24% were in Business and Management, 12% were in Education, 10% were in Multi/Interdisciplinary Studies, 7% were in Social Sciences, 6% were in Communications, 6% were in Protective Services, 4% were in

Letters, 4% were in Psychology, 3% were in Health Sciences, remainder in 21 other fields.
Faculty. About 55% of faculty hold PhD or equivalent.
Student Body. About 98% of students from in state. Average age of undergraduate student: 22.
Varsity Sports. Men (Div.I): Baseball, Basketball, Cross Country, Football, Golf, Tennis, Track. Women (Div.I): Basketball, Cross Country, Gymnastics, Softball, Tennis, Track, Volleyball.
Campus Life. About 12% of men, 205% of women live in traditional dormitories; 7% of men, 5% of women live in coed dormitories; rest live in off-campus housing or commute, according to most recent data available. Intervisitation in men's and women's dormitory rooms limited. There are 21 fraternities, 11 sororities on campus which about 10% of men, 7% of women join. About 28% of resident students leave campus on weekends.
Annual Costs. Tuition and fees, $1,624 (out-of-state, $5,704); room and board, $4,286; estimated $1,200 other, exclusive of travel. About 47% of students receive financial aid; average amount of assistance, $1,562. College reports some scholarships awarded on the basis of academic merit alone.

Southwestern College

Winfield, Kansas 67156 **(316) 221-4150**

A church-related college, located in a town of 11,400, 50 miles southeast of Wichita. Most convenient major airport: Mid-Continent (Wichita).

Founded: 1885
Affiliation: United Methodist
UG Enrollment: 268 M, 273 W (full-time); 44 M, 68 W (part-time)
Total Enrollment: 644
Cost: < $10K
% Receiving Financial Aid: 80%
Admission: Non-selective
Application Deadline: Rolling

Admission. Graduates of accredited high schools admitted according to formula based on GPA, ACT score and class rank; others admitted on condition; 63% of applicants accepted, 62% of these actually enroll. Average freshman scores, according to most recent data available: SAT, 352 M, 405 W verbal, 374 M, 430 W mathematical; ACT, 19.3 M, 22.1 W composite. *Required:* SAT or ACT; interview where possible. *Apply:* rolling admissions; priority date February 5. *Transfers* welcome.
Academic Environment. Graduation requirements: about 93% of general education requirements for graduation are elective. *Degrees:* BA, BS, BBA, BM, BPh. Unusual, new, or notable majors include resources, media management and public relations, servant leadership, church music, church music and education. About 30% of students entering as freshmen graduate eventually; 54% of freshmen return for sophomore year. *Special programs:* CLEP, independent study, study abroad, honors, undergraduate research, individualized majors, 3–2 programs in engineering, architecture, various informal cooperative programs. Adult programs: evening and weekend programs, mostly off-campus. *Calendar:* 4–1–4, summer school.
Undergraduate degrees conferred (258). 26% were in Social Sciences, 21% were in Business and Management, 10% were in Psychology, 9% were in Visual and Performing Arts, 7% were in Education, 6% were in Life Sciences, 5% were in Physical Sciences, 4% were in Letters, 3% were in Communications, 3% were in Philosophy and Religion, remainder in 5 other fields.
Faculty. About 46% of faculty hold PhD or equivalent.
Student Body. About 85% of students from in state; 90% North Central, 8% South. An estimated 71% of students reported as Protestant, 10% Catholic, 19% unaffiliated; 8% Black, 3% Hispanic, 2% other minority, according to most recent data available.
Religious Orientation. Southwestern is a church-related institution, but makes no religious demands on students; attendance at chapel services voluntary.
Varsity Sports. Men (NAIA): Basketball, Cross Country, Football, Golf, Tennis, Track. Women (NAIA): Basketball, Cross Country, Tennis, Track, Volleyball.
Campus Life. About 56% of men, 29% of women live in coed dormitories; rest live in off-campus housing or commute. Intervisitation in men's and women's dormitory rooms permitted. There are no fraternities or sororities on campus. About 35% of students leave campus on weekends.
Annual Costs. Tuition and fees, $6,500; room and board, $3,532. About 80% of students receive financial aid; assistance is typically divided 50% scholarship, 40% loan, 10% work. College reports some scholarships awarded on the basis of academic merit alone.

Southwestern University

Georgetown, Texas 78626 **(800) 252-3166; (512) 863-6511**

Long a small, regional college and school of fine arts, Southwestern is actively working to change itself into an institution of national repute. Sparked by a long-term grant from the Brown Foundation, generous support from other institutions and its own alumni, the university is actively recruiting top students from many states. It intends to remain a relatively small institution where the faculty, not graduate students, do the teaching. The university is located in a metropolitan area of 26,000, 26 miles north of Austin. Most convenient major airport: Robert Mueller, Austin.

Founded: 1840
Affiliation: United Methodist
UG Enrollment: 508 M, 669 W (full-time)
Cost: $10K–$20K
% Receiving Financial Aid: 67%
Admission: Very Selective
Application Deadline: Feb. 15

Admission is very selective. About 73% of applicants accepted, 39% of these actually enroll; 77% of freshmen graduate in top quarter of high school class, 96% in top-half. Average freshman SAT scores, middle 50% range: 480–580 verbal, 520–640 mathematical; 62% score above 500 on verbal, 18% above 600, 2% above 700; 85% score above 500 on mathematical, 42% above 600, 9% above 700; ACT, 23–28 composite. *Required:* SAT or ACT; interview highly recommended, essay. Criteria considered in admissions, in order of importance: high school academic record ranks first, while standardized test scores, recommendations, writing sample, and interview all rank second; other factors considered: special talents, alumni children, diverse student body, religious affiliation and/or commitment. *Entrance programs:* early decision, early admission, midyear admission, deferred admission, advanced placement. *Apply* by February 15; rolling admissions. About 8% of entering students from private schools, 7% from parochial schools. *Transfers* welcome; 33 enrolled 1993–94.
Academic Environment. Student leader and administration source agree a high percent of students are strongly interested in academic pursuits, but also concerned with career goals. Students report strong writing foundation, close personal attention from faculty and staff, and flexibility of degree requirements are strengths of the academic program. Freshman symposium required of all entering students. Administration reports that 39 of the 120 hours needed for graduation are required general education courses. Degrees offered: bachelors. *Majors offered* include usual arts and sciences, animal behavior, business administration, communications, computer science, drama, education, women's studies. Average undergraduate class size: 64% under 20, 32% 20–40, 4% over 40.

About 56% of students entering as freshmen graduate within four years, 72% eventually; 86% of freshmen return for sophomore year. *Special programs:* CLEP, honors, independent study, study abroad, undergraduate research, individualized majors, academic internships, 3–2 in engineering. *Calendar:* semester, summer school.
Undergraduate degrees conferred (218). 32% were in Business and Management, 14% were in Social Sciences, 14% were in Education, 12% were in Fine and Applied Arts, 10% were in Psychology, 9% were in Biological Sciences, 4% were in Letters, remainder in 5 other fields.
Graduates Career Data. Advanced studies pursued by 31% of graduates; 4% enter medical school; 1% enter dental school; 6% enter law school; 3% enter business school. Medical schools typically enrolling largest numbers of graduates include UT at Galveston, Southwestern Medical; dental schools include UTSA; law schools include UT Austin, Baylor; business schools include UT Austin. Career Development Services include assistance with resume preparation and job search, freshmen offered opportunity to begin career search.
Faculty. About 92% of faculty hold PhD or equivalent. About 77% of undergraduate classes taught by tenured faculty. About 33% of teaching faculty are female.

Student Body. About 89% of students from in state; 93% South, 4% Midwest, 2% West, 1% New England, 1% Middle Atlantic, 2% foreign. An estimated 60% of students reported as Protestant, 25% Catholic, 3% Jewish, 10% unaffiliated, 2% other; 3% as Black, 4% Asian, 13% Hispanic. *Minority group students:* special financial, academic, and social provisions.
Religious Orientation. Southwestern is a church-related institution; 32% of students affiliated with the church; 3 hours of religion required of all students (6 for AB); attendance at chapel services voluntary.
Varsity Sports. Men (Div.II): Baseball, Basketball, Cross Country, Golf, Soccer, Tennis. Women (Div.II): Basketball, Cross Country, Golf, Soccer, Tennis, Volleyball.
Campus Life. Campus is located in a small town; students report location "slows life down a bit", but call it a plus. Students are reported to be involved in organizations—service, Greek, and academic—as well as intramural sports and music rehearsals. Austin, 30 miles away, provides access to arts and entertainment. Rules governing student conduct relaxed somewhat in recent years, no student concern reported. Cars allowed for all except students on disciplinary probation. Alcohol not permitted.

About 38% of men, 47% of women live in traditional dormitories; 26% of men, 21% of women live in coed dormitories; 19% of men, 32% of women commute. Freshmen given preference in college housing if all students cannot be accommodated. There are 4 fraternities, 4 sororities on campus which about 38% of men, 38% of women join; 17% of men live in fraternities; sororities provide no residence facilities. About 26% of resident students leave campus on weekends.
Annual Costs. Tuition and fees, $11,000; room and board, $4,484; estimated $1,630 other, exclusive of travel. About 67% of students receive financial aid; average amount of assistance, $9,454 for need-based and merit aid. Assistance is typically divided 65% scholarship, 25% loan, 10% work. University reports many scholarships awarded on the basis of academic merit alone, 2 for special talents alone, many for need alone. *Meeting Costs:* university offers tuition stabilization plan, parent loan program.

Southwestern Adventist College

Keene, Texas 76059 **(817) 645-3921**

A church-related, liberal arts college, located in a community of 5,000, 25 miles south of Fort Worth.

Founded: 1893
Affiliation: Seventh-day Adventist
UG Enrollment: 302 M, 319 W (full-time)
Cost: < $10K
Admission: Non-selective
Application Deadline: 12th day of classes

Admission. Graduates of accredited high schools with 12 units in academic subjects and minimum SAT of 600 combined or ACT of 15 eligible; others admitted conditionally; 75% of applicants accepted, 58% of these actually enroll. *Required:* SAT or ACT. *Apply* by 12th day of classes. *Transfers* welcome.
Academic Environment. Degrees offered: associates, bachelors. Students report small classes, "great teachers and staff", and tutorial program are strengths of the academic program. About 50% of general education requirements for graduation are elective; distribution requirements fairly numerous. About 20–25% of students entering as freshmen graduate eventually; 69% of freshmen return for sophomore year. *Special programs:* CLEP, study abroad, individualized majors. *Calendar:* semester, summer school.
Undergraduate degrees conferred (89). 25% were in Education, 22% were in Business and Management, 11% were in Psychology, 8% were in Public Affairs, 7% were in Life Sciences, 4% were in Philosophy and Religion, 4% were in Health Sciences, 4% were in Communications, 4% were in Business (Administrative Support), remainder in 5 other fields.
Student Body. About 51% of students from in state; 59% South, 22% North Central, 6% Middle Atlantic, 3% West. An estimated 15% of students reported as Hispanic, 10% Black, 3% Asian, 7% other minority.
Religious Orientation. Southwestern Adventist is a church-related institution; all freshmen and sophomores required to register for religion course each year; attendance at dormitory worship services, Friday evening, Sabbath school, and church services required of all students.
Campus Life. Students feel campus is a "great" academic and social environment and "very peaceful", while proximity to the city provides "a variety of opportunities and activities."

About 40% of men, 34% of women live in traditional dormitories; no coed dormitories; rest live in off-campus housing or commute. No intervisitation in men's or women's dormitory rooms. There are no fraternities or sororities on campus. About 5% of resident students leave campus on weekends.
Annual Costs. Tuition and fees, $7,064; room and board, $3,466; estimated $1,518 other, exclusive of travel.

Southwestern Assemblies of God College

Waxahachie, Texas 75165 **(214) 937-4010**

A small, church-related institution, formerly a junior college, Southwestern is now accredited to confer both associate and baccalaureate degrees. .

Founded: 1927
Affiliation: Assemblies of God
UG Enrollment: 384 M, 345 W (full-time); 102 M, 63 W (part-time)
Cost: < $10K
% Receiving Financial Aid: 75%
Admission: Non-selective
Application Deadline: Rolling

Admission. About 99% of applicants accepted, 99% of these actually enroll. Average freshmen SAT scores: 409 M, 425 W verbal, 479 M, 449 W mathematical. *Required:* SAT or ACT, essay, references, transcripts, physical. Criteria considered in admissions, in order of importance: recommendations, high school academic record, standardized test scores, writing sample, extracurricular activities; other factors considered: religious affiliation and/or commitment. *Entrance programs:* early decision, early admission, midyear admission, advanced placement. *Apply:* rolling admissions. *Transfers* welcome; 181 enrolled 1993–94.
Academic Environment. Graduation requirements include 12 hours of English, 8 of science, 6 of physical education, 30 of physical education, Bible, 6 of social sciences, 3 of mathematics. Degrees offered: associates, bachelors. Average undergraduate class size: 43% under 20, 27% 20–40, 30% over 40. About 27% of students entering as freshmen graduate eventually; 53% of freshmen return for sophomore year. Adult programs: adult and continuing education, degree program.
Undergraduate degrees conferred (94). 76% were in Theology, 12% were in Business and Management, 10% were in Education, 3% were in Visual and Performing Arts.
Faculty. About 50% of faculty hold PhD or equivalent. About 28% of undergraduate classes taught by tenured faculty. About 30% of teaching faculty are female.
Student Body. About 70% of students from in state; 78% South, 7% West, 1% each New England, Middle Atlantic, Midwest, Northwest, foreign. An estimated 10% of students reported as Hispanic, 2% Black, 1% Asian, 2% other minority. Average age of undergraduate student: 25.
Religious Orientation. Southwestern Assemblies is a church-related institution; 91% of students affiliated with the church; 30 hour of religious studies required.
Campus Life. About 44% of men, 53% of women live in traditional dormitories; no coed dormitories; rest live in off-campus housing or commute. There are no fraternities or sororities on campus. About 60% of resident students leave campus on weekends.
Annual Costs. Tuition and fees, $2,900; room and board, $2,762; estimated $1,500 other, exclusive of travel. About 75% of students receive financial aid; average amount of assistance, $4,000. Assistance is typically divided 10% scholarship, 35% grant, 50% loan, 5% work. College reports 75 scholarships awarded on basis of academic merit alone, 40 for special needs alone.

Southwestern Christian College

Terrell, Texas, 75160

A small, independent college, Southwestern Christian is "chartered as a religious, co-educational institution. Since the Bible is God's revelation of the pattern of Spiritual development, daily instruction in His Word is a fundamental aspect of SwCC."

Undergraduate degrees conferred (127). 26% were in Business and Management, 20% were in Education, 17% were in Health Sciences, 7% were in Life Sciences, 5% were in Social Sciences, 5% were in Public Affairs, 3% were in Parks and Recreation, 3% were in Letters, 3% were in Communications, remainder in 8 other fields.

Southwestern College of Christian Ministries

Bethany, Oklahoma 73008 **(405) 789-76117**

A church-related college, Southwestern offers studies leading to both associate and baccalaureate degrees.

Founded: 1946
Affiliation: Pentecostal Holiness
UG Enrollment: 112 M, 49 W (full-time); 29 M, 2 W (part-time)
Total Enrollment: 191
Cost: < $10K
% Receiving Financial Aid: 98%
Admission: Non-selective
Application Deadline: Rolling

Admission. About 98% of applicants enroll. Average freshmen ACT scores: 18 composite. *Required:* ACT, telephone interview. Criteria considered in admissions: recommendations, high school academic record and standardized test scores all rank with equal importance; other factors considered: religious affiliation and/or commitment. *Entrance programs:* early decision, early admission. *Apply:* rolling admissions.
Academic Environment. Degrees offered: associates, bachelors, masters. Average undergraduate class size: 80% under 20, 10% 20–40, 10% over 40. *Special programs:* January interterm, 3–2 programs, internships and cooperative work-study programs.
Undergraduate degrees conferred (9). 89% were in Theology, 11% were in Philosophy and Religion.
Graduates Career Data. Advanced studies pursued by 60% of graduates; 40% enter graduate school; 10% enter law school; 10% enter seminary. All of 1992–93 graduates employed. Career Development Services available.
Faculty. About 80% of faculty hold PhD or equivalent. About 80% of undergraduate classes taught by tenured faculty. About 20% of teaching faculty are female; 10% Black.
Student Body. About 80% of students from Midwest; 10% South, 5% West, 5% foreign. An estimated 8% of students reported as Black, 5% Hispanic, 7% other minority.
Religious Orientation. Southwestern College of Christian Ministries is a church-related institution; 90% of students affiliated with the church; 3 courses in religious studies required.
Campus Life. About 25% of men, 25% of women live in traditional dormitories; no coed dormitories; rest commute. There are no fraternities or sororities on campus. About 50% of resident students leave campus on weekends.
Annual Costs. Tuition and fees, $7,500; room and board, $2,500; estimated $500 other, exclusive of travel. About 98% of students receive financial aid.

Southwestern Conservative Baptist Bible College

Phoenix, Arizona 85032

A small Bible college offering associates, and bachelors programs.

Founded: 1960
Affiliation: Conservative Baptist

University of Southwestern Louisiana

Lafayette, Louisiana 70504 **(318) 231-6457**

A state-supported university, located in a city of 117,000, 115 miles west of New Orleans. Most convenient major airport: New Orleans.

Founded: 1898
Affiliation: State
UG Enrollment: 5,244 M, 5,716 W (full-time); 1,080 M, 1,828 W (part-time)
Total Enrollment: 16,584
Cost: < $10K
Admission: Non-selective
Application Deadline: 30 days before beginning of semester

Admission. Louisiana graduates of accredited high schools eligible; 98% of applicants accepted, 76% of these actually enroll. *Required:* ACT. *Out-of-state* freshman applicants: university seeks students from out of state. State does not limit out-of-state enrollment. *Apply* by 30 days before beginning of semester. *Transfers* welcome.
Academic Environment. *Undergraduate studies* offered by colleges of Arts, Humanities, and Behavioral Sciences; Agriculture and Home Economics; Biological, Mathematical, and Physical Sciences; Business Administration; Education; Engineering; Nursing; and General Studies. About 15% of general education requirements for graduation are elective; distribution requirements fairly numerous.

About 45% of students entering as freshmen graduate eventually; 65% of freshmen return for sophomore year. *Special programs:* independent study, honors, study abroad, undergraduate research, 3-year degree, university year for action. *Calendar:* semester, summer school.
Undergraduate degrees conferred (1,529). 21% were in Liberal/General Studies, 19% were in Business and Management, 14% were in Education, 7% were in Health Sciences, 6% were in Engineering, 4% were in Protective Services, 4% were in Home Economics, 4% were in Communications, 3% were in Social Sciences, 3% were in Architecture and Environmental Design, 3% were in Engineering and Engineering Related Technology, remainder in 16 other fields.
Graduates Career Data. According to most recent data available, full-time graduate or professional study pursued immediately after graduation by 18% of students. *Careers in business and industry* pursued by 60% of graduates. Employers typically hiring largest numbers of graduates include Shell Oil, Electronic Data Systems, Arthur Andersen.
Student Body. About 91% of students from in state. An estimated 16% of students reported as Black, 1% Hispanic, 1% Asian, 8% other minority, according to most recent data available.
Varsity Sports. Men (Div.I): Baseball, Basketball, Cross Country, Football (IA), Golf, Tennis, Track. Women (Div.I): Basketball, Cross country, Softball, Tennis, Track, Volleyball.
Campus Life. About 12% of men, 16% of women live in traditional dormitories; no coed dormitories; rest live in off-campus housing or commute. Intervisitation in men's and women's dormitory rooms limited. There are 14 fraternities, 8 sororities on campus less than 7% of men, 5% of women join; 1% of men live in fraternities; sororities provide no residence facilities. About 65% of resident students leave campus on weekends.
Annual Costs. Tuition and fees, $1,598 (out-of-state, $3,398); room and board, $2,136. About 49% of students receive financial aid; assistance is typically divided 12% scholarship, 57% loan, 34% work. College reports some scholarships awarded on the basis of academic merit alone.

Southwestern Oklahoma State University

Weatherford, Oklahoma 73096 **(405) 774-3777**

A state-supported college, located in a community of 10,000, 75 miles west of Oklahoma City.

Founded: 1901
Affiliation: State
UG Enrollment: 1,843 M, 2,175 W (full-time)
Cost: < $10K
Admission: Non-selective
Application Deadline: 1 week prior to term

Admission. Graduates of accredited Oklahoma high schools with C average, rank in top two-thirds of class, or score in top two-thirds on ACT eligible; 99% of applicants accepted, 96% of these actually enroll; 45% of freshmen graduate in top fifth of high school class, 83% in top two-fifths. *Required:* ACT. *Out-of-state* freshman appli-

cants: university welcomes students from out-of-state. State does not limit out-of-state enrollment. Requirement for out-of-state applicants: ACT composite score of 18 or rank in top half of class. *Apply* by 1 week prior to term. *Transfers* welcome.
Academic Environment. Degrees offered: bachelors. About 25% of general education requirements for graduation are elective; distribution requirements fairly numerous. About 65% of students entering as freshmen graduate eventually; 75% of freshmen return for sophomore year. *Special programs:* CLEP, independent study, study abroad, honors, undergraduate research. *Calendar:* semester, summer school.
Undergraduate degrees conferred (672). 29% were in Education, 22% were in Health Sciences, 19% were in Business and Management, 4% were in Life Sciences, 3% were in Social Sciences, 3% were in Visual and Performing Arts, 3% were in Psychology, 3% were in Computer and Engineering Related Technology, 3% were in Physical Sciences, 3% were in Marketing and Distribution, remainder in 10 other fields.
Student Body. About 94% of students from in state; 2% South.
Varsity Sports. Men (NAIA): Baseball, Basketball, Football, Golf, Tennis, Track. Women (NAIA): Basketball, Softball, Tennis.
Campus Life. About 25% of men, 30% of women live in traditional dormitories; no coed dormitories; rest live in off-campus housing or commute. Intervisitation in men's and women's dormitory rooms limited. There are 3 fraternities, 3 sororities on campus which about 1% of each men, women join; 1% of each men, women live in fraternities and sororities. About 60% of resident students leave campus on weekends.
Annual Costs. Tuition and fees, $1,388 (out-of-state, $3,450); room and board, $1,800; estimated $1,000 other, exclusive of travel.

Southwestern Union College

(See Southwestern Adventist College)

Spalding University

Louisville, Kentucky 40203 **(502) 585-7111**

An independent, co-educational university founded by the Sisters of Charity of Nazareth, located in a metropolitan area of 850,000.

Founded: 1920
Affiliation: Independent (Roman Catholic)
UG Enrollment: 84 M, 577 W (full-time)
Cost: < $10K
Admission: Non-selective
Application Deadline: 1 month prior to registration

Admission. Graduates of accredited high schools eligible; 71% of applicants accepted, 56% of these actually enroll; 35% of freshmen graduate in top fifth of high school class, 61% in top two-fifths. *Required:* SAT or ACT; interview recommended. *Apply* by 1 month prior to registration. *Transfers* welcome.
Academic Environment. University participates in consortium of institutions in Greater Louisville area. Degrees offered: associates, bachelors. About 42% of general education requirements for graduation are elective; distribution requirements fairly numerous. About 60% of students entering as freshmen graduate eventually; 80% of freshmen return for sophomore year. *Special programs:* CLEP, independent study, study abroad. *Calendar:* semester, summer school.
Undergraduate degrees conferred (130). 32% were in Health Sciences, 18% were in Education, 18% were in Business and Management, 8% were in Public Affairs, 7% were in Communications, 5% were in Home Economics, 3% were in Life Sciences, remainder in 7 other fields.
Student Body. About 87% of students from in state; 97% Midwest.
Religious Orientation. Spalding is an independent institution in the Catholic tradition; 6 hours of religious studies required of all students as part of general education program.
Campus Life. About 10% of students live in dormitories; rest commute. There are no fraternities or sororities on campus.
Annual Costs. Tuition and fees, $7,876; room and board, $2,640; estimated $800 other, exclusive of travel. *Meeting Costs:* university offers installment payment plan, payment by credit card.

Spelman College

Atlanta, Georgia 30314 **(800) 982-2411**

An independent, liberal arts college, Spelman is located on a 32-acre campus near the business section of Atlanta. Founded as the first U.S. college for Negro women, it now admits students without regard to race or creed. The college is affiliated with the Atlanta University Center. (See also Atlanta University Center.) Most convenient major airport: Atlanta.

Founded: 1881
Affiliation: Independent
Total Enrollment: 1,708
Cost: < $10K
Admission: Non-selective
Application Deadline: Feb. 1

Admission. High school graduates with 15 units (12 in academic subjects) and C average eligible; 45% of applicants accepted, 38% of these actually enroll. Average freshman scores: SAT, 490 verbal, 520 mathematical; ACT, 23 composite. *Required:* SAT or ACT. *Apply* by February 1. *Transfers* welcome; 53 enrolled 1992–93.
Academic Environment. Students report approximate class size of 30 allows personal contact with teachers; students have personal advisors and are encouraged to meet with them regularly. Degrees offered: associates, bachelors. About 45% of general education requirements for graduation are elective; distribution requirements fairly numerous. *Special programs:* CLEP, independent study, study abroad, undergraduate research, 3–2 engineering. *Calendar:* semester, summer school.
Undergraduate degrees conferred (383). 30% were in Social Sciences, 19% were in Letters, 17% were in Psychology, 8% were in Life Sciences, 6% were in Mathematics, 4% were in Multi/Interdisciplinary Studies, 4% were in Physical Sciences, 3% were in Education, 3% were in Computer and Engineering Related Technology, 3% were in Visual and Performing Arts, remainder in 3 other fields.
Faculty. About 81% of faculty hold PhD or equivalent.
Student Body. About 22% of students from in state.
Religious Orientation. Spelman is an independent institution, but "Christian in origin"; makes no religious demands on students.
Campus Life. College is located in an urban area, close to Atlanta's many attractions; parking is, however, reported to be a problem.

About 68% of women live in traditional dormitories; rest commute. Intervisitation in women's dormitory rooms limited. There are 4 sororities on campus which about 15% of women join.
Annual Costs. Tuition and fees, $7,452; room and board, $5,250; estimated $1,600 other, exclusive of travel.

Spertus College of Judaica

Chicago, Illinois 60605

A private, nondenominational college offering a degree program in Judaic and Hebraic studies which is also open to students enrolled in cooperating institutions in the Chicago area and northern Illinois.

Founded: 1925
Affiliation: Independent

Undergraduate degrees conferred (2). 50% were in Foreign Languages, 50% were in Area and Ethnic Studies.

Spring Arbor College

Spring Arbor, Michigan 49283 **(517) 750-1200**

A church-related college, offering "Christian liberal arts education in a rural setting," located in a village of 1,800, 70 miles west of Detroit. Most convenient major airport: Detroit Metropolitan.

Founded: 1873
Affiliation: Free Methodist
UG Enrollment: 309 M, 425 W (full-time); 49 M, 136 W (part-time)
Cost: < $10K
% Receiving Financial Aid: 80%
Admission: Non-selective
Application Deadline: Rolling

Admission. High school graduates with 2.6 average and ACT composite score of 18 eligible; others accepted for "qualified admission"; 90% of applicants accepted, 45% of these actually enroll; 29% of freshmen graduate in top fifth of high school class, 56% in top two-fifths. Average freshman ACT scores: 21.3 composite. *Required:* SAT or ACT, minimum high school GPA. Criteria considered in admissions, in order of importance: high school academic record and standardized test scores rank with equal importance, recommendations, writing sample, extracurricular activities; other factors considered: alumni children, diverse student body, religious affiliation and/or commitment. *Entrance programs:* early admission, midyear admission, deferred admission, advanced placement. About 3% of entering students from private schools, 14% from parochial schools. *Apply:* rolling admissions. *Transfers* welcome; 70 enrolled 1993–94.

Academic Environment. Degrees offered: associates, bachelors, masters. About 48% of general education requirements for graduation are elective; distribution requirements fairly numerous. Average undergraduate class size: 17. About 43% of students entering as freshmen graduate eventually, 73% of freshmen return for sophomore year. *Special programs:* CLEP, independent study, January interterm, study abroad, undergraduate research. Adult programs: Adult Education Graduate Degree Completion Program. *Calendar:* 14–4–14 (2 14-week terms plus 4-week January interim).

Undergraduate degrees conferred (571). 70% were in Business and Management, 8% were in Social Sciences, 7% were in Health Sciences, 3% were in Education, remainder in 10 other fields.

Graduates Career Data. About 84% of 1992–93 graduates employed. Career Development Services include resume assistance and counseling.

Faculty. About 48% of faculty hold PhD or equivalent. About 73% of undergraduate classes taught by tenured faculty. About 29% of teaching faculty are female; 3% Black.

Student Body. About 89% of students from in state; 4% Midwest, 1% New England, 4% foreign. An estimated 86% of students reported as Protestant, 6% Catholic; 4% as Black, 1% Hispanic. Average age of undergraduate student: 31.

Religious Orientation. Spring Arbor is a church-related institution; 24% of students affiliated with the church; 3 core courses in Christian Perspective, attendance at chapel required of all students; attendance at Sunday services, regular participation in all college-related religious activities expected.

Varsity Sports. Men (NAIA): Baseball, Basketball, Cross Country, Golf, Soccer, Tennis, Track. Women (NAIA): Basketball, Cross Country, Golf, Soccer, Softball, Tennis, Track, Volleyball.

Campus Life. About 44% of men, 48% of women live in traditional dormitories; no coed dormitories; rest live in off-campus housing or commute. Freshmen given preference in college housing if all students cannot be accommodated. Intervisitation in men's and women's dormitory rooms limited. Sexes segregated in coed dormitories either by wing or floor. There are no fraternities or sororities on campus. About 50% of resident students leave campus on weekends.

Annual Costs. Tuition and fees, $8,706; room and board, $3,550; estimated $900 other, exclusive of travel. About 80% of students receive financial aid; average amount of assistance, $4,650. *Meeting Costs:* college offers monthly payment plan, AMS program.

Spring Hill College

Mobile, Alabama 36608 **(205) 460-2130**

A church-related college, conducted by the Jesuits, located in a residential area of a city of 200,000. Most convenient major airport: Mobile Municipal.

Founded: 1830
Affiliation: Roman Catholic
UG Enrollment: 1,073 M, W (full-time)
Cost: $10K–$20K
Admission: Selective (+)
Application Deadline: August 15

Admission is selective (+). About 80% of applicants accepted, 36% of these actually enroll; 40% of freshmen graduate in top fifth of high school class, 68% in top two-fifths. *Required:* SAT or ACT. *Non-academic factors* considered in admissions: diverse student body, alumni children. *Entrance programs:* early admission, deferred admission, advanced placement. About 9% of entering students from private schools, 61% from parochial. *Apply* by August 15. *Transfers* welcome.

Academic Environment. Students reported as seeking stronger voice in curriculum and faculty hiring decisions. Administration reports 5% of general education courses required for graduation are elective; distribution requirements fairly numerous. *Degrees:* AB, BGS, BS, BSCom. *Majors offered* include usual arts and sciences, business, communication arts, computer science, education.

About 50% of students entering as freshmen graduate eventually; 81% of freshmen return for sophomore year. *Special programs:* CLEP, independent study, study abroad, honors, optional January interterm, 3-year degree, individualized majors, Marine Environmental Sciences Consortium, 3–2 programs in engineering. *Calendar:* semester, summer school.

Undergraduate degrees conferred (207). 28% were in Business and Management, 16% were in Communications, 12% were in Social Sciences, 9% were in Liberal/General Studies, 8% were in Life Sciences, 7% were in Letters, 5% were in Psychology, 4% were in Visual and Performing Arts, 4% were in Education, remainder in 5 other fields.

Graduates Career Data. According to most recent data available, full-time graduate or professional study pursued immediately after graduation by 34% of students; 7% enter medical school; 2% enter dental school; 4% enter law school; 12% enter business school. *Careers in business and industry* pursued by 15% of graduates. Career Development Services include placement services, internship programs, preparing for interviews. Alumni reported as helpful in both career guidance and job placement.

Faculty. About 85% of full-time faculty hold PhD or equivalent.

Student Body. College seeks a national student body; 32% of students from in state; 78% South, 13% North Central, 4% Middle Atlantic. An estimated 75% of students reported as Catholic, 20% Protestant; 3% as Black, 3% Hispanic, 1% other minority, according to most recent data available. *Minority group students:* special financial and academic provisions including Upward Bound.

Religious Orientation. Spring Hill is a Jesuit institution; 12 hours in philosophy, theology and "respect for Catholic beliefs on which school is founded" required of all students. Places of worship available on campus for Catholics, in immediate community for Protestants and Jews.

Varsity Sports. Men (NAIA): Baseball, Basketball, Cross Country, Golf, Tennis; Sailing, Rowing. Women (Div.III): Basketball, Cross Country, Tennis; Sailing, Rowing.

Campus Life. Self-determined hours possible for all students. Use of alcohol forbidden in public places except at authorized social functions; drugs forbidden, violation results in "severe disciplinary action." Limited visitation privileges determined by each dormitory within college guidelines (noon to midnight Monday–Thursday, to 2 am Friday, Saturday). Cars allowed; parking reported as adequate for all students.

About 78% of men, 81% of women live in traditional dormitories; no coed dormitories; 4% of men, 2% of women live in off-campus college-related housing; 18% of men, 17% of women commute. There are 4 fraternities, 3 sororities on campus which about 36% of men, 46% of women join. About 20% of resident students leave campus on weekends.

Annual Costs. Tuition and fees, $11,425; room and board, $4,590. About 69% of students receive financial aid; assistance is typically divided 67% scholarship, 27% loan, 7% work. College reports some scholarships awarded on the basis of academic merit alone. *Meeting Costs:* college offers Academic Management Services.

Springfield College

Springfield, Massachusetts 01109 **(413) 788-3136**

An independent, liberal arts, teachers, and professional school located in a city of 180,000. Springfield's "distinctive task" since its founding has been to provide training for professional careers in YMCA and other youth and community service agencies. Most convenient major airport: Bradley (Hartford, CT).

Founded: 1885
Affiliation: Independent
UG Enrollment: 3,300 M, W (full-time)
Cost: $10K–$20K
Admission: Non-selective
Application Deadline: April 1

Admission. Graduates of approved high schools with 16 units in college preparatory program eligible; 54% of applicants accepted, 45% of these actually enroll. About 24% of freshmen graduate in top fifth of high school class, 50% in top two-fifths. *Required:* SAT, interview. *Non-academic factors* considered in admissions: special talents, alumni children, leadership, community activities related to intended major. *Apply* by April 1; January 15 for Physical Therapy, Athletic Training. *Transfers* welcome.

Academic Environment. *Degrees:* BA, BS, BPhEd. *Majors offered* include some arts and sciences, community leadership and development, education, environmental studies, medical technology, rehabilitation services. About 60% of general education requirements for graduation are elective; distribution requirements fairly numerous. About 85% of students entering as freshmen graduate eventually; 85% of freshmen return for sophomore year. *Special programs:* CLEP, independent study, study abroad, undergraduate research, individualized majors, International Center. *Calendar:* 3 10-week terms, January intercession.

Undergraduate degrees conferred (636). 25% were in Allied Health, 24% were in Public Affairs, 15% were in Education, 8% were in Liberal/General Studies, 7% were in Psychology, 7% were in Business and Management, 3% were in Life Sciences, 3% were in Social Sciences, remainder in 7 other fields.

Student Body. College seeks a national student body; 50% of students from New England, 30% Middle Atlantic, according to most recent data available.

Varsity Sports. Men (Div.II): Baseball, Basketball, Cross Country, Football, Golf, Gymnastics, Lacrosse (III), Soccer, Swimming, Tennis, Track, Volleyball, Wrestling. Women (Div.II): Basketball, Cross Country, Field Hockey, Golf, Gymnastics, Lacrosse, Soccer, Softball, Swimming, Tennis, Track, Volleyball.

Campus Life. About 38% of students live in traditional dormitories; 37% in coed dormitories; rest live in off-campus housing or commute. Intervisitation unlimited at discretion of individual dormitory. Sexes segregated in coed dormitories either by wing or floor.

Annual Costs. Tuition and fees, $10,368; room and board, $4,832. About 60% of students receive financial aid; assistance is typically divided 48% scholarship, 48% loan, 4% work. *Meeting Costs:* college offers payment plan, Family Education Loan Program, Co-operative Education Program.

Stanford University

Stanford, California 94305 **(415) 723-2091**

Stanford is one of the nation's most prestigious universities. Its faculty is rated among the very best in the country, ranking with Berkeley and Harvard. Stanford has overseas studies centers in Berlin, Kyoto, Moscow, Rome, Santiago, Oxford, Florence, Paris. The 8,180-acre main campus includes the main academic center, an arboretum, a small lake, a 1,200-acre biological preserve, and a research park. Stanford is located on the outskirts of Palo Alto (pop. 57,000), 30 miles south of San Francisco. Most convenient major airports: San Francisco, San Jose.

Founded: 1891
Affiliation: Independent
UG Enrollment: 3,500 M, 3,073 W (full-time)
Total Enrollment: 14,002
Cost: $10K–$20K
% Receiving Financial Aid: 67%
Admission: Most Selective
Application Deadline: December 15

Admission is among the most selective in the country. About 22% of applicants accepted, 55% of these actually enroll; 88% of freshmen graduate in top fifth of high school class, 95% in top two-fifths, 5% "unknown." Average freshman scores: SAT: 94% of freshmen score above 500 on verbal, 72% above 600, 22% above 700; 99% score above 500 on mathematical, 89% above 600, 59% above 700. *Required:* SAT or ACT, essay; 3 ACH including English strongly recommended. *Non-academic factors* considered in admissions: diverse student body, special talents, extracurricular activities. *Entrance programs:* advanced placement, deferred admission. About 30% of entering students from private schools. *Apply* by December 15. *Transfers* welcome; 120 enrolled 1993–94.

Academic Environment. Administration source characterizes students as devoted to scholarly pursuits; student leader, perhaps closer to the uncertainties of the job market, reports an overwhelming interest in pragmatic goals. Both are probably correct. Extensive study abroad program involves high percentage of sophomores and upperclassmen. University bulletin prepared by 8 freshmen for prospective applicants warns that new students should not be overly influenced "by the balmy California weather and beauty of the campus, academic competition is strenuous," but, one recent international relations student describes the student body as "diverse, smart, creative and supportive." Some student concern reported over "how to do well and have time for other activities." Administration reports 5% of courses needed for graduation are required; some distribution requirements in humanities, social sciences, and natural sciences/mathematics/technology. Requirement of 1 year of foreign language for those who did not have at least 3 years in high school. Degrees offered: bachelors, masters, doctoral. *Undergraduate studies* offered by schools of Humanities and Sciences, Earth Sciences, Engineering. *Majors offered* in humanities and sciences in addition to usual studies include African and Afro-American studies, anthropology, Chinese, communications, human biology (with Medical School), human language, Japanese, East Asian Studies, Latin American studies; individualized majors as well as inter-school majors increasingly popular.

About 77% of entering freshmen graduate within four years, 93% eventually; 98% of freshman return for sophomore year. *Special programs:* independent study, study abroad, honors, undergraduate research, 3-year degree, individualized majors, technology and society program for School of Engineering, undergraduate special courses and student-initiated courses for credit, intern programs (in Washington, Palo Alto, Sacramento; also some for business management), 3–2 programs in engineering, cross registration with Howard. *Calendar:* quarter, summer school.

Undergraduate degrees conferred (1,470). 37% were in Social Sciences, 17% were in Engineering, 11% were in Life Sciences, 7% were in Letters, 5% were in Psychology, 5% were in Computer and Engineering Related Technology, 4% were in Area and Ethnic Studies, 3% were in Physical Sciences, 3% were in Visual and Performing Arts, remainder in 6 other fields.

Graduates Career Data. Medical schools typically enrolling largest numbers of graduates include Stanford, UC-San Francisco, UCLA; law schools include Stanford, Harvard, Yale, U. of Michigan. *Careers in business and industry* pursued by 25–30% of graduates, according to most recent data available. Career Development Services include counseling, recruiting services, job fairs, resume services. Student assessment of program reported as good for both career guidance and job placement. Alumni reported by administration as active in career guidance, but not job placement.

Faculty. About 99% of faculty hold PhD or equivalent. About 16% of teaching faculty are female; 3% Black, 3% Hispanic, 7% Asian.

Student Body. University seeks a national student body; 42% of students from in state. An estimated 8% of students reported as Black, 10% Hispanic, 22% Asian, 4% ethnic minority. *Minority group students:* funds to ensure adequate cultural programs; Native American Cultural Center; meeting house for Black students; some preferential assignment to certain residences.

Varsity Sports. Men (PAC 10): Baseball, Basketball, Crew, Cross Country, Diving, Fencing, Football, Golf, Gymnastics, Lacrosse, Soccer, Swimming, Tennis, Track, Volleyball, WaterPolo, Wrestling. Women (WCAA): Basketball, Crew, Cross Country, Diving, Fencing, Field Hockey, Golf, Gymnastics, Sailing, Soccer, Softball, Swimming, Synchronized Swimming, Tennis, Track, Volleyball.

Campus Life. Student leader hails the campus environment: "Beautiful weather, exciting San Francisco close by, good restaurants, good research facilities, knowledgeable professors." Students control their own social life and lifestyles, which vary widely on this cosmopolitan campus. Students most at home on campus: "aggressive, ambitious, laid-back"; least at home: "quiet, shy." No university-wide rules on intervisitation; individual houses may establish limitation on hours if they wish. Coed housing reported to be "more mundane" than one anticipates. Rules on alcohol conform to state law; use on campus limited to interior of residence, eating clubs, and social functions in residences not occupied predominantly by freshmen. No smoking in dormitories as of 1994–95 school year. Cars allowed, but parking may be a problem. Stanford's large campus is self-contained community, independent of both Palo Alto and San Francisco.

About 94% of students live in on-campus housing; rest live in off-campus housing or commute. There are 22 fraternities, 10 sororities on campus which about 21% of men, 13% of women join; 7% of men and women live in fraternities or sororities. About 1% of resident students leave campus on weekends, according to most recent data available.

Annual Costs. Tuition and fees, $17,775; room and board, $6,535; estimated $1,300 other, exclusive of travel. About 67% of students receive financial aid. Assistance is typically divided 77% scholarship, 20% loan, 3% work. College reports 57% of scholarships awarded on the basis of need alone, 4% for special talents. *Meeting Costs:* university offers parent loan program.

Stanislaus State College

(See California State College/Stanislaus)

Stephen F. Austin State University

Nacogdoches, Texas 75962 (409) 568-2504

A state-supported university, located in a town of 31,252, 145 miles north of Houston. Most convenient major airport: Houston Intercontinental.

Founded: 1917
Affiliation: State
UG Enrollment: 4,605 M, 5,494 W (full-time); 672 M, 700 W (part-time)
Total Enrollment: 12,898
Cost: < $10K
% Receiving Financial Aid: 81%
Admission: Non-selective
Application Deadline: Rolling

Admission. Graduates of accredited high schools who rank in top half of class eligible; others must have minimum test scores of 20 (ACT composite) or 900 (combined SAT); 82% of applicants accepted, 52% of these actually enroll; 5% of freshmen graduate in top fifth of high school class, 25% in top two-fifths. *Required:* ACT or SAT. *Out-of-state* freshman applicants: university does not seek students from out of state. No special requirements for out-of-state applicants. *Apply:* no specific deadline. *Transfers* welcome.

Academic Environment. *Undergraduate studies* offered by schools of Liberal Arts, Applied Arts and Science, Business, Education, Fine Arts, Forestry, Sciences and Mathematics. General education program of communication and quantitative skills, sciences, humanities, social sciences, and physical activity required of all students. About 42% of students entering as freshmen graduate within four years; 62% of freshmen return for sophomore year. *Special programs:* honors, 3-year degree, individualized majors. *Calendar:* semester, summer school.

Undergraduate degrees conferred (1,866). 28% were in Business and Management, 20% were in Education, 7% were in Communications, 6% were in Multi/Interdisciplinary Studies, 5% were in Protective Services, 4% were in Life Sciences, 3% were in Health Sciences, 3% were in Social Sciences, 3% were in Visual and Performing Arts, 3% were in Public Affairs, remainder in 15 other fields.

Graduates Career Data. According to most recent data available, full-time graduate or professional study pursued by 17% of students immediately after graduation. *Careers in business and industry* pursued by 63% of graduates.

Student Body. College does not seek a national student body; 95% of students from in state; 40 foreign. An estimated 5% of students reported as Black, 3% Hispanic, 1% other minority, according to most recent data available.

Varsity Sports. Men (Div.IA): Basketball, Football (IAA), Golf, Track. Women (Div.IA): Basketball, Softball, Track, Volleyball.

Campus Life. About 35% of men, 40% of women live in traditional dormitories; no coed dormitories; rest commute. Freshmen given preference in college housing if all students cannot be accommodated. Intervisitation in men's and women's dormitory rooms limited. There are 19 fraternities, 13 sororities on campus which about 71% of men, 49% of women join; they provide no residence facilities. About 15% of resident students leave campus on weekends.

Annual Costs. Tuition and fees, $1,450 (out-of-state, $5,530); room and board, $3,768. About 81% of students receive financial aid. College reports some scholarships awarded on the basis of academic merit alone. *Meeting Costs:* university offers installment payment plans.

Stephens College

Columbia, Missouri 65215 (314) 876-7207

An independent, liberal arts women's college, located in a community of 65,000, 125 miles west of St. Louis. Stephens is committed to addressing change in the aspirations and roles of women, and dedicated to promote lifelong learning. Most convenient major airports: Columbia Regional, St. Louis, or Kansas City.

Founded: 1833
Affiliation: Independent
UG Enrollment: 600 W (full-time); 400 W (part-time)
Cost: $10K–$20K
% Receiving Financial Aid: 70%
Admission: Non-selective
Application Deadline: July 30

Admission. High school graduates eligible; 93% of applicants accepted, 48% of these actually enroll; 25% of freshmen graduate in top fifth of high school class, 51% in top two-fifths. Average freshman scores: SAT, 426 verbal, 444 mathematical. *Required:* SAT or ACT, essay. Criteria considered in admissions, in order of importance: high school academic record, writing sample, class rank, recommendations, standardized test scores. *Entrance programs:* early decision, early admission, midyear admission, advanced placement. *Apply* by July 30; rolling admissions. *Transfers* welcome; 25 enrolled 1993–94.

Academic Environment. Degrees offered: associates, bachelors. Candidates for BA may arrange program through many combinations of courses with an area concentration rather than traditional major. BFA candidates in fields of art, creative writing, dance, fashion design, music, theater arts must meet more specific requirements. *Majors offered* in addition to usual studies include computer science, musical theater, equestrian studies. About 75% of general education requirements for graduation are elective; distribution requirements fairly numerous. About 47% of students entering as freshmen graduate within four years; 52% eventually; 76% of freshmen return for sophomore year. Average undergraduate class size: 80% under 20, 20% 20–40. *Special programs:* CLEP, independent study, study abroad, undergraduate research, 3-year degree, individualized majors, summer programs abroad, summer stock theater, summer stock in dance, Stephens College Without Walls, legislative internships in state and city government, participation in consortium of Mid-Missouri Associated Colleges, 3–2 programs in engineering and occupational therapy, 2–2 in nursing, 3–1 in pharmacy, cross registration with MU, Columbia College, Westminster College. *Calendar:* 2 semesters each consisting of 2 7-week sessions, summer school.

Undergraduate degrees conferred (185). 20% were in Visual and Performing Arts, 14% were in Home Economics, 14% were in Communications, 10% were in Health Sciences, 9% were in Education, 9% were in Business and Management, 5% were in Psychology, 5% were in Marketing and Distribution, 4% were in Multi/Interdisciplinary Studies, remainder in 7 other fields.

Graduates Career Data. Advanced studies pursued by 20% of students.

Faculty. About 85% of faculty hold PhD or equivalent.

Student Body. College seeks a national student body; 25% of students from in state; 30% Midwest, 15% South, 15% West, 8% Middle Atlantic, 2% New England. Average age of undergraduate student: 23.

Varsity Sports. Women (Div. III): Soccer, Swimming, Tennis, Volleyball.

Campus Life. Cars allowed for all students, juniors and seniors allotted "prime parking" space; drinking not permitted at college-sponsored functions; however, students of legal age may drink in their residence hall rooms.

About 95% of women live in traditional dormitories; rest live in off-campus college-related housing or commute. Intervisitation in women's dormitory rooms limited. There are 4 local sororities on campus which about 20% of women join; they provide no residence facilities. About 20% of resident students leave campus on weekends.

Annual Costs. Tuition and fees, $13,450; room and board, $5,410. About 70% of students receive financial aid; average amount of assistance, $8,000. Assistance is typically divided 30% scholarship, 30% grant, 30% loan, 10% work. College reports some scholarships awarded on the basis of academic merit alone. *Meeting Costs:* college offers monthly payment plan.

Sterling College

Sterling, Kansas 67579 **(316) 278-2173**

A church-related college, located in a village of 2,300, 80 miles northwest of Wichita. Most convenient major airport: Wichita.

Founded: 1887
Affiliation: Presbyterian
UG Enrollment: 448 M, W (full-time)
Cost: < $10K
Admission: Non-selective
Application Deadline: August 15

Admission. Graduates of accredited high schools with 17 units who rank in top half of class eligible; 69% of applicants accepted, 39% of these actually enroll; 21% of freshmen graduate in top fifth of high school class. *Required:* SAT or ACT; interview recommended. *Apply* by August 15. *Transfers* welcome.

Academic Environment. *Degrees:* AB, BS. *Majors offered* in usual arts and sciences, education, geography, home economics, library science. All general education requirements for graduation are elective; distribution requirements limited. About 35% of students entering as freshmen graduate eventually; 45% of freshmen return for sophomore year. *Special programs:* CLEP, independent study, study abroad, honors, cooperative programs through ACCK. *Calendar:* 4–1–4.

Undergraduate degrees conferred (91). 41% were in Education, 26% were in Business and Management, 12% were in Psychology, 5% were in Social Sciences, 4% were in Life Sciences, 3% were in Philosophy and Religion, remainder in 5 other fields.

Student Body. College seeks a national student body; 60% of students from in state; 80% North Central. An estimated 80% of students reported as Protestant, 12% Catholic, 8% other; 15% Black, 3% Hispanic, 2% Asian, according to most recent data available.

Religious Orientation. Sterling is a church-related institution.

Varsity Sports. Men (NAIA): Baseball, Basketball, Cross Country, Football, Soccer, Tennis, Track. Women (NAIA): Basketball, Softball, Tennis, Track, Volleyball.

Campus Life. About 92% of men, 94% of women live in traditional dormitories; no coed dormitories; rest commute. No intervisitation in men's or women's dormitory rooms. There are no fraternities or sororities. About 30% of resident students leave campus on weekends.

Annual Costs. Tuition and fees, $7,890; room and board, $3,100. About 93% of students receive financial aid.

Stern College for Women

(See Yeshiva University)

Stetson University

DeLand, Florida 32720 **(904) 734-4121**

A church-affiliated university, Stetson is located on an 117-acre campus in a town of 16,500, 20 miles west of Daytona Beach. College of Law located in St. Petersburg. Also known as John B. Stetson University. Most convenient major airport: Daytona Beach.

Founded: 1883
Affiliation: Southern Baptist
UG Enrollment: 927 M, 1,122 W (full-time); 32 M, 30 W (part-time)
Total Enrollment: 2,830
Cost: $10K–$20K
Admission: Very Selective
Application Deadline: March 1

Admission is very selective. For all schools, 75% of applicants accepted, 44% of these actually enroll; 55% of freshmen graduate in top fifth of high school class, 82% in top two-fifths. *Required:* SAT or ACT; interview recommended. *Non-academic factors* considered in admissions: special talents, alumni children, children of Baptist ministers, diverse student body. *Entrance programs:* early decision, early admission, midyear admission, deferred admission, advanced placement. About 13% of entering students from private schools, 10% from parochial schools. *Apply* by March 1. *Transfers* welcome.

Academic Environment. Stetson was granted a chapter of Phi Beta Kappa, making it the third institution and first private one in Florida to be so acknowledged. A current student reports that the academic program is "rigorous, yet the faculty is supportive. The diversity of studies is great." Administration reports 40% of courses required for graduation are elective. *Undergraduate studies* offered by College of Liberal Arts, schools of Music, Business Administration. *Majors offered* in liberal arts in addition to usual studies include education, Russian studies, urban studies. Library and computer facilities are reported to be "good", with extended hours during finals.

About 59% of students entering as freshmen graduate eventually; 80% of freshmen return for sophomore year. *Special programs:* CLEP, independent study, study abroad, honors, undergraduate research, 3-year degree, individualized majors, Washington Semester, United Nations Semester, combined programs (forestry with Duke, 3–2 in engineering, medical technology), Roland George Investments Program. *Calendar:* 4–1–4, summer school.

Undergraduate degrees conferred (479). 48% were in Business and Management, 11% were in Social Sciences, 8% were in Education, 7% were in Psychology, 6% were in Letters, 5% were in Life Sciences, 3% were in Foreign Languages, 3% were in Mathematics, remainder in 8 other fields.

Graduates Career Data. *Full-time graduate or professional study* pursued immediately after graduation by 43% (1988–89) of students; 2% enter medical school; 2% enter dental school; 10% enter law school; 12% enter business school; 1% enter veterinary school. Medical and dental schools typically enrolling largest numbers of graduates include U. of Florida; law and business schools include Stetson, U. of Florida. *Careers in business and industry* pursued by 37% (1988–89) of graduates. Corporations typically hiring largest numbers of graduates include Barnett Bank, Martin Marietta., NCNB, Prudential. Career Development Services include career guidance, job placement, preparation for interviews. Alumni reported as actively helpful in job placement.

Faculty. About 77% of faculty hold PhD or equivalent.

Student Body. University seeks a national student body; 77% of students from in state; 84% South, 7% Middle Atlantic, 4% New England, 3% North Central.

Religious Orientation. Stetson is a church-related institution; 3 hours of religion, plus an additional 3 hours of religion or philosophy included in general education program required of all students; attendance at weekly chapel services voluntary.

Varsity Sports. Men (Div.I): Baseball, Basketball, Cross Country, Golf, Soccer, Tennis. Women (Div.I): Basketball, Cross Country, Golf, Softball, Tennis, Volleyball.

Campus Life. Strong fraternities and sororities, "social life revolves around the Greek System." University is making an effort to provide more social opportunities for non-Greeks on campus. Key privileges for women; intervisitation limited. University "does not condone the use of alcoholic beverages" on campus; illegal drugs similarly prohibited. Smoking restricted. Cars allowed. Students over 21 may be permitted to live off campus.

About 54% of men, 67% of women live in traditional dormitories; no coed dormitories; 20% of men and 23% of women live in off-campus housing or commute. Freshmen given preference in college housing if all students cannot be accommodated. There are 8 fraternities, 7 sororities on campus which about 44% of men, 42% of women join; 26% of men, 10% of women live in fraternities and sororities. About 40% of resident students leave campus on weekends.

Annual Costs. Tuition and fees, $11,995; room and board, $4,440. About 75% of students receive financial aid; assistance is typically divided 64% scholarship, 26% loan, 10% work. University reports some scholarships awarded on the basis of academic merit alone. *Meeting Costs:* university offers payment plans.

University of Steubenville

(See Franciscan University of Steubenville)

Stevens Institute of Technology

Hoboken, New Jersey 07030 **(201) 216-5000**

Founded in 1870 to provide engineering education based on scientific principles, Stevens today offers undergraduate programs in engineering, science, management, and computer science.

The 55-acre campus is located in Hoboken, N.J. on a hill overlooking the Hudson River and New York City.

Founded: 1870
Affiliation: Independent
UG Enrollment: 1,025 M, 238 W (full-time)
Total Enrollment: 2,876
Cost: $10K–$20K
Admission: Very (+) Selective
Application Deadline: March 1

Admission is very (+) selective. About 70% of applicants accepted, 30% of these actually enroll; 66% of freshmen graduate in top fifth of high school class, 96% in top two-fifths. Average freshman SAT scores: 521 verbal, 652 mathematical; 65% of freshman score above 500 verbal, 27% above 600, 3% above 700; all score above 500 mathematical, 77% above 600, 32% above 700. *Required:* SAT, 3 ACH (English, mathematics, physics or chemistry), interview. Criteria considered in admissions, in order of importance: high school academic record, standardized test scores, recommendations, extracurricular activities, interview. *Entrance programs:* early decision, early admission, advanced placement, deferred admission. *Apply* by March 1; rolling admission. *Transfers* welcome; 60 enrolled 1993–94.

Academic Environment. Common first-year program for all students. Four generalized baccalaureate programs offered in engineering, computer science, management, and science. Eight humanities courses designed as a self-contained mini-program of liberal education required. Administration reports 25–33% of courses required for graduation are elective depending on program of study. Degrees offered: bachelors, masters. Majors (concentrations) offered in engineering include chemical, civil, electrical, mechanical, metallurgical and ocean engineering, engineering physics; in science include chemical biology, chemistry, materials science, mathematics and physics; in management include management/management information systems, industrial management, statistics. Average undergraduate class size: 10% under 20, 20% 20–40, 1% over 40.

About 75% of students entering as freshmen graduate eventually; 85% of freshmen return for sophomore year. *Special programs:* summer program for qualified high school students, internships, International Scholars Program: junior year at U. of Dundee, graduate courses open to undergraduates, 3-year baccalaureate and 4-year master's programs, cross registration with NYU. *Calendar:* semester, summer school.

Undergraduate degrees conferred (226). 86% were in Engineering, 6% were in Computer and Engineering Related Technology, remainder in 5 other fields.

Graduates Career Data. According to most recent data available, full-time graduate study pursued immediately after graduation by 12% of students. Medical schools typically enrolling largest numbers of graduates include UMDNJ, Johns Hopkins, Georgetown U. School of Medicine; law schools include NY Law School, Rutgers; dental schools include Columbia. About 90% of 1992–93 graduates employed. Corporations typically hiring largest numbers of graduates include AT&T, Billcore, Allied Signal, Merck.

Faculty. About 90% of faculty hold PhD or equivalent. About 60% of undergraduate classes taught by tenured faculty. About 5% of teaching faculty are female.

Student Body. Institute seeks a national student body; 67% of students from in state; 33% Middle Atlantic, 8% foreign. *Minority group students:* Office of Educational Opportunity program funds available; pre-freshman Stevens Technical Enrichment Program and College Preparatory Program, special tutoring and counseling; Black Student Union, Latin American Club, Chinese Students Club, Indian Students Club.

Varsity Sports. Men (Div.III): Baseball, Basketball, Cross Country, Fencing, Golf, Lacrosse, Soccer, Tennis, Wrestling. Women (Div.III): Fencing, Tennis, Volleyball.

Campus Life. The Stevens honor system, established in 1907, forms the basis for a student government that gives undergraduates responsibility for all extracurricular activities, from dramatics to sports. Administration source reports "HUGE" rate of participation, including women, in intramural sports. Cars allowed all but freshmen, but parking is reported as "just barely enough" for both residents and commuters.

About 30% of students live in traditional dormitories; 35% in coed dormitories; 25% live in off-campus housing or commute, according to most recent data available. There are 10 fraternities, 3 sororities on campus which about 40% of men, 30% of women join. About 20% of resident students leave campus on weekends.

Annual Costs. Tuition and fees, $16,350; room and board, $5,290; estimated $1,000 other, exclusive of travel. About 75% of students receive financial aid; average amount of assistance, $10,000. Assistance is typically divided 58% scholarship, 21% loan, 21% work, according to most recent data available. Institute reports some scholarships awarded on the basis of academic merit alone.

Stillman College

Tuscaloosa, Alabama 35403 **(205) 349-4240**

A church-related college, located in a city of 65,800, 60 miles southwest of Birmingham; founded as a college for Negroes and still serving a predominantly black student body. Most convenient major airport: Birmingham.

Founded: 1876
Affiliation: Presbyterian
UG Enrollment: 815 M, W (full-time)
Cost: < $10K
% Receiving Financial Aid: 88%
Admission: Non-selective
Application Deadline: Aug. 1

Admission. Graduates of approved high schools with 15 units and C average eligible; graduates of nonapproved high schools must have C+ average; others admitted conditionally; 71% of applicants accepted, 53% of these actually enroll; 18% of freshmen graduate in top fifth of high school class, 39% in top two-fifths. Average freshman ACT scores, according to most recent data available: 16 M, 18 W composite. *Required:* SAT or ACT. *Apply:* by August 1; rolling admissions. *Transfers* welcome.

Academic Environment. *Degrees:* AB, BS. About 44% of general education requirements for graduation are elective; distribution requirements fairly numerous. About 35% of students entering as freshmen graduate eventually; 60% of freshmen return for sophomore year. *Special programs:* CLEP, independent study, Freshman Educational Development Program. *Calendar:* semester, summer school.

Undergraduate degrees conferred (112). 38% were in Business and Management, 13% were in Communications, 12% were in Social Sciences, 9% were in Computer and Engineering Related Technology, 7% were in Life Sciences, 7% were in Education, 4% were in Letters, 4% were in Visual and Performing Arts, 4% were in Physical Sciences, remainder in 2 other fields.

Graduates Career Data. According to most recent data available, full-time graduate or professional study pursued by 23% of students immediately after graduation.

Faculty. About 46% of faculty hold PhD or equivalent.

Student Body. College seeks a national student body; 66% of students from in state; 82% South, 10% North Central.

Religious Orientation. Stillman is a church-related institution; 12 hours of Bible required of all students.

Varsity Sports. Men (Div. III): Baseball, Basketball, Cross Country, Tennis. Women (Div. III): Basketball, Cross Country, Tennis, Track.

Campus Life. About 83% of men, 78% of women live in traditional dormitories; no coed dormitories; rest live in off-campus housing or commute. Freshmen given preference in college housing if all students cannot be accommodated. No intervisitation in men's or women's dormitory rooms. There are 4 fraternities, 3 sororities on campus which about 17% of men, 6% of women join; they provide no residence facilities. About 21% of resident students leave campus on weekends.

Annual Costs. Tuition and fees, $4,460; room and board, $2,629. About 88% of students receive financial aid. College reports some scholarships awarded on the basis of academic merit alone. *Meeting Costs:* college offers parent loans.

Stockton College of New Jersey

Pomona, New Jersey 08240 **(609) 652-4261**

A college of arts, sciences, and professional studies, Stockton provides "a distinctive alternative to . . . traditional modes of undergraduate education." The 1,600-acre wooded campus is located in New Jersey's Pine Barrens, convenient to Philadelphia, New York City, and Atlantic City. Most convenient major airport: Philadelphia International.

Founded: 1971
Affiliation: State
UG Enrollment: 2,158 M, 2,277 W (full-time); 575 M, 772 W (part-time)
Cost: < $10K
% Receiving Financial Aid: 36%
Admission: Non-selective
Application Deadline: May 1

Admission. About 39% of applicants accepted, 45% of these actually enroll; 52% of freshman graduate in top fifth of high school class, 89% in top two-fifths. "Nontraditional graduates . . . are urged to apply"; they are individually evaluated. Average freshman scores: SAT, 486 M, 493 W verbal, 567 M, 538 W mathematical; 44% of freshman score above 500 verbal, 7% above 600, 1% above 700; 79% score above 500 mathematical, 27% above 600, 4% above 700. *Required:* SAT. Criteria considered in admissions, in order of importance: high school academic record, standardized test scores, extracurricular activities, recommendations, writing sample; other factors considered: special talents, diverse student body. About 35% of entering students from private schools. *Entrance programs:* early decision, early admission, midyear admission, advanced placement. *Apply* by May 1; rolling admissions. *Transfers* welcome; 680 enrolled 1993–94.

Academic Environment. Degree offered: bachelors. Under Stockton Study Plan, student, with guidance of faculty or staff adviser, "develops and pursues own talents, interests and life goals." Only required courses (up to 3) are Basic Studies selected on basis of diagnostic testing. *Majors offered* in addition to usual studies include Physical Therapy, Speech Pathology, Radiology, environmental studies, marine science. *Special programs:* study abroad, internship/cooperative work-study programs with Washington Semester, work-study coop programs. Average undergraduate class size: 36% under 20, 54% 20–40, 10% over 40. About 41% of students entering as freshmen graduate within four years, 53% eventually; 93% of freshmen return for sophomore year.

Undergraduate degrees conferred (916). 38% were in Business and Management, 18% were in Social Sciences, 10% were in Life Sciences, 7% were in Psychology, 7% were in Health Sciences, 4% were in Computer and Engineering Related Technology, 4% were in Letters, 3% were in Public Affairs, 3% were in Visual and Performing Arts, remainder in 5 other fields.

Graduates Career Data. Advanced studies pursued by 39% of students (1990–91); 13% enter business school; 8% enter medical school; 7% enter law school; 2% enter dental school. About 74% of 1992–93 graduates employed. Career Development Services include resume and career workshops, computerized aptitude tests, career planning library, on-campus recruiting, career counseling, credential files, vacancy lists.

Faculty. About 92% of faculty hold PhD or equivalent. About 62% of undergraduate classes taught by tenured faculty. About 35% of teaching faculty are female; 10% Black, 5% Hispanic, 6% ethnic minority.

Student Body. About 97% of students from in state; 1% from New England, 1% foreign. An estimated 8% of students reported as Black, 4% Hispanic, 3% Asian. Average age of undergraduate student: 22.

Varsity Sports. Men (Div.III): Baseball, Basketball, Crew, Golf, Lacrosse, Soccer, Track. Women (Div.III): Basketball, Crew, Golf, Soccer, Softball, Track, Volleyball.

Campus Life. About 47% of students live on campus, remainder commute, according to most recent data available. There are 11 fraternities, 7 sororities on campus, which about 19% of men, 10% of women join. About 25% of resident students leave campus on weekends.

Annual Costs. Tuition and fees, $2,880 (out-of-state, $3,584); room and board, $4,225; estimated $1,836 other, exclusive of travel. About 36% of students receive financial aid; average amount of assistance, $4,252. Assistance is typically divided 8% scholarship, 51% grant, 39% loan, 2% work. College reports 293 scholarships awarded on the basis of academic merit alone. *Meeting Costs:* college offers payment plans.

Stonehill College

North Easton, Massachusetts 02357 (508) 230-1373

A church-related, liberal arts college, conducted by the Holy Cross Fathers, offering both day and evening classes, Stonehill is located on a 375-acre campus in a rural community near Easton (pop. 20,584) and 20 miles south of Boston. Most convenient major airport: Logan International (Boston).

Founded: 1948
Affiliation: Independent (Roman Catholic)
UG Enrollment: 885 M, 1,106 W (full-time)
Cost: $10K–$20K
% Receiving Financial Aid: 77%
Admission: Selective
Application Deadline: February 15

Admission is selective. About 63% of applicants accepted, 25% of these actually enroll; 58% of freshmen graduate in top fifth of high school class, 92% in top two-fifths. Average freshman scores: SAT, 470 M, 480 W verbal, 540 M, 520 W mathematical; 38% of freshman score above 500 on verbal, 6% above 600; 72% score above 500 on mathematical, 22% above 600, 2% above 700; ACT, 22 M, 24 W composite. *Required:* SAT or ACT, essay, guidance counselor recommendation, official high school transcript, 16 credits in college preparation courses. Criteria considered in admissions, in order of importance: high school academic record, advanced placement or honors courses, standardized test scores, extracurricular activities, recommendations, essay; other factors considered: special talents, alumni children, diverse student body, work experience. *Entrance programs:* early admission, midyear admission, advanced placement, deferred admission. About 2% of entering students from private schools, 28% from parochial schools. *Apply* by February 15. *Transfers* welcome; 40 enrolled 1993–94.

Academic Environment. General studies program includes three parts: Western Heritage Core Curriculum, Writing and Quantitative Techniques, and Foreign Studies. This includes 2 semesters of religious studies, philosophy, social institutions, literature and fine arts, and scientific inquiry; 1 semester writing and quantitative techniques, and 1 year of foreign language. Computer usage is incorporated into the core curriculum. Degrees offered: associates, bachelors. *Majors offered* include usual arts and sciences, accounting, criminal justice, finance, health care administration, international studies, management, managerial economics, math-computer science, marketing, medical technology, multidisciplinary studies (self designed major), public administration. Average undergraduate class size: 37% under 20, 62% 20–40, 1% over 40. Students report that small classes and supportive faculty offer personal and interactive education. Although students find the computer facilities to be adequate, they report that library facilities need improvement (which is currently in the planning stage).

About 77% of students entering as freshmen graduate within four years, 80% eventually; 87% of freshmen return for sophomore year. *Special programs:* CLEP, independent study, study abroad, undergraduate research, individualized majors, combined program in medical technology, nontraditional learning experiences for credit, cooperative engineering programs with U. of Notre Dame and U. of Hartford, cross registration with Bridgewater State, Bristol Community College, Cape Cod Community College, Dean Junior College, Massachusetts Maritime Academy, Massasoit Community College, U. of Massachusetts-Dartmouth and Wheaton College, academic international internships. *Calendar:* semester, summer school.

Undergraduate degrees conferred (540). 27% were in Business and Management, 15% were in Social Sciences, 9% were in Education, 9% were in Psychology, 9% were in Communications, 8% were in Protective Services, 7% were in Letters, 6% were in Health Sciences, 4% were in Life Sciences, remainder in 8 other fields.

Graduates Career Data. Advanced studies pursued by 17% of 1992 graduates based on a survey of 1992 graduates with a 77% response rate. Medical schools typically enrolling largest numbers of graduates include U. Mass, Chicago, U. Vermont; dental schools include Boston U., Tufts, U. Connecticut; law schools include New England School of Law, Cornell, Boston U., Boston College, Villanova; business schools include Bentley, Boston U., Suffolk. About 84% of 1991–92 graduates employed. Fields typically hiring largest numbers of graduates include business, sales, health care, human services. Career Development Services include group and individual counseling, workshops on interviewing, resume writing, computerized career guidance system, on-campus recruitment, internships, alumni career network, graduate school/career information library. Student assessment of program reported as good for both career guidance and job placement. Alumni reported as active in job placement.

Faculty. About 79% of faculty hold PhD or equivalent. About 50% of undergraduate classes taught by tenured faculty. About 29% of teaching faculty are female; 6% ethnic minority.

Student Body. College "welcomes" a national student body; 66% of students from in state; 90% New England, 7% Middle Atlantic; 1%

South, 1% foreign. An estimated 83% of students reported as Catholic, 8% Protestant, 9% other or unaffiliated; 4% ethnic minority.
Religious Orientation. Stonehill is a church-related institution; 6 hours of religion required of all students. Faculty includes members of all major faiths. Places of worship available on campus for Catholics, in immediate community for major faiths.
Varsity Sports. Men (Div.II): Baseball, Basketball, Cross Country, Football, Ice Hockey, Soccer, Tennis, Track. Women (Div.II): Basketball, Cross Country, Soccer, Softball, Tennis, Track, Volleyball.
Campus Life. An array of academic societies, clubs, varsity and intramural sports, social events and volunteer organizations on-campus are supplemented by the cultural advantages of Boston, 20 miles north, easily accessible by both public and college transportation. College residence facilities include traditional residence halls, townhouses and suite units. International experience housing and substance free/wellness housing available by application. Alcohol and drug policies reflect state law. Cars allowed.

About 3% of men, 11% of women live in traditional dormitories; 65% of men and women live in coed dormitories or townhouses; rest commute. Sexes segregated in coed dormitories by floor. There are no fraternities or sororities. About 30% of resident students leave campus on weekends.
Annual Costs. Tuition and fees, $11,485; room and board, $5,996; estimated $1,554 other, exclusive of travel. About 77% of students who apply for financial aid receive assistance; average amount of assistance, $8,460. Assistance is typically divided 48% scholarship/grant, 48% loan, 4% work. College reports 1,054 scholarships awarded on the basis of academic merit and need, 173 for special talents, 229 for need alone. *Meeting Costs:* college offers alternative financing counseling and a tuition payment plan.

State University of New York at Stony Brook

(See State University of New York)

Strayer College

Washington, D.C. 20005

An independent business school, Strayer offers associates, bachelors and masters degrees with studies in business and management, health professions, computer and information sciences, and public affairs and services.

Founded: 1904 **Affiliation:** Independent

Undergraduate degrees conferred (88). 67% were in Business and Management, 33% were in Computer and Engineering Related Technology.

Suffolk University

Boston, Massachusetts 02108 (617) 573-8460; (800) -6-SUFFOLK

An independent institution located on historic Beacon Hill in downtown Boston, close to major business, financial, and cultural centers.

Founded: 1906
Affiliation: Independent
UG Enrollment: 1,027 M, 1,175 W (full-time); 325 M, 494 W (part-time)
Total Enrollment: 4,363
Cost: < $10K
% Receiving Financial Aid: 56%
Admission: Non-selective
Application Deadline: May 1

Admission. High school graduates with 16 units (13 in academic subjects) eligible; 79% of applicants accepted, 37% of these actually enroll; 30% of freshmen graduate in top fifth of high school class, 53% in top two-fifths. Average freshman SAT scores: 402 M, 412 W verbal, 455 M, 439 W mathematical. *Required:* SAT, 3 ACH including English, essay. Criteria considered in admissions, in order of importance: high school academic record, writing sample, standardized test scores, recommendations, extracurricular activities; other factors considered: special talents, diverse student body. *Entrance programs:* early decision, early admission, midyear admission, deferred admission, advanced placement. About 20% of entering freshman from parochial schools, 5% from private schools. *Apply* by May 1; rolling admissions. *Transfers* welcome; 400 enrolled 1993–94.
Academic Environment. Degrees offered: associates, bachelors, masters. *Undergraduate studies* offered by colleges of Liberal Arts and Sciences, Business Administration. Core requirements include 2 years of English, mathematics, sciences, history, and humanities. *Majors offered* in addition to usual studies include international business, marine science, medical biophysics, radiation biology, paralegal studies. Average undergraduate class size: 23; 42% of classes under 20, 50% 20–40, 8% over 40. About 47% of entering freshman graduate within four years, 57% eventually; 89% of freshman return for sophomore year. *Special programs:* CLEP, independent study, study abroad, January term, undergraduate research, 3–2 programs in engineering, combined law degree program, combined BA/MA programs, domestic and international internship/cooperative work-study programs, cross registration with NE School of Art and Design, NE School of Braodcasting. Adult programs: evening studies office offers support and counseling. *Calendar:* semester, summer school.
Undergraduate degrees conferred (539). 46% were in Business and Management, 22% were in Social Sciences, 13% were in Communications, 5% were in Psychology, 4% were in Letters, 3% were in Education, remainder in 9 other fields.
Graduates Career Data. Advanced studies pursued by 11% of students; 4% enter law school, 2% enter business school. Business schools typically enrolling largest numbers of graduates include Suffolk, Northeastern, Bentley; law school include Suffolk, Northeastern, Boston College, NE School of Law. About 85% of 1991–92 graduates employed. Fields typically hiring largest numbers of graduates include financial services, banking, business services, government. Career Development Services and Co-op Education assist students and alumni in defining their career goals and provides the support necessary for job seekers to develop and independent, practical job search that leads to fulfilling employment.
Faculty. About 93% of faculty hold PhD or equivalent. About 65% of undergraduate classes taught by tenured faculty. About 35% of teaching faculty are female; 5% Black, 4% Hispanic, 1% ethnic minority.
Student Body. About 89% of students from in state; 90% New England, 2% Middle Atlantic, 8% foreign. Average age of undergraduate student: 22.
Varsity Sports. Men: Baseball, Basketball, Cross Country, Gold, Soccer, Tennis. Women: Basketball, Cross Country, Golf, Soccer, Softball, Tennis.
Campus Life. About 5% of men, 5% of women live in coed dormitories; rest commute. There are 3 fraternities, 1 sorority on campus which about 2% of men, 2% of women join; they provide no residence facilities.
Annual Costs. Tuition and fees, $9,860; room and board, $5,500; estimated $3,600 other, exclusive of travel. About 56% of students receive financial aid; average amount of assistance, $7,045 (includes parental loans). Assistance is typically divided 9% scholarship, 41% grant, 46% loan, 5% work. University reports 336 scholarships awarded on the basis of academic merit alone, 1,209 for need alone. *Meeting Costs:* university offers deferred payment plan.

Sul Ross State University

Alpine, Texas 79832 (915) 837-8011

A state-supported university, located in a community of 6,000, 100 miles from the Mexican border. Upper division and graduate level programs are offered through the Uvalde Study Center.

Founded: 1917
Affiliation: State
UG Enrollment: 783 M, 649 W (full-time); 70 M, 72 W (part-time)
Total Enrollment: 2,182
Cost: < $10K
% Receiving Financial Aid: 79%
Admission: Non-selective
Application Deadline: Rolling

Admission. Graduates of accredited high schools with minimum score of 800 combined SAT, or 20 ACT composite, or rank in top half of high school class; others admitted probationally; 97% of applicants accepted, 91% of these actually enroll. About 16% of freshmen graduate in top fifth of high school class, 40% in top two-fifths. Average freshman scores: SAT, 354 M, 332 W verbal, 414 M, 367 W mathematical; ACT, 17.0 M, 16.4 W composite. *Required:* SAT or ACT. Criteria considered in admissions: standardized test scores and high school academic records. *Out-of-state* freshman applicants: university actively seeks students from out of state; no limits; no special requirements; 11 out-of-state students accepted, 10 enrolled 1993–94. States from which most out-of-state students are drawn: Arizona, Colorado, Oklahoma. *Entrance programs:* early admission, midyear admission. *Apply:* no specific deadline; rolling admissions. *Transfers* welcome; 210 undergraduates enrolled 1993–94.

Academic Environment. Degrees offered: associates, bachelors, masters. *Undergraduate studies* offered by divisions of Fine Arts, Language Arts, Science, Business Administration and Social Science, Education, Vocations. Location offers excellent opportunities for studies in geological and biological fields, as well as close interaction with Mexican institutions. Core requirements include 12 hours English, 3 hours each mathematics, communications, fine arts, multicultural studies; 6 hours each, social sciences, history, political science; 8 hours science; and 2 hours kinesiology. *Majors offered* in addition to usual studies include environmental science. *Special programs:* internship/cooperative work-study programs with National Forest Service, U.S. Fish and Wildlife Services, criminal justice, and psychology. Average undergraduate class size: 39% under 20, 46% 20–40, 15% over 40. About 8% of entering students graduate within four years, 25% eventually; 46% of freshman return for sophomore year. *Calendar:* semester, summer school.

Undergraduate degrees conferred (260). 35% were in Education, 16% were in Business and Management, 8% were in Social Sciences, 7% were in Life Sciences, 7% were in Agricultural Sciences, 5% were in Protective Services, 5% were in Psychology, 3% were in Agribusiness and Agricultural Production, 3% were in Engineering and Engineering Related Technology, remainder in 8 other fields.

Graduates Career Data. Advanced studies pursued by 60% of students. About 83% of 1992–93 graduates employed. Fields typically employing largest numbers of graduates include education, business, agriculture, community service.

Faculty. About 74% of faculty hold PhD or equivalent. About 60% of undergraduate classes taught by tenured faculty. About 23% of teaching faculty are female; 7% Hispanic, 2% other ethnic minority.

Student Body. University seeks a national student body; 96% of students from in state; 2% West, 2% foreign.

Varsity Sports. Men (NAIA Div.II): Baseball, Basketball, Football, Tennis, Track. Women (NAIA Div.II): Basketball, Tennis, Track, Volleyball. (NIRA): Rodeo.

Campus Life. About 5% of men live in traditional dormitories; 19% of men, 12% of women in coed dormitories; 5% of men, 10% of women live in off-campus college-related housing; rest commute. Limited visitation in men's and women's dormitory rooms. There are no fraternities, sororities on campus. About 10% of resident students leave campus on weekends.

Annual Costs. Tuition and fees, $1,272 (out-of-state, $4,488); room and board plus 7-day meal plan, $2,980; estimated $1,049 other, exclusive of travel. About 79% of students awarded financial aid (1992–93). Assistance is typically divided 3% scholarship, 32% grant, 52% loan, 14% work. University reports 15 scholarships awarded on the basis of academic merit alone. *Meeting Costs:* university offers installment payment plan for tuition, fees, and room and board.

Susquehanna University

Selinsgrove, Pennsylvania 17870 (717) 372-4396

A comprehensive, residential undergraduate university combining traditional programs in the liberal arts and science with professional programs in business administration, the arts, and communications. The 190-acre campus is located in the Susquehanna River town of Selinsgrove (pop.5,200), 50 miles north of Harrisburg. Most convenient major airport: Harrisburg International (50 miles).

Founded: 1858
Affiliation: Evangelical Lutheran Church
UG Enrollment: 713 M, 738 W (full-time)
Cost: $10K–$20K
% Receiving Financial Aid: 75%
Admission: Selective
Application Deadline: March 15

Admission is selective. About 72% of applicants accepted, 31% of these actually enroll; 53% of freshmen graduate in top fifth of high school class, 82% in top two-fifths. Freshman SAT scores: 44% of freshmen score above 500 on verbal, 11% above 600, 1% above 700; 75% score above 500 on mathematical, 25% above 600, 3% above 700. *Required:* SAT or ACT, students with a cumulative rank in top fifth of a strong preparatory program have the option of submitting SAT/ACT scores or two graded writing samples, audition for music students; interview recommended. Criteria considered in admissions, in order of importance: high school academic record, standardized test scores or writing sample, recommendations, music audition, art portfolio, extracurricular activities; other factors considered: special talents, diverse student body, alumni children, religious affiliation and/or commitment, "desire to attend." *Entrance programs:* early decision, midyear admission, deferred admission, advanced placement. About 5% of entering students from private schools, 10% from parochial schools. *Apply* by March 15, December 15 (early decision); rolling admissions. *Transfers* welcome; 30 enrolled 1993–94.

Academic Environment. Undergraduate degrees offered by 3 schools: Arts and Sciences, Fine Arts and Communications, and the Sigmund Weis School of Business. All students complete core curriculum which includes three components: Personal Development, non-credit requirements in academic skills, library research, wellness/fitness, and career development; Transition Skills, (students may be exempted by demonstrated proficiency) using computers, basic mathematics.logic, foreign language, and writing seminar; Perspectives on the World, which includes history, fine arts, literature, sciences and social sciences, values courses from philosophy, religion or psychology, and a senior interdisciplinary seminar. More than a third of students major in business and management-related subjects. Degrees offered: associates (program offered for local adult learners), bachelors. *Majors offered* include usual arts and sciences, 3 areas of business, 3 areas of music, biology/biochemistry, environmental science, geoscience, teaching certification in elementary and numerous secondary education fields, art. Susquehanna is recognized for strong programs in business, music, biology, biochemistry and environmental science. Average undergraduate class size: 62% under 20, 37% 20–40, 1% over 40.

About 70% of students entering as freshmen graduate within four year, 75% eventually; 90% of freshmen return for sophomore year. *Special programs:* independent study, self-designed majors, study abroad, internships abroad, exchange programs in Germany, Japan and Russia, honors, undergraduate research, internships and practica in most fields, Washington and United Nations semesters, Philadelphia Urban Semester, Appalachian Semester, Film Institute, 3–2 programs in engineering, forestry and environmental management, 3–2 environmental studies with Duke, 2–2 allied health with Thomas Jefferson, Susquehanna-at-Oxford summer program. Adult programs: Evening Associate Degree Program. *Calendar:* semester, summer school.

Undergraduate degrees conferred (355). 36% were in Business and Management, 15% were in Social Sciences, 12% were in Communications, 8% were in Education, 8% were in Letters, 6% were in Psychology, 3% were in Physical Sciences, 3% were in Life Sciences, remainder in 7 other fields.

Graduates Career Data. Advanced studies pursued by 19% of students; 3% enter law school; 3% enter business school. About 71% of 1992–93 graduates employed. Corporations typically hiring largest numbers of graduates include Arthur Andersen, Hewlett-Packard, AMP, Continental. *Career Counseling Program:* all students take non-credit career planning course as part of core curriculum; other services provided include resume and interview workshops, placement service, individual and group counseling, job fair, graduate school fair, referral program. Alumni reported as active in both career guidance and job placement.

Faculty. About 90% of faculty hold PhD or equivalent. About 60% of undergraduate classes taught by tenured faculty. About 33% of teaching faculty are female; 6% ethnic minority.

Student Body. University has a regional student body; 57% of students from in state; 80% Middle Atlantic, 10% New England, 1% Midwest, 3% South, 1% West, 1% foreign. An estimated 56% of students reported as Protestant, 38% Catholic, 2% Jewish, 3% unaffiliated, 1% other; 2% Black, 1% Hispanic, 2% Asian. *Minority group students:* financial aid and academic support available.

Religious Orientation. Susquehanna is a church-related institution and follows the traditions of the Lutheran Church, but makes no religious demands on students. Places of worship available on campus and in community for Protestants and Catholics, 5 miles away for Jews.

Varsity Sports. Men (Div.III): Baseball, Basketball, Cross Country, Football, Golf, Soccer, Swimming, Tennis, Track, Wrestling. Women (Div.III): Basketball, Cross Country, Field Hockey, Lacrosse, Soccer, Softball, Swimming, Tennis, Track, Volleyball.

Campus Life. Administration reports "high emphasis on community service programs"; more than 50% of students participate before graduation. Numerous cultural events offered on campus; over 40 student organizations. Students also said to have close working relationships with faculty and are interested in arts and athletics; should enjoy rural environment. Alcohol permitted in approved areas on campus for students over 21; non-alcohol pub available.

About 9% of women live in traditional dormitories; 72% of men, 72% of women live in coed dormitories; 7% of men, 5% of women live in off-campus college-related housing; 5% of men, 5% of women commute. Freshmen given preference in college housing if all students cannot be accommodated. There are 4 fraternities, 4 sororities on campus which about 28% each of men, women join; 16% of men, 8% of women live in fraternities or sororities. About 15% of resident students leave campus on weekends.

Annual Costs. Tuition and fees, $15,580; room and board, $4,370; estimated $1,000 other, exclusive of travel. About 75% of students receive financial aid; average amount of assistance from financial aid, loan and work, $13,000. Assistance is typically divided 70% scholarship/grant, 20% loan, 10% work. College reports 125 scholarships awarded on the basis of academic merit, 10 for special talent, 250 for need alone. *Meeting Costs:* university offers monthly payment plans, extended loan programs.

Swarthmore College

Swarthmore, Pennsylvania 19081 (215) 328-8300

Swarthmore is one of the most selective undergraduate institutions in the U.S. Co-educational since its founding by the Quakers, it has long been distinguished by the excellence of its liberal arts education. An optional Honors program, with final oral examinations by visiting examiners, has been a model for other institutions for years. The 330-acre campus, officially registered as an arboretum, is located in a residential village of 6,200, 11 miles southwest of Philadelphia. Most convenient major airport: Philadelphia International.

Founded: 1864	**Cost:** $10K–$20K
Affiliation: Independent	**% Receiving Financial Aid:** 60%
UG Enrollment: 695 M, 692 W (full-time)	**Admission:** Most Selective
	Application Deadline: Feb. 1

Admission is among the most selective in the country. About 39% of applicants accepted, 33% of these actually enroll; 97% of freshmen graduate in top fifth of high school class, all in top two-fifths. Freshman SAT scores: 94% of freshmen score above 500 on verbal, 72% above 600, 23% above 700; 98% score above 500 on mathematical, 86% above 600, 45% above 700. *Required:* SAT or ACT, 3 ACH including English Composition (and mathematics for engineering applicants), essay; interview recommended. Criteria considered in admissions, in order of importance: high school academic record, recommendations and extra curricular activities, standardized test scores and writing sample; other factors considered: diverse student body, special talents, alumni children. Entrance program: early decision, deferred admission, advanced placement. About 35% of entering students from private or parochial schools. *Apply* by February 1. *Transfers* welcome; 16 enrolled 1993–94.

Academic Environment. Swarthmore's curriculum is demanding and academic achievement is a high priority with most students. The small student-faculty ratio (9.5:1) maximizes learning opportunities. The faculty is primarily committed to teaching but maintains scholarly output more typical of a research university. Students who have not read widely and intelligently, who do not write well, and who have not learned to organize their time effectively are likely to have difficulty. The administration reports, however, that only a small percentage of those who leave do so because of inability to meet academic demands. Student leader cautions, too, that despite Swarthmore's reputation, the student body is not composed solely of workaholics; the vast majority do more than study compulsively. Students represented on most faculty standing committees and are involved in the process of tenure and course evaluation. Cooperation with Bryn Mawr, Haverford, and Pennsylvania adds dimension to college's offerings. Some distribution requirements: 3 semester courses each in humanities, social sciences, natural sciences; 1 year foreign language at Swarthmore required of those who have not either passed 3 years of foreign language in high school or achieved a score of 600 on standard foreign language achievement test. Degree offered: bachelors. *Majors offered* include usual arts and sciences, astronomy, engineering; concentrations is environmental studies, peace studies; major in theater arts, women's studies.

About 89% of students entering as freshmen graduate within four years, 91% eventually; 95% of freshmen return for sophomore year. *Special programs:* study abroad, honors, undergraduate research, 3-year degree, individualized majors, 4-year 2-degree liberal arts/engineering program, cooperative programs with Bryn Mawr, Haverford, and U. of Pennsylvania. *Calendar:* semester.

Undergraduate degrees conferred (333). 35% were in Social Sciences, 15% were in Letters, 9% were in Philosophy and Religion, 8% were in Life Sciences, 8% were in Psychology, 5% were in Physical Sciences, 5% were in Visual and Performing Arts, 5% were in Engineering, 3% were in Mathematics, 3% were in Foreign Languages, remainder in 4 other fields.

Graduates Career Data. Advanced studies pursued by 32% of students; 5% enter medical school; 4% enter law school. Medical schools typically enrolling largest numbers of graduates include Harvard, Pennsylvania, Rochester, U. of Chicago, Temple, Jefferson, Stanford; law schools include NYU, Michigan, U. of Pennsylvania. About 60% of 1992–93 graduates employed. Corporations typically hiring largest numbers of graduates include Prudential, Andersen Consulting. Career Development Services include extensive interview and resume workshops, on-campus recruiting, strong alumni network, externship programs, information sessions, career library, testing programs.

Faculty. About 95% of faculty hold PhD or equivalent. About 35% of teaching faculty are female.

Student Body. College seeks a national student body; 10% of students from in state; 38% Middle Atlantic, 15% New England, 13% South, 11% Midwest, 14% West/Northwest, 7% foreign. An estimated 5% of students reported as Black, 5% Hispanic, 11% Asian, 5% foreign. Tutorial assistance, special academic advising for any student with special needs; application fees waived for applicants from families below federal poverty level; special advisors for foreign and minority students.

Varsity Sports. Men (Div.III): Baseball, Basketball, Cross Country, Diving, Football, Golf, Lacrosse, Soccer, Swimming, Tennis, Track, Wrestling. Women (Div.III): Badminton, Basketball, Cross Country, Diving, Field Hockey, Lacrosse, Soccer, Softball, Swimming, Tennis, Track, Volleyball.

Campus Life. Students have major hand in determining policies and regulations governing campus social life. Intervisitation rules permit each dormitory unit to vote on hours—up to 24 hours/day. Alcoholic beverages are permitted on campus (legal drinking age in Pennsylvania is 21). Cars discouraged; freshmen usually do not receive permission because of limited parking facilities. Interest in fraternities is moderate. Student leader emphasizes wide range of activities in which students engage. Many cultural and intellectual events and activities available on campus, supplied by visiting artists and lecturers and by students themselves. Student tastes are eclectic, and a variety of activities are offered to meet them. Black Cultural Center, Women's Center, intercollegiate and intramural sports. Nearest major cultural center, Philadelphia, is 24 minutes away by train; New York and Washington are about 2 hours away.

About 5% of men, 7% of women live in traditional dormitories; 92% of men, 90% of women live in coed dormitories; rest live in off-campus housing or commute. Freshmen given preference in college housing if all students cannot be accommodated. Sexes segregated in coed dormitories either by floor or room. There are 2 fraternities on campus which about 4% of men join; no sororities. About 5% of resident students leave campus on weekends.

Annual Costs. Tuition and fees, $18,482; room and board, $6,300; estimated $1,000 other, exclusive of travel. About 60% of students receive financial aid, need based is 45%; average amount of assistance, $17,120. Assistance is typically divided 79% scholarship/grant, 14% loan, 7% work. College reports some scholarships awarded on the basis of academic merit alone. *Meeting Costs:* college offers monthly payment plan and long term family loans.

Sweet Briar College

Sweet Briar, Virginia 24595 (800) 527-4300

Sweet Briar, an independent liberal arts college for women, enrolls students from all sections of the country, without regard to religion or race. The unusually attractive campus of over 3,300 acres is located in the foothills of the Blue Ridge Mountains, 12 miles north of Lynchburg (pop. 80,000) and 165 miles south of Washington, D.C. Most convenient major airport: Lynchburg.

Founded: 1901
Affiliation: Independent
UG Enrollment: 525 W (full-time)
Cost: $10K–$20K
% Receiving Financial Aid: 51%
Admission: Selective
Application Deadline: Feb. 15

Admission is selective. About 87% of applicants accepted, 36% of these actually enroll; 55% of freshmen graduate in top fifth of high school class, 82% in top two-fifths. Average freshman scores: SAT, middle fifty percent range, 450–550 verbal, 450–570 mathematical; ACT, 24 W composite. *Required:* SAT or ACT, 3 ACH including English, 2 recommendations, essay; interview recommended. Criteria considered in admissions, in order of importance: high school academic record, difficulty and quality of high school course work (Honors, AP, IB), standardized test scores, recommendations, writing sample, extracurricular activities; other factors considered: special talents, alumnae daughters, diverse student body. *Entrance programs:* early decision, early admission, midyear admission, deferred admission, advanced placement. About 31% of entering students from private or parochial schools. *Apply* by February 15, November 15 for early decision, January 15 to be considered for scholarship selection. *Transfers* welcome; 7 enrolled 1993–94.

Academic Environment. Students have influence on curriculum and other academic matters. Students may take full or half year for off-campus study in the U.S. and abroad. Administration reports 65% of courses required for graduation are elective; distribution requirements include 1 term each of English, social sciences, Western studies, non-Western studies; foreign language proficiency; 2 terms each literature or the arts, science (1 laboratory science), physical education. Degree offered: bachelors. *Majors offered* include usual arts and sciences, arts management, classical studies, drama, environmental studies, women and gender studies; interdepartmental and interdisciplinary majors available include mathematical physics, international affairs, environmental studies, political economy. Average undergraduate class size: 91% under 20, 9% 20–40.

About 61% of students entering as freshmen graduate within four years, 63% eventually; 80% of freshmen return for sophomore year. *Special programs:* independent study, study abroad, 4-year honors program, individualized majors, Washington Semester, cross-registration with Lynchburg and Randolph-Macon Woman's College, dual-degree programs in business and engineering, off-campus study, internship/cooperative work-study programs, January Term. Adult programs: Turning Point Program, a flexible, supportive program offering full and part-time opportunities for women over 26 years of age or out of formal schooling for at least four years. *Calendar:* 4–1–4.

Undergraduate degrees conferred (113). 44% were in Social Sciences, 15% were in Letters, 14% were in Visual and Performing Arts, 7% were in Multi/Interdisciplinary Studies, 5% were in Psychology, 5% were in Life Sciences, 5% were in Foreign Languages, remainder in 2 other fields.

Graduates Career Data. Advanced studies pursued by 26% of students. About 32% of 1992–93 graduates employed. *Career Counseling Program* designed specifically for liberal arts students. Liberal arts majors urged to seek interviews with business/industry representatives who visit campus. Help provided in preparation for interviews. Alumnae reported as active in both career guidance and job placement.

Faculty. About 95% of faculty hold PhD or equivalent. About 58% of undergraduate classes taught by tenured faculty. About 52% of teaching faculty are female; 3% ethnic minority.

Student Body. College seeks a national student body; 33% of students from in state; 62% from South, 22% Northeast, 9% Central, 5% West, 3% foreign. An estimated 4% of students reported as Black, 2% Hispanic, 2% Asian, 3% ethnic minority.

Varsity Sports. Women (NCAA Div.III): Equestrian, Field Hockey, Lacrosse, Soccer, Swimming, Tennis, Volleyball.

Campus Life. Regulations governing campus social life allow students considerable freedom. Sweet Briar makes special efforts to bring leading speakers and performing artists to campus. Fairly full schedule of intellectual and cultural events provided; student social committee provides activities during the week and on weekends. All students permitted to take unlimited overnight absences; key system available for all students. Three visitation options available, according to student's choice of residence hall. Alcohol regulations are in accordance with state law. College will stable privately-owned horses although space is limited. Cars permitted for all except those receiving substantial financial aid. About 83% of women live in traditional dormitories; rest commute. There are no sororities. About 30% of resident students leave campus on weekends.

Annual Costs. Tuition and fees, $14,015; room and board, $5,755; estimated $1,225 other, exclusive of travel. About 51% of students receive financial aid; average amount of assistance, $13,116. Assistance is typically divided 66% grant/scholarship, 27% loan, 7% work. College reports 170 scholarships awarded on the basis of academic merit alone, 13 for special talents, 224 for need alone. *Meeting Costs:* college offers loan programs.

Syracuse University

Syracuse, New York 13210 (315) 443-3611

Syracuse University is a large, independent, co-educational, teaching and research institution offering undergraduate and graduate programs of study. Eleven colleges offer over 200 undergraduate majors and graduate programs. The University also has a College of Law. Located in central New York State, the 200-acre main campus area is in a residential area of the city. The University lists 15 buildings in the National Register of Historic Places. The State University College of Environmental Science campus is adjacent to the Syracuse University campus. Most convenient major airport: Hancock International (8 miles).

Founded: 1870
Affiliation: Independent
UG Enrollment: 5,027 M, 5,115 W (full-time)
Total Enrollment: 14,743
Cost: $10K–$20K
% Receiving Financial Aid: 62%
Admission: Highly Selective
Application Deadline: February 1

Admission is highly selective for schools of Architecture, Computer and Information Science, Engineering, Management, Public Communications; very selective for Arts and Sciences, Education, Visual and Performing Arts; selective (+) for Nursing, Human Development, Information Studies, Social Work. For all schools, 69% of applicants accepted, 34% of these actually enroll; 63% of freshmen graduate in top fifth of high school class, 86% in top two-fifths. Freshman SAT scores: middle fifty percent range 990–1180 combined verbal/mathematical; 68% of freshmen score above 500 on verbal, 14% above 600, 2% above 700; 87% score above 500 on mathematical, 36% above 600, 7% above 700.

For Architecture (253 M, 108 W): 45% of applicants accepted, 36% of these actually enroll; 74% of freshmen graduate in top fifth of high school class, 96% in top two-fifths. Average freshman SAT scores: 70% of freshmen score above 500 on verbal, 24% above 600, 3% above 700; 95% score above 500 on mathematical, 75% above 600, 21% above 700.

For Arts and Sciences (1,756 M, 1,847 W): 68% of applicants accepted, 30% of these actually enroll; 56% of freshmen graduate in top fifth of high school class, 86% in top two-fifths. Average freshman SAT scores: 62% of freshmen score above 500 on verbal, 13% above 600, 2% above 700; 86% score above 500 on mathematical, 42% above 600, 6% above 700.

For Education (59 M, 244 W), 68% of applicants accepted, 28% of these actually enroll; 46% of freshmen graduate in top fifth of high school class, 83% in top two-fifths. Average freshman SAT scores: 55% of freshmen score above 500 on verbal, 8% above 600, 1% above 700; 73% score above 500 on mathematical, 28% above 600, 2% above 700.

For Engineering and Computer Science (671 M, 180 W), 58% of applicants accepted, 30% of these actually enroll; 73% of freshmen graduate in top fifth of high school class, 94% in top two-fifths. Average freshman SAT scores: 60% of freshmen score above 500 on verbal, 16% above 600, 1% above 700; 96% score above 500 on mathematical, 66% above 600, 19% above 700.

For College of Human Development (150 M, 510 W), 75% of applicants accepted, 30% of these actually enroll; 46% of freshmen graduate in top fifth of high school class, 71% in top two-fifths. Average freshman SAT scores: 43% of freshmen score above 500 on verbal, 7% above 600, 1% above 700; 72% score above 500 on mathematical, 22% above 600, 4% above 700.

For Information Studies (177 M, 64 W), 80% of applicants accepted, 28% of these actually enroll; 38% of freshmen graduate in top fifth of high school class, 69% in top two-fifths. Average freshman SAT scores: 44% of freshmen score above 500 on verbal, 6% above 600; 72% score above 500 on mathematical, 34% above 600, 1% above 700.

For Management (633 M, 377 W), 68% of applicants accepted, 30% of these actually enroll; 62% of freshmen graduate in top fifth of high school class, 90% in top two-fifths. Average freshman SAT scores: 56% of freshmen score above 500 on verbal, 9% above 600, 1% above 700; 92% score above 500 on mathematical, 54% above 600, 9% above 700.

For Nursing (29 M, 216 W), 79% of applicants accepted, 28% of these actually enroll; 42% of freshmen graduate in top fifth of high school class, 82% in top two-fifths. Average freshman SAT scores: 45% of freshmen score above 500 on verbal, 4% above 600; 58% score above 500 on mathematical, 17% above 600, 1% above 700.

For Public Communication (555 M, 579 W), 50% of applicants accepted, 43% of these actually enroll; 82% of freshmen graduate in top fifth of high school class, 98% in top two-fifths. Average freshman SAT scores: 90% of freshmen score above 500 on verbal, 34% above 600, 2% above 700; 96% score above 500 on mathematical, 60% above 600, 11% above 700.

For Social Work (25 M, 115 W), 75% of applicants accepted, 38% of these actually enroll; 52% of freshmen graduate in top fifth of high school class, 74% in top two-fifths. Average freshman SAT scores: 46% of freshmen score above 500 on verbal, 9% above 600; 66% score above 500 on mathematical, 17% above 600, 3% above 700.

For Visual and Performing Arts (790 M, 921 W), 59% of applicants accepted, 56% of these actually enroll; 47% of freshmen graduate in top fifth of high school class, 80% in top two-fifths. Average freshman SAT scores: 56% of freshmen score above 500 on verbal, 14% above 600, 1% above 700; 75% score above 500 on mathematical, 31% above 600, 5% above 700.

Required: SAT or ACT, ACH in English for those submitting SAT scores (plus mathematics and physics/chemistry for architecture; mathematics for management and systems and information science; any 2 additional for Liberal Arts), portfolio for Architecture and Art, audition for Music and Drama. Criteria considered in admissions, in order of importance: high school academic record, class rank, standardized test scores, recommendations, essay; other factors considered: special talents, alumni children, extracurricular activities. *Entrance programs:* early decision, midyear admission, deferred admission, advanced placement. About 25% of entering students from private or parochial schools. *Apply* by February 1, December 15 for early decision. *Transfers* welcome; 387 enrolled 1993–94.

Academic Environment. Degrees offered: bachelors, masters, doctoral. Pressures for academic achievement vary among the different colleges and schools, but, in general, they appear moderately intense. Students enrolled in Architecture, Engineering, Communications and some areas of the Visual and Performing Arts report spending more time in outside class preparation/studio/laboratory than others. Academic requirements vary by college but generally include the liberal arts core with distribution of course work in the humanities, social sciences, and natural sciences/mathematics. All students are required to complete a course in the Writing Program and most continue writing courses at the upper division. Professional colleges offering a common freshman year include Art and Design, Drama and Engineering. Other academic programs offer an introductory course to the profession in addition to courses in the liberal arts. Syracuse is recognized for very strong programs in journalism, art, architecture, political and social sciences, engineering, creative writing, philosophy, geography. *Majors offered* in arts and sciences in addition to usual studies include anthropology, drama, fine arts, geography, linguistics, food systems management, information studies at undergraduate level. One student finds, "there are not enough hours in the day to take advantage of all the opportunities Syracuse has to offer." Dual enrollment allows students to major in two separate colleges and receive a degree from each. Over 70 minors are offered. Approximately 900 students each year study abroad in one of the University Centers in London, Strasbourg, Madrid, or Florence or in a cooperative program in many other countries. About one-third of undergraduates participate in the community internship programs. The Honors Program offers honors sections/seminars of liberal arts courses and an upper division honors thesis. Average undergraduate class size: 58% under 20, 33% 20–40, 9% over 40. Library and computer facilities are reported to be excellent, with extended hours during finals.

About 66% of students entering as freshmen graduate within five years; 88% of freshmen return for sophomore year. *Special programs:* CLEP, independent study, study abroad, honors, undergraduate research, 3-year degree, individualized majors, credit by examination, Russian studies, variety of combined programs (6-year arts/architecture or law, 5-year arts/engineering, home economics/broadcasting, 6-year speech/law or business administration/law), 3–2 programs in law, MBA, internship/cooperative work-study programs in engineering, human development, community internship. *Calendar:* semester, summer school.

Undergraduate degrees conferred (2,783). 18% were in Business and Management, 14% were in Social Sciences, 12% were in Visual and Performing Arts, 12% were in Communications, 7% were in Letters, 7% were in Psychology, 7% were in Engineering, 4% were in Architecture and Environmental Design, 4% were in Home Economics, 3% were in Education, remainder in 12 other fields.

Graduates Career Data. Advanced studies pursued by 24% of graduates; 2% enter medical school; 5% enter law school, 7% enter business school. Medical schools typically enrolling largest numbers of graduates include SUNY Buffalo, Tufts, SUNY Health Science Center; law schools include Syracuse U., George Washington, SUNY Albany; business schools include Syracuse U., Cornell, Columbia. About 71% of 1992–93 graduates employed. Corporations typically hiring largest numbers of graduates include IBM, Price Waterhouse, Coopers & Lybrand, Gannett Newspapers. Career Development Services include individual and group counseling, career library, resume preparation, employer recruitment on campus, job bank, job fairs, resume referral to employers.

Faculty. About 84% of faculty hold PhD or equivalent. About 24% of teaching faculty are female; 12% ethnic minority.

Student Body. University seeks a national student body; 39% of students from in state; 63% Middle Atlantic, 21% New England, 5% South, 5% Midwest, 2% West, 1% Northwest, 3% foreign. Over 25 religions represented on campus. An estimated 10% of students reported as Black, 5% Hispanic, 6% Asian, 1% other minority. *Minority group students:* special financial, academic, and social provisions.

Varsity Sports. Men (Div.I): Basketball, Crew, Cross Country, Diving, Football, Gymnastics, Lacrosse, Soccer, Swimming, Track, Wrestling. Women (Div.I): Basketball, Crew, Cross Country, Diving, Field Hockey, Swimming, Tennis, Track, Volleyball.

Campus Life. Wide variety of cultural and intellectual activities on campus; university and community combine to provide a full schedule of events. Two new student centers and a new physical recreation center have encouraged more social/recreational activities on campus. A recent senior comments, "One of the best aspects of Syracuse is diversity..a multitude of diverse programs, students from all 50 states and 95 countries, and so many extracurricular opportunities that a student has to limit the amount of activities they become involved in." Intervisitation permitted. Alcohol allowed in student rooms in compliance with state regulations and may be served at university approved social events. Cars allowed on campus for juniors and seniors. Juniors, seniors and students over 21 may live off campus.

About 75% of women live in traditional or coed dormitories; 10% live in off-campus college-related housing; 5% commute. An all female option is available as well as quiet lifestyle and a health/wellness hall. Freshmen given preference in college housing if all students cannot be accommodated. Sexes segregated in coed dormitories by wing, floor or room. There are 30 fraternities, 22 sororities on campus which about 24% of men, 33% of women join; 10% of students live in fraternities and sororities. About 20% of resident students leave campus on weekends.

Annual Costs. Tuition and fees, $14,705; room and board, $6,600; estimated $1,155 other, exclusive of travel. About 62% of students receive financial aid; average amount of assistance, $12,600. Assistance is typically divided 55% scholarship/grant, 30% loan, 15% work. University reports 1,450 scholarships awarded on the basis of academic merit alone, 400 for special talents, 2,400 based on need alone. *Meeting Costs:* university offers 12-month payment plan at no interest, prepayment plan.

Utica College of Syracuse University

Utica, New York 13502 **(315) 792-3006; (800) SU-AT-UTI**

Although Utica is only one of 20 colleges of Syracuse University, its location 50 miles from the main campus gives it a unique status. The college has its own 184-acre campus in a city of 91,600. The college also has its own faculty, admissions, registrar, and business office. Most convenient major airports: Oneida County.

Founded: 1946
Affiliation: Independent
UG Enrollment: 721 M, 895 W (full-time); 173 M, 216 W (part-time)
Total Enrollment: 2,620
Cost: $10K–$20K
% Receiving Financial Aid: 79%
Admission: Selective
Application Deadline: Rolling

Admission is selective. About 80% of applicants accepted, 30% of these actually enroll. Freshman SAT scores, middle fifty percent range, according to most recent data available: 380–480 M, 370–470 W verbal, 460–580 M, 470–530 W mathematical. *Required:* SAT or ACT, interview highly recommended. *Non-academic factors* considered in admissions: diverse student body, special talents. *Entrance programs:* early decision, early admission, midyear admission, advanced placement, deferred admission. *Apply:* rolling admissions. *Transfers* welcome.

Academic Environment. Core program of 30 hours allows considerable latitude in selecting liberal arts and science courses to complement major. For BA 75% of hours required for graduation must be taken in the liberal arts and sciences, for BS, 50%. Only remaining college-wide requirement is proficiency in English composition. Degrees offered: bachelors. *Majors offered* include usual arts and sciences, accounting, business administration, child-life, construction management, criminal justice, journalism studies, international studies, medical technology, occupational therapy, public relations, urban studies, sociology-anthropology, gerontology.

About 51% of students entering as freshmen graduate eventually; 75% of freshmen return for sophomore year. *Special programs:* CLEP, independent study, study abroad, 3-year degree, combined arts/medicine or dentistry program, combined program with Syracuse College of Law, 3–2 program in engineering, field-work courses in many majors, credit by examination. *Calendar:* semester.

Undergraduate degrees conferred (427). 34% were in Business and Management, 11% were in Allied Health, 10% were in Protective Services, 9% were in Psychology, 8% were in Communications, 8% were in Social Sciences, 4% were in Life Sciences, 3% were in Public Affairs, 3% were in Computer and Engineering Related Technology, 3% were in Health Sciences, 3% were in Letters, remainder in 4 other fields.

Graduates Career Data. According to most recent data available, full-time graduate or professional study pursued immediately after graduation by 7% of students. About 91% of graduates employed by business, industry, governments and not-for-profit organizations.

Faculty. About 89% of faculty hold PhD or equivalent.

Student Body. College does not seek a national student body; 88% of students from Middle Atlantic; 7 foreign. An estimated 10% of students reported as Black, 3% Hispanic, 1% Asian, 1% American Indian, according to most recent data available. *Minority group students:* "special interest in enrolling minority students"; Black Student Union, Latin American Student Union.

Varsity Sports. Men (Div.I): Baseball, Basketball, Cross Country, Golf, Soccer, Swimming, Tennis. Women (Div. I): Basketball, Cross Country, Soccer, Softball, Swimming, Tennis.

Campus Life. Intervisitation hours set by individual residences. Enrollment is small, making for an "informal, personal atmosphere." Alcohol permitted on campus in conformity with state law; cars allowed.

About 8% of men, 42% of women live in traditional dormitories; 64% of men, 35% of women in coed dormitories; rest live in off-campus housing or commute. Freshmen given preference in college housing if all students cannot be accommodated. Sexes segregated in coed dormitories by room. There are 7 fraternities, 7 sororities on campus which about 9% each of men, women join. About 15–20% of resident students leave campus on weekends.

Annual Costs. Tuition and fees, $11,980; room and board, $4,734. About 79% of students receive financial aid; assistance is typically divided 50% scholarship, 43% loan, 7% work. College reports some scholarships awarded on the basis of academic merit alone.

Tabor College

Hillsboro, Kansas 67063 **(316) 947-3121**

A Christian, liberal arts college, located in a town of 3,000, 50 miles north of Wichita. Most convenient major airport: Wichita.

Founded: 1908
Affiliation: Mennonite Brethren
UG Enrollment: 433 M, W (full-time)
Cost: < $10K
Admission: Non-selective
Application Deadline: August 1

Admission. High school graduates eligible; 56% of applicants accepted, 72% of these actually enroll; 32% of freshmen graduate in top fifth of high school class, 62% in top two-fifths. *Required:* SAT or ACT, interview. *Non-academic factors* considered in admissions: special talents, alumni children, religious affiliation and/or commitment. *Apply* by August 1. *Transfers* welcome.

Academic Environment. *Degree:* AB. About 60% of general education requirements for graduation are elective; distribution requirements fairly numerous. About 59% of freshmen return for sophomore year. *Special programs:* CLEP, independent study, credit by examination, study abroad, cooperative programs with ACCK, 2–2 nursing. *Calendar:* 4–1–4, summer school.

Undergraduate degrees conferred (82). 18% were in Business and Management, 16% were in Education, 11% were in Public Affairs, 9% were in Physical Sciences, 9% were in Parks and Recreation, 7% were in Mathematics, 6% were in Philosophy and Religion, 5% were in Psychology, 4% were in Social Sciences, 4% were in Letters, 4% were in Computer and Engineering Related Technology, remainder in 4 other fields.

Student Body. College seeks a national student body; 57% of students from in state; 89% North Central. An estimated 92% of students reported as Protestant, 5% Catholic, 1% unaffiliated; 3% as Black, 3% other minority, according to most recent data available.

Religious Orientation. Tabor is a church-related institution; 8 hours of Bible and philosophy, attendance at convocations required of all students.

Varsity Sports. Men (NAIA): Baseball, Basketball, Cross Country, Football, Soccer, Tennis, Track. Women (NAIA): Basketball, Cross Country, Softball, Tennis, Track, Volleyball.

Campus Life. About 65% of men, 70% of women live in traditional dormitories; no coed dormitories; rest live in off-campus housing or commute. No intervisitation in men's or women's dormitory rooms. There are no fraternities or sororities. About 35% of resident students leave campus on weekends.

Annual Costs. Tuition and fees, $7,520; room and board, $3,290. About 99% of students receive financial aid. College reports some scholarships awarded on the basis of academic merit alone.

Talladega College

Talladega, Alabama 35160 **(205) 362-0206**

A church-related college, located in a town of 18,500, 50 miles east of Birmingham; founded as a college for blacks, now interracial for both faculty and student body.Most convenient major airports: Birmingham, AL or Atlanta, GA.

Founded: 1867
Affiliation: United Church of Christ
UG Enrollment: 321 M, 587 W (full-time); 105 M, 14 W (part-time)
Cost: < $10K
% Receiving Financial Aid: 93%
Admission: Non-selective
Application Deadline: Rolling

Admission. Graduates of approved high schools with 15 units eligible; in special cases, admission by examination; 36% of applicants accepted, 25% of these actually enroll; 40% of freshman graduate in top fifth of high school class, 90% in top two-fifths. Average freshman ACT scores: 17 M, 19 W composite. Criteria considered in admissions, in order of importance: high school academic record, standardized test scores, recommendations, writing sample, extracurricular activities; other factors considered: alumni children, academic. *Required:* SAT or ACT. *Entrance programs:* early decision, early admission, advanced placement. *Apply:* rolling admissions. *Transfers* welcome; 22 enrolled 1993–94.

Academic Environment. Degree offered: bachelors. Talladega is described by administrative source as "small and personable, with a family atmosphere." A remarkably high percentage of graduates go on to advanced studies. Requirements for graduation include basic liberal arts core. About 60% of students entering as freshmen graduate within four years, 80% eventually. *Special programs:* independent study, study abroad, undergraduate research, cooperative programs with Tuskegee Institute in engineering, veterinary medicine, physics, Auburn U. in engineering. Average undergraduate class size: 60% under 20, 40% 20–40. *Calendar:* semester.

Undergraduate degrees conferred (95). 27% were in Business and Management, 13% were in Public Affairs, 11% were in Letters, 9% were in Life Sciences, 8% were in Social Sciences, 8% were in Physical Sciences, 8% were in Computer and Engineering Related Technology, 7% were in Mathematics, 4% were in Education, 3% were in Psychology.

Graduates Career Data. Advanced studies pursued by 80% of students; 10% enter business school; 5% enter law school; 5% enter medical school; 5% enter dental school. Law schools typically enrolling largest numbers of graduates include U. of Alabama; medical schools include Howard; dental school include Meharry. About 35% of 1992–93 graduates employed.

Faculty. About 73% of faculty hold PhD or equivalent. About 60% of undergraduate classes taught by tenured faculty. About 45% of teaching faculty are female; 55% Black, 10% other ethnic minorities.

Student Body. College does not seek a national student body; 58% of students from in state, according to most recent data available; 60% South, 20% Midwest, 10% Middle Atlantic, 5% West, 4% New England, 1% foreign. An estimated 90% of students reported as Protestant, 5% Catholic, 5% other; 97% Black, 1% Hispanic, according to most recent data available.

Varsity Sports. Men (NAIA): Baseball, Basketball, Cross Country, Golf. Women (NAIA): Basketball, Cross Country, Golf, Volleyball.

Campus Life. About 90% of each men and women live in traditional dormitories; rest live in off-campus housing or commute. Intervisitation in men's and women's dormitory rooms limited. There are 4 fraternities, 4 sororities on campus which about 20% of each men and women join; they provide no residence facilities. About 25% of resident students leave campus on weekends.

Annual Costs. Tuition and fees, $5,584; room and board, $2,664; estimated $400 other, exclusive of travel. About 93% of students receive financial aid; average amount of assistance, $6,100. Assistance is typically divided 30% scholarship, 20% grant, 40% loan, 10% work. College reports 250 scholarships awarded on the basis of academic merit alone.

University of Tampa

Tampa, Florida 33606 **(800) 282-4773; out-of-state, (800) 237-2071)**

An independent institution, located in a city of 300,000. Most convenient major airport: Tampa International.

Founded: 1930
Affiliation: Independent
UG Enrollment: 1,961 M, W (full-time); 341 M, W (part-time)
Total Enrollment: 3,014
Cost: $10K–$20K
Admission: Non-selective
Application Deadline: Rolling

Admission. Graduates of accredited high schools eligible; others given consideration; 77% of applicants accepted, 33% of these actually enroll. *Required:* SAT, interview recommended. *Non-academic factors* considered in admissions: special talents, alumni children. *Apply:* rolling admissions. *Transfers* welcome.

Academic Environment. *Degrees:* AB, BS, BFA, BM. About 5% of general education credits for graduation are required; distribution requirements fairly numerous. About 61% of freshmen return for sophomore year. Library and computer facilities are reported to be adequate to meet student demand. A recent student finds the faculty to be accessible and supportive. *Special programs:* CLEP, independent study, study abroad, undergraduate research, Washington Semester, 3-year degree, individualized majors. *Calendar:* 4–4–1, summer school.

Undergraduate degrees conferred (411). 30% were in Business and Management, 16% were in Social Sciences, 11% were in Education, 7% were in Life Sciences, 6% were in Psychology, 6% were in Computer and Engineering Related Technology, 4% were in Health Sciences, 4% were in Communications, 3% were in Visual and Performing Arts, 3% were in Liberal/General Studies, 3% were in Letters, 3% were in Mathematics, remainder in 3 other fields.

Student Body. University seeks a national student body; 56% of students from in state; 65% South, 21% Middle Atlantic, 8% North Central, 7% New England. An estimated 4% of students reported as Black, 6% Hispanic, 1% Asian, 7% other minority, according to most recent data available.

Varsity Sports. Men (Div.II): Baseball, Basketball, Crew, Cross Country, Golf, Soccer, Swimming (I), Tennis. Women (Div.II): Basketball, Crew, Cross Country, Softball, Swimming, Tennis, Volleyball.

Campus Life About 10% of men, 7% of women live in traditional dormitories; 35% of men, 33% women in coed dormitories; rest live in off-campus housing or commute. Sexes segregated in coed dormitories by floor or room. There are 8 fraternities, 3 sororities on campus which about 20% of men, 10% of women join; they provide no residence facilities. About 2% of resident students leave campus on weekends.

Annual Costs. Tuition and fees, $12,280; room and board, $4,450. About 70% of students receive financial aid. College reports some scholarships awarded on the basis of academic merit alone. *Meeting Costs:* college offers payment plan.

Tarleton State University

Stephenville, Texas 76401 **(817) 968-9000**

A state-supported university, part of the Texas A&M University System, located in a city of 15,000, 65 miles southwest of Fort Worth. Most convenient major airport: Dallas/Fort Worth.

Founded: 1899
Affiliation: State
UG Enrollment: 2,487 M, 2,369 W (full-time); 281 M, 443 W (part-time)
Total Enrollment: 6,455
Cost: < $10K
% Receiving Financial Aid: 58%
Admission: Non-selective
Application Deadline: Aug. 7

Admission. Graduates of accredited high schools (or GED) with 15 units eligible; 92% of applicants accepted, 90% of these actually enroll. About 14% of freshmen graduate in top fifth of high school class. *Required:* minimum SAT score of 800 or ACT score of 19. Criteria considered in admissions, in order of importance: high school academic record, standardized test scores. *Entrance programs:* early admission, deferred admission. State does not limit out-of-state enrollment; no special requirements. States from which most out-of-state students are drawn: Oklahoma, New Mexico. *Apply* by August 7. *Transfers* welcome; 735 enrolled 1993–94.

Academic Environment. Degrees offered: associates, bachelors, masters. New program recently added in psychology. *Special programs:* CLEP, 3–2 program in engineering, internship/cooperative work-study programs, special degree programs may be designed to meet unusual requirements, cross registration with Texas A&M International at Laredo. About 33% of entering students graduate within four years; 61% of freshman return for sophomore year. Average undergraduate class size: 32. *Calendar:* early semester, summer school.

Undergraduate degrees conferred (835). 30% were in Education, 26% were in Business and Management, 8% were in Agribusiness and Agricultural Production, 7% were in Protective Services, 4% were in Letters, 4% were in Social Sciences, 3% were in Life Sciences, 3% were in Agricultural Sciences, 3% were in Multi/Interdisciplinary Studies, 3% were in Engineering and Engineering Related Technology, remainder in 10 other fields.

Faculty. About 62% of faculty hold PhD or equivalent. About 33% of teaching faculty are female; 2% Black, 4% Hispanic, 2% other ethnic minorities.
Student Body. University does not seek a national student body; 99% of students from in state. An estimated 3% of students reported as Black, 4% Hispanic, 1% Asian, 2% other ethnic minorities.
Varsity Sports. Men: Baseball, Basketball, Cross Country, Football, Golf, Tennis, Track. Women: Basketball, Cross Country, Tennis, Track, Volleyball.
Campus Life. About 9% of men, 7% of women live in traditional dormitories; 1% of men, 2% of women in coed dormitories; 75% of men, 72% of women live in off-campus college-related housing; rest commute. Limited intervisitation in men's or women's dormitory rooms. There are 5 fraternities, 3 sororities on campus, which about 7% men, 5% women join. About 50% of resident students leave campus on weekends.
Annual Costs. Tuition and fees, $1,420 (out-of-state, $5,500); room and board, $2,895; estimated $1,600 other, exclusive of travel, according to most recent data available. About 58% of students receive financial aid; average amount of assistance, $2,369. Assistance is typically divided 39% scholarship, 43% loan, 18% work, according to most recent data available. College reports some scholarships awarded on the basis of academic merit alone. *Meeting Costs:* college offers Parent PLUS Loans.

Taylor University

Upland, Indiana 46989 **(800) 882-3456**

A liberal arts institution, committed to a Christian perspective, Taylor is located in a village of 3,200, 50 miles southwest of Fort Wayne. Most convenient major airports: Indianapolis, Fort Wayne.

Founded: 1846
Affiliation: Independent
UG Enrollment: 845 M, 918 W (full-time)
Cost: $10K–$20K
% Receiving Financial Aid: 78%
Admission: Non-selective
Application Deadline: Rolling

Admission. Graduates of accredited high schools with 15 units with GPA of 2.8 and combined SAT of 850 or ACT of 21 composite eligible; top 40% of class; 62% of applicants accepted, 40% of these actually enroll; 28% of freshmen graduate in top fifth of high school class, 70% in top two-fifths. Average freshman scores: SAT, 521 M, 568 W verbal, 566 M, 548 W mathematical; 74% score 500 on verbal, 36% above 600; 72% score above 500 on mathematical, 35% above 600, 6% above 700. *Required:* SAT or ACT, pastor's recommendation, acceptance of standards for student life including abstinence from dancing, gambling, use of tobacco, alcoholic beverages, drugs, profane language. *Apply:* rolling admissions. *Transfers* welcome.
Academic Environment. Degrees offered: associates, bachelors. General education requirements include courses in writing, communications, Biblical literature and Christian studies, fitness, computer literacy, literature, natural sciences and mathematics, social sciences, humanities, fine arts, foreign language. New or unusual programs offered include environmental science, artificial intelligence. Practica and internships are required in some areas. About 78% of entering students graduate within four years; 97% of freshmen return for sophomore year. Average undergraduate class size: 32% under 20, 65% 20–40, 3% over 40. *Special programs:* CLEP, independent study, study abroad, honors, individualized majors, January term, 3–2 programs in pre-engineering, environmental science. *Calendar:* 4–1–4, summer school.
Undergraduate degrees conferred (344). 26% were in Education, 21% were in Business and Management, 13% were in Psychology, 8% were in Theology, 6% were in Communications, 5% were in Social Sciences, 4% were in Computer and Engineering Related Technology, 4% were in Life Sciences, 3% were in Public Affairs, 3% were in Letters, remainder in 5 other fields.
Graduate Career Data. Advanced studies pursued by 14% of students; 3% enter medical school. About 86% of 1992–93 graduates employed.
Faculty. About 70% of faculty hold PhD or equivalent. About 20% of teaching faculty are female; 2% minorities.
Student Body. University seeks a national student body; 33% of students from in state; 76% Midwest, 9% South, 3% New England, 6% Middle Atlantic, 2% West, 2% foreign. An estimated 99% of students reported as Protestant, 1% Catholic; 2% Black, 1% Hispanic, 3% Asian, 1% other minorities.
Religious Orientation. Taylor is an "evangelical Christian" institution; 12 hours of Bible and philosophy, 4 religious courses, attendance at chapel services expected of all students.
Varsity Sports. Men (NAIA): Baseball, Basketball, Cross Country, Football, Golf, Soccer, Tennis, Track. Women (NAIA): Basketball, Cross Country, Softball, Tennis, Track, Volleyball.
Campus Life. About 78% of men, 76% of women live in traditional dormitories; 13% of men, 13% of women live in off-campus college-related housing; rest commute. No intervisitation in men's and women's dormitory rooms. There are no fraternities or sororities. About 10–15% of resident students leave campus on weekends.
Annual Costs. Tuition and fees, $10,650; room and board, $3,800; estimated $1,500 other, exclusive of travel. About 78% of students receive financial aid; average amount of assistance, $5,500. Assistance is typically divided 64% scholarship, 26% loan, 10% work, according to most recent data available. College reports some scholarships awarded on the basis of academic merit alone.

Teikyo Marycrest University

Davenport, Iowa 52804 **(319) 326-9226**

A private, co-educational, Christian college with a Catholic heritage, Marycrest offers both liberal arts and career-related programs. The college overlooks a city of 102,000. As of the fall of 1994 Teikyo Marycrest University will merge with Teikyo Westmar University to form the Teikyo International University. As a multi-campus university with branches in Tokyo, Japan and Maastricht, The Netherlands, TIU's curriculum will span a broad range of traditional fields in the humanities, languages, education, nursing and social work, as well as innovative disciplines including environmental management, international communication, computer graphics, global studies and international business. Most convenient major airport: Quad-City (Moline, IL).

Founded: 1939
Affiliation: Roman Catholic
UG Enrollment: 1,065 M, W (full-time)
Cost: < $10K
Admission: Non-selective
Application Deadline: Rolling

Admission. Graduates of accredited high schools with 15 units eligible; others admitted by examination; 77% of applicants accepted, 77% of these actually enroll. *Required:* ACT; interview recommended. *Non-academic factors* considered in admissions: special talents, diverse student body, alumni children. *Apply:* rolling admissions. *Transfers* welcome.
Academic Environment. *Degrees:* AB, BS, BSN. About 50% of students entering as freshmen graduate eventually; 65% of freshmen return for sophomore year. Requirements for graduation include 39 semester hours distributed in 5 areas. Strongest programs reported to be in journalism, nursing, liberal arts. Many opportunities for study abroad. *Special programs:* CLEP, DANTES, study abroad, independent study, interdisciplinary courses, experiential learning, weekend college. *Calendar:* 8-week modules.
Undergraduate degrees conferred (204). 22% were in Liberal/General Studies, 22% were in Business and Management, 12% were in Health Sciences, 10% were in Visual and Performing Arts, 10% were in Education, 5% were in Public Affairs, 5% were in Communications, 4% were in Social Sciences, 3% were in Life Sciences, remainder in 5 other fields.
Student Body. College seeks a national student body; 67% of students from in state; 99% from North Central. An estimated 30% of students reported as Protestant, 29% Catholic, 41% unaffiliated; 4% Black, 1% Hispanic, 1% Asian, 38% other minority, according to most recent data available.
Religious Orientation. Marycrest is a church-related institution; 2 courses in philosophy and religious studies required of all students; daily Mass offered.
Varsity Sports. Men (NAIA): Basketball, Soccer. Women (NAIA): Basketball, Volleyball.
Campus Life. About 1% of men, 1% of women live in traditional dormitories; no coed dormitories; rest live in off-campus housing or commute. Intervisitation in men's and women's dormitory rooms limited. There are no fraternities or sororities.

Annual Costs. Tuition and fees, $9,800; room and board, $3,400. About 87% of students receive financial aid; assistance is typically divided 22% scholarship, 36% loan, 6% work. College reports some scholarships awarded on the basis of academic merit alone. *Meeting Costs:* college offers deferred payment plan.

Teikyo Post College

Waterbury, Connecticut 06723-2540 (203) 755-0121

Long a co-educational junior college, Teikyo Post is now accredited as a 4-year institution, part of the Teikyo International University System. Formerly known as Post College. Most convenient major airport: Bradley International (Hartford).

Founded: 1890
Affiliation: Independent
UG Enrollment: 182 M, 363 W (full-time); 354 M, 795 W (part-time)
Total Enrollment: 993
Cost: $10K–$20K
Admission: Non-selective
Application Deadline: Rolling

Admission. Graduates of accredited high schools eligible; 85% of applicants accepted, 53% of these actually enroll. *Required:* SAT, interview. *Non-academic factors* considered in admissions: special talents, diverse student body, alumni children. *Apply:* rolling admissions. *Transfers* welcome.
Academic Environment. College confers both associate and baccalaureate degrees. Programs strongly career oriented; most are in business and management, others include fashion merchandising, interior design, equine studies, therapeutic recreation. Opportunities for study abroad in The Netherlands, Germany, Russia, and Mexico. About 50% of entering freshmen graduate eventually, 60% return for sophomore year. *Calendar:* 8-week modules.
Undergraduate degrees conferred (214). 77% were in Business and Management, 14% were in Liberal/General Studies, 5% were in Architecture and Environmental Design, remainder in 4 other fields.
Graduates Career Data. According to most recent data available, full-time graduate or professional study pursued by 5% of students immediately after graduation. *Careers in business and industry* pursued by 93% of graduates.
Student Body. About 16% of students from in state; 84% New England.
Varsity Sports. Men (NAIA): Basketball, Soccer. Women (NAIA): Soccer, Softball.
Campus Life. About 15% of students live in dormitories, rest commute. Freshmen given preference in college housing if all students cannot be accommodated. There are no fraternities or sororities.
Annual Costs. Tuition and fees, $11,110; room and board, $5,450. About 75% of students receive financial aid. *Meeting Costs:* college offers tuition payment plan; family tuition discount.

Teikyo Westmar University

Le Mars, Iowa 51031 (712) 546-2611

A church-related college located in a town of 9,000, 25 miles northeast of Sioux City. Formerly known as Westmar College. As of the fall of 1994 Teikyo Marycrest University will merge with Teikyo Westmar University to form the Teikyo International University. As a multi-campus university with branches in Tokyo, Japan and Maastricht, The Netherlands, TIU's curriculum will span a broad range of traditional fields in the humanities, languages, education, nursing and social work, as well as innovative disciplines including environmental management, international communication, computer graphics, global studies and international business. Most convenient major airport: Sioux City.

Founded: 1890
Affiliation: United Methodist
UG Enrollment: 505 M, 252 W (full-time); 103 M, 43 W (part-time)
Cost: $10K–$20K
% Receiving Financial Aid: 60%
Admission: Non-selective
Application Deadline: Rolling

Admission. Graduates of approved high schools with minimum 2.3 GPA in 16 units and minimum ACT of 16 eligible; 68% of applicants accepted, 39% of these actually enroll; 19% of freshmen graduate in top fifth of high school class, 48% in top two-fifths. Average freshman ACT scores: 20 composite. *Required:* SAT score of 750, ACT score of 20. Criteria considered in admissions, in order of importance: high school academic record, standardized test scores, extracurricular activities; other factors considered: special talents, alumni children, diverse student body. *Entrance programs:* early admission, midyear admission, deferred admission. *Apply:* rolling admissions. *Transfers* welcome; 52 enrolled 1993–94.
Academic Environment. Degree offered: bachelors. About 50% of general education requirements for graduation are elective; distribution requirements limited. Average undergraduate class size: 50% under 20, 50% 20–40. About 40% of students entering as freshmen graduate within four years, 45% eventually; 66% of freshmen return for sophomore year. *Majors offered* in addition to usual studies include jazz studies. *Special programs:* CLEP, independent study, study abroad, student-designed majors, Urban Semester, program with Gulf Coast Research Laboratory, 3–2 radio/TV, internship/cooperative work-study programs with Minneapolis/St. Paul, Metro Urban internship, City Arts internship. *Calendar:* 8-week modules.
Undergraduate degrees conferred (117). 28% were in Business and Management, 16% were in Education, 11% were in Psychology, 7% were in Visual and Performing Arts, 6% were in Parks and Recreation, 4% were in Social Sciences, 4% were in Mathematics, 4% were in Life Sciences, 4% were in Engineering and Engineering Related Technology, 3% were in Computer and Engineering Related Technology, 3% were in Multi/Interdisciplinary Studies, remainder in 6 other fields.
Graduates Career Data. About 97% of 1992–93 graduates employed. Fields typically hiring largest numbers of graduates include business, education, human services. Career Development Services include graduate school information, job search strategies, job placement assistance, resume preparation, interviewing, career fairs.
Faculty. About 60% of faculty hold PhD or equivalent. About 25% of undergraduate classes taught by tenured faculty. About 46% of teaching faculty are female; 2% Black, 4% other ethnic minorities.
Student Body. College seeks a national student body; 39% of students from in state; 51% of students from Midwest, 4% South, 4% West, 1% Middle Atlantic, 40% foreign. An estimated 18% of students reported as Protestant, 10% Catholic, 72% other; 5% Black, 2% Hispanic, 1% Asian, 40% international. Average age of undergraduate student: 23.
Varsity Sports. Men (NAIA): Baseball, Basketball, Football, Golf, Soccer, Tennis, Track, Wrestling. Women (NAIA): Basketball, Golf, Soccer, Softball, Track, Volleyball.
Campus Life. About 53% of men live in traditional dormitories; 20% of men, 41% of women live in coed dormitories; 4% of men, 11% of women live in off-campus college-related housing; 23% of men, 48% of women commute. Freshmen given preference in college housing if all students cannot be accommodated. Intervisitation in men's and women's dormitory rooms limited. There are no fraternities or sororities on campus. About 20% of resident students leave campus on weekends.
Annual Costs. Tuition and fees, $12,000; room and board, $3,500; estimated $1,500 other, exclusive of travel. About 60% of students receive financial aid; average amount of assistance, $9,600. Assistance is typically divided 10% scholarship, 40% grant, 40% loan, 10% work. College reports 133 scholarships awarded on the basis of academic merit alone, 329 for special talents, 238 for need alone. *Meeting Costs:* college offers "frozen tuition", monthly payment plans.

Temple University

Philadelphia, Pennsylvania 19122 (215) 787-7200

Temple is a major, comprehensive research university which now enjoys an unusual position as a "state-related" institution, supported by both private and public funds. It is controlled by an independent, 36-member, self-perpetuating board of trustees, 12 of whom are appointed by state officials. The university offers a wide diversity of programs at both the undergraduate and graduate/professional levels on 6 campuses in metropolitan Philadelphia and abroad. Most convenient major airport: Philadelphia International.

Founded: 1884
Affiliation: Independent/State
UG Enrollment: 8,602 M, 8,733 W (full-time); 2,936 M, 3,131 W (part-time)
Total Enrollment: 30,750
Cost: < $10K
Admission: Selective
Application Deadline: June 15

Admission is selective. For all schools, 66% of applicants accepted, 58% of these actually enroll; 37% of freshmen graduate in top fifth of high school class, 69% in top two-fifths.

For Liberal Arts (2,716 M, 3,300 W), 70% of applicants accepted, 57% of these actually enroll.

For Education (160 M, 571 W), 69% of applicants accepted, 52% of these actually enroll.

For Engineering and Architecture (1,401 M, 192 W), 61% of applicants accepted, 48% of these actually enroll.

For Music (143 M, 137 W), 54% of applicants accepted, 61% of these actually enroll.

For Allied Health (85 M, 360 W), 57% of applicants accepted, 55% of these actually enroll.

For Business Administration (3,155 M, 2,120 W), 70% of applicants accepted, 59% of these actually enroll.

For Communications and Theater (1,089 M, 1,355 W), 74% of applicants accepted, 61% of these actually enroll.

For Health, Physical Education, Recreation and Dance (219 M, 306 W), 72% of applicants accepted, 71% of these actually enroll.

For Social Administration (39 M, 263 W), 66% of applicants accepted, 78% of these actually enroll.

For Tyler School of Art (226 M, 325 W), 47% of applicants accepted, 66% of these actually enroll.

Required: SAT or ACT; audition for dance and music, portfolio for art and architecture. *Out-of-state* freshman applicants: university actively seeks students from out of state. State does not limit out-of-state enrollment. No special requirements for out-of-state applicants; 58% accepted, 34% enroll. *Non-academic factors* considered in admissions: special talents, alumni children. *Entrance programs:* early decision, early admission, midyear admission, advanced placement. *Apply* by June 15. *Transfers* welcome.

Academic Environment. *Undergraduate studies* offered by colleges of Arts and Sciences, Education, Engineering and Architecture, Music, schools of Allied Health, Business Administration, Communications and Theater, Health, Physical Education, Recreation and Dance, Social Administration, Tyler School of Art. The former New School of Music merged recently with university's Esther Boyer College of Music. Core curriculum required of all undergraduates includes writing, mathematics, science, intellectual history, the arts, American culture, social science, foreign language/international studies. A new writing center has opened to provide support to all students and faculty.

Special programs: CLEP, independent study, study abroad, honors, interdisciplinary majors. *Library:* over 2 million volumes, computerized referencing, Urban Archives; open-stack privileges; hours until midnight. Planetarium and Observatory in Physics Department. *Calendar:* semester, summer school.

Undergraduate degrees conferred (3,499). 28% were in Business and Management, 13% were in Communications, 9% were in Education, 8% were in Social Sciences, 7% were in Health Sciences, 7% were in Engineering, 5% were in Visual and Performing Arts, 5% were in Psychology, 3% were in Protective Services, remainder in 15 other fields.

Graduates Career Data. According to most recent data available, full-time graduate or professional study pursued immediately after graduation by 11% of students. *Careers in business and industry* pursued by 83% of graduates. Alumni reported as active in both career guidance and job placement.

Faculty. About 85% of faculty hold PhD or equivalent.

Student Body. University seeks a national student body. An estimated 14% of students reported as Black, 2% Hispanic, 6% Asian, 4% Native American, 2% other minority, according to most recent data available.

Varsity Sports. Men (Div.I): Baseball, Basketball, Crew, Football, Golf, Gymnastics, Soccer, Tennis, Track. Women (Div.I): Basketball, Crew, Fencing, Field Hockey, Gymnastics, Lacrosse, Softball, Swimming, Tennis, Track, Volleyball.

Campus Life. University serves a largely commuter student body. Parking facilities on campus. Administration does not regulate women's hours; intervisitation unlimited. About 10% of men, 10% of women live in coed dormitories; rest live in off-campus housing or commute. Freshmen given preference in college housing if all students cannot be accommodated. There are 26 fraternities, 26 sororities on campus which about 2% of men, 1% of women join; 3% of men, 2% of women live in fraternities, sororities.

Annual Costs. Tuition and fees, $5,013 (out-of-state, $9,225); room and board, $4,950. About 65% of students receive financial aid; assistance is typically divided 44% scholarship, 53% loan, 3% work. University reports some scholarships awarded on the basis of academic merit alone. *Meeting Costs:* university offers tuition payment plan, bank loans.

Tennessee State University

Nashville, Tennessee 37209-1561 (615) 320-3131

A state-supported, land-grant university, located in the state capital; founded as a college for Negroes and still serving a predominantly Black student body.

Founded: 1912
Affiliation: State
UG Enrollment: 1,928 M, 2,855 W (full-time); 702 M, 1,132 W (part-time)
Total Enrollment: 7,851
Cost: < $10K
% Receiving Financial Aid: 83%
Admission: Non-selective
Application Deadline: Aug. 1

Admission. Tennessee graduates of approved high schools with 2.5 average and ACT composite score of 12 eligible; 46% of applicants accepted, 80% of these actually enroll. Average freshman scores: SAT, 720 combined verbal/mathematical; ACT, 19 composite. *Required:* ACT, 14 high school units. Criteria considered in admissions, in order of importance: high school academic record, standardized test scores, 14 high school units; other factor considered: alumni children. *Entrance programs:* midyear admission, advanced placement. *Out-of-state* freshman applicants: university actively seeks students from out of state. State limits out-of-state enrollment to 20% of student body. Requirement for out-of-state applicants: 2.5 average or ACT composite score of 19. About 38% of out-of-state students accepted, 20% of these actually enroll. States from which most out-of-state students are drawn: Georgia, Illinois, Michigan, Missouri, Ohio, Alabama, Indiana. *Apply* by August 1. *Transfers* welcome.

Academic Environment. Degree offered: doctoral. *Undergraduate studies* offered by schools of Arts and Sciences, Agriculture and Home Economics, Education, Engineering. About 30% of general education requirements for graduation are elective; no distribution requirements; writing proficiency and senior project required. Average undergraduate class size: 5% under 20, 67% 20–40, 28% over 40. About 45% of entering students graduate eventually, according to most recent data available. *Special programs:* honors, study abroad, degree program in correctional services, cooperative education program, internship/cooperative work-study programs in business and engineering, cross registration with Vanderbilt U., Middle Tennessee State and Meharry Medical. *Calendar:* semester, summer school.

Undergraduate degrees conferred (516). 17% were in Business and Management, 15% were in Engineering, 8% were in Education, 8% were in Protective Services, 8% were in Health Sciences, 6% were in Visual and Performing Arts, 6% were in Business (Administrative Support), 6% were in Psychology, 5% were in Social Sciences, 4% were in Life Sciences, 3% were in Liberal/General Studies, 3% were in Engineering and Engineering Related Technology, remainder in 7 other fields.

Graduate Career Data. Career Development Services include assistance in exploring a variety of career alternatives while providing career and employment information for seniors, graduates and alumni, obtaining part-time summer and cooperative education employment and internships for students.

Student Body. University does not seek a national student body; 79% of students from in state; 89% South. An estimated 62% of students reported as Black, 3% other minorities.

Varsity Sports. Men (Div.I): Baseball, Basketball, Cross Country, Football (IAA), Golf, Tennis, Track. Women (Div.I): Basketball, Cross Country, Golf, Softball, Tennis, Track.

Campus Life. About 25% of men and women live in traditional dormitories; no coed dormitories; rest live in off-campus housing or commute. Freshmen given preference in college housing if all students cannot be accommodated. No intervisitation in men's or women's dormitory rooms. There are 4 fraternities, 4 sororities on campus; they provide no residence facilities. About 25% of resident students leave campus on weekends.
Annual Costs. Tuition and fees, $1,706 (out-of-state, $8,404); room and board, $2,720; estimated $2,094 other, exclusive of travel. About 83% of students awarded financial aid. University reports 169 scholarships awarded on the basis of academic merit alone. *Meeting Costs:* university offers deferred payments for room and board.

Tennessee Technological University

Cookeville, Tennessee 38505 **(615) 372-3888; (800) 255-8881**

A state-supported university, located in a small town of 25,000, 75 miles east of Nashville. Most convenient major airport: Nashville.

Founded: 1915
Affiliation: State
UG Enrollment: 3,547 M, 2,914 W (full-time); 471 M, 439 W (part-time)
Total Enrollment: 8,341
Cost: < $10K
% Receiving Financial Aid: 62%
Admission: Non-selective
Application Deadline: July 21

Admission. Graduates of approved high schools with 2.35 average or ACT composite score of 17 eligible; 98% of applicants accepted, 70% of these actually enroll; 25% of freshman graduate in top fifth of high school class, 70% in top two-fifths. Average freshman ACT scores: 22.95 M, 21.9 W composite. *Required:* ACT. Criteria considered in admissions, in order of importance: standardized test scores and high school academic record, extracurricular activities. *Out-of-state* freshman applicants: university actively seeks students from out of state; no limits; no special requirements. About 99% of out-of-state students accepted, 97% of these actually enroll. States from which most out-of-state students are drawn: Georgia, Kentucky, Alabama, Virginia, Ohio, Illinois, and Florida. *Apply* by July 21, December 8; rolling admissions. *Transfers* welcome; 612 enrolled 1993–94.
Academic Environment. *Undergraduate studies* offered by colleges of Arts and Sciences, Agriculture and Home Economics, Business Administration, Education, Engineering and Nursing. Core requirements include 12 hours English, 8 hours sciences, 6 hours history, 3 hours mathematics, 3 hours humanities, 2 hours physical education. Degrees offered: bachelors, masters, doctoral. Campus facilities include an art gallery, radio station, television station, and 24-hour computer access. About 10% of students entering as freshmen graduate within four years, 55% eventually; 78% of freshmen return for sophomore year. Average undergraduate class size: 30% under 20, 50% 20–40, 20% over 40. *Special programs:* CLEP, honors, 3-year degree, internship/cooperative work-study programs within departments. Adult programs: night classes for non-traditional students. *Calendar:* semester, summer school.
Undergraduate degrees conferred (1,035). 29% were in Business and Management, 22% were in Engineering, 20% were in Education, 5% were in Health Sciences, 4% were in Social Sciences, 3% were in Life Sciences, 3% were in Home Economics, 3% were in Engineering and Engineering Related Technology, remainder in 11 other fields.
Graduates Career Data. Full or part-time graduate or professional study pursued by 19% of students immediately after graduation (1990–91). *Careers in business and industry* pursued by 84% of graduates (1990–91). Fields typically employing largest numbers of graduates include engineering, business and education.
Faculty. About 84% of faculty hold PhD or equivalent. About 75% of undergraduate classes taught by tenured faculty. About 44% of teaching faculty are female.
Student Body. University seeks a national student body; 94% of students from in state; 95% South; 238 foreign. An estimated 3% of students reported as Black, 3% Asian. Average age of undergraduate student: 22.
Varsity Sports. Men (Div.IA): Baseball, Basketball, Cross Country, Football (IAA), Golf, Riflery, Tennis. Women (Div.IA): Basketball, Cross Country, Golf, Riflery, Softball, Tennis, Volleyball.

Campus Life. About 42% of men, 34% of women live in traditional dormitories; no coed dormitories; 7% of men, 7% of women are married and live in apartments; 50% of men, 59% of women commute. Intervisitation in men's and women's dormitory rooms limited. There are 16 fraternities, 6 sororities on campus which about 18% of men, 12% of women join; 1% of men live in fraternities; sororities provide no residence facilities. About 70% of resident students leave campus on weekends.
Annual Costs. Tuition and fees, $1,710 (out-of-state, $5,492); room and board, $3,480; estimated $1,200 other, exclusive of travel. About 62% of students receive financial aid; average amount of assistance, $3,094. Assistance is typically divided 20% scholarship, 35% grant, 27% loan, 18% work. University reports some scholarships awarded on the basis of academic merit alone.

University of Tennessee

Knoxville, Tennessee 37996-0230 **(615) 974-2184; in-state, (800) 221-8657**

A multi-campus institution, the University of Tennessee is the state's land-grant college. On the main campus in Knoxville (pop. 181,151) are 19 schools and colleges; programs also offered in Chattanooga, Oak Ridge, Tullahoma, Memphis, Nashville, and Kingsport. Most convenient major airport: McGhee-Tyson (Knoxville).

Founded: 1794
Affiliation: State
UG Enrollment: 8,270 M, 7,481 W (full-time); 1,500 M, 1,737 W (part-time)
Total Enrollment: 25,890
Cost: < $10K
% Receiving Financial Aid: 88%
Admission: Selective
Application Deadline: July 1

Admission is selective. About 72% of applicants accepted, 56% of these enroll; 47% of freshman graduate in top fifth of high school class, 75% in top two-fifths. Average freshman scores: SAT, 468 verbal, 525 mathematical; 37% of freshman score above 500 verbal, 9% above 600, 1% above 700; 62% score above 500 mathematical, 23% above 600, 5% above 700; ACT, 23.2 composite. *Required:* ACT or SAT, minimum high school GPA of 2.0 in college preparatory program. Criteria considered in admissions, in order of importance: high school academic record, standardized test scores, writing sample, recommendations, extracurricular activities; other factors considered: special talents, alumni children. *Out-of-state* freshman applicants: university actively seeks students from out of state. States from which most out-of-state students are drawn: Virginia, Georgia, Florida, North Carolina. *Entrance programs:* early admission, midyear admission, deferred admission. *Apply* by July 1; rolling admission. *Transfers* welcome; 1,582 enrolled 1993–94.
Academic Environment. Degrees offered: bachelors, masters, doctoral. *Undergraduate studies* offered by nine colleges, students choose their college after being accepted to the University. Nationally recognized programs include accounting, transportation and logistics (College of Business Administration), and Hotel and Restaurant Management (College of Human Ecology). UT also has very strong programs in the preprofessional areas of business, architecture, and engineering; the science and technology programs benefit from a cooperative arrangement with the nearby Oak Ridge National Laboratory. *Majors offered* in liberal arts in addition to usual studies include anthropology, cultural studies, geography, medical technology, microbiology, speech pathology and audiology. General education requirements include 2 courses in English composition, mathematics, humanities, social sciences, history, natural sciences, foreign language or integrative studies; other requirements vary with specific college. Average undergraduate class size: 78% 1–30, 16% 31–50, 4% 51–100, 2% over 100. In spite of some very large introductory classes, students report that faculty is "very accessible".

About 17% of students entering as freshmen graduate within four years, 55% eventually; 81% of freshmen return for sophomore year. Library resources are ranked among the top 75 in the nation. *Special programs:* CLEP, independent study, study abroad, honors, undergraduate research, 3-year degree, individualized majors, double major, student designed major, visiting exchange student program, acceleration, credit by examination, cooperative work/study programs (in agriculture, business, chemistry, communication, engineering), binary program in engineering, pre-medicine and pre-pharmacy with UT Memphis, cross registration with Knoxville College. Adult programs: women in transition group, Mentor/Partner program, workshops to aid non-traditional student. *Calendar:* 4–1–4, summer school.

Undergraduate degrees conferred (3,168). 29% were in Business and Management, 11% were in Engineering, 9% were in Social Sciences, 7% were in Education, 5% were in Psychology, 5% were in Communications, 5% were in Letters, 4% were in Home Economics, 3% were in Life Sciences, 3% were in Health Sciences, 3% were in Multi/Interdisciplinary Studies, remainder in 15 other fields.

Graduate Career Data. According to most recent data available, full-time graduate or professional study pursued immediately after graduation by 23% of students; 2% enter medical school; 4% enter law school; 6% enter business school. Graduate and professional schools typically enrolling largest numbers of graduates include U. of Tennessee, Vanderbilt, East Tennessee, U. of Georgia. *Careers in business and industry* pursued by 70% of graduates. Corporations typically hiring largest numbers of graduates include IBM, Tennessee Eastman, Westinghouse, DuPont. *Career Counseling Program:* students urged to seek interviews with business/industry representatives who visit campus. Help provided in preparing for interviews. Alumni reported as active job placement.

Faculty. About 86% of faculty hold PhD or equivalent. About 23% of teaching faculty are female; 4% Black, 1% Hispanic, 4% other ethnic minorities.

Student Body. University seeks a national student body; 85% of students from in state; 2% foreign. An estimated 5% of students reported as Black, 2% Asian, less than 1% Hispanic. *Minority group students:* "increased sensitivity" toward helping in financial and academic areas. Average age of undergraduate student: 23.

Varsity Sports. Men (Div.I): Baseball, Basketball, Cross Country, Football, Golf, Swimming, Tennis, Track. Women (Div.I): Basketball, Cross Country, Golf, Swimming, Tennis, Track, Volleyball.

Campus Life. Administration source reports both varsity and intramural sports are popular on campus. UT's location in the foothills of the Great Smoky Mountains bordered by Fort Loudon Lake offers students abundant opportunities for outdoor recreational activities. Students may choose either personal curfew or self-regulating hours programs. Alcohol prohibited on campus; cars permitted, but parking "difficult". Students park on perimeter of campus; free bus system connects parking areas and center of campus.

About 35% of students live in traditional dormitories; 50% commute. Intervisitation in men's and women's dormitory rooms limited. Sexes segregated in coed dormitories either by wing or floor. There are 26 fraternities, 19 sororities on campus which about 11% of men, 14% of women join; 15% of students live in fraternities or sororities. About 40% of resident students leave campus on weekends.

Annual Costs. Tuition and fees, $1,982 (out-of-state, $5,762); room and board, $3,686; estimated $3,182 other, exclusive of travel. About 88% of students receive financial aid. Assistance is typically divided 49% grant, 48% loan, 3% work. University reports 1,200 scholarships awarded on the basis of academic merit alone, 215 for special talents. *Meeting Costs:* university offers prepayment plan and delayed payment plan.

University of Tennessee at Chattanooga

Chattanooga, Tennessee 37403 **(615) 755-4007**

Formerly an independent university, the institution has been part of the University of Tennessee System since 1969. The campus is located in a city of 135,000. Most convenient major airport: Lovell Field.

Founded: 1886
Affiliation: State
UG Enrollment: 2,511 M, 2,848 W (full-time); 763 M, 995 W (part-time)
Total Enrollment: 8,325
Cost: < $10K
% Receiving Financial Aid: 65%
Admission: Non-selective
Application Deadline: Aug. 15

Admission. Graduates of accredited Tennessee high schools with 10 specified academic units and minimum GPA of 2.0 and minimum ACT composite of 12 or SAT combined score of 700 eligible; 64% of applicants accepted, 74% of these actually enroll. Average freshman ACT scores: 22.1 M, 22.3 W composite. *Required:* SAT or ACT. Criteria considered in admissions, in order of importance: standardized test scores, high school academic record, recommendations, extracurricular activities; other factors considered: special talents, alumni children. *Out-of-state* freshman applicants: university actively seeks students from out of state; no limits; no special requirements. State from which most out-of-state students are drawn: Georgia. *Entrance programs:* early admission, midyear admission, advanced placement. *Apply* by August 15; rolling admissions. *Transfers* welcome; 733 enrolled 1993–94.

Academic Environment. Degrees offered: bachelors, masters. *Majors offered* include usual arts and sciences, business, dramatics, education, engineering, home economics, medical technology, social work, physical therapy. General education requirements for graduation vary by curriculum; distribution requirements fairly numerous. About 8% of students entering as freshmen graduate within four years, 38% eventually; 74% of freshman return for sophomore year. *Special programs:* CLEP, independent study, honors, study abroad, undergraduate research, forestry with Duke, 3–2 engineering. Adult programs: advisement, counseling, tutorial services, registration and other services available evenings and weekends. *Calendar:* semester, summer school.

Undergraduate degrees conferred (926). 30% were in Business and Management, 20% were in Education, 7% were in Engineering, 6% were in Psychology, 4% were in Protective Services, 4% were in Health Sciences, 4% were in Communications, 3% were in Physical Sciences, 3% were in Letters, 3% were in Home Economics, 3% were in Social Sciences, 3% were in Visual and Performing Arts, 3% were in Computer and Engineering Related Technology, remainder in 7 other fields.

Graduates Career Data. *Careers in business and industry* pursued by 52% of graduates, according to most recent data available.

Faculty. About 78% of faculty hold PhD or equivalent. About 28% of teaching faculty are female; 6% Black, 1% Hispanic, 3% other ethnic minority.

Student Body. University does not seek a national student body; 89% of students from in state; 97% South; 2% foreign. An estimated 10% of students reported as Black, 1% Hispanic, 3% Asian. Average age of undergraduate student: 24.

Varsity Sports. Men (Div.I-AA): Basketball, Cross Country, Football, Golf, Tennis, Track, Wrestling. Women (Div.I-AA): Basketball, Cross Country, Softball, Tennis, Track, Volleyball.

Campus Life. About 14% of undergraduate men and women live in coed dormitories; 86% live in off-campus housing or commute. Intervisitation in men's and women's dormitory rooms limited. There are 8 fraternities, 7 sororities on campus which about 7% of men, 7% of women join.

Annual Costs. Tuition and fees, $1,770 (out-of-state, $5,550); room and board, $3,800; estimated $600 other, exclusive of travel. About 65% of students receive financial aid; average amount of assistance, $1,000. Assistance is typically divided 28% grants, 35% scholarship, 34% loan, 3% work, according to most recent data available. College reports some scholarships awarded on the basis of academic merit alone.

University of Tennessee at Martin

Martin, Tennessee 38238 **(901) 587-7020**

The University of Tennessee's Martin campus, offering baccalaureate programs in more than 50 specialized fields, is located in a community of 9,350 in northwestern Tennessee.

Founded: 1927
Affiliation: State
UG Enrollment: 2,123 M, 2,546 W (full-time); 239 M, 436 W (part-time)
Cost: < $10K
% Receiving Financial Aid: 60%
Admission: Non-selective
Application Deadline: August 1

Admission. Graduates of accredited high schools with 16 units and 2.25 average or ACT composite score of 19 eligible for regular admission; others admitted if qualified; 91% of applicants accepted, almost all enroll. *Required:* SAT or ACT; visit to campus recommended. Criteria considered in admissions, in order of importance: high school academic record, standardized test scores, extracurricular activities, writing sample, recommendations. *Entrance programs:* early admission, midyear admission. *Out-of-state* freshman applicants: university actively seeks students from out of state; no limits; no special requirements. About 84% of out-of-state students accepted, 97% of these actually enroll. States from which most out-of-state students are drawn: Illinois, Kentucky, Missouri, Florida. *Apply* by August 1; rolling admissions. *Transfers* welcome; 450 enrolled 1993–94.

Academic Environment. Degrees offered: bachelors, masters. *Undergraduate studies* offered by schools of Agriculture and Home Economics, Arts and Sciences, Business Administration, Education, Engineering Technology, and Fine and Performing Arts, a BS in Nursing is offered through Arts and Sciences. *Majors offered* in addition to usual studies include environmental management, philosophy, international studies. Specific course and distribution requirements vary with major. About 40% of students entering as freshmen graduate within four years, 60% eventually; 63% of freshmen return for sophomore year. Average undergraduate class size: 21. *Special programs:* CLEP, honors, independent study, study abroad, undergraduate research, cross registration with Japan, internship/cooperative work-study programs. Adult programs: Off-campus Degree Program for MS in Education, non-traditional students, special counseling. *Calendar:* quarter, summer school.

Undergraduate degrees conferred (649). 31% were in Business and Management, 18% were in Education, 7% were in Protective Services, 5% were in Agricultural Sciences, 4% were in Public Affairs, 4% were in Communications, 4% were in Life Sciences, 4% were in Home Economics, 4% were in Engineering and Engineering Related Technology, 3% were in Psychology, 3% were in Social Sciences, 3% were in Physical Sciences, 3% were in Computer and Engineering Related Technology, remainder in 7 other fields.

Graduates Career Data. Advanced studies pursued by 26% of students. Professional schools typically enrolling largest numbers of graduates include U. of Tennessee at Memphis, U. of Tennessee at Knoxville, Memphis State. About 69% of 1992–93 graduates employed. Fields typically employ largest numbers of graduates include agriculture, education, engineering, business.

Faculty. About 80% of faculty hold PhD or equivalent. About 28% of teaching faculty are female; 7% Black, 7% Hispanic.

Student Body. University does not seek a national student body; 90% of students from in state; 95% South, 3% Midwest, 2% foreign. An estimated 64% of students reported as Protestant, 5% Catholic, 29% unaffiliated, according to most recent data available; 14% Black, 2% other ethnic minorities. Average age of undergraduate student: 22.

Varsity Sports. Men (Div.IA): Baseball, Basketball, Cross Country, Football (IAA), Golf, Tennis, Track. Women (Div.IA): Baseball, Basketball, Cross Country, Softball, Tennis, Track, Volleyball.

Campus Life. About 70% of men, 70% of women live in traditional dormitories; 5% of men, 5% of women live in off-campus college-related housing; 25% of men, 25% of women commute. Freshmen given preference in college housing if all students cannot be accommodated. Intervisitation in men's and women's dormitory rooms limited. There are 11 fraternities, 7 sororities on campus which about 20% of men, 18% of women join; 20% of men live in fraternities, 18% of women live in sororities, according to most recent data available. About 30% of resident students leave campus on weekends.

Annual Costs. Tuition and fees, $1,810 (out-of-state, $3,780); room and board, $2,700; estimated $2,000 other, exclusive of travel. About 60% of students receive financial aid; average amount of assistance, $2,400. Assistance is typically divided 20% scholarship, 30% grant, 30% loan, 20% work. University reports 1,628 scholarships awarded on the basis of academic merit alone, 351 for special talents, 1,060 for need alone. *Meeting Costs:* college offers 25% discount to dependents of Tennessee teachers.

Tennessee Wesleyan College

Athens, Tennessee 37371-0040 (615) 745-7504

A church-related college, located in a town of 11,800, 40 miles southwest of Knoxville. Most convenient major airports: Knoxville, Chattanooga.

Founded: 1857
Affiliation: United Methodist
UG Enrollment: 227 M, 175 W (full-time); 73 M, 164 W (part-time)
Cost: < $10K
Admission: Non-selective
Application Deadline: July 31

Admission. Graduates of accredited high schools with 16 units and C average eligible; 90% of applicants accepted, 48% of these actually enroll. About 25% of freshmen graduate in top fifth of high school class, 55% in top two-fifths. Average freshman scores: SAT, 810; ACT, 19 composite. *Required:* SAT or ACT, letter of recommendation. Criteria considered in admissions, in order of importance: high school academic record, standardized test scores, recommendations, writing sample, extracurricular activities. *Apply* by July 31; rolling admissions. *Transfers* welcome; 166 enrolled 1993–94.

Academic Environment. Degree offered: bachelors. Core requirements include 50 semester hours including English, fine arts, humanities, mathematics, sciences, social and behavioral sciences. Average undergraduate class size: 60% under 20, 40% 20–40. About 79% of students entering as freshmen graduate eventually; 75% of freshmen return for sophomore year. *Special programs:* independent study, undergraduate research, study abroad in England and Japan, individualized majors, internship program behavioral science majors. Adult programs: Evening School offers degree program in business administration. *Library:* 69,742 titles, 351 periodicals, Cooke Methodist Historical Collection; hours until 9 PM (closed Saturday). *Calendar:* 4–1–4, summer school.

Undergraduate degrees conferred (123). 46% were in Business and Management, 14% were in Education, 10% were in Multi/Interdisciplinary Studies, 7% were in Public Affairs, 6% were in Psychology, 3% were in Social Sciences, 3% were in Mathematics, remainder in 6 other fields.

Graduates Career Data. Professional schools typically enrolling largest numbers of graduates include U. of Tennessee at Knoxville. Career Development Services include a placement office, workshops on resume preparation and interviews, job fair.

Faculty. About 70% of faculty hold PhD or equivalent (1990–91). About 90% of undergraduate classes taught by tenured faculty. About 40% of teaching faculty are female; 3% ethnic minority.

Student Body. College does not seek a national student body; 94% of students from South, 1% New England, 1% West, 4% foreign. An estimated 90% of students reported as Protestant, 2% Catholic, 8% unaffiliated; 11% Black, 1% Hispanic, 1% Asian, 4% other ethnic minorities. Average age of undergraduate student: 24.

Varsity Sports. Men (Div. NAIA): Baseball, Basketball, Football, Golf, Soccer. Women (Div. NAIA): Basketball, Soccer, Softball, Tennis.

Religious Orientation. Tennessee Wesleyan is a church-related institution; 1 course in religion and philosophical studies, attendance at specified number of religious and cultural events required of all students.

Campus Life. About 34% of students women live in traditional dormitories; no coed dormitories; rest live in off-campus housing or commute. Intervisitation in men's and women's dormitory rooms limited. There are no fraternities, 2 sororities on campus which about 10% of women join. Sororities provide no residence facilities. About 30% of students leave campus on weekends, according to most recent data available.

Annual Costs. Tuition and fees, $6,520; room and board, $3,540. Financial aid assistance is typically divided 51% scholarship, 46% loan, 3% work, according to most recent data available. College reports some scholarships awarded on the basis of academic merit alone. *Meeting Costs:* college offers various payment plans.

Texas A&M University—Kingsville

Kingsville, Texas 78363 (512) 595-3907

A state-supported university, located in a community of 30,000, 40 miles southwest of Corpus Christi, 90 miles from the Mexican border. Most convenient major airport: Corpus Christi.

Founded: 1925
Affiliation: State
UG Enrollment: 2,302 M, 2,120 W (full-time); 440 M, 538 W (part-time)
Total Enrollment: 6,574
Cost: < $10K
% Receiving Financial Aid: 80%
Admission: Non-selective
Application Deadline: Rolling

Admission. Graduates of accredited high schools eligible; almost all applicants accepted, 79% of these actually enroll; 33% of freshman graduate in top fifth of high school class, 65% in top two-fifths. *Required:* SAT or ACT. Criteria considered in admissions, in order of importance: standardized test scores, high school academic record. *Out-of-state* freshman applicants: university actively seeks students from out of state; no limits; no special requirements. States from which most out-of-state students are drawn: California, Florida. *Apply*: rolling admissions. *Transfers* welcome; 531 enrolled 1993–94.

Academic Environment. Degrees offered: bachelors, masters, doctoral. *Undergraduate studies* offered by colleges of Agriculture and Home Economics, Arts and Science, Business Administration, Engineering, Education. New or unusual majors offered include restaurant food management, international business, natural gas engineering. Core requirements in liberal arts include history, mathematics, English, political science, humanities, kinesiology, fine arts. About 20% of entering students graduate within four years, 33% eventually; 50% of freshmen return for sophomore year. *Special programs:* CLEP, study abroad, internship/cooperative work-study programs. *Calendar:* semester, summer school.

Undergraduate degrees conferred (687). 36% were in Education, 19% were in Engineering, 16% were in Business and Management, 4% were in Multi/Interdisciplinary Studies, 4% were in Computer and Engineering Related Technology, 3% were in Psychology, 3% were in Agricultural Sciences, remainder in 13 other fields.

Graduates Career Data. Fields typically hiring largest numbers of graduates include teaching, engineering and agriculture. Career Development Services include resume writing, workshops, career exploration and job fairs.

Faculty. About 60% of faculty hold PhD or equivalent.

Student Body. About 95% of students from in state. An estimated 3% of students reported as Black, 62% Hispanic, 1% Asian, 5% ethnic minority. Average age of undergraduate student: 24.

Varsity Sports. Men (Div.II): Baseball, Basketball, Cross Country, Football, Tennis, Track. Women (Div.II): Basketball, Cross Country, Tennis, Track, Volleyball.

Campus Life. About 22% of men, 16% of women live in coed and traditional dormitories; 30% of men, 31% of women live in off-campus college-related housing; rest commute. Freshmen given preference in college housing if all students cannot be accommodated. There are 5 fraternities, 2 sororities on campus; they provide no residence facilities. About 80% of resident students leave campus on weekends.

Annual Costs. Tuition and fees, $1,158 (out-of-state, $4,290); room and board, $3,090. About 80% of students receive financial aid. University reports some scholarships awarded on the basis of academic merit alone.

Texas A&M University

College Station, Texas 77843 (409) 845-1060

A state-supported university, located in a metropolitan area of 100,000, 90 miles northwest of Houston. The Texas A&M University System includes Tarleton State, Prairie View A&M, and Texas A&M at Galveston. Most convenient major airports: Easterwood (College Station), Houston Inter-Continental.

Founded: 1876
Affiliation: State
UG Enrollment: 17,415 M, 13,428 W (full-time); 1,453 M, 908 W (part-time)
Total Enrollment: 38,834
Cost: < $10K
% Receiving Financial Aid: 66%
Admission: Selective
Application Deadline: March 1

Admission is selective. About 88% of applicants accepted, 62% of these actually enroll; 69% of freshmen graduate in top fifth of high school class, 93% in top two-fifths. Average freshman SAT scores, according to most recent data available: 488 M, 479 W verbal, 584 M, 536 W mathematical; 73% of freshman score above 500 on verbal, 25% above 600; 53% score above 500 on mathematical, 36% above 600, 11% above 700. *Required:* SAT or ACT; ACH in English and mathematics I or II highly recommended. *Out-of-state* freshman applicants: university seeks students from out of state. State does not limit out-of-state enrollment. Requirements for out-of-state applicants: rank in top quarter of high school class and 1,100 combined score on SAT or 27 on ACT composite. *Entrance programs:* early admission, midyear admission, deferred admission, advanced placement. *Apply* by March 1. *Transfers* welcome.

Academic Environment. *Undergraduate studies* offered by colleges of Liberal Arts, Science, Agriculture, Architecture, Business Administration, Education, Engineering, Geosciences, Medicine, Veterinary Medicine. A core curriculum required for all undergraduates emphasizing speech and writing skills, mathematical/logical reasoning, science, cultural heritage, social science, physical education and citizenship plus foreign language and computer literacy was implemented in 1988. Some student concern reported that faculty is becoming more oriented toward research than teaching. Student body reported to be very concerned with occupational/professional goals.

More than 65% of students entering as freshmen graduate within four years; 82% of freshmen return for sophomore year. *Special programs:* CLEP, honors, study abroad, independent study, cooperative education. *Library:* 1,800,000 volumes, 15,000 periodicals, 3,500,000 titles on microform, Science Fiction Collection, Range Livestock Collection; 1,000 microcomputers for class and research work available; hours until midnight. *Calendar:* semester, summer school.

Undergraduate degrees conferred (6,744). 19% were in Business and Management, 13% were in Engineering, 12% were in Education, 10% were in Social Sciences, 6% were in Agricultural Sciences, 5% were in Psychology, 5% were in Letters, 4% were in Engineering and Engineering Related Technology, 4% were in Life Sciences, 3% were in Multi/Interdisciplinary Studies, 3% were in Communications, 3% were in Agribusiness and Agricultural Production, 3% were in Architecture and Environmental Design, remainder in 11 other fields.

Graduates Career Data. According to most recent data available, full-time graduate or professional study: 2% enter medical school; 3% enter law school. *Careers in business and industry* pursued by 75% of graduates. Corporations typically hiring largest numbers of graduates include General Dynamics, Arthur Andersen, Exxon, Mobil, Texas Instruments. Career Development Services include help provided in preparation for interviews; student assessment of program reported as fair for career guidance and good for job placement. Alumni reported as active in both career guidance and job placement.

Faculty. About 77% of faculty hold PhD or equivalent.

Student Body. University accepts students from out of state; 93% of students from in state; 472 foreign. An estimated 3% of students reported as Black, 3% Asian, 8% Hispanic, according to most recent data available.

Varsity Sports. Men (Div.I): Baseball, Basketball, Cross Country, Football, Golf, Riflery, Swimming, Tennis, Track. Women (Div.I): Basketball, Cross Country, Golf, Riflery, Soccer, Softball, Swimming, Tennis, Track, Volleyball.

Campus Life. While majority of students are from Texas and commute, the size of the university means that there is still a substantial out-of-state and residential population. Campus is reported to be very attractive with a friendly atmosphere and strong student activities program. Cars allowed but parking reported to be a major concern of students.

About 25% of men and women live in traditional and coed dormitories; rest live in off-campus housing or commute. Intervisitation in men's and women's dormitory rooms limited. Small number of apartments available for married students. There are 28 fraternities, 11 sororities which about 10% of students join. Less than 1% of men and 1% of women live in fraternities and sororities. About 30% of resident students leave campus on weekends.

Annual Costs. Tuition and fees, $1,526 (out-of-state, $5,606); room and board, $4,062. About 66% of students receive financial aid; assistance is typically divided 28% grant/scholarship, 26% loan, 46% work/study. University reports some scholarships awarded on the basis of academic merit alone. *Meeting Costs:* college offers PLUS Loans.

Texas A&M at Galveston

Galveston, Texas 77553 (409) 740-4415

The Galveston campus of Texas A&M is a special purpose institution offering programs in marine and maritime related programs. Most convenient major airport: Houston.

Affiliation: State
UG Enrollment: 1,213 M, W (full-time)
Cost: < $10K
Admission: Selective (+)
Application Deadline: by registration

Admission is selective (+). About 93% of applicants accepted. *Out-of-state* freshman applicants: university actively seeks out-of-state students. State does not limit out-of-state enrollment. *Required:* SAT

or ACT; ACH (English composition, math level I or II) highly recommended. *Entrance programs:* midyear admission, advanced placement, provisional admission. *Apply* by registration. *Transfers* welcome.
Academic Environment. University offers only marine and maritime related programs. Program in Marine Engineering professionally accredited. *Special programs:* license option program, summer school at sea. Calendar: semester.
Undergraduate degrees conferred (74). 41% were in Life Sciences, 28% were in Business and Management, 18% were in Engineering, 8% were in Physical Sciences, 5% were in Renewable Natural Resources.
Graduates Career Data. According to most recent data available, full-time graduate or professional study pursued immediately after graduation by 15% of students; 4% enter medical school; 3% enter business school. *Careers in business and industry* pursued by 40% of graduates. Corporations typically hiring largest numbers of graduates include Exxon, National Marine Fisheries, Dow Chemical. *Career Counseling Program* designed for science and engineering students. Alumni reported as active in job placement but not in career guidance.
Faculty. About 75% of faculty hold PhD or equivalent.
Student Body. College has a geographically diverse student body and actively welcomes students from other areas; about 68% of students from in state. An estimated 1% of students reported as Black, 2% Asian 5% Hispanic, according to most recent data available.
Varsity Sports. Men (Independent): Sailing.
Campus Life. About 73% of men, 73% of women live in coed dorms; rest live in off-campus housing or commute. No fraternities or sororities.
Annual Costs. Tuition and fees, $1,300 (out-of-state, $5,380): room and board $3,384. About 39% of students receive financial aid, according to most recent data available. University reports some scholarships awarded on the basis of academic merit alone. *Meeting Costs:* university offers installment payment plan for tuition and fees.

Texas Christian University

Fort Worth, Texas 76129 **(817) 921-7490; 800-TCU-FROG**

Texas Christian is an independent university historically related to the Christian Church (Disciples of Christ). Students of all creeds and faiths are welcome to the 237-acre campus located in a residential area of a city of 400,000. Most convenient major airport: Dallas-Fort Worth International.

Founded: 1873
Affiliation: Independent (Disciples of Christ)
UG Enrollment: 2,103 M, 2,961 W (full-time); 234 M, 426 W (part-time)
Total Enrollment: 6,822
Cost: < $10K
% Receiving Financial Aid: 67%
Admission: Selective
Application Deadline: November 15

Admission is selective. About 75% of applicants accepted, 29% of these actually enroll; 55% of freshmen graduate in top quarter of high school class, 83% in top two-fifths. *Required:* SAT, essay, interview. Criteria considered in admissions, in order of importance: high school academic record, recommendations, extracurricular activities, standardized test scores, writing sample, geographic diversity; other factors considered: special talents, diverse student body, volunteer and work experience. *Entrance programs:* early admission, midyear admission, deferred admission, advanced placement. About 12% of entering students from private or parochial schools. *Apply* by November 15. *Transfers* welcome; 356 enrolled 1993–94.
Academic Environment. Recent student leader rates student interests as career oriented first, with academic and social interests in second place. Core studies, usually completed during first 2 years, offer students wide choices while distributing 50 semester hours among humanities, natural sciences, social sciences, fine arts, religion, physical education, writing workshop. A very substantial endowment allows TCU to offer an unusually wide variety of programs for a school this size at a very reasonable cost. *Undergraduate studies* offered by AddRan College of Arts and Sciences, Harris College of Nursing, School of Education, Colleges of Fine Arts and Communication, M. J. Neeley School of Business. Degrees offered: bachelors, masters, doctoral. *Majors offered* in 76 areas including environmental earth resources, engineering, fitness promotion, artistic diploma, performer's certificate in piano, software engineering, habilitation of the deaf, speech-language pathology, coordinated dietetics. Average undergraduate class size: 44% under 20, 30% between 20–40, 26% over 40.

About 55% of students entering as freshmen graduate in four years, 66% eventually; 79% of freshmen return for sophomore year. *Special programs:* credit by exam, independent study, informal study abroad, honors, undergraduate research, individualized majors, ranch management certificate program, cooperative work/study programs, combined work/study programs, 3–2 business, engineering, occupational therapy. Adult programs: Office of Education offers programs for part-time adult students and other non-traditional students. *Calendar:* semester, summer school.
Undergraduate degrees conferred (1,191). 22% were in Business and Management, 15% were in Communications, 13% were in Education, 10% were in Social Sciences, 5% were in Health Sciences, 4% were in Letters, 4% were in Home Economics, 4% were in Visual and Performing Arts, 4% were in Psychology, 3% were in Life Sciences, remainder in 15 other fields.
Graduates Career Data. Advanced studies pursued by 21% of students; 17% of these enter medical school; 14% enter law school, 13% enter business school, 56% enter other schools. About 62% of 1992–93 graduates employed. Fields typically hiring largest number of graduates include education, sales, medical, finance/accounting/banking. Career Development Services include career counseling, testing, self-guided computer programs, self-directed inventories, interests and skills surveys, credentials file, on-campus interviews, job listings, resource libraries, alumni contacts, career week, workshops.
Faculty. About 93% of faculty hold PhD or equivalent. About 35% of undergraduate classes taught by tenured faculty. About 33% of teaching faculty are female.
Student Body. University seeks a national student body; 70% of students from in state; 4% Foreign. An estimated 47% of students reported as Protestant, 14% Catholic, 29% unaffiliated, 10% other; 4% as Black, 5% Hispanic, 2% Asian, 4% other minority.
Religious Orientation. Texas Christian is an independent institution related to the Christian Church; 3 hours of religion required of all students; attendance at religious programs voluntary.
Varsity Sports. Men (Div.I): Baseball, Basketball, Cross Country, Diving, Football, Golf, Soccer, Swimming, Tennis, Track. Women (Div.I): Basketball, Cross Country, Diving, Golf, Soccer, Swimming, Tennis, Track.
Campus Life. Limited intervisitation in both men's and women's dorms. Alcohol restricted to dorm rooms for students over 21. Cars permitted.

About 29% of men, 34% of women live in traditional dormitories; 64% of men, 58% of women commute. Freshmen given preference in college housing if all students cannot be accommodated. There are 10 fraternities, 12 sororities on campus which about 29% of men, 38% of women join; 7% of men, 8% of women live in fraternities and sororities. About 10% of resident students leave campus on weekends.
Annual Costs. Tuition and fees, $8,970; room and board, $3,210; estimated $2,446 other, exclusive of travel. About 67% of students receive financial aid; average amount of assistance, $7,469. Assistance is typically divided 81% scholarship/grant, 6% loan, 13% work. University reports 807 scholarships awarded for academic merit, 176 for special talents. *Meeting Costs:* university offers extended payment option.

Texas College

Tyler, Texas 75702 **(214) 593-8311**

A church-related, liberal arts college, located in a city of 60,000, 100 miles east of Dallas; founded as a college for Negroes and still serving a predominantly Black student body.

Founded: 1894
Affiliation: Christian Methodist Episcopal
UG Enrollment: 410 M, W (full-time)
Cost: < $10K
Admission: Non-selective
Application Deadline: July 15

Admission. Graduates of accredited high schools with 16 units (10 in academic subjects) eligible; others admitted by examination; 92% of applicants accepted, 54% of these actually enroll; 40% of freshmen

graduate in top fifth of high school class, according to most recent data available. *Required:* ACT. *Apply* by July 15. *Transfers* welcome.
Academic Environment. *Degrees:* AB, BS. About 3–5% of general education requirements for graduation are elective; distribution requirements fairly numerous. About 70–75% of students entering as freshmen graduate eventually; 20% of freshmen do not return for sophomore year. *Calendar:* semester, summer school.
Undergraduate degrees conferred (40). 38% were in Education, 20% were in Social Sciences, 13% were in Business and Management, 10% were in Public Affairs, 8% were in Visual and Performing Arts, 5% were in Computer and Engineering Related Technology, 3% were in Mathematics, 3% were in Life Sciences, 3% were in Letters.
Student Body. College does not seek a national student body; more than 90% of students from South, according to most recent data available.
Religious Orientation. College is a church-related institution; 6 hours of religion required of all students.
Campus Life. About 55% of men, 65% of women live in traditional dormitories; no coed dormitories; rest live in off-campus housing or commute, according to most recent data available. Intervisitation in men's dormitory rooms limited; no intervisitation in women's dormitory rooms. There are 4 fraternities, 4 sororities on campus which about 10% of men, 12% of women join; they provide no residence facilities.
Annual Costs. Tuition and fees, $3,605; room and board, $2,430.

Texas Lutheran College

Seguin, Texas 78155 **(210) 372-8050**

A church-related, liberal arts college located in a town of 16,000, 32 miles east of San Antonio. Most convenient major airport: San Antonio.

Founded: 1891
Affiliation: Evangelical Lutheran Church in America
UG Enrollment: 357 M, 538 W (full-time); 31 M, 97 W (part-time)
Cost: < $10K
% Receiving Financial Aid: 89%
Admission: Non-selective
Application Deadline: August 1

Admission. About 86% of applicants accepted, 46% of these actually enroll; 45% of freshmen graduate in top fifth of high school class, 69% in top two-fifths. Average freshman scores: SAT, 435 verbal, 498 mathematical; ACT, 22 composite. *Required:* SAT or ACT, minimum H.S. GPA. Criteria considered in admissions, in order of importance: high school academic record, standardized test scores, writing sample, recommendations. *Entrance programs:* early admission, midyear admission, advanced placement. About 2% of freshmen from private schools, 10% parochial schools. *Apply* by August 1; rolling admissions. *Transfers* welcome; 54 enrolled 1993–94.
Academic Environment. Scholars Program permits selected freshmen to plan individualized curriculum that can eliminate many of the usual degree requirements. Degrees offered: associates, bachelors. *Majors offered* include accounting, business, education, secretarial sciences, collateral international studies. General education requirements for liberal arts include core of freshman English and Exploring the Arts and Sciences, as well as 45–49 hours of distribution requirements. Average undergraduate class size: 40% under 20, 55% between 20–40, 5% over 40. About 40% of students entering as freshmen graduate eventually, according to most recent data available. *Special programs:* CLEP, independent study, study abroad, honors, undergraduate research, 3-year degree, individualized majors, program in Mexican American studies, Washington Semester. *Calendar:* semester, summer school.
Undergraduate degrees conferred (211). 36% were in Business and Management, 16% were in Education, 9% were in Social Sciences, 9% were in Physical Sciences, 8% were in Communications, 5% were in Psychology, 4% were in Life Sciences, 4% were in Computer and Engineering Related Technology, 3% were in Letters, remainder in 5 other fields.
Graduates Career Data. Advanced studies pursued by 22% of students. About 48% of 1992–93 graduates employed. Fields typically hiring largest number of graduates include business, accounting, education.
Faculty. About 68% of faculty hold PhD or equivalent. About 33% of teaching faculty are female; 13% Hispanic.
Student Body. College seeks a national student body; 87% of students from South, 4% Midwest; 5% Foreign. An estimated 70% of students reported as Protestant, 18% Catholic, 12% other; 3% as Black, 13% Hispanic, 1% Asian, 6% other minority.
Religious Orientation. Texas Lutheran is a church-related institution; 6 hours of theology required of all students; chapel, providing worship services and other religious activities, is oldest college tradition.
Varsity Sports. Men (NAIA, Div.I): Baseball, Basketball, Golf, Soccer, Tennis. Women (NAIA, Div.I): Basketball, Soccer, Softball, Tennis, Volleyball.
Campus Life. As a general policy, all single students are required to live in college residence halls. Alcohol prohibited on campus; cars allowed. About 52% of men, 64% of women live in traditional dormitories; 28% men, 30% women live in on-campus apartments, rest commute. Intervisitation in men's and women's dormitory rooms limited. There are 5 fraternities, 4 sororities on campus which about 19% of men, 17% of women join; they provide no residence facilities. About 50% of students leave campus on weekends, according to most recent data available.
Annual Costs. Tuition and fees, $7,410; room and board, $3,250; estimated $1,000 other, exclusive of travel. About 89% of students receive financial aid; average amount of assistance, $6,200. Assistance is typically divided 60% grant/scholarship, 40% loan/work. College reports some scholarships awarded for academic merit. *Meeting Costs:* college offers payment plan, parental loans.

Texas Southern University

Houston, Texas 77004 **(713) 527-7070**

A state-supported university, located in Houston; founded as a college for Negroes and still serving a predominantly Black student body.

Founded: 1947
Affiliation: State
UG Enrollment: 2,143 M, 3,441 W (full-time); 1,170 M, 1,931 W (part-time)
Total Enrollment: 10,160
Cost: < $10K
% Receiving Financial Aid: 72%
Admission: Non-selective
Application Deadline: Aug. 5

Admission. Graduates of standard high schools with 15 units admitted; about 48% of applicants accepted, 77% of these actually enroll. Average freshman scores: SAT, 326 M, 325 W verbal, 384 M, 365 W mathematical; ACT, 12.1 M, 12.2 W composite, 9.6 M, 9.7 W mathematical. *Required:* SAT or ACT, minimum H.S. GPA. Criteria considered in admissions, in order of importance: standardized test scores, high school academic record, recommendations. *Out-of-state* freshman applicants: university seeks students from out-of-state. State does not limit out-of-state enrollment. About 23% of out-of-state applicants accepted, 77% of these actually enroll. States from which most out-of-state students are drawn include California, Louisiana, Illinois, Florida, Mississippi. *Entrance programs:* early decision, early admission, midyear admission. *Apply* by August 5. *Transfers* welcome; 542 enrolled 1993–94.
Academic Environment. *Undergraduate studies* offered by College of Arts and Sciences, schools of Business, Pharmacy, Technology. About 10% of general education requirements for graduation are elective; no distribution requirements. Degrees offered: bachelors, masters, doctoral. Average undergraduate class size: 20% under 20, 60% between 20–40, 20% over 40. About 9% of students entering as freshmen graduate eventually; 69% return for sophomore year. *Special programs:* independent study, honors, undergraduate research, internships, work study programs. *Calendar:* semester, summer school.
Undergraduate degrees conferred (514). 24% were in Business and Management, 15% were in Health Sciences, 15% were in Education, 9% were in Engineering and Engineering Related Technology, 6% were in Communications, 5% were in Protective Services, 5% were in Psychology, 4% were in Social Sciences, 4% were in Home Economics, 3% were in Computer and Engineering Related Technology, 3% were in Life Sciences, remainder in 12 other fields.
Graduates Career Data. Advanced studies pursued by 50% of students; 1% enter medical school; 1% enter dental school; 10%

enter law school; 17% enter business school; 1% enter other schools. Fields typically hiring largest number of graduates include business, sciences, education. Career Development Services include resume preparation, job fairs, potential employer information.
Student Body. University seeks a national student body; 84% of students from Texas; 89% South; 9% Foreign. An estimated 90% of students reported as Protestant, 10% Catholic, according to most recent data available; 90% Black, 3% Hispanic, 2% Asian, 3% other minority.
Varsity Sports. Men: Baseball, Basketball, Cross Country, Football, Golf, Soccer, Tennis, Track, Volleyball. Women: Cross Country, Golf, Softball, Tennis, Track, Volleyball.
Campus Life. About 2% of men, 3% of women live in traditional dormitories; no coed dormitories; rest commute. Freshmen given preference in college housing if all students cannot be accommodated. No intervisitation in men's or women's dormitory rooms. There are 4 fraternities, 4 sororities on campus which about 15% of men, 15% of women join; 2% of men, 3% of women live in fraternities and sororities. About 50% of resident students leave campus on weekends, according to most recent data available.
Annual Costs. Tuition and fees, $1,274 (out-of-state, $5,354); room and board, $3,300; estimated $2,000 other, exclusive of travel. About 72% of students receive financial aid. University reports 4% of scholarships awarded for academic merit, 2% for special talents, 5% for need.

Texas Tech University

Lubbock, Texas 79409 **(806) 742-3661**

A state-supported institution, Texas Tech was granted university status in 1969. Its campus of 1,839 acres, one of the largest in the U.S., is located in a city of 186,000, 300 miles west of Dallas. Most convenient major airport: Lubbock International.

Founded: 1923
Affiliation: State
UG Enrollment: 9,148 M, 7,637 W (full-time); 1,375 M, 1,405 W (part-time)
Total Enrollment: 24,007
Cost: < $10K
% Receiving Financial Aid: 46%
Admission: Non-selective
Application Deadline: Aug. 15

Admission. Graduates of accredited high schools with 15 units appropriate to area of specialization eligible; about 80% of applicants accepted, 59% of these actually enroll; 46% of freshmen graduate in top fifth of high school class, 79% in top two-fifths. Average freshman scores: SAT, 442 M, 436 W verbal, 529 M, 484 W mathematical; 21% of freshmen score above 500 verbal, 3% above 600, 54% score above 500 mathematical, 17% above 600, 3% above 700; ACT, 23 M, 22 W composite. *Required:* SAT or ACT. *Out-of-state* freshman applicants: university actively seeks students from out-of-state. State does not limit out-of-state enrollment. About 69% of out-of-state applicants accepted, 53% of these actually enroll. States from which most out-of-state students are drawn include New Mexico, California, Colorado, Oklahoma. *Entrance programs:* early decision, early admission, midyear admission, advanced placement. *Apply* by August 15; rolling admissions. *Transfers* welcome; 1,906 enrolled 1993–94.
Academic Environment. *Undergraduate studies* offered by colleges of Arts and Sciences, Agricultural Sciences and Natural Resources,, Architecture, Business Administration, Education, Engineering, Human Sciences. Degrees offered: bachelors, masters, doctoral. *Majors offered* include advertising art, computer science, biochemistry, dance, geography, geophysics, journalism, Latin American studies, microbiology, public address and group communication, restaurant, hotel and institutional management, sports medicine, social welfare, speech pathology and audiology, theater arts. Distribution requirements fairly numerous. Average undergraduate class size: 29% under 20, 51% between 20–40, 20% over 40. About 14% of students entering as freshmen graduate in four years, 39% in six years; 76% of freshmen return for sophomore year. *Special programs:* CLEP, independent study, study abroad, honors, undergraduate research, individualized majors, 3–2 in engineering, dual degree, dual major, accelerated degrees, second degrees. Adult programs: Seniors Academy. *Calendar:* semester, summer school.
Undergraduate degrees conferred (3,104). 25% were in Business and Management, 22% were in Education, 7% were in Communications, 6% were in Engineering, 5% were in Social Sciences, 5% were in Architecture and Environmental Design, 4% were in Home Economics, 4% were in Agribusiness and Agricultural Production, 3% were in Letters, 3% were in Life Sciences, 3% were in Psychology, remainder in 16 other fields.
Graduates Career Data. Advanced studies pursued by 27% of students immediately after graduation, according to most recent data available. *Careers in business and industry* pursued by 60% of graduates. Career Development Services available.
Faculty. About 87% of faculty hold PhD or equivalent. About 35% of undergraduate classes taught by tenured faculty. About 31% of teaching faculty are female; 3% Hispanic, 13% other minority.
Student Body. University seeks a national student body; 92% of students from Texas; 3% Foreign. An estimated 3% of students reported as Black, 9% Hispanic, 2% Asian, 4% other minority.
Varsity Sports. Men (Div. I): Baseball, Basketball, Cross Country, Football, Golf, Tennis, Track. Women (Div. I): Basketball, Cross Country, Golf, Tennis, Track, Volleyball.
Campus Life. Interest in fraternities/sororities and varsity athletics remains fairly strong. Drinking permitted for students over 21 in conformity with state law; cars allowed. About 15% of men, 20% of women live in traditional dormitories; 4% of men, 3% of women live in coed dormitories; rest live in off-campus housing or commute. Intervisitation in men's and women's dormitory rooms limited. Sexes segregated in coed dormitories by wing. There are 24 fraternities, 15 sororities on campus which about 12% of men, 12% of women join; they provide no residence facilities.
Annual Costs. Tuition and fees, based on 15 credit hours, $1,550 (out-of-state, $5,630); room and board, $3,688; estimated $530 other, exclusive of travel. About 46% of students receive financial aid; average amount of assistance, $2,000. College reports some scholarships awarded for academic merit.

University of Texas System

Austin, Texas 78701

The University of Texas System includes 7 liberal arts and professional universities at Arlington, Austin, Dallas, El Paso, Permian Basin (Odessa), San Antonio, and Tyler, and 4 Health Science Centers at Dallas, Galveston, Houston, and San Antonio. The System also includes the Cancer Center located in Houston, the Health Center at Tyler, and the Institute of Texan Cultures at San Antonio.

University of Texas at Austin

Austin, Texas 78712 **(512) 471-7601 for freshman; (512) 471-1711 for transfers**

One of the nation's largest universities, Texas is also one of the two or three most eminent institutions in the South and Southwest. Although its undergraduate student body is drawn largely from the region, a number of graduate departments have long attracted faculty and students from all parts of the U.S. and abroad. The university has received worldwide recognition for its special library collections in a number of fields. The campus in Austin, the state capital (pop.400,000), includes a wide range of undergraduate, graduate, and professional schools and colleges. Most convenient major airport: Robert Mueller (Austin).

Founded: 1883
Affiliation: State
UG Enrollment: 15,770 M, 14,247 W (undergraduate); 2,739 M, 2,450 W (part-time)
Total Enrollment: 48,555
Cost: < $10K
% Receiving Financial Aid: 50%
Admission: Highly Selective
Application Deadline: February 1

Admission is highly selective for Architecture; very (+) selective for Engineering; very selective for Liberal Arts, Natural Science, Business, Communications; selective (+) for Fine Arts; selective for Education, Social Work. For all schools, 65% of applicants accepted, 56% of these actually enroll; 47% of freshmen graduate in top tenth of high school class, 83% in top fourth. Average freshman scores: SAT, 523 verbal, 603 mathematical; 61% of freshmen score above 500 on verbal, 22% above 600, 3% above 700; 89% score above 500 on mathematical, 53% above 600, 17% above 700; ACT scores: 25.4 composite.

For Liberal Arts, 68% of applicants accepted, 54% of these actually enroll; 73% of freshmen graduate in top fifth of high school class, 94% in top two-fifths. Average freshman SAT scores: 537 verbal, 569 mathematical; 57% of freshmen score above 500 on verbal, 27% above 600, 4% above 700; 79% score above 500 on mathematical, 41% above 600, 8% above 700,according to most recent data available.

For Architecture, 37% of applicants accepted, 64% of these actually enroll; 92% of freshmen graduate in top fifth of high school class, all in top two-fifths. Average freshman SAT scores: 573 verbal, 647 mathematical; 87% of freshmen score above 500 on verbal, 39% above 600, 4% above 700; 98% score above 500 on mathematical, 89% above 600, 26% above 700, according to most recent data available.

For Business Administration, 65% of applicants accepted, 61% of these actually enroll; 75% of freshmen graduate in top fifth of high school class, 95% in top two-fifths. Average freshman SAT scores: 490 verbal, 569 mathematical; 50% of freshmen score above 500 on verbal, 11% above 600, 1% above 700; 81% score above 500 on mathematical, 40% above 600, 5% above 700, according to most recent data available.

For Communication, 65% of applicants accepted, 66% of these actually enroll; 78% of freshmen graduate in top fifth of high school class, 98% in top two-fifths. Average freshman SAT scores: 521 verbal, 539 mathematical; 64% of freshmen score above 500 on verbal, 18% above 600, 1% above 700; 70% score above 500 on mathematical, 25% above 600, 2% above 700, according to most recent data available.

For Education, 57% of applicants accepted, 41% of these actually enroll; 76% of freshmen graduate in top fifth of high school class, 95% in top two-fifths. Average freshman SAT scores: 482 verbal, 528 mathematical; 39% of freshmen score above 500 on verbal, 10% above 600; 64% score above 500 on mathematical, 22% above 600, according to most recent data available.

For Engineering, 68% of applicants accepted, 58% of these actually enroll; 82% of freshmen graduate in top fifth of high school class, 97% in top two-fifths. Average freshman SAT scores: 516 verbal, 632 mathematical; 59% of freshmen score above 500 on verbal, 21% above 600, 3% above 700; 94% score above 500 on mathematical, 70% above 600, 24% above 700, according to most recent data available.

For Fine Arts, 66% of applicants accepted, 63% of these actually enroll; 66% of freshmen graduate in top fifth of high school class, 95% in top two-fifths. Average freshman SAT scores: 518 verbal, 536 mathematical; 58% of freshmen score above 500 on verbal, 22% above 600, 2% above 700; 70% score above 500 on mathematical, 24% above 600, 2% above 700, according to most recent data available.

For Natural Sciences, 70% of applicants accepted, 52% of these actually enroll; 85% of freshmen graduate in top fifth of high school class, 97% in top two-fifths. Average freshman SAT scores: 506 verbal, 586 mathematical; 54% of freshmen score above 500 on verbal, 16% above 600, 2% above 700; 83% score above 500 on mathematical, 48% above 600, 15% above 700, according to most recent data available.

For Nursing, 63% of applicants accepted, 54% of these actually enroll; 80% of freshmen graduate in top fifth of high school class, 97% in top two-fifths. Average freshman SAT scores: 436 verbal, 480 mathematical; 21% of freshmen score above 500 on verbal; 47% score above 500 on mathematical, 8% above 600, according to most recent data available.

For Social Work, 46% of applicants accepted, 53% of these actually enroll; 78% of freshmen graduate in top fifth of high school class, all in top two-fifths. Average freshman SAT scores: 459 verbal, 524 mathematical; 33% of freshmen score above 500 on verbal; 44% score above 500 on mathematical, 33% above 600, according to most recent data available.

Required: SAT or ACT, and selected ACH for some students, essay, high school transcript with class rank. Criteria considered in admissions, in order of importance: standardized test scores and high school academic record, extracurricular activities, writing sample, recommendations; other factors considered: audition for music majors. *Out-of-state* freshman applicants: university welcomes students from out-of-state on a limited basis. *Out-of-state* applicants must meet some special requirements for admission. About 42% of out-of-state applicants accepted, 58% of these actually enroll. *Entrance programs:* midyear admission. *Apply* by February 1; rolling admissions. *Transfers* welcome; 1,900 enrolled 1993–94.

Academic Environment. Pressures for academic achievement appear to vary from moderate to moderately intense, depending on the school or college—likely to be most rigorous in those divisions sending substantial numbers to graduate and professional schools. As with many large state universities, the range of course offerings in professional/vocational areas is very great; it is almost as large in the arts and sciences. Student concerns reported include large classes and "red tape", but students find faculty to be accessible. Academic strengths are said to be linguistics, German, Spanish, accounting, petroleum engineering, computer sciences. Student body is said to be primarily oriented toward occupational/professional goals. Student mix is so diverse as to make it a cosmopolitan student culture. The university boasts a graduate school of increasing eminence. Texas today offers wide-ranging academic opportunities to the student—but unless the student is mature, well-directed, and persistent, he may never discover them. *Undergraduate studies* offered to freshmen in colleges and schools listed above. Distribution requirements for Liberal Arts fairly numerous: students required to complete work in 4 broad areas: 18 hours in social sciences/history, 15 hours in science/mathematics, 6 hours in humanities/area studies, 9 hours in English, foreign language proficiency, 4 semesters of physical education. Requirements vary with other degree programs. Degrees offered: bachelors, masters, doctoral.

About 31% of students entering as freshmen graduate in four years, 64% eventually; 83% of freshmen return for sophomore year. *Special programs:* CLEP, honors, study abroad, credit by examination, 6-year combined BS/BArch program, area and ethnic studies (including Asian, European, international, Middle Eastern). *Calendar:* semester, summer school.

Undergraduate degrees conferred (7,492). 21% were in Business and Management, 16% were in Social Sciences, 12% were in Communications, 9% were in Engineering, 6% were in Psychology, 5% were in Life Sciences, 5% were in Letters, 4% were in Education, 4% were in Health Sciences, 4% were in Visual and Performing Arts, remainder in 12 other fields.

Faculty. About 92% of faculty hold PhD or equivalent. About 28% of teaching faculty are female; 3% Black, 10% Hispanic.

Student Body. University does not seek a national student body; 91% of students from in state; 4% Foreign. An estimated 4% of students reported as Black, 6% Asian, 11% Hispanic, 8% other minority, according to most recent data available.

Varsity Sports. Men (Div.I): Baseball, Basketball, Cross Country, Diving, Football, Golf, Swimming, Tennis, Track. Women (Div.I): Basketball, Cross Country, Diving, Golf, Softball, Swimming, Tennis, Track, Volleyball.

Campus Life. Students have some voice in setting policies governing campus social life. Wide variety of cultural and intellectual activities on campus as well as in the city of Austin. Free shuttles and public transportation make the many resources of the area easily accessible to students. The University serves as a cultural center to the community at large as well to the students, faculty and staff. A Performing Arts Center is host to Broadway plays, the Austin Civic Opera, the Austin Symphony and visiting musical and dance groups throughout the year. University leaves students free to choose where to live. Ombudsman available to students. Limited intervisitation privileges. Cars allowed, but parking is reported to be a problem for both residents and commuters.

About 2% of men, 3% of women live in traditional dormitories; 6% of students live in coed dormitories; rest live in off-campus housing or commute. Freshmen given preference in college housing if all students cannot be accommodated. Sexes segregated in coed dormitories by wing. There are 28 fraternities, 15 sororities which about 14% of men, 14% of women join; 14% of men and women live in fraternities and sororities.

Annual Costs. Tuition and fees, $1,500 (out-of-state, $5,000); room and board, $3,600; estimated $2,800 other, exclusive of travel. About 50% of students receive financial aid; average amount of assistance, $4,200. Assistance is typically divided 23% scholarship, 22% grant, 40% loan, 15% work. University reports 7,000 scholarships awarded for academic merit, 1,500 for need.

University of Texas at Arlington

Arlington, Texas 76019 (817) 273-3275

A state-supported institution, located in a city of 250,000, 18 miles west of Dallas, Texas at Arlington has been part of the University of Texas System since 1965. Most convenient major airport: Dallas-Fort Worth International.

Founded: 1895
Affiliation: State
UG Enrollment: 5,704 M, 5,261 W (full-time); 4,278 M, 4,153 W (part-time)
Total Enrollment: 19,396
Cost: < $10K
% Receiving Financial Aid: 30%
Admission: Non-selective
Application Deadline: Aug. 1

Admission. Graduates of accredited high schools with 15 units eligible; 78% of applicants accepted, 57% of these actually enroll; 42% of freshmen graduate in top fifth of high school class, 75% in top two-fifths. Average freshman scores: SAT, 432 M, 414 W verbal, 520 M, 464 W mathematical; ACT, 21 M, 20 W composite. *Required:* SAT or ACT. Criteria considered in admissions, in order of importance: high school academic record, standardized test scores, recommendations. *Out-of-state* freshman applicants: university actively seeks students from out-of-state. State does not limit out-of-state enrollment. States from which most out-of-state students are drawn include New York, California, Oklahoma. *Entrance programs:* early admission, midyear admission, advanced placement. About 3% of entering students from private schools, 3% from parochial schools. *Apply* by August 1; rolling admissions. *Transfers* welcome; 3,730 enrolled 1993–94.

Academic Environment. Core requirements for liberal arts program include 9 hours English, 6 hours history, 6 hours political science, 6 hours mathematics, 3 hours social sciences, 3 hours fine arts. *Undergraduate studies* offered by colleges of Liberal Arts, Business Administration, Engineering, Science. Degrees offered: bachelors, masters, doctoral. *Majors offered* in addition to usual studies include architecture, social work, interdisciplinary studies.

About 28% of students entering as freshmen graduate eventually; 66% of freshmen return for sophomore year. *Special programs:* CLEP, study abroad, 3-year degree, individualized majors, credit by examination, honors in business administration, cooperative education, cross registration with UTHSC-Dallas. Calendar: semester, summer school.

Undergraduate degrees conferred (2,742). 30% were in Business and Management, 12% were in Engineering, 11% were in Social Sciences, 8% were in Communications, 8% were in Health Sciences, 5% were in Multi/Interdisciplinary Studies, 4% were in Architecture and Environmental Design, 3% were in Letters, 3% were in Visual and Performing Arts, 3% were in Life Sciences, 3% were in Psychology, remainder in 8 other fields.

Graduates Career Data. Advanced studies pursued by 45% of students; 2% enter medical school; 1% enter dental school; 2% enter law school; 20% enter business school. Business schools typically enrolling largest numbers of graduates include U. of Texas, SMU, Texas A&M. Corporations typically hiring largest numbers of graduates include General Dynamics, Texas Instruments, Vought.

Faculty. About 88% of faculty hold PhD or equivalent. About 53% of undergraduate classes taught by tenured faculty. About 30% of teaching faculty are female; 2% Black, 3% Hispanic, 11% other minority.

Student Body. University does not seek a national student body; 93% of students from Texas; 92% South; 7% Foreign. An estimated 7% of students reported as Black, 6% Hispanic, 8% Asian, 7% other minority. Average age of undergraduate student: 26.

Varsity Sports. Men (Div.I): Baseball, Basketball, Cross Country, Golf, Tennis, Track. Women (Div.I): Basketball, Cross Country, Softball, Track, Volleyball.

Campus Life. Very small percentage of students live on campus, nearly half live in off-campus housing, rest commute. Curfew only for freshmen; intervisitation limited. Alcohol prohibited; cars allowed. About 2% of men, 1% of women live in traditional dormitories; 1% each men, women live in coed dormitories; 4% each men, women live in off-campus college-related housing. There are 17 fraternities, 8 sororities on campus which about 8% of men, 4% of women join. About 33% of resident students leave campus on weekends, according to most recent data available.

Annual Costs. Tuition and fees, $1,190 (out-of-state, $4,080); room and board, $3,200; estimated $750 other, exclusive of travel. About 30% of students receive financial aid; average amount of assistance, $2,800. Assistance is typically divided 45% scholarship/grant, 40% loan, 15% work/study program. University reports some scholarships awarded for academic merit alone. *Meeting Costs:* University offers installment payment plan.

University of Texas at El Paso

El Paso, Texas 79968 **(915) 747-5576**

A state-supported university, located in a city of 382,000. Most convenient major airport: El Paso International.

Founded: 1913
Affiliation: State
Total Enrollment: 17,163
Cost: < $10K
% Receiving Financial Aid: 53%
Admission: Non-selective
Application Deadline: July 1

Admission. Graduates of accredited high schools with 16 units, rank in top half of class, and combined SAT score of 700 accepted; those who rank in lower half of class must have combined SAT score of 800; others admitted provisionally. About 82% of applicants accepted, 77% of these actually enroll. *Required:* SAT or ACT. *Apply* by July 1. *Transfers* welcome.

Academic Environment. *Undergraduate studies* offered by schools of Business, Education, Engineering, Liberal Arts, Sciences. About 40% of freshmen do not return for sophomore year. *Special programs:* CLEP, honors, undergraduate research, study abroad, independent study, Inter-American Sciences and Humanities Program. *Calendar:* semester, summer school.

Undergraduate degrees conferred (1,551). 29% were in Education, 21% were in Business and Management, 11% were in Engineering, 7% were in Health Sciences, 5% were in Protective Services, 4% were in Letters, 4% were in Social Sciences, 3% were in Communications, 3% were in Psychology, 3% were in Life Sciences, remainder in 9 other fields.

Faculty. About 89% of faculty hold PhD or equivalent.

Student Body. About 90% of students from Texas; 900 foreign students according to most recent data available.

Varsity Sports. Men (Div.IA): Basketball, Football, Golf, Riflery, Tennis, Track. Women (Div.IA): Basketball, Golf, Riflery, Tennis, Track, Volleyball.

Campus Life. About 2% of students live in coed dormitories; rest live in off-campus housing or commute.

Annual Costs. Tuition and fees, $1,408 (out-of-state, $5,488); room and board, $3,550. About 53% of students receive financial aid. College reports some scholarships awarded for academic merit alone. *Meeting Costs:* college offers installment payment plan.

University of Texas—Pan American

Edinburg, Texas 78539 **(210) 381-2011**

A state-supported school, located in a town of 30,000, 9 miles from the Mexican border, with a second campus in Brownsville. Unusual international flavor, with Spanish spoken as frequently as English. Previously known as Pan American University.

Founded: 1927
Affiliation: State
UG Enrollment: 3,047 M, 3,982 W (full-time); 2,402 M, 3,342 W (part-time)
Total Enrollment: 13,705
Cost: < $10K
% Receiving Financial Aid: 70%
Admission: Non-selective
Application Deadline: July 15

Admission. Graduates of accredited high schools with 16 units (11 in academic subjects) eligible; almost all applicants accepted, 53% of these actually enroll; 7% of freshmen graduate in top fifth of high school class, 22% in top two-fifths. Average freshman ACT scores: 17 M, 17 W composite. *Required:* ACT. Criteria considered in admissions: standardized test scores. *Out-of-state* freshman applicants: university does not seek out-of-state students. State does not limit out-of-state enrollment. About 199 out-of-state students enrolled 1993–94. States from which most out-of-state applicants are drawn include California, Michigan. *Entrance programs:* early admissions. *Apply* by July 15. *Transfers* welcome; 850 enrolled 1993–94.

Academic Environment. Degrees offered: associates, bachelors, masters, doctoral. Average undergraduate class size: 15% under 20, 80% between 20–40, 5% over 40. *Majors offered* in addition to usual studies include electrical, mechanical, and manufacturing engineering; international business, Latin American studies, Mexican-American heritage. UT Pan American is a catalyst for economic development, health care improvement, and cultural activity for the region; the campus hosts the Center for Entrepreneurship and Economic Development, the Small Business Development Center, and the Small Business Institute, and a variety of other programs, which allow students and faculty to provide services and consultation to area businesses and residents. About 26% of entering freshmen graduate in six years, 44% eventually; 63% of freshmen return for sophomore year. *Special programs:* CLEP, honors, individualized majors, study abroad. *Calendar:* semester, summer school.

Undergraduate degrees conferred (831). 41% were in Education, 27% were in Business and Management, 5% were in Social Sciences, 4% were in Life Sciences, 4% were in Protective Services, 3% were in Allied Health, 2% were in Psychology, remainder in 11 other fields.

Graduates Career Data. Career Development Services include career days, career counseling, cooperative education program.

Faculty. About 33% of teaching faculty are female, 23% Hispanic, 7% other minority.

Student Body. University seeks a national student body; 98% of students from Texas; 1.4% Foreign. An estimated 87% of students reported as Hispanic, less than 3% other minority. Average age of undergraduate student: 24.

Varsity Sports. Men (Div. I): Baseball, Basketball, Cross Country, Golf, Soccer, Tennis, Track. Women (Div. I): Basketball, Cross Country, Golf, Tennis, Track, Volleyball.

Campus Life. About 1% each of men, women live in traditional dormitories; no coed dormitories; rest commute. Intervisitation in men's and women's dormitory rooms limited. There are 2 fraternities and 1 sorority which less than 1% of students join; less than 1% of men live in fraternities. About 80% of resident students leave campus on weekends.

Annual Costs. Tuition and fees, $1,334 (out-of-state, $4,444); room and board, $3,000; estimated $2,769 other, exclusive of travel. About 70% of students receive financial aid. University reports 974 scholarships awarded for academic merit, 220 for special needs alone.

University of Texas at San Antonio

San Antonio, Texas 78249 (210) 691-4706

San Antonio is a commuting institution serving the immediate community, including a substantial Hispanic population.

Founded: 1968
Affiliation: State
UG Enrollment: 4,472 M, 4,903 W (full-time); 2,426 M, 3,031 W (part-time)
Total Enrollment: 17,097
Cost: < $10K
% Receiving Financial Aid: 22%
Admission: Non-selective
Application Deadline: July 1

Admission. Graduates of accredited high schools with acceptable class rank/test score ratio eligible; out-of-state students must have graduated in top half of high school class. About 74% of applicants accepted, 54% of these actually enroll. Average freshman scores: SAT, 425 M, 417 W verbal, 495 M, 456 W mathematical; ACT, 21 M, 19 W composite. *Required:* SAT or ACT, minimum H.S. rank. Criteria considered in admissions: standardized test scores, class rank. *Out-of-state* applicants: university does not seek students from out-of-state. State does not limit out-of-state enrollment. About 68% of out-of-state students accepted, 56% of these enroll. States from which most out-of-state applicants are drawn include California, New York, Florida, Illinois.Entrance programs: advanced placement. About 5% of freshmen from private schools. *Apply* by July 1. *Transfers* welcome; 9,697 enrolled 1993–94.

Academic Environment. Degrees offered: bachelors, masters, doctoral. University offers some 31 degree programs, 14 of which are terminal/occupational courses of study. About 21% of entering freshmen graduate in four years; 61% return for sophomore year. *Special programs:* study abroad, internships.

Undergraduate degrees conferred (1,755). 34% were in Business and Management, 18% were in Education, 9% were in Social Sciences, 6% were in Letters, 6% were in Psychology, 6% were in Life Sciences, 4% were in Protective Services, 4% were in Engineering, 3% were in Allied Health, remainder in 8 other fields.

Faculty. About 98% of tenure track faculty hold PhD or equivalent. About 52% of undergraduate classes taught by tenured faculty. About 27% of teaching faculty are female; 13% Hispanic, 10% other minority.

Student Body. About 98% of students from in state according to most recent data available. An estimated 24% of students reported as being Protestant, 41% Catholic, 3% Jewish, 1% Muslim, 11% unaffiliated, 20% other; 3% Black, 33% Hispanic, 3% Asian, 1% other minority. Average age of undergraduate student: 25.

Varsity Sports. Men (Div.IA): Baseball, Basketball, Cross Country, Golf, Tennis, Track. Women (Div.IA): Basketball, Cross Country, Softball, Tennis, Track, Volleyball.

Campus Life. About 3% of students live in coed dormitories; 5% men, 6% women live in off-campus college-related housing; rest commute. About 1% of students live in fraternities and sororities.

Annual Costs. Tuition and fees, $1,360 (out-of-state, $4,624); room and board, $5,220; estimated $8,642 other, exclusive of travel. About 22% of students receive financial aid; average amount of assistance, $5,675. Assistance is typically divided 10% scholarship, 30% grant, 57% loan, 3% work. *Meeting Costs:* university offers installment plan.

Texas Wesleyan University

Fort Worth, Texas 76105 (817) 531-4444

A church-related institution, located in a city of 400,000. Formerly Texas Wesleyan College.

Founded: 1890
Affiliation: United Methodist
UG Enrollment: 470 M, 7340 W (full-time); 144 M, 248 W (part-time)
Total Enrollment: 2,437
Cost: < $10K
Admission: Non-selective
Application Deadline: August 15

Admission. Graduates of accredited high schools with 17 units (15 in academic subjects) eligible; 85% of applicants accepted, 56% of these actually enroll; 41% of freshmen graduate in top fifth of high school class, 72% in top two-fifths. Average freshman scores: SAT, 415 verbal, 426 mathematical; ACT, 20 composite. *Required:* SAT or ACT, minimum H.S. GPA. Criteria considered in admissions, in order of importance: standardized test scores, high school academic record, recommendations, writing sample, extracurricular activities; other factors considered: special talents. *Entrance programs:* early decision, early admission, midyear admission, advanced placement. *Apply* by August 15. *Transfers* welcome.

Academic Environment. Degrees offered: bachelors, masters, doctoral. *Majors offered* include applied legal science. About 26% of general education requirements for graduation are elective; distribution requirements fairly numerous. About 68% of students entering as freshmen graduate eventually; 6% of freshmen do not return for sophomore year, according to most recent data available. *Special programs:* CLEP, study abroad, independent study, 3-year degree. *Calendar:* semester, summer school.

Undergraduate degrees conferred (225). 34% were in Business and Management, 26% were in Education, 8% were in Psychology, 8% were in Communications, 6% were in Social Sciences, 4% were in Life Sciences, 4% were in Visual and Performing Arts, 3% were in Philosophy and Religion, remainder in 6 other fields.

Graduates Career Data. Advanced studies pursued by 15% of graduates. About 89% of 1992–93 graduates employed. Employers typically hiring largest number of graduates include FWISD, City of Fort Worth, Alcon, Bank One.

Faculty. About 80% of faculty hold PhD or equivalent. About 53% of undergraduate classes taught by tenured faculty. About 26% of teaching faculty are female; 1% Black, 3% Hispanic, 2% other minority.

Student Body. College seeks a national student body; 85% of students from South, 10% Middle Atlantic. An estimated 49% of students reported as Protestant, 15% Catholic, 2% Jewish, 23% unaffiliated; 13% Black, 12% Hispanic, 1% Asian, 2% other minority. Average age of undergraduate student: 25.

Religious Orientation. Texas Wesleyan is a church-related institution; 6 hours of Bible required of all students.

Campus Life. About 17% of men, 8% of women live in traditional dormitories; 3% of men, 6% of women live in coed dormitories; rest live in off-campus housing or commute. No intervisitation in men's or women's dormitory rooms; sexes segregated by floor. There are 2 fraternities, 3 sororities on campus which about 10% of men, 10% of women join.

Annual Costs. Tuition and fees, $6,150; room and board, $3,230. *Meeting Costs:* college offers deferred payment plan.

Texas Woman's University

Denton, Texas 76204-0909 **(817) 898-2000**

A state-supported, multipurpose institution, located in a community of 45,000, 35 miles northwest of Dallas. Historically a single-sex institution, the university now accepts male students in its Institute of Health Sciences. Most convenient major airport: Dallas/Fort Worth.

Founded: 1901
Affiliation: State
UG Enrollment: 161 M, 3,630 W (full-time)
104 M, 1,857 W (part-time)
Total Enrollment: 9,702
Cost: < $10K
% Receiving Financial Aid: 57%
Admission: Non-selective
Application Deadline: July 15

Admission. Graduates of accredited high schools with 16 units (9 in academic subjects) and GPA of 2.0 eligible; 79% of applicants accepted, 61% of these actually enroll. Average freshman SAT scores: 12% of freshmen score above 500 verbal, 2% above 600, 22% score above 500 mathematical, 4% above 600. *Required:* SAT or ACT, TASP test. Criteria considered in admissions: standardized test scores; high school GPA is considered if student is first-time-in-college or has less than 12 transferable credits. *Out-of-state* applicants: university does not seek students from out-of-state. State does not limit out-of-state enrollment. About 46% of out-of-state students accepted, 49% of these enroll. States from which most out-of-state applicants are drawn include Louisiana, Oklahoma. *Entrance programs:* early decision, early admission, midyear admission, advanced placement. *Apply* by July 15; rolling admissions. *Transfers* welcome; 1,100 enrolled 1993–94.
Academic Environment. *Undergraduate studies* offered by colleges of Arts and Sciences, Education, Fine Arts, Health, Nutrition, Textiles, and Human Development, Physical Education, and Recreation, schools of Library Science, Occupational Therapy, Physical Therapy, Institute of Health Sciences. All degree programs require 12 hours of English, 6 of American history, 3 of sociology or economics, 6 of government, 4 of kinesiology, 6 in foreign language, mathematics, or science. Degrees offered: bachelors, masters, doctoral. About 14% of entering freshmen graduate in four years, 39% in seven years; 63% of freshmen return for sophomore year. *Special programs:* honors, individualized majors, 3–2 engineering, internships, cross registration with East Texas State U., U. of North Texas. *Calendar:* semester, summer school.
Undergraduate degrees conferred (1,086). 22% were in Education, 21% were in Health Sciences, 14% were in Allied Health, 8% were in Business and Management, 5% were in Social Sciences, 4% were in Life Sciences, 4% were in Home Economics, 4% were in Psychology, 3% were in Public Affairs, remainder in 16 other fields.
Graduates Career Data. Career Development Services include interest appraisals, SIGI computerized guidance system, seminars and workshops, career information days.
Faculty. About 70% of faculty hold PhD or equivalent.
Student Body. University welcomes out-of-state students; 90% of students from Texas; 4% Foreign. Average age of undergraduate student: 27.
Varsity Sports. Women (Div. II): Basketball, Gymnastics, Tennis.
Campus Life. About 6% of women live in traditional dormitories; 11% men, 8% women live in coed dormitories; rest commute. There are 5 sororities which about 3% women join. About 40% of resident students leave campus on weekends.
Annual Costs. Tuition and fees, $1,294 (out-of-state, $4,558); room and board, $2,942; estimated $450 other, exclusive of travel. About 57% of students receive financial aid; average amount of assistance, $3,854. *Meeting Costs:* university offers installment payment plan, payment by credit card.

Thiel College

Greenville, Pennsylvania 16125 **(412) 589-2345; 800-24-THIEL**

A church-related, liberal arts college, Thiel is located in a town of 10,000, 75 miles north of Pittsburgh. Most convenient major airport: Youngstown, Ohio.

Founded: 1866
Affiliation: Lutheran
UG Enrollment: 379 M, 428 W (full-time); 44 M, 96 W (part-time)
Total Enrollment: 947
Cost: < $10K
% Receiving Financial Aid: 96%
Admission: Non-selective
Application Deadline: Aug. 1

Admission. High school graduates with 16 units eligible; 82% of applicants accepted, 27% of these actually enroll; 24% of freshmen graduate in top fifth of high school class, 53% in top two-fifths. Average freshman scores: SAT, 418 verbal, 444 mathematical; ACT, 20 composite. Recommended: SAT or ACT, interview. Criteria considered in admissions, in order of importance: high school academic record, standardized test scores; of equal importance: recommendations, extracurricular activities, writing sample. *Entrance programs:* early admission, midyear admission, deferred admission, advanced placement. *Apply* by August 1; rolling admissions. *Transfers* welcome; 80 enrolled 1993–94.
Academic Environment. Administration reports 70% of general education courses required for graduation are elective; distribution requirements fairly numerous. Degrees offered: associates, bachelors. *Majors offered* include accounting, business administration, conservative biology track. Average undergraduate class size: 34% under 20, 59% between 20–40, 7% over 40. About 47% of students entering as freshmen graduate in four years, 55% eventually. Campus has Brucker Great Blue Heron Sanctuary. *Special programs:* CLEP, honors, 3-year degree, individualized majors, study abroad, Business Department Honors Seminar (students meet and dine with top executives), Thiel Enterprise Institute, Washington Semester, United Nations Semester, Appalachian Semester, Argonne Laboratory program, New York art semester, combined program in engineering with Case Western Reserve; 3–2 in engineering, forestry, environmental management. Adult programs: off-campus, Elderhostel, personal enrichment, and continuing education courses offered through Center for Lifelong Learning. *Calendar:* semester, summer school.
Undergraduate degrees conferred (145). 34% were in Business and Management, 13% were in Social Sciences, 12% were in Communications, 11% were in Health Sciences, 7% were in Psychology, 6% were in Letters, 5% were in Visual and Performing Arts, 5% were in Computer and Engineering Related Technology, 3% were in Physical Sciences, 3% were in Life Sciences, remainder in 2 other fields.
Graduates Career Data. Advanced studies pursued by 11% of students; 1% enter medical school, 1% enter law school, 1% enter business school. About 95% of 1992–93 graduates employed. Fields typically hiring largest number of graduates include nursing, management, accounting, education. Career Development Services include vocational testing, career counseling, job placement assistance, graduate school assistance, career related seminars, cooperative education program.
Faculty. About 66% of faculty hold PhD or equivalent. About 75% of undergraduate classes taught by tenured faculty. About 36% of teaching faculty are female; 1% Asian-Pacific.
Student Body. College does not seek a national student body; 82% of students from in state; 12% Midwest, 83% Middle Atlantic, 1% New England; 4% Foreign. An estimated 52% of students reported as Protestant, 27% Catholic, 1% Jewish, 18% unaffiliated, 2% other; 4% as Black, 1% Hispanic, 3% Asian.
Religious Orientation. Thiel is a church-related institution; 1 course in religion required of all students; attendance at chapel services voluntary. Places of worship available on campus and in immediate community for Protestants and Catholics, 15 miles away for Jews.
Varsity Sports. Men (Div.III): Baseball, Basketball, Cross Country, Football, Golf, Tennis, Track, Wrestling. Women (Div.III): Basketball, Cross Country, Soccer, Softball, Tennis, Track, Volleyball.
Campus Life. Rules governing student life somewhat relaxed in recent years. College has instituted program of intervisitation. Issues of particular concern to students reportedly include open house intervisitation. Beer and wine permitted in accordance with state law. Cars allowed. Students required to live in college-owned residences or at home.

About 24% of men, 34% of women live in traditional dormitories; 4% of men, 2% of women live in coed dormitories; 31% of students commute. Freshmen given preference in college housing if all students cannot be accommodated. There are 3 fraternities, 5 sororities on campus which about 15% of men, 19% of women join; 5% of men live in fraternities; sororities provide no residence facilities. About 50% of resident students leave campus on weekends.

Annual Costs. Tuition and fees, $10,446; room and board, $4,778; estimated $750 other, exclusive of travel. About 96% of students receive financial aid; average amount of assistance, $9,726. Assistance is typically divided 4% scholarship, 51% grant, 41% loan, 4% work. College reports 180 scholarships awarded for academic merit. *Meeting Costs:* college offers 10 and 12 month payment plans.

Thomas A. Edison State College

Trenton, New Jersey 08608-1176 (609) 984-1100

A state institution with no faculty or campus which awards associate and baccalaureate degrees to adults on the basis of previous college study and college-level learning acquired outside the classroom. Most convenient major airports: Newark or Philadelphia.

Founded: 1972
Affiliation: State
UG Enrollment: 5,348 M, 3,420 W (part-time)
Cost: < $10K
Admission: Non-selective
Application Deadline: Rolling

Admission is open; students may enroll at any time. *Out-of-state* freshman applicants: college welcomes out-of-state students. College does not limit out-of-state enrollment. All out-of-state applicants accepted, 50% of these actually enroll. States from which most out-of-state applicants are drawn include Pennsylvania, California, Florida, New York, Texas. *Apply:* rolling admissions.
Academic Environment. Degrees offered: associates, bachelors. Students may earn credit toward a degree at Edison in 4 ways: with transfer credit earned at other accredited institutions; by taking college-equivalency examinations such as those offered by the Thomas Edison College Examination Program, the College Level Examination Program, and the Advanced Placement Examination; by requesting individual assessment of non-classroom learning by consultants provided by the college; or by guided independent study. About 75% of bachelor degrees completed in four years or less. *Special programs:* performs experimental learning assessment for adult students enrolled at 40 other colleges. Adult programs: all programs designed to meet the adult learner.
Undergraduate degrees conferred (631). 41% were in Multi/Interdisciplinary Studies, 38% were in Business and Management, 13% were in Social Sciences, 6% were in Allied Health, remainder in Health Sciences.
Graduates Career Data. Advanced studies pursued by 44% of students.
Student Body. About 62% of students from in state; 72% from the Middle Atlantic, 5% Midwest, 9% South, 6% West, 5% New England, 1% Northwest; 2% Foreign. Average age of undergraduate student: 39.
Annual Costs. Tuition, $500 (out-of-state, $700); additional fees for examinations and individual assessments. Less than 1% receive financial aid; average amount of assistance, $900. Assistance is all from grants. College reports all scholarships awarded for need.

Thomas Aquinas College

Santa Paula, California 93060 800-634-9797

An accredited, 4-year liberal arts college, Thomas Aquinas offers studies leading to the baccalaureate degree. Most convenient major airport: Los Angeles.

Affiliation: Roman Catholic
UG Enrollment: 109 M, 99 W (full-time)
Cost: $10K–$20K
% Receiving Financial Aid: 80%
Admission: Very Selective
Application Deadline: September 1

Admission is very selective. High school graduates eligible; 53% of applicants accepted, 77% of these actually enroll; 47% graduate in top fifth of high school class, 83% in top two-fifths. Average freshman scores: SAT, 583 verbal, 589 mathematical; ACT, 27 composite. *Required:* SAT or ACT, essay, 3 letters of reference. Criteria considered in admissions, in order of importance: writing sample, recommendations, high school academic record, standardized test scores; other factors considered: religious affiliation and/or commitment. About 45% of entering students from private schools. *Entrance programs:* deferred admission. *Apply* by September 1; rolling admissions.
Academic Environment. Degrees offered: bachelors. Four-year required curriculum using the "Great Books" program of Catholic liberal education; primary sources replace textbooks, and guided conversations replace classroom lecture. Program includes 4 years of math, natural sciences, philosophy, theology, seminar; 2 years language; 1 year music. One student describes her academic experience, "..learning is an active rather than a passive process, so that reasoning skills are developed, and conclusions are known in the fullest way, because they have been reached through a natural process of question and answer. This method is so thought-provoking that it cannot be contained within the classroom; it continues on outside of class and affects every part of student life. So students are continually studying, in a way, by continual discussion, but the discussion is delightful rather than simply exhausting." Another student adds, "one of the most academically rigorous and demanding programs available—the students are expected to read and think and discuss with persistence and vigor." Average undergraduate class size: 15. About 67% of students entering as freshmen graduate in four years, more than 70% eventually; 80% of freshmen return for sophomore year.
Graduates Career Data. Advanced studies pursued by 60% of students; 4% enter medical school; 7% enter law school; 5% enter business school. *Careers in business and industry* pursued by 54% of graduates, according to most recent data available.
Faculty. About 65% of faculty hold PhD or equivalent. About 74% of undergraduate classes taught by tenured faculty. About 15% of teaching faculty are female.
Student Body. About 31% of students from California; 15% Foreign. An estimated 96% of students reported as Catholic, 2% Protestant, 1% unaffiliated; 1% Black, 3% as Hispanic, 4% Asian. Average age of undergraduate student: 22.
Religious Orientation. Thomas Aquinas is a Roman Catholic institution; four years of religious courses required.
Campus Life. A student reports, "Religion is a big part of everyday life, the focus, in fact, there are masses three times daily and twice on weekends, but students are not required to attend." The rural campus offers beautiful areas for hiking and outdoor activities; intramural sports are popular, and trips to Los Angeles, Santa Barbara, and beaches are also popular. About 99% of men, all women live in traditional dormitories; 1% men commute. About 5% of resident students leave campus on weekends.
Annual Costs. Tuition and fees, $12,790; room and board, $5,110; estimated $350 other, exclusive of travel. About 80% of students receive financial aid; average amount of assistance, $11,500. Assistance is typically divided 77% grant, 23% work. College reports scholarships awarded only on the basis of need. *Meeting Costs:* college offers early payment plan.

Thomas College

Thomasville, Georgia 31792-7499 (912) 226-1621

An independent liberal arts college, offering associates and bachelors programs in liberal studies and business fields.

Founded: 1950
Affiliation: Independent
UG Enrollment: 164 M, 278 W (full-time); 62 M, 97 W (part-time)
Total Enrollment: 601
Cost: < $10K
Admission: Non-selective
Application Deadline: Rolling

Admission. Open admissions; all applicants accepted, 74% of these actually enroll. *Entrance programs:* early admission. *Apply:* rolling admissions. *Transfers* welcome; 81 enrolled 1993–94.
Academic Environment. Graduation requirements include 45 quarter hours in English composition, history, biology, mathematics, political science, music or art, and computer science. Degrees offered: associates, bachelors. Average undergraduate class size: 73% under 20, 26% 20–40, 1% over 40. About 37% of students entering as freshmen graduate within four years, 37% of freshmen return for sophomore year. *Calendar:* quarter.
Undergraduate degrees conferred (37). 100% were in Liberal/General Studies.
Faculty. About 27% of faculty hold PhD or equivalent. About 21% of teaching faculty are female.

Student Body. About 97% of students from in state; 98% from South, 1% foreign. Average age of undergraduate student: 27.
Varsity Sports. Men: Baseball, Golf, Tennis. Women: Golf, Softball, Tennis.
Campus Life. College is a non-residential, commuter institution, there are no residence facilities.
Annual Costs. Tuition and fees, $3,024; estimated $500 other, exclusive of travel and housing.

Admission. About 74% of applicants accepted, 37% of these actually enroll; according to most recent data available 43% of freshmen graduate in top fifth of high school class, 68% in top two-fifths. Average freshman ACT scores: 22.5 composite. *Required:* SAT or ACT, minimum H.S. GPA of 2.0. Criteria considered in admissions, in order of importance: standardized test scores, high school academic record; other factors considered: special talents, diverse student body. *Entrance programs:* early admission. *Apply* by August 15; rolling admissions. *Transfers* welcome; 30 enrolled 1993–94.
Academic Environment. General requirements are constructed to encourage double majors; one for career and one for personal interest or both for career. Degrees offered: associates, bachelors. *Majors offered* include international studies, speech communications. Average undergraduate class size: 15. About 62% of freshmen return for sophomore year.

Special programs: CLEP, remedial program for educationally disadvantaged, independent study, undergraduate research, study abroad, individualized majors, credit by examination, cross-registration with Xavier U., Northern KY U., U. of Cincinnati, Cincinnati Technical, Art Academy; 3–2 in engineering. Adult programs: Associate and Bachelor programs offered in Elected Studies. *Calendar:* semester, May–June term, summer school.
Undergraduate degrees conferred (131). 35% were in Business and Management, 10% were in Liberal/General Studies, 8% were in Health Sciences, 8% were in Physical Sciences, 7% were in Computer and Engineering Related Technology, 6% were in Social Sciences, 6% were in Psychology, 6% were in Letters, 5% were in Education, 4% were in Life Sciences, remainder in 3 other fields.
Graduates Career Data. According to most recent data available, full-time graduate study pursued immediately after graduation by 37% of students; 10% enter medical school; 5% enter dental school; 12% enter law school. Corporations typically hiring largest numbers of graduates include AT&T, Procter & Gamble, General Electric.
Faculty. About 56% of faculty hold PhD or equivalent.
Student Body. College seeks a national student body; 70% of students from in state. An estimated 5% of students reported as Catholic; 5% Black, 1% Hispanic, 1% Asian, 5% other minority.
Religious Orientation. Thomas More is a church-related institution; 3 courses in theology required of all students. Places of worship available on campus for Catholics, in immediate community for major faiths.
Varsity Sports. Men (NAIA): Baseball, Basketball, Football (NCAA, Div. III), Soccer, Tennis. Women (NAIA): Basketball, Soccer, Softball, Tennis, Volleyball.
Campus Life. Large percentage of commuters influences nature of campus life. Curfew for all first-semester freshmen, both men and women. Intervisitation hours noon to midnight Sunday-Thursday, noon to 2 am Friday and Saturday. Cars allowed; alcoholic beverages prohibited. According to most recent data available about 34% of men, 27% of women live in coed dormitories; rest commute. There is 1 fraternity on campus which about 5% of men join; it provides no residence facilities.
Annual Costs. Tuition and fees, $9,072; room and board, $3,600; estimated $800 other, exclusive of travel. College reports some scholarships awarded for academic merit. *Meeting Costs:* college offers 10-month payment plan.

Thomas College

Waterville, Maine 04901 **(207) 873-0771**

An independent, professional institution, specializing in business administration and business education, located on a new 70-acre campus in a city of 19,000. Most convenient major airport: Portland International.

Founded: 1894
Affiliation: Independent
UG Enrollment: 185 M, 213 W (full-time)
Total Enrollment: 603
Cost: < $10K
Admission: Non-selective
Application Deadline: Aug. 15

Admission. Graduates of approved high schools, preferably with background in college preparatory subjects, eligible; 89% of applicants accepted, 44% of these actually enroll; 40% of freshmen graduate in top fifth of high school class, 70% in top two-fifths, according to most recent data available. *Required:* SAT; interview suggested. *Apply* by August 15. *Transfers* welcome.
Academic Environment. *Degrees:* BSBA, BSBEd. About 20% of general education requirements for graduation are elective; distribution requirements limited. *Majors offered* in addition to usual studies include computer information systems, business teacher education. *Special programs:* CLEP, individualized majors, study abroad, 5-year MBA program, some courses offered through Colby. *Calendar:* semester.
Undergraduate degrees conferred (79). 92% were in Business and Management, 8% were in Computer and Engineering Related Technology.
Graduates Career Data. According to most recent data available careers in business and industry pursued by 96% of graduates. Corporations typically hiring largest numbers of graduates include accounting firms, Scott Paper, State of Maine.
Student Body. About 91% of students from New England. An estimated 8% of students reported as Black, 2% Hispanic, according to most recent data available.
Varsity Sports. Men (NCAA, NAIA): Basketball, Golf, Soccer, Tennis. Women (NCAA, NAIA): Basketball, Soccer, Softball, Volleyball.
Campus Life. About 60% of men, 60% of women live in coed dormitories; rest live in off-campus housing or commute, according to most recent data available. Intervisitation in men's and women's dormitory rooms unlimited. About 30% of resident students leave campus on weekends.
Annual Costs. Tuition and fees, $9,050; room and board, $4,450. College reports some scholarships awarded for academic merit. *Meeting Costs:* college offers installment plan, deferred payment plan, parent loans.

Thomas More College

Crestview Hill, Kentucky 410171 **800-825-4557**

A church-related college, sponsored by the Diocese of Covington, Thomas More is located in a community of 52,500. College includes 2 units: the Division of Integrative Studies, the standard undergraduate school, and the Division of Continuing Education. The 223-acre campus is 8 miles south of the center of Cincinnati. Most convenient major airport: Greater Cincinnati.

Founded: 1921
Affiliation: Roman Catholic
UG Enrollment: 399 M, 366 W (full-time); 111 M, 382 W (part-time)
Total Enrollment: 1,258
Cost: < $10K
Admission: Non-selective
Application Deadline: August 15

Tiffin University

Tiffin, Ohio 44883 **(419) 447-6443**

A small, independent, business-oriented college offering associate and baccalaureate degrees.

Founded: 1888
Affiliation: Independent
UG Enrollment: 394 M, 268 W (full-time); 129 M, 222 W (part-time)
Total Enrollment: 1,092
Cost: < $10K
% Receiving Financial Aid: 75%
Admission: Non-selective
Application Deadline: Rolling

Admission. High school graduates eligible; 87% of applicants accepted, 35% of these actually enroll. About 20% of freshmen graduate in top fifth of high school class, 51% in top two-fifths. Average freshman scores: ACT, 18 M, 19 W composite. *Required:* ACT, minimum H.S. GPA. Criteria considered in admissions, in order of importance: high school academic record, standardized test scores, extracurricular activities, writing sample, recommendations. *Entrance programs:* midyear admission, deferred admission, advanced placement. About 20% of freshmen from private schools. *Apply*: rolling admissions. *Transfers* welcome; 94 enrolled 1993–94.

Academic Environment. Degrees offered: associates, bachelors, masters. *Majors offered* in business management, business administration and management, accounting and computing, office supervision and management, criminal justice administration, forensic psychology, hotel and restaurant management. Average undergraduate class size: 41% under 20, 58% between 20–40, 1% over 40. About 27% of students entering as freshmen graduate in four years, 35% eventually; 55% of freshmen return for sophomore year. *Special programs:* study abroad. *Calendar:* semester.

Undergraduate degrees conferred (111). 77% were in Business and Management, 13% were in Protective Services, 6% were in Business (Administrative Support), 5% were in Computer and Engineering Related Technology.

Graduates Career Data. Advanced studies pursued by 7% of students; 2% enter law school. About 94% of 1992–93 graduates employed. Employers typically hiring largest number of graduates include Whirlpool, State of Ohio. Career Development Services include counseling, placement service, on-campus recruitment, internships, library resources, resume/interview workshops, job fairs.

Faculty. About 65% of faculty hold PhD or equivalent. About 45% of teaching faculty are female; 1% other minority.

Student Body. About 89% of students from Ohio; 93% from Midwest; 3% Foreign. An estimated 9% of students reported as Black, 2% Hispanic, 4% other minority. Average age of undergraduate student: 24.

Varsity Sports. Men (NAIA): Baseball, Basketball (NAIAII), Cross Country, Football (NAIAII), Golf, Soccer, Tennis. Women (NAIA): Basketball (NAIAII), Cross Country, Soccer, Softball, Tennis, Volleyball.

Campus Life. About 25% of men, 40% of women live in coed dormitories; rest commute. There are 2 fraternities, 2 sororities, which about 1.5% of men, 1.5% of women join; 1% of men, 1% of women live in fraternities and sororities. About 70% of resident students leave campus on weekends.

Annual Costs. Tuition and fees, $7,100; room and board, $3,700; estimated $1,000 other, exclusive of travel. About 75% of students receive financial aid; average amount of assistance, $5,690. Assistance is typically divided 3% scholarship, 35% grant, 53% loan, 9% work. College reports 81 scholarships awarded for academic merit, 182 for special talents, 133 for need. *Meeting Costs:* college offers monthly payment plan and prepayment plan.

Toccoa Falls College

Toccoa Falls, Georgia 30598

A private Christian college which offers degree programs in counseling, theology, Christian education, communications, general studies, music education, missionary studies, and teacher education.

Founded: 1907 **Affiliation:** Independent

Undergraduate degrees conferred (113). 46% were in Theology, 26% were in Education, 14% were in Psychology, 12% were in Communications, remainder in Philosophy and Religion.

University of Toledo

Toledo, Ohio 43606-3390 **(419) 537-2696**

A state-supported university, formerly a municipal institution, located in a residential section of a city of 400,000. Most convenient major airports: Toledo, or Detroit.

Founded: 1872
Affiliation: State
UG Enrollment: 7,652 M, 7,776 W (full-time); 2,488 M, 2,882 W (part-time)
Total Enrollment: 24,188
Cost: < $10K
% Receiving Financial Aid: 33%
Admission: Non-selective
Application Deadline: Rolling

Admission. All graduates of Ohio high schools eligible; College of Arts and Sciences requires graduation from an accredited high school with 16 units and C average. For all schools 97% of applicants accepted, 51% of these actually enroll. Average freshman scores: SAT, 433 M, 434 W verbal, 503 M, 471 W mathematical; 33% of freshmen score above 500 verbal, 13% above 600, 3% above 700; 58% score above 500 mathematical, 29% above 600, 11% above 700; ACT, 20.9 M, 20.6 W composite.

Required: SAT or ACT, minimum H.S. GPA of 2.0, essay for academic scholarships; interview recommended. Criteria considered in admissions, in order of importance: high school academic record, standardized test scores, recommendations, writing sample, extracurricular activities; other factors considered: special talents, diverse student body. *Out-of-state* freshman applicants: university actively seeks students from out-of-state. State does not limit out-of-state enrollment. Requirements for out-of-state applicants: C average and minimum ACT composite score of 19, or 900 combined SAT. About 234 out-of-state students enrolled 1993–94. States from which most out-of-state applicants are drawn include Michigan. *Entrance programs:* early admission, midyear admission, deferred admission, advanced placement. *Apply*: rolling admissions; December 1 recommended for students desiring campus housing. *Transfers* welcome; 1,574 enrolled 1993–94.

Academic Environment. *Undergraduate studies* offered to freshmen by Colleges of Arts and Sciences, Business Administration, Education, Engineering, and Pharmacy. Degrees offered: associates, bachelors, masters, doctoral. *Majors offered* include pharmacy, physical therapy, women's studies. About 20% of general education requirements for graduation are elective; distribution requirements fairly numerous. Average undergraduate class size: 46% under 20, 41% between 20–40, 13% over 40. About 18% of entering freshmen graduate in four years, 71% eventually; 72% return for sophomore year. *Special programs:* CLEP, independent study, honors, January term, study abroad, undergraduate research, individualized majors, combined program in medical technology, cross registration with Bowling Green State U. Adult programs: Adult Liberal Studies Program, University College offers accelerated programs to students over 25 years of age. *Calendar:* quarter, summer school.

Undergraduate degrees conferred (2,348). 18% were in Business and Management, 17% were in Education, 11% were in Multi/Interdisciplinary Studies, 10% were in Engineering, 8% were in Health Sciences, 6% were in Communications, 5% were in Marketing and Distribution, 5% were in Social Sciences, 4% were in Engineering and Engineering Related Technology, 3% were in Life Sciences, remainder in 13 other fields.

Graduates Career Data. According to most recent data available full-time advanced studies pursued by 33% of students immediately after graduation. *Careers in business and industry* pursued by 65% of graduates. Corporations typically hiring largest numbers of graduates include Dana Corp., Owens Illinois, Owens Corning, Rite Aid, Toledo Hospital.

Faculty. About 88% of faculty hold PhD or equivalent. About 22% of teaching faculty are female; 4% Black, 1% Hispanic, 7% other minority.

Student Body. University seeks a national student body; 89% of students from Ohio; 95% Midwest; 4% Foreign. An estimated 9% of students reported as Black, 2% Hispanic, 1% Asian, 8% other minority. Average age of undergraduate student: 23.

Varsity Sports. Men (Div.I): Baseball, Basketball, Cross Country, Football, Golf, Swimming, Tennis, Track, Wrestling. Women (Div.I): Basketball, Cross Country, Softball, Swimming, Tennis, Track, Volleyball.

Campus Life. Campus life influenced by large number of students living off-campus. About 1% of women live in traditional dormitories; 6% of men, 7% of women in coed dormitories; 38% of men, 36% of women live in off-campus college-related housing; rest commute. Intervisitation in men's dormitory rooms unlimited; limited in women's dormitory rooms. There are 15 fraternities, 10 sororities on campus which about 10% of men, 10% of women join. About 30% of resident students leave campus on weekends.

Annual Costs. Tuition and fees, $3,236 (out-of-state, $7,758); room and board, $3,400; estimated $2,514 other, exclusive of travel. About 33% of students receive financial aid; average amount of assistance, $5,327. Assistance is typically divided 13% scholarship, 14% grant, 72% loan, 1% work. University reports 250–300 scholarships awarded for academic merit.

Tougaloo College

Tougaloo, Mississippi 39174 **(601) 977-7770**

A church-related college, located in a suburb of Jackson (pop. 205,100); founded as a college for Negroes and still serving a predominantly Black student body. Most convenient major airport: Jackson.

Founded: 1869
Affiliation: United Church of Christ, Disciples of Christ
UG Enrollment: 377 M, 743 W (full-time)
Cost: < $10K
% Receiving Financial Aid: 83%
Admission: Non-selective
Application Deadline: Rolling

Admission. Graduates of approved high schools with 16 units (9 in academic subjects) eligible; admission may be granted by examination (GED). Average freshman ACT scores, according to most recent data available: 17.7 M, 16.9 W composite, 17.0 M, 16.3 W mathematical. *Required:* SAT or ACT, minimum H.S. GPA of 2.0. Criteria considered in admissions, in order of importance: high school academic record, standardized test scores, recommendations, extracurricular activities. *Entrance programs:* early admission, advanced placement. *Apply* by no specific deadline. *Transfers* welcome.

Academic Environment. Degrees offered: associates, bachelors. About 21% of general education requirements for graduation are elective; distribution requirements fairly numerous. Average undergraduate class size: 30. About 21% of entering freshmen graduate in four years, 38% eventually; 70% of freshmen return for sophomore year. *Special programs:* CLEP, internships, exchange programs with Brown U., Tougaloo Institute for Early Childhood Education, 3–2 in engineering and physical sciences. Adult programs: The Center for Life Long Learning. *Calendar:* 4–1–4.

Undergraduate degrees conferred (98). 45% were in Social Sciences, 12% were in Psychology, 11% were in Education, 9% were in Physical Sciences, 9% were in Life Sciences, 7% were in Letters, 5% were in Mathematics, remainder in Visual and Performing Arts.

Graduates Career Data. Advanced studies pursued by 55% of students. About 37% of 1992–93 graduates employed.

Faculty. About 67% of faculty hold PhD or equivalent. About 60% of undergraduate classes taught by tenured faculty. About 26% of teaching faculty are female; 45% Black, 18% other minority.

Student Body. About 85% of students from within the state; 88% South. Almost all students are Black.

Varsity Sports. Men: Basketball, Cross Country, Track. Women: Basketball, Cross Country, Track.

Campus Life. About 51% of men, 65% of women live in traditional dormitories; no coed dormitories; rest commute. There are 4 fraternities, 4 sororities on campus. About 60% of resident students leave campus on weekends.

Annual Costs. Tuition and fees, $4,795; room and board, $2,185; estimated $1,000 other, exclusive of travel. About 83% of students receive financial aid; average amount of assistance, $1,715. Assistance is typically divided 22% scholarship, 39% grant, 32% loan, 7% work. College reports 285 scholarships awarded for academic merit, 52 for special talents, 132 for need.

Touro College

New York, New York 10036 **(212) 575-0190**

Touro is a small college of arts and sciences located on 44th Street in the Times Square area of New York City. Most convenient major airport: JFK International.

Founded: 1970
Affiliation: Independent
UG Enrollment: 5,611 M, W (full-time)
Cost: < $10K
Admission: Selective
Application Deadline: April 15

Admission is selective. About 85% of applicants accepted, 76% of these actually enroll. Average freshman SAT scores, according to most recent data available: 39% of freshman score above 500 on verbal, 10% above 600, 3% above 700; 55% score above 500 on mathematical, 16% above 600, 2% above 700. *Required:* SAT, interview. *Non-academic factors* considered in admissions: special talents. *Entrance programs:* early decision, early admission, midyear admission, deferred admission, advanced placement. *Apply* by April 15. *Transfers* welcome.

Academic Environment. *Degrees:* BA, BS. Dual requirement in College of Liberal Arts and Sciences: a 24-credit humanities core and a 24-credit Jewish studies sequence. College offers fairly wide range of arts and sciences, however, more than one-third of graduates major in business administration and management and related subjects. *Majors offered* in addition to usual studies include Judaic Studies. About 65% of students entering as freshmen graduate eventually; 20% do not return for sophomore year. *Special programs:* honors, study abroad, independent study. *Calendar:* semester.

Undergraduate degrees conferred (479). 33% were in Liberal/General Studies, 33% were in Business and Management, 8% were in Social Sciences, 7% were in Health Sciences, 6% were in Allied Health, 4% were in Psychology, 3% were in Mathematics, 3% were in Area and Ethnic Studies, remainder in 3 other fields.

Graduates Career Data. According to most recent data available full-time graduate or professional study pursued immediately after graduation by 35% of students; 5% enter medical school; 5% enter dental school; 15% enter law school; 10% enter business school. *Career Counseling Program:* student assessment of program reported as good for both career guidance and job placement. Help provided in preparation for interviews. Alumni reported as active in job placement, not active in career guidance.

Faculty. About 70% of faculty hold PhD or equivalent.

Student Body. About 75% of students from New York. An estimated 21% of students reported as Black, 12% Hispanic, 5% Asian, according to most recent data available.

Campus Life. According to most recent data available about 25% of men, 45% of women live in dormitories; remainder live off-campus or commute.

Annual Costs. Tuition and fees, $7,130; room, $3,300. College reports some scholarships awarded for academic merit alone.

Towson State University

Towson, Maryland 21204 **(410) 830-2112; in MD, (800) 225-5878)**

A state-supported university, offering a range of liberal arts and professionally-oriented programs. Towson State is located just beyond the northern border of Baltimore. Most convenient major airport: Baltimore-Washington International.

Founded: 1866
Affiliation: State
UG Enrollment: 3,787 M, 5,460 W (full-time); 1,496 M, 2,088 W (part-time)
Total Enrollment: 14,696
Cost: < $10K
% Receiving Financial Aid: 37%
Admission: Non-selective
Application Deadline: March 1

Admission. High school graduates with C+ average, preferably in college preparatory curriculum eligible; 61% of applicants accepted, 33% of these actually enroll. Average freshman SAT scores: 463 M, 470 W verbal, 528 M, 507 W mathematical; 29% of freshmen score above 500 verbal, 4% above 600, 55% score above 500 mathematical, 12% above 600, 1% above 700. *Required:* SAT (preferred) or ACT, minimum H.S. GPA of 2.5. Criteria considered in admissions, in order of importance: high school academic record, standardized test scores, recommendations, extracurricular activities; other factors considered: special talents, diverse student body. *Out-of-state* freshman applicants: university actively seeks students from out-of-state. State does not limit out-of-state enrollment. About 59% of applicants accepted, 24% of these enroll. States from which most out-of-state applicants are drawn include New York. *Entrance programs:* early admission, midyear admission, advanced placement. About 35% of freshmen from private schools. *Apply* by March 1. *Transfers* welcome; 1,544 enrolled 1993–94.

Academic Environment. Degrees offered: bachelors, masters. *Majors offered* include business administration, dance performance and education, education, geography, international studies, mass communications, medical technology, nursing, occupational therapy, speech pathology and audiology, theater arts, women's studies. About 32% of general education requirements for graduation are elective; distribution requirements fairly numerous, selection from 4 disciplines required. Average undergraduate class size: 39% under 20, 57% between 20–40, 4% over 40. About 31% of students entering as freshmen graduate in four years, 56% eventually; 82% of freshmen return for sophomore year. *Special programs:* CLEP, independent study, study abroad, honors, undergraduate research, optional January interterm, second bachelors program, College in Escrow, English Language Center, 3–2 programs in law and engineering, individualized majors, cooperative programs with other Maryland state colleges, cross-registration with University of Maryland System schools. Adult programs: Mature Adult Policy. *Calendar:* 4–1–4, summer school.

Undergraduate degrees conferred (2,458). 28% were in Business and Management, 16% were in Education, 11% were in Communications, 10% were in Social Sciences, 8% were in Psychology, 5% were in Health Sciences, 4% were in Visual and Performing Arts, 4% were in Letters, 3% were in Multi/Interdisciplinary Studies, 3% were in Computer and Engineering Related Technology, remainder in 6 other fields.

Faculty. About 81% of faculty hold PhD or equivalent. About 80% of undergraduate classes taught by tenured faculty. About 35% of teaching faculty are female; 3% Black, 1% Hispanic, 8% other minority.

Graduates Career Data. Advanced studies pursued by 44% of students. About 88% of 1991–92 graduates employed. Fields typically hiring largest number of graduates include Sales, Advertising, Nursing, Education. Career Development Services include career related workshops and clinics, personal life and career planning course (two-credits), extensive career library, computer-assisted guidance program.

Student Body. University does not seek a national student body; 84% of students from in state. An estimated 8% of students reported as Black, 1% Hispanic, 3% Asian, 3% other minority. Average age of undergraduate student: 23.

Varsity Sports. Men (Div.I): Baseball, Basketball, Cross Country, Diving, Football (IAA), Golf, Lacrosse, Soccer, Swimming, Track, Volleyball. Women (Div.I): Basketball, Cross Country, Diving, Field Hockey, Gymnastics, Lacrosse, Soccer, Softball, Swimming, Track, Volleyball.

Campus Life. Large percentage of commuters influences nature of student life. Students and administration agree that students play significant role in all aspects of policy-making except promotion and hiring faculty. Alcohol permitted in conformity with state law and regulations of university; cars allowed.

About 7% of men, 12% of women in coed dormitories; rest commute. There are 18 fraternities, 13 sororities which about 11% of men, 10% of women join. About 33% of resident students leave campus on weekends.

Annual Costs. Tuition and fees, $3,122 (out-of-state, $5,624); room and board, $4,330; estimated $1,012 other, exclusive of travel. About 37% of students receive financial aid; average amount of assistance, $1,535 (for in-state commuter). Assistance is typically divided 55% grant/scholarship, 24% loan, 20% work. College reports 588 scholarships awarded for academic merit, 339 for special talents, 1,025 for need. *Meeting Costs:* college offers AMS installment payment plan.

Transylvania University

Lexington, Kentucky 40508 (606) 233-8242; (800) 872-6798

An independent, liberal arts institution, located in a city of 226,000, Transylvania maintains ties with the Christian Church (Disciples of Christ). Most convenient major airport: Lexington.

Founded: 1780
Affiliation: Independent (Disciples of Christ)
UG Enrollment: 472 M, 509 W (full-time); 70 M, 40 W (part-time)
Total Enrollment: 1,033
Cost: $10K–$20K
% Receiving Financial Aid: 78%
Admission: Very Selective
Application Deadline: March 15

Admission is very selective. About 94% of applicants accepted, 34% of these actually enroll; 61% of freshmen graduate in top fifth of high school class, 80% in top two-fifths. Average freshman scores, according to most recent data available: SAT, 536 M, 515 W verbal, 580 M, 564 W mathematical; ACT, 26.3 M, 25.6 W composite, 25.0 M, 24.2 W mathematical. *Required:* SAT or ACT; interview recommended. *Non-academic factors* considered in admissions: special talents, diverse student body, alumni children, religious affiliation and/or commitment. *Entrance programs:* early admission, midyear admission, deferred admission, advanced placement. About 16% of entering students from private schools. *Apply* by March 15. *Transfers* welcome.

Academic Environment. Pressures for academic achievement appear moderate. Administration reports 55% of general education courses required for graduation are elective; distribution requirements fairly numerous. *Degree:* AB. *Majors offered* include usual arts and sciences, business administration (finance emphasis), computer science, drama, teacher preparation.

About 65% of students entering as freshmen graduate eventually, according to most recent data available. *Special programs:* CLEP, independent study, individually designed majors, study abroad, honors, undergraduate research, Washington Semester, 3-year degree, 3–2 programs in engineering, intercultural studies, May term. *Calendar:* 4–4–1, summer school.

Undergraduate degrees conferred (210). 29% were in Business and Management, 13% were in Social Sciences, 13% were in Life Sciences, 10% were in Education, 10% were in Psychology, 6% were in Visual and Performing Arts, 6% were in Computer and Engineering Related Technology, 5% were in Letters, 3% were in Mathematics, remainder in 3 other fields.

Graduates Career Data. According to most recent data available full-time graduate or professional study pursued immediately after graduation by 37% of students; 4% enter medical school; 8% enter law school. Medical, dental, law and business schools typically enrolling largest numbers of graduates include U. of Kentucky, U. of Louisville. *Careers in business and industry* pursued by 40% of graduates. Corporations typically hiring largest numbers of graduates include IBM, Ashland Petroleum, Ferguson Enterprises, Peat, Marwick. *Career Counseling Program:* Student assessment of program reported as fair for career guidance and good for job placement. Help provided in preparation for interviews. Alumni reported as active in both job placement and in career guidance.

Student Body. University seeks a national student body; 78% of students from Kentucky; 88% South, 7% North Central; 11 foreign students. An estimated 60% of students reported as Protestants, 15% Catholics, 1% Jewish, 23% unaffiliated, 1% other; 2% as Black, 1% Hispanic, 2% Asian, 1% other minority, according to most recent data available.

Varsity Sports. Men (NAIA): Basketball, Golf, Soccer, Swimming, Tennis. Women (NAIA): Basketball, Field Hockey, Softball, Swimming, Tennis.

Campus Life. Proximity to U. of Kentucky not only enriches library resources but also expands entertainment and cultural opportunities for students. Rules governing student conduct permit limited visitation by women in upperclassmen's dormitory. Drinking permitted in dormitory rooms for students 21 and over; cars allowed. Students under 21 required to live in dormitories.

According to most recent data available about 58% of men, 60% of women live in traditional dormitories; 19% of men, 18% of women live in coed dormitories; rest live in off-campus housing or commute. Freshmen given preference in college housing if all students cannot be accommodated. There are 4 fraternities, 4 sororities on campus which about 57% of men, 64% of women join; they provide no residence facilities. About 10% of resident students leave campus on weekends.

Annual Costs. Tuition and fees, $10,670; room and board, $4,300. University reports 25 full and 45 half scholarships awarded on the basis of academic merit alone.

Trenton State College

Trenton, New Jersey 08650-4700 (609) 771-2131

A state-supported college, the 250-acre campus is located in a suburban township of 36,000, just over an hour away form New York city, and less than an hour away from Philadelphia. Most convenient major airport: Philadelphia International.

Founded: 1855
Affiliation: State
UG Enrollment: 2,010 M, 3,155 W (full-time); 316 M, 586 W (part-time)
Total Enrollment: 7,013
Cost: < $10K
% Receiving Financial Aid: 46%
Admission: Selective (+)
Application Deadline: March 1

Admission is selective (+). About 46% of applicants accepted, 47% of these actually enroll; 90% of freshmen graduate in top fifth of high school class, 98% in top two-fifths. Average freshman SAT scores: 519 verbal, 592 mathematical; 62% of freshmen score above 500 verbal, 14% above 600, 1% above 700; 90% score above 500 mathematical, 49% above 600, 11% above 700. *Required:* SAT, essay. Criteria considered in admissions, in order of importance: high school academic record, standardized test scores, extracurricular activities, writing sample, recommendations; other factors considered: special talents. *Out-of-state* freshman applicants: college actively seeks students from out-of-state. State does not limit out-of-state enrollment. About 40% of out-of-state applicants accepted, 46% of these enroll. States from which most out-of-state students are drawn include Pennsylvania. *Entrance programs:* early decision, midyear admission, deferred admission. About 2% of freshmen from private schools, 30% parochial schools. *Apply* by March 1. *Transfers* welcome; 450 enrolled 1993–94.

Academic Environment. Degrees offered: bachelors, masters. New general education curriculum requirements include Intellectual Skills (rhetoric, mathematics, foreign language); 3-semester interdisciplinary core, Understanding Humanity; and 26 semester hours of Perspectives on the World (natural and social scientific perspectives, and humanistic and artistic perspectives). More than 40 liberal arts majors offered through five schools: Arts and Sciences, Business, Education, Nursing, and Technology. About 67% of students entering as freshmen graduate eventually; 96% of freshmen return for sophomore year, partially as a result of TSC's Expectations 4-part student orientation program. Strengths of the academic program include: small classes and excellent student-faculty ratio (15:1), no teaching assistants, and many opportunities for internships in state government, business and industry. *Special programs:* CLEP, independent study, study abroad, honors, cooperative education, 7-year BS/MD, 7-year BS/OD, cooperative programs in pharmacy and physical therapy with Philadelphia college of Pharmacy & Sciences, marine biology field stations with NJ Marine Sciences consortium. *Calendar:* semester, summer school.

Undergraduate degrees conferred (1,292). 27% were in Education, 13% were in Business and Management, 12% were in Letters, 10% were in Social Sciences, 7% were in Psychology, 6% were in Health Sciences, 6% were in Protective Services, 5% were in Visual and Performing Arts, 5% were in Engineering and Engineering Related Technology, 4% were in Life Sciences, remainder in 5 other fields.

Graduates Career Data. Advanced studies pursued 30% of students; 3% enter medical school, 2% enter law school, 8% enter business school. About 86% of 1992–93 graduates employed. Fields typically hiring largest number of graduates include business, education, human services. Career Development Services include career counseling; workshops on resume writing, interviewing skills, job search strategies; on-campus recruitment, career days, career library, internships, listings of part-time and full-time jobs.

Faculty. About 81% of faculty hold PhD or equivalent. About 34% of teaching faculty are female; 5% Black, 2% Hispanic, 5% Asian.

Student Body. College does not seek a national student body; 91% of students from in state; 98% Middle Atlantic. An estimated 23% of students reported as Protestant, 55% Catholic, 4% Jewish, 11% unaffiliated, 4% other; 7% Black, 4% Hispanic, 3% Asian, 1% other minority.

Varsity Sports. Men (Div. III): Baseball, Basketball, Cross Country, Diving, Football, Golf, Soccer, Swimming, Tennis, Track, Wrestling. Women (Div. III): Basketball, Cross Country, Diving, Field Hockey, Lacrosse, Soccer, Softball, Swimming, Tennis, Track.

Campus Life. About 10% of women live in traditional dormitories; 50% of men, 50% of women in coed dormitories; rest live in off-campus housing or commute. Freshmen and sophomores are guaranteed college housing if all students cannot be accommodated. Intervisitation in men's and women's dormitory rooms limited. Sexes segregated in coed dormitories either by wing, floor, or room. There are 14 fraternities, 13 sororities on campus which about 9% of men, 9% of women join; they provide no residence facilities. About 60% of resident students leave campus on weekends.

Annual Costs. Tuition and fees, $3,857 (out-of-state, $5,935); room and board, $5,228; estimated $1,000 other, exclusive of travel. About 46% of students receive financial aid; average amount of assistance $4,600. Assistance is typically divided 15% scholarship, 30% grant, 50% loan, 5% work. College reports 5 scholarships awarded for academic merit.

Trevecca Nazarene College

Nashville, Tennessee 37203 **(615) 248-1320**

A church-related, liberal arts college whose "students have high Christian commitment to service roles in missions, social welfare, and inner-city teaching"; located on an 80-acre campus in the southeastern section of Nashville.

Founded: 1901
Affiliation: Nazarene
UG Enrollment: 1,318 M, W (full-time)
Cost: < $10K
Admission: Non-selective
Application Deadline: September 1

Admission. Graduates of approved high schools with 15 units and C average eligible; others considered on basis of examination; 98% of applicants accepted, 75% of these actually enroll. *Required:* ACT. *Apply* by September 1. *Transfers* welcome.

Academic Environment. *Degrees:* AB, BS. About 30% of general education requirements for graduation are elective; distribution requirements fairly numerous. About 40% of students entering as freshmen graduate eventually; 35% of freshmen do not return for sophomore year. *Special programs:* CLEP, independent study, honors, undergraduate research. *Calendar:* quarter, summer school.

Undergraduate degrees conferred (229). 58% were in Business and Management, 7% were in Education, 6% were in Allied Health, 5% were in Social Sciences, 5% were in Theology, 4% were in Communications, 4% were in Public Affairs, 3% were in Visual and Performing Arts, remainder in 6 other fields.

Student Body. College seeks a national student body; 46% of students from in state; 89% South.

Religious Orientation. Trevecca Nazarene is a church-related institution; 12 hours of religion, attendance at chapel 3 days weekly required of all students.

Varsity Sports. Men (NAIA): Baseball, Basketball, Tennis. Women (NAIA): Tennis, Volleyball.

Campus Life. About 67% of men, 70% of women live in traditional dormitories; no coed dormitories; rest live in off-campus housing or commute, according to most recent data available. No intervisitation in men's or women's dormitory rooms. There are no fraternities or sororities. About 15% of students leave campus on weekends.

Annual Costs. Tuition and fees, $6,656; room and board, $3,272.

Trinity Bible College

Ellendale, North Dakota 58436

A Bible college offering associates and bachelors degree programs, as well as seminary extension courses.

Founded: 1948
Affiliation: Assembly of God

Trinity Christian College

Palos Heights, Illinois 60463 **(312) 597-3000**

A Christian liberal arts college, Trinity Christian is located in a suburban community, 25 miles from Chicago. Most convenient major airports: O'Hare International or Midway (Chicago).

Founded: 1959
Affiliation: Christian, Reformed
UG Enrollment: 527 M, W (full-time)
Cost: < $10K
Admission: Non-selective
Application Deadline: February 15

Admission. High school graduates with 16 units, 4 years English, and 2.0 GPA eligible; others admitted on probation; 96% of applicants accepted, 55% of these actually enroll. Average freshman ACT scores, according to most recent data available: 18.8 composite, 17.5 mathematical. *Required:* SAT or ACT. *Non-academic factors* considered in admissions: diverse student body, religious affiliation and/or commitment. About 77% of entering students from private schools.

Apply: recommended by February 15; rolling admissions. *Transfers* welcome.

Academic Environment. *Degrees:* BA, BS. *Majors offered* include some of the usual arts and sciences, accounting, business administration, medical technology, theology, nursing; wider selection of minors. Distribution requirements include liberal studies in social and behavioral sciences, natural sciences, fine arts, humanities. About 73% of entering students graduate eventually; 24% of freshmen do not return for sophomore year. *Calendar:* semester.

Undergraduate degrees conferred (92). 33% were in Business and Management, 24% were in Education, 17% were in Health Sciences, 10% were in Social Sciences, 7% were in Letters, remainder in 6 other fields.

Student Body. About 74% of students from in state; 95% North Central, according to most recent data available.

Varsity Sports. Men (NAIA): Baseball, Basketball, Soccer, Track. Women (NAIA): Basketball, Softball (12" fast), Track, Volleyball.

Campus Life. According to most recent data available about 59% of men, 59% of women live on campus, rest live off campus or commute.

Annual Costs. Tuition and fees, $9,460; room and board, $3,800. College reports some scholarships awarded for academic merit.

Trinity College

Hartford, Connecticut 06106 **(203) 297-2180**

Trinity is a venerable co-educational liberal arts college, located in a residential area of Hartford on an 85-acre campus "noted for its beauty," overlooking the city. Most convenient major airport: Bradley International (Windsor Locks).

Founded: 1823
Affiliation: Independent
UG Enrollment: 881 M, 856 W (full-time); 73 M, 136 W (part-time)
Total Enrollment: 2,136
Cost: $10K–$20K
% Receiving Financial Aid: 42%
Admission: Highly (+) Selective
Application Deadline: Jan. 15

Admission is highly (+) selective. About 58% of applicants accepted, 27% of these actually enroll; 70% of freshmen graduate in top fifth of high school class, 92% in top two-fifths. Average freshman SAT scores: 560 verbal, 610 mathematical; ACT, 26 composite. *Required:* SAT (preferred) or ACT, ACH in English, essay, two teacher recommendations. Criteria considered in admissions, in order of importance: high school academic record, recommendations, extracurricular activities, standardized test scores, writing sample; other factors considered: special talents, diverse student body. *Entrance programs:* early decision, deferred admission, advanced placement. About 49% of entering students from private schools, 7% from parochial schools. *Apply* by January 15. *Transfers* welcome; 34 enrolled 1993–94.

Academic Environment. This is a liberal arts college with a student body largely oriented toward professional goals, but with strong emphasis on liberal studies. Student may "use the resources of Trinity, and of the institutions with which this college has a working relationship, to construct his own program of concentration (or major)." Students hold one quarter of voting membership on Curriculum Committee and are involved, through evaluations and interviews, in faculty hiring and promotions. Core curriculum requires 5 distributional courses plus an interdisciplinary minor for all students. A selective Guided Studies Program in the humanities offered to 25 freshmen. Participants in the GSP take 13 required courses over their first 2 or 3 years at Trinity. A similar Integrated Science Program (ISP) began in 1987. Degrees offered: bachelors, masters. *Majors offered* include American studies, computer science, engineering, fine arts, theater; interdisciplinary majors including intercultural studies, urban and environmental studies; student-designed degree programs are available. Opportunities for academic internships available in virtually all areas of study. Average undergraduate class size: 18.

About 85% of students entering as freshmen graduate in four years, 88% eventually; 97% of freshmen return for sophomore year. *Special programs:* independent study, study abroad, honors, undergraduate research, individualized majors, freshman seminars, Washington Semester, student-taught courses, acceleration, internships, open semester (independent projects on or off campus), Trinity Rome Campus, Twelve College Exchange, Greater Hartford Consortium for Higher Education, which provides for cross-registration with Hartford area colleges, cooperative programs (with Hartford Conservatory of Music, with Central Connecticut State in Chinese, with Wesleyan U. and Connecticut College, Williams-Mystic Seaport Program in maritime studies), 5-year combined engineering program leading to ME from RPI, programs in classical studies in Rome, graduate courses open to undergraduates, theater arts programs at National Theater Institute of O'Neill Foundation in Waterford, Conn. Adult programs: Individualized Degree Program, self-paced for non-resident adults over 23. *Calendar:* semester, summer school.

Undergraduate degrees conferred (450). 37% were in Social Sciences, 16% were in Letters, 8% were in Visual and Performing Arts, 8% were in Psychology, 7% were in Area and Ethnic Studies, 6% were in Philosophy and Religion, 5% were in Life Sciences, 3% were in Engineering, remainder in 6 other fields.

Graduates Career Data. *Full-time graduate or professional study* pursued immediately after graduation by 25% of students; 5% enter medical school; 1% enter dental school; 10% enter law school; 5% enter business school, according to most recent data available. Medical schools typically enrolling largest numbers of graduates include U. of Connecticut, Columbia, U. of Virginia, Duke; dental schools include U. of Connecticut; law schools include Georgetown, George Washington, Northwestern, Columbia, Yale, Michigan; business schools include U. of Columbia, NYU. *Careers in business and industry* pursued by 50% of graduates, according to most recent data available. Corporations typically hiring largest numbers of graduates include Manufacturers Hanover, Chase Manhattan, Procter & Gamble, United Technologies. *Career Counseling Program:* student assessment of program reported as good for both career guidance and job placement. Help provided in preparation for interviews. Alumni reported as active in both career guidance and job placement.

Faculty. About 95% of faculty hold PhD or equivalent. About 40% of teaching faculty are female; 4% Black, 23% other minority.

Student Body. College seeks a national student body; 20% of students from in state; 45% New England, 25% Middle Atlantic, 10% Midwest, 10% West, 6% South; 2% Foreign. An estimated 7% of students reported as Black, 4% Hispanic, 6% Asian, 2% other minority, according to most recent data available.

Varsity Sports. Men (Div.III): Baseball, Basketball, Crew, Cross Country, Diving, Football, Golf, Hockey, Lacrosse, Rugby, Squash, Swimming, Tennis, Track, Water Polo, Wrestling. Women (Div.III): Basketball, Crew, Cross Country, Diving, Field Hockey, Lacrosse, Rugby, Soccer, Softball, Squash, Swimming, Tennis, Track, Volleyball.

Campus Life. Regulations governing campus social life controlled by students. No curfews; 24-hour intervisitation. Drinking permitted on campus for students over 18 in dormitories and fraternity houses; cars allowed but parking remains a problem. Active calendar of cultural and social events on campus, supplemented by those offered in Hartford and nearby colleges. Student body is reported to be informal: informal clothes, informal dating, etc.

About 90% of men, 95% of women live in coed dormitories; rest commute. Freshmen given preference in college housing if all students cannot be accommodated. Sexes segregated in dormitories by floor. There are 7 fraternities and 2 sororities on campus which about 33% of men, 12% of women join; 4% of men, 2% of women live in fraternities and sororities. About 10–15% of resident students leave campus on weekends.

Annual Costs. Tuition and fees, $18,700; room and board, $5,420; estimated $1,200 other, exclusive of travel. About 42% of students receive financial aid; average amount of assistance, $13,200. College reports all scholarships awarded on the basis of need. *Meeting Costs:* college offers alternative payment plans.

Trinity College

Washington, D. C. 20017-1094 **(202) 939-5040; (800) 492-6882**

A small, liberal arts college for women, conducted by the Sisters of Notre Dame de Namur, Trinity claims the distinction of being the first Catholic college established for women. Its location in the nation's capital is an appropriate setting for a student body of diverse geo-

graphical—though similar religious and academic—background. The 34-acre campus is located in a suburb, 2½ miles north of the Capitol. Most convenient major airport: Washington National.

Founded: 1897
Affiliation: Roman Catholic
UG Enrollment: 500 W (full-time); 500 W (part-time)
Total Enrollment: 1,112
Cost: $10K–$20K
Admission: Selective
Application Deadline: Feb. 1

Admission is selective. About 77% of applicants accepted, 46% of these actually enroll. Average freshman SAT scores, according to most recent data available: 530 verbal, 510 mathematical. *Required:* SAT or ACT; interview strongly recommended. *Entrance programs:* early decision, early admission, midyear admission, deferred admission, advanced placement. About 57% of entering students from private or parochial schools. *Apply:* by February 1; rolling admissions after February 1 if space available. *Transfers* welcome.
Academic Environment. Students reportedly have influence on faculty hiring and promotion through their class evaluations and membership on Board of Trustees as student/faculty committees. Individual programs largely developed by students with concurrence of faculty. Faculty composed primarily of lay teachers. Administration reports 47% of courses required for graduation are elective; distribution guidelines fairly numerous; most students expected to take 3 courses in each of 4 general areas. Foreign language requirement for graduation introduced recently. *Degree:* AB. *Majors offered* include usual arts and sciences, drug science, international affairs, medical technology; interdisciplinary programs include urban studies, environmental studies.

About 81% of students entering as freshmen graduate within four years. *Special programs:* independent study, individualized majors, study abroad: sophomore year at Oxford, summer in Italy, junior year in France, semester exchange in Mexico, honors, undergraduate research, cross-registration through Washington Consortium; college is host to semester program for political science majors. Adult programs: Adult Studies Program for women with work experience or previous college experience. *Calendar:* semester.
Undergraduate degrees conferred (138). 33% were in Social Sciences, 20% were in Business and Management, 10% were in Area and Ethnic Studies, 7% were in Education, 6% were in Psychology, 5% were in Letters, 4% were in Theology, 4% were in Visual and Performing Arts, 4% were in Communications, 3% were in Foreign Languages, remainder in 3 other fields.
Graduates Career Data. According to most recent data available, full-time graduate study pursued immediately after graduation by 1% of graduates; 2% enter medical school; 10% enter law school. Medical schools typically enrolling largest numbers of graduates include Georgetown, Jefferson; dental schools include Georgetown; law schools include Georgetown, Fordham; business schools include Wharton, U. of Maryland. *Careers in business and industry* pursued by 46% of graduates. Corporations typically hiring largest number of graduates include Merrill Lynch, IBM, Sun Oil.
Faculty. About 88% of faculty hold PhD or equivalent.
Student Body. About 8% of students from within district; 71% Middle Atlantic; foreign students from 14 countries. An estimated 30% of students reported as minority, according to most recent data available.
Varsity Sports. (CWAC): Crew, Field Hockey, Soccer, Tennis.
Campus Life. College is located in the heart of Washington, D.C. Varied cultural and social activities on campus, supplemented by unlimited resources of the city. Many regulations governing campus social life have been significantly modified; curfew remains only for first-semester freshmen. Alcohol allowed in residence halls, and beer and light wine permitted at college functions with consent of dean. Cars permitted.

About 90% of women live in dormitories. There are no sororities.
Annual Costs. Tuition and fees, $11,230; room and board, $6,430. College reports some scholarships awarded for academic merit.

Trinity College

Deerfield, Illinois 60015 (708) 317-7000

A private college, founded by the Evangelical Free Church, teaching liberal arts within the context of a "Biblically oriented Christian world and life view"; located in a community of 20,000, 25 miles north of Chicago. Most convenient major airport: O'Hare International (Chicago).

Founded: 1897
Affiliation: Independent (Evangelical Free Church)
UG Enrollment: 325 M, 353 W (full-time); 21 M, 40 W (part-time)
Cost: < $10K
% Receiving Financial Aid: 85%
Admission: Non-selective
Application Deadline: Rolling

Admission. Graduates of accredited high schools with 15 units (12 in college-preparatory subjects) eligible; 70% of applicants accepted, 50% of these actually enroll; 36% of freshmen graduate in top fifth of high school class, 57% in top two-fifths. Average freshman scores, according to most recent data available: SAT, 450 M, 480 W verbal, 500 M, 470 W mathematical; ACT, 19 M, 21 W composite. *Required:* ACT (SAT considered), Pastor recommendation, essay, minimum H.S. GPA of 2.5. Criteria considered in admissions, in order of importance: high school academic record, recommendations, writing sample, standardized test scores. About 4% of freshmen from private schools. *Apply:* rolling admissions. *Transfers* welcome; 132 enrolled 1993–94.
Academic Environment. Degrees offered: bachelors. About 33% of general education requirements for graduation are elective; distribution requirements fairly numerous. About 54% of students entering as freshmen graduate in four years, 61% eventually; 74% of freshmen return for sophomore year. *Special programs:* independent study, off-campus programs, study abroad, internships, cross registration with Trinity Evangelical Divinity School. Adult programs: REACH - relevant education for the Adult Christian. *Calendar:* semester, summer study tours.
Undergraduate degrees conferred (157). 41% were in Liberal/General Studies, 18% were in Education, 10% were in Philosophy and Religion, 8% were in Psychology, 8% were in Business and Management, 5% were in Social Sciences, 4% were in Communications, remainder in 6 other fields.
Graduates Career Data. Advanced studies pursued by 5% of students; 1% enter medical school; 1% enter law school; 1% enter business school. About 85% of 1992–93 graduates employed. Fields typically hiring largest number of graduates include education, business, youth ministry.
Faculty. About 50% of faculty hold PhD or equivalent. About 33% of teaching faculty are female.
Student Body. College seeks a national student body; 48% of students from Illinois; 39% Midwest, 1% Middle Atlantic, 1% New England, 4% South, 6% West; 1% Foreign. An estimated 98% of students reported as Protestant, 2% Catholic; 8% Black, 3% Hispanic, 5% Asian.
Religious Orientation. Trinity is an independent institution with a "Christian heritage"; 12 semester hours of Biblical studies, attendance at chapel services required of all students.
Varsity Sports. Men (NAIA, NCAA, Div.III): Baseball, Basketball, Cross Country, Football, Golf, Soccer, Tennis, Track, Volleyball. Women (NAIA, NCAA, Div.III): Basketball, Cross Country, Soccer, Softball, Tennis, Track, Volleyball.
Campus Life. About 80% of men, 80% of women live in traditional dormitories; no coed dormitories; rest commute. Intervisitation in men's and women's dormitory rooms limited to weekends only. There are no fraternities or sororities. About 10% of resident students leave campus on weekends.
Annual Costs. Tuition and fees, $9,600; room and board, $4,110; estimated $1,000 other, exclusive of travel. About 85% of students receive financial aid; average amount of assistance, $7,000. College reports some scholarships awarded for academic merit. *Meeting Costs:* college offers Parent PLUS Loans, 10-month payment plan with no interest.

Trinity College of Vermont

Burlington, Vermont 05401 (802) 658-0337

A church-related, liberal arts college for women, conducted by the Sisters of Mercy, located in a community of 50,000 in the Green Mountains near Lake Champlain. Most convenient major airport: Burlington International.

Founded: 1925
Affiliation: Roman Catholic
UG Enrollment: 42 M, 454 W (full-time); 135 M, 370 W (part-time)
Cost: $10K–$20K
% Receiving Financial Aid: 82%
Admission: Non-selective
Application Deadline: Rolling

Admission. Graduates of accredited high schools with 16 units who rank in top half of class eligible; 95% of applicants accepted, 91% of these actually enroll; 27% graduate in top fifth of high school class, 50% in top two-fifths. Average freshman SAT scores: 410 W verbal, 420 W mathematical. *Required:* SAT, minimum H.S. GPA, essay; campus visit recommended. Criteria considered in admissions, in order of importance: high school academic record, standardized test scores, recommendations, writing sample. *Entrance programs:* midyear admission. About 10% of freshmen from parochial schools. *Apply:* rolling admissions. *Transfers* welcome; 25 enrolled 1993–94.

Academic Environment. Cross-registration with St. Michael's and Champlain (a 2-year college in Burlington). Degrees offered: associates, bachelors, masters. About one-third of degree requirements are general education core. *Majors offered* include teacher certification as second degree, comparative cultural studies, economics, philosophy. About 60% of entering freshmen graduate in four years. *Special programs:* independent study, study abroad, January term, internships, medical technology; special, early childhood, elementary and secondary education, social work, freshman seminar for academic and peer support. Adult programs: Weekend College, Evening Degree, PACE (weekday courses). *Calendar:* semester, summer session.

Undergraduate degrees conferred (199). 38% were in Business and Management, 20% were in Education, 12% were in Psychology, 6% were in Communications, 4% were in Public Affairs, 4% were in Life Sciences, 4% were in Letters, 3% were in Mathematics, 3% were in Liberal/General Studies, 3% were in Allied Health, remainder in 4 other fields.

Graduates Career Data. Advanced studies pursued by 10% of students. About 86% of 1992–93 graduates employed. Fields typically hiring largest number of graduates include business and industry, education, human services. Career Development Services include individual and group career counseling, career library, SIGI PLUS computer, career workshops and panels, assistance with resume preparation, interviewing and developing job search strategies, alumni career network.

Faculty. About 79% of faculty hold PhD or equivalent.

Student Body. College does not seek a national student body; 82% of students from in state; 48% from New England, 2% Northwest. An estimated 50% of students reported as Catholic, remaining 50% dispersed among many; according to most recent data available 1% Black, 1% Hispanic, 1% Asian, 2% other minority.

Religious Orientation. Trinity is a church-related institution; 1 course in religious studies and 1 course in philosophy required of all students.

Varsity Sports. Women (NSCAA): Basketball, Soccer.

Campus Life. "College assumes that each student is an adult and has, therefore, made few confining regulations." Cars allowed. Seniors with consent of parents may live off campus. According to most recent data available about 75% of women live in dormitories; rest live in off-campus housing or commute. Intervisitation in women's dormitory rooms limited. There are no sororities. About 10% of students leave campus on weekends.

Annual Costs. Tuition and fees, $10,945; room and board, $5,570; estimated $550 other, exclusive of travel. About 82% of students receive financial aid; average amount of assistance, $11,000. Assistance is typically divided 62% grant, 28% loan, 10% work. College reports 65 scholarships awarded for academic merit. *Meeting Costs:* college offers tuition payment plan.

Trinity University

San Antonio, Texas 78212-7200 **(210) 736-7011; (800) TRINITY**

An independent institution with "traditional and covenant rather than legal ties to its founding church," Trinity is located on a 115-acre campus, overlooking San Antonio (pop. 1 million). Most convenient major airport: San Antonio International.

Founded: 1869
Affiliation: Independent (United Presbyterian)
UG Enrollment: 1,032 M, 1,075 W (full-time); 47 M, 54 W (part-time)
Total Enrollment: 2,465
Cost: $10K–$20K
% Receiving Financial Aid: 72%
Admission: Highly Selective
Application Deadline: February 1

Admission is highly selective. About 75% of applicants accepted, 33% of these actually enroll; 86% of freshmen graduate in top fifth of high school class, 98% in top two-fifths. Average freshman scores: SAT, 573 M, 612 W verbal, 646 M, 576 W mathematical; 83% of freshmen score above 500 on verbal, 34% above 600, 3% above 700; 95% score above 500 on mathematical, 64% above 600, 20% above 700; ACT, 28.1 M, 27.6 W composite. *Required:* SAT or ACT, essay. Criteria considered in admissions, in order of importance: high school academic record, standardized test scores, writing sample, extracurricular activities, recommendations; other factors considered: special talents, diverse student body, religious affiliation and/or commitment. *Entrance programs:* early decision, early admission, midyear admission, deferred admission, advanced placement. About 18% of entering students from private schools. *Apply* by February 1. *Transfers* welcome; 24 enrolled 1993–94.

Academic Environment. Recent student leader asserts there is a "very strong desire to become one of the premier liberal arts and sciences institutions in the country." Current data suggest university is succeeding in attracting an extremely capable student body. Undergraduate Studies offered by the Faculties of Business and Management studies, Communications and the Arts, Education, Humanities, Sciences, Mathematics and Engineering, Social and Behavioral Sciences. Degrees offered: bachelors, masters. Core requirements include courses in each of six "understandings". *Majors offered* in addition to usual studies include biophysics, communication, computing and information sciences, education, Asian studies. Students list as strengths of the academic program: small classes, professors are extremely accessible, many opportunities for undergraduate research, no teaching assistants. Average undergraduate class size: 45% under 20, 50% between 20–40, 5% over 40; student-faculty ratio of 11:1.

About 66% of students entering as freshmen graduate in four years, 77% eventually; 85% of freshmen return for sophomore year. *Special programs:* independent study, study abroad, honors, undergraduate research, 3-year degree, individualized majors, credit by examination. *Calendar:* semester, summer school.

Undergraduate degrees conferred (473). 20% were in Social Sciences, 15% were in Business and Management, 10% were in Life Sciences, 9% were in Letters, 7% were in Philosophy and Religion, 6% were in Psychology, 6% were in Communications, 5% were in Visual and Performing Arts, 3% were in Liberal/General Studies, 3% were in Computer and Engineering Related Technology, 3% were in Engineering, 3% were in Mathematics, 3% were in Physical Sciences, 3% were in Foreign Languages, remainder in 2 other fields.

Graduates Career Data. Advanced studies pursued by about 55% of students; 3% enter medical school; 3% enter dental school; 10% enter law school; 2% enter business school. Medical schools typically enrolling largest numbers of graduates include U. of Texas; law schools include G.W.U., Tulane. About 45% of 1992–93 graduates employed. Corporations typically hiring largest numbers of graduates include Arthur Andersen, IBM, Metropolitan Life, Anderson Consulting. *Career Counseling Program:* student assessment of program reported as good for both career guidance and job placement. Help provided in preparing for interviews. Alumni reported as not active in either career guidance or job placement.

Faculty. About 96% of faculty hold PhD or equivalent. About 72% of undergraduate classes taught by tenured faculty. About 21% of teaching faculty are female; 3% Hispanic, 4% other minority.

Student Body. University seeks a national student body; 63% of students from in state; 72% of students from South, 15% Midwest, 4% New England, 2% Middle Atlantic, 3% West, 2% Northwest; 2% Foreign. An estimated 54% of students reported as Protestant, 27% Catholic, 2% Jewish, 1% Muslim, 8% unaffiliated, 8% other; 2% Black, 8% Hispanic, 8% Asian, 14% other minority.

Religious Orientation. Trinity is an independent institution with some ties to the United Presbyterian Church; no religious requirements, however.

Varsity Sports. Men (Div.III): Baseball, Basketball, Football, Cross Country, Diving, Football, Golf, Skeet, Soccer, Swimming, Tennis, Track, Trap. Women (Div.III): Basketball, Cross Country, Diving, Golf, Soccer, Softball, Swimming, Tennis, Track, Volleyball.

Campus Life. Recent student leader reports those most at home on campus likely to be "strongly motivated students with middle or upper-middle class background and a broad range of interests." About 70% of students said to participate in intramural sports; varsity athletics attract far fewer students. Interest in fraternities/sororities is increasing. Student services said to be "generally excellent"; while on-campus living accommodations reportedly are "plush." One student finds that San Antonio offers multicultural experiences of a big city, with a "small town feel". Alcohol consumption limited to students 21 and over living in designated "drinking dorms."

About 4% of women live in traditional dormitories; 75% of men, 71% of women in coed dormitories; rest live in off-campus housing or commute. Freshmen given preference in college housing if all students cannot be accommodated. There are 6 local fraternities, 6 local sororities on campus which about 30% of men, 33% of women join; they provide no residence facilities.

Annual Costs. Tuition and fees, $11,720; room and board, $4,950; estimated $1,030 other, exclusive of travel. About 72% of students receive financial aid; average amount of assistance, $9,627. University reports 511 scholarships awarded for academic merit, 886 for need.

Tri-State University

Angola, Indiana 46703 (219) 665-4100

An independent institution, specializing in preparation for engineering and business careers, located in a community of 6,000, 45 miles north of Fort Wayne. Most convenient major airport: Toledo Municipal, OH.

Founded: 1884
Affiliation: Independent
UG Enrollment: 696 M, 282 W (full-time); 54 M, 44 W (part-time)
Cost: < $10K
% Receiving Financial Aid: 95%
Admission: Non-selective
Application Deadline: August 15

Admission. Graduates of approved high schools or equivalent eligible; 84% of applicants accepted, 29% of these actually enroll; 38% of freshmen graduate in top fifth of high school class, 65% in top two-fifths. Average freshman scores: SAT, 410 verbal, 510 W mathematical; 15% of freshmen score above 500 verbal, 2% above 600, 58% score above 500 mathematical, 22% above 600, 3% above 700; ACT, 22 composite. *Required:* SAT or ACT. Criteria considered in admissions, in order of importance: high school academic record, standardized test scores, recommendations, extracurricular activities; other factors considered: special talents, diverse student body. *Entrance programs:* early admission, midyear admission, advanced placement. *Apply* by August 15: rolling admissions. *Transfers* welcome; 59 enrolled 1993–94.

Academic Environment. Degrees offered: associates, bachelors. Majors include corporate English, environmental science, education, and 4-year CADD. Average undergraduate class size: 30% under 20, 69% between 20–40, 1% over 40. *Special programs:* CLEP, cooperative education. About 25% of students entering as freshmen graduate in four years, 60% eventually; 67% of freshmen return for sophomore year. *Calendar:* quarter, summer school.

Undergraduate degrees conferred (174). 57% were in Engineering, 13% were in Education, 11% were in Business and Management, 6% were in Multi/Interdisciplinary Studies, 5% were in Computer and Engineering Related Technology, remainder in 7 other fields.

Graduates Career Data. Advanced studies pursued by 20% of students; 1% enter medical school; 5% enter law school. About 90% of 1992–93 graduates employed. Fields typically hiring largest number of graduates include manufacturing, business.

Faculty. About 52% of faculty hold PhD or equivalent. About 60% of undergraduate classes taught by tenured faculty. About 17% of teaching faculty are female.

Student Body. About 52% of students from in state; 76% North Central, 9% Middle Atlantic, according to most recent data available; 18% Foreign. An estimated 2% of students reported as Black, 1% Hispanic, 2% Asian.

Varsity Sports. Men (NAIA): Baseball, Basketball, Cross Country, Fencing, Golf, Soccer, Tennis, Track. Women (NAIA): Basketball, Cross Country, Fencing, Soccer, Softball, Tennis, Track, Volleyball.

Campus Life. About 45% of men, 40% of women live in traditional dormitories; 5% of men, 20% of women live in coed dormitories; 20% of men, 10% of women live in off-campus college-related housing or commute. Freshmen given preference in college housing if all students cannot be accommodated. Intervisitation in men's and women's dormitory rooms limited. There are 9 fraternities, 4 sororities on campus which about 22% of men, 15% of women join; 20% of men live in fraternities, 10% of women live in sororities. About 20% of resident students leave campus on weekends.

Annual Costs. Tuition and fees, $9,000; room and board, $4,200; estimated $400 other, exclusive of travel. About 95% of students receive financial aid; average amount of assistance, $3,000. Assistance is typically divided 40% scholarship, 45% grant, 10% loan, 58% work. College reports 280 scholarships awarded for special talents. *Meeting Costs:* college offers monthly payment plan.

Troy State University

Troy, Alabama 36082 (205) 670-3000

A state-supported university, located in a community of 11,500, 50 miles southeast of Montgomery, with branch campuses at Montgomery and Fort Rucker, as well as at various military installations around the globe through University College. Most convenient major airport: Montgomery.

Founded: 1887
Affiliation: State
UG Enrollment: 2,040 M, 2,335 W (full-time)
Total Enrollment: 5,010
Cost: < $10K
% Receiving Financial Aid: 65%
Admission: Non-selective
Application Deadline: August 15

Admission. Graduates of accredited high schools with minimum GPA of 2.0 eligible; 79% of applicants accepted, 67% of these actually enroll; 73% of freshmen graduate in top fifth of high school class, 88% in top two-fifths. Average freshman scores: ACT, 20.1 M, 21.4 W composite. *Required:* ACT (minimum of 18), medical form. Criteria considered in admissions, in order of importance: high school academic record, standardized test scores, extracurricular activities, recommendations. *Out-of-state* freshman applicants: university actively seeks students from out-of-state. State does not limit out-of-state enrollment. About 283 out-of-state applicants enrolled. States from which most out-of-state applicants are drawn include Florida, Georgia. Entrance programs: early admission, midyear admission, advanced placement. *Apply* by August 15; rolling admissions. *Transfers* welcome; 712 enrolled 1992–93.

Academic Environment. Degrees offered: associates, bachelors, masters. Average undergraduate class size: 56% under 20, 40% between 20–40, 4% over 40. About 72% of students entering as freshmen graduate eventually; 70% of freshmen return for sophomore year. *Special programs:* CLEP, independent study, study abroad, honors, workstudy, workship programs, undergraduate research. *Calendar:* quarter, summer school.

Undergraduate degrees conferred (749). 34% were in Business and Management, 22% were in Education, 9% were in Protective Services, 5% were in Health Sciences, 5% were in Social Sciences, 5% were in Communications, 4% were in Public Affairs, 3% were in Computer and Engineering Related Technology, 3% were in Psychology, 3% were in Life Sciences, remainder in 6 other fields.

Faculty. About 75% of faculty hold PhD or equivalent. About 68% of undergraduate classes taught by tenured faculty. About 28% of teaching faculty are female; 10% Black, 4% Hispanic, 2% other minority.

Student Body. College does not seek a national student body; 76% of students from in state; 94% South; less than 1% Foreign. An estimated 6% of students reported as Protestant, 10% Catholic, 2% Jewish, 2% Muslim, 10% unaffiliated, 70% Baptist; 18% Black, 2% other minority. Average age of undergraduate student: 22.

Varsity Sports. Men (Div.I): Baseball, Basketball, Cross Country, Football (IAA), Golf, Tennis, Track. Women (Div.I): Basketball, Cross Country, Golf, Softball, Tennis, Track, Volleyball.

Campus Life. About 17% of men, 19% of women live in traditional dormitories; 3% of men, 2% of women in coed dormitories; 72% of men, 62% of women commute. No intervisitation in men's or women's dormitory rooms. There are 8 fraternities, 8 sororities on campus which about 8% of men, 17% of women join; 8% of men live in fraternities; 17% of women live in sororities. About 22% of resident students leave campus on weekends.

Annual Costs. Tuition and fees, $1,695 (out-of-state, $2,884); room and board, $2,695; estimated $700 other, exclusive of travel. About 65% of students receive financial aid; average amount of assistance, $4,000. University reports 17 scholarships awarded for academic merit, 13 for special talents, 19 for need.

Tufts University

Medford, Massachusetts 02155 (617) 627-3170

Tufts University is a complex institution built around three formerly separate colleges. The University now comprises the coeducational College of Liberal Arts and the College of Engineering, as well as the well-known Medical and Dental Schools, Sackler School of Biomedical Sciences, the School of Veterinary Medicine, a Nutrition Institute, Tufts School of Occupational Therapy, the School of the Museum of Fine Arts, and the Gordon Institute for Engineering Leadership. Finally, the prestigious Fletcher School of Law and Diplomacy completes the aggregate. The graduate schools concerned with health sciences are located in Boston, the others are housed on a 150-acre campus located in a suburban community of 64,400, 6 miles from Boston. Most convenient major airport: Logan International (Boston).

Founded: 1852	**Cost:** $10K–$20K
Affiliation: Independent	**% Receiving Financial Aid:** 39%
UG Enrollment: 2,172 M, 2,424 W (full-time)	**Admission:** Highly (+) Selective
Total Enrollment: 7,998	**Application Deadline:** January 1

Admission is highly (+) selective. For all schools, about 47% of applicants accepted, 33% of these actually enroll; 87% of freshmen graduate in top fifth of high school class, 97% in top two-fifths. Average freshmen scores SAT, 585 M, 583 W verbal, 674 M, 635 W mathematical; 93% of freshmen score above 500 on verbal SAT, 43% above 600, 3% above 700; 99% score above 500 on mathematical, 82% above 600, 29% above 700.

For Liberal Arts (1,810 M, 2,082 W), 32% of applicants accepted, 38% of these actually enroll; 89% of freshmen graduate in top fifth of high school class, 98% in top two-fifths. Average freshman SAT scores: 595 verbal, 638 mathematical; 92% of freshmen score above 500 on verbal SAT, 52% above 600, 7% above 700; 76% score above 500 on mathematical, 56% above 600, 20% above 700, according to most recent data available.

For Engineering (693 M, 207 W), 54% of applicants accepted, 36% of these actually enroll; 86% of freshmen graduate in top fifth of high school class, 95% in top two-fifths. Average freshman SAT scores: 574 verbal, 695 mathematical; 91% of freshmen score above 500 on verbal SAT, 37% above 600, 2% above 700; all score above 500 on mathematical, 99% above 600, 53% above 700, according to most recent data available.

Required: SAT and 3 ACH including English (physics or chemistry, and mathematics I or II for engineering) or ACT, essay. Criteria considered in admissions, in order of importance: high school academic record, recommendations, standardized test scores, extracurricular activities, writing sample; special talents, diverse student body, alumni children. *Entrance programs:* early decision, early admission, deferred admission, advanced placement, deferred admission. About 32% of entering students from private schools, 8% from parochial schools. *Apply* by January 1. *Transfers* welcome; 113 enrolled 1992–93.

Academic Environment. Pressures for academic achievement appear strong; student body is able; independent study is popular. Administration reports 70% of courses required for graduation under regular program are elective; some distribution requirements, however, for Liberal Arts: students must demonstrate "adequate acquaintance" with 5 broad areas (humanities, arts, social studies, mathematics, sciences) by examination, advanced placement, or by taking 2 semester courses in each area; proficiency in foreign language and college writing. "Tufts is a place where academics are taken seriously, though students generally lead well-rounded lives," according to a recent student leader. Students feel faculty is interested and accessible. University boasts a 90% retention rate. Degrees offered: bachelors, masters, doctoral. *Majors offered* include usual arts and sciences, applied physics, astronomy, chemical physics, child study, community health, computer science, mental health, drama, education, engineering psychology, fine arts, international relations, 4 fields of engineering; individualized plans of study also possible. Computer facilities reported to be adequate to meet student demand with 3 user areas, PC labs, and CAD lab. Library facilities reported as excellent. Average undergraduate class size: 68% under 20, 25% between 20–40, 7% over 40.

About 90% of students entering as freshmen graduate within four years; 99% return for sophomore year. *Special programs:* independent study, internships, study abroad, honors, undergraduate research; Experimental College offers self-achievement program permitting student to complete course from regular curriculum without formal enrollment or class attendance; 5-year arts/engineering program, 5-year BA/BFA with School of the Museum of Fine Arts; 5-year BA/BM with New England Conservatory, BA/MA with Fletcher School of Law and Diplomacy, cross registration with Boston U., B.C., Brandeis. Adult programs: REAL (Resumed Education For Adult Learners for students over 25. *Calendar:* semester, summer school.

Undergraduate degrees conferred (1,392). 35% were in Social Sciences, 13% were in Engineering, 10% were in Letters, 9% were in Visual and Performing Arts, 8% were in Psychology, 7% were in Life Sciences, 4% were in Education, 3% were in Foreign Languages, 3% were in Multi/Interdisciplinary Studies, remainder in 6 other fields.

Graduates Career Data. Advanced studies pursued by 68% of students; 10% enter medical school; 1% enter dental school; 24% enter law school; 20 enter business school; 3% enter other schools. Medical schools typically enrolling largest numbers of graduates include Tufts; dental schools include Tufts; law schools include Boston U., Georgetown, Boston College; business schools include Boston U., Wharton, Columbia. Career Development Services include career planning, on-campus recruitment, counseling, visitation form over 150 companies and organizations.

Faculty. About 99% of faculty hold PhD or equivalent.

Student Body. About 26% of students from in state; 40% New England, 29% Middle Atlantic, 7% South, 6% Midwest, 9% West/Northwest; 9% Foreign. An estimated 4% of students reported as Black, 11% Asian, 4% Hispanic, 8% other minority.

Varsity Sports. Men (Div.III): Baseball, Basketball, Crew, Cross Country, Diving, Equestrian, Football, Golf, Hockey, Lacrosse, Sailing, Soccer, Squash, Swimming, Tennis, Track. Women (Div.III): Basketball, Crew, Cross Country, Diving, Equestrian, Field Hockey, Lacrosse, Sailing, Soccer, Squash, Softball, Swimming, Tennis, Track, Volleyball.

Campus Life. Student leader writes: "Harvard Square and Boston" are nearby and "a national student body makes for a vast array of friends." Some 140 student organizations offer activities for every taste. The most popular clubs on campus include Leonard Carmichael Society, a volunteer group with over 500 members, Tufts Mountain Club, and the Environmental Conscientious Organization. Drinking allowed subject to state and local law. Cars not permitted for freshmen on campus because of limited parking space. Freshmen and sophomores required to live in university-related housing. Each dormitory sets up its own "house rules" to assure reasonable thoughtfulness of others.

About 2% of women live in traditional dormitories; 68% of men, 73% of women in coed dormitories; 21% of men, 21% of women live in off-campus college-related housing within walking distance; 3% of men, 2% of women commute. Sexes segregated in coed dormitories either by wing, floor, or room. Freshmen are given preference in college housing if all students cannot be accommodated. There are 10 fraternities, 4 sororities on campus which about 15% of men, 4% of women join; 8% of men, 2% of women live in fraternities and sororities.

Annual Costs. Tuition and fees, $18,793; room and board, $5,693. About 39% of students receive financial aid; average amount of assistance, $15,837. Assistance is typically divided 70% scholarship/grant, 22% loan, 8% work. College reports 51 scholarships awarded for academic merit, 1,450 for need. *Meeting Costs:* university offers tuition prepayment plan, Mass. Family Education Loan, AMS payment plan.

Tulane University

New Orleans, Louisiana 70118 (504) 865-5731

Tulane is not a typical Southern institution. Fewer than half its undergraduates come from the South, more are enrolled from Middle Atlantic states than from its home state of Louisiana, and substantial numbers come from other areas of the country. Many students are attracted to Tulane by its distinguished professional schools of law, medicine, social work, and business, as well as certain departments in its graduate school of arts and sciences. The undergradu-

ate colleges of Architecture, Engineering, Arts and Sciences, Newcomb, University College, and the graduate and professional schools are all co-educational except for the College of Arts and Sciences for men and Newcomb College for women. The 110-acre main campus is located in a residential section of New Orleans; Newcomb College is an integral part of the main campus. Most convenient major airport: New Orleans International.

Founded: 1834	**Total Enrollment:** 11,203
Affiliation: Independent	**Cost:** $10K–$20K
UG Enrollment: 2,540 M, 2,406 W (full-time); 668 M, 861 W (part-time)	**% Receiving Financial Aid:** 55%
	Admission: Highly (+) Selective
	Application Deadline: Jan. 15

Admission is highly (+) selective for School of Engineering, very (+) selective for School of Architecture, College of Arts and Sciences, Newcomb College.

For the undergraduate divisions, 73% of applicants accepted, 24% actually enroll; 66% of freshmen graduate in top fifth of high school class, 91% in top two-fifths.

For Architecture (170 M, 98 W), 64% of applicants accepted, 31% of these actually enroll; 64% of freshmen graduate in top fifth of high school class, 86% in top two-fifths. Average freshman SAT scores: 547 verbal, 637 mathematical; 77% of freshmen score above 500 on verbal, 25% above 600, 2% above 700; 98% score above 500 on mathematical, 73% above 600, 23% above 700.

For Engineering (585 M, 234 W), 81% of applicants accepted, 26% of these actually enroll; 83% of freshmen graduate in top fifth of high school class, 97% in top two-fifths. Average freshman SAT scores: 571 verbal, 651 mathematical; 76% of freshmen score above 500 on verbal, 40% above 600, 9% above 700; 99% score above 500 on mathematical, 77% above 600, 30% above 700.

For Arts and Sciences (1,447 M), 70% of applicants accepted, 24% of these actually enroll; 57% of freshmen graduate in top fifth of high school class, 88% in top two-fifths. Average freshman SAT scores: 553 verbal, 623 mathematical; 71% of freshmen score above 500 on verbal, 32% above 600, 6% above 700; 95% score above 500 on mathematical, 68% above 600, 21% above 700.

For Newcomb (1,866 W), 73% of applicants accepted, 22% of these actually enroll; 67% of freshmen graduate in top fifth of high school class, 94% in top two-fifths. Average SAT scores: 552 verbal, 580 mathematical; 71% of freshmen score above 500 on verbal; 29% above 600; 4% above 700; 85% score above 500 on mathematical; 41% above 600; 6% above 700.

Required: SAT or ACT, essay, guidance counselor recommendation, extracurricular activates. Criteria considered in admissions, in order of importance: high school academic record, standardized test scores, writing sample, recommendations, extracurricular activities; other factors considered: special talents, alumni children, diverse student body. *Entrance programs:* early notification, early admission, midyear admission, advanced placement, deferred admission. About 45% of entering students from private and parochial schools. *Apply* by January 15. *Transfers* welcome; 118 enrolled 1993–94.

Academic Environment. Degrees offered: associates, bachelors, masters, doctoral. *Majors offered* include environmental sciences, political economy, pre-professional programs, engineering, Latin American studies. Tulane's demanding liberal arts and sciences core curriculum draws on the university's traditional strengths in the sciences and mathematics as well as the social sciences, fine arts and the humanities. These are buttressed by the Mellon Program in Humanities and the Murphy Institute for Political Economy and Policy Analysis. Superior students enroll in the Honors Program which offers seminars, colloquia, self-designed majors, and supervised study abroad. Substantial numbers of graduates are admitted to Tulane's medical, law and business schools; others enroll at leading graduate and professional schools in all parts of the country. *Undergraduate studies* offered to freshmen by schools listed above. Average undergraduate class size: 53% under 20, 33% between 20–40, 14% over 40.

About 65% of students entering as freshmen graduate in four years, 80% eventually; 85% of freshmen return for sophomore year. *Special programs:* colloquia, early admission to Tulane Medical School, independent study, study abroad, honors, undergraduate research, 3-year degree, individualized majors, interdisciplinary studies, semester in Washington D.C., international affairs program, Latin American studies, combined arts and sciences/architecture, law, medicine, social work or business degrees, programs in public administration, teacher education, teacher–coach, pre-legal, pre-science, pre-medical, pre-social work, 3–2 engineering, cross registration with Xavier and Loyola. Computer facilities reported to be more than adequate. *Library:* 1,946,000 titles, 17,000 periodicals, 2,000,000 microforms, other materials include Latin American Library, Louisiana Collection, Jazz Archive, Newcomb College Center for Research on Women, Amistad Research Center Collection on American ethnic minorities; open-stack privileges. *Calendar:* semester, summer school.

Undergraduate degrees conferred (1,457). 30% were in Social Sciences, 12% were in Business and Management, 9% were in Engineering, 8% were in Letters, 7% were in Life Sciences, 7% were in Psychology, 5% were in Communications, 4% were in Architecture and Environmental Design, 4% were in Visual and Performing Arts, 3% were in Foreign Languages, remainder in 10 other fields.

Graduates Career Data. Advanced studies pursued by 80% of students eventually; 9% enter medical school; 16% enter law school; 7% enter business school; 12% enter other schools. Medical schools typically enrolling largest numbers of graduates include Georgetown, Loyola, Tulane, U. of Wisconsin; law schools include U. of Virginia, Tulane, Yale, Georgetown; business schools include Harvard, Tulane, U. of Texas. About 35% of 1992–93 graduates employed. Corporations typically hiring largest numbers of graduates include IBM, Shell, Exxon. Career Development Services include counseling group, placement service, resume/interview workshops, on-campus recruitment, internships, library resources, computerized guidance system, alumni assistance, job fair, career fair, graduate/profession school day, career network, community service fair, individual services.

Faculty. About 98% of faculty hold PhD or equivalent. About 23% of teaching faculty are female; 3% Black, 2% Hispanic, 6% other minority.

Student Body. University seeks a national student body; 20% of students from in state; 48% South, 28% Northeast, 11% Midwest, 7% West/Northwest. An estimated 49% of students reported as Catholic, 27% Protestant, 17% Jewish, 7% other; 10% as Black, 4% Asian, 6% Hispanic, 1% other minority.

Varsity Sports. Men (Div.I): Baseball, Basketball, Cross Country, Football, Golf, Tennis, Track. Women (Div.I): Basketball, Cross Country, Golf, Tennis, Track, Volleyball.

Campus Life. Regulations governing campus life characterized by students as "very free." As one student leader notes, "Tulane is a good place to go to school . . . and New Orleans is a beautiful, fun-loving city." Wide variety of cultural, intellectual, and social activities on campus as well as in New Orleans. Student interest in fraternities/sororities, reportedly, has decreased in recent years; intramurals still popular. Women in schools of Architecture and Engineering housed in Newcomb facilities. Freshmen who do not reside at home required to live in residence halls.

About 15% of women live in traditional dormitories; 42% of men, 25% of women in coed dormitories; 53% of men, 60% of women live in off-campus college related housing or commute. Freshmen are given preference in college housing if all students cannot be accommodated. There are 17 fraternities, 80 sororities on campus which about 32% of men, 35% of women join; 4% of men live in fraternities; less than 1% of women live in sororities.

Annual Costs. Tuition and fees, $18,760; room and board, $5,780; estimated $1,150 other, exclusive of travel. About 55% of freshmen receive financial aid; average amount of assistance, $16,500. Assistance is typically divided 75% scholarship/grant, 18% loan, 7% work. University reports 200 scholarships awarded for academic merit, 240 for special talents, 1,920 for need. *Meeting Costs:* university offers EXCEL Program, PLUS program, AMS, Variable Interest Program.

University of Tulsa

Tulsa, Oklahoma 74104 **(918) 631-2307; (800) 331-3050**

An independent institution, located in a city of 500,000, affiliated with the Presbyterian Church, U.S.A. Most convenient major airport: Tulsa International.

Founded: 1894
Affiliation: Independent (Presbyterian)
UG Enrollment: 1,404 M, 1,532 W (full-time); 163 M, 270 W (part-time)
Total Enrollment: 4,810
Cost: < $10K
% Receiving Financial Aid: 75%
Admission: Very Selective
Application Deadline: Rolling

Admission is very selective. About 90% of applicants accepted, 45% of these actually enroll; 60% of freshmen graduate in top fifth of high school class, 90% in top two-fifths. Average freshman scores: SAT, 524 verbal, 575 mathematical; 67% of freshmen score above 500 verbal, 30% score above 600, 3% above 700; 71% score above 500 mathematical, 44% score above 600, 11% score above 700; ACT, 24 M, 24 W composite. *Required:* SAT or ACT, high school counselor recommendation. Criteria considered in admissions, in order of importance: number of college prep courses taken in high school, high school academic record, standardized test scores, recommendations, writing sample, extracurricular activities. *Entrance programs:* early admission, midyear admission, advanced placement, deferred admission. About 15% of entering students from private schools and parochial schools. *Apply:* rolling admissions. *Transfers* welcome; 286 enrolled 1993–94.

Academic Environment. Administration source characterizes student body as equally concerned with scholarly/intellectual interests and career-oriented studies, with less interest in social life. Recent student leader, however, reports that students are overwhelmingly devoted to occupational/professional goals. Data on fields in which majority of recent graduates took their degrees suggests very strong interest in the acquisition of marketable skills. Strongest programs reported to be engineering (petroleum engineering, mechanical engineering, geosciences), business (accounting, finance), and arts and sciences (English, psychology). Administration reports continuing efforts to revise degree requirements to permit increased freedom of course selection "within a fixed credit requirement in specific fields of learning." Undergraduate studies offered by colleges of Arts and Sciences, Business Administration, Engineering and Applied Sciences. Curriculum requires each student to learn to write "with fluency and precision," and to acquire basic skills in foreign language and mathematics. Degrees offered: bachelors, masters, doctoral. *Majors offered* include computer science, multidisciplinary program in Law and Society, environmental policy, athletic training, international business, international studies, musical theater, women's studies certificate. Average undergraduate class size: 52% under 20, 44% between 20–40, 4% over 40.

About 40% of students entering as freshmen graduate in four years, 44% eventually; 80% of freshmen return for sophomore year. *Special programs:* independent study, undergraduate research, CLEP, advanced placement, honors, study abroad, internships, 5-year BA/MBA, law courses open to pre-law students, self-designed programs. Adult programs: non-credit programming (e.g., orientation, Adult Student Organization). *Calendar:* semester, summer school.

Undergraduate degrees conferred (521). 30% were in Business and Management, 13% were in Engineering, 8% were in Marketing and Distribution, 7% were in Social Sciences, 7% were in Communications, 7% were in Psychology, 5% were in Letters, 4% were in Education, 4% were in Visual and Performing Arts, 4% were in Health Sciences, 4% were in Life Sciences, 3% were in Physical Sciences, 3% were in Computer and Engineering Related Technology, remainder in 4 other fields.

Graduates Career Data. According to most recent data available, full-time graduate or professional study pursued immediately after graduation by 25% of students; 1% enter medical school; 4% enter law school; 3% enter business school. Medical schools typically enrolling largest numbers of graduates include U. of Oklahoma, Tufts, Arkansas; law schools include U. of Tulsa, Oklahoma, Georgetown, American U., Boston College; business schools include U. of Tulsa, Arkansas, Houston, Kansas. *Careers in business and industry* pursued by 74% of graduates. Fields typically hiring largest number of graduates include accounting, nursing, education, engineering, banking/finance. Career Development Services include interest inventory testing, assistance with major selection; workshops on resume writing, interview skills; on-campus interviews, resume registration.

Faculty. About 93% of faculty hold PhD or equivalent. About 60% of undergraduate classes taught by tenured faculty. About 33% of teaching faculty are female; 1% Black, 3% Hispanic, 4% Asian, 3% Native American, 3% other minority.

Student Body. University seeks a national student body; 58% of students from in state; 10% Foreign. An estimated 59% of students reported as Protestant, 15% Catholic, 1% Jewish, 1% Muslim; 6% as Black, 2% Hispanic, 2% Asian, 5% Native American, 11% other minority. Average age of undergraduate student: 23.

Varsity Sports. Men (Div.IA): Basketball, Cross Country, Football, Golf, Soccer, Tennis, Track. Women (Div.IA): Cross Country, Golf, Soccer, Softball, Tennis, Track, Volleyball.

Campus Life. University reports "a broad array of cultural and sports activities including lectures by nationally recognized authorities, concerts, plays, movies, intramural sports, and intercollegiate athletics." Student government is said to play an important role on campus and to provide an excellent opportunity to develop leadership skills. Social life is reported to be "important, but secondary to studies." Intervisitation limited (2 am), but not an apparent concern of students.

About 40% of students live on campus; rest commute. Freshmen are given preference in college housing if all students cannot be accommodated. There are 7 fraternities, 7 sororities on campus which about 21% of men, 22% of women join; according to most recent data available 9% of men, 11% of women live in fraternities and sororities. About 15% of resident students leave campus on weekends.

Annual Costs. Tuition and fees, $9,995; room and board, $3,800; estimated $750 other, exclusive of travel. About 75% of students receive financial aid; average amount of assistance, $9,400. Assistance is typically divided 54% scholarship/grant, 35% loan, 11% work. University reports some scholarships awarded for academic merit, in addition to a wide variety of other need-based and some merit-based aid. *Meeting Costs:* university offers parent loan program.

Tusculum College

Greeneville, Tennessee 37743 (615) 636-7300

A church-related college, located in a community of 23,000, 65 miles east of Knoxville. Tusculum considers itself a "civic arts" institution, as well as a liberal arts college. Most convenient major airport: Tri Cities—Knoxville.

Founded: 1794
Affiliation: Presbyterian
UG Enrollment: 478 M, 505 W (full-time); 16 M, 24 W (part-time)
Total Enrollment: 1,144
Cost: < $10K
% Receiving Financial Aid: 90%
Admission: Non-selective
Application Deadline: May 1

Admission. High school graduates eligible; others given individual consideration; 85% of applicants accepted, 33% of these actually enroll; 25% of freshmen graduate in top fifth of high school class, 46% in top two-fifths. Average freshman scores: SAT, 343 M, 392 W verbal, 418 M, 440 W mathematical; ACT, 18.7 M, 19.3 W composite. *Required:* SAT or ACT, minimum high school GPA, essay. Criteria considered in admissions, in order of importance: high school academic record, standardized test scores, GPA within academic core courses, writing sample. *Entrance programs:* early admission, midyear admission. *Apply* by May 1; rolling admissions. *Transfers* welcome; 40 enrolled 1993–94.

Academic Environment. Tusculum offers an unusual "Focused Calendar" in place of the more usual semester system. Students take one course at a time, allowing for longer and more intensive classes. Student reports the system "maximizes the student's attention and efforts in one class at a time. It goes very fast and keeps up interest." All BA candidates must complete a set of interdisciplinary courses, validate 15 competencies, complete a civic arts project, and fulfill the requirements of a major. Degrees offered: bachelors, masters. Unusual majors offered include museum studies, environmental studies. Average undergraduate class size: 76% under 20, 24% 20–40.

About 66% of entering freshmen graduate within four years; 80% of freshmen return for sophomore year. *Special programs:* CLEP, independent study, individualized majors, study abroad, internships and/or cooperative work-study programs in management, psychology, environmental science, education, additional travel opportunities offered both foreign and domestic. Adult programs: accelerated evening program for working adults.

Undergraduate degrees conferred (223). 83% were in Business and Management, 8% were in Education, 4% were in Psychology, remainder in 4 other fields.

Graduate Career Data. Career Development Services include resume and interviewing workshops, on-campus recruitment, library resources, individual counseling.
Faculty. About 70% of faculty hold PhD or equivalent. About 30% of teaching faculty are female; 2% Black.
Student Body. About 76% of students from in state; 93% South, 3% New England, 1% each Middle Atlantic, Midwest, West, 1% foreign. An estimated 61% of students reported as Protestant, 10% Catholic, 15% unaffiliated; 7% as Black, 1% Hispanic, 1% other minority. Average age of undergraduate student: 29.
Religious Orientation. Tusculum is a church-related institution; 7% of students affiliated with the church; no religious studies required; attendance at chapel services voluntary.
Varsity Sports. Men (NAIA): Baseball, Basketball, Cross Country, Football, Golf, Soccer, Tennis. Women (NAIA): Basketball, Cross Country, Soccer, Softball, Tennis, Volleyball.
Campus Life. Campus is located in the foothills of the Smoky Mountains. Students report campus is a "close-knit community" where "the voice of the individual (even a student) can be heard (usually)." The surrounding community is "receptive to students" but "there are few non-student activities outside the college."

About 33% of men, 18% of women live in traditional dormitories; no coed dormitories; rest commute. Intervisitation in men's and women's dormitory rooms limited. There are no fraternities or sororities on campus. About 25% of resident students leave campus on weekends.
Annual Costs. Tuition and fees, $7,100; room and board, $3,300; estimated $500 other, exclusive of travel. About 90% of students receive financial aid; average amount of assistance, $6,853. Assistance is typically divided 22% scholarship, 30% grant, 42% loan, 6% work. College reports 102 scholarships awarded on the basis of academic merit alone, 98 for special talents alone. *Meeting Costs:* college offers Parent PLUS Loans.

Tuskegee University

Tuskegee, Alabama 36088 (205) 727-8011

An independent university dedicated to preparation of students for effective service in technical, scientific, and professional fields undergirded with competence in the essentials of the arts, sciences, and humanities, located in Tuskegee (pop. 14,000), 40 miles east of Montgomery. While Tuskegee's historic commitment of service to black people remains pre-eminent, its admissions policies bar no one because of race, nationality, religion, socioeconomic status, place of residence or sex. Formerly known as Tuskegee Institute. Most convenient major airport: Dannely Field, Montgomery.

Founded: 1881
Affiliation: Independent
UG Enrollment: 1,488 M, 1,549 W (full-time); 71 M, 74 W (part-time)
Total Enrollment: 3,371
Cost: < $10K
% Receiving Financial Aid: 91%
Admission: Non-selective
Application Deadline: April 15

Admission. High school graduates eligible; 74% of applicants accepted, 46% of these actually enroll; 36% of freshmen graduate in top fifth of high school class, 81% in top two-fifths. *Required:* SAT, essay. Criteria considered in admissions, in order of importance: standardized test scores, high school academic record, recommendations; other factors considered: special talents. *Entrance programs:* early decision. About 11% of entering students from private schools, 7% from parochial schools. *Apply* by April 15; rolling admissions. *Transfers* welcome; 66 enrolled 1992–93.
Academic Environment. *Undergraduate studies* offered by College of Arts and Sciences, schools of Agriculture and Home Economics, Education, Engineering and Architecture, Nursing and Allied Health Business, Veterinary Medicine. Student reports "Professors are readily accessible and eager to help. Many incentives to do well in course work." Graduation requirements include work in English, history, and mathematics. Degrees offered: bachelors, masters, doctoral. About 20% of students entering as freshmen graduate within four years; 54% eventually; 65% of freshmen return for sophomore year. *Special programs:* CLEP, independent study, honors, internship/cooperative work-study for all technical programs. *Calendar:* semester, summer school.
Undergraduate degrees conferred (377). 25% were in Engineering, 17% were in Business and Management, 11% were in Social Sciences, 7% were in Agricultural Sciences, 7% were in Life Sciences, 6% were in Education, 4% were in Psychology, 4% were in Public Affairs, 3% were in Physical Sciences, 3% were in Health Sciences, 3% were in Mathematics, 3% were in Architecture and Environmental Design, remainder in 5 other fields.
Graduates Career Data. Advanced studies pursued by 22% of graduates; all enter graduate school. About 73% of 1992–93 graduates employed. Fields typically hiring largest numbers of graduates include federal government, public schools.
Faculty. About 62% of faculty hold PhD or equivalent. About 65% of undergraduate classes taught by tenured faculty. About 31% of teaching faculty are female; 59% Black, 24% Hispanic and other minority.
Student Body. About 27% of students from in state; 66% South, 10% Midwest, 9% Middle Atlantic, 5% New England, 4% West, 1% Northwest, 5% foreign. An estimated 91% of students reported as Black, 3% Hispanic, 1% Asian, 1% other minority.
Varsity Sports. Men (Div.II): Baseball, Basketball, Football, Swimming, Tennis, Track. Women (Div.II): Basketball, Tennis, Track, Volleyball.
Campus Life. About 50% of men, 50% of women live in traditional dormitories; no coed dormitories; rest commute. Intervisitation in men's and women's dormitory rooms limited. There are 4 fraternities, 4 sororities on campus which about 6% of men, 6% of women join; they provide no residence facilities. About 15% of resident students leave campus on weekends.
Annual Costs. Tuition and fees, $6,734; room and board, $3,394; estimated $1,725 other, exclusive of travel. About 91% of students receive financial aid. Assistance is typically divided 21% scholarship, 63% loan, 16% work. College reports 50 scholarships awarded on the basis of academic merit alone, for each freshmen class; 90 for special talents alone. *Meeting Costs:* institute offers time payment plan, short-term loans.

Union College

Barbourville, Kentucky 40906 (800) 489-8646

A church-related college, located in a town of 3,500, 60 miles north of Knoxville. Most convenient major airport: Lexington.

Founded: 1879
Affiliation: United Methodist
UG Enrollment: 343 M, 293 W (full-time); 36 M, 55 W (part-time)
Total Enrollment: 1,018
Cost: < $10K
% Receiving Financial Aid: 89%
Admission: Non-selective
Application Deadline: Aug. 1

Admission. Graduates of accredited high schools with 16 units (10 in academic subjects) and C average eligible; others admitted on probation; 79% of applicants accepted, 46% of these actually enroll; 19% of freshmen graduate in top fifth of high school class, 45% in top two-fifths. Average freshman scores: SAT, 410 M, 460 W verbal, 440 M, 440 W mathematical; ACT, 20 M, 21 W composite. *Required:* SAT or ACT, minimum 2.0 high school GPA. Criteria considered in admissions, in order of importance: high school academic record, standardized test scores, extracurricular activities, recommendations; other factors considered: special talents, alumni children, diverse student body, religious affiliation/commitment. *Entrance programs:* early admission, midyear admission, deferred admission, advanced placement. *Apply* by August 1; rolling admissions. *Transfers* welcome; 87 enrolled 1993–94.
Academic Environment. Degrees offered: associates, bachelors, masters. Student considers small class size, and "personal one-on-one relationships with professors" as strengths of the academic program. *Majors offered* include sports management, special education, athletic training. Average undergraduate class size: 88% under 20, 12% 20–40. About 56% of students entering as freshmen graduate eventually; 61% of freshmen return for sophomore year. *Special programs:* CLEP, independent study, individualized majors, study abroad, experiential education, credit for prior learning, Washington Semester, Appalachian Semester, 3–2 in engineering, May term, internships, cooperative work-study in business. *Calendar:* 4–4–1, summer school.
Undergraduate degrees conferred (107). 49% were in Education, 26% were in Business and Management, 7% were in

Social Sciences, 6% were in Life Sciences, 4% were in Psychology, 3% were in Letters, remainder in 4 other fields.

Graduates Career Data. Advanced studies pursued by 23% of graduates; 4% enter medical school; 2% enter law school; 6% enter business school; 2% enter divinity school; 2% enter pharmacy school. Medical schools typically enrolling largest numbers of graduates include U. Kentucky; law schools include U. of Cincinnati, U. Kentucky; business schools include Xavier U., U. of Cincinnati. About 88% of 1992–93 graduates employed. Fields typically hiring largest numbers of graduates include IRS, chemical firms, education. Career Development Services include job hunting skills, resume writing workshops.

Faculty. About 63% of faculty hold PhD or equivalent. About 27% of undergraduate classes taught by tenured faculty. About 54% of teaching faculty are female.

Student Body. About 69% of students from in state; 89% South, 9% Midwest, 1% West, 1% foreign. An estimated 48% of students reported as Baptist, 30% other Protestant, 6% Catholic, 16% unaffiliated; 8% Black, 1% Asian, 1% other minority. Average age of undergraduate student: 23.

Religious Orientation. Union is a church-related institution; 17% of students affiliated with the church; 2 courses in religious studies required.

Varsity Sports. Men (NAIA): Baseball, Basketball, Cross Country, Diving, Football, Golf, Soccer, Swimming, Tennis. Women (NAIA): Basketball, Cross Country, Diving, Soccer, Softball, Swimming, Tennis, Volleyball.

Campus Life. Campus is located in a very small community, but student notes Lexington, KY and Knoxville, TN are both about an hour and a half drive. Some students reportedly make regular trips to the city, while others "enjoy the beautiful natural features of the area, such as Cumberland Falls and Cumberland Gap."

About 46% of men, 21% of women live in traditional dormitories; no coed dormitories; rest commute. Intervisitation in men's and women's dormitory rooms limited. There are no fraternities or sororities on campus. About 46% of resident students leave campus on weekends.

Annual Costs. Tuition and fees, $7,000; room and board, $2,790; estimated $900 other, exclusive of travel. About 89% of students receive financial aid; average amount of assistance, $5,462. Assistance is typically divided 63% scholarship, 14% grant, 15% loan, 8% work. College reports 60 scholarships awarded on the basis of academic merit alone, 140 for special talents alone.

Union College

Lincoln, Nebraska 68506 — **(402) 486-2504; (800) 228-4600**

A church-related college, located in a city of 154,300, Union operates manufacturing enterprises and service departments to help students meet expenses. Most convenient major airport: Lincoln Municipal.

Founded: 1891
Affiliation: Seventh-day Adventist
UG Enrollment: 546 M, W (full-time)
Cost: < $10K
Admission: Non-selective
Application Deadline: Rolling

Admission. Graduates of accredited high schools with 10 units in academic subjects and C average eligible; nongraduates with 18 units considered; others admitted by examination; 87% of applicants accepted, 58% of these actually enroll. *Required:* ACT, interview. *Apply:* rolling admissions. *Transfers* welcome.

Academic Environment. *Degrees:* AB, BS, BATh, BM, BSN. *Majors offered* in addition to usual studies include institutional development, physician's assistant, pastoral care. About 30% of students entering as freshmen graduate eventually; 24% of freshmen do not return for sophomore year. *Special programs:* CLEP, independent study, study abroad, undergraduate research, individualized majors, 2–2 engineering with Walla Walla College. *Calendar:* semester, summer school.

Undergraduate degrees conferred (107). 35% were in Business and Management, 14% were in Education, 12% were in Health Sciences, 8% were in Communications, 7% were in Multi/Interdisciplinary Studies, 5% were in Public Affairs, 4% were in Physical Sciences, 4% were in Theology, 4% were in Computer and Engineering Related Technology, 3% were in Life Sciences, 3% were in Allied Health, remainder in 2 other fields.

Student Body. About 44% of students from in state; 69% North Central.

Religious Orientation. Union is a church-related institution offering "conservative Protestant Christian life integration"; 12 hours of religion, attendance at chapel services required of all students.

Campus Life. About 31% of men, 39% of women live in traditional dormitories; no coed dormitories; rest live in off-campus housing or commute. No intervisitation in men's or women's dormitory rooms. There are no fraternities or sororities.

Annual Costs. Tuition and fees, $8,100; room and board, $2,510; estimated $400 other, exclusive of travel. College reports some scholarships awarded on the basis of academic merit alone. *Meeting Costs:* college offers prepayment discounts.

Union College

Schenectady, New York 12308 — **(518) 388-6000**

The first liberal arts institution to introduce an engineering program (1845), Union College seeks to bring the social sciences and humanities into balance—both in student body and faculty—with its science and engineering programs. The college is part of Union University, which includes Albany Medical College, Albany Law School, and Albany College of Pharmacy. The 100-acre campus is located in a residential district of Schenectady (pop. 77,900), a few miles up the Mohawk River from Albany. Most convenient major airport: Albany County.

Founded: 1795
Affiliation: Independent
UG Enrollment: 1,060 M, 855 W (full-time); 91 M, 32 W (part-time)
Total Enrollment: 2,492
Cost: $10K–$20K
% Receiving Financial Aid: 51%
Admission: Highly Selective
Application Deadline: Feb. 1

Admission is highly selective. About 49% of applicants accepted, 31% of these actually enroll; 75% of freshmen graduate in top fifth of high school class, 95% in top two-fifths. Average freshman scores: SAT, 540 verbal, 620 mathematical; ACT 28 composite. *Required:* ACT or 3 ACH (including English Composition) (SAT is no longer required), essay. Criteria considered in admissions, in order of importance: high school academic record, recommendations, writing sample, extracurricular activities, interview, standardized test scores; other factors considered: special talents, alumni children, diverse student body. *Entrance programs:* early decision, early admission, advanced placement, deferred admission. About 33% of entering students from private schools. *Apply* by February 1. *Transfers* welcome; 29 enrolled 1993–94.

Academic Environment. Student reports "The academic program at Union not only enables but insists that its graduates be very well-rounded." She adds "The academics are so strong and intellectually aggressive that weaknesses are hard to pin down." Graduation requirements: combining elements of choice within a structure of requirements and incentives, the general education program consists of 3 main elements: 1) a western culture requirement (a freshman preceptorial, a 2-course sequence in history, and 2 courses in literature and "civilization" to match the history sequence); 2) a requirement designed to illustrate the approaches of various disciplines, consisting of specified courses (1 in math, 2 in science or applied science, and 1 in social science); 3) a requirement of 4 courses outside the division of one's major— with strong incentives for students to fulfill the requirement by studying a foreign culture. (Engineering students are exempt from the latter requirement.) Another student applauds the flexibility of the academic program, but wishes she had known that a "majority" of departments required a senior thesis project. College offers 7-year medical and 6-year law programs. Administration reports "great success" in preparing students for law, medicine, business, teaching and research. Degrees offered: bachelors, masters, doctoral. *Majors offered* include usual arts and sciences, 3 fields of engineering, computer science; interdepartmental majors include comparative Communist studies, industrial economics, women's studies, East Asian studies, geology, Latin American studies; individually designed thematic majors also possible. Average undergraduate class size: introductory lecture 35–50, laboratory 12–18, regular course offering 25; "numerous" upper-level arts, language, and science classes with only 2–4 students.

About 87% of students entering as freshmen graduate within five years; 95% of freshmen return for sophomore year. *Special programs:* independent study, study abroad, undergraduate research, individualized majors, variety of 5-year 2-degree programs, cross-registration with 18 other colleges in Capital District, legislative internships in Albany, NY and Washington D.C., student designed majors, Washington semester, accelerated degree programs in law and medicine. *Calendar:* 3–3.

Undergraduate degrees conferred (538). 26% were in Social Sciences, 16% were in Liberal/General Studies, 13% were in Engineering, 8% were in Life Sciences, 8% were in Multi/Interdisciplinary Studies, 8% were in Psychology, 5% were in Letters, 4% were in Mathematics, 3% were in Physical Sciences, 3% were in Foreign Languages, 3% were in Computer and Engineering Related Technology, remainder in 4 other fields.

Graduates Career Data. Advanced studies pursued by 38% of graduates; 18% enter graduate school; 8% enter medical school; 1% enter dental school; 9% enter law school; 1% enter business school. Medical schools typically enrolling largest numbers of graduates include Albany Medical College, U. of Rochester, NYU; dental schools include SUNY Buffalo, Tufts; law schools include Albany Law, Boston U., Yale; business schools include Boston U. About 61% of 1992–93 graduates employed. Corporations typically hiring largest numbers of graduates include General Electric, Bankers Trust, AT&T, Coopers & Lybrand. Career Development Services include career observation days, placement opportunities, on and off campus meetings with alumni, on-campus interviews, interview preparation assistance.

Faculty. About 96% of faculty hold PhD or equivalent. All undergraduate classes taught by tenured faculty. About 28% of teaching faculty are female; 2% Black, 4% Hispanic, 4% other minority.

Student Body. About 52% of students from in state; 63% Middle Atlantic, 30% New England, 2% each South, West, 3% foreign. An estimated 3% of students reported as Black, 5% Asian, 3% Hispanic, 2% other minority, according to most recent data available. *Minority group students:* special financial and social provisions; Academic Opportunity program.

Varsity Sports. Men (Div.III): Baseball, Basketball, Cross Country, Diving, Football, Golf, Ice Hockey (I), Lacrosse, Soccer, Swimming, Tennis, Track. Women (Div.III): Basketball, Cross Country, Diving, Field Hockey, Lacrosse, Soccer, Softball, Swimming, Tennis, Track, Volleyball.

Campus Life. Students report many "active and diverse" activities on-campus including clubs, speakers, movies, sporting events (Division I hockey games reportedly are "packed"), studying, and socializing. While surrounding neighborhood is described as "not one of NY's best", female students report no problems: "Union is almost like living in a dream world for four years, it is as though there is nothing going on outside the campus gates. Most students take the necessary safety precautions at night, but I have never felt like I was unsafe at Union." Greek organizations play a very significant role in social life; relations with independents reported as "very good": independents accepted at all Greek social events. Over three-quarters of the student body resides on campus in either residence halls or fraternities.

About 12% of men, 23% of women live in traditional dormitories; 52% of men, 55% of women live in coed dormitories; 36% of men, 22% of women live in fraternities and sororities. Coed dormitories include 7% of men and 7% of women who reside in theme houses (a substance-free house, an international house, an interdisciplinary house, and a cooperative). There are 19 fraternities, including 2 coed fraternities, 4 sororities on campus which about 45% of men, 25% of women join.

Annual Costs. Tuition and fees, $17,877; room and board, $5,940; estimated $1,483 other, exclusive of travel. About 51% of students receive financial aid; average amount of assistance, $16,350. Assistance is typically divided 65% scholarship, 10% grant, 18% loan, 7% work. College reports 863 scholarships awarded only on the basis of need. *Meeting Costs:* college offers Chester Arthur Undergraduate Support for Excellence awards, loans for students planning to enter public service forgiven at rate of 20% for each year employed in public service.

Union University

Jackson, Tennessee 38305 **(901) 661-5000; (800) 338-6466**

A church-controlled institution, located in a community of 50,000, 79 miles northeast of Memphis. Most convenient major airport: Memphis.

Founded: 1823
Affiliation: Southern Baptist
UG Enrollment: 666 M, 1,248 W (full-time); 98 M, 260 W (part-time)
Total Enrollment: 2,002
Cost: < $10K
% Receiving Financial Aid: 79%
Admission: Non-selective
Application Deadline: Sept. 1

Admission. Graduates of accredited high schools with 20 units and C average and minimum ACT of 20 eligible. About 88% of applicants accepted, 50% of these actually enroll. Average freshman ACT scores: 24 composite. *Required:* SAT or ACT. Criteria considered in admissions, in order of importance: standardized test scores, high school academic record, recommendations, extracurricular activities. *Apply* by September 1. *Transfers* welcome; 271 enrolled 1993–94.

Academic Environment. Graduation requirements include 12 credit hours of English, 8 of natural sciences, 6 each of history, social sciences, and religion, 3 of math and fine arts, and 2 of physical education. Students report small classes an asset. One says "The classes here are challenging but not unreasonable. Although lectures are used to a degree, an emphasis is placed upon class discussion and individual research as well." Degrees offered: associates, bachelors, masters. About 56% of students entering as freshmen graduate eventually; 76% of freshmen return for sophomore year. *Special programs:* CLEP, independent study, honors, study abroad, cross registration with Lambuth U., January interterm. *Calendar:* 4–1–4, summer school.

Undergraduate degrees conferred (291). 23% were in Education, 22% were in Business and Management, 11% were in Health Sciences, 7% were in Social Sciences, 7% were in Psychology, 5% were in Theology, 5% were in Communications, 4% were in Letters, 4% were in Public Affairs, remainder in 6 other fields.

Graduates Career Data. Advanced studies pursued by 37% of graduates.

Faculty. About 42% of faculty hold PhD or equivalent. About 37% of teaching faculty are female.

Student Body. About 78% of students from in state; 1% foreign. An estimated 74% of students reported as Protestant, 1% Catholic, 25% other; 6% as Black, 1% other minority.

Religious Orientation. University is a church-controlled institution; 69% of students affiliated with the church; 6 hours of religion, attendance at campus religious activities required of all students.

Varsity Sports. Men (NAIA): Baseball, Basketball, Golf, Tennis. Women (NAIA): Basketball, Softball, Tennis.

Campus Life. Campus is located on the edge of town; students call it "secluded", "protected", with "little traffic or noise." They add that "numerous organizations offer diversion for idle students" and "there is always something to do on the weekends."

About 60% of men, 54% of women live in traditional dormitories; no coed dormitories; 40% of men, 46% of women commute. Freshmen given preference in college housing if all students cannot be accommodated. No intervisitation in men's or women's dormitory rooms. There are 3 fraternities, 3 sororities on campus which about 26% of men, 27% of women join. About 50% of resident students leave campus on weekends.

Annual Costs. Tuition and fees, $5,380; room and board, $2,460; estimated $350 other, exclusive of travel. About 79% of students receive financial aid; average amount of assistance, $5,108. *Meeting Costs:* University offers payment plans.

United States Air Force Academy

USAF Academy, Colorado 80840-5025 **(719) 472-1818**

One of the nation's major service schools, the Air Force Academy offers an academic curriculum leading to the BS and specialized training for the purpose of preparing commissioned officers in the U.S. Air Force. Full information may be obtained from the Director of Admissions, U.S. Air Force Academy, 2304 Cadet Drive, Suite 200, Colorado 80840.

Founded: 1954
Affiliation: Federal
UG Enrollment: 3,687 M, 549 W (full-time)
Cost: none
Application Deadline: January 31

Admission. Admission consideration open to men and women nominated by members of Congress and those eligible in military-affiliated categories. About 17% of applicants accepted, 72% of these actually enroll; 90% of entering freshmen graduate in top fifth of high school class, 99% in top two-fifths. Average freshman scores: SAT, 568 M, 572 W verbal, 668 M, 639 W mathematical; 68% of freshmen score above 500 on verbal, 31% above 600, 2% above 700; 99% score above 500 on mathematical, 86% above 600, 33% above 700; ACT, 28.1 M, 27.9 W composite. *Required:* SAT or ACT, interview, essay; candidates must be between the ages of 17 and 22, U.S. citizens, and unmarried. Criteria considered in admissions, in order of importance: high school academic record, standardized test scores, extracurricular activities, recommendations, writing sample. About 30% of entering students from private or parochial schools. *Apply* by January 31. *Transfers* not accepted.
Academic Environment. Degrees offered: bachelors. All cadets must complete a core curriculum and an academic major. Majors are offered in 25 fields in engineering sciences, social sciences, and humanities. About 70% of students entering as freshmen graduate within four years, 72% eventually; 82% of freshmen return for sophomore year. *Special programs:* study abroad.
Undergraduate degrees conferred (977). 24% were in Engineering, 22% were in Social Sciences, 14% were in Business and Management, 10% were in Liberal/General Studies, 8% were in Psychology, 5% were in Life Sciences, 4% were in Physical Sciences, 3% were in Mathematics, 3% were in Law, remainder in 4 other fields.
Faculty. About 48% of faculty hold PhD or equivalent.
Student Body. About 5% of students from in state; 25% South Central, 20% Midwest, 18% Southeast, 16% Northeast, 15% West, 1% foreign. An estimated 56% of students reported as Protestant, 40% Catholic, 3% other; 6% as Black, 6% Hispanic, 3% Asian, 2% other minority.
Varsity Sports. Men: Baseball, Basketball, Cross Country, Diving, Fencing, Football, Golf, Gymnastics, Ice Hockey, Lacrosse, Skiing, Soccer, Swimming, Tennis, Track, Wrestling. Women: Basketball, Cross Country, Diving, Fencing, Golf, Gymnastics, Skiing, Soccer, Softball, Swimming, Tennis, Track, Volleyball.
Campus Life. All students live in coed dormitories.
Annual Costs. Federal government pays tuition, room, board costs. Cadets receive full 4-year scholarships and monthly allowance for supplies, clothing, and personal expenses. Graduates must serve in the active duty Air Force for at least six years after graduation.

United States Coast Guard Academy

New London, Connecticut 06320 (203) 444-8500

The Coast Guard Academy is the only one of the 4 Armed Forces service academies that offers appointments solely on the basis of an annual nationwide competitive examination. Graduates receive a BS and are commissioned as ensigns in the U.S. Coast Guard. Full information concerning requirements and selection examination may be obtained from the Director of Admissions, U.S. Coast Guard Academy, New London, Connecticut 06320.

Founded: 1876
Affiliation: Federal
UG Enrollment: 761 M, 169 W (full-time)
Cost: < $10K
Admission: Non-selective
Application Deadline: December 15

Admission. About 10% of applicants accepted, 6% of these actually enroll; 93% of entering freshmen graduate in top fifth of high school class, all in top two-fifths. Average freshman scores: SAT, 542 verbal, 644 mathematical. *Required:* SAT or ACT, essay; candidates must be between the ages of 17 and 22, U.S. citizens, and unmarried. Criteria considered in admissions, in order of importance: standardized test scores, high school academic record, extracurricular activities, recommendations, writing sample. *Apply* by December 15; rolling admissions.
Academic Environment. Degrees offered: bachelors. *Majors offered* include electrical, civil, and marine engineering, mathematics and computer sciences, applied sciences, management, and government. About 65% of students entering as freshmen graduate within four years; 86% of freshmen return for sophomore year.
Undergraduate degrees conferred (206). 38% were in Engineering, 23% were in Social Sciences, 19% were in Business and Management, 12% were in Mathematics, 9% were in Physical Sciences.
Faculty. About 50% of faculty hold PhD or equivalent. About 50% of undergraduate classes taught by tenured faculty. About 10% of teaching faculty are female.
Student Body. About 4% of students from in state.
Varsity Sports. Men (Div.III): Baseball, Basketball, Crew, Cross Country, Diving, Football, Soccer, Swimming, Tennis, Track, Wrestling. Women (Div.III): Basketball, Crew, Cross Country, Softball, Volleyball.
Campus Life. All students live in coed dormitories.
Annual Costs. Entrance fee, $1,500; tuition, room and board paid by federal government. Cadets also receive a monthly allowance of $525.

United States International University

San Diego, California 92131 (619) 693-4772

United States International University is an accredited university with its main campus in San Diego, California and with fully accredited associated campuses in Mexico and Kenya and one extension center in California. Most convenient major airports: Lindbergh Field, San Diego International.

Founded: 1952
Affiliation: Independent
UG Enrollment: 489 M, 512 W (full-time)
Total Enrollment: 2,462
Cost: $10K–$20K
% Receiving Financial Aid: 85%
Admission: Non-selective
Application Deadline: Rolling

Admission. About 52% of applicants accepted, 90% of these enroll. Average freshman scores: SAT, 380 M, 415 W verbal, 474 M, 457 W mathematical; ACT, 20 composite. *Required:* SAT or ACT, minimum 2.5 high school GPA, essay, recommendation. Criteria considered in admissions, in order of importance: high school academic record, standardized test scores, recommendations, writing sample, extracurricular activities; other factors considered: special talents, diverse student body. About 20% of entering students from private schools, 10% from parochial schools. *Apply*: rolling admissions. *Transfers* welcome; 48 enrolled 1993–94.
Academic Environment. Students recommended to spend at least 1 year abroad to complete degree requirements. *Undergraduate studies* offered by College of Arts and Sciences, schools of Business Management, Education, Human Behavior, International and Intercultural Studies. Degrees offered: associates, bachelors, masters, doctoral. *Majors offered* include finance, marketing, world literature, international relations, hotel/restaurant management, tourism management, international business. *Special programs:* ESOL-English for speakers of other languages, study abroad, internships/cooperative work-study programs available in senior year. *Calendar:* quarter, optional January interterm, summer school.
Undergraduate degrees conferred (332). 47% were in Liberal/General Studies, 26% were in Business and Management, 8% were in Visual and Performing Arts, 8% were in Psychology, 7% were in Social Sciences, remainder in 4 other fields.
Graduates Career Data. Career Development Services include placement office, placement files, job fairs.
Faculty. About 80% of faculty hold PhD or equivalent.
Student Body. University provides many opportunities for cross cultural experience with many international students enrolled. About 56% of students from West, 3% New England, 2% Midwest, 2% South, 1% Middle Atlantic, 1% Northwest, 35% foreign.

Campus Life. About 56% of men, 63% of women live on campus; rest commute. There are no fraternities or sororities on campus.
Annual Costs. Tuition and fees, $11,115; room and board, $4,800; estimated $500 other, exclusive of travel. About 85% of students receive financial aid; average amount of assistance, $10,000. Assistance is typically divided 30% scholarship, 40% grant, 9% loan, 21% work. College reports 4 scholarships awarded on the basis of academic merit alone, 1 for need alone. *Meeting Costs:* college offers Business/Industry Tuition Assistance Program; list of outside resources.

United States Merchant Marine Academy

Kings Point, New York 11024

Fourth of the nation's major service schools, the Merchant Marine Academy offers general and specialized programs for training future officers in the U.S. Merchant Marine. Admission is by Congressional nomination for competitive appointments which are based on CEEB tests, class rank, and leadership potential. Candidates must be between the ages of 17 and 22, U.S. citizens. Full information may be obtained from the Admissions Office, U.S. Merchant Marine Academy, Kings Point, New York 11024.

Founded: 1936
Affiliation: Federal
UG Enrollment: 936 M, W (full-time)

Undergraduate degrees conferred (160). 54% were in Military Sciences, 46% were in Engineering.

United States Military Academy

West Point, New York 10996 **(914) 938-4041**

The Military Academy is the oldest of the nation's major service academies. Graduates receive BS and commissions in the Regular Army. Full information may be obtained from the Director of Admissions, U.S. Military Academy, West Point, New York 10996-1797.

Founded: 1802
Affiliation: Federal
UG Enrollment: 4,000 M, 500 W (full-time)
Cost: none

Admission is by nomination by members of Congress (75%) or by the Department of the Army (25%). The latter category is reserved for sons and daughters of career members of the armed forces, deceased and disabled veterans, as well as members of the Regular Army and Army Reserve, and graduates of honor military schools. The academy is "making an extensive effort" to reach qualified minority group members who otherwise might not apply for admission. About 34% of applicants are nominated, 51% of these are qualified (academically and in physical aptitude), 52% of those are admitted. About 82% of freshmen graduate in top fifth of high school class, 95% in top two-fifths. Mean freshman scores: SAT, 558 verbal, 653 mathematical; 81% of freshmen score above 500 on verbal, 30% above 600, 3% above 700; all score above 500 on mathematical, 81% above 600, 29% above 700. *Required:* SAT or ACT, physical aptitude and medical testing requirements; candidates must be between the ages of 17 and 22, U.S. citizens, unmarried, have no legal responsibility to support a child, and must not be pregnant. *Non-academic factors* considered in admissions: participation in school, church, and community activities, active participation in sports.
Academic Environment. Academic program consists of a core curriculum supplemented by areas of elective concentration and an optional majors program. Programs offered in broad areas of basic sciences, applied sciences and engineering, humanities, national security and public affairs, and the independent fields of management and foreign area studies; concentration in a specific program is required. Degrees offered: bachelors.
Undergraduate degrees conferred (984). 100% were in Liberal/General Studies.
Graduates Career Data. Most graduates who remain in the service after the initial six-year obligation obtain advanced degrees at civilian universities.
Student Body. Class of 1997 includes cadets from every state, as well as 10 foreign cadets.
Campus Life. All cadets live on campus.
Annual Costs. Cadets receive full 4-year scholarships, medical and dental care, as well as an annual salary of nearly $6,500 for books, uniforms, and incidentals.

United States Naval Academy

Annapolis, Maryland 21402 **(410) 267-3507**

One of the nation's major service schools, the Naval Academy provides general and specialized studies for the professional preparation of commissioned officers in the U.S. Navy and Marine Corps. Full information may be obtained from the Dean of Admissions, U.S. Naval Academy, Annapolis, Maryland 21402.

Founded: 1845
Affiliation: Federal
UG Enrollment: 3,621 M, 504 W (full-time)
Cost: none
Application Deadline: Rolling

Admission. A candidate must obtain a nomination to be considered for an appointment as a midshipman. Nominations are made by U.S. senators and representatives, the President, the Vice-President, and the Secretary of the Navy. About 12% of applicants accepted, 83% of these actually enroll; 80% of freshmen graduate in top fifth of high school class, 93% in top two-fifths. Average freshman scores: SAT, 566 M, 583 W verbal, 664 M, 657 W mathematical; 86% of freshmen score above 500 on verbal, 35% above 600, 5% above 700; 99% score above 500 on mathematical, 88% above 600, 34% above 700; ACT, 29 M, 28 W composite. *Required:* SAT or ACT, essay, candidates must be between 17 and 22, U.S. citizens, unmarried, not pregnant, and have no children. The Admissions Board examines each candidate's school records, college board or ACT scores, recommendations from school officials, extracurricular activities, and other evidence of character, leadership potential, academic aptitude, health, and physical fitness. *Entrance programs:* early decision, early admission. *Apply:* rolling admissions; Academy states it is advisable to apply for admission during the spring of the junior year in high school.
Academic Environment. Curriculum offers 18 majors in aerospace, electrical, marine, mechanical, ocean, and systems engineering and naval architecture, as well as in chemistry, economics, English, history, physics, political science, and computer science. Degrees offered: bachelors. Average undergraduate class size: 35% under 20, 65% 20–40. About 78% of midshipmen entering as freshmen graduate eventually; 88% of freshmen return for sophomore year.
Undergraduate degrees conferred (950). 36% were in Engineering, 30% were in Social Sciences, 20% were in Physical Sciences, 7% were in Letters, 4% were in Mathematics, 3% were in Computer and Engineering Related Technology.
Graduates Career Data. All graduates required to serve six years in the U.S. Navy or U.S. Marine Corp.
Faculty. About 54% of faculty hold PhD or equivalent, 46% military faculty. About 20% of teaching faculty are female; 2% Black, 2% Hispanic, 4% other minority.
Student Body. About 7% of midshipmen from in state; 24% Midwest, 19% Middle Atlantic, 19% South, 18% West, 13% New England, 6% Northwest, 1% foreign. An estimated 43% of midshipmen reported as Protestant, 41% Catholic, 8% Jewish, 2% Muslim, 6% unaffiliated; 7% Black, 6% Hispanic, 4% Asian, 3% other minority.
Varsity Sports. Men (Div.I): Baseball, Basketball, Crew, Cross Country, Diving, Football, Golf, Gymnastics, Lacrosse, Rifle, Pistol, Sailing, Soccer, Swimming, Tennis, Track, Water Polo, Wrestling. Women (Div.I): Basketball, Crew, Cross Country, Diving, Sailing, Soccer, Swimming, Track, Volleyball.
Campus Life. All midshipmen live in coed dormitories. About 20% of midshipmen leave campus on weekends.
Annual Costs. Midshipmen receive full tuition, room and board, and military pay of $545 per month.

Unity College

Unity, Maine 04988 **(207) 948-3131**

A small, private liberal arts college located in a rural community in central Maine. Most convenient major airport: Bangor International.

Founded: 1966
Affiliation: Independent
UG Enrollment: 425 M, W (full-time)
Cost: < $10K
Admission: Non-selective
Application Deadline: Rolling

Admission. Graduates of accredited high schools or equivalent eligible; 93% of applicants accepted, 46% of these actually enroll. *Required:* interview (on- or off-campus), 2 letters of recommendation. *Non-academic factors* considered in admissions: special talents, diverse student body, alumni children. *Apply:* rolling admissions. *Transfers* welcome.
Academic Environment. *Degree:* AB. About 54% of students entering as freshmen graduate eventually; 43% of freshmen do not return for sophomore year. *Special programs:* summer institute, honors, undergraduate research, independent study. *Calendar:* semester, summer school.
Undergraduate degrees conferred (54). 57% were in Renewable Natural Resources, 26% were in Parks and Recreation, 17% were in Multi/Interdisciplinary Studies.
Student Body. About 28% of students from in state; 67% from New England, 28% from Middle Atlantic.
Varsity Sports. Men (NAIA): Basketball, Cross Country, Soccer. Women (MAIAW): Cross Country, Volleyball.
Campus Life. About 47% of men, 59% of women live in traditional dormitories; 26% of men, 19% of women in coed dormitories; 17% of men, 12% of women live in off-campus housing; 10% of men, 10% of women commute. Freshmen given preference in college housing if all students cannot be accommodated.
Annual Costs. Tuition and fees, $7,910 (out-of-state, $9,010); room and board, $4,660; estimated $1,000 other, exclusive of travel. About 57% of students receive financial aid; assistance is typically divided 40% scholarship, 37% loan, 23% work. *Meeting Costs:* college offers guaranteed tuition plan.

Upper Iowa University

Fayette, Iowa 52142 **(319) 425-3311**

An independent college, founded under the auspices of the Methodist Church, but nonsectarian since 1928. The campus is located in a town of 1,946.

Founded: 1857
Affiliation: Independent
UG Enrollment: 1,860 (full-time)
Cost: < $10K
Admission: Non-selective
Application Deadline: Rolling

Admission. High school graduates with 16 units in academic subjects and C average or rank in top half of class eligible; 53% of applicants accepted, 36% of these actually enroll; 19% of freshmen graduate in top fifth of high school class, 42% in top two-fifths. *Required:* SAT or ACT; interview recommended. *Apply* rolling admissions. *Transfers* welcome.
Academic Environment. *Degrees:* BA, BS, BGS. About 40% of students entering as freshmen graduate eventually; 32% of freshmen do not return for sophomore year. *Special programs:* CLEP, independent study, study abroad, honors, undergraduate research, 3-year degree, individualized majors, Washington Semester, United Nations Semester with Drew U., "cooperative work experience" in business. *Calendar:* 4–1–4, summer school.
Undergraduate degrees conferred (453). 74% were in Business and Management, 11% were in Education, 6% were in Public Affairs, remainder in 8 other fields.
Student Body. University seeks a national student body; 81% of students from North Central, 9% Middle Atlantic.
Campus Life. About 67% of men, 48% of women live in traditional dormitories; no coed dormitories; rest live in off-campus housing or commute. Intervisitation in men's and women's dormitory rooms limited. There are 3 fraternities, 1 sorority on campus which about 10% each of men, women join; they provide no residence facilities. About 30% of students leave campus on weekends.
Annual Costs. Tuition and fees, $8,840; room and board, $3,060; estimated $650 other, exclusive of travel. *Meeting Costs:* university offers monthly payment plan.

Upsala College

East Orange, New Jersey 07019 **(201) 266-7191**

A church-related, liberal arts college, also offering studies in business and teacher education, Upsala is named after its famous Swedish prototype. The 45-acre main campus is located in a residential area of a city of 75,500, 15 miles from New York City; a branch campus, offering 2-year programs, is located in Sussex County. Most convenient major airport: Newark International.

Founded: 1893
Affiliation: Lutheran
UG Enrollment: 1,115 M, W (full-time)
Cost: $10K–$20K
Admission: Non-selective
Application Deadline: Rolling

Admission. High school graduates with 16 units in academic subjects eligible; 63% of applicants accepted, 40% of these actually enroll; 20% of freshmen graduate in top fifth of high school class, 40% in top two-fifths. *Required:* SAT, interview. *Apply:* rolling admissions. *Transfers* welcome.
Academic Environment. Administration source characterizes student body as primarily concerned with preparation for careers. *Degrees:* AB, BS, BSW. *Majors offered* include usual arts and sciences, accounting, business administration, computer science, multinational corporate studies, human resource management; cross-disciplinary concentration also possible.

About 60% of students entering as freshmen graduate eventually; 34% of freshmen do not return for sophomore year. *Special programs:* CLEP, study abroad, honors, undergraduate research, 3–2 programs in cytotechnology, engineering, forestry, internship program in elementary and secondary education. *Calendar:* semester, summer school.
Undergraduate degrees conferred (192). 57% were in Business and Management, 13% were in Psychology, 11% were in Life Sciences, 7% were in Social Sciences, 4% were in Letters, 3% were in Communications, 3% were in Public Affairs, remainder in 3 other fields.
Faculty. About 80% of faculty hold PhD or equivalent.
Student Body. About 90% of students from in state; 95% Middle Atlantic, 5% New England.
Religious Orientation. Upsala is a church-related institution, but makes no religious demands on students; attendance at ecumenical chapel services held 2 times weekly is voluntary.
Varsity Sports. Men (Div.III): Baseball, Basketball, Cross Country, Football, Golf, Hockey, Soccer, Tennis, Wrestling. Women (Div.III): Basketball, Golf, Softball, Tennis.
Campus Life. No curfew; limited intervisitation in freshman dormitories. Alcohol permitted; cars allowed for all students. Non-commuting freshmen required to live in residence halls.

About 5% of men, 5% of women live in traditional dormitories; 45% of men, 45% of women in coed dormitories; 50% each of men, women commute. Sexes segregated in coed dormitories by floor. Freshmen given preference in college housing if all students cannot be accommodated. There are 4 fraternities, 4 sororities on campus which about 30% of men, 40% of women join; they provide no residence facilities. About 60% of students leave campus on weekends.
Annual Costs. Tuition and fees, $12,500; room and board, $5,260; estimated $600 other, exclusive of travel. About 85% of students receive financial aid; assistance is typically divided 80% scholarship, 20% loan, 20% work. College reports some scholarships awarded on the basis of academic merit alone.

Urbana College

Urbana, Ohio 43078 **(513) 653-1301**

A small, church-related, liberal arts college located in a community of about 12,000 in west central Ohio, between Columbus and Dayton. Most convenient major airports: Dayton, Columbus.

Founded: 1850
Affiliation: Swedenborgian
UG Enrollment: 476 M, 269 W (full-time); 57 M, 109 W (part-time)
Cost: < $10K
% Receiving Financial Aid: 99%
Admission: Non-selective
Application Deadline: Rolling

Admission. High school graduates in college preparatory course eligible; 83% of applicants accepted, 50% of these actually enroll; 26% of freshmen graduate in the top fifth of their high school class, 28% in top two-fifths. Average freshman ACT scores: 19 M, 20 W composite. *Required:* ACT, 2.2 minimum high school GPA, interview recommended. Criteria considered in admissions, in order of importance: high school academic record, standardized test scores, recommendations, extracurricular activities, writing sample; other factors considered: special talents, alumni children. *Entrance programs:* early admission, midyear admission, deferred admission. *Apply:* rolling admissions. *Transfers* welcome; 97 enrolled 1993–94.

Academic Environment. Graduation requirements include 9 credit hours of English/communications, 10 of math/science, 9 of humanities, 9 of social sciences, and 2 of physical education. Degrees offered: associates, bachelors. Fields of emphasis include business and economics, education, humanities, math and sciences, physical education and health, social sciences; specific majors offered in addition to usual studies include athletic training, law enforcement/corrections; marine biology offered in conjunction with Duke University. Average undergraduate class size: 40% under 20, 60% 20–40. About 77% of students entering as freshmen return for sophomore year. *Special programs:* study abroad. Adult programs: evening non-traditional programs. *Calendar:* quarter, summer school.

Undergraduate degrees conferred (100). 63% were in Business and Management, 17% were in Public Affairs, 14% were in Education, 3% were in Multi/Interdisciplinary Studies, 3% were in Letters.

Faculty. About 56% of faculty hold PhD or equivalent. About 70% of undergraduate classes taught by tenured faculty. About 20% of teaching faculty are female.

Student Body. About 97% of students from in state; 99% Midwest, 1% foreign. An estimated 25% of students reported as Black, 1% Hispanic, 1% Asian, 1% other minority.

Varsity Sports. Men (NAIA): Baseball, Basketball, Cross Country, Football, Golf, Track. Women (NAIA): Basketball, Cross Country, Softball, Track, Volleyball.

Campus Life. About 7% of men, 5% of women live in traditional dormitories; 30% each live in coed dormitories; rest commute. About 35% of resident students leave campus on weekends.

Annual Costs. Tuition and fees, $8,396; room and board, $4,140, estimated $600 other, exclusive of travel. About 99% of students receive financial aid; average amount of assistance, $6,500. College reports 75 scholarships awarded on the basis of academic merit alone, 75 for special talents alone.

Ursinus College

Collegeville, Pennsylvania 19426 (215) 489-4111

Ursinus has always been independent of church control, but continues to maintain a relationship with its founding denomination, the United Church of Christ. Changes are taking place at Ursinus with the opening of a major art museum, significant changes in the faculty, and a strong effort to attract a more diverse student body, with demonstrated interest in the humanities and the arts. The 125-acre campus is located in a borough of 3,200, 25 miles northwest of Philadelphia. Most convenient major airport: Philadelphia.

Founded: 1869
Affiliation: Independent (United Church of Christ)
UG Enrollment: 553 M, 578 W (full-time)
Cost: $10K–$20K
% Receiving Financial Aid: 80%
Admission: Very (+) Selective
Application Deadline: February 15

Admission is very (+) selective. About 73% of applicants accepted, 30% of these actually enroll; 68% of freshmen graduate in top fifth of high school class, 92% in top two-fifths. Average freshman SAT scores, middle 50% range: 460–560 verbal, 520–620 mathematical; 58% of freshmen score above 500 on verbal, 13% above 600, 1% above 700; 86% score above 500 on mathematical, 38% above 600, 3% above 700. *Required:* SAT or ACT, essay. Criteria considered in admissions, in order of importance: high school academic record, standardized test scores, extracurricular activities, recommendations, writing sample; other factors considered: special talents, alumni children, diverse student body. *Entrance programs:* early decision, early admission, midyear admission, advanced placement, deferred admission. *Apply* by February 15. *Transfers* welcome; 17 enrolled 1993–94.

Academic Environment. Student body is academically capable and students serve on committees on curriculum, student life, long-range planning, recruitment and retention of students. Administration reports requirements in mathematical science and speech as well as emphasis on career preparation; fairly numerous distribution requirements: year course in each of 3 broad divisions, 12 credit hours of courses outside division of major, proficiency in English composition and foreign language, year physical education. Degrees offered: bachelors. *Majors offered* include usual arts and sciences, business administration, health and physical education; interdisciplinary majors in applied mathematics/economics, communication arts, computer science/mathematics, anthropology and sociology recently added. Average undergraduate class size: 55% under 20, 40% 20–40, 5% over 40.

About 78% of students entering as freshmen graduate within four years; 92% of freshmen return for sophomore year. *Special programs:* CLEP, independent study, study abroad, honors, study abroad, undergraduate research, 3-year degree, Asian studies, individualized majors, 3–2 engineering, intercollege seminar, senior symposium. *Calendar:* semester, summer school.

Undergraduate degrees conferred (296). 31% were in Social Sciences, 16% were in Life Sciences, 11% were in Letters, 9% were in Business and Management, 9% were in Psychology, 5% were in Education, 5% were in Communications, 5% were in Physical Sciences, 3% were in Foreign Languages, 3% were in Mathematics, remainder in 2 other fields.

Graduates Career Data. Advanced studies pursued by 21% of graduates; 13% enter graduate school; 5% enter medical school; 2% enter law school; 1% enter business school. About 72% of 1992–93 graduates employed.

Faculty. About 76% of faculty hold PhD or equivalent. About 60% of undergraduate classes taught by tenured faculty. About 43% of teaching faculty are female; 1% Black, 1% Hispanic, 2% other minority.

Student Body. About 65% of students from in state; 92% Middle Atlantic, 2% each New England, South, 4% foreign. An estimated 40% of students reported as Catholic, 4% Protestant, 2% Jewish, 1% Muslim, 21% unaffiliated, 6% other; 3% as Black, 3% Asian, 2% Hispanic, 4% other minority. *Minority group students:* special financial, academic, and social provisions.

Religious Orientation. Ursinus is an independent institution with historical ties to the United Church of Christ, makes no religious demands on students; 3% of students affiliated with the church.

Varsity Sports. Men (Div.III): Baseball, Basketball, Cross Country, Football, Golf, Soccer, Swimming, Tennis, Track, Wrestling. Women (Div.III): Basketball, Cross Country, Golf, Field Hockey(I), Gymnastics, Lacrosse, Softball, Swimming, Tennis, Track, Volleyball.

Campus Life. Student leader characterizes student population as "moderately conservative, middle class"; administration source adds "strong academic background, well-rounded with varied interests." Significant percentage of students join fraternities and sororities. Intervisitation daily, if desired by students. Cars permitted for all students; parking is not a problem. Alcohol use regulated by state law. Nearest major cultural center is Philadelphia, 25 miles away.

About 70% of students live in traditional dormitories; 20% in coed dormitories; rest commute. Freshmen given preference in college housing if all students cannot be accommodated. There are 9 fraternities, 5 sororities on campus which about 45% of men, 40% of women join; they provide no residence facilities. About 20% of resident students leave campus on weekends.

Annual Costs. Tuition and fees, $14,265; room and board, $4,900; estimated $2,000 other, exclusive of travel. About 80% of students receive financial aid; average amount of assistance, $13,569. Assistance is typically divided 70% scholarship/grant, 20% loan, 10% work. College reports 100 scholarships awarded on the basis of academic merit alone. *Meeting Costs:* college offers monthly payment plan.

Ursuline College

Cleveland/Pepper Pike, Ohio 44124 **(216) 449-4203**

An independent, liberal arts college for women, conducted by the Ursuline Nuns of Cleveland, located on a suburban campus near a city of 800,000.

Founded: 1871
Affiliation: Independent (Roman Catholic)
UG Enrollment: 64 M, 1,536 W (full-time)
Total Enrollment: 1,600
Cost: < $10K
Admission: Non-selective
Application Deadline: Rolling

Admission. High school graduates with 11 units in academic subjects eligible; 80% of applicants accepted, 90% of these actually enroll, 10% of freshmen graduate in top fifth of high school class, 47% in top two-fifths. Average freshman scores: SAT, 430 W verbal, 444 W mathematical; ACT, 18. *Required:* SAT or ACT; essay. Criteria considered in admissions, in order of importance: high school academic record, standardized test scores, writing sample, recommendations, extracurricular activities; other factors considered: special talents, alumni children, religious affiliation/commitment. *Entrance programs:* midyear admission, deferred admission, advanced placement. *Apply:* rolling admissions. *Transfers* welcome.

Academic Environment. Graduation requirements include Ursuline Studies: a core curriculum "based in liberal arts, focusing on culture and potential student contributions to society."' Some student concern voiced about the requirements and choices offered under the curriculum. Students report small, challenging classes and caring faculty are strengths of the academic program. Degrees offered: bachelors, masters. Average undergraduate class size: 80% under 20, 20% 20–40.

About 80% of students entering as freshmen graduate eventually; 88% of freshmen return for sophomore year. *Special programs:* CLEP, study abroad, cross registration with area colleges and universities, including Baldwin-Wallace, Case Western, Cleveland St. U., Kent, Oberlin, internships/cooperative work-study programs. *Calendar:* semester.

Undergraduate degrees conferred (222). 45% were in Health Sciences, 11% were in Psychology, 10% were in Business and Management, 7% were in Marketing and Distribution, 4% were in Education, 4% were in Architecture and Environmental Design, 4% were in Social Sciences, 3% were in Multi/Interdisciplinary Studies, 3% were in Letters, remainder in 7 other fields.

Graduates Career Data. Fields typically hiring largest numbers of graduates include nursing, education, business. Career Development Services include resume-building, career counseling, job placement, internships, cooperative education.

Student Body. About 98% of students from in state; 1% foreign. An estimated 45% of students reported as Catholic; 16% Black, 1% each Hispanic, Asian, 1% other minority. Average age of undergraduate student: 31.

Religious Orientation. Ursuline is a Catholic institution; attendance at religious activities voluntary.

Campus Life. About 20% of women live in dormitories; rest commute. No intervisitation in women's dormitory rooms. There are no sororities on campus.

Annual Costs. Tuition and fees, $9,800; room and board, $4,000; estimated $750 other, exclusive of travel. About 64% of students receive financial aid; average amount of assistance, $7,930. College reports unlimited scholarships awarded on the basis of academic merit alone.

Utah State University

Logan, Utah 84322 **(801) 750-1000**

A state university and land-grant college, located in a town of 25,000, 80 miles north of Salt Lake City. Most convenient major airport: Salt Lake City International.

Founded: 1888
Affiliation: State
UG Enrollment: 5,100 M, 5,152 W (full-time); 2,235 M, 2,427 W (part-time)
Total Enrollment: 18,399
Cost: < $10K
Admission: Non-selective
Application Deadline: 30 days before quarter

Admission. Graduates of approved high schools with 2.2 average eligible; others admitted by examination; 89% of applicants accepted, 65% of these actually enroll; 47% of freshmen graduate in top fifth of high school class. Average freshman scores: SAT, 475 verbal, 500 mathematical; ACT, 22.2 composite. *Required:* SAT or ACT. Criteria considered in admissions, in order of importance: standardized test scores, high school academic record; other factors considered: diverse student body. *Out-of-state* freshman applicants: university seeks students from out of state. State does not limit out-of-state enrollment. *Apply* by 30 days before quarter. *Transfers* welcome; 1,552 enrolled 1993–94.

Academic Environment. *Undergraduate studies* offered by colleges of Humanities, Arts and Social Sciences, Agriculture, Business, Education, Engineering, Family Life, Natural Resources, Science. Average undergraduate class size: 44% under 20, 35% 20–40, 21% over 40. About 66% of freshmen return for sophomore year. *Special programs:* CLEP, independent study, study abroad, honors, 3-year degree, individualized majors, 3–2 in chemistry, cross-registration in nursing with Weber State. *Calendar:* quarter, summer school.

Undergraduate degrees conferred (1,501). 23% were in Education, 18% were in Business and Management, 6% were in Social Sciences, 6% were in Engineering, 5% were in Visual and Performing Arts, 5% were in Computer and Engineering Related Technology, 4% were in Psychology, 3% were in Liberal/General Studies, 3% were in Home Economics, 3% were in Health Sciences, remainder in 18 other fields.

Faculty. About 25% of teaching faculty are female; 8% minority.

Graduates Career Data. Career Development Services include career counseling, job placement, resume preparation, job fairs, on-campus recruitment.

Student Body. About 88% of students from Utah; 98% West/Northwest.

Varsity Sports. Men (Div.IA): Basketball, Cross Country, Football, Golf, Tennis, Track. Women (Div.IA): Cross Country, Gymnastics, Softball, Tennis, Track, Volleyball.

Campus Life. Drinking forbidden; smoking allowed in limited area; fairly strict regulation of student behavior. About 17% of men, 19% of women live in traditional dormitories; no coed dormitories; 81% of men, 79% of women live in off-campus housing or commute. Intervisitation (limited) in men's dormitory rooms only. There are 6 fraternities, 3 sororities on campus which about 5% each of men, women join; 2% of men, 2% of women live in fraternities and sororities. About 75% of students leave campus on weekends.

Annual Costs. Tuition and fees, $1,896 (out-of-state, $5,541); room and board, $2,985; estimated $2,100 other, exclusive of travel. About 70% of students receive financial aid; average amount of assistance, $4,470. Assistance is typically divided 18% scholarship, 35% grant, 45% loan, 2% work. University reports 10,419 scholarships awarded on the basis of academic merit alone, 1,812 for special talents, 64 for need alone.

University of Utah

Salt Lake City, Utah 84112 **(801) 581-7200**

Originally founded as a Mormon institution, the University of Utah is now the largest state-supported university in Utah. The 1,500-acre campus is at the eastern edge of the state capital (metropolitan pop. 726,000). Most convenient major airport: Salt Lake City International.

Founded: 1850
Affiliation: State
UG Enrollment: 7,801 M, 6,040 W (full-time); 4,073 M, 3,278 W (part-time)
Total Enrollment: 25,982
Cost: < $10K
% Receiving Financial Aid: 43%
Admission: Non-selective
Application Deadline: July 1

Admission. Utah graduates of accredited high schools with 15 units in specified areas and minimum GPA of 2.0 eligible; 90% of applicants accepted, 55% of these actually enroll. Average freshman scores: SAT, 478 M, 483 W verbal, 560 M, 510 W mathematical; ACT, 23.8 M, 23.3 W composite. *Required:* SAT or ACT (preferred), minimum high school GPA. Criteria considered in admissions: high school academic record and standardized test scores rank with equal importance. *Out-of-state* freshman applicants: university actively seeks students from out-of-state. State does not limit out-of-state enrollment. No special requirements for out-of-state applicants. States from which most out-of-state students are drawn include California, Idaho. *Entrance programs:* early admission, midyear admission, deferred admission, advanced placement. *Apply* by July 1. *Transfers* welcome; 1,851 enrolled 1993–94.

Academic Environment. *Undergraduate studies* offered by colleges of Humanities, Architecture, Business, Engineering, Fine Arts, Mines and Mineral Industries, Nursing, Pharmacy (5-year), Health, Physical Education and Recreation, Science, Social and Behavioral Science; 63 majors available. Graduation requirements include courses in fine arts, humanities, sciences, social sciences, American history, writing, and math or foreign language. Degrees offered: bachelors, masters, doctoral. Average class size: 31.

About 43% of students entering as freshmen graduate eventually; 62% of freshmen return for sophomore year. *Special programs:* CLEP, independent study, study abroad, honors, undergraduate research, internships/cooperative work-study, individualized majors. *Calendar:* quarter, summer school.

Undergraduate degrees conferred (2,818). 23% were in Social Sciences, 15% were in Business and Management, 9% were in Engineering, 8% were in Communications, 8% were in Psychology, 5% were in Education, 5% were in Visual and Performing Arts, 5% were in Health Sciences, 5% were in Letters, 3% were in Life Sciences, 3% were in Physical Sciences, 3% were in Foreign Languages, remainder in 8 other fields.

Graduates Career Data. Advanced studies pursued by 27% of graduates; 22% enter graduate school; 5% enter law and medicine. About 38% of 1992–93 graduates employed. Fields typically hiring largest numbers of graduates include business, engineering, education, nursing. Career Development Services include workshops, credit courses, interactive computer software programs (SIGI and DISCOVER), individual counseling.

Faculty. About 95% of faculty hold PhD or equivalent. About 36% of undergraduate classes taught by tenured faculty. About 20% of teaching faculty are female; 1% Black, 2% Hispanic, 5% other minority.

Student Body. About 80% of students from in state; 87% West, 3% each Northwest, Midwest, 2% South, 1% each New England, Middle Atlantic, 3% foreign. An estimated 10% of students are reported to be Catholic, 9% Protestant, 1% Jewish, 21% unaffiliated, 59% other (Mormon); 3% as Asian, 1% as Black, 3% Hispanic, 11% other minority. Average age of undergraduate student: 25. *Minority group students:* state and private funds for scholarships and grants; special counselors for individual ethnic groups; special effort to find jobs on campus for minority group members.

Varsity Sports. Men (Div.I): Baseball, Basketball, Cross Country, Diving, Football, Golf, Skiing, Swimming, Tennis, Track. Women (Div.I): Basketball, Cross Country, Diving, Gymnastics, Skiing, Softball, Swimming, Tennis, Track, Volleyball.

Campus Life. University provides almost every type of cultural activity on campus. University has more than 20 dance, theater, and musical groups presenting an extensive schedule of events. The Utah Symphony, Ballet West, and 2 professional modern dance companies started at the university and retain ties to it. Cars permitted; drinking prohibited; smoking restricted to designated areas by state law. This is primarily a commuter campus; no special rules govern residential students; intervisitation described as "very liberal."

About 3% of men, 3% of women live in traditional dormitories; 2% of men, 2% of women live in off-campus college-related housing; 94% commute. Intervisitation in men's and women's dormitory rooms limited. There are 11 fraternities, 7 sororities on campus which about 6% of men, 6% of women join; 1% of men, 1% of women live in fraternities and sororities.

Annual Costs. Tuition and fees, $2,298 (out-of-state, $6,795); room and board, $3,677; estimated $1,350 other, exclusive of travel. About 43% of students receive financial aid; average amount of assistance, $6,463. Assistance is typically divided 29% scholarship, 67% loan, 4% work. University reports some scholarships awarded on the basis of academic merit alone. *Meeting Costs:* university offers PLUS Loans.

Utica College

(See Syracuse University)

Valdosta State College

Valdosta, Georgia 31698 (912) 333-5791

A state-supported college, located in a south-central Georgia community of 45,000, 70 miles northeast of Tallahassee. Most convenient major airports: Valdosta Regional.

Founded: 1906
Affiliation: State
UG Enrollment: 5,992 (full-time)
Cost: < $10K
% Receiving Financial Aid: 45%
Admission: Non-selective
Application Deadline: Sept. 1

Admission. Graduates of accredited high schools with 16 units (13 in academic subjects) eligible; 72% of applicants accepted, 59% of these actually enroll. Average freshman scores, according to most recent data available: SAT, 397 M, 389 W verbal, 442 M, 412 W mathematical. *Required:* SAT or ACT, minimum high school GPA. Criteria considered in admissions: high school academic records and standardized test scores rank with equal importance. *Out-of-state* freshman applicants: college actively seeks students from out-of-state. State does not limit out-of-state enrollment. No special requirements for out-of-state applicants. States from which most out-of-state students are drawn include Florida. *Apply* by September 1; rolling admissions. *Transfers* welcome; 502 enrolled 1993–94.

Academic Environment. Degrees offered: associates, bachelors, masters. *Majors offered* in addition to usual studies include astronomy, sports medicine. Average undergraduate class size: 35. About 50% of students entering as freshmen graduate eventually; 60% of freshmen return for sophomore year. *Special programs:* CLEP, independent study, study abroad, honors, undergraduate research, 3-year degree, 3–2 in engineering, internships/cooperative work-study. *Calendar:* quarter, summer school.

Undergraduate degrees conferred (924). 33% were in Education, 21% were in Business and Management, 10% were in Visual and Performing Arts, 8% were in Liberal/General Studies, 7% were in Social Sciences, 4% were in Protective Services, 4% were in Health Sciences, 3% were in Psychology, remainder in 9 other fields.

Faculty. About 67% of faculty hold PhD or equivalent.

Student Body. About 87% of students from in state. An estimated 21% of students reported as Black, 2% other minority.

Varsity Sports. Men (Div.II): Baseball, Basketball, Cross Country, Football, Golf, Tennis. Women (Div.II): Basketball, Cross Country, Softball, Tennis.

Campus Life. About 15% of men, 15% of women live in traditional dormitories; rest live in off-campus housing or commute. Intervisitation in men's and women's dormitory rooms limited. No coed dormitories.

Annual Costs. Tuition and fees, $1,729 (out-of-state, $4,492); room and board, $2,940; estimated $1,000 other, exclusive of travel. About 45% of students receive financial aid. University reports 40 scholarships awarded on the basis of academic merit alone.

Valley City State College

Valley City, North Dakota 58072 (701) 845-7100

A state-supported college, located in a community of 8,500, 60 miles west of Fargo.

Founded: 1890
Affiliation: State
UG Enrollment: 440 M, 423 W (full-time)
Cost: < $10K
% Receiving Financial Aid: 79%
Admission: Non-selective
Application Deadline: Aug. 25

Admission. North Dakota graduates of accredited high schools eligible; 93% of applicants accepted, 62% of these actually enroll; 18% of freshmen graduate in top fifth of high school class, 42% in top two-fifths. *Required:* ACT. *Out-of-state* freshman applicants: college actively seeks students from out-of-state. State does not limit out-of-state enrollment. No special requirements for out-of-state applicants. About 90% of out-of-state students accepted, 31% of these actually enroll. States from which most out-of-state students are drawn include Minnesota, Wyoming, Florida. *Apply* by August 25; rolling admissions. *Transfers* welcome; 75 enrolled 1993–94.

Academic Environment. Degrees offered: bachelors. Average undergraduate class size: 59% under 20, 31% 20–40, 9% over 40. About 20% of students entering as freshmen graduate within four years, 35% eventually; 65% of freshmen return for sophomore year. *Special programs:* CLEP, independent study, individualized majors, business internships. *Calendar:* quarter, summer school.

Undergraduate degrees conferred (181). 60% were in Education, 15% were in Business and Management, 10% were in Multi/Interdisciplinary Studies, 9% were in Business (Administrative Support), remainder in 5 other fields.

Graduate Career Data. About 88% of 1992–93 graduates employed. Fields typically hiring largest numbers of graduates include public schools, small business, government. Career Development Services include counseling, job search classes, seminars and individual sessions.

Faculty. About 40% of faculty hold PhD or equivalent. All undergraduate classes taught by tenured faculty. About 34% of teaching faculty are female.

Student Body. About 89% of students from in state. An estimated 68% of students reported as Protestant, 31% Catholic; 1% Black, 1% Hispanic, 1% Asian, 5% other minority. Average age of undergraduate student: 23.

Varsity Sports. Men (NAIA): Baseball, Basketball, Cross Country, Football, Golf, Tennis, Track, Wrestling. Women (NAIA): Basketball, Cross Country, Softball, Tennis, Track, Volleyball.

Campus Life. About 17% of men, 15% of women live in traditional dormitories; no coed dormitories; rest commute. There are 2 fraternities, 2 sororities on campus which about 5% of men, 5% of women join; They provide no residence facilities. About 70% of resident students leave campus on weekends.

Annual Costs. Tuition and fees, $1,815 (out-of-state, $4,495); room and board, $2,570; estimated $2,400 other, exclusive of travel. About 79% of students receive financial aid; average amount of assistance, $4,242. Assistance is typically divided 14% scholarship, 29% grant, 63% loan, 4% work.

Valparaiso University

Valparaiso, Indiana 46383 **(219) 464-5000**

Founded as an independent institution in 1859, Valparaiso was later purchased by the Lutheran University Association in 1925. It is a liberal arts and professional/vocational university consisting of 5 undergraduate colleges, a School of Law, and a graduate division. One of its unusual units is Christ College, established for gifted undergraduates "to encourage the integration of learning, sound educational experimentation, and student involvement in the problems of modern society." The 310-acre campus is located in a town of 25,000, 44 miles southeast of Chicago. Most convenient major airport: O'Hare International (Chicago, IL).

Founded: 1859
Affiliation: Lutheran-Missouri Synod
UG Enrollment: 1,122 M, 1,418 W (full-time); 54 M, 144 W (part-time)
Total Enrollment: 2,738
Cost: $10K–$20K
% Receiving Financial Aid: 80%
Admission: Very (+) Selective
Application Deadline: Rolling

Admission is very (+) selective. For all schools, 84% of applicants accepted, 34% of these actually enroll; 49% of freshmen graduate in top tenth of high school class, 72% in top fifth, 94% in top two-fifths. Average freshman scores, middle 50% range: SAT, 470–590 verbal, 530–670 mathematical; ACT, 25–30 composite. *Required:* SAT or ACT. Criteria considered in admissions, in order of importance: high school academic record, standardized test scores, extracurricular activities, writing sample, recommendations, optional interview; other factors considered: special talents, alumni children, diverse student body. *Entrance programs:* early admission, midyear admission, advanced placement, deferred admission. About 20% of entering students from private schools. *Entrance programs:* midyear admission, advanced placement. *Apply:* rolling admissions. *Transfers* welcome; 175 enrolled 1993–94.

Academic Environment. Graduation requirements include freshman core (seminar, theology, English, and history), academic area studies (theology, literature and fine arts, philosophy and history, social analysis, natural science and math, non-Western course, and foreign language), and physical education. *Undergraduate studies* offered by colleges of Arts and Sciences, Business Administration, Engineering, as well as by Christ College (for selected students only). Students praise "excellent professors", the lack of teaching assistants, small classes, and classes that are "challenging and require student preparation and effort for success." Degrees offered: associates, bachelors, masters. *Majors offered* in addition to usual studies include Asian studies, computer science, education, journalism, communication disorders, geography, home economics, social work; special programs in humanities, interdisciplinary urban studies. Average undergraduate class size: 52% under 20, 42% 20–40, 6% over 40.

About 75% of students entering as freshmen graduate eventually; 85% of freshmen return for sophomore year. *Special programs:* CLEP, independent study, study abroad, honors, undergraduate research, individualized majors, Washington Semester, United Nations Semester, cross registration with American U., Drew U., 3-year program, internships/cooperative work study. Adult programs: bachelors completion program for registered nurses. *Calendar:* semester, mini summer session.

Undergraduate degrees conferred (716). 18% were in Business and Management, 11% were in Health Sciences, 10% were in Social Sciences, 9% were in Education, 9% were in Engineering, 9% were in Communications, 5% were in Psychology, 4% were in Multi/Interdisciplinary Studies, 4% were in Life Sciences, 3% were in Letters, 3% were in Physical Sciences, 3% were in Mathematics, remainder in 9 other fields.

Graduates Career Data. Advanced studies pursued by 20% of graduates; 12% enter graduate school, 2% enter medical school; 4% enter law school. Medical schools typically enrolling largest numbers of graduates include Indiana U., Minnesota, Wisconsin; law schools include Valparaiso, Northwestern, Indiana U. About 63% of 1991–92 graduates employed. Fields typically hiring largest numbers of graduates include nursing, engineering, accounting, education. Career Development Services include seminars, workshops, job fairs, video interviews, resume critiquing services, bi-weekly job opportunities bulletin, career service network and teacher placement office.

Faculty. About 80% of faculty hold PhD or equivalent. About 70% of undergraduate classes taught by tenured faculty. About 30% of teaching faculty are female.

Student Body. About 41% of students from in state; 84% Midwest, 5% Middle Atlantic, 3% South, 3% West, 1% each New England, Northwest, 3% foreign. An estimated 3% of students reported as Black, 2% Hispanic, 2% Asian, 3% other minority. *Minority group students:* financial aid provided; student advisers and program; Black Cultural Arts Center.

Religious Orientation. Valparaiso is affiliated with the Lutheran Church and prides itself on offering "opportunity for ethical and spiritual development within the Christian tradition"; 44% of students affiliated with the church; 9 hours of theology required; attendance at daily chapel services voluntary.

Varsity Sports. Men (Div.I): Baseball, Basketball, Cross Country, Diving, Football (IAA), Soccer, Swimming, Tennis, Wrestling. Women (Div.I): Basketball, Cross Country, Diving, Soccer, Softball, Swimming, Tennis, Volleyball.

Campus Life. Campus is located about 1 hour from Chicago and walking distance from local downtown and shopping. Students report "most" students stay on-campus on weekends; campus is "fairly self-contained". Sports (varsity and intramural), fraternity/sorority functions, union sponsored activities (lectures, movies, nightclub, etc.), and dances all reported popular. Curfew for all freshmen until midterm and then self-regulated hours. Intervisitation permitted Sunday—Thursday until midnight; Friday and Saturday until 2 am; less for freshmen. Freshmen, sophomores, and juniors (except those living in fraternity houses) required to live in university housing. Alcohol not allowed on campus (fraternities located off campus); cars permitted except for freshmen.

About 12% of men, 22% of women live in traditional dormitories; 35% of men, 24% of women live in coed dormitories; 16% of men, 11% of women live in off-campus college-related housing; 14% of men, 28% of women commute. There are 12 fraternities, 8 sororities on campus which about 40% each of men, women join; 23% of men, 15% of women live in fraternities and sororities. About 20% of resident students leave campus on weekends.

Annual Costs. Tuition and fees, $11,720; room and board, $3,090; estimated $1,300 other, exclusive of travel. About 80% of students receive financial aid; average amount of assistance, $9,286. Assistance is typically divided 54% grant, 40% loan, 6% work. College reports 300 scholarships awarded on the basis of academic merit alone, 250 for special talents alone.

Vanderbilt University

Nashville, Tennessee 37212-1700 (615) 322-2561

Vanderbilt is a co-educational institution, located in a border state, which actively seeks students from other areas of the country in an effort to make its student body "more diverse, more vital, less regional." The university's 330-acre campus is located about 2 miles from downtown Nashville, which is also the home of Fisk University, Meharry Medical College, major Black institutions, and a number of other institutions of higher learning. Most convenient major airport: Nashville Metro International.

Founded: 1872
Affiliation: Independent
UG Enrollment: 2,953 M, 2,609 W (full-time)
Total Enrollment: 9,853
Cost: $10K–$20K
% Receiving Financial Aid: 45%
Admission: Highly Selective
Application Deadline: January 15

Admission is highly selective for Arts and Science, School of Engineering; very selective for Education/Peabody College, Blair School of Music. For all schools, 60% of applicants accepted, 32% of these actually enroll; 87% of freshmen graduate in top fifth of high school class, 98% in top two-fifths. Average freshman scores: SAT, 559 verbal, 640 mathematical, 81% of freshmen score above 500 on verbal, 77% above 600, 4% above 700; 97% score above 500 on mathematical, 74% above 600, 22% above 700; ACT, 28 composite.

For Arts and Science (1,683 M, 1,630 W), 54% of applicants accepted, 32% of these actually enroll. Freshman scores: SAT, 88% of freshmen score above 500 on verbal, 32% above 600, 4% above 700; 98% score above 500 on mathematical, 77% above 600, 21% above 700.

For Blair School of Music (29 M, 58 W), 66% of applicants accepted, 47% of these actually enroll. Average freshman scores: SAT, 69% of freshmen score above 500 on verbal, 43% above 600, 3% above 700; 80% score above 500 on mathematical, 40% above 600, 14% above 700.

For Engineering (765 M, 223 W), 76% of applicants accepted, 30% of these actually enroll. Average freshman scores: SAT, 69% of freshmen score above 500 on verbal, 21% above 600, 3% above 700; 99% score above 500 on mathematical, 83% above 600, 25% above 700.

For Peabody College of Education and Human Development (159 M, 581 W), 64% of applicants accepted, 52% of these actually enroll. Average freshman scores: SAT, 50% of freshmen score above 500 on verbal, 11% above 600; 84% score above 500 on mathematical, 34% above 600, 5% above 700.

Required: SAT, ACH, essay, recommendations. Criteria considered in admissions, in order of importance: high school academic record, standardized test scores, recommendations, extracurricular activities, writing sample; other factors considered: special talents, diverse student body. *Entrance programs:* early decision, deferred admission, advanced placement. About 40% of entering students from private schools. *Apply* by January 15; rolling admissions for transfer students only. *Transfers* welcome; 78 enrolled 1993–94.

Academic Environment. Pressures for academic achievement appear to range from moderate for the Peabody College of Education to intense for the Colleges of Arts and Science and Engineering. In the College of Arts and Sciences students take about one third of their work in a major, another third in the core liberal arts program, and the final third in elective work. Large percentage of students continue graduate and professional studies after graduation. Students at Vanderbilt may take courses under a reciprocal agreement at nearby Fisk. The Blair School of Music offers "programs in all instruments of orchestra and band, piano, organ, guitar and voice." Undergraduate studies offered to freshmen by schools listed above. Degrees offered: bachelors, masters, doctoral. *Majors offered* in addition to usual studies include anthropology, business administration, computer science, drama, fine arts, molecular biology, Portuguese; interdepartmental majors also available. Average undergraduate class size: 65% under 20, 25% 20–40, 10% over 40.

About 80% of students entering as freshmen graduate within five years; 89% of freshmen return for sophomore year. *Special programs:* credit by examination, undergraduate research, independent study, study abroad, honors, joint degree programs, study at Classical Center in Rome, pre-professional advising program, cross-registration with Fisk, Meharry Medical, 3–2 in engineering. *Calendar:* semester, summer school.

Undergraduate degrees conferred (1,169). 26% were in Social Sciences, 17% were in Engineering, 15% were in Psychology, 10% were in Letters, 6% were in Mathematics, 5% were in Education, 5% were in Life Sciences, 3% were in Physical Sciences, 3% were in Multi/Interdisciplinary Studies, 3% were in Visual and Performing Arts, remainder in 4 other fields.

Graduates Career Data. Advanced studies pursued by 74% of graduates; 28% enter graduate school; 10% enter medical school; 1% enter dental school; 13% enter law school; 10% enter business school. Medical schools typically enrolling largest numbers of graduates include Vanderbilt, U. of Texas, Emory; law schools include Emory, U. of Texas, Vanderbilt; business schools include U. of Chicago, Wharton, Owen. Corporations typically hiring largest numbers of graduates include Arthur Andersen, Procter and Gamble, Merrill Lynch, Shearson Lehman Brothers. Career Development Services include assistance with career decision making, job search skills, connections with employment opportunities, counseling, testing, workshops, resume preparation, video interview training, networking, career fair, summer job fair, campus interviews, employer database, alumni career advisory network.

Faculty. About 98% of faculty hold PhD or equivalent. Over 90% of undergraduate classes taught by tenured faculty. About 23% of teaching faculty are female.

Student Body. About 14% of students from in state; 46% South, 16% Midwest, 13% Southwest, 11% Middle Atlantic, 6% New England, 5% South, 3% other. An estimated 5% of students reported as Black; 2% Hispanic, 6% Asian. *Minority group students:* increased scholarship percentage; special academic provisions in admissions only; Black Student Alliance, Black Student Center, Asian American Student Association.

Varsity Sports. Men (Div.IA): Baseball, Basketball, Cross Country, Football, Golf, Soccer, Tennis. Women (Div.IA): Basketball, Cross Country, Golf, Soccer, Tennis, Track.

Campus Life. Student Center houses a movie theater, an art gallery, the bookstore and several dining facilities. Recent dorm renovation project included adding computer networks linking residence halls to campus library system. Fraternities and sororities reported to be active, along with varsity and intramural sports. Dormitories are autonomous in setting rules in many areas, including "hours, visitation (unlimited), solicitation, alcoholic beverages (for those over 21), quiet hours, etc." Special interest housing options available. Freshmen required to live on campus and are discouraged from having cars. Parking is a problem for commuters. Students required to live in university-related housing unless approved for off-campus living.

About 86% of students live in university housing; rest commute. Sexes segregated in coed dormitories either by floor or suite. Freshmen are given preference in college housing if all students cannot be accommodated. There are 17 fraternities, 12 sororities on campus which about 67% of men, 54% of women join.

Annual Costs. Tuition and fees, $17,202; room and board, $3,930; estimated $500 other, exclusive of travel. About 45% of students receive financial aid; average amount of assistance, $17,489. Assistance is typically divided 71% scholarship/grant, 25% loan, 4% work. University reports 896 scholarships awarded on the basis of academic merit alone, 205 for special talents alone, 1,869 for need alone. *Meeting Costs:* University offers Knight Tuition Plan, Tuition Stabilization Plan, PLUS Loans.

Vandercook College of Music

Chicago, Illinois 60616

An independent, professional institution, VanderCook College specializes in preparing students for directing and teaching school orchestra, choral, and band organizations; BMEd and MMEd degrees offered.

Founded: 1909 **Affiliation:** Independent

Undergraduate degrees conferred (7). 100% were in Education.

Vassar College

Poughkeepsie, New York 12601 **(914) 437-7000**

Founded 125 years ago to be a prestigious college for young women—"what Harvard and Yale were to young men," Vassar has been co-educational since 1968. Vassar's 1,000-acre campus is located on the outskirts of Poughkeepsie (pop. 32,000), 75 miles north of New York City. Most convenient major airport: Stewart, Newburgh.

Founded: 1861
Affiliation: Independent
UG Enrollment: 841 M, 1,323 W (full-time); 23 M, 54 W (part-time)
Cost: $10K–$20K
% Receiving Financial Aid: 58%
Admission: Highly (+) Selective
Application Deadline: January 15

Admission is highly (+) selective. About 52% of applicants accepted, 34% of these actually enroll; 79% of freshmen graduate in top fifth of high school class, 97% in top two fifths. Average freshman SAT scores, middle 50% range: 570–640 verbal, 570–670 mathematical; 91% of freshmen score above 500 on verbal, 51% above 600, 4% above 700; 93% score above 500 on mathematical, 62% above 600, 11% above 700; ACT, 28 composite. *Required:* SAT, 3 ACH or ACT, essay; interview (on- or off-campus) available. Criteria considered in admissions, in order of importance: high school academic record, writing sample, recommendations, standardized test scores, extracurricular activities; other factors considered: special talents, alumni children, diverse student body. *Entrance programs:* early decision, deferred admission. About 34% of entering students from private schools, 5% parochial schools. *Apply* by January 15. *Transfers* welcome; 29 enrolled 1993–94.

Academic Environment. Requirements for graduation include completion of a major program (with at least one-quarter of total units outside division of major field), at least 1 "Fresh man Course" (small classes in a variety of disciplines intended as introductions to the collegiate experience), and demonstration of proficiency in a foreign language. Limits on electives and required courses are kept to a minimum. Student leader reports life at Vassar is marked by "Good amount of freedom with just enough guidance." Degrees offered: bachelors. *Majors offered:* students may earn a degree through concentration in a traditional discipline; an independent program (self-designed major); multidisciplinary programs (Africana studies, American culture, cognitive science, East Asian studies, Science, Technology and Society, urban studies); and interdepartmental programs (biochemistry, biopsychology, geography/anthropology, math/computer science, Medieval and Renaissance studies). Average undergraduate class size: 14.

About 89% of students entering as freshmen graduate within five years; 94% of freshmen return for sophomore year. *Special programs:* CLEP, independent study, study abroad, undergraduate research, 3-year degree, individualized majors, 4-year combined BA/MA in chemistry, French, and Hispanic studies, cross registration with Marist, 3–2 in engineering, field work for credit, freshman seminars, summer ungraded work for credit, federal intern program, Critical Languages program. *Calendar:* semester.

Undergraduate degrees conferred (628). 30% were in Social Sciences, 16% were in Letters, 12% were in Visual and Performing Arts, 11% were in Psychology, 6% were in Liberal/General Studies, 5% were in Philosophy and Religion, 5% were in Area and Ethnic Studies, 4% were in Foreign Languages, 4% were in Life Sciences, 3% were in Multi/Interdisciplinary Studies, remainder in 2 other fields.

Graduates Career Data. Advanced studies pursued by 23% of graduates; 4% enter medical school; 5% enter law school. About 65% of 1992–93 graduates employed. Corporations typically hiring largest numbers of graduates include Andersen Consulting, law firms. Career Development Services include on-campus interviews, assistance with interview preparation, alumni involvement.

Student Body. About 27% of students from in state; 46% Middle Atlantic, 18% New England, 13% West, 8% South, 7% Midwest, 3% Northwest, 4% foreign. An estimated 8% of students reported as Black, 4% Hispanic, 9% Asian. *Minority group students:* African Studies program open to all students.

Varsity Sports. Men (Div.III): Baseball, Basketball, Cross Country, Diving, Fencing, Lacrosse, Soccer, Swimming, Tennis, Volleyball. Women (Div.III): Basketball, Cross Country, Diving, Fencing, Field Hockey, Lacrosse, Soccer, Swimming, Tennis, Volleyball.

Campus Life. Students largely control their own social life; dormitories autonomous in setting and enforcing regulations. Students select living situation of their choice; corridors with limited parietals have provision for daily intervisitation hours. Virtually all students live in coed dorms, although option of sex-segregated residence remains for small number of women. Campus is 75 miles from Manhattan but one student leader has extolled the virtues of the "beautiful, calm, pastoral campus, away from the city [but with] easy access to New York City." Student leader speaks of the "widely diverse student body"; administration source agrees and adds "independent and self-motivated." Motorcycles or motorbikes may not be used on campus; cars allowed on campus weekends and evenings. Most students choose to live on campus.

About 3% of women live in traditional dormitories; 98% of men, 95% of women live in coed dormitories; rest commute. Freshmen given preference in college housing if all students cannot be accommodated. There are no fraternities or sororities on campus.

Annual Costs. Tuition and fees, $18,170; room and board, $5,750; estimated $2,000 other, exclusive of travel. About 58% of students receive financial aid; average amount of assistance, $17,200. Assistance is typically divided 83% grant, 11% loan, 6% work. *Meeting Costs:* college offers low interest loans, monthly payment plan.

Vennard College

University Park, Iowa 52595

A small Bible college located in a rural area about an hour from Des Moines. College offers associates and bachelors degree programs. Notable majors offered include missionary aviation.

Founded: 1910 **Affiliation:** Interdenominational

University of Vermont

Burlington, Vermont 05405 **(802) 656-3370**

The University of Vermont enrolls more than half of its students from outside the state, and is proud of its diverse student body. The campus is located in a community of 38,600, on the eastern shore of Lake Champlain, 95 miles south of Montreal, and 220 miles from Boston. Most convenient major airport: Burlington International.

Founded: 1791
Affiliation: State
UG Enrollment: 3,433 M, 3,822 W (full-time); 199 M, 297 W (part-time)
Total Enrollment: 10,617
Cost: < $10K
% Receiving Financial Aid: 42%
Admission: Selective (+)
Application Deadline: Feb. 1

Admission is selective (+). About 78% of applicants accepted, 29% of these actually enroll; 43% of freshmen graduate in top fifth of high school class, 81% in top two-fifths. Average freshman SAT scores: 488 verbal, 553 mathematical; 46% of freshmen score above 500 on verbal, 9% above 600, 1% above 700; 76% score above 500 on mathematical, 31% above 600, 3% above 700. *Required:* SAT, essay. Criteria considered in admissions, in order of importance: high school academic record, standardized test scores, recommendations, writing sample; other factors considered: special talents, alumni children, diverse student body. *Out-of-state* freshman applicants: university actively seeks students from out-of-state. *Out-of-state* enrollment limited only by number of in-state applicants. No special requirements for out-of-state applicants; 77% accepted, 24% of these enroll. Most out-of-state students are drawn from New England states. About 30% of entering students from private and parochial schools. *Entrance programs:* early decision, deferred admission. *Apply* by February 1. *Transfers* welcome: 331 enrolled 1993–94.

Academic Environment. *Undergraduate studies* offered by colleges of Arts and Sciences, Agriculture and Life Sciences, Education and Social Services, Engineering and Mathematics, schools of Allied Health Sciences, Business Administration, Natural Resources, Nursing. Student reports "professors are extremely knowledgeable and willing to assist students." She adds "the academics are demanding..this isn't a school that one should attend if they are looking for just a party." Degrees offered: associates, bachelors, masters, doctoral. *Majors offered* in addition to usual studies include anthropology, biochemical science, community forestry, consumer studies, computer science, geography, speech pathology and audiology, theater, recreation management, women's studies; area studies including Asia, Canada, Latin America, Russia and Eastern Europe; Environmental Studies major may be taken in any of several departments or as an interdisciplinary major. Average undergraduate class size: 25.

About 60% of students entering as freshmen graduate within four years, 77% within six years; 84% of freshmen return for sophomore year. *Special programs:* CLEP, independent study, study abroad, undergraduate research, individualized majors, credit by examination. *Calendar:* early semester, summer school.

Undergraduate degrees conferred (1,848). 21% were in Social Sciences, 10% were in Business and Management, 9% were in Education, 7% were in Letters, 6% were in Psychology, 6% were in Engineering, 5% were in Life Sciences, 4% were in Health Sciences, 4% were in Home Economics, 4% were in Agribusiness and Agricultural Production, 3% were in Visual and Performing Arts, 3% were in Mathematics, 3% were in Multi/Interdisciplinary Studies, 3% were in Foreign Languages, 3% were in Renewable Natural Resources, remainder in 8 other fields.

Graduates Career Data. Advanced studies pursued by 17% of 1991–92 graduates. About 76% of 1991–92 graduates employed. Career Development Services include alumni network, NEXUS database, on-campus recruitment, job hotline, workshops, internships, part-time jobs, skill assessment, individual counseling, testing, peer advising.

Faculty. About 87% of faculty hold PhD or equivalent. About 50% of undergraduate classes taught by tenured faculty. About 29% of teaching faculty are female; 2% Black, 1% Hispanic.

Student Body. About 44% of students from in state; an estimated 1% of students reported as Black, 1% Hispanic, 2% Asian, 1% other minority.

Varsity Sports. Men (Div.I): Baseball, Basketball, Cross Country, Golf, Gymnastics, Hockey, Lacrosse, Skiing, Soccer, Swimming/Diving, Tennis, Track. Women (Div.I): Basketball, Cross Country, Field Hockey, Gymnastics, Lacrosse, Skiing, Soccer, Softball, Swimming/Diving, Tennis, Track, Volleyball.

Campus Life. Student is enthusiastic about the beauty of Vermont, wide range of activities off-campus (skiing, hiking, etc.), and on-campus (from environmental organizations to drama to sports, and dorm programs); she likes least that "It's in Vermont! It's cold!" Students enjoy considerable freedom on campus. Each residence unit sets its own policy for intervisitation without limitation. Drinking in student rooms permitted for those of legal age. Cars allowed for all except freshmen. Freshmen and sophomores required to live on campus.

About 45% of students live in coed dormitories; 41% commute. Sexes segregated in coed dormitories either by wing, floor, or suite. There are 14 fraternities, 6 sororities on campus; 14% of students live in fraternities or sororities.

Annual Costs. Tuition and fees, $5,970 (out-of-state, $14,914); room and board, $4,376; estimated $1,360 other, exclusive of travel. About 42% of students receive financial aid; average amount of assistance, $9,725. Assistance is typically divided 39% grant, 54% loan, 7% work. University reports some scholarships awarded on the basis of academic merit alone (for in-state students only). *Meeting Costs:* university offers installment payment plan.

Villanova University

Villanova, Pennsylvania 19085 **(610) 519-4000; (800) 338-7927**

A large, church-related university, conducted by the Augustinian Fathers and Brothers, Villanova is now co-educational in all programs. The 240-acre campus is located 6 miles west of the Philadelphia city line. Most convenient major airport: Philadelphia International.

Founded: 1842
Affiliation: Roman Catholic
UG Enrollment: 3,052 M, 3,102 W (full-time); 744 M, 745 W (part-time)
Total Enrollment: 11,485
Cost: $10K–$20K
% Receiving Financial Aid: 57%
Admission: Highly Selective
Application Deadline: Jan. 15

Admission is highly selective for College of Science; very (+) selective for Arts, Engineering, Commerce and Finance; selective (+) for Nursing. For all schools, 72% of applicants accepted, 27% of these actually enroll; 57% of freshmen graduate in top fifth of high school class, 89% in top two-fifths. Average freshmen scores, middle 50% range: SAT, 470–570 verbal, 550–640 mathematical; 64% of freshmen score above 500 on verbal, 16% above 600, 2% above 700; 92% score above 500 on mathematical, 47% above 600, 10% above 700.

For Arts, according to most recent data available, (1,326 M, 1,224 W), 54% of applicants accepted, 31% of these actually enroll; 49% of freshmen graduate in top fifth of high school class, 74% in top two-fifths. Average freshman SAT scores: 517 M, 527 W verbal, 583 M, 574 W mathematical; 73% of freshmen score above 500 on verbal, 19% above 600; 91% score above 500 on mathematical, 45% above 600, 6% above 700.

For Sciences, according to most recent data available, (313 M, 280 W), 70% of applicants accepted, 23% of these actually enroll; 64% of freshmen graduate in top fifth of high school class, 76% in top two-fifths. Average freshman SAT scores: 526 M, 529 W verbal, 632 M, 593 W mathematical; 64% of freshmen score above 500 on verbal, 19% above 600, 2% above 700; 93% score above 500 on mathematical, 59% above 600, 10% above 700.

For Engineering, according to most recent data available, (631 M, 185 W), 85% of applicants accepted, 28% of these actually enroll; 51% of freshmen graduate in top fifth of high school class, 76% in top two-fifths. Average freshman SAT scores: 516 M, 522 W verbal, 630 M, 604 W mathematical; 58% of freshmen score above 500 on verbal, 13% above 600; 94% score above 500 on mathematical, 66% above 600, 13 above 700.

For Commerce and Finance, according to most recent data available, (1,024 M, 945 W), 67% of applicants accepted, 34% of these actually enroll; 55% of freshmen graduate in top fifth of high school class, 79% in top two-fifths. Average freshman SAT scores: 507 M, 515 W verbal, 617 M, 588 W mathematical; 61% of freshmen score above 500 on verbal, 9% above 600; 94% score above 500 on mathematical, 55% above 600, 7% above 700.

For Nursing, according to most recent data available, (2 M, 376 W), 77% of applicants accepted, 43% of these actually enroll; 34% of freshmen graduate in top fifth of high school class, 64% in top two-fifths. Average freshman SAT scores: 467 verbal, 516 mathematical; 30% of freshmen score above 500 on verbal, 1% above 600; 61% score above 500 on mathematical, 10% above 600.

Required: SAT, essay. Criteria considered in admissions, in order of importance: high school academic record, standardized test scores; extracurricular activities/recommendations/writing sample all rank equally, geographical location; other factors considered: alumni children, diverse student body. *Entrance programs:* early action, early admission, deferred admission. About 50% of entering students from private and parochial schools. *Apply* by January 15. *Transfers* welcome; 110 enrolled 1993–94.

Academic Environment. Both administration source and student leader list business and engineering among strongest academic programs. Technical programs are said to prevent some students from taking many electives. Pressures for academic achievement appear moderate to strong. Graduation requirements include humanities seminar, foreign language, literature, math or computer science, philosophy, religious studies, science, social sciences, ethics, and fine arts. *Undergraduate studies* offered by 5 colleges listed above. Degrees offered: associates, bachelors, masters, doctoral. *Majors offered* in addition to usual arts and sciences include astronomy, computer science, education, geography, peace and justice; program in general studies or problem area also possible. Average undergraduate class size: 24; 41% under 20, 55% 20–40, 4% over 40.

About 84% of students entering as freshmen graduate within four years; 88% eventually; 94% of freshmen return for sophomore year. *Special programs:* Freshman Humanities Seminar, independent study, study abroad, undergraduate research, cross registration with Rosemont and Cabrini, 3–2 in physical therapy and allied health areas, internships, six or seven year medical programs. Adult programs: continuing education, paralegal studies, certificates in management, advertising and public relations, human resources, payroll administration, alcohol and drug counseling. *Calendar:* semester, summer school.

Undergraduate degrees conferred (1,737). 31% were in Business and Management, 18% were in Social Sciences, 10% were in Engineering, 9% were in Liberal/General Studies, 7% were in Letters, 6% were in Health Sciences, 4% were in Communications, 4% were in Psychology, 3% were in Life Sciences, remainder in 9 other fields.

Graduates Career Data. Advanced studies pursued by 21% of graduates; 10% enter graduate school; 3% enter medical school; 1% enter dental school; 5% enter law school; 1% enter business school. Medical schools typically enrolling largest numbers of graduates include Thomas Jefferson, Hahnemann, Temple; dental schools include Boston U., Temple, Tufts; law schools include Villanova, Seton Hall, Temple; business schools include Villanova, Seton Hall, St. Joseph's U. Fields typically hiring largest numbers of graduates include public accounting, banking/insurance, hospitals, consulting. Career Development Services include career counseling, workshops, on-campus interviews, career fairs, job listings.

Faculty. About 90% of faculty hold PhD or equivalent. About 69% of undergraduate classes taught by tenured faculty. About 26% of teaching faculty are female; 1% Black, 2% Hispanic, 4% other minority.

Student Body. About 28% of students from in state; 72% Middle Atlantic, 15% New England, 5% South, 3% each Midwest, West, 2% foreign. An estimated 84% of students reported as Catholic, 7% Protestant, 1% Jewish, 8% other; 4% as Black, 3% Hispanic, 5% Asian. *Minority group students:* special financial, academic, and social provisions; fully staffed Social Action office.

Religious Orientation. Villanova is a church-related institution; 84% of students affiliated with the church; 2 courses in religious studies required of all students; daily Mass offered.

Varsity Sports. Men (Div. I): Baseball, Basketball, Crew (III), Cross Country, Diving, Football (IAA), Golf, Ice Hockey (III), Lacrosse, Soccer, Swimming, Tennis, Track. Women (Div. I): Basketball, Crew (III), Cross Country, Field Hockey, Lacrosse, Soccer, Softball, Swimming, Tennis, Track, Volleyball.

Campus Life. University governance structure permits students a significant voice in University Senate where they are equally represented with faculty and administration. On-campus residence facilities limited so most juniors and seniors live off-campus, taking much of the social life with them. High student interest reported in varsity sports (most popular: basketball, football, track, lacrosse) and intramurals (most popular: football, softball, basketball). Intervisitation limited. Rules enforced "judiciously." Drinking permitted in dormitory rooms for those over 21. Only upperclassmen and off-campus students may park on campus. Parking reported to be inadequate.

About 65% of men, 62% of women live in traditional dormitories; 6% of men, 5% of women live in coed dormitories; 24% of men, 28% of women live in off-campus college housing; 5% each commute. Freshmen are given preference in college housing if all students cannot be accommodated. There are 14 fraternities, 8 sororities on campus which about 29% of men, 48% of women join; they provide no residence facilities. About 10% of resident students leave campus on weekends.

Annual Costs. Tuition and fees, $15,200; room and board, $6,000; estimated $2,000 other, exclusive of travel. About 57% of students receive financial aid; average amount of assistance, $10,950. Assistance is typically divided 15% scholarship, 48% grant, 33% loan, 4% work. University reports 249 scholarships awarded on the basis of academic merit alone, 218 for special talents alone, 2,524 for need alone. *Meeting Costs:* University offers tuition management plans.

University of the Virgin Islands

St. Thomas, Virgin Islands 00802 (809) 776-9200

A publicly supported institution, offering 2- and 4-year programs, located on a 175-acre campus in a city of 47,000, overlooking the Caribbean Sea. University has a second campus in St. Croix. Graduate studies in 3 program areas also offered. Most convenient major airport: Cyril E. King.

Founded: 1962
Affiliation: Public
UG Enrollment: 295 M, 851 W (full-time); 407 M, 1,115 W (part-time)
Total Enrollment: 2,924
Cost: < $10K
% Receiving Financial Aid: 80%
Admission: Non-selective
Application Deadline: April 15

Admission. High school graduates with C average eligible; 80% of applicants accepted. *Required:* SAT, minimum 2.0 high school GPA, essay. Criteria considered in admissions, in order of importance: high school academic record, writing sample, recommendations, standardized test scores. *Out-of-state* freshman applicants: university welcomes students from out-of-state. State does not limit out-of-state enrollment. Required for out-of-state students: TOEFL. *Entrance programs:* early admission, midyear admission. *Apply* by April 15. *Transfers* welcome.

Academic Environment. Degrees offered: associates, bachelors, masters. Graduation requirements include English, social sciences, college algebra, 1 year of natural science, 2 years of foreign language, and 2 credits in physical education. New and unusual majors offered include marine biology, accounting, computer science, speech, communications, theater. Average undergraduate class size: 25% under 20, 55% 20–40, 20% over 40.

About 46% of students entering as freshmen graduate eventually. *Special programs:* CLEP, undergraduate research, National Student Exchange, academic assistance for students with deficiencies in English, math, and reading. *Calendar:* semester, summer school.

Undergraduate degrees conferred (116). 50% were in Business and Management, 10% were in Education, 9% were in Life Sciences, 7% were in Health Sciences, 5% were in Mathematics, 5% were in Letters, 3% were in Social Sciences, 3% were in Public Affairs, 3% were in Psychology, 3% were in Liberal/General Studies, remainder in 2 other fields.

Graduates Career Data. Advanced studies pursued by 20% of graduates; 8% enter graduate school; 3% enter medical school; 9% enter law school. Career Development Services include assistance with resume writing and interviewing techniques, job fairs.

Faculty. About 55% of faculty hold PhD or equivalent. About 40% of teaching faculty are female; 47% Black, 5% other minority.

Student Body. About 80% of students from Virgin Islands. An estimated 74% of students reported as Black, 4% Hispanic, 1% Asian, 10% other minority, according to most recent data available.

Campus Life. About 33% of men, 25% of women live in traditional dormitories; no coed dormitories; rest live in off-campus housing or commute. Freshmen given preference in university housing if all students cannot be accommodated. There are no fraternities or sororities on campus.

Annual Costs. Tuition and fees, $1,600 (out-of-state, $4,600); room and board, $4,300; estimated $1,000 other, exclusive of travel. About 80% of students receive financial aid. University reports some scholarships awarded on the basis of academic merit alone.

Virginia Commonwealth University

Richmond, Virginia 23284 (804) 367-1222; (800) 841-3638

A state-controlled university, offering liberal arts, technical, and professional programs in its Academic and Medical College campuses. Located in a metropolitan area of 500,000, Virginia Commonwealth was formed by merger of Richmond Professional Institute and Medical College of Virginia. Most convenient major airport: Richmond International.

Founded: 1838
Affiliation: State
UG Enrollment: 4,277 M, 5,955 W (full-time); 2,227 M, 2,860 W (part-time)
Total Enrollment: 21,854
Cost: < $10K
% Receiving Financial Aid: 65%
Admission: Selective
Application Deadline: Feb. 1

Admission is selective. About 70% of applicants accepted, 45% of these actually enroll; 43% of freshmen graduate in top fifth of high school class, 72% in top two-fifths. Average freshman SAT scores: 485 verbal, 525 mathematical; 40% of freshmen score above 500 on verbal, 10% above 600, less than 1% above 700; 61% score above 500 on mathematical, 19% above 600, 3% above 700. *Required:* SAT, minimum 2.2 high school GPA; portfolio for arts, audition for music and theater.

Criteria considered in admissions, in order of importance: high school academic record, standardized test scores, recommendations, writing sample, extracurricular activities; other factors considered: special talents. *Out-of-state* freshman applicants: university actively students from out-of-state. University does not limit out-of-state enrollment. No special requirements for out-of-state applicants. States from which most out-of-state students are drawn include New York, Maryland, New Jersey, Pennsylvania. *Entrance programs:* early decision, early admission, midyear admission, deferred admission, advanced placement. *Apply* by February 1. *Transfers* welcome; 1,672 enrolled 1993–94.

Academic Environment. *Undergraduate studies* offered by College of Humanities and Sciences, schools of Arts, Business, Community and Public Affairs, Mass Communications, Dentistry, Education, Nursing, Pharmacy, Social Work, and Allied Health Professions. Graduation requirements vary for undergraduate programs. Degrees offered: associates, bachelors, masters, doctoral. Average undergraduate class size: 34. About 77% of freshmen return for sophomore year. *Special programs:* CLEP, 3-year degree, honors, study abroad, 3–2 in engineering and physics, internships/cooperative work-study. Adult programs: non-traditional studies program. *Calendar:* semester, summer school.

Undergraduate degrees conferred (2,274). 18% were in Business and Management, 15% were in Visual and Performing Arts, 11% were in Health Sciences, 10% were in Education, 6% were in Psychology, 5% were in Social Sciences, 5% were in Allied Health, 5% were in Communications, 4% were in Protective Services, 4% were in Home Economics, 3% were in Computer and Engineering Related Technology, 3% were in Liberal/General Studies, 3% were in Letters, remainder in 8 other fields.

Graduates Career Data. Fields typically hiring largest numbers of graduates include banking, marketing, retail, education. Career Development Services include career search, SIGI, Virginia View, and FOCIS, interest inventory test, resume development and interviewing techniques.

Faculty. About 87% of faculty hold PhD or equivalent. About 60% of undergraduate classes taught by tenured faculty.

Student Body. About 92% of students from in state; 95% Middle Atlantic. An estimated 80% of students reported as Protestant, 10% Catholic, 1% Jewish, 9% other; 15% Black, 1% Hispanic, 5% Asian, 3% other minority. Average age of undergraduate student: 22.

Varsity Sports. Men (Div.I): Basketball, Baseball, Cross Country, Golf, Soccer, Tennis, Track. Women (Div.I): Basketball, Cross Country, Field Hockey, Tennis, Volleyball.

Campus Life. About 19% of students live in on-campus housing; rest live in off-campus housing or commute. Intervisitation in men's and women's dormitory rooms limited. There are 17 fraternities, 11 sororities on campus; they provide no residence facilities. About 30% of resident students leave campus on weekends.

Annual Costs. Tuition and fees, $3,747; (out-of-state, $10,304); room and board, $4,162; estimated $1,000 other, exclusive of travel. About 65% of students receive financial aid. Assistance is typically divided 20% scholarship, 70% loan, 10% work. University reports 185 scholarships awarded on the basis of academic merit alone. *Meeting Costs:* university offers installment payment plan.

Virginia Intermont College

Bristol, Virginia 24201 **(800) 451-1842**

A small, liberal arts college, affiliated with the Baptist General Association of Virginia and located only a short distance from downtown Bristol (pop. 45,000). Most convenient major airport: Tri-Cities.

Founded: 1884
Affiliation: Baptist
UG Enrollment: 518 M, W (full-time)
Cost: < $10K
% Receiving Financial Aid: 67%
Admission: Non-selective
Application Deadline: Aug. 15

Admission. Graduates of accredited high schools with 2.0 average eligible; 77% of applicants accepted, 35% of these actually enroll. *Required:* SAT or ACT, essay; interview recommended. *Non-academic factors* considered in admissions: special talents, alumni children. *Apply* by August 15. *Transfers* welcome.

Academic Environment. *Degree:* AB. About 70% of general education requirements for graduation are elective; distribution requirements fairly numerous. *Majors offered* in addition to usual studies include horsemanship, photography, paralegal studies, dance, sports management. About 66% of freshmen return for sophomore year. *Special programs:* CLEP, independent study, study abroad, honors, individualized majors. *Calendar:* early semester.

Undergraduate degrees conferred (66). 33% were in Agribusiness and Agricultural Production, 17% were in Visual and Performing Arts, 14% were in Law, 8% were in Liberal/General Studies, 6% were in Public Affairs, 6% were in Psychology, 6% were in Marketing and Distribution, 5% were in Education, 5% were in Business and Management, remainder in Health Sciences.

Student Body. About 45% of students from in state; 64% South, 13% Middle Atlantic, 10% North Central.

Religious Orientation. Virginia Intermont is a church-related institution, makes no religious demands on students.

Varsity Sports. Men (Div.II): Baseball, Basketball, Tennis. Women (Div.II): Basketball, Tennis, Volleyball.

Campus Life. About 68% of students live in traditional dormitories; no coed dormitories; rest commute. Intervisitation in men's and women's dormitory rooms limited. There are no fraternities or sororities. About 30% of students leave campus on weekends.

Annual Costs. Tuition and fees, $8,270; room and board, $3,980. About 67% of students receive financial aid. College reports some scholarships awarded on the basis of academic merit alone. *Meeting Costs:* college offers College Loan Association.

Virginia Military Institute

Lexington, Virginia 24450 **(703) 464-7311**

A state-supported institution for men, located in a town of 7,600, 54 miles northeast of Roanoke, VMI specializes in providing education in a military environment, together with military training. Most convenient major airport: Roanoke International.

Founded: 1839
Affiliation: State
UG Enrollment: 1,250 M (full-time)
Cost: < $10K
% Receiving Financial Aid: 61%
Admission: Selective (+)
Application Deadline: April 1

Admission is selective (+). About 76% of applicants accepted, 51% of these actually enroll; 29% of freshmen graduate in top fifth of high school class, 57% in top two-fifths. Average freshman SAT scores: 484 verbal, 542 mathematical; 43% of freshmen score above 500 on verbal, 7% above 600, 1% above 700; 70% score above 500 on mathematical, 23% above 600, 3% above 700; ACT, 22 composite. *Required:* SAT or ACT, essay. Criteria considered in admissions, in order of importance: high school academic record, standardized test scores, extracurricular activities, recommendations, writing sample; other factors considered: special talents, alumni children, diverse student body. *Out-of-state* freshman applicants: Institute actively seeks students from out-of-state. State does not limit out-of-state enrollment. No special requirements for out-of-state applicants. About 78% of out-of-state student accepted, 45% of these actually enroll. States from which most out-of-state students are drawn include New York, Pennsylvania, Maryland, New Jersey. *Entrance programs:* early decision. About 7% of entering students are from private schools, 8% from parochial schools. *Apply* by April 1. *Transfers* welcome; 48 enrolled 1993–94.

Academic Environment. Before entrance students must select one of the thirteen curricula offered by VMI; each 4-year program is highly structured. Graduation requirements include study in world civilization, chemistry, mathematics, writing composition, academic computing, ROTC, physical education. Degrees offered: bachelors. *Majors offered* in biology, chemistry, computer science, economics and business, English, history, mathematics, international studies, modern languages, physics, civil engineering, mechanical engineering, electrical engineering. Average undergraduate class size: 16; 65% under 20, 35% 20–40.

About 55% of students entering as freshmen graduate within four years, 64% eventually; 72% of freshmen return for sophomore year. *Special programs:* study abroad, honors, undergraduate research.) Calendar: semester, summer school.

Undergraduate degrees conferred (299). 44% were in Social Sciences, 34% were in Engineering, 7% were in Letters, 6% were in Life Sciences, 4% were in Computer and Engineering Related Technology, remainder in 3 other fields.

Graduates Career Data. About 36% of 1993 graduates enter the military; 11% pursue advanced studies. *Careers in business and industry* pursued by 49% of graduates. Career Development Services include career planning, placement, graduate education services.
Faculty. About 88% of faculty hold PhD or equivalent. About 85% of undergraduate classes taught by tenured faculty. About 7% of teaching faculty are female; 1% Black.
Student Body. About 63% of students from in state; 73% South, 13% Middle Atlantic, 5% Midwest, 3% New England, 2% West, 1% Northwest, 3% foreign. An estimated 61% of students reported as Protestant, 30% Catholic, 2% unaffiliated, 7% other; 7% Black, 1% Hispanic, 5% Asian, 3% other minority.
Varsity Sports. Men (Div.I): Baseball, Basketball, Cross Country, Football (IAA), Lacrosse, Soccer, Tennis, Track (Indoor & Outdoor), Wrestling.
Campus Life. Rules designed for regulation of student body as corps of cadets. All men live in barracks under military discipline. Honor system in effect; Honor Court, elected by cadets, tries all cases. Alcohol prohibited on campus; seniors with full class privileges may have cars. Only single cadets eligible for VMI; marriage during period of cadetship requires resignation. There are no fraternities.
Annual Costs. Tuition and fees (includes uniforms, laundry, pressing, and haircuts), $4,940 (out-of-state, $10,780); room and board (includes all meals and unlimited snacks), $3,690; estimated $2,050 other, exclusive of travel. About 61% of students receive financial aid; average amount of assistance, $4,500. Assistance is typically divided 50% scholarship, 50% grant. Institute reports 27 scholarships awarded on the basis of academic merit alone, 180 for special talents alone, 400 for need alone.

Virginia Polytechnic and State University

Blacksburg, Virginia 24061-0202 (703) 231-6267

Virginia Tech is a land-grant university located on a 2,600-acre campus in a town of 32,000, 38 miles west of Roanoke. Although out-of-state enrollment is limited, students from other states are "welcome" and significant numbers are attracted from New England and the Middle Atlantic states. Most convenient major airport: Roanoke International.

Founded: 1872
Affiliation: State
UG Enrollment: 10,752 M, 7,514 W (full-time); 357 M, 278 W (part-time)
Total Enrollment: 24,131
Cost: < $10K
% Receiving Financial Aid: 50%
Admission: Highly Selective
Application Deadline: Feb. 1

Admission is highly selective for Engineering; very (+) selective for Architecture; very selective for Agriculture and Life Sciences; selective (+) for Arts and Sciences, Business, Human Resources; selective for Education. About 68% of applicants accepted, 41% of these actually enroll; 66% of freshmen graduate in top fifth of high school class, 93% in top two-fifths. Average freshman SAT scores, according to most recent data available: 50% of freshmen score above 500 on verbal, 13% above 600, 2% above 700; 84% score above 500 on mathematical, 46% above 600, 11% above 700.

For Agriculture and Life Sciences (627 M, 521 W), 74% of applicants accepted, 55% of these actually enroll; 62% of freshmen graduate in top fifth of high school class, 91% in top two-fifths.

For Architecture (684 M, 266 W), 30% of applicants accepted, 53% of these actually enroll; 87% of freshmen graduate in top fifth of high school class, all in top two-fifths.

For Arts and Sciences (3,354 M, 2,969 W), 73% of applicants accepted, 40% of these actually enroll; 60% of freshmen graduate in top fifth of high school class, 94% in top two-fifths.

For Business Administration (1,757 M, 1,484 W), 65% of applicants accepted, 46% of these actually enroll; 56% of freshmen graduate in top fifth of high school class, 93% in top two- fifths.

For Education (217 M, 524 W), 58% of applicants accepted, 43% of these actually enroll; 55% of freshmen graduate in top fifth of high school class, 89% in top two-fifths.

For Engineering (3,835 M, 800 W), 53% of applicants accepted, 45% of these actually enroll; 89% of freshmen graduate in top fifth of high school class, all in top two-fifths.

For Human Resources (187 M, 924 W), 57% of applicants accepted, 46% of these actually enroll; 46% of freshmen graduate in top fifth of high school class, 89% in top two-fifths.

Required: SAT, ACH in English and mathematics. *Out-of-state* freshman applicants: university welcomes students from out of state. University policy limits out-of-state enrollment to 25% of entering class. Requirements for out-of-state applicants: "must have stronger credentials than in-state;" 59% of applicants accepted, 31% enroll. *Non-academic factors* considered in admissions: geographical distribution, alumni children, diverse student body, special talents. *Entrance programs:* early decision, early admission, midyear admission (not in all schools), deferred placement, advanced placement. *Apply* by February 1. *Transfers* welcome.
Academic Environment. Strongest academic programs reported to be engineering, business, architecture, agriculture, computer science, and theater arts. Administration source characterizes student body as pragmatically oriented. "Highly motivated, achievement oriented" students said to feel most at home. Administration reports about 25% of general education courses required for graduation are elective; new core curriculum required for all students. *Undergraduate studies* offered by colleges of Arts and Sciences, Agriculture and Life Science, Architecture, Business, Education, Engineering, Human Resources; 76 bachelor programs are offered. *Majors offered* in arts and sciences in addition to usual studies include computer science, education, geology, geophysics, hotel, restaurant and institutional management, international studies, nuclear science, statistics, technology education, theater arts.

About 68% of students entering as freshmen graduate within five years; 89% of freshmen return for sophomore year. *Special programs:* independent study, semester or summer study abroad, honors, undergraduate research, Washington program in urban studies for architecture students, cooperative work/study program in wide number of fields, credit by examination, Corps of Cadets. *Calendar:* quarter, summer school.
Undergraduate degrees conferred (3,781). 24% were in Engineering, 22% were in Business and Management, 8% were in Social Sciences, 7% were in Home Economics, 6% were in Life Sciences, 6% were in Education, 4% were in Psychology, 4% were in Communications, 3% were in Agricultural Sciences, 3% were in Letters, 3% were in Liberal/General Studies, 3% were in Architecture and Environmental Design, remainder in 10 other fields.
Graduates Career Data. According to most recent data available, full-time graduate or professional study pursued immediately after graduation by 15% of students. *Careers in business and industry* pursued by 76% of graduates. Career Development Services include career counseling, job placement assistance, on-campus interviews.
Faculty. About 87% of faculty hold PhD or equivalent.
Student Body. University seeks a national student body; 75% of students from in state; 89% South. An estimated 5% of students reported as Black, 6% Asian, 2% other minority. *Minority group students:* special financial and academic provisions.
Varsity Sports. Men (Div.I): Baseball, Basketball, Cross Country, Football, Golf, Soccer, Swimming, Tennis, Track, Wrestling. Women (Div.I): Basketball, Cross Country, Swimming, Tennis, Track, Volleyball.
Campus Life. Student leader characterizes Virginia Tech as a "very friendly campus, tough academically, though not overly competitive. Although only a minority of students join fraternities and sororities, they are active socially, and "Greeks have most leadership positions." Drinking age is 21; university-sponsored events are non-alcoholic. High interest reported in varsity sports (most popular: football, baseball, basketball, track) as well as intramurals (most popular: flag football, softball, volleyball, basketball). Cars allowed; parking available "but its getting farther away from where students want to go." Freshmen required to live in university housing.

About 25% of men, 18% of women live in traditional dormitories; 18% of men, 26% of women live in coed dormitories. Freshmen are given preference in college housing if all students cannot be accommodated. There are 33 fraternities, 16 sororities on campus which about 17% of men, 20% of women join; 1% of men, 3% of women live in fraternity/sorority dormitories. About 25% of students leave campus on weekends.
Annual Costs. Tuition and fees, $3,812 (out-of-state, $9,680); room and board, $3,196. About 50% of students receive financial aid; assistance is typically divided 50% scholarship, 35% loan, 15% work. University reports some scholarships awarded on the basis of academic merit alone. *Meeting Costs:* university offers Tuition Budget Payment Plan.

Virginia State University

Petersburg, Virginia 23803 **(804) 524-5695**

A state-supported university located in a community of 36,100, 25 miles south of Richmond; founded as a college for Negroes and still recognized in its mission as an historically black institution. Most convenient major airport: Richmond International.

Founded: 1882
Affiliation: State
UG Enrollment: 1,292 M, 1,875 W (full-time); 173 M, 153 W (part-time)
Total Enrollment: 4,589
Cost: < $10K
% Receiving Financial Aid: 84%
Admission: Non-selective
Application Deadline: May 1

Admission. Graduates of accredited high schools with 16 units (12 in academic subjects) eligible; specific requirements vary with the several schools; 88% of applicants accepted, 32% of these actually enroll; 6% of freshman graduate in top fifth of high school class, 33% in top two-fifths. Average freshman SAT scores, according to most recent data available: 450 M, 453 W verbal, 451 M, 442 W mathematical. *Required:* SAT or ACT. *Out-of-state* freshman applicants: university seeks students from out of state. State limits out-of-state enrollment to 61% of entering class. No special requirements for out-of-state applicants. *Non-academic factors* considered in admissions: special talents, alumni children. *Apply* by May 1. *Transfers* welcome; 63 M, 68 W accepted 1990–91.
Academic Environment. *Undergraduate studies* offered by schools of Business, Agriculture and Applied Sciences, Natural Resources, Education, Humanities and Social Sciences. About 18% of general education requirements for graduation are elective; distribution requirements fairly numerous. *Special programs:* independent study, study abroad, honors, undergraduate research, 3–2 programs in engineering and interdisciplinary studies. Adult programs: Interdisciplinary Studies offers credit for work experience. *Calendar:* semester, summer school.
Undergraduate degrees conferred (356). 37% were in Business and Management, 14% were in Social Sciences, 13% were in Public Affairs, 10% were in Education, 7% were in Multi/Interdisciplinary Studies, 4% were in Visual and Performing Arts, 3% were in Mathematics, 3% were in Engineering and Engineering Related Technology, remainder in 6 other fields.
Graduates Career Data. According to most recent data available: full-time graduate or professional study pursued by 31% of students immediately after graduation. *Careers in business and industry* pursued by 42% of graduates.
Faculty. About 61% of faculty hold PhD or equivalent.
Student Body. About 60% of students from Virginia; 72% from South, 18% from Middle Atlantic. An estimated 97% of students reported as Protestant, 2% Catholic, 1% other; 89% Black, 1% Hispanic, 2% Asian, 1% Native American, according to most recent data available.
Varsity Sports. Men (Div.II): Baseball, Basketball, Football, Tennis, Track, Wrestling. Women (Div.II): Basketball, Softball, Tennis, Track.
Campus Life. About 64% of men, 65% of women live in traditional dormitories; no coed dormitories; rest live in off-campus housing or commute. No intervisitation in dormitory rooms. There are 4 fraternities, 4 sororities on campus; they provide no residence facilities. About 27% of resident students leave campus on weekends.
Annual Costs. Tuition and fees, $2,913 (out-of-state, $6,315); room and board, $4,127. About 84% of students receive financial aid; assistance is typically divided 36% scholarship, 52% loan, 12% work. College reports some scholarships awarded on the basis of academic merit alone. *Meeting Costs:* college offers Parent PLUS Loans, FOCUS, The Tuition Plan, prepayment plan, Academic Management Services.

Virginia Union University

Richmond, Virginia 23220 **(804) 257-5600**

A church-related college, located in a city of 249,600; founded as a college for Negroes and still serving a predominantly black student body.

Founded: 1865
Affiliation: American Baptist
UG Enrollment: 563 M, 735 W (full-time)
Total Enrollment: 1,549
Cost: < $10K
% Receiving Financial Aid: 81%
Admission: Non-selective
Application Deadline: June 1

Admission. Graduates of accredited high schools with 16 units eligible; 86% of applicants accepted, 29% of these actually enroll; 8% of freshmen graduate in top fifth of high school class, 21% in top two-fifths. Average freshman scores: SAT, 322 M, 314 W verbal, 358 M, 332 W mathematical. *Required:* SAT, minimum high school GPA. Criteria considered in admissions, in order of importance: high school academic record, standardized test scores. *Entrance programs:* early decision, early admission, advanced placement. *Apply* by June 1; rolling admissions. *Transfers* welcome; 48 enrolled 1993–94.
Academic Environment. Graduation requirements include 49–51 general education and liberal arts courses, foreign language, and computer science. Degrees offered: bachelors, masters, doctoral. Average undergraduate class size: 30% under 20, 60% 20–40, 10% over 40. About 23% of students entering as freshmen graduate eventually; 60% of freshmen return for sophomore year. *Special programs:* independent study, Eight College Consortium, Special Opportunity Program, summer study/travel abroad, 3–2 in engineering, 3–2 in law, internship/cooperative work-study, cross registration with Virginia Commonwealth U. *Calendar:* semester, summer school.
Undergraduate degrees conferred (90). 31% were in Business and Management, 17% were in Education, 12% were in Life Sciences, 11% were in Social Sciences, 7% were in Communications, 6% were in Visual and Performing Arts, 4% were in Psychology, 4% were in Mathematics, 3% were in Philosophy and Religion, remainder in 4 other fields.
Graduates Career Data. Advanced studies pursued by 38% of graduates; 30% enter graduate school; 3% enter medical school; 2% enter law school; 3% enter business school. Career Development Services include programs and services to assist students in various areas of career development and placement.
Faculty. About 58% of faculty hold PhD or equivalent. About 40% of undergraduate classes taught by tenured faculty. About 46% of teaching faculty are female; 53% Black, 10% other minority.
Student Body. About 55% of students from in state. An estimated 62% of students reported as Protestant, 4% Catholic, 33% unaffiliated; 99% Black, according to most recent data available.
Religious Orientation. Virginia Union is a church-related institution; 1 course in religion required of all students.
Varsity Sports. Men: Basketball, Cross Country, Football, Golf, Tennis, Track, Volleyball. Women: Basketball, Softball, Track, Volleyball.
Campus Life. About 36% of men, 88% of women live in traditional dormitories; no coed dormitories; rest live in off-campus housing or commute. There are 4 fraternities, 4 sororities on campus; they provide no residence facilities. About 65–75% of resident students leave campus on weekends.
Annual Costs. Tuition and fees, $7,061; room and board, $3,494; estimated $1,950 other, exclusive of travel. About 81% of students receive financial aid; average amount of assistance, $1,888. Assistance is typically divided 42% scholarship, 14% loan, 19% work.

University of Virginia

Charlottesville, Virginia 22906 **(804) 924-0311**

The University of Virginia is today what its founder, Thomas Jefferson, wished it to be—not only the state university, but also a national institution drawing both male and female students from all parts of the U.S. and many foreign countries. Unlike many public institutions in other states, the University of Virginia continues to welcome applicants from other parts of the country. The 1,500-acre campus, designed by Jefferson, is located in a historically rich and diverse community of 110,000, 60 miles northwest of Richmond and 110 miles south of Washington, D.C. Most convenient major airports: Charlottesville, or Richmond.

Founded: 1819
Affiliation: State
UG Enrollment: 5,417 M, 5,861 W (full-time); 55 M, 59 W (part-time)
Total Enrollment: 18,073
Cost: < $10K
% Receiving Financial Aid: 36%
Admission: Highly (+) Selective
Application Deadline: Jan. 2

Admission is highly (+) selective for Arts and Sciences, Architecture, Engineering and Applied Science; very selective for Nursing. For all schools, 34% of applicants accepted, 50% of these actually enroll; 93% of freshmen graduate in top fifth of high school class, 98% in top two-fifths. Average freshman SAT scores, 50% range: 520–630 verbal, 590–710 mathematical; 83% of freshmen score above 500 on verbal, 41% above 600, 6% above 700; 94% score above 500 on mathematical, 73% above 600, 29% above 700.

For College of Arts and Sciences (3,615 M, 4,787 W), 32% of applicants accepted, 52% of these actually enroll; 92% of freshmen graduate in top fifth of high school class, 99% in top two-fifths. Average freshman SAT scores: 83% score above 500 on verbal, 43% above 600, 6% above 700; 94% score above 500 on mathematical, 70% above 600, 26% above 700.

For School of Architecture (212 M, 154 W), 24% of applicants accepted, 60% of these actually enroll; 95% of freshmen graduate in top fifth of high school class, all in top two-fifths. Average freshman SAT scores: 91% score above 500 on verbal, 43% above 600, 1% above 700; 999 score above 500 on mathematical, 84% above 600, 32% above 700.

For School of Engineering and Applied Science (1,172 M, 377 W), 40% of applicants accepted, 43% of these actually enroll; 95% of freshmen graduate in top fifth of high school class, 99% in top two-fifths. Average freshman SAT scores: 84% score above 500 on verbal, 35% above 600, 4% above 700; 99% score above 500 on mathematical, 92% above 600, 49% above 700.

For School of Nursing (12 M, 238 W), 33% of applicants accepted, 82% of these actually enroll; 91% of freshmen graduate in top fifth of high school class, all in top two-fifths. Average freshman SAT scores: 58% score above 500 on verbal, 14% above 600; 86% score above 500 on mathematical, 42% above 600.

Required: SAT, ACH, essay. Criteria considered in admissions: high school academic record ranks with highest importance; standardized test scores, extracurricular activities, recommendations, and writing sample rank equally; other factors considered: special talents, alumni children, diverse student body. *Out-of-state* freshman applicants: university actively seeks students from out-of-state. State does not limit out-of-state enrollment. No special requirements for out-of-state applicants. About 26% of applicants accepted, 36% of these actually enroll. States from which most out-of-state students are drawn include Maryland, New Jersey, New York, Pennsylvania. *Entrance programs:* early decision, advanced placement. About 21% of entering students from private and parochial schools. *Apply* by January 2. *Transfers* welcome; 475 enrolled 1993–94.

Academic Environment. Pressures for academic achievement appear to vary from moderately strong to intense, depending on the division of the university. A special Echols Scholars Program allows superior students complete freedom from area and major requirements all 4 years, while they live together as a group first year. Honors program for juniors and seniors consists of tutorials and independent study. Strong departments reported to be business, English, economics, foreign language, history. Graduation requirements include 12 hours of natural science/mathematics, 9 of social sciences (including 3 in non-Western culture), 6 of humanities; proficiency in foreign language, and 2 writing courses. *Undergraduate studies* offered to freshmen by 4 schools listed above; juniors may enter schools of Commerce, Education. Some student concern voiced about large classes. Degrees offered: bachelors, masters, doctoral. *Majors offered* in addition to usual arts and sciences include Afro-American studies, Asian studies, astronomy, cognitive studies, computer science, foreign affairs, Latin American studies, Russian studies. Average undergraduate class size: 46% under 20, 34% 20–40, 20% over 40.

About 80% of students entering as freshmen graduate within four years, 92% eventually; 97% of freshmen return for sophomore year. *Special programs:* independent study, study abroad, undergraduate research, honors, 3-year degree, individualized majors, Echols Scholars Program. *Calendar:* semester, summer school.

Undergraduate degrees conferred (2,815). 27% were in Social Sciences, 14% were in Letters, 11% were in Business and Management, 10% were in Engineering, 7% were in Psychology, 5% were in Multi/Interdisciplinary Studies, 4% were in Foreign Languages, 3% were in Life Sciences, 3% were in Architecture and Environmental Design, 3% were in Health Sciences, 3% were in Physical Sciences, remainder in 6 other fields.

Graduates Career Data. Advanced studies pursued by 65% of graduates. Medical schools typically enrolling largest numbers of graduates include U. of Virginia, Georgetown U., Duke U.; law schools include U. of Virginia, Washington & Lee, William & Mary, Georgetown, Harvard; business schools include U. of Virginia. Career Development Services include career planning and placement services providing counseling, workshops, campus recruitment, classes; resources for students, freshman through graduate, and related planning needs.

Faculty. About 90% of faculty hold PhD or equivalent. About 43% of undergraduate classes taught by tenured faculty. About 22% of teaching faculty are female; 3% Black, 1% Hispanic, 5% other minority.

Student Body. About 66% of students from in state; 81% Middle Atlantic, 8% South, 5% Midwest, 3% New England, 2% West, 2% foreign. An estimated 48% of students reported as Protestant, 24% Catholic, 4% Jewish, 18% unaffiliated, 6% other; 12% Black, 2% Hispanic, 9% Asian, 2% other minority.

Varsity Sports. Men (Div.IA): Baseball, Basketball, Cross Country, Diving, Football, Golf, Lacrosse, Soccer, Swimming, Tennis, Track, Wrestling. Women (Div.I): Basketball, Cross Country, Field Hockey, Lacrosse, Soccer, Softball, Swimming, Tennis, Track, Volleyball.

Campus Life. Campus has for many years functioned under a student honor and judiciary system code with a minimum of explicit regulations. Fraternities and sororities have long attracted a significant number of students and continue to be popular. Need for greater diversity and "more space" for social life noted. No curfew; intervisitation unlimited. Cars allowed; parking still a problem, but student asserts "you don't need a car" because most things are nearby. All first-year students required to live on campus. University provides on campus almost all types of cultural activities. Nearest major cultural center is Washington, D.C., 110 miles away.

About 50% of men, 51% of women live in coed dormitories; 36% of men, 41% of women live in off-campus housing; 1% each commute. Sexes segregated in coed dormitories by floor. Freshmen are given preference in college housing if all students cannot be accommodated. There are 39 fraternities, 22 sororities on campus which about 28% of men, 30% of women join; 13% of men, 7% of women live in fraternities and sororities.

Annual Costs. Tuition and fees, $4,350 (out-of-state, $12,254); room and board, $4,000; estimated $1,600 other, exclusive of travel. About 36% of students receive financial aid; average amount of assistance, $6,560. Assistance is typically divided 73% scholarship/grant, 24% loan, 3% work. University reports 250 scholarships awarded on the basis of academic merit alone, 400 for special needs alone, 675 for need alone.

Clinch Valley College of the University of Virginia

Wise, Virginia 24293 **(800) 468-3412**

The University of Virginia's Clinch Valley College is located in a community of 3,900, 320 miles from Charlottesville. Most convenient major airport: Tri-Cities.

Founded: 1954
Affiliation: State
UG Enrollment: 564 M, 561 W (full-time); 120 M, 302 W (part-time)
Cost: < $10K
% Receiving Financial Aid: 72%
Admission: Non-selective
Application Deadline: August 15

Admission. Graduates of accredited high schools with 16 units eligible; 81% of applicants accepted, 36% of these actually enroll. Average freshman SAT scores: 407 verbal, 452 mathematical, according to most recent data available. *Required:* SAT, high school transcript and GPA. Criteria considered in admissions, in order of importance: high school academic record, standardized test scores, recommendations. *Out-of-state* freshman applicants: university actively seeks students from out-of-state. State does not limit out-of-state enrollment. No special requirements for out-of-state applicants. States from which most out-of-state students are drawn include Kentucky. *Apply* by August 15; rolling admissions. *Transfers* welcome; 128 enrolled 1993–94.

Academic Environment. Graduation requirements include 6 hours each of English composition, math/computer science, foreign language, and Western heritage, 9 hours of social science, 8 of science, 3 each of arts, humanities, and literature, 1 hour each of physical education and orientation. Students praise the "helpful" faculty and "excellent" academic programs. Degrees offered: bachelors. About 20% of students entering as freshmen graduate within four years, 69% eventually; 65% of freshmen return for sophomore year. *Special programs:* independent study, study abroad, individualized majors, interdisciplinary major. *Calendar:* 4–1–4, summer school.

Undergraduate degrees conferred (225). 33% were in Business and Management, 24% were in Education, 20% were in Social Sciences, 4% were in Mathematics, 4% were in Computer and Engineering Related Technology, 4% were in Life Sciences, 3% were in Letters, 3% were in Physical Sciences, remainder in 4 other fields.

Graduates Career Data. Advanced studies pursued by 12% of graduates; 1% enter medical school; 3% enter law school; 4% enter business school. Medical schools typically enrolling largest numbers of graduates include Medical College of Virginia; law schools include U. of Virginia, Washington and Lee, William & Mary; business schools include Virginia Tech, U. of Tennessee. Career Development Services include placement files and job fairs.

Faculty. About 71% of faculty hold PhD or equivalent. About 35% of teaching faculty are female.

Student Body. About 96% of students from in state. An estimated 2% of students reported as Black, according to most recent data available.

Varsity Sports. Men (NAIA): Baseball, Basketball, Cross Country, Football, Golf, Tennis. Women (NAIA): Basketball, Cross Country, Tennis, Volleyball.

Campus Life. Campus is located in a small town, described by a student as "very safe and quaint." Student Government Association sponsors "all sorts of social events."

About 45% of men, 45% of women live in traditional dormitories; 7% of men, 1% of women live in coed dormitories; 47% of men, 54% of women live in off-campus housing or commute. Intervisitation in men's and women's dormitory rooms limited. There are 4 fraternities, 5 sororities on campus. About 50% of resident students leave campus on weekends.

Annual Costs. Tuition and fees, $2,988 (out-of-state, $6,826); room and board, $3,376; estimated $1,000 other, exclusive of travel. About 72% of students receive financial aid; average amount of assistance, $1,219. Assistance is typically divided 58% scholarship, 32% loan, 10% work. *Meeting Costs:* college offers installment payment plan.

Virginia Wesleyan College

Norfolk, Virginia 23502 **(804) 455-3208**

A church-related, liberal arts college, located on a 300-acre campus in a 4-city metropolitan area of 1,400,000.

Founded: 1961
Affiliation: United Methodist
UG Enrollment: 456 M, 684 W (full-time); 143 M, 264 W (part-time)
Total Enrollment: 1,547
Cost: $10K–$20K
% Receiving Financial Aid: 72%
Admission: Non-selective
Application Deadline: March 1

Admission. High school graduates with 16 units eligible; others given individual consideration; 60% of applicants accepted, 33% of these actually enroll; 35% of freshmen graduate in top fifth of high school class, 60% in top two-fifths. Average freshman SAT scores: 66% of freshmen score above 500 verbal, 31% above 600, 5% above 700; 73% score above 500 mathematical, 36% above 600, 5% above 700. *Required:* SAT, essay. Criteria considered in admissions, in order of importance: high school academic record, standardized test scores, extracurricular activities, recommendations, writing sample; other factors considered: special talents, alumni children, diverse student body. *Entrance programs:* early decision, early admission, midyear admission, deferred admission, advanced placement. About 40% of freshmen from private or parochial schools. *Apply* by March 1. *Transfers* welcome; 140 enrolled 1993–94.

Academic Environment. Degrees offered: bachelors. Core requirements for liberal arts program include 2 courses in each of the following areas: empirical knowledge, aesthetic understanding, ethical values, and historical perspectives; and one course each in communications, cultural systems, mathematics; 2 courses in English. *Majors offered* include social ecology, western cultural heritage. About 60% of students entering as freshmen graduate in four years, 70% eventually; 85% of freshmen return for sophomore year. Average undergraduate class size: 16% under 20, 60% between 20–40, 40% over 40. *Special programs:* CLEP, independent study, study abroad, honors, credit by examination, internships, cross registration with Norfolk State U., Old Dominican U., College of William and Mary. Adult programs: Adult Studies Program with majors in business, human services, and liberal studies. *Calendar:* semester, January interterm.

Undergraduate degrees conferred (206). 35% were in Business and Management, 15% were in Social Sciences, 15% were in Education, 8% were in Psychology, 6% were in Communications, 5% were in Multi/Interdisciplinary Studies, 4% were in Visual and Performing Arts, 4% were in Letters, remainder in 5 other fields.

Graduates Career Data. Advanced studies pursued by 35% of students; 5% enter medical school; 1% enter dental school; 10% enter law school; 6% enter business school; 3% enter other schools. Medical schools typically enrolling largest number of graduates include Medical College Of Virginia; law schools include College of William and Mary; business schools include Old Dominican U. About 75% of 1992–93 graduates employed. Employers typically hiring largest number of graduates include Nations Bank, Civil Service, Virginia Beach schools, WAVY TV.

Faculty. About 85% of faculty hold PhD or equivalent. About 55% of undergraduate classes taught by tenured faculty. About 28% of teaching faculty are female; 3% Black, 2% Hispanic, 2% other minority.

Student Body. College seeks a national student body; 65% of students from in state; 5% South, 15% Middle Atlantic, 10% New England; 1% Foreign. An estimated 54% of students reported as Protestant, 27% Catholic, 1% Jewish, 14% unaffiliated, 4% other; 6% Black, 3% Hispanic, 3%Asian, 1% other minority.

Varsity Sports. Men (Div.III): Baseball, Basketball, Golf, Lacrosse, Soccer, Tennis. Women (Div.III): Basketball, Field Hockey, Soccer, Softball, Tennis.

Campus Life. About 5% of women live in traditional dormitories; 59% of men, 54% of women live in coed dormitories; rest commute. Intervisitation in men's and women's dormitory rooms limited. There are 3 fraternities, 3 sororities on campus which about 15% of men, 10% of women join; 1% of men, 1% of women live in fraternities and sororities. About 15% of resident students leave campus on weekends.

Annual Costs. Tuition and fees, $10,150; room and board, $4,800; estimated $800 other, exclusive of travel. About 72% of students receive financial aid; average amount of assistance, $7,500. Assistance is typically divided 18% scholarship, 15% grant, 47% loan, 20% work.

School of Visual Arts

New York, New York 10010

An unusually large professional college of art, offering degree programs in fine and applied arts, with particular emphasis on the media and communications arts.

Founded: 1947
Affiliation: Independent

Undergraduate degrees conferred (362). 61% were in Communications Technologies, 36% were in Visual and Performing Arts, remainder in Communications.

Viterbo College

La Crosse, Wisconsin 54601 **(608) 791-0421**

An independent, co-educational college, founded by the Sisters of St. Francis of Perpetual Adoration, located in a city of 48,000, 100 miles west of Madison. Most convenient major airport: La Crosse.

Founded: 1890
Affiliation: Independent (Roman Catholic)
UG Enrollment: 257 M, 757 W (full-time); 74 M, 313 W (part-time)
Cost: < $10K
% Receiving Financial Aid: 85%
Admission: Selective
Application Deadline: May 1

Admission is selective. Graduates of accredited high schools who rank in top half of class eligible; 85% of applicants accepted, 58% of these actually enroll; 22% of freshmen graduate in top fifth of high school class, 95% in top two-fifths. Average freshman scores: ACT, 22.3 composite. *Required:* SAT or ACT (preferred), must be in top half of graduating class. Criteria considered in admissions, in order of importance: standardized test scores, high school academic record, recommendations, extracurricular activities; other factors considered: special talents, alumni children, diverse student body, letters of recommendation. *Entrance programs:* early decision, early admission, midyear admission, deferred admission, advanced placement. About 5% of freshmen from private schools, 11% from parochial schools. *Apply* by May 1; rolling admissions. *Transfers* welcome; 202 enrolled 1993–94.

Academic Environment. Degrees offered: bachelors, masters. *Majors offered* in addition to usual studies include nutrition and dietetics, nursing, art administration, art in business, music, teacher education. Core requirements in liberal arts program include 9 credits in English, 6 in history, 6 in social sciences, 8 in natural sciences, 4 in fine arts, 12 in religious studies/philosophy; English competency test required. Average undergraduate class size: 90% under 20, 10% between 20–40. About 75% of students entering as freshmen return for sophomore year. *Special programs:* CLEP, independent study, January term, study abroad, undergraduate research, internships; 3–2 in pre-physical therapy, optometry, pharmacy. *Calendar:* semester, May term, summer school.

Undergraduate degrees conferred (137). 33% were in Health Sciences, 29% were in Business and Management, 9% were in Psychology, 9% were in Education, 4% were in Social Sciences, 4% were in Home Economics, 3% were in Letters, remainder in 6 other fields.

Graduates Career Data. Advanced studies pursued by 8% of students; 1% enter medical school; 1% enter dental school; 1% enter law school; 1% enter business school. About 98% of 1992–93 graduates employed. Fields typically hiring largest number of graduates include nursing, business, psychology, education. Career Development Services include internships/fellowships, career planning class, cover letter and resume writing, career fairs and workshops.

Faculty. About 60% of faculty hold PhD or equivalent. About 80% of undergraduate classes taught by tenured faculty. About 58% of teaching faculty are female; 1% other minority.

Student Body. College does not seek a national student body; 99% Midwest; 1% Foreign. An estimated 45% of students reported as Protestant, 50% Catholic, 5% other; 2% Black, 3% other minority.

Religious Orientation. Viterbo is a church-related institution; 5–7 credits of religious studies required of all students.

Varsity Sports. Men (NAIA): Baseball, Basketball, Soccer. Women (NAIA): Basketball, Softball, Volleyball.

Campus Life. About 15% of women live in traditional dormitories; 15% of men, 30% of women live in coed dormitories; 55% men, 15% women live in off-campus college-related housing; rest commute. There are no fraternities or sororities. About 10% of students leave campus on weekends.

Annual Costs. Tuition and fees, $8,770; room and board, $4,800; estimated $1,500 other, exclusive of travel. About 85% of students receive financial aid; average amount of assistance, $8,500. Assistance is typically divided 41% scholarship, 30% grant, 21% loan, 8% work. College reports 780 scholarships awarded for academic merit, 24 for special talents, 214 for need.

Voorhees College

Denmark, South Carolina 29042

A church-related, liberal arts college, located in a town of 3,600, 50 miles south of Columbia; founded as a college for Negroes and still serving a predominantly black student body.

Founded: 1897
Affiliation: Episcopal
UG Enrollment: 298 M, 405 W (full-time)
Cost: < $10K
Admission: Non-selective
Application Deadline: August 1

Admission. High school graduates with 16 units eligible; 80% of applicants accepted, 20% of these actually enroll; 10% of freshmen graduate in top fifth of high school class, 20 in top two-fifths. Average freshman scores: SAT, 320 M, 330 W verbal, 350 M, 340 W mathematical; ACT, 15 M, 15 W composite. *Required:* SAT recommended, minimum H. S. GPA of 2.0. Criteria considered in admissions, in order of importance: high school academic record, recommendations, standardized test scores. *Entrance programs:* deferred admission, advanced placement. *Apply* by August 1; rolling admissions. *Transfers* welcome; 33 enrolled 1993–94.

Academic Environment. Degrees offered: bachelors. Core requirements for liberal arts include 55 credit hours distributed among humanities, English, fine arts, mathematics, natural sciences, social sciences, computer science. *Majors offered* in addition to usual studies include health & recreation, organizational management. Average undergraduate class size: 30% under 20, 60% between 20–40, 10% over 40. About 30% of students entering as freshmen graduate in four years, 50% eventually; 58% of freshmen return for sophomore year. *Special programs:* independent study, undergraduate research, 3-year degree, cross registration with Denmark Technical College; 3–2 in law, nursing. Adult programs: degree completion program in organizational management. *Calendar:* semester, summer school.

Undergraduate degrees conferred (74). 30% were in Social Sciences, 24% were in Business and Management, 22% were in Protective Services, 8% were in Computer and Engineering Related Technology, 7% were in Business (Administrative Support), 4% were in Mathematics, 4% were in Life Sciences, remainder in Letters.

Graduates Career Data. Advanced studies pursued by 30% of students; 5% enter medical school; 1% enter law school; 20% enter business school. Fields typically hiring largest number of graduates include business, education, corrections, social services.

Faculty. About 40% of faculty hold PhD or equivalent. About 40% of teaching faculty are female; 50% Black, 25% other minority.

Student Body. College seeks a national student body; 80% from the state; 12% of students from South; 5% Middle Atlantic, 2% Midwest. An estimated 99% Protestant, 1% Catholic; 98% Black.

Religious Orientation. Voorhees is a church-related institution; 1 course in religion required of all students.

Campus Life. According to most recent data available, about 98% of men, 98% of women live in traditional dormitories; no coed dormitories; rest live in off-campus housing or commute. No intervisitation in men's or women's dormitory rooms. There are 4 fraternities, 4 sororities on campus which about 10% of men, 20% of women join; they provide no residence facilities. About 75% of resident students leave campus on weekends.

Annual Costs. Tuition and fees, $4,250; room and board, $2,522; estimated $500 other, exclusive of travel. About 98% of students receive financial aid; average amount of assistance, $4,250. College reports 10 scholarships awarded for special talents, 25 for need.

Wabash College

Crawfordsville, Indiana 47933 **(317) 364-4225**

Wabash is recognized as a strong, traditional, liberal arts institution. It is one of the few remaining men's colleges in the Middle West. The 50-acre campus is located in a town of 13,500, 45 miles northwest of Indianapolis and 160 miles south of Chicago. Most convenient major airport: Indianapolis International.

Founded: 1832
Affiliation: Independent
UG Enrollment: 805 M (full-time)
Cost: $10K–$20K
% Receiving Financial Aid: 86%
Admission: Very Selective
Application Deadline: Rolling

Admission is very selective. About 78% of applicants accepted, 41% of these actually enroll; 68% of freshmen graduate in top fifth of high school class, 92% in top two-fifths. Freshman SAT scores, middle fifty percent range: 450–580 verbal, 540–660 mathematical; 60%

of freshmen score above 500 on verbal, 22% above 600, 2% above 700; 85% score above 500 on mathematical, 50% above 600, 14% above 700. *Required:* SAT or ACT, essay; interview strongly recommended. Criteria considered in admissions, in order of importance: high school academic record, standardized test scores, recommendations, writing sample, extracurricular activities; other factors considered: special talents, alumni children, diverse student body. *Entrance programs:* early admission, midyear admission, deferred admission, advanced placement. *Apply:* rolling admissions. *Transfers* welcome; 16 enrolled 1993–94.

Academic Environment. Students serve as voting members on some faculty committees. Student leader gives very strong endorsement of close relationship between faculty and students. Campus atmosphere is primarily scholarly/intellectual with strong pre-professional concern. College has long provided strong preparation for professional study in law, medicine, business. All freshmen participate in seminar program. Administration reports 92% of general education courses required for graduation are elective; distribution requirements, however, fairly numerous: 3 courses each in social sciences, natural sciences and mathematics, behavioral sciences, literature and fine arts, 2 from history, and philosophy and religion, and 2 courses in cultures and tradition. Seniors take both written and oral comprehensive examinations before graduation. Students now have option of departmental minor (minimum of 5 courses) or area of concentration (5–8 courses outside of major field and drawn from more than one department). Degrees offered: bachelors. *Majors offered* include fine arts, speech. Average undergraduate class size: 90% under 20, 10% between 20–40.

About 75% of students entering as freshmen graduate within four years; 89% of freshmen return for sophomore year. *Special programs:* CLEP, independent study, study abroad, programs of GLCA, Washington Semester, 3–2 in engineering and law, Far Eastern area studies, internships, marine biology studies program. *Calendar:* semester.

Undergraduate degrees conferred (231). 29% were in Social Sciences, 18% were in Letters, 13% were in Psychology, 12% were in Physical Sciences, 9% were in Life Sciences, 6% were in Philosophy and Religion, 5% were in Mathematics, 4% were in Visual and Performing Arts, 3% were in Foreign Languages.

Graduates Career Data. Advanced studies pursued by 43% of students immediately after graduation, 75% eventually; 9% enter medical school; 11% enter law school; 6% enter other schools. Medical schools typically enrolling largest numbers of graduate include Northwestern, Vanderbilt; law schools include Chicago, Indiana, Vanderbilt. About 37% of 1992–93 graduates employed. Fields typically hiring largest numbers of graduates include business, banks, sales/professional. Career Development Services include job placement service, individual and group job counseling, resume workshops, library resources, internships, on-campus recruitment.

Faculty. About 89% of faculty hold PhD or equivalent. About 63% of undergraduate classes taught by tenured faculty. About 10% of teaching faculty are female; 3% minority.

Student Body. College seeks a national student body, 75% of students from in state; 94% from Midwest; 5% Foreign. An estimated 6% of students reported as Black, 3% Hispanic, 3% Asian, 4% other minority.

Varsity Sports. Men (Div.III): Baseball, Basketball, Cross Country, Diving, Football, Golf, Soccer, Swimming, Tennis, Track, Wrestling.

Campus Life. College provides relatively wide range of cultural and intellectual activities on campus; nearest major cultural center is Indianapolis, 45 miles away. Strong student concern over absence of women on campus and some attribute transfers to this cause. Student interest in fraternities and athletics (both varsity and intramural) reported as high. Limited number of rules. No restrictions on cars except for parking regulations. Freshmen and sophomores required to live in residence halls or fraternity houses.

About 23% of men live in traditional dormitories; 6% live in off-campus college-related housing; rest commute. There are 10 fraternities on campus which about 70% of men join; 70% live in fraternities. About 50% of resident students leave campus on weekends.

Annual Costs. Tuition and fees, $12,450; room and board, $4,000; estimated $1,000 other, exclusive of travel. About 86% of students receive financial aid; average amount of assistance, $9,755. Assistance is typically divided 21% loan, 4% work, rest scholarship/grant. College reports 387 scholarships awarded for academic merit, 15 for special talents, 748 for need. *Meeting Costs:* college offers tuition payment plan, AMS Budget Payment Plan, and generous financial aid packages.

Wadhams Hall Seminary-College

Ogdensburg, New York 13669

Wadhams Hall is a fully accredited, free-standing seminary college and pre-theologate for students pursuing priesthood and other roles of leadership and service in the Catholic Church.

Founded: 1924 **Affiliation:** Roman Catholic

Undergraduate degrees conferred (9). 100% were in Philosophy and Religion.

Wagner College

Staten Island, New York 10301 **(718) 390-3411**

An independent liberal arts college, supported by the Lutheran Church in America, Wagner is located on an 86-acre campus on Staten Island, overlooking New York harbor. Most convenient major airports: JFK, LaGuardia, and Newark.

Founded: 1883
Affiliation: Independent (Lutheran)
UG Enrollment: 582 M, 742 W (full-time); 33 M, 84 W (part-time)
Cost: $10K–$20K
% Receiving Financial Aid: 70%
Admission: Non-selective
Application Deadline: February 15

Admission. About 71% of applicants accepted, 42% of these actually enroll; 23% of freshmen graduate in top fifth of high school class, 50% in top two-fifths. Average freshman SAT scores: 465 M, 490 W verbal, 520 M, 505 W mathematical; 47% of freshmen score above 500 verbal, 10% above 600, 1% above 700; 62% score above 500 mathematical, 15% above 600, 3% above 700. *Required:* SAT, essay, letter of recommendation, minimum H.S. GPA of B-. Criteria considered in admissions, in order of importance: high school academic record, standardized test scores, writing sample, extracurricular activities, recommendations; other factors considered: special talents, alumni children, diverse student body. *Entrance programs:* early decision, midyear admission, deferred admission. About 5% of freshmen from private schools, 32% from parochial schools. *Apply* by February 15; rolling admissions. *Transfers* welcome; 132 enrolled 1993–94.

Academic Environment. Wagner's academic offerings are enhanced by the Alumni Mentor Program which links accomplished alumni in the New York Metropolitan area with students. Beginning in the freshman year students have the opportunity to visit alumni in their workplace and learn first-hand the nature and responsibilities of various positions. Distribution requirements (24–30 semester hours) and broad interdisciplinary program introduced. Degrees offered: bachelors, masters. *Majors offered* include art administration, physician's assistant, public administration, musical theatre, African and Afro-American studies, bacteriology and health sciences. Average undergraduate class size: 65% under 20, 35% between 20–40.

About 60% of students entering as freshmen graduate in four years, 75% eventually; 82% of freshmen return for sophomore year. *Special programs:* CLEP, independent study, study abroad, January term, honors, undergraduate research, internships, credit by examination, graduate courses for credit, resident symphony orchestra; 3–2 in occupational therapy, speech pathology. *Calendar:* 4–1–4, summer school.

Undergraduate degrees conferred (246). 30% were in Business and Management, 16% were in Social Sciences, 15% were in Education, 12% were in Health Sciences, 11% were in Letters, 8% were in Life Sciences, 3% were in Visual and Performing Arts, remainder in 4 other fields.

Graduates Career Data. Advanced studies pursued by 25% of students; 4% enter medical school; 3% enter dental school; 3% enter law school; 15% enter business school. Career Development Services include internships, alumni mentor programs, advisement on career choices, job hunting strategies, on-campus recruitment.

Faculty. About 85% of faculty hold PhD or equivalent. About 75% of undergraduate classes taught by tenured faculty. About 48% of teaching faculty are female.

Student Body. College does not seek a national student body; 66% of students from in state; 82% Middle Atlantic, 9% New England; 6% Foreign students. An estimated 5% of students reported as Black, 1% Asian, 2% Hispanic.

Varsity Sports. Men (Div.I): Baseball, Basketball, Cross Country, Football(IAA), Golf, Tennis, Track, Wrestling. Women (Div.I): Basketball, Cross Country, Soccer, Softball, Tennis, Track, Volleyball.

Campus Life. Students enjoy convenient access to New York City with the benefits of the intimate, and relatively quiet, suburban campus. Students represented on faculty/administrative committees which formulate policies governing student life. Optional curfew and intervisitation privileges. Alcohol not permitted in public places on campus except at approved events; beer sold at snack bar. Cars not allowed for resident freshmen. Students (excluding those living at home) required to live in residence halls.

About 50% of men, 50% of women live in coed dormitories; 30% of men, 35% of women live in off-campus housing or commute. Sexes segregated in coed dormitories by suite. There are 4 fraternities, 3 sororities on campus which about 20% of men, 15% of women join; 20% of men, 15% of women live in fraternities and sororities. About 30% of resident students leave campus on weekends.

Annual Costs. Tuition and fees, $12,500; room and board, $5,450; estimated $2,000 other, exclusive of travel. About 70% of students receive financial aid; average amount of assistance, $7,580. Assistance is typically divided 25% scholarship, 25% grant, 35% loan, 15% work. College reports 300 scholarships awarded for academic merit, 200 special talents, 500 for need.

Wake Forest University

Winston-Salem, North Carolina 27109 (919) 759-5201

A small, liberal arts university, primarily undergraduate, Wake Forest is affiliated with the Baptist State Convention of North Carolina and liberally supported by the Reynolds Foundation. The 320-acre main campus is located in a city of 139,900, 4 miles from the campus housing the Bowman Gray School of Medicine. The university also includes the School of Law, the Babcock Graduate School of Management, and the Graduate School. Most convenient major airport: Greensboro/High Point/Winston-Salem Regional.

Founded: 1834
Affiliation: Southern Baptist
UG Enrollment: 1,816 M, 1,556 W (full-time); 150 M, 91 W (part-time)
Total Enrollment: 5,350
Cost: $10K–$20K
% Receiving Financial Aid: 65%
Admission: Very (+) Selective
Application Deadline: Jan. 15

Admission is very (+) selective. About 36% of applicants accepted, 44% of these actually enroll; 77% of freshmen graduate in top fifth of high school class, 84% in top two-fifths (13% not ranked). Freshman SAT scores, median range: 1150–1300 combined verbal, mathematical; 81% of freshmen score above 500 on verbal, 35% above 600, 3% above 700; 92% score above 500 on mathematical, 67% above 600, 14% above 700. *Required:* SAT, essay; interview recommended. *Non-academic factors* considered in admissions: diverse student body, alumni children, special talents, community service and extra curricular activities. *Entrance programs:* early decision, deferred admission (under special circumstances), advanced placement. About 25% of entering students from private schools, 10% from parochial schools. *Apply* by January 15. *Transfers* welcome.

Academic Environment. Students are represented on major faculty committees and on the Board of Trustees. About half of students reported to be primarily career-oriented, remainder divided between those interested in scholarly and social pursuits. Some students, reported as concerned about the "salability" of a liberal arts degree in the job market, are sacrificing electives to complete a second major more clearly related to marketable skills. Pressures for academic achievement appear moderately intense. Open curriculum permits superior students to design individualized program of study. Administration reports 41% of general education courses required for graduation are elective; distribution requirements fairly numerous: 3 courses from each of 4 major divisions (exemption possible through advanced placement), proficiency in English composition and foreign language, 2 semesters physical education. *Degrees:* BA, BS. *Majors offered* include usual arts and sciences, accounting, anthropology, computer science. *Computer Science:* computer literacy required for some majors, encouraged for all. Facilities reported as adequate to meet student demand.

About 78% of students entering as freshmen graduate eventually; 9% of freshmen do not return for sophomore year. *Special programs:* study abroad, honors, 3-year degree, Open Curriculum (freshman-designed course of study), Asian studies program, cross-registration with Salem College, combined programs (3–2 engineering with North Carolina State, forestry with Duke; medical record administration, physician assistant, and medical sciences with Bowman Gray School of Medicine), summer program in business for humanities and science majors. Adult programs: 3 MBA programs, MA in Liberal Studies. *Library:* 1,013,631 volumes, 10,870 periodicals, 1,068,170 microforms; open-stack privileges. *Calendar:* semester, summer school.

Undergraduate degrees conferred (782). 26% were in Social Sciences, 17% were in Business and Management, 10% were in Psychology, 10% were in Letters, 9% were in Life Sciences, 5% were in Communications, 5% were in Education, 4% were in Physical Sciences, 3% were in Foreign Languages, 3% were in Visual and Performing Arts, 3% were in Mathematics, remainder in 5 other fields.

Graduates Career Data. *Full-time graduate or professional study* pursued immediately after graduation by 25% of students; 4% enter medical school; 7% enter law school; 2% enter business school. Medical schools typically enrolling largest numbers of graduates include Wake Forest; law schools include Wake Forest; business schools include Wake Forest. *Careers in business and industry* pursued by 49% of graduates. Corporations typically hiring largest numbers of graduates include IBM, NCNB, Ford Motor, Eastman Kodak. *Career Counseling Program:* Student assessment of program reported as good for both career guidance and job placement. Alumni reported as "very!!" active in both career guidance and job placement.

Faculty. About 85% of faculty hold PhD or equivalent.

Student Body. University seeks a national student body; 40% of students from in state; 70% South, 17% Middle Atlantic, 8% North Central. An estimated 65% of students reported as Protestant, 15% Catholic, 1% Jewish, 20% unaffiliated or other; 6% as Black, 2% other minority. *Minority group students:* special financial and academic assistance (tutorial and advisory program).

Religious Orientation. Wake Forest is a church-related institution; 1 course in religion required of all students. University chaplain directs ecumenical program. Religious clubs on campus include Baptist, Fellowship of Christian Athletes, Methodist, Catholic, Intervarsity, Christian Fellowship. Places of worship available on campus and in immediate community for 3 major faiths.

Varsity Sports. Men (Div.I): Baseball, Basketball, Cross Country, Football, Golf, Soccer, Tennis, Track. Women (Div.I): Basketball, Cross Country, Field Hockey, Golf, Tennis, Track, Volleyball.

Campus Life. Social rules and regulations are somewhat more flexible and student body is becoming more diverse. Alcohol and intervisitation recently "deregulated" through students' efforts. State drinking age: 21. Women's dorm hours and intervisitation determined by a faculty, student and administration committee. Student leader characterizes administration as "realistic and concerned." Variety of cultural and intellectual activities offered by the resources of Winston-Salem. Cars permitted; parking reported as adequate for both residential and commuting students.

About 24% of men, 35% of women live in traditional dormitories; 52% of men, 46% of women in coed dormitories; 24% of men, 19% of women in off-campus housing or commute. Sexes segregated in coed dormitories by floor. Freshman given preference in college housing if all students cannot be accommodated. There are 12 fraternities, 9 (2 national, 7 local) sororities on campus which about 42% of men, 45% of women join.

Annual Costs. Tuition and fees, $13,000; room and board, $4,300; estimated $1,000 other, exclusive of travel. About 65% of students receive financial aid; average amount of assistance, $5,419. Assistance is typically divided 77% scholarship, 20% loan, 3% work.

Walla Walla College

College Place, Washington 99324-1198 (509) 527-2327

A church-related college, located in a community of 5,900, near Walla Walla. Most convenient major airport: Walla Walla.

Founded: 1892
Affiliation: Seventh-day Adventist
UG Enrollment: 794 M, 671 W (full-time); 76 M, 78 W (part-time)
Cost: < $10K
% Receiving Financial Aid: 70%
Admission: Non-selective
Application Deadline: by registration

Admission. Graduates of recognized high schools with C average eligible; others admitted by examination; 86% of applicants accepted, 75% of these actually enroll. Average freshman ACT scores: 22.6 M, 20.5 W composite, 20.8 M, 17.8 W mathematical. *Required:* ACT. About 75% of entering students from parochial schools. *Apply*. *Transfers* welcome.
Academic Environment. Degrees offered: associates, bachelors, masters. About 26% of students entering as freshmen complete program eventually; 39% of freshmen do not return for sophomore year. *Special programs:* CLEP, independent study, study abroad, honors, undergraduate research. Adult programs: several graduate programs offered. *Calendar:* quarter, summer school.
Undergraduate degrees conferred (202). 16% were in Business and Management, 15% were in Engineering, 15% were in Education, 8% were in Health Sciences, 6% were in Public Affairs, 5% were in Communications, 5% were in Theology, 5% were in Life Sciences, 4% were in Foreign Languages, remainder in 14 other fields.
Graduates Career Data. Graduate and professional schools enrolling largest numbers of graduates include Loma Linda U., Willamette, Washington State U. Employers typically hiring largest numbers of graduates include Boeing, Puget Sound Naval Shipyard, Microsoft, Seventh-Day Adventist Church.
Faculty. About 56% of faculty hold PhD or equivalent.
Student Body. According to most recent data available, about 41% of students from in state. An estimated 90% of students reported as Protestant, 10% other; 1% Black, 4% Hispanic, 8% Asian, 3% other minority.
Religious Orientation. Walla Walla is a church-related institution; 16 credits in religion required of all students; students expected to attend weekend services.
Campus Life. According to most recent data available, about 56% of men, 52% of women live in traditional dormitories; no coed dormitories; rest live in off-campus housing or commute. No intervisitation in men's or women's dormitory rooms. There are no fraternities or sororities.
Annual Costs. Tuition and fees, $9,978; room and board, $2,430; estimated $222 other, exclusive of travel. About 70% of students receive financial aid; average amount of assistance, $5,000. Assistance is typically divided 35% scholarship, 45% loan, 20% work. College reports some scholarships awarded on the basis of academic merit alone.

Walsh University

Canton, Ohio 44720 (216) 499-7090

A church-related, liberal arts college, conducted by the Brothers of Christian Instruction, located on a 60-acre campus, 5 miles north of Canton (pop. 100,000). Most convenient major airport: Akron/Canton.

Founded: 1960
Affiliation: Roman Catholic
UG Enrollment: 350 M, 506 W (full-time); 122 M, 378 W (part-time)
Total Enrollment: 1,578
Cost: < $10K
% Receiving Financial Aid: 56%
Admission: Non-selective
Application Deadline: Aug. 1

Admission. High school graduates with 16 units in academic subjects eligible; others given individual consideration; 90% of applicants accepted, 29% of these actually enroll; 20% of freshmen graduate in top fifth of high school class, 60% in top two-fifths. Average freshman scores: ACT 21.6 M, 21.6 W composite. *Required:* ACT or SAT, minimum H.S. GPA. Criteria considered in admissions, in order of importance: high school academic record, standardized test scores, recommendations, extracurricular activities. *Entrance programs:* early admission. About 10% of entering students from private schools, 40% from parochial schools. *Apply* by August 1; rolling admissions. *Transfers* welcome; 142 enrolled 1993–94.
Academic Environment. Degrees offered: associates, bachelors, masters. Nursing, education for handicapped recently added. Average undergraduate class size: 57% under 20, 42% between 20–40, 1% over 40. Student to faculty ratio: 19:1. Core requirements in liberal arts include foreign language, English, mathematics, science, social studies, humanities. About 60% of students entering as freshmen graduate in four years, 65% eventually; 70% of freshmen return for sophomore year. *Special programs:* CLEP, honors, undergraduate research, independent study, cross registration with Stark technical. *Calendar:* semester, summer school.
Undergraduate degrees conferred (181). 46% were in Business and Management, 18% were in Education, 5% were in Social Sciences, 5% were in Psychology, 5% were in Allied Health, 4% were in Life Sciences, 4% were in Communications, 4% were in Letters, 3% were in Physical Sciences, 3% were in Mathematics, remainder in 2 other fields.
Graduates Career Data. Advanced studies pursued by 20% of students; 2% enter medical school; 1% enter dental school; 2% enter law school; 2% enter business school. About 27% of 1992–93 graduates employed. Fields typically hiring largest number of graduates include nursing.
Faculty. About 48% of faculty hold PhD or equivalent. About 30% of undergraduate classes taught by tenured faculty. About 46% of teaching faculty are female; 4% minority.
Student Body. College does not seek a national student body; 95% of students from in state; 96% Midwest; 2% Foreign. An estimated 18% of students reported as Protestant, 80% Catholic, 1% Jewish, 1% other; 4% Black, 1% Hispanic, 1% Asian.
Religious Orientation. Walsh is a church-related institution; 12 hours of theology, 6 hours of philosophy required of all students; participation in religious activities voluntary.
Varsity Sports. Men (NAIA): Baseball, Basketball, Cross Country, Golf, Soccer, Tennis, Track. Women (NAIA, GOAC): Basketball, Cross Country, Soccer, Softball, Track, Tennis, Volleyball.
Campus Life. According to most recent data available, about 38% of men, 28% of women live in traditional dormitories; 4% of men, 5% of women live in coed dormitories; 62% of men, 72% of women commute. Intervisitation in men's and women's dormitory rooms limited. There are no fraternities or sororities. About 50% of resident students leave campus on weekends.
Annual Costs. Tuition and fees, $8,404; room and board, $3,930; estimated $1,500 other, exclusive of travel. About 56% of students receive financial aid; average amount of assistance, $7,000. Assistance is typically divided 20% scholarship, 20% grant, 40% loan, 20% work. College reports 160 scholarships awarded for academic merit, 245 for special talents. *Meeting Costs:* college offers payment plan, installment plan, grants.

Warner Pacific College

Portland, Oregon 97215 (503) 775-4366

A church-related college, located in a city of 382,600. Most convenient major airport: Portland International.

Founded: 1937
Affiliation: Church of God
UG Enrollment: 197 M, 202 W (full-time); 47 M, 51 W (part-time)
Cost: < $10K
% Receiving Financial Aid: 83%
Admission: Non-selective
Application Deadline: Rolling

Admission. Graduates of accredited high schools "who live a disciplined life in accord with Christian principles" eligible; 77% of applicants accepted, 74% of these actually enroll. Average freshmen SAT scores: 445 M, 408 W verbal, 489 M, 413 W mathematical; ACT, 22 M, 18 W composite. *Required:* SAT or ACT; interview encouraged. *Apply:* rolling admissions. *Transfers* welcome.
Academic Environment. *Degrees:* AB, BS. About 45% of freshmen do not return for sophomore year. *Special programs:* CLEP, independent study, individualized majors, study abroad. Adult programs: Adult degree-completion programs in business and human development. *Calendar:* quarter, summer school.
Undergraduate degrees conferred (66). 38% were in Social Sciences, 36% were in Business and Management, 11% were in

Education, 8% were in Philosophy and Religion, 5% were in Letters, remainder in 2 other fields.
Faculty. About 52% of full-time faculty hold PhD or equivalent.
Varsity Sports. Men (NAIA): Baseball, Basketball, Soccer. Women (NAIA): Basketball, Softball, Volleyball.
Student Body. College seeks a national student body; 69% of students from in state; 87% Northwest, 3% West. An estimated 3% of students reported as Black, 3% Asian, 2% other minority.
Religious Orientation. Warner Pacific is a church-related institution; 12 hours of religion required of all students.
Campus Life. About 13% of men, 21% of women live in traditional dormitories; no coed dormitories; rest live in off-campus housing or commute. No intervisitation in men's or women's dormitory rooms. There are no fraternities or sororities.
Annual Costs. Tuition and fees, $7,511; room and board, $3,900. About 83% of students receive financial aid. College reports some scholarships awarded on the basis of academic merit alone.

Warner Southern College

Lake Wales, Florida 33853 (813) 638-2109

A small Christian, co-educational college, Warner Southern was accredited in 1977. Most convenient major airport: Orlando International.

Affiliation: Church of God
UG Enrollment: 227 M, 242 W (full-time)
Cost: < $10K
% Receiving Financial Aid: 90%
Admission: Non-selective
Application Deadline: August 15

Admission. High school graduates with 2.0 minimum GPA or equivalent eligible; 70% of applicants accepted, 44% of these actually enroll. Average freshman scores, according to most recent data available: SAT, 364 M, 337 W verbal, 418 M, 388 W mathematical; ACT, 17.4 M, 15.7 W composite. *Required:* ACT or SAT. Criteria considered in admissions, in order of importance: high school academic record, standardized test scores, recommendations; other factors considered: special talents, religious affiliation and/or commitment. *Apply* by August 15. *Transfers* welcome; 143 enrolled 1993–94.
Academic Environment. Degrees offered: associates, bachelors. New programs include HEART (Hunger Elimination and Resources Training) a program for development work in third world settings. About 35% of students entering as freshmen graduate eventually; 52% of freshmen do not return for sophomore year. Liberal arts core requirements include freshman Composition, literature, fine arts, foreign culture, mathematics, sciences, social science, computer literacy, religion. Average undergraduate class size: 60% of classes under 20, 39% between 20–40, 1% over 40. *Calendar:* quarter.
Undergraduate degrees conferred (84). 49% were in Education, 43% were in Business and Management, 6% were in Theology, remainder in Psychology.
Graduates Career Data. Advanced studies pursued by 30% of students. Fields typically hiring the largest number of graduates include business, education, churches.
Faculty. About 52% of faculty hold PhD or equivalent. About 60% of undergraduate classes taught by tenured faculty. About 14% of teaching faculty are female; 6% minorities.
Varsity Sports. Men (NAIA): Soccer, Baseball, Basketball. Women (NAIA): Basketball, Volleyball, Softball.
Student Body. College does not seek a national student body; 88% of students from in state; 90% South; 2% foreign. An estimated 86% of students reported as Protestant, 10% Catholic, 4% other, unaffiliated; 11% as Black, 5% Hispanic, 1% Asian.
Campus Life. One student sums up what he likes best about Warner Southern, "Friends, family atmosphere, Christian fellowship." Central Florida location offers many recreational opportunities. About 11% of men, 13% of women live in traditional dormitories; rest live in off-campus housing or commute. About 20% of resident students leave campus on weekends.
Annual Costs. Tuition and fees, $6,580; room and board, $3,720; estimated $1,200 other, exclusive of travel. About 90% of students receive financial aid. College reports some scholarships awarded on the basis of academic merit alone. *Meeting Costs:* college offers cooperative payment plan.

Warren Wilson College

Asheville, North Carolina 28815-9907 (800) 934-3536

A church-related, liberal arts college, located in a rural community of 2,000, 4 miles from Asheville city limits. All students required to give 15 hours weekly to On-campus Cooperative Work Program for credit toward expenses.

Founded: 1894
Affiliation: Presbyterian
UG Enrollment: 240 M, 251 W (full-time)
Cost: < $10K
% Receiving Financial Aid: 100%
Admission: Non-selective
Application Deadline: July 15

Admission. Graduates of accredited high schools with college preparatory program and GPA of 2.4 eligible; 70% of applicants accepted, 51% of these actually enroll; 30% of freshmen graduate in top fifth of high school class, 80% in top two-fifths. *Required:* SAT or ACT; interview "often requested." Criteria considered in admissions, in order of importance: optional essay or interview, high school academic record, extracurricular activities, writing sample, standardized test scores, recommendations; other factors considered: part-time jobs during high school, environmental or outdoor interests, diverse student body, special talents, alumni children. *Apply* by July 15. *Transfers* welcome; 47 enrolled 1993–94.
Academic Environment. Degrees offered: bachelors masters. General education requirements for graduation are currently being revised; distribution requirements fairly numerous; 80 hours of non-credit voluntary service required of all students. majors offered include outdoor leadership, 3–2 programs in nursing, forestry, engineering. About 85% of students entering as freshmen graduate eventually; 25% of freshmen do not return for sophomore year. *Special programs:* CLEP, independent study, study abroad, honors, individualized majors. *Calendar:* semester, summer school.
Undergraduate degrees conferred (95). 32% were in Social Sciences, 17% were in Multi/Interdisciplinary Studies, 11% were in Renewable Natural Resources, 9% were in Education, 8% were in Life Sciences, 7% were in Letters, 5% were in Mathematics, 4% were in Visual and Performing Arts, remainder in 3 other fields.
Faculty. About 70% of faculty hold PhD or equivalent.
Varsity Sports. Men (NLCAA): Basketball, Soccer. Women (NLCAA): Basketball, Soccer.
Student Body. College does not seek a national student body; 37% of students from in state; 57% South, 11% Middle Atlantic, 5% each New England, North West, Midwest, West.
Religious Orientation. Warren Wilson is a church-related institution; makes no religious demands on students.
Campus Life. About 97% of students live in traditional dormitories. There are no fraternities or sororities. About 10% of students leave campus on weekends.
Annual Costs. Tuition and fees, $10,015 (all students participate in work program which pays $2,040, thus reducing tuition to $7,975); room and board, $2,852; estimated $600 other, exclusive of travel. College offers 12 scholarships for academic achievement, and 5 for service. *Meeting Costs:* college offers automatic quarterly payment plan, 10-month payment plan.

Wartburg College

Waverly, Iowa 50677 (319) 352-8264

A church-related, liberal arts college, located in a town of 8,500, 100 miles northeast of Des Moines. Most convenient major airport: Waterloo.

Founded: 1852
Affiliation: Evangelical Lutheran in America
UG Enrollment: 584 M, 711 W (full-time); 46 M, 59 W (part-time)
Cost: $10K–$20K
% Receiving Financial Aid: 91%
Admission: Selective (+)
Application Deadline: Rolling

Admission is selective (+). About 88% of applicants accepted, 36% of these actually enroll; 58% of freshmen graduate in top fifth of high school class, 81% in top two-fifths. Average freshman scores:

ACT, 23 M, 24 W composite. *Required:* SAT or ACT. Criteria considered in admissions, in order of importance: high school academic record, standardized test scores, recommendations, extracurricular activities; other factors considered: diverse student body, alumni children, religious affiliation and/or commitment, athletic and music abilities. *Entrance programs:* advanced placement. *Apply:* rolling admissions. *Transfers* welcome; 83 enrolled 1993–94.

Academic Environment. Degrees offered: bachelors. *Majors offered* include arts and sciences, business administration, communication arts, elementary, secondary education, music therapy, social work. New programs include leadership education, global and multi-cultural studies. Very strong biology department offers excellent preparation for medical fields. Core curriculum in liberal arts includes Human Expression, Person & Society, and Foundations of Science, with distribution requirements in behavior, expression, mathematics, natural sciences, physical education, world view, interdisciplinary study, and capstone. Average undergraduate class size: 48% of classes under 20, 44% between 20–40, 8% over 40.

About 54% of students entering as freshmen graduate within four years, 67% eventually; 77% of freshmen return for sophomore year. *Special programs:* CLEP, independent study, study abroad, 3-year degree, individualized majors, May term (for independent study and off-campus programs), internships in Denver, Washington, D.C., and abroad, combined degree programs, exchange programs with Bonn and Jena U. (Germany), International Christian U. (Japan), student-initiated courses, 3–2 programs in engineering, medical technology, occupational therapy, and public health. Adult programs: Continuing Education for John Deere employees. *Calendar:* 4–4–1, summer school.

Undergraduate degrees conferred (289). 30% were in Business and Management, 16% were in Education, 10% were in Life Sciences, 8% were in Social Sciences, 6% were in Public Affairs, 6% were in Psychology, 4% were in Mathematics, 4% were in Computer and Engineering Related Technology, 4% were in Communications, remainder in 8 other fields.

Graduates Career Data. Advanced studies pursued by 19% of graduates. About 97% of 1992–93 graduates employed. Fields typically employing largest numbers of graduates include business, industry, social sciences, education. Career Development Services include information and counseling regarding careers, employment, and graduate schools; assistance in developing search skills, resumes, letters, and interviewing techniques; credentials files service; job vacancy information; on-campus interviews. Student assessment of program reported as very good for both career guidance and job placement; student leader asserts program is "nationally noted for quality" and that a consortium with other small schools "works great." Alumni reported as helpful in both career guidance and job placement.

Faculty. About 87% of faculty hold PhD or appropriate terminal degree. About 50% of undergraduate classes taught by tenured faculty. About 39% of teaching faculty are female; 3% minorities.

Student Body. About 74% of students from in state; 94% of students from Midwest, 5% foreign. An estimated 67% of students reported as Protestant, 13% Catholic, 2% other, unaffiliated; 3% as Black, 2% other minorities.

Religious Orientation. Wartburg is a church-related institution; 2 courses in religion required of all students. Places of worship available on campus for Protestants, in immediate community for Catholics and Protestants, 20 miles away for Jews.

Varsity Sports. Men (Div.III): Baseball, Basketball, Cross Country, Football, Golf, Soccer, Tennis, Track, Wrestling. Women (Div.III): Basketball, Cross Country, Golf, Soccer, Softball, Tennis, Track, Volleyball.

Campus Life. Students report that Waverly provides enough stores and restaurants to meet student needs, and Cedar Falls and Waterloo(each about half an hour away) provide more opportunities. On-campus activities include cultural and sporting events, as well as plenty of informal "pick-up" games. Students find a diverse and friendly atmosphere. Limited daily intervisitation hours from 10 am to midnight (2 am on Friday and Saturday). Alcoholic beverages permitted in accordance with state law; no kegs allowed on campus. Cars must be registered and parked in designated areas.

About 22% of men, 31% of women live in traditional dormitories; 53% of men, 51% of women in coed dormitories; 25% of men, 18% of women commute. Freshmen given preference in college housing if all students cannot be accommodated. Sexes segregated in coed dormitories by floor. There are no fraternities or sororities. About 70% of resident students leave campus on the weekends.

Annual Costs. Tuition and fees, $11,080; room and board, $3,375–3,556; estimated $700 other, exclusive of travel. About 91% of students receive financial aid; average amount of assistance, $8,750. Assistance is typically divided 65% scholarship, 28% loan, 7% work. College reports some scholarships awarded on the basis of academic merit alone. *Meeting Costs:* college offers the low interest Wartburg Loan, Tuition Payment Plan, college employment for students.

Washburn University of Topeka

Topeka, Kansas 66621 (913) 295-6300

A municipal institution with a high proportion of commuters, located in a city of 140,000. Washburn University includes a Law School.

Founded: 1865
Affiliation: City
UG Enrollment: 1,309 M, 1,848 W (full-time); 1,026 M, 1,679 W (part-time)
Cost: < $10K
Admission: Non-selective
Application Deadline: August 1

Admission. Open admissions policy; graduates of accredited Kansas high schools eligible; 98% of applicants accepted, 66% of these actually enroll. Average freshman ACT scores: 21.7 composite. *Required:* SAT or ACT. *Out-of-state* freshman applicants: university seeks students from out of state. City does not limit out-of-state enrollment. Requirement for out-of-state applicants: 2.00 average. *Apply* by August 1. *Transfers* welcome.

Academic Environment. Degrees offered: associates, bachelors, masters. *Undergraduate studies* offered by College of Arts and Sciences, schools of Business, Nursing, Applied and Continuing Education. General education requirements for graduation vary with major; distribution requirements include courses in social sciences, humanities, mathematics and natural sciences. About 20% of students entering as freshmen graduate within four years, 50% eventually; 55% of freshmen return for sophomore year. *Special programs:* CLEP, independent study, study abroad, honors, 3–2 program in engineering. Average undergraduate class size: 20% of classes under 20, 65% between 20–40, 15% over 40. *Calendar:* semester, summer school.

Undergraduate degrees conferred (557). 24% were in Business and Management, 13% were in Education, 11% were in Social Sciences, 9% were in Health Sciences, 9% were in Communications, 6% were in Public Affairs, 6% were in Protective Services, 5% were in Psychology, 4% were in Letters, 4% were in Computer and Engineering Related Technology, 3% were in Life Sciences, 3% were in Visual and Performing Arts, remainder in 4 other fields.

Graduates Career Data. Advanced studies pursued by 15% of students. About 93% of 1992–93 graduates employed.

Faculty. About 80% of faculty hold PhD or equivalent. About 75% of undergraduate classes taught by tenured faculty.

Varsity Sports. Men (NAIA): Baseball, Basketball, Football, Golf, Tennis. Women (NAIA): Basketball, Softball, Tennis, Volleyball.

Student Body. About 95% of students from Kansas. Washburn is a municipal institution, makes no religious demands on students.

Campus Life. About 3% of students live in coed dormitories; rest live in off-campus housing or commute. Intervisitation in men's and women's dormitory rooms limited. There are 4 fraternities, 4 sororities on campus which about 4% of men, 4% of women join; 4% of students live in fraternities and sororities.

Annual Costs. Tuition and fees, $2,642 (out-of-state, $4,562); room and board, $3,100; estimated $1,500 other, exclusive of travel. *Meeting Costs:* university offers deferred tuition, MasterCard, VISA, short-term loans, PLUS loans.

Washington and Jefferson College

Washington, Pennsylvania 15301 (412) 223-6025

One of the nation's more venerable colleges and for many years a small, liberal arts college for men, Washington and Jefferson has been co-educational since 1970. Throughout its history, its gradu-

ates have made significant contributions to the leadership in business and the professions. The campus is located in a town of 19,800, 25 miles south of Pittsburgh. Most convenient major airport: Greater Pittsburgh International.

Founded: 1781	**Cost:** $10K–$20K
Affiliation: Independent	**% Receiving Financial Aid:** 70%
UG Enrollment: 603 M, 507 W (full-time)	**Admission:** Selective (+)
	Application Deadline: March 1

Admission is selective (+). About 80% of applicants accepted, 32% of these actually enroll; 56% of freshmen graduate in top fifth of high school class, 85% in top two-fifths. Freshman scores, middle fifty percent range: SAT, 460–590 verbal, 470–630 mathematical, 59% of freshman score above 500 on verbal, 11% above 600, 1% above 700, 67% score above 500 on mathematical, 22% above 600, 2% above 700; average ACT, 23.5 composite. *Required:* SAT and 3 ACH, including English or ACT; interview recommended. Criteria considered in admissions, in order of importance: high school academic record, standardized test scores, recommendations, extracurricular activities, writing sample; other factors considered: alumni children, special talents. *Entrance programs:* early decision, early admission, midyear admission, advanced placement, deferred admission. About 27% of entering freshmen from private schools. *Apply* by March 1. *Transfers* welcome; 23 enrolled 1993–94.

Academic Environment. Recent student leader characterizes student body as socially and career-oriented; but administration source insists that a large fraction of students are primarily concerned with scholarly interests. College has very strong pre-professional programs in medicine and law. Administration reports all general education courses required for graduation are elective; distribution requirements numerous: students must complete 14 credits in each of 3 broad divisions (humanities, social disciplines, sciences) according to prescribed pattern; in division of major, 4 courses in 2 departments other than major department; 4 courses in at least 2 departments of a second division; and 6 courses in at least 3 departments of a third division; proficiency in English, 2 courses physical education. Degrees offered: bachelors. *Majors offered* include usual arts and sciences, computer science, medical technology, entrepreneurial studies. Average undergraduate class size: 20; 50% of classes under 20, 50% between 20–40.

About 76% of students entering as freshmen graduate within 4 years, 84% eventually; 7% of freshmen do not return for sophomore year. *Special programs:* independent study, study abroad, 3–2 programs in engineering, 3–4 in podiatry, optometry, physical therapy. *Calendar:* 4–1–4, summer school.

Undergraduate degrees conferred (269). 40% were in Business and Management, 17% were in Social Sciences, 12% were in Letters, 11% were in Psychology, 11% were in Life Sciences, 4% were in Physical Sciences, remainder in 4 other fields.

Graduates Career Data. Advanced studies pursued by 45% of students; 17% enter law school; 20% enter medical or dental schools; 5% enter business schools. Medical schools typically enrolling largest numbers of graduates include Hahnemann, Case Western, Bowman Gray, UVA, Pittsburgh, Penn State; dental schools include Temple, U. of Pennsylvania, Case Western, Ohio State, Georgetown; law schools include Case Western, Dickinson, William and Mary, Georgetown; business schools include Case Western, Pittsburgh, RIT, Syracuse. Fields typically hiring the largest number of graduates include banking, accounting, sales, marketing. Career Development Services include mock interviews, resume development, on-campus interviewing, job bank, alumni mentoring program, individual counseling. Alumni reported as active in job placement and career counseling.

Faculty. About 91% of faculty hold PhD or equivalent. About 85% of undergraduate classes taught by tenured faculty.

Student Body. College seeks a national student body; 65% of students from in state; 80% from Middle Atlantic, 10% New England, 5% North Central, 4% South; 1% foreign. An estimated 6% of students reported as Black, 2% Asian, 1% other minority.

Varsity Sports. Men (Div.III): Baseball, Basketball, Cross Country, Football, Golf, Lacrosse, Soccer, Swimming and Diving, Tennis, Track, Wrestling. Women (Div.III): Basketball, Cross Country, Soccer, Softball, Swimming and Diving, Tennis, Track, Volleyball.

Campus Life. Administration source characterizes the student most at home on this campus as "strongly academic, socially outgoing, [with varied interests; and involved.]" Administration reportedly emphasizes self-governance for students. Some regulations remain. Intervisitation limited during week, 24-hour on weekends; alcohol prohibited in public areas; drinking age enforced. Student interest in fraternities and athletics reported as high. Nearest major cultural center is Pittsburgh, 25 miles away.

About 46% of students live in traditional dormitories; 14% live in coed dormitories; 3% live in off-campus housing or commute. Freshmen given preference in college housing if all students cannot be accommodated. There are 10 fraternities, 4 sororities on campus which about 53% of men, 65% of women join; about 37% of students live in fraternities or sororities.

Annual Costs. Tuition and fees, $15,620; room and board, $3,740; estimated $500 other, exclusive of travel. About 70% of students receive financial aid from all sources, 53% receive institutional aid; average amount of assistance, $13,000. College reports 50 scholarships awarded on the basis of academic merit alone. *Meeting Costs:* college offers commercial payment plans.

Washington and Lee University

Lexington, Virginia 24450 (703) 463-8710

The nation's sixth-oldest institution of higher learning, Washington and Lee still retains many of the academic and social traditions that have characterized it since Robert E. Lee was its president more than a century ago. It remained a relatively small men's college for more than 200 years, but went coed in 1985. The university also includes a small, rather well-known law school, which is also co-educational, and the undergraduate School of Commerce, Economics, and Politics. The 100-acre campus is located in a town of 7,600—also the home of Virginia Military Institute—50 miles northeast of Roanoke. Most convenient major airport: Roanoke (1 hour away).

Founded: 1749	**Cost:** $10K–$20K
Affiliation: Independent	**% Receiving Financial Aid:** 32%
UG Enrollment: 941 M, 636 W (full-time)	**Admission:** Highly (+) Selective
Total Enrollment: 2,000	**Application Deadline:** February 1

Admission is highly (+) selective. About 33% of applicants accepted, 40% of these actually enroll; 88% of freshmen graduate in top fifth of high school class, 99% in top two-fifths. Average freshman SAT scores: middle fifty percent range, 570–643 verbal, 608–696 mathematical; 91% of freshmen score above 500 on verbal, 36% above 600, 9% above 700; all score above 500 on mathematical, 88% score above 600, 33% above 700. *Required:* SAT, 3 ACH including English Composition or ACT; interview strongly recommended. Most important element considered in the admissions process is the applicants success in a rigorous college preparatory curriculum. *Non-academic factors* considered in admissions: special talents, alumni children, diverse student body. *Entrance programs:* early decision, advanced placement, deferred admission. About 33% of entering students from private and parochial schools. *Apply* by February 1. *Transfers* welcome.

Academic Environment. Exchange program with 6 other colleges in the area (Hampden-Sydney, Hollins, Mary Baldwin, Randolph-Macon, Randolph-Macon Woman's College, and Sweet Briar) allows students to spend junior year on any of the other campuses—including the women's colleges. Strength as a "teaching college" stressed; median class size 15, student/faculty ratio 11:1. Pre-professional programs in medicine, business, journalism, law and engineering reported to be strong. Robert E. Lee Undergraduate Research Program provides unique opportunities and support for student research on campus. Pressures for academic achievement do not appear overwhelming, but academic program is rigorous, student body is able and scholarship encouraged. Some student concern reported over grades, but relations with faculty and administration are said to be "very close." Administration reports no specific courses required for graduation; distribution requirements include English composition; foreign language; fine arts, history, philosophy and religion; science and mathematics; social sciences. Degrees offered: bachelors, doctoral. *Majors offered* include usual arts and sciences, business administration and commerce, computer science, drama, East Asian studies, journalism, public policy, Russian studies, cognitive studies, neuroscience; independent, group, and interdepartmental majors available. Program for teacher certification available. Computer facilities reported as adequate to meet student demand, with terminals accessible 24 hours a day.

About 88% of students entering as freshmen graduate within four years, 90% eventually; 4% of freshmen do not return for sophomore year. *Special programs:* independent study, study abroad, honors, undergraduate research, 3-year degree, individualized majors, 3–3 with School of Law, 3–2 engineering, 3–2 forestry, 3–2 environmental studies, 4–2 engineering and 3–3 law, spring term for independent self designed majors. *Calendar:* 2 12-week terms, 6-week spring term.

Undergraduate degrees conferred (416). 40% were in Social Sciences, 14% were in Business and Management, 9% were in Letters, 8% were in Communications, 6% were in Life Sciences, 5% were in Foreign Languages, 4% were in Physical Sciences, 3% were in Area and Ethnic Studies, remainder in 8 other fields.

Graduates Career Data. Advanced studies pursued by 25% of students; 10% enter law school; 5% enter medical school; 1% enter business school. Medical schools typically enrolling largest numbers of graduates include U. of Virginia, Medical College of Virginia, Bowman Gray; law schools include U. of Virginia, Washington & Lee, SMU, Wake Forest. About 31% of 1992–93 graduates employed. Fields typically hiring the largest number of graduates include banking, accounting, sales, business management, education. Career Development Services include advising, testing, workshops, computerized career guidance system, internships, summer jobs, resource center, on-campus interviewing, credential files service. Alumni reported as active in job placement and career guidance; pilot programs in several cities are now expanding.

Faculty. About 93% of faculty hold PhD or equivalent. About 83% of faculty tenured; all teach. About 17% of teaching faculty are female; 1% minorities.

Student Body. University seeks a national student body; 12% of students from in state; 40% South, 29% Middle Atlantic, 3% New England, 10% Midwest, 2% foreign. An estimated 32% of students reported as Protestant, 14% Catholic, 2% Jewish, 51% unaffiliated, 1% other; 2% as Black, 2% Asian, 1% other minority. *Minority group students:* financial aid available.

Religious Orientation. Washington and Lee is an independent institution, makes no religious demands on students. University chaplain is available to students for counseling and guidance. Some local churches have ministers whose primary work is with students and provide opportunities for student participation; rabbi visits campus occasionally. Chapel on campus is historical landmark. Places of worship available in immediate community for most faiths.

Varsity Sports. Men (Div.III): Baseball, Basketball, Cross Country, Football, Golf, Lacrosse, Soccer, Swimming, Tennis, Track, Water Polo (I), Wrestling. Women (Div.III): Cross Country, Lacrosse, Soccer, Swimming, Tennis, Volleyball.

Campus Life. Honor system administered entirely by Student Body Executive Committee reportedly operates effectively. Student likely to feel most at home on campus described as "one who wants a friendly campus, close relations with faculty and other students." High interest reported in intramural sports, most popular: touch football, basketball, softball; most popular varsity sports include Lacrosse, Tennis, Football, Basketball. Fraternities still important factor on campus; one student reports "social life completely revolves around the male fraternity system," other students agree more or less. Each residential unit draws up its own social regulations including those for visitation hours. Alcohol allowed in dormitory rooms if student is of legal age. Freshmen required to live in residence halls. Student center provides social and recreational activities for students. Campus offers unusual cultural opportunities, supplemented by resources of Roanoke, Lynchburg and Washington. All students may have automobiles, but parking reported to be a problem both for residents and commuters.

About 67% of students live on campus; rest live in off-campus housing or commute. Freshmen given preference in housing if all students cannot be accommodated. There are 16 fraternities on campus which about 80% of men join; 4 sororities which about 60% of women join.

Annual Costs. Tuition and fees, $13,295; room and board, $4,510. About 32% of freshmen receive financial aid; assistance is typically divided 65% scholarship, 25% loan, 10% work. University reports some scholarships awarded on the basis of academic ability alone. *Meeting Costs:* college offers tuition payment plans.

Washington Bible College

Lanham, Maryland 20706

A non-denominational Bible college offering associate and baccalaureate degree programs. Masters programs are offered though affiliation with Capital Bible Seminary.

Founded: 1938 **Affiliation:** Non-denominational

Washington College

Chestertown, Maryland 21620 (410) 778-7700

A small, liberal arts college on Maryland's Eastern Shore, Washington College is the tenth oldest institution of higher learning in the U.S. It is named after the country's first President, who contributed to the endowment of the college, served on its governing board, and consented to having his name given to it. The 104-acre campus includes waterfront boathouse and pavilion and is located in a village of 3,500, 60 miles east of Baltimore. Most convenient major airports: Philadelphia or Baltimore-Washington International.

Founded: 1782
Affiliation: Independent
UG Enrollment: 408 M, 442 W (full-time)
Cost: $10K–$20K
% Receiving Financial Aid: 68%
Admission: Selective (+)
Application Deadline: Feb. 15

Admission is selective (+). About 75% of applicants accepted, 25% of these actually enroll; 60% of freshmen graduate in top fifth of high school class, 78% in top two-fifths. Average freshman SAT scores: 516 verbal, 551 mathematical; 45% of freshmen score above 500 on verbal, 14% above 600, 3% above 700; 58% score above 500 on mathematical, 22% above 600, 2% above 700. *Required:* SAT, essay, 2 teacher recommendations, counselor recommendation, transcripts, senior grades. Criteria considered in admissions, in order of importance: high school academic record, standardized test scores and writing sample, recommendations, extracurricular activities; other factors considered: diverse student body, alumni children, special talents. *Entrance programs:* early decision, early admission, midyear admission, deferred admission, advanced placement. About 45% of entering freshmen from private schools. *Apply* by February 15. *Transfers* welcome; 30 enrolled 1993–94.

Academic Environment. Students represented equally with faculty on all college committees except those concerned with faculty appointment and tenure. Pressures for academic achievement appear moderately strong. First years of study devoted to general education background for later specialization, but students allowed considerable latitude in choosing specific course within general fields of study prescribed. Administration reports all general education courses required for graduation are elective, with exception of freshman English; distribution requirements revised recently: 12 courses in 4 broad areas (social sciences, humanities, natural sciences, "formal studies" which include languages, math, computer, music theory, logic); no specific foreign language or physical education requirements. Students may also develop, with faculty approval, completely individualized distribution or major program. Degrees offered: bachelors, masters. *Majors offered* include creative writing, international studies, Chesapeake Bay studies. Average undergraduate class size: 17; 66% under 20, 33% between 20–40, 1% over 40; student-faculty ratio of 12:1.

About 64% of students entering as freshmen graduate in four years, 67% eventually; 88% of freshmen return for sophomore year. *Special programs:* CLEP, independent study, study abroad (including junior year at Manchester College, Oxford), honors, undergraduate research, 3-year degree, individualized majors, teacher preparation program, Washington Semester, drama, apprenticeship with professional theater company, 3–2 programs in engineering and nursing. *Calendar:* semester.

Undergraduate degrees conferred (205). 30% were in Social Sciences, 17% were in Letters, 13% were in Business and Management, 11% were in Psychology, 7% were in Visual and Performing Arts, 6% were in Multi/Interdisciplinary Studies, 5% were in Life Sciences, 4% were in Area and Ethnic Studies, 3% were in Philosophy and Religion, remainder in 3 other fields.

Graduates Career Data. Advanced studies pursued by 35–50% of students eventually; 4% enter medical school; 5% enter law school; 2% enter business school. Law schools typically enrolling largest numbers of graduates include Dickinson; business schools include Maryland. About 60% of 1992–93 graduates employed. Corporations typically attracting largest numbers of graduates include Alex Brown, Inc.; U.S. government. Career Development Services include interest and vocational testing, career counseling, placement and credentials service, interview and resume workshops, alumni career mentors.

Faculty. About 93% of faculty hold PhD or equivalent. About 90% of undergraduate classes taught by tenured faculty. About 25% of teaching faculty are female; 4% minority.

Student Body. College seeks a national student body; 50% of students from in state; 75% Middle Atlantic, 5% South, 10% New England, 5% Midwest, 2% West, 1% Northwest; 2% Foreign. An estimated 35% of students reported as Protestant, 50% Catholic, 5% Jewish, 10% unaffiliated; 6% Black, 2% Hispanic, 4% Asian.

Varsity Sports. Men (Div.III): Baseball, Basketball, Crew, Lacrosse (Mid-Atlantic), Soccer, Swimming, Tennis. Women: Basketball, Crew, Field Hockey, Lacrosse (Mid-Atlantic), Softball, Swimming, Tennis, Volleyball.

Campus Life. Intervisitation hours unlimited in all campus dormitories; no curfew. Drinking permitted for students over 21 in dormitory rooms, private lounges, fraternity rooms, or at approved social events. Cars allowed on campus. Students expected to live in college residence halls. Variety of social and cultural activities provided on campus; nearest major cultural centers are Baltimore and Washington, about 60 miles from campus.

About 50% of men, 50% of women live in traditional dormitories; 35% men, 30% women in coed dormitories; rest commute. Sexes segregated in coed dormitories by floor or room. There are 3 fraternities, 3 sororities on campus which about 25% of men, 25% of women join. About 25% of resident students leave campus on weekends.

Annual Costs. Tuition and fees, $13,952; room and board, $5,318; estimated $900 other, exclusive of travel. About 68% of students receive financial aid; average amount of assistance, $11,000. Assistance is typically divided 75% scholarship, 25% loan/work. College reports 85 scholarships awarded for academic merit, 525 for need.

Washington State University

Pullman, Washington 99164-1036 (509) 335-5586

A state-supported, research and land-grant university, located in a town of 24,000 (including students), 75 miles south of Spokane. Most convenient major airports: Pullman-Moscow, Lewiston, Idaho, or Spokane International.

Founded: 1890
Affiliation: State
UG Enrollment: 7,577 M, 6,566 W (full-time); 662 M, 887 W (part-time)
Total Enrollment: 18,740
Cost: < $10K
Admission: Non-selective
Application Deadline: May 1

Admission. Graduates of accredited high schools admitted according to formula based on GPA and test scores; 89% of applicants accepted, 48% of these actually enroll. Average freshman SAT scores: 900–1000 combined verbal, mathematical, according to most recent data available. *Required:* SAT or ACT. Criteria considered in admissions, in order of importance: high school academic record, standardized tests, extracurricular activities, writing sample, recommendations; other factors considered: special talents. *Out-of-state* freshman applicants: university actively seeks out-of-state students. State does not limit out-of-state enrollment. Special admissions standards may be applied to "several special populations in order to maintain a vibrant, diverse student body." States from which most out-of-state students are drawn include California, Oregon, Idaho. *Entrance programs:* early decision, early admission, midyear admission. *Apply* by May 1; rolling admissions. *Transfers* welcome; 2,205 enrolled 1993–94.

Academic Environment. Administration reports 25% of courses required for graduation are elective; 23% are in distribution requirements. All students take 10 semester hours in the sciences, 6 each in social sciences, humanities, and communication proficiency. Degrees offered: bachelors. *Undergraduate studies* offered to freshmen in colleges of Sciences and Arts, Agriculture and Home Economics, Education, Engineering and Architecture, and the program in Nursing; upperclassmen admitted to colleges of Business and Economics, Pharmacy, and Veterinary Medicine. *Majors offered* include anthropology, bacteriology and environmental health, biochemistry, biophysics, Black studies, Chicano studies, communications, computer science, criminal justice, environmental science, fine arts, genetics, hotel and restaurant administration, music, nuclear technology, nursing, natural resource sciences, biology, zoology. Average undergraduate class size: 26% under 20, 39% between 20–40, 35% over 40.

About 23% of students entering as freshmen graduate in four years, 56% eventually; 84% of students entering as freshmen return for sophomore year. *Special programs:* CLEP, independent study, wide variety of study abroad opportunities, honors, internships/work study, undergraduate research, American minority studies, cooperative programs with U. of Washington and the University of Idaho. *Calendar:* "early start" semester, summer school.

Undergraduate degrees conferred (2,919). 22% were in Business and Management, 14% were in Social Sciences, 10% were in Engineering, 8% were in Communications, 5% were in Health Sciences, 5% were in Education, 4% were in Psychology, 4% were in Architecture and Environmental Design, 4% were in Life Sciences, 4% were in Letters, 4% were in Multi/Interdisciplinary Studies, 3% were in Home Economics, 3% were in Protective Services, remainder in 11 other fields.

Graduates Career Data. Advanced studies pursued immediately after graduation by 12% of students, according to most recent data available. *Careers in business and industry* pursued by 72% of graduates. Corporations typically hiring largest numbers of graduates include Boeing, Westin Hotels, Chevron, Marriott.

Faculty. About 96% of instructional faculty hold PhD or equivalent, according to most recent data available.

Student Body. About 78% of students from in state; 95% Northwest, 4% West. An estimated 2% of students reported as Black, 4% Asian, 2% Hispanic, 1% Native American, according to most recent data available. Average age of undergraduate student: 22.

Varsity Sports. Men (PAC 10): Basketball, Baseball, Cross Country, Football, Golf, Tennis, Track. Women (PAC 10): Basketball, Crew, Cross Country, Golf, Soccer, Swimming, Tennis, Track, Volleyball.

Campus Life. Provision for daily intervisitation; specific schedules established by each residence unit. Alcohol not allowed in public areas of residence halls or college buildings; cars permitted. Single freshmen under 20 required to live in university-related housing.

According to most recent data available, about 5% of men, 9% of women live in traditional dormitories; 8% of men, 6% of women live in coed dormitories; 9% of men, 5% of women live in fraternities and sororities; rest live in off-campus housing or commute. Sexes segregated in coed dormitories either by wing or floor. Freshmen are given preference in college housing if all students cannot be accommodated. There are 25 fraternities, 14 sororities on campus. About 20% of students leave campus on weekends.

Annual Costs. Tuition and fees, $2,667 (out-of-state, $7,269); room and board, $3,900; estimated $1,395 other, exclusive of travel. University reports some scholarships awarded on the basis of academic merit alone. *Meeting Costs:* university offers variety of non-need based loan programs.

Washington University

St. Louis, Missouri 63130 (314) 889-6000; (800) 638-0700

Washington University, a major midwestern research institution, consists of eleven schools, five of which are undergraduate and accept freshmen, the largest of which is the College of Arts and Sciences. The university attracts students from every section of the nation and from many countries abroad. It is one of the few midwestern institutions with a national student body. The 169-acre campus is located in a residential area of St. Louis. Most convenient major airport: Lambert Field (St. Louis).

Founded: 1853
Affiliation: Independent
UG Enrollment: 2,592 M, 2,248 W (full-time)
Total Enrollment: 10,164
Cost: $10K–$20K
% Receiving Financial Aid: 46%
Admission: Highly (+) Selective
Application Deadline: January 15

Admission is highly (+) selective for School of Engineering and for colleges of Arts and Sciences, Architecture, highly selective for School of Business; very (+) selective for School of Fine Arts. For all schools, 68% of applicants accepted, 24% of these actually enroll; 84% of freshmen graduate in top fifth of high school class, 98% in top two-fifths. Freshman scores, middle fifty percent range: SAT, 510–620 M, 500–610 W verbal, 630–720 M, 570–680 W mathematical; 79% of freshman score above 500 on verbal, 35% above 600, 5% above 700; 96% score above 500 on mathematical, 77% above 600, 31% above 700; ACT, 27–31 M, 26–30 W composite.

For Arts and Sciences (1,299 M, 1,623 W), 60% of applicants accepted, 25% of these actually enroll; 85% of freshmen graduate in top fifth of high school class, 99% in top two-fifths. Freshman SAT scores, middle fifty percent range: 510–620 M, 520–580 verbal, 600–710 M, 570–680 W mathematical; 80% of freshmen score above 500 on verbal, 35% above 600, 5% above 700; 95% score above 500 on mathematical, 69% above 600, 23% above 700; ACT, 28 composite.

For Architecture (129 M, 93 W), 37% of applicants accepted, 28% of these actually enroll; 95% of freshmen graduate in top fifth of high school class, 98% in top two-fifths. Freshman SAT scores, middle fifty percent range: 510–620 M, 520–580 verbal, 600–710 M, 570–680 W mathematical; 86% of freshmen score above 500 on verbal, 19% above 600; all score above 500 on mathematical, 81% above 600, 21% above 700; ACT, 27 composite.

For Business (340 M, 226 W), 50% of applicants accepted, 32% of these actually enroll; 86% of freshmen graduate in top fifth of high school class, 94% in top two-fifths. Freshman SAT scores, middle fifty percent range: 510–620 M, 520–580 verbal, 600–710 M, 570–680 W mathematical; 70% of freshmen score above 500 on verbal, 23% above 600, 2% above 700; 98% score above 500 on mathematical, 81% above 600, 36% above 700; ACT, 28.7 M, 28.0 W composite.

For Engineering and Applied Science (740 M, 187 W), 65% of applicants accepted, 25% of these actually enroll; 94% of freshmen graduate in top fifth of high school class, all in top two-fifths. Freshman SAT scores, middle fifty percent range: 510–620 M, 520–580 verbal, 600–710 M,. 570–680 W mathematical; 81% of freshmen score above 500 on verbal, 38% above 600, 5% above 700; all score above 500 on mathematical, 89% above 600, 49% above 700; ACT, 30 composite.

For Fine Arts (69 M, 219 W), 59% of applicants accepted, 34% of these actually enroll; 71% of freshmen graduate in top fifth of high school class, 98% in top two-fifths. Freshman SAT scores, middle fifty percent range: 510–620 M, 520–580 verbal, 600–710 M, 570–680 W mathematical; 75% of freshmen score above 500 on verbal, 23% above 600, 2% above 700; 90% score above 500 on mathematical, 56% above 600, 10% above 700; ACT, 27 composite.

Required: SAT or ACT; essay, rigorous college preparatory curriculum, recommendations. Criteria considered in admissions, in order of importance: high school academic record, recommendations, standardized test scores, writing sample and extracurricular activities; other factors considered: diverse student body, special talents, alumni children. *Entrance programs:* early decision, advanced placement, deferred admission. About 26% of freshmen from private schools, 4% from private schools. *Apply* by January 15. *Transfers* welcome; 178 enrolled 1993–94.

Academic Environment. Washington University is a medium-sized school with an acknowledged emphasis on undergraduate teaching. Reputation of the institution for scholarship doubtless attracts first rate talent among newly graduated scholar/teachers from nation's top graduate schools, adding strength to undergraduate instruction and advising. Research and graduate faculty are also said to spend some time teaching undergraduates. All students may take courses in any of the 5 undergraduate divisions. The geographically diverse student body is characterized by representatives of both students and administration as being equally concerned with scholarly/intellectual matters and occupational/professional career goals. Administration source reports student's concern about the "quantity" of work required and the "too structured" academic program. The pressure of 5 graduate and professional schools inevitably influences campus environment since many students enroll with an eye to later acceptance at a specific graduate or professional school. The University's very eminent Medical School, for instance, draws a substantial number of undergraduates to the campus. Degrees offered: bachelors, masters, doctoral. *Undergraduate studies* offered to freshmen by schools listed above; juniors may enter Graduate School of Business and Public Administration. *Majors offered* include anthropology, archaeology, architecture, Asian studies, Black studies, business/economy and law, Chinese, computer science, dance, drama, energy engineering and policy, Japanese, Jewish studies, Latin American studies, linguistics, Medieval and Renaissance studies, social thought and analysis, urban studies, women's studies. Average undergraduate class size: 20.

About 15% of entering freshmen graduate in four years, 85% eventually. *Special programs:* cooperative education, independent study, internships, study abroad, honors, undergraduate research, individualized majors, combined programs in arts/business, dentistry, engineering, physical therapy, or social work, 7-year architecture, engineering, MBA, 5-year fine arts/occupational therapy. Adult programs: University College - part-time evening program geared toward adults. *Calendar:* semester.

Undergraduate degrees conferred (1,492). 22% were in Social Sciences, 13% were in Engineering, 11% were in Business and Management, 9% were in Psychology, 8% were in Visual and Performing Arts, 7% were in Letters, 6% were in Computer and Engineering Related Technology, 6% were in Life Sciences, 5% were in Foreign Languages, 4% were in Architecture and Environmental Design, remainder in 10 other fields.

Graduates Career Data. Advanced studies pursued by 35% of students; 4% enter medical school; 4% enter law school; 1% enter business school; 12% enter other schools. Medical schools typically enrolling largest numbers of graduates include Washington U.; law schools include Harvard. Fields typically hiring largest number of graduates include business, medical, engineering, education. Career Development Services include career interest inventory, contacts for interviews, part-time and summer work, career placement, alumni network.

Faculty. About 99% of faculty hold PhD or equivalent. About 26% of teaching faculty are female.

Student Body. University seeks a national student body; 12% of students from in state; 36% Midwest, 18% Middle Atlantic, 11% South, 5% New England, 5% West, 2% Northwest; 5% Foreign. An estimated 30% of students reported as Protestant, 30% Catholic, 30% Jewish, 10% other; 6% as Black, 13% Asian, 2% Hispanic, 6% other minority.

Varsity Sports. Men (Div.III): Baseball, Basketball, Cross Country, Diving, Football, Golf, Soccer, Swimming, Tennis, Track. Women (Div. III): Basketball, Cross Country, Diving, Soccer, Swimming, Tennis, Track, Volleyball.

Campus Life. Campus culture is cosmopolitan, with a variety of lifestyles available; off-campus housing is available in immediate area. Downtown St. Louis is 6 miles away, provides full range of cultural opportunities. Students expected to observe state liquor laws limiting alcoholic beverages to those over 21. Cars allowed for upper-class students, but parking space may be tight. Students reported as wanting more social life, high interest reported in sponsored social activities and intramural sports (most popular: flag football, basketball). Considerable interest in fraternities/sororities, varsity sports (most popular: soccer, football, volleyball).

About 55% of men, 60% of women live in coed dormitories; rest live in off-campus housing or commute. Freshmen given preference in college housing if all students cannot be accommodated. Sexes segregated in coed dormitories by room. There are 12 fraternities, 7 sororities on campus which about 31% of men, 30% of women join, according to most recent data available; 6% of men live in fraternities; sororities provide no residence facilities. About 5% of resident students leave campus on weekends.

Annual Costs. Tuition and fees, $17,776; room and board, $5,731; estimated $2,258 other, exclusive of travel. About 46% of students receive financial aid; average amount of need-based assistance, $15,900. Assistance is typically divided 65% scholarship, 26% loan, 9% work. University reports 372 scholarships awarded for academic merit, 2,169 for need. *Meeting Costs:* university offers Tuition Stabilization Plan, monthly payment plan, SHARE Loans.

University of Washington

Seattle, Washington 98195 (206) 543-9686

The University of Washington is the largest institution of higher learning in the Pacific Northwest. It is also a major center for research and professional training for the region. Especially notable have been its contributions in the fields of oceanography, forestry, and fisheries. The university offers the only degree in fisheries in the U.S. The 690-acre main campus is located in a residential area of northeastern Seattle (pop. 500,000). Most convenient major airport: Seattle-Tacoma International.

Founded: 1861
Affiliation: State
UG Enrollment: 10,213 M, 9,801 W (full-time); 2,114 M, 2,428 W (part-time)
Total Enrollment: 38,357
Cost: < $10K
% Receiving Financial Aid: 30%
Admission: Selective
Application Deadline: Feb. 1

Admission is selective. About 75% of applicants accepted, 48% of these actually enroll. Freshman SAT scores, according to most recent data available: middle fifty percent range: 420–550 M, 410–540 W verbal, 520–650 M, 460–590 W mathematical; 39% of freshmen score above 500 on verbal, 10% above 600, 1% above 700; 73% score above 500 on mathematical, 35% above 600, 7% above 700; ACT, 22–28 M, 22–27 W composite. *Required:* SAT, ACT, or Washington Pre-College Test. *Out-of-state* freshman applicants: university welcomes students from out of state. State limits out-of-state enrollment to 26% of entering class. Special requirements for out-of-state applicants: "substantially higher GPA and test scores"; 51% of applicants accepted, 28% enroll. *Non-academic factors* considered in admissions: alumni children, underrepresented minorities, special talents (athletics, performing arts). *Entrance programs:* early admission, midyear admission, advanced placement. About 5% of entering students from private schools. *Apply* by February 1. *Transfers* welcome.

Academic Environment. Administration reports about 33% of courses required for graduation are elective; distribution requirements fairly numerous for College of Arts and Sciences. *Undergraduate studies* offered by colleges of Arts and Sciences, Engineering, Fisheries, Forest Resources, School of Nursing; upperclassmen may enter colleges of Architecture and Urban Planning, Pharmacy, Education, School of Business Administration; some undergraduate programs also available in schools of Medicine, Public Health and Community Medicine. *Majors offered* in to wide range of liberal arts studies under General Studies major include Afro-American studies, anthropology, Asian languages and literature, astronomy, atmospheric sciences, clinical health sciences, communications, computer engineering, computer science, drama, fisheries, geography, international studies, microbiology, Near Eastern languages and literature, oceanography, pulp and paper science, Russian and East European studies, Scandinavian languages and literature, biochemistry, geological sciences. Computer facilities reported as adequate to meet student demand: "access generally available"; 6,000 microcomputers available for student use in 17 sites throughout campus.

About 60% of students entering as freshmen graduate eventually; 11% of freshmen do not return for sophomore year. *Special programs:* independent study, study abroad, honors, undergraduate research, individualized majors, internships, cooperative work/study program in engineering, combined arts/medicine program. Adult programs: Women's Information Center provides counseling, support services to returning men and women. *Library:* 4.9 million titles, 50,000 serial titles, 5 million microforms; open-stack privileges. *Calendar:* quarter, summer school.

Undergraduate degrees conferred (5,471). 18% were in Social Sciences, 14% were in Business and Management, 12% were in Engineering, 11% were in Letters, 8% were in Psychology, 5% were in Visual and Performing Arts, 4% were in Communications, 4% were in Life Sciences, 4% were in Health Sciences, 3% were in Area and Ethnic Studies, remainder in 14 other fields.

Graduates Career Data. According to most recent data available, full-time graduate or professional study pursued immediately after graduation by about 20% of students.

Faculty. About 86% of teaching faculty hold PhD or equivalent.

Student Body. About 85% of students from in state. An estimated 4% of students reported as Black, 17% Asian, 3% Hispanic, 1% Native American, 8% undeclared, according to most recent data available.

Religious Orientation. Washington is a state institution, makes no religious demands on students. There are no religious clubs on campus, but Catholic, Jewish, Mormon, and most Protestant sects maintain religious centers near campus. Places of worship available in immediate community for Catholics, Protestants, Greek Orthodox, Jews, Buddhists.

Varsity Sports. Men (Div.I): Baseball, Basketball, Crew, Cross Country, Football, Golf, Soccer, Swimming, Tennis, Track. Women (Div.I): Basketball, Crew, Cross Country, Golf, Gymnastics, Soccer, Softball, Swimming, Tennis, Track, Volleyball.

Campus Life. Large percentage of commuters affects nature of campus life; "university is most inactive on Saturdays and Sundays." No university-wide regulations on dorm hours; each living group makes its own rules in these areas. Smoking permitted except in class; drinking allowed for students over 21 in dormitory rooms.

About 17% of undergraduate men, 16% of undergraduate women live in coed dormitories; 68% of men, 71% of women live in off-campus housing or commute. There are 32 off-campus fraternities, 18 off-campus sororities which about 18% of men, 14% of women join; 15% of men, 13% of women live in fraternities and sororities.

Annual Costs. Tuition and fees, $2,532 (out-of-state, $7,134); room and board, $4,086. About 30% of students receive financial aid; assistance is typically divided 31% scholarship/grant, 64% loan, 5% work. University reports some scholarships awarded on the basis of academic merit alone.

Wayland Baptist University

Plainview, Texas 79072 (806) 296-5521

A church-related university, located in a city of 25,000, 45 miles north of Lubbock. Most convenient major airport: Lubbock International.

Founded: 1908
Affiliation: Southern Baptist
UG Enrollment: 236 M, 361 W (full-time); 753 M, 406 W (part-time)
Total Enrollment: 1,456
Cost: < $10K
% Receiving Financial Aid: 85%
Admission: Non-selective
Application Deadline: Aug. 1

Admission. Graduates of accredited high schools eligible; others admitted by examination; 92% of applicants accepted, 79% of these actually enroll. Average freshman ACT scores: 21 M, 21 W composite, 17 M, 17 W mathematical. *Required:* SAT or ACT. *Apply* by August 1. *Transfers* welcome.

Academic Environment. *Degrees:* associates, bachelors, masters. About 28% of general education requirements for graduation are elective; distribution requirements fairly numerous. About 30% of freshmen do not return for sophomore year. Computer facilities reported as adequate to meet student demand. Special program: honors, independent study, 3–2 program in engineering. *Library:* 125,000 volumes, 750 periodicals. *Calendar:* 4–1–4, summer school.

Undergraduate degrees conferred (532). 46% were in Business and Management, 27% were in Military Technologies, 11% were in Social Sciences, 6% were in Education, remainder in 8 other fields.

Graduates Career Data. According to most recent data available, full-time graduate or professional study pursued by 25% of students immediately after graduation. *Careers in business and industry* pursued by 55% of graduates.

Varsity Sports. Men (NAIA): Basketball, Cross Country, Track. Women (NAIA): Basketball, Cross Country, Track.

Student Body. University seeks a national student body; 80% of students from in state; 85% South. An estimated 70% of students reported as Protestant, 5% as Catholic; 4% as Black, 3% Hispanic, 1% Asian, according to most recent data available.

Religious Orientation. Wayland Baptist is a church-related institution; 6 hours of religion required of all students.

Campus Life. About 30% of men, 30% of women live in traditional dormitories; no coed dormitories; rest live in off-campus housing or commute. No intervisitation in men's or women's dormitory rooms. There are 5 fraternities, 4 sororities on campus. About 40% of resident students leave campus on weekends.

Annual Costs. Tuition and fees, $4,766; room and board, $3,121. About 85% of students receive financial aid; assistance is typically divided 41% scholarship, 35% loan, 24% work. College reports some scholarships awarded on the basis of academic merit alone. *Meeting Costs:* university offers monthly payment plan.

Wayne State College

Wayne, Nebraska 68787 **(402) 375-2200**

A state-supported college, located in a community of 5,400, 90 miles northwest of Omaha. Most convenient major airport: Sioux City, IA.

Founded: 1910
Affiliation: State
UG Enrollment: 1,232 M, 1,503 W (full-time); 181 M, 264 W (part-time)
Total Enrollment: 3,765
Cost: < $10K
% Receiving Financial Aid: 70%
Admission: Non-selective
Application Deadline: Aug. 1

Admission. Graduates of accredited Nebraska high schools with 16 units (9 in academic subjects) admitted; almost all applicants accepted, 53% of these actually enroll; 19% of freshmen graduate in top fifth of high school class, 42% in top two-fifths. Average freshman ACT scores: 20 M, 21 W composite. *Required:* SAT or ACT for placement only. Criteria considered in admissions, in order of importance: high school academic record, standardized test scores; other factors considered: special talents, diverse student body, alumni children. *Out-of-state* freshman applicants: college seeks students from out of state. State does not limit out-of-state enrollment. *Out-of-state* applicants must have a minimum ACT composite of 18 and a minimum GPA of 2.0. About 172 out-of-state students enrolled 1993–94. States from which most out-of-state students are drawn include Iowa, Colorado, South Dakota, Florida, California. *Entrance programs:* early admission, mid-year admission. *Apply* by August 1 (priority), August 30 (final). *Transfers* welcome; 316 enrolled 1993–94.
Academic Environment. Degrees offered: bachelors, masters. General education requirements for liberal arts include 9 hours communications and literature, 9 hours mathematics and science, 4 hours fine arts, 12 hours Understanding World Heritage, 12 hours Living in the Modern

World. *Majors offered* include commercial art, food service management, exercise science/wellness. About 29% of students graduate in four years, 42% eventually; 64% of freshmen return for sophomore year. *Special programs:* CLEP, independent study, study abroad, honors, undergraduate research, internships. *Calendar:* semester, summer school.
Undergraduate degrees conferred (379). 34% were in Business and Management, 29% were in Education, 8% were in Protective Services, 8% were in Psychology, 3% were in Communications, 3% were in Parks and Recreation, remainder in 15 other fields.
Faculty. About 66% of faculty hold PhD or equivalent. About 86% of undergraduate classes taught by ranked faculty. About 48% of teaching faculty are female; 4% minority.
Student Body. College seeks a national student body; 79% of students from in state; 97% from Midwest. An estimated 53% of students reported as Protestant, 31% Catholic, 14% unaffiliated, 2% other; 2% Black, 1% Hispanic, 1% Asian, 1% other minority.
Varsity Sports. Men (NAIA, NCAA, Div.II): Baseball, Basketball, Cross Country, Football, Golf, Track. Women (NAIA, NCAA, Div.II): Basketball, Golf, Softball, Volleyball.
Campus Life. About 8% women live in traditional dormitories; 48% of men, 39% of women in coed dormitories; rest live in off-campus housing or commute. Intervisitation in men's and women's dormitory rooms limited. Sexes segregated in coed dormitories by wing. There are 2 fraternities, 2 sororities on campus which about 2% each of men, women join, according to most recent data available. About 60% of resident students leave campus on weekends, according to most recent data available.
Annual Costs. Tuition and fees, $1,690 (out-of-state, $2,838); room and board, $2,570; estimated $1,470 other, exclusive of travel. About 70% of students receive financial aid. College reports some scholarships awarded on the basis of academic merit alone.

Wayne State University

Detroit, Michigan 48202 **(313) 577-3577**

A state-supported institution, located in metropolitan Detroit, Wayne State is an urban university serving primarily residents of the Detroit area. Most convenient major airport: Detroit Metropolitan.

Founded: 1868
Affiliation: State
UG Enrollment: 4,405 M, 5,740 W (full-time); 4,777 M, 6,164 W (part-time)
Total Enrollment: 21,449
Cost: < $10K
Admission: Non-selective
Application Deadline: August 1

Admission. For all schools, 74% of applicants accepted, 55% of these actually enroll. Average freshman scores, according to most recent data available: SAT, 450 M, 410 W verbal, 530 M, 440 W mathematical; ACT, 20 M, 18 W composite. *Required:* SAT or ACT. *Out-of-state* freshman applicants: university seeks students from out of state. State does not limit out-of-state enrollment. No special requirements for out-of-state applicants. *Apply* by August 1. *Transfers* welcome.
Academic Environment. *Undergraduate studies* offered to freshmen by Colleges of Liberal Arts, Engineering, and Pharmacy and Allied Health Professions (Allied Health Programs do not admit freshmen); upper-division program in nursing offered by College of Nursing; juniors admitted to College of Education, School of Business Administration. *Majors offered* in liberal arts in addition to usual studies include Arabic, computer science, criminal justice, Hebrew, East European studies, international studies, women's studies, radiation technology, mass communications, Polish, and mortuary science. Computer literacy required for all students. Facilities reported as adequate to meet student demand; more than 600 terminals available for student use.

About 28% of freshmen do not return for sophomore year. *Special programs:* independent study, study abroad, honors, undergraduate research, study at Merrill-Palmer Institute. *Library:* 2,310,000 titles, 25,000 periodicals, 2,050,000 microforms; open-stack privileges. *Calendar:* semester, summer school.
Undergraduate degrees conferred (3,172). 15% were in Business and Management, 11% were in Education, 9% were in Psychology, 8% were in Health Sciences, 6% were in Engineering, 6% were in Visual and Performing Arts, 6% were in Social Sciences, 5% were in Communications, 5% were in Life Sciences, 4% were in Multi/Interdisciplinary Studies, 4% were in Protective Services, 3% were in Public Affairs, 3% were in Letters, 3% were in Computer and Engineering Related Technology, remainder in 11 other fields.
Graduates Career Data. *Careers in business and industry* pursued by 97% of graduates.
Faculty. About 85% of faculty hold PhD or equivalent.
Student Body. University does not seek a national student body; 96% of students from Michigan, according to most recent data available.
Religious Orientation. Wayne State makes no religious demands on students. Religious clubs on campus include Baptist Student Union, Catholic Campus Ministry, Episcopal Mission, Hillel Foundation, Wayne Christian Fellowship, Wesley Foundation.
Varsity Sports. Men (Div.II): Baseball, Basketball, Cross Country, Fencing, Football, Golf, Swimming, Tennis, Track. Women (Div.II): Basketball, Fencing, Softball, Tennis, Volleyball.
Campus Life. This is an overwhelmingly commuter campus. University provides limited on-campus housing. About two-thirds of student body work a minimum of 20 hours weekly. About 3% of students live in coed apartments; 97% commute.
Annual Costs. Tuition and fees, $2,403 (out-of-state, $5,238); room and board, $4,860; $860 estimated other, exclusive of travel. University reports some scholarships awarded on basis of academic merit alone. *Meeting Costs:* university offers AMS payment plan.

Waynesburg College

Waynesburg, Pennsylvania 15370 **(800) 225-7393**

A church-related, liberal arts college, located in a town of 5,200, 50 miles south of Pittsburgh. Most convenient major airport: Pittsburgh International.

Founded: 1849
Affiliation: Presbyterian
UG Enrollment: 550 M, 730 W (full-time)
Cost: < $10K
% Receiving Financial Aid: 86%
Admission: Non-selective
Application Deadline: Rolling

Admission. Graduates of accredited high schools with 16 units in academic subjects eligible; 82% of applicants accepted, 34% of these actually enroll. About 22% of freshmen graduate in top fifth of high

school class, 57% in top two-fifths. *Required:* minimum H.S. GPA, interview. Criteria considered in admissions, in order of importance: high school academic record, recommendations, standardized test scores, extracurricular activities, writing sample; other factors considered: special talents, alumni children, diverse student body, religious affiliation and/or commitment. *Entrance programs:* early decision, early admission, midyear admission. *Apply:* rolling admissions. *Transfers* welcome; 87 enrolled 1993–94.
Academic Environment. Degrees offered: associates, bachelors, masters. *Majors offered* include accounting, business, education, sports medicine, nursing. General education requirements for graduation include a service learning course where students are involved in community service. About 47% of students entering as freshmen graduate in four years, 60% eventually; 75% of freshmen return for sophomore year. *Special programs:* CLEP, independent study, study abroad, undergraduate research, accounting internship, interdisciplinary colloquium for selected students, 3–2 programs in engineering. *Calendar:* semester, summer school. Average undergraduate class size: 18.
Undergraduate degrees conferred (179). 38% were in Business and Management, 18% were in Health Sciences, 11% were in Letters, 9% were in Education, 6% were in Social Sciences, 5% were in Public Affairs, 4% were in Visual and Performing Arts, 4% were in Psychology, 3% were in Physical Sciences, remainder in Life Sciences.
Graduates Career Data. Advanced studies pursued by 18% of students.
Faculty. About 61% of faculty hold PhD or equivalent.
Student Body. College seeks a national student body; 89% of students from in state; 93% Middle Atlantic, 2% Midwest, 3% South; 1% Foreign. An estimated 60% of students reported as Protestant, 28% Catholic, 8% unaffiliated; 5% Black, 1% other minority.
Religious Orientation. Waynesburg is a church-related institution, one course in religion required of all students.
Varsity Sports. Men (NCAA, Div.III): Baseball, Basketball, Football, Golf, Soccer, Tennis, Wrestling. Women (NCAA,Div.III): Basketball, Soccer, Softball, Tennis, Volleyball.
Campus Life. About 45% of men, 34% of women live in traditional dormitories; rest commute. Freshmen given preference in college housing if all students cannot be accommodated. Intervisitation in men's and women's dormitory rooms limited. There are 2 fraternities, 3 sororities on campus, which about 7% men, 12% women join; about 4% of men live in fraternities; sororities provide no residence facilities.
Annual Costs. Tuition and fees, $8,560; room and board, $3,380; estimated $500 other, exclusive of travel. About 86% of students receive financial aid. Assistance is typically divided 66% scholarship/grant, 26% loan, 8% work. College reports some scholarships awarded for academic merit. *Meeting Costs:* college offers AMS, tuition payment plan.

Webb Institute of Naval Architecture

Glen Cove, New York 11542 **(516) 671-2277**

An independent, professional institution, Webb offers a single required curriculum in naval architecture and marine engineering. An all-scholarship institution at which the limited number of carefully selected students pay no tuition or fees, Webb attracts students of the highest caliber and offers a unique education. Its 26-acre waterfront campus is located in a community of 25,800, on Long Island's suburban North Shore.

Founded: 1889
Affiliation: Independent
UG Enrollment: 62 M, 20 W (full-time)
Cost: none
% Receiving Financial Aid: 100%
Admission: Selective
Application Deadline: Feb. 15

Admission Admission requirements compare to those in force at the most selective institutions in the country. About 36% of applicants accepted, 72% of these actually enroll; 24% of freshmen graduate in top fifth of high school class. *Required:* SAT, 3 ACH (English, mathematics I or II, choice of physics or chemistry), interview. *Apply* by February 15. *Transfers* not sought.
Academic Environment. *Degree:* BS.
Undergraduate degrees conferred (18). 100% were in Engineering.
Campus Life. Most students come from Middle Atlantic states. All students live in dormitories. About 25% of students leave campus on weekends.
Annual Costs. Tuition and fees, none; room and board, $5,000; estimated $600 other, exclusive of travel. Institute reports scholarships awarded on the basis of academic ability and need.

Webber College

Babson Park, Florida 33827

A private, professional institution, Webber offers both associate and baccalaureate degrees. Four-year programs offered in accounting, business management, financial management, management/law enforcement/corrections, computer information systems, marketing, retail management, resort/hotel and restaurant management, international travel and tourism.

Founded: 1927
Affiliation: Independent

Undergraduate degrees conferred (34). 74% were in Business and Management, 24% were in Marketing and Distribution, 3% were in Computer and Engineering Related Technology.

Weber State College

Ogden, Utah 84408 **(801) 626-6046**

A state-supported college, located in a city of 80,000, 30 miles north of Salt Lake City. Most convenient major airport: Salt Lake International.

Founded: 1889
Affiliation: State
UG Enrollment: 3,678 M, 3,628 W (full-time); 2,326 M, 2,364 W (part-time)
Total Enrollment: 14,495
Cost: < $10K
Admission: Non-selective
Application Deadline: 1 month before start of quarter

Admission. Graduates of accredited high schools with C average eligible; about 97% of applicants accepted, 60% of these actually enroll. *Required:* SAT or ACT. *Out-of-state* freshman applicants: college seeks students from out of state. State does not limit out-of-state enrollment. Requirement for out-of-state applicants: predicted GPA of 2.0. *Apply* by 1 month before start of quarter. *Transfers* welcome.
Academic Environment. *Degrees:* AB, BS. About 60% of general education requirements for graduation are elective; distribution requirements fairly numerous. *Majors offered* in addition to usual studies include logistics, dental hygiene, paramedics; new programs in nursing, clinical lab administration recently added. Computer facilities reported as adequate to meet student demand. About 60% of students entering as freshmen graduate eventually; 40% of freshmen do not return for sophomore year. *Special programs:* CLEP, independent study, study abroad, honors, undergraduate research, 3-year degree. *Library:* 253,326 volumes, 63,658 periodicals. *Calendar:* quarter, summer school.
Undergraduate degrees conferred (1,243). 16% were in Business and Management, 13% were in Engineering and Engineering Related Technology, 12% were in Education, 9% were in Computer and Engineering Related Technology, 6% were in Social Sciences, 6% were in Health Sciences, 4% were in Marketing and Distribution, 4% were in Public Affairs, 4% were in Liberal/General Studies, 4% were in Protective Services, 3% were in Psychology, 3% were in Communications, remainder in 11 other fields.
Graduates Career Data. *Careers in business and industry* pursued by 74% of graduates.
Varsity Sports. Men (Div.IA): Basketball, Cross Country, Football (IAA), Golf, Tennis, Track, Wrestling. Women (Div.IA): Basketball, Cross Country, Golf (IAA), Tennis, Track, Volleyball.
Campus Life. College seeks a national student body; 90% of students from in state. An estimated 3% of students reported as Black, 5% Hispanic, 3% Asian, 2% Native American, according to most

recent data available. Weber State makes no religious demands on students. About 2% each of men, women live in dormitories; rest live in off-campus housing or commute. Intervisitation in men's and women's dormitory rooms limited. There are 4 fraternities, 4 sororities on campus which about 5% of men, 5% of women join.

Annual Costs. Tuition and fees, $1,638 (out-of-state, $4,866); room and board, $3,345. About 45% of students receive financial aid. *Meeting Costs:* university offers PLUS loans.

Webster University

St. Louis, Missouri 63119 (314) 961-2660

Webster is now an independent, co-educational, liberal arts university located in suburban Webster Groves (pop. 27,000), 20 minutes from downtown St. Louis. Most convenient major airport: St. Louis.

Founded: 1915
Affiliation: Independent
UG Enrollment: 633 M, 1,106 W (full-time); 424 M, 1,126 W (part-time)
Total Enrollment: 9,794
Cost: < $10K
% Receiving Financial Aid: 50%
Admission: Non-selective
Application Deadline: Aug. 1

Admission. About 82% of applicants accepted, 49% of these actually enroll; 36% of freshmen graduate in top fifth of high school class, 66% in top two-fifths. Average freshman scores: SAT, 511 verbal, 494 mathematical; 61% of freshmen score above 500 verbal, 21% above 600, 1% above 700; 52% score above 500 mathematical, 9% above 600; ACT, 23 composite. *Required:* SAT or ACT, minimum H.S. GPA of 2.5. Criteria considered in admissions, in order of importance: high school academic record, standardized test scores, writing sample, recommendations, extracurricular activities; other factors considered: special talents, diverse student body. *Entrance programs:* early admission, midyear admission, deferred admission, advanced placement. *Apply* by August 1; rolling admissions. *Transfers* welcome; 438 enrolled 1993–94.

Academic Environment. Recent student leader reports student interests are oriented very strongly toward the arts. "Very free atmosphere here. Lots of opportunity to develop own programs." There are no general degree requirements except for Freshman Seminar for all students; each student must complete an area of concentration. Degrees offered: bachelors, masters, doctoral. *Majors offered* include business and management, computer science, education, media communications, theater and musical theater, audio production. Average undergraduate class size: 50% under 20, 50% between 20–40.

About 29% of students entering as freshmen graduate in four years, 52% eventually; 76% of freshmen return for sophomore year. *Special programs:* CLEP, 3-week January term, independent study, study abroad - Webster has 4 European campuses in Switzerland, the Netherlands, England, and Austria, undergraduate research, individualized majors, student sabbatical leave program, cooperative and 3–2 programs in engineering, architecture; cross registration with Fontbonne, Maryville U., Lindenwood, Edon Theological Seminary, Missouri Baptist. *Calendar:* semester, summer school.

Undergraduate degrees conferred (684). 40% were in Business and Management, 14% were in Health Sciences, 12% were in Communications, 8% were in Visual and Performing Arts, 7% were in Social Sciences, 5% were in Education, 4% were in Computer and Engineering Related Technology, 3% were in Letters, 3% were in Psychology, remainder in 5 other fields.

Graduates Career Data. Career Development Services include aptitude testing, counseling, placement services, on-campus recruitment, internships, library resources.

Faculty. About 68% of faculty hold PhD or equivalent. About 15% of undergraduate classes taught by tenured faculty. About 50% of teaching faculty are female; 2% Black, 2% Hispanic, 3% other minority.

Student Body. University seeks a national student body; 82% of students from in state; 93% from Midwest; 1% Foreign. An estimated 65% of students reported as Protestant, 25% Catholic, 5% Jewish, 5% other, according to most recent data available; 13% Black, 4% Hispanic, 1% Asian, 1% other minority. Average age of undergraduate student: 29.

Varsity Sports. Men (Div.III): Baseball, Basketball, Soccer, Tennis. Women (Div.III): Basketball, Cross Country, Swimming, Tennis, Volleyball.

Campus Life. University offers many types of cultural activities on campus. Cars allowed for all students; parking reported as inadequate. Out-of-town freshmen required to live in college residence halls. Residents of each dormitory select whatever intervisitation hours they desire. Campus culture influenced by high proportion of students living off-campus or commuting.

About 2% of men, 2% of women live in coed dormitories; 1% of men, 1% of women live in off-campus college-related housing; rest commute. Sexes segregated in coed dormitory by room. Freshmen given preference in college housing if all students cannot be accommodated. There are no fraternities or sororities on campus. About 50% of resident students leave campus on weekends.

Annual Costs. Tuition and fees, $8,560; room and board, $4,090. About 50% of students receive financial aid; average amount of assistance, $7,200. Assistance is typically divided 25% scholarship, 25% grant, 25% loan, 25% work. College reports 3 scholarships awarded for academic merit, 14 for special talents, 18 for need.

Wellesley College

Wellesley, Massachusetts 02181 (617) 283-2270

Wellesley is one of the original 7 Sisters which has decided to remain a college devoted to the education of women. A cross-registration program with MIT and membership in the Twelve College Exchange bring some men students to campus. One of the most sought-after colleges in the country, Wellesley is an undergraduate college stressing teaching, which contrasts with the research orientation of many larger institutions. The 500-acre campus with a lake enjoys a preferred location, 12 miles west of Boston, in a community of 28,100, where both the resources of the city and countryside are easily available. Most convenient major airport: Logan International (Boston).

Founded: 1870
Affiliation: Independent
UG Enrollment: 2,158 W (full-time)
Cost: $10K–$20K
% Receiving Financial Aid: 60%
Admission: Most Selective
Application Deadline: Jan. 15

Admission is among the most selective in the country. About 45% of applicants accepted, 46% of these actually enroll; 94% of freshmen graduate in top fifth of high school class. Average freshman SAT scores: 610 verbal, 640 mathematical; 91% of freshmen score above 500 on verbal, 59% above 600, 10% above 700; 94% score above 500 on mathematical, 72% above 600, 23% above 700. *Required:* SAT, 3 ACH including English (plus choice of 2 from among language, social studies, mathematics/science), essay, two teacher recommendations, high school transcript, guidance counselor report. Criteria considered in admissions, in order of importance: high school academic record, standardized test scores, recommendations, extracurricular activities, writing sample, interview; other factors considered: special talents, alumni children, diverse student body, intellectual curiosity, self-confidence, commitment to learning. *Entrance programs:* early decision, early admission, deferred admission. About 36% of freshmen from private schools. *Apply* by January 15. *Transfers* welcome; 26 enrolled for 1993–94.

Academic Environment. Undergraduate program is a prestigious one; student body is extremely capable; classes usually small (18–21 students) and low student/faculty ratio makes faculty quite available to students. Wellesley has deliberately maintained a faculty with a high percentage (59%) of women, in accordance with its mission as a women's college. Administration reports most courses needed for graduation are elective; distribution requirements, however, fairly numerous: 3 semester courses in each of 3 general areas (literature/languages/fine arts, social sciences/religion/philosophy, science/mathematics), foreign language proficiency, minimum of 2 physical education activities each year until requirement met. A writing course is required for all entering students. A Technologies Studies Program and a Freshman Cluster Program are offered. Exemption possible from any required studies. *Degree:* AB. Administration source reports that almost all students are primarily academically oriented. Students who feel most at home on Wellesley's campus said to be "well-motivated" and "ready to participate actively in their own education both within and outside the classroom." Degrees offered: bachelors. *Majors offered* in addition to usual studies include architecture, international relations, Latin American studies, individualized majors.

About 82% of students entering as freshmen graduate within four years, 87% eventually; 97% of freshmen return for sophomore year. *Special programs:* over 2,500 internship opportunities available during academic year, January break, or in the summer, independent study, study abroad, honors, undergraduate research, 3-year degree, Winter-session, individualized majors, cross-registration with MIT (bus service provided), Twelve College Exchange, Brandeis Exchange, Spelman Exchange, program with Babson, freshman/sophomore colloquia, 5-year BA/BS with MIT, Wellesley in Washington D.C., Los Angeles Urban Internship Program. Adult programs: Elisabeth Kaiser Davis Degree Completion Program for women over 24 years of age. *Calendar:* semester.

Undergraduate degrees conferred (558). 28% were in Social Sciences, 14% were in Letters, 10% were in Psychology, 10% were in Foreign Languages, 7% were in Visual and Performing Arts, 7% were in Area and Ethnic Studies, 6% were in Life Sciences, 5% were in Philosophy and Religion, 4% were in Multi/Interdisciplinary Studies, 4% were in Physical Sciences, remainder in 3 other fields.

Graduates Career Data. Advanced studies pursued by 39% of students; 9% enter medical school, 9% enter law school, 2% enter business school, 3% enter other schools. About 61% of 1992–93 graduates employed. Career Development Services include internships, alumni career network, staff to assist students at all levels of career exploration.

Faculty. About 93% of faculty hold PhD or equivalent. About 58% of teaching faculty are female.

Student Body. College seeks a national student body; about 21% of students from Massachusetts; 25% from New England, 25% Middle Atlantic, 13% West/Northwest, 17% South, 13% North Central, 7% foreign. An estimated 7% of students reported as Black, 4% Hispanic, 19% Asian.

Varsity Sports. Women (Div.III): Basketball, Crew, Cross Country, Diving, Fencing, Field Hockey, Lacrosse, Soccer, Swimming, Tennis, Volleyball.

Campus Life. Proximity to Boston/Cambridge makes all the cultural, intellectual, and social resources of the metropolitan area easily accessible to students. Cars permitted for all but first year students; parking is limited. Students increasingly determine their own dormitory and social lives. There are no limits on visiting hours for men or number of overnight absences. Any student may live off campus, few do. High interest reported in cultural activities, sponsored social events; somewhat milder interest in religious activities, varsity sports (most popular: crew, basketball, swimming, tennis) and intramurals (most popular: crew, volleyball, aerobics).

About 98% of women live in dormitories; 2% commute. There are no sororities. About 60% of resident students "leave" campus on weekends (to go into Boston), according to most recent data available.

Annual Costs. Tuition and fees, $17,390; room and board, $6,090; estimated $1,200 other, exclusive of travel. About 60% of students receive financial aid; average amount of assistance, $15,959. College reports scholarships awarded only on the basis of need. *Meeting Costs:* college offers deferred payment plan, four-year prepaid tuition stabilization plan, variety of loans.

Wells College

Aurora, New York 13026 (315) 364-3264

Wells is a small, independent liberal arts college which reaffirmed its mission as a women's college in February 1988. The 360-acre campus, on the shore of Cayuga Lake in central New York, is located in a village of 1,100, 26 miles north of Ithaca and 45 miles southwest of Syracuse. Most convenient major airport: Hancock International (Syracuse).

Founded: 1868
Affiliation: Independent
UG Enrollment: 396 W (full-time); 19 W (part-time)
Cost: $10K–$20K
% Receiving Financial Aid: 90%
Admission: Very Selective
Application Deadline: March 1

Admission is very selective. About 75% of applicants accepted; 55% of freshmen graduate in top fifth of high school class, 79% in top two-fifths. Average freshman scores: SAT, 54% of freshmen score above 500 verbal, 21% above 600, 1% above 700; 57% score above 500 mathematical, 13% above 600; ACT, 26 composite. *Required:* SAT or ACT, essay, minimum H.S. GPA of 82. Criteria considered in admissions, in order of importance: high school academic record, recommendations, extracurricular activities, writing sample, standardized tests; other factors considered: alumni children. *Entrance programs:* early decision, advanced placement. About 7% of entering students from private schools, 7% from parochial schools. *Apply* by March 1. *Transfers* welcome; 31 enrolled 1993–94.

Academic Environment. Students participate in determining policies governing curriculum; the board of trustees now includes one member of each graduating class who serves for 2 years. The small size of the college also makes possible close student/faculty relationships and academic flexibility. Recent student leader speaks of "small classes, excellent professors, a dedication to women in higher education." Core curriculum designed to ensure breadth of studies; each student responsible for working out own program with adviser. Academic atmosphere is serious; program focuses primarily on the arts and sciences. Wells has recently committed to the development of ethical leadership in women and has founded the Women's Leadership Institute. Independent study opportunities open to qualified students from second semester of freshman year on. Strongest academic programs reported to be languages, English, history, social studies. Wells appears to have succeeded better than most very small colleges in enjoying the advantages of "smallness" without paying a disproportionate price through limitations on program and faculty. Degrees offered: bachelors. *Majors offered* include computer science, fine arts, American studies, special majors may be developed by individual students. Dual degree programs offered in business, community health, engineering and petroleum engineering with University of Rochester, Washington University, Columbia University, Texas A&M University. Average undergraduate class size: 80% under 20, 19% between 20–40, 1% over 40.

About 74% of entering freshmen graduate in four years, 77% eventually; 76% of freshmen return for sophomore year. *Special programs:* CLEP, independent study, honors, study abroad, internships, undergraduate research, credit by examination, 3-year degree, exchange semesters, dual degree, interdisciplinary minors, 3–2 programs in engineering, BA/MS in community health with U. of Rochester, cross registration with Cornell. *Calendar:* 4–1–4.

Undergraduate degrees conferred (89). 22% were in Social Sciences, 18% were in Psychology, 15% were in Letters, 9% were in Visual and Performing Arts, 8% were in Foreign Languages, 6% were in Philosophy and Religion, 6% were in Mathematics, 6% were in Life Sciences, 6% were in Liberal/General Studies, 4% were in Area and Ethnic Studies, remainder in Computer and Engineering Related Technology.

Graduates Career Data. Advanced studies pursued by 32% of students; 5% enter medical school; 5% enter dental school; 13% enter law school; 5% enter business school. Fields typically hiring largest number of graduates include business, sales, research. Career Development Services include internships, career counseling, resume writing, interviewing skills, credentials file, alumni connections.

Faculty. About 96% of faculty hold PhD or equivalent. About 75% of undergraduate classes taught by tenured faculty. About 50% of teaching faculty are female.

Student Body. College seeks a national student body; 48% of students from in state; 58% Middle Atlantic, 20% New England, 4% Midwest, 3% South, 8% West, 5% Northwest; 2% Foreign. An estimated 5% of students reported as Black, 7% Asian, 3% Hispanic, 1% Native American, 1% other minority.

Varsity Sports. Women (Div.III): Diving, Field Hockey, Lacrosse, Soccer, Swimming.

Campus Life. Recent student leader extols the campus atmosphere as "beautiful and peaceful year round," but also adds that it is difficult to meet men and "get to know them casually." Residents of each dormitory determine social rules including visitation hours with option of 24-hour open house. Alcohol permitted in most areas on campus; beer sold in snack bar. All students may have cars on campus. Students usually required to live in residence halls. About 97% of women live in dormitories; 3% live in off-campus housing. There are no sororities. About 25% of resident students leave campus on weekends.

Annual Costs. Tuition and fees, $13,800; room and board, $5,400; estimated $600 other, exclusive of travel. About 90% of students receive financial aid; average amount of assistance, $7,900.

Assistance is typically divided 49% grant, 32% loan, 15% work; plus a varied number of scholarships. College reports about 20 4-year scholarships awarded to entering freshmen on the basis of academic merit alone. *Meeting Costs:* college offers monthly payment plan, prepayment plan, PLUS, SHELF, Wells College Loan Fund.

Wentworth Institute of Technology

Boston, Massachusetts 02115

A private technological institution offering bachelor's degrees in design, engineering, technology and management. Associate degrees are also offered in selected majors. Co-operative education is required for upperclassmen in baccalaureate programs.

Undergraduate degrees conferred (600). 64% were in Engineering and Engineering Related Technology, 12% were in Business and Management, 9% were in Computer and Engineering Related Technology, 7% were in Engineering, 7% were in Architecture and Environmental Design, remainder in Physical Sciences.

Wesley College

Dover, Delaware 19901 (302) 736-2400

Founded as a church-related 2-year college, Wesley has expanded rapidly in recent years and is now accredited as a 4-year institution conferring both associate and baccalaureate degree. Most convenient major airport: Philadelphia International.

Founded: 1873
Affiliation: United Methodist
UG Enrollment: 409 M, 446 W (full-time); 123 M, 190 W (part-time)
Cost: < $10K
% Receiving Financial Aid: 75%
Admission: Non-selective
Application Deadline: Rolling

Admission. About 77% of applicants accepted, 32% of these actually enroll; 9% of freshmen graduate in top fifth of high school class, 24% in top two-fifths. Average freshman SAT scores, according to most recent data available: 377 M, 396 W verbal, 426 M, 411 W mathematical. *Required:* SAT or ACT. *Non-academic factors* considered in admissions: special talents, diverse student body, alumni children. *Entrance programs:* early decision, early admission, midyear admission, deferred admission, advanced placement. *Apply:* rolling admissions. *Transfers* welcome.

Academic Environment. *Degrees:* BSBA, BSCIS, BSEnvSc, BSMT, BSNA, BSN. About 90% of students entering as freshmen graduate eventually; 40% of freshmen do not return for sophomore year. New programs added include economics, paralegal studies. Computer facilities reported as adequate to meet student demand. *Special programs:* independent study, study abroad. *Library:* 61,000 titles.

Undergraduate degrees conferred (73). 49% were in business and Management, 27% were in Health Sciences, 15% were in Allied Health. 7% were in Life Sciences, remainder in 1 other field.

Graduates Career Data. *Careers in business and industry* pursued by 22% of graduates.

Faculty. About 48% of faculty hold PhD or equivalent.

Varsity Sports. Men (Div.III): Baseball, Basketball, Football, Golf, Soccer, Tennis. Women (Div.III): Basketball, Field Hockey, Softball, Tennis.

Campus Life. About 40% of students from in state; 95% Middle Atlantic. An estimated 45% of students reported as Protestant, 35% Catholic, 2% Jewish, 14% unaffiliated; 9% as Black, 4% other minority. About 69% of men, 61% of women live in traditional dormitories; rest live in off-campus housing or commute. Freshmen given preference in housing if all students cannot be accommodated. There are 2 fraternities on campus. About 25% of students leave campus on weekends.

Annual Costs. Tuition and fees, $9,645; room and board, $4,100. About 75% of students receive financial aid; assistance is typically divided 45% scholarship, 37% loan, 18% work. College reports some scholarships awarded on the basis of academic merit alone. *Meeting Costs:* college offers Academic Management Systems.

Wesley College

Florence, Mississippi 39073 (601) 845-2265

A church-related Bible college offering associates and bachelors programs.

Affiliation: Congregational Methodist Church
UG Enrollment: 104 total undergraduate
Cost: < $10K
% Receiving Financial Aid: 59%
Admission: Non-selective
Application Deadline: Rolling

Admission. All applicants accepted, all enroll. *Required:* SAT or ACT. Criteria considered in admissions, in order of importance: standardized test scores, high school academic record; other factor considered: religious affiliation and/or commitment. *Apply* by no specific deadline. *Transfers* welcome; 7 enrolled 1993–94.

Academic Environment. Graduation requirements include 3 hours each in speech, fine arts, and math, 6–9 hours in English composition, 6 hours each in literature, history, and psychology/sociology, 7 hours in health/physical education/recreation, 8 hours in biology, 15 hours in Bible and theology. Degrees offered: associates, bachelors. About 30% of students entering as freshmen graduate within four years, 40% eventually; 78% of freshmen return for sophomore year. *Special programs:* pastoral internship.

Undergraduate degrees conferred ().

Faculty. About 1% of faculty hold PhD or equivalent. About 41% of teaching faculty are female; less than 1% Black.

Student Body. About 65% of students from in state. All students reported as Protestant.

Religious Orientation. Wesley is a church-related institution; 15 hours in Bible and theology required of all students.

Varsity Sports. Men: Basketball.

Campus Life. About 42% of men, 51% of women live in traditional dormitories; no coed dormitories; rest commute. There are no fraternities or sororities on campus. About 2% of resident students leave campus on weekends.

Annual Costs. Tuition and fees, $4,400; room and board, $2,200; estimated $500 other, exclusive of travel. About 59% of students receive financial aid; average amount of assistance, $1,182. Assistance is typically divided 3% scholarship, 75% grant, 15% loan, 7% work. College reports 2 scholarships awarded on the basis of academic merit alone, 11 on the basis of need.

Wesleyan College

Macon, Georgia 31297 (800) 447-6610

A church-related, liberal and fine arts college for women, located on a 240-acre campus in a city of 160,000, 90 miles southeast of Atlanta. Most convenient major airport: Atlanta.

Founded: 1836
Affiliation: Independent (United Methodist)
UG Enrollment: 387 W (full-time); 69 W (part-time)
Cost: $10K–$20K
% Receiving Financial Aid: 90%
Admission: Non-selective
Application Deadline: March 1

Admission. About 94% of applicants accepted, 47% of these actually enroll. Average freshman scores: SAT, 60% of freshmen score above 500 verbal, 32% above 600, 6% above 700; 44% score above 500 mathematical, 19% above 600, 1% above 700. *Required:* SAT or ACT, essay, minimum H.S. GPA. Criteria considered in admissions, in order of importance: high school academic record, extracurricular activities, standardized tests, writing sample, recommendations; other factors considered: special talents, alumni children, religious affiliation and/or commitment. *Entrance programs:* early decision, early admission, advanced placement. About 20% of freshmen from private schools. *Apply* by March 1; rolling admissions. *Transfers* welcome; 15 enrolled 1993–94.

Academic Environment. Degrees offered: bachelors. *Majors offered* include self-designed, interdisciplinary majors. Average undergraduate class size: 80% under 20, 20% between 20–40. About 51% of students entering as freshmen graduate within four years; 65% of freshmen return for sophomore year. *Special programs:*

CLEP, independent study, study abroad, honors, internships, 3½-year degree, 3–2 programs in engineering. Adult programs: Encore program for non-traditional students offers reduced tuition and flexible scheduling. *Calendar:* semester.

Undergraduate degrees conferred (72). 18% were in Communications, 17% were in Education, 10% were in Business and Management, 8% were in Visual and Performing Arts, 8% were in Mathematics, 7% were in Social Sciences, 7% were in Physical Sciences, 7% were in Life Sciences, 6% were in Psychology, 6% were in Letters, 3% were in Philosophy and Religion, 3% were in Foreign Languages, remainder in Allied Health.

Graduates Career Data. Advanced studies pursued by 27% of students; 10% enter medical school; 7% enter law school; 10% enter business school. *Careers in business and industry* pursued by 36% of graduates, according to most recent data available.

Faculty. About 73% of faculty hold PhD or equivalent. About 54% of teaching faculty are female.

Student Body. College seeks a national student body; 58% of students from in state; 30% South, 3% Middle Atlantic, 2% Midwest, 1% West, 2% Northwest; 4% Foreign. An estimated 68% of students reported as Protestant, 16% Catholic, 1% Jewish, 4% other; 11% as Black, 3% Hispanic, 4% Asian.

Varsity Sports. Women (Independent): Basketball, Equestrian, Soccer, Tennis, Volleyball.

Campus Life. Cars allowed; for freshmen after first three weeks. Curfew for first-term freshmen. Limited visitation only during open house. Alcohol not permitted on campus or at college functions except by special permission. About 90% of women live in traditional dormitories; rest in off-campus housing or commute. There are no sororities. About 40% of resident students leave campus on weekends.

Annual Costs. Tuition and fees, $10,850; room and board, $4,250; estimated $2,064 other, exclusive of travel. About 90% of students receive financial aid; average amount of assistance, $10,535. College reports 128 scholarships awarded for academic merit, 29 for special talents, 318 for need. *Meeting Costs:* college offers monthly payment plan, deferred loans, low interest loans.

Wesleyan University

Middletown, Connecticut 06457 (203) 347-9411

One of the so-called Little Three (with Amherst and Williams), Wesleyan is one of the most prestigious academic institutions in the country. A wealthy institution that can offer university resources to a small-college student body, Wesleyan also has a long tradition of academic innovation. The hilltop campus is located in the rural center of the state in a large town of 45,000, about midway between New York and Boston, and 30 minutes drive from Hartford and New Haven. Most convenient major airport: Hartford-Bradley International.

Founded: 1831
Affiliation: Independent
UG Enrollment: 1,378 M, 1,330 W (full-time)
Total Enrollment: 3,404
Cost: $10K–$20K
% Receiving Financial Aid: 40%
Admission: Most Selective
Application Deadline: January 15

Admission is among the most selective in the country. About 40% of applicants accepted, 37% of these actually enroll; 89% of ranked freshmen graduate in top fifth of high school class, 99% in top two-fifths. Average freshman SAT scores, according to most recent data available: 616 M, 616 W verbal, 686 M, 651 W mathematical; 94% of freshmen score above 500 on verbal, 64% above 600, 14% above 700; 98% score above 500 on mathematical, 86% above 600, 39% above 700. *Required:* SAT and 3 ACH including English, or ACT; interview strongly recommended. *Non-academic factors* considered in admissions: "strong character traits, unique background." Entrance programs: early decision, midyear admission, deferred admission, advanced placement. About 30% of entering students from private schools, 7% from parochial schools. *Apply* by January 15. *Transfers* welcome.

Academic Environment. Wesleyan has, for some years, allowed a significant measure of student self-determination in academic matters. There are no university-wide requirements for course distribution. Pressures for academic achievement, nevertheless, appear very intense; an exceptionally able and highly motivated student body seems to make competition very keen. Campus atmosphere is both scholarly and career oriented, but remains highly individual and activist "despite the conforming pressures of the 80s." Although no courses required for graduation, university guidelines include recommendation that students plan work in each of 3 broad areas: arts and humanities, social and behavioral sciences, natural sciences and mathematics. Distinctive programs include: Colleges of Letters, Social Studies and Science in Society, 3-year programs of interdisciplinary study; emphasis on tutorial approach with independent study, faculty evaluations and comprehensive examinations in lieu of classroom schedules and periodic testing and grades. The centers for Humanities, Arts, residential and performing facilities bring distinguished scholars and artists to campus for extended study and workshops as well as lectures, exhibits and performances. *Degree:* AB. *Majors offered* include usual arts and sciences, anthropology, astronomy, computer science, environmental sciences, East Asian studies, Latin American studies, linguistics, theater; interdepartmental majors including mathematics/economics, biology/psychology, sociology/psychology; student-designed interdepartmental majors also possible. New departments of Molecular Biology and Biochemistry, and Cognitive Science recently added; new program in neuroscience and behavior. Computer facilities reported as adequate to meet student demand.

About 90% of students entering as freshmen graduate eventually; 5% of freshmen do not return for sophomore year. *Special programs:* independent study, study abroad, honors, undergraduate research, Washington Semester, summer intensive language program, 3–2 engineering with Columbia, Washington U. and Cal Tech, concurrent AB and MA, African American studies, Twelve College Exchange, field work for credit, cross-registration with Connecticut College and Trinity. Adult students: MA in Liberal Studies. *Library:* 1,080,545 monographs, and periodicals; rare documents collection; Book-Sharing Program with Trinity and Connecticut College; open-stack privileges; hours vary. *Calendar:* semester.

Undergraduate degrees conferred (672). 29% were in Social Sciences, 22% were in Letters, 11% were in Area and Ethnic Studies, 10% were in Visual and Performing Arts, 7% were in Psychology, 6% were in Multi/Interdisciplinary Studies, 5% were in Life Sciences, 3% were in Philosophy and Religion, 3% were in Physical Sciences, 3% were in Foreign Languages, remainder in Mathematics.

Graduates Career Data. According to most recent data available, full-time graduate study pursued immediately after graduation by 16% of students; 3% enter medical school; 4% enter law school; 1% enter business school. Medical schools typically enrolling largest numbers of graduates include Albert Einstein, Harvard, Mt. Sinai, Yale, Columbia, U. Conn.; law schools include Columbia, NYU, Georgetown, Harvard; business schools include Harvard, Penn, Columbia, Dartmouth. *Careers in business and industry* pursued by 73% of graduates. Employers typically hiring largest numbers of graduates include ICF, Toddler U., Teach for America, Morgan Guarantee Trust.

Faculty. About 80% of faculty hold PhD or equivalent.

Student Body. University seeks a national student body; 11% of students from in state; 45% of students from Middle Atlantic; 41% New England; 11% West; 7% North Central; 5% South. An estimated 10% of students reported as Black, 8% Asian, 4% Hispanic.

Religious Orientation. An independent institution, Wesleyan makes no religious demands on students. Protestant, Catholic, and ecumenical services held Sundays in the Memorial Chapel; Jewish chaplain on campus. Places of worship and fellowship groups available on campus for 3 major faiths, in Middletown for these and other faiths.

Varsity Sports. Men (Div.III): Baseball, Basketball, Crew, Cross Country, Football, Golf, Hockey, Lacrosse, Soccer, Squash, Swimming, Tennis, Track, Wrestling. Women (Div.III): Basketball, Crew, Cross Country, Field Hockey, Ice Hockey, Lacrosse, Soccer, Softball, Squash, Swimming, Tennis, Track, Volleyball.

Campus Life. Students largely responsible for regulating their own social life. New "Area Coordinators" are enhancing and helping to direct the social life. Wesleyan can accommodate almost any lifestyle on its cosmopolitan campus. As one student leader notes, "there are virtually no rules." Wesleyan has for many years sought capable minority students who now comprise 20% of the student body. Fraternities minor factor on campus; no sororities; some women join fraternities, but "not many." Several residential units organized as living/learning centers; each of the two colleges operates in a dormitory setting. Students with grievances have access to the 3 university Ombudsmen. Cars permitted for all except students on financial aid.

About 81% of students live in coed dormitories; 14% live in off-campus housing. Freshmen given preference in college housing if all students cannot be accommodated. Sexes segregated in coed dormitories either by wing or floor. There are 8 fraternities (some coed), 1 sorority on campus which about 10% of students join; 5% of men live in fraternities.

Annual Costs. Tuition and fees, $18,780; room and board, $5,390; estimated $1,000 other, exclusive of travel. About 40% of students receive financial aid; assistance is typically divided 70% scholarship, 20% loan, 10% work. University reports scholarships awarded only on the basis of need. *Meeting Costs:* university offers installment plans.

West Chester University of Pennsylvania

West Chester, Pennsylvania 19383 (215) 436-3411

A state-supported, multi-purpose university located in a town of 22,000, 25 miles west of Philadelphia. Formerly known as West Chester State College. Most convenient major airport: Philadelphia International.

Founded: 1871
Affiliation: State
UG Enrollment: 2,920 M, 4,763 W (full-time); 906 M, 1,193 W (part-time)
Total Enrollment: 11,806
Cost: < $10K
Admission: Non-selective
Application Deadline: November 15

Admission. About 54% of applicants accepted, 39% of these actually enroll; 29% of freshmen graduate in top fifth of high school class, 68% in top two-fifths. Average freshman scores: SAT, 450 verbal, 495 mathematical. *Required:* SAT or ACT, personal essay, minimum H.S. GPA of 2.0. Criteria considered in admissions, in order of importance: high school academic record, standardized tests, writing sample, recommendations, extracurricular activities; other factors considered: special talents, alumni children, diverse student body. *Out-of-state* freshman applicants: university actively seeks students from out of state. State limits out-of-state enrollment to 35% of entering class. *Out-of-state* applicants not eligible for special admissions options. About 53% of out-of-state applicants accepted, 28% of these actually enroll. States from which most out-of-state applicants are drawn include New Jersey, New York, Maryland, Delaware. *Entrance programs:* early admission, midyear admission, deferred admission. About 21% of entering students from private and parochial schools. *Apply* by November 15; rolling admissions. *Transfers* welcome; 847 enrolled 1993–94.

Academic Environment. Degrees offered: associates, bachelors, masters. *Undergraduate studies* offered by college of Arts and Sciences, schools of Education, Health Sciences, Music, and Business and Public Affairs. *Majors offered* include communication disorders, athletic training, public health, pre-med. Average undergraduate class size: 35.

About 25% of students entering as freshmen graduate in four years, 51% eventually; 80% of students entering as freshmen return for sophomore year. *Special programs:* CLEP, independent study, January term, study abroad, National Student Exchange, undergraduate research, honors, internships, 3–2 in engineering, physics, individualized majors, oceanography program, cross registration with Cheyney U. *Calendar:* semester, summer school.

Undergraduate degrees conferred (1,526). 31% were in Education, 17% were in Business and Management, 9% were in Liberal/General Studies, 8% were in Letters, 7% were in Protective Services, 6% were in Health Sciences, 4% were in Social Sciences, 4% were in Psychology, 3% were in Life Sciences, remainder in 10 other fields.

Graduates Career Data. Advanced studies pursued immediately after graduation by 19% of students. About 76% of 1992–93 graduates employed. Employers typically hiring largest number of graduates include John Hancock, Hewlett Packard, Education. Career Development Services include on-campus recruitment, aptitude testing, counseling, placement service, resume/interview workshops, library resources, internships, career fair.

Faculty. About 67% of faculty hold PhD or equivalent. All of tenured faculty teach undergraduate classes. About 43% of teaching faculty are female; 6% Black, 2% Hispanic, 3% other minority.

Student Body. University does not seek a national student body; 82% of students from in state; 99% Middle Atlantic. An estimated 34% of students reported as Protestant, 46% Catholic, 5% Jewish, 4% Muslim; 7% Black, 1% Hispanic, 2% Asian. Average age of undergraduate student: 23.

Varsity Sports. Men (Div.II): Baseball (I), Basketball, Cross Country, Diving, Football, Golf, Lacrosse, Soccer, Swimming, Tennis, Track. Women (Div.II): Basketball, Cross Country, Diving, Field Hockey (I), Gymnastics, Lacrosse, Soccer, Softball, Swimming, Tennis, Track, Volleyball.

Campus Life. About 3% of women live in traditional dormitories; 40% of students live in coed dormitories; 57% of students commute. Sexes segregated in coed dormitories either by wing or room. There are 15 fraternities, 11 sororities on campus which about 10% of men, 7% of women join. About 50% of resident students leave campus on weekends.

Annual Costs. Tuition and fees, $2,954 (out-of-state, $7,352); room and board, $3,988; estimated $1,000 other, exclusive of travel. Average amount of financial assistance, $929– 3,098. Assistance is typically divided 35% scholarship, 65% grant. University reports 803 scholarships awarded for special talents, 823 for need. *Meeting Costs:* university offers monthly payment plan.

West Coast University

Los Angeles, California 90020 (213) 487-4433; (800) 248-4WCU

An independent, commuter institution offering only evening classes; majority of student body already employed in business, industry, or government. Main campus in Los Angeles; branch campuses in Southern California offer same curricula. Most convenient major airport: Los Angeles International.

Founded: 1909
Affiliation: Independent
Total Enrollment: 900 M, 600 W
Cost: < $10K
% Receiving Financial Aid: 25%
Admission: Non-selective
Application Deadline: Rolling

Admission. Graduates of recognized high schools, or nongraduates with evidence of comparable academic achievement, eligible; 44% of applicants accepted. *Required:* work experience of at least 3 years. *Apply:* rolling admissions; 6 admissions dates. *Transfers* welcome; most students apply as transfer students.

Academic Environment. Degrees offered: associates, bachelors, masters. WCU offers Bachelor's and Master's degrees in business and management, computer science and engineering; programs are offered at night only. Terms start every other month. About 15% of general education requirements for graduation are elective; distribution requirements fairly numerous. Special programs: certificate program in computer graphics for artists and designers, independent study. *Calendar:* 6 8-week terms.

Undergraduate degrees conferred (72). 43% were in Engineering, 26% were in Computer and Engineering Related Technology, 22% were in Business and Management, 8% were in Engineering and Engineering Related Technology.

Campus Life. University does not seek a national student body; 85% of students from in state; 325 foreign students. West Coast is an independent institution, makes no religious demands on students. No dormitories on campus.

Annual Costs. Tuition and fees, $300 per unit plus $20 term registration fee. About 25% of students receive financial aid; average amount of assistance, $7,500. College reports scholarships awarded only on basis of need.

West Georgia College

Carrollton, Georgia 30118 (404) 836-6416

A state-supported college, located in a community of 25,000, 50 miles west of Atlanta. Most convenient major airport: Atlanta.

Founded: 1933
Affiliation: State
UG Enrollment: 1,850 M, 2,688 W (full-time); 437 M, 752 W (part-time)
Total Enrollment: 7,917
Cost: < $10K
% Receiving Financial Aid: 48%
Admission: Non-selective
Application Deadline: Rolling

Admission. Graduates of accredited high schools, with 18 units (15 in academic subjects), eligible; 73% of applicants accepted, 50% of these actually enroll. Average freshman scores: SAT, 415 M, 398 W verbal, 472 M, 431 W mathematical; ACT, 20 M, 20 W composite. *Required:* SAT or ACT, minimum H.S. GPA. Criteria considered in admissions, in order of importance: high school academic record, standardized tests. *Out-of-state* freshman applicants: college does not seek students from out of state. State does not limit out-of-state enrollment. About 92% of out-of-state applicants accepted, 58% of these actually enroll. States from which most out-of-state applicants are drawn include Alabama, Florida. *Apply*: rolling admissions. *Transfers* welcome; 461 enrolled 1993–94.

Academic Environment. Degrees offered: associates, bachelors, masters. General education requirements for graduation include 20 hours in each of three areas: humanities, science and mathematics, social sciences. *Majors offered* include international economic affairs. Average undergraduate class size: 60% under 20, 34% between 20–40, 6% over 40. About 9% of entering freshmen graduate in four years, 30% eventually; 60% of freshmen return for sophomore year. *Special programs:* CLEP, Dalton External Degree Program, The Newman Center, independent study, study abroad, honors, 3–2 in engineering, cross registration with Georgia Tech., U. of Georgia. *Calendar:* quarter, summer school.

Undergraduate degrees conferred (748). 37% were in Business and Management, 22% were in Education, 8% were in Psychology, 6% were in Social Sciences, 5% were in Visual and Performing Arts, 5% were in Communications, 4% were in Protective Services, 3% were in Letters, remainder in 8 other fields.

Graduates Career Data. About 80% of 1992–93 graduates employed. Career Development Services include on-campus recruitment, resume and interview workshops, placement services, internships and co-op education, extensive library resources, counseling services.

Faculty. About 76% of faculty hold PhD or equivalent. About 46% of undergraduate classes taught by tenured faculty. About 33% of teaching faculty are female; 4% minority.

Student Body. College does seek a national student body; 96% of students from in state; 1% Foreign. An estimated 16% of students reported as Black, 1% Hispanic, 1% Asian. Average age of undergraduate student: 23.7.

Varsity Sports. Men (Div.II): Baseball, Basketball, Cross Country, Football, Golf, Tennis. Women (Div.II; NAIA): Basketball, Cross Country, Softball, Tennis, Volleyball.

Campus Life. The campus offers a unique blend of old and new architecture surrounded by a wide variety of trees, shrubs and gardens. About 7% of men, 10% of women live in traditional dormitories; 2% of men, 4% of women in coed dormitories; 79% of men, 81% of women commute. Intervisitation in men's and women's dormitory rooms limited. Sexes segregated in coed dormitories by wing or room. There are 10 fraternities, 9 sororities on campus which about 24% of men, 14% of women join; about 12% of men, 5% of women live in fraternities and sororities. About 80% of resident students leave campus on weekends.

Annual Costs. Tuition and fees, $1,766 (out-of-state, $4,528); room and board, $2,490; estimated $1,800 other, exclusive of travel. About 48% of students receive financial aid; average amount of assistance, $3,400. Assistance is typically divided 20% scholarship, 10% grant, 60% loan, 10% work. College reports some scholarships awarded on the basis of academic merit alone.

West Liberty State College

West Liberty, West Virginia 26003 (304) 336-8076

A state-supported college, located in a small village, 8 miles north of Wheeling. Most convenient major airport: Pittsburgh, PA.

Founded: 1837
Affiliation: State
UG Enrollment: 1,042 M, 1,096 W (full-time); 103 M, 124 W (part-time)
Cost: < $10K
% Receiving Financial Aid: 55%
Admission: Non-selective
Application Deadline: August 1

Admission. Graduates of accredited high schools with minimum GPA of 2.0 eligible; 91% of applicants accepted, 45% of these actually enroll. Average freshman ACT scores: 20 composite. *Required:* SAT or ACT. Criteria considered in admissions: high school academic record and standardized test scores. *Out-of-state* freshman applicants: college actively seeks students from out of state. State does not limit out-of-state enrollment. About 87% of out-of-state students accepted, 38% of these actually enroll. States from which most out-of-state students are drawn include Ohio, Pennsylvania. *Entrance programs:* midyear admission, advanced placement, rolling admission. *Apply* by August 1. *Transfers* welcome; 224 enrolled 1993–94.

Academic Environment. Graduation requirements vary for BA and BS candidates, but both include courses in communications, fine arts and humanities, natural science and mathematics, social science and history, physical education and health. Students cite "helpful" faculty and academic field work as strengths of the academic program. Degrees offered: bachelors. *Majors offered* include computer science, energy management, fashion marketing, nursing, aviation science. About 49% of students entering as freshmen graduate within five years; 66% of freshmen return for sophomore year. *Special programs:* CLEP, independent study, honors, undergraduate research. *Calendar:* semester, summer school.

Undergraduate degrees conferred (378). 35% were in Education, 26% were in Business and Management, 9% were in Allied Health, 8% were in Multi/Interdisciplinary Studies, 6% were in Protective Services, 3% were in Psychology, 3% were in Communications, 3% were in Life Sciences, remainder in 8 other fields.

Graduates Career Data. According to most recent data available, full-time graduate or professional study pursued by 15% of students immediately after graduation. *Careers in business and industry* pursued by 47% of graduates.

Faculty. About 33% of faculty hold PhD or equivalent.

Student Body. About 69% of students from in state; 99% Midwest. An estimated 25% of students reported as Protestant, 24% Catholic, 4% other; 2% as Black.

Varsity Sports. Men (NAIA): Baseball, Basketball, Football, Golf, Tennis, Wrestling. Women (NAIA): Basketball, Softball, Tennis, Volleyball.

Campus Life. Campus is located in a rural area six miles from Olgebay Park (a family resort), ten miles from Wheeling, and an hour from Pittsburgh, PA. Students report studying and sports take "a major part of students' time."

About 52% of men, 54% of women live in traditional dormitories; 48% of men, 46% of women commute. Freshmen given preference in college housing if all students cannot be accommodated. Intervisitation in men's and women's dormitory rooms limited. There are 6 fraternities, 4 sororities on campus which about 19% of men, 12% of women join. About 50% of resident students leave campus on weekends.

Annual Costs. Tuition and fees, $1,800 (out-of-state, $3,870); room and board, $2,890; estimated $800 other, exclusive of travel. About 55% of students receive financial aid; average amount of assistance, $3,034. Assistance is typically divided 15% scholarship, 39% grant, 40% loan, 6% work. University reports 122 scholarships awarded on the basis of academic merit alone, 62 for special talents alone.

West Texas State University

Canyon, Texas 79016 (806) 656-2000

A state-supported university, located in a town of 8,500, 17 miles south of Amarillo. Most convenient major airport: Amarillo.

Founded: 1910
Affiliation: State
UG Enrollment: 4,632 M, W (full-time)
Cost: < $10K
Admission: Non-selective
Application Deadline: August 22

Admission. Graduates of accredited high schools with 16 units (7 in academic subjects) with minimum SAT/ACT scores of 830/18 and rank in top half of class eligible; others admitted by examination; 84% of applicants accepted, 67% of these actually enroll; 28% of freshmen graduate in top fifth of high school class, 70% in top two-fifths. *Required:* ACT or SAT. *Out-of-state* freshman applicants: university seeks students from out of state. State does not limit out-of-state enrollment. *Apply* by August 22. *Transfers* welcome.
Academic Environment. *Undergraduate studies* offered by colleges of Agriculture, Nursing and Natural Sciences; Business; Education and Social Sciences; Fine Arts and Humanities. About 37% of students entering as freshmen graduate within four years; 52% of freshmen return for sophomore year. *Special programs:* CLEP, honors, challenge examinations. *Calendar:* semester, summer school.
Undergraduate degrees conferred (886). 30% were in Education, 24% were in Business and Management, 11% were in Health Sciences, 8% were in Liberal/General Studies, 5% were in Public Affairs, 3% were in Visual and Performing Arts, remainder in 17 other fields.
Campus Life. About 24% of men, 22% of women live in traditional dormitories; no coed dormitories; rest live in off-campus housing or commute. Intervisitation in men's and women's dormitory rooms limited. There are 6 fraternities, 3 sororities on campus which about 8% of men, 9% of women join. About 50% of resident students leave campus on weekends.
Annual Costs. Tuition and fees, $1,466 (out-of-state, $5,866); room and board, $2,588. About 35% of students receive financial aid; assistance is typically divided 55% scholarship, 29% loan, 16% work. College reports some scholarships awarded on the basis of academic merit alone. *Meeting Costs:* college offers Parent PLUS Loans.

West Virginia Institute of Technology

Montgomery, West Virginia 25136 **(304) 442-3071**

A state-supported institution, located in a town of 2,500, 25 miles southeast of Charleston; 2-year degree and 1-year certificate programs also offered. Most convenient major airport: Charleston, WV.

Founded: 1895
Affiliation: State
UG Enrollment: 1,514 M, 726 W (full-time); 248 M, 316 W (part-time)
Cost: < $10K
% Receiving Financial Aid: 43%
Admission: Non-selective
Application Deadline: August 1

Admission. West Virginia high school graduates eligible; 98% of applicants accepted, 42% of these actually enroll. Average freshman ACT scores: 21 M, 19 W composite. *Required:* ACT or SAT; minimum high school GPA. Criteria considered in admissions, in order of importance: high school academic record, standardized test scores, recommendations, extracurricular activities, writing sample. *Out-of-state* freshman applicants: institute actively seeks students from out of state. State does not limit out-of-state enrollment. Required for out of state students: 2.0 GPA, 17 ACT, 690 SAT. States from which most out-of-state students are drawn: Virginia, Maryland. *Apply* by August 1; rolling admission. *Transfers* welcome; 114 enrolled 1993–94.
Academic Environment. Graduation requirements include 4 units of English, 3 units of social studies, 2 units each of lab science, and mathematics. Degrees offered: associates, bachelors, masters. Unusual, new, or notable majors include: printing technology, printing management, nursing, industrial technology. Average undergraduate class size: 16. About 75% of students entering as freshmen graduate eventually; 70% of freshmen return for sophomore year. *Special programs:* CLEP, independent study, undergraduate research, credit by examination, cooperative work/study program. *Calendar:* semester, summer school.
Undergraduate degrees conferred (325). 44% were in Engineering, 17% were in Business and Management, 9% were in Education, 8% were in Precision Production, 6% were in Multi/Interdisciplinary Studies, 6% were in Computer and Engineering Related Technology, 4% were in Health Sciences, remainder in 6 other fields.
Graduates Career Data. Advanced studies pursued by 10% of graduates; 8% enter graduate school. Fields typically hiring largest numbers of graduates include engineering. Career Development Services include resume preparation, job fairs, referral, career counseling, careers library, job interviews, national data bank membership.
Faculty. About 46% of faculty hold PhD or equivalent. About 62% of undergraduate classes taught by tenured faculty. About 25% of teaching faculty are female; 4% minority.
Student Body. About 86% of students from West Virginia. An estimated 7% of students reported as Black, 3% Asian. Average age of undergraduate student: 22.
Varsity Sports. Men (WVAIC/NAIA): Baseball, Basketball, Football, Tennis. Women (WVAIC/NAIA): Basketball, Softball, Tennis, Volleyball.
Campus Life. About 38% of men, 50% of women live in traditional dormitories; 62% of men, 50% of women commute. Intervisitation in men's and women's dormitory rooms limited. Sexes segregated in coed dormitory by "module." There are 8 fraternities, 4 sororities on campus which about 9% of men, 8% of women join. About 50% of resident students leave campus on weekends.
Annual Costs. Tuition and fees, $1,998 (out-of-state, $4,472); room and board, $1,860; estimated $500–1,000 other, exclusive of travel. About 43% of students receive financial aid; average amount of assistance, $3,174. College reports some scholarships awarded on the basis of academic merit alone. *Meeting Costs:* institute offers cooperative education and encourages students to alternate semesters of study and work.

West Virginia State College

Institute, West Virginia 25112 **(304) 766-3221**

A state-supported college, located in a small village, 8 miles west of Charleston (pop. 71,500); founded as a college for Negroes, but now serves a fully integrated, predominantly white student body. Most convenient major airport: Charleston, WV.

Founded: 1891
Affiliation: State
UG Enrollment: 1,390 M, 1,427 W (full-time); 764 M, 1,175 W (part-time)
Cost: < $10K
% Receiving Financial Aid: 44%
Admission: Non-selective
Application Deadline: August 10

Admission. Graduates of accredited high schools with minimum 2.5 GPA eligible; 91% of applicants accepted, 25% of these actually enroll. Average freshman ACT scores: 13.2 composite. *Required:* ACT. Criteria considered in admissions, in order of importance: standardized test scores, high school academic record, recommendations, extracurricular activities, writing sample. *Out-of-state* freshman applicants: college actively seeks students from out-of-state. State does not limit out-of-state enrollment. About 61% of out-of-state applicants accepted. States from which most out-of-state students are drawn include New York, Virginia, Rhode Island. *Entrance programs:* early admission, midyear admission, advanced placement. *Apply* by August 10. *Transfers* welcome; 273 enrolled 1993–94.
Academic Environment. Degrees offered: associates, bachelors. About 23% of general education requirements for graduation are elective; distribution requirements limited. Unusual majors offered include nuclear medicine technology. About 51% of entering freshmen graduate eventually; 70% of entering freshmen return for sophomore year. *Special programs:* CLEP, study abroad, honors, independent study, internships, cooperative work study, programs for non-traditional students. *Library:* government depository since 1907. *Calendar:* semester, summer school.
Undergraduate degrees conferred (453). 24% were in Multi/Interdisciplinary Studies, 21% were in Education, 21% were in Business and Management, 10% were in Protective Services, 5% were in Communications, 4% were in Social Sciences, 4% were in Psychology, 3% were in Mathematics, remainder in 7 other fields.
Faculty. About 27% of faculty hold PhD or equivalent. About 49% of undergraduate classes taught by tenured faculty. About 45% of teaching faculty are female.
Student Body. About 96% of students from in state. An estimated 13% of students reported as Black, 1% other minority. Average age of undergraduate student: 26.
Varsity Sports. Men (NAIA): Baseball, Basketball, Cheerleading, Cross Country, Football, Track. Women (NAIA): Basketball, Cheerleading, Cross Country, Softball, Track.
Campus Life. About 9% of students live in traditional dormitories; rest live in off-campus housing or commute. Freshmen given prefer-

ence in college housing if all students cannot be accommodated. There are 6 fraternities, 4 sororities on campus.
Annual Costs. Tuition and fees, $1,894 (out-of-state, $4,294); room and board, $3,150. About 44% of students receive financial aid; average amount of assistance, $1,340. College reports some scholarships awarded on the basis of academic merit alone.

West Virginia University

Morgantown, West Virginia 26506-6001 (800) 344-WVU1

A state-supported, land-grant institution located in a community of 47,000, 75 miles south of Pittsburgh. The university also maintains several academic centers throughout the state. Most convenient major airport: Pittsburgh, PA; commuter flights to Morgantown.

Founded: 1867
Affiliation: State
UG Enrollment: 7,939 M, 6,585 W (full-time)
Total Enrollment: 23,080
Cost: < $10K
% Receiving Financial Aid: 56%
Admission: Non-selective
Application Deadline: May 1

Admission varies somewhat between individual colleges. For all schools, 81% of applicants accepted, 37% of these actually enroll. Average freshman scores: SAT, 435 M, 443 W verbal, 519 M, 491 W mathematical; ACT, 22.5 M, 21.8 W composite. *Required:* ACT or SAT; minimum high school GPA 2.0 (WV resident); for Engineering (WV resident): ACT mathematics score of 25 (SAT: 500) or GPA of 3.0 plus ACT of 21 (SAT: 450); portfolio for art; audition for music. Criteria considered in admissions, in order of importance: high school academic record and standardized test scores, extracurricular activities; other factors considered: special talents, diverse student body.

Out-of-state freshman applicants: university actively seeks students from out of state. State does not limit out-of-state enrollment. Requirement for out-of-state applicants: 2.25 average or ACT/SAT of 20/820 combined; for Engineering: ACT mathematics score of 25 (SAT: 500) (there are only a limited number of places available for out-of-state Engineering applicants, early application is "strongly encouraged"). About 76% of out-of-state applicants accepted, 68% of these actually enroll. States from which most out-of-state students are drawn include Maryland, Virginia, Pennsylvania, New Jersey, New York, Ohio. *Entrance programs:* early admission, midyear admission, deferred admission, advanced placement. *Apply* by May 1; rolling admissions. *Transfers* welcome; 804 accepted 1993–94.
Academic Environment. Graduation requirements: all students must fulfill the Liberal Studies Program requirements, which are divided into skills and distribution components. The skills component requires one course in college level math or statistics, English 1 and 2 and one course with a substantial writing component. In addition, the distribution component requires 12 credit hours in each of 3 Clusters: Humanities and Fine Arts, Social and Behavioral Sciences, and Natural Sciences and Mathematics. These 36 hours must include 1 class in international or minority cultures or issues of gender. *Undergraduate studies* offered by colleges of Arts and Sciences, Agriculture and Forestry, Creative Arts, Business and Economics, Engineering, Journalism, Mineral and Energy Resources, Social Work, schools of Dentistry (Dental Hygiene), Nursing, Pharmacy, Physical Education, Medicine (Medical Technology and Physical Therapy), upper division College of Human Resources and Education accepts limited number of freshmen in selected programs. Average undergraduate class size: 40% under 20, 38% 20–40, 22% over 40.

About 25% of students entering as freshmen graduate within four years, 50% within five years; 77% of freshmen return for sophomore year. *Special programs:* CLEP, January Term, independent study, Academic Common Market, study abroad, honors, undergraduate research, individualized majors, credit by examination. Adult programs: Board of Regents Bachelor of Arts for students out of high school at least 5 years, includes credit for life experience. *Calendar:* semester, summer school.
Undergraduate degrees conferred (2,382). 18% were in Business and Management, 10% were in Education, 9% were in Engineering, 9% were in Health Sciences, 8% were in Social Sciences, 8% were in Communications, 5% were in Liberal/General Studies, 5% were in Psychology, 4% were in Multi/Interdisciplinary Studies, 3% were in Home Economics, 3% were in Letters, 3% were in Visual and Performing Arts, remainder in 13 other fields.
Graduates Career Data. Advanced studies pursued by 33% of graduates; 12% enter business school; 5% enter law school. Business schools typically enrolling largest numbers of graduates include West Virginia U., U.of Pittsburgh, Pennsylvania State; law schools include West Virginia U. About 88% of 1992–93 graduates employed. Employers typically hiring largest numbers of graduates include Union Carbide, General Electric, Pepsi, U.S. Government. Career Services Center claims a 90% job placement rate; offers SIGI computer program, assistance with summer employment, internships, resource material, career counseling.
Faculty. About 82% of faculty hold PhD or equivalent. About 26% of teaching faculty are female; 2% Black, 2% Hispanic, 6% other minority.
Student Body. About 55% of students from in state; 60% Midwest, 30% Middle Atlantic, 5% South, 2% foreign. An estimated 3% of students reported as Black, 2% Asian, 1% Hispanic, 3% other minority. *Minority group students:* financial, academic, and social aid available.
Varsity Sports. Men (Div.I): Baseball, Basketball, Cross Country, Diving, Football (I-A), Riflery, Soccer, Swimming, Tennis, Track, Wrestling. Women (Div.I): Basketball, Cross Country, Diving, Riflery, Gymnastics, Swimming, Tennis, Track, Volleyball.
Campus Life. West Virginia reports interest in fraternities/sororities, varsity/intramural athletics and ROTC. Cars allowed, but parking is limited (a university publication warns "The easiest way to get around Morgantown is astral projection, but if you're not quite accomplished at that, try walking."). University is served by the Personal Rapid Transit. Freshmen under 21 required to live in university-supervised housing; limited intervisitation privileges, each floor determines hours within regulations. Alcohol limited by state law to those over 21.

About 15% of men, 15% of women live in traditional residence halls; 1% men, 1% women in coed residence halls; 69% of men, 71% of women live in off-campus housing; 10% of men, 10% of women commute. Freshmen given preference in college housing if all students cannot be accommodated. There are 23 fraternities, 13 sororities on campus which about 20% of men, 20% of women join; 5% of men, 3% of women live in fraternities and sororities.
Annual Costs. Tuition and fees, $2,026 (out-of-state, $5,870); room and board, $4,156. About 56% of students receive financial aid. University reports some scholarships awarded on the basis of academic merit alone. *Meeting Costs:* university offers AMS tuition pre-payment plan.

West Virginia Wesleyan College

Buckhannon, West Virginia 26201 (304) 473-8000

A church-related college, located in a community of 8,000, 138 miles south of Pittsburgh. Most convenient major airport: Pittsburgh, PA or Clarksburg.

Founded: 1890
Affiliation: United Methodist
UG Enrollment: 744 M, 765 W (full-time); 53 M, 117 W (part-time)
Total Enrollment: 1,755
Cost: $10K–$20K
% Receiving Financial Aid: 77%
Admission: Non-selective
Application Deadline: Aug. 1

Admission. Graduates of accredited high schools eligible; 82% of applicants accepted, 34% of these actually enroll. Average freshman scores: SAT, 427 M, 450 W verbal, 501 M, 479 W mathematical; ACT, 23 M, 23 W composite. *Required:* SAT or ACT, interview. Criteria considered in admissions, in order of importance: high school academic record, strength of high school curriculum, recommendations, extracurricular activities, writing sample, standardized test scores; other factors considered: special talents, diverse student body. *Entrance programs:* early admission, deferred admission. *Apply:* August 1; rolling admissions. *Transfers* welcome; 63 enrolled 1993–94.
Academic Environment. Graduation requirements include general studies program which makes up about one-third of graduation requirements. Student feels academic program is "comprehensive" and "focuses on fundamentals". Degrees offered: bachelors, masters. *Majors offered* include business administration, computer science,

education, teaching field in specific learning disabilities, electrical engineering, human ecology, nursing, public administration, public relations, sports medicine, finance. About 51% of students entering as freshmen graduate eventually; 78% of freshmen return for sophomore year. *Special programs:* CLEP, honors undergraduate research, independent study, semester or year study abroad, optional January interterm, individualized majors, acceleration, credit by examination, contract learning, 3–2 with Duke School of Forestry and Environmental Studies, 3–2 in engineering, 5-year program leading to MS in aeronautical engineering in cooperation with NASA-Langley Research Center. *Calendar:* 4–1–4, summer school.

Undergraduate degrees conferred (232). 21% were in Business and Management, 16% were in Education, 13% were in Social Sciences, 9% were in Psychology, 6% were in Health Sciences, 6% were in Life Sciences, 5% were in Engineering, 4% were in Letters, 4% were in Marketing and Distribution, remainder in 9 other fields.

Graduates Career Data. According to most recent data available, full-time graduate or professional study pursued immediately after graduation by 22% of students; 3% enter law school; 6% enter business school.

Faculty. About 62% of faculty hold PhD or equivalent.

Student Body. About 33% of students from in state; 45% Midwest, 34% Middle Atlantic, 3% foreign. An estimated 47% of students reported as Protestants, 21% Catholic, 1% Jewish, 19% unaffiliated, 1% other; 5% as Black, 1% Hispanic, 1% Asian, 13% other minority.

Religious Orientation. West Virginia Wesleyan is a church-related institution; 1 religious course required of all students.

Varsity Sports. Men (NAIA 1, NCAA Div.II): Baseball, Basketball, Cross Country, Football, Golf, Soccer, Swimming, Tennis, Track. Women (NAIA I, NCAA Div.II): Basketball, Cross Country, Soccer, Softball, Swimming, Tennis, Track, Volleyball.

Campus Life. Campus is located in a rural area; student reports students rely primarily on the school for social engagements. Students participate in clubs and organizations, sports (varsity and intramural), "many performance opportunities", including choir and drama productions.

About 70% of men, 80% of women live in traditional dormitories; 20% of men, 20% of women commute. Intervisitation in men's and women's dormitory rooms limited. There are 4 fraternities, 4 sororities on campus which about 26% of men, 26% of women join; 10% of men live in fraternities, sororities provide no residence facilities. About 10% of resident students leave campus on weekends.

Annual Costs. Tuition and fees, $13,400; room and board, $3,500; estimated $450 other, exclusive of travel. About 77% of students receive financial aid; assistance is typically divided 67% scholarship/grant, 28% loan, 5% work. College reports some scholarships awarded on the basis of academic merit alone. *Meeting Costs:* college offers tuition payment plan.

Westbrook College

Portland, Maine 04103 **(207) 797-7261**

An independent institution founded primarily as a 2-year college for women, Westbrook admits men as full-time students to both its 2- and 4-year degree programs. The campus is located in a city of 72,000. Most convenient major airport: Portland International.

Founded: 1831
Affiliation: Independent
UG Enrollment: 382 M, W (full-time)
Cost: $10K–$20K
% Receiving Financial Aid: 75%
Admission: Non-selective
Application Deadline: Rolling

Admission. High school graduates preferably with college preparatory subjects eligible; 82% of applicants accepted, 54% of these actually enroll; 21% of freshmen graduate in top fifth of high school class, 48% in top two-fifths. *Required:* SAT or ACT. *Apply:* no specific deadline. *Transfers* welcome.

Academic Environment. Westbrook offers 4-year programs in medical technology, business administration, early childhood education, nursing, dental hygiene, accounting, management, computer information systems, retail management and marketing. *Degrees:* AB, BS, BSMT. About 65% of students entering as freshmen graduate eventually; 80% of freshmen return for sophomore year. *Special programs:* independent study, individualized majors. Adult programs: Continuing Education Division offers programs in business and liberal arts. *Calendar:* semester.

Undergraduate degrees conferred (30). 67% were in Business and Management, 17% were in Allied Health, 17% were in Computer and Engineering Related Technology.

Student Body. About 90% of students from New England; 2% Middle Atlantic. An estimated 1% of students reported as Black, 4% Asian.

Campus Life. About 15% of women live in traditional dormitories; 95% of men, 45% of women live in coed dormitories; rest commute. Intervisitation in men's and women's dormitory rooms limited. There are no fraternities or sororities. About 30% of resident students leave campus on weekends.

Annual Costs. Tuition and fees, $11,000; room and board, $4,900. About 75% of students receive financial aid; assistance is typically divided 40% scholarship, 45% loan, 15% work. College reports some scholarships awarded on the basis of academic merit alone. *Meeting Costs:* college offers AMS monthly payment plan.

Western Baptist College

Salem, Oregon 97301 **(503) 375-7005**

A Christian, liberal arts college, offering professional training for church-related, teaching, business, and other vocations.

Founded: 1935
Affiliation: Independent
UG Enrollment: 229 M, 284 W (full-time)
Cost: < $10K
% Receiving Financial Aid: 86%
Admission: Non-selective
Application Deadline: Aug. 15

Admission. About 82% of freshmen applicants accepted, 58% of these actually enroll. *Required:* SAT or ACT; minimum high school GPA, essay, references. Criteria considered in admissions, in order of importance: recommendations, high school academic record, standardized test scores, writing sample, extracurricular activities; other factors considered: special talents, religious affiliation/commitment. *Entrance programs:* deferred admission. About 30% of entering students from private schools. *Apply* by August 15; rolling admissions. *Transfers* welcome; 93 enrolled 1993–94.

Academic Environment. Graduation requirements include 45 semester hours in general education, 30 hours in biblical-theological studies. Degrees offered: associates, bachelors. About 35% of entering class graduate within four years; 56% of freshmen return for sophomore year. *Special programs:* study abroad, internships, mentor program, cross registration with most Oregon private colleges. Adult programs: degree completion in management and communications, Family Studies; "MAC" program meets via computer bulletin board.

Undergraduate degrees conferred (72). 35% were in Education, 21% were in Theology, 17% were in Psychology, 13% were in Business and Management, 10% were in Multi/Interdisciplinary Studies, 3% were in Visual and Performing Arts, 3% were in Liberal/General Studies.

Graduates Career Data. Career Development Services include internships, mentoring, campus employment, field education program.

Faculty. About 33% of faculty hold PhD or equivalent. About 33% of teaching faculty are female.

Student Body. About 59% of students from in state; 85% from Northwest, 13% West, 1% foreign. An estimated 99% of students reported as Protestant, 1% Catholic; 1% Black, 2% Hispanic, 2% Asian, 3% other minority.

Religious Orientation. College is a church-related institution; 53% of students affiliated with the church; 30 semester hours in biblical-theological studies required of all students.

Varsity Sports. Men (NAIA Div.II): Baseball, Basketball, Soccer. Women (NAIA Div.II): Basketball, Soccer, Volleyball.

Campus Life. About 48% of men, 52% of women live in traditional dormitories; rest commute. There are no fraternities or sororities on campus. About 5% of resident students leave campus on weekends.

Annual Costs. Tuition and fees, $8,700; room and board, $3,700; estimated $1,400 other, exclusive of travel. About 86% of students receive financial aid; average amount of assistance, $7,170. Assistance is typically divided 42% scholarship/grant, 55% loan, 3% work.

Western Carolina University

Cullowhee, North Carolina 28723 (704) 227-7317

A state-supported university located in an unincorporated community 6 miles south of Sylvia (pop. 1,600) and 52 miles west of Asheville. Most convenient major airport: Asheville.

Founded: 1889
Affiliation: State
UG Enrollment: 5,831 M, W (full-time)
Cost: < $10K
% Receiving Financial Aid: 48%
Admission: Non-selective
Application Deadline: Aug. 1

Admission. Graduates of accredited high schools with 15 units eligible; others admitted by examination; 75% of applicants accepted, 37% of these actually enroll; 22% of freshmen graduate in top fifth of high school class, 58% in top two-fifths. Average freshman SAT scores, according to most recent data available: 410 verbal, 441 mathematical. *Required:* SAT. *Out-of-state* freshman applicants: university seeks students from out of state. State limits out-of-state enrollment to 18% of entering class. No special requirements for out-of-state applicants; 70% of applicants accepted, 26% of these enroll. *Apply* by August 1. *Transfers* welcome.
Academic Environment. *Undergraduate studies* offered by schools of Arts and Sciences, Business, Education and Psychology, Health Sciences and Services, and Technology and Applied Science. *Majors offered* include computer science, natural resource management, engineering technologies, health services management, environmental health. About 42% of students entering as freshmen graduate eventually; 70% of freshmen return for sophomore year. *Special programs:* CLEP, honors, independent study, study abroad, undergraduate research, individualized majors, 3–2 programs in forestry and engineering. *Calendar:* quarter, summer school.
Undergraduate degrees conferred (908). 28% were in Education, 20% were in Business and Management, 9% were in Health Sciences, 6% were in Visual and Performing Arts, 5% were in Home Economics, 5% were in Protective Services, 4% were in Social Sciences, 4% were in Parks and Recreation, 3% were in Computer and Engineering Related Technology, 3% were in Letters, 3% were in Public Affairs, remainder in 9 other fields.
Graduates Career Data. According to most recent data available, full-time graduate or professional study pursued immediately after graduation by 12% of students; 3% enter business school. *Careers in business and industry* pursued by 75% of students.
Faculty. About 66% of faculty hold PhD or equivalent.
Student Body. About 89% of students from in state; 98% South. An estimated 4% of students reported as Black, 3% other minority, according to most recent data available.
Varsity Sports. Men (Div.I): Baseball, Basketball, Cross Country, Football, Golf, Tennis, Track. Women (Div.I): Basketball, Cross Country, Tennis, Track, Volleyball.
Campus Life. About 44% of men, 36% of women live in traditional dormitories; 5% of men, 6% of women live in coed dormitories; 47% of men, 58% of women live in off-campus housing or commute. Freshmen given preference in college housing if all students cannot be accommodated. Intervisitation in men's and women's dormitory rooms limited. There are 15 fraternities, 9 sororities on campus which about 25% of men, 14% of women join; 4% of men live in fraternities; sororities provide no residence facilities. About 33% of resident students leave campus on weekends.
Annual Costs. Tuition and fees, $1,375 (out-of-state, $7,047); room and board, $2,310. About 48% of students receive financial aid; assistance is typically divided 51% grant/scholarship, 29% loan, 17% work. College reports some scholarships awarded on the basis of academic merit alone.

Western Connecticut State University

Danbury, Connecticut 06810 (203) 797-4347

A state-supported, comprehensive university, located in a city of 60,000, 65 miles northeast of New York City. Most convenient major airport: LaGuardia (Flushing, NY).

Founded: 1905
Affiliation: State
UG Enrollment: 1,376 M, 1,442 W (full-time); 741 M, 1,120 W (part-time)
Total Enrollment: 5,726
Cost: < $10K
Admission: Non-selective
Application Deadline: April 1

Admission. Graduates of approved high schools with 15 units in academic subjects eligible; 61% of applicants accepted, 35% of these actually enroll; 16% of freshmen graduate in top fifth of high school class, 42% in top two-fifths. Average freshman SAT scores: 13% of freshmen score above 500 on verbal, 2% above 600; 31% of freshmen score above 500 on mathematical, 6% above 600. *Required:* SAT; minimum high school GPA, interview. Criteria considered in admissions, in order of importance: standardized test scores, high school academic record, recommendations; other factors considered: special talents, diverse student body. *Out-of-state* freshman applicants: university actively seeks students from out of state. State does not limit out-of-state enrollment, however state residents have priority. About 61% of out-of-state students accepted, 33% of these actually enroll. States from which most out-of-state students are drawn include New York. *Entrance programs:* early decision, early admission, midyear admission, advanced placement. *Apply* by April 1; rolling admissions. *Transfers* welcome; 373 enrolled 1993–94.
Academic Environment. Degrees offered: associates, bachelors, masters. *Majors offered* include computer science, medical technology, meteorology. Average undergraduate class size: 30; 95% 20–40. About 35% of students entering as freshmen graduate within four years, 50% eventually; 60% of freshmen return for sophomore year. *Special programs:* CLEP, January Term, study abroad, honors, cross-registration with Connecticut State U., cooperative education programs. *Calendar:* semester, summer school.
Undergraduate degrees conferred (646). 31% were in Business and Management, 11% were in Visual and Performing Arts, 11% were in Education, 10% were in Social Sciences, 7% were in Communications, 7% were in Health Sciences, 5% were in Protective Services, 5% were in Letters, 4% were in Psychology, 3% were in Computer and Engineering Related Technology, remainder in 7 other fields.
Graduates Career Data. Advanced studies pursued by 26% of graduates; 9% enter graduate school. About 85% of 1992–93 graduates employed. Career Development Services available.
Faculty. About 95% of faculty hold PhD or equivalent. About 80% of undergraduate classes taught by tenured faculty. About 40% of teaching faculty are female; 4% Black, 4% Hispanic, 5% other minority.
Student Body. About 85% of students from in state; 95% New England, 5% Middle Atlantic.
Varsity Sports. Men (Div.III): Baseball, Basketball, Football, Golf, Hockey (field), Lacrosse, Soccer, Softball, Tennis, Volleyball. Women (Div.III): Basketball, Hockey (field), Softball, Tennis, Track, Volleyball.
Campus Life. About 8% of men, women live in traditional dormitories; 28% of men, 20% of women in coed dormitories; 22% of men, 17% of women live in off-campus housing; rest commute. Freshmen are given preference in college housing if all students cannot be accommodated. Intervisitation in men's and women's dormitory rooms limited. Sexes segregated in coed dormitories by floor. There are 3 fraternities, 4 sororities on campus. About 50% of resident students leave campus on weekends.
Annual Costs. Tuition and fees, $2,900 (out-of-state, $7,612); room and board, $3,722.

Western Illinois University

Macomb, Illinois 61455 (309) 295-1414

A state-supported institution, located in a town of 23,000, 40 miles east of the Mississippi River. Most convenient major airport: Peoria.

Founded: 1899
Affiliation: State
UG Enrollment: 4,806 M, 4,209 W (full-time); 705 M, 744 W (part-time)
Total Enrollment: 12,877
Cost: < $10K
% Receiving Financial Aid: 75%
Admission: Non-selective
Application Deadline: June 1

Admission. Graduates of accredited high schools eligible; 77% of applicants accepted, 24% of these actually enroll; 18% of freshmen graduate in top fifth of high school class, 67% in top two-fifths.

Average freshman ACT scores: 20.9 M, 20.3 W composite. *Required:* ACT. Criteria considered in admissions, in order of importance: standardized test scores, high school academic record. *Out-of-state* applicants: university actively seeks students from out-of-state. State does not limit out-of-state enrollment. States from which most out-of-state students are drawn include Iowa, Missouri. *Apply* by June. *Transfers* welcome; 1,358 enrolled Fall 1993.

Academic Environment. *Undergraduate studies* offered by colleges of Arts and Sciences, Applied Sciences, Business, Education, Fine Arts, Health, Physical Education and Recreation. Degrees offered: bachelors, masters. *Majors offered* include computer science, geography, speech pathology and audiology, BFA program. Average undergraduate class size: 28.

About 22% of students entering as freshmen graduate within four years, 45% eventually; 70% of freshmen return for sophomore year. *Special programs:* CLEP, study abroad, honors, independent study, individualized majors, credit by examination, interdisciplinary minors (African, Latin American, Middle Eastern and Asian studies). Adult programs: individualized and flexible program. *Calendar:* semester, summer school.

Undergraduate degrees conferred (2,122). 15% were in Education, 14% were in Business and Management, 12% were in Multi/Interdisciplinary Studies, 11% were in Protective Services, 10% were in Communications, 6% were in Social Sciences, 4% were in Psychology, 4% were in Home Economics, 3% were in Parks and Recreation, 3% were in Visual and Performing Arts, 3% were in Engineering and Engineering Related Technology, 3% were in Agricultural Sciences, remainder in 10 other fields.

Graduates Career Data. Advanced studies pursued by 23% of graduates. Career Development Services include occupational information and placement office offering workshops on resume preparation, interviewing, job search techniques, career fairs.

Faculty. About 44% of faculty hold PhD or equivalent. About 41% of teaching faculty (including teaching assistants) are female; 4% Black, 11% other minority.

Student Body. About 93% of students from in state; 95% Midwest, 2% South, 1% foreign. An estimated 8% of students reported as Black, 1% Asian, 2% Hispanic, 3% other minority. Average age of undergraduate student: 23.

Varsity Sports. Men (Div.I): Baseball, Basketball, Cross Country, Diving, Football, Golf, Soccer, Swimming, Tennis, Track. Women (Div.I): Basketball, Cross Country, Diving, Softball, Swimming, Tennis, Track.

Campus Life. Rules governing student life considered "very free" by student leader. Regulations for intervisitation set by residents of each floor with 24-hour option available. Special Study Floor where students agree to maintain stricter study environment.

About 50% of men, 50% of women in coed dormitories; 44% men, 44% women live in off-campus housing or commute. Freshmen are given preference in college housing if all students cannot be accommodated. There are 20 fraternities, 11 sororities on campus which about 10% of men, 5% of women join; 6% of men, 6% of women live in fraternities and sororities. About 20% of resident students leave campus on weekends.

Annual Costs. Tuition and fees, $2,548 (out-of-state, $6,244); room and board, $3,043; estimated $1,500 other, exclusive of travel. About 75% of students receive financial aid; average amount of assistance, $4,846. Assistance is typically divided 72% scholarship and grant, 40% loan, 22% work. University reports 1,000 scholarships awarded on the basis of academic merit alone, 400 for special talents alone (athletics-159, music-180, art-29, theater-30), 10 for need alone.

Western Kentucky University

Bowling Green, Kentucky 42101 (502) 745-0111

A state-supported university, located in a city of 38,000, 65 miles north of Nashville. Most convenient major airport: Nashville International (TN).

Founded: 1906
Affiliation: State
UG Enrollment: 4,678 M, 5,616 W (full-time); 991 M, 1,983 W (part-time)
Total Enrollment: 15,335
Cost: < $10K
% Receiving Financial Aid: 65%
Admission: Non-selective
Application Deadline: Aug. 1

Admission. Graduates of accredited Kentucky high schools with GPA of 2.2 or ACT of 14 eligible; others admitted under special conditions; 73% of applicants accepted, 69% of these actually enroll. Average freshman ACT scores: 21 M, 21 W composite. *Required:* ACT. Criteria considered in admissions, in order of importance: high school academic record and standardized test scores, recommendations. *Out-of-state* freshman applicants: university actively seeks students from out of state. State does not limit out-of-state enrollment. Required for out-of-state applicants: ACT composite score of 19. States from which most out-of-state students are drawn include Tennessee, Indiana, Florida, Ohio. *Entrance programs:* midyear admission, advanced placement. *Apply* by August 1 (June 1 out-of-state); rolling admissions. *Transfers* welcome; 871 enrolled 1993–94.

Academic Environment. Graduation requirements include 64 credit hours in letter, social sciences, mathematics, physical sciences, and ethics. Degrees offered: associates, bachelors, masters. Unusual, new, or notable majors include photojournalism, recombinant genetics, dental hygiene, anthropology. Average undergraduate class size: 28% under 20, 52% 20–40, 20% over 40.

About 16% of students entering as freshmen graduate within four years, 53% eventually; 65% of freshmen return for sophomore year. *Special programs:* CLEP, independent study, study abroad, honors, internships, university-wide co-ops. *Calendar:* semester, summer school.

Undergraduate degrees conferred (1,516). 22% were in Education, 14% were in Business and Management, 14% were in Communications, 8% were in Social Sciences, 5% were in Liberal/General Studies, 5% were in Psychology, 4% were in Health Sciences, 4% were in Engineering and Engineering Related Technology, 4% were in Life Sciences, 3% were in Letters, remainder in 14 other fields.

Graduates Career Data. Advanced studies pursued by 29% of graduates. Employers typically hiring largest numbers of graduates include schools, hospitals. Career Development Services include cooperative programs, interviewing skills, information on potential employers, referral services, on-campus interviews.

Faculty. About 70% of faculty hold PhD or equivalent. About 47% of undergraduate classes taught by tenured faculty. About 37% of teaching faculty are female; 3% Black, 3% other minority.

Student Body. About 82% of students from in state; 94% South, 5% Midwest, 1% foreign. An estimated 6% of students reported as Black, 2% other minority. Average age of undergraduate student: 24.

Varsity Sports. Men (Div.I): Baseball, Basketball, Cross Country, Football (IAA), Golf, Soccer, Swimming, Tennis, Track. Women (Div.I): Basketball, Cross Country, Golf, Swimming, Tennis, Track, Volleyball.

Campus Life. About 24% of men, 28% of women live in traditional dormitories; 7% of men, 5% of women live in coed dormitories; 2% of men live in fraternities; rest commute. Intervisitation in men's and women's dormitory rooms limited. There are 15 fraternities, 10 sororities on campus which about 6% of men, 7% of women join.

Annual Costs. Tuition and fees, $1,708 (out-of-state, $4,708); room and board, $2,446; estimated $1,175 other, exclusive of travel. About 65% of students receive financial aid; average amount of assistance, $3,066. Assistance is typically divided 36% scholarship, 25% loan, 10% work. College reports some scholarships awarded on the basis of academic merit alone.

Western Maryland College

Westminster, Maryland 21157 (301) 857-2230

An independent, liberal arts college, Western Maryland is located on a 160-acre campus in a town of 12,000, 28 miles from Baltimore and 58 miles from Washington. Most convenient major airport: Baltimore-Washington International.

Founded: 1867
Affiliation: Independent
UG Enrollment: 495 M, 576 W (full-time); 32 M, 66 W (part-time)
Total Enrollment: 2,109
Cost: $10K–$20K
% Receiving Financial Aid: 80%
Admission: Selective
Application Deadline: Mar. 15

Admission is selective. About 81% of applicants accepted, 30% of these actually enroll; 47% of freshmen graduate in top fifth of high school class, 70% in top two-fifths. Average freshmen scores: SAT, 484 verbal, 527 mathematical; 41% score above 500 on verbal, 12% above 600, 1% above 700; 65% score above 500 on mathematical, 23% above 600, 4% above 700. *Required:* SAT or ACT; minimum 2.5 high school GPA; essay, interview recommended. Criteria considered in admissions, in order of importance: high school academic record, recommendations, standardized test scores, extracurricular activities, writing sample; other factors considered: special talents, diverse student body. *Entrance programs:* early decision, early admission, midyear admission, advanced placement, deferred admission. *Apply* by March 15. *Transfers* welcome; 72 enrolled 1993–94.

Academic Environment. Students have some influence on academic decision-making through membership on most faculty and administration committees. Graduation requirements include cross-cultural studies, fine arts, humanities, natural sciences, quantitative analysis, and social sciences; proficiency requirements in English composition and mathematics. Degrees offered: bachelors, masters. Average undergraduate class size: 18; 60% under 20, 40% 20–40, less than 1% over 40.

About 69% of students entering as freshmen graduate within four years, 74% eventually; 71% of freshmen return for sophomore year. *Special programs:* January Term, honors, study abroad, acceleration, internship (required for some majors), program in education of the deaf, 3–2 forestry, 3–2 engineering, 3–2 occupational therapy, film studies, Washington D.C. seminar, Washington Semester, United Nations Semester. Adult Programs: non-traditional organization. *Calendar:* 4–1–4, summer school.

Undergraduate degrees conferred (306). 24% were in Social Sciences, 20% were in Multi/Interdisciplinary Studies, 11% were in Communications, 9% were in Letters, 8% were in Psychology, 8% were in Life Sciences, 6% were in Business and Management, 4% were in Visual and Performing Arts, 3% were in Education, remainder in 6 other fields.

Graduates Career Data. Advanced studies pursued by 30% of graduates; 14% enter graduate school, 4% enter business school, 2% enter law school, 3% enter medical school, 1% enter dental school. Business schools typically enrolling most graduates include West Virginia U.; medical schools include U. of Maryland; law schools include U.of Baltimore. Employers typically hiring most numbers of graduates include T.Rowe Price, USF&G, IRS, National Science Foundation. Career Development Services include on-campus interviews, career interest inventory test, resume/job search skills, alumni networking.

Faculty. About 92% of faculty hold PhD or equivalent. About 91% of undergraduate classes taught by tenured faculty. About 28% of teaching faculty are female.

Student Body. About 62% of students from in state; 93% Middle Atlantic, 3% foreign. An estimated 84% of students reported as Catholic, 4% Protestant, 3% Jewish, 13% unaffiliated, 3% other; 8% Black, 1% Hispanic.

Varsity Sports. Men (Div.III): Baseball, Basketball, Cross Country, Football, Golf, Lacrosse, Soccer, Swimming, Tennis, Track, Wrestling. Women (Div.III): Basketball, Cross Country, Golf, Hockey (field), Lacrosse, Soccer, Softball, Swimming, Tennis, Track, Volleyball.

Campus Life. Students enjoy some voice in determining campus social regulations. Cars permitted for all; drinking allowed in living units, in accordance with state laws. Intervisitation hours determined by students. Variety of cultural and intellectual activities on campus, supplemented by resources of Baltimore and Washington.

About 5% each of men, women live in traditional dormitories, 90% each of men, women live in coed dormitories; rest commute. All students are guaranteed college housing for 4 years. There are 5 fraternities, 4 sororities on campus which about 26% of men, 30% of women join. About 15% of resident students leave campus on weekends.

Annual Costs. Tuition and fees, $13,250; room and board, $5,240; estimated $1,000 other, exclusive of travel. About 80% of students receive financial aid; average amount of assistance, $12,000. Assistance is typically divided 10% scholarship, 70% grant, 10% loan, 10% work. College reports 95 scholarships awarded on the basis of academic merit alone, 60% for need alone. *Meeting Costs:* college offers monthly payment plan.

Western Michigan University

Kalamazoo, Michigan 49008 (616) 387-1000

A state-supported institution, located in a city of 85,600, (metropolitan area of 200,000) midway between Chicago and Detroit, Western Michigan occupies 2 campuses about one-half mile apart. Most convenient major airport: Kalamazoo/Battle Creek.

Founded: 1903
Affiliation: State
UG Enrollment: 7,578 M, 8,161 W (full-time); 2,010 M, 2,268 W (part-time)
Total Enrollment: 26,555
Cost: < $10K
% Receiving Financial Aid: 65%
Admission: Non-selective
Application Deadline: Aug. 15

Admission. About 78% of applicants accepted, 39% of these actually enroll; 44% of freshmen graduate in top fifth of high school class, 75% in top two-fifths. Average freshman ACT scores: 23 M, 22.4 W composite. *Required:* ACT; interview recommended. Criteria considered in admissions, in order of importance: high school academic record, standardized test scores; high school grades, ACT, mix of college prep courses, trend of grades, and class rank also considered in admissions. *Out-of-state* applicants: university actively seeks students from out-of-state. State does not limit out-of-state enrollment. About 69% of out-of-state students accepted, 28% of these actually enroll. States from which most out-of-state students are drawn include Illinois, Indiana, Ohio, Wisconsin. *Entrance programs:* midyear admission, advanced placement. *Apply* by August 15; rolling admissions. *Transfers* welcome; 2,071 enrolled 1993–94.

Academic Environment. *Undergraduate studies* offered by colleges of Arts and Sciences, Applied Sciences, Business, Education, Fine Arts, General Studies. Graduation requirements include 8 semester hours of foreign language or demonstrated proficiency, 2 semester hours of physical education, University Intellectual Skills, college writing, BA writing, and computer literacy. Degrees offered: bachelors, masters, doctoral. Unusual, new, or notable majors include agriculture, aviation, computer science, music theater performance, jazz studies, paper engineering, paper science, trade and industrial training, integrated supply management, engineering management, employee assistance, hydrology, hydrogeology. Average undergraduate class size: 7% under 20, 20% 20–40, 73% over 40.

About 15% of students entering as freshmen graduate within four years, 51% after nine years; 79% of freshmen return for sophomore year. *Special programs:* CLEP, January Term, independent study, study abroad, honors, undergraduate research, 3-year degree, individualized majors, cross-registration with Kalamazoo College and Kalamazoo Valley Community College. *Calendar:* trimester, summer school.

Undergraduate degrees conferred (3,424). 25% were in Business and Management, 17% were in Education, 7% were in Communications, 5% were in Engineering, 5% were in Engineering and Engineering Related Technology, 5% were in Marketing and Distribution, 4% were in Social Sciences, 3% were in Visual and Performing Arts, 3% were in Protective Services, 3% were in Health Sciences, 3% were in Allied Health, 3% were in Psychology, remainder in 17 other fields.

Graduates Career Data. Advanced studies pursued by 7% of graduates. About 78% of 1992–93 graduates employed. Employers typically hiring the largest numbers of graduates include the "Big 6 accounting firms". Career Development Services provide students with resources.

Faculty. About 79% of faculty hold PhD or equivalent. About 90% of undergraduate classes taught by tenured faculty. About 35% of teaching faculty are female; 4% Black, 2% Hispanic, 5% other minority.

Student Body. About 91% of students from in state; 94% Midwest, 5% foreign. An estimated 28% of students reported as Protestant, 25% Catholic, 1% Jewish, 46% unaffiliated; 6% Black, 1% Hispanic, 1% Asian, 6% other minority.

Varsity Sports. Men (Div.I): Baseball, Basketball, Cross Country, Football (IA), Gymnastics, Hockey (Ice), Soccer, Tennis, Track. Women (Div.I): Basketball, Cross Country, Gymnastics, Softball, Tennis, Track, Volleyball.

Campus Life. About 26% of men, 30% of women live in traditional dormitories and coed dormitories; rest commute. Intervisitation in men's and women's dormitory rooms limited. Sexes segregated in coed dormitories either by wing or floor. There are 21 fraternities, 14

sororities on campus which about 9% of men, 7% of women join; 1% each of men, women live in fraternities and sororities.
Annual Costs. Tuition and fees, $2,880 (out-of-state, $6,710); room and board, $3,940; estimated $1,700 other, exclusive of travel. About 65% of students receive financial aid; average amount of assistance, $3,920. Assistance is typically divided 21% scholarship, 16% grant, 42% loan, 21% work. University reports 1,476 scholarships awarded on the basis of academic merit alone, 1,409 for special talents alone, 633 for need alone. *Meeting Costs:* university offers Michigan Education Trust.

Western Montana College of the University of Montana

Dillon, Montana 59725 (406) 683-7331

A state-supported college, located in a town of 5,000, 65 miles south of Butte. Western Montana College is part of the University of Montana system. Most convenient major airport: Butte.

Founded: 1893
Affiliation: State
UG Enrollment: 1,078 M, W (full-time)
Cost: < $10K
% Receiving Financial Aid: 50%
Admission: Non-selective
Application Deadline: Rolling

Admission. Graduates of accredited Montana high schools admitted. About 98% of applicants accepted, 78% of these actually enroll. *Required:* SAT or ACT. *Out-of-state* freshman applicants: state does not limit out-of-state enrollment. *Apply:* no specific deadline. *Transfers* welcome.
Academic Environment. *Degrees:* BA, BS, BSB, BSE1Ed, BSSecEd. *Majors offered* include Bachelor of Liberal Studies with emphasis in art, music, drama, science, communication technology, social science/administrative science. About 70% of freshmen return for sophomore year. *Special programs:* CLEP, independent study, 2–2 program in business administration with U. of Montana. *Calendar:* semester, summer school.
Undergraduate degrees conferred (110). 83% were in Education, 16% were in Business and Management, remainder in Area and Ethnic Studies.
Student Body. About 90% of students from in state.
Varsity Sports. Men (NAIA): Basketball, Football, Rodeo (NIRA), Wrestling. Women (NAIA): Basketball, Rodeo (NIRA), Volleyball.
Campus Life. About 35% of students live in coed dormitories; rest live in off-campus housing or commute. Intervisitation in men's and women's dormitory rooms limited. There are no fraternities or sororities on campus.
Annual Costs. Tuition and fees, $1,780 (out-of-state, $5,336); room and board, $3,000. About 50% of students receive financial aid; assistance is typically divided 20% scholarship, 60% loan, 20% work. College reports some scholarships awarded on the basis of academic merit alone. *Meeting Costs:* college offers deferred payment schedule.

Western New England College

Springfield, Massachusetts 01119 (413) 782-3111

An independent college, located in a city of 175,000.

Founded: 1919
Affiliation: Independent
UG Enrollment: 3,459 M, W (full-time)
Cost: < $10K
Admission: Non-selective
Application Deadline: Rolling

Admission. Graduates of approved high schools or those with equivalent training eligible; academic unit requirements vary with degree programs; 93% of applicants accepted, 35% of these actually enroll; 13% of freshmen graduate in top fifth of high school class, in top two-fifths. *Required:* SAT or ACT; interview recommended. *Apply:* rolling admissions. *Transfers* welcome.
Academic Environment. *Undergraduate studies* offered by schools of Arts and Sciences, Business, Engineering. Specific course and distribution requirements vary with school. About 51% of students entering as freshmen graduate eventually; 67% of freshmen return for sophomore year. *Special programs:* CLEP, independent study, study abroad, honors, undergraduate research, individualized majors. *Calendar:* semester, summer school.
Undergraduate degrees conferred (743). 47% were in Business and Management, 14% were in Engineering, 12% were in Protective Services, 6% were in Social Sciences, 6% were in Psychology, 6% were in Computer and Engineering Related Technology, 3% were in Liberal/General Studies, 3% were in Letters, remainder in 3 other fields.
Student Body. About 71% of students from in state; 81% New England, 15% Middle Atlantic.
Varsity Sports. Men (Div.III): Baseball, Basketball, Bowling, Football, Lacrosse, Hockey, Skiing, Soccer, Wrestling, Tennis. Women (Div.III): Basketball, Bowling, Field Hockey, Skiing, Soccer, Softball, Volleyball.
Campus Life. About 33% of men, 17% women live in traditional dormitories; 10% of men, 14% of women in coed dormitories; 49% of students in nontraditional coed housing; rest live in off-campus housing or commute. Freshmen given preference in college housing if all students cannot be accommodated. Intervisitation in men's and women's dormitory rooms limited. About 35% of resident students leave campus on weekends.
Annual Costs. Tuition and fees, $9,354; room and board, $5,400. College reports some scholarships awarded on the basis of academic merit alone.

Western New Mexico University

Silver City, New Mexico 88062 (505) 538-6106

A state-supported university, located in a town of 10,000, 155 miles northwest of El Paso. Most convenient major airport: El Paso.

Founded: 1893
Affiliation: State
UG Enrollment: 1,635 M, W (full-time)
Cost: < $10K
% Receiving Financial Aid: 91%
Admission: Non-selective
Application Deadline: June 1

Admission. High school graduates with 15 units and C average eligible; others given consideration; almost all applicants accepted, 63% of these actually enroll; 22% of freshmen graduate in top fifth of high school class, 47% in top two-fifths. *Required:* ACT. *Out-of-state* freshman applicants: university seeks students from out of state. State does not limit out-of-state enrollment. No special requirements for out-of-state applicants. *Apply* by June 1. *Transfers* welcome.
Academic Environment. *Degrees:* BA, BApS, BS. *Majors offered* include international business, management information systems. About 52% of freshmen return for sophomore year. *Special programs:* CLEP, study abroad, 3-year degree. *Calendar:* early semester (fall semester begins fourth week in August), summer school.
Undergraduate degrees conferred (229). 26% were in Education, 20% were in Business and Management, 11% were in Public Affairs, 11% were in Social Sciences, 10% were in Liberal/General Studies, 7% were in Psychology, 3% were in Protective Services, 3% were in Computer and Engineering Related Technology, remainder in 8 other fields.
Student Body. About 83% of students from in state; 99% West.
Varsity Sports. Men (NAIA): Baseball, Basketball, Football, Track. Women (NAIA): Basketball, Softball, Track, Volleyball.
Campus Life. About 52% of men, 14% of women live in traditional dormitories; no coed dormitories; rest live in off-campus housing or commute. Freshmen given preference in college housing if all students cannot be accommodated. Intervisitation in men's and women's dormitory rooms limited. There are no fraternities or sororities on campus. About 20% of resident students leave campus on weekends.
Annual Costs. Tuition and fees, $1,214 (out-of-state, $4,394); room and board, $2,110. About 91% of students receive financial aid. College reports some scholarships awarded on the basis of academic merit alone.

Western Oregon State College

Monmouth, Oregon 97361 (503) 838-8211

A state-supported college, located in a town of 6,000, 15 miles southwest of Salem and mid-way between Portland and Eugene. Most convenient major airport: Portland.

Founded: 1856
Affiliation: State
UG Enrollment: 1,264 M, 1,895 W (full-time); 556 total (part-time)
Total Enrollment: 3,999
Cost: < $10K
% Receiving Financial Aid: 65%
Admission: Non-selective
Application Deadline: April 15

Admission. Graduates of standard or accredited high schools eligible; others admitted on basis of GPA, GED, or test scores; 89% of applicants accepted, 54% of these actually enroll. Average freshmen SAT scores: 429 verbal, 470 mathematical. *Required:* SAT or ACT; minimum high school GPA 2.75, high school transcript. Criteria considered in admissions, in order of importance: high school academic record, standardized test scores, recommendations; other factors considered: diverse student body. *Out-of-state* applicants: college actively seeks students from out-of-state. State does not limit out-of-state enrollment. About 79% of out-of-state students accepted, 36% of these actually enroll. States from which most out-of-state students are drawn: California, Idaho, Washington. *Apply* by April 15; rolling admissions. *Transfers* welcome; 614 enrolled 1993–94.

Academic Environment. Graduation requirements include 72 hour core curriculum in writing, math, speech, creative arts, humanities, social sciences, natural sciences, and physical education. Degrees offered: associates, bachelors, masters. Unusual, new, or notable majors include American sign language/English interpretation. Average undergraduate class size: 20% under 20, 45% 20–40, 35% over 40.

About 65% of freshmen return for sophomore year. *Special programs:* CLEP, independent study, study abroad, honors, undergraduate research, 3-year degree, individualized majors, community service internship. *Calendar:* quarter, summer school.

Undergraduate degrees conferred (708). 44% were in Education, 15% were in Business and Management, 11% were in Psychology, 8% were in Protective Services, 7% were in Social Sciences, 3% were in Visual and Performing Arts, 3% were in Multi/Interdisciplinary Studies, 3% were in Computer and Engineering Related Technology, 3% were in Architecture and Environmental Design, remainder in 4 other fields.

Graduates Career Data. Career Development Services available to all students.

Faculty. About 80% of faculty hold PhD or equivalent. About 55% of undergraduate classes taught by tenured faculty. About 47% of teaching faculty are female.

Student Body. About 94% of students from in state; 3% foreign.

Varsity Sports. Men (NAIA Div.II): Baseball, Basketball, Cross Country, Football, Track. Women (NAIA Div.II): Basketball, Cross Country, Softball, Track, Volleyball.

Campus Life. Campus is located in a rural area in the Willamette Valley. Administration reports popular student activities include student government, intramural and varsity sports, student publications and performing arts.

About 26% of men, 26% of women live in coed dormitories; 39% of men, women live in off-campus college-related housing; rest commute. Freshmen given preference in college housing if all students cannot be accommodated. Sexes segregated in coed dormitories by floor or room. There are no fraternities or sororities on campus. About 50% of resident students leave campus on weekends.

Annual Costs. Tuition and fees, $2,790 (out-of-state, $6,810); room and board, $3,720; estimated $2,490 other, exclusive of travel. About 65% of students receive financial aid; assistance is typically divided 5% scholarship, 25% grants, 60% loan, 10% work. College reports some scholarships awarded on the basis of academic merit alone. *Meeting Costs:* college offers PLUS Loans, deferred payment plans for tuition and residence hall.

Western Reserve University

(See Case Western Reserve University)

Western State College of Colorado

Gunnison, Colorado 81231 (303) 943-2119

A state-supported college, located in a village of 5,500, 210 miles southeast of Denver, Western offers an innovative academic program. Most convenient major airport: Gunnison County.

Founded: 1901
Affiliation: State
UG Enrollment: 1,374 M, 941 W (full-time)
Cost: < $10K
% Receiving Financial Aid: 70%
Admission: Non-selective
Application Deadline: April 15

Admission. Graduates of accredited high schools with minimum 2.5 GPA, ACT of 20 or SAT of 820 eligible; others admitted by examination; 77% of applicants accepted, 29% of these actually enroll; 15% of freshmen graduate in top fifth of high school class, 36% in top two-fifths. Average freshman scores: SAT, 430 M, 410 W verbal; 470 M, 470 W mathematical; ACT, 21 M, 21 W composite. *Required:* SAT or ACT; essay and interview optional. Criteria considered in admissions, in order of importance: high school academic record, standardized test scores, writing sample, interview, recommendations, extracurricular activities; other factors considered: special talents, alumni children, diverse student body. *Out-of-state* applicants: college actively seeks students from out-of-state. State does limit out-of-state enrollment. About 74% of out-of-state students accepted. States from which most out-of-state students are drawn include California, Texas, Illinois, Minnesota, Arkansas, New England states. *Entrance programs:* midyear admission, deferred admission, advanced placement. *Apply* by April 15; rolling admissions. *Transfers* welcome; 246 enrolled 1993–94.

Academic Environment. College operates under an innovative academic calendar called "Western Scholar's Year". Students choose 3 of 4 regular terms offered throughout the year: Fall (12 weeks), Winter (8 weeks), Spring (12 weeks), and Summer (8 weeks). Students take fewer but more intensive courses each term. Graduation requirements include 15 hours in Human Relations, 12 in Creative and Imaginative Arts, 12 in sciences and math, competencies in writing, math, and speech. Degrees offered: bachelors. Unusual, new, or notable majors include: biology, geology/anthropology, communication. Average undergraduate class size: 51% under 20, 41% 20–40, 8% over 40.

About 45% of students entering as freshmen graduate eventually; 47% of freshmen return for sophomore year. *Special programs:* CLEP, honors, study abroad, independent study, cross registration with consortium of state colleges, internship, National Student Exchange, capstone experience, undergraduate research, 3-year degree. Adult programs: Women in Transition (WIT). *Calendar:* quarter, summer school.

Undergraduate degrees conferred (272). 30% were in Business and Management, 17% were in Visual and Performing Arts, 13% were in Social Sciences, 8% were in Life Sciences, 7% were in Letters, 7% were in Psychology, 4% were in Education, 4% were in Parks and Recreation, 3% were in Physical Sciences, 3% were in Engineering and Engineering Related Technology, remainder in 2 other fields.

Graduates Career Data. Employers typically hiring largest numbers of graduates include marketing sales, advertising, teachers, recreation. Career Development Services include job placement, resume writing, mock interviews, on-campus recruiting, career counseling.

Faculty. About 63% of faculty hold PhD or equivalent. About 28% of teaching faculty are female; 5% minority.

Student Body. About 64% of students from in state. An estimated 11% of students reported as Protestant, 10% Catholic, 1% Jewish, 5% unaffiliated; 2% Black, 3% Hispanic, 9% other.

Varsity Sports. Men (NAIA Div.II): Basketball, Cross Country, Football, Skiing (NCSA Div.I), Track, Wrestling. Women (NAIA Div.II): Basketball, Cross Country, Skiing (NCSA Div.I), Track, Volleyball.

Campus Life. About 15% of men, 11% of women live in traditional dormitories; 29% of men, 30% of women live in coed dormitories; 1% of men live in fraternities; rest commute. Intervisitation in men's and women's dormitory rooms limited. There are 14 fraternities, 3 sororities on campus which about 5% of men, 2% of women join. About 10% of resident students leave campus on weekends.

Annual Costs. Tuition and fees, $1,819 (out-of-state, $5,918); room and board, $3,741; estimated $500 other, exclusive of travel. About 70% of students receive financial aid, average amount of assistance, $2,500. Assistance is typically 20% scholarship, 30% grant, 25% loan, 25% work. College reports 100 scholarships awarded on the basis of academic merit alone, 200 for special talents alone. *Meeting Costs:* college offers Academic Management System.

Western Washington University

Bellingham, Washington 98225 **(206) 650-3443**

Western Washington is located in a community of 46,000, 87 miles north of Seattle and 55 miles south of Vancouver, British Columbia. Most convenient major airport: Bellingham International.

Founded: 1893
Affiliation: State
UG Enrollment: 3,996 M, 4,913 W (full-time)
Total Enrollment: 10,073
Cost: < $10K
% Receiving Financial Aid: 64%
Admission: Non-selective
Application Deadline: March 1

Admission. Graduates of accredited high schools with minimum GPA of 2.5 or rank in top half of class eligible; 64% of applicants accepted, 47% of these actually enroll; 58% of freshmen graduate in top fifth of high school class, 89% in top two-fifths. Average freshman scores: SAT, 470 verbal; 530 mathematical; 38% of freshmen score above 500 on verbal, 9% above 600, 1% above 700; 66% score above 500 on mathematical, 22% above 600, 2% above 700; ACT, 24 composite. *Required:* SAT or ACT. Criteria considered in admissions, in order of importance: high school academic record, standardized test scores, writing sample, extracurricular activities, recommendations; other factors considered: special talents, diverse student body. *Out-of-state* freshman applicants: state does not limit out-of-state enrollment. States from which most out-of-state students are drawn include Alaska, California, Oregon, Idaho. *Entrance programs:* midyear admission, advanced placement. *Apply* by March 1; rolling admissions. *Transfers* welcome; 1,354 enrolled 1993–94.

Academic Environment. *Undergraduate studies* offered by colleges of Arts and Sciences, Business and Economics, Fine and Performing Arts, Fairhaven (a residential college emphasizing independent study), Huxley College of Environmental Studies, and the School of Education; the Graduate School offers masters programs. Graduation requirements include communication and critical thinking, comparative gender and multi-cultural studies, humanities, math/computer, social sciences, and science. Students cite small class size (20–21 average), "available and caring" faculty, and "freedom of opinion within class" as strengths of academic program. Degrees offered: bachelors, masters. Unusual, new, or notable majors include computer science, environmental studies, industrial technology, industrial design, recreation, visual communications, student designed majors.

About 15% of students entering as freshmen graduate within four years, 45% eventually; 84% of freshmen return for sophomore year. *Special programs:* independent study, study abroad (40 countries), honors, undergraduate research, individualized majors, credit by examination, internships, National Student Exchange, Shannon Point Marine Center, Institute for Freshwater Studies, Institute for Wildlife Toxicology, 3–2 in engineering. Adult Programs: program for students returning after time away. *Calendar:* quarter, summer school.

Undergraduate degrees conferred (1,879). 18% were in Business and Management, 13% were in Social Sciences, 13% were in Education, 7% were in Multi/Interdisciplinary Studies, 7% were in Psychology, 7% were in Visual and Performing Arts, 6% were in Communications, 5% were in Public Affairs, 4% were in Letters, 4% were in Engineering and Engineering Related Technology, 3% were in Home Economics, 3% were in Life Sciences, remainder in 11 other fields.

Graduates Career Data. About 80% of 1990–91 graduates employed. Employers typically hiring largest numbers of graduates include education, accounting, finance marketing and decision making, technology. Career Development Services include aptitude testing, placement service, resume/interview workshops, on-campus recruitment, internships, cooperative education, library resources.

Faculty. About 87% of faculty hold PhD or equivalent. About 56% of undergraduate classes taught by tenured faculty. About 30% of teaching faculty are female.

Student Body. About 94% of students from in state; 94% Northwest. An estimated 1% of students reported as Black, 6% Hispanic, 3% Asian, 1% Native American. *Minority group students:* special admission program available.

Varsity Sports. Men (NAIA): Basketball, Crew, Cross Country, Diving, Football, Golf, Soccer, Tennis, Track. Women (NAIA): Basketball, Cross Country, Crew, Diving, Soccer, Softball, Tennis, Track, Volleyball.

Campus Life. Student reports "Bellingham is a very neat small town. It is close to both Seattle and Vancouver." Many campus activities reported; strong interest reported in outdoor activities (biking, climbing, snow boarding, skiing, rollerblading). Alcohol permitted in rooms for students over 21. Motor vehicles allowed but parking "is very scarce."

About 27% of men, 29% of women live in coed dormitories; 3% of men, 5% of women live in college-owned off-campus housing; rest commute. Sexes segregated in coed dormitories either by floor or suite. There are no fraternities or sororities on campus. About 50% of resident students leave campus on weekends.

Annual Costs. Tuition and fees, $2,121 (out-of-state, $7,110); room and board, $3,956; estimated $1,970 other, exclusive of travel. About 65% of students receive financial aid; average amount of assistance, $5,340. Assistance is typically divided 23% scholarship, 34% grant, 31% loan, 12% work. College reports 200 scholarships awarded on the basis of academic merit alone, 25 for special talents alone, 5 for need alone.

Westfield State College

Westfield, Massachusetts 01086 **(413) 568-3311**

A state-supported college offering traditional liberal arts as well as career-oriented programs, Westfield State is located in a community of 35,000, in the foothills of the Berkshires, 10 miles west of Springfield.

Founded: 1838
Affiliation: State
UG Enrollment: 1,584 M, 1,693 W (full-time); 451 M, 491 W (part-time)
Total Enrollment: 4,978
Cost: < $10K
% Receiving Financial Aid: 70%
Admission: Non-selective
Application Deadline: March 1

Admission. About 65% of applicants accepted, 45% of these actually enroll; 11% of freshmen graduate in top fifth of high school class, 42% in top two-fifths. Average freshman SAT scores: 400–499 verbal; 400–499 mathematical. *Required:* SAT; minimum high school GPA 2.0; student profile; optional writing sample. Criteria considered in admissions, in order of importance: high school academic record, standardized test scores, extracurricular activities, writing sample; other factors considered: special talents, diverse student body. *Out-of-state* applicants: college actively seeks students from out-of-state. State does not limit out-of-state enrollment. States from which most out-of-state students are drawn include New England states, New York. *Entrance programs:* midyear admission, deferred admission. *Apply:* March 1; rolling admissions. *Transfers* welcome; 425 enrolled 1993–94.

Academic Environment. Graduation requirements include 41 credits in 7 categories including composition, humanities, arts appreciation, U.S. government, social sciences, math, and natural sciences. Degrees offered: bachelors, masters. Unusual, new, or notable majors include: teacher training.

About 50% of students entering as freshmen graduate within four years, 60% eventually; 75% of freshmen return for sophomore year. *Special programs:* CLEP, independent study, study abroad, honors, undergraduate research, internship, exchange with East Central Oklahoma State, Delta State (Mississippi), U.of Alaska, Arkansas Tech, U.of Wisconsin—Platteville, University of South Dakota, Northeast Missouri State, student teaching in Europe, South and Central America, cross registration with colleges of greater Springfield. *Calendar:* semester, summer school.

Undergraduate degrees conferred (783). 25% were in Education, 22% were in Business and Management, 18% were in Protective Services, 8% were in Psychology, 7% were in Social Sciences, 6% were in Communications, 4% were in Visual and Performing Arts, remainder in 9 other fields.

Faculty. About 75% of faculty hold PhD or equivalent. About 70% of undergraduate classes taught by tenured faculty. About 33% of teaching faculty are female.

Student Body. About 95% of students from in state; 99% New England. 1% Middle Atlantic. *Minority group students:* special academic provisions.

Varsity Sports. Men (Div.III): Baseball, Basketball, Football, Soccer, Track. Women (Div.III): Basketball, Diving, Hockey (Field), Soccer, Softball, Swimming, Track.

Campus Life. Students have self-determined hours and intervisitation. About 60% of students live in traditional or coed dormitories; rest live in off-campus housing or commute. There are no fraternities

or sororities on campus. About 20% of resident students leave campus on weekends.
Annual Costs. Tuition and fees, $3,060 (out-of-state, $7,200); room and board, $3,900; estimated $450 other, exclusive of travel. About 70% of students receive financial aid; average amount of assistance, $4,685. Assistance is typically divided 25% grant, 69% loan, 6% work. College reports scholarships awarded only on the basis need.

Westhampton College

(See University of Richmond)

Westmar College

(See Teikyo Westmar College)

Westminster Choir College

(See Rider College)

Westminster College

Fulton, Missouri 65251 **(314) 642-3361; (800) 475-3361**

An independent, co-educational liberal arts college, with relations by covenant with the Presbyterian Church, Westminster has an extensive program of cooperation with William Woods College for women. The 55-acre campus is located in a town of 12,100. Most convenient major airports: St. Louis (90 miles), Central Missouri Regional (Columbia, 25 miles).

Founded: 1851
Affiliation: Independent (Presbyterian)
UG Enrollment: 418 M, 284 W (full-time)
Cost: < $10K
% Receiving Financial Aid: 75%
Admission: Selective
Application Deadline: Rolling

Admission is selective. About 84% of applicants accepted, 33% of these actually enroll; 40% of freshmen graduate in top fifth of high school class, 65% in top two-fifths. Average freshman scores: SAT, 480 verbal, 520 mathematical; 40% of freshmen score above 500 on verbal, 14% above 600, 2% above 700; 72% score above 500 on mathematical, 29% above 600, 4% above 700; ACT, 24 composite. *Required:* SAT or ACT; recommendation; interview recommended. Criteria considered in admissions, in order of importance: high school academic record, standardized test scores, recommendations, extracurricular activities; other factors considered: alumni children, diverse student body. *Entrance programs:* early admission, midyear admission, advanced placement, deferred admission. About 30% of freshmen from private schools. *Apply:* rolling admissions. *Transfers* welcome; 51 enrolled 1993–94.
Academic Environment. Administration source characterizes student body as "bright, very job/goal oriented; interested in money-making majors!" Cross-registration with William Woods University brings about 350 additional students to classes at Westminster each year. Graduation requirements include 4 credits in English composition, 6 in math, 7 in a natural science, 3 in foreign language or culture, 15 credits in humanities, and 12 in social sciences. Degrees offered: bachelors. Average undergraduate class size: 75% under 20, 25% 20–40.

About 53% of students entering as freshmen graduate within four years; 77% of freshmen return for sophomore year. *Special programs:* CLEP, independent study, internships, study abroad, honors, learning disabilities program, 3-year degree, individualized majors, Washington Semester, United Nations Semester, Urban Semester, 3–2 (BS/MBA) engineering, spring short term, cooperative program with William Woods, Spring Term Consortium. *Calendar:* semester (second semester includes winter term, 3-week spring term).
Undergraduate degrees conferred (109). 39% were in Business and Management, 23% were in Social Sciences, 8% were in Psychology, 8% were in Letters, 7% were in Life Sciences, 7% were in Education, remainder in 4 other fields.
Graduates Career Data. Advanced studies pursued by 18% of graduates; 9% enter arts and science school; 5% enter law school, 2% enter medical school; 2% enter graduate school; 1% enter business school. Law schools typically enrolling largest numbers of graduates include U. of Missouri (Columbia); medical schools include U. of Missouri (Columbia). About 47% of graduates employed. Employers typically hiring largest numbers of graduates include State Farm, Purina Mills, Edward D. Jones, Boatmen's Trust. Career Development Services include aptitude testing, counseling groups, placement service, resume/interview workshops, on-campus recruitment, internships, library resources, alumni network, mock interviews, individual career exploration.
Faculty. About 66% of faculty hold PhD or equivalent. About 67% of undergraduate classes taught by tenured faculty. About 35% of teaching faculty are female; 2% Hispanic, 4% other minority.
Student Body. About 56% of students from in state; 82% Midwest, 12% South, 2% West, 2% foreign. An estimated 47% of students reported as Protestant, 20% Catholic, 1% Jewish, 22% unaffiliated; 3% Black, 2% Hispanic.
Religious Orientation. Westminster was founded by Presbyterians and "recognizes its roots in the Presbyterian and Reformed tradition of Christianity." College makes no religious demands on students; 10% of students affiliated with the church.
Varsity Sports. Men (NAIA): Baseball, Basketball, Cross Country, Golf, Soccer, Tennis. Women (NAIA): Basketball, Cross Country, Soccer, Softball, Tennis, Volleyball.
Campus Life. Campus environment influenced by close relationship with nearby William Woods and by very strong Greek system (over 70% of students join fraternities/sororities). Relations between Greeks and independents said to be "good for men; excellent among women." Intervisitation hours until midnight, 2 am on weekends. No smoking in classrooms. Alcohol not permitted in freshman residence halls; "no kegs anywhere!" Students caught with illegal drugs on campus are suspended. Cars allowed for all.

About 15% of men, 61% of women live in traditional dormitories; 24% of men, 28% of women live in coed dormitories; rest live in off-campus housing or commute. Freshmen given preference in college housing if all students cannot be accommodated. There are 6 fraternities, 3 sororities on campus which about 74% of men, 71% of women join; 56% of men live in fraternities; sororities do not provide residence facilities. About 5–10% of resident students leave campus on weekends.
Annual Costs. Tuition and fees, $9,950; room and board, $3,800; estimated $1,600 other, exclusive of travel. About 75% of students receive financial aid; average amount of assistance, $10,870. Assistance is typically divided 60% scholarship/grant, 30% loan, 10% work. College reports 4 scholarships awarded on the basis of academic merit, leadership, or athletic ability alone. *Meeting Costs:* college offers monthly payment plan.

Westminster College

New Wilmington, Pennsylvania 16172 **(412) 946-7100**

A church-related, liberal arts college, located in a town of 2,700, 60 miles north of Pittsburgh and 85 miles southeast of Cleveland. Most convenient major airport: Pittsburgh.

Founded: 1852
Affiliation: Presbyterian
UG Enrollment: 616 M, 795 W (full-time)
Cost: $10K–$20K
% Receiving Financial Aid: 91%
Admission: Selective
Application Deadline: Rolling

Admission is selective. About 87% of applicants accepted, 43% of these actually enroll; 48% of freshmen graduate in top fifth of high school class, 78% in top two-fifths. Average freshman scores: SAT, 463 M, 466 W verbal, 542 M, 506 W mathematical; ACT, 24 composite. *Required:* SAT or ACT, minimum high school GPA, essay, recommendations. Criteria considered in admissions, in order of importance: high school academic record, standardized test scores, writing sample, recommendations, extracurricular activities. *Entrance programs:* deferred admission, advanced placement. About 30% of entering students from private schools. *Apply:* rolling admissions. *Transfers* welcome; 42 enrolled 1993–94.

Academic Environment. Graduation requirements include writing, speaking, computers, religion, sciences, social sciences, humanities, literature, fine arts, and physical education. Students report challenging classes, helpful faculty, and "hands-on" work to be strengths of the academic program. Degrees offered: bachelors, masters. Unusual, new, or notable majors include: criminal justice, elementary education, industrial relations, psychobiology. Most undergraduate classes: 25–30.

About 70% of students entering as freshmen graduate within four years, 76% eventually; 90% of freshmen return for sophomore year. *Special programs:* January Term, internship, independent study, study abroad, honors, undergraduate research, individualized majors, Washington Semester, field experience, internships, 3–2 engineering. Adult programs: Lifelong Learning Program offers evening classes. *Calendar:* 4–1–4, summer school.

Undergraduate degrees conferred (299). 23% were in Business and Management, 16% were in Education, 15% were in Social Sciences, 9% were in Communications, 8% were in Letters, 7% were in Psychology, 5% were in Life Sciences, 4% were in Multi/Interdisciplinary Studies, 3% were in Mathematics, 3% were in Visual and Performing Arts, remainder in 5 other fields.

Graduates Career Data. Advanced studies pursued by 19% of graduates; 15% enter graduate school; 2% enter law school; 2% enter medical school; 1% enter business school. Law schools typically enrolling most graduates include Duquesne U.; medical schools include U.of Pittsburgh; business schools include Carnegie Mellon. About 82% 1992–93 graduates employed. Employers typically hiring most graduates include education, business, computer, health care. Career Development Services include counseling, job search assistance, internship, career workshops, on-campus recruiting, career resource library.

Faculty. About 78% of faculty hold PhD or equivalent. About 90% of undergraduate classes taught by tenured faculty. About 27% of teaching faculty are female.

Student Body. About 76% of students from in state; 90% Middle Atlantic, 8% New England. An estimated 56% of students reported as Protestant, 34% Catholic, 10% unaffiliated, 7% other; 1.5% as Black, 1% Asian, less than 1% other minority.

Religious Orientation. Westminster is a church-related institution; 24% of students affiliated with the church; 2 courses in religion required of all students; attendance at vesper and chapel services voluntary.

Varsity Sports. Men (NAIA Div.II): Baseball, Basketball, Cross Country, Football, Golf, Soccer, Swimming, Tennis, Track. Women (NAIA Div.II): Basketball, Cross Country, Soccer, Softball, Swimming, Tennis, Track, Volleyball.

Campus Life. Self-regulated hours for all students. Extended intervisitation hours on campus. Drinking prohibited on campus and at college functions. Cars or motorcycles allowed for all students. College encourages attendance at cultural and intellectual events of Liberal Arts Forum series which includes music, drama, seminars, lectures, films. Seniors permitted to live off campus, if college residence halls are filled.

About 66% of men, 90% of women live in traditional dormitories; no coed dormitories; 10% of men, 8% of women commute. Freshmen given preference in college housing if all students cannot be accommodated. There are 5 fraternities, 5 sororities on campus which about 50% of men, 50% of women join; 18% of men live in fraternities; sororities provide no residence facilities.

Annual Costs. Tuition and fees, $11,770; room and board, $3,430; estimated $1,000 other, exclusive of travel. About 91% of students receive financial aid; average amount of assistance, $8,000–9,000. Assistance is typically divided 60% scholarship/grant, 40% loan. College reports some scholarships awarded on the basis of academic merit alone.

Westminster College of Salt Lake City

Salt Lake City, Utah 84105 **(801) 488-4200**

A private co-educational, liberal arts college, located in a city of 1.1 million. Associations with Presbyterian Church and United Church of Christ still remain, but Westminster is now "fully interdenominational." Most convenient major airport: Salt Lake City International.

Founded: 1875
Affiliation: Independent
UG Enrollment: 335 M, 671 W (full-time); 270 M, 483 W (part-time)
Total Enrollment: 2,153
Cost: < $10K
% Receiving Financial Aid: 70%
Admission: Non-selective
Application Deadline: first day of semester

Admission. About 79% of applicants accepted, 30% of these actually enroll. Average freshman ACT scores: 23 M, 23 W composite. *Required:* SAT or ACT. Criteria considered in admissions, in order of importance: high school academic record, standardized test scores, recommendations, interview. *Entrance programs:* early decision, early admission, midyear admission. *Apply* by first day of semester. *Transfers* welcome; 276 enrolled 1993–94.

Academic Environment. Graduation requirements include skills requirements: computer literacy, English, foreign language, mathematics, and public speaking; distribution requirements: life sciences, physical sciences, social sciences, history, literature, arts/appreciation, arts/physical activity, and philosophy/religion. Degrees offered: bachelors, masters. Average undergraduate class size: 17.

About 35% of students entering as freshmen graduate within four years; 62% of students entering as freshmen return for sophomore year. *Special programs:* CLEP, study abroad, honors, orientation program, contractual majors, 3-year degree through credit for experiential learning, individualized majors, aviation program, degree program in nursing, cooperative work/study programs. *Calendar:* 4–4–1, summer school.

Undergraduate degrees conferred (289). 43% were in Business and Management, 13% were in Health Sciences, 9% were in Computer and Engineering Related Technology, 7% were in Social Sciences, 5% were in Psychology, 5% were in Education, 4% were in Communications, 4% were in Transportation and Material Moving, 3% were in Letters, remainder in 5 other fields.

Graduates Career Data. Advanced studies pursued by 26% of graduates; 8% enter graduate school; 7% enter business school; 4% enter law school. Career Development Services include resume writing workshops, career counseling, internships, cooperative education opportunities.

Faculty. About 83% of faculty hold PhD or equivalent.

Student Body. About 92% of students from in state. An estimated 12% of students reported as Catholic, 3% Protestant, 1% Jewish, 23% unaffiliated, 61% other and Latter Day Saints; 4% Hispanic, 6% other minority.

Varsity Sports. Men (NAIA): Soccer.

Campus Life. About 3% of men, 3% of women live in coed dormitories; rest commute. Freshmen are given preference in college housing if all students cannot be accommodated. Intervisitation in men's and women's dormitory rooms "allowed." There are no fraternities or sororities on campus.

Annual Costs. Tuition and fees, $8,820; room and board, $4,000; estimated $600 other, exclusive of travel. About 70% of students receive financial aid; average amount of assistance, $6,500. Assistance is typically divided 43% scholarship, 54% loan, 3% work. College reports 5 scholarships awarded on the basis of academic merit alone. *Meeting Costs:* college offers monthly payment plans, PLUS Loans.

Westmont College

Santa Barbara, California 93108 **(805) 565-6000; (800) 777-9011**

An independent, evangelical, liberal arts college, Westmont was founded as a school "to train Christian young men and women." The 140-acre campus is located 4 miles from Santa Barbara (pop. 75,000) and 90 miles north of metropolitan Los Angeles. Most convenient major airport: Santa Barbara.

Founded: 1940
Affiliation: Independent
UG Enrollment: 505 M, 771 W (full-time)
Cost: $10K–$20K
% Receiving Financial Aid: 80%
Admission: Selective
Application Deadline: Feb. 15

Admission is selective. About 75% of applicants accepted, 49% of these actually enroll; 64% of freshmen graduate in top fifth of high school class, 86% in top two-fifths. Average freshman SAT scores: 497 M, 504 W verbal; 567 M, 540 W mathematical; 56% of freshmen score above 500 on verbal, 13% above 600, 1% above 700; 72% score above 500 on mathematical, 25% above 600, 7% above 700. *Required:* SAT or ACT, essay. Criteria considered in admissions, in order of importance: high school academic record, standardized test scores, writing sample, religious affiliation or commitment, class rank, extracurricular activities, recommendations. *Entrance programs:* early action, midyear admission, deferred admission, advanced placement. About 2% of entering students from private schools. *Apply* by February 15. *Transfers* welcome; 112 enrolled 1993–94.

Academic Environment. Administration source reports strongest interest of student body is in economics and business, but with substantial concern also for other academic pursuits (including religious studies) and social activities. Graduation requirements include 0–16 units in competency requirements, 16 units in religious studies, 4 units in physical education, 28 units in general education distribution requirements, and 8 units in interdisciplinary studies. Degrees offered: bachelors. Unusual, new, or notable majors include communications, computer science, physics engineering. Average undergraduate class size: 59% under 20, 32% 20–40, 9% over 40.

About 81% of freshmen return for sophomore year. *Special programs:* CLEP, undergraduate research, independent study, study abroad, honors, internship/cooperative work-study, cross registration with Christian College Consortium, 3–2 engineering, combined program in medical technology, credit by examination, student designed majors. *Calendar:* semester, summer school.

Undergraduate degrees conferred (323). 37% were in Social Sciences, 11% were in Liberal/General Studies, 11% were in Letters, 9% were in Psychology, 8% were in Communications, 6% were in Philosophy and Religion, 4% were in Visual and Performing Arts, 4% were in Education, 4% were in Life Sciences, 3% were in Engineering, remainder in 5 other fields.

Graduates Career Data. Advanced studies pursued 77% of graduates. About 40% of 1992–93 graduates employed. Employers typically hiring largest numbers of graduates include: Apple Computer, Arthur Anderson, IBM, Martin Marietta. Career Development Services include counseling, computer-aided guidance programs, resource center, internships, job search strategies, resume writing and interviewing skills workshops, graduate school testing.

Faculty. About 81% of faculty hold PhD or equivalent. All undergraduate classes taught by tenured faculty. About 37% of teaching faculty are female; 7% minority.

Student Body. About 75% of students from in state; 83% West, 3% Midwest, 9% Northwest, 1% foreign. An estimated 97% of students reported as Protestant, 3% Catholic, 5% unaffiliated; 1% as Black, 4% Hispanic, 4% Asian, 4% other minority.

Religious Orientation. Westmont is an independent institution, seeking "a distinctively Christian life"; 4 courses in religion, attendance at 3 chapel services per week required of all students.

Varsity Sports. Men (NAIA): Baseball, Basketball, Cross Country, Soccer, Tennis, Track. Women (NAIA): Cross Country, Soccer, Tennis, Track, Volleyball.

Campus Life. College forbids use of alcohol or tobacco on campus; no social dancing permitted. "It is also expected that the Westmont family will avoid all forms of entertainment and any personal involvement which is spiritually or morally destructive." Intervisitation 5 nights a week, 5 PM to midnight. Cars and motorcycles not allowed for freshmen.

About 81% each of men, women live in coed dormitories; 3% of men, 5% of women live in off-campus housing; rest commute. Sexes segregated in dormitories either by wing or floor. There are no fraternities or sororities on campus. About 20% of resident students leave campus on weekends.

Annual Costs. Tuition and fees, $13,660; room and board, $5,072; estimated $1,280 other, exclusive of travel. About 80% of students receive financial aid; average amount of assistance, $10,000. Assistance is typically divided 7% scholarship, 48% grant, 35% loan, 10% work. College reports 50 scholarships awarded on the basis of academic merit alone, 116 for special talents alone, 187 for need alone.

Wheaton College

Wheaton, Illinois 60187 **(708) 752-5000**

An independent, Christian, liberal arts college, Wheaton is supported by a number of evangelical denominations. College maintains a conservative Christian faith coupled with high academic standards. Billy Graham is a well-known alumnus. The 70- acre campus is located in a suburban community of 39,000, 25 miles west of Chicago. Most convenient major airport: O'Hare (Chicago).

Founded: 1860
Affiliation: Independent
UG Enrollment: 1,036 M, 1,164 W (full-time)
Total Enrollment: 2,575
Cost: $10K–$20K
% Receiving Financial Aid: 55%
Admission: Very (+) Selective
Application Deadline: February 15

Admission is very (+) selective. About 64% of applicants accepted, 60% of these actually enroll; 79% of freshmen graduate in top fifth of high school class, 93% in top two-fifths. Average freshman scores, middle 50% range: SAT, 500–620 M, 510–620 W verbal, 570–680 M, 560–660 W mathematical; 80% of freshmen score above 500 on verbal, 38% above 600, 6% above 700; 94% score above 500 on mathematical, 58% above 600, 17% above 700; ACT, 25–30 M, 25–30 W composite. *Required:* SAT or ACT, minimum high school GPA, interview, essay, 2 recommendations. Criteria considered in admissions, in order of importance: high school academic record, standardized test scores, recommendations, writing sample, extracurricular activities; other factors considered: Christian commitment, special talents, alumni children, diverse student body. *Entrance programs:* early action, midyear admission, deferred admission, advanced placement. About 20% of entering students from private schools, 5% from parochial schools. *Apply* by February 15. *Transfers* welcome; 78 enrolled 1993–94.

Academic Environment. Pressures for academic achievement appear moderately intense. Atmosphere at Wheaton appears to be serious and dedicated primarily to academic pursuits; religious commitment of college and student body pervades both academic and Non-academic life. Graduation requirements include competency in foreign language, math, speech, and writing, area requirements in Bible, other cultures, fine arts, world history, literature, natural sciences, philosophy, physical education, and social sciences. Degrees offered: bachelors, masters, doctoral. Unusual, new, or notable majors include archaeology, elementary education, medical technology, computer science, interdisciplinary studies. Average undergraduate class size: 23.

About 70% of students entering as freshmen graduate within four years, 82% eventually; 92% of freshmen return for sophomore year. *Special programs:* Human Needs and Global Resources certificate program (requires internship in Third World country), independent study, study abroad, 3-year degree, professional quarter off campus, cross registration with Illinois Institute of Technology, 3–2 in nursing, engineering, internships. *Calendar:* quarter, summer school.

Undergraduate degrees conferred (555). 19% were in Letters, 17% were in Social Sciences, 13% were in Education, 10% were in Psychology, 8% were in Business and Management, 7% were in Theology, 5% were in Visual and Performing Arts, 5% were in Philosophy and Religion, 5% were in Life Sciences, 3% were in Physical Sciences, 3% were in Mathematics, 3% were in Foreign Languages, remainder in 4 other fields.

Graduates Career Data. Advanced studies pursued by 49% of students; 35% enter graduate school; 6% enter medical school; 6% enter law school; 5% enter business school. Career Development Services includes assistance in career planning/guidance, placement services.

Faculty. About 86% of faculty hold PhD or equivalent. About 22% of teaching faculty are female; 6% minority.

Student Body. About 22% of students from in state; 50% Midwest, 13% Middle Atlantic, 12% South, 10% West, 6% New England, 5% Northwest, 5% foreign. An estimated 99% of students reported as Protestant; 2% of students reported as Black, 2% Hispanic, 6% Asian, 1% other minority.

Religious Orientation. Wheaton is a conservative Christian institution whose central purpose is "integration of Biblical faith and learning"; 14 credit hours of religious courses; attendance at daily chapel services required.

Varsity Sports. Men (Div.III): Baseball, Basketball, Cross Country, Football, Golf, Soccer, Swimming, Tennis, Track, Wrestling. Women (Div.III): Basketball, Cross Country, Soccer, Softball, Swimming, Tennis, Track, Volleyball.

Campus Life. Student leader reports that primary interest of majority of students is religious activities. Variety of cultural activities provided on campus; nearest major cultural center is Chicago, 25 miles away. Regulations governing campus social life continue to be moderately strict. Cars permitted for all except freshmen. Except for commuting students, parking is said to be a problem. Dormitory regulations, curfew hours mildly stringent. Students must refrain "from gambling; from the possession or use of alcoholic beverages, tobacco, non-medicinal narcotic or hallucinogenic drugs, including marijuana; and from social dancing." Single undergraduate students not permitted to have their own apartments.

About 32% of men, 35% of women live in traditional dormitories; 23% of men, women live in college-related off-campus housing; rest commute; there are no fraternities or sororities. Freshmen are given preference in college housing if all students cannot be accommodated. About 5% of resident students leave campus on weekends.

Annual Costs. Tuition and fees, $10,640; room and board, $4,070; estimated $1,000 other, exclusive of travel. About 55% of students receive financial aid; average amount of assistance, $7,675. College reports 258 scholarships awarded on the basis of academic merit alone, 1,011 for need alone.

Wheaton College

Norton, Massachusetts 02766 **(800) 394-6003; (508) 285-8251**

A small, liberal arts college, Wheaton's 300-acre campus is located in a town of 10,000, 35 miles south of Boston and 15 miles north of Providence. Most convenient major airports: Providence (RI), Boston (MA).

Founded: 1834
Affiliation: Independent
UG Enrollment: 436 M, 899 W (full-time)
Cost: $10K–$20K
% Receiving Financial Aid: 58%
Admission: Selective (+)
Application Deadline: Feb. 1

Admission is selective (+). About 79% of applicants accepted, 30% of these actually enroll; 36% of freshmen graduate in top fifth of high school class, 65% in top two-fifths. Average freshman scores (tests are optional): SAT, 520 M, 530 W verbal, 560 M, 540 W mathematical; ACT, 26 M, 24 W composite. *Required:* essay; interview recommended. Criteria considered in admissions, in order of importance: high school academic record, writing sample, extracurricular activities, recommendations, standardized test scores; other factors considered: special talents, alumni children, diverse student body. *Entrance programs:* early decision, early admission, midyear admission, deferred admission, advanced placement. About 30% of entering students from private schools, 11% from parochial schools. *Apply* by February 1. *Transfers* welcome; 19 enrolled 1993–94.

Academic Environment. Graduation requirements include freshman seminar, English 101, 2 semesters of foreign language, 1 course in mathematics, computer science, or logical reasoning, 2 courses in natural sciences (1 lab), 1 course in social sciences, 1 course each in Western and non-Western history, and 1 course in cultural diversity. Wheaton Scholars Program allows outstanding students, working with 1 or more faculty advisors, to develop a 4-year program that meets their objectives without the usual degree requirements. Degrees offered: bachelors. Unusual, new, or notable majors include Asian studies, classical civilization, classics, computer science, economics, English (literature and writing), religion and philosophy, psychobiology, Russian studies. Average undergraduate class size: 77% under 20, 15% 20–40, 8% over 40.

About 70% of students entering as freshmen graduate within four years, 74% eventually; 87% of freshmen return for sophomore year. *Special programs:* CLEP, independent study, study abroad (junior year, summer and January-term programs), honors, undergraduate research, fieldwork for credit, individualized majors, career exploration internships during January-term, Twelve College Exchange, cross-registration with Brown U. and Stonehill College, Washington Semester, Mystic Seaport Semester (marine biology), National Theater Institute Program, 3–2 programs in business and management, computer science, engineering, management science, optometry, and religion, teacher certification at 3 levels. Adult programs: continuing education offers flexible requirements and scheduling for adult students. *Calendar:* semester.

Undergraduate degrees conferred (233). 39% were in Social Sciences, 18% were in Letters, 15% were in Psychology, 9% were in Visual and Performing Arts, 4% were in Philosophy and Religion, 4% were in Multi/Interdisciplinary Studies, 3% were in Life Sciences, 3% were in Foreign Languages, 3% were in Area and Ethnic Studies, remainder in 2 other fields.

Graduates Career Data. Advanced studies pursued by 21% of students; 15% enter graduate school; 4% enter law school; 1% enter medical school; 1% enter dental school. Law schools typically enrolling largest numbers of graduates include: Suffolk U. About 32% of 1992–93 graduates employed. Fields typically hiring most graduates include financial services, education, human services, retail. Career Development Services include planning services, individual advising, alumni networking, recruitment mentor and internship programs.

Faculty. About 95% of faculty hold PhD or equivalent. All of undergraduate classes taught by tenured faculty. About 50% of teaching faculty are female.

Student Body. About 41% of students from in state; 73% New England, 13% Middle Atlantic, 3% Midwest, 2% South, 3% West, 5% foreign. *Minority group students:* Multicultural Board, Union of Black Students, Asian Student Alliance.

Varsity Sports. Men (Div.III): Basketball, Cross Country, Diving, Lacrosse, Soccer, Swimming, Tennis, Track. Women (Div.III): Basketball, Cross Country, Diving, Hockey (field), Lacrosse, Soccer, Softball, Swimming, Tennis, Track, Volleyball.

Campus Life. Students have substantial degree of control over their own lifestyles. Wide variety of cultural and extracurricular activities and organizations provided on campus; resources of Boston and Providence are 35 and 15 miles away, respectively (college provides daily bus service to Boston). Cape Cod is within an hour's drive. Sports, both varsity and intramural reported popular. Cars allowed for all students; rules on alcohol conform to state law.

About 20% of women live in traditional dormitories; 84% of men, 67% of women live in coed dormitories; rest live in off campus housing or commute. There are no fraternities or sororities on campus. About 25% of resident students leave campus on weekends.

Annual Costs. Tuition and fees, $17,790; room and board, $6,050; estimated $800 other, exclusive of travel. About 58% of students receive financial aid; average amount of assistance, $16,150. Assistance is typically divided 69% grant, 23% loan, 8% work. College reports 725 scholarships awarded only on the basis of need. *Meeting Costs:* college offers short and long term payment plans.

Wheeling Jesuit College

Wheeling, West Virginia 26003 **(304) 243-2000**

A Jesuit, co-educational liberal arts college located in a small city of 43,000. Formerly known as Wheeling College. Most convenient major airport: Pittsburgh International.

Founded: 1954
Affiliation: Roman Catholic
UG Enrollment: 419 M, 552 W (full-time); 59 M, 246 W (part-time)
Total Enrollment: 1,440
Cost: < $10K
% Receiving Financial Aid: 75%
Admission: Non-selective
Application Deadline: June 1

Admission. High school graduates with 2.5 GPA, 15 academic units; 84% of applicants accepted, 28% of these actually enroll; 32% of freshmen graduate in top fifth of high school class, 62% in top two-fifths. Average freshman scores: SAT, 433 verbal, 479 mathematical; ACT, 21.5 composite. Criteria considered in admissions, in order of importance: high school academic record, standardized test scores, recommendations, extracurricular activities; other factors considered: alumni children, diverse student body. *Required:* SAT or ACT; interview recommended. *Entrance programs:* early admission, midyear admission, deferred admission, advanced placement. About 64% of entering students from parochial schools. *Apply* by June 1; rolling admissions. *Transfers* welcome; 45 enrolled 1993–94.

Academic Environment. Graduation requirements include 9 credits in English, 9 in math and science, 6 each in history, social sciences, and 15 in philosophy and theology. Degrees offered: bachelors, masters. Unusual, new, or notable majors include computer science, industrial engineering, international studies, management, nuclear medicine, respiratory therapy, professional writing, physical therapy, political and economic philosophy. Average undergraduate class size: 60% under 20, 39% 20–40, 1% over 40.

About 58% of students entering as freshmen graduate within four

years, 62% eventually; about 72% of freshmen return for sophomore year. *Special programs:* independent study, study abroad (Loyola U.-Rome), honors, individualized majors, tutorials, directed readings courses, 3–2 engineering, 5-year BA/MBA, major in technology connected with National Technology Transfer Center. Adult programs: evening programs in management and accounting; General Liberal Arts Degree; Bachelor of Human Resource Management designed for adults with 2 years of college work or equivalent experiences; BSN for nurses with RN. *Calendar:* semester, summer school.

Undergraduate degrees conferred (201). 45% were in Business and Management, 8% were in Psychology, 8% were in Health Sciences, 6% were in Liberal/General Studies, 6% were in Allied Health, 5% were in Social Sciences, 5% were in Marketing and Distribution, 4% were in Letters, 3% were in Life Sciences, 3% were in Computer and Engineering Related Technology, remainder in 6 other fields.

Graduates Career Data. Advanced studies pursued by 32% of students; 11% enter medical school; 6% enter graduate school; 1% enter business school; 1% enter law school. About 60% of 1992–93 graduates employed. Fields typically hiring largest numbers of graduates include accounting, hospitals, counseling, government. Career Development Services include job search skills, job fairs, employer recruiters.

Faculty. About 75% of faculty hold PhD or equivalent. About 95% of undergraduate classes taught by tenured faculty. About 36% of teaching faculty are female; 9% minority.

Student Body. About 40% of students from in state; 61% Middle Atlantic, 28% Midwest, 4% South, 5% foreign. An estimated 65% of students reported as Catholic, 25% Protestant, 10% other or unaffiliated. About 2% reported as Black, 2% Asian, 2% Hispanic. *Minority group students:* scholarships, loans, work/study program; Black Student Union.

Religious Orientation. Wheeling is a church-related institution; 2 academic courses in religious studies required of all students.

Varsity Sports. Men (NCAA Div.II): Basketball, Cross Country, Golf, Soccer, Swimming. Women (NCAA Div.II): Basketball, Cross Country, Soccer, Swimming, Volleyball.

Campus Life. Some provisions for daily intervisitation. Alcohol permitted for students over 21; cars allowed. No smoking in classroom buildings. Students expected to live in college-approved housing. On-campus housing available for all who want it. Freshmen and sophomores required to live on campus.

About 60% of men, 60% of women live in traditional dormitories; rest live in off-campus housing or commute. There are no fraternities or sororities on campus. About 25% of resident students leave campus on weekends.

Annual Costs. Tuition and fees, $10,000; room and board, $4,370; estimated $1,200 other, exclusive of travel. About 75% of students receive financial aid; average amount of assistance, $8,000. Assistance is typically divided 55% scholarship/grant, 35% loan, 10% work. College reports "many" scholarships awarded on the basis of academic merit alone. *Meeting Costs:* college offers private payment plans.

Wheelock College

Boston, Massachusetts 02215 (617) 734-5200

An independent, co-educational teachers college, Wheelock prepares its students to work with children in nursery school, kindergarten, primary grades and a variety of other settings. The urban campus is located in metropolitan Boston. Most convenient major airport: Logan International.

Founded: 1888
Affiliation: Independent
UG Enrollment: 23 M, 713 W (full-time)
Total Enrollment: 1,312
Cost: $10K–$20K
% Receiving Financial Aid: 74%
Admission: Non-selective
Application Deadline: February 15

Admission. High school graduates or equivalent eligible; 84% of applicants accepted, 49% of these actually enroll; 25% of freshmen graduate in top quarter of high school class; 60% in the top half. Average freshman SAT scores: 415 verbal, 440 mathematical. *Required:* SAT or ACT, essay, interview, 2 recommendations. Criteria considered in admissions, in order of importance: high school academic record, writing sample, recommendations, extracurricular activities, standardized test scores; other factors considered: special talents, diverse student body. *Entrance programs:* early decision, midyear admission, deferred admission, advanced placement. About 14% of entering students from private schools, 8% from parochial schools. *Apply* by February 15; rolling admissions. *Transfers* welcome; 83 enrolled 1993–94.

Academic Environment. Graduation requirements include 12 credits in math and science, 8 in arts, 12 in humanities, 8 in social sciences, 4 in multicultural studies, and 8 in human growth and development. Degrees offered: bachelors, masters. Average undergraduate class size: introductory lecture, 22; laboratory, 16; regular course, 16.

About 60% of students entering as freshmen graduate within 4 years; 81% of freshmen return for sophomore year. *Special programs:* honors, independent study, study abroad, cross registration with Simmons College, directed study, 4 years of internships, urban and rural teaching programs, music core program, special education, day care, infant and toddler education, children in hospitals, therapeutic tutoring program, museum education, off-campus practicum. *Calendar:* semester.

Undergraduate degrees conferred (139). 86% were in Education, 12% were in Public Affairs, 3% were in Vocational Home Economics.

Graduates Career Data. Advanced studies pursued by 7% of graduates; all enter graduate school. About 98% of 1992–93 graduates employed. Fields typically hiring largest numbers of graduates include day care centers, schools, social service agencies, hospitals. Career Development Services include resume workshops, job bank, career library, job fairs, on-campus recruitment, alumni services.

Faculty. About 78% of faculty hold PhD or equivalent. About 77% of teaching faculty are female; 14% Black, 12% other minority.

Student Body. About 52% of students from in state; 90% New England, 2% foreign. An estimated 7% of students reported as Black, 3% Hispanic, 3% other minority.

Varsity Sports. Women (NCAA Div.III): Basketball, Hockey (field, NAIA), Soccer, Softball.

Campus Life. Students represented on some college committees. Control of lifestyle by individual residential units; each residence hall determines its own rules, sets hours for visitation within existing college regulations. Rules on alcohol conform to state law. Cars not permitted for freshmen and sophomores; because of limited parking facilities, day students may drive to school only if public transportation not available.

About 60% of women live in traditional dormitories; 80% of men, 13% of women in coed dormitories; rest commute. Sexes segregated in coed dormitories by wing. There are no fraternities or sororities on campus. About 50% of resident students leave campus on weekends.

Annual Costs. Tuition and fees, $12,640; room and board, $5,360; estimated $300–500 other, exclusive of travel. About 74% of students receive financial aid; average amount of assistance, $10,500. Assistance is typically divided 54% scholarship/grant, 35% loan, 11% work. *Meeting Costs:* college offers Tuition Management systems, Academic Management Services.

College of White Plains

(See Pace University)

Whitman College

Walla Walla, Washington 99362 (509) 527-5176

Whitman is a small, highly regarded, independent, liberal arts college, located in a Pacific Northwest community of 26,000, which is also the home of two other colleges. The 45-acre campus is located in Walla Walla, 160 miles southwest of Spokane. Most convenient major airport: Walla Walla County Airport.

Founded: 1859
Affiliation: Independent
UG Enrollment: 570 M, 650 W (full-time)
Cost: $10K–$20K
% Receiving Financial Aid: 82%
Admission: Very (+) Selective
Application Deadline: Feb. 15

Admission is very (+) selective. About 61% of applicants accepted, 36% of these actually enroll; 70% of freshmen graduate in top fifth of high school class, 91% in top two-fifths. Average freshman scores:

SAT, 560 M, 530 W verbal, 640 M, 570 W mathematical; 76% of freshmen score above 500 on verbal, 32% above 600, 8% above 700; 88% score above 500 on mathematical, 51% above 600, 12% above 700; ACT, 27 M, 27 W composite. *Required:* SAT (preferred) or ACT, essay. Criteria considered in admissions, in order of importance: high school academic record, standardized test scores, writing sample, recommendations, extracurricular activities; other factors considered: special talents, alumni children, diverse student body. *Entrance programs:* early decision, advanced placement, deferred admission. *Apply* by February 15. *Transfers* welcome; 44 enrolled 1993–94.

Academic Environment. Students have some influence on curriculum matters through Student Government Committees meeting with Faculty Policy Committee. Student considers professors' "ability to relate and engage students in class activities and discussions" to be a strength of the academic program. He also felt the general education curriculum to be helpful. Pressures for academic achievement appear to be moderately intense. Whitman offers relatively flexible program with "concern for breadth of study." Specific requirements include 2 freshmen core classes, 1 senior colloquium, completion of distribution requirements, and comprehensive exams. Degrees offered: bachelors. Unusual, new, or notable majors include environmental studies, combined majors and pre-professional programs, gender studies (minor). Average undergraduate class size: 74% under 20, 23% 20–40, 3% over 40.

About 75% of students entering as freshmen graduate within four years, 77% eventually; 95% of freshmen return for sophomore year. *Special programs:* Urban semester, independent study, study abroad, honors, undergraduate research, January 1-week interterm (offers student-run "fun classes"), credit by examination, 3–2 engineering, 4–1 forestry, 3–3 law, 4–1 education, 4–2 business. *Calendar:* semester.

Undergraduate degrees conferred (306). 39% were in Social Sciences, 13% were in Letters, 11% were in Visual and Performing Arts, 10% were in Psychology, 9% were in Physical Sciences, 8% were in Life Sciences, 5% were in Foreign Languages, 4% were in Mathematics, remainder in Philosophy and Religion.

Graduates Career Data. Advanced studies pursued by 70% of graduates; 49% enter graduate school; 8% enter business school; 7% enter law school; 3% enter medical school. Medical schools typically enrolling largest numbers of graduates include U.of Washington, Oregon Health Sciences U.; business schools include U.of Chicago. Employers typically hiring largest numbers of graduates include Peace Corps, Microsoft. Career Development Services include internships, on-campus recruiting, career counseling, workshops on effective job search and attainment skills.

Faculty. About 93% of faculty hold PhD or equivalent. About 77% of undergraduate classes taught by tenured faculty. About 23% of teaching faculty are female; 6% minority.

Student Body. About 45% of students from in state; 56% Northwest, 24% West, 5% foreign. An estimated 1% of students reported as Black, 6% Asian, 1% Hispanic, 1% Native American, 2% other minority according to most recent data available. *Minority group students:* financial aid available; special academic advisers.

Varsity Sports. Men (NAIA Div.III): Baseball, Basketball, Cross Country, Golf, Skiing (Nordic and Alpine), Soccer, Swimming, Tennis, Track. Women (NAIA Div.III): Basketball, Cross Country, Skiing (Nordic and Alpine), Soccer, Swimming, Tennis, Track, Volleyball.

Campus Life. Administration source speaks of "extensive social opportunities on campus [which] promote personal development as well as intellectual growth." Student notes "There is no city life, no nightclubs or late night activities", but he adds "campus groups attempt to keep student life active daily—most activities are on campus." Sports are also reported popular. Almost 50% of students join fraternities and sororities, "but they do not shun the other 50%" according to student leader. Cars are allowed with parking space apparently no problem. Alcohol allowed in student rooms and social areas of residence halls.

About 5% of women live in traditional dormitories; 52% of men, 42% of women live in coed dormitories; 12% of men, 35% of men live in off-campus college-related housing; 2% of men, 2% of women commute. Freshmen guaranteed college housing. Sexes segregated in coed dormitories either by wing or floor. There are 5 fraternities, 5 sororities on campus which about 44% of men, 41% of women join; 34% of men live in fraternities; 16% women housed in sorority sections of women's dormitories. About 2% of resident students leave campus on weekends.

Annual Costs. Tuition and fees, $15,705; room and board, $4,790; estimated $700 other, exclusive of travel. About 82% of students receive financial aid; average amount of assistance, $10,009. Assistance is typically divided 62% scholarship, 14% grant, 14% loan, 10% work. College reports 96 scholarships awarded on basis of academic merit alone, 73 for special talents alone, 745 for need alone. *Meeting Costs:* college offers Whitman Loan Program for students and parents.

Whittier College

Whittier, California 90608 **(907) 907-4238**

An independent, liberal arts college, founded by Quakers, Whittier is located on a 95-acre campus in a suburban community of 72,900, 15 miles east of Los Angeles. Most convenient major airport: Los Angeles International or Ontario.

Founded: 1901
Affiliation: Independent
UG Enrollment: 562 M, 668 W (full-time)
Total Enrollment: 1,922

Cost: $10K–$20K
% Receiving Financial Aid: 78%
Admission: Selective (+)
Application Deadline: February 15

Admission is selective (+). About 64% applicants accepted, 32% of these enroll; 56% of freshmen graduate in top fifth of high school class, 78% in the top two-fifths. Average freshman SAT scores: 444 M, 462 W verbal, 520 M, 496 W mathematical; 30% of freshmen score above 500 on verbal, 7% above 600, 1% above 700; 57% of freshmen score above 500 on mathematical, 20% above 600, 3% above 700. *Required:* SAT, essay; interview recommended. Criteria considered in admissions, in order of importance: high school academic record, recommendations, standardized test scores, writing sample, extracurricular activities, leadership record, character and personality; other factors considered: special talents, alumni children, diverse student body. About 18% of entering students from parochial schools, 9% from private schools. *Entrance programs:* early decision, midyear admission, advanced placement, deferred admission. *Apply* by February 15 (priority); rolling admissions. *Transfers* welcome; 99 enrolled 1993–94.

Academic Environment. Graduation requirements: general education requirements are met either through the Liberal Education Program or the Whittier Scholar's Program. The Scholar's Program offers a self-designed interdisciplinary curricula. The Faculty Master's program offers out-of-classroom living and learning opportunities. Students consider the faculty to be a great strength: they "constantly go out of their way to help educate their students." Pair and team-taught courses and the mentoring and advising program are also cited as strengths. Degrees offered: bachelors, masters, doctoral. Average undergraduate class size: 20.

About 41% of students entering as freshmen graduate within four years, 54% within five years; 80% of freshmen return for sophomore year. *Special programs:* January Term, study abroad (including semester at U. of Copenhagen and January Interim Tours), internships, Washington Semester, International Negotiation Project, credit by examination, 3–2 engineering, BA/BFA with Otis Parsons, limited exchange programs. *Calendar:* flexible "4–1–4," summer school.

Undergraduate degrees conferred (199). 32% were in Social Sciences, 21% were in Business and Management, 7% were in Education, 7% were in Letters, 6% were in Life Sciences, 5% were in Visual and Performing Arts, 5% were in Psychology, 5% were in Vocational Home Economics, 4% were in Health Sciences, 3% were in Public Affairs, 3% were in Mathematics, remainder in 3 other fields.

Graduates Career Data. Advanced studies pursued by 32% of graduates; 19% enter graduate school; 5% enter law school; 4% enter medical school; 2% enter business school; 2% enter dental school. Medical schools typically enrolling largest numbers of graduates include Tufts; law schools include Whittier, Hastings; business schools include Claremont. About 41% of 1992–93 graduates employed. Employers typically hiring largest numbers of graduates include Parker/Hannifin, Bullocks/Macys, Expediturs International, Crawford & Company. Career Development Services include career planning, career preparation, job placement.

Faculty. About 89% of faculty hold PhD or equivalent. About 52% of undergraduate classes taught by tenured faculty. About 37% of

teaching faculty are female; 4% Black, 2% Hispanic, 16% other minority.
Student Body. About 68% of students from in state; 82% West, 7% Northwest, 2% New England, 3% Middle Atlantic, 2% South, 3% foreign. An estimated 4% of students reported as Black, 9% Asian, 23% Hispanic, 4% other minority. *Minority group students:* special financial assistance and academic programs; MECHA, Black Students Union.
Varsity Sports. Men (NCAA Div.III): Baseball, Basketball, Cross Country, Diving, Football, Golf, Lacrosse, Soccer, Swimming, Tennis, Track. Women (NCAA Div.III): Basketball, Cross Country, Diving, Soccer, Softball, Swimming, Tennis, Track, Volleyball.
Campus Life. Campus is located in a suburban area, 18 miles from Los Angeles, in the foothills of the San Gabriel Mountains. Student calls LA "very accessible, but being a half hour drive, it is not a major distraction." Students reported to spend on-campus leisure time with clubs, sports (formal and informal), "hanging-out" at the pool, studying, and at campus events (lectures, plays, and faculty master house events). "Uptown" Whittier offers shopping, restaurants and a movies theater. Cars allowed, but parking may be a problem. No regulations governing dorm hours or intervisitation.

About 64% of men, 59% of women live in coed-dormitories; rest live in off-campus housing or commute. Freshmen given preference in college housing if all students cannot be accommodated. There are 4 fraternities, 5 sororities on campus which about 17% of men, 24% of women join. About 15% of resident students leave campus on weekends.
Annual Costs. Tuition and fees, $16,236; room and board, $5,480; estimated $1,950 other, exclusive of travel. About 78% of students receive financial aid; average amount of assistance, $16,520. Assistance is typically divided 14% scholarship, 51% grant, 30% loan, 5% work. College reports 369 scholarships awarded on the basis of academic merit alone, 73 for special talents alone, 754 for need alone. *Meeting Costs:* college offers alternative financing programs.

Whitworth College

Spokane, Washington 99251 (509) 466-1000

A church-related, liberal arts college, located near a city of 350,000. Most convenient major airport: Spokane.

Founded: 1890
Affiliation: Presbyterian
UG Enrollment: 539 M, 732 W (full-time); 50 M, 109 W (part-time)
Total Enrollment: 1,839
Cost: $10K–$20K
% Receiving Financial Aid: 88%
Admission: Selective
Application Deadline: March 1

Admission is selective. About 83% of applicants accepted, 39% of these actually enroll; 62% of freshmen graduate in top fifth of high school class, 80% in top two-fifths. Average freshman scores: SAT, 490 verbal, 544 mathematical; ACT, 24 composite. *Required:* SAT or ACT or Washington Pre-College Test, essay, minimum high school GPA; interview recommended. Criteria considered in admissions, in order of importance: high school academic record, standardized test scores, recommendations, extracurricular activities, writing sample; other factors considered: special talents, diverse student body. Entrance Programs: early admission, advanced placement. *Apply* by March 1. *Transfers* welcome.
Academic Environment. Graduation requirements: about 50% of general education requirements for graduation are elective; distribution requirements fairly numerous. Students consider "committed" faculty to be "biggest" strength of the academic program. Degrees offered: bachelors, masters. Average undergraduate class size: 20% under 20, 60% 20–40, 20% over 40.

About 55% of students entering as freshmen graduate within four years, 65% eventually; 80% of freshmen return for sophomore year. *Special programs:* CLEP, independent study, faculty-led foreign study tours, 1,400 co-op/internship positions, 1,000 work-study positions, undergraduate research, individualized majors, 3–2 engineering, cooperative nursing program, arts administration program. *Calendar:* 4–1–4, summer school.
Undergraduate degrees conferred (296). 20% were in Business and Management, 19% were in Education, 15% were in Social Sciences, 7% were in Psychology, 7% were in Communications, 6% were in Letters, 5% were in Visual and Performing Arts, 4% were in Mathematics, 4% were in Physical Sciences, 4% were in Life Sciences, 3% were in Health Sciences, remainder in 4 other fields.
Graduates Career Data. Career Development Services include full service career planning and placement office.
Faculty. About 85% of faculty have PhD or equivalent. About 60% of undergraduate classes taught by tenured faculty. About 30% of teaching faculty are female; 5% Black, 5% other minority.
Student Body. About 50% of students from in state; 75% Northwest, 15% West, 8% foreign. An estimated 75% of students reported as Protestant, 10% Catholic, 15% other; 2% as Black, 2% Hispanic, 7% Asian, 4% other minority. *Minority group students:* Martin Luther King Fund; tutors and faculty assistance; International Club, Black Student Union.
Religious Orientation. Whitworth is a church-related institution; 25% of students affiliated with the church; 1 course in Biblical Literature required of all students.
Varsity Sports. Men (NAIA Div.II): Baseball, Basketball, Cross Country, Football, Soccer, Swimming, Tennis, Track. Women (NAIA Div.II): Basketball, Cross Country, Diving, Soccer, Swimming, Tennis, Track, Volleyball.
Campus Life. Students describe college community as "very close-knit and involved", with "a lot to do on campus for those who don't have cars." Campus events range from service projects to movies and dances; off-campus, outdoor activities (skiing, skating, hiking) are enjoyed. One student does note "It's much colder than I thought it would be." Cars permitted for all students. Alcohol prohibited on campus and at college functions.

About 10% of men, 10% of women live in traditional dormitories; 60% of men, 60% of women in coed dormitories; rest live in off-campus housing or commute. Sexes segregated in coed dormitories by floor. There are no fraternities or sororities. About 10% of resident students leave campus on weekends.
Annual Costs. Tuition and fees, $11,965; room and board, $4,300; estimated $1,100 other, exclusive of travel. About 88% of students receive financial aid, average amount received, $11,400. Assistance is typically divided 52% scholarship/grant, 37% loan, 11% work. College reports an "unlimited number" of scholarships awarded on the basis of 4 categories of merit.

Wichita State University

Wichita, Kansas 67260-0113 (316) 689-3456

A state-supported university, located in a city of 290,000. Most convenient major airport: Mid-Continent.

Founded: 1895
Affiliation: State
UG Enrollment: 3,246 M, 3,310 W (full-time); 2,534 M, 2,925 W (part-time)
Total Enrollment: 14,892
Cost: < $10K
% Receiving Financial Aid: 48%
Admission: Non-selective
Application Deadline: Rolling

Admission. Graduates of accredited Kansas high schools accepted; others admitted by examination or on conditional basis; 79% of applicants accepted, 64% of these actually enroll; 33% of freshmen graduate in top fifth of high school class, 58% in top two-fifths. Criteria considered in admissions, in order of importance: high school academic record, standardized test scores. *Out-of-state* freshman applicants: university seeks students from out of state. State does not limit out-of-state enrollment. Requirement for out-of-state applicants: rank in top half of class, 2.0 GPA or acceptable ACT scores. States from which most out-of-state students are drawn include Missouri, Nebraska, Oklahoma. *Entrance programs:* early admission, midyear admission, deferred admission, advanced placement. *Apply:* rolling admissions. *Transfers* welcome; 913 enrolled 1993–94.
Academic Environment. *Undergraduate studies* offered by colleges of Liberal Arts and Sciences, Education, Engineering, Fine Arts, Health Professions, school of Business; programs in minority studies and administration of justice. Graduation requirements include 6 hours of communication and composition, 6 hours of math, 9 of humanities/fine arts, 6 of social and behavioral sciences, 6 of math and natural sciences, and 9 hours of general studies. Degrees offered: associates, bachelors, masters, doctoral. Unusual, new, or notable majors include entrepreneurship, aerospace engineering.

About 35% of students entering as freshmen graduate eventually; 60% of freshmen return for sophomore year. *Special programs:* CLEP, independent study, study abroad, internship, credit by examination, honors, undergraduate research, 3-year degree, 3–2 accounting, 3–2 engineering, individualized majors. Adult programs: all programs designed for adult students; two-thirds of students over 22. *Calendar:* semester, summer school.

Undergraduate degrees conferred (1,626). 27% were in Business and Management, 10% were in Education, 10% were in Engineering, 10% were in Health Sciences, 8% were in Liberal/General Studies, 4% were in Communications, 4% were in Social Sciences, 4% were in Visual and Performing Arts, 3% were in Psychology, 3% were in Protective Services, 3% were in Public Affairs, 3% were in Computer and Engineering Related Technology, remainder in 10 other fields.

Graduates Career Data. Advanced studies pursued by 42% of graduates. Fields typically hiring largest numbers of graduates include health, education, engineering. Career Development Services include career counseling, employment fairs, on-campus recruitment, computerized job search lab, employment listing bulletin, part-time and summer employment opportunities.

Faculty. About 86% of faculty hold PhD or equivalent. About 30% of teaching faculty are female.

Student Body. About 86% of students from in state; 9% foreign. Average age of undergraduate student: 29.

Varsity Sports. Men (Div.I): Baseball, Basketball, Bowling, Crew, Cross Country, Golf, Tennis, Volleyball. Women (Div.I): Basketball, Bowling, Crew, Cross Country, Golf, Tennis, Volleyball.

Campus Life. About 3% of students live in co-ed dormitories; rest commute. Freshmen given preference in college housing if all students cannot be accommodated. There are 13 fraternities, 8 sororities on campus which less than 1% each of men, women join; 1% of students live in fraternities, sororities. About 96% of resident students leave campus on weekends.

Annual Costs. Tuition and fees, $1,995 (out-of-state, $6,501); room and board, $2,649; estimated $350 other, exclusive of travel. About 48% of students receive financial aid; average amount of assistance, $842. Assistance is typically divided 14% scholarship, 30% grant, 54% loan, 2% work. University reports 60% of scholarships awarded on the basis of academic merit alone, 10% for special talents alone, 30% for need alone.

Widener University

Chester, Pennsylvania 19013 (215) 499-4200

An independent, co-educational university, until 1972 Widener was known as the PMC Colleges, incorporating the Pennsylvania Military College and Penn Morton, a co-educational liberal arts institution. The college's military program has been replaced by a civilian ROTC unit. The 80-acre main campus is located in a community of 56,300, 15 miles south of Philadelphia. Most convenient major airport: Philadelphia.

Founded: 1821
Affiliation: Independent
UG Enrollment: 1,407 M, 996 W (full-time)
Total Enrollment: 4,472
Cost: $10K–$20K
% Receiving Financial Aid: 72%
Admission: Selective
Application Deadline: Rolling

Admission is selective. About 69% of applicants accepted, 37% of these actually enroll; 23% of freshmen graduate in top fifth of high school class, 61% in top two-fifths. Average freshman scores: SAT, 17% of freshmen score above 500 on verbal, 7% above 600, 1% above 700; 32% of freshmen score above 500 on mathematical, 15% above 600, 3% above 700. *Required:* SAT; essay; interview recommended. Criteria considered in admissions, in order of importance: high school academic record, recommendations, standardized test scores, writing sample, extracurricular activities. Criteria considered in admissions, in order of importance: high school academic record, standardized test scores, extracurricular activities, recommendations, writing sample; other factors considered: special talents, alumni children, diverse student body. *Entrance programs:* early decision, early admission, midyear admission, deferred admission, advanced placement. About 40% of entering students from parochial schools, 15% from private schools. *Apply:* rolling admissions. *Transfers* welcome; 255 enrolled 1993–94.

Academic Environment. University is organized into 4 learning centers: Arts and Science, Engineering, Management and Applied Economics, and Nursing. Special Exploratory Studies program for undecided students. Degrees offered: bachelors, masters, doctoral. Unusual, new, or notable majors include criminal justice, sports management, international affairs, nursing, hotel and restaurant management. Average undergraduate class size: 26; 75% 20–40, 5% over 40.

About 60% of students entering as freshmen graduate eventually. *Special programs:* CLEP, independent study, study abroad, undergraduate research, individualized majors, exploratory studies, exchange with Korean university, marine science program with summer courses and field experience, 4-year co-operative education programs (management, accounting, computer science, and engineering), urban ecology program, cross registration with Swarthmore, 3–4 programs with College of Osteopathic Medicine, College of Optometry, College of Podiatric Medicine. Adult program: University College, Weekend College. *Calendar:* 4–1–4, summer school.

Undergraduate degrees conferred (755). 49% were in Business and Management, 20% were in Engineering, 13% were in Health Sciences, 7% were in Psychology, 3% were in Social Sciences, remainder in 9 other fields.

Graduates Career Data. About 80% of 1992–93 graduates employed. Fields typically hiring largest numbers of graduates include accounting, management, hospitality, engineering. Career Development Services offered.

Faculty. About 89% of faculty hold PhD or equivalent. About 80% of undergraduate classes taught by tenured faculty.

Student Body. About 50% of students from in state; 85% Middle Atlantic, 9% New England, 4% foreign. An estimated 40% of students reported as Protestant, 50% Catholic, 5% Jewish, 2% Muslim, 3% other; 10% as Black, 2% Hispanic, 3% Asian, 4% other minority. *Minority group students:* Project Prepare program set up for educationally and financially disadvantaged students; Black Student Union.

Varsity Sports. Men (Div.III): Baseball, Basketball, Cross Country, Football, Golf, Lacrosse, Soccer, Swimming, Tennis, Track. Women (Div.III): Basketball, Cross Country, Softball, Swimming, Tennis, Track, Volleyball.

Campus Life. Students over 21 may have beer and wine in their rooms. Cars allowed; smoking restricted, not allowed in classrooms and library; drugs prohibited. Intervisitation hours unlimited unless restricted by student living group. Students expected to live on campus.

About 50% of men, 50% of women live in traditional dormitories; 5% of men, 5% of women live in coed dormitories; 37% of men, 39% of women commute. Freshmen given preference in college housing if all students cannot be accommodated. There are 8 fraternities, 6 sororities on campus which about 20% of men, 17% of women join; 8% of men, 6% of women live in fraternities and sororities. About 20% of resident students leave campus on weekends.

Annual Costs. Tuition and fees, $11,740; room and board, $5,400; estimated $100 other, exclusive of travel. About 72% of students receive financial aid; average amount of assistance, $7,200. Assistance is typically divided 50% grant, 40% loan, 10% work. College reports 45 scholarships awarded on the basis of academic merit alone. *Meeting Costs:* university offers monthly payment plan.

Wilberforce University

Wilberforce, Ohio 45384 In-state, (800) 367-8565; Out-of-state, (800) 367-8568

A church-related university, located in a rural area, 3 miles northeast of Xenia (pop. 25,400) and 20 miles east of Dayton; founded as a college for Negroes and still serving a predominantly black student body. Cooperative program, required of all students, combines alternate periods of academic instruction and employment. Most convenient major airport: Dayton.

Founded: 1856
Affiliation: African Methodist Episcopal
UG Enrollment: 796 M, W (full-time)
Cost: < $10K
% Receiving Financial Aid: 95%
Admission: Non-selective
Application Deadline: June 1

Admission. Graduates of accredited high schools with 15 units, with 2.0 GPA and rank in upper two-thirds of class eligible; 62% of applicants accepted, 36% of these actually enroll. Average freshman

ACT scores, according to most recent data available: 16 M, 16 W composite. *Required:* ACT or SAT. *Apply* by . *Transfers* welcome.

Academic Environment. *Degrees:* AB, BS. About 35% of general education credits for graduation are required; distribution requirements fairly numerous. About 50% of students entering as freshmen graduate eventually; 54% of freshmen return for sophomore year. *Special programs:* CLEP, honors, study abroad, dual degree in engineering and computer science, joint degree program in law with St. John's U., cross-registration through Dayton-Miami Valley Consortium. Adult programs: Adult Entry Program offering evening and weekend courses for adults; credit for life-learning. *Calendar:* trimester.

Undergraduate degrees conferred (107). 32% were in Business and Management, 17% were in Social Sciences, 10% were in Psychology, 9% were in Life Sciences, 9% were in Communications, 7% were in Health Sciences, 7% were in Mathematics, 3% were in Visual and Performing Arts, 3% were in Liberal/General Studies, remainder in 2 other fields.

Graduates Career Data. According to most recent data available, full-time graduate or professional study pursued immediately after graduation by 10% of students. *Careers in business and industry* pursued by 60% of graduates.

Faculty. About 23% of faculty hold PhD or equivalent.

Student Body. About 40% of students from in state; 80% North Central, 11% Middle Atlantic, 4% South. An estimated 47% of students reported as Protestant, 4% Catholic, 49% other; 97% Black, according to most recent data available.

Religious Orientation. Wilberforce is a church-related institution; 3 hours of religion required of all students.

Campus Life. About 80% of men, 83% of women live in traditional dormitories; rest live in off-campus housing or commute. Freshmen given preference in college housing if all students cannot be accommodated. Intervisitation in men's and women's dormitory rooms limited. There are 4 fraternities, 3 sororities on campus which about 20% of men, 20% of women join.

Annual Costs. Tuition and fees, $6,984; room and board, $3,562. About 95% of students receive financial aid. University reports some scholarships awarded on the basis of academic merit alone. *Meeting Costs:* university offers payment plans.

Wiley College

Marshall, Texas 75670 **(214) 938-8341**

A church-related institution, located in a city of 23,000; founded as a college for Negroes and still serving a predominantly black student body. Most convenient major airports: Shreveport (LA), Dallas.

Founded: 1873	**Cost:** < $10K
Affiliation: United Methodist	**% Receiving Financial Aid:** 92%
UG Enrollment: 432 M, W (full-time)	**Admission:** Non-selective
	Application Deadline: Rolling

Admission. High school graduates with 15 units (11 in academic subjects) eligible; 99% of applicants accepted, 33% of these actually enroll; 9% of freshmen graduate in top fifth of high school class, 37% in top two-fifths. *Required:* high school record. *Apply* by no specific deadline. *Transfers* welcome.

Academic Environment. *Degrees:* AB, BS, BBA. About 50% of students entering as freshmen graduate eventually; 80% of freshmen return for sophomore year. *Special programs:* independent study, honors, 3–2 engineering. *Calendar:* semester.

Undergraduate degrees conferred (24). 42% were in Business and Management, 13% were in Social Sciences, 8% were in Life Sciences, 8% were in Education, 8% were in Computer and Engineering Related Technology, 8% were in Communications, 4% were in Physical Sciences, 4% were in Letters, 4% were in Business (Administrative Support).

Student Body. About 65% of students from in state; 95% South, 2% each Middle Atlantic, North Central.

Religious Orientation. Wiley is a church-related institution; 2 courses in religion required of all students; attendance at church and vespers expected.

Campus Life. About 68% of men, 59% of women live in traditional dormitories; no coed dormitories; rest commute. No intervisitation in men's or women's dormitory rooms. There are 4 fraternities, 4 sororities on campus which about 23% of men, 55% of women join; they provide no residence facilities. About 80% of resident students leave campus on weekends.

Annual Costs. Tuition and fees, $3,946; room and board, $2,672. About 92% of students receive financial aid.

Wilkes University

Wilkes-Barre, Pennsylvania 18766 **In-state, (800) 572-4444; Out-of-state, (800) 537-4444**

An independent, liberal arts college, Wilkes is located in a community of 58,900, 130 miles west of New York City. Most convenient major airport: Wilkes Barre/Scranton International.

Founded: 1933	**Cost:** $10K–$20K
Affiliation: Independent	**% Receiving Financial Aid:** 80%
UG Enrollment: 3,263 M, W (full-time)	**Admission:** Non-selective
	Application Deadline: Rolling

Admission. High school graduates, preferably in college preparatory program, eligible; additional requirements in some programs; 88% of applicants accepted, 32% of these actually enroll; 36% of freshmen graduate in top fifth of high school class, 61% in top two-fifths. Average freshman SAT scores, middle 50% range, according to most recent data available: 390–490 M, 390–490 W verbal, 450–590 M, 420–560 W mathematical. *Required:* SAT, audition for music, portfolio for art; interview recommended. *Non-academic factors* considered in admissions: extracurricular activities. *Entrance programs:* early decision, early admission, midyear admission, deferred admission, advanced placement. *Apply:* rolling admissions. *Transfers* welcome.

Academic Environment. Both student leader and administration spokesman characterize student body as overwhelmingly oriented toward occupational/professional goals. *Degrees:* AB, BS. *Majors offered* include accounting, business administration, computer science, education, engineering, fine arts, nursing, urban affairs, mechanical engineering.

About 60% of students entering as freshmen graduate eventually; 78% of freshmen return for sophomore year. *Special programs:* honors, undergraduate research, study abroad, independent study, individualized studies, cooperative education, combined program in medical technology, cooperative graduate programs with Temple and Lehigh for regional teachers and businessmen, cooperative 7-year programs with Pennsylvania College of Optometry, Pennsylvania College of Podiatric Medicine, with Temple in dentistry. *Calendar:* semester, summer school.

Undergraduate degrees conferred (500). 30% were in Business and Management, 14% were in Health Sciences, 11% were in Social Sciences, 10% were in Psychology, 7% were in Communications, 6% were in Life Sciences, 6% were in Engineering, 4% were in Visual and Performing Arts, 4% were in Computer and Engineering Related Technology, 3% were in Physical Sciences, remainder in 6 other fields.

Graduates Career Data. According to most recent data available, full-time graduate or professional study pursued immediately after graduation by 23% of students. *Careers in business and industry* pursued by 85% of graduates. Corporations typically hiring largest numbers of graduates include hospitals, First Eastern Bank.

Faculty. About 70% of faculty hold PhD or equivalent.

Student Body. About 84% of students from in state; 98% Middle Atlantic. An estimated 1% of students reported as Black, 2% other minority according to most recent data available.

Varsity Sports. Men (Div.III): Baseball, Basketball, Cross Country, Football, Golf, Soccer, Tennis, Wrestling (I). Women (Div.III): Basketball, Field Hockey, Soccer, Softball, Tennis, Volleyball.

Campus Life. Alcohol prohibited on campus and at college functions; cars discouraged because of parking limitations, but no specific restrictions. Students over 21 and all upperclassmen may, with parental consent, reside off campus.

About 22% of men, 15% of women live in traditional dormitories; 12% of men, 15% of women in coed dormitories; rest commute. Freshmen given preference in college housing if all students cannot be accommodated. There are no fraternities, one sorority on campus. About 35% of resident students leave campus on weekends.

Annual Costs. Tuition and fees, $10,898; room and board, $4,830. About 80% of students receive financial aid; assistance is typically divided 55% scholarship, 41% loan, 4% work. College reports some scholarships awarded on the basis of academic merit alone. *Meeting Costs:* college offers installment payment plan.

Willamette University

Salem, Oregon 97301-3922 (503) 370-6303

Essentially a small, church-related, liberal arts college, Willamette also includes a College of Law and Graduate School of Management. The 57-acre campus is located in the heart of Salem (pop. 95,000), directly across the street from the state capital. Most convenient major airport: Portland International.

Founded: 1842
Affiliation: United Methodist
UG Enrollment: 712 M, 883 W (full-time)
Total Enrollment: 2,335
Cost: $10K–$20K
% Receiving Financial Aid: 75%
Admission: Very Selective
Application Deadline: February 1

Admission is very selective. About 79% of applicants accepted, 30% of these actually enroll; 73% of freshmen graduate in top fifth of high school class, 92% in top two-fifths. Average freshman scores: SAT, 527 M, 520 W verbal, 597 M, 561 W mathematical; 62% of freshmen score above 500 on verbal, 20% above 600, 2% above 700; 82% score above 500 on mathematical, 42% above 600, 9% above 700; ACT, 26 M, 25 W composite. *Required:* SAT or ACT, essay; interview recommended. Criteria considered in admissions, in order of importance: high school academic record, class rank, writing sample, standardized test scores, recommendations, extracurricular activities; other factors considered: diverse student body, special talents. *Entrance programs:* early decision, early admission, deferred admission. About 10% of entering students from private schools, 5% from parochial schools. *Apply* by February 1. *Transfers* welcome; 100 enrolled 1993–94.

Academic Environment. Student body is characterized as both pragmatic and scholarly. Career-oriented programs are popular. Graduation requirements include 4 semester hours in each of the following: natural sciences, social sciences, fine arts, humanities, literature, Freshman World Views Seminar, and one other interdisciplinary course; and proficiency in English language and basic math and a Senior Year Experience, which may be an internship, field study, artistic performance, or research project. Specific requirements for individual fields of study vary. Degrees offered: bachelors, masters. *Majors offered* include American studies, music therapy, rhetoric & media studies, environmental studies. Average undergraduate class size: 61% under 20, 37% between 20–40, 2% over 40. Students report faculty is "very accessible".

About 71% of students entering as freshmen graduate in four years; 88% of freshmen return for sophomore year. *Special programs:* study abroad, undergraduate research, independent study, Washington Semester, United Nations Semester, intern programs, 3–2 programs in engineering, forestry, computer science, management. *Calendar:* semester.

Undergraduate degrees conferred (340). 24% were in Social Sciences, 15% were in Business and Management, 14% were in Letters, 11% were in Psychology, 7% were in Foreign Languages, 6% were in Physical Sciences, 6% were in Life Sciences, 5% were in Area and Ethnic Studies, 4% were in Visual and Performing Arts, 4% were in Philosophy and Religion, remainder in 4 other fields.

Graduates Career Data. Advanced studies pursued by 30% of students; 3% enter medical school; 1% enter dental school; 3% enter law school; 2% enter business school, 6% enter other schools. About 50% of 1992–93 graduates employed. *Career Counseling Program:* Willamette is a member of Oregon Liberal Arts Consortium, an organization of nine schools which sponsor job fairs and recruitment with over 100 businesses. Alumni reported as active in career guidance but not in job placement.

Faculty. About 90% of faculty hold PhD or equivalent. About 45% of undergraduate classes taught by tenured faculty. About 37% of teaching faculty are female; 1% Black, 4% Hispanic, 3% other minority.

Student Body. University seeks a national student body; 45% of students from in state; 25% West, 60% Northwest, 4% New England, 3% Middle Atlantic, 3% Midwest; 5% Foreign. An estimated 44% of students reported as Protestant, 17% Catholic, 3% Jewish; 1% as Black, 3% Hispanic, 6% Asian, 1% other minority.

Varsity Sports. Men (NCAA Div.III; NAIA): Baseball, Basketball, Crew, Cross Country, Football, Golf, Lacrosse, Soccer, Swimming, Tennis, Track. Women (NCAA Div.III; NAIA): Basketball, Crew, Cross Country, Soccer, Softball, Swimming, Tennis, Track, Volleyball.

Campus Life. Recent student leader reports students, generally, find regulations governing campus life are "satisfactory." Alcohol permitted in student residences. Cars permitted for all students. All students under 21 or below junior class status must live on campus or at home. Protective environment of campus attractive to many parents.

About 60% of men, 60% of women in coed dormitories; 5% of men, 5% of women live in off-campus college-related housing; 10% of students commute. Freshmen given preference in college housing if all students cannot be accommodated. Sexes segregated in coed dormitories either by wing or floor. There are 6 fraternities, 3 sororities on campus which about 30% of men, 30% of women join; 25% of men, 25% of women live in fraternities and sororities. About 10% of resident students leave campus on weekends.

Annual Costs. Tuition and fees, $13,665 room and board, $4,420; estimated $1,115 other, exclusive of travel. About 75% of students receive financial aid; average amount of assistance, $12,000. Assistance is typically divided 50% scholarship, 5% grant, 35% loan, 10% work. University reports 153 scholarships awarded for academic merit, 151 for special talents, 991 for need. *Meeting Costs:* university offers extended payment plans, PLUS Loans.

College of William and Mary

Williamsburg, Virginia 23185 (804) 221-4223

Long popular with Northern students, William and Mary is the second oldest institution of higher learning in the country. The college desires a national student body; subject to the moderate restriction of a 35% quota for out-of-state enrollment. Phi Beta Kappa was founded at William and Mary in 1776. The 1,200-acre campus is located at the edge of historic Williamsburg (pop. 11,000). Most convenient major airport: Patrick Henry (Newport News, VA).

Founded: 1693
Affiliation: State
UG Enrollment: 2,382 M, 2,855 W (full-time); 51 M, 68 W (part-time)
Total Enrollment: 7,116
Cost: < $10K
% Receiving Financial Aid: 21%
Admission: Highly Selective
Application Deadline: Jan. 15

Admission is highly selective. About 36% of applicants accepted, 44% of these actually enroll; 91% of freshmen graduate in top fifth of high school class, 99% in top two-fifths. Average freshman SAT scores, according to most recent data available: 577 M, 583 W verbal, 649 M, 621 W mathematical; 85% of freshmen score above 500 on verbal, 45% above 600, 8% above 700; 96% score above 500 on mathematical, 72% above 600, 21% above 700. *Required:* SAT. *Out-of-state* freshman applicants: college welcomes students from out of state. State limits out-of-state enrollment to 35% of student body. No special requirements for out-of-state applicants; however SAT scores are slightly higher for out-of-state students than for Virginians; 23% accepted, 39% enroll. *Non-academic factors* considered in admissions: special talents, alumni children, diverse student body, extracurricular activities, leadership, creativity, tenacity, and character. *Entrance programs:* early decision, early admission, midyear admission, deferred admission, advanced placement. About 17% of entering students from private or parochial schools. *Apply* by January 15. *Transfers* welcome.

Academic Environment. Students characterized as somewhat career oriented, but "academically motivated," "involved," and "stimulated by competition." Curriculum offers considerable flexibility in planning individual programs, freshman seminars, and interdisciplinary studies. Especially strong programs at the graduate level offered in marine biology with neighboring Virginia Institute of Marine Science at Gloucester Point; in early American history with the Williamsburg Institute of Early American History and Culture; and in physics in cooperation with the Virginia Associated Research Center and National Aeronautics and Space Administration special development program. Students have considerable freedom in selecting academic program—distribution requirements include 3 courses each in the humanities, social sciences, and the sciences. With the emergence of graduate research facilities, some student concern expressed about " the maintenance of the high quality undergraduate program." All courses taught by regular faculty. Undergraduate degrees: AB, BS, BBA. *Majors offered* include usual arts and sciences, accounting, anthropology, business administration, education, fine arts, theater, computer science, American studies, public policy, European studies; interdisciplinary majors also possible. School attracts a wide diversity of bright, motivated students, substantial numbers of these from New England and Middle Atlantic states.

About 5% of freshmen do not return for sophomore year. *Special programs:* independent study, study abroad, honors, undergraduate research, 3-year degree, individualized majors, 3–2 engineering with Columbia, Case Western, Washington U., UVA, RPI, 4–1 forestry with Duke. *Calendar:* semester, summer school.

Undergraduate degrees conferred (1,312). 29% were in Social Sciences, 16% were in Business and Management, 11% were in Letters, 8% were in Psychology, 7% were in Multi/Interdisciplinary Studies, 7% were in Life Sciences, 5% were in Physical Sciences, 4% were in Visual and Performing Arts, 3% were in Education, 3% were in Philosophy and Religion, remainder in 3 other fields.

Graduates Career Data. According to most recent data available, full-time graduate study pursued immediately after graduation by 18% of students; 6% enter health sciences; 8% enter law school; 1% enter business school. Medical and dental schools typically enrolling largest numbers of graduates include Medical College of Virginia, UVA; law schools include U. of Virginia, William & Mary. *Careers in business and industry* pursued by 66% of graduates. Corporations typically hiring largest numbers of graduates include Arthur Andersen, KPMG Peat Marwick. Career Development Services include career guidance, help in job placement, interview preparation. Alumni reported as helpful in both career guidance and job placement.

Faculty. About 93% of faculty hold PhD or equivalent.

Student Body. College seeks a national student body; 66% of students from in state; 71% South, 16% Middle Atlantic; 176 foreign students. An estimated 46% of students reported as Protestant, 30% Catholic, 2% Jewish, 20% unaffiliated, 2% other; 6% Black, 1% Hispanic, 3% Asian, 4% other minority, according to most recent data available.

Varsity Sports. Men (Div.I): Baseball, Basketball, Cross Country, Fencing, Football (IAA), Golf, Gymnastics, Soccer, Swimming/Diving, Tennis, Track. Women (Div.I): Basketball, Cross Country, Diving, Field Hockey, Golf, Gymnastics, Lacrosse, Soccer, Swimming/Diving, Tennis, Track, Volleyball.

Campus Life. Diversity of student body demonstrated by wide variety of activities reported "of interest" to students. Fraternities/sororities attract large minority of students and tend to dominate social life, but student leader reports independent organizations also sponsor a wide array of events. Regulations governing campus social life are moderate. Some elements of college life regulated under college's honor system (oldest in the U.S.) and residence hall governance policy of self- determination. Dormitory visitation, closing hours, and related matters in hands of a governing council elected by each dormitory. Drinking not allowed in public areas on campus. Freshmen must live in campus housing. College offers wide variety of cultural and intellectual activities on campus. Nearest major cultural center, Richmond, is 52 miles away. Cars allowed for juniors and seniors, but parking reported as inadequate.

About 4% of men, 25% of women live in traditional dormitories; 46% of men, 45% of women in coed dormitories; 7% of men, 4% of women in off-campus housing; 26% of men, 21% of women commute. Sexes segregated in coed dormitories by floor. Freshmen are given preference in college housing if all students cannot be accommodated. There are 14 fraternities, 13 sororities on campus which about 40% of men, 47% of women join; 17% of men, 5% of women live in fraternities and sororities.

Annual Costs. Tuition and fees, $4,046 (out-of-state, $11,426); room and board, $3,902. About 21% of students receive need-based financial aid; assistance is typically divided 55% scholarship, 40% loan, 5% work. College reports limited number of scholarships awarded for academic merit.

William Carey College

Hattiesburg, Mississippi 39401 (601) 582-6103

A church-related college, located in a city of 40,000, 90 miles southeast of Jackson.

Founded: 1906	**Cost:** < $10K
Affiliation: Southern Baptist	**Admission:** Non-selective
UG Enrollment: 1,300 M, W (full-time)	**Application Deadline:** August 15

Admission. Graduates of accredited high schools with 15 units (11 in academic subjects) who rank in top half of class admitted; others given individual consideration; 95% of applicants accepted, 71% of these actually enroll; 35% of freshmen graduate in top fifth of high school class, 65% in top two-fifths. *Required:* ACT. *Apply* by August 15. *Transfers* welcome.

Academic Environment. *Degrees:* AB, BS, BFA, BM, BSB, BSN. About 30% of students entering as freshmen graduate eventually; 20% of freshmen do not return for sophomore year. School of Education recently added. Special programs: CLEP, independent study, study abroad, honors, undergraduate research, 3-year degree. *Calendar:* semester, summer school.

Undergraduate degrees conferred (190). 32% were in Business and Management, 29% were in Education, 10% were in Health Sciences, 7% were in Psychology, 4% were in Theology, 4% were in Allied Health, 3% were in Life Sciences, 3% were in Computer and Engineering Related Technology, remainder in 9 other fields.

Student Body. About 96% of students from in state.

Religious Orientation. William Carey is a church-related institution; 6 hours of Bible, attendance at chapel required of all students.

Varsity Sports. Men (NAIA): Baseball, Basketball, Tennis, Soccer. Women (NAIA): Basketball.

Campus Life. About 46% of men, 43% of women live in traditional dormitories; no coed dormitories; 54% of men, 57% of women commute. No intervisitation in men's or women's dormitory rooms. Freshmen are given preference in college housing if all students cannot be accommodated. There are no fraternities or sororities.

Annual Costs. Tuition and fees, $4,450; room and board, $2,110. College reports some scholarships awarded for academic merit. *Meeting Costs:* college offers deferred tuition, budget plan.

William Jennings Bryan College

Dayton, Tennessee, 37321 (615) 775-2041

An independent, nonsectarian college in the evangelical Protestant tradition, located in a community of 6,700, 38 miles north of Chattanooga. Also known as Bryan College. Most convenient major airport: Lovell Field, Chattanooga.

Founded: 1930	**Cost:** < $10K
Affiliation: Independent	**% Receiving Financial Aid:** 90%
UG Enrollment: 193 M, 217 W (full-time)	**Admission:** Non-selective
	Application Deadline: Rolling

Admission. Graduates of approved high schools with at least 20 units and C+ average eligible; 62% of applicants accepted, 52% of these actually enroll. Average freshman scores: SAT, 453 M, 437 W verbal, 497 M, 493 W mathematical; ACT, 21.5 M, 23.6 W composite. *Required:* ACT, minimum H. S. GPA. Criteria considered in admissions, in order of importance: high school academic record, standardized test scores, recommendations, writing sample, extracurricular activities; other factors considered: special talents, alumni children, religious affiliation and/or commitment. *Entrance programs:* early admission, midyear admission, advanced placement. *Apply:* rolling admissions. Transfers welcome; 37 enrolled 1993–94.

Academic Environment. Degrees offered: associates, bachelors. Liberal arts core requirements include 16 hours of Bible study, 15 hours communications, 7 hours personal development, 6 hours humanities, 7 hours natural sciences, 6 hours social sciences, competency in mathematics. Average undergraduate class size: 59% under 20, 32% between 20–40, 9% over 40. About 38% of students entering as freshmen graduate in four years, 50% eventually; 68% of freshmen return for sophomore year. *Special programs:* independent study, study abroad, undergraduate research, individualized majors. Adult programs: degree completion program in organizational management (evening). *Calendar:* semester, summer school.

Undergraduate degrees conferred (89). 26% were in Business and Management, 20% were in Education, 17% were in Theology,

12% were in Psychology, 8% were in Letters, 4% were in Social Sciences, 4% were in Multi/Interdisciplinary Studies, 4% were in Life Sciences, 3% were in Visual and Performing Arts.
Graduates Career Data. Advanced studies pursued by 18% of students; 2% enter dental school; 2% enter other schools.
Faculty. About 69% of faculty hold PhD or equivalent. All undergraduate classes taught by tenured faculty. About 12% of teaching faculty are female.
Student Body. College seeks a national student body; 35% of students from in state; 76% South, 9% Midwest, 4% Middle Atlantic; 8% Foreign. An estimated 99% of students reported as Protestant, 1% Catholic; 2% Black, 1% Hispanic, 1% Asian.
Religious Orientation. Bryan is an independent institution, "definitely committed to a Christian world view"; 16 hours of Bible, attendance at chapel services required of all students.
Varsity Sports. Men (NAIA/NCCAA): Basketball, Soccer, Tennis. Women (NAIA/NCCAA): Basketball, Tennis, Volleyball.
Campus Life. About 77% of men, 83% of women live in traditional dormitories; no coed dormitories; rest live in off-campus housing or commute. No intervisitation in men's and women's dormitory rooms. There are no fraternities or sororities.
Annual Costs. Tuition and fees, $7,690; room and board, $3,950; estimated $1,250 other, exclusive of travel. About 90% of students receive financial aid; average amount of assistance, $6,700. Assistance is typically divided 20% scholarship, 15% grant, 57% loan, 8% work. College reports 150 scholarships awarded for academic merit, 55 for special talents, 150 for need. *Meeting Costs:* college offers special payment plans.

William Jewell College

Liberty, Missouri 64068 (816) 781-7700

A private Southern Baptist liberal arts college, located in a suburban section (pop. 18,000), 14 miles from downtown Kansas City. Most convenient major airport: Kansas City (20 miles away).

Founded: 1849
Affiliation: Baptist
UG Enrollment: 550 M, 729 W (full-time)
Cost: < $10K
Admission: Selective
Application Deadline: Rolling

Admission is selective. About 83% of applicants accepted, 58% of these actually enroll; 58% of freshmen graduate in top fifth of high school class, 84% in top two-fifths. Average freshman scores: SAT, 500 M, 500 W verbal, 540 M, 540 W mathematical; 57% of freshmen score above 500 verbal, 13% above 600, 1% above 700, 75% score above 500 mathematical, 30% above 600, 7% above 700. *Required:* SAT or ACT, interview, essay. Criteria considered in admissions, in order of importance: high school academic record, standardized test scores, recommendations, writing sample, extracurricular activities; other factors considered: special talents. *Entrance programs:* early admission, midyear admission, deferred admission. About 6% of entering students from private or parochial schools, according to most recent data available. *Apply:* rolling admissions. *Transfers* welcome; 92 enrolled 1993–94.
Academic Environment. A curriculum program emphasizing personal achievement is offered whereby the student constructs his own individualized education program in consultation with a personal advisory committee. About 80% of general education requirements are elective; distribution requirements fairly numerous. The Oxbridge Alternative Honors program offers the tutorial method of instruction and one year of study in Oxford or Cambridge for qualified honors students. *Degrees:* bachelors. *Majors offered* include business administration, communications, computer science, education, nursing. Average undergraduate class size: 25–30. Students report that professors are accessible and helpful, but the work is rigorous.

About 87% of students entering as freshmen graduate within four years; 87% of freshmen return for sophomore year. *Special programs:* CLEP, independent study, January term, study abroad, honors, undergraduate research, 3-year degree, individualized majors, Washington Semester, United Nations Semester, cooperative urban teacher education project, semester in Kansas City studying urban problems, 3–2 in engineering. Adult programs: continuing education program offered at night. *Calendar:* 4–1–4, summer school.

Undergraduate degrees conferred (325). 29% were in Business and Management, 10% were in Social Sciences, 10% were in Communications, 9% were in Education, 8% were in Psychology, 7% were in Letters, 5% were in Health Sciences, 4% were in Philosophy and Religion, 3% were in Physical Sciences, 3% were in Computer and Engineering Related Technology, remainder in 7 other fields.
Graduates Career Data. Advanced studies pursued by 28% of students, according to most recent data available; 1% enter medical school; 4% enter law school; 5% enter business school; 2% enter seminary. *Careers in business and industry* pursued by 73% of graduates. Corporations typically hiring largest numbers of graduates include Hallmark, JC Penney, DST Systems.
Faculty. About 72% of faculty hold PhD or equivalent. About 73% of undergraduate classes taught by tenured faculty. About 40% of teaching faculty are female, 2% minority.
Student Body. College does not seek a national student body; 75% of students from in state; 92% Midwest, 4% South, 3% West; 1% Foreign. An estimated 74% of students reported as Protestant, 11% Catholic, 10% unaffiliated, 5% other; 2% as Black, 1% Hispanic, 1%Asian, 3% other minority.
Religious Orientation. William Jewell is a church-related institution, affiliated with the Missouri Baptist Convention and American Baptist Church; 1 course in religion required of all students, attendance at chapel/convocation not required.
Varsity Sports. Men (NAIA II): Baseball, Basketball, Cross Country, Football, Golf, Soccer, Tennis, Track. Women (NAIA II): Basketball, Cross Country, Softball, Tennis, Track, Volleyball.
Campus Life. Students and administration characterize the campus as conservative. Students have self-regulated hours; intervisitation limited. Cars permitted, but discouraged for freshman and financial aid recipients. Alcohol prohibited on campus, at college functions, and in off-campus housing. Single students required to live in residence halls. Kansas City offers easily accessible cultural and recreational opportunities

About 48% of men, 44% of women live in traditional dormitories; no coed dormitories; 6% of men, 8% of women live in off-campus college-related housing; rest commute. There are 4 fraternities, 4 sororities on campus which about 17% of men, 12% of women join; 19% of men live in fraternities; 14% of women live in sororities. About 50% of resident students leave campus on weekends, according to most recent data available.
Annual Costs. Tuition and fees, $9,720; room and board, $2,780; estimated $500 other, exclusive of travel. College reports scholarships awarded on the basis of academic merit alone. *Meeting Costs:* college offers deferred payment plan, prepayment plan (guaranteed tuition).

William Marsh Rice University

(See Rice University)

William Paterson College

Wayne, New Jersey 07470 (201) 595-2906125

A state-supported college located in a suburban area near North Haledon (pop. 7,600), 20 miles west of New York City.

Founded: 1855
Affiliation: State
UG Enrollment: 2,618 M, 3,320 W (full-time); 834 M, 1,464 W (part-time)
Total Enrollment: 9,798
Cost: < $10K
% Receiving Financial Aid: 29%
Admission: Non-selective
Application Deadline: June 1

Admission. Graduates of approved high schools with 16 units eligible; others considered individually; 59% of applicants accepted, 43% of these actually enroll; 19% of freshmen graduate in top fifth of high school class, 49% in top two-fifths, according to most recent data available. Average freshman SAT scores: 923 combined. *Required:* SAT, minimum H.S. GPA of 2.5. Criteria considered in admissions, in order of importance: standardized test scores, high school academic record, recommendations, extracurricular activities, writing sample. *Out-of-state* freshman applicants: college does no seek students from out-of-state. State does not limit out-of-state enrollment. About 41% of out-of-state applicants accepted, 18% of these actually enroll. States from which most out-of-state applicants are drawn include New York. *Entrance programs:* early decision, early admission. *Apply* by June 1. *Transfers* welcome, 1,273 enrolled 1993–94.

Academic Environment. Degrees offered: bachelors, masters. About 50% of credits required for graduation are general education courses including English, mathematics, social studies, and sciences. About 15% of students entering as freshmen graduate in four years; 78% of freshmen return for sophomore year. Average undergraduate class size: 21. *Special programs:* CLEP, independent study, study abroad, honors, undergraduate research, 3-year degree, individualized majors.

Undergraduate degrees conferred (1,281). 22% were in Business and Management, 18% were in Social Sciences, 18% were in Education, 13% were in Communications, 7% were in Visual and Performing Arts, 5% were in Health Sciences, 5% were in Psychology, 5% were in Letters, remainder in 8 other fields.

Graduates Career Data. Advanced studies pursued by 16% of students. Corporations typically hiring largest numbers of graduates include IBM, Equitable Life, Prudential Life. Career Development Services provided.

Faculty. About 79% of faculty hold PhD or equivalent. About 72% of undergraduate classes taught by tenured faculty. About 38% of teaching faculty are female; 9% Black, 4% Hispanic, 8% other minority.

Student Body. College seeks a national student body; 98% of students from in state; 98% from Middle Atlantic. An estimated 8% of students reported as Black, 9% Hispanic, 3% Asian. Average age of undergraduate student: 22.

Varsity Sports. Men (Div.III): Baseball, Basketball, Cross Country, Diving, Football, Hockey, Soccer, Swimming, Track. Women (Div.III): Basketball, Cross Country, Diving, Field Hockey, Softball, Swimming, Tennis, Track, Volleyball.

Campus Life. According to most recent data available, about 8% each of men, women live in coed dormitories; 92% each of men, women commute. There are 15 fraternities, 12 sororities.

Annual Costs. Tuition and fees, $2,745 (out-of-state, $3,614); room and board, $4,510; estimated $350 other, exclusive of travel. About 29% of students receive financial aid; average amount of assistance, $4,350. Assistance is typically divided 7% scholarship, 44% grant, 45% loan, 4% work. College reports 388 scholarships awarded for academic merit, 16 for special talents.

William Penn College

Oskaloosa, Iowa 52577 **(515) 673-1012**

A church-related college, located in a community of 12,000, 50 miles east of Des Moines. Most convenient major airport: Des Moines.

Founded: 1873
Affiliation: Friends
UG Enrollment: 299 M, 301 W (full-time); 36 M, 57 W (part-time)
Cost: $10K–$20K
% Receiving Financial Aid: 97%
Admission: Non-selective
Application Deadline: August 1

Admission. Graduates of accredited high schools eligible; 82% of applicants accepted, 48% of these actually enroll; 20% of freshmen graduate in top fourth of high school class, 55% in top half. Average freshman ACT scores: 19.4 composite. *Required:* SAT or ACT, minimum H.S. GPA. Criteria considered in admissions, in order of importance: high school academic record, standardized test scores, recommendations, alumni, writing sample, extracurricular activities; other factors considered: special talents, alumni children, diverse student body, religious affiliation and/or commitment. *Entrance programs:* early decision, early admission, midyear admission. *Apply* by August 1; rolling admissions. *Transfers* welcome; 114 enrolled 1993–94.

Academic Environment. Degrees offered: bachelors. Liberal arts core requirements include English, foreign language or English/drama/speech combination, mathematics, natural sciences, social sciences, religion, philosophy, fine arts, physical education, senior seminar, and Freshman Year Experience. *Majors offered* in addition to usual studies include industrial technology, peace studies, environmental studies. Average undergraduate class size: 70% under 20, 27% between 20–40, 3% over 40. About 45% of students entering as freshmen graduate eventually; 40% of freshmen do not return for sophomore year, according to most recent data available. *Special programs:* independent study, January term, study abroad, 3–2 in engineering, internships, individualized majors. *Calendar:* semester, summer school.

Undergraduate degrees conferred (148). 54% were in Education, 16% were in Business and Management, 7% were in Social Sciences, 5% were in Psychology, 5% were in Computer and Engineering Related Technology, 3% were in Life Sciences, 3% were in Home Economics, 3% were in Engineering and Engineering Related Technology, remainder in 2 other fields.

Faculty. About 41% of faculty hold PhD or equivalent.

Student Body. College seeks a national student body; 80% of students from in state; 90% of students from Midwest, 3% South, 4% West; 2% Foreign. An estimated 56% of students reported as Protestant, 13% Catholic, 31% unknown; 6% Black, 2% Hispanic, 2% Asian, 4% other minority.

Religious Orientation. William Penn is a church-related institution, one course in religion is required.

Varsity Sports. Men (Div.III): Baseball, Basketball, Cross Country, Football, Golf, Tennis, Track, Wrestling. Women (Div.III): Basketball, Cross Country, Golf, Softball, Tennis, Track, Volleyball.

Campus Life. According to most recent data available, about 43% of men, 23% of women live in traditional dormitories; 20% of men, 17% of women in coed dormitories; rest commute. Intervisitation in men's and women's dormitory rooms limited. There are 3 fraternities, 3 sororities on campus which about 13% of men, 8% of women join; they provide no residence facilities. About 35% of students leave campus on weekends.

Annual Costs. Tuition and fees, $10,290; room and board, $3,110; estimated $1,800 other, exclusive of travel. About 97% of students receive financial aid; average amount of assistance, $11,000. College reports 200 scholarships awarded for academic merit, 20 for music, 450 for need. *Meeting Costs:* college offers PLUS loans.

William Smith College

(See Hobart and William Smith Colleges)

William Woods University

Fulton, Missouri 65251 **(314) 642-2251**

An independent institution for women, located in a town of 12,000, 90 miles west of St. Louis. Extensive cooperative program with nearby Westminster College allows students to take courses on either campus. Formerly known as William Woods College. Most convenient major airport: St. Louis.

Founded: 1870
Affiliation: Independent, (Disciples of Christ)
UG Enrollment: 736 W (full-time); 80 W (part-time)
Cost: < $10K
% Receiving Financial Aid: 92%
Admission: Non-selective
Application Deadline: Rolling

Admission. High school graduates eligible; 92% of applicants accepted, 45% of these actually enroll; 30% of freshmen graduate in top fifth of high school class, 61% in top two-fifths. Average freshman scores: SAT, 436 verbal, 445 mathematical; ACT, 21 composite. *Required:* SAT or ACT. Criteria considered in admissions, in order of importance: high school academic record, standardized test scores; other factors considered: special talents, alumni children, diverse student body, extracurricular activities. *Apply:* rolling admissions. *Transfers* welcome; 33 enrolled 1993–94.

Academic Environment. Degrees offered: associates, bachelors, masters. General education requirements include 35 hours including English, mathematics, humanities, fine arts, natural science, behavioral or social science. *Majors offered* in addition to usual studies include equestrian science, equine administration, educational interpreting for the deaf. Average undergraduate class size: 83% under 20, 16% between 20–40, 1% over 40.

About 65% of entering freshmen graduate in four years, 85% eventually; 66% of freshmen return for sophomore year. *Special programs:* independent study, study abroad, 3-year degree, fashion design, 3–3 law, dual degree programs in engineering; 3–2 in nursing, medical technology, animal science; United Nations Semester, Washington Semester, cross-registration with Westminster College, exchange agreement with Spring Term Consortium colleges. Adult programs: evening and weekend classes leading to degrees in business, paralegal, and educational interpreting for the deaf. *Calendar:* semester, spring short term.

Undergraduate degrees conferred (136). 28% were in Business and Management, 14% were in Education, 13% were in Law, 8% were in Agribusiness and Agricultural Production, 7% were in Visual and Performing Arts, 7% were in Communications, 5% were in Multi/Interdisciplinary Studies, 4% were in Marketing and Distribution, 3% were in Psychology, 3% were in Home Economics, remainder in 7 other fields.

Graduates Career Data. Advanced studies pursued by 20% of students; 1% enter medical school; 4% enter law school; 7% enter business school; 8% other schools. About 84% of 1992–93 graduates employed. Career Development Services include job and internship searches, resume writing, interview preparation, career fairs, on-campus recruitment.

Faculty. About 70% of faculty hold PhD or equivalent. All of undergraduate classes taught by tenured faculty. About 48% of teaching faculty are female; 2% minority.

Student Body. College seeks a national student body; 53% of students from in state; 80% of students from Midwest, 12% West, 1% Middle Atlantic, 5% South, 2% New England, 1% Northwest. An estimated 59% of students reported as Protestant, 28% Catholic, 1% Jewish, 1% unaffiliated, 9% other; 1% Black, 1% Hispanic, 1% Asian.

Varsity Sports. Women (NAIA): Basketball, Equestrian, Soccer, Softball, Swimming, Tennis, Volleyball.

Campus Life. About 42% of women live in traditional dormitories; 40% of women live in sororities; 3% live in off-campus college-related housing; rest commute. Intervisitation in women's dormitory rooms determined by monthly vote for each dormitory. There are 4 sororities on campus which about 50% of women join. About 25% of resident students leave campus on weekends.

Annual Costs. Tuition and fees, $9,825; room and board, $4,200; estimated $500 other, exclusive of travel. About 92% of students receive financial aid; average amount of assistance, $8,000. Assistance is typically divided 30% scholarship, 30% grant, 50% loan, 5% work. College reports 225 scholarships awarded for academic merit, 199 for special talents, 250 for need. *Meeting Costs:* college offers PLUS loans.

Williams Baptist College

Walnut Ridge, Arkansas 72476 (501) 886-6741

A church-related liberal arts college, offering associates and bachelors degree programs.

Founded: 1941
Affiliation: Southern Baptist
UG Enrollment: 186 M, 261 W (full-time)
Total Enrollment: 604
Cost: < $10K
% Receiving Financial Aid: 82%
Admission: Non-selective
Application Deadline: Rolling

Admission. Average freshman ACT scores: 19.5 composite. *Required:* ACT, minimum high school GPA, essay. Criteria considered in admissions, in order of importance: standardized test scores, high school academic record; other factors considered: special talents. *Entrance programs:* early admission, mid-year admission. *Apply:* rolling admissions. *Transfers* welcome.

Academic Environment. Graduation requirements include 12 hours in English, 6 each in humanities, religion, history, social sciences, and natural sciences, 4 hours in health/physical education, 3 hours each in speech, and math. Degrees offered: associates, bachelors. Average undergraduate class size: 60% under 20, 40% 20–40. *Special programs:* study abroad, internships in business.

Undergraduate degrees conferred ().

Faculty. About 50% of faculty hold PhD or equivalent. All undergraduate classes taught by tenured faculty.

Student Body. About 78% of students from in state; 83% from South, 11% Midwest. An estimated 87% of students reported as Protestant, 1% Catholic, 5% unaffiliated, 7% other.

Religious Orientation. Williams Baptist is a church-related institution; 2 courses in religious studies required of all students.

Varsity Sports. Men (NAIA): Baseball, Basketball. Women (NAIA): Basketball, Volleyball.

Campus Life. About 42% of men, 38% of women live in traditional dormitories; no coed dormitories; rest commute. There are no fraternities or sororities on campus. About 80% of resident students leave campus on weekends.

Annual Costs. Tuition and fees, $3,592; room and board, $2,242; estimated $200 other, exclusive of travel. About 82% of students receive financial aid; average amount of assistance, $5,094. Assistance is typically divided 19% scholarship, 35% grant, 31% loan, 13% work. College reports 133 scholarships awarded on the basis of academic merit alone, 49 for special talents.

Williams College

Williamstown, Massachusetts 01267 (413) 597-2211

Williams College is one of the most prestigious liberal arts colleges in the country, with a national student body of substantial heterogeneity and academic capacity. Its semirural, 450-acre campus is located in a town of 8,500 in the Berkshire Hills of western Massachusetts. Most convenient major airport: Albany.

Founded: 1793
Affiliation: Independent
UG Enrollment: 986 M, 981 W (full-time)
Cost: $10K–$20K
% Receiving Financial Aid: 50%
Admission: Most Selective
Application Deadline: Jan. 1

Admission is among the most selective in the country. About 30% of applicants accepted, 42% of these actually enroll; according to most recent data available 92% of freshmen graduate in top fifth of high school class, 98% in top two-fifths. Average freshman scores: SAT, 95% of freshmen score above 500 on verbal, 76% above 600, 31% above 700; 97% score above 500 on mathematical, 87% above 600, 52% above 700; ACT, middle fifty percent: 29–32 composite. *Required:* SAT or ACT, 3 ACH; interview recommended. Criteria considered in admissions, in order of importance: high school academic record, standardized test scores, recommendations, writing sample, extracurricular activities; other factors considered: special talents, motivation, maturity and independence, alumni children, diverse student body. Entrance program: early decision, deferred admission, advanced placement. About 38% of entering students from private schools, 5% from parochial schools. *Apply* by January 1. *Transfers* welcome; 23 enrolled 1993–94.

Academic Environment. Students reported to have some influence on curriculum decisions and are consulted by all departments on selection of faculty. Close student/faculty relationship doubtless a factor in their influence. Student leader speaks of friendly atmosphere, sense of vitality, and solid academic orientation. Pressures for academic achievement appear intense. Academic program said to be "excellent, demanding." Williams allows students great freedom in selecting specific courses; college insists, however, on breadth and diversity during first 3 years in order to introduce students to the range of human knowledge. An important part of the academic environment is Winter Study, a 4-week term in January during which each student undertakes a single project. Students are encouraged to explore fields outside their usual areas of study. Experiential programs and travel are accented. Degrees offered: bachelors, masters. *Majors offered* include political economy, astronomy, biochemistry, molecular biology, neuroscience. Average undergraduate class size: 55% under 20, 35% between 20–40, 10% over 40.

About 93% of students entering as freshmen graduate in four years; 98% of freshmen return for sophomore year. *Special programs:* independent study, January term, study abroad, Williams-in-Oxford with Exeter College-Oxford, honors, undergraduate research, 3-year degree, individualized majors, Twelve College Exchange, exchange programs with MIT, RPI, Howard U., Afro-American studies, environmental studies, American Maritime studies in conjunction with Mystic Seaport, Connecticut, double and interdepartmental

majors, 3–2 in engineering. *Library:* Chapin Library of Rare Books (45,000 volumes). *Calendar:* 4–1–4.
Undergraduate degrees conferred (502). 38% were in Social Sciences, 19% were in Letters, 9% were in Visual and Performing Arts, 7% were in Psychology, 7% were in Physical Sciences, 6% were in Life Sciences, 4% were in Philosophy and Religion, 4% were in Area and Ethnic Studies, 4% were in Mathematics, remainder in 2 other fields.
Graduates Career Data. Advanced studies pursued by 22% of students; 3% enter medical school; 6% enter law school; 2% enter business school; 12% enter other schools. Medical schools typically enrolling largest numbers of graduates include U. of Rochester, law schools include Berkeley, Harvard. *Careers in business and industry* pursued by 63% of graduates, according to most recent data available. Fields typically hiring largest numbers of graduates include investment banking, consulting agencies, education, paralegal. Career Development Services include skills and interest assessment, interview strategies, help in job search and graduate school enrollment, alumni network.
Faculty. About 95% of faculty hold PhD or equivalent. All tenured faculty teach undergraduate classes including those taking introductory courses. About 34% of teaching faculty are female; 4% Black, 3% Hispanic, 5% other minority.
Student Body. College seeks a national student body; 12% of students from in state; 37% Middle Atlantic, 22% New England, 11% Midwest, 18% West/Northwest, 9% South; 3% Foreign. An estimated 8% of students reported as Black, 9% Asian, 4% Hispanic, 5% other minority, according to most recent data available.
Varsity Sports. Men (Div.III): Baseball, Basketball, Cross Country, Diving, Football, Golf, Hockey, Lacrosse, Rugby, Skiing (I), Soccer, Squash (I), Swimming, Tennis, Track, Wrestling. Women (Div.III) (NESCAC): Basketball, Cross Country, Diving, Field Hockey, Golf, Ice Hockey, Lacrosse, Skiing (I), Soccer, Softball, Squash (I), Swimming, Tennis, Track, Volleyball.
Campus Life. The Williams campus occupies an attractive location, but it is a considerable distance from any major cultural center; Boston and New York are each about 150 miles from campus. College attempts to remedy this by offering an extremely rich program of cultural and intellectual events within the campus setting. Few urban centers could compete with its current program. Enthusiastic student leader describes school: "Small college, small town, non urban atmosphere, beautiful setting in Berkshire hills." Student leader characterizes students as "preppy, outdoors-type, social." Almost half of student body participates in sports at different levels, including extensive intramural program, club and varsity sports. Competition with traditional small college rivals said to be both "friendly and intense and draws a loyal group of supportive fans." Upperclassmen housed in coed residential complex which provides dining and social facilities, and serves as centers for intramural athletics and extracurricular activities. Cars not allowed for freshmen.

About 96% of men, 96% of women in coed dormitories; rest commute. There are no fraternities or sororities. About 10% of resident students leave campus on weekends.
Annual Costs. Tuition and fees, $18,795; room and board, $5,595; estimated $1,200 other, exclusive of travel. About 50% of students receive financial aid; average amount of assistance, $16,970. Assistance is typically divided 75% grant, 15% loan, 10% work. *Meeting Costs:* college offers installment payment plan; aid-blind admissions.

Wilmington College

New Castle, Delaware 19720

A small, co-educational institution offering degree programs in business management and administration, aviation management, communications, criminal justice, behavioral science, and professional arts. Degrees: *AB, BS, BBA.*

Founded: 1967 **Affiliation:** Independent

Undergraduate degrees conferred (238). 58% were in Business and Management, 23% were in Health Sciences, 11% were in Psychology, 5% were in Protective Services, remainder in Communications.

Wilmington College

Wilmington, Ohio 45177 **(513) 382-6661**

A church-related, co-educational, liberal arts college, Wilmington offers career-oriented programs. The 65-acre campus is located in a community of 12,100, 34 miles southeast of Dayton and 47 miles northeast of Cincinnati. Most convenient major airport: Dayton International.

Founded: 1870
Affiliation: Friends
UG Enrollment: 429 M, 436 W (full-time); 57 M, 68 W (part-time)
Cost: < $10K
% Receiving Financial Aid: 95%
Admission: Non-selective
Application Deadline: Rolling

Admission. About 83% of applicants accepted, 32% of these actually enroll; 31% of freshmen graduate in top fifth of high school class, 63% in top two-fifths. Average freshman ACT scores: 20.9 composite. *Required:* SAT or ACT. Criteria considered in admissions, in order of importance: high school academic record, standardized test scores, recommendations, extra curricular activities. *Entrance programs:* early decision, early admission, midyear admission, deferred admission, advanced placement. *Apply:* rolling admissions; March 31 for financial aid. *Transfers* welcome; 76 enrolled 1993–94.
Academic Environment. Strong emphasis on international programs. Administration reports no specific general education courses needed for graduation are required; flexible core requirements cover broad range of subjects; each student plans own graduation requirements with advisor. *Degrees:* bachelors. *Majors offered* include agriculture, elementary education, industrial education, theater. Student to faculty ratio of 17:1.

About 57% of students entering as freshmen graduate within four years; 77% of freshmen return for sophomore year. *Special programs:* CLEP, independent study, study abroad, 3-year degree, individualized majors, cross-registration with SOCHE and GCCCU, freshman interdisciplinary program, medical technology, off-campus field term or cooperative work/study program (required of all students). Adult programs: evening program offering BA in business. *Calendar:* quarter, summer school.
Undergraduate degrees conferred (248). 25% were in Business and Management, 19% were in Education, 11% were in Psychology, 8% were in Agribusiness and Agricultural Production, 5% were in Computer and Engineering Related Technology, 5% were in Social Sciences, 5% were in Marketing and Distribution, 4% were in Health Sciences, 3% were in Communications, 3% were in Visual and Performing Arts, remainder in 7 other fields.
Graduates Career Data. Advanced studies pursued by 20% of graduates.
Faculty. About 52% of faculty hold PhD or equivalent. About 50% of undergraduate classes taught by tenured faculty. About 30% of teaching faculty are female.
Student Body. College seeks a national student body; 90% of students from in state; 1% Foreign. An estimated 55% of students reported as Protestant, 19% Catholic, 2% Jewish, 15% unaffiliated, 10% other; 3% Black.
Varsity Sports. Men (NAIA, Div.III): Baseball, Basketball, Cross Country, Football, Golf, Soccer, Tennis, Track, Wrestling. Women (NAIA): Basketball, Cross Country, Soccer, Softball, Tennis, Track, Volleyball.
Campus Life. Administration and student representatives agree that student body represents "a wide variety of opinions, ideas, and problems." Agreement also that college enforces "leniently" the rules governing student conduct. Variety of intervisitation options open to students including 24-hour. Alcohol not allowed on campus; and college opposed to "public display of affection if excessive." Cars allowed.

According to most recent data available about 58% of men, 54% of women live in traditional dormitories; 13% of men, 11% of women in coed dormitories; rest commute. Sexes segregated in coed dormitories either by wing, floor, or room. There are 6 fraternities, 3 sororities on campus which about 16% of men, 15% of women join; 2% of men live in fraternities. About 50% of resident students leave campus on weekends, according to most recent data available.
Annual Costs. Tuition and fees, $9,830; room and board, $3,870. About 95% of students receive financial aid; average amount of

assistance, $1,690. Assistance is typically divided 10% scholarship, 44% grant, 36% loan, 10% work. College reports 264 scholarships awarded for academic merit, 3 for special talents, 682 for need. *Meeting Costs:* college offers variety of payment plans, both in-house and commercial; PLUS loans.

Wilson College

Chambersburg, Pennsylvania 17201 (717) 264-4141

Wilson is a church-affiliated, liberal arts college for women. Situated 90 miles from Washington and 50 miles southwest of Harrisburg, the 255-acre campus is located in a residential section of historic Chambersburg. Most convenient major airport: Harrisburg International.

Founded: 1869
Affiliation: Independent (Presbyterian Church, USA)
UG Enrollment: 17 M, 182 W (full-time); 157 M, 519 W (part-time)
Cost: $10K–$20K
% Receiving Financial Aid: 81%
Admission: Non-selective
Application Deadline: Rolling

Admission. About 80% of applicants accepted, 37% of these actually enroll; 35% of freshmen graduate in the top fifth of high school class, 63% in top two-fifths. Average freshman SAT scores: 462 W verbal, 469 W mathematical. *Required:* SAT, essay. Criteria considered in admissions, in order of importance: high school academic record, standardized test scores, writing sample, extracurricular activities, recommendations; other factors considered: special talents, diverse student body. *Entrance programs:* early admission, midyear admission. *Apply:* rolling admissions. *Transfers* welcome; 10 enrolled 1993–94.

Academic Environment. Degrees offered: bachelors. *Majors offered* include computer science, equestrian studies, interdisciplinary studies, veterinary medical technology, biology, chemistry, mathematics. Core requirements include Comparative Contemporary Cultures, Roots of Western Culture, Science and Technology in Modern Culture, and Preservation of Planet Earth, as well as Skills, which include English, foreign language, computer systems, statistics, physical education. Average undergraduate class size: 70% under 20, 25% between 20–40, 5% over 40.

About 60% of students entering as freshmen graduate within four years; 80% of students entering as freshmen return for sophomore year, according to most recent data available. *Special programs:* internships, independent study, January term, honors, undergraduate research, individualized majors, medical technology, South Asian studies, Washington semester, United Nations Semester, various cooperative and combined degree programs (nursing, bio-dental, allied health sciences), cross-registration with other institutions. Adult programs: Adult Learners Program, non-residential baccalaureate program open to men and women who have earned at least 9 transferable credits; Continuing Education Program. *Calendar:* 4–1–4.

Undergraduate degrees conferred (48). 31% were in Business and Management, 19% were in Life Sciences, 15% were in Agricultural Sciences, 13% were in Letters, 8% were in Multi/Interdisciplinary Studies, 4% were in Social Sciences, 4% were in Communications, remainder in 3 other fields.

Graduates Career Data. Advanced studies pursued by 23% of students; 1% enter medical school; 1% enter law school; 1% enter business school; 20% enter other schools. About 30% of 1992–93 graduates employed. Career Development Services include resume writing, graduate school information, workshops, career fairs, job fairs, internship contacts.

Faculty. About 77% of faculty hold PhD or equivalent.

Student Body. College seeks a national student body; 48% of students from in state; 39% New England; 13% Foreign. An estimated 58% of students reported as Protestant, 15% Catholic, 27% other, according to most recent data available; 4% Asian, 4% other minority.

Varsity Sports. Women: Equestrian, Field Hockey, Gymnastics, Softball, Tennis, Volleyball.

Campus Life. College provides variety of cultural and intellectual activities; relative isolation of campus from metropolitan center stimulates this effort. Significant attempt made to draw on the facilities of Washington and Baltimore, 90 and 80 miles from campus respectively. Cars permitted for all students. Extended visitation by individual choice. About 65% of women live in traditional dormitories; rest commute. There are no sororities. About 50% of resident students leave campus on weekends.

Annual Costs. Tuition and fees, $11,546; room and board, $5,084; estimated $800 other, exclusive of travel. About 81% of students receive financial aid; average amount of assistance, $10,841. Assistance is typically divided 25% scholarship, 40% grant, 29% loan, 6% work. College reports 70 scholarships awarded for academic merit, 1 for special talents, 85 for need. *Meeting Costs:* college offers monthly payment plan.

Wingate College

Wingate, North Carolina 28174 (800) 755-5550

For many years a well-known junior college, Wingate has offered baccalaureate programs since 1977. The 300-acre campus is located in a community of about 3,000, 26 miles southeast of Charlotte. Most convenient major airport: Charlotte/Douglas.

Founded: 1896
Affiliation: Southern Baptist
UG Enrollment: 1,321 M, W (full-time)
Cost: < $10K
% Receiving Financial Aid: 75–78%
Admission: Non-selective
Application Deadline: Rolling

Admission. About 82% of applicants accepted, 40% of these actually enroll; 13% of freshmen graduate in top fifth of high school class, 45% in top two-fifths. Average freshman SAT scores, according to most recent data available: 400 verbal, 441 mathematical. *Required:* SAT or ACT; interview recommended. *Non-academic factors* considered in admissions: special talents, alumni children. *Apply:* rolling admissions. *Transfers* welcome.

Academic Environment. *Degrees:* AB, BS. Fourteen baccalaureate programs in arts and sciences and career areas. New programs include sports medicine, music and communications. About 30% of entering freshmen do not return for sophomore year.

Undergraduate degrees conferred (232). 25% were in Business and Management, 18% were in Education, 14% were in Communications, 8% were in Public Affairs, 7% were in Parks and Recreation, 6% were in Social Sciences, 5% were in Psychology, 3% were in Letters, 3% were in Health Sciences, remainder in 7 other fields.

Graduates Career Data. According to most recent data available about 14% of graduates go on to graduate or professional schools. *Careers in business and industry* pursued by 90% of graduates.

Faculty. About 82% of faculty hold PhD or equivalent.

Varsity Sports. Men (NCAA, Div II): Baseball, Basketball, Golf, Soccer, Tennis. Women (NCAA, Div II): Basketball, Soccer, Softball, Tennis, Volleyball.

Student Body. About 65% of students from in state; 85% South; 15 foreign students. An estimated 65% reported as Protestant, 20% Catholic; 7% as Black, 2% other minority, according to most recent data available.

Campus Life. About 50% of men, 50% of women live in traditional dormitories; rest commute.

Annual Costs. Tuition and fees, $7,240; room and board, $3,200. About 75–78% of students receive financial aid. *Meeting Costs:* college offers payment plans.

Winona State University

Winona, Minnesota 55987-0838 (507) 457-5100

A state-supported university, located on a bluff in the scenic Mississippi River Valley, in a community of 30,000; 110 miles from Minneapolis. Most convenient major airport: LaCrosse (WI).

Founded: 1858
Affiliation: State
UG Enrollment: 2,390 M, 3,368 W (full-time); 341 M, 535 W (part-time)
Total Enrollment: 7,156
Cost: < $10K
% Receiving Financial Aid: 72%
Admission: Non-selective
Application Deadline: Feb. 15

Admission. Graduates of accredited high schools who rank in top half of class or score 21 on ACT composite or an average SAT score of 900 eligible; others may be eligible for provisional admission; 625% of applicants accepted, 64% of these actually enroll; 20% of freshmen graduate in top fifth of high school class, 45% in top two-fifths. Average freshman scores: SAT, 460 verbal, 490 mathematical; ACT, 22 composite. *Required:* SAT or ACT; campus visit and interview recommended. Criteria considered in admissions, in order of importance: high school academic record, standardized test scores, 16 units of preparation requirement; other factors considered: special talents, diverse student body, leadership. *Out-of-state* freshman applicants: university seeks students from out-of-state. State does not limit out-of-state enrollment. About 62% of out-of-state applicants accepted, 65% of these actually enroll. States from which most out-of-state students are drawn include Wisconsin, Illinois, Iowa. *Entrance programs:* midyear admission, deferred admission, advanced placement. About 15% of freshmen from private or parochial schools. *Apply* by February 15 (priority); rolling admissions. *Transfers* welcome; 575 enrolled 1993–94.

Academic Environment. Degrees offered: associates, bachelors, masters. Specific course and distribution requirements vary with majors, but core requirements include English, speech, mathematics, humanities, sciences, social sciences, different cultures, physical education. *Majors offered* include paralegal, composite materials engineering. About 39% of students entering as freshmen graduate in four years, 52% in six years; 75% of freshmen return for sophomore year. Average undergraduate class size: 30% under 20, 60% between 20–40, 10% over 40. *Special programs:* CLEP, independent study, study abroad, 3-year degree, individualized majors, tri-college cooperative program with Saint Mary's and College of Saint Teresa, exchange with Oslo Teachers College in Norway, internship program. Adult programs: adult entry program. *Calendar:* quarter, summer school.

Undergraduate degrees conferred (1,009). 25% were in Business and Management, 22% were in Education, 8% were in Health Sciences, 7% were in Social Sciences, 6% were in Public Affairs, 5% were in Computer and Engineering Related Technology, 4% were in Law, 4% were in Communications, 4% were in Psychology, 3% were in Letters, remainder in 9 other fields.

Graduates Career Data. Advanced studies pursued by 25% of students; 2% enter medical school, 1% enter law school, 3% enter law school, 10% enter business school. Business schools typically enrolling largest number of students include Winona State University. About 80% of 1992–93 graduates employed. Employers typically hiring largest number of graduates include IBM, Mayo Clinic, 3M.

Faculty. About 65% of faculty hold PhD or equivalent. About 80% of undergraduate classes taught by tenured faculty. About 40% of teaching faculty are female; 5% Black, 3% Hispanic, 10% other minority.

Student Body. University seeks a national student body; 61% of students from in state; 35% Midwest; 4% Foreign. An estimated 40% of students reported as Protestant, 40% Catholic, 3% Jewish, 2% unaffiliated; 2% Black, 1% Hispanic, 24% Asian, 1% other minority.

Varsity Sports. Men (NCAA, Div.II): Baseball, Basketball, Football, Golf, Tennis. Women (NCAA, Div.II): Basketball, Cross Country, Golf, Gymnastics, Softball, Tennis, Track, Volleyball.

Campus Life. About 20% of men, 20% of women live in traditional dormitories; 20% of men, 20% of women in coed dormitories; 40% of men, 40% of women live in off-campus college-related housing; rest commute. Intervisitation in men's and women's dormitory rooms unlimited. Sexes segregated in coed dormitories either by wing or floor. There are 3 fraternities, 3 sorority on campus which about 3% men, 3% women join; 3% men, 3% women live in fraternities and sororities. About 40% of resident students leave campus on weekends.

Annual Costs. Tuition and fees, $2,600 (out-of-state, $5,200); room and board, $2,700; estimated $1,200 other, exclusive of travel. About 72% of students receive financial aid; average amount of assistance, $3,100. Assistance is typically divided 20% scholarship, 30% grant, 30% loan, 20% work. College reports 200 scholarships awarded for academic merit, 75 for special talents.

Winston-Salem State University

Winston-Salem, North Carolina 27110 (910) 750-2070

A state-supported university, located in a city of 161,554; founded as a college for Negroes and still serving a predominantly black student body. Most convenient major airport: Greensboro-High Point Triad.

Founded: 1892
Affiliation: State
UG Enrollment: 776 M, 1,293 W (full-time); 274 M, 474 W (part-time)
Cost: < $10K
% Receiving Financial Aid: 80%
Admission: Non-selective
Application Deadline: May 1

Admission. Graduates of accredited high schools with 12 units in specific academic areas eligible; others given individual consideration; 75% of applicants accepted, 36% of these actually enroll. About 16% of freshmen graduate in top fifth of high school class, 39% in top two-fifths. Average freshman scores: SAT, 369 verbal, 405 mathematical; ACT, 16 composite. *Required:* SAT or ACT, minimum H.S. GPA. *Out-of-state* freshman applicants: university seeks students from out-of-state. State limits out-of-state enrollment to 10%. About 72% of out-of-state applicants accepted, 35% of these actually enroll. States from which most out-of-state applicants are drawn include Maryland, Virginia, New Jersey, South Carolina. *Entrance programs:* advanced placement. *Apply* by May 1 (suggested): rolling admissions. *Transfers* welcome; 346 enrolled 1993–94.

Academic Environment. Degrees offered: bachelors. General education requirements for graduation vary with major; distribution requirements fairly numerous. *Majors offered* include nursing and allied health, business, education. About 10–15% of students entering as freshmen graduate in four years, 30–35% eventually; 70–75% of freshmen return for sophomore year. *Special programs:* CLEP, independent study, honors, undergraduate research, combined degree program in biology/microbiology with Bowman Gray School of Medicine. Adult programs: Continuing Education. *Calendar:* semester, summer school.

Undergraduate degrees conferred (331). 35% were in Business and Management, 17% were in Education, 11% were in Social Sciences, 10% were in Health Sciences, 7% were in Communications, 5% were in Psychology, 4% were in Computer and Engineering Related Technology, 3% were in Multi/Interdisciplinary Studies, 3% were in Letters, remainder in 6 other fields.

Faculty. About 73% of faculty hold PhD or equivalent. About 46% of teaching faculty are female; 61% Black, 7% Hispanic, 1% other minority.

Student Body. University does not seek a national student body; 93% of students from within state; less than 1% foreign. An estimated 78% of students reported as Black, 21% White. Average age of undergraduate student: 25.

Varsity Sports. Men: Basketball, Cross Country, Football, Tennis. Women: Basketball, Cross Country, Softball, Volleyball.

Campus Life. About 62% of men, 38% of women live in traditional dormitories; no coed dormitories; rest commute. No intervisitation in men's or women's dormitory rooms. There are 4 fraternities, 4 sororities on campus which about 4% of men, 2% of women join; they provide no residence facilities.

Annual Costs. Tuition and fees, $621 (out-of-state, $3,303); room and board, $1,450. About 80% of students receive financial aid. Average freshman award, $5,300, which includes scholarship/grant, loan and work-study.

Winthrop University

Rock Hill, South Carolina 29733 (803) 323-2191

A state-supported, coeducational, comprehensive, teaching university, located in a community of 36,000, 25 miles south of Charlotte, N.C. Most convenient major airport: Charlotte International (NC).

Founded: 1886
Affiliation: State
UG Enrollment: 1,094 M, 2,301 W (full-time); 261 M, 409 W (part-time)
Total Enrollment: 5,107
Cost: < $10K
Admission: Non-selective
Application Deadline: May 1

Admission. Graduates of accredited high schools with 18 units (12 in academic subjects) eligible; 78% of applicants accepted, 47% of these actually enroll. About 24% of entering freshmen graduate in top tenth of high school class, 48% in top fifth. Average freshman scores: SAT, 470 verbal, 516 mathematical; ACT, 18.1 composite. *Required:* SAT or ACT. Criteria considered in admissions, in order of importance: high school academic record, class rank, standardized test scores, recommendations, writing sample, extracurricular activities; other factors considered: special talents. *Out-of-state* freshman applicants: college seeks students from out of state. State limits out-of-state enrollment to 25% of student body. No special requirements for out-of-state applicants. *Apply* by May 1. *Transfers* welcome; 359 enrolled 1993–94.

Academic Environment. Degrees offered: bachelors, masters. General education requirements for graduation include 59 credit hours distributed over basic skills in English and mathematics, natural sciences, behavioral and social sciences, arts and humanities, and international understanding. About 24% of entering freshmen graduate within four years, 49% eventually; 76% of freshmen return for sophomore year.Special programs: CLEP, honors, study abroad, internships and cooperative opportunities, writing minor. *Calendar:* semester, summer school.

Undergraduate degrees conferred (749). 31% were in Business and Management, 18% were in Education, 12% were in Communications, 10% were in Visual and Performing Arts, 8% were in Social Sciences, 5% were in Psychology, 5% were in Public Affairs, 3% were in Life Sciences, 3% were in Letters, remainder in 5 other fields.

Graduates Career Data. Advanced studies pursued by 11% of students (class of '92); 1% enter law school. About 72% of 1991–92 graduates employed. Fields typically hiring the largest number of graduates include business, education. Career Development Services include individual career counseling/planning, job bank, job fairs, interviews arranged, careers library, resume preparation and referrals.

Student Body. College seeks a national student body; 86% of students from South Carolina; 93% South; 3% international.

Varsity Sports. Men (Div.I): Baseball, Basketball, Cross Country, Golf, Soccer, Tennis, Track. Women (Div.I): Basketball, Cross Country, Golf, Softball, Tennis, Track, Volleyball.

Campus Life. About 9% of men, 26% of women live in traditional dormitories; 4% of men, 7% of women live in coed dormitories; rest live in off-campus housing, fraternities or commute. Intervisitation in men's and women's dormitory rooms limited by majority vote of residents. There are 11 fraternities and 9 sororities, which 24% of men, 16% of women join. About 50% of resident students leave campus on weekends.

Annual Costs. Tuition and fees, $3,450 (out-of-state, $6,110); room and board, $3,280. About 48% of students receive financial aid; assistance is typically divided 16% scholarship, 18% grants, 56% loan, 10% work. University reports 601 scholarships awarded on the basis of academic merit alone, 145 for special talents. *Meeting Costs:* college offers PLUS loans.

University of Wisconsin System

In the fall of 1971, new legislation provided for the merger of the state's 2 large multicampus university systems, the University of Wisconsin and the Wisconsin State universities. Completion of the merger was accomplished during the 1973 legislative session. The new University of Wisconsin System includes the old University of Wisconsin System campuses at Madison, Milwaukee, Green Bay, and Parkside, as well as the 14 2-year Center System campuses, UW—Extension, and the former state universities at Eau Claire, La Crosse, Menomonie (Stout), Oshkosh, Platteville, River Falls, Stevens Point, Superior, and Whitewater.

Admission. Graduates of recognized high schools or equivalent with minimum 16 units in academic subjects who rank in top half of class eligible. *Out-of-state* freshman enrollment: university seeks students from out of state. No special requirements for out-of-state applicants, except at Madison which requires class rank in upper 20%. If number of qualified students exceeds capacity of unit to accommodate them, unit determines criteria for selection.

University of Wisconsin—Madison

Madison, Wisconsin 53706 (608) 262-3961

The original campus of one of the nation's great state universities and land-grant colleges, the University of Wisconsin—Madison pioneered the concept of the university as a resource for solving the practical problems of the people of a state by education through extension centers and services, while at the same time serving as one of the nation's leading centers for scholarship and research. The campus is located on the shore of Lake Mendota, in the state capital, a city of 173,300. Most convenient major airport: Dane County Regional.

Founded: 1849	**Total Enrollment:** 40,924
Affiliation: State	**Cost:** < $10K
UG Enrollment: 11,990 M, 12,290 W (full-time); 2,358 (part-time)	**% Receiving Financial Aid:** 55%
	Admission: Very (+) Selective
	Application Deadline: Feb. 1

Admission is very (+) selective for Engineering; very selective for Letters and Sciences, Agriculture and Life Sciences; selective for Education, Family Resources and Consumer Services, Nursing. (See also University of Wisconsin System.) For all schools, 72% of applicants accepted, 43% of these actually enroll; 66% of freshmen graduate in top fifth of high school class, 95% in top two-fifths. Average freshman scores (middle fifty percent range): SAT, 480–570 verbal, 510–660 mathematical; ACT, 23–28 composite.

For Letters and Science (8,050 M, 8,739 W f-t, 640 M, 700 W p-t), 71% of applicants accepted, 43% of these actually enroll; 59% of freshmen graduate in top fifth of high school class, 95% in top two-fifths. Average freshman scores: SAT, 509 M, 498 W verbal, 610 M, 561 W mathematical; 26 M, 24 W composite, 26 M, 23 W mathematical.

For Agricultural and Life Sciences (970 M, 733 W f-t, 93 M, 80 W p-t), 90% of applicants accepted, 59% of these actually enroll; 69% of freshmen graduate in top fifth of high school class, 98% in top two-fifths. Average freshman scores: SAT, 511 M, 505 W verbal, 584 M, 563 W mathematical; 25 M, 24 W composite, 25 M, 24 mathematical.

For Engineering (2,778 M, 471 W f-t, 174 M, 20 W p-t), 81% of applicants accepted, 49% of these actually enroll; 73% of freshmen graduate in top fifth of high school class, 97% in top two-fifths. Average freshman scores: SAT, 498 M, 515 W verbal, 648 M, 629 W mathematical; 26 M, 26 W composite, 28 M, 28 mathematical.

For Family Resources and Consumer Science (56 M, 490 W f-t, 7 M, 81 W p-t), 53% of applicants accepted, 49% of these actually enroll; 61% of freshmen graduate in top fifth of high school class, 97% in top two-fifths. Average freshman scores: SAT, 458 verbal, 504 mathematical; 22 composite, 20 mathematical.

For Nursing (24 M, 357 W f-t, 8 M, 107 W p-t), 67% of applicants accepted, 44% of these actually enroll; 64% of freshmen graduate in top fifth of high school class, 93% in top two-fifths. Average freshman scores: SAT, 513 verbal, 533 mathematical; 23 composite, 22 mathematical.

For Education (570 M, 1,830 W f-t, 116 M, 269 W p-t), 65% of applicants accepted, 68% of these actually enroll; 59% of freshmen graduate in top fifth of high school class, 95% in top two-fifths. Average freshman scores: SAT, 497 M, 463 W verbal, 579 M, 529 W mathematical; 24 M, 22 W composite, 24 M, 22 mathematical.

Required: SAT or ACT, minimum H.S. GPA; rigor of academic program and senior year class selection is very important. Criteria considered in admissions, in order of importance: high school academic record, academic rigor of course work, standardized test scores, writing sample, extracurricular activities, recommendations; other factors considered: special talents, alumni children, diverse student body. *Out-of-state* freshman applicants: university actively seeks out-of-state students. State limits out-of-state enrollment to 25% of entering class accepted. Requirement for out-of-state applicants: must be in top 20% of high school class; 62% of applicants accepted, 32% enroll. States from which most out-of-state applicants are drawn include Illinois, Minnesota, New York, Massachusetts, Connecticut. *Entrance programs:* deferred admission, advanced placement. About 25% of freshmen from private schools. *Apply* by February 1; rolling admissions. *Transfers* welcome; 1,500 enrolled 1993–94.

Academic Environment. Wisconsin has traditionally attracted large numbers of out-of-state students, including many intellectually inclined applicants from the East, and has welcomed the stimulation of students from other parts of the country. Pressures for academic achievement vary rather widely among the different programs of study. Student body at Wisconsin is extraordinarily heterogeneous. Students in upper classes generally of high caliber and pressures for academic achievement intensify in final years; pressures are most rigorous in those departments and divisions where entrance to desirable graduate and professional schools depends on the level of undergraduate performance. Distribution requirements for AB fairly numerous: 12 credits each in humanities, social studies, natural sciences; proficiency in English composition, intermediate mathematics, foreign language; semester physical education freshman year. *Undergraduate studies* offered to freshmen by 5 colleges listed above as well as School of Music included in College of Letters and Science; upperclassmen may transfer from Letters and Science to enter schools of Business, Pharmacy. Degrees offered: bachelors, masters, doctoral. *Majors offered* in over 150 fields including highly rated programs in African languages and literature, East Asian Area studies, communication arts, communicative disorders, continuing and vocational education, counseling psychology, dairy science, food science, forestry, German, journalism, meat and animal science, nuclear engineering, occupational therapy, wildlife ecology. Average undergraduate class size: 20% under 20, 60% between 20–40, 20% over 40.

About 35% of students entering as freshmen graduate in four years, 85% eventually; 94% of freshmen return for sophomore year. *Special programs:* CLEP, independent study, study abroad, honors, undergraduate research, individualized majors, credit by examination, cooperative work/study program in engineering, internships in political science, African Studies Program, certificate programs in criminal justice, environmental studies, medieval studies, Japanese for engineering majors, German studies for business students, international agriculture programs, combined degree programs (engineering with business, law, or medicine; civil engineering/city planning or construction administration). *Calendar:* semester, summer school.

Undergraduate degrees conferred (5,869). 23% were in Social Sciences, 11% were in Engineering, 9% were in Communications, 8% were in Business and Management, 6% were in Letters, 5% were in Life Sciences, 5% were in Psychology, 5% were in Health Sciences, 4% were in Education, 3% were in Visual and Performing Arts, 3% were in Foreign Languages, 3% were in Allied Health, remainder in 14 other fields.

Faculty. About 88% of faculty hold PhD or equivalent. About 97% of undergraduate classes taught by tenured faculty.

Graduates Career Data. Advanced studies pursued by 45% of students.

Student Body. University seeks a national student body; 63% of students from in state; 10% New England, 2% Middle Atlantic, 13% Midwest, 3% West; 5% Foreign. An estimated 2% of students reported as Black, 2% Hispanic, 3% Asian, 1% other minority.

Varsity Sports. Men (Div.I): Basketball, Crew, Cross Country, Diving, Football, Golf, Hockey, Soccer, Swimming, Tennis, Track, Wrestling. Women (Div.I): Basketball, Crew, Cross Country, Diving, Golf, Soccer, Swimming, Tennis, Track, Volleyball.

Campus Life. The city of Madison, long known as the Athens of the West, has benefited from the great number of cultural activities sponsored and supported by the university. It is not necessary to leave the city to experience a full cultural program. The nearest major cultural center other than Madison is Chicago, 150 miles away. Cars permitted, but discouraged by the university because of parking problems. Alcoholic beverages permitted on campus for students of legal age. Administration does not regulate women's hours; intervisitation privileges limited.

About 10% of men, 10% of women live in traditional dormitories; 20% of men, 20% of women in coed dormitories; 62% men, 50 % women live in off-campus college-related housing; rest commute. Sexes segregated in coed dormitories either by wing or floor. There are 15 fraternities, 17 sororities on campus which about 8% of men, 15% of women join; 8% of men, 15% of women live in fraternities and sororities.

Annual Costs. Tuition and fees, $2,540 (out-of-state, $8,400); room and board, $4,000; estimated $1,500 other, exclusive of travel. About 55% of undergraduate students receive financial aid. Assistance is typically divided 20% grant, 70% loan, 10% work. University reports some scholarships awarded on the basis of academic merit alone.

University of Wisconsin—Milwaukee

Milwaukee, Wisconsin 53201 (414) 229-3800

An urban institution, the University of Wisconsin—Milwaukee offers a wide range of graduate and undergraduate programs. The main campus is located close to Lake Michigan in a city of one million. A second campus, in the heart of the city, houses continuing education programs. Most convenient major airport: Milwaukee.

Founded: 1885
Affiliation: State
UG Enrollment: 5,738 M, 5,781 W (full-time); 3,292 M, 4,305 W (part-time)
Total Enrollment: 23,794
Cost: < $10K
% Receiving Financial Aid: 47%
Admission: Non-selective
Application Deadline: Rolling

Admission. (See also University of Wisconsin System.) For all schools, 73% of applicants accepted, 51% of these actually enroll; 27% of freshmen graduate in top fifth of high school class. Average freshman scores: ACT, 22 M, 22 W composite. *Required:* ACT for in-state, SAT or ACT for out-of-state. Criteria considered in admissions, in order of importance: class rank, standardized test scores, high school academic record, recommendations, writing sample, extracurricular activities. *Out-of-state* freshman applicants: university does not seek students from out-of-state. State does not limit out-of-state enrollment. States from which most out-of-state applicants are drawn include Illinois, Minnesota. *Entrance programs:* midyear admission, deferred admission, advanced placement. *Apply* as soon as possible; rolling admissions. *Transfers* welcome; 1,396 enrolled 1993–94.

Academic Environment. Degrees offered: bachelors, masters, doctoral. A total of 75 undergraduate majors offered as well as graduate studies at MA and PhD levels. An unusual program of urban studies includes urban education, urban affairs, urban planning, community health nursing, and social work. *Undergraduate studies* offered to freshmen by colleges of Letters and Science, and Engineering and Applied Science, schools of Fine Arts, Nursing, Allied Health Professions, and Architecture and Urban Planning; juniors admitted to schools of Architecture, Business Administration, Education, and Social Welfare. *Majors offered* include anthropology, biological aspects of conservation, comparative study of religion, computer science, geography, Hebrew studies, interior design and graphic arts, international relations, journalism, linguistics, mass communications, Russian; professional programs include medical technology, occupational therapy, speech pathology and audiology, peace studies, dance.

About 42% of students entering as freshmen graduate eventually; 67% of freshmen return for sophomore year. *Special programs:* CLEP, independent study, January term, study abroad, honors, undergraduate research, individualized majors, credit by examination, volunteer for credit, consortial nursing program, co-op engineering, internships including Washington internship (summer), professional theater training program, 3–1 medical technology with 8 local hospitals, cross registration with U W Parkside Nursing program. *Calendar:* semester, summer school.

Undergraduate degrees conferred (2,337). 20% were in Business and Management, 12% were in Social Sciences, 10% were in Education, 7% were in Communications, 7% were in Engineering, 6% were in Health Sciences, 5% were in Psychology, 4% were in Letters, 4% were in Visual and Performing Arts, 4% were in Allied Health, 4% were in Architecture and Environmental Design, 3% were in Public Affairs, 3% were in Life Sciences, 3% were in Protective Services, remainder in 9 other fields.

Faculty. About 79% of faculty hold PhD or equivalent. About 98% of undergraduate classes taught by tenured faculty.

Student Body. University does not seek a national student body; 97% of students from Wisconsin; 2% Midwest; 1% Foreign. An estimated 8% of students reported as Black, 3% Hispanic, 2% Asian, 4% other minority. Average age of undergraduate student: 22.

Varsity Sports. Men (Div.I): Baseball, Basketball, Cross Country, Soccer, Swimming, Tennis, Track, Volleyball. Women (Div.I): Basketball, Cross Country, Soccer, Swimming, Tennis, Track, Volleyball.

Campus Life. University provides on campus many types of cultural activities. Location 2 miles from center of Milwaukee facilitates access to broad range of additional cultural opportunities. Campus is still a commuter institution but with opening of coed dormitory complex, percentage living on campus has increased somewhat. Cars allowed; drinking permitted on campus in student union and in union facilities at residence hall complex. High proportion of students hold jobs; average age is 25.

About 8% of students live in coed dormitories; rest commute. Sexes segregated in dormitories by floor. There are 6 fraternities, 5 sororities on campus.

Annual Costs. Tuition and fees, $2,546 (out-of-state, $8,150); room and board, $3,400; estimated $1,700 other, exclusive of travel. About 47% of students receive financial aid; average amount of assistance, $2,700. University reports some scholarships awarded on the basis of academic merit alone. *Meeting Costs:* university offers PLUS Loans.

University of Wisconsin—Eau Claire

Eau Claire, Wisconsin 54701 (715) 836-5415

A state-supported institution, located in a community of more than 50,000, 80 miles east of St. Paul, Minnesota. University has expanded undergraduate programs in allied health fields. Most convenient major airport: Minneapolis (MN).

Founded: 1916
Affiliation: State
UG Enrollment: 3,731 M, 5,528 W (full-time); 430 M, 657 W (part-time)
Total Enrollment: 9,400
Cost: < $10K
Admission: Non-selective
Application Deadline: August 15

Admission. (See also University of Wisconsin System.) About 79% of applicants accepted, 54% of these actually enroll; 42% of freshmen graduate in top quarter of high school class, 77% in top half. *Required:* SAT or ACT. *Out-of-state* freshman applicants: university welcomes out-of-state students. State does not limit out-of-state enrollment. *Non-academic factors* considered in admissions: applicants out of school 2 or more years, veterans, minorities, educationally disadvantaged. *Apply* by August 15. *Transfers* welcome.

Academic Environment. *Undergraduate studies* offered by schools of Arts and Sciences, Business, Education, Nursing. About 10–30% of general education requirements for graduation are elective; distribution requirements fairly numerous. About 49% of students entering as freshmen graduate eventually; 24% do not return for sophomore year. *Special programs:* CLEP, independent study, study abroad, honors, internships, cooperative education, Educational Opportunity. *Calendar:* semester, summer school.

Undergraduate degrees conferred (1,732). 28% were in Business and Management, 15% were in Education, 8% were in Letters, 8% were in Health Sciences, 6% were in Social Sciences, 5% were in Communications, 5% were in Psychology, 5% were in Visual and Performing Arts, 4% were in Life Sciences, 3% were in Allied Health, 3% were in Public Affairs, remainder in 8 other fields.

Student Body. About 86% of students from in state; almost all from North Central.

Varsity Sports. Men (NAIA, NCAA Div.III): Baseball, Basketball, Cross Country, Football, Golf, Hockey, Swimming/Diving, Tennis, Track, Volleyball, Wrestling. Women (NAIA, NCAA Div.III): Basketball, Cross Country, Gymnastics, Softball, Swimming/Diving, Tennis, Track, Volleyball.

Campus Life. About 31% of men, 33% of women live in coed and traditional dormitories; 69% of men, 67% of women commute. Freshmen are given preference in college housing if all students cannot be accommodated. Intervisitation in men's and women's dormitory rooms limited. Sexes segregated in coed dormitories either by wing or floor. There are 4 fraternities, 3 sororities on campus which less than 1% each of men, women join; they provide no residence facilities. About 25% of students leave campus on weekends.

Annual Costs. Tuition and fees, $2,189 (out-of-state, $6,643); room and board, $3,300. About 50% of students receive financial aid; assistance is typically divided 39% scholarship, 50% loan, 11% work. University reports some scholarships awarded for academic merit. *Meeting Costs:* university offers PLUS, SELF, and Alliance loans.

University of Wisconsin—Green Bay

Green Bay, Wisconsin 54311-7001 (414) 465-2111

A 4-year, degree-granting institution since 1965, UW—Green Bay stresses interdisciplinary education. The campus is located on the shore of Green Bay in a metropolitan area of 200,000. Most convenient major airport: Green Bay.

Founded: 1965
Affiliation: State
UG Enrollment: 1,520 M, 2,302 W (full-time); 427 M, 918 W (part-time)
Total Enrollment: 5,403
Cost: < $10K
% Receiving Financial Aid: 65%
Admission: Non-selective
Application Deadline: Feb. 1

Admission. (See also University of Wisconsin System.) About 80% of applicants accepted, 40% of these actually enroll; 38% of freshmen graduate in top fifth of high school class, 80% in top two-fifths. Average freshmen scores: ACT, 22.2 M, 22.2 W composite. *Required:* ACT. Criteria considered in admissions, in order of importance: high school academic record, standardized test scores, recommendations, admissions test, extracurricular activities, writing sample. *Out-of-state* freshman applicants: university actively seeks out-of-state students. State does not limit out-of-state enrollment. About 80% of applicants accepted. States from which most out-of-state applicants are drawn include Illinois. About 15% of freshmen from parochial schools. *Apply* by February 1. *Transfers* welcome; 505 enrolled 1993–94.

Academic Environment. Degree programs offered in 4 broad areas: natural and applied sciences, arts and humanities, social sciences, and professional studies, all reflecting the university's commitment to interdisciplinary education. Degrees offered: associates, bachelors, masters. *Majors offered* include environmental science. About 57% of general education requirements for graduation are elective; distribution requirements fairly numerous. Average undergraduate class size: 36% under 20, 41% between 20–40, 23% over 40.

About 36% of students entering as freshmen graduate eventually; 77% return for sophomore year. *Special programs:* CLEP, credit by examination, independent study, study abroad, honors, undergraduate research, 3-year degree, individualized majors, 78-campus National Student Exchange, cooperative programs in engineering, business, and education; cross registration with Bellin College of Nursing. Adult programs: Extended Degree Program offers credit for life experience, off-campus study, limited on-campus sessions, leads to Bachelors of General Studies. *Calendar:* 2 semester.

Undergraduate degrees conferred (656). 25% were in Business and Management, 21% were in Psychology, 11% were in Social Sciences, 6% were in Letters, 5% were in Communications, 5% were in Public Affairs, 5% were in Health Sciences, 4% were in Visual and Performing Arts, 4% were in Multi/Interdisciplinary Studies, 4% were in Physical Sciences, 4% were in Life Sciences, remainder in 5 other fields.

Graduates Career Data. Advanced studies pursued immediately after graduation by 12% of students, according to most recent data available. *Careers in business and industry* pursued by 49% of graduates.

Faculty. About 95% of faculty hold PhD or equivalent. About 80% of undergraduate classes taught by tenured faculty.

Student Body. About 95% of students from in state; 80 foreign students 1993–94. An estimated 1% of students reported as Black, 1% Hispanic, 1% Asian, 3% other minority. Average age of undergraduate student: 22.

Varsity Sports. Men (Div.I): Basketball, Cross Country, Diving, Golf, Skiing (Nordic), Soccer, Tennis. Women (Div.I): Basketball, Cross Country, Diving, Soccer, Softball, Swimming, Tennis, Volleyball.

Campus Life. About 10% of men, 12% of women live in coed dormitories; 10% of men, 12% of women live in on-campus apartments; 80% of men, 75% of women commute, according to most recent data available. There is one fraternity and 2 sororities on campus which about 1% men, 1% women join. About 40% of resident students leave campus on weekends.

Annual Costs. Tuition and fees, $2,104 (out-of-state, $6,552); room and board, $2,800; estimated $1,750 other, exclusive of travel. About 65% of students receive financial aid; average amount of assistance, $3,300. Assistance is typically divided 10% scholarship, 40% grant, 30% loan, 20% work. University reports some scholarships awarded on the basis of academic merit alone.

University of Wisconsin—La Crosse

La Crosse, Wisconsin 54601 (608) 785-8067

A state-supported institution, located on a 160-acre campus in a community of 60,000, 120 miles west of Madison. University places emphasis on health/recreation/physical education and teacher training programs. Most convenient major airport: LaCrosse.

Founded: 1909
Affiliation: State
UG Enrollment: 3,182 M, 4,124 W (full-time); 304 M, 403 W (part-time)
Total Enrollment: 8,659
Cost: < $10K
Admission: Non-selective
Application Deadline: Rolling

Admission. (See also University of Wisconsin System); 59% of applicants accepted, 60% of these actually enroll. About 39% of freshmen graduate in top fifth of high school class, 82% in top two-fifths. Average freshman scores: ACT, 22.4 composite. *Required:* ACT. Criteria considered in admissions, in order of importance: high school academic record, high school units, standardized test scores, recommendations, extracurricular activities, writing sample; other factors considered: special talents, diverse student body. *Out-of-state* freshman applicants: university actively seeks out-of-state students. State does not limit out-of-state enrollment. States from which most out-of-state applicants are drawn include Illinois, Minnesota. *Entrance programs:* advanced placement. *Apply:* rolling admissions. *Transfers* welcome; 321 enrolled 1993–94.

Academic Environment. *Undergraduate studies* offered by colleges of Arts, Letters, and Sciences, Education, schools of Business Administration, Health, Physical Education, and Recreation, Health and Human Services. About 44% of general education requirements for graduation are elective; distribution requirements fairly numerous. Degrees offered: associates, bachelors, masters. *Majors offered* in addition to usual studies include business, physical therapy, nuclear medicine, archaeology, microbiology, medical technology, social work. About 25% of students entering as freshmen graduate within four years, according to most recent data available; 75% of freshmen return for sophomore year. *Special programs:* CLEP, study abroad, honors, internships and co-ops. *Calendar:* semester, summer school.

Undergraduate degrees conferred (1,375). 25% were in Education, 22% were in Business and Management, 11% were in Social Sciences, 7% were in Parks and Recreation, 6% were in Allied Health, 5% were in Psychology, 4% were in Public Affairs, 4% were in Communications, 3% were in Letters, 3% were in Life Sciences, remainder in 8 other fields.

Graduates Career Data. About 88% of 1992–93 graduates employed. Career Development Services include career advising, internships, co-ops, resume writing, job fairs, job bulletins, on-campus recruitment, placement service.

Faculty. About 78% of faculty hold PhD or equivalent.

Student Body. About 85% of students from in state; 99% Midwest. An estimated 1% of students reported as Black, 1% Hispanic, 1% Asian, 2% other minority.

Varsity Sports. Men (NAIA, Div.III): Baseball, Basketball, Cross Country, Diving, Football, Swimming, Tennis, Track, Wrestling. Women (NAIA, Div.III): Basketball, Cross Country, Diving, Gymnastics, Soccer, Softball, Swimming, Tennis, Track, Volleyball.

Campus Life. About 33% of students live in coed dormitories; 67% of students live in off-campus college-related housing. Intervisitation in men's and women's dormitory rooms limited. Sexes segregated in coed dormitories either by wing or floor. There are 3 fraternities, 2 sororities on campus which about 1% men, 1% women join. About 25% of resident students leave campus on weekends, according to most recent data available.

Annual Costs. Tuition and fees, $2,217 (out-of-state, $6,6655,370); room and board, $2,270; estimated $1,500–2,000 other, exclusive of travel. Assistance is typically divided 38% grant, 58% loan, 4% work. University reports some scholarships awarded on the basis of academic merit alone.

University of Wisconsin—Oshkosh

Oshkosh, Wisconsin 54901 **(414) 424-0202**

A state-supported institution, located in a community of 53,200, on the shores of Lake Winnebago. Most convenient major airports: Wittman (Oshkosh).

Founded: 1871
Affiliation: State
UG Enrollment: 3,780 M, 4,793 W (full-time); 399 M, 707 W (part-time)
Total Enrollment: 9,279
Cost: < $10K
% Receiving Financial Aid: 45%
Admission: Non-selective
Application Deadline: Rolling

Admission. (See also University of Wisconsin System.) About 76% of applicants accepted, 51% of these actually enroll; 33% of freshmen graduate in top fifth of high school class, 67% in top two-fifths. Average freshman scores, according to most recent data available: ACT, 22.2 M, 21.3 W composite, 21.7 M, 20.8 W mathematical. *Out-of-state* freshman applicants: state does not limit out-of-state enrollment. No special requirements for out-of-state students (SAT may be submitted). *Apply:* rolling admissions. *Transfers* welcome.

Academic Environment. *Undergraduate studies* offered by colleges of Letters and Science, Business Administration, Education, Nursing. All general education requirements for graduation are elective; distribution requirements in 4 broad areas. *Special programs:* CLEP, "University Learning Community" (3 semester program for new freshmen), independent study, honors, January and spring interim, Project Success, Model UN. Adult programs: Bachelor of Liberal Studies, weekend classes. *Calendar:* 2 flexible 14-week semesters with optional 3-week interims; summer school.

Undergraduate degrees conferred (1,487). 23% were in Education, 23% were in Business and Management, 9% were in Social Sciences, 7% were in Communications, 7% were in Health Sciences, 5% were in Letters, 4% were in Visual and Performing Arts, 4% were in Protective Services, 3% were in Psychology, 3% were in Public Affairs, remainder in 9 other fields.

Faculty. About 73% of faculty hold PhD or equivalent.

Student Body. About 97% of students from in state; 80 foreign students, according to most recent data available.

Varsity Sports. Men (Div.III): Baseball, Basketball, Cross Country, Football, Golf, Gymnastics, Soccer, Swimming, Tennis, Track, Wrestling. Women (Div.III): Basketball, Cross Country, Gymnastics, Softball, Swimming, Tennis, Track, Volleyball.

Campus Life. About 5% of women live in traditional dormitories; 42% of men, 52% of women in coed dormitories; 58% of men, 43% of women commute. Sexes segregated in coed dormitories either by wing or floor. Freshmen are given preference in college housing if all students cannot be accommodated. There are 5 fraternities, 3 sororities on campus; they provide no residence facilities.

Annual Costs. Tuition and fees, $2,062 (out-of-state, $6,418); room and board, $2,400. About 45% of students receive financial aid; assistance is typically divided 41% scholarship, 42% loan, 17% work. University reports some scholarships awarded for academic merit.

University of Wisconsin—Parkside

Kenosha, Wisconsin 53141 **(414) 553-2355**

A state-supported, commuter institution, located in a city of 78,000, 30 miles south of Milwaukee. Most convenient major airports: Mitchell Field (Milwaukee), O'Hare (Chicago).

Founded: 1965
Affiliation: State
UG Enrollment: 1,454 M, 1,529 W (full-time); 785 M, 1,085 W (part-time)
Cost: < $10K
Admission: Non-selective
Application Deadline: August 1

Admission. (See also University of Wisconsin System.) About 84% of applicants accepted, 95% of these actually enroll; 25% of freshmen graduate in top fifth of high school class, 54% in top two-fifths. *Out-of-state* freshman applicants: university welcomes out-of-state students. State does not limit out-of-state enrollment. No special requirements for out-of-state applicants (SAT may be submitted). *Apply* by August 1. *Transfers* welcome.

Academic Environment. *Undergraduate studies* offered by 8 academic divisions. *Degrees:* AB, BS. About 98% of general education requirements for graduation are elective from a selected list of courses; distribution requirements fairly numerous. About 50% of freshmen do not return for sophomore year. *Special programs:* CLEP, independent study, study abroad, 3-year degree. *Calendar:* semester, summer school.

Undergraduate degrees conferred (513). 32% were in Business and Management, 21% were in Social Sciences, 10% were in Psychology, 9% were in Communications, 7% were in Life Sciences, 4% were in Letters, 4% were in Visual and Performing Arts, 3% were in Mathematics, 3% were in Computer and Engineering Related Technology, remainder in 5 other fields.

Graduates Career Data. According to most recent data available full-time graduate or professional study pursued by 14% of students immediately after graduation. *Careers in business and industry* pursued by 70% of graduates.

Varsity Sports. Men (NAIA, NCAA II): Baseball, Basketball, Cross Country, Golf, Soccer, Tennis, Track, Wrestling. Women (NAIA,

NCAA II): Basketball, Cross Country, Softball, Tennis, Track, Volleyball.
Student Body. University does not seek a national student body; 95% of students from in state; almost all students from North Central. An estimated 3% of students reported as Black, 3% Hispanic, 1% Asian, less than 1% Native American, according to most recent data available.
Campus Life. About 10% each of men, women live in traditional dormitories; rest commute.
Annual Costs. Tuition and fees, $2,100 (out-of-state, $6,600); room and board, $3,650. About 30% of students receive financial aid; assistance is typically divided 45% scholarship, 45% loan, 10% work. University reports some scholarships awarded for academic merit. *Meeting Costs:* university offers tuition payment plan.

University of Wisconsin—Platteville

Platteville, Wisconsin 53818 (608) 342-1125

A state-supported institution, located in a town of 10,000, 72 miles southwest of Madison and 25 miles east of the Mississippi River and Dubuque, Iowa. Most convenient major airport: Dubuque (IA) or Madison (WI).

Founded: 1866
Affiliation: State
UG Enrollment: 3,610 M, 1,847 W (full-time); 269 M, 213 W (part-time)
Total Enrollment: 6,164
Cost: < $10K
% Receiving Financial Aid: 73%
Admission: Non-selective
Application Deadline: Jan. 1

Admission. (See also University of Wisconsin System.) About 74% of applicants accepted, 46% of these actually enroll; 39% of freshmen graduate in top fifth of high school class, 81% in top two-fifths. Average freshman ACT scores: 22.8 composite. *Required:* minimum ACT of 20 and/or rank in top half of high school class, Wisconsin English and Mathematics placement exam. Criteria considered in admissions, in order of importance: high school academic record of core preparation, standardized test scores; other factors considered: special talents. *Out-of-state* freshmen applicants: university actively seeks students from out-of-state. State does not limit out-of-state enrollment. States from which most out-of-stae applicants are drawn include Illinois, Minnesota, Iowa. *Entrance programs:* midyear admission. About 5% of freshmen from private schools. *Apply* by January 1. *Transfers* welcome; 187 enrolled 1993–94.
Academic Environment. *Undergraduate studies* offered by colleges of Arts and Sciences, Agriculture, Business, Industry and Communication, Education, Engineering. Degrees offered: associates, bachelors, masters. *Majors offered* include accounting, cartography, computer science, criminal justice, engineering technology, radio/television broadcasting, technical communication, water and land reclamation. About 35% of students entering as freshmen graduate in four years, 48% eventually; 80% of freshmen return for sophomore year. *Special programs:* CLEP, independent study, study abroad, internships/work study. *Calendar:* semester, summer school.
Undergraduate degrees conferred (896). 26% were in Engineering, 17% were in Business and Management, 11% were in Education, 11% were in Engineering and Engineering Related Technology, 6% were in Protective Services, 4% were in Agribusiness and Agricultural Production, 4% were in Communications, 3% were in Agricultural Sciences, 3% were in Letters, 3% were in Social Sciences, remainder in 11 other fields.
Faculty. About 65% of undergraduate classes taught by tenured faculty, no teaching assistants. About 25% of teaching faculty are female; 3% Black, 1% Hispanic, 7% other minority.
Student Body. According to most recent data available, about 91% of students from in state; 98% North Central; 54 foreign students 1990–91. An estimated 1% of students reported as Black, 1% Asian, 2% other minority.
Varsity Sports. Men (Div.III): Baseball, Basketball, Cross Country, Football, Golf, Soccer, Tennis, Track, Wrestling. Women (Div.III): Basketball, Cross Country, Softball, Tennis, Track, Volleyball.
Campus Life. About 29% of men, 18% of women live in traditional dormitories; 20% of men, 17% of women live in coed dormitories; 39% of men, 58% of women live in off-campus housing or commute, according to most recent data available. Freshmen are given preference in college housing if all students cannot be accommodated. There are 8 fraternities, 4 sororities on campus which about 12% of men, 7% of women join. About 50% of resident students leave campus on weekends.
Annual Costs. Tuition and fees, $2,200 (out-of-state, $6,600); room and board, $2,500; estimated $1,400 other, exclusive of travel. About 73% of students receive financial aid. Assistance is typically divided 2% scholarship, 46% grant, 48% loan, 4% work. University reports some scholarships awarded on the basis of academic merit alone.

University of Wisconsin—River Falls

River Falls, Wisconsin 54022 (715) 425-3500

A state-supported institution, located in a town of 8,000, 28 miles east of St. Paul–Minneapolis. Rivers Falls offers special programs in agricultural education and agricultural sciences. Most convenient major airport: Minneapolis/St. Paul International.

Founded: 1874
Affiliation: State
UG Enrollment: 1,858 M, 2,271 W (full-time); 96 M, 116 W (part-time)
Total Enrollment: 5,263
Cost: < $10K
% Receiving Financial Aid: 60%
Admission: Non-selective
Application Deadline: Jan. 1

Admission. (See also University of Wisconsin System.) About 62% of applicants accepted; 29% of freshmen graduate in top fifth of high school class, 64% in top two-fifths, according to most recent data available. Average freshman scores: ACT, 21.5 M, 22 composite. *Required:* minimum ACT of 22, rank in top 40% of high school class. Criteria considered in admissions, in order of importance: class rank, standardized test scores, high school academic record, recommendations, extracurricular activities; other factors considered: special talents, diverse student body. *Out-of-state* freshman applicants: university actively seeks out-of-state students. State does not limit out-of-state enrollment. States from which most out-of-state students are drawn include Minnesota. *Entrance programs:* early admission, midyear admission, deferred admission. *Apply* by January 1; rolling admissions. *Transfers* welcome.
Academic Environment. *Undergraduate studies* offered by colleges of Arts and Sciences, Agriculture, Education. About 65% of general education requirements for graduation are elective; distribution requirements fairly numerous. Degrees offered: bachelors, masters. *Majors offered* include biotechnology, hydrogeology. About 46% of students entering as freshmen graduate eventually; 71% of freshmen return for sophomore year, according to most recent data available. *Special programs:* independent study, semester study abroad, honors, individualized majors, internships. *Calendar:* quarter, summer school.
Undergraduate degrees conferred (676). 23% were in Education, 18% were in Business and Management, 14% were in Agricultural Sciences, 10% were in Social Sciences, 6% were in Letters, 5% were in Agribusiness and Agricultural Production, 4% were in Physical Sciences, 3% were in Psychology, 3% were in Life Sciences, 3% were in Computer and Engineering Related Technology, remainder in 9 other fields.
Graduates Career Data. Advanced studies pursued by 18% of students immediately after graduation, according to most recent data available; 4% enter business school; 2% enter veterinary school. *Careers in business and industry* pursued by 69% of graduates.
Faculty. About 70% of faculty hold PhD or equivalent.
Student Body. About 55% of students from in state; 98% North Central, according to most recent data available. An estimated 55% of students reported as Protestant, 43% Catholic, 2% Jewish; 1% as Black, 1% Hispanic, 1% Asian, 2% other minority.
Varsity Sports. Men (Div.III): Baseball, Basketball, Cross Country, Football, Hockey, Swimming, Tennis, Track, Wrestling. Women (Div.III): Basketball, Cross Country, Gymnastics, Soccer, Softball, Swimming, Tennis, Track, Volleyball.
Campus Life. About 11% of men, 20% of women live in traditional dormitories; 35% of men, 34% of women in coed dormitories; 53% of men, 46% of women commute, according to most recent data available. Limited and unlimited intervisitation options available. Freshmen are given preference in college housing if all students cannot be accommodated. There are 5 fraternities, 4 sororities on campus which about 10% of men, 10% of women join; 1% of men live in fraternities. About 25% of resident students leave campus on weekends.

Annual Costs. Tuition and fees, $2,145 (out-of-state, $6,593); room and board, $2,510; estimated $1,300 other (book rental included in tuition), exclusive of travel. About 60% of students receive financial aid. University reports some scholarships awarded on the basis of academic merit alone. *Meeting Costs:* university offers partial payment and extended payment plans.

University of Wisconsin—Stevens Point

Stevens Point, Wisconsin 54481-3897 (715) 346-2441

A state-supported institution, located in a town of 23,500, in the heart of the Wisconsin River Valley. Most convenient major airport: Mosinee.

Founded: 1894
Affiliation: State
UG Enrollment: 3,739 M, 3,657 W (full-time); 376 M, 543 W (part-time)
Total Enrollment: 7,890
Cost: < $10K
% Receiving Financial Aid: 60%
Admission: Non-selective
Application Deadline: Rolling

Admission. (See also University of Wisconsin System.) About 92% of applicants accepted, 50% of these actually enroll; 27% of freshmen graduate in top fifth of high school class, 57% in top two-fifths. Average freshman ACT (enhanced) scores, according to most recent data available: 20.7 composite. *Out-of-state* freshman applicants: university welcomes out-of-state students. State does not limit out-of-state enrollment. *Apply:* rolling admissions. *Transfers* welcome.
Academic Environment. *Undergraduate studies* offered by colleges of Letters and Science, Natural Resources, Fine Arts, Professional Studies; degree programs in computer science, health promotion/physical education, medical technology, natural resources, home economics, communicative disorders. About 21% of students entering as freshmen graduate within four years; 24% of freshmen do not return for sophomore year. *Special programs:* CLEP, independent study, study abroad, honors, undergraduate research, cooperative education, teacher certification, many pre-professional programs (including architecture, dental, engineering, law, optometry, veterinary). *Calendar:* semester, summer school.
Undergraduate degrees conferred (1,400). 18% were in Education, 13% were in Business and Management, 12% were in Social Sciences, 9% were in Communications, 9% were in Renewable Natural Resources, 7% were in Life Sciences, 5% were in Psychology, 5% were in Visual and Performing Arts, 4% were in Home Economics, 3% were in Computer and Engineering Related Technology, 3% were in Letters, 3% were in Allied Health, remainder in 9 other fields.
Graduates Career Data. According to most recent data available, full-time graduate or professional study pursued within 1 year of graduation by 13% of students. *Careers in business and industry* pursued by 64% of graduates.
Student Body. About 88% of students from in state; 3% foreign students, according to most recent data available.
Varsity Sports. Men (Div.III): Baseball, Basketball, Cross Country, Football (& NAIA), Golf, Hockey, Swimming, Tennis, Track, Wrestling. Women (Div.III): Basketball, Cross Country, Field Hockey, Softball, Swimming, Tennis, Track, Volleyball.
Campus Life. About 39% of students live in traditional or coed dormitories; rest live in off-campus housing or commute. Intervisitation in men's and women's dormitory rooms limited. Sexes segregated in coed dormitories either by wing or floor. Freshmen are given preference in college housing if all students cannot be accommodated. There are 3 fraternities, 4 sororities on campus which about 2% each of men, women join.
Annual Costs. Tuition and fees, $2,250 (out-of-state, $6,770); room and board, $3,030. About 60% of undergraduate students who apply for aid receive financial aid.

University of Wisconsin—Stout

Menomonie, Wisconsin 54751 (715) 232-1231

A state-supported university, located in a town of 13,000, 60 miles southeast of St. Paul.

Founded: 1891
Affiliation: State
UG Enrollment: 3,122 M, 2,940 W (full-time)
Total Enrollment: 7,198
Cost: < $10K
% Receiving Financial Aid: 51%
Admission: Non-selective
Application Deadline: Rolling

Admission. (See also University of Wisconsin System.) About 76% of applicants accepted, 53% of these actually enroll; 22% of freshmen graduate in top fifth of high school class, 57% in top two-fifths. Average freshman ACT scores: 21 composite. *Required:* ACT. Criteria considered in admissions, in order of importance: class rank, standardized test scores. *Out-of-state* freshman applicants: university actively seeks out-of-state students. State does not limit out-of-state enrollment. About 26 out-of-state students enrolled 1993–94. States from which most out-of-state students are drawn include Minnesota. *Apply:* rolling admissions. *Transfers* welcome; 551 enrolled 1993–94.
Academic Environment. *Undergraduate studies* offered by schools of Liberal Studies, Education, Home Economics, Industry and Technology. About 17% of general education requirements for graduation are elective; no distribution requirements. Degrees offered: bachelors, masters. *Majors offered* include manufacturing engineering. Average undergraduate class size: 20. About 11% of students entering as freshmen graduate in four years, 47% eventually; 69% of freshmen return for sophomore year. *Special programs:* CLEP, independent study, study abroad, mini-sessions, individualized majors, study at Merrill-Palmer Institute, internships. *Calendar:* semester, summer school.
Undergraduate degrees conferred (1,289). 34% were in Business and Management, 20% were in Engineering and Engineering Related Technology, 18% were in Home Economics, 9% were in Education, 6% were in Visual and Performing Arts, 4% were in Psychology, 3% were in Public Affairs, 3% were in Mathematics, remainder in Engineering.
Graduates Career Data. About 95% of 1992–93 graduates employed. Fields typically hiring largest number of graduates include technology and manufacturing, hospitality and tourism, computer/math/business. Career Development Services include information and counseling, placement credentials registration, on-campus interviewing, three day career conference.
Faculty. About 76% of faculty hold PhD or equivalent. About 74% of teaching faculty are female; 2% Black, 1% Hispanic, 3% other minority.
Student Body. University seeks a national student body; 74% of students from in state; 24% Midwest; 2% Foreign.
Varsity Sports. Men (Div.III): Baseball, Basketball, Cross Country, Football, Golf, Hockey, Soccer, Tennis, Track, Volleyball, Wrestling. Women (Div.III): Basketball, Cross Country, Gymnastics, Soccer, Softball, Tennis, Track, Volleyball.
Campus Life. About 35% of students live in coed dormitories; 65% of students live in off-campus college-related housing. Intervisitation in men's and women's dormitory rooms limited. Sexes segregated in coed dormitories by floor. Freshmen are given preference in college housing if all students cannot be accommodated. There are 7 fraternities, 4 sororities on campus which about 4% of men, 3% of women join; they provide no residence facilities. About 50% of resident students leave campus on weekends, according to most recent data available.
Annual Costs. Tuition and fees, $2,175 (out-of-state, $6,623); room and board, $2,544. University reports some scholarships awarded on the basis of academic merit alone.

University of Wisconsin—Superior

Superior, Wisconsin 54880 (715) 394-8230

A state-supported institution, with liberal arts and professional programs including teacher education, located in a community of 30,000, at the western end of Lake Superior.

Founded: 1893
Affiliation: State
UG Enrollment: 850 M, 875 W (full-time); 301 M, 340 W (part-time)
Total Enrollment: 2,700
Cost: < $10K
% Receiving Financial Aid: 80%
Admission: Non-selective
Application Deadline: May 1

Admission. (See also University of Wisconsin System.) About 75% of applicants accepted, 55% of these actually enroll; 30% of freshmen graduate in top fifth of high school class, 70% in top two-fifths. Average freshman ACT scores: 21.3 M, 21.8 W. *Required:* ACT. Criteria considered in admissions, in order of importance: high school academic record, standardized test scores, recommendations; other factors considered: special talents, diverse student body. *Out-of-state* freshman applicants: university actively seeks out-of-state students. State does not limit out-of-state enrollment. About 80% of applicants accepted, 50% of these actually enroll. States from which most out-of-state students are drawn include Michigan, Illinois. *Entrance programs:* early decision, early admission, midyear admission, deferred admission, advanced placement. About 12% of freshmen from private schools, 1% from parochial. *Apply* by May 1; rolling admissions. *Transfers* welcome; 325 enrolled 1993–94.

Academic Environment. *Undergraduate studies* offered by divisions of Humanities and Social Science, Sciences and Mathematics, Business and Economics, Education, Fine and Applied Arts. General education requirements for graduation vary with major; distribution requirements fairly numerous. Degrees offered: associates, bachelors, masters. *Majors offered* include art therapy, aquatic biology, public relations. Average undergraduate class size: 70% under 20, 15% between 20–40, 5% over 40. About 35% of students entering as freshmen graduate in four years, 41% eventually; 65% of freshmen return for sophomore year. *Special programs:* CLEP, independent study, cooperative programs through LSACU, 3–2 in engineering. *Calendar:* semester, summer school.

Undergraduate degrees conferred (266). 21% were in Business and Management, 16% were in Education, 12% were in Visual and Performing Arts, 11% were in Multi/Interdisciplinary Studies, 8% were in Social Sciences, 7% were in Public Affairs, 7% were in Life Sciences, 5% were in Communications, 4% were in Psychology, 4% were in Mathematics, 3% were in Letters, remainder in 3 other fields.

Graduates Career Data. Advanced studies pursued by 15% of graduates. About 80% of 1992–93 graduates employed. Fields typically hiring largest number of graduates include education, criminal justice, counseling, mass communication.

Faculty. About 80% of faculty hold PhD or equivalent. About 95% of undergraduate classes taught by tenured faculty. About 30% of teaching faculty are female; 1% Black, 1% Hispanic, 2% other minority.

Student Body. About 60% of students from Wisconsin; 92% from Midwest; 1% Foreign.

Varsity Sports. Men (NCAA, Div.II): Baseball, Basketball, Cross Country, Hockey, Track. Women (NCAA, Div.II): Basketball, Softball, Volleyball, Track.

Campus Life. About 10% of students live in traditional dormitories; 30% live in coed dormitories; 60% commute. Freshmen are given preference in college housing if all students cannot be accommodated.

Annual Costs. Tuition and fees, $2,100 (out-of-state, $6,500); room and board, $2,400; estimated $800 other, exclusive of travel. About 80% of students receive financial aid; average amount of assistance, $3,100. Assistance is typically divided 10% scholarship, 50% grant, 25% loan, 25% work. University reports 125 scholarships awarded for academic merit. *Meeting Costs:* University offers partial payment plan.

University of Wisconsin—Whitewater

Whitewater, Wisconsin 53190 (414) 472-1513

A state-supported institution, located in a town of 12,038, 51 miles west of Milwaukee, the university places special emphasis on teacher education, business education, business administration, and computer systems. Whitewater is also nationally recognized for programs which serve physically disabled and learning disabled students.

Founded: 1868
Affiliation: State
UG Enrollment: 3,635 M, 4,153 W (full-time); 708 M, 811 W (part-time)
Total Enrollment: 10,550
Cost: < $10K
% Receiving Financial Aid: 65%
Admission: Non-selective
Application Deadline: Rolling

Admission. (See also University of Wisconsin System.) About 86% of applicants accepted, 50% of these actually enroll; 34% of freshmen graduate in top quarter of high school class, 82% in top half. Average freshman ACT scores, middle fifty percent: 19–24. *Required:* SAT or ACT, class rank, academic unit pattern. Criteria considered in admissions, in order of importance: high school academic record (class rank, GPA), standardized test scores, recommendations, extracurricular activities, writing sample; other factors considered: special talents, diverse student body. *Out-of-state* freshman applicants: university actively seeks out-of-state students. State does not limit out-of-state enrollment. States from which most out-of-state students are drawn include Illinois, Minnesota, Iowa. *Entrance programs:* early admission, midyear admission, advanced placement. About 15% of freshmen from private schools. *Apply:* rolling admissions. *Transfers* welcome; 536 enrolled 1993–94.

Academic Environment. *Undergraduate studies* offered by colleges of Letters and Sciences, Arts, Business and Economics, Education. About 25% of general education credits for graduation are required; distribution requirements vary with program. Degrees offered: associates, bachelors, masters. Average undergraduate class size: 23. About 44% of students entering as freshmen graduate in four years, 60% eventually. *Special programs:* CLEP, independent study, study abroad, honors, internships, 3-year degree, individualized majors. *Calendar:* semester, summer school.

Undergraduate degrees conferred (1,557). 38% were in Business and Management, 20% were in Education, 13% were in Letters, 8% were in Social Sciences, 5% were in Public Affairs, 4% were in Psychology, 3% were in Visual and Performing Arts, 3% were in Computer and Engineering Related Technology, remainder in 7 other fields.

Graduates Career Data. Advanced studies pursued by 20% of graduates. About 94% of 1993–94 graduates employed. Fields typically hiring largest number of graduates include business, education, social sciences. Extensive Career Development Services offered.

Faculty. About 68% of faculty hold PhD or equivalent. About 29% of teaching faculty are female; 3% Black, 1% Hispanic, 6% other minority.

Student Body. About 92% of students from in state; 98% of students from Midwest.

Varsity Sports. Men (Div.III): Baseball, Basketball, Cross Country, Diving, Football, Gymnastics, Soccer, Swimming, Tennis, Track, Wrestling. Women (Div.III): Basketball, Cross Country, Diving, Gymnastics, Soccer, Softball, Swimming, Tennis, Track, Volleyball.

Campus Life. About 10% women live in traditional dormitories; 100% of men, 90% of women live in coed dormitories. Intervisitation in men's and women's dormitory rooms limited. Freshmen are given preference in college housing if all students cannot be accommodated. There are 8 fraternities, 5 sororities on campus which about 5% of men, 4% of women join. About 50% of resident students leave campus on weekends.

Annual Costs. Tuition and fees, $2,200 (out-of-state, $6,700); room and board, $2,500; estimated $2,000 other, exclusive of travel.

About 65% of students receive financial aid; average amount of assistance, $4,000. Assistance is typically divided 5% scholarship, 25% grant, 60% loan, 10% work. University reports 120 scholarships awarded for academic merit.

Wisconsin Lutheran College

Milwaukee, Wisconsin 53226 (414) 774-9367

A church-related liberal arts college offering bachelors degree programs in business fields, education, and social sciences. Most convenient major airport: Milwaukee.

Founded: 1973
Affiliation: Wisconsin Evangelical Lutheran Synod
UG Enrollment: 105 M, 180 W (full-time)
Cost: < $10K
% Receiving Financial Aid: 86%
Admission: Non-selective
Application Deadline: April 1

Admission. About 85% of applicants accepted, 62% of these actually enroll; 37% of freshmen graduate in top fifth of high school class, 58% in top two-fifths. Average freshman ACT scores: 23 M, 22.8 W composite. *Required:* SAT or ACT, minimum high school GPA. Criteria considered in admissions, in order of importance: high school academic record and standardized test scores; recommendations. About 74% of entering students from parochial schools. *Entrance programs:* early admission, mid-year admission. *Apply* by April 1; rolling admissions. *Transfers* welcome; 22 enrolled 1993–94.

Academic Environment. Graduation requirements include level 2 composition, 2–3 semesters of speech, foreign language competency, math (1 level beyond college algebra), 12–15 credits of religious studies, 12 each in humanities, natural sciences, and social sciences. Degrees offered: bachelors. Average undergraduate class size: 70% under 20, 30% 20–40. About 45% of students entering as freshmen graduate within four years, 48% eventually; 74% of freshmen return for sophomore year. *Special programs:* internships. *Calendar:* semester, summer school.

Undergraduate degrees conferred ().

Faculty. About 42% of faculty hold PhD or equivalent. About 80% of undergraduate classes taught by tenured faculty. About 26% of teaching faculty are female.

Student Body. An estimated 95% of students reported as Protestant, 1% Catholic, 1% unaffiliated; 4% Black, 1% Hispanic, 1% other minority.

Religious Orientation. Wisconsin Lutheran is church-related institution; 79% of students affiliated with the church; 12–15 credits in religious studies required of all students.

Varsity Sports. Men (NAIA): Baseball, Basketball, Cross Country, Fencing, Golf, Soccer, Tennis, Track. Women (NAIA): Basketball, Cross Country, Fencing, Softball, Tennis, Track, Volleyball.

Campus Life. About 62% of students live in traditional dormitories; no coed dormitories; rest commute. There are no fraternities or sororities on campus.

Annual Costs. Tuition and fees, $9,190; room and board, $3,800; estimated $1,625 other, exclusive of travel. About 86% of students receive financial aid; average amount of assistance, $7,410. Assistance is typically divided 21% scholarship, 22% grant, 40% loan, 15% work. College reports 144 scholarships awarded on the basis of academic merit alone, 98 for special talents, 365 for need alone.

Wittenberg University

Springfield, Ohio 45501 (513) 327-6314; (800) 677-7558

A relatively small, church-related institution, Wittenberg has traditionally drawn its students from the Midwest, but is now attracting substantial numbers from other parts of the country as it seeks a truly national student body. The 71-acre campus is located in a city of 68,000, 45 miles west of Columbus and 22 miles northeast of Dayton. Most convenient major airport: Dayton.

Founded: 1845
Affiliation: Lutheran
UG Enrollment: 928 M, 1,169 W (full-time)
Cost: $10K–$20K
% Receiving Financial Aid: 65%
Admission: Very Selective
Application Deadline: March 1

Admission is very selective. About 83% of applicants accepted, 32% of these actually enroll; 64% of freshmen graduate in top fifth of high school class, 86% in top two-fifths. Average freshman scores, middle fifty percent: SAT, 470–570 verbal, 510–620 mathematical; ACT, 21–27 composite. *Required:* SAT or ACT, essay; interview strongly recommended. Criteria considered in admissions, in order of importance: high school academic record, high school attended and trend in academic work, standardized tests, recommendations, extracurricular activities, writing sample; other factors considered: geographical distribution, special talents, alumni children, diverse student body, religious affiliation. *Entrance programs:* early decision, early admission, midyear admission, deferred admission, advanced placement. About 12% of entering students from private schools, 8% from parochial schools. *Apply* by March 1. *Transfers* welcome; 32 enrolled 1993–94.

Academic Environment. Students represented on most faculty committees and consequently have some voice in institutional decision-making. Student leader reports "close working relationships with faculty, opportunities for independent studies and off-campus study." Curriculum stresses flexibility and opportunities for independent study and internships; comprehensive examination in major field required for graduation. Administration reports no courses needed for graduation are specifically required; distribution requirements include 15 courses, writing proficiency, foreign language competency, math competency, and community service requirement. Degrees offered: bachelors. *Majors offered* include East Asian studies, Russian Studies, global studies. Average undergraduate class size: 62% under 20, 36% between 20–40, 2% over 40.

About 71% of students entering as freshmen graduate in four years, 75% eventually; 86% of freshmen return for sophomore year. *Special programs:* independent study, study abroad, honors, internships, undergraduate research, credit by examination, individualized majors, placing out of a required course; 3–2 in engineering, forestry, marine biology, occupational therapy, cross-registration through Southwestern Ohio Council for Higher Education. Adult programs: Community Education for adults over 23. *Calendar:* semester (as of fall, 1995).

Undergraduate degrees conferred (527). 22% were in Social Sciences, 12% were in Business and Management, 12% were in Letters, 9% were in Education, 9% were in Psychology, 8% were in Visual and Performing Arts, 7% were in Life Sciences, 4% were in Area and Ethnic Studies, 4% were in Multi/Interdisciplinary Studies, 4% were in Philosophy and Religion, 3% were in Liberal/General Studies, 3% were in Physical Sciences, remainder in 3 other fields.

Graduates Career Data. Advanced studies pursued by 23% of students (up to 70% eventually); 3% enter medical; 6% enter law school; 4% enter business school. Graduate and professional schools enrolling largest numbers of graduates include Ohio State, Case Western, Cincinnati, Washington U. *Careers in business and industry* pursued by 20% of graduates. Corporations typically hiring largest numbers of graduates include "Big Six" accounting firms, Federated Department Stores, Procter & Gamble. Comprehensive Career Development Services provided.

Faculty. About 98% of faculty hold PhD or equivalent. About 80% of undergraduate classes taught by tenured faculty.

Student Body. University seeks a national student body; 52% of students from in state; 66% of students from Midwest, 10% Middle Atlantic, 7% New England, 8% South, 4% West/Northwest; 5% Foreign. An estimated 57% of students reported as Protestant, 22% Catholic, 4% Jewish, 2% Muslim, 15% unaffiliated; 7% as Black, 2% Asian, 2% Hispanic, 1% other minority.

Religious Orientation. Wittenberg is a church-related institution; 1 course in religion required of all students; attendance at services voluntary.

Varsity Sports. Men (NCAC, Div.III): Baseball, Basketball, Cross Country, Football, Golf, Lacrosse, Soccer, Swimming, Tennis, Track, Wrestling. Women (NCAC, Div.III): Basketball, Cross Country, Field Hockey, Lacrosse, Soccer, Softball, Swimming, Tennis, Track, Volleyball.

Campus Life. Variety of intellectual and cultural activities offered on campus, supplemented by resources of Dayton, Columbus, and Cincinnati, 25, 45, and 75 miles away, respectively. Student interest in fraternities/sororities and varsity athletics reported as relatively high. Community service requirement provides interaction with Springfield and contributes to comfortable relationship with the community. Guidelines for limited daily intervisitation hours; 12 to 12 weekdays, 12 to 2:30 am weekends —each residence unit establishes its own schedule. Alcohol allowed only in Greek houses and dormitory rooms by those of legal age. After sophomore year, students may live off campus.

About 10% of women live in traditional dormitories; 50% of men, 50% of women in coed dormitories; 27% of men, 17% of women in off-campus housing; 3% of men, 2% of women commute. Sexes separated in coed dormitories either by wing or floor. There are 8 fraternities, 8 sororities on campus which about 30% of men, 41% of women join; 20% of men, 21% of women live in fraternities and sororities. About 10–15% of students leave campus on weekends.

Annual Costs. Tuition and fees, $15,726; room and board, $4,272; estimated $1,000 other, exclusive of travel. About 65% of students receive financial aid; average amount of need, $14,000. Assistance is typically divided 70% scholarship/grant, 18% loan, 12% work. University reports 90 scholarships awarded for academic merit. *Meeting Costs:* college offers monthly tuition payment plan.

Wofford College

Spartanburg, South Carolina 29303-3663 (803) 597-4130

A church-related, liberal arts college, Wofford is located in the Greenville-Spartanburg metropolitan area of 569,000, 76 miles southwest of Charlotte, North Carolina. The college has been coeducational since 1971. Most convenient major airport: Greenville-Spartanburg.

Founded: 1854
Affiliation: United Methodist
UG Enrollment: 627 M, 432 W (full-time)
Cost: $10K–$20K
% Receiving Financial Aid: 71%
Admission: Very Selective
Application Deadline: Feb. 1

Admission is very selective. About 60% of applicants accepted, 29% of these actually enroll; 77% of freshmen graduate in top fifth of high school class, 96% in top two-fifths. Average freshman scores: SAT, 517 verbal, 564 mathematical; 53% of freshmen score above 500 verbal, 19% above 600, 3% above 700; 91% score above 500 mathematical, 36% above 600, 6% above 700; ACT, 24 composite. *Required:* SAT or ACT, essay; interview recommended. Criteria considered in admissions, in order of importance: high school academic record, standardized test scores, extracurricular activities, writing sample (essay), recommendations; other factors considered: special talents, diverse student body. *Entrance programs:* early admission, advanced placement. About 19% of entering students from private schools. *Apply* by February 1. *Transfers* welcome; 26 enrolled 1993–94.

Academic Environment. Administration reports between one-third and one-half of courses taken by a student are basic graduation requirements. About one third of graduates go on to professional and graduate schools. Degrees offered: bachelors. *Majors offered* in addition to usual studies include interdisciplinary major in political philosophy and economy, intercultural studies, accounting, certification in secondary education, pre-professional programs in Christian ministry, dentistry, law, medicine, veterinary science, and engineering(3–2 programs). A recent student reports, "small classes, personal attention, and emphasis on writing skills are aspects I have found in all of my classes." Average undergraduate class size: 56% under 20, 40% between 20–40, 4% over 40.

About 72% of students entering as freshmen graduate in four years, 78% eventually; 91% of freshmen return for sophomore year. *Special programs:* CLEP, January Term, independent study, study abroad, January term, internships (pre-law, pre-ministerial), limited co-op education, 3-year degree, cross-registration with neighboring Converse, 3–2 in engineering, veterinary science. *Library:* rare books, art, special collection of Methodist Archives. *Calendar:* 4–1–4, summer school.

Undergraduate degrees conferred (274). 27% were in Business and Management, 19% were in Social Sciences, 12% were in Letters, 11% were in Psychology, 9% were in Life Sciences, 4% were in Physical Sciences, 4% were in Multi/Interdisciplinary Studies, 4% were in Philosophy and Religion, 4% were in Mathematics, 3% were in Foreign Languages, remainder in Visual and Performing Arts.

Graduates Career Data. Advanced studies pursued by 31% of students; 6% enter medical school; 3% enter dental school; 6% enter law school; 4% enter business school; 6% enter other schools. Medical and dental schools typically enrolling largest numbers of graduates include Medical U. of South Carolina, USC Medical School; law schools include U. of South Carolina, Wake Forest; business schools include U. of South Carolina. *Careers in business and industry* pursued by 67% of graduates, according to most recent data available. Corporations typically hiring largest numbers of graduates include Milliken, TRW Services, banks and other financial institutions.

Faculty. About 92% of faculty hold PhD or equivalent. About 71% of undergraduate classes taught by tenured faculty. About 16% of teaching faculty are female; 2% Black.

Student Body. College seeks a national student body; 70% of students from in state; 94% South; less than 1% Foreign. An estimated 73% of students reported as Protestant, 9% Catholic, 10% unaffiliated, 8% other; 8% as Black, 2% Asian, 1% Hispanic.

Religious Orientation. Wofford is a church-related institution; one course in religion is required of all students. Attendance at weekly chapel services voluntary.

Varsity Sports. Men (Div.II): Baseball, Basketball, Cross Country, Football, Golf, Soccer, Tennis. Women (Div.II): Basketball, Cross Country, Soccer, Tennis, Volleyball.

Campus Life. The "Code of Student Rights and Responsibilities" places most disciplinary powers in hands of students. Cars, alcohol, and room visitation permitted within provisions of state law and college guidelines. Upperclassmen may live off campus with permission. Nearly half of men and women join fraternities and sororities which are primarily non-residential, varsity and intramural sports are also popular.

About 90% of students live on-campus in residence halls. Freshmen are given preference in college housing if all students cannot be accommodated. There are 8 fraternities, 3 sororities on campus which about 52% of men, 54% of women join; 1% of students live in fraternities and sororities.

Annual Costs. Tuition and fees, $11,480; room and board, $4,150. About 71% of students receive financial aid; average amount of assistance, $10,465. Assistance is typically divided 20% non-need based aid, 49% need-based grants, 40% loan. College reports some scholarships awarded for academic merit. *Meeting Costs:* college offers monthly payment plans.

Woodbury University

Los Angeles, California 90017 **(213) 482-8491**

A private university offering both baccalaureate and masters degree programs in a variety of professional/vocational fields.

Founded: 1884
Affiliation: Independent
UG Enrollment: 925 M, W (full-time)
Cost: $10K–$20K
Admission: Non-selective
Application Deadline: Rolling

Admission. About 55% of applicants accepted, 41% of these actually enroll. *Apply:* rolling admissions. *Transfers* welcome.

Academic Environment. *Degree:* BS. College offers undergraduate programs in accounting, computer information systems, fashion design, fashion marketing, finance, graphic design, interior design, international business, management, marketing. *Calendar:* quarter, summer school.

Undergraduate degrees conferred (174). 55% were in Business and Management, 20% were in Architecture and Environmental Design, 16% were in Marketing and Distribution, 5% were in Visual and Performing Arts, 3% were in Home Economics, remainder in Computer and Engineering Related Technology.

Student Body. About 90% of students from California. All students commute.

Annual Costs. Tuition and fees, $12,120; room and board, $5,490.

College of Wooster

Wooster, Ohio 44691 **(800) 877-9905**

Wooster is a small, co-educational, liberal arts college that is now independent but retains voluntary affiliation with its founding church. Its strong academic program has traditionally attracted students from all parts of the country. The 300-acre campus is located in a town of 20,000, 60 miles southwest of Cleveland. Most convenient major airport: Cleveland Hopkins.

Founded: 1866
Affiliation: Independent (Presbyterian)
UG Enrollment: 830 M, 874 W (full-time)
Cost: $10K–$20K
% Receiving Financial Aid: 80%
Admission: Very Selective
Application Deadline: February 15

Admission is very selective. About 90% of applicants accepted, 30% of these actually enroll; 57% of freshmen graduate in top fifth of high school class, 82% in top two-fifths. Average freshman scores: SAT, 516 M, 526 W verbal, 572 M, 550 W mathematical; 61% of freshmen score above 500 on verbal, 21% above 600, 3% above 700; 77% score above 500 on mathematical, 33% above 600, 9% above 700; ACT, 24 M, 24 W composite. *Required:* SAT or ACT. Criteria considered in admissions, in order of importance: high school academic record, standardized test scores, recommendations, writing sample, extracurricular activities. *Entrance programs:* early decision, early admission, deferred admission. About 15% of entering students from private schools, 7% from parochial schools. *Apply* by February 15. *Transfers* welcome; 21 enrolled 1993–94.

Academic Environment. Four-year academic program includes: First Year Seminar Program which stresses critical thinking and critical writing, minimum of 5 papers plus required revisions; also attendance at the Wooster Forum, a series of lectures and events. Sophomore year includes interdisciplinary seminars and intensive research experience, on- or off-campus. Independent study compulsory for all juniors and seniors; one-sixth of student's time during junior and senior years devoted to investigation of some subject in his/her major field under supervision of faculty adviser; senior essay or project is culmination of the independent study program. Leadership and Liberal Learning program includes an interdisciplinary seminar and a symposium with recognized national leaders. Wide variety of options for extracurricular activity "allows for expression of individuality." Many academic opportunities for superior students. Through independent study all senior science majors engage in independent research. Degrees offered: bachelors. *Majors offered* include chemistry, biology, history. Average undergraduate class size: 75% under 20, 25% between 20–40.

About 67% of students entering as freshmen graduate in four years, 69% eventually; 86% of freshmen return for sophomore year. *Special programs:* independent study, January term, study abroad, study at Classical Center in Rome, programs of GLCA, study travel seminar, individualized majors, first year seminar, interdisciplinary sophomore seminar, Leadership and Liberal Learning Program, urban study centers throughout U.S., Washington Semester, internships at State Dept., Ohio Legislature; internships and practica available in American politics, ethics and society, chemical research; professional theater internships at Cleveland Play House, the Actors Theatre of Louisville, Pennsylvania Stage Co., and the Great Lakes Shakespeare Festival; GLAC Arts program in NYC; practicum in psychology; 3–2 programs in law, forestry and environmental studies, engineering, social work, architecture, nursing. *Calendar:* semester, summer school.

Undergraduate degrees conferred (448). 36% were in Social Sciences, 16% were in Letters, 9% were in Visual and Performing Arts, 9% were in Physical Sciences, 8% were in Psychology, 5% were in Philosophy and Religion, 4% were in Business and Management, 4% were in Life Sciences, 3% were in Foreign Languages, remainder in 6 other fields.

Graduates Career Data. Advanced studies pursued by 33% of students immediately after graduation; 7% enter medical school; 1% enter dental school, 8% enter law school, 5% enter business school. Medical schools typically enrolling largest numbers of graduates include Ohio State, Case Western Reserve; dental schools include Ohio State; law schools include Case Western, Ohio State, Cleveland Marshall; business schools include Northwestern, U. of Chicago. About 90% of 1992–93 graduates not attending graduate school are employed. Corporations typically hiring largest numbers of graduates include Procter and Gamble, Price Waterhouse, federal government, Peace Corps, according to most recent data available. Career Counseling Services provided. Alumni reported as helpful in both career guidance and job placement.

Faculty. About 95% of faculty hold PhD or equivalent.

Student Body. College seeks a national student body; 41% of students from in state; 8% Foreign. An estimated 6% of students reported as Black, 1% Asian, 7% other minority, according to most recent data available.

Varsity Sports. Men (Div.III): Baseball, Basketball, Cross Country, Football, Golf, Lacrosse, Soccer, Swimming, Tennis, Track. Women (Div.III): Basketball, Cross Country, Field Hockey, Lacrosse, Soccer, Swimming, Tennis, Track, Volleyball.

Campus Life. Residential self-government in all units, including open visitation option. Alcohol policy now governed by state law (legal age, 21). Cars permitted; parking reported to be adequate. Minor concern reported about interaction between local social club members and independents. College offers on campus variety of cultural activities, supplemented by full range of cultural opportunities in Cleveland, 60 miles from campus. Students expected to live in college residence halls. Housing available for all students who live on campus.

About 5% of men, 5% of women live in traditional dormitories; 90% of men, 90% of women live in coed dormitories; 1% of men, 1% of women live in off-campus college-related housing; rest commute. Sexes segregated in coed dormitories either by wing or floor. There are 7 local fraternities, 6 local sororities on campus which about 20% of men, 15% of women join; 1% of men, 1% of women live in fraternities and sororities. About 2% of resident students leave campus on weekends.

Annual Costs. Tuition and fees, $15,425; room and board, $4,450; estimated $2,000 other, exclusive of travel. About 80% of students receive financial aid; average amount of assistance, $10,000. College reports some scholarships awarded for academic merit. *Meeting Costs:* college offers installment payment plans, loan programs.

Worcester Polytechnic Institute

Worcester, Massachusetts 01609 (508) 831-5286

The third oldest engineering college in the nation, Worcester has been coed since 1968, the college is located on a 66-acre hilltop campus, a mile from downtown Worcester (pop. 176,600). WPI is part of the Worcester Consortium made up of ten institutions in Worcester area. Most convenient major airports: Worcester Municipal, Logan International (Boston).

Founded: 1865
Affiliation: Independent
UG Enrollment: 2,260 M, 542 W (full-time)
Cost: $10K–$20K
% Receiving Financial Aid: 81%
Admission: Highly Selective
Application Deadline: Feb. 15

Admission is highly selective. About 84% of applicants accepted, 30% of these actually enroll; 79% of freshmen graduate in top fifth of high school class, 98% in top two-fifths. Average freshman SAT scores: 59% of freshmen score above 500 on verbal, 18% above 600, 1% above 700; 93% score above 500 on mathematical, 72% above 600, 26% above 700. *Required:* SAT and 3 ACH, or ACT; interview recommended; optional essay. Criteria considered in admissions, in order of importance: high academic record, standardized test scores, recommendations, extracurricular activities, writing sample, interview; other factors considered: special talents, alumni children, diverse student body. *Entrance programs:* early decision, midyear admission, advanced placement, deferred admission. About 21% of entering students from private schools, according to most recent data available. *Apply* by February 15. *Transfers* welcome; 100 enrolled 1993–94.

Academic Environment. The WPI Plan provides student-designed programs that stress projects, individualized study, and tutorials with self-paced learning that balances classroom and professional experiences. Each student's program individually tailored to his or her needs and interests. Degrees awarded on the basis of demonstrated competence rather than specific course credits. Students must complete for graduation: a project in their major field of study, a project relating science to society, a qualification in a minor field of study (normally in the humanities), and a competency examination in their major area of study. Independent study and project work represent about one-quarter of student's work. In addition students complete 10 units (30 courses) specified by general topical area (not specific courses), related to their major, 2 courses in the social sciences, and 4 terms of physical education in the first 2 years. Degrees offered: bachelors, masters, doctoral. *Majors offered* in biomedical engineering, nuclear engineering, biology and biotechnology, environmental engineering and science, management, chemistry, computer science, economics, engineering (chemical, civil, electrical, management, mechanical), humanities and technology, manufacturing systems engineering, mathematics, physics; interdisciplinary program also available.

About 80% of students entering as freshmen graduate in four years; 94% of freshmen return for sophomore year. *Special programs:* CLEP, independent study (completion of 2 tutorial projects required; can include work at off-campus internship centers), study abroad, 3-year degree, individualized majors, undergraduate research, cooperative programs through Worcester Consortium, interdisciplinary courses, environmental studies program, cross-registration with neighboring institutions, 5-year BS/MS in fire protection engineering, 3–2 in engineering and science, 7-year joint program with Tufts Veterinary School. *Calendar:* 4 seven-week terms September to May, summer term.

Undergraduate degrees conferred (605). 77% were in Engineering, 6% were in Business and Management, 5% were in Computer and Engineering Related Technology, 4% were in Science Technologies, 3% were in Mathematics, remainder in 4 other fields.

Graduates Career Data. Advanced studies pursued by 60% of students; 5% enter medical school; 5% enter law school; 25% enter business school. About 80% of 1992–93 graduates employed. Corporations typically hiring largest numbers of graduates include General Electric, United Technologies. Career Development Services include interviewing skills, resume preparation, job bank, career resource library.

Faculty. About 92% of faculty hold PhD or equivalent.

Student Body. About 49% of students from in state; 76% of students from New England; 11% Middle Atlantic; 132 foreign students,

according to most recent data available. An estimated 1% of students reported as 1% Black, 5% Asian, 5% other minority.
Varsity Sports. Men (Div.III): Baseball, Basketball, Cross Country, Football, Golf, Soccer, Swimming, Tennis, Track, Wrestling. Women (Div.III): Basketball, Cross Country, Field Hockey, Golf, Softball, Swimming, Tennis, Track, Volleyball.
Campus Life. High interest reported by both administration source and student leader in fraternities/sororities, varsity sports and intramurals. Students have substantial control of their own social lives. There are no curfews or rules limiting intervisitation. No smoking allowed in classrooms, labs and many offices. Students characterized as "goal/career-oriented, friendly high achievers" who "study hard and play hard." Administration reports women's intercollegiate athletic program and a chapter of Society of Women Engineers on campus. Active calendar of cultural and intellectual events on campus, supplemented by the resources of Worcester. Students frequently visit Boston, just 50 miles away. Freshmen not allowed cars; parking for commuting students reported to be adequate, but a problem for residents.

About 50% of students live on campus. Sexes segregated in coed dormitories by wing or floor. Freshmen are given preference in college housing if all students cannot be accommodated. There are 12 fraternities, 3 sororities on campus which about 35% of men, 40% of women join. About 50–60% of students leave campus on weekends, according to most recent data available.
Annual Costs. Tuition and fees, $15,290; room and board, $5,060; estimated $1,425 other, exclusive of travel. About 81% of students receive financial aid; average amount of assistance, $11,200. Institute reports scholarships awarded only on the basis of need. *Meeting Costs:* Institute offers loan program.

Worcester State College

Worcester, Massachusetts 01602 **(617) 793-8040**

A state-supported college, primarily for commuters, located in a city of 176,600.

Founded: 1874
Affiliation: State
UG Enrollment: 1,218 M, 1,828 W (full-time)
Total Enrollment: 3,821
Cost: < $10K
Admission: Non-selective
Application Deadline: Rolling

Admission. Graduates of accredited high schools with college-preparatory program eligible; 76% of applicants accepted, 63% of these actually enroll. *Required:* SAT. *Out-of-state* freshman applicants: college welcomes students from out of state. State does not limit out-of-state enrollment. No special requirements for out-of-state applicants. *Apply:* rolling admissions. *Transfers* welcome.
Academic Environment. *Degrees:* AB, BS, BSEd. About 5% of general education credits for graduation are required; distribution requirements fairly numerous. About 40% of students entering as freshmen graduate eventually; 20% of freshmen do not return for sophomore year. *Special programs:* CLEP, independent study (in major area for seniors), contract learning, cooperative programs through Worcester Consortium. *Calendar:* semester, summer school.
Undergraduate degrees conferred (663). 23% were in Business and Management, 14% were in Psychology, 13% were in Health Sciences, 11% were in Social Sciences, 10% were in Education, 7% were in Communications Technologies, 6% were in Allied Health, 5% were in Computer and Engineering Related Technology, 5% were in Letters, 3% were in Mathematics, remainder in 4 other fields.
Student Body. College welcomes a national student body; 98% of students from Massachusetts, according to most recent data available.
Varsity Sports. Men: Baseball, Basketball, Football, Hockey, Soccer, Track. Women: Basketball, Field Hockey, Softball, Tennis.
Campus Life. Limited, but unusual residential facilities, housing 7% of men, 9% of women, available—"a loosely connected series of 26 'Town Houses' with self-contained living units in apartment style." Regulations governing lifestyle set by residents of each unit. A few students live in off-campus housing; majority commute. There are no fraternities or sororities.
Annual Costs. Tuition and fees, $2,536 (out-of-state, $6,400); room and board, $3,690.

Wright State University

Dayton, Ohio 45435 **(513) 873-2211**

A state-supported university, located in a city of 243,600. Most convenient major airport: Dayton International.

Founded: 1964
Affiliation: State
UG Enrollment: 4,643 M, 5,244 W (full-time); 1,687 M, 1,851 W (part-time)
Total Enrollment: 17,295
Cost: < $10K
Admission: Non-selective
Application Deadline: Rolling

Admission. High school graduates with 16 units eligible; 94% of applicants accepted, 59% of these actually enroll; 25% of freshmen graduate in top fifth of high school class, 51% in top two fifths. Average freshman scores, middle fifty percent range: SAT, 760–1040 combined; ACT, 18–24 composite. *Required:* ACT or SAT. Criteria considered in admissions, in order of importance: high school academic record, standardized test scores. *Out-of-state* freshman applicants: university actively seeks students from out of state. State limits out-of-state enrollment. Requirements for out-of-state applicants: must have GPA of 2.5, college preparatory program. *Apply* by no specific deadline. *Transfers* welcome.
Academic Environment. *Undergraduate studies* offered by colleges of Business and Administration, Education, Liberal Arts, Science and Engineering, School of Nursing. About 75% of general education credits for graduation are required; distribution requirements fairly numerous. Degrees offered: associates, bachelors, masters, doctoral. About 40% of students entering as freshmen graduate eventually; 70% of freshmen return for sophomore year. *Special programs:* CLEP, independent study, study abroad, internships, honors, undergraduate research, cross-registration through Dayton-Miami Valley Consortium. *Calendar:* quarter, summer school.
Undergraduate degrees conferred (1,715). 29% were in Business and Management, 13% were in Education, 10% were in Engineering, 8% were in Communications, 8% were in Social Sciences, 6% were in Health Sciences, 6% were in Psychology, 4% were in Visual and Performing Arts, 3% were in Letters, 3% were in Life Sciences, 3% were in Public Affairs, remainder in 8 other fields.
Faculty. About 80% of faculty hold PhD or equivalent.
Student Body. University does not seek a national student body; 97% of students from in state. An estimated 7% of students reported as Black, 1% Hispanic, 2% Asian, 5% other minority. Average age of undergraduate student: 24.
Varsity Sports. Men (NCAA, Div.I): Baseball, Basketball, Cross Country, Golf, Soccer, Swimming, Tennis. Women (NSC, Div.I): Basketball, Softball, Swimming, tennis, Volleyball.
Campus Life. About 10% each of men, women live in coed housing, 90% each commute, according to most recent data available. There are 9 fraternities, 7 sororities on campus which about 3% of men, 3% of women join; they provide no residence facilities.
Annual Costs. Tuition and fees, $3,084, (out-of-state, $6,168); room and board, $3,812. University reports some scholarships awarded for academic merit.

University of Wyoming

Laramie, Wyoming 82071 **(307) 766-5160; (800) DIALWYO**

Wyoming's only four-year institution of higher learning, the university is a land-grant college and state university, located in a community of 23,100, 50 miles west of Cheyenne.

Founded: 1886
Affiliation: State
UG Enrollment: 3,945 M, 3,590 W (full-time); 570 M, 918 W (part-time)
Total Enrollment: 12,012
Cost: < $10K
% Receiving Financial Aid: 68%
Admission: Non-selective
Application Deadline: Aug. 10

Admission. Graduates of accredited Wyoming high schools admitted; others must have GPA of 2.5; 75% of applicants accepted, 82% of these actually enroll; 39% of freshmen graduate in top fifth of high school class, 66% in top two-fifths. Average freshman ACT scores: 23 M, 22 W. *Required:* ACT, minimum H.S. GPA. Criteria considered in admissions, in order of importance: high school academic record, standardized test scores; other factors considered: special talents, alumni children. *Out-of-state* freshman applicants: university actively seeks students from out-of-state. State does not limit out-of-state enrollment. *Out-of-state* applicants must have a 2.75 GPA for their core curriculum average. States from which most out-of-state students are drawn include Colorado. *Apply* by August 10; rolling admissions. *Transfers* welcome; 979 enrolled 1992–93.

Academic Environment. *Undergraduate studies* offered by colleges of Arts and Sciences, Agriculture, Business, Education, Engineering, Health Sciences; programs in journalism, medical technology, wildlife conservation and game management, agro-ecology. Specific course and distribution requirements vary with major. Degrees offered: bachelors, masters, doctoral. About 17% of students entering as freshmen graduate in four years, 50% eventually; 70% of freshmen return for sophomore year. *Special programs:* CLEP, independent study, study abroad, honors, internships, work study, accelerated degree programs, specialized intercollege programs. Adult programs: special programs and residence halls for non-traditional students (over 25). *Calendar:* semester, summer school.

Undergraduate degrees conferred (1,641). 26% were in Education, 16% were in Business and Management, 8% were in Engineering, 8% were in Social Sciences, 6% were in Health Sciences, 4% were in Life Sciences, 4% were in Psychology, 4% were in Public Affairs, 3% were in Communications, remainder in 15 other fields.

Graduates Career Data. Career Development Services include resume writing, interview help, on-campus recruitment.

Faculty. About 93% of faculty hold PhD or equivalent. About 21% of teaching faculty are female; 2% Black, 1% Hispanic, 4% other minority.

Student Body. About 70% of students from in state; 4% Foreign. An estimated 1% of students reported as Black, 3% Hispanic, 1% Asian, 10% other minority. Average age of undergraduate student: 24.

Varsity Sports. Men (WAC, Div.I): Baseball, Basketball, Cross Country, Diving, Football, Golf, Lacrosse, Rifle, Rodeo, Rugby, Swimming, Track, Wrestling. Women (HCAC, Div.I): Basketball, Cross Country, Diving, Golf, Rodeo, Rugby, Softball, Swimming, Track, Volleyball.

Campus Life. About 10% of men, 7% of women live in coed dormitories. Intervisitation in men's and women's dormitory rooms limited. Sexes segregated in coed dormitories either by wing or floor. Freshmen are given preference in college housing if all students cannot be accommodated. There are 12 fraternities, 4 sororities on campus which about 10% of men, 9% of women join; 9% of men, 9% of women live in fraternities and sororities.

Annual Costs. Tuition and fees, $1,648 (out-of-state, $5,182); room and board, $3,341; estimated $1,500 other, exclusive of travel. About 68% of students receive financial aid; average amount of assistance, $3,400. Assistance is typically divided 10% scholarship, 20% grant, 50% loan, 20% work. University reports hundreds of scholarships awarded for academic merit, more than 50 for special talents, 5 for need.

Xavier University

Cincinnati, Ohio 45207 (513) 745-3301

An independent university with Roman Catholic affiliations, conducted by the Society of Jesus, Xavier is co-educational in all divisions. The suburban campus is located in a residential section of Cincinnati (pop. 500,500).

Founded: 1831
Affiliation: Independent (Roman Catholic)
UG Enrollment: 1,343 M, 1,506 W (full-time); 377 M, 730 W (part-time)
Total Enrollment: 6,279
Cost: $10K–$20K
% Receiving Financial Aid: 80%
Admission: Selective
Application Deadline: Rolling

Admission is selective. About 89% of applicants accepted, 39% of these actually enroll; 45% of freshmen graduate in top fifth of high school class, 67% in top two-fifths. Average freshman scores: SAT, 475 M, 475 W verbal, 541 M, 504 W mathematical; 45% of freshmen score above 500 verbal, 13% above 600, 1% above 700; 78% score above 500 mathematical, 45% above 600, 6% above 700; ACT, 23 M, 24 W. *Required:* SAT or ACT, minimum H.S. GPA; interview recommended. Criteria considered in admissions, in order of importance: high school academic record, standardized test scores, extracurricular activities, writing sample; other factors considered: alumni children. *Entrance programs:* early admission, deferred admission. *Apply:* rolling admissions. *Transfers* welcome; 355 enrolled 1992–93.

Academic Environment. Pressures for academic achievement appear moderate. Liberal arts core and distribution requirements include 3 hours in each of English composition, literature, fine arts; 6 hours each of foreign language, philosophy, theology, history, social sciences, mathematics, ethics/religion and society focus; and 9 hours of sciences. *Undergraduate studies* offered by colleges of arts and sciences, Business Administration. Degrees offered: associates, bachelors, masters. *Majors offered* include communication arts, elementary education, Montessori education, medical technology, occupational therapy, sports medicine/athletic training, sport management, sport marketing. Average undergraduate class size: 23.

About 63% of students entering as freshmen graduate eventually; 88% of freshmen return for sophomore year. *Special programs:* study abroad, honors, internships, undergraduate research, university scholars, Center for Adult and Part-time Students. *Calendar:* semester, summer school.

Undergraduate degrees conferred (715). 32% were in Business and Management, 12% were in Communications, 9% were in Liberal/General Studies, 7% were in Social Sciences, 7% were in Education, 6% were in Letters, 5% were in Psychology, 5% were in Computer and Engineering Related Technology, remainder in 13 other fields.

Graduates Career Data. Advanced studies pursued by 20% of students; 5% enter medical or dental school; 3% enter law school; 2% enter business school, 1% enter other schools. Medical schools typically enrolling largest numbers of graduates include U. of Cincinnati; law schools include U. of Cincinnati Law. About 6% of 1992–93 graduates employed. Fields typically hiring largest number of graduates include accounting, education, banking, marketing. Career Development Services include career counseling, career related workshops, internships, on-campus recruitment, resume referral, job fairs and other career related services.

Faculty. About 75% of faculty hold PhD or equivalent. About 59% of undergraduate classes taught by tenured faculty. About 36% of teaching faculty are female.

Student Body. University seeks a national student body; 71% of students from in state; 91% Midwest. An estimated 40% of students reported as Catholic, 4% Protestant, 1% Jewish,; 7% as Black, 2% Asian, 2% Hispanic. Average age of undergraduate student: 25.

Religious Orientation. Xavier is an independent institution with a Roman Catholic orientation; makes some religious demands on students: 12 hours of theology required of all students.

Varsity Sports. Men (Div.I): Baseball, Basketball, Cross Country, Diving, Golf, Riflery (coed), Soccer, Swimming, Tennis. Women (Div.I): Basketball, Cross Country, Diving, Golf, Riflery (coed), Soccer, Swimming, Tennis, Volleyball.

Campus Life. Expanded open house program for residence halls; priority according to class. Cars allowed, parking sometimes a problem. About 40% of men, 40% of women in coed dormitories; 9% men, 11% women live in off-campus college-related housing; 51% of men, 49% of women commute. Sexes segregated in coed dormitories by wing or floor. Freshmen are given preference in college housing if all students cannot be accommodated. There are no fraternities or sororities on campus.

Annual Costs. Tuition and fees, $10,970; room and board, $4,470. About 80% of students receive financial aid; average amount of assistance, $6,000. University reports 315 scholarships awarded for academic merit. *Meeting Costs:* university offers ten-month payment plan, Plus Loan Program, and other financial aid opportunities.

Xavier University of Louisiana

New Orleans, Louisiana 70125 (504) 483-7388

A church-related university, founded by Sisters of the Blessed Sacrament, but "operated under a combined lay/religious Board of Trustees," located in New Orleans; founded as a college for Negroes and still serving a predominantly black student body. Most convenient major airport: New Orleans International.

Founded: 1915
Affiliation: Roman Catholic
UG Enrollment: 912 M, 1,974 W (full-time)
Cost: < $10K
% Receiving Financial Aid: 86%
Admission: Non-selective
Application Deadline: March 1

Admission. Graduates of accredited high school with 16 units (10 in academic subjects), C average, and rank in top half of class eligible; 91% of applicants accepted, 36% of these actually enroll; 54% of freshmen graduate in top fifth of high school class, 77% in top two-fifths. Average freshman scores: SAT, 906 combined; ACT, 20.7 composite. *Required:* SAT or ACT. Criteria considered in admissions, in order of importance: high school academic record, standardized test scores, recommendations, extracurricular activities; other factors considered: special talents, alumni children, diverse student body. *Entrance programs:* early decision, midyear admission, advanced placement. About 32% of freshmen from private or parochial schools. *Apply* by March 1. *Transfers* welcome; 175 enrolled 1993–94.

Academic Environment. Degrees offered: bachelors, masters, doctoral. General education requirements for graduation include mathematics, English, history, social sciences, speech, sciences, fine arts, foreign language, philosophy, theology, African-American history and culture, and health and physical education. About 19% of students entering as freshmen graduate in four years, 48% eventually; 79% of freshmen return for sophomore year. *Special programs:* honors, co-op education, internships, independent study, undergraduate research, cross registration with Loyola U., Notre Dame Seminary; 3–2 programs in engineering, statistics. *Calendar:* semester, summer school.

Undergraduate degrees conferred (311). 36% were in Health Sciences, 12% were in Physical Sciences, 11% were in Life Sciences, 11% were in Business and Management, 6% were in Social Sciences, 5% were in Communications, 5% were in Education, 4% were in Computer and Engineering Related Technology, 4% were in Psychology, 3% were in Letters, remainder in 4 other fields.

Graduates Career Data. Advanced studies pursued by 36% of students; 18% enter medical or dental school; 2% enter law school; 1% enter business school. Medical schools typically enrolling largest number of graduates include LSU, Meharry Medical College. Employers typically hiring largest number of graduates include AT&T, IBM, Environmental Protection Agency. Career Development Services include on-campus interviews, resume assistance.

Faculty. About 72% of faculty hold PhD or equivalent. About 38% of teaching faculty are female; 33% Black, 12% other minority.

Student Body. University seeks a national student body; 61% of students from in state; 79% South, 11% Midwest, 3% West, 3% Middle Atlantic; 2% Foreign. An estimated 56% of students reported as Protestant, 38% Catholic, 6% other; 90% as Black, 2% Asian, 1% other minority. Average age of undergraduate: 22.

Religious Orientation. Xavier is a church-related institution; 6 hours of theology required of all students.

Varsity Sports. Men (NAIA, Div.I): Basketball. Women (NAIA): Basketball.

Campus Life. About 27% of students live in traditional dormitories; no coed dormitories; rest commute. No intervisitation in men's or women's dormitory rooms. There are 2 fraternities, 4 sororities on campus which about 5% of men, 20 of women join; they provide no residence facilities. About 73% of resident students leave campus on weekends.

Annual Costs. Tuition and fees, $6,700; room and board, $3,800. About 86% of students receive financial aid; average amount of assistance, $6,632. College reports some scholarships awarded for academic merit. *Meeting Costs:* college offers installment payment plan.

Yale University

New Haven, Connecticut 06520 (203) 432-1900

Yale is one of America's great private universities in a class ranking only Harvard and Stanford as peers. The university prides itself on remaining a university college, while boasting a prestigious group of professional schools and a first-rank graduate program. The campus of several hundred acres is located in a city of 130,000, 75 miles northeast of New York City. Most convenient major airport: Bradley International (Hartford).

Founded: 1701
Affiliation: Independent
UG Enrollment: 2,787 M, 2,430 W (full-time)
Total Enrollment: 10,954
Cost: $10K–$20K
Admission: Most Selective
Application Deadline: Dec. 31

Admission is among the most selective in the country. About 22% of applicants accepted, 55% of these actually enroll; university reports "it is safe to say most freshmen are in top tenth of their class." Required: SAT and any 3 ACH or ACT, evaluations from guidance counselors and 2 academic teachers, essay; interview recommended if local. Criteria considered in admissions, in order of importance: high school academic record, then of equal importance standardized test scores, recommendations, extracurricular activities, writing sample; other factors considered: special talents, alumni children, leadership, character. *Entrance programs:* early action, deferred admission. *Apply* by December 31 or November 1 for early action. *Transfers:* practice varies from year to year depending on space available; 24 enrolled 1993–94.

Academic Environment. Yale prides itself on being a university college where graduate faculty are involved in the direct instruction of undergraduates. However, in a major research and graduate training institution this contact will be limited. To supplement this faculty, Yale's reputation attracts to its classrooms the ablest young scholars graduating from its own departments and from other comparable graduate institutions. Students reported to be involved in curriculum policy decisions, but not in faculty selection and promotion. Pressures for academic achievement are very intense; student body is exceptionally able, and the large percentage going on to graduate and professional schools makes competition keen. Numerous opportunities for independent study and honors work. Requirements for selection of courses include only the rule that 12 courses of 36 needed for graduation must be taken outside group of major and students must take at least 2 credits in each of the following: language and literature, other humanities, social sciences, physical or biological sciences. Degrees offered: bachelors, masters, doctoral. *Majors offered* include Afro-American studies, anthropology, architecture, area studies (China, Japan, Russia, Latin America), Chinese, computer science, environmental studies, engineering and applied science, international studies, Japanese, linguistics, molecular biophysics and biochemistry, theater studies; additional special and divisional majors also available. Average undergraduate class size: 85% under 25.

About 95% of entering freshmen graduate in six years, 99% of freshmen return for sophomore year. *Special programs:* independent study, study abroad, undergraduate research, 3-year degree, double major honors program, individualized majors, non-resident enrollment for BLS degree, 4-year BA/MA in selected fields, directed studies program, early concentration (involving semi-tutorial seminars), residential college seminars. Adult programs: special students program for non-residents. *Calendar:* semester.

Undergraduate degrees conferred (1,323). 32% were in Social Sciences, 15% were in Letters, 10% were in Life Sciences, 8% were in Area and Ethnic Studies, 6% were in Multi/Interdisciplinary Studies, 6% were in Visual and Performing Arts, 6% were in Psychology, 5% were in Philosophy and Religion, 3% were in Physical Sciences, 3% were in Architecture and Environmental Design, remainder in 4 other fields.

Graduates Career Data. Advanced studies pursued immediately after graduation by 33% of 1992 graduates; 9% enter medical school; 8% enter law school; 5% enter other professional school. Medical schools typically enrolling largest numbers of graduates include Yale, NYU, Harvard; law schools include Harvard, Yale, Columbia. About 61% of 1992–93 graduates employed. *Career Counseling Program* designed specifically for liberal arts students. Liberal arts majors urged to seek interviews with business/industry representatives who visit campus. Help provided in preparing for interviews. Alumni reported as helpful in career guidance, though not active in job placement.

Faculty. About 96% of faculty hold PhD or equivalent; very high proportion earned at nation's top graduate institutions.

Student Body. University seeks a national student body; 10% of students from in state. An estimated 5% of students reported as Black, 4% Hispanic, 8% Asian, less than 1% Native American, 12% non-resident alien, according to most recent data available.

Varsity Sports. Men (Div.I): Baseball, Basketball, Crew, Cross Country, Diving, Fencing, Football, Golf, Ice Hockey, Lacrosse,

Soccer, Swimming, Tennis, Track. Women (Div.I): Basketball, Crew, Cross Country, Diving, Fencing, Field Hockey, Golf, Gymnastics, Ice Hockey, Lacrosse, Soccer, Softball, Swimming, Tennis, Track, Volleyball.

Campus Life. Few restrictions on students' social life. Many lifestyles can flourish here. Student leader reports that although the academic competition "can be keen," the "partying is also intense. Yalies tend to work hard and play hard. This makes the contrast of Sunday through Thursday to Thursday night through Saturday night very stark indeed." Most significant feature of Non-academic life for upper-class students is the existence of 12 undergraduate residential colleges (freshmen housed together on the Old Campus). These colleges are microcosms of Yale College. Although students do have contact with those in other colleges in classrooms and extracurricular activities, the group within one's "college" is closest to the student. High interest reported in cultural and sponsored social activities as well as in varsity sports (most popular: football, hockey, basketball) and intramurals (most popular: hockey, football, track, basketball). Nearest major cultural center, New York City, is 75 miles from campus. Yale has outstanding facilities for football, swimming, squash, rowing. Cars permitted, must be parked in a garage or parking lot at students' expense. Students normally expected to live in houses; upper-class students may live off campus.

About 89% of men, 91% of women live in coed college; 11% of men, 9% of women live in off-campus housing. Sexes segregated in college dormitories by floor during freshman year. About 10–20% of students leave campus on weekends.

Annual Costs. Tuition and fees, $18,630; room and board, $6,480; estimated $2,020 other, exclusive of travel. University reports scholarships awarded for need only. *Meeting Costs:* university offers budget plan, long-term loans.

Yeshiva University

New York, New York 10033-3201 (212) 960-5277

Yeshiva is a university which had its origin as a seminary for the training of Orthodox rabbis. Today it is a multi-faceted university with 5 undergraduate schools, 7 graduate and professional schools. Men attend Joel Jablonski Campus, Yeshiva College (at the Main Center in the Washington Heights section of upper Manhattan), or Sy Syms School of Business, women attend Stern College for women, located in the Murray Hill section of midtown Manhattan, or Sy Syms School of Business. Most convenient major airport: LaGuardia.

Founded: 1886
Affiliation: Independent (Jewish)
UG Enrollment: 1,029 M, 919 W (full-time)
Total Enrollment: 4,989
Cost: $10K–$20K
% Receiving Financial Aid: 75%
Admission: Very (+) Selective
Application Deadline: Feb. 15

Admission is very (+) selective. About 84% of applicants accepted, 70% of these actually enroll. Average freshman SAT scores: 559 M, 550 W verbal, 629 M, 585 W mathematical; 65% of freshmen score above 500 on verbal, 26% above 600, 7% above 700; 82% score above 500 on mathematical, 45% above 600, 14% above 700. *Required:* SAT or ACT, minimum H. S. GPA, essay, interview. Criteria considered in admissions, in order of importance: high school academic record, standardized test scores, recommendations, writing sample, extracurricular activities; other factors considered: special talents, alumni children. *Entrance programs:* early admission, midyear admission, advanced placement, deferred admission. *Apply* by February 15; rolling admissions. *Transfers* welcome; 71 enrolled 1993–94.

Academic Environment. Students represented on Academic Council of the Undergraduate Schools, the Yeshiva College Senate and Stern College Senate, with jurisdiction over many areas of academic life as well as on advisory committees for each department. Pressures for academic achievement appear moderately strong. Student leader reports "this is a college for serious students . . . . They are all Orthodox Jews and have . . . a rigorous double schedule [parallel Jewish studies] which is mandatory for all students." First 2 years consist of required courses in liberal arts and Jewish studies. Classes generally meet Monday through Friday; some Yeshiva College classes held Sunday. Student body characterized as primarily concerned with occupational/professional goals. Pass/no credit option after freshman year. Administration reports 55% of general education courses required for graduation are elective; distribution requirements fairly numerous for AB; 6–8 credits natural sciences, 6 credits social sciences/history, 14–20 credits humanities, 18–60 credits Jewish studies. Degrees offered: associates, bachelors, masters, doctoral. *Majors offered* include Jewish studies.

About 57% of students entering as freshmen graduate eventually; 80% return for sophomore year, according to most recent data available. *Special programs:* CLEP, independent study, study abroad (year long study in Israel), honors, internships, 3–2 in engineering, occupational therapy, social work, psychology; joint bachelor–master programs with University graduate schools; Stern College has combined advertising, management, and communications programs with another school, and individualized majors, cross registration with Fashion Institute of Technology. *Calendar:* semester.

Undergraduate degrees conferred (393). 25% were in Social Sciences, 14% were in Business and Management, 13% were in Psychology, 10% were in Life Sciences, 10% were in Liberal/General Studies, 9% were in Letters, 5% were in Foreign Languages, 3% were in Education, 3% were in Mathematics, remainder in 5 other fields.

Faculty. About 96% faculty hold PhD or equivalent. About 21% of undergraduate full-time teaching faculty are female.

Graduates Career Data. Advanced studies pursued by 65% of students; 20% enter medical school; 25% enter law school; 5% enter business school; 10% enter allied health schools. Medical schools typically enrolling largest numbers of graduates include Albert Einstein, Mt. Sinai, Harvard; law schools include Columbia, NYU; business schools include NYU, CUNY Baruch. All of 1992–93 graduates using placement service are employed. Fields typically hiring largest numbers of graduates include "Big Six" accounting firms, banks, utilities, government/health care, financial services. Career Development Services include self-assessment testing, career counseling, career information, educational planning, resume preparation, placement for full-time/part-time/summer and intern positions, on-campus recruitment, career fair, career forums, resume referral.

Student Body. University seeks a national student body; 57% of students from in state; 76% Middle Atlantic, 8% North Central, 4% each West, South; 86 foreign students, according to most recent data available.

Varsity Sports. Men (Div.III): Basketball, Cross Country, Fencing, Golf, Tennis, Track, Volleyball, Wrestling.

Campus Life. University provides a variety of cultural and intellectual activities on campus, which are easily supplemented by the unequaled resources of New York City. Some student concern over facilities for social activities which they feel "should be better." Student leader reports that most students come from religious backgrounds and observes, "Our conduct is governed to a greater extent by our religious principles than by campus regulations."

About 95% of men, 95% of women live in traditional dormitories; rest commute. Freshmen are given preference in college housing if all students cannot be accommodated. There are no social fraternities or sororities. About 90% of students leave campus on weekends, according to most recent data available.

Annual Costs. Tuition and fees, $12,400; room and board, $5,800; estimated $1,850 other, exclusive of travel. About 75% of students receive financial aid; average amount of scholarship assistance, $3,343. Assistance is typically divided 50% scholarship, 40% loan, 10% work. University reports 249 scholarships awarded for academic merit, 1.207 for need. *Meeting Costs:* university offers flexible payment plans.

York College

York, Nebraska 68467 (402) 362-4441

A church-related liberal arts college offering associates and bachelors degree programs.

Founded: 1890
Affiliation: Church of Christ
UG Enrollment: 215 M, 217 W (full-time)
Cost: < $10K
% Receiving Financial Aid: 91%
Admission: Non-selective
Application Deadline: Rolling

Admission. About 69% of applicants accepted, 82% of these actually enroll. Average freshman ACT scores: 21 composite. *Required:* SAT or ACT, minimum high school GPA, 2 references. Criteria considered in admissions, in order of importance: standardized test scores, high school academic record, spiritual commitment, recommendations; other factors considered: religious affiliation and/or commitment, diverse student body, moral servitude. *Entrance programs:* early admission, mid-year admission, deferred admission, advanced placement. *Apply:* rolling admissions. *Transfers* welcome; 75 enrolled 1993–94.

Academic Environment. Graduation requirements: candidates for bachelors degree must meet requirements for the Associate in Arts degree, as well as 24 hours in major concentration, 18 hours in minor concentration, 24 hours of electives and a 4 hour project. Degrees offered: associates, bachelors. New majors offered include English, Liberal Arts, business fields, Education. Average undergraduate class size: 20% under 20, 75% 20–40, 5% over 40. About 60% of students entering as freshmen graduate within four years, 70% eventually; 65% of freshmen return for sophomore year. *Special programs:* January Term. *Calendar:* semester, summer school.

Undergraduate degrees conferred ().

Faculty. About 37% of faculty hold PhD or equivalent. About 35% of teaching faculty are female.

Student Body. About 30% of students from in state; 65% from Midwest, 10% each South, West, 8% Northeast, 5% foreign. An estimated 93% of students reported as Protestant, 3% Catholic, 3% unaffiliated, 1% other; 5% Black, 4% Hispanic, 3% Asian, 1% other minority.

Religious Orientation. York is a church-related institution; 70% of students affiliated with the church; 7 courses in religious studies required of all students.

Varsity Sports. Men: Baseball, Basketball, Cross Country, Soccer, Tennis, Track. Women: Basketball, Cross Country, Soccer, Softball, Tennis, Track, Volleyball.

Campus Life. College is located in a small town of 8,000, near Lincoln. Administration reports "social clubs provide avenues for service and fun."

About 65% of men, 67% of women live in traditional dormitories; no coed dormitories; 3% of men, 4% of women live in college-related off-campus housing; rest commute. There are no fraternities or sororities on campus. About 10% of resident students leave campus on weekends.

Annual Costs. Tuition and fees, $4,760; room and board, $2,850; estimated $1,200 other, exclusive of travel. About 91% of students receive financial aid; average amount of assistance, $4,975. Assistance is typically divided 20% scholarship, 22% grant, 43% loan, 15% work. College reports 230 scholarships awarded on the basis of academic merit alone, 200 for special talents, 20 for need alone.

York College

(See City University of New York)

York College of Pennsylvania

York, Pennsylvania 17405-7199 (717) 846-7788

A private, career-oriented, liberal arts college, located in a community of 100,000, an hour north of Baltimore and in the Pennsylvania Dutch country. York offers programs leading to baccalaureate and masters degrees, as well as extensive 2-year degree programs. Most convenient major airports: Harrisburg, Baltimore/Washington.

Founded: 1787
Affiliation: Independent
UG Enrollment: 1,254 M, 1,734 W (full-time); 649 M, 1,077 W (part-time)
Total Enrollment: 4,942
Cost: < $10K
% Receiving Financial Aid: 58%
Admission: Non-selective
Application Deadline: Rolling

Admission. High school graduates with 15 units who rank in top three-fifths of class eligible; 62% of applicants accepted, 37% of these actually enroll; 39% of freshmen graduate in top fifth of high school class, 77% in top two-fifths. Average freshman SAT scores: 465 M, 475 W verbal, 534 M, 514 W mathematical; 51% of freshmen score above 500 verbal, 11% above 600, 1% above 700; 73% score above 500 mathematical, 17% above 600, 2% above 700. *Required:* SAT (ACT acceptable), minimum H.S. GPA. Criteria considered in admissions, in order of importance: high school academic record, standardized test scores, extracurricular activities, writing sample, recommendations; other factors considered: special talents, alumni children, diverse student body. *Entrance programs:* early admission, midyear admission, deferred admission, advanced placement. About 5% of freshmen from private schools, 13% from parochial schools. *Apply:* rolling admissions. *Transfers* welcome; 179 enrolled 1993–94.

Academic Environment. Degrees offered: associates, bachelors, masters. *Majors offered* include business, computer science, education, international studies, long-term care administration, medical records, medical technology, physical science, police science and corrections. About 15% of general education credits for graduation are required; distribution requirements fairly numerous. Average undergraduate class size: 52% under 20, 47% between 20–40, 1% over 40. About 62% of students entering as freshmen graduate in four years, 76% eventually; 81% of freshmen return for sophomore year. *Special programs:* January term, study abroad, independent study, internships, 3–2 engineering, premedical scholars program guarantees admission to College of Medicine at Hershey, exchange program with College of Ripon, and York St. John, York, England. *Calendar:* semester, summer school.

Undergraduate degrees conferred (588). 24% were in Business and Management, 15% were in Education, 13% were in Health Sciences, 11% were in Marketing and Distribution, 8% were in Protective Services, 6% were in Social Sciences, 5% were in Letters, 5% were in Multi/Interdisciplinary Studies, 5% were in Psychology, 3% were in Allied Health, remainder in 5 other fields.

Graduates Career Data. Advanced studies pursued by 30% of students. About 92% of 1992–93 graduates employed. Employers typically hiring largest number of graduates include AT&T, A&P, York Hospital. Career Development Services include extensive career library, self assessment of interests/values/skills on a computer guided system, career development workshops, career counseling.

Faculty. About 75% of faculty hold PhD or equivalent. About 96% of undergraduate classes taught by tenured faculty. About 37% of teaching faculty are female; 2% Black, 2% Hispanic, 5% other minority.

Student Body. College recruits majority of students from Middle Atlantic region; 60% of students from in state; 97% of students from Middle Atlantic. An estimated 41% of students reported as Protestant, 35% Catholic, 3% Jewish, 1% Muslim, 13% unaffiliated, 7% other; 2% Black, 1% Hispanic, 1% Asian, 1% other minority. Average age of undergraduate student: 25.

Varsity Sports. Men (Div.III): Baseball, Basketball, Cross Country, Golf, Soccer, Swimming, Tennis, Track, Wrestling. Women (Div.III): Basketball, Field Hockey, Softball, Swimming, Tennis, Volleyball.

Campus Life. About 37% of men, 34% of women live in traditional dormitories; 5% of men, 12% of women in coed dormitories; 25% of men, 17% of women in off-campus college-related housing; rest commute. Intervisitation in men's and women's dormitory rooms limited. There are 10 fraternities, 9 sororities on campus which about 25% of men, 20% of women join; 2% of women live in sororities. About 30% of students leave campus on weekends, according to most recent data available.

Annual Costs. Tuition and fees, $4,995; room and board, $3,350; estimated $1,500 other, exclusive of travel. About 58% of students receive financial aid; average amount of assistance, $4,232. Assistance is typically divided 7% scholarship, 30% grant, 60% loan, 3% work. College reports 339 scholarships awarded for academic merit, 1,089 for need. *Meeting Costs:* college offers deferred payment plans.

Youngstown State University

Youngstown, Ohio 44555 (216) 742-3000

A state-supported university, primarily for commuters, located in a city of 139,800, 65 miles southeast of Cleveland.

Founded: 1908
Affiliation: State
UG Enrollment: 4,816 M, 4,817 W (full-time); 1,649 M, 2,013 W (part-time)
Total Enrollment: 14,501
Cost: < $10K
% Receiving Financial Aid: 65%
Admission: Non-selective
Application Deadline: May 15

Admission. Graduates of accredited Ohio high schools with 16 units admitted; 88% of applicants accepted, 74% of these actually enroll. About 23% of freshmen graduate in top fifth of high school class, 42% in top two-fifths. Average freshman scores: SAT, 402 M, 425 W verbal, 459 M, 445 W mathematical; ACT, 20 M, 20 W composite. *Required:* SAT or ACT. Out-of state freshman applicants: university actively seeks students from out-of-state. State does not limit out-of-state enrollment. Requirement for out-of-state applicants: rank in top two-thirds of class, combined SAT of 700 or ACT composite of 17 or higher. About 89% of out-of-state applicants accepted, 81% of these actually enroll. States from which most out-of-state applicants are drawn include Pennsylvania, New York, Florida, California, West Virginia. Criteria considered in admissions, in order of importance: high school academic record, standardized test scores. *Entrance programs:* early decision, early admission, midyear admission, deferred admission, advanced placement. *Apply* by May 15; rolling admissions. *Transfers* welcome; 2,150 enrolled 1993–94.

Academic Environment. *Undergraduate studies* offered by colleges of Applied Science and Technology, Arts and Sciences, Fine and Performing Arts, schools of Business Administration, Education, William Rayen School of Engineering. Emphasis is on practical training of teachers, accountants, junior executives, engineers, laboratory technicians, social workers, and personnel in similar fields. Degrees offered: associates, bachelors, masters, doctoral. *Majors offered* include professional writing and editing, hospitality management, telecommunications, combined BS/MD program. About 98% of general education requirements for graduation are elective; distribution requirements fairly numerous. Average undergraduate class size: 49% under 20, 41% between 20–40, 10% over 40. *Special programs:* honors, January term, study abroad, 3-year degree, individualized majors, 3–2 forestry. *Calendar:* quarter, summer school.

Undergraduate degrees conferred (1,517). 21% were in Business and Management, 15% were in Education, 8% were in Social Sciences, 8% were in Engineering, 6% were in Engineering and Engineering Related Technology, 5% were in Protective Services, 5% were in Letters, 4% were in Psychology, 4% were in Health Sciences, 3% were in Life Sciences, 3% were in Visual and Performing Arts, 3% were in Physical Sciences, remainder in 11 other fields.

Graduates Career Data. Advanced studies pursued by 7–14% of students immediately after graduation, according to most recent data available. About 82% of 1992–93 graduates responding to survey are employed. Fields typically hiring largest number of graduates include medical, accounting, engineering, computer information systems. Career Development Services include career counseling, three computerized interactive career planning and job search guidance systems, on-campus interviews, credential service, mock interviews, career days on job search techniques, resume writing, interviewing techniques.

Faculty. About 71% of full-time faculty hold PhD or equivalent. About 75% of faculty are tenured. About 29% of full-time faculty are female; 3% Black, 1% Hispanic, 5% other minority.

Student Body. University does not seek a national student body; 90% of students from in state; 91% Midwest, 7% Middle Atlantic; 1.5% Foreign. An estimated 7% of students reported as Black, 1% Hispanic, 2% other minority. Average age of undergraduate student: 25.

Varsity Sports. Men (Div.I): Baseball, Basketball, Cross Country, Football (IAA), Golf, Tennis, Track. Women (Div.I): Basketball, Cross Country, Softball, Tennis, Track, Volleyball.

Campus Life. About 2% of men, 2% of women live in dormitories; rest live in off-campus housing or commute. Intervisitation in dormitory rooms limited. There are 10 fraternities, 7 sororities which about 4% of men, 3% of women join. About 97% of resident students leave campus on weekends.

Annual Costs. Tuition and fees, $2,772 (out-of state, $5,112); room and board, $3,675. About 65% of students receive financial aid; average amount of assistance, $2,000. Assistance is typically divided 35% scholarship, 40% grant, 20% loan, 5% work. College reports 3,500 scholarships awarded for academic merit, 400 for special talents, 100 for need. *Meeting Costs:* college offers grants, loans, scholarships, and work-study packages.

Comparative Listing of Majors

Listed below are the subjects in which four-year institutions conferred bachelor's degrees in 1990–91, the most recent year for which complete data are available. For disciplines offered by relatively few schools (less than 100), each school is listed along with the number of students who received degrees. For general subjects, such as English, for example, only the total number of schools offering the subject is provided.

Accounting and Computing

CONCORDIA TEACHERS COLL	1
MINOT ST U	34
NORTH TEXAS, U of	38
NORTHERN MICHIGAN U	4
QUINNIPIAC COLL	4
RIO GRANDE, U of	16
RIVIER COLL	14
TIFFIN U	5
VALLEY CITY ST U	12

Accounting, Bookkeeping, and Related Programs, General

ATLANTIC UNION COLL	1
LUBBOCK CHRISTIAN U	11
NEUMANN COLL	4
PLYMOUTH ST COLL	31
SAINT FRANCIS COLL	8
SAINT MARY PLAINS COLL	10

Accounting

Degrees in this subject were reported by 863 institutions. Consult more specific headings.

Actuarial Sciences

BALL ST U	13
BUTLER U	3
CENTRAL MICHIGAN U	2
CENTRAL OKLAHOMA, U of	2
CONNECTICUT, U of	23
DRAKE U	11
EASTERN MICHIGAN U	5
GEORGIA ST U	7
ILLINOIS URBANA CAMPUS, U of	57
INDIANA U NORTHWEST	2
IOWA, U of	28
LEBANON VALLEY COLL	9
MARYVILLE COLL—ST LOUIS	8
MINNESOTA TWIN CITIES, U of	8
NEBRASKA-LINCOLN, U of	18
NEW JERSEY INST TECH	3
OHIO ST U MAIN CAMPUS	17
PENNSYLVANIA ST U MAIN CAMPUS	3
PENNSYLVANIA, U of	12
RIDER COLL	5
TEMPLE U	22
TEXAS AT AUSTIN, U of	3
WISCONSIN-MADISON, U of	7

Administration of Special Education

WESTFIELD ST COLL	12

Adult and Continuing Education

AUBURN U MAIN CAMPUS	12
OAKLAND U	72
PURDUE U CALUMET CAMPUS	1
TRINITY COLL	1

Advertising

ABILENE CHRISTIAN U	4
ALABAMA, U of	115
ARIZONA ST U	11
ARKANSAS AT LITTLE ROCK, U of	6
ART CENTER COLL OF DESIGN	29
ATLANTIC UNION COLL	1
BRADLEY U	52
BRIDGEPORT, U of	4
DRAKE U	59
EAST TEXAS ST U	2
EMERSON COLL	61
EVANSVILLE, U of	15
FERRIS ST U	54
FLORIDA SOUTHERN COLL	7
FLORIDA, U of	180
GEORGIA, U of	164
GRAND VALLEY ST U	54
HARDING U MAIN CAMPUS	7
IDAHO, U of	24
ILLINOIS URBANA CAMPUS, U of	108
KENT ST U MAIN CAMPUS	50
KENTUCKY, U of	58
LAMAR U	4
LOUISIANA ST U & AGRI & MECH & HEBERT LAWS CTR	96
MARIETTA COLL	4
MARQUETTE U	60
MIAMI, U of	72
MICHIGAN ST U	293
MOUNT SAINT MARY COLL	9
MURRAY ST U	33
NEBRASKA-LINCOLN, U of	88
NORTH DAKOTA MAIN CAMPUS, U of	27
NORTH TEXAS, U of	25
NORTHERN ARIZONA U	43
OREGON, U of	49

PENNSYLVANIA ST U MAIN CAMPUS	92
PEPPERDINE U	40
SAN FRANCISCO, U of	3
SAN JOSE ST U	136
SETON HILL COLL	1
SIMMONS COLL	13
SOUTHEAST MISSOURI ST U	52
SOUTHERN METHODIST U	94
SOUTHERN MISSISSIPPI, U of	27
SPRING HILL COLL	2
SYRACUSE U MAIN CAMPUS	102
TEIKYO MARYCREST COLL	2
TENNESSEE-KNOXVILLE, U of	59
TEXAS AT AUSTIN, U of	232
TEXAS CHRISTIAN U	57
TEXAS TECH U	71
TEXAS WESLEYAN COLL	2
TEXAS WOMAN'S U	2
WESTERN KENTUCKY U	44
WESTERN MICHIGAN U	31
WESTMINSTER COLL	1
YOUNGSTOWN ST U	12

Aeronaturical Technology

ARIZONA ST U	46
BOWLING GREEN ST U MAIN CAMPUS	17
CENTRAL MISSOURI ST U	69
EASTERN MICHIGAN U	4
EMBRY-RIDDLE AERONAUTICAL U	661
LETOURNEAU COLL	20
NORTHEASTERN U	2
SAN JOSE ST U	22
SCHOOL OF THE OZARKS	11
SIENA HEIGHTS COLL	1
UTAH ST U	29
WESTERN MICHIGAN U	64

Aerospace Science (Air Force)

CENTRAL WASHINGTON U	3
OKLAHOMA ST U MAIN CAMPUS	1
US AIR FORCE ACAD	12

Aerospace, Aeronautical, and Astronautical Engineering

ALABAMA, U of	11
ARIZONA ST U	25
ARIZONA, U of	47
AUBURN U MAIN CAMPUS	66
BOSTON U	41
CALIFORNIA POLY-TECHNIC ST U-SAN LUIS OBISPO	45
CALIFORNIA ST POLY-TECHNIC U POMONA	55
CALIFORNIA-DAVIS, U of	12
CALIFORNIA-LOS ANGELES, U of	42
CENTRAL FLORIDA, U of	16
CINCINNATI MAIN CAMPUS, U of	45
COLORADO AT BOULDER, U of	111
DOWLING COLL	17
EMBRY-RIDDLE AERONAUTICAL U	119
FLORIDA INST OF TECH	6
FLORIDA, U of	48
GEORGIA INST OF TECH MAIN CAMPUS	72
ILLINOIS INST OF TECH	24
ILLINOIS URBANA CAMPUS, U of	96
IOWA ST U	48
KANSAS MAIN CAMPUS, U of	40
KENT ST U MAIN CAMPUS	60
MARYLAND COLL PARK CAMPUS, U of	88
MASSACHUSETTS INST OF TECH	87
MIAMI U OXFORD CAMPUS	14
MICHIGAN ANN ARBOR, U of	99
MINNESOTA TWIN CITIES, U of	98
MISSISSIPPI ST U	23
MISSOURI-ROLLA, U of	37
NORTH CAROLINA ST U AT RALEIGH	33
NORTHROP U	10
NOTRE DAME, U of	56
OHIO ST U MAIN CAMPUS	50
OHIO U MAIN CAMPUS	5
OKLAHOMA NORMAN CAMPUS, U of	19
PARKS COLL OF SAINT LOUIS U	111
PENNSYLVANIA ST U MAIN CAMPUS	84
POLYTECHNIC U	27
RENSSELAER POLYTECHNIC INST	39
SAN DIEGO ST U	56
SAN JOSE ST U	20
SUNY AT BUFFALO	44
SYRACUSE U MAIN CAMPUS	38
TENNESSEE-KNOXVILLE, U of	12
TEXAS A&M U	83
TEXAS AT ARLINGTON, U of	32
TEXAS AT AUSTIN, U of	72
TRI-ST U	4
TUSKEGEE U	7
UNITED STS NAVAL ACAD	74
US AIR FORCE ACAD	89
VIRGINIA MAIN CAMPUS, U of	44
VIRGINIA POLYTECHNIC INST AND ST U	113
WASHINGTON, U of55	
WEST VIRGINIA U	21
WESTERN MICHIGAN U	11
WICHITA ST U	22

African (Non-Semitic) Languages

WISCONSIN-MADISON, U of	2

African Studies

BRYN MAWR COLL	1
BUCKNELL U	5
COLL OF THE HOLY CROSS	1
COLUMBIA U IN THE CITY OF NEW YORK	1
KANSAS MAIN CAMPUS, U of	1
MICHIGAN ANN ARBOR, U of	5
PITZER COLL	1
WASHINGTON, U of	5
WESLEYAN U	17

Afro-American (Black) Studies

AMHERST COLL	3
BOWDOIN COLL	4
BRANDEIS U	5
BROWN U	3
CALIFORNIA ST U DOMINGUEZ HILLS	4
CALIFORNIA ST U LONG BEACH	4
CALIFORNIA ST U LOS ANGELES	3
CALIFORNIA ST U NORTHRIDGE	5
CALIFORNIA-BERKELEY, U of	7
CALIFORNIA-DAVIS, U of	1
CALIFORNIA-LOS ANGELES, U of	2
CALIFORNIA-SANTA BARBARA, U of	5
CARLETON COLL	4
COLORADO AT BOULDER, U of	2
CORNELL U-ENDOWED COLLS	2
CUNY BROOKLYN COLL	1
CUNY HUNTER COLL	16
CUNY LEHMAN COLL	2
CUNY YORK COLL	1
EASTERN ILLINOIS U	4
EMORY U	4
HOWARD U	2
INDIANA U BLOOMINGTON	4
INDIANA U NORTHWEST	1
MARYLAND BALTIMORE COUNTY CAMPUS, U of	6
MARYLAND COLL PARK CAMPUS, U of	5
MASSACHUSETTS AT AMHERST, U of	3
MASSACHUSETTS BOSTON, U of	2
MERCER U IN ATLANTA	1
MICHIGAN ANN ARBOR, U of	4
NEBRASKA AT OMAHA, U of	1
NORTH CAROLINA AT CHARLOTTE, U of	2
NORTH CAROLINA CHAPEL HILL, U of	1
NORTHERN COLORADO, U of	2
NORTHWESTERN U	2
OBERLIN COLL	11
OHIO ST U MAIN CAMPUS	2
PITTSBURGH MAIN CAMPUS, U of	2
RADCLIFFE COLL	3
RUTGERS U NEW BRUNSWICK	20
RUTGERS U NEWARK CAMPUS	1
SAINT AUGUSTINE'S COLL	1
SAN DIEGO ST U	1
SAN FRANCISCO ST U	14
SAN JOSE ST U	1
SMITH COLL	5
SONOMA ST U	3
SOUTH FLORIDA, U of	1
SOUTHERN METHODIST U	2
STANFORD U	4
SUNY AT ALBANY	19
SUNY AT BINGHAMTON	1
SUNY AT BUFFALO	6
SUNY AT STONY BROOK	4
SUNY COLL AT BROCKPORT	4
SUNY COLL AT NEW PALTZ	10
SYRACUSE U MAIN CAMPUS	4

TEMPLE U	6
VASSAR COLL	8
VIRGINIA MAIN CAMPUS, U of	3
WELLESLEY COLL	2
WISCONSIN-MADISON, U of	10
WISCONSIN-MILWAUKEE, U of	2
YALE U	6

Agribusiness and Agricultural Prod., Other

CALIFORNIA-DAVIS, U of	209
KANSAS ST U AGRI AND APP SCI	19
MAINE, U of	5
MICHIGAN ST U	218
NEBRASKA-LINCOLN, U of	30
SOUTH DAKOTA ST U	2
WESTERN MICHIGAN U	8

Agribusiness and Agricultural Production (unspecified)

Degrees in this subject were reported by 124 institutions. Consult more specific headings.

Agricultural Business and Management, Other

CENTRAL MISSOURI ST U	6
FINDLAY, U of	1
MINNESOTA TWIN CITIES, U of	1
WISCONSIN-MADISON, U of	33

Agricultural Business

ABILENE CHRISTIAN U	5
ALABAMA AGRI AND MECH U	3
ARKANSAS ST U MAIN CAMPUS	19
ARKANSAS TECH U	17
ARKANSAS-FAYETTEVILLE, U of	20
BEREA COLL	2
CALIFORNIA POLYTECHNIC ST U-SAN LUIS OBISPO	138
CALIFORNIA ST POLYTECHNIC U POMONA	7
CALIFORNIA ST U FRESNO	41
CALIFORNIA ST U-CHICO	13
CENTRAL MISSOURI ST U	7
COLORADO ST U	21
DELAWARE VALLEY COLL OF SCI AND AGRI	6
DORDT COLL	4
EASTERN NEW MEXICO U MAIN CAMPUS	3
FLORIDA AGRI AND MECH U	4
FLORIDA SOUTHERN COLL	5
ILLINOIS ST U	70
ILLINOIS URBANA CAMPUS, U of	11
IOWA ST U	82
LOUISIANA ST U & AGRI & MECH & HEBERT LAWS CTR	17
MCNEESE ST U	4
MID-AMERICA NAZARENE COLL	3
MIDDLE TENNESSE ST U	12
MINNESOTA TWIN CITIES, U of	29
MISSISSIPPI ST U	15
MURRAY ST U	4
NEW MEXICO ST U MAIN CAMPUS	44
NICHOLLS ST U	3
NORTHEAST LOUISIANA U	7
NORTHWEST MISSOURI ST U	24
NORTHWESTERN OKLAHOMA ST U	12
NORTHWESTERN ST U LOUISIANA	2
OHIO U MAIN CAMPUS	1
PANHANDLE ST U	12
PENNSYLVANIA ST U MAIN CAMPUS	43
REGIS COLL	1
SAM HOUSTON ST U	43
SOUTH CAROLINA ST COLL	16
SOUTH DAKOTA ST U	34
SOUTHEAST MISSOURI ST U	10
SOUTHEASTERN LOUISIANA U	3
SOUTHWEST MISSOURI ST U	21
SOUTHWEST TEXAS ST U	18
SOUTHWESTERN LOUISIANA, U of	7
STEPHEN F AUSTIN ST U	11
SUL ROSS ST U	9
TARLETON ST U	37
TENNESSEE TECH U	6
TENNESSEE-KNOXVILLE, U of	22
TEXAS A & I U	6
TEXAS A&M U	19
WASHINGTON ST U	15
WEST TEXAS ST U	11
WESTERN MICHIGAN U	3
WISCONSIN-PLATTEVILLE, U of	20
WISCONSIN-RIVER FALLS, U of	19
WYOMING, U of	20

Agricultural Business and Management, General

ARIZONA ST U	28
BERRY COLL	6
CALIFORNIA-DAVIS, U of	11
CHADRON ST COLL	6
CLEMSON U	4
DELAWARE, U of	25
FERRUM COLL	5
FORT HAYS ST U	10
KANSAS ST U AGRI AND APP SCI	7
KENTUCKY, U of	4
LOUISIANA TECH U	10
MICHIGAN ST U	20
MISSOURI VALLEY COLL	1
MISSOURI-COLUMBIA, U of	38
MONTANA ST U	26
NEBRASKA-LINCOLN, U of	37
NORTHWEST MISSOURI ST U	1
PERU ST COLL	1
SAM HOUSTON ST U	11
SCHOOL OF THE OZARKS	10
SOUTHERN ARKANSAS U MAIN CAMPUS	8
SOUTHWEST ST U	8
UTAH ST U	8
WISCONSIN-MADISON, U of	4

Agricultural Economics

ALCORN ST U	8
ARIZONA, U of	19
ARKANSAS PINE BLUFF, U of	10
ARKANSAS-FAYETTEVILLE, U of	2
AUBURN U MAIN CAMPUS	24
BRIGHAM YOUNG U	2
CENTRAL MISSOURI ST U	2
CLEMSON U	8
COLORADO ST U	5
CONNECTICUT, U of	2
CORNELL U-NYS STATUTORY COLLS	214
DELAWARE, U of	11
EAST TEXAS ST U	7
FLORIDA, U of	72
FORT VALLEY ST COLL	7
GEORGIA, U of	53
HAWAII AT MANOA, U of	1
IDAHO, U of	11
ILLINOIS URBANA CAMPUS, U of	85
KANSAS ST U AGRI AND APP SCI	48
KENTUCKY, U of	23
LANGSTON U	2
LOUISIANA ST U & AGRI & MECH & HEBERT LAWS CTR	1
LUBBOCK CHRISTIAN U	1
MAINE, U of	5
MARYLAND COLL PARK CAMPUS, U of	100
MASSACHUSETTS AT AMHERST, U of	31
MICHIGAN ST U	159
MINNESOTA TWIN CITIES, U of	16
MISSISSIPPI ST U	14
NEBRASKA-LINCOLN, U of	23
NEVADA-RENO, U of	7
NORTH CAROLINA AGRI AND TECHNICAL ST U	4
NORTH CAROLINA ST U AT RALEIGH	17
NORTH DAKOTA ST U MAIN CAMPUS	37
NORTHWEST MISSOURI ST U	1
OHIO ST U MAIN CAMPUS	79
OKLAHOMA ST U MAIN CAMPUS	69
OREGON ST U	46
PENNSYLVANIA ST U MAIN CAMPUS	7
PRAIRIE VIEW A & M U	6
SOUTH DAKOTA ST U	4
SOUTHERN ILLINOIS U-CARBONDALE	31
SOUTHERN U AGRI & MECH COL AT BATON ROUGE	7
TARLETON ST U	6
TEXAS A & I U	1
TEXAS A&M U	149
TEXAS TECH U	52
UTAH ST U	2
VERMONT, U of	65
VIRGINIA POLYTECHNIC INST AND ST U	24
WASHINGTON ST U	29
WEST VIRGINIA U	17

WISCONSIN-MADISON, U of	30
WISCONSIN-PLATTEVILLE, U of	7
WISCONSIN-RIVER FALLS, U of	3

Agricultural Education

ARIZONA, U of	9
ARKANSAS PINE BLUFF, U of	1
ARKANSAS ST U MAIN CAMPUS	3
ARKANSAS-FAYETTEVILLE, U of	6
CALIFORNIA-DAVIS, U of	3
CLEMSON U	1
CONNECTICUT, U of	1
DAVIS AND ELKINS COLL	1
EAST TEXAS ST U	11
FLORIDA, U of	8
GEORGIA, U of	17
IDAHO, U of	8
ILLINOIS URBANA CAMPUS, U of	2
IOWA ST U	22
KENTUCKY, U of	8
LOUISIANA ST U & AGRI & MECH & HEBERT LAWS CTR	5
LOUISIANA TECH U	1
MINNESOTA TWIN CITIES, U of	14
MISSISSIPPI ST U	11
MISSOURI-COLUMBIA, U of	10
MONTANA ST U	8
MOREHEAD ST U	3
MURRAY ST U	1
NEBRASKA-LINCOLN, U of	10
NEVADA-RENO, U of	1
NEW HAMPSHIRE, U of	1
NEW MEXICO ST U MAIN CAMPUS	13
NORTH CAROLINA ST U AT RALEIGH	11
NORTH DAKOTA ST U MAIN CAMPUS	4
NORTHWEST MISSOURI ST U	6
OHIO ST U MAIN CAMPUS	17
OKLAHOMA ST U MAIN CAMPUS	32
OREGON ST U	7
PANHANDLE ST U	4
PENNSYLVANIA ST U MAIN CAMPUS	9
PRAIRIE VIEW A & M U	6
SAM HOUSTON ST U	12
SOUTH DAKOTA ST U	11
SOUTHERN ARKANSAS U MAIN CAMPUS	2
SOUTHWEST MISSOURI ST U	9
SOUTHWEST TEXAS ST U	6
SOUTHWESTERN LOUISIANA, U of	1
STEPHEN F AUSTIN ST U	7
SUNY COLL AT OSWEGO	1
TARLETON ST U	25
TENNESSEE TECH U	2
TENNESSEE-KNOXVILLE, U of	2
TENNESSEE-MARTIN, U of	2
TEXAS A & I U	4
TEXAS TECH U	45
TUSKEGEE U	1
UTAH ST U	18
WEST VIRGINIA U	8
WISCONSIN-MADISON, U of	5
WISCONSIN-PLATTEVILLE, U of	3
WISCONSIN-RIVER FALLS, U of	12
WYOMING, U of	3

Agricultural Engineering

ARIZONA, U of	1
ARKANSAS ST U MAIN CAMPUS	1
ARKANSAS-FAYETTEVILLE, U of	3
AUBURN U MAIN CAMPUS	4
CALIFORNIA POLYTECHNIC ST U-SAN LUIS OBISPO	18
CALIFORNIA ST POLYTECHNIC U POMONA	6
CALIFORNIA-DAVIS, U of	4
CLEMSON U	4
COLORADO ST U	4
CORNELL U-NYS STATUTORY COLLS	33
DELAWARE, U of	12
FLORIDA, U of	19
GEORGIA, U of	21
IDAHO, U of	5
ILLINOIS URBANA CAMPUS, U of	16
IOWA ST U	12
KANSAS ST U AGRI AND APP SCI	3
MAINE, U of	1
MARYLAND COLL PARK CAMPUS, U of	3
MICHIGAN ST U	127
MINNESOTA TWIN CITIES, U of	5
MISSISSIPPI ST U	3
MISSOURI-COLUMBIA, U of	10
MONTANA ST U	1
NEBRASKA-LINCOLN, U of	7
NEW MEXICO ST U MAIN CAMPUS	1
NORTH DAKOTA ST U MAIN CAMPUS	7
OHIO ST U MAIN CAMPUS	28
OKLAHOMA ST U MAIN CAMPUS	2
OREGON ST U	2
PENNSYLVANIA ST U MAIN CAMPUS	15
PRAIRIE VIEW A & M U	1
RUTGERS U NEW BRUNSWICK	2
SOUTH DAKOTA ST U	5
SOUTHWESTERN LOUISIANA, U of	1
TENNESSEE-KNOXVILLE, U of	1
TEXAS A&M U	16
TEXAS TECH U	6
VERMONT, U of	2
VIRGINIA POLYTECHNIC INST AND ST U	4
WASHINGTON ST U	4
WISCONSIN-MADISON, U of	5
WYOMING, U of	3

Agricultural Mechanics, Other

KANSAS ST U AGRI AND APP SCI	9
MONTANA ST U	4
SOUTH DAKOTA ST U	3
TARLETON ST U	6

Agricultural Mechanics, General

CALIFORNIA POLYTECHNIC ST U-SAN LUIS OBISPO	11
GEORGIA, U of	7
ILLINOIS URBANA CAMPUS, U of	16
IOWA ST U	6
LOUISIANA ST U & AGRI & MECH & HEBERT LAWS CTR	17
MISSOURI-COLUMBIA, U of	12
NEBRASKA-LINCOLN, U of	14
NORTH CAROLINA AGRI AND TECHNICAL ST U	1
NORTH DAKOTA ST U MAIN CAMPUS	13
NORTHWEST MISSOURI ST U	1
OKLAHOMA ST U MAIN CAMPUS	1
PENNSYLVANIA ST U MAIN CAMPUS	3
SAM HOUSTON ST U	1
STEPHEN F AUSTIN ST U	1
TENNESSEE-KNOXVILLE, U of	1
TEXAS A&M U	32
TEXAS TECH U	2
WASHINGTON ST U	2
WISCONSIN-MADISON, U of	6
WISCONSIN-PLATTEVILLE, U of	10
WISCONSIN-RIVER FALLS, U of	7

Agricultural Power Machinery

MURRAY ST U	4

Agricultural Products and Processing, Other

KANSAS ST U AGRI AND APP SCI	9

Agricultural Products and Processing, General

KANSAS ST U AGRI AND APP SCI	19

Agricultural Production, General

EASTERN KENTUCKY U	17
HAWAII AT MANOA, U of	1
WILMINGTON COLL	20

Agricultural Sciences, General

ALCORN ST U	3
ANDREWS U	5
ARIZONA, U of	11
ARKANSAS ST U MAIN CAMPUS	5
ARKANSAS-MONTICELLO, U of	19
AUBURN U MAIN CAMPUS	2
AUSTIN PEAY ST U	14
BEREA COLL	16
CALIFORNIA POLYTECHNIC ST U-SAN LUIS OBISPO	15
CALIFORNIA ST POLYTECHNIC U POMONA	5
CALIFORNIA ST U FRESNO	106
CALIFORNIA ST U-CHICO	20
CAMERON U	19
COLORADO ST U	2
CONNECTICUT, U of	1

CORNELL U-NYS STATUTORY COLLS 60
DELAWARE, U of 13
EAST TEXAS ST U 9
FLORIDA AGRI AND MECH U 7
FORT HAYS ST U 15
GEORGIA, U of 7
HAWAII AT HILO, U of 21
IDAHO, U of 2
ILLINOIS ST U 23
ILLINOIS URBANA CAMPUS, U of 11
LINCOLN U 6
LUBBOCK CHRISTIAN U 1
MAINE, U of 1
MARYLAND COLL PARK CAMPUS, U of 2
MARYLAND EASTERN SHORE, U of 4
MCNEESE ST U 4
MCPHERSON COLL 2
MINNESOTA TWIN CITIES, U of 2
MISSISSIPPI ST U 4
MISSOURI WESTERN ST COLL 8
MISSOURI-COLUMBIA, U of 20
MOREHEAD ST U 15
MURRAY ST U 7
NEBRASKA-LINCOLN, U of 8
NEW MEXICO ST U MAIN CAMPUS 3
NORTH CAROLINA AGRI AND TECHNICAL ST U 15
NORTH DAKOTA ST U MAIN CAMPUS 6
NORTHEAST LOUISIANA U 1
NORTHEAST MISSOURI ST U 9
NORTHWEST MISSOURI ST U 12
NORTHWESTERN ST U LOUISIANA 5
OREGON ST U 14
PENNSYLVANIA ST U MAIN CAMPUS 25
RUTGERS U NEW BRUNSWICK 11
SOUTH DAKOTA ST U 4
SOUTHEAST MISSOURI ST U 5
SOUTHERN ILLINOIS U-CARBONDALE 28
SOUTHERN UTAH ST COLL 4
SOUTHWEST MISSOURI ST U 3
STEPHEN F AUSTIN ST U 1
TABOR COLL 2
TARLETON ST U 6
TENNESSEE ST U 3
TENNESSEE TECH U 1
TENNESSEE-MARTIN, U of 31
TEXAS A&M U 29
VERMONT, U of 19
VIRGINIA ST U 3
WASHINGTON ST U 8
WESTERN ILLINOIS U 65
WESTERN KENTUCKY U 33
WISCONSIN-RIVER FALLS, U of 24
WYOMING, U of 1

Agricultural Sciences, Other

ALABAMA AGRI AND MECH U 1
CALIFORNIA-BERKELEY, U of 3
IOWA ST U 7
KENTUCKY, U of 6
MARYLAND COLL PARK CAMPUS, U of 1
MISSOURI-COLUMBIA, U of 4
MONTANA ST U 2
NEW MEXICO ST U MAIN CAMPUS 5
PENNSYLVANIA ST U MAIN CAMPUS 18
STEPHENS COLL 3
WISCONSIN-PLATTEVILLE, U of 8

Agricultural Sciences (unspecified)

Degrees in this subject were reported by 127 institutions. Consult more specific headings.

Agricultural Services

WYOMING, U of 5

Agronomy

ALCORN ST U 2
ARIZONA, U of 8
ARKANSAS PINE BLUFF, U of 3
ARKANSAS-FAYETTEVILLE, U of 10
AUBURN U MAIN CAMPUS 3
BRIGHAM YOUNG U 13
CALIFORNIA POLYTECHNIC ST U-SAN LUIS OBISPO 15
CALIFORNIA ST POLYTECHNIC U POMONA 4
COLORADO ST U 6
CONNECTICUT, U of 3
CORNELL U-NYS STATUTORY COLLS 11
DELAWARE VALLEY COLL OF SCI AND AGRI 10
FLORIDA, U of 9
GEORGIA, U of 9
IDAHO, U of 3
ILLINOIS URBANA CAMPUS, U of 12
IOWA ST U 25
KANSAS ST U AGRI AND APP SCI 23
KENTUCKY, U of 8
LOUISIANA ST U & AGRI & MECH & HEBERT LAWS CTR 3
LOUISIANA TECH U 1
MARYLAND COLL PARK CAMPUS, U of 1
MCNEESE ST U 1
MICHIGAN ST U 19
MINNESOTA TWIN CITIES, U of 10
MISSISSIPPI ST U 8
MISSOURI-COLUMBIA, U of 7
MONTANA ST U 4
NEBRASKA-LINCOLN, U of 14
NEW MEXICO ST U MAIN CAMPUS 3
NORTH CAROLINA ST U AT RALEIGH 14
NORTHWEST MISSOURI ST U 2
OHIO ST U MAIN CAMPUS 28
OKLAHOMA ST U MAIN CAMPUS 13
OREGON ST U 14
PANHANDLE ST U 3
PENNSYLVANIA ST U MAIN CAMPUS 9
PRAIRIE VIEW A & M U 4
SOUTH DAKOTA ST U 12
SOUTHEAST MISSOURI ST U 3
SOUTHWEST MISSOURI ST U 7
SOUTHWESTERN LOUISIANA, U of 2
STEPHEN F AUSTIN ST U 3
TEXAS A&M U 23
TEXAS TECH U 1
VIRGINIA POLYTECHNIC INST AND ST U 17
WASHINGTON ST U 5
WISCONSIN-MADISON, U of 5
WISCONSIN-RIVER FALLS, U of 4

Air Conditioning, Heating, and Refrigeration Technology

CENTRAL MISSOURI ST U 1

Air Traffic Control

DANIEL WEBSTER COLL 9
EMBRY-RIDDLE AERONAUTICAL U 8
FLORIDA MEMORIAL COLL 4

Air Transportation, General

ANDREWS U 6
BRIDGEWATER ST COLL 45
CENTRAL WASHINGTON U 35
DELTA ST U 7
EMBRY-RIDDLE AERONAUTICAL U 282
HAMPTON U 15
LOUISIANA TECH U 74
MIDDLE TENNESSE ST U 105
NORTH DAKOTA MAIN CAMPUS, U of 98
NORTHEAST LOUISIANA U 7
OHIO ST U MAIN CAMPUS 107
ROCKY MOUNTAIN COLL 8
SALEM-TEIKYO U 6
TEXAS SOUTHERN U 2

Air Transportation, Other

FLORIDA INST OF TECH 23
LEWIS U 3
NATIONAL U 2
NORTH DAKOTA MAIN CAMPUS, U of 3
NORTHEAST LOUISIANA U 2

Aircraft Mechanics, Airframe

ANDREWS U 1
SOUTHEASTERN OKLAHOMA ST U 4

Airplane Piloting and Navigation

DANIEL WEBSTER COLL 21
DELTA ST U 17
DUBUQUE, U of 7

EMBRY-RIDDLE AERONAUTICAL U	387
HENDERSON ST U	14
JACKSONVILLE U	4
METROPOLITAN ST COLL	54
NORTH DAKOTA MAIN CAMPUS, U of	21
NORTHEAST LOUISIANA U	7
SOUTHEASTERN OKLAHOMA ST U	7
TENNESSEE WESLEYAN COLL	3
WESTMINSTER COLL OF SALT LAKE CITY	8

Alcohol/Drug Abuse Specialty

ALVERNIA COLL	8
DETROIT, U of	9
MINOT ST U	21
MISSOURI VALLEY COLL	11
PARK COLL	17
SOUTH DAKOTA, U of	10
SOUTHERN U AT NEW ORLEANS	8

Allied Health (unspecified)

Degrees in this subject were reported by 460 institutions. Consult more specific headings.

Allied Health, Other

ALABAMA AT BIRMINGHAM, U of	17
ALBANY ST COLL	20
ANDERSON U	6
BALDWIN-WALLACE COLL	8
BLOOMSBURG U PENNSYLVANIA	14
BRENAU COLL	2
CAPITAL U	5
CENTRAL MICHIGAN U	31
CHRISTIAN BROTHERS COLL	2
CUMBERLAND COLL	10
CUNY BROOKLYN COLL	19
CUNY CITY COLL	17
CUNY YORK COLL	5
DOANE COLL	2
EASTERN WASHINGTON U	18
FLORIDA, U of	22
GODDARD COLL	1
GUSTAVUS ADOLPHUS COLL	14
HEIDELBERG COLL	3
HIRAM COLL	9
HOWARD U	22
INCARNATE WORD COLL	1
INDIANA ST U	21
INDIANA U PENNSYLVANIA	8
ITHACA COLL	30
JUNIATA COLL	1
LAKE SUPERIOR ST U	6
LEBANON VALLEY COLL	2
LINCOLN MEMORIAL U	1
LONG ISLAND U BROOKLYN CAMPUS	39
LONG ISLAND U C W POST CAMPUS	6
MALONE COLL	1
MANCHESTER COLL	5
MARYVILLE COLL	4
MCMURRY COLL	5
MOLLOY COLL	7
NEW YORK U	8
NORTH DAKOTA ST U MAIN CAMPUS	16
NORTHEASTERN ST U	4
OHIO ST U MAIN CAMPUS	48
OLD DOMINION U	6
PITTSBURGH MAIN CAMPUS, U of	5
POINT LOMA NAZARENE COLL	5
PORTLAND, U of	11
ROCHESTER INST OF TECH	26
SAINT ANDREWS PRESBYTERIAN COLL	3
SAINT JOHN'S U NEW YORK	5
SAINT JOSEPHS COLL MAIN CAMPUS	31
SOUTHWESTERN ADVENTIST COLL	1
SPRINGFIELD COLL	17
ST FRANCIS COLL	1
TOURO COLL	29
UNION COLL	3
WINGATE COLL	3
YOUNGSTOWN ST U	26

American Indian Studies

ALASKA FAIRBANKS, U of	2
BEMIDJI ST U	3
CALIFORNIA-BERKELEY, U of	2
CALIFORNIA-DAVIS, U of	2
COLGATE U	1
INCARNATE WORD COLL	1
MINNESOTA TWIN CITIES, U of	5
NORTH DAKOTA MAIN CAMPUS, U of	4
NORTHEASTERN ST U	1
SCI AND ARTS OF OKLAHOMA, U of	1

American Studies

Degrees in this subject were reported by 161 institutions. Consult more specific headings.

Anatomy

ANDREWS U	30
DUKE U	1
ILLINOIS URBANA CAMPUS, U of	15

Anesthesiology

SOUTH DAKOTA, U of	5

Anesthetist

ALABAMA AT BIRMINGHAM, U of	14
EDINBORO U PENNSYLVANIA	3
LA ROCHE COLL	1
MALONE COLL	1
MINNESOTA TWIN CITIES, U of	2

Animal Health

ARIZONA, U of	5
IDAHO, U of	4
SUL ROSS ST U	5

Animal Production

BERRY COLL	4
TARLETON ST U	12
TEXAS TECH U	23

Animal Sciences, General

ABILENE CHRISTIAN U	2
ALABAMA AGRI AND MECH U	1
ALCORN ST U	4
ANGELO ST U	19
ARIZONA, U of	19
ARKANSAS PINE BLUFF, U of	1
ARKANSAS ST U MAIN CAMPUS	7
ARKANSAS-FAYETTEVILLE, U of	15
AUBURN U MAIN CAMPUS	36
BERRY COLL	2
BRIGHAM YOUNG U	13
CALIFORNIA POLYTECHNIC ST U-SAN LUIS OBISPO	40
CALIFORNIA ST POLYTECHNIC U POMONA	31
CALIFORNIA-DAVIS, U of	29
COLORADO ST U	50
CONNECTICUT, U of	37
CORNELL U-NYS STATUTORY COLLS	119
DELAWARE VALLEY COLL OF SCI AND AGRI	27
DELAWARE, U of	25
DENVER, U of	1
DORDT COLL	4
EAST TEXAS ST U	8
FLORIDA AGRI AND MECH U	2
FLORIDA, U of	31
FORT VALLEY ST COLL	1
GEORGIA, U of	28
HAWAII AT MANOA, U of	9
IDAHO, U of	12
ILLINOIS URBANA CAMPUS, U of	61
IOWA ST U	65
KANSAS ST U AGRI AND APP SCI	97
KENTUCKY, U of	33
LOUISIANA ST U & AGRI & MECH & HEBERT LAWS CTR	8
LOUISIANA TECH U	18
MAINE, U of	13
MARYLAND COLL PARK CAMPUS, U of	25
MASSACHUSETTS AT AMHERST, U of	43
MCNEESE ST U	8
MERCY COLL—MAIN CAMPUS	10
MICHIGAN ST U	43
MIDDLE TENNESSEE ST U	7
MINNESOTA TWIN CITIES, U of	11
MISSISSIPPI ST U	9
MISSOURI-COLUMBIA, U of	37

MONTANA ST U	22
MURRAY ST U	11
NEBRASKA-LINCOLN, U of	38
NEVADA-RENO, U of	6
NEW HAMPSHIRE, U of	41
NEW MEXICO ST U MAIN CAMPUS	24
NICHOLLS ST U	3
NORTH CAROLINA AGRI AND TECHNICAL ST U	1
NORTH CAROLINA ST U AT RALEIGH	53
NORTH DAKOTA ST U MAIN CAMPUS	31
NORTHEAST LOUISIANA U	1
NORTHEAST MISSOURI ST U	12
NORTHWEST MISSOURI ST U	11
OHIO ST U MAIN CAMPUS	59
OKLAHOMA ST U MAIN CAMPUS	100
OREGON ST U	15
PANHANDLE ST U	9
PENNSYLVANIA ST U MAIN CAMPUS	28
PRAIRIE VIEW A & M U	7
RHODE ISLAND, U of	24
RUTGERS U NEW BRUNSWICK	43
SAM HOUSTON ST U	10
SOUTH DAKOTA ST U	35
SOUTHEASTERN LOUISIANA U	2
SOUTHERN ILLINOIS U-CARBONDALE	10
SOUTHERN U AGRI & MECH COLL AT BATON ROUGE	2
SOUTHWEST MISSOURI ST U	13
SOUTHWEST TEXAS ST U	9
SOUTHWESTERN LOUISIANA, U of	2
STEPHEN F AUSTIN ST U	13
SUL ROSS ST U	11
TARLETON ST U	7
TENNESSEE ST U	1
TENNESSEE TECH U	5
TENNESSEE-KNOXVILLE, U of	29
TEXAS A & I U	13
TEXAS A&M U	148
TEXAS TECH U	6
TUSKEGEE U	27
UTAH ST U	18
VERMONT, U of	16
VIRGINIA POLYTECHNIC INST AND ST U	51
WASHINGTON ST U	19
WEST TEXAS ST U	8
WEST VIRGINIA U	31
WISCONSIN-MADISON, U of	11
WISCONSIN-PLATTEVILLE, U of	20
WISCONSIN-RIVER FALLS, U of	38
WYOMING, U of	16

Animal Sciences, Other

ARIZONA, U of	15
ARKANSAS-FAYETTEVILLE, U of	5
AVERETT COLL	5
CLEMSON U	16
COLORADO ST U	59
DELAWARE VALLEY COLL OF SCI AND AGRI	4
FINDLAY, U of	6
ROCKY MOUNTAIN COLL	1
SOUTHWEST TEXAS ST U	2
TARLETON ST U	3
TEXAS A&M U	70
WEST TEXAS ST U	2
WILSON COLL	7

Animal Training

WILLIAM WOODS COLL	11

Anthropology

Degrees in this subject were reported by 326 institutions. Consult more specific headings.

Apparel and Accessories Marketing, General

CENTRAL MICHIGAN U	19
MARYLAND COLL PARK CAMPUS, U of	91
NORTHEAST MISSOURI ST U	10
PHILADELPHIA COLL OF TEXTILES AND SCIENCE	14
RHODE ISLAND, U of	9
WISCONSIN-MADISON, U of	19
YOUNGSTOWN ST U	7

Apparel and Accessories Marketing, Other

WALLA WALLA COLL	3

Applied Mathematics

ABILENE CHRISTIAN U	4
AKRON, MAIN CAMPUS, U of	11
ALABAMA, U of	8
ALDERSON BROADDUS COLL	1
AUBURN U MAIN CAMPUS	41
AUGUSTANA COLL	5
BAPTIST COLL AT CHARLESTON	2
BETHEL COLL	2
BOSTON U	2
BRESCIA COLL	2
BROWN U	26
CALIFORNIA INST OF TECH	3
CALIFORNIA-BERKELEY, U of	52
CALIFORNIA-LOS ANGELES, U of	67
CALIFORNIA-SAN DIEGO, U of	51
CARNEGIE MELLON U	39
COLORADO AT BOULDER, U of	12
COLORADO-COLORADO SPRINGS, U of	8
COLUMBIA U IN THE CITY OF NEW YORK	4
CONNECTICUT COLL	1
CONNECTICUT, U of	12
DAVID LIPSCOMB U	3
DREW U	3
EASTERN ILLINOIS U	7
ELIZABETH CITY ST U	2
FERRIS ST U	3
FLORIDA INST OF TECH	2
GENEVA COLL	4
GEORGIA INST OF TECH MAIN CAMPUS	17
GRAND VIEW COLL	1
HARVARD U	19
IDAHO, U of	8
INDIANA U PENNSYLVANIA	8
JOHNS HOPKINS U	16
KENT ST U MAIN CAMPUS	9
LAMAR U	6
LONG ISLAND U C W POST CAMPUS	3
LONG ISLAND U SOUTHHAMPTON COLL	1
LOYOLA COLL	16
MASS. AT LOWELL, U of	14
MASSACHUSETTS BOSTON, U of	8
MICHIGAN ST U	9
MISSOURI-ROLLA, U of	7
MISSOURI-SAINT LOUIS, U of	10
MURRAY ST U	1
NEW JERSEY INST TECH	1
NORTHERN ARIZONA U	9
PITTSBURGH BRADFORD CAMPUS, U of	2
PITTSBURGH MAIN CAMPUS, U of	23
RADCLIFFE COLL	9
RICE U	6
RIVIER COLL	3
ROCHESTER INST OF TECH	20
ROCHESTER, U of	3
SAN FRANCISCO ST U	6
SAN JOSE ST U	4
SOUTH CAROLINA AT COASTAL CAROLINA, U of	7
STERLING COLL	2
SUNY AT STONY BROOK	84
TENNESSEE-CHATTANOOGA, U of	4
TEXAS A&M U	29
TULSA, U of	2
US AIR FORCE ACAD	27
VALDOSTA ST COLL	2
VIRGINIA MAIN CAMPUS, U of	5
WAKE FOREST U	4
WEBER ST COLL	12
WELLS COLL	2
WEST TEXAS ST U	2
WESTERN WASHINGTON U	9
WISCONSIN-STOUT, U of	40
YALE U	11

Aquaculture

AUBURN U MAIN CAMPUS	5
FLORIDA INST OF TECH	13
MAINE, U of	1

Arabic

CALIFORNIA-LOS ANGELES, U of	1
GEORGETOWN U	3
MINNESOTA TWIN CITIES, U of	1
OHIO ST U MAIN CAMPUS	3
SUNY AT BINGHAMTON	1

Archeology

BAYLOR U	3
BOSTON U	7
BOWDOIN COLL	1
BROWN U	1
BRYN MAWR COLL	6
COLL OF WOOSTER	1
COLUMBIA U IN THE CITY OF NEW YORK	3
CORNELL U-ENDOWED COLLS	1
CUNY BROOKLYN COLL	2
CUNY HUNTER COLL	2
DARTMOUTH COLL	2
EVANSVILLE, U of	2
HAVERFORD COLL	1
MISSOURI-COLUMBIA, U of	10
NEW YORK U	9
OBERLIN COLL	3
RHODE ISLAND COLL	1
RUTGERS U NEW BRUNSWICK	7
TEXAS AT AUSTIN, U of	14
TUFTS U	1
WASHINGTON AND LEE U	2
WELLESLEY COLL	2
WHEATON COLL	4
YALE U	7

Architectural Design and Construction Technology

BLUEFIELD ST COLL	4
CENTRAL MISSOURI ST U	11
CINCINNATI MAIN CAMPUS, U of	45
EASTERN KENTUCKY U	19
EASTERN MICHIGAN U	14
FAIRMONT ST COLL	14
FLORIDA AGRI AND MECH U	3
GEORGIA SOUTHERN COLL	18
GRAMBLING ST U	1
INDIANA U-PURDUE U AT FORT WAYNE	13
INDIANA U-PURDUE U AT INDIANAPOLIS	21
JOHN BROWN U	9
LINCOLN U	6
LOUISIANA ST U & AGRI & MECH & HEBERT LAWS CTR	16
MEMPHIS ST U	18
MURRAY ST U	3
NEVADA-LAS VEGAS, U of	7
NORFOLK ST U	13
NORTHEAST LOUISIANA U	26
NORTHERN IOWA, U of	10
NORTHERN KENTUCKY U	13
NORTHERN MONTANA COLL	2
PITTSBURG ST U	9
PURDUE U CALUMET CAMPUS	18
SOUTHERN MISSISSIPPI, U of	28
SOUTHERN U AT NEW ORLEANS	11
SOUTHWEST MISSOURI ST U	12
SOUTHWEST TEXAS ST U	12
TEXAS SOUTHERN U	5
TEXAS TECH U	14
VIRGINIA POLYTECHNIC INST AND ST U	34
WASHINGTON U	9
WENTWORTH INST OF TECH	49

Architectural Engineering

AUBURN U MAIN CAMPUS	103
CALIFORNIA POLYTECHNIC ST U-SAN LUIS OBISPO	36
COLORADO AT BOULDER, U of	39
DREXEL U	39
KANSAS MAIN CAMPUS, U of	27
KANSAS ST U AGRI AND APP SCI	29
MIAMI, U of	16
MILWAUKEE SCHOOL OF ENGINEERING	21
NORTH CAROLINA AGRI AND TECHNICAL ST U	20
OKLAHOMA ST U MAIN CAMPUS	6
PENNSYLVANIA ST U MAIN CAMPUS	66
TEMPLE U	69
TENNESSEE ST U	9
TEXAS AT AUSTIN, U of	31
WYOMING, U of	11

Architectural Techologies, Other

FLORIDA AGRI AND MECH U	6
FLORIDA, U of	118

Architecture and Environmental Design (unspecified)

Degrees in this subject were reported by 205 institutions. Consult more specific headings.

Architecture and Environmental Design, Other

CALIFORNIA-DAVIS, U of	11
CLEMSON U	31
KANSAS MAIN CAMPUS, U of	74
KANSAS ST U AGRI AND APP SCI	27
METROPOLITAN ST COLL	11
NEW YORK INST OF TECH MAIN CAMPUS	86
NORTH CAROLINA ST U AT RALEIGH	29
ROGER WILLIAMS COLL	19
SAVANNAH COLL OF ART AND DESIGN	15
SMITH COLL	9
VIRGINIA MAIN CAMPUS, U of	3
WASHINGTON, U of	46

Architecture and Environmental Design, General

ARIZONA ST U	1
ARKANSAS-FAYETTEVILLE, U of	6
BOWLING GREEN ST U MAIN CAMPUS	9
DRURY COLL	13
GEORGIA INST OF TECH MAIN CAMPUS	12
ILLINOIS URBANA CAMPUS, U of	135
MARYVILLE COLL—ST LOUIS	10
MASSACHUSETTS INST OF TECH	46
TEXAS A&M U	184
THE U THE ARTS	10
TUSKEGEE U	10
WASHINGTON ST U	42
WASHINGTON, U of	3
WISCONSIN-MILWAUKEE, U of	86

Architecture

ANDREWS U	15
ARIZONA ST U	40
ARIZONA, U of	68
ARKANSAS-FAYETTEVILLE, U of	40
AUBURN U MAIN CAMPUS	49
BALL ST U	60
BROWN U	2
CALIFORNIA COLL OF ARTS AND CRAFTS	14
CALIFORNIA POLYTECHNIC ST U-SAN LUIS OBISPO	113
CALIFORNIA ST POLYTECHNIC U POMONA	76
CALIFORNIA-BERKELEY, U of	194
CARNEGIE MELLON U	38
CATHOLIC U AMERICA	94
CINCINNATI MAIN CAMPUS, U of	67
COLUMBIA U IN THE CITY OF NEW YORK	31
COOPER UNION	22
CORNELL U-ENDOWED COLLS	70
CUNY CITY COLL	115
DETROIT, U of	25
DREXEL U	11
FLORIDA AGRI AND MECH U	45
FLORIDA, U of	103
GEORGIA INST OF TECH MAIN CAMPUS	66
HAMPTON U	12
HAWAII AT MANOA, U of	32
HOUSTON-U PARK, U of	64
HOWARD U	34
IDAHO, U of	32
ILLINOIS AT CHICAGO, U of	51
ILLINOIS INST OF TECH	41
IOWA ST U	53
KANSAS MAIN CAMPUS, U of	6
KANSAS ST U AGRI AND APP SCI	71
KENT ST U MAIN CAMPUS	76
KENTUCKY, U of	46
LAWRENCE INST OF TECH	79
LEHIGH U	28
LOUISIANA ST U & AGRI & MECH & HEBERT LAWS CTR	42
LOUISIANA TECH U	14
MARYLAND COLL PARK CAMPUS, U of	56
MIAMI, U of	54
MICHIGAN ANN ARBOR, U of	92
MINNESOTA TWIN CITIES, U of	55
MISSISSIPPI ST U	27
MONTANA ST U	30

NEBRASKA-LINCOLN, U of	51
NEW JERSEY INST TECH	75
NEW MEXICO MAIN CAMPUS, U of	50
NEW YORK INST OF TECH MAIN CAMPUS	56
NORTH CAROLINA AT CHARLOTTE, U of	45
NORTH CAROLINA ST U AT RALEIGH	56
NORTH DAKOTA ST U MAIN CAMPUS	38
NOTRE DAME, U of	42
OHIO ST U MAIN CAMPUS	69
OKLAHOMA NORMAN CAMPUS, U of	73
OKLAHOMA ST U MAIN CAMPUS	24
OREGON, U of	65
PENNSYLVANIA ST U MAIN CAMPUS	102
PRAIRIE VIEW A & M U	14
PRATT INST-MAIN	135
PRINCETON U	24
RENSSELAER POLYTECHNIC INST	46
RHODE ISLAND SCHOOL OF DESIGN	144
RICE U	18
ROGER WILLIAMS COLL	52
SOUTHERN U AGRI & MECH COL AT BATON ROUGE	15
SOUTHWESTERN LOUISIANA, U of	37
SPRING GARDEN COLL	24
SUNY AT BUFFALO	39
SYRACUSE U MAIN CAMPUS	79
TENNESSEE-KNOXVILLE, U of	69
TEXAS AT ARLINGTON, U of	100
TEXAS AT AUSTIN, U of	64
TEXAS SAN ANTONIO, U of	12
TEXAS TECH U	98
TULANE U LOUISIANA	65
UTAH, U of	16
VIRGINIA MAIN CAMPUS, U of	76
VIRGINIA POLYTECHNIC INST AND ST U	98
WASHINGTON ST U	38
WASHINGTON U	57
WASHINGTON, U of	72
WELLESLEY COLL	13
WENTWORTH INST OF TECH	28
WOODBURY U	18
YALE U	34

Area Studies, Other

ALASKA FAIRBANKS, U of	3
BARNARD COLL	18
BORICUA COLL	6
BOSTON U	6
BRANDEIS U	13
CALIFORNIA-LOS ANGELES, U of	3
COLBY COLL	3
COLL OF WOOSTER	2
COLUMBIA U IN THE CITY OF NEW YORK	16
CORNELL U-ENDOWED COLLS	9
CUNY CITY COLL	10
CUNY QUEENS COLL	2
DREXEL U	12
FORT LEWIS COLL	4
GANNON U	6
GEORGE MASON U	27
GEORGETOWN U	32
GEORGIA, U of	2
IDAHO ST U	1
IDAHO, U of	1
IOWA, U of	5
LOCK HAVEN U PENNSYLVANIA	11
MACALESTER COLL	2
MANHATTANVILLE COLL	15
MINNESOTA TWIN CITIES, U of	8
MISSISSIPPI MAIN CAMPUS, U of	6
MOUNT HOLYOKE COLL	1
NEW YORK U	2
NORTH CAROLINA CHAPEL HILL, U of	84
OBERLIN COLL	6
PACIFIC, U of THE	23
PITZER COLL	1
RICHMOND, U of	8
ROLLINS COLL	3
SAINT NORBERT COLL	5
SALEM COLL	4
SEATTLE PACIFIC U	4
SOUTHERN METHODIST U	3
SOUTHWESTERN LOUISIANA, U of	1
SUNY COLL AT PLATTSBURG	5
SYRACUSE U MAIN CAMPUS	1
TOURO COLL	14
TRINITY COLL	4
TRINITY COLL	23
TUFTS U	6
VIRGINIA MAIN CAMPUS, U of	27
WAYNE ST U	3
WESTERN OREGON ST COLL	5
WILLIAM JEWELL COLL	1
WRIGHT ST U MAIN CAMPUS	3
YALE U	24

Area and Ethnic Studies, Other

ANTIOCH COLL	1
AZUSA PACIFIC U	7
BRANDEIS U	3
BRIGHAM YOUNG U	12
BROWN U	4
CALIFORNIA-BERKELEY, U of	3
CALIFORNIA-SAN DIEGO, U of	8
CALIFORNIA-SANTA BARBARA, U of	9
ECKERD COLL	11
GUSTAVUS ADOLPHUS COLL	3
HAMLINE U	7
HAWAII AT HILO, U of	7
KEARNEY ST COLL	2
LORAS COLL	1
MARLBORO COLL	6
NORTHWEST CHRISTIAN COLL	1
NORWICH U	8
OBERLIN COLL	8
OGLETHORPE U	12
SAINT OLAF COLL	8
SOUTH, THE U of THE	4
SOUTHERN METHODIST U	1
TENNESSEE-KNOXVILLE, U of	18
THE PACIFIC, U of	4
TRINITY COLL	13
WILLAMETTE U	1
WILLIAMS COLL	1

Area and Ethnic Studies (unspecified)

Degrees in this subject were reported by 319 institutions. Consult more specific headings.

Art Conservation

DELAWARE, U of	1
FASHION INST OF TECH	11
REGIS COLL	4
TEXAS COLL	2

Art Education

Degrees in this subject were reported by 246 institutions. Consult more specific headings.

Art History and Appreciation

Degrees in this subject were reported by 223 institutions. Consult more specific headings.

Art Therapy

ANNA MARIA COLL	1
BOWLING GREEN ST U MAIN CAMPUS	10
CAPITAL U	2
EMMANUEL COLL	2
EVANSVILLE, U of	2
INDIANAPOLIS, U of	1
MERCYHURST COLL	1
MOUNT MARY COLL	9
SETON HILL COLL	2

Arts Management

BENNETT COLL	1
BRENAU COLL	2
BUTLER U	3
CABRINI COLL	2
CATAWBA COLL	1
EAST CAROLINA U	1
EASTERN MICHIGAN U	11
ECKERD COLL	1
ELMHURST COLL	3
GEORGIA COLL	6
KANSAS WESLEYAN U	1
KENTUCKY, U of	10
LINFIELD COLL	1
MARY BALDWIN COLL	7

MARYWOOD COLL	2
MILLIKIN U	2
NEWBERRY COLL	2
NORTHERN ARIZONA U	11
POINT PARK COLL	1
RANDOLPH-MACON COLL	6
SAINT LEO COLL	1
SALEM COLL	4
SHENANDOAH COLL AND CONSERVATORY	1
SIMMONS COLL	2
SOUTHEASTERN LOUISIANA U	1
SPRING HILL COLL	5
WHITWORTH COLL	3

Asian Studies, General

ALABAMA, U of	1
AMHERST COLL	12
ARIZONA, U of	26
BARNARD COLL	14
BAYLOR U	3
BOWDOIN COLL	8
BOWLING GREEN ST U MAIN CAMPUS	5
BRIGHAM YOUNG U	13
CALIFORNIA ST U LONG BEACH	6
CALIFORNIA-BERKELEY, U of	30
CALIFORNIA-SANTA BARBARA, U of	15
CARLETON COLL	4
CASE WESTERN RESERVE U	1
CINCINNATI MAIN CAMPUS, U of	1
COE COLL	1
COLGATE U	22
COLORADO AT BOULDER, U of	6
CONNECTICUT COLL	31
CORNELL U-ENDOWED COLLS	17
DARTMOUTH COLL	13
DEPAUW U	1
FLORIDA ST U	3
FLORIDA, U of	1
HAMILTON COLL	2
HAWAII AT MANOA, U of	20
HAWAII LOA COLL	2
ILLINOIS URBANA CAMPUS, U of	8
IOWA, U of	17
LAKE FOREST COLL	1
MICHIGAN ANN ARBOR, U of	28
MOUNT HOLYOKE COLL	7
NORTHWESTERN U	1
OKLAHOMA CITY U	1
OKLAHOMA NORMAN CAMPUS, U of	3
OREGON, U of	18
PITZER COLL	4
POMONA COLL	12
PUGET SOUND, U of	14
RANDOLPH-MACON WOMAN'S COLL	2
REDLANDS, U of	1
SAINT ANDREWS PRESBYTERIAN COLL	1
SAINT OLAF COLL	8
SAN DIEGO ST U	4
SCRIPPS COLL	1
SETON HALL U	6
SUNY AT ALBANY	1
SWARTHMORE COLL	2
TEXAS AT AUSTIN, U of	6
TRINITY U	1
TUFTS U	9
WASHINGTON ST U	2
WASHINGTON U	5
WILLIAMS COLL	7
WISCONSIN-MADISON, U of	14

Asiatic Languages, Other

ARIZONA ST U	13
BRIGHAM YOUNG U	15
CALIFORNIA-BERKELEY, U of	20
FLORIDA, U of	2
INDIANA U BLOOMINGTON	8
KANSAS MAIN CAMPUS, U of	20
LAWRENCE U	3

Astronomy

AMHERST COLL	1
ARIZONA, U of	11
BENEDICTINE COLL	2
BOSTON U	7
BRYN MAWR COLL	1
CALIFORNIA INST OF TECH	1
CASE WESTERN RESERVE U	1
CORNELL U-ENDOWED COLLS	2
FLORIDA, U of	1
GEORGIA, U of	2
HARVARD U	2
HAVERFORD COLL	4
ILLINOIS URBANA CAMPUS, U of	1
INDIANA U BLOOMINGTON	2
IOWA, U of	3
KANSAS MAIN CAMPUS, U of	1
LOUISIANA ST U & AGRI & MECH & HEBERT LAWS CTR	1
LYCOMING COLL	2
MARYLAND COLL PARK CAMPUS, U of	5
MASSACHUSETTS AT AMHERST, U of	7
MICHIGAN ANN ARBOR, U of	2
MOUNT HOLYOKE COLL	1
OHIO ST U MAIN CAMPUS	2
OKLAHOMA NORMAN CAMPUS, U of	2
PENNSYLVANIA ST U MAINCAMPUS	6
PENNSYLVANIA, U of	3
SAN DIEGO ST U	1
SMITH COLL	1
SUNY AT STONY BROOK	4
TEXAS AT AUSTIN, U of	6
VASSAR COLL	4
VIRGINIA MAIN CAMPUS, U of	3
WASHINGTON, U of	3
WELLESLEY COLL	2
WESLEYAN U	6
WYOMING, U of	1

Astrophysics

CALIFORNIA-BERKELEY, U of	2
CALIFORNIA-LOS ANGELES, U of	5
HOWARD U	1
MICHIGAN ST U	7
MINNESOTA TWIN CITIES, U of	2
MOUNT HOLYOKE COLL	3
NEW MEXICO MAIN CAMPUS, U of	5
OKLAHOMA NORMAN CAMPUS, U of	4
PRINCETON U	4
TEXAS CHRISTIAN U	3
WILLIAMS COLL	1
WISCONSIN-MADISON, U of	9

Atmospheric Sciences and Meteorology

ARIZONA, U of	6
CALIFORNIA-DAVIS, U of	4
CALIFORNIA-LOS ANGELES, U of	1
CREIGHTON U	8
FLORIDA ST U	22
HAWAII AT MANOA, U of	4
IOWA ST U	10
KANSAS MAIN CAMPUS, U of	11
LYNDON ST COLL	12
MASS. AT LOWELL, U of	18
METROPOLITAN ST COLL	6
MILLERSVILLE U PENNSYLVANIA	7
MISSOURI-COLUMBIA, U of	5
NEBRASKA-LINCOLN, U of	8
NEW YORK U	1
NORTH CAROLINA AT ASHEVILLE, U of	9
NORTH CAROLINA ST U AT RALEIGH	10
NORTH DAKOTA MAIN CAMPUS, U of	12
NORTHEAST LOUISIANA U	2
NORTHERN ILLINOIS U	11
OKLAHOMA NORMAN CAMPUS, U of	21
PARKS COLL OF SAINT LOUIS U	2
PENNSYLVANIA ST U MAIN CAMPUS	54
PLYMOUTH ST COLL	5
RUTGERS U NEW BRUNSWICK	1
SAINT LOUIS U MAIN CAMPUS	7
SAINT THOMAS, U of	2
SAN JOSE ST U	2
SUNY AT ALBANY	12
SUNY COLL AT BROCKPORT	6
SUNY COLL AT ONEONTA	4
SUNY COLL AT OSWEGO	8
SUNY MARITIME COLL	12
TEXAS A&M U	30
UTAH, U of	4
WASHINGTON, U of	9
WISCONSIN-MADISON, U of	14

Atomic/Molecular Physics

OHIO U MAIN CAMPUS 1
RADCLIFFE COLL 13

Auctioneering

CITY U 1

Audiology and Speech Pathiology, Other

CALIFORNIA-SANTA BARBARA, U of 41
COLL OF OUR LADY OF ELMS 4
MCMURRY COLL 1
SOUTH DAKOTA, U of 5
UTAH ST U 28
WORCESTER ST COLL 6

Audiology

MONTEVALLO, U of 7
NORTHERN COLORADO, U of 9
NORTHWESTERN U 2
STEPHEN F AUSTIN ST U 11
TENNESSEE-KNOXVILLE, U of 3
WASHINGTON U 5

Automotive Machanics

WALLA WALLA COLL 1

Automotive Technologoy

AKRON, MAIN CAMPUS, U of 2
GRAMBLING ST U 6
INDIANA ST U 18
NORTHERN MONTANA COLL 7
OREGON INST OF TECH 37
SIENA HEIGHTS COLL 1
SOUTHEASTERN OKLAHOMA ST U 2
SOUTHERN COLORADO, U of 9
SOUTHWEST MISSOURI ST U 2
WEBER ST COLL 6
WESTERN MICHIGAN U 13

Aviation Management

ANDREWS U 2
AVERETT COLL 3
CENTRAL MISSOURI ST U 1
DALLAS BAPTIST U 12
DANIEL WEBSTER COLL 34
DISTRICT OF COLUMBIA, U of THE 2
DUBUQUE, U of 6
EASTERN MICHIGAN U 6
EMBRY-RIDDLE AERONAUTICAL U 6
FLORIDA INST OF TECH 167
FLORIDA MEMORIAL COLL 4
JACKSONVILLE U 4
LEWIS U 28
METROPOLITAN ST COLL 53
NATIONAL U 32
NORTH DAKOTA MAIN CAMPUS, U of 84
PARKS COLL OF SAINT LOUIS U 96
PHILLIPS U 1
SAINT MARTIN'S COLL 4
SOUTHERN ILLINOIS U-CARBONDALE 278
WESTMINSTER COLL OF SALT LAKE CITY 3

Bacteriology

CALIFORNIA-DAVIS, U of 1
IDAHO, U of 1
WAGNER COLL 2

Balto-Slavic Languages, Other

NORTHWESTERN U 8
PRINCETON U 5

Banking and Finance

Degrees in this subject were reported by 376 institutions. Consult more specific headings.

Banking and Related Financial Programs, Other

MADONNA COLL 8

Banking and Related Financial Programs, General

BRYANT COLL OF BUSINESS ADMINISTRATION 9
COLUMBIA COLL 13
OKLAHOMA CHRISTIAN COLL 3

Basic Clinical Health Sciences, Other

ALABAMA AT BIRMINGHAM, U of 2
BOSTON U 3
CALIFORNIA-RIVERSIDE, U of 28
COLUMBUS COLL 18
CONCORDIA COLL AT MOORHEAD 1
FELICIAN COLL 2
GRAND VALLEY ST U 40
GWYNEDD-MERCY COLL 2
RUTGERS U NEWARK CAMPUS 3

Bible Studies

ABILENE CHRISTIAN U 15
ALASKA BIBLE COLL 4
ANDERSON U 1
ASBURY COLL 13
AZUSA PACIFIC U 1
BIOLA U 14
BLUE MOUNTAIN COLL 6
BRYAN COLL 7
CENTENARY COLL OF LOUISIANA 2
CHRISTIAN HERITAGE COLL 6
CLEARWATER CHRISTIAN COLL 6
COLUMBIA BIBLE COLL AND SEMINARY 112
COLUMBIA CHRISTIAN COLL 2
DAVID LIPSCOMB U 11
EASTERN MENNONITE COLL 8
EVANGEL COLL 21
FAULKNER U 5
FREED-HARDEMAN COLL 19
FRESNO PACIFIC COLL 13
GENEVA COLL 5
GEORGE FOX COLL 1
GORDON COLL 15
GRACE COLL 4
GRAND CANYON U 11
GRAND RAPIDS BAPTIST COLL AND SEMINARY 14
HANNIBAL-LAGRANGE COLL 10
HARDIN-SIMMONS U 5
HARDING U MAIN CAMPUS 17
HOWARD PAYNE U 5
HUNTINGTON COLL 4
JOHN BROWN U 2
JOHNSON BIBLE COLL 40
LANCASTER BIBLE COLL 49
LEE COLL 26
LETOURNEAU COLL 1
LIBERTY U 5
LUBBOCK CHRISTIAN U 2
MASTER'S COLL, THE 25
MESSIAH COLL 4
MILLIGAN COLL 8
NORTHWEST COLL OF THE ASSEMBLIES OF GOD 22
NORTHWESTERN COLL 3
OKLAHOMA BAPTIST U 1
OKLAHOMA CHRISTIAN COLL 18
OLIVET NAZARENE U 1
OUACHITA BAPTIST U 9
PATTEN COLL 4
SAMFORD U 7
SEATTLE PACIFIC U 1
SIMPSON COLL 7
SOUTHEASTERN COLL ASSEMBLIES OF GOD 39
SOUTHERN CALIFORNIA COLL 12
SOUTHWEST BAPTIST U 7
SOUTHWESTERN COLL OF CHRISTIAN MINISTRIES 3
TAYLOR U 9
TOCCOA FALLS COLL 21
WARNER SOUTHERN COLL 1
WAYLAND BAPTIST U 11
WESTERN BAPTIST COLL 10
WHEATON COLL 20
WILLIAM CAREY COLL 7
WINGATE COLL 5

Biblical Languages

ABILENE CHRISTIAN U	2
BETHANY BIBLE COLL	2
CONCORDIA COLL	2
HARDING U MAIN CAMPUS	1
SOUTHWESTERN ASSEMBLIES OF GOD COLL	2

Bilingual/Bicultural Education

BOISE ST U	10
BOSTON U	9
CHICAGO ST U	1
FINDLAY, U of	8
HOUSTON BAPTIST U	7
NORTHEASTERN ILLINOIS U	13
PAN AMERICAN U	1
SAINT EDWARD'S U	7
TEXAS A & I U	28
TEXAS SOUTHERN U	18
WASHINGTON, U of	2
WAYNE ST U	1
WESTERN ILLINOIS U	7

Biochemistry and Biophysics

Degrees in this subject were reported by 181 institutions. Consult more specific headings.

Bioengineering and Biomedical Engineering

ARIZONA ST U	12
BOSTON U	76
BRIDGEPORT, U of	5
CALIFORNIA-BERKELEY, U of	20
CALIFORNIA-SAN DIEGO, U of	58
CASE WESTERN RESERVE U	33
CATHOLIC U AMERICA	11
CEDAR CREST COLL	4
COLUMBIA U IN THE CITY OF NEW YORK	2
DUKE U	52
ILLINOIS AT CHICAGO, U of	12
ILLINOIS URBANA CAMPUS, U of	11
IOWA, U of	18
JOHNS HOPKINS U	47
LOUISIANA TECH U	8
MARQUETTE U	31
MASSACHUSETTS AT AMHERST, U of	1
MERCER U IN ATLANTA	2
MILWAUKEE SCHOOL OF ENGINEERING	16
MISSISSIPPI ST U	8
NORTHWESTERN U	45
ORAL ROBERTS U	1
PENNSYLVANIA, U of	23
RENSSELAER POLYTECHNIC INSTITUTE	19
SYRACUSE U MAIN CAMPUS	21
TEMPLE U	5
TEXAS A&M U	33
TULANE U LOUISIANA	44
VANDERBILT U	36
WESTERN NEW ENGLAND COLL	2
WRIGHT ST U MAIN CAMPUS	14

Biological Laboratory Technology

AUBURN U MAIN CAMPUS	11

Biological Technologies, Other

WISCONSIN-RIVER FALLS, U of	1
WORCESTER POLYTECHNIC INST	23

Biological and Physical Sciences

Degrees in this subject were reported by 185 institutions. Consult more specific headings.

Biology, General

Degrees in this subject were reported by 1140 institutions. Consult more specific headings.

Biomedical Equipment Technology

DAYTON, U of	2
WALLA WALLA COLL	3

Biometrics and Biostatistics

CORNELL U-NYS STATUTORY COLLS	12
IOWA ST U	1
RUTGERS U NEW BRUNSWICK	7

Blood Bank Technology

MEMPHIS ST U	1

Botany, General

ARIZONA ST U	3
ARKANSAS ST U MAIN CAMPUS	2
ARKANSAS-FAYETTEVILLE, U of	1
BRIGHAM YOUNG U	10
CALIFORNIA ST U LONG BEACH	1
CALIFORNIA-BERKELEY, U of	7
CALIFORNIA-DAVIS, U of	9
CALIFORNIA-SANTA BARBARA, U of	1
CLEMSON U	1
COLORADO ST U	2
CONNECTICUT COLL	3
EASTERN ILLINOIS U	11
FLORIDA, U of	3
HAWAII AT MANOA, U of	1
HOWARD U	1
HUMBOLDT ST U	8
IDAHO ST U	1
IDAHO, U of	2
ILLINOIS URBANA CAMPUS, U of	1
IOWA, U of	1
KENT ST U MAIN CAMPUS	1
LOUISIANA ST U & AGRI & MECH & HEBERT LAWS CTR	3
MARS HILL COLL	1
MARSHALL U	1
MARYLAND COLL PARK CAMPUS, U of	2
MASSACHUSETTS AT AMHERST, U of	5
MIAMI U OXFORD CAMPUS	5
MICHIGAN ST U	2
MINNESOTA TWIN CITIES, U of	1
MONTANA, U of	1
NORTH CAROLINA ST U AT RALEIGH	7
NORTHERN ARIZONA U	1
NORTHERN COLORADO, U of	1
NORTHWEST MISSOURI ST U	1
OHIO ST U MAIN CAMPUS	3
OHIO U MAIN CAMPUS	6
OKLAHOMA NORMAN CAMPUS, U of	1
OKLAHOMA ST U MAIN CAMPUS	2
OLIVET NAZARENE U	1
OREGON ST U	9
SAN JOSE ST U	1
SOUTH DAKOTA ST U	1
SOUTH FLORIDA, U of	1
SOUTHERN ILLINOIS U-CARBONDALE	4
TENNESSEE-KNOXVILLE, U of	1
TEXAS AT AUSTIN, U of	1
VERMONT, U of	2
WASHINGTON, U of	18
WEBER ST COLL	3
WESTERN NEW MEXICO U	1
WISCONSIN-MADISON, U of	3
WISCONSIN-MILWAUKEE, U of	1
WYOMING, U of	2

Botany, Other

CALIFORNIA-RIVERSIDE, U of	2
MINNESOTA TWIN CITIES, U of	1
NEW HAMPSHIRE, U of	2
SOUTHEASTERN LOUISIANA U	1

Business (Administrative Support) (unspecified)

Degrees in this subject were reported by 210 institutions. Consult more specific headings.

Business (Administrative Support), Other

AVILA COLL	5
EVANGEL COLL	2
HOUSTON-U PARK, U of	4
MCMURRY COLL	7

MERCYHURST COLL	4
MORNINGSIDE COLL	4
SOUTHWESTERN LOUISIANA, U of	10

Business Administration and Management, Other

ALDERSON BROADDUS COLL	1
ALVERNIA COLL	17
AMERICAN INTERNATIONAL COLL	15
BENEDICTINE COLL	2
CALIFORNIA MARITIME ACAD	16
CALIFORNIA ST U LOS ANGELES	8
CALIFORNIA ST U NORTHRIDGE	13
CALUMET COLL OF SAINT JOSEPH	80
CAMPBELL U INCORPORATED	12
CENTRAL MICHIGAN U	12
COLL OF NOTRE DAME	49
COLL OF SAINT JOSEPH	14
COLL OF SAINT THOMAS	6
CONCORDIA COLL	61
DELAWARE ST COLL	43
ELIZABETHTOWN COLL	15
EMORY U	1
FERRIS ST U	25
FORT HAYS ST U	7
FORT VALLEY ST COLL	3
GARDNER-WEBB COLL	6
GENEVA COLL	9
GEORGIA COLL	4
GRAND VALLEY ST U	4
HUNTINGDON COLL	17
JARVIS CHRISTIAN COLL	17
LAKELAND COLL	132
LESLEY COLL	202
LETOURNEAU COLL	13
LOUISVILLE, U of	8
MALONE COLL	113
MCPHERSON COLL	1
MISSOURI SOUTHERN ST COLL	8
MISSOURI VALLEY COLL	24
MOUNT MARY COLL	39
MURRAY ST U	1
NATIONAL U	48
NEW HAMPSHIRE COLL	310
NEWBERRY COLL	8
NICHOLS COLL	56
NORTH CAROLINA AT ASHEVILLE, U of	3
NORTHWESTERN COLL	5
OLIVET COLL	14
PARKS COLL OF SAINT LOUIS U	10
PENNSYLVANIA, U of	9
ROBERT MORRIS COLL	22
RUST COLL	19
SAINT AMBROSE U	3
SAINT JOSEPH'S COLL	10
SAINT MARY COLL	25
SEATTLE PACIFIC U	22
SHIPPENSBURG U PENNSYLVANIA	3
SIOUX FALLS COLL	28
SOUTHERN MAINE, U of	4
STILLMAN COLL	43
TEXAS AT AUSTIN, U of	5
TEXAS LUTHERAN COLL	25
TEXAS TECH U	2
THOMAS A EDISON ST COLL	34
TOLEDO, U of	34
UNION U	1
WARNER SOUTHERN COLL	23
WESTERN NEW ENGLAND COLL	7
WYOMING, U of	68
YORK COLL PENNSYLVANIA	17

Business Administration and Management, General

Degrees in this subject were reported by 802 institutions. Consult more specific headings.

Business Data Processing and Related Programs, Other

PONTIFICAL CATHOLIC U PUERTO RICO—PONCE CA	20

Business Data Processing and Related Programs, General

ARKANSAS AT LITTLE ROCK, U of	19
ARKANSAS COLL	1
ARKANSAS-MONTICELLO, U of	7
BELMONT COLL	3
CAMPBELL U INCORPORATED	19
CENTRAL ARKANSAS, U of	19
FLORIDA MEMORIAL COLL	5
FREED-HARDEMAN COLL	1
GANNON U	16
HENDERSON ST U	1
MARS HILL COLL	4
MCMURRY COLL	2
MISSISSIPPI ST U	20
MORRIS BROWN COLL	5
NEW ORLEANS, U of	8
NORTHERN MICHIGAN U	18
OHIO ST U MAIN CAMPUS	64
PAINE COLL	1
ROGER WILLIAMS COLL	11
SOUTH CAROLINA SPARTANBURG, U of	5
SOUTHERN ARKANSAS U MAIN CAMPUS	14
TRI-ST U	1
WISCONSIN-SUPERIOR, U of	2

Business Data Programming

AURORA U	8
COLUMBIA COLL	15
HUSSON COLL	5

Business Economics

Degrees in this subject were reported by 247 institutions. Consult more specific headings.

Business Education

Degrees in this subject were reported by 272 institutions. Consult more specific headings.

Business Home Economics

CARSON-NEWMAN COLL	13
HOUSTON-U PARK, U of	52
IDAHO, U of	1
MADONNA COLL	1
MCNEESE ST U	27
MONTANA ST U	11
NORTH TEXAS, U of	52
NORTHEASTERN ST U	18
NORTHWEST NAZARENE COLL	2
PHILANDER SMITH COLL	2
POINT LOMA NAZARENE COLL	5
SAMFORD U	2
SOUTHWESTERN LOUISIANA, U of	22
VIRGINIA ST U	7
WISCONSIN-STOUT, U of	27

Business Systems Analysis

FINDLAY, U of	3
NORTHEAST LOUISIANA U	17
SAINT VINCENT COLL	1
SHIPPENSBURG U PENNSYLVANIA	13
WESTERN ILLINOIS U	6

Business and Management (unspecified)

Degrees in this subject were reported by 1197 institutions. Consult more specific headings.

Business and Management, General

Degrees in this subject were reported by 460 institutions. Consult more specific headings.

Business and Management, Other

Degrees in this subject were reported by 129 institutions. Consult more specific headings.

Business and Personal Services Marketing, General

ASHLAND U	28
DAVID LIPSCOMB U	34
OHIO ST U MAIN CAMPUS	384
RHODE ISLAND COLL	28

Canadian Studies

BRIGHAM YOUNG U	26
VERMONT, U of	4

Cardiopulmonary Technology

BOSTON U	5
LOUISIANA ST U MEDICAL CENTER	20
NORTHEASTERN U	13
SAINT LOUIS U MAIN CAMPUS	7
SUNY AT STONY BROOK	15

Carpentry

SIENA HEIGHTS COLL	1

Cartography

EAST CENTRAL U	9
IDAHO, U of	5
SALEM ST COLL	11
WISCONSIN-MADISON, U of	5

Cell Biology

ARIZONA, U of	48
BARTON (FORMERLY ATLANTIC CHRISTIAN) COLL	1
CALIFORNIA-SANTA BARBARA, U of	10
ELON COLL	1
MINNESOTA TWIN CITIES, U of	27
SUNY COLL AT PLATTSBURG	2

Cell and Molecular Biology, Other

CALIFORNIA-BERKELEY, U of	19
CALIFORNIA-SAN DIEGO, U of	152
CALIFORNIA-SANTA BARBARA, U of	11
CONNECTICUT, U of	32
MAINE, U of	2
MICHIGAN ANN ARBOR, U of	57
SUNY COLL AT FREDONIA	12
TEXAS TECH U	4
WESTERN KENTUCKY U	12
WESTERN WASHINGTON U	6
WILLIAM JEWELL COLL	1

Ceramic Engineering

CLEMSON U	47
GEORGIA INST OF TECH MAIN CAMPUS	7
ILLINOIS URBANA CAMPUS, U of	33
IOWA ST U	12
MISSOURI-ROLLA, U of	20
OHIO ST U MAIN CAMPUS	17
PENNSYLVANIA ST U MAIN CAMPUS	37
RUTGERS U NEW BRUNSWICK	54
WASHINGTON, U of	24

Ceramics

ARTS, THE U of THE	7
CALIFORNIA COLL OF ARTS AND CRAFTS	6
CLEVELAND INST OF ART	6
DALLAS, U of	1
HARTFORD, U of	8
HOUSTON-U PARK, U of	1
KANSAS CITY ART INST	14
LOUISIANA ST U & AGRI & MECH & HEBERT LAWS CTR	1
MAINE COLL OF ART (WAS PORTLAND SCHOOL OF ART)	5
MARYLAND INST COLL OF ART	1
MCMURRY COLL	1
MICHIGAN ANN ARBOR, U of	2
NORTH TEXAS, U of	5
OHIO ST U MAIN CAMPUS	4
OREGON, U of	1
OTIS ART INST OF PARSONS SCHOOL OF DESIGN	2
RHODE ISLAND SCHOOL OF DESIGN	7
SUNY COLL AT NEW PALTZ	3
SUNY COLL AT POTSDAM	1
TEMPLE U	8
TEXAS AT EL PASO, U of	1
WASHINGTON, U of	5

Chemical Engineering

Degrees in this subject were reported by 146 institutions. Consult more specific headings.

Chemical Technology

MASS. AT LOWELL, U of	2
NORTHEASTERN U	6
WESTFIELD ST COLL	2

Chemistry Technology

SOUTH FLORIDA, U of	6

Chemistry, General

Degrees in this subject were reported by 948 institutions. Consult more specific headings.

Chemistry, Other

ABILENE CHRISTIAN U	5
BRIDGEWATER ST COLL	1
CALIFORNIA-LOS ANGELES, U of	4
CALIFORNIA-SAN DIEGO, U of	27
CHAPMAN COLL	1
CLEMSON U	4
COLL OF WOOSTER	1
EASTERN MICHIGAN U	2
EASTERN NEW MEXICO U MAIN CAMPUS	1
ELMHURST COLL	2
FLORIDA ST U	3
GEORGIA INST OF TECH MAIN CAMPUS	3
KANSAS ST U AGRI AND APP SCI	4
LOUISVILLE, U of	3
MASSACHUSETTS AT DARTMOUTH (WAS SE U OF MA, U of	1
MIAMI, U of	1
MIDLAND LUTHERAN COLL	1
MOORHEAD ST U	8
NEW HAMPSHIRE KEENE ST COLL, U of	4
NORTH ALABAMA, U of	5
NORTH CAROLINA ST U AT RALEIGH	10
NORTHERN IOWA, U of	2
OHIO WESLEYAN U	7
PHILADELPHIA COLL OF TEXTILES AND SCI-ENCE	2
PROVIDENCE COLL	1
RADCLIFFE COLL	7
SAINT ANSELM COLL	4
SCRANTON, U of	8
SOUTH DAKOTA ST U	2
SOUTHERN CALIFORNIA COLL	1
SOUTHERN MISSISSIPPI, U of	24
SUNY AT STONY BROOK	8
VIRGIN ISLANDS, U of THE	2
WESTERN MICHIGAN U	11
WIDENER U PENNSYLVANIA CAMPUS	2
WISCONSIN-EAU CLAIRE, U of	9
WISCONSIN-MILWAUKEE, U of	1

Child Care and Guidance Management and Services, Gen.

BLUFFTON COLL	1
PITTSBURGH MAIN CAMPUS, U of	33

Child Development, Care, and Guidance

ARIZONA, U of	24
BEREA COLL	13
BOWLING GREEN ST U MAIN CAMPUS	1
BRIGHAM YOUNG U	14
CENTRAL MICHIGAN U	115
DETROIT, U of	6
DISTRICT OF COLUMBIA, U of THE	2
FORT VALLEY ST COLL	3
FREED-HARDEMAN COLL	1
GALLAUDET U	11
GEORGIA, U of	22
IOWA ST U	7
LANGSTON U	1
MADONNA COLL	18
MARYGROVE COLL	4
MEREDITH COLL	47
MINNESOTA DULUTH, U of	8
NORTHEAST LOUISIANA U	11
OKLAHOMA CHRISTIAN COLL	1
PACIFIC CHRISTIAN COLL	2
PACIFIC UNION COLL	1
POINT LOMA NAZARENE COLL	12
SETON HILL COLL	3
SOUTHERN U AGRI & MECH COL AT BATON ROUGE	2
TEXAS CHRISTIAN U	1
VERMONT, U of	15
WASHBURN U TOPEKA	2
WEBER ST COLL	13

WHEELOCK COLL	4
WHITTIER COLL	9

Chinese

BRIGHAM YOUNG U	14
BROWN U	1
CALIFORNIA-LOS ANGELES, U of	4
COLORADO AT BOULDER, U of	3
CONNECTICUT COLL	2
CUNY HUNTER COLL	2
GEORGE WASHINGTON U	3
GEORGETOWN U	11
HARVARD U	18
HAWAII AT MANOA, U of	3
MASSACHUSETTS AT AMHERST, U of	7
MICHIGAN ANN ARBOR, U of	5
MICHIGAN ST U	3
MIDDLEBURY COLL	1
MINNESOTA TWIN CITIES, U of	5
OBERLIN COLL	4
OHIO ST U MAIN CAMPUS	7
OREGON, U of	1
RADCLIFFE COLL	14
ROCHESTER, U of	2
RUTGERS U NEW BRUNSWICK	1
SAN FRANCISCO ST U	5
STANFORD U	1
SUNY AT ALBANY	5
WASHINGTON U	2
WASHINGTON, U of	14
WELLESLEY COLL	6
WISCONSIN-MADISON, U of	3
YALE U	3

Cinematography/Film

ANTIOCH COLL	1
ARTS, THE U of THE	7
BRIDGEPORT, U of	3
CALIFORNIA INST OF ARTS	7
CALIFORNIA-BERKELEY, U of	14
CALIFORNIA-SANTA BARBARA, U of	53
CUNY BROOKLYN COLL	6
CUNY CITY COLL	7
CUNY COLL OF STN ISLAND	8
CUNY HUNTER COLL	13
CUNY QUEENS COLL	3
GODDARD COLL	2
ITHACA COLL	30
KENT ST U MAIN CAMPUS	1
LONG ISLAND U C W POST CAMPUS	5
MIAMI, U of	35
NEW YORK U	311
PITTSBURGH MAIN CAMPUS, U of	16
POINT PARK COLL	3
PRATT INST-MAIN	8
ROCHESTER INST OF TECH	18
ROCHESTER, U of	6
SAN FRANCISCO ART INST	7
SAN FRANCISCO ST U	62
SCHOOL OF VISUAL ARTS	29
SUNY AT BINGHAMTON	19
SUNY COLL AT PURCHASE	13
SYRACUSE U MAIN CAMPUS	9
YALE U	5

City, Community, and Regional Planning

ALABAMA AGRI AND MECH U	4
APPALACHIAN ST U	3
ARIZONA ST U	21
ARIZONA, U of	33
AUSTIN PEAY ST U	30
BALL ST U	6
CALIFORNIA POLYTECHNIC ST U-SAN LUIS OBISPO	21
CALIFORNIA ST POLYTECHNIC U POMONA	44
CINCINNATI MAIN CAMPUS, U of	15
CORNELL U-ENDOWED COLLS	19
EAST CAROLINA U	21
EASTERN MICHIGAN U	21
EASTERN WASHINGTON U	11
HOWARD U	1
ILLINOIS URBANA CAMPUS, U of	16
INDIANA U PENNSYLVANIA	2
IOWA ST U	17
MASSACHUSETTS INST OF TECH	2
MIAMI U OXFORD CAMPUS	4
MICHIGAN ST U	8
NEW HAMPSHIRE, U of	5
NORTH TEXAS, U of	2
NORTHERN MICHIGAN U	5
SOUTHERN MISSISSIPPI, U of	7
SOUTHWEST MISSOURI ST U	4
SOUTHWEST TEXAS ST U	28
SOUTHWESTERN LOUISIANA, U of	6
THE DISTRICT OF COLUMBIA, U of	20
VIRGINIA MAIN CAMPUS, U of	15
WESTERN OREGON ST COLL	18
WESTERN WASHINGTON U	8
WESTFIELD ST COLL	12

Civil Engineering

Degrees in this subject were reported by 204 institutions. Consult more specific headings.

Civil Technologies, Other

ALABAMA AGRI AND MECH U	7
MARYLAND EASTERN SHORE, U of	4
MORRIS BROWN COLL	1
OREGON ST U	30

Civil Technology

ALABAMA, U of	4
ARKANSAS AT LITTLE ROCK, U of	4
BLUEFIELD ST COLL	13
BRADLEY U	24
CLEVELAND ST U	1
DELAWARE ST COLL	2
FAIRLEIGH DICKINSON U	1
FLORIDA AGRI AND MECH U	2
GEORGIA SOUTHERN COLL	12
LOUISIANA TECH U	4
MASS. AT LOWELL, U of	2
METROPOLITAN ST COLL	13
MISSOURI WESTERN ST COLL	5
MURRAY ST U	10
NEBRASKA-LINCOLN, U of	15
NORTHERN ARIZONA U	12
OREGON INST OF TECH	47
POINT PARK COLL	18
ROGER WILLIAMS COLL	12
SAVANNAH ST COLL	3
SOUTHERN COLORADO, U of	19
SOUTHERN ILLINOIS U AT EDWARDSVILLE	13
SPRING GARDEN COLL	12
TENNESSEE-MARTIN, U of	3
TEXAS SOUTHERN U	10
WENTWORTH INST OF TECH	34
WESTERN KENTUCKY U	10
YOUNGSTOWN ST U	15

Classics

Degrees in this subject were reported by 146 institutions. Consult more specific headings.

Clinical Animal Technology

QUINNIPIAC COLL	10

Clinical Biochemistry

TEMPLE U	11

Clinical Microbiology

WISCONSIN LA CROSSE, U of	24
WISCONSIN-MADISON, U of	7

Clinical Psychology

LOYOLA U CHICAGO	41
TUFTS U	26

Clothing and Textiles

BRIGHAM YOUNG U	58

Clothing, Apparel, and Textiles Mgmt Prod and Ser Gen.

MIDDLE TENNESSE ST U	24

Clothing, Apparel, and Textiles Mgmt Prod Ser., Other

DELAWARE ST COLL	2

Coal Mining Technology

BLUEFIELD ST COLL	2
FAIRMONT ST COLL	4

Cognitive Psychology

CARNEGIE MELLON U	4
HARVEY MUDD COLL	1
MASSACHUSETTS INST OF TECH	17
SMITH COLL	1

Commercial Art

ALABAMA AGRI AND MECH U	6
CENTRAL MISSOURI ST U	28
CONCORDIA TEACHERS COLL	4
EAST TEXAS ST U	7
FORT VALLEY ST COLL	2
FRIENDS U	2
GRAND VIEW COLL	14
IOWA WESLEYAN COLL	1
JACKSONVILLE U	10
LOUISIANA COLL	1
MADONNA COLL	4
MILLIKIN U	2
MISSOURI WESTERN ST COLL	4
NORTH TEXAS, U of	66
NORTHERN KENTUCKY U	7
NOTRE DAME COLL	7
OUACHITA BAPTIST U	4
PRAIRIE VIEW A & M U	5
SALEM-TEIKYO U	1
SOUTHWEST TEXAS ST U	31
TEXAS CHRISTIAN U	14
TEXAS WOMAN'S U	5
WESTERN KENTUCKY U	4
WILLIAM CAREY COLL	2

Commercial Photography

ANDREWS U	2
CALUMET COLL OF SAINT JOSEPH	1
NORTH ALABAMA, U of	4

Communication Electronics

SIENA HEIGHTS COLL	1

Communications (unspecified)

Degrees in this subject were reported by 806 institutions. Consult more specific headings.

Communications Technologies, Other

DANA COLL	6
EASTERN MICHIGAN U	8
FRAMINGHAM ST COLL	5
HARVEY MUDD COLL	1
MADONNA COLL	5
WISCONSIN-PLATTEVILLE, U of	21

Communications Technologies (unspecified)

ABILENE CHRISTIAN U	3
AKRON, MAIN CAMPUS, U of	55
ALABAMA AGRI AND MECH U	19
ASBURY COLL	9
ASHLAND U	6
BOWIE ST U	16
CENTRAL FLORIDA, U of	10
COLL OF MOUNT SAINT VINCENT	22
COLL OF SAINT ROSE	37
CUNY BROOKLYN COLL	2
DANA COLL	9
EAST STROUDSBURG U PENNSYLVANIA	36
EASTERN MICHIGAN U	58
ELON COLL	31
FERRIS ST U	37
FRAMINGHAM ST COLL	5
GANNON U	12
GENEVA COLL	8
GEORGIA, U of	108
HARVEY MUDD COLL	1
KENT ST U MAIN CAMPUS	82
KNOXVILLE COLL	3
LEBANON VALLEY COLL	4
LYNDON ST COLL	9
MADONNA COLL	5
MANHATTAN COLL	22
MEDAILLE COLL	8
MONTEVALLO, U of	22
MOUNT SAINT MARY COLL	1
OKLAHOMA NORMAN CAMPUS, U of	70
ORAL ROBERTS U	41
OTIS ART INST OF PARSONS SCHOOL OF DESIGN	5
POINT PARK COLL	3
ROCHESTER INST OF TECH	3
SCHOOL OF VISUAL ARTS	222
SHAW U	2
SIENA HEIGHTS COLL	1
SUNY COLL AT FREDONIA	13
TEXAS CHRISTIAN U	26
TREVECCA NAZARENE COLL	1
US INTERNATIONAL U	6
WAKE FOREST U	6
WEBER ST COLL	6
WISCONSIN-PLATTEVILLE, U of	21
WORCESTER ST COLL	47

Communications, General

Degrees in this subject were reported by 544 institutions. Consult more specific headings.

Communications, Other

Degrees in this subject were reported by 124 institutions. Consult more specific headings.

Community Health Work

CENTRAL ST U	2
CENTRAL WASHINGTON U	18
CUNY CITY COLL	6
CUNY HUNTER COLL	13
DELAWARE ST COLL	3
DILLARD U	15
EASTERN KENTUCKY U	2
EASTERN WASHINGTON U	6
JAMES MADISON U	22
MANKATO ST U	29
MOORHEAD ST U	11
NEBRASKA-LINCOLN, U of	3
NORTHERN IOWA, U of	27
OHIO ST U MAIN CAMPUS	6
SAINT CLOUD ST U	16
WESTERN KENTUCKY U	6
WESTERN WASHINGTON U	6
WINONA ST U	4

Community Psychology

BEMIDJI ST U	18
NORTHERN MICHIGAN U	3
NOVA U	17

Community Services

ALABAMA ST U	5
ALASKA FAIRBANKS, U of	5
BEMIDJI ST U	4
BORICUA COLL	72
BRIDGEPORT, U of	6
CALIFORNIA ST U-CHICO	6
CENTRAL MICHIGAN U	16
COLL FOR HUMAN SERVICE	107
COLL OF NOTRE DAME MARYLAND	27
CORNELL U-NYS STATUTORY COLLS	18
CUNY JOHN JAY COLL CRIMINAL JUSTICE	3
DOANE COLL	1
ECKERD COLL	1
ELMIRA COLL	15
ELON COLL	20
LAKE SUPERIOR ST U	24
MASSACHUSETTS BOSTON, U of	13
MEDAILLE COLL	21
MISSISSIPPI COLL	4
NEBRASKA AT OMAHA, U of	3
NEVADA-LAS VEGAS, U of	11
NORTHERN ST U	4
RUSSELL SAGE COLL MAIN CAMPUS	3
SAINT JOHN'S U NEW YORK	5
SAINT MARTIN'S COLL	9
SALEM-TEIKYO U	4

SAMFORD U	17
SOJOURNER-DOUGLAS COLL	17
SOUTHERN ARKANSAS U MAIN CAMPUS	3
SPRINGFIELD COLL	153
SUNY EMPIRE ST COLL	181
TOLEDO, U of	23
WEST VIRGINIA INST OF TECH	2
WESTERN NEW MEXICO U	21
WESTERN WASHINGTON U	93

Comp. Consumer and Homemaking Home Economics

ALABAMA, U of	3
BALL ST U	7
KENT ST U MAIN CAMPUS	2
SOUTHEASTERN LOUISIANA U	3
TEXAS CHRISTIAN U	1

Comparative Literature

ALASKA PACIFIC U	1
BARNARD COLL	1
BRANDEIS U	7
BRIGHAM YOUNG U	2
BROWN U	46
BRYN MAWR COLL	1
CALIFORNIA ST U FULLERTON	3
CALIFORNIA ST U LONG BEACH	7
CALIFORNIA-BERKELEY, U of	26
CALIFORNIA-DAVIS, U of	9
CALIFORNIA-IRVINE, U of	17
CALIFORNIA-RIVERSIDE, U of	1
CALIFORNIA-SANTA BARBARA, U of	3
CASE WESTERN RESERVE U	1
CLARK U	3
COLL OF WOOSTER	2
COLORADO COLL	7
COLUMBIA U IN THE CITY OF NEW YORK	38
CORNELL U-ENDOWED COLLS	7
CUNY BROOKLYN COLL	2
CUNY QUEENS COLL	2
DARTMOUTH COLL	6
DUKE U	1
EVANSVILLE, U of	3
FORDHAM U	9
GALLAUDET U	3
GEORGETOWN U	149
GEORGIA, U of	10
GROVE CITY COLL	3
HAMILTON COLL	10
HAVERFORD COLL	1
HOBART WILLIAM SMITH COLLS	6
ILLINOIS URBANA CAMPUS, U of	5
INDIANA U BLOOMINGTON	9
IOWA, U of	2
JUDAISM, U of	3
MAHARISHI INTERNATIONAL U	5
MARLBORO COLL	6
MARYMOUNT MANHATTAN COLL	11
MASSACHUSETTS AT AMHERST, U of	10
MCKENDREE COLL	3
MICHIGAN ANN ARBOR, U of	16
MILLS COLL	1
NEW MEXICO MAIN CAMPUS, U of	1
NEW YORK U	7
NORTH CAROLINA CHAPEL HILL, U of	4
NORTH TEXAS, U of	49
NORTHWESTERN U	11
OBERLIN COLL	3
PENNSYLVANIA ST U MAIN CAMPUS	2
PENNSYLVANIA, U of	6
PRINCETON U	18
RAMAPO COLL OF NEW JERSEY	23
RUTGERS U NEW BRUNSWICK	11
SAINT EDWARD'S U	10
SAINT MARY'S COLL OF MINNESOTA	5
SAN DIEGO ST U	8
SAN FRANCISCO ST U	6
SCRIPPS COLL	2
SMITH COLL	8
SWARTHMORE COLL	3
TEXAS AT EL PASO, U of	31
TRINITY COLL	3
VIRGINIA MAIN CAMPUS, U of	6
WASHINGTON U	5
WASHINGTON, U of	45
WEST CHESTER U PENNSYLVANIA	1
WISCONSIN-MADISON, U of	19
WISCONSIN-MILWAUKEE, U of	4
YALE U	10

Composition

BAYLOR U	13
BELOIT COLL	2
BLACKBURN COLL	1
BOISE ST U	8
BRIDGEWATER ST COLL	2
CARROLL COLL	3
COLUMBIA COLL	4
DAVIS AND ELKINS COLL	3
DEPAUW U	49
EASTERN MICHIGAN U	13
EDGEWOOD COLL	1
EVANSVILLE, U of	4
GENEVA COLL	4
GRAND CANYON U	2
LA ROCHE COLL	3
LYNDON ST COLL	2
MARQUETTE U	18
NORTH TEXAS, U of	16
PITTSBURGH MAIN CAMPUS, U of	7
SAINT EDWARD'S U	7

Computer Education

ABILENE CHRISTIAN U	1
BOWLING GREEN ST U MAIN CAMPUS	1
DELTA ST U	5
GRAND CANYON U	1
LESLEY COLL	2
TOLEDO, U of	2

Computer Engineering

ARIZONA, U of	22
ARKANSAS-FAYETTEVILLE, U of	25
AUBURN U MAIN CAMPUS	25
BELLARMINE COLL	3
BOSTON U	41
BRIDGEPORT, U of	6
BUCKNELL U	16
CALIFORNIA POLYTECHNIC ST U-SAN LUIS OBISPO	9
CALIFORNIA ST U-CHICO	24
CALIFORNIA ST U-SACRAMENTO	13
CALIFORNIA-DAVIS, U of	29
CALIFORNIA-LOS ANGELES, U of	54
CALIFORNIA-SAN DIEGO, U of	33
CALIFORNIA-SANTA CRUZ, U of	48
CASE WESTERN RESERVE U	26
CENTRAL FLORIDA, U of	41
CINCINNATI MAIN CAMPUS, U of	4
CLEMSON U	21
COLORADO AT BOULDER, U of	47
COLORADO TECHNICAL COLL	5
CONNECTICUT, U of	31
EVANSVILLE, U of	4
FLORIDA INST OF TECH	45
GEORGE WASHINGTON U	22
GEORGIA INST OF TECH MAIN CAMPUS	16
HARTFORD, U of	10
HOWARD U	8
IDAHO, U of	6
ILLINOIS AT CHICAGO, U of	52
ILLINOIS URBANA CAMPUS, U of	63
IOWA ST U	55
KANSAS MAIN CAMPUS, U of	12
KANSAS ST U AGRI AND APP SCI	14
LEHIGH U	31
LETOURNEAU COLL	6
LOUISIANA ST U & AGRI & MECH & HEBERT LAWS CTR	18
LOUISIANA TECH U	1
LOUISVILLE, U of	38
MAINE, U of	3
MARQUETTE U	36
MASSACHUSETTS AT AMHERST, U of	23
MASSACHUSETTS AT DARTMOUTH (WAS SE U OF MA, U of	23
MIAMI, U of	32
MICHIGAN ANN ARBOR, U of	73
MICHIGAN ST U	16
MILWAUKEE SCHOOL OF ENGINEERING	30
MINNESOTA DULUTH, U of	21
MISSISSIPPI ST U	25
MISSOURI-COLUMBIA, U of	52
MONTANA ST U	10
NEVADA-LAS VEGAS, U of	13
NEW JERSEY INST TECH	4
NEW MEXICO MAIN CAMPUS, U of	24

NORTHEASTERN U	32
NORWICH U	3
NOVA U	4
OAKLAND U	13
OLD DOMINION U	7
OREGON ST U	16
PACIFIC LUTHERAN U	9
PACIFIC, U of THE	20
PENNSYLVANIA ST U MAIN CAMPUS	27
PENNSYLVANIA, U of	53
PORTLAND ST U	10
PRINCETON U	21
RHODE ISLAND, U of	8
ROGER WILLIAMS COLL	5
SAINT MARY'S U	1
SAN FRANCISCO, U of	1
SAN JOSE ST U	28
SANTA CLARA U	15
SOUTH FLORIDA, U of	53
SOUTHERN METHODIST U	5
SOUTHWESTERN LOUISIANA, U of	7
STEVENS INST OF TECH	19
TEXAS AT ARLINGTON, U of	85
TEXAS AT EL PASO, U of	19
TEXAS SAN ANTONIO, U of	1
TOLEDO, U of	14
TULANE U LOUISIANA	23
UTAH, U of	57
VALPARAISO U	6
VIRGINIA POLYTECHNIC INST AND ST U	36
WASHINGTON, U of	17
WEST VIRGINIA U	10
WESTERN MICHIGAN U	17
WESTERN NEW ENGLAND COLL	8
WRIGHT ST U MAIN CAMPUS	29

Computer Programming

ASBURY COLL	4
ASHLAND U	5
DAVID LIPSCOMB U	2
GONZAGA U	1
GRACELAND COLL	3
HUSTON-TILLOTSON COLL	3
KING'S COLL	7
LORAS COLL	3
MORNINGSIDE COLL	2
NATIONAL U	178
RUST COLL	3
SOUTHEAST MISSOURI ST U	1
UNION COLL	1

Computer Servicing Technology

GALLAUDET U	2
NICHOLS COLL	1

Computer Technology

ANDREWS U	2
ARKANSAS AT LITTLE ROCK, U of	3
BRIGHAM YOUNG U	113
CAPITOL COLL	10
CENTRAL FLORIDA, U of	15
CENTRAL MICHIGAN U	13
COGSWELL POLYTECHNICAL COLL	4
EASTERN MICHIGAN U	8
EASTERN WASHINGTON U	6
GEORGIA SOUTHWESTERN COLL	1
HOUSTON-U PARK, U of	31
LETOURNEAU COLL	5
MEMPHIS ST U	13
MURRAY ST U	5
NORTHEASTERN U	27
POINT PARK COLL	70
PRAIRIE VIEW A & M U	13
SAVANNAH ST COLL	8
SOUTHERN MISSISSIPPI, U of	11
SPRING GARDEN COLL	3
UTAH ST U	7
WENTWORTH INST OF TECH	27
YOUNGSTOWN ST U	25

Computer and Information Sciences, General

Degrees in this subject were reported by 882 institutions. Consult more specific headings.

Computer and Information Sciences (unspecified)

Degrees in this subject were reported by 971 institutions. Consult more specific headings.

Computer and Information Sciences, Other

ALCORN ST U	5
AMERICAN INTERNATIONAL COLL	1
AMERICAN U	20
ANDERSON U	3
BAKER U	1
BARRY U	2
BERRY COLL	3
BRIDGEWATER COLL	3
BRIGHAM YOUNG U HAWAII CAMPUS	5
CARLOW COLL	1
CARROLL COLL	2
CENTRAL MICHIGAN U	7
CENTRAL U IOWA	4
COLGATE U	2
COLL OF SAINT MARY	13
CONVERSE COLL	3
CUNY COLL OF STN ISLAND	5
CUNY JOHN JAY COLL CRIMINAL JUSTICE	3
CUNY LEHMAN COLL	41
DALLAS BAPTIST U	13
DANIEL WEBSTER COLL	7
DAYTON, U of	8
DEFIANCE COLL	3
DISTRICT OF COLUMBIA, U of THE	64
DREXEL U	44
EMBRY-RIDDLE AERONAUTICAL U	27
FERRIS ST U	54
FRANKLIN U	35
FURMAN U	8
GEORGE WASHINGTON U	10
HOLLINS COLL	1
INDIANA ST U	7
INDIANA U-PURDUE U AT INDIANAPOLIS	44
ITHACA COLL	2
LAMAR U	2
LAMBUTH COLL	4
LANE COLL	2
LEHIGH U	21
LEWIS AND CLARK COLL	3
LOYOLA U IN NEW ORLEANS	3
MARYVILLE COLL	1
METROPOLITAN ST COLL	109
MOUNT VERNON COLL	1
NORTHWEST MISSOURI ST U	6
NORWICH U	6
PITZER COLL	1
PORTLAND, U of	3
PURDUE U CALUMET CAMPUS	30
RIPON COLL	3
SEATTLE U	7
SIMPSON COLL	2
SOUTH CAROLINA SPARTANBURG, U of	3
SPRING HILL COLL	3
STANFORD U	30
TEMPLE U	31
TRINITY COLL	6
VOORHEES COLL	6
WALSH COLL	2
WELLESLEY COLL	5
WESLEY COLL	2
WEST VIRGINIA INST OF TECH	14
WESTERN MICHIGAN U	11
WILEY COLL	2
WILLIAM JEWELL COLL	7
WOODBURY U	4

Conservation and Regulation, Other

SOUTH DAKOTA ST U	2

Conservation and Regulation, General

HUMBOLDT ST U	23
MONTANA, U of	7
OHIO ST U MAIN CAMPUS	3
PRESCOTT COLL	1
RHODE ISLAND, U of	17
RUTGERS U NEW BRUNSWICK	26
UNITY COLL	15
WISCONSIN-STEVENS POINT, U of	43

Conservation

CALIFORNIA-DAVIS, U of	25
KENT ST U MAIN CAMPUS	5
LOUISIANA TECH U	7
NEW HAMPSHIRE, U of	26
NORTHERN MICHIGAN U	6
SOUTHEASTERN OKLAHOMA ST U	12
UPPER IOWA U	8
WISCONSIN-RIVER FALLS, U of	4

Construction Tech., Other

ANDREWS U	1
ARIZONA ST U	57
BOWLING GREEN ST U MAIN CAMPUS	23
CENTRAL CONNECTICUT ST U	15
EAST TEXAS ST U	8
FAIRLEIGH DICKINSON U	11
MEMPHIS ST U	10
NORTH TEXAS, U of	7
NORTHERN MICHIGAN U	2
OKLAHOMA ST U MAIN CAMPUS	14
ROGER WILLIAMS COLL	10
TEXAS A&M U	120
TUSKEGEE U	3
WENTWORTH INST OF TECH	71
WEST TEXAS ST U	1
WESTERN MICHIGAN U	13

Construction Trades (unspecified)

DISTRICT OF COLUMBIA, U of THE	17
DREXEL U	4
HAMPTON U	2
SIENA HEIGHTS COLL	1

Construction Trades, Other

DISTRICT OF COLUMBIA, U of THE	17

Consumer Education

ANDREWS U	2

Consumer Science

ALABAMA, U of	1
COLORADO ST U	10
DELAWARE, U of	50
HOWARD U	13
INDIANA U PENNSYLVANIA	13
KENTUCKY, U of	14
LOUISIANA TECH U	5
MURRAY ST U	1
NORFOLK ST U	10
RHODE ISLAND, U of	54
SEATTLE PACIFIC U	1
SOUTH DAKOTA ST U	1
SOUTHWEST TEXAS ST U	18
TEXAS WOMAN'S U	3
WISCONSIN-MADISON, U of	38

Consumer, Personal and Misc. Services (unspecified)

CENTRAL OKLAHOMA, U of	21
INDIANAPOLIS, U of	1
MINNESOTA TWIN CITIES, U of	41
POINT PARK COLL	2
SIENA HEIGHTS COLL	1
WAYNE ST COLL	3
WAYNE ST U	9
XAVIER U	1

Contract Management and Procurement/Purchasing

ALABAMA IN HUNTSVILLE, U of	16
ARIZONA ST U	164
AVILA COLL	3
BOWLING GREEN ST U MAIN CAMPUS	21
DISTRICT OF COLUMBIA, U of THE	3
GEORGE WASHINGTON U	5
GEORGIA COLL	48
MIAMI U OXFORD CAMPUS	8
NORTH GEORGIA COLL	31
NORTHERN ARIZONA U	92
ORAL ROBERTS U	30
POST COLL	28
QUINNIPIAC COLL	56
SAINT JOSEPH'S U	2
SAINT MARY'S COLL OF CALIFORNIA	6
WEST CHESTER U PENNSYLVANIA	76

Correctional Administration

LEWIS U	55
NEW MEXICO MAIN CAMPUS, U of	64
NEW MEXICO ST U MAIN CAMPUS	49
PITTSBURGH MAIN CAMPUS, U of	45
SAINT LOUIS U MAIN CAMPUS	9
TROY ST U-MAIN CAMPUS	6
WASHINGTON ST U	79

Corrections

AUBURN U MAIN CAMPUS	9
CALIFORNIA LUTHERAN U	11
CHICAGO ST U	23
DAYTON, U of	2
EASTERN KENTUCKY U	39
HARDIN-SIMMONS U	3
INDIANAPOLIS, U of	1
JACKSONVILLE ST U	13
KENT ST U MAIN CAMPUS	1
LAKE SUPERIOR ST U	5
LANGSTON U	31
LEWIS-CLARK ST COLL	1
MANKATO ST U	36
NORTHERN MICHIGAN U	17
PAN AMERICAN U	18
SCHOOL OF THE OZARKS	17
SOUTHEAST MISSOURI ST U	20
SOUTHWEST TEXAS ST U	47
STEPHEN F AUSTIN ST U	18
TENNESSEE ST U	40
WAYNE ST COLL	7
WEBER ST COLL	11
WESTERN MICHIGAN U	3
YORK COLL PENNSYLVANIA	8
YOUNGSTOWN ST U	1

Cosmetology

SIENA HEIGHTS COLL	1

Counseling Psychology

BURLINGTON COLL	2
CHRISTIAN HERITAGE COLL	15
COKER COLL	8
GENEVA COLL	2
GODDARD COLL	2
GRACE COLL	8
KANSAS WESLEYAN U	1
LYNDON ST COLL	14
MOUNT SENARIO COLL	3
NORTH TEXAS, U of	31
OAKWOOD COLL	2
OUR LADY OF HOLY CROSS COLL	14
PRESCOTT COLL	9
SAMFORD U	5
SOUTHERN CALIFORNIA COLL	9
SOUTHERN MISSISSIPPI, U of	1
TOCCOA FALLS COLL	16
WAYNE ST COLL	22

Court Reporting

CENTRAL MICHIGAN U	7
HUSSON COLL	7
MISSISSIPPI MAIN CAMPUS, U of	8
TENNESSEE ST U	28
WESTMAR COLL	2

Crafts, General

ILLINOIS URBANA CAMPUS, U of	5
INDIANA U BLOOMINGTON	5
KENT ST U MAIN CAMPUS	12
KUTZTOWN U PENNSYLVANIA	5
LOYOLA MARYMOUNT U	16
VIRGINIA COMMONWEALTH U	17
WISCONSIN-STEVENS POINT, U of	41

Crafts, Other

CALIFORNIA COLL OF ARTS AND CRAFTS	1
NORTH GEORGIA COLL	1
NORTHERN MICHIGAN U	1

Creative Writing

AGNES SCOTT COLL	4
ANTIOCH COLL	2
ARIZONA, U of	46

ASHLAND U	1
AURORA U	3
BELOIT COLL	18
BETHEL COLL	4
BOWLING GREEN ST U MAIN CAMPUS	9
BROWN U	1
BRYN MAWR COLL	1
CAPITAL U	8
CARNEGIE MELLON U	55
COLL OF SAINT CATHERINE-SAINT CATHERINE CAMPUS	12
COLUMBIA U IN THE CITY OF NEW YORK	21
CONCORDIA COLL AT MOORHEAD	15
CUNY BROOKLYN COLL	1
DENISON U	20
DENVER, U of	4
EASTERN COLL	3
ECKERD COLL	11
EMERSON COLL	42
GODDARD COLL	7
HAMILTON COLL	14
HOUGHTON COLL	6
JOHNS HOPKINS U	31
JOHNSON ST COLL	6
KNOX COLL	12
LAKELAND COLL	6
LINFIELD COLL	1
LONG ISLAND U SOUTHHAMPTON COLL	8
LORAS COLL	7
MACALESTER COLL	1
MARLBORO COLL	2
MIAMI U OXFORD CAMPUS	32
MIAMI, U of	1
MICHIGAN ANN ARBOR, U of	10
NEBRASKA AT OMAHA, U of	4
NEW MEXICO MAIN CAMPUS, U of	12
NORTH CAROLINA ST U AT RALEIGH	46
OBERLIN COLL	10
PARK COLL	6
PITTSBURGH BRADFORD CAMPUS, U of	2
PITTSBURGH MAIN CAMPUS, U of	92
PRESCOTT COLL	1
REGIS COLL	2
ROGER WILLIAMS COLL	5
SAINT LEO COLL	7
SAINT MARY'S COLL	9
SEATTLE PACIFIC U	1
SOUTHERN METHODIST U	4
SOUTHWEST MISSOURI ST U	17
SWEET BRIAR COLL	6
TAMPA, U of	4
TEXAS AT EL PASO, U of	6
WESTERN WASHINGTON U	25
WHEELING COLL	4

Criminal Justice Administration

ALVERNIA COLL	7
ANDERSON U	6
APPALACHIAN ST U	101
ARIZONA, U of	14
ASHLAND U	37
AUBURN U AT MONTGOMERY	37
AVILA COLL	1
BALDWIN-WALLACE COLL	18
BAPTIST COLL AT CHARLESTON	10
BENEDICT COLL	20
BOISE ST U	28
BRADLEY U	15
BRYANT COLL OF BUSINESS ADMINISTRATION	2
CALIFORNIA ST COLL-BAKERFIELD	12
CALIFORNIA ST U FULLERTON	121
CALIFORNIA ST U LONG BEACH	162
CALIFORNIA ST U LOS ANGELES	65
CALIFORNIA ST U SAN BERNARDINO	17
CALIFORNIA ST U-HAYWARD	57
CALIFORNIA ST U-SACRAMENTO	220
CALIFORNIA ST U-STANISLAUS	12
CAMPBELL U INCORPORATED	11
CARTHAGE COLL	13
CENTRAL MISSOURI ST U	109
CINCINNATI MAIN CAMPUS, U of	52
CLARK U	3
COLUMBIA COLL	35
CULVER-STOCKTON COLL	6
DISTRICT OF COLUMBIA, U of THE	18
DRURY COLL	6
EAST CAROLINA U	54
EAST TENNESSEE ST U	54
ELIZABETH CITY ST U	34
FAYETTEVILLE ST U	31
GEORGIA COLL	16
GOLDEN GATE U	4
GRAND VALLEY ST U	48
HOWARD U	14
LINCOLN U	14
LOUISVILLE, U of	49
MACMURRAY COLL	4
MANSFIELD U PENNSYLVANIA	52
MARIAN COLL OF FOND DU LAC	1
MASS. AT LOWELL, U of	106
MEMPHIS ST U	40
METROPOLITAN ST COLL	138
MIDDLE TENNESSEE ST U	51
MISSISSIPPI COLL	11
MISSISSIPPI MAIN CAMPUS, U of	22
MISSOURI SOUTHERN ST COLL	36
MORAVIAN COLL	20
MOUNT MERCY COLL	21
NATIONAL U	51
NEW HAVEN, U of	42
NORTH ALABAMA, U of	11
NORTH CAROLINA AT CHARLOTTE, U of	128
NORTH CAROLINA CENTRAL U	52
NORTH CAROLINA CHAPEL HILL, U of	46
NORTH CAROLINA ST U AT RALEIGH	49
NORTH CAROLINA WESLEYAN COLL	31
NORTH CAROLINA WILMINGTON, U of	25
NORTHERN ARIZONA U	58
NORWICH U	39
PARK COLL	48
PFEIFFER COLL	16
PITTSBURGH MAIN CAMPUS, U of	8
ROGER WILLIAMS COLL	88
RUTGERS U NEW BRUNSWICK	71
SAINT MARY PLAINS COLL	10
SALEM ST COLL	61
SAMFORD U	3
SAN DIEGO ST U	160
SAN JOSE ST U	103
SHIPPENSBURG U PENNSYLVANIA	75
SONOMA ST U	17
SOUTH ALABAMA, U of	41
SOUTH CAROLINA SPARTANBURG, U of	17
SOUTH CAROLINA ST COLL	38
SOUTH CAROLINA—COLUMBIA, U of	102
SOUTHERN ILLINOIS U-CARBONDALE	166
SOUTHERN VERMONT COLL	13
STONEHILL COLL	41
TENNESSEE-CHATTANOOGA, U of	41
TENNESSEE-MARTIN, U of	45
TEXAS SOUTHERN U	26
TIFFIN U	14
TRENTON ST COLL	75
VIRGINIA COMMONWEALTH U	84
VOORHEES COLL	16
WASHBURN U TOPEKA	31
WEST TEXAS ST U	19
WESTERN CAROLINA U	41
WESTERN ILLINOIS U	239
WILLIAM PATERSON COLL OF NEW JERSEY	4
WILMINGTON COLL	13
WYOMING, U of	40

Criminal Justice Studies

Degrees in this subject were reported by 203 institutions. Consult more specific headings.

Criminal Justice Technology

ARMSTRONG ST COLL	24
KENTUCKY WESLEYAN COLL	13
PENNSYLVANIA ST U MAIN CAMPUS	242
TEMPLE U	5

Criminal Justice, Other

ABILENE CHRISTIAN U	1
ALABAMA AT BIRMINGHAM, U of	55
ALASKA ANCHORAGE, U of	10
ALASKA FAIRBANKS, U of	19
AUBURN U MAIN CAMPUS	1
BEMIDJI ST U	39
BETHUNE COOKMAN COLL	32
CALVIN COLL	13
CEDARVILLE COLL	6
DALLAS BAPTIST U	20
DAVIS AND ELKINS COLL	1

ELIZABETHTOWN COLL 2
FLORIDA MEMORIAL COLL 21
FRANCISCAN U STEUBENVILLE 1
GUSTAVUS ADOLPHUS COLL 7
IOWA WESLEYAN COLL 6
JERSEY CITY ST COLL 57
LAKE SUPERIOR ST U 10
LYCOMING COLL 20
MIDWESTERN ST U 25
MISSOURI-KANSAS CITY, U of 16
MISSOURI-SAINT LOUIS, U of 68
NORTH TEXAS, U of 73
NORTHEASTERN U 2
SAINT MARTIN'S COLL 19
SAVANNAH ST COLL 14
TRINITY COLL 2
TROY ST U MONTGOMERY 1
TROY ST U-MAIN CAMPUS 1
WASHINGTON, U of 32
WESTERN MICHIGAN U 102
WILMINGTON COLL 5

Criminology

ARKANSAS ST U MAIN CAMPUS 16
AUBURN U MAIN CAMPUS 18
BRIDGEWATER ST COLL 16
CALIFORNIA ST U FRESNO 81
CAMERON U 25
CENTRAL MICHIGAN U 25
CENTRAL OKLAHOMA, U of 1
COLL OF SAINT THOMAS 29
CUNY JOHN JAY COLL CRIMINAL JUSTICE 3
DELAWARE, U of 151
DRURY COLL 7
EAST TEXAS ST U 5
EASTERN MICHIGAN U 74
GARDNER-WEBB COLL 13
GRACE COLL 4
ILLINOIS AT CHICAGO, U of 1
INDIANA ST U 95
INDIANA U PENNSYLVANIA 154
MARYLAND COLL PARK CAMPUS, U of 37
MARYWOOD COLL 1
MINNESOTA DULUTH, U of 34
MINNESOTA TWIN CITIES, U of 62
NORTHERN IOWA, U of 35
OHIO ST U MAIN CAMPUS 84
OHIO U MAIN CAMPUS 20
OLD DOMINION U 56
PONTIFICAL CATHOLIC U PUERTO RICO—PONCE CA 23
SAINT AUGUSTINE'S COLL 30
SAINT EDWARD'S U 20
SAINT JOSEPH'S U 17
SAINT LEO COLL 161
SAM HOUSTON ST U 146
SOUTHERN MAINE, U of 25
SOUTHWESTERN COLL 1
STOCKTON ST COLL 73
SUNY COLL AT BUFFALO 4
TAMPA, U of 22

Crop Production

FLORIDA SOUTHERN COLL 2

Curriculum and Instruction

KENT ST U MAIN CAMPUS 1
OREGON, U of 5
REDLANDS, U of 12
TENNESSEE TECH U 1
TEXAS A&M U 563

Cytotechnology

ALABAMA AT BIRMINGHAM, U of 1
CONNECTICUT, U of 1
INDIANA U-PURDUE U AT INDIANAPOLIS 5
JUNIATA COLL 1
LOMA LINDA U 2
LOUISVILLE, U of 2
MARSHALL U 2
MOUNT SAINT CLARE COLL 1
NORTH DAKOTA MAIN CAMPUS, U of 6
WINONA ST U 1

Dairy

ARKANSAS-FAYETTEVILLE, U of 1
CALIFORNIA POLYTECHNIC ST U-SAN LUIS OBISPO 9
DELAWARE VALLEY COLL OF SCI AND AGRI 7
FLORIDA, U of 4
GEORGIA, U of 3
IOWA ST U 16
LOUISIANA ST U & AGRI & MECH & HEBERT LAWS CTR 5
MISSISSIPPI ST U 6
OHIO ST U MAIN CAMPUS 13
PENNSYLVANIA ST U MAIN CAMPUS 5
SOUTH DAKOTA ST U 15
TEXAS A&M U 7
UTAH ST U 3
VIRGINIA POLYTECHNIC INST AND ST U 18
WISCONSIN-MADISON, U of 15

Dance Therapy

THE PACIFIC, U of 2

Dance

Degrees in this subject were reported by 127 institutions. Consult more specific headings.

Data Processing

ARKANSAS ST U MAIN CAMPUS 36
ARKANSAS-FAYETTEVILLE, U of 27
CARSON-NEWMAN COLL 5
EASTERN KENTUCKY U 22
FLORIDA AGRI AND MECH U 6
GEORGE WASHINGTON U 12
GEORGIA COLL 30
INDIANA U AT KOKOMO 3
INDIANA U NORTHWEST 9
INDIANA U-PURDUE U AT FORT WAYNE 3
IONA COLL 16
KENNESAW ST COLL 7
MOREHEAD ST U 6
NEW HAVEN, U of 17
SAGINAW VALLEY ST U 1
SAINT MARY PLAINS COLL 4
SAINT MARY'S U 2
STEPHEN F AUSTIN ST U 9
STRAYER COLL 29
TEXAS A & I U 10
THOMAS MORE COLL 9
WASHINGTON U 46
WESTBROOK COLL 3
WILLIAM CAREY COLL 6

Demography

BETHEL COLL 2
CONCORDIA COLL AT MOORHEAD 8

Dental Hygiene

ALABAMA AT BIRMINGHAM, U of 7
ARMSTRONG ST COLL 2
BRIDGEPORT, U of 9
DETROIT, U of 16
EASTERN WASHINGTON U 15
FAIRLEIGH DICKINSON U 8
HAWAII AT MANOA, U of 11
IDAHO ST U 25
INDIANA U-PURDUE U AT FORT WAYNE 1
IOWA, U of 14
LOMA LINDA U 42
LOUISIANA ST U MEDICAL CENTER 16
LOYOLA U CHICAGO 12
MARQUETTE U 7
MARS HILL COLL 3
MEDICAL COLL OF GEORGIA 11
MICHIGAN ANN ARBOR, U of 14
MIDWESTERN ST U 12
MISSOURI-KANSAS CITY, U of 24
NEW MEXICO MAIN CAMPUS, U of 7
NEW YORK U 2
NORTH CAROLINA CHAPEL HILL, U of 19
NORTHEAST LOUISIANA U 16
NORTHEASTERN U 1
NORTHERN ARIZONA U 26
NORTHWESTERN U 11

OHIO ST U MAIN CAMPUS	34
OLD DOMINION U	17
OREGON HEALTH SCI U	21
OREGON INST OF TECH	5
RHODE ISLAND, U of	12
SOUTH DAKOTA, U of	2
TENNESSEE ST U	2
TEXAS WOMAN'S U	18
VIRGINIA COMMONWEALTH U	9
WASHINGTON, U of	5
WEST LIBERTY ST COLL	25
WEST VIRGINIA U	19
WESTBROOK COLL	4
WESTERN KENTUCKY U	2
WYOMING, U of	2

Dental Laboratory Technology

LOUISIANA ST U MEDICAL CENTER	1

Dentistry, General

CASE WESTERN RESERVE U	7
ILLINOIS AT CHICAGO, U of	53
MINNESOTA TWIN CITIES, U of	13
WILKES U	2

Dentistry, Other

BAYLOR U	5
NEBRASKA-LINCOLN, U of	1

Design, Other

AKRON, MAIN CAMPUS, U of	50
BOSTON U	2
CARTHAGE COLL	8
CENTER FOR CREATIVE STUDIES COL OF ART AND DESIGN	12
DAYTON, U of	25
FASHION INST OF TECH	19
FINDLAY, U of	1
GRACELAND COLL	1
KENDALL COLL OF ART AND DESIGN	19
MARYLAND COLL PARK CAMPUS, U of	62
MASSACHUSETTS AT DARTMOUTH (WAS SE U OF MA, U of	58
MOORE COLL OF ART	17
NORTHERN MICHIGAN U	1
OKLAHOMA CHRISTIAN COLL	11
ORAL ROBERTS U	14
RINGLING SCHOOL OF ART AND DESIGN	7
SAN FRANCISCO, U of	1
SOUTHWESTERN OKLAHOMA ST U	7
WEST LIBERTY ST COLL	6

Developmental Psychology

CALIFORNIA POLYTECHNIC ST U-SAN LUIS OBISPO	89
CALIFORNIA ST U LONG BEACH	14
CALIFORNIA ST U SAN BERNARDINO	15
CALIFORNIA ST U-HAYWARD	75
EASTERN WASHINGTON U	14
ECKERD COLL	1
EMMANUEL COLL	10
KANSAS MAIN CAMPUS, U of	69
PINE MANOR COLL	21
PRESCOTT COLL	1
SAINT MARY'S COLL OF CALIFORNIA	9
UTICA COLL OF SYRACUSE	15
VANDERBILT U	108
WISCONSIN-GREEN BAY, U of	97

Diagnostic and Treatment Services, Other

ALABAMA, U of	1
LIVINGSTON U	1
LONG ISLAND U C W POST CAMPUS	7
MANHATTAN COLL	12
MEDICAL COLL OF GEORGIA	2
MIAMI, U of	1
NORTH CAROLINA CHAPEL HILL, U of	7
SAMFORD U	2
SIENA HEIGHTS COLL	1
SOUTHWEST TEXAS ST U	8
WEST CHESTER U PENNSYLVANIA	12

Dietetics/Human Nutritional Services

ALABAMA, U of	17
ANDREWS U	3
AUBURN U MAIN CAMPUS	7
BALL ST U	12
BAYLOR U	9
BEREA COLL	3
BOWLING GREEN ST U MAIN CAMPUS	18
BRIGHAM YOUNG U	1
CALIFORNIA-BERKELEY, U of	15
CENTRAL MICHIGAN U	15
CENTRAL MISSOURI ST U	4
CHICAGO ST U	10
CINCINNATI MAIN CAMPUS, U of	15
COLL OF MOUNT SAINT JOSEPH	1
COLL OF NOTRE DAME	3
COLL OF SAINT BENEDICT	18
COLL OF SAINT CATHERINE-SAINT CATHERINE CAMPUS	3
COLL OF SAINT SCHOLASTICA	5
CONNECTICUT, U of	15
DAVID LIPSCOMB U	11
DAYTON, U of	5
DELAWARE, U of	18
DREXEL U	1
EASTERN MICHIGAN U	12
FLORIDA ST U	31
FLORIDA, U of	10
FONTBONNE COLL	5
GANNON U	1
GEORGIA ST U	17
HARDING U MAIN CAMPUS	5
HOWARD U	2
IDAHO ST U	2
ILLINOIS AT CHICAGO, U of	18
IMMACULATA COLL	9
INDIANA U PENNSYLVANIA	14
IOWA ST U	22
JACKSONVILLE ST U	3
LAMAR U	9
LANGSTON U	4
LOUISIANA ST U & AGRI & MECH & HEBERT LAWS CTR	13
LOUISIANA TECH U	12
MADONNA COLL	4
MANKATO ST U	7
MARIAN COLL	3
MARSHALL U	4
MARYLAND COLL PARK CAMPUS, U of	18
MARYWOOD COLL	15
MERCYHURST COLL	3
MESSIAH COLL	9
MIAMI U OXFORD CAMPUS	10
MICHIGAN ST U	45
MINNESOTA TWIN CITIES, U of	5
MOUNT MARY COLL	9
NEW HAVEN, U of	1
NICHOLLS ST U	3
NORTH DAKOTA MAIN CAMPUS, U of	7
NORTHERN COLORADO, U of	10
NORTHERN IOWA, U of	3
NORTHERN MICHIGAN U	1
NOTRE DAME COLL	6
OKLAHOMA NORMAN CAMPUS, U of	3
OREGON ST U	20
OUACHITA BAPTIST U	3
PAN AMERICAN U	4
PENNSYLVANIA ST U MAIN CAMPUS	37
RIVIER COLL	2
SAINT VINCENT COLL	2
SETON HILL COLL	5
SOUTHEAST MISSOURI ST U	7
SOUTHERN MISSISSIPPI, U of	12
SOUTHWEST MISSOURI ST U	10
SOUTHWESTERN LOUISIANA, U of	15
SPALDING U	6
SUNY COLL AT BUFFALO	18
SUNY COLL AT ONEONTA	21
TEIKYO MARYCREST COLL	1
TEXAS AT AUSTIN, U of	13
TEXAS CHRISTIAN U	10
TEXAS SOUTHERN U	3
TEXAS TECH U	22
TEXAS WOMAN'S U	12
TUSKEGEE U	2
VALPARAISO U	2
VERMONT, U of	13
VITERBO COLL	6
WASHINGTON, U of	1
WAYNE ST U	6
WEST VIRGINIA WESLEYAN COLL	2
WESTERN MICHIGAN U	6

WESTERN WASHINGTON U	10
WISCONSIN-MADISON, U of	16
WISCONSIN-STEVENS POINT, U of	18
WISCONSIN-STOUT, U of	21

Drafting and Design Technology

CENTRAL FLORIDA, U of	21
CENTRAL MICHIGAN U	19
CENTRAL MISSOURI ST U	16
EAST TEXAS ST U	3
GRAMBLING ST U	6
HOUSTON-U PARK, U of	10
LOUISIANA ST U & AGRI & MECH & HEBERT LAWS CTR	6
NEBRASKA-LINCOLN, U of	7
NEW HAMPSHIRE KEENE ST COLL, U of	10
NORFOLK ST U	4
NORTHERN MONTANA COLL	13
PRAIRIE VIEW A & M U	5
SIENA HEIGHTS COLL	1
SOUTHEASTERN OKLAHOMA ST U	3
SOUTHWEST MISSOURI ST U	18
TEXAS SOUTHERN U	5
WESTERN MICHIGAN U	34

Dramatic Arts

Degrees in this subject were reported by 528 institutions. Consult more specific headings.

Drawing

ALBANY ST COLL	2
AUGSBURG COLL	6
BOWLING GREEN ST U MAIN CAMPUS	4
CALIFORNIA COLL OF ARTS AND CRAFTS	4
CHARLESTON, U of	1
CLEVELAND INST OF ART	2
COLUMBUS COLL	3
CONCORD COLL	2
DALLAS BAPTIST U	1
DRAKE U	1
EVANSVILLE, U of	6
FONTBONNE COLL	1
GEORGIA SOUTHERN COLL	17
GEORGIA ST U	66
HARTFORD, U of	1
LAKELAND COLL	2
MARYLAND INST COLL OF ART	9
MICHIGAN ANN ARBOR, U of	16
MONTANA, U of	19
NORTHEAST MISSOURI ST U	12
OAKLAND CITY COLL	1
PROVIDENCE COLL	2
SEATTLE U	3
SETON HILL COLL	1

Driver and Safety Education

EAST CAROLINA U	3
MONTEVALLO, U of	1
NORTHEASTERN ST U	8
NORTHERN IOWA, U of	1
WISCONSIN-WHITEWATER, U of	24

Duplicating Machine Operation

DAVIS AND ELKINS COLL	2

Earth Science

ADELPHI U	2
ADRIAN COLL	2
AKRON, MAIN CAMPUS, U of	1
ARIZONA, U of	2
ARKANSAS-FAYETTEVILLE, U of	1
BAYLOR U	2
BLOOMSBURG U PENNSYLVANIA	3
BRIDGEWATER ST COLL	2
CALIFORNIA ST POLYTECHNIC U POMONA	4
CALIFORNIA ST U NORTHRIDGE	6
CALIFORNIA U PENNSYLVANIA	8
CALIFORNIA-BERKELEY, U of	1
CALIFORNIA-SANTA CRUZ, U of	14
CENTRAL CONNECTICUT ST U	2
CENTRAL MICHIGAN U	41
CENTRAL MISSOURI ST U	2
CLARION U PENNSYLVANIA	8
DARTMOUTH COLL	13
DEPAUW U	2
DRAKE U	1
EAST STROUDSBURG U PENNSYLVANIA	2
EAST TEXAS ST U	4
EASTERN MICHIGAN U	11
EDINBORO U PENNSYLVANIA	8
FRAMINGHAM ST COLL	2
GANNON U	1
INDIANA U BLOOMINGTON	1
INDIANA U PENNSYLVANIA	1
INDIANAPOLIS, U of	2
IOWA ST U	3
KEAN COLL OF NEW JERSEY	6
KENT ST U MAIN CAMPUS	3
KUTZTOWN U PENNSYLVANIA	1
LOCK HAVEN U PENNSYLVANIA	2
LONGWOOD COLL	10
MANKATO ST U	1
MANSFIELD U PENNSYLVANIA	1
MASSACHUSETTS BOSTON, U of	13
MASSACHUSETTS INST OF TECH	7
MICHIGAN ST U	1
MILLERSVILLE U PENNSYLVANIA	6
MINNESOTA DULUTH, U of	3
MINNESOTA TWIN CITIES, U of	6
MINOT ST U	2
MOREHEAD ST U	2
MURRAY ST U	1
NEW MEXICO HIGHLANDS U	1
NORTH CAROLINA AT CHARLOTTE, U of	20
NORTH DAKOTA ST U MAIN CAMPUS	8
NORTH TEXAS, U of	5
NORTHEASTERN ILLINOIS U	2
NORTHERN ARIZONA U	3
NORTHERN COLORADO, U of	13
NORTHERN MICHIGAN U	5
NORTHLAND COLL	3
NORTHWEST MISSOURI ST U	2
NOTRE DAME, U of	2
PACIFIC LUTHERAN U	6
PENNSYLVANIA ST U MAIN CAMPUS	30
RUTGERS U NEW BRUNSWICK	12
SAINT CLOUD ST U	7
SAM HOUSTON ST U	5
SHIPPENSBURG U PENNSYLVANIA	2
SLIPPERY ROCK U PENNSYLVANIA	1
SOUTH DAKOTA, U of	1
SOUTHEAST MISSOURI ST U	3
SOUTHERN CONNECTICUT ST U	5
SOUTHERN ILLINOIS U AT EDWARDSVILLE	6
STANFORD U	12
SUNY COLL AT BROCKPORT	15
SUNY COLL AT ONEONTA	1
TEXAS A&M U	2
TEXAS TECH U	1
WASHINGTON U	2
WEBER ST COLL	1
WEST CHESTER U PENNSYLVANIA	12
WEST GEORGIA COLL	2
WESTERN CONNECTICUT ST U	1
WESTERN MICHIGAN U	3
WILKES U	9
WISCONSIN OSHKOSH, U of	1
WISCONSIN-GREEN BAY, U of	1
WISCONSIN-MADISON, U of	5

East Asian Studies

BROWN U	16
BRYN MAWR COLL	2
BUCKNELL U	2
CALIFORNIA-DAVIS, U of	5
CALIFORNIA-LOS ANGELES, U of	12
CALIFORNIA-SAN DIEGO, U of	8
CENTRAL CONNECTICUT ST U	1
CHICAGO, U of	8
COLBY COLL	11
COLL OF SAINT THOMAS	1
COLUMBIA U IN THE CITY OF NEW YORK	24
CUNY QUEENS COLL	1
DENISON U	7
DICKINSON COLL	9
EARLHAM COLL	10
GEORGE WASHINGTON U	8
HAMLINE U	1
HARVARD U	21
INDIANA U BLOOMINGTON	22
LINFIELD COLL	1
MACALESTER COLL	3
MIDDLEBURY COLL	13
MINNESOTA TWIN CITIES, U of	5

NEW YORK U	15
NORTH CAROLINA CHAPEL HILL, U of	4
OAKLAND U	3
OBERLIN COLL	16
PENNSYLVANIA ST U MAIN CAMPUS	10
PENNSYLVANIA, U of	28
PRINCETON U	14
RADCLIFFE COLL	14
RICHMOND, U of	1
RUTGERS U NEW BRUNSWICK	4
SMITH COLL	13
STANFORD U	8
VALPARAISO U	1
VANDERBILT U	6
VASSAR COLL	10
VERMONT, U of	5
WASHINGTON AND LEE U	11
WASHINGTON, U of	47
WELLESLEY COLL	11
WESLEYAN U	19
WILLAMETTE U	4
WITTENBERG U	19

Eastern European Studies

COLORADO AT BOULDER, U of	14
EMORY U	3
WASHINGTON, U of	78

Ecology

ALFRED U	3
ARIZONA, U of	20
BOWDOIN COLL	13
BRADLEY U	2
CALIFORNIA POLYTECHNIC ST U-SAN LUIS OBISPO	23
CALIFORNIA-SAN DIEGO, U of	31
CALIFORNIA-SANTA BARBARA, U of	5
CENTRAL FLORIDA, U of	1
CONNECTICUT COLL	12
EAST STROUDSBURG U PENNSYLVANIA	17
EASTERN ILLINOIS U	23
EASTERN KENTUCKY U	2
FERRUM COLL	12
GEORGETOWN COLL	2
GODDARD COLL	2
HOOD COLL	3
IDAHO ST U	4
ILLINOIS URBANA CAMPUS, U of	28
IOWA ST U	11
JOHNSON ST COLL	18
JUNIATA COLL	3
KENT ST U MAIN CAMPUS	1
LYNCHBURG COLL	8
MAINE AT MACHIAS, U of	4
MANCHESTER COLL	3
MARIST COLL	3
MASSACHUSETTS AT AMHERST, U of	13
MCNEESE ST U	7
MICHIGAN ANN ARBOR, U of	1
MINNESOTA TWIN CITIES, U of	3
MOREHEAD ST U	13
NEW HAMPSHIRE KEENE ST COLL, U of	2
NORTHEAST MISSOURI ST U	1
NORTHERN MICHIGAN U	6
NORTHWEST MISSOURI ST U	5
NORTHWESTERN U	1
OKLAHOMA ST U MAIN CAMPUS	14
PRINCETON U	42
PRINCIPIA COLL	1
RUTGERS U NEW BRUNSWICK	118
SAINT JOHN'S U NEW YORK	2
SAINT MARY'S COLL OF MINNESOTA	8
SAINT NORBERT COLL	1
STOCKTON ST COLL	36
WASHINGTON ST U	13
WESLEY COLL	6
WESTERN MICHIGAN U	4
WILLIAM PATERSON COLL OF NEW JERSEY	2
WISCONSIN-MILWAUKEE, U of	9

Economics

Degrees in this subject were reported by 662 institutions. Consult more specific headings.

Education (unspecified)

Degrees in this subject were reported by 1092 institutions. Consult more specific headings.

Education Administration, General

AKRON, MAIN CAMPUS, U of	18
FLORIDA INST OF TECH	1
NORTHEAST LOUISIANA U	8

Education Administration, Other

ASHLAND U	1

Education of the Culturally Disadvantaged

AUGUSTANA COLL	7

Education of the Deaf and Hearing Impaired

ARKANSAS AT LITTLE ROCK, U of	3
BALL ST U	20
BARTON (FORMERLY ATLANTIC CHRISTIAN) COLL	6
BOSTON U	3
BOWLING GREEN ST U MAIN CAMPUS	6
CONVERSE COLL	7
EASTERN KENTUCKY U	3
EASTERN MICHIGAN U	5
FLAGLER COLL	13
FONTBONNE COLL	4
IDAHO ST U	2
INDIANA U PENNSYLVANIA	17
KENT ST U MAIN CAMPUS	3
LENOIR-RHYNE COLL	9
MACMURRAY COLL	10
MADONNA COLL	14
MINOT ST U	3
NORTH CAROLINA AT GREENSBORO, U of	9
SOUTHERN MISSISSIPPI, U of	4
SOUTHERN U AGRI & MECH COL AT BATON ROUGE	2
TALLADEGA COLL	4
TEXAS CHRISTIAN U	13
TEXAS TECH U	19
TEXAS WOMAN'S U	28
TRENTON ST COLL	10
TULSA, U of	3

Education of the Emotionally Handicapped

BRADLEY U	12
CENTRAL MICHIGAN U	33
CENTRAL OKLAHOMA, U of	31
DETROIT, U of	1
EASTERN MICHIGAN U	21
FONTBONNE COLL	2
MACMURRAY COLL	5
MAINE AT FARMINGTON, U of	11
MISSOURI-COLUMBIA, U of	3
NORTHEASTERN ST U	6
OHIO ST U MAIN CAMPUS	3
SOUTH FLORIDA, U of	43
SOUTHEAST MISSOURI ST U	1
WESTERN MICHIGAN U	12
WRIGHT ST U MAIN CAMPUS	1

Education of the Gifted and Talented

KENT ST U MAIN CAMPUS	1

Education of the Mentally Handicapped

ADAMS ST COLL	1
AUBURN U AT MONTGOMERY	2
BELMONT ABBEY COLL	5
BENNETT COLL	3
BOWLING GREEN ST U MAIN CAMPUS	35
BRADLEY U	6
CATAWBA COLL	2
CENTRAL MICHIGAN U	32
COLUMBUS COLL	6
EASTERN MENNONITE COLL	5
EASTERN MICHIGAN U	35
FLORIDA ST U	5
FLORIDA, U of	54
FONTBONNE COLL	2

GEORGIA ST U	5
GEORGIA, U of	27
GREENSBORO COLL	5
HOUSTON BAPTIST U	6
ILLINOIS URBANA CAMPUS, U of	3
KENT ST U MAIN CAMPUS	7
LIVINGSTON U	9
MAINE AT FARMINGTON, U of	7
MERCER U IN ATLANTA	2
MINOT ST U	14
NORFOLK ST U	13
NORTHEASTERN ST U	10
NORTHERN COLORADO, U of	2
NORTHERN IOWA, U of	4
NORTHERN MICHIGAN U	3
NORTHERN ST U	17
OHIO DOMINICAN COLL	5
OHIO ST U MAIN CAMPUS	12
RADFORD U	22
RHODE ISLAND COLL	28
SAINT LEO COLL	5
SILVER LAKE COLL	2
SOUTH FLORIDA, U of	16
SOUTHEAST MISSOURI ST U	3
SOUTHWEST MISSOURI ST U	7
SOUTHWESTERN OKLAHOMA ST U	6
WEST GEORGIA COLL	11
WESTERN MICHIGAN U	18
WISCONSIN-EAU CLAIRE, U of	57
WRIGHT ST U MAIN CAMPUS	7

Education of the Multiple Handicapped

BALL ST U	24
BOWLING GREEN ST U MAIN CAMPUS	4
CENTRAL OKLAHOMA, U of	1
KENT ST U MAIN CAMPUS	4
MISSOURI-COLUMBIA, U of	8
NEBRASKA-LINCOLN, U of	2
NORTHEASTERN ST U	14
SCI AND ARTS OF OKLAHOMA, U of	7
SYRACUSE U MAIN CAMPUS	2
TOLEDO, U of	3
WRIGHT ST U MAIN CAMPUS	1

Education of the Physically Handicapped

EASTERN MICHIGAN U	9
INDIANA U PENNSYLVANIA	7
WESTERN MICHIGAN U	3

Education of the Visually Handicapped

D'YOUVILLE COLL	5
EASTERN MICHIGAN U	3
FLORIDA ST U	5
NORTHERN ST U	1
WESTERN MICHIGAN U	6

Education, General

AKRON, MAIN CAMPUS, U of	4
ALABAMA AT BIRMINGHAM, U of	4
ALASKA FAIRBANKS, U of	69
AMERICAN INTERNATIONAL COLL	7
ANTIOCH COLL	2
BAYLOR U	28
BOSTON U	1
BROWN U	12
BUCKNELL U	5
BURLINGTON COLL	5
CABRINI COLL	2
CALIFORNIA U PENNSYLVANIA	25
CALIFORNIA-RIVERSIDE, U of	1
CAMERON U	20
CARDINAL STRITCH COLL	42
CATHOLIC U AMERICA	2
CHRISTIAN BROTHERS COLL	3
CLAFLIN COLL	6
COLGATE U	13
CONCORDIA COLL	2
CONCORDIA COLL	13
CORNELL U-NYS STATUTORY COLLS	18
CURRY COLL	8
DELAWARE, U of	9
EARLHAM COLL	5
ECKERD COLL	2
ELMHURST COLL	5
EMORY U	4
FAIRMONT ST COLL	129
FITCHBURG ST COLL	9
GODDARD COLL	7
GOUCHER COLL	15
GUSTAVUS ADOLPHUS COLL	48
HERITAGE COLL	34
HUNTINGTON COLL	1
INCARNATE WORD COLL	4
KENT ST U MAIN CAMPUS	3
LESLEY COLL	115
LEWIS U	20
LINDENWOOD COLL	18
LOYOLA U CHICAGO	33
MAINE, U of	160
MARYVILLE COLL—ST LOUIS	14
MASSACHUSETTS AT AMHERST, U of	214
MICHIGAN ANN ARBOR, U of	8
MIDWESTERN ST U	1
MISSOURI-COLUMBIA, U of	59
MONTANA, U of	1
NORTH ADAMS ST COLL	2
NORTH CAROLINA ST U AT RALEIGH	26
NORTHEASTERN ILLINOIS U	8
NORTHEASTERN U	4
OGLETHORPE U	5
OUR LADY OF HOLY CROSS COLL	34
PACIFIC, U of THE	15
PANHANDLE ST U	26
PITTSBURGH MAIN CAMPUS, U of	8
REDLANDS, U of	19
RIO GRANDE, U of	1
SAINT JOSEPH'S COLL	18
SAINT LOUIS U MAIN CAMPUS	37
SIMMONS COLL	7
SMITH COLL	16
SOUTHERN NAZARENE U	7
STEPHENS COLL	5
SUNY EMPIRE ST COLL	69
TABOR COLL	1
TOWSON ST U	49
VALPARAISO U	57
VANDERBILT U	4
VERMONT, U of	1
WASHINGTON ST U	110
WASHINGTON U	3
WASHINGTON, U of	1
WEBSTER U	32
WISCONSIN-MILWAUKEE, U of	163
WYOMING, U of	2

Education, Other

ARIZONA ST U	10
AUGUSTANA COLL	1
BARRY U	24
BAYAMON CENTRAL U	5
BETHUNE COOKMAN COLL	2
BIRMINGHAM SOUTHERN COLL	4
BOSTON COLL	67
BOWLING GREEN ST U MAIN CAMPUS	10
CARROLL COLL	1
CASTLETON ST COLL	3
CENTRAL MISSOURI ST U	40
CENTRAL ST U	2
CHAMINADE U HONOLULU	2
CULVER-STOCKTON COLL	1
CUNY LEHMAN COLL	10
D'YOUVILLE COLL	5
DEFIANCE COLL	7
DELAWARE ST COLL	8
DELTA ST U	1
DOANE COLL	2
EASTERN ILLINOIS U	31
EASTERN NEW MEXICO U MAIN CAMPUS	5
FINDLAY, U of	4
FLORIDA INST OF TECH	2
FLORIDA SOUTHERN COLL	27
GANNON U	2
GEORGE WASHINGTON U	14
HAMLINE U	2
HAMPTON U	1
HANNIBAL-LAGRANGE COLL	6
HARRIS-STOWE ST COLL	7
HARTFORD, U of	4
HOFSTRA U	3
HOWARD U	25
IDAHO ST U	19
IDAHO, U of	4
KENT ST U MAIN CAMPUS	9
LA SALLE U	44
LAKE ERIE COLL	6
LEWIS AND CLARK COLL	3
LINCOLN U	9
LONG ISLAND U C W POST CAMPUS	2

LOUISIANA COLL	2
LOUISIANA TECH U	6
MANKATO ST U	1
MCMURRY COLL	1
MEDAILLE COLL	5
MEMPHIS ST U	9
MONTANA ST U	86
MOORHEAD ST U	8
MOREHOUSE COLL	1
NEW ENGLAND COLL	1
NEW HAMPSHIRE KEENE ST COLL, U of	7
NEW HAMPSHIRE, U of	1
NORTHEAST LOUISIANA U	3
NORTHLAND COLL	6
NOTRE DAME COLL	2
NOVA U	1
OHIO NORTHERN U	2
OHIO ST U MAIN CAMPUS	44
PACE U-NEW YORK	2
PACIFIC LUTHERAN U	5
PENNSYLVANIA ST U MAIN CAMPUS	90
PHILLIPS U	1
PINE MANOR COLL	4
PONTIFICAL CATHOLIC U PUERTO RICO—PONCE CA	218
PRESCOTT COLL	6
SOUTHERN CALIFORNIA COLL	3
SOUTHWEST ST U	2
SPELMAN COLL	12
STEPHENS COLL	3
SUNY COLL AT ONEONTA	3
SYRACUSE U MAIN CAMPUS	8
TAYLOR U	3
TEXAS AT AUSTIN, U of	44
TOLEDO, U of	1
TREVECCA NAZARENE COLL	3
TRINITY U	1
TULSA, U of	5
VANDERBILT U	2
WAYNE ST U	3
WEBER ST COLL	10
WEST VIRGINIA U	83
WESTMAR COLL	1
WILLIAM JEWELL COLL	8
WISCONSIN OSHKOSH, U of	35
WISCONSIN-MILWAUKEE, U of	14
XAVIER U	12
YORK COLL PENNSYLVANIA	3

Educational Media

BAYAMON CENTRAL U	19
BOWLING GREEN ST U MAIN CAMPUS	3
CENTRAL FLORIDA, U of	2
INDIANA U BLOOMINGTON	1
MIAMI U OXFORD CAMPUS	1
OHIO U MAIN CAMPUS	1
TOLEDO, U of	1
TOWSON ST U	1
WESTERN ILLINOIS U	6

Educational Statistics and Research

BUCKNELL U	3

Electrical Technology

ALABAMA, U of	19
BLUEFIELD ST COLL	15
BRADLEY U	15
CINCINNATI MAIN CAMPUS, U of	28
FAIRLEIGH DICKINSON U	40
GANNON U	12
GEORGIA SOUTHERN COLL	15
HOUSTON-U PARK, U of	6
LAKE SUPERIOR ST U	26
LETOURNEAU COLL	9
LOUISIANA TECH U	25
MAINE, U of	27
MCNEESE ST U	24
MILWAUKEE SCHOOL OF ENGINEERING	70
MURRAY ST U	11
NEW HAMPSHIRE, U of	11
NEW MEXICO HIGHLANDS U	1
NICHOLLS ST U	2
NORTHEASTERN U	93
NORTHERN ARIZONA U	17
NORTHERN MICHIGAN U	1
ROGER WILLIAMS COLL	14
SIENA HEIGHTS COLL	3
SOUTH CAROLINA ST COLL	25
SUNY AT BINGHAMTON	51
WESTERN KENTUCKY U	17
YOUNGSTOWN ST U	40

Electrical and Electronic Technologies, Other

ALABAMA AGRI AND MECH U	12
CAPITOL COLL	10
CENTRAL MISSOURI ST U	38
COLORADO TECHNICAL COLL	5
EMBRY-RIDDLE AERONAUTICAL U	13
MONTANA ST U	22
PRAIRIE VIEW A & M U	14
SAGINAW VALLEY ST U	2
SIENA HEIGHTS COLL	1
SOUTHEAST MISSOURI ST U	3
TENNESSEE-MARTIN, U of	11
TEXAS SOUTHERN U	20
TEXAS TECH U	26
WAYNE ST U	49

Electrical and Electronics Equipment Repair, General

BRIGHAM YOUNG U HAWAII CAMPUS	2

Electrical and Electronics Equipment Repair, Other

SOUTHERN ILLINOIS U CARBONDALE	157

Electrical, Electronics, and Communications Engineering

Degrees in this subject were reported by 264 institutions. Consult more specific headings.

Electroencephalograph Technology

SIENA HEIGHTS COLL	1

Electromechanical Instrumentation and Maint. Tech., Other

DISTRICT OF COLUMBIA, U of THE	10

Electromechanical Technology

HOUSTON-U PARK, U of	8
INDIANA ST U	13
SOUTHWEST MISSOURI ST U	5
SUNY AT BINGHAMTON	11
SUNY COLL AT BUFFALO	58
TEXAS SOUTHERN U	1
WAYNE ST U	1
WESTERN KENTUCKY U	2

Electronic Technology

AKRON, MAIN CAMPUS, U of	53
ARIZONA ST U	36
ARKANSAS AT LITTLE ROCK, U of	11
BOWLING GREEN ST U MAIN CAMPUS	10
CALIFORNIA U PENNSYLVANIA	12
CENTRAL FLORIDA, U of	70
CENTRAL MICHIGAN U	9
CENTRAL WASHINGTON U	23
CLEVELAND ST U	39
COGSWELL POLYTECHNICAL COLL	12
CULVER-STOCKTON COLL	1
DAYTON, U of	30
FERRIS ST U	20
FLORIDA AGRI AND MECH U	8
FORT VALLEY ST COLL	5
GALLAUDET U	2
GRAMBLING ST U	10
HARTFORD, U of	46
HOUSTON-U PARK, U of	25
INDIANA ST U	45
INDIANA U-PURDUE U AT FORT WAYNE	44
INDIANA U-PURDUE U AT INDIANAPOLIS	35
MANKATO ST U	20
MASS. AT LOWELL, U of	31
MEMPHIS ST U	30
METROPOLITAN ST COLL	43
MISSOURI WESTERN ST COLL	4
NEBRASKA-LINCOLN, U of	13
NEW HAMPSHIRE KEENE ST COLL, U of	5

NORFOLK ST U	28
NORTHERN MICHIGAN U	14
NORTHERN MONTANA COLL	8
NORTHWESTERN ST U LOUISIANA	4
OKLAHOMA ST U MAIN CAMPUS	49
OREGON INST OF TECH	44
PACIFIC UNION COLL	1
PITTSBURG ST U	17
PURDUE U CALUMET CAMPUS	40
SAVANNAH ST COLL	6
SIENA HEIGHTS COLL	33
SOUTH DAKOTA ST U	30
SOUTHEASTERN OKLAHOMA ST U	11
SOUTHERN COLORADO, U of	28
SOUTHERN MISSISSIPPI, U of	20
SOUTHERN U AGRI & MECH COL AT BATON ROUGE	20
SOUTHWEST MISSOURI ST U	7
SOUTHWEST ST U	29
SPRING GARDEN COLL	9
TOLEDO, U of	33
TRENTON ST COLL	23
US INTERNATIONAL U	2
WALLA WALLA COLL	1
WASHINGTON U	9
WEBER ST COLL	109
WENTWORTH INST OF TECH	118
WESTERN WASHINGTON U	29

Elementary Education

Degrees in this subject were reported by 883 institutions. Consult more specific headings.

Emergency Medical Technology-Ambulance

MARYLAND BALTIMORE COUNTY CAMPUS, U of	30

Emergency Medical Technology-Paramedic

CENTRAL WASHINGTON U	5
EASTERN MICHIGAN U	8
MADONNA COLL	2

Energy Conservation and Use Technology

CALIFORNIA U PENNSYLVANIA	3
EASTERN MICHIGAN U	5
FERRIS ST U	17
HOUSTON-U PARK, U of	1
MOORHEAD ST U	6
WEST LIBERTY ST COLL	1

Engineering (unspecified)

Degrees in this subject were reported by 370 institutions. Consult more specific headings.

Engineering Mechanics

CINCINNATI MAIN CAMPUS, U of	6
COLUMBIA U IN THE CITY OF NEW YORK	3
GEORGIA INST OF TECH MAIN CAMPUS	11
ILLINOIS URBANA CAMPUS, U of	13
JOHNS HOPKINS U	3
MICHIGAN ST U	1
MISSOURI-ROLLA, U of	2
NICHOLS COLL	6
US AIR FORCE ACAD	42
VIRGINIA POLYTECHNIC INST AND ST U	14
WISCONSIN-MADISON, U of	39

Engineering Physics

ABILENE CHRISTIAN U	2
ARIZONA, U of	10
AURORA U	2
BRADLEY U	1
CALIFORNIA INST OF TECH	8
CALIFORNIA-BERKELEY, U of	15
CALIFORNIA-SAN DIEGO, U of	18
CHRISTIAN BROTHERS COLL	3
COLORADO AT BOULDER, U of	10
COLORADO SCHOOL OF MINES	20
COLUMBIA U IN THE CITY OF NEW YORK	13
CORNELL U-ENDOWED COLLS	40
EASTERN MICHIGAN U	4
EASTERN NAZARENE COLL	2
EMBRY-RIDDLE AERONAUTICAL U	13
ILLINOIS AT CHICAGO, U of	4
ILLINOIS URBANA CAMPUS, U of	18
KANSAS WESLEYAN U	1
LEHIGH U	8
LOYOLA MARYMOUNT U	1
MAINE, U of	3
MIAMI U OXFORD CAMPUS	19
MICHIGAN ANN ARBOR, U of	4
MORGAN ST U	3
MURRAY ST U	10
NEVADA-RENO, U of	1
NORTH CAROLINA AGRI AND TECHNICAL ST U	1
NORTH DAKOTA MAIN CAMPUS, U of	3
NORTH DAKOTA ST U MAIN CAMPUS	8
NORTHEASTERN ST U	4
NORTHWEST NAZARENE COLL	2
OAKLAND U	1
OHIO ST U MAIN CAMPUS	6
OKLAHOMA CHRISTIAN COLL	4
OKLAHOMA NORMAN CAMPUS, U of	7
OREGON ST U	6
PACIFIC LUTHERAN U	3
PACIFIC, U of THE	6
PITTSBURGH MAIN CAMPUS, U of	1
RENSSELAER POLYTECHNIC INST	9
SAINT AMBROSE U	2
SOUTH DAKOTA ST U	2
SOUTHEAST MISSOURI ST U	2
STEVENS INST OF TECH	5
SUNY AT BUFFALO	1
TENNESSEE-KNOXVILLE, U of	7
TEXAS TECH U	1
TOLEDO, U of	1
TUFTS U	3
TULSA, U of	3
WASHINGTON AND LEE U	3
WASHINGTON U	4
WEST VIRGINIA WESLEYAN COLL	8
WESTMONT COLL	9
WRIGHT ST U MAIN CAMPUS	4
YALE U	2

Engineering Science

CALIFORNIA POLYTECHNIC ST U-SAN LUIS OBISPO	3
COLORADO ST U	11
DAVID LIPSCOMB U	2
DORDT COLL	1
DREXEL U	1
FRANCISCAN U STEUBENVILLE	5
HARVARD U	21
IOWA ST U	4
MIAMI, U of	1
MICHIGAN ANN ARBOR, U of	13
MONTANA ST U	2
NEW JERSEY INST TECH	2
NEW MEXICO INST OF MINING AND TECH	6
NEW MEXICO MAIN CAMPUS, U of	6
NORTHWESTERN U	1
PACIFIC LUTHERAN U	1
PENNSYLVANIA ST U MAIN CAMPUS	38
RADCLIFFE COLL	3
RUTGERS U NEW BRUNSWICK	21
SAINT MARY'S U	1
TENNESSEE-KNOXVILLE, U of	17
TRINITY U	15
TUFTS U	1
US AIR FORCE ACAD	14
WEST VIRGINIA INST OF TECH	7
YALE U	11

Engineering and Engineering-Related Tech

ARIZONA ST U	22
BALL ST U	8
BERRY COLL	3
CALIFORNIA POLYTECHNIC ST U-SAN LUIS OBISPO	82
CALIFORNIA ST POLYTECHNIC U POMONA	122
CALIFORNIA ST U LONG BEACH	55
CALIFORNIA ST U-SACRAMENTO	31
CAMERON U	19
CAPITOL COLL	76

CENTRAL MICHIGAN U	1
CITY U	2
COLORADO TECHNICAL COLL	53
CUNY CITY COLL	28
DAYTON, U of	8
DELAWARE, U of	15
EAST CENTRAL U	12
EAST TENNESSEE ST U	80
EAST TEXAS ST U	5
EASTERN MICHIGAN U	11
EASTERN WASHINGTON U	17
EMBRY-RIDDLE AERONAUTICAL U	74
FAIRMONT ST COLL	46
FLORIDA INST OF TECH	4
FORT VALLEY ST COLL	2
FRANCIS MARION COLL	6
FRANKLIN U	19
GANNON U	1
INDIANA ST U	59
JACKSONVILLE ST U	40
KANSAS ST U AGRI AND APP SCI	39
LANGSTON U	3
LETOURNEAU COLL	1
MARYLAND EASTERN SHORE, U of	3
MASSACHUSETTS AT DARTMOUTH (WAS SE U OF MA, U of	40
MEMPHIS ST U	11
MIDDLE TENNESSEE ST U	9
MIDWESTERN ST U	8
MONTANA ST U	46
NATIONAL U	5
NEBRASKA-LINCOLN, U of	31
NEW HAMPSHIRE KEENE ST COLL, U of	3
NEW JERSEY INST TECH	124
NEW MEXICO ST U MAIN CAMPUS	65
NEW YORK INST OF TECH MAIN CAMPUS	59
NY REGENTS COL DEG, U of THE ST OF	70
NORTH CAROLINA AT CHARLOTTE, U of	112
NORTHEAST MISSOURI ST U	28
NORTHERN ILLINOIS U	31
NORTHERN MONTANA COLL	9
NORTHROP U	5
NORWICH U	4
OKLAHOMA ST U MAIN CAMPUS	1
OLD DOMINION U	121
OREGON INST OF TECH	20
PITTSBURG ST U	28
ROCHESTER INST OF TECH	296
SAINT CLOUD ST U	47
SALEM-TEIKYO U	2
SAN JOSE ST U	70
SIENA HEIGHTS COLL	2
SOUTH FLORIDA, U of	67
SOUTHERN COLL OF TECH	396
SOUTHERN ILLINOIS U-CARBONDALE	70
SOUTHERN INDIANA, U of	18
SOUTHWEST MISSOURI ST U	1
SPRING GARDEN COLL	31
SUFFOLK U	5
TEXAS A&M U	137
VIRGINIA ST U	10
WASHINGTON U	2
WEBER ST COLL	31
WENTWORTH INST OF TECH	1
WESTERN CAROLINA U	18
WESTERN MICHIGAN U	3
WESTERN WASHINGTON U	9
WISCONSIN-STOUT, U of	1
WORLD COLL WEST	2

Engineering and Engineering Related Tech (unspecified)

Degrees in this subject were reported by 256 institutions. Consult more specific headings.

Engineering and Other Disciplines

ANDREWS U	16
ARIZONA, U of	12
BOISE ST U	19
BROWN U	3
CALIFORNIA-LOS ANGELES, U of	7
CLARKSON U	121
COLL OF SAINT THOMAS	6
COLUMBIA U IN THE CITY OF NEW YORK	4
DELAWARE, U of	1
DEPAUW U	5
FAIRFIELD U	5
FAIRLEIGH DICKINSON U	2
LEHIGH U	4
MASSACHUSETTS INST OF TECH	11
PEABODY INST OF JOHNS HOPKINS U	3
PENNSYLVANIA, U of	57
REED COLL	5
SOUTH FLORIDA, U of	29
STONEHILL COLL	2
TRI-ST U	10
TUFTS U	19
WISCONSIN-MADISON, U of	8
YALE U	1

Engineering, General

ARKANSAS ST U MAIN CAMPUS	24
ARKANSAS TECH U	9
BATES COLL	1
BAYLOR U	16
BOSTON U	1
BROWN U	86
CALIFORNIA INST OF TECH	67
CALIFORNIA ST U FRESNO	25
CALIFORNIA ST U FULLERTON	173
CALIFORNIA ST U LONG BEACH	12
CALIFORNIA ST U LOS ANGELES	133
CALIFORNIA ST U NORTHRIDGE	255
CALIFORNIA-BERKELEY, U of	1
CALIFORNIA-DAVIS, U of	96
CALIFORNIA-IRVINE, U of	184
CALIFORNIA-LOS ANGELES, U of	14
CALIFORNIA-SAN DIEGO, U of	6
CALVIN COLL	44
COLORADO SCHOOL OF MINES	91
COOPER UNION	9
CORNELL U-ENDOWED COLLS	2
CUNY COLL OF STN ISLAND	34
DARTMOUTH COLL	53
EAST CENTRAL U	5
EMORY AND HENRY COLL	1
FLORIDA, U of	9
GENEVA COLL	4
GEORGE FOX COLL	1
GRAND VALLEY ST U	5
HARTFORD, U of	4
HARVEY MUDD COLL	59
HAWAII LOA COLL	1
HOFSTRA U	15
HOPE COLL	13
IDAHO ST U	17
ILLINOIS COLL	2
ILLINOIS URBANA CAMPUS, U of	119
INDIANA INST OF TECH	2
INDIANA U-PURDUE U AT INDIANAPOLIS	1
JOHN BROWN U	7
JUNIATA COLL	2
KALAMAZOO COLL	4
KANSAS WESLEYAN U	1
KENT ST U MAIN CAMPUS	27
LAFAYETTE COLL	18
LINCOLN U	1
LOYOLA COLL	11
MANCHESTER COLL	1
MARYLAND BALTIMORE COUNTY CAMPUS, U of	64
MARYLAND COLL PARK CAMPUS, U of	22
MICHIGAN ANN ARBOR, U of	8
MICHIGAN ST U	75
MISSISSIPPI MAIN CAMPUS, U of	10
MONTANA COLL OF MINERAL SCI AND TECH	29
MORAVIAN COLL	1
NEW MEXICO MAIN CAMPUS, U of	4
OKLAHOMA NORMAN CAMPUS, U of	11
OLIVET NAZARENE U	3
PFEIFFER COLL	2
PORTLAND ST U	1
PURDUE U CALUMET CAMPUS	64
REDLANDS, U of	6
RENSSELAER POLYTECHNIC INST	2
SAINT AUGUSTINE'S COLL	1
SAINT VINCENT COLL	3
SAN JOSE ST U	3
SANTA CLARA U	1
SEATTLE PACIFIC U	4
SOUTH FLORIDA, U of	15
SOUTHWESTERN OKLAHOMA ST U	16
SPELMAN COLL	5

STANFORD U	25
SUNY AT STONY BROOK	24
SWARTHMORE COLL	15
TEMPLE U	5
TENNESSEE ST U	1
TENNESSEE-CHATTANOOGA, U of	63
TRINITY COLL	13
TUFTS U	3
TULANE U LOUISIANA	6
UNITED STS NAVAL ACAD	72
US AIR FORCE ACAD	28
VANDERBILT U	20
VIRGINIA MAIN CAMPUS, U of	5
WALLA WALLA COLL	31
WASHINGTON, U of	14
WICHITA ST U	2
WIDENER U PENNSYLVANIA CAMPUS	16
WISCONSIN PARKSIDE, U of	10
WISCONSIN-STOUT, U of	26

Engineering, Other

ARIZONA ST U	34
ARIZONA, U of	18
AUBURN U MAIN CAMPUS	66
BALDWIN-WALLACE COLL	6
BEMIDJI ST U	3
CALIFORNIA-BERKELEY, U of	4
CALIFORNIA-SAN DIEGO, U of	19
CASE WESTERN RESERVE U	2
CATHOLIC U AMERICA	1
CENTRAL ST U	8
CLAREMONT MCKENNA COLL	6
CLARKSON U	21
CLEMSON U	6
COLORADO SCHOOL OF MINES	45
COLORADO-COLORADO SPRINGS, U of	46
COLUMBIA U IN THE CITY OF NEW YORK	3
CONNECTICUT, U of	41
CUMBERLAND COLL	1
DALLAS BAPTIST U	2
DARTMOUTH COLL	25
DAVID LIPSCOMB U	2
DOWLING COLL	4
EVANSVILLE, U of	1
GEORGE WASHINGTON U	5
GMI ENGINEERING AND MANAGEMENT INST	52
HUMBOLDT ST U	19
INDIANA U-PURDUE U AT FORT WAYNE	16
IOWA ST U	57
KANSAS ST U AGRI AND APP SCI	27
KENTUCKY ST U	4
LAWRENCE INST OF TECH	43
LETOURNEAU COLL	1
MAINE, U of	5
MARYLAND COLL PARK CAMPUS, U of	23
MASS. AT LOWELL, U of	41
MASSACHUSETTS AT DARTMOUTH (WAS SE U OF MA, U of	3
MERCER U IN ATLANTA	5
MIAMI U OXFORD CAMPUS	18
MICHIGAN ANN ARBOR, U of	25
MISSOURI-ROLLA, U of	74
NEBRASKA-LINCOLN, U of	1
NEW ENGLAND COLL	1
NEW HAVEN, U of	1
NICHOLS COLL	1
NORTH CAROLINA ST U AT RALEIGH	82
NORTH DAKOTA MAIN CAMPUS, U of	4
NORTHWESTERN U	1
OAKLAND U	5
OHIO ST U MAIN CAMPUS	22
OHIO WESLEYAN U	2
POLYTECHNIC U	5
PORTLAND, U of	4
RENSSELAER POLYTECHNIC INST	56
RHODE ISLAND, U of	3
ROCHESTER INST OF TECH	62
ROCHESTER, U of	55
SAINT ANSELM COLL	2
STANFORD U	14
STEVENS INST OF TECH	12
SYRACUSE U MAIN CAMPUS	14
TENNESSEE-CHATTANOOGA, U of	6
US INTERNATIONAL U	1
WASHINGTON ST U	17
WASHINGTON U	15
WEST COAST U	1
WEST VIRGINIA INST OF TECH	24
WESTERN MICHIGAN U	28
WHEATON COLL	6
WILMINGTON COLL	4
WRIGHT ST U MAIN CAMPUS	18

English Education

Degrees in this subject were reported by 203 institutions. Consult more specific headings.

English, General

Degrees in this subject were reported by 1084 institutions. Consult more specific headings.

Enterpreneurship, General

BOISE ST U	12
HAWAII PACIFIC COLL	5
NORTH TEXAS, U of	12
OZARKS, U of THE	1
PENNSYLVANIA, U of	42

Entomology

ARIZONA, U of	1
AUBURN U MAIN CAMPUS	1
CALIFORNIA-DAVIS, U of	1
CALIFORNIA-RIVERSIDE, U of	2
CLEMSON U	3
CORNELL U-NYS STATUTORY COLLS	1
DELAWARE, U of	6
FLORIDA, U of	3
GEORGIA, U of	1
HAWAII AT MANOA, U of	2
IOWA ST U	3
KENTUCKY, U of	3
MISSISSIPPI ST U	2
NEW HAMPSHIRE, U of	2
NORTH DAKOTA ST U MAIN CAMPUS	1
OHIO ST U MAIN CAMPUS	1
OKLAHOMA ST U MAIN CAMPUS	2
PENNSYLVANIA ST U MAIN CAMPUS	1
TEXAS A&M U	6
TEXAS TECH U	3
WISCONSIN-MADISON, U of	1
WYOMING, U of	3

Environmental Control Technologies, Other

FERRIS ST U	40
FINDLAY, U of	10
FLORIDA INST OF TECH	2
ILLINOIS ST U	16
KENTUCKY, U of	3
MOBILE COLL	1
SAN FRANCISCO, U of	1

Environmental Design

ART CENTER COLL OF DESIGN	13
AUBURN U MAIN CAMPUS	13
BALL ST U	70
BOWLING GREEN ST U MAIN CAMPUS	3
CLEMSON U	90
COLORADO AT BOULDER, U of	101
CORNELL U-NYS STATUTORY COLLS	35
EASTERN MICHIGAN U	13
GEORGIA INST OF TECH MAIN CAMPUS	25
KENDALL COLL OF ART AND DESIGN	3
MASSACHUSETTS AT AMHERST, U of	13
MIAMI U OXFORD CAMPUS	47
MINNESOTA TWIN CITIES, U of	11
NEW MEXICO MAIN CAMPUS, U of	3
NEW SCHOOL FOR SOCIAL RESEARCH	36
NORTH DAKOTA ST U MAIN CAMPUS	45
NORTHERN MICHIGAN U	2
OKLAHOMA NORMAN CAMPUS, U of	30
OTIS ART INST OF PARSONS SCHOOL OF DESIGN	5
PENNSYLVANIA, U of	28
PRATT INST-MAIN	20
RUTGERS U NEW BRUNSWICK	59
SMITH COLL	1
SOUTHERN ILLINOIS U-CARBONDALE	50
SUNY AT BUFFALO	43

Environmental Health Engineering

BOISE ST U	5
CALIFORNIA POLYTECHNIC ST U-SAN LUIS OBISPO	9

CENTRAL FLORIDA, U of	15
CHARLESTON, U of	1
EAST CENTRAL U	21
FLORIDA INST OF TECH	8
FLORIDA, U of	28
MICHIGAN TECH U	19
MONTANA COLL OF MINERAL SCI AND TECH	17
NEW MEXICO INST OF MINING AND TECH	4
NORTHWESTERN U	3
PENNSYLVANIA ST U MAIN CAMPUS	4
RENSSELAER POLYTECHNIC INST	11
SYRACUSE U MAIN CAMPUS	5
TEMPLE U	7
WILKES U	1

Ethnic Studies, Other

BOISE ST U	1
BOWLING GREEN ST U MAIN CAMPUS	6
CALIFORNIA ST U FULLERTON	13
CALIFORNIA ST U-HAYWARD	2
CALIFORNIA ST U-SACRAMENTO	3
CALIFORNIA-BERKELEY, U of	13
CALIFORNIA-LOS ANGELES, U of	2
EARLHAM COLL	5
HAWAII AT HILO, U of	5
HAWAII AT MANOA, U of	8
MILLS COLL	3
TEXAS AT AUSTIN, U of	2
WICHITA ST U	1

European Studies, General

AMHERST COLL	6
BRIGHAM YOUNG U	145
CLAREMONT MCKENNA COLL	1
CORNELL U-ENDOWED COLLS	5
EMERSON COLL	3
GOUCHER COLL	2
LOYOLA MARYMOUNT U	5
MOUNT HOLYOKE COLL	3
NORTHERN IOWA, U of	1
OKLAHOMA NORMAN CAMPUS, U of	1
PHILLIPS U	4
RICHMOND, U of	9
ROSARY COLL	1
SAN DIEGO ST U	5
SCRIPPS COLL	1
SEATTLE PACIFIC U	1
SUSQUEHANNA U	1
TRINITY U	3
VANDERBILT U	13
VERMONT, U of	1
WELLESLEY COLL	8
WILLAMETTE U	3

Executive Secretarial

CENTRAL WASHINGTON U	3
EASTERN MICHIGAN U	5
HUSSON COLL	2
MAYVILLE ST U	2
OKLAHOMA CHRISTIAN COLL	1
OKLAHOMA ST U MAIN CAMPUS	2
SOUTHWESTERN LOUISIANA, U of	6
TABOR COLL	1

Exercise Physiology

CASTLETON ST COLL	6
CENTRAL MICHIGAN U	51
COLBY-SAWYER COLL	4
CONCORDIA COLL	7
CONCORDIA TEACHERS COLL	3
DAVIS AND ELKINS COLL	3
EVANSVILLE, U of	7
GORDON COLL	7
GUSTAVUS ADOLPHUS COLL	8
HARDIN-SIMMONS U	2
HOUSTON-U PARK, U of	9
LAKELAND COLL	1
MIAMI U OXFORD CAMPUS	10
MISSOURI WESTERN ST COLL	6
OHIO ST U MAIN CAMPUS	16
ROCKFORD COLL	1
ROCKY MOUNTAIN COLL	4
SOUTH CAROLINA—COLUMBIA, U of	12
SPRINGFIELD COLL	50
SUNY AT BUFFALO	23
WEST LIBERTY ST COLL	8
WESTERN MICHIGAN U	11
WINONA ST U	4

Experimental Psychology

NORTHERN MICHIGAN U	17
SOUTH CAROLINA—COLUMBIA, U of	185

Family Counseling

KANSAS ST U AGRI AND APP SCI	23
TEXAS WOMAN'S U	5

Family Living and Parenthood

BRIGHAM YOUNG U	168

Family Relations

ALABAMA, U of	6
ANDERSON U	6
BOWLING GREEN ST U MAIN CAMPUS	3
MINNESOTA TWIN CITIES, U of	66
NORTHERN ILLINOIS U	84
OKLAHOMA CHRISTIAN COLL	2
OREGON ST U	10
SOUTHEAST MISSOURI ST U	5
SOUTHERN MISSISSIPPI, U of	11
TEXAS TECH U	85
WEBER ST COLL	13
WESTERN MICHIGAN U	20

Family and Community Services, General

ADRIAN COLL	1
BOWLING GREEN ST U MAIN CAMPUS	25
IOWA ST U	21
LAMAR U	2
MARYLAND COLL PARK CAMPUS, U of	116
MICHIGAN ST U	50
NORTHERN IOWA, U of	6
SETON HILL COLL	2

Family/Consumer Resource Management, General

ARIZONA, U of	3
AUBURN U MAIN CAMPUS	5
CONNECTICUT, U of	34
CORNELL U-NYS STATUTORY COLLS	65
EASTERN MICHIGAN U	5
GEORGIA SOUTHERN COLL	3
GEORGIA, U of	32
ILLINOIS URBANA CAMPUS, U of	9
INDIANA ST U	5
IOWA ST U	15
KANSAS ST U AGRI AND APP SCI	9
KENT ST U MAIN CAMPUS	2
MARYLAND COLL PARK CAMPUS, U of	95
MICHIGAN ST U	7
MISSOURI-COLUMBIA, U of	46
NEBRASKA-LINCOLN, U of	33
NEW MEXICO ST U MAIN CAMPUS	26
NORTH DAKOTA ST U MAIN CAMPUS	3
NORTHWEST MISSOURI ST U	10
OHIO ST U MAIN CAMPUS	75
OHIO U MAIN CAMPUS	5
SOUTHERN ILLINOIS U-CARBONDALE	19
SUNY COLL AT BUFFALO	35
SYRACUSE U MAIN CAMPUS	25
TEXAS TECH U	2
UTAH, U of	23
VERMONT, U of	12
WAYNE ST U	2

Family/Consumer Resource Management, Other

CENTRAL MICHIGAN U	6

Farm and Ranch Management

IOWA ST U	46
LAKE ERIE COLL	5
MONTANA ST U	4
SOUTHWEST TEXAS ST U	2
WISCONSIN-RIVER FALLS, U of	5
WYOMING, U of	8

Fashion Design

ALBRIGHT COLL	3
AMERICAN COLL FOR THE APPLIED ARTS	23
ARKANSAS PINE BLUFF, U of	6
BAYLOR U	6
BOWLING GREEN ST U MAIN CAMPUS	1
CENTRAL MICHIGAN U	23
CINCINNATI MAIN CAMPUS, U of	31
COLL OF SAINT SCHOLASTICA	3
DELAWARE, U of	11
EASTERN KENTUCKY U	2
FASHION INST OF TECH	17
HOWARD U	14
INCARNATE WORD COLL	3
IOWA ST U	12
KANSAS ST U AGRI AND APP SCI	6
KENT ST U MAIN CAMPUS	52
MARYMOUNT U	7
MINNESOTA TWIN CITIES, U of	16
MOORE COLL OF ART	16
MOUNT MARY COLL	9
NORTH TEXAS, U of	35
OREGON ST U	6
OTIS ART INST OF PARSONS SCHOOL OF DESIGN	14
PHILADELPHIA COLL OF TEXTILES AND SCIENCE	56
RHODE ISLAND SCHOOL OF DESIGN	22
RIVIER COLL	3
ROSARY COLL	3
STEPHENS COLL	12
TEXAS CHRISTIAN U	5
TEXAS TECH U	14
TEXAS WOMAN'S U	10
URSULINE COLL	1
VERMONT, U of	9
VIRGINIA COMMONWEALTH U	87
WESTERN WASHINGTON U	12
WILLIAM WOODS COLL	1
WISCONSIN-MADISON, U of	12
WOODBURY U	5

Fashion Merchandising

ABILENE CHRISTIAN U	4
AMERICAN COLL FOR THE APPLIED ARTS	33
ASHLAND U	5
AUBURN U MAIN CAMPUS	34
BAKER U	4
BOWLING GREEN ST U MAIN CAMPUS	72
BRENAU COLL	1
BRIDGEPORT, U of	26
CENTENARY COLL	6
CENTRAL OKLAHOMA, U of	2
CENTRAL ST U	3
CENTRAL WASHINGTON U	5
CHICAGO ST U	3
COLUMBIA COLL	4
DAVID LIPSCOMB U	6
DAVIS AND ELKINS COLL	7
DELTA ST U	5
DREXEL U	34
EASTERN KENTUCKY U	16
EASTERN MICHIGAN U	43
FASHION INST OF TECH	311
FREED-HARDEMAN COLL	1
GEORGIA, U of	42
HARDING U MAIN CAMPUS	5
IMMACULATA COLL	7
INCARNATE WORD COLL	6
INDIANA U PENNSYLVANIA	44
IOWA ST U	62
LINCOLN U	1
MADONNA COLL	9
MARIAN COLL	3
MARS HILL COLL	6
MARYGROVE COLL	1
MARYMOUNT U	32
MARYWOOD COLL	29
MERCYHURST COLL	6
MEREDITH COLL	15
MINNESOTA TWIN CITIES, U of	1
MISSISSIPPI COLL	1
MOUNT MARY COLL	13
NORTH ALABAMA, U of	3
NORTH TEXAS, U of	8
NORTHERN ARIZONA U	17
NORTHERN MICHIGAN U	7
OUR LADY OF THE LAKE U SAN ANTONIO	1
PACIFIC UNION COLL	1
PHILADELPHIA COLL OF TEXTILES AND SCIENCE	59
POINT PARK COLL	4
POST COLL	1
ROSARY COLL	11
SAINT VINCENT COLL	1
SAM HOUSTON ST U	15
SAMFORD U	4
SETON HILL COLL	3
SIENA HEIGHTS COLL	3
SOUTHERN NAZARENE U	1
SOUTHWEST TEXAS ST U	62
STEPHEN F AUSTIN ST U	34
STEPHENS COLL	9
TARLETON ST U	2
TEXAS TECH U	55
TEXAS WOMAN'S U	27
URSULINE COLL	16
UTAH ST U	12
VIRGINIA INTERMONT COLL	4
WAYNE ST COLL	5
WEBBER COLL	3
WESLEY COLL	3
WEST VIRGINIA WESLEYAN COLL	10
WESTERN MICHIGAN U	60
WILLIAM WOODS COLL	6

Fiber/Textiles/Weaving

ARTS, THE U of THE	4
CALIFORNIA COLL OF ARTS AND CRAFTS	1
CENTER FOR CREATIVE STUDIES COL OF ART AND DESIGN	2
CLEVELAND INST OF ART	4
CORNELL U-NYS STATUTORY COLLS	27
KANSAS CITY ART INST	11
MARYLAND INST COLL OF ART	2
MASSACHUSETTS AT DARTMOUTH (WAS SE U OF MA, U of	5
MEMPHIS COLL OF ART	1
MICHIGAN ANN ARBOR, U of	2
MOORE COLL OF ART	1
NORTH TEXAS, U of	1
NORTHERN MICHIGAN U	5
OREGON, U of	2
PHILADELPHIA COLL OF TEXTILES AND SCIENCE	13
SAVANNAH COLL OF ART AND DESIGN	9
TEMPLE U	6
WASHINGTON, U of	12

Film Animation

CALIFORNIA INST OF ARTS	22
THE U THE ARTS	8

Film Arts, General

AMERICAN U	3
ANTIOCH COLL	3
ART CENTER COLL OF DESIGN	18
BOWLING GREEN ST U MAIN CAMPUS	7
CALIFORNIA-LOS ANGELES, U of	35
CARLETON COLL	4
CLAREMONT MCKENNA COLL	2
CLARK U	7
COLL OF WOOSTER	7
COLORADO AT BOULDER, U of	10
DARTMOUTH COLL	9
DENISON U	7
EMORY U	3
GEORGIA ST U	9
GRAND VALLEY ST U	11
GREEN MOUNTAIN COLL	5
ILLINOIS AT CHICAGO, U of	21
MASSACHUSETTS COLL OF ART	6
MIAMI, U of	9
MICHIGAN ANN ARBOR, U of	18
NEW HAMPSHIRE KEENE ST COLL, U of	3
OHIO ST U MAIN CAMPUS	52
PENNSYLVANIA ST U MAIN CAMPUS	41
PITZER COLL	3
RHODE ISLAND COLL	1
SCRIPPS COLL	2
SOUTHERN ILLINOIS U-CARBONDALE	54
SOUTHERN METHODIST U	16
UTAH, U of	17
WAYNE ST U	2
WISCONSIN-MILWAUKEE, U of	10
WRIGHT ST U MAIN CAMPUS	6

Film Arts, Other

CALIFORNIA COLL OF ARTS AND CRAFTS 7
CALIFORNIA-IRVINE, U of 17
DISTRICT OF COLUMBIA, U of THE 34
MINNESOTA TWIN CITIES, U of 2
RHODE ISLAND SCHOOL OF DESIGN 18
WAYNE ST U 2

Financial Services Marketing, General

ALLENTOWN COLL OF SAINT FRANCIS DE SALES 7

Fine Arts, General

Degrees in this subject were reported by 626 institutions. Consult more specific headings.

Fine Arts, Other

Degrees in this subject were reported by 164 institutions. Consult more specific headings.

Fire Control and Safety Technology

CENTRAL MISSOURI ST U 8
CINCINNATI MAIN CAMPUS, U of 16
COGSWELL POLYTECHNICAL COLL 4
EASTERN KENTUCKY U 32
LAKE SUPERIOR ST U 1
NEW HAVEN, U of 6
OKLAHOMA ST U MAIN CAMPUS 34

Fire Protection Administration

BRENAU COLL 1
CALIFORNIA ST U LOS ANGELES 15
CITY U 2
COGSWELL POLYTECHNICAL COLL 3
DISTRICT OF COLUMBIA, U of THE 1
HOLY FAMILY COLL 3
SALEM ST COLL 5
SOUTHERN ILLINOIS U-CARBONDALE 28
WESTERN OREGON ST COLL 5

Fire Protection, Other

HAMPTON U 7
MADONNA COLL 2

Fishing and Fisheries, General

ALASKA FAIRBANKS, U of 6
ARKANSAS PINE BLUFF, U of 1
COLORADO ST U 10
HUMBOLDT ST U 23
IDAHO, U of 8
IOWA ST U 20
MINNESOTA TWIN CITIES, U of 10
MISSISSIPPI ST U 2
OHIO ST U MAIN CAMPUS 4
OREGON ST U 17
RHODE ISLAND, U of 17
SHELDON JACKSON COLL 11
TENNESSEE TECH U 5
TEXAS A & M U AT GALVESTON 4
UNITY COLL 3
WASHINGTON, U of 15

Floriculture

ARKANSAS-FAYETTEVILLE, U of 6
BERRY COLL 1
CALIFORNIA POLYTECHNIC ST U-SAN LUIS OBISPO 39
CALIFORNIA ST POLYTECHNIC U POMONA 15
COLORADO ST U 13
DELAWARE VALLEY COLL OF SCI AND AGRI 45
EASTERN KENTUCKY U 17
FLORIDA, U of 20
IDAHO, U of 2
LOUISIANA TECH U 6
MURRAY ST U 3
TARLETON ST U 6
TENNESSEE-KNOXVILLE, U of 13

Food Marketing, General

TEXAS TECH U 4

Food Processing Technology

COLORADO ST U 2

Food Production, Management, and Services, General

BERRY COLL 2
DAVID LIPSCOMB U 2
EASTERN KENTUCKY U 1
GRAMBLING ST U 5
IMMACULATA COLL 3
INDIANA U PENNSYLVANIA 8
LAMAR U 3
MADONNA COLL 2
MISSISSIPPI COLL 6
MOREHEAD ST U 4
OHIO ST U MAIN CAMPUS 69
ROSARY COLL 1
SOUTHERN COLL OF SEVENTH-DAY ADVENTISTS 1
SOUTHWEST MISSOURI ST U 61
SOUTHWESTERN LOUISIANA, U of 5
VALPARAISO U 1

Food Products

ILLINOIS URBANA CAMPUS, U of 2
KANSAS ST U AGRI AND APP SCI 8

Food Sciences and Human Nutrition, General

Degrees in this subject were reported by 122 institutions. Consult more specific headings.

Food Sciences and Human Nutrition, Other

AUBURN U MAIN CAMPUS 13
CALIFORNIA-DAVIS, U of 7
DREXEL U 8
GEORGIA SOUTHERN COLL 11
GODDARD COLL 2
ILLINOIS BENEDICTINE COLL 3
KANSAS ST U AGRI AND APP SCI 39
LOMA LINDA U 12
RADFORD U 11
RUTGERS U NEW BRUNSWICK 3
SAINT OLAF COLL 2
SOUTH DAKOTA ST U 7
UTAH ST U 26
WISCONSIN-MADISON, U of 3
WISCONSIN-STOUT, U of 5

Food Sciences, General

ALABAMA AGRI AND MECH U 4
ARKANSAS-FAYETTEVILLE, U of 6
AUBURN U MAIN CAMPUS 3
CALIFORNIA POLYTECHNIC ST U-SAN LUIS OBISPO 10
CALIFORNIA-DAVIS, U of 39
CLEMSON U 12
CORNELL U-NYS STATUTORY COLLS 21
DELAWARE VALLEY COLL OF SCI AND AGRI 8
FLORIDA, U of 30
GEORGIA, U of 8
ILLINOIS URBANA CAMPUS, U of 10
IOWA ST U 11
KANSAS ST U AGRI AND APP SCI 4
KENTUCKY, U of 3
LOUISIANA ST U & AGRI & MECH & HEBERT LAWS CTR 6
MARYLAND COLL PARK CAMPUS, U of 6
MASSACHUSETTS AT AMHERST, U of 4
MICHIGAN ST U 17
MINNESOTA TWIN CITIES, U of 22
MISSISSIPPI ST U 1
MISSOURI-COLUMBIA, U of 18
NEBRASKA-LINCOLN, U of 2
NORTH CAROLINA AGRI AND TECHNICAL ST U 5
NORTH CAROLINA ST U AT RALEIGH 12
NORTH DAKOTA ST U MAIN CAMPUS 5
OHIO ST U MAIN CAMPUS 21
OREGON ST U 9
PENNSYLVANIA ST U MAIN CAMPUS 27
RUTGERS U NEW BRUNSWICK 17
TENNESSEE-KNOXVILLE, U of 14

TEXAS A&M U 19
TEXAS TECH U 8
VERMONT, U of 1
VIRGINIA POLYTECHNIC INST AND ST U 8
WESTERN MICHIGAN U 24
WISCONSIN-MADISON, U of 18
WISCONSIN-RIVER FALLS, U of 15
WYOMING, U of 4

Food Service

GEORGIA, U of 44
IOWA ST U 1
JACKSONVILLE ST U 2
MINNESOTA TWIN CITIES, U of 1

Food and Nutrition

DISTRICT OF COLUMBIA, U of THE 1
PITTSBURGH MAIN CAMPUS, U of 9
ROSARY COLL 1

Food/Food Sciences

ARIZONA, U of 8
DELAWARE, U of 3
ILLINOIS URBANA CAMPUS, U of 19
IOWA ST U 8
MICHIGAN ST U 6
MINNESOTA TWIN CITIES, U of 3
SAM HOUSTON ST U 4
TEXAS WOMAN'S U 2

Foreign Languages (unspecified)

Degrees in this subject were reported by 800 institutions. Consult more specific headings.

Foreign Languages Education

ANDERSON U 1
ARKANSAS ST U MAIN CAMPUS 2
ARKANSAS-FAYETTEVILLE, U of 1
ASHLAND U 1
AUBURN U MAIN CAMPUS 2
BETHUNE COOKMAN COLL 1
BOWLING GREEN ST U MAIN CAMPUS 15
CAMPBELL U INCORPORATED 1
CENTRAL ARKANSAS, U of 1
CENTRAL FLORIDA, U of 10
DELAWARE ST COLL 3
DELAWARE, U of 2
EASTERN MICHIGAN U 5
EASTERN MONTANA COLL 3
EASTERN WASHINGTON U 6
FLORIDA ST U 8
GEORGIA SOUTHERN COLL 6
GEORGIA SOUTHWESTERN COLL 1
GEORGIA, U of 10
GROVE CITY COLL 4
HAWAII AT MANOA, U of 1
IDAHO ST U 1
IDAHO, U of 1
ILLINOIS AT CHICAGO, U of 8
ILLINOIS URBANA CAMPUS, U of 19
KENNESAW ST COLL 2
LA SALLE U 1
LOUISIANA ST U & AGRI & MECH & HEBERT LAWS CTR 9
LOUISIANA TECH U 3
MANCHESTER COLL 2
MANKATO ST U 4
MARQUETTE U 5
MARYLAND COLL PARK CAMPUS, U of 9
MCMURRY COLL 1
MCNEESE ST U 1
MISSOURI WESTERN ST COLL 1
MISSOURI-COLUMBIA, U of 5
MISSOURI-KANSAS CITY, U of 2
MISSOURI-SAINT LOUIS, U of 2
MOORHEAD ST U 5
MOUNT MARY COLL 1
NEBRASKA-LINCOLN, U of 4
NEVADA-RENO, U of 1
NEW ORLEANS, U of 4
NORTH ALABAMA, U of 3
NORTH DAKOTA ST U MAIN CAMPUS 1
NORTHEAST LOUISIANA U 1
NORTHEASTERN ST U 3
OHIO ST U MAIN CAMPUS 23
OKLAHOMA BAPTIST U 2
OKLAHOMA NORMAN CAMPUS, U of 1
ORAL ROBERTS U 3
PACIFIC LUTHERAN U 2
PLYMOUTH ST COLL 1
RHODE ISLAND COLL 3
SAINT CLOUD ST U 7
SOUTH DAKOTA, U of 1
SOUTH FLORIDA, U of 9
SOUTHEAST MISSOURI ST U 3
SOUTHEASTERN LOUISIANA U 2
SOUTHEASTERN OKLAHOMA ST U 2
SOUTHERN ARKANSAS U MAIN CAMPUS 1
SOUTHERN UTAH ST COLL 5
SOUTHWEST MISSOURI ST U 5
SOUTHWESTERN LOUISIANA, U of 2
SUNY AT ALBANY 6
SUNY COLL AT BUFFALO 8
SUNY COLL AT CORTLAND 18
SUNY COLL AT FREDONIA 7
SUNY COLL AT GENESEO 6
SUNY COLL AT NEW PALTZ 9
SUNY COLL AT ONEONTA 2
SUNY COLL AT OSWEGO 19
SUNY COLL AT PLATTSBURG 5
SUNY COLL AT POTSDAM 8
TAYLOR U 3
TEMPLE U 1
TOLEDO, U of 5
VALLEY CITY ST U 3
WAYNE ST COLL 1
WAYNE ST U 1
WESTERN MICHIGAN U 18
WESTERN WASHINGTON U 2
WINONA ST U 1
WRIGHT ST U MAIN CAMPUS 5
WYOMING, U of 8

Foreign Languages, Multiple Emphasis

Degrees in this subject were reported by 137 institutions. Consult more specific headings.

Foreign Languages, Other

ALABAMA IN HUNTSVILLE, U of 2
ASBURY COLL 1
BEMIDJI ST U 3
BROWN U 1
CALIFORNIA-BERKELEY, U of 11
CALIFORNIA-LOS ANGELES, U of 8
CALIFORNIA-SANTA BARBARA, U of 2
CALVIN COLL 1
CLEMSON U 45
COLUMBIA U IN THE CITY OF NEW YORK 11
CUNY QUEENS COLL 2
DAVIDSON COLL 2
EARLHAM COLL 1
EASTERN MICHIGAN U 15
EVANSVILLE, U of 3
FERRUM COLL 1
GALLAUDET U 4
HARVARD U 25
HOLY FAMILY COLL 6
INDIANA U PENNSYLVANIA 11
MAINE, U of 1
MONTANA ST U 12
NEW YORK U 3
QUEENS COLL 2
RADCLIFFE COLL 5
SAINT ANDREWS PRESBYTERIAN COLL 1
SAINT JOHN'S U NEW YORK 1
SAINT LAWRENCE U 2
SOUTHERN ILLINOIS U-CARBONDALE 7
SOUTHWESTERN LOUISIANA, U of 1
SUNY COLL AT PURCHASE 11
WAYNE ST COLL 1
YALE U 1

Forensic Studies

BALL ST U 109
CENTRAL FLORIDA, U of 2
EASTERN KENTUCKY U 4
INDIANA U AT SOUTH BEND 18
INDIANA U BLOOMINGTON 176
INDIANA U NORTHWEST 22
INDIANA U-PURDUE U AT FORT WAYNE 19

INDIANA U-PURDUE U AT INDIANAPOLIS 40
JACKSONVILLE ST U 26
NEW HAVEN, U of 2

Forest Engineering

AUBURN U MAIN CAMPUS 1
MAINE, U of 5
OREGON ST U 10
WASHINGTON, U of 5

Forest Management

ARIZONA, U of 4
AUBURN U MAIN CAMPUS 21
CLEMSON U 15
LOUISIANA ST U & AGRI & MECH & HEBERT LAWS CTR 6
LOUISIANA TECH U 2
MONTANA, U of 13
OHIO ST U MAIN CAMPUS 2
OREGON ST U 23
STEPHEN F AUSTIN ST U 9
WASHINGTON ST U 7
WASHINGTON, U of 15
WEST VIRGINIA U 18

Forest Products Processing Technology

CLEMSON U 2
PENNSYLVANIA ST U MAIN CAMPUS 4
WASHINGTON, U of 13

Forest Products Utilization

LOUISIANA TECH U 1

Forestry Production and Processing, General

ABILENE CHRISTIAN U 4
AUBURN U MAIN CAMPUS 4
IOWA ST U 9
LOUISIANA TECH U 6
NORTH CAROLINA ST U AT RALEIGH 29
VIRGINIA POLYTECHNIC INST AND ST U 54

Forestry Production and Processing, Other

MAINE, U of 2
MIAMI U OXFORD CAMPUS 21
MICHIGAN TECH U 7
MINNESOTA TWIN CITIES, U of 24
WISCONSIN-STEVENS POINT, U of 15

Forestry Science

CALIFORNIA-BERKELEY, U of 10
IDAHO, U of 9
ILLINOIS URBANA CAMPUS, U of 11
KENTUCKY, U of 3
NORTHERN ARIZONA U 20
PENNSYLVANIA ST U MAIN CAMPUS 15
UNITY COLL 1
WASHINGTON, U of 4
WISCONSIN-MADISON, U of 6

Forestry and Related Sciences, General

ARKANSAS-MONTICELLO, U of 14
BAYLOR U 1
FLORIDA, U of 22
GEORGIA, U of 30
HIGH POINT COLL 1
HUMBOLDT ST U 22
IOWA ST U 8
MAINE, U of 29
MASSACHUSETTS AT AMHERST, U of 10
MICHIGAN ST U 18
MICHIGAN TECH U 16
MISSISSIPPI ST U 32
MONTANA, U of 5
NEW HAMPSHIRE, U of 8
NORTH CAROLINA ST U AT RALEIGH 18
OKLAHOMA ST U MAIN CAMPUS 9
SOUTH, THE U of THE 12
SOUTHERN ILLINOIS U CARBONDALE 16
STEPHEN F AUSTIN ST U 2
TENNESSEE-KNOXVILLE, U of 15
TEXAS A&M U 8
UTAH ST U 8
VERMONT, U of 10
WISCONSIN-STEVENS POINT, U of 41

Forestry and Related Sciences, Other

COLORADO ST U 20
MINNESOTA TWIN CITIES, U of 22
OHIO ST U MAIN CAMPUS 1
VERMONT, U of 4

French

Degrees in this subject were reported by 563 institutions. Consult more specific headings.

Funeral Services

CENTRAL OKLAHOMA, U of 21
INDIANAPOLIS, U of 1
MINNESOTA TWIN CITIES, U of 41
POINT PARK COLL 2
WAYNE ST COLL 3
WAYNE ST U 9
XAVIER U 1

Game Farm Management

TEXAS TECH U 23

General Marketing, Other

ALABAMA AGRI AND MECH U 18
ALLENTOWN COLL OF SAINT FRANCIS DE SALES 35
ANDERSON U 23
BAPTIST COLL AT CHARLESTON 15
BELMONT COLL 36
BENEDICT COLL 4
CALIFORNIA LUTHERAN U 21
CENTRAL ST U 21
CENTRAL WASHINGTON U 1
CLEMSON U 172
COKER COLL 15
KENNESAW ST COLL 130
LINCOLN U 9
MARS HILL COLL 2
MCMURRY COLL 7
MOBILE COLL 2
NEBRASKA AT OMAHA, U of 2
SAINT EDWARD'S U 22
SOUTH CAROLINA AT COASTAL CAROLINA, U of 37
SOUTH CAROLINA ST COLL 76
SOUTH CAROLINA—COLUMBIA, U of 204
WHEELING COLL 10
YORK COLL PENNSYLVANIA 65

General Studies

ALBERTUS MAGNUS COLL 4
ALLENTOWN COLL OF SAINT FRANCIS DE SALES 9
ARKANSAS ST U MAIN CAMPUS 9
AVERETT COLL 5
AVILA COLL 5
BRESCIA COLL 3
CAPITAL U 18
CARSON-NEWMAN COLL 6
CATHOLIC U AMERICA 1
CITY U 13
COLL MISERICORDIA 6
CONNECTICUT, U of 190
CUMBERLAND COLL 5
DALLAS BAPTIST U 2
DORDT COLL 2
DRAKE U 21
EASTERN CONNECTICUT ST U 39
EASTERN NEW MEXICO U MAIN CAMPUS 23
EMPORIA ST U 18
FAIRFIELD U 3
FRANKLIN PIERCE COLL 37
GRAND CANYON U 5
HARDING U MAIN CAMPUS 10
HOWARD PAYNE U 8
HUNTINGDON COLL 3

IDAHO ST U	3
IDAHO, U of	30
INDIANA U AT KOKOMO	16
INDIANA U AT SOUTH BEND	84
INDIANA U BLOOMINGTON	131
INDIANA U NORTHWEST	24
INDIANA U SOUTHEAST	43
INDIANA U-PURDUE U AT FORT WAYNE	53
INDIANA U-PURDUE U AT INDIANAPOLIS	140
JACKSONVILLE ST U	7
LANGSTON U	9
LEBANON VALLEY COLL	4
LEWIS-CLARK ST COLL	35
LIBERTY U	90
LOUISIANA ST U & AGRI & MECH & HEBERT LAWS CTR	371
LOUISIANA ST U SHREVEPORT	30
LOUISIANA TECH U	135
LOYOLA MARYMOUNT U	25
MAINE AT FARMINGTON, U of	14
MARY HARDIN BAYLOR, U of	28
MASSACHUSETTS AT AMHERST, U of	23
MENLO COLL	12
MISSOURI SOUTHERN ST COLL	12
NEVADA-RENO, U of	91
NEW MEXICO INST OF MINING AND TECH	5
NEW MEXICO MAIN CAMPUS, U of	257
NEW MEXICO ST U MAIN CAMPUS	7
NEW ORLEANS, U of	74
NICHOLLS ST U	79
NORTH ALABAMA, U of	2
NORTH TEXAS, U of	25
NORTHEAST LOUISIANA U	88
NORTHWEST NAZARENE COLL	4
NORTHWESTERN ST U LOUISIANA	44
OAKWOOD COLL	2
OHIO DOMINICAN COLL	19
OKLAHOMA CITY U	34
OKLAHOMA ST U MAIN CAMPUS	6
OZARKS, U of THE	9
POST COLL	29
RICE U	18
SAINT FRANCIS COLL	1
SAINT MARY'S COLL OF MINNESOTA	1
SEATTLE PACIFIC U	8
SHELDON JACKSON COLL	5
SOUTH DAKOTA ST U	11
SOUTH FLORIDA, U of	123
SOUTHEAST MISSOURI ST U	74
SOUTHEASTERN LOUISIANA U	26
SOUTHWESTERN COLL	3
SOUTHWESTERN LOUISIANA, U of	317
SPRING HILL COLL	18
SUFFOLK U	3
SUNY COLL AT BUFFALO	12
SUNY COLL AT CORTLAND	2
SUNY COLL AT ONEONTA	28
TEXAS CHRISTIAN U	24
TOLEDO, U of	7
TRINITY COLL	5
WEST TEXAS ST U	69
WESTERN NEW MEXICO U	22
WESTMAR COLL	2
WHITTIER COLL	3
WILLIAM CAREY COLL	1

Genetics, Human and Animal

CALIFORNIA-BERKELEY, U of	64
CALIFORNIA-DAVIS, U of	41
GEORGIA, U of	13
ILLINOIS URBANA CAMPUS, U of	1
IOWA ST U	10
OHIO ST U MAIN CAMPUS	25
TEXAS A&M U	10

Geochemistry

BRIDGEWATER ST COLL	2
CALIFORNIA INST OF TECH	1
HOPE COLL	1
SUNY COLL AT FREDONIA	1

Geography

Degrees in this subject were reported by 266 institutions. Consult more specific headings.

Geological Engineering

ALASKA FAIRBANKS, U of	3
ARIZONA, U of	7
COLORADO SCHOOL OF MINES	6
IDAHO, U of	2
MICHIGAN TECH U	2
MINNESOTA TWIN CITIES, U of	3
MISSISSIPPI MAIN CAMPUS, U of	3
MISSOURI-ROLLA, U of	14
MONTANA COLL OF MINERAL SCI AND TECH	1
NEVADA-RENO, U of	5
NEW MEXICO INST OF MINING AND TECH	4
NEW MEXICO ST U MAIN CAMPUS	1
NORTH DAKOTA MAIN CAMPUS, U of	1
SOUTH DAKOTA SCHOOL OF MINES & TECH	4
UTAH, U of	2
WASHINGTON ST U	1
WISCONSIN-MADISON, U of	1

Geological Sciences, Other

ARIZONA, U of	13
BOSTON U	2
BRADLEY U	1
CALIFORNIA-SANTA BARBARA, U of	2
DISTRICT OF COLUMBIA, U of THE	1
HAWAII AT MANOA, U of	5
INDIANA U PENNSYLVANIA	1
KANSAS ST U AGRI AND APP SCI	1
MIAMI, U of	1
MISSOURI-ROLLA, U of	2
MONTANA ST U	2
NORTHERN IOWA, U of	2
SHIPPENSBURG U PENNSYLVANIA	16
WESTERN WASHINGTON U	2
WISCONSIN-MILWAUKEE, U of	13
YALE U	5

Geology

Degrees in this subject were reported by 325 institutions. Consult more specific headings.

Geophysical Engineering

COLORADO SCHOOL OF MINES	9
MONTANA COLL OF MINERAL SCI AND TECH	2
ROCHESTER, U of	2

Geophysics and Seismology

BOISE ST U	1
BROWN U	5
CALIFORNIA INST OF TECH	3
CHICAGO, U of	4
DELAWARE, U of	1
HOUSTON-U PARK, U of	1
KANSAS MAIN CAMPUS, U of	1
MICHIGAN TECH U	2
MINNESOTA TWIN CITIES, U of	3
MONTANA ST U	1
NEW MEXICO INST OF MINING AND TECH	5
OKLAHOMA NORMAN CAMPUS, U of	5
SOUTH CAROLINA—COLUMBIA, U of	1
STANFORD U	1
TEXAS A&M U	2
TEXAS AT AUSTIN, U of	2
TEXAS AT EL PASO, U of	3
TEXAS TECH U	1
TULSA, U of	4
VIRGINIA POLYTECHNIC INST AND ST U	1
WESTERN MICHIGAN U	2
WYOMING, U of	1

Geriatric Services

ARKANSAS PINE BLUFF, U of	4
BOWLING GREEN ST U MAIN CAMPUS	12
CALIFORNIA ST U-SACRAMENTO	2
CALIFORNIA U PENNSYLVANIA	1
GWYNEDD-MERCY COLL	2
KENT ST U MAIN CAMPUS	5
LINDENWOOD COLL	1
LYNCHBURG COLL	4

MADONNA COLL	18
NORTHERN MICHIGAN U	3
OREGON, U of	8
QUINNIPIAC COLL	2
SAINT EDWARD'S U	2
SAINT MARY-OF-THE-WOODS COLL	3
SAN DIEGO ST U	4
SOUTH FLORIDA, U of	9
WEBER ST COLL	6

Geriatrics

NORTHERN COLORADO, U of	11

German

Degrees in this subject were reported by 368 institutions. Consult more specific headings.

Germanic Languages, Other

BETHEL COLL	2
CALIFORNIA-BERKELEY, U of	1
CALIFORNIA-SANTA BARBARA, U of	8

Glass

BOWLING GREEN ST U MAIN CAMPUS	2
CALIFORNIA COLL OF ARTS AND CRAFTS	4
CENTER FOR CREATIVE STUDIES COL OF ART AND DESIGN	1
CLEVELAND INST OF ART	1
RHODE ISLAND SCHOOL OF DESIGN	6

Graphic Design

ABILENE CHRISTIAN U	3
AMERICAN U	19
BARTON (FORMERLY ATLANTIC CHRISTIAN) COLL	5
BOISE ST U	17
BRIGHAM YOUNG U	98
CALIFORNIA COLL OF ARTS AND CRAFTS	1
CALIFORNIA POLYTECHNIC ST U-SAN LUIS OBISPO	45
CALIFORNIA-DAVIS, U of	74
CALIFORNIA-LOS ANGELES, U of	52
CENTRAL MICHIGAN U	3
COLL OF SAINT ROSE	11
CORNISH COLL OF THE ARTS	14
DAEMEN COLL	3
DUKE U	6
ILLINOIS INST OF TECH	6
IOWA ST U	44
KANSAS MAIN CAMPUS, U of	122
KENT ST U MAIN CAMPUS	15
LONG ISLAND U C W POST CAMPUS	2
MARIST COLL	11
MARYMOUNT COLL	13
MASSACHUSETTS COLL OF ART	39
MERCY COLL—MAIN CAMPUS	7
MICHIGAN ANN ARBOR, U of	38
MINNEAPOLIS COLL OF ART AND DESIGN	113
MINNESOTA TWIN CITIES, U of	67
NEW SCHOOL FOR SOCIAL RESEARCH	148
NEW YORK INST OF TECH MAIN CAMPUS	46
NEW YORK U	6
NORTHERN ST U	3
NORTHWESTERN ST U LOUISIANA	8
NOTRE DAME, U of	16
OREGON, U of	16
POINT PARK COLL	9
PRATT INST-MAIN	65
RADFORD U	66
RIVIER COLL	1
ROCHESTER INST OF TECH	152
SAGINAW VALLEY ST U	1
SAINT JOHN'S U NEW YORK	13
SAINT THOMAS AQUINAS COLL	7
SAN JOSE ST U	43
SOUTHWEST MISSOURI ST U	23
SOUTHWESTERN LOUISIANA, U of	10
SUNY COLL AT BUFFALO	67
SYRACUSE U MAIN CAMPUS	174
VIRGINIA COMMONWEALTH U	42
WINTHROP COLL	2

Graphic Design

ABILENE CHRISTIAN U	3
ANDERSON U	2
ARKANSAS ST U MAIN CAMPUS	8
ART CENTER COLL OF DESIGN	86
ARTS, THE U of THE	29
BEAVER COLL	9
BOSTON U	25
BOWLING GREEN ST U MAIN CAMPUS	53
BRESCIA COLL	5
CALIFORNIA COLL OF ARTS AND CRAFTS	30
CALIFORNIA INST OF ARTS	12
CARNEGIE MELLON U	19
CENTER FOR CREATIVE STUDIES COL OF ART AND DESIGN	44
CENTRAL MICHIGAN U	30
CENTRAL WASHINGTON U	11
CINCINNATI MAIN CAMPUS, U of	36
CLEVELAND INST OF ART	14
COLL OF SAINT MARY	4
CONNECTICUT, U of	52
CORCORAN SCHOOL OF ART	22
DELAWARE, U of	17
DENVER, U of	6
DRAKE U	15
DREXEL U	20
EAST TEXAS ST U	6
EASTERN WASHINGTON U	8
FAIRMONT ST COLL	8
FLAGLER COLL	16
FLORIDA AGRI AND MECH U	2
FLORIDA, U of	28
FRANKLIN PIERCE COLL	36
FROSTBURG ST U	11
GALLAUDET U	7
GRACE COLL	4
HARTFORD, U of	28
HENDERSON ST U	6
HOUSTON-U PARK, U of	24
ILLINOIS AT CHICAGO, U of	56
ILLINOIS URBANA CAMPUS, U of	38
IOWA ST U	52
KANSAS CITY ART INST	16
KANSAS NEWMAN COLL	1
KENDALL COLL OF ART AND DESIGN	22
KENNESAW ST COLL	9
KENT ST U MAIN CAMPUS	24
LA ROCHE COLL	19
LAMAR U	11
LINCOLN U	2
LOUISIANA ST U & AGRI & MECH & HEBERT LAWS CTR	35
LOUISIANA TECH U	20
LOYOLA U IN NEW ORLEANS	2
LYNDON ST COLL	3
MAINE COLL OF ART (WAS PORTLAND SCHOOL OF ART)	16
MARYLAND INST COLL OF ART	43
MARYMOUNT U	14
MEMPHIS COLL OF ART	1
MERCYHURST COLL	1
MICHIGAN ANN ARBOR, U of	37
MONTANA ST U	25
MOORE COLL OF ART	34
MORAVIAN COLL	9
MOUNT MARY COLL	13
MOUNT VERNON COLL	1
NEW MEXICO HIGHLANDS U	7
NORTHERN MICHIGAN U	9
NORTHWESTERN COLL	6
OHIO NORTHERN U	2
OTIS ART INST OF PARSONS SCHOOL OF DESIGN	17
PACIFIC, U of THE	11
PACIFIC UNION COLL	2
PRESCOTT COLL	1
RHODE ISLAND SCHOOL OF DESIGN	59
RINGLING SCHOOL OF ART AND DESIGN	21
SAINT CLOUD ST U	10
SAINT MARY'S COLL OF MINNESOTA	4
SAINT NORBERT COLL	11
SAINT VINCENT COLL	1
SAMFORD U	9
SAN FRANCISCO, U of	7
SAVANNAH COLL OF ART AND DESIGN	55
SETON HILL COLL	2
SOUTHWEST MISSOURI ST U	13
SUNY COLL AT NEW PALTZ	6
TEMPLE U	28
TENNESSEE-KNOXVILLE, U of	28
TEXAS AT EL PASO, U of	6
TEXAS TECH U	27
WASHINGTON U	34

WASHINGTON, U of	21
WEBER ST COLL	4
WEST TEXAS ST U	7
WESTERN CONNECTICUT ST U	37
WESTERN WASHINGTON U	34
WICHITA ST U	21
WOODBURY U	8

Graphic and Printing Communications, General

ANDREWS U	4
ARKANSAS ST U MAIN CAMPUS	7
BOWLING GREEN ST U MAIN CAMPUS	18
CALIFORNIA POLYTECHNIC ST U-SAN LUIS OBISPO	62
CENTRAL MISSOURI ST U	42
EAST TEXAS ST U	4
NORTH TEXAS, U of	25
NORTHERN IOWA, U of	5
POINT LOMA NAZARENE COLL	6
SCHOOL OF THE OZARKS	1
SIMMONS COLL	11
SOUTHWEST TEXAS ST U	4
TEXAS SOUTHERN U	1
WEST VIRGINIA INST OF TECH	25
WESTERN MICHIGAN U	30

Graphlic and Printing Communications, Other

CALIFORNIA U PENNSYLVANIA	16
DISTRICT OF COLUMBIA, U of THE	8
DREXEL U	2
SOUTH DAKOTA ST U	3

Greek (Classical)

ARIZONA, U of	1
BAYLOR U	1
BROWN U	1
BRYN MAWR COLL	5
BUTLER U	1
CALIFORNIA U PENNSYLVANIA	5
CALIFORNIA-LOS ANGELES, U of	2
CALVIN COLL	2
DICKINSON COLL	3
GETTYSBURG COLL	1
GRACE COLL	1
HAVERFORD COLL	1
INDIANA U BLOOMINGTON	2
MICHIGAN ANN ARBOR, U of	1
MILLSAPS COLL	4
MINNESOTA TWIN CITIES, U of	2
MOUNT HOLYOKE COLL	1
NORTH CAROLINA AT GREENSBORO, U of	1
OBERLIN COLL	1
OHIO ST U MAIN CAMPUS	2
OREGON, U of	1
RANDOLPH-MACON COLL	1
SAINT OLAF COLL	1
SWARTHMORE COLL	1
TEXAS AT AUSTIN, U of	1
TULANE U LOUISIANA	1
VASSAR COLL	1
YALE U	2

Health Care Administration

ALABAMA, U of	37
ALFRED U	1
ARIZONA, U of	11
ARKANSAS COLL	1
ARKANSAS ST U MAIN CAMPUS	5
AUBURN U MAIN CAMPUS	19
AUGUSTANA COLL	1
BELLARMINE COLL	7
BOWLING GREEN ST U MAIN CAMPUS	16
CALIFORNIA ST U LONG BEACH	9
CEDAR CREST COLL	2
CITY U	5
CONCORDIA COLL	16
CONCORDIA COLL AT MOORHEAD	17
CONNECTICUT, U of	19
CUNY LEHMAN COLL	32
DAEMEN COLL	2
DAVIS AND ELKINS COLL	3
DETROIT, U of	21
DOMINICAN COLL OF BLAUVELT	7
EAST CENTRAL U	1
EAST TEXAS ST U	1
EASTERN COLL	1
EASTERN KENTUCKY U	5
EASTERN MICHIGAN U	27
EASTERN WASHINGTON U	8
ELMHURST COLL	2
EMMANUEL COLL	17
FAIRMONT ST COLL	9
FERRIS ST U	27
FLORIDA AGRI AND MECH U	6
GOLDEN GATE U	5
GWYNEDD-MERCY COLL	14
IDAHO ST U	7
ILLINOIS BENEDICTINE COLL	3
IONA COLL	18
ITHACA COLL	15
KENTUCKY, U of	23
KING'S COLL	11
LANGSTON U	15
LEBANON VALLEY COLL	3
LONG ISLAND U C W POST CAMPUS	6
MARY BALDWIN COLL	9
MARYMOUNT U	5
MARYWOOD COLL	6
METROPOLITAN ST COLL	24
MILLIGAN COLL	2
MISSOURI-COLUMBIA, U of	19
MOUNT MARTY COLL	1
NEW SCHOOL FOR SOCIAL RESEARCH	44
NORFOLK ST U	8
NORTHEASTERN U	7
NORTHERN ILLINOIS U	30
OREGON ST U	25
PARK COLL	45
PENNSYLVANIA ST U MAIN CAMPUS	150
PENNSYLVANIA, U of	1
PHILADELPHIA COLL OF TEXTILES AND SCIENCE	5
PROVIDENCE COLL	18
QUINNIPIAC COLL	15
REDLANDS, U of	5
RIVIER COLL	2
ROGER WILLIAMS COLL	28
SAINT JOHN'S U NEW YORK	22
SAINT JOSEPH'S COLL	361
SAINT JOSEPH'S U	1
SAINT JOSEPHS COLL MAIN CAMPUS	47
SAINT LEO COLL	47
SAINT MARY'S COLL OF CALIFORNIA	57
SAINT PETER'S COLL	10
SALVE REGINA COLL	2
SCRANTON, U of	15
SOUTH DAKOTA, U of	19
SOUTHERN COLL OF SEVENTH-DAY ADVENTISTS	11
SOUTHERN ILLINOIS U-CARBONDALE	162
SOUTHWEST TEXAS ST U	41
SPRINGFIELD COLL	6
ST FRANCIS COLL	26
STONEHILL COLL	27
SUNY COLL AT FREDONIA	17
TENNESSEE ST U	7
TEXAS AT EL PASO, U of	1
TEXAS SOUTHERN U	10
URSULINE COLL	15
VIRGINIA COMMONWEALTH U	14
VITERBO COLL	3
WEST VIRGINIA INST OF TECH	11
WESTERN KENTUCKY U	22
WHEELING COLL	1
WICHITA ST U	8
WIDENER U PENNSYLVANIA CAMPUS	1
WISCONSIN-EAU CLAIRE, U of	28

Health Care Planning

ALASKA ANCHORAGE, U of	6
CINCINNATI MAIN CAMPUS, U of	10
WILBERFORCE U	8

Health Education

Degrees in this subject were reported by 161 institutions. Consult more specific headings.

Health Sciences (unspecified)

Degrees in this subject were reported by 758 institutions. Consult more specific headings.

Health Sciences Administration, Other

ANDERSON U	3
APPALACHIAN ST U	25
AURORA U	6
CONCORDIA COLL AT MOORHEAD	2
DETROIT, U of	21
GARDNER-WEBB COLL	5
GEORGE WASHINGTON U	2
JERSEY CITY ST COLL	30
LINDENWOOD COLL	2
MISSOURI SOUTHERN ST COLL	5
NATIONAL U	4
NORTHEASTERN U	13
NORTHERN MICHIGAN U	2
OHIO DOMINICAN COLL	2
SCRANTON, U of	15
SPRING ARBOR COLL	38
WESTERN CAROLINA U	10
WICHITA ST U	47

Health Sciences, Other

Degrees in this subject were reported by 106 institutions. Consult more specific headings.

Hebrew

CUNY BROOKLYN COLL	1
CUNY HUNTER COLL	2
GRATZ COLL	1
MICHIGAN ANN ARBOR, U of	1
SPERTUS COLL JUDAICA	1
TEMPLE U	1
TEXAS AT AUSTIN, U of	1
WISCONSIN-MADISON, U of	3
WISCONSIN-MILWAUKEE, U of	2
YESHIVA U	21

Higher Education Administration

KENT ST U MAIN CAMPUS	1

Hispanic-American Studies

ARIZONA, U of	3
CALIFORNIA ST U DOMINGUEZ HILLS	1
CALIFORNIA ST U LONG BEACH	1
CALIFORNIA ST U LOS ANGELES	5
CALIFORNIA ST U NORTHRIDGE	5
CALIFORNIA-BERKELEY, U of	18
CALIFORNIA-LOS ANGELES, U of	3
CALIFORNIA-SAN DIEGO, U of	1
CALIFORNIA-SANTA BARBARA, U of	6
LOYOLA MARYMOUNT U	1
MICHIGAN ANN ARBOR, U of	1
NORTHERN COLORADO, U of	1
RUTGERS U NEW BRUNSWICK	5
SAN DIEGO ST U	2
SAN FRANCISCO ST U	6
SONOMA ST U	7
WESTERN NEW MEXICO U	1
WILLAMETTE U	7

History

Degrees in this subject were reported by 1073 institutions. Consult more specific headings.

Home Decorating

TEXAS SOUTHERN U	1

Home Economics (unspecified)

Degrees in this subject were reported by 345 institutions. Consult more specific headings.

Home Economics Education

Degrees in this subject were reported by 115 institutions. Consult more specific headings.

Home Economics, other

ADRIAN COLL	6
ALLENTOWN COLL OF SAINT FRANCIS DE SALES	12
ARIZONA, U of	58
CHRISTIAN HERITAGE COLL	5
GEORGIA SOUTHERN COLL	1
HOWARD U	36
IOWA ST U	1
JUDSON COLL	5
MISSOURI-COLUMBIA, U of	1
MONTEVALLO, U of	10
NEW HAMPSHIRE, U of	56
NORFOLK ST U	4
NORTH ALABAMA, U of	6
OHIO ST U MAIN CAMPUS	2
OKLAHOMA BAPTIST U	7
OREGON ST U	6
SAINT OLAF COLL	2
SEATTLE PACIFIC U	2

Home Economics,General

Degrees in this subject were reported by 199 institutions. Consult more specific headings.

Home Furnishings and Equip Mgnt Prod and Ser Other

NORTHEAST LOUISIANA U	1

Home Furnishings and Equip Mgmt Production, Serv., Gen.

NORTH TEXAS, U of	12
TENNESSEE-KNOXVILLE, U of	25
TEXAS CHRISTIAN U	6

Home Management

MISSISSIPPI COLL	2
TEXAS TECH U	14

Horse Handling and Care

CENTENARY COLL	8
OTTERBEIN COLL	10
VIRGINIA INTERMONT COLL	22

Horticulture Science

ALABAMA AGRI AND MECH U	5
ARIZONA, U of	6
ARKANSAS-FAYETTEVILLE, U of	4
AUBURN U MAIN CAMPUS	22
CALIFORNIA POLYTECHNIC ST U-SAN LUIS OBISPO	6
CALIFORNIA ST POLYTECHNIC U POMONA	2
CLEMSON U	11
COLORADO ST U	6
CONNECTICUT, U of	14
DELAWARE VALLEY COLL OF SCI AND AGRI	4
FLORIDA, U of	8
FORT VALLEY ST COLL	4
HAWAII AT MANOA, U of	1
ILLINOIS URBANA CAMPUS, U of	2
KANSAS ST U AGRI AND APP SCI	21
KENTUCKY, U of	5
MARYLAND COLL PARK CAMPUS, U of	17
MICHIGAN ST U	26
MINNESOTA TWIN CITIES, U of	8
MISSISSIPPI ST U	8
MISSOURI-COLUMBIA, U of	10
NEW MEXICO ST U MAIN CAMPUS	6
NORTH CAROLINA ST U AT RALEIGH	31
NORTHWEST MISSOURI ST U	3
OHIO ST U MAIN CAMPUS	33
OKLAHOMA ST U MAIN CAMPUS	15
PENNSYLVANIA ST U MAIN CAMPUS	28
RHODE ISLAND, U of	11
SAM HOUSTON ST U	4
SOUTHEAST MISSOURI ST U	2
SOUTHWEST MISSOURI ST U	6
SOUTHWEST TEXAS ST U	3
SOUTHWESTERN LOUISIANA, U of	3
STEPHEN F AUSTIN ST U	7
TEXAS A&M U	49
UTAH ST U	2
VIRGINIA POLYTECHNIC INST AND ST U	28
WASHINGTON ST U	10
WISCONSIN-MADISON, U of	19
WISCONSIN-RIVER FALLS, U of	5

Horticulture, General

GEORGIA, U of	18
HAWAII AT MANOA, U of	9

IOWA ST U 23
LOUISIANA ST U & AGRI & MECH & HEBERT LAWS CTR 2
MARS HILL COLL 1
MONTANA ST U 11
NEBRASKA-LINCOLN, U of 9
NORTH DAKOTA ST U MAIN CAMPUS 6
OREGON ST U 28
SOUTH DAKOTA ST U 7
TEMPLE U 1
TEXAS TECH U 9

Horticulture, Other

MONTANA ST U 1

Hospitality and Recreation Marketing, General

FERRIS ST U 26

Hospitality and Recreation Marketing, Other

CENTRAL MICHIGAN U 33

Hotel/Motel Management

ARKANSAS TECH U 9
ASHLAND U 11
BELMONT COLL 4
BEREA COLL 8
BETHUNE COOKMAN COLL 21
BLACK HILLS ST COLL 6
BOSTON U 72
BOWLING GREEN ST U MAIN CAMPUS 17
BRIGHAM YOUNG U HAWAII CAMPUS 8
BRYANT COLL OF BUSINESS ADMINISTRATION 21
CENTRAL FLORIDA, U of 65
CENTRAL MISSOURI ST U 18
CHEYNEY U PENNSYLVANIA 7
CORNELL U-ENDOWED COLLS 197
CUNY NEW YORK CITY TECHNICAL COLL 26
EAST STROUDSBURG U PENNSYLVANIA 76
EASTERN MICHIGAN U 2
FAIRLEIGH DICKINSON U 23
FLORIDA ST U 104
GEORGIA ST U 63
GRAMBLING ST U 10
GRAND VALLEY ST U 21
HOUSTON-U PARK, U of 162
HOWARD U 15
IOWA ST U 49
JAMES MADISON U 26
JOHNSON ST COLL 14
LEBANON VALLEY COLL 4
MICHIGAN ST U 125
MOORHEAD ST U 15
MORRIS BROWN COLL 10
NEVADA-LAS VEGAS, U of 230
NEW HAMPSHIRE COLL 43
NEW HAMPSHIRE, U of 46
NEW HAVEN, U of 49
NEW ORLEANS, U of 21
NEW YORK INST OF TECH MAIN CAMPUS 57
NEW YORK U 14
NIAGARA U 38
NORTH CAROLINA WESLEYAN COLL 5
NORTH DAKOTA ST U MAIN CAMPUS 13
NORTH TEXAS, U of 59
NOVA U 2
OKLAHOMA ST U MAIN CAMPUS 72
OREGON ST U 35
PURDUE U CALUMET CAMPUS 43
ROCHESTER INST OF TECH 95
SAN FRANCISCO, U of 13
SIENA HEIGHTS COLL 6
SOUTH CAROLINA—COLUMBIA, U of 140
SOUTHERN MISSISSIPPI, U of 40
SOUTHWEST ST U 13
TENNESSEE-KNOXVILLE, U of 57
TEXAS TECH U 164
TIFFIN U 6
US INTERNATIONAL U 15
VIRGINIA ST U 13
WASHINGTON ST U 132
WEBBER COLL 4
WILEY COLL 4
WISCONSIN-STOUT, U of 269

Housing

MINNESOTA TWIN CITIES, U of 11
OREGON ST U 8
SEATTLE PACIFIC U 3
SOUTHEAST MISSOURI ST U 9

Human Environment and Housing, Other

ABILENE CHRISTIAN U 7
APPALACHIAN ST U 14
CAMPBELL U INCORPORATED 5
NAZARETH COLL 4
NEVADA-RENO, U of 8
NORTH CAROLINA AT GREENSBORO, U of 23
OREGON ST U 9

Human Environment and Housing, General

ARKANSAS-FAYETTEVILLE, U of 12
AUBURN U MAIN CAMPUS 31
COLORADO ST U 33
EASTERN KENTUCKY U 15
EASTERN MICHIGAN U 33
FREED-HARDEMAN COLL 1
GEORGIA SOUTHERN COLL 8
GEORGIA, U of 35
INDIANA ST U 14
INDIANA U BLOOMINGTON 21
IOWA ST U 12
KENTUCKY, U of 28
MANKATO ST U 10
MIAMI U OXFORD CAMPUS 29
MICHIGAN ST U 2
MISSOURI-COLUMBIA, U of 56
MOREHEAD ST U 12
MURRAY ST U 4
NORTHERN IOWA, U of 16
OHIO U MAIN CAMPUS 52
OKLAHOMA ST U MAIN CAMPUS 30
OUR LADY OF THE LAKE U SAN ANTONIO 2
SOUTH DAKOTA ST U 10
SOUTHERN U AGRI & MECH COL AT BATON ROUGE 1
SOUTHWEST MISSOURI ST U 16
TEXAS TECH U 1
VIRGINIA POLYTECHNIC INST AND ST U 62
WESTERN KENTUCKY U 7
WESTERN WASHINGTON U 14
WISCONSIN-STEVENS POINT, U of 18

Human Resources Development

ALASKA PACIFIC U 89
AMERICAN U 10
AVILA COLL 2
BARTLESVILLE WESLEYAN COLL 4
BAYLOR U 5
BEAVER COLL 2
BELLEVUE COLL 262
BETHEL COLL 72
BETHUNE COOKMAN COLL 2
BIRMINGHAM SOUTHERN COLL 9
BOISE ST U 45
BOWLING GREEN ST U MAIN CAMPUS 41
BRENAU COLL 14
BRIGHAM YOUNG U HA WAII CAMPUS 13
CABRINI COLL 11
CEDAR CREST COLL 5
CENTRAL WESLEYAN COLL 111
CLARK U 5
COLL OF SAINT MARY 4
COLL OF SAINT SCHOLASTICA 3
CONCORDIA COLL 80
DOANE COLL 31
EAST CENTRAL U 47
FONTBONNE COLL 2
FRIENDS U 174
GENEVA COLL 79
GEORGE FOX COLL 127
GOLDEN GATE U 41
GRAND CANYON U 5
HAWAII PACIFIC COLL 8
INDIANA U PENNSYLVANIA 37
KING'S COLL 34
LEWIS U 4

LINDENWOOD COLL	14
LORAS COLL	1
LOURDES COLL	3
MASSACHUSETTS AT DARTMOUTH (WAS SE U OF MA, U of	10
MESSIAH COLL	19
MIAMI, U of	8
MID-AMERICA NAZARENE COLL	105
MONTANA, U of	22
NATIONAL U	16
NORTHEASTERN U	11
NORTHWESTERN COLL	3
NOTRE DAME COLL	17
OAKLAND CITY COLL	36
OAKLAND U	20
OHIO ST U MAIN CAMPUS	80
PALM BEACH ATLANTIC COLL	67
PENNSYLVANIA, U of	4
POINT PARK COLL	12
QUINNIPIAC COLL	4
RHODE ISLAND COLL	13
RICHMOND, U of	7
ROCKHURST COLL	2
SAINT JOSEPH'S U	4
SAINT LEO COLL	191
SAINT LOUIS U MAIN CAMPUS	11
SAMFORD U	4
SILVER LAKE COLL	4
SIMPSON COLL	22
SOUTHERN NAZARENE U	163
SPRING ARBOR COLL	373
SUSQUEHANNA U	12
TOLEDO, U of	32
UTAH ST U	25
WESTERN NEW ENGLAND COLL	13
WESTMINSTER COLL OF SALT LAKE CITY	9
WHEELING COLL	31
WILMINGTON COLL	24
WISCONSIN-MILWAUKEE, U of	28

Humanities and Social Sciences

Degrees in this subject were reported by 213 institutions. Consult more specific headings.

Illustration Design

AMERICAN COLL FOR THE APPLIED ARTS	14
ART CENTER COLL OF DESIGN	84
ARTS, THE U of THE	30
BEMIDJI ST U	30
CALIFORNIA COLL OF ARTS AND CRAFTS	11
CENTER FOR CREATIVE STUDIES COL OF ART AND DESIGN	22
CLEVELAND INST OF ART	8
COKER COLL	2
EAST TEXAS ST U	1
HARTFORD, U of	20
KANSAS CITY ART INST	9
KENDALL COLL OF ART AND DESIGN	28
MASSACHUSETTS AT DARTMOUTH (WAS SE U OF MA, U of	1
MEMPHIS COLL OF ART	1
MOORE COLL OF ART	24
MOORHEAD ST U	12
NORTHERN MICHIGAN U	5
OTIS ART INST OF PARSONS SCHOOL OF DESIGN	19
RHODE ISLAND SCHOOL OF DESIGN	94
RINGLING SCHOOL OF ART AND DESIGN	24
SAN FRANCISCO, U of	2
SAVANNAH COLL OF ART AND DESIGN	42
TEXAS WOMAN'S U	3
WEBER ST COLL	1

Indic Languages

YALE U	3

Individual and Family Development, General

AKRON, MAIN CAMPUS, U of	39
ALABAMA, U of	21
ANDREWS U	2
APPALACHIAN ST U	28
ARIZONA, U of	51
ARKANSAS PINE BLUFF, U of	3
ARKANSAS-FAYETTEVILLE, U of	5
AUBURN U MAIN CAMPUS	19
BAYLOR U	4
CALIFORNIA POLYTECHNIC ST U-SAN LUIS OBISPO	27
CALIFORNIA-DAVIS, U of	1
CENTRAL MICHIGAN U	12
CINCINNATI MAIN CAMPUS, U of	30
COLORADO ST U	138
CONNECTICUT COLL	20
CONNECTICUT, U of	157
CORNELL U-NYS STATUTORY COLLS	125
DELAWARE, U of	29
EASTERN KENTUCKY U	12
EASTERN MICHIGAN U	15
FLORIDA ST U	51
FONTBONNE COLL	2
GEORGIA SOUTHERN COLL	2
GEORGIA, U of	33
GOSHEN COLL	1
HAWAII AT MANOA, U of	21
HOUSTON-U PARK, U of	15
IDAHO, U of	12
ILLINOIS URBANA CAMPUS, U of	20
INDIANA ST U	9
INDIANA U PENNSYLVANIA	26
KANSAS ST U AGRI AND APP SCI	14
KENT ST U MAIN CAMPUS	43
KENTUCKY ST U	2
KENTUCKY, U of	28
LOUISIANA ST U & AGRI & MECH & HEBERT LAWS CTR	35
MAINE, U of	67
MANKATO ST U	13
MASSACHUSETTS AT AMHERST, U of	7
MIAMI U OXFORD CAMPUS	3
MICHIGAN ST U	41
MISSISSIPPI U FOR WOMEN	13
MISSOURI-COLUMBIA, U of	25
MONTANA ST U	25
MURRAY ST U	12
NEBRASKA-LINCOLN, U of	84
NEVADA-RENO, U of	5
NORFOLK ST U	3
NORTH CAROLINA AGRI AND TECHNICAL ST U	8
NORTH CAROLINA AT GREENSBORO, U of	47
NORTH DAKOTA ST U MAIN CAMPUS	37
NORTHEAST MISSOURI ST U	33
NORTHERN MICHIGAN U	3
NORTHWESTERN ST U LOUISIANA	1
OAKWOOD COLL	1
OHIO ST U MAIN CAMPUS	110
OHIO U MAIN CAMPUS	24
OKLAHOMA CHRISTIAN COLL	1
OKLAHOMA ST U MAIN CAMPUS	60
OREGON ST U	46
PENNSYLVANIA ST U MAIN CAMPUS	134
PRAIRIE VIEW A & M U	2
RHODE ISLAND, U of	113
ROCKFORD COLL	40
SAINT JOSEPHS COLL MAIN CAMPUS	1
SAINT OLAF COLL	6
SAINT XAVIER COLL	2
SCRANTON, U of	5
SOUTH DAKOTA ST U	27
SOUTHEAST MISSOURI ST U	16
SOUTHERN ILLINOIS U-CARBONDALE	1
SOUTHERN NAZARENE U	15
SOUTHWEST MISSOURI ST U	13
SOUTHWEST TEXAS ST U	20
STEPHEN F AUSTIN ST U	7
SUNY COLL AT PLATTSBURG	18
SYRACUSE U MAIN CAMPUS	43
TENNESSEE-KNOXVILLE, U of	76
TEXAS AT AUSTIN, U of	11
URSULINE COLL	1
UTAH ST U	20
UTAH, U of	41
VERMONT, U of	11
VIRGINIA POLYTECHNIC INST AND ST U	114
WASHINGTON ST U	17
WISCONSIN-MADISON, U of	38
WISCONSIN-STOUT, U of	29

Individual and Family Development, Other

ASHLAND U	4
CALIFORNIA-DAVIS, U of	98

KANSAS ST U AGRI AND APP SCI 10
NORTH TEXAS, U of 7
OKLAHOMA NORMAN CAMPUS, U of 18
SOUTHWESTERN LOUISIANA, U of 24
TEXAS A & I U 3
TEXAS SOUTHERN U 10
TEXAS WOMAN'S U 8

Industrial Arts Education

Degrees in this subject were reported by 123 institutions. Consult more specific headings.

Industrial Design

ARIZONA ST U 14
ART CENTER COLL OF DESIGN 57
ARTS, THE U of THE 27
AUBURN U MAIN CAMPUS 32
BRIDGEPORT, U of 6
CALIFORNIA COLL OF ARTS AND CRAFTS 7
CALIFORNIA ST U LONG BEACH 14
CARNEGIE MELLON U 20
CENTER FOR CREATIVE STUDIES COL OF ART AND DESIGN 29
CINCINNATI MAIN CAMPUS, U of 31
CLEVELAND INST OF ART 6
DAYTON, U of 3
FASHION INST OF TECH 20
ILLINOIS AT CHICAGO, U of 26
ILLINOIS URBANA CAMPUS, U of 30
KANSAS CITY ART INST 4
KENDALL COLL OF ART AND DESIGN 4
KENT ST U MAIN CAMPUS 9
METROPOLITAN ST COLL 2
MICHIGAN ANN ARBOR, U of 6
NORTHERN MICHIGAN U 1
OHIO ST U MAIN CAMPUS 52
RHODE ISLAND SCHOOL OF DESIGN 27
SAN JOSE ST U 9
WASHINGTON, U of 10
WESTERN MICHIGAN U 12
WESTERN WASHINGTON U 14

Industrial Electronics

ANDREWS U 4

Industrial Engineering

Degrees in this subject were reported by 110 institutions. Consult more specific headings.

Industrial Equipment Maintenance and Repair, General

ANDREWS U 1
SIENA HEIGHTS COLL 1

Industrial Production Technologies, Other

ANDREWS U 1
ARIZONA ST U 48
BEREA COLL 14
BOWLING GREEN ST U MAIN CAMPUS 14
CENTRAL CONNECTICUT ST U 111
CENTRAL MICHIGAN U 3
CENTRAL OKLAHOMA, U of 32
COLORADO ST U 74
EASTERN MICHIGAN U 9
FERRIS ST U 31
GEORGIA SOUTHERN COLL 55
GRAND VALLEY ST U 21
ILLINOIS ST U 25
INDIANA ST U 58
LIVINGSTON U 3
MURRAY ST U 19
NATIONAL U 33
NEBRASKA-LINCOLN, U of 8
NORTHERN ILLINOIS U 24
NORTHERN KENTUCKY U 2
NORTHWEST MISSOURI ST U 4
OKLAHOMA ST U MAIN CAMPUS 12
PITTSBURG ST U 10
SAGINAW VALLEY ST U 1
SAINT CLOUD ST U 26
SOUTHWEST MISSOURI ST U 2
SOUTHWEST TEXAS ST U 4
TOLEDO, U of 3
WASHINGTON U 4
WEST VIRGINIA ST COLL 4
WESTERN MICHIGAN U 44

Industrial Sales

EASTERN MICHIGAN U 18
HOUSTON-U PARK, U of 32
NEBRASKA AT OMAHA, U of 1
TEXAS A&M U 136
WESTERN MICHIGAN U 79

Industrial Technology

Degrees in this subject were reported by 116 institutions. Consult more specific headings.

Industrial and Organizational Psychology

BRIDGEWATER ST COLL 5
COLL OF SANTA FE 3
CUNY BERNARD BARUCH COLL 13
DETROIT, U of 3
GEORGIA INST OF TECH MAIN CAMPUS 12
HIGH POINT COLL 10
HOLY FAMILY COLL 2
NOVA U 2
OAKWOOD COLL 1
POINT LOMA NAZARENE COLL 4
SAINT MARY'S COLL OF CALIFORNIA 9
SAINT XAVIER COLL 2
US AIR FORCE ACAD 20
WASHINGTON U 5
WESTERN WASHINGTON U 34
WESTMINSTER COLL 4

Information Sciences and Systems

Degrees in this subject were reported by 149 institutions. Consult more specific headings.

Institutional Management, Other

ALASKA PACIFIC U 3
CALIFORNIA ST POLYTECHNIC U POMONA 162
COLUMBIA COLL 3
CONCORDIA TEACHERS COLL 1
DENVER, U of 48
DREXEL U 25
FLORIDA SOUTHERN COLL 14
GEORGIA SOUTHERN COLL 1
GOLDEN GATE U 13
HAWAII AT MANOA, U of 85
INDIANA U PENNSYLVANIA 44
MARYLAND EASTERN SHORE, U of 16
MARYWOOD COLL 5
MASSACHUSETTS AT AMHERST, U of 221
MERCYHURST COLL 51
MIAMI U OXFORD CAMPUS 10
MILLIGAN COLL 42
MISSOURI VALLEY COLL 8
MISSOURI-COLUMBIA, U of 72
NEWBERRY COLL 2
NORTHERN ARIZONA U 123
REDLANDS, U of 5
REGIS COLL 124
SHEPHERD COLL 16
SIOUX FALLS COLL 1
SOUTH CAROLINA—COLUMBIA, U of 15
VIRGINIA POLYTECHNIC INST AND ST U 62
WESTERN KENTUCKY U 8
WICHITA ST U 6

Institutional, Home Mgnt and Support Serv. General

BOWLING GREEN ST U MAIN CAMPUS 4
INDIANA ST U 2
KENT ST U MAIN CAMPUS 9
OKLAHOMA CHRISTIAN COLL 1
ROCHESTER INST OF TECH 20
SOUTHERN MISSISSIPPI, U of 1
STEPHEN F AUSTIN ST U 5
SYRACUSE U MAIN CAMPUS 12

Insurance and Risk Management

ALABAMA, U of 8
ARIZONA ST U 1

ARKANSAS-FAYETTEVILLE, U of	3
BAYLOR U	7
BOWLING GREEN ST U MAIN CAMPUS	2
CONNECTICUT, U of	3
DELTA ST U	18
DRAKE U	6
EASTERN KENTUCKY U	18
FERRIS ST U	20
FLORIDA ST U	29
FLORIDA, U of	5
GEORGIA ST U	26
GEORGIA, U of	148
HARTFORD, U of	18
HOWARD U	10
ILLINOIS WESLEYAN U	7
INDIANA ST U	2
MEMPHIS ST U	7
MISSISSIPPI MAIN CAMPUS, U of	9
MISSISSIPPI ST U	11
MOREHOUSE COLL	3
NEBRASKA AT OMAHA, U of	1
NORTH TEXAS, U of	22
OHIO ST U MAIN CAMPUS	17
PENNSYLVANIA ST U MAIN CAMPUS	59
PENNSYLVANIA, U of	2
RHODE ISLAND, U of	10
RICHMOND, U of	1
SAINT CLOUD ST U	7
SAINT MARY'S U	9
SOUTH CAROLINA—COLUMBIA, U of	23
TEMPLE U	26
WAYNE ST U	1
WISCONSIN-MADISON, U of	28

Interior Design

Degrees in this subject were reported by 115 institutions. Consult more specific headings.

Intermedia

AUGUSTA COLL	2
CALIFORNIA COLL OF ARTS AND CRAFTS	30
CONCORDIA COLL AT MOORHEAD	10
INDIANA U PENNSYLVANIA	29
MASSACHUSETTS COLL OF ART	6
MERCYHURST COLL	1
OLIVET COLL	2
RAMAPO COLL OF NEW JERSEY	2
SAINT AMBROSE U	4
SHORTER COLL	1

International Agriculture

CALIFORNIA ST POLYTECHNIC U POMONA	1
CALIFORNIA-DAVIS, U of	4
EASTERN MENNONITE COLL	7
UTAH ST U	1
WYOMING, U of	1

International Business Management

Degrees in this subject were reported by 123 institutions. Consult more specific headings.

International Marketing

EASTERN MICHIGAN U	1
GANNON U	7
MIAMI, U of	64

International Public Service

BAYLOR U	28
LINCOLN U	1
PENNSYLVANIA ST U MAIN CAMPUS	90
PORTLAND ST U	27
SOUTHERN OREGON ST COLL	10
TEXAS WOMAN'S U	1

International Relations

Degrees in this subject were reported by 199 institutions. Consult more specific headings.

Investments and Securities

BABSON COLL	104
CUNY BERNARD BARUCH COLL	336
EASTERN MICHIGAN U	18
ILLINOIS BENEDICTINE COLL	8
WRIGHT ST U MAIN CAMPUS	46

Italian

ARIZONA ST U	5
ARIZONA, U of	1
BOSTON U	6
BRIGHAM YOUNG U	11
BROWN U	2
BRYN MAWR COLL	5
CALIFORNIA-BERKELEY, U of	10
CALIFORNIA-LOS ANGELES, U of	9
CALIFORNIA-SAN DIEGO, U of	1
CALIFORNIA-SANTA BARBARA, U of	3
CENTRAL CONNECTICUT ST U	1
COLORADO AT BOULDER, U of	4
CONNECTICUT COLL	6
CONNECTICUT, U of	4
CUNY BROOKLYN COLL	8
CUNY HUNTER COLL	6
CUNY LEHMAN COLL	1
CUNY QUEENS COLL	7
DARTMOUTH COLL	1
FLORIDA ST U	1
FORDHAM U	4
GEORGETOWN U	9
GEORGIA, U of	1
HAVERFORD COLL	1
HOFSTRA U	1
ILLINOIS AT CHICAGO, U of	3
ILLINOIS URBANA CAMPUS, U of	2
INDIANA U BLOOMINGTON	3
IONA COLL	5
KANSAS MAIN CAMPUS, U of	3
KENTUCKY, U of	1
LONG ISLAND U C W POST CAMPUS	1
LOUISIANA ST U & AGRI & MECH & HEBERT LAWS CTR	2
LOYOLA U CHICAGO	4
MARYLAND COLL PARK CAMPUS, U of	2
MASSACHUSETTS AT AMHERST, U of	3
MASSACHUSETTS BOSTON, U of	3
MERCY COLL—MAIN CAMPUS	1
MIDDLEBURY COLL	1
MINNESOTA TWIN CITIES, U of	3
MONTCLAIR ST COLL	2
MOUNT HOLYOKE COLL	1
NAZARETH COLL OF ROCHESTER	3
NEW YORK U	5
NOTRE DAME, U of	1
OHIO ST U MAIN CAMPUS	2
OREGON, U of	2
PENNSYLVANIA, U of	5
PITTSBURGH MAIN CAMPUS, U of	2
RHODE ISLAND, U of	3
ROSEMONT COLL	2
RUTGERS U NEW BRUNSWICK	7
RUTGERS U NEWARK CAMPUS	1
SAINT JOHN'S U NEW YORK	7
SAN FRANCISCO ST U	1
SANTA CLARA U	1
SMITH COLL	2
SOUTH CAROLINA—COLUMBIA, U of	1
SOUTH FLORIDA, U of	2
SOUTHERN CONNECTICUT ST U	3
STANFORD U	1
SUNY AT ALBANY	3
SUNY AT BINGHAMTON	4
SUNY AT BUFFALO	3
SUNY AT STONY BROOK	4
SUNY COLL AT BUFFALO	1
TEMPLE U	2
TEXAS AT AUSTIN, U of	2
TRINITY COLL	1
TULANE U LOUISIANA	1
VASSAR COLL	3
VIRGINIA MAIN CAMPUS, U of	1
WASHINGTON U	2
WASHINGTON, U of	1
WAYNE ST U	2
WELLESLEY COLL	2
WESLEYAN U	2
WISCONSIN-MADISON, U of	15
WISCONSIN-MILWAUKEE, U of	1
YALE U	2
YOUNGSTOWN ST U	2

Italic Languages, Other

BOSTON COLL	5
BRYN MAWR COLL	2

CHICAGO, U of	14
DARTMOUTH COLL	5
ILLINOIS AT CHICAGO, U of	3
PRINCETON U	22
WASHINGTON, U of	3
WHEELING COLL	1

Japanese

BRIGHAM YOUNG U	39
CALIFORNIA ST U LOS ANGELES	4
CALIFORNIA-LOS ANGELES, U of	19
CALIFORNIA-SANTA BARBARA, U of	1
CARLETON COLL	1
COLORADO AT BOULDER, U of	4
GEORGETOWN U	15
HAWAII AT MANOA, U of	19
MASSACHUSETTS AT AMHERST, U of	8
MICHIGAN ANN ARBOR, U of	9
MINNESOTA TWIN CITIES, U of	5
NORTH CENTRAL COLL	1
OHIO ST U MAIN CAMPUS	6
OREGON, U of	7
PITTSBURGH MAIN CAMPUS, U of	4
PORTLAND ST U	1
ROCHESTER, U of	2
SAN FRANCISCO ST U	12
STANFORD U	3
THE PACIFIC, U of	1
WASHINGTON U	5
WASHINGTON, U of	14
WELLESLEY COLL	1
WISCONSIN-MADISON, U of	5
YALE U	1

Jewish Studies

AMERICAN U	1
BROWN U	2
CALIFORNIA-SAN DIEGO, U of	1
CINCINNATI MAIN CAMPUS, U of	3
DICKINSON COLL	1
FLORIDA, U of	2
GEORGE WASHINGTON U	1
GRATZ COLL	4
HEBREW COLL	1
JUDAISM, U of	5
MARYLAND COLL PARK CAMPUS, U of	3
MASSACHUSETTS AT AMHERST, U of	3
MICHIGAN ANN ARBOR, U of	6
MINNESOTA TWIN CITIES, U of	4
OHIO ST U MAIN CAMPUS	2
PITZER COLL	1
SPERTUS COLL JUDAICA	1
SUNY AT ALBANY	2
SUNY AT BINGHAMTON	8
TULANE U LOUISIANA	1
WASHINGTON U	4

Journalism (Mass Communications)

Degrees in this subject were reported by 308 institutions. Consult more specific headings.

Junior High Education

ALBANY ST COLL	5
ALICE LLOYD COLL	9
APPALACHIAN ST U	29
ARMSTRONG ST COLL	14
ASBURY COLL	3
AUGUSTA COLL	11
BALL ST U	2
BARTON (FORMERLY ATLANTIC CHRISTIAN) COLL	3
BELLARMINE COLL	1
BERRY COLL	9
BRADLEY U	10
BRENAU COLL	29
CAMPBELLSVILLE COLL	9
CATAWBA COLL	4
COLUMBUS COLL	14
CUMBERLAND COLL	8
EAST CAROLINA U	32
EASTERN CONNECTICUT ST U	7
EASTERN ILLINOIS U	15
EASTERN KENTUCKY U	46
ELIZABETH CITY ST U	4
ELON COLL	2
FORT VALLEY ST COLL	12
GEORGIA COLL	15
GEORGIA SOUTHERN COLL	38
GEORGIA SOUTHWESTERN COLL	25
GEORGIA ST U	41
GEORGIA, U of	51
GORDON COLL	2
HARRIS-STOWE ST COLL	11
HIGH POINT COLL	1
ILLINOIS ST U	53
INDIANA U AT SOUTH BEND	1
INDIANA U BLOOMINGTON	1
KENNESAW ST COLL	20
KENTUCKY WESLEYAN COLL	1
KENTUCKY, U of	21
LA GRANGE COLL	8
LENOIR-RHYNE COLL	4
LESLEY COLL	1
MAINE AT MACHIAS, U of	3
MERCER U IN ATLANTA	29
MOREHEAD ST U	31
MURRAY ST U	8
NEBRASKA WESLEYAN U	2
NORTH CAROLINA AT CHARLOTTE, U of	7
NORTH CAROLINA AT GREENSBORO, U of	29
NORTH CAROLINA ST U AT RALEIGH	7
NORTH CAROLINA WESLEYAN COLL	4
NORTH CAROLINA WILMINGTON, U of	26
NORTH DAKOTA MAIN CAMPUS, U of	2
NORTH GEORGIA COLL	22
NORTHERN COLORADO, U of	28
NORTHERN KENTUCKY U	4
PAINE COLL	1
PEMBROKE ST U	5
PIEDMONT COLL	10
PIKEVILLE COLL	7
ROWAN C. OF NJ (WAS GLASSBORO ST COLL)	9
SHORTER COLL	4
TOCCOA FALLS COLL	8
TRANSYLVANIA U	4
UNION COLL	4
VALDOSTA ST COLL	37
WESLEYAN COLL	6
WEST GEORGIA COLL	34
WESTERN CAROLINA U	91
WESTERN KENTUCKY U	47
WINGATE COLL	2
WYOMING, U of	1

Labor/Industrial Relations

BOWLING GREEN ST U MAIN CAMPUS	6
BRIDGEPORT, U of	7
CALUMET COLL OF SAINT JOSEPH	1
CINCINNATI MAIN CAMPUS, U of	38
CLARION U PENNSYLVANIA	5
CLEVELAND ST U	104
CORNELL U-NYS STATUTORY COLLS	183
CUNY QUEENS COLL	13
DISTRICT OF COLUMBIA, U of THE	3
EASTERN MICHIGAN U	2
GEORGIA, U of	5
INDIANA U NORTHWEST	1
INDIANA U-PURDUE U AT INDIANAPOLIS	2
IOWA, U of	32
ITHACA COLL	11
KENT ST U MAIN CAMPUS	41
LE MOYNE COLL	21
MANKATO ST U	8
MASSACHUSETTS BOSTON, U of	4
NEW YORK U	51
NORTH CAROLINA CHAPEL HILL, U of	182
NORTH TEXAS, U of	20
NORTHERN KENTUCKY U	9
PACE U-NEW YORK	6
PENNSYLVANIA ST U MAIN CAMPUS	97
PENNSYLVANIA, U of	4
RIDER COLL	15
ROCKHURST COLL	11
RUTGERS U NEW BRUNSWICK	18
RUTGERS U NEWARK CAMPUS	1
SETON HALL U	37
SHIPPENSBURG U PENNSYLVANIA	5
SUNY COLL AT OLD WESTBURY	4
SUNY COLL AT POTSDAM	28
SUNY EMPIRE ST COLL	12
SYRACUSE U MAIN CAMPUS	11
TEMPLE U	47

WEST VIRGINIA INST OF TECH	2
WISCONSIN PARKSIDE, U of	18
XAVIER U	15
YOUNGSTOWN ST U	3

Landscape Architecture

ARIZONA, U of	12
AUBURN U MAIN CAMPUS	5
BALL ST U	23
CALIFORNIA POLYTECHNIC ST U-SAN LUIS OBISPO	52
CALIFORNIA ST POLYTECHNIC U POMONA	41
CALIFORNIA-BERKELEY, U of	16
CALIFORNIA-DAVIS, U of	25
COLORADO ST U	7
CONNECTICUT, U of	16
CORNELL U-NYS STATUTORY COLLS	21
CUNY CITY COLL	7
FLORIDA, U of	14
GEORGIA, U of	57
IDAHO, U of	8
ILLINOIS URBANA CAMPUS, U of	21
IOWA ST U	33
KANSAS ST U AGRI AND APP SCI	20
KENTUCKY, U of	17
LOUISIANA ST U & AGRI & MECH & HEBERT LAWS CTR	40
MASSACHUSETTS AT AMHERST, U of	41
MICHIGAN ST U	47
MINNESOTA TWIN CITIES, U of	15
MISSISSIPPI ST U	11
NORTH CAROLINA AGRI AND TECHNICAL ST U	4
NORTH CAROLINA ST U AT RALEIGH	4
NORTH DAKOTA ST U MAIN CAMPUS	5
OHIO ST U MAIN CAMPUS	42
OKLAHOMA ST U MAIN CAMPUS	8
OREGON, U of	17
PENNSYLVANIA ST U MAIN CAMPUS	44
RHODE ISLAND SCHOOL OF DESIGN	14
RHODE ISLAND, U of	18
TEXAS A&M U	12
TEXAS AT ARLINGTON, U of	1
TEXAS TECH U	26
UTAH ST U	15
VIRGINIA POLYTECHNIC INST AND ST U	8
WASHINGTON ST U	10
WASHINGTON, U of	13
WEST VIRGINIA U	27
WISCONSIN-MADISON, U of	29

Landscaping

FLORIDA AGRI AND MECH U	6
MAINE, U of	9
MISSISSIPPI ST U	21
MONTANA ST U	6
PENNSYLVANIA ST U MAIN CAMPUS	12
SOUTH DAKOTA ST U	10
TEMPLE U	10

Laser Electro-Optic Technology

OREGON INST OF TECH	16

Latin American Studies

ALABAMA, U of	1
AGNES SCOTT COLL	1
AMERICAN U	15
ARIZONA, U of	6
BAYLOR U	1
BRANDEIS U	1
BROWN U	7
CALIFORNIA ST U FULLERTON	2
CALIFORNIA ST U LOS ANGELES	2
CALIFORNIA ST U-CHICO	5
CALIFORNIA ST U-HAYWARD	1
CALIFORNIA-BERKELEY, U of	25
CALIFORNIA-LOS ANGELES, U of	11
CALIFORNIA-RIVERSIDE, U of	1
CALIFORNIA-SANTA CRUZ, U of	13
CARLETON COLL	7
CENTRAL U IOWA	1
CHICAGO, U of	8
COLL OF SAINT CATHERINE-SAINT CATHERINE CAMPUS	1
COLORADO AT BOULDER, U of	4
CONNECTICUT, U of	4
CUNY BROOKLYN COLL	1
CUNY HUNTER COLL	2
CUNY LEHMAN COLL	7
DENVER, U of	1
DEPAUL U	2
EMORY U	1
FLORIDA ST U	2
GEORGE WASHINGTON U	5
ILLINOIS AT CHICAGO, U of	4
ILLINOIS URBANA CAMPUS, U of	1
KANSAS MAIN CAMPUS, U of	3
KENTUCKY, U of	3
MIAMI, U of	3
MICHIGAN ANN ARBOR, U of	3
MINNESOTA TWIN CITIES, U of	4
MISSOURI-COLUMBIA, U of	2
MOUNT HOLYOKE COLL	5
NEBRASKA-LINCOLN, U of	1
NEW MEXICO MAIN CAMPUS, U of	6
NEW YORK U	4
NORTH CAROLINA CHAPEL HILL, U of	7
OBERLIN COLL	2
PITZER COLL	1
PONTIFICAL COLL JOSEPHINUM	2
PRESCOTT COLL	1
RHODES COLL	1
RICHMOND, U of	4
ROLLINS COLL	5
ROSARY COLL	1
RUTGERS U NEW BRUNSWICK	3
SAN DIEGO ST U	3
SCRIPPS COLL	1
SMITH COLL	5
SOUTH CAROLINA—COLUMBIA, U of	1
SOUTHERN METHODIST U	6
STANFORD U	2
SUNY AT ALBANY	2
SUNY AT BINGHAMTON	1
SYRACUSE U MAIN CAMPUS	1
TEXAS AT AUSTIN, U of	20
TEXAS AT EL PASO, U of	1
TEXAS TECH U	4
TOLEDO, U of	1
TULANE U LOUISIANA	15
VANDERBILT U	8
VASSAR COLL	3
VERMONT, U of	3
WASHINGTON U	1
WELLESLEY COLL	3
WESLEYAN U	8
WISCONSIN-EAU CLAIRE, U of	1
WISCONSIN-MADISON, U of	19
YALE U	8

Latin

AGNES SCOTT COLL	1
AMHERST COLL	1
BALL ST U	2
BARNARD COLL	1
BAYLOR U	3
BENEDICTINE COLL	2
BEREA COLL	1
BRIGHAM YOUNG U	3
BROWN U	2
BUTLER U	1
CALIFORNIA-BERKELEY, U of	1
CARLETON COLL	1
CHESTNUT HILL COLL	1
COLGATE U	1
COLL OF SAINT THOMAS	1
COLUMBIA U IN THE CITY OF NEW YORK	3
CREIGHTON U	2
CUNY BROOKLYN COLL	1
DALLAS, U of	1
DENISON U	1
DICKINSON COLL	11
DUKE U	2
EMORY U	1
GEORGIA, U of	3
INDIANA ST U	2
IOWA, U of	1
JOHN CARROLL U	2
KENT ST U MAIN CAMPUS	1
KENYON COLL	1
LOUISIANA ST U & AGRI & MECH & HEBERT LAWS CTR	1
LOYOLA U CHICAGO	4
MARYLAND COLL PARK CAMPUS, U of	1
MASSACHUSETTS BOSTON, U of	2
MICHIGAN ANN ARBOR, U of	5
MICHIGAN ST U	1
MINNESOTA TWIN CITIES, U of	1
MONTANA, U of	1

MOUNT HOLYOKE COLL	1
NEBRASKA-LINCOLN, U of	1
NORTH CAROLINA AT GREENSBORO, U of	3
NORTH DAKOTA MAIN CAMPUS, U of	1
OBERLIN COLL	6
PENNSYLVANIA ST U MAIN CAMPUS	1
RICHMOND, U of	1
SAINT OLAF COLL	1
SALEM COLL	1
SOUTH, THE U of THE	6
SUNY AT ALBANY	1
SWARTHMORE COLL	1
TEXAS AT AUSTIN, U of	5
TUFTS U	3
VASSAR COLL	2
VERMONT, U of	2
WAKE FOREST U	1
WASHINGTON, U of	1
WELLESLEY COLL	3
WEST CHESTER U PENNSYLVANIA	1
WICHITA ST U	1
YALE U	1

Law (unspecified)

Degrees in this subject were reported by 100 institutions. Consult more specific headings.

Law Enforcement Administration

CITY U	2
OKLAHOMA NORMAN CAMPUS, U of	48
PAN AMERICAN U	24

Law Enforcement

AUBURN U MAIN CAMPUS	29
AVERETT COLL	3
CENTRAL WESLEYAN COLL	1
CHADRON ST COLL	17
COLL OF SAINT FRANCIS	2
COPPIN ST COLL	23
DAYTON, U of	16
DRAKE U	2
EASTERN KENTUCKY U	109
FERRIS ST U	95
FROSTBURG ST U	6
GEORGE MASON U	38
HARDIN-SIMMONS U	9
INDIANAPOLIS, U of	8
JACKSONVILLE ST U	27
KENTUCKY ST U	10
LAKE SUPERIOR ST U	22
LEWIS-CLARK ST COLL	1
MANKATO ST U	66
MARYLAND COLL PARK CAMPUS, U of	194
MARYLAND EASTERN SHORE, U of	1
NORTHEASTERN U	7
NORTHERN MICHIGAN U	28
NORTHWESTERN OKLAHOMA ST U	15
OKLAHOMA CITY U	7
PRAIRIE VIEW A & M U	23
ROWAN C. OF NJ (WAS GLASSBORO ST COLL)	78
SAM HOUSTON ST U	159
SOUTHEAST MISSOURI ST U	41
SOUTHWEST TEXAS ST U	121
STEPHEN F AUSTIN ST U	34
TEMPLE U	117
WARTBURG COLL	2
WAYNE ST COLL	18
WEBER ST COLL	33
WESTERN CONNECTICUT ST U	33
WESTERN NEW ENGLAND COLL	86
YORK COLL PENNSYLVANIA	38
YOUNGSTOWN ST U	1

Law

MARYMOUNT U	1
NATIONAL U	7
NORTHERN MICHIGAN U	1
US AIR FORCE ACAD	25

Law, Other

ANNA MARIA COLL	2
BALL ST U	48
BELMONT COLL	2
CALIFORNIA-BERKELEY, U of	73
CALIFORNIA-SANTA BARBARA, U of	125
CALIFORNIA-SANTA CRUZ, U of	9
CASE WESTERN RESERVE U	2
CITY U	7
COLL OF MOUNT SAINT JOSEPH	9
COLL OF OUR LADY OF ELMS	8
COLL OF SAINT MARY	18
DETROIT, U of	11
HOOD COLL	15
MASSACHUSETTS AT AMHERST, U of	76
MASSACHUSETTS BOSTON, U of	21
MIAMI, U of	14
NOTRE DAME COLL	6
OBERLIN COLL	1
OKLAHOMA CHRISTIAN COLL	2
PITTSBURGH MAIN CAMPUS, U of	35
POINT PARK COLL	18
QUINNIPIAC COLL	28
RAMAPO COLL OF NEW JERSEY	6
RIVIER COLL	12
SCRIPPS COLL	2
TEMPLE U	25

Legal Assisting

CENTRAL FLORIDA, U of	81
COLL OF GREAT FALLS	14
CONCORDIA U-WISCONSIN	4
EAST TEXAS BAPTIST U	2
EAST TEXAS ST U	4
EASTERN KENTUCKY U	24
EVANSVILLE, U of	5
GEORGIA COLL	3
GRAND VALLEY ST U	7
HAMLINE U	18
LAKE SUPERIOR ST U	4
MADONNA COLL	33
MANKATO ST U	4
MARYMOUNT U	5
MARYWOOD COLL	9
MCMURRY COLL	4
METHODIST COLL	1
MILLIGAN COLL	3
MISSISSIPPI COLL	9
MISSISSIPPI U FOR WOMEN	33
MOORHEAD ST U	35
MOREHEAD ST U	27
MORRIS BROWN COLL	3
RICHMOND, U of	2
ROGER WILLIAMS COLL	23
SAINT MARY-OF-THE-WOODS COLL	4
SAINT THOMAS, U of	10
SAMFORD U	27
SOUTHEASTERN U	2
SOUTHERN ILLINOIS U-CARBONDALE	45
SOUTHERN MISSISSIPPI, U of	37
TEXAS WOMAN'S U	12
TULANE U LOUISIANA	22
VIRGINIA INTERMONT COLL	9
WESLEY COLL	2
WILLIAM WOODS COLL	18
WINONA ST U	45

Legal Secretarial

EASTERN MICHIGAN U	15

Letters, Other

ADRIAN COLL	1
AMERICAN U	3
BAPTIST COLL AT CHARLESTON	4
BARD COLL	39
BELOIT COLL	7
BENNINGTON COLL	47
BETHEL COLL	5
BRANDEIS U	87
BROWN U	16
CALIFORNIA-BERKELEY, U of	4
CALIFORNIA-DAVIS, U of	3
CALIFORNIA-IRVINE, U of	5
CALIFORNIA-LOS ANGELES, U of	31
CALIFORNIA-SAN DIEGO, U of	105
CALIFORNIA-SANTA BARBARA, U of	43
CALIFORNIA-SANTA CRUZ, U of	168
CASTLETON ST COLL	6
CHARLESTON, U of	1
COLL OF MOUNT SAINT JOSEPH	1
DANA COLL	2
DENISON U	1
DOMINICAN COLL OF SAN RAFAEL	7

EARLHAM COLL	1
EASTERN WASHINGTON U	6
ECKERD COLL	11
EDGEWOOD COLL	1
EMERSON COLL	18
EMMANUEL COLL	1
EMORY U	3
GEORGE FOX COLL	4
GEORGE WASHINGTON U	25
GRAND RAPIDS BAPTIST COLL AND SEMINARY	12
HARVARD U	19
HOPE COLL	17
ILLINOIS BENEDICTINE COLL	17
ILLINOIS URBANA CAMPUS, U of	51
IOWA, U of	2
JOHNS HOPKINS U	3
LENOIR-RHYNE COLL	2
LINCOLN U	1
LOYOLA U IN NEW ORLEANS	1
MADONNA COLL	4
MARYVILLE COLL	2
MICHIGAN ANN ARBOR, U of	1
MICHIGAN ST U	1
MIDDLEBURY COLL	4
MILLS COLL	3
MONTANA ST U	14
MONTEVALLO, U of	4
MOORHEAD ST U	7
MORNINGSIDE COLL	3
MOUNT MARY COLL	3
OHIO NORTHERN U	5
OKLAHOMA NORMAN CAMPUS, U of	53
PACE U-WHITE PLAINS	1
PFEIFFER COLL	6
QUEENS COLL	3
RADCLIFFE COLL	21
REED COLL	6
RICHMOND, U of	2
ROLLINS COLL	4
SKIDMORE COLL	4
STANFORD U	4
SUNY EMPIRE ST COLL	66
SWARTHMORE COLL	2
TENNESSEE-CHATTANOOGA, U of	32
VIRGINIA MAIN CAMPUS, U of	112
WESLEYAN COLL	2
WESLEYAN U	18
WESTERN KENTUCKY U	14
WILBERFORCE U	2
WILLIAMS COLL	8
WISCONSIN-GREEN BAY, U of	14
YALE U	30

Letters

Degrees in this subject were reported by 1166 institutions. Consult more specific headings.

Liberal/General Studies (unspecified)

Degrees in this subject were reported by 501 institutions. Consult more specific headings.

Liberal/General Studies, Other

Degrees in this subject were reported by 128 institutions. Consult more specific headings.

Liberal/General Studies

Degrees in this subject were reported by 322 institutions. Consult more specific headings.

Library Science

BALL ST U	5
CHADRON ST COLL	2
CLARION U PENNSYLVANIA	10
JAMES MADISON U	3
KENTUCKY WESLEYAN COLL	1
KUTZTOWN U PENNSYLVANIA	7
MILLERSVILLE U PENNSYLVANIA	6
MISSOURI-COLUMBIA, U of	3
NORTH DAKOTA MAIN CAMPUS, U of	2
NORTH TEXAS, U of	8
NORTHWEST MISSOURI ST U	5
NORTHWESTERN OKLAHOMA ST U	1
OHIO DOMINICAN COLL	8
OLD DOMINION U	1
SLIPPERY ROCK U PENNSYLVANIA	4
SOUTHERN CONNECTICUT ST U	7
SOUTHERN MISSISSIPPI, U of	6
SYRACUSE U MAIN CAMPUS	1
TEXAS WOMAN'S U	3
WESTERN KENTUCKY U	3

Library and Archival Sciences, Other

METHODIST COLL	1
THE DISTRICT OF COLUMBIA, U of	1

Library and Archival Sciences, General

LOUISIANA TECH U	2

Library and Archival Sciences

BALL ST U	5
BAYLOR U	3
CHADRON ST COLL	2
CLARION U PENNSYLVANIA	10
JAMES MADISON U	3
KENTUCKY WESLEYAN COLL	1
KUTZTOWN U PENNSYLVANIA	7
LOUISIANA TECH U	2
METHODIST COLL	1
MILLERSVILLE U PENNSYLVANIA	6
MISSOURI-COLUMBIA, U of	3
NORTH DAKOTA MAIN CAMPUS, U of	2
NORTH TEXAS, U of	8
NORTHWEST MISSOURI ST U	5
NORTHWESTERN OKLAHOMA ST U	1
OHIO DOMINICAN COLL	8
OLD DOMINION U	1
SLIPPERY ROCK U PENNSYLVANIA	4
SOUTHERN CONNECTICUT ST U	7
SOUTHERN MISSISSIPPI, U of	6
SYRACUSE U MAIN CAMPUS	1
TEXAS WOMAN'S U	3
THE DISTRICT OF COLUMBIA, U of	1
WESTERN KENTUCKY U	3

Life Sciences (unspecified)

Degrees in this subject were reported by 1173 institutions. Consult more specific headings.

Life Sciences, Other

AVILA COLL	2
AZUSA PACIFIC U	1
BELOIT COLL	8
BEMIDJI ST U	6
BLUEFIELD COLL	3
BRANDEIS U	12
BROWN U	22
BUCKNELL U	4
CALIFORNIA-LOS ANGELES, U of	115
CALIFORNIA-RIVERSIDE, U of	12
CALIFORNIA-SANTA BARBARA, U of	30
CALIFORNIA-SANTA CRUZ, U of	40
CENTENARY COLL OF LOUISIANA	4
CENTRE COLL	8
COLUMBIA U IN THE CITY OF NEW YORK	38
CORNELL U-ENDOWED COLLS	11
CUNY CITY COLL	46
DEFIANCE COLL	1
DETROIT, U of	3
EASTERN MICHIGAN U	7
FERRUM COLL	2
FINDLAY, U of	2
FRESNO PACIFIC COLL	1
GODDARD COLL	2
GRAND CANYON U	3
GRAND VIEW COLL	5
HIRAM COLL	2
JOHNS HOPKINS U	18
LEE COLL	1
LINFIELD COLL	1
LOYOLA MARYMOUNT U	2
LYNCHBURG COLL	1
MANKATO ST U	5
MANSFIELD U PENNSYLVANIA	2
MARY, U of	1

MICHIGAN ANN ARBOR, U of	37
MIDDLEBURY COLL	18
MINNESOTA DULUTH, U of	4
MINNESOTA TWIN CITIES, U of	19
MONTANA ST U	5
MOUNT SENARIO COLL	1
NEBRASKA-LINCOLN, U of	91
NEW ENGLAND, U of	8
NEW YORK U	6
NIAGARA U	1
NORTH ALABAMA, U of	10
NORTH DAKOTA MAIN CAMPUS, U of	3
NORTH DAKOTA ST U MAIN CAMPUS	10
NORTHEASTERN ST U	2
NORTHERN ST U	2
NORTHWESTERN U	1
OCCIDENTAL COLL	7
PALM BEACH ATLANTIC COLL	1
PINE MANOR COLL	1
PITZER COLL	5
PRESCOTT COLL	2
REGIS COLL	4
ROCHESTER INST OF TECH	34
SAINT JOSEPH'S COLL	1
SAINT LAWRENCE U	24
SAINT MARY'S COLL OF MINNESOTA	1
SALEM-TEIKYO U	3
SCRIPPS COLL	2
SIENA COLL	6
SIMPSON COLL	4
SKIDMORE COLL	8
SOUTHERN VERMONT COLL	3
UNION COLL	13
UTAH, U of	11
WEBSTER U	2
WISCONSIN-EAU CLAIRE, U of	3
WISCONSIN-MADISON, U of	11
WRIGHT ST U MAIN CAMPUS	9

Linguistics (Includes Phonetics, Semantics, and Philology)

ALASKA FAIRBANKS, U of	1
ARIZONA, U of	5
BARNARD COLL	2
BOISE ST U	2
BRANDEIS U	3
BRIGHAM YOUNG U	4
BROWN U	1
CALIFORNIA ST U DOMINGUEZ HILLS	5
CALIFORNIA ST U FRESNO	16
CALIFORNIA ST U FULLERTON	8
CALIFORNIA ST U NORTHRIDGE	6
CALIFORNIA-BERKELEY, U of	22
CALIFORNIA-DAVIS, U of	10
CALIFORNIA-IRVINE, U of	6
CALIFORNIA-LOS ANGELES, U of	29
CALIFORNIA-RIVERSIDE, U of	3
CALIFORNIA-SAN DIEGO, U of	9
CALIFORNIA-SANTA BARBARA, U of	8
CALIFORNIA-SANTA CRUZ, U of	10
CHICAGO, U of	10
CINCINNATI MAIN CAMPUS, U of	1
CLEVELAND ST U	4
COLORADO AT BOULDER, U of	4
CORNELL U-ENDOWED COLLS	4
CUNY QUEENS COLL	21
EASTERN MICHIGAN U	2
FLORIDA, U of	1
GEORGETOWN U	11
GEORGIA, U of	2
HAMILTON COLL	2
HARVARD U	10
ILLINOIS URBANA CAMPUS, U of	8
INDIANA U BLOOMINGTON	13
IOWA, U of	4
KANSAS MAIN CAMPUS, U of	10
KENTUCKY, U of	2
LOUISVILLE, U of	2
MACALESTER COLL	2
MARYLAND COLL PARK CAMPUS, U of	6
MASSACHUSETTS AT AMHERST, U of	8
MASSACHUSETTS INST OF TECH	5
MIAMI U OXFORD CAMPUS	2
MICHIGAN ANN ARBOR, U of	13
MICHIGAN ST U	6
MINNESOTA TWIN CITIES, U of	10
MISSISSIPPI MAIN CAMPUS, U of	1
MONTCLAIR ST COLL	1
NEW HAMPSHIRE, U of	8
NEW MEXICO MAIN CAMPUS, U of	2
NORTH CAROLINA CHAPEL HILL, U of	3
NORTHEASTERN ILLINOIS U	1
NORTHEASTERN U	2
NORTHWESTERN U	2
OAKLAND U	1
OHIO ST U MAIN CAMPUS	3
OHIO U MAIN CAMPUS	4
OKLAHOMA NORMAN CAMPUS, U of	2
OREGON, U of	12
PENNSYLVANIA ST U MAIN CAMPUS	1
PENNSYLVANIA, U of	4
PITTSBURGH MAIN CAMPUS, U of	2
PITZER COLL	1
POMONA COLL	1
PORTLAND ST U	3
RADCLIFFE COLL	3
RICE U	7
ROCHESTER, U of	1
RUTGERS U NEW BRUNSWICK	2
SAN DIEGO ST U	11
SAN JOSE ST U	2
SEATTLE PACIFIC U	3
SOUTHERN ILLINOIS U-CARBONDALE	6
STANFORD U	4
SUNY AT ALBANY	12
SUNY AT BINGHAMTON	26
SUNY AT BUFFALO	7
SUNY AT STONY BROOK	11
SUNY COLL AT OSWEGO	2
SWARTHMORE COLL	4
SYRACUSE U MAIN CAMPUS	2
TEMPLE U	3
TEXAS AT AUSTIN, U of	7
TEXAS AT EL PASO, U of	26
TOLEDO, U of	3
TULANE U LOUISIANA	1
UTAH, U of	6
WASHINGTON, U of	8
WELLESLEY COLL	4
WESTERN MICHIGAN U	1
WISCONSIN-MADISON, U of	5
WISCONSIN-MILWAUKEE, U of	7
WYOMING, U of	1
YALE U	7

Literature, American

BOISE ST U	1
CASTLETON ST COLL	4
GEORGE WASHINGTON U	14
MIDDLEBURY COLL	12

Literature, English

AGNES SCOTT COLL	13
ALBERTSON C. (WAS COLL OF IDAHO)	3
AMERICAN U	43
AURORA U	4
BELOIT COLL	11
BETHEL COLL	1
BRYN MAWR COLL	1
CAPITAL U	1
CENTRAL ST U	1
CHESTNUT HILL COLL	7
COLBY COLL	55
COLL OF SAINT CATHERINE-SAINT CATHERINE CAMPUS	5
COLUMBIA U IN THE CITY OF NEW YORK	147
DAVIS AND ELKINS COLL	2
DOMINICAN COLL OF SAN RAFAEL	2
DREW U	54
DUQUESNE U	25
EASTERN COLL	7
EASTERN MICHIGAN U	16
ELMIRA COLL	6
EMMANUEL COLL	2
GANNON U	4
GEORGE WASHINGTON U	12
GRAND CANYON U	4
HARTFORD, U of	10
HOUSTON BAPTIST U	17
ILLINOIS AT CHICAGO, U of	89
KNOX COLL	6
LYNCHBURG COLL	4
MICHIGAN ANN ARBOR, U of	468
MONTANA ST U	23
NORTH CAROLINA AT ASHEVILLE, U of	12
ORAL ROBERTS U	15
PACE U-NEW YORK	16
PACE U-PLEASANTVILLE-BROLF CAMPUS	44
PFEIFFER COLL	5

PITTSBURGH MAIN CAMPUS, U of	44
POINT LOMA NAZARENE COLL	13
ROSEMONT COLL	24
SAINT JOHN'S U NEW YORK	31
SAINT MARY'S COLL	26
SOUTHWEST ST U	4
STOCKTON ST COLL	33
SUNY COLL AT ONEONTA	44
SUNY COLL AT PURCHASE	67
SWARTHMORE COLL	40
TOURO COLL	4
TRINITY COLL	68
VOORHEES COLL	1
WASHINGTON U	88
WEST CHESTER U PENNSYLVANIA	29
WESTERN NEW ENGLAND COLL	8
WHEATON COLL	56
XAVIER U	35

Management Information Systems

Degrees in this subject were reported by 141 institutions. Consult more specific headings.

Management Science, General

BAYAMON CENTRAL U	16
CONCORDIA COLL	15
DRAKE U	36
EVANSVILLE, U of	21
GENEVA COLL	1
HEIDELBERG COLL	1
HUNTINGDON COLL	6
INDIANAPOLIS, U of	1
LOCK HAVEN U PENNSYLVANIA	63
MARYMOUNT U	1
MOUNT MERCY COLL	60
NEVADA-LAS VEGAS, U of	104
NORTHWEST CHRISTIAN COLL	19
OKLAHOMA ST U MAIN CAMPUS	36
PENNSYLVANIA, U of	76
PRESCOTT COLL	3
SAINT LOUIS U MAIN CAMPUS	5
SCRANTON, U of	10
SOUTH FLORIDA, U of	136
SOUTHEASTERN OKLAHOMA ST U	14
SOUTHERN METHODIST U	2
TEXAS WESLEYAN COLL	16
TOLEDO, U of	1
TUSKEGEE U	3
WYOMING, U of	11

Management Science, Other

ALABAMA, U of	4
AVERETT COLL	22
CALIFORNIA-SAN DIEGO, U of	146
CAPITOL COLL	2
CASE WESTERN RESERVE U	3
CHAMINADE U HONOLULU	29
CHAPMAN COLL	2
CHRISTIAN BROTHERS COLL	27
CUNY BERNARD BARUCH COLL	13
DENVER, U of	3
ELMHURST COLL	37
FRANKLIN U	5
GEORGIA INST OF TECH MAIN CAMPUS	11
GRAND VALLEY ST U	56
ILLINOIS AT CHICAGO, U of	50
IOWA ST U	146
IOWA, U of	37
KENT ST U MAIN CAMPUS	5
MADONNA COLL	1
MASSACHUSETTS BOSTON, U of	3
METROPOLITAN ST COLL	3
MIAMI U OXFORD CAMPUS	13
MIDLAND LUTHERAN COLL	12
NEBRASKA-LINCOLN, U of	58
NORTH ALABAMA, U of	57
NORTHWEST CHRISTIAN COLL	4
NORTHWOOD INST	9
PENNSYLVANIA, U of	36
PORTLAND, U of	18
RHODE ISLAND, U of	3
SOUTH CAROLINA—COLUMBIA, U of	30
SOUTHERN METHODIST U	6
SYRACUSE U MAIN CAMPUS	1
TEMPLE U	5
VIRGINIA POLYTECHNIC INST AND ST U	118
WESTBROOK COLL	6
WRIGHT ST U MAIN CAMPUS	10
WYOMING, U of	2

Marine Biology

ALABAMA, U of	2
AUBURN U MAIN CAMPUS	10
BEMIDJI ST U	10
BROWN U	2
CALIFORNIA ST U LONG BEACH	10
CALIFORNIA-SANTA CRUZ, U of	2
COLL OF CHARLESTON	11
EAST STROUDSBURG U PENNSYLVANIA	3
ECKERD COLL	13
FAIRLEIGH DICKINSON U	15
FLORIDA INST OF TECH	18
HAMPTON U	4
JACKSONVILLE U	6
LONG ISLAND U SOUTHHAMPTON COLL	24
MIAMI, U of	9
NEW ENGLAND, U of	7
NICHOLLS ST U	3
NORTH CAROLINA WILMINGTON, U of	39
RHODE ISLAND, U of	25
ROGER WILLIAMS COLL	12
SAVANNAH ST COLL	2
SOUTH CAROLINA AT COASTAL CAROLINA, U of	24
SOUTH CAROLINA—COLUMBIA, U of	28
SOUTHWEST TEXAS ST U	3
SOUTHWESTERN LOUISIANA, U of	2
STOCKTON ST COLL	30
TAMPA, U of	9
TEXAS A & M U AT GALVESTON	30
TROY ST U-MAIN CAMPUS	3
VIRGIN ISLANDS, U of THE	1
WESTERN WASHINGTON U	10

Maritime Science (Merchant Marine)

CALIFORNIA MARITIME ACAD	36
MASSACHUSETTS MARITIME ACAD	119
US MERCHANT MARINE ACAD	80

Marketing Management and Research, Other

AUGSBURG COLL	24
AZUSA PACIFIC U	9
BOWLING GREEN ST U MAIN CAMPUS	188
CENTRAL MICHIGAN U	1
CHESTNUT HILL COLL	5
CLEVELAND ST U	134
EVANSVILLE, U of	32
GEORGE WASHINGTON U	63
GEORGETOWN COLL	22
GEORGIA COLL	5
GROVE CITY COLL	28
HOWARD U	72
IOWA, U of	131
KANSAS ST U AGRI AND APP SCI	190
MONTEVALLO, U of	15
NATIONAL U	74
NORTH CENTRAL COLL	60
SAGINAW VALLEY ST U	21
SAINT JOSEPH'S COLL	5
SAINT JOSEPH'S U	72
SAINT THOMAS, U of	11
SOUTHWEST ST U	10
SUFFOLK U	54
TROY ST U-MAIN CAMPUS	49
URBANA U	2
WINONA ST U	61
WRIGHT ST U MAIN CAMPUS	146

Marketing Management

Degrees in this subject were reported by 396 institutions. Consult more specific headings.

Marketing Research

BUENA VISTA COLL	8
CARTHAGE COLL	13
EMORY U	2
MARY BALDWIN COLL	8
MARYMOUNT U	31
NEBRASKA AT OMAHA, U of	73
RUST COLL	1

Marketing and Distribution, Other

ASHLAND U	3
COLUMBIA COLL	2
FAIRFIELD U	79
GEORGIA ST U	28
HARTFORD, U of	88
MAINE, U of	11
MICHIGAN ST U	1
WOODBURY U	27

Marketing and Distributive Education

BOWLING GREEN ST U MAIN CAMPUS	10
EASTERN MICHIGAN U	9
GEORGIA ST U	11
GEORGIA, U of	13
HAWAII AT MANOA, U of	1
HOUSTON-U PARK, U of	3
INDIANA ST U	1
JAMES MADISON U	4
MIDDLE TENNESSE ST U	2
MINNESOTA TWIN CITIES, U of	11
MISSISSIPPI ST U	5
MISSOURI-COLUMBIA, U of	10
NORTH DAKOTA MAIN CAMPUS, U of	6
OHIO ST U MAIN CAMPUS	1
RIDER COLL	4
SOUTHWESTERN LOUISIANA, U of	4
TEMPLE U	6
TENNESSEE-KNOXVILLE, U of	6
UTAH ST U	10
WESTERN MICHIGAN U	4
WINTHROP COLL	5
WISCONSIN-STOUT, U of	17
WYOMING, U of	1

Marketing and Distribution (unspecified)

Degrees in this subject were reported by 156 institutions. Consult more specific headings.

Marketing of Business or Personal Services

BAYLOR U	166
CENTRAL OKLAHOMA, U of	66
HAWAII PACIFIC COLL	39

Marketing of Recreational Services

FERRIS ST U	70

Marketing, General

ARKANSAS COLL	5
AVILA COLL	13
BARRY U	17
CEDAR CREST COLL	4
EDGEWOOD COLL	2
FINDLAY, U of	11
FRANKLIN PIERCE COLL	37
KING'S COLL	23
LAKE SUPERIOR ST U	19
MARYVILLE COLL—ST LOUIS	37
NEUMANN COLL	2
NORTHEASTERN ST U	69
NORTHWESTERN COLL	13
OKLAHOMA BAPTIST U	13
OKLAHOMA CHRISTIAN COLL	17
OKLAHOMA CITY U	16
OKLAHOMA NORMAN CAMPUS, U of	114
OLIVET NAZARENE U	15
PLYMOUTH ST COLL	44
SCI AND ARTS OF OKLAHOMA, U of	1
SOUTHERN NAZARENE U	5
SOUTHWESTERN OKLAHOMA ST U	17
TOLEDO, U of	121
TULSA, U of	40
WESLEY COLL	7
WILMINGTON COLL	12

Materials Engineering

ALABAMA AT BIRMINGHAM, U of	6
ARIZONA ST U	3
AUBURN U MAIN CAMPUS	19
CALIFORNIA-BERKELEY, U of	21
CALIFORNIA-DAVIS, U of	3
CALIFORNIA-LOS ANGELES, U of	5
CASE WESTERN RESERVE U	13
CORNELL U-ENDOWED COLLS	25
DREXEL U	24
GEORGIA INST OF TECH MAIN CAMPUS	10
ILLINOIS AT CHICAGO, U of	2
JOHNS HOPKINS U	9
KENTUCKY, U of	8
LEHIGH U	13
MASSACHUSETTS INST OF TECH	31
MICHIGAN ST U	30
MINNESOTA TWIN CITIES, U of	12
NEW HAVEN, U of	4
NEW MEXICO INST OF MINING AND TECH	6
NORTH CAROLINA ST U AT RALEIGH	32
NORTHWESTERN U	12
NOTRE DAME, U of	4
PENNSYLVANIA ST U MAIN CAMPUS	20
PENNSYLVANIA, U of	11
PITTSBURGH MAIN CAMPUS, U of	16
RENSSELAER POLYTECHNIC INST	29
RICE U	13
SAN JOSE ST U	14
STEVENS INST OF TECH	7
TENNESSEE-KNOXVILLE, U of	3
UTAH, U of	14
VIRGINIA POLYTECHNIC INST AND ST U	27
WASHINGTON ST U	9
WAYNE ST U	1
WESTERN NEW ENGLAND COLL	1
WILKES U	3
WINONA ST U	6
WISCONSIN-MILWAUKEE, U of	10
WRIGHT ST U MAIN CAMPUS	9
YOUNGSTOWN ST U	5

Math and Computer Science

ANTIOCH COLL	2
AVERETT COLL	4
BARBER-SCOTIA COLL	1
BOISE ST U	1
BRIAR CLIFF COLL	1
BROWN U	4
BRYAN COLL	4
CARDINAL STRITCH COLL	1
CARLOW COLL	2
CENTRAL METHODIST COLL	1
CLARK U	3
COLL MISERICORDIA	2
COLL OF OUR LADY OF ELMS	2
COLORADO COLL	5
DREW U	2
EASTERN WASHINGTON U	6
ILLINOIS COLL	1
IMMACULATA COLL	3
LAKE SUPERIOR ST U	11
LAKELAND COLL	2
LAWRENCE U	5
MARYVILLE COLL	2
MCMURRY COLL	2
MEREDITH COLL	2
OAKWOOD COLL	3
PEPPERDINE U	5
PROVIDENCE COLL	13
PUGET SOUND, U of	23
ROCKY MOUNTAIN COLL	2
ROGER WILLIAMS COLL	6
SILVER LAKE COLL	1
URSINUS COLL	1
VIRGINIA WESLEYAN COLL	3
WESTERN CONNECTICUT ST U	10
WHEATON COLL	2

Math, Other

ALBION COLL	7
BELOIT COLL	4
BRYN MAWR COLL	1
CALIFORNIA-DAVIS, U of	19
CALIFORNIA-LOS ANGELES, U of	18
CALIFORNIA-SAN DIEGO, U of	25
CENTRAL ST U	4
CENTRAL U IOWA	11
CLAFLIN COLL	4
COLL OF SAINT BENEDICT	3
COLUMBIA U IN THE CITY OF NEW YORK	17
CUNY BERNARD BARUCH COLL	11
DANA COLL	2
DARTMOUTH COLL	4
DELAWARE ST COLL	4

DENISON U	2
DISTRICT OF COLUMBIA, U of THE	2
EASTERN NEW MEXICO U MAIN CAMPUS	2
GONZAGA U	5
GRAND CANYON U	1
HAMPDEN-SYDNEY COLL	1
INSURANCE, THE COLL OF	8
KENTUCKY, U of	6
LAFAYETTE COLL	3
LE MOYNE COLL	1
LONG ISLAND U C W POST CAMPUS	1
LOUISIANA COLL	1
MARIST COLL	3
MIAMI U OXFORD CAMPUS	2
MONTANA ST U	30
MOREHEAD ST U	7
NEW HAMPSHIRE KEENE ST COLL, U of	1
NEW HAMPSHIRE, U of	22
NEW YORK U	1
NEWBERRY COLL	4
NORTH CAROLINA CHAPEL HILL, U of	29
NORTHERN ARIZONA U	1
OCCIDENTAL COLL	3
OGLETHORPE U	5
OHIO ST U MAIN CAMPUS	6
OKLAHOMA CHRISTIAN COLL	3
PITTSBURGH MAIN CAMPUS, U of	5
QUEENS COLL	1
SAINT JOSEPH'S COLL	1
SAINT LAWRENCE U	2
SAINT NORBERT COLL	2
SOUTH CAROLINA AT AIKEN, U of	3
SOUTHERN METHODIST U	8
SPRING ARBOR COLL	1
STANFORD U	14
STONEHILL COLL	5
SUNY COLL AT FREDONIA	1
TABOR COLL	6
TAMPA, U of	4
TEMPLE U	2
TOUGALOO COLL	5
TULANE U LOUISIANA	9
UNITED STS COAST GUARD ACAD	24
VANDERBILT U	67
VASSAR COLL	2
WARREN WILSON COLL	5
WESLEYAN U	9
WHITTIER COLL	5
WILLIAM JEWELL COLL	3
WISCONSIN-MILWAUKEE, U of	3
WYOMING, U of	14

Mathematics (unspecified)

Degrees in this subject were reported by 1107 institutions. Consult more specific headings.

Mathematics Education

Degrees in this subject were reported by 202 institutions. Consult more specific headings.

Mathematics, General

Degrees in this subject were reported by 1065 institutions. Consult more specific headings.

Mechanical Design Technology

ALABAMA AGRI AND MECH U	3
ARKANSAS AT LITTLE ROCK, U of	12
BOWLING GREEN ST U MAIN CAMPUS	6
CENTRAL MICHIGAN U	4
CENTRAL WASHINGTON U	5
CINCINNATI MAIN CAMPUS, U of	34
DAYTON, U of	46
EASTERN MICHIGAN U	38
FAIRLEIGH DICKINSON U	1
FERRIS ST U	14
GANNON U	19
GEORGIA SOUTHERN COLL	19
LETOURNEAU COLL	10
MAINE, U of	31
NEW HAMPSHIRE, U of	9
NICHOLLS ST U	1
NORTHEASTERN U	59
OKLAHOMA ST U MAIN CAMPUS	25
OREGON INST OF TECH	31
PITTSBURG ST U	13
POINT PARK COLL	25
SAVANNAH ST COLL	3
SIENA HEIGHTS COLL	5
SOUTHERN COLORADO, U of	19
SOUTHERN MISSISSIPPI, U of	6
SPRING GARDEN COLL	27
SUNY AT BINGHAMTON	18
TENNESSEE-MARTIN, U of	9
TRENTON ST COLL	34
WARTBURG COLL	1
WASHINGTON U	10
WEBER ST COLL	12
WESTERN KENTUCKY U	18

Mechanical Engineering

Degrees in this subject were reported by 233 institutions. Consult more specific headings.

Mechanical and Related Technologies, Other

AKRON, MAIN CAMPUS, U of	35
ALABAMA AGRI AND MECH U	2
ANDREWS U	3
CENTRAL MISSOURI ST U	12
CLEVELAND ST U	22
COGSWELL POLYTECHNICAL COLL	2
EASTERN WASHINGTON U	5
FRANKLIN U	27
INDIANA ST U	22
INDIANA U-PURDUE U AT FORT WAYNE	19
INDIANA U-PURDUE U AT INDIANAPOLIS	34
LAKE SUPERIOR ST U	25
LETOURNEAU COLL	6
LINCOLN U	6
MASS. AT LOWELL, U of	23
METROPOLITAN ST COLL	15
MILWAUKEE SCHOOL OF ENGINEERING	32
MISSISSIPPI ST U	7
MONTANA ST U	36
NORTHEASTERN U	4
NORTHERN ARIZONA U	7
OKLAHOMA ST U MAIN CAMPUS	12
OREGON ST U	1
PRAIRIE VIEW A & M U	3
PURDUE U CALUMET CAMPUS	18
PURDUE U NORTH CENTRAL CAMPUS	8
ROGER WILLIAMS COLL	15
SAGINAW VALLEY ST U	7
SOUTH CAROLINA ST COLL	3
SOUTHERN U AGRI & MECH COL AT BATON ROUGE	12
SOUTHWEST ST U	4
TEXAS SOUTHERN U	2
TEXAS TECH U	14
TOLEDO, U of	54
WAYNE ST U	14
WENTWORTH INST OF TECH	85
YOUNGSTOWN ST U	14

Mechanics and Repairers (unspecified)

ANDREWS U	6
BRIGHAM YOUNG U HAWAII CAMPUS	2
LEWIS U	7
PARKS COLL OF SAINT LOUIS U	17
SIENA HEIGHTS COLL	2
SOUTHEASTERN OKLAHOMA ST U	4
SOUTHERN ILLINOIS U-CARBONDALE	157
WALLA WALLA COLL	1

Medical Assisting

NORTHEASTERN U	5

Medical Illustrating

BEAVER COLL	2
CLEVELAND INST OF ART	4
IOWA ST U	2
OHIO ST U MAIN CAMPUS	7
ROCHESTER INST OF TECH	25

Medical Laboratory Technology

AUBURN U AT MONTGOMERY	3
CALIFORNIA U PENNSYLVANIA	7
CINCINNATI MAIN CAMPUS, U of	6
CLARION U PENNSYLVANIA	8
COLL OF SAINT SCHOLASTICA	7
DAVID LIPSCOMB U	1
DAYTON, U of	3
EAST STROUDSBURG U PENNSYLVANIA	1
EDINBORO U PENNSYLVANIA	8
KANSAS ST U AGRI AND APP SCI	3
KUTZTOWN U PENNSYLVANIA	4
LINCOLN MEMORIAL U	2
LOCK HAVEN U PENNSYLVANIA	2
MANSFIELD U PENNSYLVANIA	2
MERRIMACK COLL	2
NEW MEXICO MAIN CAMPUS, U of	7
NORTHEASTERN U	7
OREGON INST OF TECH	10
SHIPPENSBURG U PENNSYLVANIA	1
SIENA HEIGHTS COLL	3
SLIPPERY ROCK U PENNSYLVANIA	4
WINONA ST U	4

Medical Laboratory Technologies, Other

BOSTON U	1
CONNECTICUT, U of	4
FRAMINGHAM ST COLL	6
LINFIELD COLL	1
MISSOURI-COLUMBIA, U of	3
SOUTH ALABAMA, U of	13

Medical Laboratory

AKRON, MAIN CAMPUS, U of	18
ALBANY COLL OF PHARMACY	3
APPALACHIAN ST U	2
ARKANSAS ST U MAIN CAMPUS	10
ARKANSAS TECH U	1
ARMSTRONG ST COLL	1
AUGUSTANA COLL	1
BALL ST U	5
BLACKBURN COLL	1
BRADLEY U	1
CALIFORNIA ST U DOMINGUEZ HILLS	11
CALIFORNIA ST U LOS ANGELES	5
CAMPBELL U INCORPORATED	1
CANISIUS COLL	1
CLEMSON U	5
COLL OF SAINT ROSE	2
COLUMBIA UNION COLL	2
CONCORD COLL	4
CUNY COLL OF STN ISLAND	13
CUNY HUNTER COLL	21
CUNY YORK COLL	9
D'YOUVILLE COLL	2
DAEMEN COLL	4
EAST CAROLINA U	9
EASTERN ILLINOIS U	15
EASTERN MICHIGAN U	4
FRANCIS MARION COLL	2
GARDNER-WEBB COLL	3
GENEVA COLL	1
GEORGIA ST U	10
HARDING U MAIN CAMPUS	2
HARTFORD, U of	1
HARTWICK COLL	1
HAWAII AT MANOA, U of	17
HEALTH SCIENCES-CHICAGO MEDICAL SCH, U of	21
HOUSTON BAPTIST U	2
ILLINOIS AT CHICAGO, U of	37
ILLINOIS COLL	1
ILLINOIS ST U	21
INDIANA ST U	13
JOHN BROWN U	1
KENT ST U MAIN CAMPUS	3
LONG ISLAND U BROOKLYN CAMPUS	3
LOYOLA COLL	1
MANCHESTER COLL	1
MARIST COLL	5
MARSHALL U	4
MASSACHUSETTS AT DARTMOUTH (WAS SE U OF MA, U of	9
MIAMI U OXFORD CAMPUS	4
MISSOURI SOUTHERN ST COLL	3
MORAVIAN COLL	1
MORGAN ST U	10
NEUMANN COLL	4
NEW MEXICO ST U MAIN CAMPUS	9
NEW YORK INST OF TECH MAIN CAMPUS	6
NORTH CAROLINA AT CHARLOTTE, U of	3
NORTH CAROLINA CHAPEL HILL, U of	16
NORTH CAROLINA ST U AT RALEIGH	3
NORTH CAROLINA WILMINGTON, U of	10
NORTHERN COLORADO, U of	5
NORTHERN ILLINOIS U	8
NORTHWEST MISSOURI ST U	2
OKLAHOMA NORMAN CAMPUS, U of	2
OLIVET NAZARENE U	1
ORAL ROBERTS U	1
PACE U-NEW YORK	1
PACE U-PLEASANTVILLE-BROLF CAMPUS	2
PEMBROKE ST U	1
PURDUE U CALUMET CAMPUS	1
QUINCY COLL	1
QUINNIPIAC COLL	7
RHODE ISLAND COLL	2
RIO GRANDE, U of	1
ROCHESTER INST OF TECH	6
RUSSELL SAGE COLL MAIN CAMPUS	1
SAINT BONAVENTURE U	3
SAINT JOHN'S U NEW YORK	6
SAINT THOMAS AQUINAS COLL	1
SALISBURY ST U	4
SAN FRANCISCO ST U	20
SCRANTON, U of	4
SOUTH CAROLINA—COLUMBIA, U of	1
SOUTH DAKOTA ST U	11
SOUTHERN COLORADO, U of	2
STETSON U	2
TEMPLE U	2
TOWSON ST U	3
UTICA COLL OF SYRACUSE	5
VERMONT, U of	10
VIRGINIA INTERMONT COLL	1
WASHINGTON, U of	10
WEST LIBERTY ST COLL	2
WEST VIRGINIA U	12
WESTERN CAROLINA U	6
WESTERN CONNECTICUT ST U	3
WESTERN ILLINOIS U	2
WINSTON-SALEM ST U	6

Medical Radiation Dosimetry

INDIANA U-PURDUE U AT INDIANAPOLIS	4
VIRGINIA COMMONWEALTH U	5

Medical Records Administration

ALABAMA AT BIRMINGHAM, U of	13
ARKANSAS TECH U	9
CARROLL COLL	7
CENTRAL FLORIDA, U of	10
CHICAGO ST U	5
COLL OF SAINT MARY	8
COLL OF SAINT SCHOLASTICA	19
DAEMEN COLL	1
DAKOTA ST COLL	7
DETROIT, U of	3
EAST CAROLINA U	13
EAST CENTRAL U	12
EASTERN KENTUCKY U	4
FERRIS ST U	26
FLORIDA AGRI AND MECH U	7
ILLINOIS AT CHICAGO, U of	18
ILLINOIS ST U	16
INDIANA U-PURDUE U AT INDIANAPOLIS	16
ITHACA COLL	6
KEAN COLL OF NEW JERSEY	5
LOMA LINDA U	4
LONG ISLAND U C W POST CAMPUS	4
LOUISIANA TECH U	12
MEDICAL COLL OF GEORGIA	7
NORFOLK ST U	6
NORTHEASTERN U	7
OHIO ST U MAIN CAMPUS	34
PITTSBURGH MAIN CAMPUS, U of	26
REGIS COLL	4
SAINT LOUIS U MAIN CAMPUS	14
SEATTLE U	4
SOUTHWEST TEXAS ST U	18
SOUTHWESTERN LOUISIANA, U of	15

SOUTHWESTERN OKLAHOMA ST U 13
TEMPLE U 22
TENNESSEE ST U 10
TEXAS SOUTHERN U 8
TEXAS WOMAN'S U 8
TOURO COLL 6
VIRGINIA COMMONWEALTH U 7
WESTERN CAROLINA U 2
WISCONSIN-MILWAUKEE, U of 12
YORK COLL PENNSYLVANIA 14

Medical Secretarial

PACIFIC UNION COLL 1

Medical Social Work

ALASKA FAIRBANKS, U of 1
ARKANSAS TECH U 6
KENT ST U MAIN CAMPUS 4
NEW MEXICO HIGHLANDS U 14
SLIPPERY ROCK U PENNSYLVANIA 3
SOUTHERN ILLINOIS U AT EDWARDSVILLE 27

Medical Surgical

KENT ST U MAIN CAMPUS 2

Medical Technology

Degrees in this subject were reported by 198 institutions. Consult more specific headings.

Medicine, General

BAYLOR U 3
BOSTON U 50
KENT ST U MAIN CAMPUS 27
NORTHWESTERN U 25
PONTIFICAL CATHOLIC U PUERTO RICO—PONCE CA 3
SOUTH DAKOTA, U of 8

Mental Health/Human Services, Other

AMERICAN INTERNATIONAL COLL 5
CLARION U PENNSYLVANIA 6
COLL OF GREAT FALLS 2
COLL OF SAINT JOSEPH 9
EASTERN MONTANA COLL 33
FRIENDS U 19
HURON COLL 3
LESLEY COLL 100
MANSFIELD U PENNSYLVANIA 1
MERRIMACK COLL 6
NEW ENGLAND, U of 4
NORTH CAROLINA AT CHARLOTTE, U of 26
NORWICH U 1
OLD DOMINION U 31
REGIS COLL 1
SCRANTON, U of 12
THOMAS A EDISON ST COLL 38
TRINITY COLL 5
WESTERN MICHIGAN U 8

Mental Health/Human Service Technology

COLL OF SAINT MARY 12
DETROIT, U of 12
FITCHBURG ST COLL 23
FRANCISCAN U STEUBENVILLE 23
GANNON U 12
HAHNEMANN U 11
MAINE AT MACHIAS, U of 1
MORGAN ST U 9
NORTHERN KENTUCKY U 10

Mental Health/Human Services Assisting

CENTRAL WASHINGTON U 4
GEORGIA ST U 18

Metal/Jewelry

ARTS, THE U of THE 7
BOWLING GREEN ST U MAIN CAMPUS 4
CALIFORNIA COLL OF ARTS AND CRAFTS 3
CENTER FOR CREATIVE STUDIES COL OF ART AND DESIGN 2
CLEVELAND INST OF ART 1
DRAKE U 1
HOUSTON-U PARK, U of 1
MAINE COLL OF ART (WAS PORTLAND SCHOOL OF ART) 8
MICHIGAN ANN ARBOR, U of 2
MOORE COLL OF ART 7
NORTH TEXAS, U of 7
OREGON, U of 1
RHODE ISLAND SCHOOL OF DESIGN 12
SUNY COLL AT NEW PALTZ 3
TEMPLE U 14
TEXAS AT EL PASO, U of 1
WASHINGTON U 3

Metallurgical Engineering

ALABAMA, U of 3
CALIFORNIA POLYTECHNIC ST U-SAN LUIS OBISPO 14
CARNEGIE MELLON U 28
CINCINNATI MAIN CAMPUS, U of 15
COLORADO SCHOOL OF MINES 23
COLUMBIA U IN THE CITY OF NEW YORK 6
FLORIDA, U of 60
IDAHO, U of 5
ILLINOIS AT CHICAGO, U of 1
ILLINOIS INST OF TECH 8
ILLINOIS URBANA CAMPUS, U of 14
IOWA ST U 7
MICHIGAN TECH U 34
MINNESOTA TWIN CITIES, U of 4
MISSOURI-ROLLA, U of 33
MONTANA COLL OF MINERAL SCI AND TECH 5
NEW MEXICO INST OF MINING AND TECH 3
OHIO ST U MAIN CAMPUS 16
PENNSYLVANIA ST U MAIN CAMPUS 7
PITTSBURGH MAIN CAMPUS, U of 8
POLYTECHNIC U 2
SOUTH DAKOTA SCHOOL OF MINES & TECH 11
TEXAS AT EL PASO, U of 12
UTAH, U of 2
WASHINGTON, U of 11
WAYNE ST U 2
WESTERN MICHIGAN U 5
WISCONSIN-MADISON, U of 7

Metallurgy

TRINITY COLL 1

Microbiology

ALABAMA, U of 20
ARIZONA ST U 26
ARIZONA, U of 29
ARKANSAS-FAYETTEVILLE, U of 25
AUBURN U MAIN CAMPUS 31
BOWLING GREEN ST U MAIN CAMPUS 6
BRIGHAM YOUNG U 46
CALIFORNIA POLYTECHNIC ST U-SAN LUIS OBISPO 10
CALIFORNIA ST POLYTECHNIC U POMONA 19
CALIFORNIA ST U FRESNO 7
CALIFORNIA ST U LONG BEACH 26
CALIFORNIA ST U LOS ANGELES 3
CALIFORNIA ST U-CHICO 13
CALIFORNIA-BERKELEY, U of 48
CALIFORNIA-DAVIS, U of 10
CALIFORNIA-LOS ANGELES, U of 24
CALIFORNIA-SAN DIEGO, U of 22
CALIFORNIA-SANTA BARBARA, U of 23
CENTRAL FLORIDA, U of 6
CLEMSON U 30
COLORADO ST U 63
CORNELL U-NYS STATUTORY COLLS 26
EAST TENNESSEE ST U 5
EASTERN KENTUCKY U 2
EASTERN MICHIGAN U 4
FLORIDA, U of 69
GEORGIA, U of 45
HAWAII AT MANOA, U of 2
HOWARD U 39
IDAHO ST U 10

ILLINOIS URBANA CAMPUS, U of	30
INDIANA U BLOOMINGTON	16
IOWA ST U	8
IOWA, U of	10
KANSAS MAIN CAMPUS, U of	7
KANSAS ST U AGRI AND APP SCI	10
KENTUCKY, U of	8
LOUISIANA ST U & AGRI & MECH & HEBERT LAWS CTR	59
LOUISIANA TECH U	4
MAINE, U of	5
MARYLAND COLL PARK CAMPUS, U of	43
MASSACHUSETTS AT AMHERST, U of	39
MCNEESE ST U	4
MIAMI U OXFORD CAMPUS	39
MIAMI, U of	17
MICHIGAN ANN ARBOR, U of	18
MICHIGAN ST U	26
MINNESOTA TWIN CITIES, U of	32
MISSISSIPPI ST U	19
MISSISSIPPI U FOR WOMEN	8
MISSOURI-COLUMBIA, U of	3
MONTANA ST U	16
MONTANA, U of	18
NEW HAMPSHIRE, U of	14
NEW MEXICO ST U MAIN CAMPUS	10
NORTH CAROLINA ST U AT RALEIGH	24
NORTH DAKOTA ST U MAIN CAMPUS	11
NORTHERN ARIZONA U	13
NORTHERN MICHIGAN U	1
NORTHWESTERN ST U LOUISIANA	1
OHIO ST U MAIN CAMPUS	28
OHIO U MAIN CAMPUS	4
OKLAHOMA NORMAN CAMPUS, U of	20
OKLAHOMA ST U MAIN CAMPUS	17
OREGON ST U	24
PENNSYLVANIA ST U MAIN CAMPUS	49
PITTSBURGH MAIN CAMPUS, U of	12
QUINNIPIAC COLL	2
RHODE ISLAND, U of	12
SAN DIEGO ST U	24
SAN JOSE ST U	10
SOUTH DAKOTA ST U	19
SOUTH FLORIDA, U of	15
SOUTHERN ILLINOIS U-CARBONDALE	15
SOUTHWEST TEXAS ST U	4
SOUTHWESTERN LOUISIANA, U of	12
STANFORD U	9
SUNY COLL AT PLATTSBURG	3
TENNESSEE-KNOXVILLE, U of	18
TEXAS A&M U	48
TEXAS AT ARLINGTON, U of	11
TEXAS AT AUSTIN, U of	28
TEXAS AT EL PASO, U of	12
TEXAS TECH U	10
WASHINGTON ST U	17
WASHINGTON, U of	32
WEBER ST COLL	13
WISCONSIN OSHKOSH, U of	10
WISCONSIN-MADISON, U of	46
WYOMING, U of	11
XAVIER U	4

Microcomputer Applications

MAINE AT FORT KENT, U of	2

Middle Eastern Studies

CALIFORNIA-BERKELEY, U of	8
CHICAGO, U of	6
CUNY BROOKLYN COLL	4
CUNY QUEENS COLL	4
EASTERN MICHIGAN U	3
FORDHAM U	3
GEORGE WASHINGTON U	1
MICHIGAN ANN ARBOR, U of	1
PRINCETON U	5
RUTGERS U NEW BRUNSWICK	1
SMITH COLL	1
TEXAS AT AUSTIN, U of	8
UTAH, U of	4
WASHINGTON, U of	1

Military Science (Army)

CENTRAL WASHINGTON U	1

Military Sciences (unspecified)

CALIFORNIA MARITIME ACAD	36
CENTRAL WASHINGTON U	4
CHARLESTON, U of	14
IOWA ST U	1
MASSACHUSETTS MARITIME ACAD	119
OKLAHOMA ST U MAIN CAMPUS	1
US MERCHANT MARINE ACAD	86
US AIR FORCE ACAD	12

Military Sciences, Other

CHARLESTON, U of	14
UNITED STS MERCHANT MARINE ACAD	6

Military Technologies (unspecified)

WAYLAND BAPTIST U	145

Military Technologies

WAYLAND BAPTIST U	145

Mining (Excluding Coal) Technology

CENTRAL FLORIDA, U of	9

Mining and Mineral Engineering

ALASKA FAIRBANKS, U of	1
COLORADO SCHOOL OF MINES	16
COLUMBIA U IN THE CITY OF NEW YORK	5
IDAHO, U of	7
KENTUCKY, U of	7
MICHIGAN TECH U	2
MISSOURI-ROLLA, U of	8
MONTANA COLL OF MINERAL SCI AND TECH	16
NEVADA-RENO, U of	1
NEW MEXICO INST OF MINING AND TECH	1
PENNSYLVANIA ST U MAIN CAMPUS	9
SOUTH DAKOTA SCHOOL OF MINES & TECH	6
SOUTHERN ILLINOIS U-CARBONDALE	1
UTAH, U of	6
VIRGINIA POLYTECHNIC INST AND ST U	12
WEST VIRGINIA INST OF TECH	1

Mining and Petroleum Technologies, Other

SOUTHERN INDIANA, U of	1

Miscellaneous Allied Health Service, Other

CAMPBELL U INCORPORATED	4
ELIZABETHTOWN COLL	2
MADONNA COLL	26
MONTCLAIR ST COLL	7
MURRAY ST U	13
SAINT FRANCIS COLL	1
SOUTHWESTERN OKLAHOMA ST U	3
VALDOSTA ST COLL	6
WIDENER U PENNSYLVANIA CAMPUS	1
WISCONSIN-MILWAUKEE, U of	12

Miscellaneous Construction Trades, Other

DREXEL U	4
HAMPTON U	2

Miscellaneous Physical Sciences, Other

ARIZONA, U of	10
CHADRON ST COLL	3
MARY WASHINGTON COLL	6
MASS. AT LOWELL, U of	8
MIAMI U OXFORD CAMPUS	1
MIDDLE TENNESSE ST U	8
MINOT ST U	1
NEW HAMPSHIRE, U of	2
SUNY AT STONY BROOK	7
TENNESSEE-MARTIN, U of	11
WILLAMETTE U	2

Miscellaneous Specialized Areas, Life Sciences, Other

ARIZONA ST U	14
CALIFORNIA-DAVIS, U of	21
CALIFORNIA-RIVERSIDE, U of	27
CENTRAL MICHIGAN U	7
CLAREMONT MCKENNA COLL	1
CLEMSON U	8
DENISON U	1
EMORY U	25
HEIDELBERG COLL	2
KANSAS ST U AGRI AND APP SCI	18
LOUISIANA ST U SHREVEPORT	9
MARYLAND COLL PARK CAMPUS, U of	52
MARYLHURST COLL	1
MASSACHUSETTS AT AMHERST, U of	50
MONTANA ST U	12
NORTHERN IOWA, U of	6
NORTHWEST MISSOURI ST U	3
OBERLIN COLL	4
PLYMOUTH ST COLL	6
RUTGERS U NEW BRUNSWICK	11
SAINT CLOUD ST U	34
SOUTHWEST TEXAS ST U	2
SPRINGFIELD COLL	6
SWEET BRIAR COLL	1
TEXAS AT AUSTIN, U of	4
TROY ST U-MAIN CAMPUS	4
WILSON COLL	6
WISCONSIN-MADISON, U of	2

Missionary Studies

ABILENE CHRISTIAN U	5
ASBURY COLL	4
BAPTIST BIBLE COLL OF PENNSYLVANIA	1
BARTLESVILLE WESLEYAN COLL	1
CONCORDIA COLL	4
HARDING U MAIN CAMPUS	1
LIBERTY U	7
NORTHWEST CHRISTIAN COLL	2
NORTHWEST COLL OF THE ASSEMBLIES OF GOD	4
OKLAHOMA BAPTIST U	3
OKLAHOMA CHRISTIAN COLL	3
PACIFIC CHRISTIAN COLL	5
SEATTLE PACIFIC U	4
SOUTHEASTERN COLL ASSEMBLIES OF GOD	6
SOUTHERN CALIFORNIA COLL	4
SOUTHWEST BAPTIST U	15
SOUTHWESTERN ASSEMBLIES OF GOD COLL	11
TOCCOA FALLS COLL	18
WESTERN BAPTIST COLL	2

Molecular Biology

AUBURN U MAIN CAMPUS	3
BELOIT COLL	4
CALIFORNIA LUTHERAN U	2
CALIFORNIA-BERKELEY, U of	43
CALIFORNIA-SAN DIEGO, U of	19
CHESTNUT HILL COLL	2
COLGATE U	5
COLORADO AT BOULDER, U of	76
ECKERD COLL	1
FLORIDA INST OF TECH	16
GROVE CITY COLL	6
HARVEY MUDD COLL	1
LEHIGH U	5
MARQUETTE U	12
MIDDLEBURY COLL	1
PENNSYLVANIA ST U MAIN CAMPUS	22
POMONA COLL	5
PRINCETON U	37
TEXAS AT AUSTIN, U of	15
VANDERBILT U	20
WESLEYAN U	12
WESTMINSTER COLL	3
WISCONSIN-MADISON, U of	58
WYOMING, U of	8
YALE U	43

Multi/Interdisciplinary Studies, Other

Degrees in this subject were reported by 401 institutions. Consult more specific headings.

Multi/Interdisciplinary Studies (unspecified)

Degrees in this subject were reported by 634 institutions. Consult more specific headings.

Museology

BAYLOR U	3

Music Education

Degrees in this subject were reported by 447 institutions. Consult more specific headings.

Music History and Appreciation

AKRON, MAIN CAMPUS, U of	1
BAYLOR U	1
BOSTON U	6
CENTRAL METHODIST COLL	2
CENTRAL MICHIGAN U	3
CINCINNATI MAIN CAMPUS, U of	2
COLBY COLL	1
GEORGIA SOUTHERN COLL	1
HARTFORD, U of	1
HARVARD U	11
IDAHO, U of	1
IOWA WESLEYAN COLL	1
KENTUCKY, U of	2
LOUISVILLE, U of	1
MASS. AT LOWELL, U of	2
MICHIGAN ANN ARBOR, U of	2
NORTH TEXAS, U of	2
OBERLIN COLL	3
OLIVET COLL	1
RHODE ISLAND, U of	1
SAINT AMBROSE U	1
SKIDMORE COLL	7
TEMPLE U	1
TEXAS AT AUSTIN, U of	1
VANDERBILT U	1
WASHINGTON, U of	3
WILLAMETTE U	1
WRIGHT ST U MAIN CAMPUS	3

Music Performance

Degrees in this subject were reported by 270 institutions. Consult more specific headings.

Music Theory and Composition

ALABAMA, U of	21
ARIZONA ST U	1
ARIZONA, U of	2
ARTS, THE U of THE	2
BAYLOR U	2
BERKLEE COLL OF MUSIC	3
BOISE ST U	1
BOSTON U	2
BOWLING GREEN ST U MAIN CAMPUS	1
CALIFORNIA INST OF ARTS	5
CAMPBELL U INCORPORATED	3
CARNEGIE MELLON U	3
CENTRAL MICHIGAN U	1
CINCINNATI MAIN CAMPUS, U of	4
CONNECTICUT, U of	1
DEPAUL U	4
DEPAUW U	2
EAST TEXAS ST U	2
FLORIDA ST U	1
GEORGIA, U of	1
GRAND RAPIDS BAPTIST COLL AND SEMINARY	1
HOUSTON BAPTIST U	3
ILLINOIS URBANA CAMPUS, U of	2
INDIANA ST U	1
ITHACA COLL	1
JACKSONVILLE U	1
JUILLIARD SCHOOL, THE	3
LAWRENCE U	2
LOUISIANA ST U & AGRI & MECH & HEBERT LAWS CTR	4
MANHATTAN SCHOOL OF MUSIC	5
MANNES COLL OF MUSIC	3
MIAMI U OXFORD CAMPUS	1
MIAMI, U of	5
MICHIGAN ANN ARBOR, U of	4
MICHIGAN ST U	15
MINNESOTA DULUTH, U of	3

MISSOURI-KANSAS CITY, U of 1
MONTANA, U of 1
MONTEVALLO, U of 1
NEW ENGLAND CONSERVATORY OF MUSIC 7
NEW YORK U 1
NEWBERRY COLL 1
NORTH TEXAS, U of 12
NORTHWESTERN U 5
OBERLIN COLL 8
OHIO ST U MAIN CAMPUS 4
OKLAHOMA BAPTIST U 1
OLIVET COLL 2
ORAL ROBERTS U 3
OREGON, U of 1
PACIFIC, U of THE 2
PEABODY INST OF JOHNS HOPKINS U 3
REDLANDS, U of 2
RHODE ISLAND, U of 1
ROCHESTER, U of 10
SAINT MARY'S COLL OF MINNESOTA 1
SAMFORD U 4
SAN FRANCISCO CONSERVATORY OF MUSIC 1
SOUTH ALABAMA, U of 1
SUNY COLL AT FREDONIA 2
SYRACUSE U MAIN CAMPUS 1
TEMPLE U 3
TEXAS AT AUSTIN, U of 3
TEXAS AT EL PASO, U of 2
VANDERBILT U 2
WEBSTER U 1
WESTERN CONNECTICUT ST U 3
WHEATON COLL 2
WISCONSIN-MADISON, U of 1
YOUNGSTOWN ST U 1

Music Therapy

ALVERNO COLL 1
ANNA MARIA COLL 2
ARIZONA ST U 4
AUGSBURG COLL 1
BAPTIST COLL AT CHARLESTON 3
COLL OF WOOSTER 1
DAYTON, U of 1
DUQUESNE U 5
EASTERN MICHIGAN U 5
EASTERN NEW MEXICO U MAIN CAMPUS 3
ELIZABETHTOWN COLL 2
EMMANUEL COLL 3
FLORIDA ST U 2
GEORGIA COLL 1
GEORGIA, U of 7
IMMACULATA COLL 4
INDIANA U-PURDUE U AT FORT WAYNE 2
KANSAS MAIN CAMPUS, U of 4
LOYOLA U IN NEW ORLEANS 7
MANSFIELD U PENNSYLVANIA 6
MARYVILLE COLL—ST LOUIS 3
MARYWOOD COLL 3
MIAMI, U of 2
MICHIGAN ST U 7
MINNESOTA TWIN CITIES, U of 4
MONTCLAIR ST COLL 2
PACIFIC, U of THE 7
QUEENS COLL 1
RADFORD U 6
SAINT MARY-OF-THE-WOODS COLL 3
SHENANDOAH COLL AND CONSERVATORY 8
SLIPPERY ROCK U PENNSYLVANIA 4
SOUTHERN METHODIST U 2
SUNY COLL AT FREDONIA 3
SUNY COLL AT NEW PALTZ 5
TENNESSEE TECH U 3
TEXAS WOMAN'S U 5
UTAH ST U 5
WARTBURG COLL 4
WEST TEXAS ST U 2
WESTERN MICHIGAN U 5
WILLIAM CAREY COLL 3
WISCONSIN-EAU CLAIRE, U of 12

Music, General

Degrees in this subject were reported by 611 institutions. Consult more specific headings.

Music, Other

APPALACHIAN ST U 14
ARIZONA, U of 2
BERKLEE COLL OF MUSIC 188
BIOLA U 14
BLACKBURN COLL 1
BOSTON U 3
BUTLER U 2
CAPITAL U 4
CARROLL COLL 8
CENTRAL MISSOURI ST U 12
CLARION U PENNSYLVANIA 3
DALLAS BAPTIST U 1
DEPAUL U 10
DUQUESNE U 5
EAST CAROLINA U 37
ECKERD COLL 1
FLORIDA SOUTHERN COLL 7
GENEVA COLL 2
GRACE COLL 4
GRAND RAPIDS BAPTIST COLL AND SEMINARY 2
GREENSBORO COLL 1
GREENVILLE COLL 9
HANNIBAL-LAGRANGE COLL 1
HARDIN-SIMMONS U 1
HARTFORD, U of 35
HOUSTON BAPTIST U 1
ILLINOIS BENEDICTINE COLL 1
INDIANA ST U 1
INDIANA U BLOOMINGTON 110
INDIANA U-PURDUE U AT FORT WAYNE 1
JACKSONVILLE U 3
LOYOLA U IN NEW ORLEANS 2
MACMURRAY COLL 2
MADONNA COLL 1
MANSFIELD U PENNSYLVANIA 3
MASSACHUSETTS AT AMHERST, U of 23
MIAMI, U of 48
MILLIGAN COLL 1
MONMOUTH COLL 4
MONTANA ST U 1
MOORHEAD ST U 6
MURRAY ST U 3
NEW HAVEN, U of 16
NORFOLK ST U 1
NORTH ALABAMA, U of 5
NORTH CAROLINA AT GREENSBORO, U of 9
NORTH CAROLINA CENTRAL U 1
NORTH CAROLINA CHAPEL HILL, U of 6
NORTH CAROLINA SCHOOL OF THE ARTS 22
NORTH PARK COLL AND THEOLOGICAL SEMINARY 1
OBERLIN COLL 2
OHIO ST U MAIN CAMPUS 3
PUGET SOUND, U of 7
QUEENS COLL 2
QUINCY COLL 1
SAINT MARY'S COLL OF MINNESOTA 1
SAINT OLAF COLL 2
SHENANDOAH COLL AND CONSERVATORY 14
SHORTER COLL 2
SOUTH DAKOTA ST U 3
SOUTH DAKOTA, U of 1
SOUTHWEST BAPTIST U 1
SOUTHWESTERN ASSEMBLIES OF GOD COLL 3
SOUTHWESTERN LOUISIANA, U of 1
SUNY COLL AT FREDONIA 2
TULSA, U of 3
VALPARAISO U 2
WAYLAND BAPTIST U 4
WAYNE ST COLL 3
WEBSTER U 1
WESLEYAN COLL 1
WESLEYAN U 11
WEST CHESTER U PENNSYLVANIA 3
WEST TEXAS ST U 11
WESTERN BAPTIST COLL 2
WESTERN KENTUCKY U 2
WESTMINSTER CHOIR COLL 10
WHEATON COLL 3
WINGATE COLL 1
WISCONSIN-STEVENS POINT, U of 1

Native Amercian Languages

ALASKA FAIRBANKS, U of 1
HAWAII AT MANOA, U of 4

Naval Architecture and Marine Engineering

CALIFORNIA MARITIME ACAD 25
CALIFORNIA-BERKELEY, U of 4
MAINE MARITIME ACAD 81
MICHIGAN ANN ARBOR, U of 20
NEW ORLEANS, U of 6
SUNY MARITIME COLL 27
TEXAS A & M U AT GALVESTON 5
UNITED STS COAST GUARD ACAD 19
UNITED STS MERCHANT MARINE ACAD 36
UNITED STS NAVAL ACAD 37
WEBB INST OF NAVAL ARCHITECTURE 18
WISCONSIN-MADISON, U of 5

Naval Science (Navy, Marines)

IOWA ST U 1

Neurosciences

AMHERST COLL 8
BOWDOIN COLL 2
BROWN U 17
CALIFORNIA-BERKELEY, U of 15
COLGATE U 8
NORTHWESTERN U 1
OBERLIN COLL 15
PITTSBURGH MAIN CAMPUS, U of 32
TEXAS CHRISTIAN U 6
WASHINGTON AND LEE U 1

Nuclear Engineering

ARIZONA, U of 6
CALIFORNIA-BERKELEY, U of 4
CALIFORNIA-SANTA BARBARA, U of 13
CINCINNATI MAIN CAMPUS, U of 15
FLORIDA, U of 19
GEORGIA INST OF TECH MAIN CAMPUS 11
ILLINOIS URBANA CAMPUS, U of 19
IOWA ST U 10
KANSAS ST U AGRI AND APP SCI 4
MASS. AT LOWELL, U of 7
MASSACHUSETTS INST OF TECH 4
MICHIGAN ANN ARBOR, U of 14
MISSISSIPPI ST U 2
MISSOURI-ROLLA, U of 7
NEW MEXICO MAIN CAMPUS, U of 9
NORTH CAROLINA ST U AT RALEIGH 7
OREGON ST U 12
PENNSYLVANIA ST U MAIN CAMPUS 20
POLYTECHNIC U 1
RENSSELAER POLYTECHNIC INST 7
SUNY MARITIME COLL 11
TENNESSEE-KNOXVILLE, U of 13
TEXAS A&M U 11
VIRGINIA MAIN CAMPUS, U of 7
WISCONSIN-MADISON, U of 19

Nuclear Medical Technology

ALABAMA AT BIRMINGHAM, U of 5
ALVERNO COLL 1
BARRY U 2
CEDAR CREST COLL 1
DAYTON, U of 1
FERRIS ST U 12
GEORGE WASHINGTON U 7
HOUSTON-U PARK, U of 5
ILLINOIS BENEDICTINE COLL 4
INCARNATE WORD COLL 3
INDIANA U-PURDUE U AT INDIANAPOLIS 11
IOWA, U of 3
LOUISVILLE, U of 7
MEDICAL COLL OF GEORGIA 4
MIDWESTERN ST U 11
OLD DOMINION U 5
SAINT CLOUD ST U 3
SAINT LOUIS U MAIN CAMPUS 1
SAINT MARY'S COLL OF MINNESOTA 6
SETON HALL U 1
SIENA HEIGHTS COLL 1
SUNY AT BUFFALO 11
WHEELING COLL 6
WISCONSIN LA CROSSE, U of 25
YORK COLL PENNSYLVANIA 5

Nuclear Medicine

FINDLAY, U of 1

Nursery Operation and Management

SOUTHWESTERN LOUISIANA, U of 1

Nursing Administration

COLL OF MOUNT SAINT JOSEPH 23
OTTERBEIN COLL 20
UNION U 32

Nursing, General

Degrees in this subject were reported by 565 institutions. Consult more specific headings.

Nursing, Other

ELIZABETHTOWN COLL 2
FRANKLIN U 29
HOPE COLL 14
HOUSTON BAPTIST U 38
INCARNATE WORD COLL 43
LOURDES COLL 20
LOYOLA U IN NEW ORLEANS 22
MIAMI U OXFORD CAMPUS 29
NORTHEASTERN U 2
OHIO WESLEYAN U 9
PACIFIC UNION COLL 5
ROWAN C. OF NJ (WAS GLASSBORO ST COLL) 13
SAINT ANSELM COLL 42
TEIKYO MARYCREST COLL 24
WHEATON COLL 8
WISCONSIN-GREEN BAY, U of 33
YOUNGSTOWN ST U 45

Nursing-Related Service, Other

GEORGE WASHINGTON U 2
HANNIBAL-LAGRANGE COLL 15
RIVIER COLL 6

Nutritional Sciences

ARIZONA, U of 36
CALIFORNIA-BERKELEY, U of 21
CALIFORNIA-DAVIS, U of 11
CONNECTICUT, U of 18
FRAMINGHAM ST COLL 2
HAWAII AT MANOA, U of 22
INCARNATE WORD COLL 1
LONG ISLAND U C W POST CAMPUS 11
MARYLAND COLL PARK CAMPUS, U of 2
MINNESOTA TWIN CITIES, U of 2
NEW HAMPSHIRE, U of 21
NORTH CAROLINA ST U AT RALEIGH 1
PARK COLL 14
RUSSELL SAGE COLL MAIN CAMPUS 7
RUTGERS U NEW BRUNSWICK 8
SIMMONS COLL 6
TEXAS WOMAN'S U 1
WISCONSIN-GREEN BAY, U of 5
WISCONSIN-MADISON, U of 7

Occupational Safety and Health Technology

ALLENTOWN COLL OF SAINT FRANCIS DE SALES 2
CENTRAL MISSOURI ST U 29
CENTRAL WASHINGTON U 11
GRAND VALLEY ST U 10
INDIANA U PENNSYLVANIA 51
IOWA ST U 13
MILLERSVILLE U PENNSYLVANIA 31
MONTANA COLL OF MINERAL SCI AND TECH 11
MURRAY ST U 58
NATIONAL U 8
NEW HAMPSHIRE KEENE ST COLL, U of 17
NEW HAVEN, U of 2
OREGON ST U 8
OUR LADY OF HOLY CROSS COLL 1
SIENA HEIGHTS COLL 1
SLIPPERY ROCK U PENNSYLVANIA 16

SOUTHEASTERN OKLAHOMA ST U	5
TEXAS SOUTHERN U	2

Occupational Therapy

ALABAMA AT BIRMINGHAM, U of	28
BOSTON U	35
CENTRAL ARKANSAS, U of	24
CHICAGO ST U	23
CLEVELAND ST U	20
COLL MISERICORDIA	60
COLL OF SAINT CATHERINE-SAINT CATHERINE CAMPUS	49
COLL OF SAINT THOMAS	2
COLORADO ST U	68
CREIGHTON U	33
CUNY YORK COLL	9
D'YOUVILLE COLL	17
DOMINICAN COLL OF BLAUVELT	31
EAST CAROLINA U	21
EASTERN KENTUCKY U	53
EASTERN MICHIGAN U	56
ELIZABETHTOWN COLL	28
FLORIDA, U of	31
HOWARD U	13
ILLINOIS AT CHICAGO, U of	55
INDIANA U-PURDUE U AT INDIANAPOLIS	41
KEAN COLL OF NEW JERSEY	16
KEUKA COLL	28
LOMA LINDA U	37
LOUISIANA ST U MEDICAL CENTER	51
MEDICAL COLL OF GEORGIA	28
MINNESOTA TWIN CITIES, U of	32
MISSOURI-COLUMBIA, U of	26
MOORHEAD ST U	2
MOUNT MARY COLL	49
NEW ENGLAND, U of	21
NEW HAMPSHIRE, U of	20
NEW YORK U	7
NORTH DAKOTA MAIN CAMPUS, U of	30
NORTHEAST LOUISIANA U	18
OHIO ST U MAIN CAMPUS	56
PACIFIC U	21
PITTSBURGH MAIN CAMPUS, U of	29
PUGET SOUND, U of	32
QUINNIPIAC COLL	52
SAN JOSE ST U	63
SUNY AT BUFFALO	43
TEMPLE U	17
TEXAS WOMAN'S U	63
TOWSON ST U	43
TUFTS U	1
TUSKEGEE U	7
UTICA COLL OF SYRACUSE	48
VIRGINIA COMMONWEALTH U	28
WASHINGTON U	13
WASHINGTON, U of	22
WAYNE ST U	33
WESTERN MICHIGAN U	60
WISCONSIN-MADISON, U of	39
WISCONSIN-MILWAUKEE, U of	45
WORCESTER ST COLL	41

Ocean Engineering

FLORIDA INST OF TECH	15
MASSACHUSETTS INST OF TECH	5
TEXAS A & M U AT GALVESTON	8
TEXAS A&M U	7
US NAVAL ACAD	26

Oceanographic (Physical) Technology

NORTHERN MICHIGAN U	1

Oceanography

FLORIDA INST OF TECH	6
HAWAII LOA COLL	2
HUMBOLDT ST U	8
KUTZTOWN U PENNSYLVANIA	3
MIAMI, U of	31
US COAST GUARD ACAD	18
US NAVAL ACAD	72
WASHINGTON, U of	14

Office Suspervision and Management

Degrees in this subject were reported by 101 institutions. Consult more specific headings.

Operations Research (Quantitative Methods)

ALABAMA AT BIRMINGHAM, U of	3
ALABAMA, U of	18
ANDREWS U	2
ARKANSAS AT LITTLE ROCK, U of	4
ARKANSAS TECH U	1
BABSON COLL	8
BAYLOR U	17
BOISE ST U	7
BOWLING GREEN ST U MAIN CAMPUS	1
CINCINNATI MAIN CAMPUS, U of	23
CLEVELAND ST U	24
CUNY BERNARD BARUCH COLL	3
CUNY YORK COLL	63
DREXEL U	67
FERRIS ST U	3
FLORIDA INST OF TECH	1
GEORGIA ST U	30
GONZAGA U	6
LONG ISLAND U BROOKLYN CAMPUS	8
LOUISIANA ST U & AGRI & MECH & HEBERT LAWS CTR	31
LOUISIANA TECH U	2
MARYLAND COLL PARK CAMPUS, U of	26
MASSACHUSETTS BOSTON, U of	2
NEBRASKA AT OMAHA, U of	2
NEW HAVEN, U of	1
NEW YORK U	6
NICHOLLS ST U	6
NORTHERN ILLINOIS U	61
OHIO U MAIN CAMPUS	36
OREGON, U of	7
PENNSYLVANIA ST U MAIN CAMPUS	76
RHODE ISLAND, U of	6
RIDER COLL	30
SAINT AMBROSE U	3
SAINT CLOUD ST U	50
SAINT JOHN'S U NEW YORK	10
SYRACUSE U MAIN CAMPUS	33
TEXAS A&M U	133
THOMAS A EDISON ST COLL	3
TOLEDO, U of	2
US AIR FORCE ACAD	43
WESTERN NEW ENGLAND COLL	4
WISCONSIN OSHKOSH, U of	21
WISCONSIN-MADISON, U of	4
WISCONSIN-WHITEWATER, U of	30

Optics

ALABAMA IN HUNTSVILLE, U of	10
CALIFORNIA LUTHERAN U	1
ROSE-HULMAN INST OF TECH	20
SAGINAW VALLEY ST U	1
WESTERN WASHINGTON U	4

Optometry

CALIFORNIA-BERKELEY, U of	64
FERRIS ST U	30
HOUSTON-U PARK, U of	17
ILLINOIS COLL OF OPTOMETRY	27
INDIANA U BLOOMINGTON	17
JUNIATA COLL	2
NORTHEASTERN ST U	12
OHIO ST U MAIN CAMPUS	3
WILKES U	2

Organic Chemistry

SCRANTON, U of	8

Organizational Behavior

BRIGHAM YOUNG U	47
BROWN U	16
CONCORDIA COLL	153
DANA COLL	6
ELMHURST COLL	1
HOUSTON-U PARK, U of	87
LA SALLE U	31
LOYOLA U IN NEW ORLEANS	10
MARQUETTE U	6
MIAMI U OXFORD CAMPUS	66
NEBRASKA AT OMAHA, U of	39
NORTHWEST CHRISTIAN COLL	2
NORTHWESTERN U	31

PENNSYLVANIA, U of	8
RIDER COLL	53
ROLLINS COLL	16
SAINT LOUIS U MAIN CAMPUS	35
SANTA CLARA U	12
SCRIPPS COLL	3
SIOUX FALLS COLL	32
WAYNE ST U	72

Osteopathic Medicine

MICHIGAN ST U	3
WILKES U	1

Outdoor Recreation

ARKANSAS TECH U	2
BRIGHAM YOUNG U	66
CENTRAL MICHIGAN U	7
DAVIS AND ELKINS COLL	2
LYNDON ST COLL	1
MOORHEAD ST U	1
MORRIS COLL	1
NORTHERN MICHIGAN U	6
NORTHLAND COLL	2
OREGON ST U	14
PLYMOUTH ST COLL	1
SHEPHERD COLL	6
UNITY COLL	7

Painting

ART CENTER COLL OF DESIGN	23
ARTS, THE U of THE	17
BEAVER COLL	3
BOSTON U	14
BOWLING GREEN ST U MAIN CAMPUS	2
CALIFORNIA COLL OF ARTS AND CRAFTS	15
CLEVELAND INST OF ART	12
CONNECTICUT, U of	11
EAST TEXAS ST U	4
FONTBONNE COLL	3
GUILFORD COLL	14
HARTFORD, U of	13
HOUSTON-U PARK, U of	9
ILLINOIS URBANA CAMPUS, U of	27
KANSAS CITY ART INST	27
KENT ST U MAIN CAMPUS	18
KNOX COLL	4
LOUISIANA ST U & AGRI & MECH & HEBERT LAWS CTR	13
LOUISIANA TECH U	2
MAINE COLL OF ART (WAS PORTLAND SCHOOL OF ART)	8
MARYLAND INST COLL OF ART	22
MASSACHUSETTS AT DARTMOUTH (WAS SE U OF MA, U of	11
MCMURRY COLL	2
MEMPHIS COLL OF ART	6
MILLIKIN U	6
MILLSAPS COLL	5
MOORE COLL OF ART	17
NEBRASKA AT OMAHA, U of	13
NEW ORLEANS, U of	28
NORTH TEXAS, U of	24
NORTHERN MICHIGAN U	2
OHIO U MAIN CAMPUS	33
OREGON, U of	4
PITTSBURG ST U	13
PORTLAND ST U	13
PROVIDENCE COLL	1
RANDOLPH-MACON WOMAN'S COLL	7
RHODE ISLAND SCHOOL OF DESIGN	39
SAM HOUSTON ST U	28
SAN FRANCISCO ART INST	49
SAVANNAH COLL OF ART AND DESIGN	20
SETON HILL COLL	2
SUNY COLL AT BUFFALO	7
SUNY COLL AT NEW PALTZ	10
SUNY COLL AT POTSDAM	5
TEMPLE U	24
TEXAS AT EL PASO, U of	1
TRINITY U	3
VIRGINIA COMMONWEALTH U	54
WASHINGTON U	11
WASHINGTON, U of	21

Paleontology

BROWN U	2
CALIFORNIA-BERKELEY, U of	3

Parks and Recreation, Other

ABILENE CHRISTIAN U	6
CASTLETON ST COLL	5
CENTRAL MICHIGAN U	37
CREIGHTON U	5
CULVER-STOCKTON COLL	6
GEORGE FOX COLL	2
GEORGETOWN COLL	2
GREENSBORO COLL	1
HARDIN-SIMMONS U	2
HEIDELBERG COLL	5
IOWA ST U	32
JACKSONVILLE ST U	7
MINNESOTA TWIN CITIES, U of	17
NORTH ALABAMA, U of	17
NORTHWESTERN COLL	2
NORWICH U	5
PRESCOTT COLL	1
SAMFORD U	1
SEATTLE PACIFIC U	12
SOUTHEAST MISSOURI ST U	2
SOUTHWESTERN COLL	4
TABOR COLL	7
VIRGINIA UNION U	1
WAYNE ST COLL	11
WESTMAR COLL	7
WILMINGTON COLL	2

Parks and Recreation, General

ABILENE CHRISTIAN U	2
ALABAMA, U of	3
ALCORN ST U	4
AQUINAS COLL	6
ARIZONA ST U	67
ARKANSAS PINE BLUFF, U of	2
ARKANSAS-FAYETTEVILLE, U of	7
ASHLAND U	3
AZUSA PACIFIC U	1
BARBER-SCOTIA COLL	1
BELMONT ABBEY COLL	5
BETHANY COLL	9
BOWLING GREEN ST U MAIN CAMPUS	21
CALIFORNIA POLYTECHNIC ST U-SAN LUIS OBISPO	31
CALIFORNIA ST POLYTECHNIC U POMONA	11
CALIFORNIA ST U DOMINGUEZ HILLS	5
CALIFORNIA ST U FRESNO	25
CALIFORNIA ST U LONG BEACH	35
CALIFORNIA ST U LOS ANGELES	1
CALIFORNIA ST U NORTHRIDGE	26
CALIFORNIA ST U-CHICO	88
CALIFORNIA ST U-HAYWARD	28
CALIFORNIA ST U-SACRAMENTO	28
CARSON-NEWMAN COLL	9
CATAWBA COLL	7
CENTRAL MISSOURI ST U	13
CENTRAL U IOWA	3
CENTRAL WASHINGTON U	28
DRAKE U	1
EASTERN WASHINGTON U	58
FERRUM COLL	3
FLAGLER COLL	4
FROSTBURG ST U	6
GALLAUDET U	7
GEORGE MASON U	22
GEORGIA SOUTHERN COLL	57
GRACELAND COLL	1
GREEN MOUNTAIN COLL	7
HAWAII AT MANOA, U of	5
HIGH POINT COLL	3
HOWARD U	3
HUNTINGTON COLL	5
ILLINOIS ST U	62
ILLINOIS URBANA CAMPUS, U of	68
INDIANA U BLOOMINGTON	55
KNOXVILLE COLL	1
LIBERTY U	3
MARS HILL COLL	7
MARYLAND COLL PARK CAMPUS, U of	26
MARYMOUNT U	4
MARYVILLE COLL	1
MASSACHUSETTS AT AMHERST, U of	25
MEMPHIS ST U	10
METROPOLITAN ST COLL	11
MIDDLE TENNESSE ST U	13
MIDLAND LUTHERAN COLL	5
MISSISSIPPI MAIN CAMPUS, U of	5
MISSOURI-COLUMBIA, U of	38

MORNINGSIDE COLL	9
MOUNT OLIVE COLL	7
NEVADA-RENO, U of	6
NORTH DAKOTA ST U MAIN CAMPUS	5
NORTH TEXAS, U of	15
NORTHERN ARIZONA U	1
NORTHERN IOWA, U of	5
NORTHWEST NAZARENE COLL	1
OKLAHOMA NORMAN CAMPUS, U of	4
PRESCOTT COLL	2
RADFORD U	23
SALISBURY ST U	7
SAN DIEGO ST U	79
SAN FRANCISCO ST U	27
SAN JOSE ST U	27
SHAW U	2
SOUTHEAST MISSOURI ST U	12
SOUTHEASTERN OKLAHOMA ST U	9
SOUTHERN MISSISSIPPI, U of	20
SOUTHERN NAZARENE U	1
SOUTHERN U AT NEW ORLEANS	2
SOUTHWEST MISSOURI ST U	48
SPRINGFIELD COLL	13
TEMPLE U	30
TENNESSEE-KNOXVILLE, U of	23
TEXAS A&M U	77
TEXAS TECH U	24
TEXAS WOMAN'S U	1
UPPER IOWA U	4
UTAH ST U	12
VIRGINIA COMMONWEALTH U	24
WAYNE ST U	7
WEST TEXAS ST U	1
WESTERN ST COLL COLORADO	10
WESTERN WASHINGTON U	41
WHITWORTH COLL	4
WINONA ST U	14
WISCONSIN LA CROSSE, U of	96

Parks and Recreation (unspecified)

Degrees in this subject were reported by 231 institutions. Consult more specific headings.

Parks and Recreation Management

Degrees in this subject were reported by 112 institutions. Consult more specific headings.

Pathology, Human and Animal

CONNECTICUT, U of	9

Peace Studies

BETHEL COLL	2
CALIFORNIA-BERKELEY, U of	13
EARLHAM COLL	9
MANCHESTER COLL	4
NORTH CAROLINA CHAPEL HILL, U of	3
SAINT JOHN'S U	1

Personnel Management

ALABAMA, U of	31
AMERICAN INTERNATIONAL COLL	4
ARIZONA, U of	44
ARKANSAS-FAYETTEVILLE, U of	3
AUBURN U AT MONTGOMERY	11
AUBURN U MAIN CAMPUS	25
AURORA U	2
CENTRAL MICHIGAN U	15
CENTRAL MISSOURI ST U	19
CINCINNATI MAIN CAMPUS, U of	7
COLL OF SAINT THOMAS	20
DEPAUL U	49
DETROIT, U of	2
DREXEL U	22
EAST TEXAS ST U	28
EASTERN NEW MEXICO U MAIN CAMPUS	12
ECKERD COLL	3
FERRIS ST U	16
FLORIDA SOUTHERN COLL	30
FRANKLIN U	46
GALLAUDET U	23
GEORGE WASHINGTON U	14
HAWAII AT MANOA, U of	21
HUSTON-TILLOTSON COLL	4
JUNIATA COLL	6
KANSAS MAIN CAMPUS, U of	63
KUTZTOWN U PENNSYLVANIA	71
LA SALLE U	41
LAMAR U	6
LOUISIANA TECH U	14
LOYOLA U CHICAGO	39
MANKATO ST U	19
MARIETTA COLL	4
MARQUETTE U	27
MARYLAND COLL PARK CAMPUS, U of	37
MARYMOUNT U	6
MASSACHUSETTS BOSTON, U of	13
MIAMI U OXFORD CAMPUS	32
MICHIGAN ST U	51
MILLIKIN U	5
NEBRASKA AT OMAHA, U of	4
NEW HAVEN, U of	1
NICHOLLS ST U	7
NORFOLK ST U	12
NORTH CAROLINA WESLEYAN COLL	1
NORTH TEXAS, U of	24
NORTHWEST MISSOURI ST U	14
OHIO U MAIN CAMPUS	124
QUINCY COLL	6
REGIS COLL	1
RHODE ISLAND, U of	2
ROBERTS WESLEYAN COLL	96
SAINT JOSEPHS COLL MAIN CAMPUS	16
SAINT LOUIS U MAIN CAMPUS	7
SAINT MARY'S U	13
SHIPPENSBURG U PENNSYLVANIA	53
SOUTHERN MISSISSIPPI, U of	57
SOUTHWESTERN LOUISIANA, U of	6
THE ST OF NY REGENTS COL DEG, U of	18
THOMAS A EDISON ST COLL	12
UPSALA COLL	37
URBANA U	19
UTAH ST U	21
WESTERN ILLINOIS U	16
WICHITA ST U	10
WILLIAM PENN COLL	4
WINONA ST U	14
WISCONSIN OSHKOSH, U of	39
WISCONSIN-WHITEWATER, U of	39
WRIGHT ST U MAIN CAMPUS	6
WYOMING, U of	4

Petroleum Engineering

ALASKA FAIRBANKS, U of	2
CALIFORNIA-BERKELEY, U of	2
KANSAS MAIN CAMPUS, U of	5
LOUISIANA ST U & AGRI & MECH & HEBERT LAWS CTR	6
LOUISIANA TECH U	4
MARIETTA COLL	11
MISSISSIPPI ST U	8
MISSOURI-ROLLA, U of	7
MONTANA COLL OF MINERAL SCI AND TECH	17
NEW MEXICO INST OF MINING AND TECH	11
NORTH DAKOTA ST U MAIN CAMPUS	4
OKLAHOMA NORMAN CAMPUS, U of	7
PENNSYLVANIA ST U MAIN CAMPUS	14
SOUTHWESTERN LOUISIANA, U of	6
STANFORD U	1
TEXAS A & I U	9
TEXAS A&M U	29
TEXAS AT AUSTIN, U of	15
TEXAS TECH U	14
TULSA, U of	14
WEST VIRGINIA U	4
WYOMING, U of	12

Petroloeum Technology

NICHOLLS ST U	14
OKLAHOMA ST U MAIN CAMPUS	2

Pharmaceutical Chemistry

SUNY AT BUFFALO	10

Pharmacology, Human and Animal

CALIFORNIA-SANTA BARBARA, U of	10
SUNY AT BUFFALO	13

Pharmacy

ALBANY COLL OF PHARMACY	136
AUBURN U MAIN CAMPUS	103
BUTLER U	73
CINCINNATI MAIN CAMPUS, U of	68
COLORADO AT BOULDER, U of	71
CONNECTICUT, U of	79
CREIGHTON U	52
DRAKE U	87
DUQUESNE U	124
FERRIS ST U	104
FLORIDA AGRI AND MECH U	27
FLORIDA, U of	46
GEORGIA, U of	134
HOUSTON-U PARK, U of	160
HOWARD U	56
IDAHO ST U	1
IOWA, U of	79
KANSAS MAIN CAMPUS, U of	71
KENTUCKY, U of	80
LONG ISLAND U BROOKLYN CAMPUS	185
MINNESOTA TWIN CITIES, U of	90
MISSISSIPPI MAIN CAMPUS, U of	94
MISSOURI-KANSAS CITY, U of	41
MONTANA, U of	26
NEW MEXICO MAIN CAMPUS, U of	62
NORTH CAROLINA CHAPEL HILL, U of	164
NORTH DAKOTA ST U MAIN CAMPUS	83
NORTHEAST LOUISIANA U	149
NORTHEASTERN U	74
OHIO NORTHERN U	115
OHIO ST U MAIN CAMPUS	109
OREGON ST U	93
PACIFIC, U of THE	6
PHILADELPHIA COLL OF PHARMACY AND SCIENCE	202
PITTSBURGH MAIN CAMPUS, U of	127
RHODE ISLAND, U of	100
RUTGERS U NEW BRUNSWICK	113
SAINT JOHN'S U NEW YORK	291
SAMFORD U	97
SOUTH CAROLINA—COLUMBIA, U of	83
SOUTH DAKOTA ST U	53
SOUTHWESTERN OKLAHOMA ST U	111
ST LOUIS COLL OF PHARMACY	137
SUNY AT BUFFALO	76
TEMPLE U	138
TEXAS AT AUSTIN, U of	142
TEXAS SOUTHERN U	60
TOLEDO, U of	82
UTAH, U of	45
VIRGINIA COMMONWEALTH U	101
WASHINGTON ST U	44
WASHINGTON, U of	59
WAYNE ST U	92
WEST VIRGINIA U	68
WISCONSIN-MADISON, U of	127
WYOMING, U of	38
XAVIER U	107

Philosophy and Religion (unspecified)

Degrees in this subject were reported by 778 institutions. Consult more specific headings.

Philosophy and Religion, Other

ADRIAN COLL	3
ALBERTSON C. (WAS COLL OF IDAHO)	2
APPALACHIAN ST U	9
ARKANSAS COLL	2
BAPTIST BIBLE COLL OF PENNSYLVANIA	2
BENEDICT COLL	1
BERRY COLL	4
BETHANY COLL	1
BETHUNE COOKMAN COLL	1
BLUEFIELD COLL	3
BRANDEIS U	3
BRIDGEWATER COLL	2
BROWN U	10
BUENA VISTA COLL	1
BUTLER U	1
CALIFORNIA LUTHERAN U	2
CATAWBA COLL	2
CHICAGO, U of	4
CLAFLIN COLL	4
COLGATE U	17
COLUMBIA U IN THE CITY OF NEW YORK	11
CONNECTICUT COLL	1
DALLAS BAPTIST U	9
DENVER, U of	1
EAST TEXAS BAPTIST U	24
EASTERN COLL	1
ECKERD COLL	1
EMORY U	10
EUREKA COLL	1
FISK U	1
FLAGLER COLL	6
FLORIDA MEMORIAL COLL	2
FLORIDA SOUTHERN COLL	3
GRACELAND COLL	1
GREENSBORO COLL	5
GREENVILLE COLL	3
GROVE CITY COLL	2
HAMPDEN-SYDNEY COLL	3
HENDRIX COLL	3
HOOD COLL	2
HUNTINGDON COLL	4
INDIANA ST U	2
ITHACA COLL	8
JAMES MADISON U	7
JAMESTOWN COLL	3
JUDSON COLL	7
KEAN COLL OF NEW JERSEY	2
KENTUCKY WESLEYAN COLL	2
LOUISIANA COLL	1
LOURDES COLL	3
LYNCHBURG COLL	1
MACMURRAY COLL	2
MARY BALDWIN COLL	1
MARY WASHINGTON COLL	7
MARYLHURST COLL	6
MCPHERSON COLL	1
MIDLAND LUTHERAN COLL	2
MONTANA ST U	8
MORNINGSIDE COLL	3
NEWBERRY COLL	2
NORTH CAROLINA WILMINGTON, U of	5
NORTHEAST MISSOURI ST U	7
NORTHERN IOWA, U of	4
NORTHWEST COLL OF THE ASSEMBLIES OF GOD	5
OLD DOMINION U	5
OLIVET NAZARENE U	1
PAINE COLL	1
PEMBROKE ST U	1
PHILANDER SMITH COLL	1
RADFORD U	5
REED COLL	4
ROANOKE COLL	2
ROBERTS WESLEYAN COLL	9
SAINT JOHN'S U NEW YORK	1
SAINT MARY PLAINS COLL	2
SAINT THOMAS AQUINAS COLL	7
SAN FRANCISCO ST U	7
SHENANDOAH COLL AND CONSERVATORY	1
SKIDMORE COLL	1
SPRING ARBOR COLL	7
STANFORD U	7
STOCKTON ST COLL	3
TABOR COLL	3
TENNESSEE-CHATTANOOGA, U of	7
TOCCOA FALLS COLL	2
URSINUS COLL	2
VANDERBILT U	2
VIRGINIA UNION U	3
WASHINGTON U	1
WELLS COLL	2
WESLEYAN COLL	1
WESTMAR COLL	1
WILLIAMS COLL	1
WINTHROP COLL	2

Philosophy

Degrees in this subject were reported by 600 institutions. Consult more specific headings.

Photographic Technology

KENT ST U MAIN CAMPUS	16
OTIS ART INST OF PARSONS SCHOOL OF DESIGN	5
POINT PARK COLL	3

Photography

AKRON, MAIN CAMPUS, U of	2
ART CENTER COLL OF DESIGN	60

ARTS, THE U of THE	22
BARRY U	5
BARTON (FORMERLY ATLANTIC CHRISTIAN) COLL	1
BEAVER COLL	1
BOWLING GREEN ST U MAIN CAMPUS	2
BROOKS INST OF PHOTOGRAPHY	96
CALIFORNIA COLL OF ARTS AND CRAFTS	7
CALIFORNIA INST OF ARTS	11
CARSON-NEWMAN COLL	5
CENTER FOR CREATIVE STUDIES COL OF ART AND DESIGN	19
CENTRAL MISSOURI ST U	4
CLEVELAND INST OF ART	5
CONNECTICUT, U of	11
CORCORAN SCHOOL OF ART	7
DAYTON, U of	8
EAST TEXAS ST U	14
EASTERN WASHINGTON U	4
GODDARD COLL	2
GRAND VALLEY ST U	8
HARTFORD, U of	7
HOUSTON-U PARK, U of	7
IDAHO, U of	5
ILLINOIS URBANA CAMPUS, U of	4
KANSAS CITY ART INST	10
LONG ISLAND U C W POST CAMPUS	4
LOUISIANA TECH U	3
MAINE COLL OF ART (WAS PORTLAND SCHOOL OF ART)	11
MARYLAND INST COLL OF ART	12
MEMPHIS COLL OF ART	5
MERCY COLL—MAIN CAMPUS	1
MIAMI, U of	4
MONTANA ST U	9
MOORE COLL OF ART	3
NEW SCHOOL FOR SOCIAL RESEARCH	8
NEW YORK U	25
NORTH TEXAS, U of	13
NORTHERN MICHIGAN U	5
NORTHWESTERN ST U LOUISIANA	1
OHIO U MAIN CAMPUS	9
PRATT INST-MAIN	20
PRESCOTT COLL	1
RHODE ISLAND SCHOOL OF DESIGN	23
ROCHESTER INST OF TECH	143
SAINT EDWARD'S U	6
SAINT JOHN'S U NEW YORK	1
SAINT VINCENT COLL	2
SAM HOUSTON ST U	31
SAN FRANCISCO ART INST	25
SAN FRANCISCO, U of	1
SAVANNAH COLL OF ART AND DESIGN	29
SCHOOL OF VISUAL ARTS	47
SETON HILL COLL	3
SUNY COLL AT BUFFALO	2
SUNY COLL AT NEW PALTZ	4
SUNY COLL AT POTSDAM	3
SYRACUSE U MAIN CAMPUS	28
TEMPLE U	7
VIRGINIA INTERMONT COLL	4
WASHINGTON U	9
WASHINGTON, U of	18
WEBER ST COLL	2

Physical Chemistry

HARVARD U	6
MICHIGAN ST U	2
RICE U	2

Physical Education

Degrees in this subject were reported by 672 institutions. Consult more specific headings.

Physical Sciences (unspecified)

Degrees in this subject were reported by 1015 institutions. Consult more specific headings.

Physical Sciences Technologies, Other

SOUTHWEST MISSOURI ST U	2

Physical Sciences, General

ARIZONA, U of	4
ARKANSAS TECH U	19
AUBURN U AT MONTGOMERY	14
BIOLA U	1
CALIFORNIA POLYTECHNIC ST U-SAN LUIS OBISPO	4
CALIFORNIA ST U-CHICO	19
CALIFORNIA ST U-HAYWARD	4
CALIFORNIA ST U-STANISLAUS	2
CALIFORNIA-BERKELEY, U of	12
CENTRAL ARKANSAS, U of	1
CENTRAL CONNECTICUT ST U	2
CENTRAL MICHIGAN U	6
CHRISTIAN BROTHERS COLL	10
COE COLL	3
COLORADO ST U	6
DANA COLL	3
DUQUESNE U	1
EAST STROUDSBURG U PENNSYLVANIA	2
EMPORIA ST U	4
EUREKA COLL	3
FORT HAYS ST U	3
FREED-HARDEMAN COLL	1
GALLAUDET U	1
GRACE COLL	1
GRACELAND COLL	1
HARVARD U	3
HUMBOLDT ST U	5
HUSTON-TILLOTSON COLL	1
KANSAS ST U AGRI AND APP SCI	9
KEAN COLL OF NEW JERSEY	2
LEWIS U	1
LINCOLN U	4
LORAS COLL	5
LYNDON ST COLL	2
MARLBORO COLL	2
MARYLAND COLL PARK CAMPUS, U of	21
MARYMOUNT U	4
MARYVILLE COLL—ST LOUIS	5
MEMPHIS ST U	1
MICHIGAN ST U	14
MINNESOTA TWIN CITIES, U of	9
MINOT ST U	1
MISSISSIPPI U FOR WOMEN	9
MOBILE COLL	2
MORNINGSIDE COLL	1
NEW MEXICO INST OF MINING AND TECH	1
NORTHERN ARIZONA U	19
NORTHERN COLORADO, U of	3
OKLAHOMA CITY U	2
PITTSBURGH MAIN CAMPUS, U of	4
POINT PARK COLL	1
RADCLIFFE COLL	1
RADFORD U	4
ROCHESTER, U of	2
ROWAN C. OF NJ (WAS GLASSBORO ST COLL)	38
SAINT ANSELM COLL	3
SAINT JOHN'S U NEW YORK	1
SAINT JOSEPH'S COLL	1
SAINT XAVIER COLL	3
SALISBURY ST U	11
SAN DIEGO ST U	3
SAN JOSE ST U	1
SOUTHERN ILLINOIS U AT EDWARDSVILLE	1
SOUTHERN UTAH ST COLL	1
TROY ST U-MAIN CAMPUS	1
UNITED STS NAVAL ACAD	71
VILLANOVA U	21
WALSH COLL	3
WAYLAND BAPTIST U	5
WENTWORTH INST OF TECH	3
WESLEYAN COLL	2
WESTERN NEW MEXICO U	3
WESTFIELD ST COLL	3
WISCONSIN-WHITEWATER, U of	1
YESHIVA U	3
YORK COLL PENNSYLVANIA	2

Physical Sciences, Other

AZUSA PACIFIC U	1
BELMONT COLL	1
BEMIDJI ST U	2
BENEDICT COLL	3
BOSTON COLL	15
CALIFORNIA-LOS ANGELES, U of	3
CASE WESTERN RESERVE U	1
CENTRAL ST U	3
CENTRE COLL	3
CLEMSON U	1
COLGATE U	1
CONCORDIA LUTHERAN COLL	2
CUNY JOHN JAY COLL CRIMINAL JUSTICE	9

EASTERN CONNECTICUT ST U	5
ERSKINE COLL AND SEMINARY	5
FINDLAY, U of	1
FLORIDA INST OF TECH	9
FURMAN U	11
HOBART WILLIAM SMITH COLLS	2
JAMES MADISON U	1
JOHNS HOPKINS U	1
KALAMAZOO COLL	10
LE MOYNE COLL	1
LEWIS AND CLARK COLL	4
NEW HAMPSHIRE KEENE ST COLL, U of	1
NEW YORK U	1
NORTH ALABAMA, U of	8
NORTH DAKOTA MAIN CAMPUS, U of	12
OBERLIN COLL	6
PENNSYLVANIA ST U MAIN CAMPUS	11
PENNSYLVANIA, U of	14
PHILADELPHIA COLL OF TEXTILES AND SCIENCE	3
RAMAPO COLL OF NEW JERSEY	6
RIPON COLL	1
SAINT MICHAEL'S COLL	2
SANTA CLARA U	24
SIERRA NEVADA COLL	2
SOUTH DAKOTA SCHOOL OF MINES & TECH	3
SPRINGFIELD COLL	4
SUNY EMPIRE ST COLL	75
TEXAS A & M U AT GALVESTON	6
VILLANOVA U	2
WISCONSIN-GREEN BAY, U of	11
YOUNGSTOWN ST U	3

Physical Therapy Aide

CAMPBELL U INCORPORATED	1

Physical Therapy

BEAVER COLL	1
BOSTON U	48
BOWLING GREEN ST U MAIN CAMPUS	13
CALIFORNIA ST U FRESNO	32
CALIFORNIA ST U LONG BEACH	54
CENTRAL ARKANSAS, U of	42
CLEVELAND ST U	29
CONNECTICUT, U of	67
CUNY HUNTER COLL	30
D'YOUVILLE COLL	24
DAEMEN COLL	112
DAVID LIPSCOMB U	1
DELAWARE, U of	2
EAST CAROLINA U	30
EASTERN MICHIGAN U	27
EASTERN WASHINGTON U	20
ELMHURST COLL	1
EVANSVILLE, U of	24
FLORIDA AGRI AND MECH U	28
FLORIDA, U of	33
GEORGIA ST U	34
GRAND VALLEY ST U	31
HEALTH SCIENCES-CHICAGO MEDICAL SCH, U of	25
HOWARD U	21
ILLINOIS AT CHICAGO, U of	46
INDIANA U-PURDUE U AT INDIANAPOLIS	26
ITHACA COLL	81
JUNIATA COLL	3
KEAN COLL OF NEW JERSEY	28
KENTUCKY, U of	47
LANGSTON U	25
LOMA LINDA U	68
LONG ISLAND U BROOKLYN CAMPUS	10
LOUISIANA ST U MEDICAL CENTER	50
LOUISVILLE, U of	27
MARQUETTE U	70
MARYLAND EASTERN SHORE, U of	16
MARYVILLE COLL—ST LOUIS	26
MASS. AT LOWELL, U of	54
MEDICAL COLL OF GEORGIA	39
MINNESOTA TWIN CITIES, U of	30
MISSOURI-COLUMBIA, U of	35
MONTANA, U of	20
MOUNT SAINT MARY'S COLL	37
NEW ENGLAND, U of	43
NEW MEXICO MAIN CAMPUS, U of	21
NEW YORK U	45
NORTH CAROLINA CHAPEL HILL, U of	26
NORTH DAKOTA MAIN CAMPUS, U of	42
NORTHEASTERN U	104
NORTHERN ILLINOIS U	13
NORTHWESTERN U	81
OHIO ST U MAIN CAMPUS	69
OHIO U MAIN CAMPUS	32
OKLAHOMA BAPTIST U	2
PITTSBURGH MAIN CAMPUS, U of	66
QUINNIPIAC COLL	46
ROCKHURST COLL	30
RUSSELL SAGE COLL MAIN CAMPUS	57
SAINT AUGUSTINE'S COLL	3
SAINT LOUIS U MAIN CAMPUS	63
SCRANTON, U of	36
SIMMONS COLL	33
SOUTH ALABAMA, U of	29
SOUTHWEST TEXAS ST U	24
SPRINGFIELD COLL	29
STOCKTON ST COLL	2
SUNY AT BUFFALO	50
SUNY AT STONY BROOK	25
TEMPLE U	60
TEXAS SAN ANTONIO, U of	36
TEXAS WOMAN'S U	61
TOLEDO, U of	16
UTAH, U of	24
VERMONT, U of	40
VIRGINIA COMMONWEALTH U	31
WASHINGTON, U of	32
WAYNE ST U	30
WEST VIRGINIA U	19
WICHITA ST U	21
WISCONSIN LA CROSSE, U of	55
WISCONSIN-MADISON, U of	60

Physician Assiting-Primary Care

ALABAMA AT BIRMINGHAM, U of	6
ALDERSON BROADDUS COLL	36
CREIGHTON U	11
DETROIT, U of	17
DUKE U	36
FLORIDA, U of	29
GANNON U	15
GEORGE WASHINGTON U	44
HAHNEMANN U	20
HOWARD U	2
IOWA, U of	19
KENTUCKY, U of	23
KING'S COLL	15
MARS HILL COLL	1
MEDICAL COLL OF GEORGIA	24
MEREDITH COLL	1
RUTGERS U NEW BRUNSWICK	14
SAINT FRANCIS COLL	13
SAINT LOUIS U MAIN CAMPUS	8
SIENA HEIGHTS COLL	2
SUNY AT STONY BROOK	24
TREVECCA NAZARENE COLL	14
WAKE FOREST U	1
WESTERN MICHIGAN U	17
WISCONSIN-MADISON, U of	31

Physics, General

Degrees in this subject were reported by 631 institutions. Consult more specific headings.

Physics, Other

ALABAMA AGRI AND MECH U	1
ALABAMA, U of	2
ALBION COLL	1
AUBURN U MAIN CAMPUS	6
BOWDOIN COLL	1
BRIDGEWATER COLL	1
BROWN U	12
CALIFORNIA LUTHERAN U	1
CALIFORNIA-DAVIS, U of	6
CARSON-NEWMAN COLL	1
CHRISTOPHER NEWPORT COLL	4
COLORADO COLL	8
DARTMOUTH COLL	9
DELAWARE ST COLL	3
DREXEL U	10
EAST CAROLINA U	4
FRANCIS MARION COLL	4
GEORGIA INST OF TECH MAIN CAMPUS	17
LINFIELD COLL	6
MASS. AT LOWELL, U of	5
MICHIGAN TECH U	7
MONMOUTH COLL	1
MONTANA ST U	2
NEW JERSEY INST TECH	1

NORTH CAROLINA CHAPEL HILL, U of	11
NORTHERN IOWA, U of	1
PACIFIC U	3
SAINT JOHN'S U	5
SCRANTON, U of	1
SHIPPENSBURG U PENNSYLVANIA	4
UNION U	1
WHEELING COLL	1

Physiological Psychology

ALBRIGHT COLL	6
BEAVER COLL	11
HOOD COLL	1
LEBANON VALLEY COLL	1
MIAMI, U of	5
PENNSYLVANIA, U of	70
SWARTHMORE COLL	3
WESTMINSTER COLL	4

Physiology

BOSTON U	6

Physiology, Human and Animal

CALIFORNIA-BERKELEY, U of	72
CALIFORNIA-DAVIS, U of	97
CALIFORNIA-SAN DIEGO, U of	77
CONNECTICUT, U of	3
EASTERN MICHIGAN U	17
ILLINOIS URBANA CAMPUS, U of	9
KENT ST U MAIN CAMPUS	1
MICHIGAN ST U	47
MINNESOTA TWIN CITIES, U of	14
OKLAHOMA ST U MAIN CAMPUS	18
SOUTHERN ILLINOIS U-CARBONDALE	16
SOUTHWEST TEXAS ST U	1

Planetary Science

BOSTON U	1

Plant Genetics

WISCONSIN-MADISON, U of	23

Plant Pathology

GEORGIA, U of	2
IOWA ST U	1
MASSACHUSETTS AT AMHERST, U of	2
NORTH DAKOTA ST U MAIN CAMPUS	1
OHIO ST U MAIN CAMPUS	1

Plant Protection (Pest Management)

ARKANSAS-FAYETTEVILLE, U of	1
AUBURN U MAIN CAMPUS	1
CALIFORNIA ST POLYTECHNIC U POMONA	13
IDAHO, U of	1
KANSAS ST U AGRI AND APP SCI	2
MINNESOTA TWIN CITIES, U of	1
MONTANA ST U	1

Plant Sciences, General

ARIZONA, U of	3
ARKANSAS ST U MAIN CAMPUS	7
CALIFORNIA-DAVIS, U of	14
CORNELL U-NYS STATUTORY COLLS	44
DELAWARE, U of	19
DORDT COLL	3
MASSACHUSETTS AT AMHERST, U of	14
NEW HAMPSHIRE, U of	5
NORTH DAKOTA ST U MAIN CAMPUS	9
PENNSYLVANIA ST U MAIN CAMPUS	3
RHODE ISLAND, U of	5
RUTGERS U NEW BRUNSWICK	1
SOUTHERN ILLINOIS U-CARBONDALE	31
SOUTHERN U AGRI & MECH COL AT BATON ROUGE	2
TARLETON ST U	4
TENNESSEE ST U	2
TENNESSEE TECH U	1
TENNESSEE-KNOXVILLE, U of	7
TEXAS A & I U	5
UTAH ST U	6
WEST TEXAS ST U	6

Plant Sciences, Other

ALABAMA AGRI AND MECH U	3
EAST TEXAS ST U	2
ILLINOIS URBANA CAMPUS, U of	19
MISSISSIPPI ST U	1
MONTANA ST U	15
SOUTHWEST TEXAS ST U	3
WEST VIRGINIA U	5
WYOMING, U of	3

Plastic Technology

DETROIT, U of	2
EASTERN MICHIGAN U	2
FERRIS ST U	42
PITTSBURG ST U	17

Podiatry

WILKES U	4

Political Science and Government

Degrees in this subject were reported by 921 institutions. Consult more specific headings.

Portuguese

BRIGHAM YOUNG U	12
CALIFORNIA-LOS ANGELES, U of	1
CALIFORNIA-SANTA BARBARA, U of	1
CONNECTICUT, U of	1
GEORGETOWN U	4
IOWA, U of	1
MASSACHUSETTS AT AMHERST, U of	1
MASSACHUSETTS AT DARTMOUTH (WAS SE U OF MA, U of	4
PENNSYLVANIA, U of	1
RUTGERS U NEW BRUNSWICK	2
WISCONSIN-MADISON, U of	5

Poultry

ARKANSAS-FAYETTEVILLE, U of	3
AUBURN U MAIN CAMPUS	16
CALIFORNIA POLYTECHNIC ST U-SAN LUIS OBISPO	4
CALIFORNIA-DAVIS, U of	7
FLORIDA, U of	6
GEORGIA, U of	12
MARYLAND EASTERN SHORE, U of	1
MISSISSIPPI ST U	16
NORTH CAROLINA ST U AT RALEIGH	12
OHIO ST U MAIN CAMPUS	1
OREGON ST U	3
PENNSYLVANIA ST U MAIN CAMPUS	1
TEXAS A&M U	17
VIRGINIA POLYTECHNIC INST AND ST U	2
WISCONSIN-MADISON, U of	3

Practical Nursing

SOUTHWEST BAPTIST U	14
WALSH COLL	9

Pre-Dentistry

ALABAMA, U of	2
ANGELO ST U	3
BALL ST U	2
DAYTON, U of	2
JUNIATA COLL	1
KANSAS ST U AGRI AND APP SCI	6
MCNEESE ST U	8
NEVADA-RENO, U of	1
NORTH CAROLINA CHAPEL HILL, U of	2
NORTHEAST LOUISIANA U	13
SOUTHWESTERN LOUISIANA, U of	1
TENNESSEE-MARTIN, U of	2
WAKE FOREST U	1
WEST TEXAS ST U	1

Pre-Elementary Education

Degrees in this subject were reported by 212 institutions. Consult more specific headings.

Pre-Law

ALABAMA, U of	7
ANTIOCH COLL	1

AVERETT COLL	1
BARRY U	5
BAYLOR U	9
BOWLING GREEN ST U MAIN CAMPUS	20
BRIDGEWATER ST COLL	8
CATAWBA COLL	5
CHAPMAN COLL	6
CREIGHTON U	5
EASTERN MICHIGAN U	4
FLORIDA INST OF TECH	1
FONTBONNE COLL	1
GOLDEN GATE U	5
GOUCHER COLL	1
HAMLINE U	2
JUNIATA COLL	6
LOUISIANA COLL	6
LOUISIANA ST U & AGRI & MECH & HEBERT LAWS CTR	11
LOUISIANA TECH U	14
MARYWOOD COLL	1
NEW ORLEANS, U of	1
NICHOLLS ST U	13
NORTHEAST LOUISIANA U	20
NOVA U	21
PACIFIC LUTHERAN U	12
PACIFIC, U of THE	13
PENNSYLVANIA ST U MAIN CAMPUS	35
SAINT LEO COLL	3
SOUTHWESTERN LOUISIANA, U of	8
TEIKYO MARYCREST COLL	3
US INTERNATIONAL U	2
UTAH ST U	8
WAYNE ST COLL	1
WESTERN MICHIGAN U	1
WISCONSIN-MILWAUKEE, U of	7

Pre-Medicine

ALABAMA, U of	3
ANGELO ST U	5
ARKANSAS-FAYETTEVILLE, U of	6
AUGUSTANA COLL	4
AVILA COLL	1
BALL ST U	10
BETHEL COLL	1
BOISE ST U	2
CENTRAL U IOWA	3
COLL OF SAINT SCHOLASTICA	1
DAVID LIPSCOMB U	2
DAVIDSON COLL	3
DAYTON, U of	23
ELIZABETHTOWN COLL	15
FINDLAY, U of	1
GRAND VALLEY ST U	20
IMMACULATA COLL	4
JUNIATA COLL	13
KANSAS ST U AGRI AND APP SCI	3
KENT ST U MAIN CAMPUS	12
LEHIGH U	14
LENOIR-RHYNE COLL	1
LINFIELD COLL	1
LOUISIANA ST U & AGRI & MECH & HEBERT LAWS CTR	13
MALONE COLL	2
MANCHESTER COLL	13
MASSACHUSETTS AT AMHERST, U of	1
NEBRASKA-LINCOLN, U of	1
NEVADA-RENO, U of	31
NICHOLLS ST U	3
NORTH CAROLINA CHAPEL HILL, U of	1
NORTH CAROLINA ST U AT RALEIGH	60
NOTRE DAME, U of	134
OHIO WESLEYAN U	2
OKLAHOMA CITY U	1
PENNSYLVANIA ST U MAIN CAMPUS	27
SOUTHERN NAZARENE U	3
SOUTHERN U AGRI & MECH COL AT BATON ROUGE	2
SOUTHWESTERN LOUISIANA, U of	13
TRI-ST U	2
UTAH ST U	1
WEST TEXAS ST U	4
WISCONSIN-MILWAUKEE, U of	20
YOUNGSTOWN ST U	4

Pre-Pharmacy

DAVID LIPSCOMB U	1
JUNIATA COLL	1
TENNESSEE TECH U	2

Pre-Veterinary

FINDLAY, U of	6
MARYLAND COLL PARK CAMPUS, U of	2
NEVADA-RENO, U of	7
NEW ENGLAND COLL	1
OKLAHOMA ST U MAIN CAMPUS	5
UTAH ST U	3

Precision Production

ALABAMA AGRI AND MECH U	6
ANDREWS U	6
ARKANSAS ST U MAIN CAMPUS	7
BOWLING GREEN ST U MAIN CAMPUS	18
CALIFORNIA POLYTECHNIC ST U-SAN LUIS OBISPO	62
CALIFORNIA U PENNSYLVANIA	16
CALUMET COLL OF SAINT JOSEPH	1
CENTRAL MISSOURI ST U	70
CONCORDIA TEACHERS COLL	4
DISTRICT OF COLUMBIA, U of THE	8
DREXEL U	2
EAST TEXAS ST U	11
FORT VALLEY ST COLL	2
FRIENDS U	2
GRAND VIEW COLL	14
IOWA WESLEYAN COLL	1
JACKSONVILLE U	10
LOUISIANA COLL	1
MADONNA COLL	4
MILLIKIN U	2
MISSOURI WESTERN ST COLL	4
NORTH ALABAMA, U of	4
NORTH TEXAS, U of	91
NORTHERN IOWA, U of	5
NORTHERN KENTUCKY U	7
NOTRE DAME COLL	7
OUACHITA BAPTIST U	4
POINT LOMA NAZARENE COLL	6
PRAIRIE VIEW A & M U	5
RIO GRANDE, U of	2
SALEM-TEIKYO U	1
SCHOOL OF THE OZARKS	1
SIMMONS COLL	11
SOUTH DAKOTA ST U	3
SOUTHWEST TEXAS ST U	35
TEXAS CHRISTIAN U	14
TEXAS SOUTHERN U	1
TEXAS WOMAN'S U	5
WEST VIRGINIA INST OF TECH	25
WESTERN KENTUCKY U	4
WESTERN MICHIGAN U	30
WILLIAM CAREY COLL	2

Printmaking

ARTS, THE U of THE	10
BOWLING GREEN ST U MAIN CAMPUS	1
CALIFORNIA COLL OF ARTS AND CRAFTS	8
CLEVELAND INST OF ART	3
CONNECTICUT, U of	1
DALLAS, U of	5
DRAKE U	1
HOUSTON-U PARK, U of	2
KANSAS CITY ART INST	3
MAINE COLL OF ART (WAS PORTLAND SCHOOL OF ART)	3
MEMPHIS COLL OF ART	2
MOORE COLL OF ART	4
NORTH TEXAS, U of	6
NORTHERN MICHIGAN U	2
OREGON, U of	2
RHODE ISLAND SCHOOL OF DESIGN	9
SAN FRANCISCO ART INST	5
SUNY COLL AT BUFFALO	1
SUNY COLL AT POTSDAM	1
TEMPLE U	9
TEXAS AT EL PASO, U of	1
WASHINGTON U	4

Product Management

ARIZONA ST U	61
BOWLING GREEN ST U MAIN CAMPUS	69
CLEMSON U	25
COLL OF SAINT SCHOLASTICA	1
COLL OF SAINT THOMAS	27
DOANE COLL	9
EAST TEXAS ST U	23
FLORIDA SOUTHERN COLL	15
GARDNER-WEBB COLL	3
GEORGIA INST OF TECH MAIN CAMPUS	7

LOUISIANA TECH U	5
LOYOLA U CHICAGO	12
MARYLAND COLL PARK CAMPUS, U of	2
MIAMI U OXFORD CAMPUS	15
NORTH CAROLINA WESLEYAN COLL	5
NORTH TEXAS, U of	43
NORTHEAST LOUISIANA U	3
OHIO ST U MAIN CAMPUS	126
SOUTHEAST MISSOURI ST U	5
SOUTHWESTERN LOUISIANA, U of	4
UTAH ST U	11
WESTERN ILLINOIS U	10
WINONA ST U	2
WISCONSIN-MILWAUKEE, U of	5

Protective Services (unspecified)

Degrees in this subject were reported by 381 institutions. Consult more specific headings.

Protective Services, Other

MORNINGSIDE COLL	4
NORTHWESTERN OKLAHOMA ST U	2
PROVIDENCE COLL	7
SAINT MARY'S COLL OF MINNESOTA	7
VIRGINIA COMMONWEALTH U	7

Psych., Other

ALABAMA AGRI AND MECH U	7
ANDREWS U	14
ATLANTIC UNION COLL	2
BARNARD COLL	1
BARTON (FORMERLY ATLANTIC CHRISTIAN) COLL	2
BRIDGEWATER ST COLL	3
BROWN U	6
BURLINGTON COLL	10
CALIFORNIA ST POLYTECHNIC U POMONA	74
CALIFORNIA ST U DOMINGUEZ HILLS	18
CALIFORNIA-DAVIS, U of	21
CALIFORNIA-LOS ANGELES, U of	119
CALIFORNIA-RIVERSIDE, U of	24
CALIFORNIA-SAN DIEGO, U of	43
CALIFORNIA-SANTA BARBARA, U of	44
CASTLETON ST COLL	1
CENTRAL ST U	16
CHRISTIAN BROTHERS COLL	19
CLAREMONT MCKENNA COLL	1
COPPIN ST COLL	23
CUNY JOHN JAY COLL CRIMINAL JUSTICE	52
DALLAS BAPTIST U	1
EASTERN WASHINGTON U	43
ECKERD COLL	62
EMMANUEL COLL	9
ERSKINE COLL AND SEMINARY	3
FRANKLIN U	29
GODDARD COLL	1
HAMILTON COLL	10
INCARNATE WORD COLL	6
ITHACA COLL	39
LA ROCHE COLL	4
LONG ISLAND U SOUTHHAMPTON COLL	8
MANSFIELD U PENNSYLVANIA	14
MARYMOUNT U	6
MARYVILLE COLL	1
MICHIGAN ANN ARBOR, U of	4
MINNESOTA TWIN CITIES, U of	104
MOUNT HOLYOKE COLL	8
MOUNT SAINT MARY'S COLL	7
MOUNT VERNON COLL	20
NATIONAL U	145
NEBRASKA WESLEYAN U	5
NORTHWEST COLL OF THE ASSEMBLIES OF GOD	14
OCCIDENTAL COLL	5
OKLAHOMA BAPTIST U	8
PITZER COLL	1
PRESCOTT COLL	2
REGIS COLL	1
SAN FRANCISCO, U of	7
SAN JOSE ST U	34
SCRANTON, U of	1
SCRIPPS COLL	3
SKIDMORE COLL	3
SOUTH DAKOTA ST U	1
SOUTHERN U AGRI & MECH COL AT BATON ROUGE	15
TROY ST U-MAIN CAMPUS	5
VASSAR COLL	12
WARNER SOUTHERN COLL	2
WELLESLEY COLL	11
WHEATON COLL	2
WILMINGTON COLL	27

Psychology (unspecified)

Degrees in this subject were reported by 1156 institutions. Consult more specific headings.

Psychology, General

Degrees in this subject were reported by 1131 institutions. Consult more specific headings.

Public Administration

Degrees in this subject were reported by 134 institutions. Consult more specific headings.

Public Affairs (unspecified)

Degrees in this subject were reported by 610 institutions. Consult more specific headings.

Public Affairs, General

COLUMBIA COLL	26
DENVER, U of	4
FERRUM COLL	2
FLORIDA MEMORIAL COLL	8
GEORGE WASHINGTON U	1
INDIANA U AT SOUTH BEND	17
INDIANA U BLOOMINGTON	236
INDIANA U NORTHWEST	7
INDIANA U-PURDUE U AT FORT WAYNE	16
INDIANA U-PURDUE U AT INDIANAPOLIS	57
KENNESAW ST COLL	33
LINCOLN U	8
MAHARISHI INTERNATIONAL U	2
MICHIGAN ST U	43
NORTHWESTERN U	65
OKLAHOMA NORMAN CAMPUS, U of	60
PENNSYLVANIA ST U MAIN CAMPUS	21
PRINCETON U	69
ROLLINS COLL	6
SAINT MARY COLL	1
SUNY AT ALBANY	6
TENNESSEE-CHATTANOOGA, U of	10
TENNESSEE-KNOXVILLE, U of	21
TRINITY COLL	2
WAYNE ST U	27

Public Affairs, Other

BOWLING GREEN ST U MAIN CAMPUS	12
CALIFORNIA-DAVIS, U of	20
CALIFORNIA-SANTA BARBARA, U of	2
CHATHAM COLL	4
CUNY JOHN JAY COLL CRIMINAL JUSTICE	42
ELIZABETHTOWN COLL	1
HAWAII PACIFIC COLL	16
IONA COLL	5
KENTUCKY WESLEYAN COLL	1
LINCOLN U	5
MASSACHUSETTS BOSTON, U of	3
MCMURRY COLL	14
MERCY COLL—MAIN CAMPUS	6
NEBRASKA AT OMAHA, U of	7
NEW SCHOOL FOR SOCIAL RESEARCH	100
NEW YORK U	4
NORTH TEXAS, U of	24
PORTLAND, U of	11
RHODE ISLAND, U of	16
ROBERTS WESLEYAN COLL	1
SOUTHERN VERMONT COLL	3
URBANA U	17
UTICA COLL OF SYRACUSE	13
VILLANOVA U	4

Public Health Education

COLL OF SAINT THOMAS	1
GWYNEDD-MERCY COLL	4
MORRIS BROWN COLL	5

Public Health Laboratory Science

CALIFORNIA ST U NORTHRIDGE	60
COLORADO ST U	15
GEORGIA, U of	16
INDIANA ST U	41
JOHNS HOPKINS U	10
MASSACHUSETTS AT AMHERST, U of	10
OAKLAND U	13
SAN DIEGO ST U	10
WEST CHESTER U PENNSYLVANIA	16

Public Health Practice and Mgmt.

ECKERD COLL	10
SLIPPERY ROCK U PENNSYLVANIA	33
SOUTHERN CONNECTICUT ST U	25

Public Health

BELMONT COLL	1
UTAH ST U	11

Public Health, Other

BOWLING GREEN ST U MAIN CAMPUS	9
INDIANA U BLOOMINGTON	18
INDIANA U-PURDUE U AT INDIANAPOLIS	23
LIBERTY U	16
NEW MEXICO HIGHLANDS U	2
NORTH CAROLINA CHAPEL HILL, U of	40
REGIS COLL	1
RUTGERS U NEW BRUNSWICK	16
SOUTH DAKOTA ST U	1
STOCKTON ST COLL	24

Public Policy Studies

BROWN U	35
CHICAGO, U of	42
CONCORDIA COLL	1
DICKINSON COLL	29
DUKE U	95
NEW MEXICO ST U MAIN CAMPUS	4
NORTH CAROLINA CHAPEL HILL, U of	15
NORTHERN ARIZONA U	2
OCCIDENTAL COLL	13
OREGON, U of	14
PENNSYLVANIA, U of	11
RICE U	2
SAINT PETER'S COLL	10
SIMMONS COLL	24
SMITH COLL	1
STANFORD U	21
TRINITY COLL	1
WASHINGTON AND LEE U	4

Public Relations

ABILENE CHRISTIAN U	6
ALABAMA ST U	7
ALABAMA, U of	97
ANDREWS U	1
BARRY U	3
BOWLING GREEN ST U MAIN CAMPUS	12
BRADLEY U	38
BRENAU COLL	9
CAMPBELL U INCORPORATED	11
CAPITAL U	19
CARROLL COLL	7
CENTRAL MISSOURI ST U	41
CENTRAL WASHINGTON U	25
DAVID LIPSCOMB U	2
DAYTON, U of	31
DRAKE U	14
EASTERN COLL	1
EASTERN KENTUCKY U	39
EASTERN MICHIGAN U	25
ELIZABETHTOWN COLL	7
EVANSVILLE, U of	3
FERRIS ST U	12
FLORIDA SOUTHERN COLL	21
FLORIDA, U of	147
FONTBONNE COLL	10
FREED-HARDEMAN COLL	6
GEORGIA, U of	93
GONZAGA U	26
HARDIN-SIMMONS U	5
HARDING U MAIN CAMPUS	12
HEIDELBERG COLL	5
IDAHO, U of	23
ILLINOIS ST U	164
JOHN BROWN U	3
LORAS COLL	14
LOUISIANA ST U SHREVEPORT	11
MANKATO ST U	22
MARIETTA COLL	3
MARQUETTE U	40
MARS HILL COLL	15
MARYWOOD COLL	9
MCKENDREE COLL	1
MIAMI, U of	40
MIDLAND LUTHERAN COLL	1
MISSISSIPPI COLL	1
MOUNT MARY COLL	4
MOUNT MERCY COLL	13
MURRAY ST U	22
NORTH ALABAMA, U of	14
NORTH DAKOTA MAIN CAMPUS, U of	37
NORTH TEXAS, U of	17
NORTHEAST LOUISIANA U	21
NORTHERN ARIZONA U	31
NORTHERN IOWA, U of	68
NORTHERN MICHIGAN U	8
NORTHWEST MISSOURI ST U	22
OHIO DOMINICAN COLL	6
OKLAHOMA BAPTIST U	4
OREGON, U of	36
OTTERBEIN COLL	9
PACIFIC UNION COLL	9
PEPPERDINE U	16
PITTSBURGH BRADFORD CAMPUS, U of	2
REGIS COLL	3
RIVIER COLL	3
SAINT MARY'S COLL OF MINNESOTA	12
SAN JOSE ST U	69
SHORTER COLL	4
SIMMONS COLL	8
SOUTHEAST MISSOURI ST U	21
SOUTHERN METHODIST U	32
SOUTHWEST MISSOURI ST U	67
SOUTHWESTERN LOUISIANA, U of	14
SPRING HILL COLL	4
SUSQUEHANNA U	14
TEXAS CHRISTIAN U	1
TEXAS TECH U	41
URSULINE COLL	1
WARTBURG COLL	6
WAYNE ST U	48
WEBER ST COLL	25
WEST VIRGINIA WESLEYAN COLL	5
WESTERN KENTUCKY U	37
WESTERN MICHIGAN U	23
WESTMINSTER COLL	16
WHITWORTH COLL	1
WILLIAM JEWELL COLL	17

Purchasing

MICHIGAN ST U	144

Pure Mathematics

CALIFORNIA INST OF TECH	9
DAVID LIPSCOMB U	4
DREW U	1
FRANKLIN COLL INDIANA	5
MASSACHUSETTS BOSTON, U of	11
MICHIGAN ST U	55
MONTANA COLL OF MINERAL SCI AND TECH	5

Quality Control and Safety Technologies, Other

MADONNA COLL	2

Quantitative Psychology

NORTHWEST MISSOURI ST U	1

Radio and Television Production and Broadcasting Technology

AKRON, MAIN CAMPUS, U of	55
ALABAMA AGRI AND MECH U	19
ASBURY COLL	9
ASHLAND U	6
BOWIE ST U	16
CENTRAL FLORIDA, U of	10
COLL OF MOUNT SAINT VINCENT	22
COLL OF SAINT ROSE	37
CUNY BROOKLYN COLL	2
DANA COLL	3

EAST STROUDSBURG U PENNSYLVANIA	36
EASTERN MICHIGAN U	50
ELON COLL	31
FERRIS ST U	37
GANNON U	12
GENEVA COLL	8
GEORGIA, U of	108
KENT ST U MAIN CAMPUS	66
KNOXVILLE COLL	3
MANHATTAN COLL	22
MEDAILLE COLL	8
MONTEVALLO, U of	22
MOUNT SAINT MARY COLL	1
OKLAHOMA NORMAN CAMPUS, U of	70
ORAL ROBERTS U	41
ROCHESTER INST OF TECH	3
SCHOOL OF VISUAL ARTS	222
SHAW U	2
TEXAS CHRISTIAN U	26
TREVECCA NAZARENE COLL	1
US INTERNATIONAL U	6
WAKE FOREST U	6
WEBER ST COLL	6
WORCESTER ST COLL	47

Radio/Television News Broadcast

BARRY U	1
BOWLING GREEN ST U MAIN CAMPUS	16
BRADLEY U	14
CHICAGO ST U	9
DAYTON, U of	31
DENISON U	24
DRAKE U	19
EVANSVILLE, U of	9
FONTBONNE COLL	2
GEORGIA, U of	33
ILLINOIS URBANA CAMPUS, U of	32
KENT ST U MAIN CAMPUS	32
LINCOLN U	4
LOUISIANA ST U & AGRI & MECH & HEBERT LAWS CTR	37
MAINE, U of	9
MARQUETTE U	73
MARYLAND COLL PARK CAMPUS, U of	121
MIAMI U OXFORD CAMPUS	78
MIAMI, U of	26
MIDLAND LUTHERAN COLL	2
MISSISSIPPI U FOR WOMEN	9
MORGAN ST U	42
NEBRASKA-LINCOLN, U of	47
NORTH DAKOTA MAIN CAMPUS, U of	1
NORTH TEXAS, U of	5
NORTHEAST LOUISIANA U	6
NORTHERN IOWA, U of	6
NORTHWESTERN COLL	5
OKLAHOMA CHRISTIAN COLL	13
OREGON, U of	17
PENNSYLVANIA ST U MAIN CAMPUS	167
SAINT MARY'S COLL OF MINNESOTA	6
SOUTHERN COLL OF SEVENTH-DAY ADVENTISTS	8
SOUTHERN METHODIST U	25
SOUTHERN U AGRI & MECH COL AT BATON ROUGE	38
SPRING HILL COLL	6
TEXAS CHRISTIAN U	10
WESTERN WASHINGTON U	27
WYOMING, U of	2

Radio/Television, General

Degrees in this subject were reported by 126 institutions. Consult more specific headings.

Radiograph Medical Technology

ALABAMA AT BIRMINGHAM, U of	7
AVILA COLL	5
BLOOMSBURG U PENNSYLVANIA	8
BOISE ST U	9
BRIAR CLIFF COLL	3
CENTRAL ARKANSAS, U of	9
CENTRAL FLORIDA, U of	12
CHICAGO ST U	1
COLL MISERICORDIA	7
CREIGHTON U	1
ELON COLL	4
EMORY U	2
GEORGE WASHINGTON U	1
HARTFORD, U of	4
IDAHO ST U	8
INDIANA U-PURDUE U AT INDIANAPOLIS	5
LA ROCHE COLL	10
LOMA LINDA U	5
LOYOLA U IN NEW ORLEANS	2
MADONNA COLL	1
MARIAN COLL	2
MARIAN COLL OF FOND DU LAC	1
MARS HILL COLL	1
MCNEESE ST U	13
MEDICAL COLL OF GEORGIA	4
MINOT ST U	4
MISSOURI-COLUMBIA, U of	9
NEVADA-LAS VEGAS, U of	19
NORTHEAST LOUISIANA U	25
NORTHEASTERN ST U	3
NORTHEASTERN U	2
NORTHWESTERN ST U LOUISIANA	10
OHIO ST U MAIN CAMPUS	21
OREGON INST OF TECH	30
QUEENS COLL	2
QUINNIPIAC COLL	6
SIENA HEIGHTS COLL	12
SIOUX FALLS COLL	1
SOUTHWEST MISSOURI ST U	7
WAYNE ST U	5
WILLIAM CAREY COLL	4

Radiologic (Physical) Technology

MARY, U of	9

Radiology

SAINT MARY PLAINS COLL	2

Range Management

ARIZONA, U of	5
CALIFORNIA-DAVIS, U of	3
COLORADO ST U	3
HUMBOLDT ST U	2
IDAHO, U of	3
NEBRASKA-LINCOLN, U of	1
NEW MEXICO ST U MAIN CAMPUS	4
OREGON ST U	8
SOUTH DAKOTA ST U	3
SUL ROSS ST U	2
TARLETON ST U	6
TEXAS A&M U	21
TEXAS TECH U	5
UTAH ST U	5
WASHINGTON ST U	1
WYOMING, U of	13

Reading Education

CASTLETON ST COLL	12
CENTRAL MICHIGAN U	10
EASTERN OREGON ST COLL	2
EASTERN WASHINGTON U	130
HARDIN-SIMMONS U	1
LESLEY COLL	6
NORFOLK ST U	1
NORTHERN IOWA, U of	1
SAINT CLOUD ST U	4
SEATTLE PACIFIC U	11
SOUTHWEST TEXAS ST U	1

Real EST, General

ALABAMA, U of	26
ALASKA ANCHORAGE, U of	2
AMERICAN U	14
ARIZONA ST U	45
ARIZONA, U of	14
ARKANSAS ST U MAIN CAMPUS	8
ARKANSAS-FAYETTEVILLE, U of	9
BAYLOR U	16
CINCINNATI MAIN CAMPUS, U of	19
CLARION U PENNSYLVANIA	8
CONNECTICUT, U of	5
DENVER, U of	4
EASTERN KENTUCKY U	15
EASTERN MICHIGAN U	8
FERRIS ST U	5
FLORIDA ST U	52
FLORIDA, U of	20
FRANKLIN U	3
GEORGIA ST U	30
GEORGIA, U of	40
HAWAII AT MANOA, U of	6
KENT ST U MAIN CAMPUS	5

LOUISIANA ST U & AGRI & MECH & HEBERT LAWS CTR	3
MANKATO ST U	5
MEMPHIS ST U	13
MIAMI, U of	21
MISSISSIPPI MAIN CAMPUS, U of	6
MISSISSIPPI ST U	17
MOREHEAD ST U	7
MOREHOUSE COLL	10
NATIONAL U	13
NEBRASKA AT OMAHA, U of	15
NEW MEXICO ST U MAIN CAMPUS	2
NEW ORLEANS, U of	3
NORTH TEXAS, U of	20
NORTHERN IOWA, U of	1
OHIO ST U MAIN CAMPUS	36
OKLAHOMA NORMAN CAMPUS, U of	1
PACE U-NEW YORK	6
PENNSYLVANIA ST U MAIN CAMPUS	58
PENNSYLVANIA, U of	12
RICHMOND, U of	1
SAINT CLOUD ST U	12
SHIPPENSBURG U PENNSYLVANIA	4
SOUTH CAROLINA AT COASTAL CAROLINA, U of	8
SOUTH CAROLINA—COLUMBIA, U of	9
SOUTHERN METHODIST U	4
SOUTHERN MISSISSIPPI, U of	15
TEMPLE U	33
TEXAS A & I U	2
TEXAS CHRISTIAN U	4
WESTERN MICHIGAN U	1
WICHITA ST U	5
WISCONSIN-MADISON, U of	22
WISCONSIN-MILWAUKEE, U of	23

Recreational Enterprises Management

BEMIDJI ST U	8
BOWLING GREEN ST U MAIN CAMPUS	35
COLBY-SAWYER COLL	4
COLL OF SAINT FRANCIS	1
COLL OF SAINT SCHOLASTICA	1
ELMHURST COLL	3
ELON COLL	8
FRANKLIN PIERCE COLL	10
GLENVILLE ST COLL	2
HARDING U MAIN CAMPUS	2
LYNDON ST COLL	1
MASSACHUSETTS AT AMHERST, U of	71
METROPOLITAN ST COLL	42
MISSOURI VALLEY COLL	8
MOUNT UNION COLL	19
NEW ENGLAND, U of	1
NORTHERN IOWA, U of	14
OLIVET COLL	1
PFEIFFER COLL	7
SAINT LEO COLL	7
SUNY COLL AT BROCKPORT	20
SUNY COLL AT CORTLAND	11

Recreational Therapy

ABILENE CHRISTIAN U	1
BELMONT ABBEY COLL	3
COE COLL	1
COLL OF SAINT FRANCIS	2
COLL OF SAINT MARY	4
DOANE COLL	1
EASTERN MICHIGAN U	9
GALLAUDET U	5
GANNON U	6
GRAMBLING ST U	17
GRAND VALLEY ST U	7
GREEN MOUNTAIN COLL	2
HIGH POINT COLL	3
LAKE SUPERIOR ST U	4
LINCOLN U	5
LONGWOOD COLL	11
LYNDON ST COLL	2
NEBRASKA-LINCOLN, U of	9
NORTHEASTERN U	5
NORTHERN IOWA, U of	19
SOUTHERN MAINE, U of	7
SOUTHERN U AGRI & MECH COL AT BATON ROUGE	5
SPRINGFIELD COLL	12
TEXAS WOMAN'S U	7
WISCONSIN-MILWAUKEE, U of	18

Recreational Therapy Technology

PFEIFFER COLL	5

Rehabilitation Counseling

ARIZONA, U of	30
CALIFORNIA ST U LOS ANGELES	10
EASTERN MONTANA COLL	9
EMPORIA ST U	14
FLORIDA ST U	13
LOUISIANA ST U MEDICAL CENTER	19
MARYLAND EASTERN SHORE, U of	10
MURRAY ST U	9
SPRINGFIELD COLL	53
WISCONSIN-MADISON, U of	13
WRIGHT ST U MAIN CAMPUS	20

Rehabilitation Services, Other

ASSUMPTION COLL	52
AUBURN U MAIN CAMPUS	10
BOSTON U	3
EAST STROUDSBURG U PENNSYLVANIA	16
ELMHURST COLL	5
KANSAS ST U AGRI AND APP SCI	4
MARSHALL U	29
MEMPHIS ST U	5
MONTANA, U of	4
NORTH TEXAS, U of	20
NORTHERN COLORADO, U of	19
PAN AMERICAN U	12
SAINT XAVIER COLL	14
SEATTLE U	4
SHAW U	1
STEPHEN F AUSTIN ST U	20
TROY ST U-MAIN CAMPUS	4
VIRGINIA COMMONWEALTH U	27
WEST VIRGINIA WESLEYAN COLL	5
WISCONSIN OSHKOSH, U of	6
WISCONSIN-EAU CLAIRE, U of	38
WISCONSIN-STEVENS POINT, U of	25

Religion

Degrees in this subject were reported by 409 institutions. Consult more specific headings.

Religious Education

ABILENE CHRISTIAN U	14
ANDERSON U	3
ASBURY COLL	11
AVERETT COLL	2
AZUSA PACIFIC U	3
BAPTIST BIBLE COLL OF PENNSYLVANIA	4
BETHEL COLL	1
BETHUNE COOKMAN COLL	1
BIOLA U	22
BRYAN COLL	7
CAMPBELLSVILLE COLL	3
CENTENARY COLL OF LOUISIANA	4
COLL OF SAINT SCHOLASTICA	5
COLUMBIA COLL	1
CONCORDIA COLL	8
CUMBERLAND COLL	4
DALLAS BAPTIST U	2
DEFIANCE COLL	2
ELMHURST COLL	2
GEORGE FOX COLL	4
GORDON COLL	6
GREENVILLE COLL	1
HARDIN-SIMMONS U	3
HARDING U MAIN CAMPUS	2
HOLY FAMILY COLL	2
HOWARD PAYNE U	7
HUNTINGTON COLL	10
IMMACULATA COLL	6
JOHN BROWN U	4
JUDSON COLL	3
LA GRANGE COLL	2
LA ROCHE COLL	2
LEE COLL	13
LOUISIANA COLL	1
MASTER'S COLL, THE	10
MERCYHURST COLL	2
MESSIAH COLL	6
MICHIGAN CHRISTIAN COLL	2
MID-AMERICA NAZARENE COLL	3
MISSOURI BAPTIST COLL	2
MOBILE COLL	1
MOUNT VERNON NAZARENE COLL	4
NORTH PARK COLL AND	

THEOLOGICAL SEMINARY	1
NORTHWEST CHRISTIAN COLL	7
NORTHWEST COLL OF THE ASSEMBLIES OF GOD	2
NORTHWEST NAZARENE COLL	4
NORTHWESTERN COLL	4
NORTHWESTERN COLL	5
NYACK COLL	1
OKLAHOMA BAPTIST U	1
OLIVET NAZARENE U	4
OUACHITA BAPTIST U	2
OUR LADY OF THE LAKE U SAN ANTONIO	2
OZARKS, U of THE	1
REGIS COLL	4
SAINT MARY'S COLL	2
SAINT MARY'S COLL OF MINNESOTA	1
SAINT VINCENT COLL	1
SAMFORD U	8
SEATTLE PACIFIC U	6
SHAW U	2
SIMPSON COLL	1
SOUTHEASTERN COLL ASSEMBLIES OF GOD	2
SOUTHERN CALIFORNIA COLL	11
SOUTHERN NAZARENE U	3
SOUTHWEST BAPTIST U	16
SOUTHWESTERN ASSEMBLIES OF GOD COLL	1
SOUTHWESTERN COLL OF CHRISTIAN MINISTRIES	3
TAYLOR U	17
TENNESSEE WESLEYAN COLL	2
TOCCOA FALLS COLL	12
TREVECCA NAZARENE COLL	3
UNION U	2
WAYLAND BAPTIST U	2
WESTMINSTER COLL	1
WHEATON COLL	18

Religious Music

ANDERSON U	3
AVERETT COLL	2
BAPTIST BIBLE COLL OF PENNSYLVANIA	2
BAPTIST COLL AT CHARLESTON	4
BAYLOR U	5
BETHEL COLL	1
BRYAN COLL	1
CAMPBELL U INCORPORATED	2
CAMPBELLSVILLE COLL	1
CARSON-NEWMAN COLL	3
CENTENARY COLL OF LOUISIANA	1
CENTRAL WESLEYAN COLL	3
CHRISTIAN HERITAGE COLL	2
COLUMBIA COLL	1
CONCORDIA COLL	1
CONCORDIA COLL	2
EAST TEXAS BAPTIST U	2
EASTERN NAZARENE COLL	1
FURMAN U	1
GEORGETOWN COLL	1
GEORGIA, U of	1
GRAND CANYON U	1
HARDIN-SIMMONS U	2
LEBANON VALLEY COLL	3
LOUISIANA COLL	2
MARY HARDIN BAYLOR, U of	2
MARYWOOD COLL	1
MESSIAH COLL	1
MID-AMERICA NAZARENE COLL	3
MOUNT VERNON NAZARENE COLL	1
NEWBERRY COLL	1
NORTHWEST COLL OF THE ASSEMBLIES OF GOD	2
NORTHWESTERN U	1
NYACK COLL	1
OKLAHOMA BAPTIST U	7
ORAL ROBERTS U	2
POINT LOMA NAZARENE COLL	1
SAMFORD U	6
SHORTER COLL	2
SOUTHEASTERN COLL ASSEMBLIES OF GOD	3
SOUTHWEST BAPTIST U	2
SOUTHWESTERN COLL OF CHRISTIAN MINISTRIES	2
STETSON U	3
TOCCOA FALLS COLL	1
WILLIAM JEWELL COLL	1

Renewable Natural Resources (unspecified)

Degrees in this subject were reported by 109 institutions. Consult more specific headings.

Renewable Natural Resources, Other

ALASKA FAIRBANKS, U of	13
CALIFORNIA-BERKELEY, U of	44
DELAWARE ST COLL	4
DORDT COLL	2
MICHIGAN ANN ARBOR, U of	45
NEW HAMPSHIRE, U of	13
PENNSYLVANIA ST U MAIN CAMPUS	24
PITZER COLL	5
PRESCOTT COLL	2
SHELDON JACKSON COLL	6
TEXAS A & I U	6
UNITY COLL	2
UTAH ST U	7
WISCONSIN-PLATTEVILLE, U of	3

Renewable Natural Resources, General

ALASKA PACIFIC U	2
ANTIOCH COLL	1
ARIZONA ST U	16
ARIZONA, U of	1
ARKANSAS-FAYETTEVILLE, U of	2
BALL ST U	19
BARNARD COLL	9
BEMIDJI ST U	8
CALIFORNIA POLYTECHNIC ST U-SAN LUIS OBISPO	31
CALIFORNIA-BERKELEY, U of	38
CALIFORNIA-DAVIS, U of	34
COLORADO AT BOULDER, U of	62
COLORADO ST U	35
CONNECTICUT, U of	22
CORNELL U-NYS STATUTORY COLLS	41
FROSTBURG ST U	13
GRAND VALLEY ST U	5
IDAHO, U of	12
MAINE, U of	7
MARYLAND COLL PARK CAMPUS, U of	25
MASSACHUSETTS AT AMHERST, U of	13
MICHIGAN ANN ARBOR, U of	4
MICHIGAN ST U	43
MISSOURI-COLUMBIA, U of	30
MONTANA ST U	6
MORAVIAN COLL	2
NEBRASKA-LINCOLN, U of	21
NEVADA-RENO, U of	14
NEW ENGLAND COLL	1
NORTH CAROLINA ST U AT RALEIGH	25
OHIO ST U MAIN CAMPUS	30
PENNSYLVANIA ST U MAIN CAMPUS	45
PRESCOTT COLL	3
RHODE ISLAND, U of	6
SCRIPPS COLL	1
SUNY AT BINGHAMTON	15
SUNY COLL AT PLATTSBURG	36
SUNY COLL AT PURCHASE	8
TENNESSEE TECH U	1
TENNESSEE-MARTIN, U of	14
VERMONT, U of	17
WARREN WILSON COLL	10
WASHINGTON ST U	2
WESTERN CAROLINA U	10

Resort Management

LYNDON ST COLL	3
SIERRA NEVADA COLL	3
US INTERNATIONAL U	1

Respiratory Therapy Technology

LOUISVILLE, U of	1
MISSOURI-COLUMBIA, U of	14
WHEELING COLL	7

Respiratory Therapy

BOISE ST U	4
CENTRAL ARKANSAS, U of	5
CENTRAL FLORIDA, U of	12
COLUMBIA UNION COLL	1
DAKOTA ST COLL	1
DETROIT, U of	2
FLORIDA AGRI AND MECH U	2
GEORGIA ST U	14

HARTFORD, U of	4
INDIANA U PENNSYLVANIA	17
LA ROCHE COLL	1
LOMA LINDA U	5
MARIAN COLL	5
MARY, U of	6
MEDICAL COLL OF GEORGIA	19
MIDLAND LUTHERAN COLL	3
MOUNT MARTY COLL	3
NORTH DAKOTA ST U MAIN CAMPUS	1
NORTHEASTERN U	11
OHIO ST U MAIN CAMPUS	7
QUINNIPIAC COLL	5
SALISBURY ST U	9
SIENA HEIGHTS COLL	10
SOUTH ALABAMA, U of	6
TENNESSEE ST U	8
TEXAS SOUTHERN U	2
YORK COLL PENNSYLVANIA	5

Restaurant Management

ARIZONA, U of	3
BOWLING GREEN ST U MAIN CAMPUS	3
CHICAGO ST U	6
COLORADO ST U	9
ILLINOIS URBANA CAMPUS, U of	23
IOWA ST U	49
KENDALL COLL	11
KENTUCKY, U of	12
NEW HAMPSHIRE COLL	20
RIO GRANDE, U of	1
SAINT LEO COLL	11
SOUTHWEST ST U	4

Retailing

DREXEL U	3
FERRIS ST U	23
GREEN MOUNTAIN COLL	4
LAMAR U	1
MINNESOTA TWIN CITIES, U of	28
NEW HAMPSHIRE COLL	10
PHILADELPHIA COLL OF TEXTILES AND SCIENCE	13
SIMMONS COLL	21
SOUTH CAROLINA—COLUMBIA, U of	117
WESTERN MICHIGAN U	3

Robotics Tech.

INDIANA U-PURDUE U AT FORT WAYNE	2
INDIANA U-PURDUE U AT INDIANAPOLIS	2
LAKE SUPERIOR ST U	16
PACIFIC UNION COLL	1
SIENA HEIGHTS COLL	1

Russian and Slavic Studies

ALABAMA, U of	2
ALASKA FAIRBANKS, U of	2
AMERICAN U	6
ARIZONA, U of	2
BOSTON COLL	6
BROWN U	12
CALIFORNIA ST U FULLERTON	1
CALIFORNIA U PENNSYLVANIA	2
CALIFORNIA-LOS ANGELES, U of	1
CALIFORNIA-RIVERSIDE, U of	2
CHICAGO, U of	8
COLBY COLL	3
COLGATE U	11
COLL OF SAINT CATHERINE-SAINT CATHERINE CAMPUS	1
COLL OF WOOSTER	1
CONNECTICUT, U of	3
CORNELL U-ENDOWED COLLS	9
DARTMOUTH COLL	6
DENVER, U of	2
DICKINSON COLL	1
ECKERD COLL	1
FORDHAM U	3
GRAND VALLEY ST U	5
GUSTAVUS ADOLPHUS COLL	4
HAMILTON COLL	1
HOUSTON-U PARK, U of	6
ILLINOIS ST U	3
ILLINOIS URBANA CAMPUS, U of	4
KENT ST U MAIN CAMPUS	2
KUTZTOWN U PENNSYLVANIA	2
LOUISIANA ST U & AGRI & MECH & HEBERT LAWS CTR	3
MACALESTER COLL	3
MANHATTANVILLE COLL	1
MARYLAND COLL PARK CAMPUS, U of	6
MASSACHUSETTS AT AMHERST, U of	5
MICHIGAN ANN ARBOR, U of	20
MIDDLEBURY COLL	10
MINNESOTA TWIN CITIES, U of	8
MISSOURI-COLUMBIA, U of	6
MUHLENBERG COLL	5
NEW MEXICO MAIN CAMPUS, U of	4
NORTH CAROLINA CHAPEL HILL, U of	5
NORTH DAKOTA MAIN CAMPUS, U of	1
OBERLIN COLL	6
OKLAHOMA NORMAN CAMPUS, U of	4
RANDOLPH-MACON WOMAN'S COLL	1
RICHMOND, U of	2
SAN DIEGO ST U	2
SOUTHERN METHODIST U	2
SOUTH, THE U of THE	5
SUNY AT ALBANY	1
SYRACUSE U MAIN CAMPUS	5
TEXAS AT AUSTIN, U of	1
TUFTS U	7
VERMONT, U of	5
WASHINGTON, U of	15
WELLESLEY COLL	3
WELLS COLL	1
WHEATON COLL	1
WISCONSIN-STEVENS POINT, U of	1
WITTENBERG U	2
YALE U	16

Russian

Degrees in this subject were reported by 124 institutions. Consult more specific headings.

Sales

BELLEVUE COLL	12
FERRIS ST U	53
KENNESAW ST COLL	10
MEMPHIS ST U	82
NEBRASKA AT OMAHA, U of	2
WEBER ST COLL	55

Sanitation Technology

CENTRAL FLORIDA, U of	1
EASTERN KENTUCKY U	6
MISSISSIPPI VALLEY ST U	2

Scandinavian Languages

AUGSBURG COLL	1
AUGUSTANA COLL	1
CALIFORNIA-LOS ANGELES, U of	2
LUTHER COLL	3
MINNESOTA TWIN CITIES, U of	8
SAINT OLAF COLL	4
WASHINGTON, U of	11

Scandinavian Studies

GUSTAVUS ADOLPHUS COLL	5
PACIFIC LUTHERAN U	1
WISCONSIN-MADISON, U of	4

School Psychology

ALCORN ST U	24
BRIGHAM YOUNG U	77
CASTLETON ST COLL	1
GEORGIA, U of	32
KENT ST U MAIN CAMPUS	1
MARYMOUNT MANHATTAN COLL	1
MCNEESE ST U	3
MISSISSIPPI ST U	24
SAINT MARYS COLL OF MARYLAND	28
SOJOURNER-DOUGLAS COLL	13

Science Education

Degrees in this subject were reported by 202 institutions. Consult more specific headings.

Science Technologies, Other

BARRY U	6
BETHANY COLL	3
DREXEL U	1
LAMAR U	1

MADONNA COLL	3
MARY HARDIN BAYLOR, U of	7
SIERRA NEVADA COLL	2
SLIPPERY ROCK U PENNSYLVANIA	1

Science Technologies (unspecified)

AUBURN U MAIN CAMPUS	11
BARRY U	6
BETHANY COLL	3
DREXEL U	1
LAMAR U	1
MADONNA COLL	3
MARY HARDIN BAYLOR, U of	7
MARY, U of	9
MASS. AT LOWELL, U of	2
NORTHEASTERN U	6
NORTHERN MICHIGAN U	1
SIERRA NEVADA COLL	2
SLIPPERY ROCK U PENNSYLVANIA	1
SOUTHWEST MISSOURI ST U	2
WESTFIELD ST COLL	2
WISCONSIN-RIVER FALLS, U of	1
WORCESTER POLYTECHNIC INST	23

Sculpture

ARTS, THE U of THE	11
BOSTON U	5
CALIFORNIA COLL OF ARTS AND CRAFTS	7
CLEVELAND INST OF ART	3
CONNECTICUT, U of	4
EAST TEXAS ST U	1
FONTBONNE COLL	2
HARTFORD, U of	7
ILLINOIS URBANA CAMPUS, U of	3
KANSAS CITY ART INST	11
LOUISIANA ST U & AGRI & MECH & HEBERT LAWS CTR	1
MAINE COLL OF ART (WAS PORTLAND SCHOOL OF ART)	6
MARLBORO COLL	1
MARYLAND INST COLL OF ART	14
MASSACHUSETTS AT DARTMOUTH (WAS SE U OF MA, U of	6
MEMPHIS COLL OF ART	3
MICHIGAN ANN ARBOR, U of	2
MOORE COLL OF ART	3
NORTH TEXAS, U of	8
NORTHERN MICHIGAN U	1
OREGON, U of	5
PORTLAND ST U	5
RHODE ISLAND SCHOOL OF DESIGN	19
SAN FRANCISCO ART INST	14
SETON HILL COLL	1
SUNY COLL AT BUFFALO	5
SUNY COLL AT POTSDAM	1
TEMPLE U	6
TEXAS AT EL PASO, U of	1
VIRGINIA COMMONWEALTH U	26
WASHINGTON U	9
WASHINGTON, U of	2

Secondary Education

Degrees in this subject were reported by 154 institutions. Consult more specific headings.

Secretarial and Related Programs, Other

BAPTIST BIBLE COLL OF PENNSYLVANIA	3
OKLAHOMA CHRISTIAN COLL	1

Secretarial and Related Programs, General

ALBANY ST COLL	7
ALCORN ST U	12
APPALACHIAN ST U	8
ARKANSAS AT LITTLE ROCK, U of	3
ARKANSAS ST U MAIN CAMPUS	7
BELMONT COLL	2
CENTRAL ARKANSAS, U of	11
CONCORDIA COLL AT MOORHEAD	3
CUNY BERNARD BARUCH COLL	25
EAST CAROLINA U	38
EAST TENNESSEE ST U	7
HARDING U MAIN CAMPUS	3
IDAHO, U of	3
LOUISIANA COLL	4
MANCHESTER COLL	2
MCNEESE ST U	4
MEMPHIS ST U	9
MIDDLE TENNESSE ST U	24
MORGAN ST U	5
MOUNT VERNON NAZARENE COLL	7
NEW MEXICO HIGHLANDS U	2
NORTH CAROLINA AGRI AND TECHNICAL ST U	3
NORTH CAROLINA AT GREENSBORO, U of	64
NORTH GEORGIA COLL	3
NORTHWEST MISSOURI ST U	7
OUACHITA BAPTIST U	1
ROBERT MORRIS COLL	44
RUST COLL	5
SOUTHEAST MISSOURI ST U	9
SOUTHEASTERN LOUISIANA U	7
SOUTHERN COLL OF SEVENTH-DAY ADVENTISTS	8
SOUTHERN VERMONT COLL	5
TENNESSEE ST U	2
TENNESSEE-CHATTANOOGA, U of	2
TENNESSEE-MARTIN, U of	11
TEXAS WOMAN'S U	3
TROY ST U-MAIN CAMPUS	4
UNION COLL	1
VALDOSTA ST COLL	5
WALLA WALLA COLL	3
WESTERN CAROLINA U	6
WILEY COLL	1
WINSTON-SALEM ST U	2
WYOMING, U of	9

Secretarial

BAYAMON CENTRAL U	10
BLUE MOUNTAIN COLL	3
CUMBERLAND COLL	2
EASTERN KENTUCKY U	7
GEORGIA ST U	1
LINCOLN U	1
MURRAY ST U	6
NEW ORLEANS, U of	1
NORTHERN ST U	6
OREGON INST OF TECH	9
PONTIFICAL CATHOLIC U PUERTO RICO—PONCE CA	59
SOUTHEASTERN OKLAHOMA ST U	4
WESTERN KENTUCKY U	9

Security Services

CENTRAL MISSOURI ST U	4
EASTERN KENTUCKY U	15
LAKE SUPERIOR ST U	1
MADONNA COLL	2
NORTHERN MICHIGAN U	21
SOUTHEAST MISSOURI ST U	2
WAYNE ST COLL	3
YORK COLL PENNSYLVANIA	3

Semitic Languages, Other

EMORY U	1
INDIANA U BLOOMINGTON	5
WASHINGTON, U of	1

Sign Language Interpreting

BLOOMSBURG U PENNSYLVANIA	4
MARYVILLE COLL	4
NEW MEXICO MAIN CAMPUS, U of	5

Slavic Languages (Other than Russian)

CHICAGO, U of	3
ILLINOIS AT CHICAGO, U of	3
INDIANA U BLOOMINGTON	24
LAWRENCE U	6
OHIO ST U MAIN CAMPUS	12
VIRGINIA MAIN CAMPUS, U of	17
WASHINGTON, U of	3
WAYNE ST U	1

Small Business Management

BAYLOR U	34
COLL OF SAINT THOMAS	13
FERRIS ST U	13
GALLAUDET U	6

LYNDON ST COLL	4
MARIETTA COLL	1
MIAMI, U of	7
MONTANA, U of	11
NEBRASKA AT OMAHA, U of	5
NORTHEASTERN U	15
SAINT MARY'S U	3
WAYNESBURG COLL	6
WYOMING, U of	2

Social Psychology

BARTLESVILLE WESLEYAN COLL	5
CLARION U PENNSYLVANIA	7
COLL OF MOUNT SAINT JOSEPH	3
DREXEL U	2
GRAND VALLEY ST U	3
GWYNEDD-MERCY COLL	3
KING'S COLL	4
NAZARETH COLL	8
NEVADA-RENO, U of	13
NEW ENGLAND COLL	21
NORTHWEST MISSOURI ST U	7
OUR LADY OF HOLY CROSS COLL	3
PARK COLL	123
TUFTS U	19
US INTERNATIONAL U	3
WESLEYAN U	8
WHEATON COLL	4

Social Science Education

ABILENE CHRISTIAN U	4
ALABAMA, U of	19
ADRIAN COLL	3
ALABAMA ST U	3
ALCORN ST U	1
ALVERNO COLL	1
AQUINAS COLL	16
ARKANSAS PINE BLUFF, U of	4
ARKANSAS ST U MAIN CAMPUS	21
ARMSTRONG ST COLL	1
AUBURN U MAIN CAMPUS	15
BERRY COLL	5
BETHANY COLL	2
BLACK HILLS ST COLL	12
BLACKBURN COLL	3
BOISE ST U	4
BOWLING GREEN ST U MAIN CAMPUS	3
BRIGHAM YOUNG U HAWAII CAMPUS	1
BUENA VISTA COLL	1
CALUMET COLL OF SAINT JOSEPH	1
CASTLETON ST COLL	3
CENTRAL WASHINGTON U	4
COLUMBUS COLL	1
CONCORDIA COLL	9
DANA COLL	3
DELTA ST U	9
DETROIT, U of	2
DICKINSON ST U	9
DOANE COLL	2
EAST STROUDSBURG U PENNSYLVANIA	15
EASTERN ILLINOIS U	5
EASTERN MICHIGAN U	57
EASTERN MONTANA COLL	2
EASTERN WASHINGTON U	25
FONTBONNE COLL	2
FRIENDS U	2
GEORGE WASHINGTON U	1
GEORGIA COLL	5
GEORGIA SOUTHERN COLL	14
GEORGIA, U of	25
GREENVILLE COLL	5
HAWAII AT MANOA, U of	35
HEIDELBERG COLL	6
HENDERSON ST U	5
HOUSTON-U PARK, U of	4
IDAHO ST U	11
IDAHO, U of	11
ILLINOIS BENEDICTINE COLL	1
JACKSON ST U	2
JACKSONVILLE ST U	20
LIBERTY U	10
LINCOLN U	2
LIVINGSTON U	4
LYNDON ST COLL	2
MARQUETTE U	3
MAYVILLE ST U	4
MCMURRY COLL	1
MERCER U IN ATLANTA	1
MERCYHURST COLL	2
MIDLAND LUTHERAN COLL	3
MILES COLL	1
MISSISSIPPI COLL	1
MISSOURI-SAINT LOUIS, U of	10
MOBILE COLL	1
MONTANA, U of	4
MORAVIAN COLL	5
NEBRASKA WESLEYAN U	2
NEBRASKA-LINCOLN, U of	18
NEW HAMPSHIRE KEENE ST COLL, U of	3
NORTH ALABAMA, U of	8
NORTHERN IOWA, U of	20
NORTHERN ST U	4
NORTHWEST NAZARENE COLL	4
NORTHWESTERN ST U LOUISIANA	7
OREGON ST U	27
OUACHITA BAPTIST U	4
PACIFIC LUTHERAN U	14
PLYMOUTH ST COLL	10
POINT PARK COLL	3
SAINT CLOUD ST U	5
SAINT MARY'S COLL OF MINNESOTA	2
SEATTLE PACIFIC U	13
SOUTHERN UTAH ST COLL	14
SOUTHWEST BAPTIST U	5
SOUTHWEST MISSOURI ST U	11
SOUTHWEST TEXAS ST U	13
SOUTHWESTERN OKLAHOMA ST U	14
STETSON U	1
TROY ST U-MAIN CAMPUS	6
URBANA U	2
WAYNE ST COLL	10
WEST GEORGIA COLL	8
WESTERN MICHIGAN U	51
WESTERN OREGON ST COLL	21
WESTERN WASHINGTON U	20
WINGATE COLL	6
WINONA ST U	26
WISCONSIN OSHKOSH, U of	22

Social Sciences (unspecified)

Degrees in this subject were reported by 1212 institutions. Consult more specific headings.

Social Sciences, General

Degrees in this subject were reported by 357 institutions. Consult more specific headings.

Social Sciences, Other

Degrees in this subject were reported by 187 institutions. Consult more specific headings.

Social Studies Education

Degrees in this subject were reported by 151 institutions. Consult more specific headings.

Social Work, General

Degrees in this subject were reported by 475 institutions. Consult more specific headings.

Social Work, Other

BLOOMSBURG U PENNSYLVANIA	21
CALIFORNIA ST U NORTHRIDGE	28
CARROLL COLL	9
COLL OF OUR LADY OF ELMS	20
FRANKLIN PIERCE COLL	4
GRAND VIEW COLL	13
HAMPTON U	10
HOWARD U	14
IOWA ST U	29
LA GRANGE COLL	3
MASSACHUSETTS BOSTON, U of	42
MINNESOTA TWIN CITIES, U of	3
NEBRASKA WESLEYAN U	6
OREGON, U of	43
OTTAWA U	7
PORTLAND, U of	6
RIVIER COLL	5
SAINT LEO COLL	2
SALVE REGINA COLL	7
SOUTHERN MISSISSIPPI, U of	45
TEMPLE U	14
TEXAS AT AUSTIN, U of	2
TROY ST U-MAIN CAMPUS	19

UPPER IOWA U	2
VIRGINIA UNION U	1
WASHBURN U TOPEKA	32
WEST VIRGINIA WESLEYAN COLL	3
WINGATE COLL	18
WISCONSIN-STOUT, U of	43

Sociology

Degrees in this subject were reported by 924 institutions. Consult more specific headings.

Soil Sciences, General

ALABAMA AGRI AND MECH U	1
ARIZONA, U of	1
ARKANSAS-FAYETTEVILLE, U of	1
CALIFORNIA POLYTECHNIC ST U-SAN LUIS OBISPO	7
CALIFORNIA-DAVIS, U of	8
HAWAII AT MANOA, U of	1
IDAHO, U of	1
MAINE, U of	2
MARYLAND COLL PARK CAMPUS, U of	1
MIDDLE TENNESSE ST U	5
MINNESOTA TWIN CITIES, U of	6
MONTANA ST U	4
NEBRASKA-LINCOLN, U of	2
NEW MEXICO ST U MAIN CAMPUS	5
NORTH DAKOTA ST U MAIN CAMPUS	4
OREGON ST U	3
PENNSYLVANIA ST U MAIN CAMPUS	1
TEXAS A&M U	1
TUSKEGEE U	1
UTAH ST U	1
VERMONT, U of	8
WASHINGTON ST U	2
WISCONSIN-MADISON, U of	8
WISCONSIN-RIVER FALLS, U of	12
WISCONSIN-STEVENS POINT, U of	7
WYOMING, U of	4

Soil and Water Mechanical Practices

ARIZONA, U of	1
MINNESOTA TWIN CITIES, U of	3

Sound Recording Tech.

LEBANON VALLEY COLL	4
SUNY COLL AT FREDONIA	13

South Asian Studies

BROWN U	1
CHICAGO, U of	5
MINNESOTA TWIN CITIES, U of	1
PENNSYLVANIA, U of	5
WISCONSIN-MADISON, U of	2

Southeast Asian Studies

CALIFORNIA-BERKELEY, U of	8
VERMONT, U of	1

Spanish

Degrees in this subject were reported by 649 institutions. Consult more specific headings.

Special Education, General

Degrees in this subject were reported by 281 institutions. Consult more specific headings.

Special Education, Other

ARKANSAS-FAYETTEVILLE, U of	12
BOSTON COLL	11
BOWLING GREEN ST U MAIN CAMPUS	4
CONNECTICUT, U of	6
COPPIN ST COLL	1
GRAMBLING ST U	3
GREEN MOUNTAIN COLL	7
KEAN COLL OF NEW JERSEY	25
LINCOLN U	7
LOUISIANA ST U & AGRI & MECH & HEBERT LAWS CTR	16
LOUISIANA ST U SHREVEPORT	8
LOUISIANA TECH U	3
MCNEESE ST U	11
NEBRASKA WESLEYAN U	3
NEBRASKA-LINCOLN, U of	12
NEW ENGLAND, U of	1
NICHOLLS ST U	6
NORTHERN IOWA, U of	6
NORTHWESTERN ST U LOUISIANA	6
NORWICH U	1
RHODE ISLAND COLL	13
SIMMONS COLL	1
SOUTHEAST MISSOURI ST U	1
SOUTHEASTERN LOUISIANA U	7
SOUTHWESTERN LOUISIANA, U of	18
TOLEDO, U of	28
WYOMING, U of	12

Specialty Home Furnishings Marketing

HIGH POINT COLL	22

Specific Learning Disabilities

AUBURN U AT MONTGOMERY	1
AVILA COLL	2
BETHUNE COOKMAN COLL	5
BOWLING GREEN ST U MAIN CAMPUS	4
CENTRAL WESLEYAN COLL	2
COLUMBUS COLL	6
DETROIT, U of	1
FLORIDA SOUTHERN COLL	5
FLORIDA ST U	31
FONTBONNE COLL	2
GONZAGA U	16
GRAND CANYON U	1
HARDING U MAIN CAMPUS	4
HOPE COLL	19
JACKSONVILLE U	2
KENT ST U MAIN CAMPUS	17
MACMURRAY COLL	1
MADONNA COLL	2
MAINE AT FARMINGTON, U of	12
MALONE COLL	2
MERCER U IN ATLANTA	7
MISSOURI-COLUMBIA, U of	7
MISSOURI-SAINT LOUIS, U of	3
NORTHEASTERN ST U	24
NORTHWEST MISSOURI ST U	1
NORTHWESTERN U	3
OHIO ST U MAIN CAMPUS	10
SCI AND ARTS OF OKLAHOMA, U of	2
SILVER LAKE COLL	2
SOUTH FLORIDA, U of	63
SOUTHEAST MISSOURI ST U	3
SOUTHWEST MISSOURI ST U	13
SOUTHWESTERN OKLAHOMA ST U	4
SUNY COLL AT BUFFALO	20
TOLEDO, U of	3
WRIGHT ST U MAIN CAMPUS	13

Speech Correction

ABILENE CHRISTIAN U	3
ALABAMA AGRI AND MECH U	4
ARMSTRONG ST COLL	2
ASHLAND U	2
AUGUSTANA COLL	21
BLOOMSBURG U PENNSYLVANIA	32
BOWLING GREEN ST U MAIN CAMPUS	17
BRESCIA COLL	6
CALIFORNIA U PENNSYLVANIA	17
CENTRAL ARKANSAS, U of	2
COLUMBIA COLL	12
DENISON U	1
EAST STROUDSBURG U PENNSYLVANIA	13
EASTERN KENTUCKY U	26
EASTERN MICHIGAN U	24
ELMIRA COLL	12
GRAMBLING ST U	1
HOFSTRA U	13
INDIANA ST U	6
ITHACA COLL	30
KENT ST U MAIN CAMPUS	1
KENTUCKY, U of	15
LAMBUTH COLL	3
LONG ISLAND U C W POST CAMPUS	8
LOUISIANA TECH U	1
MAINE AT FARMINGTON, U of	5
NAZARETH COLL OF ROCHESTER	20
NEBRASKA AT OMAHA, U of	4
NEBRASKA-LINCOLN, U of	22
NEW MEXICO ST U MAIN CAMPUS	11

NEW YORK U	1
NORTHERN ST U	5
NORTHWEST MISSOURI ST U	2
OLD DOMINION U	28
OUACHITA BAPTIST U	1
PACE U-NEW YORK	2
POINT LOMA NAZARENE COLL	1
RADFORD U	26
SAINT JOHN'S U NEW YORK	2
SOUTHEASTERN LOUISIANA U	9
SOUTHERN U AGRI & MECH COL AT BATON ROUGE	2
SOUTHWESTERN LOUISIANA, U of	7
SPALDING U	4
SUNY COLL AT CORTLAND	50
SUNY COLL AT FREDONIA	21
SUNY COLL AT NEW PALTZ	13
SUNY COLL AT PLATTSBURG	21
TOLEDO, U of	7
WEST CHESTER U PENNSYLVANIA	18
WESTERN CAROLINA U	7
WESTERN KENTUCKY U	18
WISCONSIN-RIVER FALLS, U of	15
WISCONSIN-WHITEWATER, U of	10
XAVIER U	1

Speech Pathology

ALABAMA AGRI AND MECH U	4
ARKANSAS ST U MAIN CAMPUS	14
CENTRAL MISSOURI ST U	13
GENEVA COLL	6
GRAMBLING ST U	2
HAMPTON U	14
HANNIBAL-LAGRANGE COLL	1
JAMES MADISON U	36
LOUISIANA ST U SHREVEPORT	5
LOUISIANA TECH U	6
MINOT ST U	30
MISSISSIPPI U FOR WOMEN	5
NEVADA-RENO, U of	5
NORTHEAST MISSOURI ST U	15
NORTHERN COLORADO, U of	8
NORTHERN IOWA, U of	26
NORTHERN MICHIGAN U	8
OKLAHOMA ST U MAIN CAMPUS	18
OUR LADY OF THE LAKE U SAN ANTONIO	5
SOUTHEAST MISSOURI ST U	8
SUNY COLL AT GENESEO	46
TENNESSEE-KNOXVILLE, U of	10
TULSA, U of	6
WILKES U	9
WILLIAM PATERSON COLL OF NEW JERSEY	13
XAVIER U	5

Speech Pathology/Audiology

Degrees in this subject were reported by 162 institutions. Consult more specific headings.

Speech, Debate, and Forensics

Degrees in this subject were reported by 252 institutions. Consult more specific headings.

Speech/Hearing Therapy Aide

CAPITAL U	2
CLEVELAND ST U	19
INDIANA U BLOOMINGTON	29
SAINT LOUIS U MAIN CAMPUS	10

Sports Medicine

ALDERSON BROADDUS COLL	7
CHARLESTON, U of	8
COLBY-SAWYER COLL	3
DETROIT, U of	1
EUREKA COLL	1
GUILFORD COLL	12
HEIDELBERG COLL	2
MALONE COLL	1
MARIETTA COLL	11
MARY, U of	1
MERCYHURST COLL	13
MESSIAH COLL	3
MOUNT UNION COLL	16
OHIO NORTHERN U	6
OTTERBEIN COLL	8
PACIFIC, U of THE	19
PEPPERDINE U	22
ROCKFORD COLL	3
SALEM-TEIKYO U	3
SOUTH DAKOTA ST U	4
WINGATE COLL	2

Ssurveying and Mapping Sciences

CALIFORNIA ST U FRESNO	20
FLORIDA, U of	18
IOWA ST U	1
MAINE, U of	12
MICHIGAN TECH U	4
NEW MEXICO ST U MAIN CAMPUS	1
OHIO ST U MAIN CAMPUS	5
SOUTHWEST TEXAS ST U	8

Statistics

AKRON, MAIN CAMPUS, U of	4
ALABAMA, U of	12
AMERICAN U	6
APPALACHIAN ST U	1
BOWLING GREEN ST U MAIN CAMPUS	10
BRIGHAM YOUNG U	20
CALIFORNIA POLYTECHNIC ST U-SAN LUIS OBISPO	1
CALIFORNIA ST U-HAYWARD	6
CALIFORNIA-BERKELEY, U of	16
CALIFORNIA-DAVIS, U of	3
CALIFORNIA-RIVERSIDE, U of	1
CARNEGIE MELLON U	1
CASE WESTERN RESERVE U	3
CENTRAL FLORIDA, U of	4
CENTRAL MICHIGAN U	1
CHICAGO, U of	5
COLORADO ST U	1
COLUMBIA U IN THE CITY OF NEW YORK	1
CONNECTICUT, U of	10
CUNY BERNARD BARUCH COLL	1
CUNY HUNTER COLL	1
DELAWARE, U of	1
EASTERN KENTUCKY U	3
FLORIDA ST U	9
FLORIDA, U of	14
GEORGE WASHINGTON U	8
GEORGIA, U of	15
HARVARD U	3
ILLINOIS AT CHICAGO, U of	4
ILLINOIS URBANA CAMPUS, U of	2
IOWA ST U	11
IOWA, U of	6
LEHIGH U	3
MIAMI U OXFORD CAMPUS	2
MICHIGAN ANN ARBOR, U of	17
MICHIGAN ST U	3
MINNESOTA TWIN CITIES, U of	15
MISSOURI-COLUMBIA, U of	7
MONTANA ST U	2
MOUNT HOLYOKE COLL	2
NORTH CAROLINA ST U AT RALEIGH	9
NORTHWEST MISSOURI ST U	1
NORTHWESTERN U	1
OAKLAND U	1
OHIO ST U MAIN CAMPUS	1
OKLAHOMA ST U MAIN CAMPUS	3
PENNSYLVANIA, U of	2
PITTSBURGH MAIN CAMPUS, U of	8
RADFORD U	7
RHODE ISLAND, U of	1
RICE U	1
ROCHESTER INST OF TECH	11
ROCHESTER, U of	6
RUTGERS U NEW BRUNSWICK	30
SAINT CLOUD ST U	2
SAN FRANCISCO ST U	3
SOUTH ALABAMA, U of	3
SOUTH CAROLINA—COLUMBIA, U of	17
SOUTHWESTERN LOUISIANA, U of	1
SUNY AT BUFFALO	16
SUNY COLL AT ONEONTA	4
TENNESSEE-KNOXVILLE, U of	12
TEXAS SAN ANTONIO, U of	3
TULANE U LOUISIANA	1
UTAH ST U	4
VERMONT, U of	4
VIRGINIA POLYTECHNIC INST AND ST U	10
WASHINGTON, U of	8
WESTERN MICHIGAN U	15
WISCONSIN-MADISON, U of	14
WYOMING, U of	2

Student Counseling and Personnel Services

KENT ST U MAIN CAMPUS 1
LOUISVILLE, U of 33
MONTEVALLO, U of 11
PRESCOTT COLL 1
WAYNE ST U 3

Surveying and Mapping Technology

ARKANSAS AT LITTLE ROCK, U of 1
FERRIS ST U 12
HOUSTON-U PARK, U of 5
METROPOLITAN ST COLL 2
SOUTHWEST MISSOURI ST U 1

Systems Analysis

CALUMET COLL OF SAINT JOSEPH 7
DAYTON, U of 5
DREXEL U 34
EASTERN MICHIGAN U 9
EASTERN NEW MEXICO U MAIN CAMPUS 11
FINDLAY, U of 10
KENT ST U MAIN CAMPUS 13
LOUISVILLE, U of 29
MIAMI U OXFORD CAMPUS 61
MIAMI, U of 4
NORTHERN MICHIGAN U 10
PRATT INST-MAIN 1
SAGINAW VALLEY ST U 9

Systems Engineering

ARIZONA, U of 21
BOSTON U 13
CASE WESTERN RESERVE U 9
FLORIDA, U of 66
GEORGE MASON U 3
OAKLAND U 6
PENNSYLVANIA, U of 27
US MERCHANT MARINE ACAD 38
US NAVAL ACAD 49
VIRGINIA MAIN CAMPUS, U of 54
WORCESTER POLYTECHNIC INST 18

Systems Science

KUTZTOWN U PENNSYLVANIA 4
PROVIDENCE COLL 7
SAINT MARTIN'S COLL 3
VALPARAISO U 11
WASHINGTON U 13
WESLEYAN U 2
YALE U 3

Teacher Assisting

OKLAHOMA CHRISTIAN COLL 1
TULSA, U of 6

Teacher Education, General Programs, Other

ARKANSAS COLL 2
BAKER U 1
BAYLOR U 1
BLOOMSBURG U PENNSYLVANIA 6
BOSTON U 6
BUCKNELL U 3
CALIFORNIA U PENNSYLVANIA 10
CARLOW COLL 2
CENTRAL MISSOURI ST U 10
CHESTNUT HILL COLL 7
CHEYNEY U PENNSYLVANIA 1
COLL OF THE SOUTHWEST 2
DREXEL U 2
DUQUESNE U 5
ELIZABETHTOWN COLL 14
GANNON U 4
GEORGE WASHINGTON U 2
HOLY FAMILY COLL 20
INDIANA U PENNSYLVANIA 35
LOCK HAVEN U PENNSYLVANIA 19
MESSIAH COLL 13
MINNESOTA DULUTH, U of 11
NEBRASKA-LINCOLN, U of 6
NEUMANN COLL 7
SPRINGFIELD COLL 2
TUSCULUM COLL 6
WESTERN ILLINOIS U 2
WHEELOCK COLL 119

Teacher Education, Specific Subject Areas, Other

Degrees in this subject were reported by 137 institutions. Consult more specific headings.

Teaching English as a Second Language/Foreign Language

BRIGHAM YOUNG U HAWAII CAMPUS 6
EVANGEL COLL 2
HAWAII AT MANOA, U of 3
HAWAII PACIFIC COLL 12
NORTHERN IOWA, U of 10
OHIO DOMINICAN COLL 2
OKLAHOMA CHRISTIAN COLL 2
SAINT MICHAEL'S COLL 7
WASHINGTON, U of 5

Technical Education

BEMIDJI ST U 10
BOWLING GREEN ST U MAIN CAMPUS 7
CENTRAL CONNECTICUT ST U 3
FERRIS ST U 23
HOUSTON-U PARK, U of 26
ILLINOIS URBANA CAMPUS, U of 17
KENTUCKY, U of 7
LOUISVILLE, U of 9
MANKATO ST U 5
MARYLAND COLL PARK CAMPUS, U of 7
MINNESOTA DULUTH, U of 2
MISSISSIPPI ST U 7
NATIONAL U 22
NEBRASKA-LINCOLN, U of 2
NEW YORK INST OF TECH MAIN CAMPUS 2
NORTHERN ILLINOIS U 1
OKLAHOMA CITY U 2
OKLAHOMA ST U MAIN CAMPUS 8
PERU ST COLL 11
RUTGERS U NEW BRUNSWICK 19
SOUTHERN MAINE, U of 10
TEXAS A&M U 7
TUSKEGEE U 10
WALLA WALLA COLL 2
WESTERN KENTUCKY U 1
WISCONSIN-STOUT, U of 25
WYOMING, U of 4

Technical and Business Writing

ALDERSON BROADDUS COLL 1
ARKANSAS AT LITTLE ROCK, U of 1
BLUEFIELD ST COLL 4
BOWLING GREEN ST U MAIN CAMPUS 7
CARLOW COLL 1
CARNEGIE MELLON U 5
CLARK U 1
DREXEL U 2
ELIZABETHTOWN COLL 12
FERRIS ST U 4
GALLAUDET U 4
GANNON U 1
LOUISIANA TECH U 3
MADONNA COLL 2
NEW MEXICO INST OF MINING AND TECH 8
NORTHEAST LOUISIANA U 1
NORTHEASTERN U 6
ROGER WILLIAMS COLL 4

Telecommunications

BAYLOR U 50
CITY U 7
COLL OF SAINT CATHERINE-SAINT CATHERINE CAMPUS 1
COLL OF SAINT THOMAS 9
GEORGE FOX COLL 9
GOLDEN GATE U 7
INDIANA U BLOOMINGTON 241
LIBERTY U 34
OKLAHOMA BAPTIST U 10
OREGON, U of 67
PEPPERDINE U 38
SAINT MARY'S COLL OF MINNESOTA 1
SALEM-TEIKYO U 2
SOUTHWEST BAPTIST U 7
WEBER ST COLL 2
WESTMINSTER COLL 8
YOUNGSTOWN ST U 13

Textile Engineering

AUBURN U MAIN CAMPUS 5
GEORGIA INST OF TECH MAIN CAMPUS 13
MASSACHUSETTS AT DARTMOUTH (WAS SE U OF MA, U of 16
NORTH CAROLINA ST U AT RALEIGH 6
PHILADELPHIA COLL OF TEXTILES AND SCIENCE 10

Textile Science

DELAWARE, U of 2

Textile Technology

FASHION INST OF TECH 33
PHILADELPHIA COLL OF TEXTILES AND SCIENCE 4
WESTERN MICHIGAN U 5

Textiles and Clothing, Other

BERRY COLL 8
ILLINOIS URBANA CAMPUS, U of 39
IOWA ST U 11
LAMAR U 9
MIAMI U OXFORD CAMPUS 36
MICHIGAN ST U 120
NEBRASKA-LINCOLN, U of 69
NORTHWEST MISSOURI ST U 12
OREGON ST U 44
RHODE ISLAND SCHOOL OF DESIGN 20
STEPHENS COLL 14
WISCONSIN-MADISON, U of 4
WISCONSIN-STEVENS POINT, U of 17
WISCONSIN-STOUT, U of 129

Textiles and Clothing, General

AKRON, MAIN CAMPUS, U of 29
ALABAMA AGRI AND MECH U 2
ALABAMA, U of 36
ALBRIGHT COLL 1
APPALACHIAN ST U 20
ARIZONA, U of 3
ARKANSAS-FAYETTEVILLE, U of 18
AUBURN U MAIN CAMPUS 6
BAYLOR U 15
BLUFFTON COLL 2
CALIFORNIA-DAVIS, U of 8
CAMPBELL U INCORPORATED 7
CENTRAL MICHIGAN U 4
CENTRAL MISSOURI ST U 10
CHEYNEY U PENNSYLVANIA 5
COLL OF SAINT CATHERINE-SAINT CATHERINE CAMPUS 7
COLORADO ST U 67
DELAWARE, U of 45
FLORIDA ST U 95
FONTBONNE COLL 2
FRAMINGHAM ST COLL 42
GEORGIA SOUTHERN COLL 7
GEORGIA, U of 3
HAWAII AT MANOA, U of 37
IDAHO, U of 5
ILLINOIS URBANA CAMPUS, U of 7
INDIANA ST U 23
INDIANA U BLOOMINGTON 107
JACKSONVILLE ST U 2
KANSAS ST U AGRI AND APP SCI 37
KENTUCKY ST U 3
KENTUCKY, U of 44
LOUISIANA ST U & AGRI & MECH & HEBERT LAWS CTR 66
LOUISIANA TECH U 20
MANKATO ST U 4
MANSFIELD U PENNSYLVANIA 9
MARYLAND COLL PARK CAMPUS, U of 16
MICHIGAN ST U 27
MINNESOTA TWIN CITIES, U of 6
MISSISSIPPI U FOR WOMEN 3
MISSOURI-COLUMBIA, U of 36
MONTANA ST U 5
MOREHEAD ST U 7
MURRAY ST U 13
NEVADA-RENO, U of 9
NEW MEXICO ST U MAIN CAMPUS 14
NORTH CAROLINA AGRI AND TECHNICAL ST U 5
NORTH CAROLINA AT GREENSBORO, U of 46
NORTH CAROLINA CENTRAL U 6
NORTH DAKOTA MAIN CAMPUS, U of 4
NORTH DAKOTA ST U MAIN CAMPUS 15
NORTH TEXAS, U of 1
NORTHEAST LOUISIANA U 14
NORTHERN ILLINOIS U 61
NORTHERN IOWA, U of 33
OHIO ST U MAIN CAMPUS 77
OKLAHOMA NORMAN CAMPUS, U of 9
OKLAHOMA ST U MAIN CAMPUS 44
PRAIRIE VIEW A & M U 4
RHODE ISLAND, U of 72
SEATTLE PACIFIC U 6
SOUTH DAKOTA ST U 13
SOUTHEAST MISSOURI ST U 15
SOUTHEASTERN LOUISIANA U 6
SOUTHERN ILLINOIS U-CARBONDALE 47
SOUTHERN MISSISSIPPI, U of 30
SOUTHERN U AGRI & MECH COL AT BATON ROUGE 7
SOUTHWEST MISSOURI ST U 20
SYRACUSE U MAIN CAMPUS 8
TENNESSEE-KNOXVILLE, U of 41
TEXAS A & I U 1
TEXAS AT AUSTIN, U of 44
TEXAS CHRISTIAN U 26
TEXAS SOUTHERN U 1
TEXAS TECH U 8
TEXAS WOMAN'S U 2
TUSKEGEE U 4
VERMONT, U of 17
VIRGINIA POLYTECHNIC INST AND ST U 41
WASHINGTON ST U 40
WASHINGTON, U of 2
WAYNE ST U 28
WESTERN KENTUCKY U 18
WESTERN WASHINGTON U 22
WISCONSIN-STOUT, U of 17

Theatre Design

BAYLOR U 1
BOSTON U 4
BUTLER U 7
CALIFORNIA INST OF ARTS 13
CINCINNATI MAIN CAMPUS, U of 7
CONNECTICUT, U of 4
CORNISH COLL OF THE ARTS 6
DAVIS AND ELKINS COLL 1
DEPAUL U 2
NORTHERN IOWA, U of 3
SUNY COLL AT NEW PALTZ 2
SUNY COLL AT PURCHASE 14
US INTERNATIONAL U 1
WRIGHT ST U MAIN CAMPUS 3

Theology (unspecified)

Degrees in this subject were reported by 199 institutions. Consult more specific headings.

Theology, Other

ATLANTIC UNION COLL 4
BAPTIST BIBLE COLL OF PENNSYLVANIA 29
BARRY U 1
BARTLESVILLE WESLEYAN COLL 2
BELHAVEN COLL 5
BOSTON COLL 2
BRIAR CLIFF COLL 8
CALVIN COLL 3
CHRISTIAN HERITAGE COLL 3
CLEARWATER CHRISTIAN COLL 3
CONCORDIA COLL 14
CREIGHTON U 1
CRICHTON COLL 8
EASTERN COLL 5
EVANSVILLE, U of 3
GENEVA COLL 1
KANSAS NEWMAN COLL 4
LEE COLL 4
MARY, U of 4
MICHIGAN CHRISTIAN COLL 1
NORTHWEST CHRISTIAN COLL 3
NORTHWEST COLL OF THE ASSEMBLIES OF GOD 16
NORTHWESTERN COLL 8
NYACK COLL 4
OAKLAND CITY COLL 5
OAKWOOD COLL 15

Institution	Number
OKLAHOMA BAPTIST U	23
OKLAHOMA CHRISTIAN COLL	2
PACIFIC CHRISTIAN COLL	18
PONTIFICAL CATHOLIC U PUERTO RICO—PONCE CA	1
ROCKHURST COLL	3
SAINT MARTIN'S COLL	1
SAINT MARY COLL	2
SAINT MARY'S COLL	2
SAINT MARY'S COLL OF MINNESOTA	4
SOUTHERN CALIFORNIA COLL	1
SOUTHWEST BAPTIST U	8
SOUTHWESTERN ASSEMBLIES OF GOD COLL	57
TENNESSEE WESLEYAN COLL	1
TEXAS LUTHERAN COLL	3
TRINITY COLL	6
UNION U	14
VITERBO COLL	2
WARNER SOUTHERN COLL	4

Theoogical Studies

Institution	Number
ALDERSON BROADDUS COLL	4
ALLENTOWN COLL OF SAINT FRANCIS DE SALES	4
ANDREWS U	2
ATLANTIC UNION COLL	5
BALTIMORE HEBREW COLL	5
BELLARMINE COLL	1
BETHANY BIBLE COLL	31
BETHEL COLL	1
BETHEL COLL	13
BUTLER U	1
CAMPBELL U INCORPORATED	7
CARLOW COLL	1
CARROLL COLL	3
CEDARVILLE COLL	24
COLL OF OUR LADY OF ELMS	2
COLL OF SAINT CATHERINE-SAINT CATHERINE CAMPUS	5
COLL OF SAINT FRANCIS	2
COLUMBIA UNION COLL	6
CONCORDIA COLL	4
CONCORDIA TEACHERS COLL	4
CONCORDIA U-WISCONSIN	12
CREIGHTON U	5
DALLAS, U of	1
DORDT COLL	2
EMMANUEL COLL	4
FRANCISCAN U STEUBENVILLE	28
GRAND CANYON U	3
HANOVER COLL	1
HARDIN-SIMMONS U	3
HARDING U MAIN CAMPUS	2
HELLENIC COLL—HOLY CROSS SCHOOL	9
HOWARD PAYNE U	4
LOUISIANA COLL	4
LOYOLA MARYMOUNT U	1
MADONNA COLL	1
MARIAN COLL OF FOND DU LAC	1
MASTER'S COLL, THE	3
MID-AMERICA NAZARENE COLL	29
MOUNT OLIVE COLL	3
NORTHWESTERN COLL	3
NOTRE DAME, U of	10
NYACK COLL	2
ORAL ROBERTS U	45
OUACHITA BAPTIST U	9
PACIFIC UNION COLL	17
PORTLAND, U of	7
QUINCY COLL	1
SAINT ANSELM COLL	1
SAINT BONAVENTURE U	2
SAINT HYACINTH COLL AND SEMINARY	2
SAINT LEO COLL	13
SAINT LOUIS U MAIN CAMPUS	4
SAINT MARY'S COLL OF MINNESOTA	2
SAINT MARY'S U	3
SAINT MARY-OF-THE-WOODS COLL	3
SAINT THOMAS, U of	3
SAINT XAVIER COLL	1
SAN FRANCISCO, U of	3
SILVER LAKE COLL	1
SOUTHEASTERN COLL ASSEMBLIES OF GOD	43
SOUTHERN COLL OF SEVENTH-DAY ADVENTISTS	12
SOUTHWEST BAPTIST U	1
SPRING HILL COLL	1
TREVECCA NAZARENE COLL	9
UNION COLL	4
WALLA WALLA COLL	10
WESTERN BAPTIST COLL	3
XAVIER U	2

Tourism

Institution	Number
DAEMEN COLL	12
DAVIS AND ELKINS COLL	3
EASTERN MICHIGAN U	19
GEORGE WASHINGTON U	6
MANSFIELD U PENNSYLVANIA	14
MICHIGAN ST U	2
NEW HAVEN, U of	9
NIAGARA U	39
ROCHESTER INST OF TECH	21
WEBBER COLL	5
WESTERN MICHIGAN U	18

Toxicology

Institution	Number
ASHLAND U	2
CLARKSON U	2
EASTERN MICHIGAN U	2
NORTHEAST LOUISIANA U	11
NORTHEASTERN U	2
PHILADELPHIA COLL OF PHARMACY AND SCIENCE	6
SAINT JOHN'S U NEW YORK	2

Trade and Industrial Supervision and Management

Institution	Number
ARKANSAS-FAYETTEVILLE, U of	10
AUBURN U MAIN CAMPUS	52
CENTRAL MICHIGAN U	22
CENTRAL WASHINGTON U	23
CHEYNEY U PENNSYLVANIA	2
EAST TEXAS ST U	15
EDINBORO U PENNSYLVANIA	3
FERRIS ST U	92
HOUSTON-U PARK, U of	39
INDIANA U-PURDUE U AT FORT WAYNE	70
INDIANA U-PURDUE U AT INDIANAPOLIS	38
KANSAS NEWMAN COLL	7
KEARNEY ST COLL	24
LAMBUTH COLL	1
LETOURNEAU COLL	9
MASS. AT LOWELL, U of	12
METROPOLITAN ST COLL	2
NORTHERN ST U	1
PITTSBURG ST U	80
PURDUE U CALUMET CAMPUS	28
PURDUE U NORTH CENTRAL CAMPUS	30
SAGINAW VALLEY ST U	1
SAINT LEO COLL	41
SOUTHEAST MISSOURI ST U	5
SOUTHERN ARKANSAS U MAIN CAMPUS	3
TEXAS A & I U	3
TEXAS SOUTHERN U	2
WARTBURG COLL	1
WAYNE ST COLL	7
WENTWORTH INST OF TECH	33
WEST VIRGINIA INST OF TECH	5

Trade and Industrial Education

Institution	Number
AKRON, MAIN CAMPUS, U of	63
BEMIDJI ST U	3
BERRY COLL	1
BOWLING GREEN ST U MAIN CAMPUS	1
CALIFORNIA POLYTECHNIC ST U-SAN LUIS OBISPO	1
CALIFORNIA ST U FRESNO	1
CALIFORNIA ST U LONG BEACH	18
CALIFORNIA ST U LOS ANGELES	2
CALIFORNIA ST U SAN BERNARDINO	6
CALIFORNIA ST U-CHICO	1
CALIFORNIA ST U-STANISLAUS	1
CENTRAL FLORIDA, U of	6
CHICAGO ST U	6
CUNY CITY COLL	19
DISTRICT OF COLUMBIA, U of THE	2
EAST TEXAS ST U	1
EASTERN KENTUCKY U	6
FITCHBURG ST COLL	13
FLORIDA AGRI AND MECH U	3
GEORGE MASON U	9
GEORGIA SOUTHERN COLL	1
GEORGIA ST U	3

GEORGIA, U of 4
HAWAII AT MANOA, U of 4
HOUSTON-U PARK, U of 10
INDIANA U PENNSYLVANIA 3
IOWA ST U 39
KENT ST U MAIN CAMPUS 2
KENTUCKY, U of 4
LINCOLN U 2
LOUISVILLE, U of 24
MANKATO ST U 1
MARYLAND COLL PARK CAMPUS, U of 47
MINNESOTA TWIN CITIES, U of 1
MOREHEAD ST U 2
MURRAY ST U 5
NEBRASKA-LINCOLN, U of 2
NEW YORK INST OF TECH MAIN CAMPUS 2
NORFOLK ST U 10
NORTH TEXAS, U of 23
NORTHERN MONTANA COLL 3
OHIO ST U MAIN CAMPUS 9
OKLAHOMA ST U MAIN CAMPUS 11
PENNSYLVANIA ST U MAIN CAMPUS 10
PITTSBURG ST U 4
PITTSBURGH MAIN CAMPUS, U of 11
PRAIRIE VIEW A & M U 2
SAN DIEGO ST U 4
SAN JOSE ST U 1
SOUTH FLORIDA, U of 17
SOUTHERN ILLINOIS U-CARBONDALE 694
SOUTHERN MAINE, U of 5
SOUTHWEST TEXAS ST U 25
TEMPLE U 4
TEXAS A&M U 7
VIRGINIA ST U 15
WEST TEXAS ST U 9
WESTERN ILLINOIS U 3
WESTERN KENTUCKY U 4
WYOMING, U of 2

Transportation Management

ARIZONA ST U 9
ARKANSAS ST U MAIN CAMPUS 5
ARKANSAS-FAYETTEVILLE, U of 13
AUBURN U MAIN CAMPUS 41
CINCINNATI MAIN CAMPUS, U of 4
ELMHURST COLL 5
IOWA ST U 119
KENT ST U MAIN CAMPUS 4
MARYLAND COLL PARK CAMPUS, U of 34
MEMPHIS ST U 39
MICHIGAN ST U 23
MISSISSIPPI ST U 10
NORTH CAROLINA AGRI AND TECHNICAL ST U 6
NORTHEASTERN U 11
OHIO ST U MAIN CAMPUS 84
PARKS COLL OF SAINT LOUIS U 10
PENNSYLVANIA ST U MAIN CAMPUS 205
ROBERT MORRIS COLL 7
SAINT JOHN'S U NEW YORK 10
SUNY MARITIME COLL 48
SYRACUSE U MAIN CAMPUS 22
TENNESSEE-KNOXVILLE, U of 128
TEXAS A & M U AT GALVESTON 6
TOLEDO, U of 1
WESTERN ILLINOIS U 12

Transportation and Material Moving (unspecified)

ANDREWS U 8
AVERETT COLL 3
BRIDGEWATER ST COLL 45
CENTRAL MISSOURI ST U 1
CENTRAL WASHINGTON U 35
DALLAS BAPTIST U 12
DANIEL WEBSTER COLL 64
DELTA ST U 24
DISTRICT OF COLUMBIA, U of THE 2
DUBUQUE, U of 13
EASTERN MICHIGAN U 6
EMBRY-RIDDLE AERONAUTICAL U 683
FLORIDA INST OF TECH 190
FLORIDA MEMORIAL COLL 8
HAMPTON U 15
HENDERSON ST U 14
JACKSONVILLE U 8
LEWIS U 31
LOUISIANA TECH U 74
METROPOLITAN ST COLL 107
MIDDLE TENNESSE ST U 105
NATIONAL U 34
NORTH DAKOTA MAIN CAMPUS, U of 206
NORTHEAST LOUISIANA U 16
OHIO ST U MAIN CAMPUS 107
PARKS COLL OF SAINT LOUIS U 96
PHILLIPS U 1
ROCKY MOUNTAIN COLL 8
SAINT MARTIN'S COLL 4
SALEM-TEIKYO U 6
SOUTHEASTERN OKLAHOMA ST U 7
SOUTHERN ILLINOIS U-CARBONDALE 278
SOUTHERN U AT NEW ORLEANS 5
TENNESSEE WESLEYAN COLL 3
TEXAS SOUTHERN U 2
WESTMINSTER COLL OF SALT LAKE CITY 11

Transportation and Material Moving, Other

SOUTHERN U AT NEW ORLEANS 5

Transportation and Travel Marketing, Other

COLUMBIA COLL 4

Transportation and Travel Marketing, General

CONCORD COLL 33

Travel Services Marketing

BRIGHAM YOUNG U HAWAII CAMPUS 17

Turf Management

MARYLAND COLL PARK CAMPUS, U of 2

Typing, General Office, and Related Programs, General

CHADRON ST COLL 4
EAST CENTRAL U 11
MCMURRY COLL 1
NICHOLLS ST U 3
NORTHEASTERN ST U 6
NORTHWESTERN OKLAHOMA ST U 1
SOUTHWESTERN OKLAHOMA ST U 5

Ultrasound Technology

MEDICAL COLL OF GEORGIA 4
SEATTLE U 12

Urban Studies

ALABAMA AT BIRMINGHAM, U of 1
BARNARD COLL 6
BAYLOR U 2
BOSTON U 7
BROWN U 12
CALIFORNIA ST U NORTHRIDGE 14
CALIFORNIA U PENNSYLVANIA 1
CALIFORNIA-SAN DIEGO, U of 44
CINCINNATI MAIN CAMPUS, U of 1
CLEVELAND ST U 18
COLL OF CHARLESTON 5
COLL OF THE HOLY CROSS 2
COLL OF WOOSTER 5
COLUMBIA U IN THE CITY OF NEW YORK 20
CONNECTICUT COLL 2
CONNECTICUT, U of 5
CUNY HUNTER COLL 8
CUNY QUEENS COLL 12
DILLARD U 5
ELMHURST COLL 4
FORDHAM U 7
FURMAN U 1
GEORGIA ST U 38
INDIANA ST U 7
JACKSON ST U 3
JOHNSON C SMITH U 2
LEHIGH U 11
LOYOLA MARYMOUNT U 5
MACALESTER COLL 4
MANKATO ST U 3
MARYLAND COLL PARK CAMPUS, U of 91
METROPOLITAN ST COLL 2
MINNESOTA DULUTH, U of 4
MINNESOTA TWIN CITIES, U of 9
MISSOURI-KANSAS CITY, U of 2

MOREHOUSE COLL	3
MORGAN ST U	5
NEW YORK U	12
NORFOLK ST U	2
NORTHWESTERN U	1
OBERLIN COLL	1
OHIO U MAIN CAMPUS	2
PENNSYLVANIA, U of	22
PITTSBURGH MAIN CAMPUS, U of	3
RHODE ISLAND, U of	4
RHODES COLL	2
RICHMOND, U of	2
ROANOKE COLL	13
RUTGERS U CAMDEN CAMPUS	8
RUTGERS U NEW BRUNSWICK	7
RUTGERS U NEWARK CAMPUS	5
SAINT CLOUD ST U	20
SAINT LOUIS U MAIN CAMPUS	3
SAINT PETER'S COLL	2
SAN DIEGO ST U	1
SAN FRANCISCO ST U	11
SEATTLE PACIFIC U	1
SHIPPENSBURG U PENNSYLVANIA	1
SOUTHERN U AT NEW ORLEANS	3
STANFORD U	12
SUNY COLL AT BUFFALO	7
TEMPLE U	9
TRINITY U	1
UTAH, U of	6
VASSAR COLL	3
VIRGINIA COMMONWEALTH U	21
VIRGINIA POLYTECHNIC INST AND ST U	17
WINSTON-SALEM ST U	1
WISCONSIN OSHKOSH, U of	3
WISCONSIN-GREEN BAY, U of	4
WORCESTER ST COLL	12
WRIGHT ST U MAIN CAMPUS	14

Vehicle and Mobile Equip Mechanics & Repairers, Other

LEWIS U	7
PARKS COLL OF SAINT LOUIS U	17

Vehicles and Petroleum Marketing, General

WESTERN MICHIGAN U	7

Veterinarian Assisting

FORT VALLEY ST COLL	3
MOREHEAD ST U	6
NORTH DAKOTA ST U MAIN CAMPUS	6

Veterinary Medicine

CALIFORNIA-DAVIS, U of	13
ILLINOIS URBANA CAMPUS, U of	50
MICHIGAN ST U	7
MINNESOTA TWIN CITIES, U of	10
SIENA HEIGHTS COLL	2
TEXAS A&M U	92
WASHINGTON ST U	22

Video Tech.

ABILENE CHRISTIAN U	3
LYNDON ST COLL	9
SIENA HEIGHTS COLL	1

Video

ECKERD COLL	1
KANSAS CITY ART INST	6
MONTANA ST U	20
SAVANNAH COLL OF ART AND DESIGN	17

Visual and Performing Arts, Other

ANDERSON U	8
BELMONT COLL	25
BELOIT COLL	5
BENNINGTON COLL	28
BERRY COLL	2
BIRMINGHAM SOUTHERN COLL	2
BOSTON COLL	10
BOSTON CONSERVATORY	19
BROWN U	12
BUTLER U	2
CALIFORNIA-SAN DIEGO, U of	69
CALIFORNIA-SANTA CRUZ, U of	1
CAMERON U	30
CASE WESTERN RESERVE U	7
CATHOLIC U AMERICA	13
CENTRAL ST U	2
CLEMSON U	28
COLL OF SAINT CATHERINE-SAINT CATHERINE CAMPUS	1
COLORADO AT BOULDER, U of	14
COLORADO ST U	4
CONCORD COLL	13
DELAWARE ST COLL	1
DEPAUW U	9
EARLHAM COLL	5
EAST CENTRAL U	3
EMERSON COLL	40
FLAGLER COLL	5
FLORIDA AGRI AND MECH U	8
GODDARD COLL	10
HAMLINE U	2
HIRAM COLL	2
INDIANA ST U	20
JACKSONVILLE U	1
JOHN BROWN U	1
JOHNSON ST COLL	3
KENDALL COLL OF ART AND DESIGN	6
KENTUCKY, U of	2
LANDER COLL	3
LEWIS-CLARK ST COLL	2
LINFIELD COLL	2
LORAS COLL	1
LOYOLA U IN NEW ORLEANS	3
MANKATO ST U	2
MARYWOOD COLL	1
MCMURRY COLL	3
MERCER U IN ATLANTA	1
NEBRASKA WESLEYAN U	1
NEBRASKA-LINCOLN, U of	1
NEWBERRY COLL	2
NORTH CAROLINA AGRI AND TECHNICAL ST U	4
OKLAHOMA CHRISTIAN COLL	3
OTTERBEIN COLL	2
PACIFIC U	1
PHILLIPS U	2
PORTLAND, U of	2
REGIS COLL	1
ROSEMONT COLL	8
SAN FRANCISCO ART INST	5
SCHOOL OF THE OZARKS	24
SEATTLE PACIFIC U	3
SIERRA NEVADA COLL	2
SIMPSON COLL	5
SIOUX FALLS COLL	6
SOUTHWESTERN OKLAHOMA ST U	5
SWARTHMORE COLL	3
TEIKYO MARYCREST COLL	1
URSULINE COLL	5
WAYNESBURG COLL	7
WEBER ST COLL	1
WEBSTER U	7
WELLESLEY COLL	7
WILLIAM CAREY COLL	1
WILLIAMS COLL	1
WILMINGTON COLL	2
WORLD COLL WEST	4

Visual and Performing Arts, General

Degrees in this subject were reported by 149 institutions. Consult more specific headings.

Visual and Performing Arts (unspecified)

Degrees in this subject were reported by 1102 institutions. Consult more specific headings.

Vocational Home Economics, Other

DELAWARE ST COLL	1
NORTHWESTERN OKLAHOMA ST U	2
SOUTHEASTERN OKLAHOMA ST U	3
SOUTHWESTERN OKLAHOMA ST U	1

Vocational Home Economics (unspecified)

ALABAMA, U of	3
ANDREWS U	2

ARIZONA, U of	24
BALL ST U	7
BEREA COLL	13
BERRY COLL	2
BLUFFTON COLL	1
BOWLING GREEN ST U MAIN CAMPUS	5
BRIGHAM YOUNG U	240
CENTRAL MICHIGAN U	115
DAVID LIPSCOMB U	2
DELAWARE ST COLL	3
DETROIT, U of	6
DISTRICT OF COLUMBIA, U of THE	3
EASTERN KENTUCKY U	1
FORT VALLEY ST COLL	3
FREED-HARDEMAN COLL	1
GALLAUDET U	11
GEORGIA, U of	66
GRAMBLING ST U	5
IMMACULATA COLL	3
INDIANA ST U	2
INDIANA U PENNSYLVANIA	8
IOWA ST U	8
JACKSONVILLE ST U	2
KENT ST U MAIN CAMPUS	11
LAMAR U	3
LANGSTON U	1
MADONNA COLL	20
MARYGROVE COLL	4
MEREDITH COLL	47
MIDDLE TENNESSE ST U	24
MINNESOTA DULUTH, U of	8
MINNESOTA TWIN CITIES, U of	1
MISSISSIPPI COLL	8
MOREHEAD ST U	4
NORTH TEXAS, U of	12
NORTHEAST LOUISIANA U	12
NORTHWESTERN OKLAHOMA ST U	2
OHIO ST U MAIN CAMPUS	69
OKLAHOMA CHRISTIAN COLL	2
PACIFIC CHRISTIAN COLL	2
PACIFIC UNION COLL	1
PITTSBURGH MAIN CAMPUS, U of	42
POINT LOMA NAZARENE COLL	12
ROCHESTER INST OF TECH	20
ROSARY COLL	2
SETON HILL COLL	3
SOUTHEASTERN LOUISIANA U	3
SOUTHEASTERN OKLAHOMA ST U	3
SOUTHERN COLL OF SEVENTH-DAY ADVENTISTS	1
SOUTHERN MISSISSIPPI, U of	1
SOUTHERN U AGRI & MECH COL AT BATON ROUGE	2
SOUTHWEST MISSOURI ST U	61
SOUTHWESTERN LOUISIANA, U of	5
SOUTHWESTERN OKLAHOMA ST U	1
STEPHEN F AUSTIN ST U	5
SYRACUSE U MAIN CAMPUS	12
TENNESSEE-KNOXVILLE, U of	25
TEXAS CHRISTIAN U	8
TEXAS SOUTHERN U	1
TEXAS TECH U	14
VALPARAISO U	1
VERMONT, U of	15
WASHBURN U TOPEKA	2
WEBER ST COLL	13
WHEELOCK COLL	4
WHITTIER COLL	9

Ward Service Management

NEW ENGLAND, U of	1

Water Resources

NEW HAMPSHIRE, U of	3
SUNY COLL AT ONEONTA	5
TARLETON ST U	5
UTAH ST U	3
WISCONSIN-STEVENS POINT, U of	34

Water and Wastewater Technology

MURRAY ST U	2

Welding Technology

FERRIS ST U	16
LETOURNEAU COLL	6

Western European Studies

AMERICAN U	10
DENISON U	1
FORDHAM U	10
GONZAGA U	1
HOUSTON-U PARK, U of	2
WASHINGTON, U of	6
WELLS COLL	1

Wildlife Management

ALASKA FAIRBANKS, U of	5
ARKANSAS ST U MAIN CAMPUS	5
ARKANSAS TECH U	22
ARKANSAS-MONTICELLO, U of	3
AUBURN U MAIN CAMPUS	21
COLORADO ST U	32
DELAWARE ST COLL	2
EASTERN KENTUCKY U	8
EASTERN NEW MEXICO U MAIN CAMPUS	2
HUMBOLDT ST U	32
IDAHO, U of	16
IOWA ST U	19
LAKE SUPERIOR ST U	8
LINCOLN MEMORIAL U	5
LOUISIANA ST U & AGRI & MECH & HEBERT LAWS CTR	4
LOUISIANA TECH U	4
MAINE, U of	31
MASSACHUSETTS AT AMHERST, U of	28
MCNEESE ST U	4
MICHIGAN ST U	41
MINNESOTA TWIN CITIES, U of	14
MONTANA ST U	22
MONTANA, U of	26
MURRAY ST U	5
NEW HAMPSHIRE, U of	16
NEW MEXICO ST U MAIN CAMPUS	19
NORTHWESTERN ST U LOUISIANA	1
OHIO ST U MAIN CAMPUS	24
OREGON ST U	13
PENNSYLVANIA ST U MAIN CAMPUS	1
SOUTH DAKOTA ST U	14
SOUTHWEST MISSOURI ST U	21
SOUTHWESTERN LOUISIANA, U of	1
STEPHEN F AUSTIN ST U	7
SUL ROSS ST U	3
TENNESSEE TECH U	4
TENNESSEE-KNOXVILLE, U of	17
UNITY COLL	10
UTAH ST U	16
VERMONT, U of	16
WASHINGTON ST U	20
WEST VIRGINIA U	22
WISCONSIN-MADISON, U of	12
WISCONSIN-STEVENS POINT, U of	27
WYOMING, U of	17

Women's Studies

AMHERST COLL	3
ARIZONA ST U	6
ARIZONA, U of	3
BOWDOIN COLL	3
BROWN U	9
BRYN MAWR COLL	4
CALIFORNIA-BERKELEY, U of	3
CALIFORNIA-DAVIS, U of	6
CALIFORNIA-LOS ANGELES, U of	4
CALIFORNIA-SANTA BARBARA, U of	1
CALIFORNIA-SANTA CRUZ, U of	12
COLL OF WOOSTER	5
CONNECTICUT, U of	2
DENVER, U of	1
EARLHAM COLL	8
EMORY U	5
GODDARD COLL	6
GOUCHER COLL	4
KANSAS MAIN CAMPUS, U of	3
MACALESTER COLL	1
MANKATO ST U	1
MASSACHUSETTS AT AMHERST, U of	20
MASSACHUSETTS BOSTON, U of	4
MICHIGAN ANN ARBOR, U of	8
MIDDLEBURY COLL	1
MILLS COLL	3
MINNESOTA DULUTH, U of	4
MINNESOTA TWIN CITIES, U of	8
MOUNT HOLYOKE COLL	7
OBERLIN COLL	9
OHIO ST U MAIN CAMPUS	4
PENNSYLVANIA, U of	2
RUTGERS U NEW BRUNSWICK	8
SAINT OLAF COLL	9
SAN DIEGO ST U	5

SAN FRANCISCO ST U	8
SCRIPPS COLL	1
SIMMONS COLL	4
SMITH COLL	17
SOUTH FLORIDA, U of	5
SUNY AT ALBANY	5
SUNY AT BUFFALO	3
SUNY COLL AT NEW PALTZ	2
TEMPLE U	3
WASHINGTON U	2
WELLESLEY COLL	5
WESLEYAN U	1
WICHITA ST U	1
WISCONSIN-MADISON, U of	15
WISCONSIN-WHITEWATER, U of	2
YALE U	5

Wood Science

CALIFORNIA-BERKELEY, U of	1
IDAHO, U of	5
MAINE, U of	2
MASSACHUSETTS AT AMHERST, U of	19
MISSISSIPPI ST U	5
OREGON ST U	11
WEST VIRGINIA U	4

Woodworking, General

RIO GRANDE, U of	2

Word Processing

BENEDICT COLL	3
EASTERN MICHIGAN U	3
NORTHWESTERN ST U LOUISIANA	6

Zoology, General

ALBERTSON C. (WAS COLL OF IDAHO)	11
ANDREWS U	11
ARIZONA ST U	27
ARKANSAS ST U MAIN CAMPUS	21
ARKANSAS-FAYETTEVILLE, U of	26
AUBURN U MAIN CAMPUS	45
BRIGHAM YOUNG U	117
BUTLER U	1
CALIFORNIA ST POLYTECHNIC U POMONA	8
CALIFORNIA ST U LONG BEACH	24
CALIFORNIA-BERKELEY, U of	26
CALIFORNIA-DAVIS, U of	52
CALIFORNIA-SANTA BARBARA, U of	7
CENTRAL FLORIDA, U of	3
COLORADO ST U	16
CONNECTICUT COLL	10
DUKE U	92
EASTERN ILLINOIS U	62
FLORIDA, U of	83
FORT VALLEY ST COLL	4
GEORGE WASHINGTON U	37
GEORGIA, U of	40
HAWAII AT MANOA, U of	29
HOWARD U	34
HUMBOLDT ST U	6
IDAHO ST U	8
IDAHO, U of	15
IOWA ST U	19
KENT ST U MAIN CAMPUS	6
KENTUCKY, U of	15
LOUISIANA ST U & AGRI & MECH & HEBERT LAWS CTR	38
LOUISIANA TECH U	23
LOUISVILLE, U of	5
MAINE, U of	16
MARSHALL U	11
MARYLAND COLL PARK CAMPUS, U of	37
MASSACHUSETTS AT AMHERST, U of	81
MCNEESE ST U	2
MIAMI U OXFORD CAMPUS	133
MICHIGAN ST U	42
MINNESOTA TWIN CITIES, U of	1
MONTANA ST U	1
MONTANA, U of	14
NEW HAMPSHIRE, U of	37
NORTH CAROLINA CHAPEL HILL, U of	1
NORTH CAROLINA ST U AT RALEIGH	60
NORTH DAKOTA ST U MAIN CAMPUS	28
NORTHEAST LOUISIANA U	3
NORTHERN ARIZONA U	20
NORTHERN COLORADO, U of	2
NORTHERN MICHIGAN U	3
NORTHWEST MISSOURI ST U	1
NORTHWESTERN OKLAHOMA ST U	1
NORTHWESTERN ST U LOUISIANA	1
OHIO ST U MAIN CAMPUS	61
OHIO U MAIN CAMPUS	111
OHIO WESLEYAN U	15
OKLAHOMA NORMAN CAMPUS, U of	55
OKLAHOMA ST U MAIN CAMPUS	15
OLIVET NAZARENE U	4
OREGON ST U	15
RHODE ISLAND, U of	27
RUTGERS U NEWARK CAMPUS	5
SAN DIEGO ST U	1
SAN JOSE ST U	4
SOUTH DAKOTA ST U	3
SOUTH FLORIDA, U of	21
SOUTHERN ILLINOIS U-CARBONDALE	41
SOUTHWEST TEXAS ST U	1
SOUTHWESTERN LOUISIANA, U of	2
SUNY COLL AT OSWEGO	16
TENNESSEE-KNOXVILLE, U of	21
TEXAS A&M U	31
TEXAS AT AUSTIN, U of	44
TEXAS TECH U	22
TEXAS WOMAN'S U	6
VERMONT, U of	19
WASHINGTON ST U	15
WASHINGTON, U of	82
WEBER ST COLL	15
WISCONSIN-MADISON, U of	121
WISCONSIN-MILWAUKEE, U of	6
WYOMING, U of	22